Oxford Dictionary of
National Biography

Volume 21

Oxford Dictionary of National Biography

IN ASSOCIATION WITH
The British Academy

From the earliest times to the year 2000

Edited by
H. C. G. Matthew
and
Brian Harrison

Volume 21
Freud–Gibberd

OXFORD
UNIVERSITY PRESS

OXFORD
UNIVERSITY PRESS

Great Clarendon Street, Oxford OX2 6DP

Oxford University Press is a department of the University of Oxford.
It furthers the University's objective of excellence in research, scholarship,
and education by publishing worldwide in

Oxford New York

Auckland Bangkok Buenos Aires Cape Town
Chennai Dar es Salaam Delhi Hong Kong Istanbul Karachi
Kolkata Kuala Lumpur Madrid Melbourne Mexico City Mumbai Nairobi
São Paulo Shanghai Taipei Tokyo Toronto

Oxford is a registered trade mark of Oxford University Press
in the UK and in certain other countries

Published in the United States
by Oxford University Press Inc., New York

First published 2004

British Library Cataloguing in Publication Data
Data available

Library of Congress Cataloging in Publication Data
Data available: for details see volume 1, p. iv

ISBN 0-19-861371-7 (this volume)
ISBN 0-19-861411-X (set of sixty volumes)

Text captured by Alliance Phototypesetters, Pondicherry
Illustrations reproduced and archived by
Alliance Graphics Ltd, UK
Typeset in OUP Swift by Interactive Sciences Limited, Gloucester
Printed in Great Britain on acid-free paper by
Butler and Tanner Ltd,
Frome, Somerset

LIST OF ABBREVIATIONS

1 General abbreviations

AB	bachelor of arts
ABC	Australian Broadcasting Corporation
ABC TV	ABC Television
act.	active
A$	Australian dollar
AD	*anno domini*
AFC	Air Force Cross
AIDS	acquired immune deficiency syndrome
AK	Alaska
AL	Alabama
A level	advanced level [examination]
ALS	associate of the Linnean Society
AM	master of arts
AMICE	associate member of the Institution of Civil Engineers
ANZAC	Australian and New Zealand Army Corps
appx *pl.* appxs	appendix(es)
AR	Arkansas
ARA	associate of the Royal Academy
ARCA	associate of the Royal College of Art
ARCM	associate of the Royal College of Music
ARCO	associate of the Royal College of Organists
ARIBA	associate of the Royal Institute of British Architects
ARP	air-raid precautions
ARRC	associate of the Royal Red Cross
ARSA	associate of the Royal Scottish Academy
art.	article / item
ASC	Army Service Corps
Asch	Austrian Schilling
ASDIC	Antisubmarine Detection Investigation Committee
ATS	Auxiliary Territorial Service
ATV	Associated Television
Aug	August
AZ	Arizona
b.	born
BA	bachelor of arts
BA (Admin.)	bachelor of arts (administration)
BAFTA	British Academy of Film and Television Arts
BAO	bachelor of arts in obstetrics
bap.	baptized
BBC	British Broadcasting Corporation / Company
BC	before Christ
BCE	before the common (*or* Christian) era
BCE	bachelor of civil engineering
BCG	bacillus of Calmette and Guérin [inoculation against tuberculosis]
BCh	bachelor of surgery
BChir	bachelor of surgery
BCL	bachelor of civil law
BCnL	bachelor of canon law
BCom	bachelor of commerce
BD	bachelor of divinity
BEd	bachelor of education
BEng	bachelor of engineering
bk *pl.* bks	book(s)
BL	bachelor of law / letters / literature
BLitt	bachelor of letters
BM	bachelor of medicine
BMus	bachelor of music
BP	before present
BP	British Petroleum
Bros.	Brothers
BS	(1) bachelor of science; (2) bachelor of surgery; (3) British standard
BSc	bachelor of science
BSc (Econ.)	bachelor of science (economics)
BSc (Eng.)	bachelor of science (engineering)
bt	baronet
BTh	bachelor of theology
bur.	buried
C.	command [identifier for published parliamentary papers]
c.	*circa*
c.	*capitulum pl. capitula*: chapter(s)
CA	California
Cantab.	Cantabrigiensis
cap.	*capitulum pl. capitula*: chapter(s)
CB	companion of the Bath
CBE	commander of the Order of the British Empire
CBS	Columbia Broadcasting System
cc	cubic centimetres
C$	Canadian dollar
CD	compact disc
Cd	command [identifier for published parliamentary papers]
CE	Common (*or* Christian) Era
cent.	century
cf.	compare
CH	Companion of Honour
chap.	chapter
ChB	bachelor of surgery
CI	Imperial Order of the Crown of India
CIA	Central Intelligence Agency
CID	Criminal Investigation Department
CIE	companion of the Order of the Indian Empire
Cie	Compagnie
CLit	companion of literature
CM	master of surgery
cm	centimetre(s)

Cmd	command [identifier for published parliamentary papers]	edn	edition
CMG	companion of the Order of St Michael and St George	EEC	European Economic Community
		EFTA	European Free Trade Association
Cmnd	command [identifier for published parliamentary papers]	EICS	East India Company Service
		EMI	Electrical and Musical Industries (Ltd)
CO	Colorado	Eng.	English
Co.	company	enl.	enlarged
co.	county	ENSA	Entertainments National Service Association
col. *pl.* cols.	column(s)	ep. *pl.* epp.	*epistola(e)*
Corp.	corporation	ESP	extra-sensory perception
CSE	certificate of secondary education	esp.	especially
CSI	companion of the Order of the Star of India	esq.	esquire
CT	Connecticut	est.	estimate / estimated
CVO	commander of the Royal Victorian Order	EU	European Union
cwt	hundredweight	ex	sold by (*lit.* out of)
$	(American) dollar	excl.	excludes / excluding
d.	(1) penny (pence); (2) died	exh.	exhibited
DBE	dame commander of the Order of the British Empire	exh. cat.	exhibition catalogue
		f. *pl.* ff.	following [pages]
DCH	diploma in child health	FA	Football Association
DCh	doctor of surgery	FACP	fellow of the American College of Physicians
DCL	doctor of civil law	facs.	facsimile
DCnL	doctor of canon law	FANY	First Aid Nursing Yeomanry
DCVO	dame commander of the Royal Victorian Order	FBA	fellow of the British Academy
DD	doctor of divinity	FBI	Federation of British Industries
DE	Delaware	FCS	fellow of the Chemical Society
Dec	December	Feb	February
dem.	demolished	FEng	fellow of the Fellowship of Engineering
DEng	doctor of engineering	FFCM	fellow of the Faculty of Community Medicine
des.	destroyed	FGS	fellow of the Geological Society
DFC	Distinguished Flying Cross	fig.	figure
DipEd	diploma in education	FIMechE	fellow of the Institution of Mechanical Engineers
DipPsych	diploma in psychiatry		
diss.	dissertation	FL	Florida
DL	deputy lieutenant	*fl.*	*floruit*
DLitt	doctor of letters	FLS	fellow of the Linnean Society
DLittCelt	doctor of Celtic letters	FM	frequency modulation
DM	(1) Deutschmark; (2) doctor of medicine; (3) doctor of musical arts	fol. *pl.* fols.	folio(s)
		Fr	French francs
DMus	doctor of music	Fr.	French
DNA	dioxyribonucleic acid	FRAeS	fellow of the Royal Aeronautical Society
doc.	document	FRAI	fellow of the Royal Anthropological Institute
DOL	doctor of oriental learning	FRAM	fellow of the Royal Academy of Music
DPH	diploma in public health	FRAS	(1) fellow of the Royal Asiatic Society; (2) fellow of the Royal Astronomical Society
DPhil	doctor of philosophy		
DPM	diploma in psychological medicine	FRCM	fellow of the Royal College of Music
DSC	Distinguished Service Cross	FRCO	fellow of the Royal College of Organists
DSc	doctor of science	FRCOG	fellow of the Royal College of Obstetricians and Gynaecologists
DSc (Econ.)	doctor of science (economics)		
DSc (Eng.)	doctor of science (engineering)	FRCP(C)	fellow of the Royal College of Physicians of Canada
DSM	Distinguished Service Medal		
DSO	companion of the Distinguished Service Order	FRCP (Edin.)	fellow of the Royal College of Physicians of Edinburgh
DSocSc	doctor of social science		
DTech	doctor of technology	FRCP (Lond.)	fellow of the Royal College of Physicians of London
DTh	doctor of theology		
DTM	diploma in tropical medicine	FRCPath	fellow of the Royal College of Pathologists
DTMH	diploma in tropical medicine and hygiene	FRCPsych	fellow of the Royal College of Psychiatrists
DU	doctor of the university	FRCS	fellow of the Royal College of Surgeons
DUniv	doctor of the university	FRGS	fellow of the Royal Geographical Society
dwt	pennyweight	FRIBA	fellow of the Royal Institute of British Architects
EC	European Community	FRICS	fellow of the Royal Institute of Chartered Surveyors
ed. *pl.* eds.	edited / edited by / editor(s)		
Edin.	Edinburgh	FRS	fellow of the Royal Society
		FRSA	fellow of the Royal Society of Arts

FRSCM	fellow of the Royal School of Church Music
FRSE	fellow of the Royal Society of Edinburgh
FRSL	fellow of the Royal Society of Literature
FSA	fellow of the Society of Antiquaries
ft	foot *pl.* feet
FTCL	fellow of Trinity College of Music, London
ft-lb per min.	foot-pounds per minute [unit of horsepower]
FZS	fellow of the Zoological Society
GA	Georgia
GBE	knight or dame grand cross of the Order of the British Empire
GCB	knight grand cross of the Order of the Bath
GCE	general certificate of education
GCH	knight grand cross of the Royal Guelphic Order
GCHQ	government communications headquarters
GCIE	knight grand commander of the Order of the Indian Empire
GCMG	knight or dame grand cross of the Order of St Michael and St George
GCSE	general certificate of secondary education
GCSI	knight grand commander of the Order of the Star of India
GCStJ	bailiff or dame grand cross of the order of St John of Jerusalem
GCVO	knight or dame grand cross of the Royal Victorian Order
GEC	General Electric Company
Ger.	German
GI	government (*or* general) issue
GMT	Greenwich mean time
GP	general practitioner
GPU	[Soviet special police unit]
GSO	general staff officer
Heb.	Hebrew
HEICS	Honourable East India Company Service
HI	Hawaii
HIV	human immunodeficiency virus
HK$	Hong Kong dollar
HM	his / her majesty('s)
HMAS	his / her majesty's Australian ship
HMNZS	his / her majesty's New Zealand ship
HMS	his / her majesty's ship
HMSO	His / Her Majesty's Stationery Office
HMV	His Master's Voice
Hon.	Honourable
hp	horsepower
hr	hour(s)
HRH	his / her royal highness
HTV	Harlech Television
IA	Iowa
ibid.	*ibidem*: in the same place
ICI	Imperial Chemical Industries (Ltd)
ID	Idaho
IL	Illinois
illus.	illustration
illustr.	illustrated
IN	Indiana
in.	inch(es)
Inc.	Incorporated
incl.	includes / including
IOU	I owe you
IQ	intelligence quotient
Ir£	Irish pound
IRA	Irish Republican Army
ISO	companion of the Imperial Service Order
It.	Italian
ITA	Independent Television Authority
ITV	Independent Television
Jan	January
JP	justice of the peace
jun.	junior
KB	knight of the Order of the Bath
KBE	knight commander of the Order of the British Empire
KC	king's counsel
kcal	kilocalorie
KCB	knight commander of the Order of the Bath
KCH	knight commander of the Royal Guelphic Order
KCIE	knight commander of the Order of the Indian Empire
KCMG	knight commander of the Order of St Michael and St George
KCSI	knight commander of the Order of the Star of India
KCVO	knight commander of the Royal Victorian Order
keV	kilo-electron-volt
KG	knight of the Order of the Garter
KGB	[Soviet committee of state security]
KH	knight of the Royal Guelphic Order
KLM	Koninklijke Luchtvaart Maatschappij (Royal Dutch Air Lines)
km	kilometre(s)
KP	knight of the Order of St Patrick
KS	Kansas
KT	knight of the Order of the Thistle
kt	knight
KY	Kentucky
£	pound(s) sterling
£E	Egyptian pound
L	lira *pl.* lire
l. *pl.* ll.	line(s)
LA	Lousiana
LAA	light anti-aircraft
LAH	licentiate of the Apothecaries' Hall, Dublin
Lat.	Latin
lb	pound(s), unit of weight
LDS	licence in dental surgery
lit.	literally
LittB	bachelor of letters
LittD	doctor of letters
LKQCPI	licentiate of the King and Queen's College of Physicians, Ireland
LLA	lady literate in arts
LLB	bachelor of laws
LLD	doctor of laws
LLM	master of laws
LM	licentiate in midwifery
LP	long-playing record
LRAM	licentiate of the Royal Academy of Music
LRCP	licentiate of the Royal College of Physicians
LRCPS (Glasgow)	licentiate of the Royal College of Physicians and Surgeons of Glasgow
LRCS	licentiate of the Royal College of Surgeons
LSA	licentiate of the Society of Apothecaries
LSD	lysergic acid diethylamide
LVO	lieutenant of the Royal Victorian Order
M. *pl.* MM.	Monsieur *pl.* Messieurs
m	metre(s)

m. *pl.* mm.	membrane(s)		ND	North Dakota
MA	(1) Massachusetts; (2) master of arts		n.d.	no date
MAI	master of engineering		NE	Nebraska
MB	bachelor of medicine		*nem. con.*	*nemine contradicente*: unanimously
MBA	master of business administration		new ser.	new series
MBE	member of the Order of the British Empire		NH	New Hampshire
MC	Military Cross		NHS	National Health Service
MCC	Marylebone Cricket Club		NJ	New Jersey
MCh	master of surgery		NKVD	[Soviet people's commissariat for internal affairs]
MChir	master of surgery		NM	New Mexico
MCom	master of commerce		nm	nanometre(s)
MD	(1) doctor of medicine; (2) Maryland		no. *pl.* nos.	number(s)
MDMA	methylenedioxymethamphetamine		Nov	November
ME	Maine		n.p.	no place [of publication]
MEd	master of education		NS	new style
MEng	master of engineering		NV	Nevada
MEP	member of the European parliament		NY	New York
MG	Morris Garages		NZBS	New Zealand Broadcasting Service
MGM	Metro-Goldwyn-Mayer		OBE	officer of the Order of the British Empire
Mgr	Monsignor		obit.	obituary
MI	(1) Michigan; (2) military intelligence		Oct	October
MI1c	[secret intelligence department]		OCTU	officer cadets training unit
MI5	[military intelligence department]		OECD	Organization for Economic Co-operation and Development
MI6	[secret intelligence department]		OEEC	Organization for European Economic Co-operation
MI9	[secret escape service]			
MICE	member of the Institution of Civil Engineers		OFM	order of Friars Minor [Franciscans]
MIEE	member of the Institution of Electrical Engineers		OFMCap	Ordine Frati Minori Cappucini: member of the Capuchin order
min.	minute(s)		OH	Ohio
Mk	mark		OK	Oklahoma
ML	(1) licentiate of medicine; (2) master of laws		O level	ordinary level [examination]
MLitt	master of letters		OM	Order of Merit
Mlle	Mademoiselle		OP	order of Preachers [Dominicans]
mm	millimetre(s)		op. *pl.* opp.	opus *pl.* opera
Mme	Madame		OPEC	Organization of Petroleum Exporting Countries
MN	Minnesota		OR	Oregon
MO	Missouri		orig.	original
MOH	medical officer of health		OS	old style
MP	member of parliament		OSB	Order of St Benedict
m.p.h.	miles per hour		OTC	Officers' Training Corps
MPhil	master of philosophy		OWS	Old Watercolour Society
MRCP	member of the Royal College of Physicians		Oxon.	Oxoniensis
MRCS	member of the Royal College of Surgeons		p. *pl.* pp.	page(s)
MRCVS	member of the Royal College of Veterinary Surgeons		PA	Pennsylvania
MRIA	member of the Royal Irish Academy		p.a.	per annum
MS	(1) master of science; (2) Mississippi		para.	paragraph
MS *pl.* MSS	manuscript(s)		PAYE	pay as you earn
MSc	master of science		pbk *pl.* pbks	paperback(s)
MSc (Econ.)	master of science (economics)		*per.*	[during the] period
MT	Montana		PhD	doctor of philosophy
MusB	bachelor of music		pl.	(1) plate(s); (2) plural
MusBac	bachelor of music		priv. coll.	private collection
MusD	doctor of music		pt *pl.* pts	part(s)
MV	motor vessel		pubd	published
MVO	member of the Royal Victorian Order		PVC	polyvinyl chloride
n. *pl.* nn.	note(s)		q. *pl.* qq.	(1) question(s); (2) quire(s)
NAAFI	Navy, Army, and Air Force Institutes		QC	queen's counsel
NASA	National Aeronautics and Space Administration		R	rand
NATO	North Atlantic Treaty Organization		R.	Rex / Regina
NBC	National Broadcasting Corporation		*r*	recto
NC	North Carolina		*r.*	reigned / ruled
NCO	non-commissioned officer		RA	Royal Academy / Royal Academician

RAC	Royal Automobile Club	Skr	Swedish krona
RAF	Royal Air Force	Span.	Spanish
RAFVR	Royal Air Force Volunteer Reserve	SPCK	Society for Promoting Christian Knowledge
RAM	[member of the] Royal Academy of Music	SS	(1) Santissimi; (2) Schutzstaffel; (3) steam ship
RAMC	Royal Army Medical Corps	STB	bachelor of theology
RCA	Royal College of Art	STD	doctor of theology
RCNC	Royal Corps of Naval Constructors	STM	master of theology
RCOG	Royal College of Obstetricians and Gynaecologists	STP	doctor of theology
RDI	royal designer for industry	*supp.*	supposedly
RE	Royal Engineers	suppl. *pl.* suppls.	supplement(s)
repr. *pl.* reprs.	reprint(s) / reprinted	s.v.	*sub verbo / sub voce*: under the word / heading
repro.	reproduced	SY	steam yacht
rev.	revised / revised by / reviser / revision	TA	Territorial Army
Revd	Reverend	TASS	[Soviet news agency]
RHA	Royal Hibernian Academy	TB	tuberculosis (*lit.* tubercle bacillus)
RI	(1) Rhode Island; (2) Royal Institute of Painters in Water-Colours	TD	(1) *teachtaí dála* (member of the Dáil); (2) territorial decoration
RIBA	Royal Institute of British Architects	TN	Tennessee
RIN	Royal Indian Navy	TNT	trinitrotoluene
RM	Reichsmark	trans.	translated / translated by / translation / translator
RMS	Royal Mail steamer	TT	tourist trophy
RN	Royal Navy	TUC	Trades Union Congress
RNA	ribonucleic acid	TX	Texas
RNAS	Royal Naval Air Service	U-boat	*Unterseeboot*: submarine
RNR	Royal Naval Reserve	Ufa	Universum-Film AG
RNVR	Royal Naval Volunteer Reserve	UMIST	University of Manchester Institute of Science and Technology
RO	Record Office	UN	United Nations
r.p.m.	revolutions per minute	UNESCO	United Nations Educational, Scientific, and Cultural Organization
RRS	royal research ship	UNICEF	United Nations International Children's Emergency Fund
Rs	rupees	unpubd	unpublished
RSA	(1) Royal Scottish Academician; (2) Royal Society of Arts	USS	United States ship
RSPCA	Royal Society for the Prevention of Cruelty to Animals	UT	Utah
Rt Hon.	Right Honourable	*v*	verso
Rt Revd	Right Reverend	v.	versus
RUC	Royal Ulster Constabulary	VA	Virginia
Russ.	Russian	VAD	Voluntary Aid Detachment
RWS	Royal Watercolour Society	VC	Victoria Cross
S4C	Sianel Pedwar Cymru	VE-day	victory in Europe day
s.	shilling(s)	Ven.	Venerable
s.a.	*sub anno*: under the year	VJ-day	victory over Japan day
SABC	South African Broadcasting Corporation	vol. *pl.* vols.	volume(s)
SAS	Special Air Service	VT	Vermont
SC	South Carolina	WA	Washington [state]
ScD	doctor of science	WAAC	Women's Auxiliary Army Corps
S$	Singapore dollar	WAAF	Women's Auxiliary Air Force
SD	South Dakota	WEA	Workers' Educational Association
sec.	second(s)	WHO	World Health Organization
sel.	selected	WI	Wisconsin
sen.	senior	WRAF	Women's Royal Air Force
Sept	September	WRNS	Women's Royal Naval Service
ser.	series	WV	West Virginia
SHAPE	supreme headquarters allied powers, Europe	WVS	Women's Voluntary Service
SIDRO	Société Internationale d'Énergie Hydro-Électrique	WY	Wyoming
sig. *pl.* sigs.	signature(s)	¥	yen
sing.	singular	YMCA	Young Men's Christian Association
SIS	Secret Intelligence Service	YWCA	Young Women's Christian Association
SJ	Society of Jesus		

2 Institution abbreviations

All Souls Oxf.	All Souls College, Oxford
AM Oxf.	Ashmolean Museum, Oxford
Balliol Oxf.	Balliol College, Oxford
BBC WAC	BBC Written Archives Centre, Reading
Beds. & Luton ARS	Bedfordshire and Luton Archives and Record Service, Bedford
Berks. RO	Berkshire Record Office, Reading
BFI	British Film Institute, London
BFI NFTVA	British Film Institute, London, National Film and Television Archive
BGS	British Geological Survey, Keyworth, Nottingham
Birm. CA	Birmingham Central Library, Birmingham City Archives
Birm. CL	Birmingham Central Library
BL	British Library, London
BL NSA	British Library, London, National Sound Archive
BL OIOC	British Library, London, Oriental and India Office Collections
BLPES	London School of Economics and Political Science, British Library of Political and Economic Science
BM	British Museum, London
Bodl. Oxf.	Bodleian Library, Oxford
Bodl. RH	Bodleian Library of Commonwealth and African Studies at Rhodes House, Oxford
Borth. Inst.	Borthwick Institute of Historical Research, University of York
Boston PL	Boston Public Library, Massachusetts
Bristol RO	Bristol Record Office
Bucks. RLSS	Buckinghamshire Records and Local Studies Service, Aylesbury
CAC Cam.	Churchill College, Cambridge, Churchill Archives Centre
Cambs. AS	Cambridgeshire Archive Service
CCC Cam.	Corpus Christi College, Cambridge
CCC Oxf.	Corpus Christi College, Oxford
Ches. & Chester ALSS	Cheshire and Chester Archives and Local Studies Service
Christ Church Oxf.	Christ Church, Oxford
Christies	Christies, London
City Westm. AC	City of Westminster Archives Centre, London
CKS	Centre for Kentish Studies, Maidstone
CLRO	Corporation of London Records Office
Coll. Arms	College of Arms, London
Col. U.	Columbia University, New York
Cornwall RO	Cornwall Record Office, Truro
Courtauld Inst.	Courtauld Institute of Art, London
CUL	Cambridge University Library
Cumbria AS	Cumbria Archive Service
Derbys. RO	Derbyshire Record Office, Matlock
Devon RO	Devon Record Office, Exeter
Dorset RO	Dorset Record Office, Dorchester
Duke U.	Duke University, Durham, North Carolina
Duke U., Perkins L.	Duke University, Durham, North Carolina, William R. Perkins Library
Durham Cath. CL	Durham Cathedral, chapter library
Durham RO	Durham Record Office
DWL	Dr Williams's Library, London
Essex RO	Essex Record Office
E. Sussex RO	East Sussex Record Office, Lewes
Eton	Eton College, Berkshire
FM Cam.	Fitzwilliam Museum, Cambridge
Folger	Folger Shakespeare Library, Washington, DC
Garr. Club	Garrick Club, London
Girton Cam.	Girton College, Cambridge
GL	Guildhall Library, London
Glos. RO	Gloucestershire Record Office, Gloucester
Gon. & Caius Cam.	Gonville and Caius College, Cambridge
Gov. Art Coll.	Government Art Collection
GS Lond.	Geological Society of London
Hants. RO	Hampshire Record Office, Winchester
Harris Man. Oxf.	Harris Manchester College, Oxford
Harvard TC	Harvard Theatre Collection, Harvard University, Cambridge, Massachusetts, Nathan Marsh Pusey Library
Harvard U.	Harvard University, Cambridge, Massachusetts
Harvard U., Houghton L.	Harvard University, Cambridge, Massachusetts, Houghton Library
Herefs. RO	Herefordshire Record Office, Hereford
Herts. ALS	Hertfordshire Archives and Local Studies, Hertford
Hist. Soc. Penn.	Historical Society of Pennsylvania, Philadelphia
HLRO	House of Lords Record Office, London
Hult. Arch.	Hulton Archive, London and New York
Hunt. L.	Huntington Library, San Marino, California
ICL	Imperial College, London
Inst. CE	Institution of Civil Engineers, London
Inst. EE	Institution of Electrical Engineers, London
IWM	Imperial War Museum, London
IWM FVA	Imperial War Museum, London, Film and Video Archive
IWM SA	Imperial War Museum, London, Sound Archive
JRL	John Rylands University Library of Manchester
King's AC Cam.	King's College Archives Centre, Cambridge
King's Cam.	King's College, Cambridge
King's Lond.	King's College, London
King's Lond., Liddell Hart C.	King's College, London, Liddell Hart Centre for Military Archives
Lancs. RO	Lancashire Record Office, Preston
L. Cong.	Library of Congress, Washington, DC
Leics. RO	Leicestershire, Leicester, and Rutland Record Office, Leicester
Lincs. Arch.	Lincolnshire Archives, Lincoln
Linn. Soc.	Linnean Society of London
LMA	London Metropolitan Archives
LPL	Lambeth Palace, London
Lpool RO	Liverpool Record Office and Local Studies Service
LUL	London University Library
Magd. Cam.	Magdalene College, Cambridge
Magd. Oxf.	Magdalen College, Oxford
Man. City Gall.	Manchester City Galleries
Man. CL	Manchester Central Library
Mass. Hist. Soc.	Massachusetts Historical Society, Boston
Merton Oxf.	Merton College, Oxford
MHS Oxf.	Museum of the History of Science, Oxford
Mitchell L., Glas.	Mitchell Library, Glasgow
Mitchell L., NSW	State Library of New South Wales, Sydney, Mitchell Library
Morgan L.	Pierpont Morgan Library, New York
NA Canada	National Archives of Canada, Ottawa
NA Ire.	National Archives of Ireland, Dublin
NAM	National Army Museum, London
NA Scot.	National Archives of Scotland, Edinburgh
News Int. RO	News International Record Office, London
NG Ire.	National Gallery of Ireland, Dublin

NG Scot.	National Gallery of Scotland, Edinburgh
NHM	Natural History Museum, London
NL Aus.	National Library of Australia, Canberra
NL Ire.	National Library of Ireland, Dublin
NL NZ	National Library of New Zealand, Wellington
NL NZ, Turnbull L.	National Library of New Zealand, Wellington, Alexander Turnbull Library
NL Scot.	National Library of Scotland, Edinburgh
NL Wales	National Library of Wales, Aberystwyth
NMG Wales	National Museum and Gallery of Wales, Cardiff
NMM	National Maritime Museum, London
Norfolk RO	Norfolk Record Office, Norwich
Northants. RO	Northamptonshire Record Office, Northampton
Northumbd RO	Northumberland Record Office
Notts. Arch.	Nottinghamshire Archives, Nottingham
NPG	National Portrait Gallery, London
NRA	National Archives, London, Historical Manuscripts Commission, National Register of Archives
Nuffield Oxf.	Nuffield College, Oxford
N. Yorks. CRO	North Yorkshire County Record Office, Northallerton
NYPL	New York Public Library
Oxf. UA	Oxford University Archives
Oxf. U. Mus. NH	Oxford University Museum of Natural History
Oxon. RO	Oxfordshire Record Office, Oxford
Pembroke Cam.	Pembroke College, Cambridge
PRO	National Archives, London, Public Record Office
PRO NIre.	Public Record Office for Northern Ireland, Belfast
Pusey Oxf.	Pusey House, Oxford
RA	Royal Academy of Arts, London
Ransom HRC	Harry Ransom Humanities Research Center, University of Texas, Austin
RAS	Royal Astronomical Society, London
RBG Kew	Royal Botanic Gardens, Kew, London
RCP Lond.	Royal College of Physicians of London
RCS Eng.	Royal College of Surgeons of England, London
RGS	Royal Geographical Society, London
RIBA	Royal Institute of British Architects, London
RIBA BAL	Royal Institute of British Architects, London, British Architectural Library
Royal Arch.	Royal Archives, Windsor Castle, Berkshire [by gracious permission of her majesty the queen]
Royal Irish Acad.	Royal Irish Academy, Dublin
Royal Scot. Acad.	Royal Scottish Academy, Edinburgh
RS	Royal Society, London
RSA	Royal Society of Arts, London
RS Friends, Lond.	Religious Society of Friends, London
St Ant. Oxf.	St Antony's College, Oxford
St John Cam.	St John's College, Cambridge
S. Antiquaries, Lond.	Society of Antiquaries of London
Sci. Mus.	Science Museum, London
Scot. NPG	Scottish National Portrait Gallery, Edinburgh
Scott Polar RI	University of Cambridge, Scott Polar Research Institute
Sheff. Arch.	Sheffield Archives
Shrops. RRC	Shropshire Records and Research Centre, Shrewsbury
SOAS	School of Oriental and African Studies, London
Som. ARS	Somerset Archive and Record Service, Taunton
Staffs. RO	Staffordshire Record Office, Stafford
Suffolk RO	Suffolk Record Office
Surrey HC	Surrey History Centre, Woking
TCD	Trinity College, Dublin
Trinity Cam.	Trinity College, Cambridge
U. Aberdeen	University of Aberdeen
U. Birm.	University of Birmingham
U. Birm. L.	University of Birmingham Library
U. Cal.	University of California
U. Cam.	University of Cambridge
UCL	University College, London
U. Durham	University of Durham
U. Durham L.	University of Durham Library
U. Edin.	University of Edinburgh
U. Edin., New Coll.	University of Edinburgh, New College
U. Edin., New Coll. L.	University of Edinburgh, New College Library
U. Edin. L.	University of Edinburgh Library
U. Glas.	University of Glasgow
U. Glas. L.	University of Glasgow Library
U. Hull	University of Hull
U. Hull, Brynmor Jones L.	University of Hull, Brynmor Jones Library
U. Leeds	University of Leeds
U. Leeds, Brotherton L.	University of Leeds, Brotherton Library
U. Lond.	University of London
U. Lpool	University of Liverpool
U. Lpool L.	University of Liverpool Library
U. Mich.	University of Michigan, Ann Arbor
U. Mich., Clements L.	University of Michigan, Ann Arbor, William L. Clements Library
U. Newcastle	University of Newcastle upon Tyne
U. Newcastle, Robinson L.	University of Newcastle upon Tyne, Robinson Library
U. Nott.	University of Nottingham
U. Nott. L.	University of Nottingham Library
U. Oxf.	University of Oxford
U. Reading	University of Reading
U. Reading L.	University of Reading Library
U. St Andr.	University of St Andrews
U. St Andr. L.	University of St Andrews Library
U. Southampton	University of Southampton
U. Southampton L.	University of Southampton Library
U. Sussex	University of Sussex, Brighton
U. Texas	University of Texas, Austin
U. Wales	University of Wales
U. Warwick Mod. RC	University of Warwick, Coventry, Modern Records Centre
V&A	Victoria and Albert Museum, London
V&A NAL	Victoria and Albert Museum, London, National Art Library
Warks. CRO	Warwickshire County Record Office, Warwick
Wellcome L.	Wellcome Library for the History and Understanding of Medicine, London
Westm. DA	Westminster Diocesan Archives, London
Wilts. & Swindon RO	Wiltshire and Swindon Record Office, Trowbridge
Worcs. RO	Worcestershire Record Office, Worcester
W. Sussex RO	West Sussex Record Office, Chichester
W. Yorks. AS	West Yorkshire Archive Service
Yale U.	Yale University, New Haven, Connecticut
Yale U., Beinecke L.	Yale University, New Haven, Connecticut, Beinecke Rare Book and Manuscript Library
Yale U. CBA	Yale University, New Haven, Connecticut, Yale Center for British Art

3 Bibliographic abbreviations

Adams, *Drama* — W. D. Adams, *A dictionary of the drama*, 1: *A–G* (1904); 2: *H–Z* (1956) [vol. 2 microfilm only]

AFM — J O'Donovan, ed. and trans., *Annala rioghachta Eireann / Annals of the kingdom of Ireland by the four masters*, 7 vols. (1848–51); 2nd edn (1856); 3rd edn (1990)

Allibone, *Dict.* — S. A. Allibone, *A critical dictionary of English literature and British and American authors*, 3 vols. (1859–71); suppl. by J. F. Kirk, 2 vols. (1891)

ANB — J. A. Garraty and M. C. Carnes, eds., *American national biography*, 24 vols. (1999)

Anderson, *Scot. nat.* — W. Anderson, *The Scottish nation, or, The surnames, families, literature, honours, and biographical history of the people of Scotland*, 3 vols. (1859–63)

Ann. mon. — H. R. Luard, ed., *Annales monastici*, 5 vols., Rolls Series, 36 (1864–9)

Ann. Ulster — S. Mac Airt and G. Mac Niocaill, eds., *Annals of Ulster (to AD 1131)* (1983)

APC — *Acts of the privy council of England*, new ser., 46 vols. (1890–1964)

APS — *The acts of the parliaments of Scotland*, 12 vols. in 13 (1814–75)

Arber, *Regs. Stationers* — F. Arber, ed., *A transcript of the registers of the Company of Stationers of London, 1554–1640 AD*, 5 vols. (1875–94)

ArchR — *Architectural Review*

ASC — D. Whitelock, D. C. Douglas, and S. I. Tucker, ed. and trans., *The Anglo-Saxon Chronicle: a revised translation* (1961)

AS chart. — P. H. Sawyer, *Anglo-Saxon charters: an annotated list and bibliography*, Royal Historical Society Guides and Handbooks (1968)

AusDB — D. Pike and others, eds., *Australian dictionary of biography*, 16 vols. (1966–2002)

Baker, *Serjeants* — J. H. Baker, *The order of serjeants at law*, SeldS, suppl. ser. 5 (1984)

Bale, *Cat.* — J. Bale, *Scriptorum illustrium Maioris Brytannie, quam nunc Angliam et Scotiam vocant: catalogus*, 2 vols. in 1 (Basel, 1557–9); facs. edn (1971)

Bale, *Index* — J. Bale, *Index Britanniae scriptorum*, ed. R. L. Poole and M. Bateson (1902); facs. edn (1990)

BBCS — *Bulletin of the Board of Celtic Studies*

BDMBR — J. O. Baylen and N. J. Gossman, eds., *Biographical dictionary of modern British radicals*, 3 vols. in 4 (1979–88)

Bede, *Hist. eccl.* — *Bede's Ecclesiastical history of the English people*, ed. and trans. B. Colgrave and R. A. B. Mynors, OMT (1969); repr. (1991)

Bénézit, *Dict.* — E. Bénézit, *Dictionnaire critique et documentaire des peintres, sculpteurs, dessinateurs et graveurs*, 3 vols. (Paris, 1911–23); new edn, 8 vols. (1948–66), repr. (1966); 3rd edn, rev. and enl., 10 vols. (1976); 4th edn, 14 vols. (1999)

BIHR — *Bulletin of the Institute of Historical Research*

Birch, *Seals* — W. de Birch, *Catalogue of seals in the department of manuscripts in the British Museum*, 6 vols. (1887–1900)

Bishop Burnet's History — *Bishop Burnet's History of his own time*, ed. M. J. Routh, 2nd edn, 6 vols. (1833)

Blackwood — *Blackwood's [Edinburgh] Magazine*, 328 vols. (1817–1980)

Blain, Clements & Grundy, *Feminist comp.* — V. Blain, P. Clements, and I. Grundy, eds., *The feminist companion to literature in English* (1990)

BL cat. — *The British Library general catalogue of printed books* [in 360 vols. with suppls., also CD-ROM and online]

BMJ — *British Medical Journal*

Boase & Courtney, *Bibl. Corn.* — G. C. Boase and W. P. Courtney, *Bibliotheca Cornubiensis: a catalogue of the writings … of Cornishmen*, 3 vols. (1874–82)

Boase, *Mod. Eng. biog.* — F. Boase, *Modern English biography: containing many thousand concise memoirs of persons who have died since the year 1850*, 6 vols. (privately printed, Truro, 1892–1921); repr. (1965)

Boswell, *Life* — *Boswell's Life of Johnson: together with Journal of a tour to the Hebrides and Johnson's Diary of a journey into north Wales*, ed. G. B. Hill, enl. edn, rev. L. F. Powell, 6 vols. (1934–50); 2nd edn (1964); repr. (1971)

Brown & Stratton, *Brit. mus.* — J. D. Brown and S. S. Stratton, *British musical biography* (1897)

Bryan, *Painters* — M. Bryan, *A biographical and critical dictionary of painters and engravers*, 2 vols. (1816); new edn, ed. G. Stanley (1849); new edn, ed. R. E. Graves and W. Armstrong, 2 vols. (1886–9); [4th edn], ed. G. C. Williamson, 5 vols. (1903–5) [various reprs.]

Burke, *Gen. GB* — J. Burke, *A genealogical and heraldic history of the commoners of Great Britain and Ireland*, 4 vols. (1833–8); new edn as *A genealogical and heraldic dictionary of the landed gentry of Great Britain and Ireland*, 3 vols. [1843–9] [many later edns]

Burke, *Gen. Ire.* — J. B. Burke, *A genealogical and heraldic history of the landed gentry of Ireland* (1899); 2nd edn (1904); 3rd edn (1912); 4th edn (1958); 5th edn as *Burke's Irish family records* (1976)

Burke, *Peerage* — J. Burke, *A general [later edns A genealogical] and heraldic dictionary of the peerage and baronetage of the United Kingdom* [later edns *the British empire*] (1829–)

Burney, *Hist. mus.* — C. Burney, *A general history of music, from the earliest ages to the present period*, 4 vols. (1776–89)

Burtchaell & Sadleir, *Alum. Dubl.* — G. D. Burtchaell and T. U. Sadleir, *Alumni Dublinenses: a register of the students, graduates, and provosts of Trinity College* (1924); [2nd edn], with suppl., in 2 pts (1935)

Calamy rev. — A. G. Matthews, *Calamy revised* (1934); repr. (1988)

CCI — *Calendar of confirmations and inventories granted and given up in the several commissariots of Scotland* (1876–)

CCIR — *Calendar of the close rolls preserved in the Public Record Office*, 47 vols. (1892–1963)

CDS — J. Bain, ed., *Calendar of documents relating to Scotland*, 4 vols., PRO (1881–8); suppl. vol. 5, ed. G. G. Simpson and J. D. Galbraith (1986)

CEPR letters — W. H. Bliss, C. Johnson, and J. Twemlow, eds., *Calendar of entries in the papal registers relating to Great Britain and Ireland: papal letters* (1893–)

CGPLA — *Calendars of the grants of probate and letters of administration* [in 4 ser.: *England & Wales, Northern Ireland, Ireland,* and *Éire*]

Chambers, *Scots.* — R. Chambers, ed., *A biographical dictionary of eminent Scotsmen*, 4 vols. (1832–5)

Chancery records — chancery records pubd by the PRO

Chancery records (RC) — chancery records pubd by the Record Commissions

CIPM	*Calendar of inquisitions post mortem*, [20 vols.], PRO (1904–); also *Henry VII*, 3 vols. (1898–1955)
Clarendon, *Hist. rebellion*	E. Hyde, earl of Clarendon, *The history of the rebellion and civil wars in England*, 6 vols. (1888); repr. (1958) and (1992)
Cobbett, *Parl. hist.*	W. Cobbett and J. Wright, eds., *Cobbett's Parliamentary history of England*, 36 vols. (1806–1820)
Colvin, *Archs.*	H. Colvin, *A biographical dictionary of British architects, 1600–1840*, 3rd edn (1995)
Cooper, *Ath. Cantab.*	C. H. Cooper and T. Cooper, *Athenae Cantabrigienses*, 3 vols. (1858–1913); repr. (1967)
CPR	*Calendar of the patent rolls preserved in the Public Record Office* (1891–)
Crockford	*Crockford's Clerical Directory*
CS	Camden Society
CSP	*Calendar of state papers* [in 11 ser.: *domestic, Scotland, Scottish series, Ireland, colonial, Commonwealth, foreign, Spain* [at Simancas], *Rome, Milan,* and *Venice*]
CYS	Canterbury and York Society
DAB	*Dictionary of American biography*, 21 vols. (1928–36), repr. in 11 vols. (1964); 10 suppls. (1944–96)
DBB	D. J. Jeremy, ed., *Dictionary of business biography*, 5 vols. (1984–6)
DCB	G. W. Brown and others, *Dictionary of Canadian biography*, [14 vols.] (1966–)
Debrett's Peerage	*Debrett's Peerage* (1803–) [sometimes *Debrett's Illustrated peerage*]
Desmond, *Botanists*	R. Desmond, *Dictionary of British and Irish botanists and horticulturists* (1977); rev. edn (1994)
Dir. Brit. archs.	A. Felstead, J. Franklin, and L. Pinfield, eds., *Directory of British architects, 1834–1900* (1993); 2nd edn, ed. A. Brodie and others, 2 vols. (2001)
DLB	J. M. Bellamy and J. Saville, eds., *Dictionary of labour biography*, [10 vols.] (1972–)
DLitB	Dictionary of Literary Biography
DNB	*Dictionary of national biography*, 63 vols. (1885–1900), suppl., 3 vols. (1901); repr. in 22 vols. (1908–9); 10 further suppls. (1912–96); *Missing persons* (1993)
DNZB	W. H. Oliver and C. Orange, eds., *The dictionary of New Zealand biography*, 5 vols. (1990–2000)
DSAB	W. J. de Kock and others, eds., *Dictionary of South African biography*, 5 vols. (1968–87)
DSB	C. C. Gillispie and F. L. Holmes, eds., *Dictionary of scientific biography*, 16 vols. (1970–80); repr. in 8 vols. (1981); 2 vol. suppl. (1990)
DSBB	A. Slaven and S. Checkland, eds., *Dictionary of Scottish business biography, 1860–1960*, 2 vols. (1986–90)
DSCHT	N. M. de S. Cameron and others, eds., *Dictionary of Scottish church history and theology* (1993)
Dugdale, *Monasticon*	W. Dugdale, *Monasticon Anglicanum*, 3 vols. (1655–72); 2nd edn, 3 vols. (1661–82); new edn, ed. J. Caley, J. Ellis, and B. Bandinel, 6 vols. in 8 pts (1817–30); repr. (1846) and (1970)
DWB	J. E. Lloyd and others, eds., *Dictionary of Welsh biography down to 1940* (1959) [Eng. trans. of *Y bywgraffiadur Cymreig hyd 1940*, 2nd edn (1954)]
EdinR	*Edinburgh Review, or, Critical Journal*
EETS	Early English Text Society
Emden, *Cam.*	A. B. Emden, *A biographical register of the University of Cambridge to 1500* (1963)
Emden, *Oxf.*	A. B. Emden, *A biographical register of the University of Oxford to AD 1500*, 3 vols. (1957–9); also *A biographical register of the University of Oxford, AD 1501 to 1540* (1974)
EngHR	*English Historical Review*
Engraved Brit. ports.	F. M. O'Donoghue and H. M. Hake, *Catalogue of engraved British portraits preserved in the department of prints and drawings in the British Museum*, 6 vols. (1908–25)
ER	The English Reports, 178 vols. (1900–32)
ESTC	*English short title catalogue, 1475–1800* [CD-ROM and online]
Evelyn, *Diary*	*The diary of John Evelyn*, ed. E. S. De Beer, 6 vols. (1955); repr. (2000)
Farington, *Diary*	*The diary of Joseph Farington*, ed. K. Garlick and others, 17 vols. (1978–98)
Fasti Angl. (Hardy)	J. Le Neve, *Fasti ecclesiae Anglicanae*, ed. T. D. Hardy, 3 vols. (1854)
Fasti Angl., 1066–1300	[J. Le Neve], *Fasti ecclesiae Anglicanae, 1066–1300*, ed. D. E. Greenway and J. S. Barrow, [8 vols.] (1968–)
Fasti Angl., 1300–1541	[J. Le Neve], *Fasti ecclesiae Anglicanae, 1300–1541*, 12 vols. (1962–7)
Fasti Angl., 1541–1857	[J. Le Neve], *Fasti ecclesiae Anglicanae, 1541–1857*, ed. J. M. Horn, D. M. Smith, and D. S. Bailey, [9 vols.] (1969–)
Fasti Scot.	H. Scott, *Fasti ecclesiae Scoticanae*, 3 vols. in 6 (1871); new edn, [11 vols.] (1915–)
FO List	*Foreign Office List*
Fortescue, *Brit. army*	J. W. Fortescue, *A history of the British army*, 13 vols. (1899–1930)
Foss, *Judges*	E. Foss, *The judges of England*, 9 vols. (1848–64); repr. (1966)
Foster, *Alum. Oxon.*	J. Foster, ed., *Alumni Oxonienses: the members of the University of Oxford, 1715–1886*, 4 vols. (1887–8); later edn (1891); also *Alumni Oxonienses … 1500–1714*, 4 vols. (1891–2); 8 vol. repr. (1968) and (2000)
Fuller, *Worthies*	T. Fuller, *The history of the worthies of England*, 4 pts (1662); new edn, 2 vols., ed. J. Nichols (1811); new edn, 3 vols., ed. P. A. Nuttall (1840); repr. (1965)
GEC, *Baronetage*	G. E. Cokayne, *Complete baronetage*, 6 vols. (1900–09); repr. (1983) [microprint]
GEC, *Peerage*	G. E. C. [G. E. Cokayne], *The complete peerage of England, Scotland, Ireland, Great Britain, and the United Kingdom*, 8 vols. (1887–98); new edn, ed. V. Gibbs and others, 14 vols. in 15 (1910–98); microprint repr. (1982) and (1987)
Genest, *Eng. stage*	J. Genest, *Some account of the English stage from the Restoration in 1660 to 1830*, 10 vols. (1832); repr. [New York, 1965]
Gillow, *Lit. biog. hist.*	J. Gillow, *A literary and biographical history or bibliographical dictionary of the English Catholics, from the breach with Rome, in 1534, to the present time*, 5 vols. [1885–1902]; repr. (1961); repr. with preface by C. Gillow (1999)
Gir. Camb. opera	*Giraldi Cambrensis opera*, ed. J. S. Brewer, J. F. Dimock, and G. F. Warner, 8 vols., Rolls Series, 21 (1861–91)
GJ	*Geographical Journal*

Gladstone, *Diaries*	*The Gladstone diaries: with cabinet minutes and prime-ministerial correspondence*, ed. M. R. D. Foot and H. C. G. Matthew, 14 vols. (1968–94)
GM	*Gentleman's Magazine*
Graves, *Artists*	A. Graves, ed., *A dictionary of artists who have exhibited works in the principal London exhibitions of oil paintings from 1760 to 1880* (1884); new edn (1895); 3rd edn (1901); facs. edn (1969); repr. [1970], (1973), and (1984)
Graves, *Brit. Inst.*	A. Graves, *The British Institution, 1806–1867: a complete dictionary of contributors and their work from the foundation of the institution* (1875); facs. edn (1908); repr. (1969)
Graves, *RA exhibitors*	A. Graves, *The Royal Academy of Arts: a complete dictionary of contributors and their work from its foundation in 1769 to 1904*, 8 vols. (1905–6); repr. in 4 vols. (1970) and (1972)
Graves, *Soc. Artists*	A. Graves, *The Society of Artists of Great Britain, 1760–1791, the Free Society of Artists, 1761–1783: a complete dictionary* (1907); facs. edn (1969)
Greaves & Zaller, *BDBR*	R. L. Greaves and R. Zaller, eds., *Biographical dictionary of British radicals in the seventeenth century*, 3 vols. (1982–4)
Grove, *Dict. mus.*	G. Grove, ed., *A dictionary of music and musicians*, 5 vols. (1878–90); 2nd edn, ed. J. A. Fuller Maitland (1904–10); 3rd edn, ed. H. C. Colles (1927); 4th edn with suppl. (1940); 5th edn, ed. E. Blom, 9 vols. (1954); suppl. (1961) [see also *New Grove*]
Hall, *Dramatic ports.*	L. A. Hall, *Catalogue of dramatic portraits in the theatre collection of the Harvard College library*, 4 vols. (1930–34)
Hansard	*Hansard's parliamentary debates*, ser. 1–5 (1803–)
Highfill, Burnim & Langhans, *BDA*	P. H. Highfill, K. A. Burnim, and E. A. Langhans, *A biographical dictionary of actors, actresses, musicians, dancers, managers, and other stage personnel in London, 1660–1800*, 16 vols. (1973–93)
Hist. U. Oxf.	T. H. Aston, ed., *The history of the University of Oxford*, 8 vols. (1984–2000) [1: *The early Oxford schools*, ed. J. I. Catto (1984); 2: *Late medieval Oxford*, ed. J. I. Catto and R. Evans (1992); 3: *The collegiate university*, ed. J. McConica (1986); 4: *Seventeenth-century Oxford*, ed. N. Tyacke (1997); 5: *The eighteenth century*, ed. L. S. Sutherland and L. G. Mitchell (1986); 6–7: *Nineteenth-century Oxford*, ed. M. G. Brock and M. C. Curthoys (1997–2000); 8: *The twentieth century*, ed. B. Harrison (2000)]
HJ	*Historical Journal*
HMC	Historical Manuscripts Commission
Holdsworth, *Eng. law*	W. S. Holdsworth, *A history of English law*, ed. A. L. Goodhart and H. L. Hanbury, 17 vols. (1903–72)
HoP, *Commons*	*The history of parliament: the House of Commons* [*1386–1421*, ed. J. S. Roskell, L. Clark, and C. Rawcliffe, 4 vols. (1992); *1509–1558*, ed. S. T. Bindoff, 3 vols. (1982); *1558–1603*, ed. P. W. Hasler, 3 vols. (1981); *1660–1690*, ed. B. D. Henning, 3 vols. (1983); *1690–1715*, ed. D. W. Hayton, E. Cruickshanks, and S. Handley, 5 vols. (2002); *1715–1754*, ed. R. Sedgwick, 2 vols. (1970); *1754–1790*, ed. L. Namier and J. Brooke, 3 vols. (1964), repr. (1985); *1790–1820*, ed. R. G. Thorne, 5 vols. (1986); in draft (used with permission): *1422–1504*, *1604–1629*, *1640–1660*, and *1820–1832*]
IGI	*International Genealogical Index*, Church of Jesus Christ of the Latterday Saints
ILN	*Illustrated London News*
IMC	Irish Manuscripts Commission
Irving, *Scots.*	J. Irving, ed., *The book of Scotsmen eminent for achievements in arms and arts, church and state, law, legislation and literature, commerce, science, travel and philanthropy* (1881)
JCS	*Journal of the Chemical Society*
JHC	*Journals of the House of Commons*
JHL	*Journals of the House of Lords*
John of Worcester, *Chron.*	*The chronicle of John of Worcester*, ed. R. R. Darlington and P. McGurk, trans. J. Bray and P. McGurk, 3 vols., OMT (1995–) [vol. 1 forthcoming]
Keeler, *Long Parliament*	M. F. Keeler, *The Long Parliament, 1640–1641: a biographical study of its members* (1954)
Kelly, *Handbk*	*The upper ten thousand: an alphabetical list of all members of noble families*, 3 vols. (1875–7); continued as *Kelly's handbook of the upper ten thousand for 1878* [1879], 2 vols. (1878–9); continued as *Kelly's handbook to the titled, landed and official classes*, 94 vols. (1880–1973)
LondG	*London Gazette*
LP Henry VIII	J. S. Brewer, J. Gairdner, and R. H. Brodie, eds., *Letters and papers, foreign and domestic, of the reign of Henry VIII*, 23 vols. in 38 (1862–1932); repr. (1965)
Mallalieu, *Watercolour artists*	H. L. Mallalieu, *The dictionary of British watercolour artists up to 1820*, 3 vols. (1976–90); vol. 1, 2nd edn (1986)
Memoirs FRS	*Biographical Memoirs of Fellows of the Royal Society*
MGH	Monumenta Germaniae Historica
MT	*Musical Times*
Munk, *Roll*	W. Munk, *The roll of the Royal College of Physicians of London*, 2 vols. (1861); 2nd edn, 3 vols. (1878)
N&Q	*Notes and Queries*
New Grove	S. Sadie, ed., *The new Grove dictionary of music and musicians*, 20 vols. (1980); 2nd edn, 29 vols. (2001) [also online edn; see also Grove, *Dict. mus.*]
Nichols, *Illustrations*	J. Nichols and J. B. Nichols, *Illustrations of the literary history of the eighteenth century*, 8 vols. (1817–58)
Nichols, *Lit. anecdotes*	J. Nichols, *Literary anecdotes of the eighteenth century*, 9 vols. (1812–16); facs. edn (1966)
Obits. FRS	*Obituary Notices of Fellows of the Royal Society*
O'Byrne, *Naval biog. dict.*	W. R. O'Byrne, *A naval biographical dictionary* (1849); repr. (1990); [2nd edn], 2 vols. (1861)
OHS	Oxford Historical Society
Old Westminsters	*The record of Old Westminsters*, 1–2, ed. G. F. R. Barker and A. H. Stenning (1928); suppl. 1, ed. J. B. Whitmore and G. R. Y. Radcliffe [1938]; 3, ed. J. B. Whitmore, G. R. Y. Radcliffe, and D. C. Simpson (1963); suppl. 2, ed. F. E. Pagan (1978); 4, ed. F. E. Pagan and H. E. Pagan (1992)
OMT	Oxford Medieval Texts
Ordericus Vitalis, *Eccl. hist.*	*The ecclesiastical history of Orderic Vitalis*, ed. and trans. M. Chibnall, 6 vols., OMT (1969–80); repr. (1990)
Paris, *Chron.*	*Matthaei Parisiensis, monachi sancti Albani, chronica majora*, ed. H. R. Luard, Rolls Series, 7 vols. (1872–83)
Parl. papers	*Parliamentary papers* (1801–)
PBA	*Proceedings of the British Academy*

Pepys, *Diary*	*The diary of Samuel Pepys*, ed. R. Latham and W. Matthews, 11 vols. (1970–83); repr. (1995) and (2000)
Pevsner	N. Pevsner and others, Buildings of England series
PICE	*Proceedings of the Institution of Civil Engineers*
Pipe rolls	*The great roll of the pipe for . . .*, PRSoc. (1884–)
PRO	Public Record Office
PRS	*Proceedings of the Royal Society of London*
PRSoc.	Pipe Roll Society
PTRS	*Philosophical Transactions of the Royal Society*
QR	*Quarterly Review*
RC	Record Commissions
Redgrave, *Artists*	S. Redgrave, *A dictionary of artists of the English school* (1874); rev. edn (1878); repr. (1970)
Reg. Oxf.	C. W. Boase and A. Clark, eds., *Register of the University of Oxford*, 5 vols., OHS, 1, 10–12, 14 (1885–9)
Reg. PCS	J. H. Burton and others, eds., *The register of the privy council of Scotland*, 1st ser., 14 vols. (1877–98); 2nd ser., 8 vols. (1899–1908); 3rd ser., [16 vols.] (1908–70)
Reg. RAN	H. W. C. Davis and others, eds., *Regesta regum Anglo-Normannorum, 1066–1154*, 4 vols. (1913–69)
RIBA Journal	*Journal of the Royal Institute of British Architects* [later *RIBA Journal*]
RotP	J. Strachey, ed., *Rotuli parliamentorum ut et petitiones, et placita in parliamento*, 6 vols. (1767–77)
RotS	D. Macpherson, J. Caley, and W. Illingworth, eds., *Rotuli Scotiae in Turri Londinensi et in domo capitulari Westmonasteriensi asservati*, 2 vols., RC, 14 (1814–19)
RS	Record(s) Society
Rymer, *Foedera*	T. Rymer and R. Sanderson, eds., *Foedera, conventiones, literae et cuiuscunque generis acta publica inter reges Angliae et alios quosvis imperatores, reges, pontifices, principes, vel communitates*, 20 vols. (1704–35); 2nd edn, 20 vols. (1726–35); 3rd edn, 10 vols. (1739–45), facs. edn (1967); new edn, ed. A. Clarke, J. Caley, and F. Holbrooke, 4 vols., RC, 50 (1816–30)
Sainty, *Judges*	J. Sainty, ed., *The judges of England, 1272–1990*, SeldS, suppl. ser., 10 (1993)
Sainty, *King's counsel*	J. Sainty, ed., *A list of English law officers and king's counsel*, SeldS, suppl. ser., 7 (1987)
SCH	Studies in Church History
Scots peerage	J. B. Paul, ed. *The Scots peerage, founded on Wood's edition of Sir Robert Douglas's Peerage of Scotland, containing an historical and genealogical account of the nobility of that kingdom*, 9 vols. (1904–14)
SeldS	Selden Society
SHR	*Scottish Historical Review*
State trials	T. B. Howell and T. J. Howell, eds., *Cobbett's Complete collection of state trials*, 34 vols. (1809–28)
STC, 1475–1640	A. W. Pollard, G. R. Redgrave, and others, eds., *A short-title catalogue of . . . English books . . . 1475–1640* (1926); 2nd edn, ed. W. A. Jackson, F. S. Ferguson, and K. F. Pantzer, 3 vols. (1976–91) [see also Wing, *STC*]
STS	Scottish Text Society
SurtS	Surtees Society
Symeon of Durham, *Opera*	*Symeonis monachi opera omnia*, ed. T. Arnold, 2 vols., Rolls Series, 75 (1882–5); repr. (1965)
Tanner, *Bibl. Brit.-Hib.*	T. Tanner, *Bibliotheca Britannico-Hibernica*, ed. D. Wilkins (1748); repr. (1963)
Thieme & Becker, *Allgemeines Lexikon*	U. Thieme, F. Becker, and H. Vollmer, eds., *Allgemeines Lexikon der bildenden Künstler von der Antike bis zur Gegenwart*, 37 vols. (Leipzig, 1907–50); repr. (1961–5), (1983), and (1992)
Thurloe, *State papers*	*A collection of the state papers of John Thurloe*, ed. T. Birch, 7 vols. (1742)
TLS	*Times Literary Supplement*
Tout, *Admin. hist.*	T. F. Tout, *Chapters in the administrative history of mediaeval England: the wardrobe, the chamber, and the small seals*, 6 vols. (1920–33); repr. (1967)
TRHS	*Transactions of the Royal Historical Society*
VCH	H. A. Doubleday and others, eds., *The Victoria history of the counties of England*, [88 vols.] (1900–)
Venn, *Alum. Cant.*	J. Venn and J. A. Venn, *Alumni Cantabrigienses: a biographical list of all known students, graduates, and holders of office at the University of Cambridge, from the earliest times to 1900*, 10 vols. (1922–54); repr. in 2 vols. (1974–8)
Vertue, *Note books*	[G. Vertue], *Note books*, ed. K. Esdaile, earl of Ilchester, and H. M. Hake, 6 vols., Walpole Society, 18, 20, 22, 24, 26, 30 (1930–55)
VF	*Vanity Fair*
Walford, *County families*	E. Walford, *The county families of the United Kingdom, or, Royal manual of the titled and untitled aristocracy of Great Britain and Ireland* (1860)
Walker rev.	A. G. Matthews, *Walker revised: being a revision of John Walker's Sufferings of the clergy during the grand rebellion, 1642–60* (1948); repr. (1988)
Walpole, *Corr.*	*The Yale edition of Horace Walpole's correspondence*, ed. W. S. Lewis, 48 vols. (1937–83)
Ward, *Men of the reign*	T. H. Ward, ed., *Men of the reign: a biographical dictionary of eminent persons of British and colonial birth who have died during the reign of Queen Victoria* (1885); repr. (Graz, 1968)
Waterhouse, *18c painters*	E. Waterhouse, *The dictionary of 18th century painters in oils and crayons* (1981); repr. as *British 18th century painters in oils and crayons* (1991), vol. 2 of *Dictionary of British art*
Watt, *Bibl. Brit.*	R. Watt, *Bibliotheca Britannica, or, A general index to British and foreign literature*, 4 vols. (1824) [many reprs.]
Wellesley index	W. E. Houghton, ed., *The Wellesley index to Victorian periodicals, 1824–1900*, 5 vols. (1966–89); new edn (1999) [CD-ROM]
Wing, *STC*	D. Wing, ed., *Short-title catalogue of . . . English books . . . 1641–1700*, 3 vols. (1945–51); 2nd edn (1972–88); rev. and enl. edn, ed. J. J. Morrison, C. W. Nelson, and M. Seccombe, 4 vols. (1994–8) [see also *STC, 1475–1640*]
Wisden	*John Wisden's Cricketer's Almanack*
Wood, *Ath. Oxon.*	A. Wood, *Athenae Oxonienses . . . to which are added the Fasti*, 2 vols. (1691–2); 2nd edn (1721); new edn, 4 vols., ed. P. Bliss (1813–20); repr. (1967) and (1969)
Wood, *Vic. painters*	C. Wood, *Dictionary of Victorian painters* (1971); 2nd edn (1978); 3rd edn as *Victorian painters*, 2 vols. (1995), vol. 4 of *Dictionary of British art*
WW	*Who's who* (1849–)
WWBMP	M. Stenton and S. Lees, eds., *Who's who of British members of parliament*, 4 vols. (1976–81)
WWW	*Who was who* (1929–)

Freud, Anna (1895–1982), psychoanalyst, was born on 3 December 1895 at Berggasse 19, Vienna, the third daughter and sixth and youngest child of Sigmund *Freud (1856–1939), the founder of psychoanalysis, and his wife, Martha (1861–1951), daughter of Berman Bernays and his wife, Emmeline. Both of Anna's parents were Jewish, but did not have any formal religious affiliations.

Education and influences When Anna was a year old the family was joined by her widowed aunt, Minna, a woman of intellectual inclinations who, unlike Martha, was interested in Freud's developing theories and liked to discuss them with him. But, for the children, as Freud himself observed, there were now, in effect, two mothers, each with distinct family roles. A Roman Catholic nursemaid, Josefine Cihlarz, warm and empathic, took an active part in the care of the three youngest children—Anna, Ernst, and Sophie. Anna felt very close, even special, to Josefine, who was very fond not only of children but of animals too: Anna was an animal lover all her life and came to share her father's particular love of dogs. The children's upbringing was firm but lenient, and disciplined behaviour and punctuality were stressed. Sigmund Freud was an affectionate father whose love and understanding of children are also reflected in his writings. Anna was deeply attached to him and remained so throughout her life.

After private elementary schooling starting at six, when she encountered antisemitism, Anna entered the Salka Goldman Cottage Lyceum (for girls) at the age of ten. In this she followed her sisters; they were not sent to the *Gymnasium*—the more likely course had a university education been envisaged for them. But Anna Freud was precocious in her ability to learn and understand, and had excellent results in all her subjects. Much of her learning was stimulated at home, where she seems to have thrived in the intellectual atmosphere surrounding her father with his highly gifted friends. Though otherwise often bored, she read a great deal, wrote poetry, and, like her father, had a remarkable memory that remained at her service all her life (she never forgot the details of any case, whether treated by her or reported by others). Sigmund Freud did not hold medical training in high regard and did not envisage it for either his sons or daughters. Anna, whose interest in psychoanalysis was evident at the age of fourteen when her father introduced her to its complexities, and who subsequently was allowed to listen to the clinical papers and discussions held every Wednesday evening, came to share her father's view (later strongly expressed in *The Question of Lay Analysis*, 1926) that medical training did nothing to prepare the student for the unique circumstances of analytic practice.

In 1914 Anna took a holiday in England but became an enemy alien when war broke out. She returned to Vienna by a circuitous route after many adventures, finally travelling with the Austrian ambassador. In the autumn she returned to the lyceum and applied her abundant energy and keen intelligence to work as an apprentice elementary school teacher, qualifying six years later and joining the school staff. She remained an exemplary teacher—in the widest sense—all her life. In the autumn of 1918 she began an analysis with her father and in 1922 read a formal paper to the Viennese Psychoanalytic Society to become an accredited member. As such she attended the International Psychoanalytic Congress of Psychoanalysis held in Berlin in October 1922, though this was not her first visit to the German capital.

The analysis of one family member by another, or even by a close friend, later became unacceptable. Yet in 1918 Freud did not set a precedent: both Carl Jung and Karl Abraham had analysed their young daughters, and Melanie Klein analysed her sons Erich and Hans, as well as her daughter Melitta, though she was very discreet about these undertakings. Unlike Freud, however, she published their analyses, albeit under pseudonyms. No records exist of Freud's analysis of Anna. But, other considerations aside, Freud was clearly aware of the difficulties attendant on such arrangements, and these would have attracted adverse comment from others even at that time. Freud's decision seems to have been influenced by a number of practical problems, including the fact that the analysts in whom he had the greatest confidence were not in Vienna (where Anna Freud was teaching) but in Berlin and Budapest. Furthermore, the Freud family's financial circumstances were straitened at this time. The difficulties included, *inter alia*, Anna's idealization of him, which he did not consider an asset. But in spite of all these complexities Freud counted the analysis a success.

In 1921 Sigmund Freud invited Lou Andreas-Salomé, a woman of quite outstanding intellect and a friend of Rilke and Nietzsche, to stay at his home, and although her first visit was short she became warmly attached to Anna, and a quasi-analytic relationship developed between them and continued in and outside Berggasse 19. Andreas-Salomé was an analyst of many years' experience and Anna learned a great deal from her, as Freud himself gratefully acknowledged. The impression that Andreas-Salomé was indeed Anna's analyst was widely held, even though some of Freud's colleagues knew that he had analysed her. In 1924, at Freud's suggestion, Anna's analysis with him was restarted. Both participants were more aware of, and prepared for, attendant problems, and Anna Freud tackled this second phase with vigour and enthusiasm. An informative discussion of these analyses, including the role of Andreas-Salomé, is given by Young-Bruehl (1988).

Child psychoanalysis Anna Freud's school career stood her in good stead for her pioneering work in child psychoanalysis. Melanie Klein, in Berlin, had already started to work in the field before moving to England in 1927 to join the British Psycho-Analytical Society at the invitation of the president, Ernest Jones. In England she became extremely influential, and though both leaders in child analysis employed a play technique with their younger patients, Klein, unlike Anna Freud, regarded this as the equivalent of free association in adults. This difference and others that became greatly intensified by the early 1930s led her to become a lifelong opponent of Anna Freud's psychoanalytic views and techniques. Exchange visits between the two capitals were arranged in an effort to resolve the differences, without appreciable success.

Anna Freud's clinical approach to children, her intellectual appeal and clarity of expression, together with her personal charm, quickly attracted a large following, and her seminars with other Viennese analysts were joined by colleagues from Prague and Budapest. Her work with pathological states of all kinds was balanced by her studies of normative development. She applied her findings to the practice of education, gave lectures on the subject to parents and teachers, and later set up with her friend and colleague Dorothy Burlingham (1891–1979) the Jackson Nurseries, for the physical and psychological care of the poorest children in Vienna. This paved the way for her future interest in paediatrics and the psychological concomitants and sequelae of physical illness in children. Her work with adults catalysed her wish to know more about adult psychiatry, and she regularly attended ward rounds at the university's psychiatric clinic, headed by the Nobel prizewinner Julius Wagner von Jauregg. She continued to publish papers, and her first book, *The Ego and the Mechanisms of Defence*, was published in English in 1937, following the German edition of 1936, which she presented to her father on his eightieth birthday. It remains a major work. It distinguishes, for the first time, between instinctual drive derivatives (already recognized), and defences against painful affects (feelings and emotions), which she had freshly discovered and described.

Anna Freud in England In 1938 the Nazis entered Vienna, and the Freud family and some of Freud's associates obtained exit visas through the good offices of Princess Marie Bonaparte of Greece (an analysand of Freud's and a family friend), while Ernest Jones secured entry permits into England. Freud was by then far from well: his cancer of the jaw was of many years' standing and he had undergone many operations. The British Psycho-Analytical Society bought a house for the family at 20 Maresfield Gardens, Hampstead, London, and Anna Freud nursed her father until his death in September of the following year. Martha Freud died there in 1951, and Anna Freud and Dorothy Burlingham remained there.

The arrival in England of the Viennese group, though welcome, sharpened the hitherto minor divisions within the British Psycho-Analytical Society, and it was clear that the differences between Anna Freud and Melanie Klein, the two leaders of child analysis, extended into the treatment of adults. The strength of disagreement led to a series of Controversial Discussions held between 1941 and 1945; the differences were never resolved, but the debate, often bitter, ended in a compromise whereby two separate training groups were organized. A split in the society, though threatened, was averted. The discussions showed plainly that there were now three broad groups of opinion: Kleinian, Freudian, and those who disagreed in some respects with both but were unprepared to accept that the differences were sufficiently important to justify a formal division. Anna Freud invariably adopted a polite, if firm, tone, and told her Viennese colleagues to keep in mind

that they were visitors, if not guests. She and her colleagues considered that Melanie Klein's views were antithetical to basic Freudian principles, but it was left to Edward Glover to make the most forceful criticisms without mincing words. The fact that Klein's daughter, Melitta Schmideberg, spoke strongly against her mother's views did nothing to help the atmosphere, nor did the fact that she was analysed by Glover help to soften the tone. For her part Klein considered that she, and not Anna Freud, was Sigmund Freud's true successor. Glover resigned from the society while the discussions were still unfinished, but Anna Freud refused to follow him.

In London, Anna Freud pursued all her old interests, but, following the outbreak of war, she was deeply concerned by the plight of children made homeless by bombing, and established the residential war nurseries in Hampstead, with a branch in the country for older children. All were carefully tended and observed by a loyal residential staff. Detailed reports of this work by Anna Freud and Dorothy Burlingham are models of clarity and meticulous observation which graphically describe revolutionary findings about child residential care. They are collected in *Young Children in Wartime* (1942) and *Infants without Families* (1944). At the end of the war many of the staff sought further training. A course in child analysis was instituted in 1947, followed in 1952 by the foundation of the Hampstead Child Therapy Clinic, to which the course became indissolubly linked. Anna Freud's work on child development, normal and abnormal, was now greatly extended, further informed, and vitally reinforced by the new facilities, which were soon the most extensive and comprehensive anywhere in the world, and resulted in a mass of important publications, many of which stemmed from the staff's own clinical research. None of this would have been possible without Anna Freud's extraordinary capacity to engage others and fire them with enthusiasm and resolve. It was largely on account of these qualities that so much was achieved at Hampstead. Many of the developmental and analytic principles arrived at through this extensive work resulted in Anna Freud's most important book, *Normality and Pathology in Childhood* (1965). Her voluminous writings reflected a vast field of study and investigation, including new and striking methods of psychoanalytic diagnosis and child assessment. Her contributions in the fields of education, paediatrics, and family law (collaborating with professors Joseph Goldstein and Albert Solnit of Yale University) won her many honours. She was appointed CBE in 1967, and was awarded many honorary doctorates and fellowships. She was especially proud of the MD which she received from the University of Vienna in 1975, and the PhD in 1981 from the Goethe Institute in Frankfurt where, fifty years before, her father had received the Goethe prize for literature.

Anna Freud's devotion to her father was unswerving, and she defended his basic theoretical principles throughout her life. However, she never followed him blindly, and rarely, if at all, spoke of the 'death instinct', preferring terms like 'destructive drive' or 'inborn aggression'; and when, at a Hampstead public meeting, a paper was read which called for significant revision of some of Freud's views on sexual development in girls, she opened the discussion by saying: 'Well! To think we have been so wrong about this for so long!'

Anna Freud's remarkable ability to draw her students and staff into her investigations, to encourage them to work on their own ideas rather than those of others, often helped them to discover resources they did not always know they possessed. It was only possible to appreciate the compelling force of these qualities if one met them face to face. She took a close interest in the welfare of her staff and kept herself unobtrusively aware of their personal problems. Although each member came to know her, often in a different way, she was, for all that, a very private person and there were limits beyond which few cared to trespass. But she would share her jokes with them and made many a point through a telling, and sometimes disconcerting, wit. When, at a diagnostic conference held at a time when the miniskirt was fashionable, a new staff member sat in the front row displaying a rather daring length of leg, the diagnostician was describing a small boy whose intense curiosity was troubling his family. The meeting was told that the boy was in the habit of repeatedly trying to get beneath his mother's skirts. 'The time is rapidly coming', said Anna Freud, 'when a child won't have much trouble doing *that*.' But she was rarely unkind in public; and her rather rare silence during discussion was the most discomforting evidence of her strong disapproval.

Leisure interests and appearance For all her major contributions to psychoanalysis, Anna Freud was a woman of wide interests. She was a keen horsewoman, and Dorothy Burlingham bought her a new horse for her seventieth birthday. She loved the Irish countryside, loved discovering new delights whether coastal or inland, and was devoted to the cottage owned by the two women in co. Cork. She was very popular there and loved by many who knew nothing of psychoanalysis. She enjoyed poetry in both German and English, and was particularly fond of Kipling. Detective novels were her favourite leisure reading, and she housed a substantial collection in both London and west Cork. She loved embroidery and crochet work, was an expert with a loom, and made the stair carpet for the Irish cottage. She knitted all her life, taught to do so by Josefine. Following Dorothy Burlingham's death in 1979 Alice Colonna took leave from the Child Study Center in Yale to keep Anna Freud company.

In both dress and appearance Anna Freud was almost timeless. She invariably wore a dirndl—the traditional long-skirted country dress—and blouse, both handmade with her usual skill, wore her straight hair in a simple bob, had enquiring eyes, and possessed an expressive warmth unimpaired by a measure of personal reserve. Anyone who spoke to her was sure of her exclusive attention. She aged almost imperceptibly until the last few years of her life. By 1981 she was already too ill to collect her Frankfurt award in person, being increasingly debilitated by a refractory anaemia of old age. She died at home on 9 October 1982. Her body was cremated at Golders Green crematorium on the 13th, when her ashes, appropriately, were put next to her father's.   CLIFFORD YORKE

Sources personal knowledge (2004) · E. Young-Bruehl, *Anna Freud: a biography* (1988) · E. Jones, *Sigmund Freud: life and work*, 3 vols. (1953–7) · private information (2004) · P. King and R. Steiner, eds., *The Freud–Klein controversies, 1941–1945* (1991)
Archives Freud Museum, London, corresp. and MSS · L. Cong., MSS | FILM BFI NFTVA, Freud, 1930–39
Likenesses photograph, Institute of Psychoanalysis, London · photograph, repro. in *The Times* (11 Oct 1982)
Wealth at death £335,980: probate, 5 Jan 1983, *CGPLA Eng. & Wales*

Freud, Sigmund (1856–1939), founder of psychoanalysis, was born on 6 May 1856 at Freiberg, Moravia, in the Austro-Hungarian empire (later Príbor, Czech republic), the first of the seven surviving children of Jacob Freud (1815–1896), wool trader, and his second wife, Amalie (1835–1931), daughter of Jacob Nathansohn and his wife, Sara. His parents were both Jewish and Freud himself went to London as a refugee in 1938.

Childhood and adolescence The Freud family occupied one large room on the first floor of a house owned by a blacksmith. His father, at one point registered as a wool merchant, made what must have been a somewhat precarious living through trade of various kinds. His mother was an attractive and strong-minded woman and by all accounts her love for Sigmund, the first-born of her eight children, was boundless. There followed two more boys, one of whom died at six months, and five girls, whose arrival stirred up intense jealousy in Freud. Freud's position in the family was unusual in that he also had two grown-up half-brothers from his father's first marriage, one of whom had a young son, so that Freud was born an uncle. This nephew, John, was Freud's closest child companion and rival. Freud remarked, in *The Interpretation of Dreams*, that his characteristic warm friendships as well as his enmities with contemporaries went back to this early relationship (Freud, *Interpretation*, 483). The two half-brothers and the young boy emigrated to Manchester at the end of Freud's third year, stimulating in him early thoughts of moving to England himself, which he was eventually to do some eighty years later.

Meanwhile, in 1860, when Freud was four, in common with many other Jews of the Austro-Hungarian empire at that time the family moved to Vienna in the wake of a recent liberalization of policy which gave Jews equal political rights and abolished ghettos. Although the family were largely non-observing Jews, ready to assimilate into Viennese society, and all his life Freud was himself an atheist, Jewishness in its religious, cultural, and political aspects was a lifelong preoccupation of his and very much a part of his identity.

The family settled in Leopoldstadt, a mainly Jewish part of the city, where they lived in straitened conditions. Little is known of these first years in Vienna and Freud's early schooling. Although it is unclear quite how Jacob Freud earned a living once there, the family seems to have

Sigmund Freud (1856–1939), by Max Halberstadt, 1921

been able to make ends meet. Freud's education at the excellent local *Gymnasium*, which he entered in 1865, proceeded without interruption and he received a classical education. He was consistently head of the class. He and his schoolfriend Eduard Silberstein, who remained a lifelong friend, formed their own 'Spanish Academy' with an exclusive membership of two, which involved corresponding in self-taught Spanish through which they divulged to each other their thoughts, fantasies, and preoccupations and developed a sort of private mythology. Their correspondence continued from Freud's mid-teens to his mid-twenties, stopping about the time that he met his future wife.

Freud's early biography is of fundamental significance to the history of psychoanalysis, as, through his own rigorous self-analysis—which he was to conduct from the mid-1890s—he effectively made himself the subject of the first psychoanalytic case-history. Freud makes thinly disguised references to his personal experience throughout his psychoanalytical writings, most notably in *Die Traumdeutung* (1900), published in English as *The Interpretation of Dreams*. A less intimately personal account is his *Selbstdarstellung* ('Autobiographical study', 1925), which was commissioned as part of a series of self-portraits by men of science, and focuses on his professional development. In a postscript of 1935 he writes: 'The story of my life and the history of psychoanalysis … are intimately interwoven … no personal experiences of mine are of any interest in comparison to my relations with that science' (p. 71). In fact Freud's most personal experience was inevitably bound up with psychoanalysis, while it is true that

outwardly his private life, typical of a bourgeois doctor, appears unremarkable.

Studies in medicine, neurology, and psychiatry In spite of the family's financial situation Freud was left by his father to make his own choice of career. He began his medical studies at Vienna University in 1873, availing himself of the considerable degree of academic freedom afforded by the curriculum to explore a variety of areas. His interest gravitated towards scientific research at the outset. He chose to supplement his studies with research in the laboratories of faculty members, undertaking such research for Ernst Brücke, a congenial teacher of physiology and histology, and he remained at Brücke's laboratory for six years. Beginning with studies of nerve cell structure in the *Petromyzon*, a primitive species of fish, and progressing to human anatomy and a minute study of the medulla oblongata, he established a solid reputation as a specialist in brain anatomy and pathology. In addition to Brücke himself, who was for Freud something of a father figure, Brücke's laboratory brought the young Freud into contact with distinguished colleagues. It was at Brücke's that Freud made the acquaintance of Dr Josef Breuer, another father figure whose personal support and professional collaboration he later acknowledged as crucial to the foundation of psychoanalysis.

It was during this period that Freud made his first long-awaited journey to England in 1875 to visit his half-brothers in Manchester, and which he acknowledged, seven years later, in a letter to his fiancée, as a decisive influence. He had dreamed of England since boyhood and had acquired an insatiable appetite for English literature, especially Shakespeare and Dickens. The trip stimulated renewed yearnings to settle there himself. Jacob Freud had hoped this stay with cousins more successful in business than himself would stimulate in Freud some enthusiasm in that line, but Freud was nurturing fantasies of pursuing a scientific career in England, for all its 'fog and rain, drunkenness and conservatism' (*Letters to … Silberstein*, 127). As a result of the excursion and his encounter with the consistent empiricism in the English scientific writings of the likes of John Tyndall, Thomas Huxley, Charles Lyell, and Charles Darwin, his own interests became more sharply focused. Correspondingly he declared himself increasingly wary of metaphysics and philosophy (ibid., 128).

Freud's studies were interrupted by military service in 1879–80, during which he translated four essays by John Stuart Mill for the German edition of the collected works. After receiving his medical qualification in 1881 he pursued his research at Brücke's laboratory, having been given a temporary post. In 1882 Freud suddenly left Brücke's laboratory and began to set himself up to pursue a clinical career, which afforded the eventual prospect of financial security by going into private practice. Significantly, the change of direction coincided with Freud's falling in love with Martha Bernays (*b.* 1861), his future wife, the daughter of an observing Jewish family well known in Hamburg. There followed a four-year engagement, during which he wrote his fiancée 900 letters while struggling to establish himself financially in keeping with conventional expectation.

In the meantime Freud somewhat belatedly began a three-year residency at the Viennese General Hospital, an internationally renowned teaching centre where the heads of department were almost invariably pre-eminent in their fields. Although Freud's career was full of promise during this period, the prospect of becoming materially secure remained remote and he was searching for new discoveries so as to make his name. One such project was concerned with the applications of cocaine, then new and relatively unknown. In 1884 Freud published an enthusiastic paper based on his experiments on himself and others. Unfortunately it was left to a contemporary, Koller, whose attention Freud had drawn to cocaine's anaesthetic qualities, to complete an investigation into such use in eye surgery and so to claim the considerable credit for the discovery.

In July 1885, a month after being appointed to the academic post of *privat-docent*, Freud left for Paris on a travelling scholarship to study at the Salpêtrière Hospital under the celebrated neurologist Jean-Martin Charcot. In contrast to the Viennese psychiatric approach Freud had so far encountered, which was concerned with physical symptoms and family pathology with little attempt to identify causes, Charcot was developing bold concepts for understanding neurosis through observing patients, in particular hysterics, with a view to characterizing disorders and establishing their aetiology. The trip to Paris was of fundamental significance to Freud's intellectual and professional development. Having arrived there primarily preoccupied with his anatomical researches, by the time of his return to Vienna his interest had turned, through Charcot's influence, to psychopathology and the applications of hypnosis.

In the wake of his formative experience in Paris, Freud gave addresses to the Vienna Medical Society championing Charcot's views on hysteria and hypnosis. These presentations met with cool receptions, to Freud's great disappointment. There was widespread scepticism concerning hypnosis and it is quite possible that Freud's youthful idealization of his French master may have rankled with his senior colleagues, reinforcing Freud's consistently held view of himself as an outsider embattled with the medical establishment.

Marriage and early career Soon after his return from Paris, Freud set himself up in private practice as a consultant in nervous diseases, of which hysteria was one of the most important. Referrals came in particular from his older friend and benefactor Breuer, with whom he was later to collaborate. After years of relative poverty, Freud had generated enough income to marry Martha Bernays on 13 September 1886 at Wandsbeck, just outside Hamburg. The couple settled down to a domestic regime typical of a Viennese doctor's family and Martha had six children, three boys and three girls, within eight years. The household also included Martha's unmarried sister, Minna, who was able to provide Freud with intellectual companionship through the initial years of relative isolation.

During the first years of married life in addition to his private practice Freud was director of neurology at the Institute for Children's Diseases, where he continued his work on brain neurology in addition to clinical duties with neurological patients, enabling him to support his young family while he pursued his greater interest in clinical psychopathology through his private practice of neurotic patients. Of the neurological papers he published as a result of the neurological post one in particular foreshadows his later work. 'Zur Auffassung der Aphasien: eine kritische Studie' ('On aphasia', 1891) reviewed the existing literature, criticizing its mechanical approach and reliance on brain mythology, which attributed mental functioning to particular parts of the brain, proposing instead a subtle relationship between anatomy and psychology.

The 'talking cure' Freud's treatment of patients by hypnosis continued for a decade after his visit to Paris, although he became increasingly aware of its limitations. A fundamental shift in his thinking evolved following his re-encounter with a case history which his older friend Breuer had related to him as early as 1882. Breuer had been treating an intelligent and lively minded young woman, known as Anna O., whose severely debilitating symptoms included paralysis, loss of speech, and a nervous cough. Taking his lead from the patient Breuer developed a cathartic method, which the patient herself called a 'talking cure'. Freud managed to persuade Breuer to revive the method, by which the doctor–patient relationship had effectively been transformed from one of passivity on the part of the hypnotized patient receiving suggestions from the doctor aimed at ridding the patient of the symptom, to that of a patient actively talking in a self-induced trance to a doctor who received information while the patient simultaneously relieved herself of the symptom, which emerged as the product of some early trauma which had not been resolved.

Implicit in the cathartic method which Freud adopted to treat his own patients were several concepts which were to be at the heart of psychoanalytic thinking: namely, that patients were suffering from 'reminiscences'—there was a causal link between hysterical symptoms and psychological trauma; that the traumatic experience had been rendered unconscious through repression, yet continued to make its presence felt; and that the unconscious experience could be made conscious, bringing relief to the patient.

An account of the case of Anna O. was eventually published by Freud and Breuer in *Studien über Hysterie* ('Studies on hysteria', 1895). Breuer had been consistently reticent about the Anna O. case, which contained elements which he found personally embarrassing, and it was left to the intrepid younger man to explore the implications of the new method which had presented itself as a viable alternative to hypnosis. It was not until 1896 that Freud used the term 'psychoanalysis'.

Freud widened the scope of the treatment by taking an interest in anything a patient might have to say, rather than inviting an account of the symptoms. Freud named this process free association and its encouragement was the object of the enduring fundamental rule of psycho-analysis, whereby a patient is asked to say whatever comes to mind. With the advent of free association came the demise of the last vestige of the hypnotic method, as Freud now refrained from applying gentle pressure to the patient's head during treatment. The setting for psycho-analysis later recommended by Freud, where the patient reclines comfortably while the analyst sits out of sight, was designed to facilitate free association. The request to patients to associate freely threw into relief resistance, a term which Freud used interchangeably with defence at that time. Listening to patients' accounts Freud became convinced that the traumas which lay behind hysterical symptoms had their origins in infancy and he was struck by their sexual content.

Family, friends, and colleagues Freud's last daughter, Anna *Freud, was born in 1895, the year of the publication with Breuer of *Studien über Hysterie*. His father died in the follow-ing year. Although he found pleasure in fatherhood and in the family home created by Martha Freud, there was no real intellectual outlet for Freud as he struggled to develop a theoretical framework for psychoanalysis and subjected himself to the emotional strain of a lengthy self-analysis. Freud's friendship with Breuer had been faltering since the late 1880s and eventually broke down, largely because Breuer was unwilling to concur with Freud's firm convic-tion about the sexual aetiology of hysteria. It was Wilhelm Fliess, a talented but ultimately discredited Berlin general practitioner, who fulfilled Freud's need for a friend, confi-dant, and critic. Fliess was closer in age to Freud and unlike Breuer could not be shocked by Freud's more auda-cious speculations. The relationship quickly developed a great intensity and the two kept up an intimate corres-pondence for fifteen years from 1887 to 1902 which sheds light on the otherwise obscure evolution of Freud's think-ing at that time and on his concurrent self-analysis. It was in a long letter to Fliess written in 1895 that Freud set out his portentous 'Project for a scientific psychology' with a view to integrating mental and physical phenomena within a single theoretical schema. Freud began work on the 'Project' in the late summer of 1895 in a rush of cre-ativity following one of his 'congresses' with Fliess. His ambition was to set out a psychology firmly grounded in neurology and biology, which he referred to as his 'Psych-ology for neurologists'. Freud likened the task to an exhausting but exhilarating mountain climb, during which more peaks to be conquered kept appearing. Exhil-aration soon gave way to frustration and dejection how-ever, and by November he wrote to Fliess that he could 'no longer understand the mental state in which I hatched the Psychology' (Freud, 'Project for a scientific psychology', 1895, 152). The undeniably abstruse draft survives only among Fliess's papers, and Freud makes no mention of this momentous effort in his autobiographical accounts. It was published posthumously in English in 1954, four years after publication in German, having been rescued from Fliess's papers by Marie Bonaparte following his

death in 1931, and edited by James *Strachey (*Standard Edi-tion*, vol. 1). As Strachey points out in his editor's introduc-tion Freud clearly regarded this ostensibly neurological work as a failure. Although it cannot be said to constitute the foundation of psychoanalytic theory as such, it con-tained the seeds of many ideas elaborated in his later psychological writings, for example drive theory, repres-sion, and an economy of mind based on mental conflict.

Freud's friendship with Fliess was destined to collapse amid recriminations, with Fliess alleging that Freud had appropriated his ideas on inherent bisexuality without acknowledgement. Ten years later Freud's friendship with Jung was also to end acrimoniously, with Jung's ques-tioning of the sexual origins of neurosis at the centre of the dispute. Long before the split with Jung, and in the period preceding his violent quarrel with Fliess in 1900, Freud reflected on the nature of his relationships to con-temporaries, which he linked to his intensely ambivalent attachment to his nephew John, who had moved to Eng-land when Freud was three.

> My emotional life has always insisted that I should have an intimate friend and a hated enemy. I have always been able to provide myself afresh with both, and it has not infrequently happened that the ideal situation of childhood has been so completely reproduced that friend and enemy have come together in a single individual—though not, of course, both at once or with constant oscillations, as may have been the case in my early childhood. (Freud, *Interpretation*, 483)

Fortunately for Freud this easily discernible pattern of tur-bulent relationships prone to eventual breakdown was restricted to close male colleagues. His family relation-ships and other friendships were contrastingly consistent and loyal. It was no coincidence that the professional dis-agreements which caused these intimate friendships to break down were concerned with Freud's insistence on the centrality of sexuality. Sexuality represented to Freud the direct and essential instinctual link between psych-ology and biology, without which he would find himself caught up in the dichotomy of mind and body which he was desperate to avoid.

Establishment of psychoanalysis Later in his career Freud recalled the 1890s as years in an intellectual wilderness. His papers on hysteria had not won the respect of the medical establishment and he was aware of his Jewish-ness in that largely Catholic milieu. In addition Freud had confessed his own surprise that 'the case histories I write should read like short stories and that, as one might say, they lack the serious stamp of science' (*Standard Edition*, 2.160).

Until the late 1890s Freud's observations of the infantile and sexual origins of hysteria had led him to believe, through listening to his patients' accounts, that his patients had fallen ill as a result of childhood sexual abuse by adults. In 1897 he modified this theory of actual child-hood seduction and proposed instead that these accounts were often derived from infantile sexual fantasies and therefore belonged in the realm of the patient's own psy-chic reality and were not, as he had previously thought, necessarily objective facts. To Freud children were no longer assumed to be innocents in a world of adult sexuality: they possessed sexual feelings and wishes of their own which were liable to repression, elaboration, and distortion during development. This shift in Freud's thinking has proved enduringly controversial. Critics have argued that patients' experiences have been denied through their reassignment by Freud to subjective reality and that he changed tack in this way only because he shied away from alienating bourgeois Vienna by reporting widespread sexual abuse in its families. In fact, Freud never denied the reality of child sexual abuse, and it was his attribution of sexual feelings to children which most shocked his contemporaries. Freud was not to be deterred from his line of enquiry. Indeed the cynicism of his medical contemporaries and outrage from members of the wider public seem to have acted as a spur to new vistas opening up. In addition to setting the scene for the detailed exposition of human development, for example in the later *Drei Abhandlungen zur Sexualtheorie* ('Three essays on the theory of sexuality', 1905), the recasting of the aetiology of hysteria in the light of childhood sexuality paved the way to a more general understanding of the role of impulse and desire in the human mind, rendered unconscious through repression.

With the publication of *Die Traumdeutung* in 1900 Freud decisively challenged the accepted limits of scientific psychology, by bringing mental phenomena generally considered beyond the pale, such as dreams, imagination, and fantasy, into the fold. The leitmotif which runs throughout the book is that dreams represent the disguised fulfilment of repressed infantile wishes and that as such 'the interpretation of dreams is the royal road to a knowledge of the unconscious activities of the mind' (Freud, *Interpretation*, 608).

Freud stated at the outset that his theory of dreams was generally applicable and not restricted to neurotic patients. Indeed, his curiosity about the nature of dreams had been aroused during his self-analysis and the bulk of the illustrative material was trawled from his own dreams and autobiographical material, along with dreams of friends and children. It was in *The Interpretation of Dreams* that Freud, drawing characteristically on his classical schooling, introduced the Oedipus complex, which asserts the universal desire of a child for the parent of the opposite sex and consequent hatred of the parent of the same sex, which must be resolved through repression in order for normal development to proceed. Although sales were slow and a second edition was not needed until 1909, Freud's explorations of normal psychological functioning did stimulate interest in a wider public.

At the time of writing his dream book Freud was planning other studies of normal psychological processes which would none the less plumb the depths of the psyche, namely *Zur Psychopathologie des Alltagslebens* ('The psychopathology of everyday life', 1901), which explored the unconscious meaning of everyday slips of the tongue and bungled actions, and *Der Witz und seine Beziehung zum Unbewussten* ('Jokes and their relation to the unconscious',

1905) for which he drew on his repertoire of 'profound Jewish stories'.

The early years of the century also saw the publication of the first of five substantial case histories which read rather like novellas, the case of Dora, under the title *Fragment of an Analysis of a Case of Hysteria* (1905 [1901]). The most important insight from the analysis of Dora, which broke down when the young woman left, came to Freud with hindsight. In a postscript, Freud reviews the analysis in the light of transference. The phenomenon of transference, whereby any individual's experience of early relationships is the blueprint for later relationships, had already been discussed in the *Studies on Hysteria* (1895) in terms of an unconscious false connection on the part of the patient between the physician and some earlier figure. Now, reflecting on Dora's inability to continue with her analysis, Freud became aware of the implications of the understanding of transference as a key factor in the therapeutic process of psychoanalysis: 'Transference, which seems ordained to be the greatest obstacle to psychoanalysis, becomes its most powerful ally, if its presence can be detected each time and explained to the patient' (*Standard Edition*, 7.117).

During this period Freud's home life remained settled. As his financial situation improved he was able to indulge his two great interests: Mediterranean travel and collecting antiquities, another natural consequence of a youth steeped in the classics. He also found time to follow the exciting archaeological discoveries being made at the time, and often cited archaeological excavation as a metaphor for psychoanalytic work, with its interest in painstakingly uncovering hidden layers and origins. In 1907 Freud made the first trip to England since his inspirational visit aged nineteen. He spent a fortnight visiting Manchester relatives who showed him Blackpool and Southport before he departed for London. He returned full of praise for the architecture and people, having seen the Egyptian antiquities at the British Museum. It was not until the hasty move to London in 1938 that Freud once again found himself in his childhood dreamland.

Freud's interests beyond the consulting room and the application of psychoanalytic theory to new areas became increasingly apparent in his writings in the years preceding the First World War. Greek literature had already yielded the Oedipus story and there followed other forays into literature and art history, with *Der Wahn und die Träume in W. Jensen's 'Gradiva'* ('Delusions and dreams in Jensen's "Gradiva"', 1907) and *Eine Kindheitserinnerung des Leonardo da Vinci* ('Leonardo da Vinci and a memory of his childhood', 1910). In *Totem und Tabu* ('Totem and taboo', 1913), Freud applied psychoanalysis to anthropological material for the first time.

The psychoanalytic movement As a *privat-docent* and from 1902 a professor extraordinarius Freud was entitled to lecture at Vienna University. These lectures attracted a small group of followers composed of both laymen and doctors. From 1902 onwards they met as the Wednesday Psychological Society, which evolved into the Vienna Psychoanalytical Society in 1908. In the meantime, to his great satisfaction, Freud's reputation began to spread beyond Vienna and he began to attract interest from foreigners, among them the well-known psychiatrist Eugen Bleuler and his young assistant Carl Jung. Others included Karl Abraham and Max Eitington, also from the Burghölzli Clinic in Switzerland, who unlike Jung were to remain loyal disciples, the Hungarian Sándor Ferenczi, and the Welshman (Alfred) Ernest *Jones, Freud's future biographer and the founder of the British Psycho-Analytical Society.

The year after the Vienna Psychoanalytical Society was founded Freud made his only trip to the United States to give a series of well-received lectures (*Five Lectures on Psycho-Analysis*, in *Standard Edition*, vol. 11) at the invitation of Clark University, Massachusetts, accompanied by Jung, Ferenczi, and Jones. The spread of psychoanalysis gained momentum and new societies were formed on the model of the Viennese. An international association was established in 1908, uniting the various groups and promising a structure which Freud hoped would facilitate the perpetuation of psychoanalysis through training. Inevitably psychoanalytic politics were in the air and Freud found himself at the centre of rivalries, jealousies, and dissenting views between individuals and groupings, notably his original Viennese colleagues and the Zürich analysts, whom he was felt to favour. Disagreements led to defection by some members, most significantly by Alfred Adler and Jung, whom Freud had thought of as his successor. In an attempt to protect the essence of psychoanalysis from distortion a 'secret committee' was formed, at the suggestion of Ernest Jones, which was intended to provide a secure setting within which theory and technique could be discussed among an inner circle of loyal colleagues which consisted of Ernest Jones, Sándor Ferenczi, Karl Abraham, Hanns Sachs, Otto Rank, and, later, Max Eitington. Although the committee met into the 1920s, its conspiratorial air set an unfortunate tone for the future functioning and reputation of the profession.

Further developments Inevitably the First World War interrupted Freud's well-established working routine. His three sons, Martin, Ernst (father of the writer and broadcaster Clement Freud and the painter Lucian Freud), and Oliver were all in active service and the real possibility of losses within the family had to be faced. Patients stopped coming, and the international psychoanalytical movement's activities came to a halt. Freud was left more time for private study, which proved very productive. There were papers which resulted from reflections on the war itself, for example 'Zeitgemässes über Krieg und Tod' ('Thought for the times on war and death'). The Vienna University lectures delivered during the war were published as the *Vorlesungen zur Einführung in die Psychoanalyse* ('Introductory lectures on psychoanalysis', 1916–17); of particular significance were his *Papers on Metapsychology* (*Standard Edition*, vol. 14), of which only five of an original twelve have survived. Dealing with five fundamental themes of psychoanalysis they are 'On narcissism', 'Instincts and their vicissitudes', 'Repression' (all 1915), 'The unconscious', and 'Mourning and melancholia' (both

1917). Freud went far beyond summing up his theories as they stood in these highly technical papers. In addition to containing new ideas they also hint at numerous revisions which would preoccupy him during the last phase of his career.

By the end of the First World War, Vienna—no longer at the centre of an empire—had become merely the capital of a small, impoverished country. After resuming his private practice Freud took on several British and American patients who proved a useful source of hard currency as a safeguard against soaring inflation. The most serious British interest in Freud came from the members of the Bloomsbury group, in keeping with their characteristic receptiveness to progressive European ideas. Frances Partridge, who lodged with the Stracheys in Gordon Square during their early years as practising analysts, recalled how psychoanalysis was very much part of the Bloomsbury scene, and that she would often recognize patients as they arrived at the house for their sessions. Among the British were the Bloomsbury couple, James *Strachey and Alix *Strachey [*see under* Strachey, James]. Introductions, through Ernest Jones, were eased by the fact that Freud admired the work of James's older brother, Lytton Strachey. Freud took James Strachey into analysis on condition that he begin translating his writings into English. Translating Freud, culminating with the publication of the complete works in twenty-four volumes by Virginia and Leonard Woolf's Hogarth Press, was to occupy Strachey for the rest of his life, and remains the standard text for the extensive scholarship on Freud in English, and for psychoanalysts without German. The Strachey translation has been criticized for its recourse to dry scientific neologisms where Freud made use of plain German. For example, Strachey's term 'cathexis', now well established as a psychoanalytic term, takes the place of Freud's 'Besetzung', a common German word with rich nuances of meaning.

The first international congress following the war was held at The Hague in 1920, which Freud attended in the company of his youngest daughter, Anna, the only one of his children to take an active interest in psychoanalysis, who was now training as an analyst herself and in analysis with her own father. Freud's three sons had survived the war, and the two elder girls, Mathilde and Sophie, were by now married. Disaster struck, though, in 1920, when Sophie, Freud's 'Sunday Child', died suddenly leaving a husband and two small boys. Three years later one of Sophie's children died of tuberculosis in the family's care in Vienna, aged four. Freud took the loss very hard—perhaps, as he reflected in a letter to his writer friend Romain Rolland, because it came soon after the shock of discovering that he was suffering from cancer of the jaw, from which he died some sixteen years later. The cancer, brought about by years of heavy cigar smoking, necessitated thirty-three operations and constant nursing attention from his daughter Anna in an attempt to contain it, and the fitting of an awkward oral prosthesis. Freud was not deterred from smoking cigars, however, and indeed remained convinced of their therapeutic qualities: 'I believe I owe to the cigar a great intensification of my capacity to work and a facilitation of my self control' (Ward, 14). The great majority of photographs of Freud show him holding a cigar. Always the perfect bourgeois, impeccably groomed throughout his life, his once well-filled features lost their softness in later years, probably as much from the illness as ageing. This has no doubt contributed to the popular image of Freud as a stern and distant figure. Less formal photographs and home movies taken on family occasions and holidays, however, convey a more relaxed and accessible family man, although his smile was rarely captured on camera.

Revisions During the 1920s Freud expanded his metapsychological theories. Two key strands can be identified in his thinking from this period onwards: a systematic study of the ego and a preoccupation with cultural and social issues in response to the crisis of humanity during the recent war. At its more speculative, psychoanalytic theory now resembled the philosophical enquiry Freud had eschewed early in his career in favour of scientific methods.

In *Jenseits des Lustprinzips* ('Beyond the pleasure principle', 1920), Freud revised his theory of the instincts by positing a death instinct. Psychic conflict could now be construed in terms of the opposing forces of love and death, as could human behaviour and interaction at large. Broadly speaking the emphasis in his thinking had shifted from the unconscious itself to the phenomenon of resistance, which he understood to exert constant pressure to keep unacceptable desires from surfacing. Freud's interest turned to the ego, the agent of this defensive activity, and to the classification of the defences at the ego's disposal. It no longer made sense to think purely in terms of conscious and unconscious, because in any case the mechanisms of defence employed by the ego were themselves unconscious. This new phase of work on the ego was initiated in *Massenpsychologie und Ich-analyse* ('Group psychology and the analysis of the ego', 1921). Freud then set out an extensively revised tripartite model of the structure and functions of the mind, in *Das Ich und das Es* ('The ego and the id', 1923). The third agency, which he termed the super-ego, was conceived to take into account the crucial internalization of parental authority and prohibition which came about with the dissolution of the Oedipus complex.

Once again new avenues had opened up to Freud as the result of an innovation, for example the possibility of classifying mental illness in terms of its origins in a conflict between parts of the personality. In a brief paper entitled 'Neurosis and psychosis' (1923), Freud offered new clarity with the following formulation: 'Transference neuroses correspond to a conflict between the ego and the id; narcissistic neuroses, to a conflict between the ego and the superego; and psychoses, to a conflict between the ego and the external world' (*Standard Edition*, 19.152). Other rewards reaped by Freud from the new structural theory were the linking of particular defences to specific mental illnesses and new insights into the nature of anxiety (*Hemmung, Symptom und Angst* ('Inhibitions, symptoms and anxiety'), 1926).

Late years Freud continued working in great pain after an initial operation for the cancer in 1923. The international psychoanalytic movement had re-established itself, with important centres elsewhere, for example in Berlin, which was presided over by Freud's disciple, Abraham. Ernest Jones had founded the London Psycho-Analytical Society in 1913, which became the British Psycho-Analytical Society in 1919. The London Institute of Psycho-Analysis was formally founded by Jones in late 1924. An international structure for training was now in place, with a training analysis as its cornerstone, conducted by Freud and a growing number of senior analysts. Among the patients to consult Freud in the mid-1920s was Princess Marie Bonaparte, wife of Prince George of Greece, a woman endowed with a lively intelligence, tremendous energy, and great material wealth. She soon began training as an analyst and went on to become a leading figure in the international movement, a patron of psychoanalysis, and a close friend of the Freud family, who secured their safe passage from Vienna in 1938.

Another woman important to Freud was his youngest child, Anna, who was by now making her name as an analyst and who increasingly acted internationally as her father's ambassador as his illness rendered him more immobile. She represented her father at the 1929 International Congress in Oxford, in difficult circumstances following a dispute with the New York analysts about whether non-medical individuals should be allowed to become analysts. Freud was exasperated, and his deep-seated antagonism to all things American was fuelled. Freud stood firm: he had already tackled this problem in 1926 in response to allegations of quackery made to a lay colleague, arguing that psychoanalysis was more than a mere offshoot of medicine and that its practice should therefore not be restricted in this way (*Die Frage der Laienanalyse*; 'The question of lay analysis', 1926; in Freud, *Standard Edition*, vol. 20).

From the publication of *Die Zukunft einer Illusion* ('The future of an illusion', 1927), which dissected religious belief, Freud's other great *bête noire*, the majority of Freud's writing dealt with cultural and wider social issues. In 1930 came *Das Unbehagen in der Kultur* ('Civilisation and its discontents'), in which he subjected civilization itself to scrutiny, asking, in the light of his experience with neurotics in clinical practice, whether instincts were unduly repressed by society. For Freud these works represented a return to his intellectual beginnings: 'My interest, after making a lifelong détour through the natural sciences, medicine and psychotherapy, returned to cultural problems which had fascinated me long before when I was a youth scarcely old enough for thinking' (*Standard Edition*, 20.72).

In the coming years Freud's consistent refusal to adopt an irrationally optimistic outlook on humanity was justified by the rise to power of Hitler in 1933. Freud's works were among thousands of books ritually burnt in Berlin that year. Freud's terse entry for 12 March 1938 in his *Brief*

Chronicle, a diary of events he kept for the final decade of his life, reads: 'Finis Austriae' (Gay, 229). Despite Chancellor von Schuschnigg's attempt to stave off Hitler through much of the 1930s Austria had been absorbed into the German Reich which in any case was congenial to popular Austrian opinion. Freud, in his eighties and too unwell even to make trips to a summer house in the Vienna suburbs, was now trapped and in fact remained adamant about not leaving. It was only when Anna Freud was briefly arrested by the Gestapo and interrogated that he agreed that the time had come for the family to flee. In a flurry of crisis diplomacy Freud's well-connected friends, Princess Marie Bonaparte, Ernest Jones, and William Bullitt, the American ambassador to Paris, began diplomatic negotiations on his behalf. Three months later bureaucratic obstacles were finally overcome and Freud was able to leave Vienna in the company of Martha, Anna, the housekeeper, a young physician, and his pet chow. Thanks to the princess an extortionate tax raised by the Nazis on Jews' possessions leaving the country could be paid, and all the apartment's contents followed on, including Freud's library and collection of antiquities, which now numbered more than two thousand objects.

Freud in England Freud arrived in London by train on 6 June 1938. His reputation had preceded him to the extent that the train had to be re-routed to another platform at Victoria, so as to avoid the enthusiastic attentions of the press. Freud was greatly heartened by the cordial welcome he received, although he wrote to friends of his sense of alienation resulting from the move and his concern over the worsening state of affairs in Europe. He was particularly anxious about four of his elderly sisters who remained in Vienna, for whom visas were being sought without success. Freud did not live long enough to know that they all perished in the camps.

Although Freud was separated from his sisters the move to London occasioned family reunions. He was now living in the same neighbourhood as his second son, Ernst, already well-established in London as an architect, having left Berlin in the early thirties. Sam Freud, his Manchester cousin, was among the first visitors. Before moving to 20 Maresfield Gardens, Hampstead (later the Freud Museum), the family lived temporarily nearby at 39 Elsworthy Road, backing on to the north side of Primrose Hill. In addition to being deluged with letters from friends, acquaintances, and complete strangers simply wishing to express their support, Freud received a stream of visitors at both addresses, regulated by his wife and daughter, Anna, with his declining health in mind. Although England had brought him respite from external persecution, the cancer was unrelenting and no longer operable by early 1939. Freud was gradually forced to withdraw from his work routine, although he continued to see a small number of patients, and to write.

Many visitors were listed by Freud in a small notebook, others in his *Brief Chronicle*. They reflect all aspects of his personal and professional life and interests as well as his preoccupations of that time, and testify to the wide variety of individuals prominent in their own fields whose work had felt the impact of psychoanalysis. In addition to visits from psychoanalysts who had been colleagues and loyal friends in Vienna, numerous members of the British Psycho-Analytical Society came, among them Melanie Klein, whose views on child analysis were at odds with the work of Anna Freud. (Melanie Klein had arrived in Britain in 1927 and had received enthusiastic support from James and Alix Strachey in particular.) A visit which gave particular pleasure was that of the president and two officials of the Royal Society, which had honoured him with membership by correspondence in 1936. Breaking with tradition the charter book was brought to Freud for signing, a privilege previously reserved for the king.

Several visitors outside the immediate psychoanalytic circles were writers, for example Stefan Zweig, who brought along Salvador Dalí, who sketched his hero, and H. G. Wells, one of the few British writers Freud had met personally in Vienna. Wells had proposed having immediate British citizenship conferred on Freud by act of parliament. Freud was interested in the idea and wrote to Wells in July 1939, with only three months to live:

> You cannot have known that since I first came over to England as a boy of eighteen years, it became an intense wish phantasy of mine to settle in this country and become an Englishman. Two of my half brothers had done so fifteen years before. But an infantile fantasy needs a bit of examination before it can be admitted to reality.   (*Letters of Sigmund Freud*, 459)

Given their shared interest in cultural matters it is likely that they would also have discussed Freud's *Der Mann Moses und die monotheistische Religion* ('Moses and monotheism', 1939), Freud's phylogenetic attempt to link the phenomenon of antisemitism to ancient inconsistencies around the identity of Moses, which was begun in 1934 soon after the rise of Hitler, and completed in London in 1938. The forthcoming publication brought Freud a number of visitors, including several from Jews urging him not to publish a work they felt would undermine the faith in their hour of need, but Freud was undeterred and pressed on with publication.

There were meetings at Maresfield Gardens with several publishers, including Leonard and Virginia Woolf. Leonard Woolf commented in his autobiography that it was

> not an easy interview. He was extraordinarily courteous in a formal, old-fashioned way—for instance, almost ceremoniously he presented Virginia with a flower. There was something about him as of a half-extinct volcano, something sombre, repressed, reserved. He gave me the feeling … of great gentleness, but behind that, great strength.   (Gay, 640)

A final paper was in hand during Freud's time in London: 'Abriss der Psychoanalyse' ('An outline of psychoanalysis', *c*.1940), an ambitious overview of his work, which he did not complete. Clinical work also continued in London for four hours a day, until Freud finally closed his practice seven weeks before the end of his life and some fifty-seven years since setting up in private practice.

Freud held Max Schur, his personal physician of many

years, to a promise he had managed to extract years previously, that he should not let him go on living when there was no longer any point. Schur duly administered a lethal injection of morphine on 23 September 1939 in Freud's study at 20 Maresfield Gardens. Freud was cremated three days later with a fittingly simple memorial service at which Ernest Jones and Stefan Zweig gave addresses, at the Jewish crematorium in Golders Green, Middlesex. His remains are there, inside one of a favourite pair of Greek urns from his collection.

The Freudian legacy In an obituary poem for Freud, W. H. Auden wrote: 'Freud is no more a person now but a whole climate of opinion' (Auden, 153). It is easy to identify Freud's language and ideas in everyday talk: human feelings and behaviour might be deemed repressed, narcissistic, or denied, whether or not an individual has read any Freud or even has any regard for his theories. Furthermore there is chronic confusion, usually unacknowledged, over what really comes from Freud. Given that people seldom react with bland indifference to his name, presumably because they feel in some way implicated by the findings of psychoanalysis, it is hardly surprising that Freud is more often than not misrepresented and misunderstood. It cannot be said that the British have responded to Freud with the same enthusiasm, regard, and affection which Freud maintained for Britain throughout his life. Psychoanalysis has never captured the imagination of the British to the extent that it did the North Americans in the post-war years, or the South Americans much later: the highest percentage of a population receiving psychoanalysis is in Argentina. British psychoanalysis and psychoanalytic psychotherapy remain largely based in London, and north London at that, although the British Psycho-Analytical Society has consistently retained its position as an innovative and influential body within the international psychoanalytic community. The *International Journal of Psychoanalysis* continues to be published in London.

Freud's impact also continues to be felt in the academic and cultural spheres, with a proliferation of postgraduate non-clinical courses in psychoanalytic studies and the widespread but often superficial application of aspects of psychoanalytic theory to academic fields such as literary and film criticism, gender studies, and politics. The death knell is regularly sounded for psychoanalysis. A frequent criticism of Freud is that he was a man of his time and psychoanalysis is therefore no longer relevant. His views on women are often cited in this connection. Indeed there are aspects of his thinking which few psychoanalysts would espouse nowadays, for example some of his ideas on female sexuality. Theoretical innovations have taken the place of those which have not stood the test of time. There has also been a deepened understanding of aspects of human experience which Freud did not fully explore—for example the complexity of the very early mother–infant relationship and its fundamental part in personality development. Yet while psychoanalysis has continued to evolve, the basic principles elaborated by Freud, such as

the concept of mind going beyond mere conscious experience, the highly dynamic nature of mental processes, and the possibility of finding psychological meaning underlying apparently meaningless symptoms or states of mind, have held good, and indeed have underpinned subsequent developments.   SUSAN AUSTIN

Sources *The standard edition of the complete psychological works of Sigmund Freud*, ed. J. Strachey, A. Freud, and others, 24 vols. (1953–74) · *Letters of Sigmund Freud*, ed. E. L. Freud (1975) · E. Jones, *Sigmund Freud: life and work*, 3 vols. (1953–7) · R. Wollheim, *Freud* (1991) · P. Gay, *Freud: a life for our time* (1988) [incl. bibliographical essay] · H. J. Ellenberger, *The discovery of the unconscious: history and evolution of dynamic psychiatry* (1970) · P. Gay, *A Freud reader* (1989) · *The diary of Sigmund Freud, 1929–39: a record of the final decade*, ed. and trans. M. Molnar (1992) [known as the *Brief chronicle*] · I. Ward, *Freud in England* (1992) · *The complete letters of Sigmund Freud to Wilhelm Fliess, 1887–1904*, ed. J. Masson (1985) · *The letters of Sigmund Freud to Eduard Silberstein, 1871–1881*, ed. W. Boehlich (1990) · H. Lange, Freud family tree, Freud Museum, 20 Maresfield Gardens, Hampstead, London [unpublished document, unpaginated] · W. H. Auden, 'Sigmund Freud', *Horizon* (1940), 151–4 · S. Freud, *Die Traumdeutung* (Vienna, 1900)

Archives Freud Museum, London, family and personal corresp. and papers · L. Cong. · Sigmund Freud Gesellschaft, Vienna | JRL, corresp., mostly with his nephew, Sam Freud | FILM BFI NFTVA, documentary footage · Freud Museum, London, home footage | SOUND BL NSA, recorded talk; performance recording

Likenesses photographs, c.1860–1939, Freud Museum, London · M. Pollock, drypoint etching, 1914, Freud Museum, London · M. Halberstadt, photograph, 1921, Mary Evans Picture Library [*see illus.*] · F. Schmutzer, chalk and mixed media, 1926, Freud Museum, London · L. Willinger, photograph, 1930–39, Wellcome L. · S. Dalí, pen-and-ink drawing on blotting paper, 1938, Freud Museum, London · O. Nemon, bronze statue, c.1970, corner of Fitzjohn's Avenue and Belsize Lane, London; maquette at Freud Museum, London

Wealth at death £22,850 3s. 2d.: probate, 1 Dec 1939, *CGPLA Eng. & Wales*

Freund [*née* Rüdiger], **Amelia Louisa** [*pseud.* Amelia Lewis] (b. **1824/5**, d. in or after **1881**), campaigner for women's rights and food reformer, was born in Prussia in 1824 or 1825, the daughter of Benjamin Rüdiger. On 18 March 1846 she married Dr Jonas Charles Herman Freund (1808–1879), a founder and honorary directing physician of the German Hospital at Dalston, London (and one of Karl Marx's doctors). They had at least eight children, who were born between 1849 and 1864.

Freund became visible in feminist circles from about 1872. She was a member of the Victoria Discussion Society established by Emily Faithfull, and her friends included Louisa Amelia Ann Stevenson, the mother of the playwright G. R. Sims, who shared her philanthropic and feminist sympathies. In January 1872 she established and edited a journal, *Woman*, 'embodying female interests from an educational, social and domestic point of view'. In August it was retitled the *Social Review* but shortly afterwards ceased. Her editorials expressed her commitment to female suffrage, equality of educational opportunity, and labour reform. Contributors included her eldest son, John Christian Freund, C. R. Drysdale, Florence Fenwick Miller, G. R. Sims, and Compton Reade. As with all her journalistic ventures, she used the pen-name Amelia Lewis.

Freund involved herself in social questions and educational reform. She attended the International Prison Congress, supported the Metropolitan Shopkeepers' Assistants' Association, and addressed the Social Science Congress in 1872. She planned a girls' school on 'Prussian' lines and was invited to lecture in Germany on the women's question. She lectured on the art of teaching at Exeter Hall, London. Her interest in food reform began at a dinner in London celebrating the Newsvendors' Benevolent and Provident Institution's anniversary in April 1872. Later she wrote that 'I am tired of writing fine things [when] I am seeing more and more that we are at fault with our plain home arrangements, and that Food and Cooking are especially neglected' (*Food and Health Leaves*, 3 Oct 1879, 165–6). Her next venture, from January to April 1874, was *Women's Opinion*, a journal (initially a weekly) that she edited, published, and printed, representing the 'social, domestic and educational interests of women'. It supported women's suffrage, covered female labour, and like *Woman* had sections on music, fine arts, and the theatre.

At the same time, Freund invented a 'reformed stove', which was designed to be fuel efficient and to promote 'scientific' cooking, and was exhibited to the public and at the Inventors' Institute, St Martin's Place, London. Later in the same year she established a National Food and Fuel Reform Association, at 420 Strand. It combated the 'state of ignorance' on food and fuel questions through an illustrated weekly journal, the *National Food and Fuel Reformer*, edited by her from November 1874 to May 1876, which featured articles on the production, marketing, chemistry, and adulteration of foods. There were departments for fuel reform and patents, and paragraphs on vegetarianism. Her stove and utensils were retailed at the offices, which also had a reading and exhibition room. She conducted cookery classes. Lectures took place in Glasgow (where her paper on food and fuel reform was admitted at the Social Science Congress), Brighton (where she again spoke at the congress), Manchester, and Oldham. In 1875 her stove won a silver medal at the Paris Exhibition.

From January to May 1876 Freund edited *The Housekeeper: A Domestic Journal*, which covered subjects similar to her *Food and Fuel Reformer*. She was too ambitious, since neither was profitable, and in May the association went into liquidation; the lease, copyright of the journal, plant, type, and the patent for the stove were auctioned. The work 'rested' for eighteen months but the cause was not abandoned since another weekly journal, *Food and Health Leaves*, was produced from May to December 1879 while she was living in Manchester. This was directed towards the local community and had a 'high artisan class' readership. She lectured on food and reformed appliances, giving practical demonstrations of her stove at the General Post Office in Brown Street, Manchester. Lectures were given across Lancashire, where she was known as the Stove Lady and Lunnun Coo-king Ooman. She spoke about the food question in a debate of the economic and trade

department of the Social Science Congress in Manchester. She established a depot at 37 Blackfriars Street.

Widowed in 1879, Freund joined her eldest son in the United States, whence he had fled to escape creditors. J. C. Freund (1849–1924) edited the magazine *Dark Blue* (1871–3) while still an undergraduate at Oxford; it featured social essays and fiction by his mother and many celebrities of the day, including Morris, Ruskin, Swinburne, and Le Fanu. Its mounting debts caused him to emigrate to America in 1873. The *New York Times* reported dinners that Amelia Freund gave in December 1880 and early January 1881, to members of the American Institute Farmers' Club and to women working at a department store. These dinners were held in her office, 704 Broadway, New York. Her tract *How to Live in Winter* was also reprinted by the Food and Health Publishing Office. After 1881 Amelia Freund fades from view.   JAMES GREGORY

Sources D. Doughan and D. Sanchez, *Feminist periodicals, 1855–1984: an annotated critical bibliography of British, Irish, commonwealth and international titles* (1987), 5–6 · G. R. Sims, *Sixty years: recollections of bohemian London* (1917) · R. Ashton, *Little Germany: exile and asylum in Victorian England* (1986) · J. Puschel, *Die Geschichte des German Hospital in London, 1845 bis 1948* (1980) · Boase, *Mod. Eng. biog.* [Jonas Charles Herman Freund; John Christian Freund] · L. R. Harlan and R. W. Smock, eds., *The Booker T. Washington papers*, 14 vols. (1981), vol. 11, pp. 450–51 · *ILN* (10 Jan 1880), 26 · census returns, 1861, PRO, RG 9/196/9, fol. 44; 1871, RG 10/436, fol. 83 · A. Lewis, *How to live in winter* (New York, 1881) · *IGI* · *New York Times* (22 Dec 1880), 8 · *New York Times* (12 Jan 1881), 8 · m. cert.

Freund, Ida (1863–1914), chemist, was born on 15 April 1863 in Austria; the names of her parents are unknown. Orphaned when she was very young, she was brought up by her maternal grandparents in Vienna. During her youth she lost a leg as a result of a cycling accident and the disease that followed. The artificial leg that replaced it was never very satisfactory. Throughout her life she moved about by means of a tricycle worked with her arms.

Freund was educated in a Vienna state school or *Bürgerschule*, and at the State Training College for Women in Vienna. She was brought to England by her maternal uncle, Ludwig Strauss, a professional violinist and member of the Joachim quartet. She had high praise for the *Bürgerschule*, which she attended by choice after her grandparents had sent her to an expensive, but not very satisfactory, private school.

Freund soon became a naturalized British subject and her sympathies and interests became very English, although she still felt an affection for her native Austria. At the suggestion of Lady Goldsmid she entered Girton College, Cambridge, in 1882, taking the natural science tripos in 1885 and 1886 and gaining first-class honours in both parts. The second part of her tripos was in chemistry. Considering that she started with only a schoolgirl's knowledge of English and with no understanding of Greek or Latin, and little if any of Euclid and the required algebra, it is a great tribute to her intelligence and diligence that she passed the required examinations within the prescribed time and obtained first-class honours.

From 1886 to 1887 Freund lectured at the Cambridge Training College for Women. The remainder of her career was spent at Newnham College, Cambridge, where she rose from demonstrator in chemistry (1887–93) to staff lecturer (1893–1912). In effect she was also director of studies in chemistry and physics at Newnham. She was an associate at Newnham College and then a member of its council (1896–1903).

Women students were not admitted to the Cambridge University Laboratory for Elementary Chemistry until they had passed part one of the tripos, and all of their practical work for the natural science tripos had to be conducted in their own laboratories. Freund arranged a course of practical work for students, held in the 'old laboratory' at Newnham. She was entirely responsible for the laboratory training of the majority of her elementary students, most of whom were entirely bereft of any knowledge of chemistry when they arrived. Once the university laboratory was opened to women students in 1910, Freund realized that the Newnham laboratory should be given up, and it was closed after her retirement in 1912. Although laboratory work was central to Freund's teaching, she did not confine herself to practical work. Laboratory experiments were combined with papers and tutorials. In the third year she added a course of lectures on chemical theory which traced and illustrated the history of chemical discovery.

Although she undertook original research in physical chemistry, Ida Freund is best-known for her interest in science education, and in particular for improving science teaching in girls' schools. Her two excellent chemistry textbooks show both the breadth of her knowledge and her ability to present it in an understandable way to students. *The Study of Chemical Composition* (1904), the substance of her third-year lectures, remained an important textbook until relatively recently, serving as a student 'source book' of chemical theory. In this book Freund demonstrated that she was aware of the 'sharp and clear' boundaries 'between facts and hypotheses', and she wanted her students to have the same awareness (I. Freund, *The Study of Chemical Composition*, v). The book

was especially important both in its own time and later for its historical outlook. She quoted extensively from classical memoirs and important writers on chemistry, allowing the creators of important discoveries to announce them in their own words. A second book, *The Experimental Basis of Chemistry*, edited by A. Hutchinson and M. B. Thomas, was published posthumously in 1920. Although she planned for the book to have twenty chapters she had only completed ten chapters at her death.

In 1897 Freund instituted a vacation course for science teachers at the Newnham College laboratory. She arranged for former natural science students who had gone to teach in schools to come to Cambridge to learn how to construct simple instruments themselves. She taught them to make the best of the conditions that they had to endure in teaching and also kept them abreast of progress in the natural sciences. Physics rather than chemistry was the subject that concerned her most in school teaching. She regarded physics as the most fundamental subject, one which was most often neglected in girls' schools, and one which, when taught, was taught badly. One of the major reasons for this neglect was the expensive equipment required for teaching physics. She strongly opposed the movement to introduce domestic science teaching in girls' schools as a substitute for fundamental scientific education. Her views were expressed in a paper to a conference on domestic science in secondary schools for girls in 1911, in which she argued that to treat these practical 'arts' as a branch of science would cause girls to acquire only a superficial level of knowledge, and would lead to a lowering of the standard of women's intellectual work ('Domestic science—a protest', *The Englishwoman*, 10, 1911, 147–63, 279–96).

Freund was recognized as a great character. Although she wrote excellent English she never mastered the spoken language. A student, H. Wilson, noted that she would break off a sentence and say: 'Have I got you wiz me in zat?' (Phillips, 72). At another time she and a student had a mild disagreement and as Freund chastised the student she said: 'Now, Miss X, have I got you wiz me in the hydrochloric acid?' (ibid., 72). Although her sense of

Ida Freund (1863–1914), by unknown photographer, 1912 [seated, with students in a laboratory at Newnham College, Cambridge]

humour became legendary, first-year students were terrorized by her sharp rebukes for silly mistakes. They soon
realized, however, that she had nothing but their best
interests at heart. Immediately before the all-important
tripos examination she would summon her chemistry students and require them to do a special study. In 1907 she
suggested that her students go to the laboratory and study
the lives of famous chemists. When they arrived they
found large boxes of chocolates with a different life history and picture of a famous chemist in each. In another
year they were to make a further study of the periodic
table. They found a large periodic table set out in the laboratory. This table, however, differed from the ordinary
periodic table: the elements were iced cakes, each with its
name and atomic weight in icing. The numbers were
made of chocolate (ibid., 72).

Freund strongly supported the women's suffrage movement and left a generous amount in her will to the
Women's University Settlement in Southwark. She had
other interests in addition to teaching. She was an excellent housekeeper, deft at knitting, crocheting, and sewing, and a fine cook. She liked to travel, was interested in
political questions, and loved literature. Gardening was
another of her interests and afforded her great pleasure.

Throughout her life Freund suffered from ill health and
this eventually forced her to give up her teaching post at
Newnham. Even with the loss of her leg she would sometimes take long excursions around the neighbourhood.
Later she lost the use of one eye, after many attempts to
save it, and she finally died of an internal problem which
necessitated an operation which her weak condition did
not allow her to survive. Following surgery she died on 15
May 1914 at her home, 7 Cranmer Road, Cambridge. In
April 1998 the 'old laboratory', where she reigned during
the early part of the twentieth century, was restored as a
memorial (now a performing arts facility) to Freund and
the other Newnham scientists who worked there.

Freund treated her students in many ways as if they
were her own children. After they left Newnham she kept
in close personal contact with many of them. Therefore,
when she resigned her students initiated a fund, which
expanded after her death, to be used for holiday courses in
girls' schools, like the successful one at Newnham which
she had taught earlier. The outbreak of the First World
War hindered the collection of further funds, but in
August 1915 a vacation course in mechanics and electricity
and magnetism for women teachers in secondary schools
was held at the Cavendish Laboratory.

MARILYN BAILEY OGILVIE

Sources I. Freund, *The experimental basis of chemistry: suggestions for a series of experiments illustrative of the fundamental principles of chemistry*, ed. A. Hutchinson and M. B. Thomas (1920) • K. T. Butler and H. I. McMorran, eds., *Girton College register, 1869–1946* (1948) • M. I. Gardiner, *Newnham College Letter* (1914), 34–8 • M. M. P. Muir, *Cambridge Magazine* (30 May 1914), 669 • A. Gardner, *Cambridge Review* (27 May 1914), 470–71 • *Nature*, 93 (1914), 327 • d. cert. • P. Gould, 'Women and the culture of university physics in late nineteenth-century Cambridge', *British Journal for the History of Science*, 30 (1997), 127–49 • A. Phillips, ed., *A Newnham anthology* (1979) • [A. B. White and others], eds., *Newnham College register, 1871–1971*, 2nd edn, 1 (1979) • M. L. Richmond, '"A lab of one's own": the Balfour biological laboratory for women at Cambridge University', *Isis*, 88 (1997), 422–55 • E. Sidgwick, 'Ida Freund memorial: vacation course for women teachers of physics', 7 Aug 1915, Newnham College, Cambridge, archive • M. B. Thomas, 'The Ida Freund memorial', *Newnham College Letter* (1911) • *CGPLA Eng. & Wales* (1914)

Likenesses photograph, 1912, Newnham College, Cambridge [*see illus.*]

Wealth at death £17,494 12s. 0d.: probate, 27 June 1914, *CGPLA Eng. & Wales*

Freund, Sir Otto Kahn- (1900–1979), jurist, was born in
Frankfurt am Main on 17 November 1900, the only child of
Richard Kahn-Freund, a merchant, and his wife, Carrie
Freund. He grew up in a cultured Jewish household and
though in religious matters he was agnostic, he himself
said that the most important fact in his life had been the
awareness of being a Jew. To this he attributed the passion
for justice and the concern for the disadvantaged which
lay at the root both of his interest in labour law and of his
socialist convictions.

Kahn-Freund studied principally at the University of
Frankfurt, where he was powerfully influenced by Hugo
Sinzheimer, who first interested him in labour law. In
1929 he entered the judiciary as a judge of the Berlin
labour court. He married in 1931 Elisabeth, daughter of
Friedrich Klaiss, mechanic. She shared his political convictions and his interests. They had an adopted daughter.

When the Nazis came to power Kahn-Freund was
already known for a small book criticizing the ideology
behind the decisions of the supreme labour court, and he
was soon in collision with the party. He refused to uphold
the dismissal of employees of the radio service who were
alleged to be communists and to have tried to sabotage
Hitler's first broadcast. The result was his own dismissal
and departure to England. There he became a student at
the London School of Economics, which for the next
thirty years was the focus of his life and which was ideally
suited to one of his temperament and views. Appointed an
assistant lecturer in 1936, he became a professor in 1951.
He was also called to the bar by the Middle Temple in 1936
and was for a time in chambers with Patrick (later Lord)
Devlin. He was naturalized in 1940.

Kahn-Freund was an outstandingly exciting lecturer,
with a command of English which any native speaker
might envy. The lecture was indeed his favourite medium
and his most brilliant work originated in that form. He
played an important part in the establishment of labour
law as an independent area of legal study in England, and
in his later years he was unquestionably its leading
authority. He also enjoyed a great reputation on the continent and in the United States (he was for many years a
visiting lecturer at the Yale law school). While he was later
unhappy with some aspects of Labour's attitude in the
1970s to the position of trade unions, he would certainly
have found much to regret in the statutory controls of
union power introduced by Margaret Thatcher's administrations. In 1965 he was appointed to the royal commission on the reform of the trade unions and employers'
associations. His hand can be seen in the legal sections of

and to write and held visiting professorships at Paris and Cambridge. He became FBA in 1965 and an honorary bencher of the Middle Temple in 1969; he was given silk in 1972 and was knighted for his services to labour law in 1976. He held many honorary doctorates. He died at Haslemere, Surrey, on 16 August 1979. He was survived by his wife.   J. K. BARRY M. NICHOLAS

Sources Lord Wedderburn, 'Otto Kahn-Freund, 1900–1979', *PBA*, 68 (1982), 579–84 · J. H. C. Morris, *Brazen Nose*, 17 (1979–82), 25–9 · M. Partington, in O. Kahn-Freund, *Selected writings* (1978), ix–xv · B. Hepple, in O. Kahn-Freund, *Selected writings* (1978), xvii–xix · private information (1986) · personal knowledge (2004) · CGPLA Eng. & Wales (1979) · F. Gamillscheg and others, eds., *In memoriam, Sir Otto Kahn-Freund* (1980)

Archives BLPES, MSS | BLPES, corresp. with Friedrich Mann
Likenesses photograph, repro. in Wedderburn, 'Otto Kahn-Freund' · photograph, BL PES [*see illus.*]
Wealth at death £129,378: probate, 27 Nov 1979, CGPLA Eng. & Wales

Sir Otto Kahn-Freund (1900–1979), by unknown photographer

its report which reflected his view that Britain possessed a reasonably well functioning system of labour relations.

Though labour law was his dominant concern, Kahn-Freund was remarkable for the range of his interests. He was a respected authority on the conflict of laws, being one of the editors of the sixth to ninth editions of *Dicey*. He was also an enthusiastic promoter of the study of family law; there, as in labour law, he constantly emphasized the need to see legal rules in terms of their social and human consequences. He was also a passionate advocate of the European ideal and vigorously advanced the study of European law.

In 1964 Kahn-Freund was persuaded to move to the chair of comparative law at Oxford and a fellowship at Brasenose College. The comparative approach was a natural concomitant of his broad interests, but he brought to the subject also a capacity for striking generalization. For anyone less youthful in spirit and less appreciative of new experiences the transition from the London School of Economics to Oxford at the age of sixty-three might have been difficult, and indeed he was genially impatient of the constraints on rapid change imposed by the collegiate and tutorial systems, but he quickly became at home and during his seven years (his tenure of the chair was, exceptionally, extended) he was influential in the establishment in the syllabus not only of comparative law, but also family law, labour law, and European law. A naturally sociable man, he also enjoyed the friendly diversity of senior common room life.

After his retirement Kahn-Freund continued to lecture

Freville, George (*d.* 1579), judge, was the second son of Robert Freville (*d.* 1521) of Little Shelford, near Cambridge, and his wife, Rose Peyton. He was educated at Cambridge and Barnard's Inn in the 1520s, and went on to the Middle Temple, perhaps in the early 1530s. In company with many other Middle Temple students who achieved distinction in the law, he was taken as a pupil by John Jenour, protonotary of the common pleas, to learn the forms of pleading. It has been conjectured that he was supported in his education by his wealthy kinsmen, the Withypoll and Fermor families. He subsequently came to the notice of Thomas Cromwell through the influence of his kinsman Richard Sampson, bishop of Chichester, and later still was befriended by Sir William Paget, who employed him on legal work. Paget was responsible for his appointment as a justice of the peace for Cambridgeshire in 1539, a position in which he served until his death; for his election to parliament as member for Preston in 1547; for his retainer as counsel to the duchy of Lancaster from 1548; and for his appointment as deputy high steward of Cambridge University in 1549. He acted as legal adviser and steward to Peterhouse and other colleges, and these appointments were followed in 1553 by the recordership of Cambridge. His seat was at Isleham in Cambridgeshire, although he also obtained the paternal manor of Little Shelford from his nephew.

In 1550 Freville became a bencher of the Middle Temple, and read on the statute 11 Hen. VII c. 20, concerning alienations of land by widows. Some notes of the reading survive in the Essex Record Office. (Dugdale recorded his name as 'Flewet', and in consequence the date of his election to the bench has usually been mistaken.) He was elected to read again in 1558 and 1559, but did not do so. In 1559 he was appointed third baron of the exchequer, becoming second baron in 1564. Together with John Birch he was one of the last barons not raised to the degree of serjeant, and was therefore not qualified to go on circuit as an assize judge. His first wife, Dorothy, died in 1568, and later the same year he married Jane, widow of Edward

Banckes of London. They are not known to have had children. Freville continued to sit in the exchequer until his death on 16 May 1579, and was succeeded by the next recorder of Cambridge, Robert Shute. J. H. BAKER

Sources HoP, *Commons, 1509–58*, 2.173–4 · R. Somerville, *History of the duchy of Lancaster, 1265–1603* (1953), 455 · *The reports of Sir John Spelman*, ed. J. H. Baker, 2, SeldS, 94 (1978), 2.130 · A. W. Franks, 'The genealogical history of the Freville family', *Miscellaneous Communications Made to the Cambridge Antiquarian Society*, 1/4 (1848), 21–9 · T. A. Walker, *A biographical register of Peterhouse men*, 1 (1927), 157, 163 · Sainty, *Judges*, 122 · Essex RO, MS D/DP L82, fols. 8v–10, 11v–12v · *CPR, 1553–4*, 468 · *VCH Cambridgeshire and the Isle of Ely*, 3.59 · Cooper, *Ath. Cantab.*, 1.407 · *N&Q*, 7th ser., 3 (1887), 203

Frewen, Accepted (*bap.* 1588, *d.* 1664), archbishop of York, was born at Northiam in Sussex, and baptized there on 26 May 1588, the eldest son of the puritan rector of the parish John *Frewen (1558–1628) and his first wife, Elinor (*d.* 1606). Traditionally his birth by caesarean section (in a farmhouse called Carriers) was used to explain his later decision to remain a bachelor and his renowned discomfort in the presence of women, even to the extent of allegedly refusing to employ female servants in his household. After education at the free school at Canterbury, Frewen was in 1604 admitted a demy of Magdalen College, Oxford, where he was taught by Richard Capel. He graduated BA in 1608 and proceeded MA on 23 May 1612, and in the same year was ordained, elected to a fellowship, and appointed divinity reader in the college. He was appointed lecturer in moral philosophy in 1614.

In 1617 Frewen was granted leave of absence by Magdalen in order to act as chaplain to Sir John Digby, created in 1618 Baron Digby, ambassador to Spain. Frewen returned to Oxford and proceeded BD in 1619, but was soon on his travels again. He appears to have accompanied Digby on an embassy to the emperor Ferdinand in 1621 and in the following year was again in Spain with Digby (now earl of Bristol) when Charles, prince of Wales, and Buckingham arrived in Madrid in the abortive pursuit of a marriage alliance with the Spanish infanta. During this visit Frewen came to Charles's notice following a sermon preached before the prince urging him to remain steadfast to the doctrines of the established church. Impressed by the sermon, Charles presented Frewen with a miniature of himself. Charles continued to show an interest in Frewen's career and, on his accession to the throne, appointed Frewen a royal chaplain, personally inserting his name into the list.

Frewen was elected vice-president of Magdalen in 1625 and was also given a canonry at Canterbury. On 24 October 1626 he was unanimously elected president of Magdalen and later that year he compounded for his DD with a thesis in support of the Calvinist doctrine of election. Frewen was elected vice-chancellor of Oxford in both 1628 and 1629, and in the latter year apparently moved his doctrinal position closer to that of his friend William Laud, whose candidature he supported, probably independently of Laud himself, as chancellor of the university during the contested election of 1630. There is no doubt that thereafter Frewen's association with Laud was close and played a part in his further promotion to the deanery of

Accepted Frewen (*bap.* 1588, *d.* 1664), by unknown artist, 1660–64 [copy]

Gloucester in 1631, procured through the offices of Secretary Dorchester, a post which he held along with the headship of his college. Frewen also benefited directly from the patronage of the college, being appointed to its rectories of Standlake in Oxfordshire and Warnford in Hampshire in 1635.

During Frewen's presidency, and partly at his own expense, Magdalen College chapel was in the forefront of the Laudian reordering of churches in Oxford; it was the first to have the communion table set altarwise, in 1631, and by 1633 it had acquired a reredos depicting the last supper. In 1635 a black and white marble pavement was laid and the following year the fellows raised £400 to beautify the body of the church. A glazing scheme of 1637 incorporated 'white glass drawn and shadowed with figures' in the ante-chapel, a 'Last Judgement' in the main west window, and panels depicting forty-eight saints in the remaining six windows, these last being the only surviving part of the scheme (*Hist. U. Oxf.* 4: *17th-cent. Oxf.*, 165–6). The changes to Magdalen chapel aroused opposition in some Oxford quarters, and the controversy surrounding sermons preached in St Mary's Church against the changes went to the privy council, with some of the preachers being removed from the university.

At the request of Laud, Frewen took on the vice-chancellorship of the university again in 1639 and was conscientious in enforcing his authority by attending academic disputations whenever he could. These years, however, not only saw increasing division within the university but also, in 1640—a period which Frewen characterized as a 'busy and inquisitive time' (*Hist. U. Oxf.* 4: *17th-cent.*

Oxf., 688)—growing disputes with the city over matters of jurisdiction. In association with his friend Gilbert Sheldon, Frewen used his experience and influence in university affairs to support the policies of Laud and the king in these years; it was probably Sheldon and Frewen who, at the suggestion of Edward Hyde, arranged for the university to lend tangible support to the king, by way of a loan and the transference of plate to his headquarters at York, in July 1642 when relations between king and parliament had reached the point where hostilities were almost unavoidable. It may be that the loan of £500 made by Magdalen came from Frewen's own pocket as that is precisely the sum which he subsequently mentioned in his will when he waived a debt owed to him by the college. As a result of this activity parliament ordered the arrest of Frewen, among others, but he was able to avoid the attention of its emissaries by going into hiding. On the outbreak of hostilities he was back in Oxford and restored to his position after the royalist occupation of the city following the battle of Edgehill. No doubt partly due to his loyalty and financial support but also on the advice of William Juxon, who thought that he was a moderate whose promotion would not arouse the hostility of the more outspoken opponents of episcopacy, Frewen was appointed bishop of Coventry and Lichfield, and was consecrated in Magdalen College chapel on 28 April 1644.

Following the end of the civil wars and the abolition of episcopacy Frewen's career disappeared 'into impenetrable obscurity' (Bosher), but he was one of five bishops with whom Eleazor Duncon, a former prebend of York sent from France at the instigation of Edward Hyde, discussed the desirability of holding episcopal consecrations abroad in 1655; Frewen agreed to go to France if it was thought helpful but nothing came of the plan and his subsequent activities and whereabouts during the interregnum remain a mystery.

At the Restoration Frewen was translated to the archbishopric of York, being nominated on 2 September and confirmed, in a ceremony at St Paul's, on 4 October 1660. By this date Frewen was already an old man and his promotion was considered a surprise in some quarters, Pepys recording how odd he and his fellow bishops seemed to the people as they left St Paul's on 4 October; doubtless Frewen's indisputable services to the new king's father, and his earlier association with Hyde, were significant. Perhaps because of his age he was not among the more aggressively episcopalian of the new regime, and Richard Baxter recalled him as a 'peaceable man', an important quality in a diocese which included, in the West Riding, one of the most entrenched areas of parliamentary support during the civil wars. Frewen's restoration of ecclesiastical discipline in the diocese was marked more by care than vigour, and he relied heavily on officials who had been in place before the civil war. His primary visitation was not held until the late summer of 1662 and his first ordination only at the beginning of July that year, when it was arranged to allow those forty or so conformable clergy active in the diocese who had not received episcopal ordination to regularize their orders, prior to the subscription required of them on the twelfth of that month. As far as national policy was concerned Frewen reacted to rather than influenced matters, exemplified by his role at the Savoy conference where, although officially in the chair, he handed over leadership of the meeting to Sheldon, who was closer to the king and Hyde, as soon as the formal proceedings were complete.

In Frewen's personal circumstances, however, the Restoration brought dramatic changes. His original promotion to Coventry and Lichfield had come too late to permit him to enjoy the material benefits of that see and so, in recompense for this and for his undoubted services to Charles I, he was permitted to hold the temporalities there after his promotion to York. Thus the archbishop was able to profit significantly from the massive reordering of ecclesiastical property in the years following the Restoration, as tenants rushed to regularize their position by taking out new leases. At York alone Frewen received over £20,000 by way of entry fines before his death in 1664 and he also profited, if not quite as much, from the Lichfield estates. This windfall, late in life, was applied by Frewen as a contribution to the restoration of Lichfield Cathedral, on which he spent £1500, and to restoring his palace at Bishopthorpe near York, notably in rebuilding the library, refitting the chapel, and repairing the roof of the banqueting hall, while other sums were directed to the augmentation of poor livings in his new diocese. However, the sheer number of property transactions in less than four years meant that he ended his life a very wealthy man.

Frewen died at his Bishopthorpe palace on 28 March 1664. Although he had asked to be interred at Northiam, he was buried at York Minster on 3 May beneath the great east window, where a substantial monument showing him lying in black gown and cap with his hands joined in prayer can be taken as a reflection of that brand of post-Reformation churchmanship he represented. By his will he left £500 to his old college for some public purpose, as well as remitting a further £500 debt; he left a ring to each of his fellow bishops, noting one in particular which had belonged to the Elizabethan bishop John Jewel, which he left to John Warner, bishop of Rochester. The rest of his fortune was left to his youngest brother, Stephen, a London merchant, who is said to have conveyed 27,000 guineas *in specie* to London after the funeral. This money was lent to Charles II and lost, except for the interest, by the closing of the exchequer, but Stephen Frewen was granted an income of £400 a year by Charles and remained wealthy enough to establish the family on an extensive property in and around Northiam. Archbishop Frewen's reputation for consistency in religious matters was questioned by Francis Drake in his *Eboracum, or, History and Antiquities of York Cathedral and City* (1736) which brought a reply, *A Just and Plain Vindication of the Late Dr Frewen*, from a descendant, Thomas Frewen, in 1743. The latter also published in the same year a collection of Frewen's speeches as president of Magdalen and vice-chancellor of Oxford.   WILLIAM JOSEPH SHEILS

Sources T. Frewen, *A just and plain vindication of the late Dr Frewen* (1743) · *Hist. U. Oxf.* 4: 17th-cent. *Oxf.* · I. M. Green, *The re-establishment of the Church of England, 1660–1663* (1978) · R. S. Bosher, *The making of the Restoration settlement: the influence of the Laudians, 1649–1662* (1951) · I. J. Gentles and W. J. Sheils, *Confiscation and restoration: the archbishopric estates and the civil war* (1981) · *Walker rev.* · probate register 46, Borth. Inst., fols. 494–5 · G. E. Aylmer, ed., *A history of York Minster*, rev. R. Cant (1977); repr. with corrections (1979) · Foster, *Alum. Oxon.* · *DNB*
Archives E. Sussex RO, papers
Likenesses portrait, 1660–64, Brickwall House School, Sussex [*see illus.*] · oils, Bishopthorpe Palace, York; repro. in J. Ingamells, *Catalogue of portraits of Bishopthorpe Palace* (1972) · portrait?, Magd. Oxf. · tomb effigy, York Minster, York; repro. in Aylmer, *History of York Minster*
Wealth at death over £30,000: Frewen, *Just and plain vindication*

Frewen, John (1558–1628), Church of England clergyman, was probably born at Earls Croome, Worcestershire, the son of Richard Frewen (*d.* 1584) and his wife, Margaret Greenwood (*d.* 1598). He apparently never attended a university. Ordained priest on 24 June 1582 by John Bullingham, bishop of Gloucester, he was presented to the rectory of Northiam, Sussex, by his father, who had leased the patronage rights from Anthony Browne, Viscount Montague. Instituted on 2 November 1583, he was almost immediately suspended for his refusal to subscribe unconditionally to the three articles of Archbishop John Whitgift, but was soon reinstated after he and other nonconforming Sussex ministers had reached a compromise agreement with Whitgift. He wrote *Certaine Fruitfull Instructions and Necessary Doctrines Meete to Edify in the Feare of God* (1587), composed of 249 mini-sermons setting forth the standard Calvinist teachings on Christian faith and practice. The book was dedicated to Thomas Coventry and Leonard Jefferies, both of Earls Croome, who had shown him 'great goodness' and probably helped to advance his career. From 1588 onwards Frewen followed the practice, then in vogue among east Sussex puritans, of baptizing children with names of 'godly signification', such as Fear-god, Faynt-not, Repent, and Be-constant, his own children among them.

In 1603 Frewen took a prominent part in organizing petitions for church reform, and was one of four Sussex ministers delegated to present them to King James at Hampton Court. When two years later some of the more militant puritans were deprived for nonconformity, many people apparently expected Frewen to be among them, and he was subsequently obliged to deny allegations that his reprieve had been due to bribery. These allegations are indications of the hostility that some local people had long felt towards him. As early as 1586, the year when he concluded the preface to his *Certaine Fruitfull Instructions* by declaring that 'if I should please men I were not the servant of Christ', he had so displeased some of his parishioners that they had reportedly indulged in 'evil speaking' against him. In 1605 he alleged that a man named John Snepp had vowed that he would 'pull me out of the pulpit', 'spit in my face', and 'make me come unto him upon my knees'. This parishioner had also 'threatened that songs should be made of me' and had declared that, since

ministers 'ought not to marry', their children were 'not legitimate' (RYE 47/67(6)).

Disagreements between Frewen and his flock took a vicious turn in the summer of 1611, when some of them tried unsuccessfully to have him indicted for nonconformity at the assizes. Soon afterwards he sought to vindicate himself by preaching at Northiam sermons published as *Certaine sermons on 2, 3, 4, 5, 6, 7 and 8 verses of the eleventh chapter of S. Paule his epistle to the Romanes* (1612), dedicated to Sir Thomas Pelham and other east Sussex JPs. In the preface he said that throughout most of his time at Northiam there had been 'as sweet an harmony between minister and people ... as in any other place', but now there was 'no minister in the land ... so contemptible in the eyes of those to whom he ordinarily preacheth the word of God'. Nevertheless Frewen was undeterred, and continued to instruct his people in the fundamentals of the faith. He published *Certaine choise grounds and principles of our Christian religion ... wherein the people of the parish of Northiam ... have been catechized and instructed for the settling of their hearts and mindes in the mysteries of salvation* (1621), dedicated to Sir Thomas Coventry, the attorney-general (and son of his former patron), and others. That same year a leading parishioner named Robert Cresswell, whose mind had evidently not been settled by the rector's sermons, insulted him on the public highway, calling him 'old fool, old ass, old coxcomb' (Lower, 48), for which offence he was subsequently excommunicated by the Lewes archdeaconry court.

Frewen's portrait, painted by Daniel Mytens in 1627, depicts him in full canonicals and a wide-brimmed hat, with his right hand on a Geneva Bible open at 2 Kings 23, a favourite passage with puritans (it describes King Josiah suppressing idolatry). On 1 June that year he made his will (East Sussex Record Office, FRE 56), being 'aged and weak in body, but of good, sound and perfect memory' and well able to sign each page of the document in a strong, clear hand. His will has an unusually comprehensive preamble, over 300 words long, expressing the hope that his body would 'have a blessed resurrection and be re-united to my soul, that they may both together enjoy everlasting glory'. In disposing of his worldly goods (valued at just over £350) he gave the same meticulous attention to detail, bequeathing to his wife 'all the swine, poultry, butter and cheese, fish and flesh as shall be remaining in my house or owing by the butcher', a load of firewood, half the fruit in the orchard, and 'two of my kine at her choice'. With similar care and caution he decreed that his scattered parcels of land in Northiam, totalling 91 acres, and his 68 acres in neighbouring parishes should pass, with certain strings attached, to his second son, Thankfull. By this date the family considered themselves gentlemen, but to the last this Frewen seems to have remained a shrewd peasant at heart.

Frewen was married three times. With his first wife, Elinor (*d.* 1606), he had seven sons (two of whom died in infancy) and a daughter: of his sons, the eldest, Accepted *Frewen, became archbishop of York; the second was

Thankfull, who entered the service of Lord Keeper Coventry; the third was John, who succeeded to the rectory of Northiam; and the fourth was Stephen, who became master of the Skinners' Company, London, and founder of the Frewen family's later fortunes. With his second wife, Elinor or Helen (d. 1619), probably daughter of Richard Hunt of Brede, whom he married on 6 October 1607, he had five sons (of whom two died in infancy). His third wife was Susan Burdon (fl. 1600–1639), whom he married in London on 29 July 1619. Frewen died at the end of April 1628 at Church House, Northiam, the house he had bought in 1593, and was buried in the chancel of the parish church on 2 May.   JEREMY GORING

Sources M. A. Lower, *The worthies of Sussex* (1865) · J. Frewen, autobiographical preface, in J. Frewen, *Certaine fruitfull instructions and necessary doctrines meete to edify in the feare of God* (1587) · J. Frewen, autobiographical preface, in J. Frewen, *Certaine sermons upon the 2, 3, 4, 5, 6, 7 and 8 verses of the eleventh chapter of S. Paule his Epistle to the Romanes* (1612) · E. Sussex RO, FRE 1, FRE 56, FRE 166, RYE 47/67 (6), PAR 431/1/1/1 · J. Goring, 'The reformation of the ministry in Elizabethan Sussex', *Journal of Ecclesiastical History*, 34 (1983), 345–66 · Burke, *Gen. GB* · BL, Add. MS 39341, fol. 61 · J. L. Chester and G. J. Armytage, eds., *The parish registers of St Antholin, Budge Row ... and of St John the Baptist on Wallbrook*, Harleian Society, register section, 8 (1883) · *DNB*
Archives E. Sussex RO, MSS
Likenesses D. Mytens, oils, 1627, Brickwall, Northiam · E. Scriven, stipple and line engraving (after D. Mytens), NPG
Wealth at death £357 5s. 4d.—goods and chattels; incl. £160 cash: will, E. Sussex RO, FRE 166

Frewen, Thomas (1704–1791), physician, was possibly the son of Thankfull Frewen, clerk, of Northiam, Sussex. After being apprenticed to George Lake in 1720 he went on to practise as a surgeon and apothecary at Rye in Sussex, and afterwards as a physician at Lewes, having obtained an MD degree from Utrecht in 1753. Frewen became known as one of the first physicians in England to adopt the practice of inoculation with smallpox. In his essay entitled *The Practice and Theory of Inoculation* (1749), he recorded information about 350 patients, only one of whom died from the smallpox so induced. The common sort of people, he said, were averse to inoculation, and 'disputed about the lawfulness of propagating diseases'—the very ground on which smallpox inoculation (but not vaccination) was made an offence in 1840. Frewen suggested that smallpox and many other diseases were propagated by means of animalcula hatched from eggs lodged in such places as the hairs and pores of human bodies. In a later essay on smallpox in 1759, he argued that many people escaped smallpox who were expected to catch it, and that, contrary to the views of Boerhaave, Cheyne, and others, medication such as aethiops mineral was irrelevant. His *Physiologia* (1780) applied the doctrines of Boerhaave to some diseases.

Frewen was married, and a son, Edward (1744–1831), was educated at Cambridge. Frewen died at Northiam in Sussex, on 14 June 1791, aged eighty-six.
                                          CHARLES CREIGHTON, rev. JEAN LOUDON

Sources R. W. Innes Smith, *English-speaking students of medicine at the University of Leyden* (1932), 90 · *GM*, 1st ser., 61 (1791), 588 · *New London Medical Journal*, 1 (1792), 116 · Venn, *Alum. Cant.* · G. Watts, A letter to Dr Frewen ... on occasion of his very extraordinary behaviour to the author, in the late unhappy case of Mr Rootes, surgeon: in which the doctrine of bleeding near the part affected, recommended by a late dissertation on the subject of revulsion and derivation is further insisted on ... (1755) · C. Creighton, *A history of epidemics in Britain*, 2nd edn, 2 (1965), 606–10 · P. J. Wallis and R. V. Wallis, *Eighteenth century medics*, 2nd edn (1988)
Archives CUL, enchiridion technicum in re medica · CUL, prescription book · RS, MSS

Frewin, Richard (1680/81–1761), physician, was the son of Susanna (1651/2–1732) and Ralph Frewin of the City of London, where Richard was born. He was sent to Westminster School (scholar, 1693), and to Christ Church, Oxford, in 1698, when he was seventeen. At Oxford he took the normal undergraduate course, reading Exodus in Hebrew, some theology, Latin and Greek classics, and Bartholin's *Physica*. He took his BA in 1702, MA in 1705 (incorporated at Cambridge, 1707), MB in 1707, and after the further statutory four years, MD in 1711. By then he was reader in rhetoric at Christ Church, and also taught chemistry. He practised as a physician in Oxford. Much respected, he was Oxford's leading physician and attended Dean Aldrich on his deathbed in Dr Radcliffe's house.

Frewin married about 1715 the rich and lively Dorothy Eyre (1678/9–1725), daughter of Sir Giles *Eyre (d. 1695), of Brickworth, Whiteparish, Wiltshire, and widow of Sir Thomas Tyrell, second baronet (d. 1714), of Hanslape, Buckinghamshire; the couple had a son and a daughter, both of whom died in infancy. The family lived first in the High Street, Oxford; from 1721 until his death Frewin rented from Brasenose College a house in New Inn Hall Lane (now Frewin Hall, New Inn Hall Street). His wife died on 26 July 1725, aged forty-six. Her connections and his 'very dashing' ('Memoir of Dr Frewin', 1) stepdaughters brought him a large county practice, though the two surviving stepdaughters became troublesome. The elder, Bel (Christabella), ran away early one morning to Magdalen College chapel, where she married John Knap, gentleman of the horse to the earl of Abingdon; her husband died two years later, in 1727, of the 'Foul Distemper' (*Remarks*, 9.351), which was probably syphilis. After that she married a rich man, who died, and then a poor Viscount Saye and Sele, and she danced away her years into her eighties. Her younger sister, Hal (Harriet or Henrietta) married twice and 'still worse' ('Memoir of Dr Frewin', 1), though Frewin was very kind to her children.

On 28 February 1727 Frewin married Elizabeth Woodward (d. 1731), niece and heir of Dr Joseph Woodward, fellow of Oriel; she had looked after her uncle in New Inn Hall Lane for many years. She was said to be Frewin's favourite wife, but they had no children. Frewin's practice was large enough for him to keep two coachmen and four horses. As well as practising from Oxford, he also had a house and patients in Bath. In his practice he 'was more exact perhaps in his Patients Cases, than many knew of—always setting down, every Night, the state of those Patients whose case required attention, that He had visited in the Day' ('Memoir of Dr Frewin', 3). However, he objected to consulting with any doctor without an Oxford or Cambridge degree, and to the granting of Oxford medical degrees to anyone not an Oxford graduate. He led the fierce opposition to Nathan Alcock (MD Leiden), a successful teacher of chemistry and anatomy, who was giving private lectures in anatomy at Jesus College.

In 1727 Frewin was elected Camden professor of history at Oxford; he was unopposed, because one candidate was a clergyman, which was contrary to Camden's requirements, and Thomas Hearne declined to stand because he felt unable to take the oath of allegiance. For most of the eighteenth century the Camden professorship was treated as a sinecure by Frewin and others, though after his appointment he did buy £100 worth of books to qualify for the post. He apparently published nothing on history or on medicine.

Frewin's second wife died on 31 August 1731, leaving him her fortune, and in March 1732 he married a widow, Ellen Graves, the daughter of Peter Cranke. They had a much loved son, Peter, who died in 1748 aged twelve. After his son's death Frewin gradually gave up practice, retiring completely when his third wife died. He lived a quiet, regular life, taking an airing every day, dining at three with James Gilpin (d. 1766) and other friends, playing a rubber of whist, and going to bed at nine. Frewin was a small man. Of the various likenesses, his bust by L. F. Roubiliac is striking, square-headed, determined, and rather forbidding-looking, though he was noted for his compassion, and described as 'one of the most pleasant and placid old Men I ever knew' ('Memoir of Dr Frewin', 3). He was also very wealthy. By his will, six codicils, and other instructions, he left money, possessions, and property to his executors, relatives, godchildren, friends, and servants. On his orders, his papers and 'numberless' (ibid.) folios of patients' cases and observations were burnt. He left 2300 books to the Radcliffe Library; over 400 were classical, historical, and antiquarian books. In May 1768 the Radcliffe trustees bought for £24 4s. a copy of Frewin's large manuscript, 'Plantes medicinales', with descriptions and notes.

Frewin left his house in New Inn Hall Street to James Gilpin for life, and then to the regius professor of physic. The income from £2000 was to be paid to the physician to be appointed to the new Radcliffe Infirmary. This was shared between the senior physicians until 1959, but because it breached National Health Service regulations, it was subsequently awarded as the Frewin prize for an essay by a registrar or senior registrar. To Christ Church Frewin left £500 for the library; and he left the income from Marriage Hill Farm, Ramsbury, Wiltshire, of which he was the mortgagor, for scholars from Westminster School who were at Christ Church. The farm was sold, but the interest on the capital continued to fund the awards.

Frewin died after a short illness on 29 May 1761 at his home in New Inn Hall Lane, Oxford, and was buried on 3 June in St Peter-in-the-East (now the library of St Edmund Hall), where a tablet was erected to his memory.

JEAN LOUDON

Sources 'Memoir of Dr Frewin', Bodl. Oxf., Radcliffe Science Library, MSS Radcliffe records, S4, FB1, H7a, H10 • *Remarks and collections of Thomas Hearne*, ed. C. E. Doble and others, 11 vols., OHS, 2, 7, 13, 34, 42–3, 48, 50, 65, 67, 72 (1885–1921), vols. 5, 8–11 • will, PRO, PROB 11/867 • memorial tablet, St Peter's in the East (now library of St Edmund Hall), Oxford • *Old Westminsters*, vol. 1; suppl. 1 • J. Burke and J. B. Burke, *A genealogical and heraldic history of the extinct and dormant baronetcies of England, Ireland and Scotland*, 2nd edn (1841); repr. (1844) • Foster, *Alum. Oxon.* • A. H. T. Robb-Smith, *A short history of the Radcliffe Infirmary* (1970), 19, 202 • C. Webster, 'The medical faculty and the physic garden', *Hist. U. Oxf. 5: 18th-cent. Oxf.*, 683–723 • I. Guest, *Dr John Radcliffe and his trust* (1991), 153–4, 161 • *Jackson's Oxford Journal* (30 May 1761) • *Jackson's Oxford Journal* (6 June 1761) • *GM*, 1st ser., 31 (1761), 284 • *GM*, 1st ser., 36 (1766), 600 [death of James Gilpin] • first account book, Radcliffe Infirmary, Oxford • private information (2004) • Dr Frewin's and Dr Jubb's trust accounts, 1762–1864, Christ Church Oxf., MS 1v.b.55 • H. M. Sinclair and A. H. T. Robb-Smith, *A short history of anatomical teaching in Oxford* (1950), 31, 33 • H. S. Jones, 'The foundation and history of the Camden chair', *Oxoniensia*, 8–9 (1943–4), 169–92 • J. K. Crellin, 'William Cullen: his calibre as a teacher, and an unpublished introduction to his *Treatise of the materia medica*, London, 1773', *Medical History*, 15 (1971), 79–87, esp. 82 • G. L'E. Turner, 'The physical sciences', *Hist. U. Oxf. 5: 18th-cent. Oxf.*, 659–81 • R. Russell, *A dissertation concerning the use of sea water … to which is added an epistolatory dissertation to R. Frewin, MD* (1753) • *VCH Oxfordshire*, 4.437–8 • A. G. MacGregor and A. J. Turner, 'The Ashmolean Museum', *Hist. U. Oxf. 5: 18th-cent. Oxf.*, 649 • Burke, *Peerage* [for Christabella Tyrell, under Saye and Sele] • *IGI*

Archives Christ Church Oxf., MSS

Likenesses miniature, before 1725, Radcliffe Science Library, Oxford • L. F. Roubiliac, marble bust, 1757, Christ Church Oxf.; repro. in R. L. Poole, *Catalogue of portraits* (1912), facing p. 227; identical bust, History Faculty Library, Oxford • M. Dahl, oils, Christ Church Oxf. • circle of J. Vanderbank, oils, Westminster School • oils, Christ Church Oxf. • oils?, Radcliffe Infirmary, Oxford

Wealth at death approx. £8700 in legacies; property in Chigwell, Essex, and Clanfield, Oxfordshire; leasehold property in Oxford, Bath, and London; over 2300 books; silver; pictures; wine; furniture; linen; clothes; horses; carriages: will, PRO, PROB 11/867

Freyberg, Bernard Cyril, first Baron Freyberg (1889–1963), army officer and governor-general of New Zealand, was born on 21 March 1889 at 8 Dynevor Road, Richmond, Surrey, the son of James Freyberg (1827–1914), a land agent and surveyor, and his second wife, Julia Hamilton (1852–1936). He was his father's seventh son, but the fifth son of his father's second marriage. Very little is known about either parent: his Scottish-born mother may have had some university education and taught her children until they went to secondary school. In 1891 James Freyberg left London and took his family to Wellington, New Zealand, where he found employment in the forestry department.

James Freyberg died in 1914 but his widow lived on until 1936 and clearly exerted a lasting influence on her son. He attended Wellington College (1897–1904), a free state school for boys, until his fourteenth year, when his father apprenticed him to a dentist. Although he was not academically inclined it was at school that he began his military career, becoming a sergeant in the cadets. A noted swimmer, he competed in the 1905 Australian championships in Sydney and Brisbane, won the New Zealand junior championship in 1906, and the senior championship in 1910. Nicknamed Tiny, a schoolboy contradiction of his height of more than 6 feet, Freyberg also played rugby,

Bernard Cyril Freyberg, first Baron Freyberg (1889–1963), by
Lenare, 1939

rowed, boxed, and sailed. His dental apprenticeship in
Wellington until 1907 was followed by employment as a
dentist in Morrinsville, Hamilton, and Levin. Unfortunately he had been unaware of the Dental Act of 1904
which introduced a four-year university degree course.
Freyberg, in 1907, joined in a petition to parliament for an
amended act. There followed a brief, unsuccessful period
at Otago University in 1910, a further petition to parliament, and final professional registration as a dentist in
May 1911.

Between 1905 and 1907 Freyberg belonged to D battery
of the New Zealand field artillery volunteers in Wellington. A more positive step in his military career was his
commission as a second lieutenant in the territorial sixth
Hauraki regiment in late 1911. A dock and shipping strike
in Wellington brought Freyberg to Wellington as a special
mounted constable in 1913 and it was during this unrest
that he crossed to Sydney several times as a volunteer
stoker. A brief return to dentistry, which he never liked
and of which he never spoke, decided Freyberg to seek a
better life overseas. At the end of March 1914 he sailed for
San Francisco, USA. What he did during the following four
months is full of uncertainty but it seems probable that
Freyberg, as a security guard for a film company, went to
Mexico where late in June 1914 he may have seen some
action in the civil war in the force commanded by General
Francisco 'Pancho' Villa. Two months later, on 5 August
1914, the First World War broke out and by the end of the
month Freyberg was in England.

Gallipoli and the western front In London Freyberg lost no
time in seeking a commission. On the advice of G. S.

Scholefield, a New Zealand press representative, he saw
Major G. S. Richardson, New Zealand's liaison officer at
the War Office, who was then on the staff of the Royal
Naval division. The latter had also been a member of
Wellington's D battery. The upshot was that Freyberg was
given a temporary commission as a lieutenant in the
Royal Naval Volunteer Reserve and posted to the Hood battalion of the 2nd Royal Naval brigade, soon to be promoted lieutenant-commander, commanding A company.
He also met Winston Churchill, first lord of the Admiralty
and champion of the naval division, who may have played
a part in securing his commission (Freyberg, 37).

In September 1914 Antwerp, covering the vital channel
ports, was threatened by advancing German forces. To
reinforce the insufficient Belgian army the Royal Naval
division was ordered to Antwerp in the first week of October. Freyberg's A company Hood battalion had its first
taste of action and joined the withdrawal on 8 October.
Freyberg, reconnoitring a route, received his first wound
from an electrified fence which severely burned his hand.
He returned to England and was at Crystal Palace and
Blandford with the Royal Naval division, regrouping and
training until 27 February 1915 when it was sent to the
Middle East for the Gallipoli campaign. It was an important period in Freyberg's development, both in a military
sense, for he lacked experience and, particularly, in the
opportunity to learn, observe, and assimilate the social
and intellectual patterns then available to him. His fellow
officers, the 'Argonauts', have often been described as the
cream of young British manhood. Arthur Asquith, Rupert
Brooke, Denis Browne, and Patrick Shaw-Stewart were A
company officers. These and others opened social and political doors that included those of Prime Minister Asquith
and First Lord of the Admiralty Winston Churchill.

As a preliminary to the action Freyberg played a part in
the burial of Rupert Brooke on the island of Skyros on 23
April 1915, helping to select the site and, with other officers, covering the grave with a cairn of marble rocks. During the action at Gallipoli itself, Freyberg won renown
with a long swim on the night of 25–26 April, towing a bag
of flares to shore at the beach below Bulair in the Gulf of
Saros, there to deceive the Turks that a major landing was
taking place. For this exceptional exploit he was awarded
the DSO. Freyberg later took part in the badly conceived
actions to capture Achi Baba and had temporary command of Hood battalion from 25 June 1915, relinquishing
it when he was shot in the stomach about a month later. A
rapid recovery in hospital in Egypt led to a return to Gallipoli in mid-August, when he was promoted commander
to lead the battalion in a reorganized Royal Naval division.
After a further three months in and out of the front line
Freyberg joined the general evacuation and left Gallipoli
with the battalion rearguard at 2.30 a.m. on 9 January
1916. The battalion was able to parade only fifteen men
from its original establishment.

Back in London Freyberg decided to pursue a permanent
career in the forces and applied for a transfer to the British
army where his new contacts opened horizons of great
opportunity. On 19 May 1916 he was gazetted captain in

the Royal West Surrey regiment and temporary lieutenant-colonel commanding the Hood battalion which was concentrated on the western front by 24 May 1916. Training and routine followed until the Royal Naval division, now transferred to the British army as 63 division, took part in the battle of the Somme in October. It was here, on 13 November 1916, during the battle of the Ancre, that Freyberg, amid quite incredible scenes of chaos and carnage, displayed conspicuous bravery and leadership during the capture of the village of Beaucourt. After two relatively minor wounds he was gravely wounded in the neck and eventually evacuated, but he refused to leave until the advanced position had been consolidated against counter-attack. For his role in the action Freyberg was awarded the Victoria Cross. It was mid-February 1917 before he was sufficiently healed to return to the Hood battalion.

For Freyberg the three-month recovery period in London was to produce two new elements that were to affect him for the rest of his life. He was introduced to the dramatist J. M. Barrie, who became one of his greatest friends and who encouraged his dormant but undoubted ability to write. And he renewed his acquaintance with Barbara McLaren (1888–1973), whose husband, Francis, was killed in August 1917 and who became his wife on 14 June 1922. As the daughter of Sir Herbert and Lady Jekyll, and widow of the son of the first Baron Aberconway, she provided not only an excellent family background but also an effective partner in all his future undertakings. Their only son, Paul, was born in 1923.

On 20 April 1917 Freyberg was posted to command 173 brigade in 58 division: at the age of only twenty-eight he was the youngest brigadier-general in the British army. Between 12 and 20 May there was severe and costly fighting at Bullecourt. Despite high casualties Freyberg felt that his careful training regime had greatly increased the morale and fighting capacity of his brigade. At the end of August 1917 his division was transferred from Third to Fifth Army in preparation for an attack at Passchendaele. After difficult preliminaries in shell-swept mud the battle of Menin Road began on 20 September. That same day Freyberg was severely wounded, penetrated in five places by a bursting shell. He was hospitalized until the end of November.

On 21 January 1918 Freyberg was appointed to command 88 infantry brigade in 29 division, then in the area south of Ypres. Here he was in and out of the line, training and reshaping his brigade until 21 March when the Germans began their last great offensive in the Somme. The brigade contested an engulfing sea of mud until 10 April, when it was ordered to halt a German thrust south of Ypres, near Bailleul. Amid the chaos Freyberg added other infantry companies, artillery batteries, engineers, and stragglers to his command and held the line. Minor but costly operations followed for the next five months. On 3 June Freyberg had been wounded for the ninth time but was not evacuated.

After a major thrust westwards from Ypres at the end of September Freyberg was awarded a bar to his DSO. By 11 November his brigade was some 10 miles short of the River Dendre. Ordered to capture the bridges at Lessines, Freyberg, on horseback with a squadron from 7 dragoon guards, achieved this just moments before the armistice. He was awarded a second bar to his DSO for this venture. On 13 December 29 division crossed the Rhine at Hohenzollern Bridge to take part in the occupation. For Freyberg the war was over.

Reverting to the substantive rank of captain, Freyberg applied for a regular commission in the Grenadier Guards in March 1919. He was sent to Staff College, Camberley, for most of 1919 and in February 1920 was posted to 1st battalion Grenadier Guards. Dogged by ill health caused by incompletely healed wounds, Freyberg left for a six-week sea journey to New Zealand in May 1921 in order to recover his health and visit his mother. Back in England he was appointed GSO2 in 44 (Home Counties) division at Woolwich.

Freyberg made his first unsuccessful attempt to enter parliament, as Liberal candidate for Cardiff South, in 1922. Soldiering had not entirely ousted his earlier ambitions, and he made three attempts to swim the English Channel, failing narrowly in August 1925, and again the following August. He was posted back to 1st battalion Grenadier Guards on 26 January 1926 and became a substantive major with a brevet for lieutenant-colonel in October 1927 when posted as GSO2, headquarters eastern command, at the Horse Guards. In March 1929 he was given command of the 1st battalion of the Manchester regiment at Shorncliffe near Folkestone. It was here that he wrote most of *A Study of Unit Administration*, published in 1923, setting out the need for a commanding officer to ensure economical and sensible administration that would have particular regard for the welfare of the troops, especially in matters of diet.

Early in 1931, as colonel, with backdated seniority to 1 January 1922, Freyberg was appointed assistant quartermaster-general southern command, then in 1933 as GSO1 at the War Office. On 16 July 1934 he was promoted major-general, soon to be on half pay until a suitable posting came up. This was in January 1935 when he was appointed general officer commanding (GOC) in the presidency and Assam district of the eastern command of India. Fate intervened when routine medical boards detected an irregular heart beat and the appointment was cancelled. After much medical discussion Freyberg was placed on retired pay in September 1937. It could have been little consolation that he was created CB in February 1936.

Freyberg failed to win the Conservative candidacy for the Ipswich constituency in 1938. Offered the candidacy for the Spelthorne division of Middlesex in 1940, he was unable to stand because of military commitment. He became a director of the Birmingham Small Arms Company in 1938, and he supervised the erection of fifteen houses on properties inherited by his wife. On 3 September 1939, under a medical grading which declared him fit for home service only, he took up appointment as GOC Salisbury Plain. Nevertheless, Freyberg got himself graded medically fit for active service by a Salisbury medical board on 11 October, and had this confirmed on 2 November by a doubtless surprised War Office medical board, with the reservation that he was fit for active service only in temperate climates, a grading he retained for the whole of the Second World War.

Commander of New Zealand forces New Zealand declared war on Germany on 3 September 1939; and Freyberg offered his services to the New Zealand government on 16 September while carrying on with his major task of preparing units for dispatch to France. On 4 November Peter Fraser, New Zealand's deputy prime minister, in London for a meeting of dominion ministers, arranged to meet Freyberg, was very favourably impressed, and after discussions with his own government, the chief of the Imperial General Staff (CIGS), General Ironside, General Gort, and Winston Churchill was able to inform Freyberg on 16 November that he would command New Zealand's expeditionary force (2NZEF).

After a short visit to France, Freyberg went to New Zealand to consult with government and to get to know as many of his senior officers as he could reach. A charter was drawn up defining his dual role as a servant of the New Zealand government, which was uppermost, and as a subordinate of the commander-in-chief of the forces to which he might be attached. He was given a great deal of discretion and, as commander 2NZEF, with its necessary non-divisional units—medical, engineering, administrative and so on—had a much greater command than that of a divisional commander in a British corps. Unlike the commander of the Australian forces, who was ranked in the Australian army, he was a British officer on loan to New Zealand.

Freyberg's effectiveness did not come into serious contention until the ill-advised campaigns in Greece and Crete in March and April 1941. Until then, from both the Middle East and England, to which about one third of the 2NZEF had been diverted in June 1940, he had assiduously consulted and advised the New Zealand government. As it became clear that the original plan of using Egypt as a staging and training base en route to action in France was no longer relevant, Freyberg's major efforts were directed to the concentration and training of his division in the Middle East. Owing largely to the political over-optimism of Anthony Eden in creating a Balkan front and the ambivalence of the service commanders, Freyberg failed to inform the New Zealand government of the risks and lack of equipment and air cover, associated with the campaign in Greece in the mistaken belief that Wavell or Eden had done this. Within the month of April 1941 the campaign in Greece, never militarily possible, was fought and lost. Freyberg, with about two thirds of 2nd New Zealand division less most of its equipment, was in Crete, with instructions from Wavell to command all allied forces there and to hold the island at all costs, a role he accepted with grave misgivings as a matter of duty.

Crete, north Africa, and Italy On 20 May 1941 the expected German onslaught on Crete began. In the three weeks available to him Freyberg had positioned his forces which lacked artillery, armour, air cover and much normal infantry equipment. The Enigma decrypts had provided generals Wavell and Wilson with most accurate information about German plans and movements during the campaign in Greece: this had been extended to Crete on 18 April 1941 and Freyberg received it disguised as information supplied by a Secret Intelligence Service agent in Athens (Hinsley, 417). He accordingly covered the areas Maleme, Khania, Retimo, and Heraklion—and the Germans assumed that espionage had divulged their plan (ibid., 420). Debate will continue over whether Freyberg had the resources in men or material to hold Crete, and over his insistence on the need to cover a possible seaborne landing that was in fact smashed by the Royal Navy. Nevertheless, for whatever reason, the failure to deny the principal landing strip, Maleme, to the German airforce proved decisive. Certainly Freyberg pondered the problem for the rest of his life. However, the importance to Freyberg of the withdrawal actions in Greece and Crete eventually centred on his relationship with Prime Minister Peter Fraser who felt that he had committed 2nd New Zealand division without adequate consultation. Freyberg was able to satisfy Fraser on this count, though neither was aware of the degree of Eden's optimism and its impact on the information given to the Australian and New Zealand governments. Any doubts about Freyberg's leadership that Fraser may have had, due to complaints by a senior officer, were swept away after very warm commendations from the CIGS, Dill, and also from Wavell. For the remainder of the war Fraser had undeviating confidence in Freyberg, who never again failed to give explicit information.

By now the Germans had effectively reinforced the Italians in north Africa, which became Freyberg's battleground for the next two years. These years may be broken down into four main periods: the relief of Tobruk, November to December 1941; the battle for Egypt, June to July 1942; the deciding battles of Alam Halfa and Alamein, August and November 1942; and the pursuit to Enfidaville in Tunisia. It was in these battles, which swayed up and down in that narrow strip of north Africa between the Mediterranean and the pathless desert, that 2nd New Zealand division became Rommel's most feared opponent and which prompted Churchill to designate Freyberg the salamander of the British empire. As in France in the First World War, Freyberg led from in front at the cost of a severe neck wound from a shell splinter on 27 June 1942 at Minqar Qaim. His division, sometimes strengthened to corps status, became expert in the three vital desert operations: the set piece break-in attack; immediate pursuit; and the outflanking movement or left hook.

For Freyberg success depended on the will to win of a fully trained force at the highest pitch of physical fitness, capable of co-operating with all other arms. He was made a KBE in the New Zealand 1942 honours list for skilled leadership in Greece and Crete and an immediate KCB in November 1942 for his historic contribution at Alam Halfa and Alamein. On 1 March 1942 he was promoted temporary lieutenant-general at the request of the New Zealand government which was prompted to this action because the GOC Australian Imperial Force, who was junior to Freyberg, had been promoted to that rank on 27 March 1942. Perhaps his greatest prize was, while temporary commander of 10 corps, to accept the surrender of the Italian Field Marshal Messe, supreme axis commander in north Africa, on 13 May 1943. On 8 July 1943 Freyberg was restored to the active list of the regular army with seniority backdated to 2 November 1939. Lady Freyberg, who made a distinguished contribution to the war effort by organizing welfare for troops, was appointed OBE in 1943. In 1953 she became a GBE.

After Africa, Italy. Here the campaign against the occupying German forces, for Italy had surrendered, fell into two phases: the hard battles culminating in the fall of Cassino on 18 May 1944 and the pursuit to Trieste, the end of the war.

The successful Sangro River crossing ended in stalemate at Orsogna and Freyberg's division, trained and organized for mobile operations, was moved from the Adriatic coast to the command of the US Fifth Army in the west. The division was to be used in a pursuit role to and beyond Rome after a successful thrust from the Anzio landing. Largely because of failure to exploit initial success at Anzio, Freyberg—who believed that this would have been an ideal role for 2nd New Zealand division (Freyberg, 455)—was again faced with a static front culminating in the battle for Cassino. For Freyberg the bombing of the Abbey Monte Cassino has attracted almost more attention than the extremely costly and only partially successful operations of his division. Organized as NZ corps on 3 February 1944 with the inclusion of 4 Indian division, this force's task became the capture of Monte Cassino and Cassino township, both rendered almost impregnable by the cover provided by the bombed ruins. Freyberg, never sanguine that a frontal attack would succeed (ibid., 457), had made it clear to General Alexander that he would withdraw 2nd New Zealand division if casualties reached 1000. Accordingly, with the road to Rome still blocked at Cassino and New Zealand casualties at 998, plans were changed and 2nd New Zealand division began an outflanking move. Cassino fell by a combined assault on 18 May 1944. Freyberg had resumed command of 2nd New Zealand division on 27 March, the corps being disbanded.

Rome was entered on 4 June by the US Fifth Army and Freyberg, ever solicitous for the welfare of his troops, acquired the best hotel, the Quirinal, in the face of keen competition, for use as the NZ forces club. Freyberg's policy during the advance on Florence was to maintain pressure but to avoid major commitment. For him the period produced three major events: the fall of Florence on 4 August, a visit by Prime Minister Churchill on 24 August, and an aircraft accident during a visit to Eighth Army headquarters on 3 September. Freyberg was incapacitated until 14 October 1944 (Freyberg, 476–9). Thereafter he reorganized and retrained his division so that it could best meet the conditions demanded by the nature of the country, riven by stop banks and swiftly flowing rivers. There remained five distinct and major river crossings requiring set-piece attacks followed by immediate pursuit, given hands-on control and making use of Freyberg's unique skill matured in so many battles from Gallipoli, Flanders, north Africa, and finally Italy. The final stages of the war in Italy saw Freyberg directing a highly mobile division and attached arms in a spectacular advance to Trieste and the enemy surrender. He was awarded a third bar to the DSO and created commander of the US Legion of Merit.

Governor-general Freyberg relinquished command of 2NZEF on 22 November 1945. He remained on the British army list with the rank of lieutenant-general until his retirement was announced on 10 September 1946. Freyberg's service to New Zealand was to continue, however. He was offered the position of governor-general of New Zealand in September 1945, being sworn in on 17 June 1946. He had received an honorary DCL from Oxford University in 1945, and became GCMG early in 1946. Freyberg later said that his six years as governor-general were the happiest of his life, combining a position of great responsibility with his pleasure in meeting—and in the case of former soldiers, greeting—very many people. Freyberg and his wife, Barbara (perhaps a little anxious that protocol would become secondary to Kiwi friendliness), constantly at his side, made a warmly appreciated and constitutionally effective pair. As well as carrying out the busy round of official duties and functions, visiting Pacific island dependencies and neighbours, including Australia, and preparing for royal visits by George VI and, after the king's illness, Princess Elizabeth, the Freybergs entertained and introduced to New Zealand many world leaders in politics, the services, and the arts. Field Marshal Montgomery, Anthony Eden, and Marie Rambert are but three examples. And with one of his wartime brigadiers, Major-General H. K. Kippenberger, a close personal friend, the editor-in-chief, he took a great and helpful interest in the preparation of the official war history. Working historians soon discovered his consuming interest in the battle for Crete. In 1951 Freyberg was created baron and took the title Baron Freyberg, of Wellington, New Zealand, and of Munstead in the county of Surrey. A final honour was bestowed on 3 July 1952 when Victoria University of Wellington conferred an honorary LLD. Amid unprecedented cheering crowds Lord Freyberg left Wellington for the final time on 15 August 1952.

Freyberg's final official position was that of lieutenant-governor and constable of Windsor Castle, which he had been asked to consider before he left New Zealand. Inspection of the Norman Tower, the official residence, revealed the need of updating, which included the provision of a lift for which Freyberg paid half the cost. Although appointed under the sign manual on 1 March 1953, the Freybergs did not occupy the Norman Tower until September 1954. Official duties included playing a leading role at Windsor Castle functions, for example, the conferring of the Order of the Garter on Winston Churchill. Freyberg also took a great interest in the proceedings of the House of Lords and spoke in some of the debates. He represented either the New Zealand services or government at such occasions as the Alamein reunion in 1952, sitting with Churchill, Alexander, and Montgomery, or at the dedication of memorials at Malta, Alamein, and Athens. Freyberg also played a role in the coronation of Elizabeth II. An event which gave him great personal satisfaction was the celebration of the centenary of the founding of the Victoria Cross when, on 26 June 1956, he commanded the Hyde Park parade of 297 holders of the award.

Reputation After the First World War—young, handsome, and much decorated—Freyberg was able to settle down and make a career for himself. As a soldier in the Second World War he fully lived up to the criteria that he had set out as necessary qualifications for the general commanding New Zealand troops: that he should be able to conduct a retreat under heavy enemy pressure; that he could make a counter-stroke, force a river line, or conduct operations in open warfare involving co-operation of all arms; that he should be able to carry out effective artillery fire plans. All these qualities were required and were amply supplied in the battles of north Africa and Italy. Freyberg himself believed that his division's most memorable days were in its part in holding the axis forces in the Middle East until the allies were organized on a war footing, that is until 'the turn of the tide' at Alamein.

Should Freyberg have been promoted to commands greater than that of 2NZEF? He did of course command 10 corps in Tunisia, and in both north Africa and Italy his command was often swelled to corps size. And command of 2NZEF was very much more than command of a single division, with ultimate responsibility for the many non-divisional troops and services and the necessary contact with a government and a prime minister. Considering Freyberg's technique as a fighting general—to lead from in front, adopted in the Hood battalion and maintained to the very end at Trieste—his ability to hold the respect and loyalty of his quite remarkably talented senior officers, together with his success in his dealings with the New Zealand government, he was ideally placed where he was.

Freyberg as a divisional commander was well supported by his brigade and services commanders. He conducted orders groups before major engagements, with maps, sand trays or plaster models, and aerial photographs. Discussion was free and vigorous. In pursuit he became known for the cry 'they've gone', and instant conferences with leading brigade commanders could result in a stream of orders and suggestions until the relevant commander seized on one thought possible and made off. It was unorthodox, but it worked. He was known by sight to the rank and file—it was Field Marshal Slim who said that a division 'is the smallest formation that is a complete orchestra of war, and the largest in which every man can know you' (Slim, 3). Freyberg was greatly respected, though few were aware of his concern that New Zealand's 'one ewe lamb' should not be exhausted of manpower.

Of the many encomiums from his superiors, that from

Montgomery spells it out: 'His example and infectious optimism were an inspiration to the whole army. Such outstanding leadership can rarely have been seen in the history of the British army' (B. L. Montgomery, introduction to Freyburg's report 'The New Zealand division in Egypt and Libya', unpublished, priv. coll.). While Montgomery was proud to have Freyberg and 2nd New Zealand division in Eighth Army, German documents reveal that they were most dreaded, and respected, by Field Marshal Rommel.

After the misunderstandings surrounding the defeats in Greece and Crete, Freyberg's relationship with the New Zealand government was excellent. Prime Minister Fraser wrote: 'We could have had no better Commander of our Expeditionary Force and never was a Commander more thoroughly and completely trusted' (Freyberg, 507). Of course he made mistakes, and his role in the débâcle in Crete will remain controversial. In addition, he failed to push ahead at Tebaga Gap in the Mareth line operations, after an easy break-in attack. Cassino, as he had advised corps and army commanders, could not be captured by frontal attack. Despite errors of judgement, which Freyberg shared with higher command, nothing can overshadow the record of the division which became synonymous with the name of its commander.

Freyberg, whose health was deteriorating with the onset of Parkinson's disease and hardening of the arteries of the brain, suffered a rupture of his Gallipoli stomach wound on 4 July 1963, and died later that night in King Edward VII Hospital, Windsor, aged seventy-four. He was buried at St Martha-on-the-Hill Church, Surrey, on the Pilgrims Way, on 10 July 1963.   IAN WARDS

Sources P. Freyberg, *Bernard Freyberg, VC, soldier of two nations* (1991) · L. Sellers, *The Hood battalion: Antwerp, Gallipoli, France, 1914–18* (1995) · *Documents relating to New Zealand's participation in the Second World War, 1939–45*, War History Branch (Wellington, New Zealand), vol. 1 (1949), vol. 2 (1951) · W. G. Stevens, *Freyberg V.C., the man, 1939–1945* (1965) · A. Hercus, *Lieutenant-General Sir Bernard Freyberg, V. C. etc* (1946) · *Official History of New Zealand in the Second World War, 1939–1945* · W. E. Murphy, *The relief of Tobruk* (1961) · F. H. Hinsley and others, *British intelligence in the Second World War*, 1 (1979) · Field-Marshal Viscount Slim, *Defeat into victory* (1972) · *New Zealand Gazette* · P. S. Gates, *General Lord Freyberg VC* (1963) · army department personal file, Archives New Zealand, Wellington, AD 36/27, pts. 1–2 · private information (2004) [Sir John White] · D. G. Stewart, *The struggle for Crete* (1991) · A. Beevor, *Crete: the battle and the resistance* (1991) · L. Barber and J. Tonkin-Covell, *Freyberg: Churchill's salamander* (1989) · b. cert. · *CGPLA Eng. & Wales* (1963) · d. cert.
Archives Archives New Zealand, Wellington, personal papers, WA 2, series 8 · NRA, papers in private possession | Archives New Zealand, Wellington, army appointments, EAI, PM 87/3/9 · Archives New Zealand, Wellington, army department personal file, AD 36/27, pts 1–2 | FILM BFI NFTVA, 'V.C. fails in attack on victorious channel', Topical Budget, 10 Aug 1925 · BFI NFTVA, 'The advance in Libya', *British News*, 28 Dec 1942 · BFI NFTVA, documentary footage · BFI NFTVA, news footage · BFI NFTVA, propaganda film footage (New Zealand Army film) · IWM FVA, 'General Clarke visits Venice', 11 May 1945, A 924/13 [incl. footage of General Freyberg receiving the Legion of Merit] · IWM FVA, actuality footage · IWM FVA, documentary footage · IWM FVA, news footage | SOUND BL NSA, documentary recordings · IWM SA, oral history interview · NZ Sound Archives

Likenesses A. McEvoy, oils, 1918, IWM · Lenare, photographs, 1939, NPG [*see illus.*] · group portrait, photograph, 1940, Hult. Arch. · I. Halliday, oils, Auckland War Memorial Museum · P. McIntyre, oils, Archives New Zealand, Wellington; copy, Ministry of Defence, Wellington · P. McIntyre, oils, Wellington College · P. McIntyre, oils, priv. coll. · O. Nemon, bronze bust, New Zealand House, London; copy, Ministry of Defence, Wellington; posthumous copy, St Paul's Cathedral, London · photographs, Archives New Zealand, Wellington · photographs, NL NZ, Turnbull L.

Wealth at death £34,620: probate, 23 Dec 1963, *CGPLA Eng. & Wales*

Freyer, Sir Peter Johnston (1851–1921), surgeon, was born in Sellerna, a village 8 miles from Clifden, co. Galway, Ireland, on 21 July 1851, the eldest son of Samuel Freyer, farmer, and his wife, Celia Burke. He was educated at Erasmus Smith's College, Galway, and Queen's College, Galway, then one of the constituent colleges of the Queen's University of Ireland. In 1872 he graduated in arts, with first-class honours and the gold medal. He then went to Dublin to study medicine at Steevens's Hospital, where he was a resident pupil of Robert McDonnell. He spent a short time in Paris, and in 1874 took the degrees of MD and MS at Queen's University, again winning the gold medal.

In 1876 Freyer married Isabella McVittie (*d.* 1914), daughter of Robert McVittie, of Dublin, and with her had a son and a daughter.

Freyer gained first place in the examination for the Indian Medical Service (IMS) in 1875, becoming surgeon-major in 1887 and lieutenant-colonel in 1895, and retiring from the service in 1896. In the Bengal army he served chiefly in the North-Western (afterwards the United) Provinces of India, and was for a time surgeon to the Prince of Wales's Hospital at Benares. Here he gained much experience in operating on cataracts and in crushing stones in the bladder by the method of litholapaxy which was introduced in 1878 by Henry Jacob Bigelow, of Boston, Massachusetts. In 1886 Freyer published *The Modern Treatment of Stone in the Bladder by Litholapaxy*, which was well received and saw a second edition in 1896.

After returning to England in 1897, Freyer was appointed surgeon to St Peter's Hospital for Stone, Henrietta Street, London, and devised the operation of total and complete removal of the prostate gland through a suprapubic incision of the bladder. He published his first four cases in 1901 (*BMJ*, 1901, 125), and the results of his first thousand cases in 1912 (*BMJ*, 1912, 869). Freyer also published two monographs on this field, *Stricture of the Urethra and Prostatic Enlargement* (1901), which had two further editions, and *Surgical Diseases of the Urinary Organs* (1908). He was awarded the Arnott memorial medal in 1904 for his work in this branch of surgery, and in 1920 was elected the first president of the newly constituted section of urology at the Royal Society of Medicine.

Freyer rejoined the Indian Medical Service (IMS) on the outbreak of the First World War, but was employed in England as consulting surgeon to the Queen Alexandra Military Hospital at Millbank, London, and to the Eastern command. He was created CB in January 1917 and made KCB

the following June. He was placed on the retired list with the rank of colonel, IMS, in 1919.

Freyer died at his home, 27 Harley Street, London, on 9 September 1921. He was buried in the protestant cemetery at Clifden, co. Galway.

D'A. POWER, *rev.* JEFFREY S. REZNICK

Sources *The Times* (10 Sept 1921) · private information (1927) · personal knowledge (1927) · *BMJ* (17 Sept 1921), 464–5 · *The Lancet* (24 Sept 1921), 677 · *CGPLA Eng. & Wales* (1921)

Likenesses W. Stoneman, photograph, 1917, NPG · oils, St Peter's Hospital, Henrietta Street, London

Wealth at death £130,053 6s. 4d.: probate, 5 Nov 1921, *CGPLA Eng. & Wales*

Frías. For this title name *see* Balfe, Victoire [Victoire Fernández de Velasco, duchess of Frías in the Spanish nobility] (1837–1871).

Fricker, Peter Racine (1920–1990), composer and music teacher, was born on 5 September 1920 in Ealing, London, the elder child and only son of Edward Racine Fricker (*d.* 1935/6), civil servant, and his wife, Deborah Alice Parr, nurse. His middle name came from his great-grandmother, who was a direct descendant of the French dramatist. He was educated at St Paul's School, London. His father died when Peter was fifteen and about to enter the merchant navy, but this plan was prevented by his poor eyesight. He began studying organ as a schoolboy with Henry Wilson, then entered the Royal College of Music in 1937, where he continued his organ studies with Ernest Bullock, and piano with Henry Wilson. He was assistant organist to Wilson while continuing his studies. Before the Second World War, he also attended classes at Morley College. An early distinction was his election as a fellow of the Royal College of Organists at the age of nineteen. He studied theory and composition with R. O. Morris.

In 1940 Fricker's studies were interrupted by the war, during which he served as a radio operator in the Royal Air Force, in signals and intelligence. It was at the Royal College of Music that he had met (Audrey) Helen, a pianist, the daughter of Raymonde William Lee Clench, chartered accountant. They married in 1943, the same year he was posted to India to serve as an intelligence officer. There were no children of the marriage.

After the war years Fricker resumed his composition studies with Mátyás Seiber, who became a strong influence and a close friend and colleague at Morley College, in London. During his years there he conducted, acted as rehearsal pianist for the choir, and, together with his wife, made a living copying and arranging music. From 1952 to 1964 he held a dual post as director of music at Morley College, where he succeeded Michael Tippett, and also as professor of composition at the Royal College of Music. His career as a composer was launched when he won the A. J. Clements prize for his wind quintet in 1947, which was quickly followed by the Koussevitzky prize for his first symphony in 1949, and by winning the Arts Council Festival of Britain competition for young composers prize for his violin concerto in 1951. These distinctions made him one of the most prominent British composers of his generation.

Fricker's music represented a departure from the nationalistic pastoralism coined by Ralph Vaughan Williams, for he was one of the first in England to assimilate the contributions of Béla Bartók, Arnold Schoenberg, and Igor Stravinsky, and to synthesize these influences with an expressively dissonant style of his own. During the 1950s he composed seven film scores and six works for radio. Other important works during this highly prolific period include two more symphonies (nos. 2 and 3), *Dance Scene* (1954), *Litany* (1955), and the large oratorio *The Vision of Judgement* (1956–8).

In 1964 Fricker was invited to the University of California at Santa Barbara, as visiting professor. He became enamoured of the school and its surroundings, and excited about the possibility of establishing a centre for compositional study at the university. In 1965 he was appointed professor. His wife joined him in Santa Barbara, and they lived in nearby Goleta for the rest of his life. He held the Dorothy and Sherill C. Corwin chair in music, and had a joint appointment in the university's innovative College of Creative Studies. He was a dedicated, patient teacher, and provided guidance to many composition students over the years. He was a tall, imposing figure of a man, but gentle and rather shy and reserved. His interests included bird-watching, word puzzles, mystery novels, travel, and cats.

His compositional output was extensive, and Fricker was steadily prolific throughout his entire career. His oeuvre included five symphonies, three string quartets, a ballet, an oratorio, concerti, various choral works, numerous chamber works, and others in all genres except staged opera, comprising a total of more than 160 works in all. His reputation was international, and he composed works for important performers and ensembles such as Julian Bream, Dennis Brain, Henryk Szering, the Amadeus Quartet, and the Royal Philharmonic Orchestra. In 1976 his symphony no. 5 was given its première by the BBC Symphony Orchestra to commemorate the twenty-fifth anniversary of the Royal Festival Hall.

Fricker's honours and awards included an honorary fellowship of the Royal Academy of Music (1966), an honorary doctorate in music from the University of Leeds (1958), the freedom of the City of London, and the order of merit of West Germany (1965). He was an honorary professorial fellow and research professor in the Institute of Creative Arts of University College, Cardiff, as well as an active member of the International Society for Contemporary Music, the Society of Composers International, and the Composers' Guild of Great Britain (of which he was elected vice-president in 1986). During the summers from 1984 to 1986 he served as president of the Cheltenham international festival.

In 1989 Fricker was appointed composer-in-residence of the Santa Barbara Symphony Orchestra, for which he had composed an orchestral work, *Walk by Quiet Waters* (1988). It was while he was working on a second work for them,

and looking forward to retirement, that he died on 1 February 1990 in Santa Barbara, of cancer of the throat and larynx.
       JOHN J. CARBON, *rev.*

Sources *New Grove* · J. Vinton, ed., *Dictionary of contemporary music* (1974) · U. Cal., Santa Barbara, Arts Library, Fricker archives · *The Times* (16 Feb 1990) · *The Independent* (8 Feb 1990) · private information (1996) · personal knowledge (1996)
Archives U. Cal., Santa Barbara, Arts Library
Likenesses M. Ambler, photograph, Hult. Arch.

Frideswide. *See* Frithuswith (*d.* 727).

Fridugisus [Frithugils, Nathanael] (*d.* 833), abbot and scholar, was called Frithugils in his native Old English and nicknamed Nathanael by his teacher Alcuin, whom he followed from York to the continent. There he sometimes served as an emissary and was later a teacher at the court school of the Frankish emperor Charlemagne. Fridugisus's distinction in the Carolingian world is revealed by his subsequent career, first as Alcuin's successor, from 804 or 806, as abbot of Tours (he was also abbot of St Bertin, St Omer, and Cormery), and later as archchancellor for Charlemagne's successor, the emperor Louis the Pious, between 819 and 833. In addition, Fridugisus was a notable—and notably controversial—speculative thinker, innovative in his application of the techniques of grammatical analysis to theological problems.

During the era of Alcuin's pre-eminence in the Carolingian intellectual world, his trusted students and assistants often appear in an understudy role, barely attested in the sources, perhaps with few securely attributed works; only their subsequent careers reveal the learning and esteem they had acquired during Alcuin's lifetime. Such is the case with the Anglo-Saxon Fridugisus. When Notker remarked on the success of Alcuin's pupils in becoming devout abbots and famous bishops, he surely had the career of Fridugisus (among others) in mind.

Fridugisus is first attested in Alcuin's letters of the late 790s, that is, during the time of Alcuin's abbacy of Tours. At this period, he seems frequently to have been employed as a messenger between Alcuin, Charlemagne, and Arno, bishop of Salzburg. At some earlier stage, however, he had been a student of Alcuin (who nicknamed him Nathanael, then understood to mean *deus meus* or *donum dei* in Hebrew). Fridugisus's own controversial work would reflect the influence of his acquaintance with grammar and dialectic as Alcuin's student.

Whether at the court, at Tours, or serving as messenger between the two, Fridugisus maintained close intellectual ties with Alcuin. His questioning was the impetus for Alcuin to write a short question-and-answer work on the Trinity which he dedicated to his pupil. Alcuin also addressed an account of the three types of vision to Fridugisus. Finally, in the dedicatory letter of his revision of Jerome's commentary on Ecclesiastes, Alcuin expressed the fear that Fridugisus and other pupils were becoming too entangled in material concerns during their service at court.

Fridugisus gradually gained respect at court and enjoyed particular intimacy with Charlemagne and the royal family; it was during this time, also, that he advanced from being a deacon to the office of archdeacon (before 15 April 800). Alcuin entrusted him with conveying Christmas greetings and presenting a volume of the New Testament to Charlemagne on Christmas day at Aachen one year, and he trusted Fridugisus to intercede for him during a painful dispute with the emperor. He commended Fridugisus's service as a teacher to Charlemagne's sister, and seems to have assumed that Fridugisus would also be engaged in teaching at least one of the emperor's daughters. (This responsibility also provoked a stern warning from Alcuin to Fridugisus against the dangers of too much familiarity with the royal womenfolk.) In court poetry, Fridugisus was remembered as a wise, learned, and dignified deacon in his youth and, in old age, as followed by a throng of students.

Charlemagne's esteem for Fridugisus is evident. When Alcuin died in 804, the emperor named Fridugisus to succeed him at Tours, one of the wealthiest and most important abbeys in the realm. Fridugisus also appears as a witness to the emperor's will in 811. Charlemagne died in 814, but Louis the Pious shared his father's high opinion of Fridugisus. He conferred additional abbacies on him (St Bertin and St Omer, 820) at a time when lay abbacy was not perceived as irregular. Louis also chose him as archchancellor in 819, in which capacity Fridugisus served until his retirement in 832. He was the first archchancellor of high rank who had not come to the post after service as a notary. During his tenure the status and professionalism of the post seem to have been enhanced; thus Fridugisus was more concerned with management and less with everyday business than his predecessors. A deputy drafted documents and attested for him, while Fridugisus himself oversaw an improvement in the Latinity and formulation of documents. He was probably responsible for the compilation of a new imperial formulary.

Modern scholarship has partially absolved Fridugisus of later medieval criticisms of his alleged tyranny and avarice as an abbot, for tenth-century writers such as Folcuin, abbot of Lobbes, had little understanding of or tolerance for the diversity of practice (monks, canons, and third orders) that characterized Carolingian religious life. The remarkable achievements of the ninth-century scriptorium at Tours, inaugurated in the time of Alcuin and brought to fruition under Fridugisus and later abbots, do not bespeak an era of abuse and neglect.

Fridugisus's contribution as a speculative thinker, on the other hand, was perceived as highly controversial even by contemporaries. In a treatise on nothing and shadows (*De nihilo et de tenebris*, c.800, ed. E. Dümmler, Monumenta Germaniae Historica, Epistolae [in quarto], 4, 552–5), Fridugisus addressed questions that had been debated at Charlemagne's court. At court the interest in the two subjects was exegetical, but Fridugisus approached the problem as a testing ground for reason and authority. For each subject he used arguments derived from grammatical analysis and then from scripture, bypassing patristic authorities entirely; he thereby purported to demonstrate that nothing was an *aliquid* and that shadows had spatial and corporeal existence

although they transcended the grasp of the human intellect. His argumentation has seemed naïve to historians of philosophy, for he conflated signs and signifiers and was apparently oblivious to the possibility of a distinction between particulars and species. Yet the arguments were novel at the time, and Fridugisus advanced them with bravado and aggression. Charlemagne was perplexed enough to consult the Irish monk Dúngal about Fridugisus's text, but Dúngal's reply does not survive. Towards the end of his life (c.830), Fridugisus was still engaged in intellectual controversy, but only the objections to his ideas by Agobard, archbishop of Lyons, survive as witness to a dispute that touched on topics such as the possible pre-existence of the soul, the salvation of the Old Testament worthies, and the relationship between *deus* and *veritas*. Fridugisus died on 10 August 833.   MARY GARRISON

Sources E. Dümmler, ed., *Epistolae Karolini aevi*, MGH Epistolae [quarto], 4 (Berlin, 1895) · O. G. Oexle, *Forschungen zu monastischen und geistlichen Gemeinschaften im westfränkischen Bereich* (Munich, 1978), 39, 40, 120, 124–9 · Agobard of Lyons, 'Contra objectiones Fredegisi', *Agobardi Lugdunensis opera omnia*, ed. L. van Acker (Turnhout, 1981), 281–300 · C. Gennaro, *Fridugiso di Tours e il 'De substantia nihil et tenebrarum'*, Pubblicazioni dell'Istituto Universitario di Magistero di Catania, Saggi e Monografie, Serie Filosofica (1963) · M. Colish, 'Carolingian debates over nihil and tenebrae: a study in theological method', *Speculum*, 59 (1984), 757–95 · E. Dümmler, ed., *Poetae Latini aevi Carolini*, MGH Poetae Latini Medii Aevi, 1 (Berlin, 1881), 483–9, and line 175 · Ermoldus Nigellus, *Poème sur Louis le Pieux et épîtres au roi Pépin*, ed. E. Faral (1964), 118, 176 · J. Marenbon, *From the circle of Alcuin to the school of Auxerre: logic, theology, and philosophy in the early middle ages*, Cambridge Studies in Medieval Life and Thought (1981) · Folcuin [Folcwinus], 'Gesta Abbatum Sithiensium', ed. O. Holder-Egger, [*Supplementa tomorum I–XII, pars I*], ed. G. Waitz, MGH Scriptores [folio], 13 (Hanover, 1881), 607–35, 614 ff. · J. Fleckenstein, *Die Hofkapelle der deutschen Könige*, MGH Schriften, 16/1 (Stuttgart, 1959) · F. J. Felten, *Äbte und Laienäbte im Frankenreich: Studie zum Verhältnis von Staat und Kirche im früheren Mittelalter*, 31 (Stuttgart, 1980), 244ff., 267, 270, 278 · J. F. Böhmer and others, eds., *Die Regesten des Kaiserreichs unter den Karolingern, 751–918*, new edn (Hildesheim, 1966) · W. Pückert, *Aniane und Gellone: diplomatisch-kritische Untersuchungen zur Geschichte der Reformen des Benediktinerordens im ix. und x. Jahrhundert* (Leipzig, 1899) · E. Lesne, *La propriété ecclésiastique et les droits régaliens à l'époque Carolingienne* (1928), vol. 2 of *Histoire de la propriété ecclésiastique en France*, 141–2 · J. Gerchow, *Die Gedenküberlieferung der Angelsachsen: mit einem Katalog der libri vitae und Necrologien* (Berlin, 1988), 311, 316 · J. A. Endres, 'Fredegisus und Candidus: ein Beitrag zur Geschichte der Frühscholastik', *Philosophisches Jahrbuch*, 19 (1906), 439–50 · J. A. Endres, *Forschungen zur Geschichte der frühmittelalterliche Philosophie* (Münster, 1915) · *Fredegis von Tours / De nihilo et tenebris*, ed. M. Ahner (Leipzig, 1878)

Friederichs, Hulda (1856/7–1927), journalist and writer, was born in Ronsdorf, Prussia, and educated in Ronsdorf and Cologne. Having moved to London as a young woman, she was living in 1881, when she was twenty-four, at Monterey, St Mary's Road, Wimbledon Park. From that address she studied English literature under an extension scheme run by the University of St Andrews to help open up higher education for women, and in 1883 passed the first part of its higher certificate.

Hulda Friederichs spent her working life as a journalist on London newspapers. In the nineteenth century journalism became a fashionable literary pursuit for women, although much of the work was freelance, and few could earn a living wage. By the 1890s significant numbers were contributing to the daily and weekly papers, albeit confined to the lighter sections. They were less evident in the mainstream press and on the news desks. Hulda Friederichs began her career on the *Pall Mall Gazette* in 1883 and served under the editorship of W. T. Stead, whose flamboyant eye and personality made the paper a leading example of the new journalism. Stead was sympathetic to the cause of women's rights, and promoted their interests and talents. Hulda Friederichs was marked out as a protégée, and given opportunities which enabled her to establish a reputation as a serious journalist. Unusually for the time, she was employed on the same terms and conditions as male reporters. She specialized in serious women's issues—uncommon in daily papers in this period—and the kind of reporting that characterized the new age of social realism. A series on women and work included a vivid, firsthand account of the 'lasses' of the Salvation Army; the investigative research on which this piece was based became the genesis for her later study *The Romance of the Salvation Army* (1907).

Not all Hulda Friederichs's colleagues approved of her success, or of her close proximity to Stead when he made her his private secretary. Stead acknowledged his affection for her and worried about the possible jealousy of his wife, but it seems unlikely that there was ever anything intimate between them. She seemed to gravitate to men of stature and to win their confidence. A friendship with Gladstone's daughter and visits to Hawarden led to *Mr. Gladstone: in the Evening of his Days* (1896), a study of his retirement, while her professional relationship with the publisher Sir George Newnes brought invitations to Wildcroft, the family home, and material for a biography (1911).

To her less admiring colleagues on the *Pall Mall Gazette*, such as Robertson Scott, Hulda Friederichs was 'the Friederichs' and 'the Prussian Governess', and Robertson Scott's waspish comments about her suggest something of the difficulties of being a woman in a man's world. She remembered her time rather differently; she recalled the heady days of the new London journalism and the sense of comradeship and enthusiasm: 'We were all young together, the whole of the editorial staff, and one and all worked for it not merely as a matter of duty, but because the paper was our pride and glory' (Friederichs, 220). The sudden sale of the paper in 1892, when E. T. Cook was editor, was a great shock to them; it was bought by W. W. Astor and became a tory organ. Along with other members of the editorial staff, Hulda Friederichs transferred to the *Westminster Gazette*, an evening penny paper which was started by Cook and Sir George Newnes. It continued the *Pall Mall*'s tradition of radical Liberalism, becoming a highly influential paper in political circles. Its stable of writers, including Friederichs, were greatly concerned with issues of social reform, and by the Edwardian years were helping to shape the climate of new Liberalism.

At Newnes's request Hulda Friederichs subsequently edited the *Westminster Budget*, an illustrated weekly digest aimed at the family market, from 1896 to 1905, and then worked on the *Saturday Westminster* as deputy to J. A. Spender. The editorship of the *Budget* was a landmark appointment, not least because it offered a woman the opportunity to put her political stamp on a mainstream paper. An additional duty, on behalf of her employer, was to administer the annual Christmas fund, dispensing money to children and the aged poor for pensions and Christmas parties, and supporting various worthy projects such as a medical mission and a convalescent home. In 1903 a day nursery at Rotherhithe in London's docklands was established, partly financed by the fund and by Lady Newnes. Some of this money was dispensed through the Salvation Army, with Hulda visiting the recipients in the poorer parts of London—a throwback, perhaps, to her days as a reporter, but also providing material for her writing.

Hulda Friederichs's other publications show that she was multilingual. She translated poems from Russian, Swedish, Spanish, and French into English and German, and translated Rudolf Martin's *The Future of Russia* (1906). She never married, and died on 12 February 1927, at her home, 2 Norfolk Mansions, Santos Road, Wandsworth, London.   LINDA WALKER

Sources WWW, 1916–28 · H. Friederichs, *The life of Sir George Newnes, Bart.* (1911) · LLA register, U. St Andr. · census returns, 1881 · d. cert. · J. W. Robertson Scott, *The story of the Pall Mall Gazette* (1950) · J. W. Robertson Scott, *The life and death of a newspaper* (1952) · J. W. Robertson Scott, 'We' and Me (1956) · R. L. Schultz, *Crusader in Babylon: W. T. Stead and the Pall Mall Gazette* (1972) · J. A. Spender, *Men and things* (1937) · J. A. Spender, *Life, journalism and politics*, 2 (1927) · A. A. Bulley and M. Whitley, *Women's work* (1894) · F. Whyte, *The life of W. T. Stead*, 2 vols. (1925)
Archives CAC Cam., W. T. Stead MSS
Wealth at death £9301 16s. 3d.: probate, 12 April 1927, CGPLA Eng. & Wales

Friel, George (1910–1975), novelist, was born on 15 July 1910, in a room-and-kitchen tenement flat at 1172 Maryhill Road, Glasgow, the fourth of the seven children (two girls, five boys) of Jimmy Friell and his wife, Sarah, *née* Toal (b. 1883). His father, born in Donegal in 1879, had left school at eleven, but had nevertheless found 'respectable' work as a salesman for the Scottish and Legal Insurance Company; he believed, though, that his true vocation was the music-hall stage, where he occasionally performed. George Friel signalled revolt by dropping the second 'l' which Jimmy had added to the family name, and later made feckless, selfish fathers a staple of his fiction. He seems to have been very close to his mother, who was an avid reader. In the Maryhill tenement hierarchy of subclasses, the Roman Catholic Friells, though cramped in their two rooms, were nowhere near the bottom. The liveliness of the area, with Maryhill army barracks and Partick Thistle football ground close at hand, would make a vivid mark on George's fiction.

George Friel's elder siblings, Cissie, Jack, and Tommy, had all impressed their teachers at St Charles's Primary, before leaving school at fourteen, and George received encouragement to proceed further. After going on to St Mungo's Academy, in 1926 he reached Glasgow University, where he fell under the spell of recent modernist writing. He became deeply interested in philosophy and in left-wing political ideas, making a lifelong friend of James Gillespie, a science student, son of a miner, who introduced him to Marxism. In autumn 1929 he published his first contribution to the *Glasgow University Magazine*, and he rose to edit the magazine in 1931; his brief tenure was curtailed by unpleasant controversy raised by his Catholic origins.

Like several other very gifted Scottish writers who attended university at this time of deep economic depression, Friel could not see beyond schoolteaching as a career: after he graduated with an ordinary MA degree in 1932 he went on to Jordanhill Teacher Training College. After a phase in 1934 when he had eleven brief supply-teaching appointments in eight different schools, he was a master at St Roch's junior school until 1940. On 9 July 1938 he married Isabella Keenan, *née* McAulay (1912/13–1985), a fellow teacher whom he had met four years previously. They had no children, and resided for the rest of their lives at 25 Brackenbrae Road in the outer suburb of Bishopbriggs. Their relationship struck outsiders as staunch and warm, though, in the Scottish manner, undemonstrative. She was a constant supporter of his writing.

In 1933 Friel had a poem published in the *Adelphi* magazine, but he abdicated his verse ambitions after several publishers rejected an offered collection. Before the Second World War disrupted literary life he had made a promising start as a writer of short stories, publishing eight, most of them involving a family called Plottel whose circumstances echoed the Friells'. From 1940 to 1946 he served in the Royal Army Ordnance Corps, where he became a warrant officer; he was posted in England, then moved to Belgium and Germany. Isabella spent most of the war in Dumfriesshire, where her family farmed. In 1947 George resumed his teaching life at St Mark's junior school, and in 1960 transferred to become assistant head teacher at St Philomena's primary school.

Friel's literary career languished. A first novel, *So I was Told*, which threaded his Plottel stories together, did not impress publishers. Late in 1946 he began to send out *Sons and Daughters*, and after this had been rejected by eight different London publishers he revised it as *No other Herald*, which incurred an identical number of rejections. He was in his late forties before his luck changed. The distinguished fiction writer Fred Urquhart reprinted one of Friel's pre-war productions in *Scottish Short Stories* (1957). *No other Herald* impressed, though it did not convince, Hutchinson's readers, and Timothy O'Keeffe of that firm wrote encouragingly to Friel early in 1958. Within six months Friel responded with another book which Hutchinson brought out in a series quixotically devoted to first novels. *The Banks of Time* (1959) is a carefully crafted story which refractedly echoes Friel's disagreements with his brothers and exasperation with their father. The protagonist,

David Heylyn, is the first of Friel's self-conscious, auto-didactic, petty-bourgeois Glaswegian aesthetes, a charmless youth with prickly integrity. Friel suppressed his splendid ear for dialogue and rendered the speech of all his characters in standard English.

Publication of *Banks of Time* did not make Friel famous, but did spur him to quest for further publication. Hutchinson rejected his second rewrite of *No other Herald*, now *Three Days with Delaney* (Friel was to rewrite and retitle this novel twice more, with consistent lack of success). In 1960 he tried out *All for Moira's Wedding*, which he set aside permanently after three rejections. Meanwhile, he had acquired an agent, James McGibbon of Curtis Brown. Friel had a new novel, *The Boy who Wanted Peace*, which unusually he had written in a rush, without pernickety revision. The raciness of this grim yet hilarious fable about juvenile corruptibility eventually prevailed. After eight publishers had rejected it, John Calder, after many months of dithering, accepted it in July 1963. This might have seemed something of a mismatch, as in the 1950s Calder had become Samuel Beckett's English publisher, and his list promoted the European avant-garde in general and the French *nouveau roman* in particular. The tenement-close, slice-of-life realism of Friel's previously published work might indeed have seemed out of place. In his reply to Calder's reservations Friel dramatized his humdrum career, making exaggerated play with brief episodes when he had tended bars, helped his father sell insurance, and appeared on stage at university, so that teaching might seem merely a retreat to a steady job after picaresque roving:

> I am not a Scottish writer at all. I am a Glasgow-Irishman, which makes writing in English feel like trying to walk in your teacher's cast-off shoes … I am old enough to have bought for a florin Samuel Beckett's Dolphin-book essay on Proust when it was first published, and I knew he was an exceptionally intelligent writer long before Waiting for Godot became a text for parsonical parables.   (G. Friel, letter, 1963, Friel MSS)

In fact Calder's was a highly apt firm to produce, in succession, Friel's further four novels, in which the writer freely indulged at last his Joycean delight in wordplay and bizarre incidents. Language itself emerged as his major theme. Glasgow became an Eliotesque 'waste land' haunted by symbolic resonances. Friel was not, as it turned out, an alien stablemate for Beckett.

The Boy who Wanted Peace appeared in October 1964, and was respectfully reviewed in major British journals—the praise of Anthony Burgess in *The Spectator* was particularly gratifying. Calder was not the most smoothly efficient of publishers, but the firm's zeal in promoting the book took Friel himself aback—he first heard about serialization in the *Scottish Daily Express* from the newspaper itself. There was much activity concerning film rights over the next few years, and, though this came to nothing, BBC Scotland broadcast a radio adaptation in March 1967, then a version for television in February 1970. Although the Calder edition sold fewer than 2000 copies before Friel's death, and a Pan paperback edition launched in February 1972 was pulped after disappointing sales eighteen months later,

Friel was now established in literary circles. Marion Boyars, Calder's partner, had handed the manuscript of *Grace and Miss Partridge* back to him early in 1965, and he had tried other publishers. Then in 1967 Boyars sheepishly asked to have it again—she had found it unforgettable. This very offbeat theological fable is narrated by an authorial persona who claims to have known the characters (indeed, has married Grace herself) and developed the story out of documents and intuitions.

Calder and Boyars published *Mr Alfred MA* early in 1972. To Friel's annoyance he had to abandon his chosen title, *The Writing on the Wall*, because Mary McCarthy brought out a book of essays with that name. It was preserved as the title of part two of the novel, in which a gentle, alcoholic Glasgow English teacher eventually loses his wits, overpowered by the ferocious graffiti now scrawled all around the city by its teenage gangs, more meaningful, as he surmises, than his own always-rejected volume of poems.

Friel himself was by now sick of teaching. St Philomena's, as a primary school, gave him less time to himself during the day than he had had at St Mark's. The discrepancy between his lowly status as an educationist and the esteem which many now had for him as a writer was expressed in an unctuous letter from Glasgow corporation's director of education, giving him one day's leave of absence—'without salary'—to represent himself at a launching event for new Pan paperbacks, and concluding 'May I congratulate you on your success.' Friel was developing a sideline in scripts for radio and television that might have become profitable. In 1973 he resigned from his teaching job on grounds of ill health. Sadly, these were not spurious. On 5 March 1975 he died of lung cancer, at home, just two months before Calder and Boyars published his last novel, *An Empty House*.

For all his natal Catholicism, Friel's personality, like his writings, had been deeply affected by the dour Scottish Calvinist tradition. He kept himself to himself, did not mix with other writers, and refused to yield any ground in argument. Immensely observant, fascinated by overheard snippets of conversation, he uttered extremely funny remarks without a smile. One radio producer who worked with him remembered a small man with rather cherubic features dominated by large spectacles—'giving nothing away, taut and tight, very quiet'. He was a heavy smoker. He relaxed after his day's teaching, then wrote after midnight, whisky and cigarettes to hand.

Friel died just before a remarkable efflorescence of fiction in the west of Scotland was signalled by William McIlvanney's *Docherty* (1975) and Alasdair Gray's *Lanark* (1981). He could have seen in these two writers, and in James Kelman who followed them, many affinities with his own work. He had written fiction exclusively about Glasgow. The tenement world of his youth dominates his novels, with its warmth and its feuding, its gossip and its violence, its pub talk and prevalent petty criminality, remembered with mingled pain and nostalgia. Pain largely comes from the discrepancy between the visions which literature, music, and art reveal to some of his characters and the dwarfish opportunities of a provincial city. Friel's belated status as an important writer was marked by two Scottish Arts Council awards for his third and fourth published novels, and the inclusion of *Mr Alfred MA* among the earliest titles in the new Canongate Classics series launched with the support of the council in 1987. Douglas Gifford, introducing the book, acclaimed it as 'one of the greatest of Scottish novels'.

ANGUS CALDER

Sources I. Cameron, 'George Friel: an introduction to his life and work', MLitt diss., U. Edin., 1987 · NL Scot., Friel MSS · private information (2004) [J. Calder, D. Campbell, S. Conn, T. Wright] · m. cert. · d. cert.
Archives NL Scot., MSS
Wealth at death £7187.47: confirmation, 14 May 1975, *CCI*

Friend [Freind], **Sir John** (*bap.* 1640, *d.* 1696), brewer and Jacobite conspirator, was baptized on 11 October 1640 at St Mary's Church, Whitechapel, the second, but first surviving, son of John Friend (*d.* 1665), brewer, of St Katharine by the Tower precinct, London, and his wife, Elizabeth, *née* Cole (*d.* 1686). A younger son died in 1665; of two or three daughters, Elizabeth survived, marrying John Phillips, described in 1662 as a minister, in 1665 as a major. John Friend married, before 1660, Joan Butcher (*bap.* 1638, *d.* in or after 1667); their two sons and two daughters predeceased him. His father's will suggests doubt about whether he would live harmoniously with his mother.

John Friend, a member of the Brewers' Company from 1662, swiftly rose 'from mean beginnings to great credit and much wealth' (*Bishop Burnet's History*, 4.316), with which 'he built the stately brew house in the Minories' (*Le Neve's Pedigrees*, 399), the Phoenix Brewery, run by a partnership in which he held almost a half share. In 1677 he joined Sir Samuel Dashwood's syndicate which farmed the excise. In 1679 he married (by a licence dated 8 October) Anne Huntington (*c.*1657–1695), a daughter of Robert Huntington of Hackney (where Friend himself now lived), an excise commissioner. From 1683, when the farm ended, until 1689, Friend was an excise commissioner and from 1684 to 1689 a commissioner for the hearth tax.

Friend served enthusiastically from 1667 in the Honourable Artillery Company, and as its colonel entertained James, duke of York, and Prince George of Denmark at its feast on 26 June 1684. From before 1680 until 1689 he was a deputy lieutenant of Tower Hamlets (of London also in 1687–8), and lieutenant-colonel of their trained bands. In 1685 he was elected MP for Great Yarmouth, defeating his uncle by marriage, and was court candidate there in 1688. James II knighted him on 3 August 1685. In December 1688 the council of peers used his trained bands to keep order in eastern London, but he concealed papers compromising to King James which were found on Lord Chancellor Jeffreys when the judge was captured at Wapping.

Friend lost his offices at the revolution and refused the oaths of allegiance and supremacy, but attended conformist religious services. The expanded wartime armed services gave his beer a wider market. He apparently at first prudently avoided direct contact with the Jacobite court and its English representatives. However, although purged in February 1690 from the Honourable Artillery Company, he claimed to retain enough influence to be able to make the Tower Hamlets trained bands declare for James (largely through their new lieutenant-colonel, John *Cass, his relative and intended heir); and, when the French invasion attempt of 1692 (for which he helped prepare the East Anglian Jacobites) exposed a vacuum in practical leadership in London, his plan to rise and seize the Tower (revived at later crises) provided a useful rallying point. In 1693 he was persuaded to start direct correspondence with James, and began meeting the aristocratic leaders of the non-compounding Jacobite faction (those who opposed James's making major constitutional concessions in order to effect a restoration), relying like them mainly on a French invasion. In their memorial of December 1693 which called for one, he even proposed 'by a stratagem' to kidnap William and Mary to France. This was ignored, but James accepted his offer to raise a cavalry regiment: he appointed as lieutenant-colonel a Catholic professional officer, Brice Blair, and recruited secretly and haphazardly in London and Kent. Among the Jacobites 'his purse was more considered than his head', as he was resentfully aware, 'and was open on all occasions, as the party'—including the compounder William Penn— 'applied to him' (*Bishop Burnet's History*, 4.316). By 1696 he had sold his Hackney home; his Jacobite expenditure had left him deep in debt and even threatened his brewing business.

In May and June 1695 Friend attended the leading non-compounders' meetings which sent Robert Charnock to press James for an immediate invasion, and promised 200 men for the rising to accompany it. Friend nevertheless displayed caution when another rising was planned in January to February 1696, intending to muster his regiment only when James and the French landed. He was not involved in the assassination plot, declaring at one meeting with its leaders 'that he fancied something was behind the curtain that was concealed from him', and, when informed indirectly, 'said … he was afraid it would ruin king James's affairs, and all his friends' (*State trials*, 12.1308, 1319).

After the plot's exposure a warrant was issued for Friend's arrest, on 29 February. Friend, found hiding in a Quaker's house, was examined on 2 March 1696 but denied everything, losing, according to the Dutch envoy, the chance of leniency offered for a confession. Rumours were spread widely that he had supplied poisoned beer to William's army and navy. His trial for high treason at the Old Bailey on 23 March before Lord Chief Justice Holt was one of three trials that the government rushed through before the Treason Trials Act (which allowed defendants counsel) came into force two days later. The accused assassins Charnock and Sir William Parkyns defended themselves ably, but Friend, being ill-educated, unintelligent, and partly deaf, was helpless, though Holt allowed him minor indulgences. George Porter, the assassin, and Blair were the main prosecution witnesses, and almost Friend's only defence was to claim, groundlessly, that as papists

they could not legally testify against a protestant. The jury convicted him in fifteen minutes. In May they were placed on the panel from which the jury to try a fellow plotter would be drawn.

Friend and Parkyns, sentenced to death, were briefly reprieved to let a House of Commons committee interrogate them. They refused to save themselves by naming accomplices, but Friend admitted the reality of Charnock's 1695 mission. The next day, 3 April 1696, they were hanged at Tyburn. Three nonjuring clergymen, Jeremy Collier, William Snatt, and Shadrach Cook, attended and absolved them: the widespread hostility this aroused sprang mainly from Parkyns's failure to repent of the assassination plot. Despite relatives' pleas, Friend's quarters were set up on Temple Bar and his head in Aldgate, arousing some pity. A paper left by Friend (but supposedly Cook's work) stressed his Jacobitism and unbigoted Anglicanism, and Archbishop Tenison commissioned clerics to answer it.

Two of Friend's Phillips nephews, excise officials, bid against each other to repurchase his forfeited estate, whose assets, particularly the brewing partnership, were worth £5000–£6000; but a spy claimed that they were Jacobites and had concealed a further (implausible) £4000 of Friend's property. The forfeiture was finally granted in 1700 to Cass and another major creditor. Friend's St Katharine's neighbour, the heraldic writer John Gibbon, 'writt a little pamphlet called the whole life & conversation of Sr Jo. friend' (*Le Neve's Pedigrees*, 399); but this apparently was never printed and is lost.

PAUL HOPKINS

Sources *State trials*, vols. 12–13 · E. Cruickshanks, 'Friend (Freind), John', HoP, *Commons, 1660–90* · E. Cruickshanks and B. D. Henning, 'Huntington, Richard', HoP, *Commons, 1660–90* · E. Cruickshanks and B. D. Henning, 'Great Yarmouth', HoP, *Commons, 1660–90*, 1.324–7 · J. Macpherson, ed., *Original papers: containing the secret history of Great Britain*, 2 vols. (1775), vol. 1 · *Le Neve's Pedigrees of the knights*, ed. G. W. Marshall, Harleian Society, 8 (1873) · J. Garrett, *The triumphs of providence: the assassination plot, 1696* (1980) · W. A. Shaw, ed., *Calendar of treasury books*, 5–15, PRO (1911–33) · N. Luttrell, *A brief historical relation of state affairs from September 1678 to April 1714*, 6 vols. (1857) · *CSP dom.*, 1687–96 · *Bishop Burnet's History*, vol. 4 · A. W. Hughes Clarke and R. H. D'Elboux, eds., *The registers of St Katharine by the Tower, London*, 7 vols., Harleian Society, register section, 75–81 (1945–52) · will of William Friend (brother), PRO, PROB 11/318, fol. 256v · will of John Friend senior, PRO, PROB 11/322, fols. 23–24 · will of Robert Huntington, PRO, PROB 11/376, fol. 180 · JHC, 11 (1693–7), 542–3 · parish register, Whitechapel, St Mary, 11 Oct 1640, LMA, P93 MY/1 [baptism] · *Report on the manuscripts of Allan George Finch*, 5 vols., HMC, 71 (1913–2003), vol. 4 · *Report on the manuscripts of the marquis of Downshire*, 6 vols. in 7, HMC, 75 (1924–95), vol. 1 · cabinet minutes, 2–9 March 1696, BL, Add. MS 72566 · Dutch diplomatic transcripts, 1696, BL, Add. MS 17677QQ · R. Beddard, ed., *A kingdom without a king: the journal of the provisional government in the revolution of 1688* (1988) · G. J. Armytage, ed., *Allegations for marriage licences issued by the vicar-general of the archbishop of Canterbury, July 1679 to June 1687*, Harleian Society, 30 (1890) · T. B. Macaulay, *The history of England from the accession of James II*, new edn, ed. C. H. Firth, 6 vols. (1913–15) · *An account of what passed at the execution of Sir Will. Parkyns, and Sir Joh. Friend* (1696) · *A letter to the three absolvers, Mr Cook, Mr Collier and Mr Snett* (1696) · DNB

Likenesses etching, 1697 (of Friend?), repro. in Macaulay, *History of England*, vol. 5

Wealth at death seven and a half of sixteen shares in the Phoenix Brewery business, with some of the auxiliary buildings and equipment, valued in 1698 at £5500; goods and jewels in his lodgings; a one-tenth share of the ship *Modena*, valued at *c.*£500; other brewing goods at Tottenham; pawned jewels; owed £500 by William Penn; it was claimed that nephews had hidden money, plate, and jewels worth (implausibly) £4000 or more; many debts, incl. £3600 to Sir Thomas Cooke, £1300 to John Cass: Shaw, ed., *Calendar*; *Report on the manuscripts of the marquis of Downshire*, HMC

Frink, Dame Elisabeth Jean (1930–1993), sculptor and printmaker, was born on 14 November 1930 at The Grange, Thurlow, Suffolk, the only daughter of Ralph Cuyler Frink (1899–1974), cavalry officer, and his wife, Jean Conway-Gordon (*b.* 1910), a colonel's daughter.

Early years Frink's early years were spent travelling with her army father, who was serving with the 4th–7th dragoon guards, to Shorncliffe, Kent, Salisbury Plain, Aldershot, and Edinburgh, but home remained at Thurlow. She had her first pony at three, and was riding at four, and then, through her father, became interested in dogs and guns. In 1940, when Frink was ten, her father was stationed at Kingston, Dorset, close to the Purbeck quarries and the magnificent ruin of Corfe Castle; both sites impressed her enough for her to make Dorset her home over thirty years later.

In 1941 Frink's mother sent her to Chypraze, near Exmouth, Devon, to stay with her godmother to avoid the planes and bombs in Suffolk, as Thurlow was surrounded by air stations. Frink started to draw when she was thirteen and her subjects were men on skeletal horses rendered in ink and wash, which she called 'apocalyptic'. At sixteen, with her father confined in the army sanatorium at Midhurst, Surrey, she applied for and won a place at Guildford School of Art. In 1947 she started in the painting school, but moved over to sculpture, where the head of department was the sculptor Willi Soukop. At this time she was given a book on Rodin, and she later remembered that 'life began for me then'.

At Guildford Frink learned to model in clay, and also to carve in wood and stone. Carving was too slow a method for her, and she abandoned it as a sculptural practice. She spent two years at Guildford and then applied to Chelsea School of Art in 1949, following Soukop, who had moved there in 1948. At Chelsea, where she studied from 1949 to 1953, she perfected her own method of modelling and carving in plaster of Paris, a practice used by the head of department there, Bernard Meadows, and also by Henry Moore, a visiting tutor who influenced her at that time. Her student sculptures were mainly men with birds and dogs, cast in cement or plaster.

Major works In 1951 Frink visited Paris for the first time and admired the recent work of Giacometti, Germaine Richier, and Picasso, all of whom made figurative sculptures in plaster. In 1952 she received her first major commission, a figure of St John Bosco (des.), for the new church of St John Bosco in Woodley, near Reading, Berkshire. Frink was brought up a Roman Catholic, and although she did not practise her religion regularly, she executed several major religious sculptural commissions throughout her career. The second work recorded in her

Dame Elisabeth Jean Frink (1930–1993), self-portrait, 1987

catalogue raisonné was a large plaster figure of *Christ at the Pillar*.

> So far as the traditional iconography of religion is concerned, with its events and characters, I have accepted commissions to make crucifixions, altar crosses, a risen Christ in Solihull, a big Head of Christ for All Saints' Church, Basingstoke, an eagle lectern for Coventry Cathedral and a walking Madonna outside Salisbury Cathedral … I also did a larger than life-size figure of Judas in 1961, not through a commission but for myself … The religious impulse or acceptance or awareness must be there, but almost at an unconscious level—and it is not only activated by commissions because the idea for Judas had absorbed me for some time as a formal, figurative embodiment of the idea of betrayal. (Shaffer, Robertson, and Kent, 33)

Her last religious commission was her last work, *The Risen Christ*, for Liverpool Cathedral, unveiled by her son on Easter Sunday, 11 April 1993, a week before her death.

In 1952, while still a student, Frink exhibited with two other sculptors at the prestigious Beaux Arts Gallery, London, and the Tate Gallery bought a small bronze, *Bird of Prey*, from the show, making her the youngest female artist to enter the national collections. In 1953 she won the student prize in the Unknown Political Prisoner sculpture competition. She taught at Chelsea School of Art from 1953 to 1961, at St Martin's School of Art from 1954 to 1962, and was visiting instructor at the Royal College of Art from 1965 to 1967. She was given her first solo show at St George's Gallery, London, in 1955 and overseas at the Bertha Schaefer Gallery, New York, in 1959. Success came early in Frink's career and she was always newsworthy as the only prominent female sculptor in post-war London.

Frink married the architect Michel Jammet in September 1955 at the new church of Notre Dame de France, Leicester Place, London, with the reception at the Cavalry and Guards' Club in Piccadilly, a reminder of her army connections. His family were French and his grandfather, a chef, started the famous Jammet's restaurant in Dublin. As a result Frink and Michel Jammet were regular visitors to the city. Her only child, Lin, was born on 11 May 1958 at St Stephen's Hospital, London.

Throughout the 1950s British sculptors such as Reg Butler, Lynn Chadwick, Kenneth Armitage, and Eduardo Paolozzi gained international acclaim for their spiky, angst-ridden male figures in bronze or iron. They were a generation older than Frink and although her contemporary work was similar, her figures had a greater sense of strength and optimism than theirs. All the sculptors at this time shared a fascination with flight and flying creatures, probably as a result of wartime experiences, but Frink was the only one to continue the theme throughout her career. Her *œuvre*, although large—about 400 editioned bronzes—kept to a small number of themes and variations, and she worked through her chosen subjects, such as birds or warriors, until their potential was exhausted.

Frink gave up her two full-time teaching jobs in 1962 in order to concentrate on work for exhibitions and commissions. One major commission was to make the eagle lectern for the new Coventry Cathedral. The eagle of St John is the usual subject for ecclesiastical lecterns, but the subject of a mighty bird was also one which fitted in with Frink's obsessions. She was the youngest artist and the only female one to be commissioned to make new work for the cathedral, and her *Eagle* elicited much admiration. About the same time Frink gained the commission to make a memorial to the aviators Alcock and Brown for Manchester airport, and she produced a large figure, *Horizontal Birdman*, which conflated bird and man. When unveiled in 1962 it received much criticism, most notably from Alcock's elderly sister, who complained that the figure of her brother was 'obscene. At least my brother had his trousers on when he landed' (Gardiner, 133).

Frink divorced Michel Jammet in 1963 and at Wandsworth register office in the spring of 1964 married Edward Pool, whose family had a butchery business in Smithfield. In 1967 they sold their Chelsea home and moved to a group of abandoned farm buildings, Le Village, in the foothills of the Cévennes, near Nîmes, France. In June 1973 Frink was divorced from Pool and returned to live and work in Britain, where she moved into a large apartment at Buckingham Gate, London. Her sculpture in the 1960s and 1970s concentrated on the nude male figure, and used it to reveal her deep concern with man's inhumanity to man. Numerous nude male figures stand or sit in postures that are both monumental and vulnerable. She also made a series of huge male heads. Living in southern France, she was very aware of the war in Algeria, and she records how a newspaper photograph of General Oufkir, a Moroccan

murderer, wearing dark glasses caught her attention. The huge heads then turned into menacing heads wearing large goggles, which shaded their eyes, and thus their emotions. About this time she joined the human rights organization Amnesty International, of which she remained a committed member all her life. She was a generous supporter of charities, and gave drawings and etchings to Amnesty International and an edition of fifty casts of a sculpture of a seated dog to Great Ormond Street Children's Hospital.

Frink made a large number of sculptures of animals, especially horses and dogs, ever favourite companions. Her horses and dogs were made with sensitivity and tenderness, and share none of the aggressiveness of the Birds series or the Goggle Head series. Although portraiture was not her favourite category of work, she did accept seven commissions between 1975 and 1984, including eminent male sitters such as Sir John Pope-Hennessy (for the British Museum), Sir Alec Guinness (for the National Portrait Gallery), and Michael Jaffé (Fitzwilliam Museum, Cambridge). Critics have remarked that in many of her sculptured male heads there is an element of self-portraiture, and her own head, with its strong features, did have a masculine aspect in her later years. The sculptor F. E. McWilliam modelled a full-length portrait of her in 1956 (priv. coll.).

Frink married Alexander Csaky, a Hungarian count and an insurance broker, in London in December 1974 and in 1976, when the lease on her Buckingham Gate studio expired, they bought Woolland House, Woolland, near Blandford Forum, Dorset, a large converted stable building with extensive gardens. In 1979 she had a studio built near the house and there made a life-size horse commissioned by the earl of March for Goodwood racecourse. This was one of her largest sculptures of a racehorse and it joined other bronze sculptures of horses, including one with a rider set on the pavement in Dover Street, London, in 1974, and one commissioned by Milton Keynes in 1978 (on Silbery Boulevard, outside Lloyds Bank).

Later years Frink became a member of the establishment in the late 1970s and early 1980s; appointed CBE in 1969, she was made DBE in 1982. She also became a trustee of the British Museum in 1975, a member of the Royal Fine Arts Commission in 1976, and a Royal Academician in 1977. She became a Companion of Honour in 1992.

Frink's career included a lifelong commitment to drawing, sometimes for its own sake and sometimes in preparation for book illustrations: *Aesop's Fables* in 1968, Chaucer's *Canterbury Tales* in 1972, the *Iliad* and the *Odyssey* in 1978, and *Children of the Gods*, a book on Greek myths, in 1983. 'My illustrations have nothing to do with sculpture; neither activity helps the other, because the illustrations are subjective and my sculpture is not. The human form is not subjective' (Shaffer, Robertson, and Kent, 36).

Frink had a solo show every year from 1967, and her work was included in group shows around the world annually. She was given a retrospective exhibition at the Royal Academy in 1985, and a major show at the National Museum of Women in the Arts, Washington, DC, in 1990.

Her work can be found in public collections throughout Britain, with a large collection of pieces at the Tate Gallery, and in major galleries in the USA, Australia, and South Africa. She died of cancer at Wooland House on 18 April 1993, two months after Alex Csaky had died of the same condition. In 1967 Frink stated that she moved to France in order 'to cut myself off from the British art scene' (Gardiner, 118). This small but significant statement reveals that she felt estranged from recent developments in British sculpture, which at that time included land art, performance art, and pieces constructed from industrial metal offcuts. Her primary theme, the human body, fell from favour as a subject for innovative sculpture in the 1960s, and Frink may have felt that her work would not have been appreciated by her native audience, or that her inspiration would be weakened by these new developments. In either case, she need not have worried. Her output remained as forceful and concentrated as ever, and as Bryan Robertson reminded the congregation in his address at her memorial service at St James's Church, Piccadilly, 'she achieved the extraordinary distinction of becoming, without compromising, a genuinely popular sculptor whose work is admired by a broad public in Britain and abroad.' Her popularity stems from that fact that she did not embrace new techniques and technologies in order to make her sculpture, and that she remained utterly committed to conveying the nature and power of the human body, an inexhaustible subject for sculptural exploration.   JUDITH COLLINS

Sources S. Gardiner, *The official biography of Elisabeth Frink* (1998) • P. Shaffer, B. Robertson, and S. Kent, *Elisabeth Frink sculpture: catalogue raisonné* (1984) • *CGPLA Eng. & Wales* (1993) • ontic.net/mk/index.htm?art.htm, 28 Jan 2002 • d. cert.

Likenesses P. M. Strickland, photograph, 1954, Hult. Arch. • F. E. McWilliam, sculpture, 1956 • L. H. Rosoman, acrylic, 1979–84, NPG • R. Clatworthy, bronze bust, 1983, NPG • E. Frink, self-portrait, bronze sculpture, 1987, priv. coll. [*see illus.*] • E. Frink, self-portrait, drawing, repro. in *The Times* (19 April 1993) • photograph, repro. in *The Times* (20 April 1993), 21 • photograph, repro. in *The Independent* (19 April 1993)

Wealth at death £5,172,374: probate, 23 Sept 1993, *CGPLA Eng. & Wales*

Frinton, Freddie [*real name* Frederick Bittiner; *later* Frederick Hargate] (1909–1968), comedian, was born Frederick Bittiner at 106 Granville Street, Grimsby, Lincolnshire, on 17 January 1909, the son of Florence Elizabeth Coo, a dressmaker. His father's name and occupation are unknown, although it has been suggested that he was a fisherman. He seems to have been fostered from an early age, and to have assumed the surname of the foster family: it is as Frederick Hargate that he is recorded taking his first job, as a fish-packer in Grimsby in 1925. He was sacked after his foreman discovered him making an extra shilling or two telling jokes and neglecting the fish.

Hargate's dismissal presented him with his true vocation: he toured the pubs and clubs of Lincolnshire, singing comic songs for half a crown a time, and as he became known in the county set up a concert party to play outdoor shows on the beach at Cleethorpes. In 1931 he was discovered by the comedian and impresario Tom Moss, who booked him for a season at the Theatre Royal, Sheffield, initially to play the Dame in pantomime; however, he appeared increasingly as a comedian and singer in variety shows. By this time, true to his seaside roots, he had taken Frinton as his stage surname.

Frinton returned to Cleethorpes as a member of Jimmy Slater's company Supper Follies in 1935, the year in which he made his London début at the East Ham Palace. In the years immediately before the Second World War he took his own roadshow around Yorkshire and Lancashire, while also appearing with Ernest Binn's Northern Concert Party. A marriage, which produced his first daughter, ended in divorce shortly after the war. He later married Norah Mary and had three further children, a daughter and two sons.

After the Second World War broke out Frinton served for eighteen months in an army searchlight unit before being discovered for a second time and seconded to George Black's forces revue *Stars in Battledress*. After demobilization he toured with three more of Black's revues, *Strike a New Note* (1946), *Strike it Again* (1947), and *Sky High* (1949), and quickly built up a successful year-round career, alternating Christmas appearances as the Dame with variety shows in the warmer months—in which he often appeared as a drunk, introducing himself with the catchphrase 'Good evening, ossifer' and brandishing his trademark broken cigarette.

Freddie Frinton made his television début in the early 1960s playing the same drunk in the *Arthur Haynes Show*, and in 1962 he appeared for the first time in a stage play, *The Best-Laid Schemes*, in which he played opposite Thora Hird. A run at Blackpool was so successful that the production, with the same team of Frinton and Hird, was booked for later summer seasons at Torquay and Bournemouth, and the two leads were reunited the following year for Frinton's first television situation comedy, *Meet the Wife*, a BBC production scripted by Ronald Woolf and Ronald Chesney. Exploiting Frinton's working-class roots, the comedy's situation was a class skirmish—typical of its time—between an upwardly mobile wife and a defiantly stationary husband. The show was popular enough to run for five series, of thirty-eight episodes, starting in April 1964 and ending with a Christmas special in December 1966, and to receive the accolade of a reference in the Beatles song 'Good Morning, Good Morning'.

Given the ease with which Frinton, the former fish-packer, could be stereotyped as this sort of working-class character, it is curious that he is best remembered at the beginning of the twenty-first century for his impersonation of a butler. Even stranger is the fact that a comedian so typical of the British variety tradition should posthumously have become a star in Germany and Scandinavia, while becoming completely forgotten at home. Nevertheless, his survival in the annals of comedy is almost entirely due to his performance in 'Dinner for One', a brief slapstick sketch about a rich old lady (Miss Sophie, played by May Warden) celebrating her ninetieth birthday at a dinner with places set for guests long since dead. Frinton, as butler, takes the part of each in toasting the health of his mistress, becoming increasingly inebriated, the charade ending with his enquiry as to whether he has to go through the same procedure every year. This attracts Miss Sophie's reply 'The same procedure as every year', a catch-phrase instantly recognized by Swedish, Danish, Norwegian, and German television audiences, among whom showings of the programme at Christmas and new year became an annual ritual.

Frinton had acquired the rights to 'Dinner for One' shortly after the Second World War. The sketch, which had been 'written by Laurie Wylie and originally performed by Bobby Howes and Binnie Hale in a West End revue' (Hudd and Hindin, 65), dated from the 1920s. After seeing it performed by a touring company, Frinton had added new material by Harry Rowson, together with some original business of his own; he presented his revised version with May Warden for the first time at Blackpool in 1945, and repeated it there and elsewhere in many of the following seasons. In the audience for a Blackpool matinée in 1963 were Peter Frankenfeld and Heinz Dunkhase, respectively compère and producer of Norddeutsche Rundfunk's variety programme *Guten Abend, Peter Frankenfeld!*, who were touring the clubs of northern England in search of British comedy suitable for a German audience. Frinton was persuaded to travel to Hamburg and record the sketch in front of the Norddeutsche Rundfunk cameras, on condition that it would be performed only in English. The eighteen-minute black and white programme that resulted—plans to re-record it in colour were thwarted by Frinton's death—does not appear to have become an instant classic. Although initially forgotten, it gradually resurfaced and became hugely popular for its embodiment of the supposed English characteristics of 'sang-froid and fondness of ritual' (Frinton).

Latterly Frinton lived in Greenford, Middlesex. After suffering a heart attack while in Bournemouth, where he was appearing in a comedy at the Pier Theatre, he died at the Central Middlesex Hospital, Park Royal, on 16 October 1968, long before the 'Dinner for One' cult established itself. There have been recurrent calls for his achievement to be commemorated in some form in his native Grimsby.   STEPHEN FOLLOWS

Sources *The Times* (17 Oct 1968) · *Grimsby Evening Telegraph* (19 March 1963) · *Grimsby Evening Telegraph* (26 Nov 1988) · *Grimsby Evening Telegraph* (4 Jan 1994) · *Grimsby Evening Telegraph* (29 Dec 1997) · newspaper cuttings, Central Library, Grimsby · R. Busby, *British music hall: an illustrated who's who from 1850 to the present day* (1976) · M. Frinton, *Daily Mail* (26 Jan 1995) · R. Geisenhanslüke, *Die Zeit* (27 Dec 2000) · R. Jenkins, *The Times* (1 Jan 1997) · R. Hudd and P. Hindin, *Roy Hudd's cavalcade of variety acts: a who was who of light entertainment* (1997) · I. MacDonald, *Revolution in the head: the Beatles records and the sixties* (1994) · b. cert. · d. cert. · will
Wealth at death £32,227: probate, 5 Feb 1969, CGPLA Eng. & Wales

Fripp, Alfred Downing (1822–1895). *See under* Fripp, George Arthur (1813–1896).

Fripp, George Arthur (1813–1896), watercolour painter, was born in Bristol on 13 June 1813, the second of the six children of the Revd Samuel Charles Fripp and his wife,

Mary Ann (1787–1843), daughter of Nicholas Pocock, the outstanding marine artist. He attended Miss Player's Quaker school at Frenchay, Bristol; Rowland Hill's school in Birmingham; and the Revd W. Field's school in Leamington. He had lessons in oil painting from James Baker Pyne and exhibited three studies from nature and a view of Tintern Abbey at the exhibition of the new Bristol Society of Artists in 1832, giving his father's address: 14 Park Row.

In July 1834 Fripp set out with the Bristol artist William James Müller on a seven-month sketching tour, visiting Belgium, travelling up the Rhine from Cologne to Schaffhausen, crossing the Alps by the Splügen Pass, and staying for two months in Venice before visiting Rome and Tivoli. He first exhibited at the Royal Academy in 1838, showing a large oil of Tivoli (Bristol Museum and Art Gallery), which had been purchased by a wealthy Bristol cousin, Charles Bowles Hare; he gave a London address but may not have settled there until 1840. He exhibited intermittently at the Royal Academy until 1854, and had a notable success in 1848 with the oil *Mont Blanc from near Courmayeur, Val d'Aosta* (Walker Art Gallery, Liverpool), which J. M. W. Turner is said to have praised; his oils were close in manner to the work of Müller. In 1841 he showed for the first time at the Old Watercolour Society, exhibiting seven watercolours of Bristol and continental scenes. In the same year he was elected an associate of the society, of which he became a full member in 1845; he was secretary of the society from 1848 until 1854, and relinquished the post only because of the demands of a very large family. He married Mary (*d*. 1887), daughter of Thomas William Percival, a merchant, on 26 March 1846; among his twelve children were Charles Edwin Fripp, artist–reporter for *The Graphic*, and Thomas W. Fripp, a watercolour painter based in Canada.

Fripp quickly became well known for his watercolours, which were mostly of scenes in Wales, Yorkshire, and Essex, and of views on the Thames and in Dorset. He continued to show views in the Avon Gorge and around Bristol. His early watercolours reflect the influence of Samuel Jackson; however, from the later 1840s the crisp drawing and even colour washes of Jackson's earlier manner gave way to a softer and warmer colouring in Fripp's watercolours. They are characterized 'by refined delicacy and tenderness of aërial effect, by truth of colour, and by the learned breadth and scrupulous balance of their composition' (Roget, 268). A slight darkening of the paper and fading of the colours over time has sometimes reduced that delicacy to mere fastidiousness. However, since the 1980s the market value of Fripp's work has risen sharply, reflecting the success of his aspiration of maintaining the traditions and standards of the finest of the early English watercolour painters. He died on 17 October 1896 at 50 Holmdale Road, Hampstead, after a long illness, and was buried three days later in Highgate cemetery.

Fripp's brother **Alfred Downing Fripp** (1822–1895), youngest of the six children, was born in Bristol and probably joined George in London in 1840, at the age of eighteen. He studied with him at the British Museum before becoming a student at the Royal Academy Schools in 1842. In 1843 he made the first of three visits to Ireland, and in the following year visited Wales. There were soon to be many watercolours of Irish and Welsh peasantry, often of one or two poor but picturesque children in a landscape setting. The more crowded and ambitious works, such as *The Irish Piper* (Bristol Museum and Art Gallery), which had been commissioned by Charles Bowles Hare, were based on innumerable diligent and delicate pencil studies and could be strongly coloured and impressively composed. In 1844 he was elected an associate of the Old Watercolour Society, and progressed quickly to full membership in 1846.

On 28 April 1849 Fripp married Anne Dalton Allies (*d.* 1850), daughter of Edwin Allies, a gentleman from Clifton. She died in the following year and Fripp moved soon afterwards to Rome. He stayed for periods in Naples, Capri, and Venice, and did not return to England until 1859. In Rome he shared premises with the painter George Hemming Mason and enjoyed the friendship of Frederick Leighton and Edward Poynter. When Ruskin reviewed his Italian subjects at the Old Watercolour Society in 1859 he hoped that Fripp might prove a worthy successor to John Frederick Lewis, the society's late president. However, after Fripp left Italy he returned to his Irish, Welsh, and English subjects, concentrating especially on Dorset scenery, particularly that at Lulworth. On 12 September 1861 he married Eliza Banister Roe (*d.* 1895), daughter of John Banister Roe of Blandford, Dorset, where, probably in that same year, he settled. In 1870 the Fripps and their children moved to London, following Alfred's election as secretary of the Old Watercolour Society, an office that he held with some interruptions until his death. He returned briefly to Italy in 1893 but, writing to his daughter from Rome, he complained that the city was now overrun with Americans. He died in London on 13 March 1895 at his home, 33 Hampstead Hill Gardens, from complications following influenza, and was buried at Tarrant Rushton, Blandford. His wife and younger son were too ill to attend the funeral and died, also of influenza, a few days later. Another son, Sir Alfred D. Fripp (*d.* 1930), was a surgeon, and a daughter, Elizabeth Jane Spencer Fripp (*d.* 1945), married Sir William Hale-White, physician.   FRANCIS GREENACRE

Sources H. Stuart Thompson, 'George A. Fripp and Alfred D. Fripp', *Walker's Quarterly*, 25–6 (1927) • J. L. Roget, *A history of the 'Old Water-Colour' Society*, 2 (1891) • MSS, Bristol Museum and AG, K 5624 [incl. obits. and ADF's notes on pictures sold 1844–61 (excluding 1854)] • F. G. Stephens, 'The late Alfred Downing Fripp', *Magazine of Art*, 18 (1894–5), 470–72 • *The Athenaeum* (24 Oct 1896), 569–70 • N. Neal Solly, *Memoir of the life of William James Müller* (1875) • Graves, *RA exhibitors* • Graves, *Brit. Inst.* • E. Morris, *Victorian and Edwardian paintings in the Walker Art Gallery and at Sudley House* (1996) • L. Lambourne and J. Hamilton, eds., *British watercolours in the Victoria and Albert Museum* (1980) • exhibition catalogues (1832) [Bristol Society of Artists] • exhibition catalogues (1834) [Bristol Society of Artists] • exhibition catalogues (1837) [Bristol Society of Artists] • exhibition catalogues (1839) [Bristol Society of Artists] • m. cert. • m. certs. [Alfred Downing Fripp]

Likenesses double portraits, photographs (with Alfred D. Fripp), Bristol City Museum and Art Gallery, family MSS, K 5624 • double portraits, photographs (with Alfred D. Fripp), repro. in Stuart Thompson, 'George A. Fripp and Alfred D. Fripp'

Wealth at death £2046 5s. 1d.: probate, 18 Dec 1896, CGPLA Eng. & Wales

Frisch, Otto Robert (1904–1979), physicist, was born on 1 October 1904 in Vienna, the only son of Justinian Frisch (1879–1949), a printer, and his wife, Auguste Meitner (1877–1951), a gifted musician who started on a career as a concert pianist but gave it up on marriage. Her sister was the physicist Lise *Meitner, who exerted a considerable influence on her nephew. Like his mother, Frisch was very musical, with the gift of absolute pitch, and later became a pianist of near-professional standard. He liked to sketch, and his doodles at meetings included portraits or caricatures of his colleagues.

There is some confusion about Frisch's first name. At home he was always called Otto Robert, as if the names were hyphenated; he later called himself Robert, until at Los Alamos there were too many Roberts and he was persuaded to become Otto. On returning to England he tried to revert to Robert, but his name appeared as Otto on many articles, and on his book of reminiscences. As a boy, when he was a pupil at Frau Schwarzwald's primary school, Vienna, and later in the Piaristen Gymnasium, he showed considerable talent for mathematics, but on entering the University of Vienna in 1922 he decided to study physics, which suited best his mechanical bent. He qualified for his DPhil (1926) with a thesis under Karl Przibram on the effect of electrons on salts, a favoured line of research at Vienna's Radium Institute. Frisch was of Jewish descent, and had declared himself 'non-confessional' while at secondary school. He was baptized as a protestant the year after he qualified for his doctorate. There is no evidence of any subsequent active religious affiliation.

Instrument design and making was a central concern for Frisch from the outset of his career, which he first intended to be in industry. After a year in a small firm which manufactured X-ray dosimeters, however, he was appointed to the optics division of the Physikalisch-Technische Reichsanstalt (PTR) in Berlin, the state metrological laboratory, with the support of Nobel prizewinning physicist James Franck, Stefan Meyer, and Przibram. At the PTR he improved photometric instruments, developed a new unit of brightness, and studied the spectral dispersion of light under different weather conditions for the German railways.

In 1930 Frisch set a foot on the academic ladder when he moved to Hamburg to assist Otto Stern in his renowned work on molecular beams. In collaboration with Stern he was able to show the diffraction of atoms by crystal surfaces and, particularly, to measure the magnetic moment of the proton, which came out as substantially larger than theory predicted.

When Hitler came to power in Germany Frisch was dismissed from his position. A grant of the recently established Academic Assistance Council allowed him to spend the year 1933–4 in the laboratory of P. M. S. Blackett at Birkbeck College, London, where he refined the cloud chamber technique, and later turned to the new subject of artificial radioactivity. This period was followed by five years in Niels Bohr's institute in Copenhagen, where he applied his technical skills to neutron physics. He collaborated with George Placzek in the study of the slowing down and capture of neutrons in matter, and with Hans von Halban and J. Koch he devised a method to measure the magnetic properties of free neutrons.

At Christmas 1938 Frisch was visiting his aunt Lise Meitner, then in Stockholm, when she was informed by Otto Hahn in Berlin of the results of his last run of experiments with Fritz Strassmann, which showed that barium was one of the products of the collision of a neutron with a uranium nucleus. Hahn knew this meant the nucleus had been split in two, but this seemed very implausible physically. Frisch and Meitner gave an explanation in terms of the excessive electric charge of the nucleus, and estimated the energy released in the process, for which Frisch proposed the term 'fission'.

In the summer of 1939 Frisch went to Birmingham for an exploratory visit but was prevented from returning to Copenhagen by the outbreak of war. The implications of fission, particularly the energy release and the possibility of a chain reaction, occupied nuclear physicists intensely. In March 1940 he and Rudolf Peierls wrote what has become known as the 'Frisch–Peierls memorandum'. This pointed out that a chain reaction was possible in separated uranium-235, that the critical mass would be reasonably small, and that such a chain reaction would release an appreciable part of the available fission energy, causing a powerful explosion. The memorandum specified many of the consequences of such an explosion. This was the start of the atomic energy project in Britain. From August 1940 Frisch pursued fission research in Liverpool with James Chadwick, focusing on isotope separation. In 1943, having been naturalized with record speed, he went to Los Alamos with other members of the British team to join in the American atomic weapon project. As a group leader in the experimental physics division Frisch worked on neutron multiplication and the determination of critical sizes of fissile material. He witnessed the first nuclear test, at Alamogordo, and he learned of the destruction of Hiroshima and Nagasaki while still at Los Alamos.

Like most of the physicists at Los Alamos, Frisch received several job offers from British and American universities immediately after the war. For eighteen months after his return to England in 1946, he was head of the nuclear physics division of the Atomic Energy Research Establishment at Harwell; in 1947 he succeeded John Cockcroft in the Jacksonian professorship of natural philosophy in Cambridge; and in 1948 he accepted a fellowship of Trinity College. In 1951 he married Ursula (Ulla), daughter of Dr Karl Blau, a civil servant, of Vienna. They had a daughter and a son, who became a physicist.

Nuclear physics still made for the largest research group in W. L. Bragg's decentralized Cavendish, yet the laboratory had not settled on a policy on the field, particularly with regard to its accelerator programme. Early in 1954, shortly after his appointment to the Cavendish chair,

Nevill Mott recommended to the nuclear physics committee of the Department of Scientific and Industrial Research that work on Cambridge's linear accelerator be discontinued. Frisch therefore pursued work on small-scale nuclear physics and taught both undergraduates and research students. His lectures managed to make abstruse problems transparent, and his training of graduates conveyed to them some of his pleasure in making things work.

Frisch's sustained interest in instrumentation culminated at the Cavendish, most of his research papers after the war being concerned with instrumentation. In 1955, shortly after the development of the bubble chamber, he set out to build a semi-automatic device to assist in the laborious analysis and recording of data from bubble chamber photographs. From 1965 on he developed a faster machine, in which the photographs were scanned by a laser beam sweeping out the tracks—'Sweepnik'. In 1969 he became chairman of a Cambridge-based scientific instrument company, Laserscan Ltd, incorporated to develop and exploit his invention. Frisch devised various constructions for the company to the end of his life. As he put it in his autobiography, 'all my life I have been interested in the design of scientific devices, even more than in the results which I or others might obtain with their help' (Frisch, 219).

Frisch was an active and successful popularizer, writing four books, and numerous articles, lectures, and broadcasts on atomic physics. He deemed communication to gain the public's support for science, which he conceived as knowledge for its own sake, to be important. In his *Letter to a Young Scientist* (broadcast in 1956), he stressed his view that 'scientists produce the tools but do not and cannot control their use … Nor do I think that scientists should form pressure groups and force the community to take heed' (*The Listener*, 56.269, 350). He did not like to recall his part in the Manhattan project and rejected invitations to lecture on the subject of 'the scientist and society'. His autobiography is admittedly sketchy about his Cambridge years.

Frisch retired from his Cambridge chair in 1972. He was appointed OBE in 1946 and elected FRS in 1948. After an accidental fall for which he was hospitalized, he died in Cambridge on 22 September 1979.

RUDOLF PEIERLS, rev. XAVIER ROQUÉ

Sources R. Peierls, *Memoirs FRS*, 27 (1981), 283–306 · O. R. Frisch, *What little I remember* (1979) · personal knowledge (1986) · Trinity Cam., Frisch MSS
Archives Archive for History of Quantum Physics, London · BBC WAC · Trinity Cam., personal and family corresp. and papers | Bodl. Oxf., Society for Protection of Science and Learning and Home Office files | FILM BBC film archives | SOUND American Institute of Physics, College Park, Maryland, Center for History of Physics · BBC sound archives
Likenesses portrait, CAC Cam., Meitner collection · portrait, Bildarchiv der Österreichischen Nationalbibliothek, Vienna, Austria
Wealth at death £55,130: probate, 1 Feb 1980, *CGPLA Eng. & Wales*

Frisell, (John) Fraser (1774–1846), writer, was educated at the University of Glasgow. He went to France, for the purpose of finishing his education, in 1792. In 1793 he was thrown into prison at Dijon, where he remained for fifteen months. He was released and returned to England following the treaty of Amiens. Frisell was again in France on the renewal of the war in 1803, and was briefly imprisoned. He took up residence at Paris, where he lived during the remainder of his life, spending, however, a portion of each year in travel.

Frisell became the intimate friend of Chateaubriand, Joubert, Fontanes, and their circle by whom he was beloved as 'a man of taste and knowledge' (Marcellus, 114). In memory of Frisell's daughter Elisa, who died at Passy in 1832, Chateaubriand composed the poem 'Jeune fille et jeune fleur', which was published in his *Mémoires d'outre-tombe*. The only work that Frisell is known to have written is *De la constitution d'Angleterre* (1820), which was praised for 'giving the clearest and most precise view of the subject' for the 'general reader' (*Athenaeum*, 175). Frisell died at Albion House while on a visit to Torquay, Devon, on 27 January 1846.   L. C. SANDERS, *rev.* MEGAN A. STEPHAN

Sources Le Comte de Marcellus, *Chateaubriand et son temps* (1859), 114, 115 · *The Athenaeum* (14 Feb 1846), 175 · P. de Raynal, ed., *Les correspondants de J. Joubert* (1883), 351 · d. cert.

Friswell, Sir Charles Ernest Hain (1871–1926), motor car distributor and manufacturer, was born on 30 December 1871 at 17 Buckingham Street, Marylebone, the son of George Friswell, advertising agent, and his wife, Jane Street. He received a private education, but little is known about his personal life. Friswell married Edith Kate Frewer in 1905; they had no children.

Like many others, Friswell entered the world of the automobile from that of the cycle, at first combining an agency for cycles with other business interests. Friswells Ltd was established in London in 1896 with a capital of £40,000 and specialized in the imported French Peugeot car. Such was his success and prominence that in 1901 Friswell was selected by the Automobile Mutual Protection Association Ltd to fight a test case against H. J. Lawson's monopolistic British Motor Traction Company Ltd. The claim, that Friswell had infringed Maybach's float feed patent by selling a car so fitted, was dismissed and an appeal dropped. By this time he was operating on a large scale: Friswell's Automobile Palace Ltd, a five-storey building, could accommodate hundreds of vehicles in garage and showroom space, with repair and paint shops, accessory sales and auction facilities, and other provisions for the convenience of the clientele.

A logical progression from the motor trade was into manufacturing, and Friswell moved into production after visiting the stand of the Standard Motor Company of Coventry at the Olympia Motor Exhibition in November 1905. He was made sole distributor for Standard cars and became chairman of the Standard Motor Company Ltd (founded 1903), a position he held until November 1912. To strengthen its financial position Friswell organized a guaranteed overdraft with Barclays Bank and the company acquired additional premises, as coachworks and repair and service centres. For nearly six years (four of which are recorded in a volume of detailed board decisions) Friswell dominated the company, both in strategy and in the detail of production. This dominance in production could be construed as undue interference and was probably a major factor contributing to his break from Standard at the end of 1912.

The board decisions show that Friswell was usually present at meetings, unless abroad, and that he was closely involved in detail as well as broad policy, for example in relation to quality control, production, and publicity. The needs of his agency seem to have impeded production runs and his attendance at morning meetings was often followed by a walk around the works before his return to London. Despite this over-close involvement, he was aware of the need to make a formal separation between manufacturer and agent, and decisions affecting his agency were transmitted in writing, even when Friswell was present at the board meeting in question.

In the wider world Friswell put his skill as a publicist to good use. In 1909 he played a prominent part in entertaining delegates to the Imperial Press Conference, attended by newspaper proprietors and editors from across the empire. In recognition for this, and also for his having arranged for hundreds of London's horse-cabmen to be retrained as motor car drivers at his own expense, he was knighted in November 1909. In 1911 his publicity secured for Standard the contract to provide all motor transport, involving some seventy vehicles, for the coronation durbar held in Delhi. During Friswell's absence in India, however, a financial crisis developed at Standard following difficulties in collecting Friswell's account for November 1911. His company subsequently dishonoured its bill for goods supplied in January 1912. Standard survived, but on short time in mid-1912 and Friswell's sole agency agreement was terminated with effect from 30 September. The ending of Friswell's connection with Standard followed soon thereafter, his offer to buy out Reginald Maudslay, founder of Standard, having failed in the face of a successful counter-bid.

In consequence, Friswell left the motor industry; his reconstructed dealership, Friswells Ltd, went into voluntary liquidation in November 1915. Friswell pursued his other business interests, in South Africa and in Sheffield, where he had manufacturing silversmiths works. He died on 15 December 1926 at Eagle House Nursing Home, Woodford Green, Essex. He was survived by his wife.

RICHARD A. STOREY

Sources J. R. Davy, *The 'Standard' car, 1903–63* (1967) · H. O. Duncan and E. Vavin, *The world on wheels* (privately printed, Paris, [1926]) · R. Church, *Herbert Austin: the British motor car industry to 1941* (1979) · R. Church, 'Markets and marketing in the British motor industry before 1914', *Journal of Transport History*, 3rd ser., 3 (1982), 1–20 · R. Storey, 'Friswell, Sir Charles Ernest Hain', *DBB* · d. cert. · U. Warwick Mod. RC, Standard Motor Company records · *CGPLA Eng. & Wales* (1927) · *WWW*

Archives U. Warwick Mod. RC, British Motor Industry Heritage Trust deposit: Standard Motor Company records

Wealth at death £156,033 5s. 5d.: probate, 14 Feb 1927, *CGPLA Eng. & Wales*

Friswell, James Hain (1825–1878), writer, was born on 8 May 1825 at Forton, near Newport, Shropshire, the youngest son of William Friswell (c.1794–1856), solicitor, of 93 Wimpole Street, London, and Henrietta Hain of Bath. He was baptized James Friswell, and it was only later that he added his mother's maiden name. Friswell was educated at Aspley College, Aspley Guise, near Woburn, Bedfordshire. His father stopped his schooling before he was sixteen, and after a year at home his wish to attend university was ignored; he was instead articled in 1842 to John Rumley, an engraver in London. On 11 September 1847 Friswell married Emma Rumley (b. 1825), his employer's daughter, and moved to live at 14 Wharton Street, Pentonville.

While working for John Rumley, Friswell devoted much of his spare time to literature; he also devoted two or three days a week to teaching in a ragged school, assisting his former schoolfriend, the Revd Warwick Wroth. His later novel *Diamonds and Spades* (1858) reflects this experience. His literary career started in 1851 when he helped to start *The Playgoer* magazine. The following year he contributed to the *Puppet Show* and in 1853 he edited the *Biographical Magazine* briefly, and wrote stories for George Cruikshank, who became a lifelong friend. These were the first steps in a long career of journalism, as editor or writer. His first major works were published in 1854, the first specially commissioned by John Cassell, *The Russian Empire: its History and Present Condition of its People*. The other work was a series of stories, *Houses with their Fronts Off* (dedicated to Thackeray), in which he 'describes what he has seen' (preface) in establishments ranging from slum dwelling to police court. His active social concerns are evident in the sympathy shown for the poor and deprived. The volume had immediate success, quickly selling 10,000 copies. Friswell followed this with a similar successful work, *Twelve Insides and One Out* (1855). In the same year he edited an anthology of Crimean War poetry, *Songs of the War*, containing some of his own verse.

In 1856 Friswell's father died, leaving his son to inherit an expensive lawsuit which had swallowed the family fortune. Friswell at this time gained employment with Hunt and Roskell, jewellers of Bond Street, where he held a responsible position for seven years. Later in 1856 Friswell and a few friends founded the Urban Club (at first jocularly named 'The Friday Knights'), which met at St John's Gate, Clerkenwell. During the 1850s Friswell contributed to a number of journals, including the *Illustrated Magazine*, *Sharpe's Magazine*, *Chambers's Journal*, *Eclectic Review*, the *Welcome Guest*, and *John Bull*. In 1859 the leader writer of the *Family Herald* died and Friswell was asked to contribute an article. He quickly established himself as a permanent writer, contributing regularly for nineteen years, except for a period of six weeks in 1876 when he was seriously ill. By 1860 he was able to report that 'the year begins, thank God, prosperously. We are settled in a new house' (Friswell, 84). This was in Southampton Street, Bloomsbury. He continued to extend the range of his periodical contributions, including *The Leader*, *Once a Week*, the *Literary Gazette*, the *Saturday Review*, and the *Illustrated London News*, in

James Hain Friswell (1825–1878), by Elliott & Fry

which he wrote 'The echoes of the week' whenever George Sala was away, often for several successive months.

In 1863, by which time he had already published eleven books, Friswell was able to devote himself full-time to writing. He became a member of the Shakespeare tercentenary committee, and he published *Life Portraits of William Shakespeare* (1864), a history of the various artistic representations of the poet and an examination of their authenticity. Friswell was able to unite here his literary and artistic skills, as an engraver. 1864 was important also for the publication of what became his most successful work, *The Gentle Life: Essays in Aid of the Formation of Character*. He chose to publish this work anonymously, to guarantee honest reviews; several works thereafter were designated simply 'by the author of *The Gentle Life*'. Its success (upwards of 20,000 copies of the 6s. edition sold within four years; Queen Victoria admired it, allowing a special edition to be dedicated to her in 1870; it reached a thirty-eighth edition in 1892) led to the publication of a series of essays and translations by Friswell, including *Half-Length Portraits* (1876), under the pseudonym Gibson Craig, the last volume he published before his death. (Three titles were published posthumously under the editorship of his daughter Laura Hain Friswell, who herself wrote children's stories in periodicals.) Ironically, Friswell sold the copyright of *The Gentle Life* to Sampson Low for just £75. His daughter in her memoir claims that between 1864 and 1866, Friswell was 'very busy, his earnings averaging £800 a year' (Friswell, 155). 1864 also saw the publication of *Familiar Words* (dated 1865), a quotations handbook. This received a severe (and inaccurate) review in *The Athenaeum* (28 January 1865, 118–19), but was welcomed by most reviewers. As well as literary success, 1864 saw the first attack of congestion of the lungs; although Friswell made a good recovery, his robust physique belied the grave state of his lungs, and much of his writing was later done from his sickbed.

As a novelist Friswell was much less successful. In addition to *Diamonds and Spades* he wrote four novels, and a final title, *Our Square Circle* (1880), was completed by his daughter. His second novel, *Sham!*, was written for serialization and produced as a single volume in 1858. Though little regarded by Friswell himself, the novel did go to a third edition. It is narrated by Plantagenet Smooth, and the disjointed account chiefly concerns his father's life, from a disapproving point of view, Plantagenet despising the empty social round. *A Daughter of Eve* (1863), in two volumes, also concerns itself with manners and morals in the family of Colonel Enscombe. The plot hinges on a matter of honour, and leads to a climax in a duel. It has a much brisker narrative to recommend it. *A Splendid Fortune* (1865) is set in country society a generation back, and *One of Two* (1871), in three volumes, borrows its main ideas and characters from the French writer Emile Gaboriau, translating his work to an English setting. By quoting from contemporary newspapers Friswell endeavours to give the impression of 'real life'.

Friswell was a vigorous campaigner against 'penny dreadfuls' as suitable reading for boys and an energetic supporter of the deprived. In 1867 he ran a campaign through his newspaper column in the *Morning Star* to start a fund for Christmas dinners for the poor in London. This was very successful, and his may be regarded as a forerunner of similar seasonal charitable projects.

Friswell died on 12 March 1878 at the home he had built for himself in 1872, Fair Home, Bexleyheath, Kent. He was buried in Crayford churchyard. His wife survived him. He was well regarded by his peers, as both man and writer; even George Sala wrote approvingly of him, although in 1871 Sala had won a libel action against Friswell's publisher of *Modern Men of Letters Honestly Criticised* (1870).

ROSEMARY SCOTT

Sources L. H. Friswell, *James Hain Friswell: a memoir* (1898) • BL, Friswell corresp., Royal Literary Fund loan no. 96: 2050, 2755 • *The Graphic* (30 March 1878) • *National commercial directory of Bedfordshire*, Pigot & Co. (1830) • *The Post Office London directory* (1861) • m. cert.
Archives BL, letters as sponsor to Royal Literary Fund, loan 96, folders 2050, 2755 • Mitchell L., Glas., corresp. and papers
Likenesses H. P. Robinson, photograph, c.1870, repro. in Friswell, *James Hain Friswell* • Elliott & Fry, photograph, NPG [*see illus.*]
Wealth at death under £1000: probate, 30 March 1878, CGPLA Eng. & Wales

Frith, Francis (1822–1898), photographer and businessman, was born on 7 October 1822 in Chesterfield, Derbyshire, the only son and the second among the three children of Francis Frith (1790–1871), cooper of Chesterfield, and his wife, Alice (1789?–1863). Born into a Quaker family, Frith's childhood combined firm morality with the indulgence given to an only son. His wanderings in the nearby Derbyshire dales laid the foundations for his lifelong love of landscape. Between 1834 and 1838 he attended Camp Hill School, a Quaker establishment in Birmingham. He was a mediocre scholar but loved poetry, science, and travel books. After he had left he was apprenticed to William Hargreaves, of a cutlery firm in Sheffield. The internal conflicts caused by his strong Quaker beliefs and lack of prospects caused a breakdown when he was twenty-one. For two years he travelled through Britain convalescing. In 1845 he started a wholesale grocery business in Liverpool, and later a printing business; hard work and a good business sense allowed him to sell these for a small fortune in 1856.

In 1853 Frith had been a founder-member of the Liverpool Photographic Society. Fascinated by photography (he also drew and painted), he embarked on the three journeys to the Middle East that were to make his reputation. Between 1856 and 1859 he travelled to Palestine and Syria and up the Nile, where he took pioneering photographs of the landscape and of monuments, often under dangerous and difficult conditions. He slept in tombs and caves and was attacked by wild dogs and brigands; inside an unventilated tent he worked in desert temperatures with collodion chemicals that were prone to boil on the glass-plate negatives. Back in London his work was praised by the Photographic Society and in *The Times*. He lectured and exhibited, and published his photographs in a series of successful books.

In 1860 Frith set up a photographic company in Reigate, Surrey (where he settled), to record on film as many locations in Britain as he could. The arrival of the railways had made cheap holidays widely available, and Frith's prints made popular souvenirs, both in postcard and folio format. For a time Frith & Co. was the largest photographic publisher in the world. Frith travelled widely and took thousands of the photographs himself, as well as commissioning many fine photographers, including Francis Bedford. The care taken in the execution and subsequent preservation of these photographs, and the wealth of period detail that they record, has made them an invaluable resource for historians.

Success allowed Frith to devote more time to leisure and to his family. On 19 July 1860 he had married Mary Ann (1837–1901), daughter of Alfred Rosling of Reigate, a timber importer; they had five sons and three daughters. Frith remained a convinced Quaker all his life and contributed a number of articles to the *Friends Quarterly Examiner*. Perhaps his most influential publication was *A Reasonable Faith: Short Religious Essays for the Times* (1844), a work of liberal theology that he co-authored with William Pollard and William E. Turner. For the last twenty years of his life bronchitis made him take holidays on the French riviera;

he said of these later years that he 'fell back upon books and art, nature, love and poetry'. He died on 25 February 1898 at his home—La Petite Bastide—in Cannes, France, where he was buried. After his death his sons Eustace and Cyril continued the business, which carried on trading until 1971.

Francis Frith's achievement was two-fold: his photographs of the Middle East set new standards in technical excellence, and his business acumen brought landscape photography to the man in the street. The Frith and Co. archive, now held at Teffont, near Salisbury, Wiltshire, remains one of the most important collections of topographical photographs of Britain in existence, and its contents have been extensively republished in book form.

T. R. SACKETT, *rev.*

Sources B. Jay, *Victorian cameraman: Francis Frith's views of rural England, 1850–1898* (1973) · records, Frith & Co., Teffont, near Salisbury, Wiltshire · 'Dictionary of Quaker biography', RS Friends, Lond. [card index] · www.francisfrith.com [incl. biographical article by M. F. Harker] · m. cert.
Archives Cambs. AS, Cambridge, prints of Cambridge area · Frith & Co., Teffont, near Salisbury, Wiltshire, records
Wealth at death £3473: probate, 30 March 1898, *CGPLA Eng. & Wales*

Frith, John (1503–1533), evangelical theologian and martyr, was born at Westerham in Kent. His family moved to Sevenoaks, where his father, Richard, became an innkeeper. He was sent as a boy to Eton College, and from there went to Cambridge, apparently as a scholar to Queens', but taking his BA at King's College in 1525. His tutor was Stephen Gardiner, later bishop of Winchester. Soon afterwards Wolsey himself, noting Frith's outstanding learning and abilities as a scholar, called him across to Oxford, with others also from Cambridge, to add lustre to his new Cardinal College (afterwards Christ Church) as one of the junior canons. Foxe reports that Frith and others (including, erroneously, Tyndale, who was then in Germany) 'held an assembly in the college, were accounted to be heretics (as they called them), and thereupon were cast into a prison of the college where salt-fish lay' (*Acts and Monuments*, 4.617). The 'stink' infected them all, and several died. Young scholars at that date, especially from Cambridge, can hardly have been unaware of the powerful reform group in that university led by Robert Barnes, fancifully called by modern historians the 'White Horse' reformers, from Foxe's statement that some 'most commonly' (ibid., 5.415) gathered in that inn. It is likely that such 'godly learned' did indeed 'infect' Wolsey's developing college.

Frith was released 'on condition not to pass above ten miles out of Oxford' (*Acts and Monuments*, 5.5). But understanding the true danger he fled, apparently to join Tyndale in Antwerp. It is highly likely that he had known Tyndale in England and it is not impossible that he worked with him on the translation of the Bible. George Joye says that Frith wrote Tyndale's *Answer to More*, which is unlikely on stylistic evidence. At some point Frith seems to have been in Amsterdam and married there (the identity of his wife is not recorded). He attended the colloquy between Luther and Zwingli in Marburg in 1529 over the nature of the presence of Christ in the sacraments. The young Scottish reformer Patrick Hamilton had also been in Marburg a little before. Hamilton, back in Scotland, had been condemned and burnt in St Andrews on 19 February 1529; his execution was to the theological faculty at Louvain a 'worthy deed'; to Knox where 'our History doth begin' (Daniell, 218). Soon afterwards Frith made a translation into English (from Latin) of Hamilton's book, *Divers Fruitful Gatherings of Scripture*, a collection of passages from scripture known to most English speaking reformed Christians as *Patrick's Places* and widely influential as a radical exposition of justification by faith in English. In July 1529 Frith published with Martin de Keyser in Antwerp (as 'H. Luft of Marlborow in the lande of Hesse'—until recently thought to conceal J. Hoochstraten) a modest octavo under the name Richard Brightwell entitled *Revelation of Antichrist*, a translation of Luther. At the end of this is joined 'a little treatise' called *Antithesis, where are Compared together Christ's Acts and our Holy Father the Pope's*. Following the example set by the *Passional* of Melanchthon and the elder Cranach (1521), it consists of seventy-eight brief records of an action or saying of Christ contrasted in each case with what is presented as one of the pope's, the latter mostly allowed to speak for themselves. As an example, take number 61:

> Christe suffered death four our synnes [in the margin Romans 4, John 11] and arose for our justification, or els we all shulde have perisshed.
> The Pope sayeth if thou bye my pardon, or els be buried in a grey fryers cote thou must nedes be saved, so that Christ hath suffered in vayn, sith a fryers coat will save a man. (*Antithesis*, sig. N.1v)

During Lent 1531 Frith paid a short visit to England, and on his return to Tyndale in Antwerp cannot have brought much comfort about developments in England. The publication of his *Disputacion of Purgatorye* in Antwerp in 1531 had made him a wanted man. By that date the first declaratory publications reaching England from abroad had received confutations, and a new wave of more subtly argued responses appeared, of which Frith's *Disputacion* is one of the finest, answering William Rastell (Sir Thomas More's nephew), More himself (whom Frith calls 'the Proctour for Purgatory' (*Whole Workes*, 6)), and John Fisher, bishop of Rochester, and showing the lack of biblical authority for, or even mention of, purgatory. Frith, who was exceptional in his powers of detailed exegesis and argument, found that the doctrine of purgatory derogated from divine grace: it was, he saw, a doctrine that cut at the roots of New Testament faith. 'If we must make satisfaction unto God for our sinnes, then would I know why Christ died' (ibid., 14). His answers to his opponents were powerful, and his book was popular; both facts put him in danger.

Frith crossed to England again in July 1531. He appeared at Reading, where he was set in the stocks as a rogue and vagabond; he was released on the intercession of Leonard Cox. An important humanist writer, Cox had been a schoolmaster in Hungary and in Poland, and was then teaching at the school in that town; he would go on in 1534 to translate the Titus section of Erasmus's *Paraphrases*, dedicated to Thomas Cromwell—the first English translation, and well ahead of Queen Katherine Parr's initiative of a decade later, which saw the whole of the *Paraphrases* put into English and published. Foxe recounts what happened. As soon as Cox approached Frith the latter, who was 'almost pined with hunger', began 'in the Latin tongue to bewail his captivity'. Cox was intrigued by 'such excellent wit and disposition unlooked for, especially in such a state and misery'. They started talking about 'the universities, schools and tongues' and 'fell from the Latin into the Greek'. Cox's admiration overflowed when Frith quoted 'by heart … Homer's verses out of his first book of the Iliad'. Cox went to the magistrats and got Frith released without punishment (*Acts and Monuments*, 5.5–6).

The chancellor, Sir Thomas More, issued a warrant for Frith's arrest on a charge of heresy. Frith tried to hide and disguise himself, but he was seized at Milton Shore in Essex while on his way to rejoin his wife and family in Antwerp, and put in the Tower. Even in prison he continued to write with passion and clarity, though at the end he was so loaded with chains that he could neither quite lie down nor stand upright. In prison he wrote on the sacraments, adopting a position which was influenced by Luther, but more by Oecolampadius. He argued first that the matter of the sacrament was no necessary article of faith under pain of damnation. Next, that Christ had a natural body (apart from sin), and could not be in two places at once. Third, that 'This is my body' was not literal. Last, that what the church practised was not what Christ instituted. These views, written down against Frith's better judgement, were carried to More by 'a tailor named William Holt' (*Acts and Monuments*, 5.6), who pretended friendship with Frith to obtain his views. More then wrote and printed a 'letter … impugnynge the erronyouse wrytyng of J. Fryth' (STC 18090). Frith was not allowed to see a printed copy of it, but obtained only a manuscript text of whose accuracy he could not be certain.

In the Tower, Frith received two letters from William Tyndale, which Foxe prints. In the first Tyndale seeks to strengthen his faith even in the likelihood of coming martyrdom. 'If the pain be above your strength … pray to your Father in that [Christ's] name, and he shall ease your pain, or shorten it.' A postscript adds, to recent news, 'Sir, your wife is well content with the will of God, and would not, for her sake, have the glory of God hindered.' The second letter, dated January 1533, is addressed to Frith 'under the name of Jacob'. Tyndale suggests that about 'Christ's body in the sacrament' he 'meddle as little as you can' but simply 'show the phrases of Scripture, and let them talk what they will' (*Acts and Monuments*, 5.131–4).

One of the royal chaplains, Dr Richard Curwen, was put up by Stephen Gardiner into attacking Frith's view on Christ's body in the sacrament in a sermon preached before the king. King Henry ordered Frith to recant or be condemned. The result was an examination in Croydon; on the way Frith was offered the means of escape, but

refused. As he would not recant he was held for examination by the bishops of London, Winchester, and Chichester, which took place on 20 June 1533 at St Paul's. He was questioned about the sacrament of the supper and purgatory and put his name to what he had said. Three days later he wrote 'The Articles wherefore John Frith dyed which he wrote in Newgate the 23 day of June the yeare of our lorde 1533'. Sentence was pronounced on him as 'guilty of most detestable heresies' and so to be punished 'for the salvation of thy soul'. On 4 July the bishop of London handed him over to the mayor and sheriffs of London, and he was taken to Smithfield and burnt. Foxe wrote:

> The wind made his death somewhat the longer, which bare away the flame from him unto his fellow that was tied to his back … but God giving him strength, that even as though he had felt no pain in that long torment, he seemed rather to rejoice for his fellow, than to be careful for himself. (*Acts and Monuments*, 5.15)

Frith's death, aged thirty, caused widespread grief in London and elsewhere in England, and also on the continent; he was mourned as a talented, modest, and good young man. His later influence was important, for the articles which he set out shortly before his execution differ little from those adopted by the reformed church in the prayer book of 1552. John Foxe, who became accustomed to martyrdoms, begins his account of Frith's end in heartfelt style: 'Amongst all other chances lamentable, there hath been none a long time which seemed to me more grievous, than the lamentable death and cruel handling of John Frith, so learned and excellent a young man' (*Acts and Monuments*, 5.3).   DAVID DANIELL

Sources *The whole workes of W. Tyndall, John Frith, and Doct. Barnes*, ed. J. Fox (1572–3) [incl. *Antithesis*] • *The acts and monuments of John Foxe*, ed. J. Pratt, [new edn], 8 vols. (1877) • Cooper, *Ath. Cantab.*, 1.47–8 • W. A. Clebsch, *England's earliest protestants, 1520–1535* (1964) • D. Daniell, *William Tyndale: a biography* (1994) • G. Latré, 'The place of printing of the Coverdale Bible', *The Bible as book: the Reformation*, ed. O. O'Sullivan and E. N. Herron (2000), 89–102 • *An apology made by George Joye, to satisfy, if it may be, W. Tundale*, 1535, ed. E. Arber (1882) • P. S. Allen, *Erasmus: lectures and wayfaring sketches* (1934) • *DNB* • R. E. Fulop, 'John Frith (1803–1533) and his relation to the origin of the Reformation in England', PhD diss., U. Edin., 1956

Frith [*married name* Markham], **Mary** [*known as* Moll Cutpurse] (**1584x9–1659**), thief, is of uncertain origins. She was perhaps the daughter of William Frith who was baptized at St Martin Ludgate, London, on 19 April 1584. This is consistent neither with her reported age ('in her seventy-fourth year') at her death in July 1659 nor with the contradictory statement of her birth in 1589, both of which come from *The Life of Mrs Mary Frith* (1662). However, while the work ostensibly contains autobiographical material, it proves to be a patchwork of legends and representations, and contains many errors and omissions. Later works have lifted information from *The Life*, and have politicized and spiced it in the retelling.

The real Mary Frith first certainly appears in the record when indicted before Middlesex justices for a crime allegedly committed on 26 August 1600. With Jane Hill and Jane Styles, two other unmarried women living in

See here the Prefidente o'th pilfring Trade
Mercuryes, fecond Venus's onely May'd
Doublet and breeches in a Uniform dreffe
The female Humurrift a Kickfhaw meffe
Here no attraction that your fancy greets
But ifher FEATURES pleafe not read her FEATS

Mary Frith (1584x9–1659), by unknown artist

London, she was accused of stealing a purse containing 2s. 11d. from a man in Clerkenwell. On 18 March 1602 two inhabitants of the parish of St Giles Cripplegate, Thomas Dobson and William Simons, apparently stood bail for her appearance at sessions on a similar accusation. The tables were turned when on 13 May 1608 'Maria Feith de Southworke' and a soldier, John Clementes, bound themselves to give evidence for the prosecution in a felony case, but on 8 September 1609 she was in the dock again, accused, as 'of St Olave, Southwark, spinster', of burglary at a house in the parish and of stealing over £10 worth of coins and jewellery. Appearing at Surrey assizes, she was found not guilty of that offence in March 1610.

On 7 August that year Frith made what may have been her début in print in *The Madde Pranckes of Mery Mall of the Bankside*. Logged in the stationers' register by its author, the playwright John Day, the jest biography has since been lost, but it depicted her going about in man's apparel and playing the lute without a licence in taverns and in the streets. She was already gossiped about across the city and was the subject of several stage plays, most notably *The Roaring Girl, or, Moll Cutpurse* (1611) by Thomas Middleton and Thomas Dekker. In April 1611 she appeared at the Fortune Playhouse in man's clothing, complete with sword, to close a play (possibly *The Roaring Girl*) with a jig. This seems to have been a publicity stunt by the playwrights and actors. On Christmas day she was arrested in Paul's

Walk when indecently dressed, and sent to Bridewell prison. Summoned to the consistory court of the bishop of London on 27 January 1612, she denied Bishop King's accusation of involvement in prostitution but he remanded her again to Bridewell pending the result of further investigation. What happened next is unclear. On 12 February John Chamberlain wrote to his friend Sir Dudley Carleton that 'Moll Cut-purse a notorious bagage' had done public penance at Paul's Cross. She was suspected of having been 'maudelin druncke' (Ungerer, 67), but none the less put on an impressive performance of tearful contrition. Thereafter she seems to have been released.

On 23 March 1614 at St Saviour's (sometimes known as St Mary Overie), Southwark, Mary Frith married Lewknor Markham, described by Mary in a 1624 lawsuit as an esquire of Nottinghamshire, but more possibly a son of Gervase Markham the London playwright. The marriage does not seem to have lasted: Mary continued to be known by her maiden name, and in a lawsuit of 1624 she indicated that they had not cohabited for a long time. For a period the relationship may have brought her a modicum of status and respectability but she was up before the Middlesex justices again in 1617.

By the time Frith appeared before star chamber in 1621 she had a fencing school in London but she seems to have used the premises to exploit her links with both criminals and respectable citizens. In 1624 she was sued in the court of requests for an unpaid bill for beaver hats, bought in defiance of both sumptuary laws and accepted female attire. The court files reveal her dropping in at ale houses, tobacco shops, and playhouses, swearing, blaspheming, mixing with lewd company, and sheltering felons. They also show her running a sort of criminal-intelligence network that helped victims such as Henry Killigrew (from the courtier family) locate their lost goods and passed on to the authorities the names of pickpockets and cutpurses. Moll Cutpurse was a law enforcer as well as a lawbreaker.

These documented activities were borrowed, exaggerated, and sometimes distorted by contemporary pamphleteers and dramatists to weave the legend of Moll Cutpurse. By now she was a staple item of story-telling and rumour-mongering, 'a notorious infamous person, and such a one as was well knowne & acquainted with all thieves & cutpurses' (Ungerer, 69). Her story possessed both an entertainment and a commercial value, as well as providing opportunities to preach about right and wrong. Her recorded lapses, particularly theft, cross-dressing, drinking, and smoking tobacco, were rising concerns in Jacobean London which in contemporary perceptions had reached near epidemic proportions. What better way to draw attention to these galloping cancers than to portray them together in the character of a source of much gossip, who had herself broken the rules? The skewed image of Moll soon included a combative element: Chamberlain mentions her challenge to a number of young men about town. In *The Witch of Edmonton* she was a bogey figure, a witch's familiar, while in *The Roaring Girl* she was a critic of predatory male sexualities.

The real Mary disappears from the record until 21 June 1644 when she was among several people discharged from the Bethlem Hospital having been judged to have recovered from insanity. She was still in the public mind. She occurs as a retriever of stolen property in Sir John Berkenhead's *Paul's Churchyard* (1651 or 1652) and in Samuel Shepherd's mock almanac *Merlinus Anonymous … for the year 1653*. When she drew up her will on 6 June 1659 she was a widow living in the parish of St Bride's, Fleet Street, 'aged and sicke and weake of body' (Ungerer, 73). She left £20 to her kinsman Abraham Robinson and the residue of her estate to her niece and executor Frances Edmondes, wife of George Edmondes. Frith died on 26 July 1659 and was buried on 10 August, as she had wished, in St Bride's.

Nowhere is the jumbling of fact and fiction in Frith's life more evident than in *The Life*, published three years after her death. It quotes wrongly the clauses of her will, makes her a resolutely single woman and thus a bad example for other women, and twists stories mentioned in court records. Her character is used to score political points: she calls the late conflict an 'unnatural war', lambasts 'precisians', and scolds troops for fighting against their king, while scenes from her 'unwomanly' life are presented as a cautionary tale for her audience. Some elements of *The Life* are at least loosely based on episodes quoted in other sources, while others match the general reality of criminal culture in seventeenth-century London. But by this time Moll's life was in the hands of those who refashioned it for their own purposes, including settling scores in the wake of the Restoration and turning her into a swashbuckling highway robber; such recasting continues today, as in Ellen Galford's *Moll Cutpurse* (1993). It is unlikely that the sixty-year-old Moll mugged General Sir Thomas Fairfax on Hounslow Heath (as *The Life* claimed): that is yet another of those inventions, embellishments, or propagandas that obscure Moll's opaque life.

PAUL GRIFFITHS

Sources PRO, ASSI 35/52/6, fol. 18 [housebreaking] · will, PRO, PROB 11/299, fols. 106–7 · consistory confession, LMA, DL/C 310, fols. 19v–20v · interrogatories, LMA, LCQS SF 113 · *The obituary of Richard Smyth … being a catalogue of all such persons as he knew in their life*, ed. H. Ellis, CS, 44 (1849), 51 · J. V. L. Pruyn, 'Weddings at St Saviour's, Southwark, from AD 1606 to 1525', *The Genealogist*, new ser., 7 (1891), 96 · *The letters of John Chamberlain*, ed. N. E. McClure, 2 vols. (1939), vol. 1, pp. 332–5 · M. Dowling, 'A note on Moll Cutpurse— "The roaring girl"', *Review of English Studies*, 10 (1934), 67–71 · G. Ungerer, 'Mary Frith, alias Moll Cutpurse, in life and literature', *Shakespeare Studies*, 18 (2000), 42–84 · J. Todd and E. Spearing, eds., *Counterfeit ladies* (1994) · E. K. Chambers, *The Elizabethan stage*, 4 vols. (1923), vol. 3, p. 297 · *The life of Mrs Mary Frith* (1662) · A. Smith, *A history of the lives and robberies of the most noted highwaymen, footpads, shop-lifts and cheats*, 2 vols. (1714) · C. Johnson, *The history of the lives and adventures of the most famous highwaymen* (1734), 88–90
Likenesses drawing, NPG [*see illus.*] · etching, BM, NPG; repro. in *Life of Mrs Mary Frith* · print, V&A; repro. in T. Middleton and T. Dekker, *The roaring girl, or, Moll Cut-Purse* (1611) · woodcut, NPG; repro. in T. Middleton and T. Dekker, *The roaring girl, or, Moll Cut-Purse* (1611) · woodcut, Bodl. Oxf.; repro. in *The woman's champion* (1662)

Frith, William Powell (1819–1909), painter, was born on 9 January 1819 at Aldfield, near Ripon, Yorkshire. His parents, Thomas Frith (1777–1837) and his wife, Jane Powell (*b.*

William Powell Frith (1819–1909), self-portrait, 1867 [with model]

1779), who married on 26 May 1814, were employed as butler and cook at Studley Royal, near Ripon.

Education and early career In 1826, when Frith was seven, his father became the landlord of the Dragon Hotel, Harrogate. Frith attended first a school at Knaresborough (1828–9) which, he claimed, resembled another Yorkshire establishment, the infamous Dotheboys Hall of Dickens's *Nicholas Nickleby*. Frith soon transferred to St Margaret's, near Dover, where he was given free rein to indulge his taste for drawing—an activity encouraged by both parents, especially his father, who took a keen interest in art and was an amateur practitioner. Caricatures and copies of Dutch low-life scenes which have survived from this period betray Frith's instinctive preference for genre, a preference which remained fundamental to his artistic achievement.

Frith's formal training began in London in March 1835 when his father entered him into the private art academy of Henry Sass at 6 Charlotte Street, Bloomsbury. Frith had little enthusiasm for drawing from the antique, nor for anatomy or perspective—'that dreadful science' (Frith, *Autobiography*, 1.37) as he called it, and which he confessed he never mastered. In 1837 he was admitted to the Royal Academy Schools, where he appreciated the life classes, but not the lax teaching system. When Frith's father died of influenza in the same year, his widow let the Harrogate hotel and moved to London with her two remaining children—Charles and Victoria Jane—the eldest, George, having died in 1831. The family made their home at 11 Osnaburgh Street, Regent's Park, where Frith set up a small painting room. Even at this early stage, he was independent and ambitious enough to seek out his own direction, and he began to make money in his second year at the academy by portrait painting. Through contacts of his uncle Scaife, a retired Brook Street, London, hotelier, he found his clientele mainly among a body of affluent farmers in Lincolnshire, earning between 5 and 15 guineas per portrait during two tours which he made in the area.

In 1838 Frith exhibited his first painting at the British Institution, *A Page with a Letter*, followed in 1839 by a portrait of one of Sass's children, and in 1840 by *Othello and Desdemona* (FM Cam.). This was a significant step. Along with other members of a group of like-minded young artists known as the Clique, which included Augustus Egg, Richard Dadd, Henry O'Neil, and John Phillip, Frith rapidly established himself as a painter of literary and historical genre. The formation of the Clique about 1840 was a signal event. Recognizing that the demands of a rapidly expanding art market were at odds with the established academic taste perpetuated at the Royal Academy, the young painters determined to cater for it in the form of accessible subjects, with the emphasis on character and incident, sparkling detail and high finish. From his earliest years these features made Frith's work eminently suited to engraving, and his close association with the print market became an essential feature of his career.

In 1840 Frith made the first of several visits to the continent, and on this occasion he recorded studying in the Louvre. In 1850 and again in 1880 he visited Belgium, the Netherlands, and the Rhine, and in 1875 made an extended tour of Italy; but although enthusiastic about Dutch art in particular he remained insular in his tastes and opinions. Also in 1840 he made his first appearance at the Royal Academy with *Malvolio before the Countess Olivia*. Although it is his paintings of contemporary life which account for his enduring fame, literature always supplied the majority of his subjects. Frith was an avid reader, and found many a paintable character and scene in novels and poems by much loved authors like Cervantes, Dickens, Goldsmith, Molière, Scott, Sterne, and in the essays of Addison and Steele in *The Spectator*. In 1845 *The Village Pastor* (priv. coll.), inspired by Goldsmith's *Deserted Village*, secured Frith's election as an associate of the Royal Academy, and in 1852, after the death of J. M. W. Turner, he was promoted to Royal Academician. In that year his exhibits included *Pope Making Love to Lady Mary Wortley Montague* (City Art Gallery, Auckland, New Zealand), one of three literary subjects which won him a second-class gold medal in the Paris Universal Exhibition of 1855; but for his diploma picture he chose a modern-life subject: *The Sleeping Model*, which includes his own self-portrait (1853; RA).

Frith also painted imaginary historical genre subjects of a nostalgic and evocative type. Some of the more ambitious works in this category show Frith at his early best. *English Merry-Making a Hundred Years Ago* (exh. RA, 1847; priv. coll.), which drew praise from Turner, and *Coming of Age in the Olden Time* (exh. RA, 1849; priv. coll.) both reveal Frith's gift for the dramatic grouping of large numbers of figures, for lively and humorous characterization, and for the telling detail. Highly successful engravings were made of both.

Modern-life subjects From an early age Frith was at the centre of literary and artistic life in London. His lifelong friendship with Charles Dickens began in 1842 when the novelist commissioned paintings of two characters from his own novels: *Dolly Varden* (1842; priv. coll.), a variation of Frith's first portrayal of the vivacious character from *Barnaby Rudge* (1841) and *Kate Nickleby* (1842; priv. coll.). Frith's acute judgement of the market meant that from his earliest years he was regularly requested for duplicates or variations of well-chosen subjects; in the case of *Dolly*, at least six. But he was anxious to break new ground and, although nervous of the difficulties involved, began to attempt subjects taken from contemporary life. These started tentatively enough in 1852 with *Bedtime* or *Prayer* (priv. coll.) and a picture of a servant girl. The latter was engraved with the saleable title *'Sherry, Sir?'* added by the publishers. At their request Frith produced a pair to it in 1854, *'Did You Ring, Sir?'* (both priv. coll.).

As Frith was well aware, the chief obstacle to modern subjects was the 'unpicturesque' nature of Victorian dress (Frith, *Autobiography*, 1.243); but in 1851, during a visit to Ramsgate, he determined to begin preparatory work on his first ambitious modern scene: *Life at the Seaside* (*Ramsgate Sands*) (Royal Collection). His diary records how he became increasingly engrossed in the subject, exploring it with typical thoroughness through numerous sketches.

Although encouraged by his artist friends—E. M. Ward, Augustus Egg, and John Leech—Frith knew that he was taking a calculated risk with *Life at the Seaside*, for it was large and elaborate enough to require a major investment of time and money. To Frith's relief, on its completion in 1854 it was bought by Messrs Lloyd, the print publishers, for 1000 guineas and popular acclaim voted it picture of the year at the Royal Academy. Its purchase by Queen Victoria (from Lloyds, who declined to make a profit on the sale) set the seal on Frith's success. The commercial possibilities of *Life at the Seaside* were patent, and in 1859 a highly successful engraving by C. W. Sharpe was published by the Art Union of London.

Frith's choice of *Derby Day* (1856–8, Tate collection) for his second important panorama was a stroke of genius; for the Derby was the major national holiday of the year when even parliament ceased to sit in order to join the exodus to Epsom Downs. It was also the one occasion when all classes mixed with a freedom unknown on any other day of the year, in what one critic called a 'temporary saturnalia of social equality' (*ILN*, 23 May 1863, 567). Frith exploited the distinctive nature of the occasion to the full. All attention is focused on a jostling, meandering crowd of almost ninety figures, each individualized in terms of character and class: itinerant acrobats, gangs of gypsies and pickpocketing boys, fraudsters with their gaming tables, aristocrats, policemen, prostitutes, and criminals.

Few paintings have ever earned such universal acclaim. It was recognized instantly as a unique historical record of a significant social event. Critics marvelled at its fidelity; as the *Morning Post* put it: 'the words needed to give an account of the copy are the very same that would be required to describe the original' (10 May 1858, 2). When it was exhibited at the Royal Academy, a policeman was called in to stand guard and a rail set up to control the spectators. It was the first time that such protective measures had been required since the exhibition of Wilkie's *Chelsea Pensioners* in 1822, and Frith wrote delightedly of the 'invidious … distinction' (Frith, *Autobiography*, 1.28) thus granted him, and the degree of envy it aroused. The painting had been commissioned by Jacob Bell, founder of the Pharmaceutical Society, at a price of £1500. On his death in 1859 he bequeathed his finest pictures to the National Gallery; but for several years while the engraving was in process *Derby Day* remained in the hands of Ernst Gambart, picture and print dealer, who had paid another £1500 for the copyright. As part of a massive publicity campaign, the picture toured the provinces and, in 1865, the major cities of Australia; but not without some protest from members of the public who complained that its display at the National Gallery was long overdue.

Derby Day was a hard act to follow but Frith found a worthy successor in *The Railway Station* (1860–62; Royal Holloway collection, Royal Holloway College, University of London). Frith had included a portrait of himself to the far right of *Ramsgate Sands*, but in *The Railway Station* he appears with his family at the very centre of it: proudly representing the self-made middle classes who were the backbone of Victorian England. Cleverly, he chose to show his family involved in that most English of customs: seeing the two elder sons off to boarding-school. Frith was sufficiently affluent to be able to send his own to Harrow; but his situation was not as harmonious as he suggests here. Frith's first marriage to Isabella Jane (1823–1880), daughter of George Baker, a stockbroker, of York, had taken place on 26 June 1845, and between 1846 and 1860 seven sons and five daughters were born to them. But during much of their marriage Frith led a double life, maintaining a mistress—Mary Alford (1834/5–1895)—with whom he had seven children. The first, Mary Powell, was born in 1856 and two more had appeared by the year of *The Railway Station*.

Frith epitomizes the success attainable to the ingenious artist who understood the market. Both pictures were conceived with an eye to commercial appeal. *The Railway Station* was from first to last a carefully calculated business venture, the format and content of the picture being planned by Frith and the dealer, Louis Victor Flatow, down to the last detail. Frith was paid a total of £5250, which included not only copyright but sole exhibiting rights—an entirely new departure. After carefully engineered advance publicity in the press over the two years when the painting was in process, in the spring of 1862 it was displayed in London at Flatow's Gallery, 7 Haymarket, and later at Messrs Hayward and Leggatt, Cornhill, before touring Britain. Visitors, who paid 1s. to see it, totalled 21,150. Henry Graves, who took over the deal from the ailing Flatow in 1863, paid more than £16,300 for it, and invited subscriptions with the aid of a thirty-one-page pamphlet written by the journalist and playwright Tom Taylor, in which every character and detail was explained.

Graves is said to have made more than £40,000 from the print (a mixed mezzotint by Francis Holl published in 1866).

In modern-life panoramas Frith found the perfect outlet for his talents. His recognition of the topical interest that attached to the modern city crowd and its anthropological components; his self-confessed interest in character and physiognomy; his aptitude for the dramatic grouping of large numbers of people into coherent units; his appeal to popular sentiment—in these pictures all are enhanced by a technique which embodies a touch so painstakingly minute as to ensure that every detail yields its full burden.

To a twentieth-century critic like Roger Fry *The Railway Station* represented the nadir of Victorian taste: 'an artistic Sodom and Gomorrah' (Fry, 109) from which more poetic painters had understandably fled. Fry complained that Frith had embraced 'the hideous present' (ibid.) all too well; but although his paintings are far from being aesthetic objects, as visual documents of Victorian society they are invaluable. Of this Frith had no doubt. He predicted that 'pictures of contemporary life and manners have a better chance of immortality than ninety-nine out of any hundred of the ideal and so-called poetical pictures produced in this generation' (Frith, *Further Reminiscences*, 9).

Having declined Queen Victoria's invitation to paint the wedding of the princess royal in 1858, Frith felt obliged to accede to a second invitation, painting *The Marriage of Their Royal Highnesses the Prince of Wales and Princess Alexandra of Denmark* in 1863 (Royal Collection). On its completion two years later, the picture aroused sufficient interest at the Royal Academy to require a policeman and a second rail; but the 139 portraits which it entailed made it the most fraught and burdensome of all the commissions Frith ever undertook. It also contributed to his failure to complete Ernst Gambart's more congenial commission for a series of three London scenes for £10,000: *The Times of Day: Morning, Covent Garden; Noon, Regent St.; Night, the Haymarket*. The remaining sketches (1862–3; priv. coll.) and *King Charles II's Last Sunday* (exh. RA, 1867; priv. coll., USA) are among the last of Frith's compositions fully to display the fluent composition and inventiveness of character and incident which distinguish his best work.

Alongside ambitious projects of this kind, Frith produced numerous potboilers in the form of characters and minor incidents from literary texts; but he was capable of major achievements in this field. *King Charles II's Last Sunday* was acclaimed by the *Art Journal* as the best of all his pictures so far. Illustrating a scene recorded by the diarist John Evelyn, this was Frith's third exhibit which required a policeman and a rail. In a luxurious apartment in Whitehall Palace, the king sits surrounded by dissolute courtiers and fawning mistresses, unaware that death will smite him within days. Another literary subject from this period, *Dinner at Boswell's Rooms in Bond St.* (exh. RA, 1869), sold for £4567 in 1875: the highest sum ever paid at that time for a work by a living painter.

Later career *The Salon d'Or Homburg* (1871; Rhode Island School of Design, Providence, Rhode Island) is a similar sensational and moralizing subject in which Frith recorded the crowded interior of the notorious gambling hall shortly before it was shut down. Predictably, it won Frith yet another protective rail at the Royal Academy. Several years later Frith returned to the dangers of gambling in two series of five paintings, the format of which was inspired by his much admired Hogarth: *The Road to Ruin* (exh. RA, 1878; priv. coll.) and *The Race for Wealth* (exh. King Street Galleries, 1880; Baroda Museum and Picture Gallery, Vadodara, Gujarat, India). The former illustrates the gradual decline into penury and ultimate death of an addict of the card-table and the racecourse; the latter the disastrous consequences of dishonest speculation in the world of high finance. The format enabled Frith to circumvent the difficulties intrinsic to large-scale composition; but these comparatively simple, stage-like scenes inevitably lack the dramatic interest which Frith had previously focused in a single powerful image. Some critics found his overt moralizing naïve and outdated by this time, but both series created a sensation; both were extensively reviewed and issued as prints. Their blatant commercialism led Harry Quilter to describe them as 'moral or social advertisements … printed in big type' (H. Quilter, *Preferences in Art*, 1892, 331) so as to be instantly comprehensible to the casual observer; and this was certainly Frith's aim. At the Royal Academy *The Road to Ruin* drew 'an excited mob [which] struggled day after day, under the guardianship of two friendly policemen' (ibid.), until yet another protective rail had been installed.

The Private View of the Royal Academy, 1881 (1883; priv. coll.) was of sufficient topical interest to earn Frith his sixth and final rail. Through a selection of prominent society figures, Frith polarized the contemporary art world, at a time when the aesthetic movement was at its height. Soulful adherents of 'the Beautiful' include Lily Langtry and Oscar Wilde, who stands in the foreground preaching the doctrine to a group of admiring females, Ellen Terry among them. The stalwart form of John Millais, to the far right, and the unpretentious Anthony Trollope are introduced as guardians of common sense: welcome antidotes to aesthetic affectation. Wilde wrought his revenge in *The Critic as Artist* (1891), satirizing Frith's memoirs as—like his art—the product of a mediocrity. Frith always remained for Wilde—as for many others, including Ruskin and Whistler—the touchstone of artistic philistinism. Frith—never slow to assert his own opinions—capitalized on this. He opposed Whistler's aesthetic stance in the trial against Ruskin in 1878, and in the articles he wrote for the *Magazine of Art* in later life he emerges as a proud and self-confessed reactionary: aestheticism, Pre-Raphaelitism (a 'ridiculous movement'); and most dangerous of all, impressionism—its 'impressions' neatly described as 'constant outrages on popular prejudice' (Frith, 'Crazes in art', 190, 191) and classed with realism as 'the fungi on the tree of [modern] art' (Frith, '"Realism" versus "sloppiness"', 7).

Frith's extraordinary gift for publicity never deserted him, and throughout a long life he was rarely out of the news. Other late paintings which aroused widespread comment include *For Better—for Worse*, intriguingly, painted in 1881, the year of his second marriage (exh. RA, 1881; priv. coll.) and *Poverty and Wealth* (exh. RA, 1888; priv. coll.); but there is no denying that on the whole his work declined in quality and interest in later years. He quite clearly grew bored, and his minor subjects—whether literary or contemporary—became increasingly limited, repetitive, and lifeless.

Final years With a second family still in tow, Frith could not afford to retire. His wife, Isabella, died on 28 January 1880, and on 30 January 1881 Frith married his mistress of long standing, Mary Alford, causing something of a rift with the children of his first marriage. As an alternative source of income, in the same decade he also took up writing, and at sixty-eight produced his two-volume *Autobiography and Reminiscences* (1887). Racy, amusing, and unpretentious, touching on the lives of many famous people and providing a fascinating insight into the Victorian art world, its success was such that Frith rapidly produced a sequel: *Further Reminiscences* (1888). He also wrote an affectionate account of *John Leech: his Life and Work* (1891), as well as short stories and articles for various magazines.

Mary died aged sixty on 7 May 1895; at his own death in 1909 Frith had made no reference in his will to his second family. Apart from his first wife's children, only his 'friend and nurse', Sarah Elizabeth Clarke, received a legacy. Five daughters and five sons from the first marriage survived their father. Of these, William Powell (1847–1876) became a playwright and novelist and Jane Ellen *Panton (Cissy) (1847–1923) a novelist and journalist. She is best-known for two volumes of memoirs, *Leaves from a Life* (1908) and *More Leaves from a Life* (1911). Walter (b. 1857), a barrister, also dabbled in journalism. According to the census, two other daughters, May Louise (b. 1851) and Mary Fanny (b. 1855) were artists. Of Frith's children by Mary Alford, Agnes Catherine (b. 1858) is also described as an artist and William Powell (b. 1862) as an architect.

Frith was a prolific painter, exhibiting 107 works at the Royal Academy between 1840 and 1906; thirteen at the British Institution between 1838 and 1857; and twelve at the Society of British Artists between 1838 and 1883. In 1890 he retired from the academy, but he continued to exhibit until 1902 and painted until the end of his life. He was admitted to membership of the Royal Belgian Academy, and the academies of Antwerp, Stockholm, and Vienna. He was a chevalier of the Légion d'honneur, and was made commander in the Royal Victorian Order by Edward VII at Buckingham Palace on 9 January 1908, his eighty-ninth birthday—an event which was widely reported in the press. Frith died of pneumonia at his home, 114 Clifton Hill, St John's Wood, London, on 2 November 1909, and was buried at Kensal Green cemetery after cremation at Golders Green.

Frith's long productive life and his unique contribution to British art were readily acknowledged in the fond obituaries which poured from the press on the occasion of his death. Although his art had become something of an anachronism in the modern world, this in no way diminished his achievement. His role as 'historian of his own age' (*The Graphic*, 7) had already ensured his immortality. In the *Art Journal's* words, Frith had become a veritable 'institution' (Jan 1910, 14) and would be sadly missed: the last great representative of his class and time.

A small exhibition of Frith's work was held at Burlington House in winter 1911, and another at Harrogate and Whitechapel in 1951. Since then, his modern-life panoramas have been represented in every major survey of Victorian art, both at home and abroad. His three most important works, *Ramsgate Sands*, *Derby Day*, and *The Railway Station*, have retained their status as veritable microcosms of mid-Victorian life. It is on this achievement that Frith's reputation rests, and in which he remains unrivalled.   Mary Cowling

Sources W. P. Frith, *Autobiography and reminiscences*, 2 vols. (1887) · W. P. Frith, *Further reminiscences* (1888) · W. P. Frith, 'Crazes in art', *Magazine of Art* (1888), 187–91 · W. P. Frith, '"Realism" *versus* "sloppiness"', *Magazine of Art* (1889), 6–8 · J. E. Panton, *Leaves from a life* (1908) · M. Cowling, *The artist as anthropologist in Victorian art* (1989) · 'British artists: their style and character: W. P. Frith, R.A.', *Art Journal* (Aug 1856), 237–40 · 'An interview with Mr W. P. Frith, R.A., C.V.O.', *The Graphic* (18 Jan 1908) · *The Times* (3 Nov 1909), 13 · *An exhibition of paintings by W. P. Frith*, Harrogate Art Gallery (1951) · R. Fry, *Reflections on British painting* (1937) · R. Parkinson, *Victoria and Albert Museum: catalogue of British paintings, 1820–1860* (1990) · J. Chapel, *Victorian taste: catalogue of paintings at Royal Holloway College* (1982) · m. certs. · d. cert. · J. Maas, *The prince of Wales's wedding: the story of a picture* (1977) · *CGPLA Eng. & Wales* (1909)
Archives V&A NAL, corresp. | Bodl. Oxf., letters to the Horsley family · JRL, letters to M. H. Spielmann · RA, letters to Royal Academy
Likenesses W. P. Frith, self-portrait, oils, 1838, NPG · A. Egg, oils, *c*.1847, Harrogate Art Gallery · W. W. Warren, watercolour drawing, *c*.1850, V&A · J. Thomas, marble bust, exh. RA 1859, Tate collection · W. P. Frith, self-portrait, oils, 1867 (with unidentified model), NPG [*see illus.*] · H. N. O'Neil, group portrait, oils, 1869 (*The billiard room of the Garrick Club*), Garr. Club · N. de Keyser, group portrait, oils, 1878 (*Les grands artistes, École du XIX siècle*), Musée des Beaux Arts Jules Chévet, Nice, France · W. P. Frith, self-portrait, oils, 1883, Aberdeen Art Gallery · J. Cassidy, bronze bust, *c*.1909, Man. City Gall. · M. D. Lapthorn, chalk drawing, 1909, NPG · Barraud, photograph, NPG; repro. in *Men and Women of the Day*, 3 (1890) · C. Baugniet, J. M. Johnstone, P. Naumann, and others, various prints (some after self-portraits by Frith), BM, NPG · H. J. Brooks, group portrait, oils (*Private view of the Old Masters exhibition, Royal Academy 1888*), NPG · Elliott & Fry, carte-de-visite, NPG · Lock & Whitfield, woodburytype photograph, NPG; repro. in T. Cooper and others, *Men of mark: a gallery of contemporary portraits* (1880) · G. G. Manton, group portrait, watercolour (*Conversazione at the Royal Academy, 1891*), NPG · H. N. O'Neil, oils, Castle Museum, Nottingham · Spy [L. Ward], chromolithograph caricature, NPG; repro. in *VF* (10 May 1873) · J. & C. Watkins, cartes-de-visite, NPG · F. R. Window, carte-de-visite, NPG · Window & Grove, cabinet photograph, NPG · ink over pencil drawing, BM
Wealth at death £1380 1*s*. 5*d*.: probate, 27 Nov 1909, *CGPLA Eng. & Wales*

Frithegod [Frithegode, Fredegaud] (*fl. c*.950–*c*.958), cleric and poet, was a deacon in the household of Oda, archbishop of Canterbury (941–58). Very little is known of Frithegod's life. From its spelling in a contemporary charter, Freðegod, it is apparent that the name is not of English origin, and is best understood as an Anglicization of a Frankish name, Fredegaud. Where in Francia he originated is unknown; he possibly met Oda on the occasion of the latter's visit to Francia in 936, and was subsequently invited to join his household. He acted as tutor to Oda's nephew, Oswald, the future archbishop of York. Frithegod's most substantial extant contribution to Anglo-Latin letters is the *Breviloquium vitae Wilfridi*, a version in hexameters of the eighth-century prose life of St Wilfrid by Stephen of Ripon, and one of the most difficult Latin poems written in pre-conquest England. The *Breviloquium* was composed on commission by Oda to celebrate Canterbury's acquisition of the relics of St Wilfrid during King Eadred's invasion of Northumbria and sack of Ripon (*c*.950); it is prefaced by a prose account in Oda's name (though, to judge by the flamboyant language, probably drafted by Frithegod) describing that notorious relic theft. Various evidence suggests that, after the death of his patron, Oda, in 958, Frithegod returned to Francia, to the canonry of Brioude in the Auvergne.

Frithegod's literary production during his stay at Canterbury was substantial, though not all of it has survived. The sixteenth-century antiquary John Bale records the existence of a manuscript, now lost, which contained the *Breviloquium vitae Wilfridi*, a life of St Ouen (whose relics Oda had also acquired for Canterbury), a poem beginning 'Dum pietate multimoda Deus', another poem on the heavenly Jerusalem (beginning 'Cives coelestis patriae'), a work entitled *De visione beatorum*, and *Contemplationes variae*. The last two works are lost, as is the life of St Ouen; but the two poems survive: the first being a hymn for Maundy Thursday focused on Mary Magdalen, the second being a poem in octosyllables consisting of sixteen six-line stanzas, based principally on Bede's allegorical explanations of the stones in Revelation found in his commentary *In Apocalypsin*. The most impressive item of Frithegod's literary estate, however, is the *Breviloquium*, consisting of some 1400 hexameters cast in Latin so difficult that its sense is not always clear, even with consultation of Stephen of Ripon's life, of which the poem is a close counterpart. Frithegod adds nothing of importance to the fund of knowledge about St Wilfrid; his sole purpose was apparently the parade of diction consisting of Greek words (some rare enough to suggest that Frithegod had some genuine knowledge of Greek) but especially of neologisms coined by Frithegod to demonstrate his poetic skill which, in the mid-tenth century, was unparalleled elsewhere in England.   Michael Lapidge

Sources M. Lapidge, 'A Frankish scholar in tenth-century England: Frithegod of Canterbury / Fredegaud of Brioude', *Anglo-Saxon England*, 17 (1988), 45–65 · *Frithegodi monachi breviloquium vitae beati Wilfredi et Wulfstani*, ed. A. Campbell (Zurich, 1950), 1–62 · *AS chart.*, S 1506 · *Willelmi Malmesbiriensis monachi de gestis pontificum Anglorum libri quinque*, ed. N. E. S. A. Hamilton, Rolls Series, 52 (1870) · W. D. Macray, ed., *Chronicon abbatiae Rameseiensis a saec. x usque ad an. circiter 1200*, Rolls Series, 83 (1886) · Bale, *Cat.*, 1.136–7

Frithestan (*d.* 932/3), bishop of Winchester, held the see from 909 to 931. Soon after his appointment, the two West

Saxon bishoprics were divided into five and Winchester lost control of what is now Wiltshire and Berkshire to the new Ramsbury diocese. Frithestan is generally presumed to be the man of that name who witnessed as deacon two charters of 904 in which King Edward granted land to Old Minster, Winchester. An eighth-century manuscript of Sedulius's *Carmen Paschale*, which was bound with the Parker manuscript containing a version of the Anglo-Saxon Chronicle, has the inscription 'Frithestan *diacon*' on its first page and is generally assumed to have once belonged to the bishop; William of Malmesbury comments that a number of books once owned by Frithestan were known in his day. Also surviving are a stole and maniples which, according to their inscription, were commissioned by Queen Ælfflæd, wife of Edward the Elder, for the bishop; these were subsequently presented by King Æthelstan to the shrine of St Cuthbert and are now preserved in Durham. The removal of the vestments from Winchester may have been linked with an apparent breach between Frithestan and Edward the Elder's eldest son and successor, Æthelstan. Frithestan is notable for his absence from the witness lists of Æthelstan's charters from the period of his coronation in 925 until 928, even on occasions when all other bishops were present. The reasons may be found in the succession disputes which followed the death of King Edward. The councillors of Wessex had chosen Ælfweard (Edward's eldest son with his second wife, Ælfflæd) as king and it was only Ælfweard's death a few weeks after his father that had enabled Æthelstan to become king in both Wessex and Mercia. William of Malmesbury records that Winchester was a centre of resistance to Æthelstan and support may have continued there for Edward and Ælfflæd's second son, Eadwine, who makes a rare appearance in a New Minster charter. Whatever Frithestan's involvement may have been, he reappears in the witness lists of royal charters in 928, which means that he was attending meetings of the king's councillors from that time, and in 929 he was recorded as a member of the confraternity of the monastery of St Gallen with other members of Æthelstan's court.

At Winchester Frithestan was remembered for establishing good relations and common regulations between the Old and the New minsters. These included the provision that when a priest of either Old or New Minster died, members of both foundations would take part in the funeral observances. Frithestan's arrangements were continued by Bishop Æthelwold (who was born in Winchester during Frithestan's episcopate) though adapted for monastic use. It was probably in Frithestan's time that a series of lateral chapels were added to the west end of the Old Minster. Frithestan resigned his position as bishop in 931 and died probably the following year, possibly 933, having continued to live in Winchester according to one tradition. He was buried in the Old Minster. There was an attempt to develop a cult of Frithestan in Winchester; he is included among the Old Minster saints in one recension of the list of saints' resting places and in some later Winchester martyrologies. However, the cult does not seem to have become well-established and William of Malmesbury records that in his day the whereabouts of Frithestan's tomb was not known.   BARBARA YORKE

Sources *AS chart.*, S 372–8, 399, 401–2, 412–13 • *Willelmi Malmesbiriensis monachi de gestis pontificum Anglorum libri quinque*, ed. N. E. S. A. Hamilton, Rolls Series, 52 (1870), 162–3 • S. Keynes, ed., *The Liber vitae of the New Minster and Hyde Abbey, Winchester* (Copenhagen, 1996) • M. B. Parkes, 'The palaeography of the Parker manuscript of the *Chronicle*, laws, and historiography at Winchester in the late ninth and tenth centuries', *Anglo-Saxon England*, 5 (1976), 148–71 • M. A. O'Donovan, 'An interim revision of episcopal dates for the province of Canterbury, 850–950 [pt 2]', *Anglo-Saxon England*, 2 (1973), 91–113 • B. Yorke, 'Æthelwold and the politics of the tenth century', *Bishop Æthelwold: his career and influence*, ed. B. Yorke (1988), 65–88 • E. Plenderleith, C. Hohler, and R. Freyhan, 'The stole and the maniples', *The relics of Saint Cuthbert*, ed. C. F. Battiscombe (1956), 375–432

Archives Durham Cathedral, vestments | CCC Cam., Parker MS 173

Frithuswith [St Frithuswith, Frideswide] (*d.* 727), abbess of Oxford, was venerated as the local saint of Oxford by at least the tenth century; her relics there are mentioned in the late Old English list of resting places and in a charter of 1004 (*AS chart.*, S 909). Traditions believed locally in the early twelfth century were recorded, apparently independently, by William of Malmesbury in summary form and in an anonymous life (life A) at greater length. Life A makes Frithuswith the daughter of Didan, king of Oxford, and his wife, Sefrida, and names her nurse as Ælfgifu. Didan founds a nunnery at Oxford for his daughter and twelve other noble maidens, and endows it with 'the estates and villages of St. Mary and a third part of the city of Oxford' (Blair, 'St Frideswide reconsidered', 75). Pursued by the lecherous King Algar of Leicester, Frithuswith flees Oxford with two of her nuns and is miraculously transported up-river to Bampton, where she hides 'in a wood called Binsey' and performs miracles (ibid., 76). Algar tries to enter Oxford but is struck blind, leaving Frithuswith free to return home and live out her life as abbess. Binsey (a mile north-west of Oxford) is not near Bampton, and the inclusion of miracle stories located at both places suggests separate traditions which life A conflates. Later in the twelfth century, the Oxford scholar and Augustinian prior Master Robert of Cricklade (*d.* 1174) reworked the story (as life B) and ironed out the confusion by adding a chapter bringing Frithuswith from Bampton to Binsey ('Thornbiri'), where she stays briefly and where a well (still in Binsey churchyard and still a place of veneration) appears in response to her prayers.

Embedded in these hagiographical fantasies may be genuine memories of the upper Thames region in the seventh and eighth centuries. Archaeology proves that Oxford, Bampton, and Binsey are Anglo-Saxon religious sites, and traffic up and down the Thames between them is consistent with other evidence for social and economic organization at the time. Frithuswith can probably be accepted as that characteristic late seventh-century figure, the king's daughter who became abbess of a royal minster: better-documented examples include Ælfflæd (*d.* 714) and Eadburh (*d.* 751).

Life A records Frithuswith's death on 19 October 727,

later observed as her feast day, and says that she was buried in St Mary's Church in Oxford, on the south side; life B adds that the church was burnt down during the massacre of Danes in 1002 and enlarged around the grave by Æthelred II. This minster was reformed as an Augustinian priory *c*.1120, and after a miraculous rediscovery of the relics they were elevated in 1180; in 1289 they were moved into a new shrine, fragments of which survive. In 1562 the bones were mixed with those of Catherine, wife of the protestant reformer Peter Martyr, and reburied in the priory church, by then Oxford Cathedral.

By the twelfth century Frithuswith was established as patron of the fast-growing city of Oxford. It was thought that no king had dared to pass the city gates since Algar's blinding, a tradition taken seriously by Henry II in 1180 and by Edward I in 1275, though the chronicler Wykes records that in 1263 Henry III 'entered St. Frideswide's church with great devotion, which no king had attempted since the time of King Algar' (*Ann. mon.*, 4.142–3). The emergent university seems quickly to have adopted Frithuswith as its patron, and the priory seal made *c*.1190 shows her holding an open book. In the thirteenth century there was a yearly procession of the scholars and parish clergy to the priory church, as the mother church of the university and city, on Ascension day (changed to mid-Lent by the mid-fourteenth century), and in 1398 the bishop of Lincoln ordered observance of the feast throughout the university and deanery of Oxford. The 1180 translation initiated a prodigious series of miraculous healings in which disturbed adolescent girls figure prominently, and in 1518 Frithuswith's reputation for gynaecological cures took Katherine of Aragon to her shrine in the vain hope of a male heir.

A cult of Ste Fréwisse in France, established at Bomy (Pas-de-Calais) by the twelfth century, may be a genuine satellite of the Oxford cult, though the attachment to it of the Oxford legends is a seventeenth-century fabrication.

JOHN BLAIR

Sources J. Blair, 'St Frideswide reconsidered', *Oxoniensia*, 52 (1987), 71–127 [incl. edns of life A, life B, and the translation narrative] · J. Blair, ed., 'St Frideswide's monastery at Oxford: archaeological and architectural studies', *Oxoniensia*, 53 (1988), 1–275; pubd separately (1988) · H. Mayr-Harting, 'Functions of a twelfth-century shrine: the miracles of St Frideswide', *Studies in medieval history presented to R. H. C. Davis*, ed. H. Mayr-Harting and R. I. Moore (1985), 193–206 · J. Blair, *Anglo-Saxon Oxfordshire* (1994), 52–4, 181–3 · *VCH Oxfordshire*, 4.70–71 · F. M. Stenton, 'St Frideswide and her times', *Preparatory to 'Anglo-Saxon England': being the collected papers of Frank Merry Stenton*, ed. D. M. Stenton (1970), 224–33 · *Acta sanctorum: October*, 8 (Brussels, 1853), 533–90 · *Ann. mon.*, vol. 4 · *AS chart.*, S 909

Likenesses priory seal, 1160–1200, repro. in Blair, ed., 'St Frideswide's monastery at Oxford' · portrait on shrine, 1289, St Frideswide's Priory, Oxford · portrait, St Frideswide's Priory, Oxford, chapter-house

Fritsch, Felix Eugen (1879–1954), algologist, was born on 26 April 1879 at 15 Princess Terrace, St Pancras, London, the second child of Ernst Theodor Hermann Fritsch, headmaster of a private school at 145 King Henry's Road, Hampstead, and his wife, Josephine Guignon (*née* Guir). He was educated at Warwick House School, Hampstead, and graduated BSc of London University in 1898. His schooldays were marred by recurrent illness, and immediately after graduation he went to Munich for his health. There he became an assistant under Ludwig Radlkofer, and obtained his DPhil in 1899. He was much impressed by the awakening ecological and physiological interests on the continent, which contrasted with the morphological outlook then dominating British botany.

After returning to England in 1901 Fritsch worked for fifteen months at the Jodrell Laboratory at Kew where he began an association with L. A. Boodle. Towards the end of 1902 Fritsch was appointed to an assistant lectureship at University College, London, where the professor of botany, F. W. Oliver (1864–1951), and his assistant, A. G. Tansley, did much to further Fritsch's developing interest in ecology. The same year he began to publish on phytoplankton and on periodicity problems, interests which he retained in later years.

On 12 July 1905 Fritsch married Hedwig, daughter of Max Lasker, a brush merchant. (The couple later had one son.) Also in 1905, he took up further lecturing work at Birkbeck College, obtained his London DSc, and began a long and fruitful collaboration with Florence Rich. In 1906 he became assistant professor at University College and in the next year began lecturing at East London (later Queen Mary) College. In 1908 Fritsch and L. A. Boodle published their translation of Solereder's *Systematic Anatomy of Dicotyledons*. In 1911 he gave up his work at University College, and became full-time head of department in botany at Queen Mary College. The department was ill-equipped and ill-staffed. However, the appointment of Edward Salisbury as his assistant lecturer (1912–19) led to a collaboration which resulted in five widely used textbooks: *An Introduction to the Study of Plants* (1914), *Elementary Studies in Plant Life* (1915), *An Introduction to the Structure and Reproduction of Plants* (1920), *Botany for Medical Students* (1921), and *Plant Form and Function* (1928).

In 1924 Fritsch received the title of university professor. In 1927, as president of the botany section at the Leeds meeting of the British Association, he emphasized the need for a British freshwater biological station. His vigorous campaign led to the formation of the Freshwater Biological Association in 1929, of the council of which he was chairman until his death, and to the foundation of the biological station at Wray Castle. He was elected FRS in 1932, served on the council in 1938–9 and 1944–6, and received the Darwin medal in 1950. In 1932 he held a visiting professorship to Stanford University, California; in 1938 he visited India and paid a second visit to Ceylon, which he had first visited in 1903. The first volume of his monumental work *The Structure and Reproduction of the Algae* appeared in 1935, the second in 1945. On his retirement from his chair in 1948 he was elected a fellow of Queen Mary College and professor emeritus of the university, on the senate of which he served in 1944–8 and from which he received an honorary LLD in 1952.

Fritsch owed his enormous output, surprising for a man of such small stature and frail constitution, to continuous industry. He was regarded by colleagues to be full of humour, genial, friendly, and unassuming. He was an ideal chairman, and thus much of his time was spent at meetings, where his sound judgement, fairness, and diplomacy were invaluable and unfailing.

Apart from walking and gardening, Fritsch's main recreation was music. His father was a singer, his wife a pianist, and his son a cellist; he was himself a violinist and an experienced ensemble player. Musical weekends were a regular feature at his home near Dorking before the outbreak of war in 1939. Thereafter he lived in Cambridge where, after his retirement, as during the war years, he was given facilities for his work at the botany school where he had initiated the national type culture collection of algae and protozoa. Here and on numerous committees in London and elsewhere he remained active and was even contemplating further books and advanced lectures right up to his last illness. He was president of the Linnean Society in 1949–52, and of the International Association of Limnology and the Institute of Biology in 1953. In 1954 he was awarded the Linnean gold medal but died at his home, 34 Causewayside, Cambridge, on 23 May, the day before the medal was to have been presented.

F. M. HAINES, *rev.* PETER OSBORNE

Sir Martin Frobisher (1535?–1594), by Cornelius Ketel, 1577

Sources private information (1971) · personal knowledge (1971) · E. J. Salisbury, *Obits. FRS*, 9 (1954), 131–40 · *WWW* · b. cert. · m. cert.
Likenesses W. Stoneman, two photographs, 1932, NPG · F. M. Haines, oils, Queen Mary College, London, Botany department · photograph, repro. in Salisbury, *Obits. FRS*
Wealth at death £11,976 13s. 10d.: probate, 6 Aug 1954, *CGPLA Eng. & Wales*

Frobisher, Sir Martin (1535?–1594), privateer, explorer, and naval commander, was descended from John Frobisher (*b. c.*1260), a Scot settled in lands near Chirk in Denbighshire granted in recognition of his services to Edward I during the Welsh wars. In the mid-fourteenth century the family crossed the Pennines to settle in west Yorkshire. The marriage of a later John (*d.* 1513) to Joan, daughter of Sir William Scargill, steward of Pontefract Castle, brought a dowry of the manor of Altofts, near Normanton. It was here that Martin Frobisher was born, the third of five children. Of his father, Bernard Frobisher, little more is known than the occasion of his burial, on 1 September 1542. Martin's mother was Margaret, *née* Yorke (*d.* 1549), of Gowthwaite. Her brother or cousin Sir John Yorke was the notable merchant adventurer, officer at the Southwark and Tower mints, and later an intimate both of Protector Somerset and the duke of Northumberland. When Margaret died in 1549, Martin was sent to London, to learn a trade at Yorke's house.

The Guinea coast and piracy As a member of a small syndicate of London merchants, Sir John Yorke had invested in Thomas Wyndham's second voyage in 1552, to the Barbary coast. The following year Yorke and others financed Wyndham once more for a projected voyage to the Guinea coast, to interlope upon the existing Portuguese to the region. Martin Frobisher sailed with this expedition as assistant to his uncle's factor, John Beryn. They were to be two of only about 40 men, from a total complement of

more than 140, to survive a fever-struck passage to the Bight of Benin, the first known English voyage to that region. Wyndham himself was one of the casualties. The expedition was profitable, however, returning with spices and some gold, and Frobisher sailed to Guinea once more in 1554, in another voyage backed by Yorke and others, and commanded by the merchant and traveller John Lok. At the town of Shamma, Frobisher volunteered as a hostage to facilitate trade with the local king. Negotiations were interrupted by the arrival of Portuguese ships; when the Englishmen fled, they left their hostage behind, and he passed thereafter into Portuguese custody, being held first at the nearby Portuguese fort of Mina, and later in Lisbon.

Released some time in 1556 or 1557, Frobisher commanded an English voyage to Barbary in 1559, but his activities for a number of years thereafter are obscure. His association with Sir John Yorke seems to have ended sourly, perhaps on a point of wages or prospects. In 1560 the pirate Henry Strangeways claimed that Frobisher and he had planned an attack upon the fort at Mina, but that the project had been abandoned. It appears that by now Frobisher was an active privateer; possibly he had learned the trade during the brief Anglo-French war of 1557–8, when the large-scale issue of letters of reprisal had encouraged Englishmen to put to sea in considerable numbers. In 1563, during a new Anglo-French conflict, Frobisher and his brother John, with another persistent privateer, Peter Killigrew, set out in three vessels with valid letters of reprisal, but the Frobisher brothers' involvement in the capture of the Spanish ship *Katherine* resulted in their imprisonment in Launceston gaol. Released in 1564, they set out on a new voyage in 1565 in the ship *Mary Flower*; by this time, however, their reputation was such that the admiralty court seized Martin on suspicion of intended piracy despite his claim that he intended a trading venture to Guinea. He was free once more at the end of October 1566, and immediately took up letters of reprisal from Cardinal Châtillon to harry French Catholic vessels in the pay of the Guises. Commanding the ship *Robert*, he persistently refused to distinguish between friendly and enemy vessels, which brought new warrants for his arrest; in July or August 1569 he was taken by admiralty officers at Aldeburgh and incarcerated, firstly in Fleet prison and then the Marshalsea, pending the payment of a £900 fine. However, he had made several powerful connections during his time as a privateer; two of these—the lord admiral Edward Fiennes de Clinton and his wife, Elizabeth—appear to have petitioned for clemency on his behalf. William Cecil himself also intervened personally, and Frobisher was free once more in March 1570.

Conditions had been attached to Frobisher's release. In 1571 he commanded a small flotilla intended to intercept unlicensed privateers. His failure to take a single vessel brought a reassignment: to provide logistical support for the land campaign against James Fitzmaurice's rebellion in Munster. With the end of the campaign, Frobisher was unemployed, though with warrants for his arrest still extant he did not return to his privateering activities. In 1571 he was briefly associated with a plot to remove the earl of Desmond from England, but he appears to have acted as a double agent on the privy council's behalf. In the following year he approached a Spanish agent in London, offering to lead disaffected English mercenaries, fresh from their failure in Montgomery's campaign to relieve La Rochelle, to seize Flushing for the Spanish king. Again, this ostensibly traitorous scheme appears to have been formulated with the knowledge of the privy council, who employed Frobisher once more in 1573 in a plot to seize the English Catholic rebel, Sir Thomas Stuckeley. With its abandonment he was unemployed once more, with few prospects and an increasingly damaging reputation for double-dealing.

The north-west passage Soon afterwards Frobisher made, or resurrected, the acquaintance of Michael Lok, London agent of the Russia Company and a notable London merchant adventurer. In the latter part of 1574 they formulated a plan to find a passage to the Far East via the north-west—the 'Strait of Anian', mooted upon contemporary charts since about 1536—far from the sea routes already dominated by the Spanish and Portuguese crowns. Lok secured support from senior figures within the Russia Company (whose patent to discover and exploit new markets via any northern sea route they were in effect attempting to infringe), while further backing—possibly

secured by Frobisher himself—came from within the privy council, with Ambrose Dudley, earl of Warwick, leading their support. In February 1575, acceding to pressure from the council, the Russia Company reluctantly provided Frobisher and Lok with the necessary patent. In 1576, partly financed by substantial loans from Lok's pocket, 2 small barks, the *Gabriel* and the *Michael*, with a 7 ton pinnace and total complement of 34 men, set out to discover the north-west passage to the fabled Cathay. Their commander was Frobisher himself. The barks departed from the Thames on 12 June. On their outward passage they touched upon the southern tip of Greenland (mistakenly supposed to be the mythical island of Friesland, thus confirming this feature in cartographers' minds for centuries to come). During a storm on their passage across the Davis Strait the pinnace sank and the *Michael* turned back to England, but the *Gabriel*, commanded by Frobisher, pressed on. Following a cursory reconnaissance of the south-eastern shoreline of Baffin Island (and a brief but fateful landing upon a small island at 62°30′ N), the *Gabriel* entered a large bay or strait. Pressing north-westwards Frobisher and his mariners made contact with Inuit parties. Initially the contacts were cautious but friendly; however, the abduction of five Englishmen by the Inuit on 20 August ended this brief period of amity. With only thirteen men remaining and the weather turning against them, at a point no more than 20 miles from the headwaters of what would become Frobisher Bay, the *Gabriel* turned for home. It is not unlikely that Frobisher intentionally allowed the passage's existence in that location to remain open, trusting to secure further backing with a partial success, rather than risk outright failure.

Frobisher's return excited public enthusiasm; in particular, the exotic prospect of an Inuit male captive, taken in reprisal for the five abducted Englishmen, and the promise of a passage to be exploited, suggested that England might be on the threshold of emulating Spain's earlier, spectacular example. Provisional plans were made for a new voyage to push on to Cathay, and the queen herself became an adventurer, donating the naval ship *Ayde* as part of her venture. Notwithstanding this, the intention to continue the search for a passage was swiftly abandoned. Upon his return Frobisher had presented a token of the new land to his friend Michael Lok. This was a small piece of black ore, taken up from the ground of Little Hall's Island during a brief perambulation by Christopher Hall, master of the *Gabriel*. Lok seems to have decided almost immediately that it had great potential value. He passed samples to several assayers until one agreed with his assumption; news of this discovery spread swiftly, despite Lok's efforts to the contrary, and by the end of March 1577 plans for the coming voyage had been adapted. Now Frobisher was to take the *Ayde*, the *Gabriel*, and the *Michael* back to Little Hall's Island to abstract large quantities of the same sort of ore, and to explore nearby shorelines for similar deposits. Only if all assays proved negative was Frobisher to send home the *Ayde* and proceed on to Cathay with his barks. The new expedition departed from Harwich on 31 May 1577. Once more the southern tip of 'Friesland' was encountered, but no landing made. Brief inspections of Little Hall's Island and the southern shores of Frobisher Bay yielded no promising deposits of ore (though a new contact with an Inuit group brought a brief skirmish, and six Inuit casualties), but samples taken in a large sound on the northern shore proved positive, and a base was established on a small island therein. This was Countess of Warwick Island. In the following days Frobisher's men mined some 160 tons of this ore, loaded it into the ships, and promptly returned to England. No attempt was made to test the passage further, though the taking of three new Inuit captives ensured that popular interest in the enterprise would remain strong.

Throughout the latter months of 1577 and into 1578 successive assays upon the ore were inconclusive, due to the failings of contemporary metallurgy and the doubtful competence of the assayers. The perceived need for new and much larger furnaces added greatly to the adventurers' expenditure, but the momentum created by the prospect of gold made a third voyage inevitable. Unfortunately, as estimates of the ore's value were steadily downgraded, it became apparent that far larger quantities of the raw material were needed to realize a profit on expenditure to date. To meet that need, a fleet of fifteen ships was assembled for the new voyage, four of which Frobisher brought in on his own authority. Sailing on 31 May 1578, the fleet passed swiftly to 'Friesland', where, finally, a brief landing was made. Storms, heavy fogs, and a remarkable prevalence of icebergs off Baffin Island that year meant that the final short leg of the voyage to Countess of Warwick Island consumed a further four weeks of the brief Arctic summer, during which time elements of Frobisher's fleet became the first English ships to enter what is now Hudson Strait. Nevertheless, Frobisher's men rose heroically to their foreshortened timetable, and by 31 August had mined and loaded some 1370 tons of mineral ore.

Frobisher's return to England should have been a triumph, but confidence in the enterprise was already collapsing. Michael Lok, who had acted as the adventurers' treasurer, was suspended for alleged dishonesty (Frobisher, increasingly antipathetic to his old friend, led the accusations). Further assays on the ore proved nothing; no gold, silver, or any other precious metal was found, and the total expenditure of some £25,000 realized nothing in the way of income. Rather than fail spectacularly, the enterprise simply disintegrated as the adventurers, most of whom still owed outstanding subscriptions, dissociated themselves from its debts. Only the hapless Lok was called to account, in a series of lawsuits and imprisonments, instigated by creditors, which effectively bankrupted him. Frobisher escaped explicit censure, but his reputation was severely damaged.

Disgrace and rehabilitation Other than in securing minor naval service—a brief voyage to Flushing in 1579 and a role in the siege of Smerwick Fort in Ireland in 1580—Frobisher remained effectively unemployed for several years,

undoubtedly a corollary of his culpability in losing some £4000 of the queen's money. In 1581 he invested in, and was chosen to lead, a voyage to the Moluccas, sponsored by a consortium led by the earl of Leicester to exploit England's support for the Portuguese pretender Dom Antonio against the *fait accompli* of the union of the Spanish and Portuguese crowns in 1580. He was removed, or stood down, from this appointment, however, and his place was taken by his lieutenant-general during the voyage of 1578, Edward Fenton. Allegations of Frobisher's dishonesty in misappropriating victualling moneys circulated, and, though not proven, they appear to be credible. In 1582–3 he was associated in a scheme led by Sir George Peckham to exploit Gilbert's patent to colonize Virginia; but the project foundered with Gilbert's death at sea and collapse of support thereafter. There is also anecdotal evidence that Frobisher accompanied, or transported, an English embassy to the Danish court in 1584, but this cannot be substantiated. Otherwise, it is possible that he returned to his old privateering trade during these years, as his penury following the collapse of the north-west enterprise was alleviated by no obvious source of income.

In 1585 Frobisher was reinstated in royal favour with his appointment as vice-admiral to Sir Francis Drake in the famous West Indies raid. Though he acquitted himself with some distinction (particularly during the attack on Cartagena and the fort at St Augustine, Florida), the voyage was personally unprofitable, and his later violent antipathy towards Drake may date from this period. In 1587 he commanded a small fleet in the channel whose brief was to support Leicester's army in the Netherlands and interrupt the flow of material and communications between Spanish forces and their king. Again he discharged his duties with diligence, though there is some evidence that he used the opportunity to despoil the cargoes of non-combatant vessels once more.

The Armada campaign With the gathering of the English fleet in the months before the Armada campaign Frobisher was one of several men brought into Lord Admiral Howard's confidence, being among 'those which I think the world doth judge to be men of greatest experience that this realm hath' (PRO, SP 12/211, 26; Laughton, 1.202), to advise him on tactics and strategy in the coming campaign. On 21 April 1588 Frobisher took command of the *Triumph*, one of the four 'great ships' of the Elizabethan navy and the largest vessel in either of the protagonists' fleets. The circumstances of his role during the Armada campaign make it one of the most visible individual contributions. At dawn on 23 July the *Triumph* and five armed merchantmen were separated from the rest of the English fleet off Portland Bill. Frobisher appears to have intended this. Attacked by the four galliasses of the Armada (probably the best-armed Spanish ships, and highly manoeuvrable in the calm waters of that morning) he conducted a master class in close-in fighting—supposedly the galliasses' forte—which had them fighting in turn for their own survival. Eventually 'rescued' by other English ships, Frobisher had in fact achieved the first tactical victory over vessels of the Armada since Drake's seizure of the *Rosario* two nights earlier. The following day Howard reorganized his fleet into four squadrons—perhaps to provide more effective local direction of its many component parts—and appointed himself, Drake, John Hawkins, and Frobisher as their commanders. In the early morning of 25 July Frobisher attempted to repeat his earlier success by overlapping the leeward wing of the Armada and attacking the Spanish flagship, the *San Martin*. However, an unfavourable wind isolated the *Triumph* and two other English ships, and over a dozen of the principal galleons of the Spanish fleet attacked them. A fortuitous turn in wind direction, and the superior ship-handling skills of the English mariners, carried the English ships safely back into their own fleet. The following morning Frobisher was knighted on the deck of the English flagship, *Ark Royal*. In the fight off Gravelines on 29 July the *Triumph* once more closed with the *San Martin* and engaged in a protracted, short-range duel. However, elements of the Armada, their mariners exhibiting great seamanship, surrounded their damaged flagship and bore away to the north. The day marked the effective end of the campaign, though the English ships followed the Armada to the latitude of the River Tyne before withdrawing.

The queen's admiral Despite his loudly expressed ire at Drake's success in taking the *Rosario*, Frobisher emerged from the campaign with his reputation greatly enhanced. Now one of the principal commanders in the English navy, he was thereafter to be among Elizabeth's most trusted officers, though he lacked the gentility that might have made him a presence at her court. For the remainder of the year and into 1589 he, Sir Henry Palmer, and Lord Henry Seymour rotated in command of the channel fleet. Later in 1589, and again in 1590 (with Hawkins), he commanded Atlantic squadrons which attempted to intercept the Spanish plate fleets. Though not successful in their principal aim, their threat disrupted the flow of New World silver and profoundly undermined Philip II's ability to pay his many creditors. Renewed accusations regarding Frobisher's taking of friendly vessels during the campaign of 1590 resulted in a brief, if useful, period of unemployment in 1591, during which he added considerably to his properties in Yorkshire; but in 1592 he replaced a reluctant Walter Ralegh in command of a new attempt upon the plate fleets. The subsequent capture of the fabulously rich Portuguese carrack *Madre de Dios* by detached elements of his fleet provided little compensation for Frobisher personally, though once more his name was associated with a notable feat. Upon his return to England, and following a further voyage in the ship *Dainty* (about which little is known), Frobisher returned to Altofts, Yorkshire. In 1594, however, he emerged from semi-retirement to command the fleet that carried an English army under Sir John Norreys to Brittany, to counter a threatened conjunction of Spanish and French Catholic league forces.

The expedition crossed to France on 27 August 1594. During the subsequent campaign Frobisher displayed great energy and initiative. After landing the English army at Paimpol he took his ships along the coast to the besieged town of Morlaix and immediately forced the surrender of the town's leaguer garrison to the army of Marshal Aumont, commander of the French royalist forces. At Crozon he pestered the reluctant French commander to agree to an all-out assault on El León, a Spanish fortress. On 7 November he personally led a force of English mariners and soldiers against the fortress's main gate. In hand-to-hand combat in which quarter was neither sought nor offered Frobisher received a pistol wound in the thigh. The ball was removed by a field surgeon, but wadding from the charge remained in his body. Following the allied victory the English fleet returned to Plymouth. There, on 22 November 1594, Frobisher died from a gangrenous infection of his lower body. His entrails were buried the following day in the churchyard of St Andrew's, Plymouth, and his cadaver brought to London, where it was buried in the south aisle of St Giles Cripplegate, on 14 December.

Frobisher married twice: first, on 30 September 1559, Isobel (*d.* 1588), widow of Thomas Rigatt of Snaith, who brought several young children from her former marriage; and second, in 1590, Dorothy, widow of Paul Withypool of Ipswich, a mature woman with a grown daughter. His marriage to Isobel was unhappy; he appears to have abandoned her and her children by the mid-1570s, and the occasion of her death in a poorhouse in 1588 brought no recorded reaction from him. His second marriage may have been contracted primarily to consolidate his estate, which by then included manors at Glass Houghton, Wasenfield, Whitewood, Finningley Grange, and Brockholes, mills at Castleford, a messuage at Heath, a house in Walthamstow, and unspecified holdings at Blackstone and Rockeley. The Walthamstow acquisition apart, these properties were located in Yorkshire and northern Nottinghamshire, within a 50 miles radius of Altofts, his main residence. His will indicates that liquid capital did not form a significant part of his total wealth—perhaps a reflection of his efforts to disguise its questionable provenance in bricks and mortar. Frobisher's principal heir was Peter, son of John Frobisher; he quickly squandered his inheritance, disappeared to London, and died there some time after 1616.

Appreciation Martin Frobisher's character is difficult to assess precisely. He was uncultured and semi-literate; throughout his career he displayed the deepest suspicion of men of business (a legacy, perhaps, of his time in the care of his rapacious uncle), and this played no small part in shaping his decades-long career as a privateer. He had an acutely violent temperament, driven in part by inner frustrations; yet he showed little tendency to outright cruelty, unlike many of his privateering contemporaries. He was fearless rather than brave, duplicitous and almost incapable of financial integrity. His reputation as a navigator was much overesteemed; he was in fact unversed in the hydrographical sciences, and relied entirely upon his subordinates' skills. He had little of the strategic appreciation exhibited by Drake and Hawkins—though his few extant comments on strategic matters (PRO, SP 12/224, 26; 12/232, 13) are not entirely unperceptive—yet he was almost certainly their superior in the application of ship fighting tactics. He often treated his officers harshly (a symptom of his uncertainly felt authority over more cultured men), but consistently engaged the affections of the common mariners under his command, whom he led by example and whose hardships he was always willing to share even as he misappropriated their victualling moneys.   JAMES MCDERMOTT

Sources R. Hakluyt, *The principal navigations, voyages, traffiques and discoveries of the English nation*, 6–7, Hakluyt Society, extra ser., 6–7 (1904) · Michael Lok's financial accounts for the 1576–8 voyages, PRO, EKR E164/35–6 · Michael Lok's financial accounts for the 1578 voyage, Hunt. L., HM 715 · T. H. B. Symons, ed., *Meta Incognita: a discourse of discovery, Martin Frobisher's Arctic expeditions, 1576–1578* (1999) · Lok's accusations against Frobisher, BL, Lansdowne MS 100/1 · narratives of Christopher Hall, Charles Jackman, and Edward Selman, 1578, BL, Harley MSS 167/40–42 · Michael Lok's narrative on the 1576 voyage, BL, Cotton MS Otho E. VIII · will, PRO, PROB 11/85, sig. 2 · PRO, SP/70/37, 72; SP/12/39, 86 · PRO, HCA 13/13–17; HCA 14/8–10 *ad finem* · BL, Add. MS 5664 · PRO, E351/2216, 2222–30 · PRO, SP/12/224, 26; 12/232, 13 · *The naval tracts of Sir William Monson*, ed. M. Oppenheim, 1, Navy RS, 22 (1902) · M. Oppenheim, *Administration of the Royal Navy* (1896) · J. K. Laughton, ed., *State papers relating to the defeat of the Spanish Armada, anno 1588*, 2 vols., Navy RS, 1–2 (1894) · E. G. R. Taylor, ed., *The troublesome voyage of Captain Edward Fenton, 1582–1583*, Hakluyt Society, 2nd ser., 113 (1959) · *An Elizabethan in 1582: the diary of Richard Madox, fellow of All Souls*, ed. E. S. Donno, Hakluyt Society, 2nd ser., 147 (1976) · K. R. Andrews, *Elizabethan privateering: English privateering during the Spanish war, 1585–1603* (1964) · M. F. Keeler, *Sir Francis Drake's West Indian voyage, 1585–6* (1981) · J. S. Nolan, 'English operations around Brest, 1594', *Mariner's Mirror*, 81 (1995), 259–74 · Fuller, *Worthies* (1840), vol. 3 · J. M. French, 'Raleigh, Frobisher and the great carack of Spain', *N&Q*, 174 (1938), 327–30

Archives BL, accounts, instructions, narratives, and other papers relating to his voyages, Add. MSS, Egerton MSS | BL, Lok's relation of the voyages with accusations against Frobisher, Lansdowne MS 100/1, fols. 1–14*v* · Hunt. L., Michael Lok's financial accounts for the 1576–8 voyages, MS HM 715 · PRO, Michael Lok's financial accounts for the 1576–8 voyages, EKR E164/35–6

Likenesses C. Ketel, oils, 1577, Bodl. Oxf. [*see illus.*] · R. Boissard, line engraving, Bodl. Oxf.; repro. in H. Holland, *Baziliωlogia: a booke of kings* (1618) · S. de Passe, line engraving, BM, NPG; repro. in H. Holland, *Heröologia* (1620) · M. Vandergucht, line engraving, NPG

Frodsham, Bridge (1734–1768), actor, was born in Frodsham, Cheshire. He became a foundation scholar at Westminster School in 1746, but ran away. In 1748 he was accepted back by the school, apparently the only instance of a boy being admitted twice on the foundation, but he ran away a second time, and joined a company of players in Leicester. He was encouraged by John Gilbert Cooper, poet and writer, to make acting his career, and joined the company at York.

At York, Frodsham was extremely popular, and became the idol of the theatre-going public; he was known as the York Roscius or the York Garrick. This early popularity 'filled him with vanity and shut up every avenue of improvement' (Wilson). Frodsham went to London but once, solely to introduce himself to David Garrick, who was astounded by his assumption of professional equality (Frodsham considered his own Hamlet to stand favourable comparison with Garrick's) and by his lack of desire for a trial on the London stage. Otherwise, he rarely left

York. Tate Wilkinson, with whom he appeared more than once, considered him a fine actor.

Frodsham died on 21 October 1768 at Hull, his early death being accelerated by drink and dissipation. He left a widow, Isabella, at least two daughters, and possibly a son. One of his daughters, Sarah Frodsham (*b.* 1761), whose married name was Reily and then Inchbald, acted on the York stage from 1769, and at the Haymarket, London, between 1783 and 1786.

ALSAGER VIAN, *rev.* K. D. REYNOLDS

Sources H. Wilson, *Wonderful characters*, 3 vols. (1821) · T. Wilkinson, *Memoirs of his own life*, 4 vols. (1790) · T. Wilkinson, *The wandering patentee, or, A history of the Yorkshire theatres from 1770 to the present time*, 4 vols. (1795) · J. Welch, *The list of the queen's scholars of St Peter's College, Westminster*, ed. [C. B. Phillimore], new edn (1852) · Adams, *Drama* · F. H. Forshall, *Westminster School, past and present* (1884) · Highfill, Burnim & Langhans, *BDA* [Sarah Frodsham]

Likenesses J. Halfpenny, etching (after an unknown artist), BM

Fröhlich, Herbert (1905–1991), theoretical physicist, was born on 9 December 1905 in Rexingen, in the Black Forest of south-west Germany, the second of three children of Julius Fröhlich (1879–1952), a cattle dealer, and his wife, Frida, *née* Schwarz (*d.* 1959). The family moved to Munich while Herbert was still young. Both parents were Jewish. Fröhlich took no interest in his mother's devout faith and soon showed his independent spirit. He chose his own school and later transferred to a technical college where he discovered the attractions of radio and mathematics. At the University of Munich he studied theoretical physics, first with Wilhelm Wien and then, after Wien's death in 1928, with Arnold Sommerfeld, gaining his DPhil in 1930. During this period he was an enthusiastic hiker, mountaineer, and skier, and until late in life would lead colleagues and students on long, fast, cross-country walks, illuminated by lively discussion of physical problems. He was always generous of time and ideas, and inspired great devotion. An appointment in 1933 as a *Privatdozent* at Freiburg University was cut short when Hitler assumed power. His father suffered a severe beating, and the whole family, except Fröhlich himself, took the first opportunity to escape to France and thence to Palestine. Fröhlich (as he was known to almost everyone, even his wife) hazarded his life for a year in Germany to rescue what he could of the family property. The local Nazi leader being absent for a day to confer with Hitler, Fröhlich slipped away to Russia and the Ioffe Institute in Leningrad. But in 1935, along with other foreigners, he was expelled, and eventually reached haven in Bristol by way of Rome and Holland, with support from the Academic Assistance Council. Apart from a few months of internment in 1940 as an enemy alien he spent the war in Bristol, and then went to Liverpool in 1948 at Sir James Chadwick's invitation, the last of his many migrations. There, on 3 July 1950, he married the much younger Fanchon Aungst, an American and a talented artist who had studied philosophy at Oxford. To his disappointment, for he loved children, the marriage was childless.

Fröhlich, who was elected a fellow of the Royal Society

in 1951, remained professor of theoretical physics at Liverpool until 1973; he was then professor of solid state electronics at Salford University from 1973 until 1976. He had wide-ranging interests in physics and a ready skill in the mathematical analysis of whatever problem took his fancy. His approach was strongly influenced by the German models of his youth, with a delight in systematic development from basic ideas until he was satisfied that his result was compatible with the known facts. For the facts themselves he was content to rely on the experimenters, having no personal interest in the practical affairs of a laboratory. One merit, to him, of Liverpool was the university's willingness to establish a separate theoretical physics department for his research students and collaborators, with only a small number of undergraduate students to teach.

Fröhlich's university career in Munich had started little more than a year after the discovery of quantum mechanics, and his professor, Sommerfeld, a master of the older quantum theory, was one of the pioneers of applying the new theory to the conduction of electricity by electrons in metals. Fröhlich's book, *Elektronentheorie der Metalle* (1936), was perhaps the first of its kind (after the ground-breaking article of Sommerfeld and Bethe in the *Handbuch der Physik*) and the first to include any discussion of semiconductors, obscure and little considered as they were then, but later dominating every aspect of electronics and computers. Between then and 1950 he set aside his interest in metals, and concentrated on insulators, their polarization by weak electric fields, and their catastrophic breakdown in stronger fields. At the same time he became fascinated by new ideas in nuclear physics, especially those of Hideki Yukawa on the as yet undiscovered mesons that bind protons and neutrons into a stable atomic nucleus. His work in this area showed his ability to master and develop the latest mathematical methods involved in the quantum theory of fields. From time to time he returned to these problems with great fertility of imagination but, as befell most other workers in particle physics, his conceptions suffered severe competition, and perhaps little of his achievement survived explicitly in the fundamental theories that later commanded assent.

By contrast Fröhlich's work on dielectrics, on which he published a small but still widely quoted text in 1949, led him to a succession of discoveries which guaranteed his place in the history of solid-state physics. In Bristol he began, with Mott, to study the motion of electrons under the influence of strong electric fields, and the collisions with vibrations of the crystal lattice which deflect their motion and hinder the growth of an avalanche of fast electrons—an important mechanism of dielectric breakdown. In examining the process further he brought to bear his expertise in quantum field theory, possibly its first application to solids, to analyse the deformation of an ionic lattice by the field of an electron. Not only did he describe the 'large polaron', moving as a free particle with the electronic mass somewhat enhanced by the locally deformed lattice, but he realized that the deformation itself could attract another electron to form a loosely bound pair. This led him to propose in 1950 the first theory of superconductivity that had the merit of a sound physical basis.

It was recognized after 1933 that the ability of certain metals to conduct electricity without resistance, at very low temperatures, depended on their expulsion of magnetic flux, and after 1936 this property of perfect diamagnetism became linked with the presence of an energy gap—unlike ordinary metals at zero temperature, an electron in a superconductor cannot be excited to a higher state without the supply of a certain minimum energy. Fröhlich showed that the attractive force resulting from lattice distortion could produce the desired gap without (as in insulators) inhibiting electron motion. While preparing his paper for publication he learned that different isotopes of mercury make the transition to superconductivity at slightly different temperatures, as his theory predicted. This was enough to convince him and others that electron lattice interaction lay at the heart of superconductivity. Fröhlich's detailed theory was not readily accepted, and it was seven years before the idea of electron pairs was incorporated into the later renowned theory of John Bardeen, Leon Cooper, and Robert Schrieffer. But Fröhlich's achievement inspired this breakthrough, and was entirely novel in that until then the ionic lattice had been treated as a rigid structure, playing at most a minor role in superconductivity.

Fröhlich's earlier work on dielectrics also seems to have inspired the ideas which from 1966 dominated his thought—a complicated system, such as a living cell, might be stimulated into organized oscillatory motion by irradiation with relatively weak electromagnetic waves. Despite the handicap of an analysis hard enough for many physicists and opaque to most biologists, he attracted an enthusiastic following who were encouraged by observations that the rate of cell division could be altered by irradiation, and that the effects were sharply dependent on the frequency used. There is no direct evidence to support Fröhlich's precise mechanism, but the occurrence of any such effect was enough to stimulate further experiments, which he supported to the last, especially at the Max Planck Institut in Stuttgart, where he was a visiting professor from 1980. He died of cancer of the bladder in Liverpool on 23 January 1991, and was cremated there a week later. He was survived by his wife.

BRIAN PIPPARD

Sources N. Mott, *Memoirs FRS*, 38 (1992), 147–62 · J. G. Powles, 'Some reminiscences of research in Liverpool in 1950', *Cooperative phenomena*, ed. H. Haken and M. Wagner (1973), 436–44 · *The Times* (30 Jan 1991) · *The Independent* (30 Jan 1991) · *WWW* · private information (2004) [A. Fröhlich] · personal knowledge (2004)
Archives Bodl. Oxf., corresp. relating to Society for Protection of Science and Learning
Likenesses F. Fröhlich, sketch, repro. in Mott, *Memoirs FRS*, 161 · photograph, repro. in *The Times* · photograph, repro. in *The Independent*
Wealth at death £164,767: probate, 21 March 1991, *CGPLA Eng. & Wales*

Froissart, Jean (1337?–*c*.1404), historian and poet, was born at Valenciennes in the county of Hainault, at a date

Jean Froissart (1337?–c.1404), manuscript illumination
[kneeling, with book]

now generally assumed to be late 1337. Details on his family and education are problematic; his father may have been a herald–painter, but it is more likely that he had an industrial or bourgeois background. Allusions in Froissart's voluminous poetry suggest a happy childhood in comfortable circumstances, but he never mentions his parents or any siblings. His contemporary fame and fortune were due to his intelligence and skill as a writer, admired by successive patrons who encouraged and sustained his endeavours.

Early patrons and early travels The first to recognize Froissart's talents was probably Jean de Hainault, seigneur de Beaumont (d. 1356), who fought in the Anglo-Scottish wars at the beginning of Edward III's reign, and whose niece, Philippa, married the king. By the age of twenty, Froissart, already under the influence of Jean le Bel, whose chronicle recounting, *inter alia*, Beaumont's exploits, he later plagiarized almost entirely, had begun to collect material for his historical work. He later did this especially by travel and conversation with those whose knightly deeds he recounted. An early journey was to Avignon towards the end of the pontificate of Innocent VI (r. 1352–62). But it was the period 1361–8 in England, where he claims to have been a *clerc de la chambre* of Queen Philippa, to whom he presented a now lost rhyming chronicle of events between 1356 and 1360, that marked a key stage in his development as a professional poet and writer. It provided him with contacts and a clientele that

remained influential throughout his life. These English links, and the value of his chronicles for the Anglo-French wars of his day, will be particularly stressed here, though Froissart was known and his works read by contemporaries throughout the medieval West.

In England Froissart met not only leading knights like Bartholomew, Lord Burghersh (d. 1369), at the royal court when Edward III was at the height of his powers, but also many important French prisoners from the battle of Poitiers and hostages for the treaty of Brétigny–Calais (1360), including Gui, count of Blois, a future patron. He personally witnessed the departure of Edward, the Black Prince, for Guyenne in 1362 and the return to captivity in London in February 1364 of Jean II of France, before accompanying the latter's body for burial in France two months later. He was at Dover in October 1364 when (a favourite ploy) he was able to interview the herald who brought news of the Anglo-Breton victory (29 September) at Auray in Brittany. These years also saw his first surviving lyrical poetry in the style of Guillaume de Machaut: *Le paradis d'amour* (c.1361–2), *Le joli mois de mai* (c.1363), the *Dit dou bleu chevalier* (written for the hostage duke of Berri), and the *Dit de la marguerite* (c.1364), in which one see reference to an unrequited love for a certain Marguerite, a theme that recurs in some later verse (for example, *L'espinette amoureuse*, c.1369–70).

An important experience was a journey to Scotland between May and October 1365. Travelling probably via Carlisle (identified later with the Caerleon of King Arthur) and Lochmaben, and returning via Berwick, Froissart stayed in 'le sauvage Escosse' with David II at Edinburgh. He then visited Dalkeith, Roxburgh, Stirling, Perth, Kildrummy, and Aberdeen, the jetty of which is described in his long Arthurian epic poem *Meliador* (30,000 lines), a first draft of which was probably penned shortly afterwards, while a humorous *Debat dou cheval et dou levrier*, in which the author's horse and dog discuss their services in Scotland, was also inspired by this journey.

In the service of Queen Philippa During a brief visit to Brabant at Easter 1366, perhaps as part of a diplomatic mission regarding Queen Philippa's family concerns, Froissart first made contact with the duke and duchess. This was followed by a tour of the west country with Edward Despenser (d. 1375), including a brief stop at Berkeley Castle in the late summer, before he set out, via Nantes and La Rochelle, for Bordeaux. Here he arrived in time to keep Christmas with the Black Prince, Princess Joan, and their court, and to witness the baptism of the future Richard II at Epiphany 1367. By then preparations were advanced for the prince's expedition to Spain in support of Pedro of Castile that culminated in their crushing defeat of Pedro's bastard brother, Enrique de Trastamara, at Nájera (3 April 1367), on which the chronicler later wrote at length. But he did not see this battle (nor, it appears, any others) at first hand since, although he accompanied the prince as far as Dax in February, he was then instructed to return to England with other messengers.

Froissart's last major journey under the patronage of Queen Philippa was again with Edward Despenser in the company of Edward III's second son, Lionel, duke of Clarence, going to Italy to marry Violante Visconti. The party reached Paris on 16 April 1368 and, passing through Bourg-en-Bresse and Chambéry, where contacts were made with the court of Savoy, finally reached Milan where the marriage took place on 5 June. Another in the party was Geoffrey Chaucer, and it is possible that they met Petrarch on this occasion. Despite Lionel's death only a few months later, Froissart seized the opportunity to see other places—Bologna (where he met Pierre de Lusignan, king of Cyprus), Ferrara, and Rome—before returning across the Alps with Guichard d'Angle, earl of Huntingdon (d. 1380). News of Queen Philippa's death on 15 August 1369, received at Brussels, forestalled his return to England and led him to seek a new patron. On 29 August the duchess of Brabant purchased 'a new book in French' (perhaps *Meliador* or *L'orloge amoureus*) from him and he spent much of the next fifteen years in Brabant. There he began, at the request of Robert de Namur, the first prose redaction of book 1 of the chronicles on which his enduring reputation stands; it was completed in 1373.

Froissart also continued to write much poetry in varied styles—one poem celebrates the release of Wenceslas of Brabant from captivity (*Entre Binch et le Bos de Haine*, after 21 June 1372); some of Wenceslas's own verses were included in *Meliador*; among his most important *dits* were *L'espinette amoureuse*, *La prison amoureuse* (1371–2), and *Le joli buisson de Jonece* (1373). References in Brabantine accounts make it possible to trace his career in some detail. In 1372 he was in debt to certain Lombards; by 19 September 1373, renouncing chances of marriage by taking holy orders, he had become *curé* of Estinnes-au-Mont in the diocese of Cambrai, worth 40 livres p.a., by gift of the duke of Brabant, and in the following year he received a further ducal grant for 'certain things which he has delivered to us' (Wilkins, 265). In 1377 a copy of *Meliador* was being bound at Brussels and a new version was prepared *c*.1380; payment in 1382 for 'a book which [Froissart] made for my lord [of Brabant]' (ibid., 265) may refer to this new edition. *Meliador* was again revised in 1389.

The historian and his work   Increasingly, however, Froissart's attention turned to his narrative of the Anglo-French wars since 1327, and this absorbed most of his remaining working life. By 1376 he had begun a revision of book 1. As time passed he also extended the work's concluding date and, besides continuing to gather oral information, he drew on other written accounts like the Chandos herald's *Life of the Black Prince* or the *Grandes Chroniques de France*, and occasionally consulted administrative or diplomatic documents. This process of compilation, adaptation, and revision (partly reflecting changes in patronage or the interests of his intended audience, and gradually moving from a position largely sympathetic to the English cause to a more French standpoint) continued for thirty years, by which time Froissart had created a gigantic panorama of (chiefly martial) events in the British Isles, France, Spain, the Low Countries, and sometimes even further afield, from 1327 to 1400, totalling about 3 million words in all. It has also created many still unresolved problems for establishing the order and chronology of the several different and overlapping recensions that survive in about 100 major manuscript copies. These pose, too, many questions about his art as a writer as well as his value as a historian of his times.

To summarize detailed arguments very crudely: it is accepted that following the completion of book 1 (1373, revised from 1376), book 2, covering the years 1377–85 (and so including Froissart's well-known account of the peasants' revolt), was written at the request of Gui, count of Blois (d. 1394), and was essentially finished in 1387; there is also a later recension of this book. Book 3, containing some of the most dazzling passages of writing in the whole work and covering 1385–9, was completed between 1390 and 1392, while book 4, for the years 1389 to 1400, was finished about 1400. At the same time, a third recension of book 1, thoroughly reworked but only covering the period 1327 to 1350, was also finished *c*.1400. By this stage Froissart's considerable skills as an inventive and imaginative writer had been honed to perfection; strict accuracy of historical detail seldom stands in his way if he could shape a pithy phrase, mould an account or make a moralistic point for dramatic effect. Thus despite an often apparently artless simplicity, combined with cleverly observed descriptive or visual detail for verisimilitude and great subtlety of characterization, his narrative is deceptively sophisticated and demands careful attention to its many different registers if its full implications and meaning are to be understood. How he achieved this result is only partly explained by what is known of the latter stages of his life.

The cosmopolitan traveller   In November 1380 Froissart accompanied Wenceslas of Brabant to Rheims for the coronation of Charles VI. Evidence for the growing popularity and knowledge of his work in French aristocratic circles comes a year later, ironically when some of his writings being copied in Paris were confiscated on the orders of Louis, duke of Anjou, possibly in revenge for Froissart's criticism of the duke's breaking parole in 1362, in his *Dit dou bleu chevalier*. Another personal loss was the death of Wenceslas of Brabant in December 1383; by 1384 Froissart had become chaplain to Gui de Blois and was appointed a canon of Chimay and, later, of Lille as well. He served the count for the next decade, frequently visiting Blois and accompanying him to family occasions like the betrothal of Louis de Blois to Marie de Berry (on 29 March 1386) and their marriage at Bourges in August. He also witnessed other important political and military developments or sought out leading participants to garner their testimony. Hence in 1386 he went to Sluys to see the fleet assembled for an invasion of England, and in 1387 he travelled to Ghent to gather material on the city's recent revolutionary past. A visit to Angers in 1388 allowed him to talk to Guillaume d'Ancenis about events in Brittany in the 1340s. In the same year, most notably, he made a prolonged tour through southern France, *en route* for the court of one of the most colourful princes of his day, Gaston de Foix (Phébus), count of Foix, arriving at Orthez in Béarn on 25 November. Here he spent ten weeks, rising at midnight to read passages of *Meliador* to the count and interviewing old soldiers like the *routier* Espan de Lion on his adventures, which are recounted in book 3, in some of the most vivid passages of the chronicles.

Renewed contact with English knights came in January 1389, when Froissart went to Bordeaux and witnessed jousts presided over by John of Gaunt, duke of Lancaster, before returning slowly northwards via Tarbes, Toulouse, and Avignon. At the latter he was robbed, an incident commemorated in one of the last of his poems, *Dit dou florin*. He was present at the marriage of the duke of Berri and Jeanne de Boulogne at Riom on 6 June 1389, and was back in Paris for the arrival of Queen Isabella of Bavaria on 22 August. After a brief sojourn in his native Valenciennes, to which he had increasingly returned in recent years, he rejoined Gui de Blois at Schoonhoven. At Middleburg in 1390 he talked to Dom João Fernandez Pacheco about recent events in Portugal, and another visit to Paris in June 1392 coincided with the attempted assassination of the constable of France, Olivier de Clisson. In June 1393 the duke of Orléans paid him handsomely for a book of his poems, which he shortly afterwards arranged in definitive chronological order (with the exception of *Meliador*). At least two fine manuscript copies of this anthology, written over thirty-four years and prepared under the author's eye, survive, one of which (Paris, Bibliothèque Nationale, MS Français 831) may be that presented to Richard II in 1395, when Froissart returned to England for the first time since 1368.

Last years and achievement Froissart arrived in England on 12 July. After paying homage next day at the tomb in Canterbury Cathedral of the Black Prince, in many respects the hero of book 1 of the chronicles, Froissart was granted an interview with the king on 25 July at Eltham, where over thirty years earlier he had seen the prince's prisoner, Jean II of France. Visits followed to Chertsey Abbey, Windsor Castle, and the duke of Gloucester's castle at Pleshey, but Froissart was cruelly disappointed by the changes that had occurred at the English court since his youth, and by the offhand treatment that he received, though some old acquaintances were renewed, most notably with the former diplomat and soldier Sir Richard Stury. Although he left England in October with a large silver goblet and 100 nobles in cash, his memories of this visit were tinged with regrets and nostalgia for a chivalric era that had passed. A last opportunity to meet leading English figures occurred in October 1396 when he attended the marriage of Richard II and Isabella of Valois at St Omer. Now about sixty years old, although continuing to work on recensions of his chronicles, Froissart largely retired from the world, possibly entering the abbey of Cantimpré at the gates of Cambrai. Still active in 1400 and probably as late as 1404, he died shortly afterwards, though the date and place of his death remain uncertain. An epitaph at Chimay was allegedly extant as late as 1873 but has since been lost, its details apparently unrecorded. But wherever 'Chivalry lifts its lance on high' (Elgar's inscription on the title page of his concert overture 'Froissart'), the *Chroniques de France, d'Angleterre et des pais voisins*, that remarkable mirror of his age, keep his name green. MICHAEL JONES

Sources J. Froissart, *Oeuvres*, ed. K. de Lettenhove, 28 vols. in 29 (Brussels, 1867–77) [vols. 26–8 contain edn of his poems by A. Scheler] · *Chroniques de J. Froissart*, ed. S. Luce and others, 15 vols. (Paris, 1869–1975) · J. Froissart, *Chroniques*, ed. G. T. Diller (Geneva, 1972) · G. T. Diller, ed., *Froissart, Chroniques, Le manuscrit d'Amiens*, 4 vols. (1991–3) · *The Chronicle of Froissart*, trans. J. Bourchier, 6 vols. (1901–3) · *Sir John Froissart's Chronicles of England, France, and the adjoining countries*, trans. T. Johnes, 5 vols. (1803–10) · G. Brereton, *Chronicles*, 2nd edn (1978) · R. S. Baudouin, ed., *Ballades et rondeaux* (1978) · P. F. Dembowski, ed., *Le paradis d'amour, L'orloge amoureus* (1986) · A. Fourrier, ed., *La prison amoureuse* (1974) · A. Fourrier, ed., *L'espinette amoureuse*, 2nd edn (1972) · A. Fourrier, *Le joli buisson de Jonece* (1975) · A. Fourrier, ed., *Dits et débats* (1979) · A. Longnon, ed., *Meliador*, 3 vols. (1895–9) · R. R. McGregor, ed., *The lyric poems of Jean Froissart* (1975) · P. F. Ainsworth, *Jean Froissart and the fabric of history* (1990) · P. F. Ainsworth, 'Collationnement, montage et jeu parti: le début de la campagne espagnole du Prince Noir (1366–67) dans les *Chroniques* de Jean Froissart', *Le Moyen Âge*, 100 (1994), 369–411 · G. T. Diller, 'La dernière rédaction du premier livre des *Chroniques* de Froissart', *Le Moyen Âge*, 76 (1970), 91–125 · A. Diverres, 'The geography of Britain in Froissart's *Meliador*', *Medieval miscellany presented to Eugène Vinaver*, ed. F. Whitehead and others (1965), 97–112 · A. Diverres, 'Jean Froissart's journey to Scotland', *Forum for Modern Language Studies*, 1 (1965), 54–63 · A. Diverres, 'Froissart's travels in England and Wales', *Fifteenth-Century Studies*, 15 (1989), 107–22 · A. Diverres, 'The two versions of Froissart's *Meliador*', *Mélanges Brian Woledge* (1987), 37–48 · M. Galway, 'The Amie of Froissart', *N&Q*, 202 (1957), 330–32 · M. Galway, 'Froissart in England', *University of Birmingham Historical Journal*, 7/1 (1959), 18–35 · M. T. de Medeiros, 'Le pacte encomiastique: Froissart, ses *Chroniques* et ses mécènes', *Le Moyen Âge*, 94 (1988), 237–55 · J. J. N. Palmer, ed., *Froissart: historian* (1981) · J. J. N. Palmer, 'Froissart et le héraut Chandos', *Le Moyen Âge*, 88 (1982), 271–92 · J. Trotin, 'Vie et oeuvre de Jean Froissart', *Valentiana. Revue Régionale d'Histoire* [Cercle Archéologique et Historique de Valenciennes], no. 4 (Dec 1989), 11–25 · F. S. Shears, *Froissart: chronicler and poet* (1930) · G. B. Stow, 'Richard II in Jean Froissart's *Chroniques*', *Journal of Medieval History*, 11 (1985), 333–45 · C. Thiry, 'Allégorie et histoire dans la prison amoureuse de Froissart', *Studi Francesi*, 61–2 (1977), 15–29 · B. J. Whiting, 'Proverbs in the writings of Jean Froissart', *Speculum*, 10 (1935), 291–321 · B. J. Whiting, 'Froissart as poet', *Mediaeval Studies*, 8 (1946), 189–216 · N. Wilkins, 'A pattern of patronage: Machaut, Froissart and the houses of Luxembourg and Bohemia in the fourteenth century', *French Studies*, 37 (1983), 257–81 · G. T. Diller, *Attitudes chevaleresques et réalités politiques chez Froissart* (1984) · D. Maddox and S. S. Maddox, eds., *Froissart across the genres* (1998) · M. Zink, *Froissart et le temps* (1998)

Likenesses manuscript drawing, 16th cent., Recueil d'Arras, Arras, Bibliothèque Municipale, MS 266, fol. 278 · manuscript illumination, BL, Harley MS 4380, fol. 233v [*see illus.*]

Fromanteel, Ahasuerus (*bap.* 1607, *d.* 1693), clockmaker and mechanic, was baptized in the Dutch Reformed church at Norwich on 25 February 1607, the eldest of five sons and two daughters of Mordecai Fromanteel, wood turner, and his wife, Leah. The Fromanteels were an armigerous family of high standing in Flanders during the sixteenth century; to escape life under Spanish rule a number of them crossed to East Anglia, to settle in Colchester, Norwich, and London. During Fromanteel's lifetime he and his children frequently passed between England and the Low Countries, though references to them simply as 'Fromanteel' make identification problematic.

Fromanteel was apprenticed as a blacksmith for seven

years, afterwards moving to London in June 1629 where he set up as a maker of steeple clocks at East Smithfield, joining the Blacksmiths' Company in 1631. He also made conventional lantern clocks with balance-wheel escapement, and spring-driven table clocks. He was made free of the Clockmakers' Company in 1632. The Fromanteels' relationship with the Clockmakers' was always contentious: in 1658 Ahasuerus and his son Louis were proceeded against for taking more apprentices than was allowed, which suggests a flourishing business, and in later years there were arguments over payments of quarterage for those years when they were out of the country.

In 1631 Fromanteel married Maria de Bruijne of Colchester. They raised six sons and two daughters, of whom Louis, Ahasuerus (1640–1703), John (d. before 1692), and Abraham (1646–1730), also became clockmakers. Ahasuerus Fromanteel senior, after a year of fruitless discussion with the elders of the Dutch Reformed church in London, was in 1646 officially proclaimed to have gone over to the Baptists, a move which he and his wife marked by having themselves rebaptized.

While on a visit to Amsterdam in 1648, Fromanteel spoke with Benjamin Worsley concerning microscopes, explaining that, having made tubes for Cornelis Drebbel's microscopes, he had been sufficiently interested to grind lenses himself, four of which he had brought to Amsterdam for sale. Worsley was impressed by their quality and persuaded Fromanteel to make him a microscope when he returned to London.

In 1657 John Fromanteel went to the Netherlands to learn the art of making pendulum clocks as invented by Huygens in 1656 and made there by Salomon Coster. On John's return in 1658 Ahasuerus Fromanteel lost no time in advertising this new method of regulation, suitable for steeple and domestic clocks, 'made by Ahasuerus Fromanteel, who made the first that were in England'. They could be had at his house in Moses Alley, Southwark, or at the sign of the Mermaid in Lothbury (for over a century a noted shop for clocks). He also advertised his 'new invented engins for quenching of fire', which were made in a variety of sizes, some small enough to be carried upstairs in a house, and which would also serve for 'the washing of vermin of Trees and Hops, & for the watering of Gardens & Cloaths, & the like' (*Mercurius Politicus*, no. 439, 28 Oct 1658). A further (undated) list of his undertakings mentions a weight-driven clock striking the quarters on two bells and the hour on another bell; a watch or clock to run for a month or a year with a single winding; a clock keeping time without a balance, instead of which 'there shall be a pleasant motion of bullets runing continually'; an engine to level the bottom of the river, taking away the shelves or sandbanks on which craft could run aground, and other engines to raise water or weights 'and many things of this kinde' (Hartlib MS 71/19/1A).

One Fromanteel clock 'to run a month or more' was sold to Dudley Palmer FRS of Gray's Inn in 1654 for £200, another to the lord protector in 1657 for £300, considerable sums at this time. John Evelyn, in 1660, saw one of Fromanteel's more elaborate clocks in the king's cabinet,

and in 1661 recorded a visit he paid in the company of Huygens to view Fromanteel's pendulum clocks. In July 1679 one of Fromanteel's fire-engines was ordered for the city of Norwich.

Fromanteel's decision to settle in the Netherlands between 1667 and 1676 may have been caused by the problems which afflicted Baptists in London at that time. His son Abraham joined him, leaving the London business in the hands of John and his own former apprentice Thomas Loomes, to whom John had been apprenticed and who was married to Ahasuerus's daughter Mary. On his return some ten years later Abraham was made free of the Clockmakers' Company at his father's urgent request; he later settled in Newcastle upon Tyne, where he died in 1730. John returned with his brother Ahasuerus to the Netherlands in 1680, where the latter settled and started an important workshop in Amsterdam.

After Maria's death, Ahasuerus married, about 1660, Sarah Winnock (d. 1665), a widow with three sons and a daughter. He was living in Whitechapel, where other members of the Fromanteel family worked as silk weavers, at the time of his death early in 1693 and was buried at St Mary Matfelon, Whitechapel, on 31 January 1693.

ANITA MCCONNELL

Sources E. G. Aghib and J. H. Leopold, 'More about the elusive Fromanteel', *Antiquarian Horology and the Proceedings of the Antiquarian Horological Society*, 8 (1972–4), 890–94 · P. G. Dawson, 'The later Fromanteels' (typescript), GL · S. E. Atkins and W. H. Overall, *Some account of the Worshipful Company of Clockmakers of the City of London* (privately printed, London, 1881), 151–2, 166 · J. Lindeboom, *Austin friars: history of the Dutch Reformed church in London, 1550–1950*, trans. D. de Iongh (1950), 56 · Hartlib MSS, University of Sheffield Library, 8/27/1A–2B; 29/4/25A; 29/6/23B; 53/35/5A; 71/19/1A · will, proved, 3 Feb 1693, GL, MS 9171/Reg. 45, fol. 44v–46v · Evelyn, *Diary*, 3.260–61, 285 · F. J. Britten, *Old clocks and watches and their makers*, ed. G. H. Baillie, C. Ilbert, and C. Clutton, 9th edn (1982), 319–20 · court books of Norwich, July 1679, Norfolk RO, vol. 153 · private information (2004) · church register (baptism), 25 Feb 1607, Norwich Dutch Reformed Church · church register (marriages), 1631, Norwich Dutch Reformed Church · parish register (burial), 31 Jan 1693, St Mary Matfelon, London

Frost, Charles (*bap.* **1782**, *d.* **1862**), antiquary, born at Kingston upon Hull, Yorkshire, and baptized there on 3 January 1782, was the son of Thomas Frost, a solicitor in that town, and his wife, Elizabeth. He followed his father's profession, and succeeded him as solicitor to the Hull Dock Company, an appointment that he held for over thirty-three years. From his father he acquired a taste for genealogical and historical research, and while still articled he gained a reputation as an expert black-letter lawyer. On 2 May 1822 he was elected FSA. In 1827 he published by subscription *Notices Relative to the Early History of the Town and Port of Hull*, in which he traced the origin of the town beyond the alleged foundation by Edward I in 1296. The work was based on original manuscript material and was well received. Frost soon published another local study, first delivered to the Hull Literary and Philosophical Society on 5 November 1830, in which he noticed the various literary societies that had been promoted in the town during the preceding half-century, giving brief biographies of most Hull authors. He was president of the society ten times between 1830 and 1855; he was also president of the subscription library on twelve occasions between 1827 and 1854. Between 1850 and 1854 he organized the amalgamation of the two organizations, and in 1853 he was one of the vice-presidents of the Hull meeting of the British Association for the Advancement of Science. Frost also published two legal pamphlets, one relating to the provision of compensation to witnesses in civil actions for loss of earnings (1815), and the other concerning the Hull poor rate (1820). Frost died at Kingston upon Hull on 5 September 1862, and was survived by his wife, Jane, and son, Percival *Frost.

GORDON GOODWIN, rev. WILLIAM JOSEPH SHEILS

Sources R. W. Corlass, 'Charles Frost, F.S.A.', Sketches of Hull authors, ed. C. F. Corlass and W. Andrews (1879), 33–4 · VCH Yorkshire, vol. 1 · C. R. J. Currie and C. P. Lewis, eds., English county histories: a guide (1994), 440–46 · GM, 1st ser., 100/2 (1830), 450–51 · GM, 1st ser., 101/2 (1831), 523–4 · GM, 3rd ser., 13 (1862), 508 · parish register, Kingston upon Hull, Holy Trinity, 3 Jan 1782 [baptism] · CGPLA Eng. & Wales (1862)
Likenesses Schmidt?, portrait
Wealth at death under £1000: probate, 13 Nov 1862, CGPLA Eng. & Wales

Frost, George (bap. 1745, d. 1821), landscape draughtsman, was, according to family tradition, the son of George Frost, a builder from Ousden in west Suffolk, and his wife, Thomasin. However, it is probable that he was born in the neighbouring village of Barrow, and he was baptized there on 21 February 1745. After beginning his career in his father's business he obtained a confidential situation in the office of the Blue Coach Company in Ipswich, where he continued until his retirement in 1813.

Recorded as a drawing-master in 1797, Frost had a natural aptitude for drawing; his first recorded watercolour is dated 1780. Early in his career he painted topographical watercolours of Ipswich but later began to sketch the countryside around the town in pencil and black chalk. He was a devoted admirer and imitator of Gainsborough and possessed many drawings and paintings by him, the best of which was The Mall (Frick Collection, New York) which he copied (Christchurch Mansion, Ipswich). Correspondence with John Constable shows that the two artists sketched amicably together along the banks of the River Orwell about 1800. He appears to have complemented his collecting activities by dealing. He died at his home, Common Quay, Ipswich, on 28 June 1821 after a long illness, and was buried at St Matthew's Church, Ipswich. After the death of his widow, Mary (b. c.1755), on 25 April 1839, his considerable art collection was sold by R. Garrod on 7 June 1839. Many of the drawings by Gainsborough he owned were bought by William Esdaile.

L. H. CUST, rev. HUGH BELSEY

Sources [J. Ford], GM, 1st ser., 91/2 (1821), 89–90 · F. Brown, Frost's drawings of Ipswich and sketches in Suffolk (1895) · J. Hayes, 'The drawings of George Frost (1745–1821)', Master Drawings, 4/2 (1966), 163–8 · M. Rosenthal, George Frost, 1745–1821 (1974) [exhibition catalogue, Gainsborough House, London] · D. Thomas, 'George Frost and the Gainsborough tradition', The Connoisseur, 178 (1971), 108–13 · I. Fleming-Williams and L. Parris, The discovery of Constable (1984) · M. Rosenthal, 'On the waterfront: Ipswich docks in 1803',
Antique Collector, 45 (1974), 40–41 · H. A. E. Day, East Anglian painters, 3 vols. (1967–9), vol. 1, pp. 41–7
Likenesses G. Frost, self-portrait, repro. in Brown, Frost's drawings

Frost, Georgina [Georgie] (1879–1939), first woman to hold public office in the United Kingdom, was born in Sixmilebridge, co. Clare, Ireland, on 29 December 1879, one of the five children born to Thomas Frost (1841/2–1938) and his wife, Margaret Kett (d. 1888). Her father was the petty sessions clerk for the district of Sixmilebridge and Newmarket-on-Fergus, as had been her maternal grandfather, John Kett, before him.

Before Thomas Frost retired as petty sessions clerk in 1915, he had for the preceding six years been assisted by Georgie in discharging the duties of the office. She sometimes acted as the clerk herself and became a familiar figure as she cycled from one village to the other (they were approximately 6 miles apart). The magistrates who presided in the courts were obviously satisfied with the way in which she carried out her duties, since they elected her to succeed her father. However, the appointment also required approval from the lord lieutenant before it became effective, and he was advised that Georgie Frost, as a woman, could not lawfully be appointed to the office.

Frost then embarked on a remarkable and protracted legal struggle to overturn that decision. She brought it under the 'petition of right' procedure, and an impressive array of counsel, led by T. M. Healy KC, appeared for her when the case came on in the chancery division of the Irish high court. It was held that she was ineligible for the appointment because of her sex, a decision that was upheld by a majority of the court of appeal. The decision was made partly on the basis that the relevant statutes made it clear that women could not be appointed to the office of clerk of the petty sessions. But the majority also relied on an alleged rule of the common law that women could not be appointed to any public office. Judges differed in their reasons for holding this to be the law: some said it was because of considerations of 'decorum' and the fact that the duties of certain offices were 'painful and exacting'. Others were quite prepared to say that it was because of 'inferiority of bodily ability and … mental inferiority'. It should be said that the majority in the court of appeal, although feeling themselves obliged to hold that the wording of the statute excluded Frost from the office, emphatically rejected the proposition that public policy required the maintenance of a rule excluding women from public office generally.

Although this was the majority view—from Chief Justice Moloney and Lord Justice Ronan—the third member of the court, the lord chancellor of Ireland, Lord Shandon, thought differently. He had retired after the hearing, but before the court gave its decision, somewhat unusually, he set out in a letter the grounds upon which he was prepared to allow the appeal. He was satisfied that neither the statutes nor the supposed principle of the common law invalidated the appointment. His dissent was important from Frost's point of view. The case might well have ended there but a London solicitor informed Healy that one of the law lords, Lord Shaw, favoured applying in the House of Lords the Scottish practice under which an appeal could be brought *in forma pauperis*. This would mean that the appellant, if found unsuccessful, could not be required to pay the costs. Apparently, the law lords would be prepared to apply the rule to a case where there had been a dissent in the Irish court of appeal.

Thus encouraged, Frost eventually made her way to the House of Lords. By the time the case was listed for hearing, however, on 27 April 1920, the Sex Disqualification (Removal) Act of 1919 had become law and the legal bar to Frost holding the office of clerk of the petty sessions no longer existed. The lord chancellor, Lord Birkenhead, saw no point in going into the old law in the circumstances and proposed to adjourn the case with a view to communicating with the lord lieutenant, who might give a retrospective approval to Frost's appointment. Counsel agreed to this course of action and she was duly appointed, thus becoming the first woman to hold public office in the United Kingdom. She retained the office through the tumultuous period in Irish history from 1920 until 1923, in which year the office of clerk of the petty sessions was abolished by statute. She died, unmarried, at her home, Garna House, Sixmilebridge, on 6 December 1939.

In December 2000 the Irish postal authorities (An Post) issued a commemorative postage stamp incorporating Frost's photograph. Her personal papers included a copy of a letter from the London solicitor to Healy recommending the appeal to the House of Lords. The courage and persistence that she showed helped to enable women to take up legal and administrative appointments at all levels in the UK and in Ireland.   RONAN KEANE

Sources *Frost v. Rex*, *Irish Reports* (1919), 1.81, 84 • J. Comyn, *Their friends in court* (1973) • *The weekly notes: being notes of cases heard in the House of Lords, the superior courts of equity and common law, the courts of probate and divorce, etc.* (1920–22), 178 • R. Keane, 'Georgina Frost and the courts: a famous victory', www.womenandlaw1919-2000. com/chief.htm, Nov 2000 • P. de Bhaldraithe, 'Sixmilebridge clerks of petty session', *The Other Clare*, 11 (1987), 22–5
Likenesses photograph, repro. in Women and Law conference papers website, www.womenandlaw1919-2000.com/chief.htm-ftn1 • photograph, repro. in Republic of Ireland commemorative postage stamp, 2000 • photograph, repro. in de Bhaldraithe, 'Sixmilebridge clerks of petty session', 24

Frost, Gualter [Walter] (*bap.* **1598**, *d.* **1652**), political agent and government official, came from a modest East Anglian background. He was baptized in Chevington, Suffolk, on 15 January 1598, the son of William Frost. He seems to have been trained as a land surveyor and had become maniciple of Emmanuel College, Cambridge, by 1628, remaining there until 1639. He was involved in constructing Hobson's conduit, or 'the new river', which provided a water supply for his own college and Christ's College. In 1639–40 he acted as a secret courier, disguised as a commercial traveller, for the English opposition leaders in their clandestine—if not treasonable—correspondence with the Scottish covenanters. One source connects him with Thomas Savile (first Viscount Savile of Castlebar), another, more reliably, with Robert Greville, second Lord Brooke. In 1642 he was acting as a commissary, or supply officer, at Chester, sending provisions for the Anglo-Scottish forces in Ireland. In 1642–3 he apparently served as an intelligence officer under the Long Parliament's committee of safety.

Frost's promotion in 1644 to the important post of co-secretary to the new committee of both kingdoms may have been partly because he was already known to, and trusted by, its Scottish members, but it also suggests more direct patronage. Since Brooke was already dead and Savile discredited, Robert Rich, second earl of Warwick (an old member of Emmanuel), and William Fiennes, first Viscount Saye and Sele (whose eldest son had been there) appear as possible links. When the Scots dropped out, Frost moved with the committee to Derby House in 1647–8, and after the establishment of the Commonwealth in 1649 he became secretary to the newly created council of state. He held this, the most senior post in the republican central executive, until his death. Presumably efficient and discreet as an administrative organizer and record keeper, his were less successful essays into political propaganda, on behalf of the regime against its radical critics, the Levellers.

It was important for the future of the English republic that Frost was succeeded not by his eldest son, who had become assistant secretary and treasurer for the council's contingencies, but by the candidate of Oliver St John and Oliver Cromwell, John Thurloe. Frost had married Phoebe Seffray in Chevington, Suffolk, in 1619. He died in London on 29 March 1652, leaving a large family and considerable debts. He showed some nepotistic, or rather patrimonial, skill in getting his sons placed in the public service; his failure to amass even a modest competence of wealth may be taken to argue either extreme probity or reckless extravagance, but more probably arose from having over-extended his credit in trying to send supplies to Ireland in 1642. The younger Walter, who seems to have succeeded his father in the service of the City of London as its official chronologer, remained on the council staff until 1660, as did one of his brothers; a third brother had died in its service earlier, and a fourth was appointed to the staff of the council in Ireland under Henry Cromwell. After being at the very centre of public affairs, the Frost family sank back into almost impenetrable obscurity.

G. E. AYLMER

Sources G. E. Aylmer, *The state's servants: the civil service of the English republic, 1649–1660* (1973) • C. Russell, *The fall of the British monarchies, 1637–1642* (1991) • private information (1993) [A. S. Bendall]

Frost, John (1625/6–1656), clergyman, was born at Langham, Suffolk, the eldest son of John Frost, rector of Fakenham in the same county. He was educated at Thetford, Norfolk, and Bury St Edmunds, Suffolk, and was admitted as a pensioner at St John's College, Cambridge, on 21 February 1642 aged sixteen. After graduating BA in 1646 Frost proceeded MA in 1649 and BD in 1656. He became a fellow of St John's in 1647, lecturing in logic and philosophy; among his students was Ashfield, son of Captain Thomas Ogle.

In 1654 Frost began to preach regularly at St Benet, Cambridge, and elsewhere in the town and county. His posthumously published sermon on 'The severitie and impartialitie of divine justice', delivered at Cambridge assizes on 25 July 1654, contained a preface addressed to his patron, Sir Henry Felton. In 1656 he was invited to become pastor of St Olave, Hart Street, London, where the congregation:

> were desirous to enjoy him, but being among themselves divided, had Mr Fenton, an hopeful pious man, put upon them, who lived but a very short season … On his death, their affections revived towards Mr Frost, they chose him to be their minister.   (Crofton, 50)

'Earnestly he desired, and studiously endeavoured an union between Episcopal and Presbyteriall divines in things relating to the discipline of the church' and 'many times', according to the presbyterian minister Zachary Crofton, 'hath he in my hearing lamented the want of discipline' (Crofton, 52–3). In a sermon preached on 29 September 1656 at the investiture of the mayor of Cambridge, Frost argued that 'a magistrate may promote the service of God, by punishing irreligion and profaneness' (Frost, 295). Later, on 27 October, Frost became very ill with smallpox, and was not apparently given the best treatment: 'I pray God pardon the preposterous course held with him by his physician' (Crofton, 58). He died in London on 2 November 1656 and was buried at St Olave's. A selection of his sermons published posthumously in 1657 refers to his widow, Theodosia, and a second John Frost, possibly the father or son of the author.

GORDON GOODWIN, rev. STEPHEN WRIGHT

Sources Z. Crofton, *The people's need of a living pastor* (1657), preface; 42–59 • Venn, *Alum. Cant.* • J. Frost, *Select sermons* (1657) • will, PRO, PROB 11/260, fols. 230–31
Likenesses R. Vaughan, line engraving, BM, NPG; repro. in Frost, *Select sermons*
Wealth at death see will, PRO, PROB 11/260, fols. 230–31

Frost, John (1750–1842), radical, was born in October 1750. His parentage remains unknown and little about his childhood, personal life, or early career has been discovered, although it is understood that he was educated at Winchester College and trained as an attorney. Like many practising lawyers Frost's occupation probably saw him actively involved in politics as an electoral agent, and it was in 1782 that he began attending meetings of a reform society at the Thatched House tavern in St James's Street, London. Here, on 18 May 1782, at a meeting chaired by William Pitt and attended by the likes of the duke of Richmond, Lord Surrey, Lord Mahon, John Wilkes, Major John Cartwright, and John Horne Tooke, a resolution was unanimously agreed which stipulated that a petition be presented to parliament calling for a reform of the House of Commons. By 1785 Frost's reformist ideas led him to join, as a paying member, the Society for Constitutional Information (SCI), where he maintained a close relationship with Horne Tooke and became acquainted with the leading reformers of the day.

Although the *Gentleman's Magazine*, in an obituary notice, stated that, 'at the breaking out of the French revolution, [Frost] … was one of the most enthusiastic of those who adopted Republican principles', it was not until 1792 that he became a truly conspicuous figure in metropolitan radicalism. In that year Frost acted at times as a patron and protector of his radical colleagues, contributing in June 1792 the sum of 1 guinea to a subscription raised in benefit of Thomas Paine. At the same time he reportedly offered his house as a secret shelter for the ill-fated Joseph Gerrald, then under sentence to be transported. It is also frequently cited that Frost was a founding member of, and one-time secretary to, the London Corresponding Society (LCS), yet it would seem that he never actually achieved such a prominent position in this organization. It is indeed difficult to determine the precise connection Frost had with the LCS, since his name does not appear on any extant membership list. However, it is known that on 15 November 1792 he was present at the Green Dragon public house in Golden Square, where Division 3 of the LCS gathered and from which meeting the spy George Munro reported that

> a Mr Frost almost the only decent Man I have seen in any of their Divisions made a long inflamatory speech, which he concluded by recomending to the members to deffend their oppinions with their lives and property; this man seem'd very popular.   (Thale, 27–8)

Eighteen months later, on 15 May 1794, just days after the arrests began of leading radicals on charges of high treason, the LCS committee of emergency convened at the house of John Thelwall, and the spy John Groves recalled Frost arriving at the door along with Horne Tooke, but since neither man was a member of the society they were not permitted to take part in the evening's proceedings. Nevertheless, Frost seems to have remained popular among certain sections of the LCS, with a toast offered in his honour at a society meeting on 20 January 1794 held in the Globe tavern. He also maintained a close connection with London's leading radicals, many of whom were in some way associated with the LCS, as depicted in the caricatured etching *Promenade in the State Side of Newgate*, where he is seen mingling with the likes of Charles Pigott, Daniel Isaac Eaton, George Gordon, James Ridgway, and Thomas Lloyd.

The prominence of Frost in the metropolitan reform movement owed much to his relationship with Horne Tooke and his role in the SCI. In September 1792 Tooke had written a letter for Jerome Pétion, the mayor of Paris, in which he advised that a sum of £1000 had been raised as a patriotic gift, and both Frost and Paine were sent to France as conveyers of this message. In a letter from Paris, Frost assured Horne Tooke of his safe arrival as well as Paine's celebrated reception in the national assembly, and he commented that the 'treachery of [King] Louis is so great, that the indignation of the people cannot be wondered at' (Wharam, 32). By 11 October 1792 Frost had returned to London where, at a meeting of the SCI, he was nominated along with the society's president and secretary, Joel Barlow, to return to Paris and deliver an address to the national convention and a gift of 1000 pairs of shoes for

French soldiers. On 28 November 1792 Barlow and Frost were admitted to the convention to read the SCI address, which in part proclaimed:

> After the example given by France, revolutions will become easy. Reason is about to make a rapid progress, and it would not be extraordinary, if in a much less space of time than can be imagined, the French should send Addresses of congratulations to a National Convention of England. (*A Collection of Addresses*, 24–5)

On the same day, a letter from the SCI, with Frost's signature alongside Barlow's, was read to the convention declaring that 'other Nations will soon follow your steps in this career of improvement, and, rising from their lethargy, will arm themselves for the purpose of claiming the Rights of Man, with that all-powerful voice which man cannot resist' (ibid., 30–31).

In his capacity as delegate of the SCI to France, Frost was afforded the opportunity in late 1792 and early 1793 to be among a large group of expatriate radicals living in Paris whose activities centred on White's Hotel, rue des Piques. Known as the British Club, this group included Thomas Paine, William Duckett, Robert Merry, Thomas Muir, John Oswald, John Hurford Stone, Henry Redhead Yorke, Helen Maria Williams, and perhaps even William Wordsworth. The sentiments of this formidable body were clearly expressed at a rally held on 18 November 1792, at which the club celebrated French military successes, and toasted the French republic and the then forthcoming British reform convention. They also resolved to draw up an address to the National Convention, which was read by Henri Grégoire on the same day the SCI address and letter were presented, suggesting 'a close union between the French republic and the English, Scotch, and Irish nations, a union which cannot fail to ensure entire Europe the enjoyment of the rights of man and establish on the firmest bases universal peace' (Roe, 81). On the day, forty-nine persons signed the address; Frost arrived in Paris on 22 November 1792 in time to add his signature. In mid-December the spy George Monro, reporting on the British Club, stated that 'Mr. Frost has left his house and seldom makes his appearance. He is, however, one of the society' (Erdman, 242). Within two weeks Monro believed, somewhat prematurely, that the club was falling apart and 'beneath the notice of any one, struggling for consequence among themselves, jealous of one another, differing in opinion, and even insignificant in a body'. Perhaps symptomatic of the club's demise was a reported incident on 11 January 1793 when Paine and Merry suggested the drawing up of another address which was strongly opposed by Frost to the extent that 'the dispute nearly ended in blows' (ibid., 242–3).

Before returning to England, Frost was present at the trial of Louis XVI in December 1792, a fact duly noted by Edmund Burke in one of his speeches. Back in London, Frost was himself brought before the courts on a charge of uttering seditious words. The incident had occurred during the autumn of 1792 when he had dined with members of the Society for the Encouragement of Agriculture at the Percy Coffee House in Marylebone. On his way out, as

Thelwall recounted in *The Tribune*, Frost was stopped by a man and engaged in the following exchange: '"Oh you are a liberty man; you are for liberty and equality and no king?"—"Yes Sir, for liberty and equality and no king"—"What are you for liberty and equality and no king in England?" Vexed and indignant … he [Frost] replied, "Yes, Sir, I am for liberty and equality and no king in England"' (Claeys, 223). At the time, a certain Colonel Bullock overheard the conversation and referred the matter to the attorney-general, which subsequently led to Frost's arrest in February 1793 and his trial the following May. Thelwall, who was present at the court, described hearing 'such a volume of horrible denunciations, and opprobrium against the culprit, that one would have imagined … that he had absolutely endeavoured to murder the king, put his sons to the torture, and violate the purity of his daughters' (ibid.). Frost was found guilty and sentenced to six months' imprisonment in Newgate, an hour in the pillory at Charing Cross, and to find two sureties of £100 each for his good behaviour for five years. The presiding judge also ordered Frost's name be removed from the roll of attorneys, 'whereby he was to be rendered infamous and to be irretrievably ruined' (Campbell, 3.50). Although he escaped his stint in the pillory when the gathering crowd demolished the platform and released the prisoner to Horne Tooke, who then escorted him back to Newgate, Frost was eventually set free from prison in an infirm state. He was reputedly paraded through the streets as a hero, with the crowd stopping outside the prince of Wales's residence to jeer before conducting Frost to his home in Spring Gardens, Westminster.

In 1794, with the treason trials looming, Frost was interviewed before the privy council on 31 May on suspicion of treasonable practices, but his five-year bond and sureties probably led ultimately to his discharge. However, with Horne Tooke less fortunate and imprisoned to await trial, Frost seems to have been appointed as guardian of his friend's family and home. Frost then abused his position in Tooke's household, an event that was recorded by Horne Tooke in his prison diary:

> A most unpleasant story about Mr. Frost and his behaviour to my maid. It has much distressed my family. The maid is gone, and a stranger come in her place. Mr. Frost has very properly been refused admittance to my House. (*Prison Diary*, 56)

Frost, however, subsequently managed to maintain a working relationship with Horne Tooke and the political circle of Sir Francis Burdett, being employed by their faction as a legal adviser in their Middlesex campaign at the general election of 1802 and again at the Middlesex by-election in 1804. Eventually, though, Frost's relationship with Horne Tooke broke down completely, an outcome which can perhaps be linked to the dispute of 1794.

For Frost himself, politics also proved momentarily alluring, and in 1802 he stood as a candidate for East Grinstead, but was defeated. In spite of a petition to the House of Commons against his opponent's election return, Frost remained unsuccessful in gaining office and his petition was dismissed as 'frivolous and vexatious' (*GM*, 443). For some time his whereabouts and activities remain unknown, until in December 1813 he received a free pardon from the prince regent and was consequently re-entered on the roll of attorneys on 8 February 1815. By this time, however, his long-term absence from the profession had made him virtually unemployable. From then on Frost passed into complete obscurity despite living to the age of ninety-one. He died on 25 July 1842 at Holly Lodge, near Lymington in Hampshire, the official cause of death recorded as old age. MICHAEL T. DAVIS

Sources GM, 2nd ser., 18 (1842), 442–3 · A collection of addresses transmitted by certain English clubs and societies to the National Convention of France (1793) · A. Wharam, The treason trials, 1794 (1992) · M. Thale, ed., Selections from the papers of the London Corresponding Society, 1792–1799 (1983) · D. V. Erdman, Commerce des lumières: John Oswald and the British in Paris, 1790–1793 (1986) · G. Claeys, ed., The politics of English Jacobinism: writings of John Thelwall (1995) · N. Roe, Wordsworth and Coleridge: the radical years (1988) · The prison diary (16 May–22 November 1794) of John Horne Tooke, ed. A. V. Beedell and A. D. Harvey (1995) · John, Lord Campbell, The lives of the chief justices of England, 3 vols. (1849–57) · d. cert.
Likenesses R. Newton, etching, 1793 (Promenade in the state side of Newgate), BM

Frost, John (1784–1877), Chartist, was born at Newport, Monmouthshire, on 25 May 1784, the son of John Frost and his wife, Sarah, landlady of the Royal Oak public house in Mill Street, Newport. His father died when John was very young and his mother remarried twice. Aged about sixteen, Frost was apprenticed to a tailor in Cardiff. In 1804 he was an assistant woollen draper in Bristol and the following year he worked in London as a merchant tailor. There he joined radical circles and sharpened his political education by reading Paine and Cobbett. On his return to Newport about 1806 he continued his business as a tailor and draper. On 24 October 1812 Frost married Mary Geach (née Morgan), widow of a timber dealer, with whom he had eight children between 1815 and 1826.

Frost published thirteen public letters on issues of Newport municipal politics during 1821–2. In 1823 he suffered six months' imprisonment for libel, as part of a twenty-year vendetta with solicitor Thomas Prothero. Frost took an active part in the struggle for reform in Newport. He helped organize a branch of the Political Union of the Working Classes in November 1831 and his A Christmas Box for Sir Charles Morgan (1831) attacked agrarian distress and advocated a widened franchise, triennial parliaments, and vote by ballot. The following year he savaged the Reform Act in A Letter to the Reformers. In 1835 Frost was elected a member of the town council of Newport and appointed a magistrate for the borough. In 1836 he was elected mayor, but he was defeated in 1837 owing to his opposition to church rates.

On 30 October 1838 Frost appeared in public in support of William Edward's Newport Working Men's Association and soon after was elected to the 1839 Chartist convention as delegate for Monmouthshire. This activity led to his removal from the commission of the peace by the home secretary, Lord John Russell, on 21 March 1839. Consequently, Frost's popularity among the Chartists increased, and he became a national leader. Throughout the spring and summer Frost acted to damp down angry and restless local Chartist groups. However, following a wave of convictions for sedition, he appeared to shift his position. On 14 September the convention, weakened in numbers by resignation and arrests, was dissolved on the casting vote of the chairman, Frost. Confusion surrounds his movements and intentions over the next six weeks but it is certain that he was present when plans were laid for a rising centred on Newport.

On 4 November Frost led a large body of armed working men, chiefly miners, into Newport. Two other groups—led by William Jones, a watch-maker from Pontypool, and Zephaniah Williams, a beershop keeper from Nant-y-glo—arrived late, or never came. Frost and his three thousand followers attacked the Westgate Hotel, where, under the direction of Thomas Phillips, the mayor of Newport, thirty-two soldiers of the 45th regiment and a number of special constables had been posted to guard existing Chartist prisoners. The relatively ill-armed and undisciplined Chartists were easily repulsed, and suffered twenty fatalities and many injuries. Frost was captured the same evening, and was tried before Lord Chief Justice Tindal, Baron Parke, and Justice Williams at a special assize that was opened at Monmouth on 10 December 1839. He was defended by Sir Frederick Pollock and Fitzroy Kelly, but after a lengthy trial was found guilty of levying war against the queen. On 16 January 1840 Frost, Williams, and Jones were sentenced to be hanged, drawn, and quartered. Appeals against the sentences by several MPs and prominent public figures and large-scale national radical protest came to nothing. However, following legal review, it was agreed by the government on 1 February 1840 that the sentences be commuted to transportation for life to Van Diemen's Land.

Several efforts were made, especially by Thomas Slingsby Duncombe in the House of Commons, to procure the release of Frost and his associates. In March 1854 Duncombe succeeded in obtaining a pardon, conditional on Frost's never returning to British territory. He went to America (reaching California in May 1855), lectured on his experiences, and published A Letter to the People of the United States Showing the Effects of Aristocratic Rule (1855). After receiving a free pardon in May 1856 as a result of the general pardon granted after the successful conclusion of the Crimean War, he returned to Britain on 12 July. He was welcomed in Newport and London but never regained his status as a radical leader. On 31 August he delivered two lectures at Padiham on the 'Horrors of convict life', which were later printed. The following year he published A letter to the people of Great Britain and Ireland on transportation, showing the effects of irresponsible power on the physical and moral conditions of convicts. Although it appears that it was his intention to write a series of letters on this subject, no more were published.

Frost moved to Stapleton, near Bristol, where he lived for many years in comparative retirement, pursuing an interest in spiritualism. He died there on 29 July 1877. The march on Newport in November 1839 for which Frost is remembered has been variously interpreted as a peaceful demonstration or as part of a national conspiracy to over-throw the government. There is strong evidence of a high degree of planning, confounded by a series of last-minute changes of plan and an ultimate divergence between intentions and execution. The Newport rising was indeed part of a wider plan of insurrection and was in fact the last on the British mainland.   MATTHEW LEE

Sources D. Williams, *John Frost: a study in chartism* (1939) · D. J. V. Jones, *The last rising: the Newport insurrection of 1839* (1985) · D. F. Schafer, 'Frost, John', *BDMBR*, vol. 2 · A. Briggs, ed., *Chartist studies* (1959) · D. Thompson, ed., *The early Chartists* (1971) · G. D. H. Cole, *Chartist portraits* (1941) · J. T. Ward, *Chartism* (1973) · *Daily News* (31 July 1877) · *Daily Bristol Times and Mirror* (30 July 1877) · *Daily Bristol Times and Mirror* (4 Aug 1877) · *DNB*
Archives Gwent RO, Newport, MSS · NL Wales, letters · PRO, treasury solicitor's papers (11/499) and Home Office papers, 40, 41 | BL, corresp. with Lord John Russell, Add. MS 34245
Likenesses W. Clark, lithograph, *c*.1840, NPG · E. Morton, lithograph, pubd 1840 (after R. R. Scanlan), NPG · W. Read, stipple, BM · portrait, repro. in *The rise and fall of chartism in Monmouthshire* (1840) · portrait, repro. in *Cornhill Magazine*, 23 (1882), 428
Wealth at death under £1500: probate, 9 Jan 1878, *CGPLA Eng. & Wales*

Frost, John (1803–1840), medical entrepreneur, was baptized at St Martin-in-the-Fields on 9 May 1803, the son of William and Mary Frost, who were in business in the Charing Cross area of London. A twin and very delicate in infancy, he was sent away to a school at Langley, near Windsor, before being apprenticed to Edward Wright, the apothecary to Bethlem Hospital in London, with a view to entering the medical profession. The two fell out, however, and he never completed his training.

At that time botany had suddenly been restored to medical curricula in Britain as a result of the Apothecaries' Act of 1815, and courses in that subject were hurriedly being introduced. So long had it ceased to be generally taught that it was conspicuously uncatered-for by any of the growing number of specialist learned societies in London, and this gap caught the notice of the botanically inclined Frost, who conceived the idea of filling it. After managing to interest several leading physicians, most notably Robert Bree, he accordingly established in 1821 the Medico-Botanical Society of London, with himself as its honorary 'director' (there was also a secretary, who may have been paid). This had for its objects the investigation of the medicinal properties of plants, the study of the materia medica of all countries, and the making of awards for original research on the subject. The well-connected Bree secured as initial president Sir James McGrigor, the director-general of the army medical department, who subsequently agreed to write to the home secretary, Sir Robert Peel, to seek his assistance in obtaining George IV as patron. Having succeeded in this Peel in turn was elected to the society's council.

This glittering start soon went to the head of the impressionable eighteen-year-old. Although the society was solidly established from the outset and appears to have had no difficulty in attracting a goodly flow of members and papers, Frost embarked on a manic drive for further aggrandizement. With irrepressible zeal, invincible bravado, and occasional subterfuges he succeeded in gaining access to many of the most prominent people in Europe and beyond—including most of the British royal family—and, having informed them that they had been elected to honorary membership, asked them to inscribe their signature in an ornate, imposing album which he carried around for this purpose. At least three foreign potentates, in return for this supposed honour, sent the insignia of one of their country's minor orders, addressed to 'the director'; these were promptly added to the accumulation of medals and ribbons which Frost increasingly delighted in wearing at the society's meetings in order to heighten the aura of pomp that he strove to cultivate.

At first people were more amused than offended by 'Jacky' Frost's pretentiousness. The society's members were doubtless prepared to indulge his vanity in exchange for his single-minded dedication to its interests and for certain concrete benefits he undeniably brought it; these included the donation of a herbarium of 5000 specimens, allegedly all collected by himself. Outsiders, however, were less charitable. John Claudius Loudon, in an editorial aside in his widely read *Gardener's Magazine* (vol. 3, 324), was sufficiently provoked to 'question his taste on the subject of adulation to certain exalted personages, who, but for their rank and fortune, would never have been heard of'. It was still a world, however, in which lofty patronage counted for much and could open doors, and Frost had become a maestro at playing on this. Despite an almost total lack of learned accomplishments he none the less contrived to be elected to several of the nation's grander scholarly societies (the Royal Society alone refusing him admittance, and that with a humiliating blackballing). The title of professor of botany, which the Medico-Botanical Society additionally conceded to him and which seems to have had his delivery of an annual oration as its sole substance, doubtless also helped to bring him other, more prestigious lecturing engagements, notably at the Royal Institution and at St Thomas's Hospital.

Meanwhile Frost was badly in need of a steady source of income. In 1824 his record in recruiting patrons among the highly placed led him to be chosen by the Royal Humane Society as its salaried secretary, with the free use of a house in Bridge Street, Blackfriars. Curiously, that did not prevent him from entering Emmanuel College, Cambridge, two years later, with a view to obtaining a medical degree and thereby qualifying as a physician; but he must quickly have found the university's requirement to go into residence difficult to fulfil, for he pursued that intention no further.

Towards the end of 1828 the docile McGrigor was succeeded as the Medico-Botanical Society's president by the more formidable and committed Earl Stanhope, a noted advocate of herbal medicine. Soon losing patience with Frost's extravagances and posturing, Stanhope played a leading part the following winter in a series of manoeuvres which culminated in effecting the director's dismissal and expulsion. The attendant ructions within the society attracted much attention from the press and the bad publicity resulting firmly put paid to Frost's fleeting new appointment as surgeon-extraordinary to the duke of

Cumberland. Worse, he had resigned from his post with the Royal Humane Society in order to take up the duke's invitation, and that society refused to have him back when he then sought to return.

For a time Frost's social wizardry nevertheless continued to be in demand in medical circles. In 1831 he was instrumental in establishing St John's Hospital in Clerkenwell, and in 1832 he obtained a grant from the Admiralty for the conversion of HMS *Chanticleer*, moored off Millbank, into a floating hospital for the treatment of Thames watermen. Back in his stride, for this latter venture he once again enlisted a distinguished body of patrons, including the king, three dukes, and an earl. But this time he overreached himself: the funds on which he had counted fell seriously short of the expenses he had incurred, and, besieged by creditors, he was forced to flee the country.

Frost went first to live in Paris, disguising himself there as 'James Fitzjames'. His Swiss wife, Harriet Yosy (probably a relation of his former Medico-Botanical Society colleague John Peter Yosy), doubtless made up for any weakness of his in French, just as her probable fluency in German may have lain behind their later decision to settle in Berlin. There Frost built up a considerable practice as a physician, aided no doubt by his assumption of a foreign knighthood earlier bestowed on him through a misunderstanding. A long and painful illness, however, ended in his death on 17 March 1840, when he was still in his thirties. There were no children of the marriage.   D. E. ALLEN

Sources GM, 2nd ser., 14 (1840), 664–6 · J. F. Clarke, *Autobiographical recollections of the medical profession* (1874), 240–1, 267–76 · *The life and letters of … Richard Harris Barham*, ed. R. H. D. Barham, 2 vols. (1870), 176–80 · *Transactions of the Medico-Botanical Society of London* (1821–37) · *Gardener's Magazine*, 3 (1828), 324 · *Gardener's Magazine*, 6 (1830), 104–5 · DNB
Likenesses J. Thomson, stipple, 1828 (after W. Derby), Wellcome L.

Frost, John Dutton (1912–1993), army officer, was born in Poona, India, on 31 December 1912, the son of Brigadier-General Frank Dutton Frost (d. 1968), army officer and later missionary, and his wife, Elsie Dora, *née* Bright (d. 1952). He was educated at Wellington College, Monkton Combe School, and the Royal Military College, Sandhurst, and was commissioned into the Cameronians (Scottish Rifles) in 1932. In September 1936 the regiment moved to Palestine, where the Arabs were rebelling against the growth in Jewish settlements and attacking the police and British troops. The Cameronians occasionally had brisk fights with terrorists, but also established friendly relationships by playing football matches against the younger Arabs. While there Frost wrote a Christmas pantomime which ran to four successful performances. At the end of this tour he returned to Hampshire before being posted in 1938 to Habbaniyyah, Iraq, where there was an RAF station. He was given command of a company of Kurds, who, as he recalled, 'despised the Arabs, distrusted the Assyrians, and took a rather poor view of the British' (Frost, *Nearly There*, 54). However, they approved of Frost.

Frost returned to Britain in 1941 and was posted to the 10th Cameronians, then engaged in preparing beach defences on the Suffolk coast. Finding the work extremely boring, he volunteered to become a parachutist. Having qualified within three days, he was appointed adjutant of the 2nd Parachute battalion (2 Para), which was just being formed. He recalled that most of the battalion were Scots who had volunteered because they thought this the quickest way to see action. 'They weren't particular who they fought and if there was no one else available as an enemy, then the English would do' (Frost, *A Drop Too Many*, 26). In February 1942 2 Para was chosen to take part in a raid on the radar station at Bruneval, near Le Havre. The station was thought (rightly) to contain new equipment which was enabling the Germans to take a heavy toll on British bombers flying over the continent. In a successful mission the raiders removed vital equipment, and destroyed much else in order to disguise the main purpose of their mission. Frost was among those called to Downing Street to brief Churchill and the war cabinet on 3 March 1942. The Bruneval raid was instrumental in the war cabinet's subsequent decision to establish an airborne division.

In November 1942 Frost and his battalion landed in Algiers, from where the First Army was planning to reach Tunis and trap the axis forces between themselves and the Eighth Army. On a reconnaissance flight Frost was shot down by Americans who mistook his aircraft for a German bomber: fortunately he was unhurt. The regiment then parachuted into Oudna, where they were heavily outnumbered. After three days' heavy fighting Frost reached the British lines at Medjez-el-Bab, with only 160 of his men. Frost 'was understandably bitter about the waste of his battalion on this ill-conceived mission. It was little consolation to be told that his wild-goose-chase had diverted considerable German strength at a critical juncture' (*The Independent*, 24 May 1993). Frost's battalion subsequently took part in much of the thickest fighting in the north African campaign, distinguishing itself in particular at Djebel Mansour, Tamera, and Sedjennane. After Tunisia 2 Para parachuted into Sicily and subsequently fought as a conventional infantry force. At the end of this campaign the battalion landed in Italy (from warships), but after some brisk fighting it was withdrawn to return to Britain, in order to prepare for the invasion of Normandy.

In September 1944 the 1st airborne division (to which Frost's battalion belonged) was allotted the task of dropping at Arnhem and capturing the road and railway bridges over the Rhine. These were bridges which the allies needed to capture undamaged in their plans to outflank the German Siegfried line. Although the bridges over the Maas and the Waal were captured without too much difficulty, the Arnhem plan proved a disaster for the lightly armed 1st airborne division, which went in by parachute and glider. Unfortunately on the day of the drop General Model, commander-in-chief of the German forces, was lunching at Oosterbeek, 6 miles from Arnhem, and was able to concentrate 9th and 10th Panzer divisions (armed with tanks and self-propelled guns), four divisional battle groups, and an infantry division in the Arnhem area. This vast numerical superiority over the 10,000 members of 1st airborne division was matched by much heavier weaponry than the British division had been able to bring in by air. Desperate attempts were made by the British 30th corps to push through the Netherlands, where the roads were narrow, the dykes flooded, and the Germans making every effort to impede them, in order to reinforce the beleaguered airborne force, but the task proved impossible in the time.

Frost, whose battalion had been dropped 8 miles from Arnhem on 18 September, had to fight through opposition to reach the road bridge (the railway bridge having been destroyed by the Germans just as Frost's men approached it), but then occupied the north end and nearby buildings. In the initial attacks on their position Frost's paratroopers managed to set on fire many of the enemy vehicles but were then assailed by shells, mortar bombs, machine-guns, and flame-throwers. To these were soon added huge Tiger tanks. The battle raged for three days and two nights. Half of the original airborne force were killed or badly wounded but as time went on they were joined by signals, sappers, and gunners who had been driven back from their original dropping zones and who now fought as infantry, inspired to heroism by Frost's encouragement and example. Snipers fired at them from the rooftops, the buildings were full of wounded or dead, and they were running short of water. Blood was everywhere but there was a clear resolve to fight to the death. Surprisingly, Frost recalled: 'We were content. Amid the din of continuous fire and crash of falling burning buildings, laughter was often heard' (Frost, A Drop Too Many, 220). When 1st airborne were eventually given orders to surrender or escape, they had had 1130 killed and 6450 (mostly wounded) captured. The Germans, who had themselves had 3300 killed and wounded, praised their opponents and treated them well. Frost, who had been wounded by a mortar bomb, only agreed to surrender when the Germans managed to set on fire the building in which the severely wounded were being sheltered. He spent the next six months in a German hospital, from which he was liberated by the American army in April 1945.

After the war Frost went to Norway to run the battle school of 1st airborne division, from which he returned to command 2 Para again, this time in Palestine on internal security duty. In 1947 he attended the Staff College, Camberley, before becoming GSO2 on the staff of 52nd Lowland division. On his 35th birthday, 31 December 1947, he married Jean MacGregor Lyle (b. 1921/2), daughter of Philip Lyle, sugar refiner. They had a son and a daughter. From 1949 to 1952 Frost attended the senior officers' school; he then spent two years in Malaya during the emergency as GSO1 in 17th Gurkha division. From 1955 to 1957 he commanded the support weapons wing of the school of infantry at Netheravon; he then commanded the 44th Parachute brigade (TA) in London, before being appointed general officer commanding 52nd Lowland division. Finally he was general officer commanding troops in

Malta and Libya and commander, Malta land forces, from 1964 to 1966. He retired from the army with the rank of major-general. He was awarded an MC in 1942, a DSO in 1943 and a bar to it in 1945, and appointed CB in 1964. On retiring from the army he bought a derelict farm in Milland, Hampshire, and with his wife worked hard for many years before making a success of it.

Frost was a quiet, unassuming man, who described himself in Who's Who as a farmer, but was one of the most effective and popular leaders of the Second World War. In his youth he had been a good oarsman who rowed at Henley regatta, was chosen for the Sandhurst modern pentathlon team, learned to fly, and played polo and golf.

Frost thought the Sicily campaign was badly planned, that the Arnhem operation was a mistake, and that the allies should have captured Rotterdam instead. He was also critical of the planning of the 1992 Falklands campaign. His forthright opinions were not popular with diplomatists or politicians and were thought to have prevented his rise to a higher rank. In retirement he was active in church and Conservative Party matters. He was deputy lieutenant for Sussex in 1982.

In the film A Bridge Too Far (1976), about Arnhem, he was portrayed by Anthony Hopkins. In 1977 the Dutch officially renamed the road bridge at Arnhem the John Frostbrug. Frost wrote two volumes of autobiography, A Drop Too Many (1980), and Nearly There (1992), and an account of his old battalion's feats in the south Atlantic campaign of 1982, Two Para—Falklands (1983). He died of prostate cancer at his home, North End Farm, Milland, on 21 May 1993. He was survived by his wife and two children.

PHILIP WARNER

Sources J. D. Frost, A drop too many (1980) · J. D. Frost, Nearly there (1992) · Parachute regiment records · G. Millar, The Bruneval raid (1974) · L. F. Ellis and others, Victory in the West, 2 vols. (1962–8), vol. 2 · I. S. O. Playfair and others, The Mediterranean and Middle East, 6 vols. in 8 (1954–88) · B. Horrocks and others, Corps commander (1977) · The Times (22 May 1993) · The Independent (24 May 1993) · The Independent (29 May 1993) · WWW · m. cert. · d. cert.
Likenesses photograph, repro. in The Times · photograph, repro. in The Independent (24 May 1993)
Wealth at death £319,901: probate, 23 July 1993, CGPLA Eng. & Wales

Frost, Percival (1817–1898), mathematician, was born at Kingston upon Hull on 1 September 1817, the second son of Charles *Frost (bap. 1782, d. 1862), a lawyer and antiquary, and his wife, Jane. He was educated at Beverley and Oakham schools and entered Gonville and Caius College, Cambridge, in October 1835, quickly transferring to St John's. He graduated BA as second wrangler in 1839 and MA in 1842. He was chosen first Smith prizeman in 1839, beating the senior wrangler, Benjamin Morgan Cowie, also of St John's College, and he was elected a fellow of the college on 19 March. In 1841 he was ordained deacon, and in the same year vacated his fellowship on his marriage, in Finchley on 2 June, to Jennett Louise, the daughter of Richard Dixon of Oak Lodge, Finchley. They had a son, Charles Frost (c.1842–1906), a clergyman, who later (1876) adopted the surname Foster, on leaving the church to take up legal training. Frost held a mathematical lectureship in Jesus

College from 1847 to 1859, and in King's College from 1859 to 1889; but his principal work consisted in the tuition of private pupils, among whom were John Rigby, William Kingdon Clifford, and Joseph Wolstenholme.

In 1854 Frost edited the first three sections of book 1 of Newton's *Principia*, and in 1863 he prepared, in conjunction with Joseph Wolstenholme, *A Treatise on Solid Geometry*, later editions of which were by Frost alone. Both of these publications became well-known textbooks. He also wrote numerous minor papers on algebra, analytical geometry, electricity and magnetism, and the theory of the solar system. In 1883 Frost was elected by King's College, Cambridge, to a fellowship (which he retained until his death) and awarded the recently established degree of DSc. On 7 June the same year he was elected a fellow of the Royal Society. He was a man of wide interests and varied attainments, an accomplished piano player, and a successful watercolour painter. He was remembered by his contemporaries as cheerful and considerate, always ready to see the humour in any situation. He died at Cambridge on 5 June 1898, at his house at 15 Fitzwilliam Street, and was buried on 10 June in the Mill Road cemetery.

E. I. CARLYLE, rev. JULIA TOMPSON

Sources H. M. T., *PRS*, 64 (1898–9), vii–viii · H. A. Morgan, *The Eagle*, 20 (1899), 445–8 · *Cambridge Review* (16 June 1898), 405 · *Men and women of the time* (1895) · Venn, *Alum. Cant.*
Likenesses Maull & Fox, sepia photograph, 1891–2, RS
Wealth at death £11,857 18s. 0d.: resworn probate, Nov 1898, CGPLA Eng. & Wales

Frost, William Edward (1810–1877), history painter, the son of James and Elizabeth Frost, was born at Wandsworth, Surrey, in September 1810 and was baptized on 4 November at All Saints' Church, Wandsworth. His father arranged drawing lessons with a neighbouring amateur, Miss Evatt, and about 1825 introduced him to the painter William Etty, who became his mentor. On Etty's recommendation he spent three years studying at the British Museum and at Henry Sass's academy in Charlotte Street, London (1826–9). He entered the Royal Academy Schools in 1829 and assiduously attended the lectures and life school while supporting himself by executing some 300 portraits over the next fourteen years. Preoccupied by academic study and potboiling portraiture, he did not exhibit publicly until 1836, his earliest contributions being portraits.

Having received the academy's gold medal in December 1839 for his painting *Prometheus Bound by Force and Strength*, Frost entered the houses of parliament competition in June 1843, winning a £100 third-prize premium for his cartoon *Una Alarmed by the Fauns and Satyrs*. That same year his academy exhibition picture, *Christ Crowned with Thorns*, was selected by a prize-holder of the Art Union Society, and in 1845 his painting *Sabrina* was engraved for the Art Union. Admiration for *Diana and Actaeon* at the 1846 Royal Academy exhibition helped secure his election as an ARA that November. He then abandoned portraiture to concentrate on imaginative paintings of mythological and allegorical themes drawn principally from John Milton and Edmund Spenser. Semi-nude female figures dominate

these works and attest to Frost's interpolation of live, undraped models with classical statuary. His landscape backgrounds show similar idealization of nature studies, such as those he occasionally exhibited at the Royal Academy and the British Institution. He commanded high prices and found ready patronage among aristocrats and middle-class industrialists alike. Queen Victoria paid £420 for *Una among the Fairies and Wood-Nymphs* (1847) and subsequently commissioned two more pictures.

Twenty-four years intervened between Frost's election as an associate and his attainment of the full rank of academician on 30 June 1870. He expressed his frustration in a watercolour captioned *All Hope Abandon Ye who Enter Here*, in which a stately audience of academicians gazes down imperiously on a riot of infighting associates. Drawings such as this retain the spontaneous energy that Frost refined away from his oil paintings. Intimately familiar with Etty's methods and ideas, he was a principal source for the older artist's biography, and critics invariably compared his work to Etty's. John Ruskin chastised Frost for 'multiplying studies of this kind, looking like Etty's with all the colour scraped off' (*Academy Notes*, 1856, 55). Other critics lauded the pearly delicacy and cold polish of his pictures for a purity absent from Etty's more robust and voluptuous imagery. Increasingly, however, critics complained of Frost's repetition of a limited number of artificial subjects and compositions. Although cloying, these conventions helped side-step the moral minefield which menaced painters of the nude. In June 1876 Frost voluntarily retired from the Royal Academy, where he had exhibited some seventy-seven works, together with thirty-three at the British Institution and two at the Society of British Artists.

Frost collected engravings after Thomas Stothard's drawings and collaborated with Henry Reeve in cataloguing the art collection of H. A. J. Munro of Novar (published 1865). 'A most amiable man', Frost was esteemed for 'modesty, gentleness, and amiability of disposition' (*Art Journal*, 1877). He never married and lived a retired existence with his unmarried sister Elizabeth, who became sole executor upon his death on 4 June 1877 at his home, 40 Fitzroy Square, London. Frost's studio sale at Christies on 14 March 1878 included 100 of his works, as well as his copies after old masters.

ROBYN ASLESON

Sources *Art Journal*, 39 (1877) · *The Academy* (16 June 1877), 543–4 · *The Times* (8 June 1877) · *The Athenaeum* (9 June 1877), 744 · O. Millar, *The Victorian pictures in the collection of her majesty the queen*, 2 vols. (1992) · W. Sandby, *The history of the Royal Academy of Arts*, 2 vols. (1862) · A. Gilchrist, *Life of William Etty, RA*, 2 vols. (1855) · D. Farr, *William Etty* (1958) · Graves, *RA exhibitors* · Graves, *Brit. Inst.* · A. Smith, *The Victorian nude: sexuality, morality and art* (1996) · C. Knight, ed., *The English cyclopaedia: biography*, 2 (1856) · R. N. James, *Painters and their works*, 3 vols. (1896–7) · 'British artists, their style and character: no. XXI, William Edward Frost', *Art Journal*, 19 (1857), 5–7 · *Art Journal*, 11 (1849), 184 · IGI · d. cert. · CGPLA Eng. & Wales (1877) · DNB
Archives York Central Reference Library, York, Etty MSS
Likenesses photograph, c.1831 (after a self-portrait by W. E. Frost), NPG · W. E. Frost, self-portrait, pencil and watercolour drawing, 1839, NPG · woodcut, c.1839–1841 (after a self-portrait by

W. E. Frost), repro. in 'William Edward Frost' · albumen photograph, c.1852, Jeremy Maas Coll.; repro. in J. Maas, *Victorian Art World in photographs* (1984) · Elliott & Fry, carte-de-visite, NPG · J. & C. Watkins, carte photograph, NPG · wood-engraving (after a photograph by J. Watkins), NPG; repro. in *ILN* (21 Jan 1871) · woodcut (after T. Scott), BM

Wealth at death under £1500: resworn probate, 25 Aug 1879, *CGPLA Eng. & Wales* (1877)

Froucester, Walter (d. 1412), abbot of St Peter's, Gloucester, presumably took his name from Frocester, some 12 miles south of Gloucester. Both the parish church and the manor pertained to the Benedictine abbey. The date of his admission to the abbey remains uncertain, as no monk of this name occurs in the surviving ordination lists, but he held the office of chamberlain at the time of his election as abbot on 17 January 1382.

According to an anonymous abbey chronicle, Froucester proved to be an able administrator, who succeeded not only in relieving his house of the greater part of a debt of 8000 florins inherited from his predecessors, but also in restoring the abbey's prosperity and enhancing its prestige. He supervised the completion of the monastery's famous cloisters, authorized repairs and additions to the manorial buildings, replenished the manorial stock, and arranged for improvements to several of the abbatial country residences. Noted for his skill in defending and promoting the abbey's rights and privileges, he successfully pleaded insufficient income for the support of a large community of monks and servants as a means of obtaining the appropriation of several churches. Moreover, on the strength of the obligations requiring him to officiate daily at the shrine of Edward II, Froucester obtained exemption for life from personal attendance at meetings of the king's council and parliament. Like other important prelates he maintained a representative at the papal curia, in his case William Bryt, one of his fellow monks, who was required to keep him informed and promote the abbey's interests. With support from Thomas of Woodstock, duke of Gloucester, Froucester received from Pope Urban VI the privileges of a mitred abbot. He was vested in the pontifical regalia for the first time on 10 April 1390, at the solemnities celebrating the translation of relics of the young virgin St Cyneburga, who had been martyred at Gloucester at an unknown date.

Froucester's initiative was responsible for a new recension of and additions to the abbey chronicle, which contains biographical accounts of the abbots from the Norman Serlo (d. 1104) down to Froucester himself, and also a record of the properties donated to St Peter's. W. H. Hart's edition of this chronicle, published in the Rolls Series (33, 1863–7) was based on two surviving manuscripts, but there is also a third, now in Gloucester Cathedral Library (MS 34), which was bought by the dean and chapter in 1879. Two contemporary registers, both compiled in the 1390s and also preserved in the cathedral library, are evidence of Froucester's personal involvement in the reorganization of the abbey muniments; Register A is a collection of charters and of documents concerning appropriations, Register B a record of the lands assigned as income for ten of the obedientiary offices.

Abbot Froucester is praised in the chronicle for his generous gifts of vestments and ornaments to the abbey church, and for presenting books to the monastic library. He died in April 1412, and his grateful community honoured his memory with a daily mass in his newly constructed chantry, dedicated to All Saints, at the south-western end of the abbey choir under the tower arch, where he is buried; a second chantry for him was established at the dependent priory of St Guthlac, Hereford. The sermon preached at his funeral by his fellow monk John Paunteley has been preserved in Bodl. Oxf., MS Laud misc. 706, fols. 13–20. As well as referring to Froucester's administrative skills, it praises him as a man of peace who was close to his brethren.

JOAN GREATREX

Sources W. H. Hart, ed., *Historia et cartularium monasterii Sancti Petri Gloucestriae*, 3 vols., Rolls Series, 33 (1863–7) · *VCH Gloucestershire*, vol. 2 · *Chancery records* · *CEPR letters*, vol. 4 · Dugdale, *Monasticon*, vol. 1 · G. R. C. Davies, *Medieval cartularies of Great Britain* (1958) · D. Walker, ed., 'A register of the churches of the monastery of St Peter's, Gloucester', *An ecclesiastical miscellany*, Bristol and Gloucestershire Archaeological Society Records Section, 11 (1976), 1–58 · C. Brooke, 'St. Peter of Gloucester and St. Cadoc of Llancarfan', *Celt and Saxon: studies in the early British border*, ed. N. K. Chadwick (1963), 258–322 · T. D. Fosbroke, *A history of the city of Gloucester* (1819) · S. M. Eward, *A catalogue of Gloucester Cathedral Library* (1972) · A. Gransden, *Historical writing in England*, 2 (1982) · R. Sharpe and others, eds., *English Benedictine libraries: the shorter catalogues* (1996) · D. Welander, *The history, art and architecture of Gloucester cathedral* (1991) · Muniments of the Dean and Chapter of Gloucester, MS 34

Froud, Ethel Elizabeth (1880–1941), feminist and trade unionist, was born on 11 April 1880 at The Willows, Loose, Maidstone, Kent, the daughter of George Christopher Froud, a butcher, and his wife, Frances Danells. Nothing is known of her education before she became a class teacher in the West Ham borough of east London. She campaigned unsuccessfully inside the National Union of Teachers (NUT) locally and nationally for the union to support the franchise for women. She was a speaker for the Women Teachers' Franchise Union and a member of its committee between 1915 and 1917. Having also joined the feminist National Federation of Women Teachers, then a pressure group inside the NUT, she became its honorary secretary in 1913, taking over from Joseph Tate. In 1917 she resigned her teaching post and became the first full-time salaried secretary of the federation. She helped to lead the breakaway of the federation from the NUT and to establish the National Union of Women Teachers (NUWT) as a feminist autonomous union.

Ethel Froud was a militant suffragist in the Women's Social and Political Union (WSPU) and a member of the fife and drum band, led by drum major Mary Leigh. She spoke for the suffrage at meetings and on one occasion was protected by railway officials from the fury of a mob by being locked into a waiting room until her train arrived. She was a 'brilliant platform speaker' (Phipps, 89), whose oratorical skills were admired even by her detractors. She addressed demonstrations of teachers campaigning for equal pay in Trafalgar Square on several occasions, as well as speaking at indoor meetings throughout the country. However, she was also a good organizer and skilled at creating harmony and a sense of unified purpose within the NUWT, which she represented in many joint campaigns with other feminist groups (particularly the Six Point Group and the Open Door Council) during the 1920s. She was the vice-chair of the Equal Political Rights Campaign committee; she spoke in this capacity at the Trafalgar Square demonstration for equal suffrage in July 1927 and led the last deputation to the prime minister on the full franchise for women under thirty. She represented the NUWT at meetings of the International Women's Suffrage Alliance in Paris in May 1926.

Ethel Froud stood unsuccessfully in an individual capacity for St Pancras borough council in November 1925 on the Labour Party platform since she believed that women should take more part in public affairs. The slogan of her election campaign was 'deeds not words', the slogan of the WSPU. She was a member of the Teachers' Labour League, although very critical of its equivocation over equal pay, and was part of a delegation organized by the league to investigate the state of education in the Soviet Union in 1926. She was impressed by the communal provision, equal pay for women teachers, and maternity leave she saw there, calling her visit 'One of the most interesting experiences in my life' (letter to Mr Hawkins, 7 Feb 1929, NUWT Archives). Although she spoke on the topic to NUWT branches she declined to write an introduction to a book produced by the league since it might offend some NUWT members.

Ethel Froud never married. She seemed to be happy with this state, writing that 'we can't have it said that we celibates are only some fraction of a human being' (letter quoted in Oram, 117). On her retirement in 1940 she moved to the Sussex Downs, naming her house in Saltdean Rhondhurst after the militant suffrage leaders Viscountess Rhondda and Emmeline Pankhurst. She died there on 21 May 1941 and was cremated at Brighton crematorium on the 24th.

Ethel Froud inspired other women, showing them that women could organize, conduct meetings, speak, and influence public opinion. She believed that hard work brought its own rewards, having the following inscription in stained glass in her office at the NUWT headquarters: 'The dreams of those that labour are the only ones that ever come true' (*Woman Teacher*, 13 June 1941, 232).

HILDA KEAN

Sources U. Lond., Institute of Education, National Union of Women Teachers archive · H. Kean, *Deeds not words: the lives of suffragette teachers* (1990) · *Woman Teacher* (28 Jan 1927) · *Woman Teacher* (5 Oct 1928), 3–4 · *Woman Teacher* (13 June 1941) · E. Phipps, *The history of the NUWT* (1928) · *The Vote* (24 April 1914) · *The Vote* (26 March 1920) · *The Vote* (2 April 1920), 4 · *The Vote* (23 Oct 1926), 340 · *The Vote* (11 Feb 1927) · *The Vote* (11 March 1927) · *The Vote* (18 March 1927) · *The Vote* (20 May 1927) · *The Vote* (16 July 1927) · A. M. Pierotti, *The story of the NUWT* (1963) · Minutes of Central Council NFWT, March 1917 · *New Schoolmaster*, 5/33 (July 1924) · A. Oram, 'Embittered, sexless or homosexual? Attacks on spinster teachers, 1918–1939', *Not a passing phase: reclaiming lesbians in history, 1840–1985*, ed. Lesbian History Group (1989), 99–118 · H. Kean, *Challenging the state: the socialist and feminist educational experience* (1990) · b. cert. · d. cert. · *CGPLA Eng. & Wales* (1941)

Archives U. Lond., Institute of Education, National Union of Women Teachers archive

Likenesses photograph, repro. in *Woman Teacher* (13 June 1941), 232 · photographs, U. Lond., Institute of Education, National Union of Women Teachers Archives [box 470] · photographs, repro. in C. Broom and D. Atkinson, *Mrs Broom's suffragette photographs* [n.d.], 14, 17

Wealth at death £1939 3s. 0d.: probate, 25 July 1941, *CGPLA Eng. & Wales*

Froude, (Richard) Hurrell (1803–1836), Church of England clergyman, was born on 25 March 1803 at Dartington parsonage in Devon. He was the son of the Revd Robert Hurrell Froude (1770/71–1859), later archdeacon of Totnes, and his wife, Margaret (1774/5–1821), daughter of John and Margaret Spedding of Armathwaite Hall, Keswick. Hurrell (the Christian name by which he was always known) was the first of eight children, most of whom died prematurely though two survived to attain distinction, William *Froude (1810–1879) as an engineer and James Anthony *Froude (1818–1894) as a historian. The latter wrote a vivid account of how he was cruelly teased as a boy by his eldest brother, Hurrell, whom he nevertheless worshipped. Despite the discipline imposed by their stern father, who banned *Pilgrim's Progress* from the house because it was vulgarly outspoken, Hurrell was no doubt a tempestuous and troublesome youth. But he learned the duty of holiness from his mother, whom he revered with all the ardour of his romantic nature.

From 1812 Froude (pronounced frood) was educated at the free school, Ottery St Mary, and in 1816 he was sent to Eton College. There, he was later ashamed to say, he never felt the notorious John Keate's birch, the headmaster having a weakness for really clever pupils. Yet Froude was not to be an outstanding scholar: in 1821 he went up to Oriel College, Oxford, as a commoner, and his devout tutor, John Keble, taught him to value moral above mental qualities. Froude graduated BA in 1824, gaining only a second class in both classics and mathematics.

Still, Froude was a bold rider over intellectual as well as rural countryside. Although his learning was varied rather than wide or deep, his 'originality of thought and brilliancy of expression' left on his contemporaries, W. J. Copeland wrote, 'the conviction that "if ever there was a genius he was one"'. And at Easter 1826 he was elected, after examination, to a fellowship at Oriel. In the following year he took his MA degree and became a college tutor. About the same time he experienced a religious crisis which took the form of corrosive self-denial and morbid self-analysis. He recorded details of his anguished condition in a penitential journal, which provoked mockery after his death among writers ranging from Sir James Stephen to Lytton Strachey. It also gave rise to unsubstantiated suspicions, notably expressed by Sir Geoffrey Faber in his book *Oxford Apostles* (1933), that the crisis stemmed from homosexual guilt. In fact, Froude became the first champion of celibacy—the revival of this and other Catholic ideals coming to constitute the Oxford Movement. By influencing another Oriel tutor, John Henry Newman, towards these ideals and bringing him into friendship with Keble, Froude became a vital catalyst in the movement.

In the 1830s, with a reforming whig government in power, when the Church of England seemed threatened by a liberal, Erastian state, Newman was especially struck by Froude's hatred of the protestant Reformation and his reverence for sacramental tradition as the basis for ecclesiastical authority. He was also charmed by the force and versatility of Froude's mind, by the grace of his character and appearance, and by his 'keen appreciation of the idea of sanctity, its possibility and its heights'.

Froude, who was ordained deacon in 1828 and priest the following year, allied with Newman in trying to augment the pastoral function of the tutor's office. The provost of Oriel, Edward Hawkins, opposed the change and in 1830 he evicted them from the tutorship, thus undermining the intellectual ascendancy of his college. The next year Froude showed the first unmistakable symptoms of the tuberculosis that would kill him. During the winter of 1832–3 he travelled to the Mediterranean, accompanied by his father and Newman, in search of health. Abroad Froude and Newman began to write religious poems, known as the 'Lyra apostolica', for the *British Magazine*. Froude's contributions were signed β and imbued, at their best, with a vehement nostalgia for the Middle Ages: attracted by the medievalism of Robert Southey and Walter Scott and (in Newman's words in *Apologia*) 'smitten with the love of the theocratic church', he looked back to an age when the church seemed to constitute an integral part of an organic and harmonious feudal society.

On his return to Oxford (before Newman) Froude opened the 'Apostolical' campaign in defence of high-church principles. He stirred up Keble, whose 'National Apostasy' sermon, in July 1833, inaugurated the Oxford Movement. Froude placed himself in its van, urging the production of what became the Tracts for the Times. He himself wrote Tracts 9, 59, 63 and possibly 8, as well as a rough draft of Tract 75, which Newman completed. However, as Dean Church noted, 'Froude was made for conflict, not to win disciples.' Although he has been described as the Tractarian leader, his chief role was to inspire Newman and Keble from a distance.

Between autumn 1833 and spring 1835 Froude vainly sought recovery in Barbados. On a final visit to Oxford, his friend Tom Mozley observed in his *Reminiscences*, he was 'full of energy and fire, sunburnt, but a shadow' (1.347). He died at Dartington parsonage on 28 February 1836 and was buried on 3 March at Dartington Old Church. Surviving only into his early thirties, Froude had not had time to shed the callowness and intolerance of his youth, but his close friends remembered only his singular attraction. 'Who can refrain from tears', Newman's sister Harriett wrote elegiacally, 'at the thought of that bright and beautiful Froude?' (Guiney, 199).

Nothing came of plans to raise a memorial to Froude, and only two sketchy likenesses of him survive. But in 1839 Newman and Keble caused a storm by publishing the first of four volumes of Froude's *Remains*, including outspoken passages from his journal. Clearly anticipating the controversy which followed, Newman (and possibly Keble too) intended the work to provide a focus and a touchstone for the Oxford Movement. Denounced by low-churchmen as papistical, it alarmed the bishops and embarrassed the 'high-and-dry' clergy who had been hitherto the lukewarm allies of the Tractarians. The *Remains* by no means proved that Froude would have converted to Rome, although some of its admirers—including W. G. Ward and Frederick Oakeley—did; indeed, some of its readers—such as J. B. Mozley and R. W. Church—were to be important liberal Anglo-Catholics. But the work certainly did impel the Oxford Movement towards daring new extremes. It also posthumously fulfilled Froude's ironic ambition to become an 'ecclesiastical agitator'.

PIERS BRENDON

Sources R. H. Froude, *Remains of the late Reverend Richard Hurrell Froude, MA fellow of Oriel College, Oxford*, ed. J. H. Newman and J. Keble, 4 vols. (1838–9) • J. H. Newman, *Apologia pro vita sua* (1864) • *The letters and diaries of John Henry Newman*, ed. C. S. Dessain and others, [31 vols.] (1961–), vols. 2–6 • P. Brendon, *Hurrell Froude and the Oxford Movement* (1974) • L. I. Guiney, *Hurrell Froude* (1904) • T. Mozley, *Reminiscences, chiefly of Oriel College and the Oxford Movement*, 2nd edn, 2 vols. (1882) • W. H. Dunn, *James Anthony Froude: a biography*, 2 vols. (1961–3) • *Cardinal Newman and William Froude, FRS: a correspondence*, ed. G. H. Harper (1933) • G. Faber, *Oxford Apostles: a character study of the Oxford Movement* (1954) • J. T. Coleridge, *A memoir of the Rev. John Keble*, 2nd edn, 2 vols. (1869) • R. W. Church, *The Oxford Movement: twelve years, 1833–1845* (1891) • P. Gauthier, *La pensée religieuse de Richard Hurrell Froude* (1977) • W. J. Copeland, 'History of the Oxford Movement', Pusey Oxf.

Archives Birmingham Oratory, corresp. with family, J. H. Newman, Samuel Wilberforce and R. I. Wilberforce, and Isaac Williams • Keble College, Oxford, Froude corresp. | Bodl. Oxf., letters to Samuel Wilberforce • LPL, William Froude MSS • LPL, Golightly MSS • Oriel College, Oxford, Hawkins corresp. • Pusey Oxf., Pusey corresp., MSS

Likenesses W. Brockedon, portrait (as a boy, unfinished), repro. in Guiney, *Hurrell Froude* • M. Giberne, pencil sketch, repro. in Brendon, *Hurrell Froude*

Froude, James Anthony (1818–1894), historian and man of letters, was born at Dartington rectory, Devon, on 23 April 1818. His father, Robert Hurrell Froude (1770/71–1859), son of Robert Froude of Walkhampton, Devon, and his wife, Phyllis Hurrell, graduated BA from Oriel College, Oxford, in 1792 and MA in 1795. He was rector of Denbury from 1798 and of Dartington from 1799, and archdeacon of Totnes from 1820 to his death on 23 February 1859 (*GM*; Boase, *Mod. Eng. biog.*). He married Margaret Spedding (1774/5–1821) of Mirehouse, Cumberland, a relative of James Spedding. They had eight children: five sons, (Richard) Hurrell *Froude (1803–1836), Robert (1804–1828), John, William *Froude (1810–1879), and James Anthony; and three daughters, Margaret, who became the wife of William Mallock, and Phillis and Mary, who died young. James Anthony was only two when his mother died (16 February 1821), and he was the youngest in the family. He was a sickly child. But the Froudes were 'a Spartan family. Whipping was always resorted to as the prompt consequence of naughtiness' (Dunn, 1.17). His brother Hurrell tried to toughen him up by holding him by the heels over a stream and stirring the mud at the bottom with his head. Archdeacon Froude had a moderate private income and

James Anthony Froude (1818–1894), by Sir George Reid, 1881

combined his religious duties with those of a landowner, but the post-war depression forced economies. James Anthony remembered his mother's carriage gathering mould in the stable. But a governess taught the children Latin and arithmetic at home in their early years.

Early life; Oxford; theological controversy In 1827 Froude was sent to the nearby Buckfastleigh School, where he made progress in Latin and Greek and was thought precocious. As his elder brother William had been a scholar at Westminster the archdeacon decided that his youngest son should go there too. The boy was not yet twelve. As a king's scholar he was cast, a rather frail boy five years younger than the rest of his class, into the roughhouse of college, along with forty other boys. He was mercilessly bullied and starved, and his health repeatedly broke down. His books were stolen, his work deteriorated. His ordeal lasted three and a half years. No authorities in the school intervened to soften the hardship he suffered. Even when his father realized that he must be withdrawn he held the boy personally responsible for his poor reports, for his depleted state, for gaps in his wardrobe, for costly bills and lost books. He was ordered to sign a confession and, when he refused to extend it, was severely beaten by his father, with brother Hurrell 'standing by and approving'. His main consolation was 'that the consumption which had proved so deadly in our family and was already working in [Hurrell's] constitution, was beginning to

show itself, and would soon take me away' (Dunn, 1.39). For two years he was kept at home, largely ignored by his father and with no companions but books. He read voraciously. His health recovered. His father told him, though 'with unchanged distrust', that he could have another chance. He was sent to a private tutor to be prepared for Oxford, and he was admitted to Oriel College in June 1835, matriculating in December.

Hurrell Froude died of consumption two months later, but his views on church and state were shared and elaborated by J. H. Newman, who naturally looked on his old friend's youngest brother as a possible recruit to the Tractarian movement. James however refused to be drawn. He respected Newman, and later contributed a *Life of St Neot* to Newman's series of lives of the English saints, but his upbringing had given him a cross-grained tenacity in his own chosen course. He saw that Tractarianism had exposed the barrenness of his father's churchmanship, but it also promoted the febrile extremism of Hurrell's views. His own sympathies went the other way: he approved of the English Reformation and its doctrine, while the German theological scholarship which Newman and Pusey feared became more and more attractive to him. Two experiences reinforced this tendency. In 1839 he fell in love with Harriet, the daughter of the Revd James Bush, and the two considered themselves engaged until the parents on both sides intervened and (for what exact reason is not clear) broke off the engagement. But it represented nevertheless a repudiation of the ideal of celibacy which some Tractarians held. Froude gave a fictional account of the affair in an autobiographical novel, *Shadows of the Clouds* (1847). In 1840 he was placed in the second class in *literae humaniores*. Soon after this he went to Ireland as a tutor to the sons of an evangelical protestant clergyman, the Revd William Cleaver, where he experienced a way of life very different from the caricature of evangelical living which prevailed in Tractarian circles, and on a tour of the south-west and west formed an impression of the conditions of the Irish peasantry and of the Catholic church the reverse of that formed by Newman and Hurrell Froude in Italy a decade previously. From this experience may be dated the views which found eventual expression in *The English in Ireland*.

Froude returned to Oxford in 1841 and took his BA on 28 April 1842. He won the chancellor's prize for an English essay and was elected a fellow of Exeter College. Outside Oriel he became bolder in his theological views, reading the German romantics and Lessing, Strauss, and Schleiermacher, and discovering the work of Thomas Carlyle. What he found liberating in Carlyle, he recalled, was the fact that he asked of every institution not whether it was true but whether it was alive. At first this seemed quite compatible with a career in the church. In 1845 Froude took deacon's orders, without which he could not retain his fellowship. But he soon realized that this was a mistake. While his brother's friends followed Newman to Rome he had more sympathy with the followers of Thomas Arnold, who wanted the Church of England to be more inclusive and more responsive to social issues. He was friendly with Mark Pattison, A. H. Clough, Matthew Arnold, and A. P. Stanley. In the summer of 1845 he went on a long tour of Ireland with George Butler, the future husband of Josephine Butler the social reformer, a trip on which both contracted an infection which they believed to be smallpox. On his return to Oxford he decided he could not take priest's orders, but must seek a more active life. He wanted to read medicine, but found that as a deacon he was barred by statute from any of the other learned professions. 'Deacon I was, and deacon I must remain, hung like Mahomet's coffin between earth and heaven' (Dunn, 1.95). For a time he considered a post as headmaster of a school in Hobart, Tasmania.

Froude's frustration and uncertainty were expressed in *The Nemesis of Faith* (1849; 2nd edn same year), part autobiography, part protest against the requirement to take orders. Its hero, Markham Sutherland, is, like Froude, the nonconformist in a large family of conformists. 'His mind was wider than theirs, little as they thought it was; and he could make allowance for the unkindness which was wounding him, while they could make none for his disappointing their hopes, and being so unlike themselves' (2nd edn, p. 82). Sutherland thinks the teachings of the church have ossified into meaningless dogmas out of touch with the modern age, but against his better judgement he allows himself to be persuaded by his father to take orders. His first parishioners note that his first sermons are Socinian and report him to their bishop, who summons him, hears him make a clean breast of his lack of vocation, and recommends that he give up his curacy and go abroad. In Italy he meets and falls in love with a young married Englishwoman. To escape from the consequences he enters the Roman church while she goes into a convent, where she dies.

The book caused a scandal in Oxford. Broad-churchmen like F. D. Maurice and J. M. Ludlow and the German Baron von Bunsen sympathized with Froude; but Archbishop Whately and Bishop Hampden seized on the book as illustrating the evil effects of Tractarianism. High-churchmen denounced it as heretical. On 27 February 1849 William Sewell, sub-rector of Exeter College, seeing it during a lecture in an undergraduate's possession, took it and put it on the fire. Froude resigned his fellowship the same day. He also gave up the post in Hobart. His father cut off his allowance. Froude was now quite alone. He considered himself a layman and asked friends not to address him as 'the Reverend', although it was not until 1872 with the passing of the Clergy Disabilities Relief Act that he formally shed his deacon's orders.

Marriage; influence of Carlyle; early works For some months after leaving Oxford, Froude was tutor to the Darbishire family in Manchester, for which he earned £150 a year. In February he visited his friend Charles Kingsley at Ilfracombe, where he met Mrs Kingsley's sister Charlotte Maria Grenfell (d. 1860), fifth daughter of Pascoe Grenfell of Taplow Court, Buckinghamshire. He also formed a warm friendship with his employer's daughter Marianne Darbishire and at one point seems to have had to choose between the two. On 3 October 1849 he married Charlotte Grenfell at St Peter's, Belgrave Square. 'I conquered my wife', he later told Clough, 'from Romanism and a convent' (Dunn, 1.162). He also encountered opposition from her family, but at least she was financially independent with her own income of £300 a year. On this together with his teaching they first thought they could live in Manchester, but neither liked the city. 'We hate Manchester', he wrote, 'Manchester in any form—Unitarian Manchester most of all' (ibid., 167). In the spring of 1850 they toured north Wales and decided to take a home, Plas Gwynant, in the valley of the Gwynant, in the shadow of Snowdon. They lived there until October 1853, and these three years were among the happiest of Froude's life: 'if any good has since come out of me, the seeds of it were planted in those years' (Dunn, 1.169), he later recalled. He began to write for a living. Visitors included the Kingsleys, Matthew Arnold, Clough, F. T. Palgrave, and Max Müller.

A new personal connection was Carlyle, to whom Froude had been introduced by James Spedding in London in June 1849. This meeting was a landmark in Froude's career. Froude's critics have portrayed him as an uncritical disciple of Carlyle, and there was certainly conscious discipleship on Froude's side and close agreement between the two men on several issues. Froude shared Carlyle's idea that societies decay when a dominant creed loses its original *élan* and hardens into mere outward forms and conventions. He thought too that the best way of delaying this decay was a candid observation of 'reality' and hard fact. Orthodoxy in the form of a list of *credenda* was a fatal mistake: 'the one great Bible which cannot lie is the history of the human race' (Froude, *Nemesis*, xii). He embraced Carlyle's 'gospel of work', sympathizing with his attack on industrialism expressed in *Past and Present*, and hating industrial cities as dehumanizing and demoralizing to the poor. Unearned wealth brought a train of disabilities no less damaging to the rich and well-born. He echoed Carlyle's disdain for parliament and for party politics. But it seems unlikely that the young man who had resisted what he called Newman's 'siren song' would have succumbed uncritically to the harsher melodies of Carlyle. Froude did not become a regular visitor to Carlyle's house until he settled in London in 1860, by which time his first major historical work on the Tudor period was half complete. Furthermore, it originated in the Tractarian *débâcle*, which in many ways provided the main themes of Froude's career as a writer. Both men thought history provided the clue to the intentions of providence, but Froude interpreted this less radically than Carlyle. He did not favour destruction for its own sake, any more than he admired authority backed by mere force. Carlyle's rough denunciation of conformity and cant made him in some ways an isolated figure in Victorian society. Froude retained a strong affection for the institutions in which he had been brought up, keeping up old contacts despite disagreement; he even returned to Exeter College in 1858 and placidly signed the Thirty-Nine Articles as an honorary fellow. He also stood aloof from the controversy which broke in 1865 over Governor Eyre, in which Carlyle was at odds with the bulk of liberal opinion. Above all Froude's writings avoided Carlyle's prophetic note. He wrote the easy fluent prose appropriate to a professional writer who covers everything from theology to travelogue, and most of his faults stemmed from haste.

At Plas Gwynant Froude embarked on the study of the English Reformation, the main labour of his life. He had also to write for periodicals as his family increased. A daughter, Georgina Margaret, was born at Taplow Court on 13 September 1850 (d. 10 May 1935). A second daughter, Rose Mary, was born on 6 May 1852. At first Froude was willing to write for any publisher who paid well. His earliest articles appeared in the radical *Westminster Review* edited by John Chapman, which took his first foray into the sixteenth century, 'England's forgotten worthies' (July 1852), and a review of Matthew Arnold's *Poems* (January 1854) which did much to establish Arnold's reputation. But Froude was not a political radical: though the European revolutions of 1848 had coincided with his own spiritual crisis he had read the early French socialists like Louis Blanc and was well aware of the ferment in European liberalism. But he was unsympathetic to its English counterpart; he could not share his brother-in-law Kingsley's enthusiasm for Chartism, and disliked the cult of material progress enshrined in the Great Exhibition of 1851. A radical in religion only, he distrusted popular opinion as the soil of superstition and priestcraft. To him the Reformation was a great liberation, but it was the achievement of two strong sovereigns, Henry VIII and Elizabeth I, 'backed by the strongest and bravest of their subjects', and, he added, 'up to the defeat of the Armada, manhood suffrage in England would have brought back the Pope' (Dunn, 1.202). Lacking any sympathy for industrialism and the economic ideals of Cobden and Bright, Froude did not see protestantism, as modern historians have, as the seedbed of capitalism; nor yet as the revival of the true faith, but as the end of cant and insincerity in England's rulers, and consequently as a prelude to the release of that energy which would enable Englishmen to conquer and colonize the world. Protestantism was not so much a doctrine as a release from doctrine, sought by simple men whose daily contact with real life made them impatient with grand impostures.

The first two volumes of Froude's *History of England from the Fall of Wolsey to the Death of Elizabeth* came out in 1856. Further volumes appeared in pairs in 1858, 1860, 1863, 1866, and 1870. Before he published volume 11 Froude decided that the defeat of the Spanish Armada would be a more appropriate end to the story of the defeat of Catholicism and he altered the title. After an uncertain début the *History of England* was a great success, to some extent emulating Macaulay's. But Macaulay's tone was brisk and materialistic; Froude's was more gentle, more diffident and elegiac, drawing on the religious controversies of his youth, but reflecting the mid-Victorian public's exhaustion with doctrinal controversy. Its main theme was anticlerical, but it was not irreligious. For its prose it soon became a classic. A second edition of the first two volumes was issued in 1858, a third edition of volumes 1–4, 7, and 8

in 1862–4, and a cabinet edition of the whole in 1870. The twelve volumes were issued in a cheaper form in 1881–2, with a new edition in 1893.

Froude's critics, however, were many. Goldwin Smith, who had just taken the regius chair in modern history for which Froude had applied, wrote a severe and anonymous review of the first four volumes in the *Edinburgh Review* for July 1858, to which Froude wrote a signed reply in *Fraser's Magazine* for September 1858. From 1860 E. A. Freeman set out on a now notorious policy, pursued over two decades, of destroying Froude's credit as a historian, in a series of articles in the *Saturday Review*, to which Froude finally wrote a dignified reply in 1879. There was also much praise, notably a eulogy by Kingsley in *Macmillan's Magazine* for January 1860, an article which contained the notorious reference to Newman which led to the composition of the *Apologia pro vita sua*. Froude's earlier career had given hostages to fortune, and he had many enemies, especially in Oxford, but in his method he was ahead of most of his critics. He was widely read, not only in the traditional ancient literature, but in German, French, and Spanish. He wrote like a man of wide culture, not as a narrow specialist, and did not hesitate to draw parallels with social and political movements of his own day. At the same time he drew his materials from sources never before used and only beginning to be catalogued and edited—in the Rolls House (later the Public Record Office); in the British Museum; and for later stages of his *History* in the Spanish archives at Simancas, where, he recalled, he had often 'found the sand glittering on the ink where it had been sprinkled when a page was turned. There the letter had lain, never looked at again since it was read and put away' (Dunn, 2.581). Froude wrote for a public with an appetite for historical detail vividly portrayed, and he applied Carlyle's dictum, 'Events should speak. Commentary ought to be sparing' (ibid.). Any critic who took exception to his views (which were not strident or obtruded) had to contend with an intimidating volume of novel evidence. They found many mistakes, for Froude did his own transcriptions and worked and wrote rapidly, but few attempted a complete critical appraisal in Froude's lifetime. Even Cardinal Gasquet's *Henry VIII and the English Monasteries* (2 vols., 1888–9) chose to criticize only a part of the *History*.

Froude found that his work drew him more and more to London, but his wife disliked town life and probably suffered from it. In October 1853 they left Wales and settled in a cottage in Babbacombe, near Torquay, where Mrs Froude had a sister. A son, Pascoe Grenfell Froude, 'with whom no good could be done' (Dunn, 2.613), was born in Torquay on 10 February 1854; he died in south Africa on 1 December 1879. In May 1854 the cottage was destroyed by fire and the Froudes moved to Northdown, near Bideford. There Froude completed the *History* up to the reign of Mary Tudor. His literary success seems to have led to a reconciliation with his father before the latter's death. But it was from Charlotte Froude's family that help came when needed. Her sister Caroline Grenfell became the third wife of John Ashley Warre MP, and when Charlotte fell suddenly and died at Taplow Court on 21 April 1860 it was Caroline and a half-sister, Henrietta, who took care of the Froude children. That summer Froude took a London house at 5 Clifton Place, near Hyde Park. He had formed a close friendship with his publisher, J. W. Parker, and his son, and he had written articles for *Fraser's Magazine*, which the Parkers owned and the younger Parker edited. But in November 1860 the son died, Froude having 'nursed him like a brother till the moment of death' (C. Kingsley, *Life and Letters*, 2.105). He was then persuaded to take over the editorship of *Fraser's*, and he held it until 1874. This not only gave him a considerable influence in London's literary culture, but it enabled him to travel in search of material for his books. In the summer of 1861 he went to Spain with his brother-in-law John Warre to work in the archives at Simancas. After his return, on 12 September 1861, he married Henrietta Elizabeth Warre (*d*. 1874), and settled into 5 Clifton Place. With his second wife he had a son, Ashley Anthony (1863–1949), and a daughter, May. In 1865 he took a house at 5 Onslow Gardens, Kensington, where he remained until he moved to Cherwell Edge, Oxford, in 1892. In the summer months he rented a house in the country, at first in Scotland and Ireland, and afterwards for many years at The Moult, Salcombe, Devon. There he built a small yacht, which he sailed himself; he was also an expert angler and excellent shot.

The growing reputation of Froude's *History* quickly brought him great social consideration. In 1859 he was elected by the committee a member of the Athenaeum. In February 1866 he was an original member of the Breakfast Club, of which Sir James Lacaita was the founder (Grant Duff); he was also a member of The Club. In November 1868 he was elected rector of St Andrews; his inaugural address, delivered on 19 March 1869, and his final address, 'On Calvinism', delivered on 17 March 1871 (Boyd), were both published in the years of their delivery and reprinted in *Rectorial Addresses*, edited by William Knight (1894).

Ireland, south Africa, and Scotland During the summer months of 1869 and 1870 Froude took a house called Derreen at Kenmare, co. Kerry, and there he began his next important book, *The English in Ireland in the Eighteenth Century*. Froude had a better firsthand knowledge of Ireland than most of his contemporaries, and he had been impressed with the fact that after the famine unplanned Irish emigration to the USA had turned Irish-American opinion against the British government—and that the latest manifestation of that opinion, Fenianism, was widely supported in the USA. Two articles on colonies in *Fraser's Magazine* in 1870 show that he set the domestic Irish problem in the wider context of British expansion overseas. He feared that the colonies might follow the same course as the Irish in America, and that the liberal view that colonies encumbered the mother country would only encourage the alienation of the colonists. If, however, they were seen as outlets for the surplus population of Britain, and people were helped to settle in them, helping others in their turn, the colonies might become extensions of England overseas, an England not of merchants seeking markets but of farmers, more loyal and more vigorous than the demoralized masses of England's great cities. Without such planned expansion England might have to yield her place as a world power to America; with it, she might hold her own. Froude's view of Ireland was therefore ultra-unionist. He thought the Irish as a race were not fit for self-government; their destiny was, he believed, bound up with England's, and they needed strong firm rule. Given that, they would be 'true as steel'. *The English in Ireland* was, as A. V. Dicey called it, 'a piece of advocacy'. All along Froude assumed that the English were a more advanced race, by which he meant not so much a genetic superiority as a cultural unity shaped by a common history and literature. He blamed the English for throwing away opportunities for ruling Ireland fairly, but also condemned Gladstone's policy in Ireland as misconceived. Even before the book's publication he was involved in controversy. When he heard that O'Donovan Rossa, the agitator, was lecturing in America against England he offered to give lectures 'on the other side'. A lecture tour was organized, and he left England in September 1872. The first volume of *The English in Ireland* appeared while he was on tour. The lectures attracted great interest in the press. Froude was controverted by a Catholic nationalist, Father Thomas Burke, and made a vigorous reply. But Irish-American opinion was inflamed, and Froude had to cut short his tour, returning to England in December 1872. Two volumes followed and the three were published in 1874; a new edition was published in 1881. The work was widely criticized during and soon after Froude's lecture tour: by the New York journal *The Nation*, by J. P. Prendergast in the *Freeman's Journal*, by Father Burke in *English Misrule in Ireland* and *Ireland's Vindication* (1873), and by John Mitchell in *The Crusade of the Period* (1873). But the most learned critic was W. E. H. Lecky, Froude's friend and neighbour in Onslow Gardens. He wrote two strong criticisms of Froude in *Macmillan's Magazine* (January 1873 and June 1874) and a more searching treatment in his *History of Ireland in the Eighteenth Century*. Froude had undoubtedly helped polarize the debate on Irish home rule into a conflict of races, and by writing of the Irish problem as what one critic called 'the white man's burden nearer home' made it inseparable from the growth of imperialism. But he also made many converts with his unsparing criticism of English rule. Fenians realized that he had done 'valuable service to the national cause', and Parnell once remarked that the book threw more light on the Irish question than any other he had read. As the land war and Catholic nationalism became more active even Lecky began to echo the views he had once condemned. To this day Froude's assumption that the protestant landowners in Ireland were 'English' is deeply rooted in the Irish outlook.

Froude's second wife died on 12 February 1874 and in the same year he gave up editing *Fraser's* and handed the task to William Allingham. Having connections with the new Disraeli ministry—notably with the foreign secretary, Lord Derby, and the colonial secretary, Lord Carnarvon—

he hoped for some patronage, and with his interest in colonies in mind he asked the latter if he could be sent on a tour of Australia. Carnarvon suggested instead that he should go to south Africa, to explore the possibility of persuading the white settlers in Cape Colony, Natal, and the two Boer republics to agree to joining a confederation. Froude was to travel as an independent observer, but he was given official letters to local dignitaries to help his travels; so his tour was a mixture of the political and personal. The idea of confederation was not acceptable to all parties. The two Boer republics had originated in dislike of British intrusion, and one of them, the Orange Free State, had a more recent grievance—the annexation by Britain of the diamond fields, officially called Griqualand West, in contravention of a treaty. Even in Cape Colony the recent grant of responsible government meant that a proposal for a confederation not conveyed in official form would be misinterpreted as a threat to a new-found independence. Froude was not an unbiased observer. His dislike of commercial greed led him to underestimate a growing source of conflict. Like Carlyle he preferred soldiers to orators and action to parliamentary discussion. Though he thought the Boers came nearest 'to Horace's description of the Roman peasant soldiers who defeated Pyrrhus and Hannibal', he assured an audience in Bloemfontein that their situation was envied by 'every ambitious and aggressive power' and that an independent south Africa would come when they 'could reply to those powers with shot and shell'. In the next decade remarks like this acquired a meaning Froude had not intended. He sailed from Dartmouth on 23 August and reached Table Bay on 21 September, sailed round to Durban and thence made his way across Natal and the Drakensberg to Harrismith. From the Free State he went on to Pretoria in November, returning to Cape Town by way of Kimberley, Bloemfontein, and Colesberg, in December. He left for England on 10 January 1875, convinced that British policy in south Africa had been characterized by a lack of wisdom and justice. He regarded the acquisition of the Griqualand diamond fields in 1871 as a culmination of the evil policy, and believed that Great Britain would be best advised to leave the south African states to work out their own future, retaining control only of Table Bay peninsula as a naval and military station. Froude duly reported his views in person to Lord Carnarvon, who seems to have been largely influenced by them. Immediately on Froude's arrival in England Carnarvon invited him to return to south Africa as a member of a conference he proposed to assemble there to deliberate upon his scheme for south African federation. Froude accepted the offer, and again landed at Cape Town on 18 June 1875. Carnarvon's dispatch embodying his scheme had preceded his arrival by a few days, but the Cape government under John Charles Molteno took umbrage at the manner in which Carnarvon laid down the details of the scheme, and on 10 June Gordon Sprigg carried a motion in the house of assembly to the effect that any movement in the direction of federation should originate in south Africa and not in England. This practically shelved the conference, and Froude on landing found the ground cut from under his feet. Nevertheless he began a political campaign in Cape Colony and the Orange Free State in favour of federation;

> he attended a public dinner at Cape Town on the day of his arrival, at which he made so ill-advised a speech that, before twenty-four hours had passed, he had put himself in a position of antagonism to the governor Sir Henry Barkly, his ministers and public feeling generally at Cape Town. (J. Martineau, *Life and Correspondence of Sir Bartle Frere*, 1895, 1.172–3; Molteno, *passim*)

Froude's intentions were no doubt excellent, but the effect of his efforts was to give the *coup de grâce* to Carnarvon's policy; the proposed conference was abandoned, and the under-secretary for the colonies disclaimed responsibility for Froude's proceedings.

Froude returned to England in the autumn of 1875 and his report was published as a parliamentary paper (*Parl. papers*, 1876, 52, C 1399). In 1876 Carnarvon assembled a conference in London to discuss south African affairs. He nominated Froude as representative of Griqualand West, a selection which that province at once repudiated. Other colonies refused to allow themselves to be represented, and the conference came to nothing. Froude defended the policy of which he had been the agent in the *Quarterly Review* for January 1877, and Frederic Rogers, Lord Blachford, replied to it in the *Edinburgh Review* for the following April. Froude was, however, opposed to the annexation of the Transvaal by the Conservative government, and in April 1879 he contributed a second article to the *Quarterly Review* suggesting doubts about the government's south African policy. Sir Bartle Frere, by this time the governor of the Cape, described it as 'an essay in which for whole pages a truth expressed in brilliant epigrams regularly alternates with mistakes or mis-statements which would be scarcely pardoned in a special war correspondent hurriedly writing against time' (J. Martineau, *Life and Correspondence of Sir Bartle Frere*, 1895, 2.367). Subsequently Froude reiterated his views on south Africa in two lectures delivered before the Edinburgh Philosophical Institute on 6 and 9 January 1880; they were published in the same year and reissued with an introduction by Froude's daughter Margaret in 1900. In 1878, again following the lead of Carlyle, he opposed Beaconsfield's policy in eastern Europe, and in the same year he contributed a preface to Madame Olga Novikoff's pamphlet *Is Russia Wrong?*. He also wrote a preface to the same author's *Russia and England*, published in 1880.

Meanwhile in 1876 Froude was appointed with Thomas Henry Huxley a member of the Scottish universities commission (Huxley, 1.330, 477, 479). In this capacity he paid frequent visits to Edinburgh, staying with John Skelton at The Hermitage. Abandoning for the moment contemporary politics he wrote in 1878 a sketch of Bunyan for Mr John Morley's English Men of Letters series, and in 1879 published his *Caesar* (new edn, 1886).

Carlyle's biographer; later works From 1866 Froude had been a close friend and confidant of Carlyle. In June 1871 Carlyle gave Froude a parcel containing the manuscript of his 'Reminiscences' which he had written after his wife's death in 1866, and the 'Letters and Memorials' of Mrs Carlyle, which he had arranged and annotated himself. In a note at the end of his manuscript he forbade his friends to publish 'any part of it' without 'fit editing' and declared that 'the fit editing of perhaps nine-tenths of it will, after I am gone, have become impossible'. In 1873 he made a will in which he said there should be no biography of himself, but that Froude should be left to decide what to do with the 'Letters and Memorials' and other 'fartherences and elucidations' relevant to it, and that his 'practical summing up and decision is to be taken as mine' (Dunn, 2.478). Soon after this, learning that various people were already, as Froude put it, 'busy upon his history', Carlyle gave Froude all his and his wife's private papers in a huge collection, thereby giving the wording of the will great additional weight by extending the duties of an editor to include those of a biographer. Froude had not sought this responsibility: he had been hoping to return to Simancas and write about Charles V and Philip II. But as his two original fellow executors of the will, John Forster and Carlyle's brother John, both died, he had to make most of the decisions himself. A codicil of the will dated 8 November 1878 named him and Sir James Stephen as executors. In the late 1870s Carlyle's niece Mary Aitken came to Cheyne Row to take care of him, and Carlyle realized that some recompense must be given her for her kindness, especially after her marriage to her cousin, Alexander Carlyle, in August 1879. He asked Froude to let Mary have the papers when he had finished with them. Froude later realized that he should at this point have insisted on a clearer written instruction. He did however have Carlyle's agreement to the separate publication of the biography and the *Reminiscences*, the latter being set up in type for his correction, though Carlyle was too weak to perform the task. By the time Carlyle died, on 5 February 1881, the *Reminiscences* was nearly ready for publication and the bulk of the first two volumes of the biography had been written. The *Reminiscences* was published a month after Carlyle's death; the first half of the biography, *Carlyle's Early Life*, appeared in 1882, the *Letters and Memorials of Jane Welsh Carlyle* in 1883; and the third and fourth volumes of the biography, *Carlyle's Life in London*, in 1884.

Almost as soon as the *Reminiscences* appeared Froude was involved in controversy. Mary Aitken Carlyle and her husband questioned the import of the will, publishing Carlyle's wish that there be no biography, as if it had not been later qualified. This dispute became entangled with another on the content of the biography. Froude was criticized both for having published too much too indiscreetly (he had in very general terms traced the unhappiness of Carlyle's marriage to his impotence) and for having disloyally exposed Carlyle's faults. Froude said that the *Reminiscences* was Carlyle's penance for his cruelty to his wife, but critics pointed out that a penance lost all its force if it was posthumous. Froude claimed that Carlyle's moral stature was if anything enhanced by the revelations of his faults, and his own candour as a biographer was consistent not only with Carlyle's contempt for the evasive respectability of the biographical conventions of the day but also by

his own practice ever since *The Nemesis of Faith*. Even here, however, biographical discretion and scholarly accuracy became confused. Froude had shocked some readers with his candour, but he had also worked fast, in part because that was his habit but also because he wanted to discharge his undertaking to Carlyle before anybody else could publish estimates and impressions. So both his ethical judgement and his scholarship were impugned, the first by Mrs Oliphant and others who approved of the conventions of Victorian biography, the second by scholars like Charles Eliot Norton and David Masson, who wanted to question Froude's veracity. Froude wrote a reply to his critics for his children's use, *My Relations with Carlyle*, published in 1903. Meanwhile the *Life of Carlyle* became a classic. It broke through the conventions of the Victorian 'life and letters'. Froude's affection for his subject was tempered by shrewd criticism, and Carlyle's personality was at its most attractive in his letters. Lord Derby told Froude that he had written 'the most interesting biography in the English language', and many would agree with the judgement of his friend John Skelton that it is among the best half-dozen biographies of the Victorian age.

The books on the Carlyles occupied most of Froude's time during 1881–4, but in 1881 he wrote a chapter on recent events in Ireland for the second edition of his *English in Ireland*, and in 1883 he published his *Luther: a Short Biography*. In 1884 he was created honorary LLD at the tercentenary of Edinburgh University. He visited Norway in 1881, and the Australian colonies in the winter of 1884–5. The result of the first tour was a poem, 'Romsdal Fiord', published in *Blackwood's Magazine* for April 1883, and his *Oceana, or, England and her Colonies* (London, two editions, 1886) grew out of the second. The latter excited much controversy, and Froude was charged with misrepresenting the views of many persons, conversations with whom he reported in his book. One of the stoutest attacks was by Mr Wakefield, a member of the New Zealand house of representatives, and appeared in the *Nineteenth Century* for August 1886. The winter of 1886–7 Froude spent in the West Indies, where he collected materials for his *English in the West Indies, or, The Bow of Ulysses, with Illustrations by the Author* (1888; 2nd edn same year). Froude's advocacy of the abolition of representative institutions in the West Indies and drastic treatment of the black population provoked many replies. Froude's next work, *The Two Chiefs of Dunboy* (1889), a historical romance, combined a romantic plot with passages of serious political and historical reflection, and represents his final views on the Irish question. In 1890 he contributed to the Queen's Prime Ministers series an essay on Beaconsfield, in which he tried 'to make out what there was behind the *mask*' (Dunn, 2.562). He wrote it to clarify his own reflections on Disraeli's *Lothair*, together with what he could learn from Disraeli's associates, but it was superseded by the major biography of Moneypenny and Buckle (1910–20). In 1891 he published *The Divorce of Catherine of Aragon* (2nd edn, 1893), in which he reiterated the views on that subject expressed in his *History of England*, with additional evidence drawn from Brewer and Gairdner's *Calendar of Letters and Papers*. This was followed by *The Spanish Story of the Armada* (1892; new edn same year).

On the death of E. A. Freeman in 1892 Lord Salisbury, whom Froude occasionally visited at Hatfield, offered Froude the regius professorship of modern history at Oxford. 'The temptation', wrote Froude to Sir John Skelton, 'of going back to Oxford in a respectable way was too much for me. I must just do the best I can, and trust that I shall not be haunted by Freeman's ghost' (J. Skelton, *Table Talk of Shirley*, 1895, 216–17). The appointment was unpopular with the high-church party, and somewhat scandalized Freeman's friends; but Froude's polished manners wore away some of this enmity, and his literary fame and gifts of elocution brought unwonted crowds to his lectures. The subjects he chose were 'Erasmus', 'English seamen in the sixteenth century', and 'The Council of Trent'. His lectures on these topics were published respectively in 1894, 1895, and 1896, and all went into second editions in the year of publication. The 'Life and letters of Erasmus', which was translated into Dutch (2 vols., 1896–7), was as bitterly attacked as anything Froude wrote, the main accusations being that he seriously garbled Erasmus's letters and misrepresented his meaning (see *Quarterly Review*, January 1895), but it was admired by no less an Erasmus scholar than P. S. Allen.

After finishing his lectures in the summer term of 1894 Froude retired to his residence, The Woodcot, Kingsbridge, Devon. His health grew worse during the long vacation and he died there on 20 October. He was buried on the 25th in Salcombe cemetery.

Froude was a strikingly handsome man, with dark brown eyes and aquiline features. His love of field sports and sailing had kept him healthy and free from the tuberculosis which ravaged his family. He seems to have enjoyed the company of men of action more than that of scholars; hence his comment that 'the silent men do the work' (Dunn, 2.846). Many found him shy and enigmatic as a young man. 'I only half like him', said Matthew Arnold in 1849, 'he comes and hangs about people' (I. Hamilton, *Matthew Arnold*, 1999, 179). The diffidence hardened into an aloofness which was not much softened by later literary fame. To intimate friends he could be a delightful companion; Sir John Skelton called him 'the most interesting man I have ever known'. A fellow passenger on his return from south Africa in 1875 found his conversation fascinating but his mind

> rather sad … sometimes pathetic and tender, usually cynical, but often relating with the highest appreciation and with wonderful beauty of language some gallant deed of one of his heroes of the fifteenth or sixteenth centuries …
> Sometimes there was something almost fearful in the gloom and utter disbelief and defiance of his mind. (Dunn, 2.442)

Froude's solitariness had its effect on his reputation. He never lost the feeling of apartness which stemmed from his unhappy childhood. He had early in his life grown accustomed to abuse, and even when he was a successful writer a certain misanthropic disharmony with the prevailing opinion made him disinclined to reap the reward.

'We Froudes', he once wrote, 'have a way of our own of laying hold of the stick by the burnt end, and making the worst rather than the best of everything' (ibid., 1.184). He did not wear the badge of any party or interest. The religious right could not forgive his heterodoxy, and the agnostic left could not understand his distrust of popular opinion and his preference for strong government. He himself concealed his private feelings behind a stoical composure, making light of his early sufferings. When Freeman accused him of dishonouring his brother Hurrell's memory, he replied that he regarded Hurrell as the most remarkable man he had ever met in his life. But in his *History* his dislike of his brother's fanatical temperament resurfaces in the portrait of Edmund Campion in what have been called 'flickering resemblances' to Hurrell Froude (Burrow, 258). Froude's reputation has therefore suffered from two sorts of obsolescence. As an essayist he covered too wide a range to be truly profound, but as a historian he revealed enough of his feelings to compromise his integrity in the eyes of the professionals. While it was dominated by religious disputes Oxford cast him out. In 1858 it preferred Goldwin Smith for the regius chair. By 1892 Froude had proved himself the finer scholar by far, but it was too late to acquire an academic reputation. Posterity has always been uncertain whether to count him as a man of letters or as a professional historian, but he attained great distinction in both roles.

A. F. POLLARD, rev. WILLIAM THOMAS

Sources W. H. Dunn, *James Anthony Froude: a biography*, 1: 1818–1856 (1961), 2: 1857–1894 (1963) • C. Ricks, 'Froude's Carlyle', *Essays in appreciation* (1998), 146–71 • D. McCartney, 'James Anthony Froude and Ireland: a historiographical controversy of the nineteenth century', *Historical Studies*, 8 (1971), 171–90 • R. Goetzman, *J. A. Froude: a bibliography of studies* (1977) • B. Willey, 'J. A. Froude', *More nineteenth century studies* (1956), 106–36 • J. W. Burrow, *A liberal descent: Victorian historians and the English past* (1981) • J. Gallagher and R. Robinson, *Africa and the Victorians: the official mind of imperialism* (1961) • C. W. de Kiewiet, *British colonial policy and the south African republics, 1848–1872* (1929) • L. P. Curtis, introduction, in W. E. H. Lecky, *A history of Ireland in the eighteenth century* (1972) • D. McCartney, *W. E. H. Lecky: historian and politician, 1838–1903* (Dublin, 1994) • I. Campbell, *Thomas Carlyle* (1974) • W. H. Paul, *Life of Froude* (1905) • M. Kelly, *Froude: a study of his life and character* (1907) • *The Times* (22 Oct 1894) • J. A. Froude, *Historical and other sketches*, ed. D. H. Wheeler (1883) • J. A. Froude, 'The Oxford Counter Reformation', *Short studies on great subjects*, 4th ser. (1871), 170–230 • J. A. Froude, 'South African journal', *Short studies on great subjects*, 3rd ser. (1871), 338–94 • J. A. Froude, *Thomas Carlyle: a history of his life in London*, 2 vols. (1884) • J. A. Froude, *The nemesis of faith* (1849); 2nd edn (1849) • A. N. Ireland, 'Recollections of James Anthony Froude', *Contemporary Review*, 67 (1895), 17–28 • A. Birrell, 'James Anthony Froude', *Scribner's Magazine*, 17/2 (Feb 1895) • G. Smith, 'Two great authors: II. Froude', *North American Review*, 159/457 (Dec 1894) • L. Stephen, 'James Anthony Froude', *Studies of a biographer* (1902) • T. R. E. Holmes, 'Mr Froude and his critics', *Westminster Review*, 138 (Aug 1892) • *CGPLA Eng. & Wales* (1894) • *GM*, 3rd ser., 6 (1859), 437 • Boase, *Mod. Eng. biog.*, 1.1110 • M. E. Grant Duff, *Notes from a diary* (1851–72), 2.4 • [A. K. H. Boyd], *Twenty-five years of St Andrews*, 2 vols. (1892), vol. 1, pp. 108, 114 • P. A. Molteno, *Life and times of Sir J. C. Molteno* (1900) • L. Huxley, *Life of T. H. Huxley* (1900), vol. 1, pp. 330, 477, 479

Archives Duke U., Perkins L., letters • Hunt. L., letters • U. Edin. L., letters | Auckland Public Library, letters to Sir George Grey •

BL, corresp. with Lord Carnarvon, Add. MSS 60798–60799 · BL, letters to T. S. Escott, Add. MS 58779 · BL OIOC, letters to Sir Mountstuart Grant Duff, MS Eur. F 234 · Bodl. Oxf., letters to Richard Bentley and George Bentley · Bodl. Oxf., letters to Friedrich Max Muller · Bodl. Oxf., letters to J. E. Thorold Rogers · CAC Cam., letters to W. T. Stead · Castle Howard, Yorkshire, letters to Lady Carlisle · Duke U., Perkins L., letters to Sir Arthur Helps · Glos. RO, letters to Sir Michael Hicks Beach · Herts. ALS, corresp. with Henry Frederick Cowper · Hove Central Library, Sussex, letters to Lord Wolseley and Lady Wolseley · Hunt. L., letters to Francis Cobbe · Mitchell L., NSW, letters to Sir William Manning · Morgan L., letters to John Ruskin · Morgan L., letters to Joan Severn · NL Scot., letters to J. S. Blackie · NL Wales, letters to Sir George Cornewall Lewis · St Deiniol's Library, Hawarden, letters to Anne Bennett · Syracuse University, New York, corresp. with Sir John Simeon · U. Birm. L., corresp. with Joseph Chamberlain · U. Edin. L., letters to Charles Butler

Likenesses G. Reid, oils, 1881, NPG [see illus.] · E. Boehm, bust effigy · H. Furniss, two caricatures, pen-and-ink sketches, NPG · J. E. Goddall, chalk drawing, NPG · S. Laurence, portrait · Lock & Whitfield, woodburytype, NPG; repro. in T. Cooper and others, *Men of mark: a gallery of contemporary portraits* (1876) · J. and C. Watkins, carte-de-visite, NPG · H. J. Whitlock, carte-de-visite, NPG · chromolithograph caricature, NPG; repro. in *VF* (27 Jan 1872) · prints, NPG · woodcut, BM

Wealth at death £12,743 3s.: probate, 29 Nov 1894, *CGPLA Eng. & Wales*

Froude, William (1810–1879), engineer and naval architect, fourth son of Robert Hurrell Froude (1770/71–1859), archdeacon of Totnes, and Margaret, *née* Spedding (1774/5–1821), was born at Dartington parsonage on 28 November 1810. (Richard) Hurrell *Froude (1803–1836) and James Anthony *Froude (1818–1894) were his brothers. He was educated at Westminster School and Oriel College, Oxford, where he graduated BA with first-class honours in mathematics in 1832, and proceeded MA in 1837. His tutors were his eldest brother, Hurrell, and John Henry Newman, who together with I. K. Brunel were, he wrote, the greatest influences on his life. He began work on the survey for the South Eastern Railway in 1833 as a pupil of the engineer Henry Palmer. In 1837 he joined the staff of Brunel, for whom he managed the last section of the Bristol to Exeter line. He demonstrated his ability by developing a new design of skew bridge, a mathematical approach to reducing the sideways force on a train entering a curve, and a theory of the expansion of steam. In 1839 he married Catherine Holdsworth (d. 1878) from Dartmouth.

At the end of 1846 Froude retired from full-time work to assist his ailing father. He then acted as harbour commissioner, magistrate, and judge of agricultural machinery. Later he improved the supply of water to the Torquay waterworks, which led him to an understanding of the friction of water. He remained a close friend of Newman and their correspondence dealt with the nature of proof in science and religion, with Froude becoming steadily more agnostic. The friendship was strained, but not broken, when, in 1857, Newman converted Catherine and the Froude children to Roman Catholicism.

In 1856 Brunel persuaded Froude to undertake a study of rolling in waves. This led to his 1861 paper to the Institution of Naval Architects which provided the first correct theory of the behaviour of a ship in a seaway. Over the next decade gaps in his theory were filled and empirical methods developed for the solution of aspects where the mathematics were too difficult. This work was enthusiastically followed by the Admiralty and influenced the design of subsequent warships; it also led to Froude's election in 1870 as a fellow of the Royal Society. Finally, it marked the beginning of a partnership with Brunel's second son, Henry. In 1869 Froude was a member of a British Association committee to improve estimates of the power required to drive a ship. The committee's report recommended a number of full-scale trials but Froude dissented, reporting the results of a series of tests of three models, of different scale, representing two very different ship forms, the *Swan* and the *Raven*. These tests showed firstly that there was no universal optimum form, as was generally believed; *Raven* was better at low speeds, *Swan* at the highest speeds. He also demonstrated that, when tested at the corresponding speed (now defined as the Froude number), the resistance per unit immersed volume of the three models of each form was the same and hence it should be possible to obtain ship resistance from models tests; this is now known as Froude's law.

Froude's approach, which was opposed by most engineers of the day, was validated by an elaborate trial in 1871, in which HMS *Greyhound* was towed and her resistance measured over a range of speeds. He proposed to Edward Reed, chief constructor of the navy, that a special tank should be built close to his (Froude's) house at Chelston Cross, Torquay, in which models could be run and their resistance measured accurately so as to develop improved hull forms for the navy. He offered his own services free to superintend the work. His proposal was approved in February 1870, and work began at once. The tank was 270 feet long, 38 feet wide at the water surface, and 10 feet deep. The model, shaped in paraffin wax, was drawn along the tank by a carriage running on rails, which was itself pulled by an endless rope, worked by a steam engine. A dynamometer on the carriage recorded speed, resistance, and the trim of the model. This was the first ship tank and there were innumerable problems in developing apparatus, including governors to ensure that the model ran at a constant speed. Calibration runs began in June 1871 and by May 1872 the tank was operational. The first task was to obtain data on frictional resistance, which had to be treated differently from the remaining residuary resistance. In 1873 Froude designed a dynamometer which would measure the performance of model propellers both in isolation and in the disturbed flow behind a ship. This machine gave good service until 1938 and later became the centrepiece of the Froude's Museum. There was a brief golden age in which he advanced both the science of hydrodynamics and its application. He was awarded the gold medal of the Royal Society in 1876 and received the degree of LLD from Glasgow the same year. He was an active member of Admiralty committees on design in 1871 and 1877 and gave lengthy evidence to a committee on scientific education and research in 1872.

Froude's work on the hydrodynamics of rolling and

powering remains valid today and his methods are only slightly changed. The influence of his work has led to the selection of hull forms which are fast and comfortable, while the cost of the model test has been repaid many times over, by the resultant fuel saving. His approach was to investigate the problem using very simple experiments which would suggest a theoretical approach. Since the mathematics was often insoluble in real cases, he would then devise empirical methods which would be validated in full-scale trials. He was a clever designer of apparatus and a skilled craftsman: he usually made the prototype himself. He was able to assemble a talented team of assistants and use their contributions. One of them, his son Edmund, continued his work for forty years after his death. He was liked by all, from admirals to shipwrights.

Froude's wife died in 1878 and the consequent distress, combined with overwork, led his friends to persuade him to take a holiday. He travelled to South Africa in HMS *Boadicea* and was about to return when he contracted dysentery and died at Admiralty House, Simonstown, on 4 May 1879. He was buried eight days later with full military honours in the naval cemetery. The majority of Froude's scientific papers were republished by the Institution of Naval Architects in a commemorative volume in 1955.

DAVID K. BROWN and ANDREW LAMBERT

Sources K. C. Barnaby, *The Institution of Naval Architects, 1860–1960* (1960) · A. D. Duckworth, ed., *The papers of William Froude, 1810–1879* (1955) · *CGPLA Eng. & Wales* (1879)
Archives Bodl. Oxf., letters to H. W. Acland · Devon RO, report to chief constructor of the Navy on tank-testing ship models · U. Glas., Archives and Business Records Centre, corresp. with James R. Napier
Likenesses photograph, Royal Institution of Naval Architects, London
Wealth at death under £50,000: probate, 20 Aug 1879, *CGPLA Eng. & Wales*

Frowde, Henry (1841–1927), publisher, was born at Southsea on 8 February 1841, the son of James Frowde (*d.* 1850) and his wife, Catherine, *née* Branscombe, of Knightsbridge, London. The Frowde family originated in Devon, and claimed an unsubstantiated connection with the historian James Anthony Froude. Frowde's father died when Henry was nine, and Frowde started working for the Post Office in his adolescence. Bookselling followed, and in 1874 Frowde was employed at Paternoster Row in London as manager of Oxford University Press's bible warehouse. In the same year, he married Mary Blanche Foster, daughter of Joel Foster Earle, and they had three daughters: Blanche, Catherine, and Anne. A son died in infancy.

Unlike Charles Cannan or Horace Hart, Frowde was not a figure who held centre stage at the press. 'Very few of us here in Oxford had any personal knowledge of him', admitted an Oxford University Press obituarist (*The Clarendonian*, 47). His reputation rested on craftsmanship, and the skill with which his workforce produced huge numbers of beautiful but exceptionally compact books. To do this, Frowde used one of the great trade secrets of the press: 'India paper'. Thin, opaque, and resilient, the paper was produced using rope fibre, and supplied exclusively to Oxford by Thomas Brittain & Son of Hanley.

Henry Frowde (1841–1927), by unknown photographer

Frowde employed it first in a small Bible in 1875. 'India paper' was used extensively in religious publications, saved warehouse space, and won the press many awards. With it, Aldous Huxley declared, one could fit 'a million words of reading matter into a rucksack and never feel the difference' (Sutcliffe, 189). The substance was essential to producing Arthur Quiller-Couch's *Oxford Book of English Verse* (1900) in a manageable form.

Frowde's greatest coup, however, was the Revised Version of the New Testament in conjunction with Cambridge University Press in 1881. The project was laborious. The perfectionist qualms of Brooke Foss Westcott, F. J. A. Hort, and J. B. Lightfoot, the Cambridge clerics who dominated the New Testament revision group, made progress towards a definitive text a difficult matter. For Frowde, once publication had been set, the book called for both efficiency and secrecy. He received a million advance orders, and rival American firms were desperate to pirate the text before British publication. They failed. Frowde opened the cramped London premises at midnight on 17 May 1881, and shipped copies all over Britain. Expectations were immense. So were the profits: one City bookseller sold 15,000 copies in a day. Frowde also published the Revised Old Testament in 1885, which proved a less volatile event. Instead of piracy, Frowde worried more about his warehouse collapsing from the sheer weight of stock that it contained.

In 1883 Frowde had received the formal title publisher to the University of Oxford, succeeding Alexander Macmillan, and he remained in this post until he retired. During his career he witnessed huge expansion of the press. Supervising Cannan's protégé, Humphrey Milford, he took on juvenile and medical publications from Hodder and Stoughton in 1906, and bought the World's Classics imprint from Blackie & Son. This became one of Oxford's best-loved lines under Milford himself. In the slump of the 1890s Frowde maintained the London business. He was rewarded by the university with an honorary MA in 1897, and as a further measure of his acumen, the delegates passed financial responsibility for Bible and prayer book publishing to him, effectively ending the Bible Press at Oxford in 1906.

Frowde retired in 1913, and was succeeded by Milford. He died in Croydon on 3 March 1927. By the end of his career, he had printed bibles, academic works, Oxford examination papers, and children's books. Some colleagues may have known little about Frowde, but their livelihoods depended on his skill.   MARTIN MAW

Sources P. Sutcliffe, *The Oxford University Press: an informal history* (1978) · *The Times* (4 March 1927) · N. Barker, *The Oxford University Press and the spread of learning, 1478–1978* (1978) · *The Clarendonian*, 4 (1927), 47 · *The Periodical* [OUP literary magazine], 12/139 (1927), 39 · *DNB* · *WWW*, 1916–28

Archives Oxford University Press, archives, letter-books | BL, letters to W. E. Gladstone, Add. MSS 44454–44526

Likenesses photograph, repro. in Sutcliffe, *Oxford University Press* · photograph, repro. in *The Periodical* · photograph, NPG [*see illus.*]

Wealth at death £12,849 8s. 7d.: resworn probate, 11 April 1927, *CGPLA Eng. & Wales*

Frowde, James Henry (1831–1899), clown and evangelical preacher, was born on 17 April 1831 at Portsea, Hampshire, the first son of James Frowde (1800–1850) and his first wife, Georgiana Margaretta Hengler (1808–1837), an equestrian performer, the daughter of the circus rope-dancer Henry Michael Hengler. His mother's early death, leaving four young children, made a vivid and lasting impression on Frowde; his father remarried within the year. He received a liberal education, while his home life was strictly religious and puritanical, under the influence of his stepmother.

Frowde's life was changed by the visit of Hengler's circus to Portsmouth in 1846. For the first time he met his mother's family, and in the summer of 1847 he joined Charles Hengler's circus at Stamford. He learned to ride, and earned his keep by cleaning out the stables and animals' quarters. He first appeared in the circus at Leicester in that year, as a supernumerary in a fête scene. One of the clowns taught Frowde all he knew, and by 1850 'Jem Frowde' appeared on the bills as 'a Man of Many Forms'—referring to his skills as a contortionist. He became one of the main attractions at Hengler's, and enjoyed immense popularity. He travelled with the company for the next ten years, and briefly ran his own company in 1859. He was principal clown at Charles Hengler's new circus which opened in Liverpool in 1857, where it was later recalled that, 'Being a good-looking young fellow, Jem had a host of female admirers and used to be daily inundated with love letters and souvenirs d'amour' (*Liverpool Citizen*, 12 Sept 1888, 12c). His dress imitated the original court jester style as closely as possible, with cap and bells, and no make-up apart from a little rouge.

The impact of his religious upbringing remained with Frowde, and in December 1856 at Chester he was presented with a valuable Bible by three clergymen, as a testimonial to his conduct in private life and his constant attendance at church services. On 4 June 1857 he married

James Henry Frowde (1831–1899), by unknown photographer, *c*.1870

Elizabeth, the youngest daughter of the Revd Christopher Hayden, at St John's Church, Liverpool. She died in childbirth the following March. The child, a daughter, also died. Frowde continued to perform as a clown until 1861, mainly with Hengler's but occasionally appearing with other companies. On 9 October 1861 he married Susan Mary, the daughter of the Revd William Harrison, at Leamington Spa, and retired from the circus.

Frowde exchanged the circus for the life of a country gentleman, purchased three estates near Newent, Gloucestershire, and became a freemason. From 1878 until 1892 he was a captain in the Gloucestershire artillery volunteers. With his second wife he had two sons and two daughters. He continued to live a religious life. His 'talking clown' experience and colloquial skills, in addition to his intimate knowledge of the scriptures, equipped him for the role of lay preacher, and he had a mission room erected at one of his properties, Walden Court, and obtained a bishop's licence to preach there. The contrast between his natural jollity and grave religious beliefs led many people to regard him as eccentric, if not actually shocking, but his character overcame the reservations of the local people.

About 1892 the Frowdes relinquished their estates and went to live in Gloucester. Following the death of his wife in 1895, James Frowde took rooms at 53 Westgate Street, where he died on 28 August 1899. He was buried in Gloucester cemetery.   JOHN M. TURNER

Sources J. M. Turner, *Gloucestershire history* (1994), 9 · *Gloucester Journal* (9 Sept 1899) · *Liverpool Citizen* (26 Sept 1888), 7a · Boase, *Mod.*

Eng. biog. • *CGPLA Eng. & Wales* (1900) • d. cert. • *Devon Notes and Queries*, 2 (1903), 124

Likenesses photograph, *c.*1870, Theatre Museum, London [*see illus.*] • engraving, repro. in *Gloucester Journal*

Wealth at death £115 14*s.* 8*d.*: administration, 23 Jan 1900, *CGPLA Eng. & Wales*

Frowde, Philip (1678/9–1738), poet, elder son of Philip Frowde, esquire (*bap.* 1645, *d.* 1715/16), and his wife, Sarah (*d.* 1704), was baptized on 28 September 1679 at St Mary Woolnoth, London. His grandfather Sir Philip Frowde (*d.* 1674) was a royalist colonel in the civil war, was knighted on 10 March 1665, and was made deputy postmaster-general and then governor of the Post Office. Of Sir Philip's children Penelope married Nathaniel, Baron Crew (1633–1722), a discreditable bishop of Durham; William rose to the rank of lieutenant-colonel in the foot guards and was friendly with Addison, Pope, Swift, and Gay; Philip, the eldest son, succeeded in 1677 to his father's lucrative positions in the Post Office with a salary, by 1687, of £1500 p.a. and occasional royal grace and favour grants, sometimes of more than £4000. He lost office in April 1689 but was wealthy enough to buy the estate of Peper Harow, Surrey, in February 1700. Ashburnham Frowde (*d.* 1735), comptroller of the foreign posts for forty-five years, was almost certainly a close relative.

Young Philip Frowde went to Eton College about 1692, then entered Magdalen College, Oxford, as a gentleman commoner (he matriculated on 17 November 1696, aged seventeen), where he was a pupil of Addison but, it seems, did not take a degree. He was admitted as a student of the Middle Temple on 16 January 1698. He is named as the author of 'Cursus glacialis, Anglicé, scating', printed in *Musarum Anglicanarum analecta*, volume 2 (1699), a collection of Oxford Latin verse edited by Addison; but Curll, who reprinted the poem in 1720, claimed that it was in fact written by Addison himself.

Frowde's uncle Colonel William Frowde was a poet. Addison wrote to him in November 1699, asking him not to say farewell to poetry; Swift listened patiently to his poems in July 1708. Pope's quotation of an epigram made by Rowe on Frowde implies that the colonel wrote the anonymous translation, from Corneille, *Cinna's Conspiracy* (1713), which is usually ascribed to Colley Cibber (*Letters of Joseph Addison*; *Correspondence of Jonathan Swift*, 1.92; Spence). He is certainly the punster referred to by Gay and Pope in a letter to Caryll of April 1715 (*Correspondence of Alexander Pope*) and is probably the 'wandring Froud' (line 147) in Gay's 'Mr Pope's Welcome from Greece', written early in 1720. He is probably also the subject of enigmatic references in Pope's 'A Farewell to London' (lines 11–12) and 'Sandys's Ghost' (lines 63–4), although it has been claimed that Pope is referring to the colonel's nephew Philip (A. Pope, *Minor Poems*, Twickenham edn, 128, 131, 173, 176).

Little certain evidence as to Philip Frowde's activities or whereabouts in the first two decades of the eighteenth century has come to light. He dined with Addison, Steele, and Swift on 29 February 1708 and it has been suggested

that it was he who introduced Swift to Addison (*Correspondence of Jonathan Swift*, 1.74 and n.). By November 1711 his father was trying to sell Peper Harow. Swift wrote that the 'old fool' was in London, 'utterly ruined, and at this present in some blind alley with some dirty wench. He has two sons that must starve, and he never gives them a farthing … I suppose [he] dare not stir out but on Sundays' (when debtors could not be arrested) (Swift, *Journal to Stella*, 2.409–19, 427). The estate was sold in 1713.

Starving or not, the younger Philip Frowde did not have recourse to writing for money until his late forties. His blank-verse tragedy *The Fall of Saguntum*, after being refused by Drury Lane, opened at Lincoln's Inn Fields on 16 January 1727 and ran for eleven nights, thus ensuring three benefits from which Frowde netted £200. During rehearsals it was unashamedly puffed in *The History of Saguntum* (1727) by A. B.—possibly Frowde himself. There was only one more performance (18 May) but three printed editions, dedicated to Frowde's one-time schoolmate Sir Robert Walpole, appeared in the next eight years. Frowde's other blank-verse tragedy, *Philotas*, ran for six nights at Lincoln's Inn Fields in February 1731; the printed edition was dedicated to the earl of Chesterfield. Both plays carried their learning heavily but did not sink entirely without trace; *Philotas* was given a favourable mention in Fielding's *Joseph Andrews* (1742), book 3, chapter 10, although some readers have mistaken Fielding's double irony for single irony.

Frowde died, unmarried, on 19 December 1738 at his lodgings in Cecil Street, Strand, London, and was buried in Lamb's Conduit Fields cemetery. He died intestate; administration was granted on 20 January 1739 to Charles Frowde, his younger brother. JAMES SAMBROOK

Sources J. Swift, *Journal to Stella*, ed. H. Williams, 2 vols. (1948), vol. 1, pp. 12, 81–2; vol. 2, pp. 409–11, 427 • *The correspondence of Jonathan Swift*, ed. H. Williams, 1 (1963), 74, 92, 120, 129 • J. Spence, *Observations, anecdotes, and characters, of books and men*, ed. J. M. Osborn, new edn, 1 (1966), 109 • *Letters of Joseph Addison*, ed. W. Graham (1941), 9 • *The correspondence of Alexander Pope*, ed. G. Sherburn, 1 (1956), 288 • Foster, *Alum. Oxon., 1500–1714* • W. Sterry, ed., *The Eton College register, 1441–1698* (1943), 132 • H. A. C. Sturgess, ed., *Register of admissions to the Honourable Society of the Middle Temple, from the fifteenth century to the year 1944*, 1 (1949), 243 • D. E. Baker, *Biographia dramatica, or, A companion to the playhouse*, rev. I. Reed, new edn, rev. S. Jones, 3 vols. in 4 (1812) • E. L. Avery, ed., *The London stage, 1660–1800*, pt 2: *1700–1729* (1960), ci, 903–5, 927 • A. H. Scouten, ed., *The London stage, 1660–1800*, pt 3: *1729–1747* (1961), 113–15 • P. Smithers, *The life of Joseph Addison* (1954), 40, 48, 132 • A. B. [P. Frowde?], *The history of Saguntum* (1727), 51 • *London Magazine*, 7 (1738), 631 • W. A. Shaw, ed., *Calendar of treasury books*, 2, PRO (1905), 159; 6 (1913), 51; 8 (1923), 1131, 1283, 2166; 9 (1931), 579 • C. Dalton, ed., *English army lists and commission registers, 1661–1714*, 2 (1894), 28, 137; 3 (1896), 382; 4 (1898), 278; 5 (1902), 42 • *VCH Surrey*, 3.51

Likenesses T. Murray, portrait, 1732 • J. Faber junior, mezzotint, 1738 (after T. Murray), BM, NPG, V&A

Frowick, Henry of (*d.* 1286?). *See under* Moneyers (*act. c.*1180–*c.*1500).

Frowick, Roger (*fl.* 1292–1327). *See under* Moneyers (*act. c.*1180–*c.*1500).

Frowyk [Frowicke, Frowyke], **Sir Thomas** (*c.*1460–1506), judge, was the son of Thomas Frowyk, gentleman mercer, and Joan (his second wife), daughter of Richard Sturgeon; his grandfather was Henry Frowyk, mercer, alderman, and mayor of London. Born at Gunnersbury in Middlesex, Frowyk was mentioned in 1464 in the will of his grandmother Isabella Frowyk. Reportedly educated at Cambridge, he was admitted to the Inner Temple, and gave readings in the autumn terms of 1492 (Westminster II cc.6–11) and 1495 (*Prerogativa regis*), readings which were often cited subsequently. He was made a common serjeant of London about 1486, serjeant-at-law in 1495, and king's serjeant in November 1501. Retained by the earls of Stafford and dukes of Buckingham, he was awarded £2 yearly by Duke Edward from the receivership of Kent and Surrey in 1502. On 30 September 1502 he was appointed chief justice of the common pleas, and was knighted later that year. With John Fisher, justice of the common pleas, and Humphrey Coningsby, later justice of the king's bench, Thomas acted as arbitrator between the university and town of Cambridge, defining their respective jurisdictions (11 July 1502). As chief justice he formulated a significant dissenting judgment in the celebrated case of *Orwell* v. *Mortoft* (1505) contributing to the development, in later years, of the action on the case as an alternative process to recover a debt.

Frowyk was married first to Joan Bardville, apparently having a son, Thomas, who probably died young, but was mentioned in the will of Frowyk's mother, and in that of John Warde (alderman and grocer of London), who bequeathed a gown to Thomas, son of Thomas Frowyk, serjeant-at-law. By 1498 Frowyk had married as his second wife Elizabeth, daughter of William Carnevyle of Tockington, Gloucestershire, and had inherited property in Hertfordshire and Middlesex where he purchased lands, holding notably a large estate called Derhams at South Mimms. He was named, with John Kingsmill, justice of the common pleas, as executor to Thomas Marow, serjeant (d. 1505), with whom he seems to have shared a chamber in the Inner Temple.

Frowyk died, still only in his mid-forties, on 7 October 1506. His memorial at Finchley (where he was buried with Joan, his first wife) was recorded in 1593, in John Norden's description of Middlesex, as having been defaced; the memorial, according to Finchley parish registers, 'which stood between the two pillars on the North side of the chancel, was took clear away to make room for a new pew to be built on the spot, October 14th., 1760'. His executors were his wife, John Kingsmill, Thomas Roberts, coroner of London, and Thomas Jakes, of the Inner Temple, clerk of the warrants. By his will of 13 August 1505, with codicil 6 October 1506, Frowyk left to Elizabeth his 'manor place and messuage at Finchley, bought of Lord Hastings' and instructed that half the profits of Derhams be applied to mend highways between London and Barnet, the remainder to go to his wife. His niece Elizabeth Frowyk married Sir John Spelman, justice of the king's bench; the marriage is commemorated on a tablet dated 1528 at Narborough Hall, Norfolk. After his death his widow, Elizabeth, married Thomas Jakes, as appears from an action against Spelman (one of Elizabeth's executors) for the

wardship of Frowyk's daughter Frideswide. Fuller describes Frowyk as having been 'accounted the oracle of law in his age' and Jakes, who died in 1516, willed that Elizabeth should 'delyver to the Company of the Inner temple' books which were 'my singuler good Lord Frowykes there to remayne in the Librarie to thentent they should the better remember my seid good lord her late husband her self and me'.   NORMAN DOE

Sources E. W. Ives, *The common lawyers of pre-Reformation England* (1983) · Baker, *Serjeants* · *The reports of Sir John Spelman*, ed. J. H. Baker, 2 vols., SeldS, 93–4 (1977–8) · A. W. B. Simpson, ed., *Biographical dictionary of the common law* (1984) · B. H. Putnam, *Early treatises on the practice of the justices of the peace in the fifteenth and sixteenth centuries* (1924) · H. K. Cameron, 'The brasses of Middlesex: Finchley', *Transactions of the London and Middlesex Archaeological Society*, 20 (1959), 2–16 · W. B. Passmore, 'Finchley Parish Church, Rectory and Rectors', *Home Counties Magazine*, 3 (1901), 127–38 · F. C. Cass, *The parish of South Mimms* (1877) · S. Gillies and P. Taylor, *Finchley and Friern Barnet* (1992) · *CIPM, Henry VII*, 3, nos. 95, 243, 279, 294, 309

Froysell, Thomas (*c.*1610–1673), Church of England clergyman, was the son of Edward Froysell (d. 1625?), vicar of Downton in Herefordshire. He matriculated as a sizar at Clare College, Cambridge, in 1623, graduated BA in 1627, and proceeded MA in 1631. Froysell was probably curate at Llanfair Waterdine in 1633, when he was among the thirteen ministers appointed to have the use of the clerical library of Thomas Pierson, rector of Brampton Bryan, after his death. He was instituted vicar of Clun in Shropshire on 27 September 1637 and in the summer of 1640 joined with a number of other mainly puritan ministers in the diocese of Hereford, who petitioned against the new church canons of that year and in particular against the 'etcetera' oath.

At the start of the civil war Shropshire and other counties in the Welsh border region were dominated by the royalists and Froysell, like several other local puritan clergy, sought safety in London. In March 1643 parliament appointed him rector of St Margaret's, New Fish Street Hill, and lecturer at St Dunstan-in-the-West. He was a member of the fourth London presbyterian classis and last attended a meeting on 2 August 1647. The previous year, at the instigation of his kinsman Sir Robert Harley, MP for Herefordshire, Froysell had been appointed preacher at Hereford Cathedral by the committee for plundered ministers and by September 1647 he had returned to Shropshire. In 1650 he preached the funeral sermon for his patron at Clun, Humphrey Walcot, later published as *The Gale of Opportunity* (1658), and looked back to the period before the wars when Walcot had been instrumental in promoting preaching in the area and in 'honoring and backing the faithfull Ministers of God' (p. 113). In 1656 Froysell was also chosen to preach at Sir Robert Harley's funeral at Brampton Bryan. *Yadidyah, or, The Beloved Disciple* (1658) characterized Harley as 'the pillar of religion among us' and linked him with Walcot and Sir Richard More of Linley as 'the triangles of our country' (pp. 97–109). Froysell's career illustrates the importance of the links between such lay patrons and the puritan clergy in this region in the civil war period.

Froysell was ejected from his living at Clun in 1662

under the terms of the Act of Uniformity and was later described by Richard Steele as 'reduced in his last years to a narrow livelihood' (Froysell, A4r). Following the indulgence of 1672 he was licensed on 25 July 1672 as a presbyterian 'teacher' at his house at Kinton in the parish of Leintwardine. He died the following year and in his will, drawn up on 20 May 1673, appointed his wife, Frances (d. in or before 1687), as his executor and Sir Edward Harley of Brampton Bryan and his brother, Thomas Harley of Downton Hall, as overseers. Froysell left his property at Kinton to his wife for her use during her natural life and thereafter to his son Jeremiah, minister at Henley-on-Thames, to whom he also left his books and papers. He left various legacies to his other son, Joseph, and his daughters Mary, Brilliana, Abigail, and Frances. In 1678 Richard Steele published as *Sermons Concerning Grace and Temptations* a collection of Froysell's sermons 'preach't in the Country', in which he described his style as a minister. Froysell was a constant scholar, 'he dwelt in his study', and he conducted a daily round of religious observance within his household including preaching to his family two or three times a week. According to Steele, he was 'greatest in the Pulpit; there his Grace and Gifts did shine … many in London, and more in the Country … received their spiritual life, growth and comfort from God by his Ministry' (Froysell, A3v–A4r).   JACQUELINE EALES

Sources Calamy rev., 215 · T. Froysell, *Sermons concerning grace and temptations* (1678) · will, proved 25 Nov 1673, Herefs. RO, wills ser., AA 20 · petitions from clergy of Hereford diocese, 1640, BL, Add. MS 70002 · will of Thomas Pierson, 1633, PRO, PROB 11/164, fol. 358 · Venn, *Alum. Cant.* · J. Eales, *Puritans and roundheads: the Harleys of Brampton Bryan and the outbreak of the English civil war* (1990)
Archives BL, letters to members of the Harley family, Add. MSS 70105, 70002–70007
Wealth at death see will, proved, 25 Nov 1673, Herefs. RO, wills ser., AA 20

Fry [married name Wilson], **Caroline** (1787–1846), author, was born in a house opposite the Pantiles at Tunbridge Wells on 31 December 1787. She was the sixth daughter and youngest but one of the ten children of John Fry, a gentleman farmer. She was taught at home by her boarding-school-educated elder sisters, with the aid of unrestricted access to circulating libraries. Her father's pride in her precocious literary ambition led him to publish her youthful composition, a *History of England in Verse* (1802). After his death in 1802 the elder sisters' marriages opened up a wider social world to the younger children, but, as an insurance against crumbling family finances, Caroline was sent, at age seventeen, to spend fifteen months at a good London school. Some of her family, meanwhile, had abandoned the high-and-dry Anglicanism of their upbringing for more fervent evangelical piety. Caroline, however, was attracted by the introduction to London society afforded by a post as companion to the family of a rich Bloomsbury solicitor. Three years there taught her the social wisdom of concealing a reputation for cleverness, and brought about a recurrence of her childhood tendency to 'nervous depression'.

A spell with a Lincolnshire clergyman's family in her mid-twenties led Caroline Fry to feel dissatisfied with her prospects; this brought about a return to her childhood enthusiasm for Edward Young's *Night Thoughts* and an evangelical conversion, the progress of which she described at the conclusion of her *Autobiography* (1848), a posthumously published account, in the third person, of the early 'history of her mental and spiritual existence'. The letters appended show that access to London society enabled her to discuss famous preachers and attend the May meetings of the missionary societies, where she was an astute observer of the millenarian debate of the mid-1820s and of the growing rift between Edward Irving and his former flock. Resuming her versifying skills she published three slim volumes (1821–3) of moralizing poems and hymns of the *vanitas vanitatum* school.

Illness prompted Caroline Fry to turn to writing as a means of earning a living. In 1823, having first secured aristocratic patronage, she launched the *Assistant of Education, Religious and Literary* (10 vols., 1823–8), intended for children aged between ten and sixteen. The monthly order placed by the Royal Library, on the recommendation of Bishop Charles Sumner, was a measure of her success. Editorial essays, offering moral and religious reflections upon the domestic mores of upper-class society, subsequently enjoyed success in anthologized form as *The Listener* (2 vols., 1830; 13th edn, 1863; Philadelphia, 1849; trans., Paris, 1844) and *Gatherings* (1839).

In December 1827 Caroline Fry's continuing social acceptability was marked by her sitting for one of Lawrence's last female portraits: despite her pose as a substantial but languorous Regency beauty, with averted gaze, the determined chin is not disguised.

The heated religious debate of this period favoured books prepared to offer authoritative definitions of the beliefs of an 'out-and-out Evangelical, a Low Churchman, a Calvinist'. The preface to the cheap edition of Caroline Fry's *Christ our Example* (1832, 1867) claimed that evangelical scholars and theologians alike recognized this as 'the best book of its kind'. The recommendation by the *Methodist Times* that it should be adopted as a textbook for class meetings resulted in 27,000 copies being printed by 1907. Although she offered the occasional glancing blow at Tractarianism, successive books of a similar kind (1837–47) owed their success to a trenchant delivery, enlivened by sketches from daily life, and nowhere enfeebled by the effects of sentimental piety. Her series of books of prayers and meditations on portions of scripture showed similar characteristics (1828–48).

In 1831 Caroline Fry married William Wilson, a merchant, and, despite her Francophobic prejudices, they spent the honeymoon in Paris. By the mid-1830s the couple had settled at The Windmills, Blackheath, before moving to Woolwich in 1844. Her letters suggest that ill health and her husband's limited income curbed their extensive social round, although she kept up her correspondence with the pious aristocracy. The recuperative powers of Hastings were tried too late and she returned to Tunbridge Wells to die of cancer and a 'congested lung' (Fry, appended letter) on 17 September 1846. She was survived by her husband.   ELISABETH JAY

Sources C. Fry, *An autobiography: letters, and remains of the author of The listener, Christ our law, &c.* (1848) • T. S. Dickson, *Caroline Fry: a story of grace* (1908) • A. M. W. Christopher, preface, in C. Fry, *Christ our example* (1907) • J. Julian, ed., *A dictionary of hymnology* (1892) • d. cert.

Likenesses T. Lawrence, oils, 1827, National Gallery, London

Fry, Charles Burgess (1872–1956), sportsman and journalist, was born on 25 April 1872 at Croydon, Surrey, the eldest son of Lewis John Fry, a civil servant who controlled the constabulary candidates' department at Scotland Yard, and his wife, Constance Isabella White. His early years were spent in Kent and east Sussex and he first made a sporting impression at Hornbrook House preparatory school in Blackheath, where he captained both the cricket and football teams, before winning a scholarship to Repton School in 1885. This was a clear indicator of the keen intellect which complemented his sporting achievements throughout his life. Fry soon showed himself to be an outstanding athlete by running under 11 seconds for the 100 yards and setting a school long jump record of 21 feet, which lasted for more than twenty years until beaten by a future Olympic champion, Harold Abrahams. Football, too, came easily to Fry. By the age of fifteen he was an integral part of the first eleven, and by the time he left Repton in 1891 he had already represented Casuals, one of the great amateur club sides of the time. Given his later reputation as a batsman of brilliant consistency, his cricketing accomplishments at Repton were modest. He was no less prominent in the classroom, and carried off prizes for Greek, Latin, French, and German.

It was Fry's flair as a classics student which earned him the top scholarship to Wadham College, Oxford, ahead of F. E. Smith (later the earl of Birkenhead). He was a dominating figure in his four years at the university and continued, for the most part, to match sporting exploits with academic excellence. He was also a keen debater and an enthusiastic member of the Oxford University Dramatic Society. He won blues for cricket, association football, and athletics and, but for injury, would probably have added a rugby blue to his laurels. In 1892 he beat the English record for the long jump with a leap of 23 feet 5 inches and a year later added another inch and a half to that mark to equal the world record set by the American C. S. Reber in 1891. Fry the raconteur embellished the achievement in later years with the claim that he had enjoyed a hearty lunch in college and had laid down his post-prandial cigar before leaping into history at Oxford's Iffley Road track. He gained a first in classical moderations in 1893, but worries over his finances and the health of his mother brought on a nervous breakdown which accounted for a disappointing fourth-class degree in *literae humaniores* in 1895.

Fry dabbled with journalism while at Oxford and after teaching at Charterhouse School from 1896 to 1898 he found that writing was the most agreeable way of subsidizing his chosen career as an amateur cricketer. He had played one match for the county of his birth, Surrey, before going up to Oxford in 1891, but it was for Sussex, his adopted home, that Fry played from 1894 to 1908. He was

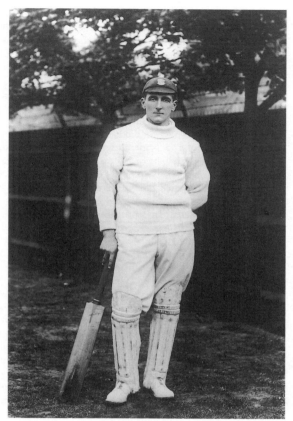

Charles Burgess Fry (1872–1956), by Thomas Henry Bolland, 1905

chosen for Lord Hawke's tour to South Africa in 1895–6, though this was in an era when many top players were unavailable for lengthy trips overseas, and played the first two of his twenty-six test matches for England. With Kumar Shri Ranjitsinhji he formed a formidable partnership for Sussex. In 1901 he enjoyed a summer of extraordinary achievement: he made 3147 runs at an average of 78.67, became the first player to hit centuries in six successive innings, and finished top of the national batting averages, a feat he was to repeat five more times in his career. He saw out the end of his career as a Hampshire player and though he turned forty at the start of the 1912 season he enjoyed huge success with the bat in both 1911 and 1912.

By comparison with his masterly form in the county championship, Fry's record as a cricketer at international level was disappointing. Despite being a man of unshakeable self-confidence, he was plainly afflicted by nerves in test matches. He made only two centuries in tests but captained England in the unique triangular series against Australia and South Africa in 1912. He did not play much after the First World War, but England's 5–0 series defeat in Australia in 1920–21, followed by continued lack of success against the same opposition the following summer, led to a panic-stricken call for a 49-year-old Fry to take over the captaincy. He accepted, with the proviso that he must make runs before taking the field at Lord's. In the event he was unable to convince himself on that score and withdrew from the game. His final first-class appearances were in India in 1921–2, and he finished with career statistics of 30,886 runs at an outstanding average of 50.22; he scored 94 centuries.

Alongside the poetic qualities of Ranjitsinhji's batting, Fry's style could seem rather mechanical, but it was a triumph for application and observation. There have been few cricketers who have applied such a resourceful intellect to mastering the principles of batsmanship and, although in the early part of his career he had the reputation for being a defensive player, he evolved a technique which enabled him to score with great fluency. He drove with immense power and his powers of concentration were huge. Fry was also a useful medium-pace bowler in the early part of his career, but he had an unorthodox action and was called for throwing on four occasions.

As a cricketer of limited personal means, Fry was grateful for the income provided by journalism. While still an Oxford student he wrote on cricket, football, and rugby for *Isis* magazine. He contributed to Ranjitsinhji's *Jubilee Book of Cricket* (1897) and collaborated with the Middlesex player-photographer George Beldam to produce two definitive works on technique, *Great Batsmen* (1905) and *Great Bowlers and Fielders* (1906). *Batsmanship* (1912) was another work of enduring value. In collaboration with his wife he also wrote a cricket-based novel, *A Mother's Son* (1907), but it was as a prolific journalist that he pioneered the style of newspaper contribution which has become commonplace: the informed comment of the active sportsman. His inventive and thought-provoking columns illuminated *The Captain*, a magazine for boys, launched in 1899, and he was also an early contributor to the *Daily Express*, which started up in 1900. The Newnes publishing house, which included *The Captain*, were so enamoured of Fry that in 1904 they launched a magazine named after him. It was the perfect vehicle for his eclectic mind and pen. He could write about everything from fishhooks to Esperanto, map reading to phrenology. The magazine's influence eventually dwindled as Fry's involvement lessened, and it expired when war broke out in 1914.

Fry's athletics career did not endure beyond his time at Oxford, but he was still much in demand as a footballer. He turned out regularly for the Corinthians, an amateur side frequently equal in quality to an international team, and also played as a speedy full-back for Southampton in the southern league. He won the first of his two international caps against Ireland in 1901 and the following year appeared for Southampton against Sheffield United in the Football Association cup final at Crystal Palace. Southampton lost 2–1 in a replay and two days later Fry was back on cricketing duty, making 82 for London counties against Surrey at the Oval.

In the mid-1890s Fry had first become aware of the training ship *Mercury*, on the banks of the River Hamble in Hampshire, which was founded in 1885 by Charles Hoare, senior partner in the family banking firm. Fry also got to know Hoare's mistress, Beatrice Holme Sumner (1862–1946), and although it appears that Hoare did not, initially, regard the relationship in a sympathetic light, their subsequent marriage protected him from damaging scandal, and he helped to subsidize Fry's cricketing career. The marriage took place at St Pancras parish church in London on 4 June 1898 and the couple, who had one son and two daughters, took over the running of the *Mercury* after Hoare died in 1908. Fry remained director of the training ship until 1950, and gained the honorary rank of captain in the Royal Naval Reserve. Under his wife's austere influence the *Mercury* gained a severe reputation for the harsh treatment of cadets, a regime which Fry did nothing to ameliorate.

Fry was also politically active between the wars. He was persuaded by Ranjitsinhji to work as his assistant when he represented the Indian princes at the League of Nations, and it was also in Geneva in 1920, so Fry claimed, that he was offered the chance of becoming king of Albania. He was also a regular visitor to India in the 1920s. Three times he stood unsuccessfully for parliament, as a Liberal candidate at Brighton and Banbury at the general elections of 1922 and 1923, and at the Oxford by-election in 1924.

In the late 1920s and early 1930s Fry was several times struck down by mental illness, but he made a triumphant return as a journalist for the *Evening Standard* in 1934 and was in constant demand for the rest of his life, in print, on radio, and latterly on television. His autobiography, *Life Worth Living* (1939), was an ebullient reflection of his multifaceted achievements, interests, and thought-provoking theories, even if it glossed over chapters and incidents which showed him in a less distinguished light. He died at the Middlesex Hospital, London, of kidney failure on 7 September 1956. A private funeral service was held at Golders Green crematorium on 11 September and his ashes were interred at Repton parish church on 28 September.

Fry, a man of medium height and build, bright-eyed and handsome, has strong claims to be regarded as the greatest sporting all-rounder of his or any era since. His sporting exploits, in themselves, were remarkable, but he also had a brilliant and original mind. His versatility of purpose, perhaps, contributed to a life which never fulfilled itself, and a stubborn conviction that he was invariably right did not always endear him to the establishment or even to his fellow journalists.　　　　CLIVE ELLIS

Sources C. Ellis, *C. B.: the life of Charles Burgess Fry* (1984) • I. Wilton, *C. B. Fry, an English hero* (1999) • A. W. Myers, *C. B. Fry: the man and his methods* (1912) • C. B. Fry, *Life worth living: some phases of an Englishman* (1939) • D. Batchelor, *C. B. Fry* (1951) • *Wisden* (1895) • *Wisden* (1957) • E. W. Swanton, *Sort of a cricket person* (1972) • R. Morris, *The captain's lady* (1985) • *CGPLA Eng. & Wales* (1956)
Archives BL, corresp. with Society of Authors, Add. MS 63243 | FILM BFI NFTVA, documentary footage • BFI NFTVA, news footage | SOUND BBC WAC
Likenesses E. Hawkins, photograph, 1894, repro. in *Wisden* (1895) • W. Rothenstein, lithograph, c.1896, repro. in W. Rothenstein, *Oxford characters* (1896) • T. H. Bolland, photograph, 1905, PRO [*see illus.*] • A. C. Taylor, lithograph, 1905 (after a photograph by G. W. Beldam), NPG • H. Coster, photographs, NPG • E. Nelson,

statuette, Marylebone Cricket Club, Lord's, London · Rotary Photo, photograph, NPG · photograph, repro. in *Wisden* (1957)

Wealth at death £9197 2s. 11d.: probate, 19 Nov 1956, *CGPLA Eng. & Wales*

Fry, Danby Palmer (1818–1903), legal writer, was born on 1 December 1818 in Great Ormond Street, London, the second son in the family of four sons and four daughters of Alfred Augustus Fry and his wife, Jane Sarah Susannah, *née* Westcott. His father was a scholar and linguist, who was accountant and for some years a partner in the firm of Thomas de la Rue & Co., wholesale stationers. He was named after his father's friend Danby Palmer of Norwich. His elder brother, Alfred Augustus Fry, was the first English barrister to practise in Constantinople.

Fry was educated at Hunter Street Academy, Brunswick Square, London, a well-known grammar school run by Jonathan Dawson. George Dawson, later a well-known Baptist preacher and lecturer, was a schoolfellow.

In 1836 Fry became a clerk in the Poor Law Board, first at Somerset House and afterwards at Gwydyr House, Whitehall. On 1 April 1848, during the Chartist riots, he was officially deputed to report to headquarters the proceedings of the agitators on Kennington Common. Each hour he received messengers to whom he delivered his hastily written reports. Called to the bar at Lincoln's Inn on 30 January 1851, he became in October 1871 inspector of audits, and on 15 October 1873 assistant secretary to the Local Government Board. From 1878 until his retirement in 1882 he was legal adviser to the board.

Fry made some reputation as author of legal handbooks. As early as 1846 he produced a work on taxes which was published officially. Several of his other works, on various legal subjects, ran to many editions and became standard works.

Through his father, whose circle of acquaintances included Lord Brougham, Leigh Hunt, and others interested in social and political reforms, Fry was friendly from an early age with Charles Knight and with Sir Rowland Hill's family. Economic and philanthropic problems occupied much of his attention, but his leisure was devoted to philology, and he became an expert student of both Old English and Old French. He helped his father in compiling in manuscript an English dictionary with the words arranged according to roots. He was an original member of the Philological Society, founded in 1842, its treasurer for many years, and a contributor of well informed papers on linguistic subjects to its *Transactions*. He was one of the original committee of the Early English Text Society, founded by F. J. Furnivall in 1864. He was joint author with Benjamin Dawson of a small book on gender in the French language. His philological studies were pursued until his death. He died, unmarried, on 16 February 1903, at his house, 166 Haverstock Hill, and was buried at Highgate cemetery.

H. B. WHEATLEY, *rev.* CATHERINE PEASE-WATKIN

Sources personal knowledge (1912)

Wealth at death £17,512 4s. 1d.: probate, 4 April 1903, *CGPLA Eng. & Wales*

Fry, Edmund (1754–1835), typefounder, was born at Bristol, the son of Joseph *Fry (1728–1787), chocolate manufacturer and typefounder, and his wife, Anna, *née* Portsmouth (1719/20–1803), daughter of Henry Portsmouth MD of Basingstoke, Hampshire. He studied medicine, took the degree of MD at Edinburgh, and spent some time at St George's Hospital, London. Already a successful chocolate manufacturer, Joseph Fry became partner in the Bristol Letter Foundry with the printer William Pine in 1764. They moved to Queen Street, near Upper Moorfields, London, about 1768, where they operated as printers and typefounders. In 1782 Joseph Fry took his two sons, Edmund and Henry, into partnership in the type foundry business.

Edmund Fry cut a type suitable for embossing words on paper for the blind in 1784, though this was not adopted then. On 19 April 1785 he married Jenny Windover (d. 1805), daughter of Nicholas Windover of Stockbridge, Hampshire. Only one of their children, Windover Fry (1797–1835), survived infancy. Joseph Fry retired in 1787 and the new firm, Edmund Fry & Co., issued their first *Specimen of Printing Types*. It was followed the next year by an enlarged edition. Several founts of the oriental type, which fill twelve pages, were cut by Fry. In 1788 the printing business was separated from the foundry and remained at Worship Street as the Cicero Press, under the management of Henry Fry. The foundry moved to premises opposite Bunhill Fields in Chiswell Street and new works erected in a street then called Type Street (now Moore Street). Homer's series of the classics (1789–94), printed by Millar Ritchie, were from the characters of the Type Street foundry.

In 1793 Edmund Fry & Co., letter founders to the prince of Wales, produced a *Specimen of Metal-Cast Ornaments Curiously Adjusted to Paper*, which gained vogue among printers. The next year Fry took Isaac Steele into partnership, and published a specimen which 'shows a marked advance on its predecessors' (Reed, 306). In 1798 he circulated a prospectus of the great work on which he had been occupied for sixteen years, published as *Pantographia, containing accurate copies of all the known alphabets of the world, together with an English explanation of the peculiar force and power of each letter, to which are added specimens of all well-authenticated oral languages, forming a comprehensive digest of phonology* (1799). The volume contains more than two hundred alphabets, including eighteen varieties of the Chaldee and thirty-two of the Greek. Many of the characters were expressly cut by Fry for his book. On the admission of George Knowles in 1799, the firm took the name of Fry, Steele, & Co. and undertook the sale of printing presses, but a year later Fry reassumed sole management of the business. At the beginning of the nineteenth century the modern-faced type supplanted the old-faced, and this is reflected in the types the company sold. The catalogue *Specimens of Modern Cut Printing Types from the Foundry of Messrs. Fry & Steele* was bound with C. Stower's *Printer's Grammar* in 1808.

Edmund Fry's wife died in 1805 and on 13 March 1807 he married Ann Hancock, with whom he had a son, Arthur

Edmund Fry
(1754–1835), by
unknown artist

(1809–1878). A catalogue, *Fry and Steele's Specimen of Printing Types*, was bound in with the 'Printing' article in Rees's *Cyclopaedia* (vol. 28, pt 2, published 16 September 1814), and in 1816 a *Specimen of Printing Types by Edmund Fry, Letter Founder to the King and Prince Regent*, was published. The firm soon after became Edmund Fry & Son, on the admission of his son, Windover. Fry cut several founts of oriental types for the University of Cambridge, the British and Foreign Bible Society, and other bodies. In a *Specimen* printed in 1824 the name is changed back to 'Edmund Fry at the Polyglot Foundry'. In 1828 he endeavoured to dispose of his business, and issued a descriptive circular, *Specimen of Modern Printing Types by Edmund Fry* (reprinted 1986). It was purchased by William Thorowgood of Fann Street and the stock removed in 1829. Some Fry type designs are still in the repertory due to a succession of amalgamations of typefounders since, which ensured the preservation of the original type matrices. Fry's Baskerville, Fry's Canon, and Fry's Ornamented were sometimes used in the 1920s and 30s by discerning printers of fine books, and a version of the Fry's Baskerville has been successfully translated for computer typesetting. In 1833 twenty designs for raised type for the blind were submitted to the Royal Scottish Society of Arts, who had offered a prize for the best example. Among them was one from Fry, to whom the gold medal was awarded.

Fry was one of the most learned among English typefounders, but he retired with very small financial means. He was a member of the Company of Stationers. Edmund Fry died at Dalby Terrace, City Road, London, at the age of eighty-one, on 22 December 1835.

H. R. TEDDER, *rev.* A. P. WOOLRICH

Sources private information (2004) · T. B. Reed, *Old English letter foundries* (1887) · T. Fry, *A brief memoir of Francis Fry* (1887) · T. C. Hansard, *Typographia: an historical sketch of the origin and progress of the art of printing* (1825) · J. Smith, ed., *A descriptive catalogue of Friends' books*, 1 (1867) · *GM*, 2nd ser., 5 (1836), 557–8 · *Transactions of the Royal Scottish Society of Arts*, 1 (1837) · introduction, *Stephenson Blake printing types* (1967) [includes a family tree tracing the descent of ownership of the various letter foundries] · W. Pincus Jaspert, W. Turner Berry, and A. F. Johnson, *The encyclopaedia of type faces*, 4th edn (1970); paperback edn (1993) · W. B. Todd, *A directory of printers and others in allied trade: London and vicinity, 1800–1840* (1972) · *DNB*

Likenesses F. Boileau, portrait, exh. 1877, repro. in G. Bullen, ed., *Caxton celebration 1877 catalogue* (1877) · silhouette, repro. in Reed, *Old English letter foundries* [see illus.]

Wealth at death small

Fry, Sir Edward (1827–1918), judge and zoologist, was born in Union Street, Bristol on 4 November 1827, the second son of Joseph Fry (1795–1879) and Mary Ann, *née* Swaine. Both his parents were Quakers. His father, a manufacturer of chocolate and cocoa, was a man with strong religious and philanthropic interests. A supporter of free trade, he continued the family tradition in business. Fry's mother, who was equally devout, also shared his father's love of reading, especially poetry. As a child, Fry was influenced by the Quaker circle, and especially by his father, to observe intensively, a habit which led him to take a lifelong interest in scenery, animals, and especially plants, and which he hoped had prevented him from 'growing into a mere lawyer'.

Fry was educated at home from an early age and his subjects included Latin, French, German, and Greek. From 1840 to 1841 he and his elder brother attended Bristol College, where at first they were ridiculed for their traditional Quaker dress and mannerisms. However, Fry was an able student, gaining a medal for English verse. After Bristol College closed in 1841, Dr James Booth, the headmaster, opened a private school which Fry attended until the end of 1842. During his time there he was greatly influenced by his reading of Berkeley's *New Theory of Vision* and by his close friendship with Walter Bagehot.

From 1843 until he went to London in October 1848, Fry worked in business and acquired a practical knowledge of accountancy and shipbroking. He did not take to a mercantile life, but he found time to read widely in the classics, literature, and history, and in 1846 at the age of nineteen wrote *A Treatise of the Elective Monarchies of Europe*, sending a paper entitled *The Osteology of the Hylobates agilis* to the Zoological Society of London the same year. This paper was published by the society, along with another entitled *The Relations of the Edentata to the Reptiles, Especially of the Armadilloes to the Tortoises*. Fry was also interested in the study of the osteology of the skull (on which he worked with William Budd) and in free trade and education. As the result of a continental tour in 1848 he published an article, 'Germany in 1848', in the *London University Magazine*. Fry worked so hard that in the London matriculation examination of 1849 he secured the prize for zoology, beating William Henry Flower who was to become the head of the Natural History Museum at South Kensington.

After his visit to the continent Fry decided to go to the bar, and it was with this in view that he entered University College, London, where Thomas Hodgkin and Walter Bagehot were fellow students. After a successful university career he took his BA degree in 1851. He spent time in the chambers of Bevan Braithwaite, the conveyancer,

Sir Edward Fry (1827–1918), by Roger Fry, 1896

Edward Bullen, the eminent special pleader in the Temple, and Charles Hall, the equity draughtsman. He was called to the bar at Lincoln's Inn in 1854. Owing to family financial difficulties and a scarcity of briefs, Fry's career at the bar started slowly; it was not until the favourable reception of his *Treatise on the Specific Performance of Contracts* (1858) that the tide began to turn. During that time Fry also produced a volume, *Essays on the Accordance of Christianity with the Nature of Man* (1857), which attracted wide approval, including that of Baron von Bunsen. After ten difficult years Fry's career started to improve on his marriage on 6 April 1859 in the Friends' meeting-house at Lewes to Mariabella (1833–1930), daughter of the Quaker barrister John *Hodgkin (1800–1875), with whom he had two sons and seven daughters, one of whom died at the age of four. They included the relief worker Joan Mary *Fry (1862–1955), the art historian and painter Roger Eliot *Fry (1866–1934), and the penal reformer (Sara) Margery *Fry (1874–1958). At about the same time as his marriage Fry discarded the external peculiarities of Quaker dress and formulations as not being essential to religious faith, issuing a pamphlet on the subject in 1859.

From 1859 until he was raised to the bench in 1877 Fry acquired a steadily growing practice, not only in Chancery and company work but at the parliamentary bar. He took silk in 1869 and joined the court of Vice-Chancellor James, competing with Richard Paul Amphlett and Edward Ebenezer Kay, who, like himself, were later to sit in the Court of Appeal. He quickly made his mark by a convincing argument in a company case in which he succeeded against Lord Westbury, Sir Roundell Palmer, and others. When James became a lord justice, Fry practised for a time

before Vice-Chancellor Bacon, but eventually migrated to the rolls court, presided over by Lord Romilly and, after 1873, by Sir George Jessel. However, pressure of work in the House of Lords made it necessary for him soon to specialize. His work continued to increase in volume, and when in April 1877 Lord Cairns offered him the additional judgeship in the Chancery Division authorized that year by statute, he accepted the offer with considerable misgivings, and characteristically set to work to put in writing his conceptions of his new duties. Fry was the first judge appointed after the Judicature Act had merged the high court of chancery in the High Court and was also the first Chancery judge to bear the title of Mr Justice and to go on circuit. He was knighted on 30 April 1877. He at first dreaded the circuit work, but came to like it, and apparently impressed the bar with his judicial versatility.

Fry's principal legal achievement dates from this period, before his move to the Court of Appeal in 1883 following the death of Sir George Jessel. The Judicature Acts of 1873 and 1875, as well as reorganizing the courts, had provided a body of rules to regulate practice in the separate divisions of the new High Court. After some years these rules needed revision as the result of experience. It was also necessary to provide a comparatively inexpensive machinery enabling trustees, executors, and beneficiaries to secure necessary judicial aid without the ruinous costs of administration suits, often undertaken merely for the sake of the costs. Fry was on the rule committee of the judges, and felt pleased with his work in addressing this problem. He was said to have invented the procedure by originating summons and was largely responsible for the development of the new system of practice, which replaced the old practice of the high court of chancery.

Between 1883 and 1892 Fry sat in the Court of Appeal with, among others, Lord Esher, lords justices Baggallay, Cotton, Lindley, and Bowen. The contributions of Lindley, Bowen, and Fry to the development of English case law in the later nineteenth century cannot be overestimated. Fry was admired for his intellectual ability, which was evinced clearly in his Court of Appeal judgment in *Robertson* v. *Hartopp* in 1899.

After fifteen years on the bench, Fry decided to retire in 1892, despite having twenty-five active years ahead of him. He felt weary of the noise and turmoil of the courts and longed to live permanently in the countryside with more leisure for reading and travel. The Frys left London for their country home at Failand, near Clifton, where the former judge sat in the local court of petty sessions, and from 1899 to 1913 took the chair of quarter sessions and an aldermanship of the Somerset county council. He was eighty-six when he retired from this work. From time to time he also sat on the judicial committee of the privy council.

Contemporaries differed in their opinion of Fry's judicial capacities, particularly since he did not follow the expected route of taking a seat in the House of Lords and was thought to have cut a promising career unnaturally short. He was renowned for his painstaking scrupulosity, for his passion for justice, and for his unusual versatility. Yet his reluctance to move beyond the known facts of any given case before him was seen by some other judges as pedantic and overly scrupulous. His legal work, undertaken at a time of transition in the courts system (1877–92), was thought to have been particularly valuable in developing a new attitude to legal matters, and he was regarded, along with Lord Cairns, as primarily responsible for the development of equity jurisprudence in the late nineteenth century.

Fry was very active in later life, taking more than four years of leisure and travel and then accepting, in 1897, the offer to preside over the royal commission on the Irish Land Acts, an office in which his services were at once widely called upon. In 1898 he acted as conciliator, under the Conciliation Act of 1896, in the colliery strike of south Wales and Monmouth, and, although the conciliation failed, his report led to the termination of the strike. In 1901 he acted as arbitrator in the Grimsby fishery dispute, and in 1902 he sat as president on the court of arbitration connected with the water companies of London, declining to receive more remuneration than would have made up his salary if he had been sitting as a lord justice. In 1906 and 1907 he acted as arbitrator between the London and North Western Railway Company and its men, refusing to accept any remuneration at all for that work.

In the meantime Fry was brought into touch with international affairs in 1902–3 by acting as arbitrator at The Hague between the United States and Mexico in the pious funds of California dispute, the first case to be brought before The Hague tribunal (created by the first Hague conference of 1899). Fry's next task was to act as the British legal assessor on the commission appointed to deal with the North Sea (Dogger Bank) incident in October 1904, when the Russian fleet in a moment of panic attacked the British herring fleet—an incident that threatened war. Fry's work on the commission—the findings of which upheld the British case—was highly commended. He played an active part at the second Hague Conference of 1907, as ambassador-extraordinary and first plenipotentiary delegate of Great Britain. Although by then an octogenarian, Fry nevertheless made his personality felt; he took a leading part in the debates, and was entrusted by the British government with the duty of raising the questions of the limitation of armaments and of the exchange of information on the subject of naval construction. In the next year he again acted at The Hague as one of the arbitrators in the quarrel between France and Germany over the Casablanca incident, which was settled in May 1909.

The remaining nine years of Fry's life were occupied with the various pursuits, literary, scientific, and educational, in which he delighted. His interest in the University of London lasted for nearly half a century. He joined the council of University College during the busiest of his years at the bar, and strove hard and successfully to secure a teaching university for London. He did much on the senate of the university to bring into the university all the institutions of high educational character in the metropolis. The scheme which was eventually adopted was not

very different from that for which he had always striven. His efforts were not limited to London. In 1906 he presided over a commission to inquire into the condition of Trinity College, Dublin, and of the Royal University of Ireland with a view to the solution of the problem of university education in Ireland. He dissented from the main report, and the view taken by himself, Sir Arthur W. Rücker, and J. G. Butcher that the ancient foundation of Trinity College should be preserved was accepted by Augustine Birrell when he became chief secretary in 1907.

Fry, who twice declined a peerage, was created GCB in 1907; he was also elected fellow of the Royal Society (1883) and honorary fellow of Balliol College, Oxford (1894). He died on 18 October 1918 at Failand House, Failand, Somerset, and was buried in Failand churchyard. He was survived by his wife.

J. E. G. DE MONTMORENCY, rev. SINÉAD AGNEW

Sources A. Fry, ed., *A memoir of the Rt Hon. Sir Edward Fry* (1921) · J. Foster, *Men-at-the-bar: a biographical hand-list of the members of the various inns of court*, 2nd edn (1885), 168 · WWW · A. T. C. Pratt, ed., *People of the period: being a collection of the biographies of upwards of six thousand living celebrities*, 1 (1897), 415 · W. P. Baildon, ed., *The records of the Honorable Society of Lincoln's Inn: admissions*, 2 (1896), 243 · Allibone, *Dict.* · J. B. Scott, *The proceedings of the Hague conferences* (1926) · A. Hopkinson, *Memoir of Sir Edward Fry* · *Law reports* · E. Kilmurray, *Dictionary of British portraiture*, 3 (1981), 73 · *Men and women of the time* (1899)

Archives King's Cam., family corresp. · U. Warwick Mod. RC, diaries and prison visits

Likenesses F. Holl, oils, 1883, NPG · R. Fry, oils, 1896, Lincoln's Inn, London [*see illus.*] · Barraud, photograph, NPG; repro. in *Men and Women of the Day* (1890), vol. 3 · Elliott & Fry, photograph, repro. in *ILN*, 113 (1898), 49 · Elliott & Fry, photograph, repro. in *ILN*, 117 (1900), 886 · Lafayette, photograph, NPG · Lock & Whitfield, woodburytype, NPG; repro. in T. Cooper, *Men of mark, a gallery of contemporary portraits*, 7 vols. (1876–83), vol. 5 · Spy [L. Ward], chromolithograph caricature, NPG; repro. in *VF* (30 May 1891) · print, NPG

Wealth at death £119,051 15s. 2d.: probate, 8 Feb 1919, *CGPLA Eng. & Wales*

Fry [*née* Gurney], **Elizabeth** (1780–1845), penal reformer and philanthropist, was born on 21 May 1780 at Magdalen Street, Norwich, the fourth of twelve children, seven daughters and five sons, of John Gurney (1749–1809), a merchant and banker, and Catherine Bell (1754–1792). Her parents were both descendants of old Quaker families, Catherine Bell being the great-granddaughter of the Quaker apologist Robert Barclay. Elizabeth's siblings included Joseph John *Gurney, Samuel *Gurney (1786–1856), Daniel *Gurney, and Louisa Gurney *Hoare. In 1786 the family moved to Earlham Hall, 2 miles from Norwich. The seven sisters received a fairly thorough education, although Elizabeth, often plagued by her 'nerves', missed many lessons and learned to spell properly only much later. Her mother, Catherine, a pious woman and serious Friend, died in 1792 aged thirty-eight. Her father, John Gurney, was a Quaker by birth and habit rather than by choice. His children in the 1790s began to share the feeling—common among the élite—that religious feeling was something to look down on.

Elizabeth Gurney, therefore, went against the ways of her immediate family when, in February 1798, she *'felt*

Elizabeth Fry (1780–1845), by George Richmond, 1844

there [was] a God' (Rose, 19). The usual tale of her religious conversion stresses the role of the travelling Quaker William Savery, who visited Norwich at the time. Yet, as her diary shows, she was equally inspired by two women Quakers, her cousin Priscilla Hannah Gurney and Deborah Darby, later in 1798 (*Memoir*, 1.58–60, 74). In 1799 Elizabeth Gurney made herself known to the world as a plain or strict Friend by adopting Quaker dress and speech. Her religious belief became the pillar of her life and pervaded all that she did.

On 19 August 1800 the strong-minded Elizabeth Gurney married Joseph Fry (1777–1861), a shy but warm-hearted young man from a family of orthodox and wealthy Quakers. The Fry business dealt in colonial wares; in 1808 Joseph started a bank as well. Between 1801 and 1816 the couple had ten children; an eleventh child was born in 1822. They first lived at St Mildred's Court in London, but, to Elizabeth's joy, in 1809 they removed to Plashet House in East Ham. Despite her busy family life, Elizabeth Fry undertook work in the community. She was a regular visitor of the so-called 'Irish colony', where she distributed clothing, food, and medicine. An advocate of vaccination, she also contributed to the near elimination of smallpox among the children of neighbouring villages. In 1811 she

was acknowledged as a Quaker minister. Although Joseph Fry supported her philanthropic activities, Elizabeth Fry felt a tension between her married state and religious ambitions most of her life.

Early in 1813 Elizabeth Fry visited the women's side of Newgate prison in London to find several hundred female prisoners—young and old, tried and untried, hardened criminals and first offenders—with their children, packed in a few crowded and poorly supervised rooms. Her interest in the treatment of prisoners was part of Quaker tradition, and was shared by other, often religiously inspired, reformers and philanthropists, who were appalled by the conditions in English prisons and by the severity of the criminal law. But if she was not alone in her concerns, she was a pioneer in her attempts to improve significantly the situation of female prisoners. During the next four years, however, family affairs prevented her from a serious involvement in the prison cause.

Education had always been high on Elizabeth Fry's social agenda. At Earlham she had improvised a Sunday school, attended by some eighty pupils. In East Ham she was co-founder of a girls' school. When she returned to Newgate prison about December 1816, her first innovation was the establishment of a little school for the prisoners' children. After discussions with the prisoners and meetings with the prison authorities, Fry and her female collaborators introduced a system of classification of the prisoners, prison dress, constant supervision by a matron and monitors (chosen from among the prisoners), religious and elementary education, and paid employment. The result was a remarkable transformation in the conduct especially of convicted prisoners (although the removal of alcohol and playing cards was not universally welcomed). Fry or one of her helpers visited Newgate daily; she herself read to prisoners from the Bible on Fridays. Her melodious voice melted her listeners, hardened criminals as well as experienced politicians, who came to see the changes for themselves. The work gained a more permanent basis in April 1817 with the creation of the Ladies' Association for the Reformation of the Female Prisoners in Newgate, extended in 1821 into the British Ladies' Society for Promoting the Reformation of Female Prisoners, with correspondents in Russia, Italy, Switzerland, and the Netherlands. The British Ladies' Society appears to have been the first nationwide women's organization in Britain.

The essence of Elizabeth Fry's religiously inspired thinking about prisoners (male and female) was that they were fellow human beings, whose treatment should be based on 'the principles of justice and humanity' (Fry, *Observations*, 74). Imprisonment, instead of contributing to the physical and moral degradation of inmates, ought to lead to their reformation in prisons operating as 'schools of industry and virtue' (Gurney, *Notes*, v). In order to 'amend the Character and change the Heart', prisoners were to be treated with kindness—Fry's watchword—instead of cruelty and neglect. Her other guiding principle was that women prisoners should be 'under the care of women'—matrons, turnkeys, visitors—and preferably in prisons of their own (Fry, *Observations*, 16–17, 22, 27–33; *Memoir*, 1.281, 292).

Impressed by the changes in Newgate, contemporaries regarded them as proof that reformation of prisoners was possible. The fact that the female inmates of Newgate had traditionally been seen as 'of all characters the most irreclaimable' (T. F. Buxton, *Inquiry whether Crime and Misery are Produced or Prevented, by our Present System of Prison Discipline*, sixth edition, 1818, 133) only added to Elizabeth Fry's fame. Beginning in 1818, she made a number of journeys through England, Scotland, and Ireland, combining her work as a Quaker minister with prison reform. She visited prisons, suggested measures for improvement to the local authorities, and established ladies' committees for visiting female prisoners. In 1827 she published her handbook *Observations on the Visiting, Superintendence, and Government, of Female Prisoners* (reprinted with additions in the same year), and in 1840 *Hints on the Advantages and the Duties of Ladies' Committees who Visit Prisons*. Two related causes taken up by her were capital punishment—in her *Observations* she presented her own system as an alternative—and the treatment of female prisoners on board convict ships to New South Wales, Australia, which she managed to improve substantially.

In 1828 Fry's husband's bank went bankrupt, a humiliating experience, especially for one as sensitive to status as Elizabeth. Joseph Fry was disowned by the Quakers and the family had to move to a smaller house, The Cedars, in Upton Lane, West Ham. In the 1830s Elizabeth was also confronted with serious opposition to her prison work, which was labelled amateurish. Never one to give up, and with the financial support of her brothers, between 1838 and 1843 Fry made five demanding journeys to the continent. There she met with fellow reformers and inspected prisons and other institutions. She was received by the highest authorities, with whom she pleaded for a more humanitarian treatment of prisoners and lunatics, the abolition of slavery (especially in Denmark and the Netherlands), and religious toleration. She also preached and distributed religious tracts, among them her own *Texts for every Day in the Year* (1839), which has since been translated into French, German, and Italian. Although prison reform was her main cause, she also established a Maternal Society in Brighton in 1813, libraries for the coastguard of England, several district visiting societies, a servant's society, and a Society of Nursing Sisters (1840), the first attempt to reform nursing in Britain. After several years of declining health, Fry died after a stroke at Ramsgate on 13 October 1845, and was buried on 20 October in the Quaker burial-ground at Barking.

Fry's is an interesting legacy. Her work undoubtedly contributed to dramatic improvements in British prison conditions and, through her collaboration with her brother-in-law Thomas Fowell Buxton, to revisions in the criminal law. Several of her ideas about the treatment of female prisoners were laid down in legislation. In Europe, the USA, Canada, and Australia her name became synonymous with the compassionate treatment of prisoners—primarily, but not exclusively, female. From Berlin (1840) and The Hague (1916) to Vancouver (1939), her example led to the establishment of societies for prison visiting and prison reform, most of them by women. Of great significance was her call on women to become active on behalf of those of 'their own sex' (Fry, *Observations*, 3, 8), which stimulated 'woman's work for woman', and thus the organized women's movement. The numerous biographies to appear in Britain and elsewhere have contributed to her status as one of the most celebrated women of the nineteenth century and ensured that her memory continued to inspire others. Florence Nightingale seems to have been one of them (but, contrary to popular myth, no hard evidence of any personal contact between the two women exists). In May 2002 she beat off competition from Jane Austen, Elizabeth Barrett Browning, and Octavia Hill to become only the second woman (after Nightingale) to appear on a Bank of England note (five pounds).

Elizabeth Fry is, however, only marginally represented in mainstream accounts of prison history. As a religiously motivated woman she was considered old-fashioned and unprofessional by later (male, professional, secular) reformers and historians. Her activities were mainly directed towards women, who are often absent from general histories of prison reform. Finally, throughout her career as a prison expert she opposed the new system of solitary confinement, denouncing it as inhumane, dangerous to the mental and physical health of the prisoners, prone to abuse by the guards, and inadequate to prepare prisoners for re-entering active life. But since this system won the day, her opposition has allowed opponents to label her work as *passé*.

FRANCISCA DE HAAN

Sources *Memoir of the life of Elizabeth Fry, with extracts from her letters and journal*, ed. [K. Fry and R. E. Cresswell], 2 vols. (1847) · E. Fry, diaries and correspondence, 1797–1845, RS Friends, Lond., Gurney MSS 255–273 · E. Fry, *Observations on the visiting, superintendence, and government, of female prisoners* (1827) · J. J. Gurney, *Notes on a visit made to some of the prisons in Scotland and the north of England, in company with Elizabeth Fry* (1819) · *A concise view of the origin and progress of the British Ladies' Society for promoting the reformation of female prisoners* [n.d., 1840?] · [J. J. Gurney], *Brief memoirs of Thomas Fowell Buxton and Elizabeth Fry* (1845) · *Elizabeth Fry's journeys on the continent, 1840–1841, from a diary kept by her niece Elizabeth Gurney*, ed. R. B. Johnson [1931] · F. de Haan and R. van der Heide, 'Vrouwen-Vereenigingen, Dames-Comité's en feministen. De zorg van vrouwen voor vrouwelijke gevangenen in de negentiende eeuw', *Tijdschrift voor Sociale Geschiedenis*, 23 (1997), 278–311 · J. Rose, *Elizabeth Fry* (1994) · A. Summers, '"In a few years we shall none of us that now take care of them be here": philanthropy and the state in the thinking of Elizabeth Fry', *Historical Research*, 67 (1994), 134–42 · F. de Haan and A. van Drenth, *The rise of caring power: Elizabeth Fry and Josephine Butler in Britain and the Netherlands* (1999) · J. Whitney, *Elizabeth Fry. Quaker heroine*, new edn (1937) · E. B. Freedman, *Their sisters' keepers: women's prison reform in America, 1830–1930* (1981) · digest registers (burials), RS Friends, Lond. · digest registers (births), RS Friends, Lond. [London and Middlesex quarterly meeting; Catherine Bell] · d. cert.

Archives BL, copy of diary made by daughter, Add. MSS 47456–47457 · BL, letters and annotated Bible, Add. MSS 73528–73533 · Bodl. RH, corresp. with Thomas Fowell Buxton and letters to her sister Hannah Buxton and niece Priscilla Buxton · Boston PL, papers and corresp. · Devon RO, family corresp. · Norfolk RO, journals, notebook, papers, and corresp. · Norfolk RO, letters and family papers · RS Friends, Lond., diaries and corresp.; extracts from journals [microfilm copy] · Swarthmore College, Swarthmore,

Pennsylvania | BL, Egerton MSS, letters with other corresp. of Fry and Gurney families · Bodl. Oxf., papers of her niece Elizabeth Gurney, incl. papers relating to continental travel and letters to queen of Denmark · Lpool RO, letters to Lord Stanley · Som. ARS, Osborne MSS, family papers incl. those relating to her death · U. Durham L., letters to Jonathan and/or Hannah Backhouse

Likenesses S. Drummond, miniature, c.1815, NPG · G. Scharf senior, pencil drawing, 1819, BM · R. Dighton, coloured etching, pubd 1820 (*In prison and ye came unto me*), BM · C. R. Leslie, portrait, 1823, NPG · G. Richmond, watercolour, 1844, priv. coll. [*see illus.*] · S. Cousins, mezzotint, pubd 1850 (after G. Richmond), BM · line engraving (after C. R. Leslie), NPG · oils (after C. R. Leslie, 1823), NPG · photograph (after albumen print of a group portrait, c.1842–1843), RS Friends, Lond. · stained glass window, St Olave's Church, Hart Street, London

Fry, Francis (1803–1886), businessman and bibliographer, was born on 28 October 1803 at Westbury-on-Trym, near Bristol, Gloucestershire, the second son of the seven children of Joseph Storrs Fry (1769–1835), manufacturer, and Ann Allen (1764?–1829). His grandfather Joseph *Fry (1728–1787) was a doctor, a manufacturer of porcelain and chocolate, and a partner in the firm of Fry and Pine, typefounders. His education began in a school at Fishponds, Bristol, run by a Quaker, Joel Lean. He then trained for business in Croydon, Surrey, before entering the family firm of J. S. Fry & Sons, chocolate and cocoa manufacturers in Bristol, at the age of twenty. In 1833 he married Matilda (1808?–1888), daughter of Daniel and Anne Penrose of Brittas, co. Wicklow. They had four sons and three daughters. After living in Bristol Fry and his family moved in 1839 to Cotham, then a rural area between Bristol and Redland; he built a house close to Cotham Tower.

Fry's business interests extended beyond chocolate manufacture, where for many years he was the most active partner in the family firm, to include, as had his grandfather's, porcelain manufacture and typefounding. He was a director of the Bristol waterworks from 1845 until his death, and chairman from 1874. He was a member of the first board of directors of the Bristol and Gloucester Railway from 1839 and served on the boards of four other railway companies. He was active in public service, though he declined to join the Bristol city council because of lack of time. In 1831 he served as a special constable in the Bristol riots. He was a member of the managing committees of the Bristol Philosophical Society and the subscription library. He suggested the introduction of a parcel post run by the railway companies well before the Post Office took up the idea.

Fry's Quakerism led him to involvement in the anti-slavery cause. In 1850 he visited northern Italy for three months as a member of a deputation from the Society of Friends to various sovereigns. He took advantage of the opportunity to visit galleries and museums. In 1852 he visited Germany and then northern Italy and Rome in 1857. A visit to Germany in 1860 was concerned largely with printing history: like many contemporary Quakers, he was a supporter of the British and Foreign Bible Society and he contributed to the formation of its collection of early bibles. He was a founding member of the first temperance society in Bristol.

Fry's chief claims to fame now are as a student of the bibliography of English versions of the printed Bible and as a collector of them. His interest in this aspect of the Bible was probably influenced by his grandfather's involvement in printing several bibles of typographical interest. His work in this field led to a number of publications; these and the knowledge that became evident in his contacts with many important contemporary collectors led to his high reputation in his day. Fry's most important publications were: a facsimile of the unique Tyndale English New Testament in the Bristol Baptist college (acquired in 1994 by the British Library) with an introduction (1862); *A Description of the Great Bible, 1539* (1865), which contained original leaves from fourteen printings to supplement the plates; *The Bible by Coverdale, MDXXXV* (1867); and *A Bibliographical Description of the Editions of the New Testament* (1878). In addition he published some short studies and facsimiles of early printed texts with introductions.

Modern scholarship, most recently that of B. J. McMullin, has rather discredited some of Fry's theories. By his enthusiasm for perfecting copies of incomplete bibles he unwittingly muddied the waters for future students of their printing history. The practice of improving imperfect copies of books by supplying missing pages from others or by carefully hand-drawn or traced facsimiles was not seriously frowned on in his day. His contemporary Robert Curzon, who bought bibles from him, described Fry as 'a Quaker, and a maker of Chocolate and Bibles, which he makes up from imperfect copies' (A. N. L. Munby, *Connoisseurs and Medieval Miniatures, 1750–1850*, 1972, 104). Fry's confidence in this area exceeded the real state of knowledge of the bibliography of the early editions of the English Bible. His studies were based on his own extensive collection, on a large number of copies which passed through his hands, on the extensive correspondence with other collectors, and on visits to libraries. He was always adamant that the substitute leaves he provided came from precisely the same printings.

Fry began the Bible collection from about 1850 and it formed the major part of his library. Some of the bibles were displayed in the Caxton celebration exhibition at South Kensington in 1877. The bulk of the English Bible collection, over 1200 volumes, was acquired by the British and Foreign Bible Society in 1890 for its library, at a cost of £6000. There were also a number of early continental bibles and a series of editions of the Book of Common Prayer and the Psalms as well as a small number of manuscripts. Tsar Alexander I presented him with a copy of the facsimile of the Codex Sinaiticus. Fry attempted also to form a comprehensive collection of Quaker literature of the seventeenth and eighteenth centuries and compiled a catalogue of the books belonging to the quarterly meeting of the Friends in Bristol. In addition to books he formed a distinguished collection of Bristol china: many pieces were described and illustrated in Hugh Owen's *Two Centuries of Ceramic Art in Bristol* (1873).

Fry died on 12 November 1886 at his home, Tower House, Cotham, Bristol, and was buried in the Quaker burial-ground at King's Weston, near Bristol. DAVID J. HALL

Sources T. Fry, *A brief memoir of Francis Fry* (1887) • *DNB* • 'Dictionary of Quaker biography', RS Friends, Lond. [card index] • J. Smith, ed., *A descriptive catalogue of Friends' books*, 2 vols. (1867); suppl. (1893) • *Biographical catalogue: being an account of the lives of Friends and others whose portraits are in the London Friends' Institute*, Society of Friends (1888) • *Annual Monitor* (1831), 14 • *Annual Monitor* (1837), 16–23 • *Annual Monitor* (1890), 75 • B. J. McMullin, 'The Bible and continuous reprinting in the early seventeenth century', *The Library*, 6th ser., 5 (1983), 256–63 • B. J. McMullin, 'Towards a bibliography of the Oxford and Cambridge University Bible presses in the seventeenth and eighteenth centuries', *Bibliographical Society of Australia and New Zealand Bulletin*, 14/2 (1990), 51–73 • D. J. Hall, 'Francis Fry, a maker of chocolate and bibles', *The book trade and its customers, 1450–1900: historical essays for Robin Myers*, ed. A. Hunt, G. Mandelbrote, and A. Shell (1997)

Archives CUL, Bible Society collection | Bodl. Oxf., corresp. with Sir Thomas Phillipps

Likenesses photograph, repro. in Fry, *Brief memoir of Francis Fry*

Wealth at death £80,028 19*s.* 7*d.*: probate, 29 Dec 1886, *CGPLA Eng. & Wales*

Fry, Joan Mary (1862–1955), relief worker and social reformer, was born on 27 July 1862 at West Hill, Highgate, Middlesex, the second daughter of the seven daughters and two sons of the judge Sir Edward *Fry (1827–1918) and his wife, Mariabella Hodgkin (1833–1930). Her distinguished younger siblings included (Sara) Margery *Fry, Ruth Fry (1879–1962), and Roger Eliot *Fry, whose children she helped to bring up. She was educated by governesses at home (1867–82) within a family that was especially interested in the natural sciences and questions of political justice, and she was imbued with a profound dedication to moral duty. In certain ways her upbringing was very restricted—by its upper-class privilege, by the Victorianism that prevented her from walking anywhere unaccompanied or unchaperoned until she was thirty, and by an internalized Quaker puritanism that forbade any visit to the theatre until she was sixty. Nevertheless, she emerged from that background an independent-minded spiritual 'seeker' and an immensely influential social interventionist.

After years of solitary study—she taught herself some Hebrew and New Testament Greek—Joan Fry became an outstanding public interpreter of a Quakerism that combined fellowship and individual freedom. In her Swarthmore lecture, *The Communion of Life* (1910), she said: 'Quakerism is nothing unless it be … a practical showing that the spiritual and material spheres are not divided, … the whole of life is sacramental and incarnational'. In *Friends and the War*, published in September 1914, she wrote: 'We believe there is something Divine in all men, which will respond *if* we call it out by acting on our belief'. An absolutist pacifist, she was appointed chaplain to imprisoned conscientious objectors during the First World War. She also attended many military tribunals and courts martial of conscientious objectors to check that justice was done. She was the only woman allowed to see and speak to these prisoners in military camps, and in one case at least she protested against a prisoner's mistreatment only just in time to save his life (F. Brockway, *Bermondsey Story*, 1949, 67).

In July 1919 Joan Fry and three other British Friends went to defeated Germany to see how they could mitigate the disastrous impact of the continued allied blockade. Her reports, for dissemination in Britain (later deposited in RS Friends, Lond.), testify to famine and the diseases of famine, including galloping consumption and epidemics of child rickets and pneumonia. In the face of Germany's distrust and outright hatred of the victorious British she organized so massive and effective a relief distribution network, focusing on the needs of women, children, and university students, that the Germans coined a new word for feeding—'Quakern'. During the occupation of the Ruhr in 1923 she reported seeing French officers walking about Duisburg with whips, and intervened on behalf of Germans imprisoned by the French military. She visited the Berlin workhouse and refuge for the homeless in September 1923 and in the following month in Nürnberg she recorded seeing '7 men in the new "Hitler" uniform'. In acknowledgement of her efforts for peace and reconstruction in defeated Germany the University of Tübingen made her an honorary doctor of political economy in 1924.

In 1926 Joan Fry turned her attention to social misery in Britain. She made many visits to the coalfields, including those in south Wales, and helped to start feeding centres for the children of unemployed miners and to encourage small community self-help industries. Her greatest contribution was her work for the Friends Allotment Committee (1928–51), which enabled the unemployed miners throughout Britain to grow vegetables on unused land without losing any part of their dole. George V wanted to confer an honour on her in recognition of this work but she refused to profit from others' misfortune. Joan Fry was not tall but she had a remarkable 'presence' and was 'austere and tender' (Fawell, 7), with white hair, one humorous, loving eye—she had lost the other in early childhood—and an eagerness to join in the good things of life with others, especially children: she would win races against them at ninety. She died, unmarried, at her London home, 40 Temple Fortune Hill, on 25 November 1955 and was cremated at Golders Green.   SYBIL OLDFIELD

Sources R. Fawell, *Joan Mary Fry* (1959) • *The Times* (28 Nov 1955) • *The Friend* (2 Dec 1955) • J. Fry, *In downcast Germany, 1914–1933* (1944) • J. Fry, *Friends lend a hand in alleviating unemployment* (1947) • O. Greenwood, *Quaker encounters* (1977) • K. Moore, *Cordial relations: the maiden aunt in fact and fiction* (1966)

Archives RS Friends, Lond., corresp.

Likenesses photograph, repro. in Fawell, *Joan Mary Fry*, frontispiece

Wealth at death £37,493 0*s.* 10*d.*: probate, 17 Feb 1956, *CGPLA Eng. & Wales*

Fry, John (*c.*1609–1656/7), religious controversialist, was the eldest son of William Fry (*d.* in or before 1631), landowner, of Iwerne Minster, Dorset, and his wife, Millicent, daughter of Robert Swaine of nearby Tarrant Gunville. His age was given in heralds' visitations of 1623 as fourteen, although the date of his admission to the Middle Temple, 11 November 1631, suggests that this may have been a slight overestimate. By about the mid-1630s he made what was probably the first of two marriages; if so, his wife's name is unknown, but at least his eldest surviving son, John, apparently of age in 1656, was her son.

In 1640, when Anthony Wood thought him 'seemingly a presbyterian' (Wood, *Ath. Oxon.*, 3.706), Fry was returned to the Long Parliament for the Dorset seat of Shaftesbury, but the election was for some reason declared void, the town's recorder, William Whitaker, and the court physician Samuel Turner sitting instead. It is likely that during the civil wars he served in the parliamentarian forces, since he was twice publicly addressed as 'Captain' and 'Colonel'. He served on the Wiltshire county committee, and in 1647, by this time apparently seen by some as an Independent, he secured the Shaftesbury parliamentary seat in the place of the deceased recruiter MP, George Starr. Fry was afterwards made a member of the committee for plundered ministers, and early in January 1649 he was named as one of a committee of two who had been commissioned to inquire into William Prynne's strident objections to the trial of the king. Appointed on 6 January to the commission to try Charles I, he attended its meetings from 20 to 25 January, but was absent from the session on 27 January when sentence was passed, his place having already been filled by someone else. He thus did not sign the warrant for the king's execution.

Fry related in an account published a month later as *The Accuser Sham'd* that on or about 15 January 1649 he was standing in the committee room of the Commons when the Independent MP Cornelius Holland asked him to use his good offices in the committee for plundered ministers to help free the Socinian John Bidle, who was in prison for questioning the Trinity. When Fry agreed, Colonel John Downes, another MP who was standing by, cried out that Bidle deserved to be hanged. Fry demurred and declared that he himself was 'altogether dissatisfied with those expressions of three distinct Persons, or Subsistences in the God-head'. In a further discussion with Downes two or three days later Fry again expressed his disbelief in the commonly accepted doctrine of the Trinity. Following a complaint of blasphemy lodged by Downes, on 26 January the Commons ordered that Fry should be suspended from sitting both in the house and on the commission for the king's trial until he gave a satisfactory account of his views. On 30 January a petition on his behalf was presented by the Leveller Thomas Prince, who spoke for 'divers Citizens of *London* and Inhabitants of the Borough of *Southwarke*' (*JHC*, 6.125). Fry then submitted an exculpatory letter affirming his belief in the Trinity, but maintaining his objection to the mode of stating it that some adopted, which he thought was tantamount to tritheism. On 3 February, probably thanks to Leveller pressure for toleration and to Fry's allies in parliament, such a paper was considered satisfactory for his readmission.

The Accuser Sham'd also contained a violent attack against 'Priests, Lawyers, Royalists, Self-Seekers, and Rigid-Presbyterians' and against 'chaffie and absurd Opinion *of Three Persons or Subsistences in the Godhead*'. It elicited at least two pamphlets in reply, the anonymous *M. Fry his Blasphemy and Error* (1649?), and the voluminous *The Divine*

Trinunity (1650), by the presbyterian Francis Cheynell, the latter intended to rebut the charge of tritheism made by Fry against some orthodox theological writers and to answer Socinian arguments on a large scale. A few months later Fry rejoined with a satirical anticlerical tract, *The Clergy in their Colours* (1650), ridiculing the doctrines and rites of the presbyterian clergy and defending the cause of a positive religion grounded on both Bible and reason against an implicit faith.

On 31 January 1651 Downes brought both books to the attention of the House of Commons, which in turn referred them to the committee for plundered ministers for examination and report. Following its report on 20 February, Fry was summoned and found to have committed a breach of privilege by printing the accusation Downes made against him *viva voce* two years before. Fry was again accused of denying the Trinity, and both his books were found to be 'against the Doctrine and Assertions of the true Religion' (*JHC*, 6.537). On 22 February the house resolved that the subject in both his books was 'erroneous, profane, and highly scandalous', that all the printed copies were to be burnt, and that he 'be disabled to sit as a Member of this House, during this Parliament' (ibid., 6.536–40). Thus ended a noteworthy 'heresy trial' against an influential MP whose old allies, the defeated Levellers and most of the Independents, now in minority in the Rump, failed to save him. Fry was condemned after a long and hard-fought parliamentary debate which saw 'conformists' prevail over 'revolutionaries' within the framework of the contemporary discussions on toleration among the main churches of the Commonwealth.

Fry was feared by his presbyterian enemies for his criticism of the religious settlement subsequent to the Westminster confession of faith (1647), and was branded as a Socinian because of his anti-Trinitarianism and his emphasis on rational biblicism and tolerance. Yet he was rather Sabellian in his christology, as he did not deny the divinity of Christ and the Holy Ghost but was convinced that the three entities were three different ways of being of the same God. In 1651 he was once again the target of polemical pamphlets: *THEIOS: divine beames of glorious light* by an unknown writer, *A Particular Answer to a Book Intituled, The Clergy in their Colours* by John Davy, and *A Discussion of Mr. Fry's Tenets* probably by Francis Cheynell. Wood states that Fry was later in touch with Bidle again, but there is no evidence for this. 'Weak in body', Fry drew up his will on 29 December 1656. He had already settled his lands in Iwerne Minster, Bursey, Gunville, and Stubhampton on his son John, and now proceeded to earmark income from lands in Dorset and Wiltshire for his sons Stephen (1649/50–1710), James, and Joseph and his daughters Anna, Elizabeth, and Martha. Special provision was made for the maintenance and education of his son Thomas from the Dorset jointure lands of his mother, 'my now wife Anna'. Fry died within the next few months: Anna obtained probate of the will on 15 June 1657. On 9 June 1660 his name occurred in a list of twenty deceased regicides excepted from the Act of General Pardon and Oblivion for their part in the trial of the king. Fry's son Stephen, who matriculated from New Inn Hall, Oxford, on 11 December 1668, aged eighteen, became a physician and was anatomy reader at Oxford between about 1695 and 1700.

DARIO PFANNER

Sources H. J. McLachlan, *Socinianism in seventeenth-century England* (1951), 239–49 · *DNB* · H. A. C. Sturgers, ed., *Registers of admissions to the Honourable Society of the Middle Temple*, 3 vols. (1949), 1.125 · H. R. Engstrom, 'Fry, John', Greaves & Zaller, *BDBR* · Wood, *Ath. Oxon.*, new edn, 3.705–8 · *JHC*, 6 (1648–51), 123, 125, 131, 529, 536–7, 539–40 · *JHC*, 8 (1660–67), 60, 286 · Foster, *Alum. Oxon.* · will, PRO, PROB 11/265, fols. 232r–232v · D. Underdown, *Pride's Purge: politics in the puritan revolution*, pbk edn (1985), 194, 242, 270 · B. Worden, *The Rump Parliament, 1648–1653* (1974) · Keeler, *Long Parliament*, 45 · *Hist. U. Oxf. 4: 17th-cent. Oxf.*, 543
Wealth at death land in Dorset and Wiltshire: will, PRO, PROB 11/265, fols. 232r–232v

Fry, John (1792–1822), bookseller and author, was born in April 1792 in Bristol. Although the names of his parents are unknown, it is recorded that his father died in 1796 while on business in Jamaica, leaving a widow and two infant sons, of whom John was the elder.

He was largely self-educated and, having shown an interest in literature, he was put to work with a bookseller in High Street, Bristol, at an early age. His work brought him into contact and correspondence with such figures as Sir Egerton Brydges, Robert Elliston, Francis Freeling, and Francis Wrangham. Two volumes of his correspondence survive at Manchester Central Library. He was the author of a number of articles, editor of five volumes of poetry, and compiler of *Bibliographical Memoranda: in Illustration of Early English Literature* (1816); a second bibliographical volume was left uncompleted on his death. His best-known work was *A Selection from the Poetical Works of Thomas Carew* (1810), although this attracted criticism for its inaccuracies. In 1811 he assumed the management of Elliston's newly opened bookshop in Broad Street, Bristol, but in 1817 illness compelled him to relinquish the post. During the five years leading up to his death he suffered from continual poor health and was confined to his bed for most of the final two years of his life. He died at Bristol on 28 June 1822. He was survived by his mother. KEITH RAMSEY

Sources 'Biographical sketch of the late Mr John Fry', *Bristol and Monmouthshire, South Wales and West of England Advertiser* (13 July 1822) · *Felix Farley's Bristol Journal* (6 July 1822) · *GM*, 1st ser., 92/2 (1822), 566 [incl. repr. of obit. in *Felix Farley's Bristol Journal* and list of Fry's works] · *DNB* · *The poems and masque of Thomas Carew*, ed. J. W. Ebsworth (1893)
Archives Man. CL, Manchester Archives and Local Studies, letters, MS Gf 091.F8

Fry, John [*formerly* Jack Freitag] (1922–1994), general practitioner and medical author, was born on 16 June 1922 in Lublin, Poland, the eldest son of Anczel Freitag (1896–1972), a young chemical engineer, and his wife, Basia, *née* Mintzman (1897–1979). The family was Jewish. In 1925 Anczel Freitag left Poland and came to Britain. He learned English, gained entry to Charing Cross Hospital medical school, and qualified in 1929. He established himself in single-handed general practice in Thornton Heath, south London. It was here that John, his younger brother, Lionel,

and his sister Margaret grew up. In the xenophobic atmosphere of wartime London the family found it expedient to change their name from Freitag to Fry; Fry's parents also changed their first names, to Ansel and Barbara. John Fry remembered his father as never off duty, but always enjoying his work. Ansel Fry was an admirer of James Mackenzie, whose vision of general practice as a fruitful but neglected field for medical research he passed on to his son.

Fry went to Whitgift Middle School, Croydon (1932–9), and then entered medicine. He trained at Guy's Hospital, where he was influenced by the teaching of John Ryle, with his original views on social medicine. He graduated in 1944, and in the same year married Joan (1921–1989), daughter of James and Catherine Sabel; there was one son and one daughter. Fry's first intention was to train in surgery, and in 1946 he gained his FRCS. In 1947 he took over a single-handed general practice in Beckenham, Kent. He was to remain there throughout his professional life. From the start he committed himself to the disciplined recording of the diseases and problems presented to him in his everyday work. Using the simplest of methods he built up a personal database for his later writings. He gained the London MD in 1955. His first book to have a wide impact was *The Catarrhal Child* (1961), in which he questioned the need for many of the tonsillectomies then being performed, basing his argument on evidence collected in his own practice. He went on to write more than fifty books. They became an important part of the literature of general practice as it developed during the middle decades of the twentieth century. He was a powerful advocate for the role of general practice in the National Health Service. In his popular book *Common Diseases* (1974) he expressed his findings in terms of an average medical list of 2500 patients, thus making them relevant to the majority of general practitioners. His publications achieved international recognition. He travelled widely, carrying out comparative studies of other systems of primary care, and was in demand as a lecturer and visiting professor.

As Fry's reputation grew, so did his involvement with the wider world of medicine. He was a long serving member of the council of the Royal College of General Practitioners (1954–90) and of the General Medical Council (1970–92), and a governing trustee of the Nuffield Provincial Hospitals Trust (1956–92). He was a member of committees of the Medical Research Council (1965–88) and a consultant/adviser to the World Health Organization (1965–91) and the British army (1968–87). He was appointed CBE in 1988, and received many professional honours and prizes. These included the Hunterian Society's gold medal in 1955 and 1956, the Charles Hastings prize of the British Medical Association in 1961 and 1964, and the foundation council award of the Royal College of General Practitioners in 1993. In 1994, the year of his death, he was elected fellow of the faculty of public health medicine of the Royal College of Physicians.

Fry possessed that essential quality for the lone researcher—a consuming commitment to his own vision and his own work. At overlong committee meetings he was sometimes noticed to be busy with his own writing under the table. He could seem aloof behind his heavy spectacles, and rather gruff in manner. But once engaged on a subject that concerned his work he became an enthusiastic and warm intellectual companion, though never one to change his opinion at all easily. He was at his best when dealing with younger people who sought his help and advice. To them he was unfailingly generous. Despite the wide range of his responsibilities he remained active in his practice until he retired in 1991. The practice grew to include four partners and assistants, but his personal commitment to his own patients never left him, even if this sometimes meant visiting them at home at 6.30 a.m. His opinions could, however, be controversial. His claim that a doctor should be able to look after three thousand patients was not popular with many who felt that smaller lists were needed if the best traditions of personal medicine were to be maintained in British general practice.

Fry's private nature made the support of his home life particularly important to him. He described his practice in the early years as consisting of two people, 'myself and my wife'. His wife, Joan, died in 1989. In September the following year he married a close friend, Gertrude Amiel (née Scher), herself recently widowed, with two daughters. She was able to be his companion on the extensive travels which he undertook in his later life, and to care for him when he became progressively disabled from the fibrosing alveolitis from which he died on 28 April 1994, in Farnborough, Kent. Cremation took place at Golders Green the following day. He was survived by his second wife, his son, daughter, four grandchildren, and two stepdaughters.   IAN TAIT

Sources BMJ (21 May 1994), 1367 · The Times (6 May 1994) · The Independent (3 May 1994) · Royal College of General Practitioners, London, archives, James Mackenzie lecture, January 1977 · private information (2004) [Lionel Fry; Gertrude Fry; J. Horder] · WWW
Archives Royal College of General Practitioners, London, archives
Likenesses photograph, Royal College of General Practitioners · photograph, repro. in The Times · photograph, repro. in The Independent
Wealth at death £44,931: probate, 27 Oct 1994, CGPLA Eng. & Wales

Fry, Joseph (1728–1787), chocolate manufacturer and typefounder, was born into a devout Quaker family in 1728, the eldest son of John Fry (d. 1775), a shopkeeper of Sutton Benger, Wiltshire. He was educated at a Quaker boarding-school in the north of England, and afterwards bound apprentice to Henry Portsmouth of Basingstoke, an apothecary and an eminent doctor. Fry set up as an apothecary in Bristol in 1753 and later married Portsmouth's eldest daughter, Anna, (1719/20–1803) in Basingstoke. He acquired a considerable medical practice but, although he continued to maintain it for charitable purposes, he abandoned medicine professionally for business pursuits and 'was led to take a part in many new scientific undertakings' (Owen, 218). As an apothecary he was making and selling chocolate at least from 1759 (in which year he moved from Small Street to Narrow Wine Street), and

in 1761, in partnership with John Vaughan, he purchased the chocolate business of Walter Churchman, together with the patent of the water-powered machine that had given the firm an advantage in the local markets. He expanded the business, and in due course a Boulton and Watt steam engine was installed. Within three years of the purchase Fry, Vaughan & Co. had agents in fifty-three towns, with a chocolate warehouse in London. In 1777 the chocolate works was moved from Newgate Street to Union Street, Bristol.

In 1768 Fry subscribed £1500 to establish the Bristol china works of Richard Champion. He was a partner, with Alderman William Fripp, in Fry, Fripp & Co., soap-boilers in Bristol, and also had chemical works at Battersea, London, in which he was assisted by one of his sons. In 1764 Fry turned his attention to typefounding and printing, entering into partnership with William Pine, the printer of the Bristol Gazette, who had a large business in Wine Street. The manager of the typefoundry of Fry and Pine was Isaac Moore, formerly a metalworker at Birmingham, and its first specimen was issued in 1766 under the name Isaac Moore & Co. The foundry then moved to London, where further specimens were issued from Queen Street, near Upper Moorfields, in 1768 and 1770. After Moore left the partnership to establish a business of his own, in 1777 the style of the firm became J. Fry & Co. Fry took his sons Edmund *Fry (1754–1835) and Henry, into partnership in 1782. The Frys bought largely at the sale of James's foundry in that year, acquiring punches and matrices of antiquarian interest that had originated with the older English typefoundries, including many for non-Latin types, which were to be of special interest to Edmund. The foundry issued further specimens from Worship Street in 1785 and 1786 under the name Joseph Fry & Co. In introductory remarks to a specimen of the foundry's types included in The Printer's Grammar, Chiefly Collected from Smith's Edition published by T. Evans in 1787, it is stated that the original plan of the foundry was 'an improvement of the Types of the late Mr. BASKERVILLE of Birmingham' (p. 271). However, having found that 'the difference in shape, from the Letters commonly used' had deterred some customers, the foundry cut a whole set of new punches, and made founts which would 'mix with, and be totally unknown from' those of William Caslon, a claim that, although strongly denied by the Caslon foundry, is largely justified. The foundry also developed an extensive range of printers' flowers or ornaments, of which a separate broadside specimen was printed by Hazard of Bath about 1790.

Fry also extended his printing business to London. In 1774 Pine had printed at Bristol a small-format Bible, in a pearl type, asserted to be 'the smallest a bible was ever printed with', and I. Moore & Co. in 1774–6 issued folio and octavo bibles, with notes 'selected from the works of several eminent divines', thus avoiding the penalty of infringing the Bible printing patent. Pine withdrew from the partnership, and the firm traded as Joseph Fry & Co. (1776–8), Frys, Couchman, and Collier (1779–84), and Frys and Couchman (1784–7).

Fry corresponded on matters of common scientific

interest with James Watt. He was an active member of the Society of Friends, making efforts to raise the moral tone of the younger Quakers in Bristol who drank and gambled, and 'flashed to chapel in gay clothes and powdered wigs' (Latimer, 178). In 1776 he wrote an account of a vision of paradise that came to him, 'being alone and under an awful exercise of mind respecting futurity'. Fry died after a few days' illness on 29 March 1787, aged fifty-nine, having retired from business a short time before, and was buried in the burial-ground of the Society of Friends at the Friars, Bristol.

After Fry's death the chocolate and cocoa business, Fry, Vaughan & Co., was carried on by his widow under the style Anna Fry & Son, and she was also associated for a short time with her sons in the typefoundry. She died at Charterhouse Square, London, on 22 October 1803, aged eighty-three. Her son Joseph Storrs Fry (1769–1835) continued the business with his three sons, Joseph, Francis *Fry (1803–1886), and Richard, as J. S. Fry & Sons, which remained the later name of the firm. During the nineteenth century it lost its dominant share of the market to more aggressively marketed products of the rival Quaker establishments of Rowntree and of Cadbury, the latter of which eventually acquired it. The typefoundry was continued by Fry's son Edmund.   JAMES MOSLEY

Sources Benevolus, 'An account of the life and character of the late Joseph Fry of Bristol', *GM*, 1st ser., 57 (1787), 385–6 • E. R. Mores, *A dissertation upon English typographical founders and founderies* (1778), with, *A catalogue and specimen of the typefoundry of John James* (1782), ed. H. Carter and C. Ricks (1961); repr. with corrections (1963) • *The printer's grammar … chiefly collected from Smith's edition* (1787) • T. B. Reed, *A history of the old English letter foundries*, ed. A. F. Johnson, new edn (1952), 298–310 • T. Fry, *A brief memoir of Francis Fry* (1887) • J. Latimer, *The annals of Bristol in the 18th century* (1893) • H. Owen, *Two centuries of ceramic art in Bristol* (1873) • M. F. Pease, 'Notes on the Fry family of Sutton Benger and Bristol, 1627–1921', typescript, 1951, Bristol Central Library, B20853 • J. Fry, 'A vision' [which he had 26th of 12th month 1776, taken from a MS made by his grandson Richard Fry], *Journal of the Friends' Historical Society*, 17 (1920), 49–58 • T. H. Darlow and J. F. Moule, *Historical catalogue of printed editions of the English Bible, 1525–1961*, ed. A. S. Herbert (1968) • I. Maxted, *The London book trades, 1775–1800: a preliminary checklist of members* (1977) • S. Diaper, 'J. S. Fry & Sons: growth and decline in the chocolate industry', *Studies in the business history of Bristol*, ed. C. E. Harvey and J. Press (1988), 33–54 • Bristol RO, J. S. Fry & Sons papers • J. Fry, letters to James Watt, Birm. CL, James Watt MSS • *IGI* • will, PRO, PROB 11/1152, sig. 166

Archives Bristol RO, records | Birm. CL, letters to James Watt
Likenesses silhouette, repro. in Fry, *Brief memoir*

Fry, Joseph Storrs (1826–1913), cocoa and chocolate manufacturer, was born in Union Street, Bristol, on 6 August 1826, the eldest son of Joseph Fry (1795–1879), cocoa and chocolate manufacturer, and his wife, Mary Ann, daughter of Edward Swaine. Initially educated at home, he went to Bristol College in 1841 for a year and, in order to learn the principles of commercial management, he joined a firm of accountants, entering J. S. Fry & Sons in 1846.

The family business had been founded by his great-grandfather, Joseph *Fry (1728–1787), an apothecary who had acquired the firm of Churchman's of Bristol, well known for a finer grade of chocolate produced by its water-powered machinery. The first Joseph Fry, an able

Joseph Storrs Fry (1826–1913), by John Beattie

and creative entrepreneur, established a number of successful businesses, including printing, pottery, and soap enterprises, and in 1777, with agents throughout the country, he moved his chocolate works from Newgate Street to Union Street, Bristol. When he died in 1787, the business was run by his wife, Anna (1719/20–1803), with their son, Joseph Storrs Fry (1769–1835), assuming control in 1795. He introduced a number of improvements to the production and roasting processes, including the installation of a Watt steam engine, and in 1822 he made his sons, Richard, Francis *Fry (1803–1886), and Joseph Fry, business partners, formally establishing J. S. Fry & Sons. In the following year, the firm accounted for 33 per cent of all British cocoa imports and, under the supervision of the first Joseph Storrs Fry, it emerged as the industry's leading business. He remained in control until his death in 1835, and it was his sons, including the father of the second Joseph Storrs, who responded to changes in Victorian consumer demand and diversified the product range.

In 1850 the firm first made eating chocolates, chocolate at that time being largely consumed as a drink rather than a solid confection. It began producing chocolate creams five years later and in 1866 it manufactured both its famous cream bar and its first pure cocoa powder, called Cocoa Essence. Joseph Fry retired in 1867, aged seventy-two, and his brothers Francis and Richard gradually relinquished management of the business, although Joseph Storrs and his cousin Francis James did not achieve formal control until 1886.

Joseph Storrs Fry inherited Britain's most successful chocolate firm, but his business had to face new competition, first Cadbury from the 1860s, and later Rowntree and Swiss companies such as Nestlé from the 1890s. As demand for cocoa essence continued to expand, he launched Fry's Concentrated Cocoa in 1883, and, unlike its predecessors, it competed successfully against rival brands. The firm benefited from the overall, long-term increase in demand for cocoa, chocolate, and confectionery. A total of 250 employees in 1869 grew to 4500 by January 1896, when the firm was transformed into a limited company with authorized capital of £1 million. Fry was appointed its first chairman and, by 1907, J. S. Fry & Sons Ltd was Britain's fifty-first largest manufacturing employer. Sales expanded from almost £150,000 in 1870 to £1.86 million in 1913, the year of his death.

Fry's business career was hardly, however, an example of vigorous leadership building upon a substantial legacy, for the company's sales were outstripped by those of Cadbury. Management at the firm was a weakness, and much of the blame must be carried by Fry himself. His brothers demonstrated little interest in cocoa and chocolate manufacture: his brother Sir Edward *Fry became a lord justice of appeal, and Lewis was the Liberal, and later Liberal Unionist, MP for Bristol. Both of them were eventually members of the privy council. In addition, J. S. Fry & Sons Ltd did not match the product innovations of rivals Cadbury and Rowntree, nor did it follow their respective examples of advanced factory organization at Bournville and York. Instead of developing a new site near Bristol, the company continued to operate in the cramped conditions of Union Street and by 1907 it was operating from no fewer than eight factories within the city.

Fry was known to be devout, gentle, reflective, kindly, and reserved, and in avoiding recreation, social contact, and marriage, he led an uneventful personal life. He was dedicated to his charitable works and to the Society of Friends and, although his brothers became very worldly Quakers, he remained plain in his devotions. Fry was a leading figure at the meeting-house at Friars, Bristol, and, as a supporter of Sunday schools, he was prominent in founding the Friends First Day Sunday Association in 1847, serving as secretary of its Bristol committee for forty years. As clerk to the London yearly meeting of the Society of Friends in 1870–75 and 1881–9, he was its leading official for a total of thirteen years. He joined the committee of the Bristol General Hospital in 1887, and became its chairman and treasurer in 1892 and its president in 1908. Until the last few years of his life, he visited every patient at the hospital on Christmas eve. He was also president of the Bristol YMCA in 1877.

Through his charitable donations and by his willingness to chair meetings, Fry was an active temperance supporter, an opponent of the opium trade and vivisection, and politically a Liberal and a believer in free trade. He employed a team of clerks to oversee his charities, and the strength of his religious convictions and charitable instincts led to paternalistic policies towards his workforce. He established the practice of a daily service in the workplace in 1854 and, until the 1890s, the partners personally interviewed all job applicants. He was generous in his charitable assistance to the workforce, but, in a reflection of general management at J. S. Fry & Sons Ltd, his beneficence was never organized through systematic welfare schemes, and cramped work conditions compared unfavourably with the staff facilities and factory gardens of Bournville and York. Unlike his contemporaries George Cadbury and Joseph Rowntree, he did not establish trusts which could continue his Quaker service to the community after his death.

In 1909, Fry was made an honorary freeman of Bristol and in 1912 he and his two brothers received honorary doctorates in law from the University of Bristol. As the first chairman of Victorian Britain's biggest cocoa and chocolate manufacturer he was a noted figure, but his talents and achievements did not measure up to his task as a business leader. He lost his sight during the last part of his life, and died on 7 July 1913 at his home, 16 Upper Belgrave Road, Clifton, Bristol. He specified numerous bequests in his will, including a sum of £42,000 which was to be distributed among all employees with more than five years' service.

There was no obvious, long-term successor, the cocoa and chocolate sides of the business were run separately with family members not on speaking terms, and the firm was merged with Cadbury to form the British Cocoa and Chocolate Company, a holding company, in 1919. Following the injection of new management, a modern factory was erected at Somerdale, near Bristol, in 1921, and in 1935 Fry Ltd became a fully fledged subsidiary of the new amalgamated concern.   ROBERT FITZGERALD

Sources S. Diaper, 'J. S. Fry & Sons: growth and decline in the chocolate industry', *Studies in the business history of Bristol*, ed. C. E. Harvey and J. Press (1988), 33–54 • P. H. Emden, *Quakers in commerce: a record of business achievement* (1939) • *Confectionery* (12 July 1913), 546 • *The Times* (8 July 1913), 11 • G. Wagner, 'Fry, Joseph Storrs', *DBB* • *DNB* • d. cert.
Archives Cadbury Schweppes Archive, Birmingham
Likenesses J. Beattie, photograph, priv. coll. [*see illus.*] • portrait, Cadbury Schweppes, Birmingham
Wealth at death £1,332,525 11s. 3d.: resworn probate, 23 July 1913, *CGPLA Eng. & Wales*

Fry, (Sara) Margery (1874–1958), penal reformer and college head, was born at Highgate, London, on 11 March 1874, the eighth child and sixth daughter of Sir Edward *Fry (1827–1918), judge of the High Court, Chancery Division, and his wife, Mariabella Hodgkin (1833–1930). Joan Mary *Fry was her elder sister. Educated at home until she was seventeen, she then spent a year at Penelope Lawrence's boarding-school (later Roedean) at Brighton. In 1892 her father retired from the bench and the family moved to Failand in Somerset. Encouraged by her brother Roger *Fry, Margery hoped initially to go to Newnham, but her Quaker parents regarded Cambridge with suspicion as a breeding-ground of agnostics. She later came to

(Sara) **Margery Fry** (1874–1958), by Claude Rogers, 1939

accept an agnostic position, but reached it by another route. Eventually she succeeded in obtaining permission to sit the entrance examination for Somerville College, Oxford, and went up to read mathematics in 1894, staying until 1897, but taking no examinations. Somerville friendships, with Eleanor Rathbone and Dorothea Scott among others, remained important through her life. For the next eighteen months she returned to the duties of a daughter at home. The opportunity for an active and independent life came with the unexpected offer of the librarianship at Somerville. There she spent five years from 1899, combining the development and rehousing of the college library with that understanding concern for the young and their problems which remained one of her outstanding qualities. Her duties included some coaching in mathematics, about which she sought advice from a family acquaintance, Bertrand Russell.

Birmingham wardenship and wartime relief work Fry's next post gave her scope to extend this interest in a new setting. Birmingham University had been granted its charter in 1900, and in 1904 she was appointed to the wardenship of a hall of residence for women students in Hagley Road, Edgbaston. Her functions were 'the superintendence of housekeeping and the maintenance of discipline' (Jones, 70): the latter she interpreted with her customary liberalism, reducing rules to a minimum and allowing students to invite their men friends to dances. In 1908 the hostel moved into new quarters at University House, for which she had worked hard, and where she used all the resources available to her—pictures, furnishings, music, play-acting, wit, and friendship—to create a living community. On the initiative of Charles Beale, the vice-chancellor, she was made a member of the university

council. During this period the range of causes in which she was interested, and of committees on which she served, became increasingly wide—the Staffordshire education committee, the county insurance committee (set up under the National Insurance Act), the county subcommittee on mental deficiency. Practical experience of the problems of social reform sharpened her tendency towards radicalism. 'Brummagem', she wrote, 'is making a first-rate democrat of me' (ibid., 75).

Shortly before the outbreak of war in 1914 she became financially independent through a legacy from her uncle, Joseph Storrs Fry, and in the summer of 1914 she resigned her post. Her Quaker background and conscience, combined with her experience of social work, made it natural that early in the war she should be drawn (with her younger sister Ruth) into work with the Friends' War Victims Relief Committee, first in the Marne and Meuse area, later in the whole of France. From early 1915 until the end of 1917 she remained based in Sermaize, with periodic journeys to other parts of France, dealing with the whole range of problems of those whose lives had been disrupted by the war, from the reconstruction of agriculture to the teaching of embroidery.

Howard League for Penal Reform Back in England in 1918 Margery Fry was uncertain where her next work should lie, although with a sense of continuing commitment to education in the widest sense. Three events particularly determined the subsequent direction of her life and activities. At the beginning of 1919 she moved to London and set up house at 7 Dalmeny Avenue, overlooking Holloway prison, with her brother Roger and his children. She thus became more deeply involved in his world, his relationships with artists and writers in particular. In May 1919 she was invited to become a member of the newly established University Grants Committee, on which she continued to serve until 1948, devoting much of her time and energies to visiting universities and gaining firsthand knowledge of their problems.

At the end of 1918 she had been persuaded by Stephen and Rosa Hobhouse to accept the secretaryship of the Penal Reform League, which in 1921 amalgamated with the Howard Association to form the Howard League for Penal Reform, housed at this period in the Frys' front sitting-room. From then on the Howard League, which she served as secretary until 1926 and later as chairman and vice-chairman, remained the most important focus of her work. Her understanding of the problems of penal reform was increased by her appointment in 1921 as one of the first women magistrates and in 1922 as the first education adviser to Holloway. In her efforts to improve prison conditions, one of the many developments which she initiated was to bring Marion Richardson in to teach painting to young prisoners. Her two main preoccupations became closely related: visits to universities were combined with visits to prisons; it was sometimes difficult to remember, she once remarked, whether students were in for crimes or prisoners in for examinations.

Principal of Somerville College In 1926, on the retirement of Emily Penrose, Margery Fry somewhat reluctantly accepted the principalship of Somerville. In spite of her strong continuing affection for the college, on whose council she had served since 1904, she genuinely doubted her suitability as a 'non-academic' woman for the post and was concerned at the limitations on her independence which it would involve. But, though finding Oxford in many ways uncongenial and obscurantist, she enjoyed this new opportunity for exercising her remarkable talent for understanding, and unobtrusively advising, the young, and opening their minds to her whole wide range of interests, from penal reform to birdwatching. At Oxford she wore a bright red coat for which she had painted large wooden buttons and there was always 'something festive' in her appearance, 'a string of fine beads, an embroidered jacket' (Jones, 138). When the Oxford tutor J. D. Mabbott called on her in 1929 he found her 'a very lively looking girl, sitting in a corner and typing furiously, with her hair all over the place', and thought at first that she was the principal's secretary (Mabbott, 81). Finding the principal's lodgings too formal, she moved to nearby Radcliffe House, where her vitality and musicality were much in evidence. She was instinctively on the side of the undergraduates, fearing not that they would work too little, but that they would work too much. At the same time she retained some of the prejudices of a world different to their own, assuming, for example, that if they sought a career it would involve unpaid social work: 'it seemed not to occur to her that an undergraduate who did not have to earn her own living should wish to do so' (Adams, 168).

Although never deeply involved in university politics, she made occasional notable incursions which left their mark, as when in 1927 she spoke in congregation with Cyril Bailey in an unsuccessful effort to resist the imposition of a quota restricting the numbers of students admitted by the women's colleges. In that year she was disenchanted over the university's treatment of her brother Roger, whose candidature for the Slade professorship of fine art was successfully opposed 'on a frivolous pretext' by those who objected to the irregularity of his private life (K. Clark, 'Fry, Roger Eliot', *DNB*). Students who came in contact with her were especially impressed by the fact that 'she knew so much about wickedness, and yet could make one believe and work for happy and rational solutions of the most tangled moral and political problems'. She continued to work on these problems—as a member of the street offences committee (concerned with prostitution and soliciting, but doomed by its composition) and the young offenders' committee, through which she tried to secure an adequate probation service and to get probation extended to cover a much wider range of offences. But above all she was deeply involved, in association with Roy Calvert, D. N. Pritt, and others, in the campaign for the abolition of capital punishment, presenting evidence on behalf of the Howard League to the abortive select committee set up by J. R. Clynes as home secretary in 1929.

Retirement and reforming causes Margery Fry had never intended to spend more than about five years at Somerville. Soon after her retirement in 1931 she established a new base in London, at 48 Clarendon Road, Notting Hill, 'absolutely on the borderline of slum and respectability' (Jones, 171), and filled it with paintings and objects of beauty collected over the years. For the remainder of her life this was her home, and a home for the homeless and wanderers of many countries, as well as a meeting place for radicals and reformers with different interests and shades of opinion. In the 1930s the worsening world situation and her own growing international reputation involved her in a new range of activities, supplementing but not displacing the old.

In 1933, shortly after the Japanese invasion of Manchuria, the Universities China Committee invited Fry to make a lecture tour of Chinese universities. Her interest in the great transformations taking place in Chinese society, as well as in its ancient civilization, remained intense, expressed both through her friendships with Chinese teachers and students and her work with the China Campaign Committee, for which she lectured and spoke at meetings throughout Britain. Her understanding of Chinese politics made her particularly concerned to ensure that aid from Britain reached the Chinese communists and was not directed solely to the Kuomintang government.

During this period Fry also became increasingly occupied with the problems of penal reform in an international setting, particularly in societies where conditions were worst and factual information most defective. She visited Geneva in 1935 to try to induce the League of Nations to adopt a convention which would lay down minimum standard rules for the treatment of prisoners. In 1936 she became a member of the Colonial Office's newly established advisory committee on penal reform, and in 1937 she took part in a Howard League mission to study the prisons and penal systems of south-eastern Europe.

In Britain during the late 1930s Fry's political sympathies lay with those of the non-communist left who were working for some form of popular front. She consequently resigned her membership of the Labour Party (which she had joined in 1918) when early in 1939 its executive expelled Sir Stafford Cripps for advocating such a policy. A more specific contribution to make radical intellectuals more effective was her sponsorship of the serious but short-lived organization For Intellectual Liberty.

When war began in 1939 Margery Fry was already sixty-five, no longer able, as in 1914, to move into some entirely different field of work. She carried on with her existing activities as far as practicable, and took on new commitments where this seemed likely to be useful. She continued to serve as a magistrate; worked on her Clarke Hall lecture, *The Ancestral Child* (never delivered, but published in 1940); visited France early in 1940 to investigate the problem of intellectual refugees; experienced the blitz; took part in a study of evacuation and evacuees; served, unwillingly, on the government committee on non-enemy interned aliens (those imprisoned under 18B); and wrote with Champion B. Russell an 'ABC for juvenile magistrates' (published in 1942 as *A Note Book for the Children's Court*), regarding 'rational occupation', for herself as for prisoners, as the best remedy for misery. Although much distressed by the prospect of leaving her sisters for so long a period, she spent the year 1942–3 in the United States, speaking on penal questions, visiting universities and prisons.

During the dozen years of life which remained to her after the war Margery Fry retained a vigorous interest in the causes with which she had become identified, withdrawing somewhat from active campaigning, but continuing to talk, write, and educate with all her old wit and understanding. During the 1930s she had discovered that she enjoyed broadcasting and was good at it, and had served as a governor of the BBC from 1937 to 1939. In 1942 she became a member of *The Brains Trust*, originally on BBC radio, and in 1948 took part in the earliest series of *Any Questions*. Her central ideas on penal reform were set out in the pamphlet, *The Future Treatment of the Adult Offender* (1944). These were further developed in her one full-length book, *Arms of the Law* (1951), in which she put together the material which she had collected over the years on the development of crime and punishment in human society and her proposals for future advance. Some of the many objectives for which she had worked, notably the abolition of the death penalty, were partially realized in her lifetime. But where she knew what ought to be done, half-measures left her unsatisfied. And at eighty she still had the freshness of mind to move into new fields and confront new problems: the importance of developing criminology and penology as academic studies; the need to work out a national scheme of compensation for the victims of violence; the problems of the aged, discussed in her address, 'Old age looks at itself' (1955), to the International Association of Gerontology.

Although any account of Margery Fry's life is bound to pay attention to causes, people mattered a great deal more to her: causes were important in so far as they were ways of trying to increase the happiness and diminish the misery of individual people. Deeply disliking all forms of dogmatism, in ethics and politics as well as religion, she believed in working for a world in which the sorts of pleasure she valued most—playing the flute, painting pictures, walking in the woods of Provence, enjoying the conversation of friends—could be made as widely available as possible. In later years her 'fine profile, framed in a huge halo of grey hair' and her 'musical and persuasive voice' became familiar to millions through her performances on the televised *Brains Trust* (*The Times*, 22 April 1958). She died at her home in Clarendon Road, where she could watch the birds in the trees at the back, on 21 April 1958 and was cremated at Golders Green on 24 April.

THOMAS L. HODGKIN, *rev.* MARK POTTLE

Sources E. H. Jones, *Margery Fry: the essential amateur* (1990) · private information (1971) · personal knowledge (1971) · *The Times* (22 April 1958) · *The Times* (23 April 1958) · *The Times* (24 April 1958) · *The Times* (25 April 1958) · *The Times* (30 April 1958) · P. Adams, *Somerville for women: an Oxford college, 1879–1993* (1996) · *WWW* · L. Radzinowicz, *Penal reform in England: introductory essays on some aspects of English criminal policy* (1940) · J. D. Mabbott, *Oxford memories* (1986)
Archives NRA, priv. coll., family papers · U. Birm. L., corresp. · U. Birm. L., papers as warden of University House, Birmingham | Bodl. Oxf., corresp. relating to Society for Protection of Science and Learning · CUL, corresp. with Sir Samuel Hoare | SOUND BL NSA, current affairs recordings
Likenesses C. Rogers, oils, 1939, NPG [*see illus.*] · photograph, c.1950–1959, NPG · R. Fry, oils, Somerville College, Oxford · photograph, repro. in *The Times* (1 Jan 1938), 10 · photograph, repro. in *The Times* (22 April 1958), 14a
Wealth at death £50,584 2s. 0d.: probate, 1958, CGPLA Eng. & Wales

Fry, (Edwin) Maxwell (1899–1987), architect, was born on 2 August 1899 at 227 Liscard Road, Liscard, Wallasey, Cheshire, the second of four children and elder son of Ambrose Fry, commercial traveller and later chemical manufacturer, and his wife, Lily Thomson. Fry was educated at the Liverpool Institute. He served in the King's Liverpool regiment at the end of the First World War and in the allied occupation of Germany. An ex-serviceman's grant enabled him to enter Liverpool University school of architecture in 1920, under Professor Charles Reilly. A distinguished graduate of 1924, Fry worked in New York before joining the office of Thomas Adams and F. Longstreth Thompson, specialists in town planning, becoming a partner in 1930, after a period away as chief assistant in the architect's department of Southern Railways. His interest in planning, an important component of the Liverpool course, was to remain with him. As a partner in Adams, Thompson, and Fry, he designed a garden village at Kemsley near Sittingbourne in 1929, and a house at Wentworth, Surrey, in 1932, in the refined neo-Georgian style typical of the Liverpool school in the 1920s.

The Canadian designer Wells Coates met Fry while working in the Adams and Thompson office in 1924, and encouraged him to set aside his classical training and follow the example of Le Corbusier, but Fry's conversion to modernism was gradual, and came principally through his membership of the Design and Industries Association, which introduced him to modern German housing. He was also influenced by the Congrès Internationaux d'Architecture Moderne, and was closely involved in its English branch, the Modern Architectural Research (MARS) Group, following its establishment in 1933. The conversion is evident at Sassoon House in Peckham (1934), a block of working-class flats he designed with the engineer Kirkwood Dodds.

Fry became well known for two of the most elegant white modernist houses of the mid-1930s: Sun House, Frognal Lane, Hampstead (1936), and Miramonte in Kingston upon Thames (1937). With the housing consultant Elizabeth Denby he carried out an extensive social housing scheme at Kensal House, Ladbroke Grove (1936), with curving blocks of flats and a circular nursery school, a model of progressive architecture well publicized by the clients, the Gas Light and Coke Company.

Fry assisted Walter Gropius (1883–1969), the former director of the Bauhaus at Weimar and Dessau, on his arrival in England in 1934, by setting up a partnership which enabled Gropius to practise in England until his emigration to the USA in March 1937. This was a distinction from which Fry benefited, and his graphic skills and sympathetic attitude helped in the realization of Gropius's ideas in an alien culture. Their designs were not fully collaborative and can be separately attributed. To reduce its cost, Fry reworked Gropius's design for Impington Village College, Cambridgeshire, and supervised its construction after Gropius's departure. In 1939 he became a fellow of the Royal Institute of British Architects, of which he was vice-president (1961–2). Fry served in the Royal Engineers from 1939 to 1944, reaching the rank of major, and ended the Second World War as town-planning adviser to the resident minister in west Africa. He worked during the early period of the war on a plan for London presented by MARS, some of which is described in his book *Fine Building* (1944), a testimony to his desire to efface the urban forms of the northern working-class suburbs known in his childhood.

In the immediate post-war period, Fry gathered a group of talented young assistants, and thereafter was to work in partnership with his second wife, the architect Jane Drew. The partnership designed Passfield Flats, Lewisham (1949), the Riverside restaurant for the South Bank exhibition (1951), and many educational buildings and offices in Ghana and Nigeria between 1946 and 1961, notably Ibadan University, Nigeria. These displayed the adaptability of modernist methods to local climatic and cultural conditions, and Fry and Drew were instrumental in the establishment of a school of tropical architecture at the Architectural Association in London.

In 1951 Fry and Drew were invited to join the design team for the new capital of Punjab at Chandigarh and were influential in causing Le Corbusier and Pierre Jeanneret to be invited as architects for the secretariat and law courts. Fry stayed in India for three years, working mainly on housing within Le Corbusier's masterplan. Fry, who was unique in his connection with two of modern architecture's masters, was content to take a less conspicuous role. He continued to work until the early 1970s, designing notable buildings such as the head offices for Pilkington Brothers at St Helens (1959–65) and the mid-Glamorgan crematorium, a romantic late design revealing Fry's attachment to Scandinavian architecture. In retirement he devoted much time to painting. *Autobiographical Sketches* (1975), the last of his many publications, revealed an emotional, even sentimental aspect of his character which could hardly be deduced from his buildings. His friends and colleagues remember him as an ebullient, optimistic, unconventional but practical man. He was slim and elegant in appearance, with a high forehead and expressive mouth. In 1964 he was awarded the RIBA Royal gold medal. He was an honorary LLD of Ibadan University. He was appointed CBE (1955), ARA (1966), and RA (1972).

On 26 June 1926 Fry married Ethel (*b.* 1887/8), a secretary, the divorced wife of Charles Leese and daughter of Walter Speakman, schoolteacher. She was his elder by twelve years; they had one daughter. The marriage was dissolved in 1942, and in the same year, on 25 April, Fry married Joyce Beverly (Jane; *b.* 1910/11), divorced wife of James Thomas Alliston and daughter of Harry Guy Radcliffe Drew, caterer. There were no children of this marriage. Having lived at West Lodge, Cotherstone, Barnard Castle, Fry died on 3 September 1987 at Darlington Memorial Hospital.   ALAN POWERS, *rev.*

Sources M. Fry, *Autobiographical sketches* (1975) · M. Fry, *Art in a machine age* (1969) · *The Independent* (8 Sept 1987) · *The Times* (5 Sept 1987) · *The Times* (25 Nov 1987) · private information (1996) · CGPLA *Eng. & Wales* (1988) · m. certs. · b. cert.
Archives RIBA, papers
Likenesses G. Hermes, bronze cast of head, 1965, NPG
Wealth at death £37,708: probate, 7 Jan 1988, CGPLA *Eng. & Wales*

Fry, Roger Eliot (1866–1934), art historian, critic, and painter, was born on 14 December 1866 at 6 The Grove, Highgate, Middlesex, the fifth of the nine children of Sir Edward *Fry (1827–1918), judge, and his wife, Mariabella (1833–1930), daughter of John *Hodgkin and his wife, Elizabeth Howard. Joan Mary *Fry and (Sara) Margery *Fry were his sisters.

Early years and education Born into a Quaker family whose affiliation to the Society of Friends could be traced back to the seventeenth century on both sides, Roger Fry received a fairly strict upbringing, which emphasized moral rectitude and intellectual rigour. There was little in his education to prepare him for a career in the visual arts. After initial years of home schooling, Fry attended St George's preparatory school, Ascot, from 1877 to 1881, and went on to Clifton College, Bristol. He achieved high results and won a science exhibition at King's College, Cambridge, in 1884, where he began studying natural sciences the following year. His father, whose own success on the bench had been achieved at the expense of an early calling in zoology, hoped that Fry would embrace a scientific profession.

At Cambridge contact with men of a freethinking turn of mind and with philosophical and artistic interests helped Fry's personality to come into its own. A close acquaintance was John McTaggart, a friend from Clifton who was to become a prominent Hegelian philosopher, and whose atheism may have contributed to dampening Fry's faith. With Goldsworthy Lowes Dickinson, a young political science lecturer, Fry maintained an intimate, lifelong friendship. All three were members of the élite Conversazione Society, also known as the Apostles. Fry's participation in the moral debates of the society and encounters with such anti-establishment figures as Edward Carpenter and George Bernard Shaw confirmed a disposition for rational analysis and a desire to challenge received opinion. Meanwhile his growing interest in art was encouraged by his friendship with Robert Ashbee, the future arts and crafts designer, who was then a regular sketching companion. Fry's contacts with the new Slade professor of fine art, John Henry Middleton, were a further influence in this respect.

Beginnings in painting and criticism After a first in both parts of his tripos (1887, 1888), but the failure of two half-hearted applications for fellowships, Fry abandoned the idea of a scientific career, choosing instead to train as a painter. He left Cambridge in 1889 and spent the next two years in London, receiving tuition from Francis Bate, who was then honorary secretary of the New English Art Club (NEAC), the main alternative exhibiting society to the Royal Academy. Early in 1892 Fry spent two months studying at the Académie Julian in Paris. Although a painting of that period, *Blythburgh, the Estuary* (exh. 1892; priv. coll.), points to some familiarity with the works of the Nabis, he remained little acquainted with the contemporary French art scene. The mediation of Walter Sickert, whose evening classes he started attending the next year, probably did more to familiarize him with certain aspects of modern French painting, notably with the work of Degas.

In London Fry moved in anti-academic circles, frequenting artists and critics like Walter and Bernhard Sickert, Philip Wilson Steer, William Rothenstein, Alfred Thornton, and D. S. MacColl. He became a member of the NEAC in 1893, exhibiting there regularly until 1908 and frequently sitting on its selection jury from 1900.

Fry's tastes then were not those of a revolutionary. He had a distrust of impressionism for its lack of structural design; he also had mixed feelings about J. A. M. Whistler, admiring his landscapes more than his free treatment of sitters. His initial ambivalence towards the doctrine of 'art for art's sake' can be felt in his first substantial article, a review of George Moore's *Modern Painting* (*Cambridge Review*, 22 June 1893, 417–19). Similarly, Fry's early practice as a painter—classical landscapes in oils and watercolours pointing back to Claude, Poussin, and Thomas Girtin— reveals a reluctance to take up a modern idiom (*The Pool*, oil on canvas, exh. 1899; priv. coll.). While the watercolours brought some success (a one-man show at the Carfax Gallery in 1903), the oils were often seen as laboured and verging on pastiche. His style was much freer in portraiture. The full-length portrait *Edward Carpenter* (exh. 1894; NPG) deserved the praise it eventually attracted. Several portraits are held in the National Portrait Gallery, London.

The classicism of Fry's painting style at this time also reflects an immersion in the works of the Italian school, the result of two long stays in Italy in 1891 and 1894. During these tours, and a third, prolonged one in 1897–8, he made the acquaintance of a number of Renaissance specialists: John Addington Symonds, Gustavo Frizzoni—a disciple of Morelli—and most importantly Bernard Berenson, who directed Fry's first steps towards connoisseurship. Berenson's own approach to works, based on a response to form, undoubtedly guided Fry in this direction. The trips also furnished him with material for lectures and articles, as well as for his first book, *Giovanni Bellini* (1899), an insightful monograph on an artist who had previously been little studied.

Much to his regret, Fry was never in a position to support himself by painting, but he had an exceptional gift for criticism, and was to be remembered as an enthralling lecturer, with a deep, mellifluous voice. His first lectures, on Italian Renaissance art, were given in 1894 in the Cambridge University extension scheme. Other courses, and

innumerable single lectures, would follow, taking him all over Britain—and occasionally abroad—and contributing to building his reputation as an authority. The venues were varied, including local art societies as well as university lecture halls; later, during the 1930s, Fry repeatedly filled the 2000-seat auditorium of the Queen's Hall. His subjects ranged from the analysis of a specific artist or school to discussions of aesthetics and of the methods of art history. The need to support a family, after his marriage on 3 December 1896 to Helen (1864–1937), a painter of some promise (the daughter of Joseph Coombe, a corn merchant), and the births of his son and daughter (1901 and 1902 respectively), had made him dependent on lecturing and publications for a regular income. This necessity became more pressing when his wife, who had begun to suffer from undiagnosed schizophrenia in 1899, was committed to an institution in 1910. Fry would remain married to her until his death.

The publication of *Giovanni Bellini* secured for Fry the job of art critic for *The Pilot* (1899). In 1901 he wrote an account of the various schools of Italian art for *Macmillan's Guide to Italy* and joined the staff of the weekly *Athenaeum*, an influential organ of British cultural life. He contributed substantial exhibition and book reviews, and commented on the policies of art institutions. Fry wrote authoritatively in a clear, flowing style, analysing technique in a lively manner and with a painter's eye. Form and composition were always important concerns, though less prominently so than later in his career, for he still mainly regarded their power as being that of expressing a given dramatic or psychological content. His interest in aesthetics comes to the fore in his annotated edition of Sir Joshua Reynolds's *Discourses* (1905).

In 1903 Fry helped to launch the monthly *Burlington Magazine*. He contributed penetrating analyses of individual works and artists, frequently suggesting new attributions. Editorial standards were high, and the articles, focusing mainly on ancient art, well illustrated. Fry helped to secure funds from American donors at an early stage; he was joint editor between 1909 and 1918, encouraging articles on modern art, and remained on the magazine's consultative committee until his death. Fry also wrote for *The Nation* from 1910 onwards, and published in a variety of other magazines on an occasional basis.

Fry and institutions Fry's evident scholarly merits and the reputation he had acquired as an expert might rapidly have made him a strong candidate for a museum directorship, or a Slade professorship at Oxford or Cambridge. However, his relations with institutions were not of a kind to attract a consensus of approval. He was outspoken in his criticism of the Royal Academy—helping, for instance, to publicize its notorious mismanagement of the Chantrey bequest in 1903–4—and regularly complained in print about the National Gallery's acquisition policy. In consequence, his hopes of a Slade chair repeatedly met resistance and it was not until 1933 that he obtained that at Cambridge. As for museums, there was a missed opportunity early in 1906, when he was unable to accept the offer of the directorship of the National Gallery, London, having already committed himself to the role of curator of paintings at the Metropolitan Museum of Art in New York. Later, when the directorship of the Tate Gallery was offered to him in 1911, he felt that the salary was too low, and declined.

Fry held his first post at the Metropolitan Museum until 1907. When family commitments became too pressing for a full-time role in New York, he became the museum's European adviser. His responsibility for developing the museum's collections, especially in Italian art, had to be reconciled with his former activism in England to resist the sale to America of works held in British private collections—the collective effort had led, in 1903, to the creation of the National Art Collections Fund. In 1910 Fry was dismissed from his post; with characteristic outspokenness, he had reproached the president of its board of trustees, the millionaire John Pierpont Morgan, for keeping for himself a work which Fry had secured for the museum. Fry's contempt for wealthy philistines, of whom he saw Morgan as the epitome, was frequently expressed in his correspondence and essays.

Post-impressionism and formalist criticism In 1910 Fry publicly embraced the cause of modern French art, organizing the famous 'Manet and the Post-Impressionists' exhibition at London's Grafton Galleries. He had coined the term 'post-impressionism' with reference to the art of Cézanne, Gauguin, Van Gogh, and their followers, who included Matisse, Derain, and Picasso, with a view to underlining the distinctiveness of the newer artists' aims. Fry's familiarity with modern French art had been gradually asserting itself from 1906 onwards, a development which coincided with his growing interest in aesthetics. In 'An essay in aesthetics' (1909, repr. in *Vision and Design*, 1920), he had set out a way of responding to art that was based on form—on the analysis of design and its constituent 'emotional' elements, including 'line', 'mass', and 'colour'. For Fry the post-impressionist artists were motivated by a similar conception of painting, favouring the expressive arrangement of form over the creation of a realistic illusion: 'They do not seek to imitate form, but to create form; not to imitate life, but to find an equivalent for life' (Fry, *Vision and Design*, 167). For Fry the post-impressionists had recovered the thread of artistic tradition, lost in the pursuit of realism.

'Manet and the Post-Impressionists' had a profound influence. Before the First World War London hosted a string of shows devoted to modern continental and British art, and Fry spared no effort to write and lecture about the new styles. In a 'Second Post-Impressionist Exhibition', also held at the Grafton Galleries, in 1912, he endeavoured to show how young British artists had responded to, and adopted, the new plastic idiom. While his formalist approach provided a theoretical legitimation of abstraction, his principal interest remained in figuration; he admired Matisse and Derain, and acknowledged the genius of Picasso, but had little interest in cubism, still less in futurism or expressionism. Fry was fascinated by

Cézanne's treatment of space; for him Cézanne had succeeded in 'us[ing] the modern vision with the constructive design of the old masters' (Fry, *Vision and Design*, 202). The appeal of Cézanne is reflected in Fry's paintings of that decade, for example *Quarry, Bo Peep Farm, Sussex* (1918; Sheffield City Art Galleries).

Fry's new role as champion of the Paris avant-garde was accompanied by major changes in his life. He found himself out of key with the critics and painters with whom he had associated through the NEAC, but was rejuvenated by close contact with the younger generation of artists, whose work he did his best to promote. Through his friendship with the painter Vanessa Bell and her husband, Clive, whom he had met early in 1910, he became a key figure of the circle of artists and writers known as the Bloomsbury group. His theories exerted a major influence on Clive Bell, whose polemic *Art* (1914) was something of a post-impressionist manifesto, and whose theory of 'significant form' was in turn to stimulate Fry's aesthetic speculations. Fry's closeness to Vanessa Bell was both artistic and sentimental. She and Fry were lovers from 1911 to 1913, and he was lastingly affected by their separation, although they remained friends.

The year 1913 also saw the launch of Fry's Omega Workshops, a decorative art venture employing some twenty artists. It was an ideal platform for experimentation in abstract design, and for cross-fertilization between fine and applied arts. Omega attracted an exceptional range of talent: besides Fry, Vanessa Bell, and Duncan Grant, artists initially associated with it included Wyndham Lewis, Frederick Etchells, and Henri Gaudier-Brzeska. However, in spite of a number of commissions for interior design, the company survived the war years with difficulty, and closed in 1919.

Maturity Fry's strong affinities with France led him to divide much of his time after the First World War between London, Paris, and Provence. Provence was a place for rest and painting, while in Paris he had numerous contacts with artists, dealers, and experts. He also sent works to the Salon d'Automne regularly between 1920 and 1926. Fry was on good terms with the artists Jean Marchand and André Derain, who both visited him in London, and enjoyed friendships with the writers Charles Vildrac, André Gide, and, above all, Charles and Marie Mauron, with whom he eventually bought a farm in Provence (1931). He had a good command of French, and his enthusiasm for French culture led him to undertake translations of poems, notably by Stéphane Mallarmé (1936), as well as of publications on art. Maurice Denis's 1907 article on Cézanne, which Fry translated for the *Burlington Magazine* (1910), was an important source for his own interpretation of the artist. Fry also translated two books on aesthetics by Charles Mauron (1927, 1935).

Vision and Design, a collection of essays which appeared in 1920, set a pattern for the format of Fry's publications—with a few exceptions, his books were revised transcripts of single or collected articles and lectures. *Vision and Design* achieved immediate popularity, and has rarely been out of print. Other important collections, also mixing aesthetics, criticism, and art history, are *Transformations* (1926) and the posthumously published *Last Lectures* (1939). Longer studies appeared in monograph form, including *Cézanne* (1927)—a justly celebrated work—and *Henri Matisse* (1930).

In the last years of his life Fry was busy writing, lecturing, painting, travelling, and sitting on committees. In 1931 a retrospective exhibition at the Cooling Galleries in London was well received, whereas his previous shows had failed to attract much praise. A series of twelve BBC broadcasts made between 1929 and 1934 shows that Fry remained an educationist at heart, taking a step-by-step approach to explanation and avoiding jargon. In line with his belief that art appreciation depends more on a 'sensibility' to form than on erudition, he encouraged receptiveness to art objects from non-Western traditions. He insisted that African sculpture was as deserving of study as Greek sculpture, and that anyone could respond to the aesthetic appeal of ancient Chinese vases. Throughout his life, however, Fry never ceased to puzzle over the status of representation, and its relation to aesthetic value. Eventually retreating from the more radical implications of formalism—which had led him, in the 1920s, to disqualify paintings seeking a narrative effect from the sphere of the visual arts—Fry came to embrace the idea that painting had a fundamentally 'double' nature. He presented Rembrandt and Giorgione, painters for whom he had the highest admiration, as 'simultaneously attaining to an extreme poetic exaltation and achieving a great plastic construction and bringing about, moreover, a complete fusion of the two' (Fry, 'The Double Nature of Painting', 1933; repr. 1969, 371).

Academic recognition came at last with the award of an honorary fellowship of King's College, Cambridge (1927), an honorary LLD of Aberdeen University (1929), and the Cambridge Slade professorship (1933). In his private life Fry found stability and happiness with Helen Anrep (1885–1965), his companion from 1926 until his death. He died at the Royal Free Hospital, London, on 9 September 1934, from complications after a fall in his flat caused a broken thigh. He was cremated on 13 September. There was no religious service, but a memorial service was held on 19 September at King's College chapel, Cambridge, where his ashes were interred.

Status and reputation In 1939 Kenneth Clark credited Roger Fry with having brought about a change in taste in Britain (introduction to Fry, *Last Lectures*, ix). By introducing post-impressionist painting, and a critical terminology to make sense of it, Fry had indeed done more than any other critic to draw British art into modernist styles. Until surrealism and abstract art imposed themselves as the new avant-garde in the 1930s with the critical support of Herbert Read, Fry remained the best-known British advocate of modern art. Readers valued his insight and independence of mind, and an approach to criticism that Fry himself characterized as 'experimental' (*Transformations*, 1), based on a receptiveness to new ideas, and a willingness to submit conclusions to continual revision.

Less positive assessments have also been made. Fry's contemporaries sometimes charged him with having used his influence within artists' societies to promote his immediate entourage, and overly favoured the imitation of French styles. Later commentators have reproached him for failing to acknowledge a specifically British school. However, it must be pointed out that even those British artists who claimed a distinctive national identity were inextricably bound up with the international avant-garde. Fry's efforts to publicize British art—including work by artists associated with vorticism—internationally (Paris, 1912, 1927; Zürich, 1918) were real enough, even if they encountered little success.

The rise of Marxist theory, and of iconology, obscured the strengths of Fry's type of formalism, while subsequent assessment of his work has been complicated by the frequent confusion, among critics of formalism, of Fry's ideas with those of Clive Bell. Serious analysis of the 'Bloomsbury' thinkers has in general suffered from the tendency to consider them as all of a piece—a coterie to be celebrated or condemned. Nevertheless, the publication of two biographies of Fry—first by Virginia Woolf, and more recently by Frances Spalding—as well as of previously uncollected writings, and the mounting, since his death, of several exhibitions examining his achievement as painter, critic, and art historian (for example 'Vision and Design: The Life, Work and Influence of Roger Fry, 1866–1934', Arts Council, 1966; 'Art Made Modern: Roger Fry's Vision of Art', Courtauld Inst., 1999), testify to the major place which twentieth-century criticism continued to ascribe to Fry.   ANNE-PASCALE BRUNEAU

Sources F. Spalding, *Roger Fry: art and life* (1999) · V. Woolf, *Roger Fry: a biography*, ed. D. F. Gillespie (1995) · *Letters of Roger Fry*, ed. D. Sutton, 2 vols. (1972) · D. Laing, *Roger Fry: an annotated bibliography of the published writings* (1979) · *DNB* · A.-P. Bruneau, 'Roger Fry, Clive Bell: genèse d'une esthétique post-impressionniste', doctoral diss., Université Paris 10–Nanterre, 1995 · R. Fry, *Vision and design*, ed. J. B. Bullen (1981) · R. Fry, 'The double nature of painting', *Apollo*, 89 (1969), 362–71 · F. Rutter, *Art in my time* (1933) · K. Clark, introduction, in R. Fry, *Last lectures* (1939) · articles on R. E. Fry as a painter, 1906–33, King's Cam., Roger Fry MSS, 10/2 · C. Green, ed., *Art made modern: Roger Fry's vision of art* (1999) [exhibition catalogue, Courtauld Inst., London, 15 Oct 1999–23 Jan 2000] · R. Shone and others, *The art of Bloomsbury: Roger Fry, Vanessa Bell and Duncan Grant* (1999) [exhibition catalogue, London, San Marino, CA, and New Haven, CT, 4 Nov 1999–2 Sept 2000] · *Vision and design: the life, work and influence of Roger Fry, 1866–1934* (1966) [with essays by Q. Bell and P. Troutman; exhibition catalogue, London and Nottingham, March–May 1966] · A. Fry, ed., *A memoir of the Rt Hon. Sir Edward Fry* (1921) · b. cert. · m. cert. · d. cert.

Archives King's AC Cam., corresp. and papers | BL, corresp. with Sidney Cockerell, Add. MS 52715 · BL, letters to George Bernard Shaw, Add. MS 50534 · Bodl. Oxf., letters to Arthur Ponsonby · Harvard U., Houghton L., letters to Sir William Rothenstein · Harvard University, near Florence, Italy, Center for Italian Renaissance Studies, letters to Bernard Berenson and Mary Berenson · King's AC Cam., corresp. with C. R. Ashbee; corresp. mainly with E. F. Bulmer; letters to John Maynard Keynes; letters to Nathaniel Wedd · LUL, letters to Thomas Sturge Moore · Tate collection, letters to Simon Bussy [photocopies] · U. Glas. L., letters to D. S. MacColl · U. Sussex, letters, literary MSS, to Clive Bell and Vanessa Bell; corresp. with Virginia Woolf · UCL, corresp. with Arnold Bennett

Likenesses photographs, *c.*1872–1901, repro. in Spalding, *Roger Fry* · photograph, *c.*1872–1932, repro. in Woolf, *Roger Fry* · group portrait, photograph, *c.*1893, repro. in Green, ed., *Art made modern* · double portrait, photograph, *c.*1897 (with Helen Fry), Tate collection · A. Broughton, photograph, *c.*1900, NPG · photograph, *c.*1911, Tate collection · W. Sickert, ink caricature, *c.*1911–1912, Islington Public Libraries, London · V. Bell, oils, 1912, repro. in R. Shone, *Bloomsbury portraits* (1976) · A. L. Coburn, photograph, 1912, NPG · double portrait, photograph, 1912 (with Sickert), repro. in R. Shone, *Bloomsbury portraits* (1976) · group portrait, photograph, 1912, Tate collection · portraits, *c.*1912–1923, repro. in Shone and others, *Art of Bloomsbury* · M. Beerbohm, pencil and watercolour caricature, 1913, King's Cam. · J. Marchand, chalk drawing, 1913, NPG · group portrait, photograph, 1913, repro. in Spalding, *Roger Fry* · photograph, *c.*1913–1919, repro. in Sutton, ed., *Letters of Roger Fry* · A. C. Cooper, photograph, 1918, NPG · R. Fry, self-portrait, oils, 1918, King's Cam. · M. Gimond, lead bust, 1920, NPG · R. Tatlock, photograph, *c.*1920, repro. in Spalding, *Roger Fry* · M. Beerbohm, pencil and watercolour caricature, *c.*1920–1921, priv. coll. · Quiz [P. Evans], pen-and-ink caricature, 1922 · H. Tonks, caricature in oils, *c.*1923, priv. coll. · R. Fry, self-portrait, oils, *c.*1926, repro. in Woolf, *Roger Fry* · photograph, *c.*1928, Tate collection · probably V. Bell, photograph, 1930–32, Tate collection · R. Fry, self-portrait, oils, *c.*1930–1934, NPG · Lenare, photograph, *c.*1930–1934, NPG · M. Beerbohm, chalk caricature, 1931, NPG · Ramsey & Muspratt, bromide print, 1932, NPG · V. Bell, double portrait, oils, *c.*1933 (with Julian Bell), King's Cam.; repro. in Shone and others, *Art of Bloomsbury* · V. Bell, oils, 1933, King's Cam. · group portrait, photograph, 1933, repro. in Q. Bell, *Virginia Woolf* (1976) · R. Fry, self-portrait, oils, 1934, King's Cam. · M. Beerbohm, caricature, Indiana University, Bloomington, Lilly Library; repro. in M.-A. Caws and S. B. Wright, *Bloomsbury and France* (2000) · Q. Bell, double portrait, photograph (with J. Bell), repro. in M.-A. Caws and S. B. Wright, *Bloomsbury and France* (2000) · W. Roberts, pencil caricature, Jason and Rhodes Gallery, London · R. Strachey, oils, NPG · caricature etching, University of Manchester · double portrait, photograph (with J. Coatmellec), King's Cam. · double portrait, photograph (with Marie Mauron), King's Cam.

Wealth at death £21,449 12*s.* 6*d.*: probate, 13 Dec 1934, *CGPLA Eng. & Wales*

Fry [*née* Pease], **Sophia**, **Lady Fry** (1837–1897), philanthropist and political activist, was born on 11 June 1837 at East Mount, Darlington, co. Durham, the first of the two daughters of John Pease (1797–1868), woollen manufacturer and director of the Stockton and Darlington Railway, and Sophia Pease, *née* Jowitt (d. 1870). Sophia Fry's outstanding contribution to philanthropy and politics was a consequence of the three main formative influences of her early life: the Quaker faith, Liberalism, and her family. The parental home at East Mount, Darlington, was run in accordance with Quaker culture and teachings, with an emphasis on philanthropy and public service. Sophia and her only sister, Mary Anna, were given an unusually well-rounded education: academic lessons from a governess were part of a regime which emphasized healthy outdoor pursuits and moral development. At the age of fourteen she spent one year at the Miss Taylors' school at Frenchay, near Bristol, where she developed a lifelong friendship with Sarah Sturge, who later married her cousin, Edward Pease, and first met her husband-to-be, Theodore Fry (1836–1912), a scion of the family of cocoa and chocolate manufacturers.

They were married on 14 August 1862, and by all accounts theirs was a compatible and companionable union, producing eight children (four girls and four boys), and with shared interests in public service and politics. After an initial four years in Bristol, they set up a permanent home at Woodburn in Darlington, where Theodore became a partner in the iron-rolling mills at Rise Carr. He subsequently served on the town council, school board, and the board of guardians, and was mayor in 1877–8. Sophia became involved in a number of religious, charitable, and educational activities in which her organizational flair and gift for public speaking began to mature.

Following family tradition, Sophia Fry had been drawn into visiting work from an early age, and developed a youthful interest in education for the poor. Her capacity for innovation was shown when, still a very young woman, she started a weekly class for pupil teachers, and set up a centre for cookery classes—well before the development of domestic skills teaching in state elementary schools. After her marriage she helped to establish the Girls' Friends Day School in Bristol, and was active in the affairs of the Darlington High School for Girls, which was attended by her daughters. She ensured that women had a responsible share in the management of the British and Foreign School Society's North of England College to train mistresses for elementary schools, established in Darlington in 1879. A supporter of the Association for the Care of Girls and the Darlington Temperance Society, her broader philanthropic work included the running of mothers' meetings and savings clubs for women at the Hopetown mission. Perhaps her most significant contribution to the civic life of Darlington was a successful campaign to raise £10,000 to build the general hospital, which was opened in 1884.

Sophia Fry was perhaps most notable for her pioneering work in encouraging women's active involvement in party politics and in establishing the national Women's Liberal Federation. The election of her husband as MP for Darlington in 1880 propelled her into campaigning and canvassing. Recognizing the valuable skills which women could bring to local constituency work, and inspired, as were others, by W. E. Gladstone's call to women during his Midlothian campaign, she set up a Women's Liberal Association (WLA) in Darlington in 1881, among the first in the country. Although the role of women in party politics was at this stage a contested one, she believed it to be their duty to work for the electoral success of the Liberal Party and thus to promote its stance on many of the great moral issues of the day. Later commentators have remarked that the experience she gained as an active philanthropist was the forerunner of her interest in politics. Aware of the need for local associations to have a national forum for communication and mutual development, she established the Women's Liberal Federation (WLF) in London in 1887, taking the position of honorary secretary, with Catherine Gladstone as a not very effective president. It quickly grew into a formidable organization of some 75,000 members and 360 local WLAs by 1892.

However, it also acquired a reputation for 'strong feminism' and its national conferences aired many of the women's issues of the time. The most divisive and controversial of these was women's suffrage which Sophia, although personally in favour, rightly viewed as a threat to the harmonious working of the federation and a deflection from their main purpose of electing Liberals to office. When a group of rebel progressives succeeded in establishing women's suffrage as one of the official aims of the federation, Sophia led a group of moderates into forming a secessionist Women's National Liberal Association in 1892, which adhered to the WLF's original aims and preserved the important principle of local WLA autonomy. She became its first vice-president (1892–7).

When her husband was created a baronet in 1894, Sophia assumed the title of Lady Fry. A serious accident while on holiday with her husband in Italy was the prelude to her untimely death the following year at the Grand Hotel, Biarritz, on 30 March 1897. She was buried in the Quaker meeting-house graveyard in Darlington on 3 April. Sir Theodore remarried in 1902. Sophia Fry is honoured for her pivotal role in bringing women to the fore of Liberal politics. LINDA WALKER

Sources E. Orme, *Lady Fry of Darlington* (1898) · E. A. Pratt, *Catherine Gladstone* (1898) · L. Walker, 'Party political women: a comparative study of liberal women and the Primrose League, 1890–1914', *Equal or different: women's politics, 1800–1914*, ed. J. Rendall (1987), 165–91 · Burke, *Peerage* · WWW · Boase, *Mod. Eng. biog.* · d. cert.

Wealth at death £4208 5s. 3d.: probate, 3 June 1897, CGPLA Eng. & Wales

Fry, Thomas (1718–1772), classical scholar and college head, was the son of Thomas Fry, of Pipe Lane, Bristol. He was educated at Bristol grammar school until 1732, and was then admitted to St John's College, Oxford, as a Bristol fellow. He took his BA degree in 1736, was MA in 1740, and took priest's orders in 1744, a BD in 1745, and a DD in 1750.

Regularly resident in college during term, Fry held most college offices, beginning as logic reader in 1737–40. He was dean of arts in 1740–44, natural philosophy reader in 1740–41 and 1745–6, the college preacher in 1743–4 and 1746–7, and dean of divinity in 1750–51. He served the college as Waple's preacher (1748–9) and the Wood bursar (1748–9, 1755–6), and became senior bursar (1751–2), junior bursar (1752–3), and rhetoric lecturer (1755). Having been twice vice-president (1754–5 and 1757–8), he was elected president of St John's College on 9 December 1757 on the resignation of William Walker. Fry was curate in three college livings between 1749 and 1757—St Giles', Oxford (1749), Fyfield until 1755, and Kirtlington (1755–7)—and so he was often an absentee incumbent. In 1757, on being elected president, he became rector of Hanborough.

Fry was determined to uphold the authority of the president; in 1766 he was upset by the appointment of a new steward (who oversaw the domestic arrangements of the college) which had been made at a meeting presided over by the vice-president. Fry persuaded eight of the senior fellows to protest at the action and overruled the appointment on the ground that the proceedings were contrary to

statute. Later the same day, with a new vice-president and the senior bursar, he elected the same man steward and clerk of accounts. However, he does not seem to have felt so strongly about public affairs, for in May 1768 he refused a seat on the bench: 'The Master of Ball. [Balliol] pressed me much to have my name inserted in the new Commissn for the Peace, but I absolutely declined it. Clergymen have no business to concern themselves with Civil affairs' (St John's College Records).

In the diary covering the last four years of his life there is little mention of books, but he had brought out an edition of Aristophanes' *Plutus* and *Clouds* in 1767. It is plain that food was one of his permanent interests, and he faithfully records details of dinners, with comments on the madeira in the common-room cellar. This perhaps accounts for the gout from which he suffered in 1771 and for which he collected prescriptions from friends.

As an old friend of John Wilkes, Fry seems to have been, if not an active radical, at least a passive sympathizer. When in 1768 action was taken against young members of the university influenced by Methodism, he commented:

The V.C. acknowledg'd that the characters of the men were very unexceptionable in every respect … but the Statutes of the Univy, he thought, obliged him to proceed in this Manner—thus is Persecution carried on under the masque of Mildness and Moderation. (St John's College muniments, 75, D7)

Fry was a tolerant man, who enjoyed solitude; he had protestant sympathies, but gave no sign of any antipathy to Catholicism. He never married and died intestate in Bristol on 22 November 1772. He was buried in the churchyard at Clifton. V. SILLERY

Sources records, St John's College, Oxford · records, St John's College, Oxford, muniments, 75, D7 [24/5/1768, 26/3/1768] · Blackwood, 213 (1923), 1287 · Oxford University matriculation register, 1732, U. Oxf. · Foster, *Alum. Oxon.*

Archives St John's College, Oxford, records

Fry, Thomas Charles (1846–1930), schoolmaster and dean of Lincoln, was born at Forest Hill, Sydenham, Kent, on 16 April 1846, the only son and youngest child of Peter Samuel Fry, solicitor, and his wife, Katherine Eliza Ann, daughter of the Revd John Charles Williams. His grandfather, the Revd Thomas Fry (1775–1860), of Axbridge, a fellow of Lincoln College, Oxford, and later rector of Emberton, Buckinghamshire, had been one of the founders of the Church Missionary Society. Fry was educated at Bedford grammar school and at Pembroke College, Cambridge, where he gained a scholarship, and obtained a second class in the classical tripos of 1868 (BA 1868, MA 1872, BD 1889, DD 1891). After two years at Durham School as assistant master, he was appointed assistant master at Cheltenham College, and was ordained deacon in 1871 and priest in 1873. In 1883 he was appointed headmaster of Oundle School, but in the following year, owing to a serious illness, he resigned, under doctors' orders, and went to the Riviera. In 1886 he took charge of the parish of Wyke Regis, Dorset.

In 1887 Fry was appointed headmaster of Berkhamsted

School. By his initiative the school was provided with modern equipment, including science laboratories, additional classrooms, a new hall, and a beautiful chapel, to which he and his wife contributed generously. He inspired his staff (whose meagre salaries he sometimes subsidized) with his own enthusiasm, and, although a strict disciplinarian, he won the esteem of the boys by his devotion and singleness of aim. Among his innovations were the establishment of a preparatory department, the foundation of an old boys' association, and the inauguration of a school rifle corps. The educational standard was raised, the numbers grew, and the school which he had found a country grammar school attained a recognized position among the public schools of the country.

Much of his success as a headmaster he owed to his marriage in 1876 to Julia Isabella (d. 1928). She was the third daughter of Edward *Greene [see under Greene family], heir to the East Anglian brewery firm and MP for Bury St Edmunds (1865–85) and for Stowmarket (1886–91). Not only did she supervise one of the boys' boarding-houses, but her family money made possible many of Fry's large benefactions to Berkhamsted School.

A man of wide interests, Fry did not confine himself to the routine of school work. A radical in politics and a liberal high-churchman, he threw himself into the task of presenting the church's spiritual and social message to the age. In sermons and in addresses at meetings and church congresses he delivered his mind on such questions as the drink traffic (he had been a total abstainer since about 1876), purity, the sanctity of marriage, the housing question, and economic and industrial problems, with impassioned earnestness, entire fearlessness, and at times with biting severity. His headmastership at Berkhamsted commenced with a purge of immorality among the boys, and he later (1920) demonstrated an unflinching harshness in the proceedings taken against John Wakeford (1859–1930), precentor of Lincoln Cathedral, for improper conduct. A contributor to Charles Gore's essays on church reform (1898), he was one of the pioneers in the work of the Christian Social Union, and was also chairman of the Church Reform League.

In 1910 Fry was appointed dean of Lincoln. He played a conspicuous part in the life of the city and of the diocese, and showed, as an active supporter of the Workers' Educational Association, a keen interest in adult, no less than in elementary and secondary education. His great achievement at Lincoln was in fund-raising when, in 1921, the fabric of the cathedral was found to be in serious danger. He quickly enlisted interest not only in England but in the British colonies and the United States of America. Twice he crossed the Atlantic on visits to Canada and the United States to collect funds. His third and last visit overseas, to South America, in his eighty-fourth year in 1929, was cut short by illness, and he was brought back to England, and died at the deanery at Lincoln on 10 February 1930. He had raised nearly £100,000 for the cathedral restoration fund. Although his task was not completed, it was due to his heroic efforts that the fabric was saved.

Fry's chief recreations were fishing and climbing, and he was a member of the Alpine Club. He was a great traveller and had a facility in acquiring foreign languages.

J. H. SRAWLEY, rev. M. C. CURTHOYS

Sources *The Times* (11 Feb 1930) · D. Winterbottom, *Doctor Fry* (1977) · B. H. G. Williams, *A history of Berkhamsted School* (1980) · J. E. Treherne, *Dangerous precincts: the mystery of the Wakeford case* (1987) · Venn, *Alum. Cant.* · *CGPLA Eng. & Wales* (1930)
Likenesses photograph, c.1883, repro. in W. G. Walker, *A history of the Oundle Schools* (1956)
Wealth at death £18,113 3s. 1d.: resworn probate, 25 March 1930, *CGPLA Eng. & Wales*

Fry, William Thomas (1789–1843), engraver, of whose parents nothing is known, was one of the first engravers to experiment with steel plates, using Jacob Perkins's steel blocks and plates by Stephen Hoole from early 1820, before conducting some of the first experiments on Charles Warren's soft plates. He found Warren's plates the most satisfactory as the burr raised by the burin parted from them more easily. Fry encouraged dialogue among manufacturers, introducing Warren to a Mr Duffy whose advice on decarbonizing steel improved his plates, and advising the plate maker Richard Hughes to consult Warren. Fry's stipple portrait of the Revd William Naylor for the *Methodist Magazine* (February 1822) was one of the first engravings to be published using Warren's plates; this was followed by portraits on steel for the *Evangelical Magazine* (1823–4), including *W. B. Collyer* after J. Rentin (1 January 1823). Fry engraved frontispieces for *The London Stage* (4 vols., 1824–7). He contributed *Lovers' Tomb* after Richard Westall and *Madonna of St Sixtus* after Raphael to Rudolph Ackermann's *Forget-me-not* (1825), the first annual to use steel plates: both engravings have the word 'steel' at the bottom.

Between 1824 and 1830 Fry exhibited various works with the Society of British Artists at Suffolk Street, including portraits after Van Dyck (1825) and a portrait of the engraver John Scott after J. Jackson (1826). In 1825 he was living at 4 Swinton Street, Gray's Inn Road, London; by 1830 he was living at 9 Constitution Row. Further portraits include eight plates engraved after Holbein, Kneller, and others for E. Lodge's *Portraits* (2nd edn, 1835), including *King Henry the Eighth*, *Queen Elizabeth*, and *Sir Isaac Newton*, and four plates for William Jerdan's *National Portrait Gallery of Illustrious and Eminent Personages of the Nineteenth Century* (5 vols., 1830–34): *Princess Charlotte* and *The Earl of Liverpool* after Sir Thomas Lawrence, *Admiral Earl Howe* after Gainsborough Dupont, and *The Rev Samuel Lee* after R. Evans. Fry also engraved eleven plates for *The National Gallery of Pictures by Great Masters* published in two volumes by Jones & Co., London [1836]. He worked mainly in stipple, but also produced aquatints and lithographs. His lithographs include *The Bird Catcher* after J. Barney, *The Favourite Bird* after H. Singleton, and *Jeune femme avec un éventail*.

Fry died, apparently unmarried, at 41 Harrison Street, London, on 5 July 1843. Plates signed 'W. T. Fry' continued to be published after his death: *Mercury and Pandora* after

J. Flaxman appeared in *Art Union* (1848), engravings of Halley and Turgot appeared in *The Imperial Dictionary of Universal Biography* (1861), and *The Royal Shakespeare* (1883–4) included his stipple portrait of Shakespeare as a frontispiece to volume 2. Examples of Fry's prints are in the British Museum and the National Portrait Gallery, London.   LOIS OLIVER

Sources B. Hunnisett, *An illustrated dictionary of British steel engravers*, new edn (1989) · B. Hunnisett, *Steel engraved book illustration in England* (1980) · J. Johnson, ed., *Works exhibited at the Royal Society of British Artists, 1824–1893, and the New English Art Club, 1888–1917*, 2 vols. (1975) · J. H. Slater, *Engravings and their value*, 5th edn (1921) · *DNB* · S. T. Prideaux, *Aquatint engraving* (1909) · B. Hunnisett, *Engraved on steel: the history of picture production using steel plates* (1998) · Graves, *Artists* · d. cert.

Fryatt, Charles Algernon (1871–1916), master mariner, was born on 2 December 1871 at 6 Marsh Lane, Southampton, the second son of Charles Fryatt, a merchant seaman, and his wife, Mary Jane Brown Percy, whose family came from Northumberland. Charles Algernon first attended the Fremantle School in Southampton and later went to school in Harwich when his father took a job there with the Great Eastern Railway Company, rising to the rank of chief officer.

Fryatt also entered the merchant service, served his apprenticeship, and worked on steam vessels until 1892 when he too joined the Great Eastern Railway Company. On 2 November 1896 he married Ethel (*b.* 1876/7), daughter of Sydney Smith Townsend, a boilermaker; they had seven children, one son and six daughters. As an able seaman he served on the paddle steamer *Colchester*, a vessel he eventually commanded in 1913 sailing between Britain, Belgium, and the Netherlands. By 1914 he was commanding the *Brussels*, a twin-screw steamer with accommodation for 164 first-class and 88 second-class passengers. Built specifically for the Harwich to Antwerp service, she normally sailed between Parkeston Quay, Harwich, and a Dutch or Belgian port and, despite the outbreak of war, she continued taking passengers and cargo to these ports. Three other vessels were assigned to this route—the *Colchester*, *Cromer*, and *Wrexham*—and it was not long before reports started coming in from these ships of harassment from German submarines. There was not only the threat of capture under the usual international law of capture and search but U-boats were now instructed by the German government to destroy any merchant vessel found in the war region without it always being possible to warn the crew and passengers of danger threatening.

On 10 February 1915 Captain Fryatt and all master mariners received secret instructions from the Admiralty on what to do when challenged by a U-boat. The orders were to steer straight at the submarine forcing her to dive: no British merchant vessel should ever tamely surrender to a submarine, but should do her utmost to escape. The *Brussels* left Parkeston Quay on 28 March 1915 bound for Rotterdam. As she was nearing the Maas lightship off the coast of the Netherlands, Fryatt sighted the submarine U33 approaching on his starboard bow. U33, under the command of the German Lieutenant-Captain Gansser, was sailing from Zeebrugge with orders to attack enemy shipping. Gansser signalled to the *Brussels* to stop but Fryatt, obeying Admiralty instructions, changed the course of the *Brussels* and then attempted to ram the U-boat. The submarine was forced to dive, and when she resurfaced the *Brussels* was 5 miles away and out of danger.

Back in England Fryatt was awarded a gold watch by the Admiralty in recognition of the example he set when attacked by a German submarine. He had previously been awarded another gold watch by the directors of the Great Eastern Railway Company for evading a U-boat on 2 March 1915 and become known as the Pirate Dodger. It was subsequently believed that this recognition made him a marked man but, if this was the case, it was over a year before the Germans exacted retribution.

On 22 July 1916 the *Brussels* sailed from the Hook of Holland with cargo, mail, and refugees bound for Tilbury. A few miles past the Maas lightship the ship was surrounded by German destroyers and boarded by their officers who, armed with revolvers, arrested Fryatt and his crew, hoisted the German flag, and sailed the ship to Zeebrugge, arriving there on 23 June. The officers and crew were first taken to Ruhleben camp in Germany, but Fryatt and his first officer, William Hartnell, were soon brought back to Bruges where they were to face three weeks of interrogation. On 27 July 1916 Fryatt stood before a German court. He was charged that although not a member of a combat force, he made an attempt on 28 March 1915 to ram the German submarine U33. The official report of the trial characterized the prisoner as a *franc-tireur* of the sea, a charge similar to piracy and an activity punishable by death.

The Foreign Office in London had asked the American ambassador in Berlin to engage a counsel for Captain Fryatt but, despite writing to the German authorities on two occasions, the ambassador received no reply until 26 July when he was informed that Fryatt was to be tried the following day. At his trial, therefore, Fryatt was defended by a German officer, Major Neuman, but he had no legal advice or assistance before the trial. Had he explained to the court that he had been acting under Admiralty instructions the charge of *franc-tireur* would not have been sustained and he probably would have been acquitted. As it was, bound by confidentiality, all he would say was 'I have done nothing wrong'. The court took only a few minutes to reach a guilty verdict and two hours later Fryatt was taken from his prison cell and shot. Before his death he spoke to the German chaplain and asked for a photograph of his grave to be sent to his wife. The chaplain also wrote to Mrs Fryatt—a letter of 400 words of which nearly half were devoted to explaining that her husband had been justly sentenced.

In Britain, Fryatt's execution aroused a storm of protest. *The Times* of 29 July 1916 wrote:

> The cold blooded murder of Captain Charles Fryatt of the Great Eastern Railway so callously announced in the German official news of yesterday is calculated to rouse the indignation of the world as nothing else has done since the assassination of Miss Cavell.

After the war memorial services were held in Antwerp and Bruges, and on 7 July 1919 Fryatt's body was brought back to England on the British destroyer *Orpheus*. His widow met the coffin on the same day at Dovercourt Bay and was given the posthumous order of St Leopold that had been awarded to her husband by King Albert of Belgium. Fryatt was buried on 7 July 1919 in All Saints' churchyard, Dovercourt, where a ward in Harwich Hospital and a public house were named after him. On 8 July a service was held at St Paul's Cathedral attended by three of his daughters and his brother. A waxwork was displayed in Madame Tussaud's until 1934, and a Claughton class London and North West Railway locomotive and a mountain in Jasper National Park, Canada, were named in his honour. A memorial plaque to Captain Fryatt was erected at Liverpool Street Station, then the headquarters of the Great Eastern Railway Company.   LIZA VERITY

Caroline Joyce Fryd (1909–2000), by Paul Caplan, 1996

Sources *DNB* · A. Hurd, *The merchant navy*, 2 (1924) · C. Winchester, ed., *Shipping wonders of the world*, 2 (1936–7) · *The Times* (29–31 July 1916) · *ILN* (12 July 1919) · C. Simpson, *Lusitania* (1972) · A. G. Jamieson, 'Martyr or pirate? The case of Captain Fryatt in the Great War', *Mariner's Mirror*, 85 (1999), 196–202 · *CGPLA Eng. & Wales* (1916) · b. cert. · m. cert.

Archives IWM, papers relating to high sea arrest, trial, and execution | FILM IWM FVA, 'Fryatt demonstration', Topical Budget, 7 Aug 1916, NTB 259–01

Likenesses memorial plaque, Liverpool Street station, London · photograph, IWM

Wealth at death £1073 16s. 7d.: probate, 20 Sept 1916, *CGPLA Eng. & Wales*

Fryd [*née* Manning], **Caroline Joyce** [Judy] (1909–2000), disability rights campaigner, was born on 31 October 1909 at 42 Falkland Road, Hornsey, London, the daughter of Harry Smith Manning, a Post Office sorter, and his wife, Carrie Aldridge. She was educated at Minchenden School, Southgate, and at Ruskin College, Oxford, where she studied economics and political science. There she met fellow student John Herbert Francis Fryd (1911/12–1981), who later became general secretary of the Trade Union Federation; they married on 29 August 1936 and moved to Leeds, where Judy gave birth to their first child, Felicity, in 1938. A second daughter, Patricia, was born in 1940, and in 1941, after the family moved to Harpenden, Hertfordshire, she had twins, Peter and Linda.

Not long after her birth Felicity showed signs of learning disability, and Judy Fryd sought help. At this time the learning disabled were usually placed in long-stay subnormality hospitals, and were labelled 'mental defectives', 'mongols', 'feeble-minded', and 'imbeciles'. Unwilling to accept this fate for her child, Judy undertook a frustrating search for help with educating Felicity. To add to her problems Felicity also had what is now known as 'challenging behaviour', and although she was found a place in a local primary school (itself an achievement, for such children were considered incapable of formal education), she was soon sent home as 'too disruptive'; at a 'special' boarding-school, she was again deemed 'not suitable' and summarily returned home within twenty-four hours.

In 1946 Judy Fryd answered a letter in the magazine *Nursery World*, in which a desperate mother asked if there were any others who were struggling to look after a learning disabled child at home. Judy's reply suggested that she and fellow parents should band together in their common cause—battling with social services, health, education, and local authorities—in an effort to receive some kind of recognition and amelioration of their unhappy plight. Within a month over 1000 parents—mainly mothers—had joined forces, and four years later the Association of Parents of Backward Children came into being. An inaugural convention, attended by 122 people, took place at the Fountain Hospital on 13 May 1950. The minutes read:

> First to speak was Mrs. Fryd who had been writing to parents all over the country and had been keeping in touch with them through her Newsletter. In giving a short account of her activities, she said how delighted she was to meet so many people with whom she has corresponded in the past.

The council met again on 19 June and then ten days later, when it was resolved (at Judy's prompting) 'that equality of educational opportunities should be made available for all children according to their needs and disabilities'. It was twenty-one years before that resolution became the law of the land. The association published an influential and ground-breaking magazine, *Parents Voice*, which became vital in promoting and researching the needs and potential of children and adults with a learning disability. Judy Fryd became editor, a role she filled for the next twenty-five years with unstinting devotion and expertise. These were the first steps of a movement which eventually led to the creation of the Royal Mencap Society, now the largest learning disability organization in the UK, employing nearly 6000 people, spending over £100 million a year, and with more than 400 affiliated local societies adding to the vast range of work undertaken by Mencap itself. People with a learning disability now also serve on Mencap's national assembly and board of trustees, making it a uniquely inclusive society.

Judy Fryd was always a political animal. She was a staunch supporter of the Labour Party, having joined the

Labour League of Youth in her teens. Indeed it was largely her campaigning that led to the Education (Handicapped Children) Act (1971), thus overturning previous thinking that children with a learning disability were ineducable. Until then parents had to find (and pay for) private education, though even then their sons and daughters were deemed not to be schoolchildren as such, being denied post-war health support, including free school milk and vitamin supplements. If this private schooling was impossible, parents had to spend their days at home looking after their learning disabled offspring, unless they were certified as mentally defective and dispatched to a National Health Service long-stay subnormality hospital, where facilities were minimal. It is perhaps ironic that, as the newly formed association came into being, Judy's daughter Felicity entered the first of her long-stay subnormality hospitals: the changes for which her mother campaigned came too late for Felicity, who died in 1993.

In 1967 Judy Fryd was appointed MBE, advanced to CBE in 1996, the occasion of Mencap's fiftieth anniversary. She was honoured by the Association of Women Clerks and Secretaries for her thirty-four years of membership and her work for the Women's Co-operative Guild throughout this time, and in 1991 she received a certificate of merit from the Labour Party for outstanding voluntary service to the party in the St Albans constituency. During this time she also received a certificate from Harpenden town council in recognition of and appreciation for services to the community. She was an active member of the Harpenden choral society for many years, as well as being an accomplished pianist.

Judy Fryd was a vice-president of Mencap for the last twenty years of her life and acknowledged as the founder member. She was the founder, too, of the Harpenden local society and died in the Field House Nursing Home, 8 Townsend Road, Harpenden, the town in which she had lived for almost sixty years, on 20 October 2000. She was cremated at the Garside crematorium, Watford, on 27 October. Although a modest person in private, in public Judy Fryd was a forthright, dynamic campaigner for people with learning disabilities. The fact that many learning disabled people now enjoy further education, independent living, and paid employment, while all are protected by anti-discrimination legislation, is due in large measure to Judy Fryd, together with her fellow parents who banded together to form the National Association of Parents of Backward Children.   BRIAN RIX

Sources personal knowledge (2004) · MSS, Royal Mencap Society, London · *The Times* (23 Oct 2000) · *The Guardian* (24 Oct 2000) · *The Independent* (26 Oct 2000) · *Daily Telegraph* (26 Oct 2000) · b. cert. · m. cert. · d. cert.
Archives Royal Mencap Society, London
Likenesses P. Caplan, photograph, 1996, Mencap, London [*see illus.*] · photograph, repro. in *The Times* · photograph, repro. in *The Guardian* · photograph, repro. in *The Independent* · photograph, repro. in *Daily Telegraph*
Wealth at death £269,604—gross; £266,492—net: probate, 14 June 2001, *CGPLA Eng. & Wales*

Frye, Thomas (1711/12–1762), portrait painter and porcelain manufacturer, was born in Edenderry, King's county,

Thomas Frye (1711/12–1762), self-portrait, 1760

Ireland, the second of the five sons and two daughters of John Fry (1670–1752) and his wife, Anne Harrington. His grandfather was a dragoon officer who fought with William III at the battle of the Boyne. Nothing is known of Frye's education and training, nor the date of his departure for London. Between 1735 and 1743 Frye and his wife, Sarah (d. 1774), had three sons and two daughters; two of his sons died while minors.

Frye's earliest known work is a pair of superb pastels, depicting two boys, one of which is signed and dated 1734 (priv. coll.). There is no evidence that these pastels were drawn in Ireland.

In London, Frye was given a prestigious commission to paint Frederick, prince of Wales, who became perpetual master of the Saddlers' Company, and who agreed to sit for a portrait for the company on 18 November 1736. The portrait was destroyed in 1940 when the company's hall fell during the blitz, though a version remains in the Royal Collection. The portrait, known today through Frye's own mezzotint made in 1741, shows the prince, full-length, seated in full regalia, wearing the collar, badge, and star of a knight of the Garter. An impression of this fine print is held in the National Gallery of Ireland, Dublin. To have acquired such a commission, Frye must have been well established, and may have moved to London earlier than 1734, the date traditionally given for his arrival. Frye's production of assured portraits is abundant. Good examples are *Sir Charles Kemeys-Tynte Bt*, signed and dated 1739 (National Gallery of Ireland, Dublin); *Sir Charles Towneley, as*

York Herald, signed and dated 1740 (College of Arms, London); and the ravishing *Mrs Wardle*, sumptuously attired, signed and dated 1742 (Yale U. CBA). He also worked as a miniature painter, in both oil and watercolour.

Frye was a founder partner, and first manager, of the Bow porcelain manufactory in London; with Edward Heylyn he took out a patent for a new method of manufacturing china on 6 December 1744 in the parish of Bow. He was living at West Ham, a short distance away from the factory. On 17 November 1749 Frye took out a second patent alone, and it has since become apparent that some of the early works from Bow were from Frye's own designs. During this period he continued to paint portraits in oil and produced some of his finest works, such as *Mr Crispe*, of Quex Park, Thanet, signed and dated 1746 (Tate collection); *Benjamin Day* and *Mrs Benjamin Day* (1751; priv. coll.).

Recent sources recount how Frye's dedication to production processes at the factory and his close supervision of porcelain designs left him completely debilitated (Yarbrough). In 1759 he went to Wales to restore his health. The factory did not long survive his departure.

In the following year in Hatton Garden, London, Frye scraped a series of eleven mezzotints with dramatic chiaroscuro, among the most powerful executed in that medium by any British or Irish artist. Together with that done in 1760 in larger size, from his self-portrait, these made up a set of 'Twelve Mezzotint Prints, from Designs in the manner of Piazetta, drawn from Nature and as large as life' (*Public Advertiser*, 28 April 1760, cited in Alexander) for which he advertised a subscription at 2 guineas a set to be closed after 200 sets had been taken. The advertisement also appeared in the *London Chronicle* (3–5 June 1760, 542). The first eight of the unnamed sitters for these diverse portrait studies have been identified. He produced a second set of *Six Ladies, in Picturesque Attitudes, and in Different Dresses of the Present Mode* which he announced in the *Public Advertiser* of 4 April 1761. Frye scraped a total of twenty-five mezzotints, including one of George III which was published shortly after the artist's death. Beset by ill health, Frye was assisted in his work on the later plates by his pupil William Pether, with whom he went into partnership in 1761. The dramatic light effects in his mezzotints influenced the work of Joseph Wright of Derby. Striking black and white drawings by Frye, showing the same sitter full-face and in profile to left, are remarkably similar to the depiction of the scientist in Wright of Derby's *An Experiment on a Bird in the Air Pump* (1768; Tate collection) (see Wynne, 'A pastel by Thomas Frye').

Esteemed and respected by all who knew him, Frye died relatively young of consumption on 2 April 1762, and was buried in Hornsey churchyard, Middlesex, five days later. Many of Frye's mezzotints and two of his etchings are in the department of prints and drawings, British Museum, London; others are in the National Gallery of Ireland, Dublin.   MICHAEL WYNNE

Sources M. Wynne, 'Thomas Frye (1710–1762)', *Burlington Magazine*, 114 (1972), 79–85 • E. Adams and D. Redstone, *Bow porcelain* (1981) • R. C. Yarbrough, *Bow porcelain and the London theatre* (1996) • J. C. Smith, *British mezzotinto portraits*, 2 (1879) • B. Nicolson, *Joseph Wright of Derby: painter of light*, 2 vols. (1968) • M. Wynne, 'A note on Thomas Frye', *Quarterly Bulletin of the Irish Georgian Society*, 13 (1970), 38–44 • M. Wynne, 'Thomas Frye, 1710–1762, reviewed', *Burlington Magazine*, 124 (1982), 624–8 • M. Wynne, 'A pastel by Thomas Frye, c.1710–1762', *British Museum Yearbook*, 2 (1977), 242–5 • *London Chronicle* (3–5 June 1760), 542 • 'Thomas Frye's epitaph', *GM*, 1st ser., 34 (1764) [repr. as appx 3 to Adams and Redstone] • W. H. P. Fry, ed., *Annals of the late Major Oliver Fry* (privately printed, London, 1909) • W. G. Strickland, *A dictionary of Irish artists*, 2 vols. (1913) • *IGI* • D. Alexander, 'Frye, Thomas', *The dictionary of art*, ed. J. Turner (1996) • A. Gabszewicz, *An exhibition of the Yarbrough collection of Bow porcelain* (1999) [exhibition catalogue, the London theatre, 11–24 March, 1999]

Likenesses T. Frye, self-portrait, oils, 1759, NPG • T. Frye, self-portrait, mezzotint, 1760, BM, NG Ire., NPG [*see illus.*] • T. Frye, etching (after his earlier work), NPG • portraits, repro. in Smith, *British mezzotinto portraits*, part 2

Frye, Walter (d. 1474/5), composer, is first recorded in 1456–7, when he joined the Confraternity of St Nicholas, the London guild of parish clerks. His fellow members included the composers John Bedyngham, John Plummer, and Richard Cox. This shared membership is especially interesting since the latter two composers and Frye were between them responsible for the five mass settings which form the original nucleus of the Burgundian court manuscript Brussels, Koninklijke Bibliotheek, MS 5557, with Frye himself the author of three masses. In the year 1464–5 Frye was paid an annuity by Anne, duchess of Exeter, sister of Edward IV. Here again the Brussels manuscript provides an interesting perspective: it was compiled for the marriage of Margaret of York, also a sister of Edward IV, to Charles the Bold, duke of Burgundy, in 1468. Limited though the direct evidence is, then, it seems clear that Frye had connections with the royal court. His will, which survives, is dated 12 August 1474. It was proved at the prerogative court of Canterbury in London on 5 June 1475, thus placing his death some time during the intervening ten months. He died in London.

While there is no evidence that Frye ever worked abroad, his fame extended throughout Europe: his brief but very beautiful *Ave regina celorum* enjoyed unparalleled popularity in the second half of the fifteenth century, turning up in sources as far away from England as Bohemia and Hungary. It is also to be found, sung by angels, in three altarpieces painted in Bruges apparently in the 1480s, and even forms part of a ceiling painting in a French château. Of the few other secular works ascribed to Frye, most have conflicting attributions to others: these include the highly popular 'Tout a par moy', which may be by the Burgundian Gilles Binchois, and 'So ys emprentid', which is more likely to be by Bedyngham.

By far the most substantial part of Frye's output are his settings of the ordinary of the mass. The survival of Brussels MS 5557, without which all his complete masses would have been lost, is therefore especially fortunate. These are works of very high quality, and at least two of them, the *Summe trinitati* and *Flos regalis*, rank among the finest mass cycles of the mid-fifteenth century. To modern ears the subtle interplay of melodic and rhythmic ideas which shape and lend a sense of structural balance to the masses offers ever deeper rewards with growing acquaintance. While these works were probably composed in the early to mid-1460s, the style of Frye's other complete mass, the *Nobilis et pulchra*, points to an earlier date, possibly in the early 1450s, and thus about the same time or slightly later than the masses of Bedyngham, who was apparently a somewhat older contemporary. A partially preserved mass based on the song 'So ys emprentid' is ascribed to Frye in the fragmentary manuscript known as the Lucca choirbook. Strong similarities between this and an anonymous mass in Brussels 5557 suggest that the latter may also be by Frye, a conclusion supported by further stylistic links with Frye's mass style generally, and with his motet *Sospitati dedit*. This piece is the only one by Frye to survive complete in a source from his native country, where most music manuscripts for this period have sadly been lost.

ANDREW KIRKMAN

Sources *Walter Frye: collected works*, ed. S. W. Kenney (1960) • G. Curtis, ed., *Fifteenth-century liturgical music*, 3: *The Brussels masses* (1989) • S. W. Kenney, *Walter Frye and the contenance angloise* (1964) • B. L. Trowell, 'Frye, Walter', *New Grove* • A. Kirkham, 'The style of Walter Frye and an anonymous mass in Brussels, Koninklijke Bibliotheek, manuscript 5557', *Early Music History*, 11 (1992), 191–221 • A. Wathey, 'More on Walter Frye' [forthcoming] • R. C. Wegman, 'New data concerning the origins and chronology of Brussels, Koninklijke Bibliotheek, manuscript 5557', *Tijdschrift van de Vereniging voor Nederlandse muziekgeschiedenis*, 36 (1986), 5–21 • R. Strohm, *Music in late medieval Bruges* (1985)
Archives Royal Library of Belgium, Brussels, MS 5557

Fryer, Alfred (1826–1912), botanist, was born at Chatteris in the Cambridgeshire fens on 25 December 1826, probably at 87 Park Street, the younger son and at least fifth child of Daniel Fryer (*d*. after 1861), a gentleman farmer and later also partner in a brewery, and Elizabeth Fortescue (*d*. after 1861), of Leighton, Huntingdonshire. Sent to a boarding-school at Billesdon, near Leicester, he formed a close friendship with Henry Walter Bates, who shared his fondness for poetry and natural history. However, Fryer could not be persuaded to join Bates and another Leicester friend, Alfred Russel Wallace, when those two left for the Amazon in 1848; by then Fryer's literary tastes were (temporarily) dominant and he was also about to marry Rose, whose surname may been Rice (*d*. 1850).

In the town reading-room at Chatteris, Fryer had come across Coventry Patmore's *Poems* (1844). He sought Patmore out at the British Museum, and won his friendship (and subsequently that of the Rossettis and other figures on the London artistic scene). Whether these connections were the product of periodic visits to London or a period of residence there is unclear: however, it was in Chatteris that his wife Rose gave birth in the spring of 1849, and he was doubtless tied to Chatteris more firmly when the child was left motherless a year later. He married for a second time, probably in 1858; his wife was Clara (1829/30–*c*.1899), and they had a family of six children.

Led to expect a substantial inheritance from an aunt, Fryer had been encouraged by his father to follow his interests and not trouble to train for a profession. Indeed, that aunt had already settled on him the freehold of 4 Wood Street in Chatteris and there he made his home for

Alfred Fryer (1826–1912), by E. E. Sheels

the rest of his life. About this time Fryer began to abandon his literary ambitions and return to studies in natural history. His initial interests in birds, molluscs, and lepidoptera were gradually replaced by a preoccupation with the local flora, resulting in his sending many records to the region's foremost botanist, C. C. Babington (1808–1895), at Cambridge. However, the list of Huntingdonshire plants he contributed to the *Journal of Botany, British and Foreign* in 1884 never grew into the book-length flora of that county that was for a time in prospect. This was because he had been diverted into studying, from 1880 onwards, the perplexing array of broad-leaved representatives of the pondweed genus *Potamogeton* which occurred in exceptional diversity in the waterways within walking distance of his home.

Potamogetons are subject to much confusing modification by subtle environmental differences and until then had defied satisfactory classification. Fryer was uniquely well placed to follow their growth over several seasons and observe their response to changing water-levels, and he supplemented prolonged fieldwork with cultivation experiments in his garden. As a result he proved that several named entities were merely impermanent growth states. After nine years he also reluctantly came to the then novel conclusion that hybrids occur in this genus, some of them even fully fertile (though, regrettably, neither he nor anyone since has proved this by synthesizing them artificially). A keen student of Darwin's work, Fryer was readier to accept this degree of plasticity in a plant group than most botanical contemporaries; unfortunately, though, his concept of a species was very narrow and almost all of the twelve new ones he described are now disregarded, subsumed within broader entities which bear prior names or else considered hybrids.

In 1898, a year after he was elected an associate of the Linnean Society, Fryer's definitive monograph, *The Potamogetons (Pond Weeds) of the British Isles*, began to appear in monthly parts. After two years, however, while the work was still only half-way, friction with the publisher caused him to break off and it was not until 1913–15, after his death, that it was taken to completion by other hands, without the benefit of his own profound knowledge of the group.

Though Fryer was invincibly buoyant and cheerful by nature, a deeper reason for that disengagement was probably the acute financial straits to which he had been unexpectedly reduced. He was bequeathed nothing by his father in the belief that the aunt would provide for him, but on her death in 1885 she proved to have left her money elsewhere. Unwilling to forfeit his independence, Fryer subsisted thereafter on the little that selling the produce of his large garden, with its five glasshouses, brought in. Luckily, his physique was equal to the hard physical labour this involved: until late in life he thought nothing of walking 12 miles to see a cricket match, standing all day, and then walking the 12 miles home again, with one ginger beer as his only sustenance. Even so the struggle for a livelihood could not help but be a distraction and, with a view to moving the monograph forward, a small grant from the Royal Society was obtained for him. Eventually, in 1909, he gave in to repeated attempts by friends to induce him to seek support from a charity, but he only lived to enjoy the resulting small pension for three years: he died on 26 February 1912 from heart failure following what was probably his first illness, an attack of influenza. He was buried in Doddington, the next village, next to his second wife. He had outlived his second wife by about thirteen years and their six children had long since moved to other parts of England, leaving him to live latterly quite alone.

Fryer's large herbarium, mainly of pondweed specimens, superlatively prepared and impeccably documented, was posthumously divided between the British Museum (Natural History), Cambridge University, and Owens College, Manchester. *Potamogeton fryeri*, an oriental species, was named in his honour by a fellow specialist in the genus, Arthur Bennett.   D. E. ALLEN

Sources C. D. Preston, 'Alfred Fryer and the study of the genus *Potamogeton* in the British Isles', *Archives of Natural History*, 15 (1988), 15–33 • C. D. Preston, 'The *Potamogeton* L. taxa described by Alfred Fryer', *Watsonia*, 17 (1988), 23–35 • A. H. Evans and J. Britten, *Journal of Botany, British and Foreign*, 50 (1912), 105–10 • G. C. Druce, *Report of the Botanical Society and Exchange Club of the British Isles*, 3 (1911–13), 195–201 • B. Champneys, *Memoirs and correspondence of Coventry Patmore*, 2 vols. (1900) • *Chatteris News and County Press* (29 Feb 1912) • census returns, 1841, 1851, 1861, 1871 • registers of births and marriages, General Register Office for England
Archives Bodl. Oxf., papers • Manchester Museum, herbarium • NHM, herbarium • U. Cam., department of plant sciences, annotated copy of *The London catalogue of British plants* • U. Cam., department of plant sciences, herbarium
Likenesses photographic print, 1901, NHM, Botany Department; repro. in Preston, 'Alfred Fryer', 16 • E. E. Sheels, photograph, Linn. Soc. [*see illus.*]
Wealth at death negligible; received charitable pension of probably £25 p.a.

Fryer, Edward (1761–1826), physician, of unknown parentage, was born in Frome in Somerset and educated at the grammar school there. He received his first medical training as apprentice to a medical practitioner in Wiltshire before going on to the London hospitals. From about 1780 he continued his studies at the University of Edinburgh before enrolling at the University of Leiden, where he proceeded doctor of medicine with the dissertation 'De vita animantium et vegetantium' on 29 January 1785. A few months later, on 11 April, he matriculated at Göttingen. How Fryer was able to finance studies at Europe's three leading medical universities is unclear, though he may well have been the beneficiary of some kind of patronage.

In November 1787 Fryer submitted *An Essay on the Vitality of the Blood* (in English) for the consideration of Johann Friedrich Blumenbach (1752–1840), then the leading natural scientist in Göttingen and one with a European reputation. The *Essay* challenged a number of Blumenbach's own views; for whatever reason, it appears to represent the end of Fryer's formal medical researches. Fryer remained in Göttingen, though in a letter written to a friend in 1788 he complains 'I am seldom out of my room, once in the course of day to see poor Mrs Volborth' (BL, C.133.9.8, 1). However, the arrival at the university of three of George III's younger sons with their entourage in the summer of 1786 had provided Göttingen's English community with a particular focus of attention, and Fryer appears to have been drawn into their circle. There is circumstantial evidence to suggest that he was the author or co-author of a series of birthday odes dedicated to the princes and printed in English in 1787 and 1788 on behalf of 'the English gentlemen at Gottingen' (Göttingen University Library, 8° P. Angl. 3651(1)). These are rare and interesting examples of English-language printing in the strongly Anglophile university town. Fryer is certainly credited with the authorship of *Ode to Health*, published in 1788 when Augustus Frederick (1773–1843), later duke of Sussex, had fallen ill and when reports of George III's own illness were giving cause for alarm. Fryer's last Göttingen production in this genre was *Ode to the Genius of Patriotism*, published on the birthday of Adolphus Frederick, later duke of Cambridge, on 7 February 1789.

Fryer appears to have left Göttingen during 1790, becoming a licenciate of the Royal College of Physicians in London on 30 September. His period in Göttingen proved a useful career move, as he was later appointed physician to the duke of Sussex, with whose outstanding collection of rare books and manuscripts he also appears to have been concerned. Fryer was a member of the Society of Arts and clearly a well-known figure in London artistic circles in this period. He edited *The Works of James Barry* (2 vols., 1809). He is also credited with a life of Barry published in 1825, as well as the epitaph on Barry's tomb in St Paul's Cathedral. Fryer died in London at his home in Charlotte Street on 9 March 1826. An anonymous obituarist summarized his character in the following terms:

> Distinguished ability, various and extensive knowledge, strict probity and unsullied honour, united with the most prompt, ardent and generous feelings, adorned by the most engaging and gentlemanly manners, combined to render him beloved and admired by all that knew him. (Munk, *Roll*)

Fryer's Göttingen productions are creditable examples of Georgian occasional verse, with the circumstances of their composition rendering their Hanoverian dynastic rhetoric of some interest. The surviving evidence for the time Fryer spent in Göttingen provides a valuable insight into aspects of the process by which British cultural influence spread in late eighteenth-century Germany.

GRAHAM JEFCOATE

Sources G. P. Jefcoate, 'Edward Fryer MD: an English gentleman and his circle in Göttingen, 1785–90', *Factotum: Newsletter of the XVIIIth-Century Short Title Catalogue*, 18 (March 1984), 28–36 • Munk, *Roll*, 2.412–13 • *Die Matrikel der Georg–August Universität* (Göttingen, 1937), 285 • BL, C.133.9.8, 1 • Göttingen University Library, 8° P. Angl.3651(1) • A. Kelly, 'A bust of James Barry for the Society of Arts', *Journal of the Royal Society of Arts*, 123 (1974–5), 819–22
Archives Göttingen University Library, cod. MS Hist. Nat. 26; cod. MS C. O. Müller, 2 II, fols. 285–6

Fryer [Freer], **John** (1498/9–1563), physician, was born in Balsham, Cambridgeshire, the son of John Fryer (*d. c.*1510), and his wife, Lettice Barnatt, daughter of Mr Barnatt of Kent. Fryer was educated at Eton College and at King's College, Cambridge, where he was admitted in 1517 aged eighteen; he was a fellow in 1520, graduated BA in 1522, and proceeded MA in 1525. An esteemed scholar, he was appointed to Wolsey's Cardinal College in Oxford, where he was incorporated on 5 November 1525.

On 3 March 1528 the bishop of Lincoln, John Longland, reported agitatedly to Wolsey that Cardinal College was a hotbed of Lutheranism. One of its members, Thomas Garret, had been dispersing Lutheran books among his friends. 'The cheefe that were famylyarly acquaynted in this mater with Master Garrott was Master Clarke, Master Freer, Sir Frith, Sir Dyott, and Anthony Delabere' (Ellis, 78). Two days later Fryer was arrested at the Black Friars in London.

According to Wood 'John Fryer was, on account of religion, committed prisoner to the master of the Savoy, where he did much solace himself with playing on the lute, having good skill in music' (Wood, *Ath. Oxon.: Fasti*, 1.72). But Wolsey dealt leniently with his protégé. On 16 September 1528 Fryer wrote to him from the Fleet prison, thanking him for restoring him to life after 'that destruction into which he had precipitated himself by his own folly' (*LP Henry VIII*, 4/2, no. 4741).

Fryer found another patron in Edward Fox, his near contemporary at Eton and King's College, formerly Wolsey's

secretary and now provost of King's. Fox sent Fryer to the University of Padua, where he studied medicine and became MD in 1535. He wrote regularly to Thomas Starkey, Henry VIII's chaplain, giving political and university news, including a mildly satirical description of Reginald Pole in Greek. (Letters from other Englishmen in Padua at this time suggest that Starkey maintained them, perhaps in exchange for intelligence.) In October 1535 Fox, now the bishop of Hereford, began a diplomatic mission to Germany. On Starkey's instructions Fryer joined him in December at the Diet of Smalcalde in Saxony, returning to England in March 1536 on a stipend.

Fryer now settled in London, and was elected a fellow of the College of Physicians in 1536. In 1539 he attended John Hilsey, the bishop of Rochester and a friend from Oxford days, in his last illness. When Hilsey died his estate reverted to the king, and on 16 August 1539 Fryer wrote to Cromwell asking for his fee, 'as I have in many other thyngs, ever fownde your Lordshype good to me'. This letter shows touches of mordant humour:

> truely if Physycyens shuld take no monye for them that they kyll, as well as for them that they save, theyr lyvyngs shuldbe very thynne and bare … I beseche your Lordshyppe it may be so motche the mor lyberall, becawse it shalbe the last payment; for of them that scape, we may take the lesse, becawse we hope they shale ons cum agayne in to our handys. (Ellis, 346–7)

Apparently Fryer had found his third patron in Cromwell, and was on fairly relaxed terms with him.

Fryer married, probably between 1536 and 1540, Ursula Castell, daughter of Robert Castell of East Hatley in Cambridgeshire. According to the visitation of London of 1568 they had eight children; one, Thomas Fryer, followed his father to Padua and into the College of Physicians. Two grandchildren also practised medicine in London. The family lived in Bishopsgate Street, in the parish of St Martin Outwich. It is often stated that John *Fryer of Godmanchester, a Catholic physician who left England for Padua *c.*1570, was a son of Fryer. Nicholas Sanders said so in 1571 (in *De visibili monarchia*, 7.700). However, this is doubtful: no son John is mentioned in Fryer's will, nor in his wife's, nor in the visitation pedigree.

In 1541 Fryer was elected as censor in the College of Physicians, and again in 1542, 1544, 1552–5, and 1559. In 1547 he became an elect, was consiliarius in 1548, and president in 1549 and 1550. He served as consiliarius again from 1555 to 1561 under John Caius.

An enthusiastic Lutheran in his youth, Fryer in later life returned to Catholicism. He did well under Mary: the visitation pedigree calls him 'Physition to Queene Mary', and he was on fairly close terms with Pole. However, under Elizabeth, Catholicism became dangerous. 'The xxiij day of June [1560] was had to the contur docthur Frere, and the next day was delevered hom' (*Machyn*, 238). In April 1561 Fryer was one of 'the prisoners for the mass' in the Tower. On 23 April 1561 his servant was questioned before the mayor of London regarding Fryer's visit to a priest and attendance at mass. On 30 September 1562 the College of Physicians noted that Fryer was in prison for the sake of his religion and temporarily replaced him as an elect (Annals, 1.22a).

In June 1563 a plague broke out in London. Fryer was released at the beginning of August, but died of this plague at his home in Bishopsgate Street on 21 October 1563 (Annals, 1.22b). He made a brief nuncupative will, and was buried in St Martin Outwich. His wife, Ursula, died soon afterwards, also of the plague. In her will, proved on 28 December 1563, she asked to be buried 'in the grave where my husbonde lieth', and directed that £3 should be distributed to 'poore folkes to pray for my sowle and for my husbande'. Some of their children also died of the plague at about the same time.

John Fryer's father died early, and Fryer had to make his way by his wits. He was a good scholar, enthusiastic for new ideas, and attracted the patronage of Wolsey, Edward Fox, and Cromwell. After an early setback he gradually rebuilt his fortunes, but even when poor he was generous to his friends. His ironic sense of humour did not offend the College of Physicians, where he rose to the highest rank. In later life he was a committed and courageous Catholic. It is regrettable that he published nothing, and speaks to us only in his intelligent and witty letters.

F. V. WHITE

Sources DNB · W. Sterry, ed., The Eton College register, 1441–1698 (1943), 130, 132 · Wood, Ath. Oxon., new edn, 1.308 · Wood, Ath. Oxon.: Fasti (1815), 72 · H. Ellis, ed., Original letters illustrative of English history, 3rd ser., 2 (1846), 78, 346–7 · LP Henry VIII, 4/1, nos. 4004, 4017; 4/2, no. 4741; 9, nos. 648, 687, 917, 1011; 10, nos. 320–21, 411, 418; 13, no. 1239; 14, no. 53; addenda, 1, no. 357 · CSP dom., 1547–80, no. 60 · CSP, addenda 1547–65, 465, 510 · annals, RCP Lond., 1.3b, 22a, 22b · J. J. Howard and G. J. Armytage, eds., The visitation of London in the year 1568, Harleian Society, 1 (1869), 82 · N. Sanders, De visibili monarchia ecclesiae (Louvain, 1571), 700 · The diary of Henry Machyn, citizen and merchant-taylor of London, from AD 1550 to AD 1563, ed. J. G. Nichols, CS, 42 (1848), 238 · will, PRO, PROB 11/47, sig. 2 · will, PRO, PROB 11/46, sig. 39 [Ursula Fryer] · Venn, Alum. Cant. · Cooper, Ath. Cantab., 1.225 · Foster, Alum. Oxon. · Gillow, Lit. biog. hist., 2.334–5
Archives BL, letters · PRO, letters
Wealth at death exact sum unknown: will, PRO, PROB 11/47, sig. 2, 1564

Fryer [Frere], **John** (b. c.1526, d. in or after 1571), physician and poet, was born in Godmanchester, Huntingdonshire. Little is known of his family, but he may have had a brother Thomas of similar age. There were still Freres in Godmanchester many years later, for in 1604 a Thomas Frere of that place was ordained deacon and priest at London. John Fryer or Frere matriculated as a pensioner at Jesus College, Cambridge, at Easter 1544, and became BA in 1545 and MA in 1548. Thomas Fryar, who matriculated at Jesus at the same time, may be his brother. John Fryer then studied medicine. He wrote verses on the death of Bucer in 1551. In 1555 he became MD and signed the Roman Catholic articles.

In 1560 the university restored to the dead protestant scholars Martin Bucer and Paul Fagius the honours which had been stripped from them under Queen Mary. 'The walls of the church and its porch were covered with verses by the academics in commendation of Bucer and Fagius'

(Cooper, Ath. Cantab., 1.102). Fryer was among the versifiers, although presumably he disliked the Germans' opinions. He was a disputant in the physic act before Queen Elizabeth at Cambridge in 1564.

Fryer combined medicine and poetry by translating Hippocrates' aphorisms from Greek prose into Latin verse in Hippocratis Coi omnis medicinae parentis aphorismi versibus scripti … per Iöannem Frerum Gormoncestrensum Anglum (1567). His purpose was to make it easier for students to learn and remember the aphorisms. His work was later incorporated into Ralph Winterton's Greek versification, Hippokratous tou Megalou hoi Aphorismoi, pezikoi te k'eumetroi (1633).

Fryer's only other extant works are commendatory verses in the publications of others, mainly his Cambridge contemporaries. These include William Alley's Ptochomyseion, the Poor Man's Library (1565, 1571), Walter Haddon's Lucubrationes (1567), Thomas Hatcher's collection of Poematum Gualteri Haddoni … libri duo (1576), and Nicholas Carr's Demosthenis orationes septem (1571). Frere was also among the many Cambridge men who wrote verses on the death of Carr in 1568.

Like some other Roman Catholics in the reign of Elizabeth, Fryer eventually left England and settled at Padua. He is mentioned by Nicholas Sanders, a co-religionist who travelled in Europe (De visibili monarchia ecclesiae ad P. Pium, Louvain, 1571). We know nothing more about Fryer's life on the continent or when he died.

Many writers have described Fryer as the son of John *Fryer MD FCP who died in 1563. However, this is unlikely. The latter's pedigree is given in the Visitation of London of 1568 and does not include a son John, nor is one mentioned in his will of 1563. His son Thomas, who matriculated at Trinity, Cambridge, in 1553, cannot be Fryer's putative brother Thomas, who matriculated at Jesus College in 1544. There is no record of the elder John Fryer living in Godmanchester in the 1520s.

Fryer was part of a closely knit group of Cambridge friends and contemporaries: Thomas Hatcher, Walter Haddon, Nicholas Carr. His peers desired his approval and admired his poetic skill. Nevertheless, his religious principles were strong enough to make him uproot himself, in his forties, from this comfortable existence and leave to start a new life abroad.

F. V. WHITE

Sources Hippocratis Coi omnis medicinae parentis aphorismi versibus scripti … per Iöannem Frerum Gormoncestrensem Anglum (1567) · Hippokratous tou Megalou hoi Aphorismoi, pezikoi te k'eumetroi: Hippocratis magni aphorismi, soluti & metrica, interprete Joanne Heurnio medico Ultrajectino, metaphrastis Joanne Frero medico-poetâ et Radulpho Wintertono medicinae & poëseos Graecae studioso, Anglis (1633) · Venn, Alum. Cant. · Cooper, Ath. Cantab., 1.102, 302 · Wood, Ath. Oxon.: Fasti (1820), 72 · Tanner, Bibl. Brit.-Hib., 37, 155–6, 297–8, 653 · W. Beloe, Anecdotes of literature and scarce books, 6 vols. (1807–12), vol. 5, pp. 17–23 · J. J. Howard and G. J. Armytage, eds., The visitation of London in the year 1568, Harleian Society, 1 (1869), 82 · DNB · N. Sanders, De visibili monarchia ecclesiae (Louvain, 1571), 676 · Gillow, Lit. biog. hist., 2.334–5

Fryer, John (1575/6–1672), physician, was the eldest son of Thomas Fryer (d. 1623), and grandson of John *Fryer (d. 1563), both of whom were fellows of the College of

Physicians, London. He studied at Padua, where he graduated MD on 6 April 1610, and was admitted a candidate of the College of Physicians on 25 June 1612.

Fryer lived in Little Britain, London, in part of his father's house. By birth a strict Roman Catholic, he was on 29 March 1626 returned to the parliamentary commissioners by the college as 'an avowed or suspected papist'. 'This', observes Munk, 'was probably the reason he was not admitted a fellow, as it was without doubt the cause of his brother, Thomas Fryer [d. 1645], having been refused admission as a candidate' (Munk, 1.72–4). After remaining a candidate for more than half a century, he was in December 1664, when honorary fellows were first created, placed at the head of the list. Fryer remained at odds with the college even after his election as honorary fellow. He is listed as one of the 'chymical physicians', critics of the classical Galenic medicine favoured by the college, who attempted to establish a rival society in the 1660s (O'Dowde).

On 5 August 1628 Fryer was admitted a member of Gray's Inn, but did not proceed to the bar. For his unfilial and unbrotherly conduct Fryer was disinherited by his father, though the latter left him £50 in token of forgiveness. He denounced, however, his son's 'many great impieties to his parents, and especially towards his tender, carefull, and mercifull mother … too horrible and shamefull to repeate', and desired the world to know that he had:

> brought his parents, against all rites and against nature, and especially me, his father, before the greatest magistrats, to our discredites, as may appear by letters sent from the highest, whch at length they, having fully ripped upp all matters, although mutch against my will, turned utterly to his utter discredit. (will, T. Fryer)

Fryer's father had purchased the manor of Harlton, Cambridgeshire, as appears from his monument in Harlton church. His second brother, Henry, who died in Little Britain on 4 June 1631, after a fall from his horse, had by his will dated 27 May of that year provided for some of his relatives, but directed his executors to settle Harlton and his other lands to such charitable uses as they thought fit. Fryer contested this will in the court of wards. The executors consented to a reference to Mr Justice Harvey, the testator's cousin and an overseer of his will, and he certified that Fryer ought to have the whole estate. The matter was eventually submitted to the arbitration of Lord-Keeper Coventry, Bishop Laud, and Secretary Coke. Fryer evidently gained the day, for by his will dated 1 September and proved 21 November 1672 he devised the property to his nephews and executors, John Peacock of Heath House, near Petersfield, Hampshire, and Andrew Matthew, carpenter, of the City of London.

Fryer died at his house in Little Britain on 12 November 1672, at the advanced age of ninety-six, and was buried on 19 November 'in the vault of St. Botolph's Church without Aldersgate, London, where his mother and eldest sister, Elizabeth Peacocke, lye buried' (Obituary of Richard Smyth, 97).   GORDON GOODWIN, rev. PATRICK WALLIS

Sources Munk, *Roll* • H. J. Cook, *The decline of the old medical regime in Stuart London* (1986) • T. O'Dowde, *The poor man's physician* (1665) • D. Lysons and S. Lysons, *Magna Britannia: being a concise topographical account of the several counties of Great Britain*, 2 (1808) • *The obituary of Richard Smyth … being a catalogue of all such persons as he knew in their life*, ed. H. Ellis, CS, 44 (1849) • private information (1998) • will, H. Fryer, PRO, PROB 11/160, sig. 104 • will, T. Fryer, proved 6 May 1623, PRO, PROB 11/141, sig. 40 • *CSP dom.*, 1631–3, 360–61; 1633–4, 376, 379 • will, proved 21 Nov 1672, PRO, PROB 11/340, sigs. 129, 150 • Harleian MS, BL, 1912, fol. 106

Fryer, John (d. 1733), traveller and writer, was the eldest son of William Fryer of London. He was educated at Trinity College, Cambridge, where he matriculated on 13 July 1664 and from where he moved on 23 July 1671 to Pembroke College as a fellow-commoner. Fryer (who also used the spellings Fryar and Friar) took two degrees in medicine (MB in 1671 and an MD twelve years later), though he was not, as is claimed in his obituary (*GM*), a member of the Royal College of Physicians.

On 9 December 1672 Fryer left from Gravesend for a lengthy tour of India and Persia undertaken in the interests of the East India Company. He did not return to England until August 1682. Sixteen years later he published *A New Account of East India and Persia … being Nine Years' Travels, Begun in 1672*, which he had been prompted to write in the wake of criticism of English expeditions in French guides. A book rich in details of natural history and local medical practice, Fryer's account was republished in Dutch in 1700.

In 1697 Fryer was elected a fellow of the Royal Society (until 1707) but did not contribute to the society's *Philosophical Transactions*. In or before June 1698 he married a niece of Rose Desborough, wife of Samuel Desborough (1619–1690), politician and keeper of the great seal of Scotland. According to the letters of administration granted to their daughter, Anna Maria Sanderson, on 14 April 1733, John Fryer outlived his wife and was resident at Bread Street, in the parish of All Hallows, London. He died on 31 March 1733.   GORDON GOODWIN, rev. PHILIP CARTER

Sources *GM*, 1st ser., 3 (1733), 214 • Venn, *Alum. Cant.*
Likenesses R. White, portrait, repro. in *New account of East India and Persia* (1698), preface

Fryer, Leonard (d. 1605), painter, whose date of birth, parentage, and place of training are unknown, was first recorded as painter to the navy in 1597. He was appointed sergeant-painter for life to Elizabeth I on 12 June 1598 at £10 p.a. with the privileges that attached to the post. From 6 May 1605 he shared this office with John de Critz the elder. His responsibilities included extensive decorative work at the royal palaces, internally and externally, notably painting walls, ceilings, beds, carriages, and numerous garden seats. Most of this work was routine and paid for by the yard; however, he is recorded as painting 'a great frame wᵗʰ turned pillers in the librarie … like to the tissewe of that roome' (PRO, E351/3234). He also painted the queen's arms over the speaker's seat in the 'Lower Parliament howse' and did some painting at the 'Offyce of the woorks' (PRO, E351/3233). Unlike his predecessor, George Gower, and successor, John de Critz the elder, Fryer is not recorded as painting portraits, but he repaired pictures and at Whitehall in 1602–3 he altered 'a picture in the Chappell and made it Joseph', as well as 'cleansing of the picture of o^ur ladie' (PRO, E351/3239). He was a mourner at Elizabeth I's funeral, for which he carried out decorative painting. None of his work survives, principally as a consequence of the destruction of Oatlands, Whitehall, and Richmond palaces and the rebuilding of that at Greenwich. He presented a chased silver cup to the Painter–Stainers' Hall inscribed 'Leonhart Fryer, Sergeaunt Painter gave this AD 1605' (Painter–Stainers' Company, London; Vertue mentioned a portrait of Fryer, formerly in the possession of this company, which is now lost). A protestant, he married Katherine (surname unknown, d. 1606?) before August 1575, had eight (or more) children, and lived in the parish of St Botolph, Aldgate, from 1575 until his burial there on 8 November 1605. His will, proved 18 December 1605, mentions his widow and three surviving children.   SUSAN BRACKEN

Sources PRO, E403/1693, fol. 72, 1597 · PRO, E403/2721, 1597 · PRO, E351/3233–3239, 1597–1604 · PRO, E351/3145 · PRO, PROB 11/106/87 · parish register, London, St Botolph, Aldgate, GL, MSS 9220, 9222/1 [marriage, burial] · PRO, LC 5/37, 259, 1601 · CSP dom., 1598–1601, no. 47; 1603–10, nos. 78, 98 · E. Auerbach, *Tudor artists* (1954) · E. Croft-Murray, *Decorative painting in England, 1537–1837*, 1 (1962) · M. Edmond, 'Limners and picturemakers', *Walpole Society*, 47 (1978–80), 60–242, esp. 184–6 · Vertue, *Note books*, 2.30

Fryers, Austin. *See* Clery, William Edward (1861–1931).

Fryon [Frion], **Étienne** [Stephen] (*fl.* 1462–1501), diplomat and spy, was a Burgundian whose precise origin and education remain obscure. By 1462 he was practising as a *procureur* of the *grand conseil* of Philip the Good, duke of Burgundy, and by 1466 was a ducal secretary. He moved to the service of Burgundy's ally, Charles, duke of Guyenne, until Charles's death in 1472, whereupon he returned to the Burgundian secretariat and served until 1480 without obtaining senior rank.

On the death of Duke Charles the Bold in 1477 Louis XI of France had overrun Burgundy's southern heartlands, and the Duchess Marie, Charles's daughter, required Edward IV's military support if she was to defend Burgundian territories in the Netherlands and north-east France against Louis's encroachments. In 1480 Edward's sister Margaret, dowager duchess of Burgundy, led an embassy to England which offered a marriage alliance between Mary's infant heir, Philip, and Edward's daughter Anne. Fryon accompanied Jean Gros, treasurer of the Golden Fleece, on a preparatory mission and then on Margaret's embassy. Margaret, observing that the office of French secretary to Edward was effectively vacant, apparently recommended Fryon for this position. He was appointed on 26 September; yet within a month he was sending back to Gros a detailed intelligence letter disclosing information about England's parallel negotiations with Louis, scarcely compatible with his new official responsibilities.

Nevertheless Fryon's ability was valued by his English employers. In 1482 he was sent on a mission to François (II), duke of Brittany, and he was reappointed to his position by Richard III and Henry VII. In 1486 he was granted a valuable property in the parish of St Giles Cripplegate, London, confiscated from Humphrey Stafford after his rebellion. In December 1488, now described as a councillor, he was an envoy to Charles VIII of France, in the company of Christopher Urswick and Thomas Ward. Henry sent him again in September 1489, with Sir John Risley and Chester herald; but this time he took the opportunity to defect to French service.

Late in 1491 Charles VIII sent Fryon to Cork to meet the leaders of the Yorkist conspiracy forming around Perkin Warbeck, who had recently assumed the identity of Richard, duke of York, and to invite Warbeck to take up residence at the French court. Warbeck was in fact the son of a boatman from Tournai. Whatever he had already learned, in Portugal, of the Yorkist court from Duarte Brandão (who had taken English nationality and served Edward IV as Sir Edward Brampton), he doubtless derived from Fryon in 1492 much of the inside knowledge he required to become a convincing impersonator. But in November 1492 Charles VIII came to terms with Henry VII at the treaty of Étaples and could no longer harbour Warbeck at court; so he secretly passed him to the custody of Margaret of York in Flanders.

Fryon was assumed by Sir Francis Bacon to have continued after this as Warbeck's 'principal counsellor' (*Works of Francis Bacon*, 6.138), but the evidence is lacking. He failed to gain entrance to the Paris *chambre des comptes* and in 1501 suffered imprisonment at the hands of the *prévôt* of Paris; but he was released on appeal. He was active as a *procureur* in the *parlement* of Paris probably as late as 1509.

The circumstances of Fryon's appointment in 1480 and the nature of his intelligence about the diplomatic activity of the Archduke Maximilian, as well as Louis XI, imply that he was then a member of Margaret of York's circle. If this allegiance continued, it would support the story of Henry VII's propagandist Bernard André that Margaret was the instigator of Warbeck's conspiracy—with Fryon as her agent—as well as his principal backer after 1492. But ostensibly Fryon cut his links with Burgundy and with Margaret. His defection to France must be seen in the context of those of more senior Burgundian officials in the 1480s, including Jean Gros and Guillaume de Rochefort; equally, his intelligence activity appears symptomatic of an era in international relations when 'diplomat' and 'spy' were regarded as opposite sides of the same coin. Nevertheless, Bacon's sketch of Fryon as 'an active man, but turbulent and discontented' (*Works of Francis Bacon*, 6.137) remains entirely apposite.   MARK BALLARD

Sources M. Ballard and C. S. L. Davies, 'Étienne Fryon: Burgundian agent, English royal secretary and "principal counsellor" to Perkin Warbeck', *Historical Research*, 62 (1989), 245–59 · I. Arthurson, *The Perkin Warbeck conspiracy, 1491–1499* (1994) · B. André, *Historia regis Henrici septimi*, ed. J. Gairdner, Rolls Series, 10 (1858), 65–7 · *The works of Francis Bacon*, ed. J. Spedding, R. L. Ellis, and D. D. Heath, 14 vols. (1857–74), vol. 6, pp. 137–57 · *Chancery records* · *Roberti Gaguini epistole et orationes*, ed. L. Thuasne, 2 (Paris, 1903), 309 · B. de Mandrot, *Ymbert de Batarnay, seigneur du Bouchage* (1886), 103 · Rymer, *Foedera*, 1st edn, 12.347–8
Archives Archives départementales du Nord, Lille, series B 18823, no. 23719

Fubister, John. *See* Gunn, Isabel (1780–1861).

Fuchs, (Emil Julius) Klaus (1911–1988), theoretical physicist, was born on 29 December 1911 in Rüsselsheim, Germany, the third child in the family of two sons and two daughters of Emil Fuchs and his wife, Else Wagner. His father, renowned for his high Christian principles, was a pastor in the Lutheran church who joined the Quakers later in life and eventually became professor of theology at Leipzig University. Fuchs's grandmother, mother, and one sister all took their own lives, while his other sister was diagnosed as schizophrenic.

Fuchs went to school in Eisenach and continued his education in the universities of Leipzig and Kiel. It was at the latter that he became involved in politics and, after some soul-searching, doubtless inspired by his father's idealistic attitude, the Communist Party. After an altercation with the Nazis in 1933 he crossed the border into France and then, with the help of family connections, travelled to Bristol, where he studied under Nevill Mott and obtained a PhD. He took a DSc at Edinburgh University under the guidance of Max Born, one of the pioneers of the new quantum mechanics. After the outbreak of the Second World War he was interned with other German refugees in camps on the Isle of Man and in Canada from June to December 1940.

In 1941 he was recruited by Rudolf Peierls to work on tube alloys, the code name for the British project to develop the atomic bomb. The following year, in spite of wartime restrictions, he was granted British nationality as a special case, and signed the Official Secrets Act. In 1943 he went with Peierls to join the Manhattan district, which was the code name given to the American atomic bomb programme. He was posted to New York and then to Los Alamos in New Mexico, where he remained until after the resulting bombs had destroyed Hiroshima and Nagasaki. In 1946 he returned to Britain, where he was appointed by John Cockcroft as head of the theoretical physics division at the newly created Atomic Energy Research Establishment at Harwell, then under the Ministry of Supply. He was given the civil service rank of principal scientific officer. He soon became senior principal and in 1949 deputy chief scientific officer. He took personal charge of the mathematical work which underpinned the development of nuclear power.

In January 1950 Fuchs was arrested for transmitting significant information about Anglo-American work on nuclear weapons, including the hydrogen bomb, to secret agents of the Soviet Union. This he had been doing continuously since 1941, after Germany invaded Russia. He had felt so strongly that the details of atomic research should be shared with the Soviet Union that he made contact with a communist colleague he had known in Germany. He had been put in touch with someone working for the Soviet embassy. He was sentenced to fourteen years' imprisonment in February and his British citizenship was revoked in December 1950. Fuchs was released on 23 June 1959 after serving nine years and four months. Immediately after leaving Wakefield prison he joined his father and one of his nephews in what had become the German Democratic Republic (GDR), where he was appointed deputy director of the Institute for Nuclear Research in Rossendorf near Dresden; he retired in 1979. He never returned to the West.

In 1959 Fuchs married a friend from his student days, a fellow communist called Margarete (Greta) Keilson, the widow of Max Keilson, president of the Association of Journalists in the GDR. They had no children. Fuchs achieved great prominence in East Germany and was elected to the Academy of Sciences and the Communist Party central committee. He was decorated with both the order of merit of the Fatherland and the order of Karl Marx. He had probably saved the Soviet Union two years' work on nuclear weapons.

Of slight build, 5 feet 9 inches in height, with fast receding hair, Fuchs was physically attractive with a warm smile, although he often seemed frail. Always tidily dressed and with impeccable manners, he could be kind and sensitive towards his friends. His legendary shyness and aloof manner, however, did not always quite succeed in concealing his innate arrogance and conceit and his belief that he was uniquely valuable. He was possessed of formidable self-control.

Short-sighted and noticeably left-handed, Fuchs was also a heavy smoker, drank quite a lot, and suffered from respiratory problems, as did his older brother, who had tuberculosis for many years. While in the USA and Britain he enjoyed social occasions and prided himself on being a good dancer. He was also keen on family life and frequently dropped in on his married friends. It is believed that he formed a relationship at Harwell with an older woman who was married to a senior colleague of his at Harwell who was also his close friend. He died in Dresden, on 28 January 1988.　　　　MARY FLOWERS, *rev.*

Sources E. Fuchs, *Mein Leben*, 2 vols. (1959) · N. Moss, *Klaus Fuchs* (1987) · personal knowledge (1996)
Likenesses photographs, 1950–59, Hult. Arch.

Fuchs, Sir Vivian Ernest (1908–1999), explorer and scientist, was born on 11 February 1908 at Recluse Lodge, Freshwater, Isle of Wight, the only child of Ernst Fuchs (1882–1957) and Violet Anne Watson (1874–1942). His father was German and his English mother was born in Australia; together they worked a smallholding in Kent during Fuchs's childhood until in May 1915 the family moved to the Isle of Man, close to Knockaloe camp, where his father was interned for the rest of the war. The family's assets were confiscated.

Fuchs was educated at Asheton preparatory school, near Tenterden, Kent, where he acquired his lifelong nickname Bunny, and then at Brighton College. He went on to read natural sciences at St John's College, Cambridge. His tutor was James Wordie, the geologist and senior scientist on Sir Ernest Shackleton's *Endurance* expedition (1914–17). Wordie took Fuchs on an expedition to Greenland in 1929, an experience that proved a major influence on his life. Fuchs was a geologist by profession but admitted that it was a means to an end, giving purpose to his love of outdoor life and hard physical exertion.

After graduation in 1930 Fuchs joined the Cambridge University expedition to the east African lakes (1930–31)

Sir Vivian Ernest Fuchs (1908–1999), by unknown photographer, 1958

where he, as the geologist, was to study the geology of the lakes, with particular reference to climate fluctuations. Back in Britain he was invited to join the anthropologist Louis Leakey's expedition to Olduvai Gorge (1931–2). He stayed for three months after the expedition to study the geology of Njorowa Gorge before returning home in April 1933.

On 6 September 1933 Fuchs married Joyce (d. 1990), his second cousin, daughter of John Connell. Fuchs had already planned his own Lake Rudolf Rift Valley expedition so they went together with the five other members. Joyce climbed Mount Meru and Mount Elgon while the expedition worked at Lake Rudolf (which was in an area closed to women). At the end of the expedition in September 1934, Fuchs and his wife drove home overland in the expedition's 1929 box-bodied Chevrolet. They covered 7687 miles in forty-six days, driving 50 miles each in turn, via Kenya, Uganda, Sudan, the Belgian Congo, Southern Cameroons and Nigeria, across the Sahara to Tangier, then through Spain and France.

The Fuchses then settled in Cambridge where he worked up his African fieldwork in the Sedgwick Museum. In 1936 their daughter Hilary was born on 17 February and he graduated PhD from Cambridge. His research was published in 1938 by the Royal Society as 'The geological history of the Lake Rudolph basin, Kenya colony'. Meanwhile he was planning an expedition to Lake Rukwa in Tanganyika to extend the geological knowledge of the Rift Valley. The expedition went into the field on new year's day 1938, complete with a car, a lorry, and

some camels. During February Joyce gave birth to their second daughter, Rosalind. The expedition was a disappointment geologically but considerable collections of plants, insects, molluscs, and reptiles were brought home in September 1938.

Fuchs's return was marred by the threat of impending war with Germany and the discovery that Rosalind suffered from cerebral palsy. She died shortly before her eighth birthday. He volunteered for the Royal Naval Volunteer Reserve but was turned down as too old at thirty and so joined the Territorial Army and was gazetted second lieutenant in the Cambridgeshire regiment. He continued to write up the expedition results until war broke out, when he was appointed adjutant to the 2nd battalion. He found that his practical skills learned in Africa had wide application in the army. On 2 June 1940 Joyce Fuchs gave birth to their son Peter Ernest Kay, a robust boy who laid their fears to rest.

Fuchs volunteered for service in east Africa, keen to use his knowledge and experience, but was posted to the Gold Coast in west Africa in 1942. This was a period of frustrating inactivity that ended in July 1943. A month's leave with his family was followed by a four-month staff course at Camberley. Afterwards he was posted to second army headquarters in London to work on civil affairs. In April 1944 the second army was transferred to Portsmouth ready for the D-day landings. Eventually he reached Germany and saw the first prisoners released from Belsen concentration camp. He stayed in Germany as a magistrate in the military government until demobilized with the rank of major in October 1946.

In 1947 Fuchs applied for a post as geologist with the Falkland Islands Dependencies survey that operated seven bases on the Antarctic peninsula. To his surprise he was appointed field commander in overall charge of field operations. The survey was run by a committee in London often at cross purposes with the governor of the Falkland Islands. Its main objective was to support Britain's claim to a sector of Antarctica, with scientific research a secondary goal. Fuchs sailed south in 1947 to a base at Stonington Island in Marguerite Bay. In February 1949, after a successful year, the ice in Marguerite Bay was still solid for 40 miles and on 1 April the governor of the Falkland Islands signalled that the ship which was due to relieve the party was unable to reach them and was returning north. Eleven men then spent an unplanned winter at Stonington Island and, for five of them, it was their third consecutive winter. They had rations for another year but coal supplies were short, and the men's fate if the ship could not reach them the next year was uncertain. In the 1949–50 summer Fuchs made a major sledge journey with the geologist Ray Adie across Marguerite Bay, along George VI Sound between Palmer Land and Alexander Island to Eklund Island. It was a round trip of some 500 miles during which much geological reconnaissance was undertaken. At the same time, while tent-bound during a storm, Fuchs began to sketch the idea of crossing Antarctica (unsuccessfully attempted by Wilhelm Filchner in 1911 and by Shackleton in 1914) with vehicles. He returned to

Stonington Island where the ice had relented and the ship was able to relieve the base but the governor decided that the base should be closed.

On his return to Britain in 1950 Fuchs was asked to set up and direct the Falkland Island Dependencies survey scientific bureau in London with responsibility for planning the scientific work in the Antarctic and arranging for the publication of the scientific results. The latter included finding suitable university accommodation for returning 'Fids' to write up their work for publication in the series of scientific reports. The job quickly expanded and kept Fuchs fully occupied, but his idea of a trans-continental journey was not dormant. He discussed the proposal with James Wordie and in 1953 the detailed planning for the Commonwealth Trans-Antarctic expedition began. In April 1955 an expedition office was established and Fuchs took three years' leave of absence. The central plan for the expedition was to cross Antarctica in 100 days from the Weddell Sea to the Ross Sea via the South Pole using Sno-Cat tractors. A full scientific programme would run alongside, including survey and geological exploration of new mountain ranges. The expedition would also have two light aircraft, two dog teams, and some additional tractors. Recruitment of some office staff, including Mrs Eleanor Honnywill, and expedition personnel began.

The advance party sailed in November 1955 and reached the Filchner ice shelf at the head of the Weddell Sea. Stores were unloaded and hut construction began but bad weather forced the ship from her mooring and many stores were lost on the sea ice. The base hut, Shackleton, was not completed and during the winter the eight men slept in tents and lived in a Sno-Cat crate. The hut was completed in the following spring, before the arrival of Fuchs and the main party in January 1957. Unloading began immediately and proceeded according to plan. Reconnaissance flights were made into the hinterland and an advance base, South Ice, 275 miles inland, was constructed and manned. After the winter, survey and geological parties with dog teams explored the newly discovered Theron Mountains, Shackleton Range, and Whichaway Nunataks. The main crossing party departed on 24 November 1957, hampered by numerous crevasses and then by large fields of *sastrugi* (ridges in the snow). Meanwhile the New Zealand support party under Sir Edmund Hillary was making good progress from the Ross Sea with modified Ferguson farm tractors towing loads from the Ross ice shelf onto the polar plateau, supported by aircraft. Hillary then, contrary to agreed plans, made a dash for the pole, arriving one month before Fuchs. The two men publicly denied that there was any disagreement between them, though this did not stop press speculation to the contrary. At the pole Hillary suggested that, as the main party was so far behind schedule, Fuchs should stop at the pole, winter his vehicles there, and fly out, returning in the spring to complete the journey. Fuchs would have none of it and continued across the continent following Hillary's outward route, and completed the crossing in 99 days on 2 March 1958, one day ahead of schedule. This was the first land crossing of the continent and its main scientific result was to establish the thickness of ice at the pole and the presence of a land mass beneath. On arrival at the New Zealand Scott Base, Fuchs received a congratulatory telegram from the queen, the expedition's patron, and was told of his knighthood.

Fuchs received awards and medals from institutions throughout the world for the expedition's achievement and he returned to be director of the Falkland Islands Dependencies survey. Over the next fifteen years and thanks in large measure to his leadership the survey grew in stature, and became the British Antarctic survey in 1961; its research achieved recognition internationally and at home where the survey's administration was transferred in 1967 from the Colonial Office to the Natural Environment Research Council. In the early 1970s he set in motion the unification of the survey in a single headquarters complex outside Cambridge. He retired in 1973 but continued to be involved with Antarctica, exploration, and the organization of science. He was president of the International Glaciological Society (1963–6), the British Association for the Advancement of Science (1972), and the Royal Geographical Society (1982–4), and was elected a fellow of the Royal Society (1974). He was also actively associated with the Trans-Antarctic Association that supports Antarctic research and exploration and the Fuchs Foundation that helps young people to join expeditions. He also chaired the committee for the Fuchs medal, established in his honour, that recognizes outstanding service by members of the British Antarctic survey.

Fuchs's wife, Joyce, died on 27 April 1990 and on 8 August 1991 he married Eleanor Honnywill, *née* Biscoe, widow of Captain Richard B. Honnywill RN, his friend and secretary since 1955. His active life was curtailed by a severe stroke in December 1997 but he fought on with characteristic determination. He died peacefully at his home at 106 Barton Road, Cambridge, on 11 November 1999.   PETER CLARKSON

Sources V. Fuchs and E. Hillary, *The crossing of Antarctica* (1958) · V. Fuchs, *Of ice and men* (1982) · V. Fuchs, *A time to speak* (1990) · B. Stonehouse, *The Independent* (13 Nov 1999) · A. Tucker, *The Guardian* (13 Nov 1999) · A. Steven, *The Scotsman* (16 Nov 1999) · *WW* (1998) · personal knowledge (2004) · private information (2004)

Archives Scott Polar RI, journals and papers · U. Cam., Sedgwick Museum of Earth Sciences, diaries and notebooks relating to geological expeditions to east Africa

Likenesses photographs, c.1947–1988, Hult. Arch. [*see illus.*] · photograph, repro. in *The Independent* · photograph, repro. in *The Guardian* · photograph, repro. in *The Scotsman*

Wealth at death £533,101—gross; £487,078—net: probate, 3 Feb 2000, *CGPLA Eng & Wales*

Fuegia Basket (*b.* 1820/21, *d.* in or after 1851). See under Exotic visitors (*act. c.*1500–*c.*1855).

Fulbecke, William (*b.* 1559/60, *d.* in or after 1602), lawyer and historian, was born in the parish of St Benedict, Lincoln, a younger son of Thomas Fulbecke, a prominent Lincoln citizen who died midway through his term as mayor in 1566. He matriculated, aged seventeen, in 1577 at St Alban Hall, Oxford, and on 6 February 1579 was admitted as a scholar to Christ Church. He graduated BA in 1581 and became probationer fellow of the college in October 1582.

Fulbecke then moved to Gloucester Hall, where he came under the influence of the noted classicist, mathematician, and antiquary Thomas Allen, and from where he proceeded MA in 1584. Fulbecke then entered Gray's Inn and he embarked on a legal career. While still a student there he turned to writing, beginning with a *Booke of Christian Ethicks or Moral Philosophie* (1587). This is written in a laborious, euphuistic style in which points are made repeatedly within the same sentence, something that would be characteristic of all his writings. The contempt for popular rule that he evinces in citing the Roman civil wars of the first century BC also provides an indication of themes fully worked out in later works. At this time Fulbecke also contributed two speeches and the conclusion to a masque usually known as *The Misfortunes of Arthur*. This was written and performed by Fulbecke and seven colleagues (among them his slightly younger contemporary Francis Bacon) before Queen Elizabeth on 8 February 1588; it was published three weeks later under the name of its principal author, Thomas Hughes, and the title *Certaine Devises and Shewes Presented by the Gentlemen of Grayes-Inn*.

Very little is known about the rest of Fulbecke's life, including the names of any spouse or children. It is possible but not certain that he spent some period of time on the continent attending a European university, which would account for his familiarity with the civil law; there is no record of his obtaining a degree in civil law at Oxford or Cambridge. Wood remarks (Wood, *Ath. Oxon.*, 1.317) that Fulbecke obtained the degree of doctor of civil laws, but there is no clear evidence for this assertion, nor does Wood specify from which place this degree was awarded. In 1600 he published his first work of legal scholarship, *A Direction or Preparative to the Study of the Lawe*. This consists mainly in suggestions to students as to study methods, but it reveals a familiarity with the civil law and a strong preference for the clarity of codified, written law in contrast with the ambiguities of custom that characterized the common law. The book also demonstrates that Fulbecke was thoroughly conversant not only with older, medieval civil lawyers, such as Bartolus of Sassoferrato, but also with newer, sixteenth-century French writers such as Guillaume Budé and François Hotman.

Fulbecke's appreciation of Roman law and his equally strong belief in the necessity of strong, though not arbitrary, government, comes through most clearly in a book he had completed by autumn 1600, but did not publish until early in the following year, his *Historicall collection of the continuall factions, tumults, and massacres of the Romans and Italians*. This was a narrative history of the last years of the Roman republic and it is significant as one of the very few attempts by a Renaissance Englishman to write such a work. In particular, Fulbecke was attempting in this book to fill in the gap that existed between the end of Livy's history of Rome and the beginning of Tacitus's *Annales*, the latter work having become very popular in the England of the 1590s. An interesting attempt to weave together such often-contradictory sources as Sallust, Dio Cassius, and Lucius Florus, the work features an extended consideration of the rebellion of the turbulent nobleman Catiline. This section was perhaps influenced by the recent troubles of a latter-day Catiline, the earl of Essex, whose execution in February 1601 would have virtually coincided with the publication of Fulbecke's book, which was dedicated to one of Essex's enemies, Thomas Sackville, Lord Buckhurst. The *Historicall Collection* is similarly full of the sorts of fears of unrest and civil dissension that characterize the literature of Elizabeth's last years.

Fulbecke's next work was his *Parallele or Conference of the Civill Law, the Canon Law, and the Common Law of England* (1601). Together with *The Second Part of the Parallele*, which appeared a year later, this represents Fulbecke's most mature and interesting work. Rendered in the form of dialogues between a canonist, a common lawyer, and a civil lawyer, it is one of the earliest attempts by an English lawyer at an essay in comparative jurisprudence, aiming to reconcile the differences that existed between the three legal systems. While his understanding of the canon law was not especially strong, his grasp of civil law rendered him much less insular than many of his contemporaries in his understanding of the historical development of English common law, within which he could discern both Anglo-Saxon and Norman influences. The survival of ancient law past the Norman conquest was an important issue to common lawyers and parliamentarians throughout the seventeenth century. In both sections of the *Parallele* and in his final work, *Pandectes of the Law of Nations* (1602), Fulbecke confirmed that the Norman conquest had been a thorough conquest, while emphasizing, nevertheless, that William I had been a wise and temperate ruler who had chosen to adopt, rather than entirely to abrogate, Anglo-Saxon law. Little is known of Fulbecke's life after 1602, nor is it known precisely where and when he died, though the Augustan bishop and scholar White Kennett believed that he had taken orders and been appointed vicar of Waldeshare in Kent.   D. R. WOOLF

Sources D. R. Woolf, *The idea of history in early Stuart England* (1990) · D. R. Woolf, 'Fulbecke, William', *Sixteenth-century British nondramatic writers: fourth series*, ed. D. A. Richardson, DLitB, 172 (1996) · Wood, *Ath. Oxon.*, 2nd edn, 1.317 · R. J. Terrill, 'The application of the comparative method by English civilians: the case of William Fulbecke and Thomas Ridley', *Journal of Legal History*, 2 (1981), 169–85 · J. G. A. Pocock, *The ancient constitution and the feudal law*, 2nd edn (1987)

Fulbourn, Stephen of (d. 1288), justiciar of Ireland and archbishop of Tuam, came from a Cambridgeshire family. A hospitaller, he became precentor and treasurer of the order's priory at Clerkenwell and in 1269 was appointed as his deputy by Roger de Vere, prior of the hospitallers in England. In 1270 the grand master of the order granted Fulbourn the personal use for life of all the property that he had acquired for Clerkenwell or might acquire in the future.

Fulbourn acted as Queen Eleanor's proctor in Ireland in 1270. He was appointed auditor of the tax of a twentieth on moveable property in England in 1273 and receiver of the tallage on the Jews in 1274. Early in 1274 he was elected bishop of Waterford by the dean and chapter at the king's request and on 25 September was appointed treasurer of Ireland, to hold office during the king's pleasure. His appointment and that of Robert of Ufford as justicar in 1276 were accompanied by measures intended to reform the administration and place control of Irish revenues in the hands of the treasurer. The level of exchequer receipts rose and considerable sums were contributed to Edward I's military activities. In 1281 Fulbourn was responsible for the issuing of a new Irish coinage, much of which was sent abroad for the king's use.

Fulbourn acted as deputy for Ufford, the justiciar, in 1280, and because of Ufford's ill health was himself appointed justiciar on 21 November 1281. He retained the office of treasurer, appointing his brother Walter as his deputy. As justiciar, Fulbourn was confronted with the problem of the Leinster Irish, which he dealt with by removing their leaders. At his instigation, Art Mac Murchadha and his brother Muirchertach were murdered at Arklow in 1282, although they had been received into the king's peace. He subsequently provided legal justification for the murders by taking inquisitions which found the Mac Murchadhas to have been felons. Despite the illegality of his actions, they achieved the desired result. Leinster became relatively peaceful and no major expedition was necessary for the next thirteen years.

Fulbourn used his official position to obtain grants of wardships and lands for himself and preferment for members of his family, whom he appointed to positions in the administration. He antagonized the earl of Norfolk by encroaching on his liberty of Carlow and by furthering the growth of Waterford at the expense of the port of Ross. The aggrandizement of the Fulbourn family gave rise to hostility and envy and led to a series of complaints to the king which came to a head in 1284. The charges included taking bribes, making illicit profits from the mint, customs, and supply of provisions for royal armies in Wales, colluding with the usurpation of royal rights by the archbishop of Armagh, and receiving and paying royal revenues outside the exchequer. Most of the accusations could not be proved, but Fulbourn was discovered to owe the king £33,000, partly because his financial records contained so many alterations and erasures that the auditors refused to allow some sums that he had expended on the king's instructions. His real debt was about £13,000, the result of inefficiency as well as of peculation.

The investigation resulted in a compromise. Fulbourn was replaced as treasurer by Nicholas of Clere, one of his principal accusers, but retained the office of justiciar and was pardoned all but £4000 of his debt to the king because of the great expenses he had incurred on war and defence in Ireland. At Edward's request the pope translated him to the vacant archbishopric of Tuam on 12 July 1286, while a disputed election to the see of Meath in which one of the parties was Walter of Fulbourn was settled by providing Walter to the now vacant see of Waterford in succession to his brother. Attempts at administrative reform after 1285 came to nothing, owing to the ineffectiveness of Fulbourn

as justiciar and the general hostility to such measures among members of the administration.

Fulbourn died on 3 July 1288, still in debt to the crown.

PHILOMENA CONNOLLY

Sources H. S. Sweetman and G. F. Handcock, eds., *Calendar of documents relating to Ireland*, 5 vols., PRO (1875–86) • H. G. Richardson and G. O. Sayles, *The administration of Ireland, 1172–1377* (1963) • *Chancery records* • R. Frame, ed., 'The justiciar and the murder of the MacMurroughs in 1282', *Irish Historical Studies*, 18 (1972–3), 223–30 • J. Lydon, 'The years of crisis, 1254–1315', *A new history of Ireland*, ed. T. W. Moody and others, 2: *Medieval Ireland, 1169–1534* (1987), 179–204; repr. with corrections (1993) • J. A. Watt, *The church and the two nations in medieval Ireland* (1970) • M. Dolley, 'Coinage to 1534: the sign of the times', *A new history of Ireland*, ed. T. W. Moody and others, 2: *Medieval Ireland, 1169–1534* (1987), 816–26; repr. with corrections (1993) • *Report of the Deputy Keeper of the Public Records in Ireland*, 37 (1905), appx 9 • G. O. Sayles, eds., *Documents on the affairs of Ireland before the king's council*, IMC (1979)
Wealth at death chattels: Sweetman and Handcock, eds., *Calendar of documents*, 180–81

Fulcher, George Williams (1795–1855), poet and writer, was a bookseller, stationer, and printer in Sudbury, Suffolk. On 6 August 1822 he married Lucy Lillie at St Gregory's in Sudbury; they had at least two sons. In 1825 he issued the first number of the *Sudbury Pocket Book*, an annual which he continued to publish during his life, and to the pages of which, besides Fulcher himself, Bernard Barton, William and Mary Howitt, James Montgomery, and other writers contributed. He was particularly good friends with Barton, with whom he corresponded for almost twenty years, and who used to tease him about his tory politics and sensibilities. A selection from the *Pocket Book* contributions appeared under the title *Fulcher's Poetical Miscellany* in 1841 and was reprinted in 1853. In 1838 Fulcher also started a monthly miscellany of prose and verse, *Fulcher's Sudbury Journal*, but this was not continued beyond the year. He made a courageous effort to treat pauperism poetically, publishing *The Village Paupers, and other Poems* (1845; 2nd edn, 1846). 'The Village Paupers' is in heroic couplets and betrays in almost every line the influence of George Crabbe and of Oliver Goldsmith's 'The Deserted Village'. Of the miscellaneous poems 'The Dying Child' is the best. He also published *The Ladies' Memorandum Book and Poetical Miscellany* (1852 and following years) and *The Farmer's Day-Book*, which reached a sixth edition in 1854.

Fulcher was throughout life a diligent student, particularly of Crabbe and William Cowper. Boswell's *Johnson* was also one of his favourite books. He was a practical botanist and was very sensitive to the beauties of nature. He took an active interest in local affairs, being one of the magistrates of the borough of Sudbury, president of the board of guardians, and several times mayor. He also donated generously to charities. He died at Sudbury on 19 June 1855 and was buried in the churchyard of St Gregory, Sudbury, the townspeople closing their shops, and the mayor, corporation, and magistrates of the borough following the bier. He was survived by his wife.

Fulcher had been working on a biography of Thomas Gainsborough at the time of his death. This work was completed by his son Edmund Syer Fulcher (*b*. 1833) and published in London in 1856. A second edition appeared in the same year.   J. M. RIGG, *rev.* REBECCA MILLS

Sources IGI • wills, PRO, PROB 11/2217, sig. 691; PROB 11/2229, sig. 201 • GM, 2nd ser., 44 (1855), 213–14 • *Selections from the poems and letters of Bernard Barton*, ed. L. Barton (1849), 76–85 • Allibone, *Dict.* **Wealth at death** considerable estate left to wife and children: will, PRO, PROB 11/2217, sig. 691, fols. 329–31; PRO, PROB 11/2229, sig. 201, fol. 6

Fulford, Francis (1803–1868), bishop of Montreal, was the second son of Baldwin Fulford of Fulford Magna, Devon, and of Anne Maria, eldest daughter of William Adams, MP for Totnes. Born at Sidmouth on 3 June 1803, he was baptized at Dunsford on 14 October 1804. He was educated at Tiverton grammar school, whence he matriculated from Exeter College, Oxford, on 1 February 1821. He was elected a fellow of Exeter on 30 June 1824 but vacated his fellowship on 18 October 1830 on his marriage to Mary, eldest daughter of Andrew Berkeley Drummond of Cadlands, Hampshire. Fulford proceeded BA in 1827 and MA 1838; he was created an honorary DD on 6 July 1850. He was ordained deacon in 1826 and became curate of Holne in Devon, afterwards moving to the curacy of Fawley. The duke of Rutland instituted him to the rectory of Trowbridge, Wiltshire, in 1832, where he lived for ten years, serving also as a justice of the peace.

In 1842 Fulford accepted the rectory of Croydon, Cambridgeshire, which he held until 1845, when he was nominated by Earl Howe as minister of Curzon Chapel, Mayfair, Westminster. He was active in the Society for the Propagation of the Gospel, and in 1848 became first editor of the *Colonial Church Chronicle and Missionary Journal*. He had some association with the Tractarians though defending the Anglican position in *The Progress of the Reformation in England* (1841); this was his only publication of substance, though many of his sermons and addresses were published. On 19 July 1850 he was appointed, by letters patent, first bishop of the new diocese of Montreal, Canada, and he was consecrated in Westminster Abbey on 25 July. He later confirmed his appointment by legislation in his synod. He was enthroned in Christ Church Cathedral, Montreal, on 15 September 1850.

Fulford's large new diocese had forty-eight clergy and, in the midst of French Canada, a mainly English-speaking congregation. Fulford quickly established a sound diocesan structure, with four rural deaneries, a cathedral chapter, and an archdeacon. Against some local opposition he set up a synod, approved by Canadian legislation in 1858 and 1859. He showed himself an adroit mover in the complex education disputes of the period, neatly solving a potential quarrel by personally presiding over the Montreal committee of the Church and School Society (a body controlled from England); the committee started teacher training in Montreal. He was also active in adult education.

On 21 May 1857 Fulford laid the foundation stone of his new gothic cathedral, designed by Frank Wills, where on Advent Sunday 1859 he preached the opening sermon. The great cost of this building involved the diocese in a

Francis Fulford (1803–1868), by William Notman, 1861

heavy debt and the bishop in much self-recrimination. On 9 July 1860 Queen Victoria caused letters patent to be issued promoting Fulford to the office of metropolitan of Canada and elevating the see of Montreal to the dignity of a metropolitical see, with the city of Montreal as its seat. On 10 September 1861 the first provincial synod of the United Church of England and Ireland in Canada was held at Montreal. It was chiefly on the representation of the synod of Canada that the archbishop of Canterbury held the pan-Anglican synod at Lambeth (24–27 September 1867), on which occasion Fulford visited England and took part in the proceedings. On this journey, however, he seems to have overtaxed his strength, and he never afterwards enjoyed good health.

In the 1860s Fulford was involved in complex legal disputes about the power of letters patent in Canada, and in a lengthy debate, mixing theology and money, with Archdeacon Isaac *Hellmuth. He died in the see house, Montreal, on 9 September 1868, survived by his wife. He was buried on 12 September, when the universal respect which his moderation had won for him was shown by the bell of the Roman Catholic church being tolled as the funeral procession passed.

G. C. BOASE, *rev.* H. C. G. MATTHEW

Sources F. Taylor, *The last three bishops appointed by the crown for the Anglican Church of Canada* (1869) • *DCB*, vol. 9 • *ILN* (3 Aug 1850) • *ILN*

(26 Sept 1868) • C. F. Pascoe, *Two hundred years of the SPG*, rev. edn, 2 vols. (1901) • *CGPLA Eng. & Wales* (1869)

Archives general synod archives, Toronto • Montreal Anglican diocese, synod office | Cadland House, Drummond MSS • priv. coll., corresp. with Drummond family

Likenesses W. Notman, photograph, 1861, NPG [*see illus.*] • wood-engraving (after photograph by Kilburn), repro. in *ILN* (24 Aug 1850) • wood-engraving, repro. in *ILN* (29 Nov 1862)

Wealth at death under £6000: probate, 20 Jan 1869, *CGPLA Eng. & Wales*

Fulford, Sir Roger Thomas Baldwin (1902–1983), author and journalist, was born on 24 November 1902 in the vicarage at Flaxley in Gloucestershire, the younger son and second of the three children of the Revd Frederick John Fulford, who was vicar at Flaxley and was later an honorary canon of St Edmundsbury and Ipswich, in Suffolk, and of his wife, Emily Constance, daughter of W. H. Ellis of Ottermouth, Budleigh Salterton, Devon. Roger's brother died young; his sister spent a happy life as a nun. He was educated at Lancing College (where he was a contemporary of Evelyn Waugh) and Worcester College, Oxford, where he took a second in modern history (1927); he was Liberal president of the union in 1927. He was called to the bar in 1931, though he never practised. He joined the editorial department of *The Times* in 1933 and remained a contributor for many years. A fervent and lifelong Liberal, he was thrice defeated in parliamentary elections (East Suffolk, 1929; Holderness, 1945; and Rochdale, 1950), and during the 1930s his third forename produced many jokes at his expense. In 1964–5 his constancy was rewarded by the presidency of the Liberal Party.

In 1932 G. Lytton Strachey died, leaving unfinished the editing of the first unexpurgated edition of *The Greville Memoirs*, on which he had been working for several years. His brother James asked Fulford to complete the editing, which he did, with the assistance of Ralph and Frances Partridge, who had already done much of the donkey work for Strachey. The first of the ten volumes appeared in 1938 with a short preface by Fulford and his name as co-editor on the title-page.

But all the time Fulford's heart was in history, particularly that of the English royal family in the late eighteenth century and all the nineteenth. His first book, *Royal Dukes* (1933; revised edn, 1973), brought him great praise. In it he gave detailed accounts of the lives of the six younger sons of George III. Lampooned and often execrated in their lifetime, to Queen Victoria they were, except for her father, unmentionable. Never before had they been treated on their merits and demerits, and Fulford did this with wit and, wherever possible, sympathy. *George the Fourth* (1935), following the same pattern of sorting good from bad, true from false, was as successful as its predecessor.

During the war Fulford was an assistant censor, a civil assistant in the War Office (1940–42), and assistant private secretary to the secretary of state for air (1942–5). After the war he returned to the royal family with *The Prince Consort* (1949) and a short life, *Queen Victoria* (1951). Next he turned aside to write a history of Glyn's Bank (*Glyn's, 1753–1953*, 1953), *Votes for Women* (1957), a history of the suffragette movement, which received a prize of £5000 from the *Evening Standard*, and *The Liberal Case* (for the general election of 1959). Then he returned once more to the royal family with *Hanover to Windsor* (1960), a study of the monarchy from William IV to George V, and his final task was the editing of five volumes of the correspondence between Queen Victoria and her eldest daughter, the Empress Frederick of Germany: *Dearest Child* (1964), *Dearest Mama* (1968), *Your Dear Letter* (1971), *Darling Child* (1976), and *Beloved Mama* (1981).

In 1937 Fulford married Sibell Eleanor Maud, daughter of Charles Robert Whorwood Adeane, of Babraham Hall, Cambridge, and widow of the Hon. Edward James Kay-Shuttleworth (*d.* 1917) and of the Revd Hon. Charles Frederick Lyttelton (*d.* 1931). There were no children of the marriage but Sibell had a son and a daughter from her first marriage and two sons from her second, of whom one died in infancy and the other of wounds in 1944. The Fulfords' married life, which was happy and lasting, was mostly spent at Barbon Manor, on a hilltop near Kirkby Lonsdale, near Carnforth. They filled the house with engaging Victoriana and established a woodland garden in which numerous Himalayan rhododendrons, including some of the large-leaved and frost-tender species, still flourish at 700 feet above sea-level.

Fulford became a great favourite with his wife's numerous relatives, who often called on his aid, and they repaid his kindness by helping to look after him in his last few years. He was a small man, always courteous and serene. His brother-in-law George Lyttelton described him as 'demure and impish', and indeed his wry humour was ever present. He was a regular attender at committee meetings of the London Library, but he never travelled all the way from Westmorland for an uneventful meeting. Often when some matter had apparently been dealt with, a quiet voice would say 'But, Mr Chairman ...' and the whole discussion would be reopened. He was a loyal and affectionate friend, the most stimulating and delightful of companions.

The death of his wife in 1980 was a terrible blow to Fulford, whose health deteriorated, and he died at his home, Barbon Manor, on 18 May 1983. He was appointed CVO in 1970 and knighted in 1980.   RUPERT HART-DAVIS, rev.

Sources *The Times* (19 May 1983) • *The Times* (26 May 1983) • personal knowledge (1990) • *CGPLA Eng. & Wales* (1983)

Archives JRL, letters to *Manchester Guardian* | HLRO, corresp. with Lord Beaverbrook • LUL, corresp. with Duckworth & Co.

Wealth at death £58,293: probate, 25 Oct 1983, *CGPLA Eng. & Wales*

Fulhame, Elizabeth [*known as* Mrs Fulhame] (*fl.* **1780–1794**), chemist, was an original chemist but little else is known of her life. Her husband, Thomas Fulhame, had come from Ireland and enrolled in the chemistry class at Edinburgh University in 1779–80. He graduated MD in 1784 and, unusually, retained a presence in the chemistry class until 1790. He travelled or lived briefly in Spain, and was a correspondent of Joseph Black, the Edinburgh physician and chemist, who in 1793 noted that Fulhame had found a new method of manufacturing white lead. Elizabeth Fulhame presumably shared her husband's interests, for in 1794 she published a remarkable monograph, *An essay on combustion with a view to a new art of dying and painting wherein the phlogistic and antiphlogistic hypotheses are proved erroneous*. This book later appeared in German translation (Göttingen, 1798) and in an American edition (Philadelphia, 1810). It was favourably noticed by Priestley, Rumford, Herschel, Woodhouse, and others and was the subject of a long review by Coindet.

In her preface the author remarked that in 1780 her husband had deemed improbable 'the possibility of making cloths of gold, silver, and other metals, by chemical processes'. In spite of such connubial discouragement and 'an expense so disproportionate to the fortune which supported it' she persevered. Such perseverance does not surprise, for the preface reveals a formidably assured woman who stated frankly: 'I published this essay in its present imperfect state, in order to prevent the furacious attempts of the prowling plagiary, and the insidious pretender to chymistry, from arrogating to themselves and assuming my invention in plundering silence'. She was well aware of the criticism she might receive from opponents, especially as a woman writing on controversial subjects, and took the robust line that

> censure is perhaps inevitable; for some are so ignorant, that they grow sullen and silent, and are chilled with horror at the sight of any thing that bears the semblance of learning, in whatever shape it may appear; and should the *spectre* appear in the shape of *woman*, the pangs which they suffer are truly dismal.

Driving the point home she went on to declare that: 'happen what may, I hope I shall never experience such desertion of mind, as not to hold the helm with becoming fortitude against the storm raised by ignorance, petulant arrogance, and privileged dulness'. It is perhaps not entirely fortuitous that her book was sold by Joseph Johnson, the publisher of Thomas Paine, Joseph Priestley, and Mary Wollstonecraft.

The body of the book details the approach Mrs Fulhame took towards the attainment of her original goal, her crowning achievement being the production of cloth 'maps, the rivers of which are represented in silver, and the cities in gold'. The lengthy, systematic study of the action of various reducing agents (hydrogen, sulphur, phosphorus, charcoal, even light) on metallic salts in aqueous, alcoholic, and ethereal solution was unusual, even unique, for its time. Several incidental observations—the passivation of iron, the production of colloidal gold, and the formation of images by the action of light—have been viewed as foreshadowing discoveries made later and assigned to others. Indeed, late twentieth-century histories of photography include Mrs Fulhame.

Perhaps the most remarkable feature of this remarkable book are Mrs Fulhame's imaginative and iconoclastic views on the nature of combustion, the central problem of late eighteenth-century chemistry. Clearly she was fully familiar with the contending phlogistic and antiphlogistic theories of those chemically revolutionary

years. She postulates a reaction sequence in which water plays the role of what would later be termed a catalyst. No wonder Rumford called her 'the lively and ingenious Mrs Fulhame'. She concludes her essay with an early statement of the ecological dogma:

> This view of combustion may serve to show how nature is always the same, and maintains her equilibrium by preserving the same quantities of air and water on the surface of our globe: for as fast as these are consumed in the various processes of combustion, equal quantities are formed, and rise regenerated like the Phenix from her ashes.

In quoting this paragraph, J. R. Partington, the historian of chemistry, added the footnote: 'The phoenix, it may be noted, was a fabulous bird regarded as sexless' (Partington, 3.708–9). Mrs Fulhame would not have been amused.

No other work by Mrs Fulhame exists, and attempts to locate her biographically have so far proven fruitless. Of her significance and interest there is, however, no doubt.

DEREK A. DAVENPORT

Sources J. F. Coindet, *Annales de Chemie*, 26 (1798), 58–85 · D. A. Davenport and K. M. Ireland, 'The ingenious, lively and celebrated Mrs Fulhame and the dyer's hand', *Bulletin for the History of Chemistry*, 5 (1989), 37–42 · J. R. Partington, *A history of chemistry*, 3 (1962), 708–9 · private information (2004) [University of Edinburgh and Mrs J. Jones]

Fulk (I) fitz Warin (d. 1171). *See under* Fitzwarine family (*per. c.*1145–1315).

Fulke, William (1536/7–1589), theologian and college head, was the son of Christopher Fulke, a prosperous citizen of London; he gave his age as twenty-nine on 30 October 1566. His mother's name is not known and only one sibling, Samuel, is certainly recorded. Both St Paul's and the Mercers' have been claimed as the London school he attended. A story that in a contest between London schools he was vanquished by the young Edmund Campion, the future Jesuit missionary and controversialist, and vowed to have his revenge, is surely apocryphal, composed in the light of the adult Fulke's success in controversy with Campion. He entered St John's College, Cambridge, in 1555, probably graduated in 1558 (though this was later doubted), and then, following his father's wish that he pursue a legal career, entered Clifford's Inn and was admitted to the Inner Temple in 1560. It may have been in this period at the inns of court that he acquired his strongly protestant religious convictions. With the intention of studying theology and oriental languages, and at the cost of his father's support, he returned to St John's in 1562 or 1563. By then he had already written two significant books which reflect his wide academic interests, especially in science. *Antiprognosticon* (1560) attacked the widely respected practice of astrology, which Fulke sharply distinguished from the science of astronomy. In denying that astrology had any truly scientific basis, Fulke's was one of the most radical attacks on astrology in this period. In his work on meteorology (*A Goodly Gallerye*, 1563) he entered another field in which superstition and appeal to supernatural forces were common. As a neo-Aristotelian scientist, Fulke explained even the most

unusual physical phenomena in terms of natural caus-
ation, while, as a theologian, he saw this as entirely compatible with belief in divine providence. These scientific
works were important in promoting a strictly rational
approach to the physical world, while denying any conflict between true science and true religion.

In 1563 Fulke commenced MA, and in 1564 became a fellow of St John's and a college preacher. His radical religious views soon became apparent when he abandoned
academic dress (gown and square cap) and the wearing of
a surplice in chapel. Such things were considered popish
remnants by the zealous protestants who regarded the
Elizabethan settlement as only a step on the way to fuller
reformation of the church. Fulke became the leader of a
puritan faction in the college, composed mostly of
younger fellows, while most of the senior fellows opposed
them. Fulke and his faction, with their inflammatory
preaching and their lively singing of metrical psalms,
were popular with undergraduates, and also gained the
support of the master, Richard Longworth, whose favouring of the puritan faction in appointments culminated in
Fulke's being made principal lecturer. By late November
1565 most members of the college, subjected to intimidation as well as persuasion, had abandoned surplices in
chapel, while the hard core of conservative fellows
merely stayed away. So alarming was this rebellion
against legal order that the university's chancellor, Sir
William Cecil, in consultation with Archbishop Parker
and even the queen, took steps to quell it. By the end of
December he had succeeded, though the bitter faction-
fighting in the college continued for years.

Fulke himself resigned his fellowship early in 1566, and
probably spent the rest of the year as a freelance lecturer
at his lodgings at The Falcon inn. In March 1567 he was
readmitted to his fellowship and his post as preacher, to
which he soon added that of Hebrew lecturer. He proceeded BTh in 1567 and became president of the college in
1568. Then, in 1569, in another acrimonious dispute
involving Cecil, Fulke and his supporters attempted to get
Longworth removed from office for misconduct, apparently with a view to electing Fulke himself as master.
Counter charges against Fulke alleged a serious crime, the
nature of which is unknown, but of which he was eventually cleared. For the sake of peace he was persuaded to
resign his fellowship; he left Cambridge to become chaplain to the earl of Leicester, well known for his patronage
of puritans. He was re-elected a fellow in March 1570, but
again resigned in the summer of 1571—this time finally,
since soon afterwards he married. His first wife (her name
is not known) bore their eldest son Christopher before her
death within two years of the wedding. Leicester obtained
for Fulke the living of Great Warley in Essex, where he resided with his family until 1574. On 16 May 1573 he married
his second wife, Margaret Cotton (d. 1604). Their children
were Mary, baptized in 1574; twin sons baptized in 1575,
who died in infancy; Hester, baptized in 1577; Elizabeth,
baptized in 1583; Anne, baptized in 1585; John, baptized in
1587, who died in infancy; and William, baptized in 1588.
After acquiring a second living, Dennington in Suffolk,

Fulke and his family moved there, leaving Great Warley to
a curate. Though he was often elsewhere, Dennington
remained his family home until his death in 1589, and his
tomb is in Dennington church, where he was buried on 28
August.

During the 1570s, under Leicester's patronage, Fulke
found a rising position in the world compatible with his
radical puritan convictions, though he was obliged to sign
a declaration that the authorized liturgies and vestments
were not contrary to scripture. He became popular as a
preacher in London churches, and in 1572 he accompanied the earl of Lincoln as his chaplain on an embassy to
Paris, receiving the Cambridge degree of DTh by special
dispensation just before the embassy left for France. The
early 1570s were also the time of his greatest commitment
to the presbyterian movement within the Church of England. But the leaders of that movement judged the book
he wrote in support of it not suitable for publication and
only published it later, anonymously and without his consent (A Brief and Plain Declaration, 1584), when Fulke had
abandoned the views expressed in it. Also in the 1570s he
was becoming well known in the role that was to be the
major concern of the rest of his career: as a theological
controversialist, exposing the errors of Roman Catholic
doctrine and defending the Church of England against
theological attacks from English Catholic polemicists. It
was his sense of the importance of arguing the common
protestant cause against Rome that led him away from a
puritan concern to cleanse the Church of England itself
from popish remnants towards a more conformist position in his later years.

In 1578 Leicester's patronage secured him the mastership of Pembroke College, Cambridge, a position he held
until his death. He was a conscientious and energetic master, during whose tenure the average number of undergraduates entering the college each year effectively
doubled, and he served as vice-chancellor of the university in 1581–2. In 1579 he would probably have been
appointed to the regius chair of divinity had he not
declined to be considered because of his parish duties.
Although he remained one of those Cambridge divines to
whom puritans looked for learning and guidance, Pembroke under his mastership did not become a puritan college, like St John's under William Whitaker or Christ's
under Laurence Chaderton. Indeed, the beginnings of the
Arminian theology of grace that would characterize the
Laudian movement, contesting the dominant Calvinism
of the Elizabethan church, can be traced to men like
Lancelot Andrewes and Samuel Harsnett who were fellows of Pembroke in the 1580s. Fulke remained an unhesi-
tating adherent of the reformed views of predestination,
grace, and assurance, but remained close to Calvin's theology in these respects, avoiding the heightened
emphasis on predestination that characterized the later
Calvinism of men like William Perkins. Amid the new
theological developments of the 1580s Fulke remained
primarily an apologist for the central doctrines of
reformed theology against the attacks of the papists. As
such, puritans continued to claim him as an authority, but

he also enjoyed the favour and co-operation of the government and the ecclesiastical authorities. It was as the acknowledged successor to John Jewel in the theological defence of the Church of England against Rome that he was admired and remembered by his contemporaries: 'that profound, ready and resolute doctor, the hammer of heretics, the champion of truth', as Bishop Joseph Hall called him in 1607 (Hall, 262).

Probably encouraged by his noble patrons and government contacts, Fulke conceived the project of answering all works of controversy written in English by papists since 1558 and of doing so by the technique of exhaustive rebuttal, answering every point, large and small, made in the writings of his opponents. In fact he published answers to twenty-one Roman Catholic works by such writers as William Allen, Thomas Stapleton, Nicholas Sander, and Robert Persons. In most cases their text was printed with Fulke's response, indicating his confidence that readers would not be led astray by the papist but rather edified by the cogency of his own response. Fulke was well equipped for this role by his vast erudition, especially in patristic literature, and his command of biblical and classical languages, as well as his painstaking concern for accurate detail and the rules of logical argument. In addition to written controversy, Fulke engaged in public disputations with recusant prisoners, most famously with Edmund Campion in the Tower before the latter's execution in 1581. The climax of his work was his vast confutation of the Rheims New Testament, the English translation of the Vulgate text produced by English Catholics with numerous annotations. To write this he lodged with two assistants for nine months in 1587–8 in the London home of his publisher, who provided living expenses and books.

As well as replying to Roman Catholic attacks on the English church, Fulke pursued his refutation of Rome in published sermons, especially a series on the Apocalypse (*Praelections*, 1573) which were first preached in the earl of Leicester's household in 1569, at the time of the northern uprising. There and in other works he propagated the dominant Elizabethan version of the apocalyptic interpretation of the Reformation as the final struggle between Christ and Antichrist, a theme that ran through the whole sixteenth-century protestant–Catholic controversy. Fulke's work is also characterized by the increasing shift in this controversy from particular doctrines to the fundamental issues of doctrinal authority and to the nature and accessibility of the biblical revelation. Most important, perhaps, were his controversy with Gregory Martin about the principles and practice of Bible translation (*A Defense of the Sincere and True Translations*, 1583) and the continuation of this in his exhaustive work on the Rheims New Testament (*The Text of the New Testament*, 1589). This controversy, with its constant demonstration of the inextricable connection between translation and interpretation, significantly influenced the King James version of the Bible.   RICHARD BAUCKHAM

Sources R. Bauckham, 'The career and thought of Dr William Fulke (1537–1589)', PhD diss., U. Cam., 1973 [incl. bibliography of Fulke's works, incl. MSS and letters] • H. C. Porter, *Reformation and reaction in Tudor Cambridge* (1958), chaps. 5–6 • W. McKane, *Selected Christian Hebraists* (1989), chap. 3 • R. Bauckham, 'Science and religion in the writings of Dr William Fulke', *British Journal for the History of Science*, 8 (1975), 17–31 • R. Bauckham, *Tudor apocalypse* (1978), esp. 321–40 • A. C. Southern, *Elizabethan recusant prose, 1559–1582* (1950) • T. E. Key, 'Dennington church', *Proceedings of the Suffolk Institute of Archaeology and Natural History*, 8 (1892–4), 65–82 [transcribes inscription on monument to Fulke erected 1621] • A. L. Attwater, *Pembroke College, Cambridge: a short history*, ed. S. C. Roberts (1936) • Venn, *Alum. Cant.*, 1/2.183; 1/4.523 • *The works of Joseph Hall, B. of Exeter* (1634) • CUL, department of manuscripts and university archives, Guard Book IV • monument, Suffolk, Dennington church

Likenesses W. Marshall, line engraving, BM, NPG; repro. in W. Fulke, *The text of the new testament of Iesus Christ, translated out of the vulgar Latine by the papists* (1633), frontispiece

Wealth at death property at Hornsey, Middlesex (inherited from his father); property at Taunton, Somerset; property at Dickleburgh, Norfolk (118 acres, purchased for £900 in 1586); books, 'antiquities', plate, etc.: will, CUL, department of manuscripts and university archives; deed of sale of land, Pembroke Cam.

Fulkherd, Quentin [Quintin Folkhard] (*fl.* **1407–1410**), alleged Lollard heretic, is identified only in two English safe conducts from 1407, as 'Quintin Folkhard of Scotland', and in a batch of his letters dated 1410 and entitled *Nova Scocie*, which are preserved in a Prague manuscript (see Haldenston); these describe him as an esquire. The safe conducts possibly imply that he was an emissary between the English and Scottish courts, for reference is made to his returning to Henry IV's presence from Scotland. If he visited the English court in this period, he may have encountered some of the evangelical (and allegedly Lollard) knights who were then active in English public life and who could have influenced him, but this is only conjecture. It may not, however, be merely coincidental that the letters were sent in a year in which contacts are recorded between Sir John Oldcastle (d. 1417), the leader of the English Lollard rising of 1414, and the Bohemian reformers. The letters, written in Latin and containing scriptural and patristic quotations, show that Fulkherd was a man of some education, although there is no evidence for his attending any university. One letter was addressed to the bishop of Glasgow, so Fulkherd might have come from that diocese. The letters were written to the whole community of Christendom, the bishop of Glasgow and the Scottish clergy, the secular lords of the country, and Fulkherd's parish priest. Their general tone is more anticlerical than heretical, and suggests that Fulkherd's principal concern was to encourage moral reform in the church. His only potentially heretical demand is that the scriptures and the articles of faith should be preached to the people in the vernacular, something which the preamble to the letters says he had actually done. He does not express any view on transubstantiation, the most significant Lollard theological deviation, and acknowledges ecclesiastical jurisdiction over heresy—in the second letter he writes that he would accept the church's correction if they could disprove his charges against the clergy. After 1410 Fulkherd disappears from the records and, although there is evidence of measures against heresy in Scotland in the following decade, the suggestion that he was the anonymous Lollard burnt at Glasgow in 1422 remains unproven.   JOHN A. F. THOMSON

Sources [J. Haldenston], *Copiale prioratus Sanctiandree: the letter-book of James Haldenstone, prior of St Andrews, 1418–1443*, ed. J. H. Baxter, St Andrews University Publications, 31 (1930) • *Chancery records* • T. M. A. MacNab, 'Bohemia and the Scottish Lollards', *Records of the Scottish Church History Society*, 5 (1933–5), 10–22 • R. Nicholson, *Scotland: the later middle ages* (1974), vol. 2 of *The Edinburgh history of Scotland*, ed. G. Donaldson (1965–75)

Fullard, George (1923–1973), sculptor, was born on 15 September 1923 at 2 Court 1 Hazel Road, Darnall, Sheffield, the youngest of the five children of George Fullard (1886–1952), a coalminer, and his wife, Henrietta Matthias (1886–1953). His early social environment considerably influenced the drawings and sculpture he produced in later life. Notably, he acknowledged this when, remarking that his growing up had been 'like living in a sculpture', he referred to the labyrinthine backyards of Darnall (Spencer). Communist politics and trade union militancy marked his early family life. In the late 1930s his father became known locally as a socialist playwright after he had been blacklisted for organizing a strike of pit deputies. Fullard's talent for drawing earned him a scholarship to the Sheffield College of Arts and Crafts, which he attended from 1937 to 1942. His student drawings of ordinary people reveal an early preoccupation with everyday life on the streets of the city. In 1942 he enlisted as a trooper in the 17/21st lancers and served in north Africa and Italy. In the final battle for Montecassino on 19 May 1944 he received severe injuries to his head, chest, and shoulder. Despite being given little hope of surviving, he made a remarkably rapid recovery.

From 1945 to 1947 Fullard studied sculpture at the Royal College of Art, in Ambleside, Westmorland, and in London, and proved to be an exceptionally gifted modeller. On graduation he was awarded a three-month travel scholarship which he spent in Paris with his wife, Irena O'Connor Corcoran (*b.* 1923), an actress, whom he had married on 1 July 1946. Until 1950 they lived in a rambling house at 44 Pembroke Road, West Kensington, London, which they shared with various Royal College graduates. In these early years Fullard undertook various commissions, including one for the Festival of Britain in 1951. Although in 1950 he and his wife moved to 11 Stanley Studios, Park Walk, Chelsea, he also shared a studio with Derrick Greaves at Fawcett Yard, a dilapidated mews near Fulham Road. In the 1950s his drawings and modelled figures and heads reflected his continuing interest in ordinary humanity. They attracted the attention of John Berger, the Marxist art critic of the *New Statesman*, who, by 1958, regarded him as Britain's best young contemporary sculptor. Fullard's first major showing of sculpture was in the 1957 'Looking at people' exhibition which toured to Moscow, despite the unfavourable cold war atmosphere. With the financial stability provided by part-time teaching at St

Albans School of Art, he devoted more energy to developing and showing his sculpture: his large *Running Woman* (bronze, 1957, Sheffield city centre) won a junior prize at the first John Moores exhibition in Liverpool.

In 1959 Fullard began to work with the idiom of 'assemblage'. Initially he meticulously assembled figures from bits of old wooden furniture and other 'junk' which he had accumulated. They displayed a distinct cubist influence but also reflected earlier concerns. The faceted profile of *Woman* (wood, 1959, Arts Council of Great Britain) has affinities with the heads of the modelled figures he made in the 1950s. However, the series of assemblages concerned with the subject of war, made from 1961 to 1964, are generally considered to be his most inventive and important work. Fullard conjured with paradoxical ideas and incongruous objects to bring out the essentially absurd nature of his subject. His work also had a personal element, as he often remarked that he was 'sculpting an autobiography' (Whiteley, *George Fullard*, 6). *Death or Glory* (1963–4, Tate collection) ironizes the noble motto of Fullard's own regiment; *War Game* (ciment fondu, 1962, Hatton Gallery, University of Newcastle upon Tyne; version in bronze) resembles the rubble at Montecassino. In these works he also amalgamated the imagery and rhetoric of the First World War, for he felt profoundly affected by the grief of his parents' generation. Above all, a key thematic concern was the loss and recovery of 'innocence', and his writings and many of his works allude, directly and indirectly, to infancy and games. In 1966 he made a seemingly radical departure, as his final group of sculptures were mainly concerned with the sea. Constructed from found objects and painted flat metal shapes, they have a picture-book quality. With sinking steamers and sailing-boats, their simplicity is deceptive. Again, Fullard's childlike vision is apparent. In particular, the folded paper helmet which featured in a number of his war assemblages became emblematic, as he transformed it into a hat, a boat, and, later, in *Dream Day* (1970–71, City of Bristol Museum and Art Gallery), a line of aeroplanes.

Fastidious about his appearance, Fullard had an elegance unmarred by his war injuries (which left scars to his forehead and poor mobility in his left arm). A raconteur who enjoyed singing and dancing, he was an inspirational teacher and a man of political conviction with no time for élitism. He believed passionately that the artist needed a personal vision which could only be gained from experience of life. George Fullard died on 25 December 1973 in St Stephen's Hospital, Chelsea, after a second heart attack; he was cremated at Golders Green, London. Although he had shown in major exhibitions of contemporary sculpture in the 1960s, had been head of sculpture at the Chelsea School of Art from 1963, and was made an ARA in 1973, his sculpture was not fully appreciated in his lifetime. His work had an idiosyncratic comic edge which was not in keeping with contemporary trends for formalism and abstraction in sculpture. His memorial exhibition at the Serpentine Gallery in London in 1974 was a major critical success, and since then his contribution to post-war art has been considerably recognized, with important retrospective shows in Wakefield, Sheffield, and Cambridge in the 1990s.   GILLIAN WHITELEY

Sources G. Whiteley, *Assembling the absurd: the sculpture of George Fullard* (1998) · J. Spalding, *George Fullard: drawings* (1982) [exhibition catalogue, Arts Council, London] · G. Whiteley, *George Fullard: a fastidious primitive* (1997) [exhibition catalogue, Yorkshire Sculpture Park] · F. Brill, *George Fullard, 1923–1973* (1974) [exhibition catalogue, Serpentine Gallery, London] · G. Whiteley, 'The impact of the survivor: the sculpture of George Fullard (1923–1973)', *The Sculpture Journal*, 1 (1997) · D. Alston, *George Fullard: from student to sculptor* (1993) [Graves Art Gallery, Sheffield, exhibition sheet] · C. S. Spencer, 'George Fullard: sculptor in search of the labyrinth', *The Studio*, 166 (1963), 8–9 · J. Spalding, *The forgotten fifties* (1984) [exhibition catalogue, Graves Art Gallery, Sheffield] · J. Berger, 'George Fullard', *New Statesman* (6 Sept 1958) · G. Fullard, 'Sculpture and survival', *The Painter and Sculptor*, 2/2 (1959), 9–12 · G. Whiteley, 'Playing with paradox', *Playing with paradox: George Fullard 1923–1973*, ed. J. Kirby and A. Middleton (1998), 5–11 · *CGPLA Eng. & Wales* (1974) · b. cert. · m. cert. · d. cert. · private information (2004) · Sheffield Central Library, Hallam University archive
Archives Arts Council of Great Britain · Henry Moore Institute, Leeds, sketchbooks, drawings, notebook · Sheffield Central Library
Likenesses J. Lewinski, photographs, 1960–69, priv. coll. · F. Monaco, photograph, priv. coll.
Wealth at death £25,428: administration, 1 April 1974, *CGPLA Eng. & Wales*

Fullarton, Adam (*d.* in or after **1595**), religious activist and civic administrator, was born in Ayrshire into the family of Fullarton of Dreghorn. His family had links with the small group of Lollards of Kyle in the 1490s and was early converted to protestantism. Adam was either the brother or cousin of the protestant laird John Fullarton of Dreghorn, who subscribed the Ayr bond in 1562 and whose son became minister of Kilmaurs in 1589 and of Dreghorn in 1590. His mother was either Elizabeth Dalrymple or Helen Chalmers.

Adam Fullarton was admitted a burgess and guild of Edinburgh on 24 December 1549, though it is not clear if this was through the familiar route for outsiders of marriage into a prominent merchant family, since the origins of his wife, Marjorie Roger (*d.* 1583), are unknown. He first appeared on the town council in 1555–6. Both he and his wife were significant figures in the capital's emerging 'privy kirk' in the mid-1550s; she belonged to John Knox's 'dear sisters' of Edinburgh, with whom he corresponded both before and after his brief visit to Scotland in 1555–6, and her testament, drawn up in 1583, reveals a remarkable library of more than thirty books. It included English works by Cranmer and Hooper published during the reign of Edward VI, demonstrating the importance of English literature in nurturing urban protestantism in Scotland.

In July 1559, when the lords of the congregation reached the capital and John Knox was appointed minister of the burgh church of St Giles, Fullarton emerged as the spokesman for the 'haill brether of the congregatioun' in the town, refusing the offer of a religious referendum made by the regent, Mary of Guise, on the grounds that 'God's truth should not be subject to the voting of men' (Marwick, 3.47–8). He was appointed a bailie on the town council brought to power in October 1559 by a purge by the

protestant lords, and became probably the most significant protestant layman in the capital during the period that Knox was minister of Edinburgh (1559–72). He was on the council from 1559 to 1562, but like other militant protestants he lost office for much of the rest of the reign of Mary, queen of Scots; he regained office in 1567, during the regency of James Stewart, earl of Moray, and retained it until 1573. He became a bailie, dean of guild, and, briefly in the absence of the provost James MacGill, president of the burgh.

Fullarton's roots may help explain Knox's close links with Ayrshire during the 1560s, when he was appointed a visiting commissioner four times. The connections of both men with Ayrshire also help to explain the militancy of the capital's protestant party. It was a letter from the uncompromising brethren of Kyle urging the rooting out of the idolatry of the mass, which led to a house to house search through the capital for Roman Catholic worshippers during Lent 1565; this resulted in the show trial and ritual beating up of a former chaplain of St Giles and provoked a riot by the burgh's Catholics on Palm Sunday. On 9 March 1566—the night on which Queen Mary's servant David Riccio was murdered—Fullarton was one of twenty-one burgesses implicated in the killing of the queen's confessor, the Dominican friar John Black. The connection between the two deaths suggests that Fullarton had foreknowledge of both plots and saw them as a means for the radicals to regain control of the town council.

After 1567 Fullarton served as a burgh commissioner: to parliament, to the convention of royal burghs, and to the general assembly, attending the important meeting at Leith in January 1572. He was a dean of guild on the council of the king's party exiled to Leith by the rival queen's party in June 1571. At Leith he was elected captain of the exiles' Edinburgh band, which he helped to provision, and he also lent sizeable sums to the king's lords, little of which seem to have been repaid. The testament of his wife, who died in 1583, recorded almost £1800 of outstanding debts owed by successive regents—Moray, Lennox, and Mar. Fullarton's house was badly damaged during the year-long siege of the burgh (1571–2), and a claim for £3667 against unspecified persons for the spoiling of his goods and property remained unsettled at the time of his wife's death. Their joint estate was then recorded as amounting to £10,717 Scots; however, all but £441 was made up of unpaid debts, many of them unrecoverable. Fullarton himself was not among the merchant élite—he was consistently assessed outside the top 20 per cent of taxpayers.

In February 1575 Fullarton's close links with Regent Morton were rewarded by the grant of a lucrative twelve-year contract for the lead mines at Glengonner, near Leadhills in Lanarkshire, and in Orkney; Fullarton shared the contract with Morton's kinsman George, later known as Douglas of Parkhead. His long devotion to the 'amity' with England, for which he claimed in 1584 to have worked 'nycht and day', brought him into contact with the highest reaches of Elizabeth's government: his 'verre good freindis' included Bedford, Burghley, Hutton, Hunsdon,

Killigrew, and Leicester (*CSP Scot.*, 1584–5, 285). In April 1560 he was sent on a secret mission to England.

In May 1577 Fullarton was appointed an emissary to pursue a series of actions by Scottish merchants against English pirates; the posting lasted over two years, proved largely fruitless, resulted in legal action against him by other Edinburgh merchants, and brought him considerable unpopularity. His uncompromising religious radicalism persisted into his last years. He suffered for his part in the welcome given to the radical minister John Durie, who had been critical of the royal court, on the latter's return to the town in September 1582, and he was himself exiled from the burgh after the Black Acts Parliament of May 1584 and incarcerated in Dumbarton Castle in August that year. By September 1585, however, when he was again sent to lobby Sir Francis Walsingham over the piracy cases, Fullarton seems to have been rehabilitated. A settlement was finally reached in December 1587. The last glimpse of Fullarton in the records comes on 23 June 1595, when his best wishes to Robert Bowes were passed on by an English agent in Edinburgh. His death is not recorded.

MICHAEL LYNCH

Sources M. Lynch, *Edinburgh and the Reformation* (1981), 260, 282, 300 (and the references therein) · M. Sanderson, *Ayrshire and the Reformation* (1997), 46 · J. D. Marwick, ed., *Extracts from the records of the burgh of Edinburgh, AD 1557–1571; 1573–1589*, [3–4], Scottish Burgh RS, 4–5 (1875–82) · *John Knox's History of the Reformation in Scotland*, ed. W. C. Dickinson, 2 vols. (1949) · *The works of John Knox*, ed. D. Laing, 6 vols., Wodrow Society, 12 (1846–64), vol. 4 · *Reg. PCS*, 1st ser., vol. 2 · *CSP Scot., 1584–1603* · Edinburgh testaments, 30 Jan 1584, General Register Office for Scotland, Edinburgh

Fullarton, John (1780?–1849), traveller and writer on currency, was the only child of Gavin Fullarton (d. 1795), a Greenock surgeon, and his wife, Anne (1744–1796), youngest daughter of Alexander *Dunlop, professor of Greek in the University of Glasgow. He went to India as a medical officer in the East India Company, became an assistant surgeon in the Bengal presidency in 1802, but resigned his appointment in 1813. During this period he became the part owner and editor of a newspaper at Calcutta. On leaving the East India Company Fullarton became a partner in the bank Alexander & Co. of Calcutta, acquired an immense fortune in a few years, and returned to England to live. In the meantime he had travelled widely over India, and about 1820 made an extensive and systematic tour through the empire, possibly the first complete progress ever made through Britain's eastern possessions. He collected copious memoranda on his travels, but they were never published.

In 1823 Fullarton purchased Lord Essex's house, 1 Great Stanhope Street, Mayfair, Westminster. During the Reform Bill crisis he contributed several articles to the *Quarterly Review* defending the tory party, and he is said to have been one of the founders of the Carlton Club. During these years he made extensive tours of Great Britain and the continent in a coach fitted up with a library and other luxuries. In 1833 he went again to India, and in the following year visited China. He returned to Europe via Egypt,

where at Memphis his wife, Charlotte, *née* Finney, of Calcutta, died in 1837 leaving an only daughter. In 1838, having lost a considerable part of his fortune through a bank failure, he moved to 12 Hyde Park Street, London.

In 1844, during the progress of the Bank Charter Act through parliament, Fullarton published *On the regulation of currencies, being an examination of the principles on which it is proposed to restrict the future issues on credit of the Bank of England*, in which he attacked the 'currency principle' and supported the views of the economist Thomas Tooke. His work was widely praised, notably in *The Economist* (28 September 1844), and was quoted approvingly in 1848 by John Stuart Mill in his *Political Economy* (bk 3, chap. 24). Robert Torrens, a supporter of the 1844 measure, addressed his pamphlet *The Principles and Practical Operation of Sir Robert Peel's Bill of 1844 Explained and Defended* (1848) in part against Fullarton's work. A fellow of the Royal Asiatic Society, Fullarton died on 24 October 1849.

L. C. SANDERS, rev. K. D. REYNOLDS

Sources private information (1889) · R. H. I. Palgrave, ed., *Dictionary of political economy*, 3 vols. (1894–9) · *The Athenaeum* (3 Nov 1849)
Archives NL Scot., letters to J. G. Lockhart

Fullarton, William, of Fullarton (1754–1808), politician and colonial governor, was born on 12 January 1754, the only son of William Fullarton (d. 1758) of Fullarton, Ayrshire, and Barbara, daughter of William Blair of Blair. While still a child he inherited considerable property in Ayrshire following the death of his father in 1758. A decade on he attended the University of Edinburgh before embarking on a grand tour (1769–71), which extended to Sicily and Malta, with Patrick Brydone for his tutor. In 1774 he entered Lincoln's Inn, but gave up law for diplomacy and in 1775–8 served as secretary to the embassy in Paris. Returning after the outbreak of hostilities with France, he was elected MP for Plympton Erle in April 1779. Though a supporter of Lord North's government he did not stand at the general election of 1780. Instead he resolved to play his part in the now general war between Britain and the continental powers. With official support, he and his best friend, Thomas Humberstone Mackenzie, *de jure* earl of Seaforth, combined in raising regiments on their estates, and Fullarton was gazetted lieutenant-colonel of the 98th on 29 May 1780. His appointment was much criticized by the parliamentary opposition, criticism which led to a duel with Lord Shelburne. The joint forces were originally meant for Mexico, to seize the annual Spanish transport of treasure. Instead, they set off for the Cape of Good Hope, only to see their design on the Dutch colony foiled by prior arrival of French reinforcements.

They continued to India, to help in the war against Haidar Ali of Mysore. Fullarton landed at Madras, and in summer 1781 commenced diversionary operations to lure the enemy out of the Carnatic. In June 1782 he was gazetted colonel a second time, in the army of the East India Company. The following winter he suppressed the Kollars of Madura, and captured Karur and Dindigul. In May 1783 he assumed general command of forces in the southernmost part of the Carnatic, invading Mysore and taking Dharapuram, Palghat, and Coimbatore. Further feats of arms were forestalled by the peace patched up with Tipu, who had succeeded his father, Haidar. Throughout the campaign Fullarton showed high abilities; James Mill in his *History of British India* (1817) praised him as the first British commander to look after his commissariat and organize intelligence. At the peace he returned home. In 1787 he published *A View of the English Interests in India* as a letter to Lord Mansfield, followed by a second letter to Lord Macartney containing an account of his campaigns. This self-advertisement did not serve to recoup the £20,000 he claimed to have spent in India, without which he had to consider entering foreign service; he got £15,750 back in the end, though only a decade later. He never took the field again, but contented himself with raising the 23rd, or Fullarton's dragoons, in 1794, and the 101st, or Fullarton's foot, in 1800.

Fullarton had meanwhile settled down to life on his Ayrshire estates. On 18 June 1792 he married Marianne Mackay, daughter of George, fifth Lord Reay; they had one daughter. He took a great interest in agricultural improvement, and published two memoirs on its progress, including a *General View of the Agriculture of the County of Ayr* (1793). At this time he was also elected a fellow of the royal societies of Edinburgh and London. In June 1787 he resumed his parliamentary career, as member for Haddington burghs (until 1790) and later Horsham (1793–6) and Ayrshire (1796–1803). As a former supporter of Lord North, he first sat with the opposition. He proved his worth as a spokesman on India with attacks on Warren Hastings, and was destined for the Board of Control if the whigs had regained power. Instead he fell victim to Henry Dundas's dominance of Scottish politics, and lost his seat in the general election of 1790. He compounded his offences by joining the Friends of the People, representing Ayrshire in their first Scottish convention in July 1792. But mayhem in France disillusioned him, and the fresh outbreak of war in the following year changed his mind decisively. Under the colours of a Portland whig, he passed over into support for the government. His patriotic zeal commended him to his native county in the general election of 1796. But it failed to win him office, after Dundas stated bluntly that he would 'never be forgiven' (Port, 3.844). Fullarton therefore had to wait five years for a change of administration. The new prime minister, Henry Addington, conceded that the eventual offer in 1802 of becoming first commissioner to Trinidad was 'inadequate to his just pretensions' (ibid., 845). An annual salary of £3000, and a condition that he could keep his seat in parliament, made it bearable. With perhaps excessive glee, Dundas had him unseated for holding an office of profit as soon as he was out of the country.

Trinidad offered little solace. Since its capture from Spain in 1797, it had been run by a military regime under Colonel Thomas *Picton. The intention was to keep him on as one member of a ruling commission of three, in which the others would be Commodore Samuel Hood of the Royal Navy and Fullarton as political officer and head. Personal difficulties with Picton, who had in effect been demoted, inevitably followed. More to the point, policy

was to change. Picton had subordinated everything to the needs, as he saw them, of making the island a redoubt in an anti-revolutionary war. He changed as little as possible in Spanish laws and usages, while welcoming aristocratic refugees with their slaves from the French islands and granting them lands. But now that peace was apparently on the way and whiggery had become respectable again, new influences bore even on distant Trinidad. Abolitionist hopes rose, so there could be no point in encouraging an economy of plantations. An alternative was to attract free settlers who would make the island a base for British trade to South America, though the continent would first have to cast off the Spanish yoke, presumably by revolutionary means. This was why General Francisco Miranda, then in London, enjoyed such official favour; Fullarton met him before departure and took along one or two of his agents to Trinidad. In major respects, the first commissioner seemed the ideal man for the job: carrying away from India a disgust with loot and pillage, and having since found no outlet for his benevolent instincts; now belonging to the right party and combining in his political outlook the patriotic, the humanitarian, and the radical.

But all was to shatter on the rock of Picton. The harshness of his rule, if legal under preserved Spanish forms, aroused Fullarton's unfavourable notice immediately on arrival in Trinidad in January 1803. When the first commissioner asked for a return of all criminal proceedings over the last six years, Picton offered his resignation to the British government. Though getting no support from Hood, Fullarton persisted in his inquiries. They fully occupied the seven months he spent on the island. Replaced by a new governor, he then went back to London to report. The eventual result was the trial of Picton for extorting confession of a certain Luisa Calderón; he had authorized her interrogation by means of the 'picket', by which she was suspended from one wrist with her weight resting only on a sharp pointed stake. The horror of this cruel punishment caused a huge sensation in Britain, fuelled by pictures and indignant pamphlets from both sides, including Fullarton's *Statement, Letters and Documents, Respecting the Affairs of Trinidad* (1804). Questions of colonial policy were overtaken by the self-justification and hatred of the two principals. The first trial before Lord Ellenborough, in February 1806, found Picton guilty. But the affair dragged on. Picton applied for a new trial, at which, supported by the war hero Hood, he was acquitted in June 1808. Fullarton had, however, already died of inflammation of the lungs at Gordon's Hotel, London, on 13 February 1808. He was buried at Isleworth, Middlesex. Miranda exclaimed: 'Murió Fullarton! Casi sin llamar la atención pública' ('Fullarton died! And the public scarcely noticed'; Naipaul, 327).   MICHAEL FRY

Sources DNB · M. H. Port, 'Fullarton, William', HoP, *Commons, 1790–1820* · V. S. Naipaul, 'The torture of Luisa Calderón', *The loss of El Dorado* (1973), 155–368 · H. B. Robinson, *Memoir of Lieutenant-General Picton* (1835) · E. A. Draper, *An address to the British public on the case of Brigadier-General Picton* (1806) · State trials, vol. 30 · R. Harvard, *Wellington's Welsh general: a life of Sir Thomas Picton* (1996)

Archives BL OIOC, corresp. relating to India · National Archives of India, New Delhi, official papers | BL, letters to Sir John Coxe Hippisley, Add. MS 41622 · NA Scot., corresp. with H. Dundas, GD 51 · NA Scot., Stirling Homes MSS, letters to Lord Kames, GD 24/584 · NRA Scotland, priv. coll., corresp. N. Macleod · PRO, Pitt MSS, letters to W. Pitt, PRO 30/8

Fuller family (*per. c.*1650–1803), gun-founders and landowners, came to prominence with John [i] Fuller (1617–1679), the son of Samuel Fuller, of Waldron, Sussex, and his wife, Joan, daughter of Stephen French, of Chiddingly, Sussex. He married Ann, the daughter of John Nutt, of Selmeston, Sussex. In 1650, together with Sir Thomas Dyke, he obtained from his maternal grandfather the lease of Stream iron furnace, Chiddingly, where ordnance was cast in the 1660s. He was succeeded by his second son, John [ii] Fuller (1652–1722), a major in the trained bands, who continued to work the furnace at Stream until 1693, when he leased land at Heathfield, Sussex, on which he built a new furnace in the same year.

John [iii] **Fuller** (*bap.* 1680, *d.* 1745), ironmaster and gun-founder, was the eldest son of John [ii] Fuller, of Tanners, Waldron, Sussex, and his wife, Elizabeth, the daughter of Samuel Fowle of London. He was baptized at Waldron on 28 July 1680. On 20 July 1703 he married Elizabeth (*bap.* 1681, *d.* 1728), daughter of Fulke Rose, of Jamaica, and his wife, Elizabeth, who later married Hans Sloane. The marriage settlement brought a large fortune from sugar plantations in St Katherine's and St John's parishes in Jamaica, the income from which formed an increasingly significant element in the family's wealth. In 1705 he took possession of Brightling Park, which he renamed Rose Hill, in honour of his wife. During the ensuing years a substantial amount of property in the Brightling and Burwash areas was purchased. It is likely that he took control of the family's furnace at Heathfield as early as 1703, when the first furnace account book was begun, and thereafter the accounts (at East Sussex Record Office) form a number of series. In 1713 he was elected MP for Sussex, but did not stand for re-election when parliament was dissolved in 1715. In 1716 he purchased Burwash forge from William Western, having worked it since 1700. During the peace of the 1720s and 1730s Fuller kept Heathfield furnace at work supplying Sussex forges with pig iron, returning to large scale ordnance production at the onset of war in 1739. Fuller favoured a protectionist policy in respect of the importation of iron, seeing the reinvigoration of the English, and not least the wealden, iron industry as a means of providing employment as well as improving the quality of iron produced. In 1734 he unsuccessfully contested one of the Sussex parliamentary seats, espousing the tory anti-excise cause. Fuller died on 4 August 1745 at Rose Hill, Brightling, and was buried on 10 August at Waldron.

John [iv] [Jacky] **Fuller** (1706–1755), ironmaster and gun-founder, was the eldest of the ten children of John [iii] Fuller and his wife, Elizabeth. He was born on 1 February 1706. In 1723 he went up to Trinity College, Cambridge, and in 1724 was admitted to the Middle Temple. He was elected FRS in 1726. On the death of his father in 1745 he took over the estate and its ironworks in a period of great

demand for ordnance. The late settlement of accounts by the Board of Ordnance, the main purchaser of the family's guns, caused Fuller much concern. The reputation of Fuller guns was such, however, that a number of orders were received from foreign states. In August 1746, at Croydon, Surrey, he married Elizabeth, daughter of Francis Dayrell, of Shudy Camps, Cambridge. There were no children from the marriage. In the same year he was appointed a justice of the peace. In 1750 he dispensed with the services of the family's Ordnance agent of more than twenty years, Samuel Remnant, concerned that he was not receiving a fair distribution of contracts compared with the other gun-founders that Remnant represented. In December 1754 Fuller was elected as MP for the duke of Newcastle's constituency at Boroughbridge, Yorkshire. He died on 5 February 1755 at Rose Hill, and was buried on 12 February at Waldron.

Rose Fuller (1708–1777), politician, gun-founder, and landowner, the second son of John [iii] Fuller, was born on 12 April 1708. He studied medicine at Trinity College, Cambridge, from 1725 to 1728, and from 1729 to 1732 at the University of Leiden. He graduated MD from Cambridge in 1732. He was elected FRS in 1732. In 1733 he was sent by his father to Jamaica, to supervise the family's sugar estates. In April 1737 he married Ithamar (*c.*1720–1738), daughter of the Hon. Richard Mill, of St Katherine's, Jamaica, and in the same year was appointed to the Jamaica council. The island's council and assembly contained strong factions for and against the governor; Fuller joined the opposition. The couple had one son, who was stillborn. Ithamar Fuller died on 22 April 1738, but the marriage had brought Rose Fuller financial security. In 1740 he was dismissed from the council by Governor Trelawny, and was elected to the Jamaica assembly. He now led the faction against Governor Trelawny and, having returned to England in 1748, used his family's friendship with the duke of Newcastle to gain support against Trelawny, with whom, however, he was reconciled in 1751. Fuller was appointed chief justice by the new governor, Admiral Knowles, in 1753, but he was soon in opposition to him over the latter's plan to move the island's capital to Kingston. He resigned as chief justice over the dismissal of a fellow judge but in 1755 returned to England on inheriting the Sussex estates. In the following year he was elected MP for New Romney, and in 1761 for Maidstone. That year he was appointed a justice of the peace. Fuller, unlike his father, had whig sympathies, and supported the duke of Newcastle's faction. In parliament he was an important spokesman for Jamaica, and spoke frequently on American affairs. In 1765 the decrease in the price offered for guns by the Board of Ordnance, occasioned by the Carron Company's low tender for orders, caused Fuller to withdraw from the manufacture of guns for the government. In the next decade, when Carron guns repeatedly failed the Ordnance board proofs (or tests of quality), Fuller and his brother Stephen tried again to tender for business but met with only limited success; within ten years, however, increased income from the Jamaica estates had almost compensated for the financial loss. As in their father's time Heathfield furnace returned to serving the needs of a diminishing number of local forges. In 1768 Rose Fuller was elected MP for Rye, the seat he held until his death on 7 May 1777, at Gerrard Street, London. At his death his landed estate amounted to 5584 acres. He was buried at Waldron on 15 May.

Stephen Fuller (1716–1799), merchant and agent for the Jamaica assembly, John [iii] Fuller's seventh son, was born on 26 November 1716. He was educated at Tonbridge School and, from 1734, at Trinity College, Cambridge, where he was a scholar, and elected fellow in 1741. On 8 July 1744 he married Elizabeth (Betsy), daughter of Laurence Noakes of Brightling. The couple had five daughters. On the death of his eldest brother, John [iv], he took charge of the Sussex estates and ironworks in the interim before his brother Rose returned from Jamaica. He continued to have a management role in both thereafter, and lived at Brightling. He was appointed justice of the peace in 1761. From 1764 until his death he was English agent for the Jamaica assembly and with his brother did much to further the Jamaica interest, being the author of several pamphlets, notably on slavery. He died on 8 September 1799 at South Stoneham, Hampshire. His wife predeceased him; she was buried on 9 March 1753. The Fuller estate was inherited, on the death of Rose Fuller, by his nephew, John [v] Fuller (1757–1834)—known as Honest John or Mad Jack Fuller—who maintained Heathfield furnace in operation, supplying local forges with pig iron, until 1787. The forge at Burwash closed in 1803.

In the diversity of their interests the Fullers were not typical of their wealden contemporaries. Long-term investment in agriculture was the basis of their wealth, and their Jamaica estates eventually made large profits; in their political activities, with the exception of Rose Fuller, they were largely unambitious; and in the manufacture of iron they were not numbered among the innovators of their age. Where their significance lies is in the wealth of letters and accounts which have survived and the light which they shed, not only on the family's interests, but on the provincial, colonial, political, and commercial life of the time.   J. S. HODGKINSON

Sources M. C. L. Salt, 'The Fullers of Brightling Park [3 pts]', *Sussex Archaeological Collections*, 104 (1966), 63–87; 106 (1968), 73–88; 107 (1969), 14–24 • [J. Fuller], *The Fuller letters: guns, slaves and finance, 1728–1755*, ed. D. Crossley and R. Saville, Suffolk RS, 76 (1991) • R. V. Saville, 'Gentry wealth on the Weald in the eighteenth century: the Fullers of Brightling Park', *Sussex Archaeological Collections*, 121 (1983), 129–47 • G. Metcalf, *Royal government and political conflict in Jamaica, 1729–1783* (1965) • HoP, *Commons, 1754–90*, 2.476–80 • R. V. Saville, 'Income and production at Heathfield ironworks, 1693–1788', *Wealden Iron*, 2nd ser., 2 (1982), 36–63 • H. Blackman, 'Gunfounding at Heathfield in the XVIII century', *Sussex Archaeological Collections*, 67 (1926), 25–54 • parish register, Waldron, 28 July 1680 [baptism, John [iii] Fuller] • E. Sussex RO, Raper papers, SAS/RF • E. Sussex RO, Fovargue papers, SAS/RAF • E. Sussex RO, PAR 254/1/1/2 [baptism, John [iv] Fuller] • parish register, Brightling, 19 April 1708, E. Sussex RO, PAR 254/1/1/2 [baptism, Rose Fuller] • parish register, Brightling, 27 Dec 1716, E. Sussex RO, PAR/1/1/2 [baptism, Stephen Fuller] • Venn, *Alum. Cant.*
Archives E. Sussex RO, family papers | E. Sussex RO, Raper and Fovargue papers, SAS/RF, RAF • Som. ARS, Dickenson papers, DD/DN

Likenesses L. Hubner, group portrait, oils, 1734, Herington's (solicitors), 1 Upper Lake, Battle, East Sussex
Wealth at death £3300—John [iii] Fuller: Saville, 'Gentry wealth', 143 • £5000—John [iv] Fuller: Saville, 'Gentry wealth', 143 • £6000—Rose Fuller: Saville, 'Gentry wealth', 143

Fuller, Andrew (1754–1815), Baptist minister and theologian, was born at Wicken, Cambridgeshire, on 6 February 1754. He was the youngest of three sons of Robert Fuller, farmer, and Philippa Gunton (*d.* 1816), daughter of Andrew Gunton of Soham, Cambridgeshire. He attended the village school at Soham, and when he was about six the family moved to that village. As a youth he worked on the land. When he was sixteen he was converted and in April 1770 was baptized in Soham Baptist Church. Soon afterwards a church member, guilty of excessive drinking, excused himself by claiming that he could not keep himself from evil. This incident made the young Fuller think out for himself the relationship between human responsibility and divine sovereignty. It also led to controversy in the church, as a result of which the hyper-Calvinist pastor left the church and Fuller took his place, encouraged by Joseph Diver, an older man with whom Fuller struck up a deep friendship. Although acting as pastor of the church he was not ordained until May 1775, when he came in touch with the Northamptonshire Association and with ministers such as the elder Robert Hall, John Sutcliff, and John Collett Ryland, whose thinking was moving in the same direction as his own. Believing that the hyper-Calvinism then widespread among Particular Baptists obscured the great evangelical truths of Christianity, he set out his thoughts in writing. Two days before Christmas, in 1776, he married his first wife, Sarah Gardiner (*bap.* 1756, *d.* 1792), daughter of Stephen and Sarah Gardiner of Burwell. Of this marriage there were eleven children, only two of whom survived their father. The closing years of Fuller's ministry at Soham were hard in the extreme, financially and spiritually, and in 1779 he almost died.

Surprisingly, therefore, Fuller was reluctant to leave Soham when he received a call to the Kettering church. Eventually, he moved there in October 1782. According to custom, he had to wait for a year until his ordination. When he went there membership was 88; by the time of his death it was 174, though his congregation was nearer 1000. He entered into Northamptonshire Association life, and on 23 June 1784 preached the association sermon 'Walking by Faith', to which he appended 'Some persuasives to united prayer for the revival of real religion' in preparing it for publication. The influence of Jonathan Edwards is clear. Fuller's thoughts now turned to his as yet unpublished manuscript, which he now, in 1785, published as *The Gospel Worthy of All Acceptation*. Its scope and overriding concerns are indicated by its subtitle: 'The duty of sinners to believe in Jesus Christ'. There followed a war of words against the critics of 'Fullerism', notably Abraham Booth, Dan Taylor, and Archibald McLean. On 30 May 1786 his six-year-old daughter Sarah died, and in his sorrow he found even preaching difficult.

Andrew Fuller (1754–1815), by J. Morrison (after Robert Bowyer)

foundations for mission at home and abroad. In his later writings he worked out the implications of his 'leading principles', which he defended against attacks from hyper-Calvinists like William Button on the one hand and the Arminian Dan Taylor on the other. He championed Christian orthodoxy in *The Gospel its Own Witness* (1799), his most outstanding work of Christian defence, written as a reply to Paine's *Age of Reason*. He also opposed Unitarians such as Priestley, Belsham, and Lindsey, and the Universalist William Vidler.

Fuller never forgot that he was a pastor. He was blessed with a powerful voice and the ability to express himself clearly. Moreover, he possessed a remarkable store of physical and mental energy which enabled him to work at his desk ten hours a day, though seldom free of headaches. Slow and deliberate in his thinking, he was accurate and thorough in everything he did. He had an intimate knowledge of affairs in the religious world. Closely in touch with influential persons in business and in parliament, he was no stranger to the group of evangelical churchmen at Clapham, which included Wilberforce. Despite his severe manner, he had a deep concern for people. Andrew Fuller was a man of remarkable achievement. His contribution to theology was recognized by the award of the degree of DD by Princeton (1798) and Yale (1805), though characteristically he declined to use the title of doctor. Worn out by his labours, he died at his home, the Baptist manse, Kettering on 7 May 1815 and was buried there on 15 May, unquestionably one of the outstanding evangelical leaders of his day.

E. F. CLIPSHAM

Sources *The complete works of the rev. Andrew Fuller, with a memoir of his life*, ed. A. G. Fuller, 5 vols. (1831–2) · J. Ryland, *The work of faith, the labour of love, and the patience of hope illustrated in the life and death of the Rev. Andrew Fuller* (1816) · G. Laws, *Andrew Fuller, pastor, theologian, ropeholder* (1942) · E. F. Clipsham, 'Andrew Fuller and Fullerism', *Baptist Quarterly*, 20 (1963–4), 99–114, 146–54, 214–25, 268–76 · E. F. Clipsham, 'Andrew Fuller and the Baptist mission', *Foundations*, 10 (1967), 1–15 · *DNB* · *IGI* · G. F. Nuttall, 'Northamptonshire and *The modern question*: a turning-point in eighteenth-century dissent', *Journal of Theological Studies*, new ser., 16 (1965), 101–23

Archives Kettering Baptist Church, Kettering, Kettering Baptist Church archives, MSS · Regent's Park College, Oxford, Angus Library, corresp. and notebook · SOAS, corresp. and notebook | Regent's Park College, Oxford, Angus Library, letters to J. Sutcliff

Likenesses N. Branwhite, stipple, pubd 1816, NPG · J. Morrison, engraving (after R. Bowyer), NPG; repro. in *Complete works of … Andrew Fuller* [*see illus.*] · engraving, repro. in Laws, *Andrew Fuller* · oils, Regent's Park College, Oxford

Further sorrows followed: in April 1792 Beeby Wallis, Fuller's senior deacon, died, and that August his wife died in childbirth, having spent her last few months mentally confused.

However 2 October 1792 saw the formation of the Baptist Missionary Society (BMS) with Fuller as its secretary. He gave himself unstintingly to the mission. While not a great administrator, his critical judgement, his firm grasp of missionary principles, and his ability to understand not only the missionaries but also the religious public enabled him to give the kind of leadership that the BMS needed in its early years. To Fuller his position was a sacred trust arising from a vow to William Carey to 'hold the rope', while he penetrated what was compared to a deep unexplored goldmine. Though supported by able men, the responsibility rested squarely on his shoulders. In 1794 his thoughts turned once again to marriage and on 30 December he married Ann Coles (1764–1825), daughter of the Revd William Coles and his wife, Anne, of Maulden, Bedfordshire. They had six children, three of whom died in infancy. Fuller preached throughout the country for the mission, corresponded with the missionaries, and pleaded their cause in high places. His *Apology for the Late Christian Missions to India* was written in 1807–8 at a critical time. When the East India Company's charter was renewed in 1813, his efforts to get permission for nonepiscopal missionaries to serve there were rewarded. However, it is as a theologian that he is chiefly remembered. His admission of the reality of human freedom without denying divine sovereignty freed his denomination from the tyranny of hyper-Calvinism, laying the

Fuller, Sir (Joseph) Bampfylde (1854–1935), administrator in India and author, was born on 20 March 1854 at Newton, Somerset. The eldest son of Joseph Fuller (1824–1903), later vicar of Ramsdale, Hampshire, and his wife, Anne Isabella, daughter of Charles Bampfylde, rector of Hemington and Dunkerton, Somerset, he was educated at Marlborough College and secured the first place in the Indian Civil Service examination of 1873. Reaching India in 1875, his first posting was in the North-Western Provinces, but in 1882 he was transferred to the Central Provinces. Here he served with distinction in the settlement and agriculture department, framing the settlement code of the Central Provinces (1891), and compiling some settlement reports. The Indian government appointed him secretary of revenue and agriculture in 1901.

In 1905 Lord Curzon partitioned Bengal, separating from Bengal the new province of eastern Bengal and Assam. Fuller, who had a brief stint as the officiating chief commissioner of Assam, was a natural choice for the lieutenant-governorship of the new province. In his new office he sought to fulfil the dual needs of the raj—playing Muslims and Hindus against each other, and suppressing the anti-partition *swadeshi* movement. When the anti-partition agitation underwent a shift towards terrorism, Fuller became a target for the revolutionaries, but assassination attempts proved abortive. Fuller did find an ally for the imperial policy of 'divide and rule' in Muslim separatism, but many Bengali Muslims supported the *swadeshi* agitations. Joint Hindu–Muslim processions during the agitations were also common. Some commentators have claimed that the press deliberately inflated reports of Fuller's measures against *swadeshi* 'lawlessness', but such conjectures seem dubious in the context of the displeasure evinced by both Lord Minto, the viceroy, and John Morley, the secretary of state, over Fuller's overreaction to the *swadeshi* turmoil: Minto privately confessed that Fuller 'lacked the qualities of patience and discretion which could alone in time abate the partition ferment'. That Fuller and Minto failed to see eye to eye on many official matters became apparent in July 1906, when Fuller shot a petulant letter to Minto, hinting that he would reconsider his position if his advice on a particular issue was rejected. Minto promptly accepted this letter as Fuller's resignation, and in parliament Morley resolutely defended Minto's actions, rebutting criticisms that the 'man on the spot' had been ill-treated. The disgruntled Fuller complained to his colleague H. Le Mesurier, on 4 August 1906, that 'the partition was launched under circumstances which we had to bring to shipwreck, either the partition or the man who was charged with its introduction. The latter has happened … Morley has sacrificed me to his noisy adherents' (Fuller to H. Le Mesurier, 4 Aug 1906, BL OIOC). Back in England, Fuller utilized occasions such as the annual Assam and Calcutta dinners to ventilate his grievances against the British Indian government. Annulment of the Bengal partition in 1911—the unsettling of what the raj had once considered a 'settled fact'—provoked Fuller's violent disapproval.

In retirement, Fuller, who had been made KCSI in 1906, travelled extensively, thrice returning to India itself. He also became a prolific author on philosophical subjects, beginning with *Life and Human Nature* (1914). Other works included *Man as he is: Essays in a New Psychology* (1916), *The Science of Ourselves: a Sequel to the 'Descent of Man'* (1921), *Causes and Consequences* (1923) and *Etheric Energies* (1928). Only a few months before his death he completed *The Tyranny of the Mind: a Commonsense Psychology* (1935). He also published a number of works about India; the first, written in 1882 with John Firminger Duthie, was entitled *Field and Garden Crops of the North-Western Provinces and Oudh*. His *Studies in Indian Life and Sentiment* (1910) and his *Empire of India* (1913) are redolent of a colonial perception of India. Justifying the repression of rising Indian nationalist sentiment, he wrote that, 'seditious opposition, if firmly encountered, loses its bitterness in respect for the state'. Fuller extolled British rule in India for its 'efficiency' and 'benevolence' that could 'surpass many European governments'. These claims—described in 1949 as 'non-controversial' (*DNB*)—have been dismissed by modern historians and nationalists, who juxtapose them to the de-industrialization of the Indian economy, the draining of Indian wealth, and the extreme racism that characterized British rule in the subcontinent. In celebrating the raj as the best guarantor of peace between contending castes and communities in India, Fuller anticipated Churchill's defence of the empire along similar lines, which was to provoke Mahatma Gandhi's retort that the British should nevertheless leave India, handing her to 'God and anarchy'.

Fuller served on the bench of magistrates at Winchester and concerned himself with municipal and philanthropic matters. During the First World War he was initially a temporary major in the Army Ordnance Corps, but subsequently became a director of timber supplies at the War Office. He was married three times, but had no children. His first marriage, in 1879, was to Maria Caldwell (*d.* 1880), fourth daughter of Colonel Henry Aston of the Bombay staff corps. In 1884 he married Sarah Augusta (*d.* 1923), fourth daughter of Arthur Wellesley Critchley. His third marriage, in 1924, was to Gabrielle Marie Adèle, daughter of Professor Eugène Rousselin. He published *Some Personal Experiences* in 1930. Fuller died at his home, the Red House, Marlborough, on 29 November 1935.

F. H. BROWN, rev. SURANJAN DAS

Sources *The Times* (30 Nov 1935) · Mary, countess of Minto, *India: Minto and Morley, 1905–1910* (1934) · J. Buchan, *Lord Minto: a memoir* (1924) · L. Fraser, *India under Curzon and after* (1911) · J. B. Fuller, *Some personal experiences* (1930) · BL OIOC, H. Le Mesurier MSS
Archives London Library, typescript of *Natural Christianity, or The Garden of Christianity* · National Archives of India, letters of Fuller and his wife to G. P. Mathur and his daughter | BL OIOC, letters to Sir Louis Kershaw, MS Eur. D 1056 · BL OIOC, H. Le Mesurier MSS · BL OIOC, Morley MSS
Likenesses portrait, Government House, Shillong, India
Wealth at death £19,961 19*s.* 9*d.*: resworn probate, 17 Jan 1936, *CGPLA Eng. & Wales*

Fuller, Sir Cyril Thomas Moulden (1874–1942), naval officer, was born on 22 May 1874 at Clarence House, West Cowes, the son of Thomas Fuller, late captain in the 18th hussars, and his wife, Mary Ada, daughter of Frederick William Fryer. Entering the Royal Navy in 1887 Fuller served in the Mediterranean as a cadet and later as midshipman in the battleship *Collingwood* from November 1889 and as a midshipman in the battleship *Trafalgar* from May 1890. He was promoted sub-lieutenant in October 1893 and, after passing first class in all his examinations and winning the Goodenough medal for gunnery, was promoted lieutenant on 14 April 1894, a few weeks before his twentieth birthday. After serving on the China station as a watchkeeper in the cruiser *Rainbow* he returned to the

United Kingdom to specialize in gunnery and was appointed gunnery officer of the battleship *Canopus* in the Mediterranean Fleet in December 1899. He joined the senior staff of the gunnery school at Portsmouth in January 1902. While there he did much of the preparation of the report of a committee on control of fire in action. On 26 July 1902 he married Edith Margaret (*d.* 1947), daughter of Charles Connell, shipbuilder, of Rozelle, Glasgow. They had two sons and two daughters.

Fuller was promoted commander in December 1903 at the early age of twenty-nine. For a short time he served as executive officer of the battleship *Majestic* but in February 1905 he joined the battleship *King Edward VII* as flag commander to Sir William May, the commander-in-chief, Atlantic Fleet. From 1908 to 1910 he commanded the dispatch vessel *Alacrity* in China. After his early promotion to captain in December 1910 he served for nearly three years on the staff of the inspector of target practice, assisting the committee on aim detector trials and later on director trials.

In May 1914 Fuller returned to sea in command of the cadet training cruiser *Cumberland*. After the outbreak of war in August 1914 the *Cumberland* was employed in the operations against German territory in the Cameroons, where Fuller was senior naval officer. In November he transferred to the light cruiser *Challenger* and in March 1915 to the light cruiser *Astraea*. He had been appointed CMG in January and in 1916 was appointed DSO in recognition of the ability and success with which he had organized the Cameroons naval operations.

On returning home Fuller was appointed, in August 1916, to the command of the new battle cruiser *Repulse* in the Grand Fleet, but in October 1917, after serving for a month in the intelligence division, became with Dudley Pound an assistant director of the newly formed plans division of the naval staff of the Admiralty. He succeeded Roger Keyes as director in January 1918 and in this capacity headed the naval section of the peace conference in Paris in 1919. In October 1919 he was gazetted CB.

Fuller's next appointment was that of chief of staff to Sir Charles Madden, the commander-in-chief, Atlantic Fleet, in the battleship *Queen Elizabeth*. In June 1921 he was promoted rear-admiral and on 1 December 1922 became a lord commissioner of the Admiralty and assistant chief of the naval staff, but in May 1923 was appointed third sea lord and controller of the navy. Then, in April 1925, he returned to sea in command of the battle-cruiser squadron with his flag in the *Hood*. He reached vice-admiral's rank in July 1926 and was appointed KCB in 1928.

In the spring of 1928 Fuller became commander-in-chief, North America and West Indies, and on his promotion to admiral two years later, in May 1930, was appointed second sea lord and chief of naval personnel. His term of office proved to be one of exceptional difficulty. It was a period of severe retrenchment following the conclusion of the London naval conference in April 1930, and it has been written that he was not a success (Roskill, 2.70). He was still in office when the financial crisis of 1931 led to the naval rising at Invergordon. Although his connection

with the incident was perhaps only nominal, as a member of the Board of Admiralty his career, like those of his brother members, suffered. When he left the Admiralty in August 1932 he was offered the command at Plymouth, but declined, and was not again employed, being placed on the retired list in 1935. During his long naval career he had received several foreign decorations: he was a commander of the Légion d'honneur and of the order of the Crown of Italy and a member of the order of the Rising Sun of Japan; he held the French Croix de Guerre, the American DSM, and the Board of Trade medal for saving the lives of two Africans at some risk in the Cameroon River. He died at Whilton Lodge, Long Buckby, Northamptonshire, on 1 February 1942.

J. H. LHOYD-OWEN, *rev.* A. W. H. PEARSALL

Sources *The Times* (3 Feb 1942) • J. S. Corbett, *Naval operations*, 1 (1920) • S. W. Roskill, *Naval policy between the wars*, 2 vols. (1968–76) • F. C. Dreyer, *The sea heritage: a study in maritime warfare* (1955), 296 • A. E. M. Chatfield, *The navy and defence: the autobiography of Admiral of the Fleet Lord Chatfield*, 2: *It might happen again* (1947), 27 • K. G. B. Dewar, *The navy from within* (1939), 243, 257 • D. Divine, *Mutiny at Invergordon* (1970), 234–7 • C. Cato, *The navy everywhere* (1919), 61–102 • record of career, PRO, ADM 196/43, p. 460 • *CGPLA Eng. & Wales* (1942) • private information (1959) • personal knowledge (1959)
Archives NMM, corresp. and papers • NMM, MSS relating to the Cameroons campaign
Likenesses W. Stoneman, two photographs, 1930, NPG • M. Bone, chalk and watercolour drawing, IWM
Wealth at death £9884 12*s*. 5*d*.: administration, 6 Aug 1942, *CGPLA Eng. & Wales*

Fuller, Francis (1636?–1701), clergyman and ejected minister, was the son of John Fuller (*d.* 1660), then vicar of Stebbing, Essex, and later rector of St Martin Pomeroy, Ironmonger Lane, London, and his wife, Dorcas. He was the younger brother of Thomas Fuller and Samuel *Fuller, both scholars and clergymen, who unlike Francis conformed at the Restoration. With a view to entering the ministry Fuller was admitted to Queens' College, Cambridge, on 18 April 1653. He graduated BA from Pembroke College in 1656 and proceeded MA from Queens' in 1660 (incorporated at Oxford in 1663). He was ordained by his uncle Thomas *Fuller, bishop of Ardfert and later archbishop of Cashel, who performed illicit ordinations in Essex during the interregnum. Francis's first ministerial appointment was as curate of Warkworth in the parish of Marston St Lawrence, Northamptonshire, to its incumbent Dr Temple; but he was unable to conform and was ejected from his living, though the date of his ejection is unclear. When he took out the licence to marry Bridget Rogers, a widow of Daventry, on 7 March 1665 he still appears as a resident of Warkworth, aged twenty-nine, but that their marriage took place in London the same day (in St Andrew by the Wardrobe) suggests that he may have moved to the capital by then. The couple had two sons, Samuel (who died young in 1682) and Francis *Fuller, the author of *Medicina gymnastica* (1705).

After his ejection Fuller became an itinerant preacher, alternating between London and the west of England, especially the cities of Bristol and Bath. He was licensed under the declaration of indulgence as a 'general Presbyterian teacher' at Bristol on 28 October 1672. On 19 April 1683 John Sherstone, a member of Bath corporation, was presented at the Bath sessions for, among other acts of disaffection, harbouring in his house 'Fuller, a Nonconformist preacher, who ought not to dwell within this city and stands presented for the same' (*Calamy rev.*, 562). In 1690 Fuller was at Bristol, a minister without a fixed charge. He finally accepted a settled ministry in 1695 when he became assistant to Timothy Cruso at the Presbyterian meeting at Crutched Friars, Mark Lane, London, where he remained until his death, becoming assistant to Cruso's successor William Harris in 1697.

Fuller was the author of a number of religious works, some of which earned the praise of the eighteenth-century Presbyterian minister Job Orton as 'very excellent, entertaining and useful' (Palmer, 3.46). His first known publication was *A Treatise of Grace and Duty*, a discourse on self-denial, published in 1684 and reprinted the following year. In 1685 he published *Words to Give the Young-man Knowledg and Discretion, or, The Law of Kindness in the Tongue of a Father to his Son*, a work of instruction dedicated to his son Francis. It had been written several years before: its dedicatory epistle, dated at Bath on 8 December 1682, movingly alludes to the death of 'Dear Sam' (sig. A3r). This was followed by *A Treatise of Grace and Duty* (1689), *Some Rules how to Use the World, so as not to Abuse either That, or Our Selves* (1695), and *Peace in War by Christ, the Prince of Peace*, a sermon preached on 26 June 1696 and published the same year. Fuller's final publication was a sermon entitled *On the Shortness of Time* (1700).

Fuller died in London on 21 July 1701 at the age of sixty-four. His funeral sermon, dedicated to his widow and his son Francis, was preached by Jeremiah White and was published the following year. Fuller was, White reminded his hearers:

> a downright Honest Englishman ... ever faithful to that Call and Interest, which asserted our Civil and Spiritual Rights. And he wisely placed our Civil Liberties in the first Order. For we never were, nor can be assaulted in our Spiritual, till we are first invaded in our Civil Liberties.   (White, 117)

M. J. MERCER

Sources *Calamy rev.*, 215, 562 · W. Wilson, *The history and antiquities of the dissenting churches and meeting houses in London, Westminster and Southwark*, 4 vols. (1808–14), vol. 1, pp. 56, 64–6 · J. White, *A funeral sermon preached upon the death of Revd. Francis Fuller* (1702), 110–17 · Venn, *Alum. Cant.*, 1/2.184 · A. Gordon, ed., *Freedom after ejection: a review (1690–1692) of presbyterian and congregational nonconformity in England and Wales* (1917), 268 · *The nonconformist's memorial ... originally written by ... Edmund Calamy*, ed. S. Palmer, [3rd edn], 3 vols. (1802–3), vol. 1, p. 159; vol. 3, p. 46 · Surman, index of nonconformist ministers, DWL · IGI

Fuller, Francis (1670–1706), medical practitioner, was born at Bristol, the second son of Francis *Fuller (1636?–1701), nonconformist preacher, and his wife, Bridget. In 1687 he entered St John's College, Cambridge, where he graduated BA in 1691 and MA in 1704. He had severe hypochondriasis following his over-vigorous external treatment of an attack of itch. The hypochondriasis was accompanied by dyspepsia, and he cured himself by exercise on horseback and by emetics. This led him to write a book on the use of exercise in the treatment of disease, called *Medicina gymnastica, or, A treatise concerning the power of exercise, with respect to the animal economy, and the great necessity of it in the cure of several distempers* (1705). A second edition was published in the same year, a third in 1707, a fifth in 1718, a sixth in 1728, and a ninth and last in 1777. Sydenham had been an advocate for fresh air and exercise as remedies in consumption and hypochondriasis, and Fuller enlarged on his suggestions. He showed limited knowledge of disease; he thought highly of millipedes in the treatment of rheumatism, and of liquorice in that of consumption, but had the merit of recommending the regular use of 'chafing', or massage, where exercise through movement is impossible. He died in June 1706.

NORMAN MOORE, *rev.* MICHAEL BEVAN

Sources T. Fuller, *Words to give the young man knowledge* (1685) · Munk, *Roll* · P. J. Wallis and R. V. Wallis, *Eighteenth century medics*, 2nd edn (1988)

Fuller, Francis (1807–1887), surveyor and land agent, was born in Coulsdon, Surrey, on 29 June 1807, the son of John and Sarah Sayer Fuller. His father was then a substantial farmer, but by 1837 was described as a land surveyor. Francis was educated at Isleworth until he was fourteen and then trained as a farmer in practical agricultural skills. Fuller married Mary Ann, daughter of George Drew, a solicitor, at Streatham on 27 July 1837; a son, Francis John, was born in 1838, followed by other children, including the suffragist Dora Frances Barrow *Montefiore.

Fuller followed the calling of a surveyor in Croydon until 1843, when he joined the Society of Arts. He became much involved in the society's agricultural committee, which he joined in 1847, interesting himself in suitable subjects for which the society could give prizes, such as research into the depredations of the turnip fly and into the role of rooks and sparrows and their benefits to agriculture. In 1845 he became a member of a committee set up to advise the society on the feasibility of staging a national exhibition of manufactures on the French model. This led, in the summer of 1849, to his being one of three members of the society who went to Paris to see the current quinquennial exhibition. The other two were the civil servant Henry Cole and the architect Digby Wyatt.

On his return Fuller met Thomas Cubitt, then building Osborne House in the Isle of Wight for Prince Albert, and spoke to him of his conviction that it would be possible to organize a still better exhibition in London. Cole also contacted the prince through his secretary, and this apparently convinced Prince Albert, who was president of the Society of Arts, that something should be done. A meeting followed at Buckingham Palace, chaired by the prince, at which the crucial decisions were made—that the exhibition should be international and that it should take place on a public site in Hyde Park. With Cole, Fuller was one of the group who visited all the manufacturing areas to generate support for the exhibition, in terms of exhibits and

Francis Fuller (1807–1887), by unknown engraver, pubd 1851 (after Richard Beard)

Brighton, and South Coast Railway for twenty-five years, Fuller built a branch between Caterham Junction and Caterham at his own expense. He was well known as a sportsman and enthusiastic horseman; it was later noted that he had seen the Derby on sixty-three occasions since he had first attended it with his father in 1821, aged thirteen, on his pony. According to one source, this was 'a fact unparalleled in turf history' (Boase, *Mod. Eng. biog.*, 1.1111).

Fuller died on 27 May 1887, at 63 St Aubyn's, Hove.

HERMIONE HOBHOUSE

Sources *The Times* (7 June 1887), 11e · Boase, *Mod. Eng. biog.* · *The Field* (4 June 1887), 769 · *ILN* (18 Oct 1851), 487, 508 · *ILN* (6 March 1852), 201–2 · H. Trueman Wood, *A history of the Royal Society of Arts* (1913) · D. Hudson and K. W. Luckhurst, *The Royal Society of Arts, 1754–1954* (1954) · Y. ffrench, *The Great Exhibition 1851* (1950) · J. T. H. Turner, *London, Brighton and South Coast railway*, 3 vols. (1978) · Royal Arch. · RS · diary of Henry Cole, V&A NAL · m. cert. · d. cert. · *Pigots directory* (1839) · *The Post Office London directory* (1846) · parish register (birth and baptism), Coulsdon parish, Surrey RO, 29 June 1807 (birth), 5 July 1807 (baptism)

Archives Royal Arch., MSS · RSA, MSS

Likenesses wood-engraving (after R. Beard), NPG; repro. in *ILN* (18 Oct 1851), 508 [*see illus.*]

of financial guarantees. They called at Balmoral in September 1849 to report to the prince, and their report convinced him that there was enough support in the country for the exhibition, and that with a royal commission it would be feasible.

Fuller rendered another service to the society and other promoters of the exhibition, who were endeavouring to get the project off the ground in under two years, by finding financial backing. A 'contractor' was identified who would be prepared to fund the exhibition, providing an office and money for prizes in return for a substantial part of the anticipated profits. These were the Mundays, uncle and nephew, who were associates of Fuller's father-in-law, George Drew. However, public opinion turned against the idea of a prestigious national exhibition's being funded privately. Fortunately, a clause had been inserted in the Mundays' contract allowing the organizers to cancel it if a royal commission were issued.

After some expense and difficulties in coming to terms the contract was cancelled, but there was a suspicion at the time that Fuller had had an interest in the contract. Though he remained a member of the executive committee, he and his father-in-law played no active part in the organization of the Great Exhibition after the issue of the royal commission. He himself explained that he needed to return to managing his own business. After the successful conclusion of the exhibition, Fuller was offered a knighthood, but refused. With Sir Joseph Paxton, Fuller subsequently played an active part as managing director in the Crystal Palace Company, which re-erected the 1851 exhibition building at Sydenham in 1854. Fuller was also later involved with the development of Alexandra park and palace for public use, and wrote two works about its future, which appeared in 1870 and 1873.

By 1854 Fuller was threatened with bankruptcy. However, he managed to satisfy his creditors, and seems to have returned to his relatively obscure role as a surveyor and land agent in Surrey. Surveyor to the London,

Fuller, Isaac (1606/1620?–1672), portrait and history painter, is said to have been born in 1606 (Redgrave) but no evidence has emerged for this date and his apparent age in the self-portrait of 1670 (Bodleian Library, Oxford) suggests that a more plausible birth date may be about 1620. He was probably born in England, but nothing is known of his early life or his parentage. He is said to have trained in France with François Perrier (1584/90–1640) (Buckeridge); this must have taken place either before 1635, when Perrier went to Italy, or after 1645, when he returned. The latter is more likely, if Fuller's later birth date is accepted. Fuller had returned to England by 1650, when his double-paged etched plate of Jewish costumes was published in Thomas Fuller's *A Pisgah-Sight of Palestine* (bk 5, p. 92; the author is not known to have been a relative). Isaac Fuller produced the earliest British drawing-book shortly after this, *Un libro di designare* (1654; based on an Italian model), with fifteen plates etched by himself; the only known copy is held in the British Museum. He also made a second book of etchings, only two plates from which survive today (British Museum).

At some point after his return from France Fuller spent a period of time in Oxford. An old label on a portrait of an unknown man, formerly identified as the poet John Cleveland (Tate collection), states that it was painted by Fuller in Oxford in 1644 but this is difficult to reconcile with the probable dates of his time in France, and the costume and hairstyle of the sitter suggest a date of c.1661–3. He probably was in Oxford, however, about 1650, when he painted a portrait of Sir William Petty (1623–1687), recorded in John Aubrey's *Brief Lives* (the portrait, or a version of it, is now in the National Portrait Gallery). Aubrey also says 'Twas he (Sir William) that putt Fuller to drawe the muscles as at Oxon gallery [the Bodleian]' (*Brief Lives*, 2.148).

Fuller must have been back in London in 1657, when the Company of Painter-Stainers commissioned him to paint

Isaac Fuller (1606/1620?–1672), self-portrait, 1670

a group portrait of their court of assistants. He clearly maintained a practice in portraiture throughout his career, but by this time his reputation was already well established primarily as a history painter. Only a year later he was listed in William Sanderson's *Graphice* as one of the native English artists who could compete with 'any now beyond the seas'; his particular specialism is given as 'story' (that is, history painting; (Sanderson, 20)).

Fuller was in Oxford again in the early years of the Restoration period, when he had a series of commissions for large religious works in college chapels. All of these have since been destroyed, with the exception of some fragments of a *Resurrection* at All Souls. His work at Magdalen College, probably the earliest of these commissions, also a *Resurrection*, was described by John Evelyn in 1664 as 'the largest piece of Fresco painting (or rather in Imitation of it, for tis in oyle [of Terpentine]) in England, & not ill-design'd … seemes too full of nakeds for a Chapell' (Evelyn, 3.385–6). The *Resurrection* and a *St Francis* in All Souls chapel, in oils on plaster, were seen in 1663 by Balthasar de Monconys; the fragments that remain are on panel and were from ceiling decorations. For Wadham College Fuller produced a *Last Supper*, with *Abraham and Melchisedek* on one side and *The Israelites Gathering Manna* on the other. This latter work was executed in the unusual medium of brown crayon heightened with white on canvas, the colours being fixed by an encaustic process.

By 1669, if not before, Fuller was back in London, living in the parish of St Giles-in-the-Fields. Here his career as a history painter seems to have taken a more secular turn;

he painted theatrical scenery and decorated at least three London taverns with large mythological scenes, none of which now survives. George Vertue, writing in the early eighteenth century, described Fuller's paintings in the Mitre tavern in Fenchurch Street—particularly the figure of Saturn—as showing some knowledge of anatomy, but the 'fiery colours, & distinct marking of the muscles make this appear like a body without a Skin' (Vertue, *Note books*, 1.102). Comment on the prominent musculature of his figures, deriving from his study of the works of Michelangelo (probably mainly in print form), is frequent among contemporary commentators. Bainbrigg Buckeridge, writing in 1706, noted that Fuller 'understood the Anatomical Part of Painting, perhaps equal to Michael Angelo, following it so close, that he was very apt to make the Muscelling too strong and prominent' (Buckeridge, 420).

Fuller's association with London taverns seems to have gone beyond the decoration of them. An epigram by John Elsum, on 'A Drunken Sot, by an Unknown Hand', begins:

> That Drinking may be better ply'd
> The Hat and wig are thrown aside:
> The Glass he holds in's palsy'd hand,
> Till he can neither go nor stand.

It ends:

> Who sees this sot in his own colour,
> Is apt to say, 'twas drawn by Fuller'.
> (Elsum, 64–5)

This may be of course simply a reflection of the style and choice of subject matter associated with Fuller but a comment attributed to Sir Peter Lely, that he 'lamented that so great a genius should besot or neglect so great a Talent' (Vertue, *Note books*, 1.126), suggests that Fuller himself had a reputation for dissipation.

The only large-scale narrative paintings attributable to Fuller that survive are a series of five scenes of Charles II's escape after the battle of Worcester, two of which are signed 'IF' (NPG). These large canvases are very unlike Fuller's surviving portraits in handling but allowance must be made for their very different function and format. The remainder of his surviving *œuvre* constitutes a handful of drawings and etchings, and a number of oil portraits, some of which are signed or documented and others attributable on the basis of style. Among the most important of these is the oil self-portrait painted for Daniel Rawlinson, the landlord of the Mitre tavern in Fenchurch Street, signed and dated 1670 (now at the Bodleian Library). This exists in several variants, some of which are probably autograph and others copies. Painted very broadly and vigorously, the figure slightly over life-size, the bravura of these portraits has led later commentators to suggest that Fuller may have shown himself drunk. Among Fuller's documented works is a portrait of a young girl (Dulwich Picture Gallery, London), formerly in the collection of the actor William Cartwright (1606–1691). Vertue also attributes a large number of portraits to Fuller in his *Note Books*, some incorrectly.

Fuller's contribution to the arts in seventeenth-century England went beyond his own paintings to the training of other artists. Charles Woodfield (1649–1724), a topographical painter, is said by Vertue to have trained under Fuller in Oxford for seven years, and Vertue also records that John Riley (1646–1691) studied under Fuller but left him when he was still very young. Fuller had at least two sons who were artists: Isaac Fuller the younger (*fl.* 1678–1709) and Nicholas. Nicholas was a talented coach painter described as 'a very ingenious Man. but liveing so irregularly. dyd young' (Vertue, *Note books*, 1.135). The work of Isaac the younger has often been confused with that of his father but was mostly completed after Isaac senior's death, including the vestry ceiling in St Lawrence Jewry (1678) and an altarpiece in St Stephen, Coleman Street (1679), both destroyed in 1940. He also worked as an etcher, producing some illustrations for the English edition of Cesare Ripa's *Iconologia*, published in 1709.

Isaac Fuller the elder died in London on 17 July 1672 at Southampton Buildings, Bloomsbury Square, and was buried the following day at St Andrew's, Holborn. The originality, even peculiarity of his style compared with that of most of his contemporaries has led to difficulties for historians and critics in assessing his achievement. The mixed response of his near-contemporary Bainbrigg Buckeridge is characteristic:

> He had a great Genius for Drawing and Designing History, yet which he did not always execute with due Decency, nor after an Historical Manner, for he was too much addicted to Modernize, and burlesque his Subjects, there being sometimes a Rawness of Colouring in them, besides other Extravagancies suitable to the Manners of the Man: But not withstanding all that a Critick may find fault with in his Works, there are many Perfections in them … he may be reckon'd among the foremost in an Account of English Painters.   (Buckeridge, 420)

CATHARINE MACLEOD

Sources [B. Buckeridge], 'An essay towards an English school of painters', in R. de Piles, *The art of painting, and the lives of the painters* (1706), 398–480, esp. 373–4 · Vertue, *Note books*, vols. 1–2, 4–6 · M. J. H. Liversidge, 'Prelude to the baroque: Isaac Fuller at Oxford', *Oxoniensia*, 57 (1992), 311–29 · E. Croft-Murray, *Decorative painting in England, 1537–1837*, 1 (1962), 43–4, 220–21 · A. Griffiths and R. A. Gerard, *The print in Stuart Britain, 1603–1689* (1998), 173–5 [exhibition catalogue, BM, 8 May – 20 Sept 1998] · D. Solkin, 'Isaac Fuller's *Escape of Charles II*: a Restoration tragicomedy', *Journal of the Warburg and Courtauld Institutes*, 62 (1999), 199–240 · E. Croft-Murray and P. H. Hulton, eds., *Catalogue of British drawings*, 1 (1960), 321–4 · W. Sanderson, *Graphice* (1658), 20 · Redgrave, *Artists*, 2nd edn, 162 · Evelyn, *Diary*, 3.385–6 · B. de Monconys, *Journal des voyages de Monsieur de Monconys*, 2 vols. (1665–6), vol. 2, p. 53 · R. Beresford, *Dulwich Picture Gallery complete illustrated catalogue* (1998), 105 · D. Piper, *Seventeenth-century portraits in the National Portrait Gallery* (1963), 275–6 · *Brief lives, chiefly of contemporaries, set down by John Aubrey, between the years 1669 and 1696*, ed. A. Clark, 2 (1898), 148 · J. Elsum, *Epigrams upon the paintings of the most eminent masters* (1700), 64–5

Likenesses by or after I. Fuller, oils, *c.*1670, Queen's College, Oxford · by or after I. Fuller, oils, *c.*1670; Sothebys, 9 April 1997, lot 21 · by or after I. Fuller, oils, *c.*1670; Sothebys, 13 April 1994, lot 14 · I. Fuller, self-portrait, oils, 1670, Bodl. Oxf. [*see illus.*] · I. Fuller, self-portrait, oils, *c.*1670, NPG · I. Fuller, self-portrait, pen and ink on paper, *c.*1670, V&A

Fuller, John (*d.* 1558/9), college head, was a native of Gloucester. He was educated at All Souls College, Oxford, where he was admitted to the degree of BCL in July 1533.

He became a notary public before February 1536 and was elected a fellow of All Souls in the same year. Fuller authenticated the protocol for admission to Corpus Christi College until 1543. He graduated DCL in January 1546, and was admitted to Doctors' Commons on 10 October of that year. On 16 July 1547 he became rector of Hanwell with Brentford, Middlesex, but resigned the charge four years later, having been appointed in 1550 (jointly with Miles Spencer) vicar-general and official-principal to Thomas Thirlby, bishop of Norwich. He became rector of Roydon, Suffolk, in the same year. On Thirlby's translation to Ely, Fuller went with him and on 14 September 1554 was constituted chancellor, vicar-general, and official-principal of the diocese. On 12 November he was collated canon of the fifth prebend, made vacant by the death of Anthony Otway.

Fuller succeeded Pierpoint as master of Jesus College, Cambridge, on 23 February 1557 and became vicar of Swaffham and rector of East Dereham and North Creake in Norfolk in that year. He was proctor for the clergy of the diocese in two convocations. In May 1558 he was elected to the prebend of Chamberlainwood in St Paul's, London. He is said to have incurred much odium for the part he took, as chancellor of Ely, in suppressing heresy; although he acquitted more heretics than did some of his fellow examiners, he seldom resorted to leniency. Those sentenced by him to be burned included William Wolsey and Robert Pigot of Wisbech St Peter and John Hullier at Cambridge, whose sentence was read by Fuller in Great St Mary's Church.

Fuller made his will on 18 September 1558, and died before 26 January 1559 when it was proved before the vice-chancellor of Cambridge University; his estate was valued at £622 15s. 6d. Fuller was a considerable benefactor: he gave to Jesus College the manor of Gravely, which had formerly belonged to Ramsey Abbey (where Fuller may at one time have been a monk) and founded four fellowships there. He left one third of his moveable goods to the college, one third to the poor of certain parishes, and the remainder to his cousins William and Margaret. He was buried, according to directions made in his will, in the choir of Jesus College chapel.   JUDITH FORD

Sources Cooper, *Ath. Cantab.*, 1.188 · Emden, *Cam.*, 221–2 · J. Bentham, *The history and antiquities of the conventual and cathedral church of Ely*, ed. J. Bentham, 2nd edn (1812), 244, 253 · *The acts and monuments of John Foxe*, ed. S. R. Cattley, 8 vols. (1837–41), vol. 7, pp. 403–5; vol. 8, p. 378 · W. Stevenson, ed., *A supplement to the second edition of Mr Bentham's history and antiquities of the cathedral and conventual church of Ely* (1817), 103 · C. H. Cooper, *Annals of Cambridge*, 2 (1843), 83, 103 · Foster, *Alum. Oxon.* · *VCH Cambridgeshire and the Isle of Ely*, vols. 2–3 · *Reg. Oxf.*, 1.169 · T. F. Shirley, *Thomas Thirlby, Tudor bishop* (1964), 135

Wealth at death £622 15s. 6d.: Cooper and Cooper, *Athenae*

Fuller, John (*bap.* 1680, *d.* 1745). See under Fuller family (*per.* *c.*1650–1803).

Fuller, John (1706–1755). *See under* Fuller family (*per.* *c.*1650–1803).

Fuller, John (1757–1834), politician and eccentric, was born on 20 February 1757 at North Stoneham, Southampton, Hampshire, the only son of Revd Henry Fuller (1713–1761), rector of North Stoneham, and his wife, Frances (1725/6–1778), his cousin, and daughter of Thomas Fuller of Catsfield, Sussex. The *Fuller family, originally cloth merchants in London, were Sussex landowners, ironmasters, and gun-founders, with sugar plantations in the West Indies. Their sources of wealth were reflected in the family motto *carbone et forcipibus* ('By charcoal and tongs'). John, who had lacked a steadying influence following the death of his father when he was still a young boy, was educated at Eton College (1767–74). On reaching adulthood he inherited a vast fortune when, on the death of his uncle, Rose *Fuller [see under Fuller family], in 1777, the family estate at Rose Hill, Brightling, near Burwash, Sussex, together with the property in Jamaica came into his possession. From this date he established himself as the local squire determined to make a name in the eyes of posterity.

Through family influence Fuller obtained the parliamentary seat of Southampton, which he held from 1780 to 1784 as a supporter of Lord North's administration. Mrs Thrale observed his rough and boisterous manner, though he rarely spoke in debates. From 1778 he was a captain in the Sussex militia, his chief interest, and he later led a troop of the Sussex yeomanry cavalry at the crucial period of the French invasion threat during the Napoleonic war. He was high sheriff of Sussex in 1796–7. After a lapse of seventeen years he was returned to parliament in July 1801 as a county member for Sussex. By then Fuller's extravagant behaviour and blunt outspokenness had become pronounced, his wild, intemperate, and frequently absurd interventions in debates making him an object of mirth. A vocal representative of the sugar planters, he declared in reply to William Wilberforce in a debate on the slave trade (30 May 1804) that the living conditions of West Indian slaves were 'equal, nay, superior to the condition of the labouring poor of this country' (*Hansard 1*, 2, 1804, 459). He defended the duke of York in 1809 and attacked sinecures, proclaiming his own independence; legend had it that he declined an offer of a peerage from Pitt as a threat to his integrity, asserting 'I was born Jack Fuller, and Jack Fuller I will die!' (*GM*, 106).

On 27 February 1810 Fuller achieved notoriety when, drunkenly entering the Commons while the inquiry into the Walcheren expedition was in progress, he interjected various absurd questions to the earl of Chatham. On being ignored he exclaimed, 'God d—n me Sir, I have as much right to be heard as any man who is paid for filling the place he holds'. It took the serjeant-at-arms and four messengers to overpower him and remove him from the chamber, on the orders of the speaker, whom he had addressed as 'the insignificant little fellow in the wig' (HoP, *Commons, 1790–1820*, 4.848). After spending two days in custody he apologized to the house, and was reprimanded, an outcome regarded by some as excessively lenient.

Fuller retired from parliament at the dissolution in 1812 and settled on his Sussex estate. There he made the contributions to the age of folly building, then already on the wane, for which he is remembered. His first such effort, a Coadestone summer house with a 'Tudor' archway, was built in 1803 (restored 1992). Seven years later, and in the churchyard at Brightling so that it was visible from his windows, he commissioned his own mausoleum, a 25 foot high pyramid with a wall tablet inside bearing Thomas Gray's lines, 'The boast of heraldry, the pomp of power'. At the same time rose the rotunda garden temple which, together with its Doric columns and dome, now forms a backdrop to the matches played by the Brightling Park cricket club. A mystery surrounds the obelisk standing 646 feet above sea level at the north-west of Brightling Park, for which no record exists except that 'Mad Jack' (as he came to be known) built it. The observatory, designed by Sir Robert Smirke, was built between 1810 and 1818 simply because the squire of Brightling was a keen amateur astronomer who previously had no adequate means for studying the heavens. About 1828 he built a tower at Brightling as an observation point from which to view the repairs to Bodiam Castle, 6 miles away, which he purchased in that year and saved from ruin. Finally he erected the Sugar Loaf, the epitome of folly building, which stands 35 feet high in a field on the Battle–Heathfield road. Fashioned in the shape of a cone (the contemporary way of retailing sugar, linked with his Jamaican interests), it was said to have been built as a result of a wager.

Anything but mad, and only mildly eccentric, Fuller had a purpose in most of his follies, not least to provide local employment, the reason for the 4 miles of stone wall he had erected around Rose Hill. He also commissioned the building of the predecessor to the Beachy Head lighthouse and donated a lifeboat to the inhabitants of Eastbourne. His patronage of the arts included several commissions to J. M. W. Turner. He was a generous benefactor of the sciences, endowing before his death two professorships, in anatomy and physiology, and chemistry, at the Royal Institution (known as the Fullerian chairs). He never married, having been rejected at the age of thirty-three by Susanna Thrale, a daughter of Henry and Hester Thrale. Fuller died at his London residence, 36 Devonshire Place, on 11 April 1834. Twenty-four private carriages attended the funeral cortège from London to his burial in the pyramid tomb in Brightling churchyard on 18 April.   J. P. J. ENTRACT

Sources GM, 2nd ser., 2 (1834), 106–7 · G. Hutchinson, *Fuller of Sussex: a Georgian squire* (1993) · A. Parks, *The Fullers' progress* (1987) · L. Namier, 'Fuller, John', HoP, *Commons* · B. Murphy and R. G. Thorne, 'Fuller, John', HoP, *Commons*
Archives E. Sussex RO, family and estate papers · Royal Institution of Great Britain, London, MSS · W. Sussex RO, family and estate papers
Likenesses F. Chantrey, bust, 1819, Brightling church, East Sussex · group portrait, 1830–70 (*The first Fullers of Brightling*), priv. coll. · Count D'Orsay, pencil sketch, 1832, repro. in Hutchinson, *Fuller of Sussex*, 101 · engraving, 1834, repro. in Hutchinson, *Fuller of Sussex*, 114 · medallion, 1834, repro. in Hutchinson, *Fuller of Sussex*, 116 · H. Singleton, oils, Royal Institution of Great Britain, London

Fuller, John (*d.* 1825), surgeon and historian, was for some years in practice as a surgeon at Ayton, Berwickshire. During that time, in 1785, he published a pamphlet, *New Hints Relating to Persons Drowned and Apparently Dead*, in which he proposed transfusion from the carotid artery of a sheep as a means of resuscitation. It does not appear that the method was tried. On 21 November 1789 Fuller, who appears to have had no previous connection with the university, received the degree of MD at St Andrews upon testimonials from Messrs N. and T. Spens, physicians of Edinburgh, Alexander Wood, a surgeon, and Andrew Wardrop, a physician. Afterwards Fuller practised at Berwick upon Tweed.

In 1794, soon after the formation of the board of agriculture, Fuller made suggestions to it for the periodic collection of county health statistics and for the formation of a central medical institution and a national veterinary college. At the request of Sir John Sinclair, president of the board, he prepared an account of Berwick for the *Statistical Account of Scotland*; but as he suggested that it required more extended treatment Sinclair agreed to its publication as a separate work, entitled *History of Berwick* (1799). Fuller afterwards lived in Edinburgh. J. Sykes, the border historian, states that in 1824 Fuller had announced the forthcoming publication of his 'Border history of England and Scotland', but that 'the work was not published during his [Fuller's] lifetime' (Sykes, 189). Fuller died at Edinburgh on 14 December 1825.

H. M. CHICHESTER, *rev.* CHRISTIAN KERSLAKE

Sources *Monthly Review*, 72 (1785), 76 · *Edinburgh Magazine and Literary Miscellany*, 96 (1825), 768 · J. Sykes, *Local records, or, Historical register of remarkable events, which have occurred in Northumberland and Durham*, 2 (1833), 189 · private information (1889)

Fuller, John Frederick Charles (1878–1966), army officer, was born on 1 September 1878 at The Pallant, Chichester, Sussex. He was the eldest son of the Revd Alfred Fuller (1832–1927) of the parish of West Itchenor, and his French wife, Selma Marie Phillipine de la Chevallerie, who had grown up near Leipzig. Fuller had a cosmopolitan background, and when he was eight the family moved to Lausanne, Switzerland. In 1889 he moved back to Sussex to attend a preparatory school, Fulmer House, West Worthing, before attending Malvern College (1893–5). Lacking ambition or direction, Fuller was placed in the army class at the suggestion of his maternal grandfather. He attended Jimmy's, a London 'crammer', (1895–6), passed into the Royal Military College, Sandhurst, in September 1897, and was commissioned into the 43rd, the 1st battalion, Oxfordshire light infantry, in August 1898.

Early years in the army Fuller was bored by the listlessness induced by regimental life. The outbreak of the Second South African War (1899–1902) offered an escape. Although forced to retire from the conflict by appendicitis, he returned to the front during the guerrilla phase of the war. In 1901–2 he spent six months as an independent intelligence officer—an episode which he later described in an entertaining book, *The Last of the Gentlemen's Wars* (1937). As a light-infantryman Fuller quickly deduced that 'mobility is of crucial importance' (Trythall, 13). He was

John Frederick Charles Fuller (1878–1966), by Elliott & Fry, pubd 1936

posted to India in 1903. He became absorbed by Indian mysticism, philosophy, and seeking out 'truth' by the elucidation of 'hidden wisdom'. Fuller subscribed to ideas later codified by the philosopher G. I. Gurdjieff. Life was governed by 'fundamental laws which lie behind all things'. The most important was the 'Law of Three', those 'three forces [which] enter into every manifestation, into every phenomenon and every event' (Ouspensky, 16). Fuller began corresponding with the bizarre occultist and sexual adventurer Aleister *Crowley. In 1907 he wrote a study of Crowley's mystical poetry, *The Star in the West*. Fuller thought Crowley a genius, a superman. His interest in the occult became all-consuming, and he helped Crowley edit an occult review, *The Equinox*. Fuller's contributions were later revised and published as *Yoga* (1925). Crowley and Fuller quarrelled in 1911 over the former's pusillanimous behaviour during a salacious libel case, and the friendship was not renewed.

Fuller's interest in things military waxed as his fascination with matters occult waned. He had been promoted captain in 1905; he married Margarethe Augusta Karnatz (*d.* 1968), known as Sonia, in December 1906. The following year he accepted the adjutancy of the 2nd South Middlesex volunteers rather than his own regiment; this became the 10th Middlesex after 1908. Dealing with keen territorials stimulated Fuller to write; he found a forum in *The Army Review*, and published two books, *Hints on Training Territorial Infantry* (1913) and *Training Soldiers for War* (1914).

He attended the Staff College, Camberley, in 1914, but was condemned by the commandant as 'lacking in military judgement' (Fuller to Liddell Hart, 16 Aug 1926, King's Lond., Liddell Hart MSS, 1/302/96). He refused to accept the shibboleths of conventional tactical wisdom, especially that all military action should be based on the envelopment of open flanks. In his essays Fuller advocated penetration of the enemy's front as well as envelopment, and analysed military history by reference to principles of war of his own devising. Confident that he was right and the authorities wrong, Fuller used these papers as the basis for four articles published in the *Journal of the Royal United Services Institution* (1914–16).

The First World War and the tank Major Fuller began the First World War in August 1914 as deputy assistant director of railway transport at Southampton, before moving to Dartmouth, and then to Tunbridge Wells as general staff officer, grade 3 (GSO3), Second Army staff. He joined the headquarters of 7th corps in France in July 1915, was promoted lieutenant-colonel, and posted GSO2 of the 37th division in February 1916. His thoughts were applied to improving conventional infantry tactics, stimulated by the challenge of setting up a senior officers' school for the Third Army in the spring. In December 1916 he was posted GSO2 to the heavy branch machine-gun corps (later the Royal Tank Corps). In January 1917 he was awarded the DSO.

Fuller's first analysis of tank tactics was embodied in 'Training note no 16'. He argued that tanks were mobile fortresses designed to reduce 'the resistance offered to the advance of the infantry bayonets'. He also called for shorter artillery bombardments. Throughout 1917 Fuller proved himself a well-organized, imaginative, and meticulous staff officer, whose methods pioneered what would later be termed 'operational research'. He was promoted GSO1 (chief of staff) of the tank corps on 1 April 1917. Almost all Fuller's career was spent on the staff. He liked to think of himself as a potential commander, but his talents were most suited to staff work. His contribution to the plan for the battle of Cambrai in November 1917 was significant, though not in the sense he later conveyed. One of the duties of a chief of staff is to provide ideas for his commander, and the translation of concepts into a practicable plan is a corporate activity during which the original source of an idea is often forgotten or overlooked. His important role was to stimulate thought during the Cambrai planning process. His critical intelligence was immediately directed towards dissecting errors that needed to be rectified, after a German counter-attack had swallowed up the initial gains. Similar qualifications need to be attached to Fuller's finest achievement as a staff officer, his memorandum, 'Tactics of the attack as affected by the speed and circuit of the medium "D" tank' (popularly known as 'Plan 1919'), completed in April and May 1918. Fuller's paper was not a plan in any formal sense, and could not be used as such, but it succeeded in formulating the essential conceptual framework of future armoured warfare, indeed manoeuvre warfare at the operational level.

Post-war life and lecturing In 1919–20 Fuller rode the crest of a wave of success. Having been promoted substantive colonel in 1920, he exerted an influence which far outshone his rank. In August 1918 he had returned to the War Office as colonel, staff duties (SD) 7, and then SD4, responsible for training throughout the army. On 1 September 1923 he secured the permanent establishment of the tank corps in five battalions, and a month later it was redesignated the Royal Tank Corps (RTC). Proselytizing on its behalf led to his composition of *Tanks in the Great War* (1920). Fuller also won the Royal United Services Institution (RUSI) gold medal (military) prize essay competition; and to the disgust of the Admiralty he won the naval prize the following year.

Fuller gave a number of brilliant lectures on future warfare, and published *The Reformation of War* (1923). The latter was his most ambitious effort to synthesize the precepts of Plan 1919 into a new theory of war. Fuller attempted to popularize as well as theorize, and the result is sometimes exaggerated. He sought also to challenge and stimulate, and he certainly succeeded. One of his most promising protégés was the young Captain B. H. Liddell Hart, who thought Fuller 'the greatest intellectual power I have ever come across, a titan among minnows' (Liddell Hart to J. M. Scammell, 22 Feb 1923, King's Lond., Liddell Hart MSS, 1/622). An exchange over infantry tactics led to a lifelong friendship—despite some quarrels—which redounded to the credit of both men, as they could so easily have become rivals. Later observers would note with interest that Fuller was the only man that Liddell Hart treated with great deference.

By the early 1920s Fuller was convinced that the restoration of mobility to the battlefield demanded nothing less than the massive task of rethinking the very nature of war and systematizing the principles of war. This quest was furthered by a posting in 1923 as chief instructor at the Staff College, Camberley. He attempted to re-organize the army staff course along university lines, and attempted to revitalize the existing syndicate (seminar) system by basing it on the mutual pooling of war experience and freedom of expression; the aim was to create a true war college and a dynamic doctrinal and educational focus rather than a training school handing down received knowledge. Fuller was encouraged by the commandant, Major-General Edmund Ironside, who henceforth became his mentor. But Fuller was bitterly disillusioned in 1924 when the chief of the Imperial General Staff (CIGS), Lord Cavan, refused him permission to publish his revised Staff College lectures, and then a year later censored a lecture he gave on mechanization at the RUSI. Fuller consoled himself with a visit to the United States in August 1924. His lifelong interest in the American Civil War dates from this trip.

A check to his career The turning point in Fuller's military career was 1926–7. In 1925 the prospects had been auspicious. With Liddell Hart's help he had stirred up public discussion of the need for a new experimental brigade to test promising developments in mechanization. His two books, *Sir John Moore's System of Training* and *British Light*

Infantry in the Eighteenth Century (1925) underpinned the project by stressing the historical parallels with Moore's experimental preparations in 1803–5 during the Napoleonic wars. Then followed *The Foundations of the Science of War* (1926), based on his Camberley lectures. It lays out the logic behind his analysis of the principles of war, summarizes the method of his concept of operational military history, and displays insight into manoeuvre warfare. Yet his attempt to universalize the principles was mistaken; even more foolhardy was mixing them up with the 'three-fold order' a mystical fancy of his own, and he suffered ridicule, especially in a sardonic review (anonymous, but actually written by Brigadier-General J. E. Edmonds) in the April issue of the *Army Quarterly*. None the less he was appointed military assistant to the CIGS and made CBE in June 1926.

The new CIGS, Sir George Milne, made progressive noises, and radicals hoped that Fuller and Milne would become close, with Fuller providing his ideas. But Milne had raised exaggerated expectations, and he found Fuller an uncomfortable nag. The CIGS liked *Imperial Defence, 1588–1914* (1926) and sent Fuller to India to consider the modernization of the Indian army. On returning Fuller was told of his appointment to command the new experimental brigade. He discovered that this involved command of a garrison with a few *ad hoc* units on Salisbury Plain. Fuller made a fuss about delegating his garrison duties and then resigned. He later withdrew his resignation and accepted transfer as GSO1 to 2nd division at Aldershot, commanded by Ironside. Fuller's career was damaged irreparably and he earned Milne's lasting animus. However, he made use of an unexpected abundance of spare time by publishing *On Future Warfare* (1928) and *The Generalship of Ulysses S. Grant* (1929). In 1929 he commanded the 2nd Rhine brigade at Wiesbaden and Catterick, and in 1930 he was promoted major-general, made CB, and then placed on half pay. In February 1931 he declined command of the second class district of Bombay. Had he accepted it perhaps his dalliance with fascism might have been avoided; certainly his re-employment in 1938–9 would have been rendered easier. It was a decisive step, and an unfortunate one.

The years on half pay, however, paid a dividend in literary effort. They began with a renewed emphasis on the technical military art with *Lectures on FSR II* (1931) and *Lectures on FSR III* (1932), the latter focusing on mechanization, though its significance is more conceptual than predictive. *India in Revolt* (1931) signalled a change of direction. Fuller became increasingly intrigued by 'warfare as a whole rather than instrumental war' (Fuller to Jay Luvaas, 8 July 1963, Luvaas MSS). *The Dragon's Teeth* (1932) related his theories to the processes of civilization, and expounded a theorem of the law of military development, that is to say, weapons reflected civil technology and thus monitoring civil progress was vital. Furthermore, he developed the notion of the 'constant tactical factor', which postulated that all advances in offensive weapons are eventually cancelled out by a protective antidote. Finally Fuller's theory of war is cemented by a cyclical device based on the never-ceasing competition between shock and projectile weapons (those that are rammed home at close quarters and those that are thrown). *War and Western Civilization, 1832–1932* (1932) forms an early attempt to relate warfare to social and economic forces. *Grant and Lee* (1933) and *Generalship: its Diseases and their Cure* (1933) reflect on command methods; the latter placed Fuller in the vanguard of those who subscribed to the unflattering interpretation of British command methods in 1914–18 that was so influential for fifty years after its publication.

On the retired list: Mosley and the British Union of Fascists
Fuller was placed on the retired list in December 1933. Even before this date he had become involved with fringe politics. In June 1934 he attended Sir Oswald Mosley's ill-fated meeting of the British Union of Fascists (BUF) at Olympia, and wrote to Mosley afterwards: 'this is the worst day of your life; you should always join a man in his worst moment' (Holden Reid, *Studies*, 185). Fuller was appointed Mosley's adviser on defence matters. Contrary to his post-war apologia, Fuller was an ideological fascist, and his dedication to Mosley's movement in 1937 cost him his friendship, albeit not permanently, with Liddell Hart, who abhorred fascism. Yet though Fuller did not take the formal step until 1934, in a very real sense he had been a proto-fascist all his intellectual life. By embracing social Darwinism, anti-materialism, mechanization, and the cult of the great man, and by rejecting mass democracy, Fuller imbibed from what Azar Gat calls the 'proto-fascist and fascist outlook or mood', since he was 20 years old (Gat, 1).

Fuller wrote a pamphlet for the BUF, *March to Sanity* (1935, 3rd edn, 1937). In 1934 he wrote a report on fascist organization. He criticized rowdyism and the wearing of political uniforms. He advocated the creation of a triumvirate with himself as chief of staff. Fuller argued that the BUF should become more respectable and not imitate the Nazis. His report caused an outcry; critics claimed that he was trying to take the movement over. Thereafter he remained rather aloof from leadership of the BUF (which became the British Union after 1936). He was adopted in 1938 as the British Union candidate to fight Duff Cooper's parliamentary seat, St George's, Westminster. Fuller withdrew after Cooper's resignation over the Munich agreement. During the late 1930s Fuller spoke to the Link and other pro-German bodies. He opposed war with Germany, advocating a policy of isolation based on rearmament and imperial consolidation.

For Fuller the 1930s were a decade of literary productivity. His books called for a complete overhaul of traditional British structures and mores; those published on the army were laced with savage wit. *Empire Unity and Defence* (1934) argued for a rationalization of imperial defence policy to ensure naval command of the oceans, the foundation of British strategy. *The Army in my Time* (1935) and *Memoirs of an Unconventional Soldier* (1936) explored the conceptual, planning, and command inadequacies of the British military system, which were rooted in an archaic social structure. *The First of the League Wars* (1936), the product of a visit to Abyssinia after the Italian invasion as the *Daily Mail's* war correspondent in 1935–6, and *Towards Armageddon* (1937), expounded a theory of 'dictatorial warfare' based on surprise and a 'war of nerves' (Holden Reid, *Studies*, 196). The only solution was for Britain to create the 'warfare state'. This could mobilize national resources for defence in the coming struggle with communism for world mastery. A centralized Ministry of Defence was required, controlled by a great general staff that would override vested service interests in pursuit of a viable strategic policy. Some of these ideas would earn Fuller new admirers in the United States in the 1950s, but in the 1930s their value was reduced by an exaggeration of the potential of strategic bombing.

Despite Fuller's attendance at Hitler's fiftieth birthday celebrations in May 1939, the coming of the Second World War which he had so adamantly opposed seemed to herald his rehabilitation. When his mentor Ironside returned as CIGS in 1939, Fuller was considered for the position of deputy CIGS. The move was vetoed, not by Leslie Hore-Belisha, the Jewish secretary of state for war, but by the prime minister, Neville Chamberlain. Fuller continued to consort with opponents of the war. In June 1940, under regulation in council 18B, 747 British Union members (including the Mosleys) were arrested, but not Fuller; his exclusion from the list remains a mystery. Winston Churchill might have protected him, and he must have acquiesced in the decision because Fuller's re-appointment was reconsidered in June 1940. There is also evidence to confirm that his main defender was General Sir Alan Brooke, commander-in-chief, home forces (1940–41) and CIGS (1941–6). 'I cannot believe', Brooke wrote in his diary, 'he [Fuller] has any unpatriotic intentions' (diary, 20 Nov 1941, Alanbrooke MSS, 5/5). His name none the less headed a list of eighty-two suspected collaborationists who were to be arrested in the event of a German invasion. Fuller was too perverse to be a convincing Pétain figure; he was temperamentally incapable of being a cringing toady. Indeed as late as 1942 the Beaverbrook press demanded his recall to oversee the procurement and deployment of British armour.

Journalism and final years   Fuller earned his living by journalism. His newspaper articles were trenchant, witty, and thoroughly individual. He published two collections of them, *Watchwords* (1944) and *Thunderbolts* (1946). In June 1942 he renewed his friendship with Liddell Hart. They both agreed that Britain's interests would have been better served by the signing of a compromise peace in the summer of 1940. Fuller was to develop his formidable indictment of Churchillian strategy over the next twenty-five years, starting with *Machine Warfare* (1942). In *The Second World War* (1948) he argued that Churchill's strategy had led to Soviet Russia's becoming the dominant military power in Europe. His thesis was buttressed by cogent criticisms of allied tactics that sacrificed operational opportunity by relying unduly on attrition and firepower. As the cold war hardened in the 1950s Fuller's gloomy conclusion that the Second World War had been barren of strategic advantage for the West did much to re-make his reputation as a military commentator. Fuller's most powerful statement of his philosophy of war and his most imaginative linking of the political, social, and ethical sources of strategy is to be found in *The Conduct of War, 1789–1961* (1961).

The last fifteen years of Fuller's life were devoted to the writing of military history. He had incorporated the nuclear equation into his *Armament and History* (1946), which, as a survey of weapons and war in short compass, has yet to be equalled. 'Actually, all this nuclear business bores me', he admitted to Liddell Hart (20 July 1958, King's Lond., Liddell Hart MSS, 1/302/507). In the early 1950s he completely recast and extended his military history, first issued in two volumes in 1939–40, pruned the fascist encrustation, and published it as *The Decisive Battles of the Western World*, 3 vols., (1954–6). Two years later *The Generalship of Alexander the Great* appeared followed by *Julius Caesar: Man, Soldier and Tyrant* (1965). They have not yet been superseded as the best military studies available of the two greatest generals of antiquity.

Fuller was awarded the RUSI's Chesney gold medal in 1963, and his final years were bathed in praise. Michael Howard described him as 'One of the greatest military thinkers of our century'; Liddell Hart in *The Tanks* (1959) claimed that no previous soldier in history could match Fuller in 'imaginative power or mental range—judged by their recorded thoughts' (Liddell Hart, 1.221). Fuller was remarkably indifferent to the opinion of posterity; he complained that he was neglected, but remained solitary—unlike Liddell Hart he made no attempt to rally a following. In the summer of 1965 Fuller's health began to decline. *En route* to Cornwall in January 1966 to visit Lieutenant-General Sir Francis Tuker, Fuller developed pneumonia; he died in Tehidy Hospital, Redruth, on 10 February.

Fuller thought of himself as a frustrated great commander and in the early 1920s as a reformer, but his true significance lay in his military thought. His reforming zeal was, in any case, blunted by the orthodoxy of the British army in the inter-war years—reflecting the 'safety' sought by successive governments. As a thinker Fuller sought to develop a system by which to evaluate ideas about war. His works were initially on subjects that were primarily of interest to soldiers, notably on the conduct of military operations; but later he extended his concepts to the relationship between war and society. These more ambitious and wide-ranging works, especially in the 1930s, attempted to define the character of the age in terms of its dynamism and political turmoil. Such an effort to divine the conditions of war, he believed, could help determine future policy. His political philosophy was unashamedly authoritarian and anti-democratic. Even though Fuller's flirtation with fascism blighted his career, his sympathies were by no means atypical as the fascist 'mood' influenced thinkers from a variety of political backgrounds. Despite his extravagances, limitations, and errors, J. F. C. Fuller ranks as one of the most significant thinkers of the twentieth century.

BRIAN HOLDEN REID

Sources B. Holden Reid, *J. F. C. Fuller: military thinker* (1990) · B. Holden Reid, *Studies in British military thought: debates with Fuller and Liddell Hart* (1998) · A. J. Trythall, *'Boney' Fuller: the intellectual general, 1878–1966* (1977) · J. Luvaas, *The education of an army: British military thought, 1815–1940* (Chicago, IL, 1964) · J. F. C. Fuller, *Memoirs of an unconventional soldier* (1936) · King's Lond., Liddell Hart C., Liddell Hart MSS · priv. coll., Luvaas MSS · King's Lond., Liddell Hart C., Alanbrooke MSS · P. D. Ouspensky, *The fourth way* (1957) · J. P. Harris, *Men, ideas and tanks: British military thought and amoured forces, 1903–1939* (1995) · B. H. Liddell Hart, *The tanks*, 1 (1959) · A. Gat, *Fascist and liberal visions of war: Fuller, Liddell Hart, Douhet and other modernists* (1998) · b. cert. · *CGPLA Eng. & Wales* (1966)
Archives King's Lond., Liddell Hart C., diaries, corresp., and military papers · Oxfordshire and Buckinghamshire Light Infantry Museum, Headington, journal · Royal Armoured Corps Museum, Bovington, diary and MSS · Rutgers University, New Jersey, Archibald S. Alexander Library, corresp., literary MSS, and papers · Tank Museum, Bovington, Dorset, diary | CAC Cam., corresp. with Monty Belgion · King's Lond., Liddell Hart C., corresp. with Sir B. H. Liddell Hart · King's Lond., Liddell Hart C., letters to N. P. MacDonald · LUL, Harry Price Occult collection · priv. coll., Luvaas MSS · priv. coll., Starr MSS
Likenesses photograph, *c.*1920, King's Lond., Liddell Hart C. · Mitzakis, photographs, *c.*1962, King's Lond., Liddell Hart C. · Elliott & Fry, photograph, repro. in Fuller, *Memoirs of an unconventional thinker*, frontispiece [*see illus.*] · cartoon (as Napoleon), Former Staff College Building, Camberley, 'The Jungle Book' · cartoon (*Extremes meet*), Former Staff College Building, Camberley, 'The Jungle Book' · photographs, Rutgers University, Sloane collection
Wealth at death £23,315: probate, 19 May 1966, *CGPLA Eng. & Wales*

Fuller, Sir Joseph (*d.* 1841), army officer, was appointed ensign, Coldstream Guards, in August 1792. He seems to have previously held the same rank in some foot regiment from 29 September 1790, but his name does not appear in the army list. He became lieutenant and captain, Coldstream Guards, on 22 January 1794, and was with the regiment at the sieges of Valenciennes and Dunkirk. Afterwards he served as aide-de-camp to Major-General Samuel Hulse in Ireland in 1798, in the Netherlands in 1799, and at home in the southern district until promoted to captain and lieutenant-colonel on 18 June 1801.

Fuller accompanied the 1st battalion of his regiment to Portugal with the expeditionary force under Major-General J. Coope Sherbrooke in December 1808; commanded a light battalion, formed of the light companies of the guards and some 60th rifles, in the operations on the Douro and advance to Oporto in 1809; and commanded the 1st battalion Coldstream Guards at the battle of Talavera. He afterwards served with the regiment at home until promoted major-general on 4 June 1813. Fuller was appointed colonel of the 95th (Derbyshire) foot at its formation in January 1824; he was made a knight bachelor in 1826, GCH in 1827, and was transferred to the colonelcy of the 75th foot in 1832. Promotion to general came in 1838.

Fuller was for many years president of the acting committee of the consolidated board of general officers, formed to inspect army clothing, investigate claims for losses, and execute other duties previously performed by separate boards of general officers, a post he ultimately resigned because of ill health.

Fuller married in 1815 Miranda, eldest daughter of General Sir John Floyd, baronet, and they had one daughter. He died at his residence in Bryanston Square, London, on 16 October 1841, and was buried at Kensal Green cemetery, Middlesex.

H. M. CHICHESTER, *rev.* ROGER T. STEARN

Sources J. Philippart, ed., *The royal military calendar*, 3rd edn, 5 vols. (1820) · C. R. Dod, *The peerage, baronetage and knightage of Great Britain and Ireland* (1841) · *GM*, 2nd ser., 17 (1842) · A. J. Guy, ed., *The road to Waterloo: the British army and the struggle against revolutionary and Napoleonic France, 1793–1815* (1990) · R. Muir, *Britain and the defeat of Napoleon, 1807–1815* (1996)
Archives Duke U., Perkins L., corresp. | BL, corresp. with Sir Robert Peel, Add. MSS 40357–40607

Fuller, Joseph Jackson (1825–1908), missionary, was born in Spanish Town, Jamaica, on 29 June 1825, a son of Alexander McCloud Fuller and another slave; his parents were unmarried. Despite being almost certainly a slave, Fuller, along with his brothers, attended school for eight years, a remarkable achievement for that time and a reflection of his family's ambitions. His father joined a pioneer Baptist Missionary Society project to evangelize Africa, travelling first to England and then to Fernando Po (west Africa) where, in 1844, he was joined by his sons Joseph and Samuel.

In 1845 the island was claimed by Spain, and Catholic missionaries came into conflict with the Baptists, whose mission, depleted by deaths (including Alexander Fuller's in 1847) and by Samuel Fuller's resignation, relocated to Victoria, the Cameroons. Joseph Fuller, ordained on 4 April 1859, was active in Baptist work in the Cameroons for over thirty years, beginning at Bimbila and ending by arranging the complete transfer of the mission to the German missionaries of the Swiss Basel Mission in 1888 after Germany claimed the Cameroons. Fuller's efforts included printing, translating (including John Bunyan's *Pilgrim's Progress* into Duala, published 1882), heading mission stations, exploring, teaching, brick making, and preaching.

Fuller had married about 1850 Elizabeth Johnson, a Jamaican school teacher on Fernando Po, and they had three children (two boys and a girl) before her death on 18 February 1859. On 1 January 1861 he married Charlotte Diboll, daughter of Joseph Diboll, an English missionary active in Fernando Po and the Cameroons from 1854 until 1865.

In 1869 Fuller made his first visit to England, travelling to the Dibolls' native Norfolk during eighteen months' leave. He spoke before audiences who were impressed by his dignity (enhanced by his height) and fascinated by his eyewitness account of the ceremony on 1 August 1838 when black Jamaicans buried slave shackles to mark their final liberation. Fuller then visited his mother in Jamaica, speaking in churches all over the island and gathering funds for the African mission. He returned to England, placing his son Joseph Fuller in an apprenticeship in a Norwich engineering company, and sailed for the Cameroons. Another son, by his second wife, was taken to England by Jamaican missionary, John Pinnock.

The relocation of missionaries to the Congo weakened

the Baptists in the Cameroons. Efforts were further diminished by tropical illnesses often leading to death, and by lengthy leaves (Fuller again toured England and Jamaica in 1884–5), which were necessary both to gather support and to recuperate. The Baptist Missionary Society's work in the Cameroons was headed by Fuller by 1886. German imperialism brought other Christian missionaries, from whom Fuller's congregations realized that Baptists had no monopoly of their new faith. Many Africans declared themselves independent Christians.

Based at Bethel and then Victoria, between 1887 and 1888 Fuller arranged the transfer to the Basel Mission. He volunteered to work in the Congo but was refused because of his age and long service. He followed his wife to England, where he spoke at Baptist and missionary gatherings, such as one in Birmingham's town hall in October 1889 before some four thousand people. In May 1890 his son Joseph Fuller, with a London-educated Jamaican missionary, Simeon Gordon, went to the Congo for the Baptist Missionary Society. After six years he worked at their London headquarters.

Fuller first lived at 2 Salisbury Villa, Cleveland Road, Barnes (on the Thames in west London) and then moved to Stoke Newington, close to the oldest Baptist congregation in London, Devonshire Square Church, where his funeral service took place (16 December 1908) after his death at 36 or 38 Sydney Road on 11 December 1908. He was interred in the nearby Abney Park cemetery, London's main nonconformist burial-ground.

Visitors to the Fullers in London had included Rose Grenfell, the Jamaican-descended widow of the Congo missionary George Grenfell, for Fuller, Pinnock, and Gordon were not the only Jamaicans to spend much of their active years as missionaries in Africa. Fuller took considerable interest in the native church in the Cameroons, and spoke of Africa and of slavery in Jamaica to British audiences. Thomas Lewis, a fellow Cameroons missionary, recalled in his 1930 autobiography, *These Seventy Years*, 'In England, pleading the cause of his African brother, nobody had a better reception from English audiences than this noble negro orator' (Lewis, 91).

JEFFREY GREEN

Sources R. Glennie, *Joseph Jackson Fuller: an African Christian missionary* (1933) · T. Lewis, *These seventy years* (1930) · E. Payne, *Freedom in Jamaica* (1933) · *North London Guardian* (25 Dec 1908) · Home Office correspondence, Baptist Missionary Society, microfilms 31, 72 · Abney Park cemetery records, Hornsey Library, Crouch End, p. 16067
Archives Regent's Park College, Oxford, Angus Library, corresp., mainly with A. H. Baynes, and papers, incl. MS autobiography
Likenesses photograph, repro. in Glennie, *Joseph Jackson Fuller* · photograph, repro. in Lewis, *These seventy years*
Wealth at death £136 10s. 11d.: probate, 30 Jan 1909, *CGPLA Eng. & Wales*

Fuller, Nicholas (1543–1620), lawyer and politician, was the son of Nicholas Fuller, a London merchant of Neat's Hall in the Isle of Sheppey. He attended Christ's College, Cambridge, from December 1560, and graduated BA in 1563. Admitted that year to Gray's Inn, Fuller was elected pensioner on 23 November 1584, and reader on 26 May 1587. By 1584 he had married Sarah, daughter of Nicholas Backhouse, alderman and former sheriff of London, and in 1586 the couple set up home at Chamberhouse, near Thatcham, Berkshire. The eldest of their seven known children, also named Nicholas (d. 1620), was born in 1592, admitted to Gray's Inn in 1601, and knighted by James I on 22 June 1619.

Legal and early parliamentary career, 1586–1604 In 1585 Fuller was offered the post of solicitor-general in Dublin, but managed to avoid the duty. On 8 February 1588 he became dean of the chapel of Gray's Inn, and in 1591 was elected to the prestigious role of treasurer. From 1588 he was often employed by the privy council in matters concerning state servants and national security. But he also began to incur official disapproval. In July 1590 the puritan minister John Udall was tried for writing a 'seditious' book, and Fuller acted for him. When Judge Clarke instructed the jury to find Udall guilty on the fact of his authorship and 'leave the felony to us', he intervened caustically, provoking a hostile response from the prosecutor and noisy scenes as Udall was removed from the chamber.

In 1591 Fuller appeared for Thomas Cartwright and other ministers whose attendance at synods and classes was said to amount to sedition. The case was dramatically altered when, at Cheapside on 16 July 1591, Edmund Copinger and Henry Arthington proclaimed Elizabeth deposed, and William Hacket the new messiah and king of Europe. This was sedition indeed. Four days later Fuller was committed to the Fleet by the same warrant which ordered Hacket's arrest, perhaps because he had offered to represent the accused. The authorities failed to secure the conviction of Cartwright and his fellow ministers; this has been attributed to 'the highly professional resistance of the puritan lawyers', which 'perhaps owed much to Nicholas Fuller' (Collinson, 420–1). He remained close prisoner until 15 August. The flow of state commissions dried up, and Fuller's indiscreet libel against the lord admiral in 1596 must have confirmed his disfavour within an increasingly conservative establishment.

In 1593 Fuller sat as MP for St Mawes. He was prominent in opposing government attempts to extend the scope of the 1581 recusancy laws to separatists, fearing that it might also be used against non-separatist puritans. On 4 April 1593 he denounced the second of two bills, sent from the Lords after the rejection of the first, as 'dangerous to good subjects': it made 'schisms to be equal with seditions and treasons, which is against the equity of the former law'. He moved in committee 'to the striking out of the title and the whole preamble. No man spake for it' (Hartley, 3.162, 167). After further hostile scrutiny the bill passed in heavily amended form.

Government critic, 1604–1607 Fuller appears not to have sought re-election in 1597–8, but he sat in the first parliament of James I, as a member for the City of London. For the next ten years he was the government's sharpest and most tenacious critic. In 1606, for example, he urged action against recusants, and spoke for deprived ministers; and he presented economic grievances over purveyance, the farming of fines, patents, various impositions, and cloth production. 'Mr Fuller of Gray's Inn, a prime man in the council of London' (Willson, 33–4) was clearly important to city merchants. But commercial issues were rarely separable from politics. Fuller helped pursue the government agent Tipper, charged with obtaining money under false pretences while in service of the revenue. He complained against impositions on currants. This was cause in Bate's case, in which the exchequer found that the king was entitled to raise customs rates in peacetime. Fuller urged that duties imposed without parliamentary consent were illegal. He was prominent in opposition to 'purveyance', under which the crown might buy supplies at less than market prices. He objected that purveyors enriched themselves at the expense of suppliers and of the state, and imposed this abuse through their own 'court of green cloth'. Efforts to abolish purveyance ran into opposition, notably from those concerned to defend or extend the limits of the royal prerogative.

Fuller was interested in other issues which bore on constitutional principles. When attending joint conferences between the two chambers, MPs were made to stand hatless, respectfully awaiting the pleasure of the Lords. In March 1607 he recommended on behalf of the committee of privileges that the Lords be asked to treat them more considerately. He appealed to a principle of equality between the two chambers: when in the past a few peers had visited the Commons to confer, 'it is not likely the whole commons did stand or were bare in reverence of so few sent down to them' (Willson, 233). On 12 April 1606 he reported that at a joint conference the judges had tried to present their views on the legality of a bill as unchallengeable by MPs. He had objected that the conference was not a court, and was rebuked for it, although subsequently cleared of fault by the House of Commons.

Constitutional battles, 1607–1610 Ministerial plans for union with Scotland aroused widespread suspicion in parliament. In February 1607 Fuller warned that impoverished Scottish artisans and feuding lairds might descend on the lush pastures of English commerce and law. The speech sought to connect both with the fears of artisans and merchants, and with resentment at Scottish courtiers, who, many felt, were showered with offices and honours. But Fuller spoke less crudely than many among the opponents of union. His main concern was with the legal issues raised by the proposals. These were not merely technical; they seemed to present political dangers. In Scotland the independence of parliament was not well entrenched; while two legal systems prevailed, the government disposed of extra discretionary powers which bypassed the statutes of either country, powers which appeared at odds with parliamentary 'liberties'. He feared the subordination of the English common law to courts operating outside the control of statute, and the extension of the royal prerogative.

Fuller's constitutional ideas led him into serious conflict with these forces. In early 1607 he agreed to act for two men, Thomas Ladd of Yarmouth and Richard Mansell of Gloucester, imprisoned by the high commission for actions subversive of the established church and its courts. Having secured a writ of habeas corpus, Fuller undertook their defence in king's bench, at hearings on 6 May and 13 June. He argued that the court of high commission had no power to arrest or imprison. Its officers were corrupt, its procedures popish and illegal. Fuller took his arguments into parliament. In June 1607 he charged that the high commission 'at every renewing increaseth and encroacheth more power and more', in breach of the laws of the land, and presented a bill which if passed would have emasculated it (Willson, 351). Despite, or because of, his public assault on the ecclesiastical courts, he seems to have retained the confidence of most MPs. On 26 June 1607, the Commons desired to elect him chairman of the committee of the whole house; Fuller modestly stood aside in favour of Hobart, the attorney-general. While the house sat, he could claim privilege against arrest. But his actions threatened the very existence of the high commission, and soon after the prorogation on 4 July, it arraigned and imprisoned him in the White Lion at Southwark.

Fuller immediately appealed to the common law judges. Fenner and Croke upheld the right of king's bench to determine whether the high commission held jurisdiction in his case. King's bench was in recess, but would hear the case when it reconvened; in the meantime, they issued a prohibition, halting the commission's legal pursuit of Fuller. In September 1607 a conference was held between the barons of the exchequer and the judges of the king's bench and common pleas. It issued a 'consultation' which enabled the high commission to proceed against Fuller on lesser charges of heresy and schism. On 20 or 21 October he was convicted, fined £200, and gaoled, but quickly secured from king's bench a new writ of habeas corpus, which challenged the authority by which he was detained.

Fuller was in effect arguing that the commissioners had no power to imprison him even in relation to cases lying within its jurisdiction. It had no coercive power at all. The full implications of his case now lay exposed. The king could only delegate powers whose limits had been defined by statute: the powers set out in letters patent, under which the commission operated, were illegal. This called into question not only the existence of the high commission but the royal prerogative itself. Ministers became alarmed. On 24 November 1607 the judges of king's bench accepted the attorney-general's view that, having conceded jurisdiction in the determination of guilt, they had no right to pronounce on sentence. Fuller was sent back to prison. Two days later he secured a second hearing, on the grounds that he had lacked counsel at the first, and the arguments were re-rehearsed.

James I had become convinced that the common lawyers were out to extend their jurisdiction at the expense of ecclesiastical authorities appointed by him. He visited Richard Bancroft, archbishop of Canterbury, and pressed him to pursue the case, urging Cecil that 'the ecclesiastical commission may not be suffered to sink besides the evil deserts of that villain [Fuller]' (*Salisbury MSS*, 19.285–6), lest the monarchy itself be harmed. James kept the case under continuous review, repeatedly urging expedition upon his ministers. When, on 24 November, the judges found against Fuller again, he thanked them, congratulating Cecil upon his discreet handling of the matter.

In the Fleet Fuller faced conflicting pressures. A prosperous lawyer and parliamentarian, he had forced the authorities to the view that the defence of both the high commission and the prerogative depended on his committal. Now, however, he vacillated, signing a submission and then withdrawing it at the behest of his wife and friends. On 5 January 1608, after signing a second submission, he was released. Earlier, however, he had passed a draft account of his argument against the commission to radical associates, who in December published it as *The Argument of N.F.*. These were not new friends. From 1604 Fuller seems to have advised clerical opponents of the bishops on how they might use the common law courts to resist deprivation. A group of these, including Mansell, circulated a series of illegal pamphlets, printed on a secret press. But in January 1608 copies of *The Argument of N.F.* were seized and on 27 February, at Star Chamber, Mansell, Fuller, and three others faced charges of sedition.

Citing both Foxe's martyrology and legal precedent, Fuller's *Argument* held that many of the powers and procedures of ecclesiastical courts were not only technically illegal but affronted the rule of equity and common justice. He proceeded to a memorable summary: 'the laws of England are the high inheritance of the realm, by which both the King and the subjects are directed'. The law 'admeasureth the King's prerogative so as it doth not extend to hurt the inheritance of the subject'. No charter or commission was legal 'unless the same charters and commissions, do receive life and strength from some Act of Parliament'. And if 'any grant or commission from the King doth tend to charge the body, lands or goods of the subjects unlawfully, the Judges will redress the same' (*Argument*, 3, 9, 11, 14–15). The last assertion reflected great faith in judicial independence, still largely untested in 1608, but it helped ensure that the judges would be so tested. Nicholas Fuller thus made his own theoretical contribution to the disintegration of the Tudor compromise on sovereignty, anticipating the pronouncements of Hakewill and Coke. It seems that *The Argument* had come to light before Fuller's release; he was rearrested and by 26 January 1608 was 'close prisoner with the Dean of Pauls'. The outcome of the case in Star Chamber is unclear; on 10 April the court ruled that Fuller might practise law, but was to be confined to the precincts of Gray's Inn pending further action, of which nothing is known.

Later parliamentary career and the final years, 1610–1620
Throughout his career Fuller remained active in his parish, and encouraged participation in its affairs by other leading laymen. The churchwardens were made to record their accounts more fully, and forbidden to lease parish property without permission. In 1608 a charge for communion bread was levied on all but the poorest. Fuller was a trustee of local charities; probably on his initiative a

legal ruling was obtained in October 1610, ensuring that their resources were used for the relief of the poor.

When Fuller returned to Westminster in 1610, the conflict with the authorities had in no way diminished his status. His basic ideas were unchanged. In principle, he continued to stand for the abolition of wardship, which would both remove a burden from many subjects and agree better with God's laws. But it was necessary to provide legal security for any agreement with the crown, and this was not easy: 'I would willingly give somewhat out of my estate, so as I might be assured to know what the rest were and enjoy it safely. But before those fears be cleared I cannot for my part have any comfort in the bargain' (E. R. Foster, 2.321). On 23 June 1610 Fuller set out his views on the prerogative with special sharpness, restating the view of his *Argument* that both king and subjects were subject to law, and attacking unparliamentary taxation. His speech was greeted by 'a great silence' (ibid., 2.165). In November he attacked again his old enemy the high commission, urging that parliament should not trust verbal promises that agencies unaccountable to it would refrain from abusing their powers. Prelatical courts 'would turn their chair into a throne, an abuse contrary to the laws of this kingdom, and (I verily think), the law of God'. He reviewed the Commons' efforts to restore deprived ministers, end non-residency, enforce the sabbath, and reform wardship and purveyance: 'there were never wiser gentlemen in the House and never less done'. If these bills 'had passed for law by joint assent of the other house and his Majesty', England might now be the happiest of states (ibid., 407–10). This came close to blaming king and Lords for the deficiencies of nation and church.

In March 1614 there was a contest over parliamentary seats in London. The city chose Sir Thomas Low as their first knight, but refused 'to admit Master Recorder [Montague], alledging only that he is the King's sergeant. Master Fuller is their first burgess.' The choice, it was rightly remarked, was 'as much subject to interpretation as the refusal of the other' (*Letters of John Chamberlain*, 2.515–16). Fuller opposed reform proposals of April 1614, by which bills of 'grace and favour' were to be granted by the king in return for early supply. When, in May, Bishop Neile accused the house of sedition in questioning the right of the king to fix duties, Fuller responded that Neile 'hath great access to the King and that he is most unworthy of it' (*JHC*, 499). With the Addled Parliament, Fuller's long career as a leading parliamentarian came to a close.

Now in his seventies, Fuller still kept up a busy schedule; he remained active in parish affairs, and audited the churchwardens' and almshouse accounts. He continued to attend meetings of the Gray's Inn benchers until 19 November 1619. He died on 23 February 1620 at Chamberhouse and was buried at Thatcham church on 2 March. In his will Fuller left much property, mostly to his wife, Sarah, and son, Nicholas; there were bequests to the poor at Newbury and to the preachers Stephen Egerton and John Dod.

Fuller left two monuments. His shield once appeared on

the south window of the Old Hall at Gray's Inn; there is a representation of it in Dugdale's *Origines juridiciales* (1671). At the Chamberhouse chapel he appears wearing a barrister's gown, with his wife, two sons, and five daughters. The inscription celebrates Fuller's piety, his fame, and his commitment to knowledge, truth, and justice.

STEPHEN WRIGHT

Sources BL, Add. MS 11402 · BL, Lansdowne MS 46 · BL, Cotton MSS, Titus Fii, Fiv; Cleo Fii · PRO, STAC 8/19/7 · *Calendar of the manuscripts of the most hon. the marquess of Salisbury*, 18–20, HMC, 9 (1940–68); 24 (1976) [see addenda 1605–12] · *Report on the manuscripts of his grace the duke of Buccleuch and Queensberry … preserved at Montagu House*, 3 vols. in 4, HMC, 45 (1899–1926), vols. 2/2–3 · *JHC*, 1 (1547–1628) · *JHL*, 1 (1509–77) · *CSP dom., 1586–1618* · *APC* · S. Barfield, *Thatcham, Berks, and its manors*, ed. J. Parker, 2 vols. (1901) · M. Curtis, 'William Jones: puritan printer and propagandist', *The Library*, 5th ser., 19 (1964), 38–66 · E. R. Foster, ed., *Proceedings in parliament, 1610*, 2 vols. (1966) · *The argument of Master Nicholas Fuller in the case of Thomas Ladd* (1641) · W. Notestein, *The House of Commons, 1604–1610* (1971) · J. P. Sommerville, *Politics and ideology in England, 1603–1640* (1986) · *The parliamentary diary of Robert Bowyer, 1606–1607*, ed. D. H. Willson (1931) · R. G. Usher, *Reconstruction of the English church* (1910) · S. B. Babbage, *Puritanism and Richard Bancroft* (1962) · *Les reportes del cases in camera stellata, 1593 to 1609, from the original ms. of John Hawarde*, ed. W. P. Baildon (privately printed, London, 1894) · W. R. Douthwaite, *Gray's Inn: its history and associations* (1886) · K. Fincham, *Prelate as pastor: the episcopate of James I* (1990) · J. Foster, *Register of admissions to Gray's Inn, 1521–1881* (privately printed, London, 1887) · B. Galloway, *The union of England and Scotland* (1986) · S. R. Gardiner, *History of England from the accession of James I to the outbreak of the civil war*, 1–2 (1883) · S. R. Gardiner, ed., *Parliamentary debates in 1610*, CS, 81 (1862) · HoP, *Commons, 1558–1603* · *State trials*, vol. 1 · *Dudley Carleton to John Chamberlain, 1603–1624: Jacobean letters*, ed. M. Lee (1972) · *The letters of John Chamberlain*, ed. N. E. McClure, 2 vols. (1939) · T. L. Moir, *The Addled Parliament of 1614* (1958) · J. E. Neale, *Elizabeth I and her parliaments*, 2: *1584–1601* (1957) · J. Peile, *Biographical register of Christ's College, 1505–1905, and of the earlier foundation, God's House, 1448–1505*, ed. [J. A. Venn], 2 vols. (1910–13) · W. R. Prest, *The inns of court under Elizabeth I and the early Stuarts, 1590–1640* (1972) · A. F. S. Pearson, *Thomas Cartwright and Elizabethan puritanism, 1535–1603* (1925) · Venn, *Alum. Cant.* · P. Collinson, *The Elizabethan puritan movement* (1967) · T. E. Hartley, ed., *Proceedings in the parliaments of Elizabeth I*, 3 vols. (1981–95) · HoP, *Commons* [draft]
Archives BL, Lansdowne MSS, corresp., Cecil papers
Likenesses statue, 1620, chapel, Chamberhouse, near Thatcham, Berkshire
Wealth at death more than £1000: Barfield, *Thatcham*, vol. 2, pp. 259–63

Fuller, Nicholas (c.1557–1623), Hebraist and theologian, was the son of Robert Fuller and Catharine Cresset. Born in Hampshire, he received his early education in Southampton. As a youth he was appointed secretary to Robert Horne and John Watson, successively bishops of Winchester. Horne had served as Hebrew lecturer at St John's College, Cambridge, in 1544–5 and during Mary's reign had found refuge in Frankfurt, where he taught Hebrew at a college established in the city to cater for the exiles. He was responsible for revising Isaiah, Jeremiah, and Lamentations for the Bishops' Bible of 1568. In Fuller's passion for the biblical languages perhaps it is not too fanciful to detect the influence of Horne, his first employer. Certainly Horne's erudition awakened in his amanuensis a love of learning and inspired him to engage in further

study. On Watson's death in 1584 Fuller opted for a scholarly rather than an administrative career. To make ends meet he became tutor to William and Oliver Wallop, whom he accompanied to Oxford, where he also pursued his own interests. He matriculated on 9 October 1584 as a member of St John's College, but soon transferred to Hart Hall, and graduated BA in 1587 and MA in 1590. After ordination to the priesthood he was appointed to the parish of Allington in Wiltshire; there he applied himself to the study of languages and their bearing on theology. He was collated as prebendary of Uffculme in the diocese of Salisbury on 14 October 1612. At an unknown date he married Catharine; they had two children, Nicholas and Catharine.

During the final decade of his life Fuller found an enthusiastic patron and admirer in Lancelot Andrewes, bishop of Winchester. According to John Aubrey, Andrewes was anxious to offer preferment to 'ingeniose persons that were staked by poore livings' and 'made it his enquiry to find out such men' (*Brief Lives*, 7). Having heard of Fuller's biblical scholarship and linguistic skills, Andrewes came to him 'as the Queen of Sheba to Solomon, to pose him with hard questions, bringing with him a heap of knots for the other to untie, and departed from him with good satisfaction' (Fuller, *Worthies*, 1.412). As a mark of respect for his learning Andrewes instituted Fuller to the Hampshire living of Bishop's Waltham on 21 February 1620 and made him a prebendary of Winchester Cathedral. Aubrey's record of the occasion highlights Andrewes's generosity and his sense of humour. The bishop apparently sent for Fuller, 'and the poor man was afrayd and knew not what hurt he had done. Makes him sitt downe to Dinner and, after the Desert was brought in, in a dish, his Institution and Induction, or the donation of a Prebend; which was his way' (*Brief Lives*, 7).

Fuller's friendship with Andrewes continued for the rest of his life. On 17 August 1622 he wrote to the bishop asking him, after his death, to support his 'desolate widow and her two young ones'. In the same letter he bequeathed to Andrewes the manuscript of a Hebrew lexicon which he knew he would never complete, 'beying now an aged man' and in failing health (Bodl. Oxf., MS Add. C.279, fol. 95). Though he died at Allington and was buried in the parish church on 13 February 1623, a manuscript signed by him and bearing the subscription 'Laus deo Walthamae … 25 Julii 1621' (Bodl. Oxf., MS Orient 476) suggests that he did spend some time in Bishop's Waltham. He may have returned to Allington because it was a smaller parish and more conducive to scholarly pursuits. He presumably held two prebends and served two parishes in different dioceses simultaneously.

While Fuller's skill in Semitic languages was recognized by his contemporaries, he has only two extant published works to his name: the *Miscellaneorum theologicorum … libri tres*, which contains a series of comments on difficult or controversial biblical texts, was first printed in Heidelberg in 1612 and reprinted several times, finally in Pearson's *Critici sacri* of 1660 (where it is referred to as

Miscellaneorum sacrorum libri); and the *Dissertatio de nomine Yaweh* was published in Reland's *Decas exercitationum philologicarum* of 1707.

Two manuscripts further attest to Fuller's knowledge of Hebrew. The first (Bodl. Oxf., MS Orient 476) is a translation of *Me'ir nativ* by the fifteenth-century French physician Rabbi Mordechai Nathan. This was the first Hebrew concordance to the Bible compiled with the intention of making it easier for Jews to respond to Christian polemic. A note attached to the manuscript but in a different hand, which suggests that it may have been copied from Fuller's will, states:

> I give and bequeath to Sir Thomas Bodley's library in Oxford my new translation of the Hebrew Concordance, with manifold notes therein, though not thoroughly perused or perfected by me; that if any good thing be found therein it may be forthcoming to the studious reader.

The second is the incomplete Hebrew lexicon which he sent to Andrewes shortly before his death. In the accompanying letter he describes his 'Linguae Sanctae Lexicon Catholicon' as

> conteyning the severall significations of the Hebrew and Chaldey Roots gathered by me owt of all the Translations both Greek and Vulgar Latin, that are now used in the Churche of Christ. And to the lexicon pertaining a little book of observations upon very many words of the Bible.

He goes on to say that it was his intention to create two lexicons out of what he had written, 'the one wonderful large' and the other an abbreviated version. But sickness and infirmity have forced him to abandon the project and he invites Andrewes to dispose of the work as he wishes (Bodl. Oxf., MS Add. C.279, fol. 95).

Fuller's writings contain ample evidence of his expertise as a Semitic scholar. It is evident from the comments he makes in *Miscellaneorum sacrorum libri* that he recognizes the importance of cognate languages such as Syriac, Arabic, and Aramaic for understanding the Hebrew Bible, and is clearly well versed in them. He also appreciates the comments of medieval rabbis for elucidating textual difficulties. While he draws much on the leading Christian transmitters of Hebrew learning such as Nicholas de Lyre, Pagninus, Muenster, Tremellius, and Fagius, he often records his debt to the principal Jewish exegetes and grammarians. He obviously had firsthand knowledge of what he calls the 'rabbinica expositio' of certain words. He cites Rashi frequently. He refers to David Kimchi as 'doctissimus Hebraeorum grammaticus' (*Critici sacri*, ix.2, 862) and quotes from his grammar and lexicon. He regards Ibn Ezra as a leading rabbinic authority and describes him as 'magni nominis rabbinus' (*Critici sacri*, ix.2, 892).

G. LLOYD JONES

Sources J. E. Bailey, *The life of Thomas Fuller, D.D.* (1874) · *Aubrey's Brief lives*, ed. O. L. Dick (1960) · *Fasti Angl., 1541–1857*, [Salisbury] · Wood, *Ath. Oxon.*, new edn · S. Andrews, 'An alphabetical index to Hampshire clergy', 1914, Winchester Cathedral Library [typescript] · Fuller, *Worthies* (1662) · Foster, *Alum. Oxon.* · Bodl. Oxf., MS Add. C. 279 · Bodl. Oxf., MS Orient 476 · J. Pearson, *Critici sacri* (1660)

Fuller, Peter Michael (1947–1990), art critic and magazine editor, was born on 31 August 1947 in Damascus, the second child and elder son in the family of two sons and a daughter of Harold William Charles Fuller, general medical practitioner, and his wife, Marjorie Dale Noyes, midwife. His childhood was largely spent in Eastleigh, a Hampshire railway town, where the family attended the Union Baptist church on Sundays. Fuller was baptized by complete immersion in 1961, just before he went away to board at Epsom College, a public school closely connected with the medical profession. Although he liked the fact that both John Piper and Graham Sutherland went to Epsom College, Fuller was unhappy there. He doubted his religious convictions and felt bewildered by the loss of earlier certainties.

The sense of confusion intensified while Fuller read English at Peterhouse, Cambridge, between 1965 and 1968. He obtained a second class (division two) in both parts of the English tripos (1967 and 1968). He later described his time at Cambridge as 'a period of personal crisis', and found his Baptist faith increasingly inadequate. Psychiatric problems aggravated his disquiet, and he consulted a psychoanalyst in his last year at Cambridge. By that time Fuller had fallen under the influence of Marxism and the far left. Revolution was in the air, and Marxist literature formed much of his reading. But he also staged an exhibition of his paintings at the Cambridge Union, and in 1967 met his future wife, Colette Marie Méjean, a French student whose father was a village postmaster. They married in 1971, and five years later their only child, Sylvia Leda, was born. After Cambridge, Fuller worked at first as a journalist on *City Press*, a City of London newspaper, whose motto was 'The voice of honest capitalism'. His interest in Marxism intensified, and he began writing for the underground press—most notably, *Black Dwarf* and *Seven Days*. A visit to Argentina allowed him to witness a struggle for national liberation, and he became an avid reader of the *New Left Review*. But his involvement with theoretical debate overlaid what he afterwards termed 'a deep sense of fragmentation'. Gambling and masochism grew into compulsive obsessions, and he began a five-year period of psychoanalysis in 1972.

Apart from editing a book entitled *The Psychology of Gambling* (1974), with Jon Halliday, Fuller became a regular contributor to *Arts Review*, *Connoisseur*, *Art and Artists*, *Art Monthly*, and *Studio International*. Some of his most substantial reviews appeared in *New Society*, to which he had been introduced by the writer who influenced him most powerfully during the 1970s, John Berger. They became friends, and Fuller also got to know the American painter Robert Natkin, about whom he wrote articles, catalogues, and finally a book (*Robert Natkin*, 1981). The most impressive outcome of his work during the 1970s was *Art and Psychoanalysis* (1980).

The advent of a new decade brought momentous changes. Colette left Fuller in 1981, and they were divorced four years later. John Berger's influence was superseded by that of John Ruskin, whose ideas dominated Fuller's book *Theoria: Art, and the Absence of Grace*

(1988). He repudiated Marxism, along with most of the friends he had made in the 1970s. Berger came under particularly virulent attack, and Fuller revised an earlier publication called *Seeing Berger* (1980) under the new, caustic title *Seeing through Berger* (1988). New friends, such as the philosopher Roger Scruton, now aligned him more with the right than the left. He became a fierce opponent of the avant-garde, calling instead for a return to the romantic and figurative tradition in British art. Marriage to the Australian sculptor Stephanie Jane Burns in 1985 brought him enormous happiness as well as a son, Laurence Ruskin Fuller, who was born in 1986. Stephanie was the daughter of Alan Robert Burns, company chairman and inventor. Two years later Fuller founded his own art magazine with the suitably Ruskinian title *Modern Painters*, as a pulpit for his views. It was an immediate success, not only because of Fuller's combative and controversial editorials, but also on account of his willingness to publish a lively range of views from novelists as well as critics. The attention attracted by the magazine helped to make Fuller more widely known, and his appointment as art critic of the *Sunday Telegraph* in 1989 gave him another public platform. A regular column there enabled him to champion artists like the painter John Bellany and the sculptor Glynn Williams, both of whom Fuller saw upholding the values he cherished.

Slight in build, and invariably pale, Fuller often looked as if he had just emerged from a long period incarcerated in his study. Behind spectacles, his eyes would often narrow as if to cope with the unaccustomed glare of daylight. Living in Bath, with a country cottage at Stowlangtoft in Suffolk, he enjoyed his greatest period of success and notoriety. But a motorway accident on 28 April 1990, when he was forty-two, cut everything short. His chauffeur-driven car crashed into a field off the M4 motorway, near Theale. Fuller died at the scene, of head and neck injuries. His wife, thirty-three weeks pregnant, broke a hip, damaged her spine, and lost her unborn child, Gabriel, as a result of the accident. Gabriel and Fuller were buried together at St George's Church, Stowlangtoft. A large sculpture called *Opening Chestnut*, by Glynn Williams, stands at the head of the grave.   RICHARD CORK, *rev.*

Sources P. Fuller, *Marches past* (1986) · J. McDonald, ed., *Modern painters: reflections on British art by Peter Fuller* (1993) · *The Independent* (30 April 1990) · *The Independent* (1 May 1990) · *CGPLA Eng. & Wales* (1990)

Archives Tate collection, corresp. and MSS

Wealth at death £155,988: administration, 22 Nov 1990, *CGPLA Eng. & Wales*

Fuller, Rose (1708–1777). *See under* Fuller family (*per. c.*1650–1803).

Fuller, Roy Broadbent (1912–1991), poet, was born at Failsworth, Lancashire, on 11 February 1912, the eldest son of Leopold Charles Fuller (1884–1920), assistant works manager at a rubber-proofing mill, and Nellie, *née* Broadbent (1888–1949), the daughter of a workhouse master's clerk. They were married in 1910. Roy's father died after an operation for bowel cancer on 18 December 1920, and shortly thereafter his widow and family began a life of living in

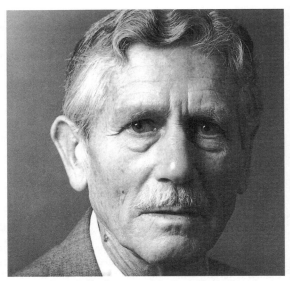

Roy Broadbent Fuller (1912–1991), by Granville Davies, 1985

rented accommodation. Roy attended Blackpool high school from 1923 to 1928 and on leaving school was articled to a firm of solicitors, T. and F. Wylie Kay. He was admitted as a solicitor in 1934. On 25 June 1936 he married Kathleen (Kate) Smith (1913–1993), a journalist with the *West Lancashire Evening Gazette*. They moved to Kennington near Ashford in Kent, where for three years he was with Flower and Pain, solicitors. Their only son, John Leopold Fuller, himself to become a distinguished poet, was born on new year's day 1937. In December 1938 they moved to Blackheath, when Fuller joined the Woolwich Equitable Building Society as assistant solicitor.

Fuller first came to public attention as a poet through publication in *Twentieth Century Verse*, edited by Julian Symons, himself later famous as poet, novelist, and critic, and a lifelong friend of Fuller. Symons initiated the series of Fortune Poets in which Fuller's first book, *Poems* (1939), appeared. Fuller's early poetry was marked by the influence of the work of W. H. Auden and (via the poetry of Norman Cameron) of Robert Graves.

With the outbreak of the Second World War Fuller was inducted into the Royal Navy in April 1941. After a course in radar, in April 1942 he left for Africa where he was promoted to petty officer in 1943. The experience of Africa in the context of the savagery of the Second World War deepened Fuller's poetry and brought to the fore that sense of incipient chaos lurking in so much of it. During the war John Lehmann, an enduring friend of Fuller, encouraged his work by publication in *New Writing and Daylight* and *Penguin New Writing*, and by bringing out his second and third books, *The Middle of a War* (1942) and *The Lost Season* (1944), from the Hogarth Press. These books established Fuller as a poet of importance.

Fuller returned to England in 1943 to serve as a lieutenant at the Admiralty in London. On demobilization in December 1945, he returned to the Woolwich, where he remained until his retirement. The end of the Second

World War brought a challenging cultural situation for Fuller, whose strongly political orientations, with a decided sympathy for communism, seemed increasingly anachronistic. His immediate post-war collections, *Epitaphs and Occasions* (1949) and *Counterparts* (1954), do not have the power of his wartime work, though his extensive reviews and broadcasts of those years contributed to a cultural ambience favourable to the Movement of the 1950s. Many of those often controversial reviews were for *The Listener*, edited by his friend J. R. Ackerley, to whom *Counterpoints* was dedicated. It was not until the publication of *Brutus's Orchard* in 1958 that Fuller found a new and abiding poetic voice. There followed a series of volumes—*New Poems* (1968), *Tiny Tears* (1973), and *From the Joke Shop* (1975), in which Fuller experimented with syllabic verse and wrote with great naturalness and fluency in a manner that was to be characteristic of him—urbane and ironic, tentative yet exploratory.

While Fuller's reputation is based on his poetry, in mid-career he published several novels. He began with crime fiction: *With my Little Eye* (1946), *The Second Curtain* (1953), and *Fantasy and Fugue* (1954), brought together in 1988 as *Crime Omnibus*. These led to his writing *Image of a Society* (1956), which reflected his experience at the Woolwich; this was followed by *The Ruined Boys* (1959), *The Father's Comedy* (1961), *The Perfect Fool* (1961), *My Child, my Sister* (1965), considered by many his best, *The Carnal Island* (1970), and *Stares* (1990). These books did not initially receive the appreciation they deserve even if they do not represent the foundation of Fuller's fame. Running through them was the theme of the relation of art to life, not inappropriate to an author who had so strong a worldly career. In 1958 he became the solicitor for the Woolwich and was a director from 1969 to 1987, and served as vice-president of the Building Societies Association from 1969 to 1987.

Fuller was elected professor of poetry at Oxford University for the period 1968 to 1973. His lectures, with their careful and sensitive exploration of the craft of poetry, were published as *Owls and Artificers* (1971) and *Professors and Gods* (1974). He was created a CBE in 1970. He served as a governor of the BBC from 1972 to 1979 and from 1976 to 1977 as a member of the Arts Council, where he was chairman of the literature panel. He resigned over what he felt was the profligate distribution of public funds. He was also a member of the Library Advisory Council for England from 1977 to 1979. Awards he received included the Duff Cooper memorial prize in 1968, the queen's gold medal for poetry in 1970, the Cholmondely award of the Society of Authors in 1980, and an honorary doctorate of literature at the University of Kent in 1986.

Handsome, moustached, with a full head of curly hair, in his later years he was said jokingly to resemble a retired major-general in appearance. His first three volumes of memoirs, *Souvenirs* (1980), *Vamp till Ready* (1982), and *Home and Dry* (1984), covering his life up to the end of the Second World War, aimed to produce an account that would not seem to be dominated by an imposed pattern. The result appeared desultory to some—including his publishers, who advised against publication. This led to changes of publisher that were ultimately less than fortunate, and he was left with problems in finding an outlet for his poetry, as he explains in his final volume of memoirs, *Spanner and Pen* (1991). The experience was extremely disturbing to him—particularly as the work that he sought to get published was his masterpiece, *Available for Dreams* (1989) which jointly won the W. H. Heinemann award.

Available for Dreams is perhaps his finest work, in which the tightly contained decency and composure that mark all his poetry come together with the unease concerning the whole enterprise of civilization that lurked behind his wartime poems. These pressures emerge movingly in a domestic ambience, often of his garden at Blackheath, through the awareness that his own life, and the lives of those close to him, are coming to an end.

In 1990 Fuller was operated on for prostate cancer and again shortly afterwards to retard the spread of the cancer in his bones. After a brief return to activity, he was confined to his home at 37 Langton Way, Blackheath, London, where he died on 27 September 1991. His body was cremated at Eltham crematorium, without benefit of clergy, as he had wished. A widely attended memorial event was held as part of the 1992 Greenwich Festival.

Fuller was described by the poet Gavin Ewart as 'one of the finest British poets of this century' (quoted on the dust jacket of *Available for Dreams*), and this is likely to remain an accepted verdict on his achievement.

A. T. TOLLEY

Sources R. Fuller, *Souvenirs* (1980) · R. Fuller, *Vamp till ready* (1982) · R. Fuller, *Home and dry: memoirs* (1984) · R. Fuller, *The strange and the good* (1989) · R. Fuller, *Spanner and pen: post-war memoirs* (1991) · N. Powell, *Roy Fuller* (1995) · A. T. Tolley, ed., *Roy Fuller: a tribute* (1992) · A. Austin, *Roy Fuller* (1979) · personal knowledge (2004) · private information (2004)

Archives State University of New York, Buffalo · U. Leeds, Brotherton L., notebooks and MSS | BL, Arts Council collection of modern literary manuscripts, Add. MS 52618 · Georgetown University, Washington, DC, letters to E. Jennings · LUL, corresp. with Douglas Foskett · U. Edin. L., letters to M. Swann · U. Leeds, Brotherton L., letters to *London Magazine*

Likenesses G. Davies, photograph, 1985, NPG [*see illus.*] · photographs, repro. in Powell, *Roy Fuller*

Wealth at death £263,758: probate, 13 Feb 1992, *CGPLA Eng. & Wales*

Fuller, Samuel (*bap.* 1635, *d.* 1700), dean of Lincoln, was baptized at Stebbing, Essex, on 16 July 1635. He was the son of John Fuller (*d.* 1660), vicar of Stebbing (and later rector of St Martin Pomeroy, Ironmonger Lane, London) and his third wife, Dorcas. Samuel's brothers were Francis *Fuller (1636?–1701), Thomas, and Matthew. Francis and Thomas also became clergymen. Samuel was admitted pensioner at St John's College, Cambridge, on 9 September 1650, aged fifteen. He graduated BA in 1655, became a fellow of St John's on 25 March 1656, and proceeded MA in 1658 (a degree incorporated at Oxford in 1663 where his name appears as Fullerton), and BD in 1665. He was created DD in 1679.

Fuller was appointed rector of Elmdon, Essex, on 8 August 1663, having been ordained during the interregnum by his uncle Thomas *Fuller, bishop of Ardfert (archbishop of Cashel from 1661 to 1667). He remained at

Elmdon until 1668, when he resigned the living to take up the rectory of Tinwell, Rutland, provided by his patron, the earl of Exeter. From this date Fuller focused his activity on the diocesan administration of Lincoln. William Fuller, bishop of Lincoln, appointed Fuller as one of his chaplains, and on 25 March 1670 appointed him chancellor of the diocese, to which the prebendary of Stoke was annexed. In 1671 he succeeded to the rectory of Knaptoft, Leicestershire, which he held until his death.

In 1677 Fuller was appointed as chaplain-in-ordinary to the king, a position he also held under Mary II; he preached before Charles II at Whitehall on 25 June 1682 on the text Matthew 22: 21 and 22, 'Render therefore unto Caesar, the things that are Caesar's'. Fuller defended both the exercise of patriarchal dominion by the crown over the subject and the royal supremacy over the church against both papal claims and dissenting objections (Fuller, *A Sermon Preached before the King*, 23–4). He asserted the 'Supremacy that belongs to Christian Princes in Right of their Crowns, in all causes, and over all Persons as well as Civil as Ecclesiastical within their own Dominions' (ibid., 41). He also attacked all those who renounced the royal supremacy, particularly protestant dissenters, 'who amidst all their Clamour against Papal Authority set up a Popular Supremacy … repugnant to Christian religion and the Rights of Princes' (ibid., 57). By contrast, Fuller concluded that it was 'impossible for a true son of the Church of England to be Disloyal' (ibid., 59) to the monarch and the principles of the reformed religion.

In 1690 Fuller published a Latin treatise, *Canonica successio ministerii Ecclesiae Anglicanae reformataetam contra pontificos quam schismaticos vindicata* (1690). On 25 June 1693, as chaplain-in-ordinary to Mary II, he delivered a sermon considering Matthew 6: 23, 'if therefore that light in thee be Darkness, how great is that Darkness?' Fuller considered the role of a divinely informed conscience in regulating human behaviour, in the form of 'a Spiritual Eye and Light within us' (Fuller, *A Sermon Preached before her Majesty*, 8). This conscience always appealed 'to God as its Judge' (ibid.) and required continual exercise, without which 'the most perfect Body of Ethics, understood, digested and believed, cannot make us Good Moralists' (ibid., 19).

On 6 December 1695 Fuller was elected dean of Lincoln, holding the post until his death in the cathedral close on 4 March 1700. Fuller was unmarried and made his nephew Francis Fuller his chief beneficiary. He left £500 to St John's College, Cambridge, to buy a benefice, stipulating that candidates bearing his surname should be offered the living 'first and before all others' (PRO, PROB 11/458, fol. 210r). He was buried in Lincoln Cathedral, to which he donated £200, and was commemorated by a mural monument and Latin inscription by Anthony Reid.

H. R. FRENCH

Sources Venn, *Alum. Cant.* · W. Kennett, *A register and chronicle ecclesiastical and civil* (1728) · J. E. B. Mayor, ed., *Admissions to the College of St John the Evangelist in the University of Cambridge*, 1: *Jan 1629/30 – July 1665* (1882) · VCH *Lincolnshire*, 2.91, 95 · *Fasti Angl., 1541–1857*, [Lincoln] · S. Fuller, *A sermon preached before the king at Whitehall, June 25, 1682* (1682) · S. Fuller, *A sermon preached before her majesty at Whitehall, June 25, 1693* (1693) · PRO, PROB 11/458, sig. 5.189 and 194, fols. 209r–210v; 249r–250r · *Calamy rev.*

Wealth at death approx. £1100 in legacies: will, PRO, PROB 11/458, sig. 5

Fuller, Stephen (1716–1799). *See under* Fuller family (*per. c.*1650–1803).

Fuller, Thomas (1593–1667), Church of Ireland archbishop of Cashel, was one of the sons of Thomas Fuller (1562–1633), vicar of Stebbing, Essex. He should not be confused with his namesake and kinsman, the church historian. His father, it seems, disinherited him for his lavish and wasteful expenditure. This disagreement drove him to Ireland, 'with the happy necessity of being sober and industrious' (Bailey, 464). He was ordained in the Church of Ireland, but evidence is lacking for his graduation from the University of Oxford, Cambridge, or Dublin. An individual of his name is found as prebendary of Cloyne, and in 1639 as chancellor of Cork. In 1641 he was consecrated bishop of Ardfert, being the last prelate who held that see as an independent diocese before it was united to the see of Limerick.

Soon after the outbreak of the 1641 rising Fuller and his family took refuge in London, and he petitioned parliament for a share of a collection raised for Irish clergy, in September 1642, presenting himself, his wife, and children as 'suffering extreme want' (Smith, 328). He probably lived in the parish of St Andrew's, Holborn, his *Sermon Preached at Grayes Inne* (1642) 'on the anniversary of the Irish rebellion' being dedicated to 'the worthy gentlemen and inhabitants of that parish who had been', he says, 'the chief preservers of me and mine since our escape out of Ireland, where we had only our lives for a prey, and those lives your bounty hath cherished'. During the civil war he retired to Oxford, where he was incorporated DD in 1645. He seems to have remained in England until the Restoration, performing illicit episcopal ordinations from 1647, mainly for clergy later found in Essex and other parts of the diocese of London. At some time he ordained his three nephews, the sons of his brother John, who had succeeded his father as vicar of Stebbing: Thomas, fellow of Christ's College, Cambridge, an acquaintance of Pepys, chaplain to Colonel Lockhart, governor of Dunkirk from 1658, vicar of the college living of Navenby, near Lincoln, and rector of Willingale Doe, Essex (1670), 'an inveterate preferment hunter', who died at Navenby in March 1701; Samuel Fuller, afterwards dean of Lincoln; and Francis Fuller the elder, later a nonconformist clergyman.

After the Restoration Fuller returned to Ireland, and was translated to the archiepiscopal see of Cashel by letters patent dated 1 February 1661. An account of the archbishop's reception at Cashel, not only by churchmen but by others, who were converted by his 'indefatigable powers and exemplary piety', is recorded by Kennett (Kennett, 312). Fuller died on 31 March 1667, in his seventy-fourth year, and was buried in the chancel of his cathedral of St John's, to which he bequeathed a silver chalice, paten, and flagon.

EDMUND VENABLES, *rev.* JASON Mᶜ ELLIGOTT

Sources H. Cotton, *Fasti ecclesiae Hibernicae*, 6 vols. (1845–78) · J. E. Bailey, *The life of Thomas Fuller, D.D.* (1874) · W. Kennett, *A register and chronicle ecclesiastical and civil* (1728) · *The whole works of Sir James Ware concerning Ireland*, ed. and trans. W. Harris, 2 vols. in 3 (1739–45, [1746]) · Wood, *Ath. Oxon.*, 2nd edn · Burtchaell & Sadleir, *Alum. Dubl.*, 2nd edn · H. Smith, *The ecclesiastical history of Essex under the Long Parliament and Commonwealth* [1933]
Archives Hunt. L., corresp.

Fuller, Thomas (1607/8–1661), Church of England clergyman, was baptized on 19 June 1608 at St Peter, Aldwincle, Northamptonshire, the eldest of two sons and five daughters of Thomas Fuller BD (*d.* 1632), who had been appointed rector there in 1602 by Thomas Cecil, second Baron Burghley, and of his wife, Judith (*d.* in or before 1620), daughter of John Davenant, a London merchant, and widow of Stephen Payne. He was educated in a local school under Arthur Smith, probably a graduate of Emmanuel College, Cambridge. According to Fuller's anonymous contemporary biographer he 'lost some time under the ill menage of a raw and unskillful Schoolmaster', but his preparation for the university was successfully completed under the supervision of his father (*Life of … Fuller*, 2–3). Two uncles were also probably significant influences on him: John Davenant, his mother's brother, professor of divinity and president of Queens' College, Cambridge, and Robert Townson, his mother's brother-in-law, former fellow of Queens' and a clergyman in Northamptonshire before becoming in 1617 dean of Westminster and in 1620 bishop of Salisbury. In the meantime Judith Fuller died, and in October 1620 the elder Fuller married Dorothy Hamond, a widow.

Cambridge, 1621–1633 On 29 June 1621, aged thirteen, Fuller entered Queens' College. Fuller's designated tutor was John Davenant, but since Davenant had been appointed to succeed the recently deceased Townson at Salisbury and was soon to leave the college the responsibility fell first on his nephew, Fuller's cousin Edward Davenant, a fellow from 1615 to 1625, and then on John Thorpe, a fellow from 1619 to 1630. The former, who was especially gifted in mathematics, had accompanied his uncle to the Synod of Dort in 1618–19; the latter was, according to Fuller, skilled in logic and divinity. Fuller graduated BA in 1625 and proceeded MA on 1 July 1628. He was not awarded a fellowship at Queens', despite Bishop Davenant's recommendation to his successor as president, John Mansell. Instead, on 5 November 1629 Fuller entered Sidney Sussex College as a fellow-commoner in order to study theology under the supervision of the master, Samuel Ward, a close friend of Bishop Davenant.

While still a resident member of Sidney Sussex, Fuller was ordained in his native diocese of Peterborough on 5 June 1631. The previous year he had already been appointed vicar of St Benet in Cambridge by its patrons, the master and fellows of Corpus Christi College. His first published work, *Davids Hainous Sinne, Heartie Repentance, Heavie Punishment* (1631), was dedicated to the three sons of Edward Montague, first Lord Montague of Boughton, whose estate was not far from Aldwincle. An extended verse narrative, it demonstrated that Fuller's talents did

Thomas Fuller (1607/8–1661), by unknown artist

not lie in English poetry, although it showed familiarity with most of the techniques of the metaphysical poets. Fuller contributed Latin poems to *Genethliacum illustrissimorum* (1631), a university collection published to celebrate the births of Prince Charles and Princess Mary, and to *Rex redux* (1633), a similar collection published to honour Charles I on his return from his coronation in Scotland. Fuller's *A Sermon of Assurance*, published in 1647, but according to the title page preached fourteen years before in Cambridge, suggests that Fuller was theologically a moderate Calvinist at the conclusion of his formal education.

Early clerical career, 1631–1642 On 18 June 1631 Fuller was appointed prebendary of Netherbury in Ecclesia in the cathedral of Salisbury and on 18 June 1633 (in which year he resigned his position at St Benet) to the living of Hilton, Dorset, which was in the gift of Bishop Davenant. Hilton was soon served by Matthew Hewett, who married Fuller's sister Margaret. In the following year, on 18 August 1634, Fuller was instituted as vicar of Broadwindsor, Dorset, a living also in the gift of Bishop Davenant, though like Hilton it was in the diocese of Bristol. Meanwhile Fuller's father had died in 1632. His will, dated 6 March 1632, named Bishop Davenant as executor, but gave his son Thomas the responsibility of providing for his sisters until they were married. Fuller's stepmother, Dorothy, was evidently deceased: there is no mention of her in the will.

Accompanied by 'four of his chief Parishioners' at Broadwindsor, who wished 'to testifie their exceeding engagements, it being the sense and request of his whole Parish' (*Life of … Fuller*, 11) Fuller journeyed to Cambridge to receive the degree of BD on 11 June 1635. While at Broadwindsor, probably in 1637, he married Eleanor Grove, daughter of Hugh Grove of Chisenbury, Enford, Wiltshire, a friend of Bishop Davenant. The Fullers' first child, Judith, was baptized on 28 April 1639 at Enford; a second child, John, was baptized on 20 April 1641. In 1639 Fuller's first major literary and historical work, *The Historie of the Holy Warre*, was published by the university press at Cambridge. The book was prefaced by commendatory verses by friends at Sidney Sussex, Queens', Corpus Christi, Jesus, and Trinity colleges. It was the first modern history of the crusades in English, aside from the account in Richard Knolles, *Generall Historie of the Turks* (1603), and was based on Fuller's extensive reading in medieval sources. He was sharply critical of the papacy for promoting the wars in the Holy Land and he analysed shrewdly the reasons for the movement's eventual failure. Fuller's *Joseph's Party-Coloured Coat* (1640), a collection of sermons, contained in its opening pages his views on how to deal with suspected heretics and schismatics, namely by using persuasion rather than imposing severe penalties. He thus by implication opposed the stringent measures being applied by officials under the direction of Archbishop William Laud and Charles I to suppress religious dissent.

Fuller attended the convocation of Canterbury in April 1640 as a proctor representing the clergy of the diocese of Bristol. When the Laudian leadership of the church introduced a new set of canons which defined more explicitly the crown's authority by divine right, forbade sectarian religious activity, and prescribed an oath against changes in the church's polity (commonly called the et cetera oath), Fuller, although a dissenter from the establishment, subscribed to the canons and took the required oath. Like other members of convocation, Fuller was fined for his actions by the House of Commons of the Long Parliament, which held that by meeting after the dissolution of the Short Parliament convocation had acted illegally. On 20 April 1641 Fuller's uncle Bishop Davenant, who had himself opposed the Laudian stress on ceremonies and discipline in the church, died.

Ministry in London, 1642–1643 One of Fuller's most important and popular literary works, *The Holy State*, was published in London in May or June 1642. It was a rich collection of characters illustrating professions and states of life, along with short biographies of historical figures. Some time in the early months of 1642 Fuller went to London to exercise his ministry on behalf of peace. Ireland was now in the midst of a massive uprising and the king and parliament were at loggerheads over the control of the country's military resources. Before leaving the west country Fuller subscribed in February 1642 to the protestation, an oath prescribed by the Long Parliament requiring the taker to promise to defend the 'true Reformed Protestant Religion' and to oppose 'Popish Innovations', as well as to profess allegiance to the king and support for parliament (Fry, 75, 88, 90). In London, Fuller soon found a position. On 15 June a petition from 'the greater part of the parishioners of the Savoy' in London to the House of

Commons asked that Fuller be made minister of the Savoy Chapel (BL, Harley MS 163, D'Ewes parliamentary diary, fol. 549). On 5 November he preached at the chapel on the anniversary of the Gunpowder Plot and afterwards dined with 'divers of the Vestry' (Westminster City Archives, Savoy churchwardens' accounts, 1586–1650). The chapel was centrally situated just off the Strand between the cities of London and Westminster, the seat of government, and Fuller proved to be a popular preacher. According to his contemporary biographer, Fuller had 'two Audiences, one without the pale, the other within; the windows of that little Church, and the Sextonry so crowded, as if Bees had swarmed to his mellifluous discourse' (*Life of … Fuller*, 15).

Fuller's *A Fast Sermon Preached on Innocents Day* (1642), delivered at the Savoy on 28 December 1642 and based on the text 'Blessed are the peacemakers' urged his hearers to petition not only the God in heaven but the gods on earth, namely the king and parliament, to resolve their differences. Both, he noted, professed the same objectives: preserving the protestant religion, the lawful prerogatives of the king, the rights and privileges of parliament, and the rights and property of the subjects. In January 1643, with Sir Edward Wardour, John Castle, John Chichley, Laurance Lisle, and Richard Dukeson, rector of St Clement Danes, he tried to get through the lines around London to reach Oxford with a petition to the king from the city of Westminster and the parishes of St Clement Danes and St Martin-in-the-Fields on behalf of an accommodation. The party was stopped and turned back. Serious negotiations did take place in February and March. They were still being pursued when Fuller delivered *A Sermon Preached at the Collegiat Church of St Peter* (1643) on 27 March 1643 in Westminster Abbey, where parliamentarians were no doubt in attendance, on the anniversary of the king's accession. Fuller reminded his hearers of the concessions the king had already made: 'Ship-mony condemned, Monopolies removed, Starre-chamber itself censured, High-commission levelled … Triennial Parliaments setled, and the present indefinitely prolonged' (p. 23). A remarriage was in order, he urged, between the king and the state. On 26 July 1643, with military operations again in full swing, Fuller preached again on behalf of peace, this time in the Savoy Chapel, where he offered his views on reforming the church, printed later as *A Sermon of Reformation* (1643). A further reformation, he asserted, should be consistent with the earlier reformation of the sixteenth century and should be based on the church's Thirty-Nine Articles. Moreover, it should not give needless offence to Roman Catholics, who were also 'professors of Christianity' (pp. 17–18).

Fuller's sermon was in part an answer to John Milton's *Of Reformation* (1641), which advocated a more radical course, but events soon made such moderate counsels unwelcome in London. In August 1643 a parliamentary covenant was imposed following an attempted betrayal of the city to the king by the poet Edmund Waller, a parliamentary commissioner in the peace negotiations in the spring. This covenant—to be distinguished from the solemn league and covenant marking the alliance between parliament and the Scots—required the taker to swear not to assist the forces of the king. Fuller took it in the vestry of the Savoy with expressed reservations; when it was urged again, he withdrew from London 'into the Kings parts', as he later explained (T. Fuller, *Church History*, 11.206–7). About this time a personal tragedy occurred. A daughter was born to the Fullers and baptized Eleanor on 21 August 1643. The infant died and was buried on the following day, and Fuller's wife, Eleanor, was buried on 26 August, evidently the victim of childbirth.

Oxford, the royalist army, and Exeter, 1643–1646 By 10 September 1643 Fuller was in Oxford, staying at Lincoln College where, he afterwards declared, seventeen weeks cost him more than seventeen years in Cambridge, namely, all he had—a reference to his necessitous condition, as well as to the inflationary effects of war on the royalist capital. He was, according to the anonymous life, soon asked by the king to preach at the university church of St Mary the Virgin. There he 'laid open the blessings of an accommodation', noting that the conflict might be allayed by making concessions on the reformation of the church (*Life of … Fuller*, 23). His proposals apparently earned him the suspicion of some of those close to the king.

About the same time Fuller's *Sermon of Reformation* was attacked in print from a puritan standpoint by John Saltmarsh, a Cambridge graduate who was rector of Heslerton in Yorkshire. Saltmarsh's *Examinations, or, A Discovery of some Dangerous Positions* (1643) argued that Fuller's proposals would so limit the process of reform as to make any thoroughgoing changes impossible. Fuller's defence, *Truth Maintained* (1643), held that reforms should be made according to the laws and customs of the country; he acknowledged that innovations had earlier been introduced in the English church and enforced 'in some places without moderation' (pp. 13–14). In a prefatory letter to his parishioners at the Savoy Chapel he declared that he hated the present war because of the 'spirituall hardnesse of hearts' that it engendered (sig. C2).

Despite his detestation of the war Fuller soon entered the service of Sir Ralph Hopton, recently named Baron Hopton of Stratton, as chaplain in Hopton's royalist army. Hopton had been a member of the Long Parliament until war threatened. He was a committed member of the church as established before 1640 and was probably a congenial commander for Fuller to serve. In the course of the war, probably in the early part of 1644, Fuller was at Basing House, near Winchester, when it was besieged; on this occasion the defenders counter-attacked and the siege was lifted. Fuller also lived for a time in the rectory of his friend John White, the 'patriarch' of Dorchester, in Dorset. There his daughter Judith, who had been born in 1639, was buried on 14 March 1644. According to the anonymous biographer the king offered to appoint him as the incumbent of this parish in Dorchester, but Fuller declined, perhaps because of his regard for White, who was attending the Westminster assembly of divines. On 10 May 1644 Fuller preached before the king and the court at the university church in Oxford, where he defended the levying of tithes for the support of the church. At the same time his sermon, published as *Jacobs Vow* (1644), called on lay owners of former monastic lands, which would include many royalists, to give up their impropriation of tithes, by which they exercised the right to collect and use the tithes at their discretion.

On 17 September 1644 Fuller took up residence in Exeter, having been appointed by the king to be chaplain to the infant Princess Henrietta, born there in mid-June to Queen Henrietta Maria. The queen had left for France at the end of June, fearing capture by the approaching parliamentary army of the earl of Essex. Fuller was associated with the queen's friend Anne Villiers, Lady Dalkeith, who was in charge of the princess. It was to Lady Dalkeith that he dedicated his first book of religious and topical meditations, *Good Thoughts in Bad Times* (1645), described in the dedication as 'the first fruits of Exeter press'. Intended partly to console those whose lives were being torn apart by the war it was subsequently reprinted in London seven times before the Restoration in 1660. Towards the end of his sojourn in Exeter, Fuller was appointed by the city corporation, on 21 March 1646, to give the lecture established by Lawrence Bodley, brother of Sir Thomas Bodley, founder of the Bodleian Library in Oxford. Fuller's sermon *Feare of Losing the Old Light*, published in London in June 1646, may have been preached on the Bodley foundation. In this sermon, in taking his leave of Exeter, he raised the question of whether the knowledge and practice of Christianity were not disappearing from England as a result of the bitterness and partisanship of the war. Following Exeter's surrender to the parliamentarian army under Sir Thomas Fairfax on 13 April 1646 Fuller made his way to London. Not long afterwards the king slipped out of Oxford and delivered himself, on 5 May, into the hands of the Scots.

Pastor and historian, 1646–1658 Fuller's career was shattered by the defeat of the royalist cause. On 1 June 1646 Fuller petitioned the committee for compounding at Goldsmiths' Hall, signifying his willingness to accept a fine according to the Exeter articles of surrender. However, property belonging to Fuller in Dorset was still under sequestration on 26 March 1647, indicating that he had not been able to find the money to compound for his estate. He first found lodging in London with his publisher, John Williams. By early July 1646 he was living at Sion College, founded twenty-three years earlier for the use of London clergy and now frequented chiefly by those of a presbyterian persuasion. In January 1647 he was a guest of Edward, second Baron Montague, a friend from Cambridge days, at Boughton House, Northamptonshire. In 1647–8 Sir John Danvers, eventually a regicide, befriended him and invited him to preach in Chelsea. In his second book of meditations, *Good Thoughts in Worse Times* (1647), Fuller expressed a doubting mood approaching despair. The obstacles to a peaceful settlement seemed 'Iron Obstructions as come not within human power or policy to take away' (p. 70). His prophetic tale—entitled *Andronicus, or, The Unfortunate Politician* (1646)—described a soldier–politician who took control of the Byzantine empire from a dissolute court only to become, finally, a notorious tyrant. Following the trial and execution of Charles I in January 1649 Fuller preached a sermon in Chelsea, published in November of the same year, under the title *The Just Mans Funeral*, which does not mention the king by name but raises the question of why God would allow the wicked to flourish while the righteous meet defeat.

Despite his association with the royalist cause Fuller found opportunities to conduct his ministry in public. In 1647 he delivered a series of sermons at St Clement Eastcheap, and he also preached at St Dunstan-in-the-East, both in London. In the following year he was appointed perpetual curate or incumbent of Waltham Abbey, Essex, by its patron, James Hay, second earl of Carlisle. There he survived the surveillance of the parliamentary commissioners for Essex, who conducted a parochial inquisition. On 9 September 1650 they found that he was regarded as 'an able godly preaching minister' (LPL, survey of church lands, 1650, Essex). While serving at Waltham Abbey, probably about 1651, Fuller married Mary Roper, daughter of Thomas Roper, Viscount Baltinglass. They had three children, two boys and a girl, though only Thomas (b. 7 May 1655) survived beyond the earliest years. Fuller's son John, from his first marriage, entered Sidney Sussex College, Cambridge, in 1657, after being prepared at St Paul's School, London.

The interregnum, which brought many radical and unwelcome changes as far as Fuller was concerned, was, paradoxically, a remarkably productive period for him as a scholar and writer. His *Pisgah-Sight of Palestine* (1650), a historical and geographical description of the Holy Land, was well received. It carried perhaps an implied message: if ancient Jerusalem and its temple could be rebuilt, so, too, could the nearly shattered Church of England. His biographical sketches of key figures in the English Reformation in *Abel redevivus* (1651) provided possible patterns for that rebuilding. Fuller was, at the same time, intent on explaining how and why the cataclysmic events of the recent past had occurred. His edition of documents from the parliamentary sessions of 1628–9, *Ephemeris parliamentaria* (1654), distinguished two parties, 'the upholders of the Royal Prerogative & the Asserters of the Subjects Liberties' (preface), which he saw at the heart of the political and constitutional struggle of his time. Fuller also participated in the controversial exchanges of the day on issues of religious practice. In *The Infants Advocate* (1653) he defended infant baptism on biblical and theological grounds and in *A Triple Reconciler* (1654) he defended a learned ministry as more able than craftsmen preachers to interpret the scriptures adequately.

The most important of Fuller's writings during the interregnum was his *The Church History of Britain* (1655), the first comprehensive English protestant account of Christianity in the island from the earliest times. In method and outlook Fuller owed much to the English antiquarian movement. He also set out to answer the interpretation of events given by English Roman Catholic historians, who,

in the late sixteenth and early seventeenth centuries, had worked out a more detailed account of the English Reformation than had adherents of the established church. Fuller's book also provided an explanation for the tumultuous religious and political events of his own time, and it included the first detailed account of the decades immediately prior to the civil wars to be published. The *Church History* suggested that the ecclesiastical policies of Archbishop William Laud and his party, supported by Charles I, provoked much of the discontent that led to the conflicts of the civil war period. At the same time, in his account of the Elizabethan and Jacobean periods, before the accession of Charles I, Fuller offered historical examples useful in a reconstruction of the church whenever the opportunity arose. The *Church History* had appended to it a substantial history of the University of Cambridge and a short history of Waltham Abbey. The volume has an extraordinary number of dedications. Each of its eleven books and each of the appended works is dedicated to a member of a noble family. There are also dedications of sections of the book to merchants and lawyers in London and gentry in the counties around London. These patrons evidently helped to support his research and the publication of the work. They comprise an extensive network of persons apparently supportive not only of Fuller's work but of the monarchy and the established church of the pre-war period.

Last years, 1658–1661 In 1658 Fuller left Waltham Abbey to serve a smaller congregation as rector of St Dunstan, Cranford, 12 miles west of London. He was appointed to the living by its patron, George Berkeley, Baron Berkeley. In the following year Peter Heylyn attacked the *Church History* in his *Examen historicum* for inaccuracies and bias in taking the side of the nonconformists against the bishops. Fuller defended himself in his *The Appeal of Injured Innocence* (1659), where he acknowledged some errors but defended his treatment of those nonconformists who were 'eminent in their Generations'. With the protectorate dissolving following Richard Cromwell's vacating of his office Fuller wrote a pamphlet entitled *An Alarum to the Counties of England and Wales* (1660) urging General George Monck to allow 'a Free and full Parliament' to decide the country's future. In *Mixt Contemplations in Better Times* (1660) he gave his advice about a religious settlement: organize a comprehensive established church that included episcopalians and presbyterians and grant toleration to sects that choose not to be included. Fuller accompanied his patron, Lord Berkeley, to The Hague in early May 1660, when delegations from both houses of the Convention Parliament went to greet the restored king, Charles II. In August 1660, as one of the consequences of the Restoration, Fuller was awarded a DD from Cambridge University by royal mandate.

Fuller was restored to his living at Broadwindsor, but in October 1660 he relinquished it to the presbyterially ordained minister, John Pinney, who had served the parish for eleven years. By February 1661 Fuller had been restored to his former position at the Savoy Chapel and by spring or summer to his prebend at Salisbury Cathedral.

In the same period he was made a chaplain-extraordinary to Charles II. But he was not to enjoy these appointments for very long. On 12 August 1661 he fell ill with a fever and on 16 August he died in his lodgings in Covent Garden. At the insistence of Lord Berkeley he was buried at Cranford church. Nathaniel Hardy, dean of Rochester, preached at his funeral on 17 August; some 200 clergymen attended. Fuller was described by his contemporary biographer as tall, erect, of considerable bulk, with curly, light-coloured hair. He was survived by his wife, Mary, who died in Enfield, Middlesex, and was buried at Cranford on 19 May 1679, and by his sons John, graduate and later fellow of Sidney Sussex College, and later vicar of Great Wakering, Essex, and Thomas, admitted to Jesus College, Cambridge, in 1672.

Fuller's *History of the Worthies of England* was edited by his son John and published in 1662. Printing had been under way for some time before Fuller's death and there seems no doubt that the contents of the book are entirely of his own composition. The *Worthies* described each county's distinctive features, including commodities and proverbial expressions, and provided short biographies of its noteworthy inhabitants in a succession going back to the Saxons. It was the first English biographical dictionary. In addition to providing valuable information, Fuller's lives are marked by pungent, telling details that effectively bring his subjects to life. Leslie Stephen in the *Dictionary of National Biography* described Fuller as one who was able to 'accommodate himself rather too easily to men of all parties', and who 'steered rather too skilful a course, perhaps, through a revolutionary time'. On the contrary, his actions and writings show that he was a person of firm political and religious convictions who took considerable risks to support the institutions he most cherished: a balanced constitution of monarch and parliament and a tolerant established church under episcopal leadership. His major historical writings were erudite, original in scope, and written with verve in a style distinctively his own.

W. B. PATTERSON

Sources *The life of that reverend divine, and learned historian, Dr. Thomas Fuller* (1661) · J. E. Bailey, *The life of Thomas Fuller, D.D.* (1874) · M. J. Fuller, *The life, times and writings of Thomas Fuller, DD, the church historian (1608–1661)*, 2 vols., 2nd edn (1886) · A. T. Russell, *Memorials of the life and works of Thomas Fuller, DD* (1844) · S. Gibson, *A bibliography of the works of Thomas Fuller, D.D.* (1936) · D. B. Lyman, *The great Tom Fuller* (Berkeley, California, 1935) · W. Addison, *Worthy Dr. Fuller* (1951) · W. E. Houghton, *The formation of Thomas Fuller's holy and profane states* (1938) · J. E. Bailey and W. E. A. Axon, eds., *The collected sermons of Thomas Fuller, D.D., 1631–1659*, 2 vols. (1891) · Venn, *Alum. Cant.* · *The nonconformist's memorial ... originally written by ... Edmund Calamy*, ed. S. Palmer, 2 vols. (1775) · J. Rushworth, *Historical collections*, 5 pts in 8 vols. (1659–1701) · *Brief lives, chiefly of contemporaries, set down by John Aubrey, between the years 1669 and 1696*, ed. A. Clark, 2 vols. (1898) · Sidney Sussex College, Cambridge, register, vol. 1: admissions, 1598–1706 · register of marriage licences, diocese of Peterborough, Northants. RO · register of ordinations, diocese of Peterborough, 1622–87, Northants. RO · churchwardens' accounts for the parish of St Mary-le-Strand alias Savoy, 1586–1650, City Westm. AC · survey of church lands, Essex, 1650, LPL, MS cod. 909, E, vol. 8 · mandates, Charles II, letters, 1660–84, CUL, department of manuscripts and university archives · subscriptions, 1613–38, CUL, department of manuscripts and university archives · parish register, Hilton, 1603–1735, Dorset RO · parish register, Holy Trinity, Dorchester, 1559–1653, Dorset RO · parish register, Waltham Abbey, Waltham Holy Cross, 1642–53, 1653–86, Essex RO · Waltham Holy Cross, churchwardens' accounts, 1642–70, Essex RO · parish register, St Benet, Cambridge, Cambs. AS [from 1539] · C. H. Mayo, ed., *The minute books of the Dorset standing committee* (1902) · institution books, ser. A, 1556–1660, PRO, MS 5/55, vol. 3, Cambridgeshire; vol. 2, Dorset · request for composition by Thomas Fuller, 1 June 1646, PRO, MS SP 23/G.85/1022 · *Report on records of the city of Exeter*, HMC, 73 (1916) · correspondence of John Davenant, Bodl. Oxf., MS Tanner 72 · H. I. Longden, *Northamptonshire and Rutland clergy from 1500*, ed. P. I. King and others, 16 vols. in 6, Northamptonshire RS (1938–52) · J. F. Fuller, 'Thomas Fuller's first wife', N&Q, 12th ser., 4 (1918), 121–2 · J. J. Hammond, 'Thomas Fuller's first wife', N&Q, 12th ser., 4 (1918), 191 · E. A. Fry, ed., *The Dorset protestation returns preserved in the House of Lords, 1641–42* (1912) · *A Perfect Diurnall of the Passages in Parliament* (2–9 Jan 1643) · *Sir Simonds D'Ewes's parliamentary diary of the Long Parliament*, BL, Harley MS 163 · court register, 1631–1716, Sion College, London · parish register, Aldwincle, St Peter, 19 June 1608, Northants. RO [baptism] · parish register, London, St Mary Strand, 26 Aug 1643, City Westm. AC [burial] · parish register, Dorchester, Holy Trinity, 14 March 1644, Dorset RO [burial] · will, Northants. RO, register of wills, 1632–7, archdeaconry court of Northampton [Thomas Fuller, father]

Archives Jesus College, Cambridge, history of Cambridge

Likenesses D. Loggan, woodcut, BM, NPG; repro. in Fuller, *Worthies*, frontispiece · oils, Berkeley Castle, Gloucestershire [see illus.] · woodcut, repro. in T. Fuller, *Abel Redevivus, or, The dead yet speaking* (1651), frontispiece · woodcut, repro. in *Life of that reverend divine*, frontispiece

Fuller, Thomas (1654–1734), physician, the son of John Fuller (d. 1678), variously described as a gentleman, yeoman, and tailor, and his wife, Mary Calverley (1631–1714), was born at Hellingly, Sussex, on 24 June and baptized at Hellingly on 6 August 1654. John Fuller built up a small estate in the parish and rented a large farm from the dowager countess of Dorset; his goods were worth over £800 when he died. Fuller was admitted as a sizar to Queens' College, Cambridge, on 19 May 1671, graduating MB in 1676 and MD in 1681. In February 1679 he was admitted as an extra-licenciate of the Royal College of Physicians. Fuller established himself at Sevenoaks in Kent. Ten years after his arrival he bought the Red House, a new brick building set back from the high street; he remained there for the rest of his life, his practice drawn from the town itself and from wealthy invalids visiting Tunbridge Wells.

On 23 September 1703 Fuller married Mary (d. 1726), daughter of Thomas Plumer of Ringmer and his wife, Mary Acton, in the chapel of Lincoln's Inn. At the time of her marriage Mary was living with her cousins at Little Horsted, and it was there that their first child, Mary Fuller, was born in 1704. With his wife Fuller received £1800 in cash, a 60 acre farm in Ringmer and a share of the manor of Iford in the Ouse valley. In 1694 Fuller bought five houses in Vine Street in St Martin-in-the-Fields, and in 1707 the lease of Lullington parsonage, which in 1720 he sold to the earl of Dorset for £875.

In August 1714 the botanist and apothecary James Petiver breakfasted with Fuller, in whose garden

> we saw many choice and curious plants, and from his summer-house, which is an octagonal structure erected on an artificial eminence, we had fair prospects of the great

If any … say I have fill'd it full of hard Words, I confess I have so, and that partly upon direct Design, that I might … keep myself close from being searched and rifled by every illiterate Quack and busy Gossip. … And those that are so mean, that they can't apprehend the language I write, ought not to read it, nor dabble in Physic. (*Pharmacopoeia extemporanea*, preface to English edition of 1710)

Extemporanea was subsequently translated into French and German and published in Venice, Lausanne, Louvain, Amsterdam, and Paris.

In 1692 Fuller had obtained confirmation from his distant cousin Major John Fuller of Tanners in Waldron, an ironmaster and ordnance contractor, of his right to bear the family arms, suitably differenced. In 1703 Major Fuller's son John Fuller of Brightling married Elizabeth Rose, the stepdaughter of Sir Hans Sloane, and Thomas Fuller developed a correspondence if not a relationship with the great physician and collector. In 1724 Fuller investigated, on Sloane's behalf, a local case of death following inoculation, a practice which they both supported. It was to Sloane that Fuller dedicated *Exanthematologia*, his most important work, and to him that he sent a rarity received from Portugal.

Exanthematologia, or, An attempt to give a rational account of the eruptive fevers, especially of the measles and small-pox, was published in 1729. Almost blind with cataracts in both eyes and compelled to read and write with other eyes and other hands, Fuller regarded it 'as 'twere a posthumous work' (preface).

I could hardly resist falling into peculiar opinions, having lead a rural life, out of all conversation with philosophers and physicians that might have informed me otherwise. And as to other my imperfections, I have good hopes that you will impute most of them to old age and weak sight: for I am not able now to read any printed book; no not with the help of the best reading glass. (BL, Sloane MS 4050, fol. 170)

Thomas Fuller (1654–1734), by George Vertue, pubd 1739 (after Joseph Tymewell)

family-seat of the Earls of Dorset … The doctor regaled us with cold venison, pastry, and extraordinary good strong beer. We were shown his study, which is well furnished with valuable, scarce and curious books. (BL, Sloane MS 3340, fol. 146)

The description matches a view of the Red House by Thomas Badeslade, engraved in 1719 for John Harris's *History of Kent*, to which Fuller subscribed. Fuller's library included an important tune book of the 1530s now known as 'King Henry VIII's Songbook' (BL, Add. MS 31922), and a collection of theatre tunes in three parts, annotated in Fuller's hand and dating from the 1680s, is perhaps evidence of his practical musicianship.

Fuller's publishing career began in 1700 with an appendix to the third edition of *Pharmacopoeia Bateana*, the prescriptions of George Bate, consisting of material given him by Bate's daughter. Fuller published three collections of prescriptions, *Pharmacopoeia extemporanea* (1702), his own edition of *Bateana* (1718), and *Pharmacopoeia domestica* (1723). All went into several editions, and in 1710 Fuller, warned of a pirated translation of *Extemporanea*, reluctantly published an English version. As well as a history of his method of accumulating the prescriptions, he gives an insight into the professional attitudes of his time:

The work, based on observations from the 1690s onwards, contains many of his own precise case notes, including those relating to the case investigated for Sloane in 1724. Like Thomas Sydenham, Fuller championed careful observation, and his clinical insight enabled him to provide the first clear account of chicken-pox as a distinct disease, and to distinguish the spots made by flea bites from those seen in eruptive fevers. Although *Exanthematologia* was not controlled by a consistent overall philosophy, Fuller was familiar with the writings of Thomas Willis, Descartes, and Robert Hooke and his theory of disease was grounded on the work of the natural philosophers.

Fuller was clearly a capable and popular physician but with a conviction, not always shared by others, that he had beneficial advice to offer in fields other than his own. *Exanthematologia* was merely one of the projects on which he engaged in a burst of activity towards the end of his life. In 1724 he took up the cause of Newhaven, and with the herald John Warburton attempted to promote a bill to construct a harbour of refuge, to be funded from a levy on ships and a tax on the Jews. The scheme, 'not for profit to my particular self but entirely for a national good' (BL, Lansdowne MS 846, fol. 15), failed to win the support of the Pelhams and remained in abeyance during Fuller's life.

In October 1725 Fuller and four local landowners agreed to share the cost of an attempt to regulate the administration of the Sevenoaks Charity. The dispute reached chancery in 1728 against the background of the virtual collapse of the new schoolhouse; by that time three of the promoters had withdrawn, but Fuller persevered and obtained a satisfactory decree in 1730. The case was not finally settled until a year after his death, but seems to have cemented his reputation in the town: as late as 1863 Dr Fuller was said to have been 'greatly esteemed by the rich and adored by the poor' (Edwards, 1863). But Fuller was not universally popular. In 1692 he had become guardian of his Calverley cousins, one of whom scrawled on a settlement that it 'was contrived by the evil counsel given to my father by that rogue Dr Fuller ..., son of John Fuller the tailor and grandson of old Fuller the blacksmith of Hellingly ... as it afterwards appeared by the confession of his mother' (Oxfordshire Health Archives, Warneford Hospital, WD 112/11a–b). In 1727 Fuller published a collection of precepts—*Introductio ad prudentiam*—for the benefit of his son John, then seventeen; it remained in print until 1819. Two similar publications, *Introductio ad sapientiam, or, The Art of Right Thinking* and *Gnomologia*, appeared in 1731 and 1732.

Fuller died at Sevenoaks on 17 September 1734. He was buried at the parish church, where a monument in the south aisle bears a Latin epitaph of his own composition, enjoining his friends to rejoice with him as he left the sadnesses of the world for the joys of heaven. But the preface of *Exanthematologia*, written five years before, provides a more telling memorial:

> time has laid its hand on me, age hath broken me and I find my imagination, judgement and memory miserably ruined. I apprehend and think slowly; and whatever I am upon, I am forced to do it over and over before I can bring it to any shape.

He was succeeded by his son John Fuller (1710–1752), who left his whole estate to his distant cousin John Fuller of Rosehill in Brightling. CHRISTOPHER WHITTICK

Sources parish registers, E. Sussex RO, SAS/RF 4/69, 4/70, 5/28–47, 82–90; AMS 6234; W/A 35.60, W/B9.30; GBN 6/2; AMS 6013; CHR 6/1/3–4; PAR 375 1/1/1 • Warneford Hospital, Oxfordshire Health Archives, WD 111/5, 112/6–12 • BL, Sloane MS 3340, fol. 146 [Petiver letter] • BL, Sloane MSS 4047–4050, 4053 [letters to Hans Sloane] • CKS, U269 T140, T141, M152 • parish register, Sevenoaks, CKS, P330 1/7 • PRO, C 11/2784/2 • 'The correspondence of James Jurin (1684–1750)', ed. A. A. Rusnock, *Clio Medica*, 39 (1996), esp. 324 • J. H. Farrant, 'The evolution of Newhaven Harbour', *Sussex Archaeological Collections*, 110 (1972), 44–60 • J. T. Dunlop, *The pleasant town of Sevenoaks* (1974), 123 • J. T. Lennox, *Sevenoaks School and its founder, 1432–1932* (1932), 53–5 • J. Harris, *The history of Kent in five parts* (1719), opposite p. 279 • J. Comber, *Sussex genealogies*, 3 vols. (1931–3), vol. 3, pp. 213–20 • J. Edwards, *Recollections and conversations of Old Sevenoaks* (1863) • Venn, *Alum. Cant.* • Munk, *Roll* • parish register, Hellingly, 6 Aug 1654, E. Sussex RO [baptism] • memorial, Sevenoaks church

Likenesses G. Vertue, line engraving (after J. Tymewell), BM, NPG; repro. in *Pharmacopoeia domestica, or, The family dispensatory* (1739), frontispiece [*see illus.*]

Fuller, Sir Thomas Ekins (1831–1910), journalist and politician in Cape Colony, was born on 24 August 1831 at West Drayton, Middlesex, of a family of Baptist ministers, the son of the Revd Andrew Fuller (son of the famous Baptist preacher and theologian the Revd Andrew Fuller, (1754–1815), of Kettering, Northamptonshire), and his wife, Esther, *née* Hobson. Fuller was educated privately and at the Bristol Baptist college. Having entered the ministry, he served as a Baptist pastor at Melksham, Lewes, and Luton, contributing occasional articles to reviews and newspapers, as he continued to do throughout his life. In 1855 he married Mary Playne Hillier (d. 1872) of Nailsworth; they had three sons and a daughter.

By 1864 Fuller was seeking information about the Cape, for he had been advised by his doctor to take his wife, who was suffering from phthisis, to a warmer climate. In that year he was introduced to Saul Solomon (1817–1892), a prominent member of the Cape legislature and proprietor of the *Cape Argus*, who was visiting England. Impressed by Fuller and his writings, Solomon offered him the editorship of the *Cape Argus*, and the Fullers emigrated later that year. Fuller edited the *Argus*, in which he later acquired an interest, from 1864 to 1873. As editor he advocated forcefully both responsible government for the Cape, which was achieved in 1872, and an examining university for Cape Town, which opened in 1873.

After the death of his wife in 1872 Fuller left the Cape the following year to become the Cape's emigration agent in London. In 1875 he married Elizabeth Mann, daughter of the Revd Thomas Mann of Cowes; she survived her husband. Offered the post of general manager of the Union Steamship Company in Cape Town, he returned to the Cape with his second wife in 1875. He remained general manager until 1898, when he resigned to become a director of De Beers (1898–1902). In both positions he had time for a wide range of public activities. He served on the town council and the council of the South African College, he was active in the chamber of commerce, and rose to become chairman of the Table Bay Harbour Board. He helped found the Art Association of Cape Town. He was a member of the first board of directors of the *Cape Times*. His most important public work, however, was as member of the legislative assembly for Cape Town. Elected in 1878, he served in the assembly from 1879 to 1900, where he was respected as an eloquent speaker and as a man of learning, moderate views, and even temper. His political philosophy was that of a traditional Cape liberal.

Fuller soon emerged as the leader in the assembly of those critical of the 'native policy' of the Sprigg government, and accused that government of actions which brought on war with the Basuto in 1880. When J. G. Sprigg fell in 1881 Fuller might have become prime minister, but he never sought high office. His liberalism was limited: he was one of the first people in Cape Town to argue for the residential segregation of Africans. Though he believed that all males who reached a certain standard of 'civilization' should have the vote, regardless of race, he accepted a secret deal with J. H. Hofmeyr of the Afrikaner Bond in 1892 which enabled franchise legislation to be passed which restricted considerably the number of African voters in the colony. He later advocated the general adoption of the Cape franchise in the forthcoming Union of South Africa.

In the 1880s Fuller became a devoted follower and close confidant of Cecil John Rhodes, who lived close to him, but he declined the offer of a cabinet post when Rhodes became prime minister. An early leader of the pro-Rhodes Progressive Party, Fuller joined the executive of the British-supremacist South African League after the Jameson raid. He served on the Cape parliamentary select committee which investigated the raid in 1896, and in 1897–8 was a member of a controversial governmental commission on the redistribution of parliamentary seats.

Fuller returned to Britain during the Second South African War to take up the post of agent-general for the Cape of Good Hope, representing the colony's interests in London. He was made a CMG in 1903 and was knighted (KCMG) in 1904; he had to give up his post in 1907 because of ill health. In 1910 he published *The Right Honourable Cecil John Rhodes: a Monograph and Reminiscence*, a substantial and well-written biography of Rhodes, which drew heavily on his memories of his friend. Fuller died on 5 September 1910 at 1 Mount Ephraim Mansions, Tunbridge Wells, a few months after the establishment of the Union of South Africa. His son Edward Barnard Fuller (1868–1946), who became medical officer of health in Cape Town, continued his father's interest in issues of public health.

CHRISTOPHER SAUNDERS

Sources T. E. Fuller, *The Right Honourable Cecil John Rhodes: a monograph and a reminiscence* (1910) · F. R. Metrowich, 'Fuller, Sir Thomas Ekins', *DSAB* · W. E. G. Solomon, *Saul Solomon* (1948) · V. Bickford-Smith, *Ethnic pride and racial prejudice in Victorian Cape Town* (1995) · *Men of the times: old colonists of the Cape Colony and Orange River Colony* (Johannesburg, 1906) · *Sir James Rose-Innes: selected correspondence, 1884–1902*, ed. H. M. Wright (1972) · J. H. Hofmeyr and F. W. Reitz, *The life of Jan Hendrik Hofmeyr (Onze Jan)* (1913) · R. I. Rotberg, *The founder: Cecil Rhodes and the pursuit of power* (1988) · *Cape Argus* (6 Sept 1910) · *CGPLA Eng. & Wales* (1910)
Archives Bodl. RH, Rhodes MSS · National Library of South Africa, Cape Town, Hofmeyr MSS
Likenesses photograph, repro. in *Men of the times* · photograph, repro. in *Prominent men of the Cape* · photograph, repro. in *The Veld* (Aug 1902) · photograph, repro. in *African Review* (28 Sept 1901)
Wealth at death £5045 4s.: probate, 10 Oct 1910, *CGPLA Eng. & Wales*

Fuller, William (*d.* 1586?), religious radical, is of origins which are unknown. The little that is known of his life derives very largely from his own book, a treatise which he prepared for presentation to Elizabeth I. This records that he began to serve Elizabeth while she was in the household of Queen Katherine Parr, and that he married at this time. His wife was Joice or Jocosa, daughter of John Butler of Aston-le-Walls, Northamptonshire, and his wife, Margaret. After Katherine's death in 1547 Fuller remained in Elizabeth's service when she was at Hatfield from 1550; he himself lived at Holwell nearby, where the princess once visited his 'godlie mother, then old and sicklie' (Fuller, 2.57). He later attended Elizabeth when she was conveyed to the Tower under suspicion of treason in 1554.

Fuller was a committed evangelical, and by July 1556 he, his wife, and three of their servants were in exile in Geneva, which he later remembered with devoted affection as an ideal Christian community. On 12 July 1556 his household was received into John Knox's congregation, in which Fuller was made an elder on 16 December following. Accounted a resident of the city on 7 January 1557 he was elected a church deacon on 17 December that year. On 15 December 1558 he was one of the signatories of a letter attacking ceremonies addressed to the city of Frankfurt-am-Main; the others included Christopher Goodman, Miles Coverdale, John Knox, and Anthony Gilby.

During his sojourn in Geneva, Fuller's wife died, and it was as a widower that he returned to England some time before 27 February 1559. He had considered remaining in Switzerland, but John Calvin persuaded him that it was his duty 'to go into my native Countrie and do what litle good I could' (Fuller, 2.58). The links he had made with Goodman in Geneva led to his being employed by his old friend Sir Thomas Parry, the treasurer of the queen's household, in the government's efforts to bring Goodman before the privy council to answer for his attack on female monarchy in *How Superior Powers Oght to be Obeyd of their Subjects* (1558). Fuller was unable to help, not least because Goodman's friends, knowing that Fuller had been critical of the book, refused to give him the necessary information. The former Genevans were far from united, and Fuller was also accused of having openly criticized Knox's *First Blast of the Trumpet Against the Monstruous Regiment of Women*, likewise published in 1558. But he was equally hostile to the Elizabethan religious settlement, and though he had brought with him from Switzerland a French Bible and New Testament to give to the queen, he now refused to be presented to Elizabeth, and the books were not handed over until 7 October 1576.

Much of the rest of Fuller's life seems to have been spent in voluntary exile from the court, unreconciled to the church order in England. At the end of 1573 an episcopal campaign against nonconformists led to his being imprisoned in the Counter; his captivity was later mitigated to house arrest. In autumn 1576 he was taken ill and 'thought to dy' and therefore sent the queen the scriptures he had brought from Geneva by the hands of Lady Stafford (Fuller, 2.60). This episode shows that Fuller still had access to Elizabeth, who clearly retained kind memories of him. Early in 1580, speaking initially to an unnamed privy councillor and then to the queen herself, he censured her alleged decision to appoint four Catholics to the privy council following opposition to her proposed marriage to the duc d'Anjou, brother of Henri III of France. Elizabeth asked him to set his criticisms down in writing, which he did, adding to them a 'book' of clauses in acts of parliament whereby 'much land and revenues and manie summes of monye were unrighteouslie had' from the crown (ibid., 62). Neither of these writings has survived. On 19 February he had a further audience with the queen—on her initiative—at which he presented Elizabeth with 'a brief, generall admonition', and then departed (ibid., 50).

Following his audience of 1580 Fuller hoped for a further meeting with the queen at which he could make his religious views known to her. No summons followed, and so on 2 July 1585, apparently moved by a near apocalyptic sense of God's imminent judgment, he made use of another of his court contacts, Lady Leighton (presumably Elizabeth, daughter of Sir Francis Knollys and wife of Sir Thomas Leighton), to present a further 'booke' to the queen. This remarkable document is an extended critical commentary on the Church of England and on Elizabeth's personal responsibility for its shortcomings. Fuller fiercely denounces the religious settlement of 1559 onwards, whereby 'but halflie by your Majestie hath God bene honoured, his Church reformed and established, his people taught and comforted, his enemies rejected and subdued, and his law-breakers punished' (Fuller, 2.52). Elizabeth must mend her own ways, not least by ceasing to countenance images, by observing the sabbath—'for if you had, things would never have gone as now thei doe' (ibid., 54)—and by refraining from swearing. Fuller is indeed a unique source for the queen's imprecatory habits:

> your gracious majestie in your anger hath used to sweare, sometime by that abhominable Idoll the masse, and often and grievouslie by God, and by Christ, and by manie parts of his glorified bodie, and by Saints, faith, troth and other forbidden things.   (ibid., 53–4)

Elizabeth is also rebuked for promoting the wrong people in the English church. In passages which constitute a priceless source for the fortunes of the Genevan exiles after their return to England, Fuller condemns her for having 'favoured, furthered, and advanced Antichristians and Neuters at home' whereas those who had suffered exile or persecution under Mary 'were so schooled, limited and stinted in their prechings and teachings, that their messages from God were not truelie and faithfullie done' (ibid., 52, 61).

Fuller was passionately serious in thus addressing the queen, but his account of the fortunes of his 'booke' after Elizabeth received it verges on the comical. She read in it, then placed it on a chair, from which Lord Burghley quietly removed it, and took care that the queen should not see it again. A lady-in-waiting, instructed to recover it, did not dare to do so. Fuller asked Lady Leighton to obtain a private audience for him with the queen, but there is no evidence that one took place. He was ill by this time, and it is possible that he was the William Fuller of St Sepulchre, London, whose will, drawn up on 18 August 1586 and proved on 14 October following, records three sons (Samuel, Daniel, and Nathaniel) and two daughters (Hester and Elizabeth). If so, he may also have been the uncle of the puritan lawyer Nicholas Fuller. William Fuller had remarried since his return from Geneva, but the identity of his second wife is unknown. His 'booke' of 1585 was published in an extended calendar by Albert Peel in 1915.

NATALIE MEARS

Sources [W. Fuller], 'A copie of Mr Fullers booke to the queene', *The seconde parte of a register*, ed. A. Peel, 2 vols. (1915), vol. 2, pp. 49–69 • C. Martin, *Les protestants: anglais réfugiés à Genève au temps de Calvin, 1555–1560: leur église, leur écrits* (Geneva, 1915) • C. H. Garrett, The *Marian exiles: a study in the origins of Elizabethan puritanism* (1938) • P. Collinson, *The Elizabethan puritan movement* (1967) • J. Fines, *A biographical register of early English protestants and others opposed to the Catholic church, part 2* (1985) • W. H. Turner, ed., *The visitations of the county of Oxford … 1566 … 1574 … and in 1634*, Harleian Society, 5 (1871) • P. Collinson, *Godly people: essays on English protestantism and puritanism* (1983) • will, PRO, PROB 11/69, fol. 414v
Archives DWL, 'A copie of Mr Fullers booke to the queene'
Wealth at death £1000 left in legacies, of which £600 was owed to him by people who had borrowed from him: will, PRO, PROB 11/69, fol. 414v

Fuller, William (1579/80–1659), dean of Ely, born in or about 1580, was the son of Andrew Fuller of Hadleigh, Suffolk. He was a sizar at Trinity College, Cambridge (BA 1600, MA 1603) and by 1606 had been elected one of the six foundation fellows of St Catharine's College under John Overall; he took the degree of BD in 1610 and became DD by royal mandate in 1628. According to David Lloyd (1668) he was a good linguist, an excellent trainer of junior clergy and was, 'with *Chrysostom*, called the *poor man's preacher*' (Lloyd, 509). In 1616 he was presented to the rectory of Weston, Nottinghamshire, by Sir Gervase Clifton, his patron: he preached at Lady Clifton's funeral. By 1621 he had been appointed a chaplain-in-ordinary to James I, serving in a June turn. He continued in his attendance for Charles I and accompanied him to Dover when the new king went to meet his French bride. Fuller's sermon on that occasion (on Ephesians 4: 7) was the first of the new reign to be printed by command. Despite this early eminence it was not until 1634 that he preached one of the Lent court sermons before the king (as he did again from 1640 to 1642). As a chaplain-in-ordinary he attended Charles on his fated journey north in the summer of 1640.

On 3 July 1628 Fuller received a dispensation to hold the vicarage of St Giles Cripplegate, London, in addition to the rectory of Weston, and he continued to hold it after July 1636 when, on the death of Henry Caesar, he was promoted to the deanery of Ely. From 1636 to 1642 he attended the annual general chapter at Ely and signed the yearly leases. In October 1641, in the wake of the parliamentary attack on Bishop Wren of Ely the previous July, some of the parishioners of St Giles petitioned parliament for Fuller's removal. They complained that, although the parish was very populous, numbering 40,000 souls, and the living worth £700 a year, Fuller had 'pluralities of livings, and thereby was a non-resident' and a 'popish innovator besides'. Altogether ten articles were exhibited against him. In addition to the charges of non-residency, and of supplying his place with the most unsuited clergy, it was objected that 'he useth superstitious cringing and bowing to the Communion table, and the name of Jesus', and that he held the communion rails about the table, which had been present since the 1580s, in such esteem that those who rested on them during sermons were forcibly evicted from the church. He was further charged with simony and with extorting exorbitant baptism and burial fees from the poor. The petitioners alleged further that Fuller's curate, Timothy Hutton, 'repaired from his pulpit to the taverne on the Lords day, and there drinking uncivilly, danced and sung most profaine, and ungodly songs and dances, to the shame and disgrace of religion' ('Articles Exhibited … Against Dr Fuller', 1641, sigs. A2v, A3v). The Commons summoned Fuller to attend in person on 3 November 1641: his failure to appear before them led to his being sent for as a 'delinquent', 'for divers dangerous and scandalous matters delivered by him in several sermons' (JHC, 2.307). On 9 November he was committed into the custody of the serjeant-at-arms, but was bailed upon good security and released two days later. News from Ireland of a potential protestant bloodbath took up more of the Commons' time. Eight months later, in July 1642, Fuller and Hutton were sent for with three other clerical 'delinquents' charged with having read the king's last declaration in church. Fuller denied having given orders for it to be read; he had in fact enjoined Hutton not to read it 'till he had received farther direction' (ibid., 2.650). Dean Fuller was discharged 'from any farther restraint without paying fees' (ibid., 2.669); however, the unfortunate curate, who confessed to having read it at the afternoon service, was committed a prisoner to the king's bench, where he remained until 4 August. Along with goods belonging to Lord Petre and Mr William Petre, and plate belonging to both the archbishop of York and the bishop of Ely, Fuller's money was on 18 February 1643 ordered to be confiscated 'for the service of the commonwealth' (ibid., 2.970). In his will Fuller claimed that the earl of Essex had unjustly seized £500 from his estate.

In 1645 Fuller was in attendance upon the king at Oxford, presumably in his monthly turn as chaplain, and was incorporated in his doctor's degree on 12 August of that year. Charles, who greatly admired his preaching, nominated him to be dean of Durham in succession to the recently deceased appointee, Christopher Potter, but it is unlikely that he was ever installed: at the Restoration, Walter Balcanquhall, who died on Christmas day 1645, was regarded as the last dean to have held office in Durham. Fuller retired to London, where he died in the parish of St Giles Cripplegate on 13 May 1659, aged seventy-nine; he was survived by his wife, Katherine, three sons, and two daughters. The intruded minister, Dr Samuel Annesley, and the authorities refused Fuller's relatives' request that he might be buried in the church of St Giles, and he was interred at the upper end of the south aisle of St Vedast's, Foster Lane, where his daughter Jane erected a monument over her father's grave. In his will, dated 14 December 1658 and proved on 30 May 1659, Fuller appointed Jane's husband, Brian Walton, later bishop of Chester, as his literary executor.

GORDON GOODWIN, rev. NICHOLAS W. S. CRANFIELD

Sources D. Lloyd, Memoires of the lives … of those … personages that suffered … for the protestant religion (1668) · list of royal chaplains, 1622, CCC Oxf., MS E 297, fol. 188 · chaplains that wait monthly, 1635–44, PRO, LC 5/134, fol. 6 · chaplains that wait monthly, 1635–44, PRO, LC 3/1, fol. 4 · dean and chapter lease book, diocese of Ely, CUL, EDC 2/2A/1 · E. E. Rich, ed., St Catharine's College, Cambridge, 1473–1973: a volume of essays to commemorate the quincentenary of the foundation of the college (1973) · PRO, LC 5/132, fol. 5r · PRO, LC 5/134, 454, 456 · PRO, LC 5/135, 32 · Fasti Angl. (Hardy) · PRO, SP 16/109/12* · JHC, 2 (1640–42), 299, 307, 309, 311, 650, 669, 703, 970 · J. E. Fagg, Deans and canons of Durham, 1541–1900 (1974) · Venn, Alum.

Cant. · Wood, Ath. Oxon., new edn, 2.79–80, 82 · monument inscription, St Vedast's, Foster Lane, London

Fuller, William (1608/9–1675), bishop of Lincoln, was born in London, the son of Thomas Fuller, possibly a city merchant, and his wife, possibly Lucy, daughter of Simon Cannow, merchant. He was educated first at Westminster School and then at Magdalen Hall, Oxford, where he matriculated about 1626. Later he moved to St Edmund Hall, where he graduated BCL in 1632. He was ordained by Bishop John Bancroft of Oxford, becoming deacon in 1635 and priest four years later, and was appointed one of the chaplains or petty canons of Christ Church Cathedral. In 1641 he was presented by the king to the rectory of St Mary Woolchurch, London, which he resigned later the same year on his institution to the rectory of Ewhurst, Surrey. When Charles I moved the royal administration to Oxford he became chaplain to Edward, Lord Lyttelton, lord keeper of the great seal. As an ardent loyalist, like his namesake the dean of Durham, who was also in the city during the 1640s, he suffered greatly in the civil war. He was sequestrated from his rectory of Ewhurst by the Surrey county committee in 1644, although in September 1645 the committee for the advance of money learned that he still had property in London, Surrey, and Sussex; in the parliamentary visitation of the university he also lost his position at Christ Church.

During the interregnum he travelled abroad in 'the Catholique countries' (Pepys, 23 Feb 1660). On returning to England he established a school at Mount Vernon, Twickenham, where he 'endeavoured to instill principles of loyalty into his scholars' (Wood, Ath. Oxon., 4.850–51). Samuel Pepys placed the twelve-year-old Edward Mountagu at school there and later found that Fuller had laid a very good foundation for the boy's Latin. Among Fuller's assistants at Twickenham were William Wyatt and Francis Drope, whom he was later able to reward with the precentorship and a canonry of Lincoln respectively.

At the Restoration Fuller obtained speedy preferment. On 3 July 1660 he was appointed to the deanery of St Patrick's, Dublin, receiving the degree of DCL from Oxford University on 2 August. After travelling to Ireland he was installed into his deanery on 22 October. As dean he was soon involved in an event which encapsulated the mood of the restored church in Ireland, the consecration at St Patrick's of twelve new bishops on 27 January 1661. Fuller not only played a major part in the ceremonial but he also composed an anthem for the occasion, Now that the Lord hath re-Advanced the Crown, whose concluding chorus expressed the sense of Anglican rejoicing:

> Angels look down, and joy to see
> Like that above, a monarchie;
> Angels look down, and joy to see
> Like that above, an hierarchie.
> (Bolton, 32)

Other preferments in the Irish church followed: he was made treasurer of Christ Church, Dublin (1661), chancellor of Dromore (1662), and finally he was consecrated bishop of Limerick on 20 March 1664, with permission to hold his deanery in commendam for two years. Wood noted that during this period much of Fuller's time was spent in England, and it has been suggested that he regarded his Irish dignities as little more than stepping stones to some more acceptable English preferment. However, evidence from St Patrick's indicates that, although he often left the subdean to preside at chapter meetings, he showed a warm interest in the repair of his cathedral, which during his tenure of office was restored from a ruinous condition to decency and stability. His absences in England were occasioned, at least in part, by the need to make representations on behalf of the whole Irish church. At a meeting of the Irish convocation in May 1661 Fuller was chosen by the lower house to be their agent in placing their affairs before the king.

In 1667 the translation of Benjamin Laney from the bishopric of Lincoln to that of Ely occasioned intricate negotiations over the fate of several concurrently vacant sees, with Fuller being promised St Asaph, and both Bishop Edward Rainbowe of Carlisle and Dean Henry Glemham of Bristol expressing a preference for moving to Lincoln. Fuller, who was then laid up with gout at the Black Bull at Chester on his way back to Ireland, wrote on 25 May 1667 to Joseph Williamson, Lord Arlington's secretary that, 'as when two contend, a third person is sometimes chosen' (CSP dom., 1667, 121), he hoped that he himself might be approved for the see of Lincoln. His application proved successful and he was elected on 17 September 1667.

Fuller proved to be an energetic diocesan. He lost no time in carrying out his primary visitation in 1668 and despite the vast extent of his diocese undertook a second one in 1671. In August of that year he reported to Williamson 'I have now passed through five counties in my visitation, and … have toiled like a horse from morning till night these 23 days' (CSP dom., 1671, 426–7). In keeping with his strong views on the interdependence of church and king he tackled the issue of nonconformity with vigour, though his willingness to license the dissenter Samuel Shaw to teach at Ashby-de-la-Zouch shows that he was prepared to show toleration in individual cases. The issue of the declaration of indulgence in 1672 reduced him to despair: 'All these licensed persons grow insolent and increase strangely' (CSP dom., 1672, 589).

Although Fuller appears initially to have envisaged that he, like his predecessors, would live at the episcopal palace at Buckden in Huntingdonshire, where he would have easy access to London, he soon changed his mind. In February 1668 the dean and chapter, 'consideringe the great benefit which would accrewe to the church and cittie and the whole dioces of Lincoln by the presence of their diocesan', reserved a house in Pottergate for the bishop's residence (Lincoln Cathedral Library, chapter acts A/3/9, fol. 261). Thus Fuller became the first bishop of Lincoln since the twelfth century to make Lincoln his main residence. Here he set about the beautification of his surroundings. Letters of 1673 show him creating a spring bulb garden, receiving tulips, auriculas, crocuses, and daffodils from John Goode in Oxford. He also co-operated with Dean Michael Honywood to repair the damage inflicted on his cathedral church during the civil war and interregnum.

He was concerned to see the sanctuary suitably adorned to reflect a proper reverence and dignity in worship. In a letter of 27 October 1668 to William Sancroft, Fuller expressed his intention of presenting the cathedral with a new altar cloth for feast days, and 'a paire of faire candlesticks' to replace 'a pitifull paire of ordinary brasse candlesticks … which I am asham'd to see, and can indure no longer' (Ornsby, 217n.). He restored the monuments of Remigius and St Hugh, supplying appropriate epitaphs in excellent Latin.

Fuller was evidently good company and he enjoyed the friendship of both John Evelyn and Pepys. The latter refers in his diaries on a number of occasions to his 'dear friend' Dr Fuller, dining with him ('very merry we were for an houre or two … I am most pleased with his company and goodness') and expressing 'great joy' at his elevation to the episcopate, finding 'the Bishopp the same good man as ever … one of the comeliest and most becoming Prelates … that ever I saw' and 'a very extraordinary good-natured man' (Pepys, 1.181, 3.86, 8.449, 7.209–10, 9.35). He enjoyed music, possessing a chest of viols and an organ. His literary talents were displayed not only in Latin epitaphs but in a series of verses later set to music by Henry Purcell. Of these the best-known is the exquisite evening hymn, Now that the Sun hath Veiled his Light.

Fuller, who was unmarried, died aged sixty-six at Kensington on 23 April 1675. His end, according to his epitaph, was as peaceful as his life had been: 'mortem obiit vita sua lenissima (si fieri posset) leniorem' (J. Monson, ed., Lincolnshire Church Notes Made by William John Monson, Lincoln RS, 31, 1936, 246). His body was conveyed to Lincoln Cathedral and was buried there under an altar tomb in the retrochoir. He bequeathed to 'the Librarie nowe preparing' at Lincoln Cathedral the choicest of his books, and to Christ Church, Oxford, his portrait and his musical instruments (PRO, PROB 11/347).   NICHOLAS BENNETT

Sources Wood, Ath. Oxon., new edn, 4.850–51 • Pepys, Diary • CSP dom., 1667–75 • PRO, PROB 11/347 • Bodl. Oxf., MS Oxf. dioc., pps.e.13, pp. 347, 444 • Walker rev., 351 • F. R. Bolton, The Caroline tradition of the Church of Ireland (1958) • H. Cotton, Fasti ecclesiae Hibernicae, 1–4 (1845–51) • W. M. Mason, History of St Patrick's Cathedral (1820) • chapter acts, Lincoln Cathedral Library, MS A/3/9 • J. Goode, letters to W. Fuller, 1673, Lincs. Arch., Vv/2/4/5–6 • 'The remains of Denis Granville, DD, dean and archdeacon of Durham', ed. [G. Ornsby], Miscellanea, SurtS, 37 (1861), pt 1 • monumental inscription, Lincoln Cathedral
Likenesses oils, 1667, Christ Church Oxf.

Fuller, William (1670–1733), government agent and controversialist, was born, according to his own account, on 20 September 1670 at Milton, near Sittingbourne, Kent, the son of Robert Fuller, a substantial local grazier, who died only a few months later, and his wife, Catherine (d. c.1682), daughter of Charles Herbert and a cousin of William Herbert, first marquess of Powis. This is confirmed to the extent that parish registers record the baptism, at Milton, of a William, son of Robert and Catherine May Fuller on 25 September 1670; and that at his admission as an apprentice Fuller was described as son of Robert Fuller, a butcher. He says that after his father's death his mother remarried, her new husband being Thomas Packman, a yeoman of Milton. The baptisms of three children of Thomas and Catherine Packman are recorded in the Milton registers.

According to Fuller, on his father's death he was placed in the wardship of a family friend, Cornelius Harflete, who sent him to school at Canterbury when he was seven and then, aged ten, at Maidstone. At fourteen he left school and, his mother having died two years earlier, lodged first with his stepfather, Thomas Packman, before moving in with Harflete, then resident in Stepney, Middlesex, who on 4 January 1688, bound him apprentice to a London skinner, James Hartley. While working for Hartley early in 1688, Fuller records, he met Sir John Burrows, a Roman Catholic relation of his mother, who introduced him to the marquess of Powis's Jesuit chaplain, Lewis Sabran. Together they persuaded Fuller to renounce protestantism, and found him places first in the London household of his supposed kinsman Lord Powis, and then in that of the earl of Melfort, secretary of state for Scotland. Here, by May 1688, he was noticed by James II's wife, Mary of Modena, then heavily pregnant with the future Jacobite claimant to the throne, James Edward Stuart. In the wake of the invasion by William of Orange the court moved in December to France, Fuller travelling with it as page to Lady Powis, governess to Prince James.

In France, Fuller, claimed he at once began to carry secret messages between the exiled court and its supporters at home. Concealing letters in his clothes (some folded up and sewn into his buttons) he travelled to England ten times and to Ireland once during the next year, staying when necessary with his former master, Hartley. However, on his eleventh visit, in autumn 1689, he was spotted and arrested by Harflete and his nephew, a Major Kitchell, who had some association with the secretary of state, Lord Shrewsbury. After withstanding Shrewsbury's interrogation Fuller was placed in the custody of John Tillotson, dean of St Paul's, whose persuasive powers, it was hoped, would turn him to the Protestant cause. Nine weeks sufficed, and in an audience with William III he revealed his methods of concealing letters and undertook to continue his missions for the Jacobites but as a double agent.

On his third mission in this capacity Fuller was accompanied by another messenger, Matthew Crone, a wanted man in England. Fuller set up a situation in which Harflete and Kitchell were able to hear Crone make treasonable oaths and then apprehend him. The ensuing trial naturally blew Fuller's cover, and he claimed to have been poisoned by a Jacobite hitman sent to prevent him giving his vital evidence. Crone was convicted in June 1690; but although he later made a confession to avoid the gallows no further prosecutions resulted and Fuller's services as a witness were not required again.

With no income Fuller fell into debt and was confined within the rules of the king's bench prison where, in summer 1691, he began to lodge in the house of Titus Oates. Shortly afterwards, however, he escaped from his warders and sailed to Flanders, where he survived for a time on the proceeds of confidence tricks before returning home in November. His claim that he had been engaged on a mission for the queen went unheeded and he was again confined. From prison he wrote to Tillotson (now archbishop of Canterbury) and the earl of Portland to say that he had firm evidence of a Jacobite plot in high places. Receiving no satisfactory response he repeated his allegations to parliament, and was summoned to appear before the bar of the Commons in December. He was also paid £50 and granted an allowance of 30s. per week by the Treasury. But whenever challenged to produce his evidence he prevaricated, either saying that his papers were detained elsewhere or feigning illness. He claimed the support of two witnesses, a Colonel Delavell and George Hayes, like him former Jacobite agents, and even obtained blank safe conducts for them, but they failed to appear. In the ensuing weeks the Commons lost patience, and on 24 February 1692 a motion was passed declaring Fuller a 'notorious Impostor, a Cheat, and a false Accuser', and recommending prosecution. He was tried and convicted on 21 November, being sentenced a week later to stand twice in the pillory and to pay a fine of 200 marks. He suffered the former part of the sentence and returned to debtor's gaol.

After two and a half years' imprisonment Fuller was able to settle his principal debts, as a result, he later stated, of a subvention from his uncle Charles Herbert. After returning to Canterbury he attempted to revive interest in the purported Jacobite plot by reporting that Delavell had landed near Romney Marsh, and had a few weeks' prosperity living on the funds intended to finance the search for his witness. It was then that he turned to the topic with which he is most closely associated: the story that James Edward Stuart, Jacobite prince of Wales, was not in fact the son of James II but a child introduced to the queen's chamber in a warming-pan. Making use of his recollections of court life at the time of the birth, in 1696 he published a short book, *A Brief Discovery of the True Mother of the Pretended Prince of Wales*, which gave the warming-pan story a new, detailed, and definitive form. In Fuller's version the child's mother was disclosed as Mary Grey, a lady-in-waiting to the countess of Tyrconnel, who had been silenced first by being removed to a Paris convent and then, it was implied, by being killed. The book was an immediate success, and was printed in the same year in Edinburgh and soon afterwards in Dutch and French translations; at least eight editions were printed by 1702 with a further version as late as 1746. Not surprisingly the controversial nature of the work drew on its author a series of vehement attacks in print. Before the end of 1696 Fuller responded with two further pamphlets in which he developed the theme of a government coverup, accusing the earl of Nottingham, as secretary of state in 1690, of concealing documents proving the substitution and conniving at the escape of Delavell and Hayes in 1692. Whether Fuller was behind the publication of one of the documents supposedly concealed by Nottingham (see *Mr De Labadie's Letter to his Daughter*, 1696) is not clear.

Fuller returned to the theme in 1700 with *A Plain Proof of* the *True Father and Mother of the Pretended Prince of Wales*, giving more specific details of the imposture and quoting letters between the principal actors. This pamphlet sold well and provoked still more vitriolic reactions in the sympathetic tory press, to which Fuller responded in kind with several pamphlets in 1701. Of these, *A Full Demonstration* (dated 1702, but actually 1701) contained a letter purporting to be from Mary of Modena to James II recounting the murder of Mary Grey, while *Twenty-Six Depositions* (stated on the title-page to be 'published by command', November 1701) included statements supposedly made by important witnesses.

In the meantime Fuller had returned to confidence trickery and the chasing of imaginary spies. In May 1698 he travelled to Newcastle, where he convinced two prominent citizens, John Clavering and William Johnson, that he was on orders from the king to appoint a commission to oversee local security. Flattered by being chosen they advanced him substantial sums. To lend credence to his story Fuller showed them letters he was sending to the earl of Portland and the king, and encouraged them to write as well. These letters, actually being dispatched, naturally led to the detection of the deceit, and Fuller fled south again, going to Hampshire, where he lived for some time off the authorities by claiming to be in pursuit of an elusive Jacobite called Thomas Jones, who had evidence of another dangerous conspiracy. He then went to France, reintroduced himself to his erstwhile mentor, Father Sabran, and spent time in Antwerp supposedly preparing for ordination as a Roman Catholic priest.

In December 1701 Fuller brought out *Original Letters of the Late King's and Others*, which included a 'deposition' by Thomas Jones. Summoned by the House of Lords and directed to produce Jones or the evidence Fuller once more prevaricated and parliament's patience again ran out. On 19 January 1702 his most recent two pamphlets were declared false and malicious by vote of the Lords and in May he was convicted of criminal libel and sentenced to stand in the pillory at three places, to be whipped at Bridewell, and to pay a fine of 1000 marks. His personal experiences in the first two parts of this sentence were recounted in *Mr William Fuller's Trip to Bridewell* (1703), which contains a recantation of his tales of Jacobite conspiracy. The confessional theme continued the same year with *The Whole Life of Mr William Fuller*, an expanded edition of a brief autobiography produced in 1701. The new edition identified the authors of the conspiracy tales as Titus Oates, John Tutchin, and others in whose hands Fuller himself was a pawn. Then, in 1704, came his *Sincere and Hearty Confession*, in which he recanted the whole story of Mary Grey and the warming-pan, presumably hoping for early release from prison, where—unable to pay his fine—he remained. A second part of the *Confession* was published in 1705.

Despite his recantation Fuller's earlier works continued to enjoy popularity, and it may have been this that prompted him to withdraw his later statement, at least in part, in a pamphlet entitled *The Truth at Last*. Undated, but probably issued about 1708, it states that the tale of Mary Grey

was true, and that he had been forced to deny it by Jacobites in authority. He also pressed his cause with members of the administration by petition, and in 1716 he published a *Letter to the Right Honourable the Earl of Oxford* and a more general address, *A Humble Appeal*, reissued the next year as *Truth Brought to Light by Time*. In these he disowned the Jacobite conspiracy theories but reasserted the warming-pan story.

This was Fuller's last public salvo, but he continued for several years to address petitions to prominent figures. His last known appeal was sent from Newgate gaol to William Wake, archbishop of Canterbury, in 1730. Wake had apparently visited Fuller in prison, but his notes on the petition indicate that he had no intention of acting to free him. The petition is of interest principally for showing that Fuller was once again firmly disavowing the warming-pan tale. He seems never to have regained his freedom, for the burial register of Christ Church, Newgate, shows that a William Fuller, prisoner, was buried on 24 March 1733. Although he claimed once to have been engaged, and one source has him married, he seems to have died a bachelor.

The main problem about reconstructing Fuller's life is that for so much of it, including his misdemeanours, one depends on his own account of 1703. In this he clearly misrepresented his family background, and his rich uncle Charles Herbert, to whom he gave an important role in his early life, may be entirely fictitious. There is no independent confirmation of Fuller's employment at court in 1688–90, and his first appearance in contemporary sources is during the trial of Matthew Crone. Thereafter, his prominence derived precisely from the brazenness of his fantasies; even this may be exaggerated in some cases by Fuller himself. He was clearly very able in deception, but his reckless attachment to certain schemes occasionally hints not so much at calculated brinkmanship as at a morbidly obsessive state of mind. The only known portrait is an engraving prefaced to several of his books, showing him aged thirty-two. This shows a characterless, slightly plump young man, and fails to confirm Fuller's account of his own comeliness.

C. E. A. CHEESMAN

Sources DNB · W. Fuller, *The whole life of Mr William Fuller* (1703) · *JHL*, 17, 12–20, 32, 116 · W. Fuller, *The life of William Fuller, Gent.* (1701) · W. Fuller, *A trip to Hampshire and Flanders* (1701) · W. Fuller, *The sincere and hearty confession of Mr William Fuller* (1704) · W. Fuller, *The second part of Mr William Fuller's last confession* (1705) · W. Fuller, letters to John Ellis, 1676–1705, BL, Add. MSS 28880; 28886, fols. 263; 28892, fols. 77; 28893, fols. 80, 107 · W. Fuller, deposition, 1701, BL, Add. MSS 28886, fol. 289 · W. Fuller, letters to the earl of Portland and William III, 1698, BL, Add. MS 40771, fols. 282–3, 302 · W. Fuller, letters to the archbishop of Canterbury, 1730, PRO, SP 36/19, fols. 91–5 · N. Luttrell, *A brief historical relation of state affairs from September 1678 to April 1714*, 6 vols. (1857), 108–9, 126–7, 129, 132–3, 140–1, 176 · *The manuscripts of his grace the duke of Portland*, 10 vols., HMC, 29 (1891–1931), 4, 28, 34 · *The manuscripts of the House of Lords*, 4 vols., HMC, 17 (1887–94), vol. 2, pp. 272–4; vol. 4, pp. 407–13 · A. Roper, *The life of William Fuller, the late pretended evidence* (1692) · *The life of William Fuller, alias Fullee, alias Fowler, alias Ellison, etc* (1701) · G. Campbell, *Impostor at the bar. William Fuller, 1670–1733* (1961) · parish register, Milton, Kent, 25 Sept 1670, Coll. Arms [baptism] · W. A. Littledale, ed., *The registers of Christ Church Newgate 1536–1754*, Harleian Society, 21 (1895)

Archives BL, letters to John Ellis, Add. MSS 28880–28893, *passim* · BL, Vernon papers, Add. MSS 40804–40850 · U. Nott. L., letters to first earl of Portland
Likenesses F. H. van Hove, line engraving, BM, NPG; repro. in Fuller, *Whole life*, frontispiece
Wealth at death was in debtor's prison for last twenty-nine years of life: Fuller, letters to the archbishop of Canterbury, PRO, SP 36/19, fols. 91–4

Fullerton [*née* Leveson-Gower], **Lady Georgiana Charlotte** (1812–1885), novelist and philanthropist, was born on 23 September 1812 at Tixall Hall, Staffordshire, the third of four children of Lord Granville Leveson-*Gower (1773–1846), diplomatist and later first Earl Granville. Her mother was Lady Henrietta Elizabeth (Harriet) Leveson-*Gower (1785–1862), second daughter of William *Cavendish, fifth duke of Devonshire (1748–1811), and his first wife, Georgiana *Cavendish (1757–1806). Granville George Leveson-*Gower, second Earl Granville and Gladstone's foreign secretary, was her brother. Georgiana and her elder sister were educated at home, first in England, and from 1824 in Paris, where her father was appointed ambassador. She spoke and wrote French from an early age and studied piano with Liszt. On 13 July 1833 she married in Paris Alexander George Fullerton (1808–1907), of Ballintoy Castle, Antrim. They continued to live at the embassy, to which he was an attaché, until 1841, and their son William Granville (1834–1855) was born there. After leaving the embassy, the Fullertons travelled for some time in France, Germany, and Italy, and eventually settled at 36 South Street, London. While in Rome in 1843 Alexander Fullerton was received into the Roman Catholic church. Although Lady Georgiana already leaned towards Catholicism, her conversion was delayed until 29 March 1846, after her father's death.

Georgiana had begun writing verses in French by the age of eleven. Her literary career commenced in 1844 with the publication of *Ellen Middleton*, a novel which hinges on the necessity of confession. Admired for its style and sentiments by Lord Brougham, Charles Greville, and Harriet Martineau, but criticized for its Roman Catholic leanings by William Gladstone, *Ellen Middleton* set the tone for Fullerton's later works. Her eight novels, which all turn on religious questions, include *Grantley Manor* (1847), *Too Strange not to be True* (1864), *Constance Sherwood* (1865), *Mrs Gerald's Niece* (1869), and *A Will and a Way* (1881). According to M. Maison, Fullerton's popularity was due largely to the elements of sensation fiction incorporated into her works, which made 'conversion exciting and theology thrilling'. R. S. Leonard and R. L. Wolff credit her with being one of the originators of the Catholic novel, and contemporary readers testified that she inspired conversions. She also published stories, a play, and some poetry, as well as biographies of eminent Catholics, including St Frances of Rome (1855), Louisa de Carvojal (1873), and Elizabeth, Lady Falkland (1883). The extensive research behind her work led to her being called as a witness in 1874 in the Cause of the English Martyrs and Confessors. She was also a close friend of Mme Augustus Craven, encouraging her to write novels, and translating them

from the French. Craven was later to publish a biography of Fullerton which was translated into English in 1888.

Fullerton wrote primarily to gain money for charity. In 1859 she reflected 'On the side of writing. Money gained, perhaps from £200 to £300 a year … How many orphans could be provided for and good works promoted with such a sum? A *little* good done also, perhaps, by such tales' (Coleridge, 387). While the Fullertons were active philanthropists before their son's sudden death from a brain tumour in 1855, thereafter their activities increased substantially. They both joined the third order of St Francis in 1857, and from their homes at Slindon Cottage in Sussex and 27 Chapel Street, Park Lane, London, they supported many charitable organizations. Lady Georgiana was instrumental in bringing the Sisters of St Vincent de Paul to England, and with Frances Margaret Taylor she also co-founded a new religious community, the Poor Servants of the Mother of God Incarnate, for women who could not afford dowries for established orders.

From 1876 the Fullertons lived mainly at Ayrfield, Bournemouth, and Lady Georgiana never left Bournemouth again after 1883. Increasingly ill, she died at Ayrfield on 19 January 1885 and was buried at the Convent of the Sacred Heart at Roehampton on 23 January. There is a memorial to her at the church of St George and the English Saints in Rome.   SOLVEIG C. ROBINSON

Sources DNB · H. J. Coleridge, *Life of Lady Georgiana Fullerton. From the French of Mrs. Augustus Craven* (1888) · R. S. Leonard, 'Lady Georgiana Fullerton', PhD diss., St John's University, Brooklyn, 1955 · *The inner life of Lady Georgiana Fullerton, with notes of retreat and diary*, ed. [F. M. Taylor] [1899] · R. L. Wolff, 'The church of Rome', *Gains and losses: novels of faith and doubt in Victorian England* (1977), 27–107 · B. R. Belloc, 'Lady Georgiana Fullerton', *In a walled garden*, 3rd edn (1896), 100–11 · H. F. Blunt, 'Lady Georgiana Fullerton', *Great wives and mothers* (New York, 1923), 341–66 · C. M. Yonge, 'Lady Georgiana Fullerton', *Women novelists of Queen Victoria's reign: a book of appreciations*, ed. M. Oliphant and others (1897); repr. (Folcroft, PA, 1969), 195–203 · A. S. Driscoll, *Tertiaries of our day: Lady Georgiana Fullerton and Lady Herbert of Lea* (1926), 5–23 · Father Gallwey, *A funeral discourse over the remains of Lady Georgiana Fullerton* (1885) · R. von Fuggar, *Lady Georgiana Fullerton: Ihr leben und ihre werke*, microfilm, 1975, 1898; History of Women Series, reel 545, no. 4196 · M. Maison, 'Fullerton, Lady Georgiana', *Dictionary of British women writers*, ed. J. Todd (1989) · Blain, Clements & Grundy, *Feminist comp.*, 403 · Gillow, *Lit. biog. hist.*, 2.336–9 · D. Mermin, *Godiva's ride: women of letters in England, 1830–1880* (1993), 7, 57–8, 81, 113 · R. Molloy, 'Fullerton, Lady Georgiana Charlotte', *British authors of the nineteenth century*, ed. S. J. Kunitz and H. Haycraft (1936), 236–7 · Burke, *Peerage* (1967) [Devonshire; Granville] · Burke, *Gen. GB* (1939) [Fullerton of Ware] · *The new Cambridge bibliography of English literature*, [2nd edn], 3, ed. G. Watson (1969), 929 · J. Sutherland, *The Longman companion to Victorian fiction* (1988) · *National union catalog, pre-1956 imprints*, Library of Congress, vols. 187, 210
Archives Society of the Sacred Heart, London, book of extracts and notes of instruction for the Children of Mary | BL, letters, as sponsor, to the Royal Literary Fund · Congregation of the Poor Servants of the Mother of God, London, letters to Sister St John · Congregation of the Poor Servants of the Mother of God, London, letters to Mother Magdalen Taylor · CUL, letters to Lord Acton · PRO, letters to Granville, PRO 30/29 · UCL, letters to Lord Brougham
Likenesses portrait, repro. in Coleridge, *Life*, frontispiece
Wealth at death £12,726 11s. 3d.: probate, 21 March 1885, CGPLA Eng. & Wales

Fulleylove, John (1845–1908), landscape painter, was born on 18 August 1845 in Leicester, the son of John Fulleylove, a coach-builder, and his wife, Elizabeth Preston. After attending the private day school of Dr Highton, in Leicester, he was apprenticed to the firm of Flint and Shenton, local architects. At the same time he took painting lessons and began to sketch local views. He turned to painting as a profession and began to exhibit in London in 1871. On 18 June 1878 he married Elizabeth Sarah, daughter of Samuel Elgood of Leicester; they had one son and two daughters.

Throughout his career Fulleylove travelled widely abroad, beginning with a trip to Italy in 1875. He was elected an associate of the Institute of Painters in Water Colours in 1879 and moved to London in 1883. As well as exhibiting at the institute, he held many exhibitions of his watercolours at The Fine Art Society's galleries in Bond Street, including 'Petrarch's Country' (1886), an exhibition of drawings of south-east France; this was followed by shows of views of Oxford (1888), views of Cambridge (1890), and Parisian subjects and studies of Versailles (1894). Following a visit to Greece in 1895, he held an exhibition, 'Greek landscape and architecture', at the Fine Art Society Gallery in 1896, when he exhibited over 100 watercolours and pencil drawings which are among the finest of his works. He exhibited drawings of the Holy Land in 1902. A frequent exhibitor at the Royal Academy, many of his paintings were of classical buildings, including *The Pantheon, Rome* (exh. 1877) and *The Acropolis, Athens* (exh. 1898), reflecting his architectural training.

Fulleylove sometimes painted in oil and, as a member of the Institute of Painters in Oil, he contributed oil paintings to the Royal Academy and exhibited a number of small panel pictures of Oxford at the Fine Art Society Gallery in 1899. He worked as an illustrator for the publishers A. and C. Black, and books illustrated by him included H. W. Nevinson's *Pictures of Classic Greek Landscape and Architecture* (1897) and J. A. McClymont's *Greece* (1906). He also contributed illustrations to various magazines, including the *English Illustrated Magazine* and the *Illustrated London News*, and he illustrated an article in the *Magazine of Art* (1898), 'Sketches of Greek landscape and ancient Greek architecture'. John Fulleylove died on 22 May 1908 at his home, 1 Denning Road, Hampstead, London, and was buried in Highgate cemetery in London. He was survived by his wife.   ANNE PIMLOTT BAKER

Sources 'Mr Fulleylove's water-colour drawings of Greek architecture and landscape', *The Studio*, 7 (1896), 77–83 · S. Houfe, *The dictionary of British book illustrators and caricaturists, 1800–1914* (1978), 311 · Wood, *Vic. painters*, 3rd edn · Graves, *RA exhibitors* · E. Morris, *Victorian and Edwardian paintings in the Walker Art Gallery* (1996) · private information, 1912 · b. cert. · m. cert. · d. cert. · *CGPLA Eng. & Wales* (1908) · DNB · WWW · J. Johnson, ed., *Works exhibited at the Royal Society of British Artists, 1824–1893, and the New English Art Club, 1888–1917*, 2 vols. (1975)

Likenesses Elliott & Fry, photograph, NPG

Wealth at death £1666 12s. 8d.: administration with will, 27 Aug 1908, *CGPLA Eng. & Wales*

Fullwood, Francis (d. 1693), Church of England clergyman, was educated at Charterhouse School and was admitted as a pensioner at Emmanuel College, Cambridge, on 14 March 1644; he graduated BA in 1647. He was minister of Staple Fitzpaine, Somerset, in 1651–2 and of West Alvington, Devon, in 1656–9 during which time he belonged to the 'associated', that is presbyterian, ministry of Devon. His opening public salvos were against religious sectaries, especially Quakers and Baptists, with whom he engaged in acrimonious public debates, such as a nine-hour disputation held to stem the 'gangrene of error' at Wiveliscombe in Somerset on 4 May 1652 (F. Fullwood, *The Churches and Ministery of England*, 1652, sig. c1r). He defended a regular clergy, tithes, infant baptism, and a learned understanding of scripture, and repudiated the dangerous doctrine of the 'inner light'. In 1660 he was made a DD at Cambridge and, notwithstanding staunchly puritan credentials, turned episcopalian at the Restoration. He was installed archdeacon of Totnes on 31 August 1660, and collated prebendary of Exeter on 15 October 1662, the latter in succession to an extruded parliamentarian. He continued in both until his death.

Fullwood was a pugnacious controversialist who published twenty works, many of inordinate length, chiefly against nonconformists and latterly against Catholics and Socinians. His enemies denounced him as a turncoat for the 'odious, egregious, and intolerable hypocrisy' of his behaviour in 1660 (*A Pretended Visitor*, 42); one critic likened his desertion to that of Archbishop Sharpe of St Andrews, who was assassinated in 1679 for his betrayal of presbyterianism. Yet Fullwood is plausible as a consistent believer in church discipline and uniformity, and he is a fascinating example of a Calvinist ecclesiastical dogmatist dressed in the clothes of Restoration Anglicanism. In a series of tracts he drew upon his puritan heritage to attack presbyterians who now dissented from the established church. He began with casuistical handbooks in 1662–3, aimed at easing the consciences of clergy reluctant to conform, in which he explained that the solemn covenant of 1643 was not binding. He turned, in 1672–3, to assault the toleration—the 'plague' and 'cancer' (*Necessity of Keeping our Parish Churches*, 1673, 4) of schism—let loose by Charles II's declaration of indulgence, notably in a tract called *Toleration not to be Abused* (1672). Fullwood constantly invoked the Elizabethan and Jacobean puritan theologians, notably William Ames and William Perkins, and stressed the conformity of the Elizabethan puritans Laurence Chadderton and John Rainolds. Indeed, in citing Calvin, Bucer, and Beza, Fullwood preserved a legacy of international Calvinism at a time when Anglican churchmanship was becoming narrowly national in temper. Arguing his case 'upon Presbyterian principles', he showed how the presbyterians of the 1640s had themselves assailed independency and sectarian schism, telling his readers to remember 'what made the thoughts of toleration so horrible to your fathers' (*Toleration not to be Abused*, 26). He claimed that Richard Baxter was now practising the sectarianism he had once deplored; Baxter replied in *Sacriligious Desertion* (1672).

Theology aside, Fullwood's tracts are revealing about the demography of nonconformity, particularly its steady urbanization. He complained of rural ministers migrating to Exeter, Bristol, and London, in order to attract congregations and richer livelihoods: 'the streets of cities and corporations, [are] the places designed, it seems, for your happier adventures' (*Toleration not to be Abused*, 29). He also disclosed fears that they 'do out preach us' (*Humble Advice to the Conforming and Non-Conforming Ministers and People*, 1672, 9). Striking, too, is his sense that the king's indulgence boosted dissent and led many people to abandon semi-conformity, thereby becoming 'totally separate' (*The Doctrine of Schism Fully Opened*, 1672, 105). He showed the crucial nature of the issue of dissenters breaching their former practice of preaching only 'out of church time', that is to say, not in direct competition with parish worship.

Never a divine-right episcopalian but rather a defender of civil authority in 'things indifferent', Fullwood made a defence of church establishment which was firmly Erastian. This was a very English Calvinism that placed authority in the hands of the godly prince. The king is not 'merely civil' but 'persona mixta cum sacerdote' ('a person partly sacerdotal'; *Doctrine of Schism*, 43). An adept in canon law and active in the use and defence of the ecclesiastical courts, Fullwood was denounced by the anticlerical Edmund Hickeringill as a tyrannical 'blackcoat' (Hickeringill, sig. A2r). At the height of the tory purges of the early 1680s, Fullwood spurred the Exeter justices to crack down on dissent, his henchmen 'smelling out their meeting places' and visiting 'apparitors, warrants, [and] constables' upon them (*Pretended Visitor*, 97, 108).

In 1689, despite having acquired high loyalist principles, Fullwood speedily accepted the revolution, being among 'the first Clergymen' to attend the prince of Orange at Exeter. He boasted that he was 'perhaps the First that in Print endeavoured to persuade my Brethren to recognise this Happy Government' (*The Socinian Controversie*, 1693, sig. A2r). Two further tracts of 1689 urged allegiance to the new regime. Whereas in 1679 Fullwood had dedicated a book to Archbishop Sancroft, who was deposed at the revolution, in 1693 he dedicated books to the revolution bishops Gilbert Burnet and John Tillotson. Fullwood was a member of the convocation of 1689 that resisted accommodation with the dissenters. Soon afterwards he became unwontedly active in exercising wide archidiaconal powers, prompting protests against his high-handedness and simoniacal extraction of fees.

In later years Fullwood lived at Litton near Dorchester, where he died on 27 August 1693. Two sons, Francis and James, born about 1650 and 1655 respectively and both educated at Exeter College and the inns of court, evidently predeceased him, for his will indicates many relations but not them. Instead he names as the principal heir his son-in-law, John Bastard, vicar of Ashburton. Fullwood left his books on canon and civil law to the cathedral or consistory court, and the rest to Bastard 'after my wife hath chosen out her own books' (will, PRO, PROB 11/417, fol. 264). Fullwood's *Roma ruit* (1679), a compendium of arguments

against popery, was sufficiently useful to be republished in 1847 at the height of the Oxford Movement's turn towards Rome. MARK GOLDIE

Sources *A pretended visitor visited* (1690) · E. Hickeringill, *The naked truth: the second part* (1681) · Venn, *Alum. Cant.* · Foster, *Alum. Oxon.* · Wood, *Ath. Oxon.*, new edn · *Fasti Angl.* (Hardy), 1.404, 424 · will, PRO, PROB 11/417, fols. 264–5
Wealth at death see will, PRO, PROB 11/417, fols. 264–5

Fullwood, William. *See* Fulwood, William (*d.* 1593).

Fulman, William (1632–1688), antiquary, was born in November 1632 at Penshurst, Kent, and baptized there on 21 December, the second of four children of William Fulman (1590–1663), carpenter, and his wife, Joan (*d.* 1675). His academic ability brought him under the patronage of Henry Hammond, rector of Penshurst, who obtained a place for him in the choir of Magdalen College, Oxford. Here he was taught by William White, master of Magdalen College School.

On 27 January 1648, again through Hammond's influence, Fulman became a scholar at Corpus Christi College, Oxford, under the tutelage of Zachary Bogan. When the parliamentary visitors expelled the college's president and fellows later that same year, Fulman, together with fellow scholar Timothy Parker, blotted out the name of the new president, Edmund Stanton, in the buttery book. Both Fulman and Parker were expelled from their scholarships on 22 July 1648.

Fulman became amanuensis to his patron, Hammond, also removed from his fellowship. It may be during this time that he acquired his exceptionally neat handwriting, renowned for its legibility. In 1654 or thereabouts Hammond found him a position as tutor to the Peto family at Chesterton, Warwickshire, where he remained until the Restoration.

In 1660 Fulman resumed his scholarship at Corpus and, along with several others ejected by parliament, successfully petitioned for the degree of MA, awarded on 23 August 1660. His first major publication followed, being an edition of the supposed works and declarations of Charles I, to which he intended to add a biographical preface. Fulman was stricken with smallpox, however, and his bookseller commissioned Richard Perrinchief to finish the task. Perrinchief took credit for Fulman's work without acknowledgement, the two volumes appearing under the title *Basilika the workes of King Charles the martyr: with a collection of declarations, treaties, and other papers* (1662).

Fulman turned next to the history of the University of Oxford, producing *Academiae Oxoniensis notitia* (1665), an account of the foundation of the university and its colleges, their principal benefactors, and noted members. This brought him into contact with Anthony Wood, and the two antiquaries enjoyed a scholarly relationship until Fulman's death. In 1674 Wood sent the pages of his *Historia* to Fulman for comment as they came off the press, and received back thirty-two pages of corrections. Such immediate access to Wood's research enabled Fulman to produce a second, fuller edition of the *Notitia* in 1675.

In 1669 Fulman left Oxford for the living of Meysey

Hampton, Gloucestershire, a rectory in his college's gift. The relative scholarly isolation of parochial life was offset by visits to Oxford every Easter, July, and Michaelmas. At other times Oxford gossip and news of English politics arrived via correspondence with Wood, John Beale (his friend at Corpus and successor at Meysey Hampton), and his bookseller Richard Davis.

On 8 August 1674 at St Mary's, Marylebone, Fulman married Hester (d. 1686), daughter of Thomas and Elizabeth Manwaring and granddaughter of Roger Manwaring (1590–1653), bishop of St David's. They had four children, of whom two sons and a daughter survived infancy; all bore the additional name Meinwaring in deference to their mother's ancestry. Fulman's hopes for preferment, perhaps amplified by his marriage, came to nothing owing to his complacent nature. Wood believed that he might have reached the rank of dean had he been more active in seeking patronage.

Fulman's output was briefly restrained by parochial and familial responsibilities. Besides the revised *Notitia*, his only published work in the 1670s was *A Short Appendix to the Life of Edmund Stanton, D. D.* (1673), a fourteen-page attack on the biased biography by Richard Mayow of the man who had displaced President Newlin at Corpus twenty-five years previously.

Fulman was a keen student of ecclesiastical history, and corresponded with the bishop of Oxford, John Fell, and the historian Gilbert Burnet. His corrections to the latter's *magnum opus* were initially well received, the author acknowledging the utility of his corrections, but when these were eventually printed in abstract form only Fulman's sense of self-importance was offended. Success was more forthcoming in his later efforts. In 1684 Fulman published the first volume of *Rerum Anglicarum scriptorum veterum* (1684), a Latin edition of five chronicles of a high standard of accuracy and presentation. The same year saw him complete *The Workes of Henry Hammond* (4 vols., 1674–84), a tribute to his mentor, with a life of Hammond provided by Bishop Fell at Fulman's request.

Fulman planned many other works. Some were beyond his abilities, such as projected 'Baronagium', an idea carried out by Dugdale. Others remained unfinished, perhaps due to his meticulous standards. His manuscripts include material for lives of John Hales (partially printed in J. Walker, *Sufferings of the Clergy*, 1714, 2.94), Bishop Robert Sanderson, and Bishop Richard Fox. Fulman's failure to publish the latter's biography led to 'grumbling among the fellows' at Corpus in 1685 who had provided a room for him 'to do something in relation to the Founder' (Wood to Fulman, 25 Oct 1685, Fulman MS 16, Corpus Christi College, Oxford).

Fulman died of a fever on 28 January 1688 at Meysey Hampton and was buried there the following day. Wood commented that 'being totally averse from making himself known … his great learning did in a manner dye with him' (Wood, *Ath. Oxon.*, 4.240). Two centuries later, however, the historian of Corpus Christi College believed that Fulman was 'saving Wood, the most indefatigable of Oxford antiquaries' (Fowler, viii).   PETER SHERLOCK

Sources Wood, *Ath. Oxon.*, new edn · T. Fowler, *The history of Corpus Christi College*, OHS, 25 (1893) · *The life and times of Anthony Wood*, ed. A. Clark, 5 vols., OHS, 19, 21, 26, 30, 40 (1891–1900) · Foster, *Alum. Oxon.* · parish register, Penshurst church [baptism], 21/12/1632 · parish register, Meysey Hampton church [burial], 29/1/1688 **Archives** CCC Oxf., collections, corresp., and papers | Bodl. Oxf., notes and criticism of Anthony Wood's *Historia et antiquitates oxon* · Bodl. Oxf., Wood MSS, letters to Anthony Wood, F 41

Fulton, Arthur George (1887–1972), rifle shot, was born at his parents' home at 57 Rosenau Road, Battersea, London, on 16 September 1887, the son of George Edmonton Fulton (1859–1944), a journeyman wood-engraver, and his wife, Isabella Lambdowne Savage. His father, who won the sovereign's prize at the National Rifle Association tournament at Bisley in 1888 and who was a finalist on thirteen occasions, gave up work as an engraver and used his winnings from shooting to set up in business as a gunsmith. Fultons, the armourers' shop at Bisley, was where Arthur spent much of his working life.

Fulton became the first man in history to win the sovereign's prize at Bisley three times, in 1912, 1926, and 1931, and shot in the final a record twenty-eight times. He came close to winning in 1914, in one of the most exciting finals ever, when he lost to Sergeant J. L. Dewar in a shoot-off after the match had been tied. He also shot for Great Britain on twenty and for England on forty-four occasions in the Kolapore cup and empire matches. In 1908 and 1912 he won silver medals with the British Olympic team. He travelled extensively with National Rifle Association teams to North America, Scandinavia, and Africa, where he was known as 'the rifle visitor'. He was extremely popular within the sport, with a reputation for unselfishness and for putting his vast experience at the disposal of younger, less experienced shots. He was appointed MBE in 1959 for his services to shooting.

Fulton enlisted in the Westminster Rifles about 1904 and went with them to France in 1914 as a machine-gun sergeant. His outstanding ability as a sniper earned him the Distinguished Conduct Medal and caused him to be 'borrowed' by other regiments. He was later recalled, along with other National Rifle Association members, to serve on Major Hardcastle's experimental team working on rifle design at the Woolwich arsenal. Too old for active service in the Second World War, he joined the Home Guard as a lieutenant.

Fulton died at his home, Oak Tree Cottage, Pirbright, Surrey, on 26 January 1972, leaving a widow, a daughter, and a son, Robin Fulton, who maintained the family tradition at Bisley, appearing in seventeen finals and winning the sovereign's prize in 1958.   TONY RENNICK

Sources *The Times* (28 Jan 1972) · *The Rifleman* (spring 1972) · S. Cornfield, *The queen's prize: the story of the National Rifle Association* (1987) · P. Matthews and I. Buchanan, *The all-time greats of British and Irish sport* (1995) · b. cert. · d. cert. **Wealth at death** £19,781: probate, 12 Oct 1972, CGPLA Eng. & Wales

Fulton, John Scott, Baron Fulton (1902–1986), university administrator and public servant, was born in Dundee on 27 May 1902, the younger son and youngest of three children of Angus Robertson Fulton, principal of University

College, Dundee, and his wife, Annie Scott. He was educated at Dundee high school, St Andrews University, and Balliol College, Oxford, where he was awarded a second class in both classical honour moderations (1924) and *literae humaniores* (1926). After two years as a lecturer at the London School of Economics (1926–8), he returned to Balliol in 1928 as a fellow and tutor in philosophy. In 1935, when 'modern Greats' (philosophy, politics, and economics) had established itself, particularly in Balliol, the 'philosophy' in his title was changed to 'politics'. Fulton remained in that position until 1947, although during the Second World War he greatly widened his political and administrative experience as principal assistant secretary in the mines department and later in the Ministry of Fuel and Power. Already a friend and admirer of Sir William Beveridge, he now added to his range of friends and colleagues Harold Wilson, who worked with him as an economist and statistician. Such personal relationships mattered greatly to Fulton and strongly influenced his career. Yet his success depended essentially on his own remarkable energy and, when inspired, his boundless enthusiasm. He demonstrated these qualities, not to universal acclaim, in his first, somewhat circumscribed, post-war field of action, as principal for twelve years (1947–59) of the University College of Swansea, with two spells, in 1952–4 and 1958–9, as vice-chancellor of the University of Wales. While in Swansea he encouraged university expansion and furthered his interest in adult education, which had been stimulated in the past by Balliol's master, A. D. Lindsay. He was chairman of the Universities' Council for Adult Education and the council of the National Institute of Adult Education (both 1952–5).

An unprecedented opportunity to bring all his gifts into play came in 1959 when he was appointed principal of the University College of Sussex, the first of seven new English university institutions. When it took in its first students in 1961 its name had happily been changed from University College to University and his own title, his second significant change of title, from principal to vice-chancellor. By then, too, Fulton had assembled a small team of academics and administrators, most of them as energetic and enthusiastic as he was, all of them sharing his vision. Together they were committed to creating a university which from the start would reshape university curricula and organizational structures and develop a strong identity of its own. Critics were sceptical—or jealous—but the new university, which was sometimes called, though it never was, 'Balliol by the sea', proved highly attractive to applicants. Indeed, it came to symbolize the spirit of the 1960s. Fulton inspired the institution rather than managed it, winning friendship as well as loyalty.

Brighton was a more useful base than Swansea had been for the 'outside' activities which Fulton enjoyed. Some of them were directly concerned with university education in Britain and abroad. He was largely responsible in 1961, for instance, for speedily bringing into existence the Universities Central Council on Admissions (of which he was chairman in 1961–4), which transformed the system of university entrance, and even before he became chairman of the Inter-University Council for Higher Education Overseas (1964–8) he had been involved in university policy making in Malta, Sierra Leone, Nigeria, and Hong Kong. In 1962 he chaired the committee that established the new Chinese University. Its pattern of four-year courses was to survive him, and he was particularly proud of the honorary degree that the university gave him and of the colourful robes that went with it.

In much of this international activity Fulton worked closely with the British Council as he did too with the BBC. He was chairman of the BBC and ITA committees on adult education (both 1962–5), seeing the two chairmanships as complementary to the chagrin of some people working in the BBC, but, despite this, he was to go on to become vice-chairman of the BBC in 1966 as successor to Sir James Duff, who had been chairman of the planning committee of Sussex University. Fulton enjoyed personal politics, and it was largely due to his strictly private intervention with Wilson, who had become prime minister in 1964, that the government did not press for the BBC to accept advertising as a source of revenue.

Fulton soon left the vice-chairmanship, but remained as a BBC governor after accepting, at Wilson's invitation, his biggest non-university public assignment—chairmanship of a committee on the civil service, then widely believed to be in need of reform. He and his colleagues produced a report which criticized the dependence of the service on generalist all-rounders and pressed for a more professional and more specialized civil service. Other influences were brought to bear upon him in reaching this conclusion, notably that of Norman Hunt (later Baron Crowther-Hunt), but the tone of the report, published in 1968, was his own. Fulton always believed in opening access and in provoking change. Much criticized in Whitehall, his report had only limited results, although it was followed by the setting up of a new civil service department and to Fulton what was even more to the point—a civil service college.

Fulton was knighted in 1964 and became a life peer in 1966. He was an honorary fellow of Balliol (1972) and Swansea (1985), and had honorary degrees from ten universities. A strong and confident believer in the claims of public service, official and voluntary, Fulton considered rightly that the various activities of his strenuous public life were all of one piece. Yet in private he owed much to the support of his wife Jacqueline, daughter of Kenneth Edward Towler Wilkinson, solicitor, of York. They married in 1939 and had three sons and one daughter. It was on his wife's initiative that, after Fulton's retirement from Sussex University in 1967, the two of them moved to Thornton-le-Dale in Yorkshire, an agreeable base, if less accessible than Brighton. He chose, however, to move frequently out of it. The motto of the University of Sussex of his own devising had been 'Be still and know', but to the end Fulton had little wish to be still. He was always full of vitality. The last of his big jobs was from 1968 to 1971 when he was a not entirely successful chairman of the British Council. In appearance he was short and wiry, and in old age he looked far younger than his years. Almost to the last he was a great traveller. He died on 14 March 1986 at his home, Brook House, Thornton-le-Dale, Pickering, North Riding of Yorkshire. He was survived by his wife.

ASA BRIGGS, rev.

Sources *The Times* (19 March 1986) · *WWW* · private information (1990) · personal knowledge (1990)
Archives CAC Cam., corresp. with A. V. Hill
Wealth at death £273,072: probate, 16 June 1986, *CGPLA Eng. & Wales*

Fulton, Margaret Barr (1900–1989), occupational therapist, was born on 14 February 1900 at Bank House, Cheetham Hill, Manchester, the youngest of the five children of Dr Andrew Boyd Fulton (1862–1919), a medical practitioner, and his wife, Elizabeth, *née* Barr (1867–1946); both parents were Scottish. After receiving private tuition at home she was educated at Manchester High School for Girls. She became interested in occupational therapy following a chance encounter on a ship to the United States, and trained at the Philadelphia School of Occupational Therapy (1922–3) where she gained her diploma. The school had been set up in 1919, initially to instruct practitioners in working with soldiers who had been physically and psychologically traumatized during the First World War. It was associated with two of the founders of occupational therapy in the United States, Eleanor Clarke Slagle and Thomas B. Kidner, who were involved with the National Society for the Promotion of Occupational Therapy, established in 1917. Fulton also worked for six months at the Metropolitan Hospital in New York, developing her interest in psychiatry, before returning to Britain, where occupational therapy was virtually unknown.

After some months looking for work, Fulton was introduced to Dr Robert Dods Brown, superintendent of the Aberdeen Royal Asylum, who persuaded the hospital board of directors to appoint her at an annual salary of £120 per year, living out. She was employed at the hospital from 1925 to 1963, being the first qualified occupational therapist to practise in the United Kingdom. By 1932, there were ten craft instructors employed in Scottish mental hospitals, who, together with Fulton, formed the Scottish Association of Occupational Therapists; Fulton was elected secretary and treasurer. The association was suspended during the Second World War, and when it was reconstituted in 1946 Fulton was elected to the chair, a position she held until 1949. She remained on the council, in various offices, almost continuously until 1971.

In 1952 Fulton was a member of the preparatory commission which drew up the constitution for the World Federation of Occupational Therapists; she was elected its first president and served for the first eight years of its existence. She was involved in the organization of the first international congress of the federation, which was held in Edinburgh in August 1954, after which she was appointed MBE for services to her profession. She was made an honorary fellow of the World Federation of Occupational Therapists in 1960.

Fulton was a strikingly handsome woman. She never married, but supported her mother until her death in 1946. As well as being an accomplished craftswoman, she was a gifted pianist. She published very little, though she was an effective, witty speaker and a prolific letter writer. She played a prominent role in the Soroptomists, an international association for professional women, through which she extended her worldwide circle of friends. After her retirement in 1963, she lived in Edinburgh, where she died after a short illness on 16 December 1989. Her body was cremated at Warriston crematorium, Edinburgh.

C. F. PATERSON

Sources private information (2004) · Z. Groundes-Peace, 'An outline of the development of occupational therapy in Scotland', *Scottish Journal of Occupational Therapy*, 30 (Sept 1957), 16–43 · M. B. Fulton, 'Review of 25 years', *Scottish Journal of Occupational Therapy*, 30 (Sept 1957), 44–8 · M. A. Mendez, *A chronicle of the World Federation of Occupational Therapists: the first thirty years, 1952–1982* (1986) · minute of the Aberdeen Royal Asylum board of directors, 15 July 1925, northern health services archives, GRHB 2/1/19 · R. K. Bing, 'Occupational therapy revisited: a paraphrastic journey', *American Journal of Occupation Therapy*, 35 (1981), 499–518 · Prospectus: the Philadelphia School of Occupational Therapy, 1925–1926, Mitchell L., Glas., Greater Glasgow health board archives, GHB/13/11/7 · personal knowledge (2004) · *British Journal of Occupational Therapy*, 53/1 (1990)
Archives SOUND priv. coll., copy of tapes of her memoirs
Likenesses photograph, repro. in *British Journal of Occupational Therapy*

Fulton, Robert (1765–1815), engineer and artist, the elder son in the family of three daughters and two sons of Robert Fulton (d. 1774?), a tailor, farmer, and tradesman, and his wife, Mary Smith (d. 1799), was born on 14 November 1765 at a farmhouse in Little Britain, Lancaster county, Pennsylvania, USA. He was educated at home to the age of eight and then attended Caleb Johnson's school in Lancaster. After this he was apprenticed to Jeremiah Andrews, a jeweller in Philadelphia, and by 1785 had become a successful miniaturist. In 1787 Fulton studied in London under the artist Benjamin West and exhibited at the Society of Artists (1791) and the Royal Academy of Arts (1791 and 1793). He developed an interest in canals and engineering and became acquainted with the inventor Lord Stanhope, who designed steam vessels, and also met the canal builder, the duke of Bridgewater. In 1794 Fulton patented (no. 1988) a machine to convey boats from one canal level to another, and then published *A Treatise on the Improvement of Canal Navigation* (1796), which advocated small canals and inclined planes and emphasized the social advantages of waterway transport.

In 1794 Fulton formed a partnership with Robert Owen, who financed some of his projects; and at about this time invented a 'mill for sawing marble or other stone', a model of which won him a medal from the Society for the Encouragement of the Arts, Manufactures and Commerce. His other inventions were a canal excavator (1796), a new method of tanning, and a rope making machine (patented 1799).

Fulton moved to France in 1797 where he met the poet and statesman Joel Barlow, who became a lifelong friend and acted as his tutor. In 1800 Fulton profitably introduced the panorama to Paris with his painting *Burning of Moscow*. He also built a submarine—*Nautilus*, which had a sail and a hand-cranked propeller, and used candlelight for illumination when submerged. It was launched in July 1800 and required a crew of three for its operation. Later it was enlarged, but the French lost interest in the vessel when it failed to sink any British ships. Subsequently Fulton offered it to the British, who declined it because it lacked mechanical propulsion. In 1802 he formed a steamboat partnership with Chancellor Robert R. Livingston, American minister to France, and the following year built and tried on the Seine a paddle wheel steamboat, which successfully towed two boats at a top speed of 4 m.p.h. He also developed two types of 'torpedoes' (really mines) for use in naval warfare. Fulton returned to England in 1804 and Pitt offered him a salary and other inducements to produce underwater mines. Fulton constructed these as partially submerged floating bombs and first used them, though with little success, against the French in October 1804. Further attempts with them were also unsatisfactory.

In 1806 Fulton returned to America, where he experimented with naval weapons and constructed a steamboat powered by a Boulton and Watt engine. With Livingston he set up the North river Steamboat Company which obtained the Hudson River monopoly. Their first vessel, known as *The Steamboat*, made her maiden passenger voyage on 17 August 1807 from New York to Albany via Clermont. After rebuilding (patented 1809) with two paddle wheels each side, she was re-registered as *The North River Steamboat of Clermont*. Passenger demand encouraged Fulton to construct further boats and start a lucrative ferry service on the wider reaches of the Hudson; later the partners obtained the steamboat monopoly on the Mississippi as well. But although Fulton prospered, he often had to defend his monopoly against competitors, who also sometimes infringed his patents.

In 1810 Fulton published *Torpedo War and Submarine Explosions* and invented a device for cutting the cables of anchored ships; in 1813 he patented columbiads, which were short-range sub-surface guns. For the Anglo-American War he designed the steam warship *Demologos*, which was launched, partially built, in October 1814. The 2475 ton fortified ship, completed after his death, was officially named *Fulton the First* but was never used in battle because the war ended soon afterwards.

Robert Fulton was a handsome man, over 6 feet tall, with a long face, high forehead, and black curly hair. He was kind, generous, and affectionate and used his great gift of eloquence to advantage. In 1808 he married Harriet Livingston (*b. c.*1786), the cousin of his partner, and their family eventually consisted of a son and three daughters. Suffering from pneumonia, he died on 23 February 1815 at 1 State Street, New York, and was buried the next day in Trinity churchyard, Broadway. He was survived by his wife. Although criticized for basing inventions on others' ideas, his work on the submarine and mines was important, but undoubtedly his greatest achievement was the successful development, introduction, and operation of steam powered vessels for transport and naval warfare.

CHRISTOPHER F. LINDSEY

Sources H. W. Dickinson, *Robert Fulton: engineer and artist, his life and works* (1913) · J. S. Morgan, *Robert Fulton* (1977) · W. S. Hutcheon, *Robert Fulton: pioneer of undersea warfare* (1981) · I. McNeil, 'Robert Fulton—man of vision', *Engineering heritage: highlights from the history of mechanical engineering*, 2 (1966), 126–32 · Graves, *RA exhibitors*, vol. 2
Archives Col. U., letters and papers · Hist. Soc. Penn., MSS and paintings · National Archives and Records Administration, Washington, DC · New York Historical Society · NMM, letters relating to steamboat design and construction · NYPL, papers · Robert Fulton Birthplace, Fulton township, Lancaster county, Pennsylvania · US Naval Academy, Annapolis, Maryland | Birm. CL, Boulton and Watt collection · CKS, letters to Lord Stanhope relating to steam navigation
Likenesses J. A. Houdon, marble bust, 1804, Detroit Institute of Arts · oils, 1806 (after B. West?), New York State Historical Association, Cooperstown, New York · C. W. Peale, oils, 1808?, Independence National Historical Park Coll., Independence Hall, Philadelphia · bronze bust, *c.*1900, City University of New York, Bronx Community College · T. O. Barlow, mixed-method engraving, NPG · engraving, Science and Society Picture Library, London · oils, Science and Society Picture Library, London · statue, U. S. Capitol, Washington
Wealth at death see details of will, J. Reigart, *Life of Robert Fulton*, 206

Fulton, Thomas Wemyss [*formerly* Wemyss Alexander Thomas Fulton] (1855–1929), fisheries authority and ocean law publicist, was born on 3 July 1855 at Cramond, near Edinburgh, the fifth son of Hugh Fulton, (*b.* 1806/7), a pier master, and Elizabeth, *née* Cumming. He was the seventh child and was named Wemyss Alexander Thomas at birth; he later adopted the name Thomas Wemyss Fulton. William Carmichael McIntosh, a colleague, wrote that '[l]ittle is known of his schooldays and earlier life', though, allegedly, 'he was reared under the care of a mother whose unselfish devotion laid the foundation of a high character' (WCM, 358). He took his MB and CM with first-class honours in 1884 from the University of Edinburgh, where he studied natural history under Sir Wyville Thompson and took the Wyville Thompson special medal in natural history. In 1887 Fulton received a thesis gold medal for his MD work, 'The maturation of the pelagic ovum of Teleostean fishes and its relation to certain phenomena in the life-history of the species'. In this period, Fulton travelled to India, and subsequently served with the *Challenger* commission under Sir John Murray, this latter post perhaps resulting from his prior connection with Thompson and his promise as a naturalist. Fulton's association with this project may have ceased because of the conclusion of relevant work, or because of the imminent cut-off of public funding for the reports.

Fulton joined the fishery board for Scotland in January 1888 as superintendent of scientific investigations, a post he held for thirty-four years. Under this aegis he organized a series of scientific fishery investigations during 1888–90. He was largely responsible for the board's test experiments in trawling and conducted early marking experiments, attaching numbered brass discs to several thousand fish tails with black silk. Fulton strongly supported co-operation with interested trawler masters in the collection of statistics. While linking a decline in fisheries to the overfishing of immature stocks, he felt that mesh size controls were impracticable and favoured supplementation of stocks from an artificial hatchery, established in Dunbar in 1893. (This was moved through his influence to Aberdeen in 1898.) From 1888 until his retirement, Fulton edited the scientific portion of the annual reports of the fishery board for Scotland, and from 1902 to 1921 he served as British government expert to the International Council for the Exploration of the Sea. Fulton and his wife, Helen Raleigh, had one son, George Alexander Wemyss Fulton, born in Aberdeen on 17 September 1900; he predeceased his parents on 20 October 1927. In 1906 Fulton was made lecturer on the scientific study of fishery problems at Aberdeen University, a post he retained until 1921. He was a member of the Scottish departmental committee on the northern fisheries in 1911 and, after his retirement, of the advisory committee on fishery research of the Development Commission (1921–7). He belonged to several national and international fishery organizations and was a fellow of the Royal Society of Edinburgh.

Fulton's position in the pantheon of Scottish fisheries experts is secure; he produced no fewer than eighty-eight papers on the topic during 1888–1913, dealing with biological, statistical, historical, legal, and administrative issues. J. Travis Jenkins claimed that 'there was hardly any branch of fishery study or investigation which he did not touch and illuminate. His knowledge of fishery literature was both wide and deep' (Jenkins, 4). Fulton was described by contemporaries as 'a man of very agreeable personality. He could both express his views, which on many subjects were very decided ones, with clearness and defend them with tenacity and all without a sign of ill feeling', and as someone 'who was always willing to help those with less knowledge and experience than himself' (ibid., 5–6). He is best known today for his book, *The Sovereignty of the Sea* (1911), dedicated to his wife, who assisted him with the transcription of records for this work. *Sovereignty* is described by Jenkins as a study which 'is, and must remain, the foundation on which all future research into the history of the British Sea Fisheries (a much neglected subject) must be based' (Jenkins, 5). This work was originally to deal with fishery claims in the British seas, but Fulton expanded its scope to include all aspects of sovereignty and to trace the evolution of Britain's territorial waters. In so doing, he made full use both of original sources and of foreign colleagues and friends, creating that rare amphibian, a book of legal and historical value by a natural scientist. *Sovereignty* proved a worthy successor to the treatises of William Welwood, *An Abridgement of All Sea-Lawes* (1613), and John Selden, *Mare Clausum* (1635), and retains its importance as a historical source for contemporary oceans law. Fulton was before his time in noting the inadequacy of the 3 mile territorial sea limit for regulating fisheries; indeed, he echoed Dr Nansen's view that fish

are not the property of any particular nation. They are, if the word may be used, international, and it would therefore be just as it would be auspicious if … [fishery] questions were dealt with in a spirit of international brotherhood, with due regard to the interests of the coast population on the one hand, and the legitimate rights of the enterprising fisherman from other nations on the other.   (Fulton, ix)

Helen Fulton died in 1929 and later the same year, on 7 October, Fulton collapsed and died of acute appendicitis and heart failure at his home, 35 Palmerston Place, Edinburgh.   SAMUEL PYEATT MENEFEE

Sources W. C. M. [W. C. McIntosh], *Proceedings of the Royal Society of Edinburgh*, 49 (1928–9), 358–60 · J. T. Jenkins, 'Thomas Wemyss Fulton: 1855–1929', *Journal du Conseil International pour l'Exploration de la Mer*, 5/1 (1930), 3–6 · *WWW* · *Aberdeen Press and Journal* (8 Oct 1929) · T. W. Fulton, *The sovereignty of the sea* (1911) · F. G. Aflalo, *The sea-fishing industry of England and Wales: a popular account of the sea fisheries and fishing ports of those countries* (1904) · E. M. Thomasson, ed., *Study of the sea: the development of marine research under the auspices of the International Council for the Exploration of the Seas* (1981), 237–42 · b. cert. · d. cert. · b. cert. [George Alexander Wemyss Fulton]
Likenesses photograph, repro. in Jenkins, 'Thomas Wemyss Fulton', 3
Wealth at death £5127 13s. 11d.: confirmation, 17 April 1930, *CCI*

Fulwell, Ulpian (1545/6–1584×6), playwright and satirist, was born in Wells, Somerset, the elder of two sons of Thomas Fulwell (d. 1563), linen-draper, and his wife, Christabel James (d. 1584). His childhood was marked by conflict over 400 acres of ecclesiastical land that his father had leased in 1539 from kinsman John Goodman, the corrupt subchanter of Wells Cathedral. When Thomas Fulwell proved too independent of Goodman the latter unleashed a decades-long campaign of violent harassment that resulted in numerous lawsuits and influenced Ulpian Fulwell's later writings. Fulwell's mother later deplored her two sons' 'unthrifty courses' and tried unsuccessfully to disinherit them from the leased land (Buchanan, x–xi).

After his father's death, in 1563, Fulwell studied to be a clergyman, and was ordained on 15 September 1566. Soon afterwards he penned his first literary work, a play called *Like Will to Like, Quod the Devil to the Collier*. This didactic morality play with satirical undertones is one of numerous similar, proverb-based plays of the 1560s. The plot centres on Nichol Newfangle the Vice, godson of Lucifer, who leads astray a series of lively stock characters such as Tom Tosspot, Ralph Roister, and Cuthbert Cutpurse. Several of these characters return at the end to lament their fate, after which Lucifer carries Nichol off to Hell on his back. Virtuous Life, Honour, and Good Fame then enter to praise the queen and sing a song about God's vengeance. The play was printed in 1568 with a chart on the title-page showing how five actors might play all the roles; Happé suggests that it was written for Paul's Boys (Happé, 56). An undated second edition survives, as does a third edition printed in 1587.

About the same time that he wrote *Like Will to Like* Fulwell became engaged to Marie Stubbard but he did not go through with the marriage after discovering that his bride-to-be was already married to William Gascoigne. Late in 1570 he became rector of Naunton, Gloucestershire, and there, on 13 May 1572, he married Eleanor

Warde (d. 1577). Fulwell does not seem to have been a very conscientious rector; in 1572 the episcopal visitation noted that the church was in a state of decay, and in 1576 he was fined for negligence because the clerk was illiterate and parents were not sending their children to learn the catechism.

Fulwell's neglect of his parish may have resulted from his concentration on literary endeavours. In 1575 he published *The Flower of Fame*, a piece of pro-Tudor propaganda dedicated to William Cecil, Lord Burghley. It consists of three parts: a chronicle of the reign of Henry VIII; a poetic 'treatise' on three of Henry's wives; and an account of the battle of Haddington, in Scotland, during the reign of Edward VI. Fulwell explicitly modelled his work on the popular *Mirror for Magistrates*, using Edward Hall's *Chronicles* as his major source. However, he also got much information from his 'faithful friend' Edmund Harman, former member of Henry VIII's household and gentleman usher to Edward VI. Harman had witnessed Henry VIII's will, and Fulwell witnessed Harman's will in 1577.

In 1576 Fulwell issued *Ars adulandi, or, The Art of Flattery*, dedicating it to Mildred, Lady Burghley. This is a biting series of eight satiric dialogues on flattery, the 'eighth liberal science', between Fulwell and a variety of adversaries. Fulwell took as his model Lucian's *The Parasite* and Erasmus's *Pseudocheus and Philetymus*, using a variety of styles and making heavy use of English proverbs. He criticizes the insincerity of courtiers in several of the dialogues but his most savage attacks are reserved for church abuses and corrupt clergy, particularly those of Wells. His Sir Simon is a transparent caricature of an archdeacon of Wells, probably John Rugge. After the book's publication Fulwell was called before the court of high commission in London, and on 7 July 1576 was ordered to make a public recantation before the bishop of Bath and Wells. Nevertheless a second edition of *Ars adulandi* was published in 1579, with revisions by the author.

Fulwell wrote no more for publication after this episode. His wife, Eleanor, died in December 1577, and on 14 April 1578 he married Marie Whorwood. The couple had six children, all baptized at Naunton: Marie (19 January 1579), Edmund (12 December 1580), John (19 July 1582; buried 14 August), Thomas (11 September 1583), Ulpian (27 November 1584), and Whorwood (buried 18 October 1585). In March 1579, at the advanced age of thirty-three, Fulwell matriculated at St Mary Hall, Oxford, where he was 'esteemed a person of ingenuity by his contemporaries' (Wood, *Ath. Oxon.*). Although there is no record of his graduation he was described master of arts in May 1584. Fulwell had died by July 1586, when there was a dispute over the advowson of the Naunton rectory, leaving his wife and children in poverty. There is no record of his burial at Naunton, suggesting that he died elsewhere.

DAVID KATHMAN

Sources R. Buchanan, introduction, in U. Fulwell, *Ars adulandi, or, The art of flattery* (1984), i–lxxx · P. Happé, introduction, *Two moral interludes* (1991), 51–7 · M. Eccles, *Brief lives: Tudor and Stuart authors* (1982), 51–3 · I. Ribner, 'Ulpian Fulwell and his family', *N&Q*, 195 (1950), 444–8 · I. Ribner, 'Ulpian Fulwell and the court of high commission', *N&Q*, 196 (1951), 268–70 · Wood, *Ath. Oxon.*, new edn, 1.540
Archives PRO, apology for Ars Adulandi, Exchequer, ecclesiastical documents, E 135/9/5
Wealth at death left his widow and children in poverty: R. Buchanan, introduction, *Ars adulandi*, xi; Eccles, 'Brief lives', 51–3

Fulwood, Christopher (d. 1643), royalist army officer, was the eldest son of Sir George Fulwood (c.1558–1624), a Gray's Inn lawyer. His family had a long association with Middleton by Youlgrave, Derbyshire. His father, who was knighted in 1606, acquired the manor by purchase in 1608 and was living there by 1611, when he served as sheriff of Derbyshire. In 1605 Fulwood was entered at Gray's Inn, of which society he was admitted ancient on 28 May 1622. In 1624 he succeeded his father as lord of the manor of Middleton. He had married Mary Johnson and two sons had been born by the time he was appointed autumn reader in 1628. He subsequently became the Gray's Inn treasurer in November 1637. Outside the legal terms he lived at Middleton. His strict impartiality as a magistrate is commemorated by the Apostle of the Peak, William Bagshaw. In 1640, at the Bakewell sessions, the curate of Taddington was charged with puritanism. Fulwood, who was chairman, 'though known to be a zealot in the cause of the then king and conformity, released him, and gave his accusers a sharp reprimand' (W. Bagshaw, *De spiritualibus pecci*, 1702, 17).

Fulwood's influence in the district was of great value to the royalist cause. He was specially employed to raise the Derbyshire miners as a life guard for the king in 1642, when the lord lieutenant of the county, the earl of Rutland, declined to appear in the service. Fulwood was soon at the head of a regiment of 1100 men, who were mustered on Tideswell Moor. His success appears to have alarmed the leaders of the parliamentarians in the neighbourhood, who, according to the local tradition, soon found an opportunity of seizing Fulwood while at his house at Middleton. The chief enemy of the king in the district was Sir John Gell of Hopton, and it was by Gell's emissaries that Fulwood was captured. It is said that while in his house he received notice of the near approach of the hostile detachment, and hid himself in a fissure separating an outlying mass of rock from its parent cliff, in the dale of the Bradford, a few hundred yards in the rear of the mansion. His pursuers saw him, and a shot from them inflicted a mortal wound. He was carried off towards Lichfield, a garrison town which had been taken by Gell on the preceding 5 March, but died on the way at Calton in Staffordshire on 16 November 1643. In the nineteenth century the rock was still pointed out at Middleton. By tradition Fulwood's two daughters, Elizabeth and Mary, were thought to have sought refuge among their friends in London, where they died in obscurity. However, Mary actually married Rowland Stevenson of Ounston, Derbyshire, with whom she had several children; her brother Audley died unmarried in 1650. Middleton apparently passed out of the hands of the Fulwood family in 1719.

GORDON GOODWIN, rev. JAN BROADWAY

Sources T. Bateman, 'Christopher Fulwood, the royalist', ed. L. Jewitt, *The Reliquary*, 1 (1860), 88–93 • J. Foster, *The register of admissions to Gray's Inn, 1521–1889, together with the register of marriages in Gray's Inn chapel, 1695–1754* (privately printed, London, 1889) • D. Lysons and S. Lysons, *Magna Britannia: being a concise topographical account of the several counties of Great Britain*, 5 (1817), cxxix, 304 • G. D. Squibb, ed., *The visitation of Derbyshire, begun in 1662*, Harleian Society, new ser., 8 (1989)

Fulwood [Fullwood], **William** (*d.* 1593), author, was the son of John Fulwood. He became a member of the Merchant Taylors' Company, to whom he dedicated his best-known work, *The Enimie of Idlenesse*, printed by Henry Bynneman in 1568. Presented as a manual 'Teaching the maner and stile how to endite, compose, and write all sorts of Epistles and Letters' (sig. A 1r), this work ranges from examples of practical letters, designed to appeal to 'the marchant' and 'the lawyer' (sig. Avr), to a sequence of six metrical love letters including a reference to Chaucer's *Troilus and Criseyde*, in which the lover remembers only Criseyde's succumbing to Troilus and requests a friend like Pandarus. These verse epistles were expanded to seven in number in Henry Middleton's editions of 1582 and 1586. The work also contains translations of letters by Cicero and 'sundry lerned men', including Poliziano, Ficino, Merula, Pico della Mirandola, as well as neutrally presented examples of papal correspondence.

The early 1560s saw Fulwood producing two works dedicated to Lord Robert Dudley, then the favourite of Elizabeth I: R. Lever's *Most Noble, Auncient & Lerned Play, called the Philosophers Game*, the description of a mathematical game 'augmented' by Fulwood (sig. A1r) published by Roland Hall in 1563; and Fulwood's translation of Gratarolus Bergomalis, entitled *Castel of Memorie* (printed by Hall in 1562), containing advice for 'the restoryng, augmentyng and conservyng of the Memorye and Remembraunce' (sig. A 1r), reprinted by W. How in 1573.

Fulwood seems to have invited contention. One of his early ballads, *A Supplication to Eldertonne, for Leaches Unlewdnes*, printed by John Alde in 1562, berates William Elderton, ballad writer and notorious tippler (also embroiled in the Davy Dicer debate between Thomas Churchyard and Thomas Camell in the 1550s) for his 'knauerie', 'whoredom', and unnecessary anger.

Fulwood himself appeared in at least four cases in the court of Star Chamber. In 1574 he was accused of conspiracy against a painter, Raphe Brooke, a case to which Fulwood returned in 1589 when he vindicated himself by publishing *A Spectacle for Perjurers*, printed by Alde, comprising a perjured deposition of one John Jones, whose earlier perjury had condemned Fulwood and his co-defendant, John Doughtie, in 1574. In 1580 Fulwood was charged with inducing one Henry Franckland to write his will in Fulwood's favour (despite Fulwood's apparent responsibility for Franckland's imprisonment in the Fleet). That year he was also accused of wrongfully acquiring the rents of properties in the London parish of St Sepulchre, where Fulwood dwelt in Long Lane. During the prolonged course of this case (which also involved proceedings in the court of wards, chancery, and Guildhall), Fulwood appeared before the queen's bench charged with the stabbing and attempted murder of the key witness, Thomas Walbutt, a defrocked minister castigated in Robert Crowley's *Apologye or defence of those Englishe wryters and prechers which Cerberus the thre headed dog of hell chargeth with false doctryne* (1566). Fulwood's hasty temper is also apparent from the fourth case brought before the Star Chamber, where in 1590 he refuted a charge of assault on London pewterer John Gaskyn. Gaskyn had been accused by Fulwood of manufacturing false-bottomed tankards, and of manhandling Fulwood's wife, Anne, daughter of the London brewer John Wood.

Despite his litigious private life, much of Fulwood's work has a moralizing tone. His description of *The Shape of Ii. Monsters* printed by Alde in 1562, transforms the birth of two prodigious pigs into God's warning 'to repent our wickednes, and faithfully to beleve his word', while *A New Ballad Against Unthrifts* (also printed by Alde in 1562), provides a vivid description of a spendthrift's descent into penury and crime. In Richard Robinson's *Rewarde of Wickednesse* (1574), Fulwood is mentioned alongside the satirist Edward Hake and Christopher Studley, translator of Seneca, as an author 'more fitter' for such a moralizing work. He died in 1593 in St Sepulchre's parish.

CATHY SHRANK

Sources W. Fulwood, *A spectacle* [sic] *for pe*[r]*ju*[r]*e*[r]*s* (1589) • Proceedings of Star Chamber, PRO, STAC 5 B 35/29; B102/28; F5/27; F.6/3; F.8/7; F.27/23; F29/39; G9/19 G37/21; S.S/24; 2.23/3; S.25/7; S.29/40; S.76/4; S.83/22 • R. Robinson, *Rewarde of wickednesse* (1574) • T. Corser, *Collectanea Anglo-poetica, or, A … catalogue of a … collection of early English poetry*, 6, Chetham Society, 100 (1877) • J. P. Collier, ed., *Extracts from the registers of the Stationers' Company of works entered for publication*, 2 vols. (1848–9), vol. 1 • E. Brydges, *Censura literaria: containing titles, abstracts, and opinions of old English books*, 2nd edn, 10 (1815) • W. C. Hazlitt, *Hand-book to the popular, poetical and dramatic literature of Great Britain* (1867) • J. Guy, *Tudor England* (1988) • DNB

Funech (*fl.* late 7th cent.). *See under* Meath, saints of (*act. c.*400–*c.*900).

Furber, Robert (*c.*1674–1756), nurseryman, established his Kensington nursery soon after 1700 near Hyde Park Gate and Kensington Gore, on the west of what became Gloucester Road. About 1706 he married Mary Everton; they had a son.

Furber and Christopher Gray both bought some of the plants collected at Fulham Palace by Henry Compton, bishop of London, after the bishop's death in 1713, and by 1724 Furber's stock was rich enough for some of his exotic trees and shrubs, including the moss rose, to be listed by Philip Miller in his *Gardeners and Florists Dictionary* (1724). Furber was also one of the Society of Gardeners, led by Miller, which published the first part of its *Catalogus plantarum* in 1730, but by then he had issued two catalogues of his own, one of English and foreign trees, the other of 'the Best and Choicest Fruit Trees' (both in 1727). About 1720 Furber had published an engraving of a tulip tree, a magnolia (then considered another species of tulip tree), and a silk-cotton tree, all from the garden of Thomas Herbert, eighth earl of Pembroke; presumably the trees had been supplied by Furber, who prefaced his tree catalogue with a pleased account of his success in propagating the tulip tree, 'notwithstanding some Writers have thought it difficult'.

Furber's pictorial catalogues, collected as *Twelve Months of Flowers*, a dozen plates based on paintings by Peter Casteels, were issued plain or coloured; the main series was issued in 1730, with a thirteenth plate, containing subscribers' names within a border of flowers, following in 1732. So popular were these annotated flower-pieces, engraved by Henry Fletcher, that they were frequently copied at the time, and later reprints kept them in circulation. Smaller versions, engraved by James Smith, were used to illustrate *The Flower-Garden Display'd* (1732), with descriptions of the flowers probably written by Richard Bradley; and another set of small copies was issued by John Bowles in 1749 as *Flora*. A similar series of *Twelve Plates with Figures of Fruit* was published in 1732, again based on Casteels's paintings, illustrating fruit in season month by month. In 1733 Furber's *Short Introduction to Gardening* appeared, 'Being several Useful Catalogues of Fruits and Flowers' introduced to supplement the large plates and to help his customers 'in furnishing their Gardens and their Tables'. The preface reminds its readers of the contents of Furber's nursery, as well as his own satisfaction with his work:

> Gardening is the Employment Providence has allotted me; and it happily falls out to be a Business the most suitable of all others to my Genius and Inclination. I have spent my Years in collecting, cultivating and improving all the different Kinds of Trees, Plants, Fruits, and Flowers, that I could possibly obtain; and in doing this, have spared neither Cost nor Pains. With intent to make the Love of Gardening more general, and the understanding of it more easy, I have from time to time published Catalogues, containing large Variety of Trees, Plants, Fruits, and Flowers, both Foreign and Domestic, cultivated by me for Sale.

Furber was an overseer of the poor in the parish of St Mary Abbots, Kensington, in 1718, and a churchwarden in 1725–6 and 1736–7. He was buried at St Mary Abbots on 1 September 1756. He left his Kensington house to his wife and a legacy to their son, William, who had been apprenticed to Philip Miller in 1722. Most of his other property was left to John Williamson, who worked with Furber during his later years and who took over the Kensington nursery, which was maintained by a succession of gardeners until the late 1840s.   SANDRA RAPHAEL, rev.

Sources J. Harvey, *Early gardening catalogues* (1972), xi, 14–15 • J. Harvey, *Early nurserymen* (1974), 78 • B. Henrey, *British botanical and horticultural literature before 1800*, 2 (1975), 341–8 • E. J. Willson, *West London nursery gardens* (1982), 27–8

Furlong, Alice Maud Mary (1871–1946), poet, was born on 17 January 1871 at Knocklaiquin Lodge, near Rathfarnham, co. Dublin, one of the four children of James Walter Furlong (*d.* 1897) and his wife, Mary Josephine Murtagh (*d.* 1897). Her father was a Wexford man and had at one stage been a leather merchant but later became the sporting editor of a Dublin newspaper. Her childhood was spent at Fernvale, Broohernabreena, Tallaght, in co. Dublin.

Furlong's sister, Mary (1866–1898) was a published poet and Alice Furlong began to publish her own poems about 1892. Throughout her career her poems appeared in a number of newspapers and journals such as the *Shan Van Vocht*, the *Irish Press*, *United Ireland*, *Sinn Féin* and the *Weekly Independent*. Much of her work was published in the *Irish Monthly*. The editor of that journal, Mathew Russell, took a keen interest in Furlong's work and was instrumental in having her first and only volume of poetry, *Roses and Rue*, published in 1899. It was well-received, one reviewer noting that it contained 'Irish poems inspired by passionate patriotism' (Russell, 393). Many of her poems were strongly nationalist and Catholic in flavour. Her second published volume was a book of Irish fairytales and mythology, *Tales of Fairy Folks, Queens, and Heroes*, which appeared in 1907. She was popular in her day; one obituarist went so far as to say that she

> was for some years supreme amongst the living poets of this century … it is not too much to claim that between the death of Yeats and her own she had a mastery of pure lyric song unequalled by any other Irish poet.   (Little, 138)

Furlong lived near the writer Katharine Tynan and was also an acquaintance of the nationalist activists Maud Gonne and Jennie Wyse Power. The family home in Tallaght was the gathering place for a number of writers such as W. B. Yeats, Dora Sigerson, and the Fenian John O'Leary. Furlong was active in the Irish nationalist movement. She was elected vice-president of the ad hoc committee, later called the Patriotic Children's Treat Committee, which had been formed in 1900 in order to organize a treat for those children who had not attended that arranged on the visit of Queen Victoria. In October 1900 Furlong was also elected as one of the four vice-presidents of Inghinidhne na hEireann (Daughters of Ireland), an organization which had a specific cultural purpose and promoted the Irish language and Irish literature. She had begun to learn the Irish language shortly after the setting up of the Gaelic League in 1893, and in July 1908 she was awarded a certificate as a teacher of Irish.

Although Furlong published in both Irish and English, after 1916 she wrote mostly in Irish, publishing under the names Eilís Ní Phartholáin and Eilís de Fhurlaing. Her Irish-language publications appeared in *Fáinne an Lae* and *An Claidheamh Soluis*, and her poem 'Dublin Easter 1916' was sold as a leaflet to support the Irish National Aid Association. She published lessons for beginners in Irish in *Nationality* in 1918, and her poems continued to appear in the *Irish Monthly* in the 1930s. Alice Furlong died, unmarried, at her home, 378 Harold's Cross Road, Dublin, on 20 October 1946, of heart disease. She was buried in Tallaght graveyard.   MARIA LUDDY

Sources M. Russell, 'Poets I have known', *Irish Monthly*, 36 (1908), 389–98 • A. Little, 'Lest we forget Alice Furlong', *Irish Monthly*, 75 (1947), 137–40 • K. O'Brennan, 'Alice Furlong: some memories', *Irish Press* (29 Oct 1946); repr. in *Irish Book Lover*, 30 (1946–8) • *United Irishman* (28 April 1900) • *United Irishman* (13 Oct 1900) • b. cert. • d. cert. • D. Breathnach and M. Ní Mhurchú, *Beathaisnéis a Trí: 1882–1982*, 3 ([Dublin], 1992)

Furlong, Thomas (1794–1827), poet, was born at Ballylough, Scarawalsh, near Ferns, co. Wexford, the youngest of the five children of a small farmer and carman. His father travelled regularly to Dublin, where he secured a job for Furlong as a grocer's assistant. Early efforts in verse drew the attention of John Jameson, the Dublin distiller, who appointed Furlong to his counting house. *The Misanthrope* (1819) was written to reclaim a friend, who, owing to early disappointments, had retired from society; it was withdrawn by the author on account of numerous typographical errors, and he issued a second edition in Dublin in 1821, with other poems.

Furlong contributed to the *New Monthly Magazine* as well as to other periodicals, and helped to found the *New Irish Magazine* in 1821. Thomas Moore, Charles Maturin, and Lady Morgan all praised his work. He was also a good friend and adviser to Daniel O'Connell, the campaigner for Catholic rights, and in 1824 Furlong published *The Plagues of Ireland: an Epistle*, a powerful indictment of the political injustices of Irish life at this time. A lively and energetic satire, steeped in the intricacies of contemporary sectarian politics, it is fiercely anti-loyalist, and strenuously advocates Catholic emancipation.

At the request of James Hardiman, editor of *Irish Minstrelsy* (1831), Furlong began to produce metrical versions in English of Turlough O'Carolan and other Gaelic poets, working from literal versions as he had no Irish. He was also engaged on a poem entitled *The Doom of Derenzie* (1829), a Gothic tale of superstition set in Wexford, when he died, unmarried, on 25 July 1827, in Dublin. He was buried in the churchyard at Drumcondra.

ROBERT WELCH

Sources S. Mythen, *Thomas Furlong: the forgotten Wexford poet* (1998) • R. Welch, *A history of verse translation from the Irish, 1789–1897* (1988) • P. Rafroidi, *Irish literature in English: the Romantic period, 1789–1850*, 2 vols. (1980) • J. Hardiman, 'Memoir of Thomas Furlong', *Irish minstrelsy, or, Bardic remains of Ireland*, ed. J. Hardiman, 1 (1831), lxix–lxxx • *DNB*

Archives NL Ire., corresp., literary MSS, and papers
Likenesses J. P. Haverty, lithograph, pubd 1829 (after his earlier work), NG Ire. • oils, repro. in Hardiman, 'Memoir'

Furly, Benjamin (1636–1714), merchant and religious writer, was born on 13 April 1636 at Colchester, Essex, the fifth son of a linen draper, John Furly (*c*.1590–1673), later alderman and mayor of Colchester, and his wife, Ann. He was admitted to Colchester School on 21 August 1643, and in 1655, with his father and at least one brother, became a Quaker after hearing James Parnell preach. By 1658 Furly had settled in Amsterdam as a merchant, though he was in London in April 1659 and was one of 164 Friends there who submitted a statement to the speaker of parliament offering to take the place of incarcerated Quakers. The same year he was a signatory of Edward Burrough's *A Declaration from the People called Quakers*, which accused England's rulers of being 'wounded with the spirit of Tyranny' (4). With George Fox and John Stubbs he published *A Battle-Door for Teachers and Professors* (1660), which employed numerous languages to justify the Quakers' use of 'thee' and 'thou' and condemned 'unsavoury Words' in textbooks. After returning to Amsterdam in 1659, Furly relocated to Rotterdam, where he spent the rest of his life,

prospering in business and becoming a naturalized citizen. For three decades commencing in 1663 he opened his house to Quaker meetings and travelling Friends.

Furly wrote and translated numerous works. With six other Quakers, in April 1662 he published *Adam Boreel Exposed by his Friends*, refuting an attack on Quakers by Mennonite Collegiants. The same year he wrote *De eere des werelds ontdeckt*, published in English as *The Worlds Honour Detected* (1663), in which he condemned such customary gestures as doffing hats, bowing, and kissing women's hands as feigned and frivolous. In the important controversy over whether hats had to be removed during prayer he sided with John Perrot, deeming this a matter of individual conscience. Seeking to resolve the issue William Caton, Stephen Crisp, and John Higgins went to Rotterdam in 1663, but not until 1669 did Furly recant, having recognized the necessity to respect the society's authority. In *Korte wederlegginge* ('A short refutation') the Dutch reformed minister Pieter Jacobsz attacked Furly's *Copye Van Eenen Brief* ('Copy of a letter', 1666), which repudiated the sacraments, and the latter responded in a preface to *Den wederlegger wederleght* ('The refuter refuted', 1670).

By April 1665 Furly had married Dorothy Graigne (*d*. 1691), a wealthy widow whose portion included land near Whitby, Yorkshire. They had five children: Benjohan (1681–1738) and John who became merchants, Arent (*d*. 1712) who became secretary to the earl of Peterborough, Johanna, and Rachel.

Furly's interests encompassed politics as well as letters. During the 1660s he supported Dutch republicans—Louvesteiners—not least because of their emphasis on the expansion of trade. Algernon Sidney often visited his home until 1677, and in the ensuing years they corresponded about public affairs and Sidney's financial interests. Sidney's *Court Maxims* may have been composed in Furly's house. As an agent for the English government Aphra Behn reported Sidney's consultations with Furly in 1675, and it was probably through Furly that Sidney and Penn became friends. Furly's house was the meeting place for the Lantern, a literary and philosophical society that was an early precursor of the Enlightenment. Among his friends were the physician Tobias Ludwig Kohlhans, who wrote tracts defending Quakers; the remonstrant theologian Philipp van Limborch; Jean le Clerc, a professor in the remonstrant seminary; the philosopher Pierre Bayle; and Franciscus Mercurius van Helmont, a student of mysticism who gave Furly books on the transmigration of souls.

During the 1670s and 1680s Furly continued to disseminate Quaker views through his writings and translations. He contributed two postscripts, one with George Keith, to the latter's *The Universall Free Grace of the Gospel* (1671), arguing for the universality of Christ's 'saving illumination' (135), and the same year he responded to a Flemish mystic in *Anthoinette Bourignon ontdeckt* ('Antoinette Bourignon discovered'). He attacked her again in *Het licht des weerelds* ('The Light of the World', 1671), but she defended her views in *Advertissement* (1672; published in English in 1708) and *Warnung durch Anthoinette Bourignon* (1683). In 1671

Furly accompanied Penn and Thomas Rudyard to Herford, where they unsuccessfully attempted to convert Jean de Labadie and his followers, who stressed the importance of the inner light, and then to Emden. Furly translated Penn's *A Trumpet Blown in … High and Low Germany* (1671), *Missive or Warning to the Netherlands* (1672), and *Christian Liberty* (1675) and Robert Barclay's *Theses theologicae* (1674) into Dutch, and in 1675 he contributed a preface to the Dutch edition of Penn's *Truth Exalted*, defending Quakers against charges by Rotterdam ministers that they were Fifth Monarchists.

When mobs threatened Rotterdam Quakers in 1675 Furly and a colleague met with magistrates to seek protection. The following year he and Barclay visited Princess Elizabeth of the Palatinate and the countess of Hoorn at Herford, and thereafter he corresponded with Elizabeth. When Fox, Penn, Keith, and Barclay arrived at Brill on 28 July 1677 Furly took them to his house in Rotterdam, where they held several meetings. There and on the ensuing tour throughout the Netherlands and the Rhineland, mostly with Penn and Keith, Furly served as a translator. In Rotterdam he hosted a disputation between Quakers and a group of Collegiant preachers led by Frans Kuyper, with whom he subsequently engaged in written debate in the mid-1670s. While Fox was in Rotterdam, Furly introduced him to Docenius, the Danish envoy, to appeal for toleration of Quakers in Denmark, and he facilitated meetings between Penn and John Dury, and correspondence between Dury and Barclay. Penn upbraided Furly for his 'Short, brittle Spirit' because he supported the Dutch government's position that all Quaker marriages be reported, whereas Dutch Friends, with Penn's support, thought this matter was best left to each Quaker (*Papers of William Penn*, 1.517). In late October Furly escorted Fox, Penn, and Keith to Brill, whence they returned to England. Furly himself visited England in 1676 and 1678.

Beginning in the 1680s, Furly recruited colonists for Pennsylvania, and by 1700 he had sold nearly 50,000 acres for Penn. He was instrumental in facilitating the emigration of Quaker, Mennonite, Labadist, and Pietist colonists from the Rhineland, and he was responsible for Dutch and German editions of Penn's *Some Account of the Province of Pennsylvania* in 1681 and 1684 respectively. Taking exception to aspects of Penn's *Frame of Government* he offered a critique in 1682, opposing the provincial council's increase in power at the assembly's expense, mandatory sabbath observance, and the provision requiring gubernatorial consent for constitutional changes. He also called for a ban on the importation of slaves from Africa and the emancipation in eight years of those brought by masters from Maryland and Virginia. Furly disappointed Penn by not emigrating to Pennsylvania, though he purchased 4000 acres and was entitled to a further 1000. In 1684 he contributed an essay on the emigration of non-Britons to *Recüeil de diverses pieces, concernant la Pensylvanie*. Two years later he provided hospitality to Penn, translated when he preached, and accompanied him to The Hague for meetings with Prince William. Furly himself periodically called on the grand pensionary at The Hague concerning

the recognition of Quaker marriages, and he hosted Fox, Alexander Parker, and William Bingley when they visited the Netherlands in 1684.

Furly may have met John Locke in 1683, and they were certainly acquainted by 1686, remaining friends until Locke's death in 1704. During this period English agents observed Furly's movements, included him on a list of enemies and fanatics in December 1683, and reported in February 1686 that he was associating with Sir Patience Ward and Philip, Lord Wharton. Like Locke, Furly had ties to Sir Walter Yonge and John Freke. By February 1687 Locke had taken up residence with Furly, where he remained until 1689 and undoubtedly availed himself of Furly's library as he wrote his *Two Treatises* and revised his *Essay Concerning Human Understanding*. Thereafter the two men corresponded frequently on current affairs, religion, finances, and book collecting. So close was their relationship that Furly reported graphic details of his health problems, including recurrent diarrhoea, constipation, and numbness in an arm. He clearly missed Locke: 'All in the Lanterne salute thee, and do regrett thy absence, which I shall not be willing to beare longer then needs must, the change is already so sensible, as if the sun were departed from our hemisphere' (*Correspondence of John Locke*, 3.570).

Furly went to London in April 1689 to plead the case for Quaker toleration with the new regime, remaining eleven months. While he was in England he and his wife independently came to the conclusion that Quaker strictures on worldly customs were excessive, and they permitted latitude to their children, seeing no reason to 'impose a yoak upon their tender necks' by insisting on such Quaker practices as eschewing hat honour, courtesy titles, and traditional names of days and months (*Correspondence of John Locke*, 4.573). He rebelled against 'anything that looks like sectism, singularitys, and authority', seeking freedom to embrace those practices he found meaningful—the very reason he had originally been attracted to the Friends (*Correspondence of John Locke*, 3.625–6). At this juncture Furly's wife died, in early 1691, and in his grief he contemplated quitting his business. Unhappy with the pomp at her funeral the general meeting expressed regret that he had deviated from his original testimony against worldly customs, but the statement was unsigned and he waited until the next general meeting to express his desire to remain a member without relinquishing his freedom regarding social practices. After some English Friends denounced him as an atheist he sought Locke's counsel. When Locke advised him not to offend weaker members Furly snapped, 'Instead of growing larger, you grow narrower' (*Correspondence of John Locke*, 4.657). Estranged from the Friends he rejected the idea of joining another religious group, finding their insistence on sacraments and doctrines intolerable.

On 10 December 1693 Furly married Susanna (*b.* 1644), daughter of Francis Huys (or House), an English merchant and his Dutch wife, and widow of Jacobus van der Tijt. Like his first wedding, this ceremony occurred at the Stadhuis in Rotterdam. He described her as 'a person of a large soule, and not to be mewed up within the wals of narrow spirited Catechisms, systems, and confessions' (*Correspondence of John Locke*, 5.2).

During his late years Furly's interests remained largely unchanged. In 1689 he published *A Copy of a Prophecy*, which Sidney had sent him in 1666. When the yearly meeting ruled against Keith in 1693, Furly, true to his liberal spirit, likened its actions to the Church of England's treatment of nonconformists. He enjoyed good relations with the third earl of Shaftesbury, who spent a year with him in 1703, and the duke of Shrewsbury, who described him in January 1706 as 'a pious Christian, but of no church, nor goes to none' (*Buccleuch MSS*, 2.798). In December 1706 he wrote to Shrewsbury, proposing an *ad valorem* tax in lieu of the high tariffs on Dutch imports, expressing the concern of Italian states about imperial aggression, and seeking assistance for Huguenots in France. Shrewsbury's response was sympathetic but not optimistic. Furly's interest in imperial aggression was also reflected in his translation from Dutch of Johann Maximilian Daut's *The Approaching Judgments of God upon the Roman Empire* (1711).

After several years of declining health Furly died in March 1714 and was interred in Rotterdam's Groote Kerk. The German bibliophile Zacharias Conrad Uffenbach described him in 1710 as tall, slender, and earnest, with a patrician demeanour despite his threadbare coat. A bibliophile himself as well as a linguist and scholar–merchant, Furly amassed a library of more than 4400 books, including works by Sidney, Locke, Bayle, Dury, Gilbert Burnet, John Saltmarsh, Henry More, Jane Leade, the Levellers, Gerard Winstanley, Muggletonians, reputed Ranters, and Cicero. Catalogued in *Bibliotheca Furliana* (1714), it was auctioned for £7638 19s. In addition to fostering the exchange of ideas on such subjects as republicanism, religious toleration, the development of trade, and mysticism, thereby helping to set the stage for the Enlightenment, Furly facilitated the development of Pennsylvania's Dutch and Germanic communities.   RICHARD L. GREAVES

Sources *The correspondence of John Locke*, ed. E. S. De Beer, 8 vols. (1976–89) • W. I. Hull, *Benjamin Furly and Quakerism in Rotterdam* (1941) • *The papers of William Penn*, ed. M. M. Dunn, R. S. Dunn, and others, 5 vols. (1981–7) • *The short journal and itinerary journals of George Fox*, ed. N. Penney (1925) • W. I. Hull, *William Penn and the Dutch Quaker migration to Pennsylvania* (1935) • *The manuscripts of his grace the duke of Buccleuch and Queensberry ... preserved at Drumlanrig Castle*, 2 vols., HMC, 44 (1897–1903), vol. 2, pp. 711–18, 798 • J. Scott, *Algernon Sidney and the English republic, 1623–1677* (1988) • J. Scott, *Algernon Sidney and the Restoration crisis, 1677–1683* (1991) • M. Cranston, *John Locke: a biography* (1957) • R. Ashcraft, *Revolutionary politics and Locke's two treatises of government* (1986) • J. Marshall, *John Locke: resistance, religion and responsibility* (1994)
Archives Bodl. Oxf., letters, mainly to John Locke • PRO, corresp. with third earl of Shaftesbury, PRO 30/24 • RS Friends, Lond., Barclay MSS • Yale U., Beinecke L., letters from Algernon Sidney
Likenesses I. Bowles, group portrait, engraving (after painting by E. van Heemskerk), RS Friends, Lond.
Wealth at death library auctioned for £7638 19s.: Cranston, *John Locke*, 281

Furneaux, Philip (1726–1783), Independent minister, was 'born of reputable but not opulent parents' (*GM*, 1063) at Totnes, Devon, where he was baptized on 28 April 1726, the son of John Furneaux. He was educated at Totnes grammar school, and in 1743 went to London to study for the ministry with a grant from the Coward Trust at the Moorfields Academy in Wellclose Square, first under John Eames and then David Jennings. He remained at the academy until 1749, probably assisting Jennings in teaching the students after 1748. After ordination in 1749 he became assistant to Henry Read, minister of the Presbyterian congregation at St Thomas's, Southwark.

Recognized as an able young man, Furneaux was appointed one of the two preachers of the Sunday evening lecture at Salters' Hall in 1752. In the following year he became the minister at the Independent congregation at Clapham, Surrey, then meeting in a wooden building in Nag's Head Lane. Furneaux increased the congregation and was a popular preacher for many years, despite his indifferent delivery and his habit of keeping his eyes fixed on his notes during his addresses. In theology he was probably an Arian, and sat lightly on the Independent and Presbyterian divide. At Clapham he exercised a considerable influence on the young William Smith, later an MP and a Unitarian, who played a key role in achieving the civil rights of dissenters in the next century. The congregation soon migrated to larger, more permanent premises, and in 1762 a substantial building was erected in Clapham Old Town, 'which he raised to one of the most opulent and considerable congregations amongst the protestant dissenters' (*GM*, 1063). Furneaux became a trustee of Coward's Fund in 1761 and took a full part in the training of Independent ministers. In 1766 he became a Dr Williams's trustee, and the same year published his edited version of David Jennings's lectures as *Jewish Antiquities*. In 1767 he was awarded the DD degree by Marischal College, Aberdeen.

This honour came to Furneaux in recognition of his exertions on behalf of the rights of nonconformists, an activity with which his name became chiefly associated. His agitation over what came to be known as the 'sheriff's case' brought his activity before a wider public. In 1748 the corporation of London devised a scheme to raise money for building the Mansion House by fining rich dissenters who refused to take the necessary oaths to become sheriff. In 1754 three nonconformists who strongly objected to paying these fines took the matter before the courts. The action was not resolved until 1767 at a hearing in the House of Lords which found in their favour. Lord Mansfield, lord chief justice of the king's bench, delivered in his speech what became the famous remark that the dissenters' way of worship was both lawful and established. Furneaux, with his remarkable memory, was able to report the speech afterwards without a single note, which Mansfield needed to correct in only a couple of minor instances.

In 1769 the eminent judge William Blackstone published the fourth volume of his *Commentaries*, in which he argued in support of the high-tory view that the suspension of legal penalties against nonconformists was not the right to toleration which dissenters claimed they possessed, and that essentially nonconformity remained a crime. Joseph Priestley responded very quickly in a book on the subject, and Furneaux replied the following year in his *Letters to the Honorable Mr Justice Blackstone*. This was a powerful and able statement of the moral arguments against enforcing religious truths by civil penalties, and was widely read and quoted. Furneaux was present on 6 February 1772 in the gallery of the House of Commons, with his fellow minister Edward Pickard, when the Feathers tavern petition for relief from subscription to the Thirty-Nine Articles by clerics was being considered. The speeches of Sir William Meredith and Sir George Savile in favour of the petition were reported by Furneaux from memory. Lord North, who opposed the petition, pointed out that if similar relief were requested by dissenting ministers there would be no reasonable objection to it.

At once Furneaux and Pickard set up a meeting of nonconformist ministers, who adopted an application to parliament, prepared by Furneaux, for relief from doctrinal subscription. A relief bill passed in the House of Commons in April 1772 but was rejected by the Lords the following month. A second bill was presented in 1773, in support of which Furneaux published his *Essay on Toleration*. Relief was eventually granted in 1779 with a new form of subscription in which a declaration of belief in the scriptures was substituted for the articles of the Church of England. According to the nonconformist historian Walter Wilson, Furneaux's '*Essay on Toleration* and *Letters to Judge Blackstone* will be read and admired as long as justice should prevail in the world' (Wilson, 4.315). These were his only published works apart from single sermons.

In the mid-1770s Furneaux was among the most highly regarded figures within English nonconformity, and was seen as the leading ministerial champion of their rights. Agitation for civil liberties often came from what is known as the Club of Honest Whigs, which consisted of twenty-five members, of whom fifteen were dissenting ministers, and included Furneaux, Price, Priestley, Kippis, and James Burgh. Furneaux and the Honest Whigs represented a fundamental change in the attitudes of many dissenters towards the state. They had admired and defended George II, but came to regard George III as a potential tyrant. Their three main targets were religious tests, the unreformed parliamentary system, and the attempt to coerce the American colonies.

Furneaux's effective end came in 1777, at the time of his greatest influence, not by death but through insanity, and he was rendered incapable of rational thought. 'Insanity seized him, and the man who had appeared with so much applause in the pulpit and from the press, was confined, during the remainder of his life, in a private madhouse' (Bogue and Bennett, 2.598). A large fund was raised for his support, to which his Clapham congregation gave £100 per annum, with Lord Mansfield being among the contributors. This trust became permanent, and in the nineteenth century its income went to the support and training of Unitarian ministers.

Furneaux died unmarried in a lunatic asylum in Hoxton, London, on 27 November 1783 and left no will. He was buried in Bunhill Fields. 'Furneaux's erudition, pulpit talents, and ardour in the cause of liberty, and worth of character, rendered him an honour to the body with which his religious principles, as a zealous and confident Protestant Dissenter, connected him' (*Protestant Dissenter's Magazine*, 128).

ALAN RUSTON

Sources *Protestant Dissenter's Magazine*, 5 (1798), 128–30 · *GM*, 1st ser., 53 (1783), 982, 1063 · *DNB* · C. Surman, index, DWL · J. Waddington, *Surrey Congregational history* (1866), 185–6 · E. E. Cleal, *The story of congregationalism in Surrey* (1908), 176–7 · D. Bogue and J. Bennett, *History of dissenters, from the revolution in 1688, to … 1808*, 2nd edn, 2 (1833), 597–602 · W. Wilson, *The history and antiquities of the dissenting churches and meeting houses in London, Westminster and Southwark*, 4 vols. (1808–14), vol. 4, p. 315 · V. W. Crane, 'The Club of Honest Whigs: friends of science and liberty', *William and Mary Quarterly*, 23 (1966), 210–33 · R. W. Davis, *Dissent in politics, 1780–1830: the political life of William Smith, MP* (1971), 7, 39 · *IGI* · J. H. Thompson, *A history of the Coward Trust: the first two hundred and fifty years, 1738–1988* (1998), 25, 26, 27, 29 · J. C. D. Clark, *English society, 1688–1832: ideology, social structure and political practice during the ancien régime* (1985), 207–8 · J. A. Jones, ed., *Bunhill memorials* (1849), 176
Wealth at death see administration, PRO, PROB 6/159, fol. 310

Furneaux, Tobias (1735–1781), naval officer, was born on 21 August 1735 on the family estate of Swilly, near Plymouth, the second son of William Furneaux (1696–1748), landowner, and his wife, Susanna (*née* Willcocks). It is not known when he joined the navy, but during the Seven Years' War (1757–63) he was employed in the West Indies, the English Channel, and the west coast of Africa. He first served as a midshipman in the *Marlborough*. On 18 October 1759 he was promoted to lieutenant for gallantry and appointed to the *Edinburgh*; he then served in the *Melampé* and *Ferret*. He was second lieutenant in the *Dolphin* (Captain Samuel Wallis), in Wallis's voyage of discovery round the world (19 August 1766–20 May 1768), during which he was described by her master as 'a Gentele Agreeable well behaved Good man and very humain to all the Ships company' (*Discovery of Tahiti*, 202). He next served briefly in the *Trident* before sailing once again with Wallis in the *Torbay*. On 28 November 1771 he was appointed commander of the *Adventure* as consort to Captain Cook's ship, the *Resolution*, in his second voyage. The *Adventure* was twice separated from the *Resolution*, and Furneaux wrote an account of events during those periods (*Journals*, 2.729–45).

During the first separation (8 February–19 May 1773) Furneaux sailed some 4000 miles alone, and explored in great part the south and east coasts of Van Diemen's Land (Tasmania), which had only been visited briefly by the French explorer Marion du Fresne in March 1772 since its first discovery by Tasman in 1642. Furneaux's manuscript and engraved charts contain much more detail than those of Tasman (David, Joppien, and Smith, 2.80–4). The names given to localities in Tasmania by Furneaux—for example, Mewstone, Swilly Isles, Fluted Head, Adventure Bay, Bay of Fires, Eddystone Point, and Furneaux Islands in what was thought to be a deep bay, but is now known as Banks Strait opening into Bass Strait—are retained in most cases in modern maps. Cook, who himself visited the same coast on his third voyage, confirms the substantial accuracy of Furneaux's survey, except in one point (*Journals*, 2.57).

Cook gave the name Furneaux Island (Marutea) to a coral atoll in Archipel des Tuamotu, visited by the two

Tobias Furneaux (1735–1781), by James Northcote, 1776

Sources R. Furneaux, *Tobias Furneaux, circumnavigator* (1960) • PRO, ADM 1/235 • PRO, ADM 1/488 • PRO, ADM 36/6060, 5481, 6138, 5593, 7528, 7683 • *The journals of Captain James Cook*, ed. J. C. Beaglehole, 2, Hakluyt Society, 35 (1961); repr. (1969) • A. David, R. Joppien, and B. Smith, eds., *The charts and coastal views of Captain Cook's voyages*, 2: *The voyage of the Resolution and Adventure, 1772–1775* (1992) • *The discovery of Tahiti: a journal of the second voyage of HMS Dolphin round the world … written by her master George Robertson*, ed. H. Carrington, Hakluyt Society, 2nd ser., 98 (1948) • J. Hawkesworth, ed., 'Captain Wallis's voyage', *An account of the voyages undertaken by order of his present majesty … by Commodore Byron, Captain Wallis, Captain Carteret, and Captain Cook*, 3 vols. (1773) • F. S. Blight, 'Capt. Tobias Furneaux RN of Swilly', *Annual Report and Transactions of the Plymouth Institution and Devon and Cornwall Natural History Society*, 22 (1952), 70–94 • PRO, PROB 6/158, 219
Archives BL, accounts of voyages, Add.MS 27890, 15500, 31360, 31363 • NL NZ, Turnbull L., journal of coastal survey, q. MS [526] • PRO, court martial proceedings, ADM 1/5309 • PRO, journal in the *Dolphin*, ADM 51/4542 • PRO, log and journal, ADM 55/1 • PRO, muster books, ADM 36/6060, 5481, 6138, 5593, 7528, 7683
Likenesses J. Northcote, oils, 1776, priv. coll. [*see illus.*]
Wealth at death see administration, PRO, PROB 6/158, 219

Furneaux, William Mordaunt (1848–1928), schoolmaster and dean of Winchester, was born on 29 July 1848 at Walton d'Eiville, Warwickshire, the eldest son of the Revd William Duckworth Furneaux, and his wife, Louisa, eldest daughter of William Dickins, of Cherrington, Warwickshire. His father, who owned a family estate at Swilly, Devonshire, was rector of Berkeley, Gloucestershire, from 1860 until his death in 1874. When he was ten years old Furneaux was sent to St Peter's College, Radley. In 1861, possibly because the future of Radley was somewhat uncertain, he was transferred to Marlborough College, where he had a successful school career under G. G. Bradley. He went up to Oxford as a scholar of Corpus Christi College in 1868. He obtained a first class in classical moderations in 1870, being in the same year *proxime accessit* for the Hertford scholarship, and graduated in 1872 with a first class in *literae humaniores*.

On leaving Oxford, Furneaux accepted an assistant mastership at Clifton College. He remained there only two years, returning in 1874 to his old school, Marlborough College, of which F. W. Farrar had become headmaster. He was ordained deacon in 1874 and priest in 1875, and in 1877 he married Caroline Octavia (*d.* 1904), youngest daughter of Joseph Mortimer of Weymouth. He remained at Marlborough for eight years, until in 1882, at the age of thirty-four, he was appointed headmaster of Repton School. Here he proved an admirable headmaster. His business capacity was considerable and it enabled him to overcome the financial and other difficulties which, at the date of his appointment, confronted the school. By judicious negotiation he obtained a secure tenure of the land which it occupied. He added many new buildings, including the hall, which was erected by subscription as a memorial to S. A. Pears, headmaster from 1854 to 1874. A vigorous and inspiring teacher, Furneaux infected his pupils with much of his own enthusiasm for both classical and English literature.

Furneaux resigned the headmastership of Repton in 1900, and in 1903 he was appointed dean of Winchester, an office which he held for sixteen years. His term as dean

ships together, and, in the same archipelago, he named another coral atoll Adventure Island (Motutunga) after Furneaux's ship. The ships again became separated off the coast of New Zealand on 30 October 1773, and Furneaux, after cruising about for some time in a vain endeavour to rejoin the *Resolution*, was ultimately obliged to return home alone, and reached Spithead on 14 July 1774. In so doing Furneaux became the first person to circumnavigate the globe from west to east and also the first to do so in both directions, for he had previously achieved an east–west circumnavigation with Wallis. The chief event occurring during this separation was the loss of a boat's crew commanded by John Rowe, master's mate. He and nine others were killed and eaten by Maori people in a cove in Queen Charlotte Sound, New Zealand. It is noteworthy that Furneaux brought home, in the *Adventure*, Omai (Mae), a native of Huahine, who remained in England for two years, and was taken back in Cook's third voyage. Omai was the first South Sea islander ever seen in England.

Furneaux was promoted post captain on 10 August 1775, and commanded the *Syren* (28 guns) in Sir Peter Parker's attack on Charles Town, South Carolina, on 28 June 1776. The *Syren* was lost on 6 November 1777 off Rhode Island and Furneaux was taken prisoner. On being released the following year he took part as a volunteer on board the *Isis* in a single ship engagement against the French ship *César*. He was not employed again and died, unmarried, aged forty-six, at Swilly, near Plymouth, on 18 September 1781. He was buried in the family vault at Stoke Damerel parish church, Plymouth, on 28 September 1781.

ANDREW C. F. DAVID

was notable for the successful renovation of the foundations of Winchester Cathedral. In 1905 it was found that the subsidence of the fabric had become so serious that, unless measures were taken at once to arrest it, the building was in danger of collapse. The magnitude of the necessary operations was such that doubts were expressed whether the saving of the fabric would be possible or was worth attempting. The dean, however, laboured unceasingly to raise the necessary funds. After seven years, in 1912, the new foundations were completed at a cost of £120,000.

Furneaux retired from the deanery in 1919. He was an honorary canon of Southwell Cathedral from 1891 to 1901, and the Lambeth degree of DD was conferred on him in 1903. He acted as examining chaplain successively to the bishops of Southwell and Winchester. His writings include *A Commentary on the Acts of the Apostles* (1912). Furneaux died at White Cottage, New Milton, Hampshire, on 10 April 1928. He had three daughters.

ALFRED COCHRANE, rev. M. C. CURTHOYS

Sources *The Times* (11 April 1928) · personal knowledge (1937) · *WWW* · *CGPLA Eng. & Wales* (1928)

Wealth at death £38,373 3s. 7d.: probate, 15 June 1928, *CGPLA Eng. & Wales*

Furnese, Sir Henry, first baronet (1658–1712), politician and financier, was born at Sandwich, Kent, on 30 May 1658, the eldest son of Henry Furnese (d. 1672) of Sandwich and his wife, Anne (d. 1696), the daughter of Andrew Gosfright of Sandwich. Augustan satirists made much of Furnese's humble origins, but his father married the daughter of a former mayor of Sandwich, and tales of a penurious upbringing seem to rest on his father's bankruptcy. In the year of his father's death Furnese was apprenticed to one of his Gosfright uncles, a London hosier. Many of the Gosfright clan traded to Flanders and Italy, and Furnese followed in their footsteps. He had prospered sufficiently to marry, on 11 November 1684, Anne (d. 1695), the daughter of Robert Brough, a linen draper of St Lawrence Jewry. The marriage, which produced one son, Robert Furnese [see below], was conducted by the prominent nonconformist divine Edmund Calamy sen., although it was recorded in the parish register of St Lawrence Jewry.

The outbreak of the Nine Years' War in 1689 increased Furnese's opportunities for making money: he clothed several regiments, lent money to the government, and even used his superior communications network on the continent to win several wagers on the progress of the war. He was knighted on 8 October 1691. He was appointed to the London lieutenancy in February 1694 and, having subscribed £3000, was elected to the first directorate of the newly formed Bank of England. Furnese gradually increased his role in public finance, particularly as an agent for remitting funds to the army on the continent. Following the death of his wife in 1695, on 1 December 1697 he married Matilda (d. 1732), the daughter of Sir Thomas Vernon and the widow of Anthony Balam; they had one daughter.

In 1698 Furnese was instrumental in ensuring that the new East India Company loan of £2 million to the government was quickly subscribed. However, it was his East India connection which cut short his first attempt at a career in parliament. Having been elected for Bramber at the 1698 election, on 14 February 1699 he was unseated on the grounds that his role as a receiver and manager of the East India loan made him a placeman. He served as sheriff of London in 1700–01 and secured election to the Commons for Sandwich in January 1701. Again his tenure of a seat in the Commons was short. On 19 February 1701 he was expelled for being a trustee for circulating exchequer bills. After resigning as a trustee he was re-elected for Sandwich in December 1701, and voted consistently with the whigs.

Following the succession of Anne and the renewal of the war with France, Furnese was regularly used as a remittancer of funds to the army. Indeed, in 1705 he negotiated a six-month contract granting him a monopoly of all remittances to the Netherlands, Germany, and Portugal. His commission was 11s. per £100. A further reward for this service was a baronetcy, created on 27 June 1707. Such was his dominance of the remittancing business that in 1709 James Craggs the younger thought it 'not only a difficult, but a dangerous matter to oppose his schemes' (Craggs to J. Stanhope, 3 Aug 1709, Kent Archives Office, Stanhope MS U1590/0139/9/71/3).

The fall of the Godolphin administration in August 1710 placed Furnese in a quandary, as he came under whig pressure not to deal with the incoming tory ministry. But the new ministry had already begun to ease him out of the remittance business, and he signed his last contract in November 1710. Meanwhile he was re-elected to parliament, where he continued to vote with the whigs. As a prominent supporter of the previous ministry and a moneyed man to boot, Furnese was an obvious target for those tories intent on investigating the misdeeds of whig finance. However, he avoided any such attacks before his death, his accounts being passed by his son in 1718. Furnese died of a 'violent colic', at his seat at Waldershare, Kent, on 30 November 1712. His will instructed that he be buried at St Peter's, Sandwich, and that a monument be erected to 'God's great goodness to me in advancing me to a considerable estate from a very small beginning', and his son duly saw to it, commissioning a 'towering mass of marble, with its seated female figures, cherubs, and ammonite-like volutes' (*Archaeologia Cantiana*, 62, 1949, 69).

Furnese was succeeded as second baronet by his only son, **Sir Robert Furnese** (1687–1733), politician, who was born on 1 August 1687. He was educated at Eton College and then travelled in Germany. He was licensed to marry his stepsister Anne (d. 1713), the daughter of Anthony Balam, on 1 October 1708; they had one daughter. Having been abroad during the 1708 election, Furnese secured a seat in the Commons at a by-election for Truro on 16 December 1708. He voted for the impeachment of Sacheverell in 1710. In the election that year he was returned for New Romney, and again voted with the whigs. The death of his father left Furnese a very rich man, and his second marriage (on 8 July 1714), to Arabella Watson (1693–1727), the daughter of the third Baron Rockingham, reflected his increased status. The couple had a son (who eventually became the third baronet) and a daughter. Furnese was not much interested in trade or finance, being content to live off his extensive inheritance. He continued to support the whigs, but joined Robert Walpole in opposition in 1717. With Walpole in power he returned to the government fold, and in 1727 was elected knight of the shire for Kent. He was married for a third time on 15 May 1729. His new wife was Lady Anne Shirley (d. 1779), the daughter of Robert, first Earl Ferrers; they had two daughters, one of whom predeceased her father. Furnese died on 14 March 1733 of a cold, made worse by a bout of heavy drinking 'that he was not sober for ten days before he was taken ill' (Hastings MSS, 3.15). His monument paid tribute to his parliamentary service, as well as his 'affable behaviour and liberal spirit' (Parsons, 402–3).   STUART HANDLEY

Sources HoP, *Commons* [draft] · W. Boys, *Collections for an history of Sandwich in Kent* (1792, [1892]) · IGI · D. W. Jones, *War and economy in the age of William III and Marlborough* (1988) · P. Parsons, *Monuments and painted glass in east Kent* (1794) · parish register (marriage), London, St Lawrence Jewry, 11 Nov 1684 · A. Boyer, *The political state of Great Britain*, 2nd edn, 4 (1718), 368 · *Report on the manuscripts of the late Reginald Rawdon Hastings*, 4 vols., HMC, 78 (1928–47), vol. 3, p. 15 · CKS, Stanhope papers, U1590/0139/9/71/3 · R. Gunnis, 'Signed monuments in Kentish churches', *Archaeologia Cantiana*, 62 (1949), 57–86, esp. 69 · W. A. Shaw, *The knights of England*, 2 vols. (1906)
Archives CKS, letters to James Stanhope

Furnese, Sir Robert, second baronet (1687–1733). *See under* Furnese, Sir Henry, first baronet (1658–1712).

Furness, Christopher, first Baron Furness (1852–1912), shipowner and industrialist, was born on 23 April 1852 at West Hartlepool, the seventh son of John Furness (1808–1885), provision merchant, and his wife, Averill, daughter of John Wilson of Naisbet Hall, co. Durham. John Furness worked as a coal trimmer on the local railway line until 1850 when he founded a grocery and provisioning business in Lynn Street. His sons ran the enterprise, which under his eldest son, Thomas (b. 1836), became known as Thomas Furness & Co. and developed into one of the largest of its kind in north-eastern England. John Furness died in 1885 leaving an estate sworn at £460.

After attending Anderson School in West Hartlepool, Furness joined the family firm and in 1870 went to Sweden as a buyer. During the blockade of the Elbe by the French fleet, he secured a corner on the grain market and made an estimated profit of £50,000–60,000 for the firm. He became a partner two years later and in 1876 married Jane Annette, only daughter of Henry Suggitt, of Brierton, co. Durham, a builder.

Thomas Furness & Co. won large provisioning contracts in the mid-1870s and chartered ships to import foodstuffs from the USA and Europe. Furness wanted to develop the shipping side of the business further and in 1877 the firm bought sailing vessels and inaugurated a regular service between Boston, Massachusetts, and West Hartlepool. Differences concerning the future policy of the firm arose between the eldest and youngest brothers and in 1882

Christopher Furness, first Baron Furness (1852–1912), by Sir Benjamin Stone, 1902

they divided the assets of the firm between them. Thomas retained the provisioning operations, while Christopher embarked on a career as a shipowner by forming Christopher Furness & Co. as a private concern with a capital of £100,000.

During the 1880s, Furness extended his transatlantic liner operations and built up a substantial fleet of tramping vessels. Having made a large fortune in speculative shipbuilding during the preceding boom, in 1891 he amalgamated his fleet of eighteen wholly-owned steamers and investments in twenty-one other ships with the West Hartlepool shipbuilding firm of Edward Withy & Co., in which he had acquired an interest in 1882. The new concern, Furness Withy & Co., had capital of £700,000.

In the 1890s, Furness founded a series of new transatlantic lines in conjunction with other shipowners and financiers. To these ventures Furness contributed capital and management services, while Withy's yard supplied many of the required vessels. The growing size of his fleet (he ordered nearly 100 ships between 1898 and 1901) enabled Furness to use his purchasing power to acquire interests in numerous steel, engineering, and shipbuilding companies in the north-east. He also acquired four large coalmining firms to build up a large coal export business.

After 1901, Furness did not enlarge his industrial interests significantly but instead focused his attention on shipping projects. During 1902 and 1903, he and Alfred Jones attempted to form a shipping combine to contest the north Atlantic passenger trade with J. P. Morgan's recently formed International Mercantile Marine. The £20 million Furness–Jones venture depended on government postal subsidies and Admiralty subventions, which proved inadequate, and with Furness unable to secure the confidence of the other parties involved, his plan collapsed. As a result, it was Cunard which benefited from the government funds, enabling the *Mauretania* and the *Lusitania* to be built.

After this setback, Furness concentrated on expanding his tramping and bulk carrying operations, while building a network of UK coastal lines. Beginning in 1910, Furness Withy expanded aggressively by acquiring four trans-atlantic lines, companies involved in the Argentinian frozen-meat trade, and eleven firms operating on the Great Lakes. By 1914, the Furness group of companies controlled over 1 million gross tons of shipping.

Furness was keenly interested in commercializing new technology. He built Britain's first motor ship, *Eavestone*, and the first turbine-powered vessel to cross the Atlantic was his yacht, *Emerald*. His most ambitious project was the reconstruction of the Cargo Fleet Iron Company's works, which incorporated the most advanced equipment of the period and a new steel making process invented by Benjamin Talbot. Furness's hunting lodge, Cundall Manor, North Riding of Yorkshire made experimental use of stressed metal construction.

Furness also had an active political career. In 1891, he defeated William Gray to become Liberal MP for Hartlepool. He lost the seat in 1895 to the Unionist candidate, Thomas Richardson, and unsuccessfully ran in York in 1898, but was re-elected for Hartlepool in 1900 and returned unopposed in 1906. Although Furness won again in 1910, he was unseated on petition because of the irregular practices of an agent. One month later he was raised to the peerage as first Baron Furness of Grantley, having been knighted in 1895. His nephew, Stephen Wilson Furness won the consequent by-election. Furness was a radical Liberal who favoured electoral registration reform, 'one man one vote', and the abolition of the hereditary principle of the House of Lords, and who supported Lloyd George's budget of 1909. He had experimented with profit-sharing at the Wingate Coal Company and Irvine's Shipbuilding and Dry Dock Company in 1908, and his maiden speech in the Lords called for a parliamentary commission to investigate the broader application of co-partnership.

Furness displayed remarkable energy in both business and political affairs. He considered the suggestions of trusted advisers, Frederick W. Lewis (later Lord Essendon) and Stephen (later Sir Stephen) Wilson Furness who succeeded him as chairman of Furness Withy & Co., but displayed authoritarian characteristics. He had a short temper, especially when dealing with those who prevaricated, but afterwards behaved in a conciliatory manner. He was unfailingly loyal to trusted associates and was extremely interested in the development of young people. He attracted criticism for some of his methods and political views, but he expected and gave no quarter. He was of solid build and sported a large moustache and mutton chop whiskers.

Furness died at Grantley Hall, Grantley, near Ripon, in Yorkshire, on 10 November 1912, after a lengthy and painful illness during which he was attended by a United Methodist minister. He left an estate of £1 million. His landed property of some 30,000 acres and the greater part of his estate he left to his only son Marmaduke (*b.* 1883), later first Viscount Furness. He left his shares in Furness Withy & Co. in trust to ensure that they were retained by the family.   GORDON BOYCE

Sources G. Boyce, 'The growth and dissolution of a large-scale enterprise: the Furness Interest, 1892–1919', PhD diss., London School of Economics, 1984 · Redhill, Surrey, Furness Withy MSS · NMM · private information (2004) · *WWW* · Burke, *Peerage* · G. Boyce, *Information, mediation and institutional developments: the rise of large-scale enterprise in British shipping, 1870–1919* (1995) · d. cert.
Archives Furness Withy Co. Ltd, Redhill, Surrey · NMM | U. Glas., Alexander Stephen's MSS
Likenesses B. Stone, photograph, 1902, NPG [*see illus.*] · Spy [L. Ward], caricature, Hentschel-colourtype, NPG; repro. in *VF* (21 Oct 1908) · oils, Furness Withy Ltd, London · photograph, repro. in *DBB* · photograph, repro. in W. G. Willis, *The history of South Durham Steel and Iron Co* (1969)
Wealth at death £1,000,000: probate, 2 Dec 1912, *CGPLA Eng. & Wales*

Furness, Jocelin of (*fl.* 1199–1214), Cistercian monk and hagiographer, is known only through the four saints' lives that he composed in the late twelfth and early thirteenth century. The manuscripts describe him as 'monk of Furness', the Cistercian abbey on the coast of Lancashire, and three of his works have associations with the adjoining regions of southern Scotland, Man, and northern Ireland.

Jocelin's *Vita sancti Kentigerni episcopi* is dedicated to his namesake Jocelin, bishop of Glasgow (1175–99), who had been monk and prior of the Cistercian monastery of Melrose. For this account of the founding father of the diocese, Kentigern, he drew on earlier lives, one that had been produced in the episcopacy of Bishop Herbert (1147–64), the other older and, in Jocelin's opinion, composed in a barbaric Scottish style. His *Vita sancti Patricii episcopi* was undertaken at the request of John de Courcy, ruler of Anglo-Norman Ulster, Malachy, bishop of Down, and Thomas, archbishop of Armagh, and is datable to 1180–1201. Furness had links with Ulster, being the mother house of the abbey of Inch, which John de Courcy founded with Bishop Malachy's support in the 1180s. Jocelin's life of Patrick draws on the so-called *Vita tertia* and the tripartite life but adds new material, including the earliest claim that St Patrick expelled poisonous reptiles from Ireland. Jocelin's *Vita sancti Waldevi abbatis* is dedicated to William the Lion, king of Scots, and to the king's son and brother, and is datable to 1207–14. Waldef, abbot of Melrose (*d.* 1159), was a kinsman of the Scottish royal family, and Jocelin's portrayal provides a conventionally saintly figure in which the dedicatees might feel 'exultation through the common stock and descent you share' (Bartlett, 42). Finally, his *Vita et translatio sancte Helene regine* was composed, at an uncertain date, at the request of 'religious persons who dedicate themselves to obedience to Christ under the yoke of the rule and the patronage of saint Helen' (translated from Gotha, Forschungs- und

Landesbibliothek, MS I 81, fol. 204). In his preface Jocelin explains that he has constructed this account of the mother of the emperor Constantine from scattered references in various histories and chronicles, including a life in English translated from 'Britannic', probably Welsh. He tells of Helen's activities, including the discovery of the true cross, and relates how her relics were brought from Rome to Hautvilliers in the ninth century. Jocelin's style is rhetorical and rich in biblical allusions, citations, and echoes. He frequently engages in explicit moralization, using his saintly subjects as models by which to judge and castigate the sins and shortcomings of contemporaries. He transmitted much legendary material about early Celtic saints as well as providing, in his life of Waldef, a more nearly contemporary source of some historical importance.   ROBERT BARTLETT

Sources Jocelin of Furness, *Vita sancti Kentigerni*, *Lives of S. Ninian and S. Kentigern*, ed. A. P. Forbes (1874), 159–242 · Jocelin of Furness, 'Vita sancti Patricii', *Acta sanctorum: Martius*, 2 (Antwerp, 1688), 540–80 · Jocelin of Furness, 'Vita sancti Waldeni', *Acta sanctorum: Augustus*, 1 (Antwerp, 1733), 241–77 · [Jocelin of Furness], 'Translatio S. Helenae', ed. P. Grosjean, *Analecta Bollandiana*, 58 (1940), 199–203 [contains only a pt of the life, which as a whole remains unpubd] · G. McFadden, 'The *Life of Waldef* and its author, Jocelin of Furness', *Innes Review*, 6 (1955), 5–13 · R. Bartlett, 'The hagiography of Angevin England', *Thirteenth century England: proceedings of the Newcastle upon Tyne conference* [Newcastle upon Tyne 1993], ed. P. Coss and S. D. Lloyd, 5 (1995), 37–52 · K. H. Jackson, 'The sources for the Life of St Kentigern', in N. K. Chadwick and others, *Studies in the early British church* (1958), 273–358 · A. Boyle, 'St Servanus and the manuscript tradition of the life of St Kentigern', *Innes Review*, 21 (1970), 37–45 · A. Macquarrie, 'The career of Saint Kentigern of Glasgow: Vitae, lectiones and glimpses of fact', *Innes Review*, 37 (1986), 3–24 · L. Bieler, 'Did Jocelin of Furness know the writings of St Patrick at first hand?', *Studies on the life and legend of St Patrick*, ed. R. Sharpe (1986) · L. Bieler, 'Jocelin von Furness als Hagiograph', *Studies on the life and legend of St Patrick*, ed. R. Sharpe (1986) · G. McFadden, 'An edition and translation of the life of Waldef, abbot of Melrose, by Jocelin of Furness', PhD diss., Columbia University, 1952 · J. B. P. Bulloch, 'Saint Waltheof', *Records of the Scottish Church History Society*, 11 (1951–3), 105–32 · D. Baker, 'Legend and reality: the case of Waldef of Melrose', *Church, society and politics*, ed. J. Bulloch, SCH, 12 (1975), 59–82 · M. Lapidge and R. Sharpe, *A bibliography of Celtic-Latin literature, 400–1200* (1985), 283–4
Archives Forschungs- und Landesbibliothek, Gotha, MS 181, fol. 201

Furness, Richard (1791–1857), poet, was born on 2 August 1791, the son of Samuel Furness, a small farmer at Eyam, Derbyshire, and his wife, Margaret. He left school at the age of fourteen and was apprenticed to a currier at Chesterfield, although he soon displayed poetic tendencies and a great love of learning. From some French officers on parole he learned French and mathematics, and he also became proficient in music.

When Furness was seventeen years old he joined the Wesleyan Methodists, and undertook the duties of local preacher. Four years later he walked to London, and on his arrival enlisted as a volunteer soldier; he also continued to preach, once at the City Road Chapel. After a year he returned to his native county. He separated from the Methodists about this time over a conflict regarding a patriotic song he had written which was sung at a meeting in a public house.

In 1813 Furness started business on his own account at Eyam as a currier, but he neglected the trade, focusing instead on his interest in music, poetry, and mathematics. His prospects were not improved when in 1816 he ran away with Frances Ibbotson of Hathersage whom he married on 29 December that year. In 1821 he became schoolmaster in the free school of the small village of Dore, Derbyshire. He also acted as vestry and parish clerk, but showed his independence of mind and action by invariably closing his book and resuming his seat at the recitation of the Athanasian creed. He practised medicine and surgery, and when the ancient chapel of Dore was pulled down in 1828, his plans for a new one were adopted. He not only superintended the erection of the building, but carved the ornamented figures which adorn the structure.

Furness's first publication was a satirical poem, 'Rag Bag' (1832). His next was *Medicus-Magus, a Poem, in Three Cantos* (1836), in which he depicted the idiosyncrasies of residents of the more remote parts of Derbyshire, and included a glossary of local dialect. The title was afterwards altered to *The Astrologer*. Many of his miscellaneous poems were printed in the *Sheffield Iris*. One of his short pieces, the 'Old Year's Funeral', was thought by James Montgomery to be worthy of comparison with Coleridge's ode 'On the Departing Year' (Holland and Everett, 6.232).

Furness's first wife died in 1844, and on 17 October 1850 he married Mary (*b*. 1802/3), the daughter of Godfrey Swift, a farrier, and the widow of John Lunn, of Staveley, Derbyshire. On a change of incumbent at Dore, Furness retired as schoolmaster on a pension of £15. The only duties left to him were those of the district registrar of births and deaths, which yielded him £12 a year. In no year of his life did his income exceed £80. Furness suffered from asthma for much of his later life; he died at Dore on 13 December 1857, and was buried at Eyam church. A collection of his *Poetical Works* was published posthumously in 1858.

                              C. W. SUTTON, *rev.* MEGAN A. STEPHAN

Sources G. C. Holland, 'Biographical sketch', in *The poetical works of the late Richard Furness* (1858), 1–84 · S. T. Hall, *Biographical sketches of remarkable people* (1873), 334–40 · *Memoirs of the life and writings of James Montgomery*, ed. J. Holland and J. Everett, 7 vols. (1854–6), vol. 6, p. 232 · Boase, *Mod. Eng. biog.*, 1.1113 · Colvin, *Archs.*, 384 · Allibone, *Dict.* · *IGI* · m. cert., 1850 · d. cert.

Furniss, Henry [Harry; *pseud.* Lika Joko] (1854–1925), caricaturist and illustrator, was born on 26 March 1854 in Wexford, Ireland, the first child of the second family of James Furniss, civil engineer, and his second wife, Isabella Cornelia, a miniature painter, daughter of Eneas *Mackenzie (1777–1832), author, topographer, politician, publisher, and newspaper proprietor. His father was from Hathersage, Derbyshire, his mother from Scotland.

Furniss was educated at the Wesleyan College, St Stephen's Green, Dublin, the Royal Hibernian School, and the Hibernian Academy. At the academy his restless temperament rebelled against the tedium of drawing from

Henry Furniss [Lika Joko] **(1854–1925)**, by Walery, pubd 1890

classical sculpture. He sketched from life whenever possible and always claimed to be self-taught. At school he edited the *Schoolboys' Punch*. Years later he wrote revealingly, 'I resolved to use the columns of *The Schoolboys' Punch* not so much in the interest of the schoolboy world as to attract the headmaster's favourable notice to the editor' (Furniss, *Confessions*, 1.7). Throughout his life Furniss assiduously sought, and usually found, favourable notice. In 1873 his early, tentatively drawn cartoons appeared in *Zozimus*, the Irish *Punch*, and in the same year at the age of nineteen he moved to London where his reportorial drawings were commissioned by the *Illustrated Sporting and Dramatic News* and the *Illustrated London News*. His confidence and abilities increased and a wider range of commissions for a large number of periodicals soon followed, among them *The Graphic*, *Black and White*, *Good Words*, *Pall Mall*, *Pearson's*, and, in particular, *Punch*, to which he began contributing on 30 October 1880. Furniss joined the staff in 1884 not as a full-time member but on a retainer, a more flexible and profitable arrangement. During his fourteen years there he drew some 2600 cartoons and illustrations, most notably the full-page, multi-figured caricatures for Sir Henry Lucy's *Essence of Parliament*, made from sketches taken on the spot and remarkable for their vitality and spontaneity. Furniss's parliamentary sketches were usually drawn in the Victorian mode of (fairly) gentlemanly politics. His firm political and social opinions—he was a strong unionist—sometimes intruded into his cartoons but most of his subjects made no complaint, partly

because Furniss lacked malice and partly because 'If we must confess it, [politicians] are quite offended and downcast when the cartoons stop', as Winston Churchill observed (D. Low, *Ye Madde Designer*, 1935, 20). Furniss gave Gladstone hilarious collars (the drawings, intrinsically comic, still raise a smile), and in presenting the reader with similarly recognizable '"tabs" of identity' (ibid.), for example, a collar, multiple chins, a monocle, Furniss, more than any other cartoonist of his day, set an example for later generations of newspaper caricaturists to emulate.

A genuine amiability could not always disguise Furniss's dog-worrying-a-bone business tactics. After fourteen years he quit *Punch* following a protracted exchange of correspondence in which he paraded himself, not always convincingly, as hard done by. During this turbulent period he also claimed that the commercial use of one of his cartoons had degraded his name and reputation. The drawing, published throughout the world and several times plagiarized, depicted a filthy tramp writing a letter: 'Two years ago I used your soap, since when I have used no other.' From the proprietors of *Punch* the makers of Pears Soap obtained the right to use the drawing in a long-running advertising campaign which paradoxically added its recurring mite to the artist's growing international fame.

After leaving *Punch* Furniss began publishing his own humorous journal, *Lika Joko* (1894)—a name sometimes used as a pseudonym—a successful but short-lived venture followed by the *New Budget* (1895) and *The Cartoon* (1915).

Furniss was 'a most fertile delineator of the Victorian and Edwardian scene' (*The Times*, 16 Jan 1925, 14). When, in the 1880s, the new photo-mechanical means of reproduction began replacing laborious wood-engraving, Furniss took full advantage of the greater technical flexibility in order to produce a huge range of drawings, both comic and serious. A frenetic energy was his most notable characteristic which, in his rush to meet deadlines and fulfil commissions, and to complete his own many projects, left no time for reflection. His style suffered. Brilliant at its frequent best it was also often uneven in quality; David Low noted, 'at his zenith [Furniss] was almost a factory' (Low, 34). Furniss also found time to write and produce entertainments by limelight—*Art and Artists*, *The Humours of Parliament*, *Portraiture—Past and Present*—which he gave throughout Britain, often travelling several hundred miles overnight from one venue to another. Visits to Australia and America in turn produced their own entertainments. He wrote and illustrated twenty-nine books of his own and illustrated thirty-four works by other authors, including the complete works of Charles Dickens—eighteen volumes, 500 full-page illustrations (1910)—and Thackeray (1911).

One of Furniss's happiest enterprises was the talk of 1887 when *Harry Furniss's Royal Academy: 'An Artistic Joke'*, a series of huge monochrome paintings wickedly parodying the works of well-known Royal Academicians, was shown to amused crowds and bemused members of the academy at the Gainsborough Gallery in Bond Street. A large format, almost comically luxurious volume of the paintings, limited to 1000 copies, was published at the artist's own expense. Individual copies sold for 5 guineas: an expensive joke indeed.

Artists are not always the best judges of their own work and in his *Confessions of a Caricaturist* Furniss wrote: 'Caricature pure and simple is not the art I either care for or succeed in practising as well as I do my less well known more serious and more finished work' (Furniss, *Confessions*, 1.91). The drawings so casually dismissed are superior to and more compelling than his 'serious' illustrative works, which, for all their sterling qualities, are stubbornly unmemorable. Even so, he was disappointed, after a seven-year collaboration, with Lewis Carroll's *Sylvie and Bruno* (1889), and in the following year, with *Sylvie and Bruno Concluded*. The stories lacked the magic of *Alice* and Furniss was ruefully aware that his illustrations also lacked the imaginative grasp of John Tenniel in the earlier works. Furniss was sustained through success and failure by his marriage to Marian (b. c.1853), daughter of Alfred Rogers, which began on 11 December 1877 and lasted his lifetime. Of his four children, Dorothy became an artist and a collaborator on some of his later book illustrations. All four served in and survived the First World War of 1914–18. In a brief wartime propaganda exercise, *Peace and War: Pencillings by Harry Furniss* (1914), Furniss appears briefly on camera: a sturdy, stocky, ebullient man, smiling and self-confident, his balding head and beard well groomed and, typical of the period, he wore a sober suit and tie while, in this instance, sketching with brush and black ink at a vertical drawing board. Furniss's 'pleasant carrying voice of great power' was noted by a journalist watching one of the entertainments (*Harry Furniss at Home*, 118). An active member of the Savage, Garrick, Beefsteak, and the Two Pins clubs, he enjoyed the company of successful men. The comforting thud of dropped names fills his later writings and he unblushingly boasted that the Garrick 'is not a school for budding geniuses. It is an academy for the elect' (Furniss, *The Two Pins Club*, 75).

In 1912, at the age of fifty-eight, Furniss visited the United States where for two years he worked in the studios of Thomas Alva Edison. There he wrote and acted in early film shorts and produced cinema storylines which were 'prepared to be given in conjunction with phonographic rendering of the actors' speeches' in which he was too far ahead of his time (*New York Times*, 16 Jan 1925, 17, col. 3). Furniss returned to Britain in time for the First World War.

Responding to concern among family and friends who had for years worried about his health being destroyed by overwork, Furniss retired to Hastings, joined the Author's Club, the Hastings Golf Club, and the Literary Society, and found time to write a stream of reminiscences and anecdotes—wordy but worth reading—songs of praise to himself in his prime among the distinguished friends and colleagues of his heyday. Little heed was taken of the postwar world.

Harry Furniss died at The Mount, 8 High Wickham,

Hastings, on 14 January 1925, aged seventy, and was buried on 17 January at All Saints' Church, Hastings. His wife survived him. After a lifetime of industry he left an estate valued at £2566 gross, £1475 net. His considerable correspondence with Lewis Carroll was auctioned shortly after his death. A memorial exhibition of his work was held at the Fine Art Society in 1925 and the National Portrait Gallery, London, mounted an exhibition of his work in 1983.

JOHN JENSEN

Sources A. Opyrchal, *Harry Furniss, 1854–1925: confessions of a caricaturist* (1983) [exhibition catalogue, NPG, 8 July – 25 September 1983, and elsewhere] · H. Furniss, *The confessions of a caricaturist*, 2 vols. (1901) · H. Furniss, *Catalogue of a collection of drawings, political and pictorial*, ed. E. J. Milliken (1894) [exhibition catalogue, Fine Art Society, London, 1894] · *Catalogue of a memorial exhibition of drawings and cartoons by the late Harry Furniss* (1925) [exhibition catalogue, Fine Art Society, London; incl. introduction by M. H. Spielmann] · M. H. Spielmann, *The history of 'Punch'* (1895) · *Harry Furniss at home* (1904) · H. Furniss, *How to draw in pen and ink* (1905) · [H. Furniss], *Harry Furniss's Royal Academy: 'An artistic joke'* (1887) [exhibition catalogue] · H. Furniss, *Garrick Gallery caricatures* (c.1923) · H. Furniss, *My bohemian days* (1919) · H. Furniss, *The Two Pins Club* (1925) · *The Times* (16 Jan 1925), 14 · *The Times* (5 March 1925), 17 · J. A. Hammerton, *Humorists of the pencil* (1905) · A. Opyrchal, 'Harry Furniss caricaturist', *Antiquarian Book Monthly Review*, 11 (1984), 88–93 · C. Veth, *Comic art in England* (Amsterdam, [1929]) [introduction by J. Greig] · H. Furniss, *Pen and pencil in parliament* (1897) · D. Low, *British cartoonists, caricaturists and comic artists* (1942) · M. Bryant and S. Heneage, eds., *Dictionary of British cartoonists and caricaturists, 1730–1980* (1994) · B. Hillier, *Cartoons and caricatures* (1970) · J. Geipel, *The cartoon: a short history of graphic comedy and satire* (1972) · W. Feaver, *Masters of caricature: from Hogarth and Gillray to Scarfe and Levine*, ed. A. Green (1981) · C. R. Ashbee, *Caricature* (1928) · S. Houfe, *The dictionary of British book illustrators and caricaturists, 1800–1914* (1978) · A. Horne, *The dictionary of 20th century British book illustrators* (1994) · M. Horn, ed., *The world encyclopedia of cartoons* (1980) · m. cert. · d. cert.

Archives BM, MSS, photographs, cuttings, etc. · House of Commons, MSS · Hunt. L., letters · NPG, MSS, photographs, cuttings, etc. · Punch, MSS and drawings | BL, corresp. with Macmillans, Add. MS 55230 · JRL, letters to M. H. Spielmann | FILM BFI NFTVA, *Peace and war: pencillings by Harry Furniss*, 1914

Likenesses Walery, photograph, pubd 1890, NPG [*see illus.*] · E. J. Sullivan, pen-and-ink drawing, 1891, NPG · M. Beerbohm, caricature, exh. 1911, Princeton University, New Jersey · W. H. Bartlett, group portrait, oils (*A Saturday night at the Savage Club*), Savage Club, London · Bassano, photographs, NPG · Elliott & Fry, cabinet photograph, NPG · H. Furniss, self-portrait, caricature, repro. in Opyrchal, 'Harry Furniss caricaturist' · H. Furniss, self-portrait, pen-and-ink drawing, NPG · H. Furniss, self-portraits, caricatures, pencil drawings, NPG · S. P. Hall, pencil drawing, NPG · woodcut, BM

Wealth at death £2566 7s. 0d.: probate, 27 Feb 1925, *CGPLA Eng. & Wales*

Furniss, Henry Sanderson, Baron Sanderson (1868–1939), college head, was born in London on 1 October 1868, the elder son of Thomas Sanderson Furniss (1833–1912), JP and barrister, of Stratford St Mary, Suffolk, and his wife and second cousin, Mary (d. 1899), daughter of Edward Fisher Sanderson, of New York. His greatgrandfather Thomas Sanderson went into partnership with a Sheffield steel maker, Naylor, thus founding the firm which eventually became Sanderson Brothers and

Henry Sanderson Furniss, Baron Sanderson (1868–1939), by Sir Stanley Spencer, 1921

Newbould. One of the earliest partners was Lord Sanderson's paternal grandfather, Henry Furniss, who had married a daughter of Thomas Sanderson.

Furniss had extremely poor eyesight from birth and was almost completely blind towards the end of his life. After attending a boys' day school for five years until the age of thirteen he was taught by private tutors in the country until the age of twenty-one, when he entered Hertford College, Oxford (1889). He read modern history, assisted by a reader and an amanuensis, and obtained a second-class degree in 1893.

Furniss's first real employment came in 1907, but before then he lived for several years at Clifton, Bristol, with a barrister friend. He did charitable work with the Bristol Charity Organization Society, his father having worked with the London body. Otherwise he spent much time reading (with a reader), especially economics, which had attracted him during his undergraduate course: 'Economics is a very good subject for a blind man … it is by no means necessary to read everything' (Furniss, 62). His Clifton friend was a son of Louis Mallet, who had been close to Richard Cobden. Furniss was a free-trader as well as a supporter of the theory, then exercising many minds, of bimetallism.

Although Furniss later thought that 'the years I spent at Clifton … were to a large extent wasted' (Furniss, 70), one valuable consequence of his time there was his marriage on 23 January 1902 to Averil Dorothy, the only daughter of

Henry Frederick Nicholl, of Twyford, Berkshire. In London he worked for a short period for the secretary of the royal commission on alien immigration (the secretary was his wife's uncle) and visited Jewish tailors' outwork places in Whitechapel. He became engrossed in the free trade versus fair trade controversy, writing pamphlets for the Free Food League. Unlike his family and that of his wife, who were staunch Conservatives, his first ever vote was for a Liberal candidate in 1906.

By then settled in Oxford, Furniss studied there for the new diploma in economics; his aim was to be qualified to become a teacher. He obtained his diploma in 1906 and a year later he was invited by an acquaintance, H. B. Lees Smith, to become a tutor in economics at Ruskin College. The college had been founded in 1899 as a residential college for working men and Lees Smith, the vice-principal, had been associated with it from the start. He was leaving for a post at Bristol University and Furniss took his place as tutor in economics.

Furniss himself thought he was an unusual choice for the position for he had little knowledge of working people and had done very little teaching. This was true also of another new appointment, Charles Sydney Buxton, the son of the cabinet minister Sydney Buxton. It proved to be a difficult introduction for both of them: despite their inexperience they comprised two-thirds of the teaching staff and did most of the teaching. Their appointment coincided with the effects of major influences on the college. Many Ruskin students, mostly active trade unionists, were affected by growing militancy in the union movement as well as by the ideas of sundry varieties of socialism. Furniss had moved from Conservatism to Liberalism but was clearly out of sympathy with many of the ideas and attitudes of the students. Moreover, there was friction between the two new tutors and the college principal, James Dennis Hird (1850–1920), formerly a Church of England priest but now virtually an atheist. There were accusations that Hird was teaching both socialism and atheism under the guise of sociology.

Furniss stated in his autobiography that Hird undermined the two new tutors by his criticisms and that under him there was a lack of order in the college. Hird also sided with the students in their disagreements with the college, which were primarily over two issues. Many of them objected to the economics they were taught, which was in no sense geared to the interests of working people. Some wanted it to be overtly Marxist. Furniss did include some Marxism in his lectures but merely concentrated on a critical examination of the labour theory of value. The second disagreement related to the organization and control of the college. It was run by a combination of trade-union leaders, Oxford academics, and philanthropists. The 'revolting' students wanted it to be run solely by the labour movement. At the same time a number of reforming Oxford academics, wishing *inter alia* to widen the university's intake, tried to bring Ruskin and the university into closer contact. This was interpreted by the students as the university taking over the college.

On 17 November 1908 the college executive set up a subcommittee of inquiry into the problems troubling the college. Its report, which found many faults, was considered by the executive on 6 March 1909. Furniss related in his autobiography that he was quite sure that he and Buxton would be sacked. However it was the principal, Hird, who was asked that day to resign. The grounds were essentially his lack of control in the college rather than the content of his teaching. Three weeks later, on 26 March, the students went on strike in favour of the principal, although a number remained loyal to the college. After a week's strike the students were sent home and the college reopened on 20 April. The dissident students and outside sympathizers opened their own labour college in Oxford on 8 September, later transferring to London. There followed a half-century of antagonism between the two adult education providers: the Workers' Educational Association and Ruskin against the National Council of Labour Colleges. The former regarded the latter as peddling dogmatic Marxism; the latter said that the former were mere reformists. Furniss was on the central executive of the Workers Educational Association from 1915 to 1935.

Ruskin College settled down after the strike, and during the First World War, when the college was closed, Furniss was appointed principal in 1916, without pay; he remained in that post until 1925. He and his wife travelled extensively in Australia, South Africa, and the United States, and they were brought into contact with the labour movement and educational developments in those countries. At home they had become even closer to the trade union movement by supporting a strike in 1914 in the Oxfordshire village of Chipping Norton. Politically they both came to support the Labour Party, and in 1918, when it first became possible for individuals to join the party, they both became members. In 1918 Furniss stood, unsuccessfully, as the first Labour candidate for Oxford University.

In Furniss's few years as principal, the college's reopening in 1919 saw women admitted as students, but soon the economic depression told, reducing the number of students as well as the college's finances. Furniss suffered from ill health and had some lengthy periods away from the college. In October 1924 he sent in his resignation, which took effect in April 1925.

Furniss was raised to the peerage as Baron Sanderson of Hunmanby, Yorkshire, on 18 June 1930, and he was an active member of the House of Lords. He represented the Labour peers on the parliamentary executive of the Labour Party and was also a member of the national executive. But as a pacifist he quarrelled with the party over foreign policy and resigned from the national executive in 1936 and from the party two years later. In October 1938 he supported the Conservative candidate at the Oxford City by-election, when the Munich agreement was the predominant issue.

Furniss died suddenly at the Lansdowne Club, Berkeley Square, London, on 25 March 1939; he was buried on 28 March at Headington cemetery, Oxford. He was survived by his wife, and there were no children of the marriage.

The portrait of Sanderson by A. K. Lawrence at Ruskin College was a testimonial he received on his retirement from past and present students and from the general council of the Trades Union Congress. Furniss was close to his students and a conscientious and meticulous teacher. His successor as principal, Alfred Barratt Brown, noted 'his essential kindness and generosity' (*DNB*).

HAROLD POLLINS

Sources H. S. Furniss, *Memories of sixty years* (1931) · *DNB* · GEC, *Peerage* · H. Pollins, *The history of Ruskin College* (1984) · B. Jennings, 'Revolting students: the Ruskin College dispute, 1908–9', *Studies in Adult Education* (1977), 1–16 · H. S. Furniss, *Charles Sydney Buxton: a memoir* (1914) · J. Beatson-Hird, *Dennis Hird, socialist educator and propagandist, first principal of Ruskin College* (1999) · W. W. Craik, *The Central Labour College, 1909–1929: a chapter in the history of working-class education* (1964) · A. Ockwell and H. Pollins, '"Extension" in all of its forms', *Hist. U. Oxf. 7: 19th-cent. Oxf. pt 2* · J. Mabro, *I ban everything: free speech and censorship in Oxford between the wars* (1985) · *The Times* (27 March 1939) · *The Times* (28 March 1939) · *The Times* (29 March 1939) · *CGPLA Eng. & Wales* (1939) · m. cert.
Archives Ruskin College, Oxford, strike records | Bodl. Oxf., letters to Lord Ponsonby
Likenesses W. Stoneman, photograph, 1917, NPG · S. Spencer, drawing, 1921; Christies, 13 March 1981, lot 72 [*see illus.*] · A. K. Lawrence, oils, Ruskin College, Oxford
Wealth at death £60,842 7s. 9d.: probate, 23 June 1939, *CGPLA Eng. & Wales*

Furnival, Elizabeth [Fanny; *known as* Mrs Kemble] (*fl.* 1731–1752), actress and singer, took her first known role as Lady Grace in John Vanbrugh's and Colley Cibber's *The Provok'd Husband* on 10 February 1731 at the Haymarket Theatre, London, where she and her husband, Thomas Furnival (*d.* 1773), were engaged for the 1730–31 season. According to William Chetwood, while playing at York, in 1736 Mrs Furnival was noticed by a noble person who arranged for her Drury Lane début in the title role of Beaumont's and Fletcher's *The Scornful Lady* on 17 March 1737. Despite performing several other parts that season, including Lady Townly in *The Provok'd Husband* for a benefit she shared with her husband and Charles Macklin, she was given little opportunity to act tragic roles and was advised to try to make a name for herself in Dublin. Following two more Drury Lane seasons, during which she performed Portia, Goneril, and Lady Fidget in William Wycherley's *The Country Wife*, she moved to the Smock Alley Theatre in Dublin, where she played over thirty parts from 1739 to 1742, including Hamlet in 1741. She also toured during this time. From 1742 to 1744, when her husband left Ireland and they presumably separated, she acted at the Aungier Street theatre in Dublin. She was performing with the United Company in 1744–5; the following season the company began at Aungier Street but moved to Smock Alley in December 1745.

It was during this season that Furnival shared a celebrated rivalry with George Anne Bellamy. The latter wanted Furnival's role as Constance in *King John* and schemed with her influential patroness Mrs Butler to ensure poor houses until she got her way. Fanny's ill-judged revenge occurred after George Anne again took one of her parts, Cleopatra in John Dryden's *All for Love*. Relegated to Octavia (and jealous of George Anne's notices), Furnival stole the diamond-studded costume borrowed from Mrs Butler (in some accounts the dress had been given to George Anne by the princess of Wales). When she appeared on stage Thomas Sheridan was astounded by her 'borrowed plumes' (Bellamy, 1.83) and Mrs Butler exclaimed, 'Good heaven, the woman has got on my diamonds!' (ibid.). The audience cried 'No more Furnival!' until she 'very prudently called fits to her aid, which incapacitated her from appearing again' (ibid., 1.84). The part was taken over by Mrs Elmy.

Fanny Furnival returned to Drury Lane, replacing Mrs Macklin as Lady Macbeth opposite Spranger Barry on 10 November 1746. During the rest of the season her parts included Lady Upstart in William Taverner's *The Artful Husband* and Gertrude in *Hamlet*, and she also replaced the ailing Mrs Cibber in Nicholas Rowe's *Jane Shore* at Covent Garden. She is mentioned only once in the Drury Lane bills for 1747–8 but the play was not performed. Chetwood wrote that Mrs Furnival was in England in 1749 but that she would be better remembered in Dublin for her Alicia, Hermione in *The Distrest Mother* by Ambrose Philips, Lady Macbeth, and Zara in William Congreve's *The Mourning Bride*.

In 1752 Furnival was the leading lady in Smith's troupe at Canterbury and began a relationship with Roger *Kemble (1722–1802) with 'the promise of making an actor of him'. She was billed as Mrs Kemble (or Mrs Campbell), although it is unlikely that the couple ever married, and played a variety of parts as well as singing in *Romeo and Juliet* and providing entr'acte songs. Charles Lee Lewes, though writing of events before his career began, considered her 'far superior to any of her predecessors, possessing an elegant figure, an uncommon share of beauty, a perfect knowledge of every part she undertook and an execution scarcely excelled by any actress of that day' (Lewes, 1.87). After the 1751–2 season the pair applied to John Ward at Birmingham but there was no room in the company for Fanny and she joined Quelch's Coventry troupe instead. After apparently rejecting Kemble for another man she disappears from theatrical records.

ROBERTA MOCK

Sources W. R. Chetwood, *A general history of the stage, from its origin in Greece to the present time* (1749) · G. A. Bellamy, *An apology for the life of George Anne Bellamy*, ed. [A. Bicknell], 3rd edn, 6 vols. (1785) · C. L. Lewes, *Memoirs*, 4 vols. (1805) · J. Doran, *'Their majesties' servants', or, Annals of the English stage*, 2nd edn, 2 vols. (1865) · La T. Stockwell, *Dublin theatres and theatre customs, 1637–1820* (1938) · J. C. Greene and G. L. H. Clark, *The Dublin stage, 1720–1745: a calendar of plays, entertainments, and afterpieces* (1993) · E. K. Sheldon, *Thomas Sheridan of Smock-Alley: recording his life as actor and theater manager in both Dublin and London* (1967) · S. Richards, *The rise of the English actress* (1993) · J. Knight, *David Garrick* (1894) · Highfill, Burnim & Langhans, *BDA*

Furnivall, Frederick James (1825–1910), textual scholar and editor, was born on 4 February 1825 in Egham, Surrey, the eldest of the nine children of George Frederick Furnivall (1781–1865) and Sophia Hughes Barwell (1794–1879). Furnivall's father, descended from a family of Cheshire yeoman farmers, was trained at St Bartholomew's Hospital and briefly served as an assistant surgeon in the 14th

Frederick James Furnivall (1825–1910), by Charles Haslewood Shannon, 1901

foot but, at his mother's request, adopted a civil practice in Egham. George Frederick Furnivall attended Shelley's wife at Marlow in 1817 during her confinement (as his son often boasted in later years), married Sophia Barwell on 10 February 1825, and amassed a considerable fortune (some £200,000) through the founding of the Great Foster House Lunatic Asylum.

Early years and education Frederick Furnivall attended private schools at Englefield Green, Turnham Green, and Hanwell. In his earliest diaries one catches glimpses of a conventionally religious adolescent (sitting through two or three services each Sunday, and faithful in his attendance at family prayers) who is remarkable only for his physical and intellectual restlessness: when he is not taking strenuous walks, he is reading Dickens, the Robin Hood tales, and Tennyson's 'Morte d'Arthur' (the latter of which kindled his lifelong interest in older literatures). He matriculated at University College, London, in 1841 and in October of the following year enrolled at Trinity Hall, Cambridge.

At Cambridge Furnivall spent much of his time on the river, and boating remained a passion throughout his life. He gained a place in the college eight, and in 1845 he built a sculling vessel, a 12-inch wager-boat, that brought him local fame. Furnivall (always a man of strong convictions) was persuaded of the superiority of sculling to rowing and publicly championed that view for many decades.

During his Cambridge years Furnivall also became a close friend of Daniel Macmillan, then the owner of a local bookshop. He later recalled that Macmillan opened his 'boating mind' and stimulated historical and literary interests, so that by the time he took his BA in 1846 (the MA followed in 1849), he asked his father for a few thousand pounds to go into partnership with Macmillan. George Furnivall firmly declined, and his son entered Lincoln's Inn in January 1846 and was called to the bar at Gray's Inn in January 1849. Somewhat unenthusiastically, he practised law as a conveyancer in London from 1850 until 1872.

Philological Society and Working Men's College In 1847 Furnivall joined the Philological Society and in 1853 became its honorary secretary—a position he held until three weeks before his death—in which capacity he laid the foundations for the *Oxford English Dictionary*. The dictionary had a slow and convoluted genesis, and the editor who was chiefly responsible for its success was of course Sir James Murray; but, as Murray himself acknowledged, the conception of a completely new dictionary (rather than merely a supplement to Johnson's work), the initial organization, and much of the preliminary research had originated with Furnivall. At a meeting of the society in 1858 Furnivall presented a *Proposal for the Publication of a New English Dictionary by the Philological Society*, and he served on the committee that designed the basic format of the dictionary. Furnivall then organized an army of mostly amateur scholars to record instances of usage on slips of paper that in time found their way into the pigeon-holes of Murray's celebrated 'scriptorium' at Oxford. Clearly Furnivall did not possess Murray's organizational skill and iron self-discipline, and no doubt would have been incapable of bringing the work on the dictionary to fruition, but his contributions to its early development were more significant than any other person's.

Meanwhile, Furnivall's religious attitudes were shifting in a Liberal direction. His first separate publication was a pamphlet entitled *Association a Necessary Part of Christianity* (1850). In London he fell into the company of John Malcolm Ludlow, F. D. Maurice, Charles Kingsley, and Thomas Hughes, and soon became involved in various Christian socialist schemes, particularly the founding of the Working Men's College in 1854. At the college's opening he arranged for the distribution of a private reprint of the chapter entitled 'On the nature of Gothic' from *The Stones of Venice* (1851–3) by John Ruskin, with whom he had become acquainted a few years earlier. 'Ruskin was one of the most generous and honourable of men, with the most pretty manners and delightful ways', Furnivall declared in old age, 'and I retain of him recollections more pleasant than of any other man'; Ruskin, for his part, claimed that he learned what little he knew about philology from Furnivall (Munro, 20, xxiii). Furnivall—who by now thought of himself as a disciple of Ruskin and Maurice—was a popular teacher of English grammar and literature at the Working Men's College, served on the college council, and was informally put in charge of college social life. He summarized his experiences in these words: 'We studied and took exercise together, we were comrades and friends, and helpt one another to live higher, happier, and healthier lives, free from all stupid and narrow class humbug' (Davies, 60). Furnivall's personal religious views continued to evolve, however, and he soon found himself in conflict with Maurice over such questions as college dances and Sunday rural excursions. Furnivall loved his relaxed friendships with pupils and saw no possible objection to a weekend ramble or a trip on the river with them, but Maurice was offended by these practices and wrote a pamphlet entitled *The Sabbath-Day: an Address to the Members of the Working Men's College* (1856). Despite these differences, Furnivall never fully broke his connection with the Working Men's College and always in later years spoke of it with affection and respect, though inevitably he became less heavily involved in its day-to-day activities. Nevertheless, the college as Furnivall envisioned it—a jolly, classless community characterized by democratic comradery and a love of learning—is a key to understanding his subsequent life, for in all his later endeavours he was inspired by a conviction that scholarship could be pursued by quite ordinary people in a spirit of good-humoured enthusiasm.

Furnivall's father deplored this drift away from the legal profession. 'Lawism, not Socialism, Schoolism, or any other ism, ought to be your End and Aim, your Duty, your Pleasure, and Pursuit', he wrote to his son in 1851. 'Don't play at Law and work at school teaching' (Munro, xx). But despite parental pressure, Furnivall continued to move toward a literary and scholarly career.

Marriage and domestic life In 1862 Furnivall married Eleanor Nickel Dalziel (1838?–1937), sister of W. A. Dalziel, one of Furnivall's students at the Working Men's College. It was rumoured that she had been a maid, but family tradition suggests a more conventional middle-class background. The Furnivalls had two children: Ena, who died in infancy in 1866, and Percy (1867–1938). One likely reason for his prolonged bachelorhood is that he lived in near-poverty for decades. He then lost his inheritance with the collapse of the Overend and Gurney Bank in 1867, and thereafter he was compelled to exist on what little money he could bring in by writing and editing.

Societies and controversy Furnivall is probably most often remembered today as a founder of a series of literary and philological societies: the Early English Text Society (1864), the Chaucer Society, the Ballad Society (1868), the New Shakspere Society (1873), the Browning Society (1881, with Miss Emily Hickey), the Wyclif Society (1882), and the Shelley Society (1885). Some of them, at least, were created as a direct result of Furnivall's work on the *Oxford English Dictionary*, which had revealed to him the need for editing and publishing the primary documents of early English literature. He displayed a prodigious amount of energy in running these societies: he set up committees for them, chaired most of the public meetings, arranged for the production of concerts and plays (such as the first performance of Shelley's *Cenci* in 1886), recruited members, and above all organized ambitious programmes of publication (the Early English Text Society alone issued approximately 250 volumes during his lifetime, and it was estimated that he raised and expended more than £40,000 on printing). The Browning and Shelley societies had comparatively short lives, perhaps because Furnivall's formula was less successful for modern writers, but certainly also because their typically grandiose publishing schemes led to financial collapse.

Furnivall's societies were all weakened by exceptionally acrimonious controversies. E. A. Freeman—in the pages of the *Saturday Review* during the 1860s—attacked the editions of the Early English Text Society, provoking a characteristically aggressive response from Furnivall. The Browning Society became the scene of fierce debates about whether Browning was to be regarded as an essentially Christian poet; one member brought a libel suit against Furnivall. Furnivall complained publicly that Henry Bradshaw was hindering the work of the Chaucer Society. And when the committee of the Shelley Society declined to accept as a member the common-law husband of Karl Marx's daughter, William Michael Rossetti, the honorary secretary, threatened to resign, pointing out that on the same grounds the committee would have refused membership to Shelley himself.

Despite their extraordinarily contentious atmosphere, Furnivall's societies were primarily textual publishing ventures, and it is on this basis that their ultimate success or failure must be judged. Furnivall, unfortunately, placed ammunition in the hands of his enemies by his chatty, self-deprecating 'Forewords' (a word he much preferred to the latinate 'Preface') and by his public pose of breezy carelessness. In a foreword published in 1866, for example, he offered this typically pragmatic theory of textual editing:

> the time that it takes to ascertain whether a poem has been printed or not, which is the best MS. of it, in what points the versions differ, &c., &c., is so great, that after some experience I find the shortest way for a man much engaged in other work, but wishing to give some time to the [Early English Text] Society, is to make himself a foolometer and book-possessor-ometer for the majority of his fellow members, and print whatever he either does not know, or cannot get at easily, leaving others with more leisure to print the best texts. He wants texts, and that at once. (Peterson, *Browning's Trumpeter*, xxvi)

All of Furnivall's societies operated on such oddly casual principles.

Though Furnivall's occasional attempts at literary criticism are mawkishly sentimental, his pioneering editorial achievements are so massive that they cannot be easily dismissed. To this day there is no universal agreement among scholars about his merits as an editor, but Donald C. Baker, who collated Furnivall's *Six-Text Print of Chaucer's Canterbury Tales* (1869) against some of the original manuscripts, offered this summary judgement:

> He made all modern editions possible ... Whether we condescend in our own day of supersophisticated (perhaps too sophisticated) concepts of editing even to admit Furnivall into our ranks, he is the giant upon whose shoulders we all stand—enthusiastic, genial, enormously hard-working, quick to judgment and quick to admit error, encouraging all who followed and criticized and bettered his own work. (Baker, 169)

Certainly the parallel text *Canterbury Tales*, which has some claim to being Furnivall's most important editorial achievement, represents him at his best: the use of multiple columns for printing the best surviving Chaucer manuscripts was a brilliant conception, Furnivall's transcriptions were full and accurate, and his work led directly to the later achievements of Skeat, Manly, and Rickert.

Much of the work published by his societies was carelessly done, either by Furnivall himself or by the untrained amateurs that he casually recruited. John Gross has remarked that Furnivall was 'one of the great rock-blasting entrepreneurs of Victorian scholarship, the kind of man who if his energies had taken another turn might have covered a continent with railways' (Gross, 169); when he became interested in a historical or philological subject, Furnivall threw himself into it with a ferocious intensity and rarely paid much attention to the nuances of scholarly technique. Alois Brandl observed that 'he was not a philologist of thorough linguistic training: I should not even care to assert too positively that he could conjugate an Anglo-Saxon verb' (Munro, 10). Furnivall himself cheerfully admitted his technical deficiencies: in 1910, near the end of his life, he declared that 'I have never cared a bit for philology: my chief aim has been throughout to illustrate the social condition of the English people in the past' (ibid., 43). Furnivall's work as a textual scholar, though impressive in its sheer bulk (a search under his name in the online version of the British Library catalogue produces 164 titles), must be regarded as decidedly uneven.

Furnivall also wrote a large number of pamphlets ('on Rowing and kindred subjects', as his bibliographer put it) and was a frequent contributor to journals such as *The Athenaeum*, *The Academy*, and *Notes and Queries*. His financial difficulties continued, however. 'I go on as before', he commented to a friend in 1876, 'Chaucer & Early English—always busy, always earning nothing' (Peterson, *Browning's Trumpeter*, xxvii). There were unsuccessful applications for the secretaryship of the Royal Academy (1873), the principalship of University College, Bristol (1877), and several librarianships.

The New Shakspere Society It was within the New Shakspere Society that the most heated disputes developed. Furnivall at first alarmed his officers, members, and speakers by announcing that he wanted the society to focus its energies primarily on statistical analyses of metre and rhyme; then he raised the level of discord by entering into a public quarrel with Swinburne—an extraordinarily abrasive dispute even by Furnivall's usual standards—from which the society never fully recovered. 'Shakspereans are touchier folk than I fancied', he remarked in 1873. 'Our friend A[lgernon] S[winburne] is regular powder barrel' (Spevack, 133).

In 1876 Swinburne offered a satirical view of its activities entitled 'The Newest Shakespere Society' in *The Examiner* which infuriated Furnivall; then James O. Halliwell-Phillipps, an active member of the society, became the second target of Furnivall's wrath when he allowed Swinburne to dedicate *A Study of Shakespeare* (1879) to him. Furnivall regarded the pair as in collusion and published a scurrilous pamphlet, *The 'Co.' of Pigsbrook & Co.* (1881), thus translating Swinburne's name into Anglo-Saxon in the most insulting fashion possible. (The 'Co.' was Halliwell-Phillipps, whose name Furnivall always thereafter rendered as 'Hell.-Phillipps.'.) Swinburne replied with his own grotesque translation of Furnivall's name ('Brothels-dyke'), and for months the ugly exchange filled the columns of *The Athenaeum*. (A contemporary poem summed up the tone of the dispute by describing it as 'Furnivallos Furioso! and "The Newest Shakespeare Society"'.)

Meanwhile, Halliwell-Phillipps appealed to Robert Browning, the president of the society, to keep Furnivall's tongue under control. An embarrassed Browning protested that his leadership of the society was purely nominal, but he acknowledged privately that Furnivall was behaving with reckless abandon. Browning, in common with other friends, regarded Furnivall as a charming, good-natured man who from time to time made a complete fool of himself in public controversies. Browning, moreover, had reason to be grateful to Furnivall: 'His peculiarities and defects are obvious—and some of his proceedings by no means to my taste', he wrote: 'but there can be no doubt of his exceeding desire to be of use to my poetry, and I must attribute a very great part indeed of the increase of care about it to his energetic trumpet-blowing' (Collins, 38).

Furnivall, unusually pugnacious (contemporary reports indicate that he was just as vigorously self-assertive in a boat as in his scholarship), defended his aggressive tactics by appealing to a Victorian ideal of 'manliness', but his opponents were more inclined to interpret his behaviour as ill-tempered and malicious. 'As to objectors, all I require of 'em is evidence of work, insight, and thought', Furnivall wrote in 1887.

> When I see imposters like ... Swinburne, [and F. G.] Fleay, who know as much early English as my dog, & who fancy they can settle Chaucer difficulties as they blow their noses, then I ridicule or kick them. But earnest students I treat with respect, & am only too glad to learn from them.   (Peterson, *Browning's Trumpeter*, xxvii)

He enjoyed many warm friendships—with German philologists in particular—and to younger scholars and to a handful of established writers (such as Browning and Ruskin), Furnivall was remarkably generous, but towards his numerous enemies he behaved with alarming ferocity.

Furnivall's great preoccupation in Shakespearian studies—as can be seen in his popular *Leopold Shakespeare* (1879)—was to establish the exact chronology of the plays in order to discover the personality of the playwright behind them. Although his suggestions about dating were often shrewd, few later scholars or critics have shared his enthusiasm for interpreting Shakespeare's writings as primarily autobiographical documents.

Later years In June 1883 Furnivall and his wife were legally separated. 'A wife's want of sympathy with her husband's work ruined Dickens's married life, mine, too, & hundreds of others besides', Furnivall remarked later (Peterson, *Browning's Trumpeter*, xxviii), but the marriage probably collapsed because of his open relationship with Mary Lilian ('Teena') Rochfort-Smith, a young woman who was active in several of his societies. When Miss Rochfort-Smith died in 1883, Furnivall published an effusive tribute to her and announced her death to his societies, no doubt to the bewilderment of some of their members. He never

remarried but managed to surround himself with attractive young women the rest of his life.

In his later years Furnivall supported himself primarily with a modest stipend associated with the trusteeship of a family estate and with the civil-list pension awarded him in 1884. Honours, on the other hand, came more readily: a PhD from the University of Berlin, a DLitt from Oxford University, and an honorary fellowship from Trinity Hall, Cambridge.

In 1896 Furnivall founded the Hammersmith Sculling Club, initially intended for working-class girls though it later admitted male members as well. Furnivall entered into its activities with his usual boyish enthusiasm, for it brought together two of his favourite activities: vigorous outdoor exercise and enjoyment of the company of young women.

Throughout most of his adult years Furnivall followed a highly regular daily schedule. He lived at 3 St George's Square, Primrose Hill, but he normally spent the greater part of the day in either the reading-room or the manuscripts department of the British Museum, with a long break for tea at his favourite ABC tea-shop on New Oxford Street, where, especially in the final decades of his life, he was likely to be surrounded by admirers and friends. With his bright pink neckties, baggy suits, and long, white beard, he was a familiar sight to both British and foreign scholars in Bloomsbury. On Sundays he sculled 14 miles with his working girls from Hammersmith to Richmond and back, usually punctuated with a leisurely picnic on an island near Richmond. Until a few months before his death in London on 2 July 1910, Furnivall retained his youthful vigour of mind and body. His editing activities never slackened until the end. His remains were cremated at Golders Green on 5 July 1910.

Furnivall's achievements Frederick Furnivall was a man of diverse causes, all based on passionately held beliefs: vegetarianism, sculling, spelling reform, atheism (in his later years), socialism, egalitarianism, teetotalism, and above all the supreme importance of editing historic and literary texts that could shed light on the cultural and social life of England's past. He was an occasionally annoying and irascible figure, prone to carelessness in his scholarship, often outrageous in his personal behaviour, but he never wavered in his lifelong devotion to the cause of preserving and editing English written records. He must also be seen as one of a small group of Victorian scholars who persuasively made the case for the investigation of English literature in an academic setting; the rise of English studies in the universities coincided with his lifetime, and that is more than a chronological accident.

WILLIAM S. PETERSON

Sources J. Munro, ed., *Frederick James Furnivall: a volume of personal record* (1911) · W. S. Peterson, ed., *Browning's trumpeter: the correspondence of Robert Browning and Frederick J. Furnivall, 1872–1889* (1979) · W. S. Peterson, *Interrogating the oracle: a history of the London Browning Society* (1969) · W. Benzie, *Dr F. J. Furnivall: Victorian scholar adventurer* (1983) · DNB · *An English miscellany presented to Dr Furnivall in honour of his seventy-fifth birthday* (1901) [includes a bibliography of his writings by H. Littlehales] · *The Times* (4 July 1910), 12 · genealogical information in Furnivall family Bible, King's Lond., library · T. J. Collins, ed., 'Letters from Robert Browning to the Rev. J. D. Williams, 1874–1889', *Browning Institute Studies*, 4 (1976), 1–56 [editor assisted by W. J. Pickering] · D. C. Baker, 'Frederick James Furnivall', *Editing Chaucer: the great tradition*, ed. P. G. Ruggiers (1984), 157–79 · J. L. Davies, ed., *The Working Men's College, 1854–1904* (1904) · K. M. E. Murray, *Caught in the web of words: James Murray and the Oxford English dictionary* (1977) · M. Spevack, 'James Orchard Halliwell and friends: X. Frederick James Furnivall; XI. William Aldis Wright and William George Clark', *The Library*, 6th ser., 20 (1998), 126–44 · J. O. Halliwell-Phillipps, *A letter from Mr J. O. Halliwell-Phillipps to the members of the New Shakspere Society* (1881) · J. Gross, *The rise and fall of the man of letters: aspects of English literary life since 1800* (1969) · *Selected correspondence of William Michael Rossetti*, ed. R. W. Peattie (1990) · private information (2004) · B. J. Myers, 'F. J. Furnivall. Lexicographer, philanthropist, oarsman', *Journal of the William Morris Society*, 9 (1992) · S. M. Naiman, 'Frederick James Furnivall', *Nineteenth-century British book-collectors and bibliographers*, ed. W. Baker and K. Womack, DLitB, 184 (1997), 121–37 · Furnivall family Bible, King's Lond., library

Archives Baylor University, Waco, Texas, corresp. relating to the Browning Society · BL, corresp., Add. MSS 34813, 43798 · Bodl. Oxf., diaries · Hunt. L., corresp., papers · King's Lond., corresp. and papers, personal library | BL, letters to W. H. Griffin, Add. MSS 45563–45564 · BL, letters to W. C. Hazlitt, Add. MSS 38898–38913, *passim* · Bodl. Oxf., letters to A. S. Napier · Bodl. Oxf., letters to Sir Thomas Phillipps · Folger, corresp. relating to the New Shakespeare Society · Harvard U., Houghton L., postcards to G. L. Kittredge · King's AC Cam., letter to Oscar Browning · U. Edin. L., corresp. with James O. Halliwell-Phillipps · U. Edin. L., letters to David Laing · University of Illinois, Chicago, corresp. with Edith Rickert, MS 64-152 · University of Lancaster, Ruskin Library, papers relating to John Ruskin

Likenesses photograph, 1862, repro. in Benzie, *Dr F. J. Furnivall* · photograph, 1876, repro. in Peterson, ed., *Browning's trumpeter* · N. K. Munday, photograph, *c.*1890, repro. in Munro, ed., *Frederick James Furnivall* · W. Rothenstein, pencil drawing, 1901, NPG · C. H. Shannon, pencil and chalk drawing, 1901, NPG [*see illus.*] · G. C. Beresford, photograph, NPG · C. W. Carey, photograph, NPG · Elliott & Fry, photograph, NPG · H. Furniss, pen-and-ink caricature, NPG · W. Rothenstein, oils, Trinity Hall, Cambridge · A. A. Wolmark, oils, Working Men's College, London · heliogravure print (aged sixty-four; after photograph), BM · photograph, NPG · platinotype print (aged sixty-four; after photograph), BM · platinotype print (aged seventy-six; after photograph), BM

Wealth at death £796 19s. 2d.: probate, 15 July 1910, CGPLA Eng. & Wales

Furphy, Joseph (1843–1912), writer, was born on 26 September 1843 at Yering, north-east of Melbourne, in the colony of Port Phillip (Victoria), the second of the eleven children of Samuel Furphy (1816–1891), farm labourer, and his wife, Judith Hare (1818–1917), daughter of William Hare and his wife, Anne. His parents had arrived in the colony in 1841 as free immigrants from co. Armagh, where both families were tenant farmers. Taught to read and write by his mother, Furphy was reputed to be able to recite fluently pages of Shakespeare and chapters of the Bible by the time he was seven. His formal education was very limited (he attended state schools briefly in 1851–2 and 1856–7), but he early acquired a lifelong love of what he called 'ignorance-shifting' (Furphy to W. Cathels, 9 Sept 1895). Furphy's youth was spent mainly in farm work. On 27 May 1867, at the age of twenty-three, he married Leonie Celina Germain (1850–1936), a sixteen-year-old girl, born in New York of French parents, whom he had

met only three weeks earlier. The couple were ill-matched but remained together until Furphy's death in 1912. Of the six children born of the marriage three survived childhood. In 1877, having failed as a 'selector' (small farmer), Furphy began working as a carrier with a team of bullocks. He moved across the border of Victoria to the sparsely settled plains of the Riverina district of New South Wales in 1880, remaining there until 1883 when, his bullocks having died in the drought, he moved back to Victoria.

For the next twenty-one years Furphy worked in the Shepparton foundry of his successful elder brother, John, helping to make farm machinery and the famous Furphy water-carts (from which the twentieth-century word 'furphy', signifying rumour, derives). He had long cherished literary ambitions, and from 1889 he contributed verse and prose to the radical Sydney weekly *The Bulletin*, using the pen-name Tom Collins. In 1897 he wrote to the editor of *The Bulletin*: 'I have just finished writing a full-sized novel: title, "Such is Life"; scene, Riverina and northern Vic; temper, democratic; bias, offensively Australian' (Stephens MSS). On reading the highly original novel, which purports to be the diary of a former bullock-driver, the literary editor of *The Bulletin*, A. G. Stephens, pronounced it 'to be fitted to become an Australian classic, or semi-classic' (ibid.). After significant revision *Such is Life* was published, by *The Bulletin*, in 1903. Furphy received good reviews but no royalties, and he continued to work in the foundry. In 1905 he moved to Perth in Western Australia where his sons had established a foundry, and he was working for them when he died suddenly of a cerebral haemorrhage on the morning of 13 September 1912; he was buried in the Karrakatta cemetery in Perth the following day.

Furphy's fame as a leading Australian writer was posthumous. *Such is Life* sold only 1100 copies in his lifetime, and recognition of his literary achievement came slowly. However, when *Such is Life* was republished in full for the first time, in 1944, writers and critics praised his surprisingly modern narrative strategies and placed him, along with Henry Lawson, at the centre of 'an Australian literary tradition'. Two novels based on excised chapters of *Such is Life* were subsequently published, *Rigby's Romance* in 1946 (an abridged version had appeared in 1921) and *The Buln-Buln and the Brolga* in 1948, but only *Such is Life* has remained continuously in print. There is now general consensus that Furphy is 'one of the most significant writers of Australian fiction before the First World War' (Wilde, Hooton, and Andrews, 305).

In appearance Furphy was, as he said, 'the usual lanky Australian' (Franklin MSS). His heavy-lidded eyes bore witness to the effect of the ophthalmia from which he suffered in the Riverina. Shy, self-effacing, and slow of speech, his manner was that of the bushmen with whom he identified, but in its learning and philosophical depth, his talk—like his writing—revealed him to be a most unusual and bookish bushman.   JOHN BARNES

Sources J. Barnes, *The order of things: a life of Joseph Furphy* (1990) · *Bushman and bookworm: letters of Joseph Furphy*, ed. J. Barnes and

L. Hoffmann (1995) • W. H. Wilde, J. Hooton, and B. Andrews, *The Oxford companion to Australian literature*, 2nd edn (1994), 305 • A. G. Stephens MSS, Mitchell L., NSW • Miles Franklin MSS, Mitchell L., NSW • letters to William Cathels, Mitchell L., NSW • baptismal records, St James's, Melbourne, Australia • m. cert. • d. cert. • parish register, Shankill, Lurgan, co. Armagh, Ireland • baptismal cert. [Leonie Celina Germain] • d. cert. [Leonie Celina Germain] **Archives** Mitchell L., NSW, letters to William Cathels • Mitchell L., NSW, Miles Franklin MSS • Mitchell L., NSW, A. G. Stephens MSS • NL Aus., Kate Baker MSS • State Library of Victoria, Melbourne, letters to Cecil Winter **Likenesses** photographs, repro. in Barnes, *Order of things*

Fursa [St Fursa, Fursey] (*d.* 649), missionary monk, was of Irish birth but his precise origins are unknown. In his life (the *Vita Fursei*) he is said to have been nobly born but this is an entirely conventional background for a saint of this period. Although the names of his parents are known— Fintan, son of Findloga, and Gelges, daughter of Áed Find—the region of Ireland from which he came is not. Nearly all the information about Fursa comes from his seventh-century life, which either in the version which has survived or a text close to that version, also formed the basis of Bede's knowledge of Fursa and of his activity in England. In addition to the life there is an account of Fursa's miracles which appears to add further details about his career in Francia and about events after his death there. This work, however, is from the ninth century, and though it contains a great deal of interest in its description of the ways in which disputes over the burial of Fursa were settled, these details reveal more about the ninth-century imagination of exotic dispute settlement than about the seventh-century events themselves. Later Irish legend about Fursa, that in his throat lived a beast which could only be kept in check if the saint ate three pieces of bacon each morning, is in the realm of the bizarre rather than the exotic.

According to Fursa's life, he was dedicated to religion at an early age. He established a monastery, identified as Louth (Ireland) and there he had the first of two visions. The second vision occurred as he returned to his native area to preach and it is the details of this which make up the bulk of the life. In this vision Fursa was taken out of his body and led by angels into the space above the earth where he could see souls in torment. It is the earliest of a series of early medieval visions through which purgatory would be imagined; and the fact that Bede chose to relate it in some detail ensured that it would have an influence on the development of vision texts.

The annals of Ulster say that the vision took place in the year 627, and the life of Fursa recounts that ten years after the vision (thus about 637), he left his monastery. This he did not only because he needed to escape the crowds of people who flocked to the place, but also because he understood that certain people, 'stirred up by envy [*invidia*]' were against him. In the hagiography of this period the term *invidia* usually denotes some kind of rivalry within institutions. Later tradition has it that Fursa was forced out of Louth to make way for Abbot Ultán. This cannot be substantiated, although there are indications that both Louth and Péronne (the monastery in Francia in which Fursa was buried and which was known as *Peronna Scottorum*, 'Péronne of the Irish') were subject in some way to the monastery of Slane.

After leaving Louth, Fursa travelled with at least four companions to 'Britain' (probably Wales), after which the party made its way to East Anglia, where Fursa was welcomed as a missionary by King Sigebert. After a third vision Fursa was prompted to found another monastery. This he did at Cnobheresburg (Burgh Castle in Suffolk), receiving help from Sigebert and gifts from the latter's successor, Anna. After some time Fursa left one brother, *Foillan, in charge of the monastery and went to join another brother, Ultán, as a hermit. But when East Anglia was attacked by the pagan Penda, Fursa fled to Francia where he was welcomed by the king, Clovis II (*r.* 638–57), and the mayor of the palace, Erchinoald. Fursa's choice of destination is an indication of Erchinoald's links with England: it may have been at this time that the mayor of the palace acquired the future Frankish queen, Balthild, as another casualty of Penda's invasion of East Anglia.

Fursa founded yet another monastery, at Lagny on the River Marne, and there he died shortly after. The *Vita et virtutes Fursei* have the date 16 January 649 for his death and given that he died fairly soon after arriving in Francia, his stay in East Anglia would have lasted roughly ten years (638–48). After his death there was clearly some sort of dispute over Fursa's remains, with Erchinoald keeping them unburied for a couple of weeks until he had completed a new monastery at Péronne on the River Somme. There they were finally interred; but four years later they were translated by two bishops opposed to Erchinoald. Translation in contexts of dispute over bodies often means the transfer of control over cults; and in this case loss of control over Fursa's cult may have promoted Erchinoald to drive the Irish, including Foillan, out of Péronne. Nevertheless, within a generation they were back there.

Fursa's career demonstrates that Irish monastic foundations abroad were not solely influenced by St Columbanus. There was more than one group of Irish active in Francia in the seventh century, just as there were several different groups in England in the same period. In Francia different political factions and, in England, different kingdoms, each supported their 'own' group of Irish. A certain degree of competition for the services of these prestigious holy men ensured that travellers like Fursa would receive a warm welcome in both England and Francia, as his life attests. By the same token, holy men were vulnerable to any fall in their protectors' fortunes. Fursa's career nicely reflects such vicissitudes. Erchinoald's treatment of Fursa when alive reveals the magnate's desire to control sanctity to enhance and to legitimate his power. The struggle over Fursa's body, on the other hand, demonstrates the value placed on dead holy men: they were certainly more tractable then. By contrast, English society was still in the process of conversion and seems at this date to have valued ministry over relics. Both alive and dead, Fursa was held in very high regard. His life reports that he was famous for his visions and was accustomed to tell of them until he dripped with sweat, suggesting that his reputation as a visionary preceded him to both England and Francia and ensured that he would be received with great honour. PAUL FOURACRE

Sources W. W. Heist, ed., 'Vita s. Fursei', *Vitae sanctorum Hiberniae ex codice olim Salmanticensi nunc Bruxellensi*, Subsidia Hagiographica, 28 (Brussels, 1965), 37–55 · 'Vita et virtutes Fursei', *Passiones vitaeque sanctorum aevi Merovingici*, ed. B. Krusch, MGH Scriptores Rerum Merovingicarum, 4 (Hanover, 1902), 434–49 · Bede, *Hist. eccl.*, 3.19 · Ann. Ulster · *Félire Óengusso Céli Dé / The martyrology of Oengus the Culdee*, ed. and trans. W. Stokes, HBS, 29 (1905) · P. O'Riain, ed., *Corpus genealogiarum sanctorum Hiberniae* (1983) · J. M. Wallace-Hadrill, *Bede's Ecclesiastical history of the English people: a historical commentary*, OMT (1988) · K. Hughes, *The church in early Irish society* (1966) · F. Prinz, *Frühes Mönchtum im Frankenreich* (1965)

Fursdon [alias Breton], **John** [name in religion Cuthbert] (d. **1638**), Benedictine monk, was born at Thornverton, Devon, the eldest son of Philip Fursdon of Fursdon, Cadbury, Devon. Under the influence of Augustine Baker, chaplain to his father, he entered St Gregory's Priory, Douai, as a novice of the English Benedictines. He was professed on 25 November 1620 and took the name in religion of Cuthbert. Living as a mission priest in England he worked in the south province of the English Benedictine congregation and seems often to have lived with the families of Viscount Montagu and Lady Elizabeth Falkland. He assisted in the conversion to Catholicism of Lady Falkland's four daughters and of Hugh Paulinus (in religion Serenus) Cressy.

Fursdon translated *The second book of the dialogues of S. Gregorie the Greate … containing the life and miracles of our holie father S. Benedict, to which is adioined the rule of the same holie patriarche translated into the English tongue by C. F. priest and monke of the same order* (2 parts, 1638). The work was completed and seen through the press by his fellow Benedictine Anthony Batt who signed the dedicatory epistle to 'Mrs Anne Carie, daughter to the Lord Viscount of Faukland'. 'A short treatise touching the confraternitie of the scapular of St Benedict's order' (1639) forms part of some editions of the work. The attribution to Fursdon of the translation from Latin of *The Life of Lady Magdalen, Viscountesse Montague* by Richard Smith, has been discounted (Allison and Rogers, *Contemporary Printed Literature*, vol. 2: *Works in English*). Fursdon, who frequently used the alias Breton, died in Lady Falkland's house in London on 2 February 1638. He was 'a living example of Baker's teaching' (Lunn, 205) and was 'a most exemplary recollected Religious living in great abstraction both in his convent and on the mission' (Allanson, 1.66).

THOMPSON COOPER, *rev.* DOMINIC AIDAN BELLENGER

Sources A. Allanson, 'Biography of the English Benedictines', 1850, Downside Abbey, 2 vols., vol. 1 · D. Lunn, *The English Benedictines, 1540–1688* (1980) · A. F. Allison and D. M. Rogers, eds., *The contemporary printed literature of the English Counter-Reformation between 1558 and 1640*, 2 vols. (1989–94)

Furse, Charles Wellington (1868–1904), painter, born at Staines, Middlesex, on 13 January 1868, was the fourth son of Charles Wellington Furse (1821–1900), vicar of Staines, principal of Ripon Clergy College (1873–83), rector of St John the Evangelist, Westminster, and canon of Westminster (1883–94), and from 1894 to his death in 1900 canon and archdeacon of Westminster. The artist's mother also came from an ecclesiastical background: Jane Diana, second daughter of John S. B. Monsell, vicar of Egham, was granddaughter of Thomas Bewley Monsell of Dunbar, archdeacon of Derry. After an undistinguished school career at Haileybury College, Furse entered the Slade School of Fine Art, London, at the age of sixteen. Then under Alphonse Legros, the Slade was growing in importance as the home of avant-garde thinking in painting and sculpture. Furse won the Slade scholarship within a year of entrance, and became one of Legros's favourite pupils. Even at this early stage, however, he was consumptive and was forced to interrupt his studies to spend a winter at St Moritz. His most intimate friend at this time was a fellow pupil, Charles Holroyd, with whom he spent his holidays on the borders of the Lake District or near Maidstone, Kent, sketching and reading. In 1887 he took the channel packet and studied for some months at the Académie Julian in Paris. Although some of the work of fellow students impressed him, it was far outstripped by the experience of Titian in the Louvre. There he met William Rothenstein, with whom he became friends. On his return in 1888 Furse registered with Fred Brown, whose teaching at the Westminster School of Art was regarded as the most radical in London. There he would have encountered D. S. MacColl, David Muirhead, and Jack B. Yeats.

At the same time Furse exhibited *Cain*, a large biblical composition, at the Royal Academy. However, his first success was a portrait of Canon Burrows shown at the Royal Academy in the following year. This, and a head of his uncle, William Cory, shown at the first exhibition of the Society of Portrait Painters in 1891, secured his recognition as one of the leading portraitists of the day and brought him into contact with such luminaries as Whistler and Sargent. In 1891 he also began to show at the New English Art Club (NEAC). Moving now in the circle of W. E. Henley and the writers of the *National Observer*, and participating in the discussions at the Art Workers' Guild, Furse submitted his thoughts on impressionism to *The Albemarle* magazine the following year. Comparing Luke Fildes's popular *The Doctor*, shown at the previous Royal Academy exhibition with Whistler's portrait of Rosa Corder, Furse commended the selection and sensitivity of the latter, declaring that 'pictures are never interesting as a journalist's catalogue of facts, but as an appeal to the imagination from the mind of the painter' (*Illustrated Memoir*, 48). Furse then embarked upon a discussion of Titian and Velázquez, the two most distinguished precursors of the modern movement. Furse was one of the most active, but least accredited, participants in the debate about impressionism in Britain in the 1890s. Like Walter Sickert, Philip Wilson Steer, D. S. MacColl, and George Moore, he was anxious to relate impressionism to ongoing traditions in British and European art and as part of this élite he was pictured in Rothenstein's *A Group of Friends* (c.1893; priv. coll.).

Furse had, however, succumbed even more to the lure of

portrait painting and had taken a large studio at 33 Tite Street, Chelsea, close to that of Sargent. This enabled him to carry out the commissions for equestrian portraits which were now returning to fashion. The first of these, *R. Allison Esq., Master of the North Hereford*, was shown at the NEAC in 1893 to great acclaim. Furse immediately embarked upon *Field Marshal Earl Roberts on Volonel*, for the Royal Academy exhibition of 1894, and an even more ambitious but ultimately unfinished picture of Roberts on Saracen (both Tate collection). This second canvas, 11 by 15 feet, shows Roberts commanding regiments of Sikh lancers in a composition which emulates Velázquez's *Surrender of Breda*. His knowledge of the masters was undoubtedly enhanced by being asked to give lectures on Velázquez, Rembrandt, and Van Dyck at the Oxford University Extension Society summer school in 1894. As work progressed, however, Furse suffered the sudden death of Eleanor Butcher, the young woman to whom he had recently become engaged. Progress on the picture was further interrupted by the return of his tuberculosis, and he was advised to spend winter 1895 in South Africa.

Arriving shortly after the Jameson raid, Furse seized the opportunity to portray the event in a lost picture which was shown to President Kruger. Kruger, apparently disdainful of perspective, protested that he had made the Boers too small. Furse was nevertheless captivated by the experience of Africa and had some thoughts of volunteering for the Matabele (Ndebele) campaign. However, he returned to England in 1896 to resume his career as a painter and by the following year he exhibited equestrian and female portraits at the Royal Academy, the NEAC, and the Society of Portrait Painters.

In 1898 Furse went to Italy, where he toured the galleries and churches of Florence and Siena with the art collector and historian Herbert Horne. These experiences confirmed his predilection for the work of high Renaissance and mannerist painters over the primitives, and to some extent this taste is reflected in his *Orpheus*, an unfinished sketch of which was shown at the first exhibition of the International Society of Sculptors, Painters, and Gravers that year. About this time he accepted a commission, obtained for him by his friend Professor F. M. Simpson, to execute decorative paintings to fill four pendentives under the dome over the staircase in the Liverpool town hall. The evolution of this cycle was extraordinary for two reasons. First, there were significant changes in the subject matter of the scheme. Furse switched from the theme of the history of Liverpool trade, to that of produce such as Sugar, Corn, and Cotton. These then became focused in the activities of Liverpool docks, which Furse visited as part of his research. Second, Furse pondered the appropriate style for work on this scale. He rejected the 'flat' mural manner of Puvis de Chavannes, derived from the primitives. There was much talk of Tintoretto and the desire for theatrical lighting and bold forms. Sargent, whom he consulted, approved. These paintings, which occupied him for nearly three years, were enormously influential for the later work of muralists like Frank Brangwyn.

Furse by this stage was reported to be highly successful, his portrait practice in 1900 alone returning him £1000. Rothenstein recalled that his studio was 'usually full of generals, admirals, distinguished and admiring ladies, painters and poets; while he strode up and down, working away with huge brushes and boisterous energy' (Rothenstein, 172). The state of his health was now giving cause for concern and from 1900 he was compelled to pass each winter at Davos. There, in February 1900, he became engaged to Katharine (1875–1952) [*see* Furse, Katharine], the youngest daughter of John Addington Symonds. They were married in October that year and during the following year they moved to a new house in Camberley designed by Reginald Blomfield. Here Furse constructed a formal eighteenth-century-style garden. Intensely happy in his marriage and settled in congenial surroundings, he worked harder than ever, and in these last years produced successful pictures like the *Return from the Ride* (1903), purchased by the trustees of the Chantrey bequest for the National Gallery of British Art (Tate collection). In the same year he was elected associate of the Royal Academy. This was followed by *Diana of the Uplands* (1904; Tate collection), a picture for which Katharine posed and which was regarded as the epitome of the Edwardian grand manner. It was hailed as a 'breezy and masterly portrait' set in a 'wind filled sky and a windswept landscape' (*The Academy*, 7 May 1904, 530).

Furse's condition was, however, getting worse. Much of 1903 and 1904 was spent travelling in the Alps and the Riviera, eventually hurrying to Madrid, where he bumped into C. Lewis Hind, who recalled that in the Velázquez rooms in the Prado he was 'unable to control his enthusiasm' (Lewis Hind, 7). Still full of hope and enthusiasm, he gradually grew weaker, and died at his home, Yockley House, Camberley, Surrey, on 16 October 1904. He was buried in Frimley churchyard. He left two sons, Peter and Paul, the second of whom was born three days before his death. The artist's widow, later Dame Katharine Furse, saw active service in the First World War in the Women's Royal Naval Service and between 1928 and 1938 was director of the World Bureau for Girl Guides and Girl Scouts. Her memoir *Hearts and Pomegranates* was published in 1940. In its obituary on Furse, *The Times* (18 October 1904), not only praised the painter, but also paid tribute to his 'gift of speech', explaining that few painters could talk so convincingly on the theory and practice of their craft. It was this power of advocacy, seen in his occasional papers, which led some of his friends to predict his eventual candidature for the presidency of the Royal Academy.

KENNETH MCCONKEY

Sources D. S. MacCool, trans., *Illustrated memoir of Charles Wellington Furse, ARA, with critical papers and fragments, a catalogue of the pictures exhibited at the club in 1906, and a chronological list of works* (1908) [exhibition catalogue, Burlington Fine Arts Club] · K. Furse, *Hearts and pomegranates* (1940) · C. W. Furse, 'The Grafton Gallery: a summary', *The Studio*, 1 (1893), 33–4 · C. Lewis Hind, *Days with Velasquez* (1906), 6–8 · W. Rothenstein, *Men and memories: recollections of William Rothenstein*, 2 vols. (1931–2), vol. 1, pp. 172–3 · L. Robinson, *Palette and plough: a pen-and-ink drawing of Dermod O'Brien PRHA* (1948), 63 · *The Times* (18 Oct 1904), 5 · *Catalogue of British impressionist and post-impressionist paintings and drawings … property of Mrs Paul Furse*

(1982) [sale catalogue, Sothebys, 10 March 1982] · *CGPLA Eng. & Wales* (1904)

Archives University of Bristol Library, corresp. and papers
Likenesses photograph, 1903, NPG; repro. in MacColl, *Illustrated memoir* (1908) · W. Rothenstein, group portrait (*A Group of Friends*), repro. in Rothenstein, *Men and memories*
Wealth at death £3184 5s.: administration, 14 Dec 1904, *CGPLA Eng. & Wales*

Furse [*née* Symonds], **Dame Katharine** (1875–1952), nurse and nursing administrator, was born at Clifton, Bristol, on 23 November 1875, the fourth daughter of the author John Addington *Symonds (1840–1893) and his wife, Janet Catherine, sister of the painter and traveller Marianne North (1830–1890) and daughter of Frederick North, squire of Rougham, Norfolk, and Liberal member of parliament for Hastings. Owing to her father's ill health Katharine spent most of her youth at Davos, Switzerland, with frequent visits to Italy. She grew up the youngest of a loving and gifted family in surroundings ideally suited to her enterprising and energetic nature, and in close contact with many famous literary and artistic figures. Her father's sister had married the philosopher Thomas Hill Green; Henry Sidgwick, philosopher, his wife, and Benjamin Jowett, master of Balliol College, Oxford, were regular summer visitors; and her two surviving sisters were later to marry Walter Leaf, banker and classical scholar, and William Wyamar Vaughan, a well-travelled schoolmaster. Educated by governesses, with somewhat spasmodic additions by her father, Katharine owed to her mother her intimate knowledge of flowers and she developed natural artistic gifts in various forms of handicraft, including exquisite embroidery and wood-carving. Tall and strong, with a beauty of the Venus de Milo type, she was always full of energy; while still a child she was winning ladies' tobogganing events in competition with adults.

An inherited tradition of social service showed itself early and Katharine was a frequent visitor of the sick in Davos. A few months at a school in Lausanne, abruptly terminated by the death of her father, gave her lessons in first aid and home nursing, which she afterwards followed up by studying massage in London. She had decided to train as a hospital nurse when she met Charles Wellington *Furse (1868–1904), the painter. They were married in 1900, but he died four years later; Katherine was left with two sons, both of whom entered the navy.

Soon after the formation in 1909 of the first Red Cross voluntary aid detachments attached to the Territorial Army Katharine Furse enrolled, and she joined enthusiastically in training, camps, and studies. In September 1914 Arthur Stanley sent her to France with other representatives for preliminary discussions, and the following month she headed the first official VAD unit (twenty in number) to be sent abroad. The unit was instructed to install rest stations on the lines of communication, first at Boulogne. Many thousands of wounded men were ministered to before the end of 1914, when Furse was recalled to London to start a VAD department. The organization was gradually built up into an enormous service whose members were invaluable assistants in hospitals at home and

Dame Katharine Furse (1875–1952), by Elliott & Fry, 1919

abroad. In 1916 Furse was decorated with the Royal Red Cross, and when a joint committee was set up to co-ordinate the VAD work of the British Red Cross Society and the order of St John of Jerusalem, Furse was appointed commandant-in-chief, and became a lady of grace of the order. In 1917 she was one of five women appointed dame grand cross in the newly created Order of the British Empire.

But Dame Katharine had for some time not been happy in her work. She lacked the power to institute various reforms which she felt necessary, both in administration and in conditions of work. In November 1917 she and a number of her colleagues resigned. Several posts were immediately offered to her, and in the same month she became director, with the equivalent rank of rear-admiral, of a new organization, the Women's Royal Naval Service. Although the new service saw only one year of war and never exceeded some seven thousand in number, her creation earned a fine reputation and before it was disbanded had established a tradition—of which the officers' tricorn hat was not the least important detail—for the vast service that was to be formed twenty years later.

After the war Dame Katharine joined the travel agency of Sir Henry Lunn, working mainly in Switzerland, where in winter she was a skiing representative of the Ski Club of Great Britain. Although in her youth she had been one of the first to experiment with skiing, in company with Sir

Arthur Conan Doyle, it was not until after the war that she took it up seriously. She was the second British woman to be awarded the gold badge for passing the first-class ski-running test, and the second president of the Ladies' Ski Club. She also took up Girl Guide work, and at her suggestion the Association of Wrens, of which she was president, affiliated to the Girl Guides Association; Dame Katharine became head of the Sea Guides, later known as Sea Rangers. She was also for ten years director of the World Association of Girl Guides and Girl Scouts. She died at University College Hospital, Grafton Way, London, on 25 November 1952.   V. L. MATHEWS, rev.

Sources K. Furse, *Hearts and pomegranates* (1940) • V. L. Matthews, *Blue tapestry* (1948) • *British Ski Year Book* (1953) • *The Times* (26 Nov 1952), 10d • *The Times* (28 Nov 1952), 10e • *The Times* (29 Nov 1952), 8b • *The Times* (11 Dec 1952), 8e • *The Times* (12 Dec 1952), 10f • *The Times* (17 Dec 1952), 8b • personal knowledge (1971) • *CGPLA Eng. & Wales* (1953)
Archives NMM, papers • University of Bristol Library, corresp. and papers • University of Bristol Library, corresp. and family papers | BL, corresp. with Sir Sydney Cockerell, Add. MS 52715 • JRL, letters to the *Manchester Guardian* • PowerGen Library, corresp. relating to M. P. Follett
Likenesses C. W. Furse, oils, c.1903–1904, Tate collection • C. G. Beresford, photograph, 1918, NPG • Elliott & Fry, photograph, 1919, NPG [*see illus.*] • M. Morley, oils (in Women's Royal Naval Service uniform), Women's Royal Naval Service headquarters, Furse House, London • G. Philpot, oils, IWM
Wealth at death £10,996 13s. 7d.: probate, 17 Feb 1953, *CGPLA Eng. & Wales*

Furse, Sir Ralph Dolignon (1887–1973), civil servant, was born at 8 Gloucester Street, London, on 29 September 1887, the only child of John Henry Monsell Furse, sculptor, of Halsdon, Dolton, Devon, and his wife, Ethel (d. 1887), daughter of the Revd John William Dolignon, rector of Cockley Clay, Norfolk. The religious strain was prominent in the family. His grandfather Charles Wellington Furse had been archdeacon of Westminster, two of his great-grandfathers were in holy orders, and an uncle, Michael Bolton, became bishop of Pretoria. Furse's Christian principles of duty and service were to inform his forty years of judging applicants for the colonial service. Educated at Eton College, he graduated from Oxford in 1909 with third-class honours in *literae humaniores*. He played for Balliol College cricket eleven and rugby fifteen and was secretary of the Chatham Society. While at Oxford he joined King Edward's Horse and was placed on the special reserve, but incipient deafness ruled out hopes of an army career. Instead, in 1910 he became assistant private secretary (appointments) to the secretary of state for the colonies.

On 2 June 1914 Furse married Margaret Cecilia (Celia; 1890–1975), daughter of the poet Sir Henry Newbolt. He was on active service throughout the war with King Edward's Horse, being wounded in 1917. Winning the DSO and bar, he was twice mentioned in dispatches. On demobilization in 1919 in the rank of major, Furse resumed his unestablished post in the Colonial Office, serving six secretaries of state up to 1930. Following the recommendations of the landmark Warren Fisher committee on colonial service appointments (1929–30), in 1931 he became

director of recruitment in the new personnel division of the Colonial Office. He held this position until 1948, continuing as adviser on colonial service training until 1950.

Furse is recognized as 'the father of the modern Colonial Service'. Before the First World War there was no unified colonial service and officers were appointed to individual colonial governments. In the 1920s it became evident that such an arrangement could not provide an attractive career, least of all in smaller territories. The Colonial Office conference of 1927 recommended the unification of all the territorial services and functional branches into a single HM colonial service. This was followed in 1929 by the appointment of a committee under Sir Warren Fisher, head of the civil service, to review the system of appointments. Despite its vulnerability to the charge of patronage, the committee endorsed Furse's recruitment procedures, supporting the Colonial Office preference for selection by references and interviews over the written examination required for the Indian Civil Service and the Colonial Office's eastern cadetships. However, to safeguard the principle of open competition, a colonial service appointments board was established, responsible to the civil service commissioners.

Furse was instrumental in opening up the colonial service to the dominions. As a result of visiting Canada in 1922 and Australia and New Zealand in 1928, the dominion selection scheme was initiated, with preliminary interviews of local candidates now taking place in their own country. In 1926 Furse persuaded Oxford and Cambridge (and later the London School of Economics) to organize training courses for cadets similar to those already operating for Indian Civil Service probationers. He was proud of his 'recruiting spies' among Oxbridge dons, notably Claude Elliott at Cambridge and H. Sumner, W. T. S. Stallybrass, Sir John Masterman, K. Bell, and P. A. Landon at Oxford. The master of Balliol, his own college, was at the bottom of his list of reliable referees. Again, Furse was the moving spirit behind plans for the post-war colonial service. His 1943 memorandum became a plank in the deliberations of the committee under the tenth duke of Devonshire, parliamentary under-secretary at the Colonial Office, and much of his thinking was incorporated into the new training programmes. Known as the Devonshire courses, they were essentially Furse's brainchild.

Although Furse's greatest influence was on the formation of the colonial administrative service, his enthusiasm extended to the training of the agriculture, veterinary, and—in particular—the forest services. He was a member of the Lovat committee, from 1925 to 1928, on their professional training and was largely responsible for the founding of the Imperial Forestry Institute at Oxford, where his portrait now hangs. For a Colonial Office official he travelled unusually widely in the colonies.

Furse was an intuitive judge of character, and with what a colleague called 'his keen eye for men' (Parkinson, 103) he chose his own staff—chief among them his brother-in-law and successor A. F. Newbolt—as unerringly as he selected his field officers. His aim was to raise the colonial service to the level of the Indian Civil Service among undergraduates seeking a crown career overseas. It was said that Furse's beau idéal of the colonial administrator was a man who had been a prefect at a public school and had captained a team at college: granted that such a personal triumph was but a floating distinction, it could also, Furse argued, be both a test and a presage of character. Another colleague recalled his charm and courtesy, 'an ever fertile imagination and a forthright personality' (DNB).

Colonial Office lore abounded of how Furse turned his increasing deafness to good account when the going became hard at meetings. The title of his autobiography, Aucuparius (1962), in which he expounded his uncannily successful and ebulliently subjective 'hunches', encapsulated the shrewd skill of the eponymous bird-catcher who netted birds of the highest quality. The chapter entitled 'Our system' is complemented by the in-house 'Appointments handbook', a confidential exposition of the Fursian code on the art of interviewing in search of what he roundly called the 'spiritual', with its focus on 'the imponderables of character and personality' (Furse, Aucuparius, 228). One colonial service historian, an American (perhaps on safer ground reading Colonial Office files than grasping the nuances of the English class system), depicted Furse as 'largely an unreconstructed Victorian country gentlemen. ... his convictions about people socially are simple, straightforward and unshakable' (Heussler, 68), yet his admiration for the efficacy of the Furse system against the needs and conditions of the time is transparent: confident in his conception of the English gentleman, Furse brought the colonial service to 'a peak of prestige' (ibid., 198). In Lord Salisbury's opinion, Furse built up 'by his own efforts and his own vision' a recruitment system second to none (Furse, Aucuparius, vii).

Furse spent his retirement on his family estate at Halsdon in Devon. A firm Christian, when in London he looked on St Michael Cornhill as his parish church. He died at the Withymead Nursing Home in Exeter on 1 October 1973. There were two sons from his marriage, and two daughters, each of whom in turn married the engraver Laurence Whistler.

Furse won the DSO in 1918, was appointed CMG in 1935, and advanced to KCMG in 1941. In 1949 Oxford University made him an honorary DCL.   A. H. M. KIRK-GREENE

Sources R. D. Furse, *Aucuparius: recollections of a recruiting officer* (1962) · R. Heussler, *Yesterday's rulers: the making of the British colonial service* (1963) · Bodl. RH, Furse MSS · *The Times* (5 Oct 1973) · *Corona Club Bulletin* (1973) · *DNB* · C. Parkinson, *The colonial office from within* [1947] · A. H. M. Kirk-Greene, '"Taking Canada into partnership in the white man's burden": the British colonial service and the dominion selection scheme of 1923', *Canadian Journal of African Studies*, 15/1 (1981), 33–54 · A. H. M. Kirk-Greene, *On crown service: a history of HM colonial and overseas civil services, 1837–1997* (1999) · Colonial office, 'Appointments handbook', 1948, Foreign Office Library, London · *WWW* · C. Jeffries, *The colonial office* (1956) · N. Gardiner, 'Sentinels of empire: the British colonial administrative service, 1919–1954', PhD diss., Yale U., 1998 · *CGPLA Eng. & Wales* (1974) · b. cert. · m. cert. · d. cert. · private information (2004) [F. Whistler]

Archives Bodl. RH, corresp. and papers | Bodl. RH, corresp. with R. H. Heussler · Bodl. RH, corresp. with Margery Perham and related papers
Likenesses G. C. Beresford, photograph, 1913, NPG · B. Craig, portrait, 1950, U. Oxf., Forestry Institute · studio of S. Ward, photograph, c.1950, NPG
Wealth at death £467,805: probate, 18 March 1974, *CGPLA Eng. & Wales*

Fury, Billy [*real name* Ronald Wycherley] (**1940–1983**), singer and songwriter, was born on 17 April 1940 at 126 Smithdown Road, Garston, Liverpool, the elder son of Albert Edward Wycherley, a shoe repairer, and his wife, Sarah Jane (known as Jean), *née* Homer. He first attended St Silas's infant school and, after leaving Wellington Road secondary modern school at the age of fifteen, worked as a rivet thrower in an engineering factory and as a deckhand on a tugboat in the Mersey estuary. He was fascinated by rock'n'roll music and taught himself to play guitar and to write songs. He occasionally performed in public as part of the Formby Sniffle [*sic*] Group under the name Stean Wade.

In 1958 Ronald sent a tape of six compositions to the rock'n'roll impresario Larry Parnes, who invited him to play them backstage at the Birkenhead Essoldo to the singer Marty Wilde. As a result he was given a spot in that night's show and was signed to a contract by Parnes, who gave him the stage name Billy Fury. After being turned down by Marty Wilde's recording company, Philips, he was given a recording contract by Decca and in 1959 made his first hit recording, his own composition 'Maybe tomorrow'. This was followed by three more self-written hits: 'Margo', 'Colette', and 'That's love'. But the most acclaimed of his early recordings was *The Sound of Fury* (1960), a long-playing album that featured Fury's singing and Joe Brown's guitar playing in a convincing imitation of the American rockabilly sound.

Recognizing the potential impact of Fury's Elvis Presley-influenced, hip-swivelling, and at times highly suggestive stage act, the television producer Jack Good featured him on his shows *Oh Boy!*, *Boy Meets Girls*, and *Wham!* In 1959 he made his acting début, playing a Teddy boy in *Strictly for Sparrows*, a television play by Ted Willis. Fury undertook concert tours frequently in the early 1960s but toned down his stage act after the curtain was dropped during his performance at the Theatre Royal, Dublin, in October 1959, swapping his bomber jacket and cowboy boots for a gold lamé suit and smart shoes. At one stage Parnes briefly considered hiring the Beatles as Billy Fury's backing group. Instead, Parnes formed the Blue Flames, led by pianist and organist Georgie Fame. After leaving Fury in 1962, the Blue Flames became a pioneer of the rhythm and blues movement in London. Fury's later supporting groups were the Tornados and the Gamblers.

From 1960 Decca decided that Fury should record versions of American hits rather than his own compositions. Among these were 'One thousand stars' (1961), 'Halfway to paradise' (1961), 'Jealousy' (1961), and 'It's only make believe' (1964). With musical arrangements by Ivor Raymonde, both 'Halfway to paradise' and 'Jealousy' earned

Billy Fury (1940–1983), by Harry Hammond, 1960

Fury had suffered intermittent health problems following a bout of rheumatic fever at the age of six which damaged his heart valves. In the latter part of his life he spent much of his time on his farm on the Surrey–Sussex border, turning a swimming pool into a bird sanctuary. In the 1970s he purchased a 100 acre farm near Llandovery in north Wales, where he bred horses and sheep and indulged his interest in ornithology. His personal life was somewhat complicated: an eight-year relationship with Audrey Valentine (Lee) Middleton (*b.* 1937) ended in 1967 (she subsequently married the disc jockey Kenny Everett). There followed a short-lived marriage (from 31 May 1969) to Lee's friend Judith Hall, a fashion model. The last twelve years of his life were shared with Lisa Rosen, a music publisher.

During the 1970s Fury twice underwent major heart surgery, and in March 1982 he collapsed, suffering from paralysis and temporary blindness. He recovered, but died of a heart attack in St Mary's Hospital, Harrow Road, Westminster, London, on 28 January 1983 and was buried on 4 February at Paddington new cemetery, Mill Hill, London. A tribute concert was held at the Beck Theatre, Hayes, to raise funds for the Billy Fury Memorial Fund for Research into Heart Disease. Fury was one of Britain's first rock'n'roll stars, and his music, which has had numerous CD reissues since his untimely death, continues to inspire a loyal following.   DAVE LAING

Sources P. Hardy and D. Laing, *Faber companion to 20th-century popular music* (1995) · S. Leigh and J. Firminger, *Halfway to paradise: Britpop, 1955–1962* (1996) · D. McAleer, *Hit parade heroes: British beat before the Beatles* (1993) · J. Rogan, *Starmakers and Svengalis: the history of British pop management* (1988) · b. cert. · d. cert. · *DNB* · *The Times* (29 Jan 1983) · 'The Billy Fury Story', www.billyfury.co.uk, Nov 2001

Archives FILM BFI NFTVA, *Omnibus*, BBC1 12 Oct 1998 · BFI NFTVA, performance footage |SOUND BL NSA, 'Like I have never been gone: the Billy Fury story', BBC Radio 2, 25 Jan 1998, H9642/1 · BL NSA, documentary recording · BL NSA, performance recording

Likenesses H. Hammond, photograph, 1960, NPG [*see illus.*] · photographs, 1962–8, Hult. Arch.

Wealth at death under £40,000: probate, 21 July 1986, *CGPLA Eng. & Wales*

silver discs for sales of 250,000 copies. His last major hit was the romantic ballad 'In thoughts of you' in 1965, the year in which he made his only appearance on television in the United States and his only appearance in pantomime—*Aladdin* at the New Theatre, Oxford. He starred in two light comedy musical films, *Play it Cool* (1962, directed by Michael Winner) and *I Gotta Horse* (1965, directed by Kenneth Hume).

Fury's popularity, and that of many contemporaries, was affected by the arrival of a new generation of Liverpool musicians led by the Beatles. In an attempt to capitalize on their success he recorded versions of two songs associated with the new groups ('Glad all over' and 'Hippy hippy shake') for the US market. He signed a new recording contract with EMI's Parlophone label and issued eleven singles between 1966 and 1968. Most were undistinguished. He formed his own record company, Fury, in 1971 to release his own work and that of rock'n'roll singer Shane Fenton (later Alvin Stardust) and others. He returned to the stage in the next decade, appearing at the London Rock'n'Roll Festival in August 1972. In the same year he starred with David Essex and Ringo Starr in *That'll Be the Day*, a nostalgic film set in a 1950s holiday camp in which Fury played a rock star named Stormy Tempest. In 1974 he took part in a rock'n'roll revival tour with Marty Wilde and others and in 1978 he re-recorded his early hits for the K-Tel company in order to raise money following his being declared bankrupt, having apparently become the victim of unscrupulous management. He returned to recording in 1981 and his final album, *The One and Only*, was released posthumously.

Fuscincelli, Octaviano. *See* Baldwin, William (1562–1632).

Fuseli, Henry [*formerly* Johann Heinrich Füssli] (1741–1825), painter and writer, was born Johann Heinrich Füssli at Zürich, Switzerland, on 6 February 1741, although he later regularly mis-stated his true birth date. He was baptized on 7 February 1741 at the Grossmünster, Zürich, the second of the three surviving sons and two daughters (of eighteen children) of Johann Caspar Füssli (1706–1782), Zürich city clerk, portrait painter, writer on art, and collector of Renaissance and Swiss old-master drawings and prints, and his wife, Anna Elisabeth Waser (1714–1759). Johann Caspar's correspondence with painters and art theorists, including Jean-Georges Wille (1715–1808) and Johann Joachim Winckelmann (1717–1768), made him an important conduit for the diffusion of new ideas on art.

Henry Fuseli (1741–1825), self-portrait, *c.*1780

All five children were talented artists, but Johann Caspar—having experienced the uncertain life of a peripatetic portrait painter—opposed Henry's becoming an artist and intended him for the clergy, apparently for the educational advantages and opportunities for advancement. Henry received no practical instruction in art but gained a good grounding in art history from participation in his father's projects, reputedly editing, perhaps even ghost-writing, most of the *History of the Best Painters in Switzerland* (1755) and other works published under Johann Caspar's name, although the extent of such collaboration has been questioned.

Early career Fuseli began his long career as an artist aged about eight, covertly copying and imitating drawings and woodcuts by Gotthard Ringgli and other Swiss mannerists in his father's collection, using his left hand to avoid detection. Many faults in his later style can be traced to these models. He drew and painted left-handed throughout his life (the shading in his drawings characteristically runs from upper left to lower right) and many figures in his drawings, such as Achilles lopping off his hair at the funeral pyre of Patroclus (1800–05; Kunsthaus, Zürich), are represented as left-handers. His surviving juvenile productions include a cycle of earthy *Till Eulenspiegel* illustrations and an impressive series of imaginary portraits of Swiss artists, humanists, and reformers. Fuseli signed his early works, but his later practice was limited to noting the place and date of execution of any given drawing.

Fuseli's early education was imparted at home by his mother. When he was twelve, her health obliged the family to move to the country. From this period dates his life-long interest in entomology: the form of the beetle or the butterfly was 'the only one in which he can hold infinity in the palm of his hand' (Mason, 332). He even introduced life-size moths into his paintings *The Oath on the Rütli*, *The Weird Sisters*, and the *Sleeping Shepherd and Shepherdess at Dawn* from *Lycidas*, while in his seventies he 'reared, perhaps for the first time in England, two beautiful moths from pupae of *Sphinx euphorbiae*' (*Collected Letters*, 372). When he was fifteen the family returned to Zürich and Fuseli was sent to the Caroline College where he studied literature, aesthetics, Greek, and Latin under Johann Jakob Bodmer and Johann Jakob Breitinger, the intellectual progenitors of the *Sturm und Drang* ('Storm and Stress') movement. Bodmer instilled in Fuseli a love of the *Iliad* and *Odyssey*, the *Nibelungenlied*, Dante's *Divina commedia*, Shakespeare's tragedies, and Milton's *Paradise Lost*. These and the Bible always remained staples of his art.

In 1761 Fuseli was ordained a Zwinglian minister, taking as the text of his first sermon the verse 'What will this babbler say' (Acts, 17: 18). In 1766 he 'renounced the last trappings of the Altar' (*Füssli: Briefe*, 132). His friendships with Johann Caspar Lavater and Felix Hess date from this period of his studies. In autumn 1762 the three friends, inspired by Bodmer's political teachings, wrote a pamphlet exposing the corrupt Zürich magistrate Felix Grebel. Forced to leave Switzerland to avoid retaliation from Grebel's powerful friends, they travelled in March 1763 to Prussia with Johann Georg Sulzer, the Swiss art theorist. In Berlin they met the leading figures of the German Enlightenment, who were working to free the creative consciousness from its rationalistic fetters. About a month later they proceeded to Barth in then-Swedish Pomerania to stay with the protestant theologian Johann Joachim Spalding; there Fuseli completed his German translation of Mary Wortley Montagu's *Turkish Letters* and painted a group portrait of the family and guests in grisaille on the walls of Spalding's summer house. In October 1763 Fuseli returned to Berlin to assist Sulzer with his *General Theory of the Fine Arts* (1772), to which he contributed articles on allegory, the sublime, and related topics. Fuseli also prepared twelve illustrations for Bodmer's epic poem *Die Noachide* (1765), although four of these were replaced with designs by Bernard Rode. Written on his 'banishment' from Lavater, the 'friend of my soul', Fuseli's rhapsodic prose poem the *Complaints* marks the birth of the Romantic spontaneous lyrical confession: 'It was decided! *Then* I sank upon your countenance! *Then* I laid my hand upon your bared, softly-beating heart—and … swore upon that altar' (Mason, 99, 100). His Klopstockian odes were disproportionately admired by the members of the Herder circle among whom they circulated in manuscript. After 1770 Fuseli almost abandoned poetry, apart from his two famous love poems of 1779, but resumed about 1800 following the French invasion of Switzerland and the death of Lavater. Some forty of his productions, including reworked versions and two or three poems in English, survive.

In spring 1764 Sir Andrew Mitchell, the British chargé d'affaires in Berlin, took Fuseli to London, where he resided with a Mrs Green in Cranbourn Alley. He was expected to promote a broader knowledge in England of the literature of the German-speaking countries. But his efforts in this direction appear to have been very limited. Mitchell introduced him to Joseph Johnson, the 'radical' bookseller, the banker Thomas Coutts (whose daughters, particularly Susan, the future countess of Guilford, and granddaughters would contribute so much to the happiness of Fuseli's later years), and others who became lifelong friends and supporters. Through Mitchell he also met Earl Waldegrave, becoming travelling tutor to his fourteen-year-old son on a tour through France. But after a physical altercation Fuseli left his unruly pupil to his own devices, returning alone, ten months later, in October 1766 to England, remarking of the experience, '[He] took me for a bear-leader, but found me the bear' (Knowles, 1.42).

Fuseli's exposure to the London theatre and stage performances of Shakespeare had an impact on him like 'an operation for cataract', according to David Garrick (Tomory, 15). In later life he often dismissed his classes at the Royal Academy early in order to indulge his passion for the playhouse. But surprisingly few of his Shakespeare representations are based on actual performances.

In Fuseli's first months in London, Sulzer at least once arranged credit for him with Millar (Sulzer to Bodmer, 21 July 1764; MS correspondence of S— and B—, Zentralbibliothek, Zürich). Fuseli was kept afloat financially during these first years by his journalistic work and his book illustrations, although Allan Cunningham's estimate of his early London periodical productions is exaggerated. But even when his literary activities occupy the foreground, they never completely overshadow his art. Some thirty of his designs were engraved before his departure for Rome, including four for Smollett's *Peregrine Pickle* (1769) and eleven for Willoughby's *Practical Family Bible* (1772). Fuseli mentions a commission in 1765 for fifty quarto drawings at £2 apiece that would clearly have exceeded returns on his translations: Winckelmann's *Reflections on the Painting and the Sculpture of the Greeks* (1765) and Giacinto Dragonetti's *Treatise on Virtues and Rewards* (1769). His *Remarks on J. J. Rousseau* (1767), written after meeting Rousseau at Paris during his tour in France, represents an important gloss on Fuseli's developing aesthetic, particularly his endorsement of Rousseau's subversive views on the separation of art from morality, but the work's eccentric English baffled contemporary readers. Neither Winckelmann nor Rousseau seems ever to have been aware of Fuseli's efforts on their behalf. David Hume attributed the *Remarks* to 'one Fuseli, an Engraver … as mad as Rousseau himself' (*Letters of David Hume*, 2.136).

In spring 1768 Fuseli met Sir Joshua Reynolds, who encouraged him to become a painter and study in Italy, rekindling his 'unshakeable passion' for art (*Füssli: Briefe*, 154), and inspiring him to create his first oil painting on canvas, *Joseph Interpreting the Dreams of the Pharaoh's Baker and Butler* (priv. coll.). Over the next two years he made considerable progress as a painter, although much of the artistic output of this transitional period between dilettantism and the dedicated study of art, including paintings, drawings, books, and literary papers, and in particular the manuscript of his 'History of German poetry', was destroyed in a fire in Joseph Johnson's house where he lodged. He did not, however, allow this disaster to delay his planned journey to Italy. The three history paintings he dashed off for Coutts in the first three months of 1770 were intended to make up for these losses. Notwithstanding his poor handling of his raw materials, the painterly intelligence of Fuseli's prolific productions during the early 1780s and references in unpublished letters from Rome to works now missing suggest that the number of his paintings during the 1770s (including *A Scene from Macbeth*, probably *The Witches Show Macbeth Banquo's Descendants*, that he sent to the Royal Academy in 1777, telling his correspondent to hold it back so that 'it will … produce a greater effect by coming unexpectedly upon the public') has been greatly underestimated (*Collected Letters*, 16). Even so, the statement that Fuseli received £1300 in commissions in 1772–3 may be overblown.

Residence in Rome After a three-week journey by sea via Genoa in the company of the irascible physician–poet John Armstrong, in late May 1770 Fuseli reached Rome, where he adopted the Italianate form and pronunciation of his name. His journey was made possible through the generosity of Thomas Coutts. He resided in the via Babuino until 1777, when he moved to the strada Felice, where he lived with John Rouby. Fuseli's eight-and-a-half-year residence in Rome, under the intoxication of Michelangelo and the ceiling of the Sistine Chapel, was the most formative event in his artistic development. The enduring impression left on him by Michelangelo's 'sublimity of conception, grandeur of form, and breadth of manner' (Knowles, 2.84) was strengthened by Fuseli's discovery of the painter's pervasive 'imitations' of Dante in the *Last Judgment* (ibid., 2.164–6 n.). Other stylistic influences upon him were the mannerists Parmigianino, Giovanni Battista Rosso, and Baccio Bandinelli. Rome itself with its superabundance of antiquities and historical associations was 'classick ground' and a trigger to the imagination. That Pompeii, which Fuseli visited in 1775, could stir the imagination in similar fashion is reflected in such drawings as *Satyr and Boy* (Öffentliche Kunstsammlung, Basel) and *The Selling of Cupids* (Yale U. CBA). Unlike many foreign students during their stay at Rome, Fuseli did not spend time in formal studies, although he may have attended the Roman schools of anatomy and even performed partial dissections.

Meanwhile Lavater kept Herder and Goethe abreast of Fuseli's growing fame, describing him in 1773 as 'one of the greatest imaginations in Rome … everything in extremes … hurricane and tempest' (*Füssli: Briefe*, 168). Herder likened his genius to 'a mountain torrent' (Mason, 69). Among his artistic peers in Rome, Thomas Banks ranked him 'the Greatest figure … among the Students in

Painting' (*Collected Letters*, 14), while Richard Chapple Whalley was convinced, like William Blake three decades later, that Fuseli was 'a full age before all his brethren of the brush' (ibid., 15, 347). Fuseli soon became the acknowledged leader of an international group of artists that included John Brown, Thomas Banks, James Barry, James Jefferys, James Northcote, Alexander Runciman, and the Scandinavians Johan Tobias Sergel and Nicolai Abilgaard. They favoured similar subject matter, and their style was characterized, like Fuseli's, by its pursuit of the sublime and its emotionally expressive approach, by its dramatically simplified forms, and, in their drawings, by the suggestive use of wash. Copies made by Thomas Kerrich, Prince Hoare, and James Northcote after Fuseli's drawings suggest the special working intimacy that members of Fuseli's circle shared. Indeed, James Jefferys executed his own versions after Fuseli's drawings directly on the verso of Fuseli's originals (see, for example, Christies sale catalogue, 14 April 1992, lots 55, 57; Jefferys's copies identified by Nancy Pressly). Another member of this group was George Romney, whose drawings of subjects from Milton's poetry with their atypical fervour were obviously produced under Fuseli's influence.

Despite his growing cosmopolitanism, Fuseli never entirely freed himself from his Zwinglian puritanism—but his years in Rome, where proverbially 'Venus reigned as second sovereign after St Peter' (Andrieux, 109), certainly softened its hard edges. He liked to relate that the time he spent lying on his back musing on Michelangelo's *Last Judgment* was often as much a recuperative necessity 'for a body fatigued like his with the pleasant gratifications of a luxurious city' as it was an aesthetic joy to the mind (Cunningham, 2.269). The hard-living Sergel, well funded by a Swedish government grant, also contributed significantly to this other part of Fuseli's studies. He undoubtedly participated in the frequent 'bacchanals with young girls' orchestrated by Sergel (Pressly, 15) and vividly captured in Antoine Esprit Gibelin's reportage drawing *Roman Bacchanal with Sergel* (*c*.1771; Nationalmuseum, Stockholm, illustrated in Jørgen Andersen, *De År i Rom*, 1989, 255). These retreats were also fictionalized in Wilhelm Heinse's *Ardinghello* (1787), 'one of the earliest manifestoes of aesthetic immoralism' (G. Schiff, ed., introduction, *German Essays on Art History*, 1988, xviii). Fuseli's erotic drawings now in the Horne Foundation Museum, Florence, may be reminiscences of his own experiences at Sergel's entertainments.

Return to London On his way back to England Fuseli returned to Switzerland for the first and last time, spending six months in Zürich (October 1778–April 1779), where he was fêted as a celebrity. During his stay Fuseli painted his two large-scale pictures, *The Oath on the Rütli* and *The Artist in Conversation with J. J. Bodmer* (both Kunsthaus, Zürich), although these were completed in London. The latter work, cited by Klaus Lankheit as an example of the genre of Romantic 'friendship painting', was conceived as homage to his old teacher, but the arrogance and lack of humility evinced in Fuseli's self-portrait suggest a reversal of the two men's previous roles of student and teacher rather

than the image of a self-effacing disciple. Indeed, in his illustrations of *Macbeth* over the next two decades Fuseli demonstrates a mischievousness verging on malice by giving the witches the features of Bodmer. To date, he had had no serious emotional attachments, although on leaving Rome he assured 'Nanina' of the Bolognette Palace that he was not 'capable of forgetting her friendship' (*Collected Letters*, 19). In Zürich, however, he experienced the most shattering crisis of his life when he fell violently in love with the 21-year-old niece of J. C. Lavater, Anna Landolt (Lavater), even as he flirted outrageously with Magdalena Hess, the coquettish wife of the affluent 'projector' Johann Caspar Schweizer, and her younger sister Martha. But Fuseli's love was doomed from the start. Motivated by what Fuseli saw as 'infernal Zürich family humbug' about money (Mason, 155), Anna's father rejected Fuseli's application to marry her. Fuseli may never in fact have declared his feelings directly to Anna, reflecting what Gert Schiff interprets as a repeated pattern of 'fear of commitment' (Schiff, *Füssli*, 1973 1.86). In fervid letters to Lavater from London in summer 1779 Fuseli poured out his passion for Anna: 'Last night I had her in bed with me … fused her body and her *soul* together with my own … Anyone who touches her now commits adultery and incest! She is *mine* and I am *hers*' (Mason, 155). Fuseli's unrequited love for Anna is also enshrined in his two best poems in German, 'An Nannas Lieblingsreh' ('Alcaics—to Nanna's pet fawn') and 'Nannas Auge' ('To Nanna's Eye') (ibid., 150–51, 153–4), and may also have inspired Fuseli's notorious painting *The Nightmare* (Detroit Institute of Arts, Michigan). On the reverse of the painting, exhibited in 1782, is an unfinished portrait of a beautiful young woman, identified by H. W. Janson as Anna Landolt. The woman oppressed by the nightmare on the front of the canvas has Anna's features, while the incubus-demon squatting on her chest bears a striking likeness to the artist himself, thus suggesting the strong personal element that seems to underlie the broader metaphorical structure of the work.

The London art scene to which Fuseli returned in spring 1779 was dominated by face painters, and competition among history painters for patrons was correspondingly intense, but the twenty-one paintings Fuseli exhibited at the Royal Academy between 1780 and 1786 soon established his reputation as a history painter. The most impressive of these, *Satan Starting at the Touch of Ithuriel's Spear* (Staatsgalerie, Stuttgart), *The Death of Dido* (Yale U. CBA), *Lady Macbeth Sleepwalking* (Louvre, Paris), and *Queen Katharine's Dream* (town hall, Lytham St Anne's), formed part of the seven works commissioned by Sir Robert Smyth, his major patron during this period, whom Fuseli had met at Rome.

Back in London, where he lived at 1 Broad Street on the corner of Portland Street, Fuseli re-established contact with his old mentor Sir Joshua Reynolds, becoming a regular guest at his dinner table and visitor to his studio—although for Fuseli the relationship was always a competitive one. Over the years he challenged Reynolds by painting a number of pictures on subjects already undertaken by the president of the Royal Academy. The earliest and most striking manifestation of this strategy was Fuseli's *Death of Dido*, exhibited in 1781 at the Royal Academy. Executed on the same scale as Reynolds's version (Royal Collection), Fuseli's vertically oriented picture was hung directly opposite Reynolds's with its horizontal orientation, inevitably inviting comparison between the two works and garnering Fuseli much publicity and favourable reviews in the newspapers. The exhibition 'Art on the Line' (2001–2) held in the restored Great Room of the Royal Academy at Somerset House and the accompanying book *Art on the Line* (2001) edited by David Solkin provide invaluable information about how exhibitors' pictures were hung at this time. (For locations of Fuseli's paintings in the exhibitions of 1784 and 1792 see also figs. 17, 207, 14, and 27.) Both Reynolds and Fuseli subsequently contributed versions of *Puck*, the mischievous fairy from *A Midsummer Night's Dream*, to Boydell's Shakspeare Gallery. In an anonymous critique in the *Analytical Review* (4, 1789, 106), Fuseli ridiculed Reynolds's figure as 'a fairy whom fancy may endow with the creation of a midnight mushroom, a snow-drop, or a violet; but [who] cannot be mistaken for the Robin [Goodfellow] of Shakespeare or Milton'. This would not be Fuseli's last criticism of Reynolds as a history painter. In unpublished remarks written in 1813 on the *Death of Beaufort* Fuseli labelled him 'a Painter [who] has not Left One genuine Specimen of Invention himself' (MS, priv. coll.). Fuseli's *Ugolino* was conceived with a similar intent.

But it was *The Nightmare* (perhaps commissioned by Brooke Boothby) that sealed Fuseli's celebrity status, prefiguring the shape of Romanticism to come. Described by Horace Walpole as 'Shockingly mad, madder than ever, quite mad', it took London by storm (Whitley, 2.377). In its engraved form it became an icon of the age's insecurities and Gothic terrors, earning John Raphael Smith over £500. Smith's mezzotint of 1785 after Fuseli's *Weird Sisters* similarly demonstrated Fuseli's power to capture the popular imagination and the vital role of the engraver in creating an audience for the painter's work. The grotesque sublimity of Fuseli's imagery lent itself to comic exaggeration and was regularly exploited by James Gillray and other political cartoonists such as Thomas Rowlandson and Robert Seymour.

Shakespeare's painter The 1780s ushered in a spate of 'literary' and 'historic' galleries, intended to capture the sublimity of the great national poets on canvas and create a demand for history painting. Fuseli was present at the dinner given by John Boydell in November 1786 when the creation of what became the Shakspeare Gallery was discussed, and he undoubtedly played a significant role in the discussions that made Boydell's ambitious project a reality. Fuseli was already widely recognized as 'Shakespeare's painter'. While at Rome he had conceived the idea of a room dedicated to Shakespeare's genius, modelled on the Sistine Chapel and decorated with scenes from the plays in imitation of Michelangelo's *Last Judgment*. (These designs are in the British Museum and a Swiss private collection.) Apart from his nine paintings for Boydell and five

for James Woodmason's *Irish Shakespeare Gallery*, he also contributed to Thomas Macklin's *Poets' Gallery* and illustrated Bible, and to Robert Bowyer's *Historic Gallery*, illustrating David Hume's *History of England*. In 1791 Joseph Johnson and Fuseli issued proposals (MSS, Beinecke Library, Yale) for a magnificent edition of Milton's complete poems, supervised by William Cowper and embellished with thirty plates (plus vignettes) executed by eminent engravers such as Francesco Bartolozzi, William Sharpe, Thomas Holloway, and William Blake. In contrast with the arrangements in other such galleries Fuseli was the only painter involved. When a new fit of insanity sidelined Cowper as editor, Johnson withdrew from the scheme, but Fuseli decided to press ahead alone with his own more ambitious and at this point still evolving Milton Gallery, discarding all previous plans to publish a new edition. For the rest of the decade, 'goaded by the furies of Enterprise and despair', he struggled to realize a project that even 'Michelangelo … would in my Situation perhaps not have dared to undertake' (*Collected Letters*, 153). It was only the generosity of William Roscoe, who financed him during these years to the tune of £700 (eventually repaid in the form of paintings), that enabled Fuseli in 1799 to exhibit his first cycle of forty-one paintings devoted to Milton's life and works. A second enlarged exhibition, displaying forty-seven works, followed in 1800. Both were financial failures. Only minor support was ever forthcoming from wavering patrons like William Seward, George Steevens, and even Joseph Johnson. A few large paintings were purchased from the exhibitions by John Julius Angerstein and other wealthy friends but almost half the Milton pictures languished in Fuseli's studio until his death. No plates were engraved to sell to subscribers. Fuseli sought to rectify this blunder with the eleven large plates retrospectively engraved by Moses Haughton after the most sublime of the Milton Gallery paintings (in particular, the *Lazar House*) and jointly published as 'from the Royal Academy' between 1803 and 1813. In the late 1780s and 1790s Fuseli found time to assist Cowper in his translation of Homer, although by the end he was 'deadly Sick of revising his foul Linen' (ibid., 47). He also contributed more than sixty anonymous critiques of books and exhibition reviews to Johnson's *Analytical Review* (1788–98). In 1788 Joseph Johnson published Lavater's *Aphorisms on Man*, translated (and, indeed, often adapted) with pith and point by Fuseli from Lavater's *Vermischte physiognomische Regeln*. This work became the direct inspiration for his own *Aphorisms on Art*. Although this was already half printed in 1800, Fuseli suspended plans for publication, fearing he would be considered 'a man of fancy rather than of explanation' (Farington, *Diary*, 4.1539), and the work was not published until after his death. He also undertook supervision of the re-engraving of the illustrations to the English edition of Lavater's *Essays on Physiognomy* (1789–98).

After the collapse of Boydell's gallery the London booksellers became the history painters' new patrons. Although Fuseli complained about the small-format paintings they solicited to illustrate their books, the estimated £700 he received for almost sixty such 'puny' productions was a welcome windfall after the financial fiasco of the Milton Gallery (*Collected Letters*, 290). Half of these were for Francis Isaac Du Roveray, the Huguenot publisher of nine illustrated editions of the eighteenth-century English poets, including Pope's translation of Homer; another thirty-seven designs were destined for Alexander Chalmers's nine-volume *Shakespeare* (1805, 1809, and 1811).

Marriage On 30 June 1788, shortly after his election as an associate of the Royal Academy, Fuseli married at St Mary's, St Marylebone, the beautiful, fashion-conscious Sophia Rawlins (1762/3–1832) of Batheaston, over twenty years younger than him, of whom over the next two decades he executed a remarkable gallery of some 150 fantasized 'portraits' in pen and ink with watercolour washes, many of which merge into his erotic *œuvre* (examples in BM, V&A, AM Oxf., Kunsthaus, Zürich, and City of Auckland Art Gallery, New Zealand). The couple lived at 72 Queen Ann Street East (now Foley Street), London. In the latter part of 1787, about the same time that he was courting his future bride, Fuseli also became acquainted with Mary *Wollstonecraft (1759–1797), probably at one of Joseph Johnson's weekly dinners. Early in 1788 with the assistance of his cousin Heinrich Füssli (1751–1829), who was living in Paris, he helped make arrangements for Mary's sister Everina to stay with a French family to improve her French. Their friendship was already close at this period, for Fuseli also made Mary a gift of an unidentified painting (*Letters of Mary Wollstonecraft Shelley*, 3.103). Mary's feelings did not long remain purely platonic. 'I love the man and admire the artist', she declared to William Roscoe (*Collected Letters*, 79). Her constant letters became irksome to Fuseli, who put them aside without even reading them, but Mary's correspondence with Roscoe with its insights into Fuseli's state of mind (she 'made light to him' of his lack of subscribers to the Milton Gallery but was acutely aware that 'the comfort of his life in every sense of the word' depended on the success of the project; ibid., 80) suggests that she offered Fuseli much-needed moral support and advice at this critical time. In her infatuation, as Fuseli distanced himself from her, Mary avowed her passion to Mrs Fuseli, requesting her permission to share her husband's life and home. When her unconventional overture was rebuffed, Mary set out alone in early December 1792 for France (determined 'no longer to struggle with a rational desire' (ibid., 83)). Fuseli refers to her on only two other occasions. In 1797 he informed Roscoe of the marriage of 'the assertrix of female Rights' and 'the Balanciere of political Justice' (William Godwin) (ibid., 170), only to report her death to Roscoe the same year in a two-word postscript: 'Poor *mary*!' (ibid., 75). The 'Klage um Maria' ('Lament for Maria') (MS, Kunsthaus, Zürich) that Mason assumes may be in memory of Mary Wollstonecraft, written on paper watermarked 1807, was probably for Maria Riddell (1772–1808), who had also set her sights on the painter. Apart from the snippets published

by his biographer John Knowles, no correspondence between Fuseli and Mary Wollstonecraft has survived.

Royal Academy Fuseli was elected Royal Academician in 1790 and professor of painting in 1799, his candidacy buoyed by his Milton Gallery. Other academicians seem to have shared William Hamilton's opinion that 'Fuseli's Milton pictures prove him … an extraordinary man' (Farington, *Diary*, 4.1232). His first three lectures on painting were published in 1801; all twelve were published in Knowles's *Life and Writings* in 1831. In 1804 Fuseli also became keeper of the Royal Academy, the only individual ever simultaneously to hold both these positions in the institution, and took up residence at Somerset House. As a teacher Fuseli was well liked by the students in the academy's schools, who in an unprecedented gesture showed their appreciation by presenting him in 1807 with an inscribed silver cup designed by the sculptor John Flaxman. Knowles extolled him for raising the level of drawing in England, but Fuseli could be caustic about a bad drawing ('take it out and shoot at it'), and would slash a student's drawing if he did not get in the wearer's foot and toes before starting on the sandal, or otherwise subordinated accuracy to mere finish (Smith, 2.348). Fuseli made no attempt in his teaching to inculcate his personal practice and had already allayed most fears about this before his election as professor of painting. Outstanding students like B. R. Haydon, William Hilton, William Etty, Edwin Landseer, C. R. Leslie, William Mulready, and David Wilkie were thus enabled to develop in directions which had little in common with his own artistic principles. As a result, apart from Theodore von Holst, who served as a bridge linking Fuseli and the Pre-Raphaelites, and his fellow disciple Thomas Griffiths Wainewright, the dilettante artist and writer who probably encouraged Fuseli to illustrate De la Motte Fouqué's *Undine*, he had no direct disciples. But his paintings for the Shakspeare Gallery and, subsequently, his book illustrations strongly influenced younger history painters like William Hamilton, Richard Westall, and Henry Howard, as well as Flaxman and William Blake, who was not yet known for his poetry. Blake's close personal and professional relationship with Fuseli began about 1787. Of the sixteen plates he engraved after Fuseli, only three came to Blake after 1800. The ways these stand out from the 'perfect routine-work' of Fuseli's other engravers may explain why he 'discarded his graver', preferring the stylistic and tonal uniformity and control he could impose on Moses Haughton, by then his resident engraver (Weinglass, review, 669). Blake acquired such a familiarity with Fuseli's Roman drawings in the early 1780s that the extent of his borrowings from the older man should not be surprising. Fuseli returned the compliment, noting that Blake was 'damned good to steal from'—although his figurative borrowings all date from after the turn of the century (A. Gilchrist, *Life of William Blake*, ed. R. Todd, New York, 1945, 45). The two men were particularly close during the 1790s, and Blake considered Fuseli:

The only Man that eer I knew
Who did not make me almost spew.
(Johnson and Grant, 200)

But although they shared many mythographic concerns Blake's mysticism (like Lavater's religiosity) strained their friendship. When Blake remarked of one of his works that 'The Virgin Mary had appeared to him and praised it', Fuseli rejoined that 'her ladyship has not an immaculate taste' (Cunningham, 2.309).

Written works Like many of Joseph Johnson's authors, Fuseli had at first welcomed the French Revolution and in 1792 had even planned a visit to Paris with Johnson and Mary Wollstonecraft to see its effects. In 1802 Fuseli, no longer politically so impressionable, was persuaded to accompany the landscape painter and diarist Joseph Farington on a six-week trip to Paris (27 August to 11 October) to view the paintings looted from Italy and to prepare a critical account of them and other important pictures in the Louvre for English travellers. Fuseli had been reluctant to 'quit the English shore' (Farington, *Diary*, 5.1810), and after five weeks he was chafing to leave 'this paradise of Mud and fricandeaus' (*Collected Letters*, 254–5). He found the poorly lit gallery of the Louvre 'little Superior to a huge auction room' and the French restorers' treatment of the Renaissance masterpieces displayed there insensitive and destructive (ibid., 256). He visited the studios of J. L. David, but remained unimpressed by what he saw, including the *Sabine Women*. He admired, however, the works of François Gérard, A.-L. Girodet, and Baron Guérin. Fuseli's guide to the artworks in the Louvre was never published separately, although Knowles included a selection of his commentaries in the *Life* (1.262–76). Fuseli also incorporated some in his new edition of Mathew Pilkington's *Dictionary of Painters*, published in 1805 and reissued in a wholly reworked form in 1810. As a reference work this is notable for its biographical accuracy and pungency—occasionally seasoned with unabashed personal prejudice against such painters as Dürer and his circle. He included biographies of his father and two brothers but, while less stringent about the selection of male flower painters, deliberately omitted any reference to his two sisters, Anna and Elisabeth.

In 1805 Fuseli made the acquaintance of John Knowles, his future executor and biographer. In 1818 Knowles helped him make a final collation of the manuscript of his *Aphorisms on Art* begun thirty years earlier. This was published by Knowles in 1831, after Fuseli's death. The concept may have represented a refinement of an earlier, less sophisticated plan for a collection of observations and anecdotes to be entitled 'Wahrheiten' ('Truths') which he was compiling in 1763. In September 1816 Fuseli, together with Sir Thomas Lawrence and John Flaxman, was unanimously elected as honorary academician of the Accademia di San Luca at Rome, undoubtedly at the suggestion of the great neo-classical sculptor Antonio Canova, who had visited the Royal Academy the previous December. Canova told Haydon that in art 'Raphael has the fire, Fuseli the flame' (*The Diary of Benjamin Robert Haydon*, ed. W. B. Pope, 1960, 1.485).

There was thematically little new in Fuseli's late work. He was, however, the first to illustrate the *Nibelungenlied*, his interpretation of which sometimes brilliantly anticipates the conclusions of nineteenth-century German scholarship. His illustrations of De la Motte Fouqué's *Undine*, like his sensual 'kiss-drawings' and sketches of Lavinia de Irujo and other young girls with whom he surrounded himself at this time, mark the transition to 'the new lyrical and elegiac components of his late style' (Schiff, *Füssli*, 1973, 1.375). Known for the chiaroscuro effect of so many of his paintings, Fuseli insisted he had 'courted … Colour as a despairing lover courts a disdainful mistress' (Knowles, 2.333). Yet throughout his writings he constantly refers to the dangers of colour and the 'insidious foundation' it provides painters who 'debase themselves to be the debauchers of the senses' (ibid., 332). As late as 1821, in his annual report to the council on progress in the Royal Academy Schools, he complains bitterly that 'the Lure of Colour [has eclipsed] the sterner tints of History [painting]' (Zürich, Zentralbibliothek).

Death and reputation Fuseli always enjoyed robust health, although he seems to have suffered from depressions in his last dozen years, and remained productive to the end, leaving an unfinished painting, *Lady Constance* (priv. coll.), on his easel. He died on 16 April 1825 at the home of the countess of Guilford at Putney Hill, Surrey, and was buried in St Paul's Cathedral on 25 April. He was never naturalized in England and in 1798 had had to register with the alien office. Following his death, his widow was taken into the household of Moses Haughton. She died at Brighton on 18 March 1832, aged sixty-nine.

Fuseli was about 5 feet 2 inches in height. He had expressive large blue eyes that never required the aid of spectacles, a large and rather aquiline nose, and hair that had turned prematurely white after a bout of fever in Italy. He was rather dapper in appearance. He seems never to have worn a wig, but had his hair styled and powdered every morning by a hairdresser. The 'little white-headed, lion-faced man in an old flannel dressing gown' whom Haydon encountered in 1805 on his first visit to Fuseli in his 'gallery' of images of 'terror, blood, and murder' was a disconcerting contrast to the 'giant [Haydon] fancied him to be' (*Autobiography*, 18).

Fuseli was the most learned painter of the age, with a remarkable command of Greek and Latin rivalling that of the great classical scholar Richard Porson, whom he once fooled with an invented Greek quotation. He was equally familiar with Dante's *Divina commedia*, the *Nibelungenlied*, Shakespeare's plays, and Milton's *Paradise Lost*. His uncommonly tenacious visual memory helped him become one of the most perceptive art historians of the eighteenth and nineteenth centuries. He enunciated sophisticated theories about the history and changing role of art in society, narrowly scrutinized prevailing art historical method in order to harness 'novelty [to the task of] enlarging the circle of fancy' (Knowles, 2.11), and rethought many concepts governing artistic composition and design, thereby introducing scores of new art historical terms into the language. A superb and intensely dramatic draughtsman, although this has often been allowed to overshadow the virtues of his paintings, he was notorious for his sensational, demonic, irrational, and bizarre subjects (categorized by S. T. Coleridge as 'Convulsia & Tettanus upon innocent Canvas'; *Notebooks*, 954). His exploration in his art of the unconscious and his claim that 'One of the most unexplored regions of art are [*sic*] dreams' (Aphorism no. 231, Knowles, 3.145) have led the surrealists to claim him as a forerunner. His documented œuvre comprises close to 3000 known works in all media, but his drawings have fared better both critically and physically than his paintings, many of which are marred, or have disintegrated, owing to the destructive effect of the bituminous brown pigment he added to his paint. Many of his surviving works have come down to us through the families of his closest friends: Lady Susan North, countess of Guilford (1771–1837), eldest daughter of Thomas Coutts, and her two daughters, Susan, later Lady North (1797–1884), to whom over 800 of Fuseli's drawings descended (sold by Sothebys on 14–15 July 1885), and Lady Georgina North (1798–1835) (who had owned the fourteen paintings by him sold by Pippings from Wroxton on 7 May 1933, lots 749–62); and Dr James and Harriet (Carrick-)Moore and their daughters, Harriet, Jane, and Louisa, who donated many of Fuseli's drawings, particularly the so-called Roman Album, to the British Museum. More drawings (and letters) from the same source were sold at the Anthony Heath sale (Christies, 6 March 1973, lots 19–21, 29), while another trove of fifty-seven drawings assembled by Harriet was sold at Christies on 14 April 1992, for a total of £750,000. Many of the other paintings owned by Coutts's descendants were eventually consolidated in the hands of John Herbert Dudley, fifth earl of Harrowby, who took advantage of the opportunity offered by the great Fuseli exhibition in Zürich in 1926 to dispose of them to a syndicate of Swiss collectors, eager to take them home to Switzerland, in exchange for what his lordship considered more desirable old masters.

D. H. WEINGLASS

Sources G. Schiff, *Johann Heinrich Füssli, 1741–1825*, 2 vols. (Zürich, [1973]) · G. Schiff and W. Hofman, *Henry Fuseli, 1741–1825*, trans. S. Twohig (1975) [exhibition catalogue, Tate Gallery, London] · J. Knowles, *The life and writings of Henry Fuseli, Esq. M.A. R.A.*, 3 vols. (1831); repr. with a new introduction by D. H. Weinglass (1982) · *The collected English letters of Henry Fuseli*, ed. D. H. Weinglass (1982) · *Heinrich Füssli: Briefe*, ed. W. Muschg (Basel, 1942) · E. C. Mason, *The mind of Henry Fuseli* (1951) · *Unveröffentlichte Gedichte von J. H. Füssli*, ed. E. C. Mason (1951) · *J. H. Füssli: sämtliche Gedichte*, ed. M. Bircher and K. S. Guthke (Zürich, 1973) · N. L. Pressly, *The Fuseli circle in Rome: early Romantic art of the 1770s* (New Haven, CT, 1979) [exhibition catalogue, Yale U. CBA, 12 Sept – 11 Nov 1979] · L. Stainton, *British artists in Rome, 1700–1800* (1974) [exhibition catalogue, Greater London Council] · D. H. Weinglass, *Prints and engraved illustrations by and after Henry Fuseli: a catalogue raisonné* (1994) · D. H. Weinglass, F. Licht, and S. Tosini Pizzetti, *Füssli pittore di Shakespeare: pittura e teatro, 1775–1825* (Milan, 1997) [exhibition catalogue, Milan] · C. Becker and C. Hattendorff, *Johann Heinrich Füssli: das verlorene Paradies* (Stuttgart, 1997) [exhibition catalogue, Gerd Hatje and Staatsgalerie Stuttgart] · P. Tomory, *The life and art of Henry Fuseli* (1972) · J. Ingamells, ed., *A dictionary of British and Irish travellers in Italy, 1701–1800* (1997) · J. Barrell, *The political theory of painting from Reynolds to Hazlitt* (1986), 258–307 · Y. Boerlin-Brodbeck, 'Johann Caspar Füssli und sein Briefwechsel mit Jean-Georges Wille: Marginalien zu Kunstliteratur und Kunstpolitik in der zweiten Hälfte des 18. Jahrhunderts', *Jahrbuch 1974–1977 des Schweizerischen Instituts für Kunstwissenschaft* (1978) · D. A. Brenneman, 'Self-promotion and the sublime: Fuseli's *Dido on the funeral pyre*', *Huntington Library Quarterly*, 62/1–2 (1999), 68–87 · G. Schiff, 'Füssli, puritain et satanique', *L'Œil*, 63 (March 1960), 22–9 · K. Schulthess, 'Vorfahren von Johann Heinrich Füssli, Dichter und Schriftsteller', *Genealogie*, 12/10 (Oct 1975), 689–95 · M. Vogel, 'Johann Heinrich Füssli als Maler: Gedanken zu seiner Ausdrucksqualität', in P. Pfister, *Von Claude Lorrain bis Giovanni Segantini: Gemäldeoberfläche und Bildwirkung* (Zürich, 1996), 77–104 [exhibition catalogue, Kunsthaus, Zürich] · W. H. Friedman, *Boydell's Shakespeare gallery* (New York, 1976) · O. R. Pinelli, 'La lezione italiana', *Füssli: art dossier* (Florence, 1997), 14–25 · IGI · D. Solkin, *On the line* (2001) [exhibition catalogue, Courtauld, 2001–2] · M. Andrieux, *Daily life in Rome in the eighteenth century* (1968) · A. Cunningham, *The lives of the most eminent British painters, sculptors, and architects*, 2nd edn (1829–33) · M. Myrone, 'The sublime as spectacle', *Art on the line*, ed. D. H. Solkin (2001), 84, 86–7 · *The letters of Mary Wollstonecraft Shelley*, ed. B. T. Bennett, 3 vols. (1980–88), vol. 3, p. 103 · [B. R. Haydon], 'To the artist', *The Artist*, 14 (13 June 1807), 19–20 · D. H. Weinglass, review, *Art Bulletin*, 42 (Dec 1980), 665–9 · M. L. Johnson and J. E. Grant, eds., *Blake's poetry and designs* (1979), 200 · J. T. Smith, *Nollekens and his times*, ed. W. Whitten (New York, 1920) · K. Lankheit, *Das Freundschaftsbild der Romantik* (Heidelberg, 1952), 77–8 · *The Times* (20 March 1832), 4 · *The notebooks of Samuel Taylor Coleridge*, ed. K. Coburn, 1 (1957), 954 · *The autobiography and memoirs of Benjamin Robert Haydon, 1786–1846*, ed. A. P. D. Penrose (1927) · W. T. Whitley, *Artists and their friends in England, 1700–1799*, 2 (1928), 377 · *The letters of David Hume*, ed. J. Y. T. Greig, 2 (1932), 136 · W. Wartmann, *Johann Heinrich Füssli [Henry Fuseli], 1741–1825: Ausstellung von Gemälden, Zeichnungen und Kupferstichen* (Zürich, 1926) [exhibition catalogue, Zürcher Kunstgesellschaft und Kunsthaus, Zürich] · G. Schiff, *Johann Heinrich Füssli, 1741–1825: Gemälde und Zeichnungen* (Zürich, 1969) [exhibition catalogue, Kunsthaus, Zürich, and Swiss Institute for Art Research, Zürich]

Archives McGill University, Montreal, McLennan Library, corresp. and papers · RA, corresp. and papers | RA, corresp. with Thomas Lawrence

Likenesses H. Fuseli, self-portrait, pen-and-ink drawing, 1761–2, repro. in Bircher and Guthke, eds., *J. H. Füssli*; priv. coll. · C. B. Rode, chalk and wash, 1763, Zentralbibliothek, Zürich; repro. in Schiff, *Johann Heinrich Füssli*, vol. 1, pt 2, p. 49 [1973] · J. T. Sergel, terracotta bust, *c.*1772–1776, Nationalmuseum, Stockholm; repro. in *Henry Füssli: Briefe*, ed. Muschg, frontispiece · J. T. Sergel, caricature, 1774–6, Nationalmuseum, Stockholm; repro. in J. Andersen, *De Är i Rom* (1989) · J. Northcote, oils, 1778, NPG · H. Fuseli, self-portrait, 1778–81, Kunsthaus, Zürich · J. H. Lips, stipple and line engraving, 1779, BM, NPG; repro. in Lavater, *Physiognomy* (1783) [French edn] · H. Fuseli, two self-portraits, chalk studies, 1779–*c.*1780, V&A [*see illus.*] · W. Bromley, engraving, 1792 (after Lips), repro. in Lavater, *Physiognomy* (1783) [English edn] · J. Opie, oils, 1794, NPG · W. Ridley, engraving, 1801 (after J. Opie, 1794) · W. Evans, stipple, 1808 (after M. Haughton, before 1808), BM, NPG · M. Haughton, miniature, before 1808, repro. in P. Ganz, *The drawings of Henry Fuseli* (1949), frontispiece; priv. coll. · G. H. Harlowe, oils, 1817, Yale U. CBA; priv. coll. · R. W. Sievier, engraving, 1820 (after G. H. Harlowe, 1817) · E. H. Baily, marble bust, *c.*1824, NPG · G. North, portrait, 1824 (in old age), Bodl. Oxf., Georgina North papers · T. Lawrence, oils, 1825, Musée Bonnat, Bayonne · T. Thomson, stipple, 1825 (after E. H. Baily, *c.*1824), BM, NPG · T. A. Dean, engraving, 1831 (after G. H. Harlowe, 1817) · W. Bromley, engraving (after Lawrence), repro. in Lavater, *Physiognomy* (1789) [English edn] · W. Etty, portrait (in old age), priv. coll. · attrib. J. Flaxman, marble relief, Staatliche Museen zu Berlin, Preussischer Kulturbesitz; repro. in

M. Knuth, 'Korrigierte attributionen: zu Zuschreibungs-problemen bei Berliner bildwerken', *Museums Journal aus den Museen, Schlössern und Sammlungen in Berlin und Potsdam*, 13/1 (Jan 1999), 45 · M. Haughton, miniatures, AM Oxf., FM Cam. · C. J. Hullmandel, engraving (after G. S. Newton) · G. S. Newton, portrait (in old age), Bodl. Oxf., Georgina North papers · E. Scriven, engraving (after G. H. Harlowe) · white glass cameo (after E. H. Baily), priv. coll.

Fust, Sir Herbert Jenner- (1778–1852), judge, was born on 4 February 1778 in the parish of St Gregory by Paul, London, in the City of London, the second son of Robert Jenner, proctor, of Chislehurst, Kent, and his second wife, Ann, eldest daughter of Peter Birt of Wenvoe Castle, Glamorgan. He was educated at a school in Reading run by Dr Valpy before going on to Trinity Hall, Cambridge, where he graduated LLB in 1798 and LLD in 1803. He was called to the bar at Gray's Inn on 27 November 1800, admitted an advocate in the ecclesiastical and admiralty courts, and a fellow of the College of Doctors of Law on 8 July 1803. On 14 September 1803 he married Elizabeth (1784–1828), daughter of Lieutenant-General Francis Lascelles.

On 28 February 1828 Jenner was appointed king's advocate-general, and knighted on the same day by George IV. He became vicar-general to the archbishop of Canterbury in 1832, but resigned both his posts on 21 October 1834, when appointed official principal of the arches and judge of the prerogative court of Canterbury. He was sworn of the privy council on 29 October 1834.

Jenner assumed the additional surname of Fust on 14 January 1842 on inheriting Hill Court, Gloucestershire, and Capenor Court, Somerset, which had belonged to his cousin Sir John Fust. He was elected master of Trinity Hall, Cambridge, in February 1843, but never resided there, although he remained master and dean of the arches until his death.

Fust is best remembered for his involvement in the controversial case, *Gorham v. Bishop of Exeter*, which divided evangelical and Tractarian parties within the Church of England, lasted for three years (1847–50), and caused heated controversy within the Anglican community over both the degree to which the state should be allowed to interfere in ecclesiastical matters and the nature of theological opinion to be espoused by members of the church. The case turned on baptismal regeneration. Bishop Henry Phillpotts accused George Cornelius Gorham of heresy and refused to appoint him vicar of Brampford Speke, Devon. On 2 August 1849 Fust was carried into court by two footmen to deliver his decree, which found that an infant was regenerated by baptism, thus finding against Gorham. Fust's decree threatened to lead to an exodus of evangelicals from the Church of England, but on appeal the judicial committee of the privy council set Fust's judgment aside. Fust's decree led to the publication of no fewer than eighty pamphlets.

Fust's opinions and cases, reported under Fust and Jenner-Fust, include: a letter to the archbishop of Canterbury on *Breeks v. Woolfrey*, on praying for the dead (1839); on unauthorized baptism, (*Mastin v. Escott*, 1841); the will of W. Brayne (1848), and Gorham, clerk, against the bishop of Exeter; the judgment delivered in the arches court (1849),

and his judgment in the prerogative court in *Cursham v. Williams and Chouler* (1851). His judgments led to commentaries such as *Gorham v. Bishop of Exeter* by J. King (1849) and *The Sacrament of Baptism* by H. Phillpotts, bishop of Exeter (1849); another review of *Gorham v. Bishop of Exeter* came from the editor of the *Christian Observer*, William Goode jun. (1850).

Jenner-Fust died at 1 Chesterfield Street, Mayfair, Westminster, on 20 February 1852, and was buried six days later in the family vault at St Nicholas, Chislehurst, Kent.

G. C. BOASE, rev. HUGH MOONEY

Sources GM, 2nd ser., 37 (1852), 408 · *Law Times* (28 Feb 1852), 216 · *Christian Observer* (1849), 809–56 · *Christian Observer* (1850), 698–713 · G. W. Thornbury and E. Walford, *Old and new London: a narrative of its history, its people, and its places*, 6 vols. (1873–8), vol. 1, pp. 288, 292 · E. Foss, *Biographia juridica: a biographical dictionary of the judges of England … 1066–1870* (1870) · J. C. S. Nias, *Gorham and the bishop of Exeter* (1951)
Likenesses W. Walker, mezzotint, pubd 1835 (after F. Y. Hurlstone), BM, NPG

Fust, Herbert Jenner- (1806–1904), cricketer, born on 23 February 1806 at 38 Sackville Street, Piccadilly, London, was the eldest son and one of fourteen children of Sir Herbert Jenner (1778–1852) [see Fust, Sir Herbert Jenner-], dean of arches, and his wife, Elizabeth (1784–1828), daughter of Lieutenant-General Francis Lascelles. A younger brother, Henry Lascelles Jenner (1821–1898), played cricket for Cambridge University in 1841 and was the first bishop of Dunedin (1866–71). Jenner was educated at Eton College from 1818 to 1823, spent a year at a private tutor's, and matriculated in 1824 at Trinity Hall, Cambridge, where he gained a scholarship and afterwards a fellowship. In 1827 he was third in the law honours list; he graduated LLB in 1829 and proceeded LLD in 1835. He was called to the bar at Lincoln's Inn in 1831 and admitted an advocate in the ecclesiastical court of Doctors' Commons in 1835. He practised there until 1857/8, when that court was abolished and its business transferred to Westminster. In 1833 he married Maria Eleanora (d. 1891), third daughter of George Norman and sister of George Warde Norman; with her he had a son and two daughters. After living successively at Beckenham, at Carshalton, and at Sidcup, he finally settled on the family property, Hill Court, at Falfield, Gloucestershire, in 1864, when he adopted the additional surname of Fust on taking over what had once been the estate of a cousin, Sir John Fust.

Jenner, best known as a cricketer, was rather generously described by Lord Harris as 'the first gentleman player in the country' (*Lord's and the MCC*). At Eton he had been captain of the eleven in 1823, when his opposite number at Harrow was Charles Wordsworth. Four years later, the two men were respectively captains of Cambridge and Oxford. A challenge from Wordsworth to Jenner led to the inauguration of the university match at Lord's in 1827. Jenner scored 47 out of Cambridge's 92 in a rain-ruined game. Fifty years later he spoke at the jubilee dinner of the match and he eventually lived to be the last survivor of the original encounter.

Jenner represented the Gentlemen against the Players

at Lord's on nine occasions between 1827 and 1836 in matches in which his team were usually allowed more players or, in 1832, defended smaller stumps. He also played for Kent over the same period. He kept wicket to Alfred Mynn recalling that 'pads were not heard of in my days and the player would be laughed at who attempted to protect his shins' (Pullin). A contemporary verse declared:

Wicket-keeper, or bowler, or batter in all
He is good, but perhaps, shines most with the ball.
(Haygarth)

In 1833 Jenner was elected the president, for the year, of the MCC at the age of twenty-seven—not unusual in an era of playing presidents. He was also president of the West Kent cricket club (1882–1904). After 1836 he often took part in local matches, proving himself an admirable captain and once making 173 runs. In 1880, at the age of seventy-four, he played for his parish of Hill in a match against Rockhampton, scoring 11 (run out by his substitute runner), and as bowler and wicket-keeper taking ten wickets. A curiosity of his life—for such an enthusiast—was his admission that he never saw W. G. Grace play, despite the fact that his son, Herbert Jenner-Fust (1841–1940), played a match with Grace for Gloucestershire in 1875. On that occasion all three Grace brothers played, making most of the runs and taking all but three of Yorkshire's wickets.

When Jenner-Fust died at Hill Court on 30 July 1904, in his ninety-ninth year, he was the oldest first-class cricketer—as was his son in his turn, who lived until his hundredth year. Father and son spanned an era from one month after the death of William Pitt the younger to the battle of Britain.

PHILIP NORMAN, rev. GERALD M. D. HOWAT

Sources [A. Haygarth], *Frederick Lillywhite's cricket scores and biographies*, 1 (1862) · *Wisden* (1898) · *Wisden* (1905) · A. W. Pullin, *Talks with old English cricketers* (1900) · Lord Harris, ed., *The history of Kent county cricket* (1907) · Lord Harris and F. S. Ashley-Cooper, *Lord's and the MCC* (1914) · P. Bailey, P. Thorn, and P. Wynne-Thomas, *Who's who of cricketers* (1984)
Likenesses F. Cox, oils, *c.*1870, Lord's, London, Marylebone Cricket Club Pavilion · photograph (after portrait), Lord's, London, Marylebone Cricket Club Library · photograph (after portrait), repro. in Harris and Ashley-Cooper, *Lord's and the MCC*
Wealth at death £43,464 3*s.* 5*d.*: probate, 9 Sept 1904, CGPLA Eng. & Wales

Fychan, Roger (d. 1415). See under Vaughan family (*per.* c.1400–c.1504).

Fychan, Simwnt [Simon Vaughan] (d. **1606**), poet, was one of the last great practitioners of the traditional bardic skills in Wales. He gave his paternal pedigree as Simwnt Fychan ap John ap Jenkin ap Hywel ab Ieuan Fychan. As his forebear was named Ieuan Fychan, it would probably be best to assume that Fychan (small, little) was Simwnt's inherited surname, although Thomas Evans, his nephew and disciple, described him in his elegy as being of small stature. In a rental for 1465 his grandfather Jenkin ap Hywel is listed as a bondman in the commote of Llannerch (which comprised the parishes of Llanfair Dyffryn Clwyd and Llanelidan).

A long-standing oral tradition claims that Simwnt resided in a house called Tŷ-brith in Llanfair. There is, however, contemporary evidence that from 1580 onwards he dwelt in a house in Ruthin on the Thelwall estate. Thomas Evans seems to confirm that Simwnt continued to live in Ruthin up to the time of his death. Although he was not of aristocratic stock on his father's side, Simwnt claimed descent on his mother's side from the princes of Powys; his mother was Jonet, daughter of Marfred. He records that his wife was Lowri, widow of Thomas ap Gruffudd of Bodliwydd in the parish of Llanelidan.

Simwnt is reputed to have been one of the pupils of the bard Gruffudd Hiraethog, and at the second Caerwys eisteddfod (bardic congress), probably held in 1567, he was one of four who gained the highest bardic degree of *pencerdd* (chief of song). Copies of his graduation certificate have been preserved (for example Thomas, facsimile facing 81). He composed a very large number of poems, most of which were eulogies and elegies to his patrons in the northern half of Wales. His datable poems show that he was a practising poet for over fifty years, from 1551 until 1603–5.

All of Simwnt's poems were written in the Welsh strict metres. One of the best-known is a biting satire on the contemporary law courts. Another unusual offering from a Welsh bard of the period was a rather free translation of Martial's epigram on the happy life (book X, epigram 47), undertaken at the request, and with the help, of his patron, Simwnt Thelwall. This, according to a current classical scholar, was 'the earliest version of a classical work put into Welsh' (Davies, 67). Simwnt's poem, together with the Latin version and an anonymous English translation, was printed as a broadside in 1571. Another popular poem by Simwnt was his ode to Pirs Mostyn, which is said to have been exhibited at the Caerwys eisteddfod. It contains examples of each of the twenty-four strict metres of Welsh prosody.

There is ample evidence that Simwnt Fychan had mastered the curriculum of the bardic schools. He left a large collection of genealogical material (Cardiff County Library, MS 4.265, and other MSS). The Cardiff manuscript also contains his version of a medieval treatise on heraldry (edited by E. J. Jones in *Medieval Heraldry*, 1942). Simwnt Fychan's grammar, 'Pum llyfr kerddwriaeth' ('Five books of prosody'), preserved in his autograph in Jesus College MS 15, is the most comprehensive of all the Welsh bardic grammars (reprinted in G. J. Williams and E. J. Jones, *Gramadegau'r penceirddiaid*, 1934, 89–142). At the end of his version of the bardic grammar Simwnt included a copy of William Salesbury's treatise on rhetoric, dated 1551, and this copy was annotated and emended by Salesbury himself.

Simwnt died on 5 April 1606 and was buried eight days later in the chancel of Llanfair Dyffryn Clwyd church. Each of his three elegists, Siôn Phylip, Edward ap Raff, and Thomas Evans, lamented the passing of a major poet and a leading authority on Welsh bardic learning.

W. GERALLT HARRIES

Sources Cardiff County Library, MS 4.265 [in the hand of Simwnt Fychan] · P. C. Bartrum, ed., *Welsh genealogies, AD 1400–1500*, 18 vols. (1983), vol. 10 · Bodl. Oxf., Jesus College MS 15 · E. J. Jones, *Medieval heraldry* (1942) · W. A. Mathias, 'Llyfr rhetoreg William Salesbury', *Llên Cymru*, 1 (1950–51), 259–68 · W. A. Mathias, 'Llyfr rhetoreg William Salesbury', *Llên Cymru*, 2 (1952–3), 71–81 · E. J. Jones, 'Martial's epigram on the happy life: Simwnt Vychan's translation', *BBCS*, 3 (1926–7), 286–97 · M. Richards, 'The lordship of Dyffryn Clwyd in 1465', *Transactions of the Denbighshire Historical Society*, 15 (1966), 15–54 · G. Thomas, *Eisteddfodau Caerwys* (1968) · C. Davies, *Welsh literature and the classical tradition* (1995) · E. ap Raff, elegy to Simwnt Fychan, NL Wales, Llanstephan MS 36, fol. 201 ff. · *DWB* · M. Stephens, ed., *The new companion to the literature of Wales*, rev. edn (1998), 680 · T. Evans, 'Elegy', *Blodeugerdd barddas o'r ail ganrif ar bymtheg*, ed. N. Lloyd (1993), 135–7 · NL Wales, Wyanstey MS 86
Archives Cardiff Central Library, MS 4.265

Fyche [Fich], **Thomas** (*d.* 1518), Augustinian canon and ecclesiastical writer, was almost certainly Irish by origin. He is said by Anthony Wood to have studied at Oxford, but is first recorded in 1468 as a canon of Holy Trinity Cathedral priory, Dublin. He was probably related to other men named Fyche who occur in connection with the churches of Dublin, notably Richard Fyche (*d.* 1482), who was receiver-general to the archbishop of Dublin, and Geoffrey Fyche, who was dean of St Patrick's when he died in 1537. Thomas Fyche was increasingly involved in the administration of his house: in 1478, for instance, he acted as Holy Trinity's proctor at a parliament held at Trim; in 1490 he made a rental for some of its properties; and in 1494 he was said to be the priory's proctor-general at an inquest into its claims to tithes of salmon from the River Liffey. By August 1503 he had become sub-prior, an office he held until his death.

It was doubtless for administrative purposes that Fyche made two compilations relating to Holy Trinity's interests and responsibilities. The so-called *Liber albus*, a collection of charters, papal bulls, leases, rentals, and other memoranda, made between November 1504 and January 1518, declares on folio 57 that 'I am the book of the cathedral church of the Holy Trinity of the city of Dublin, made by Brother Thomas Fyche, canon of the same' (Lawlor, 30). A book of obits, which also includes a list of the cathedral's relics (of particular value since these were destroyed in 1538), although it continued to receive entries until 1558, has been attributed in its original form to Fyche, on the strength of the similarity of its handwriting to that of the *Liber albus*. It records the names of benefactors going back to the twelfth century, along with members of the priory's confraternity, and also the cathedral canons. The latter include Thomas Fyche himself, who died on 17 January 1518 and was buried in the cathedral. His book of obits was published in 1844, a calendar of the *Liber albus* in 1908.

HENRY SUMMERSON

Sources H. J. Lawlor, 'A calendar of the *Liber niger* and *Liber albus* of Christ Church, Dublin', *Proceedings of the Royal Irish Academy*, 27C (1908–9), 1–93 · J. C. Crosthwaite, ed., *The book of obits and martyrology of the cathedral church … Dublin*, Irish Archaeological Society, 4 (1844) · H. F. Berry, ed., *Register of wills and inventories of the diocese of Dublin … 1457–1483* (1898) · *Report of the Deputy Keeper of the Public Records in Ireland*, 20 (1888), appx 7 [calendar to Christ Church deeds] · Emden, *Oxf.*, 2.735 · Wood, *Ath. Oxon.*, new edn, 1.21

Fyfe, Andrew (1752–1824), anatomist, was born on 30 August 1752 and baptized on 6 September 1752, at Corstorphine, near Edinburgh, the second son of John Fyfe, tenant there, and Agnes Alexander, his wife, who had married at Corstorphine in 1750. Fyfe served a surgical apprenticeship with a Mr Anderson and a number of matriculations in medicine in the archives of the University of Edinburgh suggest that he took classes in medical subjects in the academic sessions of 1775, 1776, 1779, 1780, and 1781 but did not take a degree. Fyfe was a talented artist and won a medal in 1775 for the best drawing in the academy for improvements in Scotland. He succeeded John Innes about 1777 as principal janitor and macer in the university, a post then usually held by a student, which provided free living quarters. He was appointed dissector jointly with Innes in the same year. Innes died shortly afterwards, and Fyfe remained in the triple post for forty years. Anatomy was a compulsory subject within the medical curriculum, so that Fyfe, who served under Professor Alexander Monro Secundus, and then his son Alexander Monro Tertius, must have known many of the luminaries of eighteenth- and nineteenth-century medicine, both as teachers and as students. Sir Astley Cooper, a student in 1777–8, said:

> Fyfe I attended, and learned much from him. He was a horrid lecturer, but an industrious, worthy man, and good practical anatomist. His lecture was, 'I say—eh, eh, eh, gentlemen; eh, eh, eh, gentlemen—I say, etc.;' whilst the tallow from a naked candle he held in his hand ran over the back of it and over his clothes: but his drawings and depictions were well made and very useful. (Cooper, 172)

Sir Robert Christison, who attended in 1815–16, remembered the 'prosector', 'one of the last in Edinburgh to wear the pigtail', every afternoon going over what every student had done with his dissected part. 'Duty over, we all gathered round him at the fireside, where he entertained us with anecdotes of the departed medical worthies who had adorned the University in his day' (*Life*, 68).

Fyfe married, on 19 October 1787, Agnes Ord Williamson, daughter of the late principal gardener at the university's botanic garden, and was described as 'surgeon' in the register. At least five sons and one daughter were baptized to the couple, another three children dying in infancy. Following the example of his predecessor, John Innes, Fyfe began to work on a series of anatomical textbooks. *A System of Anatomy and Physiology* was published in 1784, with the approbation of Alexander Monro Secundus. It contained many illustrations by Fyfe and was amended in several subsequent editions to suit the needs of students, and to save them expense. *A Compendium of the Anatomy of the Human Body* appeared in two volumes in 1800, and was improved in later editions; the seventh edition included directions for dissecting the different parts of the human body.

It is not known when Fyfe's appointment terminated, but his ceasing to teach or dissect in the university must have been a staggered event, as he is reported as teaching well after 1815, and Monro Secundus's death in 1817 brought a new superintendent of the university dissecting rooms. Fyfe had also acted as curator of a collection of anatomical figures given to the university by Monro Secundus in 1800, and which became the subject of some debate in 1813, when it was found to be in disorder. Fyfe was admitted a fellow of the College of Surgeons of Edinburgh on 23 October 1818. He was occupied until his death with numerous improved editions of his works. Fyfe died in Edinburgh on 31 March 1824. The consensus of opinion of the medical journals of his day was expressed by the *Edinburgh Medical and Surgical Journal*: 'In this country it is impossible to number any other works professedly systematic than the matter-of-fact volumes of Fife, the work of John and Charles Bell, and the *Outlines* of Dr Monro' (24, 1825). Four of Fyfe's sons followed him into the medical profession, including his namesake, Andrew *Fyfe (1792–1861), professor of chemistry at Aberdeen.

JO CURRIE

Sources parish register, Corstorphine, 1750, General Register Office for Scotland, Edinburgh · matriculation records, U. Edin. L., special collections division, university archives · A. Grant, *The story of the University of Edinburgh during its first three hundred years*, 2 (1884), 389 · A. G. Fraser, *The building of Old College: Adam, Playfair, and the University of Edinburgh* (1989), 234, 241 · B. B. Cooper, *The life of Sir Astley Cooper*, 2 vols. (1843) · *The life of Sir Robert Christison*, 2 vols. (1885–6) · private information (2004) · *Edinburgh Medical and Surgical Journal*, 24 (1825)

Fyfe, Andrew (1792–1861), chemist, was born, probably in Edinburgh, on 18 January 1792, the eldest son of Andrew *Fyfe (1752–1824), dissector in anatomy at the University of Edinburgh, and his wife, Agnes Ord Williamson. He graduated MD from that university in 1814, and he was elected fellow of the Royal College of Surgeons of Edinburgh in 1818 (he was also president in 1842–3) and fellow of the Royal Society of Edinburgh in 1823. Despite this recognition, for thirty years Fyfe could earn only a precarious living as an extramural private teacher of practical chemistry in Edinburgh. Several young chemists who were later to occupy established chairs had to start in this way; that it was possible for them to make a living at all arose from the popularity of Thomas Charles Hope's chemistry classes at the university, together with Hope's unwillingness to give practical instruction himself and his opposition for many years to the appointment of an official university instructor, which might have reduced his own income.

During these years Fyfe published a successful (albeit rather old-fashioned) *Elements of Chemistry* (3 edns, 1827–33), whose subtitle, ending 'for the use of pupils of mechanics' institutions', pointed to the new market he was trying to tap. He also wrote some twenty journal papers in experimental chemistry, mostly concerned with the illuminating power of coal gas and the heat obtainable from different coals. His utilitarian emphasis can hardly have helped his academic ambitions, for 'pure' chemistry was becoming increasingly the fashion in universities, following the lead of Justus Liebig in Germany. Fyfe was an unsuccessful candidate for the chair of materia medica at Edinburgh in 1832, and again for the chair of chemistry in 1844. The successful candidate, William Gregory, an

ex-student of Liebig's, left vacant the post of mediciner at King's College, Aberdeen (a post dating from the university's foundation in 1495, and later devoted to the teaching of chemistry); this Fyfe managed to obtain.

In his inaugural lecture at Aberdeen, as reported in the local press, Fyfe certainly caught the new mood:

> The doctor ... inculcated upon the minds of the students the duty of endeavouring to be something more than mere practitioners—to enter upon their scientific studies as an expansive field for philosophical research and reflection, rather than with views merely professional; and thus ... become better and more enlightened men. (*Aberdeen Journal*, 20 Nov 1844)

However, it is not known if he lived up to his own expectations, since no notes survive from his lectures (in itself, perhaps, a measure of ordinariness). His obituarist in Aberdeen noted his pre-eminence in the chemistry of coal, clearly a continuing preoccupation, and recorded how 'In private life Dr Fyfe was much esteemed for his genial kindly character and Christian worth' (*Aberdeen Journal*, 8 Jan 1862). When the two universities of Aberdeen were merged in 1860, Fyfe was chosen as the one professor of chemistry to continue. However, his health failed almost immediately, and for the last fifteen months of his life his class was taught by a substitute.

Fyfe was married twice: first to Eliza Charles, and second to Margaret Johnstone. The first marriage produced a daughter, the second a son, who became a physician. He died on the last day of 1861, at his home, 4 Windsor Street, Edinburgh, and was buried at the city's new Calton cemetery.

In retrospect, Fyfe's most intriguing work lay in early photography. Shortly after Fox Talbot's first announcement of paper negative photographs in 1839, Fyfe read a short series of papers before the Society of Arts for Scotland, in which he examined the chemistry of Talbot's process. He went on to show that positive prints were possible: paper soaked in silver phosphate solution blackens with exposure to light, owing to the deposition of metallic silver. If this is further soaked in potassium iodide solution and selectively exposed to light, the silver redissolves where the light strikes, giving a positive print. Fyfe himself only took images of ferns on the paper (technically 'heliographs') and investigated the possibilities of reproducing engravings, but he does have a claim as an inventor of positive photographic prints. However, since he did not pursue these researches, he remains little more than a footnote in the history of photography.

NICHOLAS FISHER

Sources A. Findlay, *The teaching of chemistry in the universities of Aberdeen* (1935) · R. G. W. Anderson, *The Playfair collection and the teaching of chemistry at the University of Edinburgh, 1713–1858* (1978) · H. Gernsheim and A. Gernsheim, *The history of photography* (1955) · *Aberdeen Journal* (20 Nov 1844) · *Aberdeen Journal* (8 Jan 1862) · *Catalogue of scientific papers*, Royal Society, 2 (1867), 748–9 · DNB
Likenesses photograph, repro. in Findlay, *The teaching of chemistry*, facing p. 58

Fyfe, David Patrick Maxwell, earl of Kilmuir (1900–1967), politician and lawyer, was born on 29 May 1900 at 60 Morningside Drive, Edinburgh, the only child by his

David Patrick Maxwell Fyfe, earl of Kilmuir (1900–1967), by Elliott & Fry, 1954

second marriage to Isabella Campbell (b. c.1860), a schoolteacher, of William Thomson Fyfe (b. c.1857), an inspector of schools, former headmaster, and author. Sir Cleveland Fyfe (1888–1959), general secretary of the National Farmers' Union (1932–44) was his half-brother. He was educated at George Watson's College before going up to Balliol College, Oxford, in the autumn of 1917. At Oxford his priorities were, by his own later admission, first Conservatism, second the union, third his studies, and fourth sufficient athletic activity to maintain his fitness. In the circumstances it was not entirely surprising that he secured only a third in Greats in 1921.

Liverpool lawyer and MP After coming down from Oxford Maxwell Fyfe began work for the British Commonwealth Union, whose main function was to carry out the parliamentary work of the Federation of British Industries. This involved acting as a political secretary to Sir Patrick Hannon MP. In his spare time he studied law and was called to the bar at Gray's Inn in June 1922, joining the Liverpool chambers of George Lynskey. He married on 15 April 1925 Sylvia Margaret (d. 1992), daughter of William Reginald Harrison, a civil engineer from Liverpool, and sister of the actor Rex Harrison [see Harrison, Reginald Carey]. They had three daughters. He became a bencher (1936) and treasurer (1949) of Gray's Inn.

But Maxwell Fyfe was already committed to combining his legal work with a political career. Many years later it was revealed that he had set himself the ambition of taking silk in his thirties, becoming a government minister in

his forties, and reaching the top of the legal profession in his fifties. He contested the hopeless seat of Wigan in the Conservative interest in the general election of 1924. By 1927 he had been adopted for the more promising Spen Valley division in Yorkshire, and he nursed this constituency until 1929 when he was obliged to withdraw as the Conservatives agreed to allow the sitting Liberal, Sir John Simon, a free run in view of his long-term absence as head of the statutory commission on India. Finally, he was returned unopposed for the West Derby division of Liverpool in a by-election in July 1935, at a time when working-class Conservatism remained strong in that city. He successfully defended the seat in the general election later that year. In the meantime his legal career continued to prosper. He took silk in February 1934 and served as recorder of Oldham from 1936 to 1942.

Along with Patrick Spens and Derrick Gunston, Maxwell Fyfe joined a ginger group of about a dozen back-benchers which was intended to offer support to the National Government in the wake of the Hoare–Laval crisis of December 1935. He also endorsed Neville Chamberlain's settlement of the Czechoslovakian problem at the Munich conference of September 1938. When Hitler marched into Prague in March 1939 he joined the Army Officers' Emergency Reserve, but at the outbreak of war six months later he was sent by the army to the judge-advocate-general's department. In September 1940 he was badly injured when the car in which he was travelling was hit during an air raid.

Nevertheless, it was an indication of the high regard Maxwell Fyfe already enjoyed inside the Conservative Party that when, in May 1941, R. A. Butler was invited to chair the party's central committee on post-war problems, Maxwell Fyfe was appointed as his deputy. By July 1943 Butler had resigned to focus on his work at the Board of Education and Maxwell Fyfe took his place as chairman, although by then the work of the committee had been downgraded and in any case his own interests were more in the area of devising party propaganda than in creating policy.

Law officer and Nuremberg prosecutor Meanwhile, in March 1942, Churchill, at the prompting of Brendan Bracken, had appointed Maxwell Fyfe solicitor-general. He was also knighted and made a privy councillor. It was at this stage of his career that his enormous industry and apparently insatiable appetite for paperwork first became apparent. One of his last but most significant acts in the coalition government was to assist William Jowitt to introduce the Children's Allowance Bill. In Churchill's caretaker government, formed when the Labour and Liberal parties withdrew from the coalition in May 1945, he served briefly as attorney-general.

The Labour Party swept to power in the July 1945 general election, but this event did not immediately interrupt Maxwell Fyfe's period of public service. As solicitor-general he had been involved from the beginning in discussions as to the procedure to be adopted for trying war criminals at the end of hostilities. As the new Labour attorney-general, Sir Hartley Shawcross, now designated the chief British prosecutor, wished to emphasize that the activities at Nuremberg had no party political implications, he invited Maxwell Fyfe to serve as his deputy. In practice, Shawcross's political duties in London largely excluded him from the trials and he came to Nuremberg only to deliver the opening and closing speeches of the British prosecution. Maxwell Fyfe thus became the day-to-day head of the British legal team, while also being in charge of all British personnel at Nuremberg. In this way he combined the roles of 'capable lawyer, efficient administrator and concerned housemaster' (Tusa and Tusa, 136).

Maxwell Fyfe's appointment occasioned some misgivings. He was not regarded as among the most brilliant cross-examiners of the English bar. But he made up for any lack of talent through sheer hard work and by making sure that he was always fully prepared when confronting the accused. His cross-examination of Goering, who had scored heavily in his verbal exchanges with the American prosecutor Robert Jackson, and who Maxwell Fyfe later conceded was the ablest man he had ever interrogated, was one of the highlights of the trial. 'Faced with sustained and methodical competence rather than brilliance, Goering … crumbled' (Tusa and Tusa, 287). His overall performance at Nuremberg, his conscientiousness, and his commitment to fair play, won the confidence of the various allied teams as well as the respect of the German defence lawyers. It was one of the high points of his career.

Conservative Party after 1945 Returning to England, Maxwell Fyfe began to advance through the depleted ranks of the parliamentary Conservative Party. His stamina was extraordinary. During the years of opposition he enjoyed a full-time career at the bar, where his average annual earnings were in excess of £25,000. He usually arrived at the Commons at about 5 p.m. and would regularly stay through all-night sittings. Between December 1946 and June 1947 he made 178 Commons speeches on the government's Transport Bill. As one newly elected MP recalled, 'I often saw him, quickly shaved and breakfasted, going from the House straight on into Court. He spoke incessantly in the country, and did everything he was asked by the Party' (J. Boyd-Carpenter, *Way of Life*, 1980, 261). 'He is the blue-eyed boy of our Party and is unquestionably very able', noted another (Cuthbert Headlam) of longer experience, in 1947. 'I like him personally and hope that he will be as successful as people expect him to be and he intends' (Ball, 502–3). In sustaining this prodigious workload Maxwell Fyfe was greatly assisted by his wife, who herself became active in Conservative politics, emerging as a competent public speaker; she was invited to become a party vice-chairman in 1950, and was created DBE in 1957.

As a member of the industrial policy committee set up in the autumn of 1946, Maxwell Fyfe played an important part in drafting the industrial charter. He is perhaps best remembered for chairing a committee of inquiry into the Conservative Party organization, though his input was very limited. What became known as the Maxwell Fyfe

report was presented in two parts, in October 1948 and July 1949. The report ended the payment of electoral expenses by candidates and MPs, while limiting their contributions to £25 for the former and £50 for the latter. The clear intention was to broaden the social basis of any future intake of Conservative MPs, and the report has often been represented as a landmark in the democratization of the party. In practice, however, its impact was far less dramatic, not least because in encouraging constituency selection committees to follow their own instincts it probably made the parliamentary party of the following generation less rather than more representative of the nation as a whole. Certainly, the hope that there might now emerge a substantial body of working-class Conservative MPs remained unfulfilled.

Maxwell Fyfe's other great interest in this period was the movement towards European integration. In 1947 he accepted Churchill's invitation to join the committee of the united European movement and, as a member of the assembly of the Council of Europe, he was closely involved in drawing up the European convention on human rights. When he came to write his memoirs he claimed that his own enthusiasm for British involvement in the European movement, and therefore any chance of British leadership of that movement, had been thwarted in the first weeks of the new Conservative government by a negative statement from Eden in Rome on 28 November 1951. Eden contemplated legal action, and Maxwell Fyfe certainly seems to have exaggerated the polarization of opinion within Churchill's cabinet.

Home secretary and lord chancellor Having shadowed the Ministry of Labour during the years of opposition and made a study of industrial relations in other countries, Maxwell Fyfe was widely expected to receive this portfolio in a future Conservative government. An injudicious remark during a radio broadcast in September 1951, however, in which he appeared not to rule out the possibility of legislation caused uproar in the ranks of the unions and seems to have caused Churchill to change his plans. When, therefore, the party returned to office that October, he was made home secretary. His tenure was not a period of conspicuous reform, but he piloted several complicated measures through the Commons, including the introduction of commercial television. In the words of its historian, 'if anyone deserves the title of hero of the enterprise, it must surely be he', for he 'had the commanding role in Parliament. He was at the height of his reputation and displayed at all times a cool, articulate competence' (Sendall, 36). 'He was so useful in the House of Commons,' commented Churchill, 'where he was most industrious' (Moran, 605). His reputation developed as an able and reliable debater and as a hard-working member of cabinet committees. He was believed to have handled the problems caused by the east coast floods of January 1953 with efficiency and sensitivity, though his refusal in the same month to reprieve the convicted murderer Derek Bentley caused great controversy. On most issues he was on the progressive wing of his party and he opposed the re-introduction of corporal punishment during discussion of the Criminal Justice (Amendment) Bill of 1953. His Home Office duties included responsibility for Wales, which he visited regularly, though few policy initiatives resulted.

Maxwell Fyfe may at one time have wanted to rise even higher in Conservative politics. A *Daily Mirror* poll published in the summer of 1954 suggested that he was third favourite to succeed Churchill, behind Eden and Butler but significantly ahead of Macmillan. But as Eden's succession became increasingly inevitable his ambitions turned to the woolsack and he succeeded Lord Simonds as lord chancellor in the reshuffle of October 1954, taking the title of Viscount Kilmuir, the name of a village east of Invergordon near where his mother was born. As lord chancellor he remained, unlike his predecessor, very much a political figure, and he was given a large amount of cabinet work outside his specific departmental brief. In the autumn of 1955, for example, he chaired a round table conference on the constitutional future of Malta, which proposed that the island should be treated as an integral part of the United Kingdom. In the following year he was involved with the president of the Board of Trade in setting up the restrictive practices court. He had published a short book on monopolies and restrictive practices eight years earlier.

The question of capital punishment remained prominent, with Kilmuir opposing Sidney Silverman's private member's bill to abolish the death penalty in the summer of 1956. It was, he said, 'an unwise and dangerous measure, the presence of which on the statute book would be a disaster for the country and a menace to the people' (*House of Lords Debates*, vol. 198, col. 586). Nevertheless, a cabinet committee under his chairmanship recommended limited abolition and led to the Homicide Act of 1957. Immigration was another issue to engage his attention. His report, presented to the cabinet in July 1956 but not implemented, warned of the progressively serious implications of uncontrolled immigration and called for restrictive legislation for the whole Commonwealth. His legal opinions were still valued, especially when, in the wake of Colonel Nasser's nationalization of the Suez Canal Company in July 1956, he sought to justify the use of force on the grounds of self-defence under article 51 of the United Nations charter.

Kilmuir undertook no major reconstruction of the legal system during his time on the woolsack, though the Occupiers' Liability Act (1957), the Tribunal and Inquiries Act (1958), and the Law Reform (Husband and Wife) Act (1962) brought about useful reforms. During his eight years as lord chancellor he sat in only twenty-four appeals to the House of Lords, emphasizing the still largely political role which he played in the Eden and Macmillan governments. High office brought traditional honours. He was awarded the knight grand cross in the Royal Victorian Order in the coronation honours list of 1953, and received honorary degrees from an array of universities, including those of Oxford, Manitoba, Edinburgh, and Wales. He was installed as rector of St Andrews in April 1956 and became visitor of St Antony's College in 1953.

Termination of political career Kilmuir's ministerial career came to an end in controversial circumstances. By the early 1960s Macmillan's government was declining rapidly in public esteem and, in a move apparently designed to reinvigorate a tired administration but which smacked unmistakably of panic, the prime minister dismissed a third of his cabinet in the infamous 'night of the long knives' on 12–13 July 1962. Kilmuir was one of the victims who believed that he had been misled and badly treated. He had in fact indicated his willingness to stand down but had anticipated that any change would not come until well into 1963. Indeed, Macmillan had already said that government business commitments early in the new year would rule out the absence abroad for which he had requested permission. The ruthlessness of Macmillan's actions clearly hurt the lord chancellor, who complained to friends that his cook would have been given more notice than he had received. An earldom did little to assuage him. Ironically, he had recently told a political researcher that 'loyalty was the tories' secret weapon', a phrase which, despite repeated evidence to the contrary, still enjoys common currency. In later years Macmillan suggested that Kilmuir, saddened by the effective breakdown of his marriage, had become a liability to the government and 'hopeless in Cabinet' (Horne, 346). But there is little evidence for this assertion. Kilmuir was only sixty-two.

After leaving office Kilmuir caused some surprise by accepting appointment to the board of Plesseys, an unusual step for a former lord chancellor. His memoirs, *Political Adventure*, were published in 1964. He made only occasional speeches in the Lords and his health soon began to decline. He died at Hardings, Withyham, Sussex, on 27 January 1967. He was cremated and his ashes were buried at the church of St Michael and All Angels, Withyham. One of his daughters had predeceased him. His widow married in 1968 Herbrand Edward Dundonald Brassey *Sackville, ninth Earl De La Warr.

Kilmuir was not among the great lord chancellors of recent history, but his political career was important and he developed into one of the Conservative Party's most formidable parliamentary performers. His appearance has been described as 'unusual for a man seeking advancement on the Tory political ladder' in the mid-twentieth century: 'His body was pear-shaped, and beneath a large square bald head there were dark heavy eyebrows and a face of middle-eastern pallor and swarthiness' (*DNB*). But he employed his talents, including a prodigious memory, to the full. His speaking style was sometimes considered dull, but he was capable of considerable passion. One spontaneous attack on Lord Salisbury, in defence of Iain Macleod (7 March 1961), silenced and awed the House of Lords. Above all he will be remembered for his part in conducting the Nuremberg trials and in preparing the European convention on human rights.

D. J. DUTTON

Sources R. F. V. Heuston, *Lives of the lord chancellors, 1940–1970* (1987) • Lord Kilmuir, *Political adventure* (1964) • *The Times* (28 Jan

1967) · *DNB* · A. Tusa and J. Tusa, *The Nuremberg trial* (1983) · A. Seldon, *Churchill's Indian summer* (1981) · J. Ramsden, *The age of Churchill and Eden, 1940–1957* (1995) · *The Guardian* (28 Jan 1967) · *Parliament and politics in the age of Churchill and Attlee: the Headlam diaries, 1935–1951*, ed. S. Ball, CS, 5th ser., 14 (1999) · B. Sendall, *Independent television in Britain*, vol. 1: *Origin and foundation, 1946–62* (1982) · Lord Moran, *Winston Churchill: the struggle for survival* (1966) · K. Alderman, 'Harold Macmillan's "Night of the long knives"', *Contemporary Record* (1992) · A. Horne, *Macmillan*, 2: *1957–1986* (1989)

Archives CAC Cam., diaries, speeches, corresp., and papers | Bodl. Oxf., conservative party archives · Bodl. Oxf., letters to A. L. Goodhart · Bodl. Oxf., corresp. with Lord Monckton · CUL, corresp. with Sir Samuel Hoare · NL Wales, corresp. with Huw T. Edwards

Likenesses W. Stoneman, photograph, 1946, NPG · Elliott & Fry, photograph, 1954, NPG [*see illus.*] · W. Bird, photograph, 1962, NPG · A. C. Davidson-Houston, portrait, St Ant. Oxf. · S. Elwes, portrait, Gray's Inn, London · H. Knight, portrait, priv. coll. · L. Knight, pastels, IWM · C. Sanders, portrait, Balliol Oxf.

Wealth at death £22,202: probate, 5 April 1967, *CGPLA Eng. & Wales*

Fyfe, Henry Hamilton (1869–1951), writer, was born in London on 28 September 1869, the eldest of the three sons of James Hamilton Fyfe (1837–1880), barrister and journalist, and his wife, Mary Elizabeth Jonas. Sir William Hamilton *Fyfe was his younger brother. He was educated at Fettes College, Edinburgh. At seventeen he joined the staff of *The Times*, where his father had earlier served as a parliamentary correspondent. Fyfe was employed as a reporter, then sub-editor, contributing occasional reviews and dramatic criticism. Finally, he was appointed secretary to the editor, G. E. Buckle.

In 1902 Fyfe was appointed editor of the *Morning Advertiser*, the long-established newspaper of the Licensed Victuallers' Association. Unfortunately his efforts to refurbish the paper's image did not please the proprietors, whose only real interest was to improve the sales of beer. The unavailing efforts of the young editor had been noticed by Alfred Harmsworth (later Lord Northcliffe), who had been impressed. In 1903 he invited Fyfe to take over editorship of his recently launched *Daily Mirror*. Designed to attract mainly women readers, and edited by a woman, Mary Howarth, the *Mirror*'s circulation had plummeted disastrously. Fyfe soon set the *Daily Mirror* upon its path to unprecedented popularity and profitability, sacking most of the existing staff and exploiting the latest innovations and improvements in print technology. Within four months he had turned the *Mirror* around and transformed it into the first halfpenny, newspicture daily.

In 1907, the year of his marriage to Eleanor, daughter of William Kelly of the War Office, Fyfe transferred from the *Daily Mirror* to the *Daily Mail*. There he was to distinguish himself as an outstanding reporter. He had considerable affection as well as admiration for Northcliffe. They shared an enthusiasm for pioneer aviation. Fyfe wrote memorably of the first channel crossing by Louis Blériot in 1909, and the exciting contest between Claude Graham White and Louis Paulhan in 1910, to be the first to fly 200 miles. He was amused by Northcliffe's various stunts designed to promote the sales of the *Daily Mail*. He was amazed to discover that George Curnock, responsible for running most of Northcliffe's campaigns, actually believed in the supposed merits of 'standard' bread. Perhaps it was as well for his continued good relations with Northcliffe that Fyfe spent most of his time 'scouring the world in search of picturesque copy' (Clarke, 44). In 1911 he paid his first visit to Russia; in 1913, on behalf of *The Times*, now owned by Northcliffe, he was sent to Mexico to report the Carranza revolution. Wherever there was a trouble-spot in the world, he was dispatched there to file a report. From Mexico he went to Ulster, only almost immediately to be sent to France in August 1914.

Despite the difficulties imposed upon all journalists by the military censorship, within three weeks Fyfe secured a memorable success with his account of the retreat from Mons. He honestly prefaced his unvarnished description of a totally unexpected British military defeat with the reluctant avowal, 'Would to God I had not to tell this story' (*Daily Mail*, 24 Aug 1914). His story's impact was made greater by the censor's erasures and amendments which suggested that even more dire intelligence had been suppressed.

In 1915 Fyfe was transferred from the western to the eastern front. He travelled from Petrograd through Galicia to Bucharest. Back in Russia in 1916, he reported Rasputin's murder. His journeyings continued in 1917; he had to report successively from Spain, Portugal, and Italy before his appointment as an honorary attaché to Northcliffe's war mission brought him to the United States of America. His post amounted to being Northcliffe's major-domo, a title that Fyfe would certainly have resented. In July 1918 he accepted a much more important appointment, replacing H. G. Wells at Crewe House, where he made his contribution to the British propaganda campaign in enemy territories.

Fyfe's political sympathies were broadly left-wing. He had greeted the emergence of an independent Parliamentary Labour Party in a *Daily Mirror* editorial that hailed socialism as 'the philosophy of the future' (Cudlipp, 38). As Northcliffe's and Fyfe's political sympathies were diametrically opposed, there were increasing tensions in their relationship, exacerbated by the press magnate's violent changes of mood. Yet Fyfe always admired and liked Northcliffe, whereas for Rothermere he had little respect and less affection.

In 1922 Fyfe accepted the editorship of the *Daily Herald*. Arthur Henderson, the one leading Labour figure convinced that his party required a national newspaper constantly to promote its views, had offered a three-year contract together with the promise of a free hand. Fyfe stayed for four years, almost quadrupling the *Herald*'s circulation from 120,000 to 450,000 copies. But from the first there were difficulties in reconciling editorial demands with the aspirations of an editorial board dominated by Trades Union Congress members with neither knowledge, interest, nor understanding of running a national newspaper. His urbanity and invariable cheerfulness were tested beyond endurance by his board members, who were 'foolish and silly … an hindrance rather than a help' (Fyfe, *Sixty*

Years, 193–4). Shortly after the general strike of 1926, during which he had edited the trade union paper the *British Worker*, he resigned and joined the Liberal *Daily Chronicle*. He left in 1930, when the *Chronicle* was amalgamated with the *Daily News*. He was angry and dispirited by changes in the press, especially the 'murder' of the *Daily Chronicle*. He saw the *Chronicle*'s closure, described by the proprietors as 'rationalization', as symptomatic of a revolution in Fleet Street, where business interests increasingly took precedence over newspapermen's values. He continued to make freelance contributions to newspapers, particularly *Reynolds News*, but increasingly he devoted his time to independent authorship and working for the Labour Party. Twice he stood unsuccessfully for parliament in hopeless constituencies: at Sevenoaks in 1929, and at Yeovil in 1931.

An unusually versatile writer, Fyfe, in addition to his journalism, regularly produced novels, plays, travel books, contemporary political studies, biographies, and a number of engaging volumes of reminiscences. His style was clear and uncluttered, he was very well informed, and his judgements were thoughtful and delivered without fear or favour. As an editor he was skilled and versatile. Though he was unusually even-tempered, inefficiency would arouse his impatience. He had a deep aversion to pomposity, and because he supposed the name Henry pretentious, insisted upon being called Harry. As he grew older, he grew increasingly hostile to any form of established authority. He cultivated a vision of himself as a rebel to the left of labour. Certainly there was nothing he enjoyed more than twigging Labour Party leaders about 'the dangers of relishing the privileges you were elected to destroy' ('The house of Rimmon', *Socialist Review*, 24; quoted in C. A. Cline, *Recruits to Labour*, 1963, 117).

Fyfe's writing for the stage included *A Modern Aspasia*, produced first in 1909 to wide critical acclaim; *The Pool* (1912); *The Borstal Boy* (1913); and *The Kingdom, the Power and the Glory* (1920). He wrote biographical studies of a playwright, *Arthur Wing Pinero* (1902); of a young colleague at the *Daily Mail*, *Twells Brex* (1920); and an intimate portrait, *Northcliffe* (1930); his admirable study *T. P. O'Connor* (1934) was a panegyric also to the old Fleet Street ways and men. The changing scenes and personalities of his professional life he captured admirably in his *Sixty Years of Fleet Street* (1949), part memoir, part history, with a dash of polemic to add savour.

Fyfe's great hobby was gardening. Such was his enthusiasm and almost obsessive passion, on several occasions he moved house just for the pleasure of constructing a new garden. He died at the Berrow Nursing Home, Carew Road, Eastbourne, Sussex, on 15 June 1951. He had no children.

H. B. Grimsditch, rev. A. J. A. Morris

Sources H. H. Fyfe, *My seven selves* (1935) · H. H. Fyfe, *Sixty years of Fleet Street* (1949) · *The Times* (19 June 1951) · *WW* · S. E. Koss, *The rise and fall of the political press in Britain*, 2 (1984) · R. Pound and G. Harmsworth, *Northcliffe* (1959) · T. Clarke, *My Northcliffe diary* (1931) · H. H. Fyfe, *Northcliffe: an intimate biography* (1930) · H. Cudlipp, *Publish and be damned! The astonishing story of the 'Daily Mirror'* (1953) · *CGPLA Eng. & Wales* (1951)

Archives BL, corresp. with Lord Northcliffe, Add. MS 62206 · BL, corresp. with Society of Authors, Add. MS 63244 · Ransom HRC, Garvin MSS, corresp. with J. L. Garvin
Wealth at death £29,039 8s. 2d.: probate, 6 Oct 1951, *CGPLA Eng. & Wales*

Fyfe, John (1830–1906), granite quarry master, was born at Goodhope, Bucksburn, Aberdeenshire, the eldest son of James Fyfe (d. 1846), quarry master, and his wife, Elizabeth Strachan. The region had for over two centuries been associated with the extraction of granite, and quarrying reached its peak in the latter half of the nineteenth century, when John Fyfe was the dominant figure. Fyfe was educated at the local school until he was sixteen, when he had to take over the family business following the death of his father. He continued operations at Newhills until 1857 when he moved to Kemnay and opened two adjacent workings on Paradise Hill, on land belonging to John Burnett. It had long been known that good surface deposits of granite abounded in the Kemnay area, but until the advent of the Great North of Scotland Railway into the Alford valley, the cost of extracting this stone and then transporting it by cart or even canal to Aberdeen made it uneconomic to quarry so far from an immediate market. Fyfe quickly secured an agreement with the railway company for transporting stone to Aberdeen, and, as the railway extended its network further into the Alford valley, he subsequently opened workings at Tom's Forest, Tillyfourie, and Corrennie on the outlying hills of the Grampians.

Fyfe's quarrying empire grew quickly and, while continuing to exert a high level of managerial control over his business, he was nevertheless forced to delegate the daily operations of his workings to foremen and quarry managers, the latter being recruited from the former. Fyfe's primary contribution to quarrying lay in developing the technology involved. Efficiency in granite quarrying depends very much on the speed at which stone can be blasted from the master joints, broken down, and then lifted to the quarry surface. Delays at any of these stages could (and still does) hinder a working's productivity. Fyfe's innovations had a positive impact on all these processes. Until the 1860s it was normal to drill blast-holes using hand drills—a long, slow, physically laborious process; rock penetration would typically average 4 feet a day. Fyfe replaced hand drilling with steam-power drilling both for boring the blast-holes and for breaking up large blocks of stone. Once broken, the granite was raised to the quarry loading banks with steam-powered cranes but, because of their fixed jibs, their range and lifting power were limited. This problem was partially overcome by Fyfe through the introduction of the Scotch steam derrick with its movable jib, but the need for greater speed still remained. It was said that after watching a display of tight-rope walking by the most famous of all tight-rope walkers, Charles Blondin (1824–1897), in 1872, Fyfe invented the 'Blondin', a suspension cableway with a travelling carriage that could be lowered to any part of the quarry from a fixed position. This new machine quickly proved its worth as the quarries became deeper, as it reduced the time taken to raise stone from the quarry floors from as much as an hour to a matter of minutes.

An equally important contribution to the growth of his operations was Fyfe's ability to attract and retain his labourers. Besides recruiting workers from the local agricultural labour force, he enticed skilled men from Aberdeen by offering them high wages and cheap building stone to enable them to build their own houses in Kemnay village. At the more distant Corrennie quarries he built blocks of tenement flats, known as barracks. As an employer he was generally regarded as being firm but approachable. By the end of the century, Fyfe ran the largest single firm in the industry, employing almost 600 men, and producing almost 100,000 tons of stone per annum. Fyfe was also extremely active within the industry as a whole, serving on the committees of both the Aberdeen Granite Quarrymasters' Association and the Aberdeen Granite Manufacturers' Association. He became a director of the Aberdeen Lime Company and the local branch of the London and Lancashire Insurance Company, and was a partner in another nineteen firms in the north-east.

Fyfe was married to Barbara Stevenson, daughter of the grocer in Dalmadilly, Aberdeenshire; they had two sons and eight daughters. In his public life he served as a magistrate, and was a member of Aberdeen University's building committee as well as being a significant figure in the city's business life. An 'In memoriam' in the *Aberdeen Free Press* said after Fyfe's death:

> Aberdeen itself owes Mr Fyfe a lasting debt of gratitude, not only for the distinct lead he has consistently given in fostering the artistic development of architecture in granite work, but for his public-spirited generosity in making it possible on more than one occasion to retain inviolate the most striking aspect of Aberdeen as the Granite City. (*John Fyfe*, not paginated)

Fyfe died of heart failure and Bright's disease at his home, Beechgrove House, King's Gate, Aberdeen, on 18 July 1906; his wife had predeceased him. His business was continued by his two sons.   THOMAS DONNELLY

Sources T. Donnelly, 'The development of the Aberdeen granite industry, 1750–1939', PhD diss., U. Aberdeen, 1975 • W. Diack, *The rise and progress of the Aberdeen granite industry* (1948) • G. Harris, *Granite and our granite industries* (1886) • 'Kemnay Quarries', *The Builder*, 23 (1865), 852 • *DSBB* • *John Fyfe: one hundred and fifty years, 1846–1996* (1996)
Likenesses J. S. Sargent, portrait, City of Aberdeen Art Gallery

Fyfe, William Baxter Collier (*c.*1836–1882), painter, was born in Dundee and was brought up in the nearby village of Carnoustie. Although discouraged by his family, at the age of fifteen he entered the Royal Scottish Academy, where he was awarded prizes for his crayon portraits. He studied in Paris from 1857 to 1858. His first important picture, *Scene in Loch Leven Castle—Queen Mary Compelled by the Nobles to Resign her Crown*, was shown at the Royal Scottish Academy in 1861. After spending a year in France, Italy, and Belgium, he settled in London, but passed most of his summers in Scotland.

The Death of John Brown of Priesthill and *Jeanie Deans and the Laird o'Dumbiedykes* attracted attention, and in 1866 Fyfe began to show at the Royal Academy, exhibiting twenty-six pictures in all, including *A Girl of the Period* (which became very popular), *On Household Cares Intent*, and *What can a Young Lassie Dae wi' an Auld Man?*. Several of his paintings were engraved and appeared in the illustrated newspapers in Europe and the United States, and even Asia. About 1874 he returned to Italy and painted several Italian subjects. His best-known later works included *A Good Catholic*, *Wandering Minstrels*, *The Love Letter*, *A Quiet Christmas*, *The Fisherman's Daughter*, and *A Chelsea Pensioner*. *The Raid of Ruthven*, his most important historical picture, was exhibited at the Royal Academy in 1878, and afterwards at the Royal Scottish Academy. Among his portraits are those of the earl and countess of Dufferin, Lord Houghton, Peter Lorimer, first principal of the English Presbyterian College, and his friend the artist John Faed. Fyfe died suddenly on 15 September 1882 at his home, 62 Abbey Road, St John's Wood, London, and was buried in Willesden cemetery, London. His son, the architect George Peters Collier Fyfe, survived him.

R. E. GRAVES, *rev.* ANNE PIMLOTT BAKER

Sources *The Times* (18 Sept 1882) • Boase, *Mod. Eng. biog.* • *ILN* (30 Sept 1882) • *The exhibition of the Royal Academy* (1866–82) [exhibition catalogues] • C. B. de Laperriere, ed., *The Royal Scottish Academy exhibitors, 1826–1990*, 4 vols. (1991) • P. J. M. McEwan, *Dictionary of Scottish art and architecture* (1994) • B. Stewart and M. Cutten, *The dictionary of portrait painters in Britain up to 1920* (1997) • Wood, *Vic. painters*, 3rd edn • Bryan, *Painters* (1903–5) • *CGPLA Eng. & Wales* (1883)
Likenesses wood-engraving, NPG; repro. in *ILN*
Wealth at death £4836 1*s.* 11*d.*: administration, 25 Jan 1883, *CGPLA Eng. & Wales*

Fyfe, Sir William Hamilton (1878–1965), headmaster and university administrator, was born in London on 9 July 1878, youngest of the three sons of James Hamilton Fyfe (1837–1880), a barrister and journalist, and his wife, Mary Elizabeth Jonas. Henry Hamilton *Fyfe was his eldest brother. His father died young, and his mother had little on which to bring up the family. Fyfe won a scholarship to Fettes College, Edinburgh, and then in 1897 went on to Oxford with a postmastership at Merton College, being placed in the first class both in classical honour moderations (1899) and in *literae humaniores* (1901). After taking his degree, he taught at Radley College for two years. William Sewell's lavish foundation had by then settled down to quieter ways, but in retrospect Fyfe found his Radley time an idyllic existence.

In 1904 Fyfe returned to Merton as a fellow and principal of the postmasters, the senior disciplinary officer of the college. There he remained until 1919, being also tutor in classical honour moderations, and producing translations of Tacitus' *Dialogus*, *Agricola*, and *Germania* (1908), and of *The Histories* (1912). During this pre-war period he was one of a number of younger dons clustering on William Temple, who was then a fellow of Queen's. They were active as propagandists for university reform, particularly for a wider opening of the university to members of the working class. He married in 1908 Dorothea Hope Geddes (d. 1977), daughter of John Forbes White LLD, flour-miller in Aberdeen, and a local patron of the arts. From this singularly happy marriage there were three children—two sons

Sir William Hamilton Fyfe (1878–1965), by Olive Edis, *c*.1931

(the elder of whom, Maurice, became a Canadian QC), and a daughter.

In the First World War Fyfe was commissioned in the Territorial Force (unattached list) in February 1915, and after service in training officer cadets and in intelligence, he ended the war (with the rank of major) in resettlement work, having been posted to the general staff in 1917. He was also made officier of the Académie Française.

In 1919 Fyfe left Merton to become headmaster of Christ's Hospital, at Horsham, Sussex. The old (and original) Christ's Hospital (in the City of London) had entered the English tradition with Charles Lamb. That gave it appeal to Fyfe, but even more attractive was the fact that it admitted only those boys whose parents were unable to meet the fees normally paid elsewhere. As he was later to put it: 'Poverty cuts diagonally across classes. So the boys came from very different backgrounds—an educational advantage which other Public Schools are seeking to acquire.' Fyfe soon became known as a new and unexpected type of headmaster, approachable and humorous, ready to experiment and encourage sensible change. Older hands might grouse, but the younger—boys and masters alike—gave him their devotion. To this period belong his Loeb translations of Aristotle's *Poetics* and Longinus's *On the Sublime* (1927).

In 1930 a party of British headmasters (including Fyfe)

visited Canada. One result was the offer to him of the post of principal and vice-chancellor of Queen's University, Kingston, Ontario, which he accepted, and held until 1936. The Scottish Presbyterian ethos of Queen's was still much as T. R. Glover had experienced it thirty years earlier (T. R. Glover and D. D. Calvin, *A Corner of Empire*, 1937). Now also came the depression of the 1930s; but Fyfe raised money for his university, and initiated a kind of intra-Canada 'Rhodes scholarship' system that brought it many able students from other provinces.

In 1936 Fyfe left Canada for Scotland to be principal of Aberdeen University. He thought the outlook 'a bit dour'. That was true politically but not otherwise, for, though the Second World War was soon to freeze expansion plans, he quickly won over and brought the best out of the shyer (and perhaps prouder) Scottish students, who could well have begun thinking (with many of their professors) that so unconventional a principal was not quite *sérieux*.

The years in Scotland (until Fyfe's retirement in 1948) were increasingly devoted to public work. As chairman of the Advisory Council on Education in Scotland, as member of the Scottish Advisory Council on the Treatment of Offenders, and perhaps above all as a member of the Inter-University Council for Higher Education in the Colonies, he found stimulus and interest in subjects which appealed to his liberal temperament. He had a major part in the founding of the institutes which became the universities of Ibadan (Nigeria) and of Ghana. He also brought out an edition of Aristotle's *Poetics* (1940), prefacing it with a characteristic note: 'The translation … is that of Ingram Bywater which the editor, a Satyr to his Hyperion, has ventured to alter slightly in a few places'.

Fyfe spent his years of retirement in Blackheath, and he was developing there a new and very successful career as a broadcaster until failing eyesight compelled him to give it up. Fyfe was a great educator, and his liberal outlook (grounded on a simple Christian faith) made him an ardent advocate of a type of society in which abilities of all kinds could flourish without privilege unfairly tipping the scales. He was also possessed of a gracious informality of manner, and a very considerable verbal felicity and style that, allied to humour, was at once arresting and could in a flash put a case in a wholly new light. Three lines on a postcard from him said more than many a man could say in a long letter. Few of his calling can in recent times have so unobtrusively and effortlessly had so sane and pervasive an influence on so many over so great an area of the world.

Fyfe was knighted in 1942, held honorary doctorates from Canadian, British, and American universities, was elected a fellow of the Royal Society of Canada in 1932, and became an honorary fellow of Merton College in 1948. He was chairman of the governors of Gordonstoun School from 1945 to 1948. He died at his home, 10 St Germans Place, Blackheath, London, on 13 June 1965.

A. H. K. SLATER, rev.

Sources *The Times* (15 June 1965) · *The Times* (18 June 1965) · *Postmaster*, 3/4 (Dec 1965) · *Oxford*, 9/1 (1945) · *The Blue*, 42/3 (Sept 1965) · *Proceedings and Transactions of the Royal Society of Canada*, 4th ser., 5

(1967) • *Aberdeen Chamber of Commerce Journal*, 44 (1962–3) • *Aberdeen University Review*, 41/134 (1965) • *Aberdeen Press and Journal* (16 June 1965) • personal knowledge (1981) • private information (1981) • d. cert. • *CGPLA Eng. & Wales* (1965)

Archives Queen's University, Kingston, Ontario, corresp. and papers | Bodl. Oxf., corresp. with Sir J. L. Myres |

Likenesses O. Edis, photograph, *c*.1931, NPG [*see illus.*] • T. B. Huxley Jones, bronze bust, 1945, Aberdeen Art Gallery • M. Ayoub, oils, Christ's Hospital, Horsham • M. Ayoub, oils, Rowett Research Institute, Buckburn, Aberdeen • J. K. Green, oils, U. Aberdeen • L. T. Newton, oils, Queen's University, Kingston, Ontario • J. B. Souter, pencil drawing, priv. coll.

Wealth at death £41,815: probate, 20 Oct 1965, *CGPLA Eng. & Wales*

Fyffe, Charles Alan (1845–1892), historian, the son of Lawrence Hay Fyffe, MD, of Blackheath, and Mary Prudence, daughter of John Urd, was born at Lee Park, Blackheath, on 3 December 1845, and was educated at Christ's Hospital, after which he obtained an open exhibition at Balliol College, Oxford, in 1864. He graduated BA in 1868, with a first class in *literae humaniores*, and proceeded MA in 1870. From 1869 he was a fellow of University College; he was also a tutor (1870–74) and librarian (1872–4), and from 1885 until 1891 acted as bursar and steward for estates. Fyffe had a strong interest in politics, with pronouncedly liberal views, and was president of the Oxford Union in 1867. As special correspondent to the *Daily News* during the first part of the Franco-Prussian War, he was reportedly responsible for dispatching the first account to appear in print of the capitulation of Napoleon III at Sedan. He was in Paris during the commune, where he narrowly escaped execution, being taken for a spy.

Fyffe entered as a student at Lincoln's Inn (10 June 1873), but was transferred to the Inner Temple (26 May 1876). He was called to the bar on 10 May 1877 and subsequently joined the south-west circuit, but never practised. In 1875 he published a small school history of Greece, which sold well and was reprinted. His more significant work was the *History of Modern Europe* (3 vols., 1880–89), which covered the period from the outbreak of the French Revolutionary war in 1792 to the accession of Louis XVIII in 1814. It was written using the unpublished records of the English Foreign Office and other European archival papers. It was critically well regarded and popular, passing through several editions. He was active in the Royal Historical Society, of which he was vice-president in 1885.

Fyffe was in favour of land-law reforms and was one of the founders of the Free Land League; he was a member of the National Liberal Federation and an unsuccessful radical candidate for the city of Oxford at the general election in 1885. He was preparing to be a candidate for Devizes at the time of his death.

Fyffe married, on 7 June 1883, Henrietta Frances Arnaud, only child of Waynflete Arnaud Blagden of Holmbush Ashington, Sussex, with whom he had three children. Late in 1891 a charge was brought against him; he was eventually cleared by a grand jury, but did not recover after a suicide attempt and died on 19 February 1892 at Laughton Hall, Edinburgh. He was buried at Buncton in Sussex.   WILLIAM CARR, *rev.* MYFANWY LLOYD

Sources *The Times* (23 Feb 1892) • *Oxford Magazine* (2 March 1892), 203 • *The Academy* (27 Feb 1892), 205–6 • Boase, *Mod. Eng. biog.* • Allibone, *Dict.* • G. P. Gooch, *History and historians in the nineteenth century*, 4th edn (1928) • Foster, *Alum. Oxon.*

Archives King's AC Cam., letters to Oscar Browning

Wealth at death £4862 18s. 8d.: probate, 10 Aug 1892, *CGPLA Eng. & Wales*

Fyffe, Edward Wathen (1853–1935), tea and fruit importer, was born on 31 December 1853 in Woodchester, Gloucestershire, the younger son of Ebenezer Wathen Fyffe and his wife, Martha, *née* Dunn. His father was head of a long established tea trading business in London, which became E. W. Fyffe, Son & Co. Fyffe was brought up in the Gloucestershire village of Box, near Minchinhampton. After an attempt at farming, he entered the family firm and on his father's death was left in sole charge, his elder brother having taken holy orders.

Fyffe appears to have been reasonably successful, undertaking a trip to Ceylon to establish personal contacts with the growers at the start of his career. He married Ida Stanton Brown (1859–1911), daughter of a Baptist minister, in 1884. They had two daughters within a very short time of each other, which led to a sharp deterioration in Ida's health, diagnosed as tuberculosis. As was customary in those days, a sojourn in a warmer climate such as that of the Canary Islands was advised. The family spent most of 1887 there with the result that Ida recovered completely, becoming well enough to enjoy social life and travel. In that way Edward became acquainted with the recent traumatic downturns in the islands' economy and was able to assess its potential.

Sir Alfred Jones, of the Elder Dempster Line, had already been encouraging the growing and export of bananas and tomatoes, to replace the islands' former main export, cochineal, now obsolete owing to the invention of aniline dyes. Elder Dempster's coal-carrying vessels picked up the fruit as cheap deck cargo on their return journey to Liverpool, but there was no organized distribution network in the UK for bananas and in the London fruit market they were regarded as an expensive luxury. Fyffe investigated the possibility of shipping the fruit directly to London himself. The problem, of which Elder Dempster and other shippers were equally aware, was the difficulty of bringing the fruit to Britain in good condition. Fyffe decided to confine himself to providing an import agency in London. It was a skilfully negotiated arrangement, in which the responsibility for the provision of fruit in reasonable condition fell on the grower. Evidence is lacking regarding its precise terms, but it is clear that Fyffe's long stay in the Canaries secured for him the confidence of a number of expatriate Britons who had become large landowners there. They agreed to back his venture and he sold their consignments on a commission basis. The first cargo of fruit arrived in September 1888, realized a reasonable profit, and from then on regular shipments were made. Most was sold in Covent Garden, with a small quantity being sold directly to the better class of London fruiterer. He met little competition in London until 1892, when Elder Dempster extended its activities from Liverpool.

By 1897 the growers' 'syndicate' decided to buy Fyffe out, even though they had enjoyed great prosperity on his account. The reasons for this are obscure. Fyffe had taken a partner, James Hudson, in 1896 and the firm had changed its name to Fyffe, Hudson & Co. This now became a private limited company in which the Canary Island expatriate growers held all the preference and ordinary shares.

After he was bought out, Fyffe retired from business altogether, apart from a brief period as chairman of Hilliers Bacon Curing Factory, whose founder was related to his wife. During his brief involvement with the trade, he had seen banana imports grow from 10,000 to nearly a million hands a year. He left the company in sound enough shape to induce Elder Dempster to merge its fruit department with it in 1901 under the style of Elders and Fyffes Ltd. By that time Jamaica had become a major source of supply.

Fyffe enjoyed a long retirement. He lived at Trullwell, Box, until his death, indulging his golfing interests and working for the National Trust. He does not appear to have been a man of great business ambitions. He took an opportunity that came his way quite fortuitously and built on it as far as he could, but was quite happy to retire gracefully at the age of forty-four. After his wife died in 1911 his daughters, both unmarried, continued to live with him. He died at Trullwell on 17 October 1935, leaving an estate of £38,493, which, in its time, and considering his long retirement, represented a considerable amount of wealth.

J. GORDON READ

Sources P. N. Davies, *Fyffes and the banana, Musa Sapientum, a centenary history* (1990) • P. N. Davies, 'Fyffe, Edward Wathen', *DBB* • *Banana Budget* (16 Aug 1922) • d. cert. • *CGPLA Eng. & Wales* (1935)
Likenesses photograph, repro. in Davies, *Fyffes and the banana*, facing p. 30
Wealth at death £38,493 7s. 4d.: probate, 22 Nov 1935, *CGPLA Eng. & Wales*

Fyffe, William [Will] (1885–1947), comedian and actor, was born on 16 February 1885 at 36 Ferry Road, Dundee, the eldest child of John Fyffe (1864–1928), ship's carpenter, and Janet Rhynd Cunningham (1858–1949), music teacher. Shortly after Will was born his father left his job to form a touring company of actors who performed in a portable wooden theatre, called a geggy, which was assembled and dismantled at every venue. Will Fyffe started playing Little Willie in the stage version of Mrs Henry Wood's *East Lynne* but soon graduated to adult roles, appearing as Polonius when just fifteen. Geggy actors had to be versatile and quick learners because programmes changed nightly and in later life Will Fyffe attributed much of his success, especially in films, to this early training. He married Lily Wilcock (c.1884–1917?), an actress, on 13 November 1905; they had two daughters. Fyffe left his father's company to gain experience in companies touring England and Wales but, as live theatre lost out to touring moving picture shows, decided to switch to the variety stage. His act followed the pattern set by earlier Scottish performers with songs in character interspersed with comic patter, and the years spent in England ensured that he was as readily understood there as he was in Scotland.

About 1920 Fyffe offered his most famous song, 'I belong to Glasgow', to Harry Lauder, and when Lauder turned it down Fyffe performed it himself at the Glasgow Pavilion. It was a huge success and led to a booking at the London Palladium. By 1921 he was topping the bill in London and in 1922 appeared in the first of his five royal command performances. His first wife had died in a shipping tragedy, and on 23 February that year he married the singer Emmeline Eugenie Pooley (1896–1979); they had a daughter and son. In 1927 he made the first of many successful visits to North America and tours of Australia and South Africa followed. Not since Harry Lauder more than twenty years earlier had a Scottish comedian gained such acclaim; Fyffe and Lauder never performed together, but were friendly off-stage with shared passions for fishing and golf. Fyffe added quality of material and meticulous attention to detail to his flair for characterization. His widow wrote of his 'genius for living all his characters … which was shared by his genius for make up and dress to which he gave a lot of thought and attention' (Fyffe, 20 June 1955).

A young simpleton, Daft Sandy, was Fyffe's greatest creation, in whom he combined comedy and pathos to telling effect. His characters such as the drunk working man were drawn from life and it was a habit of his to go incognito into public places just to observe his fellow men. He was also a supreme pantomimist and co-starred with Harry Gordon in a series of productions at the Glasgow Alhambra in the 1940s which are considered classics of their kind. Fyffe was the main comic lead, always named Willie, while Gordon took the part of the dame. Throughout his career Fyffe took pride in the fact that his material could never be considered suggestive or offensive and famously walked out of a production on New York's Broadway after the first night because it was 'a dirty show' (House, *Music Hall Memories*, 46).

Fyffe made a number of films of which *Owd Bob* (1938), *The Brothers* (1947), and *Rulers of the Sea* (1939) are perhaps the pick. He completed the last in Hollywood and turned down a number of lucrative offers to remain in America in order to return to Britain at the outbreak of the Second World War. By December 1939 he was entertaining troops in France; he was appointed CBE in 1942 for his war work and efforts for charities over many years.

After an operation on his right ear in December 1947 Fyffe went to recuperate at the hotel he had bought in St Andrews. On 14 December he fell from the window of his suite and died in the local cottage hospital from the shock and injuries received. He was buried at the Western Necropolis in Glasgow on Wednesday 17 December 1947.

ARCHIE L. FOLEY

Sources E. Fyffe, 'Will Fyffe', *Evening Citizen* [Glasgow] (June–July 1955) • J. House, *Music hall memories* (1986) • J. House, *Comics in kilts* (1945) • *The Scotsman* (15 Dec 1947) • b. cert. • m. cert. • d. cert. • J. Moore, *Ayr Gaiety: the theatre made famous by the Popplewells* (1976) • private information (2004) [family]

Archives U. Glas., Scottish Theatre Archive, press cuttings, programmes | FILM BFI NFTVA, news footage · BFI NFTVA, performance footage · Glasgow, Scottish Screen Archive | SOUND BL NSA, performance recordings
Likenesses oils, U. Glas. L., Scottish Theatre Archive · photographs, U. Glas. L., Scottish Theatre Archive
Wealth at death £53,295 7s. 10d.: confirmation, 25 Feb 1948, CCI

Fyge, Sarah. *See* Egerton, Sarah (1670–1723).

Fyleman, Rose Amy (1877–1957), children's writer, was born at The Park, Standard Hill, Basford, on the outskirts of Nottingham on 6 March 1877, the third child of John Feilmann and his wife, Emilie, *née* Loewenstein, who was of Russian extraction. Her father was in the lace trade, and the family were freethinking Jews who had come from Jever in Oldenburg in Germany some seventeen years previously. Rose was educated at a private school, and first got into print at the age of nine, when one of her school compositions was published in a local paper. She entered University College, Nottingham, but failed in the intermediate, thus frustrating her ambition to become a schoolteacher. She had, however, a fine voice, and her paternal aunt gave her £200 to study singing. She studied in Paris, then in Berlin under Etelka Gerster, and finished at the Royal College of Music in London, where she took her diploma as associate of the Royal College of Music. She received encouragement from Henry Wood and made her first public appearance in London at the Queen's Hall in 1903. Subsequently she returned to Nottingham, teaching singing and helping in her sister's school. With other members of her family she Anglicized her name at the outbreak of war in 1914.

Rose Fyleman was forty when it was suggested to her that she send some of the verses she had been writing to *Punch*. Her first contribution, 'There are Fairies at the Bottom of our Garden!', appeared on 23 May 1917. This evoked immediate response and five publishers wrote to her within a week. It was followed by 'The Best Game the Fairies Play' (13 June) and a succession of other fairy poems. Readers of *Punch* were soon looking for the initials R. F., and she became a regular contributor. Her verses enjoyed a similar success in book form, the first collection *Fairies and Chimneys* (1918) being reprinted more than twenty times during the next ten years. It was followed by *The Fairy Green* (1919), *The Fairy Flute* (1921), and *Fairies and Friends* (1925). These verses were eventually gathered together in *A Garland of Rose's* (1928).

During the twenties and early thirties Rose Fyleman held a firm place in nursery affection throughout the English-speaking world, and she kept her name alive with a flow of new publications of which *Forty Good-Night Tales* (1923), and *Twenty Teatime Tales* (1929) were particularly successful. She founded (1923), and for two years edited, a children's magazine, the *Merry-Go-Round*, and as time went on devoted an increasing amount of attention to juvenile drama, writing among others *Eight Little Plays for Children* (1924), *Nine New Plays for Children* (1934), and *Six Longer Plays for Children* (1936). She had a Christmas play produced at the Old Vic in 1926, and, with Thomas Dunhill, a children's opera at Guildford in November

Rose Amy Fyleman (1877–1957), by Howard Coster, 1920s

1933. She was also a linguist who translated books from French, German, and Italian; and an inveterate traveller visiting most European countries, and making two lecture tours in the United States, in 1929–30 and 1931–2. She never married, and although she lived most of her final years in the Inverness Court Hotel, London, she died at a nursing home at 17 Lemsford Road, St Albans, Hertfordshire, on 1 August 1957. She was cremated at the Golders Green crematorium, Middlesex, on 7 August.

Like other successful writers for children, Rose Fyleman had not much time for them. Of medium height, with dark hair, large brown eyes, and strong features, she was outwardly a somewhat formidable character, and not the type of person likely 'to see fairies everywhere'. In fact she admitted that she did not believe in them. She was none the less a kindly person who could arouse affection, a cultivated and amusing conversationalist, and one who had a professional attitude to her work and was vitally interested in her craft. Her verse has a clear lyrical quality which makes each of her poems memorable, and ideal for recitation. Although she maintained herself with her pen for forty years, and lived to hear lines of her poetry become proverbial, she had to contend with the knowledge that her best work was her first, and that it was becoming dated. She rarely repeated the simple magic of her early fairy poetry.   IONA OPIE

Sources S. J. Kunitz and H. Haycraft, eds., *Twentieth century authors: a biographical dictionary of modern literature* (1942) · *The Times* (2 Aug

1957) • *The Times* (3 Aug 1957) • private information (1971) • *WW* • d. cert. • *CGPLA Eng. & Wales* (1957) • b. cert.

Archives BL, corresp. with Society of Authors, Add. MSS 63245–63247

Likenesses H. Coster, photograph, 1920–29, NPG [*see illus.*] • H. Coster, photographs, NPG • photograph, repro. in DLitB, 160 (1996)

Wealth at death £11,097 11s. 8d.: probate, 1 Nov 1957, *CGPLA Eng. & Wales*

Fynch [Finch], **Martin** (1628/9–1698), clergyman and ejected minister, was admitted from Norfolk as a pensioner at Trinity College, Cambridge, on 23 January 1646, and graduated BA in 1647. He took the engagement on 18 October 1649. In June 1654 he was vicar of Aby and Belleau, Lincolnshire, and on 3 August 1654 was admitted as vicar of Tetney, in the same county. In 1656 he was also vicar of Humberstone, also in Lincolnshire. In 1654 he was named as an assistant to the commissioners into the ministry in the county. He was ejected under the Act of Uniformity in 1662 and his successor was instituted at Tetney on 26 August.

Soon after his ejection Fynch moved to Norwich, and on 9 November 1663 he was cited before the mayor, with fifty-six others, for meeting in a private house in the city; officers of the corporation launched a search for arms. In 1668 Fynch was a teacher to 300 Independents meeting in the house of a grocer, John Tofts, and elsewhere, in St Clement's parish, Norwich. In 1669 he was reported as preaching, again to about 300, at the houses of John Hooker, Henry Brett, and Richard Clements at Woodnorton, at William Bell's house in Oulton, and at the Lammas house of Thomas Church, an excommunicate worsted weaver, all in Norfolk. He was licensed on 10 June 1672 as an Independent teacher at the house of Nicolas Withers in the parish of St Clement's, Norwich. Soon afterwards he returned to Lincolnshire; he was licensed on 5 September 1672 to teach in his own house at Great Grimsby. From there, on 26 August 1674, he signed the preface to *The Way of the Spirit in Bringing Souls to Christ* by Thomas Allen.

By 1685 Fynch was back in Norwich, as pastor of the Independent church meeting at the West Granary, in succession to John Cromwell. The church moved, first to a former brewery in St Edmund's parish, and in 1693 to a new building in St Clement's. Fynch and his assistant John Stackhouse were reported in early 1690 to be in receipt of £130 per annum. In that year he and John Collinges implemented the union between Presbyterians and Independents in Norwich. When Collinges died soon after, Thomas Grantham issued an attack upon him, *A Dialogue between the Baptist and the Presbyterian*. Fynch had also come under fire from Grantham, and thought it his duty to respond, although his Baptist opponent had:

> put me to a great deal of pains to answer his book, considering my age, and what bad eyes I have had some years, whereby both reading and writing are made hard to me; if he write again I do not intend to meddle with him any more. (Fynch, 163)

He rejected the charge of unfriendliness, and defended his reserved attitude: 'one of your own judgement about Baptism had charged you in print that you set the Houses

of God on fire, wherever you came, and that you pretended to be an Archbishop, and to have jurisdiction over other churches' (ibid., 146). Fynch died aged sixty-nine on 13 February 1698 and was buried at his St Clement's meeting-house, where a monument was erected recording that he:

> laboured abundantly in the ministry of the gospel 49 years, and guided this church of Christ 12 years with great wisdom and integrity, diligence and faithfulness, and many years desired to depart hence, and to be with Christ; being worn out with the pains of the stone. (Browne, 265)

STEPHEN WRIGHT

Sources *Calamy rev.* • A. Gordon, ed., *Freedom after ejection: a review (1690–1692) of presbyterian and congregational nonconformity in England and Wales* (1917) • Venn, *Alum. Cant.* • J. Browne, *A history of Congregationalism and memorials of the churches in Norfolk and Suffolk* (1877) • M. Fynch, *An answer to Mr Thomas Grantham's book called a dialogue between the Baptist and the Presbyterian* (1691)

Fyncham, Eleanor (*fl.* 1447). *See under* Women traders and artisans in London (*act. c.*1200–*c.*1500).

Fyneux [Fenex], **Sir John** (d. 1525), judge, was born into an old but obscure Kentish family seated at Swingfield; there was another John Fyneux (*fl.* 1435–1450) of Sandwich. The judge was the son of William Fyneux, esquire, of Swingfield, and Alice Monynges. The surname (sometimes spelt Fenex) was probably pronounced like 'phoenix'; a descendant spelt his name thus in 1593, and a drawing of a phoenix adorns some of Sir John's plea rolls. Fyneux was a member of Gray's Inn and acted in numerous legal employments from 1472 onwards. From 1475 until he took the coif he was steward of all the manors of Christ Church Priory, Canterbury. In 1478 he served in parliament for Bodmin, and from 1480 to 1481 he held the office of deputy justice of Chester, though there is no evidence that he exercised it in person. He was counsel to Prince Edward (later Edward V), was granted an annuity by Richard III, and was created serjeant in the first year of Henry VII's reign. (His descendants possessed a gold ring with the motto 'Suae quisque fortunae faber', said to have been made for the serjeants' call of 1486; but it seems more likely to have been a personal posy-ring.)

In 1489 Fyneux was appointed one of the king's serjeants, and began to ride the Norfolk circuit as justice of assize. Raised to the bench as a justice of the common pleas in February 1494, he became chief justice of the king's bench in November 1495 and received his knighthood in 1497. Lloyd said that he left twenty-three folios of notes and 3502 cases. Whether or not he was a law reporter, he was certainly renowned for his learning, regularly participating in the readings in Gray's Inn after he became chief justice, and his own legal opinions were keenly reported. By the end of his life he must have been seventy-five, if not eighty, years of age; and yet, although he was described as 'aged and sickly' in 1521, he remained active. In that year he gave an eloquent charge to the grand jury which sat on the duke of Buckingham, on the theme that the realm was a body politic with the king as head and the law as its sinews, and also a rhetorical speech (which survives) to the new serjeants-at-law. A seventeenth-century biographer recorded from family tradition 'a freedom of converse' and 'a gay and cheerful humour', and set down a number of philosophical precepts attributed to him.

Fyneux presided over the king's bench during a period of resurgence and reform to which he himself contributed significantly. The court had lost much of its importance during the fifteenth century, and Fyneux had a material interest in its recovery, especially through the appointment of his son-in-law as chief clerk in 1498; but there are no known contemporary complaints of his motives, and most of the legal innovations in his time were inherently sound and passed into the common law. The decision that the trespass action called *assumpsit* lay to recover damages for failing to perform a service undertaken, without proof of physical harm, was announced by Fyneux in Gray's Inn in 1499 and was never again judicially questioned. It was avowedly intended to save occasional litigants the inconvenience of resort to chancery, but it brought a swelling tide of commercial and consumer litigation into the king's bench and began the development of the modern law of contract. Fyneux at first doubted whether *assumpsit* could also be used to recover contract debts, thereby avoiding the older procedure which allowed debtors to swear themselves out of liability. But the remedy was soon established, and in 1520 his court sanctioned its use against a deceased debtor's executors, who until that time had been immune in the absence of a document under seal. Although the common pleas did not approve of these developments, the debt jurisdiction of the king's bench increased steadily, and in the early seventeenth century Fyneux's doctrines were upheld by all the judges of England. In an *assumpsit* action which he brought himself in 1517 he went still further, relying on a purely consensual theory of contractual liability which was not to become orthodox for another generation.

During the same period, the two benches opened their gates to some new torts. The most notable was slander, which had previously belonged exclusively to the church courts. Even more important in the long term was the bold decision by the king's bench in 1500 that possession of land could be recovered in the trespass action called ejectment. Intended to improve the legal position of leaseholders, this piece of judicial legislation bore fruit two generations after Fyneux by enabling the archaic real actions to be almost completely replaced. Fyneux was equally progressive in the sphere of public law. His reputed opposition to the machinations of Empson and Dudley is borne out by his having allowed actions based on Magna Carta for parties treated unconstitutionally in the name of the king's council. But his best-known achievement was his victory over the church authorities in the struggle to curtail the abuses of sanctuary and benefit of clergy, a conflict of some significance in the story of the English Reformation. Fyneux played a prominent part in two famous debates arising from notorious murders, both held in the king's presence, the first at Baynard's Castle in 1515 concerning benefit of clergy, and the other

in the inner Star Chamber in 1519 concerning the sanctuary of the priory of St John of Jerusalem. His arguments persuaded king and parliament. He was convinced that the abuses were against the spirit of the original privileges and that preserving them was against the interests of the church; indeed, it was his own choice to be buried near the altar of St Thomas in Canterbury Cathedral.

In 1494 Fyneux moved from Faversham to Herne, where he rebuilt the moated manor house of Hawe. He had another house in Canterbury, and was a prominent citizen there; he built a gate for Christ Church Priory in 1517 and was a benefactor in other ways. In London he lived in a house near St Bride's, but was also a member of Serjeants' Inn, Fleet Street. For a time he was proprietor of New Inn, the inn of chancery in the parish of St Clement Danes which was let to attorneys and students. His first wife, Elizabeth, was daughter and heir of William Apuldrefield (d. 1487) of Faversham and Lynsted. Their son Richard (d. 1520) twice served as member of parliament for Dover; another son, John, became an Austin canon. One of their daughters, Jane, married John Rooper (d. 1524) of Eltham, whom Fyneux appointed as chief clerk of his court; their grandson John (d. 1618) sold the chief clerkship to become Baron Teynham in 1616. At the time of Fyneux's death, on 17 November 1525, his only surviving son, and thus his heir, was William (d. 1557), the child of Fyneux's second wife, also Elizabeth (d. 1539), daughter of Sir John Paston and widow of William Clere. William Fyneux's son John (d. 1592) was member of parliament for West Looe in 1571; John's only child, Elizabeth, married Sir John Smythe (d. 1608) of Westenhanger, and their son Sir Thomas (d. 1635) was created Viscount Strangford in the peerage of Ireland in 1628. The peerage became extinct on the death of the eighth viscount in 1869.

J. H. BAKER

Sources M. Sparks, 'Sir John Fyneux', *Hoath and Herne*, ed. K. H. McIntosh and H. E. Gough (1984), 40–50 • E. W. Ives, *The common lawyers of pre-Reformation England* (1983) • *The reports of Sir John Spelman*, ed. J. H. Baker, 2 vols., SeldS, 93–4 (1977–8) • A. W. B. Simpson, ed., *Biographical dictionary of the common law* (1984) • Baker, *Serjeants* • Sainty, *King's counsel* • Sainty, *Judges* • M. D. Harris, ed., *The Coventry leet book*, 4 vols., EETS, 134, 135, 138, 146 (1907–13) • F. Hull, ed., *A calendar of the white and black books of the Cinque Ports, 1432–1955*, Kent Archaeological Society Records Branch, 19 (1966) • C. R. Councer, 'Heraldic notices of the church of St Martin, Herne', *Archaeologia Cantiana*, 53 (1941), 81–100 • D. Lloyd, *State worthies* (1670), 84 • E. Williams, *Early Holborn and the legal quarter of London*, 2 vols. (1927) • will, PRO, PROB 11/22, sig. 1 • D. J. Clayton, *The administration of the county palatine of Chester, 1442–85*, Chetham Society, 3rd ser., 35 (1990), 159 • PRO, C142/45/2 • PRO, E356/25 m.45
Wealth at death see will, PRO, PROB 11/22, sig. 1

Fysher, Robert (*bap.* 1698, *d.* 1749), librarian, was baptized on 30 December 1698 at Grantham, Lincolnshire, the son of Robert Fysher of Grantham. Nothing further is known of his family background or early life. He matriculated from Christ Church, Oxford, on 25 February 1715, aged sixteen, and graduated BA on 11 October 1718. He was elected to continue with his studies at Oriel College, but was not admitted until 19 April 1723 because the provost of Oriel opposed the bishop of Lincoln. Fysher proceeded MA in

1724 and BM in 1725. He was admitted a probationary fellow of Oriel on 18 July 1726 and in perpetuity the following year.

On 2 December 1729 Fysher was elected Bodley's librarian in the university, beating Francis Wise by 100 votes to 85. The antiquary Thomas Hearne gleefully reported how the whigs in the university, led by the vice-chancellor, had been defeated by Fysher's election: 'The Whiggs were all, as it were, to a Man against Fysher, insomuch that Merton, Wadham, Exeter, & Jesus were in a combination for Wise. As far as I can understand, it was a party cause, & they rather contended in the score than for merit' (*Remarks*, 207). With his friend Emmanuel Langford of Hart Hall, Fysher completed work on the catalogue of printed books in the Bodleian Library that had been started by his predecessor Joseph Bowles, and published it as *Catalogus liborum impressorum Bibliothecae Bodleiannae* (2 vols., 1738). Although Hearne and Moses Williams were in large part responsible for the 'remarkable accuracy, and … the abundance and minuteness of its cross-references' (Macray, 212–13) of the catalogue, Fysher incurred much work in organizing and editing the whole catalogue, which remained in use until the next century.

Fysher served three terms as dean of Oriel (1727, 1731–2, 1734–5) and acted as both junior and senior treasurer of the college on several occasions. He died, unmarried, on 4 November 1749 at Mr Warneford's house in Sevenhampton, Wiltshire, and was buried on 7 November in Adam de Brome's chapel in the university church of St Mary the Virgin, Oxford. He had been in poor health in his final years and was accused of failing to catalogue new acquisitions. Richard Rawlinson defended him in a letter, dated 15 April 1751, to Fysher's successor, Humphrey Owen, on the grounds 'that Dr Fysher's indisposition disabled him much from the duty of his office, and that I did not think every small benefaction ought to load the velom register' (Macray, 222).   DOROTHY M. MOORE

Sources W. D. Macray, *Annals of the Bodleian Library, Oxford* (1868) · *Remarks and collections of Thomas Hearne*, ed. C. E. Doble and others, 10, OHS, 67 (1915) · Foster, *Alum. Oxon.* · G. C. Richards and C. L. Shadwell, *The provosts and fellows of Oriel College, Oxford* (1922) · C. D. Frost, 'The Bodleian catalogues of 1674 and 1738: an explanation in the light of modern catalog theory', *Library History*, 46/3 (1976), 248–70 · IGI

Gabell, Henry Dison (1764–1831), headmaster, was born at Winchester and baptized there on 13 March 1764, the son of the Revd Timothy Gabell (*c*.1737–1803), a minor canon of Winchester Cathedral. He was elected a scholar of Winchester College in 1779, and subsequently of New College, Oxford, where he matriculated in 1782 and held a fellowship from that year until 1790. He graduated BA in 1786, incorporated at Cambridge in 1807, where he graduated MA, and was made DD Canterbury in 1811.

On 11 January 1790 Gabell married Anne Gage, daughter of a clergyman of Holton, Oxfordshire. Soon afterwards he was appointed a master of Warminster School, where he had twenty boys to teach, with a salary of £30, and liberty to take private pupils. He was presented to the rectory of St Lawrence, Winchester, in 1788, and in 1793 was appointed second master of Winchester College, where he succeeded William Goddard as headmaster in 1810. His insistence upon accurate scholarship established a high reputation for his pupils, who included Thomas Arnold. But his headship was marred by a rebellion among the boys in May 1818, precipitated by the encroachments of his assistant, John Williams, upon the customary independence of the prefects. Gabell's disciplinary methods, which were said to include the use of spies, were considered underhand. His conduct during the rebellion, when the boys surrendered on the offer of a holiday but were then confronted by soldiers, exposed him to charges of duplicity. Among those boys subsequently expelled was William Page Wood. He resigned the headmastership of Winchester College in December 1823, receiving a present of richly engraved plate from the scholars.

In 1812 Gabell was presented to the rectory of Ashow, Warwickshire and in 1820 to that of Binfield, Berkshire; he continued to hold these livings, together with St Lawrence, until his death at Binfield on 18 April 1831. Gabell was a friend of Samuel Parr, with whom he corresponded on points of classical scholarship. His publications were a pamphlet on the parliamentary bounty to encourage the import of wheat (1796) and a fast-day sermon (1799).

J. M. RIGG, rev. M. C. CURTHOYS

Sources GM, 1st ser., 60 (1790), 84 · GM, 1st ser., 101/1 (1831), 469 · Venn, *Alum. Cant.* · Foster, *Alum. Oxon.* · T. F. Kirby, *Winchester scholars: a list of the wardens, fellows, and scholars of … Winchester College* (1888) · A. Bell, 'Warden Huntingford and the old conservatism', *Winchester College: sixth-centenary essays*, ed. R. Custance (1982), 351–74 · R. C. Hoare, *The history of modern Wiltshire*, 3 (1834–5), 40 · *The works of Samuel Parr … with memoirs of his life and writings*, ed. J. Johnstone, 8 vols. (1828), vol. 7, pp. 470–501 · J. D'E. Firth, *Winchester College* (1949)

Gabháin, Seoirse Ui. *See* Duffy, George Gavan (1882–1951).

Gabhánach Ní Dhufaigh, Luise. *See* Duffy, Louise Gavan (1884–1969), *under* Duffy, George Gavan (1882–1951).

Gable, Christopher Michael (1940–1998), dancer, actor, and ballet director, was born on 13 March 1940 in Hackney Hospital, London, the younger of the two sons of Denis Gable (1901–1976), a dental technician, and his wife, Hylda, *née* Knights (1906–1987). As a child he entered diverse talent competitions; watching the great film musicals encouraged him to dance, and at eleven he won a scholarship to the Royal Ballet School. After graduation and a year's stage experience with Sadler's Wells Opera Ballet, he had no offer of a permanent contract, but shrewdly contrived to be seen in class by the director of the Royal Ballet's touring company, John Field, impressing him enough to be given the next vacancy, in 1957. Fairhaired, with a lively, rugged face and outgoing personality, he soon obtained small roles. His big chance came in 1960 when his contemporary Lynn Seymour, who had found that they went well together dancing in an opera-ballet, urged the young choreographer Kenneth MacMillan to cast Gable in a work he was making for her. All three made their names with *The Invitation*, its story of rape and

Christopher Michael Gable (1940–1998), by unknown photographer, 1989

sexual initiation unusual then in ballet. Three months later Gable (replacing a sick colleague) and Seymour confirmed their star quality in an entirely different new work, Frederick Ashton's poetically romantic *The Two Pigeons*. Later that year, on 16 December 1961, he married a fellow dancer, Carole Judith Needham (*b.* 1940); they had a daughter and a son.

Gable's further progress was rapid as he took on a range of new and old roles where his strong technique, acting skills, and powerful stage presence encompassed a variety of moods: heroic in *Sylvia*, glamorous in *Cinderella*, lyrical with Margot Fonteyn in *Daphnis and Chloe*, dramatic with Rudolf Nureyev in *Images of Love*, or comic in *Card Game*, to name only a representative few. On tour and at Covent Garden he was one of the Royal Ballet's strongest and most popular talents. However, in 1965 the management decided that Fonteyn and Nureyev must dance the première of *Romeo and Juliet*, which MacMillan had created for Seymour and Gable. The success of Seymour and Gable when they performed the roles a few days later did not overcome the resentment Gable understandably felt at this. That, coupled with foot pain from osteoarthritis, prompted him to leave ballet in 1967, after less than ten years, for drama (although he first gave some memorable guest performances with Ballet Rambert).

One of Gable's first acting roles was as Lysander in Peter Brook's acclaimed *Midsummer Night's Dream*, and what he learned from that experience influenced all his subsequent career, both in drama and when he returned in a different capacity to ballet. Although not repeating as an actor the eminence he achieved in dance, he successfully took a range of leading roles (including parts in Shakespeare, Molière, Ibsen, and Wilde) for companies including the Royal Shakespeare, Manchester Royal Exchange, Bristol Old Vic, and Chichester. He was greatly enjoyed on film and television, too, especially in Ken Russell's musical *The Boy Friend* (1971) playing opposite Twiggy, and, with the same director, as Delius's assistant Fenby in a documentary about the composer.

In 1982, after giving guest classes at the Rambert Ballet

School, Gable responded to the suggestion of some students there by opening, with his wife and an administrator, Ann Stannard, his own Central School of Ballet, dedicated to training dancers in a seriously dramatic approach to their work. Five years later the choreographer Gillian Lynne persuaded him to play the painter L. S. Lowry in her new ballet *A Simple Man* for Northern Ballet Theatre, first on television, with the long-retired ballerina Moira Shearer also making a comeback as his mother, then on stage with Seymour. The company's dancers liked Gable's way of working so much that when, during rehearsals, their director Robert de Warren suddenly resigned to take another engagement, they and the board unanimously begged him to take over. Accepting this unexpected career move, he found himself faced, coincidentally, with the proposed withdrawal of the company's Arts Council grant. He overcame that threat by winning 20,000 letters of support through speaking to audiences after every performance (even though he much preferred home life to touring) and taking part in a television documentary.

Gable set about improving the company's standards through teaching and a new repertory of specially made big productions, comprising both radical new versions of popular classics and works started from scratch. He was never the sole choreographer, leaving that function partly or wholly to others. His main contribution was, like that of the director of a play, to develop the collaboration of composers, choreographers, designers, and performers (even in tiny roles) in quest of complete conviction. He listened to his audiences (who generally proved more enthusiastic than critics) and responded to their comments, often completely revising productions. The best of his stagings were a highly theatrical and original *Romeo and Juliet* and a lively, popular treatment of *A Christmas Carol*, both of them repeated often by public demand and long surviving their creator.

Gable was appointed CBE in the 1996 birthday honours list. He had already developed cancer, but a long struggle against the illness did not stop him from continuing to run both the Central School in London and Northern Ballet in Yorkshire, planning further productions; these were completed by others after he died, survived by his wife, on 23 October 1998 at his home, The Barn, Little Park Farm, Park Lane, Mytholmroyd, Hebden Bridge, Yorkshire. He was cremated at Elland, Yorkshire.   JOHN PERCIVAL

Sources A. M. D. Izza, ed., *Northern Ballet Theatre, 1987–1997* (1997) · L. Seymour, *Lynn* (1984) · *The Times* (26 Oct 1998) · *The Independent* (26 Oct 1998) · *The Guardian* (27 Oct 1998) · *Daily Telegraph* (26 Oct 1998) · personal knowledge (2004) · private information (2004) [Carole Needham, widow] · b. cert. · m. cert. · d. cert.
Archives FILM The amazing adventures of Christopher Gable (documentary film, BBC, 1989)
Likenesses photograph, 1989, repro. in *The Independent* (26 Oct 1998) [*see illus.*] · A. Crickmay, photograph, Theatre Museum, London · K. Money, photograph, Theatre Museum, London

Gabo, Sir Naum [*formerly* Neyemiya Borisovich Pevzner] (1890?–1977), sculptor, was born on 5 August, probably in

Sir Naum Gabo (1890?–1977), by Nina and Graham Williams [at Carbis Bay studio]

1890 and also probably in Klimovichi, Mogilev, in provincial south-west Russia (now in Belorussia), the seventh of the eight children of Boris Grigoryevich Pevzner (*c.*1850–*c.*1929), the owner of a foundry in nearby Bryansk which produced alloys and machinery, and his wife, Fanny Borisovna, *née* Ozerskaya (*c.*1855–*c.*1930). His parents, who were both Jewish, may have amended his year of birth in order that he might later avoid military service. The privileges which accompanied the flourishing of the Pevzner business meant that, when he was aged about eight, the entire family was able to join the father in the industrial town of Bryansk, outside the pale of settlement to which Russian Jews were normally confined. His father seems to have preserved a sense of his Jewish roots and religion in private, but Neyemiya Pevzner had a Russian Orthodox nanny and was baptized, a common practice among assimilated families.

Youth and early career in Russia Pevzner seems to have been a rebellious youth. He was expelled from two local schools, and then was sent to Tomsk in Siberia, where his eldest brother, Mark, was studying. Between 1907 and 1910 he attended the *Gymnasium* in Kursk, south-east of Bryansk, where his principal love was literature. In his teens he developed a strong commitment to radical politics, especially after the failed 1905 revolution. He was particularly attracted to Peter Kropotkin's *Mutual Aid* (1902), a key text of communist anarchism. His interest in art was inspired by his elder brother Antoine Pevsner (Natan Pevzner), then an art student in Kiev, and his early drawings were mainly influenced by the work of the Russian symbolist painter Mikhail Vrubel.

Pevzner was under strong family pressure to pursue a career in medicine and in 1910 he enrolled at Munich University, where he attended courses in anatomy, physics, and chemistry. Although he remained fascinated with science, in 1912 he changed his registration to philosophy,

and began to study logic and the ideas of Kant. He also started following courses in civil engineering at the Technische Hochschule in Munich (though he may not have been officially enrolled) and studying art history at the university, notably with Heinrich Wölfflin, under whose guidance he visited Italy in the summer of 1913. He also discovered avant-garde art and theory. He read Wilhelm Worringer's *Abstraktion und Einfühlung* (1908) and Kandinsky's *Über das Geistige in der Kunst* (1912), and had opportunities to view the latest art in Munich, home of the Blaue Reiter group, and in Paris, which he visited in 1912 and 1913 to stay with Antoine.

The outbreak of the First World War compelled Pevzner to leave Germany without graduating. He and his younger brother Alexei settled in Christiania, where they were subsequently joined by Antoine. In these relatively tranquil circumstances he began experimenting with figurative sculptures which were constructed by joining together flat planar elements (initially of cardboard, later of wood and metal) so that form is permeated by space (such as *Constructed Head No. 1*, *c.*1916–17, Städelsches Kunstinstitut, Frankfurt am Main), in contrast to the solid volumes produced by the traditional methods of carving and modelling. His early works reflected the artistic examples of cubism and Russian icon painting, but also ideas of open-work structure and the separation of material strength from mass which were implicit in modern engineering structures. As a sign of his new sense of identity as a sculptor, he coined the pseudonym Gabo, to distinguish himself from his artist brother Antoine.

The brothers returned to Russia in the spring of 1917, after the February revolution. They settled in Moscow, and Gabo, like many avant-garde artists, was seized by enthusiasm for the new political order. In August 1920 he organized a small group exhibition in a bandstand on Tverskoy bulvar, which included more permanent realizations of the sculptures which he had begun to develop in Norway, such as the *Head No. 2* (iron, *c.*1916–20, priv. coll.). To accompany the show he wrote *The Realistic Manifesto*, a polemical justification of his art, which was printed in the form of a poster and pasted up all over Moscow. He argued that the cubists and futurists had laid the foundations for a new art but had failed to convey the essence of the 'new age', whereas his works offered a distillation of the modern scientific world-view:

> With a plumb line in the hand, with eyes as precise as a ruler, with a spirit as taut as a compass, we build them in the same way as the universe builds its own creations, as the engineer his bridges, as the mathematician his formulae of the orbits. (*Gabo*, 1957, 151)

Gabo proclaimed that art should be based on 'kinetic rhythms' rather than static form. As an experiment in this direction, he produced *Kinetic Construction: Standing Wave* (1920, Tate collection), comprising a thin metal rod which is caused to vibrate by a motor, and through its oscillations describes a virtual volume or wave form in space. He also declared that art should be placed in the 'squares and streets', communicating progressive values to a mass audience. This attitude underlay a subsequent series of highly architectonic constructions, built up from geometrical elements, which he hoped would eventually be enlarged to a monumental scale and sited in the modern urban environment (for example, *Column*, *c*.1923, Solomon R. Guggenheim Museum, New York).

All Gabo's subsequent work was affected by the idealistic ethos of revolutionary Russia, and by the experimentation with purely abstract styles which he had encountered in the work of Russian avant-garde artists such as Kazimir Malevich and Vladimir Tatlin. By 1922, however, he was becoming disillusioned with the increasingly authoritarian character of the Soviet regime, the government's growing preference for realism in art, the erosion of avant-garde influence over artistic affairs, and the trend towards practical design, at the expense of art, among hardline Marxist artists such as Aleksandr Rodchenko. Gabo had been involved in artistic administration, and his contacts enabled him to leave Russia for Berlin in the spring of 1922, to help organize the 'Erste Russische Kunstausstellung' (first Russian art exhibition) which opened that October. He settled in Berlin, where he encountered a sympathetic circle of artists and critics, and had ready access to modern materials such as glass, plastic, and metals, which had been hard to obtain in Moscow. He also met Elisabeth Richter (*c*.1900–1929), the estranged wife of the artist Hans Richter, with whom he lived until her tragic death in childbirth in 1929.

Years in Germany In the West Gabo became a leading representative of constructivism. The term suggested an art in tune with social, political, and scientific progress, as expressed by precise impersonal techniques, and geometric forms and materials more redolent of engineering structures, machinery, or scientific laboratories than the traditional artist's studio. By 1924 his work had been widely reproduced in avant-garde journals, and he had exhibited at the Galerie Percier in Paris alongside his brother Antoine, who had moved to Paris in 1923. In 1928 Gabo wrote an article for *Bauhaus* magazine denouncing the growing assimilation and vulgarization of constructivism by the worlds of fashion and design. His first one-man show, at the Kestner-Gesellschaft in Hanover in 1930, displayed the extensive body of sculpture which he produced in the 1920s, including *Construction in Space with Balance on Two Points* (*c*.1925, Yale University Art Gallery, New Haven, Connecticut) and *Construction in Space: Soaring* (*c*.1929–30, reassembled 1985, Leeds City Art Gallery).

Gabo's ambitions extended beyond the traditional sculptural object. In 1927, assisted by Antoine, he created the highly successful set and costumes for Serge Diaghilev's production of the ballet *La chatte*. The design was notable for its purely abstract forms and its use of transparent, reflective plastics, the visual impact of which was enhanced by dark backdrops and strong lighting. In 1931 he submitted an architectural design to the competition in Moscow for a new Palace of the Soviets (Shchusev Architectural Museum, Moscow). This reflected his long-standing interest in architecture, but also his continuing commitment to the Soviet experiment and his desire at this stage to establish an artistic reputation in his homeland.

France, Britain, and the United States After the Nazis came to power in 1933, Gabo decided that it was imperative for him to leave Germany, and he subsequently spent three years in Paris, in conditions of profound poverty and depression, during which time he produced very little work. His career and spirits revived when he moved to London in the spring of 1936. He soon met and married Miriam Franklin, *née* Israels (1907–1993), with whom he lived very happily for the rest of his life. Moreover, England was currently a principal centre of the modern movement in art and design. Gabo encountered other émigrés from Germany and also became good friends with the critic Herbert Read, abstract artists such as Ben Nicholson and Barbara Hepworth, and the architect Leslie Martin. In England he was able to exhibit and sell a significant number of sculptures, and with Nicholson and Martin he embarked upon the creation of *Circle*, a book-length celebration of the international 'constructive spirit' which underpinned progressive architecture, painting, and sculpture, and foreshadowed the enlightened cultural values of society in the future. His opening essay, 'The constructive idea in art', indicated his prestigious position within the *Circle* grouping. He asserted the fundamental affinity between art and science, as explorations of the 'hidden forces of nature'. In 'Sculpture: carving and construction in space', which introduced the sculpture section for which he was responsible, he emphasized his fundamental aim of heightening the viewer's sensation of space:

> Our task is to penetrate deeper into its substance and bring it closer to our consciousness; so that the sensation of space will become for us a more elementary and everyday emotion the same as the sensation of light or the sensation of sound. (Martin, Nicholson, and Gabo, 107)

Gabo's English constructions, such as *Spheric Theme* (1937–8, Solomon R. Guggenheim Museum, New York) and *Construction in Space: Crystalline Centre* (1938, Tate collection), revealed a new transparency and curvilinearity. Both effects depended upon his discovery and aesthetic exploitation of the recently marketed type of plastic known in Britain as perspex, which was less brittle and so more easily malleable than its predecessors.

In 1938 Gabo spent six months in the United States. Thereafter he was constantly thinking about moving across the Atlantic, to escape a war which was first imminent and then actual, but he ultimately stayed in England until November 1946. He spent the years of the Second World War in the relatively peaceful surroundings of Carbis Bay, Cornwall, in close proximity to Nicholson, Hepworth, the critic Adrian Stokes, and the studio potter Bernard Leach. Younger artists such as Peter Lanyon and John Wells were drawn to this grouping, which formed the basis of the post-war St Ives school. Gabo was frequently tormented by events in the wider world, especially during the German invasion of western Russia where he had grown up. He wrote several articles, kept a diary, produced an interesting group of paintings (for example, *Construction in Depths*, 1944, Solomon R. Guggenheim Museum, New York), and in 1944–5 devoted considerable energy to designing a new car for the Jowett company, a project which eventually collapsed. His major sculptural innovation, announced by *Linear Construction in Space No. 1* (1942–3, Kettle's Yard, Cambridge), was the introduction of closely spaced threads of nylon filament (another brand-new form of plastic) which he wound around a framework to create the illusion of curving planes permeated by space. The technique of stringing, recurrent in his subsequent work (such as *Linear Construction in Space No. 4*, 1958–9, Art Institute of Chicago), was probably inspired by the mathematical models which he had encountered as a student in Munich, and in the Science Museum in London.

Gabo's career in the United States was never quite as successful as he had hoped, partly because the pristine forms and optimistic message of constructivism lost some of their resonance in the gloomy aftermath of the war. He and Miriam settled in Woodbury, Connecticut, and moved to nearby Middlebury in 1953. He exhibited and sold works, lectured widely, and executed a commission for a large-scale stairwell sculpture in the Baltimore Museum of Art (1950–51). His greatest public project stemmed, however, from his first return visit to Europe in 1954, when he was commissioned to produce an outdoor sculpture for Marcel Breuer's austere Bijenkorf department store in Rotterdam. The 85 foot construction was unveiled in 1957. The soaring verticality of the form provided an effective and accessible visual metaphor for the rebirth of Rotterdam, destroyed by Nazi bombing, while the materials and structure evoked the cranes which were so vital to the economic life of the city, and which littered the docks just a few minutes' walk away. The spatial openness of Gabo's design produced a structure which was relatively lightweight in relation to its spatial volume, while the twist of the planes through 90 degrees served to prevent any dangerous build-up of wind pressure.

Last years Gabo's fame was at its height in the years that followed. A major monograph appeared in 1957, illustrating his work to date and reprinting some of his major theoretical texts. In 1959 he delivered the prestigious A. W. Mellon lectures at the National Gallery of Art in Washington, DC, which were subsequently published as *Of Divers Arts* (1962). A string of prizes and official honours culminated in Gabo becoming KBE in 1971. Major retrospectives of his work were mounted in both Europe and the United States. Whereas he had been a relatively marginal figure during his initial ten years in the United States, which coincided with the heyday of abstract expressionism, his critical reputation from the 1960s onward benefited from the emergence of kinetic art and a more geometric idiom of abstract art, as well as from the increasing interest in the Russian avant-garde, of which he was one of the few surviving witnesses.

Gabo's late constructions were frequently large, and employed as material various kinds of metal, in the form of both sheets and linear springs (for example, *Vertical Construction No. 2*, 1965–6, Julia A. Whitney Foundation, Connecticut). The boom in the market for contemporary art produced a degree of financial security which enabled Gabo to use these more lasting materials and to employ studio assistants from the early 1960s onward. Assistance was essential for executing the commissions for public sculptures he regularly began to receive. The most impressive of these was the fountain, unveiled in 1976, installed in the grounds of St Thomas's Hospital, London, directly across the Thames from the houses of parliament. The form was adapted from *Torsion* (c.1929, Berlinische Galerie, Berlin), but the incorporation of a rotating movement and of linear jets of water, evoking diaphanous planes curving through space, served to dematerialize the steel structure.

When presenting a group of small works to the Tate Gallery in 1977, Gabo explained his continuing affection for the country he had left thirty years earlier:

> I have lived in England through the most tragic years of her history and the most glorious period in the life of her people and I have learned to know and to love that country.
>
> I have found a spirit of humanity in England which I carry with me in spite of my having to take citizenship in another country due to circumstances—but I never, in my heart, lost my attachment to England.
>
> I have acquired more personal friends in England than anywhere and any time in the wandering years of my life.
> (Gabo to Lord Bullock, 14 April 1977, New Haven, Connecticut, Yale University, Beinecke Rare Book and Manuscript Library, Gabo MSS)

Gabo's health slowly declined, and in his final years he was mainly confined to working on wood engravings, a medium he had first taken up in 1950. On 23 August 1977 he died in Waterbury Hospital, Waterbury, Connecticut. Following cremation, his ashes were scattered in front of his studio in Middlebury. He was survived by his wife and daughter.   MARTIN HAMMER and CHRISTINA LODDER

Sources M. Hammer and C. Lodder, *Constructing modernity: the work and career of Naum Gabo* (1999) · *Gabo on Gabo: texts and interviews*, ed. and trans. C. Lodder and M. Hammer (1999) · C. Sanderson and C. Lodder, 'Catalogue raisonné of the constructions and sculptures of Naum Gabo', *Naum Gabo: sixty years of constructivism*, ed. S. A. Nash and J. Merkert (Munich, 1985) · J. L. Martin, B. Nicholson, and N. Gabo, eds., *Circle: international survey of constructive art* (1937) · N. Gabo, *Gabo: constructions, sculpture, paintings, drawings, engravings* (1957) · A. Pevsner, *A biographical sketch of my brothers Naum Gabo and Antoine Pevsner* (1964) · Yale U., Beinecke L., Gabo papers · Tate collection, Gabo MSS · Berlinische Galerie-Archiv, Berlin, Gabo MSS · private information (2004) [Miriam Gabo]

Archives Berlinische Galerie, Berlin, MSS · Tate collection, corresp., papers, print-making archive, woodblocks, and drawings · Tate collection, letter and list of colours · Tate collection, papers relating to construction of revolving torsion fountain · Yale U., Beinecke L., MSS | Solomon R. Guggenheim Museum, New York · University of East Anglia Library, Norwich, corresp. with J. C. Pritchard | SOUND Yale U., Beinecke L., Gabo MSS

Likenesses N. Williams and G. Williams, photograph, Tate Gallery archive [*see illus.*] · photographs, Tate Gallery archive

Gabor, Dennis [*formerly* Dénes Gábor] (**1900–1979**), electronics engineer and humanist, was born Dénes Gábor on 5 June 1900 in Budapest, Hungary, the first of three sons of Bertalan Bartholomew Gábor, formerly Günsberg (1867–

Dennis Gabor (1900–1979), by Dr Lessing

1942), engineer, and director of Hungarian General Coal-mines, and his wife, Adrienne Kálmán (1879–1967), actress and daughter of a watchmaker. All the children were multilingual and accomplished in arts and sciences and were encouraged by their parents to buy many books and equipment for experimental work. In 1915 Gábor and his brother George built an epidiascope and a Tesla coil and made X-ray experiments at home. Because of his advanced intellectual development Gábor was seen as a demanding pupil by his teachers at the grammar school in Budapest. At sixteen, his knowledge of physics and mathematics was of degree level. Before university, however, military service intervened; a posting to Italy instilled in him a life-long appreciation of that country.

Gábor entered the technical university in Budapest in 1918 for a four-year mechanical engineering course. When called up again in his third year, he transferred to the Technische Hochschule, Berlin–Charlottenberg, where he attended seminars on statistical mechanics given by Einstein in 1921–2. He gained his diploma in 1924 and in 1927 obtained his doctorate in engineering for work on transient waveforms. His inventions during this period led to the development of the first practical electron lens. His later inventions included holography and the flat television tube, besides his numerous contributions to physics and electronics such as communication theory, electron optics, electromagnetic interactions, and plasma theory, and his resolution of Langmuir's paradox relating to electron interactions. Many inventions did not come to fruition until many years after his first discoveries. He just missed developing the laser, although he had discussed a pulsed laser with a colleague in 1950. He later admitted that this was a disappointment.

From 1927 to 1933 Gábor worked for Siemens and Halske, Berlin, on a gas discharge lamp and on the plasma state and its applications. His plasma work continued when, because of the election of Hitler, he moved to England in 1934 to work for British Thomson-Houston (BTH) in Rugby. He also worked on electron beam properties in lamps, television tubes, and electron microscopes, on speech compression, on three-dimensional cinema image projection, and on an early warning system for aircraft approach. Much of his work was done in a hut close to the security fence of BTH because, after the outbreak of war in 1939, as a registered alien with special qualifications, he could not contribute directly to war work projects. He devised a moral code for scientists, hoping their work would be used to end the war quickly. This he promoted through the local branch committee of the Association of Scientific Workers. The national executive committee dismissed his ideas and his branch resigned *en masse* from the association. The code was a portent of his later work, writings, discussions, and lectures on the proper use of science for the good of humanity. He Anglicized his forename from Dénes to Denis in the 1930s and finally to Dennis.

On 8 August 1936 Gabor married Marjorie Louise Butler (1911–1981), daughter of Joseph Butler, an engine driver. She was a tracer who also worked at BTH and shared an interest in amateur dramatics and music. They had no children, but shared a warm home life with their families, friends, and colleagues. When Gabor's brother Andrè, an economist, visited them in 1938, Gabor refused to let him return to Hungary because of the threat of war. In 1946 Dennis Gabor became a naturalized British citizen. He and Andrè published joint papers on mathematics and social science in the 1950s.

Gabor invented holography in 1947 but this did not flourish until the development of lasers in 1961 when it was applied usefully in many sciences, and embraced by the arts as can be seen in several museums of holography. For that invention he was awarded the Nobel prize for physics in 1971. Gabor described himself as 'an ideas man' (Allibone, *Memoirs FRS*, 133), was astute enough to take out early patents on his work, and said that he was 'never interested in inventions which were not difficult' (J. Brown, *The Times*, 16 Nov 1979). In 1949 Gabor was offered the Mullard readership in electronics at Imperial College, London. There he continued his inventive work, telling a bemused colleague of his methods: 'First you have to know the answer, logic comes afterwards'. He regarded his research students as his most precious products, and his laboratory as his 'Heaven on Earth' (Allibone, *Memoirs FRS*, 123, 126).

In 1958 Imperial College appointed Gabor to a personal chair of applied electron physics. His inaugural lecture was entitled 'Electronic inventions and their impact on civilization', in which he invoked the 'nightmare of a leisured world for which we are socially and psychologically unprepared'. A book on that theme followed: *Inventing the Future* (1963), then further development of his thoughts in *Innovations: Scientific, Technological and Social* (1970) and, in 1972, *The Mature Society*, which advocated the growth of quality of life over materialistic developments. In 1968 he became a founder member of the Club of Rome, begun by a group of concerned leaders in science, industry, and the arts who were keen to explore ways to mitigate the world's problems relating to the use of natural resources, the environment, and economics. Gabor contributed a chapter on energy in the report to the club on the use of science in the exploitation and regeneration of natural resources. It was translated into English as *Beyond the Age of Waste* (1978 and 1981).

When Gabor retired from Imperial College in 1967 his great friend Peter Goldmark invited him to take the post of staff scientist (for life) at CBS Laboratories, Connecticut, but Gabor declined and worked only as a part-time consultant so that he could continue to research and write. He bought a house near Anzio in Italy, where he spent the summer months. He produced over 150 papers between 1925 and 1978, despite a severe stroke in 1974. He was appointed CBE in 1970, seven honorary degrees from British and American universities between 1970 and 1975, and membership and medals of learned societies, including fellowship of the Royal Society in 1956 and its Rumford medal in 1968; its Gabor medal has been awarded biennially since 1989. He was the first émigré to receive honorary membership of the Hungarian Academy of Sciences (1964). He had two streets named after him, one in Nottingham and one in Munich, and a high school in Budapest. Gabor died in a nursing home at 7 Knaresborough Place, Kensington, London, on 9 February 1979. He had 'invented a future,—and a good one,—that preserves the values of civilization and yet is in harmony with man's nature—based on hope and love of life' (Allibone, *Memoirs FRS*, 107, quoting D. Gabor, *Inventing the Future*, 1963).

ANNE BARRETT

Sources T. E. Allibone, *Memoirs FRS*, 26 (1980), 107–47 · E. Ash, *Nature*, 280 (1979), 431–3 · T. E. Allibone, 'Technological world of the future', 23 April 1985 [Denis Gabor memorial lecture, Cybernetics Society] · ICL, archives, Dennis Gabor MSS, B/Gabor · 'The wide range of a creative mind', *New Scientist* (3 Aug 1961), 274–5 · T. E. Allibone, address at the memorial service for Dennis Gabor, 15 March 1979, ICL, archives, Gabor MSS, B/Gabor/A/3 · *WWW* · m. cert. · d. cert.
Archives ICL, corresp. and papers | ICL, corresp. with Lord Jackson · ICL, corresp. with J. D. Mcgee · Sci. Mus., corresp. with Gordon L. Rogers
Likenesses photographs, 1912–75, ICL, Gabor MSS · N. Ferenc, photograph, 1970, Budapest, Hungary · Keystone New York, photograph, 12 Nov 1971, Hult. Arch. · Svenska Dagbladet Stockholm, photograph, 13 Dec 1971 (with King Gustav Adolf of Sweden), Hult. Arch. · Lessing, hologram, NPG [*see illus.*]

Gabrán (*d. c.*558). *See under* Dál Riata, kings of (*act. c.*500–*c.*850).

Gabriel, (John) Beresford Stuart (1888–1979), machine tool manufacturer, was born on 1 August 1888 at Twickenham, Middlesex, the elder son of the three children of John William Wright Gabriel and his wife, Eleanor, *née* Broad. That year J. W. W. Gabriel sold his interest in the family drug manufacturing company of Gabriel and Troke and joined the partnership of Charles Churchill (1837–1916) and his eldest son, Charles Henry Churchill, formed in 1865 to import the new machine tools of the American system of interchangeable manufacture, which led to mass production. In 1889 the firm was registered as Charles Churchill Ltd, a private company with a capital of £5500.

Beresford Gabriel, as he was known, went to Mill Hill

School (1902–7) and then read mechanical and applied sciences at Emmanuel College, Cambridge, graduating with a second class degree in 1910. He then gained practical engineering experience, successively in the works of R. W. Munro & Co. and the Churchill Machine Tool Company, and afterwards as overseas representative for the Cincinnati Milling Machine Company. During the First World War he served with the Royal Engineers, working on searchlight defences for London and reaching the rank of captain.

Gabriel returned to the Churchill family firm as assistant managing director in 1920. Demand for machine tools, traditionally cyclical and derived from the machine making industries, was dented first by the post-war sale of surplus government machine tools and then by the slump of 1921–2. Moreover, during the war years Charles Churchill and two of his sons had died. Gabriel, appointed a joint managing director in 1923, reduced the network of warehouses to those in Birmingham, Glasgow, Manchester, Newcastle, and London (the location of headquarters). Manufacturing was sited in two plants, one near Salford, which made grinding machines under a subsidiary company, the Churchill Machine Tool Company. The other was a third share (purchased in 1919) in C. Redman & Sons' Pioneer ironworks at Halifax, a small firm which made a variety of planers and lathes.

Some recovery came in the late 1920s but in 1931 the national economic crisis hit the company with a peculiar severity, cutting demand and introducing 20 per cent duties on imported machine tools. Gabriel, sole managing director from 1932, responded by securing manufacturing licences from a number of Churchills' American suppliers. Secondly he negotiated the formation in 1933 of an English subsidiary of the Cincinnati Milling Machine Company, with himself as chairman. At this point boardroom divisions split the firm between a sales agency and a manufacturing business (named the Churchill Machine Tool Company). Gabriel stayed with the former, Charles Churchill & Co., as managing director, under F. P. Burnage, son-in-law of Charles Churchill, chairman. In December 1934 Gabriel restored the firm's manufacturing base by purchasing complete control of the Redman firm, renamed the Churchill-Redman Company, which grew to a turnover of £141,773, with pre-tax profits of £23,415, and 300 employees in 1939. The basic technology still originated in the USA. From the Jones and Lamson Company of Springfield, Vermont, a manufacturing licence was secured in 1937 for the Fay lathe, an automatic lathe noted for its versatility, suitability for mass production, and relative ease of operation.

Still, neither Churchill-Redman, nor the British machine tool industry as a whole, met effective demand. This grew with the expansion of the motor industry in the early 1930s. The Ford Motor Company placed the first of its many orders with Churchill-Redman in 1931 and Gabriel set up a new machine tool headquarters at South Yardley in the midlands' motor manufacturing region in 1938. Demand for machine tools was augmented by rearmament after 1936 and then by the outbreak of war in 1939.

For much of the Second World War Gabriel was controller of machine tools, in charge of the Ministry of Supply's programme for mobilizing the industry which had to meet 83 per cent of home demand, the rest coming from the USA under 'cash and carry' and lend-lease arrangements. Targets were reached in November 1943. Gabriel returned to Churchills in 1944.

When peacetime released pent-up demand for machine tools, Gabriel expanded the firm's output. In 1945 he visited the USA to negotiate arrangements under which Churchills would manufacture hobbing and gear shaving machines, required by the motor industry particularly. Capacity was then increased by purchasing the Longfield foundry in Halifax and by leasing from Vickers Armstrong part of the extensive Admiralty works in Scotswood Road, Newcastle upon Tyne. At Halifax, Gabriel launched the search for technical improvements in machine tool performance. Higher cutting speeds and faster times in sizing work pieces, setting up work, and transferring it to another machine were the objectives which led the firm's engineers to develop a new heavy-duty copying lathe, forerunner of the CR P5 range of fully automatic, multi-tool and profiling lathes. A lathe with an automatic feed and delivery heralded an automatic machine tool production line.

The growth in machine tool demand, stemming from the expansion in motor car manufacture, was reflected in Churchill-Redman turnover, which rose from just over £200,000 in 1946 to over £1 million in 1955. To meet demand, new capacity and new products were sought in the mid-1950s. The Scotswood operation moved to a purpose-built factory at Blaydon on the other side of the Tyne in 1957. This plant made machine tools for the motor industry, including the Vertimax vertical spindle production lathe, invented in the war by James Anderson, a Glasgow garage proprietor.

Anderson's company was one of a number of innovative firms in the industry which Gabriel brought into the Churchill Group in the 1950s and early 1960s. Gabriel preferred to run these acquisitions as separate operating companies, to which he added a selling firm, Charles H. Churchill Ltd, in 1962. The firm's headquarters were moved in 1950 from London to Birmingham, though he kept his chairman's office at Caxton Street, London, until 1960. The parent company's capital was increased to £1.26 million in 1955. A decade later the Churchill Group was one of the largest in the machine tool industry, with group sales of £14 million and employing 2000. However, rising German and Japanese competition, and the concomitant needs to increase investment and to cut labour costs drastically, persuaded him to recommend a take-over of the Churchill Group by Tube Investments. When this happened in 1966 Gabriel retired.

Gabriel belonged to both the Institution of Mechanical Engineers and the Institution of Civil Engineers. In 1949–51 he served as president of the Machine Tool Trades Association. Early in life he enjoyed rowing and later took up golf. Raised as a Methodist, he later attended the Church of England, but could not always agree with Anglican doctrines. Politically, he regarded socialism as a false paradise. He married in 1914 Elfrida Ianthe Mary Griffith Clarke, daughter of Edward Clarke, a merchant. They had three sons, the youngest of whom, Ralph, read engineering at Cambridge, served in the REME in the Second World War, and afterwards joined the management of the Churchill Group. Gabriel died at his home, Robin Hill, Forrest Road, Kenilworth, on 7 July 1979.

DAVID J. JEREMY

Sources D. J. Jeremy, 'Gabriel, John Beresford Stuart', *DBB* • D. H. Aldcroft, 'The performance of the British machine-tool industry in the interwar years', *Business History Review*, 40 (1966), 281–96 • T. R. Gourvish, 'Mechanical engineering', *British industry between the wars*, ed. N. K. Buxton and D. H. Aldcroft (1979) • L. T. C. Rolt, *Charles Churchill, 1865–1965* (1965) • L. T. C. Rolt, *Tools for the job: a short history of machine tools* (1965) • S. B. Saul, 'The machine tool industry in Britain to 1914', *Business History*, 10 (1968), 22–43 • d. cert.
Likenesses photograph, repro. in Jeremy, 'Gabriel'
Wealth at death £80,971: probate, 31 Oct 1979, *CGPLA Eng. & Wales*

Gabriel [married name March], (**Mary Anne**) **Virginia** (1825–1877), composer, was born in Banstead, Surrey, on 7 February 1825, the daughter of Robert Gabriel, an Irish colonel of the 7th dragoon guards. She was educated in Italy, and studied the piano with J. P. Pixis, Theodor Döhler, and Sigismund Thalberg, and composition with Saverio Mercadante and Bernhard Molique. She went on to compose more than 300 songs and thirty piano works, many of which achieved popularity and were widely performed in the 1860s. They included the songs 'Forsaken' (1855), 'The Skipper and his Boy' (1865), and 'Lost Dreams' (1876), and *La gondola* (1855) and *Long Ago* (1861) for piano. She also wrote about a dozen operettas, which were performed by the German Reed Company at the Gallery of Illustration, London, and on their tours of the provinces. *Widows Bewitched* (1865) was produced by the Bijou Operetta Company at St George's Hall on 13 November 1867 and went on to enjoy a lengthy and successful run. Other similar works, including *Who's the Heir?* (1870), *Grass Widows* (1873), and *Graziella* (1875), were also popular. Her cantata on Longfellow's poem *Evangeline* was a great success after its première at William Kuhe's Brighton festival on 13 February 1873, and was heard again that year at Rivière's Covent Garden concerts on 24 November and 1 December. Another cantata, *Dreamland*, appeared in 1875.

On 4 November 1873 Virginia Gabriel became the second wife of George Edward March (1834–1922), a Foreign Office official who also wrote some of her librettos, including those for *Grass Widows* and *Who's the Heir?*. She died on 7 August 1877 in St George's Hospital, London, from injuries, including a fractured skull, sustained after being accidentally thrown from her carriage in Lower Belgrave Street. L. M. MIDDLETON, *rev.* DAVID J. GOLBY

Sources P. Fox and J. R. Gardner, 'Gabriel, Mary Anne Virginia', *The new Grove dictionary of women composers*, ed. J. A. Sadie and R. Samuel (1994) • *MT*, 18 (1877), 443 • Brown & Stratton, *Brit. mus.* • d. cert. • m. cert.
Likenesses print, Harvard TC
Wealth at death under £12,000: probate, 29 Nov 1877, *CGPLA Eng. & Wales*

Gace, William (*fl.* 1568–1580), translator, was admitted to Clare College, Cambridge, as a sizar in Michaelmas term 1568, where he read for a BA. Having taken his degree in 1572, he proceeded to devote his linguistic skills to translating continental evangelical tracts into English. His motivation for making the Latin works of a number of German and Danish Lutheran reformers known in England was 'that those my godly country-men which are ignorant of the Latine tongue may become partakers of such Christian doctrine' (Hemmingsen, sig. Aiiiv).

Gace was a convinced evangelical, and by his translations sought to sustain the consolidation of Reformation doctrine in England 'for the common good both of Church and state' (Luther, *Thirtie Foure Special and Chosen Sermons*, sig. A8r). A rather eclectic selection of popular Lutheran theological works formed the basis for his translations. For Gace, Martin Luther stood out as 'a miracle among men' (ibid., sig. A2r), and so he compiled a significant anthology of homilies on justification by faith alone from Luther's works 'for the commodity and use of our English nation' (ibid., sig. Aa7r), which he published as *Thirtie Foure Special and Chosen Sermons of D. Martin Luther* in 1578. Two years later Gace translated another of Luther's writings, published as *A right comfortable treatise conteyning sundrye pointes of consolation for them that labour & are laden*. He also selected for translation a commentary on the epistle of James from the exegetical work of the Danish reformer Niels Hemmingsen (1513–1600), a man whose orthodoxy was seriously questioned by contemporary Lutherans, as well as a guide to life in a Christian society by the Saxon Johannes Rivius (1500–1553).

J. ANDREAS LÖWE

Sources M. Luther, *Thirtie foure special and chosen sermons of D. Martin Luther … discovering most clearly … to every ordinary capacity: the difference betwixt faith and workes … Englished by W. Gace* (1578), sigs. A2r, A8r, Aa7r • M. Luther, *A right comfortable treatise conteyning sundrye pointes of consolation for them that labour & are laden. Written by D. Martin Luther to Prince Friderick, duke of Saxonie; being sore sicke. … Englished by W. Gace* (1580), sig. *vv • N. Hemmingsen, *A learned and fruitefull commentarie upon the epistle of James the apostle … and newly translated into English by W.G.* (1577), sig. Aiiiv • J. Rivius, *A guide unto godliness, moste worthy to bee followed of all true Christians* (1579) • Cooper, *Ath. Cantab.*, 2.22–3 • Venn, *Alum. Cant.*, 1/2.187 • J. Venn and J. A. Venn, eds., *The book of matriculations and degrees … in the University of Cambridge from 1544 to 1659* (1913), 276

Gadbury, John (1627–1704), astrologer, was born on 31 December 1627 in Wheatley, Oxfordshire, the son of William Gadbury, a farmer, and his wife, who was the daughter of Sir John Curzon of Waterperry and seems to have been disinherited as a result of the union. Her forename is unknown. Gadbury was briefly apprenticed to an Oxford tailor before a partial reconciliation with his maternal grandfather enabled him to take up studies with Nicholas Fiske at Oxford in 1644. This did not last for long, however; by 1648 he was working for a merchant adventurer living near Strand Bridge in London—very near the residence of the leading astrologer of the day, William Lilly, with whom he became acquainted in this period.

Gadbury's astrology and politics, c.1648–c.1690. Gadbury threw himself into the religious and political turmoil of

John Gadbury (1627–1704), by Thomas Cross, pubd 1658

the time, joining up successively with the presbyterians, the Independents, the Levellers, and finally the notorious 'Family of Love' under Abiezer Coppe. About this time he also married. His wife's name is not known. In 1652 he returned to Oxford, mended his fences with his grandfather, and took up the serious study of astrology under the mathematician and astrologer Nicholas Fiske. That year saw his first publication, *Philastrogus Knavery Epitomized*, which defended 'Mr. Culpepper, Mr. Lilly and the rest of the students in that noble Art' against an attack by William Brommerton. Two years later, he published *Animal cornutum, or, A Brief Method of the Grounds of Astrology*.

In 1655 (for the following year) there appeared *Speculum Astrologicum*, the first of his annual almanacs and ephemerides. After two issues it was replaced by *An Astrological Prediction* (1658), and for 1659 the title became *Ephēmeris, or, A Diary Astronomical and Astrological*, which he continued to produce annually until the year before his death. About this time he moved back to London; he eventually settled in Brick Court, College Street, off Dean's Yard in Westminster, very close to St Margaret's Church, where he attended services.

Gadbury occasionally supplemented his regular almanac with special issues, as *The Jamaica Almanack, or, An Astrological Diary* (1673), *The West-India or Jamaica Almanack* (1674), and *Diarum astronomicum, or, A West India Almanack* (1675). In 1672 he also issued *Ephemerides of the Celestial*

Motions for X Years, 1672–81—which listed all the planetary positions, movements, and events without any prognostication—and followed this up in 1680 with *Ephemerides of the Celestial Motions for XX Years, 1682–1701*.

As these publications imply, Gadbury's interests extended beyond judicial astrology to other aspects of the seventeenth-century intellectual ferment: navigation and exploration, astronomy, and natural philosophy. His books thus also included *Natura prodigiorum, or, A Discourse Touching the Nature of Prodigies* (1662) and *De cometis, or, A Discourse on the Natures and Effects of Comets* (1665). In another such work, *Nauticum astrologicum, or, The Astrological Seaman* (1689), he confessed that:

> My inclinations aim at a certainty in Science: and I can truly say, that I have found more in Astrology, than in all others put together. But such is my ill Fortune … that I want Parts to Demonstrate that to be certain and true to others, which by assiduous Experience I am myself convinced of. (*Nauticum astrologicum*, 1689, A3r)

The thread uniting these concerns thus remained astrology. Indeed Gadbury, together with Lilly and John Partridge, was one of the three best-known English astrologers of the second half of the seventeenth century. But his attitude towards his subject changed radically in close parallel to the transformation in his religious and political opinions. Thus in 1658 he published a thoroughly traditional textbook of judicial astrology: *Genethlialogia, or, The doctrine of nativities … together with the doctrine of horarie questions*. Building on William Lilly's *Christian Astrology* of 1647, it appeared with that master's imprimatur. By the Restoration two years later, however, he had broken with the radicalism of Lilly, and set out his stall as a royalist and high Anglican. Indeed, he was frequently accused of being a Jacobite and crypto-Catholic, in whose opinion 'the Coelestial Orbs disown all Anti-Monarchical, Disloyal and Rebellious Principles' (*Diary*, 1689). Accordingly, in 1659 he attacked Lilly rancorously in *The Novice-Astrologer Instructed* and issued a regretful analysis of *The Nativity of the Late King Charls*, while *Britain's Royal Star* (1661) found promising portents in the planetary positions at the accession of Charles II.

In this capacity Gadbury became Lilly's bitterest enemy and rival, as he was later to become that of the radical whig astrologer John Partridge. He also formed friendships with the more conservative and (as they would now be termed) scientifically inclined astrologers, such as Vincent Wing, whom he commemorated in *A Brief Relation of the Life and Death of … Mr Vincent Wing* (1669), Sir George Wharton, whose works he saw into print in 1683 after the latter's death two years earlier, and, later, George Parker. Gadbury continued feuding with Lilly until the latter's death in 1681; in 1675 he published *Obsequium rationabile, or, A reasonable service performed for the coelestial sign Scorpio … against the malitious and false attempts of that grand (but fortunate) IMPOSTOR, Mr William Lilly* (who had used Gadbury's Scorpio ascendant to cast aspersions on his character). In addition to Lilly's barbs he also had to endure the scandalous speculations of Partridge's *Nebulo Anglicanus* (1693). In 1687, he seems to have married again, although no details of this are known.

Gadbury's contemporary reputation and influence Gadbury's impact was not limited to the astrological world. Thanks to his uncompromising views together with the extensive contemporary readership of astrological almanacs, he became a nationally notorious figure, and one occasionally in danger of his life. He was arrested on 2 November 1679 during the furore over the Popish Plot, and imprisoned for supposedly conspiring with Thomas Dangerfield and Mrs Elizabeth Cellier to assassinate the king and bring in a Catholic succession. He was examined by the privy council in the presence of Charles II, who apparently asked him sardonically whether he could predict to which prison he would be sent. After fifteen weeks, however, want of evidence—and possibly the intercession of Wharton—compelled his release, and £200 compensation was paid in 1681.

Gadbury was also accredited with writing the popular narrative *A Ballad upon the Popish Plot Written by a Lady of Quality* (1679). Publicly rebuked by the bishop of London for pointedly failing to include the anniversary of the discovery of Guy Fawkes's plot in his almanac, he was even twice burnt in effigy, along with the pope, by a London street mob.

In 1690 Gadbury was again arrested, accused (falsely, but more plausibly) of plotting against William III, and detained for eight or nine weeks before being released. Having quite failed to foresee the revolution of 1688, and also in the interests of discretion, he had written in his almanac for that year that 'my muse hath of late been planet-struck, and I must waive predictions for a season' (*Diary*, 1690).

In tandem with the transformation of his original political and religious views, Gadbury's astrology also changed drastically. From his early traditional position, he moved to a markedly more sceptical outlook. This led to his becoming the leader of an ambitious programme to reform astrology along natural philosophical lines. From the early 1650s until the late 1680s, he carried this out in parallel with Joshua Childrey and John Goad, with the knowledge of the Royal Society and the encouragement of some of its fellows (John Aubrey, Jonas Moore, John Beale, John Collins, and Elias Ashmole). Gadbury and Goad in particular were close friends and colleagues though neither belonged to the Royal Society.

The social and political character of this reform was uniformly Anglican (usually high) and tory (with suspicions of Jacobitism), and its intellectual approach élitist, experimental, and rational, in a Baconian sense. These commitments placed it in direct opposition to both the political radicalism, populism, and magic of earlier astrologers such as Lilly, Nicholas Culpeper, and John Booker—now widely felt to be no longer tenable—and the radical whiggism and Aristotelian rationalism of later astrologers such as Partridge and John Whalley. The reformers' attempted alliance with the Royal Society, which was itself a focus of attempts to define and create 'certain' experimental truth as a way to overcome the recent excesses of antinomian sectarianism and fend off new bouts, was thus quite natural.

Some fellows were more sceptical of Gadbury's efforts, probably because of his reputation as a judicial (rather than natural) astrologer. John Flamsteed was not encouraging, Robert Hooke dismissed him as 'mad' (Hooke, 248), and when Aubrey suggested to Edmond Halley that he look into astrology more closely, Halley replied that 'it seems a very ill time for it, when the Arch-conjuror Gadbury is in some prospect in being hanged for it' (Ronan, 47).

Gadbury's research programme in astrology Although there was no firm consensus yet among natural philosophers, Halley's unflattering epithet accurately reflects the sharp decline in the opinion of astrology among the middle and professional classes since 1660. This was something of which Gadbury, whose fervent hope was that 'the Astrologer will not be esteemed a Witch or Conjurer, but a friend to Natural Philosophy' (*Diary*, 1680, B2) was painfully aware, and he blamed principally the magical and populist astrology of Lilly and others that included such things as prophecies attributed to Mother Shipton and Merlin, stuff 'fit only for laughter' (*Diary*, 1670, C3–4). According to him (writing in 1666), it was 'by reason of the apocryphal part of astrology that the sound part so extremely suffers'. He later added the melancholy reflection that between those who will believe nothing of it and those who believe everything, 'I know not which of the two doth Astrology the greatest injury: I conceive she is equally indebted to them both' (*Diary*, 1668, A3).

However, Gadbury was also aware of the pressures of popular demands for astral drama. In common with several other almanac writers he discussed recent scientific discoveries and theories, but remarked sharply in 1692 that it would have pleased many readers more if, like some, he had 'told them a story of dragons seen in the air in Sussex … some ignus fatuus haunting Clerkenwell … killed a king or two, destroyed an army' (*Diary*, 1692).

Central to Gadbury's research was his belief that 'the influences of the Stars are purely natural, and directed by Natural Beams, or Aspects Geometrical' (*Astrological Predictions*, 1679, 3–4). His proposed solution to the crisis in astrology was therefore to adopt the Baconian programme also embraced by the early Royal Society, and reform astrology along experimental lines. Thus he argued that 'Astrology wanteth its History', using the term history in Bacon's sense of a careful tabulation of past events and their comparison with the relevant conditions, 'as much (if not more) than any other Science; That being the via regia to its Perfection'. Accordingly 'One real experiment is of greater worth and more to be valued than one hundred pompous predictions' (*Diary*, 1676, C7–8). Of course, 'experiment' did not necessarily mean then what it does today; for Gadbury it included the detailed analysis of nativities and their comparison with the chief 'accidents' (events) of the person's life to check, in particular, the vexed question of the best methods of timing.

(This was also Aubrey's chief motive for compiling, at the same time, his *Brief Lives*.) This research resulted in Gadbury's study *Collectio generarum* (1662), the first such collection of nativities in English. (In 1693 it was challenged by Partridge's *Defectio geniturarum*.)

Gadbury's research also took a more comparative and quantitative turn. In his almanacs for 1664 and 1665, for example, he asked his readers to send him the birth data and then the major events of all children born on 4 and 5 September 1664. The object was to separate what such time twins had in common, what was necessarily true, from what was merely contingent and personal. To this end he called for closer co-operation among astrologers in gathering data, exchanging information, and co-ordinating research.

Recognizing the difficulties presented by observing fellow human beings (something that still exercises social scientists today), Gadbury also had great hopes for astrometeorology. To that end he encouraged the labours of his friend and colleague John Goad, and he himself took extensive weather records, comparing each day's meteorological and astronomical–astrological conditions. The object was to find the key that would constitute a means of distinguishing between 'chance' and 'necessity'.

Unfortunately, the weather, too, offers methodological problems of extraordinary complexity, ones which naturally left others unimpressed by, for example, Gadbury's unpublished 'Catalogue of more than 270 new and full moons, which apparently brought Rain'. Late in life Gadbury himself admitted that:

> I have been a daily observer of Aireal Variety for almost 35 Years, as the Noble Lord Bacon directs as necessary: And though I have met with several Similitudes of Verity … yet I must freely own to have met with other Arguments too hard for me to bring under a Regimental Order of Experience. (Gadbury, A3)

By the end of his life, Gadbury came close to admitting the failure of his programme, though not to surrendering his hopes for its eventual success. Introducing his last almanac, for 1704, he wrote that 'the brink of the Grave become the desk we write upon', and poignantly reflected, with characteristic honesty, that:

> I am very much ready to part with any Errors, upon an assured Conviction they are such; yet, I shall not, cannot, wholly Renounce, or bid Good Night to Astrology: Lest in so doing I should Espouse a far greater Error, than any I am willing to part with. For Astrology is the language of the Heavens. … Howbeit, for my Great Creator's Honour, the Welfare of the Church and Nation, and Benefit of true Philosophy, I wish this Noble Art were well corrected. (Gadbury, A1)

Gadbury died on 24 March 1704 and was buried in the vault of St Margaret's Church, Westminster, four days later. He left a widow, and a professional successor in George Parker, another tory high-churchman and a respected observational astronomer, who saw Gadbury's last twenty-year ephemeris into print in 1709. His almanac was briefly continued by his cousin Job, and then others appointed by the Company of Stationers, but it steadily lost the interest of readers, and circulation.

PATRICK CURRY

Sources B. S. Capp, *Astrology and the popular press: English almanacs, 1500–1800* (1979) · P. Curry, *Prophecy and power: astrology in early modern England* (1989) · *DNB* · J. Gadbury, *Ephemeris, or, A diary astronomical, astrological, meteorological, for the year … 1704* (1704) · *The diary of Robert Hooke … 1672–1680*, ed. H. W. Robinson and W. Adams (1935) · C. Ronan, *Edmund Halley: genius in eclipse* (1969)
Archives U. Durham L., meteorological observations | NL Wales, letters to Edward Lloyd of Llanforda
Likenesses T. Cross, line engraving, NPG; repro. in J. Gadbury, *The doctrine of nativities* (1658), frontispiece [*see illus.*] · engraving, repro. in *Ephemeris, or, A Diary Astronomical and Astrological* (1673–5) · line engraving, BM, NPG; repro. in J. Gadbury, *Collectio genituarum, or, a collection of nativities* (1662)

Gadbury, Mary (*b. c.*1619). *See under* Franklin, William (*b. c.*1610).

Gadderar, James (*c.*1655–1733), Scottish Episcopal bishop of Aberdeen, was a younger son of William Gadderar, a tenant in Trowes, Moray, and Margaret Marshall, heir of a portion of the lands of Urquhart, Moray. He graduated MA at Glasgow on 20 July 1675. Following his brother Alexander, minister of Girvan, into the ministry, he was recommended for his licence by the presbytery of Glasgow on 23 March 1681. In October he was presented to the parish of Kilmacolm, to which he was collated on 12 January and admitted on 15 January 1682.

Gadderar was presbytery clerk of Paisley when rabbled from his charge by the presbyterians during the winter of 1688–9. Active in Glasgow until about 1692, he is said to have farmed with his dispossessed brother, but probably during the 1690s moved to London, where he was a close friend of fellow nonjuring Scots Dr Alexander Monro and the Hon. Archibald Campbell. In 1703 he published *Concerning the Right of Succession to the Kingdom of England*, a translation of Sir Thomas Craig of Riccarton's Latin treatise. In his dedication to the Faculty of Advocates, Gadderar emphasized the duty of subjects to their prince, and struck at John Toland's attacks on religion and the monarchy. An active friend to Scottish nonjurors in London, in 1711 Gadderar was the candidate of Bishop Alexander Ross or Rose of Edinburgh to become their agent, but was passed over, allegedly because he regarded the Church of England as schismatic.

In London, on 24 February 1712, Campbell, George Hickes, and John Falconer secretly consecrated Gadderar bishop to maintain the English nonjurors' succession. At first, like Campbell, with whom he shared a house, he did not act episcopally in Scotland, instead assisting Hickes in consecrating Jeremy Collier, Nathaniel Spinckes, Samuel Hawes, and others, and peacemaking in the disputes between the English nonjurors sparked by the restoration of certain usages in their liturgy of 1718. He himself had long used the mixed cup (wine and water), express invocation of the Holy Spirit, and the prayer of oblation when administering communion in nonjuring congregations

and noble households. He believed the 1637 Scottish liturgy (containing the latter two usages) to be more authentic than the 1662 prayer book, and esteemed William Laud the greatest post-Reformation churchman. Between 1717 and 1722 he participated in the nonjurors' abortive negotiations of a concordat with the Eastern churches.

After Bishop Rose's death in 1720 Gadderar and Campbell supported the creation of episcopal districts instead of a college of bishops without dioceses. Although consulted as Scottish bishops over the royal nominations in 1720–21, they were estranged from the college by their declaration of non-communion with brethren who were not usagers. The breach grew in May 1721, when the Aberdeen clergy elected Campbell as their temporary superintendent, and he refused to promise the college not to make or allow liturgical innovations. The college and George Lockhart of Carnwath feared a damaging division and attempted to curb the Aberdeen clergy, who were mainly pro-usager. In response Campbell dispatched Gadderar north in November 1722, then the following January nominated him his suffragan. Gadderar assured the college of his loyalty to James Edward Stuart and parried moves to suppress the usages. His pastoral work began in Lent 1723 with the first confirmations in the diocese since the revolution of 1688–9, followed by another visitation in June.

However, by a concordat in July 1724 Gadderar agreed to cede the public use of the mixed cup, to receive the unmixed cup conditionally, and not to introduce the usages without the consent of the college bishops, who thereby recognized his title by virtue of their authority, not Campbell's. The resultant rupture with Campbell over the apparent betrayal of the usagers' cause was healed in March 1725 when Gadderar declared his intention never to omit the usages. Campbell resigned his title as superintendent, and Gadderar was elected bishop of Aberdeen on 24 May by the clergy of Aberdeen diocese, and bishop of Moray on 17 June by the Moray presbyters. He visited Moray in 1726, but soon passed the burden to William Dunbar, whom he helped to consecrate in 1727. Gadderar was a wise, zealous, and beloved bishop, who revitalized the church throughout the north-east by his extensive confirmations and many ordinations.

In 1724 Gadderar reprinted a version of the 1637 communion office, the first of the 'wee bookies' containing the developing Scottish use, for which he did much to gain the church's acceptance. He was also distinguished for supporting the church's intrinsic rights and the electoral rights of the presbyters. He lived at Arbuthnott under the viscount of Arbuthnott's patronage until about winter 1726, when George Skene of Skene provided him with a house near Aberdeen. After 1729 he lived in Old Aberdeen, where he died unmarried of 'the epidemicall cold then raging' (*Remarks*, 11.166) on 23 January 1733, and was buried in Bishop Patrick Scougall's grave in St Machar's Church.

TRISTRAM CLARKE

Sources *Fasti Scot.*, new edn, vol. 3 · G. Grub, *An ecclesiastical history of Scotland*, 4 vols. (1861), vols. 3–4 · letters of and papers concerning J. Gadderar, 1688–1733, NA Scot., CH 12/12 · A. Campbell, letters to Thomas Brett, 1721–5, Bodl. Oxf., MS Eng. th. c. 27–8 · letters to J. Mackenzie of Delvine, 1715–21, NL Scot., MSS 1108–1109 · J. Dowden, *The annotated Scottish communion office* (1884) · T. Clarke, 'Nurseries of sedition? The episcopal congregations after the revolution of 1689', *After Columba—after Calvin: community and identity in the religious traditions of north-east Scotland*, ed. J. Porter (1999), 61–9 · *Remarks and collections of Thomas Hearne*, ed. C. E. Doble and others, 11, OHS, 72 (1921), 166

Archives NA Scot., letters, the Episcopal Chest, CH 12/12 · NL Scot., letters to Mackenzie family · University of Dundee, Brechin Diocesan archives, copy list of ordinations, Br. MS.3.DC/115(19)

Wealth at death £232 17s. od. Scots; incl. books to value of £180; debts of £371 17s. od.: testament, including inventory of moveable estate, Aberdeen commissary court, 6 July 1733, NA Scot., CC 1/6/14

Gaddesden, John (d. 1348/9), physician, took his name from Little or Great Gaddesden, Hertfordshire. He was later enrolled in the confraternity of nearby St Albans Abbey, in order to secure the benefits of spiritual fellowship with the monks; perhaps he had formerly attended the school there. The fact that he held an Oxford MA degree by 1307 suggests a birth date in the early 1280s. Several John of Gaddesdens are recorded in the reign of Henry III, most notably one who served as Queen Eleanor's chamberlain from 1236 to 1242, but no descent can be traced from any of them to the physician. His parents are unknown, but his father lived into John's adulthood, for John operated to remove a 'stone' from under his father's tongue.

Recorded as a fellow of Merton College in 1305 and 1307, Gaddesden next occurs in December 1316 when, as Master John de Gatesden, acolyte, he obtained the rectory of St Nicholas, Abingdon, Berkshire. Between 1307 and 1316 he apparently studied medicine at Oxford and wrote his most famous work, the *Rosa anglica medicine*. He reports that he compiled this text in the seventh year of his *lectura*, probably the seventh year since his inception as a master of arts, which presumably had marked the beginning of his medical studies. If Gaddesden incepted c.1307, that would date the *Rosa* to c.1313. He probably remained in Oxford until the 1330s. On 24 February 1317 he presented John Ely, priest, to the vicarage of Abingdon and on 3 March 1321 he exchanged the rectory there for that of Chipping Norton, Oxfordshire (valued in 1336 at 40 marks). Bishop Henry Burghersh of Lincoln (d. 1340) granted him licence on 4 March 1321 to study at an English university for one year, and renewed this for two years on 4 April 1323, and again on 10 May 1328. On 22 May 1323 Burghersh also licensed Gaddesden to have mass celebrated in his lodgings while studying at Oxford and on 23 February 1330 licensed him to let his rectory to farm for two years. Emden's assertion that Gaddesden had obtained the degree of doctor of medicine by 1332 is unsubstantiated; he was described in 1336 as master of arts and medicine and bachelor of theology.

By 1332 Gaddesden had entered royal service. On 16 December 1332 John de Catesdene, master of arts and medicine and king's clerk, received, at the king's petition, the provision of a canonry of St Paul's, London, with reservation of a prebend, notwithstanding his rectory of Chipping Norton. On 4 December 1333 the pope granted him the provision of a canonry of Chichester with reservation of a prebend, again despite his rectory, and on 22 September 1334 the reservation of a dignity in the gift of the bishop and chapter of London, though on condition that he resign the rectory. Gaddesden may have resigned his canonry instead. He attended the monks of Abingdon in 1334–5 (for a fee of 13s. 6d.), and on 5 July 1336 the pope ordered the bishop of Winchester to provide Gaddesden with a canonry of London with reservation of a prebend, again on condition that he resign his rectory. Gaddesden, however, continued to hold Chipping Norton until his death.

By 1338 Gaddesden had entered the service of Edward, prince of Wales (the Black Prince), receiving from him gifts of winter robes and a barrel of wine. In the spring of 1341 he attended Edward III's second daughter, Joan. In August 1342 he obtained the prebend of Weldland in St Paul's, London, and on 25 October 1342 he received a licence of non-residence at Chipping Norton for one year. In 1347 or 1348 the Black Prince gave him a rose of gold, probably an allusion to the *Rosa*, as a new year's gift, in addition to his annual fee of £10. Gaddesden's licence for non-residence was renewed on 23 January 1348 for two years while he was in the Black Prince's service, but according to Emden he had died by July 1349, perhaps of plague.

Gaddesden left a considerable reputation. He was the first major medical scholar to have been trained wholly in England, and the only Oxford-trained medieval physician to achieve recognition on the continent. His *Rosa anglica* was a distillation of the works of more than forty-six medical authorities, ancient and recent, although it ignored the near contemporary works from the northern Italian universities. In it Gaddesden claims to have saved the king's son (presumably either Thomas or Edmund, sons of Edward I from his second marriage) from smallpox by wrapping him in scarlet cloth in a bed with red hangings. He also, unusually, admits to practising the arts of the surgeon and barber–surgeon as well as the physician, proclaiming his skills at setting bones, letting blood, drawing teeth, and even cutting corns and killing lice. Money was probably a factor: Gaddesden boasts of his fees, suggests expensive remedies for the rich and cheap ones for the poor, and notes that mental illnesses are seldom lucrative for the physician.

Gaddesden chose the title because the five books of the *Rosa* recalled the five sepals of the rose; it also echoed the *Lilium medicine* of Bernard de Gordon. Gaddesden claims that, just as a rose excels every other flower, so the *Rosa* excels all previous medical works, and that poor surgeons and physicians can substitute it for many other books. Matthaeus Sylvaticus mentioned Gaddesden in his *Pandectae* (1317), and although the illustrious Montpellier surgeon, Gui de Chauliac, sniffed in 1363 that the *Rosa* was a foolish compendium of stale material, Chaucer included Gaddesden with Galen, Avicenna, and the other great medical authorities. Numerous Latin copies of the *Rosa* survive and it was partially translated into Middle English and Irish in the fifteenth century. The first printed edition appeared at Pavia in 1492; three more followed, the first two at Venice and the third at Augsburg, in 1502, 1516, and 1595 respectively. The only modern English translation of the *Rosa*, published in 1929, was made from an Irish version of the fifteenth century.

John Bale lists six additional medical works by Gaddesden: *De regimene acutorum et dietarie*, *De simplicibus medicinis*, *De digerentibus et euacuantibus*, *De instrumentis sue artis*, *Quid pro quo*, and *De fleubotomia*, all with incipits, and two others, *Practica medicinae* and *Pro dietariis*, without incipits. However, these attributions have been challenged by Wickersheimer. A brief treatise on the pestilence in English, attributed in a rubric to Gaddesden, survives in a manuscript dated 1472 (BL, Sloane MS 3866, fols. 90–92).

MARTHA CARLIN

Sources Emden, *Oxf.*, 2.739 · C. H. Talbot and E. A. Hammond, *The medical practitioners in medieval England: a biographical register* (1965), 148–50 · W. Wulff, ed. and trans., *Rosa anglica sev Rosa medicinae Johannis Anglici*, ITS, 25 (1929) · F. M. Getz, 'The faculty of medicine before 1500', *Hist. U. Oxf. 2: Late med. Oxf.*, 373–405 · L. Thorndike and P. Kibre, *A catalogue of incipits of mediaeval scientific writings in Latin*, rev. edn (1963), nos. 85, 552, 577, 721, 823, 1218 · H. P. Cholmeley, *John of Gaddesden and the Rosa medicinae* (1912) · T. Hunt, *Popular medicine in thirteenth-century England: introduction and texts* (1990), 26–33, 67, 349–50 · H. H. Bashford, *The Harley Street calendar* (1929), 15–22 · CEPR letters, 2.372, 399, 406, 535 · R. Barber, *Edward, prince of Wales and Aquitaine: a biography of the Black Prince* (1978), 22, 30, 93 · *The registers of Roger Martival, bishop of Salisbury, 1315–1330*, 1, ed. K. Edwards, CYS, 55 (1959), 64, 77 · M. C. B. Dawes, ed., *Register of Edward, the Black Prince*, PRO, 4 (1933), 69 · R. E. G. Kirk, ed., *Accounts of the obedientiars of Abingdon Abbey*, CS, new ser., 51 (1892), 4 · Bale, *Cat.*, 1.389 · Bale, *Index*, 206 · *National union catalog, pre-1956 imprints*, Library of Congress · *Fasti Angl., 1300–1541*, [St Paul's, London], 66 · F. M. Powicke, *The medieval books of Merton College* (1931), 141n.; nos. 379, 603, 800 · G. Dock, 'Printed editions of the *Rosa Anglica* of John of Gaddesden', *Janus*, 12 (1907), 425–35 · W. G. Lennox, 'John of Gaddesden on epilepsy', *Annals of Medical History*, 3rd ser., 1 (1939), 283–307 · C. H. Talbot, *Medicine in medieval England* (1967), 107–15, 146, 201, 208 · J. Freind, *The history of physick*, 4th edn, 2 (1750); repr. (1973), 264, 277–93 · E. Wickersheimer and D. Jacquart, *Dictionnaire biographique des médecins en France au moyen âge*, new edn, ed. G. Beaujouan, 3 vols. (Geneva, 1979), vol. 1, pp. 404–5; vol. 3, p. 158 · J. Freind, *Opera omnia* (1733), 550–55 · J. H. Talbott, *A biographical history of medicine* (1970), 32–3 · L. E. Voigts, 'Multitudes of Middle English medical manuscripts, or, The Englishing of science and medicine', *Manuscript sources of medieval medicine*, ed. M. R. Schleissner (1995), 187, 190 · L. Thorndike, 'Unde versus', *Traditio*, 11 (1955), 163–93 · H. E. Ussery, *Chaucer's physician: medicine and literature in fourteenth-century England* (1971) · W. Feldhaus, 'Zahnärztliches bei John of Gaddesden', diss., University of Leipzig, 1922 · M. A. E. Green, *Lives of the princesses of England*, 3 (1851), 242 · G. C. Brodrick, *Memorials of Merton College*, OHS, 4 (1885), 176–7 · J. R. L. Highfield, ed., *The early rolls of Merton College, Oxford*, OHS, new ser., 18 (1964), 77 · VCH Hertfordshire, 2.203, 208; pl. facing 204 · Tout, *Admin. hist.*, 1.253–4 and note

Archives BL, Sloane MS 3866, fols. 90–92

Gaddum, Sir John Henry (1900–1965), pharmacologist, was born on 31 March 1900 at Hale, Cheshire, the eldest child in the family of four boys and two girls of Henry Edwin Gaddum, a silk importer who was made an honorary MA of Manchester University for his devotion to charitable work, and his wife, Phyllis Mary, daughter of Alfred Barratt, a first cousin of Sir Samuel Hoare (later Lord

Templewood), and of Richard D. Acland, bishop of Bombay, by whom Gaddum was married in 1929 to Iris Mary (1894–1992), daughter of the zoologist Sir Sidney *Harmer. Miss Harmer did outstanding clinical research under Sir Thomas Lewis and became a consultant dermatologist. There were three daughters of the marriage.

At Rugby, Gaddum won prizes in mathematics, physics, and astronomy. He entered Trinity College, Cambridge, in 1919 on an entrance scholarship, later won a senior scholarship, read medicine and obtained first-class honours in part one of the mathematical tripos (1920), and second-class honours in part two of the natural sciences tripos in physiology (1922). Among his teachers were the physiologist John Newport Langley, the neurophysiologist Edgar Douglas Adrien, and the biochemist Frederick Gowland Hopkins. In 1922 Gaddum entered University College Hospital, London, qualified MRCS LRCP in 1924, but in his final MB in Cambridge failed twice in medicine. Later Cambridge gave him a ScD.

In 1925 Gaddum was initiated into pharmacological research by J. W. Trevan at the Wellcome Physiological Research Laboratories in Beckenham. This collaboration initiated Gaddum's interest in the mathematical analysis of biological data. In 1927 he was accepted as assistant to Henry Dale at the National Institute for Medical Research in Hampstead, where he spent six extremely fruitful years of research. He became keen to take charge of a department of his own and, when he did not succeed in getting the chair at Birmingham University, in 1934 he accepted the chair of pharmacology at the Egyptian University of Cairo where his friend G. Anrep was professor of physiology. His stay there was short, but made a deep impact lasting long after he had left. He was appointed professor of pharmacology at University College, London, in 1935. Two years later he accepted the chair at the School of Pharmacy, University of London. During the Second World War he worked at Porton Camp and was in part responsible for deciding on the drug to be carried by British agents to be used for suicide in case of serious emergency. For a short time he served as a temporary lieutenant-colonel in the army, and if gas warfare had started he would have been physiologist to the Twenty-First Army group when France was invaded. In 1942 he succeeded Alfred Joseph Clark in the chair of materia medica in the University of Edinburgh and acted as director of the Medical Research Council endocrinological research unit.

In 1958 Gaddum became director of the Agricultural Research Council Institute of Animal Physiology in Babraham, Cambridge, and within a few years the institute became one of the great international centres for research in physiology and pharmacology. Gaddum's work at the institute brought him wide national and international recognition. He became corresponding and honorary member of scientific societies and academies in France, Italy, Germany, and South and North America. He was elected fellow of the Royal Society in 1945; was a fellow of the Royal Society of Edinburgh; was knighted in 1964; and was awarded an honorary LLD at Edinburgh.

The two main lines of research Gaddum pursued

throughout his life were the mode of action of drugs and the development of specific and sensitive methods for biological assay. The modern development of bioassay owes much to him. He stressed and demonstrated the need for making parallel estimates on different assay preparations in order to identify an unknown pharmacologically active substance in a tissue extract. He formulated the concept of competitive inhibition. An important statistical contribution was his report, in 1933, to the Medical Research Council on methods of biological assay depending on a quantal response, and he was instrumental in getting a mathematical and statistical approach to bioassay accepted in this country.

Gaddum developed new methods of bioassay for acetylcholine, adrenaline, 5-hydroxytryptamine (5-HT), substance P, and thyroxin, and introduced a new method for extracting histamine from blood. With this method he showed that the blood histamine rises after extensive cutaneous burns. He constructed new pieces of apparatus, such as a flow recorder, an outflow recorder, a micro-bath, and his famous push-pull cannula, a device to perfuse small regions of tissue in brain and to detect substances liberated from them by appropriate stimuli.

A few fundamental discoveries stand out among Gaddum's many contributions to problems of internal secretions and autopharmacology. They include the discovery in 1931, with von Euler, of substance P, a vasodepressor peptide in extracts of brain and intestine; the demonstration in 1933, with Wilhelm Feldberg, of the role of acetylcholine as synaptic transmitter in sympathetic ganglia; three major contributions in the 1950s to the pharmacology and physiology of 5-HT—(1) evidence for specific tryptamine receptors, M and D receptors, in smooth muscle, (2) the finding that lysergic acid diethylamide (LSD) was a specific potent 5-HT antagonist on smooth muscle, (3) the mapping out, together with A. H. Amin and T. B. B. Crawford, of the distribution of 5-HT in brain, and demonstrating a different distribution in brain of the enzymes for its formation and destruction. Gaddum was the first who tried to explain the schizoid changes that LSD produces by interference with the 5-HT metabolism of brain.

In 1936 Gaddum wrote a book which appeared in German (translated by Wilhelm Feldberg): *Die gefässerweiternde Stoffe der Gewebe*, which summarized the knowledge of vasodilating substances occurring in the tissues. A fiftieth anniversary edition in English was published in 1986. He also wrote a textbook on pharmacology which appeared in 1940; it had its emphasis on principles of drug action, was written with a remarkable feeling for essentials, and was unsurpassed in its charm when, as so often, his sense of humour broke through. It passed through five editions and was translated into German, Spanish, and Japanese.

Gaddum was tall, rather ungainly, and looked as if he didn't care how he was dressed. He had a moustache which looked as if it had been accidentally stuck to his lip. When watching him carry out an experiment one was struck by the delicate skill of his large, rather clumsy looking hands. What endeared him to his friends was that he was completely unprejudiced; that he was open to unorthodox ideas put forward by colleagues, giving them the benefit of the doubt until further work should clarify the issue; that he was ready to admit ignorance. He had a gift for clear and concise expression, loved to play with figures, and possessed a quizzical sense of humour with a fondness for light and nonsense verse.

Gaddum died after a long illness at his Cambridge home, 10 Fendon Close, on 30 June 1965. In 1966 the British Pharmacological Society created the Gaddum Memorial Trust to commemorate Sir John's services to pharmacology in the form of the Gaddum memorial lectures.   W. FELDBERG, *rev.* M. P. EARLES

Sources W. Feldberg, *Memoirs FRS*, 13 (1967), 57–77 • *BMJ* (10 July 1965), 114; (17 July 1965), 176 • *The Lancet*, 2 (1965), 86 • G. Buttle, 'A full circle', *Trends in Pharmacological Sciences*, 1 (1980), 443–5 • *WWW, 1961–70* • B. Hulmstedt and G. Liljestrand, *Readings in pharmacology* (1963) • R. D. Mann, *Modern drug use: an enquiry on historical principles* (1984) • private information (1981) • personal knowledge (1981) • *BMJ* (27 March 1993) [obit. of Lady Gaddum] • *CGPLA Eng. & Wales* (1965)

Archives Medical Research Council, London, corresp. and papers • NRA, priv. coll., diaries • RS, corresp. and papers • Wellcome L., corresp. and papers • Wellcome L., notes | Wellcome L., corresp. with Henry McIlwain

Likenesses R. Tollast, drawing, repro. in *The Lancet*, 86 • photograph, repro. in *BMJ*, 2 (1965), 114

Wealth at death £38,192: probate, 17 Nov 1965, *CGPLA Eng. & Wales*

Gadesden [Gadsden], **Florence Marie Armroid** (1853–1934), headmistress, was born in Paris on 15 May 1853, the second daughter of John Burnett Gadsden (she spelt her surname thus until about 1883), gentleman, and of his wife, Esther Elizabeth, *née* Atlee, originally from Lewisham, where the couple were married in February 1850, John Gadsden giving his occupation as professor of music and his address as St George's, Hanover Square. Nothing is known of the place or circumstances of her early upbringing (she was always noticeably reticent about her parents) or of any siblings, with the important exception of her elder sister Lizzie, whose teaching career ran parallel to her own. It seems, however, that Florence attended more than one school, of which the last, incontrovertibly, was the Anglican boarding establishment at Sandwell Hall in Staffordshire directed by Frances Laetitia Selwyn (sister of Bishop Augustus Selwyn), which she left about 1872 with passes in the Cambridge senior local examinations, including a distinction in French. Shortly afterwards she joined the household of Edward North Buxton, to whom she was already known, as governess to his older children, latterly combining her duties with study for the Cambridge higher locals. Having secured three good passes, in May 1880 she was admitted to Girton College, Cambridge, where although older than most of her year group she participated fully in college life, as conductor of the Choral Society, organist, champion tennis player, and co-founder of the *Girton Review*. Among the earliest Girtonians to read for the historical tripos, she was placed in 1883 at the top of the second class, and was immediately appointed to the staff of Oxford high school, founded by the Girls' Public Day School Company (GPDSC). One of the prime movers in the formation early in 1884 of the Assistant Mistresses' Association, and already renowned for her energy and efficiency, she was made honorary secretary. Within a few months, however, she had risen from the rank of assistant to that of headmistress, having been recruited as 'a suitable, discreet and sufficiently learned person' to launch a new high school for girls being opened in Leamington Spa. In her two years there (1884–6) she established Leamington high school (known since 1949 as the Kingsley School) on a sound footing; described by one former pupil as 'most engaging, attractive, electrifying', she is remembered by another 'holding the alto part in a strong firm voice against our girlish trebles' (Parry, 12).

In 1886 Florence Gadesden was chosen by the council of the GPDSC to succeed Sarah Allen Olney as headmistress of its school in the London suburb of Blackheath, founded in 1880 but already numbering some 300 pupils; within a decade of her arrival the total had increased to about 450. Here over the next three decades Florence Gadesden demonstrated that she was indeed, as was said later, 'a pioneer it was safe to follow' (Major, 17). She brought science from its hitherto peripheral position into the mainstream of the curriculum and ensured that chemistry, at least, was taught in a purpose-made and properly equipped laboratory. She transformed physical education by abolishing 'drill' in favour of modern gymnastics, performed in the abbreviated 'gym slip' which was also worn, to the initial astonishment of other headmistresses, for the organized games, hockey, netball, lacrosse, and tennis, in which Blackheath soon excelled. In her scheme of things intellectual effort, physical fitness, development of the team spirit, charitable endeavours in aid of deprived children and the elderly infirm, supplemented ideally by a comprehensive post-school course in the domestic arts such as she established in 1904 at Blackheath, all had a part to play in the school's overall purpose, which was to prepare girls as individuals—'everyone must be allowed to be herself'—for a life of service in the common good, an aim amply fulfilled by Blackheathans in their later careers. Accounts of the school in her time dwell on the spirit of freedom and air of excitement she generated, evidently without detriment to her personal and professional authority. Well-groomed, modishly dressed, and trim of figure, she made a point of being accessible, moving constantly about the school followed as often as not by her Aberdeen terrier.

Florence Gadesden's influence was widespread, disseminated most immediately through the network of schools in membership of the GPDSC, within which she was an acknowledged pacemaker. In addition, nearly thirty members or former members of her staff were promoted to the headship of girls' schools, independent and maintained, and women's colleges—Edith Major became mistress of Girton. A keen member from 1885 of the Association of Head Mistresses (AHM), as president from 1905 to 1907 she backed a resolution demanding women's suffrage in terms which avoided support for militancy, and

she proposed reforms to the public examination system designed to give more weight to 'a pupil's capacity as a whole', anticipating by many decades the eventual introduction of the school-based record of achievement. Her clear-headed interventions in difficult discussions were greeted with sighs of relief, and she captivated all audiences, whether of adults or schoolgirls, by the exceptional power and beauty of her speaking voice. From 1911 she represented the AHM on the Teachers' Registration Council, and in 1918 was among the members of the latter chosen to serve on the Board of Education's newly established Secondary Schools Examinations Council. Her paper 'The secondary education of girls and the development of girls' high schools', presented to the education section of the Cambridge University extension meeting in August 1900, was printed in *Education in the Nineteenth Century* (ed. R. W. Roberts, 1901). She contributed the chapter on examinations to the book edited by S. A. Burstall and M. A. Douglas, *Public Schools for Girls* (1911).

Other organizations and causes which benefited from Florence Gadesden's active support included the Victoria League, the University Extension Movement, and closer to home the Reading Room for Ladies in Blackheath village, as well as the local branch of the London Society for Women's Suffrage. During the First World War she did voluntary work for the Red Cross and in a canteen for munition workers; as treasurer of the Girls' Patriotic Union she helped to co-ordinate the voluntary work of schoolgirls, to which Blackheath pupils made a substantial contribution.

In her private life, Florence Gadesden enjoyed a mutually rewarding friendship, dating back to Leamington days, with Professor John Massie, a New Testament scholar prominent in public affairs, and his wife, Edith. The person closest to Florence was her sister Lizzie, headmistress from 1884 to 1907 of Norwich high school, a sister school to Blackheath, who when she died in 1917 was living in Gresham, the Norfolk village to which Florence herself retired two years later. Public-spirited as ever, Florence served as president of the Women's Institute and manager of the village school, started a bowling club for men and revived the annual flower show, in both cases on her own premises, and devoted some of her capital to the building of modern, labour-saving cottages. She died after a brief illness on 19 May 1934 at the Nursing Home, Cromer, Norfolk; three weeks later the London church of St Martin-in-the-Fields was filled to overflowing for her memorial service.   JANET SONDHEIMER

Sources M. C. Malim and H. C. Escreet, eds., *The book of the Blackheath High School* (1927) • A. B. Parry, *The Kingsley School* (1994) • *Girton Review*, 1–5 (1882–3) • *Girton Review*, 7 (1884) • J. Kamm, *Indicative past: one hundred years of the Girls' Public Day School Trust* (1971) • E. H. Major, *Girton Review* (1934) • R. Haig Brown, *School Record* [Blackheath High School] (1934) • *Journal of Education*, 66 (1934), 434, 438 • Blackheath high school, Vanbrugh Park, London, Archives • F. M. H. Gadesden, *Testimonials* (1886) • register of births, British Consulate, Paris, 15 May 1853 • d. cert.

Likenesses group portrait, photograph, 1919, Blackheath high school, Vanbrugh Park, London • photograph, Blackheath high school, Vanbrugh Park, London

Wealth at death £6152 15s. 5d.: probate, 18 July 1934, *CGPLA Eng. & Wales*

Gadsby, Henry Robert (1842–1907), organist and composer, was born in Hackney, Middlesex, on 15 December 1842, the son of William Gadsby. From 1849 to 1858 he was a chorister at St Paul's, where he learned harmony from the vicar-choral William Bayley; otherwise he was self-taught. In 1863 he started work as a piano teacher, and, having taught himself the organ, became organist of St Peter's, Brockley; he held this post until 1884. He was also professor of harmony and piano at Queen's College, London. In 1880 Gadsby was appointed one of the original professors of harmony at the Guildhall School of Music, where he taught until his death. He was a member of the Philharmonic Society and fellow of the College of Organists.

Gadsby's published works include cantatas, incidental music, an organ concerto, a string quartet, and numerous partsongs, services, and anthems. His works were always well received but seldom heard a second time. His *Treatise on Harmony* (1883) was probably the first in England that, instead of working from figured bass, provided melodies to be harmonized. He also wrote *A Technical Method of Sight-Singing* (1897). Gadsby was one of a number of distinguished musicians who sang at the open-air service for Queen Victoria's Diamond Jubilee in 1897. He died on 11 November 1907 at 53 Clarendon Road, Putney, and was buried in Putney Vale cemetery. His widow, Jessie Adela, died on 21 November 1909, leaving two daughters.

FREDERICK CORDER, rev. JOHN WARRACK

Sources *New Grove* · Grove, *Dict. mus.* · *MT*, 48 (1907), 806 · T. Baker, *A biographical dictionary of musicians* (1900) · personal knowledge (1912)
Likenesses portrait, repro. in *MT* · portrait, repro. in Baker, *Biographical dictionary*
Wealth at death £691 3s. 8d.: administration, 3 Dec 1907, *CGPLA Eng. & Wales*

Gadsby, William (1773–1844), Strict and Particular Baptist minister, was born at Attleborough, Nuneaton, on 3 January 1773. His father was a poor road mender. As a boy he had a scanty elementary education until he was thirteen, then led a particularly wild life, but was converted at the age of seventeen. At first he worshipped with the Independents at Bedworth, but on 29 December 1793 he was baptized at Cow Lane Baptist Chapel, Coventry. Until he was twenty-two he worked as a ribbon weaver, and then went to Hinckley, Leicestershire, as a stocking weaver. In 1796 he married Elizabeth Marvin (d. 1851) and began business on his own account. Two years later he commenced preaching regularly at Bedworth and Hinckley, but he continued in business, and used to carry his wares to market on his back. He first preached in Back Lane Chapel, off Rochdale Road, Manchester, in 1803. His bucolic appearance and dialect aroused much comment, but he was nevertheless called there in 1805. At Rochdale Road he remained pastor until his death. At first he met with considerable opposition, but gradually his sterling qualities were appreciated and he drew vast crowds. He had a quaint humour and was an earnest and persuasive

William Gadsby (1773–1844), by William Barnard (after F. Turner)

speaker, though he would often startle his hearers with some coarse or eccentric remark. He preached passionately a high Calvinism, contrasting strongly law and gospel and refusing to usurp the Spirit's work by offering the gospel to sinners. His enemies called him a hyper calvinist and an antinomian. He was a tireless evangelist and it is calculated that in the exercise of his ministry he travelled nearly 12,000 miles, preached nearly 60,000 sermons, and founded more than thirty churches. Politically he was a radical and a generous friend of the poor.

Between 1806 and 1843 Gadsby wrote frequently on religious subjects, and published a number of pamphlets, most of which were later issued in a collected form in two volumes (1851) by his son, John, who also in 1884 edited and published his father's *Sermons and Letters*. Gadsby wrote many hymns and other verses and published them in *A Selection of Hymns* (1814), *The Nazarene's Songs* (1814), and elsewhere. In 1835 he and his son began the *Gospel Standard Magazine* as an organ for those Strict and Particular Baptist churches which followed his teachings. The Gospel Standard denomination (comprising in 1993 about 150 churches) still generally uses Gadsby's hymnbook and holds to the articles of 1878, which he adumbrated in his magazine in 1835 and 1841. Gadsby, whose last years were clouded by his wife's insanity, died at Manchester on 27 January 1844 and was buried in the Rusholme Road cemetery. His body was later reinterred at Charlesworth, Derbyshire.

IAN SELLERS

Sources J. Gadsby, *A memoir of ...William Gadsby* (1844) · J. C. Philpot, *A tribute of high esteem and love* (1844) · B. A. Ramsbottom, *History* *of the Gospel Standard Magazine* (1985) · *The Evangelical Library Bulletin*, no. 50 (May 1973) · *The Gospel Standard Magazine*, no. 1902 (Jan 1994) · *Manchester City News* (24 March 1881) · *Manchester City News* (31 March 1881)

Likenesses J. H. Lynch, lithograph, pubd 1844 (after E. Benson), BM · W. Barnard, mezzotint (after F. Turner), BM, NPG [*see illus.*]

Gadsden, Christopher (1724–1805), merchant and revolutionary politician, was born on 16 February 1724 in Charles Town, South Carolina, the fourth and only surviving son of Thomas Gadsden (1688–1741) and Elizabeth (1694–1727), daughter of Christopher Terrey, a man of Irish extraction. Thomas Gadsden served in the Royal Navy during the War of the Spanish Succession and later became a captain in the merchant service. After his marriage to Elizabeth Terrey in Barbados in 1715 the couple moved permanently to Charles Town, South Carolina, where Thomas became the collector of customs. Christopher's mother died in 1727. His first stepmother, Collins Hall, died in 1730; his second stepmother, Alice Mighells, the mother of his two half-brothers, James and Thomas, died in 1741, also the year of his father's death.

From 1732 to 1740 young Christopher, also known as Kittie, lived with relatives in England while he attended grammar school near Bristol. He returned to America to enter a mercantile apprenticeship in Philadelphia, then to serve as a purser on the British man-of-war *Aldborough* during King George's War from 1745 to 1746. In 1748 he became a small merchant, or factor, who bought rice, furs, and indigo from large planters and resold them to merchants involved in transatlantic trade. Very successful, partly because of a substantial inheritance from his father, he eventually owned two plantations, a fleet of small boats, a large wharf on the Cooper river, a subdivision in Charles Town named Gadsdenboro, more than 100 slaves, and a townhouse in Charles Town. As a man of wealth and distinction he rendered public service in both politics and the military.

Elected to the Commons house of assembly from St Philip's parish, Charles Town, in 1757, Gadsden served there for the next twenty-seven years. His political career encompassed all the major events that led to the British North American colonies' war for independence, the war itself, and the establishment of an independent nation. Virtually a madman on the subject of independence, Gadsden used profane language, graphic imagery, and erratic personal behaviour to condemn Britain for acting like a 'stepmother' towards her colonies where she treated her faithful subjects as 'slaves'. A devout Anglican, he often argued that God favoured American independence. Like other leaders of the revolution, he justified his stance with the English whig philosophy that had condoned parliament's victory over the crown in 1649 and the revolution of 1688.

Gadsden first defied royal authority during the French and Indian War of 1756–63. In a series of passionate letters to the *South-Carolina Gazette* he vilified the royal governor for meddling in elections for the Commons house of assembly. The celebrated Gadsden election controversy of 1762 ignited a power struggle between the Commons and the royal governor. When St Philip's parish elected Gadsden to the Commons in 1762, Governor Thomas Boone, who thought Gadsden a trouble-maker because of his criticism of royal authority during the Indian wars, denied him his seat on the grounds that the churchwardens who had conducted the election had not been properly certified. In a new election, which the wardens conducted properly, the voters again chose Gadsden. He then led the Commons in a two-year-long condemnation of the governor for having interfered with the election. The battle raged in the newspapers and finally reached the lords of trade in 1764. They recalled Boone to England, thus handing the colony an early triumph over royal authority.

Emboldened by his success in the election controversy, Gadsden proceeded to prod his colony and its sisters towards independence. During the Stamp Act crisis of 1765, he attended the protest congress in New York and organized the Sons of Liberty in South Carolina, who resorted to violence to prohibit the sale of the stamps. When parliament repealed the Stamp Act he warned the celebrants under the Liberty Tree in Charles Town that the mother country should not be trusted. He organized the boycott of British goods after the Townshend Acts of 1767, supported the whig politician John Wilkes, who accused George III of tyranny, and served in the first two sessions of the continental congress. He spoke in favour of independence during the first session, and during the second he designed the bright yellow flag with a coiled rattlesnake and the words 'DONT TREAD ON ME' for the commander of the continental navy.

During the revolution Gadsden played both military and political roles. Early in 1776 he commanded the 1st South Carolina regiment, helped William Moultrie repel a British invasion in May and June, and in September accepted the continental congress's appointment as brigadier-general. As vice-president of the province he refused to retreat to safety when the British captured it in 1780. For ten and a half months the British held him prisoner at their fort in St Augustine, Florida. After the war he endorsed the constitution of the United States and championed the federalist presidencies of George Washington and John Adams. With the help of his sons he recouped the fortune he had lost during the war.

Gadsden was married three times: on 28 August 1746 to Jane Godfrey (1729?–1755), on 29 December 1755 to Mary Hasell (1734–1769), and on 17 April 1776 to Ann Wragg (1732–1805). With Mary Hasell he had four children, including Philip, whose son James Gadsden, army officer, politician, and railway executive, became Christopher's most famous descendant. Christopher Gadsden died in Charles Town on 28 August 1805, the victim of old age and an accidental blow to the head from a fall. He was buried the following day in St Philip's churchyard near the graves of his parents.   E. STANLY GODBOLD JR.

Sources E. S. Godbold and R. H. Woody, *Christopher Gadsden and the American Revolution* (1982) · C. C. Gadsden, 'Thomas Gadsden, 1688–1741', South Carolina Historical Society, Charleston, South Carolina · *The writings of Christopher Gadsden, 1746–1805*, ed. R. Walsh

(1966) • J. P. Greene, *The quest for power: the lower houses of assembly in the southern royal colonies, 1689–1776* (1963) • P. Maier, *From resistance to revolution: colonial radicals and the opposition to Great Britain, 1765–1776* (1972) • R. Middlekauff, *The glorious cause: the American Revolution, 1763–1789* (1982) • J. J. Nadlehaft, *The disorders of war: the revolution in South Carolina* (1981) • D. D. Wallace, *The life of Henry Laurens* (1915) • R. Walsh, *Charleston's Sons of Liberty: a study of the artisans, 1763–1789* (1959) • E. S. Godbold, 'Gadsden, Christopher', *ANB*

Likenesses J. Theus, oils, 1766, priv. coll. • R. Peale, oils, 1797, Independence National Historical Park Coll., Philadelphia, Pennsylvania • portraits, repro. in Godbold and Woody, *Christopher Gadsden*, 8, 46, 240 • watercolour, priv. coll.

Wealth at death over $250,000: Charleston county will book, 1800–07, pp. 594ff.; inventories D, 1800–10, Charleston district, equity court, report book, 19 May 1800–25 May 1808, pp. 274, 305, 511–29, both in South Carolina Archives and History Center, Columbia

Gaekwar, Sayaji Rao. *See* Gaikwar, Sayaji Rao, maharaja of Baroda (1863–1939).

Gage, Francis (1621–1682), Roman Catholic priest, was born on 1 February 1621, probably in Clerkenwell, Middlesex, the son of John Gage (*c.*1580–1626) of Haling, Surrey, and his second wife, Anne Barnes, *née* Shelley (*d.* 1630), a widow. He was the half-brother of Sir Henry *Gage, royalist governor of Oxford, of George *Gage (*c.*1602–1652) [*see under* Gage, George (*c.*1582–1638)], priest and agent at Rome, and of Thomas *Gage (1603?–1656), missionary and traveller. A student at the English College at Douai from 1630 to 1641, he was then sent to the Collège de Tournai at Paris, which had recently been handed over by Louis XIII for the education of the English Catholic clergy. In 1646 he was ordained priest, and in 1648 appointed tutor to Thomas Arundel, then living in Paris. He graduated BD at the Sorbonne in 1649, and DD in 1654. He then returned to England, was appointed archdeacon of Essex, and lived with Lady Herbert, whom he afterwards accompanied to France with Lady Talbot. Appointed clergy agent in 1659 he went to Rome and remained there until 1661. According to his detailed personal journal, in which he recorded the chief events of his life to 1677 (Westminster Archdiocesan Archives, vol. 34, no. 125), he then lived with various Catholic families in England for the next six years. In November 1667 he returned to Paris as tutor to young Philip Draycot of Painsley, Staffordshire. On 23 January 1676 he was nominated president of Douai College in succession to Dr John Leyburn. Under his direction the college prospered until the Popish Plot in 1678 made the English Catholics fearful of sending their sons to the colleges abroad. But after the storm had subsided the number of students at Douai increased, largely due to Gage's reputation. He is widely believed to be the F. G. who edited *The Spiritual Exercises of Gertrude More*, published at Paris in 1658, though the attribution is not certain. Dodd, in 1742, described him as

> a person of extraordinary qualifications, both natural and acquired. His memory was of late years very fresh in the university of Paris, where upon several occasions he had distinguished himself, especially by his flowing eloquence. In regard of his brethren he behaved himself with remarkable discretion in several controversies which required management. (Dodd, 3.296)

Gage died at the English College, Douai, on 2 June 1682 after a short fever and was buried there, with his heart placed under the high altar of the college chapel.

THOMPSON COOPER, rev. D. MILBURN

Sources G. Anstruther, *The seminary priests*, 2 (1975), 119–20 • Gillow, *Lit. biog. hist.*, 2.354–6 • C. Dodd [H. Tootell], *The church history of England, from the year 1500, to the year 1688*, 3 (1742), 296 • *The memoirs of Gregorio Panzani*, ed. and trans. J. Berington (1793), 298, 301–2 • P. Guilday, *The English Catholic refugees on the continent, 1558–1795* (1914), 330 • E. H. Burton and T. L. Williams, eds., *The Douay College diaries, third, fourth and fifth, 1598–1654*, 2, Catholic RS, 11 (1911), 288, 571 • T. A. Birrell, 'English Catholics without a bishop, 1655–1672', *Recusant History*, 4 (1957–8), 142–78 • F. Gage, 'Journal of the chief events of his life from his birth in 1621 to 1677', Westm. DA

Archives Westm. DA, 'Journal of the chief events of his life from his birth in 1621 to 1677', vol. 34, no. 125

Likenesses oils, Douai Abbey, Woolhampton, Reading

Gage, George (*c.*1582–1638), diplomat and businessman, was the son of Edward Gage (*b.* 1539), gentleman, of Firle, Sussex, and Margaret, daughter of Sir John Shelley of Michelgrove. Educated overseas, he became skilled in the Italian, French, and Spanish languages. During 1612–16 he was a companion of Toby Matthew (1577–1655) on a European tour and in Rome in 1614 he witnessed the ordination of Matthew by Cardinal Bellarmine. In 1615 and 1616 they were seen in Leipzig and the Spa, where Matthew wrote of Gage's familiarity with works of art. At this time Matthew composed a series of twenty-nine religious sonnets, which he dedicated to Gage, whose visible loyalty inspired Chamberlain to write of him as Matthew's '*fidus Achates*' (*Letters of John Chamberlain*, 2.306, 452).

In May 1621 James I asked Gage to visit Rome as a representative English Catholic to learn the reaction of the new pope, Gregory XV, to a request for a dispensation for the infanta to marry his son. In his interviews the pope warned Gage that James must be ready 'to do many things not taken into account' thus far (Gardiner, 164–6) but details were left to a small committee of cardinals who stressed the need of better treatment of Catholics. After his report to the king Gage was sent again to Rome, in September 1622, with an official credential to Gregory, signed by James, Prince Charles, and the duke of Buckingham, 'to explain these things more fully' (*CSP dom.*, 1619–23, 451). His itinerary led him first to Madrid to inform the young king Philip IV of James's intentions and then, after lengthy meetings with the cardinals in early 1623, he returned to London; he was convinced that he had succeeded, for he watched the ceremony of the signing of the articles of marriage and joined in the plans for changes in the penal laws, but his diplomatic career ended when Charles and Buckingham began to oppose the match.

The last decade of Gage's life was concentrated on commerce. In 1628 he was associated with Sir Edward Stradling and others in the New River project, which intended to construct an aqueduct from Hoddesdon, Hertfordshire, to London. Early in 1632, by order of Charles I, Gage, together with Sir Richard Weston, Sir Basil Brooke, and others, were incorporated as the Society of Soapmakers of Westminster, with Gage as the governor. By this charter English soap should be made with vegetable oil, and its production was confined to the society and those it licensed. The new formula was a failure, for no one in the society was 'bred up in the trade', and they were relieved to surrender their monopoly for a sum of money. In 1637 Gage with Sir Kenelm Digby and others petitioned the City of London for a market and fair to be located in his own parish of St Martin-in-the-Fields but was refused. On 14 August 1638 Gage prepared his will, naming as his chief beneficiary his 'worthy frend', Lady Jane Gardner, who received £2000 and the residue of his properties. He died shortly afterwards and his will was granted probate on 12 September. As there is no contemporary evidence that Gage was ordained a priest by Cardinal Bellarmine together with Toby Matthew, the career of his second cousin, with the same name, is a clue to how a misunderstanding about him arose.

George Gage (*c*.1602–1652), Roman Catholic priest, was one of the sons of John Gage (*c*.1580–1626) of Haling, Surrey, and his first wife, Margaret (*c*.1580–*c*.1630), daughter of Sir Thomas Copley, and brother of Sir Henry *Gage (1597–1645) and Thomas *Gage (1603?–1656), and a half-brother of Francis *Gage (1621–1682). His recusant parents sent him to St Omer, after which in 1625 he entered Douai College; he was ordained in 1626. In 1628 he was arrested in London and kept in the Clink prison for two years. Upon release he lived for a time at the Portuguese embassy while serving Catholic families in the Middlesex area. By 1647 George Gage was agent in England for Douai and then in June 1649 vicar-general for London and south-east England. However, his leading role led to his arrest in 1650 and he died in prison in the summer of 1652.

A. J. LOOMIE

Sources P. Revell and F. W. Steer, 'George Gage I and George Gage II', *BIHR*, 31 (1958), 141–58 · F. Francisco de Jesus, *El hecho de los tratados del matrimonio pretendido por el principe de Gales con la serenissima infante de España, María / Narrative of the Spanish marriage treaty*, ed. and trans. S. R. Gardiner, CS, 101 (1869) · A. G. Petti, 'Unknown sonnets by Sir Toby Matthew', *Recusant History*, 9 (1967–8), 123–58 · E. Simpson, *The economic history of England*, 3 vols. (1931), vol. 3 · *The letters of John Chamberlain*, ed. N. E. McClure, 2 vols. (1939) · *CSP dom.*, 1619–37 · *Report on the manuscripts of the marquis of Downshire*, 6 vols. in 7, HMC, 75 (1924–95), vol. 5 · G. M. Bell, *A hand-list of British diplomatic representatives, 1509–1688*, Royal Historical Society Guides and Handbooks, 16 (1990) · will, PRO, PROB 11/177, fol. 455
Likenesses A. Van Dyck, oils, 1620–1621? (of Gage?), NPG; repro. in O. Millar, *Van Dyck in England* (1982), 40–41 [exhibition catalogue, NPG, 19 Nov 1982 — 20 March 1983]
Wealth at death see will, PRO, PROB 11/177, fol. 455

Gage, George (*c*.1602–1652). *See under* Gage, George (*c*.1582–1638).

Gage, Sir Henry (1597–1645), royalist army officer, was born in London on 29 August 1597, the eldest son of John Gage of Haling Manor, Surrey, and his wife, Margaret, daughter of Sir Thomas Copley. Initially educated at home, he entered the English College of St Omer at the age of twelve to study the humanities for five years and then, in October 1615, he enrolled in the English College in Rome for a three-year course of lectures in philosophy.

Sir Henry Gage (1597–1645), by Weesop, 1640s

To protect their families in England it was a practice of students at the college to adopt a pseudonym as a surname and Gage selected 'Howard' (Kelly, 177), perhaps an ironical salute to Charles Howard, earl of Nottingham, who had lived at the Gage family's Haling Manor since 1592, for it had been forfeited to Elizabeth I after a priest was arrested on its premises.

Since Gage did not wish to follow an ecclesiastical career, he left for England in September 1618. In 1620, at the end of the twelve years' truce with the Dutch republic, Gage enlisted in Spain's army of Flanders in Antwerp. He was commissioned a captain by the Archduchess Isabella on 10 April 1622, at the request of Archibald Campbell, seventh earl of Argyll, who was one of the commanders of English and Scottish troops in Flanders. His company's first task, starting in August, was to assist Spinola's costly and unsuccessful siege at Bergen op Zoom in Brabant. Later, after August 1624, again under Spinola's command, Gage's company joined the protracted siege at Breda, which surrendered after ten months in a scene brilliantly painted by Velázquez.

With the outbreak of war between the England of Charles I and Spain and France, Gage returned to London in 1626. Fascinated by military strategy, he published in 1627 his translation of Herman Hugo's detailed narrative of the recent victory: *The Siege of Breda Written in Latin*. Dedicating it 'to the Souldiers of our Nation in General', he said he was 'a Workeman whose profession is to manage the pike not the pen', but he trusted that soldiers were 'able to judge the worth of it'. Some time later he married

Mary Daniel, daughter of John Daniel of Daresbury, Cheshire, who accompanied him to Flanders after the peace of 1630 and who eventually survived him. In Flanders Sir Edward Parham appointed him the captain-commandant of an English regiment, which he led from 1631 to 1643 in what is aptly called an 'Ageing Land War' (Israel). A high point for him occurred in July 1638 when he led the successful defence of St Omer against repeated French assaults.

By 1639 this Hispano-Dutch stalemate assumed a lower priority for Gage and for the advisers of Philip IV, but for different reasons. Madrid, confronted by crises, first in Catalonia, then later in Portugal, had far fewer funds for the war in the north. Meanwhile Gage was alert to the declining authority of Charles I, at first in Scotland, then later in England. Accordingly he tried, but failed, to secure a loan of £150,000 from Spain in return for English naval protection for its convoys to Flanders. Ironically he was vindicated in October 1639, when Admiral Tromp inflicted great damage on Oquendo's ships in the battle of the Downs near Dover. Arguably Gage gave more significant aid to the royalists from 1641 to 1643, when he used his authority in Flanders to deprive the roundheads' forces of 30,000 arms—presumably pikes, pistols, and muskets—and capture 8000 more for the use of troops loyal to King Charles.

While his family stayed in Flanders Gage had leave in early 1644 to travel to the king's headquarters at Oxford. On 3 June he was appointed to the military council, which aroused the anger of the ambitious governor of Oxford, Sir Arthur Aston. However, his military expertise was vindicated on 12 June, when he led a thousand men to recapture Boarstall House, Buckinghamshire, near Aylesbury. Here, after a brief siege, the enemy surrendered; he allowed them to retain their arms. His most famous exploit was his skilled deployment of soldiers and cavalry on 11 September to bring ammunition, food, and forage to Basing House, Hampshire, where the defenders, under the marquess of Winchester, were in desperate straits after a siege of three months. Although his men were fatigued by a 40-mile march from Oxford, Gage guided them around the lines of the besiegers and enabled them to rush the supplies into the garrison while suffering few casualties. After setting fire to the roundheads' quarters Gage evaded pursuit by a new route back to Oxford. On 25 October Gage's regiment was sent to Banbury, Oxfordshire, where another royalist garrison faced starvation, to leave provisions before winter made the roads impassable.

For these achievements the king conferred a knighthood on Gage on 1 November 1644. A second relief mission to Basing House proved easier to accomplish, for the roundheads had decided to leave in frustration shortly before he was reported to be on the way. There was widespread approval when Gage was appointed governor of Oxford on 25 December after the unpopular governor Aston had been incapacitated by an injury. Unfortunately Gage's tenure of office was destined to be brief. On 10 January 1645 he led his troops to Culham Bridge, a vital

crossing of the Thames on the edge of Oxford, which he planned to seize and tear down in order to build a fort near it and repel any offensive actions by troops from Abingdon. Here the following day, during a violent skirmish on the bridge, he was mortally wounded by a musket shot and died while attended by his chaplain, the Jesuit Peter Wright. On 13 January, after a funeral attended by notables from the court, he was buried in Christ Church Cathedral, Oxford. Several years later Clarendon, in his *History of the Rebellion*, wrote a lengthy encomium of Gage as a 'man of extraordinary parts'. He recalled that he was 'a large and very graceful person, of an honourable extraction' and 'a great master in the Spanish and Italian tongues, besides the French and the Dutch, which he spoke in great perfection'. Gage had been welcomed for many years at Brussels 'which was a great and very regular court at that time'. Later at Oxford 'the lords of the council had a singular esteem' of him and 'consulted frequently with him, whilst they looked to be besieged'. Clarendon narrated in detail the striking success at Basing House and noted that Gage's death was a great loss to the cause of Charles I, for he had proved in many ways to be: 'a man of great wisdom and temper, and among the very few soldiers, who made himself to be universally loved and esteemed' (Clarendon, *Hist. rebellion*, 3.407, 443).

A. J. LOOMIE

Sources W. Kelly, ed., *Liber ruber venerabilis collegii Anglorum de urbe*, 1, Catholic RS, 37 (1940) · P. Revell and F. W. Steer, 'George Gage I and George Gage II', *BIHR*, 31 (1958), 141–58 · A. J. Loomie, 'Gondomar's selection of English officers in 1622', *EngHR*, 88 (1973), 574–81 · J. Israel, *The Dutch republic and the Hispanic world, 1606–1661* (1982) · G. Parker, *The army of Flanders and the Spanish road, 1567–1659* (1972) · *VCH Buckinghamshire*, vol. 4 · *VCH Hampshire and the Isle of Wight*, vol. 5 · E. Walsingham, *Alter Britanniae heros, or, The life of … Sir Henry Gage* (1645) · Clarendon, *Hist. rebellion* · *DNB* · Gillow, *Lit. biog. hist.*, 2.357–9

Likenesses Weesop, oils, 1640–45, NPG [*see illus.*]

Gage, Sir John (1479–1556), military administrator and courtier, was born on 28 October 1479 at Burstow, Surrey, the only son of William Gage of Burstow (*d.* 1497) and Agnes (*d.* 1501), daughter of Bartholomew Bolney, of Bolney, Sussex. He was baptized the same day at St Michael's Church, Burstow. The Gages later transferred their residence to Firle, near Lewes. The tradition that after his father's death John became a ward of the third duke of Buckingham, based on recollections of a son, seems to have no basis, and in 1499 his wardship was acquired by Robert Tate, alderman of London. By a contract dated 14 April 1502 he was married to Philippa, daughter of Sir Richard Guildford of Cranbrook, Kent, comptroller of the royal household; she predeceased him.

It was probably through the patronage of Guildford that Gage entered the royal household as esquire of the body during the lifetime of Henry VII and continued in that post under Henry VIII. In local affairs he served as justice of the peace for Sussex from 1514 and for Surrey from 1528 and on various other local commissions. His first major post came some time before 1522, by which time he had been appointed deputy to Sir Nicholas Vaux, captain of

Sir John Gage (1479–1556), by Hans Holbein the younger

Guînes in the Calais pale. It seems that Vaux wished to replace him, and Sir William Sandys, treasurer of Calais and an early patron, pressed hard for a new office, repeatedly praising Gage's 'wisdom, personage and hardiness' and adding that he 'has done the king good service' (*LP Henry VIII*, vol. 3, pt 2, nos. 2222, 2326, 2413). On 17 August 1522 Gage was granted the survivorship of the office of comptroller of Calais during the infirmity of Sir Robert Wotton, and he succeeded him in 1524. He plainly gained experience in the French wars of 1512–13 and 1522–5 and by 1525 was a knight.

In April 1526 Gage exchanged his post of comptroller of Calais for that of vice-chamberlain of the household when his patron Sandys became lord chamberlain. In 1529 he was elected to parliament for Sussex (sitting in all the subsequent Henrician parliaments), and in April 1530 wrote to Cromwell from Windsor about Wolsey's ostentatious journey to the north, advising it would be wise for him to 'in godde avatte vatte vordeys passeys hyme' (*LP Henry VIII*, vol. 4, pt 3, no. 6335). In 1529–30 he received grants of wardship, portions of Wolsey's property, a manor in Lincolnshire, and the deer park at Burstow from Archbishop Warham. Appointed commissioner to survey the lands of Calais in 1532, in December he went north on important royal business, staying until the spring of 1533.

Thus far Gage's rise, if slow, had been smooth and successful, but it seems the impending royal divorce caused problems. Gage was conventionally pious, but had signed the petition for divorce to the pope in July 1530, and was at Cranmer's court at Dunstable on 12 May 1533. In August,

though, he left the court. His friend Sir William Fitzwilliam (alongside whom he had fought when the latter was captain of Guînes in 1524) reported that 'Master vice-chamberlain departed from the king in such sort as I am sorry to hear; the king licensed him to depart hence, and so took leave of him, the water standing in his eyes' (*LP Henry VIII*, vol. 6, no. 965), adding, in a letter asking Cromwell to intervene, that though he was a man 'more ready to serve God than the world ... there is so much honesty in him that I dare warrant that, next God, he loves the king above all things' (*LP Henry VIII*, vol. 6, no. 966). Chapuys reported in January 1534 that Gage, 'who is of the Council, and one of the wisest and most experienced in war of the whole kingdom has renounced his office and gone to the Charterhouse intending, with the consent of his wife, to become a Carthusian' (*LP Henry VIII*, vol. 7, no. 14). Indeed he did write from the Sheen Charterhouse in December (probably 1534) on court matters to his son James (a member of the household, first in the pitcher house, then as clerk of the green cloth, and master of the household by 1540).

The deaths of Katherine and of Anne Boleyn may have resolved any conflict of loyalties; Gage was summoned to the council in the crisis of July 1536 and attended both the baptism of Prince Edward and the funeral of Jane Seymour in 1537. He had been appointed to the commission for the survey of church tenths in Sussex in January 1535, played a part in the dissolution of Battle Abbey, and accepted extensive grants from its lands (he was to be a great dealer in church lands). In 1537–8 he was active in the arrest in Sussex of dissidents and examinations for the Exeter conspiracy trials, and in 1539 in the organization of coastal defence. It is therefore incorrect to suppose that he remained aloof because of the king's religious policies. Cromwell had made a note to 'remember Sir John Gage to the King' in October 1533 (*LP Henry VIII*, vol. 6, no. 1371) and in May 1536, while Fitzwilliam had appealed to the 'old friendship' between them in 1533 (*LP Henry VIII*, vol. 6, no. 965). There is ample evidence of extensive business dealings between them in 1529–30. Their religious leanings, though, could not have been more divergent, and in 1540 Gage was drawn into the complex manoeuvres surrounding the minister's fall, appointed with the earl of Sussex to the investigative commission at Calais. However, by the time they returned in July Cromwell had been executed, and Gage the following year received the grant of some of Cromwell's offices and lands in Sussex.

As a religious conservative, Gage was more than ever in favour; in October 1540 he succeeded Kingston as comptroller of the royal household and constable of the Tower and was sworn of the privy council. In May 1541 he was installed KG. He was now at the centre of power, involved for instance in the arrest and execution of Katherine Howard. In October 1542 Fitzwilliam died at Newcastle during preparations for an attack on Scotland. Hertford was sent north to replace him, accompanied by Gage in order to assure the loyalty of Fitzwilliam's men, 'being a dere freende and allyance to the said lord Privy seale' and designated to succeed to the chancellorship of the duchy of

Lancaster (Bain, 1.272). Gage's main task was the supply of the army. In the following year he formed part of the commission to negotiate the marriage of Prince Edward to the infant Mary Stuart and signed the treaty of Greenwich in July. Above all, in 1544 he played a pivotal role in the organization of transport and supplies for the army for the invasion of France, his presence on the expedition being specifically requested by Suffolk. He had already been organizing supplies through his contacts in the Low Countries and left in June to complete arrangements. His role both in the siege of Boulogne and in diplomatic negotiations was prominent, and after the fall of the town, and until the king's death, he was preoccupied with the maintenance of the English military establishment at Calais and Boulogne. In 1544 he became a knight banneret.

Henry VIII appointed Gage a councillor for Edward VI, but though he knew Somerset well during the late Henrician wars, their religious views diverged. In June 1547 Gage was ousted from his council position and his offices as comptroller and chancellor of the duchy of Lancaster. He sided with Warwick in the crisis of 1549, signed the council letter declaring Somerset's treason, and resumed his role as co-ordinator of military supplies for Calais. However, though his wife and Warwick's were related, he had little sympathy with the new head of the council and attended only infrequently in 1551 and never in 1552–3, supposedly being too ill to attend the Garter chapter in April 1553. He refused to side with Northumberland's attempt in July to set up Jane Grey as queen (thus being suspended as constable), and he received the duke a prisoner into the Tower. Restored as constable of the Tower by Mary I, he was created lord chamberlain of the household. He welcomed the return of Catholicism and took part as captain of the guard in the resistance to the Wyatt rebellion; as related by Edward Underhill, at Charing Cross 'old Gage fell downe in the durte, and was foul arrayed ... and ... came in amoungst us alle durt, and so fryghted that he coulde not speke to us' (Nichols, *Narratives*, 165–7). Train-bearer at Mary's marriage to Philip of Spain, Gage supported Gardiner in council politics during this period. As constable he received Princess Elizabeth into the Tower and was thought to have treated her severely 'more for love of the pope than for hate of her person' (Heylyn, 2.259).

Gage died at his Sussex house of Firle Place on 18 April 1556 and was buried on 25 April beside his wife at West Firle church. His income (estimated for the subsidy in 1527 at £73 6s. 8d.) then stood at £309 p.a., derived, apart from his offices, from the profits of livestock rearing and timber production (his contacts with merchants such as the Johnson brothers were close, and he was a founder member of the Russia Company). He had built up extensive holdings in Sussex and Surrey and owned a house in Southwark, where he was king's steward by 1542. He left four sons, Edward (d. 1567), James (the household official), Robert (c.1518–1587), and William, and four daughters. One of his daughters married Sir Anthony *Browne (d. 1548), master of the horse, another the heir of Christopher Baynham. The family continued in the Catholic faith

and were excluded from office and punished as recusants; one grandson was executed for complicity in the Babington plot.   DAVID POTTER

Sources E. Sussex RO, Gage papers, 3/37, 39, 42; 4/9, 26, 31, 85, 96; 5/8, 16, 31; 6/6; 7/20; 16/5, 8–9; 19/1–6, 12; 21/3–4, 5–8, 11–12; 36/4–5 · charters, E. Sussex RO, Gage papers, 321, 326 · W. D. Budgen, notebooks, Sussex Archaeological Society, Barbican House, Lewes, vol. 135 · will, PRO, C142/110, 144, PROB 11/38, sig. 9 · PRO, SP1, SP3 · BL, Harleian MS 283 · BL, Add. MS 32648 · BL, Cotton, Calig. E II · *CClR, 1500–09* · *CIPM, Henry VII*, 2 · *CPR, 1494–1509* · *CSP dom.*, rev. edn, *1547–58* · J. G. Nichols, ed., *The chronicle of Queen Jane, and of two years of Queen Mary*, CS, old ser., 48 (1850) · H. Ellis, 'Commissions of the sewers for the Lewes levels', *Sussex Archaeological Collections*, 10 (1858), 95–9 · E. Hall, *Henry VIII*, ed. C. Whibley, 2 vols. (1904) · J. Bain, ed., *The Hamilton papers: letters and papers illustrating the political relations of England and Scotland in the XVIth century*, 2 vols., Scottish RO, 12 (1890–92) · *LP Henry VIII* · R. G. Rice, 'The household goods, etc. of Sir John Gage, of West Firle, co. Sussex, KG, 1556', *Sussex Archaeological Collections*, 45 (1902), 114–27 · J. C. Heylyn, *Ecclesia restaurata, or, History of the Reformation*, ed. J. C. Robertson, 2 vols. (1849) · J. G. Nichols, ed., *Narratives of the days of the Reformation*, CS, old ser., 77 (1859) · J. E. Ray, ed., *Sussex chantry records*, Sussex Records Society, 36 (1931) · W. B. Bannerman, ed., *The visitations of the county of Sussex ... 1530 ... and 1633–4*, Harleian Society, 53 (1905) · *The diary of Henry Machyn, citizen and merchant-taylor of London, from AD 1550 to AD 1563*, ed. J. G. Nichols, CS, 42 (1848) · R. Cavendish, 'Firle Place, East Sussex (historic estate of the Gage family)', *History Today*, 48/6 (1998), 62–3 · J. Gage, *The history and antiquities of Hengrave, in Suffolk* (1822) · E. H. Harbison, *Rival ambassadors at the court of Queen Mary* (1940) · D. E. Hoak, *The king's council in the reign of Edward VI* (1976) · A. Oswald, *Firle Place, Sussex* (1955) · T. S. Willan, *The Muscovy merchants of 1555* (1953)
Archives E. Sussex RO, MSS
Likenesses G. Johnson, alabaster tomb effigy, 1595, St Peter's Church, West Firle, Sussex · oils, c.1620–1630, Royal Collection; version, Firle Place, Sussex · H. Holbein the younger, chalk and ink drawing, Royal Collection [*see illus.*]
Wealth at death £309 p.a.: assessment of court of wards, feodary (June–July 1556), E. Sussex RO, Gage MSS 19/12, 7/20

Gage, Joseph Edward (c.1687–1766), adventurer, the younger son of Joseph Gage (1652–1700) and his wife, Elizabeth Penruddock (d. 1693), was born about 1687. His father, the third son of Sir Thomas Gage, of Firle, Sussex, inherited Shirburn Castle, Oxfordshire, about 1682 on the death of his aunt Elizabeth, Lady Abergavenny, but died in 1700, leaving his two sons under the tutelage of Sir Henry Goring. Joseph Edward and his elder brother, Thomas, were educated at the Jesuit college of La Flèche, near Le Mans, where they went under the alias of Donne. Whereas Thomas later conformed to the Church of England, became an MP, and acquired a viscountcy in 1720, Joseph remained a Catholic and sought his fortune abroad. By 1718 he was a professional gambler in Paris, where he made the acquaintance of John Law, the Scottish financier and economic adviser to the regent, Philippe, duc d'Orléans. In November 1718 he, Law, and the Irish banker Richard Cantillon formed a syndicate to buy one of the tracts of land in Louisiana put on sale for colonial development. In partnership with Lady Mary Herbert (1686–1775), the eldest daughter of the second marquess (and Jacobite duke) of Powis, he became one of the new millionaires who amassed paper fortunes on the Paris stock market, speculating in Mississippi Company shares. By the end of 1719 the sieur de Gueche (as he was known in

Paris) was reputed to be a 'Croesus' (PRO, SP 78/166, fol. 88a) who maintained a lavish lifestyle at his residence on the faubourg St Germain, and through the ambassador, Lord Stair, he made overtures to the British government with a view to transferring his capital to London in return for a peerage and the right to buy an estate (from which Roman Catholics were legally debarred).

The collapse of the Mississippi Company and Law's 'system' in May 1720 left Gage and the Herberts financially ruined, owing vast sums to their creditors, notably to Richard Cantillon. In an attempt to recoup their losses they sued Cantillon for usury, initiating legal proceedings which dragged on until Cantillon's mysterious death in 1734. To evade imprisonment Gage went into hiding in the Parisian underworld, where he orchestrated a campaign to discredit Cantillon. In 1727 he and Lady Mary decided to seek their fortune in Spain, where, on the basis of the reputation of the Herberts' lead mines in Wales, they won a concession to drain and rework the disused silver mines of Guadalcanal, Cazalla, and Galaroza, on the borders of Andalusia and Extremadura. Lady Mary and her aunt Anne, Lady Carrington, took up residence in Seville, while Gage managed operations in the sierra, rendered difficult by shortage of a skilled workforce and adequate machinery. The Guadalcanal mine was drained in 1732, but a legal dispute delayed its exploitation, and Gage prospected elsewhere, at Casares for copper, and at Oropesa for gold. Pressing his advantage, he wrote to the marquess of Powis to seek his daughter's hand in marriage, but Lady Mary, by now a confirmed spinster, evaded his suit by procrastination while retaining his services. In 1740 she was granted full control of the silver mines, and of the potentially even more valuable copper mines at Rio Tinto, but was unable to exploit her advantage for want of capital. She and Gage returned to Paris in 1743 to raise funds, but these did not materialize.

On 23 December 1747 Gage married Catherine Caryll (1716–1748), the younger daughter of John Caryll, of Ladyholt, Sussex. She died little more than three months later, on 4 April 1748. Gage spent his remaining years in Paris, where he died at his lodgings near St Germain-des-Prés on 31 May 1766. He named Lady Mary Herbert as one of the executors of his will, in which he left her an annuity of £100.

The confusion about Gage's career can be traced back to Alexander Pope, who, in his *Epistle to Bathurst* (lines 129–34), launched the legend that, at the height of his fortunes, Gage bid 'three millions' for the crown of Poland, and that he and Lady Mary Herbert—'congenial souls'—later repaired to the mines of Asturias in search of gold. This myth, founded on poetic commonplace and fancy rather than on historical fact, was taken up by Horace Walpole. Confusion was further compounded by reports in the *Gentleman's Magazine* which attributed to Joseph Gage the military exploits of the Walloon general Joseph Bonaventure Thierry du Mont (*d.* 1753), created conde de Gages for his services to the Spanish crown. The error may be explained by the fact that Joseph Gage frequently, but without justification, styled himself as a count. The

legend was perpetuated in the *Dictionary of National Biography* by H. M. Chichester, who also invented a marriage between Gage and Herbert. Mary Herbert died, unmarried, at her apartment in the Temple, Paris, at the age of eighty-nine, in September 1775.   G. MARTIN MURPHY

Sources M. Murphy, 'Pope's "congenial souls": Joseph Gage and Lady Mary Herbert', *N&Q*, 237 (1992), 470–73 • M. Murphy, 'Maria's dreams: Lady Mary Herbert, 1685–1775', *Montgomeryshire Collections*, 85 (1997), 87–100 • M. Murphy, 'Maria's dreams: the reckoning', *Montgomeryshire Collections*, 86 (1998), 65–80 • A. E. Murphy, *Richard Cantillon: entrepreneur and economist* (1986) • A. Pope, *Epistles to several persons*, ed. F. W. Bateson (1961) • J. H. Pollen, ed., 'Bedingfield papers', *Miscellanea, VI*, Catholic RS, 7 (1909), 1–245, esp. 132 • parish registers, Shirburn, Oxon. RO • A. Parry, *The Carylls of Harting: a study in loyalty* (1976) • *Scots Magazine*, 28 (1766), 389 • VCH Oxfordshire, 8.184
Archives PRO, SP 78/165–166 | BL, Caryll MSS • NL Wales, Powis Castle MSS
Wealth at death see will, PRO, PROB 11/941

Gage, Thomas [*name in religion* Tomás de Santa María] (1603?–1656), Dominican friar and writer, was the son of John Gage (*c.*1580–1626) of Haling Manor, Surrey, and his first wife, Margaret (*c.*1580–*c.*1630), daughter of Sir Thomas Copley; he was probably their third son. The Gage and Copley families, both established in Surrey, were prominent among the recusant Roman Catholic community. Both Gage's parents had been condemned to death (but reprieved) for harbouring priests, one of his uncles had been executed with Robert Babington, and a cousin was the Jesuit martyr Robert Southwell. Among Gage's brothers and half-brothers four became Roman Catholic priests, while his eldest brother, Sir Henry *Gage, was an able royalist commander during the civil war. Gage was educated at the Catholic academy in St Omer from about 1615 to about 1620 and then in Spain at the College of San Gregorio in Valladolid, a Dominican establishment, until about 1625. His father had intended him for the Society of Jesus; upon learning that his son had taken Dominican orders instead his father disowned him.

As a young man, under his religious name of Tomás de Santa María, Gage volunteered for a mission to the Philippines. On 2 July 1625 he sailed from Cadiz—smuggled aboard in a barrel of dry biscuit, according to Gage, because his order had designated all English friars for work in England, and the Spanish crown had barred foreigners from America. (Based on Dominican records, Godfrey Anstruther argues that Gage sailed in 1627, but Gage's statements and documents strongly support the earlier date.) After landfall on Guadeloupe the mission party reached Vera Cruz on 12 September 1625 and proceeded overland, intending to sail from Acapulco for Manila. From Mexico City, Gage and four other young friars slipped away and rode south, heading for the Dominican missions in Guatemala. Gage later wrote that the New World offered better pickings than the Philippines, and that he meant 'to gain out of Potosí or Zacatecas treasure that might counterpoise that child's part of which, for detesting the four-cornered cap and black robe of Jesuits, my father had deprived me' (Gage, 11). This cynicism may have been a pose. Gage vividly evokes his youthful break for freedom: the howls of wolves and jaguars on an unknown upland; a mountain crossing attempted on scant provisions; how the young friars fought a 'snowball' fight with lemons and oranges in the Dominican cloister in Chiapas in southern Mexico; how the kindly provincial there welcomed them.

After some months in Chiapas Gage travelled on to Guatemala—'my second *patria*', he fondly wrote—where he spent the next ten years (Gage, 159). In April 1627 he was named reader of arts in the local Dominican college. For three years he lived in the capital city, now known as Antigua (not the present Guatemala City, to which the capital was moved after a devastating earthquake in 1773).

In early 1630 Gage ventured into southern Yucatan with an abortive mission to the Indians of the Petén country. His party found deserted villages and withstood a night-long attack by Chol Maya archers. The return trip took Gage to the Caribbean coast and overland through what is now Honduras. Gage had begun learning Maya in the Petén. In June 1630 he was assigned to serve Indian communities near Antigua, and from early 1635 in Amatitlán. Gage claimed that he had grown wealthy from parishioners' offerings. He was clearly an active priest—ready to defend Indian servants against Creole masters, quarrel with mayors, smash in crocks of home-brewed liquor, and publicly hew to pieces an idol hidden by Maya converts. In Mixco he reconstructed a church; in Amatitlán he oversaw the building of a cloister.

On 6 January 1637, without the approval of his order, Gage began his trip home. He first travelled on muleback, through what are now El Salvador and Nicaragua, to the eastern coast, where Dutch pirates relieved him of £8000 in coins and jewels. After recrossing to the Pacific, Gage travelled by boat to Panama and crossed the isthmus to Portobello. From there he worked a passage to Spain as chaplain to a sea captain. In December 1637 he returned to England, barely able to speak English after more than two decades abroad.

For the next three years Gage was an active but increasingly discontented member of the recusant underground. In 1639 he travelled to Italy, wintered at Rome, was captured by French privateers on the way home, and was back in England by October 1640. Gage continued to feel religious misgivings. Finally, on 28 August 1642 he preached a sermon announcing his defection to the Church of England, published that year as *The Tyranny of Satan Discovered in the Tears of a Converted Sinner*. In December 1643 parliament rewarded him with the living of St Martin in Acrise, Kent. In October 1648 he moved to a more prominent pulpit at St Leonard's in Deal. By then he had married, about 1643, a woman variously identified as either Ellen Yatt, or Mary, and fathered at least three daughters, of whom at least two survived him.

In these surroundings Gage wrote *The English-American his Travail by Sea and Land, or, A New Survey of the West Indias* (1648). This was the first book by an English writer—in fact, the first book not by a Habsburg subject—portraying daily life in Spanish America. It sold well and has often been reprinted. Gage took from others his account of the conquest of Mexico; wholly his own were the strong narrative line and his gift for observation. He wrote of the volcanoes overlooking Antigua (Agua, Fuego, and Acatenango) and the bustle of Portobello when the treasure fleet was in, with silver ingots piled in the street like paving-stones. He zestfully recalled the cuisine of the New World—the tortillas, beans, and tamales of the poor, the strange new fruits of the Indian market, and delicacies like the iguana. To chocolate, with an addict's obsessiveness, he devoted an entire chapter. He denounced the blending of Mayan ceremony and Catholic rites, but seldom condescended to his Indian parishioners, whom he found civil, gentle, industrious, and long-suffering.

Gage played an informant's role in the ugly religious strife of the civil war years. His testimony sent to the gallows at least three Roman Catholic priests: Father Thomas Holland, his schoolmate at St Omer, in October 1642; Father Arthur Bell, a relative's chaplain, in December 1643; and Father Peter Wright, the Jesuit military chaplain in whose arms Gage's brother, Sir Henry Gage, had died, in May 1651. He even testified against his own brother, Father George Gage. Ironically Gage's rancour may reflect a bitterly divided psyche. Tried with Father Wright was Father Thomas Middleton, alias Dade, the Dominican provincial for England. While Gage denounced Wright he testified on behalf of Middleton that one could be a friar without being a priest, thus winning his old superior's acquittal. When Gage defended his conduct in a short mean-spirited pamphlet titled *A duell between a Jesuite and a Dominican … victoriously ended at London upon Fryday, 16 May, 1651*, he identified himself as 'preacher of the Word at Deal in Kent'. This puritan title punned, obscurely but proudly, on Gage's membership in the famed *orden predicante* of St Dominic. Intriguingly, a master at Douai later reported to Rome that Gage had 'returned to a better state of life, whose fall from the faith of Christ was the worst and most vile of all' (Anstruther, 193).

Whatever his private crises of faith Gage gave notable public service to the Commonwealth. He defended the Cromwellian religious establishment in *A Full Survey of Sion and Babylon* (1654). Sponsored by regicide Thomas Chaloner, Gage submitted to Oliver Cromwell a plan to attack the Spanish Caribbean. Both the Venetian ambassador and Bishop Gilbert Burnet report secret meetings between Gage and the protector and credit Gage with inspiring this 'Western design'. When, in late 1654, General Robert Venables and Admiral Sir William Penn led an expeditionary force to the Caribbean, Gage sailed with the force as Venables's chaplain. The English fleet was rebuffed at Haiti—where Indian peasants and escaped slaves failed to aid the English in spite of Gage's hopeful predictions otherwise—but sailed on to seize Jamaica. Spanish sources place Gage among the English officers at the conference table, taking a characteristically vocal part.

In early 1656 Gage died in Jamaica, amid the epidemic dysentery and malaria which killed half of the English garrison. On 18 July 1656 his widow was voted arrears of pay and a pension of 6s. 8d. a week. No will has been traced nor any details of his burial discovered. His widow and daughters apparently prospered sufficiently to contribute, in 1671, toward ransoming English prisoners held by Moorish pirates, with whose misfortunes Gage would have sympathized.

Gage's career and character were stained by the conflicts of his day. To relieve his virulent attacks on the Church of Rome and the high-church Anglican archbishop William Laud later editors have excised whole chapters of *The English-American*. Despite such bias the book remains a colourful, surprisingly sensitive account of early Central America. One of Gage's modern editors has entertained

> a picture—perhaps entirely false—of Gage in later years … on the cold English Channel, longing with all his maimed soul for a view of Fuego from the cloisters of Antigua, or a morning cup of chocolate in the company of old friends. (Gage, xxxii)

The image has something memorable in it.

ALLEN D. BOYER

Sources T. Gage, *Thomas Gage's travels in the New World*, ed. J. E. S. Thompson (Oklahoma, 1958) · G. Anstruther, *A hundred homeless years: English Dominicans, 1558–1658* (1958) · A. P. Newton, introduction, in T. Gage, *The English-American: a new survey of the West Indies* (1928) · S. A. G. Taylor, 'The western design': an account of Cromwell's expedition to the Caribbean* (Kingston, Jamaica, 1965) · P. Revell and F. W. Steer, 'George Gage I and George Gage II', *BIHR*, 31 (1958), 141–58 · *DNB*
Wealth at death £80 p.a. from church living; plus second living: *DNB*; Gage, *Gage's travels*, introduction

Gage, Thomas (1719/20–1787), army officer and colonial governor, was probably born at Highmeadow, Wye valley, Gloucestershire. He was the second of three children of Thomas Gage, first Viscount Gage (d. 1754), and his first wife, Benedicta Maria Theresa Hall (d. 1749). His parents were both Catholics, but his father joined the established church in 1715 and in 1721 was elected MP for Tewkesbury. John, Baron Hervey, described Viscount Gage as 'a petulant, silly, busy, meddling, profligate fellow', while Philip, duke of Wharton, promised to pay his debts when 'Lady Gage grows chaste' (Alden, 6–7). The unhappy marriage, which had united considerable wealth, ended with her death in 1749.

Eight years at Westminster School (1728–36), to which he was sent at the age of eight, were followed in 1741 by a lieutenancy purchased in Cholmondeley's (later the 48th) foot. After several exchanges Gage was captain by 1743, aide to William Anne Keppel, second earl of Albemarle, at Fontenoy in 1745, and was also at Culloden in 1746. His elder brother, William, second Viscount Gage, after their father's death in 1754, married Elizabeth, daughter of the financier Sampson Gideon, and aided by her wealth and his own connections with Thomas Pelham-Holles, first duke of Newcastle, actively furthered his younger brother's military rise. After the war Gage served in Ireland with the 44th foot, becoming lieutenant-colonel in 1751. The important stage of his career began in late 1754, when the 44th was ordered to America under Major-

Thomas Gage (1719/20–1787), by John Singleton Copley, c.1768–9

General Edward Braddock as part of a plan imposed by the duke of Cumberland on an uncertain Newcastle to counter a French advance into the Ohio River valley.

Twice during the ensuing war Gage was at the forefront of major military actions, commanding Braddock's advance guard in the march toward the forks of the Ohio River in July 1755, and three years later when he led the light infantry screen in Abercromby's attack on Ticonderoga. Both actions rank among the worst defeats in the history of the British army, and in neither did Gage distinguish himself except by personal bravery. Slightly wounded in Braddock's defeat, he defended himself in Benjamin Franklin's *Pennsylvania Gazette* against published criticism of his handling of the advance guard. Other chances also slipped past him. Ordered by Amherst in 1759 to move into the upper St Lawrence valley from Lake Ontario, thus aiding Wolfe's desperate venture against Quebec by bringing pressure from the west, Gage concluded that he was too weak to cope with the French forces blocking his path. His boldest stroke came in 1757 when he won approval of his proposal to form a corps of light infantry (80th foot) that could perform many of the functions then assigned to the mutinous and unreliable American rangers, but the aim appears to have been to secure a colonelcy for himself, and there is little evidence that the 80th ever fulfilled its tactical promise. In the final campaign on the continent, in 1760, Gage commanded the rearguard of Jeffrey Amherst's army. Regarded as a capable and conscientious officer by all who knew him, including the hero of Quebec James Wolfe, Gage as a wartime commander had proved to be 'certainly none of the

Sons of Fortune' (Dr Richard Huck to the earl of Loudoun, 3 Dec 1759, Loudoun MS 6153).

At the end of the Seven Years' War, promoted major-general (1761), Gage became military governor of Montreal, where he was popular for tactful dealings with civilians, French, and British and for keeping strict discipline in the garrison. The outbreak of a major Indian war (the Pontiac War) in 1763 occasioned the recall of Amherst, and Gage succeeded him at New York as commander-in-chief for North America. The government's decision to maintain a large peacetime garrison of regular troops in the new provinces of Canada and Florida as well as along the transappalachian frontier would keep Gage in America for the next decade, nor did he ever forget the reasons for Amherst's recall. Much of his correspondence with successive secretaries of state, and privately with his personal friend William, second Viscount Barrington, secretary at war from 1755 to 1761 and 1765 to 1778, concerned the use of the American garrison to reduce the likelihood of another American Indian outbreak, whether by regulating white settlement of the vast western territories acquired in 1763 or by policing the Indian trade, notorious for abusive practices by white traders. At the same time growing political trouble in the eastern port towns gave reason to enlarge the small regular garrisons at New York and Philadelphia and, in 1768, to send troops to Boston. Gage was well aware, however, as his Whitehall correspondents were not, that small regular forces could not suppress American disorder. In the 1765 New York riots against the Stamp Act the royal governor declined to call for military aid from the 100 regulars at Fort George as being insufficient to quash the insurgency. Similarly, in 1770, after the guard at the customs house had fired on a menacing crowd, killing five people in the Boston 'massacre', both the provincial governor and Gage's local commander, faced by the threat that thousands of New England militia would march on the town, agreed to withdraw both regiments of regulars from Boston to an island in the harbour.

Gage was a capable, honest administrator, minimizing the heavy costs of the American garrison while dealing tactfully with Americans, but he was extremely cautious in offering advice to his superiors. Only in his private letters to Barrington can his own opinions about a deteriorating, perhaps irremediable British position in the American colonies be detected. The decision of 1768 to withdraw regulars from all the western posts save Niagara, Detroit, and Michilimackinac (on the strait connecting lakes Michigan and Huron) was made with no more than a self-protective, equivocating report from Gage. He never suggested redeployment of the large regular garrison in the St Lawrence valley, where the French Canadian population had been docile, nor did he show any interest in Barrington's idea of removing all troops from the older mainland colonies in order to cut costs while eliminating a cause of future trouble. Charged with supervising the conduct of Indian affairs, he rarely ventured beyond budgetary management and the occasional expression of an opinion, doing little to support a promising plan of 1764 to regulate the Indian trade, and permitting his nominal subordinates to revise westward the boundaries for white settlement in ways that undercut the aim of reducing trouble along the frontier.

Imaginative leadership may be too much to ask of a senior military commander faced with a complex political situation, both in London and in America, but as a virtual viceroy, the only man on the spot able to deal with a dozen fractious colonial governments and to keep Whitehall abreast of all that was happening, Gage rarely ventured beyond the limits of routine. Commanding from his New York headquarters, with years of experience in the colonies and good personal connections there, Gage was singularly unenterprising, privately outraged by American challenges to royal authority, but officially bent on no more than keeping himself and his army out of the line of fire.

Granted leave to return to England in 1773, Gage arrived at a moment of crisis in American affairs. Protesting the tax on a large shipment of East Indian tea, a Boston mob had dumped the tea in Boston harbour. After an audience with George III, the king reported Gage as saying the Americans 'will be Lyons, whilst we are Lambs but if we take the resolute part they will undoubtedly prove very meek' (George III to North, 4 Feb 1774, *The Correspondence of George III*, ed. Fortescue, vol. 3, no. 1379). Gage returned to America with a commission as governor of Massachusetts, orders to enforce a set of new, draconian laws for the governance of the colony, and promises of both large military reinforcements and strong political support at home. In advising the king, Gage apparently had dropped his habitual caution, but later claimed that the king had misunderstood him. Even at the climax in 1774–5, when compelled to play a decisive role in the opening battles of an imperial civil war, Gage was seldom the object of American hatred, though many of his own officers considered him unsuited for the challenge, and argued for his recall. Most historians would agree that nothing that Gage might have done could have averted the outbreak of rebellion, although he should have known and told the government that rebellion was not confined to Boston or even New England; and yet a more aggressive commander-in-chief of the American garrison might well have made matters worse. But as a decade of political crises had swirled around him, the most notable feature of General Gage's performance had been his passivity.

Gage's last acts as a field commander were as unfortunate as his record in the Seven Years' War. In Boston he saw that growing opposition posed a formidable military challenge, and begged Whitehall for more troops. Government's confidence in him dropped with the receipt of each negative dispatch, and in mid-April 1775 he received secret orders 'to arrest and imprison the principal actors & abbettors' of rebellion (Dartmouth to Gage, 27 Jan 1775, *Correspondence*, 2.181).

After nightfall on 18 April Gage sent a large column to Concord, a town 20 miles from Boston where the rebel congress had met and munitions were known to be secreted. Lightly armed for rapid movement, the column skirmished with militia at Lexington, half way, destroyed stores, but captured no one of importance after a confused battle at Concord, and then ran a terrible gauntlet of rebel militia fire until being rescued by a more heavily armed brigade sent out by Gage early on the 19th. Before regaining the shelter of Boston, the original column lost almost a third of its force. Within a few days Gage and his army were penned on the Boston peninsula by thousands of militia from the New England provinces. When three junior generals—William Howe, Henry Clinton, and John Burgoyne—arrived in May with more troops, Gage knew his days were numbered. But he saw a chance in June to teach the rebels a lesson when they fortified a hill on Charlestown peninsula, opposite Boston. Instead of using the navy to cut off his enemy at Charlestown neck, he ordered Major-General Howe to attack frontally. Meeting ferocious resistance, Howe carried the rebel works at the cost of well over 1000 casualties in an attacking force of about 2500. Gage reported privately to Barrington that 'These People Shew a Spirit and Conduct against us, they never shewed against the French' (26 June 1775, *Correspondence*, 2.686). In October Gage sailed for England.

On 8 December 1758, a few months after the defeat at Ticonderoga, Gage had married Margaret Kemble or Kembal (*c*.1734–1824), eldest daughter of a wealthy and politically important family in the province of New Jersey, and closely related to the most aristocratic families of New York. Known facetiously as the Duchess of Brunswick for her cool beauty and social position, she would give him eleven children, and he found employment in his army for her brothers and cousins. Their youngest son was the naval officer Sir William Hall *Gage. The marriage cooled with time, and soured after their first, brief visit to England in 1773–4, when Gage was directed to crush the American rebellion, by force if necessary. Evidence indicates that Margaret Gage, sympathetic to her countrymen, revealed the secret plan of the march to Concord to his American enemies (Fischer, 96). The magnificent portraits of Gage and his wife by John Singleton Copley are especially valuable because personal evidence for their lives is meagre. Painted about 1768–9 in New York, he surveys a battlefield, dignified yet curiously benign and complacent, while she is beautiful, pensive, and apparently bored.

Gage did not cultivate his earliest contacts with other important Americans, neither an acquaintance with Benjamin Franklin who assisted Braddock's army, nor a promising friendship with young Colonel George Washington who was a comrade in that army. Instead, his grasp of the American political situation derived chiefly from a narrow circle of appointed officials and his wife's relations, who, unlike Mrs Gage, showed no sympathy for the rebel cause. Gage seems to have had as little gift for human relationships as for warfare. Like battles, people appeared to him less as opportunities than as a set of responsibilities and problems.

Residing in London after his return, Gage suffered the benign neglect of the government, which continued his salary as governor of rebel-held Massachusetts but gave him no other reward for twenty years of American service. Old friends did not neglect him, nor did the American loyalists emigrating to England. In 1781 he briefly commanded the defences of Kent against French invasion, and a report circulated that he had taken a mistress. When the North government fell after the news of the defeat at Yorktown, Gage was promoted full general. He died at his home in Portland Place, London, on 2 April 1787, after a prolonged 'inflammation of the bowels' (Alden, 292), and was buried with his ancestors at Firle Place, Sussex. A harsh but fair epitaph might read 'Good soldier but no warrior'.   JOHN SHY

Sources J. R. Alden, *General Gage in America* (1948) · L. H. Gipson, *The British empire before the American revolution*, 6–12 (1946–65) · *The correspondence of General Thomas Gage*, ed. C. E. Carter, 2 vols. (1931–3) · 'Confronting rebellion: private correspondence of Lord Barrington with Thomas Gage, 1765–1775', ed. J. Shy, *Sources of American independence*, ed. H. Peckham, 1.1–139 · J. Shy, *Toward Lexington* (1965) · J. Shy, 'Thomas Gage', *George Washington's opponents*, ed. G. Billias (1969), 3–38 · D. H. Fischer, *Paul Revere's ride* (1994) · S. Pargellis, ed., *Military affairs in North America, 1748–1765: selected documents from the Cumberland papers in Windsor Castle* (1936) · S. F. Wise, 'Gage, Thomas', *DCB*, vol. 4 · *Collections of the New York Historical Society*, 17 (1884), xvii–xviii
Archives BL, corresp., orders and MSS, Add. MSS 21656–21657, 21662–21665, 21677, 21680–21683, 21697 · Detroit Public Library, Michigan, corresp. and MSS · E. Sussex RO, MSS as commander-in-chief, North America · Harvard U., Houghton L., letters · NA Canada, corresp. relating to American rebellion · U. Mich., Clements L., corresp. and MSS | American Antiquarian Society, Worcester, Massachusetts, corresp. with John Bradstreet · BL, Newcastle, Haldimand, and Bouquet MSS · CKS, corresp. with Lord Amherst · Hunt. L., Loudoun and Abercromby MSS · PRO, Amherst MSS, corresp. with commander-in-chief, North America, WO 34/46A · U. Mich., Germain and Henry Clinton MSS
Likenesses J. S. Copley, oils, *c*.1768–1769, Yale U. CBA, Paul Mellon collection [*see illus.*] · D. Martin, oils, Firle Place, Sussex · J. Meyer, miniature, NPG · R. Pollard, line engraving, NPG
Wealth at death not inconsiderable wealth: Alden, *General Gage in America*, 293

Gage, Sir William Hall (1777–1864), naval officer, sixth and youngest son of General the Hon. Thomas *Gage (1719/20–1787) and his wife, Margaret (*c*.1734–1824), daughter of Peter Kembal, president of the council of New Jersey, was born in Park Place, St James's, London, on 2 October 1777. He entered the navy on the guardship *Bellona* at Plymouth in November 1789. After serving in several ships on the home, West Indian, and Mediterranean stations, including the *Princess Royal* (flagship of Rear-Admiral Goodall in the actions off Toulon on 13 March and 13 July 1795) and the *Bedford* (in the defence of the convoy against Richery off Cadiz), he was appointed to the *Victory*, flagship of Sir John Jervis, and was promoted from her lieutenant of the frigate *Minerve* (42 guns), in which he took part in the engagement with the *Sabina* on 20 December 1796, in the battle of Cape St Vincent on 14 February 1797, and in the cutting out of the brig *Mutine* on 29 May of the same year. On 13 June he was made commander, and on 26 July was posted captain of the frigate *Terpsichore* (32 guns), which for the next three years served in the Mediterranean, and notably in the blockade of Malta. Having returned to England, the *Terpsichore* was one of the frigates which detained the Danish ships under the convoy of the *Freja*, an affair which proved one of the main causes of the second armed neutrality and of the battle of Copenhagen.

In March 1801 Gage was appointed to the *Uranie* (38 guns), and on 21 July he took part in the cutting out of the French 20-gun corvette *Chevrette* from under the batteries in Camaret Bay. From 1805 to 1808 he commanded the frigate *Thetis* (38 guns) in the North Sea and Mediterranean, and in 1813 and 1814 the *Indus* (74 guns) off Toulon under Sir Edward Pellew. In July 1821 he became rear-admiral. He was commander-in-chief in the East Indies from 1825 to 1830, and in the Downs from May to July 1833. He was made a GCH on 19 April 1834, became a vice-admiral on 10 January 1837, was commander-in-chief at Lisbon from April to December 1837, was a member of the Board of Admiralty between 1842 and 1846, and became an admiral on 9 November 1846. From 1848 to 1851 he was commander-in-chief at Plymouth.

This was the end of Gage's long service, though in 1853 he was appointed rear-admiral of the United Kingdom, and vice-admiral in 1854. In 1860 he was made a GCB, and in 1862 admiral of the fleet. During his later years he lived at Thurston, near Bury St Edmunds, Suffolk, where he freely contributed both time and money to the restoration of the parish church and to local charities, and where he died on 4 January 1864.

J. K. LAUGHTON, rev. ROGER MORRISS

Sources J. Marshall, *Royal naval biography*, 1/2 (1823), 836–40 · O'Byrne, *Naval biog. dict.* · *GM*, 3rd ser., 16 (1864), 388 · A. B. Rodger, *The war of the second coalition: 1798–1801, a strategic commentary* (1964) · P. Mackesy, *The war in the Mediterranean, 1803–1810* (1957) · R. Muir, *Britain and the defeat of Napoleon, 1807–1815* (1996) · Boase, *Mod. Eng. biog.*

Archives NMM, corresp. with Lord Minto

Wealth at death under £30,000: probate, 28 Jan 1864, *CGPLA Eng. & Wales*

Gager, William (1555–1622), Latin playwright and poet, was born on 24 July 1555, possibly in Long Melford, Suffolk, the son of Gilbert Gager (d. 1590) and Thomasine, sister of Sir William Cordell, master of the rolls. He had a sister, Mary, who was born in 1560, and a brother, John, who died in 1630. William Gager was educated at Westminster School and from there was elected to Christ Church, Oxford, in 1574. He graduated as BA on 4 December 1577, MA on 5 June 1580, and took his BCL and DCL on 30 June 1589.

At Oxford Gager became well known both as a Latin poet and as a playwright. His autograph manuscript book (BL, Add. MS 22583) contains not only his juvenilia but also many poems which he wrote during his period at Oxford. These include occasional poems to contemporaries and friends such as the playwright George Peele, the philosopher and Aristotelian commentator John Case, and Martin Heton, later bishop of Ely, and short epigrams on the members of Christ Church. In the 1580s Gager wrote poems on the Babington conspiracy against the life of Queen Elizabeth, the *In catilinarias proditiones ac proditores*

domesticos, odae 6, soon reprinted with three additional odes as *Odae 9* (1586). These poems were printed on the newly established press of Joseph Barnes, the Oxford University printer. Gager was also asked to edit the university's tribute on the death of Sir Philip Sidney, the *Exequiae D. Philippi Sidnaei* (1587), an early commemorative volume to which he also contributed, along with numerous Oxford contemporaries. He also wrote verses for the university anthologies of chiefly Latin verse on the deaths of Sir Henry Unton in 1596 and Queen Elizabeth I in 1603. A later lengthy poem on the Gunpowder Plot was not printed, but is extant in the British Library (Royal MS 12A LIX).

Gager has more claim to fame as a playwright than as a poet. His commonplace book contains some short dramatic treatments of episodes from the story of Oedipus, dating from the 1570s. From the early 1580s onwards he was in demand as a university dramatist, writing plays for the entertainment of distinguished visitors to the university. *Meleager*, printed at Oxford in 1593 and dedicated to the earl of Essex, was first performed at Christ Church in February 1582. It was performed again there in January 1585 in the presence of the earls of Pembroke and Leicester and Sir Philip Sidney. Gager wrote an extra prologue and epilogue for that occasion. The play is based on the well-known classical story of Meleager, narrated by Ovid, among others, in *Metamorphoses*, book viii, and tells of the jealousy of Meleager's uncles at Atalanta's success in hunting the Calydonian boar. When Meleager angrily slays his uncles, his own life is in return brought to an end by his mother, Althaea, to avenge the deaths of her brothers. Gager's comedy 'Rivales', which is lost apart from the prologue, was performed at Christ Church in June 1583 in honour of the visiting Polish prince Albertus Alasco, as was his play 'Dido', a dramatization of the tale of Dido and Aeneas which draws heavily on the *Aeneid* and was spectacularly produced for this occasion. This was not printed, but two acts were copied out in Gager's manuscript book, and a manuscript of the whole survives at Christ Church (MS 486).

The year of Gager's greatest dramatic triumph was 1592. On 6 February his new play, *Ulysses Redux*, a tragicomedy based on the *Odyssey* and describing Ulysses' return to Ithaca and his vengeance on the suitors of his wife, Penelope, was performed at Christ Church. On 7 February his 'Rivales' was revived; later that year Gager was a member of the committee charged with overseeing the theatrical performances for the queen's visit to Oxford, and the play was performed before her in September. On 8 February 1592 there was a performance of Seneca's *Hippolytus* with additional scenes written for the production by Gager. At the end of this performance, Gager brought on to the stage the figure of Momus, the carping critic, who objected to the performance of academic drama on grounds of expense and waste of time, and because for young men to act in public and in particular dressed as women was injurious to morality, and contrary to the precepts of the Bible and Roman law. Following Momus was an 'Epilogus responsivus' who countered his arguments one by one. *Ulysses Redux* was printed in 1592, dedicated to Lord Buckhurst, chancellor of Oxford University, with one surviving copy being dedicated to the countess of Pembroke. The printed edition contains the prologue and epilogue written for the production of *Hippolytus* and the speeches for and against plays of Momus and the 'Epilogus responsivus'.

Dr John Rainolds, president of Corpus Christi College, who had previously declined an invitation to attend the Christ Church plays in a letter using many of the same anti-theatrical arguments as Momus, believed he was being satirized by this portrayal. A lengthy correspondence in English between Gager and Rainolds developed which throws much light on contemporary puritan attitudes to the theatre; it also expounds in unusual detail Rainolds's objections to stage transvestism. When Gager gave up replying to Rainolds's lengthy missives, his part was taken by Alberico Gentili, regius professor of civil law at Oxford, who continued to debate the issues raised in Latin letters with Dr Rainolds. Rainolds's letters to Gager, and the first four letters exchanged between himself and Alberico Gentili, were printed under Rainolds's name as *Th'Overthrow of Stage-Playes* (1599). The whole correspondence is extant in Corpus Christi College, Oxford, MS 352.

Not much is known of Gager's activities in the 1590s, apart from those as a playwright at the beginning of the decade. In 1599 his friend Martin Heton was appointed bishop of Ely and, no doubt through his influence, in 1601 Gager was appointed surrogate to the vicar-general of Ely, Dr Richard Swale. On the death of Swale in 1606 Gager was himself appointed chancellor and vicar-general of the diocese of Ely. In 1609, when Martin Heton died, Gager composed the Latin elegiacs which are still to be seen on Heton's tomb in Ely Cathedral. The last Latin verses which Gager is known to have written are those in the Cambridge University anthology celebrating the marriage of King James's daughter Princess Elizabeth to Frederick, count palatine of the Rhine. This anthology was not printed but is extant in the Vatican Library (MS Palat. Lat. 1736). Some of the verses which he had written for the death of Sir Philip Sidney were printed in some seventeenth-century editions of Sidney's *Arcadia*.

Late in life Gager married a widow, Mrs Mary Tovey, who had two children, Edmund and Humphrey. They lived in Chesterton, on the outskirts of Cambridge. Gager made his will in July 1615. He died in 1622 and was buried on 1 September of that year in All Saints' Church, Cambridge.

J. W. BINNS

Sources C. F. T. Brooke, 'The life and times of William Gager', *Proceedings of the American Philosophical Society*, 95 (1951), 401–31 · W. Gager, *The complete works*, ed. D. F. Sutton, 4 vols. (1994) · F. S. Boas, *University drama in the Tudor age* (1914) · J. W. Binns, *Intellectual culture in Elizabethan and Jacobean England: the Latin writings of the age* (1990) · W. Gager, commonplace book, BL, Add. MS 22583 · Foster, *Alum. Oxon.*
Archives BL, commonplace book, Add. MS 22583 | CCC Oxf., letters to Rainolds, MS 352
Wealth at death described self as 'poor scholar': will, Brooke, 'Life and times', 430–31

Gagnier, John (*c*.1670–1740), orientalist, was born in Paris. His father was attaché to the French ambassador to Denmark, and his sudden death about 1680 led to his widow's decision to enter the nunnery of St Élisabeth. Her three sons were farmed out to Génovefains, and subsequently John was enrolled in the prestigious College of Navarre, where his tutor was the Augustinian monk René le Bossu. Le Bossu used Brian Walton's polyglot Bible to fire his pupil's enthusiasm, and although this text hastened the decline of Arabic's ancillary role in Old Testament studies le Bossu presided over the birth of a committed Arabist and Christian Hebraist, if not a devoted Catholic priest. Graduating from the influence of le Bossu as apologist of Descartes, Gagnier became a canon regular at the university abbey of St Geneviève du Mont, where the philosopher's bones had been reburied.

Whether motivated by Cartesian doubt or antipathy to celibacy Gagnier abandoned both Catholicism and France in 1702, finding an asylum in Anglicanism, and powerful patronage in London. He won the support of John Sharp, archbishop of York, Sir Thomas Parker (later Lord Chancellor Macclesfield), and William Lloyd, bishop of Worcester and lord almoner; a Cambridge MA was conferred by royal mandate in 1703. Attracted by the superior manuscript holdings of the Bodleian Library, Gagnier was introduced to Oxford by Lloyd, who appointed him his personal chaplain. A zealous scholar himself, Lloyd's friendship to oriental learning and to distressed foreign protestants was demonstrated in Gagnier's first published works of 1706. The *Josephus Ben-Gorion*, printed in Oxford at Lloyd's expense, was a scholarly edition, with Latin translation and notes, of a Hebrew chronicle based on Josephus but erroneously ascribed to Ben Gorion. Gagnier's second publication, *L'Église Romaine convaincue de dépravation, d'idolatrie, et d'antichristianisme, en forme de lettre*, published at The Hague, might suggest a profound doctrinal dimension to his conversion; it was also exactly the kind of work to endear him to his anti-papist patron. Through the considerable efforts of Bishop Lloyd and his nephew Benjamin Marshall, a Christ Church Arabic scholar, to promote Hebrew studies and secure another foreigner to succeed Rabbi Levi as Hebrew lecturer, by late 1709 the antiquary Thomas Hearne could announce Gagnier 'is now a Teacher of the Hebrew Language in Oxford, and is esteem'd by able Judges to be a compleat Master of it' (*Remarks*, 2.308). Gagnier was simultaneously developing his skills in Arabic by assisting John Ernest Grabe to settle a scholarly dispute with the Cambridge scholar William Whiston.

By 1715 Gagnier was deputy for the regius professor of Hebrew, Robert Clavering, and three years later he was appointed deputy to the absentee Laudian professor of Arabic, John Wallis. In the same year he published an accomplished Hebrew elegy on the death of John Radcliffe, and soon numbered the young John Wesley among his pupils. In 1723 he produced an Arabic edition of the fourteenth-century Syrian Prince Abu'l-Fida's life of Muhammad, with Latin translation and notes. This first complete Muslim account of the prophet established an enlightened historicist objectivity after the Eurocentrism of Humphrey Prideaux and Henri de Boulainvilliers. Appointed to the Lord Almoner's professorship of Arabic in the following year, Gagnier drew upon Abu'l-Fida and al-Jannabi for his own, two-volume *Vie de Mahomet*, published in Amsterdam in 1732, a pioneering yet accessible work of historiography which found Muhammad neither impostor nor hero. Gagnier had produced in 1727 a specimen of Abu'l-Fida's *Taqwim al-buldan*, but publication of this Arabic geography was delayed by financial constraints, his *Descriptio peninsulæ Arabum* not appearing until 1740. Contemporary assessments varied like Hearne's opinions, but his splenetic dismissal of Gagnier as 'a very mean piddling Author' was not endorsed by fellow antiquary Richard Mead, for whom Gagnier translated a medical treatise by Rhasis. George Sale acknowledged Gagnier's edition as his chief source of information on Muhammad's career, and Edward Gibbon praised 'the honest Gagnier' as 'the best and most authentic of our guides'.

Prompted by a prize of £200 Gagnier even aspired to master Persian and become the first European translator of the *Zend-Avesta*, but Cambridge refused to lend him three manuscript Persian dictionaries. Having resigned his chair he died in Oxford, probably late in 1740, leaving a widow and a son John (or Thomas), born in 1721, who had just graduated from Wadham College and entered holy orders.

MICHAEL J. FRANKLIN

Sources *Remarks and collections of Thomas Hearne*, ed. C. E. Doble and others, 11 vols., OHS, 2, 7, 13, 34, 42–3, 48, 50, 65, 67, 72 (1885–1921) • B. Lewis and P. M. Holt, eds., *Historians of the Middle East* (1962) • P. M. Holt, 'The treatment of Arab history by Prideaux, Ockley, and Sale', *Studies in the history of the Near East* (1973), 50–63 • P. J. Marshall, 'Oriental studies', *Hist. U. Oxf.* 5: *18th-cent. Oxf.*, 550–63 • D. Patterson, 'Hebrew studies', *Hist. U. Oxf.* 5: *18th-cent. Oxf.*, 535–50 • L. S. Sutherland, 'The origin and early history of the lord almoner's professorship in Arabic at Oxford', *Bodleian Library Record*, 10 (1978–82), 166–77 • A. Tindal Hart, *William Lloyd, 1627–1717* (1952) • G. J. Toomer, *Eastern wisedome and learning: the study of Arabic in seventeenth-century England* (1996) • M. Feingold, 'Oriental studies', *Hist. U. Oxf.* 4: *17th-cent. Oxf.*, 449–503 • G. A. Russell, ed., *The 'Arabick' interest of the natural philosophers in seventeenth-century England* (Leiden, 1994) • *Dictionnaire de biographie française*, 15, ed. M. Prevost, R. D'Amat, and H. Tribout de Morembert (Paris, 1982) [cols. 49–50] • H. Hall, 'The origin of the lord almoner's professorship of Arabic', *The Athenaeum* (16 Nov 1889), 673–4 • J. Fück, *Die arabischen Studien in Europa bis in den Anfang des 20. Jahrhunderts* (Leipzig, 1955) • DNB

Archives Bodl. Oxf., MS Ballard • Bodl. Oxf., MS Rawl., letters 96, fol. 31 • Christ Church Oxf., Wake MSS, papers and letters, vol. 21, fol. 49 • NL Wales, Clemenstone papers

Wealth at death valuable library: NL Wales, Clemenstone papers, 5, Daniel Durrel, letter to Mrs Gagnier, 25 July 1741

Gahagan, Usher (*d.* 1749), classical scholar and coiner, came from a family in co. Westmeath, Ireland, but nothing more is known about his background or early life. He attended Trinity College, Dublin, with the intention of entering the law but his conversion to Catholicism while a student prevented him from being called to the bar. He left without taking a degree and was disowned by his parents. He married a wealthy heiress, whom he treated cruelly, and they soon separated. His conduct alienated his remaining friends, and with mounting debts he moved to London, where he hoped to make a living from writing. He was a more than competent classical scholar and found employment editing J. Brindley's beautiful editions of the works of Horace, Cornelius Nepos, Sallust, Juvenal, Persius, Virgil, and Terence, all published in 1744. His edition of Quintus Curtius appeared in 1746 and those of Catullus, Propertius, and Tibullus in 1749. He also translated into Latin verse Pope's *Essay on Criticism*, published with a dedication to the earl of Chesterfield as *Tentamen de re critica* (1747).

In London Gahagan fell into the company of a fellow Irishman, Hugh Coffey, and together they agreed a plan for making money by filing pieces off silver and gold coins. They took into partnership Gahagan's lodger Terence Connor, another well-educated Irishman, and for some months the scheme appears to have worked well. Suspicions arose when they began buying gold coins known as Portuguese pieces from a bank, with the intention of filing them. Coffey was arrested and, promised a lenient sentence, turned informer. Gahagan and Connor were arrested in a public house at Chalk Farm early in January 1749 and placed in Newgate gaol. At their trial at the Old Bailey on 16 January both men were found guilty of 'diminishing the coin of the realm' and were sentenced to death.

While awaiting execution in Newgate, Gahagan translated into Latin verse two more works by Pope, 'The Temple of Fame' and 'The Messiah', both of which were dedicated to the prime minister, the duke of Newcastle, in the hope of obtaining a pardon. He also addressed some verses to Prince George, and Connor wrote a poetic appeal to the duchess of Queensberry, but their pleas were in vain. They were hanged at Tyburn on Monday, 20 February 1749 with five other criminals, all of whom 'behaved with great decency' (*London Magazine*).

SIDNEY LEE, rev. M. J. MERCER

Sources GM, 1st ser., 19 (1749), 43, 90, 96 • *N&Q*, 5th ser., 1 (1874), 482–3 • A. Knapp and W. Baldwin, *The Newgate calendar, comprising interesting memoirs of the most notorious characters*, 4 vols. (1824–6), vol. 2, pp. 27–30 • D. J. O'Donoghue, *The poets of Ireland: a biographical dictionary with bibliographical particulars*, 1 vol. in 3 pts (1892–3) • *London Magazine*, 18 (1749), 99

Gahan, William (1730?–1804), Roman Catholic priest and writer, was born in Old Broad Street, Dublin, probably in June 1730, though several sources record a birth date of 1732. He was of a Leinster sept, the original name of which was Ó Gaoithín, Anglicized Gahan. He was educated in Dublin, where he became a member of the Augustinian order, and in 1747 he entered the Roman Catholic University of Louvain, where he studied for eleven years and received the degree of doctor of divinity. Gahan returned to Ireland in September 1761, was appointed curate of the parish of St Paul, Dublin, and subsequently, on being appointed as Irish provincial, retired to the house of his order in that city, where he devoted much of his time to the composition of works for the use of Roman Catholics on subjects connected with religion and morality. In 1777 he established a school in John's Lane, Dublin, near to his own birthplace. In 1786 he travelled through England, France, and Italy, and wrote what remains an unpublished account of his tour. Gahan narrowly escaped with his life during the rising of 1798, when he was seriously injured by soldiers in search of the rebel leader, Lord Edward Fitzgerald.

The most important public incident in Gahan's career occurred in connection with John Butler, Roman Catholic bishop of Cork, of whom he had been a close friend since 1783. In 1786, following the death of his nephew Pierce Butler, Bishop Butler became twelfth Lord Dunboyne and inherited extensive estates. Anxious to prevent the extinction of the direct line of his family he resigned the bishopric of Cork on 12 December of that year. In late April 1787 he married, and on 9 August he took the required oaths to become a member of the established Church of Ireland. While suffering from his last illness, in May 1800, Dunboyne addressed a letter to the pope, requesting readmission to the Roman Catholic church; he also executed a will by which he bequeathed one of his estates to the Roman Catholic college of Maynooth. The letter to the pope was transmitted through John Troy, Roman Catholic archbishop of Dublin, who expressed his disapproval of any of the Dunboyne estates being alienated from the family. With Troy's permission Gahan, in company with a friend of Dunboyne, attended on his lordship, received him into the Roman Catholic church, and urged, in vain, the revocation of the will. After Dunboyne's death on 7 May 1800 the validity of the bequest to Maynooth was challenged by his sister in the court of chancery, and Gahan underwent several examinations there. The case came to trial at the assizes at Trim, co. Meath, on 24 August 1802, before Viscount Kilwarden, the chief justice.

John Philpot Curran was one of the counsel for the college of Maynooth. In the course of the trial Gahan was required by the court, under penalty of imprisonment, to state certain details of his relations with Lord Dunboyne. These he held to have been confidential, in connection with his duties as a priest, and he firmly declined to disclose them. He was then sentenced to a week's imprisonment for contempt of court. Gahan's confinement was brief, however, since after the jury had returned their verdict the court ordered his discharge. A subsequent compromise between the litigants led to the endowment of a department of the college of Maynooth, designated the Dunboyne Establishment.

Gahan died in Dublin, in the house of his order, on 6 December 1804 and was buried in St James's cemetery. His published works consist of *Sermons and Moral Discourses* (6th edn, 1847), a history of the Christian church (Catholic Book Society, c.1839), translations from the sermons of Louis Bourdaloue, and several devotional books.

J. T. GILBERT, rev. J. FALVEY

Sources C. Costello, *In quest of an heir* (1978) · J. Kingston, 'Lord Dunboyne', *Reportium Novum*, 3/1 (1961–2) · J. J. Delaney and J. E. Tobin, *Dictionary of Catholic biography* (1962) · F. X. Martin, 'Provincial rivalries in eighteenth-century Ireland', *Archivium Hibernicum*, 30 (1972), 117–35
Likenesses Maguire, stipple, NPG

Gaikwar [Gaekwar], **Sayaji Rao** [Sayaji Rao III], **maharaja of Baroda** (1863–1939), social reformer, was born on 11 March 1863 at Kavlana in Nasik district of Bombay presidency, and named Gopal Rao, the second son of Kashi Rao, a village headman, who belonged to the Maratha family which had created the state of Baroda in Gujarat during the eighteenth century. After the British government of India had deposed Maharaja Malhar Rao as ruler of Baroda in 1875 for misconduct (which reputedly included attempting to poison the British resident with diamond dust) and misgovernment, the maharani, Jamnabai (1863–1898), widow of his brother and predecessor, was permitted to adopt a collateral relative as heir. Her choice was the twelve-year-old Gopal Rao, who took the name Sayaji Rao III when he was installed on the *gadi* or throne of Baroda in May 1875. F. A. H. Elliott, an Indian Civil Service officer and member of the Minto family which had a long tradition of imperial service in India, was appointed as tutor for the new heir and established a rigorous regime of literary education in English, Gujarati, Marathi, and Urdu as well as practical training in administration. At the same time, the British government of India secured the appointment of Sir T. Madhav Rao, a Maratha administrator reputed to be both progressive and loyal to the British, as *diwan* or chief minister. During the minority of the young prince, the *diwan* reformed the court system and state police while building schools, hospitals, and roads, and achieving a balanced budget.

Invested with governing powers in December 1881, shortly before his nineteenth birthday, Sayaji Rao, short, stocky, and socially reserved, was an administratively active ruler. He soon earned a reputation as a model prince for his attention to duty and social programmes. His first priority was to make educational institutions available in all segments of his state of about 8000 square miles, which consisted of four provinces dispersed within the Gujarat and Kathiawar areas of the British Indian province of Bombay and had a population of slightly more than 2 million (1881). In 1893 free compulsory primary education was inaugurated in Amreli district as an experiment; in 1907 it was extended throughout Baroda state. Although the legal sanctions against parents who did not send their children to school were not strictly enforced, especially during periods of famine or floods when parents found it difficult to withdraw their children from economic production, the positive effect of this initiative was reflected in higher literacy rates in Baroda than in the surrounding Bombay presidency by 1921. Sayaji Rao viewed education as a precondition for effective social changes and developed a comprehensive library system, including mobile units in rural areas, to reinforce classroom instruction. A second concern was to enhance the legal rights of women through legislation such as the Hindu Widow Marriage Act in 1902, the Infant Marriage Prevention Act in 1904, and the Hindu Divorce Act in 1930. A third focus was to end discrimination based on caste status. Institutional provisions for depressed castes, the so-called untouchables, included special scholarships, schools, and hostels, and the maharaja himself undertook a public

Sayaji Rao Gaikwar, maharaja of Baroda (1863–1939), by
unknown photographer

relations campaign, speaking at many public functions of
associations both within his state and in India advocating
changes in social attitudes. In the tradition of princely patronage he granted scholarships to B. R. Ambedkar, the
prominent scheduled caste leader, to study in India and
later law at Columbia University.

Reflecting his commoner birth and later education,
Sayaji Rao was a complex synthesis of populist and paternal autocrat. To staff his administration and educational
institutions he recruited talented Indian nationalists as
well as bureaucrats. They ranged from Romesh Chander
Dutt, an Indian Civil Service officer who formulated the
theory that the British drained India of its economic
resources, to Aurobindo Ghose, eventually a mentor to
radical Bengali students. In 1908 the ruler inaugurated a
legislative council (Dhara Sabha) which was mainly advisory and had no budgetary oversight. Desirous of being a
modernizer while still retaining his authority, he promoted social mobility and political consultation but not
political responsibility or democracy among his subjects.

Sayaji Rao's relations with the British government of
India followed a tortuous path. He owed his *gadi* to British
policy which, after the uprising of 1857, was to refrain
from annexing princely states where there was no natural
heir. After his installation he was carefully groomed to be
an enlightened ruler and socialized into British imperial
culture, beginning with his presentation to the prince of
Wales (later Edward VII) during his Indian tour in 1875 and
his participation in the imperial durbar in 1877 in Delhi. In
order to relieve health problems reputedly brought on by
overwork and variously described as neurasthenia or

nervous prostration, sleeplessness, and gout, he made his
first trip to England in 1887 despite the spiritual and social
ostracization which orthodox Hindus then endured after
crossing the ocean. Received by Queen Victoria, he was
viewed as an exemplary imperial collaborator. However,
as he sought greater personal and public autonomy,
points of tension arose with the imperial authorities.
Plagued by continuing ill health and curious about modern institutions abroad, he extended his stays in England,
where he purchased several residences including the former home of Lord Tennyson at Aldworth, Haslemere,
Surrey, during the 1890s. His absences from Baroda were
one factor leading the viceroy, Lord Curzon, in 1900 to
order that Indian princes seek viceregal permission
before leaving their states. On a personal level, Sayaji Rao
deeply resented this imperial interference, while his continued employment of Indian critics of the British and toleration within his territory of presses that published
material which the British deemed seditious caused some
British officials to question his loyalty. This friction
reached a climax in 1911 when he allegedly insulted
George V at the imperial durbar in Delhi by turning his
back on the king–emperor while walking away after being
presented. The British and Indian press debated his
motives, and some called for his deposition. Sayaji Rao
apologized, and his relations with the British improved as
he generously supported Britain during the First World
War. Appointed GCSI in 1887, he became GCIE in 1919.

After 1919 Sayaji Rao travelled and lived in Europe and
Britain for several months each year. Capable *diwans*, especially Sir Manubhai Mehta (1916–26) and Sir V. T. Krishna-
machari (1926–44), oversaw a centralized administration
which implemented social and economic reforms, including industrial projects, and acquiesced in controlled demonstrations of popular support for Indian nationalists,
especially Mahatma Gandhi. Recognized as an elder
statesman among the Indian princes, Sayaji Rao participated in the first and second round-table conferences on
constitutional reform in London during the early 1930s,
when the princes enunciated their support for a federation with British Indian provinces. During the first
round-table conference his dinner with a scheduled caste
guest at his West End hotel occasioned perhaps even more
publicity than his speeches.

The maharaja was married twice: first on 6 January 1880
to Lakshmibai (*c*.1864–1885), daughter of Haibatrao
Mohite, of the Maratha princely family of Tanjore, who
took the name of Chimnabai. They had one son (who predeceased the maharaja) and two daughters before
Chimnabai's death on 7 May 1885. On 28 December 1885
he married Gajrabai (1871–1958), daughter of Bajirao
Amritrao Ghatge, subsequently named Chimnabai II,
from a branch of the Maratha Ghatge family settled in
Dewas state. In 1914 Chimnabai II publicly ceased to
observe purdah in Baroda after returning from her tenth
trip to Europe, co-authored with S. M. Mitra *The Position of
Women in Indian Life* (1911), and was the first president of
the All India Women's Conference in 1927. The couple had
three sons (the elder two predeceased their father), and

one daughter, who became the maharani of Cooch Behar and a well-known hostess in London during the 1920s and 1930s.

After spending most of the 1930s travelling to seek relief for health problems at various European spas, Sayaji Rao III returned to India in November 1938. Too ill to travel to Baroda, he died in Bombay on 6 February 1939 of a heart attack complicated by uraemia; his remains were cremated the following day in Baroda. He was succeeded by Pratapsinh, his grandson from the son of his first marriage.   BARBARA N. RAMUSACK

Sources F. P. Gaekwad, *Sayajirao of Baroda* (1989) · P. S. Rice, *Life of Sayaji Rao III, maharaja of Baroda*, 2 vols. (1931) · *Speeches and addresses of his highness Sayaji Rao III, maharaja of Baroda*, 2 vols. (1927) · *The Times* (7 Feb 1939) · *DNB* · D. Hardiman, 'Baroda: the structure of a progressive state', *People, princes and paramount power*, ed. R. Jeffrey (1978), 107–35 · I. Copland, 'Sayaji Rao Gaekwar and "Sedition"', *Rule, protest, identity*, ed. P. Robb and D. Taylor (1987), 28–48 · M. B. Bhagavan, 'Higher education and the "modern": negotiating colonialism and nationalism in princely Mysore and Baroda', PhD diss., U. Texas, 1999 · S. Bottomore, '"Have you seen the Gaekwar Bob?": filming the 1911 Delhi durbar', *Historical Journal of Film, Radio and Television*, 17 (1997), 309–45 · C. W. Nuckolls, 'The Durbar incident', *Modern Asian Studies*, 24 (1990), 529–59 · P. W. Sergeant, *Ruler of Baroda* (1928) · I. Copland, 'The Baroda crisis of 1873–77', *Modern Asian Studies*, 2 (1968), 97–123

Archives Gujarat State Archives, Southern Circle, Vadodara, Gujarat, India, MSS · priv. coll., MSS | Bodl. Oxf., Wodehouse MSS · CUL, Hardinge MSS

Likenesses M. R., cartoon, repro. in *VF* (3 Jan 1901) · equestrian statue, near Maharaja Sayajirao University, Baroda · four photographs, repro. in Rice, *Life* · photograph, repro. in Gaekwad, *Sayajirao* · photograph, NPG [*see illus.*]

Gailhard, Jean (*fl.* 1659–1708), writer and religious controversialist, was a protestant Frenchman whose roots are unknown: a tract of his, published at Geneva in 1663, was addressed to 'les pasteurs et anciens des eglises Reformées en France' ('the ministers and elders of the Reformed church in France') in vindication of the 'Puritains d'Angleterre'. His first known work, in French, dates from 1659. He moved to England probably about 1660, the year when his first English publication appeared, in which he apologizes for 'my unskilfulness in the English tongue (for I am a stranger)'. He then plunges into an eloquent defence of presbyterianism against prelacy, on the authority of the 'incomparable' Calvin (*The Controversie between Episcopacy and Presbytery*, 1660, 2, 34). In all he published some eighteen tracts, largely in divinity and many of them signed J. G. G. (Jean Gailhard, gentleman). He was a dogmatic predestinarian Calvinist, virulently hostile to Arminianism and Socinianism, and he despised Catholicism—the religion of 'wafer-idol-worship' and 'brazen-faced whoredom' (*The Blasphemous Socinian Heresy Disproved*, 1697, sig. A3r; *God's Truth Vindicated Against Man's Lies*, 1703, 13).

In 1668–9 Gailhard fed public interest in travel literature with accounts of Italy and Venice, respectively dedicated to the earl of Sunderland and Sir John Trevor. Writing in the 'reason of state' tradition, he provided assessments of the 'politic strength' of those states, their armies, manners, and fiscal systems, spiced with tales of Latin lasciviousness. He wrote that he had travelled 'into most parts of Europe'; that travel completed a gentleman; and that, when travelling, gentlemen needed 'wise counsel, a director' (*The Present State of the Princes and Republicks of Italy*, 1668, p. 8, sig. A7v). This last was a naked job application. He wrote ingratiating letters to Theophilus, earl of Huntingdon, from Angers in 1670–71 on Huguenot affairs, and from Paris in 1673. From about 1671 to 1675 he travelled as tutor to Sir Thomas Grosvenor in France, Italy, Hungary, Bohemia, Germany, and Switzerland.

In 1676 Sir Robert Southwell appointed Gailhard tutor to his nephew Sir Philip Percival (1656–1680). Tutor and pupil embarked on a sightseeing tour to the west of England, then visited the Percival seats in Ireland, and then went to Angers. Here Gailhard tried to induce Percival to study civil law seriously, but found him lazy and spendthrift with a preference for dancing, fencing, the guitar and flute, and carousing instead. Gailhard had no objection to physical prowess, but hated debauchery and inattention to books. Exasperated, he told Southwell that 'there is in him things to be rooted out, others levelled, and some others to be polished'; he would try to 'bring him to the practice of Christian and moral virtues' (BL, Add. MS 46953, fols. 112, 207). Gailhard read his pupil Livy and Suetonius in Latin, and made him read the *London Gazette* with an atlas alongside.

Gailhard's most sustained work was *The Compleat Gentleman, or, Directions for the Education of Youth*, published in two parts in 1678, with two further parts appearing in 1682; the four parts were dedicated to the earl of Huntingdon, Sir Thomas Grosvenor, Dr Thomas Coxe, and Sir Joseph Williamson respectively. The first two had been written at Angers about 1671. Comparisons have been made between this work and John Locke's *Some Thoughts Concerning Education* (1693). Gailhard's emphasis is not upon erudition, but upon character, manners, disposition, civility; in a word, virtue. He cites, as Locke did, the Aristotelian maxim that a child is 'a smooth table upon which anything can be written', and he says 'let nature be what it will it may be changed by education' (pp. 4–5). Gailhard warns against undue corporal severity, and against tutors who 'would frighten young men into learning, instead of enticing them to it' (p. 19). He is keen on physical exercise and a capacity for hardship, and deplores the 'effeminacy' of the age. He encourages the virtuosity of gentlemen, rather than bookish pedantry and rote learning, and recommends riding, fencing, dancing, drawing, languages, and music. He is concerned for conversation and oratory, and takes care over posture and demeanour. As to reading, what he commends is almost wholly classical. Gailhard's originality is exhausted in his first discourse. The work then turns to the grand tour and becomes an extended travelogue and itinerary, laced with classical tags and tales to illustrate virtues and vices. Supposing a tour of three years, he recommends eighteen months in France (including nine or ten in Angers), six weeks in Geneva, nine months in Italy, and five in Germany and the Low Countries, rounded off with four months more in Paris.

In the 1690s Gailhard wrote prolifically on behalf of

theological orthodoxy and moral reformation. His intellectual intolerance shines forth, yet he was politically a firm whig. True to his presbyterian roots, in 1694 he defended the Long Parliament's civil war against the popish and persecuting Charles I, though not the regicide itself, and repudiated as an idolatrous fetish the continuing high-church cult of Charles the Martyr. He roundly condemned Charles II's regime, its pensioner parliament, its ambitious and tyrannizing churchmen who preached *jure divino* monarchy, its persecution of nonconformity, its tolerance of vice and debauchery. Gailhard was in the forefront of the assault on John Toland's *Christianity not Mysterious* and Locke's *Reasonableness of Christianity*, publicizing the Middlesex grand jury's presentment against them for blasphemy. He gave a copy of his *Epistle and Preface to the Book Against the ... Socinian Heresie* (1698) to his friend the presbyterian judge Sir Thomas Rokeby, who had spurred the grand jury into action. Gailhard and Rokeby shared a passionate providentialist commitment to the campaign for moral reformation. Gailhard was also a whig enemy of the new freedom of the press following the lapse in 1695 of the Licensing Act. What use was it, he asked, if 'Popery or Idolatry [be] expell'd, if Socinianism or Blasphemy be let in?' 'Extream remedies' were needed against 'Atheism, Deism, Prophaneness, Immorality [which] brazen-faced walk in our streets' (*Blasphemous Socinian Heresy*, sigs. A2v, A3r). He demanded the death sentence for heretics, approving of Calvin's burning of Servetus, and commending recent Scottish exertions in hanging Thomas Aikenhead for blasphemy. An attack upon Gailhard, *An apology for the parliament, humbly representing to Mr John Gailhard some reasons why they did not at his request enact sanguinary laws against protestants in their last session*, was published in 1697. His last known work is *Discources on Several Useful Subjects*, dated 1708.   MARK GOLDIE

Sources BL, Add. MSS 46953–46954 · J. A. I. Champion, 'Making authority: belief, conviction and reason in the public sphere in late seventeenth century England', *Libertinage et Philosophie au XVIIe Siècle*, 3 (1999), 143–90 · *Report on the manuscripts of the late Reginald Rawdon Hastings*, 4 vols., HMC, 78 (1928–47), vol. 2 · *An apology for the parliament, humbly representing to Mr John Gailhard ...* (1697)
Archives BL, Add. MSS 46953–46954

Gaimar, Geffrei (*fl.* 1136–1137), Anglo-Norman poet and historian, is of unknown origins, and nothing is known of his background except that he enjoyed the patronage of Constance, wife of Ralph Fitzgilbert who held lands in Lincolnshire and Hampshire, while Robert, earl of Gloucester (*d.* 1147), Walter Espec (*d.* 1153), and Walter, archdeacon of Oxford (*d.* 1181), are mentioned as having provided him with access to his source books, which, he specifies, were in English and French as well as Latin. Gaimar was the author of a rhymed history of Britain, *L'estoire des Engleis*, probably written in 1136 and 1137. Made up of 6526 rhyming octosyllables—all that survives of a much longer and more ambitious chronicle which, according to its epilogue, had originally opened with the mythical Trojan origins of British history, and which closes with the death of William Rufus in 1100—Gaimar's *Estoire* is the oldest surviving work of history in the French vernacular. The popularity of Wace's *Roman de Brut* (1155) is assumed to account for the loss of the first part of Gaimar's poem, which in its four manuscripts extant today begins *in medias res* with the arrival of Cerdic in Britain in 495. Up to the accession of Edgar in 959, its narrative follows the annalistic model of the Anglo-Saxon Chronicle, which Gaimar seems to have known in its northern recension, in an archaic version which he refers to as the 'Washingborough book'. He accommodates this unpromising material to the requirements of a verse chronicle destined for a predominantly secular audience, first by consistently suppressing all reference to ecclesiastical history, and second by introducing narrative interludes from more popular sources. From the Old French epic tradition he introduces the viking Gormund in the guise of a ninth-century Danish king who invades France from England. Two more substantial interpolations are clearly selected for inclusion by virtue of their human interest: Haveloc's adventure-packed and ultimately triumphant struggle against disinheritance, and Buern Bucecarle's feud against Osberht and the vengeance exacted for the latter's rape of Buern's wife. Human interest also accounts for his extended treatment of the love affair between King Edgar and Ælfthryth.

Although he does not hesitate to take liberties with chronology, and is neither exempt from error nor averse, on occasion, to creative rewriting, Gaimar's is in general a conscientious historical narrative. Several of his descriptions of royal deaths, for example (those of Edward the Martyr, Edmund Ironside, Alfred Ætheling, and William Rufus), introduce incidental details which, even though unrecorded elsewhere, are not necessarily to be dismissed as gratuitous fiction. At the same time, his skill as a writer of literature was to accommodate his material to the tastes of his audience, and this in itself can provide valuable insights into attitudes and mentalities current in the 1130s. He restricts his account of the battle of Hastings to a literary set piece based on the heroic exploits of the *jongleur* Taillifer (viewed by Gaimar from the English standpoint). Hereward figures prominently in the post-conquest part of Gaimar's chronicle, where he is unambiguously portrayed as a freedom fighter against Norman oppression. Gaimar's positive portrayal of Cnut, Robert Curthose, Earl Hugh of Chester, and Rufus, and his account of courtesy and chivalry at the latter's court, all provide an alternative secular voice to those of monastic and church chroniclers of the twelfth century. Gaimar signs off his poem enigmatically by an evocation of the court of the recently deceased Henry I as a place of amorous dalliance, unending festivity, and courtly splendour. As a pioneering work of secular historical literature which 'set the pattern for popular history for something like three centuries' (Legge, 29), the *Estoire des Engleis* marks a significant, early stage in the dual processes of cultural symbiosis and the vernacularization of learning that so uniquely characterize twelfth-century Anglo-Norman Britain.   IAN SHORT

Sources *L'estoire des Engleis by Geffrei Gaimar*, ed. A. Bell, Anglo-Norman Texts, 14–16 (1960) · A. Bell, 'Maistre Geffrei Gaimar', *Medium Ævum*, 7 (1938), 184–98 · M. D. Legge, *Anglo-Norman literature and its background* (1963), 27–36 · A. R. Press, 'The precocious courtesy of Geoffrey Gaimar', *Court and poet: selected proceedings of the third congress of the I. C. L. S.*, ed. G. S. Burgess (1981), 267–76 · I. Short, 'Gaimar's epilogue and Geoffrey of Monmouth's *Liber vetustissimus*', *Speculum*, 69 (1994), 323–44

Gainford. For this title name *see* Pease, Joseph Albert, first Baron Gainford (1860–1943).

Gains, Lawrence Samuel [Larry] (**1900–1983**), boxer, was born in Sumach Street, Toronto, Canada, on 12 December 1900 (although some sources say 1901), the third of three sons and one daughter of Manny Gains and his wife, Alice Henderson. After a successful amateur boxing career in Canada, he turned professional, and as a result lost the opportunity to box in the 1924 Paris Olympics. His first professional contest was in Britain in June 1923, when he was easily defeated by Frank Moody in London. He immediately went to France to gain more experience. After boxing mainly in Paris, but also in Belgium and Sweden, he settled in Cologne, Germany, in 1924. It was here that he had the vast majority of his early fights, one of which, a second-round knock-out of a young Max Schmeling in August 1925, singled him out as a more than capable boxer. While in Cologne he married early in 1926, at a register office, Lisa, with whom he had four children.

Gains's reputation spread to his home country and he returned there in 1926. In February 1927 he became Canadian heavyweight champion, and was already being talked of as a potential world champion. However, an unofficial colour bar, invoked after Jack Johnson's reign as heavyweight champion in the 1910s, prevented black boxers from fighting for the world title, and Gains had to make do with the 'coloured' version of the title, which he first won in Toronto in August 1928 by defeating the black American heavyweight George Godfrey. It was a 'title' Gains held until 1935 when, owing to the rise of Joe Louis, it ceased to be relevant.

In 1929 Gains returned to Europe to live first at Market Bosworth, Leicestershire, until 1936, and then in Palmers Green, London. An extremely popular boxer, he appeared in Italy, France, and Germany, as well as in Britain, over the next ten years. He had already defeated a number of Europe's top heavyweights, most notably Schmeling, George Cook, the Australian contender, and Britain's Harry Crossley and Don Shortland, before he met Phil Scott, another leading British contender, in his most important fight to date in June 1931. The contest, watched by over 35,000 at Leicester Tigers' athletics ground, was for the British empire heavyweight title, the first time a black boxer had been allowed to contest the title. The British boxing authorities were conciliatory in allowing Gains to contest the empire title, though they also stressed the fact that this concession did not mean that black boxers would be allowed to contest British titles (the British ban was not lifted until 1947).

Gains held the empire title until 1934, during which time he met such top-class boxers as Don McCorkindale, Primo Carnera, Walter Neusal, Reggie Meen, and Jack London. After losing the title, however, he was still good enough to meet boxers as competent as Ben Foord, Maurice Strickland, Len Harvey, and Tommy Farr. However, although he remained in Britain for most of the remainder of his life, Gains was never allowed to contest the British title. This situation was the opposite of that experienced by two non-British but white 1930s heavyweights: George Cook (of Australia) and Ben Foord (of South Africa). Cook lost four British empire title fights between 1922 and 1934, while Foord won the title in 1936. Both were allowed to contest the British national title because they had lived in Britain for the requisite three years. By the end of 1933 Gains also met this requirement, but was not allowed the same dispensation owing to his colour, even though he had also beaten Cook twice. He continued to box until 1941, by which time he had joined the RAF as a physical training instructor; he eventually became a sergeant.

Tall and powerfully built, Gains was one of only a handful of highly talented black boxers active in Britain before the Second World War. He was extremely unlucky to come to the fore in a period when racial prejudice operated against black boxers. Despite being one of the world's leading heavyweights, rated in the top ten for much of his career, he was denied the opportunity to fight for the world title by the unofficial colour bar which was in place at the time. This misfortune was compounded by his move to Britain, where the world's only official colour bar for all championship boxing contests lasted from 1911 until 1947. Joe Louis's rise to fame saw the unofficial ban on black heavyweight world champions lifted in the late 1930s, though by then Gains's career was in decline. Similarly, by the time the British ban was lifted in 1947, Gains had not boxed for six years. In retirement he lived in Surrey but he later returned to Cologne, where he died on 26 July 1983.

GARY SHAW

Sources L. Gains, *The impossible dream* (1991) · G. Shaw, 'The rise and fall of the colour bar in British boxing, 1911–1947', *2000 British Society of Sports History conference* [Liverpool 2000] [2000] · G. Odd, *The Hamlyn encyclopedia of boxing* (1987) · S. Shipley, 'Boxing', *The history of sport in Britain*, ed. T. Mason (1988)
Archives FILM BBC WAC
Likenesses photographs, 1931–51, Hult. Arch. · photographs, repro. in Gains, *Impossible dream*

Gainsborough, Thomas (**1727–1788**), painter and printmaker, was probably born in Sudbury, Suffolk, and was baptized there at the Independent Meeting-House in Friars Street on 14 May 1727, the fifth son and ninth child of John Gainsborough (*c*.1683–1748), publican, clothier, and postmaster, and his wife, Mary (*c*.1690–1755), daughter of the Revd Henry Burroughs. He attended Sudbury grammar school, where his uncle the Revd Humphrey Burroughs was headmaster, and Fulcher refers to stories of him playing truant in order to draw in the fields around the town. Gainsborough's paternal uncle Thomas (1678–1739) bequeathed a total of £30 to his nephew; this must have encouraged him to travel, about 1740, to London, where he stayed with an unidentified silversmith.

Thomas Gainsborough (1727–1788), self-portrait, c.1787

Early years William Hogarth had been taught engraving by a silversmith twenty years before, and Gainsborough may have thought this a natural means of learning his craft; however, the laborious process did not suit his temperament and, although he experimented with the medium in the 1750s, he did not form a serious interest in printmaking until the 1770s. Rather more important were the influence of William Hogarth and Francis Hayman, who were at the centre of so much artistic activity at the time.

Hogarth's revival, in 1735, of the St Martin's Lane Academy, where Hubert-François Gravelot was employed as the drawing-master until 1745, must have provided a framework for Gainsborough's education. It has been said that the young artist helped Gravelot design the decorative surrounds for Jacobus Houbracken's engravings for *Heads of Illustrious Persons of Great Britain*, though it is difficult to discern his contribution. At St Martin's Lane he would have come into contact with other pupils such as Charles Grignion and Nathaniel Smith, but more importantly he was in the current of artistic discussion and could experiment with his ideas. Under the influence of French draughtsmanship he adopted the use of black and white chalks on coloured (generally blue) paper for his figure drawings. The use of drawings as a means to nurture his hungry visual memory was essential to his development as an artist.

Although Francis Hayman masterminded the decorations for the supper boxes in Vauxhall Gardens commissioned by the enterprising Jonathan Tyers, there is some stylistic evidence that the young Gainsborough had a hand in the decorative scheme. If Gainsborough was involved, the Vauxhall pictures would have provided him with an opportunity to learn more about the techniques of painting and the pecking order of a busy makeshift studio. It has been suggested that one of the paintings, *The House of Cards*, designed by Gravelot, shows Gainsborough's contribution in at least two of the figures. Similarly Hogarth supervised the scheme for decorating the Court Room at the Foundling Hospital and took the opportunity to raise the profile of history painting by basing the scheme on four large canvases of biblical subjects painted by established artists (Hogarth, Joseph Highmore, Hayman, and the Revd James Wills). In order to promote the work of young landscape painters in the wake of Canaletto's recent visit to Britain, Edward Haytley, Richard Wilson, and Samuel Wale were invited to donate topographical roundels depicting London hospitals. Gainsborough must have been delighted at the invitation to participate. In November 1748 the last to be presented, his view of the Charterhouse hospital, the most accomplished of the group, was installed, and there it remains. Gainsborough approached the commission in a novel way, using an unusual view with great originality and flair. The painting deliberately uses a red rather than a buff ground, which helps it stand out from the others; it has a daring composition that uses a large chimney stack on the right to anchor the design. Its strong lighting, which divides the causeway in the centre, highlights the top of a gateway on the right and a belfry on the left.

Gainsborough's earliest work demonstrates a joy and an ability to use paint similar to that of Hogarth. His ability to describe texture and tone with a clarity of light he may have learned from the landscapes of George Lambert. He may have lodged in London with Hayman (*GM*, 199), but this apparently did not work out, and by 1744 he was renting rooms from John Jorden in Little Kirby Street, Hatton Garden, where he set up in practice as an independent artist, dividing his time between London and Sudbury. The surviving fragments of a portrait of a boy and girl (Gainsborough's House, Sudbury) of about 1744, despite its defects in anatomy, is exceptional in its energy and skilful handling of paint. This portrait's ambitious scale gave way to painting small-scale full-length portraits (conversation pieces) and landscapes. The latter, which sometimes have a topographical basis at this date, combine extraordinary powers of observation with an intense ability to interpret the play of light on the landscape. Like the fragmentary portrait in Sudbury, however, the larger canvases, for example, divide up into well-rehearsed sections, and Gainsborough is less able to manage larger compositions such as *Cornard Wood* (*c*.1748; National Gallery, London; Hayes, *Landscape*, no. 17). They demonstrate the influence of Dutch seventeenth-century artists such as Jan Wynants. Similarly Gainsborough had probably encountered the work of Jacob van Ruisdael in the London auction rooms and copied in chalk his *La forêt* (*c*.1660; Louvre, Paris, deposited at Musée de Douai; Gainsborough's copy, 1746–7; Whitworth Art Gallery, University of Manchester). Gainsborough's proven ability as a landscapist encouraged other artists to collaborate with him. A documented example is Francis Hayman's portrait of the Bedford children (1746; priv. coll.), and stylistic evidence points to similar collaborative ventures with Gravelot in his *Couple in the Park* (c.1746; Louvre, Paris) and with Joshua Kirby, an Ipswich drawing-master, in his topographical view of St Mary's Church, Hadleigh (priv. coll.; Hayes, *Landscape*, no. 28), commissioned by the Revd Dr Thomas Tanner about 1748.

Marriage; return to Suffolk In 1746 Margaret Burr (c.1728–1798) became pregnant by Gainsborough and on 15 July of that year they married in the clandestine chapel of St George's, Curzon Street, London. An illegitimate daughter of Henry, third duke of Beaufort, Margaret was provided with a settlement of £200 per annum. The young couple moved out of lodgings and took a house in Little Kirby Street, London. Their first child, Mary, is shown in a family group by Gainsborough (1748?; National Gallery, London) shortly before she died. She was buried on 1 March 1748 at St Andrew's, Holborn. In Sudbury, Gainsborough's father died on 29 October 1748; the rate accounts show that the artist had moved to the town early the following spring, by which time he seems to have been renting a house in Friars Street from a cousin. Soon afterwards two more daughters were born in Sudbury: Mary, baptized on 3 February 1750 at All Saints', Sudbury, and Margaret, baptized on 22 August 1751 at St Gregory's, Sudbury.

Away from the artistic crucible of London, Gainsborough's style became more relaxed and he was able to impose overall design on excessive detail. The double portrait *Mr and Mrs Andrews* (c.1750; National Gallery, London) includes an accurate topographical view of the Stour valley from the Auberies, the couple's estate situated 2 miles to the south-west of Sudbury. Aesthetically the portrait was his greatest achievement to date. The balance of colour, the complex cloudscape, and the way in which the trees part in the centre to reveal the church of All Saints, Sudbury, where the couple married on 10 November 1748, produce a perfectly balanced composition. It is tempting to interpret the unusual use of topography and the exceptional quality of the painting as the product of particular demands placed on the artist by the sitters.

About 1752 Gainsborough rented a house from Mrs Raffe in Foundation Street, Ipswich. The town offered greater intellectual stimulus than Sudbury with a town library, a musical club (Gainsborough was an active member), lively theological discussion, and an argumentative political life. Ipswich provided more opportunity for commissions. Although he continued to paint a number of conversation pieces, notably the *Gravenor Family* (c.1754; Yale U. CBA), the genre lost its appeal for Gainsborough and he soon began to concentrate on painting uncompromising head-and-shoulders portraits. These experiments honed his ability to paint a good likeness which, in his own words, was 'the principal beauty & intention of a portrait' (*Letters*, 90). They satisfied a conservative clientele and served as a valuable means of learning the craft of a portraitist. Occasionally Gainsborough added a landscape background to

vary the limitations of the design. Privately, unrestricted by the expectation of his patrons, he was able to indicate the extent of his ambition and talent in exceptional portraits such as *The Painter's Daughters Chasing a Butterfly* (c.1756; National Gallery, London), which, in its sensitivity and rapid technique, ranks as one of the most remarkable paintings of the eighteenth century. Among his best landscapes from the period are the two commissioned by John, fourth duke of Bedford (1755; Hayes, *Landscape*, nos. 50 and 51), which are remarkable in their high finish and in the relative importance of the figures. At least one of the Bedford landscapes was painted as an overmantel, and many other landscapes from the 1750s, such as that formerly in the Howe collection (Hayes, *Landscape*, no. 62), are of unusual proportions which probably indicate their original location in prescribed architectural settings. The style of the paintings had changed too. Instead of a tightly knit verisimilitude, they had become a more imaginative amalgam of elements arranged so that (as he put it) 'a Picture [is] like the first part of a Tune that you can guess what follows, and that makes the second part of the Tune' (*Letters*, 71). It was possibly with the encouragement of Joshua Kirby and the engravers Thomas Major and Joseph Wood that Gainsborough learned to etch. With the help of Wood he contributed an illustration to Kirby's *Dr Brook Taylor's Method of Perspective Made Easy*, published in Ipswich in 1754. However, the laborious technique tried his patience, and from that date there remains only one other complete print, *Philip Thicknesse's Cottage*, and a more complex but incomplete plate, *The Suffolk Plough* (Hayes, *Landscape*, no. 39). Another, *The Gipsies* (Hayes, *Printmaker*, no. 2), known in several states, was eventually finished by Wood and proved a popular success.

Move to Bath In autumn 1758 Gainsborough, perhaps to address the financial problems which beset him in the mid-1750s, felt sufficiently pleased with his development to search for work further afield. Showing considerable confidence, and charging 5 guineas a head, he moved to Bath, where his arrival was recorded in the *Bath Advertizer* (7 Oct 1758). There he painted the portraits *George Bussy, Viscount Villiers* and *William Villiers, 3rd Earl of Jersey* (depicting Bussy's father; both priv. colls.), and by the time he painted *Mr and Mrs William Lee* (priv. coll.) in April 1759, he had raised his price to 8 guineas for a head-and-shoulders portrait. Having tested the market, he felt the journey had been worth while, and returned to Ipswich; there he sold the contents of his studio and Mrs Raffe advertised for a new tenant. With his family Gainsborough moved to Bath and rented a large house owned by the duke of Kingston in Abbey Street. The seven-year renewable lease was signed on 24 June 1760. The size of the house enabled Gainsborough to provide a home for his family, to diversify and take in lodgers, and arrange a studio and a showroom. Eventually Gainsborough's sister, Mrs Mary Gibbons, took over a portion of the building and complemented the artist's studio with a millinery shop. Recently discovered evidence suggests that the portrait of the amateur musician Ann Ford (1760; Cincinnati Art Museum, Ohio) was painted to display in the 'Shew' room. Apparently Gainsborough painted it as an outstanding advertisement to display his special abilities. He chose a sitter well known not only through her liaison with Lord Jersey but also as a result of her public musical performances, an unladylike activity which caused much comment. Gainsborough employed an unusual and dramatic pose for a woman that was intended to show off his skill in painting drapery. Mary Delany in a letter dated 23 October 1760 remarked that she would have been 'very sorry to have any one I loved set forth in such a manner' (*The Autobiography and Correspondence of Mary Granville, Mrs Delany*, ed. Lady Llanover, 1861, 3.605). While the painting shares the ambition of his *Daughters Chasing a Butterfly*, it lacks the latter's eloquence of composition.

In 1761 Gainsborough sent the portrait *Sir Guy Nugent* (priv. coll., on loan to the Holburne Museum of Art, Bath) to the second exhibition of the Society of Artists in London. Nugent's confident pose sitting before a window was repeated, less successfully, in several other male portraits produced by Gainsborough in the early 1760s. Slightly later in the decade, perhaps after he had visited Wilton House near Salisbury in 1764, he painted a series of female portraits employing the pose of Lady Anne Sophia Herbert from Van Dyck's huge *Pembroke Family* at Wilton House. The best of them is *Lady Carr* (c.1764; Yale U. CBA).

Bath provided Gainsborough with artistic companionship, a constantly changing source of wealthy and leisured clients, easy access to print dealers, and remarkable collections of paintings near the city. He was nervous about composing figure groups and full-length portraits, and several figurative compositions from the period are rehearsed in preparatory drawings. For instance, the sketches of his great friend the viola da gamba player Carl Friedrich Abel (c.1762; NPG) and the *Portrait of the Artist's Daughters* (c.1763; Gainsborough's House, Sudbury) are adapted in the finished oil portraits (NPG and Worcester Art Museum, Massachusetts, respectively). The surviving preparatory sketches must represent only a small proportion of what once existed, for the early years of the decade were exceptionally busy. Commissions included the portrait of Sir William St Quintin (priv. coll.), who proved a friend as well as a generous patron; the vast portrait *George Byam and his Wife Louisa* (Andrew Brownsword Foundation, on loan to the Holburne Museum of Art, Bath), to which Gainsborough added their daughter Selina in 1766; the portrait of the actor James Quin (exh. Society of Artists, 1763; NG Ire.), which like the portrait of Ann Ford was perhaps painted for Gainsborough's 'Shew' room; and *Dr Rice Charlton* (exh. Society of Artists, 1764; Holburne Museum of Art, Bath). A series of full-length portraits of women charts the swift progress in his work in the early 1760s: *Lady Alston* (c.1762; Louvre, Paris), *Lady Howe* (1762; Iveagh Bequest, Kenwood House, London), and *Mrs Portman* (c.1764; priv. coll.) demonstrate how Gainsborough was able to overcome the compositional awkwardness that concerned him in his earliest works in Bath.

Gainsborough continued to paint landscapes, though in smaller numbers, as portrait commissions took priority.

He appears to have been friendly with those of a tory persuasion, perhaps reflecting his wife's links with the Beaufort family. The Prices of Foxley, Herefordshire, counted among Gainsborough's sitters, as did Coplestone Warr Bampfylde of Hestercombe House, Kingston, Somerset, whose interest in garden design may have helped Gainsborough reassess his approach to landscape painting and further distance him from any residual interest in topography. The influence at this time of a succession of great old-master painters such as Rubens, Claude, and Gaspard Dughet made this an experimental period for Gainsborough. The influence of the heavily wooded landscapes of Dughet is evident in the painting at Worcester Art Museum, there entitled *A Grand Landscape* (exh. Society of Artists, 1763?; Hayes, *Landscape*, no. 80); the St Quintin landscape (1766; priv. coll.; Hayes, *Landscape*, no. 87) is closer to Rubens, while *Harvest Waggon* (exh. Society of Artists, 1767; Barber Institute of Fine Arts, University of Birmingham; Hayes, *Landscape*, no. 88) has an openness more akin to the work of Claude.

In autumn 1763 Gainsborough became ill from overwork, and the situation was compounded by his anxiety about venereal disease which he may have contracted during visits to London. His illness was so severe that the *Bath Journal* (17 Oct 1763) reported his death, but, after being, as Gainsborough himself put it, 'kept [in] my Bed 5 weeks … of a most terrible Fever', he recovered (*Letters*, 22). This health scare made him take stock and he decided that he should move to a house 'about three quarters of a Mile in the Lansdown Road' but retain the 'House in the Smoake' for his painting and 'shew' room, and he took a second lease in 1767 (ibid., 23). In 1768 he became the first tenant of a house in the newly built Royal Circus. He continued to respond to the stream of visitors requesting portraits throughout the 1760s, and raised his prices again, this time to 20 guineas a head, 40 for a half-length, and (presumably) 80 for a full-length. He worked hard and played hard. Among his friends were the actor David Garrick, James Unwin (the agent who secured his wife's annuity from the Beaufort estate), and the musician Samuel Linley. (Linley was born at the duke of Beaufort's house at Badminton, Gloucestershire, a circumstance that may have facilitated his friendship with the painter.) William Jackson, from 1777 organist at Exeter Cathedral, was also a friend, but Gainsborough's heavy drinking led to their estrangement. Occasionally a commission would require special attention. Great care was taken with the series of portraits of the duke of Bedford's family (1764–5, 1769; Woburn Abbey, Bedfordshire, and National Gallery of Victoria, Melbourne). In 1764 the demands of General Honywood's equestrian portrait (Ringling Museum of Art, Sarasota, Florida) led to Gainsborough's visiting Wilton House to draw horses, presumably those trained in dressage. (As noted this visit would have given him the opportunity to study the Van Dyck portraits there.) Following the success of his portrait of George Pitt (Cleveland Museum of Art, Ohio) at the Royal Academy exhibition in 1769, in the following year he travelled to Stratfield Saye in Hampshire to paint his host's daughter and son-in-law, Lord and Lady

Ligonier (Hunt. L.). In 1771 he travelled to Wootton Lodge in Staffordshire to see his friend and correspondent James Unwin, and two years later he visited Longford Castle, Wiltshire, to paint a series of portraits of the Bouverie family, where he would have seen a varied collection of paintings including works by Teniers (which he had already copied), Van Dyck, and Claude.

Royal Academician The political manoeuvrings which led to the foundation of the Royal Academy of Arts in December 1768 and the resulting marginalization of his friend Joshua Kirby must have been upsetting for Gainsborough. None the less, he accepted the invitation to become a founder Royal Academician and submitted two of his greatest works to the first exhibition in May 1769. *George Rivers, later Lord Pitt* (Cleveland Museum of Art, Ohio) and *Isabella, Viscountess Molyneaux, later Countess of Sefton* (Walker Art Gallery, Liverpool) 'in elegance must have conquered everything else in the exhibition' (Waterhouse, 'First Royal Academy exhibition', 946). By 1770 Gainsborough had united in his portraiture the realism first seen in the head-and-shoulders likenesses painted during his Ipswich years with a bravura technique and elegant grandeur learned so well from Van Dyck. There were few academicians living outside London, and it was important that his work was seen to compete with that of his rivals based in the more competitive environment of the capital.

Several contemporary commentators noted that Gainsborough made model landscapes, fashioned out of broccoli, mirrors, and coal, from which to draw. His landscape drawings had now become studies in balanced composition, reflections of a rural idyll rather than real representations of a given place. For Gainsborough they were like his music-making, a form of relaxation. Correspondence with Lord Mulgrave and the artist's friend William Jackson shows that he shared his gift for drawing and was keen to discuss new graphic techniques that obviously fascinated him. In a letter to Lord Mulgrave dated 13 February 1772 he says, 'Methinks I would fain have you join a little Drawing to your valuable accomplishments … I am sure I shall be proud of being your Master' (*Letters*, 94). He appears to have acted as an informal tutor to a number of amateur artists including his daughters and, in the 1780s, members of the royal family.

About 1770 Gainsborough began to explore new subject matter in his landscapes. *Going to Market* (Iveagh Bequest, Kenwood House, London; Hayes, *Landscape*, no. 95), dating from the late 1760s, includes a group of peasant women gathered round a cottage door with a group of horsemen riding off to market in the morning light. Nostalgic admiration for simplicity of life pervades the work. Some scholars have interpreted the cottage dwellers, market traders, and beggars as illustrating the different levels of rural poverty which had been exacerbated by recent enclosures of common land for farming. Similar sentiments are reflected in the poetry of Oliver Goldsmith and William Shenstone written towards the end of the decade. In other works such as the mixed-media landscape of travellers begging at the door of a nobleman's house of

about 1772 (Indianapolis Museum of Art; Hayes, *Landscape*, no. 99), Gainsborough anticipates the subject matter of the 'fancy' pictures he produced during the next decade. This is just one interpretation of his work which has challenged the common theory that Gainsborough, as a natural genius and an artist who spurned foreign travel, was unaffected by the work of earlier artists or contemporary aesthetic theories.

In the early 1770s, under the presidency of Sir Joshua Reynolds, the character and future direction of the Royal Academy developed. Each annual exhibition had a growing number of exhibitors, inevitably leading to crowded hanging conditions in the exhibition room as well as a strong competitiveness among the exhibitors. The president's discourses delivered to the academy's students did much to define the canon of subject matter, but despite this academic encouragement history painting largely failed to attract patrons. Commissions for portraiture continued to dominate. Another of Gainsborough's show pictures, the portrait perhaps of Jonathan Buttall (known as 'The Blue Boy', Hunt. L.), was exhibited at the academy in 1770. It has been argued that Gainsborough's dominant use of blue in the painting was in direct opposition to the view that Reynolds later expressed in his eighth discourse of 1778, where he wrote that 'blue [should be] used only to support and set off … warm colours; and for this purpose, a small proportion of cold colour will be sufficient' (*Discourses on Art*, 158). The portrait is undoubtedly also the most overt homage paid by Gainsborough to Van Dyck, an artist he was anxious to emulate in opposition to Reynolds's admiration for the Italian school. This would appear to be at odds with his disdain, expressed in a letter to Lord Dartmouth, about 'the foolish custom of Painters dressing people like scaramouches, and expecting the likeness to appear' (*Letters*, 90). With the exhibition in 1771 of the Ligonier portraits (Hunt. L.), which make visual sense only when hung as a pair, and the dashing portrait *Captain Wade* (Bath City Council), which was shown in the same year and presented by the artist to the newly built Assembly Rooms in Bath (*in situ*), Gainsborough was yet again emphasizing his strengths and pointing out the very obvious differences between his work and that of Reynolds. Certain of his worth, he increased his prices further to 30, 60, and 100 guineas, and on 14 January 1772 he took his nephew Gainsborough *Dupont as an apprentice. In the same year, like Nathaniel Dance, he failed to be included in Johann Zoffany's group portrait *Academicians in the Life Class of the Royal Academy* (Royal Collection), and in the following year a disagreement with the academy led to his refusal to exhibit there.

Move to London The lease expired on the duke of Kingston's house in Abbey Street in Bath in summer 1774, and there is some evidence that portrait commissions were also waning, perhaps because of Gainsborough's recent increase in prices. He was falling out of sympathy with Bath and had become, according to the Irish artist John Warren, 'uncommonly rude & uncivil to artists in general, & was even haughty to his employers, which with his proud prices caus'd him to settle in London'

(McEvansoneya, 165). These were all factors which, coupled with developments at the academy, contributed to his decision to move to London. From midsummer 1774 he rented the western third of Schomberg House in Pall Mall. Shortly afterwards he built a two-storey building in the garden which provided him with a studio and a show-room. With his move to London, Gainsborough reassessed his position, particularly as regards the Royal Academy. Through his friendship with Joshua Kirby he gained access to the court, and was quick to realize the influence of the press. Sir Henry Bate (later Bate-Dudley), the propri-etor of the *Morning Chronicle*, became a friend and sup-porter. Perhaps the first notice he wrote in support of Gainsborough is that dated April 1775: 'The Duke and Duchess of Gloucester [*recte* Cumberland] are often going to a famous painters in Pall Mall; and 'tis reported that he is now doing both their pictures.' The duke and duchess had already sat to Reynolds for portraits that had been exhibited at the Royal Academy in 1773. The date of Bate's report, timed to appear just before the opening of the 1775 exhibition, was designed to fuel rivalry between the two artists and suggests a change in preference in the taste of the Cumberlands. About the same time Gainsborough was painting the ravishing portrait *The Hon. Mrs Graham* (NG Scot.).

Nathaniel Dance, who had known Gainsborough since the 1740s and who too had withdrawn from the academy, persuaded Gainsborough to exhibit there again in 1777, and he responded by showing an outstanding group of paintings including the portraits of the duke and duchess of Cumberland, already noted (Royal Collection), *Carl Friedrich Abel* (Hunt. L.), *The Hon. Mrs Graham*, and *The Water-ing Place* (National Gallery, London; Hayes, *Landscape*, no. 117) which Horace Walpole described in his copy of the catalogue (priv. coll.) as 'By far the finest Landscape ever painted in England'. One critic, whose remarks must have pleased Gainsborough greatly, commented that ''Tis hard to say which Branch of the Art Mr. Gainsborough most excels, Landscape or Portrait painting' (*Public Advertiser*, 26 April 1777). He continued to court the press. Bate founded the *Morning Post* in 1780 and to underline the relationship between the new proprietor and the artist Gainsborough exhibited Bate's portrait (priv. coll., on loan to Tate Brit-ain) at the Royal Academy exhibition that year.

Gainsborough also found time to make prints. His fas-cination with new techniques encouraged him to explore a combination of soft-ground etching and aquatint, both of which had only recently been discovered. His reasons for expending so much time on printmaking, which pro-vided no income, remain unclear though he evidently admired the technique of imitating chalk lines with soft-ground etching and wash with aquatint. In 1780 he com-pleted three prints that were inscribed with a publication date. The publication of these large soft-ground etchings with aquatint was aborted for some unknown reason. Michael Rosenthal has argued that the subjects of the three prints were selected to demonstrate the variety of his landscape work (Rosenthal, *The Art of Thomas Gainsbor-ough*, 258–62).

There was some diversity in his subject matter, and in 1781 Gainsborough submitted rather more varied works to the Royal Academy. In 1781 and 1783 he exhibited sea-scapes (priv. coll. and National Gallery of Victoria, Mel-bourne) which brought a fresh energy to his work. In 1781 he also exhibited *King George III* and *Queen Charlotte* (both Royal Collection), which became the successors to the state portraits painted twenty years earlier by Allan Ram-say. The portraits of the monarch and his consort pro-vided Gainsborough's nephew Gainsborough Dupont with a welcome opportunity to supplement his living by making numerous copies of them.

'Fancy pictures' The landscape theme to which Gainsbor-ough continually returned was the cottage door, a motif first seen in the background of *Going to Market* (Iveagh Bequest, Kenwood House, London) painted some ten years earlier. *The Cottage Door with Children Playing* (exh. RA, 1778; Cincinnati Art Museum, Ohio; Hayes, *Landscape*, no. 121) is perhaps the most narrative representation of the theme with a mother caring for a group of wild children at the door of a hovel while the father provides for the basic needs of the group with bundles of sticks for cooking. Two years later the upright version, *The Cottage Door* (Hunt. L.; Hayes, *Landscape*, no. 123) was shown at the Royal Acad-emy. Here there are fewer children. The figures are of a degree of beauty at odds with their humble origins and the wooded splendour of their surroundings almost con-sumes the humble cottage. They represent a noble, honest simplicity of rural living.

In 1781 Gainsborough exhibited *A Shepherd* (dest.), which one critic described as 'equal to any picture produced by any modern artist; and superior to most' (*Morning Chron-icle*, 28 April – 1 May 1781, 416). It shows a beleaguered shep-herd boy with his dog sheltering from lightning. Gains-borough commissioned Richard Earlom to make a mezzo-tint of it in an attempt to exploit its critical success. The inspiration for the image came from the work of the Span-ish painter Murillo, and it provided a new form of subject picture which, in a posthumous description by Reynolds, was described as a 'Fancy picture', a term which may have been intended to have pejorative overtones. The purpose of a 'fancy picture' was to elicit a response, a 'sensibility', in the beholder. The idea had developed from Gainsbor-ough's landscape of the early 1770s, already mentioned, in the Indianapolis Museum of Art, showing travellers beg-ging at the door of a house, and the same sentiment is most clearly expressed in *Charity Relieving Distress* (priv. coll.) exhibited at Schomberg House in 1784. This modern subject matter interested Reynolds, who purchased Gainsborough's *Girl with Pigs* (priv. coll.) for 100 guineas; with some satisfaction, Gainsborough felt that he had 'brought [his] Piggs to a fine market' (*Letters*, 147).

Drawing the line In 1783 Gainsborough submitted his paintings to the Royal Academy so late that the only avail-able space for the head-and-shoulders portrait *Lady Anna Horatia Seymour* (Detroit Institute of Arts, Michigan) was the chimney-board in the fireplace of the Great Room. In the following year he forcefully insisted that if his portraits of the king and queen with thirteen of their children (Royal Collection) were shown above the 'line' (a moulding about eight feet from the floor which separated larger from smaller works) he would 'never more [send] another picture to the Exhibition' (*Letters*, 150). Immediately after the exhibition ended he travelled to the Lake District with his Ipswich friend Samuel Kilderbee and made a number of sketches that were to transform the mountains of coal in his table-top models to more realistic and romantic representations. Between July and September he visited Antwerp, his only continental trip, where he found the 'florid Gothic architecture like a cake all plumbs' (Asfour, Williamson, and Jackson, 28), and he presumably spent much of his time studying the work of Rubens and Van Dyck.

In the following year Gainsborough asked the hanging committee of the Royal Academy for a second dispensation, making the same request that he had made in 1783: he wanted his portrait *The Three Eldest Princesses* (Royal Collection) shown no more than five and a half feet from the ground. Perhaps the height was chosen with reference to its intended position at Carlton House, or it may have been chosen to cause maximum disruption to the hanging plan at the Royal Academy. The request was refused and, rather than opt for the threatening tone of his earlier correspondence, with a cold courtesy Gainsborough asked for all his paintings to be returned. He never exhibited at the Royal Academy again. With considerable support from the press, he instead displayed a selection of his work each year at Schomberg House to coincide with the Royal Academy exhibition. It is hard to see these altercations as anything but posturing by Gainsborough: the requests he made to the academy were unreasonable and led to the inevitable consequence. It is likely that he had orchestrated this response because his work was unsuited to the competitive nature of group exhibitions, and he wished to control the manner and lighting in which his work was hung. Support from Henry Bate helped him save face, although other journalists were more critical of his behaviour.

The 'fag End of Life' The events of 1784 provided Gainsborough with an opportunity for redirection. He took on fewer portrait commissions, concentrating instead on producing landscape paintings and 'fancy' pictures and experimentation with prints using pure aquatint. Without the need to pander to patrons' egos, he was able to 'walk off to some sweet village where I can paint Landskips and enjoy the fag End of Life' (*Letters*, 68). He was developing something of a new style as first revealed in *The Mall* (1783; Frick Collection, New York; Hayes, *Landscape*, no. 148), a landscape full of fashionable promenading women later described as 'all in motion, and in a flutter like a lady's fan' (W. Hazlitt, *Conversations of James Northcote, R.A.*, 1894, 213). His late portraits, such as *Mr and Mrs Hallett* ('The Morning Walk', 1785; National Gallery, London) and *Mrs Sheridan* (National Gallery of Art, Washington, DC), manage a balance of tone, which in his *Discourses* Reynolds

commented on with some surprise: 'his manner of forming all the parts of his picture together; the whole going on at the same time, in the same manner as nature creates her works' (*Discourses on Art*, 251), and provide an equilibrium between the subjects and their landscape backgrounds that Gainsborough had never before achieved. Many of the landscapes, especially those in the National Gallery of Art, Washington, DC (for example: Hayes, *Landscape*, no. 151) and his single mythological subject *Diana and Actaeon* (Royal Collection; Hayes, *Landscape*, no. 160), have a freedom and mastery of handling that, compared with the finish of the works of his contemporaries, would have been difficult for many patrons to accept. Not surprisingly, both works remained in the artist's studio until after his death. Of the series of 'fancy' pictures he also produced, many remained in Gainsborough's studio, but the best of them, such as *Cottage Girl with Pitcher* (NG Ire.), were sold. This particular canvas was bought by Sir Francis Bassett in 1785. *The Woodman*, now known only from a print by Peter Simon, a painting that Gainsborough considered his best, was completed in 1787. It was shown to George III at Buckingham House, and Reynolds also viewed it shortly before Gainsborough died.

Death and reputation Gainsborough noticed a cold spot on his neck at the trial of Warren Hastings in April 1788, and it proved to be a cancerous growth. Despite the attentions of Dr John Heberden, Gainsborough's neighbour, and the surgeon John Hunter, nothing could be done to cure him. He took refuge in his summer house at 2 The Terrace, Richmond, and died at Schomberg House on 2 August 1788. He was buried beside his old friend Joshua Kirby at St Anne's, Kew. Six artists were pallbearers: Sir William Chambers, Sir Joshua Reynolds, Benjamin West, Francesco Bartolozzi, Paul Sandby, and Samuel Cotes. Other mourners included his nephew Gainsborough Dupont and his friends Samuel Linley, Jonathan Buttall (supposedly the sitter for 'The Blue Boy'), Isaac Gosset (the frame maker), James Trimmer (Kirby's son-in-law), and Jeremiah Meyer. His widow, Margaret, held a private exhibition and sale of pictures in March 1789. Further auction sales at Christies on 2 June 1792, 10–11 April 1797, 10–11 May 1799, and 25 February 1831 continued the process of dispersing the contents of Gainsborough's studio. The lease on Schomberg House expired in June 1792, and early in the following year Mrs Gainsborough moved to 63 Sloane Street, London. Gainsborough Dupont, who had remained at Schomberg House, moved to 17 Grafton Street, Fitzroy Square, London, where he continued to work as a painter. Margaret Gainsborough died on 18 December 1798. The artist's daughters, Margaret and Mary, moved in the following summer to Michael's Place, Brompton Road, then to Brook Green, Hammersmith, and finally to Acton, where they were protected, perhaps not entirely altruistically, by the amateur painter Henry Briggs. Margaret died on 18 December 1820 and was buried at Hanwell. Mary, by then deranged, was cared for by her cousin Sophia Lane, and died on 2 July 1826. She was buried with her sister.

The most distinguished of Gainsborough's siblings, the

Revd Humphrey Gainsborough (1718–1776), was an engineer of note who balanced his nonconformist ministry at Henley-on-Thames with improvements to the navigation of the River Thames and the construction of a steam engine which caused some concern to his rival, James Watt. His sister, Mary Gibbons (1713–1790), a lodging-house keeper in Bath, showed considerable entrepreneurial skill.

Gainsborough was a mercurial character with a clear understanding of his own abilities and a stubbornness inherited from his East Anglian nonconformist roots. His artistic training (he was mostly self-taught) exaggerated his temperamental opposition to the studio system operated by so many of his rivals and posed a problem which he was able to address by adopting a speedy technique of 'all those odd scratches and marks' that Reynolds found so difficult to understand (*Discourses on Art*, 257–8). Drawing at speed was the means by which he recorded what he saw around him. Reynolds was moved to comment with some disbelief about his:

> habit of continually remarking to those who happened to be about him, whatever peculiarities of countenance, whatever accidental combination of figures, or happy effects of light and shadow, occurred in prospects, in the sky, in walking the streets or in company … he neglected nothing which could keep his faculties in exercise, and derived hints from every sort of combination.   (ibid., 250)

He did not suffer fools gladly and hated humbug. Like so many other artists, he found the regimented order of a portrait practice difficult to bear:

> now damn Gentlemen, there is not such a set of Enemies, to a real Artist, in the World as they are, if not kept at a proper distance[.] *They* think (& so may you for a while) that they reward your merit by their Company & notice; but I, who blow away all the chaff & by G[od] in their Eyes too if they don't stand clear, know that they have but one part worth looking at, and that is their Purse; their Hearts are seldom near enough the right place to get a sight of it.   (*Letters*, 42)

He was a *bon viveur*, with some musical ability and a lively wit—'I have done nothing but fiddle since I came from London so much was I unsettled by the continual run of Pleasure with my Friend Giardini and the rest of you engaged me in' (ibid., 123). He was liberal-minded—'I would have every body enjoy, unmolested, their own opinions' (ibid., 131); considerate though prone to drinking which disrupted his work—Joseph Farington noted a conversation with the artist's daughter which recorded that he 'often exceeded the bounds of temperance & His health suffered from it,—being occasionally unable to work for a week after' (Farington, *Diary*, 1149). He was also charitably minded; in this he was supported by a firm religious belief. Although William Jackson states that he never read a book, recent research has done much to show that this was far from the truth. Connections have recently been made between Gainsborough's work and illustrations in books by Richard Bentley and Joseph Spence. His interest in the works of Sir Anthony Van Dyck, Sir Peter Paul Rubens, and David Teniers is demonstrated by the copies he made of their paintings, but he was also inspired by works, often known only through prints, by

such varied artists as Claude, Adriaen de Vries, Philips Wouvermans, Karel Dujardin, Rembrandt, Filippo Lauri, Salvator Rosa, Bartholomew Dandridge, and William Hogarth. No doubt future research will further demonstrate the extraordinary wealth of his visual memory and the inventive way in which he was able to adapt his sources.

The importance of the Royal Academy and the standards that Reynolds prescribed for it did much to suppress Gainsborough's reputation after his death. The prices achieved at his posthumous sales were disappointing and the publication of a set of prints by Joseph and Josiah Boydell in 1797 was surprisingly unsuccessful. Although he was regarded as 'one of the greatest ornaments of our Academy' and one of the founders of the English school (*Discourses on Art*, 248), the exhibition of a large selection of his work at the British Institution in 1814 did little to redress this decline. Interest in his landscape painting was encouraged by this exhibition and by the early acquisition of both *The Watering Place* and *The Market Cart* by the National Gallery in 1827 and 1830 respectively. John Constable in a lecture at the British Institution on 16 June 1836 provided the most touching tribute:

> The landscape of Gainsborough is soothing, tender, and affecting. The stillness of noon, the depths of twilight, and the dews and pearls of the morning, are all to be found in the canvases of this most benevolent and kind-hearted man. On looking at them, we have tears in our eyes, and know not what brings them.   (*Constable's Discourses*, 67)

However, the real turn in opinion occurred after the publication of George Williams Fulcher's monograph in 1856 and when his portraits of the Hon. Mrs Graham and 'The Blue Boy' were included in the 'Manchester Art Treasures Exhibition' in 1857. Their exhibition encouraged the press to compare favourably his portraiture with that of Reynolds. By the 1870s a number of wealthy bankers and industrialists, particularly Baron Lionel de Rothschild, Sir Michael Bass (later Lord Burton), and Lord Iveagh, began to collect (mostly female) portraits. In 1876 Gainsborough's portrait *Georgiana, Duchess of Devonshire* (priv. coll.) was sold for the world-record sum of 10,000 guineas and was stolen ten days later. These extraordinary events made the portrait famous beyond its merit. Its recovery in 1901 made the portrait even better known, and it was frequently reproduced in a variety of media. From about 1910 Lord Duveen successfully encouraged American clients, particularly Henry Clay Frick, Henry E. Huntington, George Elkins, and Andrew Mellon, to purchase portraits by Gainsborough. The most famous purchase through Duveen was Mr Huntington's of 'The Blue Boy' in 1921 from the duke of Westminster for a reputed £120,000, which fuelled a similar public adoration to that spawned by the sale of the *Duchess of Devonshire*. British artists were never more esteemed, and Gainsborough was represented as the pinnacle of their achievement.

A series of exhibitions organized by Sir Philip Sassoon at 45 Park Lane, London, in the 1930s and Sir Sacheverell Sitwell's book *Conversation Pieces* of 1936 led to a general re-evaluation of Gainsborough's early work. After twenty years' research Sir Ellis Waterhouse's pioneer catalogue raisonné of Gainsborough's paintings was published in 1958. The taste for the artist's earliest work mostly painted in Suffolk was especially favoured by Paul Mellon in the 1960s and 1970s and was most clearly marked by the acquisition of *Mr and Mrs Andrews* by the National Gallery in 1960. This painting is now so well known that it has entered the public's imagination as the quintessential illustration of middle England, and is frequently used as the basis of political cartoons. Waterhouse's predominant interest in Gainsborough's portraiture left an imbalance in the study of his work that was redressed when John Hayes published his catalogues of Gainsborough's landscape drawings (1970 and 1983), prints (1971), and paintings (1982). Hayes also curated a number of exhibitions including that at the Tate Gallery (1980) and another in Ferrara in 1998.

In the United States there is a long-standing appreciation of Gainsborough's work; an exhibition was held in Cincinnati in 1931 and another, of Gainsborough's drawings, toured the country in 1983. In 2003 the monograph exhibition organized by the Tate also travelled to Washington, DC, and Boston. Exhibitions in Europe include that held at the Grand Palais, Paris (transferred from the Tate Gallery exhibition of 1980), and that at Ferrara. In the last fifteen years there has been evidence that the popularity of Gainsborough's early works has waned and, in parallel with the rising interest in the work of Reynolds, there are signs, borne out by the Tate exhibition in 2002, that the taste for Gainsborough's grander, later works is returning.

HUGH BELSEY

Sources B. Allen, *Francis Hayman* (1987) [exhibition catalogue, New Haven and London] · A. Asfour and P. Williamson, 'William Jackson of Exeter: new documents', *Gainsborough's House Review* (1996–7), 39–144 · A. Asfour, P. Williamson, and G. Jackson, 'A second sentimental journey: Gainsborough abroad', *Apollo*, 146 (Aug 1997), 27–30 · A. Asfour and P. Williamson, *Gainsborough's vision* (1999) · R. Asleson and S. M. Bennett, *British paintings at the Huntington* (2001) · J. Barrell, *The dark side of the landscape* (1981) · H. Belsey, 'A visit to the studios of Gainsborough and Hoare', *Burlington Magazine*, 129 (Feb 1987), 107–9 · H. Belsey, *Gainsborough's family* (1988) · H. Belsey, 'Two works by Gainsborough', *National Art Collections Fund Review* [year ending] (31 Dec 1992), 6–12 · H. Belsey, 'Thomas Gainsborough as an Ipswich musician, a collector of prints and a caricaturist', *East Anglia's history: studies in honour of Norman Scarfe*, ed. C. Harper-Bill, C. Rawcliffe, and R. G. Wilson (2002) · H. Belsey, *Gainsborough at Gainsborough's House* (2002) [exhibition catalogue, Sudbury and London] · H. Belsey, *Gainsborough: a country life* (2002) · H. Belsey and C. Wright, *Gainsborough pop* (2002) · D. Brenneman, 'Thomas Gainsborough and the picturesque sketch', *Word and Image*, 13/4 (autumn 1997), 392–404 · D. Brenneman, 'Thomas Gainsborough's Wooded landscape with cattle by a pool: art criticism and the Royal Academy', *Gainsborough's House Review* (1995–6), 37–46 · H. S. Brown, 'Gainsborough's classically ambivalent wife', *British Art Journal*, 3/1 (autumn 2001), 78–9 · J. Burke, *English art, 1714–1800*, Oxford History of English Art, 9 (1976) · *John Constable's discourses*, ed. R. B. Beckett (1970) · J. Derow, 'Thomas Gainsborough's varnished drawings', *Master Drawings*, 26/3 (autumn 1998), 259–71 · J. Egerton, *National Gallery catalogues: the British school* (1998) · Farington, *Diary* · G. W. Fulcher, *Life of Thomas Gainsborough R.A.* (1856) · J. Hayes, 'Gainsborough and Rubens', *Apollo*, 78 (1963),

89–97 · J. Hayes, 'Gainsborough and the Bedfords', *The Connoisseur*, 147 (April 1968), 217–24 · review of Fulcher's biography, *GM*, 3rd ser., 1 (Aug 1856), 199 · J. Hayes, *The drawings of Thomas Gainsborough*, 2 vols. (1970) · J. Hayes, *Gainsborough as printmaker* (1971) · J. Hayes, *The landscape paintings of Thomas Gainsborough*, 2 vols. (1982) · J. Hayes, 'Gainsborough drawings: a supplement to the catalogue raisonné', *Master Drawings*, 21/4 (winter 1983), 367–91 · J. T. Hayes, *British paintings of the sixteenth through nineteenth centuries* (1992) · *The letters of Thomas Gainsborough*, ed. J. Hayes (2001) · R. Jones, 'Gainsborough's materials and methods: a "remarkable ability to make paint sparkle"', *Apollo*, 146 (Aug 1997), 19–26 · M. J. Levy, 'Gainsborough's Mrs Robinson', *Apollo*, 136 (1992), 152–4 · P. McEvansoneya, 'An Irish artist goes to Bath: letters from John Warren to Andrew Caldwell, 1776–1784', *Irish Architectural and Decorative Studies*, 2 (1999), 146–73 · O. Millar, *The later Georgian pictures in the collection of her majesty the queen*, 2 vols. (1969) · M. Pointon, 'Gainsborough and the landscape of retirement', *Art History*, 2/4 (Dec 1979), 441–55 · M. Postle, 'Gainsborough's "lost" picture of Shakespeare', *Apollo*, 134 (1991), 374–9 · M. Postle, *Thomas Gainsborough* (2002) · *Sir Joshua Reynolds 'Discourses on art'*, ed. R. R. Wark (1959) · M. Rosenthal, 'Gainsborough's Diana and Acteon', *Painting and the politics of culture: new essays on British art, 1700–1850*, ed. J. Barrell (1992), 167–94 · M. Rosenthal, *Glorious nature: British landscape painting, 1750–1850* (1993), 13–30 [exhibition catalogue, Denver Art Museum] · M. Rosenthal, 'The rough and the smooth: rural subjects in later eighteenth-century British art', *Eighteenth-century life*, 18 (May 1994), 36–58 · M. Rosenthal, 'Testing the water: Gainsborough in Bath in 1758', *Apollo*, 142 (Sept 1995), 49–54 · M. Rosenthal, 'Ann Ford', *Art Bulletin*, 90/4 (Dec 1998), 649–65 · M. Rosenthal, *The art of Thomas Gainsborough: 'a little business for the eye'* (1999) · M. Rosenthal and M. Myrone, *Gainsborough* (2002) [exhibition catalogue, Tate Britain] · S. L. Sloman, 'Gainsborough and "the lodging-house way"', *Gainsborough's House Review* (1991–2), 23–44 · S. L. Sloman, 'Gainsborough in Bath, 1758–59', *Burlington Magazine*, 137 (Aug 1995), 509–12 · S. L. Sloman, 'Mrs Margaret Gainsborough, "a prince's daughter"', *Gainsborough's House Review* (1995–6), 47–58 · S. L. Sloman, 'The Holloway Gainsborough: its subject re-examined', *Gainsborough's House Review* (1997–8), 47–54 · S. L. Sloman, *Gainsborough in Bath* (2002) · D. H. Solkin, 'Gainsborough's classically virtuous wife', *British Art Journal*, 2/2 (2000–01), 75–7 · G. Sawyer, 'A note on Thomas Gainsborough and Adriaen de Vries', *Journal of the Warburg and Courtauld Institutes*, 14 (1951), 134 · P. Thicknesse, *A sketch of the life and paintings of Thomas Gainsborough* (1788) · D. D. Tyler, 'Thomas Gainsborough's daughters', *Gainsborough's House Review* (1991–2), 50–66 · D. D. Tyler, 'The Gainsborough family: births, marriages and deaths re-examined', *Gainsborough's House Review* (1992–3), 38–54 · D. D. Tyler, 'Out from the shadows: Robert Gainsborough, the artist's eldest brother', *Gainsborough's House Review* (1997–8), 55–69 · E. K. Waterhouse, 'The first Royal Academy exhibition, 1769', *The Listener*, 43 (1 June 1950), 944–6 · E. K. Waterhouse, 'Preliminary check-list of portraits by Thomas Gainsborough', *Walpole Society*, 34 (1953) [whole issue] · E. K. Waterhouse, *Gainsborough* (1958) · G. Walkley, *Artists' houses in London, 1764–1914* (1994) · W. T. Whitley, *Gainsborough* (1915) · M. Woodall, 'Gainsborough's use of models', *Antiques*, 70 (Oct 1956), 363–5 · will, PRO, PROB 11/1169, fols. 29v–32r

Archives BL, letters and drafts, Add. MS 48964 · Gainsborough's House, Sudbury, papers · RA, letters · V&A NAL, notes relating to Allan Cunningham's *Life of Gainsborough*, and papers

Likenesses T. Gainsborough, group portrait, oils, 1751–2, Houghton Hall, Norfolk · T. Gainsborough, self-portrait, oils, 1754, Houghton Hall, Norfolk · T. Gainsborough, self-portrait, oils, c.1758–1759, NPG · attrib. W. Hoare, oils, 1763–7, Museum of Art, Santa Barbara, California · J. Zoffany, oils, c.1772, NPG · T. Gainsborough, self-portrait, oils, after 1782, Holkham Hall, Norfolk · T. Gainsborough, self-portrait, oils, c.1787, RA [*see illus.*] · E. Ortner, medal, 1859, NPG · J. Scott, mezzotint (after T. Gainsborough), BM, NPG

Gainsburgh [Gainsborough], **William** (*c*.1260–1307), diplomat and bishop of Worcester, was of unknown origins, but is presumed to have come from Gainsborough, Lincolnshire, because in 1300 he interceded with the king for some of its inhabitants arrested at York for homicide. He is first in evidence at the Oxford house of the Franciscans, and is said to have graduated MA during the academic year 1284–5, while on 1 August 1285 he is mentioned as vicar-general of the provincial minister of the English Franciscans. Shortly afterwards, on 8 September, he was himself elected twelfth provincial minister at the Cambridge chapter, and attended the general chapter at Assisi in 1289. By reason of his office he has been given credit for launching Duns Scotus on his scholastic career, but there was no more definite connection between them. From 1292 to 1294—by then a doctor of theology—he was twenty-fifth regent master of the Oxford Franciscans. A sermon attributed to him survives in Worcester Cathedral, MS Q. 46, fols. 298*v*–299*v*.

Gainsburgh's regency was interrupted by royal service. In October and November 1292 he was at Berwick with Edward I, as member of a commission to establish the king's rights over Scotland. Two years later he joined the former provincial of the Dominicans, Hugh of Manchester, to protest to Philippe IV of France against the latter's seizure of Gascony. In 1295 he again attended the general chapter at Assisi, bearing instructions from the king, who paid his expenses. Being sworn of the king's council he was summoned to attend the Westminster parliaments of 1295 and 1297. For some years he was engaged with John de Pontoise, bishop of Winchester (whose executor he became), in negotiations that culminated in the treaty of Montreuil in 1299 and Edward I's marriage to Margaret, King Philippe's sister. In that year he accompanied Hugh of Hartlepool, the provincial minister, to the Franciscan general chapter at Lyons. He was one of the envoys appointed in 1300 to receive the papal arbitration between France and England. Boniface VIII (*r.* 1294–1303) subsequently retained him at Rome, where he lectured in theology in the papal palace, and also continued to act as proctor and *nuncius* for his king, who had paid £68 from his wardrobe towards his expenses.

Following the death of Bishop Giffard of Worcester on 26 January 1302, the cathedral priory monks elected John of St Germans, but John was induced to resign at the curia. Boniface then provided Gainsburgh in his stead by bulls dated 24 October 1302, and he was consecrated at Rome on 25 November. In February 1303 he appeared before the king at Windsor, where he was made to renounce that part of his provisory bulls which claimed to grant the temporalities of his bishopric and was condemned to pay 1000 marks for his contempt in accepting that grant, but in 1306 the fine was remitted. Lack of money delayed his enthronement, which eventually took place on 9 June 1303. The *sede vacante* register has a full account of the proceedings, held on a hot day and attended by the bishops of Hereford and Llandaff and a huge crowd.

Continued royal service hampered Gainsburgh in the performance of his diocesan duties. He visited his cathedral chapter on 26–27 September 1303 and issued injunctions later entered in the register of Bishop Montagu (1334–7). Of the proceedings that followed little is recorded. According to the Worcester *Liber albus*, he gave warning of a further visitation in September 1306, but his itinerary does not reveal his activity in the parishes. He held some seventeen ordinations, and also acted as conservator, or protector, of the privileges of the Franciscans and Dominicans.

For five months in 1305 and 1306 Gainsburgh was absent on an embassy to the newly elected Clement V, an absence that gave rise to the first recorded commission to a vicar-general in the Worcester registers. It was issued on 17 October 1305 to Master Walter Wotton, who opened a special register on the 21st. Earlier that year, before his departure for the curia, Gainsburgh had attended the Westminster parliaments of February and September. On his return to his diocese his continued poverty is suggested by the fact that he had to beg a horse from the prior, who provided one called Hoel, described as small and thin. He was again outside the diocese from Christmas 1306 until the following Easter, during which time he attended the parliament summoned to Carlisle. He departed for the curia in July 1307 but according to the Lanercost chronicle died at Beauvais on 17 September during his return journey, and was buried in the Franciscan convent there.

Although his reputation stood high, Gainsburgh's quality as a scholar cannot now be judged. Bale ascribes to him *Questiones subtiles*, *Disceptationes quaedam*, and *Sermones ad utrumque statum*, but provides no incipits, while Leland in his *Collectanea* records *Questiones* formerly at Buckfast Abbey.   ROY MARTIN HAINES

Sources CEPR letters, vols. 1–2 · Chancery records · J. Stevenson, ed., Chronicon de Lanercost, 1201–1346, Bannatyne Club, 65 (1839) · wardrobe expenses, 28 Edw. 1, Society of Antiquaries, MS 119 · W. Gainsburgh and S. de Montacute, registers, Worcs. RO · J. W. Willis Bund, ed., Register of Bishop William Ginsborough, 1303 to 1307, Worcestershire Historical Society (1907); rev. edn with introduction by R. A. Wilson, as The register of William de Geynesburgh, Bishop of Worcester, 1302–1307 (1929) · J. W. W. Bund, ed., The register of the diocese of Worcester during the vacancy of the see, Worcestershire Historical Society, 8 (1893–7) · The 'Liber albus' of the priory of Worcester, ed. J. M. Wilson, Worcestershire Historical Society, 35 (1919) · The Worcester 'Liber albus', ed. J. M. Wilson (1920) · R. M. Haines, The administration of the diocese of Worcester in the first half of the fourteenth century (1965) · Ann. mon., 4.554–6, 559 · J. S. Brewer, ed., Monumenta Franciscana, 1, Rolls Series, 4 (1858), 537, 553, 560 · A. G. Little, Franciscan papers, lists, and documents (1943), 193–4, 212 · A. G. Little, The Grey friars in Oxford, OHS, 20 (1892), 157, 159, 160–62, 218 · A. G. Little and F. Pelster, Oxford theology and theologians, OHS, 96 (1934), 81, 88, 95, 157, 174, 176, 178, 182, 185–6, 239, 244, 272n., 280 · P. A. Callebaut, 'A propos du Bx. Jean Duns Scot de Littledean', Archivum Franciscanum Historicum, 24 (1931), 305–29, esp. 326 · P. Glorieux, 'Le manuscrit d'Assise, Bibl. Comm. 158', Recherches de Théologie Ancienne et Médiévale, 8 (1936), 294 · H. G. Richardson, 'The origins of parliament', TRHS, 4th ser., 11 (1928), 164–5 · Fasti Angl., 1300–1541, [Monastic cathedrals] · Emden, Oxf., 2.750–51 · Joannis Lelandi antiquarii de rebus Britannicis collectanea, ed. T. Hearne, 6 vols. (1715)

Archives Worcester Cathedral, MS Q. 46, fols. 298*v*–299*v* · Worcs. RO, register

Gainsford, Thomas (*bap.* 1566, *d.* 1624), soldier and historian, from a Surrey gentry family, was baptized on 16 December 1566, the son of Henry Gainsford (*d.* 1574), London goldsmith, and his wife, Mary Johnson. Gainsford has often been confused with other members of the Surrey family with the same name, but he probably matriculated at Peterhouse, Cambridge, in Easter term 1582 and was tutored there by a Greek scholar. He entered the Inner Temple in 1586, although he appears in the Surrey muster roles for 1583 and at some time between 1584 and 1588 served with the English army under Sir John Norreys in the Low Countries.

Gainsford inherited the spendthrift ways of his grandfather. Always in need of money he was known as 'a poore Captaine about London' (Gardiner, 143–4). In 1587 he sold his inherited property except for Scrope Place, opposite St Andrew's, Holborn, which he rented to musicians and actors of the royal household, among others. However, this property was seized in 1588 for a debt of £500 owed to a grocer and a merchant tailor. Gainsford had married a woman named Constance by 1590, but his financial situation was not thereby improved; further judgments were made against him for debt in 1593 and 1599.

Gainsford was back in military service in the Netherlands 1594–6, and from 1597 he served with the English army in Ireland under Richard de Burgh, fourth earl of Clanricarde. Late in 1600 at Moyerie Pass, Gainsford was wounded in the back. Subsequently he was with the troops that drove the Spanish out of Kinsale in 1601 and the company that brought the imprisoned Tyrone to England in 1603. He may have been in Ireland as late as 1605, but thereafter travelled on the continent, in 1606 from Geneva to Turin, Venice, and Pisa, delivering official documents to English exiles there for his kinsman Sir Henry Wotton. By August 1607 Gainsford had reached Constantinople, and visited Alexandria, Cyprus, and Greece. Early the next year at Milan he encountered his old foe Tyrone, headed for exile in Rome. In 1610 Gainsford was granted land in Ulster, and may have lived there for a time, though from 1611 to 1614 he fought under Maurice of Nassau in the Jülich–Cleves conflict.

After this active military career Gainsford turned to literary work. *The Vision and Discourse of Henry the Seventh*, a historical poem supporting James I's plan to unify England and Scotland published in 1610, is often attributed to him, but this is debatable. His authorship of *The Rich Cabinet*, a commonplace book; *The Secretaries Studie* (1616), a guide for writing letters which claims to be his first literary venture; and *The Historie of Trebizond* (1616), a prose romance modelled on Sidney's *Arcadia*, is certain. In 1616 he also contributed an elegy to the ninth edition of *Sir Thomas Overbury his Wife*, all the contributors having been in Overbury's circle at the Inner Temple. *The Glory of England*, dedicated to the marquess of Buckingham in 1618, was his most popular book, running to four editions by 1622. In 1619 Gainsford's *The True and Wonderfull History of Perkin Warbeck*, dedicated to the earl of Arundel, was published by Nathaniel Butter, and has been identified as a source for John Ford's *Perkin Warbeck* and (with Thomas Dekker) *The Witch of Edmonton*. In 1619 Gainsford published *The True Exemplary, and Remarkable History of the Earle of Tirone*, dedicated to his old commander Clanricarde.

The dedications in these works and the author's prefaces make it clear that Gainsford sought a patron to support him as a writer. Unsuccessful both in securing the support of the nobles he addressed, and in an approach to the East India Company for a post in 1619, he soon took employment with the publisher Nathaniel Butter as a writer and editor of news. In November 1620 Gainsford was investigated by the privy council as a 'suspitious person' (Adams, 141), believed to have authored the notorious *Vox populi*. His house was searched and Camden noted his arrest, although this pamphlet was ultimately shown to be the work of Thomas Scott. The council nevertheless confiscated Gainsford's manuscript 'Vox spiritus, or, Sir Walter Ralegh's ghost', unpublished until the late twentieth century.

Gainsford's actions and writings indicate that his political and religious beliefs were, like those of Butter, Calvinist and anti-Spanish. Butter's newsbooks championed the palatine cause in the Thirty Years' War and Palatinate officials possibly engaged Gainsford to write propaganda for them. He published in 1623 *The Friers Chronicle* and may have left Butter's operation that same year. But although a letter of Joseph Mead indicates a change in Butter's editor in 1623, Butter's newsbooks appeared regularly until 3 July 1624, after which time there was a two-month lapse. It is possible that Gainsford continued to edit the corantos right down to the moment that he fell victim to an outbreak of spotted fever that devastated London that summer. Gainsford was buried in St Martin Ludgate on 26 August 1624, his death and its cause reported in John Chamberlain's newsletter of 4 September 1624.

Gainsford was well known as a news writer and he appeared in a number of works both before and after his death. Three references to him occur in epigrams by Ben Jonson, namely 'An Execration upon Vulcan', 'Epigram to Captaine Hungry', and 'To True Soldiers'. Gainsford also appears in Jonson's dramatic works *Neptune's Triumph* (1624) and *The Staple of News* (1626). He is referred to by Abraham Holland in *A Scourge for Paper-Persecutors* (1625); by John Fletcher in *Fair Maid of the Inn* (1626); and by James Shirley in *Love Tricks, or, The School of Compliment* (1631). The last known contemporary reference is in *Mercurius anti-Britanicus, or, The Second Part of the 'King's Cabinet Vindicated'* (1645). One of Gainsford's works, *An Answer to Wither's Motto* (1625), a satire, was published posthumously by his son William, a student at Oxford. Thomas Gainsford left three unpublished manuscripts besides 'Vox spiritus': a work on state military affairs based on Tacitus, a history of Warwick the kingmaker, and a poem about women.

S. A. BARON

Sources M. Eccles, 'Thomas Gainsford, "Captain Pamphlet"', *Huntington Library Quarterly*, 45 (1982), 259–70 • W. H. Phelps, 'Thomas Gainsford (1566–1624), the "grandfather of English editors"', *Papers of the Bibliographical Society of America*, 73 (1979), 79–85 • J. F. Erath, 'The life and works of Thomas Gainsford: a Jacobean hack writer', PhD diss., Rutgers University, 1968 • S. Adams, 'Captain Thomas Gainsford, the "Vox spiritus" and the *Vox populi*',

BIHR, 49 (1976), 141–4 • *The Fortescue papers*, ed. S. R. Gardiner, CS, new ser., 1 (1871) • *CSP dom.* • PRO, SP 14, SP 16 • *The letters of John Chamberlain*, ed. N. E. McClure, 2 (1939), 579 [Chamberlain's news-letter, 4 Sept 1624]

Gairdner, James (1828–1912), archivist and historian, was born in Edinburgh on 22 March 1828, the second son of John *Gairdner MD and Susan or Susanna, *née* Tennant. A maternal great-grandfather was William Dalrymple (1723–1814). Gairdner was educated privately in Edinburgh, and in 1846 at the age of eighteen was appointed to a clerkship at the Public Record Office. He became an assistant keeper in 1859, a position which he continued to occupy until his retirement in 1893. Recognition of his work was generous, but came late in his life. Edinburgh University conferred the honorary degree of LLD upon him in 1897 (the first degree of any kind which he obtained). He was made a CB in 1900, and received the honorary degree of DLitt from the University of Oxford in 1910.

Although Gairdner wrote a number of historical works, his main service to scholarship was as an editor and collator of documents. In 1856 the master of the rolls commissioned John Sherren Brewer to prepare a calendar of manuscripts relating to the reign of Henry VIII, in the Public Record Office and elsewhere, and Gairdner became first his assistant and then his associate. Brewer died in 1879, when the first four volumes of the *Letters and Papers, Foreign and Domestic, of the Reign of Henry VIII* had been published. Gairdner then took over as editor, completing the work in twenty-one volumes, the last of which appeared in 1910. For volumes 14 to 21 he was assisted by R. H. Brodie, but the *Letters and Papers* were Gairdner's monument. It was not, however, his only large project. In 1858 he edited the *Memorials of Henry VII* for the Rolls Series, and in 1861 and 1863 two volumes of the letters and papers of Richard III and Henry VII in the same series. Gairdner married on 19 June 1867 Annie Maria, the daughter of Joseph Sayer of Carisbrooke, Isle of Wight, with whom he had one daughter.

In 1876 Gairdner processed *The Historical Collections of a Citizen of London in the Fifteenth Century* (CS, 2nd ser., 17), and in 1880 *Three Fifteenth-Century Chronicles* (CS, 2nd ser., 28). He also published a number of individual documents, mainly in the *English Historical Review*, and three editions of *The Paston Letters* (1872–5, 1901, and 1904), with an introduction which was thought by some contemporaries to be his best work. Gairdner's industry as an editor was immense, and his efficiency set new standards, but a calendar such as the *Letters and Papers* presented him with problems which he was unable to overcome. Some passages he transcribed, some he paraphrased, and some he omitted altogether, in accordance with his own perception of their interest and value. Consequently, although his great work remains an indispensable starting-point for any serious study of the period, it cannot necessarily be relied upon to provide the full sense of any document. It is remarkable that over 100,000 manuscripts in many languages could be calendared at all, but if the intention was to obviate the need to resort to the originals, then it did not succeed.

Gairdner's original writings were almost equally voluminous. He published *A History of the Life and Reign of Richard III* in 1878, a popular study of Henry VII in 1889, the volume covering the years 1509 to 1559 in *The History of the English Church* in 1902, and his main work, *Lollardy and the Reformation in England* (4 vols.), commencing in 1908. The last volume of the latter appeared after his death, in 1913, with a biographical preface by W. Hunt. He also wrote several lesser pieces, over a dozen learned articles, and the equivalent of a whole volume of the *Dictionary of National Biography*, covering almost every figure of importance between 1450 and 1550. His work as a historian was less satisfactory than that as an archivist and editor, and has not worn particularly well. This was partly the result of his unswerving Conservatism in politics, and his strict high Anglicanism. As the author of his obituary observed, 'for the historical period in which circumstances led him to specialize, he felt a profound distaste' (*The Times*, 6 Nov 1912). He had little skill in narrative presentation, no imagination, and less humour. J. P. Whitney, reviewing the first volume of *Lollardy and the Reformation* in 1909, pointed out that Gairdner's skill in the presentation and criticism of evidence was not matched by similar powers of historical analysis, or clarity of expression. Nor did he attempt to conceal his strong prejudices against heresy, resistance to lawful authority, and (most particularly) Henry VIII. As Whitney justly observed, 'Such an expression as that Henry was "in a more fiendish disposition than ever ..." really prejudices the ordinary reader'. Gairdner's objective was to be scientific and clinical in his presentation of historical material, and as an archivist and editor he was largely successful, leaving generations of scholars immensely in his debt. However, his larger and more ambitious original works fall significantly short of such high standards of objectivity, and are now little consulted except by historiographers. Gairdner died at his home, West View, Pinner, Middlesex, on 4 November 1912, and was buried in London; his wife survived him.

DAVID LOADES

Sources *The Times* (6 Nov 1912) • J. Gairdner, *Lollardy and the Reformation in England*, ed. W. Hunt, 4 (1913) • J. P. Whitney, review, *EngHR*, 18 (1903), 790–92 • J. P. Whitney, review, *EngHR*, 24 (1909), 780–84 • *DNB* • *CGPLA Eng. & Wales* (1912) • m. cert.
Archives BL, corresp. with Macmillans, Add. MS 55076 • CUL, letters to Lord Acton, 6443, 8119
Likenesses F. Baxter, plaster bust, 1900, NPG
Wealth at death £10,550 16s. 8d.: administration, 14 Dec 1912, *CGPLA Eng. & Wales*

Gairdner, John (1790–1876), surgeon, eldest son of Captain Robert Gairdner (d. 1795) of the Bengal artillery and J. Macrae Smith, was born at Mount Charles, near Ayr, on 18 September 1790. When he was only five years old his father was killed by the kick of a horse, and the care of five sons and a daughter fell upon his widowed mother. He received his school education at Ayr Academy, but when he and his brother William *Gairdner (1793–1867) decided upon a career in medicine his mother moved with her family to Edinburgh, in 1808, and there he took his degree of MD in 1811 with a thesis entitled 'De enteride'. He spent the winter of 1812 in London, studying anatomy under Charles Bell.

In 1813 Gairdner began practice in Edinburgh in partnership with Dr Farquharson, one of the leading physicians there. In the same year he became a fellow of the Royal College of Surgeons of Edinburgh, and four years later he began to act as examiner for the college, an office he performed until a few years before his death. He always took a close interest in the affairs of the college, of which, besides being for many years treasurer, he was president from 1830 to 1832. This appointment occurred at a politically sensitive time, for it gave him a seat in the unreformed town council of Edinburgh as 'deacon of the chirurgeon barbers'. The election for the parliament of 1831 was entirely in the hands of the town council, and Gairdner, being a staunch reformer, seconded the nomination of the popular candidate, Francis Jeffrey, then lord advocate under Earl Grey's government. The majority of the council, however, ignoring the popular fervour and a monster petition presented to them in Jeffrey's favour, elected Robert Adam Dundas, and had immediately to escape through back streets while an infuriated mob attacked the lord provost and threatened to throw him over the north bridge.

The reforms in which Gairdner took a more efficient part were those connected with the medical profession. With the zealous co-operation of William Wood, a lifelong friend though of opposing political beliefs, Gairdner added his support to the movement for obtaining for medical undergraduates at Edinburgh the right to receive some part of their professional training from extramural lectures—a change which, instead of weakening the university, as was feared by some, very greatly strengthened it. Gairdner also gave evidence before parliamentary committees in London on behalf of the Royal College of Surgeons of Edinburgh in support of the reforms in medical licensing eventually secured by the Medical Act of 1859.

Gairdner wrote little on medical subjects, but produced a large number of antiquarian memoirs, continuing these until shortly before his death. Among them were lectures, published separately, on the history of the college of surgeons, and on the early history of the medical profession in Edinburgh. Historical subjects had a great attraction for Gairdner, and as an aid to chronological research he published in his later years a *Calendar*, printed on cardboard with a cardboard slide, for the verification of past or future dates and their correspondence with days of the week and month. He was also interested in the life of Robert Burns. He was the author of some letters published anonymously at the time in the *Scotsman* newspaper in answer to certain statements that had appeared elsewhere relating to Burns's life. Gairdner's family ties and personal memories of Ayrshire in his early days made him an important witness, and his letters on Burns were reprinted after his death and privately published, though still anonymously, in 1883, as *Burns and the Ayrshire Moderates*.

Gairdner's independence of mind and deep religious convictions led him to join a small body of Unitarians at a time when that sect was very unpopular, especially in Scotland. There is no doubt that, though he had a fair professional practice, this step did hinder his professional progress. He took an active part in the setting up of a new Unitarian chapel in Edinburgh; but after many years, failing to find in that sect what he considered to be pure Christianity and freedom, he returned once more to the Church of Scotland. His revolt against the established church in his youth had been caused mainly by the prevalence of a narrow Calvinism; but in his later years he was more inclined to look for breadth and freedom to national churches than to sects. He married on 8 August 1817 his cousin Susanna (d. 1860), a daughter of William Tennant, a merchant of Edinburgh, and a granddaughter of Dr William Dalrymple (1723–1814) of Ayr. Gairdner survived his wife by sixteen years, and died on 12 December 1876, leaving three sons, one of whom was Sir William Tennant *Gairdner (1824–1907), and two daughters. Gairdner's entry in the *Dictionary of National Biography* was written by his son, the historian James *Gairdner (1828–1912).

JAMES GAIRDNER, rev. PATRICK WALLIS

Sources The Scotsman (14 Dec 1876) · Edinburgh Courant (14 Dec 1876) · BMJ (23 Dec 1876), 841–2 · The Lancet (23 Dec 1876) · Caledonian Mercury (May 1831) · Nomina eorum, qui gradum medicinae doctoris in academia Jacobi sexti Scotorum regis, quae Edinburgi est, adepti sunt, ab anno 1705 ad annum 1845, University of Edinburgh (1846) · bap. reg. Scot., Ayr, 18 Sept 1790 · m. reg. Scot., Edinburgh, 7 Aug 1817 · personal knowledge (1889)
Likenesses J. M. Barclay, oils, 1867, Royal College of Surgeons, Edinburgh
Wealth at death £6339 14s. 10d.: confirmation, 8 Jan 1877, CCI

Gairdner, William (1793–1867), physician, son of Robert Gairdner (d. 1795), captain in the Bengal artillery, and his wife, J. Macrae Smith, was born at Mount Charles, Ayrshire, on 11 November 1793, the fourth of five sons born before their father's untimely death from a kick by a horse (a daughter was born posthumously). William followed his elder brother John *Gairdner (1790–1876) into a medical career; from Ayr Academy he went in 1810 to the University of Edinburgh, where he graduated MD on 13 September 1813, taking dysentery as the subject of his inaugural dissertation. After further study in London he went abroad as physician to Frederick William Hervey, eighth earl of Bristol. He married on 12 January 1822 Cecilia Bordier, daughter of a banker of Geneva. She predeceased him; their daughter Clara married Julius Bordier and died in 1911.

After his marriage Gairdner settled in London. He took a house in Piccadilly at 12 Bolton Street, where he was to remain for the rest of his life. In 1823 he was admitted a licentiate of the Royal College of Physicians, and in the following year he published *An Essay on the Effects of Iodine on the Human Constitution*. Dr Coindet of Geneva had in 1820 proposed to treat goitre and other glandular enlargements by the internal administration of iodine, and Gairdner's essay was written in support of Coindet's views and to improve the understanding of this new treatment. While advocating the use of iodine it described more minutely than any previous English book the ill effects of large doses.

Gairdner's practice grew slowly, and he did not attain success until after long struggles. In 1849 he published *On Gout, its History, its Causes, and its Cure*, a work which went through four editions, the last published in 1860. This book essentially comprised a succession of cases, presented to demonstrate Gairdner's clinical skills. As one of the last of the old-school bedside doctors, he regarded the malady in a holistic manner, considering it to be the consequence of disordered blood. He also believed it to be hereditary, though not necessarily appearing in every generation. He nevertheless denied the popular view that attacks of gout gave relief; indeed he insisted that these were the result of excess, the best remedy being a moderate diet, to which he added bloodletting and purging. The older he grew, the author says, the more his confidence in drugs abated.

Gairdner was a small man with a florid complexion, and his hair became white at an early age. He was a new whig in politics, and had an independent, inflexible spirit, which, if it sometimes increased the difficulties of his life, also enabled him to conquer them. He continued his practice almost to the end of his life, and died at Avignon, after spending a winter in the south of France, on 28 April 1867.   NORMAN MOORE, rev. DAVID SOUDEN

Sources G. A. Gibson, *Life of Sir William Tennant Gairdner* (1912) · List of the graduates in medicine in the University of Edinburgh from MDCCV to MDCCCLXVI (1867), 47 · R. Porter and G. Rousseau, *Gout, the patrician malady* (1998) · bap. reg. Scot.
Wealth at death under £9000—effects in UK: resworn probate, Aug 1875, *CGPLA Eng. & Wales* (1867)

Gairdner, William Henry Temple (1873–1928), missionary, was born on 31 July 1873 in the family's summer home at Ardrossan, Ayrshire, the eldest of four sons and four daughters of Sir William Tennant *Gairdner (1824–1907), professor of medicine at the University of Glasgow and Glasgow's chief medical officer, and his wife, Helen Bridget Wright. James Gairdner, the Tudor historian, was his uncle. He was educated first at St Ninian's preparatory school in Moffat, Dumfriesshire, and subsequently at Rossall School from 1887 to 1892. In October 1892 he entered Trinity College, Oxford, as an exhibitioner, emerging in 1896 contrary to his own and his friends' higher expectations with a second-class BA degree in both classical moderations and Greats.

In Trinity Gairdner's circle of close friends included J. H. Oldham, and while there, in reaction to the death of his brother Hugh, he became very actively involved, through the strongly evangelical Oxford Inter-Collegiate Christian Union, in the work of the Student Volunteer Missionary Union. He declared his intention to become a missionary at the annual Keswick Convention of 1893, and his enthusiasm was further fired there the following year by the American student leaders J. R. Mott and R. G. Speer, with their challenge to 'the evangelization of the World in this generation'. On leaving Oxford he spent twelve months as a lay brother assisting the Oxford pastorate clergy, while also studying theology with F. J. Chavasse, principal of

Wycliffe Hall. This was preparation enough to secure his acceptance as a missionary by the Church Missionary Society (CMS) in November 1897.

Gairdner had no doubt that his destination lay in Egypt and the Sudan, his thoughts crystallizing in response to several influences. Thrilled by the royal jubilee celebrations of 1897, he was prompted to declare 'I should like to serve my Queen. Can I do it better than by taking Christ to her Empire?' (Padwick, 51). Like many of his contemporaries Gairdner had also been brought up a great admirer of General Gordon, whom he regarded as the embodiment of heroism and Christian service; as the reconquest of the Sudan went slowly ahead, the opportunity to complete Gordon's work there seemed very real. There was also a more general preoccupation with Islam at this time, especially in evangelical Anglican circles where eschatological reflections on Christianity's confrontation with 'Mohammedanism' resonated with the student movement's commitment to a missionary strategy which would hasten Christ's second coming.

From 1897 to 1898, based in London, Gairdner worked as travelling secretary for the British College Christian Union (forerunner of the Student Christian Movement), and then in 1899 spent a final two terms at Wycliffe Hall preparing for ordination and starting to learn Arabic. Ordained deacon in St Paul's Cathedral by the bishop of London early in October 1899, he left England six weeks later under instructions from the CMS to join his Oxford friend Douglas Thornton for work with students and educated Muslims in Cairo. With missionaries barred from the Sudan by the British authorities, Gairdner became steadily more settled in Cairo. Ordained priest there in February 1901 by G. F. P. Blyth, bishop of Jerusalem, and abandoning earlier thoughts of a celibate life, on 16 October 1902 he married an old Glasgow friend, Margaret Dundas Mitchell (b. 1874/5), who had joined the CMS in Palestine the previous year. They had three sons and two daughters.

Increasingly convinced of Cairo's importance as the publishing and literary centre of the Islamic world, Gairdner came to share Thornton's belief that their task was not only to expound Christianity to Muslims but to stimulate Anglican understanding and sympathy for Islam. The creation of an educational, apologetic literature thus became his principal concern, a literature at once imaginative and wide-ranging in content and rid of its traditional yet ever more lifeless trading of theological argument. For Muslims, Gairdner produced a steady stream of lectures, leaflets, and pamphlets in Arabic, and in 1905 with Thornton set up a regular Arabic and English paper, *Orient and Occident*, which flourished unbroken until 1942. With similar inspiration he turned his own considerable musical talents to the adaptation of traditional local music for Christian worship. For readers at home, two of his books became of particular importance: *D. M. Thornton: a Study in Missionary Ideals and Methods* (1908), a biography of his friend who died of typhoid in 1907, was immediately followed by his survey for students, *The Reproach of Islam* (1909). Appearing in the setting provided by the Pan-Anglican Congress of 1908 and the Edinburgh World Missionary Conference of 1910, which paid considerable attention to the expansion of Islam, both books were widely read. Gairdner's prominence in the early twentieth-century encounter between Christianity and Islam was finally confirmed by his commission to write the popular report of the Edinburgh conference. 'Edinburgh 1910': an Account and Interpretation of the World Missionary Conference (1910), written in only eight weeks, in part restated for a new generation the challenge presented by Islam and its centrality in what he interpreted as a major turning point in world history.

The lines of Gairdner's career were now well established. After Edinburgh he visited the United States, Germany, and Hungary to update his knowledge of Arabic scholarship, before returning to Cairo. Continuing his own study and writing, he also acquired an outstanding reputation as a linguist and teacher of Arabic, activities concentrated in the Cairo Study Centre which he set up in 1912. However, administrative obligations constantly intruded, never more so than for the duration of the First World War, when he was obliged to take over the secretaryship of the Cairo mission. Ever anxious to influence the growing nationalist movement, Gairdner also fostered the YMCA in Cairo. He worked constantly to improve relations both with other churches, such as the Copts, and between the different missionary societies.

Gairdner was tall, athletic, and clean-shaven, and somewhat short-sighted. An impulsive, versatile, warm, and unpretentious man, he was much loved, and much mourned when he died on 22 May 1928 of septicaemia in Cairo's Anglo-American Hospital. He was buried in Cairo. A memorial appeal made possible the building of a new church in Old Cairo, completed in 1934 as home to the Egyptian Episcopal church.   ANDREW PORTER

Sources C. E. Padwick, *Temple Gairdner of Cairo*, rev. edn (1930) · G. Hewitt, *The problems of success: a history of the Church Missionary Society, 1910–1942*, 2 vols. (1971–7) · E. Stock, *The history of the Church Missionary Society: its environment, its men and its work*, 4 (1916) · L. L. Vander Werff, 'The strategy of Christian missions to Muslims: Anglican and reformed contributions in India and the Near East from Henry Martyn to Samuel Zwemer, 1800–1938', PhD diss., U. Edin., 1967 · *The Rossall register, 1881–1954* (1956) · *CMS Register of Missionaries and Native Clergy* (CMS, privately printed, c.1904) · *WWW* · L. R. Murphy, 'W. H. T. Gairdner: an Englishman in Egypt', *Personalities and policies: essays on English and European history presented in honor of Dr Marguerite Potter*, ed. E. D. Malpas (1977), 76–93 · G. K. A. Bell, *Randall Davidson, archbishop of Canterbury*, 3rd edn (1952)
Archives U. Birm. L., Church Missionary Society archive
Likenesses photographs, 1902–26, repro. in Padwick, *Temple Gairdner of Cairo*

Gairdner, Sir William Tennant (1824–1907), physician and university professor, born in Edinburgh on 8 November 1824, was the eldest son of John *Gairdner (1790–1876), physician, and his wife, Susanna (d. 1860), daughter of William Tennant and granddaughter of the religious writer Dr William Dalrymple (1723–1814). William *Gairdner (1793–1867) was his uncle and James *Gairdner his brother. Educated at the Edinburgh Institution, in 1840

Gairdner became a medical student at Edinburgh University, where he had a brilliant career. Immediately after graduation as MD in 1845, he went to the continent with Lord and Lady Beverley as their medical attendant and spent the winter in Rome. On his return to Edinburgh in 1846 he became house physician and house surgeon to the Royal Infirmary. At this time, typhus was rampant in the larger Scottish towns, and the experience for Gairdner was a dominant influence, leading him to work in the field of public health in later life.

Gairdner was appointed pathologist to the Edinburgh Royal Infirmary in 1848, and full physician in 1853, shortly before he began a series of private lectures entitled 'Principles and practice of medicine'. His *Public Health in Relation to Air and Water* was published in 1862. In this he discussed the dangers of overcrowding, and insufficient and impure water supplies. He suggested that these problems could be overcome by investigation, education, moral suasion, and occasionally legal compulsion. His *Clinical Medicine* was also published in 1862, and was well received by the profession. In the same year, Gairdner was appointed professor of medicine at the University of Glasgow. From 1863 to 1872 he was also medical officer of health to the city. During that period he remodelled the city's sanitary arrangements, despite meagre resources. In 1870 he married Helen Bridget Wright, daughter of Mr Wright of Norwich; they had four sons and four daughters. Their eldest son was the missionary William Henry Temple *Gairdner (1873–1928).

Gairdner's lectures did not appeal to everyone. He was too slow for those students only interested in passing exams, and the lectures were marked by select, rather than wide, reading. His contributions to the medical literature were many. In 1848, while he was pathologist to the infirmary, he contributed a series of papers to the *Monthly Journal of Medical Sciences*. The most valuable of these was an early description of the 'waxy' kidney. In 1850 his *Pathological Anatomy of Bronchitis and the Diseases of the Lung connected with Bronchial Obstruction* expressed an original viewpoint. Other notable works included *Insanity: Modern Views as to its Nature and Treatment* (1885), and *The Physician as Naturalist* (1889), which contained his presidential address to the section of medicine of the British Medical Association. His other publications, numerous pamphlets, reports, and papers, dealt with various subjects. These included the connection between arterial supply and myocardial changes; the reciprocal influence of the heart and lungs; hypertrophy and dilatation; the system of representing the sounds and murmurs of the heart by means of diagrams; and the recognition of tricuspid obstruction, aneurism, and angina pectoris. With William Stokes, George Balfour, and C. H. Fagge, Gairdner helped to make certain the diagnosis of mitral obstruction. His last contribution to circulatory disease was the article on aneurism in the sixth volume of Clifford Allbutt's *System of Medicine* (1889). Gairdner also gave many public addresses. Some of his later ones were published in *The Three Things that Abide: Faith; Hope; Love* (1903).

In 1876 Gairdner might have taken the chair in medicine at Edinburgh. However, he hesitated too long in his application, and it was passed over. Many distinctions were granted him. He was awarded the honorary degrees of LLD from Edinburgh in 1883, and of MD from Dublin in 1887; he became FRS in 1893, honorary FRCP (Ireland) in 1887; physician-in-ordinary to Queen Victoria in 1881; honorary physician to King Edward VII in 1901; president of the Royal College of Physicians of Edinburgh in 1893–4; and president of the British Medical Association when it met in Glasgow in 1888. He was made a KCB in 1898.

Gairdner resigned his professorship at Glasgow University in 1899 and returned to his old haunts in Edinburgh. He was a man of strong religious conviction. He gave support to the abolition of abuses in the army and the disestablishment of the church in Ireland. During the last seven years of his life, Gairdner presented the typical symptoms of Stokes–Adams disease, an obscure affliction of the heart. During this time, he suffered from nervous seizures. He made careful record of these symptoms and an account of the clinical and pathological conditions of his disease was duly published. He died suddenly at his home, Bracondale, Colinton, Edinburgh, on 28 June 1907, and was survived by his wife.

G. A. GIBSON, rev. TIM O'NEILL

Sources BMJ (6 July 1907), 53–9 · The Lancet (6 July 1907), 58–61 · G. Gibson, Life of Sir William Tennant Gairdner (1912) · PRS, 80B (1908) · A. Thomson and H. Littlejohn, 'The late Sir William Tennant Gairdner', Edinburgh Medical Journal, new ser., 22 (1907), 97–100 · W. T. Gairdner, 'The physician as "naturalist"', Scottish Medical and Surgical Journal, 21/2 (Aug 1907), 99–130 · Glasgow Medical Journal, new ser., 68 (1907), 113–18 [incl. catalogue of his work in the library of the Faculty of Physicians and Surgeons of Glasgow, 7/1907] · CGPLA Eng. & Wales (1907)
Archives NRA Scotland, priv. coll., lectures and reports
Likenesses G. Reid, oils, before 1893, U. Glas. · G. Reid, oils, 1912, U. Glas. · Maull & Fox, photograph, RS

Gairy, Sir Eric Matthew (1922–1997), prime minister of Grenada, was born on 18 February 1922 near Grenville, Grenada, the son of an estate foreman and his wife, a domestic servant. He was educated at a Catholic elementary school. He emigrated to Aruba, where he worked as a clerk in the oil refinery before returning home at the end of 1949. He first came to public attention in 1950, when he negotiated a cash compensation for estate tenants evicted by a new owner. With this intervention he was viewed as the champion of rural workers. He capitalized on this goodwill by establishing the first trade union for agricultural workers, the Grenada Manual and Mental Workers' Union (GMMWU), in July 1950. Within a month of the union's registration Gairy launched a strike on behalf of the sugar workers which resulted in substantial wage increases. His efforts to secure wage increases for workers on the cocoa and nutmeg estates succeeded only after a month-long, island-wide general strike in 1951.

The loyal following of rural workers created by Gairy's trade union militancy formed the core of support for his Grenada People's Party (by 1953 the Grenada United Labour Party), which he established in 1951. In the first general elections under adult suffrage in October that year Gairy's party won six of the eight seats. By 1951 he had emerged as the major trade unionist and political figure in Grenada. His success challenged the prevailing economic and political order. As a trade unionist he established the power of organized labour in its confrontation with capital. His electoral victory represented a shift of political power from the white and brown élite that had controlled government under a restrictive franchise. The basis of his popular appeal was his identification with the interests of the working class. Thus he presented himself as 'the little black boy' who had forced the 'upper brackets' to come to terms with him (Thorndike, 33). To his supporters he brought a new level of class consciousness by drawing their attention to the domination of a small economic élite in the main export industries, the inadequate compensation of workers, and the existence of colour prejudice which shaped employment practices.

In his first term in office as minister of trade and production from 1956 to 1957 (following an increased measure of self-government granted by Britain) Gairy introduced reforms which benefited his rural constituency, including land reform and security of tenure for tenants. There were, however, signs that the purpose of the organizations that he led was to sustain his political career rather than to promote social and economic change. The GMMWU lost its early momentum as Gairy used his trade union mainly for political support. He made, moreover, no attempt to develop a party organization, but relied instead on his personal appeal. In the period 1954–7 his electoral support declined with the formation in 1954 of the Grenada National Party (GNP), led by Herbert Blaize. In 1957 the GNP won the general elections, and shortly afterwards Gairy was disfranchised after disrupting a GNP meeting. His franchise was restored in 1961, when he became chief minister under a new constitution with a ministerial system. Gairy's tenure had lasted only ten months when the British government suspended the constitution after a 1962 commission of inquiry charged him with violating the regulations governing expenditure. He subsequently lost the 1962 election.

On his return to office as chief minister in 1967 Gairy consolidated his power by dispensing concessions to a new class of businessmen and benefiting from their loyalty and financial kickbacks. He centralized decision making in the cabinet, assumed control over civil service appointments, and suppressed dissent by making it difficult for a parliamentary opposition to operate. He thus established an alternative power base to the rural workers, from whom he distanced himself. By the early 1970s organized opposition to his rule grew with the return of professionals who had studied abroad. These individuals emphasized political mobilization outside the electoral cycle. In March 1973 the New Jewel Movement (NJM) was established and by 1973–4 had co-ordinated a broad alliance of political, trade union, business, and religious organizations in opposition to Gairy, who became prime minister of Grenada, and minister of external affairs, planning and development, lands, tourism, information service, public relations, and natural resources, following independence, in 1974.

Gairy responded to this growing opposition by repression and intimidation. He relied increasingly on the use of paramilitary forces (including the notorious 'Mongoose Gang') to terrorize opponents, and on legislation to close the opposition's access to the media. By 1979 his government had alienated important sections of Grenadian society, including the businessmen, who regarded his corrupt and authoritarian government as a hindrance to economic activity. On 13 March 1979 the NJM seized control of the government during his absence in New York, where he had gone to address the United Nations on one of his favourite topics, unidentified flying objects. He remained in the United States for the four years of the NJM's Marxist regime. After American forces invaded the island in October 1983 and established control, he returned to Grenada and contested the December 1984 elections. His party won only one seat but gained 36 per cent of the popular vote. However, he failed to regain power in the 1990 and 1995 elections. Gairy, who was knighted in 1977, died at Grand Anse, Grenada, on 23 August 1997. He was survived by his wife, Cynthia, née Clyne, whom he had married in 1949 and who had served as a minister in his cabinet, and two daughters. He had begun his public career as a champion of the working class, but by the late 1970s he had become a repressive tyrant, having used his popular support to advance his political ambitions and financial interests.

HOWARD JOHNSON

Sources G. Brizan, *Grenada, island of conflict: from Amerindians to people's revolution, 1498–1979* (1984) · M. G. Smith, 'Structure and crisis in Grenada, 1950–1954', *The plural society in the British West Indies* (1965), 263–303 · G. K. Lewis, *Roots of revolution: Gairy and Gairyism in Grenada* (1986) · T. Thorndike, *Grenada: politics, economics and society* (1985) · A. W. Singham, *The hero and the crowd in a colonial polity* (1968) · W. R. Jacobs and I. Jacobs, *Grenada: the route to revolution* (1980) · J. R. Mandle, *Big revolution, small country: the rise and fall of the Grenadian revolution* (1985) · C. Searle, ed., *In nobody's backyard: Maurice Bishop's speeches, 1979–1983. A memorial volume* (1984) · A. Payne, P. Sutton, and T. Thorndike, *Grenada: revolution and invasion* (1984) · *The Independent* (25 Aug 1997) · *The Times* (25 Aug 1997) · *Daily Telegraph* (25 Aug 1997) · WWW

Likenesses photograph, repro. in *The Independent* · photograph, repro. in *Daily Telegraph*

Gaisberg, Frederick William (1873–1951), recording engineer and record company executive, was born on 1 January 1873 in Washington, DC, the second of four children of Wilhelm Gaisberg and his wife, Emma, née Klenk. His father was the son of German émigrés and worked at the United States Federal Printing Office. His mother encouraged the young Gaisberg to learn the piano, for which he had a natural talent. Gaisberg was educated in Washington, DC, until the age of sixteen, and was a chorister at St John's Episcopal Church.

The piano remained Gaisberg's first love, and as a schoolboy he earned pocket-money playing piano accompaniments for singers, comics, and others making cylinder records for the Columbia Phonograph Company. His name was announced on these records as 'Professor Gaisberg'. In 1889 he met Charles Sumner Tainter, who had

invented the cylinder graphophone, and through his influence he was sent to the American Graphophone factory at Bridgeport, Connecticut, where he was trained as a precision engineer. Returning to Washington, Gaisberg worked for the Columbia Phonograph Company, recruiting performers and accompanying them at recording sessions.

In 1894 Gaisberg met Emile Berliner, inventor of the gramophone, which used disc records. Upon first hearing a Berliner record Gaisberg was, in his own words, 'spellbound by the beautiful round tone of the flat gramophone disc', which was, even in its infancy, far superior to the cylinder records. Gaisberg joined Berliner initially as an impresario and accompanist, but later as a Berliner-trained sound engineer, a training that formed the basis of his later career and achievements.

In 1898 Berliner sent Gaisberg to London where he established a recording studio making the first European disc records for the Gramophone Company, Berliner's British and European licensees. In 1899 this business was reconstructed and expanded. As a consequence, Gaisberg went on the first of his many European tours making records for the various distinctive local markets. As the company's principal recording engineer, he then travelled further afield, capturing on record the music of artists in Russia, India, and the Far East. However, Gaisberg's most important contribution to the Gramophone Company's success came in 1902, when he recorded the Italian tenor Enrico Caruso in Milan. These recordings not only enhanced Gaisberg's own reputation but also established the gramophone as an important means for spreading art and culture around the world. This was how Gaisberg viewed the gramophone record itself: as a means to an end. Years later, he told a colleague that he saw his task simply as one of making as many sound photographs or gramophone disc sides as possible during each recording session. Thus, Gaisberg did not view the recording process as an art form in itself, nor, modestly, did he view himself as an artist.

When Gaisberg made his first recording of Fyodor Chalyapin, the great Russian bass, he began a lifelong friendship which was to see him help Chalyapin escape Russia after the Bolshevik revolution. In the decades after the first Caruso recordings, Gaisberg built up the HMV label's classical catalogue, signing and recording important international performers such as Beniamino Gigli, Nellie Melba, John McCormack, and Fritz Kreisler. Gaisberg briefly considered quitting the business in 1918 after the death of his brother William from influenza after a recording expedition to the western front, but his determination kept him going. In 1921 Gaisberg became HMV's artistic director in the newly formed international artistes department, and, after the introduction of electrical recording in 1925, he abandoned recording in favour of artiste and repertoire management. Electrical recording nevertheless provided Gaisberg with the opportunity to both re-record many artistes and extend the range of music available on record. He remained artistic director after the formation of Electric and Musical Industries

(EMI) in 1931, a depression-led merger between the Gramophone and Columbia Graphophone companies, and supervised the international artistes department during the dark days of the great depression, keeping faith in the viability of the recording industry even as the company's American affiliates RCA Victor and American Columbia were dissolving their catalogues and allowing Gaisberg to sign their artistes to the HMV and Columbia labels. Throughout the 1930s Gaisberg continued to develop newer artistes like the violinist Yehudi Menuhin, and deepened his working relationship with established performers, particularly the British composer and conductor Sir Edward Elgar.

At the age of sixty-six, in 1939, Gaisberg retired, allowing the men he had trained—Walter Legge and David Bicknell—to pick up the baton. Gaisberg remained a consultant to EMI for the rest of his life, and continued to have an important influence on the recording industry as a whole. In particular, in the late 1940s he argued in favour of longplay and stereophonic recording, both of which were introduced the following decade. Gaisberg never married and, apart from war enforced moves, he lived out the remainder of his life with his sister Carrie in London. During this time he wrote his memoirs, published in London as *Music on Record* in 1946, and he continued to travel extensively, particularly to his native USA.

The enormous regard and affection in which Fred Gaisberg was held was displayed at a banquet held at the Savoy Hotel on 21 April 1939 to honour his fifty years in the recording business and to mark his formal retirement. It was appropriately attended by figures from the world of recorded music which Gaisberg had helped to create, such as Sir Thomas Beecham, Gracie Fields, Richard Tauber, and Artur Rubinstein. Throughout his career, Gaisberg combined an artistic sensitivity with a friendly, modest, diplomatic nature which won him the respect and friendship of many. His dedication to and ingenuity within the recording industry remain legendary.

Gaisberg died in his sleep in the early hours of 2 September 1951 at his home, 42 Crediton Hill, Hampstead, London, and was buried in London later that month.

PETER MARTLAND

Sources F. W. Gaisberg, *Music on record* (1946) · J. N. Moore, *A voice in time* (1974) · *The Voice* (Oct 1951) · *The Gramophone*, 58/689 (Oct 1951) · CGPLA Eng. & Wales (1952) · d. cert.
Archives EMI Music Archive, Hayes, Middlesex, Central Research Laboratories, MSS
Likenesses photographs, EMI Music Archive, Hayes, Middlesex, Gaisberg coll.
Wealth at death £1388 0s. 9d.: administration with will, 1952, CGPLA Eng. & Wales

Gaisford, Thomas (1779–1855), classical scholar and dean of Christ Church, Oxford, was born at Iford Manor in Wiltshire on 22 December 1779. He was the eldest son of John Gaisford, a wealthy clothier of Bradford, Wiltshire, from whom he inherited a valuable house and estate; his mother was Sarah, daughter of a clergyman named Bushall. He was educated at Hyde Abbey School, Winchester, under the Revd Charles Richards before entering Christ

Thomas Gaisford (1779–1855), by Henry William Pickersgill, exh. RA 1847

Church, Oxford, as a commoner in 1797. He was made student by the dean, Cyril Jackson, in 1800, and graduated BA in 1801 and MA in 1804.

For a time Gaisford served as tutor, and had Sir Robert Peel among his pupils. In 1809–11 he served as examiner in the newly instituted honour schools, but in the words of a not unsympathetic obituary notice he 'never suffered the instruction of his pupils to interfere with the pursuit of his own studies' (*GM*). In 1812 the regius chair of Greek was vacant, and it might have been expected that another Christ Church man, Peter Elmsley, would have been preferred. Elmsley, who was six years older, had achieved more, and his intellectual gifts were greater than those of Gaisford. But Elmsley as a whig and a contributor to the *Edinburgh Review* was not acceptable to Christ Church. The first draft of Gaisford's reply to the prime minister's letter offering the chair is said to have run 'My Lord, I have received your letter and accede to its contents', but Dean Jackson made Gaisford substitute a letter of his own dictation (Tuckwell, 123). This is one of many anecdotes that touch on his marked deficiency in urbanity and sociability, but this seems to have been accompanied by a remarkable persuasive power.

On 11 May 1815 Gaisford married Helen Margaret (d. 1830), second daughter of the Revd Robert Douglas, who was not only a beauty but a niece of Dr William Van *Mildert, later bishop of Durham; they had three sons and two daughters. When she died in 1830, Gaisford replaced her on 1 May 1832 with Jane Catharine (1787–1863), a sister of Dr Richard *Jenkyns, master of Balliol College, and of Dr

Henry *Jenkyns, professor of Greek at Durham University. This second marriage seems to have been childless.

One of the many probably apocryphal sayings attributed to Gaisford was the remark, in one of his cathedral sermons, that the study of Greek literature 'not only elevates above the vulgar herd, but leads not infrequently to positions of considerable emolument' (Tuckwell, 124). Christ Church had presented him in 1815 to the living of Westwell, Oxfordshire, which he retained until 1847. A member of the royal commission on ecclesiastical revenues and patronage (1832–5), he held canonries at Llandaff and St Paul's from 1823 until his death, and a canonry at Worcester from 1825 to 1829. In 1829, after rejecting the bishopric of Oxford as a post that would have interfered with his studies, he received the golden stall at Durham. Two years later he was able to exchange this with Dr Samuel Smith for the deanery of Christ Church, taking the degrees of BD and DD in April 1831. Gaisford held the deanery from October 1831 until his death in 1855, while continuing to hold the chair of Greek, which he thus occupied for forty-three years.

In W. E. Gladstone's view Gaisford was 'a splendid scholar, but a bad Dean' (J. Morley, *Life of Gladstone*, 1, 1903, 49). Under Jackson, who was dean from 1783 to 1809, Christ Church had flourished as never before or since; but the next two deans, Charles Henry Hall and Samuel Smith, were unworthy of the post, and their inertia contributed to the decline which then set in. Gaisford tried by the enforcement of strict discipline to reverse the downward trend—John Ruskin in his autobiography gives a dramatic description of how he terrified the undergraduates—but he could not alter the prevailing trend among the sons of the nobility and gentry. Further, Gaisford's own behaviour in discouraging Christ Church men from reading for the honour schools and in refusing to allow anyone who had been a servitor to become a student did not encourage industry. Gaisford did not approve of university reform, and when almost at the end of his life the first university commission was appointed, he wrote to his eventual successor, H. G. Liddell, that he felt, in common with almost everyone both at Oxford and Cambridge, that it was 'a measure which can be productive of no good, and may eventually breed discord and disunion, and destroy the independence of those bodies' (H. L. Thompson, *Christ Church*, 1900, 197).

Gaisford did not believe that lecturing was part of the duties of the regius professor; yet it can be argued that he did more good as professor than his rival Elmsley could have done. As professor he was *ex officio* a curator of the Bodleian Library and a delegate of the Clarendon Press, and he rendered very great services to both these institutions. As early as 1806 he brought out the first catalogue of the university's collection of Greek manuscripts, adding a supplement when in 1809 the university bought the collection of Edward Daniel Clarke; later he encouraged H. O. Coxe to compile the catalogue that was still in use at the end of the twentieth century, brought up to date by N. G. Wilson. As a curator Gaisford was responsible for the purchase of the Canonici collection in 1817 and the Saibante

collection in 1820, and in 1824 he travelled to The Hague to secure important items from the Meerman sale. He seems to have taken as active an interest in the purchase of books as in the acquisition of manuscripts; the lean years in the library's classical and patristic holdings in the nineteenth century are those between his death in 1855 and the election of Ingram Bywater as curator in 1884.

Since 1795 the Clarendon Press had been bringing out successive volumes of the great edition of Plutarch by Daniel Wyttenbach, and after the fire in that scholar's library Gaisford travelled to Holland to help him rearrange his papers and finish off his work. Gaisford caused the Press to publish the edition of Plotinus by F. Creuzer and G. H. Moser (1835), to reprint Immanuel Bekker's text of the whole of Aristotle (1837), and to employ Wilhelm Dindorf to edit Homer, the scholia on the Odyssey, the Venice scholia on the Iliad, the Greek dramatists (with scholia and notes), Demosthenes (with same), the scholia on Aeschines and Isocrates, the lexicon of Harpocration, and the works of Clement of Alexandria. Gaisford encouraged J. A. Cramer to publish his *Anecdota Oxoniensia* and *Anecdota Parisina*, Henry Fynes Clinton to compile his two great works on Greek and Roman chronology, and H. G. Liddell and Robert Scott to compile their Greek lexicon.

Gaisford was a scholar of the eighteenth century, of a kind not uncommon in Germany and Holland but rare in England, and he continued to practise a kind of scholarship characteristic of that period until his death. The scientific study of an author's textual tradition was not widely prevalent before the publication of Lachmann's *Lucretius* in 1850. Before then an editor improved the text by conjectural emendation or by the use of whatever manuscript or manuscripts might come to hand, sometimes advancing beyond his predecessors by making use of manuscripts not known to previous editors. Gaisford lacked the gift of divination, and seldom improved the text of an author he edited except by the use of new manuscript material. He relied largely on collations made by others, who sometimes let him down. But with astonishing industry he made available many texts not previously accessible, often bringing new manuscripts to light. Though he lacked flair, he possessed good sense, and scholars have reason to be grateful for his massive contribution.

The list of Gaisford's publications begins with school editions of Euripides and revisions of other scholars' editions of Euripides and Cicero that contain little of his own. But in 1810 he brought out the first edition of the Greek metrical writer Hephaestion to appear since 1726 and the first competent edition of him since 1553. His subsequent edition of the Latin metrical writers (1837) was an undistinguished work, but was not superseded until forty years later. He was the first to publish a complete text of the grammatical canons of Theodosius from the only complete manuscript, but did so from an inaccurate collation.

The *Poetae Graeci minores* (4 vols., 1814–20) adds little to knowledge, but includes new manuscript material for Hesiod and Theocritus, and for the scholia on Hesiod.

Similarly his *Herodotus* of 1824 has nothing new but the recollection of a single manuscript. For his edition of Aristotle's *Rhetoric* (1820) Gaisford obtained collations of five manuscripts in Paris, one of which was later seen to be important, but he did little to improve the text. His edition of the Laurentian scholia on Sophocles (1825) and of the poet's text (1826) had the merit of making public Elmsley's collations and the part of the edition that he had finished.

More important were Gaisford's editions of the anthology of Stobaeus (4 vols., 1822), of the lexicon of Suidas (1834), and of the Greek collections of proverbs (1836); but again the value of the work resulted from the provision of new manuscripts or new collations, and not from the editor's critical acumen. His edition of the vast compilation called the *Etymologicum Magnum* (1848) was still in use 150 years later. 'It is easy', wrote the great scholar Richard Reitzenstein in 1897,

> to find fault with Gaisford's edition; the perversity, the apparatus related not to his own text but to that of Sylburg [1594], the awkward long-windedness of the annotation, the constant failure to distinguish between a source and a parallel—all this easily affects one's attitude towards the greatness of the concrete achievement, the careful demonstration of a large number of borrowings and the generally sound justification of the transmitted text.
> (*Geschichte der griechischen Etymologika*, 1897, 222)

Gaisford also brought out an edition of the Septuagint (1848), and edited patristic texts, including the *Graecarum affectionum curatio* of Theodoret in 1839 and the same author's church history (1854), the *Eclogae propheticae* of Eusebius in 1842 (the first edition of that work, and, like his edition of Choeroboscus's commentary on the Psalms which he published in the same year, still not superseded at the end of the twentieth century), the fifteen books of the same author's *Praeparatio evangelica* in 1843 and the ten books of his *Demonstratio evangelica* (1852), and his polemical works against Hierocles and Marcellus (1852).

Gaisford died at Christ Church, Oxford, on 2 June 1855, and was buried in the nave of the cathedral. His portrait by H. W. Pickersgill hangs in the hall of Christ Church. His widow, who died in 1863, is commemorated by a tablet in Wells Cathedral.

After Gaisford's death a sum of money raised for a memorial was spent on an object most characteristic of the time but most inappropriate to him, the establishment of prizes for translations from English into Greek verse and prose. As, during the 1960s, it was observed that undergraduates were no longer interested, it was decided that part should go towards essay prizes and part towards an annual lecture.   HUGH LLOYD-JONES

Sources *GM*, 2nd ser., 44 (1855), 198–200 · Barrow, *Literary Churchman* (16 June 1855) · *The Crypt*, 2 (1827), 169 · *The Crypt*, 3 (1828), 201 · *Classical Journal*, 24 (1821), 121 · J. Ruskin, *Praeterita* (1885–9), ch. 11 · W. Tuckwell, *Reminiscences of Oxford*, 2nd edn (1907) · J. E. Sandys, *A history of classical scholarship*, 3 (1908), 395–7 · V. von Wilamowitz-Moellendorff, *Geschichte der Philologie* (1927), 38 · H. H. E. Craster, *History of the Bodleian Library, 1845–1945* (1952) · H. Lloyd-Jones, *Blood for the ghosts* (1982) [ch. 6] · private information (2004)

Archives Christ Church Oxf., corresp. and papers · priv. coll., corresp. | BL, corresp. with Sir Robert Peel, Add. MSS 40254– 40568, *passim* · Bodl. Oxf., corresp. with Sir Thomas Phillipps · LPL, letters to Christopher Wordsworth

Likenesses H. W. Pickersgill, oils, exh. RA 1847, Christ Church Oxf. [*see illus.*] · plaster bust, exh. RA 1847, Christ Church Oxf.

Gaitens, Edward (1897–1966), short-story writer and novelist, was born on 26 February 1897 at 104 South Wellington Street, in the Gorbals, Glasgow, probably fourth of six surviving children of Edward Gaitens, stationer, and his wife, Mary, *née* Colwell. Gaitens was educated locally and left school at the age of fourteen, taking up a succession of unskilled jobs. During the First World War he spent two years in Wormwood Scrubs prison as a conscientious objector. He was homosexual and never married.

Gaitens began writing in his middle thirties. His first short story, 'Growing Up', was published in the *London Mercury* in 1938 on the recommendation of the playwright Osborne Henry Mavor (James Bridie), to whom he later dedicated his only novel. His first book, *Growing Up and Other Stories* (1942), was well reviewed. H. G. Wells wrote to the author, 'I do not exaggerate when I say that at least two of these stories are among the most beautiful in the English language' (Gaitens, *Dance of the Apprentices*). These ten lively, social-realist pieces depict a sensitive boy observing and responding to his Glasgow background—family, shipyard work, unemployment—and discovering transcendental moments of beauty, as in 'The Sailing Ship'. They appear to draw their inspiration from Gaitens's own experience. His long-term companion (and later literary executor) Charles Turner has been quoted as saying that 'he put his life into his writings' (Urquhart and Gordon, 203).

Gaitens lived in London during the Second World War and served for four years as a firewatcher. He returned to Glasgow after the war, working as a night telephonist. Encouraged by an Atlantic award in literature (1946) for *Growing Up*, he wrote *Dance of the Apprentices* (1948), the novel for which he is best-known today. It is episodic in structure, six stories from *Growing Up* appearing, with minor alterations, as chapters in the novel. Again the book seems to be semi-autobiographical, charting the adolescent experiences of Eddy Macdonnel and his friends, the apprentices of the title. Part 1 closes as they go gladly to prison as conscientious objectors at the outbreak of the First World War. Part 2 covers the next twenty years as they come to terms with the unsatisfactory 'world fit for heroes' to which they have returned, but the last chapter is a strikingly detailed and bitter depiction of Eddy's— or Gaitens's—experiences in prison.

Gaitens published little else during his lifetime and his work was neglected for some years, perhaps owing to the restricted scope of his subject matter, perhaps to the ephemeral nature of his true medium, the short story. During the early 1960s, renting a basement flat in Edinburgh in poor health and considerable poverty, he sublet a room to the poet George Mackay Brown, who later wrote 'I think his gift had deserted him, but he kept still a bright eye and an eager spirit … He had long abandoned Catholicism, but men must be believing something and Edward's religion was art' (Brown, 159). Gaitens died of a heart attack in Deaconess Hospital, Edinburgh, on 16 December 1966. MOIRA BURGESS and HAMISH WHYTE

Sources H. Whyte, 'Edward Gaitens: a short bibliography', 1977, Mitchell L., Glas. · electoral rolls, Glasgow, 1920–25 · G. M. Brown, *For the islands I sing* (1997) · F. Urquhart and G. Gordon, eds., *Modern Scottish short stories* (1978) · E. Gaitens, *Dance of the apprentices* (1948) [book jacket] · b. cert. · d. cert.
Likenesses photograph, repro. in *Holiday Book* (1946)
Wealth at death under £1000: probate, CGPLA Eng. & Wales

Gaitskell [*née* Creditor; *other married name* Frost], **(Anna) Dora**, Baroness Gaitskell (1901–1989), politician, was born on 25 April 1901 near Riga in Latvia, then part of imperial Russia, the eldest in the family of four daughters and one son of Leon Creditor, a Hebrew scholar and writer, and his wife, Tessa Jaffé. Her father emigrated to Britain in 1903 and, when his wife and daughter followed shortly afterwards, they settled in Stepney Green, in the East End of London. Dora Creditor won a scholarship to Coborn High School for Girls, Bow Road. She would have preferred to become a teacher, but was persuaded to study medicine, although she abandoned it when she married on 15 March 1921 Isaac (David) Frost, a lecturer in physiology, the son of Louis Frost, a mechanical engineer. A son, Raymond, was born in 1925, but the marriage ended in divorce in 1937, having continued only because of what she was later to call 'the utterly shameful and disgraceful' state of the divorce laws.

Dora Creditor joined the Labour Party at sixteen and became politically active. She met Hugh Todd Naylor *Gaitskell (1906–1963) at the Fitzroy tavern in Soho, then a popular haunt of artists, writers, journalists, dons, and aspiring politicians. Hugh Gaitskell had recently arrived in London to take up a teaching post at University College and was living a Bohemian social life in and around Fitzrovia, a milieu with which Dora Frost was already familiar. Gaitskell, who was five years younger than Dora, soon made her his confidante and, when he went to Vienna in 1933 on the eve of the climax of the counter-revolution against the Viennese socialists, led by Engelbert Dolfuss, she followed him. They lived together until marrying at Hampstead town hall on 9 April 1937.

Dora Gaitskell settled easily into domestic life. Her first child by this marriage, a daughter, Julia, was born in 1939, and a second, Cressida, in 1942. She proved an affectionate and caring mother, creating a family life of a fairly traditional kind. She was confident in her husband's love and ultimate loyalty and, in turn, became a devoted wife, a tigress in defending him from his political enemies, and committed and affectionate towards his friends.

Having been elected as MP for Leeds South East in 1945, Hugh Gaitskell was chosen as leader of the Labour Party ten years later. This was a stormy period in Labour's history, and Gaitskell was frequently the object of bitter personal attacks. His wife was fierce in her defence of her husband and was thought, even by some of his friends, to exacerbate rather than soften his more extreme sentiments. During his lifetime, her political views were not easily distinguishable from his, but after his death she

(Anna) **Dora Gaitskell, Baroness Gaitskell (1901–1989)**, by Godfrey Argent, 1970

supported the 'yes' campaign in the European referendum of 1975, despite her husband's earlier opposition to Britain's membership of the EEC. But she did not break with the Labour Party when, in 1981, most of the remaining Gaitskellites left to form the Social Democratic Party.

By that time Dora Gaitskell had enjoyed a substantial career of her own. Shortly after her husband's death, she was made a life peer in 1963, on the recommendation of the prime minister, Harold Macmillan. When Harold Wilson became prime minister in 1964, he arranged for her to become a member of the UK delegation to the general assembly of the United Nations. She became an outspoken champion of human rights, critical of the double standards of some Afro-Asian nations, but strong in her advocacy of the needs of the third world. She caused some anxiety in Foreign Office circles through her firm commitment to the state of Israel—but she was not an unthinking Zionist and was critical of the policies of right-wing Likud governments.

Dora Gaitskell was active in the House of Lords, and never afraid of controversy or of crossing swords. Plump of figure, a redhead in her earlier years, and only a little over 5 feet tall, she was spirited in her advocacy of libertarian causes and as direct as ever in personal relationships. At the time of her husband's death, on 18 January 1963, Dora Gaitskell had every reason to believe that she would shortly accompany him to No. 10 Downing Street. It would be easy to see the remaining quarter century of her life as a pianissimo coda to the excitement and expectations of those earlier years. Yet, while continuing to grieve for her lost husband, she established herself as a public figure in her own right and contributed bravely to causes which were both his and her own. She died on 1 July 1989 at her home, 18 Frognal Gardens, Hampstead, London.

WILLIAM RODGERS, *rev.*

Sources P. M. Williams, *Hugh Gaitskell: a political biography* (1979) · *The Guardian* (3 July 1989) · *The Times* (5 July 1989) · *The Independent* (4 July 1989) · personal knowledge (2004) · private information (2004)

Likenesses Suschitzy, photograph, 1951, Hult. Arch. · G. Argent, photograph, 1970, NPG [*see illus.*] · photograph, repro. in *The Guardian*

Wealth at death £27,157: probate, 6 Feb 1990, *CGPLA Eng. & Wales*

Hugh Todd Naylor Gaitskell (1906–1963), by Judy Cassab, 1957

Gaitskell, Hugh Todd Naylor (1906–1963), politician, was born at 3 Airlie Gardens, Kensington, London, on 9 April 1906, the youngest of the three children of Arthur Gaitskell (1870–1915), of the Indian Civil Service, and his wife, Adelaide Mary (d. 1956), the daughter of George Jamieson, who had been consul-general in Shanghai. They met on the boat to Japan. Hugh, known as a child as Sam, was born into a comfortable upper-middle-class English family with strong roots in the empire. After attending the Dragon School, a preparatory school at Oxford (1912–19), he was educated at Winchester College (1919–24), and New College, Oxford (1924–7), following his elder brother, Arthur, who was an academic star at both.

University teacher and Labour Party adviser For Gaitskell the general strike of 1926 was a transforming experience, which drew him to the left (he joined the Labour Party about this time). At Oxford he took part in activities in support of the strikers, and came into contact with G. D. H. Cole, under whom he studied and wrote an extended essay on chartism, arguing that a successful working-class movement needed middle-class leadership. This was published as a Workers' Educational Association booklet in 1928. After graduating with a first in philosophy, politics, and economics in 1927, he spent a year as a Workers' Educational Association tutor in the Nottinghamshire coalfield. It was a formative experience for him, both personally and politically. Personally, he lived briefly with a local woman and enjoyed his first mature relationship. Politically, he developed a less romantic view of the working class and learned much more about the practical aspects of socialism. In 1928 he was appointed to a lectureship in political economy at University College, London, and he remained there until 1939, becoming head of the department of political economy and university reader in 1938. He was adopted as prospective Labour Party candidate for Chatham in autumn 1932, but was defeated when he stood there in the general election of 1935.

Gaitskell developed his ideas, and had his first impact on Labour policy, when he moved to London, becoming heavily involved in policy groups and the political and cultural activism centred on Fitzrovia, near Bloomsbury. From its formation by Cole in March 1931, Gaitskell helped to run the New Fabian Research Bureau, which influenced the drafting of *Labour's Immediate Programme* of 1937 and the unused policy documents for the election that was due in 1939 or 1940. From 1934 he belonged to the XYZ Club, a select dining club which brought City figures, such as Nicholas Davenport, into contact with Labour's financial experts, such as Hugh Dalton, Evan Durbin, and Douglas Jay. Gaitskell absorbed the Keynesian analysis as it emerged, and with Durbin and Jay politicized its implications for policy, feeding these ideas to an often reluctant Dalton. Gaitskell's political economy entailed fiscal and monetary planning along Keynesian lines and physical planning where these policies proved inadequate. The programme of 1937 endorsed some of these ideas, but Dalton's crucial paragraph committing the party to 'plan the economic life of the nation, both industry by industry, and district by district, and on a co-ordinated whole' was dropped from the published version. There were commitments to nationalization in the programme, though not of the joint-stock banks or the steel industry, and the wording was ambiguous in places and left the party freedom of manoeuvre. Gaitskell never wavered in his conviction that the economy could and should be planned.

During his apprenticeship Gaitskell stood out from the small group of advisers gathered around Dalton in two ways. First, his economic analysis was always grounded in a political analysis, which recognized the electoral dimension of policy making but which was realistic about voter aspirations; and second, he consistently opposed appeasement, both before and after Munich. His firsthand experience of helping Austrian socialists escape from the seizure of power by a right-wing, authoritarian government in 1934, when he was studying in Vienna as the holder of a Rockefeller scholarship, ensured that he had few illusions about the nature of the enemy. Dalton became his patron, and was among those recommending him for selection as a candidate for the Labour seat of South Leeds in November 1937.

Election to parliament and office in the Attlee government On the outbreak of war Gaitskell was recruited into Whitehall, working for Dalton as a temporary civil servant in the Ministry of Economic Warfare from May 1940, and from February 1942 at the Board of Trade, which brought him into contact with the miners' leaders. His period in the civil service demonstrated his aptitude for administration. It also meant that, following his return for South Leeds in Labour's general election landslide in 1945, he was unusual among the new intake of Labour MPs in having seen Whitehall from the inside. A short but significant illness prevented his immediate inclusion in the government, but he was made parliamentary secretary to Emanuel Shinwell at the Ministry of Fuel and Power in May 1946. Gaitskell's first task was to help the passage of the Coal Nationalization Bill through the House of Commons, and he carried the brunt of the committee stage, winding up both the final debate on nationalizing this industry and the second reading debate on electricity nationalization. He also shouldered much of the ministerial burden of the fuel crisis of 1947. Jay and James Meade had been warning Gaitskell for months of the possible problems and Gaitskell had tried to get this through to Shinwell, who dismissed him as a Wykehamist who did not know the miners. Finally on 6 February 1947 Shinwell had to ask the cabinet for permission to implement daily shutdowns of the power stations in several regions, blaming the minister of transport for the crisis. Gaitskell ran the key committee that decided where the coal should go, and his administrative decisiveness and skill made a considerable impression throughout the department and the cabinet.

Gaitskell's first major task as a politician was to create and then deal with the shortcomings of nationalized industries. He believed in nationalization on grounds of efficiency, economies of scale, and rationalization of production, and considered it to be morally right. He also recognized its limitations. Although in public he defended the structure of the nationalized industries to the hilt, he was privately somewhat ambiguous about how the public corporation had been devised. The problem was that Gaitskell, like the rest of the Labour government, put far too much faith in the nationalization programme. The result could hardly be presented as the socialization of industry or indeed as having anything very much to do with socialism. Management structures and the exercise of authority in the workplace were largely unaltered. At best the change of ownership produced an enhancement of the unions' status. Gaitskell's hope for the industries was that the relationship between workers and employers would be transformed. That aspiration was never realized.

In October 1947 Gaitskell replaced Shinwell as minister of fuel and power, though he remained outside the cabinet. He was obliged to defend unpopular policies of fuel economy, including the abolition of the basic petrol ration for private motorists. Less publicized, but more crucial in the long term, was his far-sighted encouragement for the building of oil refineries and the development of a petrochemical industry in Britain. During the devaluation crisis in the summer of 1949, when the illness of the chancellor of the exchequer, Sir Stafford Cripps, left a space in the government for economic policy making, he was among a triumvirate of young ministers who were crucial in bringing to a head a debate on changing the value of sterling. Gaitskell was the rock of the group and, backed by Douglas Jay, held Harold Wilson, the president of the Board of Trade, to the line agreed on the economic benefits of the change. The prime minister, Clement Attlee, and other senior ministers took note.

Chancellor of the exchequer, 1950–1951 In February 1950 Gaitskell was promoted to minister for economic affairs, though he was still outside the cabinet, and in October 1950, when Stafford Cripps resigned, Gaitskell was appointed to succeed him as chancellor of the exchequer. This was a dramatic leap to one of the most senior positions in the government. The major feature of Gaitskell's short period as chancellor was the controversy over the imposition of National Health Service (NHS) charges, known as the 'teeth and spectacles row'. No other political crisis in Gaitskell's career better illustrated how far his greatest strength—political courage and confidence—could turn into his singular weakness, stubbornness. His budget of 1951 did not lose the Labour government the election, but it did little or nothing to help the government win. There have been election-winning budgets, but Gaitskell was not in the business of delivering a reflation package. When he presented the outline of his proposals to Attlee, the prime minister's response was that there were not going to be very many votes in it. Gaitskell replied that he could not expect votes in a rearmament year. However, with the benefit of hindsight it is too easy to see the Labour administration as one that was running out of steam: a successful budget, a unified party, and careful timing could have produced a different result in 1951.

The most damaging feature of Gaitskell's budget, which sought to raise additional taxation to meet the cost of the rearmament programme resulting from the Korean War, was the imposition of the charges on teeth and spectacles. These charges were originally accepted by the cabinet in February 1951 but the debate was reopened in the budget cabinets in April. The initial agreement was critical to Gaitskell's case but the imposition of the charges was completely irrelevant to the short-run economic well-being of the country, to its capacity for fulfilling the rearmament programme, and even to the terms of the Treasury's own forecasts. This episode raised two substantial policy issues. First, could the NHS have been sustained without the imposition of charges? Second, should charges have been imposed to help finance the rearmament programme for the Korean War, alongside an overall budget that proposed wide-ranging tax increases? Here Gaitskell represented the consensus in the cabinet as agreed in 1949 and in February 1950: welfare expenditure could not be an open-ended commitment. This assessment reflected the importance which the Labour government attached to production or supply problems as well as to welfare provision. A further question was whether these charges had to be implemented at this point, in this budget, in this way, with the possible political fall-out. Gaitskell forced the cabinet to back him. Herbert Morrison repeatedly offered a compromise whereby the budget would contain a ceiling on NHS spending but would not mention charges. Gaitskell consistently refused and made this the sticking point. He believed that it was necessary to adopt charges and that merely setting a ceiling was insufficient; politically, he needed to be backed by the cabinet to assert his ascendancy over his main political rival and the champion of the left, Nye Bevan. Attlee had little option but to back his chancellor: resignation the week before a budget by a chancellor would never have been accepted.

Though he genuinely seems not to have counted on such an outcome during the budget crisis, Gaitskell was the principal beneficiary in personal political terms. He established his position as a political actor in his own right, in effect forcing his two main opponents (Bevan and Wilson) out of the government, and consolidating his standing among the leadership, who suspected that Bevan was looking for a pretext to resign. Paradoxically perhaps, Gaitskell, supporting a rearmament package in support of an anti-communist war in Asia, emerged as the loyalist and Bevan, supporting the idea of a free health service and opposing an over-ambitious rearmament package which squandered much of the post-war recovery in export trade, was seen as the splitter. The whole affair brought Gaitskell close to a physical and emotional collapse, but it also placed him ahead of Bevan in terms of popularity with the Parliamentary Labour Party, in which loyalty counted above almost anything else.

In opposition: the Labour leadership Following Labour's defeat in the general election of 1951, Gaitskell's house in Frognal Gardens, Hampstead, became the centre for a long and successful campaign for the leadership of the Labour Party. Initially it seemed that the leadership would pass naturally to Morrison for a period before moving to Gaitskell's generation. However, Morrison's reputation had been undermined by his weak performance as foreign secretary, and his support from right-wing unions declined. A movement of opinion on the right developed in favour of someone of Gaitskell's age-group who would take a tough line against left-wing critics. As a former chancellor Gaitskell was able to lead the attack on the Conservative government's economic policies. He attacked his Conservative successor as chancellor, R. A. Butler, thereby producing evidence against those who employed the epithet 'Butskellism' to suggest ideological continuity.

In a speech at Stalybridge on 5 October 1952, following an acrimonious party conference at Morecambe in which the Bevanites effectively took over the constituency section of the national executive committee, Gaitskell

attacked communist infiltration in the party, and spoke of 'mob rule' got up by 'frustrated journalists' (Brivati, 176). His stand as a patriotic anti-communist and critic of the broader left gained him a powerful network of backers among the leadership of the right-wing trade unions, including at this time the Transport and General Workers' Union (TGWU). Although they did not have votes in the election for leader, figures such as Arthur Deakin could bring pressure to bear on their sponsored MPs. Having effectively courted union support, Gaitskell defeated Bevan in the election for Labour Party treasurer in October 1954, a victory he repeated more decisively a year later. The backing of the unions had its price, and he felt obliged to do some of what he termed the 'dirty work' (*Diary*, 401, 2 April 1955) for them. Most notably he took the lead in the unsuccessful attempt to have Bevan expelled from the party in March 1955. This toughness consolidated Gaitskell's hold over the right.

Attlee finally retired as Labour Party leader after losing the general election in 1955. In the ensuing leadership election, held in December 1955, Gaitskell won an emphatic victory at the first ballot, gaining 157 votes against 70 for Bevan and 40 for Morrison. Between 1951 and 1955 Gaitskell had consolidated his national reputation, made some strong alliances but also some powerful enemies, and often displayed a sure political touch, sense of timing, and acumen. It was a political performance that has not received the credit it deserves, for energy, for strategy, and for sheer nerve.

The first major challenge which Gaitskell faced as leader was the Suez crisis, and his political touch, timing, and judgement failed him momentarily. He has been criticized for this ever since. In his first speech on the crisis, in the House of Commons on 2 August 1956, he clearly stated his view that he would support armed intervention only if it was endorsed by the United Nations. Although this was his line throughout the crisis, it occupied only a minor part of his first speech, the emphasis of which was more anti-Nasser than pro-United Nations. The speech, which could be cited selectively to create the impression that the Labour Party was not opposed to the use of force, was even welcomed by some Conservative die-hards. But on 31 October he attacked the military intervention by Britain, France, and Israel, calling it 'an act of disastrous folly' (Brivati, 273–4) which compromised the three principles of bipartisan foreign policy: solidarity with the Commonwealth, the Anglo-American alliance, and adherence to the charter of the United Nations. When it became clear that the prime minister, Anthony Eden, had been lying to him in private, he reacted with characteristic passion and emotion, broadcasting a powerful attack on Eden (4 November 1956) in reply to an earlier ministerial broadcast. In doing so, however, he was exposed to the Conservative charge that he had changed his position in response to the clamour of his own party's left wing. Gaitskell was in fact consistent throughout the crisis, and spoke for an internationalist tradition that was deeply rooted in British politics. It was arguably at odds with the views of some core Labour voters, but he attracted support from sections of Liberal opinion who in other respects might have found a Labour Party based on trade unions and sentiments of class solidarity unattractive.

The internationalism of Gaitskell's stance on Suez and the emphasis he placed on the central role of the United Nations connected him with a broader movement in colonial development and disarmament, which had a constituency of support that was much wider than Labour's traditional strongholds. He had no sense of this during the crisis, but afterwards it tended to reinforce his instincts, which were further supported by the evidence produced by the pollster Mark Abrams, that Labour needed to become more open and less sectarian in its search for electoral support. But he presented his position badly, and his performance deteriorated because of the depth of his distaste for Eden: his call for Conservative opponents of the Suez operation to join with the opposition to oust Eden was a serious miscalculation, for it served only to rally that party behind its leader. Gaitskell committed errors during the Suez crisis and was made to pay for them in the House of Commons and in the press.

Family and private life The emotion and passion shown by Gaitskell during the Suez crisis and later in his conference speeches in 1960 and 1962 were the key to the personality that lay behind his otherwise dry public image. He was an engaging and warm person away from the political stage, with a love of dancing, an enjoyment of life, and a liking for high society. At university he had worked and studied hard with one set of friends centred on Evan Durbin. Serious-minded, politically engaged, and rather earnest, they expressed the side of Gaitskell's character that insisted that his suits were bought from the Co-op. But he had another set of friends at Oxford, including his old schoolfriend John Betjeman, who were members of Maurice Bowra's salon. Their world was altogether more frivolous and bohemian. Gaitskell was comfortable in both groups.

On 9 April 1937 Gaitskell married Dora (1901–1989) [see Gaitskell, (Anna) Dora], the divorced wife of David Frost. She was the daughter of Leon Creditor. They had two daughters. When Gaitskell first met Dora in Bloomsbury, she belonged to a group of artists and intellectuals who seemed to bring the two sides of Gaitskell's Oxford life together. From 1946 their home was at Frognal Gardens, Hampstead, which became the focus of his 'Hampstead set' of younger MPs, notably Tony Crosland, Douglas Jay, and Roy Jenkins.

In the middle of the 1950s Gaitskell met and had an intense affair with the society hostess Ann *Fleming (1913–1981), the wife of the writer Ian Lancaster Fleming. Friends and close colleagues worried both that the liaison would damage Gaitskell politically and that the kind of society life that Fleming lived was far removed from the world of Labour politics. Widely known in journalistic circles, though never reported, his attachment did not outwardly affect his marriage, but it did show the streak of recklessness and the overpowering emotionalism in his character that so diverged from his public image.

Revisionism and clause 4 The early years of Gaitskell's leadership saw some blurring of the Labour Party's factional alignments. Frank Cousins became general secretary of the TGWU in 1956; gradually this loyalist union shifted to the left. Bevan, on the other hand, became shadow foreign secretary in 1956 and broke spectacularly with the left at the party conference in 1957 with his attack on unilateral nuclear disarmament. Gaitskell's early leadership was reconciliatory; his opposition to the Suez invasion strengthened his standing within the party, not least on the left. Within this relatively consensual environment the party rethought its policies in the aftermath of a second successive general election defeat. The most controversial policy document, *Industry and Society*, was endorsed at the party conference in 1957. This supplemented the existing conception of the public corporation as the method of nationalization by more flexible forms of social ownership, including state purchase of shares in private firms. The policy was a compromise not least between Gaitskell, Bevan, and Cousins, but the superficiality of the new-found unity was quickly made clear when *Industry and Society* was loudly condemned by Bevan's wife, Jennie Lee, and by Michael Foot in the pages of the Bevanite paper, *Tribune*.

Nevertheless, the Labour Party appeared to enter the general election in 1959 more united and more confident than in 1955. Its campaign was better organized and its appeal on international and domestic questions was more positive. Yet the election came at the end of a long hot summer and in a context of national well-being. 'Life's Better with the Conservatives. Don't let Labour Ruin it' was the claim against which Gaitskell had to make his party's case. He appeared in all Labour's television broadcasts and undertook a strenuous national tour. The campaign increased his standing but an apparently innocuous comment at Newcastle arguably inflicted decisive damage on the party's chances. A pledge that in normal circumstances Labour would not raise income tax seemed reasonable in the light of the party's plans for economic expansion. But the Conservative counter-attack against 'fiscal irresponsibility' proved effective. The result showed an increase in the Conservative majority to over 100 seats.

The implications for Gaitskell and the Labour Party were potentially devastating. Commentators suggested that the party—at least in an unreformed state—would be doomed to long-term opposition due to the spread of postwar affluence and the resulting transformation of working-class experiences. In one sense Labour was seen as a victim of its own success in creating extensive welfare provision and a climate in which large-scale unemployment was politically unacceptable. Despite the defeat Gaitskell's position within the party was initially strong. Both Richard Crossman and Tony Benn thought that this credibility would allow him considerable scope to advocate party reform.

Gaitskell felt that the Conservatives' campaign had exposed ambiguities in Labour's proposals for nationalization. *Industry and Society*, with its share-buying proposals, allowed both cautious and radical interpretations. His own views on the status of public ownership within party strategy had been presented in a Fabian pamphlet, *Socialism and Nationalisation*, written in 1953 and published in 1956. This rejected the view that the achievement of a socialist society required the gradual extension of public ownership. There was no such necessity; the contributions of specific public ownership proposals to full employment, industrial democracy, and the transfer of economic power were matters not of assertion but of investigation. In effect Gaitskell rejected public ownership as the most efficient means of transforming the market economy into a socialized one. In particular he rejected the Morrisonian model. However, he retained a faith in physical controls to correct market failure and advocated flexibility about the form but not the existence of public ownership. In this Gaitskell was, and remained, a little to the left of his closest ideological partner, Tony Crosland, author of the classic statement of what became known as the revisionist case, *The Future of Socialism* (1956). Both men, however, believed that the ritual endorsement of public ownership needed to be replaced by a commitment that the Labour Party would maintain a mixed economy which operated with more efficiency and greater fairness because of government intervention, especially to stimulate demand. This position was shared in its essentials by Gaitskell's closest allies within the party. Socialism was not an end state to be achieved by gradual transformation, but the reform of institutions and practices for the more effective realization of preferred values. The roots of Gaitskell's position on these basic issues could be found in the 1930s, not least in his association with Evan Durbin, whose book *The Politics of Democratic Socialism* (1940) was a seminal text.

Goodwill towards Gaitskell within the party diminished rapidly in the aftermath of defeat. An impromptu gathering of his close associates at his Hampstead house three days after the election sparked rumours of radical change, and these inevitably fed criticism. Inept public comments by allies meant that when he addressed the postponed party conference in November 1959 the party was already divided. Faced with this challenge, he abandoned the reconciling strategy that had served him and the party well for four years. Ignoring prudential advice from some close allies, he advocated replacing clause 4 of the party constitution, which was a commitment to the public ownership of the means of production, distribution, and exchange. To urge its replacement with a new statement of party aims was to combine his pragmatic view of public ownership with a desire to revise the party's socialist commitment.

Gaitskell was receiving detailed polling evidence from Mark Abrams that the image of the party and its association with nationalization was disillusioning younger voters. He therefore decided that the party had to break with the strongest statement of that commitment, clause 4. He decided on this because he believed it would address directly Labour's electoral weakness and allow a more modern presentation of the party's message. How far the removal of clause 4, in isolation from other more wide-ranging reforms, would have improved Labour's electoral position, is debatable. What was clear was that the attempt to remove it carried obvious political costs. The removal of clause 4 aroused not just the predictable hostility of the left, but a much broader opposition. Much was pragmatic. Clause 4 was irrelevant to the party's activities; division over its removal was therefore unnecessary. Even on the right of the party there were many normally loyal supporters of Gaitskell for whom the broad outlook which clause 4 embodied, if not its precise detail, was integral to their political identity. This was true in particular of the older trade union loyalists both inside the parliamentary party and on the industrial wing of the labour movement. Gaitskell risked rejection; he was inspired by a sense that he could re-educate the party by a frontal assault on a significant, if rarely cited, party symbol, a Labour equivalent of the Thirty-Nine Articles of the Church of England.

Initially it appeared that a compromise had been reached. The party's national executive in March 1960 endorsed a new statement of aims as an addition to clause 4, not a replacement. But through the summer the verdicts of union conferences showed that this settlement would probably be rejected by that party's autumn conference. To avoid such a dénouement, the new statement was demoted to the status of a 'valuable expression'. Clause 4 remained intact and alone. Four of the six largest trade unions had in effect opposed the party leader. Pragmatism and cultural conservatism combined with ideological opposition to the proposed change; some trade union rule books contained the equivalent of clause 4.

Britain's nuclear deterrent The controversy suggested that one relationship that had dominated Labour Party politics for decades was coming under pressure. Gaitskell's rise to the leadership had owed much to the backing of significant trade union leaders. Once elected leader, he had depended on such support for his control of the party conference, an alliance that had sustained his predecessors. The clause 4 controversy demonstrated that this backing was not guaranteed. Changes in internal union politics—most notably in the TGWU—and Gaitskell's tactical mistakes had produced a rebuff. Moreover clause 4 was intertwined increasingly with a second party crisis over defence. The issues were complex. From 1959 the unilateral abandonment of Britain's nuclear deterrent became an increasingly popular cause, not least among trade union activists. Those union conferences that addressed the clause 4 controversy in spring and summer 1960 also debated the defence issue. Gaitskell and a large majority within the parliamentary party favoured defence through the NATO alliance involving both nuclear and conventional weapons. Disarmament should be multilateral. By late summer it became apparent that the party conference might reject this policy and declare for unilateralism. The evidence of a likely clash eventually encouraged Gaitskell to abandon the battle over clause 4.

The issue's complexities provided sufficient scope for face-saving compromises but Gaitskell once again favoured a combative strategy, not least against Cousins. In effect the defence issue served as a focus for broader concerns about the continuation of Gaitskell's leadership and the character of the party. As in 1951 Gaitskell sought an outcome that in his view would present Labour as a party of government, rather than of principled protest.

The Scarborough conference of October 1960 produced the dramatic spectacle of a Labour Party leader faced with the rejection, albeit narrowly, of a key policy. Two unilateralist resolutions, from the transport workers and the engineers, were carried; the official policy document on defence was rejected. Gaitskell's moving peroration that he and his allies would 'fight and fight and fight again to save the party we love' passed into party folklore. Less remembered was an echo of the Stalybridge speech, that his opponents included not just pacifists and unilateralists but fellow travellers.

As Gaitskell publicly recognized, his leadership was at stake; so was the effective operation of the party constitution. The arrival of a sizeable parliamentary Labour Party in 1906 had soon raised the question of the relationship between the Labour MPs and party conference decisions. The established constitutional interpretation emphasized the ultimate sovereignty of conference but left to MPs significant autonomy as to timing and priority. Historically, significant conflict had been avoided through the operation of an alliance between the parliamentary leadership and loyalist trade union leaders. At Scarborough in 1960, this alliance failed, and for the first time on a significant issue the parliamentary party and the conference were at odds with one another.

The crisis was addressed initially within the parliamentary party. When Wilson challenged Gaitskell for the leadership he was defeated by 166 votes to 81. Within parliament the Labour Party advanced a defence policy that effectively rejected the Scarborough decisions. Yet it would be simplistic to see Gaitskell's position as an unqualified assertion of the position of the parliamentary Labour Party over the extra-parliamentary party. He and his allies sought to reverse the unilateralist commitments of the trade unions. They were sufficiently successful, though sometimes by only narrow margins, to secure a decisive vote in favour of multilateralism at the Labour Party conference held at Blackpool in October 1961. In the aftermath of Scarborough pro-Gaitskellite activists in the constituency parties and in the unions had come together in the Campaign for Democratic Socialism, a strongly revisionist group. Its impact on the complex shifts in trade union positions was small, but its long-term significance was in influencing the selection of parliamentary candidates. Much more weight should be attached to how Gaitskell re-established his position after Scarborough, aided by the difficulties of the Macmillan government. By summer 1961 a desire for a united party was the dominant emotion and Gaitskell reverted to his earlier, more conciliatory style of leadership.

Britain and Europe This reversion was evident in his handling of the party's response to the Macmillan government's decision in July 1961 to apply for entry to the European Economic Community. Although the European issue did not fit easily into established partisan alignments, most of Gaitskell's closest allies were in favour of Britain joining; many on the Labour left and the traditional right of the party were hostile or sceptical. In summer 1962 Gaitskell shifted from a relatively non-committal position to one of opposition. He felt that any terms achievable by a Conservative government would be unacceptable. The economic consequences for the Commonwealth would be damaging; the community would be resistant to reform. Moreover Gaitskell was concerned that Macmillan envisaged the issue as a means of restructuring the political agenda, allowing the Conservatives to present themselves as a modernizing party. However, Gaitskell's conference speech at Brighton in October 1962 demonstrated a visceral response to what he acknowledged to be a complex question. Thus he characterized the prospects for a federal Europe as amounting to 'the end of Britain as an independent European state. I make no apology for repeating it. It means the end of a thousand years of history' (Brivati, 414). Summoning the images of Vimy Ridge and Gallipoli, he articulated a national identity in which a sense of empire was integral. In his last major speech he had returned to his own origins.

Gaitskell's Brighton speech dismayed many of his closest friends. 'All the wrong people are cheering', his wife observed (Williams, 736). Yet his allies remained loyal, and many critics and doubters were committed to his leadership. Although his initial handling of the European issue marked a shift back from his post-election confrontational style, his conference speech demonstrated his capacity for decisive leadership. That the speech further united the party was not the decisive reason for making it.

Legacy and historical reputation Hugh Gaitskell died at the Middlesex Hospital, London, of the rare disease lupus erythematosus, on 18 January 1963, 108 days after the Common Market speech. He left the Labour Party united and on the threshold of power, though it took the greatest performance by a leader of the opposition this century, Harold Wilson, to achieve a narrow victory. Gaitskell's legacy to the Labour Party was a style of confrontational leadership and a political approach of brutal frankness. He was intellectually and emotionally woven into the Labour Party and labour movement even though he enjoyed a social life far removed from the experience of ordinary Labour members.

The political ideas which dominated Gaitskell's life were rooted in an emotional response to the inequality he saw as a young man first at Oxford and then as a Workers'

Educational Association lecturer teaching miners working in the Nottinghamshire coalfield. His socialism was based on a desire to change the structure of society so that it promoted equality rather than inequality. The means for achieving this were of secondary importance, though he firmly believed to the end of his life that state intervention was a more efficient way of organizing society and promoting social welfare, and that the free market was wasteful. This marked him out from most Liberals, except the very interventionist phases of new Liberalism personified by Lloyd George, and it is a widespread mistake to see Gaitskell's political heritage in the progressives of the period before the First World War. The intellectual and political liberation Gaitskell offered the Labour Party on domestic policy was actually a distinctive one. It was to focus on the ends for which the party had been created and stop being obsessed with the means. He failed to teach his party the lesson, but his leadership was a heroic failure.

Gaitskell's leadership was the defining event of the post-war history of the British Labour Party. The force of his personality and the immense personal loyalty of his followers resulted in prolonged factional fighting that switched, somewhat ironically, from unilateralism to Europe. The Gaitskellites, with the important exceptions of Douglas Jay and Tony Crosland, became committed supporters of British membership of the European Economic Community and were ultimately the basis for the Social Democratic Party. His opponents formed the opposition to the community and learning the lessons of 1960–61, they dedicated themselves to taking over the constituency Labour parties and transferred power in the party from the leadership and the national executive committee to the activists. This process culminated in the Wembley conference in 1980, when even the election of the leader was transferred from the MPs to an electoral college of activists, trade unions, and parliamentarians. This 'democratization' contributed to the left's domination of the party's programme and a long run of election defeats.

Until the 1990s Gaitskell's legacy to his party appeared both negative and doubly ironic. Thereafter the picture began to change. The return to revisionism under Neil Kinnock, the attempt to break the stranglehold of the left on the apparatus of the party, and the adoption of more centrist macro-economic, foreign, and defence policies opened a space for a re-evaluation of Gaitskell's leadership. The election of Tony Blair and the launching of the 'new' Labour project speeded up this process of reappraisal. Gaitskell's revisionism was compatible with a commitment to the future of the Labour Party as an independent political entity. He did not toy with coalition or merger with Liberals but advocated, in his attempt to replace clause 4, the modernization of the Labour Party so that it absorbed the radical centre. His brand of economic intervention and his central belief in equality were not easily reconciled with economic liberalism. He did not believe that the destruction of the historic Labour Party was necessary for the formation of a revisionist Labour

Party: the integrity of the Labour Party as an independent political force was not negotiable, and he believed that the market economy was a less efficient and equitable means of distributing wealth than a mixed economy. This model of modernizing leadership was one of his legacies. Above all, however, the quality that Gaitskell brought to British politics was an almost reckless honesty and courage when he felt that an issue of principle mattered.

BRIAN BRIVATI

Sources B. Brivati, *Hugh Gaitskell* (1996) · P. M. Williams, *Hugh Gaitskell: a political biography* (1979) · *The diary of Hugh Gaitskell, 1945–1956*, ed. P. M. Williams (1983) · M. Foot, 'Hugh Gaitskell', *Loyalists and loners* (1986) · D. Marquand, 'Hugh Gaitskell', *The progressive dilemma* (1991) · J. Vaisey, 'Hugh Gaitskell', *In breach of promise* (1983) · S. Haseler, *The Gaitskellite* (1969) · G. McDermott, *Leader lost* (1972) · W. T. Rodgers, ed., *Hugh Gaitskell, 1906–1963* (1964)
Archives UCL, corresp. and papers · W. Yorks. AS, Leeds, constituency corresp. | Bodl. Oxf., corresp. with William Clark · Bodl. Oxf., corresp. with R. R. Stokes · HLRO, corresp. with Lord Beaverbrook · King's Lond., Liddell Hart C., corresp. with Sir B. Liddell Hart · London School of Economics, Tony Crosland papers · London School of Economics, Hugh Dalton papers · NL Wales, letters to Desmond Donnelly · PRO, treasury and other departmental papers · U. Sussex, corresp. with *New Statesman* magazine | FILM BFI NFTVA, Profile, 8 June 1959 · BFI NFTVA, *Reputations*, 30 Sept 1979 · BFI NFTVA, 'Walden on Gaitskell', 3 March 1997 · BFI NFTVA, current affairs footage · BFI NFTVA, news footage · BFI NFTVA, party political footage · IWM FVA, actuality footage | SOUND BL NSA, *Reputations*, T2533 W BD1 · BL NSA, current affairs recordings · BL NSA, party political recordings · IWM SA, oral history interview
Likenesses photographs, 1951–63, Hult. Arch. · P. Halsman, bromide print, 1955, NPG · J. Cassab, oils, 1957, NPG [*see illus.*]
Wealth at death £80,013 10s.: probate, 23 April 1963, CGPLA Eng. & Wales

Galbraith, Robert (d. 1544). *See under* College of justice, procurators of the (act. 1532).

Galbraith, Vivian Hunter (1889–1976), historian, was born on 15 December 1889 in Sheffield where his father, David Galbraith, who came from Belfast, was secretary at the Hadfield steelworks. His mother was Eliza Davidson McIntosh. He was the youngest of a family of four sons and a daughter. His family moved first to London, where he was educated at Highgate School from 1902 to 1906, and then to Manchester. He went to the university there in 1907 and attended the lectures of T. F. Tout, whose warm support, destined to be lifelong, was a turning point in his career. Galbraith's other teachers were James Tait and F. M. Powicke, with whom he also retained a lifelong friendship. He was later to write the notices of both Tout and Tait for the *Dictionary of National Biography*. In 1910 he obtained a first class in modern history at Manchester University and gained a Brackenbury scholarship to Balliol College, Oxford. He did his first piece of serious research for the Stanhope prize, which he won in 1911 with an essay on the chronicles of St Albans. He received, however, a severe academic reverse by getting a third class in *literae humaniores* in 1913—a subject to which he was wholly unsuited. It was a bitter blow which set back his prospect of an academic career for many years despite another first class in modern history which he obtained in 1914.

Tout immediately persuaded Manchester University to

Vivian Hunter Galbraith (1889–1976), by unknown photographer, 1966

make Galbraith the Langton research fellow for three years, and he plunged with enthusiasm into the records of the abbey of Bury St Edmunds in the British Museum. War took him by surprise. So far as he thought about it during its early months, he was against it; but not to the point of declining to join up, which he did in January 1915. He served as a company commander in the Queen's regiment with impetuous courage in Palestine in 1917 and France in 1918, being awarded the Croix de Guerre avec palme.

Galbraith returned to academic life in January 1919, first as a temporary lecturer at Manchester and then with a renewed Langton research fellowship which allowed him to live in London and pursue his former research. In January 1921 he joined the Public Record Office as an assistant keeper, and this position determined the shape of his later historical development by giving him daily access to the records of English medieval government. Meanwhile, he began his first important piece of editorial work, an edition of the Anonimalle chronicle of St Mary's, York, which appeared in 1927. In June 1921 he married a fellow medievalist, whom he had met at Manchester, Georgina Rosalie, daughter of Lyster Cole-Baker MD; they had one son and two daughters, including (Georgina) Mary Moore, later principal of St Hilda's College, Oxford.

In 1928 Galbraith returned to Oxford to succeed R. L. Poole as reader in diplomatic; he was also elected a tutorial fellow of Balliol. Thus began the golden years of his life. His effervescent vitality, and his intimate knowledge of documents, gave his pupils the feeling that this was the real thing in historical scholarship. His bold judgements on historical issues and his uninhibited comments on contemporary masters of the subject brought a breath of freedom to the most timorous pupils. In the intervals of teaching, lecturing, talking, and golfing he continued his work on chronicles and charters, including the important edition of the St Albans chronicle 1406–20, in 1937. In 1934 he published his readable and stimulating *Introduction to the Use of Public Records*. In 1937 he became professor of history at Edinburgh; in 1939 he was elected a fellow of the British Academy; and in 1940 he was Ford's lecturer at Oxford. In 1944 he succeeded A. F. Pollard as director of the Institute of Historical Research, and in January 1948 Sir Maurice Powicke as regius professor at Oxford.

Galbraith brought to all these posts the same unflagging zest. The main themes of his historical interests never changed, though he extended his range in two ways. First he undertook a fundamental reappraisal of the purpose of Domesday Book. Next he initiated a series of critically edited texts and translations of medieval sources. His detailed study of Domesday Book had its origin in the discovery of a late twelfth-century annotated copy of the Herefordshire portion of the survey in a manuscript in the Balliol Library. From this, he was led to challenge the accepted orthodoxy about the purpose and method of compilation of the great survey which had been formulated by J. H. Round. Galbraith's views were expressed in a series of works from 1942 to 1974 culminating in *Domesday Book: its Place in Administrative History*. The series of medieval texts arose from discussions with H. P. Morrison, the managing director of the Edinburgh publishing firm of Nelson, and it developed into one of the most successful attempts to make original sources of medieval history widely available to students.

Galbraith retired in 1957 and died on 25 November 1976 in Oxford, where his home was 20A Bradmore Road. He was an honorary fellow of Balliol (1957) and Oriel (1958), and he received many honorary doctorates.

Galbraith was the last important representative of the modern history school at Oxford in the period when it concentrated on the continuous institutional and constitutional development of England from the early middle ages. His talk and presence suggested his power as a teacher. His early white hairs and stooping gait would have suggested premature old age if they had not been contradicted by a general appearance of intense vitality. Next to the study of medieval charters, golf was the activity which gave him most pleasure. His features were mobile and striking, and his outspoken judgements were without malice. His family life was exceptionally harmonious and hospitable, and he found a deep satisfaction in his son and two daughters. His appearance is best preserved in photographs of which two good examples can be found in *Facsimiles of English Royal Writs to A.D. 1100*, the volume presented to him on his retirement in 1957, and in the *Proceedings of the British Academy*, 1978.

R. W. SOUTHERN, *rev.*

Sources R. W. Southern, 'Vivian Hunter Galbraith, 1889–1976', *PBA*, 64 (1978), 397–425 · JRL, T. F. Tout and J. Tait MSS · Bodl. Oxf.,

MSS Galbraith · personal knowledge (1981) · private information (1981) · *CGPLA Eng. & Wales* (1977)
Archives Bodl. Oxf., MSS | GL, corresp. with M. B. Honeybourne · U. Glas. L., letters to E. L. G. Stones · U. Reading, letters to Sir Frank Stenton and Lady Stenton · University of Manchester Library, J. Tait MSS · University of Manchester Library, T. F. Tout MSS
Likenesses photograph, 1966, British Academy [*see illus.*] · G. Spencer, drawing, Balliol Oxf. · bust, U. Oxf., modern history faculty · photograph, repro. in T. A. M. Bishop and P. Chaplais, eds., *Facsimiles of English royal writs to A.D. 1100, presented to Vivian Hunter Galbraith* (1957) · photograph, repro. in Southern, 'Vivian Hunter Galbraith'
Wealth at death £22,225: probate, 18 April 1977, *CGPLA Eng. & Wales*

Galdric. *See* Waldric (*d.* 1112).

Gale, Dunstan (*fl.* 1596), poet, was the author of a 480-line poem entitled *Pyramus and Thisbe*. Nothing is known of his life, although given his unusual name it is certainly tempting to identify him with the Dunstan, son of Edward Gale, baptized at St Giles Cripplegate in London on 7 November 1568. *Pyramus and Thisbe* was first entered on the Stationers' register on 22 July 1616, and printed in 1617 seemingly as an appendix to an edition of Robert Greene's romance *Arbasto*, which describes it as 'a lovely poem'. However, a dedication in the text 'to the worshipfull his verie friend, D. B. H.', dated 25 November 1596, suggests that the poem may have been written twenty years earlier. It was reissued, again with *Arbasto*, in 1626.

Pyramus and Thisbe is written in pentameter couplets, broken into twelve-line stanzas, the last couplet of which always has a feminine rhyme. Its florid conceits jar with unexpectedly homely language. Described by Kenneth Muir as 'both dull and bad' (Muir, 146), Gale's poem is now generally thought unlikely to have been a source for the playlet in *A Midsummer Night's Dream*. It may, however, be rather more interesting as a specimen of the Elizabethan epyllion. Influenced by Shakespeare's *Venus and Adonis* and possibly even by *A Midsummer Night's Dream* itself, it can be seen as an extreme example of the deliberately comic and self-destructively parodic aspects of the form.

MATTHEW STEGGLE

Sources G. Stanivokovic, 'Shakespeare, Dunstan Gale, and Golding', *N&Q*, 239 (1994), 35–7 · K. Muir, '*Pyramus and Thisbe*: a study in Shakespeare's method', *Shakespeare Quarterly*, 5 (1954), 141–53 · parish register, St Giles Cripplegate, 7 Nov 1568, GL [baptism]

Gale, Frederick (1823–1904), writer on cricket, was born at Woodborough rectory, Pewseyvale, near Devizes, Wiltshire, on 16 July 1823, the son of Thomas Hinxman Gale (*d.* 1864), rector of Woodborough and afterwards vicar of Godmersham, near Canterbury, and his wife, Elizabeth, daughter of Dr Poore of Andover, Hampshire. After attending the preparatory school run by Dr Buckland at Laleham, he was at Winchester College (1835–41), of which a great-uncle, Dr W. S. Goddard, had been headmaster. While at Winchester he played against both Eton and Harrow at Lord's in 1841. One of the great disappointments of his life was the decision in 1854 of the headmaster of Winchester to end these fixtures at Lord's, and Gale campaigned fruitlessly for their restoration. In 1845 he

played a few games for Kent, appearing for the county against the Gentlemen of England at Lord's. He was a hard-hitting batsman who later captained Mitcham, in Surrey, and who played his last match in 1883. Work and his writing on cricket, however, restricted his appearances.

Gale was articled to a member of the London firm of Messrs Bircham & Co., solicitors, and worked with them as a parliamentary clerk, and afterwards as a parliamentary agent on his own account. But he gradually abandoned legal business for the work of an author and journalist, usually employing the pseudonym of 'the Old Buffer'. He contributed to *The Globe and Traveller*, *Punch*, the *Cornhill Magazine*, *Sporting Life*, *Bell's Life*, and *Baily's Magazine*. Of his many books, the best-known remain *Echoes from Old Cricket Fields* (1871), *The Life of the Hon. Robert Grimston* (1885), and *The Game of Cricket* (1887). In a long life, Gale was coached by Fuller Pilch, played with Felix (Nicholas Wanostrocht), watched Alfred Mynn in a single-wicket contest in 1838, and saw the young wicket-keeper Herbert Strudwick at the Oval in 1903. Through his brother-in-law Arthur Severn he became a friend of John Ruskin, to whom he dedicated his book *Modern English Sports: their Use and Abuse* (1885). Ruskin had written the preface and the two men had watched together the Australians beating England by 7 runs at the Oval in 1882.

Gale married in 1852 Claudia Fitzroy (*d.* 1874), daughter of Joseph *Severn, with whom he had two sons and four daughters. From 1865 to 1882 he lived in Mitcham, where he helped to discover some future Surrey professional cricketers. In 1891, before going to live with a son in Manitoba, Canada, he had his collection of cricketing memorabilia auctioned at Sothebys in London. Within a year he had returned home to live in Kent, before becoming (1899) an almsman of the Charterhouse, London, where he died on 24 April 1904. He was buried beside his wife at Mitcham. *Cricket* described him as a journalist with 'a quaint and racy humour'.

GERALD M. D. HOWAT

Sources A. Haygarth, *Arthur Haygarth's cricket scores and biographies*, 14 (1895), 1010 · *Cricket* (28 April 1904) · *Wisden* (1905) · *Cricket* (9 Sept 1889), 373–4 · *Cricket Field* (5 Aug 1893) · F. Gale, *The game of cricket* (1887) · Lord Harris, ed., *The history of Kent county cricket* (1907) · T. F. Kirby, *Winchester scholars: a list of the wardens, fellows, and scholars of ... Winchester College* (1888) · DNB
Likenesses Banraud, photograph, *c.*1865, repro. in Gale, *The game of cricket* · line drawing, *c.*1875, repro. in *Cricket* (5 Sept 1889) · H. B. Collis, photograph, *c.*1890, repro. in *Cricket Field*
Wealth at death £129 4s. 10d.: probate, 26 May 1904, *CGPLA Eng. & Wales*

Gale, George Burcher (1794–1850), balloonist, is believed to have been born at Fulham in May 1794. Originally an actor in small parts in London minor theatres, he became a great favourite of the theatre proprietor Andrew Ducrow. In 1831 he went to America, where he played Mazeppa for 200 nights at the Bowery Theatre in New York, and also first encountered a balloonist (Arnand Robert). He brought back six Native Americans with their chief, Ma Caust, to London, where they were exhibited at the Victoria Theatre until their popularity declined. Thanks to Sir Augustus Frederick D'Este, who had become interested in them, Gale became coast blockade inspector in the north of Ireland for seven years on the strength of which he assumed the title of lieutenant. When he tired of this, he made an unsuccessful attempt to return to the London stage, and then took to ballooning. Gale had a balloon manufactured at the old Montpelier Gardens in Walworth, and made his first ascent with success from the Rosemary Branch tavern at Peckham on 7 April 1847. He advocated the dispatch of balloons to search for Sir John Franklin in 1849, and attempted innovations, such as a balloon with a double car, which after his death was demonstrated to the Prussian army as a bombing machine. On 8 September 1850 he made his 114th ascent, with the Royal Cremorne balloon, seated on the back of a pony suspended from the car. He descended at Auguilles, and the pony was released, but owing either to Gale's 'imperfect knowledge of the French language' (*Gentleman's Magazine*) or (the less charitable have suggested) to his intoxication, his rope holders mistakenly let go, and he was carried out of sight. His body was found several miles away on the morning of the 9 September, with 'limbs all broken'. He was buried on 11 September at the protestant cemetery at Bordeaux. He left seven children and a widow, who was also an active balloonist.

JAMES BURNLEY, rev. JULIAN LOCK

Sources GM, 2nd ser., 34 (1850), 668 · J. E. Hodgson, *The history of aeronautics in Great Britain, from the earliest times to the latter half of the nineteenth century* (1924), 236–8 · L. T. C. Rolt, *The aeronauts: a history of ballooning, 1783–1903* (1966) · private information (1889)
Likenesses lithograph, repro. in Hodgson, *History of aeronautics*, 236

Gale, Sir Humfrey Myddelton (1890–1971), army officer and administrator, was born in London on 4 October 1890, the elder son and eldest of the five children of Ernest Sewell Gale, architect, of Liphook, and his wife, Charlotte Sarah, daughter of Eugene Goddard, surgeon. He was educated at St Paul's School, and from 1908 to 1910 studied at the Architectural School, Westminster. During this time he served with the Artists' Rifles, a Territorial Army regiment, and then decided to try for the Indian army and applied for the Royal Military College, Sandhurst. He was successful and became a cadet there in September 1910.

Gale did not pass out high enough to join the Indian army, and instead was gazetted second-lieutenant in the Army Service Corps in September 1911. There followed peacetime soldiering at Woolwich and Aldershot, where he improved his horsemanship and learned something about supply and transport. During the First World War he served in France both at regimental duty and as a staff captain. He was awarded the MC and was twice mentioned in dispatches. In 1917 he married Winifred (d. 1936), second daughter of William Cross, farmer. They enjoyed a very happy marriage and had two daughters.

Between the wars Gale served at regimental duty and on the staff both at home and in Egypt. In 1934 he became an instructor at the Staff College, Camberley, where he also hunted with the drag, and while on holiday enjoyed fishing and painting. In 1937 Gale became a staff colonel in the War Office, and then soon after the start of the Second

World War he was appointed brigadier, deputy assistant quartermaster-general in 3rd corps, which went to France in 1940. During the withdrawal to Dunkirk, Gale was responsible for all administrative arrangements for 70,000 men. By his energetic leadership and practical improvisation Gale was able to keep the supply system working and morale high. He was appointed CBE in 1940 for his service.

Back in Britain, Gale became major-general, administration, Scotland, and in 1941 he was in charge of administration for all home forces. Here his cheerfulness, experience, and planning ability did much to prepare for the offensives which the joint Anglo-American forces were soon to undertake. In 1942 he was appointed chief administrative officer to General Eisenhower for the north-west African operation, and it was as Eisenhower's principal administrative expert that Gale made his great contribution to allied victory. In 1942 Gale was also appointed CB. Apart from successfully organizing support for the huge and complex operation Torch, Gale's gift for running a happy, efficient allied team was invaluable. After the successful conclusion of the north African campaign, Gale was appointed CVO (1943) and awarded the American Legion of Merit. Eisenhower then appointed him deputy chief of staff (administration) for the invasions of Sicily and Italy, both of which depended on the smooth assembly and movement of troops and stores at a time when the shortage of shipping was critical. In August 1943 Gale was created KBE.

In January 1944 Gale left allied force headquarters, Algiers, to accompany General Eisenhower to Britain for the intended invasion of Normandy. Never before in the history of warfare had there been such an administrative problem of landing and distributing supplies to support the invading forces and then moving on from the beachheads. Gale's responsibilities were to advise the supreme commander on all administrative matters and to ensure that operational plans were viable. He co-ordinated resources between army groups and generally oversaw all supply, military and civil. Until the very end of the war in Europe, Gale continued to be Eisenhower's administrative right-hand man.

With the war over, Gale was awarded the American Distinguished Service Medal, and in July 1945 he supervised distribution of resources between the allied armies. In this year he also married Minnie Grace (d. 1970), daughter of Count Gregorini-Bingham, of Bologna, and widow of Prince Charles Louis de Beauvau-Craon.

In September 1945 Gale was appointed European director for the United Nations Relief and Rehabilitation Administration. He stayed there until July 1947, when he retired from the army to hold further positions with the Anglo-Iran Oil Company. From 1954 to 1964 he was chairman of the Basildon New Town Development Corporation. It was Harold Macmillan who persuaded him to do this job and who described Gale as one of the most efficient officers he had ever known. Gale was also colonel-commandant of the Royal Army Service Corps from 1944 to 1954 and of the Army Catering Corps from 1946 to 1958.

He received foreign awards from France, Panama, and Morocco.

Gale and his second wife had made their home in La Tour de Peilz, Vaud, Switzerland, and it was there that he died on 8 April 1971. It is not only as a superbly successful administrative soldier that Gale is remembered, but as a man devoted to his family, deeply religious, a talented linguist, sportsman, and artist, a fine leader, and a sure friend. JOHN STRAWSON, *rev.*

Sources *The Times* (10 April 1971) • *Daily Telegraph* (10 April 1971) • W. D. H. Ritchie, 'Lieutenant General Sir Humfrey M. Gale KBE CB CVO MC', *The Waggoner* [journal of the royal corps of transport] (March 1982) [supplement] • personal knowledge (1986)
Archives Berks. RO, letters to Lord Glyn • IWM, corresp. with Sir Thomas Riddell-Webster • King's Lond., Liddell Hart C., papers and diaries of services at supreme headquarters allied expeditionary force • NL Wales, corresp. with Sir George Rendel
Likenesses H. Carr, oils, 1943, IWM • W. Stoneman, photograph, 1946, NPG • W. Bird, photograph, 1959, NPG

Gale, John (1680–1721), General Baptist preacher, was born in London on 26 May 1680, the son of Nathaniel Gale, 'an eminent citizen' who owned property in the West Indies. Gale was educated under Richard Claridge, presumably the Quaker schoolmaster of Tottenham, and when he entered Leiden University on 7 December 1697 he was already proficient in Latin, Greek, and Hebrew. On 3 July 1699 he received the degrees of MA and PhD; the latter, which had not been conferred within memory, was revived especially for him. He dedicated his graduation thesis, *De ente ejusque conceptu* to his uncles, Sir John and Sir Joseph Wolf. He proceeded to Amsterdam, where he studied under Limborch, and met Locke's friend Le Clerc, who became his correspondent. After returning to England he pursued his studies in private, examining particularly the earliest Christian writers. In 1703 the University of Leiden offered him the degree of DD on condition that he subscribe to the articles of Dort. This he declined on principle as a violation of religious liberty.

In 1705–6 Gale wrote a series of letters which, when published in 1711 as *Reflections on Mr. Wall's History of Infant-Baptism*, established his reputation as a scholar. William Wall, the vicar of Shoreham, Kent, had written in 1705 what was considered an unanswerable defence of infant baptism, for which convocation had thanked him. In the course of his review of Jewish and early Christian practice, Gale characteristically chided Wall for dispensing with the rules of charity over mere differences of opinion. Prominent clergymen like William Wotton applauded Gale's handling of the controversy. The biblical commentator Daniel Whitby conceded that his 'learned letters prove it to be … doubtful whether [infant baptism] did constantly obtain among the primitive Christians' (Crosby, 4.367–8). James Foster and Hubert Stogdon, two heterodox dissenters from Exeter, rejected infant baptism upon reading Gale's work. It is said that Whiston's reading of Gale's *Reflections* first led him to examine the Baptist views which he eventually embraced. It was at Whiston's home in Cross Street, Hatton Gardens, London, that William Wall met Gale for a discussion of the subject.

Gale preached his first sermon in February 1706 at Paul's Alley, Barbican. Its pastor, Richard Allen, recommended him to the congregation as a possible assistant. Although his services were acceptable, owing to a 'heavy burden of domestick affairs' and his own modesty he was prepared to offer no more than occasional sermons (Burroughs, 27). After 1715 he did assist Allen and Joseph Burroughs at Paul's Alley. He never undertook a pastoral charge and was never ordained. In addition to his work at the Barbican, he preached to Baptist societies at Virginia Street, Ratcliff Highway, and at Deptford, Kent, not far from Blackheath where he lived.

Gale was a member of Whiston's 'society for promoting primitive Christianity', which sought to discover genuine Christianity 'abstracted from all party notions and human determinations' (Whiston, 54). He acted as its first chairman from 3 July 1715 until 10 February 1716. Thomas Emlyn, the noted Arian, was the third and final chairman. Despite his association with Whiston, Emlyn, and Burroughs, who was later reputed a Socinian, no heterodoxy can be inferred from Gale's writings. His commitment to the non-subscribing principle, rather than any doctrinal heterodoxy, accounts for his taking the liberal side in the Salters' Hall dispute, as did all the General Baptists except Abraham Mulliner. John Shute Barrington's *Account of the Proceedings of Salter's Hall* was published in 1719 as an anonymous letter to Gale. To Barrington he probably owed his introduction to Lord Chancellor Peter King and the whig bishops Benjamin Hoadly and Samuel Bradford of Rochester, who commended his 'learning, candour, and largeness of mind' (Wilson, 3.249).

In spite of a good constitution Gale died in his prime. In December 1721 he was attacked by a fever, and died three weeks later. Funeral sermons were preached by Burroughs on 24 December and John Kinch the following week. He left little to his family. A subscription enabled his widow to open a coffee house in Finch Lane to support herself and her several children. Gale was tall in stature and had a striking countenance. In addition to his *Reflections*, Gale published three separate sermons, of which *A Thanksgiving Sermon Preached November 5* (1713) went through five editions that year. After his death appeared four volumes of *Sermons* (1724–6); prefixed to the first volume is a life of the author. A second edition followed in 1726. ALEXANDER GORDON, *rev.* JIM BENEDICT

Sources J. Burroughs, *A sermon preached at Barbican in London December 24 1721 upon the death of the Rev. Dr. John Gale* (1722) • J. Kinch, *A sermon occasioned by the death of the late Rev. and learned Dr. John Gale, preached December 31, 1721* (1722) • 'Life', J. Gale, *Sermons preached upon several subjects*, 1 (1726) • T. Crosby, *The history of the English Baptists, from the Reformation to the beginning of the reign of King George I*, 4 vols. (1738–40), vol. 4, pp. 366–75 • W. Wilson, *The history and antiquities of the dissenting churches and meeting houses in London, Westminster and Southwark*, 4 vols. (1808–14), vol. 3, pp. 242–9 • W. Whiston, *Historical memoirs of the life of Dr Samuel Clarke*, 2nd edn (1730), 54–8 • J. Ivimey, *A history of the English Baptists*, 4 vols. (1811–30), vol. 3, pp. 149–66; vol. 4, pp. 204, 207, 212–17 • N. Billingsley, *Sermon preached on the occasion of the death of Hubert Stogdon* (1728) • J. T. Rutt, letter, *Monthly Repository*, 19 (1824), 712–14 • J. Evans, letter, *Monthly Repository*, 20 (1825), 74 • R. Brown, *The English Baptists of the eighteenth century* (1986), 75 • T. S. James, *The history of the litigation and legislation respecting Presbyterian chapels and charities in England*

and Ireland between 1816 and 1849 (1867), 704 • M. R. Watts, *The dissenters: from the Reformation to the French Revolution* (1978), 381–2 • *The epistolary correspondence, visitation charges, speeches, and miscellanies of Francis Atterbury*, ed. J. Nichols, 5 vols. (1783–90), vol. 3, p. 858
Likenesses attrib. J. Highmore, oils, DWL • G. Vertue, line engraving (after an oil painting attrib. J. Highmore), BM, NPG; repro. in Gale, *Sermons*

Gale, Miles (1647–1721), antiquary and Church of England clergyman, was the eldest son of John Gale (1601–1686) and his wife, Joanna, daughter of Miles Dodson of Kirkby Overblow. After serving in the Netherlands and as a captain against the Scots, John Gale refused a commission from Cromwell and retired to Farnley Hall in Yorkshire where his son was born on 19 June 1647. Miles Gale matriculated at Trinity College, Cambridge, in 1663 where his first cousin, Thomas Gale (1605–1732), was his tutor. He graduated BA in 1667 and MA in 1670 and took holy orders. In 1680 he became the rector of Keighley, a post he held for forty-one years. His marriage to Margaret, daughter of Dr Christopher Stones, the chancellor of York, brought them five sons and a daughter. He was a friend of Henry Gyles (1646–1709), glass painter, and was one of the 'York virtuosi' who met at Gyles's house in York to discuss techniques and find patrons for him.

Gale was a trustee of the new school in Keighley, the foundations of which were laid in 1716, but he soon fell out with the other trustees, six 'illiterate and ill bred country fellows' (Gale, 95). He left an account of the disputes in his 'History of the free school in Kighley' (1713), a work 'freely interlarded with strong invective and personal abuse, more calculated to injure than promote good morals' (Keighley, 214). He was a man of many talents and donated to Ralph Thoresby's museum in Leeds, among other items, 'a reel with silk and silver twist wound upon it, after it was inclosed in a small Bottle; the Cork is also fastened on the In-side with three Wood Pins, by the ingenuity of the Rev. Mr. Miles Gale, Rector of Kighley' (Thoresby, *Ducatus Leodiensis*, catalogue 46). He also gave the museum a copy of his short *Account of Kighley* and his *Memoirs of the Family of Gale*. 'For the Credit of Leeds and honour of the country it is to be hoped that his memoirs of the family of Gale survived the wreck of Thoresby's Museum [in 1764] where they had been confidently deposited as in a secure place' (Keighley, 147). They did not survive, although three different versions of his *Account of Kighley* were published posthumously. His Keighley school history is lodged in Keighley Library, and two other examples of his writing survive in the British Library: a short account of a morbid premonition dreamt by his cousin's butler, and a curious piece of verse describing a conversation with the ghost of his friend Thomas Kirke.

Gale died during the night of 2 January 1721 'a pious man and fit for death how sudden ever' (*Diary of Ralph Thoresby*, 308). According to Nichols he was the author of the Latin inscription on his own monument which described him as being 'enemy to no one'. The monument was removed from the church in 1805 and lost. His eldest son, Christopher Gale (b. 1680), emigrated to the New World and married Sarah Harvey, the widow of the governor of North

Carolina. With a brief interlude as chief justice of Providence and the Bahamas, he served as the chief justice of North Carolina for over twenty years, and in 1728 was a commissioner for running the line between Virginia and North Carolina.   PIERS WAUCHOPE

Sources M. Gale, 'The history of the free school in Keighley', 1713, Keighley Library • W. Keighley, *Keighley past and present* (1879) • I. Dewhurst, *A history of Keighley* (1974) • *The diary of Ralph Thoresby*, ed. J. Hunter, 2 vols. (1830) • R. Thoresby, *Ducatus Leodiensis, or, The topography of … Leedes*, ed. T. D. Whitaker, 2nd edn (1816) • Nichols, *Lit. anecdotes* • Nichols, *Illustrations* • W. W. Rouse Ball and J. A. Venn, eds., *Admissions to Trinity College, Cambridge*, 2 (1913) • *Magna Britannia et Hibernia Antiqua et Nova*, 6 (1731), 426–7 • T. Gent, *The antient and modern history of the loyal town of Rippon* (1733) • *GM*, 1st ser., 85/1 (1815), 495–6 • BL, Add. MS 4457, fol. 45; Add. MS 4458, fol. 151 • T. D. Whitaker, *The history and antiquities of the deanery of Craven, in the county of York*, 3rd edn, ed. A. W. Morant (1878), 202–3 • *CSP col.*, 1717–18; 1728
Archives BL, holographs, Add. MSS 4457, fol. 45; 4458, fol. 151 • W. Yorks. AS, Bradford, notebooks • York Minster, notes on the parish
Likenesses M. Gale, self-portrait, pen-and-ink, repro. in 'History of the free school in Keighley', 1713, Keighley Library

Gale, Sir Richard Nelson (1896–1982), army officer, was born in London on 25 July 1896, the only child of Wilfred Gale, a merchant from Hull, and his wife, Helen Webber Ann, daughter of Joseph Nelson of Townsville, Queensland, Australia. After early years in Australia and New Zealand, the family returned to England when Richard was ten. He entered Merchant Taylors' School, London, by his own account a 'day-dreamer'. He then went to Aldenham School and in 1913 began work in the City. Keen to become a regular army officer, he attended a crammer and passed the entrance examination for the Royal Military College, Sandhurst, in 1915. From a shortened war course he was gazetted to the Worcestershire regiment in the same year.

A particular interest in the Vickers machine-gun carried Gale into a unit of what was to become the machine-gun corps. He took part in the major battles in France and Flanders from the Somme, through Passchendaele, to the defeat of the final German offensive in 1918, winning an MC as a company commander in that year. He remained in the corps until, to his vexation, it was disbanded in 1922, when he reverted to his peacetime seniority. He served in India from 1919 to January 1936, attending the Staff College at Quetta in 1930–32. In 1924 Gale married Ethel Maude Larnack, daughter of Mrs Jessie Keene, of Hove, Sussex.

Although Gale was graded above average in his annual reports and selected for the staff, he was a subaltern for fifteen years until accelerated to captain in the Duke of Cornwall's light infantry in 1930. These reports remarked upon 'a strong personality and leader with plenty of ambition … a readiness for hard work, practicality, and great keenness on the polo field'. Gale was promoted major in 1938 in the Royal Inniskilling Fusiliers but never served with this regiment, for he had become a GSO2 in the War Office and was advanced on the outbreak of war to GSO1. In 1940 he was given command of a Territorial Army battalion, the 5th Leicesters.

General Sir Alan Brooke, commander-in-chief, home forces, was much impressed by the high morale and standards of Gale's battalion. In September 1941 he promoted him to form and command the 1st Parachute brigade, raised by direction of the prime minister. His height and weight were not well suited to parachuting, but his earthy humour and direct methods appealed to the men who volunteered for this duty. With a threefold expansion of airborne forces in view, a specialist director was required in the War Office. Gale was ordered to take up this post in 1942. He was thus well fitted in practical experience, including acquaintance with the Royal Air Force and the development of glider aircraft, for command of the 6th airborne division on its formation in April 1943.

Gale's task was to make his division ready for the invasion of Europe in June 1944. No British airborne division had ever taken to the battlefield as an entity by air; the technical and concomitant tactical options had to be tried out. In the subsequent training and planning he drew shrewdly on the ideas of able subordinates, but his was the binding influence throughout the division. He made friends with the American air transport forces. The result was an outstanding operational success in the airborne assault, transcending that of the two United States airborne divisions involved.

Because of its spirit and operational skill, Gale's division was chosen to help counter the German Ardennes offensive at the end of 1944. It repeated its earlier airborne success in the Rhine crossing in March 1945. In the remaining months of the war Gale was given command of the British Airborne Corps.

After the war many of Gale's contemporaries were retired or reverted to lower permanent ranks. Valued by Field Marshal Viscount Montgomery of Alamein, he was selected for a series of senior appointments: command of 1st division in the Palestine operations (1946–7), command of British troops in Egypt (1948–9), director-general of military training (1949–52), and commander-in-chief of the British army of the Rhine and the NATO northern army group (1952–6), a unique extension of that post. Gale's first wife died in 1952, and in 1953 he married Daphne Mabelle Eveline, daughter of Francis Blick, of Stroud, Gloucestershire.

Almost two years after retirement Gale returned to succeed Montgomery as deputy to the NATO supreme allied commander in Europe. There was no command function, which fell to the American principal alone. Gale wisely made no attempt to follow his predecessor's ways; rather, he made his own reputation among the alliance, relying on his experience in training and international co-operation, and playing up to the continental image of a British general. He took pains to manifest loyalty to the supreme allied commander. These accomplishments overcame international resentment about the continuous British tenure of the post, the final achievement of a career in which a simple intelligence combined fruitfully with an instinctive understanding of those with whom he worked.

Gale was appointed GCB in 1954 (CB, 1945; KCB, 1953), KBE in 1950 (OBE, 1940), DSO in 1944, commander of the American Legion of Merit, and grand officier de la Couronne (Belgium). He was awarded the Croix de Guerre with palm (France). He was aide-de-camp (general) to the queen (1954–7), colonel, the Worcestershire regiment (1950–61), and colonel-commandant, the Parachute regiment (1956–67). Gale's second wife died after a candle overturned in her flat in Hampton Court Palace in March 1986, burning down part of the palace. Gale died in Kingston upon Thames General Hospital on 29 July 1982. He had no children.   ANTHONY FARRAR-HOCKLEY, rev.

Sources R. Gale, *Call to arms* (1968) · *The Times* (30 July 1982) · WWW · CGPLA Eng. & Wales (1982)
Archives FILM BFI NFTVA, documentary footage · IWM FVA, 'General Omar Bradley presents awards to senior British Army commanders', Army Film Unit, 13 July 1944, A700/80/182 · IWM FVA, actuality footage · IWM FVA, documentary footage | SOUND IWM SA, oral history interview
Likenesses portrait, priv. coll.
Wealth at death £20,837: probate, 12 Oct 1982, CGPLA Eng. & Wales

Gale, Roger (1672–1744), antiquary, was born at Impington, Cambridgeshire, on 27 September 1672, the eldest son of Thomas *Gale (1635/6–1702), regius professor of Greek at Cambridge and later dean of York, and his wife, Barbara (1639/40–1689), daughter of Thomas Pepys of Impington. Samuel *Gale was his younger brother. He was educated at St Paul's School, London, where his father had been high master since 1672, and at Trinity College, Cambridge, whence he matriculated in 1691, obtained a scholarship in 1693 and a fellowship in 1697. He graduated BA in 1695 and MA in 1698, and was incorporated at Oxford University in 1699, registering as a reader in the Bodleian Library on 6 March that year. On the death of his father in 1702 he inherited the family estate at Scruton, Yorkshire, and settled there intending, according to his friend and brother-in-law William Stukeley, to pursue a 'rural life of learned leisure' (Bodl. Oxf., MS Eng. misc. e. 396, fol. 33). He was plucked from this retreat on being returned member of parliament for Northallerton in a by-election of 1705. He continued to represent the same borough until 1713, voting as a whig, acting as teller on several occasions, and serving on committees which considered the exclusion of placemen from the House of Commons, the naturalization of foreign protestants, and the regulation of servants' wages. In 1714 he was appointed commissioner of stamp duties, then of excise, a post he held until 1735, when he was displaced by Sir Robert Walpole in favour of one of Walpole's friends. He retired once more from public life in 1736 and retreated to Scruton, where he spent his time running his estate, rebuilding his house, cataloguing his library, and maintaining an extensive correspondence with fellow antiquaries. Gale married Henrietta (d. 1720), daughter of Henry Roper of Cowling, Kent. Their only son, Roger Henry, was born in 1710.

Among his contemporaries Gale enjoyed a high reputation as scholar and antiquary, though his publications were few. His first was a translation into English of Louis Jobert's *La science des médailles*, a treatise designed to

Roger Gale (1672–1744), by John Vanderbank, 1722

instruct the amateur numismatist and to protect the inexperienced collector from unscrupulous dealers. Published anonymously in 1697 as *The Knowledge of Medals*, its usefulness as a beginner's guide to the study of coins and medals is attested by the appearance of a second edition in 1715. Gale himself collected coins and bequeathed his fine collection to Cambridge University. His second publication was an edition of his father's commentary on the Antonine itinerary, with additional notes, in 1709. It provided a summary of the available evidence for the course of roads and the position of posting stations in Roman Britain. His own notes linked the historical text to topographical evidence surviving in the landscape, and provided his contemporaries with a framework within which to conduct their own archaeological researches. Their enthusiasm for so doing is illustrated in the survival of many annotated copies of Gale's work. His edition of the *Itinerary* was followed by an essay tracing the course of the four main Roman roads in Britain, published as an appendix in the sixth volume of Thomas Hearne's edition of Leland's *Itinerary* (1712). Gale's last publication of any size was an edition of a twelfth-century register of the honour of Richmond from the Cotton Library, accompanied by a long appendix of important early charters. It was published in 1722 under the auspices of the Society of Antiquaries, of which he was first vice-president. He was for many years treasurer of the Royal Society, and the papers he contributed to its *Philosophical Transactions* reflect his interest in field antiquities. He was also an active member of both the Gentlemen's Society of Spalding and the Brazen Nose Society of Stamford.

Although Gale's publications were slight, compared with those of his father and of the great antiquaries of the previous generation, his correspondence on antiquarian matters was voluminous. Many of his letters survive in library collections. He himself copied over a hundred letters received or sent by him into three quarto volumes (Bodl. Oxf., MSS top. gen. d. 74–6), but the bulk was made known through publication, first by John Nichols in *Bibliotheca Topographica Britannica* (vol. 3, *Reliquiae Galeanae*, 1790), subsequently in several volumes of Nichols's *Literary Anecdotes*, and finally in volumes 73, 76, and 80 of the Surtees Society, edited by W. C. Lukis as *The family memoirs of the Rev. William Stukeley M.D. and the antiquarian and other correspondence of William Stukeley, Roger and Samuel Gale etc.* (1882, 1883, and 1887).

Gale's correspondence provides a vivid picture of the antiquarian pursuits of country gentlemen and clergy energetically travelling around the country (as Gale did frequently, often in Stukeley's company), scouring their neighbourhood for traces of ancient times, meticulously recording inscriptions, monuments, artefacts, and sites and enthusiastically speculating on the significance of each other's finds. It reveals Gale as an indefatigable receiver and purveyor of antiquarian information and one of the principal participants in the learned letter-writing which was so notable a feature of the revival of antiquarian studies in the first half of the eighteenth century.

John Nichols in the second volume of his *Bibliotheca Topographica Britannica* (1781) hailed Gale as 'one of the most learned men of his age'; but this verdict did not survive the passage of time. D. C. Douglas, contrasting Gale with his more scholarly father, described him as a 'cultured country gentleman' who attained to 'greater distinction than he deserved' (Douglas, 174). Gale's contribution to antiquarian studies does not lie in the scholarly editing of historical texts, except indirectly as he made his fine collection of manuscripts available to others in his lifetime, and presented them to Trinity College, Cambridge, in 1738. His correspondence places him firmly in the ranks of the new generation of antiquaries, who turned their attention from texts to topography and antiquities in the field, recorded much that has since been lost, and laid the foundations for the development of scientific archaeology. He died at Scruton on 25 June 1744 and was buried in the churchyard there.

MARY CLAPINSON

Sources M. Clapinson, 'Roger Gale, an eighteenth-century antiquary', *Bodleian Library Record*, 12/2 (April 1986), 106–18 · Nichols, *Lit. anecdotes*, 4 (1812), 543–50 · J. Nichols, ed., *Bibliotheca topographica Britannica*, 3 (1790), no 2, *Reliquiae Galeanae* · D. C. Douglas, *English scholars, 1660–1730*, 2nd edn (1951) · Gale, Roger, HoP, *Commons, 1690–1715* [draft] · M. R. James, *The western manuscripts in the library of Trinity College, Cambridge: a descriptive catalogue*, 4 vols. (1900–04), vol. 3 · S. Piggott, *William Stukeley: an eighteenth-century antiquary* (1950) · William Stukeley's eulogium, read to Society of Antiquaries 5 June 1760, Bodl. Oxf., MS Eng. misc. e. 396 · Venn, *Alum. Cant.* · *DNB*

Archives AM Oxf., letters [transcripts] · Bodl. Oxf., corresp. and papers · Trinity Cam., MSS.O | Bodl. Oxf., MSS Top.gen.d.74–76 ·

Bodl. Oxf., letters to T. Hearne • Bodl. Oxf., corresp. with W. Stukeley, MSS Eng. lett c.9–10 • NA Scot., corresp. with J. Clerk

Likenesses J. Vanderbank, oils, 1722, S. Antiquaries, Lond. [see illus.] • I. Whood, oils, 1738, Trinity Cam. • J. Van den Berghe, stipple, 1799 (after unknown portrait), BM, NPG • oils, Old Schools, Cambridge

Gale, Samuel (1682–1754), antiquary, was born on 17 December 1682 in the parish of St Faith, London, the youngest surviving son of the four sons and one daughter of the antiquary Thomas *Gale (1635/6–1702), dean of York, and his wife, Barbara Pepys (1639/40–1689), daughter of Thomas Pepys of Impington, Cambridgeshire. He was baptized on 20 December, with the diarist Samuel Pepys as one of his godfathers. He was educated at St Paul's School, London, where his father was then high master, but his father's death in 1702 prevented him from following his brother Roger *Gale (1672–1744) to Trinity College, Cambridge. Instead, about 1702 he obtained a position in the custom house in London, where he became 'searcher of the books and curiosities imported into this kingdom, and land surveyor of the customs' (*GM*). Like his father and his brother Roger, Samuel Gale was a keen antiquarian, with a particular interest in ecclesiastical history. At his death his manuscripts included a history of York Minster, but the only work published in his lifetime was *A History of Winchester Cathedral* (1715). He made a 'Tour through several parts of England' in 1705, including Oxford, Stonehenge, Salisbury, and Sussex, which, together with several other pieces by him and his brother, appeared as 'Reliquiae Galeanae' in the third volume of John Nichols's *Bibliotheca Topographica Britannica* (1790).

Gale was one of the founders of the revived Society of Antiquaries in January 1718, and served as its first treasurer until 1739–40. With his brother Roger he accompanied their friend the antiquarian Dr William Stukeley on the latter's first visit to the Avebury stone circle in Wiltshire in 1719. In 1739 Stukeley would marry Gale's sister Elizabeth. Samuel was also a close friend of Dr Andrew Coltee Ducarel, with whom he made excursions every August for a number of years into the English countryside exploring antiquities, taking William Camden's *Britannia* as a guide. The two men travelled *incogniti*, journeying between 15 and 20 miles a day, staying in inns from which they would explore the surrounding countryside. They were accompanied only by their footman and coachman, the latter being directed, in the spirit of his employers' playful anonymity, to tell any enquirers 'it was *a job*; and that he did not know their names, but that they were civil gentlemen' (Nichols, *Lit. anecdotes*, 6.402). He amassed what Nichols described as 'a very valuable library' (Nichols, *Bibliotheca Topographica Britannica*, xiii), as well as a collection of prints by Wenceslaus Hollar, Collet, and others, and assisted the researches of other antiquarians, including Francis Drake, the author of *Eboracum* (1736), and Thomas Hearne of Oxford.

Although Stukeley frequently encouraged his brother-in-law to purchase a house in the countryside, Gale lived his entire life in London, residing at a number of different lodgings in the city, including at Bedford Row, Holborn,

with a 'Mr Pyke a watchmaker', and at Gray's Inn. His brother Roger ran the family estates in Scruton, Yorkshire, where Samuel was often a visitor. He died, unmarried, of a fever on 10 January 1754 in his lodgings at The Chicken-house, Hampstead. He was buried on 14 January 1754 in the burial-ground, near the Foundling Hospital in London, belonging to St George the Martyr, Queen Square, Bloomsbury, where Stukeley was rector. Ducarel described him as a 'worthy and amiable' man (*DNB*), while Nichols referred to him as 'a man of great learning and uncommon abilities' (Nichols, *Lit. anecdotes*, 4.552).

DAVID BOYD HAYCOCK

Sources *Reliquiae Galeanae, or, Miscellaneous pieces by the late learned brothers Roger and Samuel Gale* (1781), no. 2, pt 1 [3/2] of *Bibliotheca topographica Britannica*, ed. J. Nichols (1780–1800) • Nichols, *Lit. anecdotes* • *GM*, 1st ser., 24 (1754), 47 • S. Gale and W. Stukeley, correspondence, Bodl. Oxf., MS Eng. misc. c. 538 • *DNB* • *The family memoirs of the Rev. William Stukeley*, ed. W. C. Lukis, 3 vols., SurtS, 73, 76, 80 (1882–7)

Archives Bodl. Oxf., corresp. and papers • Bodl. Oxf., MS collections | Bodl. Oxf., corresp. with Stukeley and others

Likenesses school of G. Kneller, oils, S. Antiquaries, Lond. • attrib. I. Whood, oils, S. Antiquaries, Lond.

Gale, Theophilus (1628–1679), ejected minister and theologian, was born at Kingsteignton, Devon, where his father, Theophilus Gale DD (d. 1639), was vicar as well as a prebendary of Exeter Cathedral. His mother, Bridget (née Walrond), was the elder Gale's second wife. Gale was educated by a private tutor and at a grammar school. In 1647 he entered Magdalen Hall, Oxford, as a commoner, and in 1648 was appointed a demy of Magdalen College, Oxford, by the parliamentary visitors. He graduated BA on 17 December 1649, and in 1650 was appointed by the visitors a fellow of the college. Gale proceeded MA on 18 June 1652. Also in 1652 he was logic lecturer at Magdalen, and in 1657 he was junior dean of arts and in 1658 senior dean of arts. Gale adopted the Independency and high Calvinism of Thomas Goodwin, then the president of Magdalen, and of Goodwin's close associate John Owen, vice-chancellor of Oxford. Gale preached frequently within the university. In November 1657 he was appointed preacher in Winchester Cathedral, while retaining his fellowship. At the Restoration in 1660 he lost his position at Winchester, and his fellowship reverted to its prior ejected incumbent.

Not conforming to the new order in the Church of England, in early 1662 Gale took a position (at £40 per annum) as tutor to the sons of Philip, fourth Baron Wharton, who had been a supporter of parliament against the king. By August 1662 Gale was settled with his pupils in Caen, France, where they attended the protestant college, and there Gale became acquainted with the Huguenot scholar Samuel Bochart. In July 1664 Gale was dismissed as a tutor because of his strictness. He travelled on the continent for a while, but by late 1665 he had returned to Wharton's estate at Quainton, Buckinghamshire. In 1666 he went to London, where he had deposited his manuscripts, arriving at the time of the great fire to find that they had been preserved. At Newington Green he established an academy for the education of the children of dissenters, eventually training some for the ministry (among his pupils was a son of his cousin John Rowe, Thomas Rowe, who succeeded Gale as head of the academy). Gale also assisted John Rowe in the latter's Independent congregation in St Andrew's, Holborn. When John Rowe died in 1677 Gale succeeded him as pastor of the congregation with Samuel Lee as co-pastor. In May 1670 Gale was fined 5*s.* for attendance at an illegal meeting. He died suddenly at Newington Green in February 1679 and was buried in Bunhill Fields. He bequeathed much of his estate to various ejected ministers (a group of beneficiaries including John Owen and Thomas Goodwin) and to a trust for the education of needy nonconformists preparing for the ministry, while almost 1000 books, including a valuable collection of Hebraica, went to Harvard College. Gale never married.

Gale's writings were published between 1669 and his death. Several of them were devotional in character: *Theophilie, or, A Discourse of the Saints Amitie with God in Christ* (1671) cited classical authors on friendship and then advised friendship with God in Christ, and *The Anatomie of Infidelitie* (1672) analysed the sin of unbelief. In *A Discourse of Christ's Second Coming* (1673) Gale turned from the political eschatology characteristic of puritans in the 1640s and 1650s to the encouragement of conversion and a holy life in readiness for the last day. Gale also contributed to the dissenting literature detailing holy lives: his preface to a biography of his uncle, a layman and magistrate, *The Life and Death of Mr. John Rowe of Crediton in Devon* (1673), asserted that the reality of God's grace was illustrated by such lives. Gale himself recounted *The Life and Death of Thomas Tregosse* (1671), a Cornwall minister whom he had converted.

In other writings Gale joined contemporary theological discussions. *The True Idea of Jansenisme* (1669), with a commendatory preface by John Owen, was probably the first English book on the subject. It presented the Jansenists, like Calvinists, as opponents of Pelagian heresy, which Gale thought the Arminians had revived. In other writings too Gale cited Cornelis Jansen, whose thought influenced him. Gale also edited for publication and wrote a prefatory summary for a work by William Strong, *A Discourse of the Two Covenants* (1678), illustrating Gale's commitment to double-covenant federal theology.

However, Gale's reputation as one of the great savants of his time rested on his monumental *The Court of the Gentiles*, published in four parts and four volumes between 1669 and 1678, with revised editions of various portions of it appearing in 1672, 1676, and 1682. This learned work was inspired by Gale's reading of Hugo Grotius, and argued, especially on the basis of philological evidence, that all truth and knowledge had been derived from the ancient Jews, the gentiles having (metaphorically) resorted to the court of the gentiles in the Jewish temple for it. Eventually the gentiles, through sin, corrupted this knowledge. Gale's theory thus accounted both for such truth as the gentiles had and for its imperfections. Accordingly, the adumbrations of divine truth in Plato, Pythagoras, and Zoroaster were survivals of the original truth first known by Adam. Gale regarded Greek and other myths as garbled versions of biblical history. Some of the ancient sages were in fact just other names for biblical figures, the Greek Atlas being Enoch, and Hermes Trismegistus either Joseph or Moses, or both (Gale ignored Isaac Casaubon's disproof of the antiquity of the hermetic literature). The arts and sciences also traced back to biblical sources: geometry came from the division of the land of Canaan, navigation from Noah, and architecture from Solomon's temple. Gale followed the Hellenistic Jews Philo and Josephus in believing that Greek philosophy was borrowed from the writings of Moses. Even the philosophy of the Brahmans and Buddhists had been derived from the Jews. For Gale the Phoenicians often served as the middlemen in this cultural diffusion.

This mélange of ideas was not new to Gale: it reflected the Euhemerism (that is, the argument that the gods of antiquity were deified men and women) and 'ancient theology' which had been employed apologetically by the church fathers and which had later flourished as a legitimation of the ancient wisdom for Renaissance thinkers such as Marsilio Ficino, also a source for Gale. Gale too used these ideas to legitimate ancient pagan books, but his version of 'ancient theology' had a high Calvinist intent: it not only proved that all truth had come through divine revelation, but also exalted grace and divine sovereignty and took account of the disastrous impact of original sin.

The recommendation and presentation of Platonism in the latter part of *The Court of the Gentiles* was another purpose of this work. True philosophy, Gale thought, went back to Adam's naming of things under God's direction, which established correspondences between the essences of things and their names, all the arts and sciences being originally in the divine mind and then communicated through Hebrew, the primordial language. Gale considered his to be a reformed Platonism, for true philosophy had been corrupted by the sin of pride, and needed to be cleansed of many errors, especially those that had crept in through Aristotle, the Gnostics, and the medieval scholastics. Gale's Platonism paralleled the revival of Platonism among the Cambridge Platonists and such fellow protestant dissenters as John Howe, although he criticized the latter for being insufficiently predestinarian. Modern philosophers such as Descartes and Gassendi, Gale thought were mere imitators of Plato. Much of the latter portion of *The Court of the Gentiles* was also devoted to moral theology, and in this Gale rejected the Aristotelian notion of natural virtues, since true virtue could only result from divine grace.

Several Latin treatises of Gale, *Ideae theologiae* (1673) and *Philosophia generalis* (1676) dealt with aspects of what he had treated in *The Court of the Gentiles*. When he died Gale had finished a lexicon of the Greek New Testament as far as 'iota'.

Gale, highly regarded by his contemporaries for his erudition, exemplifies the systematizing impulse in seventeenth-century learning. His unifying scheme for all knowledge enabled him to retain and yet criticize the culture of the ancient pagans. That he did this as a Calvinist theologian and spiritual writer illustrates the variety of Calvinist expression at his time. He also illustrates the persistence of Platonism in seventeenth-century England.

DEWEY D. WALLACE, JUN.

Sources E. Calamy, ed., *An abridgement of Mr. Baxter's history of his life and times, with an account of the ministers, &c., who were ejected after the Restauration of King Charles II*, 2nd edn, 2 vols. (1713), vol. 2, pp. 64–6 • E. Calamy, *A continuation of the account of the ministers … who were ejected and silenced after the Restoration in 1660*, 2 vols. (1727), vol. 2, pp. 97–8 • Calamy rev. • Foster, *Alum. Oxon.* • DNB • *The Rev. Oliver Heywood … his autobiography, diaries, anecdote and event books*, ed. J. H. Turner, 2 (1883), 258–9 • Wood, *Ath. Oxon.*, new edn, 2.1149–51 • Bodl. Oxf., MSS Rawl. letters 49, 52, 54 • N. Fiering, *Moral philosophy at seventeenth-century Harvard* (1981), 279–94 • D. D. Wallace, *Puritans and predestination: grace in English protestant theology, 1525–1695* (1982), 179–80 • S. E. Morison, *The tercentennial history of Harvard College and University, 1636–1936*, 3–4: *Harvard College in the seventeenth century* (1936), 290–91 • J. W. Ashley Smith, *The birth of modern education: the contribution of the dissenting academies, 1660–1800* (1954), 41–6 • J. R. Bloxam, *A register of the presidents, fellows … of Saint Mary Magdalen College*, 8 vols. (1853–85), vol. 2, pp. 204–7 • will, PRO, PROB 11/360, sig. 70 • A. G. Mathews, 'The Wharton correspondence', *Transactions of the Congregational Historical Society*, 10 (1927–9), 53–65
Archives Bodl. Oxf., MSS Rawl. letters 49, 52
Wealth at death £281; almost 1000 books, many valuable, given to Harvard College; residue to fund to educate poor scholars: will, PRO, PROB 11/360, sig. 70

Gale, Thomas (*c*.1507–1567), surgeon, was born in London, one of at least three sons. In his youth he served a lengthy apprenticeship under Richard Ferris, an important London barber-surgeon, who later served as sergeant-surgeon to Elizabeth I. By the time he was twenty Gale was practising independently. He worked primarily in London, though he served as a surgeon with the army of Henry VIII at the siege of Montreuil in September 1544, and under Philip II of Spain in the battle of St Quentin on 10 August 1557.

Gale was closely associated with the London Company of Barber-Surgeons, probably from its foundation in 1540. He is mentioned as holding the office of warden and master in 1555 and 1561 respectively. The company also received a legacy in Gale's will of 1567 on condition that its masters carried his corpse to church on the day of his funeral. Gale's defence of the interests of barber-surgeons is evident as early as 1542 when he sued and was counter-sued by London empirics concerning their remedies. His most enduring contribution to the profession was his *Certaine Workes of Chirurgerie* which was published in 1563. Dedicated to Lord Robert Dudley it consisted of four separate works, each of which was intended to teach barber-surgeons about a specific aspect of their profession. The first, 'The institution of chirurgerie', presents the theory of surgery in the form of a dialogue with Thomas Yates, a student of surgery, Gale, and his longtime friend and fellow member of the company, John Field. The second work, 'The enchiridion of surgery', is a treatise on surgical practice concerned with wounds, fractures, and dislocations. It also includes details of a powder to staunch bleeding. Gale claimed that he and a Master Pierponte had invented the powder and that it eliminated the need for cauterizing irons. Gale's claim was disputed on both counts: the powder was said to have been invented by another, and his fellow barber-surgeon William Clowes claimed the powder generated gangrene. The third treatise concerns gunshot wounds, in which he shows that gunpowder is not a poison. The fourth is an antidotary or collection of prescriptions.

Three years later Gale published translations and abridgements of the Latin versions of Galen's *De naturalibus facultatibus* and *De humoribus prater naturam*, though later commentators question whether Gale's Latin was good enough to undertake the task. Gale was said to have partially written treatises on tumours and ulcers, a new translation and commentary on a work of the French physician Guy de Chauliac (*d*. 1368), and several other unidentified works. Gale also planned to produce a herbal specifically for surgeons. Gale's death in 1567 appears to have prevented the completion of any of these projects.

Gale made his will on 6 August 1567 and was buried at St Dionis Backchurch, London, nine days later. He was survived by his wife, Joan, and his son Thomas, who also became a barber-surgeon, admitted to the company in 1597. The family was evidently living in straitened circumstances. Joan, the principal beneficiary of the will, received a house in the parish of St Dionis Backchurch, London. The largest cash legacy, a paltry £4, was divided between Gale's brothers, William and Roger. Gale's books and manuscripts appear to have been given in lieu of unpaid wages; 220 copies of his printed works went to a literate maidservant, Katherine, and all his 'written books of surgery in the English tonge and all the pamflitts and peces of written books or any written books of Surgery wherin any englishe is written, bundells of Examinations etc' went to a former manservant (PRO, PROB 11/49, sig. 255). While writing and the practice of surgery may have generated only modest returns for Gale during his lifetime, his complaints about unregulated practice, his published works, and his ambitious plans for further works to aid barber-surgeons demonstrate the importance of his role in the struggle of his profession to establish itself and to raise the standards of English surgical practice.

MAX SATCHELL

Sources T. Gale, *Certaine workes of chirurgerie* (1563) • T. Gale, *Certaine workes of Galens called Methodus medendi* (1586) • PRO, PROB 11/49, sig. 255 • *LP Henry VIII*, 17.1225 • J. L. Chester, ed., *The reiester booke of Saynte De'nis Backchurch parishe … begynnynge … 1538*, Harleian Society, register section, 3 (1878), 190 • S. Young, *The annals of the Barber-Surgeons of London: compiled from their records and other sources* (1890), 5–6 • N. Moore, *The history of St Bartholomew's Hospital*, 2 vols. (1918) • V. Nutton, *From Democles to Harvey* (1988)
Likenesses woodcut, 1563, BM, NPG; repro. in Gale, *Certaine workes of chirurgerie*, frontispiece • woodcut, 1563, Wellcome L.
Wealth at death negligible: will, PRO, PROB 11/49, sig. 255

Gale, Thomas (1635/6–1702), dean of York and antiquary, was born at Scruton in the North Riding of Yorkshire, the only surviving child of Christopher Gale of Scruton and his wife, Frances Conyers, of Holtby, also in Yorkshire. Educated at Westminster School, he was admitted as a king's scholar to Trinity College, Cambridge, in 1655, graduating BA in 1659 and proceeding MA in 1662 (a degree incorporated at Oxford in 1669). He became a fellow of his college in 1659 and was tutor there from 1663 to 1672. He contributed verses to the university's volumes on the death of Oliver Cromwell in 1658 and the deaths of Mary, princess of Orange, and Henry, duke of Gloucester, in 1661. He was ordained in 1666 and became vicar of Barrington, Cambridgeshire, the following year.

Gale's record as a scholar earned him the regius professorship of Greek at Cambridge in 1672, a post he resigned in October that year to become high-master of St Paul's School, London. He married Barbara (1639/1640–1689), daughter of the physician Thomas Pepys of Impington; the first of their eleven (or more) children was born on 27 September 1672. She was buried in St Augustine with St Faith, London, on 5 June 1689, aged forty-nine. Samuel Pepys was her cousin, and he and Thomas Gale became good friends; Pepys greatly respected Gale for his company and his intellectual interests. In 1675 Gale proceeded BD and DD at Cambridge; the following year he was appointed a prebendary of St Paul's Cathedral. He was responsible for the Latin inscription on the monument (1671–7) commemorating the great fire of London. Gale remained head of St Paul's School until 1697, during which time its reputation grew, attracting the sons of the nobility and gentry to be educated there, notable pupils including the astronomer Edmond Halley and Samuel Knight, author of the *Life of Dr John Colet, Dean of St Paul's* (1724).

Gale was an active member of the Royal Society, to which he was elected in December 1677, serving as its secretary between 1679 and 1681 and again from December 1685 to 1693, this time with Edmond Halley as assistant secretary. Like others, Gale failed to match the high standards set by the society's first secretary, Henry Oldenburg, and on his appointment he had to be instructed on the kind of information to send correspondents. Gale has been described as one of the society's 'active nucleus', and although his activity dwindled after the mid-1680s, he always retained his interest in its affairs, being made vice-president in 1690.

In September 1697, with the backing of Archbishop John Sharp, Gale was appointed dean of York. He had retained strong links with his county, in 1688 buying the manor and advowson of his native Scruton. As early as 1679 it appears that he had plans to 'perfect' the life of St Wilfrid, the seventh-century bishop of York. Nevertheless, while York provided scope for his antiquarian interests, Gale rapidly came to regret the move, complaining to Pepys of his social and intellectual isolation. "'Tis realy too long … to tell you what an impertinent, unscholarlike, unstudying, bookeless sort of life I live here', he moaned in March 1699 (*Private Correspondence*, 1.170). 'We often desire what we shortly dislike', he wrote in December the following year, 'I am here less able to correspond or study than I was at St Paul's' (ibid., 2.146). His hope of returning to Cambridge as master of Trinity was dashed when the place went to Richard Bentley in February 1700.

Nevertheless, his private complaints belie Gale's

achievements at York. As at St Paul's School, the intellectual and scholarly distinction of the chapter quickly improved under his care. Noted for his hospitality, Gale was also an able administrator, obtaining for the deanery in 1699 the dean's right to be a canon residentiary. He was also keen to protect his own position; in March 1701 he was offered the prebend of Botevant by Sharp, a position he accepted but then quickly declined on the realization that if he obtained a prebend or living he would automatically forfeit the deanery. During his time at York, Gale developed a strong interest in the cathedral, compiling a three-part manuscript history from its foundation to his own time. In this he generously put aside his dislike of parliamentarians in praising Sir Thomas Fairfax for 'strictly and vigourously' forbidding soldiers to damage the building during the civil war, 'an Honourable and Noble act, which few, if any of the Rest in that Cause had so much as conscience to consider' (Bodl. Oxf., MS Gough Yorks. 22, fol. 37). Similarly, by allowing the leases on the shops and dwellings attached to the south side of the cathedral to expire, Gale 'cleaned this part of the church from the scurf it had contracted by the smoke proceeding from these dwellings' (Drake, 486), while in the north aisle of the choir he erected a large tablet 'with the names and dates of the several founders and benefactors to this church' (ibid., 527).

Gale's numerous published and unpublished works pay testimony to his wide-ranging interests and the breadth of his knowledge. His most important works as a classicist include *Opuscula mythologica, ethica et physica* (1671), *Historiae poeticae scriptores antiqui* (1675), and *Rhetores selecti* (1676). His *Scriptores quindecim* (1691) contains the first published version of Nennius's eighth-century *Historia Brittonum*, and his transcription with emendations of John Leland's *Itinerary* was used by Thomas Hearne in his nine-volume edition of 1710–12. Gale's interest in prehistory is reflected in his additions to John Aubrey's *Monumenta Britannica*, and in Roman antiquities not only in *Antonini iter Britanniarum*, published posthumously in 1709, but in the many manuscript notes he left, including those made after his move to York, which were drawn upon by Francis Drake in his *Eboracum* (1736). Throughout his adult life Gale corresponded regularly (often in Latin) with other scholars and antiquaries at home and abroad, including Edward Bernard, John Evelyn, Ralph Thoresby, Thomas Smith, William Worth, Paulus Baldri, and Jean Mabillon.

Gale died at York, aged sixty-six, on 7 April 1702 and was buried on 15 April in the middle of the cathedral choir, where he is commemorated by a plain tomb slab behind the high altar. He was survived by four sons, two of whom, Roger *Gale (1672–1744) and Samuel *Gale (1682–1754) themselves became notable antiquaries; and by a daughter, Elizabeth (1687–1757), who in 1739 became the second wife of William Stukeley. Roger inherited his father's vast library (catalogued in *Catalogus librorum*), which he in turn donated to Trinity College, Cambridge, in 1738, the college already having acquired a large collection of Arabic, Persian, and Turkish manuscripts direct from Gale in 1697. Apart from editing *Antonini iter Britanniarum*, Samuel Gale published his father's *Sermons Preached upon Several Holydays Observed in the Church of England* (1704).

Gale's interests are characteristic of the late seventeenth-century scholarly community, his scientific, theological, and historical pursuits typical of a period when it was still possible to 'move with relative ease from one kind of intellectual enterprise to another' (B. Shapiro, *Probability and Certainty in Seventeenth-Century England*, 1983, 152).

NICHOLAS DOGGETT

Sources M. Hunter, *The Royal Society and its fellows, 1660–1700: the morphology of an early scientific institution*, 2nd edn (1994), 45, 81, 82, 89, 246 • Venn, *Alum. Cant.* • M. Hunter, *Establishing the new science: the experience of the early Royal Society* (1989), 155 • T. Gale, 'Historicall view of the severall foundations and buildings of the cathedrall church of York', Bodl. Oxf., MS Gough Yorks. 22, fols. 18–42 [copy made in 1712 from Gale's own MS notes] • *Old Westminsters*, 1.361 • A. Tindal Hart, *The life and times of John Sharp, archbishop of York* (1949), 143 • M. Hunter, *Science and the shape of orthodoxy* (1995), 174 • F. Drake, *Eboracum* (1736); repr. with a new introduction by K. J. Allison (1978), 21, 23, 25, 26, 27, 486, 527 • D. Owen, 'From the Restoration until 1822', *A history of York Minster*, ed. G. E. Aylmer and R. Cant (1977), 240, 248, 270 • G. Parry, *The trophies of time: English antiquarians of the 17th century* (1995), 81, 336 • Nichols, *Lit. anecdotes*, 4.536–55 • *Private correspondence and miscellaneous papers of Samuel Pepys, 1679–1703*, ed. J. R. Tanner, 2 vols. (1926) • Evelyn, *Diary*, vol. 5 • M. J. F. McDonnell, *A history of St Paul's School* (1909) • M. McDonnell, ed., *The registers of St Paul's School, 1509–1748* (privately printed, London, 1977) • R. B. Gardiner, ed., *The admission registers of St Paul's School, from 1876 to 1905* (1906) • R. Ollard, *Pepys: a biography* (1974) • *DNB*

Archives BL, corresp., Add. MSS 4277, 4292, 34727, 38849 • GL, draft of ordinances for Christ's Hospital Grammar School | BL, corresp., Sloane MSS 4037, 4059 • Bodl. Oxf., corresp., Smith MSS 8, 45, 50

Likenesses G. Kheller, oils, 1689, New York City Art Gallery • J. Riley, oils, RS; repro. in N. H. Robinson, *The Royal Society catalogue of portraits* (1980), facing p. 124 • attrib. J. Riley, oils, RS • oils, TCD

Galensis, John (*fl.* 1210), canon lawyer, was of Welsh origin but took up residence at Bologna where he studied at the university. His principal accomplishment was the compiling of the *Compilatio secunda* (between 1210 and 1212 or 1215 at the latest). Chronologically the third of the *Quinque compilationes antiquae* to be made, this collection contains selections from papal decretals chiefly from the pontificates of Clement III (1187–91) and Celestine III (1191–98), that is, decretals which fall between those in the *Compilatio prima* and those in the *Compilatio tertia* of 1210, and was thus known as the second compilation or the *Decretales medie seu intermedie*. The selections are arranged systematically in five books. The collection drew heavily on the works of Gilbert the Englishman and Alan the Englishman. A measure of the work's significance is that of its 330 chapters nearly 75 per cent were included in the greatest of medieval canonical collections, the *Decretals* of Gregory IX (1234). Galensis also wrote a partial summary and a gloss for his own collection, as well as glosses and an *apparatus* for the *compilatio tertia*. He is to be distinguished from the Franciscan theologian of the same name, who died about 1285.

F. DONALD LOGAN

Sources E. Friedberg, ed., *Quinque compilationes antiquae* (1882), 26–33, 66–104 • S. Kuttner, *Repertorium der Kanonistik, 1140–1234* (1937), 345–6, 355–6, 361 • A. van Hove, *Prolegomena ad codicem iuris canonici*, 2nd edn (1945), 356, 444–5 • A. M. Stickler, *Historia iuris canonici latini* (1950), 234 • F. Gillmann, 'Johannes Galensis als Glossator, insbesondere der Compilatio III', *Archiv für katholisches Kirchenrecht*, 105 (1925), 488–565 • F. Gillmann, 'Des Johannes Galensis Apparat zur Compilatio III in der Universitätsbibliothek Erlangen', *Archiv für katholisches Kirchenrecht*, 118 (1938), 174–222 • G. Post, 'Additional glosses of Johannes Galensis and Silvester in the early Tancred or so-called Laurentius-Apparatus to Compilatio III', *Archiv für katholisches Kirchenrecht*, 119 (1939), 365–75

Galeon, William (*d.* 1507), theologian and Augustinian friar, was probably born in Norfolk about 1455. He entered the order at the Bishop's Lynn convent, and may have studied arts at the Oxford convent from 1472. He continued his studies in Cambridge in the 1480s, and in 1484–5 he was granted a grace there to oppose in theology, the second stage of qualification as a bachelor, on the strength of twelve years' study. So long a period of study for a scholar who was not yet a bachelor was unusual, and may indicate that he had studied in one of his order's studia before he went up to Oxford. He incepted as doctor of theology early in 1488; his promotion to the doctorate was confirmed by the general chapter of his order on 8 April. It is not clear whether he remained in Cambridge or returned to Norfolk, but on 19 August 1496 he was appointed vicar-general of the English province. On 4 July 1498 he was appointed prior provincial, an office which, unusually, he held for over five years. Galeon probably retired to Bishop's Lynn at the turn of the century; he died there in 1507, and was buried in the convent.

Although he held high office for much of his career, Galeon did not achieve renown in public life. He was none the less active as a theologian and preacher. A collection of his disputations and sermons was known to Bale but no longer survives, and he seems to have owned a considerable library, which he left at his death to his convent at Bishop's Lynn.

JAMES G. CLARK

Sources Emden, *Oxf.*, 2.740 • Bale, *Cat.*, 1.633 • Bale, *Index*, 125 • Tanner, *Bibl. Brit.-Hib.*, 304

Gales, Joseph (1761–1841), newspaper proprietor and radical, was born at Eckington in north Derbyshire on 4 February 1761, the eldest son of Thomas Gales, a village school teacher. His early years were spent assisting his father, after which he was apprenticed to a printer in Manchester. He absconded after he was attacked by his master's wife and returned to Eckington. In the early 1780s he completed his apprenticeship with James Tomlinson, a printer of Newark-on-Trent, Nottinghamshire. On 4 May 1784 he married Winifred Marshall (1761–1839), novelist and political writer, who was a daughter of John Marshall, an innkeeper of Newark and a cousin of Lord Melbourne. His lifelong companion, Winifred was a woman of considerable ability and learning who studied Latin as a child and by the age of fourteen had read the works of Shakespeare, Milton, and Adam Smith. In adult life she contributed passages of political analysis to her husband's newspaper, together with commentaries for Gales's edition of the Bible and a novel, *Lady Emma Melcombe*. The marriage produced eight children, five daughters and three sons.

Following his apprenticeship Gales moved to Sheffield,

where in 1787 he established a reformist weekly, the *Shef-field Register* (first number 8 June), in partnership with David Martin. Like many publishers of that era, Gales was also a printer, stationer, auctioneer, and insurance agent. The valuation on his own property in the Hartshead area of the town shows that he possessed buildings and equipment worth £500 in 1787.

As an editor Gales pursued a reformist agenda for the abolition of slavery, educational improvements, canal building, and, especially, the removal of legal constraints on religious dissenters. Gales was himself a Unitarian and, in line with his religious beliefs, regularly condemned the 'evils' of popular recreations such as bull-baiting, cock-fighting, and boxing. Under his editorship the *Register* became the voice of the Sheffield Society for Constitutional Information, an artisan-based political club founded in late 1791 and comprising up to 2000 members. Gales held no office in the organization but was a founder member who once chaired one of its larger public meetings in 1793. Like many similar radical clubs, the Sheffield society advocated a radical extension of the franchise as a means to secure political reform. Such was the support for reform in Sheffield that demonstrations organized by the society could attract 5000–10,000 supporters, while the *Register*, with its innovative coverage of local news and reprints of the writings of liberal thinkers, often sold 2000 copies of individual issues during the early 1790s. Gales also published the first cheap edition of Thomas Paine's *Rights of Man* (6 *d.*) and a short-lived fortnightly periodical, *The Patriot* (1792–4), which included political essays, extracts from reformers such as Paine, Joseph Priestley, and James Mackintosh, and correspondence with and the addresses of other reform societies. Gales himself had links to these wider circles of dissenters and political radicals including Priestley and Thomas Walker of Manchester. He may also have met Paine during the latter's visit to Yorkshire in the late 1780s. In March 1792 Gales, along with several other members of the Sheffield society, was elected an associate member of the London-based Society for Constitutional Information.

Gales's profile also brought him to the attention of Pitt's government, especially during the period of state trials in 1794. At the start of that year he was accused of writing an anonymous letter to Thomas Hardy, secretary of the London Corresponding Society, which discussed the possibility of distributing arms (pikes) to supporters of political reform. Facing arrest, Gales left Sheffield for Derby and thereafter left the country. Winifred Gales was left behind to arrange the sale of the *Sheffield Register* to his former assistant, James Montgomery, before joining her husband in exile.

The family went first to Hamburg in Germany before sailing for America. While in Europe, Gales studied several languages and learned shorthand, a skill he used to good effect in later political journalism. After arriving in Philadelphia in 1795, he worked first as a printer, reporter, and bookkeeper before starting his own paper, the *Independent Gazetteer*. Following advice from members of the Republican Party, he re-established himself in North Carolina and in October 1799 started the *Raleigh Register*. Through this publication he continued his political career as a liberal reformer in the Jeffersonian mould. He served as the mayor of Raleigh for nineteen years and was state printer for several decades. An abolitionist who owned slaves, Gales also promoted the cause of Unitarianism as well as publishing his newspaper until retirement in 1832. His son Weston continued as editor and maintained the family's publishing interest in the *Congressional Record*.

Gales lived for several years in Washington with his eldest son, also Joseph, who was a journalist and was mayor of Washington between 1827 and 1830. The elder Joseph Gales died in Raleigh, North Carolina, on 21 July 1841.

FRED DONNELLY

Sources W. H. G. Armytage, 'The editorial experience of Joseph Gales, 1786–94', *North Carolina Historical Review*, 28 (1951), 332–61 · W. S. Powell, 'The diary of Joseph Gales, 1794–5', *North Carolina Historical Review*, 26 (1949) · J. Stevenson, *Artisans and democrats: Sheffield in the French Revolution, 1789–97* (1989) · E. J. Evans, 'Gales, Joseph', *BDMBR*, vol. 1 · W. E. Smith, 'Gales, Joseph', *DAB* · M. Durey, *Transatlantic radicals and the early American republic* (Lawrence, KS, 1997) · *Memoirs of the life and writings of James Montgomery*, ed. J. Holland and J. Everett, 7 vols. (1854–6) · C. Eaton, 'Winifred and Joseph Gales, liberals of the old south', *Journal of Southern History*, 10 (1944), 461–74 · J. Graham, *The nation, the law and the king: reform politics in England, 1789–1799*, 2 vols. (Lanham, Maryland, 2000) · F. K. Donnelly, 'The foundation of the Sheffield Society for Constitutional Information', *Labour History Review*, 56/2 (1991), 51–3 · Royal Exchange fire policy no. 101787, Joseph Gales and David Martin, 1787, GL, MS 7253/12 · minute book of Society of Constitutional Information, 1792, PRO, treasury solicitor's papers, T.S.11/962/3508 · E. P. Thompson, *The making of the English working class* (1963) · A. Goodwin, *The friends of liberty: the English democratic movement in the age of the French Revolution* (Cambridge, Massachusetts, 1979) · G. A. Williams, *Artisans and sans-culottes: popular movements in France and Britain during the French Revolution* (1968) · W. Noblett, 'From Sheffield to North Carolina, 1795', *History Today*, 26 (1976), 23–31 · E. Harrison, *A reply to a letter addressed to Dr. Stevenson of Newark* (1782) · *Creswell and Burbage's Nottingham Journal* (8 May 1784)

Archives University of North Carolina, Chapel Hill, family MSS | GL, Royal Exchange fire policy no. 101787, MS 7253/12 · PRO, treasury solicitor's papers, minute books of Society for Constitutional Information, T.S.11/962/3508

Likenesses portrait, North Carolina Division of Archives and History, Raleigh; repro. in Graham, *The nation, the law and the king*, vol. 1, p. 449

Galfridus Anglicus. *See* Vinsauf, Geoffrey of (*fl.* 1208–1213).

Galgacus. *See* Calgacus (*fl. c.*AD 83/4).

Galignani, (John) Anthony (1796–1873), bookseller and publisher, and his partner, **William Galignani** (1798–1882), were the two eldest sons of Giovanni Antonio Galignani (1757–1821), a bookseller and publisher presumably born in Brescia, and his wife, Anne Parsons (1776–1822), the daughter of a London printer. John Anthony Galignani was born in London on 13 October 1796 and his brother William was born in London on 10 March 1798. A third son, Charles (1811–1829), was born in Paris.

The Galignani family had been in the book trade in Italy until at least the end of the seventeenth century. Giovanni

(John) Anthony Galignani (1796–1873), by unknown engraver, pubd 1874 (after Bingham)

Antonio Galignani is said to have been a many-talented man, able to speak several languages fluently, who probably came to France about 1790, then moved to London, where in 1796 he published twenty-four lectures on the Italian language. He returned to Paris with his wife, his two sons, and his father-in-law towards the end of the century. In 1800 he opened a bookshop in the rue Vivienne, soon to become an extensive circulating library for the English nobility and gentry under the management of his wife and offering 'a numerous catalogue of the most approved British authors in every branch of literature … altogether with the principal periodical publications' (advertisement in the *Argus, or, London Review'd in Paris*, 6, 8 Nov 1802). Galignani and his wife published what seems to have been their first book in 1804: Hester Lynch Piozzi's *British Synonymy, or, An Attempt at Regulating the Choice of Words in Familiar Conversation*. They also started the British Library in Verse and Prose, a duodecimo cheap reprint issued in numbers and, as an unauthorized printing, sold at well under the London price.

On the fall of Napoleon in 1814, Giovanni Galignani launched an English newspaper entitled *Galignani's Messenger*. A small four-page paper, it was published three times a week, on Tuesdays, Thursdays, and Saturdays, but its publication was interrupted during Napoleon's Hundred Days. When it reappeared in August 1815, it became a daily paper, circulated among English residents all over Europe, who appreciated all the news crammed into it. Galignani thus became a well-known name, especially in Britain, appearing in the correspondence of writers such as Sir Walter Scott, Lord Byron, Dickens, and George Eliot. Thomas Moore co-operated with the Galignanis on the publication of his works in French and William Makepeace Thackeray actually worked on the paper for a short period.

After their father's death in 1821, John Anthony and William Galignani took over the firm and continued to publish a new edition every year of the successful *New Paris Guide*, first launched as the *Picture of Paris* in 1814. Probably acting as agents for Colburn and Bentley, they also issued reprints of many successful English books, in a series called Standard Modern Novels and Romances. Scott

visited the Galignani brothers in 1826, and they offered him 100 guineas for the translation and publication in Paris of his *Life of Napoleon*. The Galignani brothers' books had then a reputation for textual accuracy and completeness. Meanwhile the bookshop continued to thrive, serving as a club for English residents and visitors, who paid 6 francs a month to use the reading-room, which contained English and continental newspapers and 18,000 books. In 1856 the establishment was moved to its final location, 224 rue de Rivoli.

The Galignani brothers were also well known for their great hospitality and generosity. In 1866 the British government presented them with a silver epergne in recognition of their benevolent efforts. Anthony Galignani (he had dropped his first name) was made chevalier and William Galignani officer of the French Légion d'honneur. The former remained a British subject until his death, but his brother was naturalized in 1832 and became the mayor of Étiolles, a village where they had bought a country house as early as 1827. The brothers founded a girls' school and a hospital in the adjoining town of Corbeil, where a fine sculpture of them, by Chapu, was erected in the garden of the town hall. They were also liberal donors to British charities in Paris.

Anthony Galignani, who was unmarried, died in France on 29 December 1873, and William Galignani, a widower since 1862, died on 11 December 1882. Both brothers were buried in the Père Lachaise cemetery, in Paris. William Galignani and his wife had had no children, and in his will he bequeathed a site and funds for the erection at Neuilly of the Retraite Galignani frères for a hundred inmates of both sexes, who were connected with the world of letters, arts, and sciences. The Galignani bookshop in the rue de Rivoli was still in the family's hands at the end of the twentieth century. MARIE-FRANÇOISE CACHIN

Sources *A famous bookstore: the Galignani Library* (brochure, Paris, 1920) · G. Barber, 'Galignani's and the publication of English books in France from 1800 to 1852', *The Library*, 5th ser., 16 (1961), 267–86 · J. J. Barnes, 'Galignani and the publication of English books in France: a postscript', *The Library*, 5th ser., 25 (1970), 294–313 · *Argus, or, London Review'd in Paris* (8 Nov 1802) [advertisement]
Likenesses engraving, pubd 1874 (after Bingham), NPG [*see illus.*]

Galignani, William (1798–1882). *See under* Galignani, (John) Anthony (1796–1873).

Gall [St Gall, Gallus] (*fl.* **615**), supposed monastic founder, is reported by Jonas of Bobbio, the seventh-century biographer of Columbanus (*d.* 615), as a companion of that saint. Gall may have been a Frank or an Aleman, but his lives, written much later, suggest an Irish origin. They relate that he became a disciple of Columbanus at the monastery of Bangor (Down) and followed him in his *peregrinatio* to the continent. When the party of Columbanus and his twelve companions arrived in the region of Lake Constance, having been expelled by the Frankish king Theuderic II from Luxeuil in Burgundy, Gall's missionary zeal proved too vehement for the local pagan communities. Although said to be able to converse with the local people in their own language, he did not endear himself to them when he set about destroying their pagan idols. When the missionaries were banished again, Gall refused to follow Columbanus across the Alps into Lombard Italy, feeling too sick to travel. Angered by Gall's obstinacy, Columbanus forbade him to say mass during his own lifetime. Some three years later, shortly before his death, Columbanus sent Gall his abbot's staff as a sign of reconciliation.

In the meantime, Gall was nursed back to health at Arbon, and proceeded into the wilderness to find a place suitable for a hermitage. Near the River Steinach he founded a church which was later to become the celebrated monastery of St Gall (or St Gallen, now in Switzerland), and then gathered to him from among the local populace twelve young men whom he educated to become his disciples. As Gall's fame spread, he was offered the abbacy of Luxeuil and the bishopric of Constance, but refused both. During a visit to Arbon he died in his ninety-fifth year, and his body was brought back to his church to be buried. His feast day is 16 October, that of his translation 20 February.

This narrative is drawn entirely from the three surviving recensions of Gall's life, of which the later versions by Wettinus (c.816–824) and Walahfrid Strabo (c.833), both from the nearby monastery of Reichenau, are based on a common text. This is the *Vita vetustissima*, which survives in fragmentary form in a ninth-century manuscript but is thought to date from c.771. Whether an even older recension, dating to the beginning of the eighth century, existed, is open to question, as is the theory that an earlier version may have been composed by an Irishman.

The only contemporary source for Gall is Jonas of Bobbio's life of Columbanus, written c.643. This at least proves his existence, but adds nothing to Gall's biography. It mentions him only once, and then not in the context of Columbanus's sojourn on the shores of Lake Constance. In an anecdote which he claims Gall had told him personally, Jonas relates how, during their early years at Luxeuil, Columbanus had rebuked Gall for fishing in a river different from the one that he had recommended.

An early tenth-century St Gallen codex incorporating Jonas's life of Columbanus and that of Gall by Wettinus (St Gallen, Stiftbibliothek, MS 553) also contains genealogies of Brigit, Patrick, and of Gall, attributed by the scribe to certain 'venerable Irishmen'. According to this, Unuchun, an Irish king, was succeeded by his son Kethernach, father of Gall. The latter's native name is given as Callech, in Latin Gallus. Brigit's genealogy states that she was of the same royal lineage as Gall.

On the basis of this evidence, it is not clear that the Gall mentioned in the life of Columbanus is identical with the founder of the hermitage near the River Steinach. Although the Irish descent of the monastic founder had never been previously doubted, the most modern commentators have suggested both that he may not have been a follower of Columbanus, and that he may not have been Irish, but a native of the region in which he founded his church. These suggestions have arisen to account for various difficulties with the sources. Gall receives no mention in the Irish annals, and the life of Columbanus is silent

concerning the sojourn of the saint's disciple Gall in Switzerland. Added to this, there is confusion as to the proper form of his name. The generally used form Gall (Gallus in Latin) does not appear in an authenticated document of his church before 771. Earlier charters and privileges refer to the establishment as *monasterium Sancti Galloni*, and even earlier ones as *ecclesia Sancti Caliani* or *Giliani*. This, together with the testimony of the genealogy, suggests that the accredited founder of St Gallen may first have been known under some form of the Irish name Cellach, or Cellianus, which became transformed via Callech, or Gallech, to Gall. The abbey's attested history suggests a context for the emergence of such a name. It begins about 720 with the abbacy of Otmar, one of a group of Alemannian landholders who founded it, apparently on the site of Gall's hermitage. During his troubled period of office, culminating in his death in exile in 759, Otmar tried to maintain his abbey's independence both from Frankish expansion and from control by the bishop of Constance. The lives of Gall can best be understood in this context, stressing as they do the antiquity and independence of the foundation. It may well have been that the life of Columbanus was utilized to provide the abbey with a founder saint, who was then accredited by the hagiographer with deeds deemed to be useful for the position of the monastery. While uncertainty remains as to whether its saintly founder ever existed, there is no doubt that, from Carolingian times onwards, the abbey was considered to be an Irish foundation.

DAGMAR Ó RIAIN-RAEDEL

Sources 'Vitae sancti Galli', *Passiones vitaeque sanctorum aevi Merovingici*, ed. B. Krusch, MGH Scriptores Rerum Merovingicarum, 4 (Hanover, 1902) · Jonas, 'Vita sancti Columbani abbatis', *Passiones vitaeque sanctorum aevi Merovingici*, ed. B. Krusch and W. Levison, MGH Scriptores Rerum Merovingicarum, 4 (Hanover, 1902), 61–108 · J. F. Kenney, *The sources for the early history of Ireland*, 2nd edn (1993) · D. Bullough, 'The career of Columbanus', *Columbanus: studies on the Latin writings*, ed. M. Lapidge (1997), 1–28 · J. Duft and P. Meyer, *Der irischen Miniaturen der Stiftsbibliothek St Gallen* (1953) · J. M. Clark, *The abbey of St Gall as a centre of literature and art* (1926)

Gall, Richard (1776–1801), poet, was born at Linkhouse, near Dunbar, in December 1776, the son of a notary. Having attended the parish school of Haddington, he was apprenticed at the age of eleven to his maternal uncle, a carpenter and builder. He afterwards became an apprentice of a printer in Edinburgh, Mr Ramsay, and he later became his travelling clerk, giving all his leisure to study. His powers attracted considerable attention during his lifetime, and he enjoyed the friendship of Burns and Thomas Campbell.

Several of Gall's songs were set to music, and became popular. Two of these, 'The Farewell to Ayrshire' and 'Now bank and brae are clad in green', were falsely assigned to Burns; the former was sent by Gall to Johnson for his *Scots Poetical Museum*, with Burns's name prefixed, and the latter appeared in Cromek's *Reliques of Burns*. Most of Gall's verse was rendered in Scottish dialect. He also composed some patriotic pieces while he was a volunteer in a Highland regiment. He remained in Ramsay's employment until his death, on 10 May 1801, in Edinburgh, and he spent the last weeks of his illness, a breast abscess, writing poetry. An edition of Gall's *Poems and Songs* was published at Edinburgh in 1819.

WILLIAM BAYNE, *rev.* S. R. J. BAUDRY

Sources C. Rogers, *The modern Scottish minstrel, or, The songs of Scotland of the past half-century*, 6 vols. (1855–7) · A. Cunningham, ed., *The songs of Scotland, ancient and modern*, 4 vols. (1825) · J. Stark, *Biographia Scotica* (1805) · Anderson, *Scot. nat.*

Gallacher, Patrick [Patsy] (**1891–1953**), footballer, was born at Ramelton, co. Donegal, on 16 March 1891, the son of poor Irish parents named Gallagher, who emigrated to Clydebank in Scotland when he was three years old. The Scottish spelling of his surname was adopted when misspelt on the nameplate on the door of the family home. His father, William Gallacher, became a shipyard foreman; his mother was Margaret (*née* Gallacher). On leaving Our Holy Redeemer School in Clydebank in 1906 Gallacher was apprenticed as a carpenter in John Brown's shipyard, where he worked until 1918. He married, on 28 June 1915, Mary Josephine Donegan (*d.* 1929), who was in domestic service as a housekeeper, the daughter of Thomas Donegan, a shopkeeper. They had five sons and a daughter.

Gallacher began his playing career in 1907 with Renfrew St James, and he moved to Clydebank Juniors in June 1910 before joining Glasgow Celtic on 25 October 1911. Although extremely slight of build, barely 5 feet 4 inches and 7 stones when he played his first senior game in 1911, and never gaining more than a couple of inches in height or 2 stones in weight, the Mighty Atom proved that he could hold his own in the toughest company.

It was with the Catholic-Irish Glasgow Celtic club that Patsy Gallacher made his reputation as a complete footballer, renowned above all for his tactical vision and dribbling skills, though he also had a powerful shot that belied his slight stature. The goal which he scored in the 1925 Scottish cup final for Celtic against Dundee entered the folk legends of the club: a mazy dribble in which a variety of tricks took him through a thick wall of opponents until, when it looked as though he would lose possession, he fell backwards with the ball held between his feet and somersaulted into the net. But in one of the decisions for which the club became notorious, the Celtic manager, Willie Maley, believing that Gallacher was nearing the end of his career, sold him to Falkirk in October 1926. He went on to play another six seasons before retiring on 30 April 1932. In his professional career Gallacher played more than 600 league and cup games in Scotland, and made twelve international appearances for Ireland.

Always his own man Gallacher had a shrewd assessment of his own worth, whether he was dictating orders on the field of play or making deals beneficial to himself off it. In the lunchtime kick-around games at the shipyard he preferred to practise by himself rather than to join in with the others. During the First World War his combination of professional football with employment in the shipyard led to his being brought before a sheriff, in November 1916, and fined for absenting himself from work without leave, contrary to wartime regulations intended to maximize the output of munitions and other fighting materials. After the war his club allowed him to own a public house when this was forbidden to the other Celtic players. His involvement in the drink trade enabled him to give up work in the shipyard. He did not train with his Celtic team-mates when this clashed with his business interests, and he was paid substantially more than others in the team, although by how much was never revealed. There was a probably apocryphal story that when selected to play for Ireland against England in 1920, and a crowd of 50,000 had turned up at Windsor Park, Belfast, he refused to get changed until his personal terms for the game had been met. When the management threatened to drop him, he challenged them to go out and tell the expectant crowd, swollen by the promise of his making an appearance, that Patsy Gallacher would not be playing that day.

When he stopped playing Gallacher retired from the game altogether to concentrate on his business interests which included a wine and spirit shop and The International bar in Clydebank. He was too demanding to be a coach for, like most gifted players, he was unable to comprehend why others could not perform the tricks that came so naturally to him. After the death of his wife in 1929 he brought up their children with the aid of a housekeeper; two of his sons went on to play professional football, Willie for Celtic and Tommy for Dundee. His grandson Kevin Gallacher played in the English premier league and became a Scottish international. Gallacher died of cancer at his home, Celfal, 50 Lennox Avenue, Scotstoun, Glasgow, on 17 June 1953 and was buried at Arkleston cemetery, Paisley. After his death another side of his character was revealed: a heap of IOU's amounting to hundreds of pounds, which he had never pursued.   BILL MURRAY

Sources R. Kelly, *Celtic* (1971) · T. Campbell and P. Woods, *The glory and the dream: the history of Celtic F.C., 1887–1986* (1986) · T. Campbell and P. Woods, *A Celtic A–Z* (1992) · W. Maley, *The story of Celtic* (1939) · D. W. Potter, *The mighty atom: the life and times of Patsy Gallacher* (2000) · d. cert. · G. R. Rubin, 'When Patsy Gallagher was prosecuted for playing for Celtic', 1984 [unpublished typescript]
Likenesses photographs, repro. in D. W. Potter, *The mighty atom* (2000)
Wealth at death £17,802 5s. 11d.: confirmation, 2 Oct 1953, *CCI*

Gallacher, William (**1881–1965**), political activist and politician, was born on 25 December 1881 at 39 Back Sneddon Street in the Irish ghetto of Sneddon, Paisley, the eighth-born child of Scottish parents, John Gallacher (*c.*1839–1889), a labourer and formerly a soldier, and his wife, Mary, *née* Sutherland (1845–1901). He was a pupil at St Mirin's Roman Catholic School, where he was frequently beaten for failing to attend Sunday mass. His mother moved him, at the age of nine, to the local board school at Camphill. He left when he was twelve to work full time as a grocery boy.

At fifteen Gallacher was apprenticed as a brass finisher at Doulton's, a sanitary engineering works in Paisley. Despite his lack of secondary schooling, he was serious-minded, largely self-educated, and well read; he was also a churchgoer and member of the Good Templars. A stocky

William Gallacher (1881–1965), by Howard Coster, 1936

figure, 5 feet 5 inches tall, Gallacher the man was always respectably dressed. He was an inveterate pipe smoker from an early age but, more significantly, he remained a lifelong teetotaller, acutely aware of the ruinous effects of excessive alcohol consumption on male members of his family.

Gallacher was in his twenties before he rejected the temperance movement and religion, finding both incompatible with socialism. He joined the local Independent Labour Party in 1905 and was a member of the Social Democratic Federation by 1906. Inspired by its Marxist perspective, and influenced by the example of the Glasgow-based revolutionary teacher John Maclean, Gallacher became an open-air propagandist and was a local election candidate. Moreover, from 1907 he was a trade union activist within the Amalgamated Society of Engineers and the National Union of Brassfounders and Finishers.

Gallacher left Doulton's in 1909, victimized for socialist activities. Thereafter he held several short-lived jobs until, in early 1914, he found work as a lathe operator at the Albion motor works, Glasgow. On 9 January 1913 he married Jean Roy, the manageress of a Co-op dairy shop. Their two sons died soon after birth, in 1916 and 1920, and two adopted nephews (Gallacher's brother's sons) died in 1944 on war service. Jean, a dearly loved and devoted companion, died in July 1962.

From 1912 Gallacher was an active member of the British Socialist Party, a Marxist party committed to winning parliamentary elections. However, until his participation in founding the Communist Party in 1920 his conception of revolutionary strategy for workers' power was fundamentally syndicalist. While he was in the USA during 1913 he was influenced by the militant direct action stance of the Industrial Workers of the World. His perspective on industrial unionism and workers' control of industry was also close to that of the Socialist Labour Party, a De Leonite organization which had a significant Glasgow base and, before and during wartime, included many fellow militants in the Clydeside shop stewards' movement.

Gallacher was already leading shop steward in the Albion works in 1914, before he became chairman of the unofficial co-ordinating Clyde Workers' Committee. In this capacity he gained a reputation as an industrial agitator in the wartime militancy of red Clydeside. Although an anti-conscription campaigner, he was careful to avoid an outright war resistance stance. In 1915, after the government failure to quell unrest against dilution of labour schemes on Clydeside, he was a marked man. In April 1916 he was falsely convicted on sedition charges and imprisoned for twelve months, the first of four spells as a political prisoner.

Following his release in March 1917, Gallacher threw himself into the Shop Stewards' and Workers' Committee movement and, in the aftermath of the October revolution in Russia, campaigned for the direct establishment of Soviet power via workers' councils throughout industry and the wider community. The pamphlet by Gallacher and J. R. Campbell, *Direct Action* (1919), encapsulates this standpoint.

On 31 January 1919, implicated in the strike movement for a forty-hour week, Gallacher was arrested and later sentenced to three months for alleged incitement to riot during 'the battle of George Square', Glasgow. Again, in early 1921, he was imprisoned for three months, the victim of a government raid on leading Communist Party militants. Finally, from October 1925, arrested along with the whole Communist Party leadership, he spent a year in prison.

In July–August 1920 Gallacher participated in the Second Congress of the Communist International in Moscow. Here, after conference decisions and extensive discussion with Lenin, who had criticized him earlier in '*Left Wing*' *Communism, an Infantile Disorder* (1920), Gallacher was persuaded to drop his anti-parliamentary views, and instead to pursue the policy of direct affiliation to the Labour Party and election of revolutionaries to the British parliament.

Gallacher returned to play an important role in founding the Communist Party of Great Britain in 1920–21, especially in Scotland. He served on the central committee from 1921 until 1963. As a leading member of the Communist Party he was both revolutionary agitator and paid party functionary. His first major task was to help centralize the party structure, and in the early 1920s he was frequently abroad on Communist International missions. As secretary of the British bureau of the Red International of Labour Unions in 1923, he was also involved in building a revolutionary base among the trade unions. He contested Dundee as Communist candidate in the general elections of 1922 and 1923. Implementing the united front policy until the class against class turn in 1928, he offered critical support to the left wing of the ILP and struggled, without success, to win Communist Party affiliation to the Labour Party.

In the early 1930s Gallacher concentrated on promoting the *Daily Worker* and, as a national council member of the national unemployed workers' movement, was a peripatetic activist, mainly in the mining areas. In the 1935 general election he won the predominantly mining constituency of West Fife as a Communist candidate, after two previous attempts in 1929 and 1931. Here his political base was among the left-wing breakaway United Mineworkers of Scotland, which was strongest in Fife. From 1935 until his defeat in 1950 Gallacher was the Communist Party's most public figure and, for ten years, its single spokesperson in parliament. He was a conscientious constituency MP, campaigning assiduously for pit baths and coal nationalization, and pioneered the pensioners' movement.

Although he was never a yes-man, Gallacher's political behaviour was consistent with the demands of Communist Party orthodoxy. From the mid-1920s he implemented the policy line of the Stalin-dominated Communist International. From 1935 he campaigned for the popular front programme and later pushed for a British–Soviet alliance to defeat fascism at home and abroad. On 28 September 1938 he stood alone in the Commons to voice direct opposition to Chamberlain's meeting with Hitler at Munich. However, in September 1939, following the Nazi–Soviet pact and outbreak of war in Europe, he initially opposed but reluctantly followed the new directive from Moscow to condemn the war as an imperialist one. After the Nazi invasion of the Soviet Union in June 1941, however, Gallacher had no difficulty in accepting the latest Moscow line as ultimate authority, and he became fervently pro-war. He was elected chairman of the Communist Party in 1943, when he reached the height of popularity inside and outside the party.

Gallacher retained West Fife in 1945 but lost out to the Labour challenge and cold war pressures in 1950. Though nearly seventy, he did not retire from political life. Between 1956 and 1965 he was honorary president of the Communist Party, and was still in demand as a speaker.

To the end Gallacher remained an unrepentant Stalinist, a virulent anti-Trotskyist, and in denial over the crimes of the regime in the Soviet Union. In common with policy and practice of the Communist Party, his abandonment of revolutionary politics dated from the mid-1930s. Thereafter his political stance may at best be characterized as left reformist.

Gallacher was not a first-rate theorist, but he excelled as organizer and agitator. He had a loud speaking voice and was a lively, witty, and engaging speaker and raconteur.

He was also an able and copious writer. As political journalist, pamphleteer, and polemicist he was a long-standing contributor to the left-wing press from his early days on the shop stewards' paper *The Worker* right through his career in the Communist Party. He wrote four volumes of memoirs, including *Revolt on the Clyde* (1936) and *Last Memoirs* (1966)—also an important testimony.

Gallacher died of prostate cancer on 12 August 1965, in his native Paisley, in the same council house, 68 Rowan Street, where he had lived modestly since 1929. The funeral service, held at Woodside crematorium, Glasgow, on 21 August was preceded by a massive procession which paid tribute to his lifelong struggle as a working-class agitator. ROBERT DUNCAN

Sources W. Knox, 'Gallaher, William', *Scottish labour leaders, 1918–1939*, ed. W. Knox (1984), 113–21 • J. McKay, 'William Gallacher, 1881–1965', 1993, Glasgow Caledonian University, Gallacher Memorial Library • *DNB* • *The last memoirs of William Gallacher*, ed. N. Green (1966) • J. McKay, 'William Gallacher: from infantile disorder to Stalinist order', *Scottish Labour History Review*, 5 (1991), 4–6 • J. McKay, 'Communist unity and division, 1920: Gallacher, Maclean and "the unholy Scotch current"', *Scottish Labour History Journal*, 29 (1994), 84–97 • W. Gallacher, *Revolt on the Clyde: an autobiography* (1936) • J. Hinton, *The first shop stewards movement* (1973) • I. McLean, *The legend of red Clydeside* (1983) • J. Klugmann, *History of the communist party of Great Britain*, 1 (1968) • F. King and G. Matthews, eds., *About turn: the British communist party and the Second World War* (1990)

Archives Glasgow Caledonian University, Gallacher Memorial Library, MSS and memorabilia • JRL, Labour History Archive and Study Centre, corresp., diary, MSS and transcripts of plays, poetry, etc.; papers • Marx Memorial Library, London, papers re casework for unemployed • Paisley Central Library, file and photographs | People's History Museum, Manchester, Communist Party of Great Britain archive • U. Hull, Brynmor Jones L., corresp. with R. Page and Olive Arnot; MSS | FILM BFI NFTVA, documentary footage | SOUND BL NSA, party political recordings

Likenesses H. Coster, photograph, 1936, NPG [*see illus.*] • F. Brilliant, bust, 1955, Paisley Arts Centre • I. Walters, sculpture, 1981, People's Palace, Glasgow • H. Coster, photographs, NPG • photograph, repro. in Klugmann, *History of the communist party*, facing p. 169 • photographs, repro. in Green, ed., *Last memoirs*

Wealth at death £3688 17s.: confirmation, 11 Oct 1965, NA Scot., SC 58/42/232, 1237–40

Gallagher, James [Séamus Ó Gallchoir] (c.**1690–1751**), Roman Catholic bishop of Kildare and Leighlin, was a native of the diocese of Kilmore; the names of his parents, like the year and place of his birth, are uncertain. After ordination at home he went abroad for ecclesiastical studies at the Irish College, Paris, and took his MA degree at the University of Paris on 2 August 1715. Two years later he was a student at the Irish College in Rome, where he took the customary oaths on 15 August 1717. Instead of returning to Kilmore after his studies, he went to the diocese of Raphoe in co. Donegal, ancestral homeland of the Gallagher clan. There he soon became vicar-general, and on 21 July 1725 was named bishop of Raphoe, a diocese that had been vacant for fifty years. He was consecrated at Drogheda by Hugh MacMahon, archbishop of Armagh, on 14 November 1725.

Since Raphoe had been heavily settled by Scottish Presbyterians, there were few Catholics in the diocese, and among them scarcely any of substance to offer the bishop bed and board. The *Report on the State of Popery* compiled in 1731 shows that there were only twenty-three priests in Raphoe, assisted by several itinerant friars. Mass was usually celebrated in the open air, for only six parishes out of twenty-one could boast a mass-house, a cabin, or even a shed for religious services. Gallagher's activity can be noticed in the entry for Glencolumbkille: three young priests, lately ordained there, had gone to France for their education. This and other attempts to improve the diocese came to an end in March 1734 when the civil authorities attempted to arrest him. While he escaped, one of his priests was shot dead and three others had to flee the diocese. Gallagher soon resumed his work from a base on the southern borders of his diocese, but he was pitiably poor, lived in the greatest danger, and could no longer effectively function in Raphoe. Hugh MacMahon, archbishop of Armagh, remarked at this juncture on his extraordinary zeal and youthful vigour.

According to tradition, Gallagher took refuge on the northern shores of Lough Erne and there composed the book by which he is chiefly remembered: *Sixteen Irish sermons, in an easy and familiar style, on useful and necessary subjects: in English characters, as being the more familiar to the generality of our Irish clergy.* This was first published at Dublin in 1736, proved very popular, and went through almost twenty editions before 1912. It was the only devotional book in Irish to be printed in Ireland itself until the closing decades of the eighteenth century. In the main it was directed at priests and contained the basic tenets of Catholic teaching. The spelling used, as the author explained in his preface, 'kept nearer to the present manner of speaking, than to the true and ancient orthography'; it reveals a pronunciation still characteristic of Donegal Irish.

The exiled Stuart James III, who had nominated Gallagher for Raphoe in 1725, again nominated him for Kildare and Leighlin in 1737, considering that his situation made him useless to Raphoe, while his long experience enabled him to be more serviceable elsewhere. By papal brief dated 18 May 1737, Gallagher was accordingly translated to the diocese of Kildare and Leighlin. Even in this more settled and wealthy diocese, he was still in danger of persecution, particularly after 1743, and seems to have spent much of his time at Dublin, going perhaps only in summer to what local tradition claims to have been his residence: a cabin on the road from Allen to Robertstown, co. Kildare, facing the vast moor called the Bog of Allen.

Gallagher went abroad in 1741, and visited both Paris and Brussels. At Paris he wrote a formal letter of approval for the publication of Andrew Donleavy's *An teagasg Críosduide*, which duly appeared in 1742 with the full text of the bishop's letter. At Brussels, accompanied by three other Irish bishops, he took part in discussions with the papal nuncio on the state of the Irish mission. On 12 May 1741 these prelates wrote a joint letter to Rome outlining the four chief needs of the mission. They wished particularly to reduce the number of clergy and asked for a papal subsidy to establish Catholic schools as a bulwark against the Charter Schools which, in their opinion, constituted the greatest danger to the faith in Ireland.

As bishop of Kildare, Gallagher had sometimes to censure individual priests or deprive them of their parishes. They in turn were apt to appeal to the archbishop of Dublin. These cases were handled by Patrick Fitzsimons, vicar-general of Dublin, who often overruled not only Gallagher's decision but those of two other suffragans as well. The prompt complaints made to Rome on this head by Gallagher and others delayed for many years Fitzsimons' promotion to the archbishopric. The most important record of Gallagher's work in Kildare and Leighlin is a set of diocesan regulations framed in 1748 to correct prevalent abuses. Their aim was to ensure the validity of marriage, to put a stop to obscene games of pagan origin then often played at wakes, and to insist on the Easter duty of receiving the sacraments of confession and communion.

Although Gallagher was listed in 1750 with nine other bishops who were prevented from living in their dioceses, local tradition claims that he closed his days at Allen, co. Kildare, in May 1751 and was buried near by at Cross Patrick, an ancient burial-ground.   HUGH FENNING

Sources *DNB* · C. Giblin, ed., 'Catalogue of material of Irish interest in the collection *Nunziatura di Fiandra*, Vatican archives [pt 5]', *Collectanea Hibernica*, 9 (1966), 7–70, esp. 40, 46–7, 69–70 · L. W. B. Brockliss and P. Ferté, 'Irish clerics in France in the seventeenth and eighteenth centuries: a statistical study', *Proceedings of the Royal Irish Academy*, 87C (1987), 527–72, esp. 570 · J. Hanly, 'Records of the Irish College Rome under Jesuit administration', *Archivium Hibernicum*, 27 (1964) · 'John Kent's report on the state of the Irish mission, 1742', ed. H. Fenning, *Archivium Hibernicum*, 28 (1966), 59–102, esp. 74–6, 94 · H. Fenning, 'Documents of Irish interest in the *Fondo Missioni* of the Vatican archives', *Archivium Hibernicum*, 49 (1995), 11–12 · C. Eubel and others, eds., *Hierarchia Catholica medii et recentioris aevi*, 5, ed. P. Ritzler and P. Sefrin (Passau, 1952) · U. J. Bourke, *Sermons in Irish-Gaelic by … James Gallagher … with a memoir of the bishop* (1877) · M. Comerford, *Collections relating to the dioceses of Kildare and Leighlin*, 3 vols. (1883) · S. Ó Neill, 'Bishop Gallagher's sermons', *Éigse*, 17 (1977–9), 209–13 · L. Swords, 'History of the Irish College, Paris, 1578–1800', *Archivium Hibernicum*, 35 (1980), 3–233, esp. 70 · E. Maguire, *A history of the diocese of Raphoe*, 2 vols. (1920) · P. Fagan, ed., *Ireland in the Stuart papers*, 2 vols. (1995) · 'Report on the state of popery, 1731', *Archivium Hibernicum*, 1 (1912), 20–23

Gallagher, John Andrew (1919–1980), historian, was born at the maternity hospital, Birkenhead, on 1 April 1919, the only child of Joseph Gallagher and his wife, Mary Adeline, *née* Welsh. His father, a working-class Irishman, had fought in the 1st Canadian contingent during the First World War, and subsequently worked in Liverpool as a warehouseman and then a railwayman during the depression. In 1937 a major open scholarship took Gallagher from the Birkenhead Institute to Trinity College, Cambridge, where he took a first class in part one of the historical tripos (1939) before his studies were interrupted by the outbreak of the Second World War. He enlisted in the Royal Tank regiment and saw action as a sergeant tank driver (he refused a commission) in north Africa, Italy, and Greece. Returning to Cambridge after the war, he took a first in part two of the tripos (1946) and by 1948 had completed a dissertation, 'The British penetration of west

Africa', resulting in his election to a prize fellowship at Trinity in the same year. In 1950 he was appointed as lecturer in colonial studies at Cambridge.

Gallagher migrated to Oxford in 1963 to become Beit professor of the history of the British Commonwealth. Though he developed many friendships in Oxford and was impressed by the quality of his students, he never really settled at Balliol, and eagerly returned to Trinity and Cambridge in 1971 to accept the Vere Harmsworth professorship of imperial and naval history. Trinity, in particular, he adored, as the college in turn adored him. From 1960 to 1963 he served as its dean, and from 1972 until his death as its vice-master. Many of the most moving tributes to Gallagher came from his Trinity colleagues.

Gallagher was an inspirational figure. A powerful historical imagination, a prodigious memory seasoned by extensive reading and travel, and a natural facility of expression all made for exhilarating conversation. Moreover, though in many ways a secretive and lonely man— he never married—he gave unstintingly of himself: he was patient with undergraduates, generous to research students, and loyal to colleagues. His company was thus highly sought after, as indeed were his opinions. In an era when there was less pressure to publish, he was able to write sparingly. But when he did put pen to paper the results were always luminous and transformative. Though he is mainly (and justifiably) known as a half of an internationally famous partnership with Ronald Robinson [see below], equally important work was published under his sole name. Two fields of research merit particular attention, the first being his Ford lectures of 1973, the second his contribution to modern Indian historiography.

The publication of the Ford lectures—*The Decline, Revival and Fall of the British Empire* (1982)—owed much to his Trinity colleague, Anil Seal, with whom Gallagher worked in collaboration on modern India. Cited far less frequently than the work published jointly with Ronald Robinson, in many ways it is the Ford lectures that provide the key to Gallagher's thinking. Indeed, such was the importance he attached to the lectures that they were given a trial run in Cambridge seminars during the previous year. With typical economy of expression, the period from the Napoleonic Wars through to the Suez crisis is covered in a mere eighty pages, testimony to what has since been described as Gallagher's 'all-embracing global range' (Hyam, 84). The empire is presented as a dynamic 'system of power' whose decline was by no means a continuous process. We are told of its shifting geographical centre, the multiple techniques of expansion by which it was sustained, the sources of its fragility, and the way its history interlocked with events elsewhere in the world. Organized with beautiful simplicity around the categories of domestic, international, and colonial factors impinging on expansion, the lectures are also full of fun—literary allusions and a variety of metaphors provide the vehicles for an irreverent yet sympathetic sense of humour. They remain one of the most accessible, the most enjoyable, and the most

rewarding introductions to the history of the modern British empire.

Gallagher's second solo contribution was to the historiography of modern India. Later in his career he gradually turned his attention away from colonial Africa toward the raj, which he had long regarded the nerve centre of the British imperial system—a mainstay of its military and economic power. The so-called Cambridge school of Indian historiography drew deeply on the ideas elaborated in two of his essays—'Congress in decline' (*Modern Asian Studies*, 7, 1973) and 'Nationalisms and the crisis of empire' (*Modern Asian Studies*, 15, 1981). While Gallagher had already pointed to the security of the Indian empire as the reason for the creation of an east African empire in the late nineteenth century, and a Middle Eastern empire after the First World War, he now began to explore the bases of Indian nationalism and the effect of government intervention thereon. He was particularly fascinated by the complex web of relationships which linked locality, province, and nation, the ways in which resources were bargained for and distributed in each of these spheres, and the part played (unintentionally) by the British in inducing Indians to organize themselves in ever larger groups.

Gallagher's thesis was that after 1918 financial imperatives impelled increasing levels of bureaucratic meddling in Indian social life, thus breaking the unwritten rule of colonial administration—'salutary neglect'. In self-defence Indians had to mobilize politically; once they had done so, policy-making became more constrained by indigenous opinion, and 'collaborators' (that is, 'moderate' and constitutionally-minded nationalists) more necessary than ever before. Gallagher was extremely sceptical regarding the inflated claims of Congress: Gandhi and Nehru constantly talked up the representativeness of the movement, but they spoke of a unity which neither it, nor India, in fact possessed. None the less he had a sharp eye for the circumscriptions which colonial politics imposed on the working of imperialism in the subcontinent, not least over the use of the Indian army. Hitherto deployed freely overseas as an 'imperial mobile reserve', by 1939 the Indian army was being bankrolled by the British taxpayer rather than by the Bombay merchant or Bengali ryot. This, as Gallagher wryly remarked, was to be the true test of Britain's will for empire.

Ultimately, however, Jack Gallagher's name will always be linked with his collaborator, **Ronald Edward Robinson** (1920–1999). Robinson was born at 18 Anhalt Road, Battersea, London, on 3 September 1920, the son of William Edward Robinson, a commercial traveller, and his wife, Ada Theresa, *née* Goldsmith. After attending Wix's Lane elementary school and Battersea grammar school, he was awarded a major scholarship to St John's College, Cambridge, where he matriculated in 1939. Sporting prowess won him a blue as a goalkeeper of the university soccer eleven in 1941; he also captained the college cricket team. From 1941 he trained as a pilot in southern Africa, to be posted as a flight lieutenant of the 58th bomber squadron flying missions over Germany, for which he was given the Distinguished Flying Cross in 1944; later in life he regularly had his old air crew at his Cambridge home for a new year singsong. After graduating in 1946 with upper seconds in both parts of the historical tripos (1941, 1946), he worked as a research officer (on the subject of trusteeship) in the African studies branch of the Colonial Office from 1947 to 1949, when he completed his PhD.

Robinson returned to St John's with a fellowship in 1949, and was appointed to a university lectureship in 1953. From 1966 to 1971 he was Smuts reader in the history of the British Commonwealth at Cambridge, and from 1971 to 1987 Beit professor of the history of the British Commonwealth at Oxford and a fellow of Balliol College, as well as chairman of the modern history faculty at Oxford (1974–6). Unlike Gallagher he enjoyed Balliol and almost, perhaps, became an 'Oxford man'. He was also very much a family man, with a very happy marriage to the American newspaper correspondent Alice Josephine Denny, whom he wed at Wandsworth Unitarian Church, London, on 12 August 1948; she was the daughter of Ludwell Howard Denny, a newspaper editorial writer. They had two sons and two daughters, of whom he was extremely proud. Alice Denny's role in the publication of *Africa and the Victorians*—acknowledged on the book's front cover—should not be underestimated. It was she who took charge of the project and gave the two men a timetable—Gallagher, in particular, did not relish the discipline of sitting down to write.

In appearance Jack Gallagher and Robbie, as Robinson was known, could not have been more different. Gallagher presented a well-rounded figure; 'the Living Buddha' was how some described him. The don Johnson Fruylen ('all big-headed and baldy, with spindle-shanks and a bit of a tummy') in the novel *My Friend Judas* by Andrew Sinclair, is modelled on Gallagher. Robinson, by contrast, was a beanpole—tall and straight of back. But their similarities are perhaps equally striking. They were both ebullient and enthusiastic, well known for their conviviality and generous hospitality; equally elusive, both men could make themselves invisible when they wished (something that frustrated administrators in particular); they were both innately conservative, while at the same time being anti-establishment, a tendency perhaps born of their working-class roots; and they were both born communicators, with a fund of choice phrases, who delighted in words and revelled in controversy. None the less, this was a partnership of thought as much as (or more than) it was a matter of sympathetic personalities. From the beginning they shared an intense interest in Africa, its partition, and the interplay of nationalism and imperialism in the continent; they also shared an impatience with Marxist scholarship, and were eager to refute the theory that imperialism was simply the economic exploitation of the wider world by European powers.

The Robinson and Gallagher 'thesis' Robinson and Gallagher first came together in their seminal essay 'The imperialism of free trade', published in the *Economic History Review* in 1953. How far the ideas and themes elaborated in this essay were truly original, or had in fact been anticipated by others and merely given a new 'spin' by Robinson and Gallagher, is a moot point for future historians to decide. Either way, it is justly acclaimed as a landmark in the study of the British empire, and remains one of the most widely cited and influential articles in any field of post-war British history. It portrayed the nineteenth century as a period of relentless expansion, taking many different forms, whereby Victorian governments worked to establish British paramountcy by whatever means seemed locally most appropriate. The preferred mode of expansion was *informal*, resulting from the forces of economic and cultural attraction; the actual annexation of overseas territory (*formal empire*) was always a last resort—a departure from the normal pattern of securing British interests in the wider world, undertaken not in response to organized opinion or electoral pressures, but in response to the perceptions of a policy-making élite (the *official* or *collective* mind). Yet this policy-making élite did not have an entirely free hand. If the limits on the independent action of statesmen in foreign and imperial policy were far looser than in other areas of policy, Britain's pursuit of profit and power was none the less constrained by a variety of external forces, which often obstructed overseas expansion. Central to the calculations of this official mind was India. Indeed, the early nineteenth century witnessed a major and conscious shift in British imperial policy—a 'swing to the East'—whereby India became the nucleus of the British empire. Its unique political, economic, and strategic value meant that Victorian statesmen were prepared not only to intervene much more directly in its affairs than in those of other colonies, but to contemplate the acquisition of territory in other parts of the world to ensure its future safety and stability.

These themes were elaborated in Robinson's and Gallagher's co-authored book *Africa and the Victorians: the Official Mind of Imperialism*, first published in 1961, reprinted seven times, and issued in a second edition twenty years later. The book was a fearless and frontal assault on the Marxist interpretation of the late nineteenth-century partition of Africa. As one right-wing scholar later remarked, 'it annoyed all the right people' (Norman Stone in the preface to C. Bayly, ed., *Atlas of the British Empire*, 1989, 6). Robinson and Gallagher argued that the main impulse for Britain's involvement in these events was not to be found in the metropolitan economy but in local crises and proto-nationalisms on the periphery and in the colonial pretensions and policies of other European powers, in particular France. Rather than a new, industrially or financially motivated drive to empire at the end of the Victorian era, Robinson and Gallagher insisted that British imperialism was, if anything, more cautious, tentative, and defensive. Certainly, public opinion played little part in producing a more forward policy, as the main calls for expansion did not emerge until the 1890s when partition was already well under way. Similarly, the records of the Foreign, India, and Colonial offices gave no ground for thinking that business or commercial opinion was capable of pressuring government into taking new territory overseas. Rather, the motives of the official mind were first and foremost strategic. It was the defence of India which provided the key to understanding when, where, and why Britain reluctantly decided to extend its African empire.

The idea that imperialism needed to be redefined in terms of the interconnections between its European and extra-European components was revisited by Robinson in two important essays, 'Non-European foundations of European imperialism' (published in R. Owen and R. B. Sutcliffe, eds., *Studies in the Theory of Imperialism*, 1972), and 'The excentric idea of imperialism' (published in W. J. Mommsen and J. Osterhammel, eds., *Imperialism and after: Continuities and Discontinuities*, 1986). These essays were typical of Robinson's social scientific frame of mind. His *modus operandi* was to test hypotheses, to probe for the general principle, and to generalize from detailed case studies. This brought both clarity and analytical rigour to his work.

In Robinson's writing on 'collaboration' two main propositions were advanced. The first was that the longevity of imperialism ultimately depended on working out a basis of co-operation (or collaboration, as Robinson preferred to call it) with the local population. The second stated that not only was collaboration inherent in the imperial relationship, but the choice of collaborators determined the organization, depth, and character of colonial rule. Though the word 'collaboration' suggested that Europe was able to profit from the divisions and rivalries which riddled African and Asian societies, this was no mere theory of 'divide and rule'. To be sure, the balance of terms between indigenous collaborators and their imperial masters was always unequal. But if terms became too unequal, they could not for long be sustained: either collaborators were alienated from their rulers, and withdrew their co-operation, or they were alienated from their subjects, and thus of little value. In many ways, therefore, the strength of imperialism rested on identifying and encouraging an influential yet pliable collaborating élite. This was no easy task. As Britain found to its disappointment, and sometimes cost, in Turkey, China, and parts of Africa, such collaborators were not always forthcoming, and even when they were, their improved organization frequently turned the terms of co-operation progressively in their favour. Moreover, the British public's notorious parsimony meant that it was extremely difficult to commit the resources to these relationships that might have helped to shore them up.

It would be difficult to overestimate the scholarly impact of Robinson and Gallagher. Dubbed by one scholar the 'Morecambe and Wise' of imperial history (Clarke), they were said by another to have 'a sort of Laurel and Hardy quality to them' (Louis, 17). The most appropriate analogy for their importance may arguably lie, however, not in the field of comedy but in another sphere of the arts. It would probably not be an understatement to say that Robinson and Gallagher were to Commonwealth-imperial history what the Beatles were to popular music. Their multifaceted theory, first outlined in 1953, set the agenda for everyone else; after the publication of 'The imperialism of free trade' the discipline could never be the same again. Indeed, in many ways it was Robinson and Gallagher who created the subject that we know today. Hence the shift in emphasis toward periphery-based, area studies from the 1960s onwards. Hence the proliferation of essays and books which have explicitly or implicitly set out to review (and revise) their work. Hence the inclusion of regions of informal empire (the Middle East, China, and Latin America) in the new *Oxford History of the British Empire*. And hence the way in which the discipline of Commonwealth-imperial history has in recent years been developing rather differently in the USA and in the UK: the former more open to new post-colonial perspectives, but concentrating on culture (in particular race) at the expense of the material and political dimensions to Britain's imperial past; the latter so steeped in the ideas and idioms of Robinson and Gallagher that it perhaps runs the risk of ignoring some of the more innovative areas of research.

Gallagher, who from humble beginnings rose to become one of the twentieth century's most distinguished and most cherished historians, died tragically, of acute cardiac and renal failure, at Trinity College, Cambridge, on 5 March 1980. Much of his research on India was still to be written up. Robinson, a self-assured character who made a powerful impression on the people who knew him, died of cancer at his home, 79 Mill Road, Cambridge, on 19 June 1999. At the time of writing, several scholars are trying to chart a new course for Commonwealth-imperial history for the twenty-first century, but the future of the discipline remains uncertain. It cannot yet be said whether anyone will succeed in stepping into their shoes.

ANDREW S. THOMPSON

Sources A. Seal, introduction, in J. A. Gallagher, *The decline, revival and fall of the British empire* (1982) · R. Robinson, *Balliol College Annual Register* (1980), 28–37 · R. Cobb, *Balliol College Annual Record* (1980), 28–37 · W. R. Louis, 'Historians I have known', *Perspectives* [journal of American Historical Association] (May 2001), 15–18 · H. A. Williams, funeral address, *Trinity College annual record* (1980) · *The Times* (7 March 1980), 19 · R. A. B., *The Times* (11 March 1980), 14 · Trinity Cam. · b. cert. · d. cert. · *WWW* · P. Lineham, *The Independent* (25 June 1999) · P. Clarke, *The Guardian* (26 June 1999) · St John Cam., Archives · *WWW* · R. Hyam, 'Imperial and commonwealth history at Cambridge', *Journal of Imperial and Commonwealth History* (Sept 2001) · b. cert. [Ronald Edward Robinson] · m. cert. [Ronald Edward Robinson] · d. cert. [Ronald Edward Robinson]

Wealth at death £73,818: probate, 4 June 1980, *CGPLA Eng. & Wales* · under £200,000—Ronald Edward Robinson: probate, 1999, *CGPLA Eng. & Wales*

Gallagher, Patrick [*known as* Paddy the Cope] (1870/71–1966), co-operative pioneer in Ireland, was born on 25 December 1871 (or possibly, given the lack of reliable sources, 1870) at Cleendra in the Rosses in the west of co. Donegal, the eldest son and the second of the nine children of Patrick (Pat Bán) Gallagher and Nancy (Seán Óg) Boyle. His parents were poor farmers in a mountainous district where the rocks protruded like bare bones through the starved skin of the earth. It was a region of high emigration, and six of his sisters emigrated to America. Until he was ten Gallagher attended Roshine primary school, and then economic necessity forced him to hire himself for six months a year to farmers in the more prosperous Lagan region in the east of co. Donegal. For six years he remained at this occupation before emigrating in 1889 to Scotland, where he worked as a farm hand and afterwards as a miner, principally in Roxburghshire and Lanarkshire.

In West Calder, Gallagher and his wife, Sally, née Gallagher, a farmer's daughter from Dungloe, co. Donegal, whom he married on 8 May 1898, bought their supplies from a co-operative store based on the Rochdale model, and when they returned to Ireland in 1902 he determined to introduce co-operative trading to his native region. Thus in 1906 the Templecrone Co-operative Society was formed under his chairmanship, with fourteen farmers each contributing capital of half a crown. The Co-op, or 'Cope' as it was known, was based in Mrs Gallagher's kitchen. The store was bitterly opposed by the traders and moneylenders ('gombeenmen') who controlled business in the region. At one point Gallagher spent three days in Derry gaol as a result of an action brought against him, but eventually his integrity and enthusiasm won through, and the Templecrone Co-operative Society soon moved to more spacious headquarters in Dungloe village, co. Donegal. From 1908 to 1911 Gallagher served as a Donegal county councillor, and he was also a JP.

The Templecrone Co-operative received substantial support from the Scottish Co-operative Wholesale Society and was affiliated to the Co-operative Union in Manchester. It was also affiliated to the Irish Agricultural Organisation Society, founded by Horace Plunkett in 1894, and Gallagher developed close relations with R. A. Anderson, its secretary. Others of his close connections were Father Tom (Thomas Aloysius) Finlay, the economist, and, in particular, the writer and mystic George William Russell (A. E.).

In 1945 the Dungloe premises, and Gallagher's house, were destroyed by fire, but new premises were opened in the following April, and the Templecrone Co-operative Society continued to prosper. By 1965 it had six branches and seventy-five employees, and was exporting lace, knitwear, and fish besides its normal trade in groceries, seeds, manures, flour (which was milled by the Co-op), and agricultural requisites. The turnover was £300,000; ten years later it had reached £1 million. Patrick Gallagher led the society from its inception, and it remains a monument to his vision and business ability. He served on the commission for vocational education and as a director of the Irish Agricultural Wholesale Society. The history of the Templecrone Co-operative Society is graphically recounted in his autobiography My Story: Paddy the Cope (1939), which has been reprinted many times on both sides of the Atlantic. In it, Gallagher was happy to admit to his shortcomings and mistakes; he was, according to his biographer, a 'consummate storyteller' (Scanlon, 136).

Patrick Gallagher died in Main Street, Dungloe, on 24 June 1966, having been predeceased by his wife, Sally, in 1948.   TREVOR WEST

Sources P. Gallagher, My story: Paddy the Cope (1939) • P. Bolger, The Irish co-operative movement: its history and development (Dublin, 1977) •

L. Scanlon, The story he left behind him: Paddy the Cope (1994) • homepage.tinet.ie/ndungloens/stair.htm [local history web page for Dungloe] • m. cert. • d. cert.
Archives Templecrone Co-operative Society, co. Donegal, Ireland, records

Gallaher, Thomas (1840–1927), tobacco manufacturer, was born on 27 April 1840 in the townland of Templemoyle, near Eglinton, co. Londonderry, the fourth of the ten children of Thomas Gallaher (d. 1855), corn miller, and his wife, Martha. Both his parents were Irish. The younger Thomas was educated privately, and at an early age helped in the substantial family business. He later recalled that, aged twelve, he had been 'gaffer' in charge of fifty men. On the death of Thomas senior, the mill passed to his second son, John, the eldest son, Alexander, having entered the Anglican church. Unwilling to accept a subsidiary role within the firm, Thomas established himself independently.

During an apprenticeship with Osborne and Allen, general merchants, of Londonderry, Gallaher learned the techniques of tobacco manufacture. In 1857, with £200 borrowed from his mother at 5 per cent interest, he established his own business in the city. It was an opportune period: from the early 1850s tobacco consumption per capita in Ireland rose steadily, doubling by 1900. Through energy and hard work—Gallaher later claimed to have worked seventeen hours a day—he earned a reputation for producing pipe tobacco far superior to the adulterated product common in Ireland, and built a small export trade to Britain. In 1863 he moved to Belfast, which offered an expanding market and better port facilities. The firm prospered, and in 1873 Thomas married Robina Mitchell (d. 1930), with whom he had five daughters and a son, who predeceased him. In 1881 a factory employing 600 workers was constructed in Belfast, replacing hand-operated methods of production with power-driven machinery. During the next decade, following visits by Thomas to America, the firm acquired plantations and stemming factories in Kentucky and Virginia, which he personally supervised. In 1888 premises were established in London, employing 200. In 1896 a new factory was built in Belfast and the company acquired limited liability status. Gallahers had become the largest tobacco firm in Ireland and was one of the biggest in the United Kingdom.

In 1898 Thomas's position in the industry was recognized when he became chairman of the National Association of Tobacco Manufacturers. Yet he refused to join the Imperial Tobacco Company founded in 1901 to combat American competition. Gallaher believed the firm's interests were still predominantly Irish, and Imperial was seen as a British organization. Furthermore, Thomas did not relish playing second fiddle to the Wills family. The decision had no adverse effects, though Gallahers had to beat off a challenge from the American Tobacco Company by producing (under the 'Park Drive' brand) machine-made cigarettes, which Thomas had originally despised.

During the years before 1914 the firm expanded its markets in Britain, the empire, America, and Scandinavia. The 1920s saw difficulties for the company, however, and

Gallaher was, by then, old and troubled by heart problems. There were losses in the southern Irish market following boycott and partition, and increased competition in Britain. After Thomas's death the company's position improved. In 1928 it became public when the Gallaher family sold its holding to a consortium. The move proved decisive in the firm's fortunes, its share of the tobacco market increasing throughout the 1930s.

Gallaher's business interests were not confined to tobacco. He was for a period chairman of the Belfast Steamship Company. In this capacity he came into conflict with James Larkin, the radical Irish trade union leader, who had been sent from Liverpool to organize dock labourers into trade unions. Gallaher was recognized as a good employer, even by the Belfast socialists like William Walker, but he was against trade unions—'Do not argue' was one of the mottoes displayed in his Belfast factory—and resisted Larkin's attempt to unionize the labour force. The ensuing conflict escalated into a bitter industrial struggle, involving most of the workers employed in unloading and transporting goods in Belfast. The dispute spilled over into Gallaher's tobacco factory. Seven girls who attended one of Larkin's meetings were suspended from work, and 1000 walked out in sympathy. The strike eventually petered out, however, and the labour force returned to work.

Gallaher never claimed to be a technical innovator, attributing his success to hard work and an ability to grasp market opportunities; but, as his dealings with Larkin showed, he could be ruthless. He was, nevertheless, the first employer in the tobacco industry to reduce the working week from fifty-four to forty-seven hours. Perhaps his greatest achievement was to create, in Belfast, a non-sectarian workforce, something requiring both moral and physical courage. On one occasion he kept an agitator out of the factory only by acquiring a pistol and threatening to shoot him. Gallaher died on 3 May 1927 at his home, Ballygoland House, Greencastle, near Belfast, aged eighty-seven. He was buried at Belfast city cemetery.

DAVID JOHNSON

Sources D. S. Johnson, 'Gallaher, Thomas', *DBB* · papers and photographs, PRO NIre., Gallaher MSS, D 3624/3/1–4 · *Gallaher Ltd. and subsidiary companies* (Gallaher Ltd., 1956) · *Belfast News-Letter* (4 May 1927) · *Belfast Telegraph* (4 May 1927) · *Irish News and Belfast Morning News* (4 May 1927) · *Irish Times* (4 May 1927) · *Northern Whig and Belfast Post* (4 May 1927) · J. Gray, *City in revolt, James Larkin and the Belfast dock strike of 1907* (1985) · B. W. E. Alford, *W. D. & H. O. Wills and the development of the UK tobacco industry* (1973) · *Northern Whig and Belfast Post* (23 April 1923) [interview with Thomas Gallaher] · M. Corina, *Trusts in tobacco* (1975) · D. Johnson, 'The Belfast boycott, 1920–1922', *Irish population, economy and society. Essays in honour of the late professor K. H. Connell*, ed. L. Clarkson and J. M. Goldstrom (1982), 287–307
Likenesses photograph, repro. in *Belfast Telegraph* · photograph, repro. in R. M. Young, *Belfast and the province of Ulster in the twentieth century* (1909) · photographs, PRO NIre., Gallaher MSS and photographs
Wealth at death £503,954: Irish probate sealed in London, 26 April 1928, *CGPLA Eng. & Wales*

Gallduf, Teabóid. *See* Stapleton, Theobald (1589–1647).

Gallenga, Antonio Carlo Napoleone [*pseud.* Luigi Mariotti] **(1810–1895)**, journalist and writer, was born on 4 November 1810 in the duchy of Parma, the eldest son of Celso Gallenga, a Piedmontese soldier in the Napoleonic army, and Marianna Lombardini. He probably attended the local *liceo* (grammar school) in Parma. While reading classics at the University of Parma, Gallenga came into contact with the radical groups who were plotting for national independence in the wake of the French Revolution of 1830. In January 1831 he headed a students' protest against the dismissal of mathematics professor Macedonio Melloni on political grounds. Imprisoned for sedition, Gallenga was released by the rebels in February, but had to flee when the Austrians restored the duchess to the throne a few weeks later. After an adventurous escape, related in his fictional autobiography, *Castellamonte* (1855), he led a precarious life under the name of Luigi Mariotti, earning his living as a private tutor in southern Europe and northern Africa. At the same time he joined the newly established Young Italy, waiting for an opportunity to fight for his country. However, the spirit of revolt had come to a standstill in Italy. After a lapse of time, he decided to seek his fortune overseas. In the autumn of 1836 he left for New York, and then went to Cambridge, Massachusetts. John Madison Leib, American minister in Tangier, had supplied him with letters of introduction to Edward Everett, the governor of Massachusetts, and to Josiah Quincy, the president of Harvard University. Both assisted him in finding employment as teacher of Italian at Harvard Young Ladies' Academy, where he remained for two years. In the 1830s Harvard was a flourishing American centre for Italian studies under the guidance of Longfellow, George Ticknor, and William Prescott. With the help of Prescott, whom he had a chance to meet, Gallenga started to write about his country for the *North American Review* as soon as his English was proficient enough. But this occupation did not fulfil his ambition, and he waited in vain for an opportunity to get an appointment at the university. Eventually, he first tried his fortune in Philadelphia and later in Nashville, before returning to Europe. He landed in Britain on 2 June 1839 at Portsmouth.

While Gallenga's American experiment ended in failure—spiritedly recounted in the first volume of his *Episodes of my Second Life* (1884)—his move to Britain proved to be a success. He arrived in London with an aura of martyrdom, created by fellow exiles who had taken shelter there. Lady Blessington, Henry Crabb Robinson, and the Carlyles, who backed Mazzini and his followers, sponsored him in the capital. The interest in all things Italian was then at its height: Gallenga had an easy pen and was a good social mixer, in spite of occasional bursts of temper. He thus became a prosperous freelance writer and teacher. Among his most distinguished pupils he counted Dickens who, on the eve of leaving for Italy (1 November 1843), wrote to John Forster 'A blessing on Mr Mariotti, my Italian master' (*The Letters of Charles Dickens*, ed. M. House, G. Storey, and others, 12 vols., 1965–2002, 3.587).

On 12 July 1847 Gallenga married Juliette Schunck

Antonio Carlo Napoleone Gallenga (1810–1895), by Camille Silvy, 1861

(1826–1855), the daughter of Martin Schunck, a wealthy Manchester merchant, thus securing a comfortable financial situation for himself. Their only living son, Romeo, returned to live in Italy. Romeo and his family settled in Perugia. Their home, the Palazzo Gallenga, is now the seat of the Italian University for Foreign Students. It was donated to the Italian state by Romeo Adriano Gallenga Stuart (Antonio's grandson), a Mussolini-era politician and art critic of some renown.

The Harvard experience was a decisive factor in Gallenga's formation as a professional writer. In the 1840s he contributed to reviews and magazines, such as the *Metropolitan Magazine*, the *Foreign Quarterly*, and *New Monthly Magazine*. He also published several volumes, including a collection of poems, an Italian grammar, and some collections of articles on English and Italian customs. In 1846 the first romantic history of Italian literature, *Italy, Past and Present*, established him as a scholar. The following year he was appointed to the chair of Italian at University College, London, which he held until 1858.

When the first Italian war of liberation broke out in 1848, Gallenga returned to Italy and settled at Turin, determined to help in the national cause. He resumed the full use of his family name, while using Mariotti as a pen name until 1855. The Piedmontese government, whose policy was to incorporate refugees from Italian states into public life, sent him to Frankfurt in 1849 for the signing of the peace between Austria and Piedmont after the defeat at

Novara. However, his real gift was for writing. For about eight years Gallenga shuttled between Piedmont and England, promoting the cause of Savoy in English and Italian journals. He became a regular contributor to the nationalistic paper *Il Risorgimento* and was appointed Italian correspondent for the *Daily News* in 1855. He also published two successful histories: *Fra Dolcino* (1853), the tragic story of a thirteenth-century heretical movement in Piedmont, and *History of Piedmont* (1855), a well-documented chronicle of the little kingdom, which was largely *terra incognita* to the English. The appearance of this book during the Crimean War made it particularly timely.

In 1854 Gallenga was elected to the subalpine parliament in the ranks of the Cavourian right. He distinguished himself by championing the English: in his speeches he loved to compare the probity of the British constitution with the laxity of Italian politics. Though the claims he made had some foundation, his Anglomania made him extremely unpopular. Hence, when an unknown episode of his earlier life came to light by his own folly, not only his political adversaries but also his party colleagues were glad to be rid of him. As a newly staunch conservative, he had become a fierce enemy of his former friend Mazzini. In the middle of a violent campaign by the supporters of the Savoy cause against Young Italy in 1856, Gallenga revealed how he had plotted regicide with the assistance of Mazzini in the summer of 1833. The intended victim was King Charles Albert of Savoy, who had abandoned the patriots with whom he had consorted as a young prince upon taking the throne. After meeting Mazzini in Geneva, Gallenga proceeded to Turin, but lacked the heart to commit the crime. He stayed for a short time, but then left Piedmont and his fellow patriots. The confession provoked a general outcry. Monarchists and Mazzinians alike considered him a traitor and a hypocrite. In London echoes of the scandal put an abrupt end to his acquaintance with Henry Crabb Robinson and the Carlyles. A period of public disgrace ensued. Gallenga resigned his seat in parliament, returned to Britain, and took refuge in his beloved studies. His first wife died of scarlet fever in 1855 and he married a widow of Irish origin, Anna Robinson (b. 1822), daughter of Captain Charles Johnson, on 21 June 1858. Together they had a son, Guy Hardwick, and a daughter, Ann.

When the second Italian war of liberation broke out in 1859, memories of the scandal were on the wane and *The Times*'s manager, Mowbray Morris, had the right man for the occasion when he appointed Gallenga his war correspondent with the Piedmontese army. As soon as this became known, many who had turned their backs on Gallenga welcomed him again. Camillo Cavour himself, in spite of his personal reservations, had him re-elected to parliament, but his second term was brief: he resigned in 1864, as *The Times* kept sending him on various missions.

Working for *The Times* was the greatest achievement of Gallenga's life. Soon he could say 'It was not long before I felt that *The Times* was a power—a power greater than any of the most colossal European Empires; and I found out that of that power I was the mouthpiece, and—so to say, the accredited Ambassador' (Gallenga, 2.313). In 1863 he went to the United States to cover the civil war. In 1864 he moved to Denmark to do the same for the conflict with Prussia over Schleswig and Holstein. In the same year he was also sent to Spain, where civil conflict was becoming endemic and where he was to return on separate occasions in 1869 and 1879. When not abroad, Gallenga wrote a large number of leading articles on foreign affairs. Though a brilliant journalist, he retained a literary style in depicting the countries he visited. His first travel report was from Cuba and Jamaica in 1864, but it was in his two-year stay in Constantinople (1875–7), during the Russo-Turkish conflict, that travel writing took the upper hand over politics. As his skill as a reporter began to decline with age, *The Times* preferred to employ him for general services. Most of his later articles form a collection of remarkable travel literature, notably those on South America and Russia. From time to time he was sent back to Italy to report on its progress after unification. His last books on Italy, *Italy Revisited* (1875) and *The Pope and the King* (1879), written during his years at *The Times*, as well as *Italy, Present and Future* (1887), written in retirement, offer a bitter portrayal of the new nation.

By the time he was seventy, Gallenga's star began to decline at *The Times*. In 1884 he was refused a mission to Morocco because of his age. In the same year the publication of *Episodes of my Second Life*, in which he did not scruple to relate details of his connection with the London newspaper, brought the collaboration to an end, as he found himself accused of having violated the secrecy expected from *Times* leader writers. Once again Gallenga had to pay for his indiscretion. He retired to live at Chepstow, in Monmouthshire, where he had earlier acquired a property, The Falls. He kept up an active correspondence with eminent Italian politicians and visited his country occasionally. He continued to write the odd piece for the papers and even tried his hand at fiction in *Jenny Jennett* (1886) and *Thecla's Vow* (published posthumously in 1898), with mediocre results. In his old age he was distressed by the death of his daughter in a road accident in 1885, by his wife's poor health, and by constant quarrels with his son Guy. Latterly, the novelist Mary Mackay (Marie Corelli), who was a family friend, tried to revive his reputation. When he died at his Chepstow home on 17 December 1895, a few obituaries paid a belated homage to one 'of the most gifted and most distinguished members of his craft' (G. A. H. Sala, *His Life and Adventures*, 1895).

Gallenga's literary output covered a wide range of genres from politics to literature, from verse to novelettes; but his reputation rests on his writings on the Italian question. His works reflect the making of modern Italy as seen through the eyes of a strong conservative who was at the same time a rebel. Moreover, his volumes on Italian literature and historiography, though not particularly original in their romantic outlook, are extremely valuable as source material for intellectual history, as they bear witness to a national vitality at a time when international esteem of the Italian character was at a low ebb. In his later works, the crude realism with which he depicted the post-risorgimental situation tells more about the country than the apologetic celebrations of the period. In *Italy Revisited* several memorable pages on the carnage of the battle of Solferino in 1859 and the bitter commentary on the growing social conflict in the south after the reunification of the country were at odds with the heroic myth of national unity. More than once, he provoked nationalistic anger not only in his own country but also elsewhere, as when he called New York a 'one-way-street city' in 1863. In spite of his prejudices and idiosyncrasies, Gallenga had an immediate perception of realities, even of those he barely knew, which made him an acute and reliable witness of events. With Henri de Blowitz and George Augustus Sala, he belongs to that Victorian generation of foreign journalists who assured the primacy of Printing House Square in international affairs.

TONI CERUTTI

Sources A. C. N. Gallenga, *Episodes of my second life*, 2 vols. (1884) · A. Garosci, *Antonio Gallenga: vita avventurosa di un emigrato dell'Ottocento*, 2 vols. (Turin, 1979) · T. Cerutti, *Antonio Gallenga: an Italian writer in Victorian England* (1974) · A. Garosci, *Antonio Gallenga: avventura, politica e storia nell'Ottocento italiano* (1964) · [S. Morison and others], *The history of The Times*, 1–4 (1935–52) · *Men and women of the time* (1895), 325–6 · A. Bertolotti, *Passeggiate nel Canavese: Castellamonte*, 5 (1867–8), 408–27 · *The Times* (19 Dec 1895) · *The Athenaeum* (21 Dec 1895) · P. Vayra, 'Documenti di un episodio della vita di Antonio Gallenga', *Rivista Storica del Risorgimento*, 1 (15 May 1896), 551 · H. N. Gay, 'Mazzini e Antonio Gallenga, apostoli dell'indipendenza italiana in Inghilterra', *Nuova Antologia*, 338 (16 July 1928) · I. Raulich, 'Mazzini e la trama del Gallenga', *Nuova Antologia*, 290 (16 June 1920) · M. C. W. Wicks, *The Italian exiles in London, 1816–1848* (1937) · M. Menghini, *Gallenga: enciclopedia Italiana* (1932), 289

Archives Athenaeum Club, London, records · Biblioteca Labronica, Leghorn, MSS · Biblioteca Nazionale Centrale, Florence, MSS · Museo del Risorgimento, Milan, MSS · Museo del Risorgimento, Rome, MSS · Museo del Risorgimento, Turin, MSS · News Int. RO, papers | Archivio di Stato, Turin, lettere ai Ministri di Allemagna 1848 · Archivio di Stato, Turin, Registri Segreteria Estera · Biblioteca Civica, Turin, Carteggio Giobertiano · BM, Panizzi MSS · DWL, letters to Henry Crabb Robinson · priv. coll., E. Mayer MSS · Providence, Rhode Island, Ann Brown Memorial MSS · Turin, rapporti parlamentari di stato

Likenesses O. Manara, oils, 1850, *Times* Newspapers Ltd, London · photograph, c.1855, repro. in Cerutti, *Antonio Gallenga* · C. Silvy, photograph, 1861, NPG [*see illus.*]

Wealth at death £7267 3s. 7d.: probate, 15 Feb 1896, CGPLA Eng. & Wales

Galli, Caterina (1719x24–1804), singer, was said to come from Cremona, in Lombardy, Italy, when she made her first recorded appearance, at Bergamo, in spring 1742. She was then engaged to sing secondary male roles, as a mezzo-soprano, with the Italian opera company at the King's Theatre, London, in the 1742–3 season. Despite having 'something spirited and interesting in her manner' (Burney, *Hist. mus.*, 4.449), she was not re-engaged. In spring 1745 she sang in an Italian pastoral at the Little Theatre in the Haymarket and appeared at a benefit concert for the Decayed Musicians' Fund. Her career was revived by Handel, who engaged her for the première of his oratorio *Judas Maccabaeus* on 1 April 1747, and gave her the air ''Tis liberty alone'. According to Charles Burney, 'she was not only encored in it every night, but became an important personage, amongst singers, for a considerable time afterwards' (ibid.). Handel wrote a series of fine parts for Galli in his subsequent oratorios: Othniel in *Joshua* (9 March 1748), the title roles in *Alexander Balus* (23 March 1748) and *Solomon* (17 March 1749), Joacim in *Susanna* (10 February 1749), Irene in *Theodora* (16 March 1750), and Storge in *Jephtha* (26 February 1752). She sang in Handel's Lent oratorio seasons until 1754 and in his *Messiah* performances at the Foundling Hospital. Galli also sang with the opera company at the King's Theatre in 1747–8, appearing in operas by Johann Adolf Hasse and Vincenzo Ciampi as well as in the Handel pasticcio *Lucio Vero* and in *Rossane* (a version of his *Alessandro*), where she was advertised as singing 'all the Original Songs of Signor *Senesino*' (*General Advertiser*, 8 March 1748). That August she was reported as earning nearly £200 from her benefit concerts at Scarborough, then a fashionable spa. She sang in Thomas Augustine Arne's *Judgment of Paris* (1751) and his *Alfred* (1753) and appeared regularly in the annual benefit concerts for the Decayed Musicians' Fund. Galli was the composer of a song, published in *Twelve Duets or Canzonets … by Sig^r Hasse &c.* (1748) with the Italian words 'Se son lontana'. As 'When first I saw thee graceful move', it was republished several times, appearing finally in the *Universal Magazine* of September 1763.

After singing in the Foundling Hospital *Messiah* in May 1754, Galli returned to the continent, where she sang as prima donna in opera houses in northern Italy and in Prague, being also in the service of Francesco III, duke of Modena, at least for the period between 1756 and 1767. Although Galli's last known appearance in Italy was at Alessandria in October 1769, she did not reappear in London until 1773, when she sang in *Messiah* in February and in Samuel Arnold's oratorio *The Prodigal Son* in March. For the two seasons 1773–5 she took male roles in Italian operas at the King's Theatre. In October 1775 Fanny Burney was pleased that 'the squalling Galli' (*Early Journals and Letters*, 2.160) was dismissed and replaced by the castrato Gaspero Savoi, but Galli sang in one more opera at that theatre, making her last stage appearances in Mattia Vento's *La vestale* in spring 1776. Galli continued as a concert singer at least until May 1777, when she sang with the young Samuel Harrison at her benefit concert. She had taught singing since the 1750s, when Lady Caroline Russell was her pupil, and gave lessons to Martha Ray, the mistress of John Montagu, fourth earl of Sandwich, singing with her in oratorio performances at Sandwich's seat, Hinchingbrooke, Huntingdonshire. She was not Ray's paid live-in companion, as sometimes stated, but was with Martha Ray when she was murdered by James Hackman as they left Covent Garden Theatre on 7 April 1779.

By 1792 Galli had declined into poverty and was granted 10 guineas by the Royal Society of Musicians, who were to give her relief payments annually from 1798 and to pay her funeral expenses. In an attempt to earn money she sang in the 1797 Lent oratorio performances at Covent Garden, performing a Handel aria on each occasion. Two years later, on 15 March 1799, she made a final appearance

there, to sing 'He was despised'. Richard Edgcumbe, second earl of Mount Edgcumbe, remembered that 'her voice was cracked and trembling, but it was easy to see her school was good; and it was pleasing to observe the kindness with which she was received, and listened to' (Edgcumbe, 19–20). In the same month, the *Monthly Mirror* reported the death of Mr Galli, her husband, 'in an advanced age, and in extreme indigence'. This seems to be the only mention of him. Galli, remembered as 'the last of Handel's scholars' (*GM*), died at her lodgings in Woods Rents, Chelsea, London, on 23 December 1804; the *Gentleman's Magazine* stated that she was then in her eighty-first year, but the register recording her burial on 30 December 1804 at St Luke's, Chelsea, gave her age as eighty-four.

OLIVE BALDWIN and THELMA WILSON

Sources A. H. Scouten, ed., *The London stage, 1660–1800*, pt 3: 1729–1747 (1961) • G. W. Stone, ed., *The London stage, 1660–1800*, pt 4: 1747–1776 (1962) • C. B. Hogan, ed., *The London stage, 1660–1800*, pt 5: 1776–1800 (1968) • C. Sartori, *I libretti italiani a stampe dalle origini al 1800*, 7 vols. (Cuneo, 1990–94) • *General Advertiser* (8 March 1748) • *Morning Chronicle* (19 Feb 1773) • *Public Advertiser* (5 March 1773) • *Public Advertiser* (30 May 1777) • *London Chronicle* (10 April 1779) • Burney, *Hist. mus.*, vol. 4 • O. E. Deutsch, *Dokumente zu Leben und Schaffen*, vol. 4 of (1985) *Händel-Handbuch*, ed. W. Eisel and M. Eisel (1978–85) • W. Dean, *Handel's dramatic oratorios and masques* (1959) • R. Edgcumbe, *Musical reminiscences of an old amateur* (1824) • *The early journals and letters of Fanny Burney*, ed. L. E. Troide, 2: 1774–1777 (1990) • D. Burrows, 'The autographs and early copies of *Messiah*: some further thoughts', *Music and Letters*, 66 (1985), 201–19 • D. J. Reid, 'Some festival programmes of the eighteenth and nineteenth centuries [pts 1–2]', *Royal Musical Association Research Chronicle*, 5 (1965), 51–79; 6 (1966), 3–23 • *Music and theatre in Handel's world: the family papers of James Harris, 1732–1780*, ed. D. Burrows and R. Dunhill (2002) • 'Galli, Caterina', *The catalogue of printed music at the British Library to 1980*, ed. G. Balchin, 22 (1983) • *The case and memoirs of the late Rev. Mr James Hackman* (1779) • *The Cumberland letters*, ed. C. Black (1912) • private information (2004) [secretary, Royal Society of Musicians] • *GM*, 1st ser., 74 (1804), 1250 • *Monthly Mirror*, 7 (1799), 192 • parish register, Chelsea, St Luke, 30 Dec 1804 [burial]

Likenesses Lady C. Russell, pen-and-ink drawing, c.1753, repro. in G. S. Thomson, *The Russells of Bloomsbury 1669–1771* (1940)

Galliard, John Ernest [*formerly* Johann Ernst Galliard] (*c*.1666/1687–1747), composer and musical performer, was probably born in Celle, Germany, probably about 1666 (according to Highfill, Burnim & Langhans, *BDA*), but possibly about 1687 (Hawkins), the son of Jean Galliard, a French wig maker. He received musical training in the flute and oboe from Pierre Maréchal, a French member of the Celle court orchestra, before joining the orchestra in 1698. When the orchestra was disbanded in 1706, Galliard went to London to become chamber musician to Prince George of Denmark. It is not clear whether he was awarded the post some years earlier, while still in Germany, or was appointed upon his arrival in London.

In 1710 Galliard was awarded the sinecure post of organist of Somerset House, London, which had been vacant since the death of Giovanni Battista Draghi in 1708. He wrote a number of pieces to English words soon afterwards, demonstrating his quick grasp of the language; these included three anthems. He also wrote his Te Deum and Jubilate at this time. He soon began to make his mark, both as an oboist, performing at the Queen's Theatre under George Frideric Handel (who wrote obbligato parts for him in *Teseo*), and as a secular composer. His connection with the stage began in 1712, with his setting of John Hughes's opera *Calypso and Telemachus*, performed at the Queen's Theatre in the Haymarket. Unfortunately, English opera was going out of fashion at the time, and despite its obvious merit the work was given only five times. It was the last English opera to be staged at the Queen's Theatre.

Between 1717 and 1730 Galliard was employed by John Rich to compose music for his theatrical entertainments at Lincoln's Inn Fields and later Covent Garden, many of which were in collaboration with the Shakespeare scholar and writer Lewis Theobald. First, in the 1717–18 season, came two masques, *Pan and Syrinx* and *Decius and Paulina*, and then, in 1719, another opera, *Circe*, but the real success began when Galliard composed the music (to Theobald's words) for Rich's pantomimes between 1723 and 1730, in which Rich himself mimed the part of Harlequin. After 1730 Rich rarely risked staging new productions, so many of the performances were revivals of earlier pantomimes. *Jupiter and Europa*, first performed in 1723 with music by several different composers, was revived in 1736 under the name *The Royal Chace*, with much new music by Galliard. It was enormously successful, and the hunting song 'With Early Horn' helped to make the reputation of the young tenor John Beard.

Galliard was not just a composer of theatre music. His *Hymn of Adam and Eve*, first published in 1728, a setting of a section from Milton's *Paradise Lost*, was enormously popular, as was demonstrated by its revival (in a heavily revised format) by Benjamin Cooke in 1733. His musical output also included six English cantatas, and six sonatas each for the bassoon and the flute. Galliard appeared regularly in concerts, mainly performing his own new works, such as his *Choruses to the Tragedy of Julius Caesar* (referring to the play by John Sheffield, duke of Buckingham) of 1723 and the serenata *Love and Folly* of 1739. He put on another full-scale opera, *The Happy Captive*, at Lincoln's Inn Fields in 1741.

A major figure in London musical society, Galliard was a founding member of the Academy of Ancient Music about 1710, of the Academy of Vocal Music (of which he directed the first performance) in 1727, and of the Royal Society of Musicians in 1738. He also made a fluent translation of Pier Francesco Tosi's Italian singing manual, under the title *Observations on the Florid Song*, which was published in 1742. Further evidence of his status in London musical society can be seen by his inclusion in the poem 'The session of musicians' (an imitation of John Suckling's 'The session of the poets', 1637), published in 1724, which relates Apollo's attempt to award the prize to the best musician in England:

His Fate soft G[a]ll[ia]rd with Care attends,
In Sounds and Praise they still prov'd equal Friends,
Shewing his Hautboy and an Op'ra Air,
He gently whisper'd in his Godship's Ear:
So oft he was distinguish'd by the Town,

That without Vanity, he claim'd the Crown.
The God replied—your Musick's not to blame,
But far beneath the daring Height of Fame;
Who wins the Prize must all the Rest out-strip,
Indeed you may a Conjurer equip;
I think your Airs are sometimes very pretty,
And give you leave to sing 'em in the City.
(quoted in Highfill, Burnim & Langhans, *BDA*)

Other contemporary commentators apparently agreed with the tepid praise expressed in the poem. Dr Charles Burney remarked that Galliard was 'an excellent contrapuntist; but with respect to his compositions in general, I must say, that I never saw more correctness or less originality in any author that I have examined, of the present century, Dr Pepusch always accepted' (Burney, *Hist. mus.*, 2.990). However, Burney was more generous elsewhere in his book, and Charles Dibdin said that Galliard had 'considerable genius' (Dibdin, 59).

Despite the misconception, held since Sir John Hawkins's time, that Galliard died in London in 1749, his burial record in fact clearly states that he was buried on 21 February 1747 at Chelsea, suggesting he died about three days before that. He never married. Administration of his estate was granted to his sister Margaret in March 1748. Many of his compositions exist in manuscript in the British Library (Add. MS 31588); other surviving manuscripts include that of *The Happy Captive* at the Paris Conservatoire, and that of *The Rape of Proserpine*, at the Guildhall Library, London.   VICTORIA HALLIWELL

Sources Burney, *Hist. mus.* · J. Hawkins, *A general history of the science and practice of music*, 5 vols. (1776) · C. Dibdin, *A complete history of the stage*, vol. 5 (1800) · R. Fiske and R. G. King, 'Galliard, John Ernest', *New Grove*, 2nd edn, vol. 9, pp. 451–3 · Highfill, Burnim & Langhans, *BDA* · G. Linnemann, *Celler Musikgeschichte bis zum Beginn des 19. Jahrhunderts* (Celle, 1935) · T. Gilliland, *The dramatic mirror, containing the history of the stage from the earliest period, to the present time*, 2 vols. (1808) · [J. S. Sainsbury], ed., *A dictionary of musicians*, 2 vols. (1825) · *DNB* · E. L. Avery, ed., *The London stage, 1660–1800*, pt 2: 1700–1729 (1960) · A. H. Scouten, ed., *The London stage, 1660–1800*, pt 3: 1729–1747 (1961) · R. Fiske, *English theatre music in the eighteenth century*, 2nd edn (1986) · administration and estate records · burial record, LMA

Archives BL, letter to William Duncombe, Add. MS 31588

Galliardello, Caesar (*bap.* 1568, *d.* 1627), musician, was baptized in the London liberty of Holy Trinity Minories on 1 July 1568, second but only surviving son of Mark Anthony *Galliardello (*d.* 1585) and his wife, Margery (*d.* 1611). In 1585 Caesar inherited his father's place among the royal viols and violins, remaining in place until his death. He also inherited his father's trenchant protestant convictions, and was at once accepted into the ruling vestry of Holy Trinity. Though only seventeen, he was a signatory to the confirmation of new churchwardens in January 1586. In 1590 he was chosen one of the two collectors for the poor, but by January 1592 had left the parish, probably on his marriage to Elizabeth Cosyn (*b. c.*1570), sister of the composer Benjamin Cosyn. Three children, Mark Anthony, Mary, and Judith, had been born by 1599, when Caesar and Elizabeth settled in Camberwell, Surrey. Here four more children were baptized: Susan, Martha, Edmund, and lastly Benjamin, on 23 October 1608.

Caesar Galliardello was one of the seven violinists who played at the funeral of Elizabeth I in 1603. Thereafter he climbed steadily through the ranks of the royal violins. With the death of Joseph Lupo in 1616 he may have become their leader.

By 21 May 1611, when a daughter was baptized there, the Galliardellos had returned to the Minories. Although Caesar was at once accepted back into the ruling vestry, serving as churchwarden in 1612, the ensuing years proved tragic. By 1627, when he made his will, Caesar had only two children living, Mary and Benjamin. Elizabeth, too, had died and Caesar had remarried.

Galliardello maintained links with Camberwell, however, in the process becoming a friend of the actor Edmund Alleyn, who founded Dulwich College within the parish in 1619. Alleyn's diary twice records the Galliardello family dining at Dulwich. It was presumably this friendship which led to Benjamin Cosyn's appointment as organist of Dulwich College in 1622.

Galliardello played at the funeral of James I in 1625, was again elected churchwarden of Holy Trinity, on 11 October 1626, and died in office in 1627. His will, drawn up on 14 September, begins with a trenchant protestant preamble. Like Shakespeare, he describes himself only as 'gentleman', making no reference to his profession, to musical instruments, or to manuscripts. His estate was divided between his second wife, Alice (d. 1641), and his son Benjamin. The will's principal witness was the veteran preacher Josias Nicholls, who thereafter lived on in the parish until 1635. Caesar Galliardello was buried in the churchyard of Holy Trinity on 15 November 1627. His will was proved on 10 December following.   BRETT USHER

Sources B. Usher, 'The Cosyns and the Galliardellos: two Elizabethan musical dynasties', *The Consort*, 50 (1994), 95–110 · parish register, Holy Trinity Minories, GL, MS 9238 · churchwardens' accounts and vestry minutes of Holy Trinity Minories, LPL, MS 3390 · W. L. Woodfill, *Musicians in English society from Elizabeth to Charles I* (1953) · R. Prior, 'A second Jewish community in Tudor London', *Jewish Historical Studies*, 31 (1988–90), 137–52 · E. M. Tomlinson, *A history of the Minories, London*, 2nd edn (1922) · A. Ashbee, ed., *Records of English court music*, 3 (1988); 4 (1991); 6 (1992) · P. Holman, *Four and twenty fiddlers: the violin at the English court, 1540–1690*, new edn (1993) · W. Young, *The history of Dulwich College*, 2 vols. (1889) · will, GL, MS 9052/10
Wealth at death had earned £46 p.a. as royal musician since 1585; £10 p.a. to second wife: will, GL, MS 9052/10

Galliardello, Mark Anthony (d. 1585), musician, was born in or near Venice into a Jewish musical dynasty whose Italian surname was probably Alberti. When at the end of the 1530s Henry VIII authorized Thomas Cromwell to effect an improvement in his musical establishment at court, Cromwell recruited a branch of the Lanier family from France and many musicians from the Venetian families of Lupo, Ferrabosco, Bassano, and (as they came to be known in England) Galliardello.

The Galliardellos specialized in playing, and probably also making, viols and violins. Mark Anthony 'Gagiardell' entered the royal service on 1 May 1545 and was in 1549 living in a large alien colony in East Smithfield. By the beginning of Elizabeth's reign he had moved to the liberty of

Holy Trinity Minories, next to the city parish of St Botolph Aldgate, having apparently just married his wife, Margery. A daughter, Lucretia, was baptized at Holy Trinity on 8 April 1563, followed by Mark Anthony in 1565 (d. 1566), Frances in 1566, and Caesar *Galliardello in 1568. One month before Caesar's birth Mark Anthony was granted letters of denization as queen's servant, born a subject of the duke of Venice.

By this time Galliardello had abandoned his Jewish faith and espoused protestantism—with a vengeance, it may be said. He became churchwarden of Holy Trinity Minories in December 1568, keeping scrupulous accounts and carefully compiling a list of visiting preachers and the sums paid to them. His conscientious drudgery provides historians with vital clues to the development of nonconformist activity in London in the aftermath of the vestiarian controversy which divided the capital after March 1566. It is plain that he was prominent in encouraging the activities of such radical clergymen as John Field, William Bonham, and Nicholas Crane.

Although Galliardello's successors after 1570 did not continue the tradition of listing their visiting preachers, one of them noted in 1575 that he and others were to be thanked for their 'liberality towards the preachers … or else it would cost us more money' (Tomlinson, 398). Galliardello served again as churchwarden for two years from December 1576 and was associated with Crane and Thomas Wilcox in the regulation of poor relief.

Galliardello's daughter Lucretia married another royal musician, Henry Troches, in 1580 and gave birth to three children before dying aged twenty-one in September 1584. Mark Anthony did not long survive her, dying on 15 June 1585 in Holy Trinity Minories. He was buried at the church two days later, in 'most good name and fame and godly report of all his neighbours' (ibid.), a comment unique in the Minories' records. He was survived by Margery, by Caesar, and by Frances, who on 12 October 1585 married the musician John Lanier (d. 1616). Their son, Nicholas *Lanier, first master of the king's music, was baptized in the parish on 10 November 1588. Margery Galliardello long survived her husband, dying in 1611.

                                                        BRETT USHER

Sources B. Usher, 'The Cosyns and the Galliardellos: two Elizabethan musical dynasties', *The Consort*, 50 (1994), 95–110 · parish registers, Holy Trinity Minories, GL, MS 9238 · churchwardens' accounts and vestry minutes, Holy Trinity Minories, LPL, MS 3390 · W. L. Woodfill, *Musicians in English society from Elizabeth I to Charles I* (1952) · R. Prior, 'A second Jewish community in Tudor London', *Transactions of the Jewish Historical Society of England*, 31 (1988–90), 137–52 · E. M. Tomlinson, *A history of the Minories London*, 2nd edn (1922) · A. Ashbee, ed., *Records of English court music*, 9 vols. (1986–96), vols. 6–7 · P. Holman, *Four and twenty fiddlers* (1993)
Archives LPL, churchwardens' accounts of liberty of Holy Trinity Minories, London, MS 3390

Gallini, Sir John Andrew [formerly Giovanni Andrea Battista Gallini] (1728–1805), dancer and theatre manager, was born in Florence, Italy, on 7 January 1728. He was trained in Paris by François Marcel and emigrated to England at an unknown date, though he had been performing at the Académie Royale de Musique. By 17 December 1757 he was dancing at Covent Garden Theatre. Between 1758 and 1766 he performed and served as director of dances at the King's Theatre, Haymarket (the opera house), except for an interval at Covent Garden in late 1763 and 1764. He ceased to perform in public at the end of the 1766 season.

In a campaign to raise the intellectual respectability of dance, on 3 March 1762 Gallini published *A Treatise on the Art of Dancing*, which was followed by *Critical Observations on the Art of Dancing* (1770?). Dance historians agree that these elegantly printed volumes were largely derivative, citing Weaver, Cahusac, and other sources, but were important statements of philosophy that helped gain Gallini entrée into society. While teaching dance, at which he was expert, he courted and married privately, on 23 February 1763 at St James's, Westminster, Lady Elizabeth Peregrine Bertie (d. 1804), the daughter of the third earl of Abingdon. She gave birth to twin sons on 13 October 1766 and later to two daughters. Notwithstanding outrage in parts of the fashionable world, her family accepted the match. However, the marriage eventually broke down, and in later years the couple lived apart.

In addition to the money and property his wife brought him, Gallini, who was famously parsimonious, accumulated a substantial fortune. On 28 June 1774, with J. C. Bach and Karl Friedrich Abel, he purchased premises in Hanover Square, where the three men built a splendid concert room 95 feet by 30. Gallini bought out his partners on 12 November 1776 and continued to operate the hall successfully for the rest of his life, making large sums from series such as the Professional Concert and Academy of Ancient Music, and from masquerades held there.

Not content, in the spring of 1778 Gallini attempted to buy the opera at the King's Theatre, Haymarket. Xenophobia against him coalesced into a bidding war won by Richard Brinsley Sheridan and Thomas Harris, who paid the outlandish price of £22,000 for the enterprise (all of it borrowed). Unfamiliar with opera, they began losing large sums; meanwhile, Gallini embarked on an aggressive campaign to force them out. After seven years of transfers of authority, forced declarations of bankruptcy, feuding trustees, and sheriff's sales, he achieved his wish, though the conditions were far from ideal. He served as trustee for William Taylor, who loathed him, harassed him, and sued him year after year, and he had to operate under a budget cap of £18,000 enforced by the court of chancery. The lord chamberlain, who regarded him as an undesirable foreigner, made him struggle to get a licence to perform. Surprisingly, Gallini paid more attention to opera than to dance, mounting highly creditable seasons. To supplement the Italian repertory he began to import both works and performers from German houses, and he drew to England such major performers as Giovanni Maria Rubinelli, Luigi Marchesi, and Gertrud Mara. Dance required more than a single star, however. Without a major choreographer, even Auguste Vestris's performance seemed less brilliant, and although Jean Georges Noverre returned at the end of 1787 the talent provided for him to work with was so limited that in February 1789 a riotous audience demanded that better dancers be imported. Even after

Marie Madeleine Guimard consented to a short visit for exorbitant fees, Gallini somehow managed to run up a profit of £4000 in four seasons—though the money went to the theatre's innumerable creditors.

All along, rent from concerts continued to increase Gallini's personal fortune, and he acquired real estate in England and abroad. Money probably also changed hands when he was awarded the knighthood of the order of the Golden Spur by the pope in the spring of 1788. He was then popularly styled Sir John Gallini, but English society proved more willing to joke about the title than to recognize it.

The opera burnt down in June 1789. Although Gallini schemed to take full control of the business in a new space with a new partner, Robert Bray O'Reilly, by December he had broken away and joined forces with his nemesis William Taylor, who was rebuilding the old theatre. Defying the lord chamberlain, they reopened without a licence in the spring of 1791, with Gallini responsible for artistic direction. Despite the presence of Haydn, the great tenor Giacomo Davide, and the Vestris, father and son, the company lost £9700 in five months. Gallini thereafter dropped out of opera management and contented himself with teaching, at which he was recognized to be superb, and running Hanover Square. He probably lost very little on the new opera venture, since he did collect most of the money he was owed from Taylor. He died abruptly at his home in Hanover Square on the morning of 5 January 1805 at the age of seventy-six, survived by a son and two daughters, among whom an estate said to be £150,000 was divided. He was buried at Yattendon church, Berkshire. Having sought his fortune in England in 1757, Gallini had led the opera ballet, taught a generation of aristocrats to dance and married one of them, made a substantial fortune as impresario of the chief concert venue in London, and proved to be one of the most successful opera managers of the eighteenth century.   JUDITH MILHOUS

Sources R. Ralph, 'Sir John Gallini', *About the House* (summer 1979), 30–37 • C. Price, J. Milhous, and R. D. Hume, *Italian opera in late eighteenth-century London*, 1: *The King's Theatre, Haymarket, 1778–1791* (1995) • *GM*, 1st ser., 75 (1805), 89 • *DNB* • Highfill, Burnim & Langhans, *BDA* • S. J. Cohen, ed., *International encyclopaedia of dance*, 6 vols. (1998) • *IGI* • will, PRO, PROB 11/1420, sig. 95
Likenesses C. Bretherton, engraving, 1781
Wealth at death approx. £150,000: *GM*

Galloway. For this title name see Fergus, lord of Galloway (d. 1161); Roland, lord of Galloway (d. 1200); Alan, lord of Galloway (b. before 1199, d. 1234); Balliol, Dervorguilla de, lady of Galloway (d. 1290); Douglas, Archibald, lord of Galloway and third earl of Douglas (c.1320–1400).

Galloway, Alexander (1776–1847), radical and engineer, is of unknown parentage and background; by the age of eighteen he emerged from obscurity to assume an influential role in the London Corresponding Society (LCS). According to Francis Place, Galloway was one of 'the cleverest men' of the LCS (*Autobiography of Francis Place*, 142), and in 1794 he appeared at several divisional and committee meetings of the society. The following year he was signing its official correspondence as assistant secretary, and in July 1795 he was one of the society's representatives who tried in vain to present a reform address to the secretary of state for the Home Office. Galloway's prominence in the LCS soon brought him to the attention of the authorities, and on 31 July 1797 he was arrested along with five other members at a meeting at St Pancras but was released on bail after several hours of questioning; no charges were ever filed.

Galloway's radical enthusiasm was not dampened by the incident, and that same year he became president of the LCS and a member of the revolutionary United Englishmen. Although as president of the LCS he tried to distance the society from implication in the naval mutinies of 1797, his own private sympathies were with the mutineers, and he was one of numerous radicals caught in a government campaign of repression in 1798. He surrendered himself on 20 April 1798 after learning of his impending arrest, and under the suspension of habeas corpus he remained imprisoned in Newgate until 2 March 1801. Within nine months of his release he was struggling to establish an engineering business in High Holborn, but he had lost none of his political conviction. Along with his brother-in-law Thomas *Evans, an ultra-radical, Galloway was reputedly part of a new 'national committee' of United Irishmen and United Britons formed in late 1801, and his private correspondence around this time suggests an affiliation with the revolutionary cause: 'We have only to rest on our oars for a short time, to strike with more force and intrepidity' (quoted in McCalman, 17).

In early 1802 Galloway was part of a committee, which had suspected links with the French directory, organized to raise money in support of John Nicholls, a member of the united movement, and he was an active supporter of Colonel Edward Marcus Despard in 1803 in the lead-up to his trial. With the resumption of war with France in May 1803, he was suspected of being involved in the publication of a piece of anti-war propaganda by Arthur Seale called *Are you Right?* Eight years passed before Galloway once more appeared to take an active role in the burgeoning radical reform movement. In 1811 he was one of the collectors for a subscription raised to assist the family of John Gale Jones, and the Regency crisis and the apparent demise of George III aroused his democratic hopes that 'such a change in our Government … would not only obtain us a Peace with Europe, but would grant us that of all things we most stand in need of a Parliamentary Reform' (Hone, 202). On 16 October 1811 Galloway was made free of the Worshipful Company of Leathersellers by redemption, and he was afterwards elected to the livery. By this time he had probably married (details of his wife are unknown), and in the years between 1818 and 1825 he bound five sons apprentice to him in the Leathersellers' Company; three were subsequently admitted to the livery. Galloway himself maintained a distinguished association with the Leathersellers' Company, serving as fourth warden in 1834–5 and being elected to the court of assistants on 15 June 1841, and although he later came to disapprove of the operations of the livery corporations of

London he nevertheless used livery meetings as a forum to promote his political campaigns.

In 1813 Galloway was chairman of a committee which campaigned for improved working conditions through an abolition of the apprenticeship clauses of the Statute of Artificers; he also became a member of Joseph Lancaster's West London Lancasterian Association. When Galloway's nephew Thomas John Evans and Arthur Thistlewood travelled to France in 1814 they carried with them letters of introduction from Galloway to Jacobin émigrés in Paris, and in September of that year Galloway commissioned commemorative busts of Thomas Spence to be made following his death. His Spencean commitments also involved him in raising a subscription for his imprisoned colleagues in 1816; in the following year he probably financed the *Forlorn Hope* published by Robert Wedderburn and Charles Jennison. At much the same time he was one of the subscribers to a fund organized by the Friends of the Liberty of the Press under the management of Robert Waithman for the support of the embattled William Hone. In January 1818 he was part of a committee organized to administer money collected in support of imprisoned radicals, although he subsequently faced some scathing criticism from the likes of Gale Jones, Henry Hunt, and John Gast implicating him in the unfair distribution of the money raised and in favouritism for Thomas Evans. As a member of the Metropolitan and Central Committee founded in August 1819, Galloway sought a legal redress for the Peterloo massacre, and he made public his sympathy for Queen Caroline in 1820 as part of the queen's plate committee. By this time he was well acquainted with Francis Burdett and had a genuine interest of his own in City of London politics. Between 1821 and 1823 he was elected as common councilman for Farringdon Without; he was returned for the same ward in 1825 and served fifteen years in the position.

As an engineer, Galloway was by the mid-1820s one of London's largest employers, and in 1824 he gave evidence before the select committee on artisans and machinery. While his obituarist referred to him as 'the eminent civil engineer' (*GM*, 103), his professional reputation was tainted, albeit temporarily, through his association with the Greek loan affair of 1826. Galloway's firm, which by this time was located at West Smithfield, was engaged to supply the machinery for six vessels to serve the Greeks in their revolution. The work was not completed on time and the workmanship was allegedly of a very poor quality. William Cobbett led the public attack on Galloway in the pages of *Cobbett's Weekly Political Register*. He alleged that while Galloway was preparing the engines for the Greek vessels, one of his sons was supplying weapons to the Turks to counter the Greek revolution and that Galloway was 'employed by, and has, for a long time past, had a son at Alexandria, in the pay of the Pacha of Egypt' (*Cobbett's Weekly Political Register*, 28 Oct 1826, 297). Galloway's later life was relatively inactive compared with his early radical years, and he by and large contented himself with official City politics as a common councilman. Galloway died on

20 November 1847 in Claremont Street, Smithfield, London, at the age of seventy-one. His place of burial remains unknown.

MICHAEL T. DAVIS

Sources J. A. Hone, *For the cause of truth: radicalism in London, 1796–1821* (1982) • I. McCalman, *Radical underworld: prophets, revolutionaries, and pornographers in London, 1795–1840* (1988) • J. Graham, *The nation, the law and the king: reform politics in England, 1789–1799*, 2 vols. (2000) • E. P. Thompson, *The making of the English working class*, new edn (1968) • M. Thale, ed., *Selections from the papers of the London Corresponding Society, 1792–1799* (1983) • *The autobiography of Francis Place, 1771–1854*, ed. M. Thale (1972) • *GM*, 2nd ser., 29 (1848), 103–4 • W. Cobbett, *Rural rides*, ed. G. D. H. Cole and M. Cole, 3 vols. (1930), 3.433, 497, 980 • *Cobbett's Weekly Political Register* (16 Sept 1826) • *Cobbett's Weekly Political Register* (7 Oct 1826) • *Cobbett's Weekly Political Register* (28 Oct 1826) • *Cobbett's Weekly Political Register* (11 Nov 1826)
Archives BL, letters to E. Ellice, Add. MS 36463 • BL, letters to J. C. Hobhouse, Add. MSS 36461–36462 • BL, letters to Francis Place, Add. MSS 35149, 35151, 37950

Galloway, Sir Alexander (1895–1977), army officer, was born at Minto manse, Hawick, Scotland, on 3 November 1895, the second son and youngest of the four children of the Revd Alexander Galloway, Presbyterian minister of Minto, and his wife, Margaret Rankin Smith. Educated at King William's College, Isle of Man, he was at a peak of schoolboy success academically and at games, and about to go up to Cambridge, when war broke out in 1914. Galloway volunteered immediately, and was commissioned on the basis of his service in the school Officers' Training Corps into the Cameronians (Scottish Rifles), but he first saw active service with 4th King's Own Scottish Borderers at Gallipoli, where he earned a high reputation for bravery. Among the last to leave the Peninsula, he then took part in the campaigns in Egypt and Palestine before being posted to the western front. There he was awarded the MC in 1918.

Galloway became a regular officer in 1917 and after the war was one of the many experienced junior officers who served long years without promotion. In 1920 he married Dorothy Hadden, daughter of Frank Hadden White, stockbroker, of Norham, Northumberland. They had three sons, one of whom died in 1955. After service abroad, Galloway's quick brain, energy, and regimental reputation earned him entry to the Staff College at Camberley. He was then thirty-three, noted by his contemporaries as a man of hot temper, a generous friend, and a deadly fast bowler. Almost ten years later he returned to Camberley to instruct before commanding 1st Cameronians, an appointment cut short by promotion to command the Staff College at Haifa in February 1940.

When the war in the western desert began in earnest Galloway was picked as brigadier, general staff—chief staff officer—to Sir H. M. Wilson. He made an important contribution to the desert victory of 1940 and equally to the evacuation from Greece in 1941. Back in Egypt he became chief staff officer to the newly forming Eighth Army under Lieutenant-General Sir Alan Cunningham, whose task it was to destroy the combined German–Italian army. Operation Crusader began to this end in November 1941 with high success but the German command then reversed the situation. Exhausted and ill, Cunningham decided to break off the battle and withdraw. With extraordinary resolve, Galloway decided to withhold the order, convinced that such a move would be disastrous. He told the commander-in-chief, Sir Claude Auchinleck, that they must fight on though very weak in armour. His advice was taken and proved sound. A British success resulted. Galloway, having risked removal and perhaps disciplinary action, was promoted and sent to the United States to select equipment for the Eighth Army. However, the incident brought him to the attention of General Sir Alan Brooke. At the time Brooke needed a major-general for the exacting post of director of staff duties and ordered Galloway to London, much to his vexation, for he was commanding a division in battle.

At last, in 1944, Galloway was sent to 1st armoured division in the Mediterranean; but it remained in reserve during the campaign through the Italian mountains. He took temporary command of 4th Indian division at Cassino before being recalled to the staff, this time at the wish of Field Marshal Sir B. L. Montgomery. Thus he was in north-west Europe at the end of the war when he was promoted and, paradoxically, given a series of commands: 30th corps, the army in Malaya, and in 1947 high commissioner and commander-in-chief, British forces in Austria.

As Galloway arrived the Soviet Union was seeking to establish Austrian communists as police and local government authorities in the western occupation zones. The skill of Galloway and his American colleague in preventing this earned the praise of the foreign secretary, Ernest Bevin. When Galloway left Austria in 1949 the struggle to institute an independent democratic state was largely won.

Galloway was too old to hold another appointment in an army over-full of senior officers. By mischance his talents as a dynamic and courageous leader had been sacrificed to his reputation as a staff officer. He retired in 1950 but remained active in several commercial activities until 1965. He was appointed CBE and to the DSO in 1941. Created CB in 1946 and KBE in 1949, he was twice mentioned in dispatches, besides being awarded the first class Military Cross of both Greece and Czechoslovakia, the orders of Merit and the White Lion of Czechoslovakia, and the order of Orange-Nassau of the Netherlands. Galloway died on 27 January 1977 at Norham, Northumberland.

ANTHONY FARRAR-HOCKLEY, rev.

Sources *The Times* (1 Feb 1977) • *WWW* • private information (1986) • I. S. O. Playfair, *The Mediterranean and the Middle East*, 1–2 (1954–6)
Archives CAC Cam., corresp.

Galloway, Sir Archibald (bap. 1780, d. 1850), army officer in the East India Company and writer, was baptized at Blairgowrie, Perthshire, on 12 February 1780. He was the son of James Galloway and Margaret, née Forester, of Perth. He obtained a cadetship in 1799, and on 29 October 1800 was appointed ensign in the 14th Bengal native infantry. He was promoted lieutenant on 18 May 1802, serving as regimental adjutant and quartermaster. During the Second Anglo-Maratha War he took part in the defence of

Delhi and distinguished himself greatly at the siege of Bharatpur. Galloway subsequently wrote an influential work on Indian sieges, as well as treatises on aspects of Indian law and custom. On 12 October 1812 he was made brevet captain, and on 19 December the same year regimental captain.

On 28 November 1815, in Calcutta, Galloway married Adelaide, née Campbell (d. 1832), with whom he had three sons and six daughters. He was promoted major on 1 May 1824, and on 6 March 1826 was made lieutenant-colonel of the 2nd native infantry, transferring to the 10th on 26 April 1830 and to the 55th on 14 September 1833. From 1830 to 1835 Galloway served as a member of the Bengal military board, on the appointment of Lord William Bentinck. He was made brevet colonel on 18 June 1831 and colonel on 22 September 1836, and was nominated a CB on 20 July 1838.

On 24 September 1840 Galloway was elected a director of the East India Company, becoming chairman in 1849. He received the rank of major-general on 23 November 1841, and was decorated with the KCB on 25 August 1848. He died in Upper Harley Street, London, on 6 April 1850, aged seventy.

G. F. R. BARKER, rev. ALEX MAY

Sources *Indian Army List* · V. C. P. Hodson, *List of officers of the Bengal army, 1758–1834*, 4 vols. (1927–47) · Chambers, *Scots.* (1835) · *GM*, 2nd ser., 33 (1850), 660–62 · *Dod's Peerage* (1850), 222
Archives BL, letters to John Cam Hobhouse, Add. MSS 36479–36480
Likenesses Dickinson of New Bond Street, engraving, 1850

Galloway, Christopher (*fl.* 1621–1645), architect and engineer, was sometimes known as Halloway and Holloway, and in Russian as Khristofor Khristoforov Galovey, Alavey, or Khalove. He worked in Moscow for over twenty years, but nothing is known about his early life or career; it is possible, however, that he was descended from Christopher Galloway, a burgess of Haddington, who died in 1570, or that he was related to John Holloway, the early seventeenth-century maker of an iron lantern clock in Market Lavington, Wiltshire, who was the first of a family of clockmakers.

In 1621 Galloway was hired, through the agency of the merchant Fabin Ulyanov, by Muscovy's embassies department. His most important work was the construction of the superstructure over the saviour's gate, the imperial portal to the Moscow Kremlin (1621–8), then known as St Florus's tower. He followed this with essential repairs and alterations to the Kremlin's patriarchal cathedral of the Assumption (1626), the construction of a water supply system to the Kremlin (1633), and a steeple to the new Moscow printing house (1643–5). On most of these projects he worked in collaboration with the Russian builder Bazhen Ogurtsov. He is reputed to have discovered silver and copper ore in the Urals in 1644, and in 1645, together with the English smelter 'Rytser Still', checked stones brought from Siberia to Moscow for copper content.

For the saviour's gate Galloway conceived and built a structure unprecedented in Russia, 70 metres and ten storeys high. The top four storeys comprised a triumphal crown, with gallery, octagonal belfry, and green-tiled spire. The fusion of Gothic and Renaissance motifs and forms included an openwork parapet with ogee gables and arches, carved botanic and geometric decorations, and stone sculptures of bears, lions, and gargoyles. This composition was copied for the capping of the Kremlin's important Trinity Tower in 1672–87. Galloway's celebratory design—which led to the capping of all the other towers—inaugurated the Romanovs' attempt to give the citadel, as the sacred heart of Muscovy, a distinctly spiritual and regal aureole. It was to become the most enduring and popular architectural emblem of Russia, and survived the obfuscation of its creator's identity which occurred in the twentieth century.

The clock (des.) that Galloway built for the saviour's tower was a feat of ingenuity for which he was richly rewarded. The striking mechanism sounded thirteen bells cast in the Poganny Prud ironworks in Moscow by Kirill Samoylov and others commissioned from Holland. It had two dials, one facing the Kremlin and the other facing the city, both of which measured over 16 feet in diameter. Made from oak panels held together by iron clasps, these were painted azure blue and covered with gold and silver stars, and the sun and moon. The dials rotated and the time was indicated by a single pointer. This innovatory mechanism worked until 1705, when it was replaced. In 1626, upon his first completion of the saviour's tower (after a fire he had to rebuild it), Galloway received from Tsar Michael and the Patriarch Filaret a silver goblet, forty sables, forty martens, ten arshins of scarlet satin, ten arshins of sky-blue damask, five arshins of dark red taffeta, and four arshins of crimson brocade. His other major work in Moscow was the first pressure water supply system in Russia, operated by an apparatus which he installed in the Kremlin's water pumping tower (previously known as the Sviblov tower) at the confluence of the Moscow and Neglinnaya rivers in 1633. Using cogs, cisterns, lead pipes, and a large external iron wheel, it drew water from the river. Via an intricate canal arrangement this was then raised to the Kremlin and distributed twenty-four hours a day to the service quarters, imperial apartments, and palace gardens. This much needed supply replaced the earlier, extremely limited, hand-drawing processes.

JEREMY HOWARD

Sources J. Howard, *The Scottish Kremlin builder: Christopher Galloway* (1997) · J. Howard, 'The Scottish Kremlin: Christopher Galloway and the saviour's tower', *British East–West Journal*, 109 (April 1998), 4–5 · J. Howard, 'Clocks in the Kremlin', *Horological Journal*, 141 (1999), 275–9, 297–9 · B. Brodskiy, *Serdrse-rodiny-Kreml* (1996), 69, 83, 141 · I. Zabelin, *Istoriya goroda Moskvy* (1905), 181–93 · M. Pylyaev, *Staraya Moskva* [1891] (1990), 278–9 · A. Voyce, *The Moscow Kremlin* (1971), 26–31 · Thieme & Becker, *Allgemeines Lexikon*, 20.130 · *Bol'shaya Sovetskaya entsiklopediya* (1952), 10.151 · D. Fedosov, *The Caledonian connection* (1996), 52
Archives RGADA (Russian State Archive of Early Acts), Moscow, fonds 141, 150, 396

Galloway, Janet Anne (1841–1909), promoter of higher education for women in Scotland, was born at Birdston Cottage, Birdston, parish of Campsie, Stirlingshire, on 10 October 1841, the elder daughter of Alexander Galloway (1802–1883), estate factor, and his wife, Anne, née Bald, of

Carsebridge, Alloa (d. 1858). The family moved to Glasgow in 1844, where Alexander commenced business as land agent, valuator, and accountant, residing at 59 Bath Street, Glasgow, from 1857. Janet was the only one of their four children to survive to adulthood; two brothers died in infancy and a sister, Eliza Margaret, died in 1855 aged eight.

Janet Galloway was educated in Scotland and then sent abroad to schools in France, Germany, and Holland, her father believing that 'as much pain should be taken about girls as boys' (Jardine, 56). On her return, she was trained by her father in bookkeeping, office work, and business methods. Finding by experience the limited range of employment open to women, which was due to their restricted education, she became an ardent supporter of the movement to provide higher education for women. In 1877 she became honorary secretary of the newly established Glasgow Association for the Higher Education of Women, founded by Jessie Campbell and others, to offer women opportunities of study at university level. She earnestly worked to provide teaching for women in university arts subjects, drawing up schemes of instruction, devising standards and methods of teaching, and securing lecturers and examiners. In 1883 the association was incorporated as Queen Margaret College, and she became its first secretary, continuing to refuse any payment for her duties. She had been her father's constant companion and housekeeper, and after his death in 1883 she moved into rooms in the college, the former North Park House in Hamilton Drive, Glasgow, donated by Isabella Elder.

Queen Margaret College amalgamated with Glasgow University in 1892 after the Scottish universities commissioners issued an ordinance empowering Scottish universities to make provision for the instruction and graduation of women. Janet Galloway became a university official, and although new duties were placed on her she still refused to be paid. She helped to promote a corporate life among the students, organizing social gatherings and encouraging the formation of societies and a union. She would keep in touch with them after they left the college, taking a very keen interest in their careers, and promoted the formation of a women graduates association. She helped to found and run the Queen Margaret Guild (1885) which provided lectures for the university extension movement, was a founder of the students' residence, Queen Margaret Hall (1894), and was a prominent member of the executive committee of the Queen Margaret Settlement Association (1897), a social work programme carried out by students. She was also a member of the Teachers' Guild and from 1905 was one of the university's representatives on the Glasgow Provincial Committee for the Training of Teachers. Although baptized into the Church of Scotland she was a devoted member of St Mary's Episcopalian Cathedral in Glasgow. She was also an accomplished pianist and had a deep love of music.

Janet Galloway, who was unmarried, was described as being blunt and having a 'ready fearless wit and kind eye'. Her personality was a mixture of conservative instinct and progressive act. She did not intend at first that Queen Margaret College should equip women to compete professionally with men but that it should better prepare them for their traditional roles. She personally preferred single-sex education for women but welcomed the changes that opened universities to women and eventually to co-education. She was a Conservative in politics and disapproved of women's suffrage, as well as being thoroughly opposed to the idea of female lecturers working in the college. Initially doubtful about the wisdom of establishing a medical school for women, she then spent years planning its proper layout and was very proud that she helped produce the first two female medical graduates from a Scottish university in 1894.

Janet Galloway followed closely educational trends in Great Britain, Europe, and North America, and in 1893 represented Queen Margaret College at the Chicago Great Exhibition. In 1907 she received the honorary degree of doctor of laws from Glasgow University in recognition of her lifetime of gratuitous service to the higher education of women. She died in harness at Queen Margaret Drive, Glasgow, on 23 January 1909, having continued in her duties despite failing health. She would not hear of resting and attended an educational conference in Edinburgh the evening before her death. She was buried in Lennoxtown cemetery, Campsie, on 26 January. A fund was raised and a memorial window entitled *The Pursuit of Ideal Education* was installed in the Bute Hall, Glasgow University, in honour of a woman who had unselfishly devoted her life to the advancement of education, the pursuit of learning, and the fulfilment of women's potential.

LESLEY M. RICHMOND

Sources records, U. Glas., Archives and Business Records Centre, Glasgow Association for the Higher Education of Women • U. Glas., Archives and Business Records Centre, Queen Margaret College archives • M. B. Jardine, *Janet A. Galloway, L.L.D.: a book of memories* (1914) • D. Murray, *Miss Janet Ann Galloway and the higher education of women in Glasgow* (1914) • *Glasgow University Magazine: special supplement containing tributes to the late Miss Janet A. Galloway, L.L.D.*, 21/11 (1909) • J. McLintock, 'Janet Galloway', in J. E. Thomas and B. Elsey, *International biography of adult education* (1985), 191–6 • J. Cameron, 'Mr Alexander Galloway', in J. Cameron, *The parish of Campsie* (1892), 223–6 • *Englishwoman's Review*, 40 (1909), 133–4 • parish records (birth/baptism), Campsie, Stirlingshire, Scotland, No. 475, vol. 4, p. 153 (10 Oct 1841/28 Oct 1841) • *Glasgow Herald* (27 Jan 1909)

Archives U. Glas., Queen Margaret College archives, MSS and corresp. | U. Glas., Glasgow Association for the Higher Education of Women, MSS

Likenesses photograph, 1907, U. Glas., archives

Wealth at death £4628 6s. 2d.: confirmation, 10 May 1909, *CCI*

Galloway, John (1804–1894), iron-founder and engineer, was born on 14 February 1804 at his father's house, 37 Lombard Street, Manchester, the second son of William Galloway (1768–1836) and his wife, Elizabeth. His father had moved to Manchester in 1790 from Coldstream, his birthplace, and by the time John was born his father was in business in Manchester as a millwright. John was educated at a local school in Mosley Street until at the age of fourteen he became apprenticed for seven years in his father's firm, Galloway and Bowman, millwrights, engineers, and iron-founders.

John completed his time in 1825 and remained with the firm of Galloway, Bowman, and Glasgow for another ten years. When the Liverpool and Manchester Railway opened in 1830 he became interested in the construction of locomotives and by 1833 had completed the *Manchester*, the first locomotive to be built in that city. The firm, however, built only about four or five locomotives in all. In 1835 Galloway, in partnership with his elder brother, William (1796–1873), hived off from the original family business and established the firm of W. and J. Galloway at the Knott Mill ironworks, on the site of a former foundry.

The elder William Galloway died in 1836 and by 1839 the firm of Galloway, Bowman, and Glasgow had been wound up; but by this time William the younger and John Galloway had begun to make their mark as iron-founders and engineers. William and his wife, Elizabeth, had a son, **John Galloway** (1826–1896), iron-founder and engineer, who was born on 18 July 1826 at Great Jackson Street, Manchester. In 1840 he was apprenticed for seven years to his father and uncle.

In the early 1840s the use of gas was expanding rapidly and the firm of W. and J. Galloway began to execute increasing numbers of orders for gasworks equipment and gas pipes. At the same time the Galloway brothers were developing an early version of the double-fire flue boiler, a smoke consuming variation of the Lancashire boiler patented in 1844 by their great rival William Fairbairn. From 1848 the two brothers took out frequent patents for improvements to boilers and other parts of the steam engine, and by 1851 the 'Galloway boiler' had been developed to the stage where it could be patented. In the next forty years the firm made nearly 9000 boilers based on the design.

From about 1850 most of the firm's business consisted of the manufacture of boilers, steam engines, and mechanical equipment for local cotton mills, but from 1852 it exported equipment for gunpowder mills in Turkey and cotton mills in Russia and India, in some cases also supplying cast-iron columns for the erection of the spinning and weaving sheds. At the same time the firm undertook some work in what would now be regarded as civil engineering, building a viaduct on the Ulverston and Lancaster Railway in 1857 and erecting the pier at Southport in 1860. These works, executed under the supervision of James Brunlees, were notable for the first successful use of high-pressure water-jetting in the sinking of cast-iron piles into sand.

One of the brothers' most percipient and profitable associations was with Henry Bessemer, a customer of the firm for twelve years before he asked them in 1855 to make the special equipment required for trials of his new steel-making process. It is very likely that, in the course of extensive testing carried out by Bessemer and the Galloways at the Knott Mill ironworks, the first ingots of Bessemer steel in the world were produced there. In 1856 John Galloway and Charles John, son of the elder John Galloway, entered the business as partners, the firm becoming W. and J. Galloway & Sons. Three years later John Galloway senior and his brother William became partners with Bessemer, along with others in the company he formed, to erect a Bessemer steelworks in Sheffield, for which they supplied the converters and other special equipment. Galloways subsequently supplied converters and equipment to a number of other firms making Bessemer steel under licence.

In 1872 a separate boilerworks was opened in Hyde Road, Ardwick, and thereafter Knott Mill works was devoted entirely to the manufacture of engines. The firm's largest engine was one of 10,000 indicated horsepower, supplied in 1888 to Palmers shipyard in Jarrow. In 1889 the partnership was turned into a private company, with a capital of £250,000, and ten years later Galloways became a public limited liability company.

For more than thirty years from 1856 John Galloway the younger had been increasingly involved in the management of the rapidly expanding business, but after 1889 it was Charles John Galloway, the chairman and managing director, who effectively held the reins. John had acquired many other business and financial interests; he was also a JP for over thirty years, and with his wife, the daughter of William Crippin, he devoted much time to philanthropic and charitable undertakings.

John Galloway senior died in Manchester at Coldstream House, Old Trafford, on 11 February 1894 at the age of almost ninety. He was known in commercial circles as the father of the Manchester iron trade; Galloways has been described as the oldest of the large Lancashire engineering firms, and at the time of his death Hyde Road works employed 800 men and Knott Mill works 500. He never took an active part in public movements, though he was known as a Liberal in politics and a member of the United Presbyterian church.

John Galloway junior died on 16 December 1896 at his Manchester home, The Cottage, Seymour Grove, Stretford, Lancashire. He was survived by one son, William J. Galloway, at the time the MP for Manchester South-west, who was also involved in the family firm.

RONALD M. BIRSE

Sources W. H. Chaloner, 'John Galloway, 1804–1894, engineer, of Manchester and his reminiscences', *Transactions of the Lancashire and Cheshire Antiquarian Society*, 64 (1954), 93–116 · *The Engineer* (18 Dec 1896) · *The Engineer* (1 Jan 1897) · *Engineering* (18 Dec 1896) · *Journal of the Iron and Steel Institute*, 51 (1897), 311 · D. A. Collier, 'Galloway, John', *DBB* · *The Times* (13 Feb 1894), 10 · *DNB* · *CGPLA Eng. & Wales* (1894) · d. cert. [John Galloway junior] · *CGPLA Eng. & Wales* (1927)
Archives Chetham's Library, Manchester · Hick, Hargreaves & Co. Ltd, engine records of W. & J. Galloway & Sons; Galloway Ltd, company files · NRA, priv. coll., notebooks and diary
Likenesses portrait, repro. in *Transactions of the Lancashire and Cheshire Antiquarian Society*, pl. VIII
Wealth at death £143,117 3s. 2d.: probate, 1894, *CGPLA Eng. & Wales*

Galloway, John (1826–1896). *See under* Galloway, John (1804–1894).

Galloway, Joseph (c.1731–1803), colonial politician and author, was born at West River, Anne Arundel county, Maryland the son of Peter Bines Galloway, a substantial landowner in Maryland and Pennsylvania, and his wife, Elizabeth Rigbie. After his father's death Galloway moved to Philadelphia, where he began to practise law in 1747. In the following year he was elected to the Colony in Schuylkill, Philadelphia's exclusive gentleman's club comprising the city's aristocracy. In 1753 he gave up his privileged position as a Quaker in order to marry an Episcopalian woman, Grace Growden, daughter of Laurence Growden. Galloway was a highly intelligent, self-taught man, a future vice-president of the American Philosophical Society (1769–75), and his success as a lawyer opened up possibilities in politics. In 1756 he was elected to Pennsylvania's provincial assembly but, along with Benjamin Franklin, lost his seat in 1764 after his abortive attempt to replace the current proprietary administration with a directly appointed royal government. Galloway's proposed reforms were opposed by John Dickinson, a prominent pro-proprietary member of the assembly, whom Galloway defeated to regain his seat in September 1765. In the following year he was appointed to the important position of speaker of the assembly, which he held until 1775.

Galloway had long been convinced of the need to establish a system of colonial government that provided American subjects with sufficient representation while preserving British sovereignty. It was a message he took to the first continental congress in 1774, which rejected his proposal for an American assembly separate from but subordinate to the British parliament. An invitation to join the second congress was refused by Galloway, then occupied in writing the defence of his proposal *A Candid Examination of the Mutual Claims of Great Britain and the Colonies* (1775).

In May 1775 Galloway resigned from the provincial assembly and in December 1776 he joined the British army, then under General William Howe's command, on a salary of £200 p.a. In the winter of 1777–8 he served as superintendent-general for the maintenance of peace in Philadelphia, on a salary of £300 p.a., before being evacuated to New York with his family and other city loyalists in June 1778. Attempts to salvage the family's confiscated property, valued at some £40,000, failed, and the Galloways were dispossessed in March of the following year.

By this date Galloway and his family were resident in London, where he spoke for the loyalist cause. He was a critic of the British army's handling of the war and at a Commons enquiry spoke out against General Howe's conduct, which he also censured in *Letters to a Nobleman on the Conduct of the War in the Middle Colonies* (1779). In 1780 he published his *Historical and Political Reflections on the Rise and Progress of the American Rebellion*, which influenced John Wesley, whom he had met in the previous year, to write his own *Reflections on the Rise and Progress of the American Rebellion*. Wesley's press was also responsible for many of the reprints of these and later pamphlets on similar themes, including Galloway's *Letter to [Lord Howe] on his Naval Conduct* and *Cool Thoughts on the Consequences … of American Independence*. In 1790 he secured compensation of £500 p.a. for the loss of his American property.

In the final years of his life Galloway turned from military and political analyses to a study of church history and biblical prophecy. He died in Watford on 29 August 1803 and was buried in Watford churchyard, survived by his daughter Elizabeth.   JAMES TAIT, rev. PHILIP CARTER

Sources F. Baker, 'Galloway, Joseph', *ANB* · J. P. Boyd, *Anglo-American union: Joseph Galloway's plans to preserve the British empire, 1774–1788* (1941) · O. C. Kuntzteman, *Joseph Galloway, loyalist* (1941) · J. E. Ferling, *The loyalist mind* (1977)
Archives L. Cong., corresp. and papers

Galloway, Patrick (*c.*1551–1626), Church of Scotland minister, was born in Dundee, the son of Thomas Galloway, a baker of that town, and his wife, Christian Nicoll. After studying at St Mary's College, St Andrews, by 1576 he had become the minister at Fowlis Easter, Forfarshire, with responsibility as well for Longforgan. In April 1581 the general assembly approved his transfer to Perth, where his forthright preaching and opposition to Robert Montgomery, archbishop of Glasgow, offended the duke of Lennox, the king's favourite, who had him summoned before the privy council; it found no cause to punish him, and the general assembly appointed him to its delegation to present the church's grievances to King James and the council in July and October 1582. Although Galloway was suspected of having had advance knowledge of the palace revolution known as the Ruthven raid in August 1582, led by William Ruthven, first earl of Gowrie, there is no proof of this. On 1 May 1583 Galloway married Matilda (or Matillo) Guthrie (*d.* 1592); they had four children, James (created Baron Dunkeld on 15 May 1645), William, Dorothy, and Christian.

Galloway's opposition to episcopacy and the alleged urging of the earl of Gowrie to mount an insurrection made him a target of James Stewart, fifth earl of Arran, who led the reaction against the Ruthven raiders. When Gowrie's allies failed in their attempt to recover power in April 1584, the king ordered the apprehension of Galloway and three fellow ministers. Galloway evaded arrest, and on 10 May the government ordered him to appear before the privy council, failing which he was denounced as a rebel on the 28th. That month he was at Berwick, and on 20 June, with Andrew Melville and James Carmichael, he conferred with Sir Francis Walsingham in London. Thereafter he joined James Melville as co-minister to a congregation at Newcastle that followed the strict Genevan model and included exiled Scottish lords. He defended his actions in an 'Apology', published a century later by David Calderwood in 1678. With the earls of Angus and Mar, and with Andrew Melville, Walter Balcanquhall, and others, Galloway returned to Scotland in October 1585, and the next month, following the *coup d'état* against Arran, he resumed his ministry at Perth. In May 1586 the general assembly appointed him to commissions to establish presbyteries and hear charges brought against the archbishop of St Andrews and the bishop of Dunkeld, and also sent him with two others to confer with the king regarding the assembly's insistence that bishops must be subject to trial and censure by presbyteries and synods. The following year Galloway declined an invitation to succeed James Lawson as minister in Edinburgh, and in June Andrew Melville defeated him in the election for moderator of the general assembly; he was, however, assigned to advise the moderator. The general assembly appointed him in February 1588 to the delegation that exhorted James to purge Scotland of Roman Catholics, and in August to thank the king for his concern about the defence of protestantism. In 1588 he published in London *A Catechisme: Conteyning Summarely the Chief Points of Christian Religion*, which he had originally prepared for the exiled Scottish lords in Newcastle.

After his return from exile Galloway had been critical of the king, but by 1588 his views of James had altered, as may be seen in the prefaces he wrote to the latter's *Ane Fruitfull Meditation* (1588) and *Ane Meditatioun on 1 Chronicles 15* (1589). Regarding James now as the church's nursing father, he accepted an appointment as royal chaplain in June 1589, having earlier in the year accompanied the king in his expedition against the Roman Catholic earls of Huntly and Erroll. As moderator of the general assembly in August 1590 he had little success persuading James to accept articles dealing with the kirk's liberties, the repression of Catholicism, and the provision of a qualified minister with an adequate stipend for every church. In November 1592 he was appointed to a council established to monitor Catholic activities and deal with other weighty matters between sessions of the general assembly, and in October 1593 he was one of the ministers who exhorted James to act against the Catholic northern earls.

Although Galloway was again defeated by Andrew Melville in the election for moderator in May 1594, he was one of three ministers the general assembly dispatched to confer with James about the Catholic threat, and with James Melville and James Nicolson he drafted the rationale for a general fast. He also preached at the opening of parliament in June and at the baptism of Prince Henry in August, and in the autumn again accompanied the king against Huntly and Erroll. In June 1595 the assembly made him a commissioner to oversee the church's benefices and rents. Sent with Nicolson and James Melville in March 1596 to remonstrate to the king about immorality at court, he was with Andrew Melville at Falkland in September when the latter warned James not to indulge the excommunicated northern lords. In November he offended the king by accusing him of offering the church nothing but empty promises. On 20 December James ordered Galloway to sign a bond recognizing the pre-eminence of the king's judgment and the wrongfulness of preaching sedition, but Galloway refused unless the assembly first approved it. James countered by suspending the pensions of ministers who refused to sign. When James sought to resolve outstanding issues with the church, however, and recommended the establishment of a council of ministers to discuss problems, Galloway was one of fourteen clergy selected in March 1597, and in May the council consulted with the king about the appointment of ministers in Edinburgh, St Andrews, and Dundee. In March 1598, at the assembly's request, he and John Duncanson conferred with James about the trial of witches.

Galloway's first wife having died in June 1592, in 1600 he married Katherine, daughter of the minister James Lawson and widow of Gilbert Dick, merchant and burgess of Edinburgh. On 11 August that year, less than a week after the Gowrie conspiracy, Galloway preached on Psalm 124 at the market cross in Edinburgh, in the king's presence, averring that the earl of Gowrie and his brother had conspired to assassinate the king and exhorting the people to remain loyal; he subsequently preached a similar sermon in Glasgow, and set out the case against Gowrie in *A short discourse of the good ends of the higher providence, in the late attempts at his majesty's person* (1600). His anti-Catholicism deeply offended Queen Anne, however. In November 1602 Galloway was elected moderator of the general assembly, which convened at Holyrood. In that capacity he continued to push for adequate clerical maintenance and pressed James to compel Roman Catholics to conform outwardly, but he was later criticized for silencing the more zealous presbyterians in the assembly.

When James succeeded to the English throne Galloway accompanied him to London; he was rewarded in February 1604 with a pension of £200 per annum. During the summer of 1603 he and Lewis Pickering were leading organizers of a puritan campaign calling for church reform and urging James not to rely exclusively on the bishops. When Thomas Bilson, bishop of Winchester, attempted to dissuade James from holding the Hampton Court conference, Galloway argued to the contrary; to the puritans he recommended moderation as the best means to further a preaching ministry, reform church discipline, and mitigate subscription. He attended the conference, took notes, which James edited, and sent a copy to the Edinburgh presbytery. Notwithstanding Galloway's long friendship with the puritans, after the conference the Brownist Henry Jacob denounced him as an instrument of the bishops.

By December 1606 Galloway had returned to Scotland, where he opposed the king's desire to have a permanent moderator in each presbytery, believing that such a system would undermine the presbyteries' election rights, enable moderators to become tyrants, and lead to general assemblies composed exclusively of bishops and moderators. In June 1607 he was appointed minister of St Giles, Edinburgh, but at the request of the king, who still wanted permanent moderators, he refused to serve as moderator of the synod of Lothian in October. At the general assembly in July 1608 Galloway refused a demand for the expulsion of nobles who had not been sent by presbyteries, and according to Calderwood took the innovative step of permitting bishops to vote for a moderator. As the assembly neared an end, ten presbyterians and ten episcopalians were chosen for a conference about policy. Calderwood was incensed that the presbyterian contingent included Galloway and John Hall, 'two pernicious instruments circumveening many of the Ministery with their pretences' (Calderwood, 599). When the conference convened at Falkland in May 1609 Galloway submitted articles recommending that disputes be laid aside and attention directed to the Roman Catholic threat, and that imprisoned ministers be freed and exiled clergy allowed to return to their churches.

James appointed Galloway to the high commission for the province of St Andrews on 15 February 1610, and to the unified high commission on 21 December 1615. At the general assembly in August 1616 Galloway was assigned to committees to codify the disciplinary canons, prepare a uniform order of worship, draft a catechism, and provide clerical maintenance. With four other Edinburgh ministers, he was summoned before the privy council on 22 January 1617 to account for the tumults that had accompanied the election of new ministers, but they disclaimed responsibility. About the same time he helped to block plans to place gilded wooden statues of the apostles and evangelists in Holyrood Chapel. On 27 June Galloway was one of fifty-five ministers who protested against a parliamentary bill proposing to grant the king power to impose binding decisions on the church after consulting the bishops and selected ministers; James subsequently withdrew the bill. Summoned before the high commission on 12 July, three signatories were deprived, but Galloway and three other Edinburgh clerics sought and received the king's forgiveness. At a gathering of ministers the following day, Galloway assured James that the clergy would accept the five articles of Perth, embodying the king's innovations in worship, but proposed a number of modifications, suggesting that private baptism and communion were acceptable in some cases; proposing kneeling in prayer before and after communion, but taking the elements while seated; and averring that holy days which fell during the week should be observed on the ensuing Sundays.

When his proposed compromise proved unacceptable Galloway defended the articles of Perth. He preached regularly at Christmas, sparking dissension in Edinburgh. His endorsement of the articles in the general assembly of August 1618 prompted Edinburgh presbyterians to accuse him of apostasy in March 1619. James renewed Galloway's appointment to the high commission on 15 June 1619, but became concerned about the unrest in Edinburgh, and in late July instructed Archbishop John Spottiswoode and the earl of Melrose to seek a reconciliation between Galloway and his opponents. The tension continued, manifesting itself in debates in the Edinburgh kirk session in April 1620 over kneeling at communion; Galloway reluctantly agreed that kneeling would be optional. In October he successfully opposed the appointment of three additional ministers in Edinburgh to bolster opposition to the articles, and in May 1621 he blocked ministers, elders, and burgh officials in Edinburgh who proposed to petition James that the articles were Catholic in origin.

One of Galloway's last noteworthy acts was a request of about 1624 for a commission to try witches in the presbyteries of Duns and the Merse. On 8 November 1625 Charles I ordered him to provide the privy council with documentation for his pension, which he did three weeks later, showing that it was now 20 marks sterling. On that occasion it was noted that he was not expected to live long, and by 10 February 1626 he was dead. For thirty-six years he

had served James, fired by a Knoxian vision of a ruler intent on uniting England and Scotland as one English-speaking, protestant polity, but his willingness to compromise and his flattering comments about the king in his sermons brought opprobrium from the more zealous presbyterians.   RICHARD L. GREAVES

Sources *Fasti Scot.*, new edn, 1.53–4; 4.229, 332; 5.351, 357; 7.439–40 · T. Thomson, ed., *Acts and proceedings of the general assemblies of the Kirk of Scotland*, 3 pts, Bannatyne Club, 81 (1839–45) · *Reg. PCS*, 1st ser. · *CSP Scot. ser.*, 1589–1603 · D. Calderwood, *The true history of the Church of Scotland, from the beginning of the Reformation, unto the end of the reigne of King James VI* (1678) · *The autobiography and diary of Mr James Melvill*, ed. R. Pitcairn, Wodrow Society (1842) · W. Scott and D. Laing, eds., *The Bannatyne miscellany*, 1, Bannatyne Club, 19 (1827) · E. Cardwell, *A history of conferences and other proceedings connected with the revision of the Book of Common Prayer*, 3rd edn (1849) · *CSP dom.*, 1603–10, 31, 77 · J. Row, *The history of the Kirk of Scotland, from the year 1558 to August 1637*, ed. D. Laing, Wodrow Society, 4 (1842) · J. Spottiswood, *The history of the Church of Scotland*, ed. M. Napier and M. Russell, 3 vols., Bannatyne Club, 93 (1850) · P. Collinson, *The Elizabethan puritan movement* (1967) · M. Lee, *Government by pen: Scotland under James VI and I* (1980) · *DNB* · G. Donaldson, 'Scottish Presbyterian exiles in England, 1584–8', *Records of the Scottish Church History Society*, 14 (1960–62), 67–80 · A. R. Macdonald, *The Jacobean kirk, 1567–1625: sovereignty, polity and liturgy* (1998) · *DSCHT*

Galloway, Robert (1752–1794), bookseller and poet, was born in Stirling in June 1752. Little is known about him; the earliest biographical reference is in James Robertson's *Lives of Scottish Poets* (1822). Some information can be gleaned from his only book, *Poems, epistles and songs, chiefly in the Scottish dialect: to which are added, a brief account of the revolution in 1688, and a narrative of the rebellion in 1745–46, continued to the death of Prince Charles in 1788* (1788). He presumably had some elementary education, though he claimed in the preface to be 'an entire stranger to the learned languages, and little acquainted with the refinements of science'. Judging by the poems he was no stranger to his own languages, Scots and English. If 'A Bard's Soliloquy' is autobiographical, Galloway had a hard early life, 'opprest wi' others' care' until he was nineteen. He married about 1772 and by 1788 he and his wife had seven children, all daughters. In 1783 he was listed in the Glasgow trade directory as 'shoe maker, high street'.

According to Robertson, Galloway found shoemaking 'too sedentary for a weak habit of body' and turned to bookselling and running a circulating library (Robertson, 3.128). From his shop on the south side of the Bridgegate (no. 24) he published his book of poems in 1788, perhaps encouraged by the success of Robert Burns two years previously, the title of whose collection his own echoed. A second edition appeared in 1792 (with fifteen extra poems) in which he described himself as 'bard and bookseller'. The only other known instance of his bookselling activities was in 1793, when he was listed in the imprint as one of those selling *The Trial of the Rev. Thomas Fyshe Palmer*. The publisher of that work, William Skirving, was a member of the Friends of the People, and Palmer was tried for sedition: this may offer some indication of Galloway's political inclinations.

Galloway was certainly a Scottish patriot, as evinced in the epigraph to his book:

> To love my country, and to read her tale,
> Was all the height my fancy did aspire.

In Richard Sher's words, 'Galloway's is a strong voice for Whig cultural nationalism and the common man' (Sher, 200). His subjects were local and national: 'The Beauties of Stirlingshire', 'Glasgow Fair', 'On the Recovery of the Highland Dress', 'Lunardi's First Flight from Glasgow'. The remarkable 'Glasgow Reviewed and Contrasted' deserves notice for its use of different registers of speech and its defence—in Scots and by a ghost of Glasgow past—of the old, honest, frugal ways against the prevailing get-rich-quick mentality:

> For riches then were got by slow degrees,
> Now handsome fortunes are procur'd with ease.

For Galloway, the prosperity of the new merchant city was not progress. He saw himself in the vigorous Scots tradition of Robert Fergusson and Burns: his poems lack their wit and technique but are still worth reading for their contemporary comment, rough humour, and humanity. Galloway died on 4 March 1794.   HAMISH WHYTE

Sources [J. Robertson], *Lives of Scottish poets*, 3 (1822), pt 6, 128 · R. B. Sher, 'Glasgow in late eighteenth-century popular poetry', *The Glasgow Enlightenment*, ed. A. Hook and R. B. Sher (1995), 190–213 · R. Galloway, 'A bard's soliloquy' and 'On the birth of a seventh daughter', *Poems, epistles and songs, chiefly in the Scottish dialect* (1788), 67, 120 · IGI

Galloway, Thomas (1796–1851), mathematician, was born on 26 February 1796 at Symington, Lanarkshire, the eldest of the five sons and one daughter of William Galloway and his wife, Janet Watson. His father and grandfather were mechanical engineers who occupied Symington mill. He attended parish schools at Symington and Biggar and the New Academy, Lanark, where he studied mostly classics. He is said to have received instruction in mathematics from French prisoners billeted locally about 1811, thereby gaining some insight into French methods of analysis. In 1812 he entered Edinburgh University. In the mathematics class of 1815–16 he gained a prize for the solution of some problems and became the favourite student of Professor William Wallace. He did not take his MA until March 1824, and despite further theological studies abandoned his original intention of the ministry of the Church of Scotland. Wallace assisted him in finding two years' employment in teaching and editing in Edinburgh, then in 1823 he was appointed teacher of mathematics at the Royal Military College, Sandhurst, where 'his accuracy of knowledge and business-like habits rendered him both efficient and popular' (PRS, 6, 1850–54, 120). On 9 January 1831 he married Margaret, Wallace's eldest daughter.

In November 1832 Galloway became one of the five candidates for the chair of natural philosophy at Edinburgh, made vacant by the death of Sir John Leslie, but stood little chance against James David Forbes. At the end of 1833 he was appointed registrar, or actuary, to the Amicable Life Assurance Company of London, a post he held for the rest of his life. In February 1829 he was elected a fellow of the Astronomical Society and in 1834 fellow of the Royal Society. He served on the council of the Royal Society from 1843 and contributed to the *Philosophical Transactions* (1847) a memoir on 'The proper movement of the solar system' from a study of the proper motions of southern stars. Although he concluded that data were still insufficient, he deduced the apex of the sun's motion to be at r.a. 259°46′2″, dec. +32°29′6″, close to earlier estimates. He was awarded a royal medal on 30 November 1848.

Galloway was a member of the council of the Royal Astronomical Society in 1834 and 1851, a vice-president in 1837 and 1848, foreign secretary in 1842, and one of the two secretaries in 1847, and was noted for his efficiency. He wrote *A Treatise on Astronomy* (1831) and numerous papers for *Monthly Notices*, *Memoirs of the Royal Astronomical Society*, the *Philosophical Magazine*, the *Edinburgh New Philosophical Journal*, and the *Edinburgh Review* on topics as diverse as the application of the method of least squares to the determination of the most probable errors of observation in part of the Ordnance Survey of England; the determination of longitude by meteor observations; the recent history of astronomical science; double stars of the southern hemisphere; the dodo and its kindred; and the statistics of coal. He wrote the article 'Pendulum' for the *Edinburgh Encyclopaedia* (1830) and contributed to the 7th edition of *Encyclopaedia Britannica* (1831) articles on 'Astronomy', 'Balance', 'Calendar', 'Chronology', 'Comet', 'Figure of the earth', 'Precession of the equinoxes', and 'Probability', the last being issued as a separate volume. The Royal Astronomical Society preserves an undated manuscript memoir of his on the recent progress of astronomy. He possessed a small but valuable library, including nineteen works of Kepler.

Thomas Carlyle described Galloway as 'hirsute', 'a small dogmatical teacher of Mathematics—a wrangler of the first order—of brutal manners, and a terror to those embryo philosophers … who … frequent the backshop of [Edinburgh bookseller] David Brown' (*Early Letters*, 1.191). Galloway died, following some months of illness, of a heart attack on 1 November 1851 at his home, 45 Torrington Square, London, and was buried in Kensal Green cemetery. On his deathbed he implored that 'neither strength nor length of eulogy' should be reported of him in the Royal Astronomical Society's obituary, read on 13 February 1852.   DAVID GAVINE

Sources *Monthly Notices of the Royal Astronomical Society*, 12 (1851–2), 87–9 · *Abstracts of the Papers Communicated to the Royal Society of London*, 6 (1850–54), 120 · Boase, *Mod. Eng. biog.* · R. Grant, *History of physical astronomy, from the earliest ages to the middle of the nineteenth century* (1852), 557 · *Early letters of Thomas Carlyle*, ed. C. E. Norton, 2 vols. (1886) · DNB · Index of parish records, Lanarkshire · catalogue of graduates, U. Edin. [March 1824]

Archives RAS, corresp. | RS, corresp. with Sir John Herschel

Galloway, Sir William (1840–1927), mining engineer, born on 12 February 1840, was the eldest son of William Galloway, JP, of Paisley, owner of a Paisley shawl factory and colliery owner, and his second wife, Margaret Lindsay. He was educated at a private school, the University of Giessen, the Bergakademie at Freiberg, Saxony, and University College, London. He became a junior inspector of mines in west Scotland, and was later transferred to south Wales. He early directed his attention to the causes of explosions in mines, and in 1873 won the Hermon prize for an essay on this subject. At this time Galloway still accepted the orthodox view that the most serious explosions were occasioned by the combustion of fire-damp; he subsequently altered this opinion, and in a series of papers published in the *Proceedings of the Royal Society* between 1875 and 1887 contended that floating coal dust was the means of extending the area of explosions. From an analysis of the evidence afforded by actual explosions he demonstrated that fire-damp could not have been present in appreciable quantities along most of the track in the cases examined. He also conducted experiments in galleries specially constructed for the purpose in a south Wales colliery, in which he was able to get ignition and very violent explosions from coal dust without the presence of fire-damp. He showed that an initial explosion raised dust elsewhere in the mine, causing further explosions.

For many years, however, Galloway's conclusions were received with scepticism, and, owing to the conflict of views between him and his senior colleagues he was compelled to resign his inspectorship. Eventually, however, his theory was confirmed by the testimony of mining engineers and of junior inspectors of mines, and by Henry Hall, who was appointed to experiment and report to the royal commission of 1893 on coal-dust explosions in mines. As a preventive of such explosions Galloway first recommended the wetting of the roads in mines, a method which was not found to be wholly effective; later, in 1896, he advocated the spreading of stone dust. This method, which was independently initiated and developed by William Garforth, proved very successful and was generally adopted from 1908, with the result that the death-rate resulting from colliery explosions was considered to have been lowered to 10 per cent of the figure prevailing when Galloway began his investigations.

Galloway married twice: first, in 1874, Christiana Maud Mary, daughter of William Francis Gordon, of Milrig, Ayrshire, (they had two sons); second, in 1900, Mary Jane Gwennap Douglas Killick, *née* Wood, daughter of Captain James Wood, Royal Marines, of Nunlands, Surrey.

From 1891 to 1902 Galloway was professor of mining at University College, Cardiff. He also carried on until his death an extensive business at Cardiff as a consulting mining engineer. He received many awards for his investigations, was president of the South Wales Institute of Civil Engineers in 1912, and was knighted in 1924. Galloway published twenty-one papers based on his research into colliery explosions, and nineteen other papers on mining subjects, and patented a number of safety devices, including twin guide ropes and improved counter-balanced doors to cover the shaft top. He died on 2 November 1927

at his home, 17 Park Place, Cardiff. An obituary in *Nature* described him as 'an outstanding figure in the development of scientific coal mining' (*Nature*, 777).

E. I. CARLYLE, rev. ROBERT BROWN

Sources *Nature*, 120 (1927), 776–7 • *The Times* (4 Nov 1927) • *Journal of Education*, 59 (1927), 870, 872 • R. Church, A. Hall, and J. Kanefsky, *Victorian pre-eminence: 1830–1913* (1986), vol. 3 of *The history of the British coal industry* (1984–93) • 'Royal commission on explosions from coal dust in mines', *Parl. papers* (1893–4), 20.535, C. 7185 • W. N. Atkinson and J. B. Atkinson, *Explosions in coal mines* (1886) • m. cert.
Archives Glos. RO, report, corresp., and MSS relating to Forest of Dean collieries | CUL, letters to Sir George Stokes, Add 7342, 7656
Likenesses photograph, repro. in *The Times* (5 Nov 1927)
Wealth at death £5972 18s. 3d.: probate, 1 Dec 1927, CGPLA Eng. & Wales

Gallwey, Peter (1820–1906), Roman Catholic priest and Jesuit, was born on 13 November 1820 at Killarney, Ireland, the son of Christopher Gallwey, agent to the earl of Kenmare, and his wife, Lucinda (*née* Groham). They had at least three children, including two other sons, Christopher and Thomas. When Gallwey was six years old he was sent to a school in Boulogne and then in 1829, with his brothers, to the Jesuit Stonyhurst College in Lancashire. In 1836 he entered the Society of Jesus and underwent the usual noviciate. Between his philosophy course at St Mary's Hall, Stonyhurst (1840–43), and theological studies at St Beuno's College, north Wales (1849–53), he also taught at the recently opened College of St Francis Xavier, Liverpool, and at Stonyhurst. On 21 September 1852 he was ordained priest at St Beuno's College and, after further training, was put in charge of the studies at Stonyhurst for two years, during which time he infused the department with his own energy and enthusiasm. In 1857 he was transferred to the Jesuit church in Farm Street in London, where he was made rector. It was during this period, about 1864, that he urged successfully that the English Jesuits should take over the periodical *The Month*. In 1869 he was appointed director of the Jesuit novices at Manresa House, Roehampton, and he held this post until 1873, when he was named provincial superior of the Society of Jesus in Great Britain. It was during his tenure that the decision to open a Jesuit college in Manchester in March 1875 led to controversy with the then bishop of Salford, Herbert Vaughan, who believed it would damage an existing college. In June 1875 the appeal to Rome by the bishop went in his favour and against the Jesuits, so the college had to be closed. In 1876 Gallwey was appointed rector and lecturer in moral theology at St Beuno's College, but a year later returned to the church of the Immaculate Conception, Farm Street, where he remained for the rest of his life. For four years (1877–81) he was again rector at Farm Street and in 1892 he visited the Holy Land. He died in London on 23 September 1906, and was buried in the churchyard of St Thomas's, Fulham.

Gallwey was an energetic and eloquent preacher and lecturer and his success is said to have been due to his ability to convey sincere and profound conviction. Among his published sermons were *Convent Life and England in the Nineteenth Century* (1869), *The Beatified Martyrs, or, Prayers for the Conversion of England* (1888), *Salvage from the Wreck: a Few Memories of Friends Departed, Preserved in Funeral Discourses* (1889), *Centenary Sermon Preached at Stonyhurst, July 25th, 1894* (1894), *The Golden Jubilee of the Church of the Immaculate Conception, Farm Street* (1896), and many funeral discourses on persons of note. As well as editing and contributing forewords to other books, he published controversial and devotional works, including *The Committee on Convents* (1870), a reply to a demand in parliament for the inspection of convents, *Twelve Lectures on Ritualism* (2 vols., 1879), *Thoughts on Apostolic Succession* (1889), *The Watches of the Sacred Passion, with before and after* (3 vols., 1894), and *Mr Birrell's Education Bill: Selections from the Objections Urged Against it* (1906).

Less well known in his lifetime was Gallwey's work for the poor and for those with spiritual problems. A contemporary described him when young as dark-eyed, sallow or ivory skinned, with black glossy hair and round shouldered; in later years he was almost bent double. When he was about thirty years of age Gallwey was warned that, because it was believed his lungs were affected, he might have only a short time to live. He was eighty-six when he died.

GEOFFREY HOLT

Sources *Letters and Notices* [Society of Jesus], 29 (1907–8), 45–54 · *DNB* · P. Fitzgerald, *Father Gallwey, a sketch* (1906) · E. F. Sutcliffe, *Bibliography of the English province of the Society of Jesus, 1773–1953* (1957) · baptism cert., 15 Nov 1820, Killarney, Ireland
Archives Archives of the British Province of the Society of Jesus, London | Stonyhurst College, Lancashire
Likenesses H. G. Jones, portrait, Stonyhurst College, Lancashire · photograph, Archives of the British Province of the Society of Jesus, London

Gally, Henry (*bap.* 1696, *d.* 1769), Church of England clergyman and writer, son of the Revd Peter Gally, a French Huguenot refugee, was born at Beckenham, Kent, and baptized on 13 August 1696. He was admitted a pensioner of Corpus Christi College, Cambridge, under the tuition of a Mr Fawcett (8 May 1714), and became a scholar in the following July. He graduated BA (1717), MA (1721), and was on the king's list for the degree of DD, which he received on 25 April 1728, when George II visited Cambridge. In 1721 he was chosen lecturer of St Paul's, Covent Garden, and on 23 November in the same year was instituted to the rectory of Wavendon or Wandon, Buckinghamshire, on the presentation of his father.

In 1723 Gally published *The Misery of Man*, the product of two sermons delivered at St Paul's, Covent Garden, followed by *The Moral Character of Theophrastus* with an essay on character writing (1725). In the same year he was appointed domestic chaplain to the lord chancellor, Peter, Baron King of Ockham, who later preferred him to a prebend in the church of Gloucester (15 May 1728), and to another in the church of Norwich in 1731. Lord King also presented him to the rectory of Ashney or Ashton, Northamptonshire, in 1730, and to that of St Giles-in-the-Fields, London, two years later. Gally then resigned the rectory of Wavendon, in which he was succeeded by his father.

George II made him one of his chaplains-in-ordinary in October 1735.

Earlier that decade Gally had published *The Reasonableness of Church and College Fines Asserted* (1731), written when the House of Commons was considering a bill to alter the tenure of church and college estates, and to ascertain the fines payable on the renewal of their leases. Gally's essay was a direct response to a treatise by Samuel Burroughs who, under the pseudonym Everard Fleetwood, had written *An enquiry into the customary-estates and tenant-rights of those who hold lands of church and other foundations*, a work which also prompted replies from the Cambridge astronomer Roger Long and the principal of St John's College, Oxford, William Derham. In 1739 Gally preached a sermon before the House of Commons on the anniversary of the king's accession, and in 1750 offered *Some Considerations upon Clandestine Marriages*. In this influential pamphlet Gally called for an end to what he saw as the increasing practice of clandestine marriages, especially those at the Fleet prison. Recent well-publicized cases in which spouses were discovered to have previously married were, he argued, raising fears that even the most respectful marriage might be declared bigamous or be open to allegations of bigamy, an unacceptable feature of a supposedly civilized society with serious consequences for participants and their children. Gally's pamphlet, bolstered by several subsequent scandals, did much to prompt Lord Hardwicke in 1753 to introduce his successful Marriage Act banning clandestine marriages. Gally followed this publication with two dissertations (1754 and 1768) 'against pronouncing of the Greek language according to accents', the second essay being a reply to John Foster's *Essay on the Different Nature of Accent and Quality*; all three titles were reprinted in 1820. Henry Gally was married to Elizabeth and they had two sons. He died on 7 August 1769, survived by his wife.

THOMPSON COOPER, *rev.* PHILIP CARTER

Sources Nichols, *Lit. anecdotes*, 2.274 · Venn, *Alum. Cant.* · *GM*, 1st ser., 39 (1769), 414 · *IGI* · H. Gally, will, PRO, PROB 11/952, fols. 264r–264v · L. Stone, *Road to divorce: England, 1530–1987* (1990)
Archives BL, corresp. with duke of Newcastle, Add. MSS 32699–32975, *passim*

Galmoye. For this title name *see* Butler, Pierce, styled third Viscount Galmoye, and Jacobite earl of Newcastle (1652–1740).

Galpin, Francis William (1858–1945), Church of England clergyman, musicologist, and antiquary, was born on 25 December 1858 in Dorchester, the eldest of three children of John Galpin (1813–1883), an ironmaster, and his wife, Emily, *née* Hamsford (*d.* 1899). He is remembered for his outstanding contributions to the scholarship of musical instruments, although these were not achieved at the expense of his pastoral work. Because of his ecclesiastical title he is generally referred to in musical circles as Canon Galpin.

Galpin's early interest in music was encouraged at home and fostered at King's School, Sherborne, Dorset,

Francis William Galpin (1858–1945), by unknown photographer

where he was a student until he matriculated at Trinity College, Cambridge, in 1877. Although his degree was in classics and he intended to become a clergyman, his leisure was devoted to musical activities—as an accomplished clarinettist (he was the dedicatee of Sir Charles Stanford's *Three Intermezzi*); as the organizer of an 82-strong amateur orchestra; and as a librarian to the Cambridge University Musical Society. He graduated BA in 1883, the year in which he was ordained and took up the curacy of Redenhall with Harleston, Norfolk. From 1887 to 1891 he was a curate at St Giles-in-the-Fields, London. In 1889 he married Mary Maude, *née* Hawkins (d. 1942), who shared his musical interests and soon became an accomplished lutenist. They had four children: Christopher (1892–1964), Bernard (1897–1977), Stephen (1898–1966), and Ursula (1903–1980?), who married J. C. T. Willis.

The rest of Galpin's working life was spent in Essex. From 1891 to 1915 he was vicar of Hatfield Regis. In this time he made his mark with perhaps his best scholarly writings and, as usual, was active in encouraging community music-making. Like Thomas Hardy, Galpin regretted the passing of the old 'west-gallery' church bands; rather than trying to turn the clock back by forming a new church band, however, he organized music in an unprecedented variety of forms, frequently exploring early repertoire using original instruments from his own collection. A feature of parish life was the annual 'paraffin concert' (in aid of a lighting fund) of both old and new music. Galpin enlivened these and other occasions by performing on the viol, recorder, serpent, baryton, marimba, nyastaranga, his own reconstruction of the ancient hydraulis or water-organ, and other unusual instruments.

Galpin continued his ecclesiastical career as vicar of Witham (1915–21) and rector of Faulkbourne (1921–33). During the First World War he served as an honorary chaplain to the forces. He was made an honorary canon of Chelmsford in 1917 and, after his retirement in 1933, canon emeritus. As well as being a musician, Galpin was a keen archaeologist. He contributed many papers to the Essex Archaeological Society and served as its president from 1921 to 1926. As a botanist and writer on flora of some distinction, he was elected a fellow of the Linnean Society in 1877. He moved to a house just opposite Kew Gardens, at 164 Kew Road, in order to share experiences (and, it was rumoured, exchange specimens) with the authorities; he was a personal friend of the curator. He wrote a little book on the flora of Palestine that combined his botanical and religious interests, *In the Garden of the Lord*. When war broke out in 1939 he went to live in Cheltenham, but on his wife's death in 1942 he returned to spend his final years at Kew.

Galpin's amateur pursuits resulted in significant contributions to a number of fields, but particularly to that of the history of music. His achievements in music complemented those of his contemporary Arnold Dolmetsch (1858–1940): both felt that to perform early music one needed to use instruments appropriate to the period. Dolmetsch, a trained professional musician, pioneered public performances on early instruments, carrying out the necessary research and even acquiring the skills to make instruments. Galpin's interest developed through his collection of instruments, which he used to become a musicologist and author with a worldwide reputation, receiving a DLitt from Cambridge in 1936 and serving as president of the (London) Musical Association (later the Royal Musical Association) 1938–42.

Galpin's career as a musical collector began when he acquired his first serpent as an undergraduate. By 1890 he was able to lend forty-five wind instruments to the Royal Military Exhibition; his contribution to the Crystal Palace International Exhibition of 1900 included both exhibits and the scholarly arrangement. For the Worshipful Company of Musicians Loan Exhibition of 1904 he also wrote the catalogue and was made an honorary freeman of the company in 1905. By 1914 Galpin had in his possession more than 400 instruments, the first British didactic collection of European instruments to demonstrate their historical development. He realized that his collection would be more appropriately housed in a public museum than in a rural vicarage, and endeavoured to find an institution where his instruments could form the nucleus of a national collection. To his lasting regret he failed in this, and the greater part of his collection went to Boston, USA, in 1916. He retained some of the more important items, however, most of which were auctioned after his death. A group of scholars and collectors who had known him purchased most of these and also, a year after his death, formed the Galpin Society in his memory.

Galpin's major works on music include: *The Sackbut*

(1907; for sixty years the most authoritative work on the history of the trombone); *Old English Instruments* (1910); *The Music of the Sumerians, Babylonians and Assyrians* (1937); *A Textbook of European Musical Instruments* (1937); and sixty articles for *Grove's Dictionary of Music and Musicians* (1928 and 1940). Galpin also catalogued several major collections, including the Van Raalte collection and those of museums in New York (1902) and Stockholm (1903). He was an accomplished lecturer, not hesitating in his eightieth year to tackle a lecture on electrophonic instruments. Galpin died in London on 30 December 1945 and was buried close to the scene of much of his work, in the churchyard at Hatfield Regis.　　　　　　　　ARNOLD MYERS

Sources F. G. Rendall, 'F. W. G. 1858–1945', *Galpin Society Journal*, 1 (1948) [incl. bibliography of Galpin's musical writings, and articles on his collection], 3–8 • *The Times* (2 Jan 1946) • *WWW*, 1941–50 • S. Godman, 'Francis William Galpin: music maker', *Galpin Society Journal*, 12 (1959), 8–16, pl. 1 • B. Galpin, 'Canon Galpin's Check lists', *Galpin Society Journal*, 25 (1972), 4–21, pl. 1 • G. Melville-Mason, ed., *European musical instruments* (1968) [exhibition catalogue, Reid School of Music, U. Edin., 18 Aug – 16 Sept 1968] • N. Bessaraboff, *Ancient European musical instruments…* (1941) [with a forward by Francis W. Galpin] • C. Lindahl, 'Galpin's copy of his *Textbook*', *Galpin Society Journal*, 29 (1976), 123–4 • F. W. Galpin, *Old English instruments of music* (1910) • personal knowledge (2004)
Archives Boston University, musical instruments
Likenesses photograph, repro. in Galpin, *Old English instruments of music*, pl. 19 • photograph, repro. in Godman, 'Francis William Galpin: Music maker', pl. 1 [*see illus.*] • photograph, repro. in Melville-Mason, ed., *European musical instruments* • portrait, priv. coll.
Wealth at death £11,724 15s. 6d.: probate, 2 July 1946, *CGPLA Eng. & Wales*

Galpine, John (1771–1806), nurseryman, was born at Blandford Forum, Dorset, the son of John Kingston Galpine (1741–1786), nurseryman of Blandford Forum, whose business he inherited. On 2 October 1797 he married Kitty Clapcott (1771–1849) at Blandford. They had two children, one of whom was called John Kingston Galpine (*b.* 1800). He was elected an associate of the Linnean Society of London in 1798, when his address was given as Great Portland Street. His distinguished sponsors were founder member and vice-president Aylmer Bourke Lambert, botanist, vice-president William George Maton, physician to Queen Charlotte, and the Revd Thomas Rackett, vicar of Spetisbury, Dorset, botanist and antiquary.

On 1 January 1806 Galpine published *A Synoptical Compend of British Botany*, his translation of *Compendium florae Britannicae* (1800) by Sir James Edward Smith (the abridgement of Smith's *Flora Britannica*, 1800, 2 vols.). Galpine's *Compend* comprised all Smith's genera, including those in the third volume of *Flora Britannica* (1804), except the cryptogams. It gave references to illustrations, mostly in *English Botany* (1790–1814, 36 vols.) by J. Sowerby and J. E. Smith, and was designed for taking on botanizing excursions, using its tabular check-list arrangement in the new, pocket-size, duodecimo format. Galpine's death at Blandford Forum on 6 January 1806 delayed republication. The publisher Samuel Bagster undertook a second

edition (1819), augmented with 200 cryptogams by a member of the Linnean Society. There were two further editions in 1829 and 1834. Galpine was buried at Blandford on 10 January 1806.　　　　　　　　ENID SLATTER

Sources J. Harvey, *Georgian garden* (1983) • Desmond, *Botanists*, rev. edn • J. E. Smith, *Compendium florae Britannicae* (1800) • J. E. Smith, *Flora Britannica*, 3 vols. (1800–04) • J. E. Smith, J. Sowerby, and others, *English botany*, 36 vols. (1790–1814) • J. Britten and G. S. Boulger, eds., *A biographical index of deceased British and Irish botanists*, 2nd edn, ed. A. B. Rendle (1931) • *DNB*

Galsworthy, John (1867–1933), novelist and playwright, was born at Parkfield, Kingston Hill, Surrey, on 14 August 1867, the second of the four children and eldest son of John Galsworthy (1817–1904), solicitor and company director, of Old Jewry, London, and Blanche Bailey (1837–1915), the daughter of Charles Bartleet, needle maker, of Redditch. His father's family originated from Wembury, near Plymouth, and he retained a close association with Devon. He was educated from the age of nine at Saugeen, a preparatory school in Bournemouth, and Harrow School (1881–6), where he distinguished himself as an athlete. From there he entered New College, Oxford, to read law, gaining second-class honours in 1889. After Lincoln's Inn, he was called to the bar in 1890. In 1895 Galsworthy began a ten-year affair with Ada Nemesis Pearson (1866–1956), wife of his first cousin Arthur John Galsworthy and daughter of Emanuel Cooper, an obstetrician of Norwich. The relationship was kept secret from his father during his lifetime, and eventually culminated in marriage on 23 September 1905. The marriage, which was childless, lasted until Galsworthy's death.

Reluctant to practise as a barrister, Galsworthy was sent by his father on trips to Vancouver Island, Australia, and South Africa, to look after the family's business interests and to learn maritime law. On a memorable occasion in 1893, boarding the sailing-ship *Torrens* at Adelaide, bound for Cape Town, he met its first mate, Joseph Conrad, the future novelist, who was angry and black with coal dust. Conrad became a lifelong friend. Galsworthy's writing career began in 1897 with a volume of short stories, *From the Four Winds*. Like the succeeding volume, *A Man of Devon* (1901) and the novels *Jocelyn* (1898) and *Villa Rubein* (1900), it was published under the pseudonym John Sinjohn. The first novel to appear under his own name was *The Island Pharisees* in 1904, a novel of social observation with touches of satire and propaganda, held together by the loosely autobiographical character Shelton. It was published by Heinemann, with whom Galsworthy remained.

The publication of a major novel and a theatrical triumph in the same year, 1906, underlined Galsworthy's maturity as a writer. *The Man of Property* (which became the first volume of *The Forsyte Saga*, but was a separate novel in itself), was widely regarded by contemporaries as confirming the end of Victorianism. It is a typically Edwardian novel in its focus on the conflict between property and art, and draws its emotional power to some degree from Galsworthy's own family relationships, particularly his affair with Ada Galsworthy. It drew praise from Conrad as

John Galsworthy (1867–1933), by Olive Edis, 1929

'indubitably a piece of art' (Gindin, 171), and although D. H. Lawrence lamented its capitulation to the wealthy and clannish Forsytes, and its timid treatment of sexuality, he described it as potentially 'a very great novel, a very great satire' (Lawrence, 540). Galsworthy's play *The Silver Box*, produced at the Court Theatre by Harley Granville Barker, concerns the different treatment of rich and poor criminals, and examines the complexity of individual experience behind social façades. It was warmly received in the press for its compelling realism, and the prince and princess of Wales attended its final performance.

At this point in his career Galsworthy's reputation rested on his work as a playwright. Some of his novels during this period possess an uncertainty of focus. For instance, *The Country House* (1907), a satire on the county set, is thinly characterized, with an air of ironic detachment, while *Fraternity* (1909), which explores connections between the urban social classes, offers an unconvincing portrayal of lower-class Londoners. *The Freelands* (1915), which again takes up the topic of the land, does not move much beyond discussions of the effects of capitalism on the rural economy. Instead Galsworthy became established, with Granville Barker and Shaw, as one of the new dramatists, whose plays debating social issues were directed towards a small, literate, and politically aware audience. Galsworthy's drama is realistically muted, visually static, and simply structured to produce moments of arresting theatre. His instinct for dramatic balance is also evident in the popular play *Strife* (1909), which explores

the postures of the main antagonists in a strike at a Cornish tin mine with both sympathy and irony. *Justice* (1910), a moving attack on the use of solitary confinement in prisons, excited the first-night audience, caught the contemporary liberal mood, and received an approving response from the home secretary, Winston Churchill. Although apolitical, Galsworthy at this period became associated in the public mind with the Liberal establishment. It was not until 1920 that he had his first commercial triumph with *The Skin Game*, a melodrama that deals with ethical issues, and also matters of property and class. The popular success of *Loyalties* (1922) was based on its powerfully ironic treatment of the confusions inherent in class allegiances. His last popular play was *Escape* (1926), about a gentleman convict on the run from Dartmoor. His writing throughout his career as a dramatist is uneven, however, and the number of successful plays is small. His *Collected Plays* was published by Duckworth in 1929.

Galsworthy's place in the history of English literature rests on the vast social chronicle comprising his three trilogies, *The Forsyte Saga* (1922), *A Modern Comedy* (1929) and *End of the Chapter* (1935). He returned to the Forsyte family in 1918 with a short story 'Indian summer of a Forsyte' (in *Five Tales*). A chance remark by his god-daughter, Dorothy Ivens, on reading the story led to *In Chancery* (1920). A study of the effects on English society of the imperial vision and the Second South African War, it was described by Katherine Mansfield, reviewing it in *The Athenaeum*, as a 'fascinating, brilliant book' (Gindin, 439–40). *In Chancery* concludes at a clearly defined point of change with the funeral of Queen Victoria. *To Let* (1921), set in 1920, is placed precisely in the contemporary historical moment, and written in a more impressionist style, capturing the post-war atmosphere of restless gaiety, with its undercurrent of nihilism.

The single-volume edition of *The Forsyte Saga* has been extremely popular, while the BBC television dramatization in 1967, the centenary of Galsworthy's birth, attracted an extraordinary number of viewers. The Forsyte family represents the distinctive ideology of the English commercial upper-middle class. Its instinct of possession, its sole means of self-definition and evolution, is distilled in the portrait of the dry solicitor and art collector Soames Forsyte and his tortured relationship with his wife, Irene. Soames's obsessive love for his daughter Fleur is pursued in the second trilogy, *A Modern Comedy* (1929), comprising *The White Monkey* (1924), *The Silver Spoon* (1926), and *Swan Song* (1928). Galsworthy's fiction centres on his own social class, whose instincts and ideology he largely repudiates. He is critical of its insularity, materialism, aesthetic deficiency, chauvinism, restrictive moral codes, and imperialism. His exploration of the febrile world of 1920s society includes his treatment of the general strike, in which Fleur and her friends are caught up, and culminates with the death of Soames. Though critical interest had waned, this second trilogy was extremely popular, and *Swan Song*, with its greater social depth, emotional range, and narrative subtlety, is among the best of Galsworthy's writing. The final, less successful trilogy, *End of the Chapter* (1935), occupied his last years. *Maid in Waiting* (1931), *Flowering Wilderness* (1932), and *Over the River* (1933) are less coherent works, linked by a satirical treatment of the old-established Charwell family, and increasingly preoccupied with the condition of contemporary English life.

Galsworthy was also an accomplished writer of short stories, the most popular collection being *Five Tales* (1918). He possessed little talent for poetry, however. A single volume of *Collected Poems* was published posthumously in 1934, but his meditations on the nature of the universe, love, and social issues rarely transcend the conventional. Similarly, his essays and lectures are thoughtful but unremarkable.

Photographs of Galsworthy portray a handsome, dignified, and fastidiously dressed figure. Instinctively reserved, he had a strong sense of propriety, and little humour. Not conventionally religious, his guiding values were love, beauty, and justice. His unusual capacity for compassion involved him in a variety of causes, including reforms of the penal system, the House of Lords, and theatrical censorship. He denounced the Second South African War, supported the aims of the suffragette movement, and campaigned for the protection of animals. His moral confusion at the outbreak of the First World War was partly resolved, emotionally, by pledging his American earnings to fund relief, and after rejection for military service, by several months spent as a masseur in a hospital for wounded soldiers in France. In 1921 he was elected president of the International PEN Club. At his death he left cottages in Bury, his Sussex retreat, to his astonished tenants.

Galsworthy declined a knighthood in 1918, but accepted the Belgian Palmes d'Or in 1919. He also received honorary degrees from the universities of St Andrews (1922), Manchester (1927), Dublin (1929), Cambridge (1930), Sheffield (1930), Oxford (1931), and Princeton (1931). He was elected an honorary fellow of New College, Oxford, in 1926. In 1929 he was appointed to the Order of Merit. He was awarded the Nobel prize for literature in 1932.

Galsworthy died of a stroke at his London home, Grove Lodge, The Grove, Holly Bush Hill, Hampstead, on 31 January 1933. On 3 February, in accordance with his will, he was cremated at Woking, and his ashes were scattered by aeroplane over the South Downs.   GEOFFREY HARVEY

Sources J. Gindin, *John Galsworthy's life and art* (1987) · H. V. Marrot, *The life and letters of John Galsworthy* (1935) · R. H. Sauter, *Galsworthy the man* (1967) · R. H. Mottram, *For some we loved: an intimate portrait of Ada and John Galsworthy* (1956) · C. Dupré, *John Galsworthy* (1976) · D. Barker, *The man of principle: a view of John Galsworthy* (1963) · H. Ould, *John Galsworthy* (1934) · *DNB* · D. H. Lawrence, 'John Galsworthy', *Phoenix: the posthumous papers of D. H. Lawrence* (1936) · d. cert.

Archives BL, autograph MSS, Add. MSS 41752–41759, 42178–42179 · Brandeis University, Waltham, Massachusetts, letters · Forbes Magazine, corresp. and literary papers · Harvard U., Houghton L., corresp. and papers · Hunt. L., corresp. and papers · Indiana University, Bloomington, Lilly Library, corresp. and literary papers · Morgan L., corresp. and papers · NRA, priv. coll., corresp. and literary papers · Ransom HRC, literary MSS and letters · U. Birm. L., corresp. and literary papers · U. Birm. L., letters | BL, corresp. with W. Archer, Add. MS 45291 · BL, letters to G. K. Chesterton, Add. MS 73237, fols. 63–76v · BL, corresp. with Society of Authors, Add. MS 56708 · Bodl. Oxf., letters to J. L. Hammond · Bodl. Oxf., letters to Gilbert Murray · Bodl. Oxf., letters to Lord Ponsonby · Harvard U., Houghton L., letters to Horley Granville Barker · JRL, letters to Basil Dean · JRL, letters to *Manchester Guardian* · Ransom HRC, Pen archive, letters · Royal Society of Literature, London, letters to Royal Society of Literature · Stanford University Library, California, MSS and letters to Leon Lion and Sheila Kaye-Smith · U. Reading L., letters to R. L. Mégroz · University of Rochester, New York, Rush Rhees Library, letters to Leon Lion · W. Yorks. AS, corresp. with Bradford English Society

Likenesses G. Sauter, oils, c.1905–1906, U. Birm. L. · M. Beerbohm, caricature, 1909, U. Birm. L. · A. L. Coburn, photogravure, 1909, NPG · K. Kennet, bronze mask, c.1910, Man. City Gall. · E. O. Hoppé, photograph, 1911, V&A · W. Rothenstein, crayon drawing, 1916, New College, Oxford · J. Russell & Sons, photograph, before 1917, NPG · W. Strang, etching, 1920, NPG · T. Spicer-Simson, bronze head, 1921, NPG · R. H. Sauter, oils, 1923, U. Birm. L., Galsworthy papers · M. Beerbohm, caricature, drawing, 1924 (*Breezy Jack of Biarritz*), Indiana University, Bloomington, Lilly Library · W. Stoneman, photograph, 1924, NPG · D. Low, caricatures, sketches, 1927, NPG · H. Coster, photograph, 1929, NPG · O. Edis, photograph, 1929, NPG [*see illus.*] · D. Evans, bronze bust, 1929, NPG · R. S. Sherriffs, ink and pencil caricature, c.1930, NPG · E. J. Sullivan, pencil drawing, 1930, BM · R. H. Sauter, charcoal drawing, 1932, U. Birm. L. · R. H. Sauter, oils, c.1932–1933, U. Birm. L. · R. H. Sauter, charcoal drawing, U. Birm. L. · R. H. Sauter, photographs, U. Birm., Galsworthy papers · R. H. Sauter, sketches, U. Birm., Galsworthy papers · photographs, U. Birm. L.

Wealth at death £95,283 12s. 11d.: resworn probate, 5 April 1933, CGPLA Eng. & Wales

Galt, Sir Alexander Tilloch (1817–1893), businessman and politician in Canada, was born on 6 September 1817 in Chelsea, London, the youngest of the three sons of John *Galt (1779–1839), author and colonizer, and his wife, Elizabeth (d. 1851), the daughter of the publisher Alexander *Tilloch. Galt was strongly influenced by his father, a prominent Scottish novelist and the founder of the first major Canadian land company, as well as by his deeply religious mother, who joined him in Canada after her husband's death. He spent his early years in the London and Edinburgh areas before in 1828 entering an Anglican seminary in Chambly, Lower Canada, while his father managed the Canada Company in Upper Canada. The family returned to Britain after John Galt's dismissal in 1829, but in 1835 Alexander went back to Canada to become a clerk in the office of the newly created British American Land Company, in the town of Sherbrooke, Lower Canada. After investing much of its development capital in access routes to remote, infertile parts of the American-settled Eastern townships region, where it had acquired vast tracts of land, the company was faced with a sudden decline in British immigration due to the rebellions of 1837–8. It survived only by completely changing its economic strategy during the early 1840s.

In 1844 Galt was appointed company commissioner after having convinced the London directors to focus on developing the promising water-power sites in Sherbrooke. Among the industries he was instrumental in establishing was the Sherbrooke Cotton Factory, the first cotton mill and joint-stock industrial company in the province. This strategy proved successful largely because Galt was able to convince Montreal and London financiers to invest in a railway passing through Sherbrooke *en route* from Montreal to the ice-free port of Portland, Maine. Nor would this project have been completed without Galt's application of the strategy he would follow throughout his life, namely the skilful exertion of political pressure in order to extract financial backing from the government. While he was closely tied to the pro-development Conservative Party throughout much of his career, Galt nevertheless sat as an independent in the legislature, representing Sherbrooke from 1849 to 1850 and from 1853 to 1872.

In the 1840s Galt also became involved in promoting a rail link from Montreal to Upper Canada, a project which ultimately emerged as the Grand Trunk Railway, Canada's first trunk line. When the Montreal–Portland line was absorbed by the Grand Trunk company, Galt and the other investors benefited from the artificial inflation of the value of their shares. This manoeuvre, and continuing government subsidy of the unprofitable railway company, earned Galt the lasting hostility of the reform-orientated opposition party even though he shared many of its basic ideas, particularly pertaining to the separation of church and state. On 9 February 1848 Galt married Elliott, the daughter of John Torrance, a wealthy Montreal merchant, but she died in 1850 shortly after having given birth to their first child. In 1851 Galt married her sister, Amy Gordon.

After the fall of the short-lived Reform government in 1858, Galt declined to form a new administration. Instead, he accepted the finance portfolio in the reconstituted Cartier–Macdonald ministry on condition that it accept his plan for the federation of the British North American colonies, including the annexation of Rupert's Land. The Colonial Office expressed little interest at the time, but the details of Galt's proposal anticipated the centralized federation established by the British North America Act of 1867. Galt was made KCMG in 1869 for his role in establishing confederation. In the meantime, he took steps to consolidate the public debt and to increase state revenues during this period, when economic depression coincided with mounting government obligations to make the interest payments on railway bonds held by defaulting companies and municipalities. By substantially raising the import duties in the face of British and American objections in 1859, Galt solved the government's financial problem as well as protecting fledgeling Canadian manufacturers from external competition during this free-trade era.

During the early 1860s the province's politics became increasingly polarized between Reform-dominated Upper Canada and Conservative-dominated Lower Canada, which made government increasingly unstable. When a virtual deadlock was reached in 1864 a coalition ministry, which included the Conservatives and George Brown's Upper Canadian Reformers, quickly moved towards the incorporation of the Atlantic colonies in a federal union. Galt's chief roles were to resolve the impasse over the size of the federal subsidy to the provinces and, as representative of an English-speaking protestant region of Lower Canada, to secure the inclusion of a clause protecting the existing educational rights of religious minorities.

Galt became the new country's minister of finance, but soon resigned when the prime minister, John A. Macdonald, failed to support his proposal to assist a failing bank. He then became a vocal critic of the government's transcontinental railway policy, arguing that its all-Canadian route would be financially ruinous for Canada. Freedom from political office also gave Galt the opportunity to express his views candidly on issues such as Canada's right to sign commercial treaties and the Roman Catholic ultramontane threat to civil liberties in Quebec. On the latter issue he published two controversial pamphlets in 1876, *Civil Liberty in Lower Canada* and *Church and State*.

In 1878 Galt was made GCMG in recognition of his role as Canada's representative on the Halifax commission which awarded a favourable settlement to Canada in the inshore fisheries dispute with the United States. Friendly relations were restored with Macdonald after the latter's return to power the same year, and Galt's skills as a negotiator were put to the test with foreign missions. He felt increasingly frustrated by his lack of authority to act independently of British authorities, but agreed to become the first Canadian high commissioner to London in 1880. His chief roles were to raise investment capital for the transcontinental railway and promote European immigration, but he could not overcome the competition from more attractive countries, and he preferred profit-orientated colonization companies to the government's proposal for the mass removal of Irish families to the Canadian west. Galt constantly complained that his limited means kept him from the necessary socializing with the political and financial élites. Furthermore, skilful though he may have been as a negotiator, his effectiveness as a diplomat was limited by his somewhat impatient and outspoken nature.

After returning to Canada in 1883, Galt attempted to recoup his fortune by directing his energies to the exploitation of his coal mine in the arid western region which later became Lethbridge, Alberta. This was a risky undertaking, given the widespread distribution of coal deposits in the region and the heavy reliance on the Canadian Pacific Railway (CPR) as customer, but Galt used his political influence to win generous land concessions from the government. Profits from land sales later subsidized the company's costly rail links north to the CPR line and south to Montana. Galt was also ruthless in laying off miners and cutting wages to meet competition, but after 1890 his failing health forced him to leave development of Lethbridge to his eldest son, Elliott. Galt died of throat cancer on 19 September 1893, in or near Montreal, and was buried in Montreal's Mount Royal cemetery.

Left in somewhat straitened circumstances were Galt's shy but firmly supportive second wife and the younger of their eight surviving daughters and two sons. Despite his many absences, Galt had had a very strong bond with his wife and children, whom (a daughter later recalled) he dominated, as he did other people, with a quiet charming assurance. He also expressed a strong personal sense of religious mission, though he was apparently not a great churchgoer, and he switched from the Presbyterians to the Anglicans after his mother's death in 1851.

Galt was aptly described by a recent biographer as a practical visionary (den Otter, ch. 2), and his greatest skill lay in raising and applying the capital for ambitious and financially risky development projects. Although at different times he advocated Canadian annexation to the United States, autonomy from Britain, and imperial federation, his vision was consistently of a strong, independent northern nation carved out of what he considered to be a wilderness wasteland. When he signed the annexation manifesto in 1849, he was clearly motivated by the desire to see the industries he had recently established in Sherbrooke gain ready access to the American market, but he paradoxically also appealed to a nascent sense of Canadian nationalism by arguing that 'a Union with the United States will give Canada a place among the nations' (*Stanstead Journal*, 15 Nov 1849). In 1869 Galt candidly informed the Colonial Office that he felt Canada should move towards complete autonomy from Britain, for, if Canadians failed 'to look forward to an independent existence as a nation' (Galt to Sir John Young, 15 May 1869, Galt MSS, 2794), they would inevitably fall under the control of the United States. Galt felt the situation was particularly urgent at that time because the sacrifices needed to incorporate the north-west 'will only be cheerfully borne under the idea that we are building up an Empire *for ourselves*' (Galt to Mr Cardwell, 17 May 1869, Galt MSS, 2801). Finally, in his promotion of imperial federation a few years later, Galt envisaged Canada and the other dominions as equal partners with Britain.

Galt was a large, imposing figure with a calm look of self-assurance, who excelled as a master salesman on account of his energetic enthusiasm and his ability to convey complex ideas in simple terms. His political and financial careers were clearly also hindered to some extent by his impatient optimism, but it did make him the ideal nineteenth-century nation-builder.   J. I. LITTLE

Sources A. A. den Otter, *Civilizing the west: the Galts and the development of western Canada* (1982) · H. B. Timothy, *The Galts: a Canadian odyssey*, 2 (1984) · J. P. Kesterman, 'Galt, Sir Alexander Tilloch', *DCB*, vol. 12 · O. D. Skelton, *Life and times of Sir Alexander Tilloch Galt* (1920) · E. C. Springett, *For my children's children* (1937) · NA Canada, Alexander Tilloch Galt collection, MG27-ID8 · *DNB* · M. E. McCulloch, 'English-speaking liberals in Canada East, 1840–54', PhD diss., University of Ottawa, 1986 · J. I. Little, *State and society in transition: the politics of institutional reform in Eastern Townships, 1838–1852* (1997) · J. I. Little, 'The short life of a local protest movement: the annexation crisis of 1849–50 in the eastern townships', *Journal of the Canadian Historical Association*, new ser., 3 (1992), 45–67 · *Stanstead Journal* (15 Nov 1849)

Archives NA Canada, MSS | Bodl. Oxf., corresp. with Lord Kimberley · NA Canada, Gzowski MSS, Macdonald MSS

Likenesses photograph, 1871, NA Canada · photograph, repro. in Springett, *For my children's children*, facing p. 17 · wood-engraving, NPG; repro. in *ILN* (18 Feb 1860) · wood-engraving, NPG; repro. in *ILN* (12 Nov 1864)

Galt, John (1779–1839), novelist, was born on 2 May 1779 in Irvine, a port on the west coast of Scotland. His father, also John Galt (d. 1817), was the captain and owner of a ship

John Galt (1779–1839), by Robert Graves, pubd 1833 (after John Irvine)

trading to the West Indies. He is described by the son in his *Autobiography* (2 vols., 1833) as 'one of the best, as he was one of the handsomest of men' but of 'easy nature' and 'only passable ability'. On the other hand Galt speaks very highly of his mother: 'a very singular person with great natural humour', who indulged 'in queer metaphysical expressions'. She discouraged, fortunately without success, Galt's 'bookish propensities', for his poor health kept him from the usual pursuits of boys of his age (Galt, *Autobiography*, 1.16–7). It was probably from her and from the conversation of the old ladies of the neighbourhood, to which Galt listened avidly, that he acquired his mastery of Scots speech and knowledge of human character which are the great strengths of his novels. She lived until 1826.

Education and early life Galt's early education was at home because of the state of his health, but he went later to the grammar school of Irvine. When he was about nine years old the family moved to Greenock, a more important port on the Clyde estuary, about 30 miles from Irvine. It was in this corner of Scotland, between these two places, that Galt was to place the most successful of its novels, which he called Tales of the West. He spent the next fourteen or fifteen years in Greenock and he retired there in 1834 for the last five years of his life.

In Greenock, too, Galt joined a subscription library which became in effect his university. It was, he says in the *Autobiography*, 'a selection of books formed with uncommon judgement and taste. The useful predominates in the collection and to this circumstance, probably, should be attributed my habitual partiality for works of a solid character' (1.17). It included the standard works of the Scottish Enlightenment, Robertson, Hume, Smith, Ferguson, Reid, Beattie, and the *Statistical Account* (later an important source for his *Annals of the Parish*), as well as Malthus, Bentham, Godwin, Burke, Condorcet, Voltaire, Rousseau, Montesquieu, and Franklin. When the fear of intellectual contagion from revolutionary France was at its height Galt successfully led a revolt against a proposal to remove 'dangerous' books from the shelves.

Like Burns, Scott, and Stevenson, Galt followed the practice of joining a society for debate and intellectual exercise. It is to this society that we owe the first reference in literature to the young Galt. Early in 1804 Galt and his friends invited James Hogg to a dinner in his honour. Hogg, a remarkable self-taught genius, had by this time published only his first collection of poems. He recorded his impressions of Galt in his 'Reminiscences of some of his contemporaries'. Galt, he says:

> managed his part in the conversation with such good nature and such strong emphatic reasoning, that my heart whispered to me again and again, 'this is no common youth'. Then his stories of old-fashioned and odd people were so infinitely amusing, that his conversation proved one of the principal charms of that enchanting night.   (Hogg, cxv)

At about this time Galt first ventured into print. He wrote an essay on John Wilson as an introduction to an 1808 edition of his poems. Galt's own verse, including extracts from *The Battle of Largs: a Gothic Poem*, began to appear in the *Scots Magazine*. He also wrote a tragedy about Mary, queen of Scots. He continued to write verse and plays at various times in his life, but work in neither genre represents his enduring work. He remarked in his *Autobiography* that it was a 'curious coincidence' that he had the idea of 'illustrating Scottish history by tales and poems' at about the same time as Walter Scott. There was, he added, a 'still more singular anticipation' (1.58). This was a reference to the historical novels, set in Scotland in the recent past, which he started to write shortly before Scott.

London experiences and European travels Galt at first directed his ambitions mainly to commerce. In the *Autobiography* he is dismissive of writing as a livelihood: 'a poor trade … It has been only when I had nothing else to do, that I have had recourse to this secondary occupation' (1.84–5). This may have been a fashionable pose; Walter Scott at times said much the same. Galt between the ages of seventeen and twenty-five was a junior clerk with a firm of merchants in Greenock. After a brush with a client, whom he thought rude and insulting, he suddenly decided in June 1804 to try his fortune in London. He arrived there with a pile of letters of introduction which did him little good. His account of hawking them around the recipients is strongly reminiscent of the well-known painting on the subject by Sir David Wilkie, which may well be more than a coincidence, as the two men were in London at the same time and they corresponded and no doubt met. Certainly contemporaries perceived a link: Lord Byron told Lady Blessington, for instance, that the characters in Galt's novels reminded him of Wilkie's pictures (Blessington, 74).

Galt spent three years trying to establish himself in business in London. One of his partners was his brother,

Thomas, who had inherited, Galt said, their mother's 'relish of the ridiculous and her … incomparable Scottish phraseology' (Galt, *Autobiography*, 1.112). John's novels were to prove that he had done so as well, but he was still engaged in writing of a different kind, beginning at this time a life of Wolsey. For the *Philosophical Magazine* he wrote 'An essay on commercial policy' and, in unconscious anticipation of his later involvement, a 'Statistical account of Upper Canada'. The magazine was edited by another émigré Scot, Alexander Tilloch, whose daughter, Elizabeth, Galt married on 20 April 1813.

Meanwhile the business venture failed. Galt thought that he might make a career at the bar and he entered Lincoln's Inn. Again he made a sudden change of direction and he set off in 1809 to travel around the Mediterranean. He says in the *Autobiography* that this was for health reasons, but he also speaks rather vaguely of an attempt to break the Napoleonic blockade by exploring the prospects of exporting British goods into central Europe through Turkey. His leisurely progress of nearly three years sounds more like a prolonged holiday than anything else, financed presumably by his father. At Gibraltar he made the acquaintance of Lord Byron, of whom he later wrote one of the first biographies. He sailed in the same ship with him to Malta and met him again in Athens and some years later in London.

This acquaintance with Byron provides another view of Galt as he appeared to a contemporary. Lady Blessington in her *Conversations with Lord Byron* (249–50) reports that he said about Galt:

> I am pleased at finding he is as amiable a man as his recent works prove him to be a clever and intelligent author. When I knew Galt some years ago, I was not in a frame of mind to form an impartial opinion of him; his mildness and equanimity struck me even then; but, to say the truth, his manner had not deference enough for my then aristocratical taste, and finding I could not awe him into a respect sufficiently profound for my sublime self, either as a peer or as an author, I felt a little grudge towards him that has now completely worn off … There is a quaint humour and observance of character in his novels that interest me very much … he shows a tenderness of heart which convinces one that *his* is the right place.

Galt was aware of the impression he made. In the *Autobiography* he says that Byron 'claimed more deference than I was disposed to grant' (1.231).

First publications and novels Galt was back in London by 1811 and in the following year the first of his books were published: *Life of Cardinal Wolsey*, *Voyages and Travels*, and a collection of plays in blank verse. He was sent by a merchant in Glasgow to open a branch in Gibraltar, but within a year he had to return to London for surgery. Since all his business ventures had come to nothing, he decided to try to earn his living by his pen. He also accepted appointment as what should now be called a lobbyist on behalf of the company promoting the Union Canal between Edinburgh and Glasgow. This gave the familiarity with Westminster and Whitehall which was the basis subsequently both of his involvement in Canadian affairs and of his political novels.

At this point in his life, after much miscellaneous writing and many false starts, Galt suddenly found his métier. For some years he had been thinking about an idea which eventually became *Annals of the Parish*. In 1813 he made a proposal to the publisher Archibald Constable, but he rejected the notion of a novel about life in rural Scotland. Soon after, however, the literary climate changed with the dramatic success of Walter Scott's *Waverley* (1814). Galt had been writing articles for the Edinburgh magazine *Blackwood's*, and in 1820 it started to publish in monthly parts *The Ayrshire Legatees*, his epistolary novel about the visit of the family of an Ayrshire minister to London to collect a legacy. For the first time Galt was drawing on his knowledge of life in the west of Scotland, his comic invention, and his exuberant Scots dialogue.

In the next two years Galt produced other Tales of the West at an astonishing pace: *The Steamboat* and *Annals of the Parish* in 1821, and *Sir Andrew Wylie*, *The Gathering of the West*, *The Provost*, and *The Entail* all in 1822. In that year alone Blackwoods published ten volumes of Galt in seven months. At least three of these novels were masterpieces. Both *Annals* and *The Provost* were 'imaginary biographies' in which a character writes in the first person and reveals himself with greater frankness than he realizes. They are so accurate in their account of social change that historians such as G. M. Trevelyan have recommended them as authentic social history. Left to himself Galt might have continued to write short novels of this kind, compact, coherent, and without a surplus word or episode. The publisher, William Blackwood, however, wanted three-volume best-sellers with an involved plot and striking episodes. As Galt himself said, *Sir Andrew Wylie* was marred by the inclusion of events 'too romantic and uncommon to my taste' (Galt, *Literary Life*, 1.244). The same is true of *The Entail*, although it is a novel of great emotional depth and wealth of characters; it was admired by both Scott and Byron.

Galt gave his next novel, *Ringan Gilhaize* (1823), which he regarded as his finest work, to another Edinburgh publisher, Oliver and Boyd. This is an account of the Scottish Reformation and religious wars of the seventeenth century, in which the imaginary narrator spans nearly two centuries by recalling conversations in his boyhood with his grandfather. It was a conscious riposte to Walter Scott's handling of the covenanters in *Old Mortality*. To Galt they were heroes in the Scottish tradition of the right of resistance to unjust authority, and he thought that Scott had treated them 'with too much levity' (Galt, *Literary Life*, 1.254). To emphasize his point Galt quoted as an appendix the declaration of Arbroath of 1320, the classic text of Scottish independence.

Canadian projects In spite of the success of his novels Galt had not abandoned his ambitions in other directions. His parliamentary lobbying experience and his childhood interest in Canada came together in his next venture. Canadians who had suffered losses when the United States invaded in 1812 had been trying in vain to extract compensation from the British government. In 1820 Galt had

agreed to act on their behalf, but after two years of effort the government still evaded payment. He then produced another scheme, a proposal for a company to raise capital for the development and settlement of land in Ontario. This could earn revenue which could be used to meet the claims. The company was formed in 1824 with Galt as secretary. He sailed to Canada in 1826 to direct operations there, leaving with Blackwood another novel in his best manner, *The Last of the Lairds*.

For just over two years, from 1827 to 1829, Galt threw his energy into the development of 1 million acres of largely virgin land between Lake Huron and Lake Ontario. He organized the clearing of forests, the building of roads, bridges and canals, the sale of land to settlers, and the foundation of the towns of Guelph and Goderich. Galt was clearly very happy in this work and, in his own view at least, successful. Part of his character was not satisfied with the 'secondary pursuit' of literature and longed for the satisfaction of involvement in practical affairs on a substantial scale. He said in his *Autobiography* that he felt that he was now 'entering seriously the avenue of life' (2.1). His family joined him in Canada and two of his sons afterwards had distinguished careers there. The youngest, Alexander Tilloch *Galt (1817–1893), became finance minister of Canada, and his elder brother, Thomas, chief justice of the court of common pleas of Ontario. Both were knighted.

The Canadian career of John Galt himself, however, came to an abrupt and distressing end. For reasons which are obscure, the board of the company, which was Galt's own idea and creation, evidently lost confidence in him. There was talk of a whispering campaign. The board sent out an accountant with instructions to report directly to them. This became, Galt says, an 'affliction' (Galt, *Autobiography*, 2.124) and he decided to return to London to have the matter out with the directors. He sailed from New York but before he went on board he was informed that a new man had been appointed in his place. Afterwards he said in a letter to his friend D. M. Moir: 'It has fallen to the lot of few to have done so much for any country and to be so used' (Moir, xcvii).

This was not the end of Galt's misfortunes. He arrived in Liverpool on 20 May 1829. On 15 July he was arrested for a debt of £80 for school fees and spent several months in king's bench prison. In his *Autobiography* and *Literary Life* Galt plays down this episode; but R. P. Gillies in *Memoirs of a Literary Veteran* says that he was 'irretrievably injured in mind, body and estate' by his imprisonment (3.61). Certainly his health, which had never been robust, deteriorated badly at about this time. Moir attributes this to a fall in Canada which injured his spine (Moir, cix). Whatever the reason, Galt for the rest of his life suffered from attacks of paralysis which at times even deprived him of sight.

Later years According to his own account Galt now largely withdrew from society, but he continued to write, producing in rapid succession a novel entitled *Southennan* (1830), set in the Scotland of Queen Mary, and two further novels, which were set in contemporary North America, *Lawrie Todd* (1830) and *Bogle Corbet* (1831), as well as his *Life of Lord Byron* (1830). In 1832 he wrote two political satires as contributions to the controversy over parliamentary reform, *The Member* and *The Radical*. Both are 'imaginary autobiographies', but are quite different in style. *The Radical* is entirely in English and is a somewhat abstract exercise on the theory that radical thought was liable to lead to anarchy. *The Member* returns to Galt's best manner in an account of a self-made man using the unreformed House of Commons for his own profit. In the *Autobiography* Galt professes surprise that it was resented by the tories as an attack, because he had always regarded himself as a tory. This is a paradox, because Galt's instincts and attitudes were anything but tory. He was no respecter of the established order and inherited privilege, and his novels give an unfavourable view of landowners. He says that most of his friends were whigs and that when he was for a time editor of a newspaper, *The Courier*, he set about alleviating its 'ultra toryism' (Galt, *Autobiography*, 2.196–8).

In January 1832 Thomas Carlyle met Galt and recorded his impressions in his notebook:

> Galt looks old, is deafish; has the air of a sedate Greenock Burgher; mouth indicating sly humour, and self-satisfaction; the eyes old and without lashes, gave me a sort of *wae* interest for him. He wears spectacles, and is hard of hearing: a very large man; and eats and drinks with a certain west-country gusto and research. Said little; but that little peaceable, clear and gutmüthig. Wish to see him also again. (*Two Notebooks*, 249–51)

Towards the end of 1832 Galt had a stroke which left him for a time unable to hold a pen. In this state he dictated his *Autobiography* and shortly afterwards his *Literary Life*. In 1834 he retired to Greenock for, as Katherine Thomson said, he 'was never in his element out of Scotland' (Thomson, 2.97). He continued to write short stories with his usual zest and humour and perfect command of the Scots tongue. In one of them, 'The Seamstress', he made explicit his enthusiasm for the language. The Scots, he said, were fortunate in having their own language as well as English and therefore 'an unusually rich vocabulary'. His own work was an ample demonstration of this richness. Galt died on 11 April 1839 in Greenock, survived by his wife, and was buried in the new burying-ground there.

PAUL HENDERSON SCOTT

Sources J. Galt, *The autobiography of John Galt*, 2 vols. (1833) · J. Galt, *Literary life*, 3 vols. (1834) · D. M. Moir, 'Biographical memoir', in J. Galt, *'The annals of the parish', and, 'The Ayrshire legatees'*, new edn (1841) · J. Hogg, 'Reminiscences of some of his contemporaries', *Poetical works*, 5 (1840), cxiv–cxv · *Two notebooks of Thomas Carlyle*, ed. C. E. Norton (1898), 249–50 · M. Gardiner, countess of Blessington, *Conversations of Lord Byron* (1834), 6, 74, 249–50 · R. P. Gillies, *Memoirs of a literary veteran*, 3 vols. (1851), vol. 3, pp. 57–61 · K. Thomson, *Recollections of literary characters*, 2 vols. (1854), vol. 2, pp. 99–107 · I. A. Gordon, *John Galt: the life of a writer* (1972) [incl. full bibliography] · C. A. Whatley, ed., *John Galt, 1779–1979* (1979) · P. H. Scott, *John Galt* (1985) · E. Waterston, ed., *John Galt, reappraisals* (1985)

Archives NL Scot., corresp. and letters · NL Scot., MSS · Public Archives of Ontario, Toronto, corresp. | Derbys. RO, letters to Sir R. J. Wilmot-Horton · NA Canada, corresp. and genealogical MSS · NL Scot., corresp. with Blackwoods · NL Scot., letters to Richard Bentley · NL Scot., corresp. with Archibald Constable · NL Scot., letters to D. M. Moir

Likenesses Count A. D'Orsay, pencil drawing, 1823, Scot. NPG · T. Woolnoth, stipple, 1824 (after E. Hastings), BM, NPG; repro. in *Ladies' Monthly Museum* (1824) · W. Brockedon, pencil and chalk, 1834, NPG · J. Fleming, oils, Greenock Art Gallery · R. Graves, line engraving (after J. Irvine), BM, NPG; repro. in Galt, *Autobiography*, frontispiece [*see illus.*] · C. Grey, oils, Scot. NPG · D. Maclise, lithograph (The Fraserians), BM; repro. in *Fraser's Magazine* (1830) · G. B. Shaw, engraving (after oil painting by W. J. Thomson), repro. in J. Galt, *'The annals of the parish', and, 'The Ayrshire legatees'* (1841) · J. Smith, oils, Guelph, Canada

Wealth at death granted £50 in 1838 by Literary Fund; British Government granted 1200 acres in Canada in 1838: Gordon, *John Galt*, 140–41

Galton, Dorothy Constance (1901–1992), university administrator and apiculturist, was born on 14 October 1901 at 66 Rathcoole Avenue, Edmonton, Middlesex, the daughter of Frank Wallace Galton, secretary to the Fabian Society and to Sidney and Beatrice Webb, and his wife, Jessie Jane Townsend, *née* Cottridge. She grew up in a political atmosphere, and was a lifelong supporter of the Labour Party. As a young woman she had critical surgery which deprived her of the ability to have children and altered the shape of her life. She was educated at home before going to secondary school at Wood Green, London, and then to Bedford College, London. She soon decided that university was not for her, and left after a few months, but she developed privately her gifts for the Slavonic languages. She worked for a time in Transport House and then for Count Mihaly Karolyi, the exiled socialist president of Hungary, travelling with the count and his wife to France, where she tasted the aristocratic life and at the same time developed her east European interests.

In 1928 Galton returned to London as secretary to Professor Sir Bernard Pares, who was reputed not to be an easy man to get on with. He was a leading expert on Russia and director from 1922 to 1939 of the School of Slavonic and East European Studies, then based at King's College, London. The school was founded in 1915 by Robert Seton Watson and T. G. Masaryk. In 1932 it became an independent university institute with Galton, although lacking a formal academic training, promoted to be its administrative secretary. At the school her gifts for languages and administration, and her warm personality, stood her in good stead, particularly during the difficult years of the Second World War. She was able to make several visits to the Soviet Union, building valuable personal contacts.

In 1939 Pares retired from the directorship, going to live in the USA where he remained until his death in 1949. Galton continued as secretary of the School of Slavonic and East European Studies under his successors Professor William Rose (1939–47) and Dr George Bolsover (1947–75) until her retirement in 1961. During the Second World War part of the school was evacuated to Oxford, with Galton the link between the sections. Onto her capable shoulders fell the work of maintaining an organization that lost its records during the bombing of central London. In 1941 she organized a seminal summer school in Oxford attended by some eighty students and in 1945, at the invitation of the Rockefeller Foundation, she visited several universities in the USA to further the cause of Slavonic studies. It then fell to her to reintegrate the institute as a single unit in London.

Galton's other great interest, beekeeping, commenced in 1954 and was for a time a purely practical activity. Her leaving present from her colleagues at the School of Slavonic and East European Studies in 1961 was a honey extractor. After her retirement and move to Norfolk she brought her considerable intellect to bear on research into beekeeping in Russia. It was natural for her to use the resources of the London-based Bee Research Association, whose director, Eva Crane, was another *grande dame* of the apicultural world. The fruit of her research was published by the association in 1971 as *A Survey of a Thousand Years of Beekeeping in Russia*, with a foreword by Professor Robert E. F. Smith. The International Bee Research Association in 1987 awarded her an honorary membership in recognition of her contribution to the Russian section of its library, through the translation of Russian apicultural materials. Her second book, *The Bee-Hive: an Enquiry into its Origins and History* (1982), was an etymological study that ranged far beyond the borders of eastern Europe and Russia. Finally, she assembled in her closing years an unpublished study, 'Bees, honey and beeswax in early historical times'. Although her books were without doubt her major occupations, she also contributed to the beekeeping press on a wide range of topics, including studies of the Russian wax trade into Kings Lynn, Norfolk.

Galton maintained her political interests until late in life, being active in the local Labour Party and involved with other voluntary bodies. It was an odd turn of the wheel of fortune that in her latter years she, who gave a low priority to wealth, had never owned a home, and had never had a bank account, inherited a house and capital, and thus found herself a minor capitalist. She never married, and died on 27 August 1992 at her home, 3 Hooks Hill Road, Sheringham, Norfolk, of cancer of the stomach. She donated her body to medical research.

KARL SHOWLER

Sources *The Times* (6 Oct 1992) · *Beeworld*, 73/4 (1992), p. 223 · I. W. Roberts, *History of the School of Slavonic and East European Studies* (1991) · E. Hill, *The mind's eye: memoirs of Dame Elizabeth Hill* (1999) · b. cert. · d. cert. · personal knowledge (2004)
Archives UCL, school of Slavonic and east European studies, diary of a visit to USA
Likenesses photograph, repro. in Roberts, *History of the School*
Wealth at death under £125,000: probate, 14 Oct 1992, *CGPLA Eng. & Wales*

Galton, Sir Douglas Strutt (1822–1899), engineer, was born on 2 July 1822 at Spring Hill, Worcestershire, the second son of John Howard Galton of Hadzor House, Droitwich, and his wife, Isabella, eldest daughter of Joseph Strutt of Derby. He was educated at Birmingham, Geneva, and at Rugby School under Thomas Arnold, where he was

Sir Douglas Strutt Galton (1822–1899), by unknown photographer, 1899

a contemporary of R.A. Cross and of the author Thomas Hughes. He graduated with distinction from the Royal Military Academy, Woolwich, and was commissioned second lieutenant in the Royal Engineers on 18 December 1840.

After further training in engineering at Chatham, Galton was appointed by Major-General Charles William Pasley in 1841 to oversee the removal of the wreck of the *Royal George* from the anchorage at Spithead, using the first electrically fused explosives. He then went to the Mediterranean, where he served at Malta and Gibraltar. He was promoted lieutenant on 1 October 1843. In 1846 he returned to Britain and joined the Ordnance Survey. In 1847 he was appointed secretary to the newly formed railway commission. On 26 August 1851 he married Mary Anne, daughter of George Thomas Nicholson of Waverley Abbey, Farnham, Surrey. She was the sister of General Sir Lothian Nicholson. They had two daughters. He was made second captain on 31 August 1851 and first captain on 14 March 1855. In 1854 he became secretary to the railway department of the Board of Trade, and in 1856 he visited the United States, together with Robert Lowe MP, to inspect the railways there. In 1860 he was appointed to the War Office as temporary assistant inspector-general of fortifications, for barracks. In May 1862 Palmerston made him assistant permanent under-secretary for war, a position he occupied for nearly eight years, and on 2 July he was placed on the permanent half pay list of the army. In 1865 he was made a companion in the Order of the Bath, civil division. In 1869 he transferred from the War Office to the office of works, where he was made director of public works and buildings. He retired in 1875.

During his years of government service Galton was employed on a great many routine engineering investigations and served on numerous royal commissions and other official committees. His work covered issues as diverse as the application of iron to railway structures, the main drainage of London, the sanitary condition of military barracks and hospitals, and the laying of underwater telegraph cables. He was a member of the army sanitary committee from 1862 until his death. He had a strong interest in railways, was an active member of the royal commission on railways in 1866, and served as judge of railway equipment at the Philadelphia exhibition in 1876 and at the Paris Universal Exhibition in 1878. His experiments with railway brakes were published in his *Memorandum on Brake Experiments* (1879) and *Report on Brake Experiments* (1880), which became standard reference works at the time.

Galton also had varied scientific and humanitarian interests. He was elected a fellow of the Royal Society in 1859 and served on its council. He joined the British Association for the Advancement of Science in 1860 and was one of their general secretaries from 1871 to 1895, when he was elected president. Having previously visited the *Reichsanstalt* at Berlin, he used his position as president to support the project for a national physical laboratory in London. His energy in negotiations with the government and the Royal Society led to success but he did not live to see the completion of the project. He was a member of the first committee to advocate the higher education of women, and was one of the original founders of the Girls' Public Day School Company. He was president of the senate of University College, London, vice-president of the Society of Arts, a member of the council of the Royal Drawing Society, and a member of the council of the Princess Helena's College at Ealing. It was through his efforts that the Childhood Society was established. Appearing before a committee of the education department, Galton strongly argued that special classes in elementary schools should be provided for children with learning disabilities, and advocated their placement in foster homes if they were being subjected to unhealthy or criminal environments. He was an active member of the Society for the Aid to the Sick and Wounded in War (now the Red Cross); during the Franco-Prussian War he was sent by the society as commissioner to the sick and wounded of both nations. He was especially active in visiting German hospitals, and in recognition of his efforts the imperial order of the crown of Prussia was conferred upon him by the German emperor.

Perhaps Galton's most important work, however, was in the development of sanitary engineering. The Herbert Hospital at Woolwich was designed by him when he was at the War Office, and many improvements in barracks and hospitals were due to his initiative. He invented a ventilating fire grate, known as the Galton grate, in the early 1860s; this was adopted for all military barracks and hospitals. General Arthur Jules Morin, of the French artillery, head of the Conservatoire des Arts et Métiers, considered it the best arrangement for perfect warming and ventilating with the open fireplace that had been produced during the nineteenth century. Galton published several books on the role of sanitary engineering in the construction of hospitals and homes, as well as several reports on sewage and drainage. He was among the first and strongest supporters of the Parkes Museum and was chairman of its council from 1882 to 1888. He was also a member of the Sanitary Institute of Great Britain, and acted as chairman of its council from 1885 to 1887. After the merger of the two bodies, he served as chairman from 1888 to 1892 and 1897 to 1899. He was elected vice-president in 1892 and also became treasurer in 1894. He was for many years chairman of the institute's board of examiners, and took a great interest in the training of sanitary officers, to whom he often lectured, both in London and in the provinces. His last lecture to them in London was given on 17 October 1898, when he urged that their motto should be that 'prevention is better than cure'.

At Queen Victoria's jubilee in 1887 Galton was made a knight commander in the Order of the Bath, civil division. In 1889 he was made an officer of the Légion d'honneur and a knight of grace of the order of St John of Jerusalem. He also received the Turkish order of the Mejidiye.

He was also a member of many other learned societies in Britain and elsewhere. Oxford University made him an honorary DCL in 1875, and both Durham and Montreal universities made him an honorary LLD. He was a member of the Institution of Electrical Engineers, serving on their council from 1888 to 1890, and was vice-president of the Institution of Mechanical Engineers. In 1891 he acted as chairman of the executive committee of the International Congress of Hygiene and Demography held in London. In 1894 the Institution of Civil Engineers made him an honorary member. During the last decade of his life he was also associated with some of the metropolitan electrical industries. In his own county of Worcestershire he was a JP and a county councillor.

Despite the apparent diversity of his activities, almost all of Galton's work was connected with the improvement of public health and safety. While not one of the most significant engineers of the nineteenth century, he is notable for his role in the establishment and promotion of sanitary engineering as an important element of nineteenth-century industrial development. He died at his London home, 12 Chester Street, Grosvenor Place, on 10 March 1899. Although a prominent advocate of cremation, he was buried at Hadzor, Worcestershire, for family reasons. He was survived by his wife.

R. H. VETCH, *rev.* DAVID F. CHANNELL

Sources *Journal of the Sanitary Institute* (April 1889) · *Nature*, 59 (1898–9), 512–13 · *Science*, 9 (1899), 421 · *PICE*, 137 (1898–9), 413–7 · d. cert. · *CGPLA Eng. & Wales* (1899)
Archives BL, corresp. with Florence Nightingale, Add. MSS 45759–45767 · Bodl. Oxf., letters to H. W. Acland · UCL, corresp. with E. Chadwick

Likenesses photograph, 1899, National Physical Laboratory Museum, Teddington [*see illus.*] · T. Brock, bust, Shire Hall, Worcester · photograph, repro. in *Journal of the Sanitary Institute*

Wealth at death £92,804 1s. 9d.: resworn probate, Nov 1899, *CGPLA Eng. & Wales*

Galton, Sir Francis (1822–1911), statistician, now called human geneticist, and eugenicist, was born in Birmingham on 16 February 1822, the youngest of the seven children of Samuel Tertius Galton (1783–1844), a very successful banker, and his wife, Frances Anne Violetta Darwin (1783–1874), one of the many daughters of Erasmus *Darwin (1731–1802). The older Galtons, like the older Darwins, had been Quakers but by the time of Francis Galton's birth Samuel Galton had joined the Church of England. Both of Francis Galton's paternal and maternal grandfathers had been founding members of the Birmingham Lunar Society and Galton considered himself to be heir to the scientific and intellectual tradition which that society represented.

Childhood and education According to his older siblings Galton was a child prodigy: they claimed that he learned the alphabet at eighteen months, read at two and a half years, memorized lengthy poems at five, and discussed the *Iliad* at six. However, despite this auspicious beginning, his school record was relatively undistinguished. At King Edward's School (the Birmingham Free School) he showed little aptitude for classical studies and chafed at the limitations that were placed upon him, occasionally becoming something of a disciplinary problem. At sixteen he was removed from school, much to his joy. His parents had decided that he should become, like his eminent grandfather, a physician; he became a pupil at Birmingham General Hospital in 1838 and, a year later, enrolled in King's College medical school in London. Medical education did not, however, suit him; after much discussion—and over some parental objections—he was allowed to proceed to Trinity College, Cambridge, in 1840 to read mathematics.

At Cambridge Galton read mathematics under William Hopkins. However, his academic record was again undistinguished. Although his circle of friends included some of the most notable scholars of his day—among them H. S. Maine and Henry Hallam—he was never able to equal their academic success. In his autobiography Galton made much more mention of the social activities in Cambridge—reading parties, hiking parties, boating parties, and drinking parties—than of books or professors. During his third year, while preparing for his final set of examinations, he suffered what was probably a nervous breakdown and was forced to leave Cambridge with a pass ('poll') degree. He spent another term or two studying medicine, but this desultory progress toward a medical degree came to an abrupt end when, in the autumn of 1844, his father died, leaving an enormous inheritance.

Travel and marriage 'Being much upset and craving for a healthier life' (Galton, 82) Galton set out on a year-long tour of the Middle East. During this trip he learned to speak Arabic. Between 1846 and 1850 he divided his time

Sir Francis Galton (1822–1911), by Eveleen Myers, 1890s

between London and Scotland, pursuing a sporting life. However, this did not satisfy either his restless spirit or his intellect. Thus, in 1850 he undertook a journey of exploration (at his own expense but under the auspices of the Royal Geographical Society) to south-west Africa—an area which was, at that time, largely unknown to Europeans. Two books resulted: *Tropical South Africa* (1852) and *The Art of Travel* (1855). The first of these was rewarded with a gold medal from the Royal Geographical Society, a fellowship of the Royal Society, and membership of the Athenaeum; the second (a how-to book) was reprinted several times over the next four decades.

On 1 August 1853 Francis Galton married Louisa Jane Butler (d. 1897), daughter of George *Butler (1774–1853), dean of Peterborough and formerly headmaster at Harrow School. The London residence that the Galtons established soon after, in an elegant Georgian terraced house on Rutland Gate in South Kensington, was emblematic of the life they would lead in London for the next half century: active, central, wealthy, and intellectual.

Having settled in London, Galton became involved in various aspects of scientific administration. He belonged to and played an active role both in the Royal Society and in the Royal Geographical Society. In addition he was regularly involved in the governance of the British Association for the Advancement of Science; he served as secretary from 1863 to 1867. Having published some important meteorological investigations (Galton is credited with discovery of the anti-cyclone effect), he served on the governing committee of the Meteorological Office from 1868 to 1900 and as a member of the Kew committee of the Royal Society (chairman, 1889–1901). The Athenaeum was another important locus for his social and intellectual life.

'Hereditary talent and character' Galton's fame rests on his long series of enquiries—spanning more than three decades—into the nature of heredity in general and human heredity in particular. With a few exceptions most of these investigations were numerical or statistical in character. Early in his adult life Galton had demonstrated an idiosyncratic appetite for counting and quantifying. When travelling in Africa, for example, he had come across some African women with extremely large breasts and had devised a method for estimating the size of their chests by triangulation. Later, when he was bored at scientific meetings, he counted the frequency with which people were fidgeting—and published the figures. He invented a little pocket ticker which would enable him to count without being noticed and, when taking long walks in various cities, he would count the frequency of attractive women he passed (he published those results also). Thus it is hardly surprising that when he decided to study heredity systematically his studies would be quantitative; somewhat more surprising is the fact that Galton, who was not a sophisticated mathematician, laid the foundation for the science of biostatistics as a result of his investigations into heredity.

Galton's first publication on the subject was an article, 'Hereditary talent and character', which appeared in *Macmillan's Magazine* in 1865. Inspired by his reading of the *Origin of Species* (published in 1859), and most probably by the fact that Charles Darwin was his first cousin, Galton became interested in the question of whether human mental traits could be inherited, and if they were, whether they could be made susceptible either to natural or to artificial selection. To this end he undertook a statistical analysis of the entries in biographical dictionaries, trying to determine the frequency with which eminent people were related to other eminent people and comparing this with the frequency with which eminent people arose within average, or undistinguished families. Using some data that today seem quite problematic, as well as some estimates which now seem quite crude, Galton concluded that 'talent and peculiarities of character are found in the children, when they have existed in either of the parents, to an extent beyond all question greater than in the children of ordinary persons' (F. Galton, 'Hereditary talent and character', *Macmillan's Magazine*, 12, June, 1865, 158). He had concluded, to put the matter another way, that mental traits were more the product of heredity than of environment, more the product of nature than of nurture. This belief led Galton to what appeared a simple and logical conclusion. That, if even 'a twentieth part of the cost and pains were spent in measures for the improvement of the human race that is spent on the improvement of the breed of horses and cattle' it could produce 'a galaxy of genius' (ibid., 165–6). Galton believed selective breeding (the cultural equivalent of Darwin's natural selection) to be the only hope for improving the human race, precisely because heredity was a more important determinant than environment. This was the fundamental idea behind the eugenic political programme that he subsequently espoused.

Researches in inheritance After 1865 Galton became actively engaged in researches which explored various aspects and corollaries of his initial insights. During the 1870s he disproved Darwin's theory of pangenesis, which held that inheritance could be affected by environmental conditions because hereditary particles were carried in the circulatory system. Galton created an experiment in which he transfused the blood of several black rabbits and several white rabbits. He then bred each of the rabbits to see whether changing the blood of the animals would change the colour of their offspring. Since this did not happen Galton was able to argue (much to his cousin's displeasure) that on this crucial point Darwin was wrong.

Galton also carried out several series of investigations on inheritance patterns in sweet peas (ironically, the same plant used experimentally, a few years earlier, by Gregor Mendel). Galton wanted to find out whether the plants that grew from extremely large seeds also produced extremely large seeds, whether, and to what extent, seed size was inherited. During this series of experiments Galton made two crucial discoveries that eventually formed the basis of biostatistics. He had long understood that the characteristics of populations could be described by the features and mathematics of normal curves, but in the sweet pea analysis Galton came to the further conclusion that the relationship between two populations could also be described by the laws of probability (then called the laws of frequency of error). Second, he realized that when the data for one characteristic (say for the weight of sweet pea seeds) were analysed probabilistically (to derive, for each seed, its unit of deviation from the population mean), and when the data (in units of deviation) for the parental generation were plotted against similar data for the offspring generation, a sloping line resulted. The slope of that line provided a measure, Galton thought, of the strength of the hereditary relationship between the two generations. That measure, generalized beyond genetic relationships, subsequently came to be called a regression coefficient and came to be used daily in thousands of different statistical investigations.

Galton completed the sweet pea studies in 1877. At that time he had for several years been trying to collect similar data from human populations, for example, by asking the headmasters of several schools to send him information about the height, weight, and health of their students. These human data had been helpful to him in some ways (the studies that he published form part of the basis of psychometrics, the quantitative analysis of human mental and physical characteristics) but they lacked the generational dimension that had proved so fruitful and interesting in the sweet pea studies. In order to gather intergenerational data Galton created, at his own expense, what he called an anthropometric laboratory at the International Health Exhibition at the South Kensington Science Museum. The booth was equipped with instruments which allowed various measurements to be taken (height, weight, chest span, head size, arm strength, hearing, visual acuity, and colour sense) and was staffed with people to take the measurements. During the life of this laboratory 9337 persons, parents and children, were measured. In addition Galton had published a pamphlet, *Record of Family Faculties*, and had offered cash prizes to families that sent it back to him with complete sets of data inscribed.

Biostatistics In his effort to analyse the data that he had now collected Galton made another important contribution to the sciences of human genetics and biostatistics. He had constructed elaborate graphs on which he had entered mid-parental height (an average of the mother's and the father's height) on one axis and offspring height on the other. At the point of intersection, however, he had placed a number corresponding to the number of children of that height that had been, according to his data, produced by parents of the corresponding height. Galton immediately noticed that if he drew lines connecting the points of equal frequency (for example, all the '4s' on his chart) they formed concentric ellipses, reminding him of meteorological charts that he had prepared years earlier. Furthermore, the straight line that connected the tangent points of those ellipses had a slope identical to the regression coefficient for his data. His knowledge of mathematics was sufficient to suggest to Galton that his graphs could be constructed from only three pieces of information: the probable error for each generation and the regression coefficient. When a professor of mathematics (J. D. Hamilton Dickson of Cambridge University) was able to do this construction without the original data, simply as a problem in analytic geometry, Galton realized that he had discovered a way to measure the relationship between the characteristics of two bodies of data, whether or not the two populations being studied were biologically related to each other—that he had discovered what was later called the measurement of correlation.

Galton was enthusiastic about these discoveries. There was, he wrote, 'scarcely anything so apt to impress the imagination as the wonderful form of cosmic order expressed by the "Law of Frequency of Error" … The law would have been personified by the Greeks, and deified, if they had known of it' (F. Galton, *Natural Inheritance*, 1889, 66). Unfortunately, after 1889, when his summary book, *Natural Inheritance*, was published, he no longer had the energy to collect additional data and analyse them. However, his writings had inspired several younger people to take up both the study of human heredity and the analytical tools of statistical analysis, and Galton was able to use both his financial resources and his prestige to further their endeavours. In the last decades of his life (and in his will) he worked to create several institutions in which biostatistical and genetic research would be pursued: the scientific journal *Biometrika* (founded in 1902 with Galton's disciples Karl Pearson and W. F. R. Weldon as co-editors), the Galton Laboratory for National Eugenics, and the Galton Eugenics Professorship. (Both of these latter were at University College, London; after Galton's death, and Karl Pearson's accession to the Galton professorship, they were combined into the department of applied statistics.)

Although the study of inheritance was his main focus Galton also undertook many investigations of human mental and physical abilities. He asked mathematicians to make drawings of the ways in which they visualized the number system. He used superimposed photographs to create composite portraits of various groups of people. In the 1890s he investigated the use of fingerprinting for personal identification, establishing that the pattern of a person's fingerprints did not change from youth to old age and creating a taxonomic system by which the variations in fingerprint patterns could be described and catalogued. Although he never succeeded in developing a system for measuring intelligence, his various attempts provided the stimulus for the research which, in the early decades of the twentieth century, resulted in standardized tests for both intelligence and emotional states.

Final years and lasting influence During the last years of his life Galton devoted himself to promoting the political programme of eugenics. In 1883 he had created the word eugenics out of the Greek roots for 'beautiful' and 'heredity'. He meant the word to denote both the science and the practice of improving human stock 'to give the more suitable races or strains of blood a better chance of prevailing speedily over the less suitable' (F. Galton, *Inquiries into Human Faculty*, 1883, 24–5). Most of his practical eugenic suggestions were for forms of what might be called positive eugenics: research programmes for discovering which diseases were hereditary; tax schemes for encouraging intelligent people to marry each other and to have large families. However, many of the people who took up the eugenic cause (and there were thousands of such people in many countries) were more interested in negative eugenic measures (for example the sterilization of persons deemed 'unfit'). Particularly after the lengths to which the Nazi regime in Germany took eugenic practice the word developed ugly connotations and was subsequently dropped from the title of all the institutions that Galton had helped to found.

Galton's ultimate contribution to human genetics is somewhat more difficult to explain than his contributions to biostatistics and psychometrics. In genetics he did not discover any law, enunciate any theory, nor reveal any body of facts which were later considered valid. What he did do, however, was provide an operational and quantitative definition for a process—heredity—which was, in his day, both ill-defined and very ambiguous. According to Galton heredity is the measurable relationship between two generations. This definition may seem obvious to us today, but it is only obvious because Galton was able to demonstrate not only how that measurement could be taken, but also how fruitful a scientific enterprise the exploration of the measurements could be.

Galton died on 17 January 1911 at Grayshott House, Haslemere, Surrey, and was buried in the Galton family vault at Claverdon, near Warwick. Louisa Galton had predeceased him by several years; she died on 13 August 1897.

Ironically, given the fact that both Galtons belonged to intellectually eminent families and that Francis Galton had devoted himself both to the study of human heredity and to the cause of eugenics, the Galtons had no children.　　　　　　　　　　　　　　　　RUTH SCHWARTZ COWAN

Sources R. S. Cowan, *Sir Francis Galton and the study of heredity in the nineteenth century* (1985) • R. S. Cowan, 'Francis Galton's statistical ideas: the influence of eugenics', *Isis*, 63 (1972), 509–28 • R. S. Cowan, 'Francis Galton's contribution to genetics', *Journal of the History of Biology*, 5 (1972), 389–412 • R. S. Cowan, 'Nature and nurture: biology and politics in the work of Francis Galton', *Historical Studies on the Biological Sciences*, 1 (1977), 133–208 • K. Pearson, *The life, letters and labours of Francis Galton*, 3 vols. in 4 (1914–30) • D. J. Kevles, *In the name of eugenics* (1985) • F. Galton, *Memories of my life* (1908) • *CGPLA Eng. & Wales* (1911) • *DNB*
Archives McGill University, Montreal, notebook • MHS Oxf., papers • RGS, astronomical observations • RS, letters and papers • UCL, corresp. and papers | Air Force Research Laboratories, Cambridge, Massachusetts, letters to Lord Rayleigh • BL, corresp. with Macmillans, Add. MS 55218 • CUL, letters to Charles Darwin • CUL, letters to G. Stokes • Keele University Library, LePlay Collection, corresp. • King's AC Cam., letters to Oscar Browning • RGS, letters to RGS • UCL, letters to A. G. Butler • UCL, letters to Millicent Lethbridge • UCL, letters to James Sully
Likenesses O. Oakley, watercolour drawing, 1840, NPG • Maull & Polyblank, photograph, c.1856, NPG • G. Graef, oils, 1882, NPG • E. Myers, platinum print, 1890–99, NPG [*see illus.*] • C. W. Furse, oils, 1903, NPG • G. Frampton, bronze bust, c.1910, UCL • F. S. Baden-Powell, drawing silhouette, NPG • English school, oils, Down House, London • J. C. Fisher, chalk drawing, NPG • Graham's Art Studios, photograph, NPG • H. J. Whitlock, carte-de-visite, NPG
Wealth at death £104,487 3s. 1d.: resworn probate, 7 March 1911, *CGPLA Eng. & Wales*

Galway. For this title name *see* Massue de Ruvigny, Henri de, earl of Galway, and marquess of Ruvigny in the French nobility (1648–1720).

Galway, Mary (1864/5–1928), trade unionist, was born in Moira, co. Down, the daughter of a linen weaving family. Nothing else is known about her early life, but the family moved to Belfast about the 1870s and Mary Galway worked as a machinist in the city's linen industry for at least eleven years.

Mary Galway became involved in trade unionism from the 1890s and by the summer of 1897 she was appointed general secretary of the Textile Operatives' Society of Ireland (1893), a position she held until her death. In 1894 the Irish Trade Union Congress (ITUC) was formed in Dublin. Mary Galway first attended the congress in 1898 and was the only woman delegate consistently to attend the congress in its first two decades. From 1907 Galway was elected annually to the parliamentary committee, which was also the congress executive. She became vice-president of the ITUC in 1910, the only vice-president never to become the president the following year.

Through the Textile Operatives' Union Mary Galway attempted to organize linen workers, the majority of whom were women, often the main breadwinners for their families. This was an extremely difficult task owing to the nature of the relationship between employers and employees in the north. Often employers were paternalistic, providing houses and other services for their workers, expecting absolute loyalty in return. Linen strikes tended to result in a lock-out or the replacement of workers by machinery or by other workers from the area. Mary Galway became the sole organizer for women linen workers in the city of Belfast. It was a demanding role, as only about five per cent of linen workers had joined the union by 1910. Her greatest success was in organizing skilled weavers rather than the unskilled workers in the linen mills. The fact that Galway targeted the more skilled linen weavers led to lack of support for her among the unskilled women workers, who eventually asked James Connolly (1868–1916) to organize them, much to Mary Galway's anger.

Mary Galway was regarded as a moderate in trade union circles and she strongly opposed the radical trade unionism of James Larkin (1876–1947) and James Connolly. She was a close political ally of the Belfast trade unionist William Walker (1871–1918). Her union was strong in some small Belfast factories and succeeded in improving working conditions. However, in the larger factories, where the union was weak, threatened strike action produced lock-outs.

When Connolly arrived in Belfast in 1910 as an organizer for Larkin's Transport Union, Mary Galway, along with Walker and a number of other Belfast trade unionists, was suspicious of the political agenda which lay behind the union's activities. Galway and Connolly became embroiled in an inter-union dispute during the linen strike of 1911. Those unskilled workers who did not belong to Galway's union had approached Connolly to organize them. Connolly told the girls to seek Galway's advice but she showed little sympathy for their cause. Connolly therefore began to organize them, which led to the formation of a rival union for women in Belfast. Mary Galway believed this to be detrimental to the workers' cause and, accusing Connolly of poaching, she took her case to the trades council. The debate in council exposed the political differences between the Belfast trade unionists and Connolly. Galway called Connolly 'an adventurer … coming to a city to wreck a trade union that has done incalculable good' (Belfast Trades Council minutes, 2 Nov 1911). The council came to no decision on the dispute.

Mary Galway was a well-known figure in Belfast and acted as a negotiator during the 1906 linen strike and also in the campaign to improve home workers' pay and conditions in 1910–11. Between 1908 and 1912 she contributed to a number of parliamentary committees investigating the linen trade, most notably the inquiries into truck payments (1908) and conditions in the linen industry (1912) which resulted in the setting up in 1915 of a trade board for outworkers or home workers. She was also instrumental in having the first woman factory inspector appointed to Ireland.

After 1913 Mary Galway ceased to hold a prominent position in the Irish TUC, although she remained general secretary of the Textile Operatives' Union. She died at 31 Crocus Street, Belfast on 26 September 1928.　　MARIA LUDDY

Sources P. Collins, 'Mary Galway', *Labour History News*, 7 (summer 1991), 14–15 • T. Moriarty, 'Work in progress': episodes from the history of

Irish women's trade unionism (1995) • Irishman (6 Oct 1928) • Weekly Belfast Telegraph (6 Oct 1928) • M. Galway, 'The linen industry in the north', The voice of Ireland, ed. W. G. Fitzgerald (c.1924), 295–8 • Irish TUC, annual reports of the Irish Trade Union Congress (1898–1913) • Belfast trades council minutes, 2 Nov 1911, PRO NIre. [microfilm copy] • d. cert.
Likenesses photograph, repro. in Collins, 'Mary Galway', 14–15

Gamage, Albert Walter (1855–1930), retail entrepreneur and department store owner, was born on 14 July 1855 at Hereford, the seventeenth child of Henry Gamage, a plumber and glazier, and his wife, Tryphina Carr. After leaving the local school he was apprenticed to a draper at Winslow, Buckinghamshire. At the age of nineteen he went to London, finding work initially with the drapery firm of Spencer Turner and Boldero of Lisson Grove, and then at the wholesale drapery warehouse of Hitchcock, Williams & Co. at St Paul's Churchyard. As was usual at that time he lived in at both his early jobs.

After gaining some experience in the drapery business Gamage joined with a young colleague Frank Spain, and in 1878 the pair used their savings of £150 to lease a small hosiery shop, with a tiny frontage of just 5 feet, at 128 Holborn. Years later Gamage told how his career as a shop owner and the location of his business were both determined by a chance remark from a local trader who told him that Holborn needed a good hosiery shop. The pair's first success came with the sale of special hairbrushes, which they sold far more cheaply than any of their competitors. This gave Gamage the idea of bulk buying goods of reasonable quality and then lowering profit margins to undersell rival shopkeepers. Gamage was ambitious and by 1881 he had bought out his partner and set about reorganizing the small but highly competitive business for further growth. Gamage brought about this expansion by widening his merchandise and selling new products. He left no stone unturned in his search for new products, travelling extensively throughout Europe and North America. In later years his travels to seek out new goods became legendary: tales were told of how he battled through blizzards in the wilds of Michigan in search of a new toy gun for his store. He became the largest importer of Steiff toys, including the now famous Steiff bear, after visiting Frau Steiff's toy factory in the Black Forest. Gamage was always quick to spot new products and related consumer booms. He was quick, for instance, to exploit the popularity of cycling following the introduction of the new safety bicycle in 1885: he promptly made arrangements for cycles to be manufactured under the Gamage label, and because of his direct bulk purchasing, was able to undercut all competitors. His business maxim was 'Always be satisfied with small profits.'

The increased range of goods sold by Gamage necessitated changes in the size and arrangement of the store. Both were achieved in something of a piecemeal fashion as Gamage spread his business by buying up adjoining premises, creating by the turn of the century a department store which covered almost 2 acres of floorspace housed behind an impressive neo-Gothic façade. Unlike many of London's other department stores, Gamage's was oriented less toward the female shopper and more at the men working in the nearby City. But of course many of these office workers were family men who at weekends came on shopping trips to Gamages with their wives and children. Indeed the store's Christmas bazaar was a children's dream, always presenting new toys often searched out by Gamage himself.

Gamage was always a retail innovator. He developed strong links with his suppliers, often using small manufacturers, who produced exclusively for him, in a bid to bypass those firms that disapproved of his price cutting. When cars started to become more widely available he sold cars manufactured under the Gamage name and opened a new motoring department in the store. His thousand-page mail-order catalogue was one of the first of its kind and the range of products on offer provides an interesting insight into Edwardian consumer society. Gamage's penchant for advertising was strong, and although not a showman like his rival William Whiteley, he originated many ideas. He was the first to take out full-page newspaper advertisements, using the whole front page of the Daily Mail on 12 July 1904 to announce enlargements to his store, which he named the People's Popular Emporium.

The store's development of sporting goods strongly reflected Gamage's own love of games. He became president of many athletic clubs, as well as the donor of a large number of challenge cups and shields. He was also a strong supporter of working men's clubs. In 1888 Gamage married the second daughter of J. G. Murdoch. There were two sons and one daughter from the marriage. One of Gamage's other passions was his home at Grange Farm, Charteridge, Buckinghamshire, which he acquired during the 1920s. Despite such diversions he never neglected the store, which grew from strength to strength, having a turnover in 1930 of over £1 million per year and employing some 2000 people. The business was a family-run affair, with Gamage's son Eric becoming managing director. The firm was closed in 1972 and the building demolished.

Gamage died at Charteridge after a long illness, on 5 April 1930. He was 'laid in state' in the store's motor department with his staff standing guard, encouraged to do so by the unprecedented offer of a Saturday afternoon holiday.   GARETH SHAW

Sources A. Adburgham, Shopping in style: London from the Restoration to Edwardian elegance (1979) • T. C. Bridges and H. H. Tiltman, Kings of commerce [1928] • The Times (7 April 1930) • The Times (15 March 1972) • W. H. Beable, Romance of great businesses, 2 vols. (1926) • B. Lancaster, The department store: a social history (1995) • d. cert.
Likenesses photograph, repro. in Beable, Romance of great business
Wealth at death £28,766 4s. 9d.: probate, 25 June 1930, CGPLA Eng. & Wales

Gambarini [married name Chazal], **Elizabeth** [Elisabetta de Gambarini] (1730–1765), composer, keyboard player, and singer, was born on 7 September 1730 in Holles Street, St Marylebone, Middlesex, the third of the four children of

Charles Gambarini (d. 1754) and his wife, Joanna (Giovanna Paula) Stradiotti (d. 1774). She seems to have been the only sibling to have survived to maturity. Her parents had probably arrived in London from Italy by 1726, when a sale of 'Mr Gambarini's entire collection' was advertised (BL, S.C. 222 (4, 5)). The baptismal records for the Gambarini children are unusually helpful in revealing the parents' origin and social status, Elizabeth's showing that her father was a nobleman from Lucca and her mother a woman of similar status from Dalmatia. She described her father as 'Librarian, Antiquarian and Counsellor to the late Landgrave of Hess Cassel' (Gambarini, proposal to the Royal Society and accompanying letter to Dr Birch, BL, Add. MS 4308, fol. 13); he is almost certainly the 'Conte Carlo Gambarini' who published *A Description of the Earl of Pembroke's Pictures* (1731), and the 'G-mb-r-ni, the Picture-monger' mentioned in the anonymous pamphlet *Do you know what you are about, or, A protestant alarm to Great Britain* (1733, 21). Her mother may have been a tutor to the nobility: a letter from Elizabeth to Lord Bute in 1761 notes, 'My Mamma had the honour of teaching Lady Bute [Mary Wortley Montagu] when she was about fourteen years of age' (BL, Add. MS 5726 D, fols. 22–23v).

Elizabeth began her career in the mid-1740s as a singer in Handel's oratorio productions. By 1748 her developing reputation enabled her to promote her own benefit concert, in which she sang and played some of her own compositions on the organ, and to issue her first two volumes of music. The *Six Sets of Lessons for the Harpsichord* was the first collection of keyboard music to be published by a female composer in Britain, and contains a lengthy and illustrious list of subscribers. The music is charming, in the new Italian mould rather than traditionally Handelian, and full of imaginative strokes. The success of this volume seems to have prompted the production of the second later in the year. As a frontispiece to *Lessons for the Harpsichord Intermix'd with Italian and English Songs* there is an engraving of Gambarini by Nathaniel Hone, showing her sitting at a desk composing. This engraving is the source of the usual, incorrect, date of birth for the composer.

Gambarini issued her final publication, *XII English & Italian Songs*, in 1750; after this there is little indication of public musical activity until 1760 and 1761, when she gave a number of benefit concerts, appearing as composer, harpsichordist, organist, and singer. Her letter to Lord Bute quoted above shows that at the same time she sought a court appointment, and she later attempted to sell her father's collection of paintings to the Royal Society.

On 20 March 1764 Elizabeth married Etienne Chazal at St Martin-in-the-Fields. She gave one concert as Mrs Chazal in May, but died at her home in Castle Court, Strand, in the parish of St Martin-in-the-Fields, Westminster, less than a year later, on 9 February 1765. She was buried at St James's, Westminster, on 14 February. Her mother's will reveals that Elizabeth had a daughter, Giovanna Georgiana Chazal. Elizabeth may have died in or as a result of childbirth. Nothing more is known of either her husband or her daughter.

Henry Bromley's *Catalogue of Engraved British Portraits* (1793, 310) and a note against Gambarini's signature in BL, Add. MS 5726 B, fol. 31v claim that Elizabeth was also a painter. In recording her death, the *Gazetteer and New Daily Advertiser* (11 February 1765) observed that she used to exhibit pictures at her home.   ANTHONY NOBLE

Sources A. F. G. Noble, 'A contextual study of the life and published keyboard works of Elisabetta de Gambarini', PhD diss., King Alfred's College, Winchester (U. Southampton), 2000 · parish register, Middlesex, St Marylebone, 7 Sept 1730 [birth] · parish register, Middlesex, St Marylebone, 1 Nov 1730 [baptism] · parish register, Middlesex, Westminster, St James, 30 March 1754 [burial: Charles Gambarini, father] · parish register, Middlesex, Westminster, St James, 22 Oct 1774 [burial: Giovanna Paula Stradiotti Gambarini, mother] · parish register, Middlesex, Westminster, St Martin-in-the-Fields, 20 March 1764 [marriage] · parish register, Middlesex, Westminster, St James, 14 Feb 1765 [burial] · *Gazetteer and New Daily Advertiser* (11 Feb 1765) · W. Dean, *Handel's dramatic oratorios and masques* (1959); repr. (1990) · S. McVeigh, *Calendar of London concerts, 1750–1800* [unpublished computer database, Goldsmiths' College, London] · E. Gambarini, proposal to the Royal Society and accompanying letter to Dr Birch, 17 Nov 1763, BL, Add. MS 4308, fol. 13 · E. Gambarini, letter to the earl of Bute from 'Miss Gambarine Aug. 1761', BL, (on back of 2nd sheet, fol. 23v) Add. MS 5726 D, fols. 22–23v, Add. MS 5726 B, fol. 31v · will of Giovanna Paula Stradiotti Gambarini, PRO, PROB 11/1008, fols. 315v, 316 · sale catalogues (1726) [Mr Gambarini's library; London, 26 May, 3 June 1726; BL, SC 222(4), 222(5)] · H. Bromley, *A catalogue of engraved British portraits* (1793) · *Do you know what you are about, or, A protestant alarm to Great Britain* (1733) · W. Dean, 'Gambarini, Elisabetta de', *The new Grove dictionary of women composers*, ed. J. A. Sadie and R. Samuel (1994), 181–2 · S. McVeigh, *Concert life in London from Mozart to Haydn* (1993) · L. Lindgren, 'Handel's London—Italian musicians and librettists', *The Cambridge companion to Handel*, ed. D. Burrows (1997), 78–91 · St Marylebone, rate books: poor rate, vol. 1, 1683–1731; vol. 2, 1732–7, LMA [1736 missing] · rate books, St James, Westminster, City Westm. AC, D474, D481, D488, D501, D509, D516 [watch rate collector's books, Golden Square ward] · rate books, St George, Hanover Square, City Westm. AC, C291–C311 [poor, highway, and scavengers' rates collector's books, Dover Street ward] · rate books, St George, Hanover Square, City Westm. AC, C218, C219, C262–C267 [poor rate collector's books, Dover Street ward]
Archives BL, letter to the earl of Bute, Add. MS 5726 D, fols. 22–23v; date, address, and signature, Add. MS 5726 B, fol. 31v · BL, proposal to the Royal Society, and accompanying letter to Birch, Add. MS 4308, fol. 13
Likenesses N. Hone, engraving, 1748, repro. in E. Gambarini, *Lessons for the harpsichord intermix'd with Italian and English songs* (1748), frontispiece

Gambier, Sir Edward John (1794–1879),

judge in India, was born on 24 April 1794, the third son of Samuel Gambier (1752–1813), commissioner of the navy from 1796 to 1813, and his wife, Jane, youngest daughter of Daniel Mathew of Felix Hall, Essex, and the nephew of Admiral James *Gambier, Baron Gambier. He entered Eton College in 1808 and went on to Trinity College, Cambridge (matriculated 1813, scholar 1815), and was president of the Union (1815). He was ninth senior optime, junior chancellor's medallist (1817), BA in 1817, MA in 1820, and fellow in 1819. He was admitted to Lincoln's Inn on 31 August 1815 and called to the bar on 7 February 1822. He published *A Treatise on Parochial Settlement* (1828, 2nd edn 1835). In 1828 he married Emilia Ora, daughter of C. Morgell MP, she died on 25 February 1877.

Gambier was one of the municipal corporation commissioners in 1833. He was appointed recorder of Prince of Wales Island (Penang) in 1834, and was knighted by William IV at St James's Palace on 6 August. He was appointed on 28 November 1836 a puisne judge of the supreme court, Madras, and chief justice there on 11 March 1842 (sworn in on 22 May). He reportedly discharged his duties with ability and efficiency until he retired in 1849, when he received from the Hindu community of Madras a testimonial silver centrepiece weighing 550 ounces, and Lady Gambier was presented with a handsome tripod centrepiece by the European ladies of Madras.

Gambier died at his home, 22 Hyde Park Gate, South Kensington, London, on 31 May 1879, in his eighty-sixth year.   G. C. BOASE, rev. ROGER T. STEARN

Sources *The Times* (14 June 1879) • *Law Times* (7 June 1879), 105 • H. E. C. Stapylton, *The Eton school lists, from 1791 to 1850*, 2nd edn (1864) • Venn, *Alum. Cant.* • *Dod's Peerage* (1858) • Kelly, *Handbk* (1879) • W. P. Baildon, ed., *The records of the Honorable Society of Lincoln's Inn: admissions*, 1 (1896) • Boase, *Mod. Eng. biog.* • J. M. Collinge, *Navy Board officials, 1660–1832* (1978)
Wealth at death under £14,000: probate, 28 June 1879, *CGPLA Eng. & Wales*

Gambier, James (1723–1789), naval officer, was the son of James Gambier, the warden of the Fleet prison, and his wife, Mary, *née* Mead. His grandfather, Nicolas Gambier, was a Huguenot from Caen who came to England after the revocation of the edict of Nantes (1685). James Gambier doubtless gained his start in the navy from his maternal uncle, Captain Samuel Mead. He was made lieutenant in 1743 and on 3 April 1746 was promoted to command the sloop *Speedwell*, employed in the North Sea. On 5 December 1747, just before the end of the 1739–48 war, he was promoted captain, and briefly commanded the *Flamborough* and *Squirrel*, both of 24 guns, before they were sold at the end of hostilities. It was at this time that Gambier gained notoriety when he lost a law suit over an adulterous affair with Maria de Bouget, the second wife of Admiral Sir Charles Knowles. At the beginning of the Seven Years' War he commanded small ships, and in 1758 he was appointed to command the *Burford* (70 guns), which assisted at the capture of Louisbourg and, in the following year, at the capture of Guadeloupe and the unsuccessful attack on Martinique. He returned to take part in the battle of Quiberon Bay, from which time until the end of the war the *Burford* was part of the Channel Fleet. Gambier's career to this point was undistinguished; there was, for example, a disagreement with Admiral Sir Edward Hawke, who in December 1760 did not allow Gambier to return to Plymouth from the blockade of the French coast to repair a list of fictitious defects which he had submitted.

Always short of money, Gambier nevertheless had connections who ensured that he found peacetime employment. His sister Susan was married to Vice-Admiral Sir Samuel Cornish, at that time an MP; another sister, Margaret, was married to Captain Charles Middleton, while a niece was to marry into the Pitt family. Gambier commanded the guardship *Yarmouth* (64 guns) at Chatham

from 1766 to 1770, after which he was commander-in-chief of the North American station as commodore for ten months. His main task was to move the naval base from Halifax to Boston, which was not easy in view of the increasing hostility of the inhabitants whom he tried to conciliate. He was recalled at the change of government, the Treasury being unhappy about his level of expenditure, and replaced by a rear-admiral. Lord Sandwich, in order to make amends to a well-connected officer, appointed Gambier to the Navy Board as commissioner of victualling accounts and soon afterwards, on 2 September 1773, resident commissioner of Portsmouth Dockyard. He was notably ineffective in this post. On 23 January 1778, by means of seniority, Gambier was appointed rear-admiral; Sandwich sent him to America as second-in-command to Vice-Admiral Lord Howe, and he arrived at Sandy Hook on 27 May. It was his task to supervise the refitting and repair of ships at New York and he took no active part in the parrying of the French threat under D'Estaing in 1778. After Howe resigned his command and sailed for England, Gambier was briefly commander-in-chief until superseded by Vice-Admiral John Byron, who arrived on 1 October. Gambier's performance in New York showed him unable to withstand the pressures of a wartime command. There were problems over promotions made by him and over his issuing of privateering commissions, while his reputation among the loyalists of New York was very low. When he left on 6 April 1779 one loyalist remarked that there was 'Universal joy in all rank and conditions. I believe no person was ever more generally detested than this penurious old reptile' (Wilcox, 265–6). Gambier later defended his conduct in *A narrative of facts relative to the conduct of Vice-Admiral Gambier during his late command in North America* (1782).

Unemployed during the rest of the war and advanced to vice-admiral on 26 September 1780, Gambier had a last, short period of active service as commander-in-chief, West Indies; he left Spithead in the *Europa* (64 guns) on 20 October 1783 and returned on 25 August 1784. Gambier was twice married. Details of his first wife are unknown; his second, whom he married possibly in 1788, was Sarah Newcombe. He died at Burlington Street, Bath, on 8 January 1789. His nephew was James *Gambier, later Baron Gambier.   ROGER KNIGHT

Sources D. Syrett, '"This penurious old reptile": Rear-Admiral James Gambier and the American war', *Historical Research*, 74 (2001), 63–76 • W. B. Wilcox, 'Arbuthnot, Gambier and Graves: "Old women" of the navy', *George Washington's opponents*, ed. G. A. Billias (1969), 264–6 • N. R. Stout, *The Royal Navy in America, 1760–1775: a study of enforcement of British colonial policy in the era of the American revolution* (1977) • R. Buel, jun., *In irons: Britain's naval supremacy and the American revolutionary economy* (1998) • R. J. B. Knight, *Portsmouth dockyard papers, 1774–1783: the American war* (1987) • N. A. M. Rodger, *The wooden world: an anatomy of the Georgian navy* (1986) • J. M. Collinge, *Navy Board officials, 1660–1832* (1978) • lieutenants' logs, NMM, ADM/L/E/15 and 18 • *The Royal Navy and North America: the Warren papers, 1736–1752*, ed. J. Gwyn, Navy RS, 118 (1975) • *GM*, 1st ser., 59 (1789), 182 • will, PRO, PROB 11/1175
Likenesses J. S. Copley, portrait, 1773, Museum of Fine Arts, Boston
Wealth at death very little: will, PRO, PROB 11/1175; *GM*

Gambier, James, Baron Gambier (1756–1833), naval officer and evangelical activist, was born at New Providence in the Bahamas on 13 October 1756, the second son of the lieutenant-governor John Gambier and Deborah, née Stiles. He was brought up in England by his aunt Lady Middleton, the wife of Sir Charles Middleton (later Lord Barham). Another uncle, James *Gambier (1723–1789), was also a naval officer. He went to sea at an early age, was promoted lieutenant in 1777, and became a post captain on 9 October 1778. While in command of the frigate *Raleigh* (32 guns) during the American War of Independence he captured several prizes and took part in the reduction of Charlestown. In July 1788 Gambier married Louisa, second daughter of Daniel Matthew of Felix Hall, Essex. The couple, who lived at Iver, Buckinghamshire, had no children.

After a decade on half pay Gambier commissioned the *Defence* (74 guns) for war service in 1793. The skill and courage with which he fought in her in the battle of 1 June 1794 earned Lord Howe's admiration, the award of the king's gold medal, and, exactly a year later, promotion to flag-rank with a seat at the Board of Admiralty where he served for three periods, 1795–1801, 1804–6 and 1807–8, interspersed with a two-year governorship of Newfoundland (1802–4) and experience as a flag-officer with the Channel Fleet. In 1807, rightly fearing French intentions to take over the neutral Danish navy, the British government sent Gambier's fleet to Copenhagen with an army under Lord Cathcart to secure the ships peaceably or with force if opposed. Danish resistance led Gambier to bombard Copenhagen until terms were sought in the face of the overwhelming force of the attackers. The whole Danish navy was brought over to Britain as a prize of war but at the price of turning Denmark into an ally of Napoleon. Gambier was rewarded with a peerage. In 1808 he became commander-in-chief of the Channel Fleet for a three-year term.

Further controversy attended Gambier in 1809. A strong French squadron destined for the West Indies escaped from Brest and slipped into the Aix Roads anchorage off Rochefort, where natural defences such as shoals and islands were further strengthened by shore gun-batteries and a boom. To the Admiralty this seemed an opportunity to strike at the French fleet away from its base and they pressed a reluctant Gambier to consider an attack by fire-ships under Lord Cochrane, a junior captain with a genius for war. The Admiralty's choice was perceived as an insult by Gambier's second-in-command, Admiral Harvey, who turned his fury into a public denunciation of Gambier's fitness for command, an outburst which led inevitably to Harvey's court martial and dismissal.

Cochrane's daring attack proved devastating to the French. In the confusion of the night many vessels cut their cables and went aground. By dawn a jubilant Cochrane counted eleven ships ashore and looked to Gambier to send in his big ships to destroy them. The commander-in-chief, however, was unwilling to risk his battlefleet in confined waters, and it was mid-afternoon before he sent in a powerful division of four ships of the line to support Cochrane's two frigates and smaller craft. Gambier was satisfied enough with the losses inflicted on the French—three ships of the line destroyed, soon to be joined by a fourth, and a 56-gun Indiaman burnt to a wreck with her cargo of military stores. Furthermore, since several ships which escaped up the River Charente had jettisoned their guns, the whole squadron was effectively neutralized for months to come and the French West Indies starved of assistance. Cochrane, however, was maddened by what he saw as a lost opportunity to achieve a complete victory. When he learned that Gambier was to be given the thanks of parliament he announced his intention of opposing it—as an MP rather than a naval officer—on the grounds of the admiral's culpable delay and inactivity. Faced with public criticism from a relatively junior officer, Gambier felt he must demand a court martial to judge his own handling of the action.

Gambier's statements at the hearings reflected his awareness that the battlefleet was the mainstay of national defence and not to be put at hazard. He spoke of his conviction that once large vessels had negotiated the channel between the Aix and Boyart shoals they would have been exposed to fire from shore batteries with little room to manoeuvre. In his autobiography Cochrane expressed his outrage over the composition and procedures of the court, and its unwillingness to accept a captured French chart as evidence. He underestimated the risk to the big ships—one went aground for some hours and two others touched bottom—and the benefits he had received from Gambier's support, reluctant and tardy as it may have been. For his part Gambier overestimated the strength of the shore batteries and the extent of shallow water, but he based his decision upon a cautiously responsible assessment of risks. Excessive caution, not cowardice or incompetence, had been his failing. Cochrane's vendetta was regarded with distaste by the Admiralty, by the captains of the Channel Fleet, by the court martial which honourably acquitted Gambier, and by parliament which voted him their thanks.

Reliable competence marked Gambier's record in naval administration. For a total of six years at the Admiralty he shared in the collective direction of the war at sea. His personal contribution was in ship design, in signalling (each ship given her own identification number), and—with his uncle Lord Barham—in the publication of the revised *Regulations* in 1806, with detailed instructions for each grade of officer. Nor was this the full extent of his public service. Appointed a peace commissioner to treat with the USA he helped to end the Anglo-American War of 1812–14. Through longevity and the ordinary process of naval promotion he became admiral of the fleet in 1830.

Fundamental to Gambier's life were deep Christian convictions, openly professed at a time when religious observance at sea was unusual and evangelical belief extremely rare. Officers of this stamp were known as 'blue lights', and he is usually regarded as the most prominent of them. From the first he encouraged church services and chaplains as *Regulations* required, but once made aware that the lower deck needed evangelization even more than compulsory religious observance, he gave strong support to the distribution of bibles and tracts. Earlier writers stress how old-fashioned he was in enforcing the religious provisions of the 1731 *Regulations*; it would be more appropriate to acknowledge how forward-looking he was in recognizing the spiritual needs of the lower deck and in championing a form of seaboard piety which became standard for the Royal Navy in the nineteenth century.

In retirement Gambier became the first president of the Church Missionary Society. Among the many Christian and philanthropic causes which he championed the interests of seamen were paramount, including the Naval and Military Bible Society and the Episcopal Floating Church Society. After the war he perceived that the most effective ways to evangelize the wider maritime community were through dedicated missions, floating chapels, and hostels ashore. Although a staunch Anglican, he gave public support to the evangelistic enterprises of 'Bo'sun' Smith, a Baptist minister, and he may justly be regarded as a pioneer advocate for seamen's causes. A writer in the *Naval Chronicle* once described him as 'the sailor's friend', a title he might have valued as much as any public distinction. Gambier died on 19 April 1833 and was buried at Iver churchyard.

Gambier's reputation has remained as controversial as his career, partly because he has lacked a competent biographer, but also because his major contributions to history were in the two disparate areas of church life and high command in war. The *Dictionary of National Biography* ignored his later evangelistic and philanthropic concerns. RICHARD C. BLAKE

Sources DNB · J. Marshall, *Royal naval biography*, 1 (1823), 74–86 · J. Ralfe, *The naval biography of Great Britain*, 2 (1828), 82–90 · W. H. Dillon, *A narrative of my professional adventures, 1790–1839*, ed. M. A. Lewis, 1, Navy RS, 93 (1953) · W. James, *The naval history of Great Britain, from the declaration of war by France in 1793, to the accession of George IV*, [5th edn], 6 vols. (1859–60) · E. P. Brenton, *The naval history of Great Britain, from the year 1783 to 1836*, 2 (1837) · [W. B. Gurney], *Minutes of a court martial taken in shorthand by Mr. W. B. Gurney* (1809) · Thomas, tenth earl of Dundonald [T. Cochrane], *The autobiography of a seaman*, 2 vols. (1860) · H. G. Chatterton, *Memoirs personal and historical of Admiral Lord Gambier*, 2 vols. (1861) · A. N. Ryan, ed., 'Documents relating to the Copenhagen operation, 1807', *The naval miscellany*, ed. N. A. M. Rodger, 5, Navy RS, 125 (1984) · *Letters and papers of Charles, Lord Barham*, ed. J. K. Laughton, 3 vols., Navy RS, 32, 38–9 (1907–11) · *Regulations and instructions relating to his majesty's service at sea* (1806) · *Naval Chronicle*, 22 (1809), 107–30, 215–42 · *Report of Proceedings of the Naval and Military Bible Society* (1806) · GEC, *Peerage*
Archives BL, letters and dispatches to Lord Nelson *passim*, Add. MSS 34925–34936, *passim* · NMM, Keats MSS, KEA · NMM, corresp. with Lord Sandwich · NMM, Yorke MSS, YOR · PRO, ADM
Likenesses Bartolozzi, Landseer, Ryder, and Stow, group portrait, line engraving, pubd 1803 (*Naval victories, Commemoration of the victory of June 1st 1794*), BM, NPG · G. Clint, mezzotint, pubd 1808 (after W. Beechey), BM, NPG; photograph, NMM · W. Beechey, oils, 1809, NMM · J. Slater, pencil drawing, 1813, NPG · J. G. Murray, group portrait, stipple, pubd 1823 (after J. Stephanoff; *Trial of Queen Caroline, 1820*), BM

Gamble, Sir David, first baronet (1823–1907), chemical manufacturer, was born in Dublin on 3 February 1823, the only son of Hannah, daughter of Henry Gower, a Dublin solicitor, and **Josias Christopher Gamble** (1775–1848), chemical manufacturer, who was born at Enniskillen, co. Fermanagh. The elder Gamble, having been educated at Glasgow University (MA 1797), served from 1799 to 1804 as a Presbyterian minister in his native town. He also valued earthly promotion, however, and, perceiving the recent but growing demand for chloride of lime for bleaching Irish linen, he is said to have become interested in its manufacture in the adjacent co. Monaghan. He certainly was active as a chemical manufacturer in Dublin in 1806; there in due course he came to know James Muspratt, and may have had business relations with him. Muspratt pioneered the Leblanc soda-making process in Liverpool in 1823 in order to supply the expanding soap industry of the area, but was soon driven out of the borough because of the extreme atmospheric pollution caused by his factory. In 1828 he moved a dozen miles or so to the east, to the small but growing town of St Helens, which still lacked any form of restrictive local government. He invited J. C. Gamble, then in his early fifties, to join him as junior partner. When Muspratt moved on again after two years, Gamble found other partners, and eventually John Crosfield, then in business in Warrington.

David Gamble was educated at a private school in St Helens. His father, then unusual in being a university graduate in business, resolved that his son should benefit from the best training in chemistry available. He sent him for a year, aged sixteen, to University College, London, and then (1840–43) to the Andersonian Institution in Glasgow. In 1843 David joined his father (aged sixty-eight) in a small new chemical works which they opened, as J. C. Gamble & Son, close to the original Muspratt premises. He inherited the business at his father's death on 27 January 1848 and built it up so successfully that by 1865 its rateable value had caught up with that of the earlier factory, which itself had grown fourfold in the interim.

Gamble married Elizabeth, daughter of James Haddock, a prominent local coal owner, at St Helens parish church on 26 February 1847. They lived comfortably in Windle township on the north side of St Helens until the 1860s, when he was in a position to build himself an impressive mansion, Windlehurst, in its own grounds not far from Windle Hall, where the senior member of the Pilkington glass-making family lived. He needed the large house for his growing family. Of eleven children, the four older sons (born 1848, 1852, 1856, and 1858) eventually joined him in the business which, besides the manufacture of Leblanc soda and bleaching powder, developed markets for by-products as well as potassium chlorate and magnesium sulphate (Epsom salts). Although the chemical industry was concentrated on Widnes, a few miles to the south on the Mersey, because of canal transport cost advantages, J. C. Gamble & Son remained at St Helens and became the main chemical manufacturers there, developing a flourishing export trade, especially to the United States. When Parr's Bank was formed into a limited company in 1865, Gamble was made a director, with authority 'to examine the customers' accounts at St Helens from time to time …

and to report thereon', though he was specifically forbidden from seeing any of the accounts of other chemical manufacturers. From 1883 he was paid £150 a year 'for St Helens duty' and remained on Parr's board for the rest of his life.

Although he was a convinced free-trader, Gamble did not hesitate to combine with other manufacturers where this was to their common advantage. In 1867 he joined in the formation of the Tharsis Sulphur and Copper Company to ensure sulphur supplies. In 1883 he was involved in creating the Lancashire Bleaching Powder Manufacturers' Association in an attempt to maintain profitability within the industry against the lower cost ammonia-soda process, worked in Britain by Brunner, Mond & Co. This competition, however, caused the Leblanc manufacturers to merge their businesses into the United Alkali Company Ltd in 1891. J. C. Gamble & Son was then valued at £320,000, considerably more than the next largest chemical concern in St Helens.

All this business activity did not prevent Gamble from playing a leading part in local government from its inception. In 1845 he became one of the original St Helens improvement commissioners and served as their chairman from 1856 to 1862. When the town was incorporated in 1868, he served as the first mayor, and was re-elected for two further terms in 1882/3 and 1886/7. When the volunteers were formed in 1860, he became their lieutenant-colonel—until 1887—and built the local Volunteer Hall. Colonel Gamble, as he then liked to be called, stood for parliament as a Liberal when the town first obtained independent representation in 1885, but was narrowly defeated. When a new grammar school, Cowley School, was opened in 1882, he contributed £1000 towards it and saw that laboratory facilities were provided. In 1883 he contributed towards University College, Liverpool, together with other chemical manufacturers, who all wished to see higher education facilities available in the region for present and future employees. In 1893 he gave £25,000 to enable a technical institute and library to be built in the town centre 'for the purpose of assisting our people to make themselves equal or superior to those countries where technical education has been an institution for a great number of years'.

For his many public services Gamble was made a CB in 1887, a baronet in 1897 and a KCB in 1904. He died at Windlehurst on 4 February 1907.   THEO BARKER

Sources T. C. Barker and J. R. Harris, *A Merseyside town in the industrial revolution: St Helens, 1750–1900* (1954); repr. with corrections (1993) · *St Helens Newspaper and Advertiser* (6 June 1885) · *St Helens Newspaper and Advertiser* (8 Feb 1907) · *The Times* (10 May 1907) · 'Industrial celebrities VI: Josias Christopher Gamble', *Chemical Trade Journal* (1 March 1890), 139–42 · records of Parr's Banking Co, National Westminster Bank Ltd Archives, London · U. Glas., Archives and Business Records Centre · register of students, UCL · m. cert. · d. cert. · d. cert. [Josias Gamble]

Likenesses H. Herkomer, portrait, St Helens town hall, Lancashire

Wealth at death £388,265: PRO

Gamble, John (d. 1687), composer and musician, was born to parents who are unknown. According to Anthony

VERA EFFIGIES IOANNIS GAMBLE PHILOMUSICI

This to the Graver owes ;
But read and Find
T. Cross sculpsit

By his owne hand ,
a most Harmonious Mind.
I. S.

John Gamble (*d.* 1687), by Thomas Cross, pubd 1656

Wood he was apprenticed to Ambrose Beeland (a court and theatre musician), afterwards becoming 'a musician belonging to a playhouse in London' (Ashbee and Lasocki, 459), probably that of the King's Company of Players. His name appears in various theatrical records prior to the outbreak of the civil war, and in 1641 he was associated with a group of musicians hired by the Middle Temple. He was probably the John Gamble who, on 18 November 1634, married Elizabeth Harrison at St Bride, Fleet Street; John, almost certainly a son of this couple, was baptized there on 9 June 1639.

Gamble seems to have maintained himself during the later 1640s and 1650s by teaching and giving concerts. Wood heard Gamble play with Thomas Pratt in Oxford on 14 July 1658, and recorded that Gamble won great renown among Oxford musicians for his two books, *Ayres and Dialogues*, the first in two editions of 1656 and 1657 (with an engraved portrait), the second in 1659, despite their disappointing quality. A third book seems to have been planned, though it remains in manuscript (BL, Add. MS 32339). His style was modelled on that of Henry Lawes but he shows much less ability, sometimes to the point of downright incompetence. Instead his claim to fame, such as it is, rests on a large manuscript collection of songs inscribed 'John Gamble his booke amen / 1659 / an[no] domine' on the flyleaf (New York Public Library, Drexel MS 4275). It comprises a total of 327 song titles, though only 240 are notated complete with treble and bass. Many are unattributed, but the principal composers represented are Henry Lawes (with fifty-two), William Lawes (twenty), and John Wilson (eighteen), with twenty-six by Gamble himself—six of which lack music. Other composers include Nicholas Lanier (eight), William Webb (eight), and Robert Johnson (five). These numbers take account of attributions known from other sources, but may be underestimates. Three different hands are discernible, the first of which has been identified with that of the City poet Thomas Jordan, who contributed a commendatory poem to Gamble's 1659 *Ayres and Dialogues*, and referred to him as 'Honest friend and Old Acquaintance'. None of the hands seems to match the inscription of the flyleaf, however. The contents of this manuscript form a representative anthology of English continuo song from the middle of the seventeenth century. Most are solo songs, with a few dialogues. The period over which they were entered is difficult to determine. It is not impossible that the earliest songs could have been entered in the 1630s, but most of the evidence suggests that the manuscript dates from the 1650s. Although the political tone of many of the songs is strongly royalist, there is no sign that the restoration of the monarchy had taken place.

Soon after the Restoration, Gamble entered the king's wind band as a cornet player (3 January 1661), and in 1662 he was asked to set songs for John Tatham's lord mayor's pageant, *Aqua triumphalis*, but by October 1666 he was petitioning for salary arrears 'haveing lost all hee had by the late most dreadfull fire in London' (Ashbee and Lasocki, 460). Despite the fact that he had already increased his income by obtaining a place among the London waits on 30 May 1665, and served as a member of the king's band of violins between 1674 and 1676, he seems to have been beset by financial problems throughout his life, and was at one stage imprisoned for a debt. On the accession of James II his court appointments were not renewed, perhaps because he was already 'crazed and infirm of body', when, as of St Bride's, London, he drew up his will on 30 June 1680. He was living at the Two Black Posts, Salisbury Court, Fleet Street, when he died, about 29 November 1687; he was buried at St Bride's a day later. His will, proved on 3 December by his widow, Elizabeth, mentioned a son and a grandson, both also called John Gamble. IAN SPINK

Sources Highfill, Burnim & Langhans, *BDA*, 5.450–52 · A. Ashbee and D. Lasocki, eds., *A biographical dictionary of English court musicians, 1485–1714*, 1 (1998), 459–61 · *IGI* [St Bride, Fleet Street, London]
Likenesses T. Cross, line engraving, NPG; repro. in T. Stanley, *Ayres and dialogues to be sung … by J. Gamble* (1656) [see illus.] · pen-and-ink drawing (after engraving), NPG

Gamble, John (1761/2–1811), Church of England clergyman and writer on telegraphy, was born at Bungay, Suffolk, the son of Dixon Gamble, wool dealer. He was admitted to Pembroke College, Cambridge, in 1780, graduating BA in 1784, and taking his MA in 1787. He became a fellow of his college, was chaplain to the duke of York, and chaplain-general of the forces. In 1795 he published in London a small twenty-page pamphlet entitled *Observations on telegraphic experiments, or, The different modes which have been or may be adopted for the purpose of distant communication*. This caused some stir in the scientific world, and encouraged him to produce a more ambitious *Essay on the Different Modes of Communication by Signals* in 1797. This contained a number of elaborate and ingenious illustrative plates. The book gave a concise history of developments in the art of communication from the first beacon light to telegraphy, with many valuable suggestions. Gamble is said to have been highly thought of in scientific circles. He married, in 1805, a Miss Lathom of Madras. He was rector of Alphamstone, Suffolk, and also of Bradwell-juxta-mare in Essex; the latter providing a significant income. He died at Knightsbridge, London, on 27 July 1811.

JAMES BURNLEY, rev. R. C. COX

Sources *GM*, 1st ser., 81/2 (1811), 193 · R. Sabine, *History and progress of the electric telegraph* (1869) · Venn, *Alum. Cant.*

Gamble, Josias Christopher (1775–1848). *See under* Gamble, Sir David, first baronet (1823–1907).

Gambold, John (1711–1771), bishop of the Moravian church, was born on 10 April 1711 at the rectory, Puncheston, Pembrokeshire, the eldest of the five children of William Gambold (1672–1728), rector of Puncheston with Llanychâr, and his wife, Elizabeth (d. 1744). Initially educated by his father, he entered Christ Church, Oxford, as a servitor in 1726. His father's death and deathbed exhortations in 1728 profoundly affected Gambold, turning a vivacious teenager who loved reading poetry and drama into a religious melancholic concerned only about his salvation. For over a year he was 'in a despairing mood and totally neglected all care of his person and clothes' ('Memoir', Moravian Church House, AB95.A3.27D).

By March 1730 Gambold was sufficiently improved to desire like-minded company. He introduced himself to his fellow Christ Church undergraduate Charles Wesley and became one of the Oxford Methodists. Although he participated in their meetings and prison visiting, he preferred to remain in his room, reading and meditating on the fathers, especially mystical writers. Ordained in September 1733, in 1735 he became vicar of Stanton Harcourt, Oxfordshire, where he was looked after by his sister Martha (1713–1741) and, for about two years (1736–8), by the Wesleys' sister Kezziah. He performed his parochial duties conscientiously, but otherwise shut himself away, devoting himself to the Greek fathers, philosophical speculation, and mysticism. By October 1738 he had even given up the fathers, and described himself as 'almost swallowed up with melancholy', 'peevish … by an hypochondriac constitution, and an internal religion ending in despondency' (Gambold to [J. Hutton], 31 Oct 1738, Moravian Church House, AB87.A3.10.2).

It was moving from Oxford Methodism, with its emphasis on fasting, liturgical prayer, and good works, to a Lutheran reliance on justification by faith alone, as taught by the Moravian church, which was to rescue Gambold from melancholy. He had read Luther in the

John Gambold (1711–1771), by Jonathan Spilsbury, pubd 1771 (after Abraham Louis Brandt)

mid-1730s, but his gradual change of position was prompted by the Moravian Peter Böhler, when he visited Oxford in February 1738. In 1739 Gambold met the Moravian leader Count Zinzendorf in Oxford. By now he 'thought the Brethren peculiarly happy and their Doctrine true but could not apply it to myself' ('Memoir', AB95.A3.27D). In April 1740 he described himself as still 'mostly pensive and dejected, surrounded with solitude, sickness and silence, … contracting an abjectness, that blunts every finer sentiment, and damps every nobler ardor of the soul' (*Works*, 225). That year he did, however, compose a dramatic poem, *The Martyrdom of Ignatius* (published in 1773).

In December 1740 Gambold's brother Hector (1714–1788) gave him an attractive account of his life in London with members of the Moravian-led Fetter Lane Society. Gambold went and experienced it for himself, and was drawn into the Moravian circle. This resulted in July 1741 in a breach with the Wesleys. Despite occasional meetings, the friendship was never restored. In Gambold's December 1741 university sermon, published as *Christianity, Tidings of Joy*, he spoke of baptismal regeneration in high Anglican fashion, but the Moravians' emphasis on faith, their spirituality, and community life were the answer to his depression. In October 1742 he finally resigned his living and moved to London. On 31 October he was received, as a founder member, into the London Moravian congregation. Writing to his parishioners, he stressed that his resignation did not imply criticism of the Church of England's liturgy or constitution. It was simply that he needed the sort of daily fellowship and pastoral care which the Moravian church offered and which he could find nowhere else.

In December 1742 Gambold became a teacher at the Moravian boarding-school at Broadoaks, a manor house near Thaxted, Essex, where he married Elizabeth Walker (1719–1803) on 14 May 1743. Of their five children, one son and one daughter reached adulthood. In the autumn they moved to Haverfordwest, where Gambold kept a school and preached in local churches. Gambold had felt happy in the gentle but intense atmosphere of the Moravian school, describing himself in April 1743 as 'at peace' (Gambold to Hutton, 21 April 1743, Moravian Church House, AB87.A3.10.5), but was not suited to schoolmastering. By his own admission he had never loved children, found their concerns trivial, and preferred silent solitude. In Haverfordwest he was 'too feeble' to keep order and unwilling to punish (Gambold to Hutton, 13 Feb 1744, Moravian Church House, AB87.A3.10.7). The venture failed.

In November 1744 Gambold returned to London. It helped the Moravians' image to have a learned Anglican priest as the stated preacher at their Fetter Lane Chapel, which Gambold remained until 1768. He also interpreted when Zinzendorf preached; his translation was both precise and praised by the count as of 'heavenly beauty' ('Special-Diarium', 7 April). In the autumn of 1746 Gambold was Zinzendorf's intermediary in abortive negotiations with Archbishop John Potter for recognition of the Moravians as a society within the Church of England under Potter's personal oversight, helping to develop the proposals. A visit to the Moravian centre at Herrnhaag in Wetteravia for the 1747 general synod served to seal his commitment to the current Moravian spirituality and community life.

In 1742 Gambold had published anonymously an edition of the Greek text of the New Testament. His editing and translation skills were now employed in the service of the Moravian church. Beginning with *Acta fratrum unitatis in Anglia* (1749) he became the chief translator and editor of a series of books designed to promote the Moravians' image in England, including Zinzendorf's *Maxims* (1751). Assisted by James Hutton, he was responsible for most of the literary defence mounted when they came under attack between 1753 and 1755. He was the editor of *Peremtorisches Bedencken* (1753), *A Modest Plea for the Church of the Brethren* (1754), *The Representation of the Committee of the English Congregations in Union with the Moravian Church* (with Hutton, 1754), and probably also *The Plain Case of the Representatives of the People Known by the Name of the Unitas Fratrum* (1754). Hutton's *Essay towards Giving some Just Ideas of the Personal Character of Count Zinzendorff* (1755) included a letter about the count by Gambold. Later Gambold revised the translation of David Cranz's *History of Greenland* (1767). He also used his editorial skills commercially, acting as proofreader and editor for the publisher William Bowyer.

Gambold also played a considerable part in the preparation of the Moravians' *Londoner Gesangbuch* of 1754, and edited *A Collection of Hymns* (2 vols., 1754), to which he contributed eleven translations and twenty-eight original hymns, *A Hymnbook for the Children* (1756), and *A Collection of Hymns* (1769). Assisted by Ludolf Ernst Schlicht, he also edited the 1759 *Litany Book*. His sermon *The Reasonableness and Extent of Religious Reverence* was published in 1756, and his *Short Summary of Christian Doctrine* in 1765.

In November 1754 Gambold was consecrated the first English Moravian bishop. As such he consecrated chapels in Bristol and Kingswood (1757) and Leominster (1761). In 1764 he attended the Moravian church's constitutive general synod (following Zinzendorf's death), and inaugurated the congregations in Haverfordwest in 1763 and Cootehill, co. Cavan, during a visitation to Ireland in 1765. When his health failed in 1768 Gambold returned to Haverfordwest as minister of the congregation there. Despite breathlessness, dropsy, and increasing pain he remained in office until his death in Haverfordwest on 13 September 1771.

Lewis Morris said of Gambold, 'Such were the bishops of primitive times' (*Letters*, 2.224). In becoming a Moravian, Gambold had embraced poverty; in 1759 Richard Morris even thought he 'delights in appearing poor and slovenly' (ibid., 141). To John Wesley, Gambold was one of the 'most sensible men in England' (31 Aug 1770, *Journal*, 5.383). In his edition of Gambold's *Works* (1789) Benjamin La Trobe wrote

> Such a Bishop would have been justly esteemed an honor to any church, whether ancient or modern, if disinterestedness of spirit, humility of mind, devotion of heart, a benevolent disposition to all men, and a voluntary submission to the service not only of the church in general, but of every member thereof though in their most inferior status, be the proper qualifications and distinguished ornaments of the christian episcopacy   (*Works*, xvi)

Gambold was much loved.   C. J. PODMORE

Sources *Works of the late Rev. John Gambold*, ed. B. La Trobe (1789) · D. Benham, *Life and labours of the Rev. John Gambold* (1865) · L. Tyerman, *The Oxford Methodists* (1873) · 'Lebenslauf des Bischofs der Brüderkirche John Gambold', *Nachrichten aus der Brüder-Gemeine*, 1 (1863), 286–305 · [J. Hutton (?)], 'Memoir of John Gambold', Moravian Church House, AB95.A3.27D, AB77.A1.B1 · J. Gambold's letters, Moravian Church House, AB87.A3.10, AB108.C18 · MSS, Moravian Church House · *DWB* · J. Walters, *An English-Welsh dictionary* (1794), preface · private information (2004) · *The journal of the Rev. John Wesley*, ed. N. Curnock and others, 8 vols. (1909–16) · 'Des Jüngers Special-Diarium von 1754', Utrechts Archief, archiv Broedergemeente Zeist, PA I R.9.B.3 · *The letters of Lewis, Richard, William and John Morris of Anglesey*, ed. J. H. Davies, 2 vols. (1907–9), vol. 2 · *DNB*
Archives Moravian Church House, London, letters, AB87.A3.10, AB108.C18 · NL Wales, corresp.
Likenesses J. Spilsbury, mezzotint, pubd 1771 (after A. L. Brandt), BM, NPG, Unitätsarchiv, Herrnhut [*see illus.*] · Hibbart, engraving, 1789 (after J. Spilsbury), Unitätsarchiv, Herrnhut · Topham, engraving, 1816 · Bath, etching (after drawing by Hibbart), NPG

Game, Sir **Philip Woolcott** (1876–1961), air force officer, colonial governor, and commissioner of the Metropolitan Police, was born at Streatham, London, on 30 March 1876, the second son in the family of eight children (five boys and three girls) of George Beale Game, a member of the Baltic exchange, of Broadway, Worcestershire, and his wife, Clara Vincent. After education at Charterhouse School and the Royal Military Academy, Woolwich, he joined the Royal Artillery in 1895. He saw action in South Africa (1901–2), during which time he was promoted captain, mentioned in dispatches, and awarded the queen's medal with five clasps. On 11 August 1908 he married Gwendolen Margaret (d. 1972), the daughter of Francis Hughes-Gibb; they had two sons (one of whom died on active service in 1943) and one daughter.

Game graduated from the Staff College in 1910 and won the Chesney gold medal of the Royal United Service Institution for that year with a wide-ranging essay on imperial defence policy. From then on he was caught up in the succession of staff appointments from which he scarcely escaped during his subsequent service. From the general staff at the War Office he went to France in November 1914 as a major on the staff of the 4th army corps. He soon made his mark, and was appointed to the DSO in April 1915, then in July moved to the staff of 46th division as temporary lieutenant-colonel.

The decisive change in Game's career came in March 1916 when, in order to meet the urgent need to strengthen the staff of the Royal Flying Corps, of which Brigadier-General Hugh Trenchard was then in command, he was transferred by general headquarters as general staff officer I, much against his will. At first he was extremely unhappy. He was less likely to achieve his ambition of active command, and he found the atmosphere of this new and highly technical service entirely uncongenial. He felt that 'General Trenchard would prefer someone of his own type—a hustler'. But in fact Game provided exactly the support that Trenchard needed, turning his 'mysterious thought processes' into clear and persuasive language; as mutual confidence grew, Game was able to stand up to his chief when necessary. Trenchard was to refer to him as 'the best staff officer I have ever had or ever seen'.

Promoted temporary brigadier-general in October 1916, Game remained at Trenchard's right hand and gradually became fully committed to the air arm. He learned to fly, and became a member of the Royal Air Force on its establishment in 1918. After a brief period as general officer commanding south-western area he became director of training and organization (air commodore) in March 1919 after Trenchard's reappointment as chief of air staff. He was closely concerned with the white paper of December 1919 on the future of the RAF and with the continuing battle to secure the RAF's independent role. After promotion to air vice-marshal in January 1922 he was in 1923 at last given a chance to command, as air officer commanding RAF India. But he had been in India only a few months when he was called home urgently, as indispensable, for what the Air Ministry in a formal letter called his 'unique administrative qualities'. Appointed air member for personnel, he remained one of the senior members of the Air Council until he retired at his own request in 1929.

Game was still only fifty-two, and in 1930 he was appointed governor of New South Wales. He arrived in Sydney in May, and soon found himself in a turmoil of political and constitutional controversy. The depression had hit Australia very hard, with the collapse of wheat and wool prices. In October J. T. Lang, the explosive leader of the Labor Party of New South Wales, won a general election on a programme of resistance to orthodox measures for dealing with the slump, and attacked the payment of interest to the 'bondholders'. Game was determined to maintain the neutrality appropriate for the king's representative. As a result he was roundly abused by the anti-Labor forces, especially when he eventually agreed to Lang's demand for the appointment of additional members to the second chamber. To compel Lang to fulfil the state's obligations, the commonwealth government, acting under hastily passed legislation which was upheld by the courts, tried to require that taxes should be paid direct to the commonwealth of Australia and not to the state. Lang directed that state officials should ignore the commonwealth proclamation. Game held that this was a direct breach of the law, and dismissed Lang (13 May 1932). An election followed and Lang was decisively defeated. The governor's action was the subject of bitter controversy. Its critics maintained that it was for the courts, not for the governor, to resolve disputes between state and commonwealth. But the circumstances in which prerogative action of this kind could be taken were not clearly defined. There can be no doubt about the gravity of the situation. Game acted against Lang with the utmost reluctance, but he felt that things could not be allowed to drift. The argument continues. The rest of Game's tenure, until January 1935, was uneventful and happy.

On his return home Game was offered and accepted the succession to Lord Trenchard, whose brief period as commissioner had transformed the Metropolitan Police. No doubt Trenchard felt that his most trusted staff officer could be relied on to carry his changes through. Ironically they soon fell out over the future of Trenchard's most cherished project, the Metropolitan Police College at Hendon. Game did not accept Trenchard's strongly held view that the higher ranks in the police, as in the services, should be filled by young men recruited direct as officers and trained for responsibility. Further experience only strengthened Game's early views, and when the post-war national police college was being considered he asserted strongly that 'we have, and will have, in the ranks, the material to fill all senior posts'. Game was consistent: his own most trusted adviser was not one of the officers brought in by his predecessor but George Abbiss, the only one of the assistant commissioners who had risen from the ranks.

Game's calm judgement fitted him admirably for the impartial maintenance of public order in the East End during the clashes between the Fascists and their opponents. The organization of the force for its manifold wartime duties, and the reshaping required to meet constantly changing wartime conditions, gave full scope for his administrative talents, and he himself gave an outstanding personal example by being out and about in the heaviest air raids. Genuinely unassuming, he did not attempt to make an impact on the general public, who were content to accept that everything was under control, but he gained the respect of all who came in contact with him. Urged on by his sense of duty and of the personal integrity which shines through every account of him, he was a fanatically hard worker, sometimes criticized for doing too much himself. He went to great trouble to improve relationships with the Police Federation, and his deep feeling for the individual came out clearly in his handling of individual cases. He was in fact sometimes misled by his inclination to think that he would get better information and advice from the constable he met on his rounds than from those higher up.

Despite his continuing physical activity Game was remarkably prone to accident. He had acquired a limp from a serious skating accident in the 1920s. His assumption of office as commissioner was delayed by a broken kneecap, and he suffered three fractures of the leg during his period of office. Despite poor health in the later stages of the war he characteristically deferred his retirement until the selection of his successor could be made with the end of the war in sight. He retired in 1945, and lived in retirement until his death, at his home, Blakenhall, Wildernesse Avenue, Sevenoaks, Kent, on 4 February 1961.

Game was slight in build and quiet in speech—a striking contrast to his predecessor as commissioner, Boom Trenchard. He was unpretentious in his habits, for example, often taking public transport in preference to his official car. A good horseman, he was an execrable driver. His many high distinctions reflect his responsibilities: DSO (1915), CB (1919), KCB (1924), GBE (1929), KCMG (1935), GCVO (1937), and GCB (1945).   KENNETH PARKER, rev.

Sources *The Times* (6 Feb 1961) · A. Boyle, *Trenchard* (1962) · B. Foott, *Dismissal of a premier* (1968) · H. V. Evatt, *The king and his dominion governors* (1936) · Metropolitan Police records, London · IWM, Game correspondence · private information (1981) · AusDB · CGPLA Eng. & Wales (1961)

Likenesses W. Stoneman, two photographs, 1935–42, NPG · H. Coster, photographs, NPG · R. G. Eves, oils, Government House, Sydney · M. Mulvey, oils, Scotland Yard, London

Wealth at death £47,460 11s. 2d.: probate, 11 April 1961, CGPLA Eng. & Wales

Gamelin (d. 1271), bishop of St Andrews, was of illegitimate birth, probably Scottish and possibly a sprig of the Comyns; a French origin associated with Queen Marie de Coucy has also been suggested. His place of study is unknown, but was probably Oxford or Paris university. He collected various benefices in Scotland, and was already a master and clerk of Alexander II when he first obtained a pluralist's dispensation at the papal curia at Lyons in 1245, not long before the council there. He seems to have been a protégé of Bishop William of Bondington of Glasgow until the latter died in 1258.

On the death of David of Bernham, bishop of St Andrews, in 1253, the Comyn-dominated government of the young Alexander III nominated Gamelin to the chapter, which, however, elected the dean of Dunkeld. The government then sent Master Abel of Gullane, archdeacon of St Andrews, to Rome; he successfully had the election quashed, but was himself provided and consecrated in the see, only to die late in 1254. On 14 February 1255 the chapter elected Gamelin, again the government's nominee, and papal approval was obtained. He was described at this time as the king's chancellor, although only a small seal of regency was in use. The Comyns and their supporters, including Gamelin and Bondington, were swept from office on 20 September 1255, before Gamelin had been consecrated, but the new government was unable to prevent his consecration on 26 December.

When the revenues of Gamelin's see were seized, he went to the curia, and various letters in his favour were issued in 1256 and 1257. After another coup in Scotland on 29 October 1257, he was able to return there in 1258, despite a threat by Henry III to arrest him. He was a member of the compromise council of 1258, and his ally William Wishart (his successor as bishop) became chancellor when Alexander III assumed power about 1260. In the following decade he was busy with ecclesiastical matters, including raising funds to pay the expenses of Abel's and his own promotion. He pursued the rights of his see and of his cathedral priory with vigour, to the extent of excommunicating those who had been friends, and, having himself been instructed to implement papal provisions, he excommunicated others so instructed for infringing his own rights of collation. Towards 1268 his health began to decline and he was confined to bed long before his death at Inchmurdo, near St Andrews, on 29 April 1271. He was buried in his cathedral.

Gamelin offers little as a role model for a bishop. A pluralist, a safe pair of hands, able and fairly vigorous in the discharge of his duties, particularly where his own rights were concerned, he was unfortunate in the political circumstances of his early episcopate; a conservative, he is not found supporting the mendicant orders, but showed sympathy for the monastic houses of his diocese.

A. A. M. DUNCAN

Sources J. Dowden, *The bishops of Scotland … prior to the Reformation*, ed. J. M. Thomson (1912), 17–18 • D. E. R. Watt, *A biographical dictionary of Scottish graduates to AD 1410* (1977), 209–14 • A. O. Anderson, ed. and trans., *Early sources of Scottish history, AD 500 to 1286*, 2 (1922), 579–606, 644, 656, 662 • A. A. M. Duncan, *Scotland: the making of the kingdom* (1975), vol. 1 of *The Edinburgh history of Scotland*, ed. G. Donaldson (1965–75), 562–73
Likenesses seal, U. Durham L., dean and chapter archives, misc. ch. no. 1297

Games, Abram (1914–1996), poster artist and graphic designer, was born on 29 July 1914 in Whitechapel, London, the second of three children of Joseph Gamse (1877–1974), portrait and commercial photographer, and Sarah, *née* Rosenberg (1885–1969), seamstress, whose emigrant family were woollen merchants from Łódź on the Russo-Polish border. Joseph Gamse was born in Latvia and served in the imperial Russian army before emigrating to England in 1904. In 1926 he changed the family name from Gamse to Games. Abram's early education was in the East End of London, at Millfields Road primary school, Clapton, and the Grocers' Company's (Hackney Downs) School (1925–9).

Games was largely self-taught as a designer, leaving St Martin's School of Art after two terms in 1930 and thereafter attending evening classes in life drawing. His career was launched after winning first prize in a London county council poster competition to promote evening classes in 1935. After a brief and unproductive period with the Askew Young studio, he slowly established himself as a freelance poster designer and attracted clients including Shell, the General Post Office, and London Transport. He joined the infantry as a private in 1940 and designed a recruiting poster for the Royal Armoured Corps (1941); thereafter he was appointed official war poster designer (1942–6) with Frank Newbould as his assistant. He designed approximately one hundred educational and instructional wartime posters which included many memorable images cajoling soldiers about personal cleanliness, warning against careless talk, and encouraging civilians to grow food, give blood, and even knit socks. Some of these campaigns excited fierce controversy; a recruitment poster for the Auxiliary Training Service (1941) which portrayed a glamorous, blonde female soldier in uniform (*The Blonde Bombshell*) was withdrawn after the MP Thelma Cazalet questioned its suitability in parliament. In 1942 his set of three posters for the 'Your Britain … fight for it now' campaign juxtaposed images of 1930s squalor and poverty with symbols of modern public architecture, revealing Games's socialist sympathies. The political message of these posters, which acknowledged the darker side of social inequality in Britain, infuriated some members of the war cabinet, including the prime minister, Winston Churchill, and the Labour minister, Ernest Bevin. Bevin had a poster from the campaign removed from an Association of International Artists' exhibition 'Poster design in wartime Britain', and Churchill ordered its destruction. Games expressed his personal design philosophy in the phrase 'maximum meaning, minimum means', revealing an approach to design which was concerned with creating a form of visual shorthand. Wartime poster designs including *Your Talk may Kill your Comrades* (1942) and *He Talked … they Died* (1943) gain their power and immediacy through a paring down of the message to a direct and simple symbolic form. Games acknowledged the influence of European modernism upon his work, in particular the posters of Lucian Bernhard and Julius Klinger in Germany, of Cassandre and Paul Colin in France and of the American McKnight Kauffer, who worked in Britain between the wars. In later life he recalled how important the German graphic design journal *Gebrauchsgraphik* was in introducing him to European developments.

Having acquired the skills of airbrushing as a young boy in his father's studio, Games generally preferred to hand-render his images—although he could also incorporate photographic elements with startling effect. In 1945 he was among the first at the War Office to see the photographic evidence of Nazi atrocities in the Belsen concentration camp, harrowing images which were to remain with him and inform his subsequent practice as a designer.

As a Jew, Games worked for the Jewish relief unit and for many Jewish and Israeli organizations, producing posters, including *Give Clothing for Liberated Jewry* (1945), based upon an image of a starving victim of Belsen.

Games was rather austere looking, with a gaunt appearance which seemed appropriate for a designer whose life and work exuded great discipline. In 1945 he married Marianne Salfeld (1919–1988), a textile designer born in Mainz, Germany. They had two daughters and a son. Games re-established his commercial design practice in the family home in north-west London and throughout the 1950s created advertising campaigns for the British Overseas Airways Corporation, British European Airways, Guinness, Murphy Television, and the *Financial Times*, for whom he produced the series 'Top people read the *Times*'. He designed famous symbols for the 1951 Festival of Britain (1948), BBC television (1953), and the queen's award to industry (1965). In 1957 he became OBE and, in 1959, was appointed royal designer for industry (RDI). He was a visiting lecturer at the Royal College of Art, London (1946–53), and in Israel.

In addition to graphic design, Games had a passion for product innovation. He designed the Cona coffee new table model (1957, manufactured in 1959), which soon became a design classic. *Over my Shoulder* (1960) is his personal account of his working methods and career, up to that point. In his later years he worked for a number of public service and charitable organizations. In recognition of a lifetime's achievement he received the Designers and Art Directors Association president's award in 1991. Games died in London on 27 August 1996. Examples of his work may be seen at the Victoria and Albert Museum and the Imperial War Museum, London.

ALAN LIVINGSTON and ISABELLA LIVINGSTON

Sources D. Gentleman, *The Guardian* (29 Aug 1996) • A. Livingston and I. Livingston, *The Independent* (29 Aug 1996) • A. Games, *Over my shoulder* (1960) • *Abram Games* (1990) [exhibition catalogue, Howard Gardens Gallery, South Glamorgan Institute of Higher Education, March 1990] • private information (2004)
Archives priv. coll.
Likenesses A. Games, self-portrait, photograph, 1943, repro. in *Abram Games* • A. Games, self-portrait, photograph, 1995, repro. in Livingston and Livingston, *The Independent*

Gamgee, Arthur (1841–1909), physiologist, born in Florence on 10 October 1841, was youngest of the eight children of Joseph Gamgee (1801–1894), veterinary surgeon and pathologist, and Mary Ann West. Joseph Sampson *Gamgee (1828–1886) and John *Gamgee were elder brothers.

Gamgee spent his early boyhood in Florence, where he acquired a lifelong love of art and literature. When he was fourteen his family returned to England and he entered University College School, London. Afterwards he proceeded to the University of Edinburgh, where he studied physics under Peter Guthrie Tait. After taking his MD there in 1862, he was appointed house physician to the Royal Infirmary. Physiology, especially on its chemical side, interested him; his inaugural thesis for the MD, 'Contributions to the chemistry and physiology of foetal nutrition', won the gold medal in 1862.

From 1863 to 1869 Gamgee was assistant to Douglas Maclagan, professor of medical jurisprudence at Edinburgh, and was at the same time lecturer on physiology at the Royal College of Surgeons there and physician to the Royal Hospital for Sick Children. But his interests were centred in research, and later he published various papers elucidating problems of physiological chemistry and of the pharmacological action of chemical bodies. The most interesting of these were 'The action of the nitrites on blood' *PTRS*, 1868, and 'The constitution and physical relations of cystine' *Journal of Anatomy and Physiology* 1870, issued jointly with James Dewar.

In 1871 Gamgee worked with W. Kühne, professor of physiology at Heidelberg, and with Carl Ludwig at Leipzig; and in the same year he was admitted MRCP (Edin.), becoming FRCP in 1872. In the latter year he was also elected FRS. In 1873 he was appointed the first Brackenbury professor of physiology at Owens College, Manchester. He held this post for twelve years, having Henry Roscoe, Balfour Stewart, and Stanley Jevons among his colleagues, and with them helped to make Owens College one of the most conspicuous scientific schools in the country. He worked with tireless enthusiasm as dean of the medical school, and established a working arrangement between the purely scientific and the applied aspects of medicine. In 1875 he married Mary Louisa, daughter of J. Proctor Clark; they had a son and two daughters. In 1882 he was president of the biological section of the British Association which met at Southampton, and from 1882 to 1885 he was Fullerian professor of physiology at the Royal Institution, London. While in London he was admitted MRCP in 1885, and FRCP in 1896.

Gamgee resigned his chair in Manchester in 1885 and practised for a time as a consulting physician at St Leonards, Sussex. In 1887 he was appointed assistant physician to St George's Hospital, London, where he was also a lecturer on pharmacology and materia medica in the medical school. On resigning these appointments in 1889 he resumed his scientific work at Cambridge for a year, and then left England for Switzerland, residing first at Bern, then at Lausanne, and finally at Montreux, where he engaged in active practice as a consulting physician, devoting all his spare time to research in his own laboratory. In 1902 he visited the United States by invitation to inspect various physiological laboratories where the work was chiefly directed towards the study of nutrition in health and disease. In the same year he delivered the Croonian lecture before the Royal Society on 'Certain chemical and physical properties of haemoglobin'. He revisited America in 1903, and at the celebration of Haller's bicentenary at Bern he represented the Royal Society.

Gamgee died of pneumonia on 29 March 1909 in Paris and was buried in the family vault in Arnos Vale cemetery, Bristol. His widow was granted a civil-list pension of £70 in 1910.

Research was Gamgee's main interest throughout his life. His intimate knowledge of physics and chemistry was linked with experience of German methods, which he had gained especially in the laboratories of his lifelong friend, Kühne. While lecturing at Manchester, Gamgee prepared a translation of Ludimar Hermann's *Grundriss der Physiologie des Menschen* from the fifth German edition. This book, which appeared in 1875, together with the publication of Michael Foster's textbook of physiology in 1876, powerfully influenced the development of physiological research in England. In 1880 Gamgee published the first volume of *A Textbook of the Physiological Chemistry of the Animal Body*; the second volume appeared in 1893. The publication of this book marked an epoch in the progress of English physiological study.

Certain parts of physiology possessed a peculiar fascination for Gamgee. Knowledge of the physical and chemical properties of haemoglobin was largely due to him. He was engaged for many years on an elaborate research upon the diurnal variations of the temperature of the human body, with specially devised apparatus for obtaining a continuous record throughout the twenty-four hours. The subject had always been in his mind since he had worked at Edinburgh under Tait. The paper recording his method and results appeared in the *Philosophical Transactions of the Royal Society* (200B, 1908), but his death cut short the investigation. Gamgee believed that physiology stood in an intimate relation to the practice of medicine and that scientific training in a laboratory was essential to the advance of medicine. An excellent linguist, he could lecture fluently in French, German, and Italian.

D'A. POWER, rev. RACHEL E. DAVIES

Sources *The Lancet* (17 April 1909), 1141–5 · *BMJ* (10 April 1909), 933–4 · private information (1912) · personal knowledge (1912) · Munk, *Roll*

Gamgee, John (1831–1894), veterinary surgeon and inventor, was born in the via de Pizzacotti, Florence, Italy, the fourth of the eight children of Joseph Gamgee (1801–1894) and his wife, Mary Ann, daughter of John and Sarah West of Honiton, Devon. His elder brother, Joseph Sampson *Gamgee (1828–1886), achieved fame as a surgeon in Birmingham; his younger brother, Arthur *Gamgee (1841–1909), was an eminent biochemist; and his nephew, D'Arcy Wentworth *Thompson (1860–1948), was the celebrated scholar and naturalist. His father had built up a flourishing veterinary practice in Florence and was able to provide the best education for his children. After private tuition and schools in Florence, John and his elder brother were sent to Switzerland and Germany to complete their education and to become fluent in French and German as well as Italian.

In 1849 John Gamgee was entered for medical school in Italy when he heard that his brother Sampson, as he now chose to call himself, who had qualified as a veterinary surgeon, was about to enter University College, London, to train as a medical surgeon. Thereupon Gamgee changed his plans and decided to become a veterinary surgeon. He qualified from the Royal Veterinary College, London, in 1852, and then spent two years touring the continental veterinary schools and making a study of contagious diseases. On his return to London in 1854 he gave a series of extramural lectures and at some time after that was in

practice for a brief period in Thirsk, Yorkshire. In 1856 he went to Edinburgh as an assistant to William Dick, who had founded the veterinary school there in 1823. Dick was sixty-three years of age and set in his ways. He was well regarded for his practical, clinical acumen but he was in no sense a scientist. By comparison Gamgee was aged twenty-five, a determined, cultured, well-travelled man who had firm ideas about the need for science in the training of veterinary students. They were incompatible and the appointment lasted for only one year.

Within a few months of his arriving in Edinburgh, Gamgee married, on 5 December 1856, Adeline (*b.* 1830/31), an actress and the daughter of Thomas Hartley, lieutenant in the Royal Welch Fusiliers, and his wife, Belinda Payne. Following his marriage Gamgee began to establish himself in the cultural and scientific life of the city. On leaving Dick's college he decided to set up a veterinary school of his own. He had no funds, but his enthusiasm to promote a scientific veterinary training won him influential support and he opened the Edinburgh New Veterinary College on 4 November 1857 in Drummond Street. William Dick was outraged and was further antagonized when he heard that Gamgee had applied for his school to be recognized by the Royal College of Veterinary Surgeons. The college was the governing body of the profession and was nominally responsible for the examinations of the students of the London and Edinburgh schools. Dick had spurned that arrangement and although he himself wanted nothing to do with the governing body he was determined that the Gamgee school should not be recognized. It took Gamgee two attempts before the New Veterinary College was granted the royal sign manual on 31 March 1859.

Gamgee had a passionate interest in matters of public health and contagious disease. In 1862 he was appointed by the privy council to conduct an inquiry on cattle diseases. He urged the government to reform the cattle trade and to create an effective system of veterinary inspection. Looking for professional support he convened the first international veterinary congress, which was held at Hanover in July 1863. By now he was convinced that the uncontrolled importation of cattle would lead to disaster, and in two prophetic letters to *The Times* in November 1863 he warned that if cattle were imported from a Baltic port then Britain could expect rinderpest, a highly contagious, virulent disease of cattle. Eighteen months later the great cattle plague of 1865 broke out in the London dairies; it had been imported from the Baltic port of Revel. The plague was not recognized as rinderpest until Gamgee came down to London on 29 July, one month after the outbreak had started. The government had no effective statutory powers to control it and the royal commission that was set up in October failed to provide a solution. It was the Cattle Diseases Prevention Act of February 1866 that led to the eventual control of the epidemic by means that were essentially those advocated by Gamgee.

At the time of the cattle plague Gamgee was transferring his school to London, where it was known as the Albert Veterinary College. Unfortunately it failed in 1868, probably owing to Gamgee's not giving it the attention it required—in that year he was in the United States investigating Texas fever. On his return to Britain he severed his connections with veterinary science and turned to thermodynamics. His interest in refrigeration led to his building ice-skating rinks in London and Southport and, for seven years from 1878, to consultancy work in the United States on the cooling of mines and offices and the building of refrigerator ships. Another of his projects was the 'zeromotor', a device for powering the ships of the United States navy from the thermal energy in sea water. It aroused much interest and even President Garfield inspected a model of it, but it was bound to fail because it violated the second law of thermodynamics, which Gamgee never could accept. The rest of his life was spent in promoting the zeromotor, which brought him nothing but disappointment and financial anxiety. He died at his home, 13 Springfield Road, Wimbledon, Surrey, on 19 December 1894, from heart failure, and was buried in Wimbledon cemetery. He was survived by his wife; there were no children.

Gamgee's erratic change of career was a great loss to the veterinary profession. He had made a distinguished contribution as an author of several books and numerous articles. He had founded the *Edinburgh Veterinary Review*, which set a new standard for a scientific periodical and foreshadowed the duty of a state veterinary service by publishing national disease statistics. Had he persisted he would surely have reached the pinnacle of his profession.

SHERWIN A. HALL

Sources R. D. Thompson, *The remarkable Gamgees* (1974) · S. A. Hall, 'John Gamgee and the Edinburgh New Veterinary College', *Veterinary Record* (16 Oct 1965), 1237–41 · S. A. Hall, 'The cattle plague of 1865', *Medical History*, 6 (1962), 45–58 · Gamgee MSS, priv. coll. · F. Smith, *The early history of veterinary literature and its British development*, 4 vols. (1919–33); repr. (1976), vol. 4 · S. W. Angrist, 'Perpetual motion machines', *Scientific American*, 218 (1968), 114–22 · *Veterinary Record*, 7 (1894), 365–6 · m. cert. · d. cert. · *CGPLA Eng. & Wales* (1895) · R. D'Arcy Thompson, *D'Arcy Wentworth Thompson: the scholar-naturalist, 1860–1948* (1958), 9

Archives priv. coll., family MSS | PRO, MSS relating to the Edinburgh New Veterinary College, HO 45/056672

Likenesses W. Mallyon, portrait, 1865, U. Glas., veterinary school

Wealth at death £4005: probate, 7 May 1895, *CGPLA Eng. & Wales*

Gamgee, Joseph Sampson (1828–1886), surgeon, eldest son of Joseph Gamgee (1801–1894), veterinary surgeon and pathologist of Edinburgh, and Mary Ann West, was born on 17 April 1828 at Leghorn, Italy, where his father was living. Arthur *Gamgee and John *Gamgee were his brothers. In 1829 the family moved to Florence, where the young Gamgee later went to school. In 1847 he went to London, and became a student at the Royal Veterinary College, his father wanting him to follow his own profession. However, Moncreiff Arnott, professor of surgery at University College, and later Professor William Sharpey and Professor C. J. B. Williams, admitted him to classes and lectures. Williams was pleased with Gamgee's work and suggested he become a doctor. This he did, first obtaining a veterinary diploma. At University College medical school

Gamgee was a most successful student, gaining several gold medals. In 1854 Gamgee became MRCS, and later FRCS (Edin.) and FRSE. Early in 1855 he was appointed surgeon to the British Italian Legion, and had charge of the hospital at Malta during the Crimean War.

In 1857 Gamgee was appointed surgeon to the Queen's Hospital, Birmingham, and he served the hospital and medical school well. He was actively concerned with public health and medical reform, and with his help the hospital was extended and improved and its funds were raised. In 1860 Gamgee married Marion Parker, of Edgbaston, Warwickshire; they had seven children, of whom two sons, both medical students in 1886, and two daughters, survived him. His wife wrote all his works from his dictation, and helped substantially with his writing.

During the Franco-Prussian War (1870–71) Gamgee was secretary of the Birmingham Society for Aid to the Wounded, and he turned his surgery into an ambulance depot. In 1873 he was one of the main initiators of the Hospital Saturday collections in Birmingham, especially in factories and workshops; for this he was presented with 400 guineas and an address by residents of Birmingham.

Gamgee was at various times president of the Birmingham and midland branch of the BMA and of the Birmingham Medical Institute. He was strongly opposed to indiscriminate hospital relief, and he advocated the thorough reorganization of hospital out-patient departments. He vigorously supported the claims of the members of the Royal College of Surgeons to direct representation on its council, and of the members of the profession to direct representation on the General Medical Council.

Gamgee was a surgeon of practical skill and marked individuality. He was said to be the first person in Birmingham to wash his hands before as well as after operating or dressing a wound (Dickens, 27). He was a strenuous advocate of the treatment of wounds by dry and infrequent dressing, rest, and immobility, and he was an opponent of the extremes of Lister's antiseptic system.

In 1853 at Florence, Gamgee had met the eminent Belgian surgeon, Baron Seutin, who had introduced the treatment of fractures by starched apparatus and bandages, which was the subject of Gamgee's Liston prize essay in 1853. In 1854 Gamgee introduced plaster of Paris to England, replacing starched bandages. The idea of using cotton wool came to him from reading Mathias Mayor's *La chirurgie simplifiée* (1842). In 1880 he described 'Gamgee tissue'; this was composed of cotton wool padding which was absorbent because it was free from fat and grease, and which was covered with bleached gauze that could also be medicated. The pads were also used in obstetrics and then in gynaecology, and it was Gamgee's suggestion in 1880 to Robinson & Sons, Chesterfield, Derbyshire, that led to the first manufacture of absorbent sanitary towels. According to the *British Medical Journal* several of his surgical appliances and his Gamgee tissue were adopted, especially by the army medical department; his millboard and paper splints were very widely used for a long time, and Gamgee tissue continued to be used in the National Health Service.

Gamgee wrote much, including pamphlets. His major works were on the treatment of fractures and wounds: *On the Advantages of the Starched Apparatus* (1853); *On the Treatment of Fractures of the Limbs* (1871); *On the Treatment of Wounds* (1878); and *On the Treatment of Wounds and Fractures* (1883). He also wrote on medical and hospital reform: *Medical Reform, a Social Question* (1857); *Hospital Reform* (1868); and *Medical Reform* (1870).

Sampson Gamgee was a fine linguist, who read widely and knew many continental medical men. For many years he was a frequent contributor to *The Lancet*, which said of him that he loved the working men of Birmingham, but had a keen sympathy with intellect. He never took part in affairs outside his profession (*The Lancet*, 590, 607). A lively speaker, Gamgee had great influence on general and professional audiences. A Conservative and a churchman, he was tolerant and liberal-minded, helpful to younger practitioners, and a benefactor to the poor.

In 1881, after a severe attack of haematuria, Gamgee retired from active hospital work, and was appointed consulting surgeon; but he continued to carry on a considerable private practice. While staying at Dartmouth, Devon, he slipped and fell, fracturing the neck of his femur; this was followed by uraemic poisoning, and he died at home, 22 Broad Street, Birmingham, on 18 September 1886, his wife surviving him.   G. T. BETTANY, rev. JEAN LOUDON

Sources *BMJ* (25 Sept 1886), 604–5 · *The Lancet* (25 Sept–2 Oct 1886) · A. J. G. Dickens, 'J. S. Gamgee and "Gamgee tissue"', *The Black Bag*, 18/3 (1962), 27–9 · J. C. Lawrence, 'A century after Gamgee', *Burns, including thermal injury*, 13/1 (1987), 77–9 · *Birmingham Daily Gazette and Daily Post* (20 Sept 1886) · *Birmingham Daily Gazette and Daily Post* (23 Sept 1886) · private information (1889) · *Monthly Index of Medical Specialities* (June 1996), 345 · H. H. Bellot, *University College, London, 1826–1926* (1929), 293 · W. J. Bishop, *A history of surgical dressings* (1959)
Likenesses photograph, repro. in Lawrence, 'A century after Gamgee', 77
Wealth at death £817 14s. 6d.: probate, 1 Nov 1886, *CGPLA Eng. & Wales*

Gammage, Robert George (*c*.1820–1888), Chartist, was born at Northampton. Following education at the Central national school and the Blue Coat charity school at Northampton, he was, at the age of twelve, informally apprenticed to a coach builder. He began his political career in 1837, when he joined the Working Men's Association. He was a deputy to the national convention of 1838, and lectured in support of Chartist principles between 1842 and 1844. He settled at Northampton in 1844, and became Chartist secretary for that district; he thus came into frequent contact with Feargus O'Connor, whom he opposed. At this time Gammage earned his living as shoemaker. In 1848, after losing his employment at Northampton on account of his political propagandism, Gammage moved to Birmingham. In 1852 he achieved national prominence by his nomination as Chartist parliamentary candidate for Cheltenham (though he did not go to the poll), and his election to the paid executive of the National Charter Association. Following a number of speaking tours in 1852–3, he failed to secure re-election, having clashed with Ernest Jones, when he rejected the latter's support for a labour parliament and co-operative enterprises on the land. In 1854 he published his *History of the Chartist Movement* (repr., ed. J. Saville, 1969), a work reflecting his bias against O'Connor and Jones, and his indebtedness to Bronterre O'Brien's social thought. The work is dominated by a one-sided interpretation of the tensions within the Chartist movement but remained a standard account for many years.

In May 1854 Gammage moved to Sunderland, where he worked as an insurance agent and lived with his brother Thomas Gammage (secretary of the Garibaldi committee). He joined the Newcastle foreign affairs committee (1854), the Newcastle committee for watching the war (1855), the National Reform Union, and the Northern Reform Union, and in 1866–7 he shared political reform platforms with Jones and Edmond Beales. In 1864 he qualified as a doctor, and he went on to practise medicine at Newcastle and then Sunderland. He retired to Northampton in 1887, where he died at his home, 155 Wellingborough Road, on 7 January 1888, four days after falling from a tram. He left a widow, Sarah.   E. C. K. GONNER, rev. MATTHEW LEE

Sources *DLB* · F. D. Barrows and D. B. Mock, *A dictionary of obituaries of modern British radicals* (1989), 165 · J. Burnett, *The autobiography of the working class*, ed. D. Vincent and D. Mayall, 3 vols. (1984–9), 117–18 · M. Taylor, *The decline of British radicalism, 1847–1860* (1995) · *CGPLA Eng. & Wales* (1888)
Wealth at death £365: probate, 7 Feb 1888, *CGPLA Eng. & Wales*

Gammans [*née* Paul], **Annie Muriel**, **Lady Gammans** (1898–1989), politician, was born on 6 March 1898 at 61 Marmion Road, Southsea, Hampshire, the daughter of Frank Paul, a master grocer, and his wife, Annie Eliza Adams. She was educated at Portsmouth high school. On 21 November 1917 she married, at the Victoria Wesleyan Chapel, Southsea, Leonard David Gammans (1895–1957), the son of David Gammans, an iron founder. They had no children. After her husband finished his service with the Royal Field Artillery in France, his career involved many years of overseas postings, starting with two years in Canada. From 1920 until 1934 his career in the colonial service took them to Malaya, Sarawak, and Japan, where he was seconded to the British embassy and she learned some of the language. In 1941 Captain Gammans was elected Conservative MP for Hornsey, Middlesex. When he served as assistant postmaster-general from 1951 until 1955 (when he was created a baronet), she assumed most of his constituency duties. It was said that constituents preferred dealing with her and there was little surprise when she was chosen to stand in the by-election necessitated by his death on 8 February 1957. Since the 1920s the death of an MP husband had been a frequent route for women into parliament, but at the time of the by-election the Conservative government was being assailed over its Rent Bill, which among other controversial provisions removed wartime rent controls, and consequently her husband's 1955 majority of 12,000 fell to 3000.

As an MP, Gammans raised such issues as her constituency's housing problems with members of the government. Although she was diligent in her attendance she rarely addressed the House of Commons, preferring to meet privately with ministers or submit written questions. When she did speak it was often on various difficulties faced by British companies and individuals abroad or colonial and foreign affairs, issues which had also interested her husband in parliament. She supported continuing aid to newly independent Commonwealth countries despite criticisms of the seeming ingratitude of some beneficiaries, and felt that the Commonwealth offered a potential model for world government. She raised issues of concern to her constituents such as cheaper goods and services for pensioners, and traffic problems in north London. In 1963 she unsuccessfully sought to amend the London Government Bill by redistributing the boundaries of the new borough to which Hornsey would belong on a north-south axis rather than an east-west axis. She argued that Hornsey had better road connections and more in common with Wood Green and Southgate than the two boroughs with which it was scheduled to be amalgamated. The following year she and several other Conservatives abstained on a three-line whip over the Resale Prices Bill, which abolished most resale price maintenance, and a few weeks later she voted against the government over the inclusion of drugs and medicine in the bill.

Yet it was not the debates and divisions of the House of Commons but rather the social aspect of an MP's responsibilities on which Gammans focused, participating in Inter-Parliamentary Union events and the 1961 Commonwealth Parliamentary Conference. She also enjoyed attending innumerable teas in her Hornsey constituency; it was said that she could not hear the tinkle of teacups without being present. At election time she preferred canvassing one to one to debates or stump speeches, which were not her forte, but in 1964 her 'Maginot Line of tea cups', as described by the local press, began to crack and her previous majority (from 1959) was sharply reduced. With the social and ethnic complexion of Hornsey changing through immigration the local party decided that a more political and less social worker type of MP was needed and she agreed to stand down in 1966. Even at the end of her career contemporaries noticed her lack of basic knowledge on many issues, and she made little mark in parliament or the constituency, despite being well liked in Hornsey. She was probably better suited to the role of a political wife than that of a politician in her own right. In 1966 she became a fellow of the Royal Society of Arts and five years later she received the order of the Sacred Treasure (second class) from the emperor of Japan. She settled in southern England and died at her home, Fitzhall, Iping, Midhurst, Sussex, on 28 December 1989.

DUNCAN SUTHERLAND

Sources *Hornsey Journal* (1957–66) · *The Times* (1957–66) · private information (2004) · *Hansard 5C* (1957–66) · J. Mann, *Woman in parliament* (1962) · *WWW* · b. cert. · m. cert. · d. cert. · *CGPLA Eng. & Wales* (1990)

Archives Bodl. RH, Gammans diary · LMA, David Gammans papers
Wealth at death £1,068,265: probate, 13 March 1990, *CGPLA Eng. & Wales*

Gammon, James (*fl.* 1653–1670), engraver, was apprenticed to William Faithorne the elder in 1653. He is known by a few works, which are for the most part poor copies of better-known engravings: Joseph Strutt justly described him as 'a very indifferent engraver' (Strutt, 1.319). Gammon lived in London, and his plates seem to have been made as frontispieces to books rather than as single-sheet prints. Among his recorded engravings are portraits of James I, Charles I, Charles II, Catherine of Braganza, James, duke of York, Henry, duke of Gloucester, Mary, princess of Orange, the duke and duchess of Monmouth, Richard Cromwell, George Monck, the duke of Albemarle (a copy from David Loggan's print), Sir Tobias Mathew (prefixed to his *Letters* of 1660), and Edward Mascall the painter. A portrait of Ann, duchess of Albemarle, was engraved by a Richard Gammon 'against Exeter House in the Strand', probably a relative of James.

L. H. CUST, *rev.* ANTONY GRIFFITHS

Sources G. Vertue, BL, Add. MS 23078, fol. 23 · J. Strutt, *A biographical dictionary, containing an historical account of all the engravers, from the earliest period of the art of engraving to the present time*, 1 (1785), 319 · T. Dodd, 'Memorials of engravers in Great Britain, 1550–1880', BL, Add. MS 33401 · Goldsmiths' Company, London, Goldsmiths' Company Records

Gamon, Hannibal (*bap.* 1582, *d.* 1650/51), Church of England clergyman, was baptized at St Matthew's, Friday Street, London, on 19 March 1582. He was the son of a London goldsmith, also Hannibal Gamon, and his wife, Frances Galis, daughter of Richard Galis of Windsor, although the Gamon family originated from Padstow, Cornwall. Gamon matriculated at Broadgates Hall, Oxford, in October 1599, graduating BA in 1603 and MA in 1607.

On 10 February 1619 Gamon was presented to the living of Mawgan in Pyder, Cornwall, by Elizabeth Peter on the assignment of the Catholic recusant Sir John Arundell of Lanherne, who owned the advowson. Two months later, on 7 April 1619, Gamon married Elizabeth Peter at Mawgan in Pyder. She had married before and brought children from her previous marriage. When Hannibal signed the herald's visitation in 1620 he gave her maiden name only: Eliza Rilston, daughter of the Reverend James Rilston of St Breock, Cornwall. In his will of 1650 Gamon left bequests to his stepdaughters Grace and Avis Peter (including providing for the latter the £80 marriage portion intended by her late father) and to his stepson, Thomas Peter, daughters and son of Thomas Peter, though the identity of Thomas Peter is uncertain. It is possible that Elizabeth's first husband was a member of the powerful merchant dynasty of Fowey which produced the puritan ministers Thomas and Hugh Peter. Hannibal and Elizabeth's first son together, Hannibal, was baptized on 30 January 1620; Gamon's will also records the existence of another son, Philip, and a daughter, Jane.

Gamon also became associated with the puritan Robartes family of Lanhydrock, Cornwall, preaching at the funeral of Lady Frances Robartes in August 1626. He dedicated the funeral sermon, published the following year, to Lady Robartes's eldest son, John, later second Baron Robartes, counselling him to:

> Abandon then I beseech you in the name of Christ, all iniquitie, yea abominate the sweetest sin, to which your youthfull affections are most endeared, else you will never be able to encline and enlarge them to the pursuit and practise of so excellent and Glorious a Grace as the Feare of the Lord. (Gamon, *Praise of a Godly Woman*, sig. A2)

Gamon particularly commended Lady Robartes's influence upon the religious education of her children and her care 'to fit them with worthy Matches out of Religious Families'. He also praised her religious conversation; many had received 'spiritual Helpe and refreshment' by 'conversing with Her in the choicest passages of sanctification'; he concluded with the proclamation that 'this Elect Lady' was certain of salvation (ibid., 27–30). Gamon was later appointed Robartes's chaplain, establishing an extensive collection of puritan tracts at Lanhydrock. The library he collected is still there in the long gallery, and includes some of his manuscript notebooks containing collections of theological and medical notes.

Gamon delivered sermons to the Launceston assizes in 1621 and 1628. The first of these, entitled *God's Just Desertion of the Unjust, and his persevering Grace to the Righteous*, was published in 1622. The second, *Gods Smiting to Amendment, or, Revengement with Preservatives Against Revolting* (published in 1629), was dedicated to the sheriff, Jonathan Rashleigh of Menabilly, and 'the vertuous Gentlewoman his wife'. The dedication was full of puritan phraseology: 'For the end of God's electing, calling, justifying, and correcting mercy is this, that we should be holy' and the sermon itself attacked 'popery', reciting various offences committed against the state by Catholics, including the Spanish Armada and the Gunpowder Plot (Gamon, 'Gods smiting', dedication, Cornwall RO, R(S) 1/461).

In May 1641 Gamon signed the protestation as rector of Mawgan in Pyder. On 20 April 1642 he was nominated, with Gaspar Hickes of Landrake, as Cornish representative to the Westminster assembly of divines. On 23 October 1643 the House of Commons ordered him to attend the assembly within fourteen days, but he never appears to have attended. Old age, distance, and the difficulties of travel in wartime may be enough to explain his non-appearance, though John Walker described him as 'so miserably harrass'd that it broke his heart' (*Walker rev.*, 97). To Walker, Gamon was a puritan who had suffered for not sharing the extremism of his godly brethren. Nevertheless Gamon was not ejected and when he made his will on 9 April 1650 he could still describe himself as 'minester of the gospell of Jesus Christ and parson of St Maugan in pider', requesting burial 'in a decent and clene manner' and 'expectinge a Joyfull resurrection at the last day' (will, Cornwall RO, FS3/792/1). 'In remembrance of my love' he left to Thomas Peter a two-volume edition of Cardinal Bellarmine's works (an influence on puritan casuistry) and to his niece Elizabeth Peter, Bishop Joseph Hall's works. On 14 November that year his eldest son, Hannibal,

was presented to the rectory of Mawgan in Pyder in his place. Gamon died shortly afterwards. His will was proved on 19 May 1651.

ANNE DUFFIN

Sources A. Duffin, *Faction and faith: politics and religion of the Cornish gentry before the civil war* (1996) · H. Gamon, *The praise of a godly woman: a sermon preached at the solemne funerall of the right honourable ladie, the Ladie Frances Roberts, at Lanhide-rock-church in Cornwall, the tenth of August, 1626, by Hannibal Gamon, minister of the word of God, at St Maugan in the same countie* (1627) · H. Gamon, *Gods smiting to amendment, or, Revengement with preservatives against revolting in a sermon preached at the assises in Launceston, the 6 of August, 1628 by Hannibal Gamon minister of Gods word at St Maugan in Cornwall* (1629) [MS copy, Cornwall RO, R(S) 1/461] · J. L. Vivian, ed., *The visitations of Cornwall, comprising the herald's visitations of 1530, 1573, and 1620* (1887) · will, Cornwall RO, FS3/792/1 · will, PRO, PROB 11/217, fol. 8r · *Walker rev.* · Boase & Courtney, *Bibl. Corn.* · M. Coate, *Cornwall in the great civil war and interregnum, 1642–1660* (1933) · *DNB* · PRO, E331 [presentation to living] · T. L. Stoate, ed., *The Cornwall protestation returns, 1641* (1974) · Foster, *Alum. Oxon.* · A. M. B. Bannerman, ed., *The register of St Matthew, Friday Street, London, 1538–1812, and the united parishes of St Matthew and St Peter Cheap*, Harleian Society, register section, 63 (1933) · *IGI* · R. P. Stearns, *The strenuous puritan: Hugh Peter, 1598–1660* (1954)

Wealth at death see will, PRO, PROB 11/217, fol. 8r

Gamwell, (Anne) Hope (1893–1974). *See under* Gamwell, (Antonia) Marian (1891–1977).

Gamwell, (Antonia) Marian (1891–1977), volunteer ambulance driver and commanding officer of the FANY, was born on 28 July 1891 at 169 Knight's Hill Road, West Norwood, the eldest daughter of Frederick Robison Gamwell (1835–1901), an East India merchant, and his wife, Marian Antonia Bankart (1864–1922). Her sister **(Anne) Hope Gamwell** (1893–1974), who was also a senior member of the FANY during the Second World War, was born at Innisfail, 79 Beulah Hill, Upper Norwood, on 15 May 1893.

Both the Gamwell sisters were educated at Roedean School. They had a very strict upbringing but they inherited a sense of adventure from their mother, a qualified nurse, who was always encouraging the girls to go ahead and do things. Mrs Gamwell was one of the first people in England to own a car and the two girls learned to drive about the age of fifteen. Marian and Hope used to spend hours stripping the engine to repair faults and putting it together again. In these early years they wore their hair in thick, long plaits, but later, in 1914, had it cropped in the style which remained a characteristic of the two sisters for the rest of their lives.

During her youth Marian developed an interest in farming and when she left school in 1910 she sought to study agriculture. However, none of the agricultural colleges would accept a woman as a student. Instead, she went to work on poultry and dairy farms in Gloucestershire and Berkshire and eventually travelled to Saskatchewan in Canada where she worked on a dairy-cum-wheat farm. She sailed home about December 1912 on the British liner *Lusitania* (sunk in 1915).

By this time Marian's mother had moved to Llanbedr, north Wales, and was living in a country house called Aber Artro, which during the First World War became a British Red Cross auxiliary hospital. After the war broke out in 1914, Mrs Gamwell took her two daughters to France at the suggestion of Dr Elsie Inglis, who founded the Scottish Women's Hospitals for Foreign Service, to prepare a hospital for the French army at the Abbaye de Royaumont, near Viarmes, 30 miles from Paris. Marian described the old abbey, which had been used as stables, as filthy (Gamwell and Albrecht). They set about cleaning it and while Marian drove ambulances Hope worked in the X-ray room. They worked there until May 1915 when the two sisters went to Calais where they joined the FANY, which had been founded in 1907 as a corps of nurses on horseback 'tending Britain's soldiers on the field' (Terry, 25). Their mother returned to north Wales.

Marian and Hope were set to work at the first FANY hospital, Lamarck, which had 100 beds and was housed in a convent school in the rue de la Rivière, Calais. Their patients consisted mainly of cases of typhoid which was then raging in the Belgian army. Thanks to the generosity of their mother the sisters were able to provide an ambulance and a mobile bath for Lamarck transport. The mobile bath was an enormous Daimler car fitted with six canvas baths on each side. Water was heated by Primus stoves inside the body of the car. It gave 250 baths a day and disinfected the men's clothes (Ward, 47).

On 1 January 1916 the Calais convoy came into being to relieve the men ambulance drivers and for the first time women were officially driving ambulances for the British army. Thus the FANYs became the guinea pigs for women at war. Their vehicles were ill-equipped for the weather and the conditions. They had rudimentary windscreens, inefficient springs, unreliable engines, no self-starters, and tyres which punctured easily. The women drivers had to maintain the vehicles and during the winter months they had to crank the engines at hourly intervals to warm them up. On Good Friday 1916 Marian broke an arm when the engine backfired and the starting-handle smashed into her right arm.

In April 1918 Marian, suffering from appendicitis, returned to England leaving Hope to take over her task as sergeant responsible for stores for the servicing of the vehicle fleet. She spent the rest of the war working for Rolls-Royce as a member of the aircraft inspection department.

After the war Hope returned to England in 1919 to become a member of the newly formed FANY headquarters staff committee and played a decisive part in the development of the corps. Marian, while retaining membership of FANY, spent some time in Greece. Apart from their many other pursuits, the two sisters were keen sailors and found time to cruise from Bangor in Marian's yawl, Boudja. They sold the house in Wales after their mother's death and went to Africa to prospect for land on which to farm. On 6 November 1928 they set off from Nairobi in a Rugby car to drive across Kenya and Tanganyika (Tanzania). The roads in Africa at that time consisted mainly of cattle tracks, and bridges across the streams and rivers were rudimentary. However, the intrepid Gamwell sisters allowed nothing to impede their progress and they arrived at Abercorn (now called Mlala) in Northern Rhodesia (Zambia) on 19 December 1928. Here they

acquired what Marian called 'a plot of land' (Gamwell and Albrecht) consisting of 999 acres at the southern tip of Lake Tanganyika which they called Chilongolwelo.

The two sisters with their team of workers hacked a farm out of the virgin Rhodesian bush, built their home, and planted coffee. They had to battle against predators, locusts, tsetse flies, and malaria. During trips to England, Marian and Hope trained as pilots at the London Aeroplane Club at Hanworth. Marian says in her manuscript autobiography that she was the first woman to drive a motor car in Dresden, the first to ride a motor bicycle in Athens, and the first to cycle in Majorca.

When they were ready for the first picking of coffee, the Second World War broke out and the FANYs sent an urgent request to the Gamwell sisters to return. Hope flew home immediately while Marian set about burning the crop because it was against the law to leave the coffee untended. When Marian returned to London in 1940 she found herself embroiled in a battle to maintain the autonomy of the FANYs against the formidable opposition of Helen Gwynne-Vaughan, director of the Auxiliary Territorial Service. Part of the FANYs formed the basis of the driver training centre at Camberley under Mary Baxter-Ellis while the Gamwell sisters, referred to by a certain brigadier as 'the thick one [Hope] and the thin one [Marian]' (Popham, 134), took over the running of the corps unit. Marian became commandant of the independent FANYs and Hope went to Scotland to command the corps unit attached to the Polish forces before returning to London to recruit for the special operations executive (SOE), which infiltrated agents into occupied territory in Europe. This, according to Marian (Gamwell and Albrecht), was undoubtedly the most important work that the FANYs undertook during the war. In April 1942 the first women to join SOE as agents were selected and sent for training. By 1944 just over fifty had been sent into France, thirty-nine of them FANYs, or members of the Women's Auxiliary Air Force who became FANYs on recruitment to SOE. Of these thirty-nine, thirteen died in concentration camps. Three of these women agents were awarded the George Cross, two posthumously. Some 2000 other FANYs provided the backbone of SOE, working with ciphers and signals, as agent-conducting officers, and administering the special training schools. In all the FANYs served in forty-four countries with Hope playing a prominent part in the organization of SOE in Egypt and Italy (FANY Gazette, 18).

During the war both Marian and Hope travelled extensively visiting FANY outposts abroad. An illustration of Marian's spirit of adventure is the story of one of her wartime trips when, needing to get to Baghdad, with no other form of transport available from Cairo, she seriously suggested that she might take a camel (Popham, 134). Marian became an OBE in the 1946 new year's honours and was mentioned in dispatches.

Hope Gamwell returned to their Abercorn farm in December 1945 and Marian followed in June 1946. Instead of coffee they embarked on growing rice, wheat, and millet and Marian took up bee-keeping. They remained on their farm until October 1964 when Marian, aged seventy-three, and Hope, aged seventy-one, returned to the United Kingdom to live in Jersey.

While Hope was shy, reserved, and self-effacing, Marian was the born leader, a competent administrator, a strategist, a builder who never shirked responsibility. Both sisters were tall with a martial bearing, emphasized by their crisp, no-nonsense manner, their cropped hair, and the khaki drill they wore which became almost a Gamwell trade mark. Dr F. O. Albrecht in a foreword to Marian's autobiography says they formed a perfect team working in a kind of symbiotic unity, each knowing the other's mind without actually saying a word (Gamwell and Albrecht, iii). The contribution of the two sisters was immense and stories of their wartime experiences are an integral part of FANY lore. Both died in Jersey, Hope on 25 April 1974 and Marian on 13 May 1977.   ROY TERRY

Sources M. Gamwell and F. O. Albrecht, 'An adventurous heart', unpublished autobiography, c.1977, FANY Archives, London · H. Popham, *FANY: the story of the women's transport service, 1907–1984* (1984) · I. Ward, *FANY invicta* (1955) · R. Terry, *Women in khaki* (1988) · *FANY Gazette*, autumn (1974) · b. cert. [Antonia Marian Gamwell] · b. cert. [Anne Hope Gamwell]
Archives FANY Archives, London
Likenesses G. Harcourt, oils, Women's Transport Service (FANY), Duke of York's Headquarters, London · photographs, Women's Transport Service (FANY), Duke of York's Headquarters, London

Gandell, Robert (1818–1887), orientalist and biblical scholar, was born in the parish of St Michael, Crooked Lane, London, the sixth and youngest son of Thomas Gandell. He was educated at Mill Hill School and at King's College, London, before going to Oxford where he matriculated in 1839 at St John's College. He graduated BA in 1843 at Queen's College, Oxford; remaining there as Michel scholar from 1843 to 1845 and as fellow from 1845 to 1850. He proceeded MA in 1846. He was tutor at Magdalen Hall from 1848 to 1872, chaplain at Corpus Christi in 1852, and fellow at Hertford from 1859 to 1861, and was senior proctor in 1860. In 1861 he was appointed Laudian professor of Arabic at Oxford, in 1874 prebendary of Ashill in Wells Cathedral, and in 1880 canon of Wells Cathedral. He lectured on Hebrew for E. B. Pusey for many years. In 1859 he published an edition in four volumes of John Lightfoot's *Horae Hebraicae*, a New Testament commentary originally published in the second half of the seventeenth century. American editions of this scholarly work were issued in 1859 and 1979. He further contributed a commentary (on conservative lines) on the books of Amos, Nahum, and Zephaniah to the Speaker's Commentary. He lived at Holywell Lodge, Oxford, and at The Liberty, Wells, Somerset, where he died on 24 October 1887. He left two sons, but nothing more is known of his private life.

D. S. MARGOLIOUTH, rev. ELIZABETH BAIGENT

Sources Foster, *Alum. Oxon.* · *CGPLA Eng. & Wales* (1887) · J. W. Burgon, *Lives of twelve good men*, 6th edn, 2 vols. (1889)
Wealth at death £2425 17s. 4d.: probate, 30 Dec 1887, *CGPLA Eng. & Wales*

Gandhi [née Nehru], **Indira Priyadarshini** (1917–1984), prime minister of India, was born on 19 November 1917 at Allahabad, Uttar Pradesh, the only child of Jawaharlal *Nehru (1889–1964), one of the principal leaders of the

Indira Priyadarshini Gandhi (1917–1984), by Derry Moore, 1976

Indian nationalist movement and India's first prime minister, and Kamala (c.1899–1936), daughter of Atal Kaul, a businessman of Delhi. Both her parents were Kashmiri Brahmans. Indira was an only child, brought up in the wealthy, Westernized, politicized, and bustling household of Motilal *Nehru, her grandfather, one of the most prominent lawyers of the province.

Childhood and education Three generations of the Nehru family, several aunts, and many family retainers and political activists resided in or engaged in political work in the grand family residence, known as Anand Bhavan ('Happy Home'). Indira was a favoured child in this household, though she recalled unkind treatment and devastating remarks about her made by her aunt Vijayalakshmi *Pandit, whom she never forgave. Moreover, in the midst of this bustle of family and political activity Indira was often alone and lonely, especially during the periods of intense nationalist activity, when many of her family, including at times both her mother and father, were in gaol.

Long and frequent periods of separation from one or both parents and prolonged travel and residence away from home contributed to the development of several of Indira's characteristic personality traits: a strong sense of self-reliance and personal responsibility for her own fate, those of others, and later the country; personal courage; mistrust of others and detachment, manifested in a lifelong inability to maintain close relationships with people other than her nearest family members; the frequent use of silence in her private and public relations as a means of obtaining her wishes, and of withdrawing from conflict temporarily in order to bide her time for later action; a tendency to blame others for difficulties and misfortunes; a determination in the face of a perceived hostile world to prevail nevertheless against all odds in the attainment of her goals. A gangly child, she became in maturity an attractive woman, who carried herself with great poise and dignity.

Although Indira was often with her father and from her twenties onward became his personal confidante and hostess, she was closer in her formative years to her mother. The disparate character and lives of her father and mother, the former a thoroughly Westernized and modern man, an agnostic, and an intellectual, the latter a simple, traditional, and religious woman, were reflected also in their daughter's personal and private views on life. Publicly she projected her father's outlook, privately her mother's faith.

Indira's formal education was obtained at numerous schools and universities in India and abroad, including the École Nouvelle at Bex in Switzerland, St Mary's Convent School in Allahabad, the Pupil's Own School in Poona, Rabindranath Tagore's Visva-Bharati University at Santiniketan, Badminton School near Bristol, and finally Somerville College, Oxford. Her education at most of these places was interrupted by travel with her father, her own discontent, and at Oxford by academic failure. Although she became proficient in French, she was otherwise an indifferent student.

Contrary to social custom and against her father's wishes, Indira married on 16 March 1942 Feroze Gandhi, a Parsi, who had for long been a part of the Nehru household and a trusted intimate of her mother. Although Indira and Feroze became estranged from each other within a few years and she spent more and more time with her father while Feroze spent more time with other women, they had two children, Rajiv, born on 20 August 1944, and Sanjay, born on 14 December 1946. Feroze died in 1959, after which Indira remained a widow, though there were at times unconfirmed rumours of liaisons with other men.

Early political career Indira Gandhi was, of course, a dedicated nationalist, who had seen her parents and other relations move in and out of gaol in pursuit of the goal of Indian independence and who had herself spent nine months in gaol in 1942–3. She was also in her soul a political person, deeply involved in 'power politics' and committed to the attainment of specific goals, though without the overall vision of a new society which guided her father. From her youth she demonstrated an abiding interest in activities and programmes for the benefit of children, the low castes, and the poor, which was ultimately reflected in concrete policies for these groups when she came to power.

However, the most dramatic and consequential actions in Mrs Gandhi's political career arose primarily out of political combat and international conflict. Of these, the first in a long series occurred when she was elected president of the Indian National Congress in 1959, while her father was prime minister. Initially against her father's wishes, she helped instigate a protest movement in the state of Kerala against policies of a duly elected communist government with a majority in the legislature, then used that movement as a pretext for actions—legal in form, but against the constitution in spirit, and deceptive in practice—which led to the dismissal of the government and the establishment of president's rule (rule by the central government) in the state.

Indira Gandhi was passed over in the succession to her father in 1964, which was handled by a group of state party bosses known as the syndicate, who chose instead Lal Bahadur Shastri as Nehru's successor. Inducted into Shastri's cabinet as minister for information and broadcasting, a relatively minor portfolio, she made little mark or impression. Even when she was chosen as prime minister in January 1966 to replace Lal Bahadur after his sudden death in Tashkent, it was not because of her achievements or her political support, but because the still politically dominant syndicate members saw her as a manageable person whose selection would prevent the ascendance of Morarji Desai, perceived as a dangerous and unmanageable rival to them. Nor did she display at first any of the self-assurance and political skill for which she later became famous.

Prime minister Mrs Gandhi's dynamism, combativeness, and assertiveness only became evident when she began to feel threatened by fears that the syndicate was trying to control her and then displace her from power, and by the disastrous results of the first general elections held while she was prime minister, in 1967, during which the Congress failed for the first time to win a two-thirds majority in parliament, and in the aftermath of which the Congress lost power in half the Indian states. Her first decisive act came in the midst of these dangers in 1969, when the president of India died in office. Fearing the election as president of a man chosen by the syndicate, she defied her own party, lobbied for another candidate, who succeeded as a consequence of her efforts, and was expelled from the Congress. In the midst of this conflict she became head of a rival Congress, which ultimately became in effect her party, called the Indian National Congress (Indira), or for short the Congress (I).

In national elections called at her request in 1971 Indira's Congress prevailed against the syndicate-dominated Congress with a two-thirds majority in parliament. In the March 1972 state legislative assembly elections which followed, the Congress (I) again emerged triumphant, winning large majorities in all the larger states of the union, establishing definitively her personal political dominance and that of her party in the country.

In the midst of the internal struggle to establish her power base India and Indira had to face the consequences of the civil war in Pakistan between the East and West wings, which led to an influx of an estimated 9 to 10 million refugees from the East wing. Failing to win support from Western countries to force a peaceful settlement of the struggle on Pakistan and the return of the refugees, she turned to the Soviet Union, signing a treaty of peace, friendship, and co-operation in August 1971 with the understanding that its terms implied Soviet support to prevent US involvement in opposition to any Indian action against Pakistan. In December 1971 India invaded East Pakistan, defeated the Pakistan army there, and thereby brought independence to the new state of Bangladesh.

Consolidation of power Despite India's triumph in war under her leadership, and the massive character of the victory against all her rivals in the 1971–2 elections, as well as the absence of significant opposition to her leadership in her own party, Mrs Gandhi never felt secure in power. She always felt threatened by both domestic and international forces, which she saw as bent on thwarting her policies and displacing her from power. She took numerous measures, therefore, to deal with what she perceived as the remaining opposition to her authority—measures including challenges to the independence of the judiciary through judicial appointments, and the assertion of the supremacy of parliament over the supreme court, as well as the enactment of measures additional to the already extensive armoury of laws to control domestic dissent through preventive detention of persons without trial.

Mrs Gandhi also took measures to prevent the rise of strong opposition parties and to control dissent within her own party in the states through the use or threat of president's rule and by removing from the Congress state legislature parties the power to elect their leaders, whom she chose herself. Elections to party positions in the Indian National Congress itself were stopped, and all important party appointments and decisions were made directly by her or in her name by her closest advisers. Within the central government all cabinet ministers were either people without independent power bases or saw their power bases undermined while they served under her leadership. Increasingly, Mrs Gandhi took her own decisions independently of the cabinet, in consultation only with a shifting clique of high-level bureaucrats personally loyal to her, former retainers from the Nehru household, and her younger son, Sanjay.

Emergency rule A few voices were raised from among the opposition parties and from some non-party figures contending that Mrs Gandhi was bent upon establishing personal, authoritarian rule in the country. Charges were also made that under her rule corruption, endemic in Indian politics, had become so massive as to constitute a qualitative change, including such matters as the buying and selling of the loyalty of members of the state legislatures to undermine opposition parties and the collection of large monetary contributions for the party coffers from state party leaders and businessmen. Domestic food shortages and price rises in 1973–4 precipitated discontent in the states of Bihar and Gujarat, where popular movements were launched to displace the Congress from power. At this time also an old and highly respected nationalist leader, Jayaprakash Narayan, emerged from political retirement to take up the leadership of all the forces opposed to the authoritarian tendencies and the corruption which had been spreading under Mrs Gandhi's leadership.

An unexpected fillip was suddenly provided to the opposition to Mrs Gandhi when an election petition, filed in a local court and alleging the use of corrupt practices in her own election to parliament in 1971, succeeded in June 1975, and her election was declared invalid. Under the laws she would have been disbarred from contesting an election for six years, which would have terminated her position as prime minister and threatened her future political career. Mrs Gandhi responded, as always in the face of a major threat, by buying time through an appeal to the supreme court while she gathered the internal strength for decisive action. That action came on 25 June 1975 in the form of a declaration of emergency for the entire country, and the arrest of thousands of opposition leaders and activists and of hundreds of people from her own party, including Congress members of parliament and of the state legislatures. Complete press censorship was imposed, the laws under which her election was declared invalid were themselves invalidated, the powers of the prime minister's office were strengthened, the terms of the national parliament and of the state legislatures were extended, and the preventive detention laws were fortified further to nullify even the use of the right of habeas corpus in the courts.

During the succeeding two-and-a-half years of emergency rule Mrs Gandhi allowed her son **Sanjay Gandhi** (1946–1980), who held no elected position in government, to exercise power and authority in her name in relation to party members and government bureaucrats. He in turn recruited into the party thousands of younger people, many of them hooligans and ruffians, who used threats and force to intimidate rivals and those who opposed Mrs Gandhi's authority or his own. Many of Sanjay Gandhi's actions and those of his followers, as well as the zealousness of bureaucrats determined to prove their loyalty to the leaders of the new regime, produced popular discontent and fears, which lingered below the surface during the emergency rule. These measures included forced sterilizations of men as part of Sanjay Gandhi's family planning programme, destruction of squatter settlements in the cities, and the police firing on crowds which gathered to protest such actions.

Defeat and re-election When Mrs Gandhi decided to seek to legitimize her rule by releasing virtually all political prisoners and holding an election in January 1977, this discontent provided an important basis for her defeat by a new force, called the Janata Party, formed by most of the important opposition parties and leaders in the country. During the two-and-a-half years of Janata rule, most of the emergency laws and measures were rescinded and the basic features of the constitutional order were restored. Attempts to convict Mrs Gandhi and her son for illegal acts committed during the emergency foundered, as did the Janata government itself in July 1979, when, as a consequence of internal divisions and the efforts of Sanjay Gandhi, the Janata Party split, the government fell, and no new majority could be found in parliament. The failure of efforts to arrest and convict Mrs Gandhi, followed by the disintegration of the Janata Party, brought her public sympathy and renewed political support as she became seen as the political leader most likely to bring stability to the country.

Prime minister again and assassination In an election called for January 1980 to replace the parliament Congress (I) prevailed and Mrs Gandhi again became India's prime minister. Most of the opposition-controlled state legislatures were soon dismissed and new state legislative assembly elections called, which restored the Congress to power in most of the states once again. Mrs Gandhi's gratification over her triumph was marred by personal tragedy in the sudden death of her favoured son and political heir apparent, Sanjay, in a plane crash on 23 June.

Mrs Gandhi governed for the next four years for the most part without resort to the extreme measures adopted during the emergency. However, her attempts to consolidate her power anew everywhere in the country led to interventions which precipitated turmoil in the north-east, in Kashmir, and in Punjab. The latter proved to be the most serious, where violent terrorist groups overshadowed the routine politics of the state, which had to be placed under president's rule. After the leader of the Sikh militants and his followers had taken refuge in the Golden Temple at Amritsar, the holiest site of the Sikh religion, Mrs Gandhi ultimately ordered the Indian army to launch an assault within the temple precincts to remove them, during which many hundreds of defenders, soldiers, and visitors to the shrine were killed. Far from settling the Punjab conflict, this action embittered virtually the entire Sikh population of the world and led to an insurrection which lasted for a decade thereafter. On 31 October 1984 Mrs Gandhi was assassinated by two of her own Sikh bodyguards in the garden of her residence in New Delhi. During her funeral in Delhi organized mobs took vengeance in the slaughter of thousands of Sikh residents. Her body was cremated near her father's and son's cremation sites at Raj Ghat in Delhi and her ashes were scattered by her surviving son, Rajiv, from a plane over the Himalayan mountains.

Rajiv Gandhi Indira Gandhi was succeeded immediately after her death by her son **Rajiv Gandhi** (1944–1991), who had been groomed for the succession after the death of Sanjay. Aided by a great wave of sympathy for his bereavement, Rajiv led the Congress to a landslide victory in the general elections held in December 1984. He remained prime minister for a full term, until the Congress was defeated in the general elections held in November 1989, after which he became leader of the opposition in parliament. In the midst of mid-term elections in May–June 1991 he, too, was assassinated in a suicide bomb blast in Madras, carried out on 21 May under the orders and by a member of the Liberation Front of Tamil Eelam, the Sri Lankan secessionist organization whose leader had become hostile to Rajiv because of his withdrawal of support to the movement. Rajiv's death brought to an end the dynastic succession in the prime minister's office of three generations of the Nehru family, who, in or out of office, were the central figures in Indian politics throughout the post-independence era.

Indira Gandhi's reputation During the two decades in which she dominated Indian politics, Indira Gandhi left a mixed legacy of highly controversial actions and policies, some of them long-lasting, others short-lived. In her early years as prime minister she adopted policies consistent with the then socialist bent of the Indian state: bank nationalization and abolition of the privy purses of the princes, which persisted, and nationalization of the wholesale trade in wheat, which was withdrawn. The green revolution in agriculture also began during her first years in office. Most of the institutional changes introduced during the emergency lasted only as long as the emergency itself. During her last four years in office she shifted the Congress stance from its historic position of protector of minorities, particularly Muslims, towards one more identified with Hindu pride, thereby laying the basis for the rise of contemporary militant Hindu nationalism and the associated upsurge of Hindu–Muslim riots. In her struggles to undermine her rivals and build new bases of support for herself and her party she patronized new leaders from among the middle (so-called 'backward') castes, lower castes, and tribals, which permanently altered political and social alignments in several of the Indian states. During her stewardship of the Indian National Congress the party organization became virtually defunct and dependent overwhelmingly on her personal appeal for its electoral success. Corruption in public office reached previously unheard-of proportions and became systematized.

In international relations she departed from Nehru's policy of non-alignment, and moved towards an alliance with the Soviet Union, formalized in the treaty of 1971. Even before this alliance relations with the United States had become embittered as a consequence of her criticism of US actions in Vietnam, her desire to free India from dependence upon US foreign aid, and the government of India's continued identification with the Palestinian cause and hostility to Israel. The lowest point in US–Indian relations was reached during the Bangladesh crisis and the Third Indo-Pakistan War of 1971, when the United States threatened India with the dispatch of the nuclear-powered aircraft-carrier *Enterprise* into the Bay of Bengal. On 18 May 1974 she announced to the world that India had succeeded in carrying out an underground nuclear explosion, which she described as a 'peaceful nuclear test'. In all these matters and many others Mrs Gandhi stood her ground against foreign criticism and objections and asserted calmly, proudly, and sometimes defiantly India's right to take an independent position in international politics.

Indira Gandhi in life and death was the most controversial Indian political personality of her times. Even members of her own family and her in-laws polarized around her. She remained an immensely popular figure for tens of millions of Indians, especially among the poor and other-wise disadvantaged groups and classes. However, although she retained the loyalty of many intellectuals identified with the left, the predominant image of Mrs Gandhi among most of the literate and especially the Westernized intellectual classes has become that of a paranoid personality, a political opportunist with no consistent or coherent political views, a wrecker of Indian political institutions, and a demagogue.

Mrs Gandhi's international reputation (aside from feelings towards her in the United States) was much more favourable, especially among the non-aligned countries, who looked to India and to her for leadership and defence of their economic interests against the industrialized powers. She was particularly favoured in the Soviet Union; honorary doctorates from Moscow State University and the Soviet Academy of Sciences were awarded to her in life as well as the Lenin prize after her death. Numerous other honours and awards of this type were also granted to her in Europe, including degrees from Oxford and the Sorbonne, in developing countries, and from international organizations. She received as well many such awards in her own country, including its highest honour after her successful prosecution of the Bangladesh war as prime minister, the bharat ratna.

PAUL R. BRASS

Sources P. Jayakar, *Indira Gandhi: an intimate biography* (1992) · N. Sahgal, *Indira Gandhi: her road to power* (1982) · I. Malhotra, *Indira Gandhi: a personal and political biography* (1989) · M. C. Carras, *Indira Gandhi in the crucible of leadership* (1979) · U. Vasudev, *Indira Gandhi: revolution in restraint* (1974)
Archives Indira Gandhi Memorial Trust, New Delhi | FILM BFI NFTVA, *The dynasty: 'The Nehru–Gandhi story'*, BBC2, 2 Aug 1997 · BFI NFTVA, current affairs footage · BFI NFTVA, news footage · IWM FVA, actuality footage · IWM FVA, documentary footage · IWM FVA, home footage | SOUND BL NSA, 'A tribute to Indira Gandhi', T7 308/7308 RO1 TR2 · IWM SA, documentary recording · IWM SA, oral history interview
Likenesses Y. Karsh, bromide print, 1956, NPG · D. Moore, photograph, 1976, Camera Press Ltd, London [*see illus.*] · photographs, Hult. Arch.

Gandhi, Mohandas Karamchand [*known as* Mahatma Gandhi] **(1869–1948)**, political leader and religious and social reformer, was born in Porbandar, Kathiawar, western India, on 2 October 1869, to Karamchand Uttamchand Gandhi and his fourth wife, Putlibai: he was the youngest of the one daughter and three sons of the marriage.

Childhood and marriage Karamchand Gandhi, like his father and brother, served various princely states in Kathiawar, being prime minister in Rajkot and Vankaner. As was customary among Hindus, he arranged his son's marriage when he was still a child. In 1882 Mohandas married a child bride of about his own age, Kasturbai Makanji (d. 1944), daughter of a Porbandar merchant. Their first child died; but they had four surviving sons, Harilal (b. 1888), Manilal (b. 1892), Ramdas (b. 1897), and Devadas (b. 1900). The marriage to Kasturbai lasted until her death on 22 February 1944, while she was sharing imprisonment

with her husband, but Gandhi was a difficult husband and father and it was a turbulent relationship at times. At least once in South Africa Kasturbai threatened to leave him because he made her do religiously polluting work, and the relationship became platonic after he took a vow of celibacy in 1906. But it developed into a deeply affectionate partnership, as he later acknowledged: he taught his wife to read and write in Gujarati, and to participate in his domestic and public reform experiments. The eldest son rebelled totally against his father's ideals, and the scandals surrounding him were a considerable embarrassment when Gandhi became a notable public figure in India.

Education, and legal studies in England Gandhi was exposed to the piety of his Vaishnavite Hindu family, particularly the intense devotion of his mother; and, more unusually, to a tolerant atmosphere encouraged by his father, who welcomed into his home not just fellow Hindus, but Jains as well as Muslims and Parsis. Gandhi admitted that as a youth he had no real religious faith and disliked the glitter of temple worship. Nothing suggested his future religious vision or qualities of leadership. He recorded that he was terrified of the dark, of thieves, ghosts, and snakes; and reacted with horror to a friend's attempt to make him eat meat and frequent a brothel. He was not outstanding at school in Porbandar and Rajkot, nor, after matriculating in 1887, as a student at Samaldas College in Bhaunagar, which he left after one term, unable to follow lectures. This failure came soon after his father's death, when Mohandas was only sixteen: but it was to be a turning-point in his life. A family friend encouraged his mother and brother to let him go to England to study law, to enable him to succeed his father in princely service. His mother eventually agreed, provided he vowed not to touch wine, women, and meat. Although family and friends supported his enterprise, the members of the Modh Bania caste, to which he belonged, opposed the plan on grounds of potential religious pollution, and outcasted him when he persisted. Gandhi spent three years in London, from 1888 to 1891. He completed his primary purpose of studying law, in the meantime becoming fluent in English and familiar with Western ways, in contrast to his experience on the voyage to England, when he hid in his cabin because he was ignorant of Western table manners and did not dare to ask if the menu contained meat. He enrolled in the Inner Temple, and was called to the bar in 1891. He also embarked on a long journey of personal exploration. After a brief attempt to live the fashionable life, taking French, elocution, and dancing lessons, and dressing elegantly, he settled to a seriously disciplined and frugal lifestyle, and began to study both Hinduism and Christianity, and to read their scriptures (he embarked on the whole Bible and found that much of the Old Testament sent him to sleep; while the New Testament, and the Sermon on the Mount in particular, touched him profoundly). He began to overcome his shyness and made like-minded friends among other Indian students, and with non-Indians for the first time, particularly through the Vegetarian Society.

South Africa and political action The earnest young lawyer who returned to India found that he was too shy to practise in the Bombay courts: release from petty legal work in his home town, Rajkot, came with an offer through his brother from a Porbandar Muslim firm trading in South Africa, in need of a lawyer for a year. South Africa transformed Gandhi, though he is remembered more for his work and influence in India. He lived almost continuously in South Africa from 1893 to 1914: here he raised his family, established himself as a lawyer and then as a political activist, and evolved the religious, social, and political vision which was to inspire him on his return to India and distinguish him from his Indian political contemporaries.

The most obvious change in Gandhi in South Africa was the unexpected making of a public figure, first as a successful lawyer and then as the political spokesman and leader of Indians in Natal and the Transvaal. Within days of arriving he was thrown out of a train on the cold winter night of 7 June 1893 at Pietermaritzburg Station, because a white passenger objected to sharing a compartment with an Indian, even though Gandhi had a first-class ticket. He recorded that this was a seminal experience: he resolved not to run away, back to India, but to stay and fight the colour prejudice of which this episode was a mild symptom. There was a sizeable Indian community in Natal and Transvaal by this time, composed of 'free' Indians, mostly in trade, and indentured labourers and their descendants. Despite their economic contribution to the area they faced legal restrictions as well as social discrimination:

restrictions on entry, franchise, places of trade and residence, a tax on ex-indentured labourers and their children who stayed in Africa, and attempts to enforce registration of Asians, as a means of controlling migration and settlement. When Gandhi's initial year's contract expired in 1894, he decided to stay on and combat growing pressure on Indians while earning his living as a lawyer. So began his two decades of campaigning against the many forms of anti-Indian discrimination. He took his stand on the moderate grounds that Indians were equal citizens of the British empire, following a royal proclamation of 1858; and he urged Indians to live clean and decent lives worthy of that status. He showed his own 'citizenship' by working as a stretcher bearer and organizing Indians in an ambulance corps in the Second South African War. His political work took the form of petitions and deputations, even to London in 1906 and 1909; publicity through pamphlets and letters to the press, and his own journal, *Indian Opinion*, launched in 1903; and the organization of Indian political activity through the Natal Indian Congress and the Transvaal British Indian Association. It became clear that imperial citizenship availed Indians little, as the London government was reluctant to intervene in domestic colonial affairs on their behalf. Gandhi eventually concluded that principled, peaceful resistance was the way to oppose the 'wrong' done to Indians, particularly the so-called Black Act of 1907, requiring Indian registration in the Transvaal. In South Africa such resistance took various forms between 1907 and 1914, including bonfires of registration certificates and deliberate courting of arrest for illegal border crossing. Gandhi himself was gaoled several times, and spent a total of nearly 250 days in gaol. He became known as the Indian spokesman,

Mohandas Karamchand Gandhi [Mahatma Gandhi] **(1869–1948)**, by Margaret Bourke-White, 1946

and a formidable opponent, and was in 1915 honoured by the government of India with the kaisar-i-Hind gold medal for services to Indians in South Africa. Yet his campaigns did little fundamentally to change their situation. His African experience was more important for what it did to him, creating a man not only of public experience, but of principles and religious vision. This became increasingly clear as he abandoned his comfortable, Westernized home and dress, and simplified his lifestyle (even doing his own washing and cutting his own hair). His inner transformation was clearest when he took a vow of celibacy in 1906, to free himself to care for the whole of humanity as his family, and in the two communities he founded on the lines of Hindu ashrams, Phoenix near Durban in 1904, and Tolstoy Farm near Johannesburg in 1910. These became his home, his political base, and the site of his experiments with a simple religious life which would enable him and his associates, now both European and Indian, to follow what he perceived as Truth.

Gandhi's political beliefs When Gandhi left South Africa the core of his religious vision had taken shape, though he always went on learning, 'experimenting with Truth', as he subtitled his autobiography. His main piece of extended political analysis, *Hind Swaraj* ('Indian home rule') was written in 1909, on a return voyage from England to South Africa: and his autobiography (1927) and *Satyagraha in South Africa* (1928) related primarily to his African experience. In India he wrote copiously—letters, speeches, articles in his two papers, *Young India* and *Navajivan*: but he had neither time nor temperament for extended literary activity and what he did write was for specific audiences and occasions, such as his *Discourses on the 'Gita'* (1926)—a collection of his ashram prayer discourses—and his pamphlet *The Constructive Programme* in 1941. He saw himself as pre-eminently a practical man, a truth-seeker, and insisted that his life was his real message.

Although Gandhi was not a systematic thinker, nor did he originate any belief system (though people sometimes later referred to 'Gandhism'), there is an internal consistency in his thought. At its centre were the concepts of *satya* (truth) and *ahimsa* (non-violence), both deeply embodied within Hindu tradition. In later life Gandhi often said that Truth was God, rather than that God was Truth. For him Truth was the central moral principle undergirding all existence, and infusing all life. It also demanded a personal pursuit or pilgrimage, involving discipline and devotion: a human life without such a pilgrimage was essentially subhuman. However, like the Jains from whom he drew inspiration, he saw Truth as many-faceted, incapable of total perception by any one person or religious group. It flowed from this that the pursuit of Truth, and particularly all situations and relationships of conflict, must be conducted in a non-violent way so as not to coerce the opponent or deny the opponent's vision of Truth. If Truth was the goal, then non-violence was inevitably the means. He always insisted that means and ends were inextricable: that evil means always produced evil, and that men must choose good means if they wished for

a good end. When English-speakers in South Africa called his non-violent resistance 'passive resistance' and a weapon of last resort for the weak, he replied that it was truth force, *satyagraha*, and demanded immense courage and self-discipline of its exponents, or *satyagrahis*. His own experiments with simple living, meagre diet, and sexual control were designed to create the truly non-violent yet strong and courageous individual, by decreasing wants and building inner strength and discipline.

From Gandhi's understanding of Truth flowed conclusions vital for his work in India, over and above his refinement of techniques of non-violent resistance to perceived wrong. He believed that true religion was the individual's search for Truth, and that all 'religions' were equal pathways towards Truth. Although he remained a Hindu all his life, he drew personally on the inspiration, devotion, and scriptures of other religious traditions, including Islam and Christianity. One of his favourite sayings was 'One step enough for me', taken from J. H. Newman's hymn 'Lead kindly Light': and he often referred to the inspiration of the Sermon on the Mount. He also insisted that religious tolerance was essential, not just for the individual religious pilgrimage, but for India with its many religious traditions and minority groups. His understanding of true religion also enabled him to encourage reform both of religious tradition itself and of social customs sanctioned by religious tradition. Where religious tradition stood condemned by reason and conscience, he argued for change—most clearly in India for change in the position of women, and for a revolution in the social system of caste, and particularly for the abolition of the practice of untouchability.

In the realm of political analysis Gandhi's understanding of religion drew him ultimately to oppose British rule in India and to evolve an idiosyncratic vision of *swaraj* or home rule for India. By the time he wrote *Hind Swaraj* he had come to believe that British rule was wrong, not because the raj was a colonial state as such, but because it was the means by which modern, and in his eyes materialistic and irreligious, civilization was taking root in India, replacing what he perceived to have been India's essentially religious civilization. Colonial rule had, he believed, succeeded in enthralling India not because of British might, but because of India's moral degradation—a theory Gandhi shared with many sensitive and self-critical Hindus. For him true self-rule would mean not just the departure of the British, but the radical moral transformation of Indians, manifested in changed relations among them, including religious harmony, the end of untouchability, and a return to *swadeshi*, using things made in India rather than foreign products. The external symbol of a simple Indian life was the *charkha*, or spinning-wheel; and he devoted hours daily to spinning and encouraged people to follow his example. Having abandoned Western dress in Africa, he wore *khadi*, or handspun material, loincloth and shawl, and for many of the generation influenced by him, *khadi* clothes became a nationalist uniform. Gandhi maintained resolute hostility to the modern state, manned by colonial or Indian politicians, because of its potential for organized violence, and because he felt it deprived people of the moral duty of self-regulation. His political vision of a morally renewed India after the end of the British raj was of a rural country, whose political system would be based on self-governing groups of villages: and in this sense he delighted in being considered an advocate of anarchy, or minimal government. Always for him moral self-ordering individuals, rather than political systems, were the key to genuine, radical change.

Return to India and opposition to the raj Gandhi returned permanently to India early in 1915, travelling via London, where he and his wife stayed for nearly six months in late 1914, when their visit coincided with the outbreak of the First World War. For much of this time Gandhi was exhausted and ill, and at times bedridden, the strains of his African work having taken their toll of him. But even so he was the moving spirit behind the formation of a field ambulance training corps, mainly for Indians in London. In this project he followed the pattern of non-violent, humanitarian service in wartime which he had initiated in Africa, and argued in the face of some Indian opposition that they should serve in this way because they were protected by British arms.

Gandhi was deeply moved at the thought of his eventual return to India, which he saw as his spiritual home. But he had no plans for what he would do on his arrival, believing that divine guidance would show him the road ahead. Given his priorities, his lifestyle, and appearance it was hardly surprising that on his return to India many Indians thought him strange and unmodern. Throughout his Indian career, and despite his political influence, many criticized what Jawaharlal Nehru called 'the Mahatma's fads', and were unconvinced by his vision of a rural, loosely governed country. Many, including the great poet Rabindranath Tagore, were profoundly worried about the long-term implications of non-violent resistance to government, his use of the fast as a moral weapon (V. S. S. Sastri called it 'whitemail'), and his turning away from a cosmopolitan culture which valued the artistic and material creations of the West. At a pragmatic level most of his associates in the Indian National Congress, India's oldest and most powerful political organization, felt that his 'constructive programme' deflected his own and the country's attention from the primary and urgent task of reforming and ultimately ending colonial rule. Gandhi sadly reflected on how few shared his ideals, how most preferred to leave his reform schemes as bits of paper on the floor of political meetings; but his own commitment to practical constructive work remained paramount. It was manifested in his two ashram communities, first at Sabarmati, in Ahmadabad, Bombay presidency, and then from the mid-1930s in Sevagram, near Wardha in central India. These were home to him and his wife and closest adherents, as well as temporary resting-places for the host of Indian and Western admirers and enquirers who increasingly gathered round him. They were also the environments in which he attempted to solve in microcosm many of India's health, religious, and social problems, and to train *satyagrahis* for their country's service.

Increasingly he devoted himself to hand-spinning, and to nurturing it and other village industries; to the cause of public cleanliness and simple but sound sanitation; and to the use of natural health cures and simple diet to improve the lives of the truly poor, who were in his eyes the key to India's future, and in whose service he said he found God and his own salvation. None of Gandhi's apparently 'social' work was divorced from politics. For him radical social and economic change were the basis of true *swaraj*; and his campaign against untouchability was partly religious—saving Hinduism from its internal evils—but also a recognition of the harm that would be done to India's polity in the face of the British if untouchable political separation reinforced the fracture of the body politic between Muslims and Hindus.

It was not until 1919 that it became clear that Gandhi would involve himself in Indian politics and in opposition to British rule. From his return to India until 1919 he was more involved in establishing the Sabarmati ashram, and using *satyagraha* on various local issues, such as the exploitations of indigo planters in Bihar, land revenue levels in the Kaira district, and mill-workers' wages in the Ahmadabad cotton mills. His experience of these local *satyagrahas* in 1917–18 encouraged him to attempt to organize a national *satyagraha* against the Rowlatt bills, by which the British tried in 1918, contrary to unanimous Indian political opinion, to arm themselves against political terrorism after wartime controls had lapsed. Gandhi's attempt failed, as he had no political organization of his own and was not supported by Congress. When violence broke out during the campaign, he admitted to a 'himalayan miscalculation' in suggesting *satyagraha* before people were prepared for it and called it off. But by late 1920 he had clearly decided that he must throw his weight and expertise into Congress and oppose the British raj, which he now described as 'satanic'. The turning-point of his nationalist commitment and participation was the combination of two 'wrongs'—the allied treatment of the defeated sultan of Turkey or Muslim caliph, despite Indian Muslim sensitivity, and the notorious incident in the Punjab at Jallianwalla Bagh, Amritsar, when on 10 April 1919 General Dyer ordered the shooting of unarmed civilians in a walled area from which there was no escape.

Campaigns against the raj Gandhi's subsequent political career and influence followed an unusual trajectory: it was no simple, increasing accretion of popularity and power, and for most of the time he held no formal position in Congress, and was at times not even a member. He led three major all-India *satyagraha* campaigns against the British, in 1920–22, 1930–34, and 1940–42, during each of which he was eventually imprisoned. But none of these fatally eroded British power; and when independence came in 1947, it was the result of many world-wide as well as domestic factors, and Gandhi felt increasingly isolated and inconsequential in Indian politics, while younger men negotiated with each other and the British and achieved freedom but at the price of the country's partition into India and Muslim Pakistan.

This pattern of apparent influence and power as the leader of *satyagraha* and setter of Congress priorities, and seeming isolation and inactivity in between the three big *satyagraha* movements, and his eventual impotence in politics, is explicable only if one understands Gandhi's own motivation and his power base. He believed that in *satyagraha* he had an unfailing and matchless technique, for Indian moral renewal and for opposition to the raj (for he saw that the raj ultimately relied on the paid or voluntary collaboration and acquiescence of Indians). Yet he was unwilling to risk its use if there was danger of mass violence, and if his colleagues in Congress would not submit to his direction. As in 1934, he chose to 'retire' from Congress when his compatriots preferred constitutional politics within British structures of collaboration to *satyagraha*. So for him the apparent ebbs and flows of his political power and leadership were of little import, and he felt that by small-scale constructive work he was building the foundations of *swaraj* and a new India, and keeping *satyagraha* pure and 'burnished' for use when opportunity offered. His power base reflected the nature and ambiguity of the Indian National Congress. It was a confederation of political activists from the many diverse parts of India, who had both to consider and consolidate their local power bases, and to confront their rulers in a nationalist movement. Their choices of strategy were made the trickier in the period from 1919 to 1947 by the substantial political reforms of 1919 and 1935, which offered politicians very real power through enlarged consultative structures in Delhi and the provinces, and control of large parts of the provincial administrative machinery. Few wished to engage in all-out opposition to the British, which would deprive them of the power now on offer, power that would advance their careers (even to ministerial level) and would give them access to the patronage and decision making with which to satisfy their followers. Therefore, there were only limited situations when Gandhi's *satyagraha* offered productive politics—a means of gaining more power from the British while still maintaining their local support. These were situations where the politics of constitutionalism seemed to have reached an impasse in the face of British determination to control the pace of political change—as in 1920, when the Muslim and Punjab issues seemed to nullify constitutional reform, and in 1930, when the prospect of major constitutional advance seemed unlikely after the Simon commission, or during the Second World War, when the British refused to countenance major political change during the conflict which threatened their world-wide empire, in which India was a critical base. However, few politicians were committed Gandhians; and despite the high personal regard in which he was held, and the knowledge that he had an unrivalled hold on the popular mind, most were anxious to release themselves from *satyagraha* and the Mahatma's moral politics if the mundane politics of constitutionalism seemed more productive, as they did in 1922, 1934, and again after the war ended, when ultimate political power was in sight.

Gandhi's contribution to nationalist politics Gandhi's major significance in nationalist politics was to provide Indians with a form of resistance to imperial control which generated unprecedented popular support yet did not threaten the social, economic, and political fabric of India or raise the spectre of violent struggle, which experience showed would only elicit imperial violence and coercion in return. Although he brought from Africa the core of the idea and some practical experience of non-violent resistance, in India he elaborated and refined the technique, making it infinitely more flexible and inclusive. It could take the form of withdrawal from government institutions, such as the legislatures, the law courts, or government schools, as in 1920–21. It could focus on particular issues symbolic of imperial power and public disquiet, as in opposition to the salt tax in 1930. Often it took the form of opposition to aspects of government revenue, such as land revenue or excise from liquor sales, or to foreign interests which bolstered the raj, such as Lancashire cotton imports. Gandhi was the master of communication and symbol in a society where literacy was low and there were few modes of mass communication—campaigning on issues with moral resonance, capable of generating mass understanding. For example, in 1920 he urged Indians to turn their backs on imperial 'honours' as a sign of non-co-operation with the government, and himself returned his kaisar-i-Hind medal with his Boer and Anglo-Zulu War medals. He was also a superb master of strategy—finding flexible modes of non-violent action suitable for rich and poor, educated and illiterate, men, women, and children, in striking contrast to the politics of the legislatures and the established political organizations such as Congress, which demanded high levels of education and considerable leisure. For example, women could participate in the new politics of moral protest and reconstruction, by walking in processions, helping in political organizations when their male relatives were gaoled, picketing liquor and foreign cloth shops, and donating their jewellery to finance Gandhi's work. Many women and men testified to the exciting and liberating effect Gandhi had on their previously closed worlds, how he gave them new forms of action, made them believe in a new India, and encouraged them to believe in their own strength and cast away fear of the British, which enabled tiny numbers of foreigners to rule over them.

Yet the unprecedented public response to Gandhi's campaigns also raised the critical problem of potential violence, either between Indians, which would rend apart the nationalist movement and play into British hands, or against the British, which would invite repression and mar the international repute of the movement. For this reason Gandhi searched for unifying issues on which to launch *satyagraha*. Opposition to the government's monopoly and taxation of salt, for example, was intended (unsuccessfully) to unite Hindus and Muslims in 1930. He also attempted to avoid issues and actions which would set the Indian poor against the more privileged and powerful, as with his strict instructions in the 1920–22 campaign to peasants in the United Provinces, where there was profound anti-landlord unrest intermingled with the all-India campaign of non-co-operation. He was also prepared to delay or even call off *satyagraha* rather than risk its wreck in violence, as in 1919, or in 1922 after the murder of twenty-two Indian policemen at Chauri Chaura. Ultimately in 1940–41 he hand-picked the people who were to protest against participation in the war, in an attempt to safeguard the protest's peaceful and moral nature. But in 1942, when he took the risk of the mass Quit India movement in the face of possible Japanese invasion, he knew that violence was indeed likely; but he was prepared to take that risk rather than let the political nation remain paralysed and inactive, provided that the core of his adherents remained non-violent.

Assessment of the effect of the campaigns In retrospect in the later 1940s Gandhi felt (and rightly) that Indian experiments with *satyagraha* had not been true *satyagraha*, but merely strategic uses of his suggested programmes. Had Indians shared his total principled commitment to non-violence, then the violence of 1942–3 and the horror of Hindu–Muslim carnage would not have occurred. In retrospect, too, historians can properly doubt whether *satyagraha* did much directly to change British policy. It never made administration impossible, though on occasion it sorely depleted government coffers and stretched the gaol organization to breaking-point. And in 1942, faced with the worst challenge to the raj in parts of India since 1857, the government was prepared to crack down with ferocity behind a wall of wartime secrecy. What *satyagraha* did do was help to generate a new sense of Indian identity and to legitimize the idea of the new nation both in India and abroad, and this itself was significant in British calculations about the long-term viability of the raj. It is difficult from a later perspective, but essential, to remember that the Indian nationalist movement was the first such movement in Asia or Africa in the twentieth century against a European empire: there were no precedents for the interaction between rulers and ruled in such a situation. Here Gandhi's stance as a *satyagrahi* was highly significant. He always maintained that a *satyagrahi* must be open to negotiation with the opponent and prepared to compromise on inessentials, because the goal was not necessarily the defeat of the opponent but his conversion, and the mutual enlargement of the vision of truth. In South Africa he had marked the struggle with a personal stance of courtesy throughout his negotiations with J. C. Smuts, for example. In India he was willing to talk whenever possible to the protagonists and to achieve warm personal relations with political opponents.

The most famous of these 'talks' was with Lord Irwin, viceroy in 1931, which resulted in a negotiated settlement or truce in the current *satyagraha* campaign, and enabled Gandhi in the autumn of 1931 to visit London for the second round-table conference on constitutional reform. This was the one time during Gandhi's Indian career when he travelled abroad; and he used his visit to publicize India's cause to a British and world public beyond the conference table. He stayed in a settlement in the East End of London, identifying himself with the poor rather than the privileged. He visited the cotton manufacturing areas of Lancashire, which had suffered from his campaign to use Indian goods; and went to a number of prominent educational institutions, including schools and universities—his name still adorns the visitors' book of the master of Balliol, marking the weekend he spent in the college. He took time from the conference negotiations to address MPs, church leaders, and other groups interested in India.

The transfer of power in India When war ended in 1945 the British began to negotiate the transfer of power to Indian hands, as promised in 1942 under the offer made by Sir Stafford Cripps during his abortive mission to India to achieve wartime political co-operation. At this juncture the main Congress leaders who negotiated with successive viceroys, Lord Wavell and Lord Mountbatten, were younger men than Gandhi—such as Vallabhbhai Patel, Jawaharlal Nehru, and A. K. Azad for the Indian National Congress, and M. A. Jinnah for the Muslim League. To Gandhi's intense distress these months of negotiation until independence in August 1947 were marked by increasing tension between Hindus, Muslims, and Sikhs, horrific communal violence particularly in Bengal, Bihar, and the Punjab, and the eventual partition of the country. Here, in his eyes, lay one of his greatest failures. Not only had Indians not seen the virtues of non-violence: they had ignored his exhortations about the nature of true religion and the requirement of religious tolerance if there was to be true *swaraj*. Since his South African experience Gandhi had believed that Hindus and Muslims and their religious and cultural inheritances were integral to Indian culture and India's body politic, and he denied that nationality and religious identity were synonymous. He had tried in India to repeat his African pattern of close co-operation with Muslims on issues which concerned them. But Indian Muslims were very diverse in their nature and interests, with little unity in their political goals until very near the end of colonial rule, when 'Pakistan' became a potent symbol and demand. Increasingly after the collapse of the Khilafat movement in the 1920s Gandhi saw Muslim politics develop outside his control and in growing antagonism to Congress—an antagonism which was manifested in calls for separate voting arrangements, and increasingly in actual violence. The nature of Muslim political aspiration, the precise vision Jinnah had of 'Pakistan', and the balance of responsibility for partition between the British, Congress, and the Muslim League are among the most controversial areas of historical debate. Many have argued that Gandhi's Hindu style and his use of Hindu symbol and metaphor exacerbated communal feeling, though this was certainly not his intention. His distress at the escalating communal violence led him in 1946 to a personal, unarmed walking pilgrimage through the violent areas of Bengal, in an attempt to control fear and hatred; and in 1947 to a fast in Calcutta, which soothed communal violence and caused Mountbatten to call Gandhi his one-man boundary force. He also engaged in a seemingly bizarre experiment in sexual control by sleeping naked with his young female attendants, an episode which reflected his wish to test his spiritual strength as a *satyagrahi*, in the hope that one firmly non-violent person could change a devastating situation.

Gandhi's other great sadness in the final months of his life was the failure of the new independent Indian government to change its style and structures so as to become radically different from the imperial regime. As he had feared, there was little to choose between the old and new regimes: one of his last acts was to write out a suggested new role for Congress, advising it to abandon the pursuit of power and to turn itself into an organization of social workers who would carry out the work of reconstruction he considered essential for a new India.

Assassination and cremation Gandhi was assassinated on 30 January 1948 in the grounds of Birla House in New Delhi, by a young Hindu, Nathuram Godse, who, ironically in view of Gandhi's passion for communal unity, held him responsible for the partition of the country. True to his vision of *ahimsa*, Gandhi ignored threats of violence and was convinced that death, far from being a catastrophe, might in some circumstances signify the triumph of the human quest for truth. He had been physically assaulted in South Africa, and threats had been made to his life in India. Now, late in life and despite the concern of his Congress colleagues in government, who knew that his life might be in danger, he was reluctant to accept security measures for his own protection, and insisted on walking openly without guards to his public prayer meetings, supported only by two young women on either side. He was therefore an easy target for his assailant, who pushed his way through the throng and shot him at point blank range. The tiny, frail body slumped to the ground; and the Mahatma died instantly, with the words 'He Ram' on his lips, invoking God by the name taught him by his nurse when he was a tiny, frightened child. News swept quickly through Delhi and Congressmen flocked to see the body in silent mourning: they were joined by Mountbatten, who had stayed on as governor-general of the new dominion, and who now firmly quashed any rumours that the assassin might have been a Muslim, knowing full well what carnage that would precipitate. As Gandhi had requested, his body was neither revered nor preserved; and according to Hindu custom it was cremated the next day on the banks of the Jumna River, while thousands flocked to line the streets in stunned and silent grief, the mood which Nehru articulated in a broadcast on 30 January in the words 'the light has gone out of our lives and there is darkness everywhere'. But, as he continued, 'In his death he has reminded us of the big things of life, the living truth, and if we remember that, then it will be well with India'. The site where the body was burned remains to this day, Raj Ghat, on the Delhi ring road, a place of pilgrimage and memory.

Retrospect Gandhi's assassination evoked a wave of emotion and a reaction against communalist politics in India. The manner of his death made him a martyr for the new India, and he became known in India and abroad as the father of the new Indian nation. There is no doubt that he was profoundly important in moulding the style and tone of Indian nationalist activity over more than twenty years. He gave Indians a practical technique to use in the specific circumstances of British rule, and he elicited unprecedented popular support for the national movement, while inspiring and touching the lives of many individuals. Yet recent research has shown that many of his contemporaries failed to share his ideals, despite their personal loyalty to him; and that both leaders and grass roots activists were prepared to use his appeal and techniques only when it suited their particular purposes. Many of the British thought him a tricky lawyer who used religion to cloak a drive for political power: but his willingness to divest himself of power, to suffer and ultimately to die for his beliefs, suggests that they underestimated his religious vision and motivation.

In retrospect, less immediate judgements rightly raise doubts about Gandhi's leadership and political sagacity. His experience of co-operation with Muslims in South Africa, his personal understanding of religion and eclectic tolerance, made it difficult for him to understand, let alone control, the passions which swept India towards partition on religious lines. His moderate and inclusive appeal evaded some of the hardest socio-economic issues facing the new India, while the popular support he elicited absolved Congress of the need to take seriously and appeal to the most underprivileged in Indian society, with lasting consequences for the post-independence Congress Party and the new Indian state. Moreover, his insistence on the power of *satyagraha* and the importance of the moral individual, combined with his profound hostility to the modern state, stood in the way of a political analysis and commitment which could have translated his idealism into the realm of modern politics, thus leaving his country the poorer in terms of political ideology and practice.

When the generation of his associates had died, it became clear that he was not the architect of a new India, nor the mind behind a new political strategy either for India or for the world. Rather, he had become an international symbol and inspiration for those who search for peaceful means to resolve conflict and create change. He remains, therefore, a towering figure of the twentieth century, despite his immediate failure: a symbol of anti-colonialism, and of the potential nobility of the human spirit.   JUDITH M. BROWN

Sources *The collected works of Mahatma Gandhi*, 90 vols. (1958–84) · R. Iyer, ed., *The moral and political writings of Mahatma Gandhi*, 3 vols. (1986–7) · M. K. Gandhi, *An autobiography, or, The story of my experiments with truth*, trans. M. Desai, 2 vols. (Ahmadabad, 1927–9) [Gujarati orig., *Satyana prayogo athara atmakatha* (1927)] · M. K. Gandhi, *Satyagraha in South Africa* (1928) · J. M. Brown, *Gandhi: prisoner of hope* (1989) · J. M. Brown, *Gandhi's rise to power: Indian politics, 1915–1922* (1972) · J. M. Brown, *Gandhi and civil disobedience: the Mahatma in Indian politics, 1928–34* (1977) · M. Chatterjee, *Gandhi's religious thought* · B. Parekh, *Colonialism, tradition and reform: an analysis of Gandhi's political discourse* (1989); rev. (1999) · B. Parekh, *Gandhi's political philosophy: a critical examination* (1989) · J. Nehru, *An autobiography* (1936) · M. Swan, *Gandhi: the South African experience* (1985) · M. K. Gandhi, *Hind Swaraj and other writings*, ed. A. J. Parel (1997)

Archives Gandhi National Museum and Library, New Delhi, India · Sabarmati Ashram, Ahmadabad, India | National Archives of India, New Delhi, Home Department MSS, government of India · Nehru Memorial Museum and Library, New Delhi, Nehru and Indian National Congress MSS | FILM BFI NFTVA, 'Gandhi in England', Channel 4, 2 Oct 1989 · BFI NFTVA, 'Mahatma Gandhi Noakhali March', 1947 · BFI NFTVA, current affairs footage · BFI NFTVA, documentary footage · BFI NFTVA, news footage · IWM FVA, 'Mahatma: the life of Gandhi', 1970, MGH 749-1 to 748-33 · IWM FVA, actuality footage · IWM FVA, documentary footage · IWM FVA, news footage | SOUND IWM SA, oral history interview · IWM SA, recorded talk

Likenesses photograph, 1930, Hult. Arch.; *see illus. in* Naidu, Sarojini (1879–1949) · screen print, 1932 (after J. Kramer), NPG · M. Bourke-White, photograph, 1946, Rheinisches Bildarchiv, Cologne [*see illus.*] · statue, 1993, near town hall, Pietermaritzburg, Natal, South Africa · portraits, Gandhi National Museum, New Delhi

Wealth at death virtually nothing, except clothes (minimal), spectacles, pen, and spinning-wheel

Gandhi, Rajiv (1944–1991). *See under* Gandhi, Indira Priyadarshini (1917–1984).

Gandhi, Sanjay (1946–1980). *See under* Gandhi, Indira Priyadarshini (1917–1984).

Gandolphy [Gandolphi], **Peter** (1779–1821), Roman Catholic priest, born in London on 26 July 1779, was the second of the three sons (Francis, Peter, and Joseph) of John Vincent Gandolphy or Gandolphi (c.1739–1816?) of Sheen and his second wife, Jane (c.1751–1825?), daughter of John Hyde of Hyde End, Berkshire. With his first wife, Anna Maria Hinde, John Vincent had a son, another John Vincent, and a daughter, Anne. Peter Gandolphy was educated by the English Jesuits at Liège Academy and then, in 1794, moved to Stonyhurst College in Lancashire, where in 1801 he was appointed to teach humanities. He held this post until 1804, when he was ordained priest by Bishop John Douglass, vicar apostolic of the London district, at the Spanish Chapel, Manchester Square, London. Despite the claims of the *Dictionary of National Biography* article, there is no evidence that Gandolphy was a Jesuit.

Gandolphy's first appointment as a priest was to the mission at Newport, Isle of Wight, in the early summer of 1804. In 1806 he became a chaplain at the Spanish Chapel. In appearance he is said to have been short in stature and unprepossessing, owing to a distortion of the neck, but he was ardent and intense, with a good command of language both as a preacher and writer. These qualities were to lead him into trouble with Bishop William Poynter, the successor to Bishop Douglass. Gandolphy published letters to the press and pamphlets on matters of controversy, and in 1810 began to publish volumes of his sermons, the first of which was entitled *A Defence of the Ancient Faith*. Two years later appeared *Liturgy, or, A Book of Common Prayer, and administration of sacraments, with other rites and ceremonies of the church*. It seemed from the title and from the manner in which he dealt with the subject that he was trying to assimilate his language to that of the Church of England.

The book sold well and, when a second edition was called for, Gandolphy asked the vicars apostolic in 1813 for permission to dedicate it to them. Except for Bishop John Milner of the midland district, they took exception to the title and the language used (the mass, for instance, was referred to as the sacrament of the Lord's Supper), noted that there were theological errors, and refused to allow publication. Milner, who thought the book 'orthodox' and 'valuable' despite 'some looseness of expression' (Ward, 2.208–9), allowed the book in his district, and the second edition was printed in Birmingham with a slight change of title and many corrections in the text. Bishop Poynter forbade its use in the London district, and the sale of the third and fourth volumes of Gandolphy's sermons, which he considered to contain theological errors and unclear statements. Gandolphy submitted and stopped the sale of his books for a time, but decided to appeal in person to Rome. There he obtained in 1816 an approbation, after some minor corrections had been made, by two censors appointed by the master of the Sacred Palace. Nevertheless, Poynter called on Gandolphy to withdraw the books from sale in the London district until the Congregatio de Propaganda Fide in Rome had pronounced on the text. On his failure to do so the bishop suspended him in September 1816 for disobedience. Gandolphy replied on 5 October with his *Address to the Public*, of which the bishop complained to Rome. It was decided in Rome that Gandolphy should apologize to Poynter and express his willingness to make the necessary corrections in his books as soon as any errors were definitely pointed out, while refraining in the meantime from circulating the books. The bishop would then be obliged to return his faculties. Gandolphy apologized in 1817 but the bishop declared the apology insufficient. In July Gandolphy made another unconditional apology and received back his faculties.

After examination in Rome, Gandolphy's books were condemned in 1818 and he was ordered to withdraw them from circulation. This, he said, he was unable to do as he had sold the copyright some years before. In February 1820 he made a final apology to the bishop. By then he had retired from the Spanish Chapel to live with his relatives at East Sheen, where he died on 9 July 1821. He was buried in St Pancras old churchyard, London.

Gandolphy's friend Milner wrote of his good qualities: 'whatever inaccuracy there was in some of the writer's expressions, there was no heterodox or dangerous principle in his mind' (Gillow, *Lit. biog. hist.*, 2.366). But he thought him wrong-headed, since 'he generally asks my advice but in no instance has he followed it' (Milner's letters, 2.128, Jesuit Province Archives, London). George Oliver, who had known Gandolphy from Stonyhurst days, believed 'all his friends must admit that he wrote too much and published too rapidly not to err against theological precision' (Oliver, 83), but he admired his zeal, charity, and submission. Gandolphy's *Lessons of Morality and Piety; Extracted from the Sapiential Books of Holy Scripture* was published posthumously in 1822, revised and approved by Milner.   GEOFFREY HOLT

Sources Gillow, *Lit. biog. hist.*, 2.365–8 · B. N. Ward, *The eve of Catholic emancipation*, 3 vols. (1911–12), vol. 2, pp. 205–20 · *DNB* · H. Foley, ed., *Records of the English province of the Society of Jesus*, 7/1 (1882), 286 ·

G. Oliver, *Collections towards illustrating the biography of the Scotch, English and Irish members, SJ* (1838), 83 · P. Gandolphy, 'Forma Declarationis a R. D. Petro Gandolphy Eliciendae', *Orthodox Journal and Catholic Monthly Intelligencer*, 5/49 (June 1817), 269–70 · Burke, *Gen. GB* · Milner's letters, 2, 128, Jesuit Province Archives, London · Westm. DA, 017/81 938 3580
Archives Archives of the British Province of the Society of Jesus, Stonyhurst College, Lancashire | Archives of the British Province of the Society of Archives, London, Milner MSS · Westm. DA, Bramston MSS · Westm. DA, Poynter MSS · Westm. DA, Gradwell MSS
Wealth at death all personal property to sister: will, 1821, PRO

Gandon, James (1742–1823), architect, was born on 20 February 1742 in New Bond Street, London, at the house of his grandfather Peter Gandon, a French Huguenot refugee. He was the only son of Peter Gandon (*b*. 1713), a gunmaker, and Jane Burchall (possibly *née* Wynne), a widow. A second child, Mary, was born in 1743. The architect's father neglected his affairs to dabble in alchemy and was declared a bankrupt in 1754, thereby curtailing his son's education at a boarding-school in Kensington. James continued his studies at home (principally classics and mathematics) and enrolled in evening classes at William Shipley's drawing academy. Gandon spent two years there, acquiring the skills of a draughtsman and a 'theoretic knowledge of architecture' (Gandon and Mulvany, 12).

About 1757 the architect William Chambers took on Gandon as his first apprentice 'at a very moderate fee' (Gandon and Mulvany, 14); one of his clients, the earl of Charlemont, gave Gandon particular encouragement in his studies. In 1764–5 he began to practise independently but his architectural output over the following sixteen years, before he moved to Ireland, was rather limited. Gandon exhibited in 1762 and 1763 at the Free Society of Artists where he was a member, at the Society of Artists from 1765 to 1773, and at the Royal Academy from 1774 to 1780. From 1762 he competed for Society of Arts premiums, beating Thomas Cooley in 1764 with a design for a 'Country-house and Offices … decorated in the Palladian Style'. In 1769 he entered the Royal Academy Schools as a rather mature student, and was awarded their gold medal in architecture. This ultimately resulted in a belated offer by the academy in 1790 to send him to Rome, which he declined. Gandon never made the grand tour and his knowledge of European architecture came secondhand from Chambers and from James Stuart, with whom he had a brief professional association.

In 1767 Gandon published *Six Designs of Frizes*, before collaborating with the Irishman John Woolfe, of the office of works, in the production of two volumes of *Vitruvius Britannicus*, issued in 1767 and 1771 as successors to Colen Campbell's publications of a generation earlier. More than half the plates were drawn by Woolfe but the later volume included two versions of one of Gandon's own designs, the county hall at Nottingham, built in 1769–72. In this competent if unspectacular building his use of Roman themes, notably triumphal arches and motifs from the interior of the Pantheon, anticipated his mature work: he favoured Roman over Greek sources. In 1768–9 he took part in the competition to design the royal

exchange, Dublin, but was beaten into second place by Cooley, who moved to Ireland on the strength of his win. Third premium was awarded to Gandon's great friend and promoter the artist and draughtsman Paul Sandby. Gandon's designs do not survive. In 1777 Gandon won first premium for the rebuilding of St Luke's Hospital, London, but lost the commission to the incumbent architect George Dance. Other projects of these years include designs for two Irish buildings—the deanery at Killaloe, co. Clare (1768; unexecuted) and Heywood, Queen's county (1771; dem.), built to a modified design by its proprietor, the amateur architect Frederick Trench.

On 26 July 1770 Gandon married Eleanor Smullen (*d. c*.1790?) at St Paul's Church, Covent Garden. In the following year he bought a house in Broad Street. Their eldest child, Mary Anne, was born in July 1771. She was followed by a boy and three girls: James (1772), Eleanor (1774), Anne, who died in infancy (1775), and Elizabeth (1776).

Through Sandby, Gandon met, around 1779, the Russian Princess Dashkova, who invited him to St Petersburg 'to conduct the erection of some public buildings' (Gandon and Mulvany, 41). She may have seen some of Gandon's classical capriccios in the manner of Charles-Louis Clérisseau, whose work was collected by her friend Catherine the Great. Gandon declined the invitation, but soon received another offer, this time from Lord Carlow, who proposed to set up a syndicate to employ him in Ireland. Nothing came of this but a year later, in November 1780, through Carlow's good offices, Gandon received an invitation from John Beresford, chief commissioner of the Irish revenue, to consider a 'new plan for a building of a public nature in Ireland' (ibid., 43). Beresford's potentially contentious scheme, developed in secrecy, was for a new Dublin custom house, docks, and stores, to be constructed downstream from the established city centre. Following his arrival in the city in April 1781, Gandon developed his designs but the works were delayed and he returned to England, where his wife was in poor health. The *Life of James Gandon* claims that this illness proved fatal but there is evidence that she was still living in London at the end of the 1780s. When he returned to Dublin in March 1782 he took his three children with him.

The political and technical obstacles to Beresford's scheme were eventually overcome, with Gandon taking particular pride in his method of forming foundations in the riverbank. The elevations, apparently based on a proportioning system, reflected his interests in antiquity and Franco-Roman neo-classicism, coupled with English influences such as Wren and Chambers. Gandon also paid attention to craftsmanship and championed the local carver Edward Smyth. Construction took ten years, with the dock and several blocks of stores (dem.) following in 1792–1803. In the meantime he had undertaken another project for the revenue, the construction of Carlisle Bridge (1791–5, replaced 1880). For Beresford's son John Claudius he designed a crescent of five houses facing the north front of the Custom House (1788–93). Through Beresford's brother Lord Tyrone, Gandon obtained the commission for a court house (a stylistic development of the scheme for Nottingham) and gaol at Waterford (1784–7; dem.). An earlier Waterford commission, the design of the model town of New Geneva (1783–4), proved abortive.

Gandon's second major public building in Dublin was the Four Courts, also on the Liffey, on which he worked from 1785. The site had been allocated to the public law offices and King's Inns, and two western ranges of offices had been constructed by Cooley before his death in 1784. Gandon modified the layout in order to insert the court accommodation in a domed centre block, completed in 1796: symmetrical eastern ranges were added in 1798–1802. Like the custom house, the Four Courts was an eclectic design, though its effect relies more on massing than refinement of detail. In the event the King's Inns were built elsewhere, in Henrietta Street, and although Gandon was involved in their development from 1794, construction did not begin until 1800. Earlier Gandon had been separately approached by the building committees of the Irish House of Lords (in 1782) and House of Commons (in 1786) to prepare designs for altering their respective sections of the parliament house on College Green. The most significant element constructed was the House of Lords' Corinthian portico (1784–7). For the barrack board he designed (in 1786) the Royal Military Infirmary, overlooking Phoenix Park, which was completed, with some modifications, by a superintending architect, William Gibson. He worked for the governors of the lying-in hospital between 1784 and 1791, designing a new entrance block to its assembly rooms and embellishing the elevations of the rotunda proper. Gandon's success engendered resentment in some quarters and he was attacked by an anonymous though well-informed critic in a series of vituperative letters to a Dublin newspaper in 1785–86, later reprinted in pamphlet form. The King's Inns was to be Gandon's last Dublin undertaking: frustrated by delays, he resigned c.1808 in favour of his assistant Henry Aaron Baker and retired to his estate at Canonbrook, near Lucan.

As well as his public buildings, Gandon worked for a number of individual patrons. Designs for several villas survive, a few of which were built, but he was responsible for only one major country house, Emo Court in Queen's county, commissioned by Lord Carlow and begun in the early 1790s but not completed until the 1850s. The nearby parish church at Coolbanagher was built from Gandon's designs c.1782–5. Gandon also designed a villa for Sir William Gleadowe-Newcomen at Carricklass, co. Longford, c.1790 but only the triumphal-arch entrance gates, stable, and farmyards were built. In co. Dublin, Gandon's villa work included extensions to Abbeville, Kinsealy, for John Beresford (c.1790), Emsworth, Malahide, for James Woodmason (1794), and a house at Sandymount for the painter William Ashford (c.1788). In the city he added a library (1789) to Lord Charlemont's house in Rutland Square.

Slim in his youth, by his late thirties Gandon was both overweight and balding. He suffered for most of his life from gout. He was a member of the London Architects' Club and was elected a fellow of the Society of Antiquaries

in 1797. In 1823 he was offered membership of the newly incorporated Royal Irish Academy, but declined on the grounds of age and infirmity. He died on Christmas eve of that year and was buried in Drumcondra churchyard, Dublin, alongside his friend the antiquary Francis Grose. While sheltering in London during the Irish rising of 1798 Gandon began work on a book of his life and work. It was not, however, until after his death that *The Life of James Gandon* was edited by his son James and the artist Thomas John Mulvany. It was published in 1846 with two of Gandon's essays as appendices.

Gandon was the most significant Irish-based architect of the neo-classical era and his impact on the architectural development of Dublin was unparalleled. His major buildings survive, though both the custom house and the Four Courts were destroyed by fire in the 1920s and reconstructed with modifications, including much simplified interior decoration.   FREDERICK O'DWYER

Sources J. Gandon and T. J. Mulvany, eds., *The life of James Gandon* (1846) • J. Gandon and T. J. Mulvany, eds., *The life of James Gandon* (1846); repr. with introduction by M. Craig (1969) • E. McParland, *James Gandon: Vitruvius Hibernicus* (1985) • H. Duffy, *James Gandon and his times* (1999) • J. Woolfe and J. Gandon, *Vitruvius Britannicus*, 4, 5 (1767–71) • J. Malton, *A picturesque and descriptive view of the city of Dublin* (1799) • E. McParland, 'James Gandon and the Royal Exchange competition', *Journal of the Royal Society of Antiquaries of Ireland*, 102 (1972), 58–72 • E. McParland, 'The early history of James Gandon's Four Courts', *Burlington Magazine*, 122 (1980), 727–35
Likenesses P. Sandby, wash drawing, c.1770, Royal Library, Windsor Castle • P. Sandby, group portrait, wash drawing, 1780, Yale U. CBA • P. Sandby, group portrait, wash drawing, 1780 (as part of composition *Garden of the British Museum during the encampment*), Royal Collection • H. Hone, watercolour miniature, 1799, FM Cam. • J. Comerford, drawing, 1805 • H. Hone, watercolour miniature, NG Ire. • T. Kettle and W. Cuming, oils, NG Ire. • H. Meyer, stipple (after J. Comerford), BM, NG Ire., NPG • H. Meyer, stipple and etching (after H. Hone), BM, NG Ire. • engraving (after H. Hone), repro. in Gandon and Mulvany, *Life* (1846), frontispiece
Wealth at death under £14,000; property in Dublin city; estate at Lucan, co. Dublin: Gandon and Mulvany, *Life*, 232–3

Gandy, Henry (*bap.* 1649, *d.* 1734), bishop of the nonjuring Church of England, was baptized at St Paul's, Exeter, on 23 September 1649, the son of John Gandy (1604/5–1672). His father, vicar of South Brent in Devon, had been ejected from his living and suffered a period of imprisonment in 1644; from 1652 he held the living of Bridford in the same county and was restored to South Brent in 1660. Educated at Merchant Taylors' School from 1663, Gandy matriculated from Oriel College, Oxford, on 15 March 1667, graduating BA in 1670 and MA in 1674. Ordained to the ministry at the conclusion of his studies he served in several capacities at Oriel College, including senior proctor (1683), senior treasurer (1687), and dean (1679–80, 1686–9). He also held the living of St Leonard's, Exeter, a position he lost at the revolution of 1688. He was married to Anne, with whom he had at least one daughter, Anne, baptized on 28 October 1717 at St Andrew's, Holborn, London.

After Gandy refused to take the oaths to William and Mary in 1689 the provost of Oriel College declared his place vacant, and Gandy joined the nascent nonjuring community. A strong advocate of divine right monarchy he wrote several anonymous pamphlets against rebellion and schism, including *An Answer to some Queries Concerning Schism, Toleration &c. in a Letter to a Friend* (1700), and *Old England, or, The Government of England Prov'd to be Monarchical and Hereditary* (1705). In another anonymous tract entitled *Remarks on a Sermon, Preached January the 31st 1703/4* (1704) he rebuked White Kennett, then rector of Shottesbrooke, for abandoning his divine right principles in the pursuit of preferment. He also edited a compilation of seventeenth-century tracts entitled *Bibliotheca scriptorum Ecclesiae Anglicanae* at the suggestion of George Hickes, which defended the orthodoxy and catholicity of the Church of England against the challenges of non-conformity.

A strong defender of both divine right monarchy and episcopacy, Gandy strongly supported continuing the separation from the established church even after the last of the deprived bishops, Thomas Ken, returned to the Church of England. In his *A Conference between Gerontius and Junius* (1711), Gandy offered an anonymous rebuttal to Henry Dodwell's *A Case in View now in Fact*, arguing that Dodwell had betrayed his earlier principles in returning to the established church. Gandy remained a leading member of the nonjuring community until his death, being consecrated bishop in 1716, with Thomas Brett, by Jeremy Collier, Nathaniel Spinckes, and Samuel Hawes, at his oratory at Scroop's Court in the parish of St Andrew's, Holborn.

Soon after his consecration Gandy broke with Brett and Collier over the question of the usages, a series of four ancient liturgical acts that Brett and Collier sought to restore to the liturgy, preferring to remain true to the established liturgy. Gandy remained steadfast in his opposition to the usages, rebuffing Brett's overtures for reunion in 1727, arguing that any alterations in the sacraments must await a lawfully called convocation. Reunion of Gandy's non-usages party with Brett and most of the usages party finally came in 1732 when Brett agreed to abandon the usages and use the established liturgy.

Gandy did not long survive this reunion: he died of a palsy at Scroop's Court on 26 February 1734 at the age of eighty-four. He was buried at St Pancras churchyard, where the curate was acquainted with the nonjurors. Nonjuring bishop Richard Rawlinson, whom Gandy and two others consecrated as bishop in 1728, officiated. Gandy was survived by his wife and daughter. A notice of his death in the *Daily Post* described him as 'a person of great piety, singular modesty, extremely temperate, diligent and regular through the whole course of his life' (Overton, 152).   ROBERT D. CORNWALL

Sources G. C. Richards and C. L. Shadwell, *The provosts and fellows of Oriel College, Oxford* (1922) • Foster, *Alum. Oxon.* • *Remarks and collections of Thomas Hearne*, ed. C. E. Doble and others, 11 vols., OHS, 2, 7, 13, 34, 42–3, 48, 50, 65, 67, 72 (1885–1921) • H. Broxap, *The later nonjurors* (1924) • J. H. Overton, *The nonjurors: their lives, principles, and writings* (1902) • G. V. Bennett, *White Kennett, 1660–1728* (1957) • 'The memoirs of the life of Mr. John Kettlewell', *A complete collection of the works of the reverend and learned John Kettlewell, B. D.*, 2 vols. (1719), vol. 1, pp. 1–188 • J. Carter, *The life and times of John Kettlewell*, ed. T. T. Carter (1895) • *A biographical history of England, from the revolution to*

the end of George I's reign: being a continuation of the Rev. J. Granger's work, ed. M. Noble, 3 vols. (1806) • IGI • *Walker rev.* • will, PRO, PROB 11/664, sig. 60
Archives Bodl. Oxf., MSS Rawl.
Wealth at death £50 to daughter on coming of age: will, PRO, PROB 11/664, sig. 60

Gandy, James (1618/19–1689), portrait painter, was of obscure origins. He was the father of William *Gandy (d. 1729), also a portrait painter. Probably the most reliable commentator on James Gandy is Matthew Pilkington. He informs us that the artist died in 1689 aged seventy and that he was:

> instructed by Vandyck, and his works are proof of the signal improvement he received from the precepts and example of that great master. The cause of his being so unknown, was his being brought into Ireland by the old Duke of Ormonde, and retained in his service … There are at this time in Ireland, many portraits painted by him, of noblemen and persons of fortune, which are very little inferior to Vandyck's either for expression, colouring, or dignity: and several of his copies after Vandyck, which were in the Ormonde collection at Kilkenny, were sold for original paintings of Vandyck. (Pilkington, 208)

It may be that James Gandy was the anonymous painter recommended to Ormond's agent as a copyist, by Sir Peter Lely in 1663: 'Mr Lilly tells me that there is one very good at cappeinge in Dublin' (*Ormonde MSS*, 3.55). Later writers on the artist, such as James Northcote, C. H. Collins Baker, and G. Pyecroft all drew on Pilkington as their source. Pyecroft was the first to suggest that James Gandy was born in Exeter, although this is probably a loose interpretation of Pilkington's information (Pycroft, 46). The Irish writer Walter Strickland also based his text on Pilkington's work and provided a list of paintings that he attributed, incorrectly in some cases, to James Gandy (Strickland, 1.394–5). Pilkington's assertion of a link between Gandy and Van Dyck forms the basis for attributing two well-painted portraits of Charles I and Henrietta Maria (Dúchas, Kilkenny Castle) to that artist. James Gandy's portrait of Elizabeth Bourke, Viscountess Dillon (who later married Sheffield Grace, esquire), listed by Strickland, was engraved by Robert Graves before 1822; a damaged version of this portrait (c.1660; priv. coll.) came to light at the end of the twentieth century. An oval portrait of Charles Cutliffe (c.1670; St James's Church, Swimbridge, Devon), painted on copper and inserted into Cutliffe's monument, has been attributed to James Gandy (Hoskins, 483). There is a stylistic link, however, between this work and the early portraits of Gandy's son, William. These similarities and the superficial Van Dyckian qualities of William's early work suggest that James Gandy was his son's earliest teacher. The portraits in Exeter, Devon, attributed to the elder Gandy by C. H. Collins Baker and also that of Deborah Hopton and child (Royal Albert Memorial Museum and Art Gallery, Exeter) bear little resemblance to the aforementioned works. James Gandy died in 1689.

L. H. CUST, *rev.* T. J. FENLON

Sources M. Pilkington, *A dictionary of painters: from the revival of the art to the present period*, ed. H. Fuseli, new edn (1805), 208 • W. G. Strickland, *A dictionary of Irish artists*, 1 (1913), 394–5 • C. H. C. Baker, *Lely and the Stuart portrait painters: a study of English portraiture before* *and after van Dyck*, 2 (1912), 56–63 • W. G. Hoskins, *Devon* (1954), 483 • T. J. Fenlon, 'The idle and talented Mr William Gandy in Ireland', *Irish Arts Review Yearbook*, 12 (1996), 130–38 • *Calendar of the manuscripts of the marquess of Ormonde*, new ser., 8 vols., HMC, 36 (1902–20), vol. 3, p. 55 • G. Pycroft, *Art in Devonshire: with the biographies of artists born in that county* (1883), 4–5, 46–50 • J. Northcote, *Memoirs of Sir Joshua Reynolds*, 1 (1813), 338–43 • *Catalogue of oil paintings, watercolours, drawings, and sculpture in the permanent collection*, Royal Albert Memorial Museum and Art Gallery, Exeter, ed. [C. J. Baker] (1978) • S. Grace, *Memoirs of the family of Grace* (1823)

Gandy, John Peter. *See* Deering, John Peter (1787–1850).

Gandy, Joseph Michael (1771–1843), architect and artist, was born on 2 September 1771 in Aldgate, London, and baptized on 29 September 1771 at St Botolph, Aldgate, one of the ten children of Thomas Gandy (*d.* 1814), a butler and waiter at White's Club, and his wife, Sophia, *née* Adams. It was at White's that Gandy, at the age of fifteen, was discovered by the prominent and fashionable architect James Wyatt, who took him in as a pupil in 1787. Joseph's younger brothers Michael *Gandy and John Peter *Deering later followed him in pursuit of architectural careers that also began in Wyatt's office. In November 1788 Gandy entered the Royal Academy Schools, where in 1790 he was awarded a gold medal for a design of a triumphal arch. From 1794 until 1797 he travelled and studied in Italy, most notably competing in the student architectural *concorso* sponsored by the Accademia di San Luca in Rome, which awarded a special premium to Gandy's design for a sepulchral chapel in 1795. The French invasion of the Papal States ended his Italian sojourn and he returned to London uncertain and anxious about his professional prospects. Gandy's rapidly developing skills as a designer and draughtsman fluent in the most grandiloquent neo-classical style were recognized by the architect Sir John Soane, who in 1798 hired him as a paid assistant. Although Gandy left Soane's office in 1801 to establish his own practice, he continued to serve as Soane's draughtsman in preparing impressive watercolour perspective drawings of Soane's architecture for the annual Royal Academy exhibitions.

Gandy never truly succeeded in establishing his own architectural practice. Residing for most of his career in a series of rented houses in Soho, which also accommodated makeshift studios and offices, he led a life of persistent financial distress. In 1801 he married Eleanor Webb, with whom he had a family of nine children. Gandy was twice incarcerated in debtors' prison, at Fleet Street prison in 1816 and at Whitecroft Street prison in 1830. From 1809 until 1810 he settled in Liverpool and entered into an unsuccessful partnership with the sculptor and furniture designer George Bullock. His letters and the comments of contemporaries suggest a temperament at once exceedingly prideful and paranoiac. Gandy was alternately guarded and impolitic in his dealings with clients and colleagues; the painter John Constable noted Gandy's reputation as 'a "bad-mannered" man … rude to any gentleman or nobleman who found fault with his designs' (Lukacher, 'Joseph Michael Gandy', 81). He briefly tutored Soane's eldest son in architecture and two of his own

children undertook artistic careers: Thomas as a portraitist and Hannah as a still-life painter.

Among Gandy's few commissioned buildings, the most significant include the Phoenix Fire and Pelican Life Insurance Office, Charing Cross, London (1804–5; dem.), Storrs Hall on Lake Windermere (1804–11), and Doric House, Bath (1816–18). Gandy favoured a severe neo-classical style with an innovative approach to the application of the orders and Graeco-Roman ornament in modern architecture. He supplemented his limited practice with publishing ventures, including two pattern books of model cottages in a simplified picturesque style, *Designs for Cottages … and other Rural Buildings* (1805) and *The Rural Architect* (1806). Gandy also prepared drawings for antiquarian and topographical publications on medieval architecture by John Britton that were engraved in *Architectural Antiquities of Great Britain* (1807–14) and *Cathedral Antiquities of Great Britain: Exeter* (1825–7).

Throughout his career Gandy exhibited his architectural perspective drawings at the Royal Academy. Elected as an associate of the RA in 1803, his ambition to gain election as a full academician on the basis of his architectural watercolours was never fulfilled (six nominations for this academic promotion failed between 1809 and 1820). Gandy's exhibits presented epic designs for imperial palaces and national monuments, literary illustrations inspired by Ovid, Ariosto, and Milton, and, most frequently, imaginative reconstructions of ancient Greek architectural monuments and temple precincts. Often emulating the scale of history paintings, these elaborate watercolours received critical praise in contemporary reviews of the RA exhibitions: the critics often classified Gandy as a poetical and historical landscapist comparable to J. M. W. Turner and John Martin. Reviewers also alluded to Gandy's unfortunate failure as a practising architect, as a critic for the *Morning Chronicle* observed in 1832: 'Modern times have given birth to no such genius in design as this man, as extraordinary in his talent as in the neglect he has experienced' (cited in Lukacher, 'Joseph Michael Gandy', 84).

Gandy was fascinated by architectural theory and the comparative study of ancient religion and mythology. He published two short papers on architectural symbolism entitled 'On the philosophy of architecture' in the *Magazine of the Fine Arts and Monthly Review of Painting* (1821). His study of mythography, archaeology, and architectural theory resulted in a voluminous unpublished treatise that he wrote in the 1830s, 'The art, philosophy, and science of architecture'. From 1836 to 1838 (the last year in which he exhibited at the Royal Academy) Gandy showed a series of watercolours entitled Comparative Architecture, incorporating a pictorial world history of architecture and its religious cultures. In the 1841 census he was listed as a patient at the Plympton House Asylum, Plympton St Maurice, Devon, where he died on Christmas day, 1843. His wife survived him.

BRIAN LUKACHER

Sources B. Lukacher, 'Joseph Michael Gandy: the poetical representation and mythography of architecture', PhD diss., University of Delaware, 1987 • B. Lukacher, 'Joseph Gandy and the mythography of architecture', *Journal of the Society of Architectural Historians*, 53 (1994), 280–99 • J. Summerson, 'The vision of J. M. Gandy', *Heavenly mansions and other essays on architecture* (1949), 111–34 • Colvin, *Archs.* • *Joseph Michael Gandy (1771–1843)* (Architectural Association, 1982) • B. Lukacher, 'John Soane and his draughtsman Joseph Michael Gandy', *Daidalos: Berlin Architectural Journal*, 25 (Sept 1987), 51–64 • F. Salmon, 'An unaccountable enemy: Joseph Michael Gandy and the Accademia di San Luca in Rome', *Georgian Group Journal*, [5] (1995), 25–36 • *IGI* • J. Ingamells, ed., *A dictionary of British and Irish travellers in Italy, 1701–1800* (1997)

Archives NRA, priv. coll., 'Gandy Green Book', letters, autobiographical writings, and family history • Sir John Soane's Museum, 'G' corresp. packet | RIBA BAL, corresp. with his father Thomas Gandy [copies]

Likenesses H. W. Pickersgill, pencil drawing, *c.*1820–1822, NPG

Wealth at death £200: administration, PRO, PROB 6/220/96

Gandy, Michael (*bap.* **1773**, *d.* **1862**), architect, was baptized at St Botolph, Aldgate, London, in October 1773. He was the son of Thomas Gandy (*d.* 1814), who was employed at White's Club, St James's, and his wife, Sophia, *née* Adams. His five brothers included Joseph Michael *Gandy and John Peter *Deering, and he also had four sisters. Following his marriage, he and his wife, Susannah, had several children, including two sons, Michael Gandy (*bap.* 21 Jan 1810) and Charles Deering Gandy. Gandy was a pupil of his elder brother Joseph Michael Gandy, and from 1793 of James Wyatt, whose assistant he was from 1796. In 1796 he was admitted to the Royal Academy Schools, and exhibited at the Royal Academy from 1795 to 1797. He left Wyatt for a post in the Indian naval service, and served in India and China for some years. On his return to Britain he worked as a draughtsman for Edward Hall, civil architect to the navy, and later for the architect Francis Goodwin. In 1812 he exhibited *The Burning of Onrust and Kupers Island, Batavia, in 1800, Drawn on the Spot* at the Royal Academy. He worked for Sir Jeffry Wyatville from 1807 until Wyatville's death in 1840. In 1842 he published with Benjamin Baud *Architectural Illustrations of Windsor Castle*, with a historical account by John Britton. Gandy died in April 1862.

L. H. CUST, rev. ANNE PIMLOTT BAKER

Sources Colvin, *Archs.* • S. C. Hutchison, 'The Royal Academy Schools, 1768–1830', *Walpole Society*, 38 (1960–62), 123–91 • *IGI* • Graves, *Artists* • [W. Papworth], ed., *The dictionary of architecture*, 11 vols. (1853–92)

Archives RIBA, London, corresp. with his father • RIBA, London, treatise on architecture

Gandy, William (*d.* **1729**), portrait painter, was the son of James *Gandy (1618/19–1689), also a portrait painter. George Vertue's notes inform us that 'Mr. Gandy of Exeter received instruction from Caspar (or Gaspar) Smitz in London' (BL, Add. MS 23072, fol. 21*v*). As Caspar Smitz is known to have been in Ireland by 1681 and to have remained there until his death in 1688, it is assumed that Gandy was in London before Smitz's arrival in Dublin. By 1687 Gandy was also in Dublin, shortly after he had painted a portrait of *James Butler, 2nd Duke of Ormonde, when Lord Ossory* (*c.*1686, NMM). He painted at least three other Irish sitters during the 1690s, including Richard Parsons, first earl of Rosse (*c.*1698, Oxmantown Settlement Trust, Birr Castle, King's county). His portraits from his Irish

period demonstrate knowledge of the work of Willem Wissing and his assistant Jan Vandervaart.

Gandy must have moved to Exeter at the turn of the century, because there is a fine signed portrait, *Master Willcock, Son of the Sheriff of Exeter* (*c.*1700, priv. coll.). The Willcock portrait should be regarded as his masterpiece, and in works such as this can be seen some basis for Sir Joshua Reynolds's reported admiration of his painterly technique. His later career in south-west England is well documented by the number of portraits to be found in that area. He painted several Exeter worthies, including a strikingly confident portrait of Sir Henry Langford, bt (*c.*1710, Royal Albert Memorial Museum and Art Gallery, Exeter). The portrait of William Jane, dean of Gloucester and chanter of Exeter (1706, Bodleian Library, Oxford) was originally signed and dated on the back; his portrait of the Revd John Gilbert was engraved by Vertue. Gandy moved in 1714 to Plymouth, where he painted members of the Northcote family and other prominent families. By then an old man, he was difficult in manner and careless in his work. James Northcote RA later described Gandy's rendering of the drapery in his grandmother's portrait as slovenly and painted 'from a print after Kneller' (Northcote, 343). An illustration of such practice is the double portrait of Elizabeth and Sarah Gould (priv. coll.), which is obviously based on Sir Godfrey Kneller's portrait, *Henrietta Churchill, Duchess of Marlborough, and Anne Churchill, Countess of Sunderland* (1688, Althorp, Northamptonshire), engraved by John Smith. William Gandy was buried on 14 July 1729 in St Paul's churchyard, Exeter.

T. J. FENLON

Sources T. J. Fenlon, 'The idle and talented Mr William Gandy in Ireland', *Irish Arts Review Yearbook*, 12 (1996), 130–38 • J. Northcote, *Memoirs of Sir Joshua Reynolds*, 1 (1813), 338–43 • C. H. C. Baker, *Lely and the Stuart portrait painters: a study of English portraiture before and after van Dyck*, 2 (1912), 56–63 • George Vertue's notebooks, BL, Add. MS 23072, fol. 21*v* • BL, Ellis MSS, Add. MS 28938, fols. 444–5 • BL, Ellis MSS, Add. MS 28876, fols. 1 and 3 • Mrs R. Lane Poole, ed., *Catalogue of portraits in the possession of the university, colleges, city and county of Oxford*, 3 vols. (1912–25), vol. 1, p. 77 • J. D. Stewart, *Sir Godfrey Kneller and the English baroque portrait* (1983) • *Catalogue of oil paintings, watercolours, drawings, and sculpture in the permanent collection, Royal Albert Memorial Museum and Art Gallery, Exeter*, ed. [C. J. Baker] (1978) • *Concise catalogue of oil paintings in the National Maritime Museum* (1988), 529 • T. J. Fenlon, 'The painter stainers companies of Dublin and London craftsmen and artists, 1670–1740', *New perspectives*, ed. T. J. Fenlon, N. Figgis, and C. Marshall (1987), 101–8 • *DNB* • M. Pilkington, *A dictionary of painters: from the revival of the art to the present period*, ed. H. Fuseli, new edn (1805)

Ganga Govind Singh [Ganga Gobinda Sinha] (*fl.* **1750–1795**), revenue administrator in Bengal, wielded great power and influence under Warren Hastings, accumulating in the process a huge fortune which enabled his descendants to become one of the most notable families in nineteenth-century Bengal. He was one of four sons of Bihari Singh, a silk merchant and descendant of a Kayastha family, settled at Kandi near Murshidabad, the capital of Mughal Bengal. Members of his family were engaged in trade and revenue administration under the nawabs of Bengal. Ganga Govind Singh was adopted by his uncle Gouranga Singh, and he and his elder brother Radhakanta were brought up as *kanungos*, keepers of revenue records.

When the East India Company took control of the Bengal revenues in 1765, they urgently needed the expertise of men like Ganga Govind Singh. By 1771 he was being employed in the company's central treasury, and in 1773 became *diwan*, or agent, to a committee managing the revenues of the Calcutta area. By then he had attracted the notice of Warren Hastings, who appointed him in 1778 to a commission to survey the revenue resources of Bengal and in 1781 made him *diwan* to a committee responsible for the revenue of the whole province. The next four years, until Hastings left Bengal in 1785, were the apogee of Ganga Govind Singh's career. Hastings paid both public and private tributes to his 'fidelity, diligence, and ability' and to his faithful support of the governor-general (*Writings and Speeches*, 440). Hastings's enemy Philip Francis called Ganga Govind Singh 'prime minister to Mr Hastings and I believe the only man he really trusts' (MS Eur. G5, p. 431). It was said that he 'was looked upon by the natives as the second person in the government, if not the first' (Marshall, 112). All the great *zamindars* (revenue payers) in Bengal felt obliged to deal with the government through him and it is clear that they had to pay heavily for his favour. There was said to be 'hardly a Native family of credit … whom he has not some time or other distressed or afflicted', or a *zamindar*'s estate 'that he has not dismembered and plundered' (*Writings and Speeches*, 442). He built up an enormous fortune, estimated at over £3 million by 1785 (Marshall, 112), and acquired much land.

There were, however, dangers in being the governor-general's protégé, since Hastings's enemies also became Ganga Govind Singh's enemies. As soon as Hastings had left India, charges were laid against Ganga Govind Singh, which he fought off, but he felt obliged to resign in 1786. At Hastings's impeachment Edmund Burke excoriated Ganga Govind Singh for his 'wickedness, barbarity and corruption' (*Writings and Speeches*, 443). Ganga Govind Singh appealed to the new governor-general, Lord Cornwallis, for further employment: 'From the first establishment of the Company I have been in their Service and expended my Life' (Cornwallis MSS, PRO 30/11/12, fol. 352). The climate of opinion among the British had, however, turned irrevocably against men like him. He retired to his family lands at Kandi, where he lived the life of a devout Vaishnavite Hindu, distributing his wealth in acts of piety, founding temples, giving alms to Brahmans and pilgrims, and performing a spectacular *sraddha* (memorial festival) for his mother, said to have cost £200,000. Hastings in retirement received occasional reports about Ganga Govind Singh, the last apparently being a message of congratulation in 1795 on the ending of Hastings's impeachment. The date and manner of his death are unknown. His son Santiram Singh, also active in revenue business and as the personal agent of prominent Europeans, predeceased him. Ganga Govind Singh then adopted Santiram's son Prankrishna Singh, who also became a *kanungo* and acted as his adopted father's deputy. Ganga Govind Singh's descendants came to be known as the Paikpara family, the name of their great house in Calcutta.

P. J. MARSHALL

Sources 'The territorial aristocracy of Bengal, no. 6: the Kandi family', *Calcutta Review*, 58 (1874), 95–120 · P. J. Marshall, 'Indian officials under the East India Company in eighteenth-century Bengal', *Trade and conquest: studies on the rise of British dominance in India* (1993) · enclosure in P. Francis to W. Ellis, 2/1/1778, BL OIOC, MS Eur. G5, fol. 431 · PRO, Cornwallis MSS, memorial, PRO 30/11/12 [fols. 352–63] · F. W. Torrington, ed., *Trial of Warren Hastings: minutes of the evidence*, 10 vols. (Dobb's Ferry, NY, 1974) · S. Lambert, ed., *House of Commons sessional papers of the eighteenth century* (1975), vol. 58 · *The writings and speeches of Edmund Burke*, ed. P. Langford, 6: *India: the launching of the Hastings impeachment, 1786–1788* (1991) · S. C. Nandy, *Life and times of Cantoo Baboo* (*Krisna Kanta Nandy*), *the banian of Warren Hastings*, 2 vols. (1978–81) · BL, Add. MS 29173, fol. 532 [letter of J. H. Harrington, 10/3/1795]

Archives BL OIOC, East India Company records, Bengal revenue proceedings and Calcutta committee of revenue proceedings | BL, Warren Hastings MSS

Wealth at death approx. 320 lakhs of rupees [approx. £3 million]: evidence by hostile witness to House of Commons

Ganguly [*née* Basu], **Kadambini** (*c.*1862–1923), physician and political activist, was born in Bhagalpur, a town in eastern India (now in the state of Bihar) where her father, Brajakishore Basu, was headmaster of a school. He was an active member of the reformist Brahmo Samaj, a religious movement based on the philosophy of the *Upanishads* and influenced by Sikhism, Islam, and Unitarianism, which stressed intellectual freedom and women's rights. There is no information on Kadambini's mother or siblings, though her mother's brother, Monomohan Ghose, a barrister, was instrumental in persuading Brajakishore to send Kadambini to the progressive Banga Mahila Vidyalaya, the closest approximation to a girls' boarding-school in Calcutta. Monomohan and other Brahmos, including Dwarakanath Ganguly (1844–1898), who was later to marry Kadambini, were the founders of this unique school and continued to be very active in the running of the institution. In 1878 Dwarakanath had to expend considerable energy and time in getting permission for Kadambini to sit for the entrance examination to the University of Calcutta, after she had passed a preliminary test. As there were no girls' colleges at that time the Bethune School in Calcutta added special classes in 1879, and in 1882 Kadambini and Chandramukhi Basu became the first women graduates of the University of Calcutta. Due to the proscriptions of female seclusion it soon became essential to introduce training for women in nursing and medicine; while the missionaries were the first to enrol, these professions started recruiting Indian women by the 1880s. After her graduation Kadambini decided to study medicine at the University of Calcutta, where a BA degree was adequate for admission to the course. Despite an official commitment to expand medical education among women the authorities granted her a place grudgingly: clearly, those in charge of women's education were not unaffected by the prejudices against its dissemination.

On 12 June 1883, shortly after entering medical college, Kadambini married Dwarakanath, by now a 39-year-old widower with six adult children. Dwarakanath had been her teacher, and clearly the two had become very close during Kadambini's later school years. The marriage caused a stir even among the reformist Brahmo Samaj; while there is no information on family responses, Dwarakanath's close friends and associates apparently disapproved and refused to attend the marriage ceremony. The leading women's journal *Bamabodhini Patrika*, which usually carried information on Brahmo Samaj marriages, made no mention of this interesting match and it is possible that Dwarakanath was viewed as having taken advantage of the emotions of a young woman assigned to his charge. By all accounts the marriage was an extremely successful one, and Dwarakanath fully supported Kadambini's further education and professional career.

In 1886 Kadambini passed in all the written papers of the final medical examination but failed in an essential component of the practicals; deliberate bias against her for being a woman was suspected. Instead of an MB degree she was awarded that of a GBMC (graduate of Bengal medical college), which enabled her to practise. In 1885 the Dufferin Fund (later known as the National Association for Supplying Female Medical Aid to the Women of India) was set up; the fund was the first systematic attempt at institutionalizing Western medicine and its use among Indian women. Clearly Kadambini was quick to take advantage of the facilities being made available for Indian women in the field of medicine and in 1888 was appointed a doctor at the Lady Dufferin Medical College on a monthly salary of Rs300. Kadambini soon had a flourishing practice and among her patients were women of the Nepalese royal family; the queen mother loaded her with gifts, which included a pony. In no time pony rides became popular with her two children and step-grandchildren, to whom Kadambini was a remote and busy figure, different from all the other women they knew. Kadambini's clinic-cum-study held many mysteries for them, including a human skeleton. As she commuted between patients in a horse-drawn carriage she occupied herself with the ubiquitous feminine occupation of the times—making fine lace, for which she gained some reputation.

Soon after the establishment of the Indian National Congress in 1885, Dwarakanath Ganguly began agitating for women's representation at the annual sessions and the 1889 Bombay session had a delegation of six women including Kadambini. The following year, at the Congress session at Calcutta, she delivered the vote of thanks in English, becoming the first Indian woman to speak at such occasions. Not unexpectedly, orthodox Hindus viewed Kadambini's career with deep misgivings. Fearing that their own women might emulate her, a section of conservatives launched a slander campaign, and in 1891 *Bangabasi*, a journal of the traditionalists, accused Kadambini of being a whore. Dwarakanath and other eminent Brahmos committed to women's emancipation launched a counter-offensive in the columns of a Brahmo publication, the *Indian Messenger*, where articles strongly criticized those who felt that the 'maintenance of female virtue is incompatible with their social liberty' (Kopf, 126). Dwarakanath was vindicated when the editor of the *Bangabasi*, Mohesh Chandra Pal, was fined Rs100 and sentenced to six months' imprisonment.

In 1892 Kadambini went to the United Kingdom for higher medical education and was made LRCP (Edin.), LRFPS (Glasgow), and DFPS (Dublin); at a time when women of her own class had barely started coming out in mixed company Kadambini's sojourn abroad further marked her out as an exceptional woman, intelligent, tenacious, and self-confident. During her long widowhood (Dwarakanath died on 27 June 1898), Kadambini continued to combine wider community activities with her professional life. At the beginning of the twentieth century she became the president of the Indian branch of the Transvaal Indian Association, established by Henry Pollack, a co-worker of M. K. Gandhi. A year before her death Kadambini became a member of a commission to enquire into the working conditions of women workers in Bihar and Orissa. Though little is known about her later years, family sources reported Kadambini's tireless commitment to her profession and to the cause of women in fast changing times. She died on 3 October 1923.

MALAVIKA KARLEKAR

Sources M. Karlekar, *Voices from within: early personal narratives of Bengali women* (1991), ch. 4 • S. Sengupta and A. Basu, eds., *Samsada Banali caritabhidhana*, 2 vols. (Calcutta, 1994), 79–80 • P. Chakravarti, *Chele belar din guli* [Childhood days] (1956), 3–7 • G. Murshid, *Reluctant debutante: response of Bengali women to modernization, 1849–1905* (1982), 106–7 • M. Borthwick, *The changing role of women in Bengal, 1849–1905* (1984) • B. Bandyopadhyay, *Dwarakanath Ganguly*, 2nd edn (1962) [in Bengali] • D. Kopf, *The Brahmo Samaj and the shaping of the modern Indian mind* (1979) • K. Nag, ed., *Bethune School and College centenary volume, 1849–1949* (1949) • P. Gangopadhyay, *Banglar nari jagaran* [The awakening of Bengali women] (1945) • D. Arnold, *Colonizing the body: state medicine and epidemic disease in nineteenth-century India* (1993) • G. Forbes, 'Medical careers and health care for Indian women: patterns of control', *Women's History Review*, 3 (1994), 515–30 • M. Lal, 'The politics of gender and medicine in colonial India: the Countess of Dufferin's Fund', *Bulletin of the History of Medicine*, 68 (1994), 29–66

Likenesses photograph (in her early thirties), repro. in Karlekar, *Voices from within*

Ganley [*née* Blumfield], **Caroline Selina** (1879–1966), co-operative movement activist and politician, was born on 16 September 1879 at 33 Admiralty Street, East Stonehouse, Plymouth, the daughter of James Blumfield and his wife, Selina Mary (*née* Norgrove). Her father was a bombardier at the time of her birth, and later a tailor. She attended Plymouth church and national schools, and Ottershaw School, Chertsey. On 24 July 1901 she married James William Henry Ganley, a tailor's cutter; the couple lived in Westminster before settling in Battersea, and raised two sons and a daughter.

Mrs Ganley became active in left-wing politics in opposition to the Second South African War, and in response to the poor social conditions of the working-class communities in which she lived. She joined the Social Democratic

Federation in 1906, campaigned for the suffrage, and was instrumental in setting up a socialist women's circle in Battersea and developing it into a branch of the Women's Labour League (later the Labour Party women's sections). In 1914 she was involved in the British committee of the International Congress, anti-war suffragists who detached themselves from the more patriotic National Union of Women's Suffrage Societies to work with European women for peace.

After the war Mrs Ganley's politics gradually became more moderate and geared to reformism but she was no less energetic. Having campaigned for citizenship rights, she made every effort to ensure that they were put to good use. She joined the co-operative and Labour parties, and in November 1919 won a seat on Battersea borough council; she chaired the health committee, and it was mainly through her efforts that a well-equipped maternity home was opened in Battersea in 1921. In 1920 she became one of the first women magistrates in London, and for twenty years sat in juvenile courts. She also served as a London county councillor and as a member of the London county education committee.

In the 1930s Mrs Ganley set her sights on Westminster, seeking nomination as a Co-operative Party candidate. In 1935 she stood unsuccessfully for Paddington North but in 1945 she was elected Co-operative-Labour MP for Battersea South, delivering a maiden speech on the subject of national health care. In 1950 she held the seat with a margin of 368, and the next year her golden wedding anniversary was marked at Westminster when her female colleagues made her a presentation. In the 1951 general election she was defeated. Mrs Ganley was appointed CBE in 1953, and in the same year was re-elected to Battersea borough council where she continued to serve until 1965.

An outstanding figure in the consumers' co-operative movement, Mrs Ganley was an elected director of the West London Society from 1918, and after its merger with the London Society in 1921, of the London Co-operative Society, which position she retained until 1946. In 1942 she became the first woman president of the London Co-operative Society, the largest retail society in the world with 792,000 members in that year. In the early 1940s she appeared as the presenter in an educational film about its work.

Mrs Ganley was also prominent in the labour and co-operative women's movements. She sat on, and chaired, the standing joint committee of industrial women's organizations, and chaired the national conference of Labour women. She belonged to the Lavender Hill branch of the Women's Co-operative Guild and held a number of official positions in the guild's national committee structure including a place on the south-eastern sectional council. She was an experienced and respected guildswoman, knowledgeable on such diverse subjects as tariffs and the consumer, married women's nationality rights, and the supply of milk to schoolchildren. Although she avoided the politically sensitive issue of birth control, and was in agreement with Labour's opposition to family allowances between the wars, the care of maternity

remained one of her chief concerns; in a speech at the 1928 national guild congress, for example, she urged that more co-operative women should get elected onto local authorities in order to promote measures to combat the high maternal mortality rates. In June 1943 she was honoured by the guild as one of the speakers at its diamond jubilee demonstration at the Royal Albert Hall.

Mrs Ganley died in London at the Bolingbroke Hospital, Battersea, on 31 August 1966, aged eighty-six. Her husband, who predeceased her, had worked for the co-operative movement prior to his retirement.

GILLIAN SCOTT

Sources DLB · Co-operative News (3 Sept 1966) · The Times (1 Sept 1966) · Co-operative News (9 April 1921) · Co-operative News (16 June 1928) · Co-operative News (22 April 1933) · WW (1966) · b. cert. · m. cert. · d. cert.
Archives FILM Co-operative College, Loughborough, National Co-operative film archive, London Co-operative Society educational feature
Likenesses photograph, repro. in The Times
Wealth at death £3245: probate, 1 March 1967, CGPLA Eng. & Wales

Ganly, Patrick (1809–1899), geologist, was born in the Rotunda Hospital, Dublin, on 15 October 1809, the son of Patrick Ganly (c.1783–1865), a bricklayer, and his wife, Ann (c.1779–1855). A Roman Catholic, he probably went to Eugene Finnerty's school in Cork; in 1827 he joined the boundary survey being organized by Richard *Griffith (1784–1878) as an adjunct to the Ordnance Survey. Between 1830 and 1832 he worked as a civilian employee of the Ordnance Survey itself, and in 1833 he rejoined Griffith, this time in the office for the general survey and valuation of rateable property. In 1846–9 he was seconded to the board of works, for famine relief projects, and he may have worked in the United States during 1851–2. By 1853, the probable year of his marriage to Mary Elizabeth (Eliza; c.1828–1894), he was back in the valuation office, and he remained there until he was declared redundant in May 1860.

Within the valuation office Ganly was variously described as 'valuator' or as 'cartographer'. The true nature of his activities there over many years is rendered clear by a series of more than 600 of his letters (three volumes of letters in the Royal Irish Academy and one in private hands) addressed to Griffith and dating from between 1837 and 1847. The letters reveal that throughout the greater part of that period Griffith used Ganly as his geological field factotum. He clearly proved himself to be a painstaking and conscientious field geologist, inured to the problems of year-round fieldwork in an often harsh environment.

Some of the detail on Griffith's pioneering quarter-inch (1:253,440) geological map of Ireland of 1839 is based upon Ganly's studies, and most of the revisions introduced into the map between 1839 and 1855 are the fruit of Ganly's investigations. Similarly, many of the geological papers published by Griffith owed much to Ganly's field activities, but for a variety of reasons Griffith chose not to acknowledge his indebtedness to Ganly.

In 1841 Ganly entered Trinity College, Dublin, as an

external student, and he graduated BA in 1849. During 1856 he joined the Geological Society of Dublin, and in a paper read there on 11 June that year he explained his discovery that cross-stratification might be used to indicate whether strata had been inverted. The paper was published in 1857, but its importance was overlooked by the geological world, and his discovery had to be remade some seventy years later.

Of Ganly's life after 1860 little is known, but he seems to have practised as a civil engineer. Ganly's wife died in 1894, and he himself died at 52 Main Street, Donnybrook, Dublin, on 29 October 1899. He was buried in Glasnevin cemetery two days later. The grave is unmarked.

JEAN B. ARCHER

Sources Archives of the Valuation Office, Dublin · G. L. Herries Davies, *Sheets of many colours: the mapping of Ireland's rocks, 1750–1890* (1983) · J. B. Archer, 'Patrick Ganly', *Irish Naturalists' Journal*, 20/4 (1980), 142–8 · R. C. Symington and A. Farrington, 'A foreign pioneer: Patrick Ganly, geologist, surveyor, and civil engineer', *Journal of the Department of Agriculture of the Republic of Ireland*, 46 (1949), 36–50 · d. cert. [Mary Elizabeth Ganly] · d. cert. · *Irish Times* (30 Oct 1899)
Archives Geological Survey of Ireland, Dublin, field maps · National University of Ireland, Galway, field maps · Royal Irish Acad.

Gann, Thomas William Francis (1867–1938), colonial medical officer and archaeologist, was born at Murrisk Abbey, Westport, co. Mayo, his mother's family home, on 13 May 1867, the son of William Gann, later of Whitstable, Kent, and his wife, Elizabeth Rose Garvey. He was educated at the King's School, Canterbury, and the medical school of the Middlesex Hospital in London, where he qualified MRCS and LRCP in 1890. He practised in London and Yorkshire, but after a spell in Guatemala on earthquake relief joined the colonial service, and in 1894 was appointed district medical officer in Corozal, British Honduras. He played a full role in local administration as a JP, member of the legislative council, and sometimes acting district commissioner, and remained in the crown colony well after his retirement as chief medical officer in 1923, continuing to engage in the archaeological investigations which he had pursued throughout his career, and which provided the first substantial collection of Maya materials from British Honduras. 6 feet tall, slim, and moustached, Gann looked like a guards officer, although dressed for comfort rather than appearance.

The Corozal hospital lay close to the ruins of Santa Rita, and Gann rapidly developed an interest in Maya remains. His first major find was a building there decorated with polychrome murals in what is now called the International Style of the Late Postclassic, indicative of the impact of central Mexican culture across the whole of Mesoamerica in the immediate pre-conquest period. The murals were destroyed by local Maya who believed the plaster to be medically efficacious, and Gann's careful drawings, published by the Society of Antiquaries of London and subsequently the Smithsonian Institution, are the only, and invaluable, record.

In 1903 Gann was sent to investigate reported ruins on the Rio Grande in the far south of British Honduras; these,

Thomas William Francis Gann (1867–1938), by Elliott & Fry

which he subsequently named Lubaantum ('place of fallen stones'), he re-'discovered' in 1924, when he carried out excavations in company with the self-proclaimed 'explorer' Frederick Mitchell-Hedges and with Lady Richmond Brown. Their work stimulated official British Museum expeditions in 1926–7, continued at the Pusilhà site to the south-west in 1928–30, with Gann's aid.

Over the first two decades of the twentieth century Gann carried out sporadic investigations throughout the colony, usually at sites where he could anchor his boat. In 1918 his accumulated notes, together with observations on Maya ethnology in British Honduras and Yucatán, were published by the Smithsonian Institution (*The Maya Indians of Southern Yucatan and Northern British Honduras*). He was the first to draw attention to a number of important sites in Quintana Roo, including Cobá, Ichpaatun, and Tzibanché, and in 1918 made an extended voyage along that coast in company with Sylvanus G. Morley of the Carnegie Institution which resulted in further discoveries, described in *In an Unknown Land* (1924), the first of a series of popular books drawing on his memories and diaries, and retailing with relish the hardships of life in the bush. The others were *Mystery Cities* (1925), which described work at Xunantunich and Lubaantun; *Ancient Cities and Modern Tribes* (1926), detailing the discovery of Ichpaatun and Cobá; *Maya Cities* (1927), that of Tzibanché; *Discoveries and Adventures in Central America* (1928), documenting the exploration of Pusilhà by the British Museum; and *Glories of the Maya* (1938), all except the first and last published by Gerald Duckworth within a few months of the experiences described. Despite his amateur standing, some of Gann's notions about the ancient Maya turned out to be more presciently accurate than those of his professional contemporaries, though others were wildly wrong.

Gann also wrote, in collaboration with J. Eric S. Thompson, *The History of the Maya from the Earliest Times to the Present Day* (1931), the first general book on ancient Maya civilization, and pieces for the *Illustrated London News* and *Morning Post* describing his own and others' work. Although not an archaeologist, Gann helped to make Maya archaeology accessible to the public. His excavations were usually carried out by hired labourers under distant and occasional supervision, and his lack of training resulted in a paucity of formal records, but no other or better archaeology was being carried out in British Honduras at the time.

The colony had no archaeological administration or law until long after Gann's time, nor a museum: Gann's collections went during his lifetime variously to the Museum of the American Indian in New York, to the Liverpool Free Museum (he was honorary lecturer in Central American archaeology at Liverpool University from 1919 to 1938), and to the British Museum, the latter receiving his superb personal collection of Maya jades. On 2 October 1930 he married Mary (1901/2–c.1974), daughter of Robert Wheeler of Hazlemere, Buckinghamshire, who worked with him on his last excavation, at Nohmul, in 1936. She survived him after his death at the London Clinic, Harley Street, London, on 24 February 1938; his funeral was held at Golders Green crematorium on 28 February.

NORMAN HAMMOND

Sources DNB · *The Times* (25 Feb 1938) · J. E. S. Thompson, 'Bibliografías de antropólogos, Thomas William Francis Gann, 1867–1938', *Boletín Bibliográfico de Antropología Americana*, 4 (1940), 158–63 · CGPLA Eng. & Wales (1938)
Likenesses Elliott & Fry, photograph, NPG [*see illus.*] · photographs, Museum of Mankind, London · portrait, repro. in T. Gann, *Glories of the Maya* (1938), frontispiece
Wealth at death £5093 12s. 8d.: probate, 22 June 1938, CGPLA Eng. & Wales · English probate resealed in Belize, 9 Dec 1938, CGPLA Eng. & Wales

Gant, Gilbert de, earl of Lincoln (c.1123–1155/6), magnate, lord of Folkingham, Lincolnshire, and Hunmanby, Yorkshire, was the son of Walter de Gant (d. 1139) and Maud, daughter of Stephen, count of Brittany and lord of Richmond. Gant had three brothers, Robert, Geoffrey, and Baldwin, and two sisters. He was born, baptized, and brought up at Bridlington Priory, Yorkshire, founded by his father. At the battle of Lincoln on 2 February 1141, while still a young man, he fought with King Stephen against Robert, earl of Gloucester, Ranulf (II), earl of Chester, and William de Roumare, earl of Lincoln. He was captured in battle and forced by Ranulf to marry his niece Rohese, daughter of Richard de Clare. With her he had a daughter, Alice (d. 1185). About 1143 Gant fought with Ranulf against William, earl of York, who seized and fortified Bridlington Priory. At some point thereafter, and probably in 1146 when King Stephen arrested Ranulf and confirmed Gant's gifts to Rievaulx Abbey, Gant established his local ascendancy. Between October 1149 and 1150 he was created earl of Lincoln by Stephen in opposition to Roumare, and at about the same time received the honour of the royal constable. This provoked a war between Gant and Roumare in which the latter was supported by Ranulf and William, earl of York. During the fighting Gant captured the earl of York's Lincolnshire castle and *caput* of Bytham, Roumare's son was slain (c.1151), and the earl of York and the constable of Chester, Eustace fitz John, destroyed Hunmanby Castle. Gant also fought in the 1140s against Henry de Lacy, lord of Pontefract, inflicting serious damage on the priory of Pontefract, for which he was excommunicated and later made recompense. This war probably resulted from the retention of Lacy lands by Gant's sister, Alice, after the death of her husband, Ilbert de Lacy (c.1141). Gant appears to have lost the earldom of Lincoln officially by 1153 or 1154, but continued to use the comital style.

Gant was a generous patron of the church. He founded the abbey of Rufford in 1146–7, and was a benefactor of the abbeys at Bardney, Crowland, Kirkstead, Rievaulx, and Thornton, the priories at Sempringham and Spalding, and the hospital of St Peter, York. He provided the monks of Bytham with a better site for their abbey at Vaudey, near Edenham, Lincolnshire. He desired to spend his last days as a canon at Bridlington, and gave his body to be buried there. He died in 1155 or 1156, being succeeded by his daughter, Alice, then a minor, who married Simon (III) de Senlis, earl of Northampton and of Huntingdon (d. 1184).

PAUL DALTON

Sources GEC, *Peerage* · M. R. Abbot, 'The Gant family in England, 1066–1191', PhD diss., U. Cam., 1973 · W. Farrer and others, eds., *Early Yorkshire charters*, 12 vols. (1914–65), vol. 2 · R. M. Sherman, 'The Ghents: a Flemish family in Norman England', PhD diss., University of Pennsylvania, 1969 · P. Dalton, *Conquest, anarchy, and lordship: Yorkshire, 1066–1154*, Cambridge Studies in Medieval Life and Thought, 4th ser., 27 (1994) · P. Dalton, 'Aiming at the impossible: Ranulf II earl of Chester and Lincolnshire in the reign of King Stephen', *Journal of the Chester Archaeological Society*, 71 (1991), 121–5 [G. Barraclough issue, *The earldom of Chester and its charters*, ed. A. T. Thacker] · Symeon of Durham, *Opera*, vol. 2 · C. J. Holdsworth, ed., *Rufford charters*, 1, Thoroton Society Record Series, 29 (1972) · *The chronicle of Pierre de Langtoft*, ed. T. Wright, 2 vols., Rolls Series, 47 (1866–8)
Archives BL, Harley charters · Lincs. Arch., charters | BL, Add. MS 40008 · BL, Cotton MS Vespasian E.xx · PRO · PRO, charters [copies]

Gant [Ghent], **Maurice de** [Maurice fitz Robert, Maurice Paynel] (c.1185–1230), magnate, was heir to two major estates: the barony of Beverstone in Gloucestershire inherited from his father, Robert fitz Robert (d. 1194), a younger son of *Robert fitz Harding, lord of Berkeley; and the barony of Hooton Pagnell in Yorkshire, which came to Maurice from his mother, Avice, daughter of Alice Paynel and Robert de Gant. Together these brought Maurice land in half a dozen counties, focused upon the honours and castles of Beverstone in Gloucestershire and Leeds in Yorkshire. Maurice's maternal grandfather, Robert de Gant (d. 1191), was the younger brother of Gilbert de *Gant (c.1123–1155/6), a knight of Flemish descent created earl of Lincoln by King Stephen, and it was the name Gant (or Ghent) which was adopted by Maurice's father, Robert fitz Robert, and by Maurice himself.

Maurice de Gant was a minor at the death of his father in 1194 when his wardship was purchased for 500 marks by William de Ste Mère-Église (d. 1224), afterwards bishop of London. Although in January 1205 he unsuccessfully sued the prior of Holy Trinity, York, for the restoration of a third of the advowson of the church of Leeds, his lands were still in the custody of Bishop William as late as August 1205, which suggests that he had not yet achieved his majority, and hence that he cannot have been born before 1184. He had come of age by 12 November 1207 when as Maurice Paynel he granted a charter of liberties to the men of Leeds, the first step towards the establishment of a borough there. In the following year he went to law against numerous subtenants in Yorkshire and Lincolnshire. For the royal writs initiating these suits, and for a promise of royal support in respect of his litigation and his rights, Gant was fined 100 marks. Despite this, the majority of cases were decided against him in court. Gant married twice: first, in 1213, Matilda, daughter of Henry d'Oilly, baron of Hook Norton in Oxfordshire, in return for which alliance Gant assumed responsibility for £800 of Jewish debt which d'Oilly owed at the royal exchequer. Matilda died before 1220, and Gant married second, c.1229, Margaret, widow of Ralph de Someri, through whom he acquired a temporary interest in the barony of Dudley in Worcestershire. He left no children from either marriage.

Gant participated in the Irish campaign of 1210, sent knights to the king's army in 1213, and in 1214 served on King John's ill-fated expedition to Poitou, but in the following year he joined the assembly of the barons at Stamford, perhaps spurred on by the king's failure to honour his fine for special treatment, perhaps because of another fine that he had been forced to undertake in 1214, when he assumed the massive Jewish debts of his father-in-law, Henry d'Oilly. As a result of his rebellion Maurice was excommunicated and his estates were confiscated by the crown. He fought on the side of Louis of France at the battle of Lincoln in May 1217 and was taken prisoner by Ranulf (III), earl of Chester. By December 1217 he had obtained his release, and his estates were restored to him, except for the manors of Leeds and Bingley which were retained by Chester despite extended litigation. In 1225 he was sent into Wales to assist William (II) Marshal, earl of Pembroke. Two years later he was engaged in fortifying his castle at Beverstone, and in 1228 he was appointed royal justice on eyre. In 1230 he sailed with Henry III for Brittany, but died in France that July; his body was divided for burial between the Dominicans and the canons of St Augustine's in Bristol. He had earlier made an extensive grant of property to St Augustine's, to establish an almonry for paupers, and in exchange for prayers for his soul.

Before Gant sailed for Brittany in 1230 he had surrendered his rights in Beverstone to the king. None the less his nephew, Robert de Gournay, son of his half-sister, Eve, was allowed to succeed to most of his manors in Somerset and Gloucestershire, and Gant reserved various subsidiary rights to another nephew, Thomas of Berkeley. His manor of Irnham together with the remainder of the barony of Hooton Pagnell passed to Andrew Lutterell, a descendant of the Paynels. NICHOLAS VINCENT

Sources Chancery records • Pipe rolls • Calendar of the manuscripts of the dean and chapter of Wells, 1, HMC, 12 (1907) • I. H. Jeayes, Descriptive catalogue of the charters and muniments in the possession of the Rt. Hon. Lord Fitzhardinge at Berkeley Castle (1892) • I. J. Sanders, English baronies: a study of their origin and descent, 1086–1327 (1960) • J. Le Patourel, ed., Documents relating to the manor and borough of Leeds, 1066–1400, Thoresby Society, 45 (1956) • Ann. mon. • Paris, Chron. • Coll. Arms, Glover MSS, A fol. 111v

Ganzoni, (Francis) John Childs, first Baron Belstead (1882–1958), politician, was born at The Cottage, Clapham Common, on 19 January 1882, the only son of Julius Charles Ganzoni (d. 1949), a colonial broker and later chairman of C. Czarnikow Ltd, and his wife, Mary Frances Childs, daughter of Major James Childs of the 3rd Royal Fusiliers. John Ganzoni, as he was known, had the opportunity to see the world in his youth as his grandfather, who was Swiss but became a naturalized British subject, was in the sugar trade. His travels instilled in him the ambition to bond the dominions and the United Kingdom, and in later life he travelled widely to this end, becoming a fellow of the Royal Geographic Society. These overseas trips interrupted his formal education; he never attended in the spring term when at Tonbridge School, and did so only from his second year at Christ Church, Oxford, where, as an undergraduate from 1900 to 1904, he was more interested in sport than in public speaking. After graduating with a third in modern history in 1904, he was called to the bar (Inner Temple) in 1906, and joined the south-eastern circuit, but came to dislike legal practice.

In 1911 Ganzoni was adopted as the Unionist parliamentary candidate for Ipswich, which traditionally had been a Liberal seat and with which he had no connection. In May 1914 a by-election was called, following the death of Charles Silvester Horne, one of the sitting Liberal members; C. F. G. Masterman was 'carpet-bagged' into Ipswich by the Liberals, but Ganzoni won, to his own surprise. It was during this campaign that he earned the name Union Jack Ganzoni. He had been in the Commons for only three months when the First World War began, and he was commissioned in the 4th battalion of the Suffolk regiment, serving in France from 1914 to 1916 with the rank of captain, then at the quartermaster-general's services in York in 1917, returning to the British expeditionary force in 1918 as a staff officer. He was gassed twice, but was at home on account of frostbite when many of his relatives died at the Somme. He claimed that the tin helmet that he wore was responsible for his early baldness; a more significant result of his experiences in the trenches was to generate a genuine interest in people, which assisted him in his political career.

In the general election of 1918 Ganzoni won with almost twice the number of votes as his long-standing opponent from the Labour Party, Robert Frederick Jackson. For the next three contests Ipswich followed the 'Right, left, right' swings of government that knocked out the Liberal Party. He retained the seat in 1922, lost it in the unexpected election of 1923, when protection was rejected in both country districts and the cities, but recovered it in 1924 as a result of one of several Unionist–Liberal pacts in East Anglia. Ganzoni himself spoke out for co-operation between opponents of socialism. From 1924 until 1929 he was unpaid parliamentary private secretary to the postmaster-general. Knighted in 1921, he was created a baronet in March 1929.

Ganzoni married, on 31 May 1930, Gwendoline (Gwen)

Gertrude (1893/4–1962), the elder daughter of Arthur Turner, a partner in an Ipswich leather manufacturing firm. She became president of the Royal Midwives' Society. After their late marriage both devoted much time to their son, John, and daughter, Jill.

Ganzoni's majority of 12,292 in 1931 was the biggest in Ipswich during the twentieth century. His final victory, with Jackson still the opponent, was in 1935, and he remained an MP until December 1937. He encapsulated the successful Conservative adaptation to a democratic electorate: like Baldwin, he was moderate, charming, and an unpolitical animal, and at ease with MPs of all parties.

In his late fifties Ganzoni said that he would not fight another election, and accepted a peerage as Baron Belstead of Ipswich in January 1938, forcing MPs to find a new chairman for the kitchen committee of the Commons, a post that he had enjoyed for six years, and for which MPs would remember him. A gourmet who later possessed a large figure, he introduced MPs to exotic dishes, and was proud that they began to drink more empire wine; in 1932, when asked if the Tabasco pepper sauce might be obtained from Yorkshire rather than the United States, Ganzoni replied, amid much laughter, that no more would be purchased after the present supply was exhausted. The dining rooms were often called Chez Ganzoni.

From 1939 to 1942 Belstead was a local army welfare officer (AWO) in Ipswich, and his organization of activities for army camps meant that his house was full of dartboards; he continued as the county AWO until 1949, with rank of lieutenant-colonel. From 1940 he served as the chairman of the private bills committee in the Lords, having carried out the same duties in the Commons from 1923 until 1937. He also became a magistrate and deputy lieutenant for Suffolk.

Ultimately Ganzoni's interests were local, and he was active in every branch of Ipswich life. He indulged his main sporting interests as the president of Suffolk County Cricket Club and a founder director of Ipswich Town Football Club. But the sport at which he excelled was tennis, and he was president of the Suffolk Lawn Tennis Association from 1929; he had been a member of the Lawn Tennis Association Council from 1910 until 1923, and a member of the House of Commons team. In his later days, he was frequently an umpire at local tournaments, and his enthusiasm lives on in the many trophies that were donated to clubs and schools in his name.

Ganzoni was not disappointed that he never held higher office: he lived according to his motto, *Fidelitas vincit* ('faithfulness conquers') by loyally serving the constituents of Ipswich, where he died at Ipswich Nursing Home, 57 Fonnereau Road, on 15 August 1958. He was succeeded as second Baron Belstead by his son, John Julian Ganzoni (*b.* 1932), who held office in Conservative governments between 1970 and 1992.   DANIEL CREWE

Sources *Chronicle & Mercury* (22 Aug 1958) [Ipswich] • *WWW*, 1951–60 • Burke, *Peerage* (2000) • GEC, *Peerage* • Kelly, *Handbk* (1939) • private information (2004) [Jill Ganzoni, daughter] • *The Times* (13 March 1923) • *The Times* (11 Oct 1924) • *The Times* (15 Oct 1924) • *The Times* (31 Oct 1924) • *The Times* (14 Dec 1932) • *The Times* (16 Nov 1935) • *The Times* (16 Aug 1958) • *Evening Star* (24 Feb 1962) • *East Anglian Daily Times* (24 Aug 1997) • b. cert. • m. cert. • d. cert. • B. Harrison, *The transformation of British politics, 1860–1995* (1996) • R. Clarke, *Hope and glory: Britain, 1900–1990* (1997) • C. L. Mowet, *Britain between the wars, 1918–1940* (1956) • M. Pugh, *State and society: British political and social history, 1870–1992* (1994) • *CGPLA Eng. & Wales* (1958)
Archives FILM BFI NFTVA, news footage
Wealth at death £716,467 19s. 5d.: probate, 28 Aug 1958, *CGPLA Eng. & Wales*

Gaposchkin, Cecilia Helena Payne- (1900–1979), astronomer, was born at Holywell Lodge, Wendover, Buckinghamshire, on 10 May 1900, the eldest of the three children, two girls and a boy, of Edward John Payne (*d.* 1904), a London barrister, and his German-born wife, Emma Leonora Pertz, an art copyist. Her father died when she was only four years old. She received her early education at a small private school in Wendover; while at home she imbibed a love of art, music, and literature that never left her. When Cecilia was twelve the family moved to London, where she attended St Mary's College, Paddington, before being sent for a final year to St Paul's Girls' School, from which she won a scholarship in natural sciences to Newnham College, Cambridge. She went up to Cambridge in 1919 at the age of nineteen. A high point in her student life was a lecture by A. S. Eddington describing observations of the deflection of light by the sun during the total eclipse of 1919, the confirmation of Einstein's theory of relativity. Cecilia Payne determined there and then to become an astronomer. She received kindly encouragement from Eddington himself, as well as E. A. Milne and others; her first published piece of research, on a problem of stellar motions set by Eddington, was carried out in those undergraduate days. However, the traditional avenue to a career in astronomy in Britain, through mathematics, was not open to her. L. J. Comrie advised that the United States would be her best chance, and after a lecture in London he introduced her to Harlow Shapley, director of the Harvard College observatory at Cambridge, Massachusetts, who agreed to accept her.

Cecilia Payne took part two of the Cambridge tripos in physics in 1923 and, supported by a fellowship, moved to Harvard in the same year to begin research under Shapley. She was to remain at Harvard for the rest of her life. Using the observatory's collection of spectrograms taken at Harvard and at its southern station in Peru, she re-examined stellar spectra in the context of current theoretical predictions. In 1925 she became the first astronomer at the observatory to be awarded a PhD degree (from Radcliffe College) with a thesis on *Stellar Atmospheres*, published as the first of the Harvard Monographs (1925). The work demonstrated that, contrary to generally held ideas, the abundances of the chemical elements in the universe of stars are essentially uniform.

Cecilia Payne stayed on at Harvard in an undefined post attached to the famous group of women workers headed by Annie J. Cannon: the appointment of a woman at a more senior level would not have been countenanced by the university authorities. It was only in 1938 that she and

Miss Cannon were appointed to the rank of 'astronomer', her own official designation being 'Phillips astronomer of the Harvard observatory'. She continued her spectroscopic work with research on luminous stars, described in her second book, *Stars of High Luminosity* (1930).

Cecilia Payne's later career was taken up almost entirely with the subject of variable stars, on which she published numerous papers, chiefly in the observatory's own bulletins, and several books. From the time of her marriage in 1934 most of this work was carried out in collaboration with her husband, Sergei Illarionovich Gaposchkin (1898–1984), a Russian astronomer whom she had met in Germany in 1933 and whom she had helped to obtain entry into the United States. Between them the Gaposchkins performed an enormous volume of research on variables of all kinds. Their book *Variable Stars* (1938) became a standard reference in this field. They masterminded a huge programme, carried out with the help of a team of assistants, of identifying and measuring variable stars on photographic plates, a task that required well over a million individual observations. This was followed in the 1960s by a similar project, entailing two million brightness estimates, on the variable stars of the Magellanic clouds.

Throughout this period Cecilia Payne-Gaposchkin was actively involved in university teaching. She was made a full professor in 1956, the first woman to achieve this rank, but, though the appointment represented a landmark in the history of academic women at Harvard, it was a long overdue promotion in her case. After retirement from her university chair in 1966 she remained affiliated to the Smithsonian Astrophysical Observatory (as the observatory was called following reorganization) and continued her research until 1976. She published her last scientific paper and her last book in 1979.

In 1936 Cecilia Payne-Gaposchkin was elected a member of the American Philosophical Society. Other honours and prizes followed, including the Henry Norris Russell lectureship of the American Astronomical Society in 1977. Among several honorary degrees was an ScD from the University of Cambridge in 1952. Cecilia Payne-Gaposchkin was a tall woman, dignified in bearing, awe-inspiring to her students, but described as warm and generous by her colleagues. She combined an intensely busy scientific life with the hectic activities of home and family. The Gaposchkins had two sons and a daughter; the daughter and one of the sons became astronomers. In her last years Cecilia Payne-Gaposchkin recorded a small volume of highly readable memoirs, published after her death by her daughter. She died in Cambridge, Massachusetts, on 7 December 1979. She bequeathed her body to science and was buried in the graveyard of the Tufts medical school, Tewksbury, Massachusetts.
M. T. BRÜCK

Sources *Cecilia Payne-Gaposchkin: an autobiography and other recollections*, ed. K. Haramundanis, 2nd edn (1996) [incl. biography of annotated works] · *Quarterly Journal of the Royal Astronomical Society*, 23 (1982), 450–51 · [A. B. White], ed., *Newnham College register, 1871–1950*, 2 vols. (1964) · J. B. Hearnshaw, *The analysis of starlight: one hundred and fifty years of astronomical spectroscopy* (1986), 229–31

Archives American Institute of Physics, New York, Niels Bohr Library, typescript of interview with Owen Gingerich | Harvard U.
Likenesses photograph, 1919, Newnham College, Cambridge · photograph, 1948, repro. in Haramundanis, ed., *Cecilia Payne-Gaposchkin*

Garakonte [Daniel Garakontié] (*d.* **1677**), Native American leader, is of unknown parentage. He first appears in Euro-American documents in May 1654, when he led a delegation of Onondaga Iroquois to Montreal. By that time he had already achieved prominence as an orator, or ritual specialist who spoke for hereditary chiefs on public occasions. There is no evidence that he himself held a hereditary title or was a clan headman. Yet in the general ferment caused by European colonization, orators often achieved influence far beyond their traditional role.

Garakonte's career spanned a crucial period in Iroquois–French relations. Since long before the French arrived, the five nations of the Iroquois league had been at war with Native American peoples of the St Lawrence valley and Great Lakes region. When the latter became trading partners of New France, they involved colonists in their struggles, and low-grade Franco-Iroquois warfare became almost constant. In the 1640s and 1650s the conflicts entered a deadly new phase, as Iroquois in search of furs and captives to be adopted to replenish disease-ravaged populations relentlessly attacked French allies, many of whom were Christian converts. Most notable among these were the Hurons, whose villages were overrun in 1648–9. Hundreds of the survivors were forcibly resettled among Garakonte's Onondagas.

In this context Garakonte had three goals: to keep peace with the French and so free Iroquois forces to attack Native American enemies; to open trade with New France as an alternative to New Netherland; and to encourage French Jesuits to establish a mission in his country to serve Christian Huron captives and convince others to join them voluntarily. Pursuing these goals, he courted personal relationships with missionaries—in 1654 inviting Father Simon le Moyne, the first Jesuit to visit Onondaga country, to lodge in his nephew's house; in 1656 helping to settle some fifty priests and lay workers at a mission in Iroquoia; and in 1658, when Iroquois sentiment turned against the mission, warning the Jesuits to escape before they could be attacked. By 1661 Garakonte had brokered a truce with the French, and in 1665 a formal treaty with four of the Iroquois nations followed. After a French invasion of the Mohawk country in 1666, that nation also made peace, and Jesuits opened missions throughout Iroquoia. None of the five nations had much choice. They were engaged in desperate wars with various Algonquian-speaking peoples to the east and Susquehannocks to the south, and their source of weapons and trade goods had been disrupted by the 1664 English conquest of New Netherland. Most Iroquois seemingly agreed that peace on their northern flank and secure trade with the French were necessary, but Garakonte and his followers envisaged far more than a marriage of convenience. To them an economic, political, and religious alliance with the French was the best hope for restoring Iroquois power.

Although at first Garakonte's relationships with French Jesuits were primarily political, by the late 1660s he had become a genuine convert to their faith. Befitting his diplomatic importance to the French, he was baptized at the Quebec cathedral in 1670, taking the Christian name of his godfather, Governor Daniel de Rémy de Courcelles. From that time forward he was a vocal proponent of Christianity, and his opponents accused him not only of surrendering to Europeans but of disrupting the sacred ceremonies that defined his people. None the less, he sought to blend Christian and traditional customs—never more so than as he lay dying of a gastrointestinal ailment in 1677. Although too weak to speak and so prone to vomiting that he could not receive the sacrament during the last rites of his adoptive church, he arranged a traditional death feast, at which a speech delivered in his name encouraged his followers not only to become Christians and strengthen the French alliance but to continue their wars against Native American enemies. He was buried in Onondaga, probably in the autumn of 1677.

In ironic testimony to the influence Garakonte wielded during his lifetime, his policies did not long survive him. By the mid-1680s anti-French Iroquois factions with strong ties to a newly expansionist English New York regime had forced the Jesuits to close their missions and resumed warfare against the French and their Native American allies. None the less, Garakonte left an enduring legacy. His pro-French political faction remained a major force until the British conquest of Canada, and his style of leadership based on the shrewd exploitation of ties with Europeans became a hallmark of Iroquois diplomacy.

DANIEL K. RICHTER

Sources R. G. Thwaites, ed., *The Jesuit relations and allied documents* (1896–1901), vols. 41–61 · D. K. Richter, *The ordeal of the longhouse: the peoples of the Iroquois league in the era of European colonization* (1992) · W. N. Fenton, *The great law and the longhouse: a political history of the Iroquois confederacy* (1998), 282–6 · E. B. O'Callaghan and B. Fernow, eds., *Documents relative to the colonial history of the state of New York* (1853–87), vol. 9 · L. H. Leder, *The Livingston Indian records* (1956) · B. G. Trigger, 'Garakontié', *DCB*, vol. 1 · S. S. Webb, *1676: the end of American independence* (1985), 251–302 · N. Clermont, 'Une figure iroquoise, Garakontié', *Recherches Amérindiennes au Québec*, 7 (1978), 101–7 · S. S. Webb, 'Garaconsté, Daniel', *ANB*

Garald (d. 732). *See under* Connacht, saints of (*act. c.*400–c.800).

Garba-Jahumpa, Ibrahima Momodou (1912–1994), schoolteacher and politician in Gambia, was born in Bathurst (Banjul), capital of the British colony of Gambia, in 1912, the son of Momodou Jahumpa, a shipwright and senior figure in the local Mohammedan Society, whose family had emigrated to Gambia from Senegal in 1816. Although a Wolof, Garba-Jahumpa claimed Mauritanian ancestry. He attended Koranic, primary, and secondary schools in Bathurst and qualified as a teacher in 1936, taking up teaching posts in Bathurst and Georgetown, McCarthy Island division, save for a brief period during the Second World War when he worked for the British

Overseas Airways Corporation in Bathurst. Initially enjoying the patronage of Edward Small, the colony's leading politician, Garba-Jahumpa served as assistant secretary of the Bathurst Rate Payers' Association and as secretary of the Gambia Labour Union from 1942 to 1945. He was also nominated by the governor, Sir Thomas Southorn, to serve on the Bathurst advisory town council in 1941, to which he would be elected after the Second World War and become the first chairman of the Bathurst town council in 1959.

After 1945 Garba-Jahumpa broke with Small and sought to establish an independent power base to promote his political career. He created a short-lived Gambia Amalgamated Trade Union from 1947 to 1948, but his route to political office was to be through organizing the Muslim community in Bathurst. Already active in the Bathurst Young Muslim Society, an offshoot of the Mohammedan Society in which his father had been prominent, Garba-Jahumpa sought to play on the grievances of Bathurst Muslims, particularly regarding the dominance of the smaller Christian community in public life and modern-sector employment. Unsuccessful against Edward Small in the 1947 legislative council election, Garba-Jahumpa went off to teach in Georgetown until he returned to contest the next legislative council election in 1951. With Bathurst Young Muslim Society support he came second in the polls, which gave him a seat in the legislative council and, together with the Revd J. C. Faye, the new status of 'member of government', a proto-ministerial appointment created by the governor, Sir Percy Wyn-Harris. In January 1952, Garba-Jahumpa sought to strengthen his position politically by forming the Gambia Muslim Congress out of some forty Muslim societies, including the Bathurst Young Muslim Society. He was returned to the legislative council in the elections of 1954 and was given the agriculture and natural resources portfolio by Wyn-Harris, who was widely seen as favouring Garba-Jahumpa over the Revd J. C. Faye, leader of the Gambia Democratic Party, and P. S. N'Jie, the United Party leader, the other two elected members for Bathurst. The Gambia Muslim Congress entered into a loose alliance with the United Party against the Gambia Democratic Party in the mid-1950s, but the personal animosity between the two leaders and the growing strength of the United Party, led Garba-Jahumpa to abandon N'Jie in order to merge the Gambia Muslim Congress with his earlier rival Faye's Gambia Democratic Party to form the Democratic–Congress Alliance, ahead of the 1960 elections to the new house of assembly. Notwithstanding the new alliance, Jahumpa lost his seat and the Democratic–Congress Alliance won only one seat. In 1961, the Democratic–Congress Alliance formed a tactical alliance with the new force in Gambian politics, the rural-based People's Progressive Party, which was eager to obtain a foothold in the Gambian capital. Neither Garba-Jahumpa nor the Democratic–Congress Alliance fared any better in the 1962 general elections, doing no more than hanging on to their one seat. Breaking with other elements in the Democratic–Congress Alliance over his opposition to a republican constitution, Garba-

Jahumpa created his own Gambia Congress Party, allied with the United Party. He succeeded in winning a seat in parliament in the elections of 1966, only to disband the Congress Party two years later in order to join the People's Progressive Party. He was rewarded with ministerial office at health and social welfare. He held on to Half Die (Bathurst South) constituency in the general elections of 1972 and was subsequently promoted to the prestigious finance ministry, which he retained until his defeat in the general elections of 1977. He never stood for parliament again and faded from public life long before his death. He was married with several children. He died on 4 September 1994 in Banjul, Gambia, and was buried in the Muslim cemetery at Kanifing, Greater Banjul.

Garba-Jahumpa was the ultimate political chameleon, changing his political colour as the pursuit of his political career dictated. At one time he posed as a radical pan-Africanist, cultivating links with Ghanaian president Kwame Nkrumah, having previously been a loyal member of the Wyn-Harris administration; he sought early to exploit religious divisions and yet was prepared to enter into tactical alliances with both his Christian rivals in Bathurst; and, finally, though spokesman for the colony (Bathurst), he readily subordinated himself to the People's Progressive Party in the late 1960s in order to ensure himself a political future. ARNOLD HUGHES

Sources A. Hughes and H. A. Gailey, *Historical Dictionary of The Gambia* (1999), 82–4 · A. Hughes and D. Perfect, 'Trade unionism in The Gambia', *African Affairs*, 88/349 (Dec 1989), 557–9 · 'The Gambia's first minister?', *West Africa* (12 Dec 1953), 1157

Likenesses photographs, National Archives of Gambia

Garbet, Samuel (*b.* 1684/5, *d.* in or after 1751), schoolmaster and topographer, was born at Norton in the parish of Wroxeter, Shropshire, the son of Francis Garbet of Walcot. He was educated at Donnington School and, in June 1700, aged fifteen, matriculated from Christ Church, Oxford, whence he graduated BA on 23 May 1704 and proceeded MA on 5 July 1707. Ordained deacon on 22 September 1706, he became curate of Great Ness. On 11 March 1712 he was elected second master of the free school at Wem in Shropshire, and was appointed curate of Edstaston, Shropshire, in 1713. He married Anna, daughter of John Edwards of Great Ness, Shropshire, on 16 May 1714 and they had one son, Samuel, who was baptized at Wem on 17 July 1716.

In 1724 Garbet was offered, but declined, the headmastership of Wem School. After working for thirty years at the school, and finding himself in comfortable circumstances, he retired in 1742 and devoted his time to compiling his *History of Wem, and the Following Villages and Townships*. The book was published posthumously in 1818. He had published a translation of books 1 and 2 of Phaedrus's fables in 1715.

Garbet was still curate of Edstaston in 1751 and died some time in or after that year. His son graduated BA from Christ Church, Oxford, in 1737, proceeded MA in 1743, and became curate of Wem, and later of Newtown, Shropshire. He shared his father's topographical interests, and according to Richard Gough was the principal contributor to Valentine Green's *Survey of the City of Worcester* (1764), but published nothing under his own name. He died in 1768 and was buried at Stoulton near Worcester.

W. W. WROTH, *rev.* DAVID BOYD HAYCOCK

Sources S. Garbet, *The history of Wem* (1818), 208–9, 280 · Foster, *Alum. Oxon.* · IGI · R. G. [R. Gough], *British topography*, [new edn], 2 vols. (1780) · T. Nash, *Collections for the history of Worcestershire*, 2 (1782), 25

Garbett, Cyril Forster (1875–1955), archbishop of York, was born on 6 February 1875 at Tongham, Surrey, the eldest among the five children of the Revd Charles Garbett (1813–1895) and his second wife, Susan Charlotte Bowes (1843–1934), who was thirty years younger than her husband. Charles Garbett was the brother of two of the leading evangelical opponents of the Tractarians, James *Garbett (1802–1879) and Edward *Garbett (1817–1887), but was himself a broad-churchman. He was a chaplain in the East India Company for twenty-five years before returning home as vicar of Tongham.

Education and ministry Cyril Garbett was educated at Farnham grammar school before being sent to board at Portsmouth grammar school in 1886. A gangly, nervous, hypochondriac adolescent, he was known as Bunny because of his long ears. He was not especially academic, and failed to get into Keble College, Oxford, at his first attempt, but in 1895 he was awarded the Gomm scholarship to the college, by dint of a distant family connection. During his time in Oxford Garbett's father died, leaving his mother with little money, but a benefactor enabled him to finish his studies, and he took a second in modern history in 1898. Oxford gave him two lasting interests. He became politically active, finding an outlet for his radical views in the Oxford Union, of which he was president in 1898. He also became increasingly drawn to Anglo-Catholicism and decided to be ordained. He trained for ordination at Cuddesdon Theological College, which he found unbearably stuffy, but where he developed the daily discipline of reading and prayer which he observed rigidly throughout his life.

In 1900 Garbett was ordained to the curacy of St Mary, Portsea, a huge dockyard parish of 40,000 people served by a college of sixteen celibate clergy. Garbett was appointed by Cosmo Gordon Lang, who departed to be bishop of Stepney after a year and was replaced by Bernard Wilson. Portsea was a notable pastoral experiment, which emphasized house-to-house visiting and the provision of classes and clubs for working-class parishioners. It was described in *The Work of a Great Parish*, which Garbett edited in 1915. Garbett visited the poor for four hours each weekday. He was also a doughty controversialist, taking on the local brewing interest. When he accused the local magistrates of being in the pockets of the brewers he was threatened with a libel action. He also clashed with local nonconformists over church schools, and with Winchester College, which was unwitting landlord to a number of brothels in the parish. Such was Garbett's reputation as a curate that when Bernard Wilson died suddenly in 1909, he was the obvious choice to replace him as vicar.

Cyril Forster Garbett (1875–1955), by David Jagger, 1951

The transition from curate to vicar was not easy for Garbett, who felt that he had to assert himself over the other curates and became a martinet. He insisted that his curates submit their sermons in advance for his approval, that they provide a weekly account of how they had spent every hour of the day, and what books they had read. A chilly, maladroit figure, he had no small talk, and could not achieve familiarity with his junior colleagues. He was in fact extremely lonely, but his brusqueness discouraged them from the intimacy which he craved. He suffered bouts of depression, and was given to unprovoked tantrums. His only close relationship (he never married) was with his widowed mother, who lived in a cottage close to the vicarage. But even she was not permitted to dine in the vicarage.

Southwark and Winchester In 1919 Garbett was appointed bishop of Southwark in place of Charles Burge. He had two great priorities. The first was to provide churches for the new housing estates of south London. Complaining that after six years as bishop he still had not been called upon to consecrate a single new church, he began an energetic campaign for £100,000 to build twenty-five new churches. Within three years he had exceeded this sum. Garbett's other priority was to visit the clergy of his diocese, and to improve their pastoral work. He successfully developed the use of diocesan synods for consultation. His asperity with errant clergy was legendary, and he would conclude his interviews with them by saying, 'I'm sorry for you when the Day of Judgment comes' (Smyth, 165). Even lateness was a cardinal sin, and he once refused to license a curate because he had arrived three minutes late.

But Garbett took an enlightened view of ritualist clergy, and averted confrontation with them. As a central-churchman with moderate Anglo-Catholic leanings, Garbett himself wore vestments, and cope and mitre in his cathedral. He also took great pains with young clergy, whom he would take on his country walks, and with sick clergy. Every summer he would embark on a 'pilgrimage', walking from parish to parish in the southern, rural part of his diocese.

Garbett was an expeditious administrator, brutally swift in his conduct of meetings. Such administrative acumen was soon in great demand outside his diocese. He was actively involved in drafting the revised prayer book. Working with his kindred spirit John Reith, he was influential in developing religious broadcasting as first chairman of the religious advisory committee of the BBC (1923–45).

Southwark also made Garbett into an expert on the housing and other social problems of south London. In his book *In the Heart of South London* (1931) and his 1933 pamphlet *The Challenge of the Slums*, he urged government to act to cure the overcrowding of south London. As a young curate Garbett had supported the Labour candidate in a local by-election, and he remained loosely left-wing as a bishop. On the first day of the general strike he co-wrote a letter to *The Times* calling for a government subsidy for the coal industry. During the depression he championed the unemployed, and in his later career he frequently spoke out on all areas of government policy in the House of Lords. But he was more aware than some of his episcopal colleagues of the clergy's limited competence to address political and social questions.

In 1932 Garbett became bishop of Winchester. He initially refused this offer, but was assured that it was part of a bigger plan that he should eventually replace Arthur Winnington-Ingram as bishop of London. Garbett could not resist the challenge of remedying Winnington-Ingram's derelictions and reforming the London diocese, so he agreed to go to Winchester as a rest-cure while he waited his turn. But he was robbed of his prize by Winnington-Ingram's stubborn refusal to retire until 1939. Instead he remained at Winchester, where he felt underemployed and frustrated. In the early years of the Second World War this frustration gave way to acute depression and insomnia. This was caused partly by the suffering of his clergy in the Southampton blitz and in the Nazi occupation of the Channel Islands (part of his diocese). But Garbett was also lonely, especially after the departure of his chaplain, Gerald Ellison, to fight in the Royal Navy. After his chauffeur was called up, the uncoordinated bishop resolved to learn to drive, a development which terrified his friends and passengers.

York When William Temple became archbishop of Canterbury in 1942, Garbett was chosen to succeed him as archbishop of York. He went reluctantly, being unwilling to leave his beloved Winchester (and particularly his garden there) for the cold north and the notoriously draughty Bishopthorpe. But he settled to his new role with alacrity.

Garbett's brusque style caused some tensions with his suffragan bishops, and he inevitably suffered in comparison with his more emollient predecessor. He maintained good relations with Temple, and the two primates made an effective double-act, with Garbett reining in Temple's more naïve political enthusiasms. There were occasional tensions, and Garbett felt that Temple had given away too much of the church's influence over schools in the Education Act (1944). But the two remained good friends, and Temple's sudden death in 1944 was a grievous blow to Garbett.

Garbett was as punctilious an administrator at York as at Southwark and Winchester. But he also acquired two new public roles. The first was as a popular Christian apologist. Though it was once rightly said of him that he had never had an original thought in his life, he became an extremely effective expositor of Anglicanism, producing a succession of guides such as *The Claims of the Church of England* (1947) and *Church and State in England* (1950). In the latter book he argued that reform of the establishment was necessary if a clash between church and state was to be averted. Garbett had a canny appreciation of the possibilities of the popular media, writing for tabloid newspapers and always ensuring that his speeches were well publicized. Throughout his life he remained an omnivorous reader of books and newspapers of all sorts.

The second role was as an international ambassador for the Church of England. Garbett was a compulsive traveller, making a succession of visits to Russia, Australia and the Pacific, the United States, the Balkans, and Palestine. These visits did much to promote ecumenism, but there was another reason for them, which became public only after his death. Garbett's trip to Soviet Russia in 1943 had been made at the behest of the Ministry of Information, as part of a campaign to cement allied relations, and he sent back detailed reports on Soviet morale to the ministry. In 1944 and 1945 he made trips to the United States and to the allied troops in the Low Countries. The Foreign Office spotted his usefulness, and encouraged him to act as a sort of roving anti-communist ambassador after the war. This Garbett did willingly, travelling to Yugoslavia and Czechoslovakia in 1947, and meeting Marshal Tito. On all his subsequent tours abroad, Garbett publicly denounced communism. This semi-official role perhaps pandered to his self-importance, and he got a rather childlike thrill from being met by dignitaries as he got out of aeroplanes. But as his book *In an Age of Revolution* (1952) showed, his anti-communism was genuine and heartfelt. He was no hawk, though, and was hesitant in his support for the atom bomb.

Final years Garbett was by no means the greatest twentieth-century archbishop of York. He lacked the brilliance, charisma, and ability to inspire devotion of either his predecessor, Temple, or his successor, Michael Ramsey. Garbett recognized (and was pained by) his limitations. 'I have always felt that I should like to be a man to whom people would come instinctively with their troubles,' he said, 'but I find that I am not much more than a rather able administrator' (Smyth, 119). At least in his

years at York some of the old *froideur* began to thaw, and he even unwound enough to enjoy visits to a York City football match and a Butlin's holiday camp. Though still lonely at Bishopthorpe (where his sister Elsie kept house for him, as at Winchester), he found solace in the hills and dales of north Yorkshire.

Garbett was clerk of the closet to the king (1937–42) and was sworn of the privy council in 1942. He had been made an Oxford DD in 1921, and subsequently received eleven honorary doctorates from British and North American universities. By mid-1955 failing health meant that Garbett had reluctantly resolved to resign, but in the event death pre-empted him. He had become unwell during an ill-advised trip to Palestine in spring 1955, and his condition worsened on his return to England. He died at Bishopthorpe on 31 December 1955, hours before he was due to be made a baron in the new year's honours list. His ashes were buried at York on 4 January 1956.

MATTHEW GRIMLEY

Sources C. Smyth, *Cyril Forster Garbett* (1959) · D. Kirby, *Church, state and propaganda: the archbishop of York and international relations* (1999) · A. Hastings, *A history of English Christianity* (1985) · E. Norman, *Church and society in England, 1770–1970* · York Minster Library, Garbett papers [incl. MS autobiography] · *The Times* (2 Jan 1956) · Prioress of Whitby, *Archbishop Garbett, a memoir* (1957) · CGPLA Eng. & Wales (1956)

Archives Borth. Inst., corresp. and papers · York Minster Library, corresp., papers, and diaries | BL, corresp. with Albert Mansbridge, Add. MS 65255A–B | FILM BFI NFTVA, current affairs footage; news footage

Likenesses W. Stoneman, photographs, 1919–45, NPG · D. Jagger, oils, 1951, Bishopthorpe Palace, York [*see illus.*] · H. Coster, photographs, NPG · photograph, NPG

Wealth at death £36,673 4s. 1d.: probate, 17 April 1956, CGPLA Eng. & Wales

Garbett, Edward (1817–1887), Church of England clergyman, journalist, and evangelical apologist, was born at Hereford on 10 December 1817, the sixth son of James Garbett (1775–1857), prebendary of Hereford Cathedral, and brother of James *Garbett (1802–1879), archdeacon of Chichester. He was educated at Hereford Cathedral school, from where he won a scholarship to Brasenose College, Oxford; he matriculated on 19 May 1837, graduated BA in 1841, and proceeded MA six years later. Ordained deacon in 1841 and priest the following year, he was curate to his father at Upton Bishop, Herefordshire, before moving to Birmingham in 1842 to be curate at St George's under his cousin, John Garbett. In 1844 he became vicar of St Stephen's, Birmingham, and five years later minister of St Bartholomew's, Gray's Inn Road, London.

In 1854 Alexander Haldane appointed Garbett as the editor of *The Record*, a position he filled with marked ability until his resignation in 1867, after which he continued to be a regular contributor. Under him the paper became rather less militantly evangelical and shifted its controversial attention from the high to the broad church, especially after the appearance of *Essays and Reviews* (1860). Indeed, E. B. Pusey published a protest at the acquittal of the essayists in *The Record*, and Garbett was later to advocate that evangelical and high-churchmen should join forces to counter the threat from liberal teaching. Garbett also founded and edited the *Christian Advocate* (1861–74).

Journalism did not, however, disqualify Garbett from wide-ranging activity in other spheres. He delivered the Boyle lectures in 1860–63, and those for 1861 were published as *The Bible and its Critics* (1861), an attack on *Essays and Reviews*. The following year his *The Pentateuch and its Authority* took issue with Bishop Colenso. His Bampton lectures were published as *The Dogmatic Faith* (1867). He played a key role both in the foundation of the Church Association in 1865 and in the establishment of the Evangelical Union of Clerical and Lay Associations throughout the country, and he was one of the first evangelicals, from 1866, to participate regularly in church congress meetings alongside churchmen of other schools of thought. Garbett was vicar of Christ Church, Surbiton, Surrey (1863–77), and rector of Barcombe, near Lewes, Sussex, from 1877, having previously declined invitations to more influential parishes such as St Martin's, Birmingham, and St Paul's, Onslow Square, London. In 1875 he was appointed an honorary canon of Winchester, and in the same year he became chaplain to the earl of Shaftesbury.

Garbett's health was much impaired by his work at Barcombe, and on 11 October 1886 he was stricken with paralysis. He died a year later during the night of 10–11 October 1887 at the rectory in Barcombe; he was buried in Barcombe churchyard on 15 October. He was survived by his wife, Elizabeth, whom he had made his sole executor, and by a son and a daughter. A clever controversialist and a vigorous and able champion of the evangelical party through his numerous books and pamphlets, his journalism, and lectures, he never achieved the high office which many contemporaries anticipated for him.

A. R. BUCKLAND, rev. STEPHEN GREGORY

Sources J. S. Reynolds, *The evangelicals at Oxford, 1735–1871: a record of an unchronicled movement* (1953) · D. M. Lewis, ed., *The Blackwell dictionary of evangelical biography, 1730–1860*, 2 vols. (1995) · Boase, *Mod. Eng. biog.* · Foster, *Alum. Oxon.* · J. L. Altholz, *The religious press in Britain, 1760–1900* (1989) · *The Record* (14 Oct 1887) · *The Record* (21 Oct 1887) · *Clergy List* (1842) · *Clergy List* (1845) · *Clergy List* (1850) · Crockford (1887) · D. W. Bebbington, *Evangelicalism in modern Britain: a history from the 1730s to the 1980s* (1989) · private information (1889) [widow] · *CGPLA Eng. & Wales* (1887)
Wealth at death £4680 9s. 7d.: probate, 5 Nov 1887, *CGPLA Eng. & Wales*

Garbett, James (1802–1879), Church of England clergyman and university professor, born at Hereford, was the eldest of six sons of the Revd James Garbett (1775–1857), prebendary of Hereford. Edward *Garbett (1817–1887) was his brother. He passed from the Hereford Cathedral school to Brasenose College, Oxford, where he was elected to a scholarship in 1819. He obtained a first class in classics in 1822 and throughout his life retained a high reputation as a classical scholar. He graduated BA in 1822 and MA in 1825; he was fellow of Queen's College (1824–5), fellow of Brasenose College (1825–36), tutor (1827), Hulmeian lecturer in divinity (1828), junior dean (1832), and Latin lecturer (1834). The college living of Clayton-cum-Keymer,

Sussex, was conferred on him in 1835, and he held it until his death. Garbett was a representative evangelical, and strongly opposed the Tractarian movement at Oxford. In 1842 he was Bampton lecturer. In his lectures, published as *Christ as Prophet, Priest, and King* (2 vols., 1842), while respecting the significance and import of the visible church, he none the less attacked the Tractarians as being in their very essence Roman Catholic, alleging that they substituted human forms for Christ himself. In the same year, although he was only a critic of poetry, he was elected professor of poetry, in opposition to Isaac Williams, the Tractarian candidate. Garbett's election marked the beginning of the decline of the Tractarian movement in Oxford. Garbett again denounced the Tractarians in a university sermon delivered in 1844. He was re-elected professor in 1847, and held the post until 1852. Some of his lectures, all delivered in Latin, were published, and illustrated his finished scholarship. He was said to have declined the Ireland professorship of exegesis in 1847. He certainly refused a seat on the university commission in 1853. He explained in a published letter to B. P. Symons, warden of Wadham (1853), that he took the latter step not because he was unfriendly to the commission but because he objected to the mode of its appointment. He became a prebendary of Chichester in 1843, and archdeacon of the diocese, in succession to Henry Manning, in 1851. Garbett, who seems never to have married, died at his house, 7 Belgrave Place, Brighton, on 26 March 1879.

RONALD DENT KUYKENDALL

Sources *Manchester Guardian* (2 April 1879) · *Manchester Guardian* (23 April 1879) · *The Times* (27 March 1879) · *The Times* (28 March 1879) · Boase, *Mod. Eng. biog.* · W. R. Ward, *Victorian Oxford* (1965) · P. Toon, *Evangelical theology, 1833–1856: a response to Tractarianism* (1979) · [C. B. Heberden], ed., *Brasenose College register, 1509–1909*, 2 vols., OHS, 55 (1909)
Likenesses wood-engraving, NPG; repro. in *ILN*, 74 (1879), 373
Wealth at death under £5000: probate, 24 May 1879, *CGPLA Eng. & Wales*

Garbett, Samuel (1717–1803), industrialist and ironmaster, was born in humble circumstances in Birmingham; nothing else is known about his early life. In August 1735 he married Anne Clay (d. 1772) of Aston. They had four children, two of whom died in infancy. Francis, his son, was associated with his father in some of his business enterprises, as was Charles Gascoigne, husband of Garbett's eldest child and only daughter, Mary.

Garbett was probably almost entirely self-taught but he soon made his mark as a brassworker and became an agent for a London merchant in the purchase of Birmingham ware. He entered into partnership with John Roebuck as a refiner of gold and silver and a consultant chemist to local industries in Birmingham. This early work gave them both the technical skill and the financial resources to begin the manufacture of sulphuric acid in Birmingham and from 1749 at Prestonpans in Scotland. Ten years later the Scottish interests took a major leap forward with the start of the ironworks at Carron, Stirlingshire, in which Garbett and Roebuck each held 25 per cent of the initial capital of the Carron Company. William *Cadell (*bap.* 1708, *d.* 1777) and his son William *Cadell (*bap.* 1737, *d.* 1819) [*see under* Cadell family (*per. c.*1740–1934)] were also financially involved.

Roebuck's wayward genius could not be restrained even by Garbett's commercial acumen. The Carron works was soon greater than anyone had expected and Garbett was called on to finance much of the expansion. The strain was worsened by the activities of Francis Garbett in a shipping company and by those of Gascoigne. The latter took control of most of the family's Scottish interests and eventually ousted his father-in-law before going to Russia to set up a major iron foundry. Such commercial expansion, usually initiated by others, called for financial support beyond Garbett's means. The general financial crisis of 1772 deepened his difficulties and ten years later Garbett was declared bankrupt. His friend Matthew Boulton was a trustee and his loyal supporter in all his difficulties. Boulton especially encouraged him to re-establish his business in Birmingham; Garbett was eventually able to leave more than £12,000 on his death, though with creditors not fully discharged.

From the crisis of 1772 Garbett's financial affairs were in such complex disarray in a mass of interlocking and intricate legal actions that Boulton deemed them beyond his comprehension. While Garbett gave them much attention, at the same time he became a pioneering political lobbyist on behalf of manufacturers and a commentator on political and economic affairs. The key figure in his political contacts was the second earl of Shelburne and first marquess of Lansdowne (1737–1805), but Garbett corresponded widely with the result that letters from him are to be found in many manuscript collections.

In 1783 Garbett promoted the Birmingham Commercial Committee to look after the city's interests, especially of its manufacturers, and was its chairman until 1782. Though concerned initially with local industries, he was convinced of the need to be able to exert wider influence by collective action. In 1785 the threat of reciprocal trading privileges for Ireland led him to co-operate uneasily with Josiah Wedgwood (1730–1795) in promoting a general chamber of manufacturers to lobby parliament on behalf of all manufacturers. Local jealousies ensured that the general chamber did not survive the test of the commercial treaty negotiated with France in 1786 by William Eden, first Baron Auckland. Though influenced by the growing acceptance of free trade views among some of his close friends, Garbett showed traits of a lingering mercantilism in his reluctance to allow free movement overseas of men and machinery. His liberal sympathies are evident in an investigation into the Royal Mint, undertaken with his son, Francis, at the request of Shelburne in 1782. The report, published in 1837, shows the authors' intimate knowledge of the trade in precious metals, offers suggestions for more economical methods of coinage, and pointedly draws attention to the proliferation of sinecures.

Garbett's public life centred on Birmingham. He helped set up the city's assay office in 1773 and was warden from 1796 to 1800. He was active in the Birmingham General Hospital and was chairman of a commission of 1769 to widen and clean the streets. He pioneered the campaign for the abolition of slavery and took part in work on poor relief, excessive consumption of alcohol, and public order. On issues where extremes dominated, he was often a moderating influence. He adhered to the Church of England, but in Scotland associated with the established (Presbyterian) church there, and he defended Joseph Priestley and other dissenters when they were attacked by a mob in 1791.

After Garbett's death Boulton offered the best assessment of his character: 'I have always found his principles unfailingly just, honourable and liberal' (M. Boulton to W. Davies, 12 Dec 1803; Matthew Boulton MSS). His personal misfortunes arose chiefly from the reckless schemes of others, notably of Roebuck and Gascoigne. Garbett died in Birmingham on 5 December 1803 and was buried in the grounds of St Philip's Church (now the cathedral), of which he had been a churchwarden.   R. H. CAMPBELL

Sources P. S. Bebbington, 'Samuel Garbett, 1717–1803, a Birmingham pioneer', MCom diss., U. Birm., 1938 · J. M. Norris, 'Samuel Garbett and the early development of industrial lobbying in Great Britain', *Economic History Review*, 2nd ser., 10 (1957–8), 450–60 · J. Money, *Experience and identity: Birmingham and the west midlands, 1760–1800* (1977) · *Autobiography of the Rev. Dr. Alexander Carlyle ... containing memorials of the men and events of his time*, ed. J. H. Burton (1860); repr. as *Anecdotes and characters of the times*, ed. J. Kinsley (1973) · J. Redington and R. A. Roberts, eds., *Calendar of home office papers of the reign of George III*, 1: 1760–1765, PRO (1878) · J. Redington and R. A. Roberts, eds., *Calendar of home office papers of the reign of George III*, 2: 1766–1769, PRO (1879) · C. Gill, *Manor and borough to 1865* (1952), vol. 1 of *History of Birmingham* (1952–74) · Birm. CL, Matthew Boulton MSS
Archives Birm. CA, Matthew Boulton MSS · Birm. CA, Boulton and Watt MSS · Birm. CA, letters to the marquess of Lansdowne · NA Scot., Carron Company MSS
Likenesses medallion, Assay Office, Birmingham
Wealth at death over £12,000: Bebbington, 'Samuel Garbett', 42

Garbrand, Herks. *See* Harkes, Garbrand (*fl.* 1539–1590), *under* Garbrand, John (1541/2–1589).

Garbrand, John (1541/2–1589), Church of England clergyman and literary executor, was the third surviving son of **Garbrand Harkes** [*later* Herks Garbrand] (*fl.* 1539–1590), bookseller, who fled from religious persecution in the Netherlands and settled in Oxford. On 3 April 1539 the state authorities recorded that Harkes and others had eaten meat during the fast of Lent, evidently an expression of religious dissent. During the reign of Edward VI, he bought much literature from suppressed monasteries, and Wood also reports his role in saving 'a cart load of' manuscripts which 'contained the lucubrations ... of divers of the learned fellows' of Merton College. These had been removed from the college library by 'certain ignorant and zealous coxcombs', but happily, 'some that were lovers of antiquity, interposing themselves, recovered divers of them from ruin' (Wood, *History*, 2.107). In 1551, as one of the two leading booksellers in the town, Harkes was reported to have supplied psalters to Magdalen College. The following year he became a freeman of Oxford. Like others in the local book trade, he diversified his business: in 1554 he took an apprentice as a mercer.

Another later apprentice was Joseph Barnes (d. 1618), who revived printing in Oxford in the later years of the century.

In 1556 Harkes's Oxford house 'now or lately called Bulkley Hall in St Mary's parish, was a receptacle for the chiefest of the Protestants, where, for their privacy, they exercised their religion in a large cellar belonging thereto' (Wood, *History*, 2.132). From 1563 Harkes was the leading supplier of books to the colleges of the university, and in 1566 he was licensed to sell wine. He seems after 1570 to have retired, or at least taken a less prominent role in the business; his son Richard was licensed as an Oxford bookseller in his own right from December 1573 and traded in his father's parish, St Mary's. In 1570 Garbrand Harkes apparently acquired the advowson of the rectory of North Crawley from Sir William Dormer. He was still alive in 1590, when, following the death of his son John Garbrand, the rector, he presented Roger Hackett as successor in the living. After this, nothing is known of him, but the manuscripts from Merton were bought by others and given eventually to the Bodleian Library.

John Garbrand was born in Oxford, and was a student of Winchester College in 1556 at the age of fourteen. He was admitted as a probationary fellow of New College, Oxford, on 24 March 1560, and was a perpetual fellow from 1562 to 1570. He graduated BA on 22 April 1563, proceeded MA on 25 February 1567, and was incorporated at Cambridge the following year. Through Bishop John Jewel, who was friendly with his father, the bookseller, Garbrand was presented to a succession of prebends in the diocese of Salisbury. These were Minor Pars Altaris (where he was installed by proxy on 19 July 1564), Yatesbury (installed 10 November 1565), and Chisenbury and Chute (installed 21 March 1569); Garbrand held this last canonry until his death. Concurrently with it he held another prebend, Taunton, in the diocese of Wells, where he compounded for the first fruits on 21 September 1571 and resigned by 22 August 1578. From 1572 to 1579 he also held the rectory of Farthingstone, Northamptonshire. But it was from another rectory, that of North Crawley, Buckinghamshire, that he signed the preface, dated 27 January 1582, to his edition of Jewel's *A View of a Seditious Bull*. Garbrand was rector from 1567, and died at North Crawley, so it may be that he was ordinarily resident there. On 5 July 1582 he graduated BD and DD at Oxford. Wood called him 'an eminent theologist and a noted preacher, but withal a severe puritan', and in these respects he followed his patron (Wood, *Ath. Oxon.*, 1.556–7). When in 1571 Bishop John Jewel was dying, 'his discourse and prayer on his death bed … were taken from his mouth by John Garbrand, who was always about him … and set down by him' (Strype, 146–7). Jewel bequeathed his papers to Garbrand, who in his own will entrusted them to the keeping of Dr Robert Chaloner and Dr John Reynolds. Garbrand also edited from Jewel's manuscripts *A Short Treatise of the Holie Scriptures* (1582) and *Certaine Sermons Preached before the Queen's Majestie and at St Paul's Crosse* (1583), in which his dedication to Lord Burghley and Robert Dudley, earl of Leicester,

urged 'that all particular churches may be furnished with sufficient, learned and godly ministers, and therefore that tender and due care be had to increase the numbers of them.' To Jewel's *An Exposition upon Paul's Two Epistles to the Thessalonians* (1583) he contributed Latin verses and a dedication to Sir Francis Walsingham. John Garbrand died at North Crawley on 15 November 1589, and was buried in the church there two days later. His will of 10 December 1587, proved by his widow, Elizabeth, and nephew Richard Garbrand on 5 February 1590, gave several books to the library of New College and left funds for a scheme whereby the local poor might borrow money to tide them over in times of particular need. STEPHEN WRIGHT

Sources A. Wood, *The history and antiquities of the University of Oxford*, ed. J. Gutch, 2 vols. in 3 pts (1792–6) · E. Duff, *A century of the English book trade* (1905) · H. G. Aldis and others, *A dictionary of printers and booksellers in England, Scotland and Ireland, and of foreign printers of English books, 1557–1640*, ed. R. B. McKerrow (1910) · VCH Buckinghamshire, vol. 4 · Wood, *Ath. Oxon.*, new edn, vol. 1 · *Fasti Angl., 1541–1857*, [Salisbury] · *Fasti Angl., 1541–1857*, [Bath and Wells] · J. Jewel, *The works of John Jewel*, Parker Society (1850), vol. 4 · Cooper, *Ath. Cantab.* · J. Strype, *Annals of the Reformation and establishment of religion … during Queen Elizabeth's happy reign*, new edn, 2/1 (1824) · Foster, *Alum. Oxon.* · H. I. Longden, *Northamptonshire and Rutland clergy from 1500*, ed. P. I. King and others, 16 vols. in 6, Northamptonshire RS (1938–52) · J. R. Bloxam, *A register of the presidents, fellows … of Saint Mary Magdalen College*, 8 vols. (1853–85) · T. F. Kirby, *Winchester scholars: a list of the wardens, fellows, and scholars of … Winchester College* (1888) · *Hist. U. Oxf. 3: Colleg. univ.* · will, PRO, PROB 11/75, sig. 7 · F. Madan, *The early Oxford press: a bibliography of printing and publishing in Oxford, 1468–1640*, OHS, 29 (1895), vol. 1 of *Oxford books: a bibliography of printed works* (1895–1931)
Wealth at death see will, PRO, PROB 11/75, sig. 7

Garbrand, John (b. 1646/7), political writer and barrister, was born at Abingdon, Berkshire, the son of **Tobias Garbrand** (d. 1689), physician and college head, and Susanna Garbrand (d. 1688). His father, a puritan, was principal under the parliamentary regime from 1648 to 1660. On the restoration of Charles II he was expelled and retired to Abingdon where he practised medicine and died on 7 April 1689. John Garbrand's grandfather was probably **Tobias Garbrand** (1579–1638), college administrator, who was educated at Magdalen and graduated BA in 1602 and MA in 1605. He was a fellow of the college between 1605 and 1619, and was appointed vice-president in 1618. On 5 March 1619 he became vicar of Findon, Sussex, and remained there until his death in 1638. This Tobias was grandson of Garbrand Harkes, a Dutch bookseller of Oxford.

John Garbrand became a commoner of New Inn Hall, Oxford, in midsummer term 1664, aged seventeen, and proceeded BA on 28 January 1668. He was called to the bar at the Inner Temple in November 1673. He may have been the John Garbrand who married Dulcebella Becke of Eaton Hastings, Berkshire, on 12 January 1674, with whom he had at least one son and two daughters. He wrote three books, *The Grand Inquest* (1680), *The Royal Favourite Clear'd* (1682), and *Clarior e tenebris* (1683), discussing the religion of James, duke of York, in 1682–3; by writing these books 'and his endeavours in them to clear the Duke of York from being a papist, he lost his practice, and could get nothing by it' (Wood, 4.786-7).

GORDON GOODWIN, *rev.* M. E. CLAYTON

Sources Foster, *Alum. Oxon.* • F. A. Inderwick and R. A. Roberts, eds., *A calendar of the Inner Temple records*, 3 (1901), 94 • *IGI* [Berkshire] • Wood, *Ath. Oxon.*, new edn • *VCH Berkshire*

Garbrand, Tobias (1579-1638). *See under* Garbrand, John (b. 1646/7).

Garbrand, Tobias (d. 1689). *See under* Garbrand, John (b. 1646/7).

García, Manuel Patricio Rodriguez (1805-1906), singer and singing teacher, was born in Madrid on 17 March 1805 into a prominent family of Spanish musicians. His father, Manuel del Popolo Vicente Rodriguez García (1775-1832), made a reputation as a singer, impresario, composer, and teacher of singing. His mother, Maria Joaquina Sitchès (1780-1854), was an accomplished singer and actress. Manuel, the only son, had two sisters, Maria Felicia (Madame *Malibran) (1808-1836) and Michelle Ferdinande Pauline (Madame Viardot) (1821-1910), who achieved great success as operatic singers. All three children were educated by their parents. At the age of fifteen Manuel was studying harmony with François-Joseph Fétis in Paris and singing opera with his father in Madrid. In 1825 the family migrated to America, and in New York the father founded an opera house; Manuel sang in its first season as Rossini's Figaro. After eighteen months of success the company toured to Mexico, where it is reported they were robbed of their earnings—some £6000 in gold. They then returned to Paris, where the father pursued his career, but Manuel retired from the stage in 1829 and became a teacher.

In 1830 Manuel García temporarily interrupted his musical work to accept an appointment in the commissariat of the French army at Algiers, and on his return studied the physiology of the voice in the military hospitals of Paris and became the first to study voice production. In 1840 he presented to the Académie des Sciences his *Mémoire sur la voix humaine*, which was published in 1841 and became the foundation of all later investigations into the voice. His *Traité complet de l'art du chant* (1840) was also extremely well received, and appeared in a third edition in 1851 and an enlarged English translation in 1894. He had married, in Paris on 22 November 1832, Cécile Eugénie Mayer (1815-1880), a soprano and teacher, and a pupil of her husband. They had two sons, Manuel (1836-1885) and Gustave (1837-1925), a well-known baritone and teacher, and two daughters, Maria (1842-1867) and Eugénie (b. 1844).

After being appointed to a professorship at the Paris conservatory in 1847 García attracted many distinguished pupils, including Jenny Lind, whom he had taught in Paris from 26 August 1841 to July 1842. He was prominent in both literary and artistic circles in the city. Early in 1848 he resigned his position at the conservatory and in June moved to London. On 10 November he was appointed a professor of singing at the Royal Academy of Music. Having closely studied the physiology of the voice, in 1854, for the purpose of examining his own larynx and that of some of his pupils, he invented the instrument since known as the laryngoscope. On 24 May 1855 he presented a paper to the Royal Society of London, through Dr William Sharpey, entitled 'Observations on the human voice', which explained his invention (*Proceedings of the Royal Society of London*, 7, 1855, 399). The opening of this dissertation is given in the *Musical Times* (46, 1905, 228-9). After undergoing some modification in 1857 by Johann Czermak of Pest (1828-1873), the laryngoscope came into universal use as a medical and surgical appliance and brought García world fame. His *Observations physiologiques sur la voix humaine* was published in Paris in 1861. He held his professorship at the Royal Academy of Music for forty-seven years, having been elected a member of the committee of management on 5 July 1869 and a director in 1878, and finally retired in September 1895, at the age of ninety. However, he appears to have remained remarkably fit, both physically and mentally, and he continued to teach privately and maintained an interest in musical affairs until his death.

On 17 March 1905, his hundredth birthday, García was received at Buckingham Palace by Edward VII, who made him a CVO. The German emperor, Wilhelm II, conferred on him the gold medal for science; the king of Spain admitted him to the order of Alfonso XII; the king of Sweden made him *chevalier de l'ordre de mérite*; a banquet, attended by many distinguished persons, was held in his honour; and his portrait, painted by John S. Sargent RA, was presented to him. This was left to the Laryngological Society.

For more than half a century García held, by general consent, the position of premier singing teacher in the world, his school being based on an extension of his father's methods. His pupils, other than Lind, included Frezzolini, M. Marchesi, and Charles Santley. In person he was, from youth to old age, extremely handsome, with all his father's fiery and impetuous disposition. His main recreation appears to have been chess; C. E. Hallé owned a sketch by Richard Doyle of García and his friend Sir Charles Hallé playing a game, which is reproduced in the *Musical Times* (46, 1905, 229). García died at his home, Mon Abri, Shoot-up Hill, Kilburn, on 1 July 1906, and was buried in the private Roman Catholic burial-ground at St Edward's, Sutton Place, near Woking.

FREDERICK CORDER, *rev.* DAVID J. GOLBY

Sources 'Manuel Garcia: the centenarian', *MT*, 46 (1905), 224-32 • A. Fitzlyon, 'García, Manuel (Patricio Rodríguez)', *New Grove* • M. Sterling-Mackinlay, *Garcia the centenarian and his times* (1908) • J. Levien, *The Garcia family* (1932) • J. M. Levien, *Six sovereigns of song* (1948) [lectures] • private information (1912) • personal knowledge (1912) • A. G. Tapia, *Manuel García: su influencia en la laringología y en el arte del canto* (1905) • J. Warrack and E. West, *The Oxford dictionary of opera* (1992)

Likenesses M. F. P. Viardot, crayon sketch, *c.*1855, repro. in 'Manuel Garcia: the centenarian'?, 228 • R. Lehmann, portrait, exh. RA 1869 • J. S. Sargent, oils, exh. RA 1905, Rhode Island School of Design; repro. in 'Manuel Garcia: the centenarian', 224 •

R. Doyle, double portrait, sketch (with Charles Hallé), repro. in 'Manuel Garcia: the centenarian', 229 **Wealth at death** £4362 7s. 6d.: probate, 28 Aug 1906, CGPLA Eng. & Wales

Garcke, Emile Oscar (1856–1930), company director and constructor of electric tramways, was born in Saxony. He came early to Britain, and was naturalized on 17 March 1880, but details of his early background and education have not survived. Their outcome was to provide him with a grasp of the commercial potential of electrical power, and his single-minded application to business enabled him to become the prime mover in the establishment of the British Electric Traction Company (BET), of which he was to be chairman from 1911 to 1920.

Appointed secretary of the Brush Electrical Engineering Company in 1883, Garcke subsequently became managing director, and by the 1890s he had become known in the City for his business acumen, as well as for his command of the new technology. He represented the London chamber of commerce at a conference called by the Board of Trade which led to the passing of the Light Railways Act 1896. This statute enabled tramways to be constructed without the restrictive provisions of the Tramways Act 1870, and thus offered new opportunities for investment, which he was able to exploit.

Registered on 26 October 1896, BET became the chief promoter of tramway schemes throughout the country. The first to be developed were at Hartlepool, Kidderminster, Oldham, and Stoke-on-Trent; and forty were operating by 1899. Two years later BET was responsible for 124 miles of electric tramway.

Garcke was to become the object of criticism from the left wing of politics, BET being attacked as 'the octopus' by the *Daily News* and *Daily Chronicle*, and regarded with animosity by proponents of municipal socialism, including George Bernard Shaw. But the policy of constructing tramways in order to utilize the unused day-time generating capacity of the company's power stations proved successful; and despite some early financial problems BET emerged from the First World War in a strong position.

Garcke had a sophisticated understanding of business management, and adroitly managed the relationship between BET and its eighty or so tramway operating companies. The latter all had separate accounts, as Garcke was insistent that each subsidiary should stand or fall on its own balance sheet. In essence, BET was a holding company, and Garcke summarized the firm's structure as one of 'independence and autonomy of the separate companies in regard to their own affairs, but solidarity in regard to the general questions of principle and policy' (Fulford, 33).

Although Garcke's confidence in the electric tramway played such a great part in the growth of BET he recognized the potential of the motor bus as early as 1900, and by 1906 a subsidiary company was running buses in London. However, Garcke conceived of buses as feeders to the tramway network, and the development of the bus companies owed more to his son, Sidney Emile *Garcke. The

latter, indeed, later remarked that 'I have spent a lot of time taking up the tramways my father laid' (*DBB*).

Garcke's genius was recognized by the financial world, and after a reconstruction in 1915, under his chairmanship, BET attracted men well suited to carry on his policies. In 1920 he was succeeded as chairman by J. S. Austin, continuing as deputy chairman and chief executive until he retired in 1929, handing the reins to R. J. Howley.

In 1882 Garcke married Alice, daughter of John Withers, a brush manufacturer; and the couple had at least one son. Garcke was the author, together with J. M. Fells, of *Factory Accounts, their Principles and Practice* (1887), which was one of the first systematic discussions of cost accounting for a British readership. He was elected a fellow of the Royal Statistical Society, and also became a member of the Institute of Actuaries.

Garcke's commitment to electrical engineering led him to be instrumental in forming the electrical section of the London chamber of commerce, and he was a member of the executive committee of the Federation of British Industry. He was a member of the Institution of Electrical Engineers, and also founded the Tramways and Light Railway Association. In 1896 he launched the annual *Manual of Electrical Undertakings*, often known as 'Garcke's Manual'. He was a founder member of the Institute of Transport.

Garcke died of a heart attack on 14 November 1930 at his home, Ditton Meads, at Pinkneys Green, Cookham, near Maidenhead; his wife survived him. The company he founded remained a leading power in the bus industry under the chairmanship of Howley and H. C. Drayton, until J. S. Wills, who had married Garcke's granddaughter, sold the operating companies to the state-owned Transport Holding Company in 1968.　　　　JOHN HIBBS

Sources R. Fulford, *Five decades of BET: the story of the British Electric Traction Company, Limited* (privately printed, London, 1946) • R. Fulford, *The sixth decade, 1946–1956* (1956) • G. E. Mingay, *Fifteen years on: the B.E.T. group, 1956–1971* (privately printed, London, 1973) • R. Roberts, 'Garcke, Emile Oscar', *DBB* [see also J. Hibbs, 'Garcke, Emile Sidney'] • *Railway Gazette* (21 Nov 1930) • d. cert. • *CGPLA Eng. & Wales* (1931) • *The Times* (15 Nov 1930)
Archives Sci. Mus., ref. Lee-G, Box 6
Likenesses portrait, repro. in Fulford, *Five decades of BET*
Wealth at death £67,150 14s. 5d.: resworn probate, 21 Feb 1931, CGPLA Eng. & Wales

Garcke, Sidney Emile (1885–1948), road transport administrator, was born on 6 January 1885 at 52 Bassein Park Road, Shepherd's Bush, London, the son of Emile Oscar *Garcke (1856–1930), founder of the British Electric Traction company, and his wife, Alice, *née* Withers. He attended the University of London before starting work with BET. He was invited to join the board in 1907 and in 1908 he married Clare Lorraine. They had at least one son and one daughter.

BET interests in the west midlands, where they owned or operated numerous tramways, included a bus company in Birmingham which had been experimenting with motors. Garcke was sent to help deal with the problems of running buses in a big city, and when it was decided to revert to horse-drawn transport he persuaded his board to let him transfer the motor vehicles to a less demanding area. In due course this led to the formation of the East Kent Road Car Company, and, more importantly, to the system of 'area agreements', designed to avoid competition, which Garcke negotiated with Walter Wolsey of Thomas Tilling. These agreements generated a closer working relationship, and Garcke became chairman of the joint holding company, Tilling and British Automobile Traction, formed in 1928. His relationship with Sir J. F. Heaton, the chairman of Tillings, was an uneasy one; none the less he supported Heaton's settlement with the railway companies, which prevented them from acquiring control of the major British bus operators.

Garcke was a member of the first council of the Institute of Transport, founded in 1919, and was awarded the institute's Road Transport (Passenger) medal in 1923. He was also a member of the Institution of Mechanical Engineers. He unsuccessfully contested the Kingswinford division of Staffordshire as a Conservative in the general election of 1929. In line with BET policy, he served from time to time as chairman or director of several of the company's bus operating subsidiaries. In 1943 he joined the board of Dennis Brothers, bus and coach manufacturers, becoming chairman in 1945. When H. C. Drayton succeeded R. J. Howley as chairman of BET, Garcke retired from the board.

Garcke played a significant part in the establishment of the motor bus industry, and is said to have remarked that whereas his father laid down tram lines, he was responsible for digging them up, as BET moved from electric traction to the internal combustion engine. He was made a CBE in 1941 in recognition of his contribution to the establishment of the bus industry, to which he bequeathed the system of agreed territorial monopolies which the leading companies have sought to maintain ever since, with varying degrees of success. He died at his home, Felhurst, Grand Avenue, Hove, Sussex, on 3 October 1948.

JOHN HIBBS

Sources *Modern Transport* (18 Jan 1930) • R. Fulford, *Five decades of BET: the story of the British Electric Traction Company, Limited* (privately printed, London, 1946) • R. Fulford, *The sixth decade, 1946–1956* (1956) • J. Hibbs, 'Garcke, Sidney Emile', *DBB* • b. cert. • d. cert. **Archives** Kithead Trust, Droitwich Spa, Worcestershire, British Electric Traction Company MSS • National Tramway Museum, Crich, Derbyshire, British Electric Traction Company MSS **Wealth at death** £258,627 19s.: probate, 22 Dec 1948, *CGPLA Eng. & Wales*

Gard, William Henry (1854–1936), naval architect, the son of William James Gard, a master painter at Chatham Dockyard, and his wife, Jane (*née* Usher), was born at Lower Briton Street, Gillingham, Kent, on 23 October 1854. He entered Chatham Dockyard as a shipwright apprentice in 1869 and in 1875 studied naval architecture at the Royal Naval College, Greenwich. He was enrolled in the Royal Corps of Naval Constructors when that body was founded in 1883. He was then ordered to the Admiralty, where he assisted in examining and classifying the merchant ships of the United Kingdom, to determine their suitability for conversion into armed auxiliary cruisers in the event of war. His first independent work as a designer came with the *Archer* class torpedo cruisers of 1885. When Sir William White became director of naval construction he came to rely for the detailed design of his ships on a small group of four men, among whom Gard was prominent. He was promoted to assistant constructor, first class, in 1887, and designed the successful first-class cruisers of the *Edgar* class in 1889, and the pioneer torpedo-boat-carrying ship *Vulcan* in 1888. The hull form of the last ship became an accepted standard, and the basis of R. E. Froude's methodical series of hull forms.

In 1894 Gard became chief constructor at Chatham, before moving to Bermuda in 1896 and Malta in 1897 in the same capacity. At Malta he came into contact with Admiral Sir John Fisher, then commander-in-chief of the Mediterranean Fleet. Fisher was impressed by his work in maintaining the Mediterranean Fleet at a time when Fisher's high-speed cruises and manoeuvres were making increasing demands on mechanical reliability. The two men began work on innovative big battleship designs in 1900. Gard provided technical expertise to keep Fisher's ideas within the limits of contemporary shipbuilding technology. In 1902 Gard became chief constructor at Portsmouth, then the finest warship building centre in the world, and renewed contact with Fisher, who was then commander-in-chief. The combination of Fisher's vision and Gard's ability led to a series of pioneering designs, which, although not adopted at once, formed the basis for the epoch-making battleship *Dreadnought*, the battle cruiser *Invincible*, and the ocean-going destroyer. On 31 October 1903 Gard was made a member in the Royal Victorian Order by Edward VII, in recognition of his prompt action in saving Nelson's flagship, the *Victory*, from sinking after a collision. When Fisher became first sea lord in October 1904, Gard was immediately moved to the post of additional chief constructor, and in 1906 rose to be assistant director of naval construction, under Sir Philip Watts. In 1912 Watts resigned, and Gard was considered for the senior post of director, and favoured by Fisher, who was then out of office, despite limited design experience. It may be that his bluff and direct manner did not endear him to Churchill. In the event Gard was passed over, but there was a period without a director, in which he served as acting head of the department. The new director, Sir Eustace Hugh Tennyson-D'Eyncourt, who had been brought in from the private sector by his friend Churchill, paid tribute to the way in which Gard helped him to take control of a large body, over which Gard himself could have hoped to be placed. Gard made a major contribution to the design of successive classes of dreadnought battleship, culminating in the outstanding *Queen Elizabeth* class of 1913 and the *Royal Sovereign* of 1914.

Having reached the age of sixty in October 1914, Gard was due to retire, but the outbreak of war led to his remaining in service until 1919. During the war his experience and resourcefulness were constantly employed, notably in the design of the monitors ordered by Fisher and Churchill for inshore operations, in the adoption of the underwater bulge for protection against mines and torpedoes, and in the remedial work necessary in the aftermath of Jutland. His work on underwater defences at Chatham earned him the commendation of the Admiralty in 1916. In 1917 he was promoted deputy director of naval construction. Like Fisher, Gard was an early convert to the use of oil fuel, leading Admiralty study of the design implications and, of particular value, the safety aspects of bunker design. Gard also pioneered the use of welding in ship repair and construction, and published the first British paper on the subject, 'Some experiences with welding', in the *Transactions of the Institution of Naval Architects* in 1919.

In 1919 Gard finally retired, having been created CB in 1916. He remained a member of the Institution of Naval Architects to the end, but gradually gave up his other professional interests. After a period of ill health he died at his home, Bearsden, Dunheved Road South, Thornton Heath, Surrey, on 29 January 1936, and was buried on 1 February at Mitcham Road cemetery, Croydon.

ANDREW LAMBERT

Sources D. K. Brown, *A century of naval construction: the history of the Royal Corps of Naval Constructors, 1883–1983* (1983) • K. C. Barnaby, *The Institution of Naval Architects* (1960) • *Shipbuilder and Marine Engine Builder*, 43 (1936), 148–9 • E. H. W. Tennyson-D'Eyncourt, *A shipbuilder's yarn* [1948] • *Fear God and dread nought: the correspondence of Admiral of the Fleet Lord Fisher of Kilverstone*, ed. A. J. Marder, 2 (1956) • private information (2004) • b. cert. • d. cert.
Wealth at death £6990 5s. 1d.: resworn probate, 6 March 1936, CGPLA Eng. & Wales

Gardelle, Théodore (1722–1761), murderer and painter, was born in Geneva on 30 November 1722, the son of Elie or Giovino Gardelle of Ravenna. He came of a family of goldsmiths and jewellers that probably also included the miniature painter Daniel Gardelle (1679–1753), who was also born in Geneva. Gardelle was educated at Turretine's charity school and apprenticed to M. Bousquet, a miniaturist and printseller. At the age of sixteen he ran away to Paris but he eventually returned to Geneva, where his conduct, considered immoral, forced renewed visits to Paris. There he studied from 1744 to 1750. He left Geneva finally in 1756, taking with him a young woman whom he called his wife and whom he deserted in Paris with their two young children. He travelled on to Brussels and eventually to London, where he arrived in 1759 and found work as a miniature painter. A life of Gardelle (published in 1761) narrates that he became acquainted with Voltaire at Geneva, drew his portrait and enamelled it on a snuffbox, went to Paris with a recommendation from Voltaire to Louis Surugue, chief engraver to the king, and was advised by the duc de Choiseul to try his fortune in London.

Having arrived in London Gardelle lodged at 37 Leicester Fields, a house kept by Mrs Anne King, a 'gay, showy woman, of a doubtful character, who dressed fashionably, and was chiefly visited by gentlemen' (*GM*, 172). On 19 February 1761, when, according to Gardelle's own account, they were alone in the house together they had an argument over her portrait, which Gardelle had painted; this ended in physical violence, with Mrs King eventually

(according to Gardelle) falling against a bedstead and hitting her head. To silence her screams he, in terror, cut her throat with an ivory comb fitted with a sharply tapered curling iron that lay on her toilet table. Having concealed the body for some days while he arranged for the departure of Mrs King's maid, he eventually cut it up and attempted to dispose of the parts in a variety of ways, which included burning. A horrific and detailed account of the murder and its aftermath, based on Gardelle's own memoir written in French, appears in the *Gentleman's Magazine*. Gardelle was arrested on 27 February 1761. In prison he made an unsuccessful attempt at suicide with laudanum before being convicted and then executed at the corner of Panton Street, Haymarket, on 4 April 1761. A frequenter of Old Slaughter's in St Martin's Lane, Gardelle came into contact there with several artists, including Hogarth. An aquatint by Samuel Ireland (of which a colour proof impression is in the Royal Collection, reproduced in Ireland's *Graphic Illustrations to Hogarth* (vol. 1, facing p. 172) and based on a sketch by John Inigo Richards, shows Gardelle in a white cap reading from a book. The sketch was made as Gardelle was seated in a cart on his way to execution; the artist told Ireland that 'Hogarth came into the room while he was drawing the portrait and added the strong touches' (Oppé, 64). Gardelle's body was hung in chains on Hounslow Heath. Gardelle was notorious at the time for the murder of his landlady, which presumably attracted such lengthy notice in the *Gentleman's Magazine* because of his social status as a gentleman. *The Life of Theodore Gardelle* is presumably identical with Théodore Gardelle, *The Life, Trial and Last Words of Théodore Gardelle*, published by Holborn E. Smith (n.d.), of which a copy is held in the law library reading room of the Library of Congress, Washington. No other published life of Gardelle has been traced. Gardelle appears to have painted portraits in oils, as well as miniatures and enamels. Schidlof states that a miniature on parchment signed 'T. G.', then in the F. Wallop Collection, London, is probably by him.

L. H. CUST, rev. EMMA RUTHERFORD

Sources B. S. Long, *British miniaturists* (1929) • D. Foskett, *A dictionary of British miniature painters*, 2 vols. (1972) • L. R. Schidlof, *The miniature in Europe in the 16th, 17th, 18th, and 19th centuries*, 4 vols. (1964) • Bénézit, *Dict.*, 3rd edn • E. Lemberger, *Meisterminiaturen aus fünf Jahrhunderten* (1911) • J. J. Foster, *Dictionary of painters of miniatures* (1926) • H. Clouzot, *Dictionnaire des miniaturistes sur émail* (Paris, [1924]) • P. F. Schneeberger, *Les peintres sur émail genevois au XVIIe siècle* (1958) • R. Paulson, *Hogarth*, 3 (1993), 20–21 and n. 42 • T. Taylor and R. Owen, *Leicester Square: its associations and its worthies* (1874) • C. Pelham, *The chronicles of crime*, 2 vols. (1841) • S. Ireland, *Graphic illustrations of Hogarth*, 1 (1794), 172 and illustration facing p. 172 • A. P. Oppé, *The drawings of William Hogarth* (1948), 64 [catalogue] • *GM*, 1st ser., 31 (1761), 171–8
Likenesses S. Ireland, aquatint impressions, pubd 1794 (after J. I. Richards and W. Hogarth), BM, NPG • S. Ireland, engraving, impression (after W. Hogarth), BM

Garden [Gardyne], **Alexander** (c.1585–1642?), poet, was probably born in Banchory, Aberdeenshire. The designation of the author as 'Mr.' in a work of his published in 1609 shows that he had graduated with the degree of MA, probably from Marischal College, Aberdeen, before that date. His name appears in 1633 on a list of advocates sworn before the sheriff principal of Aberdeen, and in 1638 as one of a committee of four appointed to choose a new sub-principal. He is not mentioned in any records after 1642, which was probably the year of his death.

Four substantial works are attributed to Alexander Garden: *A Garden of Grave and Godlie Flowers* (1609), *The Theatre of the Scotish Kings*, *A Theatre of Scottish Worthies*, and *The Lyf, Doings and Deathe of William Elphinstoun* (1619). The first of these is a curious miscellany of elegies, prayers, meditations, and poems in praise of King James and of various public figures and personal friends. The two *Theatres* are sequences of short poems, the first covering every monarch from the legendary Fergus to James VI and ending with a lament for Prince Henry, the second (probably incomplete) praising mostly knights and warriors. Garden's attempts to pack a maximum of historical information and moral commentary into each rigidly metrical and highly alliterative poem give to some an almost cryptic air. Finally, the poem on Bishop Elphinstone is a translation of a Latin life by Hector Boece into jingling poulter's measure.

Garden is in no respect a major poet: the elevated moral tone of his works, and their technical adroitness and abundance of erudite allusions, mask a lack of imagination and originality of style. His reliance on polished technique and his insistence on the national history as a theme illustrate in different ways the growing unease regarding Scotland's cultural identity in the period following the union of the crowns.

J. DERRICK MCCLURE

Sources W. B. D. D. Turnbull, 'Prefatory remarks', in A. Gardyne, *A garden of grave and godlie flowers*, Abbotsford Club (1845), ix–xxvi • D. Laing, 'Introduction', in A. Garden, *A theatre of Scottish worthies*, Hunterian Club, 41 (1878), vii–xvi • M. Spiller, 'Poetry after the Union', *The history of Scottish literature*, ed. C. Craig, 1: *Origins to 1660*, ed. R. D. S. Jack (1987), 141–62
Archives NL Scot., Advocates' Library, MSS • U. Edin., MSS

Garden, Alexander (1730–1791), naturalist and physician, was born at Birse, Aberdeenshire, in January 1730, the son of the Revd Alexander Garden (d. 1778), a clergyman of the Church of Scotland. From about 1743 to 1746 he studied medicine at Marischal College, Aberdeen, under the instruction of James Gordon, who encouraged his interest in natural history. Failing to obtain an appointment in the Royal Navy in 1746, Garden continued his medical studies at Aberdeen until 1748. After two years as a surgeon's first mate in the navy he resumed his medical education in 1750 at the University of Edinburgh, where he studied under Charles Alston and John Gregory. As the king's botanist Alston was keeper of the garden at Holyrood and professor of botany and medicine at the university, and it was largely through his influence that Garden developed his enthusiasm for botany.

Soon after completing his training, Garden accepted an offer to join the medical practice of Dr William Rose in Prince William parish, South Carolina. Garden arrived in Charles Town, South Carolina, in April 1752, and his degrees of AM and MD were granted to him by Marischal College in 1753 and 1754. In 1755 Garden moved from Prince William parish to Charles Town where he bought into a prosperous medical partnership, and married Elizabeth (1739–1805), daughter of Henry Peronneau, a prominent Huguenot merchant. Though serving a large practice and having a delicate constitution, Garden managed to devote considerable time to the study of botany and zoology. He had a wide range of correspondents, including, after 1755, Linnaeus. In his letters he expressed disgust and indignation at the inaccuracy of Catesby's *Natural History of Carolina* (2 vols., 1731–43), and showed himself 'a zealous and classical Linnaean' (Smith, 1.282). By 1756 Garden was sending to his European associates large collections of natural history material, including birds, fish, reptiles, amphibia, insects, and plants. Many of his specimens represented new species, genera, or classes of organisms, which were subsequently described in the scientific literature. Although most of his collecting was done in the vicinity of Charles Town, he extended his explorations into Florida, the Cherokee Indian territory, and north to Pennsylvania and New York. One of his correspondents, Thomas Pennant, incorporated some of Garden's information into his *Arctic Zoology* (1784).

In the twelfth edition of Linnaeus's *Systema naturae* (1766–7) Garden's name was subjoined to many new or little-known species of fish or reptiles. He sent many new plants to Europe, including several magnolias and the *Gordonia*, which was, at his request, to have been named after him. Ellis had, however, already named this tree for James Gordon, a London plant nurseryman, and so bestowed the name *Gardenia* upon the Cape jasmine. In 1763 Linnaeus nominated him for membership of the Royal Academy of Uppsala and in 1773 he was elected fellow of the Royal Society. He was also a member of the Royal Society of Arts, the Philosophical Society of Edinburgh, the American Philosophical Society, the Philadelphia Medical Society, and the American Society for Promoting and Propagating Useful Knowledge. In 1764 he published an essay on the medical properties of the Virginia pink-root (*Spigelia marilandica*), and in the following year he described the genera *Stillingia* and *Fothergilla*, dedicated to Benjamin Stillingfleet and John Fothergill respectively.

In the American War of Independence Garden sided with Britain, sending a congratulatory address to Cornwallis on his success at Camden in 1780. In 1782 his properties were confiscated and, having been banished from South Carolina for his loyalist sentiments, he returned the following year to England with his wife and two daughters. He settled in Cecil Street, Westminster, became generally respected for his benevolence, cheerfulness, and pleasing manners, and was chosen vice-president of the Royal Society. Already weak in health, Garden contracted tuberculosis and, despite several tours abroad in search of a cure, died at his home on 15 April 1791.

Garden's son, **Alexander Garden** (1757–1829), was born on 4 December 1757 at Charles Town. He was educated at Westminster School and graduated MA at the University of Glasgow in 1779. In 1784 he married Mary Anna Gibbes. He joined the American army, rising to the rank of major, and received a grant of his father's confiscated estates. He afterwards published *Anecdotes of the Revolutionary War in America* (1822) and *Anecdotes of the American Revolution* (1828). He died on 24 February 1829, at Charles Town.

G. S. BOULGER, *rev.* MARCUS B. SIMPSON JUN.

Sources E. Berkeley and D. S. Berkeley, *Dr. Alexander Garden of Charles Town* (1969) · M. Denny, 'Linnaeus and his disciple in Carolina: Alexander Garden', *Isis*, 38 (1947–8), 161–74 · *A selection of the correspondence of Linnaeus, and other naturalists, from the original manuscripts*, ed. J. E. Smith, 2 vols. (1821) · D. Ramsay, *The history of South Carolina: from its first settlement in 1670, to the year 1808*, 2 vols. (1809) · C. L. G. Gunther, 'Presidential address', *Proceedings of the Linnean Society of London*, 2 (1848–55), 15–38 · W. Darlington, *Memorials of John Bartram and Humphry Marshall: with notices of their botanical contemporaries* (1849) · C. Linnaeus, *Systema naturae* (1766–7) · M. Catesby, *The natural history of Carolina, Florida, and the Bahama Islands* (1731–43) · T. Pennant, *Arctic zoology* (1784) · D. C. Peattie, 'Garden, Alexander (1757–1829)', *DAB*
Archives Linn. Soc., herbarium | Hist. Soc. Penn., Bartram MSS · Linn. Soc., corresp. with John Ellis · Linn. Soc., Linnean corresp. · NHM, description of *Gordoniana* · RS, letters to Royal Society

Garden, Alexander (1757–1829). *See under* Garden, Alexander (1730–1791).

Garden, Francis, Lord Gardenstone (1721–1793), judge, was born at Edinburgh on 24 June 1721, the second son of Alexander Garden of Troup, Banffshire, and his wife, Jane, daughter of Sir Francis Grant, Lord Cullen. He was educated at Edinburgh University and was admitted an advocate in 1743. During the 1745 Jacobite rising, while serving as a volunteer under Sir John Cope, Garden and his companion Colquhoun *Grant (d. 1792) tarried overlong in a bar at Musselburgh and were captured by an enemy patrol. About to be hanged, they were released when they were seen to be completely drunk and incapable.

In 1748 Garden was appointed sheriff-depute of Kincardineshire, and on 22 August 1759 was elected one of the assessors to the magistrates of Edinburgh. On 30 April 1760 he was appointed with James Montgomery joint solicitor-general, but both were denied the privilege of sitting within the bar. He was employed in the celebrated Douglas cause, concerning the right of Archibald James Edward Stewart to inherit the Douglas estates, appearing before the *chambre criminelle* of the parliament of Paris, where he distinguished himself by his legal knowledge and his fluency in French. He was appointed an ordinary lord of session, taking his seat on the bench on 3 July 1764 with the title Lord Gardenstone, and holding this appointment until his death. He also became a lord of justiciary, a post in which he was accused of being swayed by personal or political convictions, and from which he retired in 1787 with a yearly pension of £200.

Gardenstone purchased in 1762 the estate of Johnston at Laurencekirk, Kincardineshire, a parish bisected by the road from Edinburgh to Perth, and in 1765 began to build a new village, which so rapidly increased in size that in 1779 it achieved the status of a burgh of barony. By the time of his death it contained 500 houses with a population of several thousand. To encourage settlement, he offered land on very easy terms. He built an inn, founded a library and

museum for the use of the villagers, and endeavoured to establish various industries based on the production of linen textiles. This philanthropy brought him into considerable debt, relieved when in 1785, on the death of his elder brother, Alexander, he succeeded to the family estates in Banffshire and Aberdeenshire, as well as to a large fortune. Gardenstone improved the road passing through the village, and its bridge, and in May 1789 he paid for a Doric temple to be erected over St Bernard's Well, near Edinburgh, having derived benefit from its waters. He went abroad in September 1786 for the sake of his health, travelling in France, Germany, and Italy, and returning in the summer of 1788. He described this journey in his *Travelling memorandums, made in a tour upon the continent of Europe in the years 1786, 1787 and 1788*. Two volumes were published in 1791 and 1792; the third, with a memoir of him, was published in 1795.

Gardenstone never married. He was a man of many peculiarities, one of which was an extreme fondness for pigs. It is related that a visitor called on him early one morning before he was up, and being shown into the bedroom, in the dark stumbled against something which gave a terrible grunt. At this Gardenstone said 'It is just a bit sow, poor beast, and I laid my breeches on it to keep it warm all night' (Kay, 1.24). His convivial habits as a young advocate were the subject of anecdote, but to Tytler he was 'an acute and able lawyer, of great natural eloquence, and with much wit and humour, [and] had a considerable acquaintance with classical and elegant literature' (Tytler, 3.293n.). In his final years Gardenstone was weakened in mind and body, his inheritance spent, and again encumbered with debt. He died at Morningside, near Edinburgh, on 22 July 1793, and was buried in Greyfriars churchyard on 24 July, in an unmarked grave.

G. F. R. BARKER, *rev.* ANITA McCONNELL

Sources J. Sinclair, *Statistical account of Scotland*, 1 (1791), 475–7; 14 (1795), 163–9 · *Scotland and Scotsmen in the eighteenth century: from the MSS of John Ramsay, esq., of Ochtertyre*, ed. A. Allardyce, 1 (1888), 369–80 · F. Garden, *Travelling memorandums*, 3 vols. (1791–5) · G. Brunton and D. Haig, *An historical account of the senators of the college of justice, from its institution in MDXXXII (1832)*, 526–8 · J. Kay, *A series of original portraits and caricature etchings … with biographical sketches and illustrative anecdotes*, ed. [H. Paton and others], new edn [3rd edn], 1 (1877), 22–5, 61, 350, 419; 2 (1877), 8, 71, 163 · Chambers, *Scots.* (1835) · A. F. Tytler, *Life and writings of the Honourable Henry Home of Kames*, 2nd edn (1814), 3.293–304 · Anderson, *Scot. nat.* · *N&Q*, 3rd ser., 5 (1864), 95 · *GM*, 1st ser., 63 (1793), 769, 803 · *Scots Magazine*, 10 (1748), 155 · *Scots Magazine*, 21 (1759), 446 · *Scots Magazine*, 51 (1789), 653–4 · *Scots Magazine*, 55 (1793), 362
Archives NL Scot., misc. corresp. and MSS · U. Edin., journal
Likenesses J. Kay, caricature, etching, NPG

Garden, Francis (1810–1884), Church of England clergyman and theologian, son of Alexander Garden, a Glasgow merchant, and his wife, Rebecca, daughter of Robert Menteith of Carstairs, Lanarkshire, was educated partly at home and partly from 1825 at Glasgow University; from there he passed in 1829 to Trinity College, Cambridge, where he graduated BA in 1833 and MA in 1836. In 1833 he obtained the Hulsean prize for an essay, 'Advantages accruing from Christianity'. At Cambridge he belonged to the broad-church set of which R. Chenevix Trench, F. D.

Maurice, and John Sterling were among the leaders, and had a close friendship with them and with Edmund Lushington and G. Stovin Venables. His name occurs frequently in Trench's early letters, and he was Trench's companion in Rome in January 1835. He was ordained deacon in 1836, as curate to Sir Herbert Oakeley at Bocking in Essex. In 1837 he married Virginia, the daughter of Admiral Dobbie; she died young, leaving one daughter. The maiden name of his second wife was Boucher; she probably predeceased him. In 1838 Garden became curate to Julius Charles Hare at Herstmonceaux in Sussex, succeeding after an interval his friend Sterling. At this time Garden showed Tractarian sympathies and this soon led to difficulties with Hare. In 1839 Garden became curate of St James's, Piccadilly, from which he became successively the incumbent of Holy Trinity Church, Blackheath Hill (1840–44); junior incumbent of St Paul's, Edinburgh (1845–9); curate of St Stephen's, Westminster; and assistant minister of the English chapel at Rome (1851–2). Finally, in 1859, he succeeded Dr Wesley as subdean of the Chapel Royal, an appointment which he held until his death in 1884. From 1841, also until his death, he edited the *Christian Remembrancer*, a monthly periodical which, in a period of intense church-party partisanship, succeeded in being relatively impartial. Despite his brush with Tractarianism in the late 1830s, Garden was predominantly a broad churchman, adopting the teaching of F. D. Maurice on the incarnation, the atonement, and other chief Christian doctrines, and contributing several thoughtful essays to the series Tracts for Priests and People. The bent of his mind was essentially philosophical, disinclined to accept dogmatic statements without probing them to the bottom to discover the intellectual basis on which they rested. In 1848 he published *Discourses on Heavenly Knowledge and Heavenly Love*, followed in 1853 by *Lectures on the Beatitudes*. A pamphlet on the renunciation of holy orders, then beginning to be debated, appeared in 1870 under the title *Can an Ordained Man Become a Layman?* He published *An Outline of Logic* in 1867, with a second edition in 1871. He was also the author of *A Dictionary of English Philosophical Terms* (1878), and works on the atonement and baptism. He was a contributor to Smith's *Dictionary of the Bible*, the *Contemporary Review*, and other periodicals. Garden died on 11 May 1884 at his home, 67 Victoria Street, Westminster, London.   EDMUND VENABLES, *rev.* H. C. G. MATTHEW

Sources Venn, *Alum. Cant.* · Boase, *Mod. Eng. biog.* · R. Chenevix Trench, *Letters and memorials*, 2 vols. (1888) · *CGPLA Eng. & Wales* (1884)
Archives LPL, corresp. with A. C. Tait
Wealth at death £24,555 8s. 8d.: probate, 25 June 1884, *CGPLA Eng. & Wales*

Garden, George (1649–1733), Scottish Episcopal clergyman and religious controversialist, was born at Forgue, Aberdeenshire, the younger son of Alexander Garden (1611–1674), minister of Forgue, and his wife, Isobel Middleton (*d.* in or after 1696). At about thirteen he followed his elder brother, James [*see below*], to King's College, Aberdeen, graduating MA in 1666. He disappears from the records until 1673, when upon Henry Scougall's

appointment as professor of divinity he was made regent of King's College. He was ordained a minister at Forgue in September 1674 in succession to his father. He was translated to the old cathedral church of St Machar, being installed on 29 June 1679. At some point before his removal there Garden had married Anna Crichton (*d.* 1695), for a son was baptized at St Machar on 22 September 1679. Two sons and two daughters followed. By now a DD Garden was translated to St Nicholas, Aberdeen, on 22 November 1683.

Following the revolution of 1688–9 in Scotland and the re-establishment of presbyterianism Garden continued to preach at St Nicholas, but he declined to pray for King William and Queen Mary, or to read proclamations which referred to them. Accordingly he was called before the Scottish privy council and deprived of his benefice in February 1693. Garden had been in correspondence with some of the members of the Royal Society, and had published on medical topics in the society's *Philosophical Transactions* in 1677 and 1693, so when he set out from Edinburgh to visit Bath in July 1695 he also intended to visit London and Oxford. Indeed, Garden was approved on 19 November 1695 as a fellow of the Royal Society, but he was never formally elected. The previous month, on 23 October, his wife had died.

Garden was much influenced by the work of the French mystic Antoinette Bourignon (*d.* 1680), and in 1699 he published *An Apology for Madame Antonia Bourignon*. This work was formally condemned at the general assembly on 5 March 1701 and he was deposed from exercising any ministerial office. In 1702–3 he published in Amsterdam the collected works of John Forbes, *Opera Johannis Forbesii*. In 1703 there appeared *The Case of the Episcopal Clergy*. In 1710 he was residing in semi-monastic retreat at Rosehearty. However, the new ministry in London evinced considerable sympathy for the plight of Scottish episcopalians and in 1712 a Toleration Act was passed in favour of those ministers willing to pray for the sovereign. Garden appears to have accepted this for following the peace of Utrecht in 1713 both he and his brother were selected to present an address to Queen Anne from the episcopalian clergy of the diocese of Aberdeen. Garden was also a promoter of the use of the English prayer book in Scotland, and eventually preferred to use the Laudian version rather than that favoured by the Church of England. Both Garden brothers were presented to Queen Anne by the earl of Mar on 14 April 1714, when they were in London for his brother's hearing before the House of Lords.

Garden was a committed supporter of the Jacobite rising in 1715. In September he took possession of St Nicholas on Jacobite authority and on 29 December 1715 he and his brother went to Fetteresso, Kincardineshire, and presented James Stuart, the Old Pretender, with an address from the episcopalian clergy of Aberdeen. This was subsequently printed. Following the collapse of the rising Garden was arrested, in March 1716, and deposed again by the Aberdeen presbytery on 27 June 1716. He eventually escaped and arrived in the Netherlands at the beginning of October 1716. Exile gave Garden the chance to take up another long-standing interest and later that month he matriculated at Leiden as a medical student.

While abroad Garden became increasingly influenced by the work of another French pietist, Madame Guyon, actually attending her deathbed in 1717. Garden returned to north-east Scotland in 1720, where his support for Bourignon was held to disqualify him from a bishopric. He described himself as 'minister of the Gospel in Aberdeen' when he drew up his will on 11 February 1730. By this time his children seem to have died: a total of 5500 merks was left to his nephews, nieces, and grandnieces, 300 merks to Archibald Seton, minister, and £400 to 'pious uses' at the discretion of the executor. By 1732 it was reported that his mind had gone, but he survived until 31 January 1733. He was buried at Old Machar Cathedral, Aberdeen.

James Garden (1645–1726), elder brother of George Garden, was born on 3 May 1645 in the castle of Frendraught, where his mother had taken refuge from the war. He was educated at King's College, Aberdeen, graduating MA and DD. He was minister successively at New Machar, Aberdeen (before 1672), Maryculter, Kincardineshire (1675), Balermino (1676), and Carnbee (1678). In 1680 he became professor of divinity at King's College. Probably about this time he married Margaret Irvine (d. 1704), as a son was baptized on 5 April 1682; they had six further sons and four daughters. In October 1690 he appeared before the visitation commissioners, but avoided taking the oaths of allegiance and subscribing to the confession of faith by challenging the jurisdiction of the commissioners. He was eventually deprived of his professorship in January 1697. In 1700 he published *Comparative Theology*, which was republished in 1735 and 1756. In 1703 Garden tried to reclaim his professorship citing the recent Act of Indemnity. He even took the case to the House of Lords in 1714. He died at Old Aberdeen on 8 April 1726.

STUART HANDLEY

Sources G. D. Henderson, *Mystics of the north-east*, Spalding Club (1934) · *Fasti Scot.*, new edn, 6.2, 254; 7.371; 8.526, 590, 713 · C. A. Gordon, 'Professor James Garden's letters to John Aubrey, 1692–1695', *The miscellany of the third Spalding Club*, 3 (1960) · M. K. Ritchie and C. Ritchie, eds., 'An apology for the Aberdeen evictions', *The miscellany of the third Spalding Club*, 3 (1960) · G. Grub, *An ecclesiastical history of Scotland*, 4 vols. (1861), vol. 3 · M. Hunter, *The Royal Society and its fellows, 1660–1700: the morphology of an early scientific institution* (1982), 58, 137 · *Calendar of the Stuart papers belonging to his majesty the king, preserved at Windsor Castle*, 7 vols., HMC, 56 (1902–23), vol. 3, p. 23 · *The book of bon-accord, or, A guide to the city of Aberdeen* (1839), 322 · R. W. Innes Smith, *English-speaking students of medicine at the University of Leyden* (1932), 91 · *Scottish Notes and Queries*, 3rd ser., 10 (1932), 65–6, 130–31 · *Scottish Notes and Queries*, 3rd ser., 11 (1933), 26 · B. Lenman, 'The Scottish episcopalian clergy and the ideology of Jacobitism', *Ideology and conspiracy: aspects of Jacobitism*, ed. E. Cruickshanks (1982) · [P. Bell], ed., *Ministers of the Church of Scotland from 1560 to 1929: an index to Fasti ecclesiae Scoticanae*, 2: E–K (1999) · will, NA Scot., Ex CC 1/6/14

Garden, James (1645–1726). *See under* Garden, George (1649–1733).

Gardenstone. For this title name *see* Garden, Francis, Lord Gardenstone (1721–1793).

Gardiner. For this title name *see* individual entries under Gardiner; *see also* Box, (Violette) Muriel [(Violette) Muriel Gardiner, Lady Gardiner] (1905–1991).

Gardiner. *See also* Gardner, Gardnor.

Gardiner, Sir Alan Henderson (1879–1963), Egyptologist and linguistic scholar, was born on 29 March 1879 in Eltham, Kent, the younger son of Henry John Gardiner (1843–1940), director (later chairman) of the textile company Bradbury, Greatorex & Co., and his wife, Clara Elizabeth, *née* Honey (d. 1879), of Irish descent. She died in Gardiner's infancy; he and his elder brother, the composer (Henry) Balfour *Gardiner (1877–1950), were brought up by their father's housekeeper, Sophia Hawkins. Gardiner was educated at a boarding-school in Margate, at Temple Grove, East Sheen, and at Charterhouse (1892–5). There he developed an interest in ancient Egypt, especially after his father moved to Tavistock Square, near the British Museum and the office of the Egypt Exploration Fund, where Gardiner met, and was encouraged by, W. E. Crum and F. Ll. Griffith. He wrote his first article on Egypt when he was only fifteen ('The Reign of Amen-em-hat I', *Biblia*, 7, 1895). He became an admirer of Gaston Maspero after reading one of his books on Egyptian history, and persuaded his father to send him to study under Maspero in Paris (1895–6) at the Collège de France and the École des Hautes Études. In 1897 he went to Queen's College, Oxford, with a scholarship; Egyptology was not then taught at Oxford, and his father wanted him to have a classical education, but after narrowly failing to achieve a first in classics moderations (1899), he changed to Hebrew and Arabic, gaining a first in 1901. He then spent three months in his father's office learning business methods.

In the autumn of 1901 he married, in Vienna, Hedwig (d. 1964), daughter of Alexander von Rosen, king's counsellor for Hungary, whom he had met in Paris in 1896; they were to have two sons and a daughter; one of their sons was (Henry) Rolf *Gardiner (1902–1971), ecological campaigner and youth leader. Gardiner saw Egypt for the first time on their honeymoon. In 1902 he moved to Berlin, to help gather material for the great Egyptian dictionary project sponsored by four German academies and directed by Adolf Erman. In 1905 he made prolonged stays in Turin and Leiden to examine unpublished material for the dictionary, and from 1906 to 1908 he served as a sub-editor. In 1908 he visited the excavations of D. Randall-MacIver in Nubia, and on his return journey stopped at Thebes and was persuaded by A. E. P. Weigall, then chief inspector of antiquities in Upper Egypt, of the need to survey the private tombs in the Theban area. Accordingly in 1909 he returned to Thebes and over the next two seasons helped Weigall to explore 252 tombs and publish the findings as the *Topographical Catalogue of Private Tombs at Thebes* (1913). He also commissioned Nina M. Davies to make full-colour copies of the most important tomb paintings; her excellent work appeared in the Theban Tombs series (5 vols., 1915–33) and *Ancient Egyptian Paintings* (1936), both edited by Gardiner.

In 1911 Gardiner moved back to England, eventually settling at 9 Lansdowne Road, Holland Park, London, his home until 1940. From 1906 to 1912 he had been Laycock student of Egyptology at Worcester College, Oxford, and from 1912 to 1914 he was reader in Egyptology for Manchester University, but thereafter he avoided academic posts—despite being offered the Oxford chair more than once. His wealthy father had made him financially independent. He was, however, research professor of the University of Chicago (1924–34), without visiting America. He took little part in the First World War, but did some work for the Ministry of Information. From 1922 to 1929 he collaborated on the project, started by P. Lacau, to collate and publish the important funerary texts inscribed on Middle Kingdom coffins, completed by A. de Buck (*The Egyptian Coffin Texts*, 7 vols., 1935–61). From 1928 he supervised and edited the monumental publication of the scenes from the great temple of Abydos (*The Temple of King Sethos I at Abydos*, 4 vols., 1933–58). In 1947 he moved to his final home, Court Place, Iffley, Oxford.

Gardiner considered that his father's generosity placed him under an obligation to spend all his time and energy on his studies, and his approach to research and publishing was businesslike and thorough; his published output was accordingly substantial in both quantity and quality. (A full bibliography up to 1949 is given in the *Journal of Egyptian Archaeology*, 35, 1949, 1–12.) Much of his time was devoted to the publication of previously unpublished Egyptian texts, which he attempted to make available in reliable editions at a reasonable price. To this end he often subsidized works (including ones by other scholars) from his own resources. His editions were usually accompanied by detailed commentaries which made them enduring standard works. His most important titles in this area were his first book, *The Inscription of Mes* (1905), *The Admonitions of an Egyptian Sage* (1909), *Egyptian Letters to the Dead* (1928, with Kurt Sethe), *Hieratic Papyri in the British Museum* (2 vols., 1935), *The Wilbour Papyrus* (3 vols., 1941–8), and *Ancient Egyptian Onomastica* (1947). These all exhibit the wide knowledge of Egyptian texts and vocabulary, particularly of the cursive script of the New Kingdom, which he had gained from his work on the Berlin dictionary.

In 1915, while he was working on some inscriptions found by W. M. Flinders Petrie at Serabit al-Khadim in the Sinai peninsula, Gardiner noticed an otherwise unknown hieroglyphic script which was clearly not Egyptian and which he correctly identified as the earliest known Semitic alphabet, probably the ancestor of all later Semitic and European ones. His theory was long disputed but eventually won general acceptance. Gardiner's other major works were mostly in the field of grammar and linguistics. Dissatisfaction with existing grammars led him to produce his own *Egyptian Grammar* in 1927, in which he discussed not only forms but also meaning and usage. It combined a detailed account of the language with graded exercises for beginners and invaluable sign-lists and vocabularies. Attractively produced and priced, it immediately became the standard work on Middle Egyptian. It

also aroused his interest in general linguistics, first apparent in an article, 'Some thoughts on the subject of language' (*Man*, 1919), and in 1932 he published *The Theory of Speech and Language*. He regarded this as his most important work, and was disappointed when it was poorly reviewed. In 1940 he published *The Theory of Proper Names*. Perhaps his best-known work was *Egypt of the Pharaohs* (1961), an account of Egyptian history based mainly on the written evidence.

Gardiner exercised an influence on Egyptology, particularly in Britain, far beyond his publications. Although he held no important academic post he was universally respected as a senior member of the academic community, and few major appointments were made without his being consulted. He was a leading figure in the Egypt Exploration Fund which, as honorary secretary for 1917 to 1920, he helped reorganize as the Egypt Exploration Society in 1919. He was also instrumental in founding the society's organ, the *Journal of Egyptian Archaeology* (the principal British Egyptological periodical), in 1914, and edited it from 1916 to 1924, in 1934, and from 1941 to 1946. He was largely responsible for improving the conventions governing the transcription of hieratic into hieroglyphs, and commissioned a new hieroglyphic typeface (required for his *Grammar*), subsequently presented to Oxford University Press. He also launched the careers of several budding Egyptologists who lacked his financial advantages, employing as his assistants Battiscombe Gunn in 1915–21, Raymond Faulkner in 1924–39, and Jaroslav Černý in 1934–9. Gardiner obtained the DLitt at Oxford in 1910 and in 1929 he was elected FBA. He received honorary degrees from Durham and Cambridge and was an honorary or corresponding member of many foreign learned bodies. He was an honorary fellow of his old Oxford college, Queen's, from 1935, and in 1948 he was knighted.

Gardiner had a powerful physique and took brisk daily walks. His other interests were mainly tennis (at which he showed some skill), the violin, and foreign travel—although a disciplined worker, he normally took long summer vacations, especially before his wife was immobilized by a stroke in 1955. His own health deteriorated after 1961, and he died at home on 19 December 1963. He was cremated at Oxford and his ashes were interred in Iffley churchyard.   R. S. SIMPSON

Sources DNB · A. Gardiner, *My working years* (1963) [privately printed] · A. Gardiner, *My early years* (1986) [privately printed] · J. Černý, 'Sir Alan Gardiner, 1879–1963', *PBA*, 50 (1964), 263–74 · *Year Book of the American Philosophical Society* (1965), 156–61 · *Journal of Egyptian Archaeology*, 35 (1949), 1–12 [bibliography of works] · WWW
Archives U. Oxf., Griffith Institute, papers, incl. notebooks, copies, transcripts, photographs, indexes, corresp. · UCL, MSS | BL, corresp., with Sir H. Idris Bell, Add. MS 59510 · Bodl. Oxf., corresp. with Sir J. L. Mynes · Egypt Exploration Society, London, corresp. with the Egypt Exploration Society · U. Oxf., Griffith Institute, corresp. with Jaroslav Černý; corresp. with B. G. Gunn and copy of his Egyptian grammar
Likenesses W. Stoneman, two photographs, 1930–45, NPG · T. Styka, oils, 1933, U. Oxf., Griffith Institute · Lafayette, photograph, 1938, NPG; repro. in Černý, 'Sir Alan Gardiner, 1879–1963',

pl. 33 · A. Chappelow, photograph, 1963, repro. in *Journal of Egyptian Archaeology*, 50 (1964), pl. 18 · A. Chappelow, photograph, 1963, repro. in *ILN* (4 Jan 1964), 27
Wealth at death £194,670: probate, 16 March 1964, *CGPLA Eng. & Wales*

Gardiner, Alfred George (1865–1946), newspaper editor and journalist, was born at Rainsford Road, Chelmsford on 2 June 1865. He was the youngest of the eight children of Henry James Gardiner, a cabinet-maker, and his wife, Susannah, *née* Taylor. Like his brothers before him he left school at fourteen to join the *Chelmsford Chronicle*. He was apprenticed as a shorthand writer and reporter. His elder brother Arthur proved a benign mentor. In 1886 he moved to the *Bournemouth Directory*, but within a year left for Blackburn, where he joined the staff of a recently launched Liberal newspaper, the *Northern Daily Telegraph*.

On 21 May 1888 Gardiner married his childhood sweetheart, Ada (1864/5–1948), daughter of Peter Claydon of Witham, Essex. Their happy marriage produced four daughters and two sons. Gardiner, who never found it easy to express personal emotions, was invariably relaxed and happy when with his family. Professional not personal confidence was the source of the assurance he affected in public. In his later years Gardiner's home increasingly became his sanctuary from the world's woes.

T. P. Ritzema, chief proprietor of the *Northern Daily Telegraph*, was a radical zealot. The paradox was that despite an Anglican tory background Gardiner, an instinctive puritan, could not have been happier dispensing nonconformist, radical remedies. He was a confirmed temperance reformer, opposed privilege and monopoly, abominated corruption, and frowned upon any vulgarity. As a journalist, in his *Telegraph* years he mastered the arts of political and descriptive writing. Rapidly he became chief leader writer, assistant editor, and in 1899, editor of the newspaper's weekly edition. The loyalties he forged during the Second South African War significantly determined his attitude towards leading Liberal politicians up to the outbreak of the First World War: for Harcourt and Morley, reverence; for Lloyd George's progressivism, praise; but distrust for the Liberal imperialism of Asquith and Edward Grey. Gardiner was a passionate Little Englander. He despised imperialism not only because he thought it affronted international morality, but also because it distracted Liberals from their most important task, domestic social reform.

In 1901, at Lloyd George's instigation, George Cadbury had become chief proprietor of the oldest, most widely read Liberal newspaper, the *Daily News*. Gardiner's appointment as editor in February 1902 was fortuitous and unexpected. Many knowledgeable critics doubted whether Gardiner was suitable. Because he had no previous Fleet Street experience they supposed that his independence would be easily undermined by ministerial blandishments. There were some initial difficulties with his staff, but Gardiner soon established his position, and his influence was immediate upon the paper's literary and political content. Gardiner was Sir Henry Campbell-

Alfred George Gardiner (1865–1946), by James Russell & Sons

Bannerman's most powerful ally in opposition, and in government his ardent and persuasive spokesman. His commitment to the full radical programme of 'peace, retrenchment, and reform' was absolute, and Sir Henry he supposed was its best guarantor. But when Asquith succeeded as prime minister Gardiner proved more critical, and in matters concerning foreign naval and military policy, distrustful.

Gardiner made the *Daily News* a natural forum for the expression of the hopes and fears of that awkward, conscience-stricken group of radicals, later felicitously dubbed 'the Troublemakers' by A. J. P. Taylor. It became increasingly difficult for Gardiner as editor to satisfy the political and religious scruples of his proprietor, afford support to the Liberal administration, and publish the advanced and critical opinions of brilliant, impatient, young colleagues he had himself recruited to the staff of the *Daily News*. When in 1912 the *Morning Leader* was merged with the *Daily News*, Gardiner's influence was circumscribed. C. P. Scott speculated in his diary that because the former editor of the *Morning Leader* had been made a board member and Gardiner had not, he was now effectively editor in name only and reduced to little more than chief leader writer. Actually, the only hands strengthened by the changes were those of Cadbury. Gardiner, who had never particularly interested himself in the organizational side of the *Daily News*, was not unduly concerned.

'We did what we could to prevent the war', Cadbury

wrote to Gardiner in November 1914. 'Now … it is impossible to stop it … [but] we must secure restitution to Belgium for the injuries inflicted' (A. G. Gardiner, *Life of George Cadbury*, 1923, 273). Though he earned the disapproval of many former friends, Gardiner supported the government's declaration of war against Germany. The bloody stalemate on the western front extinguished hopes of a swift and easy victory and placed an unendurable strain upon old as well as new allegiances and friendships. Gardiner and Lloyd George became estranged, and their alienation was exacerbated when, late in 1916, the Welshman succeeded Asquith as prime minister. Gardiner had once described himself to G. B. Shaw as a 'timid' editor, and certainly his usual disposition was pacific, temperate, and conciliatory. But when he did lose control, self-restraint was forgotten and proportion ignored.

Fighting to save his beloved Liberal Party's soul and principles, Gardiner grew ever more obsessive in his vendetta with Lloyd George. The earlier intimacy of politician and editor was ignored. Standing shoulder to shoulder with Asquith and Grey in the years of Liberal decline, Gardiner chose to laud legislation that earlier he had criticized. He had always viewed international relations as a conflict between good and evil, right and wrong. Their shared admiration for Gladstone helps to explain why President Wilson now seemed to Gardiner the saviour of liberal values. This simplistic perception prompted his moral certitude but blinded him to the fact that his uncompromising opposition to the Versailles peace settlement helped to promote a climate of opinion which nurtured the appeasement that he later condemned.

Gardiner's appointment as editor of the *Daily News* had been unexpected; his resignation in 1919, effectively his dismissal, surprised no one. George Cadbury, a convinced Georgite, not unreasonably objected to his editor constantly nagging and deriding Lloyd George. Cadbury's personal affection and regard for Gardiner remained undiminished. The former editor was given a seat on the board and a very generous pension. He was also allowed to retain his weekly column, though this too fell foul of Gardiner's attacks on the prime minister, and the last links with the *Daily News* were finally severed in February 1921. Journalists commenting on Gardiner's departure saw it as evidence of the changes overtaking their profession: the surrender of editorial independence to proprietorial whim, of principle and conscience to the pursuit of profit. Twice president of the Institute of Journalists, Gardiner had not been slow to express contempt for proprietors who mistook journalism for a trade and who ran newspapers as they might a brewery. Further, pointing a finger at Northcliffe, Rothermere, and Beaverbrook rather than at Cadbury, Gardiner censured proprietors for their irresponsible incursions into politics that demonstrated their desire to make Downing Street an annexe of Fleet Street. H. W. Nevinson listed Gardiner among those editors who had been 'deposed on account of their excellence' (H. W. Nevinson, *Last Changes, Last Chances*, 1928, 273n.). Another former colleague, H. W. Massingham, bluntly asserted that with Gardiner's resignation the *Daily News* lost 'the last pen that seemed to have a definite political creed and the force of conviction behind it' (*The Nation*, 26 March 1921).

Gardiner was not alone in his fate. Everywhere in Fleet Street the opinionated, omnipotent, independent prophets and publicists who had occupied the editors' chairs now yielded place to business managers and accountants. To Gardiner, writes Koss, 'journalism was much more a public service than a career', and for him Liberalism 'was much more a mission than a party affiliation' (Koss, *Fleet Street Radical*, 16). Personally Gardiner suffered few regrets. He had long wearied of the stresses and strains inseparable from editing a daily newspaper, and welcomed a quieter life with more time for his family. Far from abandoning journalism, in the quarter-century coda to his editorship he was a successful, highly paid, regular contributor to several disparate journals on both sides of the Atlantic: *Passing Show*, *Atlantic Monthly*, *The Nation*, and *John Bull*.

Most of Gardiner's writing was undertaken during the three days of most weeks that he spent in London. There, in a committee room of his beloved Reform Club, he competed with Hilaire Belloc for a particular table that both writers found a source of inspiration. Gardiner had always been two kinds of writer: the combative, disputatious controversialist who signed himself A. G. G., and the gentle, discursive essayist, Alpha of the Plough, who, from 1915 contributed to *The Star*. Gardiner was a vivid writer in both moods, although his style perhaps lacked something in distinction when compared with the best of his contemporaries such as Brailsford or Massingham. But his unique gift was an ability to observe and delineate, accurately and without malice, the characters of leading contemporary figures. His skill was best displayed in the four published collections of pen portraits: *Prophets, Priests and Kings* (1908), *Pillars of Society* (1913), *The War Lords* (1915), and *Certain People of Importance* (1926). He never attempted to sketch Lloyd George. G. P. Gooch unreservedly praised Gardiner's portraits as 'a precious contribution to the history of the British post-Edwardian age' (G. P. Gooch, *Under Six Reigns*, 1958, 201). However, Gardiner's three full-length biographies, of which the best is his two-volume *Life of Sir William Harcourt* (1923), were less successful.

Gardiner died at his home, The Spinney, Whiteleaf, Princes Risborough, Buckinghamshire, on 3 March 1946. His editorship of the *Daily News* was, by then, 'already regarded as an episode in the history of British journalism and a chapter in the closed book of Liberal politics' (Koss, *Fleet Street Radical*, 311).   A. J. A. MORRIS

Sources S. E. Koss, *Fleet Street radical: A. G. Gardiner and the 'Daily News'* (1973) · A. J. Lee, *The origins of the popular press, 1855–1914* (1976) · P. Clarke, *Lancashire and the new liberalism* (1971) · P. Clarke, 'British politics and Blackburn politics, 1900–1910', *HJ*, 12 (1969), 302–27 · S. E. Koss, *The rise and fall of the political press in Britain*, 2 (1984) · T. Wilson, *The downfall of the liberal party* (1966) · S. E. Koss, *The pro-Boers* (Chicago, 1973) · b. cert. · m. cert. · d. cert.
Archives BLPES, corresp. and papers | BL, corresp. with G. K. Chesterton and F. A. Chesterton, Add. MSS 73232A, fols. 29–39, 43, 47; 73454, fol. 42; 73455, fol. 227 · BL, corresp. with Lord Gladstone, Add. MSS 46059–46070 · Bodl. Oxf., letters to Herbert Asquith · Bodl. Oxf., letters to William Montgomery Crook · U. Leeds,

Brotherton L., letters to Clement Shorter · University of Arkansas, Fayetteville, Frank Swinnerton papers
Likenesses J. Russell & Sons, photograph, NPG; repro. in Koss, *Fleet Street radical*, frontispiece · J. Russell & Sons, photograph, NPG [*see illus.*] · R. S. Sherriffs, caricature, ink drawing, NPG
Wealth at death £68,569 14*s.* 8*d.*: probate, 13 Aug 1946, *CGPLA Eng. & Wales*

Gardiner, Allen Francis (1794–1851), naval officer and missionary, was the fifth son of Samuel Gardiner of Coombe Lodge, Oxfordshire, and his wife, Mary, daughter of Charles Boddam of Capel House, Bull's Cross, Enfield, Middlesex. He was born on 28 January 1794 in the parsonage house at Basildon, Berkshire, where his parents were temporarily living. He had a religious education, and in May 1808 entered the Royal Naval College, Portsmouth. On 20 June 1810 he went to sea as a volunteer on board HMS *Fortune*, and then on HMS *Phoebe*, on which he served as midshipman until August 1814, when, having distinguished himself in the capture of the American frigate *Essex*, he was sent to England as acting lieutenant of the prize ship. Being confirmed as lieutenant on 13 December 1814, he afterwards served in the *Ganymede*, the *Leander*, and the *Dauntless* in various parts of the world, and returned, invalided, to Portsmouth on 31 October 1822. On 1 July 1823 he married Julia Susanna, second daughter of John Reade of Ipsden House, Oxfordshire; she died on the Isle of Wight on 23 May 1834.

As second lieutenant of the *Jupiter*, Gardiner was at Newfoundland in 1824, and in 1825 came back to England in charge of the *Clinker*. He obtained his promotion as commander on 13 September 1826, after which, although he often applied for employment, he never succeeded in obtaining any other appointment. Long before this, however, he had developed an interest in missions, and he therefore decided to become a missionary. In 1833 he published *Outlines of a Plan for Exploring Australia*, but in 1834 he went to Africa instead, explored Zululand, and started the first missionary station at Port Natal. From 1834 to 1838 he attempted to establish Christian churches in Zululand, but political events and native wars combined to prevent any permanent success; he described his experiences in his *Narrative of a Journey to the Zoolu Country* (1836). On 7 October 1836 he married, as his second wife, Elizabeth Lydia, eldest daughter of Edward Garrard Marsh, vicar of Aylesford, Kent. From 1838 to 1843 he worked among the Indians of Chile, and went from island to island in the South American archipelago, but his efforts were foiled by the opposition of the various governments, as described in his *Visit to the Indians on the Frontiers of Chili* (1840).

His first visit to Tierra del Fuego took place on 22 March 1842, when, coming from the Falkland Islands in the schooner *Montgomery*, he landed in Oazy harbour. The Church Missionary Society was now under pressure to send out missionaries to Patagonia but declined on the ground of shortage of money. Similar proposals were unsuccessfully made to the Wesleyan and London Missionary societies. Eventually in 1844 a special society was formed for South America—the Patagonian Missionary

Allen Francis Gardiner (1794–1851), by unknown engraver, pubd 1857

Society—and Robert Hunt, a schoolmaster, was sent out as the first missionary, accompanied by Gardiner. This attempt to establish a mission failed, however, and they returned to England in June 1845. Gardiner, not discouraged, left England again on 23 September 1845, and, in company with Federico Gonzales, a Spanish protestant, from whom he learnt Spanish, went to Bolivia, where he distributed bibles to the Indian population despite much opposition from the Roman Catholics. Having established Gonzales as a missionary at Potosi, Gardiner came back to England, landing at Southampton on 8 February 1847. That same year he published *A Voice from South America*.

Gardiner spent 1848 in making a survey of Tierra del Fuego with a view to a mission, and suffered great hardships. He then tried to interest the Moravian Brethren and the Foreign Missions of the Church of England in this enterprise, but neither was in a position to help. In the end, a lady from Cheltenham having given £700, the mission was dispatched. Accompanied by Richard Williams (surgeon), Joseph Erwin (ship's carpenter), John Maidment (catechist), and three Cornish fishermen—Pearce, Badcock, and Bryant—Gardiner sailed from Liverpool on 7 September 1850 in the *Ocean Queen*, and landed at Picton Island on 5 December. He had with him two launches, each 26 feet long, in which had been stowed provisions to last for six months. The Fuegians were hostile and ready to plunder, the climate was severe, and the country barren. Six months passed without the arrival of further supplies, which were stuck at the Falkland Islands. The missionaries gradually died of starvation, Gardiner, the last survivor, dying, it is believed, on 6 September 1851. The *John Davison*, sent to assist them, arrived on 21 October, and HMS *Dido* called at the island on 6 January 1852, but all that could be done was to bury the bodies and bring away Gardiner's journal. Two years later, in 1854, the *Allen Gardiner* was sent out to Patagonia as a missionary ship, and in 1856 Captain Gardiner's only son, Allen W. Gardiner, went to Patagonia as a missionary.

G. C. BOASE, rev. H. C. G. MATTHEW

Sources GM, 2nd ser., 38 (1852), 92–4 · J. W. Marsh, *A memoir of Allen F. Gardiner* (1857) · J. W. Marsh, *The story of Commander Allen Gardiner* (1874) · A. Canclini, *Allen F. Gardiner, marino, misionero, martir* (1979) · A. Canclini, *Ultimos documentos del Capitan Allen F. Gardiner* (1959)
Archives Oxon. RO, journal at Tierra del Fuego [transcript] · SOAS, journals · U. Birm. L., letters from him
Likenesses engraving, repro. in Marsh, *Memoir* [*see illus.*]

Gardiner, Arthur (*b.* in or before **1715**, *d.* **1758**), naval officer, seems to have had an Irish background, though no details of his parents are known. His executors came from Dublin, and he had some property in co. Wicklow. He entered the navy as a volunteer per order on 24 August 1730 in the *Falmouth* (Captain John Byng), with Thomas Griffin as first lieutenant, on the Mediterranean station. After five years in her, and short spells in the *Newark*, the *Bridgwater*, and the *Alborough*, in the last two under Captain George Pocock, he passed for lieutenant on 3 November 1737, his age then given as 'more than 21', but he had to go as able seaman in the *Hampton Court*, flagship of a squadron under Commodore Charles Brown bound for Jamaica. The commodore gave him his lieutenant's commission to the *Falmouth* on 4 July 1738, and he served in her until she paid off in 1741. Most of the rest of his service was to be in the Mediterranean, first with the *Sutherland*, and then the *Captain*, again with Griffin, until he was given command of the bomb-vessel *Lightning* in 1744. He reached post rank on 27 May 1745 as flag-captain to William Rowley, the commander-in-chief, in the *Neptune*, and then had an independent command, the *Feversham* (1746–8) during which time he visited the Adriatic.

From 1749 to 1754 Gardiner commanded the *Amazon* on the coast of Ireland, and on paying her off applied, on 15 May 1754, for leave to go to France for eight or ten months. In May 1755 he was appointed to the *Colchester*, but he left her in September to join the *Ramillies* as flag-captain to his old commander, now Admiral Byng. In this capacity he accompanied Byng to the Mediterranean; and when, after the action off Minorca, Byng was recalled, Gardiner too was superseded from his command. According to the journals of Augustus, Lord Hervey, Gardiner remained a friend of Byng's and provided him with helpful advice during his trial.

In February 1757 Gardiner was appointed to the *Monmouth* (64 guns) and again sent to the Mediterranean. In February 1758 he was with the squadron under Admiral Henry Osborn, shutting up M. De la Clue in Cartagena, when on 28 February the Marquis Du Quesne, with three ships, attempted to raise the blockade. The ships were immediately chased, and took different courses. The *Foudroyant*, carrying Du Quesne's broad pennant, was the ship in which M. de La Galissonnière had hoisted his flag

in the battle of Minorca, and, notwithstanding her enormous size, Gardiner had been heard to say that if he fell in with her, in the *Monmouth*, he would take her or perish in the attempt. It is, perhaps, more probable that the story was invented afterwards; for it was by the mere accident of position that the *Foudroyant* was chased by the *Monmouth*, these being followed by the 70-gun ships *Swiftsure* and *Hampton Court*. As night closed in, however, the *Monmouth*, the best sailer, ran the chase out of sight of the other two ships, and, having partially disabled the *Foudroyant*'s rigging, brought her to close action about seven o'clock. In the very beginning of the fight Gardiner was wounded in the arm by a musket bullet, though not so seriously as to compel him to leave the deck. About nine o'clock, however, he fell, shot through the head; he died a few days afterwards, probably on 2 March, and was buried at sea, south-east of Cape de Gata, on 3 or 4 March. The fight was gallantly continued by the first lieutenant, Robert Carkett, and on the *Swiftsure*'s coming up about one o'clock, the *Foudroyant* hauled down her colours. The fact that the *Foudroyant* was an unusually large and heavily armed ship of 80 guns, and that the *Monmouth* alone had beaten her almost to a standstill before the *Swiftsure* came up, as well as the circumstances of Gardiner's death, have combined to render the action one of the most celebrated in eighteenth-century naval history.

Hervey said of Gardiner that he was a very brave officer and a worthy good man (*Hervey's Journal*, 272). He was evidently popular, with many followers, and attained almost continuous employment, though his family commitments were few, for he never married. He left bequests of £1790 and had some property, much of which went to three sisters and two brothers.

J. K. LAUGHTON, rev. A. W. H. PEARSALL

Sources [earl of Bristol], *Augustus Hervey's journal*, ed. D. Erskine (1953) · B. Tunstall, *Admiral Byng and the loss of Minorca* (1928) · J. S. Corbett, *England in the Seven Years' War: a study in combined strategy*, 2 vols. (1907) · R. Beatson, *Naval and military memoirs of Great Britain*, 2 (1790), 153 · J. Charnock, ed., *Biographia navalis*, 5 (1797), 383 · letters, PRO, ADM 1/232 (Brown's), 384 (Osborn's), 1832 · logs, PRO, ADM 51/373 *Feversham*, ADM 52/657 *Monmouth* · muster books, PRO, ADM 36/55 *Alborough*; 330, *Bridgwater*; 1106, 1107, 1113 *Falmouth*; 1423 *Hampton Court*; 2156 *Newark* · pay books, PRO, ADM 33/330 *Hampton Court*; 355 *Diamond* · passing certificate, PRO, ADM 107/3, p. 316 · PRO, PROB 11/840, fol. 146
Archives PRO, ADM MSS 1/232, 384, 1832; 51/373; 52/657; 36/55, 330, 1106, 1107, 1113, 1413; 2156 33/330; 355 107/3, p. 316
Likenesses Benoist, line engraving, NPG
Wealth at death approx. £1200—some property: PRO, PROB 11/840, fol. 146

Gardiner, (Henry) Balfour (1877–1950), composer, was born on 7 November 1877 at 6 Orsett Terrace, London, the elder son of Henry John Gardiner (1843–1940), director of a textile company, and his wife, Clara Elizabeth Honey (*d.* 1879), who died soon after giving birth to their second son, Sir Alan Henderson *Gardiner (1879–1963), later well known as an Egyptologist. Educated at Charterhouse School (1891–4), Gardiner joined the Hoch Conservatorium, Frankfurt-am-Main, in 1894, where he formed lifelong friendships with fellow students and composers Percy Grainger, Cyril Scott, Roger Quilter, and Norman

O'Neill, sometimes collectively known as the Frankfurt Group. Although Gardiner intended to become a concert pianist, partial paralysis of his hand muscles through over-practice forced him to change course to composition. His professor was the kindly Iwan Knorr, who encouraged pupils' individuality, something the independently minded Gardiner greatly appreciated. Gardiner was less happy at New College, Oxford, which he entered in October 1896, obtaining a second class in honour moderations (1898) and a fourth in *literae humaniores* (1900). Between terms and afterwards he returned to Frankfurt for further private study with Knorr. In 1901 he studied conducting at Sondershausen, where he received his first orchestral performances, of a symphony and an overture, neither of which has survived.

Gardiner first became known in England in 1903 with a string quintet, soon followed by a string quartet (1905). For a short while he was active as a collector of folk songs and, despite his considerable inherited wealth, undertook a spell of teaching at Winchester College that resulted in his best-known work, the anthem *Te lucis ante terminum* (*Evening Hymn*, 1908). Up to the war he produced a small corpus of choral and orchestral works, including a second symphony, which in most cases achieved only single performances before his highly self-critical nature either withdrew them for revision or rejected them. The few that passed his scrutiny were an *Overture to a Comedy* (1906, revised 1911), *News from Whydah* (a setting of John Masefield's poem, 1911), and *April* (words by Edward Carpenter, 1913). The tone poem *A Berkshire Idyll* (1913) and the choral *Philomela* (a setting of Matthew Arnold's poem, 1923) were not performed during his lifetime. In 1911 he was working on a one-act opera based on Thomas Hardy's *The Three Strangers*, but the only outcome was his one popular orchestral success, *Shepherd Fennel's Dance* (1911), which exemplifies Gardiner's fondness for dance-like rhythms. He also produced a few piano pieces and some songs among which are to be found Gardiner's finest musical expressions.

The two series of Balfour Gardiner choral and orchestral concerts arguably represent his greatest achievement. Each of their four programmes, consisting almost exclusively of British music, he organized, financed, and in part conducted in the Queen's Hall, London, in 1912–13. These concerts not only helped to establish the reputations of Arnold Bax, Gustav Holst, Ralph Vaughan Williams, Grainger, and others, but gave British music a standing that the Musical League (1908–13) had signally failed to do. Plans for a further series were abandoned because of the outbreak of the First World War, during which Gardiner served first as a censor in Calais and Boulogne and then as an interpreter at prisoner-of-war camps in England and Wales. When in 1918 he learned that Holst was to be posted to Salonika, as a parting gift he paid for the first performance of *The Planets* before an invited audience at the Queen's Hall.

His musical patronage continued for a short while after the war through the financial and artistic support he gave to the Royal Philharmonic Society. Thereafter, friends

were the chief objects of his remarkable generosity. His close friendship with Frederick Delius, with whose music his own harmonic language had much in common, made him question his own output. Composition, despite his very considerable skills, had never been easy for him, and it became increasingly difficult. In the post-war climate he found his music jarred with the prevailing mood, which sought austerity rather than romanticism, and in the mid-twenties he effectively ceased composition altogether. He destroyed many works with which he was dissatisfied and turned instead to other pursuits. First was architecture and, with the aid of a business partner, he bought and restored old country properties. In 1930 he moved from a delightful cottage in Ashampstead, Berkshire, to a house he designed for himself at Iwerne Minster, Dorset. There he embarked on a grand scheme of reafforestation, buying up the barren slopes which through lack of care were fast becoming an ecological wilderness and gradually reclothing them with trees. In his later years he was looked after by a faithful valet and divided his time between Dorset and Oxford, where he had a flat.

Gardiner's opinions and almost childlike sense of humour delighted his many friends. His generosity nearly always benefited the individual, and ranged from the financial support he gave to composers like Delius and Holst to gifts to close friends. He enjoyed travelling abroad, especially to Spain, always in the company of friends. His surviving music, brief in duration but warm and impassioned in feeling, is influenced by Wagner, Tchaikovsky, and Grieg, and firmly rooted in English folk song. He died unmarried in a hospital at Salisbury on 28 June 1950 and his ashes were buried on the north Dorset downs among the trees that he himself helped to plant.

STEPHEN LLOYD

Sources private information (2004) · S. F. S. Lloyd, *H. Balfour Gardiner* (1984) · *CGPLA Eng. & Wales* (1950) · DNB
Archives priv. coll., MSS · University of Melbourne, Grainger Museum, letters, MSS, etc.
Likenesses photograph, repro. in Lloyd, *H. Balfour Gardiner* · photograph, priv. coll.
Wealth at death £312,931 15s. 8d.: probate, 12 Dec 1950, *CGPLA Eng. & Wales*

Gardiner, Bernard (1668–1726), college head, was born at Roche Court, Hampshire, and baptized at Fareham, Hampshire, on 25 September 1668. He was the younger son of Sir William Gardiner, first baronet (*c*.1618–1690/91), barrister and politician, and Jane (*b*. 1642/3), only daughter of Robert Brocas and Jane Bodley, and heir of Beaurepaire and Roche Court in Hampshire. In November 1684 Gardiner matriculated from Magdalen College, Oxford, where he was a demy and whence he was ejected during the struggle with James II. He graduated BA in 1688 and was elected fellow of All Souls in 1689; he subsequently proceeded BCL in 1693 and DCL in 1698. He was elected warden of All Souls in 1702, on the nomination of Archbishop Thomas Tenison, he became keeper of the archives in 1705, and he was vice-chancellor of the university from 1712 to 1715. He held the vicarage of Ambrosden, Oxfordshire, from 1708 and the rectory of Hawarden, Flintshire, from 1714. On 29 February 1712 at Horspath, Oxfordshire, he married Grace, daughter of Sir Sebastian Smythe of Tackley Park and Cuddesdon, Oxfordshire.

Gardiner's principal preoccupation both as warden and as vice-chancellor, was trying to end the abuses of fellows, particularly those not in residence and those not receiving ordination when required to do so by college statutes. He was only partially successful in his campaigns. In 1710–11, for example, he sought to require William Blencowe to take orders and reside but Blencowe appealed to Tenison and Lord Sunderland, who supported him. While Gardiner also had powerful supporters they could not force the government to pursue the issue. All Souls was subject to two visitations by Archbishops Tenison and Wake during Gardiner's wardenship but neither secured the wholesale reform that Gardiner sought. The second of these, in 1717, forced Gardiner to concede archiepiscopal visitational authority over the college, despite nineteen pages of counter-argument that he submitted to Wake.

Gardiner was a whig and anxious to ensure that the Hanoverian succession of 1714 was peaceful, even though he was a founder of the extreme whig Constitution Club. In 1712 he opposed Lord Harcourt's attempt to arrange his son's election as MP for Oxford University, fearing the rise of sectarianism, and backed instead the re-election of Sir William Whitlock. Equally, in 1713 he suppressed the extreme whig *terrae filius* speech by an undergraduate that might have sparked violence. Later published as *The Speech that was Intended to have been Spoken by the Terrae-Filius* it denounced Gardiner's 'bespattered' reputation and claimed that 'not only his honesty and learning, but even his manhood' had been questioned. Gardiner struggled to persuade the university publicly to denounce the author by burning the pamphlet. In 1714 he prosecuted John Aycliffe in the vice-chancellor's court for attacking the privileges of the university in *Ancient and Present State of the University of Oxford* and forced him to resign his fellowship. On the Hanoverian succession Gardiner presented an address to George I and ensured that the succession occurred without undue violence in Oxford, even requiring the mayor of Oxford to ignore threats against him for proclaiming the new king. Despite Gardiner's sympathy for Thomas Hearne's bid to become beadle of civil law in 1715 he supported his ejection from the university as a non-juror in 1716. Hearne unsurprisingly denounced Gardiner as dishonest and grasping in his ambition.

Gardiner gradually became unpopular with the whig government that took power in 1715. He opposed Lord Sunderland's scheme for university reform and supported a moderate tory, George Clarke, who was also a fellow of All Souls, for election as MP for the university in 1717. Though Gardiner defended himself from suggestions of disloyalty in *A Plain Relation of some of the Late Passages at Oxford*, in 1718 he was struck from the commission for the peace for Oxford. He none the less remained intransigent in his views. In 1723 he opposed Thomas Wharton's re-election as professor of poetry because Wharton had accused Gardiner of deliberately concealing some statutes. Fellowship elections remained a cause of conflict; in

1723 Gardiner joined the fellows of All Souls in protesting against Archbishop Wake's imposition of a fellow on the college on the claim of 'founder's kin', and in 1725 he refused to accept the election of three Balliol College fellows at All Souls. He played a significant role in the major renovation of All Souls by George Clarke and Nicholas Hawksmoor, and raised funds for the restoration of the chapel.

Gardiner died in Oxford on 22 April 1726. His daughter, Grace, who married Dr Robert Whalley of Clerk Hill, Lancashire, on 29 July 1742, inherited the Brocas estates of Roche Court. WILLIAM GIBSON

Sources Foster, *Alum. Oxon.* · W. R. Ward, *Georgian Oxford: university politics in the eighteenth century* (1958) · *The speech that was intended to have been spoken by the Terrae-Filius* (1713) · *Reliquiae Hearnianae: the remains of Thomas Hearne*, ed. P. Bliss, 2nd edn, 3 vols. (1869) · J. R. Green and G. Roberson, *Studies in Oxford history*, ed. C. L. Stainer, OHS, 41 (1901) · E. Carpenter, *Thomas Tenison, archbishop of Canterbury* (1948) · A. D. Godley, *Oxford in the eighteenth century* (1908) · N. Sykes, *William Wake, archbishop of Canterbury*, 2 vols. (1957) · *Hist. U. Oxf.* 5: *18th-cent. Oxf.* · GEC, *Baronetage* · DNB

Archives All Souls Oxf., papers relating to the archiepiscopal visitations · LPL, papers relating to the archiepiscopal visitations

Gardiner, Bertha Meriton (1845–1925). *See under* Gardiner, Samuel Rawson (1829–1902).

Gardiner [*née* Kempe], **Dorothy** (1873–1957), writer, was born on 31 August 1873 at 197 Piccadilly, London, the eldest among the six children of Sir John Arrow Kempe (1846–1928), an official in the Treasury, and his wife, Mary Jane, *née* Edwards (d. 1926). She was the niece of the mathematician Sir Alfred Bray *Kempe (1849–1922). She was educated, as were her two younger sisters, at the Francis Holland Church of England School for Girls, London. She excelled in drama and music, and in November 1890 launched and edited a magazine entitled, at her father's suggestion, *Chips and Sparks from Graham Street*. Her article 'A school of the past' anticipated her later interest in the history of education. She studied at Lady Margaret Hall (LMH), Oxford, from 1895 to 1896 and in 1898, taking a third class in English. She was temporary librarian of LMH from 1899 to 1900 and then travelled widely, visiting a brother in New Zealand. Her first notable publication was a scholarly pamphlet for the Early English Text Society entitled *The Legend of the Holy Grail, its Sources, Character and Development* (1905). From 1906 to 1910 she was honorary secretary and editor of the LMH *Brown Book* and editorial secretary to the committee of women's work of the Society for the Propagation of the Gospel. Her interest in social work led her to teach at the LMH settlement in Lambeth, of which she was head from 1908 to spring 1911. Her report of 1909 expresses hopes for 'a Lambeth that is clean and wholesome and roomy, sober, thrifty and *employed*'. In 1911 she was a vice-president of the Workers' Educational Association and from 1912 to 1913 she was an assistant inspector in the south-west division of the National Insurance Council. In 1912 she published *A Social History of Sussex*.

On 30 December 1913 Dorothy Kempe married Thory Gage Gardiner (1857–1941), rector of Lambeth, who shared her social and educational interests. In 1917 he became a residential canon of Canterbury Cathedral and they moved from Lambeth rectory to 14 The Precincts, Canterbury. There were no children. The verse she had previously published in periodicals was collected under her maiden name in *Mary in the Wood with other Lyric Poems* (1917). An editorial note states that 'In social work she finds the chief business of her life; in writing, and in Nature, its chief delight'. Dorothy Gardiner also published a number of distinctive guidebooks, including *Canterbury* (1923) and *Companion into Kent* (1934). Their vivid topographical description is secondary to their thorough account of historical and literary associations, presented in an engaging style.

Gardiner's major work, ten years in preparation, was *English Girlhood at School* (1929), a pioneering contribution to women's studies. An ambitious survey of girls' education in England over twelve centuries, Gardiner's study has enjoyed lasting significance for its unrivalled chronicling of the educational opportunities and experiences of girls before the reforms of the nineteenth and early twentieth centuries. Acutely aware of how greatly she had benefited from the improvements in girls' education, Gardiner memorably compared 'the long struggle, the hope deferred' that characterized female education in previous centuries with 'the fairy-tale' of achieving access to higher education in her own day (*English Girlhood at School*, 484). *The Story of Lambeth Palace* (1930), written at the invitation of Archbishop Davidson, was also thoroughly researched. She then edited, with detailed annotation, *The Oxinden Letters, 1607–1662* (1933) and *The Oxinden and Peyton Letters, 1642–1667* (1937).

In Canterbury Dorothy Gardiner was involved in voluntary work, and was a justice of the peace, chairman of the Canterbury Archaeological Society, a city councillor, and a member of the education committee. Her husband retired in 1937 and died in 1941. Dorothy Gardiner died at her home, Cogan House, 53 St Peter's Street, Canterbury, on 23 January 1957.

JOHN D. HAIGH

Sources *The Times* (25 Jan 1957) · C. Avent and H. Pipi, eds., *Lady Margaret Hall register, 1879–1990* · B. Dunning, ed., *Francis Holland Church of England School for Girls: Graham Street memories* (1931) · J. A. Kempe, *Reminiscences of an old civil servant, 1846–1927* (1928) · D. Kempe, *Mary in the wood with other lyric poems* (1917) [ed.'s note] · D. Gardiner, *Historic haven: the story of Sandwich* (1954) [biographical note on dust jacket] · D. Kempe, ed., *The Brown Book: Lady Margaret Hall Chronicle* (1906); (1907); (1908); (1909), 41–2; (1910) · *The Times* (31 Oct 1941) [obit. of T. G. Gardiner] · *The Times* (6 Nov 1941) · *The Times* (5 April 1928) [obit. of J. A. Kempe] · *The Times* (19 May 1928) · *The Times* (29 June 1928)

Archives Canterbury Cathedral, archives, journals, travel notes, local history notes, and papers | Save the Children, London, archives, corresp. with E. Jebb

Wealth at death £4707 11s. 1d.: probate, 1 Nov 1957, CGPLA Eng. & Wales

Gardiner, Evelyn Grace Rochfort

Gardiner, Evelyn Grace Rochfort [Eve] (1913–1992), beautician, was born on 14 November 1913 at Garfield, Albert Road, Clevedon, Somerset, the daughter of Edward Cecil Gardiner and his wife, Dorothy Frances Elizabeth, *née* Rochfort. She wanted to study art at the Slade School, but her father's finances had suffered during the depression and he could not afford to pay her fees, so she became a hairdresser and qualified while working at a hair and beauty salon in London. In 1936 she heard that Max Factor was planning to open a London branch. He had become well known on the west coast of the United States in the 1920s for his development of make-up for Hollywood film stars, and had moved into the wider cosmetics world in 1929 when he founded Max Factor & Co., with its headquarters in Hollywood. Eve Gardiner applied for a job, and was trained as a make-up artist at the new Bond Street salon, which was opened by the actress Merle Oberon amid a blaze of publicity in 1937. She remained with the company throughout her career.

Because of Max Factor's reputation in the film and theatrical world, the BBC, which then had no make-up artists of its own, asked the London salon in 1938 to help at the Radio Show in London, and Eve Gardiner did the make-up for all the artists appearing in the pioneering television shows presented at the exhibition. She continued to work with television later in her career, developing new techniques to cope with the transition from black and white to colour television; when the television companies started their own make-up departments, the make-up artists were often trained at Max Factor.

During the Second World War, when the Max Factor salon was closed, Eve Gardiner worked as an aero-engine inspector, and when the salon reopened in 1945 she was appointed *directrice*. Already, before the war, she had become interested in cosmetic remedial work; Max Factor, shortly before his death in 1937, on his last visit to London, passed on to her his experience of working with soldiers severely burnt by poison gas during the First World War, together with his techniques for disguising facial disfigurement and scarring. From the earliest days of the London salon, the plastic surgeon Sir Harold Gillies (1882–1960) sent many of his patients to her for remedial camouflage make-up, and after the war Archibald McIndoe (1900–1960), another famous plastic surgeon, worked with her to develop better techniques for disguising the scarring. McIndoe had built up a centre for the treatment of burns and facial injuries at the Queen Victoria Hospital, East Grinstead, in Sussex, where his patients were severely burnt RAF pilots: many of these formed the 'Guinea Pig Club' and kept in touch after the war, and Eve Gardiner was able to help them. She was approached after the war by St Dunstan's Institute for the Blind and asked to help women who had been blinded during the war who had become depressed because, as they could not see to apply their make-up, they thought they were no longer attractive. She became an expert on make-up for the blind, and worked in schools for the blind, teaching girls the techniques of make-up and skin care. She later brought out an audio cassette, *A Touch of Beauty*, for blind women, and she was asked to demonstrate her method of teaching the blind at the National Congress of Esthetics held at Versailles in 1970. As the importance of cosmetic remedial work became recognized through her efforts, the British Red Cross and other organizations began to train volunteers to do this work.

Another aspect of Eve Gardiner's work at Max Factor after the war was her involvement in the London theatre world, where she arranged the make-up for a number of stage productions, including the Festival of Britain productions in 1951 of *Caesar and Cleopatra* and *Antony and Cleopatra*, starring Laurence Olivier and Vivien Leigh, who became a close friend. Her services were also in demand for state occasions, including the 1953 coronation.

After the profits of Max Factor & Co. declined in the early 1970s, the London salon was closed in 1974, but Eve Gardiner continued to work part-time for the company as an adviser, and she became a popular lecturer to women's clubs. In 1988 she was the main speaker at the Esthetics World Expo 88 in Dallas, Texas, where she was appointed to the Academy of Legends.

A beautiful and glamorous woman herself, Eve Gardiner remained single until 1990, when she married her cousin Lieutenant-Colonel Michael David Gardiner, a retired Canadian army officer, whose first wife had died a short while before. She died two years later, on 1 June 1992, in Ealing Hospital, London.

ANNE PIMLOTT BAKER

Sources M. Allen, *Selling dreams: inside the beauty business* (1981) · L. Mosley, *Faces from the fire: the biography of Sir Archibald McIndoe* (1962) · *The Times* (8 June 1992) · *The Independent* (9 June 1992) · b. cert. · d. cert. · *Daily Telegraph* (11 June 1992)
Likenesses photograph (aged sixty), repro. in *The Times* · photograph, repro. in *The Independent*
Wealth at death £156,970: probate, 18 Nov 1992, *CGPLA Eng. & Wales*

Gardiner, George (d. 1589), dean of Norwich, son of George Gardiner, was born at Berwick. He was a scholar of Christ's College, Cambridge, where he graduated BA in 1554 and proceeded MA in 1558, having in the meantime become a fellow of Queens' College; however, he was deprived of this position on 6 August 1561 by reason of his continued absence from Cambridge. In December 1560, at the instigation of Lord Robert Dudley, who was always a firm friend, he was presented by the crown to the living of Chatton, Northumberland. In or about 1562 he became a minor canon of Norwich Cathedral, and was appointed minister to the church of St Andrew in the same city. Through the patronage of bishops Parkhurst of Norwich and Grindal of London he was promoted prebendary in 1565 and introduced improvements in record keeping, including the beginning of a register of leases and a minute book of chapter meetings. During Parker's metropolitical visitation of 1569 he complained of poor discipline at the cathedral, a charge which he repeated to a royal commission the following year, alleging that he was the only resident preacher. But he may have been himself partly responsible for the disorder; during the metropolitan visitation, articles had been lodged against him charging him with having been 'a man very unquiet, troublesome, and dissenting, setting debate between man and man'. It was also said that in Queen Mary's time he had persecuted persons supposed to favour the gospel at the universities. In 1570 he was one of those who broke into the choir of the cathedral and, among other outrages, broke down the organ. He always disapproved of elaborate cathedral music, but in later years he abandoned many of his radical views. In 1571 Gardiner gave up his Norwich living on being presented by the Merchant Taylors' Company to the rectory of St Martin Outwich, London, which he resigned in 1574, and in the same year he was collated to the living of Morley, Norfolk.

Meanwhile Gardiner had been seeking preferment at Norwich. Dean John Salisbury died in September or October 1573, and on 22 November following, undeterred by the fact that Archbishop Parker was also supporting a candidate, Gardiner petitioned to succeed him. He was presented six days later, and was first recorded in chapter on 24 December. But even before that he was also endeavouring to obtain the archdeaconry of Norfolk. The office was already in dispute between two other candidates, John Rugge and Thomas Roberts, who went to law about it. Gardiner claimed that the titles of both men were invalid, and that the presentment had reverted to the queen, and he persuaded Dudley, now earl of Leicester, to support him. He was also rumoured to have claimed that he had the backing of Bishop Parkhurst, even though the bishop's own son was Roberts's patron. Parkhurst was indignant, and when Gardiner secured presentment, on 25 July 1573, put pressure on him to relinquish his new office; he also prevented him from exercising jurisdiction and enjoying the fruits. Gardiner finally reached an agreement with Roberts in September 1574, and he eventually became good friends with Parkhurst. When the bishop died, on 2 February 1575, Gardiner erected a monument to his memory, with an inscription describing him as a good, learned, and godly man, and a most vigilant bishop.

In 1573 Gardiner had also been appointed chaplain to the queen, and in the following year he was in attendance at court. In the same year he was on a commission of oyer and terminer for the county of Norfolk to examine into offences against the Act of Uniformity. In 1578 he was vicar-general of Norwich, apparently for only a short period. In 1575 he obtained the vicarage of Swaffham by gift of the queen, in 1579 the rectory of Haylesden, in 1580 that of Blofield, in 1583 that of Ashill, and in 1584 that of Forncett, all in Norfolk. He held as well the rectory of West Stow, Suffolk. He also had duties in London, and in February 1587 a formal complaint was made against him, among others, for neglecting to preach at Paul's Cross according to a monition.

As dean of Norwich he had the opportunity to institute the better management practices he had earlier advocated, but in fact he was involved in complicated political manoeuvres, the details of which remain obscure, which included three leases of large estates for the exceptionally long period of 100 years. Litigation over this issue continued as late as 1617. There was also a serious dispute over lands held by Lord Wentworth and later leased to Sir Thomas Shirley. Private bills to establish the cathedral's rights, introduced in parliament in 1584 and again in 1589, failed to pass. A settlement arranged by Lord Burghley proved disadvantageous to the cathedral. While Gardiner was dean the lead was stripped from the roof of the lady chapel, and the old library was demolished in 1574. The chapter act books reveal continued laxity and neglect of duties by the petty canons and singing men.

In the later years of his life Gardiner was much troubled by gout. He died about June 1589, and was buried in the south aisle of his cathedral, where his tomb, with its Latin inscription, still remains. He is described by Strype as 'a man of learning and merit and a hearty professor of the gospel'. Many of his letters are extant, and a number of them are printed in Strype's *Annals*. Gardiner was married to a woman named Dorothy, who outlived him; they had at least four children.

ALSAGER VIAN, *rev.* STANFORD LEHMBERG

Sources I. Atherton and others, eds., *Norwich Cathedral: church, city and diocese, 1096–1996* (1996) · *The letter book of John Parkhurst, bishop of Norwich*, ed. R. A. Houlbrooke, Norfolk RS, 43 (1974–5) · *VCH Norfolk*, vol. 2 · J. F. Williams and B. Cozens-Hardy, eds., *Extracts from the two earliest minute books of the dean and chapter of Norwich Cathedral, 1566–1649*, Norfolk RS, 24 (1953) · chapter book I, Norfolk RO, MS DCN, R229A · *Articles to be enquired of within the diocese of Norwiche* (1567) · BL, Lansdowne MSS, MS 443, fol. 144 · Cooper, *Ath. Cantab.*, 2.55 · *Fasti Angl., 1541–1857*, [Ely] · J. Strype, *Annals of the Reformation and establishment of religion … during Queen Elizabeth's happy reign*, new edn, 4 vols. (1824) · J. Strype, *The life and acts of Matthew Parker*, new edn, 3 vols. (1821) · administration, PRO, PROB 6/4, fol. 94r

Archives Norfolk RO, dean and chapter of Norwich papers · Norwich Cathedral, muniments

Gardiner, Gerald Austin, Baron Gardiner (1900–1990), lord chancellor, was born on 30 May 1900 at 67 Cadogan Square, London, the second of three sons (there were no daughters) of Sir Robert Septimus Gardiner, a businessman with interests in the theatre and shipping, and his wife, Alice Marie, daughter of Hermann von Ziegesar, a Prussian officer. He was educated at Harrow School and served briefly in 1918 as a second lieutenant in the Coldstream Guards. At the end of the First World War he joined the Peace Pledge Union. He then entered Magdalen College, Oxford, where he became president of the union and of the Oxford University Dramatic Society (both 1924). Acting remained a lasting attraction. He was rusticated for two terms in 1921, and was again threatened with rustication in November 1922, for publishing a pamphlet attacking restrictions on women undergraduates. He gained a fourth class in jurisprudence (1923) and was called to the bar at the Inner Temple in 1925.

Initially supported financially by his father, by the end of the 1930s Gardiner had a busy practice. His success lay in meticulous preparation of his cases and in the clarity and courteous, unrhetorical style with which he addressed judge, jury, or witnesses, although with the last he could, if necessary, be icy. In the Second World War he was not called up for active service, but, unhappy with a practice expanding at the expense of absent colleagues, joined the Friends' Ambulance Unit and served with, and finally commanded, its sections on the western front.

In 1947 Gardiner was appointed a member of the committee on Supreme Court practice and procedure chaired by Sir Raymond Evershed, but the fact that virtually no

Gerald Austin Gardiner, Baron Gardiner (1900–1990), by Walter Bird, 1965

action was taken to implement the recommendations formulated over a period of six years helped convince Gardiner that more effective methods of achieving law reform were needed. This view was reinforced by his ten years' service on the lord chancellor's Law Reform Committee. Gardiner took silk in 1948, and rapidly became a fashionable advocate. His notable cases included the prosecution in 1960 under the Obscene Publications Act (1959) of Penguin Books for publishing *Lady Chatterley's Lover* by D. H. Lawrence, in which the acquittal Gardiner won for the defendants led to a significant widening of the permissible boundaries in literature; in 1961 the proceedings against the Electrical Trades Union, in which he exposed the ballot rigging of its communist officials; and in 1964 the successful defence of the author Leon Uris in the first Holocaust trial in the English courts, a libel action brought by the Auschwitz doctor Dr Wladislaw Dering. Gardiner had been chairman of the bar council in 1958 and 1959.

Gardiner had begun his law reform campaign in his own practice before the war by circularizing solicitors on how they could shorten litigation procedures. On leaving for the Friends' Ambulance Unit he wrote to the lord chancellor, Lord Simon, about the legal aid crisis arising from the departure for war service of the volunteers who provided the minimal aid then available. His initiative ultimately led to the Legal Aid and Advice Act of 1949. He had also joined the Haldane Society, which supported law reform. In 1945, when the society was threatened with a takeover by communist sympathizers, Gardiner led a secession to form the Society of Labour Lawyers, of which he became chairman. He was also one of the founders of Justice, the British branch of the International Commission of Jurists and an effective law reform pressure group. Justice made the proposals leading to the Parliamentary Commissioner ('Ombudsman') Act and the Rehabilitation of Offenders Act, the latter's spirit being very close to Gardiner's own view of human nature as redeemable. Under the auspices of the International Commission of Jurists Gardiner had travelled to South Africa, Portugal, Tunisia, and Greece investigating alleged breaches of the 'rule of law'. In 1971 he was elected a member of the International Commission of Jurists. He served on its executive committee from 1971 to 1981, and on his retirement in 1986 remained an honorary member until his death. In 1963, with a member of the Society of Labour Lawyers, Andrew Martin, he co-edited and jointly contributed to *Law Reform Now*, which proposed a full-time permanent law commission making recommendations for law reform to parliament.

Gardiner had joined the Labour Party in the 1930s. In the 1951 general election he stood unsuccessfully for parliament at West Croydon. In 1963 Harold Wilson nominated Gardiner for a life peerage and, after the Labour victory in 1964, chose him for lord chancellor. He was sworn of the privy council in the same year. He was inexperienced in the ways of Whitehall, and found some difficulty in getting the Law Commissions Act (1965) onto the statute book. But the commission proved to be profoundly influential in the development of English law and is a lasting monument to Gardiner's commitment to law reform. However, it is possible to argue that his most remarkable achievement was in securing radical reform of the court system. He was responsible for setting up a royal commission on assizes and quarter sessions under Lord Beeching; and its far-reaching recommendations—including the abolition of the assizes and many other historic features—were implemented by the Courts Act (1971). Gardiner was also responsible for the Administration of Justice Act (1970), transforming the Probate, Divorce, and Admiralty Division into the Family Division of the High Court, and thus laying the foundations for what may be regarded as an integrated family court system. Gardiner's restructuring of the court system greatly increased the responsibilities and influence of civil servants in the Lord Chancellor's Department—not least in appointments to what increasingly seemed to be becoming a career judiciary—and was a major factor in transforming what had been a small cabinet of officials into a major department of state. He also appointed the first woman High Court judge.

Gardiner had long been a committed believer in the need for reform of the divorce laws. His action in referring the report of the archbishop of Canterbury's group, *Putting Asunder*, to the Law Commission ultimately led to the publication of the commission's report *The Field of Choice*, and a formal agreement between the archbishop's group and the commission made possible the enactment of the Divorce Reform Act (1969). This established 'irretrievable breakdown' as (in theory at least) the sole ground for divorce. He was also responsible for legislation reducing the age of majority from twenty-one to eighteen, and for a number of other reforms of family law. But the reform from which Gardiner drew the greatest satisfaction was the suspension of the death penalty for murder in 1965 and its final abolition in 1969. He had argued against capital punishment in his book *Capital Punishment as a Deterrent: and the Alternative* (1956), and had been joint chairman of the National Campaign for the Abolition of Capital Punishment. He retired as lord chancellor when the Labour government fell in 1970.

As lord chancellor Gardiner laid great emphasis on the quality of judges at all levels. He introduced systematic training for justices of the peace and sought to ensure that they were drawn from as wide a cross section of the community as possible. His reforming zeal stopped short when considering the legal profession, and especially the division between barristers and solicitors. He feared that in a single profession it would be more difficult to maintain the professional standards generally observed in a bar of limited size, and that, if the selection for the higher judiciary extended to the whole legal profession, there would be practical difficulties in ensuring candidates were all of the calibre required.

In 1972 Gardiner was one of three privy councillors (the other being the lord chief justice and a Conservative politician) appointed to investigate the alleged abuse of interrogation procedures in Northern Ireland. The majority were prepared to condone the practices complained of, but it was Gardiner's minority report which, in a remarkable tribute to his legal and moral authority, was accepted by Edward Heath's government. Nevertheless he could make practical compromises, as when as chairman of another committee on Northern Ireland in 1975 he approved the continuation for the time being of detention without trial.

Gardiner received honorary degrees from Southampton, York, London, Upper Canada, Manitoba, Birmingham, the Open University, Melbourne, and Surrey. In 1975 he was appointed CH. Gardiner's standing as one of the great reforming lord chancellors of the twentieth century remains secure. Probably only Lord Birkenhead (with whom Gardiner has otherwise nothing at all in common) would be a plausible rival for the accolade of the greatest.

Gardiner was a tall, thin man, of upright bearing, with finely chiselled features. His shy courtesy and painful inability to engage in small talk could be taken for coldness, but on closer acquaintance he soon revealed his warm spirit. He supported a very large number of liberal, humanitarian, and charitable causes. When he accepted the chancellorship of the Open University (1973–8) he himself enrolled for, and successfully completed, a three-year degree course in the social sciences (1977).

On 3 December 1925 Gardiner married Doris (Lesly; d. 1966), daughter of Edwin Trounson, company director and later mayor of Southport; they had one daughter, Carol (b. 1929). On 28 August 1970 he married Mrs Muriel Violette *Box (1905–1991), a distinguished film producer and writer, who survived him. She was the daughter of

Charles Baker, railway clerk, and divorced wife of Sydney Box, of J. Arthur Rank. Gardiner died on 7 January 1990 at his home, Mote End, Nan Clark's Lane, Mill Hill, London.

NORMAN S. MARSH, *rev.*

Sources *The Times* (9 Jan 1990) · *Daily Telegraph* (9 Jan 1990) · *The Guardian* (10 Jan 1990) · *The Independent* (10 Jan 1990) · M. Box, *Rebel advocate* (1983) · papers, CAC Cam. · private information (1996) · personal knowledge (1996)
Archives BL, corresp. and papers relating to campaign for the abolition of capital punishment, Add. MSS 56455–56463 · CAC Cam., papers
Likenesses W. Bird, photograph, 1965, NPG [*see illus.*] · N. Hepple, portrait, Inner Temple, London

Gardiner, James (1636/7–1705), bishop of Lincoln, was the second son of Adrian Gardiner, an apothecary of Nottingham, and his second wife. He was admitted to Emmanuel College, Cambridge, as a pensioner in 1649, graduating BA in 1653 and proceeding MA in 1656 and DD in 1669. He incorporated at Brasenose College, Oxford, in 1665. At some point he became a chaplain to the duke of Monmouth. He was collated to the prebendal stall of Stow in Lincoln Cathedral by Bishop Robert Sanderson in 1661, and installed in person. He was presented by the crown to the rectory of Epworth in Lincolnshire in 1668, and collated to the subdeanery of Lincoln Cathedral by Bishop William Fuller in 1671. He married Anne Hale (*d.* 1705) of Kettlethorpe in Lincolnshire in 1677. He restored the subdeanery, which had been badly damaged during the sack of the close in 1644, building a fine great hall to replace the medieval hall. Despite Archbishop Sancroft's commendation of Gardiner, Charles II granted the deanery in 1681 to Daniel Brevint. Gardiner was critical of Brevint as dean, reporting to Sancroft in 1685 Brevint's illness, and added that things had been in an

> ill ... state ... since the coming in of that Dean who in the space of 4 years ... has never taken one weeks paines to peruse our Statutes or Chapter Acts, or any other Records of our Church which might inform him of his office, and direct him of the conduct of his Government. (Bodl. Oxf., MS Tanner 130, fol. 121)

Gardiner was in general a caustic critic of churchmen who did not apply themselves to their tasks.

When Thomas Tenison was translated from Lincoln to Canterbury in 1695 he commended Gardiner to the ecclesiastical commission established by William III as his successor. Gardiner was consecrated bishop of the diocese with which he had such a long association on 10 March 1695, and was enthroned in Lincoln Cathedral in person. By royal warrant he was permitted to retain his prebendal stall *in commendam* for three years, presumably to help his finances. He was a close ally of Tenison, and joined in the call for a 'national reformation of manners' to combat the influence of freethinking 'libertines' and Roman Catholics; the latter, he suggested, were using 'libertines' and dissenters to undermine the Church of England (*Twenty Sermons*; Gardiner, *A Sermon*). However, in February 1700 he was the only one of the seventeen bishops in the court of delegates not to endorse Tenison's decision to deprive Thomas Watson, bishop of St David's, for simony. In 1702

James Gardiner (1636/7–1705), by Mary Beale, in or after 1695

he acted as Tenison's commissary in proroguing convocation when the lower house attempted to defy Tenison's authority to prorogue convocation against its will. He supported Tenison and bishops Gilbert Burnet of Salisbury and William Lloyd of Worcester in successfully opposing an occasional conformity bill in 1703.

As a diocesan bishop Gardiner was exemplary. He normally conducted ordinations in his diocese, at the canonical seasons, usually at Buckden in Huntingdonshire, the main episcopal residence, relatively centrally situated in that vast diocese. He conscientiously checked the letters of orders of clergy presented to livings, and in 1700 detected an incumbent with forged letters of orders. He was sympathetic to the poverty of many of his clergy, and their heavy burden of the clerical taxes of first fruits and tenths. He undertook triennial visitations in 1697, 1700, and 1703. Rather than delivering a charge at his primary visitation he issued an 'Advice' to the clergy prior to the visitation. This 'new Method' meant that he would not be tired when he delivered the charge, could give more time for confirming, and enable those prevented from attending the visitation by 'Sickness or very Old age' or 'unavoidable and necessary business' to 'know his mind' (Gardiner, *Advice*, 3–4). He emphasized the importance of attending visitations in order to hear the sermon, to meet fellow clergy, for intellectual stimulation, and for mutual encouragement. He hoped that they might 'direct one another in the Knowledge of Modern Books and Treatises of Religion' and encourage one another to 'vigorously oppose the Vices and Factions of the Age' (ibid., 5). He regretted the lack of rural deans, whom he envisaged might assist the bishop by reporting 'the ignorant, the

Factious, the Scandalous, the Negligent, and the Dissenting' to the archdeacons, who themselves ought to be resident in their archdeaconries. He quoted the example of his thirteenth-century predecessor, Robert Grosseteste, as a conscientious diocesan. He encouraged clergy to say the daily services and perform occasional offices audibly and with dignity, and to resist requests for private baptisms, and to give notices of fasts and feasts that people might at least forbear from 'Labour and Work' at the hours of worship (ibid., 13). He emphasized explaining scripture and 'fundamental doctrines' in preaching and catechizing (ibid., 18). People should be warned of the dangers of not receiving holy communion or of receiving it unworthily. He discouraged the reception of holy communion by people in their seats, and advocated using chancels for its celebration, even if it provoked accusations of popery. He criticized the practice of clandestine marriages. He warned the clergy against generosity in signing testimonials of ordination candidates, or providing them with false titles, and required that all curates should be examined by the bishop before being admitted to a curacy; he criticized incumbents with considerable incomes who paid curates £20, £25, or £30 a year. He emphasized the need to lead exemplary lives and to avoid drunkenness. In all this he echoed the royal injunctions of 1695.

Gardiner was a noted antiquary, some of which knowledge he put to good use in his pastoral policy as a bishop. He consulted White Kennett after reading Kennett's *Parochial Antiquities* in 1699 to gather information about rural deans and the form of their appointment, and subsequently appointed Kennett archdeacon of Huntingdon, in 1701.

Gardiner died on 1 March 1705, aged sixty-eight, at his house in Dean's Yard, Westminster, following the sudden death of his wife, and was buried in the retrochoir of Lincoln Cathedral. His fine Latin inscription praises him as an imitator of the best of the fathers of the church. Among his children were his younger sons James *Gardiner (d. 1732) and William Gardiner, who was admitted scholar at Trinity Hall, Cambridge, in 1699 and became vicar of Hambleton, Rutland.   W. M. JACOB

Sources J. Gardiner, *Advice to the clergy of the diocese of Lincoln* (1697) · *Twenty sermons preached upon several occasions by William Owtram DD by the Revd Dr James Gardiner*, 2nd edn (1697) · bishops registers, 1691–1704, Lincs. Arch., 35 · letter to Gardiner from William Kirke, 11 Feb 1703, Lincs. Arch., COR/B/4/16 · clergy call books 1697 visitation, Lincs. Arch., LCXIV · Venn, *Alum. Cant.* · *Fasti Angl., 1541–1857*, [Lincoln] · E. Carpenter, *Thomas Tenison, archbishop of Canterbury* (1948) · M. Bowker, 'Historical survey, 1450–1750', *A history of Lincoln Minster*, ed. D. Owen (1994), 164–209 · G. Jones, K. Major, and J. Varley, *The survey of ancient houses in Lincoln*, 2 (1987) · G. V. Bennett, 'King William III and the episcopate', *Essays in modern English church history: in memory of Norman Sykes*, ed. G. V. Bennett and J. Walsh (1966), 104–31 · N. Luttrell, *A brief historical relation of state affairs from September 1678 to April 1714*, 6 vols. (1857) · R. Thoroton, *The antiquities of Nottinghamshire* (1677) · J. Gardiner, *A sermon preached before the House of Lords* (1695)
Likenesses M. Beale, oils, in or after 1695, LPL [*see illus.*] · oils, Emmanuel College, Cambridge · portrait, Bishop's House, Lincoln

Gardiner, James (d. 1732), Church of England clergyman, was the younger son of James *Gardiner (1636/7–1705)

bishop of Lincoln, and his wife, Ann Hale (d. 1705) of Kettlethorpe, Lincolnshire. He was educated at Westminster School, and admitted pensioner of Emmanuel College, Cambridge, in 1695, proceeding BA, as sixteenth wrangler, in 1699 and MA in 1702. He was elected a fellow of Jesus College, Cambridge, in 1700 and incorporated into the University of Oxford in 1703. He was ordained deacon by the bishop of Lincoln in 1702. In Lincoln Cathedral, in 1704, his father preferred him as prebendary of Asgarby, as subdean of the cathedral, and as master of St John's Hospital, Northampton, and of Bedford Hospital, Nottingham, all of which posts he held until his death.

In *A Practical Exposition of the Beatitudes*, published in 1712, Gardiner noted a parallelism between the giving of the ten commandments and the sermon on the mount in Matthew's gospel, and compared it with the version in Luke's gospel. Gardiner also published a sermon which he had preached in Lincoln Cathedral in 1713, entitled *The Duty of Peace amongst the Members of the Same State*, against faction and party, commenting that as there was peace abroad so there ought to be peace at home. In 1715 he published *A practical exposition of the latter part of our saviour's sermon on the mount from the beatitudes to the end of the sermon*. He noted that in his earlier volume he had been criticized for lack of oratory, but he pointed out that these two volumes were not intended to be sermons but practical expositions. He contributed to the *Oxford and Cambridge Miscellany Poems*, published in 1709, and translated *Rapin of Gardens*, published in 1718.

Gardiner appears to have kept his full residence at Lincoln and to have continued the work of his father, who had been subdean from 1671 to 1695, in rebuilding and renovating the subdeanery after its sack by the military in 1644. His expenditure on the house was considerable, and it was thought by contemporaries to be the best house belonging to the cathedral. During Gardiner's time as a subdean successive deans were largely absentee. In 1729 a new chancellor, the nephew of Bishop Reynolds, pointed out that the dean was no longer entitled to a share of the cathedral's common fund. This was because under the cathedral's statutes the dean was required to be in residence for 119 days per year and he had been absent for two years. The bishop, as visitor, upheld the statutes, and in doing so gave additional recognition to the enhanced role of the subdean. During Gardiner's subdeanship the dean and chapter were very conservative in their management of their estates, resisting raising their rents, as were other capitular bodies at this time, which may have avoided opposition and anti-clericalism but reduced the residentiaries' income and, more importantly, reduced the amount spent on the cathedral fabric. In fact very little was spent on the cathedral between 1701 and 1719. In 1725 a visitor commented that it was in very poor condition and James Gibbs was called in to survey the building and advise on its repair. He recommended the removal of the spires on the western towers; this provoked opposition in the city and the county. In September 1726, when work was about to begin on taking down the spires, rioting broke out in the cathedral precincts, and Gardiner and the chancellor of the cathedral had to negotiate with the mayor to preserve the peace and decided to retain the spires. Gardiner died at Lincoln on 24 March 1732 and was buried in the retrochoir of the cathedral, next to his father. His wife, Dinah, died on 4 September 1734.

W. M. Jacob

Sources Venn, *Alum. Cant.* · M. Bowker, 'Historical survey, 1450–1750', *A history of Lincoln Minster*, ed. D. Owen (1994), 164–209 · F. Hill, *Georgian Lincoln* (1966) · G. Jones, K. Major, and J. Varley, *The survey of ancient houses in Lincoln*, 2 (1987) · *DNB*
Likenesses G. Vertue, line engraving (after J. Verelst), BM, NPG; repro. in *Rapin of Gardens*, 2nd edn, trans. J. Gardiner (1718)

Gardiner, James (*bap.* 1686, *d.* 1745), army officer, was baptized on 10 January 1686 at Carriden parish church, Linlithgowshire, the eldest son of Captain Patrick Gardiner of Torwoodhead and his wife, Mary Hodge, of Gladsmuir. Educated at Linlithgow grammar school, he entered service as a cadet in a Scots regiment in Dutch service, and was made a colour ensign in 1702. He shortly afterwards transferred to Borthwick's regiment on the Scottish establishment. He took an active part in Marlborough's campaigns during the War of the Spanish Succession, and on 23 May 1706 was wounded at the battle of Ramillies, where he was shot in the mouth and left for dead.

On 31 January 1714 Gardiner became lieutenant in Kerr's dragoons (7th hussars), and captain in Stanhope's dragoons (disbanded 1718) on 22 July. During the 1715 Jacobite rising Gardiner fought at the battle of Preston (12 November 1715) and had command of a storming party which rushed the Jacobite barricades. On 14 January 1718 he was promoted major, and subsequently he became aide-de-camp to John Dalrymple, second earl of Stair. As Stair's master of horse Gardiner arranged his entry into Paris as British ambassador in 1719. On 20 July 1724 Gardiner was made major in Stair's dragoons (6th Iniskillings), and on 24 January 1730 lieutenant-colonel in that regiment. It was probably during this stage in his career that Gardiner, who until then had been noted for his dissolute life, experienced a religious conversion, and he thereafter led an abstemious life.

Gardiner married Lady Frances Erskine, daughter of David, ninth earl of Buchan, in Edinburgh on 11 July 1726. They had thirteen children, of whom only two sons and three daughters survived their father.

On 18 April 1743 Gardiner succeeded to the command of Bland's dragoons (13th hussars), based in Haddingtonshire. During the 1745 rising Gardiner was not reinforced and was obliged to evacuate Perth at the approach of the Jacobite army. He withdrew first to Stirling, and then Edinburgh. Both Gardiner and his regiment seem to have been in poor spirits at this time. He fought at the battle of Prestonpans (21 September 1745) close to his own house, Bankton in Haddingtonshire. Gardiner's soldiers mostly fled but, though shot and wounded, he dismounted to fight on foot to encourage the infantry. He was eventually disabled by a blow from a lochaber-axe, and died at Tranent manse the following morning, 22 September. On 24 September Gardiner was buried in the churchyard at Tranent, where he had been a regular worshipper. He was survived by his wife.

Described, rather ambiguously, as 'a weak, honest, and brave man' (*Autobiography of Dr Alexander Carlyle*, 1860, 132), James Gardiner was a man whose slow rise as a junior officer in the army indicates a lack of influential friends. He was fortunate in his connection with the earl of Stair from 1719 onwards, and in his ability to marry well, while only a major of dragoons. His bravery at Prestonpans had wide popular notice at the time, and his reputation as a sincere and devout Christian led to his being presented as an example of a reformed life by Philip Doddridge, whose *Some Remarkable Passages in the Life of … Colonel James Gardiner* (1747) was frequently republished until 1864. The dramatic way in which he died and his appearance in devotional literature have attracted attention to an officer whose career was otherwise unspectacular.

James Falkner

Sources *DNB* · N. B. Leslie, *The succession of colonels of the British army from 1660 to the present day* (1974) · R. Cannon, ed., *Historical record of the thirteenth regiment of light dragoons* (1842) · J. Ferguson, ed., *Papers illustrating the history of the Scots brigade in the service of the United Netherlands, 1572–1782*, 3 vols., Scottish History Society, 32, 35, 38 (1899–1901) · notes, NAM, 13th Hussars, Army Museums Ogilby Trust files, box 1 1730–1781 · C. Petrie, *The Jacobite movement*, 3rd edn (1959) · J. Home, *The history of the rebellion in the year 1745* (1802) · C. Sinclair-Stevenson, *Inglorious rebellion: the Jacobite risings of 1708, 1715 and 1719* (1971) · B. Lenman, *The Jacobite risings in Britain, 1689–1746* (1980) · F. Maclean, *Bonnie Prince Charlie* (1988)
Archives NL Scot., letters
Likenesses J. T. Wedgwood, line engraving, pubd 1815, BM, NPG · T. Kitchin, line engraving (after Van Deest), NPG

Gardiner, Luke, first Viscount Mountjoy (1745–1798), politician and property developer, was born on 7 February 1745, the eldest son of Charles Gardiner (*c.*1712–1769), landowner and MP, and Florinda Norman (*b.* 1722). As the scion of a family that had become extremely wealthy as a consequence of shrewd land purchases and urban development on Dublin's north side, Gardiner enjoyed a privileged upbringing. Educated at Eton College (1759–62) and St John's College, Cambridge, he and his brother William Neville *Gardiner made their grand tour to France and Italy between 1770 and 1771. While still a student Luke demonstrated a keen aesthetic sensibility by commissioning Francis Cotes to paint his portrait. Further commissions ensued while he was in Rome, and following his election to the exclusive Society of Dilettanti in 1773 he sat for Joshua Reynolds. In the same year Reynolds painted the famous portrait of the three Montgomery sisters—the 'Irish Graces'—at Gardiner's request. Gardiner married the eldest sister, Elizabeth Montgomery (1751–1783), daughter of Sir William Montgomery, first baronet, and Hannah Tomkyns, on 3 July 1773, and the couple established a reputation as enthusiasts of the private theatricals that were then very fashionable in Ireland. Elizabeth died in childbirth on 7 November 1783; their only surviving son, Charles John Gardiner (1782–1829), later earl of Blessington, married the author Marguerite Power [*see*

Gardiner, Marguerite, countess of Blessington (1789–1849)].

Gardiner was not content to be a dilettante. Following in the footsteps of his father and grandfather he pushed ahead with the development of the Gardiner estate and was responsible in the 1770s for the development of Temple, Eccles, and North Great George's streets. He was also possessed of political ambitions, and he secured his return to parliament for the co. Dublin constituency in a by-election in 1773. On entering the House of Commons he 'profess'd great attachment to government' (Hunt, 22), not least because, like his father who had sought the honour from Lord Townshend, he aspired to a peerage. Criticism of his unwillingness to go along with the agenda of the vocal reform-minded electorate of Dublin caused him to claim subsequently that he was not attached to any party, whereas in reality he was an independent whose primary disposition was to support the administration. Thus, while he opposed the suggestion that four thousand troops on the Irish army establishment should serve in America in 1775, he believed that Ireland should 'assist' (Black, 2.202) the crown. To this end he opposed the attempts by the patriots at the beginning of the 1777–8 session to exploit the issue and denied their claim that the economic downturn that the country experienced was attributable to the wartime embargo on Ireland's freedom to trade.

Gardiner's critics in the Dublin press would, had they been aware, have related his political conduct to his desire for a peerage whereas his stand was entirely in accordance with his convictions. He was instinctively cautious on constitutional issues. He was no less convinced of the importance of public order and eager to foster economic advancement, and it was these factors rather than electoral advantage that caused him to promote the interests of Dublin and its environs. Similar convictions informed his decision to introduce legislation aimed at repealing the bulk of the economic disabilities against Catholics in 1778. Convinced that economic concessions did not pose a threat to the security of the protestant interest in Ireland, and encouraged by the administration, he shrugged off the 'misrepresentations' (Freeman's Journal, 25 July 1780) to which he was subject as further examples of the 'monstrous abuses' (Black, 2.325) perpetrated by the popular press. He was, he informed the House of Commons in November 1779, 'one of those persons who will always do what I think right, let the consequence be what it may' (ibid., 2.265). Guided by this principle, and notwithstanding his colonelcy of the co. Dublin light dragoons volunteer corps, he did not decline to express his unease at the formation of independent corps of volunteers in the late 1770s. His preference was for an official militia, and he further displayed his political moderation by declining to support the demand of the patriots for a six-month money bill in 1779 and by opposing calls for an Irish mutiny act in 1781. His stand pleased the Irish administration, which, unable to give him a peerage, made him surveyor-general of the customs for life, appointed him to the Irish privy council, and, in recognition of his and his family's influence in Dublin, appointed him to the Wide Streets commission.

In keeping with the moderate position he had adopted in the 1770s, Gardiner kept the demand for constitutional reform at a distance in the early 1780s. He was silent, significantly, on the subject of legislative independence though his endorsement of simple repeal, his support for a financial grant to Grattan, and his public praise for the volunteers indicated that he was not unaffected. His priority was 'to give such relief to the Roman Catholics as would advance the prosperity and gratify the wishes of the whole nation' (Parliamentary Register, 1.197) and, as a result of the tactful, accommodating, and flexible manner with which he pursued the subject, he was able to secure the ratification of a number of enactments in 1782 that substantially enhanced the civil and economic rights of Catholics.

Gardiner's willingness to support the Irish administration in the early 1780s was influenced, but not determined, by his conviction that successive lords lieutenant supported his request for a peerage. So when it emerged in 1783 that the current viceroy, Lord Northington, was disinclined to advance his claims Gardiner distanced himself from the administration and advocated the introduction of a regimen of protecting duties as a solution to the high unemployment in the textile sector in Dublin. However, when distress escalated into violence in the spring of 1784 he promptly 'abandon[ed] the cause' (Parliamentary Register, 3.167), and he had no hesitation in supporting controversial legislation aimed at curbing the 'licentiousness of the press' (ibid., 3.162) in 1784.

Promised by the Rutland administration that he would be raised to the peerage, for which he lobbied intensely in the winter of 1784–5, 'at the first convenient opportunity' (Bolton MS 15921/1), Gardiner aligned himself more closely with the Irish administration from 1785. He supported William Pitt's proposed commercial union without any enthusiasm, but he welcomed the proposal to replace the volunteers with an official militia on 18 February 1785. He confined his remarks, thereafter, to non-controversial Dublin issues, to the need for proper gaols, and to the house of industry. He made his last recorded speech in the House of Commons in February 1789 when he spoke against disfranchising revenue officers, as he had done previously in 1782, on the grounds that it would not be to the advantage of the protestant interest in Ireland. Seven months later he was raised to the peerage as Baron Mountjoy, and six years later he was made a viscount.

Mountjoy's ennoblement coincided with his intensified pursuit of his plans for urban development in Dublin. His most noteworthy achievements were Mountjoy Square (1790) and Rutland Square (1791). Urban development on this scale produced a healthy economic return for Mountjoy, and his financial position was further improved by his second marriage, to Margaret Wallis (d. 1839), daughter of Hector Wallis and Sarah Drope, on 20 October 1793, and by successful litigation that brought him extensive lands in co. Tyrone. Politically, Mountjoy eschewed both the conservative and revolutionary extremes into which Irish politics became polarized in the 1790s. At the same time his founder membership of an association for the protection of property in 1795 indicated that he remained as concerned as ever to maintain public order. It was thus entirely in character for him to hasten to Wexford at the head of his regiment of militia on the outbreak of the rising in 1798. His death at the battle of New Ross on 5 June 1798 elicited little sympathy from ultra-conservatives, but their unforgiving judgement did little justice to a man who had conducted himself honourably during his lifetime, and who is rightly remembered for his important contributions to the cityscape of Dublin and to the cause of Catholic relief.   JAMES KELLY

Sources J. Porter, P. Byrne, and W. Porter, eds., *The parliamentary register, or, History of the proceedings and debates of the House of Commons of Ireland, 1781–1797*, 17 vols. (1784–1801) · *The manuscripts of his grace the duke of Rutland*, 4 vols., HMC, 24 (1888–1905), vol. 3 · J. Coleman, 'Luke Gardiner (1745–98): an Irish dilettante', *Irish Arts Review Yearbook*, 15 (1999), 161–8 · GEC, *Peerage* · *An edition of the Cavendish Irish parliamentary diary, 1776–1778*, ed. A. R. Black, 3 vols. (Delavan, WI, 1984–5) · W. Hunt, ed., *The Irish parliament, 1775* (1907), 22–3 · J. R. Hill, *From patriots to unionists: Dublin civic politics and Irish protestant patriotism, 1660–1840* (1997) · H. Cavendish, parliamentary diary, 1776–89, L. Cong. · NL Ire., Bolton MSS, MS 15921/1 · M. R. O'Connell, *Irish politics and social conflict in the age of the American revolution* (1965) · E. McParland, *James Gandon: vitruvius Hibernicus* (1985) · B. Burke, *A genealogical history of the dormant, abeyant, forfeited and extinct peerages of the British empire*, new edn (1883) · *Kearsley's complete peerage of England, Scotland and Ireland* (1811) · Venn, *Alum. Cant.*
Archives BL, Northington letterbook, Add. MS 38716 · NA Ire., Townshend MSS, MS 5040 · NL Ire., Bolton MSS · NL Ire., Domvile MSS
Likenesses F. Cotes, pastels, 1765, priv. coll. · J. Reynolds, oils, 1773, priv. coll. · engraving, repro. in *Hibernian Magazine* (June 1778)

Gardiner [*née* Power; *other married name* Farmer], **Marguerite** [Margaret], **countess of Blessington** (1789–1849), author, was born on 1 September 1789 at Knockbrit, near Clonmel, co. Tipperary, Ireland, the second daughter and third of the six children of Edmund Power (1767–1837), a small Roman Catholic landowner, and Ellen, daughter of Edmund Sheehy, whose family was excessively proud of its very old Roman Catholic ancestry. As a girl Margaret was chiefly noticeable as the one plain member in a singularly handsome family. Feeling out of place among her boisterous, handsome siblings, Margaret was miserable until Miss Anne Dwyer, a kind-hearted neighbour, a spinster, and friend of her mother's, took pity on her and taught her reading and the love of story-telling. When she was eight, her father moved his family to Clonmel, where he was appointed magistrate, both in Waterford and Tipperary.

In 1804 Margaret, then only fourteen and a half, was proposed to by two officers of the 47th regiment of foot, then stationed at Clonmel. Her parents forced her to marry one of them, Captain Maurice St Leger Farmer (*d.* 1817) of Poplar Hall and Laurel Grove, co. Kildare, a man who indulged in such ungovernable outbursts of passion as to suggest

insanity. They were married in the parish church of Clonmel in the United Church of England and Ireland on 7 March 1804. Three months later Margaret refused to accompany her husband when he was ordered to join his regiment, and she returned to her father's house at Clonmel. Because of a serious argument with his colonel, Captain Farmer soon sold his commission and went to India, ending his relationship with Margaret. He returned from India in 1816 and was killed during a drunken orgy in a fall from a window in the king's bench prison on 21 October 1817.

After she left her husband Margaret stayed for almost three years with her parents, who treated her as an unwanted stranger; in 1807 she moved to Cahir and then in 1809 to Dublin. In that year she formed a close relationship with Captain Thomas Jenkins, an officer in the 11th light dragoons, and began a five-year residence with him in Hampshire. The ugly duckling had by now turned into a swan, whose beauty had become so well known that her portrait was painted by Sir Thomas Lawrence. It was also during this time that she met Charles John Gardiner, second Viscount Mountjoy and first earl of Blessington (1782–1829). With the approval of Jenkins, who received £10,000 from Lord Blessington as a reimbursement for the jewels and clothing that he had purchased for Margaret, and only four months after the death of her first husband, she married Gardiner. He was a widower seven years her senior with four children, two legitimate. The wedding took place at a church in Bryanston Square on 16 February 1818. On her marriage she changed both her birth name and surname: Margaret Farmer became Marguerite, countess of Blessington. Gardiner drew on his annual income of £30,000 from his estates in Ireland and spent lavishly on his bride. After honeymooning in Ireland, the couple settled at a newly leased town mansion at 11 St James's Square. This soon became a centre of social attraction, with its spacious drawing-rooms and splendid furnishings, excellent food and wine, its famous guests, such as Thomas Moore and John Galt, the writers, and William Jerdan, editor of the influential *Literary Gazette*, and its beautiful and witty hostess. When Lawrence's portrait of her was shown at the Royal Academy in 1821, P. G. Patmore, father of Coventry Patmore, wrote:

> I have seen no other so striking instance of the inferiority of art to nature as in this celebrated portrait of Lady Blessington. As the original stood before it, she fairly 'killed' the copy, and this no less in the individual details than in the general effect.   (Sadleir, 41)

The famous classical scholar Dr Samuel Parr was the first to attribute to her the 'most gorgeous' appellation (ibid., 40). In autumn 1821, at one of her soirées, Lady Blessington met the twenty-year-old Alfred, Count D'Orsay [*see* D'Orsay, Gédéon Gaspard Alfred de Grimaud], reputedly the handsomest man of his time, who was later fictionalized in Clyde Fitch's 1902 play *Last of the Dandies*. From the date of that meeting until her death Count D'Orsay became closely associated with Lady Blessington.

Early in 1822 Lady Blessington published anonymously her first work, *The Magic Lantern, or, Sketches of Scenes in the*

Metropolis, four essays about her attendance at an auction, at the Italian opera, a visit to the Egyptian tomb, and a walk in Hyde Park. In that year she also published *Sketches and Fragments* and *Journal of a Tour through the Netherlands to Paris in 1821*.

On 25 August 1822 the Blessingtons—accompanied by Marguerite's youngest sister, the twenty-one-year-old Mary Anne, and servants—started on a continental tour, meeting D'Orsay in Avignon on 20 November. The Blessingtons settled on 31 March 1823 in Genoa, where they met Lord Byron, whom they saw daily for approximately two months. From their conversations Lady Blessington gathered material for her most famous book, *Journal of Conversations with Lord Byron*, which she published in one volume eleven years later, after initially publishing it in instalments in the *New Monthly Magazine* from July 1832 to December 1833. The last meeting between Lord Byron and Lady Blessington was on 2 June, at which they exchanged gifts. He gave her an Armenian grammar with his annotations, and she gave him a ring from her finger. Touched by this personal gift, Lord Byron impulsively presented to Lady Blessington a small cameo pin of Napoleon that he treasured; he regretted the gesture, however, and sent a letter the next day requesting its return. The Blessingtons remained in Italy for over another five years, settling for the most part in Naples but spending time in Florence with their friend Walter Savage Landor, whose *Imaginary Conversations* Lady Blessington greatly admired. It was there on 1 December 1827 that Count D'Orsay married Lord Blessington's fifteen-year-old daughter Harriet, thus strengthening the tie between the count and Lady Blessington. After moving to Paris towards the end of 1828, the Blessingtons and the D'Orsays took up their residence in the Hôtel Maréchal Ney, where the earl of Blessington died suddenly from a stroke of apoplexy on 25 May 1829, aged forty-six.

In November 1830 Marguerite, along with her sister Mary Anne and Count and Countess D'Orsay, returned to London, subletting the mansion in St James's Square, which would revert to Lord Blessington's family at the expiration of the present lease, and renting a house in Seamore Place, Park Lane. Here she resumed her old social pre-eminence, gathering around her a court of many of the most distinguished literary men of the time, such as Edward Bulwer-Lytton, John Forster, Benjamin Disraeli, Charles Dickens, and the American journalist Nathaniel Parker Willis, whose detailed and extravagant descriptions of Lady Blessington in his *Pencillings by the Way* (1835) praised her wit, her beauty, her maturity, and her intelligence. To him she was 'one of the most lovely and fascinating women I have ever seen' (Sadleir, 200). On her husband's death Lady Blessington's income was restricted to her jointure of £2000 a year. Besides living expensively, she had many members of her own family dependent on her. In order to supplement her income she returned to writing, publishing her first three-volume novel, *The Repealers* (1833), retitled *Grace Cassidy, or, The Repealers* in its second edition (1834), and contributing articles, verse, and fiction to periodicals and magazines. She started to edit

The Book of Beauty, an annual gift-book, for which she continued as editor and contributor until 1849, and in 1841 she started the editorship of another annual, *The Keepsake*. Other three-volume novels and non-fiction works followed in quick succession. These included *The Victims of Society* (1837), *The Governess* (1839), one of the earliest Victorian novels dealing with this much discussed subject, *The Lottery of Life and Other Tales* (1842), *The Memoirs of a Femme de chambre* (1846), *Lionel Deerhurst, or, Fashionable Life under the Regency* ('edited by her', 1846), and the four-volume *Strathern, or, Life at Home or Abroad*. Although only 400 copies of this last mentioned novel were sold, she realized nearly £600 since it had first appeared as a serial in the *Sunday Times*. Lady Blessington's novels fall within the fashionable or 'silver-fork' school, whose heyday had passed before she began her writings. Not very imaginative, her novels, however, had occasional realistic details of the mundane and domestic duties and conditions of the 1830s: she had a 'good visual sense' (Jenkins, 170).

Among her non-fiction works the most popular ones were her three-volume *Idler in Italy* (1839–40) and the two-volume *Idler in France* (1841), books containing reminiscences of her sojourn in those countries, bits of gossip, and clever anecdotes. In 1838 an American publisher in Philadelphia issued a two-volume *The Works of Lady Blessington* containing her novels written to that date, her *Conversations with Lord Byron*, and items that she had published in the annuals. Her literary legacy lies with her *Conversations with Lord Byron*, which has became a major nineteenth-century source for later biographers of Lord Byron, being praised for its grasp of the complex Byron and being valuable for its gossipy record of Byron's opinions of many of his intimates.

In 1836 Lady Blessington's lease at Seamore Place expired, and she moved to Gore House, Kensington, where for the next thirteen years she gathered around her the most distinguished men of intellect. Although her writings earned her between £2000 and £3000 a year, she suffered financial problems. In 1845 the potato disease seriously affected her jointure; after rapidly dwindling, it disappeared in 1848. Her annual expenditure at Gore House exceeded £4000. In April 1849 to escape their creditors she and Count D'Orsay, whose wife had left him in 1831, fled to Paris, he on 1 April and she on 14 April. She rented a small apartment in the rue du Cirque, near the Champs Elysées. Not quite two months later, on 4 June 1849, Lady Blessington died aged fifty-nine from an apoplectic seizure, complicated by heart disease. She was buried at Chambourcy, near St Germain-en-Laye, the residence of her long-time friends the duke and duchess de Grammont. D'Orsay erected as a mausoleum a massive granite pyramid containing two stone sarcophagi placed side by side. A little over three years later D'Orsay joined her in the mausoleum at his death on 4 August 1852 at the age of fifty.

WILLIAM H. SCHEUERLE

Sources R. R. Madden, *The literary life and correspondence of the countess of Blessington*, 3 vols. (1855) · M. Sadleir, *Blessington–D'Orsay: a masquerade* (1933); new edn (1983) · J. F. Molloy, *The most gorgeous*

Lady Blessington [n.d., *c.*1897] • E. J. Lovell, ed., *Lady Blessington's conversations of Lord Byron* (1969) • E. Jenkins, *Ten fascinating women* (1968) • D. L. Moore, *The late Lord Byron: posthumous dramas* (1961) **Archives** NYPL, Carl H. Pforzheimer Collection of Shelley and His Circle, papers • Princeton University Library, New Jersey, papers • U. Edin. L., corresp. | BL, letters to Sir Robert Peel and others • Bodl. Oxf., letters to Benjamin Disraeli • Bodl. Oxf., letters to C. E. de Michele • Herts. ALS, corresp. with Lord Lytton • Lambton Park, Chester-le-Street, co. Durham, letters to Lord Durham and Lady Durham • Mitchell L., Glas., letters to William Beattie • NL Scot., letters to William Blackwood & Sons **Likenesses** P. E. Ströhling, chalk drawing, 1812, BM • T. Lawrence, oils, *c.*1820, Wallace Collection, London; copy, Hughenden Manor, Buckinghamshire • R. J. Lane, lithograph, 1833 (after E. Landseer), BM • W. Gilles, mezzotint, pubd 1835 (after E. T. Parris), BM, NPG • watercolour, *c.*1836 (after A. E. Chalon), NPG • C. Martin, pencil drawing, 1844, NPG • G. Cattermole, pencil drawing, BM • J. Cochran, stipple (after Count D'Orsay), BM, NPG • R. J. Lane, lithograph (after Count D'Orsay, 1841), NPG • D. Maclise, lithograph, BM; repro. in *Fraser's Magazine* • B. W. Rand, portrait, repro. in Sadleir, *Blessington-d'Orsay*

Gardiner [Gardyner], **Richard** (1590/91–1670), Church of England clergyman and benefactor, was born in Hereford of unknown parents. After attending grammar school in the city he matriculated as a poor scholar of Christ Church in 1607, graduated BA in 1611, proceeded MA in 1614 (and was incorporated at Cambridge in 1620), and was licensed to preach in June 1627. After pleasing James VI and I with a speech 'in the Scotch tone' (Wood, *Ath. Oxon.* 3.921), he was made deputy orator at Oxford as well as given reversion of the next Christ Church canonry. He was installed as canon in 1629 and the next year received a doctorate in divinity and was made a chaplain to Charles I. About this time he delivered a convocation sermon (dedicated to William Laud) in which he mentions both his benefactor, Edward, earl of Dorset, and the martyred duke of Buckingham (*Concio ad clerum*, 1631, sig. A3).

Gardiner became both vicar of Flore, Northamptonshire, and rector of Westwell, Oxfordshire, in 1632. But his outspoken defence of religious festivals (sermons published 1638 and 1639), of Charles I (an oration on the king's safe return to Oxford from Edge Hill, 29 October 1642), and his attacks on sectaries (*A Sermon Appointed for Saint Pauls Crosse*, 1642, 11, 25–6) led to his being sequestrated. In May 1646 another was admitted into his place at Flore and he was removed from Westwell before 1652. Parliamentary visitors ejected him from his canonry in 1647 or 1648, and he perhaps preached before other ejected loyalists at Magdalen parish church, Oxford, in 1649. According to Wood, he 'lived obscurely' in Oxfordshire during the 1650s, but he continued his defence of church and crown in print. In 1653 he published his *Specimen oratorium* which included his oration thanking James I for donating his *Works* to the university library, his oration to convocation (11 November 1640), and his Edge Hill oration. In 1659 he brought out *XVI Sermons Preached in the University of Oxford, and at Court* ('together with his Sermon Preached ... on the Anniversary Meeting of Hereford-shire Natives, June 24. 1658') which he prefaced by taunting that though 'the Powers ... shut up his tongue in silence ..., he is not denied the liberty to hold forth a Transcript of what he formerly taught and preach'd' (sig. A2).

In more conciliatory fashion Gardiner was, in April 1660, one of the thirty-nine signatories to the Oxfordshire manifesto of royalist nobility, gentry, and clergy who disavowed revenge and submitted to future parliamentary settlement. A good friend of Gilbert Sheldon, he was restored that year to both his livings and his canonry at Christ Church. During the next decade he made a number of donations to the college for rebuilding and for the support of students. He died at Christ Church on 20 December 1670, aged seventy-nine, and was buried the same day in Christ Church Cathedral. By his will, proved on 28 December, he made further benefactions to the college.

NEWTON E. KEY

Sources *Walker rev.* • Wood, *Ath. Oxon.*, new edn, 3.921–2 • Foster, *Alum. Oxon.* • *Hist. U. Oxf.* 4: *17th-cent. Oxf.*, 814, 827 • R. Gardiner, *XVI sermons preached in the University of Oxford, and at court* (1659) • R. Gardyner, *A sermon appointed for Saint Pauls Crosse, but preached in Saint Pauls Church, on the day of his majesties happy inauguration. March 27. 1642* (1642) • R. Gardiner, *Concio ad clerum habita in Templo Beatae Mariae Oxon: Feb: 14* (1631) [1632?] • *BL cat.*

Gardiner, Richard (1723–1781), writer and army officer, was born on 4 October 1723 at Saffron Walden, Essex, the son of the Revd John Gardiner (*d.* 1770) and Hannah (*d.* 1759), daughter of John Turner of Saffron Walden, Essex. He was a pupil at Eton College from 1738 to 1739, and was admitted on 15 January 1742 to St Catharine's College, Cambridge. He appears to have left university to serve as a volunteer in Flanders in 1744, in the company of George Townshend (later fourth Viscount and first Marquess Townshend). By September 1744 he was serving as a volunteer in the navy at Florence, and attempting to pass himself off as the natural son of George, Lord Walpole (later second earl of Orford) in order to secure a lieutenant's commission. In 1747 he was taken prisoner by a French privateer on his way to serve as a volunteer under William, duke of Cumberland.

Gardiner was released in 1748 and spent the next few years as a deacon, but he resigned in 1751. He then went abroad to the University of Göttingen, returning in the winter of 1751–2 to Ireland with the son of Speaker Walsingham. In 1753 he was used to write political satire in the run-up to the elections of 1754 in Norfolk, and in 1754 he published an autobiographical novel, *The History of Purdica, a Lady of N—rf—lk, with an Account of her Five Lovers*, one of whom was 'Dick Merryfellow', identified by his anonymous biographer as Gardiner himself. The outbreak of war in 1756 saw him join the army. He secured a lieutenancy of grenadiers in the 12th foot in March 1757 and eventually sailed in command of a company of marines to the Caribbean. He served at St Pierre, Martinique, and the siege of Guadeloupe. On his return to England he published *An Account of the Expedition to the West Indies* (1759).

Gardiner married, on 3 May 1761, Ann (*bap.* 1734), daughter of Benjamin Bromhead of Thirlby, Lincolnshire. In 1763 Gardiner retired on half pay, and settled at Swaffham, Norfolk. In the 1768 general election he was again employed as a political propagandist, on this occasion in support of Wenman Coke in the Norfolk contest. He was made a captain in the 16th light dragoons in 1773, but shortly thereafter he retired and bought a house at Ingoldisthorpe, Norfolk. The death of Wenman Coke in 1776 saw Gardiner secure appointment from Thomas Coke in August as auditor-general of the Holkham estates. He was not a success, being dismissed in February 1777. Gardiner blamed Sir Harbord Harbord for his plight, and subsequently vented his spleen against him during the general election campaign of 1780, when Harbord stood with Coke. Gardiner also contributed some of the articles on local hundreds to a history of Norfolk completed in 1779, presumably that of Mostyn John Armstrong published in 1781. Gardiner died on 14 September 1781, aged fifty-seven, and was buried at Ingoldisthorpe church.

STUART HANDLEY

Sources Memoirs of the life and writings (prose and verse) of R—ch—d G—rd—n—r esq., alias Dick Merry-Fellow (1782) • R. W. Ketton-Cremer, Norfolk portraits (1944), 110–39 • Venn, Alum. Cant. • R. A. Austen-Leigh, ed., The Eton College register, 1698–1752 (1927), 136 • Walpole, Corr., 2.120; 18.507, 522, 543–4, 562 • A. M. W. Stirling, Coke of Norfolk and his friends (1912), 118–24 • IGI

Gardiner, Sir Robert William (1781–1864), army officer and writer, was born on 2 May 1781, second son of Captain John Gardiner, senior, 3rd Buffs, and his wife, Mary, daughter of J. Allison of Durham. He entered the Royal Military Academy, Woolwich, on 13 July 1795, and passed out as a second lieutenant Royal Artillery on 7 April 1797. His subsequent commissions were: first lieutenant, 16 July 1799; second captain, 12 October 1804; first captain, 18 November 1811; brevet major, 27 April 1812; brevet lieutenant-colonel, 8 March 1814; brevet colonel, 22 July 1831; regimental colonel, 24 November 1839; major-general, 23 November 1841; lieutenant-general, 11 October 1851; general, 28 November 1854; and colonel-commandant, 23 March 1853.

In October 1797 Gardiner embarked for Gibraltar, then partially blockaded by the French and Spanish fleets, and in 1798 was present at the capture of Minorca. He commanded a detachment of twelve guns with the force under General Don sent to Stade and Cuxhaven in November 1805, as the advance of the army proceeding to Hanover under command of Lord Cathcart. The troops having returned to England in January 1806, Gardiner effected an exchange to Sicily, which he reached just after the battle of Maida. He served in Sicily, part of the time as aide-de-camp to General Fox and afterwards to Sir John Moore, returning with Moore to England from Gibraltar in December 1807.

As regulations prevented Gardiner from serving on Moore's staff on the expedition to Sweden, he exchanged in order to accompany Sir Arthur Wellesley to Portugal. He was present at Roliça and Vimeiro. He was brigade-major of the artillery in the Corunna retreat. In the Walcheren expedition he was present at the siege of Middelburg and Flushing, and was invalided with fever. On his recovery he went to Cadiz, and his battery took a prominent part in the battle of Barossa.

Gardiner joined Wellington's army in February 1812, and received a brevet majority for his services at the siege

and capture of Badajoz. He commanded a field battery at the battle of Salamanca, the capture of Madrid, the siege of Burgos (where he volunteered to serve in the siege batteries), and in the Burgos retreat. Early in 1813 he was appointed to the command of E troop Royal Horse Artillery, then attached to the 7th division, with which he fought at Vitoria in the Pyrenees, at Orthez, Tarbes, and Toulouse. He was made KCB in 1814.

In 1815 Gardiner's troop was stationed in front of Carlton House during the corn riots in London, and subsequently was sent to the Southern Netherlands, where he commanded it through the Waterloo campaign and entered Paris. Gardiner married, on 11 October 1816, Caroline Mary, eldest daughter of Sir John Macleod, adjutant-general Royal Artillery, and granddaughter on the maternal side of the fourth marquess of Lothian. They had one daughter and one son, General Henry Lynedoch Gardiner, Royal Artillery, for some years equerry in ordinary to Queen Victoria. Gardiner was appointed principal equerry to Prince Leopold of Saxe-Coburg-Saalfeld on the prince's marriage with the Princess Charlotte of Wales, and held the post until Leopold became king of the Belgians, after which Gardiner continued to reside at Claremont in Esher. He was governor and commander-in-chief at Gibraltar from 1848 to 1855.

In 1844 Gardiner published a brief memoir of Admiral Sir Graham Moore, brother of Sir John Moore. Between 1848 and 1860 he published twelve pamphlets on military organization, artillery, and national defence. In 1854 the committee of merchants at Gibraltar protested to Lord Aberdeen's government against Gardiner's interference with the Gibraltar trade, which he described as contraband and sought to render more reputable. The correspondence, together with a long report by Gardiner entitled 'Gibraltar as a fortress and a colony', was printed as a parliamentary paper (Parl. papers, 1854, 43). A polemical pamphlet, replying to the report, was distributed gratis by the committee of merchants in 1856. Gardiner was also the author of many reports on professional subjects, which contributed to the improvement in the artillery service which began after 1848.

Gardiner was a GCB and KCH, and had the decoration of St Anne of Russia for his services in the Southern Netherlands and France. Gardiner died at his residence, Melbourne Lodge, Claremont, Esher, Surrey, on 26 June 1864.

H. M. CHICHESTER, rev. JAMES LUNT

Sources J. Kane, List of officers of the royal regiment of artillery from 1716, rev. edn (1869) • GM, 3rd ser., 17 (1864), 383–5 • Army List • The dispatches of … the duke of Wellington … from 1799 to 1818, ed. J. Gurwood, 5: Peninsula, 1790–1813 (1836), 580 • Supplementary despatches (correspondence) and memoranda of Field Marshal Arthur, duke of Wellington, ed. A. R. Wellesley, second duke of Wellington, 15 vols. (1858–72), vol. 11, p. 515 • 'Copy … of a despatch from the governor of Gibraltar', Parl. papers (1854). 43.82, no. 130 [Gibraltar as fortress and colony] • F. Duncan, ed., History of the royal regiment of artillery, 2 (1873) • Boase, Mod. Eng. biog. • Dod's Peerage

Archives Bodl. Oxf., papers relating to Gibraltar • Royal Artillery Institution, Woolwich, London, corresp. and papers | BL, corresp. with Liverpool, Add. MSS 38264–38289, 38474, 38573, passim • BL, corresp. with Sir Robert Peel, Add. MSS 40406–40582, passim • Bodl. Oxf., corresp. with Sir William Napier • NAM, letters to Lord Raglan · NL Scot., letters to Lord Lynedoch · NMM, letters to Sir William Parker · U. Durham L., letters to third Earl Grey · U. Nott., corresp. with duke of Newcastle

Likenesses oils, *c.*1860, Convent, Gibraltar · W. Salter, oil study (for *Waterloo banquet at Apsley House*), NPG · W. Salter, oils (*Waterloo banquet at Apsley House*), Wellington Museum, Apsley House, London

Wealth at death under £18,000: probate, 10 Oct 1864, *CGPLA Eng. & Wales*

(Henry) Rolf Gardiner (1902–1971), by Maxwell Armfield, 1928

Gardiner, (Henry) Rolf (1902–1971), ecological campaigner and youth leader, was born on 5 November 1902 at 56 FitzGeorge Avenue, Fulham, London, the son of the Egyptologist Sir Alan Henderson *Gardiner (1879–1963) and his wife, Hedwig von Rosen (*d.* 1964). After spending part of his childhood in Berlin, Rolf Gardiner was educated at Rugby and Bedales schools and, from 1921, St John's College, Cambridge, where he read modern and medieval languages, gaining a third in the tripos in 1923 and graduating BA in 1924.

Gardiner became a heterodox inter-war prophet of moral, communal, and ecological regeneration, leading a series of youth groups, work camps, folk-dances, and organic farms. Shaped partly by his childhood experience of Berlin, partly by the Scandinavian and Austrian Jewish background of his mother, Gardiner's vision of cultural renewal was tied to a geopolitical project aimed at bringing together English with German and Scandinavian peoples.

The land was the principal site for the reintegration of work, art, and religion in Gardiner's life and the source of social, economic, cultural, and national life. In the early 1920s he joined the craze for folk-dancing and rambling, but quickly came to criticize their becoming commercial leisure activities. Instead, he advocated the sword dance as a solar cult and morris dancing as a masculine group activity for the communal cleansing of the soul. In 1923, together with Arthur Heffer of the bookselling family, he founded the Travelling Morrice. At Cambridge he had become interested in the social credit movement, and between 1923 and 1925 he was involved in one of the movement's offshoots as an officer in John Hargrave's Kibbo Kift Kindred, but he eventually found even this brew of Native American culture and boy scouts too intellectual and materialist, and insufficiently in 'blood contact with the living past of the English earth' (Gardiner to Hargrave, 27 June 1925, Gardiner papers, C6/1/51).

Gardiner's vitalist anti-modernism found a more convenient outlet through his contacts with the German youth movement, the *Bünde*, and the voluntary work camps springing up across central Europe. Between 1926 and 1932 Gardiner oversaw a series of Anglo-German folk-lore tours and exchanges. He collaborated closely with Georg Goetsch, who directed the *Musikheim* at Frankfurt an der Oder, a centre of adult education. In 1928 he acquired Gore Farm in Dorset from his uncle (Henry) Balfour Gardiner, the composer, and in the next few years extended it into the Springhead estate. Springhead became the model estate in Gardiner's fight against modernity and brought together organic farming, communal folklore, and voluntary work camps that sought to reintegrate nature and culture and labour and leisure. The 'Springhead Ring' brought together youth workers, folklorists, and other supporters of his movement. Several camps attracted unemployed miners. Cultural exchange between the young generation in Germany and Britain would, Gardiner hoped, purge both societies of the worst aspects of their national character: an inflexible mentality in Britain and a self-centred intolerance in Germany.

While Gardiner's thinking drew on an eclectic though not atypical brew of vitalism, neo-Romanticism, and anti-liberalism current in Europe, the particular direction of his anti-positivist mentality was shaped by several intellectual encounters. D. H. Lawrence, whom Gardiner first met in 1926, became his 'hero-poet' and urged him to establish a 'holy centre' for a new generation. C. H. Becker, the Prussian minister of education in the Weimar period, championed community art colleges and supported Gardiner's initiatives. Gardiner was also in contact with Eugen Rosenstock Huessy, the intellectual and promoter of adult education.

The world depression (1929–32) appeared to bear out Gardiner's prophecy that the suicide of western materialist civilization was approaching, but it created a political climate which marginalized his influence in Britain and doomed his project of a new cultural and territorial order under Anglo-German auspices. Gardiner's attack on liberal values reached its peak in the early 1930s. In *World without End: British Politics and the Younger Generation* (1932) and other writings he presented Britain with a stark choice: a spiritually impoverished British people and an obsolete parliamentary system consumed by American materialism and vulnerable to the 'Soviet menace', or a nation resuscitating Saxon traditions and willing to play its historic part in a regional federation (Hansa) of German and Scandinavian power. The empire, international free trade, and plans for a united Europe were all pathological forms of international organization that needed to be superseded by what Gardiner called 'interlocality'. In a north European federation, Britain was to provide the religious sources for a revival of European civilization, Germany the political power. The urgency of this project was reinforced by his reading of works on ecology and geopolitics, including James Westfall Thompson's *Feudal Germany* (1928) and Paul von Sokolowski's *Die Versandung Europas* (1929), which presented the Baltic and Germany as the bulwark against an expanding Slavic Soviet dune of wasteland and barren soil.

Gardiner's ambitious project for a Baltic youth expedition in 1932 was designed to weave the cultural ties for a future *Hansa*, but many in the *Bünde* now turned towards an autarchic *Mitteleuropa* and abandoned the project. At home his dismissal of parliamentary democracy, his romantic disdain for the Conservatism of Baldwin and Beaverbrook 'with its mania for petrol and profits', and his equally strong élitist distaste for the football hooliganism of Oswald Mosley's British Union of Fascists, left Gardiner politically homeless, increasingly turning to German developments for hope. On 24 September 1932 he married, in Southwark Cathedral, Mariabella Honor (Marabel) Hodgkin (*b.* 1907/8). They had two sons (one of whom, John Eliot Gardiner, *b.* 1943, became a conductor) and a daughter.

In April 1933, three months after the Nazi seizure of power, Gardiner wrote to Goebbels congratulating the new leaders on ushering in a national renewal and promising the co-operation of English youth. Advertising the work of the *Musikheim* and the *Bünde*, he recalled the Anglo-German youth exchanges as a 'spiritual battle' for the new Germanic order. English youths would bring 'Nordic wisdom and Germanic tradition' to the new order (Gardiner to Goebbels, 25 April 1933, Gardiner papers, A2/6). The letter offered a welcome propaganda tool to Goebbels, who published it. In Britain, it further undermined Gardiner's credentials.

Criticism at home and the growing militarization of life in Germany, however, did little to weaken Gardiner's belief that national socialism would act as the vehicle of a peaceful renewal of culture and conservationist land reform. Beneath the excesses of the Nazis Gardiner perceived the spontaneous coming of a new order of life, freed of un-European elements and firmly rooted in the traditions of the soil. In 1933 he defended the expulsion of Jews from office as a legitimate act of collective renewal (see his 'Die deutsche Revolution von England gesehen' in *Nationalsozialismus von Ausland gesehen*, 1933). He admired Richard Darré, the Nazi minister of agriculture (1933–42), who combined Nordic eugenics with organic family farms

and led the *Reichsnährstand* (national food estate). Continuing to regard these groups as successors to the German youth movement, Gardiner failed to see their intrinsic connection to territorial militarism and aggressive racism. In July 1936 he showed the *Reichsnährstand* round Springhead.

In November 1936 Gardiner attended a conference of the *Reichsnährstand* at Goslar, one of two British participants. He admired its work for retrieving agriculture as 'holy soil' and restoring a peasant world capable of withstanding both commercial erosion and the nomadic threat of Bolshevism. Germany, he believed, had a historic mission to colonize and cultivate lands in eastern Europe. What was 'exceedingly bitter' to him was Britain's insensitivity and unresponsiveness to the danger of 'Bolshevism and anarchy'. For it was this that apparently drove German leaders to turn to lesser nations which had no place in Gardiner's Europe, including Italy and Japan (Gardiner to his wife, 27 Nov 1936, Gardiner papers, B4/6/12). If Gardiner was 'deeply moved, and not unnaturally disturbed' by Goering's powerful speech on destiny and unity at that conference, it did not deter him from further contacts, including a trip in early 1939 when he taught ceremonial dances to 100 members of the Sturm-Abteilung and Schutzstaffel at the *Reichssportschule*. At the same time, Gardiner's hospitality at Springhead continued to extend to non-fascist members of the now suppressed youth movement, such as Adolf Reichwein, a former *Wandervogel* and Social Democrat, who was executed for his role in the resistance of 1944.

The outbreak of war in 1939 severed Gardiner's Anglo-German connections. He now turned more intensely to organic farming and ecology. He was a member of the Dorset county council between 1937 and 1946, and ran a series of work camps at the Springhead estate in 1938–40. His vision of rural regeneration was strengthened by the work of (Reginald) George Stapledon, the proponent of grassland improvement, and a band of conservative conservationists led by Lord Lymington (Gerald Vernon Wallop) and (Harold) John Massingham. Together they campaigned for national service along regional lines to revive 'English memory'. They formed the Kinship in Husbandry, from which developed the Soil Association. One of Gardiner's pamphlets advocating organic farming sold 40,000 copies among servicemen and prisoners of war. At Springhead his efforts to stem the tide of modernization centred on two projects during the war, described in his *England Herself: Ventures in Rural Restoration* (1943): a massive reforestation project involving over 1 million trees to renew soil fertility, and the re-establishment of the flax industry along traditional lines.

Gardiner's campaign for sustainable agriculture and organic farming continued after the Second World War, but now along broader European and global lines. In 1947 he undertook his first trip to Nyasaland in central Africa, where he assumed control of 1500 acres of the family company's estate, planting tea and peanuts and promoting forests. Having unleashed industrialization on the world,

Gardiner insisted, Europe was obliged to lead an ecological campaign. In Africa this meant greater reliance on communal traditions and reforestation. In Europe it called for reclaiming the countryside and woodland, both as an organic part of the economy and as a lifestyle integrated into society. Recreational incursions had to be limited. Acquisitive consumerism had to be replaced by a greater awareness of real needs. The global population explosion threatened the exhaustion of natural resources and called for sustainable 'post-modern farming' (*Organischer Landbau*, 1969, 97). Organic farming could reconstruct bonds of mutual responsibility between town and country.

In the 1960s Gardiner campaigned widely against factory farming, drawing attention to the dangers of disease, including foot-and-mouth disease, as well as to soil erosion and the declining nutritional yield of foodstuffs. In 1963 he became the founding chairman of the European working party for landscape husbandry. In 1967 he joined the national executive of the Council for the Preservation of Rural England. Gardiner continued to insist that England was the natural leader in the international battle against commercial farming and EEC plans for agricultural rationalization. He was high sheriff of Dorset in 1967–8. In 1971 he was awarded the Peter Joseph Lenné gold medal by the Goethe Foundation for services to European youth and for his work on landscape husbandry in Dorset and Malawi. He died suddenly on 26 November 1971, at Lansdown Nursing Home, Bath, before seeing many of his prescient criticisms of modern agriculture more widely recognized.   FRANK TRENTMANN

Sources CUL, Gardiner MSS · M. Chase, 'Rolf Gardiner: an inter-war cross-cultural case study', *Adult education between cultures*, ed. B. J. Hake and S. Marriott (1992), 225–41 · F. Trentmann, 'Civilization and its discontents: English neo-Romanticism and the transformation of anti-modernism in twentieth-century Western culture', *Journal of Contemporary History*, 29 (1994), 583–625 · A. Best, ed., *Water springing from the ground: an anthology of the writings of Rolf Gardiner* (1972) · *The letters of D. H. Lawrence*, ed. A. Huxley (1932) · H. Massingham, *Remembrance: an autobiography* (1941) · W. Laqueur, *Young Germany* (1962) · A. Bramwell, *Ecology in the twentieth century: a history* (1989) · R. Griffiths, *Fellow travellers of the right: British enthusiasts for Nazi Germany, 1933–9*, pbk edn (1983) · P. J. Atkins, 'The pasteurisation of England', *Food, science, policy and regulation in the twentieth century*, ed. D. F. Smith and J. Phillips (2000), 37–51 · M. Chase, 'North Sea and Baltic: historical conceptions in the youth movement and the transfer of ideas from Germany to England in the 1920s and 1930s', *Historikeriadaloge: Geschichte, Mythos und Gedaechtnis im deutsch-britischen kulturellen Anstausch, 1750–2000*, ed. S. Berger, P. Lambert, and D. Schumann (2003), 309–30 · *CGPLA Eng. & Wales* (1972) · b. cert. · m. cert. · d. cert.
Archives CUL, corresp. and papers | CUL, letters to his sister Margaret
Likenesses M. Armfield, portrait, 1928, repro. in K. Sager, *The life of D. H. Lawrence* (1980) [see illus.]
Wealth at death £163,585: probate, 1972, *CGPLA Eng. & Wales*, (1972)

Gardiner, Samuel (1564–1632?), Church of England clergyman and writer on angling, was born in Norwich, but nothing is known of his parents. After attending Eton College he matriculated at King's College, Cambridge, in 1581, and graduated BA in 1585–6. After ordination he became in 1588 vicar of Ormesby in Norfolk, proceeding MA in 1589 and BD in 1596. From 1599 he emerged as a Calvinist polemicist, some of whose theological writings employed angling metaphors. Two in particular, *A Booke of Angling, or Fishing* (1606), dedicated to a number of Norfolk gentry of like persuasion, and *The Scourge of Sacriledge* (1611), use a limited range of angling allusions, drawn from his own recreations, to prop up virulent attacks on spiritual and political corruption among the opponents of Calvinism in the Church of England. His other theological pieces share their turgid prose but do not employ his contrasts between Satan's wiles as an angler for souls and the weaknesses of those called to be the true fishers of men. The sporting analogies led some late Victorian angling antiquarians to give him an undeserved reputation as a key early writer on fishing but his works were never republished and only one copy of *A Booke of Angling* is known to survive, in the Bodleian Library.

Continuing as vicar of Ormesby, Gardiner was in 1620 made lecturer of St Peter Mancroft, Norwich. He served at the former until 1631 and remained lecturer until 1632, when he is assumed to have died. He was married by 1595. His son Thomas Gardiner, educated at Cambridge and ordained in 1619, held livings in Norfolk and Hertfordshire before being ejected in 1662. He was licensed as a Presbyterian minister in 1672.   J. R. LOWERSON

Sources S. Gardiner, *A booke of angling, or fishing* (1606) · S. Gardiner, *The scourge of sacriledge* (1611) · *DNB* · Venn, *Alum. Cant.* · K. Fincham, *Prelate as pastor: the episcopate of James I* (1990) · N. Tyacke, *Anti-Calvinists: the rise of English Arminianism, c.1590–1640* (1987) · *The angler's notebook and naturalist's record* (1888), 5–6 · T. Westwood and T. Satchell, *Bibliotheca piscatoria* (1883), 103 · W. Hone, *The yearbook of daily recreation and information* (1878), 801ff. · *Calamy rev.*, 217

Gardiner, Samuel Rawson (1829–1902), historian, was born on 4 March 1829 at Ropley, near Alresford, Hampshire, the eldest son of Rawson Boddam Gardiner (1788–1863), an East India civil servant from Whitchurch, Oxfordshire. His mother, Margaret (1803–1853), was daughter of William Baring Gould. Samuel's paternal grandfather, also Samuel, was high sheriff of Oxfordshire in 1794. His paternal grandmother, Mary Boddam, could claim descent from Bridget, eldest daughter of Oliver Cromwell, from her marriage to Henry Ireton. Samuel Gardiner, at Winchester College from 1841, matriculated as a commoner at Christ Church, Oxford, in October 1847. Awarded a studentship in 1850, he graduated BA in 1851, but did not proceed MA until 1884. As a result of his theological position his studentship had long lapsed. His parents were Irvingites, members of the Catholic Apostolic church founded principally by Edward Irving (1792–1834). Ritualistic and millenarian, the Irvingites lacked any connection with the nonconformity of the seventeenth century or, indeed, of the nineteenth, but were conservative and deeply suspicious of the democratic trends of the early Victorian period. That Rawson Gardiner became an elder of the nascent church in 1834 was evidently a matter of significance in the early life of his son, who on 8 January 1856 married Isabella (1834/5–1878), Irving's youngest daughter, and was himself from 1851 to 1866 a deacon.

Samuel Rawson Gardiner (1829–1902), by James Russell & Sons

Samuel Gardiner's first published work (1856) was a translation of an Irvingite work, *Christian Family Life*, from the German of W. G. Thiersch. However, his name was deleted from the church register some time before 1872 and for the last thirty years of his life he was a regular communicant of the established church. Essentially reticent about his private life, Gardiner never explained his defection, even to his close friend C. H. Firth, but no doubt this religious experience had an impact on his approach to history.

Early career; the History begun After marriage the young Gardiners settled in London and Samuel began serious research into English history. Lacking a steady comfortable income, he maintained his family by miscellaneous teaching. Admitted a reader of the British Museum on 8 November 1856 and at the Public Record Office on 1 July 1858, he soon settled on the early seventeenth century as a likely fruitful subject. Perhaps respondent to the sharp controversies of his own time, he turned to those of the civil wars and interregnum but strived, he claimed, to deal intelligently and objectively with people, events, and trends without passion or favour, evolving his own sort of 'scientific history', extracting 'the facts' from primary sources and letting them speak for themselves. Dissatisfied with existing explanations of the conflicts of the 1640s and 1650s, he came quickly to believe that if 'studied for the mere sake of understanding', they would assume 'a very different appearance from that which [they] had in the eyes of, say, Macaulay and Forster' (S. R.

Gardiner, preface, *History of England, 1624–28*, 1875). He decided on an emphatically narrative approach, beginning with the accession of James I and accepting that 'it was the duty of a serious enquirer to search into the original causes of great events, rather than for the sake of catching at an audience, to rush unprepared upon the great events themselves' (S. R. Gardiner, preface, *History of England, 1603–1640*, 1863). This was, then, from the start a narrative with a purpose, produced systematically over four decades and finally comprising eighteen volumes.

After some preliminary articles in *Notes and Queries* (1860) on James's parliaments and their attitudes towards papists, and a documentary volume on the parliamentary debates in 1610 for the Camden Society (1862), Gardiner brought out in 1863 *A History of England from the Accession of James I to the Disgrace of Chief Justice Coke* in two volumes quarto. Tepidly reviewed, *inter alia* by Lord Acton, who would later come to admire Gardiner's scholarship, the set sold only 100 copies: the rest of the small edition went to waste paper. The next two volumes, on Prince Charles and the Spanish marriage, had a circulation of 500 but made no profit for the author. The third instalment, on the duke of Buckingham and Charles I—the subject evidently more significant than the sovereign—and covering 1624–8, actually paid its costs. The fourth, *The Personal Government of Charles I*—Gardiner's coinage for the 1630s, still current a century later (2 vols., 1877)—and two more, *The Fall of the Monarchy of Charles I*, a somewhat premature summation (1882), brought Gardiner his first financial reward, but more importantly clinched academic recognition of the quality of his 'one-man' achievement. Somewhat revised, particularly the first two volumes, the series was reissued in 1883–4 as *The History of England, 1603–1640*. Gardiner had now arrived at the period and problems which had from the start most excited his interest and between 1886 and 1891, in three volumes separately issued but collectively entitled *The Great Civil War*, he embraced the 1640s down to the execution of the king. *The History of the Commonwealth and Protectorate* took three further instalments, in 1895, 1897, and 1901. Later editions of the whole *History*, only lightly revised, were issued in a 'cabinet format'. By then ill health had enforced a modification of the intended terminal date from the Restoration of 1660 in favour of the protector's death in 1658. In the event Gardiner broke off at 1656, leaving his friend, almost a disciple, C. H. Firth, who described him as 'the most trustworthy of nineteenth-century historians' (*DNB*), to tackle *The Last Years of the Protectorate* (2 vols., 1909). Firth's own research student Godfrey Davies in effect rounded off a history begun nearly a century earlier with the publication of *The Restoration of Charles II, 1658–1660* (1955).

The *History*—with other works along the way—is Gardiner's tribute to what he saw as a major formative and destructive period and force in English, and British, development, one which he set out to make as absorbing to other historians as it was to himself. Deep research into it called for and found in him remarkable qualities of method, organization, and endurance, sustained over years of growing confidence in his own powers. In its pursuit he acquired languages and sought out and exploited primary sources, both printed and manuscript, over a wide range of type and location, thereby bringing to attention the riches of archives in several European countries, which enabled him to pioneer the study of Stuart diplomacy and foreign policy, and to give a fresh European dimension to the whole *History*. That achievement was recognized by honorary degrees and membership of foreign and learned institutions, some of them long before English universities accorded him similar honours (Bohemia, 1870; Massachusetts, 1874; Copenhagen, 1891; Uppsala, 1893; Göttingen, 1887; Utrecht, 1900; Edinburgh, 1881; Oxford, 1895; Cambridge, 1899). But his main work was done in London from his Gordon Square home and in forays from later residences in Bromley, Bedford, and finally Sevenoaks.

Methodology; the *History* continued; other works Travelling by train and cycle (or rather tricycle—his only recreation), Gardiner visited civil war locations, especially battlefields, all over England, Scotland, and Ireland, in an effort to establish and understand strategy and tactics. He was not unaware of the uses to which historians can put landscape, maps, buildings, and other artefacts. All the while the *History* was in the writing, he was supporting it by teaching, notably in schools. According to his richer Oxford friend and obituarist Firth, Gardiner found pleasure in the grind of teaching and was an admirable popular lecturer, which Firth himself was not. Like Cromwell in his speeches to the protectorate parliaments, Gardiner generally dispensed with notes, sure of what he wanted to say and how to say it to diverse auditories. Even his Ford lectures—which inaugurated the series—in 1896 were not written down until he was invited to publish them as *Cromwell's Place in History*. Earlier he had augmented his income to support his research and a growing family by drawing on his teaching experience to write textbooks, notably *The Thirty Years' War* (1874) and *The Puritan Revolution* (1876); the latter title, a term of his own invention, may suggest that long before he reached the 1640s in the *History* Gardiner already had an interpretation in mind. These two books, written for Longman's short Epochs of Modern History series, were still in print in the early twentieth century, as was his *Outline of English History for Children* (1881) and the three-decker, copiously illustrated *Students' History of England* (1890). An anonymous hand added a supplement covering the period to 1919 for a 1920 edition. A *School Atlas of English History* (1895) was a useful offshoot of these books.

Gardiner's major incidental work, however, was *Constitutional Documents of the Puritan Revolution* (1899), initially covering 1629–60 but later extended back to 1625. Solid and thoughtfully selected, it was by no means narrow in its view of 'constitutional' and was kept in print, eventually in paperback, and widely used in universities and sixth forms. Boundless energy and zeal for the discipline led to much original work in the form of articles and annotated documents. Gardiner was a prolific book reviewer, for example in the *Contemporary Review* and The

Athenaeum, where he displayed a keen interest in current affairs, particularly the Irish question (a Gladstonian, he supported home rule), imperial policy, and the burgeoning nationalisms of central and eastern Europe. For the *Revue Historique* he produced over several years surveys of contemporary English historical writing. During three fruitful decades (1869–97) he was director of the Camden Society's publications fostering collections of unedited documents, a dozen by himself, besides contributing to the *Miscellany* volumes. Similar work was done for the Naval Records Society and the Scottish History Society— Gardiner always took a wide historical swathe, topically and topographically. Involved from the outset with the *English Historical Review*, he was co-editor from 1891 to 1901 and turned what had begun as a sort of magazine into a truly professional journal. *En passant*, he wrote scores of entries for the *Dictionary of National Biography*, including those on Francis Bacon (in collaboration), Archbishop Laud, and John Pym, whose dominance and that of the Commons he sat in during the early years of the Long Parliament had been, in effect, 'created' by the *History*. Gardiner was prolific, too, in the ninth edition of the *Encyclopaedia Britannica*, where he provided a succinct survey of English history and articles on many historical themes well outside his special field, perceptively on George III. Moreover, as Firth reported from his own experience, Gardiner's love of the subject made him ever ready to encourage, advise, and assist other scholars, not least those on the threshold of research.

Distinguished product of the university though he was, Gardiner never held an Oxford teaching appointment, though an All Souls research fellowship came in 1884 and Merton gave him another when that lapsed in 1892. He had fared better in London: he lectured at King's College from 1872 and replaced J. S. Brewer as professor of modern history there in 1877. He was an extra-mural tutor for the Society for the Extension of University Teaching and taught at Toynbee Hall. Lord Acton's effort in 1878 to secure him the deputy keepership under the master of the rolls came to nothing, but Acton did persuade Gladstone to give Gardiner a civil-list pension of £150 p.a. He was passed over in 1892 for the regius chair of modern history, which went to Froude, a rather less conscientious historian. On Froude's death in 1894 Lord Rosebery, admirer of Cromwell and of Gardiner's view of him, offered him the chair. Gardiner declined, not out of pique—life's experience had raised him above that—but because, his health beginning to fail, he preferred to stay in London, near the holdings of the British Museum, among them the Thomason Tracts, whose source value he had long recognized. Even so, his dedication to the *History* itself was faltering, and he allowed himself to be distracted for the production of a 'life' of Cromwell in the lavishly illustrated Goupil series of biographies (1899) and, returning to an earlier interest, to respond sharply to Father Gerard's query *What was Gunpowder Plot?* with *What Gunpowder Plot was* (1897), which was not a conspiracy hatched by the government to entrap Catholics. He saw volume 3 of *The Commonwealth and Protectorate* through the press in January 1901, but

March found him partially paralysed. A year later (23 February 1902) he died, a few days before his seventy-third birthday, at 7 South Park, Sevenoaks, where he had been living latterly. He was buried in Sevenoaks. Memorial plaques were later put up in Winchester Cathedral and Christ Church Cathedral.

Gardiner's first wife had died in 1878, and four years later, on 15 July 1882, he had married Bertha Meriton Cordery [**Bertha Meriton Gardiner** (1845–1925)], daughter of John and Henrietta Cordery of Hampstead. She shared his historical interests, having already—in collaboration with her brother-in-law James Surtees Philpotts—published *King and Commonwealth* (1875), a work which dealt particularly with the strategy and tactics employed during the civil war. After their marriage she edited a collection of documents from the Tanner manuscripts concerning the secret negotiations made by Charles I in 1643 and 1644 (*Camden Miscellany*, vol. 8, 1883). In the same year appeared her short history of the French revolution in the Epochs of Modern History series, which passed through a number of editions. She was said to have been 'a real helpmeet' to Gardiner in his work, and to have fully concurred in his decision to refuse the Oxford regius professorship (*The Times*, 16 Jan 1925). After his death (from 1903) she received a civil-list pension of £75. She died on 5 January 1925 at the Red House, River, Dover. Gardiner's two marriages produced six sons and two daughters.

Legacy and reputation Though the many obituaries at home and abroad were laudatory, Gardiner's work in all its aspects was already under fire. First, his style, which was certainly rather monotonous and pedestrian, hardly conveyed either the sheer excitement of his subject or his own enthusiasm for it. He was perhaps most moving in elaborating his maturing portrait of Oliver Cromwell, which led some to see him as an out-and-out hero-worshipper. He was not. Gardiner's Cromwell is a warts-and-all figure, seen as he pushed on into the protectorate as a military despot, much of whose achievement was doomed to failure. This 'most typical of all Englishmen' was not the most admirable of Englishmen; nor was he, for all that could be said of 'the puritan revolution' God's Englishman, but at least he was human.

The first large-scale attack on the whole Gardiner canon came from R. G. Usher in 1915, who, after a preliminary shot in 1910, exposed without much difficulty inconsistencies in the *History*'s dealing with characters such as Charles I, who were, of course, inconsistent themselves. Usher went on with some satisfaction to argue that Gardiner's claim that by pursuing his strict chronological course he had not gone beyond the facts was false. He had, indeed, 'decided a great issue of history, by no means clear to the men of the time'—of course, it never is—'by applying to it his later knowledge, deceiving himself along with his readers' (Usher, 195). In 1919 an anonymous correspondent in the *Times Literary Supplement* went further, claiming that every reference of 'the subtle and dangerous partisan' Gardiner needed to be checked. That sparked off a lively, increasingly unmannerly debate in which Gardiner's admirers, particularly Firth, rushed to his defence,

but the broader issues got lost in trivialities. As the century wore on, it became increasingly apparent that despite Gardiner's genuine efforts to write what he called 'scientific history'—by which he seems to have meant factually based unbiased history—his conclusions were very much what might have been expected of an honest late Victorian liberal, open to the political, social, and cultural influences of his times, yet convinced of his own objectivity in approaching Stuart England. Gardiner, in truth, never sought to hide his concern for, and positions on such matters as House of Lords reform and public worship, while asserting that when it came to the *History* he worked from the facts of the early seventeenth century and those facts alone. But he would certainly have bridled at Lytton Strachey's sneer that all he had done was to make 'a sawdust heap of facts' (Strachey, 170).

Newer interpreters of Gardiner's period came along, as confident of their own impartiality as he was of his. Time, the mother of truth, showed that they in their turn reflected the values and controversies of their own age. For them Gardiner's picture seemed too sharp, too clear, too complete, a pattern imposed more than one emerging naturally from the facts. Yet, though the vital role of narrative was more and more stressed, no historian came forward with the conviction and courage to replace the *History* on anything like the same scale. Rather, intense professional study of the period, posing more questions than answers, produced bright jigsaw pieces, discrete, incapable of sitting together. No serious student, however critical, could yet ignore Gardiner. During the later 1990s the volumes of the *History* covering 1640 to 1656 were reissued in paperback to meet a current need. A long review of these by J. S. A. Adamson in the *Historical Journal* (vol. 33, 1990), dwelt lovingly on their deficiencies, most of them real enough, yet concluded that the reprint was justified, *faute de mieux*. Just so. IVAN ROOTS

Sources C. H. Firth, 'Dr. S. R. Gardiner', *PBA*, [1] (1903–4), 294–301 · *DNB* · T. Lang, *The Victorians and the Stuart heritage* (1995) · J. S. A. Adamson, 'Eminent Victorians: S. R. Gardiner and the liberal as hero', *HJ*, 33 (1990), 641–57 · R. G. Usher, *Critical study of the historical method of S. R. Gardiner* (St Louis, 1915) · J. Kenyon, *The history men: the historical profession in England since the Renaissance*, 2nd edn (1993) · W. C. Abbott, *A bibliography of Oliver Cromwell* (1929); repr. (New York, 1969) · R. C. Richardson, *The debate on the English revolution*, 3rd edn (1998) · L. Strachey, *Portraits in miniature* (1931) · A. Faher, 'Gardiner and Usher in perspective', *Journal of Historical Studies* (1968) · W. A. Shaw, *A bibliography of the works of … Dr S. R. Gardiner* (1903) · *The Times* (16 Jan 1925) [obit. of Bertha Meriton Gardiner] · S. Baring Gould, *Early reminiscences 1834–1864* (1923) · *IGI* · m. certs. · d. cert.

Archives BL, state papers, Add. MSS 31112, 31998–32004, 34486, 35352, 38490–38491 [transcripts] · Bodl. Oxf., historical collections and papers · Bodl. Oxf., notebooks of extracts from Venetian dispatches and state papers · Hunt. L., letters | All Souls Oxf., letters to Sir William Anson · BL, speeches and other compositions, Lansdowne MS 236 · Bodl. Oxf., letters to Richard Bentley and George Bentley · CUL, letters to Lord Acton · King's Cam., letters to Oscar Browning · LUL, letters to J. H. Round · University of Toronto, Thomas Fischer Rare Book Library, notes on Thurloe papers

Likenesses J. Russell & Sons, photograph, NPG [*see illus.*]

Wealth at death £10,064 0s. 3d.: resworn probate, April 1903, *CGPLA Eng. & Wales* (1902)

Gardiner, Stephen (*c.*1495x8–1555), theologian, administrator, and bishop of Winchester, was born, according to John Bale, at Bury St Edmunds, and thus was probably the son of that name mentioned in the will of John Gardiner, a clothmaker from Bury, of 18 January 1507. His mother's name was probably Agnes. By 1511, still a boy, he was in Paris, where, as he recalled in a letter of 1527, he met Erasmus. His recollections included making a salad for the great man, and receiving an invitation through Gerard, the Cambridge bookseller, to take a position in Erasmus's service.

Education and introduction to government Gardiner almost certainly went to Cambridge in 1511 (counting back from the seven years' study there acknowledged in his grace for the degree of BCnL in 1518), presumably to Trinity Hall, very much a lawyers' college, of which he was eventually elected master in 1525. He graduated DCL in 1521 and DCnL in 1522, and served the university in various capacities (such as auditor) during these years. His pupils at Trinity Hall included his future colleagues Thomas Wriothesley and William Paget. During the early part of his career he was sometimes known as Dr Stevyn or Dr Stevyns.

Gardiner was educated in a Cambridge which was already stirring to the currents of humanism. Many of his books were written in an elegant Latin, and his theological writings display familiarity with Greek as well as Latin fathers—though not to the exclusion of scholastic learning. However, Gardiner has been portrayed as hostile to humanism on account of his controversy with John Cheke and others in the early 1540s over the pronunciation of Greek at Cambridge. Cheke was introducing a new, more classical pronunciation, which Gardiner (by then chancellor of the university) forbade. In fact Gardiner conceded the academic merits of Cheke's pronunciation, opposing it for the pragmatic reason that the received pronunciation was prevalent in the wider academic world, and that the reform would therefore simply sow confusion. He even displayed his own humanist pretensions by quoting Erasmus against Cheke. At the time Gardiner's decision was not seen as that of an obscurantist. One of Cheke's supporters, the Catholic humanist Thomas Watson, joined Gardiner's household as a chaplain soon afterwards, as did another leading Cambridge humanist, John Seton. Another of Cheke's supporters, Roger Ascham, one of the greatest English humanists, besought Gardiner's patronage in the reigns of both Henry VIII and Mary. During the latter's reign, Gardiner helped Ascham to the position of the queen's Latin secretary—notwithstanding Ascham's association with Cheke in the quarrel over the pronunciation of Greek in the early 1540s, and his affiliation with protestantism under Edward VI. Gardiner himself became less sympathetic to Erasmus in that reign, writing to Protector Somerset in 1547 to criticize the general use of an English translation of Erasmus's paraphrases of the New Testament. But even here it was Erasmus's theology, rather than his humanist scholarship, to which he objected.

In 1523 Gardiner was a member of a Cambridge delegation to Cardinal Wolsey, the lord chancellor. Perhaps this brought him to the attention of his first major patron, for he appears to have entered Wolsey's service in the following year, and soon began accumulating an impressive portfolio of ecclesiastical preferment. To the mastership of Trinity Hall (in which he succeeded Thomas Larke, another Wolsey client), he added the archdeaconries of Taunton (1526), Worcester (1528), Norfolk (1530), and Leicester (1531), together with a prebend at Salisbury (about 1526).

Gardiner rapidly became indispensable not only to Wolsey but also to Henry VIII himself. He accompanied Wolsey on his embassy to France in 1527, and when Henry tried to summon him back for his own reasons (perhaps connected with his plans to divorce Queen Katherine), Wolsey held onto him, protesting that Gardiner was his only help and instrument. The king's Great Matter (Henry VIII's divorce) soon provided full scope for Gardiner's talents as a canon lawyer and diplomat, and opened for him the path to high office. Gardiner was present at the formal inauguration of the proceedings for the divorce on 17 May 1527, and early in 1528 he was sent on embassy to the pope in the company of another rising Cambridge don, Edward Foxe (later bishop of Hereford). Having passed through Calais in February, they had reached Orvieto by the end of March and there they found Clement VII, who had taken refuge in the town after the sack of Rome. Gardiner reported to Wolsey that various 'incommodities' kept the pope 'and all his straightly as he was ever kept in Castle Angel' (Pocock, 1.89). After protracted and sometimes bitter negotiations (at one point Gardiner complained that 'his holiness handled the king's highness as though he had been the most ingrate man' (ibid., 132)), a commission was obtained on the Wednesday in Holy Week 1528 empowering Wolsey and a papal legate, Cardinal Campeggi, to decide the case in England. This commission, Gardiner believed, was 'as good as can be devised' (ibid., 134). After a brief mission to Venice, Gardiner returned to England.

Gardiner had to return to Italy in 1529, in a fruitless attempt to rule out as a forgery a recently rediscovered papal brief of Julius II which remedied defects in the original dispensation authorizing Henry's marriage to Katherine. False rumours of Clement VII's death led Henry to instruct Gardiner to lobby for the election of Wolsey as his successor. Gardiner did at least secure a new papal commission for the legatine court which was to try the divorce case. In the following month Gardiner reported to Henry that the pope wished Katherine was in her grave.

Royal secretary and bishop of Winchester After returning to London in June 1529, Gardiner moved a month later from Wolsey's service to that of the king, as his principal secretary. His appointment is unsurprising. Gardiner had made himself useful to the king in the matter of the divorce, and Henry had tried two years before to secure the services of the young master of Trinity Hall. His star was clearly in the ascendant: in August Wolsey advised Edmund Bonner to consult Gardiner before speaking with the king. Just as clearly, Wolsey's star was waning. Late in August Brian Tuke told Wolsey that Gardiner was inclined towards his former master. Yet by September Gardiner was writing to Wolsey to inform him of the king's reluctance to give an audience to the cardinal. Gardiner was present at Wolsey's surrendering of the great seal in October. Yet although it was suspected in Wolsey's circle that Gardiner had been disloyal to him, the cardinal sought Gardiner's assistance throughout the following year.

In his new capacity as secretary, Gardiner remained closely involved with the king's Great Matter. At this stage he appears still to have believed that the divorce would be granted by the Holy See, thus averting, of course, the danger of Anglo-Roman conflict or even schism. Campeggi wrote on 20 May 1529 that Gardiner and Wolsey still believed that the pope would grant a divorce even though he (Campeggi) had told them of the impossibility of their demands. During the summer of 1529 Gardiner met Thomas Cranmer, who suggested that Henry might consult the theology faculties of the continental universities about the validity of his marriage. With Edward Foxe, Gardiner was sent to Cambridge to consult the theologians there. However, to some observers his zeal in the cause was far from clear, perhaps because he had begun to doubt the possibility of securing a favourable sentence from the pope. Eustace Chapuys, the new imperial ambassador, felt in June 1531 that Gardiner had some sympathy with Queen Katherine, and believed that Anne Boleyn was hostile to him. In January 1532 a Spanish diplomat reported from Rome that Gardiner had intimated to the papal nuncio in France that he hoped that some expedient might be found to bring an end to the divorce proceedings.

Stephen Gardiner was nominated by Henry VIII as Wolsey's successor in the see of Winchester in September 1531, and was enthroned by proxy on 27 December following. Still only in his thirties, he was now one of England's wealthiest and most important bishops, and his promotion marked him as one of Henry's leading servants. However, he was not destined to become one of the great pastoral bishops: within a few days of his installation he was on his way to France on a diplomatic mission. When foreign affairs did not keep him out of the country, public affairs tended to keep him at court, and although his normal residence, Southwark Palace, was within his diocese, diocesan administration was throughout his episcopate chiefly in the hands of his chancellor and vicar-general, Dr Edmund Steward, who took up these duties in December 1531.

Gardiner returned in March 1532 to face the first great crisis of his career. In April 1532 Archbishop Warham presented to the southern convocation the 'supplication against the ordinaries', which had been drawn up by the House of Commons. The task of responding to this attack upon the legal powers and privileges of bishops and ecclesiastical officials was entrusted to Gardiner, and his draft was approved by convocation's upper house on 15 April and by the lower house on 19 April. His reply affirmed the divine origin of the church's right to make laws and denied that such laws were contingent upon royal approval. Henry's response to this was not welcoming. Gardiner's letter of apology only made matters worse, as

he tactlessly excused himself on the grounds that his argument was in line with Henry's own arguments in the *Assertio septem sacramentorum* against Luther. Chapuys, with a characteristic excess of optimism, now numbered Gardiner among Queen Katherine's supporters, reporting that he was refusing to preach in favour of the king and that Henry was pressing him to return to court to assist in dealings with the papacy. What lay at the root of this episode was the underlying conflict of loyalties between church and crown that ran like a fault-line through Gardiner's career in the 1530s and 1540s.

Even in disgrace, though, Gardiner was well-nigh indispensable, and he was soon back at court. However, his defiance of the king may well have cost him his chance of the see of Canterbury, where Cranmer succeeded Warham in spring 1533. It was therefore Cranmer who presided in April 1533 at the court that annulled Henry's marriage to Katherine: despite Chapuys's opinion, Gardiner appeared there as counsel for Henry himself, and attended Anne's coronation in June.

Diplomacy was the obvious employment for a man who was indisputably able, yet no longer entirely trusted by the king. In autumn 1533 Gardiner led a delegation to François I at Marseilles to give formal notice of Henry's intention to appeal to a general council against the pope's judgment in his matrimonial cause, which upheld Katherine's side. Gardiner's conduct on this mission displeased the French king—an early indication of the bad relations with the French that characterized most of the rest of his career. Despite the deepening schism between England and Rome, Gardiner continued to hedge his bets: he was included with several other clerics and noblemen in a papal dispensation permitting the celebration of mass even in the event of a papal interdict.

De vera obedientia Gardiner no longer enjoyed the full confidence of his master. By April 1534 he had been formally replaced as royal secretary by Thomas Cromwell (who, as his substitute in his absence, had in practice been gradually displacing him since 1532), and after his return from France he resided mostly in his diocese until late 1535. This was one of his few extended periods of residence at his see (although he spent much of his life at his episcopal palace in Southwark, which was part of his diocese), and saw the only priestly and lesser ordinations he appears to have conducted in person. In the spring of 1535 he protested against Cranmer's visitation of the diocese of Winchester. While this showed his thoroughly old-fashioned 'prelatical' attitudes, it also revealed that he was adjusting to Henry's new church order, for he based his protest on the claim that the metropolitical powers under which Cranmer proposed to act were of papal origin and therefore contrary to the royal supremacy.

Gardiner sought his way back into the king's favour by writing in defence of the royal supremacy and of the execution of John Fisher; both works were ready by September 1535. The defence of Fisher's execution was a response to a papal brief denouncing Henry VIII, and is known from its opening words as 'Si sedes illa'. His elegant Latin defence of the royal supremacy, the best-known of his writings, was published as *De vera obedientia*. It came as something of a surprise to Chapuys, who commented in December 1535 that Gardiner had hitherto been thought to have upheld papal authority. But Chapuys seems never to have understood the way in which the bishop was pulled between loyalty to church and crown. *De vera obedientia* was soon reprinted in Strasbourg, with a preface probably drafted by Martin Bucer commending Gardiner as a model bishop. A further edition appeared at Hamburg, and an unauthorized English translation was produced by protestants in Mary Tudor's reign with the intention of embarrassing its author. Among Gardiner's most important published writings, *De vera obedientia* is the only one to have received a modern edition, and has been justly described as 'the most original work of theory to be associated with the Henrician settlement' (McConica, 128). Gardiner's contemporaries were equally alert to the book's significance. On Cromwell's instructions, Edward Foxe (bishop of Hereford) took a copy with him on his mission to Germany late in 1535.

De vera obedientia is unequivocal in its assertion and defence of royal power, which it derives from divine grace and gift, and not in any sense from popular or communal consent. It extends royal power to ecclesiastical governance on the basis of dense scriptural citation, especially from the Old Testament, adducing the relations between the kings and princes of ancient Israel to support its thesis. The king represents God's image among men, and the king, as head of his realm, is a fortiori head of the church when both he and the realm are Christian. However, while arguing robustly for the validity of both the divorce and the supremacy, the tract is not without subtlety. Gardiner argues that the role of the head of the church is to defend it as well as to govern it, 'even as the headde maynteneth and defendeth the body' (*Obedience*, ed. Janelle, 119). Thus by glossing the king's new title of 'supreme head' with the slightly older title of *fidei defensor*, he seeks to ensure that the supremacy does not become a threat to the essential interests of the church. Moreover, Gardiner is careful to leave some room for a papal primacy of honour, hedging his bets against the possibility of a reconciliation. The virtue of obedience is, obviously enough, the common thread: in the version of its near contemporary translator,

> to obeye truly
> is nothing elles
> but to obey unto the truthe
> (ibid., 72)

Gardiner's case for the content and character of this virtue is also predominantly scriptural, though this time drawing more upon the New Testament, and he shrewdly deploys and develops the concept of obedience in understated opposition to the concept of 'faith alone'.

Ambassador to France These literary endeavours earned Gardiner, if not a return to royal favour, then at least a return to royal service. September 1535 saw him set out once more as ambassador to France, where he remained for three years. But as Henry VIII's ecclesiastical policy was about to enter its least conservative phase, this embassy may have been a form of exile. The papal nuncio in France, Rodolfo Pio (bishop of Faenza), was initially unsure what to make of Gardiner's appointment, as he knew that Gardiner had recently been out of favour. After arriving at the French court, Gardiner seems to have informed the nuncio that *De vera obedientia* had been written under compulsion. In May 1536 the nuncio reported the joy with which Gardiner and his colleague Sir John Wallop greeted the news of Anne Boleyn's execution, and their hopes that a reconciliation with Rome would soon follow. There is no evidence that Gardiner's contacts with the papal nuncio (which continued into 1538) were made known to Henry himself, or in any sense authorized by him.

Early in 1537 Gardiner once more managed to cut across Henry's bows. In the wake of the Pilgrimage of Grace, he apparently advised the king to make concessions to his subjects. Henry's response was furious. He accused Gardiner of returning to his old opinions, and complained that a faction was seeking to win him back to their 'naughty' views. Although much later (in 1554) Gardiner claimed that Henry had considered a reconciliation with Rome at this time, there is every sign that this was really Gardiner's initiative, rather than that of Henry, who dismissed it brusquely.

A little later Gardiner was instructed to ask the French king to apprehend Cardinal Reginald Pole, who was then passing through France on a papal mission to Flanders, and extradite him to England. Henry wrote to Gardiner approving of his conduct of this affair on 8 April, yet a week later was complaining that Gardiner had asked François I merely for the expulsion of Pole, and not for his arrest. Subsequently, Henry continued to harass Gardiner about his failure to secure Pole's capture, and even urged him to consider kidnapping the cardinal and taking him to Calais. Since it seems to have been about this time that Cromwell engaged one Peter Mewtas to spy upon Gardiner, there may have been suspicions as to his loyalty. A few years earlier Gardiner had delayed reporting the flight from England of the conservative priest John Helyar, in whose parish dwelt Pole's mother, Margaret, countess of Salisbury. Then, as in this case, he seems to have dragged his feet—to the benefit of the Poles. While Gardiner certainly did approach François to act against Pole, there is also record of a message from Gardiner to Pole's colleague the bishop of Verona, expressing his regret (and that of his fellow envoy, Sir Francis Bryan) that he could not speak to Pole in person and maintaining that Henry himself had been misinformed about Pole.

Gardiner's prevarication in this affair testifies to what might be called his 'crypto-papist' tendencies—public support of the royal supremacy combined with a private preference for reconciliation with the papacy. Much of the rest of Gardiner's mission in France was occupied in abortive negotiations for a marriage between Princess Mary and one of François I's sons. Gardiner's problems with the French came through in Cromwell's lament to the French envoy in England about the bishop's personal irritability and clumsiness. By April 1538 it had been decided to recall Gardiner, but his successor, Edmund Bonner, was not chosen until July, so it was not until September that Gardiner actually returned, having already managed to quarrel with Bonner. He did not return to office or especial favour, and spent most of his time at his palaces in Southwark and Winchester, although he was briefly active on the king's council in 1539, and helped in drafting the penalty clause of the Act of Six Articles—perhaps in concert with the duke of Norfolk. He was also involved in enforcing the new act. In 1540 a priest described as 'of the new sect' was reported as having hanged himself while in confinement at Gardiner's house awaiting interrogation (Wriothesley, 1.115).

What paved the way for Gardiner's return to the centre of events was the fall of Thomas Cromwell, following the fiasco of Henry's marriage to Anne of Cleves. The extent of Gardiner's role in Cromwell's fall is not clear, but contemporaries saw his hand therein; there may have been a connection with the destruction of the protestant reformer Robert Barnes earlier in 1540. Following a pulpit controversy with Gardiner in Lent 1540, Barnes was arrested in April. Cromwell was arrested in June, and after summary proceedings was executed for treason on 28 July 1540—the very day of Henry's marriage to his fifth wife, Katherine Howard, Norfolk's niece. Barnes went to the stake two days later. Gardiner's expertise in canon law was called upon during the proceedings to annul the marriage to Anne, and contemporaries such as the French ambassador Marillac credited him with a vital role in arranging the new one. In a letter to Heinrich Bullinger, the evangelical merchant Richard Hilles claimed that Gardiner had provided entertainments and feasts at his Southwark palace in order to advance the courtship. If true, this story suggests that Gardiner was close to the duke of Norfolk, and when Norfolk was disgraced in 1546 efforts were made to bring down Gardiner with him.

One immediate benefit to Gardiner from the fall of Cromwell was his election, in succession to the fallen minister, as chancellor of the University of Cambridge. This office remained his until Edward VI's reign, when he was dispossessed in favour of the duke of Somerset in 1547, and he regained it under Mary Tudor. Cambridge made many demands upon his time. He disputed with John Cheke and Thomas Smith on the question of the pronunciation of Greek; he was vexed by breaches of the Lenten fast in the university; and he even turned his attention to the performance of the German protestant play *Pammachius*. About half of the relatively few letters of Gardiner's which survive from Mary's reign concern university business.

Anglo-imperial relations, 1540–1541 According to one source, Gardiner had been removed from the king's council in 1539 because Cromwell disapproved when he opposed the use of Robert Barnes on a diplomatic mission to Germany. Cromwell's downfall led to Gardiner's return not only to the council (he was a member of the privy council when it was established on a formal footing in August), but also to diplomatic work. Towards the end of 1540 he set off with Sir Henry Knyvett, a gentleman of the

privy chamber, on an embassy to Emperor Charles V. Their mission is poorly documented, but their main task was to notify the emperor that reconciliation with Rome could not be made a precondition of Anglo-imperial *rapprochement*. Reconstructing the work of this embassy largely depends on foreign reports from the time and on subsequent English recollections. Marillac told François I that the embassy was planned first to explain the divorce from Anne of Cleves; second to defend England from the charge of religious innovation; and third to sow discord between France and the empire. The pomp accompanying the bishop on his embassy was, Marillac supposed, designed to show that in England the church had not been despoiled. Chapuys, however, reported to Charles that Henry wanted to be reconciled to him but feared that two obstacles could not be surmounted—the divorce, and the break with Rome. Richard Pate, the envoy whom Gardiner and Knyvett were to replace, wrote that the embassy was seen as being concerned with either matters of religion or some marriage project.

The bishop of Aquila reported to Cardinal Farnese from Speyer on 25 January 1541 that Gardiner had arrived there with great pomp, and feared that the English bishop's purpose was to cause trouble. In February the papal nuncio in Speyer reported a conversation between Gardiner and the imperial minister Nicolas de Perrenot, sieur de Granvelle, in which the latter urged that England return to Rome. Gardiner appeared to agree, but said that to raise such matters with the king was a capital offence. Late in March the bishop of Modena wrote that Gardiner had received a letter from Henry in which the king had thanked Granvelle for his offer to mediate in such a reconciliation. No such letter survives, but it is noteworthy that the duke of Norfolk was asked in December 1546 about a letter on this subject allegedly received by the king at Dover. Norfolk denied all knowledge of it, but Henry was at Dover in March 1541. Meanwhile Sir John Wallop, once again envoy at the French court, informed Henry that he had urged Gardiner to be wary against a possible Franco-imperial *rapprochement* at papal instigation. By the end of February the English ambassadors had reached Ratisbon, where the imperial diet was to be held.

The principal purpose of the diet was to reconcile the differences between protestants and Catholics in the empire. The divines assembled there failed to achieve this; had the diet succeeded, then England would have been left still more isolated in diplomatic terms. Fear of isolation may have encouraged Gardiner in his efforts to reconcile England and Rome. The papal legate Giovanni Morone reported that Granvelle still found Gardiner positive in his responses to proposals for reunion, but that he had said that for him it was a capital crime to speak or write on such matters. Another papal official reported to Farnese later in May that Henry would permit Granvelle to mediate; meanwhile Gardiner and Knyvett were said to have spoken again to Granvelle, asking him to secure a proposal from Charles V concerning the fate of church lands in England in the event of reunion. Indeed, a Venetian diplomat noted that Gardiner and Granvelle were often together, speculating that if the diet itself failed, Charles might form an alliance with Henry. In June Chapuys told Mary of Hungary (regent of the Netherlands and the emperor's sister) that Gardiner and Knyvett had been negotiating for an alliance between the emperor and Henry.

May 1541 saw the collapse of the diet's efforts to achieve religious reconciliation. Gardiner received news of his recall early in July—at about the same time that news arrived of the execution of Margaret, countess of Salisbury. Coming at this moment, the execution was clearly a gesture on Henry's part designed to show his commitment to the royal supremacy and his refusal to have any truck with the papacy. It was small wonder, then, that (as the bishop of Modena told Cardinal Farnese on 4 July) Gardiner's recall made him fear for his life, as he had tried to persuade the king to consider reconciliation with Rome. Knyvett, the bishop observed, had given contrary advice. The papal nuncio in France believed that Gardiner was in disgrace and would rather flee to Rome than return to England. The likelihood is that Gardiner's informal soundings about reconciliation had been made on his own initiative, for Henry's instructions to Gardiner and Knyvett (17 June 1541) make it clear that he had no interest in such a project. At Gardiner's trial in 1551 it was alleged that he had been in contact with Cardinal Contarini at Ratisbon, and had received at his hands a letter from the pope. Knyvett, suspicious of Gardiner's actions, had informed on him to the king, but had been told to cease disputing with his fellow ambassador. Notwithstanding his fears, Gardiner managed to retain the king's favour, perhaps because he had proven his worth by reaching an understanding with the imperial representatives at Ratisbon, or perhaps because he convinced the king that he had not been negotiating with representatives of the papacy. After returning to England in October, he was soon attending the privy council, and according to Chapuys was well received by the king.

On his way back from Ratisbon, Gardiner visited Louvain, the seat of one of the great Catholic and humanist universities of northern Europe, where he was received honourably by the faculty of theology. However, when the members of the faculty challenged him over his *De vera obedientia*, he defended it, and was in consequence denied the privilege of celebrating mass in St Peter's Church. The day after his departure, the dean of the faculty delivered an oration against him. Interestingly, the Louvain theologians viewed Gardiner as a schismatic rather than as a heretic, and the quarrel between the churches of England and Rome as a matter of jurisdiction rather than of doctrine.

Defender of Catholicism In the following years Gardiner established a reputation for himself at home and abroad as a defender of orthodoxy against the Reformation. In the course of his mission to Ratisbon he had disputed with the protestant theologians Osiander and Bucer, on justification and clerical celibacy respectively. He went on to publish two Latin treatises on the latter subject against Bucer in Henry VIII's reign (*Stephani Winton episcopi Angli ad*

Martinum Bucerum, de impudentia eiusdem pseudologia conquestio, Louvain and Cologne, 1544; and *Stephani Winton episcopi Angli ad Martinum Bucerum epistola, qua cessantem hactenus et cunctantem ac frustratoria responsionis pollicitatione*, Louvain and Ingolstadt, 1546), and followed these with a third written in Edward VI's reign but not published until Mary's (*Exetasis testimoniorum, quae Martinus Bucerus ex sanctis patribus non sancte edidit*, Louvain, 1554). Yet another assault on Bucer, his 'Contemptum humanae legis', remained in manuscript until published by Pierre Janelle in 1933. But his published Latin works, which were frequently cited by other Catholic polemicists, made him the most important English Catholic theologian between John Fisher and the Elizabethan Louvainists.

Bucer was not Gardiner's only target. Before Henry VIII died, Gardiner published a series of English polemics, the first against George Joye on the question of justification, *A Declaration of such True Articles as George Joye hath Gone about to Confute* (London, 1546), and the next in defence of the real presence in the eucharist, *A Detection of the Devils Sophistry* (London, 1546). During the reign of Edward VI the eucharist became Gardiner's principal theological preoccupation.

The 1540s also saw Gardiner involved in ecclesiastical politics within England. He was active in the convocation of 1542, which set out to scrutinize the English version of scripture known as the Great Bible. Gardiner himself paid for a Great Bible, which was cut up into sections and distributed for scrutiny. He was also asked by Cranmer to take part in the compilation of some English homilies. However, he failed to deliver his contribution, and when an official book of homilies was finally published under Edward VI, it contained none of his work. He was not involved in the preparation of the doctrinal formulary commonly known as the King's Book, which was published in 1543.

In 1543 Gardiner was more preoccupied with moves against Thomas Cranmer, increasingly his greatest rival, after Dr John London (dean of the cathedral at Osney, which served the new diocese of Oxford) had furnished him with evidence of protestant heresy at Windsor. A number of arrests were made, and Gardiner himself took part in the interrogation of the protestant musician John Marbeck. He then turned his attention to Cranmer's own diocese of Canterbury, where his conservative allies produced a dossier on heresy for him shortly before Easter 1543. In May the king, too, ordered an investigation into the diocese, and there is evidence that at this time Gardiner was also trying to hunt out heresy in Henry's privy chamber.

Gardiner's plans came to nothing. An attempt to have Cranmer arrested for heresy in November 1543 ended with Henry's commissioning Cranmer himself to investigate the charges relating to his diocese, and a number of religious conservatives were arrested, among them Dr London (who died in prison in 1544) and Germaine Gardiner, the bishop's nephew and secretary. Germaine, of whom his uncle was very fond, was executed in 1544 on charges of denying the royal supremacy, and the duke of Suffolk later recalled that Stephen Gardiner himself came close to arrest at this time, saving himself only by begging the king's pardon. There may be some corroboration for this in a report of Chapuys, dating from 1546, that some years earlier Gardiner had been saved from arrest thanks only to the intervention of the duke of Norfolk.

Diplomacy and war, 1542–1546 Gardiner had proved his worth as a diplomat at Ratisbon. He was the architect of the Anglo-imperial understanding that took shape after his return to England. Throughout his career he preferred an imperial to a Francophile policy: François I had been offended by his manner at Marseilles in 1533; and Bonner, his successor as envoy to the French court in 1538, had complained that Gardiner had made

> incomparably more of the Emperor's, the King of Portugal's, Venetian, and the Duke of Ferrara's ambassadors, than of any Frenchmen in the Court, which with his pride, caused them to disdain him, and to think that he favoured not the French king but was imperial. (Foxe, ed. Cattley, 5.159–60)

Marillac, the French ambassador to the English court, wrote in 1542 that Gardiner was 'aussi bon impérial que mauvais françoys' (Kaulek, 420). Gardiner's imperialist leanings were probably intensified by his profound religious conservatism and underlying attachment to notions of a united Christendom.

It had been arranged at Ratisbon that an Anglo-imperial treaty should be concluded within ten months. This period expired at the end of April 1542. In the following month, however, Gardiner opened negotiations with Chapuys, and found him favourably inclined to the idea of an alliance between England and the emperor. Chapuys reported to Charles V that he was in agreement with Gardiner, and wrote to one of his master's ministers that Gardiner would be the best person to be sent to the emperor as an ambassador. Eventually a treaty was concluded with the empire on 31 December 1543, with Gardiner as one of the commissioners. It provided for a joint Anglo-imperial invasion of France.

In the ensuing war Gardiner played a major part in organizing the provisioning of English forces both on the continent and in Scotland; indeed he earned the sobriquet Simon Stockfish thanks to his work organizing supplies of food. Although his competence in this field was questioned at the time both by his friend and colleague Sir Anthony Browne and by Edward Seymour, earl of Hertford, who commanded the English invasion of Scotland in 1544, the planning of the latter campaign, in which Gardiner played a large part, has been described by a modern historian as 'extremely thorough' (Davies, 245). In September 1544 Gardiner led a delegation (which also included Hertford and Sir William Paget, his sometime pupil at Trinity Hall) to negotiate with the French. Charles V was already negotiating a separate peace. Chapuys commented on Gardiner's sharp and pointed manner in his dealings with the leader of the French delegation, Cardinal du Bellay, who himself observed that Gardiner always wanted to speak and shout and gain the upper hand. Relations with the representatives of the emperor

worsened as well. Early in October Gardiner complained that the emperor wanted Boulogne to be handed back to the French because he was jealous of Henry VIII's success in the war. After joining Hertford on a brief mission to Charles V at Brussels, Gardiner returned home in November having failed to persuade the emperor to resume hostilities.

In October 1545 Gardiner returned to Europe with two objectives: to make terms with the French and to renew the Anglo-imperial alliance. Talks with the French commenced in November at Bruges. Gardiner was worried at this time about England's international position: at war with France and Scotland, at enmity with the pope, and without a firm friendship with the empire. He told Paget that he thought Boulogne a drain on English resources, although he had also remarked that if it were to be abandoned, 'it shuld not be thought it wer bycause we coulde not kepe it, but because his Highnes wold not' (*Letters*, ed. Muller, 179–80). The French delegation left Charles V's court at the end of November, but Gardiner remained there, and in January 1546 concluded a treaty with the emperor. He returned to England in March, and left the country only once more, for a brief trip to Boulogne in June, to inspect the fortifications.

The end of Henry VIII's reign For the rest of 1546 Gardiner was preoccupied with domestic affairs. He was involved in the examination of Anne Askew, a protestant gentlewoman of the court, who was executed for heresy in July 1546. He also took part in proceedings against other reformers such as Edward Crome and Hugh Latimer. According to Foxe, Gardiner tried to turn these investigations against Katherine Parr, Henry's last queen, who was suspected of protestant inclinations. These efforts failed, and, if Foxe is to be believed, the king berated Gardiner: 'knave! arrant knave! beast! and fool!' (Foxe, ed. Cattley, 5.561). Foxe also maintained that it was Gardiner who, in this last year of the reign, dissuaded Henry from accepting certain religious innovations proposed by Cranmer.

Gardiner's period of favour was brief. As late as August 1546 Van der Delft (the new imperial ambassador) identified him, Paget, and Baron Wriothesley as the king's leading councillors. When John Dudley, Lord Lisle (later earl of Warwick and duke of Northumberland), struck Gardiner in the face at the council table, he was banished from court for a month. Towards the end of November, however, Gardiner unwisely declined a proposed exchange of lands with the king: at least, Henry believed that Gardiner had refused to comply. Gardiner was obliged to apologize, writing to Paget on 2 December that 'I here no specialte of the kings Majesties myscontentement in this matier of lands, but confusely, that my doinges shuld not be wel taken' (*Letters*, ed. Muller, 247). When Gardiner claimed never to have denied any request for the lands, Henry upbraided him, declaring that he had 'utterly refused any conformity' (Foxe, ed. Cattley, 6.138). The incident may well have been manipulated by Hertford and his allies in order to 'unhorse Winchester' (Scarisbrick, 490).

About the same time the duke of Norfolk was disgraced and arrested. He was questioned about a letter sent to the king by Gardiner and Knyvett in 1541, outlining Granvelle's proposals for reconciliation with Rome, and was also interrogated about remarks allegedly made by Sir Francis Bryan on Gardiner's views concerning reunion. On Christmas eve Van der Delft reported to the emperor that many people (perhaps those associated with the court) wanted to see Gardiner in the Tower with Norfolk.

The day after Christmas, Henry called for the draft of his will and ordered Paget (according to the latter's testimony at Gardiner's trial in 1551) to remove Gardiner's name from the list of executors and councillors who were to rule during his son's minority. Paget claimed that he and others tried to persuade Henry to restore Gardiner's name, but the king was adamant in his refusal, for he 'had the same bishop of suspicion of misliking his highness's proceedings in some things of religion'. Henry thought him 'too wilful in his opinion, and much bent to the pop-ish party', 'a wilful man and not meet to be about his son' (Foxe, ed. Cattley, 6.163). Somerset testified at the same time that Henry had said that 'the said bishop was a troublesome man; and that he would trouble all the rest if he were named among them' (ibid., 170). Much the same message came from Sir Anthony Denny, who recalled Henry's words to him that if Gardiner:

> were in my testament, and one of you, he would cumber you all, and you should never rule him, he is of so troublesome a nature. Marry, I myself could use him, and rule him to all manner of purposes as seemed good to me; but so shall you never do, and therefore talk no more of him to me in this behalf. (ibid., 5.691–2)

The king's will was signed on 30 December 1546, with Gardiner's name omitted from the list of executors and councillors. Gardiner was still attending the privy council as late as 16 January 1547, but his exclusion from power under Edward VI had been assured.

The reign of Edward VI: combating protestantism Early in the new reign Gardiner received some marks of favour from the council, but none of any great moment. He presided over the arrival of Henry's corpse at Windsor on 15 February 1547, and preached at the requiem mass. At Edward's coronation, he and Tunstall flanked Cranmer. Of greater political importance was the invitation to address the ambassadors of Scotland and France and the emperor at the residence of Protector Somerset, who assured Gardiner that there would be no innovations in religion until the king attained his majority.

Despite this assurance Gardiner was concerned about the religious tendencies of the new regime from almost the earliest days of the reign. On Ash Wednesday (23 February), he heard Nicholas Ridley preach a sermon at court against the use of images and holy water (which itself may have been following the lead Cranmer had probably set in his sermon at the coronation, which extolled Edward as a second Josiah, a royal iconoclast). Writing to Ridley, Gardiner defended these usages, appealing to the King's Book as embodying 'the doctrine set forth by our late soveraine lord' (*Letters*, ed. Muller, 259). He wrote to Somerset to complain of another sermon, given by William Barlow

(bishop of St Davids), enclosing a copy of his letter to Ridley.

Gardiner also clashed with Paget, over the wording of the royal commission renewing episcopal jurisdiction, writing to him in the hope that he would 'maynteyne Goddes truth against that they call Goddes worde' (*Letters*, ed. Muller, 272). Soon afterwards he retired to his diocese, only for trouble to follow him. On 3 May he wrote to the captain of Portsmouth, Edward Vaughan, demanding to know more about incidents of image-breaking there. A few weeks later he was complaining to Somerset about the circulation of John Bale's books and breaches of Lenten observance, once more resting his case on Henry's religious settlement. In reply, Somerset (who had by now been informed about the correspondence about Portsmouth by Vaughan) accused Gardiner of scaremongering and tried to blacken his name by association with the leading conservative theologian from Oxford, Dr Richard Smyth (who had recently been induced to recant a number of his opinions). Somerset's increasing suspicions and anxieties about Gardiner are corroborated by a report that the council wanted to prevent the bishop from meeting with Wriothesley (now earl of Southampton), the recently displaced lord chancellor. In his turn, Gardiner urged Somerset to resist religious innovation during the royal minority, and denied all knowledge of Smyth.

By now Gardiner was aware of Cranmer's plan to issue a book of homilies, and was swift to lodge his objections with Somerset, protesting 'I can admit no inovacions' (*Letters*, ed. Muller, 298). Just a month previously he had reminded the protector of the latter's assurance that he would 'suffer no innovacion' (ibid., 278). He continued the offensive with two letters to Cranmer, contesting the latter's claim that Henry had been tricked into assenting to the King's Book, and charging the homilies with contradicting that formulary by promoting justification by faith alone. And in due course he laid his complaints before the privy council in further letters, turning his fire also onto the injunctions issued in association with the homilies. He warned in particular that the injunction against liturgical processions would prejudice relations with the empire. He also observed that the King's Book had been authorized by a statute still in force. When Sir John Mason was appointed as a visitor for Winchester diocese, Gardiner wrote to him pointing out that the injunctions and homilies were contrary to Henry VIII's religious laws and advising him that he would be welcome providing he did nothing in breach of statute.

Thus far Gardiner had tried to counter religious innovation with four arguments: first, he warned of the inadvisability of change during a royal minority; second, he argued that innovation was contrary to Henry's express wishes; third, he raised technical and legal objections; and finally he offered theological objections. The publication of the homilies goaded him into open defiance, as he appealed to the Act for the Advancement of True Religion of 1543 during the visitation of his diocese. As a result he was summoned to appear before the privy council on 25 September, and his refusal to accept the new injunctions unconditionally led to his incarceration in the Fleet prison. Paget defended this action to the imperial ambassador on the grounds that Gardiner had become intractable.

Gardiner himself reckoned that he had been imprisoned in order to keep him away from the parliament that proceeded to repeal the Henrician religious legislation on which he based his resistance. Nevertheless, he continued his campaign against religious change, turning his attention to the *Paraphrases on the New Testament*, a translation of Erasmus, the use of which was imposed by the new injunctions. He was not released from the Fleet until January 1548, safely after the closure of parliament. Brought once more before a group of councillors headed by Somerset and Cranmer, he was invited, and refused, to subscribe to a statement on the doctrine of justification, upon which he was placed under house arrest in his Southwark palace. He spelt out his objections in another letter to Somerset, but was set at liberty after giving a qualified subscription to the statement.

On his release Gardiner returned to his diocese, but trouble followed him once more. He declined to surrender the mastership of Trinity Hall. John Philpot put about rumours concerning his conduct in his diocese. Matters worsened with the arrival in Winchester of two committed protestants, Roger Tonge and Giles Ayre, to take up canonries at the cathedral. They were soon complaining that Gardiner prevented them from preaching, and that his chaplain, Thomas Watson (later the Marian bishop of Lincoln), had preached against them. Gardiner was once more hauled before the council in May to answer their charges. He was required to prove his good faith by preaching a sermon endorsing the regime's religious policy, and specifically covering papal authority, the dissolution of the monasteries, the suppression of shrines and images, the prohibition of various ceremonies, and the lawfulness of religious change notwithstanding the king's minority. He got away with refusing to provide an advance copy of his text, by dint of undertaking not to touch upon 'doubtful matters'—although he rather cheekily stated that he would preach on 'the very presence of Christ's most precious body and blood in the sacrament, which is the Catholic faith, and no doubtfull matter, nor yet in controversy' (Foxe, ed. Cattley, 6.70).

The sermon was delivered on St Peter's day (29 June), and sailed close to the wind. Gardiner spoke of the sacrifice of the mass (contrary to his instructions) as designed 'to continue us in the remembrance of his [Christ's] passion suffred for us' (Foxe, ed. Cattley, 6.89). Although, modifying his own earlier views, he granted the permissibility of communion under both kinds and duly attacked papal authority, he defended religious ceremonies in principle as serving 'to move men to God', censured preachers who spoke against the mass, and upheld clerical celibacy (ibid., 6.92–3).

Imprisonment and deprivation This audacious protest against possible future change led next day to Gardiner's confinement in the Tower, where he remained for the rest of the reign. This may not have been entirely unexpected—according to Van der Delft, Gardiner had made provision for his servants before preaching his sermon, though not all of them can have left his service at this time, since the council made provision for maintaining his servants and house in July 1550 after his temporary sequestration from his see. Nor was Gardiner without hope of release. In common with other conservatives, he looked to the earl of Warwick to reverse Somerset's religious policies when the protector was brought down, and wrote to him petitioning for justice in October 1549. Van der Delft was hopeful of Gardiner's release at this point, but both men were deceived. Religious change continued, and Gardiner remained incarcerated.

During this period of enforced retirement, Gardiner's main occupation was theological controversy, mostly on the subject of the eucharist. His first effort was a refutation of Peter Martyr Vermigli's *Tractatio de sacramento eucharistiae* (London, 1549). Gardiner's response, *In Petrum Martyrem Florentinum malae tractationis querela sanctissimae eucharistiae* (BL, Arundel MS 100, fols. 1–182), written in 1549–50, was a sturdy defence of transubstantiation. He followed this with *An Explication and Assertion of the True Catholique Fayth* (Rouen, 1551), replying to Cranmer's *Defence of the True and Catholique Doctrine* (London, 1550). Essentially a defence of the real presence in general and of the doctrine of transubstantiation in particular, this work is notable chiefly for its claim that Cranmer's prayer book of 1549 was 'not distant from the Catholique fayth in my jugement' (*Explication*, fol. 38v). Nevertheless, Gardiner insisted that in allowing only for the real presence, rather than for the full doctrine of transubstantiation, it was still defective. He returned to the subject yet again in another unpublished manuscript (PRO, SP 10/12, fols. 2–68), an answer to John Hooper's *An Oversight and Deliberacion upon the Holy Prophete Jonas*.

The Edwardian regime remained keen to secure Gardiner's conformity. In June 1549 he was brought a copy of the new prayer book and warned of the dangers of defying the Act of Uniformity. He replied guardedly to the effect that he felt safe from being troubled under the terms of the act so long as he was not indicted. Then a high-level delegation visited him in June 1550 to demand a clear answer about the prayer book. He was persuaded to say that he could use the new liturgy himself, and allow its use in his diocese, but he declined to give anything in writing. He may have hoped thus to gain his freedom, but in vain. Warwick and some others came back in due course with articles for him to sign. Finally, he was summoned before the council and, refusing to subscribe to articles put before him, was sequestered from his temporalities for three months.

The next act began on 15 December, when Gardiner was brought to trial before royal commissioners headed by Cranmer at Lambeth. Tried on nineteen charges, Gardiner put up a vigorous defence, and proceedings were further drawn out by a substantial body of witnesses summoned by the commissioners. But the inevitable conclusion was reached on 14 February 1551, when Gardiner was deprived of the see of Winchester.

Despite a council decision the following day that Gardiner should be denied pen, ink, and paper during his continued imprisonment, he somehow carried on his activities as a controversial theologian. His *Confutatio cavillationum* (a reply to Cranmer's *An Answer unto a Craftie and Sophisticall Cavillation*, London, 1551) was published at Paris in 1552 under the name Marcus Antonius Constantius. Its authorship was an open secret, despite the pseudonym, and it was later reprinted under his own name. Further treatises on the eucharist followed: *Annotationes in dialogum Oecolampadii* (LPL, MS 140, fols. 225–333) and a defence of criticisms of John Hooper made by two priests of his diocese, Henry Joliffe and Robert Johnson.

The reign of Mary: the Spanish match Gardiner's long imprisonment came to an end with Mary Tudor's triumphant entry into London on 3 August 1553, when he was released together with the old duke of Norfolk and the young Edward Courtenay (soon restored as earl of Devon). Within a week he was once more sworn of the privy council and resumed possession of his Southwark palace, and on 23 August he was appointed lord chancellor. About the same time he was restored to his see.

Any analysis of Gardiner's actions under Mary needs to take into account the fact that many of the sources are non-English, most notably the reports of the imperial ambassadors of the period. About half of his surviving letters from these years are concerned with university business. And the principal literary work ascribed to him from this time, the so-called 'Machiavellian treatise', is unlikely to be entirely his. A further note of caution has to be sounded concerning the diplomatic sources, namely that Simon Renard, the principal imperial envoy, was deeply and consistently hostile to Stephen Gardiner. How far this hostility was reciprocated cannot be known. It is clear, however, that Renard sometimes reported false information about the chancellor as well as his own negative opinions of him. For example, on 22 March 1554 Renard told Charles V that Gardiner never cared to attend the council unless he was sent for, thus intending, presumably, to portray the bishop as an isolated and insignificant figure. The reverse was in fact the case: not only did Gardiner attend most meetings of the council in the early months of 1554, but he was present at over three-fifths of all meetings between his readmission to the council and his last appearance about a month before his death.

Two questions dominated the early years of Mary's reign, and therefore the career of Gardiner during that period: the restoration of Catholicism in England, and the matter of the queen's choice of husband. The tensions that arose from both issues became evident early on. Both created difficulties between Gardiner and his main rival (and former protégé), Baron Paget.

The question of the queen's marriage proved troublesome. As early as September 1553, ambassadors were reporting Gardiner's preference that Mary should marry Edward Courtenay, and commenting that the bishop

seemed to have established some sort of personal ascendancy over the young man while they were fellow prisoners in the Tower. Simon Renard related Gardiner's view that England would never abide a foreigner as the queen's consort, and that Courtenay was the only alternative. This set Gardiner, hitherto a firm ally of the empire, at loggerheads with the imperial ambassadors, who were pressing for Mary to marry Philip of Spain, Charles V's son. It also tended to throw him into the arms of the French ambassador, Antoine de Noailles, who did his best to convince him of the dangers of the Spanish match.

On 17 November 1553 Renard reported to Charles V that the speaker of the House of Commons, Sir John Pollard, had appeared before the queen accompanied by, among others, the duke of Norfolk, the earl of Arundel, Gardiner, and Paget, to urge her to marry an Englishman; he also claimed that Pollard had been briefed by supporters of Courtenay and Gardiner. Mary rebuked Pollard, and Arundel (according to Renard) told Gardiner that he had lost the chancellorship that day. Three days later Renard added that Mary had accused Gardiner of having inspired Pollard—a charge which the chancellor denied, adding that he would obey the man whom she chose as her husband.

Gardiner's supporters on the council included Sir Robert Rochester, Sir Francis Englefield, and Sir Edward Waldegrave. His main opponent was Paget, and their rivalry was obvious from the start to the ambassadors at court. But Paget read the queen's mind better than Gardiner. Although by the end of the year Gardiner had reconciled himself to the inevitable, co-operating with Paget in the drafting of the treaty which would regulate the marriage of Mary and Philip, his early misreading of the situation may have undermined the queen's trust in him. After the treaty had been concluded, Gardiner's attitude to Philip became more positive. On 6 May 1554 Renard told Charles V that Gardiner had had a genealogical tree drawn up to demonstrate Philip's descent from John of Gaunt. Paget thought that this was meant to constitute a claim to the English throne on Philip's behalf. And Gardiner's ingrained Francophobia was soon in evidence once more: on 29 May the council wrote to Dr Wotton about a violent argument between Gardiner and de Noailles at court. Moreover, it was Gardiner who presided at the royal marriage in July 1554, which took place at his own cathedral in Winchester.

Catholic restoration Gardiner's determination to proceed speedily with the restoration of Catholicism was clear from the start, and gave rise to discomfiture both at home and abroad, even among his co-religionists. The papal nuncio in Brussels reported that Antoine de Perronet (bishop of Arras and later Cardinal Granvelle), one of Charles V's leading ministers, disapproved of Gardiner's decision to celebrate a requiem mass for Edward VI. The chancellor (who was praised by Pole for having celebrated mass even during his incarceration) was confident in his own rectitude, but his actions were technically illegal, as the Act of Uniformity had not yet been repealed.

Gardiner's opening speech in Mary's first parliament

struck a similarly urgent note, making it clear that a Catholic restoration was to be undertaken expeditiously, and even touched on the subject of reunion with Rome. That first parliament duly repealed most of the religious legislation of Edward's reign, but the outbreak of Wyatt's rising in January 1554 weakened Gardiner's position. Not only did he apparently panic, and advise the queen to flee the city, but when order had been restored, he also found that blame for the rebellion was being laid at his door on account of his enthusiasm for reversing religious change. Nor was he helped by the involvement of his protégé Courtenay in the Wyatt affair, which he tried to cover up as best he could. This further complicated his relationship with Renard, who wished to see Courtenay executed. Renard continued to believe that Gardiner was proceeding with excessive haste in religious affairs, and lobbied both the queen and the emperor against Gardiner's plans to abrogate the royal supremacy in the next parliamentary session. In fact, the main issue in the next session was the reintroduction of a statute against heresy. This was frustrated in the Lords, thanks to the machinations of Paget—who this time had read the situation less shrewdly than Gardiner, and had to beg the queen's pardon.

Gardiner was also at one with the queen over the need to welcome the new papal legate, Cardinal Reginald Pole, into England as soon as possible. Notwithstanding Renard's misgivings, Pole arrived at Westminster on 24 November 1554 and, in response to a parliamentary petition addressed to Philip and Mary, formally absolved the realm (as represented in the two houses of parliament) from the sin of schism on 30 November. Gardiner marked this on the first Sunday of Advent (2 December) with a sermon at Paul's Cross celebrating England's reconciliation with Rome. This did not end his political difficulties, however. He was said to have been jealous that it was not he but Paget who was chosen to escort Pole from Brussels to England, and there were rumours that Pole would displace him as chancellor. According to Renard, Gardiner felt towards the end of 1554 that Philip was communicating affairs to him only when decisions had already been taken, and early in 1555 he continued to face opposition on the council.

Although Renard thought Gardiner all too keen to protect Courtenay, he found the chancellor more ready to act against Princess Elizabeth. On 3 April 1554 he reported to the emperor that when he told Gardiner that he had better prepare to have Elizabeth tried, the bishop told him that so long as the princess lived he could not hope to see the kingdom at peace; earlier Gardiner had been the main advocate on the council of sending Elizabeth to the Tower (whither she was consigned on 18 March 1554). According to Renard's dispatch of 21 December 1554, Gardiner wanted her declared a bastard (and thus excluded from the succession) during that parliamentary session—a wish which went unfulfilled. Gardiner's hostility to Elizabeth gives some plausibility to Foxe's story that Gardiner's servant James Basset went to Bladonbridge near Woodstock (where the princess resided after her release from the Tower) in company with 'twenty or thirty privy

coats' (that is, gentlemen of the privy chamber) in order to murder her (Foxe, ed. Cattley, 8.618). A murder plot is unlikely, but Gardiner may have intended to intimidate her or provoke her into some act of indiscretion. Foxe also claimed that Gardiner and other councillors sent a writ to the Tower ordering Elizabeth's execution, and that this was frustrated by the lieutenant of the Tower's decision to consult the queen before taking any action. But this story is less likely, since Elizabeth was never put on trial—a trial being a common preliminary, even in Tudor England, to execution. After her return to Woodstock in 1555, Gardiner examined her at Hampton Court and urged her to submit to the queen.

In May 1555 Gardiner seemed to be back at the heart of affairs, when with Pole, Paget, and Arundel he was sent to France to broker a deal between France and the empire, and Gardiner acted as spokesman for the English delegation. It probably did him no harm with the imperialists that he was so forceful in urging the French to restore the duke of Savoy to his lands that his English colleagues thought he was exceeding his brief as a mediator. After negotiations broke down in June, and the English returned home, Gardiner was still active in drafting further proposals to send to the king of France.

August saw Gardiner busy with preparations for the next parliament. According to Philip, he was trying to ensure the return of sound Catholics to the Commons (as well as to improve enforcement of the heresy laws), and the two men had by now seemingly established a good working relationship. Furthermore, the advice Gardiner appears to have given Philip on religion throws considerable doubt on Foxe's assertion that Gardiner grew disillusioned with efforts to suppress heresy. In early 1555 he had taken part in the trials and examinations of (among others) John Hooper, Rowland Taylor, John Rogers, and Robert Ferrar, all of whom were burnt. He was also present in the summer of 1555 at meetings of the privy council which approved the execution of heretics.

Professor P. S. Donaldson, the editor of the so-called 'Machiavellian treatise' (properly the *Ragionamento dell'advenimento delli Inglesi et Normanni in Britannia, or, A Discourse on the Coming of the English and Normans to Britain*), has seen in this work further signs of Gardiner's growing support for Philip. However, it is something of a conundrum. A dialogue combining political advice with an account of English history, it also contains extensive (though unacknowledged) quotations from Machiavelli. Its translator, one George Rainsford, who presented the work to Philip, claimed to have produced the Italian from an English original by Gardiner. Scholarly objections to Gardiner's sole authorship are cogent. Most notably, the author of the treatise was strikingly ignorant of English statute law—an unlikely failing in Gardiner. However, there are undeniable parallels between this dialogue and other writings of Gardiner's, and at the same time differences between it and the accompanying text (*Ritratto dell'Inghilterra*) by Rainsford which the latter sent Philip along with it, which would be difficult to account for if both were the work of a single author. While on balance it is unlikely that the *Ragionamento* is wholly Gardiner's work, it remains possible that some of it was originally his, even if most of it came from the pen of Rainsford.

Death By early autumn 1555 Gardiner's health was failing. He appears to have attended the council for the last time on 25 September 1555, and the diplomatic correspondence is full of reports about his condition and his treatment. He struggled out to speak at the opening of parliament on 21 October, and apparently spoke again a couple of days later, but the end was near. His will was dated 8 November (with a codicil added the next day), and he died about the middle of the night on 12–13 November. Rumours of poisoning circulated, but the protracted nature of his final illness (perhaps dropsy) makes this unlikely. It was later said by Thomas Stapleton, the Elizabethan Catholic theologian, that Gardiner listened on his deathbed to the gospel narrative of Peter's betrayal of Christ. Weeping bitterly, the bishop said 'Ego exivi sed non dum flevi amare' ('I have gone out, but I have not yet wept bitterly'; Muller, 291–2). Next day his bowels were removed for burial in St Mary Overy, Southwark. Bonner, bishop of London, sang the requiem mass for Gardiner on 14 November, and the sermon was preached by John White (then bishop of Lincoln, and soon to succeed Gardiner at Winchester). There were dirges and masses for his soul in every parish in London. Gardiner's body was taken to Winchester and buried in the cathedral on 28 February 1556 in a splendid chantry tomb. Anthony Browne, now Viscount Montagu, and Thomas Thirlby, bishop of Ely (his executors) rode to his interment at the head of 200 gentlemen and yeomen. The head of the recumbent stone effigy was later removed. The chantry itself is a remarkable edifice, the fluted Ionic colonnettes of the reredos among the earliest of their type in England. 'Far from homogeneous' (Pevsner, 679), it combines elements of Gothic and both early and high Renaissance styles, and is perhaps a suitable memorial to Gardiner's own blend of humanist and scholastic learning.

It is hard to say how much difference Gardiner's death made to the course of Mary's reign. Certainly Mary's council lost its most dominant (and divisive) figure. However, Gardiner's Francophobia would doubtless have led him to support English intervention in the war between France and the empire. There is no reason to suppose that the consequent loss of Calais could have been avoided if Gardiner had still been in office as lord chancellor. And as he had always been profoundly hostile to protestantism, his survival would probably have made little difference to the burnings, which continued until the end of the reign.

Assessment Gardiner was one of the giants of Tudor politics. Among the English statesmen of the sixteenth century, only Wolsey, Cromwell, Cecil, and perhaps Walsingham exceeded him in stature. Few other politicians of the age had a career of comparable duration. Gardiner was a figure of the first rank for almost thirty years, surpassing the records of his first patron, Wolsey, and his great rival,

Cromwell. Moreover, as the leading English religious conservative of his time, Gardiner bulks large in political, intellectual, and ecclesiastical history. He enjoyed a European reputation as a theologian, second only to Fisher among his English contemporaries.

It is because of his importance as a politician, diplomat, and theologian that Gardiner's reputation has always been so controversial. To the protestant martyrologist John Foxe, he was 'a man hated of God and all good men' (Foxe, ed. Cattley, 7.585). Foxe had no doubts about Gardiner's significance: several hundred pages of the *Actes and Monuments* (in its nineteenth-century edition) feature the bishop of Winchester, and it was Foxe who dubbed him 'wily Winchester' (ibid., 7.592), a nickname still sometimes used to this day. Not even Foxe could deny him his 'wit, capacity, and memory' (ibid., 7.585). Other contemporaries and near contemporaries had a less jaundiced view of Gardiner. The Elizabethan humanist Gabriel Harvey wrote of him as a 'crafty, deceytfull fox' but also referred to his 'singular perfection, experience and cunning practis in the affairs of the world', summing him up as a man 'reputed singularly wise, politique & learned: especially in *Lawe*, and matters of *State*' (Stern, 154–5).

Opinions about Gardiner divided along fairly predictable lines. Protestants hated him and Frenchmen despised him; Catholics and imperialists admired and respected him. Protestant hatred of the bishop surfaced as early as Henry's reign, with William Turner describing him as 'the Romysh fox', and Henry Brinklow going so far as to accuse him of murder. Among Catholics his reputation was for the most part quite the reverse. The long-serving Chapuys held Gardiner in generally high regard, as did his successor, Van der Delft. Renard, the imperial ambassador in Mary's reign, had his differences with Gardiner, notably over her marriage to Philip, and continued to distrust him even after he had solemnized that marriage. Yet their differences may have been personal as much as political, because Gardiner seems to have had a good relationship with Philip himself.

Gardiner's detractors often spoke of his irascibility. There is something in Elton's observation that he 'always made enemies more readily than friends' (Elton, *Reform and Reformation*, 328). But he was not without friends. He retained the loyalty of his household even during his trial. And he had his protégés, men such as Edward Courtenay and Thomas Watson. What is also clear, though, is that he came close to wrecking his own career on more than one occasion, whether out of principle or personal arrogance.

Gardiner can hardly be dismissed as an opportunist. His commitment to Catholic doctrines on the eucharist, justification, and clerical celibacy is beyond doubt. He testified to his religious convictions in lengthy polemics, published and unpublished. Critics have charged him with insincerity on the grounds of his attachment to the royal supremacy under Henry and his subsequent return to the papal obedience under Mary. But even here an underlying consistency can be discerned. Gardiner's doubts about the wisdom of the divorce (if foreign diplomatic sources are to be trusted on this score); his opposition to the submission of the clergy in 1532; his concession of a papal primacy of honour even in *De vera obedientia*; his frequent contacts with the papal nuncio while ambassador to the French court; his efforts at Ratisbon to promote Anglo-Roman reconciliation—all these suggest where his true loyalties lay. Gardiner was indeed at heart a papist (albeit a crypto-papist), as so many of his enemies alleged. Yet his loyalty to the crown was equally sincere. It was not simply fear of the prince's wrath that kept his papal sympathies in check. It was only under Edward VI, and far from willingly, that he came to see that his divided loyalties could no longer be reconciled.

It is hard to dissent from Elton's judgement of Gardiner: that he had 'an energetic, ranging, fertile mind with an eye to self-advancement' (Elton, *Reform and Reformation*, 118). That he was arrogant is clear. But he had much to be arrogant about: learning, a ready pen, fluency in extemporary oratory, gifts as an advocate and polemicist. Nor was he without humour. As he wrote to Somerset from the Fleet prison in November 1547:

> I wrot to your Grace out of this prison as I was wont to wryte to our late soveraign lord, whose soul God pardon, when I was ambassador, refreshing my self somtime with a mery tale in a sad mater; which his Highnes ever passed over without displesure, as I trust your Grace wil do the semblable. For though some accompt me a Papist, yet I cannot play the pope holy, as thold term was. (*Letters*, ed. Muller, 419)

Few Tudor statesmen rose so far and so fast. Born of humble stock, Gardiner was bishop in one of England's richest sees by his mid-thirties. Had it not been for the break with Rome he might have achieved under Henry the chancellorship that he attained under Mary. As it was, he became one of the dominant figures of mid-Tudor England, in favour a capable official and out of it a formidable opponent. So it was that Cromwell kept him out of office, out of the council, and indeed out of the country for all but a short part of his own heyday, while the Edwardian regime ensured that Gardiner remained out of London or in prison for most of the time between Henry's death and Mary's accession.

Gardiner's training in civil and canon law, his humanist education, and his theological learning gave him an intellectual ascendancy over most of his contemporaries. Disputatious by nature, he used his training to hone his talents. His gifts were those of a controversialist and (except perhaps in France) a diplomat. What he was not was 'wily' in the sense that Foxe meant. He was not as adept in court politics as some of his contemporaries. His disputes with Henry VIII in 1532 and 1546 show this as much as his failure to destroy Cranmer in 1543 and Katherine Parr in 1546. His lack of political 'wiliness' perhaps also accounts for his defeat over Queen Mary's marriage plans. In the final analysis, Gardiner's wiles were too much those of the scholar, too little those of the politician.

C. D. C. ARMSTRONG

Sources J. A. Muller, *Stephen Gardiner and the Tudor reaction* (1926) · G. Redworth, *In defence of the church catholic: the life of Stephen Gardiner* (1990) · C. D. C. Armstrong, *In defence of the church Catholic: the life of Stephen Gardiner*, review of G. Redworth, *Journal of Ecclesiastical History*, 44 (1993), 311–13 · *The letters of Stephen Gardiner*, ed. J. A. Muller (1933) · *LP Henry VIII*, vols. 3–21 · *State papers published under ... Henry VIII*, 11 vols. (1830–52) · *CSP Spain, 1509–58* · *CSP Venice, 1520–80* · N. H. Nicolas, ed., *Proceedings and ordinances of the privy council of England*, 7 vols., RC, 26 (1834–7), vol. 7 · *APC, 1542–1546* · *Opus epistolarum Des. Erasmi Roterodami*, ed. P. S. Allen, 12 vols. (1905–58) · 'Will of John Gardener of Bury, 1506', *Proceedings of the Bury and W. Suffolk Archaeological Institute*, 1 (1853), 329–30 · D. MacCulloch, *Thomas Cranmer: a life* (1996) · *Registra Stephani Gardiner et Johannis Poynet, episcoporum Wintoniensium*, ed. H. Chitty, CYS, 37 (1930) · A. Oswald, 'Stephen Gardiner and Bury St Edmunds', *Proceedings of the Suffolk Institute of Archaeology*, 26 (1955), 54–7 · G. Scott Thomson, 'Three Suffolk figures: Thomas Wolsey, Stephen Gardiner, Nicholas Bacon: a study in social history', *Proceedings of the Suffolk Institute of Archaeology*, 25 (1952), 149–63 · D. N. J. MacCulloch, 'Two dons in politics: Cranmer and Stephen Gardiner, 1503–1533', *HJ*, 37 (1994), 1–22 · J. Kaulek, ed., *Correspondance politique de MM. de Castillon et de Marillac, ambassadeurs de France en Angleterre (1537–1542)* (Paris, 1885) · L. Cardauns, ed., *Berichte aus Regensburger und Speierer Reichstag, 1541, 1542, Nuntiaturberichte aus Deutschland*, pt 1, vol. 7 (1912) · H. Laemmer, ed., *Monumenta Vaticana historiam ecclesiasticam saeculi XVI illustrantia* (1861) · P. Janelle, 'Select documents XI: an unpublished poem on Bishop Stephen Gardiner', *BIHR*, 6 (1928–9), 12–25, 89–96, 167–74 · R. Pogson, 'God's law and man's: Stephen Gardiner and the problem of loyalty', *Law and government under the Tudors: essays presented to Sir Geoffrey Elton*, ed. C. Cross, D. Loades, and J. J. Scarisbrick (1988), 67–89 · V. F. Stern, *Gabriel Harvey: his life, marginalia, and library* (1979) · P. Gwyn, *The king's cardinal: the rise and fall of Thomas Wolsey* (1990) · E. W. Ives, *Anne Boleyn* (1986) · J. J. Scarisbrick, *Henry VIII* (1968) · N. Pocock, *Records of the Reformation: the divorce, 1527–1533* (1870) · M. J. Kelly, 'The submission of the clergy', *TRHS*, 5th ser., 15 (1965), 97–119 · H. Gee and W. J. Hardy, eds., *Documents illustrative of English church history* (1921) · *Obedience in church and state: three political tracts by Stephen Gardiner*, ed. P. Janelle (1930) · T. F. Mayer, 'A diet for Henry VIII: the failure of Reginald Pole's 1537 legation', *Journal of British Studies*, 26 (1987), 305–31 · P. Janelle, 'La controverse entre Étienne Gardiner et Martin Bucer sur la discipline ecclésiastique (1541–1548)', *Revue des Sciences Religieuses*, 7 (1927), 452–66 · *Henry Brinklow's 'Complaynt of Roderyck Mors'*, ed. J. M. Cowper, EETS, extra series, 22 (1874) · G. R. Elton, 'Thomas Cromwell's decline and fall', *Studies in Tudor and Stuart politics and government: papers and reviews, 1946–1972*, 1 (1974) · *Life and letters of Thomas Cromwell*, ed. R. B. Merriman, 2 vols. (1902) · H. de Vocht, *Monumenta humanistica Lovaniensia: texts and studies about Louvain humanists in the first half of the XVIth century* (Louvain, 1934) · H. O. Evennett, *The cardinal of Lorraine and the Council of Trent: a study in the Counter Reformation* (1930) · P. Polman, *L'élément historique dans la controverse religieuse du XVIe siècle* (Gembloux, 1932) · S. E. James, *Kateryn Parr: the making of a queen* (1999) · S. R. Gammon, *Statesman and schemer: William, first Lord Paget, Tudor minister* (1973) · *Henry VIII to his ambassadors at the diet of Ratisbon, 17 June 1541*, ed. C. J. Black and C. E. Challis (1968) · D. Loades, *Mary Tudor: a life* (1989) · D. M. Loades, *The reign of Mary Tudor: politics, government and religion in England, 1553–58* (1979) · D. E. Hoak, 'Two revolutions in Tudor government: the formation and organization of Mary I's privy council', *Revolution reassessed: revisions in the history of Tudor government and administration*, ed. C. Coleman and D. Starkey (1986) · *The diary of Henry Machyn, citizen and merchant-taylor of London, from AD 1550 to AD 1563*, ed. J. G. Nichols, CS, 42 (1848) · D. M. Loades, *Two Tudor conspiracies* (1965) · H. Lutz, *Friedenslegation des Reginald Pole zu Karl V und König Heinrich (1553–1556)*, Nuntiaturberichte aus Deutschland, 15 (Tübingen, 1981) · *CSP dom., 1553* · A. Weikel, 'The Marian council revisited', *The mid-Tudor polity, c.1540–1560*, ed. J. Loach and R. Tittler (1980), 52–73 · J. G. Nichols and J. Bruce, eds., *Wills from Doctors' Commons*, CS, old ser., 83 (1863) · P. S. Donaldson, ed., *A Machiavellian treatise* (1975) · S. Anglo, 'Crypto Machiavellianism in early Tudor England: the problem of the *Ragionamento dell'advenimento delli Inglesi et Normanni in Britannia*', *Renaissance and Reformation*, 2 (1978),

182–93 • M. A. R. Graves, *The House of Lords in the parliaments of Edward VI and Mary I: an institutional study* (1981) • E. H. Harbison, *Rival ambassadors at the court of Queen Mary* (1940) • G. R. Elton, *Reform and Reformation: England, 1509–1558* (1977) • A. Lutz, ed., *Nuntiatur des Girolamo Mazzarelli, Sendung des Antonio Agustin, Legation des Scipione Rebiba* (1554–1556), Nuntiaturberichte aus Deutschland, 14 (Tübingen, 1971) • *Nuntiaturen des Pietro Camaini und Achille de Grasse. Legation des Girolamo Dandino* (1552–1553), ed. H. Lutz, Nuntiaturberichte aus Deutschland, 13 (Tübingen, 1959) • W. B. Robison, 'The national and local significance of Wyatt's rebellion in Surrey', *HJ*, 30 (1987), 769–90 • S. Alford, *Kingship and politics in the reign of Edward VI* (2002) • G. S. Thomson, 'Background for a bishop', in J. Conway Davis, *Studies presented to Sir Hilary Jenkinson* (1957), 414–22 • G. A. Lemasters, 'The privy council in the reign of Queen Mary I', PhD diss., U. Cam., 1972 • R. Rex, 'The crisis of obedience', *HJ*, 39 (1996), 863–94 • A. Theiner, ed., *Vetera monumenta Hibernorum et Scotorum historiam illustrantium* (1864) • J. K. McConica, *English humanists and Reformation politics under Henry VIII and Edward VI* (1965) • C. Wriothesley, *A chronicle of England during the reigns of the Tudors from AD 1485 to 1559*, ed. W. D. Hamilton, 2 vols., CS, new ser., 11, 20 (1875–7) • C. S. L. Davies, 'Provisions for armies, 1590–50: as study in the effectiveness of early Tudor government', *Economic History Review*, 2nd ser., 17 (1964–5), 238–48 • *Hampshire and the Isle of Wight*, Pevsner (1967) • H. Robinson, ed. and trans., *Original letters relative to the English Reformation*, 1 vol. in 2, Parker Society, [26] (1846–7) • W. G. Searle, ed., *Grace book Γ* (1908) • J. Foxe, *Actes and monuments* (1563) • *The acts and monuments of John Foxe*, ed. S. R. Cattley, 8 vols. (1837–41)

Archives BL, corresp. and papers relating to his embassy to France • Hants. RO, household account book | BL, Cotton MSS, papers • BL, Harley MSS, papers

Likenesses oils, Trinity Hall, Cambridge; version, Plas Newydd, Anglesey • portrait, Bodl. Oxf.

Gardiner, Thomas (*b. c.*1479, *d.* after **1528/9**), Benedictine monk and chronicler, was born in London. He is first recorded in 1493/4, when he became a monk in Westminster Abbey. He was then probably about fifteen years old. He studied at Oxford in 1497–9 (probably living at Gloucester College, in the abbey's Oxford house of residence) and was at both Oxford and Cambridge in 1499/1500. He was ordained priest in 1501. He was never prominent in the administration of the abbey, although he perhaps had a minor position in the prior's household about 1502–3. In 1507, however, Henry VII (as duke of Lancaster) presented him as prior of the Benedictine priory of Blyth, Nottinghamshire. He resigned this in 1511 and returned to Westminster, where he was shortly afterwards appointed one of the three monks who said mass daily at the chantry established by Henry VII.

In 1512 Gardiner completed a short chronicle of English history, 'The flowers of England', from Brutus down to that year. The best-known copy of this, MS Otho C. vi in the Cotton Library, was destroyed by fire in 1731, but the full text can be obtained by combining two manuscripts in the library of Trinity College, Dublin, parts of MSS E.1.15 (no. 513) and E.5.22 (no. 633); the former appears to have been Gardiner's own copy and has summary entries for a further two years. Another copy, reaching 1516 but damaged and very imperfect, is in the Bodleian Library, MS Rawlinson D. 1020, fols. 1–32. It is a partisan little treatise, written to show that Henry VIII was the right inheritor, by all lines of descent, of the crown of England. It is not, and does not claim to be, a work of authority and originality, although it contributes a few snippets of information drawn from Gardiner's own knowledge of his contemporary world.

Gardiner also compiled another minor historical work, a pedigree of the kings of Wales, France, and England, to exhibit Henry VIII's ancestry. A mid-sixteenth-century copy is Bodleian Library, MS Eng. hist. e. 193, and excerpts are in British Library, Cotton MS Julius F.ix, fol. 24; it may date from 1515–16.

In middle age Gardiner held positions of some responsibility within Westminster Abbey—he is mentioned as kitchener in 1521–2, master of the novices at some stage between 1519 and 1527, and as chamberlain in 1528–9—although these could not compare with the priorate of Blyth. It is not known when he died.   NIGEL RAMSAY

Sources Emden, *Oxf.*, 2.743 • E. H. Pearce, *The monks of Westminster* (1916), 28, 175 • J. G. Smyly, 'Thomas Gardiner's history of England', *Hermathena*, 43 (1922), 235–48 • B. F. Harvey, 'The monks of Westminster and the University of Oxford', *The reign of Richard II: essays in honour of May McKisack*, ed. F. R. H. Du Boulay and C. M. Barron (1971), 108–30 • B. Harvey, *Living and dying in England, 1100–1540: the monastic experience* (1993), 120 • TCD, MSS E.1.15, E. 5.22 • Bodl. Oxf., MS Eng. hist. e. 193 • BL, MS Harleian, fol. 9v • Westminster Abbey muniments, MS 33288, fol. 21v • GL, MS 9531/8, 2nd ser., fols. 178–9; MS 1951/10, 2nd ser., fols. 3r, 4v

Gardiner, Sir Thomas (1591–1652), barrister, was the third son of Michael Gardiner (*fl.* 1570–1620), rector of Littlebury, Essex, and Greenford, Middlesex, and his wife, Margaret (*fl.* 1570–1620), daughter of Thomas Brown, merchant tailor of London. Gardiner began his legal studies at Clifford's Inn before being admitted to the Inner Temple on 15 May 1610. He was called to the bar on 16 April 1618. His marriage about this time to Rebecca Child brought them numerous children.

In 1623 Gardiner was protonotary and clerk of crown for Carmarthen, Cardigan, and Pembroke. Two years later he became a bencher of the Inner Temple and he was sworn in as recorder of London on 25 January 1636. His eldest son and heir, Thomas, was admitted to the Inner Temple in 1637, and two younger sons, George and Henry, followed in 1640. In 1638 Gardiner advocated the collection of ship money, and also about this time he purchased Cuddesdon Manor in Oxfordshire from his brother-in-law John Child. In November 1639 he became treasurer of the Inner Temple, serving until November 1641 when Nicholas Cholmley succeeded him.

During the period from the calling of the Short Parliament in the spring of 1640 to the commencement of the first civil war in the summer of 1642, Gardiner emerged as a partisan of the royalist cause and a staunch defender of episcopacy in the established church. His role was highly significant because, as recorder, Gardiner was the City's chief legal adviser occupying an office that traditionally served as the crucial link between the court and the City of London during a period of heightening tensions. He was returned for Callington, Cornwall, in the Short Parliament but appears to have played no significant role in that brief assembly's proceedings. In spite of his increasing identification with the unpopular policies of the personal rule he maintained the respect of many in the City of London and was admitted to the freedom on 6 October 1640. He stood for election in the City of London in the Long Parliament and was reputedly the king's choice as speaker for the House of Commons. However, the City franchise rejected him and William Lenthall became speaker in his stead.

On 1 March 1641 Gardiner was among those named in Archbishop Laud's petition for counsel during his impeachment in the Long Parliament. On 4 March Laud again specifically requested that Gardiner be named as one of his counsel 'in regard that … Mr Recorder of London hath been of his Counsel in divers Business heretofore' (*JHL*, 176). The Long Parliament, however, declined to appoint him. The king, having withdrawn to Hampton Court Palace in the face of disturbances in London, visited the City on 25 November 1641 and Gardiner presided at a banquet in his honour. On this occasion he delivered a speech of welcome that earned him the king's commendations and later a knighthood. On 3 December 1641 he led a delegation of aldermen to visit the king at Hampton Court Palace asking him to return to the City. In December 1641 he joined the lord mayor, Sir Richard Gurney, in denouncing and obstructing the petition organized by Alderman John Fowke against the votes of bishops in the House of Lords. Early in 1642 he served as counsel to the impeached attorney-general Sir Edward Herbert, a contemporary from the Inner Temple. He was imprisoned on 9 March for refusing the Lords' order to open his defence of Herbert and on 12 March he petitioned for Herbert's release.

The Commons subsequently impeached Gardiner for his support of ship money and conscription during the bishops' wars of 1638–40, his alleged hindering of the calling of parliaments, his obstruction of the December 1641 petition against the bishops, and his assertion that the citizens would be bound to support the king were he to set up his standard. On 18 May 1642 the Commons sent up to the Lords a charge in seven articles which were published five days later. Shortly after this Gardiner wrote to the king, then at York, reassuring him of his loyalty. The Long Parliament ordered his goods to be sold on 29 January 1643 and by 30 October, when he was nominated as solicitor-general, he had joined the king at Oxford. In 1644 he drew up a royal pardon for Laud which the Long Parliament disregarded, proceeding to attaint the archbishop by parliamentary ordinance in January 1645. In October 1644 he was possibly a prisoner of the Long Parliament. In January 1645, however, he served as one of the king's commissioners at the failed Uxbridge negotiations and on 3 November 1645 the king appointed him attorney-general. In 1646 Gardiner compounded for his delinquency with the Long Parliament for the sum of £942 13s. 4d. which he paid on 23 September 1647. At that point he retired to Cuddesdon Manor.

Gardiner died at Cuddesdon in poor financial circumstances on 15 October 1652, having in 1648 declared in his will that his 'temporal estate' had been 'broken and wasted in exceeding great measure' (*VCH Oxfordshire*, 5.102). He left his lands at Cuddesdon, Denton, and Wheatley to his colleague Hugh Audley of the Inner Temple to dispose of in discharge of his debts and provide for his surviving family. His eldest son, Thomas, a royalist captain whom the king had knighted in 1643, had died in the king's cause near Oxford in late July 1645 and one of his younger sons, Henry, had also perished in the king's service, shot dead during a royalist reconnaissance near Thame on 7 September 1645. Both were buried in Christ Church Cathedral, Oxford. Gardiner's surviving kin included his wife, at least one daughter, Mary (1627–1664), and possibly a son George whose fate is uncertain. Clarendon, writing after the Restoration recalled that he was, 'a man of gravity and quickness, that had somewhat of authority and gracefulness in person and presence' (Clarendon, *Hist. rebellion*, 1.220).

D. A. ORR

Sources DNB · F. A. Inderwick and R. A. Roberts, eds., *A calendar of the Inner Temple records*, 2 (1898) · W. R. Prest, *The rise of the barristers: a social history of the English bar, 1590–1640* (1986), 234–82, 363 · J. Bruce, ed., *Verney papers: notes of proceedings in the Long Parliament*, CS, 31 (1845), 167–9 · *JHL*, 4 (1628–42), 174, 176 · *Articles of impeachment by the Commons assembled in parliament, in the name of themselves and all the Commons in England against Sir Thomas Gardiner, recorder of the Citie London, for severall great crimes and misdemeanours committed by him* (1642) · *VCH Oxfordshire*, 5.102 · C. Russell, *The fall of the British monarchies, 1637–1642* (1991), 429, 431–2 · V. Pearl, *London and the outbreak of the puritan revolution: city government and national politics, 1625–43* (1961), 66–7 · K. Lindley, *Popular politics and religion in civil war London* (1997), 102–3, 170, 205 · Clarendon, *Hist. rebellion*, 1.220 · R. Ashton, *The city and the court, 1603–1643* (1979)

Gardiner, Sir Thomas Robert (1883–1964), civil servant, was born at Cork on 8 March 1883, the son of Matthew John Gardiner, a Post Office surveyor, who held appointments in Ireland and subsequently in Scotland, and his wife, Elizabeth Granger. He was educated at Lurgan College, in co. Armagh, and subsequently at the Royal High School, Edinburgh. He went to Edinburgh University, and graduated MA with first-class honours in history and economic science in 1905. The university was later to give him an honorary LLD degree (1949). His Irish and Scottish provenance was always a source of great pride, and he never lost his rich and highly individual brogue.

Gardiner entered the Post Office in 1906 and after service as an assistant surveyor went to its headquarters in London in 1913, serving from 1914 to 1917 as private secretary to the secretary of the Post Office, Q. E. C. Murray, an aristocratic figure and an autocrat of great ability. Gardiner's own autocratic style, though partly inborn, no doubt owed something to his close contact with Murray during his formative years. He then had a short period in the Ministry of Reconstruction, followed by fifteen years in the London postal service, the last eight as controller, probably the most exacting managerial post in the Post Office. Following the Bridgeman report, which was critical of what it regarded, with some justice, as an ivory tower mentality in the headquarters administration, Sir H. Kingsley Wood brought Gardiner back to headquarters in 1934 to serve as deputy director-general, under Donald Banks, former controller of the Post Office Savings Bank.

As deputy director-general Gardiner chaired the reorganization committee, which was responsible for the replacement of the old surveyors, in charge of the postal service and the commercial side of the telephone and telegraph services, by regional directors, heading an integrated organization embracing the regional engineering service. In 1936 he succeeded Banks as director-general of the Post Office, a post he held until his retirement in 1945.

The testing of the civil preparations to deal with air attack at the time of the Munich crisis in 1938 showed that they could not all be left to be handled by the small air-raid precautions department set up in 1935. Sir John Anderson (later Viscount Waverley) was appointed lord privy seal, with responsibility for civil preparations against air raids: and he asked Gardiner to serve as head of the small office that was to co-ordinate the work of all the departments now enlisted to make adequate preparations. The respect in which Gardiner was already held in Whitehall made him an ideal choice for this difficult task. His outstanding managerial ability, coupled with Irish charm, enabled him to organize and push forward, in the short time available before war broke out, preparations covering not only air-raid precautions services but also the police and fire brigades, emergency hospital arrangements, evacuation plans, and liaison with the fighting services. He became permanent secretary of the Ministry of Home Security, which was created on the outbreak of the Second World War in 1939.

In the autumn of 1940 Gardiner returned to his post of director-general of the Post Office, where he directed the vital communication services of the nation during the war years. There can have been few holders of the top position in the Post Office who have stamped the impact of their personality on it as Gardiner did. He combined great natural ability with a down-to-earth practicality, reinforced by his experience as an assistant surveyor and as assistant controller of the London postal service, and he changed the whole style of management in the Post Office. When he retired the British postal service indisputably led the world, and the telecommunications services, if not perhaps equally pre-eminent, enjoyed an enviable reputation.

After his retirement Gardiner's services were greatly in demand. He confined himself to public work, but within this field the range of his activities was wide. In 1946 he became a member of the royal commission which examined the organization and pay of the senior ranks of the Canadian civil service. In 1947–8 he did pioneering work as chairman of the Stevenage New Town Development Corporation; and from 1949 to 1951 he was vice-chairman, and for a time acting chairman, of the National Dock Labour Board. He was also a government director of the Anglo-Iranian Oil Company from 1950 to 1953. The postal service being highly labour-intensive, Gardiner had been necessarily heavily involved in staff matters, and he was a natural choice as chairman of the committee of three appointed in 1948 by the prime minister to deal with cases of civil servants removed from confidential work because of alleged association with subversive organizations. He chaired a committee on the organization and pay of architects, engineers, and surveyors which reported in 1951, and in 1952 he chaired a similar committee dealing with accountants. He was a member of the royal commission on Scottish affairs from 1952 to 1954 and served from 1953 to 1956 on a committee chaired by Lord Waverley on the medical and dental services of the armed forces.

Despite Gardiner's wide range of experience and achievement, he always felt himself to be a Post Office man first and foremost. Almost to the end of his life, he was wont to drop in on his successors as director-general and tell them, more in sorrow than in anger, of what he regarded as instances of failing to meet his own exacting standards for Post Office services. The surveyors of the Post Office, the predecessors of the present directors of the postal regions, have a proud history, counting among their number Anthony Trollope, and Gardiner was conspicuous among heads of the Post Office for his recognition of the importance of provincial managerial experience for the men and women who were to hold the highest offices in the service. For the administrative class in the Post Office at that time he had something less than unqualified admiration, though this did not prevent him from recognizing outstanding ability wherever it was to be found.

Gardiner was appointed KBE in 1936, KCB in 1937, GBE in 1941, and GCB in 1954. In 1919 he married Christina Stenhouse; they had no children. Away from work his main interest was his family, including those who remained in Ireland. For recreation he most enjoyed walking, and was a keen golfer in his younger days; later his delight was to spend summer or autumn holidays in the Scottish highlands. Physically Gardiner was an imposing figure, tall and upright; and he had a dominating personality, combined with natural charm but also with a capacity to be ruthless when he judged it necessary.

Until the age of fifty-five Gardiner's experience had been confined to the Post Office, and in the main to the postal service, but it came as no surprise to those who knew him that, having moved within five years of normal retiring age into Whitehall, he quickly became a dominating figure in fields where he was previously unknown, and earned such wide respect and admiration as to be in great demand in so many different fields on his retirement. He died on 1 January 1964 at the Hospital of St John and St Elizabeth, 60 Grove End Road, London. He was survived by his wife.   DONALD SARGENT, *rev.*

Sources *The Times* (2 Jan 1964), 10d · private information (1981) · personal knowledge (1981) · *CGPLA Eng. & Wales* (1964)
Wealth at death £6665: probate, 18 March 1964, *CGPLA Eng. & Wales*

Gardiner, William (1770–1853), composer and author, was born in Leicester on 15 March 1770. His father, a Leicester manufacturer, was an amateur musician and composed at least one hymn tune (preserved in the first volume of his son's *Sacred Melodies*, 1812), yet he did little to encourage William's precocious talents, and judged that the smallest possible amount of general knowledge would be sufficient for a career in the hosiery trade. However, the young Gardiner's enquiring mind led him to the meetings of the Adelphi Philosophical Society, formed in Leicester by Richard Phillips. He wrote some striking papers for the society, including 'Whether all the celestial bodies naturally attract each other?', 'What are those bodies called comets?', and 'On matter and its properties'. In 1790, the second year of the society's existence, this gathering of 'philosophical infants' (fourteen out of the seventeen members were under twenty-one) was prohibited by the authorities on account of its political radicalism.

Subsequently it was chiefly musical matters which claimed Gardiner's attention during his leisure hours. His artistic taste was provided with direction by the arrival in Leicester of the Abbé Dobler with the latest works of Haydn and Beethoven. Gardiner consequently acquired a copy of Beethoven's E♭ string trio, op. 3, in Bonn, and in 1794 played the viola in a performance in Leicester, three years before the work was published in London. Having thus introduced Beethoven's music to England, he was asked, at the unveiling in 1848 of Beethoven's statue in Bonn, to sign the inauguration parchment beneath the names of Victoria and Albert. Gardiner's familiarity with the works of the most revered composers led to such 'barbarous compilations' (*DNB*) as *Sacred Melodies* (vols. 1–6, 1812–38), which contains extracts from religious works by Haydn, Mozart, Beethoven, and others, adapted to English words, *The Universal Prayer* (1840), which sets Pope's words to music by Haydn, Mozart, and Beethoven, and *Judah* (1821), an oratorio 'written, composed and adapted to the works of Haydn, Mozart, and Beethoven'. Garbled fragments out of masses, symphonies, quartets, and even operas, were here patched up with original matter by the compiler; the first subject of the andante in Beethoven's seventh symphony does duty as a march of the Philistines. Gardiner is reported to have written to Beethoven offering 100 guineas for an overture to the work, but his letter went astray (as had some stockings, woven with themes, which he had sent to Haydn some years previously). All these works were popular for many years. Gardiner's independent compositions consist of anthems, glees, and songs. He also provided annotations to C. Berry's translation of H. Beyle's version of Carpani's biography of Haydn (1817) and to R. Brewin's translation of Schlichtergroll's biography of Mozart (1817). *The music of nature, an attempt to prove that what is passionate and pleasing in the art of singing, speaking, and performing upon musical instruments is derived from the sounds of the animated world, with illustrations* (1832) is interesting as an attempt to combine the scientific with the artistic.

Gardiner trained a 100-voice chorus for the 1827 Leicester festival and was a member of the semichorus at Queen Victoria's coronation. After his retirement from commercial life he wrote and published *Music and Friends, or, Pleasant Recollections of a Dilettante* (1838–53), which contains observations on contemporary musical, literary, and artistic life. His travels and correspondence, extending over a long period, had brought him into contact with many well-known musicians, including Paganini and Weber. A last work, *Sights in Italy, with some account of the present state of music and the sister arts in that country* (1847), was the outcome of a tour made at the age of seventy-seven, yet it is written with great freshness of interest in pictures, persons, and performances. Gardiner was a foreign member of the Accademia di Santa Cecilia and attended one of its meetings in Rome. He was also a corresponding member of the Institut Historique de France. At the age of eighty-three he was reported to have been in remarkably good health, but he died after a week's illness in Leicester on 16 November 1853, and was buried in a new cemetery there. An article in the *Musical World* (10 December 1853) describes how 'a few months before his decease a bust of him was modelled in clay, by a foreign gentleman then residing in Leicester' and claims that 'the likeness is perfect'. His portrait, by a Miss M. A. Hull, was published by Messrs Allen of Leicester, and another portrait, attributed to Artaud, is in the Leicester Museum Collection. He appears to have been a very lively and popular figure, and an obituary highlights how he was 'moral and temperate in his habits, and without a spark of malice in his nature' (*Musical World*, 3 Dec 1853).

L. M. MIDDLETON, rev. DAVID J. GOLBY

Sources *Musical World* (3 Dec 1853), 765 · J. Wilshere, 'Gardiner, William', *New Grove* · J. Wilshere, *William Gardiner of Leicester, 1770–1853* (1970) · *Musical World* (10 Dec 1853), 784
Archives Leics. RO, corresp.
Likenesses attrib. W. Artaud, oils, Leicester Museum and Art Gallery · M. A. Hull, portrait · clay bust, repro. in *Musical World*, 31/50 (10 Dec 1853), 784

Gardiner, William Nelson

Gardiner, William Nelson (1766–1814), engraver and bookseller, born at Dublin on 11 June 1766, was the son of John Gardiner, 'crier and factotum' to Judge William Scott, and Margaret Nelson, his wife, a pastry-cook. He was educated at Sisson Darling's academy. After his mother's death, *c*.1776, Gardiner was, with his father, attached to the suite of Sir James Nugent of Donore, co. Westmeath. In 1781 he was placed for three years at the Dublin Society's School, where he obtained a silver medal. He then went to London and was at first employed by Mr Jones, a silhouettist on the Strand. Gardiner also supported himself by portrait painting, but gave it up for the stage, both as scene painter and actor. Eventually he worked for Mrs Beetham in Fleet Street, also a silhouettist. Through his acquaintance with the antiquary Captain Francis Grose, Gardiner was placed with R. Godfrey, the engraver to *The Antiquarian Repertory*. At the same time he acquired some considerable skill as an engraver in stipple. Having taken an original engraving of his own to Messrs Sylvester and Edward Harding, the publishers in Fleet Street, he was employed by them in engraving plates for their publications in company with Bartolozzi and others. For them he worked on their *Shakespeare Illustrated*, *The Oeconomy of Human Life*, *The Biographical Mirror*, *The Memoirs of Count de Grammont*, Lady Diana Beauclerk's illustrations of Dryden's *Fables*, and other works. His style was similar to that of Bartolozzi, and Gardiner claimed some of the plates bearing Bartolozzi's name as his own work. He subsequently worked for Bartolozzi. Of this work, Gardiner said that really he was 'gay, volatile, and lively as a lark [and] the process of the copper never really suited me' (*GM*, 623). He occasionally painted, and between 1787 and 1793 exhibited pictures at the Royal Academy. Abandoning his profession as an engraver, he returned to Dublin, where he spent all his money and injured his health.

Gardiner returned to England with the intention of entering the church, and was entered at Emmanuel College, Cambridge. Finding that as an Irishman he had no chance there of a fellowship, he moved to Corpus Christi College and took his degree in 1797 as sixth senior optime. He remained at Cambridge for some time in the hope of obtaining a fellowship, but, being unsuccessful, relinquished all idea of taking holy orders and returned to London, where he obtained employment in copying oil portraits in watercolour for his former patron, E. Harding. However, his eyesight began to fail, and subsequently he set up as a bookseller and publisher in Pall Mall, with financial assistance from his wife, *née* Seckerson, about 1801. From his eccentricities of dress, behaviour, and conversation, he became a well-known figure at sales, and his shop was often visited by people out of curiosity. He avowed his political views as a whig with great freedom. The Revd Thomas Frognall Dibdin introduced him in his *Bibliomania* under the character of Mustapha. Gardiner resented this characterization, and retaliated in his published catalogues. Dibdin, in his *Bibliographical Decameron*, refers again to this controversy. Gardiner did not meet with great success in his new profession. His wife and child having died, he lost interest in his appearance and became a recluse, attached to his tabby cat. His will reveals an honest and generous man who had given up on life. He committed suicide at his home, 48 Pall Mall, London, between 8 and 18 May 1814, in consequence, as he described it, of unbearable misery. He left a brief autobiography, printed in the *Gentleman's Magazine* (June 1814). A collection of Gardiner's engravings is in the National Library of Ireland, Dublin.

L. H. CUST, rev. E. M. KIRWAN

Sources PRO, PROB 11/1556, fols. 238r–239r · 'Memoir of the late William Gardiner, bookseller', *GM*, 1st ser., 84/1 (1814), 622–3 · W. G. Strickland, *A dictionary of Irish artists*, 1 (1913) · Graves, *RA exhibitors* · Thieme & Becker, *Allgemeines Lexikon* · Bénézit, *Dict.*, 3rd edn · R. M. Elmes, *Catalogue of engraved Irish portraits mainly in the Joly collection* [1938] · F. G. Stephens and M. D. George, eds., *Catalogue of political and personal satires preserved … in the British Museum*, 6 (1938) · Bryan, *Painters* (1903–5) · J. S. Crone, *A concise dictionary of Irish biography* (1928) · Redgrave, *Artists* · A. Le Harivel, ed., *National Gallery of Ireland: illustrated summary catalogue of prints and sculpture* (1988)

Likenesses stipple, BM, NPG

Wealth at death over £22 10s.: will, PRO, PROB 11/1556

Gardiner, William Neville (1748–1806), army officer and diplomatist, was born on 23 October 1748, the second son of Charles Gardiner (c.1712–1769), MP, of Dublin, and his wife, Florinda (b. 1722), the daughter of Robert Norman of Lagore, co. Meath. He was the younger brother of Luke *Gardiner, first Viscount Mountjoy. On 9 January 1779 he married Harriet Wrottesley, the youngest daughter of the Revd Sir Richard Wrottesley, seventh baronet (c.1721–1769), and Mary Leveson-Gower (d. 1778), and the sister of Elizabeth, duchess of Grafton. They had one son and four daughters.

Gardiner commenced his military career on 31 December 1767, when he was gazetted cornet in the 18th light dragoons. He was promoted to the command of a company in the 45th foot on 31 March 1770, at first in Ireland and then in America. After serving in the campaigns of 1775–6, partly as an aide-de-camp to the commander-in-chief, Sir William Howe, he brought home the dispatches following the battle of Long Island. He returned to America as a major in the 10th foot and was wounded in action at Freehold, New Jersey, on 28 June 1778. Having been appointed lieutenant-colonel of the 45th foot, he sailed to join his regiment in England. He was given command of the 88th foot in January 1782 and was made colonel of the 99th foot in February 1783, although his service as aide-de-camp to the lord lieutenant in Ireland seems to have prevented him from joining his new regiment before it was disbanded following the peace of Paris. He remained on half pay until December 1789, when he was sent to report on the condition of the fortress of Luxembourg following the outbreak of revolution in the Austrian Netherlands. He subsequently became a special envoy in Brussels, but his mission was essentially one of information-gathering. His passive role led Richard Burke, while visiting Brussels, to deem him 'but a man of straw' (*The Correspondence of Edmund Burke*, ed. T. W. Copeland and others, 10 vols., 1958–78, 6.328).

On 5 January 1792 Gardiner was nominated minister-plenipotentiary to the king and republic of Poland on the recommendation of his friend James Bland Burges, under-secretary of state at the Foreign Office, with whom he maintained an extensive private correspondence separate from (and frequently more informative than) his dispatches. His appointment marked the end of serious British interest in Poland, following the collapse the previous spring of Pitt's plans for armed intervention against Russia by the Anglo-Prussian-Dutch alliance. Grenville's instruction to Gardiner on 4 August 1792 excluded any possibility of British assistance to Poland. Because the previous incumbent, Daniel Hailes, delayed his departure to Copenhagen, Gardiner did not arrive in Warsaw until 13 October 1792. Burges had privately charged him with assuaging the slights rendered by Hailes to Burges's personal friends King Stanislaus Augustus and his brother, Primate Michał Poniatowski. Gardiner swiftly won their lasting approbation, trust, and friendship. However, by the time of his arrival in Warsaw, Poland's new constitution (of 3 May 1791) had been overthrown by the Russian army, fronted by the aristocratic confederacy of Targowica. Gardiner's job was simply to report on the dramatic events attending the second and third partitions of the republic, which he did scrupulously. However, during the Kościuszko insurrection of 1794 he took on a more active and independent role, winning the respect of all sides and emerging as the unofficial leader of the diplomatic corps in Warsaw. Gardiner insisted that the insurrectionary council uphold his accreditation to the king as well as the republic, and he participated in regular conferences with both the king and the council. He stood up for the imprisoned personnel of the Russian embassy and also successfully demanded that the Prussians allow diplomatic correspondence to pass through their blockade of Warsaw. He then sheltered 300 refugees in his residence following General Suvorov's bloody storming of the suburb of Praga on 4 November 1794. Consequent on the Russian occupation of Warsaw Gardiner fought a noble rearguard action in defence of his diplomatic prerogatives, even attempting to escort Stanislaus Augustus to his exile in Grodno. His final departure from Warsaw was delayed until the end of 1797 or beginning of 1798 by his inability to settle the debts he had contracted during the insurrection. George III pitied his situation but took a dusty view of his expenses, and when the funds were finally forthcoming they were to be repaid in instalments from his pension as governor of Hurst Castle.

Having meanwhile been promoted major-general (April 1794) and appointed colonel commandant of the 99th foot (21 March 1795; it was disbanded in 1796), Gardiner finally arrived in Ireland in March 1799. Lord Cornwallis, who knew him of old, remarked that he was 'much the same as to manner and action, but much graver' (*Correspondence of … Cornwallis*, 3.81)—and that he had lost his teeth; he later commented that he took 'rather too much wine' (ibid., 3.353).

Nevertheless Cornwallis strongly but unsuccessfully pushed him for next in command to General Lake in Munster. Gardiner also sought the protection of the prince of Wales, and the duke of York recommended him to the king for the 1st battalion of the 60th foot. He was shortly given the newly raised 6th battalion and promoted lieutenant-general. As a reliable government man, he sat in the last Irish parliament for Thomastown, King's county. Cornwallis continued to support his protégé, even recommending him for the post of commander-in-chief in Ireland, before finally securing the governorship of Kinsale Castle for him on 22 August 1801. From 1803 he commanded the north inland district of England, then in 1805 he was appointed commander-in-chief in Nova Scotia and New Brunswick. He died on 25 June 1806.

RICHARD BUTTERWICK

Sources B. Dembiński, *William Gardiner, ostatni minister Wielkiej Brytanii na dworze Stanisława Augusta* (1936) • Z. Libiszowska, 'Insurekcja kościuszkowska widziana z Anglii', *200 rocznica powstania Kościuszkowskiego* (1994) • DNB • *Correspondence of Charles, first Marquis Cornwallis*, ed. C. Ross, 3 vols. (1859) • *The later correspondence of George III*, ed. A. Aspinall, 5 vols. (1962–70), vol. 1, no. 741; vol. 2, no. 1279; vol. 3, nos. 1826, 1935, 2503 • *The correspondence of George, prince of Wales, 1770–1812*, ed. A. Aspinall, 8 vols. (1963–71) • GEC, *Peerage* • (Poland), PRO, FO 62, 5–9 • Bodl. Oxf., MSS Bland Burges, 35, 45 • N. Davies, *God's playground: a history of Poland* (1981), vol. 1, pp. 543–6 • J. Rose, *William Pitt and the great war* (1911), 54 • *GM*, 1st ser., 49 (1779), 47 • *GM*, 1st ser., 76 (1806), 682–3, 771 • private information (2004) [E. Johnson–Liik]

Archives BL, letters to Lord Auckland and Lord Grenville, Add. MSS 34435–34453 *passim* • BL, letters to Lord Grenville, Add. MS 59020 • BL, letters to duke of Leeds, Add. MSS 28064–28066 • BL, corresp. with Sir A. Paget, Add. MS 48394 • Bodl. Oxf., corresp. with Sir James Burges • CKS, letters to duke of Dorset • priv. coll.,

corresp. with Francis Wilson • PRO, Foreign Office/Flanders, Poland

Likenesses J. Reynolds, oils, exh. RA 1773, Petworth House, West Sussex

Gardner, Alan, **first Baron Gardner** (1742–1808/9), naval officer and politician, was born at Uttoxeter, Staffordshire, on 12 April 1742, the son of Lieutenant-Colonel William Gardner of the 11th dragoon guards, and Elizabeth, daughter of Valentine Farington of Preston. In his passing certificate (dated 15 February 1760) he is said to have spent upwards of six years at sea, 'part whereof in the merchants' service'. He joined the *Medway*, under the command of Captain Peter Denis, in May 1755, and in January 1758 was moved into the *Dorsetshire*, also commanded by Denis, in which he was present at the battle of Quiberon Bay. On 7 March 1760 he was promoted lieutenant of the *Bellona*, again with Denis, but he remained in the ship after Denis had been superseded by Captain Robert Faulknor, and took part in the capture of the *Courageux* on 14 August 1761. On 12 April 1762 he was promoted commander of the fireship *Raven*, and on 19 May 1766 he was advanced to post rank, and appointed to command the *Preston*, going to Jamaica as flagship of Rear-Admiral Parry. On 20 May 1769 at Kingston, Jamaica, he married Susannah Hyde, daughter and heir of Francis Gale and widow of Sabine (or Samuel) Turner; the couple had seven sons and one daughter.

In 1768 Gardner was removed into the frigate *Levant*, which he commanded on the same station until 1771. In 1775 he was appointed to the *Maidstone* (28 guns), also sent to the West Indies, from where in 1778 he was sent to join Lord Howe on the coast of North America, to whom he carried the first intelligence of the approach of the French fleet. On 3 November 1778 Gardner captured a large and heavily armed French merchant ship, which he brought with him to Antigua, when he was appointed by Admiral John Byron to the *Sultan* (74 guns). In her he played an important role in the battle of Grenada (6 July 1779) as one of the seconds of the admiral; and in the following year he was sent to England in charge of convoy. In December 1781 he commissioned the *Duke* (98 guns), and accompanied Sir George Rodney to the West Indies, where he took part in the battle of the Saints (12 April 1782). He returned to England at the peace, and in 1786 was sent to Jamaica as commander-in-chief, with a broad pennant in the *Europa*. After holding the command for three years he returned to England, and on 19 January 1790 he was appointed to a seat at the Board of Admiralty, which he held until March 1795.

On 1 February 1790 Gardner was returned to parliament as MP for Plymouth, which he represented until 1796, when he was returned for Westminster. During the Spanish armament in 1790 he commanded the *Courageux* for a few months; and in February 1793, being advanced to flagrank, he went to the West Indies, with his flag in the *Queen*, and in command of a considerable squadron. However, with insufficient troops he achieved little against the French colonies. On his return to England in the autumn he was attached to the Channel Fleet under Lord Howe, and took part in the Glorious First of June (1794), when the losses on the *Queen* were exceptionally severe. For his services on this occasion Gardner, appointed major-general of marines on 28 June, was created a baronet, and on 4 July advanced to the rank of vice-admiral. His conduct also earned him the praise of Lord St Vincent who considered him 'a zealous and brave man', though a prime exemplar of the 'deficiency of nerve under responsibility' that St Vincent detected in many of his fellow admirals (Corbett and Richmond, 3.295; Brenton, 2.327–8). He was again with the fleet under Lord Bridport off Lorient, on 23 June 1795, but had little share in the action. In April 1797, at the time of the mutiny at Spithead, he was second in command of the Channel Fleet, with his flag in the *Royal Sovereign*, and on 14 February 1799 he was promoted admiral of the blue.

In May 1800 Gardner's career suffered what he believed to be a significant setback when he was not chosen to succeed Lord Bridport as commander of the Channel Fleet. Instead the appointment went to Lord St Vincent on the recommendation of Lord Spencer, who fully believed that Gardner had no wish to take on the post. Gardner now embarked on an acrimonious correspondence with both men in which he claimed that his failure to receive promotion would 'disgrace me in the eyes of the fleet', and demanded an 'enquiry … in order to clear my character' (Gardner to Spencer, 24 April and 28 April 1800, Corbett and Richmond, 3.304, 308). Relations quickly cooled between Gardner and his two superiors and were only partially salvaged when, in August 1800, Spencer offered him the position of commander of the Irish station. Gardner held this post until 1805 and appears to have gained many admirers, including Captain Thomas Francis Fremantle who wrote of his eventual departure as a source of 'national grievance' (Fremantle, 3.182).

In December 1800 Gardner was created Baron Gardner in the Irish peerage. He continued, however, to represent Westminster in parliament until in November 1806 he was raised to a peerage of the United Kingdom, with the title Baron Gardner of Uttoxeter. In 1807 he was appointed to the command of the Channel Fleet, the source of his earlier dispute with Spencer and St Vincent, but poor health compelled him to resign in the following year, and he died a few months later on either 31 December 1808 or 1 January 1809. His titles now passed to his eldest son, Alan Hyde Gardner.

J. K. LAUGHTON, *rev.* CHRISTOPHER DOORNE

Sources J. Charnock, ed., *Biographia navalis*, 6 (1798), 583–8 • J. Ralfe, *The naval biography of Great Britain*, 1 (1828) • commission of warrant books, PRO, ADM 6/19–20 (1758–63); ADM 6/22 (1779–82); ADM 6/24–5 (1789–96); ADM 6/27 (1799–1801); ADM 6/29 (1804–7) • N. Tracy, ed., *The Naval Chronicle: the contemporary record of the Royal Navy at war*, 5 vols. (1998–9), vols. 1–4 • M. H. Port and D. R. Fisher, 'Gardner, Alan', HoP, *Commons, 1790–1820*, 4.3–4 • W. L. Clowes, *The Royal Navy: a history from the earliest times to the present*, 7 vols. (1897–1903); repr. (1996–7), vols. 4–5 • *Steel's Original and Correct List of the Royal Navy* (1793–1807) • *Private papers of George, second Earl Spencer*, ed. J. S. Corbett and H. W. Richmond, 3, Navy RS, 58 (1924), 295, 304, 308 • E. P. Brenton, *Life and correspondence of John, earl of St Vincent*, 2 vols. (1838) • *The Wynne diaries*, ed. A. Fremantle, 3 vols. (1935–40)

Archives BL, letters to Lord Hardwicke, Add. MSS 36728–36763, *passim* • BL, letters to Hood, Add. MSS 35194–35201, *passim* • NL Scot., letters to Viscount Melville • NMM, corresp. with Sir Charles Middleton • Yale U., Beinecke L., letters and memoranda to Sir John Duckworth

Likenesses A. Hickel, oils, 1794, NMM • Pierson, stipple, pubd 1794, BM, NPG; repro. in *European Magazine* (1794) • T. Clarke, oils, *c.*1799, NPG • Bartolozzi, Landseer, Ryder & Stow, group portrait, line engraving, pubd 1803 (*Commemoration of the victory of June 1st 1794*; after *Naval victories* by R. Smirke), BM, NPG • W. Daniell, etching, pubd 1809 (after G. Dance), BM, NPG • oils (after W. Beechey), NMM

Gardner, Alice (1854–1927), historian, was born on 26 April 1854 at Hackney, London, one of the six children of Thomas Gardner, stockbroker, and his wife, Ann, *née* Pearse. Educated privately at first, she went to Hannah Pipe's celebrated school at Laleham in 1869. Then in 1876, at twenty-two, she went up to Newnham College, Cambridge, where she read for the history tripos. In 1879 she and her fellow student Sarah Marshall, later Mrs Harry Toynbee, were both placed in the first class, well ahead of the male competition.

Alice went immediately into teaching, then the only respectable occupation for a middle-class woman who had to earn her own living. She taught at Plymouth high school (1880–82) and then at Bedford College, London (1883–4). In 1884 she returned to Newnham, where she taught and directed studies in history until she retired in 1914. Following the outbreak of the First World War she did a short stint in the historical department of the Foreign Office, then in 1915 came decisively out of retirement to take charge of the history department at Bristol University while the professor and lecturer were both on war service. Bristol was able to recognize her contribution more generously than the Cambridge of the day, awarding her an honorary degree of MA in 1918 and appointing her as reader in Byzantine studies in 1920.

It is not clear when and how Alice acquired the formidable linguistic skills she brought to bear in this field or how her interest was first triggered. It was sustained and supported by travels in Asia Minor and Bulgaria and she appreciated the encouragement to research and write provided by Newnham's first principal, Anne Jemima Clough. In her contacts and fieldwork she helped and was helped by two of her brothers, Percy *Gardner (1846–1937) and Ernest Arthur *Gardner (1862–1939), both distinguished classical archaeologists. Besides two history books for children and many articles in learned journals, she published *Synesius of Cyrene: Philosopher and Bishop* in 1885, *Julian: Emperor and Philosopher* in 1895, *Studies in John the Scot* in 1900, *Theodore of Studium: his Life and Times* in 1905, and *The Lascarids of Nicaea* in 1912. Her translations remain in use. She was a vice-president of the Historical Association, a fellow of the Royal Historical Society, and a member of its council.

The range and importance of Alice Gardner's intellectual contribution, making the period from the fall of Rome through to Byzantium in the lands of the eastern Mediterranean significantly more accessible to an English-speaking audience, are the more striking as much of her Cambridge teaching had to be of English medieval history. Its scope and distinction must also at first have seemed at odds with her personal style. She was a small, shy, reticent woman, with a poor lecture delivery and was renowned at Newnham for her dowdiness. The frail Winnie Seebohm, briefly her student in 1885, never penetrated the shyness and found her uninspiring. But others, including the future novelist Flora Macdonald Mayor, saw further, and appreciated the quiet energy and determination, the intellectual clarity, the endless taking of pains, and the unobtrusive but perceptive kindness. Alice herself, recalling an occasion when she had gone back to consult her old headmistress about a dilemma, recorded with approval the advice, 'Don't do anything heroic' (Stoddart, 221). Yet while entirely sharing the distaste felt for denominational conflict by both Hannah Pipe and A. J. Clough, she was clear about her own standards and values: she was a regular contributor to Newnham's Sunday Society and published two collections of her papers to them, *The Conflict of Duties* (1903) and *Within our Limits* (1913). Her Bristol students warmly appreciated her quiet insistence that 'a young university must not fall below the standards set by the older ones' (*Newnham College Roll Letter*, 36).

Alice settled in Clifton when she began to teach at Bristol, although retaining many links with Cambridge. In 1921 she contributed *A Short History of Newnham College, Cambridge*, to the college's fiftieth birthday celebrations, scrupulously precise and non-triumphalist to the point of understatement. Then, shortly before her death, as her memory began to fail, she moved to Oxford, where her brother Percy and his wife lived, and where she died, at the Warneford Hospital, on 11 November 1927.

GILLIAN SUTHERLAND

Sources [A. B. White and others], eds., *Newnham College register, 1871–1971*, 2nd edn, 1 (1979) • *Newnham College Roll Letter* (1928), 35–40 • V. Glendinning, *A suppressed cry: life and death of a Quaker daughter* (1969) • A. M. Stoddart, *Life and letters of Hannah K. Pipe* (1908) • Alice Gardner to B. A. Clough, 8 Sept 1896, BL, Clough–Shore Smith papers, Add. MS 72824A, fols. 128–37 • tripos letters, Newnham College, Cambridge, archive • d. cert.
Archives BL, Clough–Shore Smith MSS • CUL, letters to Lord Acton • Newnham College, Cambridge, archives
Likenesses pencil drawing, 1913, Newnham College, Cambridge
Wealth at death £4002 0s. 11d.: probate, 29 Dec 1927, CGPLA Eng. & Wales

Gardner, Daniel (c.1750–1805), portrait painter, born in Kendal, Westmorland, was the only son of a master baker. His mother was the sister of an upholsterer and alderman called Redman, an acquaintance and business associate of George Romney's father. She was artistic and had some skill in watercolours and gave George Romney early encouragement, which he repaid by teaching her son to draw. Gardner was educated at the local grammar school, where he made lasting friendships with William and Joseph Pennington, who later became patrons; his *Self-Portrait with William Pennington* is in the Abbot Hall Art Gallery, Kendal. Romney had left for London in 1762, and Gardner followed in either 1767 or 1768, and lived at 11 Cockspur Street, very close to the Royal Academy Schools in Pall Mall which he joined in 1770. He studied under such teachers as G. B. Cipriani, Benjamin West, and Johan Zoffany and in 1773 won a silver medal for a drawing of an academy figure. That same year he had a drawing, *Portrait of an Old Man* accepted for exhibition, the only time he ever exhibited. On leaving the schools, Gardner joined Reynolds's studio as an assistant in exchange for further tuition. His oil paintings tend to be of a rough and heavy texture, as for example *Members of the Heathcote Family* (1779; Montacute House, Somerset). He also produced idealized pastel group portraits of women and children combining oil, gouache, and pastel on paper later laid on canvas, unvarnished but glazed. This technique, where shadow is replaced by tone, maintains a lasting freshness and vivacity, for example *Mrs Justinian Casamajor and Eight of her Children*, (1779; Yale U. CBA), and was also used for small whole lengths in landscape, a decorative approximation of Reynolds's 'grand style'. Gardner refused to take on any pupils and would admit no visitors to his studio. Concerned to prevent sitters from seeing their portraits prior to completion, he had a special frame constructed that fitted over his easel with which he hid the painting immediately the sitting was finished until the sitter left the room; it was fastened with a lock and key.

In 1776 or 1777 Gardner married Ann Haward, sister of the engraver Francis Haward. Their first child, George, was born in 1778, but their happy marriage ended abruptly with her death and that of their second son in 1781. A portrait by Gardner of his wife and children, *Mrs Gardner and her Two Sons*, is at Lehigh University, Pennsylvania. Gardner retained strong links with his home town of Kendal, sending his surviving son George to be educated there, under the care of the Pennington family. He purchased considerable property in the town; by 1780 he had an income of £200 per annum from The Elephant inn and surrounding cottages. That same year he purchased the estate of Braithwaite and in 1787 his parent's former home and some adjoining property. He continued to accumulate land and property in the area until the year of his death, buying the estate of Haverbrach in 1796 and adjacent land in 1805.

Towards the end of his life and during the peace of Amiens, in 1802–3, Gardner travelled to Paris with his son, George. He sketched in the Louvre Museum, particularly the antique sculpture looted from Italy, and narrowly escaped imprisonment at the resumption of hostilities. A proud and blunt man, he did not mix well and was not very active socially but maintained a few lasting friendships, including one with the young John Constable, whom he painted in 1796 and whom he introduced to Lakeland scenery. He was described by Joseph Farington as 'extremely parsimonious. His great delight was in arguing in which He occasionally brought upon Himself severe animadversions, which generally caused him to be more respectful to His opponent afterward' (Farington, *Diary*, 8.2929). Gardner moved from his rooms in New Bond Street to lodgings in Beak Street, Golden Square, and as a contemporary noted 'gave up the pursuit of every art, except that of improving his fortune, in which he is said to have been adept, not without a degree of penury which injured his health' (Williamson, 34). Farington also records that Gardner had 'been much accustomed to quack himself' (Farington, *Diary*, 8.2929) and had been ill for about six months before he died from a liver complaint on 8 July 1805. He died intestate, his son inheriting less than £10,000.   EVELYN NEWBY

Sources H. Kapp, *Daniel Gardner, 1750–1805* (1972) [exhibition catalogue, Iveagh Bequest, Kenwood, London, 16 May – 26 June 1972] · G. D. Williamson, *Daniel Gardner* (1921) · Farington, *Diary*, 8.2928–9 · S. C. Hutchison, 'The Royal Academy Schools, 1768–1830', *Walpole Society*, 38 (1960–62), 123–91 · *400 years of Cumbrian portrait painting* (privately printed, Kendal, 1982) [exhibition catalogue, Abbot Hall Art Gallery, Kendal, 8 July – 5 Sept 1982]
Archives Cumbria AS, MSS
Likenesses D. Gardner, oils, NPG · D. Gardner, self-portrait, oils (with William Pennington), Abbot Hall Art Gallery, Kendal
Wealth at death under £10,000: administration, PRO, PROB 6/181, fol. 134*v*

Gardner, (John) Edmund Garratt (1869–1935), Italian scholar, was born on 12 May 1869 at 3 St James's Terrace, Kensington, the first child of John Gardner (1839–1887), member of the stock exchange, and his wife, Amy Vernon, *née* Garratt (*d.* 1937). Monica Mary *Gardner (1873–1941) was his sister. After Beaumont College, Windsor, he matriculated for a science degree at University College, London, then transferred to Gonville and Caius College, Cambridge, in 1887. He intended to read medicine, but this proved so stressful and damaging to his health that he interrupted his course in 1890 to winter in Florence. While there he took Italian lessons from a bookseller, the only formal instruction in the subject he later taught at university. After being awarded an *aegrotat* in part one of the natural sciences tripos at Cambridge in 1891 and graduating BA, he abandoned his medical degree in favour of literary studies, and by 1893 he was teaching Shakespeare to the Cambridge Extension School. In the same year he published in *Nature* a short article on Dante's *Quaestio de aqua et terra*.

Like Thomas Okey, Gardner became involved in the popular city guides published by Dent, contributing volumes on *The Story of Florence* (1900), which ran to eleven editions, and *The Story of Siena and San Gimignano* (1902). His scholarly reputation was secured by *Dante's Ten Heavens* (1898), then the best English guide to Dante's third cantica, and *Dante and Giovanni del Virgilio* (1902), written with his friend and mentor Philip Wicksteed. His popularizing writing continued with a *Dante Primer* (1900) for Dent, which went through numerous editions. Wicksteed, who was a reader for Constable, persuaded Gardner to write a study of Ariosto and the Este court, *Dukes and Poets in Ferrara* (1904), which dealt with cultural life up to the League of Cambrai (1508). A companion volume, *The King of Court Poets*, concentrating more heavily on Ariosto, came out two years later. Both volumes show Gardner's keen eye for document, rather than venturing into psychological or literary analysis. By this time his Roman Catholicism (he was known to friends only half-jocularly as Saint Edmund) led him increasingly towards the mystic tradition; he wrote on *Saint Catherine of Siena* (1907) and republished devotional pamphlets from the sixteenth century, *The Cell of Self Knowledge* (1910). This vein continued with *Dante and the Mystics* (1913), a fundamental reassessment of the role

of Joachim of Fiore, Richard of Saint Victor, Celestine V, and even Augustine in Dante's thought, and was again shadowed at a popular level by yet another Dent imprint, *The Book of Saint Bernard* (1916).

Gardner's growing academic standing brought him recognition as Barlow lecturer on Dante at University College, London (1910–26), while during the First World War the absence of Italian staff, called to the trenches, meant that he was able to obtain more consistent teaching duties. Appointed reader in 1918, he moved to Manchester to occupy the newly created Serena chair of Italian studies in 1919. His inaugural lecture, 'The national idea in Italian literature', amply demonstrated the Mazzinian sentiment prevalent among British Italianists of his generation. After promotion, honours followed regularly: an officer of the crown of Italy in 1921, and nominated commendatore in 1929, he achieved the highest rank, grand officer, in 1935. More importantly, he was awarded the recently instituted Serena medal in 1922, and made a fellow of the British Academy in 1925.

In 1923 Gardner moved to University College, London, to a personal chair in early Italian language and literature, and after two years transferred to the established Serena chair in Italian studies. Here his interests took a new direction, towards Tommaso Campanella's poetry (the subject of his inaugural lecture), and towards the influence of the *matière de Bretagne* in Italian literature, on which he published an important reassessment, *The Arthurian Legend in Italian Poetry* (1930). His work for others was characterized by meticulousness, particularly as editor of the *Modern Language Review*, and by tireless work as a reviewer. His late work began to show signs of an ingenuous enthusiasm for fascism, as the preface to *Italy: a Companion to Italian Studies* (1934) demonstrates. This admiration for Mussolini was, however, shared by other Italianists, such as Cesare Foligno, whose obituary of Gardner praises him for his fascist credentials (Foligno, 474–5). He retired from the Serena chair in 1934.

Though unworldly, and suffering from bad eyesight and poor health, in retirement Gardner concealed twin passions: for birdwatching, perhaps the motivation for *Saint Francis and the Birds* (1935), and for detective stories. Indeed, his pet project, combining his religiosity with his delight in whodunnits, was to be a thriller entitled *Blood in the Beadle's Box*. It was never realized. He died, from complications following an operation, at the Middlesex Hospital, Mortimer Street, London, on 27 July 1935. He was unmarried. His extensive scholarship, both on Ariosto and Dante, was swiftly superseded as the discipline professionalized between the wars, but he decisively introduced two distinct audiences to Italian studies: undergraduates and the lay reader.   JONATHAN USHER

Sources C. Foligno, memoir, *PBA*, 21 (1935), 464–79 · E. R. Vincent, *Enciclopedia dantesca*, ed. U. Bosco, 3 (Rome, 1973), 96–7 · *Edmund Garratt Gardner, 12 May 1869 – 27 July 1935: a bibliography of his publications, with appreciations by C. J. Sisson and C. Foligno* (1937) · b. cert. · Venn, *Alum. Cant.* · J. R. Tanner, ed., *The historical register of the University of Cambridge* (1917) · CGPLA Eng. & Wales (1935)
Wealth at death £7625 8s. 4d.: resworn probate, CGPLA Eng. & Wales

Gardner, Ernest Arthur (1862–1939), classical scholar and archaeologist, was born at Clapton, London, on 16 March 1862, the sixth and youngest child of Thomas Gardner, of the stock exchange, and his wife, Ann Pearse. Percy *Gardner was his eldest brother and Alice *Gardner his sister. He was educated at the City of London School under E. A. Abbott and at Gonville and Caius College, Cambridge, which he entered as a scholar in 1880. He obtained a first class in both parts of the classical tripos (1882 and 1884). In 1882 he appeared as Athene in the Cambridge Greek play *Ajax*. He was a fellow of his college from 1885 to 1894 and Craven student from 1887 to 1890.

By the time that Gardner started upon his career British scholars had already embarked on scientific field archaeology in classical lands. He continued Flinders Petrie's excavations at Naucratis in Egypt for the Egypt Exploration Fund in 1885–6, and was subsequently admitted as the first student at the British School at Athens, arriving in December 1886, under the first director Francis Penrose. He was shortly joined in Athens by David Hogarth, Oxford Craven fellow, and another future director. In 1887 Gardner was appointed director of the British School, a post he held until 1895. In the same year he married Mary (*d.* 1936), daughter of Major John Wilson, of the Scots Greys; they had one son and two daughters, the elder of whom predeceased her father. His appointment at Athens coincided with the creation of the Cyprus Exploration Fund, largely at the instigation of F. H. H. Guillemard (1852–1933), university reader in geography at Cambridge and also a fellow of Gonville and Caius College. This led to a series of excavations at a number of sites on Cyprus, such as Old Paphos and Salamis, by Gardner and members of the British School including Hogarth and M. R. James. In 1891 Gardner's appointment as director of the British School at Athens was renewed through the generosity of the master and fellows of Gonville and Caius College, who agreed to extend his college fellowship for another three years if it 'was of consequence to the cause of archaeology' (*The Caian*, 1, 1891–2, 82). This allowed Gardner to excavate at Megalopolis in the Peloponnese. This was an influential period in the life of the British School, and students at this time included J. G. Frazer, J. A. R. Munro, and J. L. Myres.

In 1896 Gardner was elected Yates professor of archaeology in the University of London, where he soon established a school of classical archaeology at University College: he also became Yates lecturer in 1927. His students in London included Mortimer Wheeler, who was later to acknowledge that it was Gardner's 'teaching that drove me ultimately and not unwillingly into professional archaeology' (Wheeler, 33). In addition to teaching he organized a number of successful vacation tours to Greece and the eastern Mediterranean. These experiences were to appear as a handbook for travellers, *Greece and the Aegean* (1933). He also collaborated with his brother Percy in arranging vacation courses in archaeology for schoolteachers and others in Britain.

Gardner was one of the editors of the *Journal of Hellenic Studies* from 1897 to 1932 and president of the Hellenic Society from 1929 to 1932. He was also active in university

Ernest Arthur Gardner (1862–1939), by unknown photographer

administration, serving as dean of the faculty of arts from 1905 to 1909 and from 1913 to 1915, as vice-chancellor from 1924 to 1926, and as public orator from 1910 to 1932. As lieutenant-commander in the Royal Naval Volunteer Reserve he saw active service as naval intelligence officer at Salonika from 1915 to 1917. During this campaign he ensured that archaeological remains were protected and collected together in the White Tower. For this service he was awarded the gold cross of the Greek order of the Redeemer in 1918. From the autumn of 1917 to early 1919 he was transferred to the Admiralty, where he continued to work in naval intelligence.

The wide scope of Gardner's archaeological interests is attested by his numerous publications. The earliest of these are the chapters on inscriptions in *Naucratis I* (1886) and *Naucratis II* (1888). He wrote *A Handbook of Greek Sculpture* (1896–7), of which a revised and enlarged edition appeared in 1915. *The Catalogue of the Greek Vases in the Fitzwilliam Museum, Cambridge* appeared in 1897, *Ancient Athens* in 1902, *Six Greek Sculptors* and *Religion and Art in Ancient Greece* in 1910. In 1905 he collaborated with E. S. Roberts, master of Gonville and Caius College, Cambridge, in the *Introduction to Greek Epigraphy*, of which he wrote part 2, 'The inscriptions of Attica'. His later works include *The Art of Greece* (1925).

Gardner retired from his chair in 1929, but retained his lectureship until 1933. Among the distinctions which he received were the honorary fellowship of Gonville and Caius College (1926) and the honorary degree of LittD of Trinity College, Dublin. He died at his home, Recess, Boyn Hill, Maidenhead, Berkshire, on 27 November 1939, and was buried on 1 December at Stubbings church, Maidenhead.

J. M. C. TOYNBEE and H. D. A. MAJOR, rev. DAVID GILL

Sources *The Times* (29 Nov 1939) · *The Caian*, 48 (1939–40), 72–4 · H. Waterhouse, *The British School at Athens: the first hundred years* (1986) · J. Venn and others, eds., *Biographical history of Gonville and Caius College*, 2: 1713–1897 (1898) · *The Caian*, 1 (1891–2), 5, 82–3 · *The Caian*, 6 (1896–7), 4–5 [farewell address from the British School at Athens] · M. Wheeler, *Still digging* (1955) · personal knowledge (1949) · *The Times* (4 Dec 1939) · J. Hawkes, *Mortimer Wheeler: adventurer in archaeology* (1982)
Archives UCL, diaries and notebooks | BL, corresp. with Macmillans, Add. MS 55130
Likenesses S. Carline, oils (as vice-chancellor), U. Lond., Senate House · R. E. M. Wheeler, caricature, priv. coll.; repro. in Hawkes, *Mortimer Wheeler* · photograph, repro. in Waterhouse, *British School* · photograph, British School at Athens [see illus.]
Wealth at death £11,443 14s. 8d.: probate, 18 March 1940, CGPLA Eng. & Wales

Gardner [*married name* Qvist], **Dame Frances Violet** (1913–1989), cardiologist and teacher of medicine, was born on 28 February 1913, the youngest of three daughters of Sir Ernest Gardner (1846–1925), a farmer and Conservative MP for Wokingham and then Windsor, and his second wife, Amy Inglis, daughter of Lieutenant-General Laurie. Educated at Headington School, Oxford, and Westfield College, University of London, Frances Gardner graduated BSc in 1935 and then studied medicine at the Royal Free Hospital School of Medicine for Women, beginning an association which would form the mainstay of her whole career. She graduated MB BS in 1940, with distinctions in three parts of the final, followed by the MD and membership of the Royal College of Physicians in 1943. These achievements were made despite the heavy bombing raids on London in the Second World War during which Frances organized both the reception of casualties and morale-boosting activities for her colleagues. The latter was a joint venture with her future husband George Qvist (1910–1981), surgeon to the hospital since 1941, the son of Emil and Emily Qvist, whom she eventually married in 1958 to the delight of friends and students. This was a lifelong and devoted, if argumentative, medical partnership and, in the absence of children, their students were treated as an extended family.

Immediately after the war Frances Gardner was awarded a travelling fellowship, visiting Harvard where she learned the diagnostic technique of angiocardiography, which she then introduced to Britain on her return in 1946. Enabling the radiographic visualization of the heart and arteries through the injection of suitable contrast material into the blood, this technique provided for a more sophisticated and accurate diagnosis of heart disease which had previously relied on bedside examination, chest X-rays, and electrocardiographs. The same year saw her appointment as consultant physician in the department of cardiology at the Royal Free Hospital, a post that she held until her retirement in 1975, while she was also for some years on the consulting staff of the Royal National Throat, Nose and Ear Hospital, the Hospital for Women in Soho, and the Mothers' Hospital, Clapton. Her election as a fellow of the Royal College of Physicians came in 1952 and she was honoured in a similar fashion in 1983 by the Royal College of Surgeons of England, where she had endowed the Qvist curatorship of John Hunter's Museum and, also in memory of her late husband, sponsored evenings during which students were entertained with clinical demonstrations and excellent dinners.

Frances Gardner made as equal a contribution to medical education as she did to her clinical speciality. As well as being a gifted and effective teacher respected and loved by her students, she was dean of the medical school from 1962 to 1975, weathering the upheavals of the Todd report on medical education and the Flowers report on the University of London, while also negotiating the protracted planning over a decade of the move to a new site in Hampstead where the hospital and its school of medicine would be combined for the first time. The move was finally accomplished when she was no longer dean.

Beyond the immediate sphere of the Royal Free Hospital and her valued contributions to the committees of the University of London and the General Medical Council, Frances Gardner received the unusual distinction of being invited by King Feisal to Saudi Arabia. There, in 1966, she was an influential adviser on the establishment of the medical faculty at the new University of Riyadh, served as visitor to the University of Khartoum medical faculty and as chairman of the London–Riyadh universities medical faculty.

Retirement as dean in 1975 did not end Gardner's connection with the school; she was created DBE in that year and served as president until her death. Even so, retirement allowed more time for her other passion of gardening and the tending of her allotment, close to home but reached by the somewhat eccentric conveyance of an electric milk float. Dame Frances Gardner died at her home, Fitzroy Lodge, Fitzroy Park, Camden, London, on 10 July 1989, and was buried in her local church of St Anne's, Highgate, nine days later.

JANET FOSTER

Sources *The Times* (22 July 1989) · *BMJ* (29 July 1989), 318 · *The Lancet* (5 Aug 1989), 341 · E. Lyle and S. Taylor, eds., *Lives of the fellows of the Royal College of Surgeons of England, 1983–1990* (1995) · *WW* (1981) · *WW* (1983) · d. cert.
Likenesses photographs, Royal Free Hospital Archives
Wealth at death £1,634,761: probate, 16 Aug 1989, CGPLA Eng. & Wales

Gardner, George (1812–1849), botanist, was born in Glasgow in May 1812. He studied medicine at Glasgow University and gained his MD in 1835. After graduation he decided to undertake botanical travel, and with the assistance of his teacher, W. J. Hooker, obtained the support of the duke of Bedford and others as subscribers for the plants that he might collect. In May 1836 he sailed for Brazil. Before starting he issued a pocket herbarium of about

250 species of British mosses, *Musci Britannici* (1836). In Brazil he first explored the Organ mountains, and subsequently the Pernambuco, Rio, São Francisco, Aracaty, Ceara, and Piauhy areas, returning to Rio de Janeiro on 2 November 1840. He sent home 60,000 specimens, representing 3000 species, and his entire collection comprised twice that number of species of flowering plants alone. When he arrived at Liverpool in July 1841 he brought with him six large Wardian cases of plants, although many of these were found to have died during the voyage.

Gardner described several new genera in a series of papers published in Hooker's *London Journal of Botany*, and also provided lists of Brazilian plants. In the *Journal of the Horticultural Society* he published his reflections on the relation between climate and vegetation. In 1842 he became a fellow of the Linnean Society. In 1843 he was employed by H. B. Fielding, who owned an extensive private herbarium at Lancaster, to help prepare an illustrated descriptive work entitled *Sertum plantarum* (8 vols., 1844). Gardner also investigated the geology and fossil fishes of Brazil. In 1844 he was appointed superintendent of the botanical garden at Peradeniya, Ceylon, and devoted the voyage out to the preparation of the journal of his Brazilian travels, some accounts of which had already appeared, in letters to Sir W. J. Hooker, in the *Companion to the Botanical Magazine*, and in the *Annals of Natural History*. The detailed journal (the proof-sheets of which were revised by John Miers and Robert Heward) appeared in 1846 as *Travels in the interior of Brazil, principally through the northern provinces and the gold and diamond districts, during the years 1836–1841* (2nd edn, 1849). At Peradeniya he made a rapid start in the improvement of the garden with the strong support of the colonial secretary Sir James Emerson Tennent. In 1845 he visited Madras, and botanized in the Nilgiri hills with Dr Robert Wight, with whom he became associated as part editor of John McClelland's *Calcutta Journal of Natural History* (vols. 6–7, 1846–7).

At the time of his death Gardner had fully prepared for publication a manual of Indian botany, which, however, never appeared. In addition to official reports, he published over thirty-two papers, all but three of which—on geology and fossil fishes—concerned botany. Nineteen of these appeared in Hooker's botanical journal between 1840 and 1850. He died of apoplexy at Neura Ellia, Ceylon, on 10 March 1849. His herbarium, comprising about 14,000 specimens, was mostly purchased for the British Museum.   G. S. BOULGER, rev. ANDREW GROUT

Sources *Proceedings of the Linnean Society of London*, 2 (1848–55), 40–44 · W. J. Hooker, 'Information respecting Mr Gardner', *Journal of Botany*, 4 (1842), 199–206 · *Hooker's Journal of Botany and Kew Garden Miscellany*, 1 (1849), 154–6 · *Hooker's Journal of Botany and Kew Garden Miscellany*, 3 (1851), 188–9 · R. Desmond, *The European discovery of the Indian flora* (1992) · F. A. Stafleu and R. S. Cowan, *Taxonomic literature: a selective guide*, 2nd edn, 1, Regnum Vegetabile, 94 (1976), 915–16 · 'Death of Dr Gardner', *Gardeners' Chronicle* (28 April 1849), 263 · 'The Gardnerian herbarium', *Gardeners' Chronicle* (31 May 1851), 343–4 · 'Gardener's [sic] British mosses', *Companion to the Botanical Magazine*, 1 (1835), 20, 226 [Hooker] · A. M. Coats, *The plant hunters* (1969), 355

Archives Bodl. Oxf., papers · RBG Kew, archives, drawings and catalogues | NHM, Botany Library, plant catalogue · RBG Kew, archives, letters to Sir William Hooker

Gardner, Gerald Brosseau (1884–1964), publicist of the Wicca religion, was born on 13 June 1884 at Serpentine North, Great Crosby, Lancashire, the third of four sons of a Liverpool timber merchant, William Robert Gardner (*d.* in or after 1927), and his wife, Louise Barguelew Ennis (*d.* 1920). It is significant that in his memoirs Gardner never named his parents, recalling instead his nursemaid Josephine McCombie to whom he was handed over in early childhood. He was a sickly youngster, with chronic asthma, and received no formal schooling, teaching himself to read and write. In 1900 McCombie married a tea planter in Ceylon and took the boy with her. He remained in the Far East for the whole of his working life.

Until 1908 Gardner stayed in Ceylon, working for two successive tea plantations and then managing one of rubber. Between 1908 and 1911 he oversaw rubber plantations in British North Borneo and central Malaya. In 1923 rubber prices fell and he became a government inspector of plantations in the same region, being later promoted to principal customs officer of Johore. During one of his rare visits to England, on 16 August 1927 he married a nurse, Dorothea Frances Rosedale (*d.* 1960), usually called Donna. They returned to England on his retirement in 1936.

Gardner's memoirs depict a hardy, lonely, temperate, and self-contained man, distinguished by three traits. One was his conversion to naturism. Another was his interest in antiquities which resulted in his becoming a pioneer of Malayan archaeology and numismatics and a collector of Malay weapons. The third was his study of esoteric religion. Having been brought up in no faith, he took a keen interest in freemasonry, Buddhism, spiritualism, and tribal animism and shamanism. Most unusually, however, it was to be his hobbies in retirement which were to make him a national figure.

In 1938 Gardner rented a house at Highcliffe on the Hampshire coast, and added a flat in Ridgmount Gardens, London, in 1946. In 1954 he moved to Castletown in the Isle of Man, which became his home until his death. During the late 1930s he visited archaeological sites in the Near East, and joined the Folklore Society in London, the Co-Masons, and the Rosicrucian Fellowship of Crotona, in Hampshire. During the early 1940s he served as an air raid warden, and from 1944 to 1945 was co-president of the Bournemouth Historical Association. In 1946 he was elected to the council of the Folklore Society and also to that of the Druid Order. In 1947 he visited the famous ritual magician Aleister Crowley and was chartered by the latter to revive his magical society, the Ordo Templi Orientis, in Britain. By 1948 Gardner had failed to do this, and committed himself to the witch religion of Wicca which was to dominate the rest of his life.

Gardner's account of it depended on the thesis—most notably associated with Margaret Murray, the Egyptologist and author of *The Witch-Cult in Western Europe* (1921)—that the people persecuted as witches in the early modern period had been pagans practising the old religion of Europe. His claim was that through the Fellowship of Crotona he had met members of a coven at Highcliffe which had survived the persecutions and persisted in secret until the present. He was initiated into this in 1939, and obtained permission to publish its rituals ten years later, first in fictional form and then as fact. The collapse of the Murray thesis has removed the historical context for the story, and the existence of the coven concerned has not so far been proved or disproved. What is certain is that in 1939 Gardner published a novel, *A Goddess Arrives*, which displayed no knowledge of Wicca, and a second in 1949, *High Magic's Aid*, in which key Wiccan rites were printed. His beliefs were fully elaborated by 1948, but the extent to which he personally devised the religion is unclear.

The Wicca religion as expounded by Gardner was focused on a goddess, identified with the night sky and with wild nature, and a horned god who represented the fertilizing powers of the natural world. It was organized into covens, through which members were initiated through three ascending degrees of competence and authority and which were governed by a high priestess, supported by a high priest. This pattern of management mirrored that in the cosmology of the tradition, in which the goddess was the senior partner; it was a religion which gave a superior margin of power to the feminine. It placed a heavy emphasis on direct experience of divinity, the two deities being invoked into the bodies of their worshippers and speaking through them, and on the practical working of magic. The latter was bound by an ethic, that all humans were entitled to express, develop, and indulge themselves to the limit of their wills, providing that they did no harm to others. The religion was practised in private, as a series of mysteries, and the practitioners worked nude, except for jewellery. It infused sexuality with sanctity, although the former was much more commonly present in Wiccan rites in symbolic than in actual form.

Gardner was certainly the person who publicly promoted Wicca, circulating details of its beliefs among London occultists in 1950. Early in 1951 he began a campaign of interviews in newspapers and in radio and television programmes which continued until his death. Also in 1951 he became associated with the first Museum of Witchcraft in the British Isles, at Castletown, and bought the premises on moving there in 1954. He published two books on Wicca: these were *Witchcraft Today* (1954) and *The Meaning of Witchcraft* (1959), while a ghosted autobiography, *Gerald Gardner: Witch*, written by Idries Shah under the name Jack Bracelin, appeared in 1960. He lectured at University College, Accra, in present-day Ghana, in 1952–3, and attended the congress of world religions in 1954. He certainly co-wrote some of the later Wiccan rituals, in collaboration with the most talented author among his initiates, Doreen Valiente, and founded a network of covens which by his death spanned the British Isles and had reached America. All the modern branches of Wicca are either based on or influenced by his teachings. It is the only complete religion (as opposed to sect or denomination) which England has ever given the world.

Gardner was clearly a man of considerable charm and kindness, an excellent raconteur with a love of jokes and a zest for life. He also had a taste for mischief, and at times for duplicity. His status as a scholar remains controversial. His wife, Donna, died in 1960. He himself died on 12 February 1964 at sea off the Tunisian coast from a cerebral haemorrhage while on a Mediterranean cruise aboard the *Scottish Prince*. He was buried in the public cemetery at Tunis, the nearest port, on 13 February.

RONALD HUTTON

Sources Wiccan Church of Canada, Gardner papers · J. Bracelin [I. Shah], *Gerald Gardner: witch* (1960) · Museum of Witchcraft, Boscastle, Williamson papers · D. Valiente, *The rebirth of witchcraft* (1989) · private information (2004) [Doreen Valiente newspaper collection] · *Christchurch Times* (1938–44) · *Daily Mail* (1 Oct 1964) · R. Hutton, *The triumph of the moon: a history of modern pagan witchcraft* (1999) · b. cert. · m. cert. · d. cert.
Archives Wiccan Church of Canada, MSS | FILM BFI NFTVA, documentary footage
Likenesses photographs, repro. in Bracelin, *Gerald Gardner*
Wealth at death £21,688: administration with will, 26 Aug 1964, *CGPLA Eng. & Wales*

Gardner, Dame **Helen Louise** (1908–1986), literary scholar and university teacher, was born at Brookfield, Dukes Avenue, Church End, Finchley, Middlesex, on 13 February 1908, the middle child and only daughter of Charles Henry Gardner (*d.* 1919/20), journalist, and his wife, Helen Mary Roadnight Cockman. Helen was eleven when her father died and the family thereafter made their home with her grandparents. Mrs Gardner, a very musical woman, was ambitious for her gifted daughter and her encouragement was stimulating and sometimes a strain. Helen's education was at the North London Collegiate School for Girls, where she benefited from the excellent teaching of her English mistress, Florence Gibbons. In 1926 she went to St Hilda's College, Oxford, and in 1929 obtained first-class honours in English language and literature. Amateur dramatics revealed talents that could be discerned later in her style of lecturing and lively conversational habits.

Helen Gardner accepted a temporary post at the University of Birmingham. After three years (1931–4) as an assistant lecturer at the Royal Holloway College, London, she seized the chance of returning to Birmingham, as a member of the English department (1934–41). She extended the scope of her lecturing beyond the university audience; canvassed for Labour in a Conservative area; agonized over the Spanish Civil War and refugees from Nazi Germany. It was on a dreary March day in 1940 that her spirits were roused by a first contact with T. S. Eliot's 'East Coker'. In 1941 she sought and took good advice and left Birmingham for Oxford to become a tutor (1941–54), and later fellow (1942–66), at her old college. The next thirteen years she regarded as her 'golden years'. She was memorably steady in her concern for the welfare of her own pupils. To the less able her tutorials were formidable, but to those who could take the wit and severity of her criticism of their essays the experience proved rewarding. In 1954 she was made reader in Renaissance studies and after one set-

Dame Helen Louise Gardner (1908–1986), by Walter Bird, 1959

back was elected in 1966 Merton professor of English language and literature, with a fellowship at Lady Margaret Hall. The distinction of being the first woman to hold this chair gave her special satisfaction. She exerted herself as a supervisor and was as successful as she was strict. Forewords in many publications bear witness to her influence. From 1961 to 1963 she served on the committee on higher education chaired by Baron Robbins. She relished the discussion and travel involved and remained unabashed by some of the criticism of the extent of university expansion which was recommended. She served on the Council for National Academic Awards (1964–7) and enjoyed being a trustee for the National Portrait Gallery (1967–78). As a delegate to the Oxford University Press (1959–75) she made herself felt to the benefit of English studies. On subjects outside her range her judgements were sometimes less happy.

Meanwhile Helen Gardner's work on the two poets with whom she will chiefly be associated—John Donne and T. S. Eliot—went on concurrently. Her masterly edition of Donne's *Divine Poems* appeared in 1952 and was revised in 1978. The parallel edition of his *Elegies and Songs and Sonnets* followed in 1965. It was her declared intent to supersede Herbert Grierson's text, believing that she had the advantage of more manuscripts to subject to the rigorous method of collation she favoured. The introductions and commentaries manifest the industry and intelligence she brought to this work. Against subsequent criticism she continued to defend the readings and reorderings she proposed.

Helen Gardner's tribute to the genius of T. S. Eliot took a different form. In *The Art of T. S. Eliot* (1949) she provided a way into an originality in thought and prosody in the poems which both fascinated and perplexed many readers. It was gratifying for her to learn that she had her author's approval. This book was written *con amore* and shows to advantage her critical enthusiasm. Later, in 1978, she took advantage of the publication of the drafts of *Four Quartets* to demonstrate a poem in the making (*The Composition of 'Four Quartets'*, 1978). She also wrote on Shakespeare and on Milton's *Paradise Lost*. The British Academy lectures on Othello ('The noble Moor', 1955) and on King Lear (1967) draw out her best. The introductions to the World's Classics selections of metaphysical poets (1961) and of George Herbert are admirable. She collaborated with Timothy Healy in selecting from Donne's sermons (*Selected Prose*, 1967), and with G. M. Story in an edition of William Alabaster's poems (1959).

The popularity of Helen Gardner as a lecturer in Britain, the United States, European capitals, and the Far East owed as much to her style as to her subject. Her enthusiasm could be infectious. She had a clear, strong voice and was aware of its attraction. The phrasing and rhythms of her prose echo in some measure their oral delivery. Her favourite unit of composition was about the length of a lecture, essay, long obituary, or university sermon. Criticism she regarded as a serving art. She was not an innovator but chose rather to consolidate and conserve. Her endeavour was to increase the understanding and enjoyment of the best to be found in the literature of her own language. Later in life she was dismayed to realize how strong was the current of new methods of analysis, in the valuation of poetry and the style of theatrical production, and the effect it had on the teaching of English. She advertised her disapproval with fierce irony and then in more positive chapters reasserted her own beliefs in *In Defence of the Imagination* (1982). As a reviewer she was thorough, conscientious, severe, and open: everything was signed. She dealt with many of the most important publications of her peers and risked making enemies in the process. Twice she took on the thankless task of an anthologist with good will. The *Faber Book of Religious Verse* (1972) was followed in the same year by a more ambitious undertaking, The *New Oxford Book of English Verse*. To her Oxford DLitt (1963) and Cambridge honorary LittD (1981) she added honorary degrees from eight other universities. She was appointed CBE in 1962 and a DBE in 1967. She was made a fellow of the British Academy in 1958, twice won the Crawshay prize (1952 and 1980), and was made a fellow of the Royal Society of Literature in 1962.

In person Helen Gardner was small and sturdy. Vivacious, temperamental, and occasionally overbearing, she appreciated good food and drink, liked to dress well, and revelled in parties where she talked well but, as she herself knew, too much. She was kinder in her actions than in her wit. No feminist, she liked to be a woman in a man's world, game to compete and reckoning that she could match anyone for scholarly hard work and tough argument. She made no secret of her satisfaction in her success. She was brave in a number of illnesses and limped a little after a repeated hip replacement. She was a devout Anglican in the tradition of the seventeenth-century divines. Retirement at Myrtle House, 12 Mill Street, Eynsham, near Oxford, in 1975 did not greatly change her way of working except that she had more time to give to her pleasure in gardens and foreign travel. She died, unmarried, on 4 June 1986 in a nursing home at Bicester, Oxfordshire, after many months of a distressing illness.

K. M. LEA, *rev.*

Sources K. Lea, 'Helen Gardner, 1908–1986', *PBA*, 76 (1990), 394–409 · *The Times* (6 June 1986) · personal knowledge (1996) · private information (1996) · b. cert. · *CGPLA Eng. & Wales* (1986)
Archives Bodl. Oxf., working papers for her *Divine poems of John Donne* · University of Bristol, corresp. and statements relating to trial of *Lady Chatterley's Lover* | Bodl. Oxf., letters to T. S. Eliot [copies]
Likenesses W. Bird, photograph, 1959, NPG [*see illus.*]
Wealth at death £336,563: probate, 9 July 1986, *CGPLA Eng. & Wales*

Gardner, (Leslie) James (1907–1995), designer and graphic artist, was born on 29 December 1907 at 26 Stacey Road, Hendon, Middlesex, the son of Frederick James Gardner, a commercial traveller, and his wife, Flora May, formerly Jarvis. He was brought up in somewhat unhappy family circumstances in suburban London. Awarded a council scholarship to Westminster School of Art, where his teachers included Randolph Schwabe and E. McKnight Kauffer, he was taken on in 1923 as an apprentice at Cartiers the jeweller of Bond Street, London, where he remained for six years. After a period travelling abroad for much of the 1930s he was employed at Carlton Studios, a leading London-based commercial design consultancy. On 20 February 1935 he married (Violet) Mary, daughter of William John Williams, at Brentford, Middlesex. During the 1930s he came into contact with Jack Beddington of Shell, for whom he carried out poster production and early work in exhibition design, the field in which he was to become a defining practitioner.

Gardner established his reputation after the Second World War, during which he had been involved with the Camouflage Training School, working alongside the couturier Victor Stiebel and the set designer Oliver Messel. He was appointed as chief designer for the landmark 'Britain Can Make It' exhibition of 1946, the first of a series of commissions for the Council of Industrial Design; these included the 'Enterprise Scotland' exhibition of 1947 and the 'Festival of Britain' of 1951. For the latter he served as a design panel member and the design co-ordinator of the whimsical Battersea pleasure gardens. A number of other important official commissions followed, including the British government pavilion at the Brussels World Fair of 1958 and the British contribution to the Montreal World Fair of 1967. In the latter he portrayed the dynamic, creative side of life in Britain in the 1960s, including in his display Carnaby Street fashions and an Austin Mini decorated with the union flag. One of his most significant achievements in museum design was the Evoluon

(Leslie) James Gardner (1907–1995), by Lewis Morley, 1961

Museum (1966) for Philips in Eindhoven. His pioneering work on museum displays was remarkable in the ways in which the complexities of science, technology, and history were made accessible without being patronizing. As well as working on a series of important commissions including the Pilkington Glass Museum (1965), the 'Story of the Earth' exhibition (1972), and the 'Britain before Man' exhibition (1977) at the Geological Museum, London, in 1972, Gardner was involved in mainstream industrial design and interior design commissions. These included a prestigious commission from Cunard to design the superstructure and interior for their ocean liner *QE 2*, for which he supervised work in 1966.

For much of the rest of his productive life Gardner worked on a wide range of significant national and international projects, such as the Museum of the Diaspora in Tel Aviv (1978), though for a while the recession of the 1980s constrained his prolific output. None the less, with the assistance of Martin Pyant and Eve Harrison he won further important commissions, including the Museum of Natural Science in Taiwan (1988) and the Museum of Intolerance, Los Angeles (1993). In 1989 he was awarded the medal of the Chartered Society of Designers for outstanding achievement in industrial design.

Although never self-consciously stylish in his dress in the manner of many designers in the later twentieth century, Gardner's appearance in later life perhaps singled him out as 'arty'. He was a pipe-smoker who often looked out quizzically over his black, thick-rimmed glasses, his brushed-back hair longer than that of many of his contemporaries. He also often sported a polo-neck sweater beneath a corduroy jacket with pens, emblematic of his profession, visible in its breast pocket. His autobiographical writings, *Elephants in the Attic* (1983) and *James Gardner, the ARTful Designer: Ideas off the Drawing Board* (1993), reveal both his strengths and his weaknesses. Evident in both is a complete belief in his own professional abilities as a designer, together with an absolute reluctance to 'suffer fools'. An air of irreverence and, at times, flippancy pervaded the prose that G (as he was known to many fellow designers) produced. Its somewhat raffish, casual, and throwaway style made light of the genuine importance of his contribution to design, though the many drawings that accompanied the text revealed the eloquence and facility of his draughtsmanship. These books also reveal his general sense of self-containment, a strong sense of living for his work, and a reluctance to give away significant details about his private life. Similarly, his sketches and designs have not been systematically preserved since, after completing work, Gardner was prone to give them—or even throw them—away, their immediate purpose having been fulfilled. Gardner was also capable of writing a very good book about the profession itself, as in *Exhibition and Display* (1960), which he co-wrote with Caroline Heller.

James Gardner died in the Middlesex Hospital, London, on 25 March 1995. It was within the museum and exhibition design profession that he was best known and where the true originality of his design solutions has been recognized. He was considered by Hugh Casson as 'perhaps the most inventive, versatile and prolific designer in the UK' for more than half of the twentieth century. Although a highly significant figure in the history of design, unlike an increasing number of designers in the latter half of the twentieth century he rejected the cult of personality and devoted himself to his work.   JONATHAN WOODHAM

Sir James Tynte Agg-Gardner (1846–1928), by James Russell & Sons, 1887

Sources *The Times* (21 April 1995) · *The Independent* (29 March 2001) · *Chartered Designers' Newsletter*, 1 (July–Aug 1995) · *Design Week*, 10/15 (14 April 1995) · information files, V&A NAL · University of Brighton, Design History Research Centre Archives, James Gardner Archive · S. Pendergast, ed., *Contemporary designers*, 3rd edn (1997) · J. Gardner, *Elephants in the attic: the autobiography of James Gardner* (1983) · J. Gardner, *The ARTful designer: ideas off the drawing board* (1993) · P. Maguire and J. M. Woodham, eds., *Design and cultural politics in postwar Britain: the Britain Can Make It exhibition, 1946* (1997) · B. Hillier and M. Banham, eds., *A tonic to the nation: the Festival of Britain* (1976) · 'Giles Velarde interviews James Gardner', *Did Britain make it? British design in context, 1946–86*, ed. P. Sparke (1986) · J. Gardner and C. Heller, *Exhibition and display* (1960) · Festival of Britain collection, V&A NAL, Central Office of Information, Council of Industrial Design [700 photographs] · B. Peppin and L. Micklethwaite, *Dictionary of British book illustrators: the twentieth century* (1983) · b. cert. · m. cert. · d. cert. · H. Casson, 'The last of the herbivores', *Blueprint: London's Magazine of Design, Architecture and Style*, 10 (Oct 1993), 45

Likenesses L. Morley, photograph, 1961, NPG [*see illus.*]

Wealth at death £226,761: probate, 1997

Gardner, Sir James Tynte Agg- (1846–1928), brewer and politician, was born on 25 November 1846, at Cheltenham, the elder son of James Agg-Gardner (1804–1858) and his wife, Eulalie Emily (1819–1901), the fifth daughter and coheir of William Richard Hopkins-Northey. He had one brother and a sister. His father took the additional surname after his patronymic of Agg as the nephew and heir of John Gardner (*d.* 1836), a country banker and Cheltenham brewer. Agg-Gardner senior was an astute businessman who purchased the manor of Cheltenham in 1843 for £39,000 from Lord Sherborne; he unsuccessfully contested Cheltenham (then a pocket borough of the whig Berkeley family) as a Conservative in 1841 and 1848. James, his heir, was brought up in a Calvinist atmosphere; he became a ward in chancery on his father's death and was 'carefully reared, watched over by his widowed mother'

(*Cheltenham Chronicle*). He went to Harrow School in 1861 and was coached privately at Hedsor in 1864 by the chaplain of his uncle, Lord Boston, before matriculating at Trinity College, Cambridge, in 1865. At the age of nineteen he became a freemason. Owing to his first parliamentary candidature at Cheltenham in 1868 he took no degree, but became a student of the Inner Temple in that year and was called to the bar in 1873. He never practised.

Agg-Gardner was lord of the manor of Cheltenham until 1862, when his interest was sold for £33,000, and again from 1872, when he bought back the manorial rights. His property in the town was developed after his coming of age. New malthouses were built in the 1870s, and £75,000 was spent on improving head premises and brewery houses. He bought a wine and spirit shop in Cheltenham High Street, and had a pecuniary interest in the Plough Hotel, where he lived before acquiring Evesham House at Pittville about 1888. Agg-Gardner's brewery enjoyed 'the highest possible character' for a radius of 50 miles, and was 'the largest brewery in England, and probably therefore in the world, which is the sole and entire property of one man' (*Licensed Victuallers Gazette*). It suffered by this, for Agg-Gardner was not a keen-minded entrepreneur and the business needed a committed managing director to impose policy. In 1888 it was turned into the Cheltenham Original Brewery Company Ltd (with Agg-Gardner as chairman until his death). The brewery was encumbered by heavy borrowings, and a collapse in profits about 1905 was reversed only by the appointment of a professional brewer to direct the business.

The young lord of the manor was first elected Conservative MP for Cheltenham in 1874. Defeated in 1880, he was returned in 1885 and held the seat until the general election of 1895, when he did not stand 'for reasons unconnected with politics' (Agg-Gardner, 58). Agg-Gardner never married, and H. Montgomery Hyde, without giving evidence, stated he was homosexual (Hyde, 201). He had intimated in 1894 that he would not seek re-election, and conceivably his decision was influenced by the libel actions brought in 1893–4 by Charles Gatty who, as parliamentary candidate for West Dorset in 1892, had been sexually traduced by opponents. There may have been financial or other explanations for his temporary political retirement: he had lost about £15,000 invested in Horatio Bottomley's Anglo-Austrian Printing and Publishing Company. Agg-Gardner was returned unopposed in 1900, but was defeated in 1906. He did not contest the seat in 1910, but after Richard Mathias, the successful Liberal, was unseated on petition, Agg-Gardner was returned for the town in a by-election of April 1911, defeating Mathias's brother by four votes. He retained the seat until his death.

Although regular in attendance, Agg-Gardner seldom intervened in the chamber. He introduced bills on fire escapes (1891) and hire purchase (1928). He voted for women's suffrage as early as the 1870s and always maintained his support, most notably on 28 March 1912, when he moved the second reading of the Parliamentary Franchise (Women) Bill. After this was defeated, Robert Sanders, later Lord Bayford, noted: 'a very poor effort. He was frightened out of his life all through' (Ramsden, 45). Agg-Gardner's votes in support of bills to permit marriage with a deceased wife's sister strained his relations with high-church constituents. He resisted the Licensing Bill in the 1870s, and opposed the reduction of liquor licences in *The Times* (31 March 1883). He attended the inaugural meeting in Paris of the Inter-Parliamentary Union in 1887, and was later treasurer of the British group. He joined the kitchen committee of the House of Commons in 1886 and was chairman from 1917 until his death. In *The Times* (5 May 1904) he complained that evening adjournments were too short for members who wished to dine in South Kensington.

Agg-Gardner served in the Gloucestershire militia when young, and sat on the Gloucestershire bench of magistrates from 1875. He supported Cheltenham's incorporation as a borough, and sponsored the necessary parliamentary private bill. He was appointed its first freeman in 1896, and was generous to the town in both public and private charities. After selling Evesham House in 1907, he lived at the Queen's Hotel in Cheltenham. Twice he was mayor of Cheltenham (1908–9, 1912–13). He was chairman of the Cheltenham Newspaper Company (which owned the *Cheltenham Chronicle and Gloucester Graphic*) from its inception in 1912 until the sale of the business in 1928. He was knighted in 1916 and sworn of the privy council in 1924.

Agg-Gardner was a short, bald man with a toothy smile, sagging moustaches, and ugly features, but gentle, unassuming manners. It was difficult to quarrel with him. In 1927 he published *Some Parliamentary Recollections*, 'a modest, kindly and discursive little book' (*TLS*). He died of heart failure on 9 August 1928 at the Carlton Club, Pall Mall, London, and was interred in the family vault at Prestbury cemetery, Cheltenham.

RICHARD DAVENPORT-HINES

Sources J. Agg-Gardner, *Some parliamentary recollections* (1927) · *Cheltenham Chronicle and Gloucester Graphic* (11 Aug 1928), 2, 15 · The *Times* (10 Aug 1928) · *The Times* (14 Aug 1928) · *TLS* (16 Feb 1928), 115 · *Real old tory politics: the political diaries of Robert Sanders, Lord Bayford, 1910–35*, ed. J. Ramsden (1984) · H. M. Hyde, *The other love* (1970) · *Licensed Victuallers' Gazette and Hotel Courier* (13 Feb 1875) · T. R. Gourvish and R. G. Wilson, *The British brewing industry, 1830–1980* (1994) · E. Clarke, *The story of my life* (1918)

Archives Glos. RO, parliamentary notebooks, election papers, and misc. papers; corresp.

Likenesses J. Russell & Sons, photograph, 1887, NPG [see illus.] · oils, 1895, Cheltenham town hall · photograph, *c.*1910, Whitbread Brewery; repro. in Gourvish and Wilson, *British brewing industry*, pl. 32 · photograph, repro. in *The Times* (10 Aug 1928) · photograph, repro. in *Cheltenham Chronicle and Gloucester Graphic* · photographs, repro. in Agg-Gardner, *Some parliamentary recollections*

Wealth at death £66,627 4s.: probate, 14 Sept 1928, CGPLA Eng. & Wales

Gardner, John (1804–1880), general practitioner, was born in Great Coggeshall, Essex, and was possibly the son of Matthias Gardner (d. 1835?), probably a carpenter, and Rosemond Warner. His medical training was in London and consisted of an apprenticeship with James Russell of Golden Square, for five years from 1825, with hospital attendances at St George's Hospital and St James's Dispensary. He became a licentiate of the Society of Apothecaries, London, in 1829, and later by examination in 1860 a licentiate of the Royal College of Physicians of Edinburgh. He practised medicine in London as a general practitioner at 49 Portland Street from 1839, 51 Mortimer Street from 1847, and 23 Montague Street from 1860 to 1870.

In 1843 Gardner translated and edited *Familiar Letters on Chemistry* by the great German chemist Justus Liebig, editing further series in 1844 and 1854. This led to his making Liebig's personal acquaintance at Giessen University, where Gardner was made MD in 1847. Gardner was instrumental in forming the Royal College of Chemistry, in 1844; he was its secretary until 1846. He helped to secure the services of its first professor, A. W. Hofmann. The Royal College of Chemistry later became part of Imperial College, London. Gardner was himself a fellow of the Chemical Society and the Ethnological Society, and he was described as a professor of chemistry and materia medica to the General Apothecaries' Company. While connected with this company, which he had helped to found, he was involved with the preparation and sale of pure drugs under the supervision of scientific chemists. In this capacity he introduced medical practitioners in England to many drugs from the USA, including podophyllin, which was used as a cholagogue and purgative.

Gardner's principal publication was *The Great Physician: the Connexion of Diseases and Remedies with the Truths of Revelation* (1843). It is a theological treatise, except for the final chapter, which contains a brief history of epidemics and plagues. *The Great Physician* is a reference to Christ as the divine healer, and the book posits that medical science and Christian scriptures reflect similar principles and that this provides a new argument for the truth inherent in God. Gardner proposes that diseases and their remedies are component parts of God's spiritual government. He cites numerous examples from the Bible to demonstrate his beliefs concerning disease, remedies, and natural law.

The reader, whether lay or professional, is urged to study medicine in order to discover more of the workings of God, and also to study scripture the better to elucidate nature. Gardner's *Household Medicine* (1861) reached thirteen editions by 1898. Although aimed at the lay reader the book was intended to aid and not supersede a doctor's services. Written in eight parts, it includes general anatomy and physiology, principles of disease, nursing, and treatments of local and systemic disease. There is also a section on gynaecology. Gardner also wrote *Longevity: the Means of Prolonging Life after Middle Age* (3rd edn, 1874). This book examines old age, said to begin at sixty-three, and promotes the desirability and possibility of living a long life, the normal lifespan being one hundred years. It proposes that disease should be detected early and treated, and that care of the elderly demands specialist attention. The commoner diseases of old age are discussed as is their treatment, and also a suitable diet and way of life.

In 1834 Gardner married Julia Emily Barton, who later wrote *Marriage and Maternity, or, Scripture Wives and Mothers* (1881). They had a large family. John Gardner was a highly religious man, energetic in his working life and enthusiastic in promoting the study of chemistry and the production of pure pharmaceuticals. He died in London on 14 November 1880 at 29 Lansdowne Crescent, Kensington, as a result of bronchitis and of enlargement of the prostate gland. He was survived by his wife.

CHARLOTTE MENDES DA COSTA

Sources DNB · records, Society of Apothecaries, London · *London Medical Directory* (1846) · *London Medical Directory* (1847) · *London and Provincial Medical Directory* (1861) · *Medical Directory* (1871) · *Medical Directory* (1882) · medical registers, 1863 · medical registers, 1874 · *The Lancet* (19 April 1862), 418 · T. G. Chambers, *Register of the associates and old students of the Royal College of Chemistry, the Royal College of Mines and the Royal College of Science* (1896) · IGI · marriage register, 1834, Coggeshall, Essex · d. cert.
Archives ICL, college archives
Likenesses group photograph (after daguerreotype, *c*.1842), ICL, archives; repro. in R. G. Williams and A. Barrett, *Imperial College: a pictorial history* (1988)
Wealth at death under £500: probate, 24 Jan 1881, *CGPLA Eng. & Wales*

Gardner, Martin John (1940–1993), medical statistician, was born on 25 July 1940 at 253 Coventry Road, Ilford, Essex, the eldest child in the family of two sons and two daughters of Thomas Murray Gardner, marine superintendent, and his wife, Nellie, *née* Jackson. Educated at Palmer's Boys' School, Grays, Essex, he graduated from the University of Durham in 1961 with a first-class degree in mathematics. In 1962, after a year at Cambridge University working for the diploma in mathematical statistics, he joined the social medicine unit of the Medical Research Council at the London School of Hygiene and Tropical Medicine, and spent a year teaching at the University of California from 1966 to 1967. While in California, in 1967 he married Linda Claire Fritz, daughter of Edward C. Fritz, lawyer, of Dallas, Texas; they had two sons and one daughter. He moved to the University of Southampton in 1972 as senior lecturer in medical statistics, and reader from 1979, and was appointed professor of medical statistics in 1985.

He also held a post at the environmental epidemiology unit of the Medical Research Council at Southampton General Hospital from 1980.

Gardner's research centred on the geographical distribution of major diseases, and he published an *Atlas of Cancer Mortality in England and Wales, 1968–78* (1983) and an *Atlas of Mortality from Selected Diseases in England and Wales, 1968–1978* (1984). Much of his time was spent teaching medical scientists the importance of a study's initial design, and his success in raising the quality of statistical methods used in medical studies led to his appointment in 1980 as the main statistical adviser for the *British Medical Journal*.

In November 1983 Gardner was asked to join the committee chaired by Sir Douglas Black examining cases of childhood leukaemia around British Nuclear Fuels' nuclear-fuel reprocessing plant at Sellafield, in west Cumbria. The committee had been set up by the government in response to the television documentary *Windscale—the Nuclear Laundry* (1983), which argued that the cluster of children's deaths from leukaemia in Seascale could be attributed to contamination from radioactive waste discharged from the plant into the Irish Sea. The programme caused much public concern about the safety of nuclear plants. The Black report (1984) concluded that while there did seem to be an excess of childhood leukaemia in the Sellafield area, this could not be explained by an excess of environmental radioactivity, since not enough radioactive material had been released, and recommended further study. Gardner directed the research commissioned by the Department of Health and Social Security, setting up a study of all children born or attending schools in Seascale between 1950 and 1983. This showed that leukaemia occurred only in children born in the village, and that these cases were statistically related to their fathers' exposure to radiation while working at Sellafield before the children's conception. These findings were published in the *British Medical Journal* in 1990 in an article, 'Results of a case-control study of leukaemia and lymphoma among young people near Sellafield plant in west Cumbria'. In the same article Gardner stated his hypothesis that exposure to very low levels of radiation, previously thought safe, could have damaged the sperm of men working at Sellafield, introducing a mutation passed on to their children, who would have been born with a susceptibility to leukaemia. This became known as the Gardner hypothesis, and led to further studies both in England and abroad to see whether childhood cancer could be linked to fathers' exposure to radiation. Gardner's study was highly controversial, and leading medical scientists began to question his hypothesis, asking why, if childhood leukaemia was linked to fathers' employment in the nuclear industry, it should be confined to children born in Seascale and not elsewhere in Cumbria, and to develop the theory that infection could be a cause of childhood leukaemia. Nevertheless Gardner's work stimulated some of the most thorough investigations of childhood cancer ever undertaken, and expanded the understanding of its causes. In its report in 1996 the Committee on Medical

Aspects of Radiation in the Environment found no evidence to support Gardner's hypothesis.

Gardner died on 22 January 1993 in Countess Mountbatten House, Moorgreen Hospital, West End, Eastleigh, Hampshire. After his death *Childhood Cancer and Nuclear Installations* (1993), a collection of papers, letters, and reports, edited by Valerie Beral, Eve Roman, and Martin Bobrow, was dedicated to his memory. He was survived by his wife, Linda, and their three children.

ANNE PIMLOTT BAKER

Sources V. Beral, E. Roman, and M. Bobrow, eds., *Childhood cancer and nuclear installations* (1993) · *The Independent* (1 Feb 1993) · *The Guardian* (5 Feb 1993) · *The Times* (16 Feb 1993) · D. Barker, 'Martin Gardner', *BMJ*, 306 (1993), 387 · H. Inskip, 'Martin Gardner', *The Lancet*, 341 (1993), 429 · private information (2004) [daughter and son] · b. cert. · d. cert.
Likenesses photograph, repro. in Beral, Roman, and Bobrow, eds., *Childhood cancer and nuclear installations*, frontispiece · photograph, repro. in Barker, 'Martin Gardner', 387 · photograph, repro. in Inskip, 'Martin Gardner', 429
Wealth at death £84,503: probate, 14 April 1993, *CGPLA Eng. & Wales*

Gardner, Monica Mary (1873–1941), writer on Poland and Polish literature, was born on 26 June 1873 at Subiaco Lodge, Roehampton Lane, London, the fifth of the six children of John Gardner (1839–1887), a stockjobber, and his wife, Amy Vernon, *née* Garratt (d. 1937). (John) Edmund Garratt *Gardner (1869–1935) was her brother. Monica Gardner, who was a devout Roman Catholic (her originally Anglican parents having converted), was educated at the Sacred Heart Convent, Roehampton Lane. Her interest in Poland originated while she was still at school, when she participated in a competition in which each entrant had to write an essay on a favourite historical figure. Having chosen to write on Bonnie Prince Charlie, she discovered that his mother, Clementina Sobieska, was Polish and so decided to probe further into Polish history. Subsequently she decided to teach herself Polish and, with the assistance of Edmund Naganowski (1853–1915), a Polish writer and Anglophile who lived in England from 1899 to 1903, became sufficiently proficient to read Polish books.

Monica Gardner began publishing articles on Polish literature and soon became the leading British scholar in the field. Her ability to make full use of critical studies in Polish, already manifest in her first book, *Adam Mickiewicz: the National Poet of Poland* (1911), was the more impressive in view of her complete lack of academic training. She published at least seven more books including *Poland: a Study in National Idealism* (1915), *The Anonymous Poet of Poland: Zygmunt Krasiński* (1919), and *The Patriot Novelist of Poland: Henryk Sienkiewicz* (1926), and many articles and translations. Writing for an audience unfamiliar with the authors under discussion, she did not aspire to scholarly analysis, but as a pioneer introducing Polish literature to the English-speaking public she was unequalled in her lifetime. Although her commitment to the Polish cause was uncompromising and her enthusiasm was said to be 'sometimes bordering on exaltation' (Krajewska, 52), in literary matters she was capable of impartial discernment.

Monica Gardner never married. During the 1920s and 1930s she lived with her brother Edmund Garratt *Gardner (1869–1935), a distinguished scholar of Italian literature, and their mother at 5 Ruskin Close, Meadway, London. Accompanied by Edmund she spent a few weeks in Poland in August and September 1922, visiting Poznań and Cracow. This was probably her only visit to the country to which she devoted her life's work, but there is slender evidence to suggest a second brief visit in 1930. Her house in London was a well-known port of call for Polish visitors, and she corresponded with many prominent Poles, including the statesman Roman Dmowski, the composer Feliks Nowowiejski, the poet Kazimiera Iłłakowiczówna, and the literary historians Wacław Borowy, Julian Krzyżanowski, and Roman Dyboski. In 1927 the cross of officer of the order of Polonia Restituta was conferred on her by the president of the republic of Poland and she was elected to membership of the literary history commission of the Polska Akademia Umiejętności (Polish Academy of Sciences) in Cracow. In appearance she was tall and angular with looks that were distinctive and intelligent but without pretension to either elegance or beauty. She had rather thin wispy hair, which she wore in a bun, kept up precariously by hairpins. Though austere in face and manner, she was neither intolerant nor intimidating. One account describes her as having 'the face of a visionary' (Kuncewiczowa, 121). She looked not unlike Virginia Woolf, to whom she was distantly related.

Following the outbreak of the Second World War in September 1939, and especially after the establishment of the Polish government in London in 1940, Gardner's work acquired a new topicality and she was much in demand. She was working on an English translation of O. Halecki's *History of Poland* (1942). Her family and friends pleaded with her, in view of the German air raids, to leave London, but she refused, asserting that her Polish interests kept her in London and that her literary work was her way of fighting Hitler. 'This is my war work', she used to say. She was killed in the early hours of 17 April 1941 by a German land-mine falling on the house where she was then living at 8 Fellows Road, Hampstead, London. Some of her possessions, including books and manuscripts, were recovered from the ruins by her friend Mary Corbridge-Patkaniowska, who completed the translation of Halecki and saw it through the press, but the manuscript of a book on the poet Juliusz Słowacki, which Monica Gardner was known to have been writing, was never found. The funeral, arranged by the Polish embassy with almost military honours, took place on 23 April in the presence of representatives of the Polish government, including the president. She was buried at Kensal Green Roman Catholic cemetery, London.

GERALD STONE

Sources private information (2004) · priv. coll. of G. Stone, Oxford, Monica Gardner MSS · M. Corbridge-Patkaniowska, 'Monica Gardner', *Slavonic and East European Review*, 23 (1945), 150–52 · S. Helsztyński, 'Anglofil Edmund Naganowski', *Poradnik dla pracowników świetlic żołnierskich*, 8/36 (Aug 1943), 234–5 · M. Kuncewiczowa, *The keys: a journey through Europe at war* (1946) · Z. Krajewska, *Roman Dyboski, 1883–1945* (1968) · Archives of the Polska Akademia Umiejętności, Cracow · G. Stone, 'Z historii

polonistyki angielskiej na przeomie XIX i XX wieku (W. R. Morfill i M. M. Gardner)', *Slawistyka na przełomie XIX i XX wieku* [Warsaw 1987], ed. M. Basaj and others (1990), 91–100 · *Dziennik Polski* [Polish Daily] (23 April 1941)
Archives priv. coll.
Likenesses photograph, 1938, priv. coll. · photograph, c.1939, priv. coll.
Wealth at death £13,066 2s. 5d.: probate, 7 Aug 1941, CGPLA Eng. & Wales

Gardner, Percy (1846–1937), classical archaeologist and numismatist, was born at Wells Street, Hackney, Middlesex, on 24 November 1846, the third child and eldest son of Thomas Gardner, of the stock exchange, and his wife, Ann, daughter of Peter Pearse. Ernest Arthur *Gardner, classical scholar and archaeologist, was his brother and Alice *Gardner, historian, his sister. Gardner described his mother as 'of a high order of intelligence, and pronounced character', and she and his uncles—one an ardent Christian, the other widely read in European literature—were the major influence on his early intellectual development. He was educated at the City of London School which he left at the age of fifteen in order to enter his father's stockbroking business. This work, however, proved uncongenial, and at the end of two years he was released. In 1865 he matriculated at Christ's College, Cambridge, and immediately found his level with undergraduates who had enjoyed a full classical training at school. He had, however, a strong speculative bent and found the Cambridge emphasis on exact scholarship barren and pedantic. In his spare time, almost unaided, he read philosophy, and in 1869 obtained a low first class in the classical tripos and the top first class in the moral sciences tripos. The next year he won the Whewell university scholarship in international law. After a period of depression and uncertainty he was appointed in 1871 assistant in the department of coins and medals at the British Museum, and there he discovered his life's work, the scientific study of Greek coins and art in relation to Greek history. He collaborated with R. S. Poole and B. V. Head in compiling the first of the British Museum catalogues of Greek coins, the volumes for which he was eventually responsible being those on Italy (1873), Sicily (1876), Thrace (1877), the Seleucids (1879), Thessaly to Aetolia (1883), and the Peloponnesus (1887). Other numismatic works of this period included *Samos and Samian Coins* (1882), *The Types of Greek Coins* (1883), a general work based upon his detailed researches, and *A Numismatic Commentary on Pausanias* in collaboration with F. Imhoof-Blumer (1887), in which he revealed the contribution made by coins to the study of texts on ancient sculpture.

Meanwhile, in 1872, Christ's College elected Gardner into a fellowship, which in 1874 he forfeited on his marriage to Agnes (d. 1933), daughter of John Reid and sister of J. S. *Reid. In 1877 he had what was perhaps the most exciting experience of his life when he paid his first visit to Greece, witnessed the progress of the German excavations at Olympia, and saw the newly revealed treasures of Mycenae. Under this stimulus he became an enthusiastic promoter of the Hellenic Society, founded in 1879, and edited the *Journal of Hellenic Studies* from 1880, when he was appointed to the Disney chair of archaeology at Cambridge, until 1896.

In 1887 Gardner was elected to the recently founded Lincoln and Merton professorship of classical archaeology at Oxford, where he lived and worked for the remainder of his long life. A researcher *par excellence* and accustomed while at the British Museum to almost daily contact with the world of international learning and discovery, he was inevitably somewhat impatient of the Oxford of that day, with its concentration on the teaching and formation of youth at the expense of knowledge pursued for its own sake. The story of his early struggles for the admission of archaeology as a subject in the classical schools is told in *Classical Archaeology at Oxford* (1889) and *Oxford at the Cross Roads* (1903). The latter work also contains an eloquent plea for the reinstatement of learning and research as the primary function of a university. Gradually, however, his scholarship, devotion, and energy prevailed. In the university galleries (Ashmolean Museum) he freed the Arundel marbles from modern restoration and proceeded to build up a major collection of casts. With Arthur Evans he established an archaeological library and founded a school of pupils, some of whom became leading archaeologists. His work in the museum, together with that of John Beazley, his successor, determined the university's continuing international reputation as a centre for the study of Greek vase painting, and for the application of archaeology to the problems of history and literature.

Gardner's literary output kept pace with his teaching activities. *New Chapters in Greek History* appeared in 1892, *A Manual of Greek Antiquities* (with F. B. Jevons) between 1895 and 1898, *The Sculptured Tombs of Hellas* in 1896, *The Grammar of Greek Art* in 1905 (republished as *The Principles of Greek Art* in 1914), and *A History of Ancient Coinage 700–300 B.C.* in 1918. He was a most thorough, painstaking, and helpful, if not pre-eminently stimulating, teacher, always conscious of the need to explain his subject to a wider audience. He was no less appreciative of the work of his women, than of his men, pupils, but he remained unrepentantly hostile to the admission of women to full membership of the university.

Gardner's general position as an archaeologist can best be gathered from his last substantial work, *New Chapters in Greek Art* (1926). For him classical Greek art between 600 BC and 300 BC was the ideal norm: on the one hand, he mistrusted any tendency to specialize in prehistoric studies, while, on the other, the great advances in realistic portraiture, historical relief sculpture, and landscape painting made by artists of the Roman age were, in his eyes, little more than degenerate and puerile deviations from the fixed standards of earlier times. By his own admission, his approach to ancient monuments was always more historical than aesthetic, and he feared that the detailed study of artistic style pursued by some of the ablest of his pupils might lead to neglect of the spirit and content of Greek sculptures and vase paintings. But by insisting that archaeological work must always be firmly anchored in historical, literary, and linguistic knowledge he rendered enduring service to the essential unity of classical studies.

Brought up in a devout Christian home, Gardner possessed a strong moral and spiritual nature. In his younger manhood he was much attracted by positivism and asserted that he had read every word of Auguste Comte's exposition of his positivist philosophy. He became increasingly aware, however, of a religious need which positivism failed to satisfy. This religious need was eventually satisfied for him by 'evolutional', not static, Christianity, and the last half of his life was devoted to critical and constructive study and exposition of the Christian religion. This bore fruit in some ten publications between 1899 and 1931, of which the earliest, *Exploratio evangelica* (1899), was undoubtedly the greatest of Gardner's achievements in this sphere. His scientific criticism of religion, united to his strong and practical faith in the supreme value of Christianity both for the individual and for society, gave his religious life a dual aspect which was reflected in his will, in which he gave £200 to Ripon Hall and an equal amount to the Salvation Army.

Gardner was elected an honorary fellow of Christ's College, Cambridge, in 1897 and a fellow of the British Academy in 1903; he was a corresponding member of several continental academies, as well as a member of various foreign archaeological institutions. He retired from his professorship in 1925 and died at 12 Canterbury Road, Oxford, on 17 July 1937. He had no children.

J. M. C. TOYNBEE and H. D. A. MAJOR, rev. JOHN BOARDMAN

Sources P. Gardner, *Autobiographica* (1933) · G. Hill, 'Percy Gardner, 1846–1937', *PBA*, 23 (1937), 459–69 · *CGPLA Eng. & Wales* (1937) **Archives** Bodl. Oxf., corresp. | AM Oxf., academic/administration · BL, corresp. with Macmillans, Add. MS 55128 · Bodl. Oxf., corresp. with J. L. Myres **Likenesses** Elliott & Fry, photograph, 1916, repro. in Gardner, *Autobiographica*, frontispiece · W. Stoneman, photograph, 1917, NPG · D. Smith, photograph, Christ's College, Cambridge **Wealth at death** £10,781 4s. 7d.: probate, 19 Aug 1937, *CGPLA Eng. & Wales*

Gardner [née Cheney], **Sarah** (*fl.* **1763–1795**), actress and playwright, first appeared at Drury Lane Theatre on 1 October 1763 under her maiden name, Miss Cheney, playing Miss Prue in William Congreve's *Love for Love*. A diary entry by the prompter Hopkins recorded: 'a Pretty Figure, play'd with Spirit, very Awkward, & Speaks too much at the top of her Voice' (Highfill, Burnim & Langhans, *BDA*). On 13 January 1764 she played Rose in George Farquhar's *The Recruiting Officer*, and on 20 October 1764 she performed Miss Prue again. She was the original actress to play Mrs Mechlin in Samuel Foote's comedy *The Commissary*, at the Haymarket on 10 June 1765. In the same summer she married William Gardner (*d.* 1790), 'an inferior actor' (Baker, 1.260) at Covent Garden Theatre, where she made her début as Mrs Gardner on 19 October 1765, as Polly in George Colman's *Polly Honeycombe*. On 19 November she played her favourite part of Miss Prue, on 15 March 1766 she was Belinda in George Etherege's *The Man of Mode*, on 15 April Jenny Private in *The Fair Quaker of Deal*, and on 26 April the original Fanny in Thomas Hull's *All in the Right*. In the seasons that followed at Covent Garden

(1767–74) she performed a modest repertory of comic roles, which were not well received by the critics.

However, Mrs Gardner achieved a reputation from working with Foote in his summer companies at the Haymarket (1766–77), acting a variety of roles which included original performances of Foote's plays, such as Margaret in *The Devil upon Two Sticks* (30 May 1768), Mrs Circuit in *The Lame Lover* (22 June 1770), Mrs Matchem in *The Nabob* (29 June 1772), and Mrs Simony in *The Cozeners* (15 July 1774). By all accounts it appears that her reputation degenerated after Foote's death in 1777: 'having had Foote for a teacher she had picked up his mannerisms, and she did not have his genius' (Highfill, Burnim & Langhans, *BDA*), and Colman (the new manager) was asked to 'use some means to prevent Mrs Gardner's *bouncing* and bawling' (ibid.).

Mrs Gardner wrote a comedy, *The Advertisement, or, A Bold Stroke for a Husband*, which was performed at the Haymarket on 9 August 1777. However, there were various difficulties with both Colman and the actors in relation to this performance. The *Morning Chronicle* of 11 August 1777 described the event: 'Her feelings as an author entirely possessed her; in fact, she spoke, walked and moved, as if she had lost her senses'. *The Female Dramatist* has been attributed to Mrs Gardner, and also to George Colman the younger.

By 1777 Mrs Gardner had a young family but was estranged from her husband. She went to the West Indies in 1777 and stayed there until 1781 or 1782. On 13 August 1782 she played Mrs Cadwallader in Foote's *The Author* at the Haymarket, which may have been her first London stage appearance for some years. In 1783 she was in conflict with the managers of the Capel Street Theatre, Dublin, over one of her comedies. John Bernard (who knew her in Dublin) described her as 'a lady of extravagant habits' and as a 'chambermaid actress of great merit' (Bernard, 1.281). According to Bernard, in order to avoid her creditors in Dublin, she arranged a mock illness: 'at noon she was quite dangerous; at evening past recovery, and at night—dead'. The funeral comprised 'a long train of mourners, who carried onions in their handkerchiefs, whilst a lady … two days afterwards was drinking to Mrs Gardner's repose in lodgings near the Strand' (ibid., 1.303–5).

It appears that in 1783 Mrs Gardner gave a series of lectures in Dublin and in Liverpool. She returned to Jamaica in 1785, then travelled to North America, and made her début in New York during November 1789. Her appearance at the Haymarket in *Mrs Doggrell in her Attitudes, or, The Effects of a West India Ramble*, apparently from her own pen, on 22 April 1795 was announced as her first performance since returning from the West Indies. After Everard's benefit in 1795 Mrs Gardner was not heard from again.

ALISON ODDEY

Sources Highfill, Burnim & Langhans, *BDA* · J. Bernard, *Retrospections of the stage*, ed. W. B. Bernard, 1 (1830) · F. Grice and A. Clarke, 'Mrs. Sarah Gardner', *Theatre Notebook*, 7 (1952–3), 76–81 · G. Greene, 'Mrs. Sarah Gardner: a further note', *Theatre Notebook*, 8 (1953–4), 6–10 · D. E. Baker, *Biographia dramatica, or, A companion to the playhouse*, rev. I. Reed, new edn, rev. S. Jones, 3 vols. in 4 (1812)

Likenesses Walker, line engraving (as Lady Plyant in *The double dealer*; after D. Dodd), BM; repro. in *New English Theatre* (1777) · engraving (after Walker), repro. in *Hibernian Magazine* (April 1778)

Gardner, Thomas (*bap.* 1690, *d.* 1769), antiquary, was probably the second of four sons of John Gardner and Mary, his wife (*née* Randall), of Ombersley, near Worcester, baptized there on 3 September 1690. A sibling was baptized Thomas five years later, but no infant Thomas Gardner was buried there in the interim. It seems likely that he was brought up by Thomas Gardner, gentleman, bailiff of Southwold in 1695, who made his will that year and died the next; he and his wife Susan had no children of their own, and the will mentions a living brother John, perhaps John of Ombersley. A letter written to Gardner about 1755 by his elder brother John, then living at Evesham, strongly indicates the Worcestershire origins of the antiquary of Suffolk. It is not known where he received his considerable education; although he was not a graduate, he was a competent Latinist.

On 11 June 1713 at St Michael, Cornhill, London, Gardner married Rachel Redshaw (*bap.* 1693, *d.* 1729), daughter of John Redshaw and his wife, Mary Beck. They had ten children, only four of whom lived to maturity. In London, Gardner trained and practised as an engraver, publishing 100 road maps in the first small-scale edition of John Ogilby's *Britannia*, originally published in 1675, as *The Pocket-Guide for the English Traveller* in 1719. He moved his family back to Southwold by 1726, probably earlier, and there Rachel died, aged thirty-six, on 9 March 1729. Gardner then married Mary Jordan, *née* Millburn, the widow first of John Reeder, then of Jonathan Jordan, who twice had been bailiff of Southwold. Perhaps because they were all from Southwold they chose to be married in Reydon church, to which Southwold was a chapel of ease, on 2 September 1733. Mary was sixty-seven when she died on 3 May 1759. Both marriages advanced Gardner's social standing.

Gardner was collector of the duties on salt at Southwold and from 1748 deputy patent controller of the port in the excise; his cottage in Park Lane in the town still bears an identifying inscription. In 1754 he published *An historical account of Dunwich, antiently a city, now a borough; Blithburgh, formerly a town of note, now a village; Southwold, once a village, now a town corporate*. It was the decline of Dunwich which really intrigued him and was the spur to his writing the book. In the preface he suggests the fate of Dunwich 'will afford speculation sufficient to ruminate on the vicissitude and instability of sublunary things' (*An Historical Account of Dunwich*, 1754, preface). He gathered oral evidence from the oldest inhabitants, and coins, seals, and other antiquities taken away by the sea and eventually washed up on the shingle beach. Looking for written records, he 'found [the town's] archives ransacked of all records except the common court books, and those too close confined for my due inspection' (ibid.). Welcomed by Martin Folkes and introduced by Joseph Ames at a meeting of the Society of Antiquaries in July 1745, he exhibited his treasures, which included the 'true and exact platt' (minute book of the Society of Antiquaries of London, 1745, 5.25) of Dunwich which Radulph Agas drew in 1589;

Ames and Ducarel, whom he met then, later subscribed to his book. The Agas survey was his, and his book includes the accompanying report on the state of the town and harbour; the frontispiece map of Dunwich was drawn by Joshua Kirby from the Agas map but with the 1753 shoreline indicated. Despite the dearth of local records, other antiquaries were generous with help: Thomas Martin lent collections made by Le Neve, and John Revett of Brandeston his own, both including original documents. Gardner was meticulous in giving references. He was churchwarden in 1756, elected bailiff in 1757, and served as chamberlain in 1759 and 1764.

When Gardner made his will he had been a widower again for nearly ten years. He owned eight dwellings and a share in the sloop *John and Sarah*. His property and their rents were shared between his son George Redshaw Gardner (who was childless) and his two widowed daughters. Ten grandchildren shared over £600, and he made provision for their education, and in case another son, William, should return from abroad. He died on 30 March 1769 in Southwold and was buried on 2 April near the south aisle in Southwold church; there his headstone stood between those of his wives with an epitaph based on the first words of theirs:

> Between Honour and Virtue here doth lie
> The remains of old antiquity.

J. M. BLATCHLY

Sources will, of Thomas Gardner, 1695, Suffolk RO, Ipswich, IC/AA1/126/28 · will, 1768, Suffolk RO, Ipswich, IC/AA1/190/20 · minute books, 1745, S. Antiquaries, Lond., 5.25, 25 July 1745 · BL, Le Neve/Thomas Martin Dunwich collections, Add. MS 34653 · BL, John Revett collections, Add. MS 34757 · gravestone, Southwold church, 1769 · parish register, Ombersley, Worcestershire [baptism], 3 Sept 1690 · parish register, Ombersley St Martin, Worcestershire [marriage], 22 April 1684 · parish register (baptism), Southwold, 25 Dec 1683 · parish register (marriage), London, Cornhill, St Michael, 11 June 1713 · parish register (marriage), Reydon, 2 Sept 1733 · IGI · GM, 1st ser., 39 (1769), 215
Wealth at death over £600; plus property and rents: will, 1768, Suffolk RO, Ipswich, IC/AA1/190/20

Gardner, William (1844/5–1887), inventor of a portable machine-gun, was a native of Toledo, Ohio, USA, who as a volunteer during the civil war rose to the rank of captain. In 1874 he designed the first portable machine-gun, but he lacked the capital to develop it and turned the prototype over to Pratt and Whitney, who brought it into production. Although the gun passed the required tests, the United States government declined to purchase it, and Gardner was therefore pleased to accept an invitation to demonstrate his weapon to the British Admiralty. He took part in competitive trials at Shoeburyness firing range in January and February 1881, where his gun was commended. Gardner established a manufactory at 49 Curtain Road in Shoreditch, east London, and produced large numbers of machine-guns for the British army and navy before their adoption of the Maxim gun.

Gardner died suddenly at his home, Henley Lodge, Maze Hill, St Leonards, Sussex, on 20 January 1887, aged forty-two, of delirium tremens, gastritis, and syncope. He left a widow, Sallie Howell Gardner, of whom nothing is known.

ANITA MCCONNELL

Sources G. M. Chinn, *The machine gun*, 1 (Washington, DC, 1951), 79–88 · M. M. Johnson and C. T. Haven, *Automatic Weapons of the world* (1945), 89–90 · 'Result of experiments with machine-guns at Shoeburyness', *Parl. papers* (1881), 20.1–39, no. 223 · *CGPLA Eng. & Wales* (1887) · d. cert. · census returns for Henley Lodge, 1881
Wealth at death £1749 os. 8d.: administration, 29 April 1887, *CGPLA Eng. & Wales*

Gardner, William Linnaeus (1771–1836), army officer, was the eldest son of Major Valentine Gardner (b. 1739), 16th foot. His father was elder brother of Alan Gardner, first Baron Gardner, and served in the 16th foot in America from 1767 to 1782. Gardner's mother was his father's first wife, Alicia, third daughter of Colonel Robert Livingstone of Livingstone Manor, New York. He was brought up in France, and when still a boy was commissioned ensign in the old 89th foot on 7 March 1783; he was placed on half pay on its disbandment some weeks later. He was brought on full pay as ensign in the 74th Highlanders in India on 6 March 1789, and promoted lieutenant in the 52nd foot in India in October 1789. He became captain in 30th foot in 1794, and at once exchanged to half pay of a disbanded independent company.

Of the circumstances under which Gardner retired various stories have been told. All that is known is that he appeared afterwards in India as a military adventurer in the aftermath of the collapse of the Mughal empire when the Marathas were fighting to achieve paramountcy. For some time he was in the service of Jaswant Rao Holkar, the Maratha ruler of Indore. Holkar sent him on a mission to the princes of Cambay, where he married an Indian princess, on whose ancestors the emperors of Delhi had conferred high hereditary honours. Holkar afterwards sent Gardner to treat with Lord Lake, and, suspecting treachery, grossly insulted him on his return. Gardner replied by attempting to cut down the maharaja. Failing, he escaped in the confusion, and reportedly went through a succession of wild adventures. Eventually in 1804 he made his way into Lake's camp disguised as a grass cutter. His wife and her attendants were allowed to depart unmolested from Holkar's camp through her family influence. Gardner served as a leader of irregular horse (captain) under Lake, and in the same capacity (lieutenant-colonel) performed important services under Sir David Ochterlony in Kumaon and Nepal in 1814–15. In the latter connection Gardner (whose name, like that of his father, is spelt Gardiner in many army lists) has been confused by some writers with the first British resident in Nepal, the Hon. Edward Gardiner, Bengal civil service. He also rendered valuable service under Ochterlony in the settlement of Rajputana in 1817–18. He was rewarded in 1822 with an unattached majority in the king's service antedated to 25 September 1803.

Gardner's name first appears in the East India Company army lists in January 1819, as a local lieutenant-colonel commanding irregular cavalry, afterwards described as Gardner's local horse, and as the 2nd local horse, with

which he was stationed at Kasganj in 1819, at Saugor in 1821, at Bareilly in 1821–3, in Arakan in 1825, and at Kasganj again in 1826–7. In January 1828, when the 2nd local horse was again at Bareilly, Gardner is described as on leave, and his name does not again appear in either the British or Indian army list. His regiment was taken on the regular establishment after the mutiny as the 2nd Bengal cavalry, later the 2nd lancers (Gardner's horse).

Gardner resided at Kasganj, his private property near Agra, and died there on 30 July 1836, aged sixty-five. His begum died a month after him. Gardner, a skilled rider and swordsman in his prime, was described in his latter years as a tall, soldierly old man, courteous and dignified, and kind to his ailing wife.

H. M. CHICHESTER, rev. JAMES LUNT

Sources F. Parkes, *Wanderings of a pilgrim, in search of the picturesque*, 1 (1850) · J. Foster, *The peerage, baronetage, and knightage of the British Empire for 1883*, 1 [1883] · *Hart's Army List* · J. Gaylor, *Sons of John Company* (1992) · P. Mason, *A matter of honour: an account of the Indian army, its officers and men* (1974) · C. C. Grey and H. L. O. Garrett, *European adventurers in northern India* (1929) · D. E. Whitworth, *History of the 2nd lancers (Gardner's horse), 1809–1922* (1924) · Burke, *Peerage*
Archives U. Cam., Centre of South Asian Studies, corresp. and papers [copies] | BL OIOC, letters to Edward Gardner, MS Eur. C 304

Gardnor, John (1728/9–1808), painter and Church of England clergyman, of whose family background or education nothing is known, and who does not appear to have married or have had children, is first known as an annual exhibitor at the Free Society of Artists from 1763 to 1769. In 1769 Gardnor gave up his drawing academy in Kensington, where he taught painting, drawing, and calligraphy, and took orders in the Church of England, becoming a curate and then in 1778 vicar of Battersea in Surrey where he remained until his death.

Gardnor is remembered as the author of a book of aquatint prints by various artists with a commentary, entitled *Views Taken On and Near the River Rhine*, published in 1788 and again, in a smaller edition, in 1792. This was based on a journey through France, Germany, and the Netherlands that he made with his nephew (later Major) Richard Gardnor [see below] who, together with his uncle, executed the aquatints. Both the images and the language in the commentary are heavily influenced by the contemporary vogue for the poetry of James Thompson, and the taste for the 'pittoresque' (Gardnor, 30).

Richard Gardnor (fl. 1766–1793), drawing master, appears to have been the pupil of his uncle. He exhibited with the Free Society of Artists in 1766 and at the Royal Academy between 1786 and 1793. His contributions were landscapes and views.

John Gardnor published in 1794 *The History of Monmouthshire*, with aquatints after his own views made by himself and J. Hill and text by David Williams. The initiative for this work was Gardnor's; the diarist Joseph Farington recorded on 22 June 1800 that Gardnor and Williams argued about the profits, 'Gardnor professing to understand that Williams undertook to assist him as *a friend*, the other declaring that he looked for a reward' (Farington,

Diary, 4.1408). Gardnor seems to have had a strong personality, and lost more than one friend as a result; Farington also noted a litigious argument between Gardnor and a neighbour, over a folly in the latter's garden.

From 1778 to 1796 Gardnor exhibited a total of sixty-one paintings and drawings at the Royal Academy as an honorary exhibitor. Gardnor's exhibited paintings reflect his publishing interests after 1788; before this, his subjects are domestic landscapes. He appears to have been on close terms with a number of Royal Academicians, including Richard Hamilton and Paul Sandby, and Farington himself, who procured him a place at the exhibition of 1795. He died in the first week of January 1808, aged seventy-nine, leaving £300 and 'all the furniture of my bed chamber' to his housekeeper, Hannah Black, and almost £1500 to four relatives and a colleague (will). He was buried in Battersea church on 8 January.

L. H. CUST, *rev.* NICHOLAS GRINDLE

Sources J. Gardnor, *Views taken on and near the River Rhine, at Aix-la-Chapelle, and on the River Maese* (1788) · D. Williams, *The history of Monmouthshire ... illustrated and ornamented by views of its principle landscapes, and residences; by John Gardnor, vicar of Battersea* (1794) · Farington, *Diary* · Graves, *RA exhibitors* · will, PROB 11/1472, fol. 26 · Waterhouse, *18c painters*

Wealth at death approx. £1800: will, PRO, PROB 11/1472, fol. 26

Gardnor, Richard (*fl.* 1766–1793). *See under* Gardnor, John (1728/9–1808).

Gardyne, Alexander. *See* Garden, Alexander (c.1585–1642?).

Gardyne, John [Jock] **Bruce-**, **Baron Bruce-Gardyne** (1930–1990), journalist and politician, was born on 12 April 1930 at Hazelwood, Thorpe, Chertsey, Surrey, the second of the three sons of Captain Evan Bruce-Gardyne (*b.* 1885), laird of Middleton, naval officer, and superintendent of the Royal Hospital school, Holbrook, Suffolk, and his wife, Joan, only child of Charles Edward McLaren, barrister, of Rosehill, Alderley Edge, Cheshire. He was educated at Winchester College (1943–8), from where he won an exhibition to Magdalen College, Oxford, which he entered in 1950 after the then compulsory two years national service, in his case in the army. Leaving Magdalen in 1953 with a second-class degree in history he joined the foreign service and in September the following year was posted to Sofia, where he spent most of his time playing bridge—a lifelong passion, second only to fly-fishing—with his opposite numbers from other Western embassies.

Temperamentally unsuited to the caution and dissembling required of a career with the Foreign Office, and soon recognizing, in his own words, that 'life in a gilded cage did not greatly appeal' (unpublished autobiography), Bruce-Gardyne resigned in 1956 to become a journalist, joining the *Financial Times* as a feature writer at a time when it had just embarked on its transformation from a somewhat parochial City news-sheet to the world's foremost economic and business newspaper. Three months later, on the strength of his fluent French, he was sent to Paris, his favourite city, as the paper's first ever full-time

Paris correspondent, where he rapidly made a name for himself with his lucid, well-informed, and penetrating dispatches, written at great speed—a facility he retained to the end of his life. On 24 January 1959 he married Sarah Louisa Mary (Sally) Maitland (*b.* 1932), only daughter of Sir John Francis Whitaker Maitland, of Harrington Hall, Spilsby, Lincolnshire, Conservative MP for Horncastle from 1945 to 1966. There were two sons and a daughter of the marriage. In 1960 Bruce-Gardyne was recalled from Paris to succeed William Rees-Mogg as the editor of the *Financial Times*'s gossip column, 'Men and matters'. This was less to his liking, and in 1961 he left the paper to join the weekly magazine *The Statist*, as its foreign editor (which he was to remain until 1964).

In 1962 the sitting member of parliament for the then safe Conservative seat of South Angus, where the Gardyne family roots had lain since at least the fourteenth century, decided to retire, and Bruce-Gardyne, without any previous political activity of any kind, threw his hat in the ring. To his surprise and delight he was narrowly (if slightly dubiously) selected, and after the general election of October 1964, which brought to an end thirteen years of Conservative government, he found himself, at the very suitable age of thirty-four, in the House of Commons. Effective though he was as an opposition back-bencher, the role provided neither sufficient outlet for his abundant energies nor an adequate income to support and educate his growing family, and in 1966 he accepted the invitation of the newly appointed editor of *The Spectator*, his old friend and former *Financial Times* contemporary Nigel Lawson, to double up as the paper's foreign editor, in which capacity he also contributed a characteristically shrewd column under the pseudonym of Crabro. Meanwhile his parliamentary career quietly progressed. In 1967 he was elected secretary of the Scottish Conservative MPs' group and in 1970, shortly after the Conservatives, led by Edward Heath, had been returned to office in the general election of June that year, he left *The Spectator* on his appointment as parliamentary private secretary to the secretary of state for Scotland, Gordon Campbell.

A Thatcherite before Margaret Thatcher, it did not take long for Bruce-Gardyne to become increasingly disillusioned with the Heath government's economic policies. In 1972, when the government, in one of a series of U-turns, bowed to trade union threats and provided the increased subsidies to the upper Clyde shipyards it had previously refused, he decided he had had enough and resigned as parliamentary private secretary in order to regain his freedom of speech and action—keeping the reason for his resignation private out of a misplaced sense of loyalty which he soon regretted. But his robust free market economic views became increasingly known as he made good use of his new-found freedom, not least by getting himself elected vice-chairman of the Conservative Party's back-bench finance committee.

By 1974, however, a tidal wave of nationalism was engulfing much of Scotland, and in the general election of October of that year Bruce-Gardyne, defending his once safe seat of South Angus, was its most spectacular victim.

He decided to waste no time in returning to the Commons—this time for an English seat—but the process proved to be far more difficult than he had expected, and it was not until March 1979, in the dying days of the Callaghan Labour government, that he was returned in a by-election as member for the ultra-safe seat of Knutsford in Cheshire. He made the best use he could of his enforced absence from the House of Commons, first by rapidly writing a series of books (*Whatever Happened to the Quiet Revolution?*, a perceptive post-mortem on the Heath government, published in 1974; *Scotland in 1980*, a projection of the trend that had cost him his parliamentary seat, published in 1975; and—jointly with Nigel Lawson—*The Power Game*, a highly readable study of decision making in government, published in 1976), and subsequently by returning to journalism: in 1977 William Deedes, the then editor, invited him to become a leader writer on the *Daily Telegraph*, a position he was to occupy (except for a short break as a Treasury minister) until his death in 1990, most of the time coupled with contributing an economic column to its Sunday stablemate.

Despite his considerable qualities and impeccable proto-Thatcherite credentials, Bruce-Gardyne was passed over when the Conservatives, led by Margaret Thatcher, regained office in May 1979. It was not until the watershed reshuffle of September 1981, when the prime minister purged the cabinet of most of the Heathite opponents of her economic policies, that Bruce-Gardyne at long last, seventeen years after first entering the House of Commons, became a minister, as economic secretary to the Treasury (for the first few weeks, until this traditional title was revived for him, he was minister of state). He greatly enjoyed the job, the most junior in the Treasury team, and filled it with distinction; but it was to be his last, as well as his first, ministerial post. For once again he was to lose his parliamentary seat. This time it was at the hands of the boundary commissioners, who decided that his constituency of Knutsford should be abolished and its territory distributed among the five neighbouring constituencies. Bruce-Gardyne hopefully applied to be the candidate for one of these, only to be rejected for lesser men. It must be said that he had not helped himself by imprudently writing to an old friend, Samuel Brittan, at the outset of the Falklands War in May 1982 expressing some scepticism about the wisdom of the enterprise. The letter was stolen from its recipient and, the following month, gloatingly published by the *New Statesman*. This made it easy for his opponents in Cheshire to question his loyalty and even his patriotism.

So, following the general election of June 1983, which saw the Conservatives, led by Margaret Thatcher, returned with a greatly increased majority, Bruce-Gardyne once again found himself ejected from the House of Commons—and, this time, from office, too. The prime minister lost no time in sending him to the House of Lords, where he assumed the title of Baron Bruce-Gardyne, of Kirkden in the district of Angus; but although he was a regular attender and a provocative and witty back-bencher whose interventions were always savoured on both sides of the house, that was effectively the premature end of his political career. He returned to his old trade as a journalist and to writing books—notably *Mrs Thatcher's First Administration: the Prophets Confounded* (1984), an admirable account which presciently concluded with the words 'History's verdict on Mrs Thatcher could yet be that she saved the nation and dished her party. It might be a verdict that all three deserved' (p. 188); and (perhaps his best book) *Ministers and Mandarins: Inside the Whitehall Village* (1986), an outstanding and entertaining ministerial memoir. He also took on a non-executive directorship of the Trustee Savings Bank, in which capacity he was able benignly to watch over its privatization, and—as the father of a deaf child himself—agreed to become an active and energetic vice-president of the National Deaf Children's Society.

In the autumn of 1988 Bruce-Gardyne was struck down with a brain tumour, and despite submitting to all the ghastly forms of treatment the doctors recommended, within eighteen months, on 15 April 1990, he was dead. During that time he went on with his writing, his verve and insight undiminished—and the account he wrote for *The Spectator* of his own fatal illness, with total frankness and without the least trace of self-pity, drove strong men to tears. His funeral took place on 20 April 1990 at St Helen's Church, Aswardby, Lincolnshire. He was survived by his wife and three children.

Bruce-Gardyne was of average height, with a pronounced beak of a nose and (being himself hard of hearing) possessed of an unusually loud voice, in which he would freely give his opinions on the people and issues of the day. Those opinions were always worth listening to, for his views were shaped neither by intellectual fashion nor by sectarian loyalty: they were always his own, always thought through, and frequently prophetic. He combined a generally gloomy approach to public affairs—he was an inveterate pessimist about the likely course of public events and tended to assume the lowest motives for public acts—with an abundance of energy, exuberance, and zest for life, the whole mixture heavily seasoned with wit and supreme irreverence. An endearing eccentric who insisted, even as a government minister, on travelling the streets of central London on a series of battered old bicycles (they were regularly stolen), he was, although somewhat short of tact and at times excessively cynical, devoid of malice and possessed of unshakeable honesty and integrity. With these qualities the relative failure of his political career in conventional terms did not prevent him either from exercising a considerable influence over the political debate of his day or from accumulating an extraordinary number of genuinely devoted friends. It was no surprise that his memorial service in St Margaret's, Westminster, on 6 June 1990 attracted a larger and more sincere congregation than most public figures, far more prominent than Bruce-Gardyne, ever command.

NIGEL LAWSON

Sources J. Bruce-Gardyne, *Ministers and mandarins* (1986) · J. Bruce-Gardyne, autobiography, priv. coll. · *The Times* (16 April 1990) · *The*

Times (26 April 1990) • The Independent (16 April 1990) • Daily Telegraph (16 April 1990) • Financial Times (17 April 1990) • The Guardian (22 April 1990) • K. Leyses, 'Jock Bruce-Gardyne', Magdalen College Record (1990), 84–5 • Burke, Peerage • Burke, Gen. GB • WWW • b. cert. • d. cert. • personal knowledge (2004) • private information (2004)

Likenesses photograph, repro. in The Times (16 April 1990) • photograph, repro. in The Independent • photograph, repro. in Daily Telegraph • photograph, repro. in The Guardian

Wealth at death £373,221: probate, 3 Dec 1990, CGPLA Eng. & Wales

Garencières, Theophilus (1610–c.1680), physician, was born in Paris. After mastering the primer he was made to read The Prophecies of Nostradamus, and retained a love for them throughout his life. He graduated MD at Caen in Normandy in 1636. Garencières came to England with the French ambassador, was incorporated MD at Oxford on 10 March 1657, and admitted a candidate at the College of Physicians, London, on 23 March in the same year. In 1647 he published Angliae flagellum, seu, Tabes Anglica, a work which owed its reputation to the error deduced from its title-page, that it is a treatise on rickets, three years earlier than Francis Glisson's work on the subject. The tabes Anglica of Garencières is pulmonary phthisis, not rickets. In 1665 he published A Mite Cast into the Treasury: the book, dedicated to the lord mayor of London, contains thirty-five aphorisms, and recommends Venice treacle taken early as the best internal remedy for the plague, while poultices are to be applied externally to the glandular swellings. A second edition, enlarged to sixty aphorisms, appeared in the same year, and a third, containing sixty-one aphorisms, in 1666.

While in England, Garencières left the Roman Catholic church, and in 1670 produced The famous conclave, wherein Clement VIII was elected pope: with the intrigues and cunning devices of that ecclesiastical assembly. In 1672 he published The True Prophecies or Prognostications of Michael Nostradamus, Translated, and in 1676 The admirable virtues and wonderful effects of the true and genuine tincture of coral in physick. Ten authors are quoted as praising coral, and it is stated to cure more than thirty separate diseases, but no cases or personal experience are given. Garencières lived for more than ten years in Clerkenwell, and was on friendly terms with Francis Bernard, the apothecary and afterwards physician to St Bartholomew's Hospital. He died poor about 1680. NORMAN MOORE, rev. MICHAEL BEVAN

Sources Wood, Ath. Oxon. • Munk, Roll

Likenesses W. Dolle, line engraving, pubd 1672, BM, NPG, Wellcome L. [see illus.]

Garfield, Leon (1921–1996), writer, was born on 14 July 1921 in Brighton, the younger son of David Kalman Garfield (d. 1951), businessman, and his wife, Rose, formerly Blaustein (d. 1964). He had one brother, David (c.1916–1980). Of Jewish origin, the family lived in Brighton and Garfield was educated at Brighton grammar school (1932–8), followed by a brief period of art studies at Regent Street Polytechnic, London, in 1939. His father, who was unable to pay the fees, arranged for him to work in a London office. This was cut short by the Second World War.

Garfield served as a private in the Royal Army Medical

Theophilus Garencières (1610–c.1680), by William Dolle, pubd 1672

Corps, 1940–46, including time with the war crimes investigation team. He acquired a position with the latter by falsely claiming he was an interpreter to avoid being sent to the Far East. His work included a period at Bergen-Belsen concentration camp retrieving evidence for trial. He married Lena Leah Davies (b. 1918/19), a saleswoman and ARP worker, on 27 April 1941 at Golders Green synagogue. They separated after a few months. During wartime service in Belgium he met his second wife, Vivien Dolores Alcock (b. 1924), a commercial artist and later an established children's writer herself. Garfield divorced his first wife about 1946 and married Vivien Alcock at Hampstead register office, London, on 23 October 1948. They settled in Highgate in north London. His father disapproved of Garfield divorcing his first, Jewish, wife, to marry a non-Jew, and this led to a family rift. This fracture, in what was already a difficult father–son relationship, affected Leon Garfield deeply, and was to surface in his writing. Garfield had trained in biochemistry and haematology during the war, and worked as a biochemical technician at the Whittington Hospital, Islington, north London, from 1946 to 1966. In 1964 the Garfields adopted a baby daughter, Jane Angela.

From 1969 Garfield worked as a full-time writer. His first book, Jack Holborn (1964), a story of adventure and piracy, was originally written as an adult novel. However, in the

Leon Garfield (1921–1996), by unknown photographer, *c.*1980

mid-1960s many promising new children's writers were being published, and Grace Hogarth, an editor at Constable, saw its potential as a children's story. This launched a writing career of three decades and more than thirty published works. In *Devil-in-the-Fog* (1966), which won the first *Guardian* award for children's fiction in 1967, George Treet, from a family of strolling players, searches for his own identity amid conflicting loyalties and surprise revelations. In *Smith* (1967), one of Garfield's best books, a London pickpocket's quest to decipher a stolen document leads him from a life of solitary deception to one of companionship and trust. In the macabre *Black Jack* (1968), in which an apprentice falls under the spell of a survivor of the gallows, Garfield diversified his output.

Garfield's versatility during this period is clear from his collaboration with Edward Blishen on two retellings of Greek myths, *The God Beneath the Sea* (1970), a Library Association Carnegie medal winner in 1971, and its sequel *The Golden Shadow* (1971). Garfield experimented with the ghost story in *Mr Corbett's Ghost* (1968) and the Faustian chiller *The Ghost Downstairs* (1972). He also produced shorter works, such as the series *The Apprentices* (1976–8), a dozen linked stories, beginning with *The Lamplighter's Funeral*, about the sometimes bizarre lives and trades of young Londoners.

The *Apprentice* series, which many critics regard as Garfield's crowning achievement, consolidated many of his themes and techniques. Most of Garfield's children's books, atmospherically illustrated by Antony Maitland, are usually categorized as historical fiction. However, his history is more a matter of impressions than of precise dates and details. His characters are rarely linked to actual historical events but are often to be found in the richly realized miasma of an eighteenth- or nineteenth-century London slum. History in these works is used as an environment in which characters and plots can be developed, and Garfield evokes a sense of period through inventive, expressive language but without recourse to hindsight—this is history as experienced by his characters, with no authorial presence. Themes of relationships, loyalties, and the search for identity recur often. Garfield's own difficult, ambivalent relationship with his father surfaces in various forms. His childhood memories of his father, and his adult revision of that understanding after his father's death, provided a double perspective which influenced the way Garfield wrote about relationships. This can be seen in *Devil-in-the-Fog*, where George's understanding of his father's identity and their relationship shifts and changes in the course of the book. Illusion is also a dominant motif—fathers are absent, or appear in unexpected, sometimes unwelcome guises; villains and criminals may turn into friends and allies, and it is hard to discern the truth in a world of shifting perceptions. For his young heroes the getting of wisdom sometimes begets disillusion but stories generally end on a note of optimism, if not always of tidy closure. Garfield was a natural story-teller. His narratives, richly textured, entertaining, and inventive, demonstrate his command of language and plot.

Although the distinction between 'adult' and 'for children' often broke down in Garfield's novels, his later work was infused with a new, allegorical, often religious tone, most notable in *The Pleasure Garden* (1976) and *The Confidence Man* (1978). Garfield returned to the themes and successes of his early fiction with the Whitbread prizewinner *John Diamond* (1980), a story about a young boy dealing with problems inherited from his swindler father (David Kalman Garfield's lack of success in business, and rumours surrounding his financial dealings, possibly inspired this portrait). In *Blewcoat Boy* (1988) Nick's and Jubilee's fading memories of a real father are exchanged gradually for a new relationship with a substitute father.

In the latter part of his career, however, Garfield moved further away from children's fiction. In 1980 he produced a successful completed version of Charles Dickens's unfinished novel *The Mystery of Edwin Drood*, compounding critical opinion that in the combination of comedy, eccentricity, and tragedy, Garfield was comparable with Dickens. In 1982 he published his only 'adult' novel, *The House of Cards*. His love of Shakespeare resulted in the critically acclaimed *Shakespeare Stories* (1985) and *Shakespeare Stories II* (1994); in the early 1990s he completed scripts for a television series of animated tales from Shakespeare. Garfield was elected a fellow of the Royal Society of Literature in 1985.

Known for his erudition, generosity, and talkativeness (particularly on the subject of Shakespeare), Garfield, who often wore bow ties and velvet jackets, is said to have had a dandified appearance. He died of cancer on 2 June 1996, at the Whittington Hospital, Islington, where he had once worked. He had been preparing a dramatization of *The Odyssey* for BBC radio at the time of his death.

Leon Garfield was one of the most prominent writers for children in the second half of the twentieth century. His novels, fast-paced and full of incident, owe much to the classic adventure story as epitomized by Robert Louis Stevenson. They have also been read and admired by adults, as he intended: he always said he wanted 'to write that old-fashioned thing, the family novel, accessible to the 12-year-old and readable by his elders' (*The Independent*). Several of his novels were adapted for television; *Black Jack* was made into a film directed by Ken Loach (it shared the International Jury award at Cannes in 1979) and the director John Huston made his last appearance in film in *Mr Corbett's Ghost* in 1987.   BELINDA COPSON

Sources R. Natov, *Leon Garfield* (New York, 1994) · D. L. Kirkpatrick, ed., *Twentieth-century children's writers*, 3rd edn (1989) · M. Fisher, *The bright face of danger* (1986), 387–8 · *The Guardian* (June 1996) · H. Carpenter and M. Prichard, *The Oxford companion to children's literature*, pbk edn (1999) · m. certs. · d. cert. · *Daily Telegraph* (4 June 1996) · *The Independent* (4 June 1996)
Likenesses photograph, *c.*1980, Hult. Arch. [*see illus.*] · photograph, repro. in *The Independent*
Wealth at death under £180,000: probate, 21 Aug 1996, *CGPLA Eng. & Wales*

Gargan, Denis (1819–1903), college head, was born in Duleek, co. Meath, in June 1819. He was the second son of Patrick Gargan and Jane Branagan. Destined by his parents for the priesthood, Gargan was sent at an early age to St Finian's seminary, Navan. On 25 August 1836 he entered St Patrick's College, Maynooth, in co. Kildare, where he showed much promise, especially in physics and astronomy. He was ready for ordination before the canonical age. Ordained by Archbishop Daniel Murray on 10 June 1843, he was sent to the Irish College, Paris, where he taught physics and astronomy until 1845.

In 1845 Gargan was appointed professor of humanity in Maynooth, and in 1859 he succeeded Matthew Kelly as professor of ecclesiastical history at the college. In 1885 he was made vice-president of the college, and in 1894 became its president. Two historic events happened during Gargan's presidency, namely, the centenary celebration of the college foundation in 1895, and the visit of Edward VII and Queen Alexandra in 1903. His management of both ceremonies was dignified and impressive. He was chiefly responsible for organizing the construction of the college's chapel and tower. He died at Maynooth on 26 August 1903, after almost sixty years' association with the college.

Though a man of wide and accurate scholarship, Gargan published only two books, *The Charity of the Church a Proof of its Divinity*, a translation from the Italian of Cardinal Balluffi (1885), and *The Ancient Church of Ireland, a Few Remarks on Dr Todd's 'Memoirs of the Life and Times of St Patrick'* (1864).
                        D. J. O'DONOGHUE, rev. C. A. CREFFIELD

Sources J. F. Hogan, *Irish Ecclesiastical Record*, 4th ser., 14 (1903), 481–92 · *The Times* (28 Aug 1903) · J. Healy, *Maynooth College: its centenary history* (1895) · *Freeman's Journal* [Dublin] (27 Aug 1903)
Wealth at death £1760 7s. 4d.: probate, 23 Sept 1903, *CGPLA Ire.*

Gargill, Anne (*b. c.*1625, *d.* in or after **1659**), Quaker and writer, was born in Swine in the East Riding of Yorkshire. It is not known when she became a Quaker; however, in 1659 Katharine Evans, who knew her, told the inquisition in Malta that Anne Gargill before her conversion to Quakerism was a Catholic. Three years earlier Anne herself declared to the inquisition authorities in Lisbon that before her conversion to Quakerism she had not held any kind of belief.

Charles Leslie asserts that when George Fox first went to London in 1654 Anne Gargill 'threw her self upon her Knees, betwixt his Feet; and cry'd out to him, Thou art the Son of the Living God!' and adds that S. B. (who may be the Quaker Susannah Blandford) 'was struck with that Blasphemous Expression' (Leslie, 114). The story was repeated in 1702 by John Stillingfleet in his *Seasonable Advice Concerning Quakerism*, to which the Quaker Daniel Phillips replied in 1703 with *Vindiciae veritatis*. Phillips rejects this story, saying that the Quaker S. B. told him that Anne Gargill 'did not throw her self between G[eorge]. F[ox].'s Feet'. He adds that Anne Gargill 'was a *Ranter*, and reputed as such' before the supposed episode and that 'she was publickly disowned' by the Quakers a 'few Weeks after'. Phillips connects Anne Gargill with the 'Set of Women tinctured with the Spirit of Ranterism' rejected by the Friends, with the exception of James Nayler, who afterwards 'was deluded by them' (Phillips, 40–41). Phillips, who wrote his account about fifty years after the event, is probably wrong in asserting that she was disowned by Friends at that time.

In January 1656 Anne Gargill published the short pamphlet *A Warning to All the World*. Shortly afterwards she went to Plymouth with the intention of travelling to Spain. Her ship reached Lisbon at the end of April. She landed and made her way to the king's palace, but when she discovered that he was not there she returned to the ship. On 2 May two inquisition officials went aboard the ship and spoke with her. Three days later she was taken to the inquisition palace in Lisbon and interrogated. The inquisition decided to release her, fearing that her detention would cause diplomatic problems with England, but ordered her to return to England on the first available ship. In September that year Gargill published *A Brief Discovery of that which is Called the Popish Religion*. In 1659 Katharine Evans and Sarah Cheevers told the Maltese inquisitor that Anne Gargill had founded Quaker congregations in Spain. In a letter dated September 1656 Edward Montague wrote to John Thurloe and mentioned a ship full of Quakers; this could perhaps refer to a further voyage of Anne Gargill in the Iberian peninsula.

In the spring of 1657 Anne Gargill was in Holland. There are several references to her in letters written from Holland by William Ames, William Caton, and George Rofe to London Friends between 1657 and November 1659. From these it is known that she caused discord and dissent in the Quaker community of Amsterdam, that for this reason she was disowned by the Quaker leaders, and that for a short time a small group formed around her. A woman of strong spirituality and keen intelligence (as can be gleaned from her writings and from the reports of the Lisbon inquisition), she was probably opposed to the process of organization of Quakerism that followed James Nayler's entry into Bristol. Nothing is known of her after November 1659. She was unmarried.

STEFANO VILLANI

Sources 'Ana Gargim', Arquivo Nacional da Torre do Tombo, Lisbon, *Inquisição de Lisboa*, no. 13011 · C. Leslie, *The snake in the grass* (1697), 114 · J. Stillingfleet, *Seasonable advice concerning Quakerism* (1702), 17–18 · D. Phillips, *Vindiciae veritatis* (1703), 40–41 · G. Bishop, *New England judged by the spirit of the Lord* (1661), 22–4 · *The journal of George Fox*, ed. N. Penney, 2 (1911), 326, 468n. · W. I. Hull, *The rise of Quakerism in Amsterdam, 1655–1665* (1938), 123, 275–8, 292 · 'Examen Sarah Cheevers, Catherina Evans', Mdina, Archivum Inquisitionis Maltae [Maltese Inquisition Archives], Sezione Processi Criminali, vol. 70 A, caso 3, fols. 23–35 · *A journal of the life of … Will. Caton* (1839), 60–64 · W. Sewel, *Histori van de opkomste, aanwas, en voortgang der Christenen, bekend by den naam van Quakers* (1717), 206 · S. Villani, *Tremolanti e Papisti: missioni quacchere nell'Italia del seicento* (Rome, 1996)

Gargrave, George (1710–1785), mathematician, was born at Leyburn, Yorkshire. He was educated by an uncle, John Crow, a schoolmaster in Leyburn, from whom he acquired a considerable knowledge of the classics and mathematics. His natural bent was towards astronomy, and in later life he was reputedly one of the most proficient astronomers in the north of England. By 1736 he was established as a teacher of writing and accounts in Briggate, Leeds; four years later he was also teaching the use of globes and maps. In 1745 he was employed in Joseph Randall's outstanding academy at Heath, near Wakefield, which at one time had more than 200 pupils. The academy, though of good repute, did not pay, and in 1754 Randall fled, leaving his teachers to shift for themselves.

Gargrave then started at Wakefield a mathematical and commercial school in partnership with Godwin, with such success that in 1768 he retired on a handsome competency. He married on 14 December 1775 Jane Forster of Wensley. Gargrave was a musician of some skill, and his handwriting was remarkably clear and fine. He possessed a large and well-selected library and an excellent collection of astronomical and other scientific apparatus. He contributed to the *Gentleman's Magazine* several astronomical articles and a memoir of the mathematician, mechanic, and astronomer Abraham Sharp, who had been his neighbour; he also left a manuscript treatise on the doctrine of the sphere. Gargrave died at Wensley, Yorkshire, on 7 December 1785 and was buried in Wensley churchyard.

J. M. RIGG, rev. ANITA MCCONNELL

Sources P. J. Wallis, *George Gargrave and his manuscript book* (1970) · *GM*, 2nd ser., 16 (1841), 36–7

Gargrave, Sir Thomas (1494/5–1579), administrator, was born in 1494 or 1495 in Wakefield, the son of Thomas Gargrave and Elizabeth, daughter of William Levett of Normanton. He received a legal education at either Gray's Inn or the Middle Temple, and by 1521 had entered the service

Sir Thomas Gargrave (1494/5–1579), after unknown artist, 1570

of Thomas, Lord Darcy, whom he served as steward until his patron's execution in 1537. After Darcy's disastrous involvement in the Pilgrimage of Grace, Gargrave attached himself to Francis Talbot, fifth earl of Shrewsbury. His administrative acumen earned him a place on the council of the north on the death of Sir Thomas Tempest in 1544, but to his chagrin he received only the reduced fee of £50 instead of 100 marks because he had not yet been knighted. Shrewsbury became president of the council of the north in 1549 and Gargrave's career prospered: it was at his patron's instigation that he received his knighthood the same year. He became a formative influence in the institutional development of the council, of which he became vice-president in 1557, heavily involved in the revision of its operations in 1556 and 1561. The provision of 1561 that the vice-president with one or more of the legal members, a secretary, and pursuivant should always be resident at York enabled the council to develop as a court of summary jurisdiction in both civil and criminal cases.

By this stage Gargrave had established himself as a near-ubiquitous presence in the government of the north, a JP for the West Riding from 1542, and from 1547 for the other ridings; he served on numerous government commissions, and was member of parliament for York in 1547 and for Yorkshire in March 1553, November 1554, and 1555. His influence with Shrewsbury ensured that he acted as a conduit for local concerns, the city of York mobilizing his support on several occasions, 'as ye have always ben … our frend … to our very specyall good lord, the lorde president' (Raine, 5.164). His religious sympathies may have put him at odds with Mary's government, for he offended the queen in the parliament of 1555, possibly for his opposition to the Exiles Bill. Although he complained then that he 'should be so reported in religion' (Bill, 704), his later association with godly archbishops of York suggests that, however strong his service ethic, his sympathies were with the reformed. His election as speaker to Elizabeth's first parliament in 1559 indicates his acceptability to the new regime, and he enjoyed close relations with Cecil. If anything his influence in northern administration was consolidated as he maintained the essential continuity between successive presidents. He continued to represent Yorkshire in the parliaments of 1563, 1571, and 1572. In 1568 the earl of Sussex noted him as 'a great stay for the good order of these parts' (CSP dom., addenda, 1566–79, 60), and he played an important role in stabilizing Yorkshire in the crisis of the following year. Noted as a 'favourer of religion' in 1564, he became increasingly preoccupied with the need for religious conformity in the north as a guarantee of security. He saw the key to stability as lying in the alliance of a godly archbishop and president, and he welcomed the appointments of Edmund Grindal in 1569 and of the third earl of Huntingdon in 1572.

In January 1570 Gargrave suggested to Cecil that parliament should pass a:

stricter law for Religyon & agaynst papysts ... yf any refuce the servyce or communyon, I wold wyshe them convyncyd by opyn disputation in every shyre before Commyssyoners and yf they will not relent to the truth, I wold wyshe them attayntyd in premunire for one yer, and yf they stycke at the yeres end, then to be dethe for herysey or treson.
(Cartwright, 46)

In another letter later in the year he opined that although he disapproved of bloody laws in matters of conscience, nevertheless in Henry VIII's reign 'sharpe lawes kept the evyll quiett and in dew obedyence' (ibid., 50). But he was concerned by the indiscriminate reprisals taken against the participants in the rising of the northern earls, reporting that 'the common people say the poor are both spoiled and executed, and the gentlemen and rich escape' (CSP dom., addenda, 1566–79, 271–2). Gargrave himself was appointed to replace the disgraced Richard Norton as sheriff in 1569–70, leading him to complain to Cecil that he had been forced to take on this onerous charge twice within the space of four years, and begging for some further remuneration from the queen. Although his rewards from Elizabeth were not overwhelmingly generous, he had nevertheless built up a comfortable estate around Wakefield by the time of his death. Residing in the early years of Elizabeth's reign in Kinsley, in 1567 he acquired Nostell Priory from James Blunt, Lord Mountjoy, for £3560. He married twice. His first wife (by 1540) was Anne, daughter of William Cotton of Oxenheath, Kent; his second wife (by 1549), who survived him, was Jane, daughter of Roger Appleton of Dartford, Kent, and widow of John Wentworth of North Elmshall. There was one son from the first marriage, Cotton Gargrave (d. 1588). Gargrave died on 28 March 1579 at Nostell Priory and was buried at Wragby.   IAN W. ARCHER

Sources J. J. Cartwright, *Chapters in the history of Yorkshire* (1872) · J. Hunter, *South Yorkshire: the history and topography of the deanery of Doncaster*, 2 (1831) · *LP Henry VIII*, 3/1.16–21 · *CPR, 1547–78* · *CSP dom., 1553–8*, with addenda, *1547–79* · R. R. Reid, *The king's council in the north* (1921) · HoP, *Commons, 1509–58*, 2.188–9 · N. M. Sutherland and P. W. Hasler, 'Gargrave, Sir Thomas', HoP, *Commons, 1558–1603*, 2.167–9 · A. Raine, ed., *Yorkshire records*, 5–7; Yorkshire Archaeological Society, 110 (1946); 111 (1948); 115 (1950) · E. G. W. Bill, ed., *Calendar of the Shrewsbury papers in the Lambeth Palace Library*, Derbyshire Archaeological Society, 1 (1966) · R. Strong, *Tudor and Jacobean portraits*, 2 vols. (1969)

Likenesses oils, 1570 (after unknown artist), NPG [*see illus.*] · oils, second version, Selby Hall, North Yorkshire

Garioch. For this title name *see* David, earl of Huntingdon and lord of Garioch (1152–1219).

Garioch, Robert. *See* Sutherland, Robert Garioch (1909–1981).

Garland, Alison Vickers (1862–1939), suffragist and political activist, was born on 10 April 1862 at 1 Village Road, Oxton, Cheshire, the daughter of Alfred Stephen Garland, master silversmith, and his wife, Isabella, *née* Priestley. She combined suffragism with an active role in Liberal politics, and lectured on subjects as diverse as bimetallism and infant welfare. It was as a Liberal that she spoke in Devon and Cornwall at meetings of the Central and West of England Society for Women's Suffrage in 1897. In the following year she joined the executive committee of the Union of Practical Suffragists, a ginger group within the Women's National Liberal Federation (WNLF) that aimed to persuade women's Liberal associations not to work on behalf of Liberal parliamentary candidates who were anti-suffrage. In 1899 she was elected president of the Devon Union of Women's Liberal Associations and in December of that year she attended the Indian National Congress held in Lucknow, as a delegate of the British Indian parliamentary committee. While in India she travelled, made speeches, and collected some thousands of pounds for famine relief on the subcontinent, work that she continued on her return to Britain.

In 1904 Garland joined the executive of the WNLF. Her involvement in suffrage societies continued and on 9 February 1907 she participated in the 3000-strong march from Hyde Park to Exeter Hall in the Strand organized by the National Union of Women's Suffrage Societies, and dubbed the 'mud march' because of the state of the demonstrators' clothing at the finish. The decision of the WNLF in 1903 to seek from Liberal parliamentary candidates a commitment to women's suffrage led to the voluntary dissolution of the Union of Practical Suffragists in that year. But when the 'test' question resurfaced in 1905, the decision to disband seemed premature, and in 1908 the Forward Suffrage Union emerged to renew the pressure. Garland was again involved, and represented the group on the suffrage deputation received by Asquith and Lloyd George on 17 November 1911. The deputation sought to persuade the government to give parliamentary time to the Conciliation Bill introduced earlier that year. That bill, however, seemed likely to enfranchise many more Unionist than Liberal women, and Garland showed political realism by proposing instead that an extensive suffrage amendment be included in the government's own Franchise Bill, scheduled for 1912. It was a course of action that Asquith had indicated would have government support, though when it was tried in January 1913 the speaker of the Commons unexpectedly ruled the suffrage amendment out of order, and a settlement of this vexed issue was further delayed.

Garland is sometimes credited (Crawford, 236) with the authorship of a suffrage play, *The Better Half*, which was performed at the King's Hall, Covent Garden, on 6 May 1913 to an audience principally consisting of members of the Actresses' Franchise League. The drama promoted 'the cause' by depicting an imaginary society where only women possessed the vote and could make laws, and where men, supported by some of the women members of parliament, were campaigning for the vote (*The Times*, 7 May 1913, 10). However, both the play, and a novel published in 1888, *By the Tide*, appeared over the name of Alison L. Garland.

Enabled by the 1918 Franchise Act, for which she had so long campaigned, Garland stood for parliament on three occasions. Her best performance was her first, at Portsmouth South in 1918, when she came second to the Conservative, after winning nearly 19 per cent of the vote. But at Dartford, Kent, in 1922 she lost her deposit in a three-way fight, and at Warrington in 1929 she fared no better. The Liberals were specially weak in Lancashire, and Garland, who came last with barely 7 per cent of the vote, again lost her deposit. She nevertheless played an active role in post-war public affairs and at the women's international housing congress at Caxton Hall, in July 1924, identified a lack of tradesmen as a factor in the housing shortage in Britain. 'If you clothe me suitably', she said, 'I will undertake to learn bricklaying in four months', a bold promise that was met with laughter and cheers from the audience (*The Times*, 24 July 1924).

Towards the end of her life Garland played a central role in the affairs of the WNLF, and served as its president from 1934 to 1936. At the annual conference at Scarborough on 17 May 1933 she moved a resolution urging an international solution to the problem of war debts and reparations, which she believed caused the stagnation of world trade. And in her first speech as president, at Kingsway Hall in May 1934, she warned of the dangers of political extremism in England, at a time of fascist and communist dictatorship abroad. This presented both a challenge, and an opportunity, to Liberalism. The possibility of fascist candidates standing in urban constituencies at the next election, she suggested, might take votes away from Conservatives, allowing the Liberals to win seats: 'It was the unexpected that happened in politics. An international situation might arise that would dominate the election, and the Liberal attitude to that situation might sweep the field' (*The Times*, 2 May 1934). Such optimism for her party proved to be ill-founded.

At the WNLF conference at Blackpool in 1935 Garland was re-elected president. The conference gave enthusiastic support to the policies of the 'New Deal' being pursued

in the United States and Garland advocated a similarly positive response to the continued high levels of unemployment in Britain. She followed the line given by the party leadership in recommending a 'prosperity loan' to attract industrial investment: 'This is the brilliant idea of Mr Lloyd George, and we entirely agree' (*News Chronicle*, 22 May 1935, 13c). Garland, who in her day was styled 'a Lloyd George in petticoats' (*The Times*, 9 Dec 1918, ELS 3d), died on 26 September 1939 at her home, 21 Ferndale, Tunbridge Wells, Kent. She was unmarried.   MARK POTTLE

Sources E. Crawford, *The women's suffrage movement: a reference guide, 1866–1928* (1999) · *The Times* (7 May 1913), 10e; (9 Dec 1918), ELS 3d; (24 July 1924); (25 May 1929); (31 May 1929), 7d; (18 May 1933), 9d; (2 May 1934) · *News Chronicle* (22 May 1935), 13c · F. W. S. Craig, *British parliamentary election results, 1918–1949*, rev. edn (1977) · P. Rowland, *The last liberal governments: unfinished business, 1911–1914* (1971) · b. cert. · d. cert.
Wealth at death £3428 13s. 8d.: probate, 10 Jan 1940, CGPLA Eng. & Wales

Garland, Augustine (*bap.* 1603, *d.* in or after 1677), regicide, son of Augustine Garland (*d.* 1637/8), attorney, of Coleman Street, London, and his first wife, Ellen (*bap.* 1579), daughter of Jasper Whitteridge of London, was baptized on 13 January 1603 at St Antholin's, Budge Row, London. In 1618 he was admitted a pensioner of Emmanuel College, Cambridge, and became a member of Lincoln's Inn in 1631. Four years later Garland was among the ringleaders of a riot got up by the students of the inn in defence of one of their number who had recently been expelled. The controversy, which led to Garland's detention in the prison of king's bench, did not, however, seriously damage his career prospects, and he was called to the bar in 1639.

By the death of his father Garland succeeded to some property in Essex at Hornchurch and Waltham Holy Cross, and at Queenborough in the Isle of Sheppey. In his account of himself at his trial Garland says: 'I lived in Essex at the beginning of these troubles, and I was enforced to forsake my habitation. I came from thence to London, where I behaved myself fairly in my way' (*Trials of the Regicides*, 264). On 26 May 1648 Garland was elected member for Queenborough in place of Sir Edward Hales, second baronet, expelled. Garland later claimed to have withdrawn from the Commons in the wake of Pride's Purge. However, he was clearly present on 20 December 1648, when he signed the protest against the acceptance of the king's concessions. He was appointed one of the king's judges, and acted as chairman of the high court of justice at its first meeting on 8 January 1649. On 13 January he reported the recommendation of a committee of the court that the trial take place in the great hall at Westminster. 'I could not shrink for fear of my own destruction', pleaded Garland at his own trial. 'I did not know which way to be safe in anything—without doors was misery, within doors was mischief' (ibid., 265). He attended seventeen meetings of the court, was present when sentence was given, and signed the death warrant [*see also* Regicides].

Garland continued to sit in the Long Parliament until its

expulsion by Cromwell. At Westminster, Garland attended more debates than anyone other than the speaker and toiled incessantly over the drafting of legislation. He is also credited as having been in the van of 'republican' reformists. Sitting for Queenborough once more in the lord protector's first parliament, he is said to have moved a motion to offer Cromwell the crown. That his proposal fell without a division may have told Garland all he needed to know about the influence of the army officers over the new constitution, and he subsequently withdrew from public life. He was recalled to his place in the restored Long Parliament in May 1659.

On 9 May 1660 Garland appeared before the lord mayor of London and claimed the benefit of the king's declaration. Nevertheless he was put on his trial, and on 16 October 1660 condemned to death. Besides his share in the trial he was accused of spitting in the king's face as Charles was led away from Westminster Hall after being sentenced. Garland strenuously denied the charge, saying, 'If I was guilty of this inhumanity I desire no favour from God Almighty' (Trials of the Regicides, 264). The death sentence was not put into execution, but Garland's property was confiscated, and he was kept prisoner in the Tower of London. A warrant for his conveyance to Tangier was issued on 31 March 1664. He was still there on 16 September 1676, when he was ordered to be brought from Tangier to Plymouth, the order being repeated on 3 February 1677, according to which he was to be brought to Southsea Castle and imprisoned there, 'upon account of his contributing to the many present disagreements and animosities' at Tangier (Tanner, 4.399). Joseph Williamson, secretary of state, was directed to provide a warrant for Garland's reception at Southsea, but Garland's eventual fate is unclear.   C. H. FIRTH, rev. SEAN KELSEY

Sources DNB · W. P. Baildon, ed., The records of the Honorable Society of Lincoln's Inn: the black books, 2 (1898), 327–9, 350 · J. G. Muddiman, The trial of Charles I [1926] · D. Underdown, Pride's Purge: politics in the puritan revolution (1971) · B. Worden, The Rump Parliament, 1648–1653 (1974) · Trials of the regicides (1660) · J. Nalson, A true copy of the journal of the high court of justice, for the tryal of K. Charles I (1684) · M. Noble, The lives of the English regicides, and other commissioners of the pretended high court of justice, appointed to sit in judgment upon their sovereign, King Charles the First, 2 vols. (1798) · C. Walker, The compleat history of Independency (1661), vol. 2, p. 48 · CSP dom., 1663–4, 536 · Cobbett, Parl. hist., 21.375 · parish register, London, St Antholin's, Budge Row, 13 Jan 1603 [baptism] · IGI · PRO, PROB 11/176, fols. 67r–67v · PRO, PROB 11/176, sig. 9 [Augustine Garland, father] · private information (2004) [R. Ollard] · J. R. Tanner, ed., A descriptive catalogue of the naval manuscripts in the Pepysian Library at Magdalene College, Cambridge, 4, Navy RS, 57 (1923), 351, 399, 403

Garland, John of (b. c.1195, d. in or after 1258), grammarian, lexicographer, and poet, was born in England, in a place he calls by its Latin name Gingia, perhaps Ginge in the Wantage hundred in Berkshire.

Education and career Garland studied at Oxford University under one John of London about 1210–13, which would suggest a birth date c.1195, and probably took up residence in Paris shortly thereafter, taking his surname, as he relates in both Parisiana poetria and Exempla honestae vitae, from the clos de Garlande where he lived and taught.

Though there is no record of it, he may have earned the degree of master of arts at Paris. He was chosen in 1229 to be master of grammar in the new university in Toulouse, but returned to Paris in 1232, and probably stayed there for the rest of his life, teaching grammar and literature at the university and writing, though he made at least one trip to England. He lived at least until 1258, the date of Exempla honestae vitae. Virtually all that is known about the details of his career comes from obiter dicta in his poems. He achieved a certain stature in his day; this is clear from the appointment in Toulouse, from the number of significant people with whom he was acquainted, from his own reports of public recognition accorded his work, and perhaps above all from the modest yet unmistakable air of authority with which he speaks about his work and about literary issues. His works were copied widely, and were still being copied in the fifteenth century; a few were printed.

Lexicographic and grammatical work Garland's earliest work was lexicographic, the prose Dictionarius (c.1218, revised c.1230), which he says he wrote pene puer pueris ('for boys though almost a boy himself'). Its title is the first recorded use of the word 'dictionary'. It helps boys learn the Latin names of things by grouping them by topic. He accompanied it with a commentary, and the result is still of interest for what it reveals not only about Latin vocabulary but about Garland himself and social practices. With it belong the much later Commentarius (1246), a similar work in prose devoted to the details of noble life; Unus omnium, a poem of just over 3000 hexameters on derivatives and compounds; and works on deponent verbs, composite terms, words with defective endings, homonyms, synonyms, and equivocal terms, although his authorship has not been clearly established in every case.

Garland's major grammatical work is the Compendium grammatice (probably c.1230), a complete treatment of Latin grammar in over 4000 hexameters, meant to rival and correct the widely used Graecismus of Eberhard de Béthune and Doctrinale of Alexandre de Ville-Dieu (of which he also published a revised version), and drawing numerous examples of usage from the works of the Roman writers Virgil, Horace (including the Odes and Epodes), Ovid, Juvenal, Persius, Lucan, Statius, Terence, and Claudian; the Compendium grammatice bears out Garland's commitment to making the classical authors the basis of instruction. He also wrote a key to it, the Clavis compendii (probably c.1234), itself extending to more than 2300 hexameters. Finally, in 1246–9, to supplement these he wrote the Accentarium, or Ars lectoria ecclesie, in 1560 hexameters, treating quantity and accent, and not simply for their importance in ecclesiastical services. Throughout he relies rather deftly on the hexameter line to indicate quantity. In all three works Garland regularly denounces Eberhard's and Alexandre's shortcomings, though apparently without convincing many, since these two works continued to hold the field. None of these works is edited; Lester Born's articles indicate that he prepared editions of all three, but they were never published.

John of Garland's grammatical writings display a strong

commitment to the liberal arts in general and to poetry in particular, at a time when logic and dialectics were gaining ascendancy in the university curriculum. The commitment to poetry is evident in his *Parisiana poetria* (*c*.1220, revised *c*.1235), a composition book that covers prose but is largely devoted to poetry, both quantitative and accentual, and is filled with original poems as examples, including a 'tragedy' in which jealousy arises between two washerwomen confined in a castle under siege with sixty soldiers; one kills the other and her lover, then to hide the crime lets in the enemy, who proceed to kill all the sleeping soldiers. Since tragedies are hard to come by in the middle ages, this poem has attracted some attention, as have various of Garland's doctrines, particularly his remarks on levels of style, on genres, and on accentual verse. With the *Parisiana poetria* may be grouped Garland's last known poem, dated from internal evidence to 1258, *Exempla honestae vitae*, in elegiacs, which combines rhetorical with moral instruction by couching moral advice for a young friend in the complete set of the figures of words and thought laid out in the *Rhetorica ad Herrenium*. He had earlier done a similar thing in the *Poetria*, and indeed some couplets from there reappear here.

Poems The truest measure of Garland's commitment to literary art is provided by the major poems: the *Stella maris* (1248–9), which recounts sixty-one miracles of the Virgin in 192 rhyming stanzas; three works in hexameters: *Georgica spiritualia*, an early poem (probably *c*.1215) of which only fragments survive, which superimposes Alain de Lille on Virgil and the Bible in order to treat the ploughing of the soul—a tradition of spiritual agriculture not irrelevant to *Piers Plowman*; *Morale scholarium* (1241), a satiric poem meant (naïvely enough) to improve the behaviour of students; and *De mysteriis ecclesie* (1245), which explains the allegorical significance of various rites, hymns, prayers, and sacred objects, including the parts of a cathedral; and three in elegiacs, the form in which he seems to have been most at home. Of these there is the short *Integumenta Ovidii* (probably written before 1241), which offers allegorical interpretations of various figures and stories in the *Metamorphoses*; and two poems so ambitious that they can only be called epics.

The earlier of these is the *Epithalamium beatae Mariae Virginis* (or *Virginis Mariae*), which Garland clearly considered his masterpiece. He recited it before a group of scholars and dignitaries, including the bishop of Paris, at its completion in 1221, and a copy of it was chained to the altar in the church of St Julien-le-Pauvre. George Rigg has called it 'a superb example of the allegorical epic' (Rigg, 171). It is written in the tradition of Martianus Capella's *De nuptiis Mercurii et Philologiae*, Bernard Sylvestris's *De mundi universitate*, and Alain de Lille's *Anticlaudianus*, and it depends for its key idea on the allegorical interpretations of the Song of Songs as celebrating the mystic marriage of Christ and Mary. Its aim is to praise the Virgin, but at the same time to teach theology, canon law, and the liberal arts. Its epic plot is that of salvation history: mankind is redeemed from sin by means of the mystic marriage of Christ and the church, of which Mary is the mystical type,

or of Christ and the human soul, of which she is also the type. Garland clearly saw himself

> as one in a direct line which begins with Homer and Virgil and extends unbroken to the twelfth century in Bernard Sylvester and Alan of Lille. He saw in the *De mundi universitate* … an epic of the Creation, and in the *Anticlaudianus* … an epic of the Incarnation; and he intended, doubtless, to make the *Epithalamium* an epic of the Virgin, the third of a trilogy. (E. F. Wilson, 'Study of the epithalamium', 219–20)

The extent of secular material in the poem, and its influence on such romantic conventions as the love court, have also been emphasized. A. Saiani published in 1995 a complete and magisterial edition of the poem, including in his thorough introduction a nuanced exposition of the deep cultural connections between Garland and Dante.

John of Garland's second epic is *De triumphis ecclesie*, completed in 1252, a celebration in eight books of the victories of the church in the crusades: *Arma crucemque cano*, he announces boldly in the eleventh line. It spends almost as much energy denouncing heretics and infidels as celebrating the victories of the faithful. Since it has survived in only one manuscript, it seems not to have reached the wide audience Garland no doubt hoped for, and its literary interest is indeed smaller than that of the *Epithalamium*, but it has historical value because of the firsthand information it offers about the Albigensian wars.

For a long time Garland was thought to be the same Johannes de Garlandia who wrote several important treatises on music. In 1972, however, Erich Reimer studied all the evidence and concluded that evidently two men called John of Garland were teaching simultaneously in the early and middle decades of the thirteenth century in the clos de Garlande (where the faculty of arts had been located since 1213), one the musician and one the grammarian.

Reputation, death, and assessment Garland's frequent mention in his poems of English personages suggests that he maintained a strong interest in the country of his birth, and the number of manuscripts of his work in English collections indicates that his country was interested in him. There are at least thirty manuscripts in England that contain one or more of his works, of which three are particularly important: BL, Cotton Claudius A.x, the unique copy of *De triumphis ecclesie* and the most complete of the four copies of the *Epithalamium* (of which two others are also in England); Cambridge, Gonville and Caius College, MS 385, which has the three major grammatical works, the *Commentarius* and *Dictionarius*, and *De mysteriis ecclesie*; and Lincoln Cathedral Library, MS 132, which has the last two works plus the *Accentarium*. The fullest resource for the study of John of Garland, however, is the richly glossed anthology of his work, MS 546 of the public library in Bruges. It includes, in this order, *Morale scholarium*; *Dictionarius*; *Clavis compendii*; *De mysteriis ecclesie*; *Ars lectoria ecclesie*; *Commentarius*; *Stella maris*; *Compendium grammatice*; and *Parisiana poetria*. The last two long works take up half the book of 174 folios. It may well have once had a companion volume, like Cotton Claudius A.x, containing the *Epithalamium* and *De triumphis ecclesie*. Since many of the glosses seem to be by Garland himself, and many show a grasp of certain poems that only the author could have, the anthology must have been put together by John himself or one of his students. It seems clear that he lectured on his own works—he says in the *De triumphis* that he lectured on the *Epithalamium* in Toulouse—'Virgine de sacra sponsalia carmina legi'—and that he thought of his poems as extensions of his teaching vocation, and his students as his prime audience. Though various scholars have examined this manuscript, a patient reading of all the glosses has yet to be made; it may reveal more biographical information about this not altogether private author.

The date of Garland's death is unknown. It may have been not long after 1258, the date of *Exempla honestae vitae*. Roger Bacon in 1272, correctly insisting that the word for brass in Latin is *orichalcum*, not *auricalcum*, said that of the many who wrote the latter 'Magister Johannes de Garlandia vituperavit omnes, sicut ego ab ejus ore audivi' ('Master John of Garland has denounced them all, as I have heard from his own mouth'; Bacon, 453). Paetow, claiming, apparently on the basis of the present perfect tenses, that the words 'distinctly give one [the] impression' that Garland was still alive, says, 'Tentatively we may say that John of Garland probably was still alive in Paris about 1272' (*Morale scholarium*, 96). But this is not an inevitable interpretation, and fourteen years of silence are virtually unthinkable for him; it seems equally probable that he died soon after completing the *Exempla*.

In some respects, John of Garland's significance is slight. His hope to replace the grammar texts of Eberhard and Alexandre with his own was vain. If he ever wished to equal Alain de Lille (whom he greatly admired) in poetry, he failed there as well—though Saiani's devoted labours on the *Epithalamium* may bring at least those who can still read the *Anticlaudianus* to read it as well, and they will find much to admire. Similarly, the grammatical and lexicographical works are filled with interest for the student of the Latin language. The rhymed stanzas of the *Stella maris* share in the charm that all medieval rhymed poetry continues to exert. And the *Poetria* remains one of the richest sources for knowledge of how medieval poets thought about their craft. If nothing else, the part Garland played in the tradition inherited by Dante would give him a valued place in literary history. His work is of immense value in the history of education; the glossed manuscripts of his works in particular evoke the atmosphere of the medieval classroom. Finally what is to be valued is the life and urgency of the poetic voice; pedant though he was, Garland put himself and his passions, convictions, and experience of reading and teaching into his poems, and their vitality is still to be felt. TRAUGOTT LAWLER

Sources '*Morale scholarium*' *of John of Garland*, ed. L. J. Paetow (1927) · Giovanni di Garlandia, *Epithalamium Beate Virginis Marie*, ed. A. Saiani (Florence, 1995) · E. F. Wilson, 'A study of the epithalamium in the middle ages: an introduction to the *Epithalamium Beatae Mariae Virginis* of John of Garland', PhD diss., U. Cal., 1930 · E. F. Wilson, 'The *Georgica spiritualia* of John of Garland', *Speculum*, 8 (1933), 358–77 · *The 'Stella maris' of John of Garland*, ed. E. F. Wilson, Mediaeval Academy of America (1946) · L. K. Born, 'The manuscripts of the major grammatical works of John of Garland: *Compendium grammatice, Clavis compendii, Ars lectoria ecclesie*', *Transactions and Proceedings of the American Philological Association*, 69 (1938), 259–73 · T. Hunt, *Teaching and learning Latin in thirteenth-century England*, 3 vols. (1991) [incl. edns of *Dictionarius* and *Commentarius*] · Johannes de Garlandia, *De mensurabili musica*, ed. E. Reimer, 2 vols. (Wiesbaden, 1972) · G. L. Bursill-Hall, 'Johannes de Garlandia—forgotten grammarian and the manuscript tradition', *Historiographia Linguistica*, 3 (1976), 155–77 · A. G. Rigg, *A history of Anglo-Latin literature, 1066–1422* (1992) · *The 'Parisiana poetria' of John of Garland*, ed. T. Lawler (1974) · E. Habel, 'Die *Exempla honestae vitae* des Johannes de Garlandia: eine lateinische Poetik des 13. Jahrhunderts', *Romanische Forschungen*, 29 (1911), 131–54 · John of Garland, *De mysteriis ecclesiae*, ed. F. W. Otto, *Commentarii critici in codices Bibliothecae Academicae Gissensis* (1842), 131–51 · John of Garland, *De triumphis ecclesiae*, ed. T. Wright, Roxburghe Club (1856) · R. Bacon, *Compendium philosophiae*, ed. J. S. Brewer, vol. 3 of *Rogeri Bacon opera quaedam hactenus inedita*, Rolls Series, 15 (1859)
Archives BL, Cotton MS Claudius A.x · Gon. & Caius Cam., MS 385 · Lincoln Cathedral, MS 132 · Public Library, Bruges, MS 546

Garland [*née* McHarg], **Madge** (1898–1990), fashion journalist and teacher, was born on 12 June 1898 in Melbourne, Australia, third child of Andrew McHarg, international shipper, and his wife, Henrietta Maria Aitkin. Brought up in St John's Wood in London, she was sent to the International School in Paris in 1912 and this initiated her interest in travel, French art, and fashion. Her family prevented her from completing her degree course at Bedford College, London, but she fought against their attempts to restrain her ambitions and left home at twenty-one. She progressed from Fleet Street errand girl to assisting *Vogue* fashion editor Dorothy Todd in 1922. Todd was turning *Vogue* into a champion of avant-garde art and literature, with Aldous Huxley and Raymond Mortimer on the staff. Garland honed her skills, as well as developing friendships with Virginia Woolf, whom she advised on clothing, Rebecca West, and Ivy Compton-Burnett. However, in 1926 Todd was sacked, as *Vogue's* management wanted to change direction to focus more closely on fashion. Garland left, spending the next two years as a successful freelance writer for New York's influential *Women's Wear Daily*, and in 1928–32 writing the *Illustrated London News*'s women's section, while also contributing to *Eve* and *Britannia*.

Garland returned to *Vogue* (1932–41), but spent most of the Second World War at the London department store Bourne and Hollingsworth, where she became an excellent businesswoman. She advised the British fashion industry in various capacities, helping to form the London Fashion Group and going on a government-sponsored trip to Paris in 1947 to buy 'new look' accessories for British manufacturers to copy. She continued to act as consultant to fashion firms, notably West Cumberland Silk Mills, who benefited from her expertise in colour and texture.

In 1948 Garland was made the Royal College of Art's first professor of fashion, as part of the scheme of the principal, Robin Darwin, to reinvigorate the college. Although not from a design background herself, Garland, an expert publicist, was able to develop a groundbreaking course, bringing together a teaching staff from diverse aspects of the industry. She studied American teaching methods and

Madge Garland (1898–1990), by Sir Cecil Beaton, 1927

used these as a basis to set up the college's School of Fashion, while maintaining and exploiting her connections within the fashion world. She fought for fashion to be taken seriously within the art school context, and demanded high standards from her students, whom she expected to dress smartly, read widely, and develop a sharp critical eye to produce designs appropriate to the contemporary market. She responded to British consumers' changing needs, especially to the newly growing youth market, which demanded new types of fashion. She presided over the end of year fashion show, inviting fashion insiders as well as college staff to raise the profile of the course and expose her students, who included Gina Fratini and David Sassoon, to potential employers. She was determined to raise fashion design above the status of dressmaking and when she handed over her title to Janey Ironside in 1956, the course's reputation was cemented. After her retirement she wrote a series of popular books about fashion, as well as travelling widely. Always impeccably dressed, she retained the hauteur of a *Vogue* editor. Ironside described her in her autobiography as an imposing figure, very well groomed and clad in couture by Michael, Balenciaga, or Balmain. Her marriages, to Captain Ewart Garland in 1922 and Sir Leigh Ashton (1897–1983), director of the Victoria and Albert Museum, London, in 1953, both ended unhappily in divorce, but she was surrounded by friends and remained active until well into her eighties. In her final years she was cared for in a convent and died in London on 15 July 1990.

REBECCA ARNOLD

Sources J. Ironside, *Janey: an autobiography* (1973) · 'Madge Garland, British fashion editor', *Annual Obituary* (1990), 424–6 · D. Scarisbrick, 'Artist in life of fashion', *The Guardian* (19 July 1990), 39 · H. Spurling, *The Independent* (17 July 1990), 30 · *The Times* (18 July 1990), 14 · M. Garland, 'Artifices, confections and manufactures', in R. Moynihan and others, *The anatomy of design: a series of inaugural lectures by professors of the Royal College of Art* (1951) · C. Frayling, *The Royal College of Art: one hundred and fifty years of art and design* (1987) · G. Howell, *In Vogue: sixty years of celebrities and fashion from British Vogue* (1978) · A. McRobbie, *British fashion design: rag trade or image industry?* (1998) · *CGPLA Eng. & Wales* (1991)

Likenesses E. Wolfe, portrait, 1926, Geffrye Museum, London · C. Beaton, photograph, bromide print, 1927, NPG [*see illus.*] · M. Laurencin, oils, 1937

Wealth at death £142,751: probate, 26 Feb 1991, *CGPLA Eng. & Wales*

Garland, Will (b. 1878, d. after 1938), theatrical entertainer, was born in Keokuk, Lee county, Iowa, USA, on 30 December 1878. Little is known of his early life. He worked in Cuba from 1899 to 1900 in a band directed by composer William C. Handy, who recalled him in his autobiography, *Father of the Blues* (1941). Following the success of *In Dahomey*, a review that took London by storm in 1903, Garland moved to England, where by October 1906 his *A Trip to Coontown* was touring the Empire Theatre circuit. Most of 1907 was spent in Germany, and continental touring took Garland and his troupe, numbering eighteen to thirty, to Hungary, Austria, France, Russia, and Belgium into 1910. Managing a song-and-dance troupe had additional problems when the billing was 'coloured': illness or resignation caused recruitment problems, for the black population of Europe was far from numerous. Garland's Negro Operetta Company, which toured from London far into imperial Russia, in 1913 numbered six black Americans, and three black and five white British. Their contact in London was the daughter of the Sierra Leonean author and doctor Africanus Horton.

Britain's entertainment press detailed Garland's *A Trip to Coontown* in Dublin in May 1915, then in London, Aldershot, Manchester (now as *In Dahomey*), and Bury into 1916. His *Coloured Society* was reported in Cowdenbeath, Lancashire, Newcastle, and Birmingham through to 1917, when it appeared in Wolverhampton, Liverpool, Lancashire, and suburban London. His *All Black* show appeared in 1917 and early 1918. Little is known of Garland's further movements until 1921, when *All Black* appeared in Salisbury, Weymouth, and Norwich, with Christmas at Portsmouth 'with 25 Coloured Performers and A Chorus of Creole Belles' (*Portsmouth Evening News*, 12 Dec 1921). Garland, and the popular success of his *Coloured Society*, angered the Actors Association, which in 1922–3 unsuccessfully sought police investigation.

Down South took Garland to the Netherlands in 1923. In 1924, after a week at the Granville in Walham Green, west London, he went to Germany, where he recorded two discs, the rare survivor exhibiting a quintet of genuine African-American singing. In late 1925 he took *Coloured Lights* to the Hammersmith Palais, London. The summer of 1926 was spent in Switzerland, followed by months touring Britain. A problem faced by Garland was that continental touring took him far from his base, and as absence became lengthy, memories faded among employers and managers. His base was in London, where, with his second wife, Rosie, he kept in contact with newcomers. He knew of American imports, such as *Blackbirds*, and from 1927 his *Brownbirds* toured Britain, presenting a mixture of popular song, the latest American dances, jazzy music, and comedy. The American theme of Garland's song-and-dance shows was again evident in *Down South* (1936) and *Brownbirds, 1937*, which was billed as 'all-American'.

The Garlands knew many black people in Britain in the 1920s and 1930s: the singer Evelyn Dove (whose father was a barrister from Sierra Leone, and whose brother was a war hero and Oxford graduate), the pianist Lilly Jermott (born in Cardiff of a Barbados father), the singer–trumpeter Arthur Dibbin (another black from south Wales), the Jamaican former military band musician Leslie Thompson, fellow American singer John C. Payne, and Charlie Woods (a Londoner) and his wife, Aurora Groves (from Wales).

The files of the BBC contain *Mississippi Nights*, a radio programme broadcast on 8 May 1938, in which Garland led the choir in 'My Old Kentucky Home'. Colleagues included Payne, Rollin Smith (who had worked with Louis Armstrong), and Ida Shepley, the English-born daughter of a west African, whose radio career developed in the 1940s. That this radio programme was preserved when almost all others of the era were not suggests that the show was regarded as valuable. In the summer of 1938 a Garland show was billed at the Empire Theatre, Woolwich (southeast London), but after that nothing further is known of him.

In an age when people of African birth or descent were widely regarded as inherently inferior and lacking leadership or skills, opportunities provided by Garland gave hope to British-born black people. The shows he presented amused the masses, and simultaneously revealed qualities that deserved respect. That he earned a living in the entertainment business shows that he was a skilled operator. That major theatrical chains employed him over decades reveals that he had a solid professional approach. Aided from the 1920s by his English wife, Rosie, he managed to be successful in a highly volatile business.

JEFFREY GREEN and RAINER E. LOTZ

Sources US passport office, Washington, DC · R. E. Lotz, *Black people: entertainers of African descent in Europe, and Germany* (Bonn, 1997), 199–223 · *Mississippi nights*, BL NSA, BBC sound archive, T.86218, reel 1 · R. E. Lotz, 'Will Garland's Negro Operetta Company', *Under the imperial carpet: essays in black history, 1780–1950*, ed. R. E. Lotz and I. Pegg (1986), 130–44
Archives SOUND BL NSA, BBC sound archives, T.86218, reel 1 · priv. coll., Lotz Collection, 1924 recording
Likenesses two photographs, *c.*1906–1914, repro. in Lotz, *Black people*, 102, 205

Garment, Joshua (*fl.* 1631–1660). *See under* Robins, John (*fl.* 1641–1652).

Garneau, François-Xavier (1809–1866), poet and historian of Canada, was born on 15 June 1809 at Quebec, Lower Canada, the eldest of the four children of François-Xavier Garneau (1781–1831), successively a saddler, carter, captain of a merchant schooner, and innkeeper, and Gertrude Amiot-Villeneuve (1781–1835), the daughter of François Amiot, called Villeneuve, and Louise Drolet. After receiving his primary education at a local school, from 1821 to 1823 he attended the Lancastrian school of Joseph-François Perrault, a prominent teacher, and from 1823 worked as an assistant to Perrault, who was also clerk of

the court of king's bench. In 1825 Garneau began acting as clerk to the leading notary at Quebec, Archibald Campbell, and in 1828 Campbell enabled him to travel for two months in Upper Canada, Acadia, and the northern United States, where he observed American democracy in action. Garneau obtained his notary's licence on 23 June 1830 but continued to act as clerk to Campbell until 1831, when he travelled to London and to Paris. He observed approvingly the first anniversary celebrations of the revolution of 1830 in France, and in London he acted as secretary to Denis-Benjamin Viger, agent of the Lower Canadian house of assembly, and was introduced to various prominent British and Canadian liberal leaders.

Garneau returned to Quebec in 1833 and began practising, without conviction, as a notary. His marriage on 25 August 1835 to Marie-Esther Bilodeau (1812–1893) and the birth of ten children, seven of whom died in childhood, kept him for a decade in search of material security. In addition to practising as a notary, at least sporadically until 1842, he was a cashier from 1837 to 1842 at the British North American and then at the Quebec Bank, served as a translator at the legislative assembly from 1842 to 1844, and finally found security as city clerk at Quebec from 1844. In 1834 he was secretary of the constitutional committee, which promoted the nationalist *patriote* party, and he was among the founders of the nationalist Société St Jean-Baptiste at Quebec in 1842. In addition to two short-lived newspapers, the *Abeille Canadienne* (1833–4) and *L'Institut, ou, Journal des Étudiants* (1841), Garneau published some thirty poems, largely inspired by nationalist sentiment, between 1831 and 1841. His poetry, although today considered for the most part mediocre and derivative of contemporary French romantic writing, was outstanding for the time and occasionally original in its efforts to express Canadian nature and traditions through the prism of Romanticism.

Considering the union of the Canadas in 1841 as potentially disastrous for French Canada, Garneau virtually ceased writing poetry to concentrate on a history of Canada. Previous histories had been written from the British perspective, or were poor, uninspiring accounts, or school textbooks. Influenced by numerous French authors, particularly Thierry, the *Histoire du Canada depuis sa découverte jusqu'à nos jours* galvanized the nationalist movement by offering an inspired historical synthesis from the perspective of contemporary French-Canadian liberal professional thought. It was published in three editions during Garneau's lifetime (1845–9, 1852, and 1858), was constantly revised and improved, and reflected the transformation of mainline bourgeois nationalist thought under pressure by the Roman Catholic clergy, from the doctrinaire liberalism of Papineau in the 1830s to the pragmatic reformism and even conservatism of the 1840s incarnated in the person of Louis-Hyppolyte LaFontaine.

Although the *Histoire*, the greatest single work of literature to come out of French Canada in the nineteenth century, was his crowning achievement, Garneau contributed to the development of French-Canadian culture in other ways. He was a founder member of the Institut Canadien at Quebec in 1847. Nineteen of his poems were included in the anthology *Répertoire national, ou, Recueil de littérature canadienne*; he published, and then immediately withdrew from sale because of editorial errors, *Voyage en Angleterre et en France dans les années 1831, 1832, et 1833* (1855); and he wrote a small textbook on Canadian history. The remarkably successful English translation of the *Histoire*, first published in 1860 by Andrew Bell, was too liberally adapted to anglophone sensibilities for Garneau, who denounced it.

Garneau had a passion for politics but, hampered by his personality, never entered political life. He enjoyed an enormous capacity for work, but abused it to the detriment of his health. For the last twenty years of his life he suffered from epilepsy. In 1859 he had been appointed one of the original members of the provincial council of public instruction, but in 1869 he was obliged to resign, and two years later he retired as city clerk of Quebec. He died at 2 rue Sainte Famille, Quebec, on 2 February 1866 of epilepsy complicated by pleurisy, and was buried in the city on 6 February. The following year a monument was erected in his honour in Belmont cemetery. Textbooks on, and anthologies of, Canadian and French-Canadian literature underline Garneau's position as the greatest French-Canadian writer of the nineteenth century. A college and numerous streets, parks, schools, rivers, and lakes throughout French Canada named after him testify to the enduring reverence for the man who gave his compatriots a proud heritage on which to build a national determination first to survive and then to prosper.

JAMES H. LAMBERT

Sources G. Lanctot, *Garneau: historien national* (1946) · G. Bergeron, *Lire François-Xavier Garneau, 1809–1866: 'historien national'* (1994) · P. Savard and P. Wyczynski, 'Garneau, François-Xavier', *DCB*, vol. 9 · S. Gagnon, *Quebec and its historians* (1982), 9–43 · P. Savard and P. Wyczynski, 'Histoire du Canada depuis sa découverte jusqu'à nos jours de François-Xavier Garneau', *Dictionnaire des œuvres littéraires du Québec*, 1, ed. M. Lemire and others (Montréal, 1978), 347–55 [incl. bibliography] · F.-X. Garneau, *Voyage en Angleterre et en France dans les années 1831, 1832 et 1833*, ed. P. Wyczynski (1968) [introduction and notes] · [Société Historique de Montréal], *Centenaire de l'histoire du Canada de François-Xavier Garneau: deuxième semaine d'histoire à l'Université de Montréal, 23–27 avril, 1945* (1945) · P. Wyczynski and P. Savard, *François-Xavier Garneau, 1809–1866* (1977) · H.-R. Casgrain, *Œuvres complètes*, 2 (1897), 84–156 · A. Lauzière, *François-Xavier Garneau* (1965) · G. Robitaille, *Études sur Garneau: critique historique* (1929)

Archives Archives Nationales du Québec · Bibliothèque Municipale de Montréal · University of Ottawa, Ottawa, Centre de Recherche en Civilisation Canadienne-Française | University of Ottawa, Ottawa, Centre de Recherche en Civilisation Canadienne-Française, Alfred and Hector Garneau MSS

Likenesses lithograph, after 1866 (after photograph by J. Livernois), University of Ottawa, Ottawa, Canada, Centre de Recherche en Civilisation Canadienne-Française · P. Chèvre, statue, 1942, Grande-Allée, Quebec, Canada · J. Livernois, photograph, Archives Nationales du Québec, Quebec, Canada

Garner, Margaret, Lady Garner (1917–1994). *See under* Garner, (Joseph John) Saville, Baron Garner (1908–1983).

Garner, Richard (*d.* in or after 1415), merchant and master of the mint, was born in Piedmont, Italy, but had migrated to London by 1400–01 where he began an eventful career as a resident alien merchant. He exported wool, for instance, on the Venetian Peter Meany's galley in 1404, and petitioned Henry IV for a seven-year monopoly of exports of block and piece tin outside the staple. Membership of the Vintners' Company enabled him to deal in Gascon wine, which he sometimes sold to the royal wardrobe; he also imported from La Rochelle, where he was represented by his brother. Extending beyond the English foothold on the continent into Spain and Portugal, his import business also included iron, Seville oil and white soap, and Portuguese fruit, wines, oxhides, and wax. These additional interests abroad were looked after by fellow Piedmontese.

His habitual use of Spanish boats to bring these imports north meant that Garner's goods were often intercepted by west-country and Calais-based shipmasters, even when sailing under English safe conduct. However, his royal connections enabled him to invoke the king's protection, permitting him to reclaim his belongings and bring his antagonists before the council. Notably, he petitioned with the Florentine Filippo Alberti concerning four Spanish ships which had been seized and taken to Plymouth in October 1403; Garner and Alberti were able to obtain restitution by indicating the merchants' marks to be found on their goods. But such incidents were not always resolved to Garner's satisfaction, and altogether he alleged losses worth over £2000 at the hands of various English shipmasters. Even less happily, two of his employees were held to ransom at Calais; another, Peter King of London, was imprisoned and his money and goods confiscated while he was on business at Dartmouth. It may have given Garner some small satisfaction in 1404 to have brought a case in the mayor's court to recover a £12 debt against Richard Spicer, MP for Portsmouth and a well-known pirate.

Garner was granted letters of denization, at a cost of £20, on 4 March 1409, perhaps in anticipation of his appointment as keeper of the king's exchange and master of the mint in London and Calais in July of that year. However, his adoption of English nationality soon proved an unforeseen disadvantage: having sent merchandise worth £4000 to Italy, he could obtain neither a return cargo nor financial compensation because of his changed allegiance, while other Italians joined forces to sue him for debt 'on account of the odium against him for becoming the king's liege man' (*CPR, 1408–13*, 212–13). Consequently, in July 1410, he sought and gained royal protection for seven years. He may also have attempted to find a short-term solution to his business problems by exploiting his position as master of the mint; a commission for his arrest was issued in March 1413 on the grounds that he had made money contrary to ordinance, and in April his offices were granted to Louis John. By May he had taken sanctuary at Westminster, apparently somewhat hastily as he left behind some of his personal property, including wine, at the Tower of London. He was pardoned two years later.

Garner made his will on 14 October 1415, when, as a citizen and vintner of London, he was living in the parish of

St Benet Fink. Although he did not specify a place of burial, he left £20 to pay for masses to be said for him at Westminster Abbey. His only other particular bequests were for masses and prayers in the city, where he gave £5 to the Augustinian friars—increasingly popular among the resident Italian community—and £2 to each of the other orders of friars. He divided the residue of his estate into third shares, according to London custom: one third went to his executors, the mercers Laurence Hampton and Thomas Bataille; one third was devoted to pious works for the welfare of his soul and those of his Italian relatives and benefactors; the remaining third was set aside to buy lands to support a perpetual chantry at Westminster Abbey, although he instructed his executors to distribute this sum in charitable works if it proved insufficient for his original purpose. Garner's will, which covered only his possessions in England, made no provision for a wife or children. His death is not recorded.

H. L. BRADLEY

Sources GL, 9171/2 fol. 336v · CLRO, MC 1/2/199 · Harley MSS, BL, 1878, fol. 7 · PRO, Exchequer, King's Remembrancer, Customs Accounts, E 122/72/8 · GL, 15/190 · PRO, Exchequer, King's Remembrancer Accounts Various, E 101/404/21 · CPR, 1402, 1405–9 · PRO, Exchequer of Receipt, Receipt Rolls, E 401/658 · C. E. Challis, ed., A new history of the royal mint (1992), 708
Wealth at death left a third of estate to found chantry at Westminster Abbey: will, GL, London commissary court, wills and administrations

Garner, (Joseph John) Saville [Joe], **Baron Garner** (1908–1983), civil servant and diplomatist, was born in Muswell Hill, Middlesex, on 14 February 1908, the second of three sons of Joseph Garner (1861–1940), draper, of Highgate, and Helena Maria (d. 1939), daughter of John Culver, of London. He was brought up in Highgate, and was educated at Highgate School and Jesus College, Cambridge, where he obtained a first in modern and medieval languages in 1929. He worked briefly as a schoolmaster at Haileybury, teaching modern languages, and published in 1930 *The Books of the Emperor Wu Ti*, a translation of Walter Meckauer's *Die Bücher des Kaisers Wutai* (1928).

In 1930 Garner entered the Dominions Office, with the rank of assistant principal. In 1935 he was appointed assistant private secretary to the secretary of state for the dominions, J. H. Thomas, who reputedly refused to call him by his customary forename Saville ('What sort of fancy name is that?'), calling him instead Joe, by which name he came to be known thereafter (*DNB*). Garner served in the same capacity under Thomas's successor, Malcolm MacDonald, with whom he forged a lasting personal and professional friendship. MacDonald found that Garner 'in fact did almost all the day-to-day work of both the private secretary and the assistant private secretary' (Garner, xi), the principal private secretary, Sir Edward Marsh, being one of Whitehall's last great intellectual dilettantes. On 28 May 1938 Garner married Margaret (Peggy) Beckman [see below]. They had two sons, Christopher (b. 1939) and Jonathan (b. 1940), and one daughter, Helena (b. 1947).

Garner succeeded Marsh as principal private secretary

(Joseph John) Saville Garner, Baron Garner (1908–1983), by Howard Coster, 1956

in 1940, serving under viscounts Caldecote and Cranborne, and Clement Attlee. This was at a time when relations between Britain and the dominions were crucial to the war effort, but also strained. Garner was assiduous in promoting the interests of the dominions within Whitehall. In 1943 he took up his first overseas post, following MacDonald to Canada, as deputy high commissioner. Canada's gradual loosening of its constitutional ties with Britain, notably by the Canadian Citizenship Act of 1946, was a process which Garner regarded as both natural and necessary for continuing good relations.

On MacDonald's return in 1948, Garner was appointed assistant under-secretary of state in the Dominions Office, and made CMG. In 1951 he was again posted overseas, to India, as deputy high commissioner. He returned to London in 1953 as deputy permanent under-secretary of state in what had by now become the Commonwealth Relations Office, charged in particular with liaising with the Foreign Office. He was advanced to KCMG in 1954. (He subsequently served as registrar from 1962 to 1966 and secretary from 1966 to 1968 of the Order of St Michael and St George.) In 1956 he returned to Canada, as high commissioner. His appointment coincided with a nadir in Anglo-Canadian relations, caused by the Suez crisis and its aftermath. Suez horrified Garner and prompted him to offer his resignation, but he was persuaded to stay. His integrity, informality, and friendliness endeared him to Canadians, and enabled him to do much to repair the damage.

In 1962 Garner succeeded Sir Alexander Clutterbuck as permanent under-secretary at the Commonwealth Relations Office, serving under three prime ministers and four secretaries of state. His years as permanent under-secretary were marked by a transformation of the administrative structures through which Britain dealt with the Commonwealth. In 1965, the creation of an independent Commonwealth secretariat ended the anomaly of Britain's control of inter-Commonwealth diplomacy, a development which Garner supported. In 1966 the Commonwealth Relations Office was amalgamated with what was left of the Colonial Office, and Garner became the first permanent under-secretary of the combined Commonwealth Office. Concurrently, he was also the head of the diplomatic service, following the merger of the foreign service, the Commonwealth service, and the trade commissioners' service. He retired in February 1968, shortly before the amalgamation of the Foreign and Commonwealth offices. He was appointed GCMG in 1965, and created a life peer, as Baron Garner, of Chiddingly in the county of Sussex, on 21 February 1969.

Garner's interest in the Commonwealth was reflected in his chairmanship of the board of governors of the Commonwealth Institute (1968–74), the Commonwealth Scholarship Commission (1968–77), the committee of management of the Institute of Commonwealth Studies, University of London (1971–9), and the Joint Commonwealth Societies Council (1981–3). He was also a member of the security commission (1968–73), the body charged with investigating security lapses and advising on security arrangements in the public service, and of the council of Voluntary Service Overseas (1969–74), the board of governors of the School of Oriental and African Studies, University of London (1968–73), and the Royal Postgraduate Medical School (1971–80). He received honorary doctorates from the universities of British Columbia (1958) and Toronto (1959), and was made an honorary fellow of Jesus College, Cambridge, in 1967. He was also a governor of Highgate School from 1962, and treasurer and chairman from 1976. In 1978 he published *The Commonwealth Office, 1925–68*, a thoughtful history of the Dominions Office and its successors. His account of the structure, personalities, and politics of the office was enlivened by personal recollection, and by his enthusiastic regard for the Commonwealth as a vehicle for international peace and co-operation.

Colleagues remembered Garner not only as a gifted administrator, but also as an exceptionally lively and personable individual. His advice was frequently sought, not only by his fellow administrators and by politicians in Britain, but also by his many friends in the Commonwealth overseas. His career spanned the emergence of the dominions from satellites of the United Kingdom into independent states, the decolonization of vast tracts of the British empire, and the transformation of the Commonwealth from a white man's club into a multiracial association of twenty-eight equal members. With all three trends he was in complete sympathy.

Garner died in Bournemouth while visiting his family,

on 10 December 1983. A memorial service was held in his honour at Westminster Abbey on 14 February 1984.

Garner's wife, **Margaret** [Peggy] **Garner**, Lady Garner (1917–1994), hostess, was born in Berwyn, Illinois, USA, on 6 April 1917, the daughter of Herman Beckman, an inventor with the DeLaval Separator Company of Chicago. She was brought up in Cedar Lake, Indiana, and after leaving school travelled to London, where through family connections she met Joe Garner. 'I came over to be finished', she said, 'and I sure was!' (*The Times*, 7 July 1994). She felt keenly the difficulties and isolation of a diplomatist's wife, and while in Delhi formed the Delhi Commonwealth Women's Association. Once the family was back in Britain she was a moving spirit behind the formation of the Commonwealth Relations Office Wives (Crows) in 1955. This was a forerunner of the Diplomatic Service Wives' Association, formed in 1960, in whose affairs she took great interest after the family's return from Canada in 1962. Loyally supportive of her husband, she was a noted hostess, and reinforced his interest in the welfare of individual diplomatists and their families. She outlived him by more than ten years, dying on 23 June 1994. She was survived by their three children.   ALEX MAY

Sources *The Times* (12 Dec 1983) · *DNB* · Burke, *Peerage* · J. Garner, *The commonwealth office, 1925–1968* (1978) · J. A. Cross, *Whitehall and the commonwealth: British departmental organisation for commonwealth relations, 1900–1966* (1967) · J. D. B. Miller, 'The CRO and commonwealth relations', *International Studies*, 2 (1960–61), 42–59 · M. J. Macdonald, *People and places: random reminiscences* (1969) · C. Sanger, *Malcolm MacDonald: bringing an end to empire* (1995) · *CGPLA Eng. & Wales* (1984) · *Dod's Parliamentary Companion* · *The Times* (7 July 1994) · *CGPLA Eng. & Wales* (1994)
Archives Bodl. Oxf., corresp. with Attlee
Likenesses H. Coster, photograph, 1956, NPG [*see illus.*] · photograph, repro. in *Dod's Parliamentary Companion*
Wealth at death £29,831: probate, 6 June 1984, *CGPLA Eng. & Wales* · £224,593—Margaret Garner: probate, 28 Oct 1994, *CGPLA Eng. & Wales* (1994)

Garner, Thomas (1789–1868), engraver, was born in Birmingham, and was possibly the son of the engraver J. Garner (*fl.* 1829–1831). He received instruction in the art of engraving from Samuel Lines and entered the Royal Academy Schools in 1817. In the 1820s he joined Charles Heath's studio and produced work anonymously for the annuals. After returning to Birmingham he became an active promoter of the study of art and was one of the founders of the city's Antique Academy, later known as the Birmingham Society of Arts. As an engraver he produced topographical subjects and portraits of local interest; from time to time he worked as assistant to William Radclyffe. His longest series of plates appeared in S. W. H. Ireland's *England's Topographer* (1828–30). He is best-known, however, for his plates for the *Art Journal* published in the 1850s and 1860s, which included, in 1854, *The Grecian Vintage*, after Thomas Stothard, *HRH Princess Charlotte*, after Sir Thomas Lawrence, and, in 1866, *Chastity*, after William Edward Frost. All his *Art Journal* plates (except that after Lawrence) appeared in the 1877 exhibition of engravings by Birmingham men together with seventeen others. Garner served for many years on the hanging committee of the Birmingham Society of Arts, and acted as director of the life academy until obliged to retire through failing health. He was also an accomplished violinist. When he died, on 14 July 1868, at 145 Lee Bank Road, Edgbaston, the school of Birmingham engravers became extinct.

L. H. CUST, rev. GREG SMITH

Sources *Art Journal*, 30 (1868) · B. Hunnisett, *A dictionary of British steel engravers* (1980) · B. Hunnisett, *An illustrated dictionary of British steel engravers*, new edn (1989) · d. cert.

Archives BM, department of prints and drawings

Garner, Thomas (1839–1906), architect and designer, was born at Wasperton Hill, Wasperton, Warwickshire, on 12 August 1839, the son of Thomas Garner (1795–1880), farmer, and his wife, Louisa Savage (*b. c.*1815). Brought up in country surroundings, he acquired as a boy a love of riding and a knowledge of horsemanship which he retained through life. In 1856, at the age of seventeen, he entered as a pupil the office of George Gilbert Scott, where he was a fellow student with T. G. Jackson, Somers Clarke, and J. T. Micklethwaite. He had already made the acquaintance of George Frederick *Bodley RA, who had served articles in the same office in 1845–50. After completion of his pupillage Garner returned to Warwickshire, and there began architectural practice, partly on his own account, partly as an assistant to Scott. His principal work in these years was the restoration of the chapel of Lord Leycester's Hospital, Warwick (1864–5). Garner married on 4 October 1866 Rose Emily, daughter of the Revd J. N. Smith of Milverton, Warwickshire; she survived him but there were no children. Their residence from about 1867 to 1893 was 20 Church Row, Hampstead, London.

In 1867 Bodley sought Garner's collaboration, and in 1869 the two became partners, without any legal deed of association. A series of beautiful works in ecclesiastical, domestic, and collegiate architecture was the result of this combination. The fine churches of St Michael and All Angels, Folkestone (1870–78; dem. 1953), St Augustine, Pendlebury (1870–74), and Holy Angels, Hoar Cross, Staffordshire (1872–6), are the chief buildings of definitely united authorship. As the partnership developed, it became the practice of the two to give separate attention to separate works, and among the buildings which under this system fell mainly if not entirely to Garner's share the chief were the small tower in the south-east angle of Tom quad, Christ Church, Oxford (1872–8), St Michael's Church, Camden Town (1879–81), St Swithun's quadrangle at Magdalen College, Oxford (1879–84), Hewell Grange, Worcestershire, a house for Lord Windsor, designed in 1883, the reredos in St Paul's Cathedral (1886–7), the monuments of the bishops of Ely and Lincoln in their respective cathedrals, and the monument of Canon Liddon in St Paul's. Other designs in which it appears that Garner's authorship was either sole or predominant were: churches at Bedworth, Warwickshire (1889–90), and Peasdown St John, Somerset (1892–4); classrooms and the chapel at Marlborough College, Wiltshire; the altar of King's College, Cambridge; and from 1893 the restoration of Garner's own Jacobean home, Fritwell Manor, Fritwell,

Oxfordshire, of which a full photographic record by Bedford Lemere is preserved in the National Monuments Record. In 1896 Garner and his wife converted to Roman Catholicism. This prompted the perfectly friendly dissolution of the partnership with Bodley in 1897, after which Garner carried out as his own work exclusively the restoration of Yarnton Manor, Oxfordshire (1897); Moreton House, Hampstead (1896); the restoration of the chapel at St Catharine's College, Cambridge (1898); and the Empire Hotel, Buxton (1898–9; dem. 1964). His office remained in Gray's Inn. In 1902 Garner designed the cope worn by the dean of Westminster at the coronation of Edward VII. Following the death of Edward Hansom, he was in 1899 appointed architect to Downside Abbey, Bath, where he designed the choir in which his own interment was to take place. It is said that when J. F. Bentley, the architect of the cathedral at Westminster, became aware of his own fatal illness, he suggested in answer to the question who should be his successor, 'Garner, for he is a man of genius.'

It is difficult to form a clear picture of Garner's artistic personality, since he spent most of his career in the shadow of Bodley, who was responsible for all the partnership's correspondence. (Lord Windsor recalled that the designs for Hewell Grange were well advanced before Bodley informed him they had been prepared by Garner.) Unlike Bodley, he was a skilful draughtsman, as is demonstrated by a group of drawings for stained glass in the collection of the Royal Institute of British Architects. With Bodley and George Gilbert Scott junior he founded in 1874 the church and house furnishers Watts & Co., for which he made designs for textiles and ecclesiastical furnishings.

Garner died on 30 April 1906 at Fritwell Manor and his collection was sold in January 1907; his widow presented his library to the Architectural Association, London. He was buried at Downside Abbey on 4 May 1906, and his estate was valued for probate at £13,194. *The Domestic Architecture of England during the Tudor Period*, a joint work by Garner and Arthur Stratton, was published in 1908, after Garner's death, under Stratton's editorship.

PAUL WATERHOUSE, rev. MICHAEL HALL

Sources *The Builder*, 90 (1906), 523, 531 · private information (2004) · E. Green, 'In memoriam Thomas Garner: artist, architect and archaeologist', *Downside Review*, 25 (1906), 116–21 · *CGPLA Eng. & Wales* (1906)

Wealth at death £13,194 15s. 3d.: probate, 20 July 1906, *CGPLA Eng. & Wales*

Garner, William Edward (1889–1960), chemist, was born at Hugglescote, Leicestershire, on 12 May 1889, the eldest son of William Garner, baker, and his wife, Ann Gadsby. Sir Harry Garner and Professor F. H. Garner were younger brothers. He was educated at Market Bosworth grammar school and at the University of Birmingham where he studied under P. F. Frankland and obtained honours in chemistry in 1912. He was awarded an 1851 Exhibition scholarship in 1913 to work with Gustav Tammann at the University of Göttingen and returned to England only just before the outbreak of war in the following year. He joined the scientific staff of Woolwich arsenal (1915–18) where he carried out some outstanding research work with Robert Robertson on the calorimetry of high explosives.

In January 1919 Garner was appointed assistant lecturer at Birmingham but in October moved to University College, London, where he enjoyed a close and happy association with F. G. Donnan and a fruitful period of research; he became reader in physical chemistry in 1924. Three years later he was appointed to the Leverhulme chair of physical and inorganic chemistry at Bristol and until his retirement in 1954, except for the war period, carried out a series of experimental studies of far-reaching practical and theoretical importance. In particular he made a systematic study of the kinetics of solid reactions and of heterogeneous catalysis and the mechanism of interface reactions and nucleation processes; as with much of his other work on the solid state he was a pioneer in applying the newer ideas of quantum physics.

On the outbreak of war in 1939 Garner established an extramural research team in the University of Bristol to assist the government ordnance factories in explosives and munitions research. Although never losing contact with the work of this group, he moved to Fort Halstead in Kent in 1943 to become superintendent of chemical and explosives research for the Ministry of Supply; he later became deputy chief, then chief superintendent of armament research. His enthusiasm, wise guidance, and inspiration were of paramount importance. He served on many high-level committees and was associated with notable developments in new armaments and munitions. He was appointed CBE in 1946.

On the cessation of hostilities Garner returned to his university work, although until his retirement he was actively engaged in the work of the Scientific Advisory Council of the Ministry of Supply with which he had been associated since its inception. During this period he built around him in Bristol one of the strongest research groups in the country. He continued with increasing vigour his studies of heterogeneous catalysis. After his retirement he organized a symposium on 'Chemisorption' at the University College of North Staffordshire which was published by the Chemical Society (1957), and edited a large volume on the *Chemistry of the Solid State* (1955).

Garner was a man of charm and kindness who won the affectionate admiration of all who came into contact with him. He was quiet, unobtrusive, and entirely devoid of personal ambition, devoted to his work whether in the laboratory or the councils of the university. These qualities did not obscure his greatness—he was an enthusiastic and inspiring leader of research, conscientious in the discharge of his duties. His interests were wide; he was a collector of paintings and china, had a critical appreciation of art, and was an enthusiastic gardener. He was a man of great tenacity and courage and no problem ever daunted him. He was a well-known figure at scientific gatherings and gave generously of his time to scientific societies and government committees. He served on the council of the Royal Society, having been elected FRS in

1937, and of the Faraday Society, over which he presided in 1945–7. He was senior scientific adviser for civil defence in the south-west region, and in 1948 a member of the joint services mission to the United States and Canada. He was a fellow of University College, London, an honorary member of the Polish Chemical Society, and a correspondent councillor of the Patronato 'Alfonso el Sabio', Madrid (1959). He died, unmarried, at his home, Oakwood, 168 Westbury Road, Westbury-on-Trym, Bristol, on 4 March 1960.   C. E. H. Bawn, *rev.*

Sources C. E. H. Bawn, *Memoirs FRS*, 7 (1961), 85–94 · C. E. Bawn, *Proceedings of the Chemical Society* (1960), 230–32 · *The Times* (7 March 1960), 14b · *The Times* (10 March 1960), 16a · *The Times* (11 March 1960), 12e · *CGPLA Eng. & Wales* (1960)
Likenesses W. Stoneman, photograph, 1948, NPG · W. T. Monnington, chalk drawing, University of Bristol
Wealth at death £9985 18s. 5d.: probate, 13 April 1960, *CGPLA Eng. & Wales*

Garnett [*married name* Crow], **Alice** (1903–1989), geographer, was born at 83 Cicada Road, Wandsworth, London, on 15 May 1903, the daughter of George Garnett, publisher's clerk and later company secretary, and his wife, Alice, *née* Brooks. After studying geography at University College, London (1920–23), under Professor Lionel William Lyde, she took the London diploma in pedagogy before embarking in 1924 on a lifelong career at Sheffield University, where she was initially appointed assistant lecturer in geography, as assistant to Rudmose Brown. Her appointment enabled an honours school in geography to be established. In contrast to her own experience as a student at University College, where geography students attended lectures in the departments of geology, botany and zoology, anthropology, and civil engineering, the two lecturers at Sheffield were responsible for delivering all aspects of the undergraduate course. There was little relief from Garnett's enormous teaching load until the 1930s, when she was able to give more time to research and publication, and she subsequently gained her PhD from London in 1937.

During the Second World War Garnett's university post was a reserved occupation, and she taught the condensed degree course, based on four terms a year, for deferred call-up students. Some of the courses were modified to meet the needs of the armed and intelligence services and included climatology, meteorology, landscape analysis, map interpretation, surveying, and map-making. She also worked part-time for the naval intelligence department at Cambridge (1941–5), working on two volumes of the geographical handbook of Yugoslavia. In addition she provided the inter-service intelligence department with information on landing conditions on the Adriatic coast, as well as giving lectures to troops prior to postings abroad. Her work at Sheffield University also included the role of dean of women students (at a time when female lecturers were scarce). She was promoted senior lecturer in the late 1940s, in an expanding department. On 25 March 1948 she married Colin Arthur Crow (b. 1896/7), a steelworks manager, whose former marriage (to Beryl

Russell) had been dissolved, but she remained professionally known by her former name. In 1962 she was appointed professor of physical geography at Sheffield, becoming only the second woman to hold a chair of geography in the United Kingdom. She formally retired in 1968, after teaching geography at Sheffield for forty-four years.

Garnett's first book, *The Geographical Interpretation of Topographical Maps* (1930), was innovative in its approach and highly valued by students and lecturers for more than two decades. Her other research work was to follow this model, being renowned for its meticulous representation of data and analysis on map, table, and diagram. Her monograph *Insolation and Relief: their Bearing on the Human Geography of the Alpine Regions* (1937), based on her PhD research, established her academic reputation. Always keen to update geographical information and critically apply appropriate new methods such as quantitative techniques and remote sensing, she was none the less deeply committed to an approach to her subject that integrated physical and human geography. While physical geography grounded her understanding, she is credited with avoiding the simple geographical determinism not uncommon in the inter-war years. She took a possibilist stance, influenced by her early mentor L. W. Lyde, who believed in regions primarily as political phenomena rather than physically or climatologically founded.

Garnett thought it a duty of academics to support teachers of their subject in schools. She joined the Geographical Association (GA) in 1926, following in the footsteps of her own secondary school teacher, who had brought geography alive to her following the unreflective recitation of 'capes and bays' under which she had suffered geography in her early school life. Garnett succeeded Herbert John Fleure as honorary secretary of the GA (1947–67), was made president in 1968, and chaired its council from 1970 to 1973. In 1950 she helped to negotiate the association's move from Manchester to Sheffield. She was also a founder-member of the new Institute of British Geographers (established in 1933 to disseminate academic geography), eventually becoming its president, in 1966, and was vice-president of the Royal Geographical Society from 1969 to 1971, acting as a significant link between the three geographical institutions.

Having retired from her chair, and while nursing her terminally ill husband, Garnett continued her research with the Air Pollution Unit that she had set up in Sheffield. The findings from this research influenced planning policy in Sheffield and gained her international recognition. In 1977 her contribution to geography, the university, and the city were recognized when she was awarded the honorary degree of DSc at Sheffield. Promotion to a chair and academic honours had come very late in her career, but she was gracious in her acceptance of the acknowledgement and treated it as a privilege. She was a person of indomitable energy, incisive argument, good cheer, organization, and willingness to help others, her actions influenced by her humanist ethics. She championed geography throughout the whole educational spectrum, from post-doctoral research to the primary-school curriculum.

A member of the first generation of degree-qualified geographers, taught by some of the earliest lecturers in the subject, she was a significant link with the modern foundation of the discipline. Having settled at Ferndown, in the New Forest, she died at Poole General Hospital, Dorset, on 5 March 1989, her husband having predeceased her.   AVRIL M. C. MADDRELL

Sources M. Wise, *Transactions of the Institute of British Geographers*, new ser., 15 (1990), 113–16 · R. Ellis and A. Hunt, *Geography*, 74 (1989), 274–5 · D. Linton, *University of Sheffield Gazette*, 48 (1968), 67–8 · A. Garnett, 'Teaching geography: some reflections', *Geography*, 54 (1969), 385–400 · b. cert. · m. cert. · d. cert. · *CGPLA Eng. & Wales* (1989)
Archives RGS
Likenesses L. Garnett, photograph, Geographical Association, Fullwood Road, Sheffield
Wealth at death £246,588: probate, 1989, *CGPLA Eng. & Wales*

Garnett, Arthur William (1829–1861), army officer and engineer, was born on 1 June 1829, the younger son of William *Garnett (1793–1873) and his first wife, Ellen (*d.* 1829), daughter of Solomon Treasure. He was educated at Addiscombe College from 1844 to 1846, was commissioned second-lieutenant on 12 June 1846, and went to India in 1848 to join the Bengal Engineers. Assistant field engineer with the army before Multan during the Second Anglo-Sikh War (1848–9) he was wounded in attendance on Sir John Cheape. He joined the army under Lord Gough, held the fords of the Chenab during the victory of Gujrat, and went forward with Sir Walter Raleigh Gilbert's flying column in pursuit of the Afghans. Having taken part in the first survey of the Peshawar valley with Lieutenant James T. Walker, on 31 May 1850 Garnett was placed in command of the engineers in the department of public works at Kohat. Later that year the sappers employed under his command in making a road to Landi Kotal were surprised in their camp by Afridis. Garnett and his party were surrounded, but held their position until Sir Colin Campbell (Lord Clyde), with General Charles J. Napier, arrived from Peshawar and forced the Kohat Pass.

Garnett reconstructed and strengthened the fort of Kohat, and designed and built the fort at Bahadur Khel for guarding the salt mines, as well as barracks, forts, and defensive works at other points on the frontier, including Fort Garnett, named after him. He planted forest trees wherever practicable, and constructed bridges, roads, and other works in circumstances of extreme difficulty. He was constantly interrupted by being called upon to take the field with expeditions such as those in the Derajat region, the Miranzai valley, Yusufzai country, the Kurram valley, and Peiwar Kotal, where there was frequently hard fighting. During the mutiny Garnett was kept at his post on the frontier, where his experience and influence with the hillmen were of the greatest value. He was promoted lieutenant on 15 February 1854 and second-captain on 27 August 1858.

Garnett went to England on leave in 1860, studied dockyard works with a view to the needs of Bombay, and married Mary Charlotte Burnard of Crewkerne, with whom he had a posthumous daughter. After returning to India he died of pleurisy in Calcutta on 1 May 1861, while temporarily assisting Colonel Henry Yule, secretary to the government of India in the department of public works. He was buried in St Paul's Cathedral, Calcutta, where a monument was erected by his fellow officers. He was also commemorated by other monuments placed in the church at Kohat, which he had built, and in that of Holy Trinity at Brompton.   F. B. GARNETT, *rev.* ALEX MAY

Sources *Indian Army List* · E. J. Thackwell, *Narrative of the Second Seikh War, in 1848–49* (1851) · H. C. B. Cook, *The Sikh wars: the British army in the Punjab, 1845–1849* (1975) · J. G. Elliott, *The frontier, 1839–1947* (1968) · A. H. Swinson, *North-west frontier: people and events, 1839–1947* (1967)
Wealth at death £200: administration, 2 April 1862, *CGPLA Eng. & Wales*

Garnett [*née* Black], **Constance Clara** (1861–1946), translator, was born at 58 Ship Street, Brighton, Sussex, on 19 December 1861, sixth of the eight children of the solicitor David Black (1817–1892), afterwards town clerk and coroner, and his wife, Clara Maria (1825–1875), daughter of the portrait painter George *Patten (1801–1865). Her grandfather Captain Peter Black (1783–1831) designed a steamer for the Russian government but died on delivering it to Kronstadt. Her eldest sister was Clementina *Black (1853–1922), the novelist and social reformer.

Constance had an unhappy childhood. A perhaps unnecessary operation at the age of three for tuberculosis of the hip left her an invalid for years; she suffered from headaches and rheumatism, and was extremely short-sighted; her moody, irascible father became paralysed in 1873; and two years later her mother died, having ruptured herself by lifting him. Constance became a lifelong sceptic and atheist. Taught at first by her family, she went to Brighton high school and achieved examination distinctions in arithmetic, French, and especially English, for her top marks in which she was awarded a scholarship to Newnham College, Cambridge. On taking up residence there in October 1879 this shy and fragile figure, rather small, with fair hair, blue eyes, and steel spectacles, threw off her Victorian yoke and lived intensely. She read classical languages and philosophy, and particularly enjoyed Greek unseens; in her final examinations in 1883 she obtained a first class, and qualified for (but as a woman could not take) the Cambridge BA degree.

In her last year at Newnham, Constance gave tutorials, and was considered businesslike, if too lenient. She afterwards taught privately in London before becoming co-librarian of the new People's Palace, Mile End, in 1887; she was later its head librarian, and published its catalogue, but resigned to marry at Brighton register office on 31 August 1889 Edward William *Garnett (1868–1937), editor and book reviewer. In 1891 the couple rented a cottage at Henhurst Cross in Surrey. There the pregnant Constance entertained guests such as W. B. Yeats and the Russian exile F. V. Volkhovsky; the latter taught her Russian and supervised her first translation exercise, Goncharov's *Obyknovennaya istoriya* (*A Common Story*). Through him she met other revolutionaries, including Stepniak (S. M. Kravchinsky), with whom she was in love for a time, and who

Constance Clara Garnett (1861–1946), by unknown photographer, 1903 [with her son, David Garnett]

helped to edit her work. He encouraged her to move on to Turgenev, already a favourite of hers, but Heinemann, whom Edward persuaded to accept the Goncharov, asked her to tackle next Tolstoy's *Tsarstvo bozhiye vnutri vas*, translated as *The Kingdom of God is within you*.

Following the difficult birth of her son, David *Garnett, born at Brighton on 9 March 1892, Constance had no more children and virtually no sexual relations with Edward. He assisted her professionally, writing prefaces as required, but they agreed to live together yet apart—as would be confirmed by his liaison with Nellie Heath. Constance, who hated scenes, overcame her frustration by a will to work and be independent.

An early test of Constance's self-sufficiency was her first trip to Russia. Carrying messages from her revolutionary friends, she left on the last day of 1893 for St Petersburg, where she accepted an invitation to travel to Tver, Moscow, Nizhniy Novgorod, and on by sledge to the Arzamas district. In Moscow she called on Tolstoy, who praised her current translation and encouraged her to attempt others. In Nizhniy she saw the writer V. G. Korolenko, whom she had met previously at Stepniak's. In the remote countryside she witnessed the poverty and sickness of the peasantry, tempered by their intelligence and dignity. Her seven-week tour gave her valuable first-hand experience of Russian life and ways of thinking, and improved her facility with the language.

The Goncharov and Tolstoy translations came out in 1894, followed by Constance's first two Turgenev volumes, *Rudin* and *Dvoryanskoye gnezdo* (*A House of Gentlefolk*), each with an introduction by Stepniak (despite Heinemann's misgivings). Stepniak's participation was such that Constance intended to give him twenty per cent of her receipts. His untimely death in 1895 came as a serious blow, but the Turgenev set in fifteen volumes was completed in 1899.

In 1896 the Garnetts settled at The Cearne, their mock-ancient house near Limpsfield Chart on the Surrey–Kent border north of Edenbridge. Its visitors included Conrad, Galsworthy, D. H. Lawrence, Ford Madox Ford, and H. E. Bates. David Garnett recalled that, as his mother translated, Russian words turned into expressions on her face before being Englished onto paper. D. H. Lawrence watched rapt while she filled page after page, throwing them to a pile on the floor. Books lay open everywhere, when not propping up furniture.

After an interlude for Duckworth with Ostrovsky's *Groza*, translated as *The Storm* (1899), Constance reverted to Heinemann and to Tolstoy, beginning with *Anna Karenin* (1901). But work on *War and Peace* (1904), by which she most wished to be judged, damaged her eyesight and caused her great difficulties. In 1904 she was somewhat revived by a second journey to Russia, with David; her enthusiasm for things Russian was also sustained by the political ferment of the times. She had long promoted socialism; in 1894, rather to the chagrin of her friend Bernard Shaw, she had even been elected to the executive of the Fabian Society. In London in 1907 she saw and was impressed by Lenin, but mistrusted the other bolsheviks. She rejoiced in the triumph of the Russian people in 1917, but thereafter became more conservative.

Constance found that she could continue to pursue her career by dictating to assistants. In 1910 Heinemann, following critical demand, invited her to translate Dostoyevsky, thinking him a gamble worth taking despite the commercial failure of the Tolstoy series. Beginning with *The Brothers Karamazov*, their comprehensive Dostoyevsky (12 vols., 1912–20) actually provoked a literary craze. However, disagreements over royalties led Constance to switch to Chatto and Windus for her next project, Chekhov, whom she had wanted to translate as early as 1893, and with whom she had corresponded. The *Tales* (13 vols., 1916–22) and *Plays* (2 vols., 1923–4) set off another craze in Britain. For Chatto, Constance also undertook the works of Gogol (6 vols., 1922–8) and, concurrently, Alexander Herzen's *Byloye i dumy* (*My Past and Thoughts*; 6 vols., 1924–7).

By now Constance was frail, white-haired, and half-blind. She retired from translating after the publication in 1934 of *Three Plays* by Turgenev, and after Edward's death on 19 February 1937 she became quite reclusive. She developed a heart condition, with attendant breathlessness, and towards the end had to walk with crutches. She died at The Cearne on 17 December 1946.

Constance Garnett's requirements for a good translation were sympathy for the author and a love of words and their meanings. She herself had faults: her dialogues are sometimes stiff; her transliteration of Russian names is illogical and inconsistent; she makes many errors. But the speed at which she worked, which was partly to blame for these, allowed her to maintain stylistic unity. Her descriptive passages are often exquisitely done and she eschews linguistic fads or slang. Conrad, for whom Turgenev *was* Constance Garnett, compared her to a great musician interpreting a great composer. For Katherine Mansfield, Constance Garnett transformed the lives of younger authors by revealing a new world. Without her translations, H. E. Bates believed, modern English literature itself could not have been what it is (Bates, 120).

PATRICK WADDINGTON

Sources R. Garnett, *Constance Garnett: a heroic life* (1991) · G. Jefferson, *Edward Garnett: a life in literature* (1982) · C. G. Heilbrun, *The Garnett family* (1961) · D. Garnett, *The golden echo* (1954) · C. Garnett, 'The art of translation', *The Listener* (30 Jan 1947), 195 · A. Tove, 'Konstantsiya Garnet—perevodchik i propagandist russkoy literatury' [Constance Garnett—translator and propagandist of Russian literature], *Russkaya Literatura*, 4 (1958), 193–9 · B. C. Johnson, ed., *Tea and anarchy! The Bloomsbury diary of Olive Garnett, 1890–1893* (1989) · *Olive and Stepniak: the Bloomsbury diary of Olive Garnett, 1893–1895*, ed. B. C. Johnson (1993) · E. Crankshaw, 'Work of Constance Garnett', *The Listener* (30 Jan 1947), 195–6 · G. Turton, 'The Garnett translations', in G. Turton, *Turgenev and the context of English literature, 1850–1900* (1992), 183–200 · L. G. Leighton, 'Chekhov in English', *A Chekhov companion*, ed. T. W. Clyman (1985), 291–309 · C. A. Moser, 'The achievement of Constance Garnett', *American Scholar*, 57 (1988), 431–8 · A. N. Nikoliukin, 'Dostoevskii in Constance Garnett's translation', *Dostoevskii and Britain*, ed. W. J. Leatherbarrow (1995), 207–27 · R. Rubenstein, 'Genius of translation', *Colorado Quarterly*, 22 (1974), 359–68 · H. E. Bates, *The modern short story* (1972) · G. Jean-Aubry, *Joseph Conrad: life and letters*, 2 vols. (1927) · IGI · d. cert.

Archives priv. coll., unfinished MS autobiography and family corresp. · Ransom HRC, letters | Eton, letters to Edward Garnett · Eton, letters to Nellie Heath

Likenesses photograph, *c*.1894, repro. in Garnett, *Constance Garnett*, facing p. 82 · photograph, 1903, priv. coll. [*see illus.*] · photograph, 1920–1929?, repro. in Heilbrun, *Garnett family*, facing p. 176 · D. Garnett, photograph, 1937, repro. in Garnett, 'The art of translation', p. 195 · E. L. Mahomed (Black), portrait (as young woman), repro. in D. Garnett, *Great friends: portraits of seventeen writers* (1979), 17 · group photograph (*Newnham Hall, 1880*), Newnham College, Cambridge · portraits, repro. in Garnett, *Constance Garnett*

Wealth at death £8181 5s. 6d.: probate, 5 May 1947, *CGPLA Eng. & Wales*

Garnett, David (1892–1981), writer and publisher, was born on 9 March 1892 at Brighton, Sussex, the only child of Edward William *Garnett (1868–1937), author and publisher's reader, of The Cearne, near Edenbridge, Kent, and his wife, Constance Clara *Garnett (1861–1946), distinguished translator of Russian classics and the daughter of David Black, town clerk and coroner. His grandfather was Richard *Garnett (1835–1906), prolific man of letters and keeper of printed books at the British Museum. David Garnett was educated at University College School and at the Royal College of Science, South Kensington, London, where he studied botany, and fungi in particular. At the age of twelve he paid a memorable visit to Russia with his mother, while through his father's gift for discovering literary talent he became friendly from boyhood with such

David Garnett (1892–1981), by Vanessa Bell, 1915

writers as Joseph Conrad, D. H. Lawrence, and W. H. Hudson. Later he got to know the Stracheys, J. M. Keynes, Duncan Grant, and the rest of the Bloomsbury group, with whom he was associated all his adult life.

During the First World War Garnett went to France with the Friends' War Victims' Relief Mission, and afterwards worked on the land. After the war he opened a bookshop in the heart of Bloomsbury with his friend Francis Birrell, but writing had already become his chief interest. On 30 March 1921 he married Rachel Alice (Ray; 1892–1940), the daughter of William Cecil Marshall, architect; the couple had two sons. Ray illustrated her husband's books as well as those of other writers, and wrote and illustrated children's books. Garnett's marriage and the outstanding success of his first serious novel, *Lady into Fox* (1922; Hawthornden and James Tait Black memorial prizes for 1923), persuaded him to buy Hilton Hall, an early seventeenth-century house near Huntingdon, and devote himself entirely to literature. His output of over a dozen novels included *The Sailor's Return* (1925), *Aspects of Love* (1955), and *Up she Rises* (1977). Among his other works were *A Rabbit in the Air*, a delightful account of learning to fly (1932); and three volumes of autobiography, *The Golden Echo* (1953), *The Flowers of the Forest* (1955), and *The Familiar Faces* (1962). He also wrote *Pocahontas* (1933), *Beany-Eye* (1935), and *Great Friends* (1979). He was also responsible for editing *The Letters of T. E. Lawrence* (1938), *The Novels of Thomas Love Peacock*

(1948), and Dora Carrington's *Letters and Extracts from her Diaries* (1970), as well as being involved in two successful publishing ventures: the Nonesuch Press—with Francis Meynell—in 1923, and Rupert Hart-Davis Ltd in 1946.

Garnett was literary editor of the *New Statesman* from 1932 to 1934. He continued to write its leading review until the outbreak of the Second World War, when he joined the Air Ministry with the rank of flight lieutenant Royal Air Force Volunteer Reserve, and subsequently was an intelligence officer in the political warfare executive, whose secret history he wrote. After the death of his first wife in 1940, on 8 May 1942 he married the painter and writer Angelica Vanessa Bell (*b.* 1918), daughter of Duncan James Corrowr *Grant (1885–1978) and Vanessa *Bell (1879–1961), both painters, of Charleston, Sussex. They had four daughters, the two youngest of whom were twins. They later separated.

Garnett's was a large and vigorous output, based on a variety of interests and wide reading. On first starting as a novelist he had taken Daniel Defoe as his model, and the same combination of an imaginative or fantastic premiss with a sturdy, objective, and masculine style can be seen in the work of both writers. Many of his plots were markedly original and have attracted the interest of artists in other media. Ballets founded on *Lady into Fox* (1939, with music by Arthur Honegger) and *The Sailor's Return* (1947) were successfully staged by the Ballet Rambert with Sally Gilmour in the leading roles, while the latter novel and *A Man in the Zoo* (1928) were made into films and shown on television. Most successfully, *Aspects of Love* was made into a musical by Andrew Lloyd Webber in 1989 and ran for some time posthumously in London and abroad. In 1996 *Lady into Fox* was produced as an opera, with music by Nicholas Bloomfield, at the Lyric Theatre, Hammersmith, London.

As a young man Garnett, known as Bunny to his friends, was good-looking, fair-haired, and blue-eyed. His energy and enterprise—and perhaps a streak of recklessness—found an outlet in learning to fly, among other outdoor activities such as fishing, swimming (he could be seen diving into cold water when he was over eighty), and beekeeping. For a time he kept a small herd of Jerseys at Hilton, and he took a sympathetic interest in most agricultural processes and liked to describe them. As he said himself: 'I believe I can write about grass growing as well as anyone'. Indeed he had always been more at home in the country than in town, from his days as a rather solitary child exploring the woods around his parents' house and developing an enthusiasm for the wild flowers and creatures he saw there until his discovery in middle age of the attractions of the Yorkshire dales. Travel was another source of pleasure, particularly in France, but he also paid several visits to the United States, where he made many friends and sometimes gave lectures. A lover of life, gregarious, and a genial host, he gave and received much affection and was an excellent letter-writer. He spent the last ten years of his life in France in a modest stone cottage in Charry, Montcuq (Lot), surrounded by his fine library and a small collection of Bloomsbury paintings. Here he bottled wine and cooked for his many visitors, and could be seen sitting out of doors under a large straw hat typing away at his latest book.

Garnett had been appointed a CBE in 1952, was elected a fellow of the Imperial College of Science and Technology in 1956, and became CLit in 1977. In 1977 he received the honorary degree of DLitt at Birmingham University. He died of a cerebral haemorrhage on 17 February 1981 at his home in France. There was no funeral, and his body was given to a French teaching hospital.

FRANCES PARTRIDGE

Sources D. Garnett, *The golden echo* (1953) · D. Garnett, *The flowers of the forest* (1955) · D. Garnett, *The familiar faces* (1962) · C. G. Heilbrun, *The Garnett family* (1951) · R. Garnett, *Constance Garnett: a heroic life* (1991) · m. certs. · personal knowledge (2004) · private information (1990) · *CGPLA Eng. & Wales* (1981)
Archives U. Texas, papers | CUL, letters to Geoffrey Keynes · Eton, corresp. with Constance Garnett and Edward Garnett · King's Cam., letters to Clive Bell and copies of letters to Julian Bell · King's Cam., corresp. with Vanessa Bell and Angelica Garnett; letters to John Hayward; letters to John Maynard Keynes · U. Reading, corresp. with Jonathan Cape Ltd; letters to Herbert E. Herlitschka · U. Sussex, letters to Leonard Woolf
Likenesses photograph, 1903 (as a child, with his mother, Constance Garnett), priv. coll.; *see illus. in* Garnett, Constance Clara (1861–1946) · V. Bell, oil and gouache, 1915, NPG [*see illus.*] · M. Gerson, photograph, 1953, NPG · N. Garnett, oils, *c.*1970, NPG · D. Grant, oils, Hilton Hall · S. Tomlin, stone bust, Hilton Hall
Wealth at death £11,170—in England and Wales: probate, 28 Sept 1981, *CGPLA Eng. & Wales*

Garnett, Edward William (1868–1937), publisher's editor and writer, was born on 5 January 1868 at 3 St Edmund's Terrace, London, the third of the six children of Richard *Garnett (1835–1906), keeper of the printed books at the British Museum, and his wife, Olivia Narney Singleton (1842–1903). His father's family came from Otley in Yorkshire, his mother's from co. Clare in Ireland. Garnett was educated at the City of London School, and then, at the age of nineteen, after three years of idleness—and voracious reading—he took a menial job with T. Fisher Unwin, the publisher. There he soon graduated to reading manuscripts for publication. This was to be his vocation for the rest of his life, successively with Unwin, Heinemann, Duckworth, John Lane, and finally with Jonathan Cape. Once he had recommended an author for acceptance, Garnett felt responsible for developing his talent and promoting his interests. His methods were intuitive. He had a quick eye for character and a ready sympathy, and he took great pains to cajole, or if necessary to browbeat, his authors into revising or even abandoning work that did not reach his high standards.

Garnett married on 31 August 1889 Constance Clara Black (1861–1946) [*see* Garnett, Constance Clara], translator of Russian and the daughter of David Black, coroner, and Clara Maria Patten. They had one son, David *Garnett (1892–1981), who became a novelist. In 1895–6 they built themselves The Cearne, near Limpsfield, Surrey, a house in the medieval manner, full of raw stone and unpainted wood, where they provided frugal entertainment and intellectual encouragement to several generations of

writers. This remained their home, and they on affectionate terms, when two years later Garnett began a lifelong liaison with the painter Ellen Maurice (Nellie) Heath (1872–1962).

Meanwhile, in 1894 Garnett accepted Joseph Conrad's first book, *Almayer's Folly*, and persuaded him not to go back to sea but to write another. Conrad, though eleven years his senior, nevertheless deferred to Garnett's authority; and Garnett's considerable influence on Conrad's work, which is revealed in *Letters from Conrad* (1928), is perhaps his greatest contribution to literature. His influence on another writer is recorded in *Letters from John Galsworthy* (1934), and his friendship with W. H. Hudson, whose letters he published in 1923, was also of literary importance.

In 1912 Garnett provided D. H. Lawrence with a haven at The Cearne when he ran off with Frieda Weekley and was an outcast in English society. When Lawrence was still unknown Garnett took trouble to place his poems and stories in journals. He guided Lawrence's rewritings of his early novels, was trusted by him to prune the prolixities of *Sons and Lovers*, and defended him against attacks by moralists.

At Cape, Garnett revived C. M. Doughty, published T. E. Lawrence, and fostered the careers of many younger writers, notably H. E. Bates, Henry Green (Henry Yorke), and Liam O'Flaherty. William Plomer, who succeeded him at Cape, maintained that Garnett's work with other writers was 'creative in a special sense, far more creative, I consider, than most writers' (Jefferson, 287).

Garnett wrote numerous book reviews and critical articles in which he championed contemporary authors: a selection of these was published as *Friday Nights* (1922). He promoted the cause of the Russian writers translated by his wife and wrote books such as *Tolstoy* (1914) and *Turgenev* (1917). But his acute critical sense failed him in his own creative writing. His three early fictions are not particularly memorable. His four published plays reveal the pessimistic side of his nature, and while aiming at tragedy, offer little but pain. One of them, *The Breaking Point* (1907) was refused a licence for performance and became a *cause célèbre* in the campaign against stage censorship.

Garnett never cared for worldly success, and began to lose interest in his authors once they became popular. He lambasted the reading public for its poor taste, but maintained that there was still a 'residuum of educated folk' (Jefferson, 285) who appreciated good literature. He considered himself an outsider and was sceptical of all politics and religion. He supported the Boers at the time of the Second South African War of 1899–1902, and during the First World War wrote savage satires against it, collected as *Papa's War* (1919). He also served in 1915 with the first British ambulance unit for Italy. He scorned the establishment and refused all honours, including a Companionship of Honour, which he dismissed as 'that thing they give dentists'.

Garnett had great physical courage, and was undaunted by picking up a live adder or confronting a mad odd-job man wielding an axe. He was well over 6 feet tall, slight and sensitive when young, ponderous and formidable when old. His face looked sad in repose, especially when he took off his thick-lensed spectacles, and he was apt to be melancholy when alone. But in company he was often witty and mischievous, and loved to tease those of whom he was fond. He died of a cerebral haemorrhage at his London flat, 9 Pond Place, on 19 February 1937 and was cremated at Golders Green crematorium.

RICHARD D. C. GARNETT

Sources G. Jefferson, *Edward Garnett: a life in literature* (1982) · R. Garnett, *Constance Garnett: a heroic life* (1991) · H. E. Bates, *Edward Garnett* (1950) · B. McCrimmon, *Richard Garnett: the scholar as librarian* (1989) · D. Garnett, 'Edward Garnett: a biographical note', in J. Conrad, *Conrad's prefaces to his Works* (1937), v–viii · personal knowledge (2004) · private information (2004)
Archives Eton, letters to John Galsworthy · JRL, letters to Allan Monkhouse · King's School, Canterbury, corresp. with Arnold Bennett · NL Scot., letters to R. B. Cunninghame Graham · NL Wales, letters to Geraint Goodwin · NL Wales, corresp. with Thomas Jones · NYPL, reader's reports, Berg collection · Ransom HRC, corresp. · U. Birm. L., letters to Francis Brett Young, 1915–19 · U. Reading L., letters to the Bodley Head · U. Reading L., letters to Jonathan Cape
Likenesses E. M. Heath, oils, 1896, repro. in K. Gänzl, *The complete 'Aspects of love'* (1990); priv. coll. · S. Bussy, pastels, c.1914, repro. in Bates, *Edward Garnett*; priv. coll. · F. Dodd, charcoal drawing, c.1926, Tate collection · L. Moholy, photograph, 1936, NPG
Wealth at death largely in books and MSS

Garnett [*née* Hart], **Elizabeth** (1839–1921), missionary to navvies and author, was born on 23 September 1839 in Otley, Yorkshire. The first and apparently only child of Joshua Hart, vicar of Otley from 1837 until his death in 1867, and his wife, Hannah, she was educated at home. A strong Anglican as a result, she claimed that her interest in the navvies began when her father consecrated a memorial to those killed while building the nearby Bramhope railway tunnel. She married an Anglican clergyman, Charles Garnett (1834–1862), the son of Peter Garnett, paper manufacturer in Otley, on 13 November 1861, but he died within a year of the marriage, on 13 October 1862, apparently while the couple were still on their honeymoon.

Nearly ten years later Garnett found a 'new vista of interest in a lonely life' (Garnett, 'Navvy Mission Society', 94) after a friend took her to see the navvy settlement at Lindley Wood, in Wharfedale, a few miles above Otley, where a reservoir was being built for the city of Leeds. After running a Sunday school for navvy lads there for nearly a year, Garnett moved to the settlement, despite family opposition. In 1874 Lewis Moule Evans, newly appointed vicar of nearby Leathley, also began missionary work at Lindley Wood. The Christian Excavators' Union (popularly known as the Navvies' Mission) was established in November 1877 after Evans, along with the eight teachers of the Navvy Sunday School, including Garnett, sent out some 400 letters of appeal to high-placed Anglicans throughout the nation. As a result Evans is recorded on his grave in Leathley parish churchyard as being the union's founder, but Garnett must be considered its co-founder, both because of her earlier work and because it was the royalties from her first publication, a 'navvy novel' entitled *Little Rainbow* (1877), that provided the financial support for this appeal. Through her missionary work, a further eight navvy novels, and her lively reports on the mission in *Our Navvies*, *Women's Mission*, and the *Quarterly Letter to the Navvies*, which she edited from 1878 until 1917, Elizabeth Garnett was the spirit of the union from Evans's premature death in 1878 until her own in 1921.

While Garnett held no official role within the union save that of a lady section head, her zeal brought much support to it. Commencing with a membership of thirty-seven, including seven navvies, in 1877, the union boasted a total of 700 supporters by 1917. Of course its first aim was that of evangelizing the navvies and their families. This was accomplished not just through the provision of some thirty-nine mission rooms and missionaries, these often being navvies who had come to faith through the union, but in the day and night schools and libraries which the union established in these isolated settlements. It also introduced various welfare measures such as sick clubs and savings banks, while harsh winters prompted it to provide soup kitchens, first for navvy children, then for the families, and, during one outbreak of smallpox, a hospital and attendant nurse. Few navvies may have become Christians through all this work, but the union did make a significant improvement in navvies' working and living conditions and in their moral outlook.

It was in the union's subsidiary but highly necessary role of gaining publicity and support for its work that Garnett proved most successful. Through her writings she gained a huge audience, some 155,000 copies of the *Letter* being distributed during every quarter of 1904 when the publication was at its height. More significantly, her readers gained a sympathy for the navvies, and a 'strong-jawed and strong-willed little woman' (Sullivan, 204) accused of possessing a 'mingy sanctity' by Sullivan found a great deal of love among 'her navvy family'. Garnett died at 6 Canning Road, Croydon, Surrey, on 22 March 1921. A memorial was erected in her honour in Ripon Cathedral in 1926.

D. K. DRUMMOND

Sources D. Sullivan, *The navvymen* (1983) · T. Coleman, *The railway navvies: a history of the men who made the railway*, new edn (1968) · Mrs C. Garnett [E. Garnett], 'How and why the Navvy Mission Society was formed', *Woman's mission: a series of congress papers on the philanthropic work of women*, ed. Baroness Burdett-Coutts [A. G. Burdett-Coutts] (1893), 92–105 · Mrs C. Garnett [E. Garnett], *Our navvies: a dozen years ago and today* (1885) · papers relating to Elizabeth Garnett, the Garnett family and the Rev. Joshua Hart, Otley Museum, West Yorkshire · parish registers, Otley, W. Yorks. AS, Leeds · b. cert. · m. cert. · d. cert.
Archives Otley Museum, West Yorkshire, papers relating to Elizabeth Garnett, *née* Hart, and to Joshua Hart and the Garnett family | LPL, copies of the *Quarterly Letter to the Navvies*, after 1893 *The Quarterly Letter to those on Public Works*
Likenesses illustrations, repro. in Coleman, *Railway navvies* · line drawing (after photograph), Otley Museum, West Yorkshire · photograph, Otley Museum, West Yorkshire
Wealth at death £4859 4s. 1d.: probate, 12 May 1921, CGPLA Eng. & Wales

Garnett, Henry (1555–1606), Jesuit, was born at Heanor, Derbyshire, the son of Brian Garnett (*d.* 1576), schoolmaster, and his wife, Alice Jay. He was born in the second half of 1555, perhaps about the time of the feast of St Henry (15 July). His father became master of the grammar school in Nottingham in 1565. Garnett had at least two brothers, Richard (father of Thomas *Garnett SJ) and John, and at least three sisters: Margaret and Eleanor, both of whom became nuns in Louvain, and Anne. Henry's family conformed to the religious changes introduced by Elizabeth I.

Early life Garnett was a student at the grammar school in Nottingham when his father was appointed master. On 24 August 1567 he was elected a scholar at Winchester College, which he entered the following year. Because of the lack of earlier contact between the Garnetts and Winchester College, some biographers, including Philip Caraman, speculate that the family selected Winchester because of its lingering allegiance to Catholicism. Thomas Stanney, a Jesuit who served under Garnett in England for many years, testified to his academic prowess—he was:

> the prime scholar of Winchester College, very skilful in music and in playing upon the instruments, very modest in his countenance and in all his actions, so much that the schoolmasters and wardens offered him very great friendship, to be placed by their means in New College, Oxford.   (Gerard, *Contributions towards a Life of Father Henry Garnet, SJ*, 62)

But Garnett did not move on to New College. Jacobean authors, including Robert Abbot, seeking to blacken his reputation because of the Gunpowder Plot, asserted that (in the summary of the Victorian Jesuit John Gerard) 'Garnet was guilty at Winchester not only of the grossest immorality, but of a precocious display of his aptitude for plots, probably unique in schoolboy annals [to cut off the right hand of the headmaster]' (ibid., 6). More likely, religious reasons prompted his departure from Winchester for London in late 1571.

Richard Tottell, the celebrated publisher of legal works, employed Garnett as a proof-reader and corrector. At Tottell's, Garnett met Sir John Popham, attorney-general, with whom he often dined and to whom he confessed his interest in legal studies. But for reasons unknown, Garnett abandoned that career and sailed for Portugal in 1575 with fellow Wykehamist Giles Gallop to enter the Society of Jesus. Passing through Santiago de Compostela, they went overland to Rome and were accepted into the Jesuit novitiate at Sant' Andrea on 11 September 1575. Garnett did his philosophical and theological studies at the Roman College. Among his professors were the mathematician Christopher Clavius and the theologian Robert Bellarmine, both of whom praised his virtues and abilities. Ordained about 1582, Garnett remained in Rome to lecture in Hebrew, metaphysics, and mathematics; and to serve as English confessor at St Peter's. In May of 1584 Robert Persons asked the Jesuit General Claudio Acquaviva to send Garnett to England. Because Clavius wanted Garnett to succeed him at the Roman College, Acquaviva refused.

Henry Garnett (1555–1606), by Johan Wierix

Moreover, Acquaviva believed Garnett 'more suited to the quiet life rather than the unsure and worrisome one that must be lived in England' (McCoog, 'Correspondence', 170). On 2 May 1586 Acquaviva finally granted permission to Garnett and to Robert Southwell to travel to England. In his instructions, Acquaviva appointed Garnett superior during the journey and successor to William Weston, Jesuit superior in England, if anything should happen to Weston. Among the faculties and privileges granted was permission to print books for defence of the faith and edification of Catholics. The two departed on 8 May, embarked at Calais, and landed not far from Folkestone on 7 July (by English reckoning).

Life on the English mission There were five Jesuits in England in the summer of 1586: Thomas Pounde, Thomas Metham, Ralph Emerson, William Crichton (all in prison), and Weston. Garnett and Southwell met Weston at a London inn on 13 July. Because the intense surveillance and renewed persecution caused by the discovery of the Babington plot made London too dangerous for any prolonged discussion, the three departed the following day for Harlesford (or Hurleyford), Berkshire, home of Richard Bold, former favourite of Robert Dudley, earl of Leicester, and recent convert of Weston. For eight days they prayed, heard confessions, sang masses (including some by William Byrd), exhorted each other to the mission at hand, and discussed procedures and strategies. Important for the survival of the mission, Weston provided Garnett and Southwell with names of Catholic households who would receive them, and explained the financial system he had established with Catholic laity. On 23 July guides conducted Garnett either to Harrowden, the Northamptonshire residence of William, Lord Vaux; or to Shoby, the residence of Vaux's daughter Eleanor Brooksby, in Leicestershire. This was his introduction to the Vaux family whose members supported and succoured him until his execution. Southwell returned to the London area to receive incoming priests at Vaux's house in Hackney, Middlesex. Weston, meanwhile, travelled to Oxford on business before continuing on to London. On 3 August, outside Bishopsgate, Weston was captured. In England for less than a month, Garnett was now superior.

Spies kept the government informed of the movements of Garnett and Southwell and both were often nearly captured. In February 1587 the two met in London. Drawing on his experience and taking advantage of his contacts acquired from his work for Tottell with the Stationers' Company, Garnett advised Southwell on the establishment of a secret press. Its exact location is unknown but it was within a house owned by Anne Howard, countess of Arundel, and most likely within the precincts of a former Augustinian hospital near Spitalfields. Between spring 1587 and the press's closure in late 1588, it published *A Consolatory Letter to All the Afflicted Catholikes in England* by the still unidentified H. B., and Southwell's *An Epistle of Comfort*.

Perched in a window of a friend's house in Ludgate Hill, Garnett watched the triumphal procession to a service of thanksgiving at St Paul's for victory over the Spanish Armada on 24 November 1588. Fearful of assassination attempts, the government ordered that no spectators be allowed to observe the proceedings from any window unless the householders pledged their lives and fortunes for the spectator's loyalty. 'Because they [his friends] are of the opinion that we are more interested in the safety of the Queen than her Calvinist ministers are', Garnett wrote to Acquaviva, many were willing to pledge for him (McCoog, *Society of Jesus*, 257). A consequence of the scare surrounding the Armada was the first attempt to formulate an oath whereby Catholics could proclaim their allegiance to the queen. The version proposed by the government required denial of papal deposing power, and the spiritual power of the pope in England. The Catholic version insisted that they would show her the same obedience owed to any secular prince by a Catholic and proposed to do so on the basis of the 'apostolic concession whereby it is licit to recognize her as queen until the public execution of the bull [of her excommunication]' (ibid.). Garnett submitted both to Acquaviva with a request for guidance, but the matter died when the privy council rejected the Catholic version.

Garnett steadily expanded the network of Catholic households where priests could be accommodated, but raids remained a persistent problem. Nine Jesuits and an unknown number of secular clergy met at a house rented by the Vaux sisters, Anne and Eleanor Brooksby, traditionally believed to be Baddlesley Clinton in Warwickshire, in October 1592. On the 19th, after the departure of four Jesuits, pursuivants arrived at the house. As they searched the premises, five Jesuits and an unknown number of secular clergy hid in a tunnel, ankle deep in water. If the pursuivants had arrived a day earlier they could have captured every Jesuit within the realm.

After, and probably because of, the raid in Warwickshire, Garnett asked to be relieved of the burden of superiorship. The capture of Southwell in June 1592 added to his worries: 'While I cannot help myself in my sadness and anxiety … deprived as I am now of my companion, my dearest father and my helper [I await] his greatest achievements yet' (Caraman, *Garnet*, 151). Southwell was executed at Tyburn on 21 February 1595. Garnett beseeched Acquaviva for a qualified assistant who would eventually succeed him as superior. Henry Walpole was sent. Captured almost upon arrival in December 1593, Walpole was executed in York on 7 April 1595.

At Southwell's trial Sir Edward Coke attacked the Jesuit for his use of the controversial doctrine of equivocation. Some time thereafter, Garnett composed a treatise on the subject to defend his associate's reputation and to explain fully the proper use and limitations of the practice. Garnett's work remained unpublished until the nineteenth century.

About the same time Garnett addressed a second controversial issue, occasional conformity (the practice whereby Catholics attended services of the established church to avoid persecution and financial ruin) which surfaced again in the early 1590s. Thomas Bell, an influential diocesan priest in northern England, justified the practice in sermons and manuscripts. Despite his acceptance of the established church in 1593 and his subsequent persecution of his former colleagues, many still accepted his arguments.

Garnett's *An Apology Against the Defence of Schisme* ([1593]) attacked Bell's theological interpretation of several scriptural passages. Contrary to Bell's claims no pope had granted a dispensation to attend heretical services. In fact, because attendance at a protestant service involved contempt for the Roman Catholic church, a pope could not grant a dispensation. Garnett continued his battle with *A Treatise of Christian Renunciation* ([1593]), a collection of quotations from the writings of the fathers and the canons of the church regarding what each believer must be prepared to renounce for the faith. To strengthen Catholics, Garnett established the Dominican Sodality of the Holy Rosary for men, and the Jesuit Sodality of the Blessed Virgin for women. On his secret printing press, Garnett published *The Societie of the Rosary* ([1593–4]).

During the first week of November 1593, Garnett visited Weston and other imprisoned priests at Wisbech in Cambridgeshire. Supported at considerable expense by Catholics, priests in Wisbech lived a style of life that shocked their protestant contemporaries. Although there were periodic searches and the occasional disputation with a visiting protestant cleric, priests had their own dining room and makeshift chapel where they were generally able to celebrate daily mass. Catholics flocked to Wisbech for spiritual direction and the sacraments. In a letter to Acquaviva, Garnett referred to Wisbech as a 'college of venerable confessors' (Caraman, *Garnet*, 169). He even celebrated his visit by singing a solemn high mass.

Conflict and compromise Tension between diocesan clergy and Jesuits lurked beneath the surface for years before the outbreak of the so-called 'Wisbech stirs' in late 1594. Scandalized by lack of proper decorum and the introduction of frivolous practices (nothing more serious than morris dancers and a hobby horse at Christmas according to Weston's principal opponent Christopher Bagshaw), Weston withdrew from communal life and refused to return until common rules governed the life of the community. His opponents accused him, and the Jesuits, of seeking to dominate the secular clergy and of diverting communal funds for their own use. Garnett sought to defuse the situation. With his concurrence, delegations of Catholic clergy visited the prison to confer with both sides. By the end of 1595, they reached a compromise. Garnett, however, feared that stories of student discontent at the Jesuit-administered English College, Rome, and reports of tension between some English exiles (Charles Paget, a few Jesuits in Brussels, and William Holt) would circulate in England and stir up the still smouldering embers at Wisbech. In the summer of 1596, Robert Fisher, a student opposed to Jesuit involvement in the English College, arrived in England to establish contact between Jesuit foes in Brussels and Rome with Jesuit opponents in Wisbech. The issues were now much more serious. Jesuit opponents accused the English members of the society of administrative incompetence and financial irregularities in Rome; of exploiting their control of the Spanish purse in Brussels to deprive their opponents of much needed financial assistance; of attempting to dominate the secular clergy in England and preserving more comfortable chaplaincies for themselves and their secular clerical supporters; and of such uncompromisingly strong support for Spain and her machinations against England that Catholics were generally considered disloyal traitors. The remedy was removal of the society from the administration of English seminaries on the continent, if not from the mission itself—a move that some believed would result in the crown's conceding some form of religious tolerance—and the restoration of ordinary episcopal governance in England. Opposition of Belgian and Spanish Jesuit superiors to the existence of quasi-ecclesiastical peculiars within their provinces (English Jesuit institutions over which they had little jurisdiction) compounded the problems for the English Jesuits. Throughout Garnett defended his subjects in England.

In spring 1598 both Rome and the Jesuit curia acted. On 7 March, Rome appointed George Blackwell archpriest with limited jurisdiction within England. He was provided with twelve assistants and exhorted to obtain the advice of the Jesuit superior in serious matters. A month later, on 16 April, Acquaviva established a prefecture for the English Jesuits. Persons was prefect, with Joseph Creswell and Holt vice-prefects in Spain and Flanders, and Garnett superior in England. Neither novel form of governance satisfied critics. Coincidentally Garnett pronounced his final vows as a Jesuit somewhere in London, perhaps his house near Spitalfields, on 8 May.

Not everyone was satisfied with the Roman decision. Some secular clergy challenged the novel structure because it was founded not on papal authority but on the questionable authority of a cardinal protector. They accused the English Jesuits of foisting their puppet upon the English church and appealed to Rome. Meanwhile, with support from Richard Bancroft, bishop of London, they escalated their attacks on English Jesuits. These 'appellants' presented themselves as loyal Catholics, as opposed to the Jesuit traitors. They later obtained assistance from the crown and from Henri IV of France. Supporters of the archpriest labelled the appellants schismatics. The subsequent controversy endured until October 1602: a papal brief ratified the ecclesiastical structure, exonerated appellants from charges of schism, and deleted the original clause requiring consultation with the Jesuit superior, but did not remove Jesuits from the mission. Any hope that the English government would reward the appellants was dashed by a royal proclamation of 5 November which distinguished between traitorous Jesuits and disloyal and disobedient appellants, but ordered both out of the kingdom.

The Gunpowder Plot Enthusiastic about Catholic prospects upon the accession of James I, Garnett wrote to Persons on 16 April 1603: 'Great hope [there] is of toleration: and so general a consent of Catholics in the [King's] proclaiming [that] it seemeth God will work much' (Caraman, *Garnet*, 305). Moreover, any attempt to press the claims of any foreign competitors would harm the Catholic cause. In his pursuit of the English throne, James had courted English Catholics and insinuated, if not actually promised, religious tolerance. Expectation quickly turned to disappointment and anger. Rumours of Catholic plots and conspiracies even reached Rome and Acquaviva ordered Garnett to do everything he could to prevent Catholics from resorting to violence. On 25 July 1605, in confession and under the seal thereof, Garnett learned of a plot from the Jesuit Oswald Tesimond. With the permission of his penitent, Robert Catesby, Tesimond wished to discuss a 'case of conscience' with his confessor and superior. Garnett's threats, admonitions, and warnings failed to prevent the Gunpowder Plot. England would long remember the fifth of November. The discovery of the plot ended any chance of religious toleration of Catholics and unleashed a frenzied search for the conspirators and their associates.

Garnett was at Coughton Court near Alcester, Warwickshire, the home of the Throckmortons, when he heard of the plot's discovery on 6 November. Some time before the end of November he moved to Hindlip Hall near Worcester, home of the Habingtons. On 30 November, he, 'being newly charged, as I understand, with the late most horrible attempt, as if I had been accessory thereunto', protested his innocence in a letter to the privy council (Foley, 4.66). On 15 January 1606 the government issued a proclamation for his arrest along with Tesimond and John Gerard. It described Garnett as:

of a middling Stature, full Faced, Fatte of body, of Complexion faire: his Forehead high on each side, with a little thinne Haire comming down upon the middest of the forepart of his Head: the Haire of his Head and Beard griseled: of Age betweene fiftie and threescore: his Beard on his Cheekes cut close, on his Chinne but thinne, and somewhat short: his Gate upright, and comely for a Fatte man. (Larkin and Hughes, 133)

The search began on 20 January: Nicholas Owen and Ralph Ashley were discovered on the 23rd at Hindlip Hall, and Garnett and Oldcorne on the 27th. Garnett appeared for his first examination on 13 February. He was transferred from the Gatehouse prison to the Tower of London the next day. In early March he was charged with complicity in the Gunpowder Plot and tortured. His trial in the Guildhall began on 28 March. Among those on the bench was Popham, now chief justice of the king's bench. According to Coke, Garnett, the instigator of the plot:

hath many gifts and endowments of nature, by art learned, a good linguist and, by profession, a Jesuit and a Superior as indeed he is Superior to all his predecessors in devilish treason, a Doctor of Dissimulation, Deposing of Princes, Disposing of Kingdoms, Daunting and deterring of subjects, and Destruction. (Caraman, *Garnet*, 403)

Garnett defended himself against all Coke's charges and explained Catholic teaching on papal power and equivocation, on which Coke had attempted to place a sinister construction during the trial. The court found Garnett guilty as charged and sentenced him to death. He was hanged, drawn, and quartered on 3 May 1606 in St Paul's Churchyard, London. His remains were dispersed.

Almost immediately after Garnett's death London theatregoers were reminded of the sinister reputation his defence of equivocation had brought him in protestant eyes, when the porter in Shakespeare's *Macbeth*, welcoming imaginary visitors at the gate of hell, alias Inverness Castle, exclaimed 'Faith, here's an equivocator that could swear in both the scales against either scale, who committed treason enough for God's sake, yet could not equivocate to heaven' (*Macbeth*, II.iii, 7–11). English Catholics venerated Garnett as a martyr. Among the many relics associated with him, was the famous 'straw', a small husk on which a drop of Garnett's blood bore a strong resemblance to his face. Eventually smuggled out of the kingdom and kept at the English Jesuit college in Liège, the 'straw' was lost during the French Revolution. According to Caraman, Acquaviva allowed Garnett's cause for canonization to be introduced but the suppression of the Jesuits in 1773 halted its slow progress. His name was originally included in the list of martyrs submitted to Rome in 1874 by the archdiocese of Westminster, but eventually deleted because of fear of possible political involvement. It has not yet been reintroduced. THOMAS M. McCOOG

Sources A. F. Allison and D. M. Rogers, eds., *The contemporary printed literature of the English Counter-Reformation between 1558 and 1640*, 2 vols. (1989–94) • P. Caraman, *Henry Garnet, 1555–1606, and the Gunpowder Plot* (1964) • P. Caraman, *A study in friendship: Saint Robert Southwell and Henry Garnet* (1995) • H. Foley, ed., *Records of the English province of the Society of Jesus*, 7 vols. in 8 (1875–83) • A. Fraser, *The Gunpowder Plot* (1996) • J. Gerard, 'Contributions towards a life of Father Henry Garnet, SJ', *The Month*, 91 (1898), 6–21, 121–30, 238–46, 356–67, 458–67, 603–10; 92 (1898), 144–52; pubd separately (1898) • L. Hicks, ed., *Letters and memorials of Father Robert Persons*, Catholic RS, 39 (1942) • D. Jardine, ed., *A treatise of equivocation* (1851) • J. F. Larkin and P. L. Hughes, eds., *Royal proclamations of King James I, 1603–1625* (1973) • T. G. Law, ed., *The archpriest controversy: documents relating to the dissensions of the Roman Catholic clergy, 1597–1602*, 2 vols., CS, new ser., 56, 58 (1896–8) • T. M. McCoog, *The Society of Jesus in Ireland, Scotland, and England, 1541–1588* (1996) • T. M. McCoog, *English and Welsh Jesuits, 1555–1650*, 2 vols., Catholic RS, 74–5 (1994–5) • T. M. McCoog, ed., *Monumenta Angliae*, 1–2 (1992) • T. M. McCoog, 'Robert Parsons and Claudio Acquaviva: correspondence', *Archivum Historicum Societatis Iesu*, 58 (1999), 79–182 • P. Milward, *Religious controversies of the Elizabethan age* (1977) • P. Milward, *Religious controversies of the Jacobean age* (1978) • J. H. Pollen, *The institution of the archpriest Blackwell* (1916) • A. Pritchard, *Catholic loyalism in Elizabethan England* (1979) • P. Renold, ed., *The Wisbech stirs, 1595–1598*, Catholic RS, 51 (1958) • A. Walsham, *Church papists: Catholicism, conformity, and confessional polemic in early modern England* (1993)

Archives Archivum Romanum Societatis Iesu, Rome, corresp., 651/624 • Hatfield House, Hertfordshire, corresp., Hatfield MS 110 • Inner Temple, London, corresp., Petyt MS 538, vol. 47 • PRO, corresp., SP 12/271, 287; SP 14/1, 19, 20 • Westm. DA, corresp., VIII | Archives of the British Province of the Society of Jesus, London, Anglia MSS and Grene's Collectanea P, corresp., 46/12/1–2 • Archives of the British Province of the Society of Jesus, London, Stonyhurst MSS, philosophical notes, A.V. 15

Likenesses portrait, 18th cent.; Sothebys, 27 Feb 1963, lot 107 • A. Lommelin, line engraving, NPG • C. Weld, drawing (after portrait, 17th cent.), Stonyhurst College, Lancashire; repro. in Foley, *Records of the English Province of the Society of Jesus*, vols. 4 and 7 • J. Wierix, line engraving, BM [*see illus.*] • line engraving, BM, NPG • line engraving, BM, NPG; repro. in Endamon-Jones, *Apologia* (1619)

Garnett, Jeremiah (1793–1870), journalist, younger brother of Richard *Garnett, was born on 2 October 1793 at Wharfeside, Otley, in Yorkshire, where his father, William Garnett, was a paper manufacturer. His mother was Mary, *née* Rhodes, and his younger brother was Thomas *Garnett (1799–1878). After attending Rawdon School in Leeds and being apprenticed to a printer at Barnsley he entered the office of *Wheeler's Manchester Chronicle*, a tory newspaper, about 1814. A breach came in 1819 when he wrote a first-hand account of the Peterloo massacre, in which a working-class crowd, gathered to hear the orator Henry Hunt, was violently dispersed by a force of yeomanry; eleven persons were killed and some hundreds wounded. The *Chronicle* omitted most of his report and Garnett immediately resigned, moving to Huddersfield to edit the town's first newspaper, the *West Yorkshire Gazette*. A group of Manchester reformers subsequently called on his evidence in a legal action seeking to place responsibility for the casualties on the military.

Garnett returned to Manchester after six months, renewing his association with the *Chronicle*, but soon afterwards joined John Edward Taylor in establishing the *Manchester Guardian* on 21 May 1821. The first days of that journal were days of struggle. Garnett was printer, business manager, and sole reporter at a salary of £120. He took his notes in a rough shorthand extemporised by himself, and on occasions set them directly into type. As the paper gained ground his share in the editorial management increased. In 1826 he became a partner in the publishing firm, with a third share of the profits, and in January 1844 he became sole editor on the death of his partner, a position which he held until his retirement in 1861.

Partly under Garnett's influence before Taylor's death, and certainly so after, the paper became increasingly whig and reformist rather than radical. Garnett supported libertarian causes including Roman Catholic emancipation and the Divorce Bill of 1857. He opposed restrictions on Sunday trading. He joined the Manchester Anti-Corn Law League a week after its foundation in 1838 by, among others, John Bright. Although the two men had many aims in common their association did not last. Garnett was prepared to see the corn laws ameliorated short of abolition and supported Peel's tariff reductions of 1842. They disagreed more fundamentally in the following decade. Garnett reluctantly supported Bright's successful candidature in 1847 and 1852 for one of the two Manchester seats in parliament, but took the lead in securing his defeat in 1857. As a Palmerstonian Liberal, Garnett argued that Bright was unrepresentative of Manchester opinion, not least in his opposition to the Crimean War.

Garnett was active as a police commissioner, and in obtaining a charter of incorporation for Manchester. His writing was lucid and influential but his public appearances were rare. He was regarded by contemporaries as upright and benevolent. He was tall and strong, devoted to field sports, and widely read. He was twice married. After his retirement Garnett lived in Scotland and at Sale in Cheshire, where he died on 27 September 1870, survived by one of three daughters.

RICHARD GARNETT, *rev.* GEOFFREY TAYLOR

Sources *Manchester Guardian* (28 Sept 1870) · D. Ayerst, *Guardian: biography of a newspaper* (1971) · W. H. Mills, *The Manchester Guardian: a century of history* (1921) · personal knowledge (1889) · *Manchester Free Lance* (1 Oct 1870)
Archives Birm. CL, letters to Harriet Martineau
Likenesses photograph, repro. in Mills, *Manchester Guardian*, 92
Wealth at death under £50,000: probate, 10 Jan 1871, *CGPLA Eng. & Wales*

Garnett, John (1707/8–1782), Church of Ireland bishop of Clogher, was born at Lambeth, Surrey, the son of John Garnet (*d.* 1735), rector of Sigglesthorne, in the East Riding of Yorkshire. He was educated at a school in Beverley, Yorkshire, and matriculated at St John's College, Cambridge, on 21 May 1725. In September 1728 he moved to Sidney Sussex College where he graduated BA (1729) and MA (1732), becoming a fellow of the college and Lady Margaret preacher to the university.

In 1751 Garnett went to Ireland as chaplain to the duke of Dorset, lord lieutenant, and in 1752 became bishop of Ferns, from where he was translated to Clogher in 1758. A patron of the Church of Ireland clergyman and author Philip Skelton, Garnett received warm praise from Skelton's biographer, Samuel Burdy, who drew particular attention to the bishop's interest in literature, his good nature, and kindness to his domestic staff. Burdy's assessment was reiterated by Thomas Campbell in his *Philosophical Survey of the South of Ireland* (1777). In addition to several sermons Garnett published a *Dissertation on the Book of Job* (1749; 2nd edn, 1752), which he dedicated to the duke of

Newcastle. Described by Lord Morton as 'a very proper book for the ante-chamber of a prime minister', it offered, in addition to a statement on the virtues of patience, a strikingly original thesis.

Garnett died, aged seventy-four, at his home in Leinster Street, Dublin, on 1 March 1782. His son, **John Garnett** (1747/8–1813), was appointed dean of Exeter in February 1810, and died in Exeter on 11 March 1813, aged sixty-five.

RICHARD GARNETT, *rev.* PHILIP CARTER

Sources Venn, *Alum. Cant.* · *The complete works of the late Rev. Philip Skelton, to which is prefixed Burdy's life of the author*, ed. R. Lynam, 6 vols. (1824) · H. Cotton, *Fasti ecclesiae Hibernicae*, 1–2 (1845–8) · *GM*, 1st ser., 52 (1782), 150 · *GM*, 1st ser., 83/1 (1813), 389 · F. Ross, *Celebrities of the Yorkshire wolds* (1878)
Archives BL, corresp. with duke of Newcastle, Add. MSS 32710–33070 · BL, letters to earls of Hardwicke, Add. MSS 35596–35612 · Representative Church Body Library, Townshend MSS, letters to Lord Townshend
Likenesses J. Macardell, mezzotint (after Gainsborough), BM · oils, St John Cam. · oils, Sidney Sussex College, Cambridge

Garnett, John (1747/8–1813). *See under* Garnett, John (1707/8–1782).

Garnett, (William) John Poulton Maxwell (1921–1997), industrial relations officer, was born on 6 August 1921 in Hampstead, London, into the family of four sons and three daughters of (James Clerk) Maxwell *Garnett (1880–1958), educationist and peace campaigner, and his wife, Margaret Lucy (1887–1965), second daughter of Sir Edward Bagnall *Poulton, Hope professor of zoology at Oxford. William *Garnett, physicist and educational administrator, was his paternal grandfather, and Margaret Christian (Peggy) Jay (*d.* 1996), first wife of Douglas Patrick Thomas Jay, Baron Jay, politician, was the eldest of his three sisters. He was educated at Rugby School and at Kent School in the USA before becoming an undergraduate at Trinity College, Cambridge, in 1940. In 1941 he volunteered to join the Royal Navy and served briefly as a rating on the battleship *Malaya*. He was asked to volunteer for special service and joined the inshore patrol as a lieutenant. The patrol was engaged in difficult and dangerous work, taking agents and supplies to and fro across the English Channel. These experiences introduced him to the problems and opportunities of leadership, to which he was to devote the rest of his life. On 7 April 1943 he married (Kathleen) Barbara Rutherford Smith (*b.* 1918/19), schoolteacher, daughter of Reginald Rutherford Smith, medical practitioner. There were two sons and two daughters of the marriage, including Virginia (*b.* 1948), who in 1967 married Peter Bottomley and was secretary of state for health (1992–5) and for national heritage (1995–7). After the war Garnett returned to Cambridge and was awarded an upper second-class degree in economics. He then joined Imperial Chemical Industries in Glasgow as a clerk, and in due course was promoted to be personnel manager at their plastics factory in Blackpool. For a short time he was in charge of the communications unit at the head office in London.

In 1962 Garnett became director of the Industrial Welfare Society (later renamed the Industrial Society). The

(William) **John Poulton Maxwell Garnett** (1921–1997), by Dod Miller, 1985

society provided him with the platform and opportunity he needed. For twenty-five years he developed the style, the ideas, and the convictions which influenced so many managers and supervisors throughout the 1960s, 1970s, and 1980s. In the words of one observer, 'he lit a torch for management'. The Industrial Society proved to be the ideal vehicle for the propagation of his ideas about management and industrial relations, which, although not entirely original, were innovatory at the time. When he joined as director 48 staff were employed with a turnover of £165,000; in 1986, when he retired, 380 staff managed a £10 million turnover. He was appointed CBE in 1970.

Garnett's messages were simple, clear, direct, and forceful. He believed in managers 'walking the job', and communicating regularly through 'team briefings' in groups with no more than fifteen people. He emphasized the accountability of leaders for involving people in their work. He hated waste of any kind—by which he meant the underutilization of people's skills and experience. He had a special regard for the role and function of the supervisor, whose importance he never forgot. All this and more he set out in detail in his book *The Work Challenge* (1973) and summarized on a plastic card listing leadership action points. In his own words:

> the leader's job is to call forth the gifts of people and help them to work for a common task … A crucial function of the leader is to take decisions. It is not just a question of taking the best decision but also taking it in a way which will obtain the best possible cooperation of the people who have to carry it out … We shall fulfil our place in history if we carry out the common sense actions contained in this book with

courage, humility and hope.   (Garnett, *The Work Challenge*, 1973, 11, 53, 105)

All along Garnett was driven by his Christian faith and by his belief in the ability of the individual.

Garnett was a handsome man with a classical profile and a shock of unruly hair which in later life was still present, though white. He held his audiences by the force and charm of his personality and the appeal of his ideas. At conferences he could be relied on to inspire and energize the participants. There were many firms and individuals who had reason to be grateful to him. Throughout a life of exceptional commitment, he proclaimed tirelessly the significance and importance of work in industry and commerce. Essentially an evangelical Christian, he was a crusader for the causes and the messages he believed in. He was a passionate man with strong yet practical ideas, which he expressed in thousands of speeches he made throughout the country. Both during his working life and in retirement he was asked to serve on many public bodies. He was a member of the Wilberforce inquiry into the miners' strike in 1972; arbitrator for a long-running Transport and General Workers' Union lorry drivers' strike in 1979; a member of the Churches' Council on Gambling (chair 1965–71); and chair of the West Lambeth Health Authority from 1986 to 1990 (being largely responsible for saving St Thomas's Hospital).

Garnett's first marriage was dissolved in 1985, and on 2 April that year he married Julia Charity (*b.* 1950), industrial relations officer, daughter of (Thomas) Douglas James *Cleverdon, BBC producer and publisher, and former wife of Martin Christopher Ollard. She had joined the Industrial Society in 1975, and was head of its common purpose campaign from 1977 to 1979, director of its communications and publicity division from 1979 to 1981, and founding head of its Pepperell department for inner cities and education work from 1981 to 1988; she was subsequently chief executive of Business in the Community from 1992. There were two daughters of this second marriage. With his second family Garnett continued to enjoy holidays on the Isle of Wight, where he was able to indulge his passion for sailing, and where he had built with his own hands a house (Stone House) and a Greek amphitheatre. In later life he became a regular visitor to the Greek islands, where he died on holiday on 14 August 1997. He was survived by his second wife and his six children. A memorial service was held at St Martin-in-the-Fields on 4 December 1997.   RICHARD O'BRIEN

Sources J. Cleverdon, memorial service address, 4 Dec 1997 · *The Times* (15 Aug 1997) · *Daily Telegraph* (16 Aug 1997) · *The Scotsman* (16 Aug 1997) · *The Independent* (18 Aug 1997) · *The Guardian* (18 Aug 1997) · 'John Garnett: memoirs of a communicator', *Personnel Management* (Aug 1986), 24–7 · *WWW* · personal knowledge (2004) · private information (2004) · m. certs.
Archives Archives of the Industrial Society, 3 Carlton House Terrace, London
Likenesses D. Miller, photograph, 1985, News International Syndication, London [*see illus.*] · photograph, repro. in *Personnel Management*, 24 · photograph, repro. in *The Times* · photograph, repro. in *Daily Telegraph* · photograph, repro. in *The Scotsman* · photograph, repro. in *The Independent* · photograph, repro. in *The Guardian*

Garnett, Lucy Mary Jane (1849–1934), folklorist and traveller, was born in Sheffield, the daughter of Thomas Garnett, surgeon, and his wife, Lucy Sarah, *née* Roberts. Lucy Garnett travelled extensively in the Balkans and Middle East, recording the customs of the people among whom she lived. In Smyrna, and later in Salonica, she learned Greek and Turkish; her familiarity with demotic Greek led to a collaboration with the folklorist John Stuart Stuart-Glennie, with whom she translated and published her first compilation, *Greek Folk-Songs from the Turkish Provinces of Greece*, in 1885. Later books included *The Women of Turkey and their Folk-Lore* (1890), *Mysticism and Magic in Turkey* (1912), *Ottoman Wonder Tales* (1915), and *Balkan Home-Life* (1917). She also published in reviews and magazines such as the *Fortnightly Review*, *Good Words*, *The Nation* (New York), the *Scottish Review*, and the *Nineteenth Century*. In the 1890s she lived for a while in Manila, and published several articles on the ethnography of the Philippines.

Lucy Garnett's most important achievement was the documentation and comparative study of Balkan folk literature, which is still valuable when detached from the dubious theories of 'scientific' folklore with which Stuart-Glennie tended to preface and gloss her work. She was particularly interested in the lives and status of women, and took advantage of her access to the women's quarters of remote Christian and Muslim communities to supplement the accounts of earlier travellers for whom, as she noted, 'the female sex may be said not to have existed … at all' (*The Women of Turkey*, 1, 1890, lxxvii). She was also drawn to Gypsies, monks, and dervishes, observing them with a crisp protestant detachment. In 1893 she was granted a civil-list pension for services to literature. She died at St Margaret's Nursing Home, Twickenham, Middlesex, on 24 February 1934. ROWENA FOWLER

Sources *WWW* · E. Martell, L. G. Pine, and A. Lawrence, eds., *Who was who among English and European authors, 1931–1949*, 2 (1978) · R. M. Dorson, *The British folklorists: a history* (1968), 312 · D. C. E. Swanson, *Modern Greek studies in the west* (1960) · B. Melman, *Women's orients: Englishwomen and the Middle East, 1718–1918* (1990) · *Wellesley index* · *CGPLA Eng. & Wales* (1934) · d. cert. · b. cert.

Garnett, (James Clerk) Maxwell (1880–1958), educationist and peace campaigner, was born at Cherry Hinton, Cambridge, on 13 October 1880, the eldest of the five children of William *Garnett (1850–1932), physicist and educationist, and his wife, Rebecca Samways (1853–1945). The career of Maxwell Garnett, as he was always known, has striking resemblances to that of his father, from whom he inherited his height (over 6 feet), commanding presence, religious beliefs, and most significantly also his academic brilliance, interest in administration, and confidence in his own policy judgements. A Congregationalist, who became secretary of the Public Schools' Scripture Union, he was educated at St Paul's School and from 1899 at Trinity College, Cambridge, where he won a major

(**James Clerk) Maxwell Garnett** (1880–1958), by Karl Pollak, c.1948

scholarship and the Sheepshanks astronomical exhibition, rowed in the university's trial crew, became joint-sixteenth wrangler in 1902, and gained a first class in the first division of part two of the mathematics tripos in 1903. Thereafter he lectured briefly in mathematics at University College, London, and became a Smith's prizeman at Cambridge in 1904 and a junior research fellow of his college (a six-year position without residential obligation) in 1905.

For eight years after 1904 Garnett worked as an examiner at the Board of Education, and he was called to the bar in 1908 by the Inner Temple. He married Margaret Lucy (1887–1965), second daughter of Professor Edward Bagnall *Poulton of Oxford, in 1910: they were to have four sons and three daughters. The eldest son died in infancy and another, John *Garnett (1921–1997), was to be director of the Industrial Society and father of the Conservative politician Virginia Bottomley; the eldest daughter, Margaret, known as Peggy, served on the London county council and was the first wife of the Labour politician Douglas Jay.

In 1912, at the young age of thirty-one, Maxwell Garnett was appointed to the dual position of principal of the Municipal School of Technology at Manchester, a former mechanics' institute which had been taken over by the city council twenty years previously, and dean of the faculty of technology, which was part of the University of Manchester. He moved his family to Westfield, Victoria Park, Manchester, and found himself at the centre of tension between the local need for trained artisans and the national need for graduates in technology and science. He wanted the municipal school to concentrate on higher education, and had considerable success in pursuing this policy: it was redesignated the Manchester College of Technology in 1918, and he was made CBE and rewarded with an increased salary the following year. But his determination to get his own way won him enemies, and in 1920 the city council's education committee reversed his policy, at least for twelve months, by cutting the number of degree students and admitting boys from technical schools as full-time students. In an attempt to put pressure on the education committee, Garnett wrote to applicants for degree courses informing them of the reduction in the number of places available to them; but the education committee censured him publicly for what it saw as an act of disloyalty. After the county council endorsed the committee's action, Garnett resigned in July 1920. The *Times Educational Supplement* (22 July 1920), though sympathetic to his attempt to create a northern counterpart of London's Imperial College of Science and Technology, criticized his 'unwise letter' for giving the 'parochial party' its chance to force him out.

However, Maxwell Garnett had, even before his resignation, been appointed to the job which made him a national figure—the general secretaryship of the League of Nations Union (LNU), an association to mobilize support in Britain for the pioneering international organization which had come into existence at Geneva in January 1920. He was drawn to this work not only by his Christianity but also by a scholarly interest in educational psychology which convinced him that a science of peace was possible: he received a ScD degree for his book *Education and World Citizenship* (1921). He must also have been influenced by the deaths caused by military service of his two brothers, Stuart and Kenneth (both first-class Cambridge mathematicians and muscular Christians, the former the founder of the Sea Scouts, the latter a rowing blue), and of his brother-in-law, Ronald Poulton Palmer (an English rugby international).

As in his previous job, Garnett had a clear vision for his institution which he maintained in face of objections from those officially responsible for determining its policy: he wanted the LNU to be an educational body and not a pressure group. This approach, coupled with his intellectual power and personal drive, helped it develop into a peace association of unprecedented respectability and size: it attracted an unusually large minority of Conservative supporters, persuaded virtually all party leaders to become vice-presidents, received a royal charter in 1925, and collected more than 400,000 annual subscriptions at its peak in 1931. However, Garnett was obstructive when members of the LNU's executive committee wished to press successive British governments to give greater support to the League of Nations. As early as 1926 leading LNU members were attempting to find him another post, so he could depart with dignity; and in 1929 he signed a secret agreement to leave if he could obtain either a university headship, a major post at Geneva, or a knighthood. None of these could be procured for him, however—the last of

them was refused by Ramsay MacDonald, who had a long-standing grudge against the LNU—and Garnett remained at his post for a further nine years.

As strains increased after 1931 between the LNU's activists (who mostly supported the Liberal or Labour parties) and the National Government (which was dominated by the Conservatives), Garnett saw himself as an increasingly embattled defender of the non-partisan nature of the LNU against those wishing to commit it to left-wing politics. A number of his fellow staff members believed that he not only exceeded his remit as a salaried administrator, but also lacked political sense and behaved in a didactic manner: an office joke was that his initials stood for 'Just Call Me God' (private information). However, everyone in the LNU respected his ability; and the issue over which matters came to a head was one on which many members of both executive committee and staff privately agreed with him. Early in 1936 the LNU's acknowledged leader, Viscount Cecil of Chelwood, began insisting that it co-operate with the Rassemblement universel pour la paix (international peace campaign), a continental movement for collective security which not only had close links with the communists but in Britain duplicated the position of the LNU, which was in any case experiencing financial difficulties as the reputation of the League of Nations declined. The LNU's executive committee deferred to Cecil and endorsed the international peace campaign; but Garnett and some of his colleagues appeared to be obstructive. Cecil and his supporters forced Garnett to take six months' sick leave in January 1938 and dismissed him shortly before he was due to return.

Although only fifty-seven Garnett did not obtain further paid employment, though he received a pension from the LNU. During the remaining twenty years of his life he wrote more books about internationalism, and 'used *The Times* as his parish magazine' (private information). Having lived during his LNU years in Hampstead, first at 1 Foley Avenue and then at 21 Well Walk, he moved early in the Second World War to 37 Park Town, Oxford. From 1956 he lived at his holiday home since 1946, Horestone Cottage, at Seaview on the Isle of Wight, where he had loved to sail since boyhood. He died at Seaview on 19 March 1958, in the Fairy Hill Nursing Home.

MARTIN CEADEL

Sources DNB · WW · WWW · J. R. Tanner, ed., *Historical register of the University of Cambridge … to the year 1910* (1917) · D. S. Birn, *The League of Nations Union, 1918–1945* (1981) · Venn, *Alum. Cant.* · *The Times* (13 July 1920) · *The Times* (20 March 1958) · *Times Educational Supplement* (22 July 1920) · H. B. Charlton, *Portrait of a university, 1851–1951: to commemorate the centenary of Manchester University* (1951) · private information (2004) [J. Garnett, M. Jay, C. A. Macartney] · B. M. Allen, *William Garnett: a memoir* (1933) · E. B. Poulton, *The life of Ronald Poulton* (1919) · M. L. Garnett, *Kenneth Gordon Garnett, MC, RFA, 30 July 1892–22 August 1917* (1917)
Archives BL, corresp. with Lord Cecil, Add. MS 51136 · BLPES, League of Nations Union MSS · Bodl. Oxf., Gilbert Murray MSS, corresp. with Gilbert Murray · JRL, *Guardian* archives, letters to *Manchester Guardian*
Likenesses K. Pollak, photograph, c.1948, NPG [*see illus.*]

Wealth at death £3013 5s. 4d.: probate, 22 May 1958, *CGPLA Eng. & Wales*

Garnett, Richard (1789–1850), philologist, was born at Otley in Yorkshire on 25 July 1789, the eldest son of William Garnett, paper manufacturer at Otley, and his wife, Mary, *née* Rhodes. His younger brothers were Jeremiah *Garnett (1793–1870) and Thomas *Garnett (1799–1878). He was educated at Otley grammar school, and afterwards at Leeds learned French and Italian from an Italian gentleman named Facio, with a view to working in a mercantile house. This plan was abandoned, and he remained at home, assisting his father in the works, and teaching himself German, in order to read a book on birds in that language. In 1809, convinced that trade was not his vocation, he became assistant master in the school of the Revd Evelyn Falkner at Southwell, Nottinghamshire, devoting his leisure hours to preparing himself for the church. Within two years he had taught himself sufficient Latin, Greek, and divinity to obtain ordination from the archbishop of York, whose chaplain regarded him as the best prepared candidate he had ever examined. After a brief settlement at Hutton Rudby in Yorkshire he became curate at Blackburn in 1815 and assistant master of the grammar school, and continued there for several years, occupied in incessant study and research. On 15 October 1822 at Southwell, Nottingham, he married his first wife, Margaret (*d.* 1828), daughter of the Revd Godfrey Heathcote of Southwell, and granddaughter of the Revd Ralph *Heathcote (1721–1795), and in 1826 was presented to the perpetual curacy of Tockholes, near Blackburn. He had earlier met and corresponded with Southey, who in a letter to Rickman of 10 April 1826 calls him:

> a very remarkable person. He did not begin to learn Greek till he was twenty, and he is now, I believe, acquainted with all the European languages of Latin or Teutonic origin, and with sundry oriental ones. I do not know any man who has read so much which you would not expect him to have read. (*Selections from the Letters*, 3.540–41)

About this time Garnett made his name as a writer on the Roman Catholic controversy, contributing numerous articles to the *Protestant Guardian*, the most remarkable of which were extremely humorous and sarcastic exposures of the apocryphal miracles attributed to St Francis Xavier. He was, however, in favour of Roman Catholic emancipation. He also began and largely completed an extensive work in reply to Charles Butler on the subject of ecclesiastical miracles; but the deep depression caused by the deaths of his wife in October 1828 and his infant daughter in January 1829 compelled him to lay it aside. Seeking relief in a change of residence, he became priest-vicar of Lichfield Cathedral in 1829, and absorbed himself in the study of comparative philology, then just beginning to be recognized as a science. He obtained an introduction to Lockhart, and contributed in 1835 and 1836 three articles to the *Quarterly Review*, dealing respectively with English lexicography, English dialects, and Prichard's work on the Celtic languages. These papers attracted great attention, and were almost the first introduction of German philological research to the English public. He made the Celtic

question peculiarly his own. His conviction of the extent of the Celtic element in European languages, and of the importance of Celtic studies in general, was to have been expressed in an article in the *Quarterly Review* on Skene's 'Highlanders', which for some reason never appeared.

On 15 May 1834, at Norton in Derby, Garnett married his second wife, Rayne, daughter of John Wreaks, of Sheffield. In 1836 he was presented to the living of Chebsey, near Stafford, which he relinquished in 1838 on succeeding H. F. Cary, the translator of Dante, as assistant keeper of printed books at the British Museum. Though exemplary in his attention to his duties, he took little part in the great changes then taking place in the library under Panizzi, but was an active member of the Philological Society, founded in 1842. To its *Transactions* he contributed numerous papers, including two long and important series of essays entitled 'On the languages and dialects of the British Islands' and 'On the nature and analysis of the verb'. Besides his philological essays, edited in 1859 by his eldest son, Richard *Garnett (1835–1906), and his theological writings, which were uncollected, he was author of some graceful poems and translations, and of a remarkable paper entitled 'On the formation of ice at the bottoms of rivers' in the *Transactions of the Royal Institution* for 1818, containing a most graphic account based on personal observation. It was republished along with the essays of his brother Thomas Garnett.

From 1848 Garnett's health declined and he died on 27 September 1850 and was buried in Highgate cemetery. He was survived by his second wife. This tribute was paid by a colleague in the museum: 'Seldom has a man left behind him so fragrant a memory' (Cowtan, 105). As a philologist he is thus characterized in the preface to Kington-Oliphant's *Sources of Standard English*:

> It is a loss to mankind that Garnett has left so little behind him. He seems to have been the nearest approach England ever made to bringing forth a Mezzofanti, and he combined in himself qualities not often found in the same man. When his toilsome industry is amassing facts, he plods like a German; when his playful wit is unmasking quackery, he flashes like a Frenchman. He it was who first called attention to the varying dialects of England and who first endeavoured to classify them. (Kington-Oliphant, ix)

RICHARD GARNETT, *rev.* JOHN D. HAIGH

Sources R. Garnett, ed., 'Memoir', in *The philological essays of the late Rev. Richard Garnett*, ed. R. Garnett (1859), i–xvi · *Selections from the letters of Robert Southey*, ed. J. W. Warter, 4 vols. (1856), vol. 3, pp. 540–41 · T. L. Kington-Oliphant, *Sources of standard English* (1873), ix · *The Athenaeum* (23 April 1859), 544–5 · R. Cowtan, *Memories of the British Museum* (1872), 104 · J. C. Prichard, *The Eastern origin of the Celtic nations*, ed. R. G. Latham (1857), 371–2 · Ward, *Men of the reign* · J. W. Donaldson, *The new Cratylus* (1839), chap. 2 · J. F. Waller, ed., *The imperial dictionary of universal biography*, 3 vols. (1857–63)

Garnett, Richard (1835–1906), librarian and author, was born in Beacon Street, Lichfield, on 27 February 1835, the elder son (he also had a brother and a sister) of the second marriage of Richard *Garnett (1789–1850), then priest-vicar of Lichfield Cathedral, and his wife, Rayne, daughter of John Wreaks of Sheffield. In 1838 the father moved with his family to London, to become assistant keeper of printed books at the British Museum. The younger Richard was educated mainly at home, but also at the Revd C. M. Marcus's school in Caroline Street, Bedford Square, London, and for one term in autumn 1850 at Whalley grammar school, Lancashire. He was a precocious student who inherited his father's facility in acquiring languages. Before he was fourteen he had read widely in the classics and in Italian literature, as well as the stories of Hofmann and Tieck. Throughout his life he maintained his reading in the classics, and in French, German, Italian, and Spanish literature, with a keen interest in European politics.

At the British Museum library Garnett's father died on 27 September 1850, and the young Richard resisted his family's suggestions that he should prepare for admission to Oxford or Cambridge, from a mistrust of their educational efficiency. On 1 March 1851, through the introduction of his father's colleague Anthony Panizzi, then keeper of printed books, he was appointed an assistant in the British Museum library, where he was to spend his entire career. He began by copying titles for the catalogue, but was soon promoted to revising the catalogue entries. Panizzi's opinion of his protégé was confirmed, and Garnett was soon entrusted with cataloguing new acquisitions and placing them on the shelves. The new reading room was opened in 1857 and the superintendent Thomas Watts took on Garnett as assistant placer to W. B. Rye. The experience of refreshing his powerful memory each working day with the systematic handling of new stock in many languages gave Garnett a body of bibliographical knowledge that made him a walking guide to the collections before an actual subject-index was published. After missing some promotions he became senior assistant in November 1869, and in July 1875 succeeded George Bullen as assistant keeper of printed books and superintendent of the reading room. In that post he became a well-known

figure in literary London, much respected for his knowledge and helpfulness. In 1882 he was an unsuccessful candidate for the librarianship of the Bodleian Library, Oxford, but his metropolitan renown was secure and his achievements at the museum were to take him more appropriately to the headship of his own department.

From 1881 a project was revived to print the general catalogue, which had become gross and inefficient in over 2000 volumes of mounted handwritten slips. The work began with current accessions and was in 1884 extended retrospectively. The project was placed under Garnett's supervision, with the assistance of A. W. K. Miller, and late in 1884 Garnett was moved from the reading room to concentrate on the heavy burden of editorial work. He succeeded in building work on the printed catalogue into the library's administrative structure, rather than leaving it to be dispensed with as an additional project. Even more importantly, his nine years in the reading room had earned him an enduring reputation for helpfulness to readers, and they set a standard for the future development of the post. By 1890, when as keeper of the department he again succeeded George Bullen, work on the catalogue (which was completed in 1905, covering in 4.5 million entries all accessions to the end of the century) had to be delegated to others. As keeper, in spite of unwelcome restrictions on expenditure, Garnett was responsible for many important acquisitions, especially in early English books (described with others in the volume on *Three Hundred Notable Books* with which colleagues marked his retirement in 1899). He had interested himself in technical innovations, such as the application of photography for copying rare books, and electric lighting for the reading room, which led to an extension of opening hours; in 1887 he had introduced sliding, suspended book-presses to economize on storage space. In spite of such achievements there are grounds for thinking that Garnett, who

Richard Garnett (1835–1906), by unknown photographer, 1902

had not been able to defend his department from the full effects of financial restrictions ordained by central government, 'was on the whole rather less successful as Keeper than he had been as Superintendent' (Harris, 441). He resigned the keepership on 11 February 1899, on the grounds of his wife's poor health; his retirement broke the direct link with Panizzi, and with the Panizzian concept of universality in the collections. Garnett had also been a significant figure in the rapidly evolving profession; in 1877 he was one of the organizers of the conference that led to the foundation of the Library Association. He was its president in 1892–3, and in 1897–8 he served a year as president of the Bibliographical Society. He collected his various articles on professional subjects in *Essays in Librarianship and Bibliography* (1899), published in a series of which he was general editor, and in *Essays of an ex-Librarian* (1901).

Garnett's writings Throughout his long career at the British Museum the routines of library work did not quash Garnett's own literary ambitions. At first he worked on translations from the Spanish and German, and published essays in the *Manchester Guardian*, edited by his uncle Jeremiah Garnett. In 1858 there appeared anonymously, and at the author's expense, a first volume of poems, *Primula: a Book of Lyrics*, slim but well received. It was incorporated in *Io in Egypt, and other Poems*, with his name on it, published in 1859, when an edition of his father's *Philological Essays* also appeared, with a prefatory memoir. His poetic output was sustained throughout his life but, though fastidious and cultivated in a literary way, it is derivative in style and has not generally survived well; but 'Where corals lie' has endured in Elgar's musical setting—originally for Clara Butt. Garnett's translations include an early selection of *Idylls and Epigrams* from the Greek anthology (1869). *Poems* (1893) preserves his own selection of his earlier verse.

By his prose writings Garnett supplemented his professional income with much literary journalism, for papers including the *Literary Gazette* and *The Examiner*. He was deft and industrious in preparing introductions to reprints of literary classics, and made many contributions to the ninth edition of the *Encyclopaedia Britannica*, and contributed 196 articles (including those on Percy Bysshe and Mary Shelley, and several Garnetts) to the *Dictionary of National Biography*. He wrote short lives of Milton, Carlyle, and Emerson for the Great Writers series, and also a biography of Edward Gibbon Wakefield (1898) and W. J. Fox, the social reformer (completed by his son Edward and published in 1910). In retirement Garnett wrote a *History of Italian Literature* (1897), and was one of four editors who assembled the twenty-volume *International Library of Famous Literature*, a popular compilation commissioned by American publishers and published in Britain in 1901. He also collaborated with Edmund Gosse in the first two of four volumes of *English Literature: an Illustrated Record* (1903).

Io had included a poem to the memory of Shelley, which appears to have given Garnett an introduction to the poet's son Sir Percy Florence Shelley, and his wife, Jane,

who was protective of her father-in-law's reputation and strongly in favour of his second wife against his first. From 1859, when he first visited them, Garnett proved himself all too willing a collaborator in their partial view of Shelley, and in Lady Shelley's long-drawn-out quarrel with the poet's own friends T. J. Hogg, Thomas Love Peacock, and E. J. Trelawny, especially over Shelley's conduct towards his first wife. Garnett, over-impressed by Lady Shelley's patronage, was drawn into dispute with Peacock, and in periodical articles and in *Relics of Shelley* (1862), which included unpublished fragments, he expressed himself in bitter terms that he later regretted and retracted. The Shelleys invited Garnett to write the authorized life, but attached though he had become to their position, he prudently declined the commission, quite plausibly claiming that pressure of work at the British Museum would not allow it; Edward Dowden was chosen instead. He did, however, remain on friendly terms with the Shelley family, and later edited selections of Percy Bysshe Shelley's poetry and letters (1882, 1898), and in 1891 a collection of Mary Shelley's stories from the *Keepsake*. His correspondence with Dowden and W. M. Rossetti was edited by his son R. S. Garnett in *Letters about Shelley* (1917).

More unusual than his work on Shelley is Garnett's set of short stories *The Twilight of the Gods, and other Tales* (1888; expanded in 1903). Some have seen parallels with Anatole France, some with Peacock, but it is really an unplaceable book, pagan in tone and disrespectful of all religions, wry and subversive in humour, and mannered, but not unpleasantly so, in expression. Some of its stories had appeared in the *Yellow Book*. Garnett's tales, inspired by the classics, have worn better than his poetry. It was little remarked when it first appeared, but in time gained an enthusiastic readership.

Garnett had married on 13 June 1863 Olivia Narney (1842–1903), daughter of Edward Singleton of Kilmadean Castle, co. Clare, who had been brought up by her mother in England. They had four sons (of whom one died in infancy) and three daughters. They set up home within walking distance of the museum, at 4 St Edmund's Terrace, Primrose Hill, and entertained a circle of literary friends, both there and from June 1890 in the east residence at the museum, into which they had moved when Garnett was promoted to the keepership. Several of their children had literary careers, especially Edward *Garnett (1868–1937), who became a notable editor and publisher's reader and the husband of Constance *Garnett, the translator from the Russian.

Narney Garnett died on 24 June 1903. Her husband had always been susceptible to intelligent young women he met in the course of his museum duties, not least the German refugee poet Mathilde Blind. In his widowerhood he was consoled by the insistent presence of Violet Eveleen Neale (1873–c.1950), an enthusiastic woman less than half his age, who shared his interest in Shelley. It was under her influence that he produced anonymously a collection of 'thoughts and fancies on love', called *De flagello myrteo* (1905), inspired by a myrtle sprig she had sent him from a bush planted by the poet. These classical reflections on emotional and physical love were characteristically free from prudery or prurience, but they were an odd emanation, owing more perhaps to Garnett's ardour for Violet Neale than to his literary skill. The collection was expanded to 360 apophthegms (thus matching the degrees of the zodiac); a third edition, in 1906, issued by Violet Neale, was the first to bear his name.

Astrology; physical description   To the puzzlement of many of his literary friends Garnett had long been a convinced exponent of astrology, rejecting imputations of 'occultism' and seeing it as an exact science; perhaps, as an autodidact, he was all too readily susceptible to such studies. As A. G. Trent he expounded his beliefs in an essay, 'The soul and the stars' (*University Magazine*, 1880, 334–46; later reprinted separately). Trent cast hundreds of horoscopes for friends and for literary eminences; his own, from his birth at 5.51 p.m., was published with full technicalities in A.J. Pearce's *Star Lore* (December 1889, 54–7). The prognosis was of overall vitality, and of strength and generosity of mental and literary powers. Fellow astrologers later published respectful obituaries of specialist tenor.

Garnett has been well portrayed, from strong family literary tradition, by his great-grandson Richard as

> a tall man with a scholar's stoop, and he wore an old frock-coat pulled out of shape by the books in its large pockets. His face was short and square, with a short nose and a short beard, and he wore the usual gold-rimmed spectacles of his day. His manner of speech was gentle and humorous, with the remains of a Yorkshire accent, and so measured that one could tell where each mark of punctuation was due to fall.
> (R. Garnett, *Constance Garnett*, 1991, 48)

In 1883 he had been made an LLD of Edinburgh University (and was thereafter known as 'Dr Garnett'), and he was created CB in the new year's honours of 1895. He died of nephritis at his home, 27 Tanza Road, Hampstead, London, on Good Friday, 13 April 1906, and was buried at Highgate cemetery four days later. A sale at Sothebys on 6 December 1906 dispersed in 395 lots most of his own library, including three of the four volumes of Shelley's notebooks that he had been given by the family in gratitude for his literary advice.   ALAN BELL

Sources DNB · B. McCrimmon, *Richard Garnett: the scholar as librarian* (1989) · B. McCrimmon, *Power, politics and print* (1981) · *The Library* (July 1906) · *The Bookman* (June 1906) · P. Curry, *A confusion of prophets: Victorian and Edwardian astrology* (1992), 113–21 · P. R. Harris, *A history of the British Museum library, 1753–1973* (1998)
Archives priv. coll., family papers | Ransom HRC, corresp., literary MSS and papers | BL, corresp. with Mathilde Blind, Add. MSS 61927–61929 · BL, corresp. with James Dykes Campbell, Add. MSS 49525 A · BL, letters to W. A. Copinger, Add. MS 62551 · BL, letters to his brother John William Garnett, Add. MS 37489 · BL, letters to John Lane, MS 71496 · BL, Ashley MSS, letters to T. J. Wise · Bodl. Oxf., letters to Edith Clarke · Bodl. Oxf., letters to Sidney Lee · CUL, letters to Lord Acton · JRL, letters to W. E. A. Axon · Ransom HRC, corresp. with John Lane · Royal Literary Fund, letters as sponsor to Royal Literary Fund · U. Leeds, Brotherton L., letters to Edmund Gosse · U. Reading L., letters to George Bell & Sons
Likenesses G. Frampton, bust, exh. RA 1889 · J. Collier, portrait, presented in 1899, priv. coll. · W. Strang, etching, 1899 (after his earlier work), BM; NPG · photograph, 1902, NPG [*see illus.*] · H. Furniss, caricature, pen-and-ink sketch, NPG · E. M. Heath, portrait, priv. coll. · M. Morris, etching, BM · Spy [L. Ward], chromolithograph, caricature, repro. in *VF* (11 April 1895)
Wealth at death £2734 7s. 2d.: administration, 23 May 1906, CGPLA Eng. & Wales

Garnett, (Frances) Theresa (1888–1966), suffragette, was born on 17 May 1888 at 33 Stanningley Road, Armley, Leeds, the daughter of Joshua Garnett (b. 1862), an iron planer, and his wife, Frances Theresa, *née* Armstead. Theresa Garnett was educated at a convent school and was for some time a teacher.

In 1907 Theresa Garnett joined the Women's Social and Political Union (WSPU), the organization formed in 1903 by Emmeline Pankhurst to lobby for women's enfranchisement. She claimed to have inherited her fighting spirit from Irish ancestors (*Votes for Women*, 2 July 1909, 877). In April 1909, with four others, including Alys Russell (first wife of Bertrand Russell), Theresa Garnett chained herself to a statue in the central lobby of the houses of parliament to protest against the so-called Brawling Bill, which was intended to penalize anyone found guilty of disorderly conduct within the confines of the Palace of Westminster while parliament was in session. She suffered no punishment on this occasion but on 29 June, by now a seasoned protester, after having taken part in a WSPU deputation from Caxton Hall to the houses of parliament she was arrested in Whitehall while participating in the ensuing stone-throwing at government offices. She was sentenced to a month's imprisonment in Holloway, where she went on hunger strike and was, in addition, charged with biting and kicking a wardress. Her defence was that she had not bitten but that the wardress might have been scratched by her WSPU brooch. She was found guilty of assault, sentenced to a further term of imprisonment, again went on hunger strike, and was released within a few days. In August 1909, as Annie O'Sullivan, Theresa Garnett was sentenced after taking part in a demonstration in Liverpool on the roof of the Sun Hall, in which building R. B. Haldane, the Liberal minister, was holding a meeting. She was imprisoned in Walton gaol, went on hunger strike, and was released on 26 August.

In Bristol in November 1909, wearing a 'merry widow' hat and with a whip in her hand, Theresa Garnett accosted Winston Churchill. The account in the WSPU newspaper, *Votes for Women*, on 19 November 1909, mentions that she struck him several times but in an interview, recorded in 1964, Theresa Garnett was adamant that she had not touched him. She was, in the end, charged with disturbing the peace, sentenced to a month's imprisonment in Horfield gaol, and went on hunger strike. As a protest against being forcibly fed she set fire to her cell, and was then placed in a punishment cell, in solitary confinement, for eleven of the fifteen remaining days of her sentence. After being found unconscious, she spent the rest of her sentence in a hospital ward. By the end of 1910, however, suffragette militancy had increased to a level that she could no longer support; she left the WSPU and did not join any other suffrage group, although she kept in touch with her erstwhile comrades. Theresa Garnett was a sister at the London Hospital and nursed at the front during the First

World War. She was an active member of the Suffragette Fellowship after the Second World War and in 1960 was honorary editor of the Women's Freedom League *Bulletin*. In 1962 Theresa Garnett gave to the National Portrait Gallery a wooden head of Frederick Pethick-Lawrence, which had been sculpted by Albert Moroder in 1949. She died on 24 May 1966, virtually penniless, in Whittington Hospital, near her home in north London. She was unmarried.

ELIZABETH CRAWFORD

Sources *Votes for Women* (1907–10) · 'The blaze of day': the suffragette movement, a documentary survey (1992) [two interviews recorded in 1964 with Theresa Garnett; CD] · b. cert. · E. Crawford, *The women's suffrage movement: a reference guide, 1866–1928* (1999) · CGPLA Eng. & Wales (1966)

Likenesses Blathwayt, photograph, 1909, repro. in B. M. Willmott Dobbie, *A nest of suffragettes in Somerset* (1979) · photograph, repro. in *Votes for Women* (6 Aug 1909)

Wealth at death £120: probate, 3 April 1967, CGPLA Eng. & Wales

Garnett, Thomas [St Thomas Garnett] (**1575–1608**), Jesuit, was born in London in 1575, the son of Richard Garnett, who had been a fellow of Balliol College, Oxford, and his wife (*née* Sawyer). He was educated at Horsham grammar school in Sussex, in the college of the English Jesuits at St Omer (1594–6), and in the English College of St Alban's at Valladolid, where he was ordained priest about 1599. Soon afterwards he came to England on the mission, and was admitted into the Society of Jesus on 29 September 1604 by his uncle, the provincial superior, Henry Garnett. In the following year he was arrested, committed to the Gatehouse, and thence transferred to the Tower. As he was a nephew of the superior he was examined by secretary Cecil concerning the Gunpowder Plot, but as nothing could be proved against him he was set free at the end of eight or nine months, and banished for life in 1606. Having completed his Jesuit noviciate in Louvain, he returned to England but was apprehended and tried at the Old Bailey on 19 June 1608 on an indictment of high treason for having been made priest by papal authority and remaining in England, contrary to the statute of 27 Elizabeth. He was sentenced to death and was executed at Tyburn on 23 June 1608. Some parts of his body were taken to St Omer. He was canonized by Paul VI on 25 October 1970.

THOMPSON COOPER, *rev.* G. BRADLEY

Sources T. M. McCoog, *English and Welsh Jesuits, 1555–1650*, 2, Catholic RS, 75 (1995), 189 · G. Holt, *St Omers and Bruges colleges, 1593–1773: a biographical dictionary*, Catholic RS, 69 (1979), 111 · H. Chadwick, 'Blessed Thomas Garnet S.J.', *Stonyhurst Magazine*, 27/352 (1944) · Gillow, *Lit. biog. hist.*, 2.395 · R. Challoner, *Memoirs of missionary priests*, ed. J. H. Pollen, rev. edn (1924), 296 · D. H. Farmer, *The Oxford dictionary of saints* (1978), 163 · G. Anstruther, *The seminary priests*, 1 (1969), 127 · H. Foley, ed., *Records of the English province of the Society of Jesus*, 2 (1875), 475–592

Likenesses portrait, *c.*1620, St Alban's College, Calle Don Sancho, Valladolid, Spain

Garnett, Thomas (**1766–1802**), chemist and physician, was born on 21 April 1766 at Casterton, near Kirkby Lonsdale, Westmorland, the elder of the two sons of Joseph Garnett (1726?–1812). He learned the rudiments of English, Latin, French, and mathematics at the village school of Barbon, where his parents moved soon after his birth to occupy a small landed property, Bank House, that remained in the family for many years. At the age of fifteen he was apprenticed to John Dawson, of Sedbergh, who taught him mathematics and science and prepared him for entry to the University of Edinburgh. He is also recorded as having attended Sedbergh School. After matriculating at Edinburgh in 1785 Garnett attended lectures on all aspects of medicine, including those of the chemist Joseph Black, and in 1788 he submitted a thesis on vision, published as *De visu*, for the degree of MD. While in Edinburgh he also became president of both the Royal Physical Society and the Natural History Society and was active in the Royal Medical Society of Edinburgh.

Following a brief period of further study and practical experience in London, Garnett returned to his parents' house in Barbon, where he wrote parts of a substantial unsigned article on optics for the third edition of the *Encyclopaedia Britannica*. In 1790 he set up as a physician in Bradford, and there, in addition to practising medicine, he gave lectures on natural philosophy and chemistry and published the first of several works on the nature and medicinal properties of the spa waters of Yorkshire. He moved to Knaresborough in 1791 and soon afterwards to the emerging spa resort of Harrogate, and he continued his analyses of mineral waters and applied the results in his remedies.

In Harrogate Garnett prospered. By 1794 he had strengthened his reputation among his fashionable clients by securing the patronage of Alexander Wedderburn, Lord Loughborough, who settled him in a house on land he owned in High Harrogate. Here Garnett received guests who had come to take the waters, among them Catherine Grace Cleveland, whom he married in 1795. But for someone of his sociable disposition and ambition, the excitement of the summer season contrasted too markedly with the languor of the winter months, and he decided to emigrate to America, which promised not only a wider scope for his talents, in particular as a lecturer, but also a more congenial environment for what appear to have been his moderately republican sympathies. While he awaited a passage in Liverpool, however, he was persuaded to unpack his demonstration instruments and offer a course of public lectures. The clarity of the lectures, an extensive digest of which was subsequently published as *Outlines of a Course of Lectures on Chemistry* (1797), immediately won him further invitations, and in 1796, after giving courses in Manchester, Warrington, and Lancaster, he was appointed professor of natural philosophy at the newly founded Anderson's Institution in Glasgow.

In Glasgow, Garnett resumed practice as a physician and in 1798 he undertook a tour of north-west Scotland, which he described in his topographical and historical *Observations on a Tour through the Highlands and Part of the Western Isles of Scotland*. Published in two volumes in 1800 and embellished with plates by Walter H. Watts, who had accompanied him, the work enjoyed considerable success and was translated into German in 1802. By the time it appeared, however, Garnett's spirit had been irretrievably broken by the loss of his wife, who had died on 25

December 1798 in giving birth to the second of his two daughters, Catherine Grace, later Catherine *Godwin (1798–1845). A move to London, to become professor of natural philosophy and chemistry at the Royal Institution in December 1799, only aggravated his physical disability and melancholy. After two winters of strenuous lecturing and worsening relations with Count Rumford (who, as a manager of the Royal Institution, had been instrumental in Garnett's appointment but who now proved an uncompromising employer), he resigned in June 1801. In the same month, he leased a house in Great Marlborough Street, built a room in which to give private lectures, and set up once again as a physician. The arrival of his children from Kirkby Lonsdale, where they had been living with a close friend of his deceased wife, raised his spirits, and in May 1802, after another winter of lecturing, he was pleased to be appointed physician to the St Marylebone Dispensary. It was while practising there that he contracted typhus fever; he died at his house in Great Marlborough Street, London, on 28 June 1802. He was interred in the burial-ground of St James's parish, Westminster.

The posthumous volume of Garnett's *Popular Lectures on Zoonomia*, published in 1804 for the benefit of his orphaned daughters (with a portrait of a visibly depressed Garnett and the names of over 1000 subscribers), is marked by the erudition and balanced opinions that characterized all his writing. Although committed to the medical doctrines of John Brown (1735–1788), which he had encountered in Edinburgh, he recognized the need for further elaboration of the central Brunonian categories of sthenic and asthenic diseases and the associated theory of stimulant remedies. In other fields of science he was responsive to new ideas rather than truly original. Nevertheless, he was elected to the Manchester Literary and Philosophical Society and to the Royal Irish Academy, and he was well-connected in the scientific world, notably with Thomas Percival and Erasmus Darwin. It was typical of his openness that he promptly endorsed the chemistry of Antoine Laurent Lavoisier and followed closely the early continental work on the electric pile. With Britain and France at war, Garnett's opinion (advanced in a lecture in May 1800) that the pile owed more to the French than it did to the Italian physicist Alessandro Volta was regarded as mischievous by Rumford, and the public retraction that Garnett was required to make seems to have contributed to the souring of relations between the two men. By now, however, Garnett's illness had probably made him a difficult colleague, and his powers as a lecturer were in the decline that helped to ensure the rapid demise of his scientific reputation. Only his analyses of the mineral waters of Yorkshire, which continued to be cited well into the nineteenth century, were seen as having lasting value.   ROBERT FOX

Sources 'An account of the life of the author', T. Garnett, *Popular lectures on zoonomia* (1804), vi–xxii · *Public characters of 1799–1800* (1799), 4.405–14 · S. G. E. Lythe, *Thomas Garnett (1766–1802): highland tourist, scientist and professor, medical doctor* (1984) · *GM*, 1st ser., 72 (1802), 690, 777–8 · J. Muir, *John Anderson, pioneer of technical education and the college he founded* (1950), 96–107 · K. D. C. Vernon, 'The foundation and early years of the Royal Institution', *Proceedings of the Royal Institution of Great Britain*, 39 (1962–3), 364–402 · minutes of the meetings of managers, vols. 1 and 2, 1799–1802, Royal Institution of Great Britain, London · private information (2004) [Isobel German] · DNB
Likenesses engraving, c.1795, U. Edin. · J. Hopwood, stipple, 1800 (after J. R. Smith), Wellcome L. · S. Phillips, stipple, pubd 1 May 1801 (after T. Phillips), BM, U. Edin. · J. Gillray, etching, pubd 1802, NPG · W. S. Lenney, stipple, 1805 (after J. R. Smith), Wellcome L. · Lenney, engraving, pubd 1805 (after a drawing by J. R. Smith) · D. Wilke, oils, Royal Technical College, Glasgow · mezzotint, Wellcome L. · mezzotint (after an unknown artist), BM, NPG · portrait, repro. in Garnett, *Popular lectures*, frontispiece
Wealth at death 'philosophical apparatus' sold for £455

Garnett, Thomas (1799–1878), textile manufacturer and naturalist, was the son of William Garnett, paper manufacturer, and Mary, *née* Rhodes, and the younger brother of Richard *Garnett (1789–1850) and Jeremiah *Garnett (1793–1870). He was born at Otley, Yorkshire, on 18 January 1799. In his early days he supported himself by weaving pieces on his own account, but about 1820 he obtained employment in the cotton-spinning establishment of Garnett and Horsfall, Low Moor, Clitheroe, Lancashire, founded and then directed by his uncle, Jeremiah Garnett. He successively became manager and partner, and at the time of his death had for many years been head of the firm. Garnett is said to have possessed an enquiring and speculative intellect, and was an unwearied observer and experimenter in agriculture, medicine, and natural history. He was one of the first to propose the artificial propagation of fish, on which he wrote in the *Magazine of Natural History* in 1832; he also first discovered the economic value of wool from the alpaca llama, although he failed in inducing his partners to take it up, and he was one of the earliest experimenters with guano. His papers on natural history were collected and privately printed, under the editorship of his nephew, in 1883. Garnett's character was said to be strong and decided; he was active in civic life and several times mayor of Clitheroe. He died on 25 May 1878 at Low Moor, Clitheroe. Nothing is known of Garnett's wife, but two sons, William and James, survived him.   RICHARD GARNETT, rev. GILES HUDSON

Sources T. Garnett, *Essays in natural history and agriculture*, ed. R. Garnett (1883) · personal knowledge (1889) · *CGPLA Eng. & Wales* (1878)
Wealth at death under £35,000: probate, 6 Aug 1878, *CGPLA Eng. & Wales*

Garnett, William (1793–1873), civil servant, born in London on 13 November 1793, was the second and posthumous son of Thomas Garnett of Old Hutton, Kendal, who married Martha Rolfe, and died in 1793. The care of William and his elder brother, Thomas, from an early age became the responsibility of their cousin Thomas Constantine Brooksbank, an official in the Treasury, who educated them and found them appointments in government employment. William was appointed to the office for licensing hawkers and pedlars in 1807, at the age of only thirteen and a half, and afterwards transferred to the tax office, in which he rose to the highest positions. He was deputy registrar and registrar of the land tax from 1819 to 1841. Together with John Wood, the chairman of the board of stamps and taxes, he gave evidence to the select committee on agricultural distress in March 1836, showing how the tax was collected and demonstrating the striking inequalities in its incidence in different parts of the country.

Garnett was made assistant inspector-general of stamps and taxes in 1835, and inspector-general in 1842. He took a leading part in the introduction of income tax in Great Britain in 1842, and was author of *The Guide to the Property and Income Tax*, of which several editions were published. He was also mainly instrumental in the successful establishment of income tax in Ireland in 1853, and author of *The Guide to the Income-Tax Laws as Applicable to Ireland*. In 1851 he made a special visitation of all the assay offices in the United Kingdom, on which he reported to parliament. He gave evidence to the select committee of the House of Commons on 'gold and silver wares' in 1855 and 1856.

In private life Garnett was an admirable artist and musician. In 1827 he married Ellen, daughter of Solomon Treasure, under-secretary for taxes. She died, aged twenty-three, in June 1829, shortly after the birth of their second son, Arthur William *Garnett, who became a military engineer. Their elder son, Frederick Brooksbank Garnett (1828–1896), became surveyor-general of the Inland Revenue. William Garnett remarried in 1834; his wife was Priscilla Frances Smythe, who survived him by ten years. He died at his home, 4 Argyll Road, Kensington, London, on 30 September 1873.

F. B. Garnett, rev. M. C. Curthoys

Sources Boase, *Mod. Eng. biog.* • *Parl. papers* • Treasury and inland revenue records • *CGPLA Eng. & Wales* (1873)

Wealth at death under £16,000: probate, 23 Oct 1873, *CGPLA Eng. & Wales*

Garnett, William (1850–1932), physicist and educational administrator, was born at 183 Queen Street, Portsea, on 30 December 1850, son of William Garnett, auctioneer, and his wife, Selina (*née* Webb). He was baptized at King Street Chapel in the following March. Four years later, the family moved to Hoxton, London. After attending a dame-school, and elementary schooling where his enthusiasm was aroused by demonstration lectures given by Lewis M. Stewart, science master at Charterhouse School, he attended City of London School. He became head boy in mathematics, his opposite number in classics being H. H. Asquith. Thereafter Garnett gained scholarships at the Royal School of Mines at South Kensington from 1867, and from 1869 at St John's College, Cambridge, where he supported himself while reading mathematics. He rowed, joined the rifle volunteers, and graduated fifth wrangler in 1873.

The following year Garnett began lecturing at evening classes. He became a fellow of his college and was invited by James Clerk Maxwell to become his demonstrator in the newly opened Cavendish Laboratory. Maxwell, whose biography Garnett later helped to write, became his beau ideal of a physicist and professor. Garnett took the keenest delight in choosing apparatus in conjunction with Maxwell, and in 1876 was appointed lecturer: he was thus Maxwell's right-hand man both in the laboratory and in the lecture theatre, where he made great use of the magic lantern. He published standard textbooks on various branches of physics. As college steward he attempted to reform the kitchens and the purchasing of food: meals at St John's became known as 'Garnett's sixpenny blowouts', but this experiment in scientific domestic administration was not altogether successful.

On 21 August 1879, at the Missionary College, Richmond, Surrey, Garnett married Rebecca Samways (1853–1945) of Portsea, and therefore relinquished his fellowship. That winter Maxwell died: Garnett, who was grief-stricken, had high hopes of becoming the next Cavendish professor but Lord Rayleigh was appointed, and wanted no lecturer. Garnett needed a job and was appointed professor of physics, mathematics, and mechanics at the new University College established by the town council at Nottingham, in 1882. In 1884 he accepted an invitation to be principal of the Durham College of Science being established in Newcastle upon Tyne.

Garnett demanded proper buildings: the longer-established College of Medicine made difficulties about moving to the new site chosen by him; but a foundation stone was laid in 1887, and within six years three of the four planned blocks were completed. They form the nucleus of the campus of the University of Newcastle today. Garnett used the enthusiasm for Queen Victoria's golden jubilee to raise funds; his energy was indomitable, and he even assisted with the building works, as well as giving Christmas lectures to children. He secured one of the first government grants for university colleges in 1888. Newcastle's reputation stood high, and Garnett served on a scientific committee in London where he encountered T. H. Huxley, Lord Kelvin, Norman Lockyer, and Henry Roscoe.

In 1893 Garnett was chosen as secretary to the new technical education board of the London county council, under the chairmanship of Sidney Webb. Garnett became responsible for twelve London polytechnics, and played an important part in reorganizing the University of London. Altogether, 50,000 students, including those at art schools, came within his purview. Secondary education became at this time an area of contention between school boards and county councils, as various education acts (culminating in that of 1902) were debated in parliament. Garnett's influence and experience were very important in the eventual victory of the county councils, but his memorandum of 1903 to MPs was leaked to *The Times*, which weakened his position thereafter. After retiring in 1915 he chaired the Educational Reform Council in 1916–17, and organized wartime courses for Britons interned in Switzerland. In 1919–23 he was secretary of the London District University Committee, which placed over 7000 ex-servicemen on courses.

Garnett was affable and charming, alert and vigorous, and retained a firm Christian faith. He enjoyed alpine holidays, notably at Riffelalp above Zermatt. Himself the fruit of competitive scholarship examinations, he became a pioneer in scientific and technical education, at the Cavendish Laboratory, at new redbrick universities, and finally in London. Two of his sons were killed in the First World War; the eldest (James Clerk) Maxwell *Garnett, his wife, and his two daughters survived him when he died peacefully at his home, Horestone Point, Seagrove Bay, Isle of Wight, on 1 November 1932. He was buried at St Helen's Church on the Isle of Wight.   DAVID KNIGHT

Sources B. M. Allen, *William Garnett: a memoir* (1933) · *The Times* (2 Nov 1932), 17 · St John Cam. · *The Eagle*, 47 (1932–3), 184–6
Likenesses Lafayette, photograph, repro. in Allen, *William Garnett*, frontispiece · engraving, repro. in *Monthly Chronicle of North Country Lore and Legend*, 2 (Nov 1888), 575
Wealth at death £6148 1s. 9d.: probate, 13 Jan 1933, CGPLA Eng. & Wales

Garneys, Sir Christopher (d. 1534), courtier and soldier, is of unknown origins. A gentleman usher of the king's chamber from the beginning of Henry VIII's reign, attending the coronation in that capacity, he participated in court entertainments and was among those intimates of the king who played cards with him in his chamber. In 1509 the king granted him an annuity of £10, increased a year later to £20, and then, in 1515, to £30 in recognition of his services. His position at court enabled him to petition for such spoils as came available: in 1511 he received grants of the Sussex manors of Barkham, Wiggenholt, and Greatham forfeited to the crown on the attainder of Edmund Dudley, and later received the manors of Saxlingham in Norfolk and Wellington in Shropshire. He also received the wardship of the son and heir of Thomas Kebill, a London merchant, as well as the offices of bailiff of Stockton Socon, Suffolk, and keeper of the new park of Nottingham Castle, both of which he probably exercised through deputies. In 1513 he served as sergeant of the tents in the royal army which invaded France. He was knighted at the mass held in Tournai Cathedral on 25 September to celebrate Henry VIII's capture of the town. Afterwards he returned to Greenwich and served on the Kent commission of the peace from 1514 until 1521.

In 1514 Garneys went on the embassy to Louis XII to arrange the marriage of the French king to Princess Mary, and in the following year went north with a present of a dress from Henry VIII to his other sister, Margaret, queen of Scotland. By December 1518 he was serving in Calais when he and the other royal officials there wrote to Wolsey, explaining the precedence dispute between the mayor of Calais and the mayor of the town's wool staple. In August 1519 he took up the office of chief porter of Calais, of which he had been granted the reversion in October 1516. This was part of a general shift of office holding in Calais masterminded by Wolsey. In 1520 Garneys prepared the lodgings for the court at the Field of Cloth of Gold.

Garneys spent the remainder of his life discharging his duties as porter in Calais, an important post which involved primarily keeping the keys of the main gates into the town and monitoring the influx of merchants, particularly strangers, through the town gates. He also served as a commissioner of sewers for the Calais pale, while maintaining his links with the court and Wolsey, for instance by supplying the king with artichokes. He died in

Calais on 25 October 1534 and was succeeded by Thomas Palmer, then lieutenant of the Newnhambridge, who had been granted the reversion of Garneys's office in June 1526. In a letter to Thomas Cromwell, Palmer contrasts his own lack of reward in royal service with that of his predecessor, describing how Garneys had been allowed by the king to marry a wealthy widow, Joan, some time before 1514, and had made £800 from the wardship of Thomas Kebill on top of the grants of land and annuities. Garneys thus exemplifies the substantial rewards available in royal service for even relatively minor servants of the Tudors. He left no heir on his death.

DAVID GRUMMITT

Sources LP Henry VIII, vols. 1–7, addenda · D. I. Grummitt, 'Calais, 1485–1547: a study in early Tudor politics and government', PhD diss., U. Lond., 1997 · M. St C. Byrne, ed., *The Lisle letters*, 6 vols. (1981) · DNB
Archives PRO, letter to Henry VIII, SP 1/49, fols. 58–9 · PRO, letter to Cardinal Wolsey, SP 1/39, fols. 147–8 · PRO, letter to Viscount Lisle, SP 3/3/72 · PRO, letters to Thomas Cromwell, SP 1/77, fols. 75–6; SP 1/80, fols. 27–8; SP 1/80, fols. 168–9; SP 1/82, fols. 192–3

Garnier, Thomas (1776–1873), dean of Winchester, was born at Rookesbury, Hampshire, on 26 February 1776, the second son in the family of six sons and three daughters of George Charles Garnier (1739–1819), and his wife, Margaret (d. 1807), daughter of Sir John Miller, bt. Members of his family, which was of Huguenot origin, long held the office of apothecary to Chelsea Hospital. Isaac Garnier (1631–1712) was appointed in 1686; his son Isaac (1672–1736) succeeded in 1702, and his son Thomas Garnier held the post from 1723 to 1739. The dean's grandfather, George Garnier (1703–1763), addressed by Lord Chesterfield as 'Garnier my friend' (Garnier, 22) in a poem published in Dodsley's collection, was appointed to the lucrative sinecure of apothecary-general to the army by William, duke of Cumberland. The sinecure patent, 'a most unjustifiable one', the dean used to say, was passed down, in spite of hostile attacks, to the dean's father, who held it until his death. George Charles Garnier purchased the Rookesbury estate from the lucrative proceeds of the family salt mine, which supplied Epsom salts to the army, and served as high sheriff of Hampshire in 1766. His London house was regarded as one of the best for meeting celebrities. At his Hampshire residence he also used to entertain a distinguished literary society, including Garrick, Churchill, Foote, and Sotheby.

Thomas Garnier was educated at Hyde Abbey School, a celebrated private academy near Winchester, under 'Flogging Richards', where he had as his schoolfellow George Canning. He proceeded to Worcester College, Oxford, in 1793, was elected fellow of All Souls in 1796, and took his degree of BCL in 1800 and DCL in 1850. His tutor at Worcester, Dr Jacob, inspired his interest in horticulture, and in 1798 he was elected a member of the Linnean Society. In the same year he commanded a force of militia raised by his father to repel the French invasion threat. During the short peace of 1802–3 Garnier went abroad with Dr Halifax, physician to the prince of Wales. He attended a levee of Napoleon, then first consul, to whom he was presented,

Napoleon 'smiling and looking very gracious'. He saw General Dumouriez, Marmont, and other marshals of the staff, and heard Napoleon tell C. J. Fox that he was the 'greatest man of the greatest country in the world'. He was fortunately summoned to Oxford in November 1802, and thus escaped a long detention in France.

In 1800 Garnier was ordained by Brownlow North, bishop of Winchester, whose daughter had married one of Garnier's elder brothers. A steady flow of lucrative preferment came his way. His uncle, Sir Thomas Miller, presented him to the living of Froyle, Hampshire, which he held until 1803. At about this time he lost the use of one eye after an attack of fever. From 1803 to 1806 he held the rectory of Wickham. He married, on 8 May 1805, Mary (1781–1849), youngest daughter of Caleb Hillier *Parry, the physician. In 1807 the bishop of Winchester presented him to the rectory of Bishopstoke, Hampshire, which he held for over sixty years, indulging his taste for botany by collecting rare plants and flowers, and considerably extending the rectory garden. He became rector of North Waltham, Hampshire, together with, in 1820, Brightwell, Berkshire, both in the gift of the bishop of Winchester; he resigned them following his appointment to a stall in Winchester Cathedral in April 1830. Lord Melbourne nominated him in 1840 the successor to Dr Rennell as dean of Winchester.

A staunch whig in politics, Garnier was a prominent backer of Palmerston, his friend, neighbour, and shooting companion, in contests for the South Hampshire parliamentary seat. Later, he was said to have influenced Palmerston's ecclesiastical appointments. He was of an amiably charitable disposition, his propensity for almsgiving attracting crowds of mendicants outside the cathedral. Of one bad-tempered acquaintance he remarked, 'His heart is all right, it is his liver that is at fault' (Garnier, 57). He resigned his Bishopstoke living in 1869 and the Winchester deanery in 1872, dying at 4 Dome Alley, The Close, Winchester, on 29 June 1873. With the exception of one daughter, he outlived all his family of four sons—including Thomas *Garnier (1809–1863)—and four daughters.

EDMUND VENABLES, rev. M. C. CURTHOYS

Sources A. E. Garnier, *The chronicles of the Garniers of Hampshire* (1900) · Boase, *Mod. Eng. biog.* · Burke, *Gen. GB* · Desmond, *Botanists*, rev. edn
Archives Bodl. Oxf., corresp. with Sir Thomas Phillipps
Likenesses portrait, 1830, repro. in Garnier, *Chronicles of the Garniers*, facing p. 38 · R. C. Lucas, wax medallion, 1850, NPG · C. Silvy, carte-de-visite, NPG · carte-de-visite, NPG · photograph, repro. in Garnier, *Chronicles of the Garniers*, facing p. 52 · portrait, repro. in *The Church of England photographic portrait gallery* (1859) · stipple and line engraving, NPG
Wealth at death under £40,000: resworn probate, June 1874, *CGPLA Eng. & Wales*

Garnier, Thomas (1809–1863), dean of Lincoln, was born at Bishopstoke, Hampshire, on 15 April 1809, the second son of Thomas *Garnier (1776–1873), dean of Winchester, and his wife, Mary, *née* Parry (1781–1849). He was educated from 1820 to 1822 at Twyford School, near Winchester,

under Revd J. G. Bedford, before entering Winchester College, from where, in 1826, he was admitted to Worcester College, Oxford. In 1828 he accompanied his uncle, Captain William Edward *Parry, the Arctic explorer, on a tour of the continent of Europe. He rowed for Oxford in the first boat race against Cambridge, at Henley in 1829, and in 1832, with his brother John Garnier, played for the university cricket eleven against the MCC. He graduated BA in 1830, was elected a fellow of All Souls in that year, proceeding to the degree of BCL in 1833, and was ordained to the title of Old Alresford, Hampshire. He published a pamphlet, addressed to 'the labouring classes', *Plain Remarks upon the New Poor Law Amendment Act* (1835), disputing the idea that it was damaging to their interests, for which he was thanked by the poor-law commissioners. On 23 May 1835 he married Lady Caroline Elisabeth (1814–1898), younger daughter of William Charles Keppel, fourth earl of Albemarle. She shared her husband's strong evangelical religious inclinations. The couple had seven sons and seven daughters.

Garnier was presented by All Souls to the college living of Lewknor, Oxfordshire, in 1835, where he established parochial schools and was so successful as a preacher that he drew away the congregation of a nearby dissenting minister. In 1840 his brother-in-law, the earl of Leicester, presented him to the rectory of Longford, Derbyshire, where he restored the parish church, built and endowed an additional church, and expanded the parish schools. He resigned the living in 1847 and became minister to the chapel of the Lock Hospital, which cared for sufferers from venereal disease. In 1849 Charles Shaw Lefevre nominated him chaplain to the House of Commons, and in the following year Lord John Russell nominated him to the crown living of Holy Trinity, Marylebone, where he became conspicuous for his work among the poor. During his ten years there he raised some £35,000 for charitable objects, including a penitentiary and a large school. His zeal in suppressing brothels in his parish attracted death threats. He supported the Church Missionary Society and maintained good relations with nonconformists. Socially he was well connected. At a party given by the Misses Waldegrave his prompt action saved Lady Blandford (wife of the seventh duke of Marlborough) from incineration; engrossed in conversation with Garnier at the fireside, her crinoline dress ignited, but by wrapping her in the hearthrug he succeeded in putting out the flames.

In August 1859, on Palmerston's recommendation, Garnier was made dean of Ripon, but finding the accommodation there inadequate, he was transferred to the deanery of Lincoln in March 1860. A serious fall shortly afterwards exacerbated an existing illness, and he became paralysed in a wheelchair. He was not considered narrow in his evangelicalism; he established daily services and weekly communions in his church at Marylebone, and instituted a Sunday evening service at Lincoln. He attended the meets of the Burton hounds and was known to peruse *Bell's Life*, the sporting paper. In 1847 he published a sermon on the Irish and Scottish famines and in 1851 a series of sermons on domestic duties. Garnier died at the deanery, Lincoln, on 7 December 1863, and was buried at Bishopstoke, Hampshire. In 1889 his body was reinterred in the churchyard of Quidenham, Norfolk, the parish of his fifth son, the Revd Edward Southwell Garnier.

M. C. CURTHOYS

Sources *Some account of the life and character of ... Thomas Garnier, dean of Lincoln* [1861] • A. E. Garnier, *The chronicles of the Garniers of Hampshire* (1900) • Boase, *Mod. Eng. biog.* • D. M. Lewis, ed., *The Blackwell dictionary of evangelical biography, 1730–1860*, 2 vols. (1995)
Likenesses photograph, repro. in Garnier, *Chronicles of the Garniers*, facing p. 79
Wealth at death under £6000: probate, 20 Jan 1864, *CGPLA Eng. & Wales*

Garnock, Robert (*c*.1660–1681), covenanter, was the son of Robert Garnock, of Stirling, a 'hammerman' or blacksmith; the identity of his mother is unknown. He was baptized by James Guthrie (*c*.1612–1661), minister of Stirling and presbyterian martyr, who was executed for treason in 1661. Garnock received an elementary education, probably as an apprentice to his father, as he later followed the same trade. He never married.

From an early age Garnock attended conventicles with his uncle, at which he was regarded as something of a child prodigy, since the company 'thought [he] had religion'. But, as he recorded later, 'the hidden things of godliness was yet a mystery to me' (Howie, 459). As a young man—and in common with all apprentices—Garnock completed his practical education as a journeyman, perfecting his skills while working at various sites across the country. In this capacity he travelled to Glasgow, Falkirk, and Bo'ness, pursuing his trade as he found opportunity. At temporary lodgings in these towns he debated the issues of the day with his fellow craftsmen, and became convinced that episcopacy was 'directly wrong, and contrary to scripture'. Thereafter, he pledged never to 'own that perjured adulterous wretch [Charles II] as head of the church', or to acquiesce in the authority of 'those bloody thieves', the bishops (ibid., 458).

The itinerant life suited Garnock, since it meant that he could search out like-minded souls at illegal 'field preachings', which served to reinforce his uncompromising presbyterianism. In April 1677 he attended a large gathering at 'East Nisbet on the Merse', Lothian, and in August 1678 he was one of 'thousands' who attended communion at Maybole, Ayrshire. Here, he listened avidly to a sermon of the 'lion of the covenant', Richard Cameron (1648–1680), author of the Sanquhar declaration of 1680. It was almost inevitable that Garnock's activities would lead to conflict with the authorities, and on 8 May 1679 he was present at Fintry, near Stirling, when a company of dragoons surprised the meeting. The young man escaped, but on attempting to enter Stirling was apprehended and thrown into prison, where he lay until July.

Eventually Garnock was removed with a number of other prisoners, and confined in Greyfriars churchyard at Edinburgh. On 25 October 1679 his case was considered by the privy council, who found that he was 'a most obstinate and malicious person', who disowned the king's authority, and 'will neither enact himself not to take up armes,

nor will he say that the murder [of Archbishop James Sharp] was a murder' (*Reg. PCS*, 6.356). He was incarcerated in the Tolbooth of Edinburgh, where he remained a prisoner for two years. On 7 October 1681 he was re-examined, but his opinion that the 'king and council [were] tyrants, murderers, perjured and man-sworn' was unchanged (Wodrow, 3.285). He was convicted of treason, and condemned to death.

While in prison Garnock wrote a short account of his life which is largely concerned with his 'protest against Prelacy', and contains little personal detail. He was, by his own beliefs, a pious and principled young man, whose notoriety was considerably increased by rumours of his sufferings at the hands of his jailers. On 10 October 1681 he was hanged at the 'Gallow-lee, betwixt Edinburgh and Leith', rather than at the 'cross and grassmarket', in order that as small a crowd as possible would be influenced by his demeanour and dying testament (Wodrow, 3.287). His head and hands were cut off and placed on spikes at the Pleasance port of the town, which act served only to grant his last wish, that 'Mr Guthrie's head [be] on one port of Edinburgh, and mine on another' (Howie, 474). Garnock's body was recovered by sympathizers—among whom was James Renwick (1662–1688), the noted covenanter—and interred at the West Church, Edinburgh. He had apparently few possessions or ready cash, and left no will.

VAUGHAN T. WELLS

Sources J. Howie, *The Scots worthies*, ed. W. H. Carlaw, [new edn] (1870) • R. Wodrow, *The history of the sufferings of the Church of Scotland from the Restoration to the revolution*, ed. R. Burns, 4 vols. (1839–41) • *Reg. PCS*, 3rd ser., vol. 6 • *Extracts from the records of the burgh of Stirling, 1667–1752* (1887) • Anderson, *Scot. nat.* • A. Smellie, *Men of the covenant* (1960) • *Fasti Scot.*, new edn, vol. 4 • *DNB*

Garnsey, Sir Gilbert Francis (1883–1932), accountant, was born on 21 March 1883, the fifth son of William Samuel Garnsey, a butcher in Wellington, Somerset, and his wife Emily, *née* Gibbings. He was educated locally at Wellington School, and his headmaster later recalled that Garnsey learned bookkeeping and had an uncanny way of getting very high marks in mathematics. He began to study for his accountancy qualifications during his final years at Wellington. The Revd E. C. Harries, the second master, introduced him to the Walsall firm of chartered accountants, Muras, Harries, and Higginson, where he became an articled clerk. Garnsey's intelligence and aptitude were revealed in 1903 when, at the age of twenty, he came first in the intermediate examination; he repeated this achievement two years later in his finals. Between 1902 and 1904, he played soccer for Aston Villa's second eleven as an amateur, though it is possible he was financially rewarded by the club, and used the money to pay for his articles.

Being of an ambitious disposition, Garnsey wrote to three of the leading accountancy firms in the City of London for a position. Price Waterhouse engaged him in 1905 at a salary of £2 per week. Initially, he worked almost exclusively for Nicholas Waterhouse, the most recent admission to the partnership, and made an excellent impression. Waterhouse considered his investigation of

Cornells, a Smithfield business seeking public flotation, masterly. Although only in his early twenties, Garnsey detected irregularities which resulted in a prolonged but successful litigation. Shortly after joining Price Waterhouse, Garnsey was sent to Paris to assist with an investigation of the New York Life Insurance Company, and his ability to work efficiently under pressure drew him to the attention of other partners.

Inexhaustible energy, combined with high intelligence and a natural skill for accountancy, resulted in Garnsey's being made a partner in 1913, aged thirty—a remarkable achievement in an era when experience and family connections were valued. He had developed an uncanny skill with numbers and once observed: 'to me figures have always possessed individuality. I can remember a figure connected with an individual long after I may have forgotten his features and form' (obituary, *Evening News*). In the years before the First World War, Garnsey travelled extensively on the continent on audits and investigations for Price Waterhouse. In 1914 he volunteered for military service but was rejected on health grounds. In 1915 he married Miriam Howles BSc, daughter of John Howles, a cotton-mill manager; they had a son and a daughter. The following year he joined the finance department of the Ministry of Munitions in an honorary capacity and in 1917 was appointed director of internal audits and controller of munitions accounts. He eventually served as chairman of the finance committee and the finance member of the Munitions Council, and in June 1918 he was made a KBE for his war work.

While controller of munitions accounts, Garnsey met leading politicians, including Churchill, and had an opportunity to demonstrate his administrative and financial expertise to senior civil servants. As a result, he was in demand to serve upon government committees and investigations; in 1919 these included the Demobilization Board, the Munitions Council for the liquidation of contracts, the Ministry of Health committee on the government housing scheme, and the Treasury committee of inquiry into the accounts of aerodrome construction works. He was later a member of the Ministry of Health inquiry into the affairs of the Metropolitan Water Board (1920), the Lawrence committee on the administration of accounting for army expenditure (1922), and (in 1924) the Treasury committee on the accounting methods of government departments, the Board of Trade committee on the Assurance Companies Acts, and the court of inquiry into the remuneration of doctors under the National Health Insurance Acts. In 1925 he was appointed a member of the National Food Council, and in 1930 he served as chairman of the marketing and distribution consumable commodities committee of the Economic Advisory Council. He became chairman of the British industries fairs, sites, and buildings committee in 1931.

This public role reflected not only his own eminence, but the increasing significance of the accountancy profession. The network of connections that Garnsey had established led to Price Waterhouse being entrusted with a succession of special assignments. The companies with which the firm had close links included: Marconi Wireless Telegraph Company; Farrow's Bank; Armstrong, Whitworth & Co.; Liptons; Cable and Wireless; Spillers' Milling and Associated Industries; and William Beardmore & Co. Appointment as a company's auditor often followed intensive work on a prospectus or reorganization. As a result, Price Waterhouse flourished throughout the 1920s, generating sustained growth: its fee income rose from £102,398 in 1918 to over £300,000 by 1930, making it one of the largest practices in the UK.

Appreciating the limitations of the Companies Acts, Garnsey was one of the first accountants in Britain to call for reform of reporting procedures. In December 1922 he read a paper entitled 'Holding companies and their published accounts' to the London members of the Institute of Chartered Accountants, publishing the text in the same year. He recommended the presentation of 'a consolidated balance sheet of the whole undertaking amalgamating the assets and liabilities of all the subsidiaries with those of the holding company and a consolidated profit and loss account embracing the profits and losses of all the companies' (Garnsey, *Holding Companies*, 1923, 10).

An exceptionally hard worker himself, Garnsey demanded the most of his assistants, whom he chose with care. He was also ambitious for Price Waterhouse and in 1929 put pressure on Sir Albert Wyon, the senior partner, to surrender some of his shares in the firm. Length of service governed the principle of succession and Garnsey had no immediate hope of executive authority. However, he continued to challenge Wyon and it was agreed that from 1 July 1932 the latter would retire to become a consultant and Garnsey would assume the senior partnership. Then on 26 June, five days before he was to take the post, Garnsey collapsed and died, aged forty-nine, of a pulmonary embolism, at Saint Hill House, his home at East Grinstead. A brilliant career was thus ended just when its greatest potential was about to be realized. Lengthy obituaries in the financial press and national newspapers nevertheless fittingly described him as a 'business doctor', a 'master of figures', and an 'unusual man of destiny'. He was survived by his wife.

EDGAR JONES

Sources E. Jones, *True and fair, a history of Price Waterhouse* (1995) • J. R. Edwards, 'Garnsey, Sir Gilbert Francis', *DBB* • *Somerset County Gazette* (2 July 1932) [obituary] • *Evening News* (27 June 1932) • *The Times* (28 June 1932) • d. cert.
Archives Price Waterhouse, London, archives
Wealth at death £151,466 10s. 11d.: probate, 17 Aug 1932, *CGPLA Eng. & Wales*

Garran [*formerly* Gamman], **Andrew** (1825–1901), journalist and politician in Australia, was born at Wilmot Square, London, on 15 November 1825, the third of thirteen children of Robert Gamman, a coal merchant of Flemish ancestry, and his wife, Mary Ann, daughter of Henry Matthews, architect and engineer. He went to boarding-school when five, having already been taught to read by his grandfather, and in 1834 to Hackney grammar school. Having decided to enter the ministry, he went to a Congregational theological coaching college in Norfolk before proceeding in 1842 to Spring Hill College, Birmingham, where he studied under Professor Henry Rogers. The next year he matriculated at London University, graduating with a first-class BA in 1845, and an MA in mental, moral, and political philosophy at University College in 1848.

Suffering from acute pleurisy (and suspected consumption), Garran, as he always styled himself, went to Madeira for eighteen months to recover, but, recommended to seek a still warmer climate, in October 1850 he sailed for South Australia, receiving a free passage in the *Ascendant* as 'Christian instructor', thanks to fellow Congregationalist, George Fife Angas. After arriving in Adelaide in January 1851, he preached, edited the short-lived *Austral Examiner*, campaigned for the abolition of state aid to religion at that year's elections, refused a government sinecure in the commissariat, and finally tutored a Victorian squatter's son for a year before returning to Adelaide to edit the *South Australian Register* from 1853 to 1856. While so engaged, on 1 December 1854 he married Mary Isham (1829–1923), daughter of John Sabine, a chemist (who had also migrated to South Australia for his health), and Adelaide, daughter of Captain William Eppes RN—all four devout Congregationalists. Looking for a higher income, Garran offered to act as Adelaide correspondent of the *Sydney Morning Herald* and again found the Congregational network useful when the paper's Congregationalist proprietor, John Fairfax, having heard of him from Professor Rogers, invited him to become assistant editor to the Congregationalist clergyman, John West. Garran decided to be a journalist and not a minister, and moved to Sydney, to be assistant editor from 1856 to 1873 and then editor from 1873 to 1885, while also acting as a correspondent for the *Adelaide Register* and the London *Times*. He graduated LLB at Sydney University in 1868, and LLD in 1870.

Garran undoubtedly made *The Herald* a great newspaper. His editorials, 2520 between 1873 and 1885, always lucid and impartially argued (if occasionally a little self-righteous), maintained a steady defence of English liberal principles, although in Sydney these were at times conservative enough to irritate colonial radicals. A moderate free-trader, he was also a defender of *laissez-faire* against the growing activities of the state. While criticizing the short-sighted selfishness of many squatters, he opposed the selection of their land for small farms, which took away their property; but, more radically, he supported a land tax, state-managed primary schools against the existing sectarian ones, and scientific enquiry in opposition to contemporary religious dogmatism—although his 'Leaves from a layman's notebook' in the *Sydney Mail* between 1884 and 1887 showed that he remained firmly attached to the basic principles of Christianity and he continued as a deacon of the Pitt Street Congregational Church.

Poor health forced Garran's retirement from *The Herald* in 1885, although he continued to contribute to it and to the London *Times*. He was a commissioner for the international exhibitions in Philadelphia in 1876 and in Sydney in 1879 and after his retirement he edited the comprehensive three-volume *Picturesque Atlas of Australia* (1886). He was appointed to the legislative council in 1887 and sat on inquiries into noxious trades in 1888 and strikes in 1890. The latter led to his becoming president of the resultant arbitration council from 1892 to 1894. He became more radical with age, and in the legislative council helped to carry a divorce law reform bill in 1892. As a member of George Reid's cabinet from 1895 to 1898, he supported that government's many social and political reforms. He also supported federation.

'A long, lanky, ungainly figure, with dreamy faraway eyes and benevolent features, flapping coat-tails and a wind-tossed beard', according to a former assistant, F. J. Broomfield, writing in *The Bulletin* (15 June 1901), a lover of cricket and fine music, Garran died of bronchitis at his home in Roslyn Avenue, Darlinghurst, Sydney, on 6 June 1901, survived by his wife, one son (Sir Robert Garran GCMG), and five of his seven daughters. He was buried on 7 June in the Congregationalist section of Rookwood cemetery in Sydney, a man to be praised as 'a leader of the people by his counsels' (Ecclesiasticus 44: 4).

A. G. L. SHAW

Sources R. R. Garran, *Prosper the Commonwealth* (1958) · E. K. Bramsted, 'Garran (Gamman), Andrew', *AusDB*, 4.233 · R. B. Walker, 'Andrew Garran: Congregationalist, conservative and liberal reformer', *Australian Journal of Politics and History*, 18 (1972), 386–401 · G. Souter, *Company of Heralds* (1990) · T. A. Coghlan, *Labour and industry in Australia, from the first settlement in 1788 to the establishment of the commonwealth in 1901*, 4 (1918); repr. (1969) · J. A. Froude, *Oceana, or, England and her colonies* (1886) · D. Pike, *Paradise of dissent: South Australia, 1829–1857* (1957) · *Sydney Morning Herald* (7 June 1901) · G. Woolnough, *Daily Mail* [Brisbane] (23 April 1927) · F. J. Broomfield, *The Bulletin* [Sydney, NSW] (15 June 1901) · *Sydney Morning Herald* (8 June 1901)
Archives NL Aus.

Garrard, Apsley George Benet Cherry- (1886–1959), polar explorer, was born in Bedford on 2 January 1886, the only son (there were five daughters) of Major-General Apsley Cherry-Garrard CB (1832–1907), and his wife, Evelyn Edith, daughter of Henry Wilson Sharpin. Major-General Cherry-Garrard, a distinguished soldier, inherited from his elder brother the Cherry estate of Denford Park, Berkshire, and in 1892 that of his mother's family also, Lamer Park, Hertfordshire, with the added name and arms of Garrard. He leased Denford and made Lamer his residence; it became to his son the dearest place on earth. Short-sightedness handicapped the young Cherry-Garrard in games at his preparatory school and at Winchester College, where he was lonely. But at Oxford he found congenial friends and interests as well as rowing—a sport to which bad eyesight was no bar: he helped the Christ Church eight to win the Grand Challenge cup at Henley in 1908. In the same year he obtained a third class in modern history.

On his father's death in 1907 Cherry-Garrard found himself the heir to a double fortune, and two years later went for a cruise round the world on cargo boats. Hearing when at Brisbane that Captain Robert Falcon Scott proposed a second expedition to the Antarctic in 1910, he wrote to Edward Wilson, whom he had met previously at a shooting party in Scotland, volunteering his services. Every member of the expedition was a specialist of some sort

Apsley George Benet Cherry-Garrard (1886–1959), by Frank Debenham

and he was accepted by Scott on Wilson's recommendation alone: he duly enlisted as 'assistant zoologist'. Yet from the outset, despite his youth and inexperience, he won the affectionate regard of his more seasoned comrades, and before the close of the expedition had more major sledge journeys to his credit than any other surviving member.

On the Depôt Journey to lay stores at stages along the southern route, as far as to One Ton Depôt 140 miles from base, Cherry-Garrard was warmly commended by Scott for his efficiency and unselfishness as a sledger and tent-mate. In the comparative comfort of life at the base he edited the *South Polar Times*, a unique periodical afterwards reproduced in facsimile. Wilson chose 'Birdie' Bowers and Cherry-Garrard—'the pick of the sledging element' (Scott, quoted in *South Pole Odyssey*, 81)—as his companions for a Winter Journey in 1911 to obtain specimen eggs from the emperor penguin rookery at Cape Crozier. This entailed a hazardous round trip of 120 miles in darkness, at temperatures in excess of −70 °F, an exploit which is still without parallel in the annals of polar exploration. An unbreakable bond was forged between the three men and on their return five weeks later Scott described their journey as 'the hardest that has ever been made'—a phrase which later suggested to Cherry-Garrard the title of his narrative of the fortunes of the whole expedition: *The Worst Journey in the World* (1922).

The Winter Journey was the climax of the whole expedition for Cherry-Garrard, so much so that even the outward marches of the great southern journey, despite their gruelling nature, were a picnic by comparison. He accompanied the polar party as far as the summit of the Beardmore Glacier whence he was sent back, because of his youth, with the first of the two supporting parties. Early in March 1912 he set out with dog teams and Dimitri, the Russian dog driver, to speed the return of the polar party. Having reached One Ton Depôt on the night of the third, the date approximately timed for their arrival, he was beset by a four days' blizzard which prevented movement, but stayed on until there remained only just enough dog food for the return. Although his decision to return was the only possible one, he never ceased to reproach himself

afterwards for not having attempted the impossible. He was a member of the search party eight months later which found the bodies of Scott, Wilson, and Bowers, who had died within only 11 miles of One Ton Depôt (which they reached on 21 March), and learned of the heroic self-sacrifice of Lawrence Oates a few marches behind, and of Petty Officer Edgar Evans's earlier collapse below the Beardmore Glacier. It was at Cherry-Garrard's suggestion that the last line of Tennyson's *Ulysses* ('To strive, to seek, to find and not to yield') was inscribed on the cross surmounting the cairn of snow which covered them, as well as the epitaph commemorating Oates.

The rest of Cherry-Garrard's life was anticlimax. During the First World War he commanded a squadron of armoured cars in Flanders from 1914 until invalided out two years later, and during long convalescence wrote *The Worst Journey*, a classic of Antarctic literature. First published in December 1922 it went through several editions before being republished in 1951, with a postscript written in 1948. Years later he also wrote introductions to biographies of Wilson and Bowers. He cultivated friendships with men of letters, including George Bernard Shaw, H. G. Wells, and Arnold Bennett; and with men of action, especially Mallory of Everest and Lawrence of Arabia. To the latter he paid tribute in the symposium *T. E. Lawrence by his Friends* (1937).

In the early 1920s Cherry-Garrard recovered some strength but the Scott tragedy continued to haunt him, altering and even reversing many of his interests: 'He gave up shooting, became almost hostile to fox-hunting, and disappointed the churchmen who had been accustomed to his support in the parish' (*The Times*). Later he cruised the Mediterranean and collected books, first editions where possible, but 'he still lived with the Polar expedition and would talk of little else' (ibid.). He married, on 6 September 1939, Angela Katherine, daughter of Kenneth Turner, of Fairfields, Ipswich. In 1947 income tax demands and ill health obliged him to sell Lamer, which was demolished, and he moved into a London flat. After many years of intermittent illness he died at the Berkeley Hotel, Piccadilly, London, on 18 May 1959. He was survived by his wife; there were no children.   MARK POTTLE

Sources *The Times* (19 May 1959), 13a · L. Huxley, ed., *Scott's last expedition*, 2 vols. (1913) · A. Cherry-Garrard, *The worst journey in the world: Antarctic, 1910–1913* (1951) · personal knowledge (1971) [*DNB*] · S. Wheeler, *Cherry: a life of Apsley Cherry-Garrard* (2001) · *WWW* · G. Seaver, *'Birdie' Bowers of the Antarctic* (1938) · G. Seaver, *Edward Wilson of the Antarctic* (1933) · *South Pole odyssey: selections from the Antarctic diaries of Edward Wilson*, ed. H. King (1982) · F. Spufford, *I may be some time: ice and the English imagination* (1996) · Burke, *Gen. GB* (1937) [Cherry-Garrard of Lamer] · *CGPLA Eng. & Wales* (1959)

Archives Scott Polar RI, corresp., journals, and notebooks

Likenesses F. Debenham, photographs, c.1911–1912, Scott Polar RI · H. C. Ponting, photographs, c.1911–1912, Scott Polar RI · I. Roberts-Jones, bronze statuette, 1962, Wheathampstead parish church · F. Debenham, photograph, Scott Polar RI [*see illus.*] · group portrait, photograph (with Bowers and Wilson; after return from the 'Winter Journey'), repro. in Huxley, *Scott's last expedition*, vol. 2, p. 73 · photograph, repro. in Huxley, *Scott's last expedition*, vol. 1, p. 426

Wealth at death £481,158 6s. 8d.: probate, 14 July 1959, *CGPLA Eng. & Wales*

Garrard, George (1760–1826), animal painter and sculptor, was born on 31 May 1760, and baptized on 26 June at St Lawrence Jewry, London, the son of Robert Hazlewood (Haselfoot) Garrard and his wife, Miriam. After studying with the animal painter Sawrey Gilpin (whose daughter Matilda he later married), Garrard enrolled at the Royal Academy Schools on 31 December 1778. He came to public notice in 1784 when the Royal Academy president purchased one of his paintings (F. Broun, 'Sir Joshua Reynolds' collection of paintings', PhD diss., Princeton University, 1987). In 1786 Garrard documented Colonel Thomas Thornton's outlandish 'sporting tour' of northern England and Scotland. About the same time he began painting for the eighth duke of Hamilton, who ultimately regarded Garrard as his favourite artist. From 1796 to 1815 he worked extensively for the brewer Samuel Whitbread (1764–1815), producing portrait busts, paintings of family properties, and architectural relief sculptures of animal themes similar to those he produced at Woburn Abbey for another steady patron, the duke of Bedford.

Fiercely protective of his interests, Garrard successfully sued a negligent patron in 1797. In the following year he secured a copyright act for the protection of sculptors (38 Geo. III c. 71). In 1800 he became an associate of the Royal Academy, where he exhibited 215 works, principally portraits and animal compositions in marble, bronze, and plaster. The models he displayed at the 'Agricultural Museum' in his George Street home were considered to rival 'the greatest statuaries of Greece' (Gunnis, 163). Garrard also worked in watercolour, oil, and engraving, and produced landscapes, city views, and genre scenes.

This prolific and multifarious practice eclipsed Garrard's early promise. Joseph Nollekens dismissed him as 'a Jack of all trades' and Joseph Farington noted his acceptance of commissions insufficiently remunerative for George Stubbs or Gilpin (Farington, *Diary*, 4.1569). Both artists influenced Garrard's proto-Romantic groups of frenzied and savage beasts. His anatomical studies possessed real scientific value, and under the auspices of the board of agriculture he published a volume of aquatints after his own plaster models, *A Description of the Different Varieties of Oxen Common in the British Isles* (1800).

Ambitious and somewhat vain, Garrard betrayed his pretensions in *The Woburn Sheep-Shearing* (1804) at Woburn Abbey, a painting he subsequently engraved with an explanatory text. Teeming with over 100 animals and 200 human figures (including several agricultural celebrities), the picture shows Garrard surrounded by props emblematic of his knowledge and social standing. He angled unsuccessfully for prestigious public commissions, exhibiting numerous models for equestrian statues and entering competitions for monuments honouring William Pitt (1806), Sir John Moore (1811), and the duke of Wellington (1814). Despite steady employment by several aristocratic patrons and a large sale of his works at 23 Old Bond Street, London, in June 1813, Garrard left an impoverished widow on his death at Queen's Buildings, Brompton, London, on 8 October 1826. On application to the Royal Academy, Mrs Garrard received an annual pension of £45 for herself and an invalid daughter. Garrard's son, Charles, exhibited portrait sculpture at the academy from 1816 to 1829.

ROBYN ASLESON

Sources E. Croft-Murray, *George Garrard* (1961) · S. Deuchar, *Paintings, politics, and porter: Samuel Whitbread II (1764–1815) and British art* (1984) [exhibition catalogue, Museum of London, London, 21 Feb – 29 April 1984] · G. Garrard, *A description of the different varieties of oxen common in the British Isles* (1800) · D. Spargo, *This land is our land: aspects of agriculture in England* (1989) · J. Egerton, ed., *British sporting and animal paintings, 1655–1867* (1978), 161–6 · Graves, *RA exhibitors* · Farington, *Diary* · R. Gunnis, *Dictionary of British sculptors, 1660–1851* (1953), 163–4 · T. Thornton, *A sporting tour through the northern parts of England and great part of the highlands of Scotland* (1804) · J. Blore, *A guide to Burghley House, Northamptonshire, the seat of the marquis of Exeter* (1815) · W. S. Sparrow, *British sporting artists: from Barlow to Herring* (1922), 232–3 · G. Lyster, ed., *A family chronicle, derived from notes and letters selected by Barbarina, the Hon. Lady Grey* (1908), 15–17 · S. C. Hutchison, 'The Royal Academy Schools, 1768–1830', *Walpole Society*, 38 (1960–62), 123–91, esp. 143–4 · *IGI* · 'Getty provenance index', piedi.getty.edu, 17 Nov 1998 · J. C. Wood, *A dictionary of British animal painters* (1973), 32
Archives Beds. & Luton ARS, letters to Samuel Whitbread · Ches. & Chester ALSS, receipts, etc. for sums received for his pictures · Woburn Abbey, Bedfordshire, corresp. with fifth duke of Bedford
Likenesses G. Garrard, self-portrait, oils, *c*.1815, priv. coll. · S. W. Arnold, marble bust, 1828 · J. Constable, oils; Hearn sale, New York, 25 Feb – 4 March 1918

Garrard, Sir Samuel, fourth baronet (1651–1725), politician and merchant, was the sixth child and fourth son of Sir John Garrard, second baronet (*d*. 1686), of Lamer, landowner, and his wife, Jane (1617–1692), daughter of Sir Moulton Lambard of Westcombe, Kent, and his wife, Jane (1593–1673), who after 1636 was Sir John's stepmother. The exact date of Samuel's birth is not known, but the ages given at his first marriage (24) and his death (73) suggest that it took place between 10 March and 16 October 1651. The family had come from Sittingbourne in Kent in the sixteenth century and Garrard's ancestors had settled in Lamer, near Wheathampstead, in Hertfordshire. His grandfather was made a baronet in 1622, and his father became high sheriff during the civil war and a supporter of parliament. The Garrards had also been deeply involved in the City of London. Samuel's great-great-grandfather Sir William (*d*. 1571) and three of his great-grandfathers served in the office of mayor. Samuel went up to London—possibly as early as the late 1660s—and in time became established in the parish of St John the Evangelist, where he lived at least until 1695 and had a business in Watling Street. He clearly prospered. A Samuell Gerard, lately apprenticed to William Savage jun., was admitted and sworn to the Company of Grocers in 1674–5. On 8 July 1678 Garrard was made a liveryman in the company. He was sworn second warden on 28 August 1700 and master a year later.

By a licence dated 16 October 1675 Samuel married Elizabeth (1656–1677), daughter of George Poyner of Codicotebury, Hertfordshire. They had no children. Later, by a licence dated 22 January 1689, he married Jane (1669–1746), daughter of Thomas Benet of Salthrop, Wiltshire, and they had three surviving sons. The eldest, Sir Samuel

Sir Samuel Garrard, fourth baronet (1651–1725), by unknown artist

(1692–1761), served as a lieutenant-colonel in Marlborough's regiment of guards and succeeded his father in the baronetcy; Thomas (1699–1758) became recorder of St Albans in 1727 and common serjeant of the City of London in 1729; and Sir Benet (1704–1767) succeeded as the sixth and last baronet.

On 13 January 1701 Garrard's elder brother Sir John died, and he succeeded as the fourth baronet and inherited the family estate at Lamer. He succeeded his brother also as an MP. In a by-election at Agmondesham (Amersham) in March 1701 Samuel was returned to serve in William's fifth parliament. He was not re-elected to William's sixth and last parliament in 1701–2, but under Anne he served continuously from 1702 to 1710 for the same borough. He was a tory and supported the tack, a high-church tory attempt to attach anti-occasional conformity legislation to a supply bill. He survived a petition against his election in 1705, no doubt to the distress of Lord Treasurer Godolphin, who described him as the most 'perverse man against us in the whole House' (HoP, *Commons, 1690–1715*).

Garrard was also active in City politics. On 7 March 1702 he was chosen alderman for Aldersgate, and on 27 June he was elected sheriff. He continued on the aldermanic bench for the rest of his life, representing Aldersgate until 1722, when, being then the senior alderman, he moved to Bridge Without. In 1709–10 he served as lord mayor, and in the course of that year he set in train a series of events which hastened the downfall of the whig ministry.

Garrard began by inviting the notorious Dr Sacheverell to deliver the Guy Fawkes sermon at St Paul's on 5 November 1709. Sacheverell took advantage of this formal City occasion to expound the doctrine of non-resistance and to denounce in colourful and provocative terms false, and clearly whig, brethren in church and state. Afterwards Garrard congratulated the preacher and said he would be happy to see his sermon in print. He was, however, unable to get the court of aldermen to support him in this. Sacheverell went ahead with the publication anyway, claiming the backing of the lord mayor. He was hauled before the House of Commons to answer an impeachment. When questioned he cited as excuse the encouragement of the lord mayor, but from his place in the house Garrard totally denied that he had ordered or encouraged the printing, and the house accepted the denial. During the trial there was growing unrest, which culminated in serious riots on the night of 1–2 March 1710. The mob roamed the streets of London destroying dissenting chapels and houses, and the lord mayor was slow to act. In the end, when Sacheverell's sermon came to be burnt by the hangman, the lord mayor did not attend.

Honours and responsibilities descended on Garrard in his latter years. He was made an honorary DCL at Oxford in 1707 and colonel of the White regiment of the city militia in 1711. He became deputy lieutenant of the county of Hertford, and in 1721 president of the Bridewell and Bethlem hospitals. One of his last appearances on the national stage was in 1721 when he was sent by the City to ask parliament to do something about the South Sea Bubble.

Garrard died on 10 March 1725 aged seventy-three, leaving considerable property in land and securities, including a London dwelling in Warwick Place, Christ Church, and extensive premises in Watling Street near the Old Exchange. He was buried on 17 March in the parish church of Wheathampstead, where a monument was erected to his memory. His wife survived him, and died in August 1746.

DAVID C. ELLIOT

Sources GEC, *Baronetage*, 1.188–9 • A. B. Beaven, ed., *The aldermen of the City of London, temp. Henry III–[1912]*, 2 vols. (1908–13), vol. 1, pp. 7, 67, 252, 303–4, 319, 324; vol. 2, pp. 120, 125, 195 • *VCH Hertfordshire*, 2.299, 434 • D. Warrand, ed., *Hertfordshire families* (1907), 10–11, 283 • G. Holmes, *The trial of Dr. Sacheverell* (1975) • Cobbett, *Parl. hist.*, 6.806–7, 813 • A. Kingston, *Hertfordshire during the great civil war* (1894), 28, 40, 52, 56, 62, 145, 148–9, 182 • R. Clutterbuck, ed., *The history and antiquities of the county of Hertford*, 1 (1815), 51, 513–15, 521–2 • N. Luttrell, *A brief historical relation of state affairs from September 1678 to April 1714*, 6 (1857), 404, 498, 523, 640 • H. Chauncy, *The historical antiquities of Hertfordshire* (1700); repr. in 2 vols. (1826), vol. 1, p. 49; vol. 2, pp. 409, 427 • J. L. Chester and J. Foster, eds., *London marriage licences, 1521–1869* (1887), 529 • D. V. Glass, introduction, *London inhabitants within the walls, 1695*, ed. D. V. Glass, London RS, 2 (1966), 116 • wardens' accounts, 1674–5, GL, Grocers' Company MSS, 11571/15; minute book, 11588/5, 11588/6 • 'Garrard, Sir Samuel, 4th bt', HoP, *Commons, 1690–1715* [draft] • will, PRO, PROB 11/602, sig. 86

Archives Herts. ALS, Garrard MSS, ref. 26933–27422
Likenesses T. Athow, drawing (after school of G. Kneller), AM Oxf. · J. Thornhill, oils, Guildhall Art Gallery, London · portrait; Phillips, June–July 1977, formerly owned by Bridewell Hospital, London [*see illus.*]
Wealth at death owned house at Warwick Court in parish of Christ Church, London; extensive premises in Watling Street; landed property incl. Lamer and adjoining manors in Hertfordshire; land near Exall and Bedworth in Warwickshire and round about Flore in Northamptonshire, as well as securities: *VCH Hertfordshire*, 2.299–301, 434; *DNB*; will, County Hall, Hertford, Garrard MSS, ref. 27156

Garrard, Thomas (1498–1540), clergyman and protestant reformer, is first recorded in 1517, when at the age of nineteen he was admitted to Corpus Christi College, Oxford. He graduated BA in 1518 and became a fellow of Magdalen College in 1519. He incepted MA in 1524, and was BTh (probably of Oxford) by 1535. By 1526 he was curate of All Hallows, Honey Lane, London (then precociously moving towards reform under its rector, Robert Forman), and was subsequently admitted rector there on 22 June 1537.

At Oxford Garrard made an abiding enemy in the vigilant Bishop John Longland of Lincoln (a future chancellor of the university), in whose diocese Oxford stood. Until the late 1520s Longland and his officers congratulated themselves that due to their habitual watchfulness Oxford had largely escaped the Lutheran contagion that had swept through Cambridge. Then a book-smuggling enterprise was discovered in which Garrard was a linchpin. He had been sending heavy fardels of Luther's books from London booksellers to the universities, and distributing small (and easy to hide) copies of William Tyndale's illicit New Testament. Garrard 'corrupted' the monastery of Reading, selling the prior over sixty books. At Easter 1527 Garrard was in Oxford, lining up Greek and Hebrew scholars as potential customers, and was back again from Christmas 1527, 'lurking' at the university until mid-February 1528, when he was seized by Longland's commissary and held in his chamber at Lincoln College. But Garrard picked the lock, and disguising himself in the tawny coat of a friend, fled in the hope of reaching Wales and sailing to Germany. Ports were watched, and he was captured at Bedminster near Bristol on 29 February. Examined by Longland and Cuthbert Tunstall, bishop of London, Garrard retracted his belief in justification by faith alone, with other Lutheran tenets.

Within a few years Garrard became chaplain to Sir Francis Bigod, a Yorkshire landowner who was then an enthusiastic supporter of the royal supremacy, who on 6 June 1535 obtained a licence under the royal seal from the archiepiscopal faculty office for him to preach throughout the realm. Bigod sent Garrard to preach at Jervaulx Abbey in July 1535, and one of the monks, George Lazenby, interrupted him openly to defend the powers of the papacy. The investigation that followed resulted in Lazenby's execution for treason the next month.

By June 1536 Garrard had become chaplain to Hugh Latimer during his short-lived tenure as bishop of Worcester, rising to become Latimer's chancellor. In June 1539 he became rector of Hartlebury, near Kidderminster. Garrard contributed to contentious divisions in the diocese. Latimer's promotion of evangelical reforms pitted his friends among the local gentry against conservative gentlemen and long-time diocesan officials. Latimer's opponents claimed that he kept none but 'heretic knaves' in his service, and Garrard was particularly marked as one of the most pernicious examples of the new bishop's intrusive influence. These years were the busiest period of Garrard's life, as his duties required him to take part in investigations to protect Latimer, as well as to make extensive preaching tours throughout the diocese and across southern England. As John Foxe said, Garrard was continually 'flying from place to place' (*Acts and Monuments*, 5.428). Although his sermon notes have not survived, it is clear that he emphasized Christ's passion as the only means of salvation, at the expense of the traditional economy of good works. At Rye in 1537, he was noted for criticizing purgatory, masses for the dead, offerings to saints, and pilgrimages, inculcating about twenty men with his views. The next year at Kidderminster his sermon dealt with 'the righteousness that cometh by Christ and of the righteousness of works', and he was interrupted by a member of the audience, who denounced him as 'a foolish knave priest come to preach of the new learning' (PRO, SP 1/134, fols. 298r–300r; *LP Henry VIII*, vol. 13, pt 1, no. 1509). Before mid-1539 he had become chaplain to Archbishop Cranmer, who sent him to preach in Calais, an especially risky assignment, as the tide was now turning against the reformers.

Cromwell could afford to protect Latimer and his men until the king turned his back on limited doctrinal experimentation, endorsing the six articles in 1539, which invested new confidence in traditional tenets, including transubstantiation and masses for the dead. At issue was the ultimate control of the English church, and whether further reforms would be pursued. Protestant reformers were losing their influence over the king (especially in his eventual repudiation of his marriage to Anne of Cleves) while conservative bishops, led by Stephen Gardiner of Winchester, pressed their advantages. When Latimer refused to work for the passage of the act in parliament, he was forced to resign his see. Ever watchful of his old enemy, Longland complained of Garrard's disrespectful breaking of a holy fast in Oxfordshire in the summer of 1539.

The prolonged, shifting crisis which resulted in the fall of Cromwell was triggered by an unusually stormy series of sermons at Paul's Cross during Lent 1540. Gardiner opened the attack against Lutheran opinions on 15 February, arguing that those who said good works were not necessary for salvation were misinterpreting scripture. In succeeding weeks he was answered in highly contentious terms by Robert Barnes, William Jerome, and Garrard. Barnes attacked Gardiner by name, but subsequently he admitted he had 'overshot' himself, and was 'confuted by scriptures', conceding that good works were allowed of God as a means to salvation, concessions which were also endorsed by Garrard and Jerome (*Acts and Monuments*, 5, appx 7).

During Easter week the three men made highly equivocal recantations at the preaching cross at St Mary Spital, mouthing prepared retractions while convincing onlookers that, in reality, they maintained their old opinions. On 3 April they were admitted to the Tower at Henry's command, but only briefly, for Cromwell regained the upper hand over his enemies in the tumultuous weeks that followed. But on 10 June came the ultimate defeat with Cromwell's arrest. Charged with heretical opinions and licensing known heretics to preach, as well as with treason, he was beheaded on 28 July.

Barnes, Garrard, and Jerome were exempted from a general pardon and had no trial. On 30 July 1540 they were drawn from the Tower through London and burnt in one fire at Smithfield, while three long-time prisoners, Thomas Abell, Richard Fetherstone, and Edward Powell (Catholic priests who had been supporters of Katherine of Aragon) were hanged, drawn, and quartered as traitors. At the stake, Garrard and his fellows maintained that they did not know why they were being burnt, and that they died guiltless. Foxe records that Garrard said he never knowingly preached anything 'against God's holy word, or contrary to the true faith' (*Acts and Monuments*, 5.437). Richard Hilles, who observed the executions, reported to Heinrich Bullinger that they 'remained in the fire without crying out, but were as quiet and patient as though they felt no pain' (Robinson, *Original Letters*, 1.209).

Although Garrard and his companions deliberately created the impression that they were yielding their lives as martyrs, their execution marked a critical juncture in defining the late Henrician church as conservative in doctrine yet estranged from Rome, dependent upon a mercurial supreme head who was the final arbitrator of matters of faith in his realm. Garrard and the others perished in 1540 in a ruthless demonstration of King Henry's religious even-handedness.   SUSAN WABUDA

Sources *The acts and monuments of John Foxe*, new edn, ed. G. Townsend, 5 (1846), 421–9, 430–39, 448; appx 6–8 · PRO, SP 1/115, fols. 116r–167r · *LP Henry VIII*, 12/1, no. 308; 13/1, no. 1509 · PRO, SP 1/134, fols. 298r–300r · Emden, *Oxf.*, 4.228–9 · A. G. Dickens, *Lollards and protestants in the diocese of York, 1509–1558*, 2nd edn (1982), 58–9, 76, 79–83, 103–6 · S. Brigden, *London and the Reformation* (1989), 114–15, 235, 265–6, 311–19, 322, 324, 350, 391, 407 · H. Robinson, ed. and trans., *Original letters relative to the English Reformation*, 1 vol. in 2, Parker Society, [26] (1846–7), 200–15, 616–17 · S. Wabuda, '"Fruitful preaching" in the diocese of Worcester: Bishop Hugh Latimer and his influence, 1535–1539', *Religion and the English people, 1500–1640*, ed. E. J. Carlson (1998), 49–74

Likenesses woodcut, repro. in Townsend, ed., *Acts and monuments*

Garrard, Thomas (1787–1859), biographer, was the eldest son of Thomas Garrard of Lambourne, Berkshire. In 1822 he was elected chamberlain of Bristol, and on 1 January 1836, under the provisions of the Municipal Reform Act, he became city treasurer, an office which he held until March 1856. In 1852 Garrard published a book entitled *Edward Colston, the Philanthropist, his Life and Times, Including a Memoir of his Father*, which was edited by Samuel Griffiths Tovey; the latter issued in 1862 a second edition under a slightly different title. Colston, who had been MP for Bristol from 1710 to 1713, helped finance the building of schools and hospitals in the city, and donated money to other charities.

Garrard died at 8 Springfield Place, Bath, on 18 December 1859. He was twice married and left a family.

B. H. BLACKER, *rev.* MARK CLEMENT

Sources J. Latimer, *The annals of Bristol in the nineteenth century*, [1] (1887) · *Bristol Times* (24 Dec 1859) · *GM*, 3rd ser., 8 (1860), 196 · d. cert.

Garrard, Sir William (*c.*1510–1571), merchant, was born in the parish of St Magnus the Martyr near London Bridge, the son of John Garrard, a London grocer. He became a haberdasher and merchant adventurer, growing rich on the cloth-export trade to Antwerp. He bought the manor of Dorney, Buckinghamshire, in 1542, but continued to live mainly in London and remained an active merchant all his life. When the Antwerp market began to contract, he diversified into more risky ventures. In 1552 he exported linen and woollen cloth, coral, amber, and jet to the Barbary coast in return for sugar, dates, almonds, and molasses. He was involved in a number of voyages to Guinea in the 1550s and 1560s, shared in two of the slaving expeditions of Sir John Hawkins, and was a leading promoter of the expedition of Richard Chancellor to Russia in 1553. Garrard was named a consul of the Russia Company when it was founded about 1553, and from 1561 until his death was almost continuously either sole or joint governor of the company. He was also a governor of the Mineral and Battery Works founded in 1568.

An alderman by 1547, Garrard was elected sheriff of the City of London in 1552, mayor in 1555—being knighted during his term of office—and one of London's MPs in the last parliament of Mary I's reign. But his major contribution to the corporate life of the City was his work for the relief of the poor. In 1545 he was one of those appointed to devise new means of tackling the problem and in the 1550s he took a leading part in drawing up constitutions for the City's new or refounded hospitals. He was a governor of Christ's Hospital in 1553–4, of Bridewell in 1558–9, and of St Bartholomew's from 1559 until his death, surveyor of all the City's hospitals in 1566–7 and their comptroller-general from 1568. He maintained his interest until the end, bequeathing to Christ's Hospital £20, 'which they owe me that I lent them', with an additional £6 13s. 4d., besides £20 each to St Bartholomew's and St Thomas's. He also left money for prisoners in the City's prisons and the Gate House at Westminster and for poor householders in his ward and in two London parishes—St Magnus and St Christopher-le-Stocks, where he was then living—and in the parishes of Dorney and Burnham in Buckinghamshire and Sittingbourne in Kent, where he owned property.

Garrard died on 27 September 1571 and was buried, as he had requested, in the church of St Magnus the Martyr. He was survived by his wife, Isabel, daughter of Julian Nethermill, a Coventry draper, and their four sons and one daughter. The eldest son inherited Dorney and became a country gentleman, but John, the third son, followed his father as a City merchant and, in 1601, lord mayor. Sir Samuel Garrard, lord mayor in 1709, was a descendant of this son, providing a rare example of continuity in the mercantile élite of London.   HELEN MILLER, *rev.*

Sources HoP, *Commons, 1509–58* • T. S. Willan, *The Muscovy merchants of 1555* (1953) • R. Hakluyt, *The principal navigations, voyages, traffiques and discoveries of the English nation*, 2nd edn, 3 vols. (1598–1600); repr. 12 vols., Hakluyt Society, extra ser., 1–12 (1903–5) • will, PRO, PROB 11/54, sig. 3

Garratt, Geoffrey Theodore (1888–1942), administrator in India and author, was born on 7 November 1888 at The Grange, Little Tew, Oxfordshire, the sixth and youngest son of Charles Foster Garratt, who was vicar of Little Tew from 1858 to 1880, and his wife, Agnes Mary Percival, who came from a banking family. He was educated at Rugby School, and won a scholarship worth £100 and tenable for five years at Hertford College, Oxford, where he obtained a first class in mathematical moderations (1908) and a second in modern history (1911). He succeeded in the Indian Civil Service examination in 1912, and arrived in India in 1913, serving in Bombay as assistant collector and magistrate. His work involved close contact with rural society, and he was impressed by the abject poverty of Indian cultivators. During the First World War he joined the Indian army reserve of officers, and fought in the Mesopotamia campaign from 1916 to 1919. On 3 April 1920 he married Annie Beryl (1895/6–1949), daughter of Charles Francis Benthall, an Anglican clergyman, of Benthall Hall, Shropshire.

Garratt tendered his resignation from the Indian Civil Service in 1921, protesting against the squandering of money on building unnecessary amenities, including a costly fountain at Government House, while the Indian people lacked basic necessities. The resignation took formal effect in August 1922. During 1921–2 he was Berlin correspondent of the *Westminster Gazette*. He joined the Labour Party and in 1924 stood unsuccessfully as Labour parliamentary candidate for Cambridgeshire. He bought a farm at Barrington, Cambridgeshire, and was a member of the county council from 1925 to 1931. In November 1927 he sailed for India, and he stayed there until February 1928. After returning home, he published *An Indian Commentary* (1928), on which Edward John Thompson, another writer and Indian specialist, wrote a review. Garratt and Thompson became close friends and collaborators. Philip Rattray, the protagonist in *So a Poor Ghost* (1933), a novel written by Thompson, was modelled on Garratt. He supported the cause of Indian nationalism, but was not wholeheartedly sympathetic to the leadership of the Indian National Congress. At the general election of 1929 he again failed to win the Cambridgeshire seat.

In 1930, as reporter for *The Nation*, Garratt covered the first round-table conference in London, where representatives of the government and various strands of Indian political opinion discussed possible constitutional advance for India. He then planned to go to India to organize welfare work for jute mills of Bird & Co., Calcutta, of which his brother-in-law Edward Charles Benthall was partner. On hearing this, Edward Taylor Scott, the editor of the *Manchester Guardian*, approached Garratt and arranged that he should contribute articles to the paper from India. Garratt arrived in India in March 1931, met Gandhi, by now chief spokesman of Indian nationalism, and Irwin, the viceroy, in Delhi, and attended the Congress session in Karachi. He observed that an early resolution of political conflict between the Congress and the British raj, giving elected Indian ministers real responsibility in a new constitutional arrangement, was urgently needed. By October he had returned to Britain (being defeated for a third time as candidate for Cambridgeshire) and attended the second round-table conference as adviser to the Labour Party group. In December he returned to India, as he was invited by the diwan of Baroda, a princely state, to become *naib diwan*—secretary to the prime minister—of that state. However, the appointment was not realized, owing to the objection of the government of India. After working out the welfare scheme for Bird & Co., he went back to Britain in April 1932.

Garratt settled in Bishopsteignton House, near Teignmouth in south Devon, and contributed a number of reviews and articles to journals. In 1932 he published *The Mugwumps and the Labour Party*, in which he discussed the uneasy relationship within the Labour Party between socialist intellectuals and trade union leaders. In 1934 Garratt and Thompson published *The Rise and Fulfilment of British Rule in India*, which came to be regarded as the first British attempt to understand the Indian nationalist movement on its own terms. In the general election of 1935 he unsuccessfully stood for Wrekin, Shropshire. Meanwhile, preparing a biography of Lord Brougham, published in 1935 and followed in 1936 by another historical study, *The Two Mr Gladstones*, he contemplated an academic career, but developments in international relations drew him back into journalism and politics. In 1936 he went to Ethiopia as correspondent for the *Manchester Guardian* to cover the war. He saw the raising of sanctions against Italy by Britain as 'a lunacy', as Italy's real aims in Ethiopia were 'only too blatant' (Garratt to Thompson, 22 June 1936, Bodl. Oxf., MS Eng. C 5289/125).

Garratt's keen sense of public duty and radical sympathies were displayed during the Spanish Civil War. He became a leading member of the National Joint Committee for Spanish Relief. He spent most of 1937 in Spain and organized transport to and from the besieged Madrid, bringing food in and evacuating children. In May he was temporarily back in Britain, as he was persuaded to fight a by-election as a Labour candidate at the Plymouth Drake constituency, but was defeated by his Conservative opponent. During the campaign he attacked 'Eden and his foul and fascist foreign office' (Garratt to Thompson, 9 May 1937, Bodl. Oxf., MS Eng. C 5289/133), and afterwards was 'ticked off' by the Labour Party for having said too much about Spain (Garratt to Thompson, 10 Sept 1937, Bodl. Oxf., MS Eng. C 5289/137). His despair with the party was deep. In 1938 he joined the co-ordinating committee for refugees and became temporary secretary for the organization. On the basis of his first-hand experiences in Ethiopia and the Spanish Civil War, he wrote *Mussolini's*

Roman Empire (1938), in which he tried to convince readers that Mussolini was more dangerous than most Englishmen believed, and alleged that British foreign policy was dictated by pro-fascists in high places.

When the Second World War broke out Garratt was keen to enlist, but was not called up immediately. In January 1940 he went to Finland as correspondent for the *Manchester Guardian* to cover the Russo-Finnish War. After a long wait, in July 1940 he joined the Pioneer Corps. By February 1941 he was appointed captain and second in command of a company of German volunteers removing the debris of buildings hit by German bombs in London. By September they moved to Pembroke Dock, where they built defences as well as doing anti-invasion exercises. Garratt felt irritated by the reluctance of the British government to use people like himself or Thompson in the critical situation in India. In April 1942 he sought to make contact with Sir Stafford Cripps, who was leading a cabinet mission to India in an attempt (vain as it turned out) to enlist Congress co-operation in the war in return for radical political change in peacetime.

Garratt died at the Defensible Barracks at Pembroke Dock on 28 April 1942 'from multiple injuries accidentally sustained through the explosion of a beach mine during a military lecture' (d. cert.). A fortnight before his death he was appointed MBE. He was an individual of ability, energy, and public spirit. A tall man (about 6 foot), he was known for his modesty and the charm of his character; according to his wife, he had a peculiarly peaceful expression even in times of stress. Garratt and his wife adopted two sons in 1938.   TAKEHIKO HONDA

Sources Thompson MSS, Bodl. Oxf. · *Guardian* archives, Manchester University · Cecil of Chelwood papers, BL · BL, D'Abernon papers · *Manchester Guardian* (2 May 1942) · *The Times* (1 May 1942) · *Hertford College Magazine*, 31 (May 1943) · *India office lists* · *The Labour who's who* (1927) · b. cert. · m. cert. · d. cert. · M. Lago, 'India's prisoner': a biography of Edward John Thompson, 1886–1946 (2001)
Archives BL, Cecil of Chelwood papers · BL, D'Abernon papers · Bodl. Oxf., letters to E. J. Thompson · JRL, letters to the *Manchester Guardian*
Wealth at death £7523 2s. 11d.: resworn probate, *CGPLA Eng. & Wales*

Garratt, Herbert William (1864–1913), locomotive engineer, was born on 8 June 1864 at 11 Loddiges Road, Hackney, London, the son of William Garratt, umbrella manufacturer, and his wife, Emma Hunt. He was educated at private schools in London, then served his apprenticeship from 1879 to 1882 in the locomotive works in Bow. From there he went to Doxford's marine engine works in Sunderland, after which he served at sea as fourth and third engineer on several steamships. From 1885 to 1889 he acquired more railway-engineering experience, first as an inspector of engines and railway materials for C. Douglas Fox and Alexander Rendel respectively, then on the London and South Western Railway in conjunction with the Vacuum Brake Company.

From 1889 to 1906 Garratt worked on railways in many other countries: the Central Argentine Railway appointed him district locomotive superintendent in 1894, but in 1897 he was summarily dismissed for being late in returning from leave in England; in 1900 he went as locomotive superintendent to the Cuban Central Railways, in 1902 to the Lagos Government Railway, and in 1904 to the Lima Railways in Peru. In this way he acquired an unusually wide experience of railway engineering and management under difficult conditions. During those periods of service on overseas railways he made a special study of existing types of articulated locomotive, such as the Fairlie, Meyer, and Mallet, and the problems involved in achieving, especially on narrow-gauge track, adequate stability, traction, and speed. His first sketches of the Garratt articulated locomotive show that he appreciated the advantages of mounting the boiler centrally between a pair of driving bogies carrying the fuel and water tanks. He applied for a patent for his design on 26 July 1907.

After his ideas had been rejected by Kitsons, the locomotive builders of Leeds, Garratt was fortunate in gaining the support of Beyer, Peacock & Co. in Manchester, who saw the inherent superiority of his design concept. After some initial problems had been overcome the Garratts were outstandingly successful, running on all gauges from 2 feet to 5 feet 6 inches on gradients up to 1 in 20 or more, usually at modest speeds on heavily curved and graded routes, but capable of 75–80 m.p.h. on the Algerian expresses which were headed by probably the fastest articulated locomotives (4–6–2+2–6–4) ever built. A total of 1636 Garratts ran on eighty-six railways in forty-eight countries: of these, Beyer Peacock built just over 1000. Between November 1885 and February 1913 he took out nine patents, eight relating to locomotive engines and one for 'an improved egg-opener'.

Garratt was elected a member of the Institution of Mechanical Engineers in 1902. He died at his home, 9 Ellerker Gardens, Richmond, Surrey, on 25 September 1913.   RONALD M. BIRSE, rev.

Sources R. L. Hills and D. Patrick, *Beyer Peacock, locomotive builders of Gorton: a short history* (1982) · R. L. Hills, 'The origins of the Garratt locomotive', *Transactions* [Newcomen Society], 51 (1979–80), 175–92 · *Railway Gazette* (3 Oct 1913), 374 · *Engineering* (3 Oct 1913), 461 · A. E. Durrant, *Garratt locomotives of the world* (1981) · L. Wiener, *Articulated locomotives* (1930) · b. cert. · d. cert. · *CGPLA Eng. & Wales* (1913)
Wealth at death £3314 11s. 2d.: probate, 24 Dec 1913, *CGPLA Eng. & Wales*

Garraway, Sir Henry. *See* Garway, Sir Henry (*bap.* 1575, d. 1646).

Garraway, Thomas (d. 1692?), coffee-house keeper, is of unknown parentage. He married his first wife, Elizabeth, in the 1650s, and their first recorded residence was a house in Sweeting's Rents in the parish of St Bartholomew by the Exchange, London, the registers of which record the baptisms of their first son, Philip, early in 1658, and of a daughter, Susanne, and a second son, Henry, both in 1668. Garraway opened one of the earliest coffee houses in London at his house in Sweeting's Rents, and he may well have been the first retailer of tea in England. An advertisement for Garraway's tea was placed in the *Mercurius Politicus* (23–30 September 1658), and in 1660 he published a broadside, *An Exact Description of the Growth, Quality and Vertues of the Leaf Tea.*

The Garraway family moved from the parish of St Bartholomew to that of St Mary Woolnoth some time between 1668 and 1670. Elizabeth Garraway was buried on 5 April 1674. Thomas Garraway appears to have remarried some time thereafter, but the identity of his second wife is not known. Garraway's new residence was located in Exchange Alley on the south side of Cornhill ward, and it was here that his famous coffee house began to flourish as an important centre of mercantile activity.

Beginning in the 1670s, auction sales of ships, bulk goods, and rare books were held at Garraway's Coffee House, and these sales became a regular occurrence in the eighteenth century. Garraway expanded his business in coffee and tea to include wine sales in 1679, but it was as the favoured resort for City stock-traders that Garraway's made its fame. Along with Jonathan's Coffee House, which was also located in Exchange Alley, Garraway's Coffee House can rightly be regarded as one of the birthplaces of the British stock exchange and a key nexus in the development of the City of London as a centre for world finance. In 1692 John Houghton remarked that Londoners 'may, every noon and night on working days, go to Garraway's Coffee-House, and see what prices the actions bear of most companies trading in joynt-stocks' (*Collection for the Improvement of Husbandry and Trade*, 1/2, 6 April 1692).

Apart from its role as a mercantile centre, Garraway's was also an important gathering place for London's social élite. Virtuoso members of the Royal Society, such as Robert Hooke and James Brydges, gathered at the coffee house to engage in learned discourse with each other as well as the merchants in the house, and to inspect the newly published books on display there, as did prosperous physicians such as Dr John Radcliffe. James Mackay noted in the early eighteenth century that Garraway's was frequented by 'the people of quality, who have business in the city, and the most considerable and wealthy citizens' (Mackay, 112).

In 1672 Garraway joined with more than 140 other coffee-house keepers to sign a remarkable petition to Thomas Osborne, earl of Danby and the lord high treasurer of England, in which they complained of their harassment by agents of the crown despite their possession of licences obtained in good faith and by virtue of statutory authority. Garraway's Coffee House did not escape official suspicion, however, and it was associated with the circulation of a wide variety of illicit literature during the Restoration era. A servant of Garraway's was called before the privy council in September 1677 to answer for his role in circulating unfounded rumours about foreign policy. Garraway was chastened well enough by this near miss to advise one of his news suppliers, the Roman Catholic Edward Sing, to forbear thenceforth from sending him any further news manuscripts. The crisis soon passed, however, and Garraway's remained an important centre for the circulation of news of all sorts in the later decades of the seventeenth century.

Garraway himself was one of the most prosperous coffeemen in the City of London. The London poll taxes of the 1690s assessed Garraway's Coffee House at the considerable value of £150. Although it is not known when Garraway died or left his business, the poll tax list of Langbourn ward for 1692 replaces the assessment of Garraway's residence and coffee house for that of one Jeremy Stoakes. Garraway's Coffee House, however, remained a flourishing London institution, and continued to host traders and financiers until its demolition about the year 1897.   BRIAN COWAN

Sources B. Lillywhite, *London coffee houses* (1963), 216–24 · B. Cowan, 'The social life of coffee: commercial culture and metropolitan society in early modern England, 1600–1720', PhD diss., Princeton University, 2000 · A. Ellis, *The penny universities: a history of the coffee houses* (1956) · H. B. Wheatley and P. Cunningham, *London past and present*, 3 vols. (1891), vol. 2, pp. 85–7 · CLRO, Alchin box H/103, 12 · session minutes, CLRO, 47 · PRO, E 179/147/617, fol. 68v · PRO, PC 2/66, 108 · *True Domestic Intelligencer*, no. 25 (30 Sept 1679) · *Collection for the Improvement of Husbandry and Trade*, 1/2 (6 April 1692) · [J. Mackay], *A journey through England in familiar letters from a gentleman here, to his friend abroad* (1714), 112 · *Dr. Radcliffe's life and letters*, 4th edn (1724), 41, 45–6 · *CSP dom.*, 1677–8, 339, 627–78 · J. Brydges, London journal, 2 vols., 1697–1702, Hunt. L., Stowe MS 26 · *The diary of Robert Hooke ... 1672–1680*, ed. H. W. Robinson and W. Adams (1935) · J. M. B. Alexander, 'The economic and social structure of the City of London', PhD diss., London School of Economics, 1989 · P. G. M. Dickson, *The financial revolution in England: a study in the development of public credit, 1688–1756* (1967), 490, 503–6 · L. Neal, *The rise of financial capitalism: international capital markets in the age of reason* (1990), 22–5, 33, 46 · R. Steele and others, *The Guardian*, ed. J. C. Stephens (1982), 610 · D. F. Bond, ed., *The Tatler*, 3 vols. (1987), vol. 2, pp. 333, 486; vol. 3, pp. 198, 300 · R. Steele and J. Addison, *The Spectator*, ed. D. Bond, 5 vols. (1965), vol. 2, p. 46; vol. 3, p. 509; vol. 4, p. 113 · vestry minutes, St Mary Woolchurch, 25 Aug 1715, GL, MS 1001/1 · *The manuscripts of his grace the duke of Portland*, 10 vols., HMC, 29 (1891–1931), vol. 5, p. 620

Garrett family (*per.* 1778–1884), agricultural engineers, came to prominence with **Richard** [i] **Garrett** (1757–1839), who founded the business in Suffolk in 1778. Richard came from a family that had been bladesmiths since the late seventeenth century at least. He was born at Woodbridge, Suffolk, on 12 October 1757, and at the age of twenty-one set up on his own account at nearby Leiston as a bladesmith. It was a small-scale business, making principally sickles and employing at most eight to ten men. He married Elizabeth Newson in 1778, and they had at least one son. In 1805 Garrett retired from this business and worked as a farmer until his death at Leiston, on 20 September 1839.

His son **Richard** [ii] **Garrett** (1779–1837), who was born on 4 August 1779 at Leiston, took over the management of the forge in 1805. In 1806 he married Sarah, daughter of John Balls of Hethersett, near Norwich. This match was of great significance for Garrett's business, for John Balls was the designer of improved threshing machines that used an open drum with beater bars, a principle of operation that became standard. The couple had three sons, Richard [*see below*], Balls, and Newson. Garrett and his father-in-law began to manufacture threshing machines at Leiston and the firm began to grow. By the time Garrett died (on 6 June 1837 at Leiston) there were about sixty employees.

Richard [iii] **Garrett** (1807–1866) was born on 1 February 1807, also at Leiston. Aged only nineteen he took over responsibility for the finances of the engineering works in 1826. Ten years later he took over general management of the business from his father. Under his direction the firm became one of the leading agricultural engineers of East Anglia, employing about 500 people in the 1850s. In consequence the family advanced from being well-to-do tradesmen to respectable gentlemen-manufacturers. The design of threshing machines continued to develop, with the introduction of portable machines. Garretts started to produce steam engines to provide power for their threshing machines. Two other products for which Garretts became especially noted during the mid-nineteenth century were seed drills and horse hoes. Later machinery included traction engines for ploughing, and also steamrollers; the latter began to carry the distinctive Garrett trade mark on their funnels: a prancing horse in gleaming brass. Machinery from the Leiston works was exported worldwide, and sales were particularly good in Germany and Russia.

Leiston, near the Suffolk coast, was fairly isolated as the base for an agricultural engineering concern of national renown, and to counteract this Richard [iii] Garrett joined the promoters of the East Suffolk Railway. This railway company built the branch line, opened in 1859, that connected Leiston to the national network. Another of his business interests was the Camden Brewery, in north London, which he had founded. He was also involved in the discussions that led to the foundation of the Royal Agricultural Society of England and served as a member of the society's council from 1846 to 1856. Garrett married Elizabeth Dunnell in 1828. They subsequently moved from Leiston to live at Carlton Hall, Saxmundham. He served as justice of the peace and as deputy lieutenant for the county. In 1855 he retired from management of the engineering works, though remaining a partner, and moved to St John's Wood, London. He died on 26 June 1866 at Carlton Hall and was buried in Carlton churchyard.

Garrett and his wife had nine children, four sons and five daughters. The eldest son, **Richard** [iv] **Garrett** (1829–1884), became senior manager of the engineering firm, and brought as much vigour to its direction as his father had done. He was born on 22 July 1829 at Works House, Leiston, and was educated at a private school in Woodbridge. He was apprenticed to the Leiston works at the age of fourteen, appointed works manager when he was twenty-one in 1850, made a partner in 1853, and became senior partner on the death of his father in 1866. He was a first-rate engineer who made many practical contributions to the development of his firm's portable steam engines and threshing machines. Most notable was a threshing machine in which one fan provided all the blasts needed for the operation of threshing, dressing, and finishing; the principle was patented in 1859 in the names of Richard Garrett and James Kerridge. Garrett was

a member of the Institution of Civil Engineers and of the Institution of Mechanical Engineers.

Garrett became a noted agriculturist and sportsman at his Carlton Hall estate, and he also leased an estate of 2000 acres near Brandon, from William Angerstein. He was well known as a breeder of shorthorn cattle, Suffolk sheep, and Suffolk horses. His Suffolk stallions Cupbearer I and Cupbearer III won many prizes. He served on the committees of the Suffolk Stud-Book Association. As a young man he regularly rode to hounds, and in later years he turned to shooting as his main sporting recreation. He joined the Leiston rifle corps on its foundation in 1860, and retired with the rank of major from the 3rd battalion Suffolk rifle volunteers in 1870. He was a governor of Framlingham College, in the foundation of which his father had been active. Also with his father he founded the Leiston Mechanics Institute in 1861. Garrett contracted heart disease and, after a period of illness, died suddenly at Leiston on 30 July 1884; he was buried in Carlton churchyard. He never married, and the ownership of the firm passed to his brother Frank (1845–1918).

By the 1850s the seed drills and horseshoes manufactured by Garretts of Leiston were the best-known in England. Garretts were also pioneers of steam engines and threshing machines for agricultural use, and they succeeded through a combination of inventiveness and productive energy in overcoming the natural isolation of their Suffolk coastal location to create an engineering firm of international renown. By the early twentieth century the firm had about 1200 employees. In the process, Leiston had grown from a small village to a small town, and the Garretts themselves had become a family of reasonable substance in local society, in farming, in horse breeding, and in sporting activities. The ramifications of the family's interests and activities were far-reaching, for Richard [iii] Garrett's brother, Newson *Garrett (1812–1893), operated the maltings at Snape (later a major concert hall); among his six daughters were Elizabeth Garrett *Anderson, Millicent Garrett *Fawcett, and Agnes *Garrett. JONATHAN BROWN

Sources R. A. Whitehead, *Garretts of Leiston* (1964) · *The Engineer*, 58 (1884) · *Farmer's Magazine*, 3rd ser., 12 (1857), 1–2 · R. A. Whitehead, *Garrett 200* (1978) · J. Manton, *Elizabeth Garrett Anderson* (1965)
Archives Suffolk RO, business records of Garretts of Leiston
Likenesses oils (Richard Garrett, 1829–1884), priv. coll.; repro. in Whitehead, *Garrett 200*
Wealth at death under £80,000—Richard Garrett: resworn probate, 1868, CGPLA Eng. & Wales · £70,053 1s. 7d.—Richard Garrett: probate, 1884, CGPLA Eng. & Wales

Garrett, Agnes (1845–1935), interior designer and suffragist, was born on 12 July 1845 at The Uplands, Aldeburgh, Suffolk, the seventh of eleven children of Newson *Garrett (1812–1893), merchant, and his wife, Louisa (1813–1903), daughter of John Dunnell of Marylebone, Middlesex. She was educated at a boarding-school in Blackheath, near London.

The Garrett family played a pivotal role in the development of women's rights in Britain: Agnes, with her cousin Rhoda, established the first interior design business run by women and thereby contributed to the opening up of the professions to women; Agnes's older sister Elizabeth Garrett *Anderson (1836–1917) was the first British woman to qualify as a doctor; and her younger sister Millicent *Fawcett (1847–1929) was president of the National Union of Women's Suffrage Societies from its foundation in 1897 until 1918 when the vote was secured for women.

Rhoda Garrett (1841–1882) was born on 28 March 1841 at Elton in Derbyshire, the daughter of the Revd John Fisher Garrett and his first wife, Elizabeth Henry Pillcock. Her father married again, and his second wife was said to have 'practically turned her predecessor's children out of the house to fend for themselves' (Smyth, 7). Rhoda had a 'terrible struggle' to support herself and her younger brothers and sisters, and was 'dogged by ill-health as well as poverty' (ibid.). Rhoda's younger half-brother was Fydell Edmund *Garrett (1865–1907), an associate of Cecil Rhodes.

Rhoda Garrett went to London in 1867 intending to train as an architect, an intention shared by Agnes. As this was not a profession considered suitable for women, it took several years before they found an architect prepared to take them on as clerks. Eventually, in 1871, J. M. Brydon, who was later to design the new women's hospital in Euston Road, London, for Elizabeth Garrett Anderson, employed them as apprentices for eighteen months.

This training was followed by a walking tour around England, visiting and sketching old buildings and interiors, after which the Garretts set up their own interior decorating business, designing furniture, chimney-pieces, and wallpapers in the Queen Anne style and aiming at middle-class people with moderate incomes. Among their commissions were the new women's university colleges and in 1874 they advised on the furnishings of Elizabeth Garrett Anderson's new home in 4 Upper Berkeley Street. These were among a number of projects that established them as leaders in their field.

The composer Ethel Smyth became friends with the two designers, whom she described in her memoirs, *Impressions that Remained* (1919). Smyth recalled 'The beauty of the relation between the cousins', and the sanctuary they gave to 'waifs and strays of art' in their home at 2 Gower Street, London. However, it was with Rhoda that Ethel Smyth formed a particular bond:

> How shall one describe that magic personality of hers, at once elusive and clear-cut, shy and audacious?—a dark cloud with a burning heart—something that smoulders in repose and bursts into flame at a touch … though the most alive, amusing, and amused of people, to me at least the sombre background was always there—perhaps because the shell was obviously too frail for the spirit.   (Smyth, 7)

The work of Agnes and Rhoda Garrett was considered as influential as that of Morris & Co. in spreading new and artistic ideas of taste in the home from the 1870s. In 1876 they published *Suggestions for House Decoration in Painting, Woodwork and Furniture*, one of the Art at Home series published by Macmillan and edited by the journalist W. J. Loftie. Enormously successful, the book had gone into six editions by 1879. In 1878 the Garretts exhibited furniture

and a cottage room at the Universal Exhibition in Paris and ten years later Agnes designed a complete interior consisting of carpets, furniture, metalwork, wallpaper, and woodwork for the first exhibition of the new Arts and Crafts Exhibition Society. Alongside this work they also ran a school of interior decoration. In addition to their Gower Street house they rented an old thatched cottage at Rustington in Sussex. A friend later recalled their 'art-y clothes' (Smyth, 54). Rhoda was a member of the Royal Archaeological Institute, and also served on the committee of the Society for the Preservation of Ancient Buildings.

The Garretts were not only the best-known women designers and decorators of the period, but they also campaigned actively for women's rights. They were both active in the London National Society for Women's Suffrage set up in 1867. They spoke regularly at meetings in support of the cause of women's rights and Rhoda was considered to be one of the most effective of the early suffrage speakers. In 1871 they both joined the central committee of the National Society for Women's Suffrage when it was set up to campaign both for women's suffrage and for the repeal of the Contagious Diseases Acts, and Agnes for a time was one of its honorary secretaries.

Neither Agnes nor Rhoda married and they shared a house together until Rhoda's early death from typhoid fever and bronchitis on 22 November 1882 at 2 Gower Street, London. Her death certificate was, fittingly, signed by Elizabeth Garrett Anderson; she was buried in the churchyard at Rustington. Agnes continued with the interior decorating business; after the death of her husband, Harry Fawcett, Millicent moved in to share the Gower Street house. Agnes died on 19 March 1935 at 2 Gower Street, London, having outlived all of her siblings.

SERENA KELLY

Sources D. Rubenstein, *A different world for women: the life of Millicent Garrett Fawcett* (1991) · J. Manton, *Elizabeth Garrett Anderson* (1965) · I. Anscombe, *Woman's touch: women in design from 1860 to the present day* (1984) · J. Attfield and P. Kirkham, eds., *A view from the interior: feminism, women and design* (1989) · A. Callen, *Angel in the studio: women in the arts and crafts movement, 1870–1914* (1979) · M. D. Conway, *Travels in South Kensington, with notes on decorative art and architecture in England* (1882) · R. Garrett and A. Garrett, *Suggestions for house decoration in painting, woodwork and furniture* (1876) · Boase, *Mod. Eng. biog.* · L. Collis, *Impetuous heart: the story of Ethel Smyth* (1984) · E. Smyth, *Impressions that remained*, 2 vols. (1919) · E. T. Cook, *Edmund Garrett: a memoir* (1909) · *Englishwoman's Review*, 13 (1882), 547–8 [Rhoda Garrett]
Likenesses photograph, 1865 (with Millicent Fawcett), repro. in R. Strachey, *The cause: a short history of the Women's Movement in Great Britain* (1978) · photograph, 1872 (Rhoda Garrett), *ILN* Picture Library; repro. in Callen, *Angel in the studio* · photograph (Rhoda Garrett, with her younger sister), repro. in Smyth, *Impressions that remained*, vol. 2, p. 55
Wealth at death £25,163 17s. 5d.: probate, 27 May 1935, *CGPLA Eng. & Wales*

Garrett, Daniel (d. 1753), architect, was a subordinate figure in the circle of the third earl of Burlington. Nothing is known of his background and little of his career before the 1730s, when he acted as Burlington's personal clerk of works, assisting in the realization of a number of his projects; later in that decade he began to develop a practice of his own, mainly in the north of England through the patronage of Lord Burlington's fellow Palladian Sir Thomas Robinson. In 1736, in connection with the first of these commissions (the steps and outer wall to the mausoleum at Castle Howard, Yorkshire), Robinson wrote:

My Ld. Burlington has a much better opinion of Mr. Garret's knowledge and judgement than of … any person whatever, except Mr. Kent, he lives in Burlington House and has had care and conduct of … all my Lds designs he ever gave. (Webb, 160)

In the following year he added that 'all those I have recommended Mr. Garrett to have thanked me for doing it' (ibid., 161). Previously, in 1727, Garrett had been appointed to a minor post in the office of works, as labourer in trust at Richmond New Park Lodge, and two years later to the parallel position at Windsor Castle, but in 1737 he was dismissed for 'not attending his duty' (Colvin, Archs., 393).

Garrett's approach to architecture is encapsulated in his comment on a drawing of his showing two versions of a Doric column: 'Vitruvius says if anyone alter this he is a great Block head' (Rowan, 25–6, 46). His Palladian orthodoxy is confirmed by designs such as Nunwick, Northumberland (1745–52), and, if the attribution to him is correct, his most important work, Foots Cray Place, Kent (c.1752), a derivative of the Villa Rotonda. But he was in addition a pioneer in the design of Rococo decoration in England, as in his interiors at Raby Castle, co. Durham, and Temple Newsam, Yorkshire (both c.1745); while for his remodelling of Kippax Park, Yorkshire (c.1750), and his banqueting house at Gibside, co. Durham (1751), for example, he followed the gothick manner of William Kent. A strongly practical cast is also evident, notably in the volume of farmhouse designs he published in 1747. Occasioned by 'the great complaint of Gentlemen, who have built Farm-Houses, that they were irregular, expensive and frequently too large for the Farms they were intended for' (Designs and Estimates of Farm Houses, &c. for the County of York, Northumberland, Cumberland, Westmoreland, and Bishoprick of Durham, 1), it was the first publication in which the principles of order and symmetry were applied to this type of building.

At Stanwick Park, Yorkshire, as well as assisting the owner Sir Hugh Smithson in designing estate buildings, Garrett was on friendly terms with the family; he took part in fishing and shooting expeditions and on one occasion acted as master of the revels at a family party. He died intestate early in 1753—when he was described as of the parish of St Martin-in-the-Fields, London—leaving an only daughter. His practice was evidently taken over by the architect James Paine.   PETER LEACH

Sources P. Leach, 'The architecture of Daniel Garrett [pts 1–3]', Country Life, 156 (1974), 694–7, 766–9, 834–7 • Colvin, Archs. • H. Colvin and J. Harris, 'The architect of Foots Cray Place', Georgian Group Journal, 7 (1997), 1–8 • E. Harris and N. Savage, British architectural books and writers, 1556–1785 (1990) • G. F. Webb, 'The letters and drawings of Nicholas Hawksmoor relating to the building of the mausoleum at Castle Howard, 1726–1742', Walpole Society, 19 (1930–31), 111–64 • A. J. Rowan, 'Gothick restoration at Raby Castle', Architectural History, 15 (1972), 23–50 • PRO, PROB 6/129, fol. 162 • London Evening-Post (3–6 March 1753) • R. Wittkower, Palladio and English Palladianism (1974)

Archives Alnwick Castle, Northumberland, Northumberland MSS • Glamis Castle, Angus, Strathmore MSS • Raby Castle, co. Durham, Raby Castle MSS

Garrett, (Fydell) Edmund (1865–1907), journalist and newspaper editor, was born on 20 July 1865 at Elton, Derbyshire, the son of John Fisher Garrett (1803–1878), rector of Elton. He was the third child of his father's second marriage, to Mary (d. 1872), daughter of Godfrey Gray. His mother died of consumption when he was seven, and his father died six years later. His half-sister Rhoda *Garrett [see under Garrett, Agnes], an interior decorator, also died while he was still at school, and thereafter his cousin Agnes *Garrett was responsible for his upbringing, assisted by another cousin, Millicent Garrett *Fawcett. He was educated at a private school in Spondon, Derbyshire, before obtaining a scholarship at Rossall School. There he was a leading member of the essay and debating societies, and edited the school magazine, Rossallian; in the school holidays he visited the gallery of the House of Commons, hearing Gladstone speak on the Affirmation Bill in 1883. In 1884 he went up to Trinity College, Cambridge, graduating in 1887 with a third class in classics. Debating was more important to him than studying for his degree, and in 1887 he was president of the Cambridge Union. His brother-in-law J. H. Badley recalled that he shone as a debater 'thanks to the fearlessness of his convictions, no less than to his readiness as a speaker' (Cook, 11). While at Cambridge he also wrote verse, some of which was published in Rhymes and Renderings (1887), a collection of undergraduate verse to which five of his friends contributed.

On leaving Cambridge Garrett joined the staff of the Pall Mall Gazette, under the editorship of W. T. Stead. He rapidly made his name as a journalist, but in 1889 he began to suffer from consumption, a disease which was to plague him for the rest of his life, and was sent to South Africa to restore his health. During this visit he became friendly with Cecil Rhodes, and met many other leading figures in South Africa, including Jan Hofmeyr and President Kruger. The result was a series of articles in the Pall Mall Gazette, later published in book form as In Afrikanderland and the land of Ophir: notes and sketches in political, social and financial South Africa (1891). These articles conveyed a lively picture of the area at an important point in its history, including a vivid character sketch of Kruger and an entertaining if not entirely accurate account of the court of Lobengula, king of the Matabele (Ndebele), and the granting of the Rudd mineral rights concession of 1888.

For the next four years Garrett was again based in London, writing first for the Pall Mall Gazette and then, from 1893, for the Westminster Gazette. In 1894 he also produced a translation of Ibsen's Brand. In 1892 he visited Egypt, and there met Alfred Milner, who was to play a significant role in South Africa as high commissioner (1897–1905). In April 1895 he returned to Cape Town to become editor of the Cape Times, the leading English newspaper in southern

Africa. He was not only the editor of the paper, but also the principal writer in it, and campaigned vigorously on behalf of a wide range of causes, including the need for better education for all races, slum clearance, the rebuilding of St George's Cathedral, and the preservation of the old buildings of Cape Town and a greater appreciation of Cape Dutch architecture. Unusually for the time, he also initiated a column giving the viewpoint of the black population.

Garrett was a firm believer in Britain's imperial mission, and he supported Rhodes's ideas of expansion to the north. This led him to support the claims of the Uitlanders in the Boer republic of the Transvaal, and at the time of the Jameson raid he appears to have made attempts to minimize the effect of the high commissioner's condemnation of Jameson which he correctly feared would weaken the resolve of the revolutionaries in Johannesburg. Privately, he may have known more of the conspiracy than is apparent from his editorials in the *Cape Times*, but in these, after initially showing his strong sympathy with the Rand revolt, he offered a more measured response to the crisis, advising Rhodes to own up to his part in the affair. His conduct of the paper during 1896 is generally regarded as having enhanced its reputation. Garrett subsequently published his own version of events as *The Story of an African Crisis* (1897).

In 1898 Garrett decided to stand for parliament, and in the Cape general election he was returned as member for Victoria East, combining the job of editor of the *Cape Times* with a political career. This was a mistake as his health was unable to take the strain of this dual career and he rapidly became unfit to undertake either. Initially he backed Cecil Rhodes's Progressives, but as Rhodes's political star began to fade, he associated himself more with the policies of the new British high commissioner in South Africa, Sir Alfred Milner. He supported Milner's aggressive diplomacy towards the Boer republics in the period leading up to the Second South African War, arguing that they would back down under pressure. Once war had broken out he took the line that Milner had had to act to ensure British supremacy in South Africa, which would otherwise have been dominated by the gold-rich, Boer-ruled Transvaal. As the war progressed, however, he became disturbed by some aspects of its conduct, for which he held the military commanders rather than Milner responsible.

In July 1899 Garrett suffered a severe haemorrhage. After treatment in sanatoria in Kimberley and Germany, he returned to England in the autumn of 1900 and from then until 1903 remained under the medical charge of Dr Jane Walker, first at Maltings Farm, and then in her sanatorium at Wiston, near Colchester. He had already in January 1900 resigned the editorship of the *Cape Times*, and in 1902 he gave up his seat in the house of assembly. He wrote a farewell letter to the electors of Victoria East in which he reiterated his call for a united South Africa, but called also for reconciliation between Briton and Boer. From the sanatorium he continued to write articles, of which the most notable was his character sketch of Cecil

Rhodes (*Contemporary Review*, June 1902). He also wrote political verse, including 'The Last Trek', written for the funeral progress of President Kruger through Cape Town (*The Spectator*, 10 Dec 1904), and epitaphs for Frank Rhodes and Alfred Beit.

On 26 March 1903 Garrett married Ellen (*b.* 1865), eldest daughter of James Haworth Marriage. They had met as fellow patients at the sanatorium. It was a happy marriage, but Garrett's health continued to decline. In June 1904 they moved to a cottage, Wiverton Acre, near Plympton, Devon, where Garrett continued to write, chiefly on South Africa. Two questions in particular concerned him. One was the position of the black population in the proposed new constitutions for the Transvaal and the Orange River Colony. Aware that they were being largely ignored, he devoted much of his remaining strength to the cause of what he called 'the unheard helot' (*Westminster Gazette*, 31 July 1906). Rather than give them the vote, he proposed a scheme of indirect representation through an advisory council of 'leading natives and experts in native affairs', which he developed in a memorandum entitled 'Natives and the new constitutions' (*The State*, February 1909). The second question concerning him was the principle of 'one vote, one value'. Garrett was in favour of the grant of responsible government, but disliked the way the constituencies were being drawn to favour rural districts (where the Afrikaners were in a majority) against the towns (where English speakers predominated). His very last article, 'The Boer in the saddle' (*The Standard*, 12 April 1907) was devoted to this issue.

Garrett died of phthisis at Wiverton Acre on 10 May 1907, and was buried three days later in the nearby churchyard of Brixton. A memorial was subsequently erected in St George's Cathedral, Cape Town, and a library of books on colonial subjects was presented to the Cambridge Union Society in his memory.   JOHN PINFOLD

Sources E. T. Cook, *Edmund Garrett: a memoir* (1909) · G. Shaw, ed., *The Garrett papers* (1984) · G. Shaw, *Some beginnings: the 'Cape Times'* (*1876–1910*) (1975) · F. E. Garrett and E. J. Edwards, *The story of an African crisis* (1897) · G. Shaw, 'South African Telegraph' versus 'Cape Times' (1980) · b. cert. · m. cert. · d. cert.
Archives Bodl. RH, MS Afr. s 2005 | BL, letters to his cousin and Lord Milner, Add. MS 45929 · CAC Cam., letters to W. T. Stead · King's AC Cam., letters to Oscar Browning
Likenesses photograph, 1895, repro. in Cook, *Edmund Garrett*

Garrett, Edward. See Mayo, Isabella (1843–1914).

Garrett, George William Littler (1852–1902), clergyman and submarine designer, was born on 4 July 1852 at 45 Waterloo Road, Lambeth, London, the third son of John Garrett (*d.* 1893), an Irish curate, and his wife, Georgina. The Garretts moved to Manchester in the early 1860s, and George attended Rossall School in Fleetwood until 1867, when the family was financially ruined and he was moved to Manchester grammar school. From 1869 he worked as a schoolteacher and studied chemistry at Owens College, Manchester. The combination of work and study reflected the financial pressures on his father. At Owens he developed an effective system for self-contained breathing, using caustic potash to remove carbon dioxide from the

George William Littler Garrett (1852–1902), by unknown photographer

exhaled air. Work on this device probably damaged his lungs, and brought about his early death. In 1871 he went to work and study in Ireland, and graduated from Trinity College, Dublin, with an honours degree in experimental sciences in 1875. After a year travelling in the south seas Garrett married Jane Parker of Waterford—they had four children—took the Cambridge theology examination, and in 1877 became curate to his father.

The Russo-Turkish War of 1877–8 and the war scare that gripped the British empire inspired Garrett to develop a simple one-man submersible, built in Birkenhead and demonstrated by the autumn of 1878. This secured support for a company from a mystery backer, possibly the Swedish armaments magnate Thorsten Nordenfelt, for the construction of a larger, 33 ton, steam-driven version. This craft, the *Resurgam*, was completed at Birkenhead in November 1879. Extensive trials were conducted at Liverpool and at sea, demonstrating that it could be submerged, if only briefly, and propelled underwater. This was the first time any vessel had been mechanically propelled below the surface. In February 1880, while on a voyage to Portsmouth for Royal Navy inspection, the boat was lost off Rhyl in a storm.

In August 1882 Garrett travelled to Sweden to work for Nordernfelt's Submarine Torpedo Boat Company. Here the interests of inventor and owner clashed; Garrett sought an effective submersible, while Nordenfelt wanted a torpedo boat that could submerge. While Nordernfelt's name graced the product, the design was essentially Garrett's. The new boat carried a single locomotive torpedo. The boat was completed in August 1883, but underwater trials were hampered by the poisonous fumes from the steam plant. However, public trials were held in September 1885. Despite Garrett's best efforts the flawed design did little more than show that it could operate on the surface and run briefly underwater. It was sold by Nordenfelt's agent Basil Zaharoff to the Greek navy, and delivered in January 1886. While trials in Greece were a failure the Turks were persuaded otherwise, and bought two boats. These were badly built, inferior, if larger, versions of the prototype, and did not work when completed in 1887, though Garrett did manage to carry out the first submerged launch of a torpedo. In their efforts to make the boats work the Turks even commissioned Garrett as commander, though on an honorary basis. A fourth boat was built at Barrow in Furness to an improved design, but the hectic schedule of work in Britain and Turkey finally caught up with Garrett, never in good health, who suffered a breakdown. He recovered in time to demonstrate the latest craft at Portsmouth in May 1887, and at the jubilee naval review in July. Eventually the Russians agreed to try the vessel on a sale-or-return basis, but it was wrecked, *en route* on the Danish coast. Garrett, who was living in some style at Southampton, continued to work on enclosed steam systems, but when the Nordenfelt company was subsumed into the new Barrow Shipbuilding concern, which eventually became Vickers, Garrett lost his major backer. The Germans built two Garrett/Nordenfelt submarines, but paid no royalties. Not surprisingly, they also made them work rather better than the originals.

In 1890, after discussions with John Jacob (IV) Astor, Garrett moved to the United States to become a farmer in Florida. He was already seriously ill with the pulmonary disease that was to kill him. Farming proved disastrous, and after a spell as a railway fireman in New York, and an American soldier during the Spanish-American War of 1898, when he became an American citizen, he died of tuberculosis in New York Metropolitan Hospital on 26 February 1902, aged forty-nine. He was buried in Mount Olivet cemetery, Maspeth, New York on 1 March.

Garrett's career combined innovation, triumph, absurdity, and failure in a way that quickly obscured his real contribution. By creating a submersible, though it failed, he spurred the work of others, notably the American John Holland, which resulted in effective submersible warships entering service within a decade of Garrett's death. The Garrett family remained in the United States, and subsequently prospered. At the time of writing the *Resurgam* had been located by divers, with the possibility of being raised.

ANDREW LAMBERT

Sources W. S. Murphy, *The father of the submarine: the life of the Reverend George Garrett Pasha* (1987) · R. Gardiner and A. Lambert, eds., *Steam, steel and shellfire: the steam warship, 1815–1905* (1992) · W. L. Clowes, *The Royal Navy: a history from the earliest times to the present*, 7 vols. (1897–1903), vol. 7

Likenesses photographs, repro. in Murphy, *Father of the submarine* [see illus.]

Garrett, Jeremiah Learnoult (1764–1806?), dissenting minister, was born at Horsleydown, in the Borough, Southwark, near the Old Stairs, on 29 February 1764. His parents were boat builders, respectable people, but by no means evangelically religious. The evangelical habit of mind, however, showed itself early in Jeremiah. When only five he had, he writes, 'views of the last day', and before he was eight had 'strict views of the world being burnt up, and the wicked being turned into hell'. Soon after this time his father died. He was then sent to school, first at Christ's Hospital, Hertford, and afterwards at Jackson's academy, Hampton.

After a year or two Garrett was set to learn the tailoring trade, but disliking it he was apprenticed to a builder of ships' boats at Wapping, who treated him badly. His master absconded for debt, and he was apprenticed to another in the same line of business, from whom he met with better treatment. At the age of fourteen or fifteen he had 'a vision of an ancient form with more majesty than ever was or can be seen in mortality', which laid its hand upon him, and which he took to be Christ. A dissenting minister at his earnest request was called in to see him, to whom he confessed his sins, the most flagrant of which was that seven years previously he had stolen a halfpenny. The minister thereupon 'pointed him to the blood of Christ', which gave him great relief. Subsequently, however, he took to vicious courses, had a man-of-war's man who had assaulted him arrested, frequented theatres, fought with his fellow apprentice, and contracted debts and a venereal disease for which he was treated in the Lock Hospital. On emerging from the hospital he attended both Wesleyan and Anglican services, used 'to go out into the fields, and rave hell and damnation to sinners' to the detriment of his lungs, and came to be called a second George Whitefield by the old women in Moorfields. A mysterious find of £80 in his bed enabled him to pay his debts. At a somewhat later date he held forth at the old Rectifying House and the old Soap House, Islington, and in 1788 he laid the foundation-stone of the chapel later known as Islington Chapel in Church Street.

Having thus established a certain reputation Garrett was received into the Countess of Huntingdon's Connexion and ordained. About this time he married, but was sorely tempted by love for a young woman of his congregation, whom he had saluted, according to the primitive Christian custom, with a 'holy kiss'. He moved to Basingstoke, and from there to Wallingford, and afterwards spent some three years in Guernsey. On returning to England he ministered for a time at Ashby-de-la-Zouch, but, developing lax views on baptism, was ejected from the Countess of Huntingdon's Connexion and went into business as a cotton dyer at Leicester. He soon, however, resumed preaching, and after ministering for some time at Nottingham established himself about the close of the eighteenth century at Lant Street Chapel in the Borough, Southwark, having also a lecture at Monkwell Street Chapel, London. His views seem latterly to have inclined to antinomianism. The date of his death, according to John Ward, the mystic, was 1806.

Of Garrett's various polemical works his anti-Southcottian pamphlet *Demoncracy Detected, Visionary Enthusiasm Corrected* (1804) was the best-known, and evoked from the prophetess an *Answer*. Garrett's *The Songs of Sion* (1804?) includes an engraving of his head and autobiographical sketch.

J. M. RIGG, rev. TIMOTHY C. F. STUNT

Sources J. L. Garrett, 'Preface', in J. L. Garrett, *The songs of Sion* (1804?) · J. Nelson, *The history, topography and antiquities of the parish of St Mary Islington* (1811), 273 · 'Ward, John (1781–1837)', *DNB*

Garrett, John Walter Percy (1902–1966), educationist, was born on 30 May 1902 at 28 Wingfield Road, Trowbridge, Wiltshire, the son of Percy Edgar Thorne Garrett, hairdresser, and his wife, Florence Emily Cray (d. 1953). He was educated at Trowbridge high school and, from 1921, at Exeter College, Oxford, where he took a degree in modern history in 1924 and the diploma in education in 1925. His first post was at Victoria College, Jersey. Though he reorganized all the history teaching in the school, English was becoming his main interest. He undertook a drastic revision of the library and was responsible for a great bonfire of what he judged to be 'smug nineteenth-century trash' (*The Victorian*).

After six months as master of history and English at the Royal Naval College, Dartmouth (1929–30), and a year at the Crypt School, Gloucester, Garrett became senior English master at Whitgift School in September 1931. Here he attracted attention through extra-curricular activities, founding the Fanatics, a discussion group which met fortnightly to respond to distinguished speakers, who included John Gielgud and A. L. Rowse, organizing theatre parties to London, and inviting the Balliol Players to perform in Greek in the open air.

Garrett's headmaster at Whitgift was Ronald Gurner, who, in his novel *The Day Boy* (1924), expounded the theory that a public school atmosphere could be reproduced in non-boarding secondary institutions. In September 1935 Garrett took up the post of headmaster of Surrey county council's new secondary school at Raynes Park, which he set about making both welcoming and challenging to the sons of (in his view) the unduly conventional inhabitants of a new but uninspiring south-west London suburb. Most of his assistant masters were from Oxford and Cambridge; his school was probably the only one in England with a Balliol man teaching woodwork. He again set about opening up the school to an array of well-known figures in the arts, including Benjamin Britten, Nevill Coghill, T. S. Eliot, C. Day Lewis, Louis MacNeice, Stephen Spender, L. A. G. Strong, and Sybil Thorndike. W. H. Auden wrote the school song, and Garrett secured reviews of the annual Shakespeare production in national newspapers. For the arts sixth he had a special eye: these were to be the pupils who forged the link between his school and the ancient universities. By 1942 this aim had been achieved: some twenty boys had won places at Oxford and Cambridge. Raynes Park had now been compared with Eton College as one of the two best schools in the country. 'The traditions of the English County Secondary School are being made', Katherine Chapman (a parent) wrote in 1942, 'and Mr Garrett has set his mark upon them' (*The Spur*, 3).

Much to the regret of Surrey county council's former chairman, Chuter Ede, Garrett resigned in December 1942, abandoning the state sector to become headmaster of Bristol grammar school, which he had attended as a student teacher eighteen years before. An early devotee of the performance culture which was soon to grip the fee-paying schools of the country, he galvanized his pupils to attain new levels of academic and sporting distinction. Economics was introduced, the science sixth tripled in size, and playing fields were expanded. His cultural activities continued. Distinguished public figures delivered Monday morning lectures, and Shakespeare was vigorously promoted. In January 1943 the school had 770 boys; in 1960, the year in which Garrett retired through ill health, there were over 1100. The sixth form increased from 80 to 298 pupils. Over seventeen years 244 boys won open awards to Oxford and Cambridge.

Garrett compiled *Scenes from School Life* (1933), *The Poet's Tongue* with W. H. Auden (1935), and edited *Talking of Shakespeare* (1954). He was awarded the degree of DLitt by the University of Bristol in 1960.

Tall, with a drooping eyelid and a peremptory voice, Garrett was throughout his career a vigorous, outspoken, and inspiring figure. As Robert Robinson (the author and broadcaster) recalled, 'he tirelessly rallied boys, parents, governors with his radical assessment of the empowering nature of education' (Robinson, 22). Unmarried, he died on 23 December 1966 at St George's Hospital, Tooting, London, and was cremated on 29 December after a funeral service at St Mary's, Wimbledon, London.

ROBIN BETTS

Sources P. Vaughan, *Something in linoleum* (1994) · R. Robinson, *Skip all that* (1996) · P. Harris, *Raynes Park high school, 1935–1985: a jubilee history* (1985) · *Bristol Grammar School Chronicle*, 28 (1960) · *Bristol Grammar School Chronicle*, 29 (1967) · *The Spur*, 6/1 (1942), 3 · *Whitgiftian* (Jan 1967) · *The Times* (24 Dec 1966) · *The Times* (29 Dec 1966) · *The Victorian* (Dec 1929) · A. L. Rowse, *The road to Oxford* (1978) · J. C. Ede, diary, BL, Add. MS 5969 · b. cert. · WWW · Exeter College records
Likenesses C. Rogers, oils, Raynes Park county grammar school · J. Whitlock Codner, oils, priv. coll.
Wealth at death £55,271: probate, 6 March 1967, *CGPLA Eng. & Wales*

Garrett, Newson (1812–1893), maltster and brewer, was born on 31 July 1812 at Leiston, Suffolk, the third son of Richard *Garrett (1779–1837) [see under Garrett family], agricultural engineer, and his wife, Sarah, daughter of John Balls, engineer, of Hethersett, Norfolk. Educated at Grundisburgh School, near Woodbridge, Suffolk, Newson had little interest in his studies.

An ambitious young man, determined not to be overshadowed by his eldest brother, Richard *Garrett (1807–1866) [see under Garrett family]—who was to inherit the family business—Newson Garrett subsequently moved to London. Here he was befriended by Richard's father-in-law, John Dunnell, landlord of The Beehive inn, Crawford Street, Marylebone. On 5 April 1834 Garrett married his younger daughter, Louisa (1813–1903) and for seven years managed Dunnell's pawnbrokers shops; first at 1 Commercial Road, Whitechapel, then, from 1838, at 142 Long Acre, off St Martin's Lane, Westminster. However, after the death in 1838 of their third child, Garrett decided to return to the healthier climate of Suffolk. Three years later he purchased the Snape corn and coal merchant's business and shipping interests of Robert Fennel and settled his wife and young family at The Uplands, in Aldeburgh.

Newson Garrett's business grew apace. Within three years he was sending about 17,000 quarters of barley to London and Newcastle. He was soon building his own barges and in 1848 was appointed agent for Lloyds. He constructed a gasworks, acquired a local brickworks and built numerous cottages. In 1852 he built Alde House, an impressive mansion overlooking the town of Aldeburgh (complete with ice-house and turkish bath), and two years later designed and built maltings at Snape Bridge. In 1859 the capacity of the maltings was doubled, and the adjoining Bridge House, the family's winter residence during the malting season, completed. Despite his substantial shipping interests—he owned half the twenty-four ships in the port—Garrett was keenly aware of the potential of the railways and, by guaranteeing regular freight, persuaded the East Suffolk Railway Company to extend a private line to his maltings. Finally, to consolidate his interests, he became a partner in the Bow brewery, London. When in 1882 the brewing company (one of the earliest to take company status) was registered as Smith, Garrett & Co. Ltd, with a capital of £450,000, Newson and his son Edmund (who managed the brewery), were among its first directors. Shortly after, the malting business of Newson Garrett & Son was similarly incorporated, with Garrett and his youngest son, George (the manager) as directors.

Newson Garrett, fair-haired and blue-eyed, was strikingly handsome, self-confident, and impetuous. Indeed, according to one contemporary, 'none of his virtues were passive' (Manton, 29). Intense rivalry with his brother Richard, fuelled by the shift in Garrett's political allegiance from Conservative to Liberal radical, culminated in a bitter rift. Despite the fact that their wives were sisters, they are said not to have spoken to each other for thirty years. Newson Garrett's involvement in civic life was equally stormy. He served the Aldeburgh corporation (a self-elected body until 1885) as burgess and, for forty years, as bailiff. Many of the older members resented the pushy newcomer; in particular his altercations with the rector of Aldeburgh and frequent defection to the Union Chapel were both a scandal and delight to the town. Yet he was regarded with affection and respect. When, following the report on the 1880 Municipal Corporation Act, the corporation was reformed, Garrett was elected its first mayor, serving again in 1886 and 1890 and as alderman, 1888–93. He was also Aldeburgh's first county councillor and alderman, 1889–92. He was a justice of the peace, commanding-lieutenant of the local volunteer company, branch-chairman of the Royal National Lifeboat Institution, and founder of the Adair Lodge of freemasons.

Newson and Louisa Garrett's large family of ten surviving children inherited intellect and determination in full measure. Three of their six daughters achieved notable firsts: Elizabeth Garrett *Anderson was Britain's first legally qualified woman doctor; Millicent *Fawcett, first president of the National Union of Women's Suffrage Societies; and Agnes *Garrett, London's first woman interior designer. Notably, their brother Sam, president of the Law Society, was the first to employ female pupils. Among Garrett's grandchildren, Millicent's daughter,

Phillippa, and Alice's son, Philip Cowell, were both senior wrangler at Cambridge University. To them all, Newson gave his wholehearted support and was fiercely proud of their success. At every opportunity he gathered them round him. Typically, he laid out the 35 acres surrounding Alde House as a private estate of large houses and gardens for his children. Newson Garrett died at Alde House on 4 May 1893 following a heart attack and was buried four days later in the family vault at Aldeburgh churchyard. The maltings at Snape subsequently formed the venue for the Aldeburgh music festival founded by Benjamin Britten and Peter Pears. CHRISTINE CLARK

Sources J. Manton, *Elizabeth Garrett Anderson* (1965) · *East Anglian Daily Times* (6 May 1893) · *Brewing Trade Review* (July 1893) · R. Simper, *Over Snape bridge: the story of Snape maltings* (1967) · J. P. Bristow, *Aldeburgh diary* (1980) · V. B. Redstone, *The Suffolk Garretts* (1916) · *Brewers' Journal* (15 Aug 1882) · *CGPLA Eng. & Wales* (1893)
Likenesses photograph (after an oil painting), repro. in Manton, *Elizabeth Garrett Anderson*
Wealth at death £50,605—net · £57,801 7s. 6d.: probate, 1 June 1893, *CGPLA Eng. & Wales*

Garrett, Rhoda (1841–1882). *See under* Garrett, Agnes (1845–1935).

Garrett, Richard (1757–1839). *See under* Garrett family (*per.* 1778–1884).

Garrett, Richard (1779–1837). *See under* Garrett family (*per.* 1778–1884).

Garrett, Richard (1807–1866). *See under* Garrett family (*per.* 1778–1884).

Garrett, Richard (1829–1884). *See under* Garrett family (*per.* 1778–1884).

Garrett, Sir Robert (1794–1869), army officer, was the eldest son of John Garrett of Ellingham, Isle of Thanet, and his wife, Elizabeth, daughter of J. Gore of St Peter's, Isle of Thanet. He was educated at Harrow School, and on 12 March 1811 became ensign by purchase in the 2nd Queen's foot. With them he was present at Fuentes d'Oñoro, and in the attack on the forts of Salamanca, where he was the only surviving officer of his party and received two wounds. He was promoted to a lieutenancy in the 2nd garrison battalion on 3 September 1813, and on 2 October was transferred to the 7th Royal Fusiliers, with which he served in the campaigns of 1813–14, and was again severely wounded in the Pyrenees. On 7 July 1814 he became captain by purchase in the 97th (Queen's Own), and served with it in Ireland until it was disbanded, as the 96th foot, in 1818, when he was put on half pay. He married, in 1814, Charlotte Georgina Sophia, daughter of Lord Edward Bentinck and granddaughter of the second duke of Portland; she died in 1819. In 1821 he married Louisa, widow of Mr Devaynes; they had a son and a daughter. He purchased an unattached majority in 1826, and in 1834, after nearly fifteen years on half pay, was brought into the 46th foot, as major, and became regimental lieutenant-colonel in 1846. He served with the regiment, much of the time in command, at Gibraltar, in the West Indies and

North America, and at home. He became brevet colonel in January 1854.

When the 46th was doing duty, with Garrett in command, at Windsor in the summer of 1854, after the departure of the guards for the East, courts martial on two young officers of the regiment on charges arising from coarse practical joking at the expense of an unpopular subaltern attracted much attention. The first case gave much offence, as it supposedly showed that a poor officer had no security against persecution by men of higher rank or wealth. A clamour for further inquiry was met by the dispatch of the regiment, under Garrett's command, to the Crimea, where it landed three days after Inkerman, and served throughout the siege of Sevastopol.

Garrett, a familiar figure in the trenches, commanded a brigade of the 4th division from November 1854 to November 1855, from which time he commanded that division until the troops left the Crimea the next year. He served as a brigadier at Gibraltar and in the China expedition of 1857, and, becoming major-general in 1858, commanded a division in Bengal and afterwards in Madras until 1862, when he returned home. He was appointed to command the south-eastern district with headquarters at Shorncliffe in 1865, but resigned on promotion to lieutenant-general in 1866. In that year he was transferred to the colonelcy of the 43rd light infantry from that of the 4th West India regiment, to which he had been appointed in 1862.

Garrett was a KCB (January 1857) and KH (1863), and had the orders of the Légion d'honneur and of the Mejidiye. He was a JP and deputy lieutenant for Kent. A tough veteran of the old school, Garrett died on 13 June 1869, aged seventy-five, at his residence, 40 Pall Mall, London.

H. M. CHICHESTER, *rev.* JAMES LUNT

Sources Walford, *County families* · *Army List* · R. Cannon, ed., *Historical record of the second, or queen's royal regiment of foot* (1838) · R. Cannon, ed., *Historical record of the seventh regiment, or the royal fusiliers* (1847) · R. Cannon, ed., *Historical record of the forty-sixth, or the south Devonshire regiment of foot* (1851) · *The Times* (27 July 1854) · *The Times* (1 Aug 1854) · *The Times* (7 Aug 1854) · *Naval and Military Gazette* (26 Aug 1854) · W. H. Russell, *The war*, 2 vols. (1855–6) · *Army and Navy Gazette* (19 June 1869) · *ILN* (29 Aug 1869) · A. W. Kinglake, *The invasion of the Crimea*, [new edn], 9 vols. (1877–88) · Boase, *Mod. Eng. biog.* · *Dod's Peerage*
Archives CKS · East Kent Archives Centre, Dover, corresp. and papers | W. Sussex RO, letters to duke of Richmond
Wealth at death under £30,000: resworn probate, Oct 1869, *CGPLA Eng. & Wales*

Garrick, David (1717–1779), actor and playwright, was born on 19 February 1717 at The Angel inn in Hereford, the third of the seven children of Peter Garrick (1685–1737), an army officer, and his wife, Arabella (*d.* 1740), the daughter of Anthony Clough, a vicar-choral of Lichfield Cathedral. His paternal grandfather, David de la Garrique, was among the many Huguenots to leave France after the revocation of the edict of Nantes in 1685. There was a distinct community of émigré Huguenots in London at the end of the seventeenth century, and the sparse journal kept by David de la Garrique (rewritten initially as Garric, and then as Garrick) from 1685 to 1701 bears witness to his

David Garrick (1717–1779), by Sir Joshua Reynolds, 1767 [as Kitely in *Every Man in his Humour* by Ben Jonson]

devoutness. Imprecisely described as a merchant, he seems to have been prosperous enough to have purchased for his son Peter a commission in a regiment of foot in April 1706. It was his army service that took Peter Garrick to the garrison at Lichfield, Staffordshire, where the growing family lived close to the cathedral, in Bird (later Beacon) Street.

Early years and education Lieutenant Peter Garrick was on a recruiting mission in Hereford when the future actor was born, but it was in Lichfield that the boy spent his formative years. The family was not, by contemporary standards, poor, but it was a struggle for Peter Garrick to maintain his wife and children, particularly after, as a career officer during a period of peace, he was reduced to half pay. The habitual prudence in financial matters that would earn for David Garrick a reputation for meanness owed something to family circumstance during his boyhood. There was, however, no social deprivation. As an officer in a garrison town Peter Garrick had easy access to the cream of Lichfield society, and the young David's close interest in many of the most prominent citizens is evident in his earliest surviving letters. The first of these, written when he was not quite sixteen, dates from the mid-point of Peter Garrick's prolonged absence in Gibraltar. Now with the rank of captain, and presumably under financial pressure, Peter had, in 1729, entered active service under Major-General Percy Kirke, with the Queen's Own 2nd regiment of foot. With his elder brother, also called Peter, serving as an ensign in the navy, and his mother and elder sister, Magdalen, in consistently poor health, David was, precociously, the virtual head of the household until his

father's return in May 1736. To judge from the tone of his letters to his father, it was a job he generally relished, although his enjoyment of it was delayed by a curious episode. It was not only David's father who left home in 1729. At some time during that year he himself was sent to Lisbon to learn the wine trade from his uncle and namesake, who prospered as a vintner in that city. The decision to interrupt young David's schooling must have been taken for financial reasons, and it may have been his son's unhappiness in Portugal that persuaded Captain Garrick to volunteer for the Gibraltar posting. Within a year David was back at Lichfield grammar school.

There is presumptive evidence, despite the Portuguese venture, that Garrick's parents hoped to see their sons well educated. The regimen at the grammar school, under its headmaster Dr John Hunter, was a stern one, and it was probably outside school hours that the twelve-year-old Garrick first involved himself in theatrical activity. He was the prime mover in a children's performance of George Farquhar's *The Recruiting Officer* at the bishop's palace, himself playing the role of the hard-drinking professional soldier Sergeant Kite. If the choice of play was Garrick's, it fairly represents his humorous but respectful relationship with his father, to whose recruiting activities he owed his place of birth. As a boy he was already displaying the extraordinary social energy that he sustained throughout his life. Looking back on his own early years in Lichfield, and contrasting David with his older brother, Dr Johnson observed to Boswell, 'I don't know but if Peter had cultivated all the arts of gaity as much as David has done, he might have been as brisk and lively. Depend upon it, Sir, vivacity is much an art, and depends greatly on habit' (Boswell, *Life*, 2.462). It was in Johnson's short-lived school, Edial Hall, that Garrick completed his Lichfield education. Less than eight years older than his pupil, Johnson was a friend as well as a mentor, but there has been a tendency to overstate his influence on Garrick. It was Gilbert Walmesley (1680–1751), registrar of the ecclesiastical court in Lichfield, who did most to stimulate, and sometimes to satisfy, the curiosity of the future actor. The scholarly Walmesley, a bachelor until his fifty-seventh year, opened his library to both Johnson and Garrick, and continued to interest himself in their careers long after they had left Lichfield. Learning of Garrick's intention to move to London, and believing him worthy of a university education, he pressed John Colson, headmaster of a free school in Rochester, to tutor him: 'He is now nineteen, of sober and good disposition, and is as ingenious and promising a young man as ever I knew in my life' (Stone and Kahrl, 13).

In London, 1737–1741 When Johnson and Garrick set off from Lichfield to London on 2 March 1737, neither had clearly mapped out a future. Captain Garrick had hopes of a legal career for his confidently loquacious son, who dutifully enrolled at Lincoln's Inn on 9 March. There is, however, no evidence of enthusiasm behind the enrolment, and the prospect of legal studies was summarily abandoned when Captain Garrick died untimely on 19 March (the date is disputed, though not the month). The captain's brother, David the vintner, had died the previous December, leaving £1000 to the nephew who bore his name 'to be put out at interest by the Executors ... until he is of age, or to be paid before in case there is a good place that offers in given money' (Oman, 19). Knowing of this legacy, Captain Garrick left fairly substantial sums to six of his children, but only a shilling to David, a disparity which has given rise to unnecessary speculation. There is no evidence at all that the family suspected David of a duplicitous preference for the stage over the law, though it is possible that he harboured one. He later admitted to his brother Peter, in a letter probably written on 20 October 1741, that 'My Mind (as You must know) has been always inclin'd to the Stage' (Letters, 1.28). But his first moves, after his father's death, were not in that direction. During the summer of 1737, responsive to Walmesley's advice, he studied with John Colson in Rochester, dependent on gifts and loans to pay his way. It may have been in the hope of releasing his uncle's legacy in advance of his twenty-first birthday that he joined with his brother Peter, in the autumn of 1737, in a commercial enterprise to which he was only moderately suited, but one in which they could exploit some of Uncle David's business connections. As Garrick & Co., wine traders, they established a London office and cellars in Durham Yard, between the Strand and the River Thames. Peter Garrick remained a vintner for the rest of his working life, but in Lichfield, not London. To begin with, though, the brothers shared lodgings in the capital, working together to further the trade. Garrick had many of the attributes of an effective businessman, as he would prove during his thirty years of theatre management. The problem was that his professional engagement with wine had to give room to his amateur passion for the theatre.

The only asset Dr Johnson had brought with him to London was the manuscript of his tragedy *Irene*. Peter Garrick, who had some connection, perhaps through his naval career, with Charles Fleetwood, the manager of the Drury Lane theatre, pressed him to read Johnson's play. That is the only known evidence of Peter's interest in the theatre. Before his elder brother Garrick was consistently defensive, perhaps secretive, about his own involvement with the stage, and it was probably a relief to him when Peter entrusted the London end of the business to him while he set about establishing the Lichfield branch. Among his new London friends were two uncommonly forceful actors, Henry Giffard and Charles Macklin. It was for Giffard's benefit night at Drury Lane on 15 April 1740 that Garrick wrote his first play, *Lethe, or, Esop in the Shades*, little more than a *jeu d'esprit*, but clear evidence of the keenness of his observation. Short as it is, *Lethe* gave the leading players of the company rich opportunities to display their tricks. Kitty Clive and Henry Woodward made the greatest impression, but Macklin's drunkard was enjoyed too. The success of *Lethe* advanced Garrick's interest in the theatre. In the summer of 1740 he involved himself in Giffard's attempts to obtain a licence for his theatre in Goodman's Fields, even to the extent of pressing his brother Peter to

use his influence on Giffard's behalf. In a devious letter of 5 July 1740 he reported to Peter some good news of their business enterprise: 'I have the Custom of the Bedford Coffee House, one of the best in London by Giffard's means; I would help him all in our power, as I dare answer you would' (Letters, 1.23–4). If he was already in rehearsal for an amateur production of Henry Fielding's *The Mock Doctor*, he neglected to mention it.

The performances of *The Mock Doctor*, with Garrick in the title role, took place in the early autumn of 1740, in an upstairs room of the St John's gatehouse, Clerkenwell. It was probably Dr Johnson who enticed Garrick into the project. Since 1731 the gatehouse had been the editorial base of the *Gentleman's Magazine*, for which Johnson was reporting parliamentary debates. The amateur theatricals there were sponsored by the magazine's eccentric founder, proprietor, and editor, Edward Cave. Garrick wrote an epilogue, the first of the many for which he was famous, which was published in the September issue of the *Gentleman's Magazine*. The episode seems to have been concealed from Peter Garrick, who was occupied during September with the last illness, death, and burial on 28 September 1740 of their mother. Increasingly obsessed by the theatre, Garrick was meanwhile gaining a reputation as an entertainer among his London friends: 'He loved to indulge in a vein of criticism on the several performers, and, to illustrate his remarks, he mounted the table, and displayed those talents for mimickry, for which he has been much celebrated in the character of Bayes' (Murphy, 1.15). His dislike of rant in tragedy, and of 'airs, affectation, and Cibberisms' (Letters, 1.44) in comedy, was shared by Macklin, whose iconoclastic performance of Shylock in February 1741 Garrick saw. Macklin later claimed: 'I have often advised you upon many circumstances of your acting; which you have allowed to be right, and have accordingly adopted my advice' (Appleton, 57). Together they challenged the prevailing artifice of Augustan acting, and it was Macklin's encouragement, as much as Giffard's entrepreneurial interest, that finally eased Garrick into acting.

Garrick's first professional appearance was almost accidental. In March 1741, at his still unlicensed playhouse, Giffard staged a pantomime, with Richard Yates as Harlequin. In December of that year, responding shamefacedly to his brother's reproaches, Garrick confessed that 'Yates last Season was taken very ill & was not able to begin the Entertainment so I put on the Dress & did 2 or three Scenes for him, but Nobody knew it but him & Giffard' (Letters, 1.34). It was not in Garrick's interest to let it be known that he had made his theatrical début in a vulgar pantomime. He preferred it to be believed that his first professional engagement was with Giffard's summer company in Ipswich, where he played Aboan in black-face in Thomas Southerne's *Oroonoko*. According to Murphy, 'He used to say, that, if he had failed there, it was his fixed resolution to think no more of the stage' (Murphy, 1.20). East Anglian audiences were satisfied with the performances of Mr Lydall (a pseudonym chosen because it was the maiden name of Giffard's wife) in Southerne's tragedy, and even more so in George Farquhar's comedy *The Inconstant*. The versatility that made him exceptional was already in evidence, and Garrick returned to London resolved to make his bid as an actor.

Making a reputation, 1741–1747 Garrick made his sensational London début as Richard III in Giffard's unlicensed Goodman's Fields Theatre on 19 October 1741. It was nearly two months before the playbills admitted that the unnamed 'gentleman' was David Garrick, but the public was undeterred: 'From the polite ends of Westminster the most elegant company flocked to Goodman's Fields, insomuch that from Temple Bar the whole way was covered with a string of coaches' (Murphy, 1.25–6). The vitality of the young actor, his expressive features, and his vivid eyes were the talk of the town. It was the aim of leading tragedians to express the universality of human passions, but the dynamic Garrick dared to break the mould by portraying Richard III in his particularity. Fumbling for definitions, audiences were gripped by a sense of newness; soon they would be agreeing that this young man embodied in performance the scope of the sympathetic imagination. In that first season they saw him in comedy too: as Clodio in Colley Cibber's *Love Makes a Man* on 28 October 1741 and as Bayes in the duke of Buckingham's *The Rehearsal* on 3 February 1742. But only those in the know realized that the new idol was also the author of the two-act farce *The Lying Valet*, first staged at Goodman's Fields on 30 November 1741 and destined for durable popularity. The plot was French, but the language was Garrick's, as was the title role of the mendacious Sharp. It was always his acting rather than his writing that singled him out. As a playwright, and as an adapter of old plays, he served the taste of the time; as an actor he was startlingly innovative. There is no exaggeration in the letter Garrick wrote to his brother five weeks after his London début: 'I have the Judgment of the best Judges (Who to a Man are of Opinion) that I shall turn out (nay they Say I am) not only the Best Trajedian [sic] but Comedian in England' (*Letters*, 1.32). He could cite the elder Pitt, George Lyttelton, and Alexander Pope, among many others.

Garrick continued at Goodman's Fields until towards the end of May 1742 and then embarked for a season at the Smock Alley playhouse in Dublin. Just before leaving he gave three special performances at Drury Lane—Bayes on 26 May, King Lear on 28 May, and Richard III on 31 May—tokens of his agreement to play there during the 1742–3 season. The Dublin triumph was shared with the fine Irish actress Margaret (Peg) *Woffington (1720?–1760). By the time they returned to England, Garrick was in love with her. They are thought to have lived together at 6 Bow Street, in a house that belonged to Charles Macklin. Macklin had aspirations as a trainer of actors, and Garrick may briefly have shared them. But the demands of Drury Lane came first. Garrick's contract was a lucrative one (£500 for the season), and the company was strong: not only Garrick, Macklin, and Woffington, but also Hannah Pritchard and Kitty Clive. The rival house at Covent Garden had only one actor of comparable status, James Quin, the leading tragedian of the suddenly 'old' school. All should have

been well for Charles Fleetwood, the manager of Drury Lane. Garrick's Hamlet drew crowds, and it was during this season that London first saw him in two of his finest comedy parts, Abel Drugger in a reshaping of Jonson's *The Alchemist* and Archer in Farquhar's *The Beaux' Stratagem*. But Fleetwood was a feckless housekeeper, and the season ended with actors unpaid. Garrick became their spokesman in a protracted dispute with Fleetwood and also the man deputed to petition the lord chamberlain for a licence to set up a rival company. To his dismay, the duke of Grafton dismissed the application outright. Fleetwood had meanwhile opened the new season on 13 September 1743, with a makeshift company, leaving the rebellious actors without employment. It fell to Garrick to make peace with Fleetwood, who expressed his willingness to welcome back all except Macklin. The outmanoeuvred Garrick agreed, and Macklin launched a ferocious pamphlet campaign against the friend who had betrayed him. Although the ferocity diminished over time, Macklin was never securely an ally again. When Garrick finally returned to the Drury Lane stage in December 1743 it was to confront a claque of Macklin's supporters. The idol of London was hissed off the stage.

The beneficial aspect of this experience was that it forced Garrick to take stock of himself. His lack of height (he was about 5 feet 6 inches tall) was compensated by fine proportions and physical grace, and he had a capacity, both on and off stage, to charm. He was better read, and had more business acumen, than most of his fellow actors, and he was making a lot of money. Having committed himself to the theatre, he found himself ambitious to improve it. There was shrewdness, as well as self-confidence, in the determination, arrived at in his twenties, to enter into management. Over the coming years, particularly in the prologues and epilogues through which he talked directly to his audience, he would develop an unrivalled skill in public relations. In the more private dealings that are the stuff of management, it was his natural inclination to be even-handed. He made enemies, sometimes he got things wrong, but the many extant letters to and from him place him predominantly in a good light. At the end of 1743, though, there were still storms ahead. Early in the new year (7 January 1744) he made his first appearance as Macbeth, a part which he found the most demanding in his repertory. Only in partnership with Hannah Pritchard as Lady Macbeth, after their first appearance together on 19 March 1748, did he feel at ease in it. The relationship with Peg Woffington was uneasy, too, though posterity has only hints and rumours to rely on. It was probably the quarrel with Macklin that led Garrick to move his lodgings to James Street, Covent Garden, but Woffington's suspected infidelity concerned him more. They were both sufficiently in the public eye to attract the attention of high society. In the summer of 1744, when Woffington was being courted at her Teddington villa by Sir Charles Hanbury-Williams, Garrick was visiting the wealthy William Windham and Lord Rochford in Suffolk and assisting the duke of Bedford with some private theatricals at Woburn Abbey. They played together at Drury Lane through the 1744–5 season, with Garrick challenging Quin's possession of the part of Sir John Brute in Vanbrugh's *The Provoked Wife* opposite Woffington's Lady Brute. As Shakespeare's King John, though, Garrick played for the first time with Susannah Cibber, an actress with whom he would sustain a sentimental friendship until her death in 1766. Like Othello, which he played first on 7 March 1745, King John was a part soon dropped from Garrick's repertory. In the continuing turmoil of Drury Lane, he had his eye on management.

At the end of the 1744–5 season Fleetwood surrendered the management of Drury Lane to the pugnacious James Lacy, who immediately taxed Garrick with a failure to meet the terms of his contract. Indignantly, Garrick protested his April illness and the exhaustion of playing tragic roles on successive nights. From December 1745 to May 1746 he was in Dublin, sharing the management and the profits of two playhouses with Thomas Sheridan. Before leaving England he had made the final break with Peg Woffington: 'What she does now, so little affects me, that, excepting her shewing my letters of nonsense and *love* to make me ridiculous, she can do nothing to give me a moment's uneasiness' (*Letters*, 1.65). The fear of ridicule, which was Garrick's besetting weakness, was the final threat to his resolve. Whispers of a love child were revived in 1755 when Garrick assumed the guardianship of Samuel *Cautherley (*c*.1747–1805), and it is certainly odd that Garrick never formally dispelled the rumours that he was Cautherley's father. But green-room gossip more often named Jane Hippisley (later Mrs Green) as the mother than Peg Woffington. The date of Cautherley's birth is not known for certain, and there is no mention of him in Garrick's correspondence until March 1759. There is scant information about Garrick's private life before his marriage, but 1745 was clearly a year of decision for him. In the autumn he was ready to volunteer for Lord Rochford's regiment, hastily assembled to meet the Jacobite invasion. As a precaution he entrusted his financial interests to James Clutterbuck, one of a number of lifelong friends from London's business community. The Dublin engagement was to be a first step on the road to management, and it was time to put his personal life in order.

In Dublin, Sheridan and Garrick collaborated warily, but the season was a financial success. Engraved plates of Hogarth's expressive portrait of Garrick as Richard III had helped to monumentalize his fame there as well as in London. He would become the most painted man in England, and a noted connoisseur and collector. Contemporaries drew comparisons between Hogarth and Garrick, masters of the informal and everyday. For Christopher Smart, in *The Hilliad*:

> While thinking figures from the canvas start,
> ... Hogarth is the Garrick of his art.
> (*Collected Poems*, 1.184)

The two men were convivial friends and mutual admirers, although Hogarth complained that the constant and complete mobility of Garrick's face made him a difficult subject for a portraitist. It was an essential part of Garrick's art to visualize himself in performance, as is very clear in the advice he gave to Francis Hayman, another artist friend, on the choice of apt Shakespearian scenes for illustration. Benjamin Wilson, Zoffany, Gainsborough, and, more circumspectly, Reynolds were also included in Garrick's unusually diverse circle of friends. Although he was alert to the commercial value of publicity portraits and prints, his friendships were motivated by more than self-interest. He made an art of sociability, and painters are prominent among those who repaid him. Garrick's career was the major inspiration to the extraordinary growth of interest in actors and acting during the second half of the eighteenth century.

Garrick returned from Dublin with an enhanced sense of his own value on 10 May 1746, and immediately engaged with John Rich, the manager of Covent Garden, for six end-of-season performances on a profit-sharing basis. Garrick had the management of Drury Lane in mind, but was not yet ready to show his hand. Instead, he contracted with Rich for the 1746–7 season at Covent Garden, confident that Lacy would feel his absence at Drury Lane. The company was a strong one. It included three of the actors Garrick most trusted, Hannah Pritchard, Henry Woodward, and Susannah Cibber. But Rich's particular coup was to bring together, for the first time, James Quin, the old king of the tragic stage, and the young pretender. In the event, they performed together in only three plays, Nicholas Rowe's two tragedies, *The Fair Penitent* (14 November 1746) and *Jane Shore* (2 January 1747), and *I Henry IV* (6 December 1746). As Falstaff, Quin held his own with Garrick's Hotspur, but the verdict of the town, which read the performances as a contest rather than a collaboration, was that Garrick had outfaced Quin in Rowe's tragedies. For the fourteen-year-old future playwright Richard Cumberland the contrast was thrilling: Lothario, 'young and light and alive in every muscle and in every feature', bounding onto the stage to meet a 'heavy-paced Horatio'—'It seemed as if a whole century had been stept over in the transition of a single scene' (Cumberland, 59–60). Garrick's prestige was further increased by the success of his two-act farce *Miss in her Teens*, which opened on 17 January 1747 and ran for forty nights during the season. It was also at Covent Garden that, on 12 February 1747, he first appeared as Ranger in Benjamin Hoadly's *The Suspicious Husband*. A philandering rake, Ranger licensed Garrick to display himself at his most seductively charming. Over the next thirty years he played it 120 times, more often than any other role in his repertory. There is no surer evidence of his awareness of the female vote in his theatrical constituency.

We know from their correspondence that Susannah Cibber had been urging Garrick to share with her in the management of Drury Lane. She had written to him in Ireland, 'I desire you always to be my lover upon the stage and my friend off it' (*Private Correspondence*, 1.38–9). Garrick baulked at the idea, not least because he feared the intervention of her meddlesome husband, Theophilus Cibber. Through the spring of 1747 he negotiated with Lacy towards their joint purchase of the patent. Finally, and not without suspicion on both sides, a contract was signed on 9 April 1747. Garrick's share of the purchase price was £12,000. In return he was to be paid annually £500 as proprietor and 500 guineas as an actor. According to a division of responsibility finally agreed in 1750, Lacy was to manage the property and Garrick was to manage the stage. Despite occasional disagreements, that remained essentially true until Lacy's death in 1774.

First years of management, 1747–1751 While Garrick was engaged in the glittering Covent Garden season of 1746–7, the woman who was to become his wife was Lacy's principal dancer at Drury Lane. They are likely to have met first at one of the formal events in which London society delighted. Eva Maria Veigel (1724–1822) [see Garrick, Eva Maria] was born into a Roman Catholic family in Vienna. Exactly seven years Garrick's junior, she had travelled to England in 1746 to dance with the Italian Opera at London's King's Theatre, where she was initially known by her stage name of Violette. When Garrick met her, and fell in love, she was living with the earl and countess of Burlington, celebrated patrons of the arts. The countess initially opposed her charge's marriage to a player, and it was not until 22 June 1749 that the thirty-year partnership formally began. Garrick settled £10,000 on her, with a promise of £70 per annum. The Burlingtons awarded her the annual interest on their Lincolnshire estates. She made no attempt to resume her stage career, content to be identified as Garrick's wife for thirty years, and then, for more than forty, as his widow. Whatever his bachelor reputation, Garrick took his marriage seriously, and no scandal was ever attached to it.

Garrick was serious about his theatre management, too. He selected and contracted actors with care (over his period in management he would engage nearly 300 of them), and always with an eye to establishing a stable company and a high standard of performance. There were, inevitably, rivalries and desertions, but Garrick earned and cherished the loyalty of many of the finest actors: Woodward, Susannah Cibber, Catherine Clive, Hannah Pritchard, Thomas King, Jane Pope, James Love, John Moody, James Dodd. He had the good sense to recognize that, in serving the interests of the individual performers, he was also serving the interests of Drury Lane's managers. What his detractors called meanness was managerial prudence, what they called vanity was awareness of his own value. Over his first sixteen seasons as manager he averaged about ninety personal appearances, far more than most leading actors, but only half of the playing nights. Under Garrick, Drury Lane became unquestionably the leading theatre in Britain, but it was not, like Henry Irving's Lyceum, a one-man show. Sometimes he quarrelled with actors more temperamental than himself, and the antics of leading ladies such as Elizabeth Younge and, particularly, Frances Abington exasperated him into pronouncing, shortly before his retirement:

the present race of Theatrical Heroines with all their Airs, indispositions, tricks & importances which have reduc'd the Stage to be a dependant upon the Wills of our insolent, vain, & let me add insignificant female trumpery—there must be a

revolution, or my Successors will Suffer much. (*Letters*, 3.1063)

His genuine feeling for his fellows is better represented by his foundation, in 1766, of the Theatrical Fund for the relief of actors in retirement or disability.

Garrick's relations with playwrights were, from the start, more contentious. His closest friend among them was George Colman, with whom he collaborated in *The Clandestine Marriage* (1766), one of the best eighteenth-century comedies, though the two were briefly estranged in 1767, when Colman bought into a share of the management of Covent Garden, the rival playhouse. With Arthur Murphy, later his biographer, he had a love–hate relationship of real complexity. It was, in general, the playwrights whose work he rejected who turned most savagely against him, but Garrick's letters to them were characteristically detailed and patient in explaining his decision. Political and sentimental material, he told John Home, is 'of the least dramatic kind' (*Letters*, 1.269), and he wrote to Edward Thompson, 'I would not write a line till I had fix'd upon a good Story & consider'd it well upon paper—If you don't you will sail without rudder, compass or ballast' (ibid., 2.542). The most vitriolic encounter was with William Kenrick, against whom Garrick instituted a suit for libel in July 1772, in response to Kenrick's scurrilous lampoon *Love in the Suds*. The affair ended in November 1772 with Kenrick's abject apology and promise to suppress sale of the lampoon, but he remained a voluble antagonist.

In keeping with his new status as manager, Garrick had moved his lodgings to King Street, Covent Garden. He had also taken under his wing his improvident younger brother George, who remained at Drury Lane as a company go-between for actors and managers for the rest of his life (he died two weeks after Garrick). Drury Lane had been refurbished ready for its opening on 15 September 1747. Garrick recited Dr Johnson's subsequently famous prologue:

The drama's laws the drama's patrons give,
For we, who live to please, must please to live.

The Lichfield friends had clearly colluded in its composition, for, if the language is Johnson's, the theatrical sentiments are Garrick's. The opening play was *The Merchant of Venice*, featuring Macklin's Shylock. In an implied statement of managerial policy, Garrick delayed his own appearance in a favourite role until 15 October 1747, when he played Archer in *The Beaux' Stratagem*. Before that there was a revival of *The Beggar's Opera* and a chance to see the Hamlet of the handsome Spranger Barry, later to be more often a rival than a colleague of Garrick, who would soon offer his audience the contrast of himself in the part. Comparisons of this kind kept tongues wagging and furnished material for a growing journalistic interest in the theatre. With the assumption of management Garrick was moving towards a proprietorial interest in Shakespeare, whose cause he would increasingly promote. By 1751 he was ready to call Drury Lane 'the house of William Shakespeare' (*Letters*, 1.172). He was not so foolhardy as to present unimproved versions of Shakespeare, but his *King*

Lear of 1747–8 pared away some of Nahum Tate's refinements and restored the Fool. Lear was considered, by many contemporaries, Garrick's finest tragic role. Sir Joshua Reynolds is said to have taken three days to recover from it. His recorded performances of it in London throughout his career number eighty-five, five less than Hamlet, two more than Richard III. Of his other roles in Shakespearian tragedy, he played Romeo sixty times, Macbeth thirty-seven, Falconbridge in *King John* twelve, King John and Iago nine, Antony in *Antony and Cleopatra* six, Mercutio in *Romeo and Juliet*, the Ghost in *Hamlet*, and Othello three. In all of these the text was arranged by, or with the sanction of, Garrick himself. His activity as an adapter of plays was a constant factor in his working life.

By the spring of 1748 Garrick was 'often troubled with Pains in my Breast, arising from Colds' (*Letters*, 1.93). The strains of management were exacerbated by anxiety about his marriage prospects. Lady Burlington was pressing Eva Maria to marry the superannuated earl of Coventry, and Garrick sought solace at Chatsworth House, where he was the guest of the Burlingtons' son-in-law, the marquess of Hartington. Despite the inequality of rank, this was a genuine friendship. Without Hartington's support it is unlikely that Garrick would ever have gained the consent of Lady Burlington to pursue his courtship. Now in his thirty-second year, he opened his second season in management as the bachelor Benedick in a revival of *Much Ado about Nothing*. His Beatrice was the commanding Hannah Pritchard, notably taller than he when fully wigged. The partnership was a popular triumph, and Benedick became Garrick's favourite role in Shakespearian comedy. He performed it 113 times in London, making it a close second to Ranger in *The Suspicious Husband*. His other favoured comic roles were non-Shakespearian eccentrics: Sir John Brute in Vanbrugh's *The Provoked Wife* (105 times), Archer in *The Beaux' Stratagem* (100), Bayes in *The Rehearsal* (91), Kitely in his own adaptation of Jonson's *Every Man in his Humour* (81), Abel Drugger (80), and Don Felix in Susannah Centlivre's *The Wonder* (70), the part in which he took his final farewell in 1776. In comedy Garrick relished opportunities for virtuoso display and inspirational improvisation. His management policy was less showy. For the 1748–9 season he featured Spranger Barry and Mrs Cibber in *Romeo and Juliet* and Robert Dodsley's musical entertainment *The Triumph of Peace*, a celebration of the treaty of Aix-la-Chapelle, which signalled a lull in hostilities between England and France. Dodsley was soon to join the number of playwright complainants against Garrick, whose record in the staging of new plays is easy to defend. Drury Lane, during his seasons in management, presented sixty-one premières of full-length plays and ninety-six new afterpieces. Covent Garden, over the same period, premièred, respectively, forty-nine and forty-two. In general Garrick effectively balanced novelty and the well-tried in his repertory. The two new mainpieces for 1748–9 were both hazardous: Johnson's stodgy *Irene*, staged out of friendship rather than conviction, barely survived its nine performances, and Aaron Hill's *Merope*, well puffed, soon languished.

The marriage of Garrick and Eva Maria Veigel on 22 June 1749 was discreetly managed, combining an Anglican ceremony in Bloomsbury with a Roman Catholic blessing in the chapel of the Portuguese embassy. The couple honeymooned in Mereton, Surrey, and were, for several years, regular guests of the reconciled Burlingtons, both on their Palladian estate in Chiswick and in their Yorkshire residence at Londesborough. There was much repair work to be done in the house at 27 Southampton Street, which Garrick bought for 500 guineas in July 1749, and it was not until 14 October that they moved in. It remained their city home for twenty-three years, its four storeys tastefully furnished by Mrs Garrick and its walls decorated by Garrick's growing collection of books and pictures. His unique dramatic library was eventually bequeathed to the British Museum. His purchases of play-texts served both to enhance Drury Lane's repertory and to satisfy his bibliomania. He bought volumes on the fine arts, too, and collected emblemata, engravings, and a variety of prints. Among the paintings at his houses, originals as well as copies, were works by artists as various as Watteau, Andrea del Sarto, Hals, Poussin, Lely, and Gainsborough. Pride of place went to the four great oils of Hogarth's *Election* sequence, which Garrick bought from the artist in 1762.

The Garricks, to David's certain regret, were childless. Had he had children, he would have lavished on them the kind of attention he paid to his books and pictures. Fanny Burney was one of many to comment on the lack: 'How many pities that he has no children; for he is extremely, nay passionately fond of them' (*The Early Diary of Frances Burney, 1768–1778*, ed. A. E. Ellis, 2 vols., rev. edn, 1907, 1.144). He was uncle and playmate to his brother George's children, an active governor of London's lying-in hospital from 1756, a solicitous guardian to Samuel Cautherley, and, over the last years of his life, a fatherly friend to Hannah More. There is an indicative passage in a letter to George Colman, dating from 30 June 1766. Colman had gone to Paris, leaving his four-year-old son in the charge of nannies:

> I must tell, that yr sweet boy is at this instant as happy & as well as Ever I knew him. … We have work'd very hard in the Garden togeather, & have play'd at Ninepins till I was oblig'd to declare off. (*Letters*, 2.520)

Having last played Benedick as a bachelor, Garrick determined to open his third season in the same part: a public statement that the bachelor had reformed to respectability. He explained the decision to Lady Burlington on 19 September 1749: 'I shall open with Benedick *the Married Man*; I have so resolv'd, & I find the People are very impatient to laugh with Me & at Me' (*Letters*, 1.128). Marriage had confirmed Garrick's resolution to raise the moral and social status of himself and, by association, his profession. He had a taste and a talent for brilliant society, as did his young wife, and enjoyed being a celebrity. There is an ill-concealed delight in his narration of an episode, in September 1749, when, while walking in the Strand, he found that the sign being erected outside a bookseller's was his own portrait, '& My Name written about it, in Letters as tall as Myself' (ibid., 1.124). The season, though successful, ended disconcertingly with Barry, Macklin, and Mrs Cibber announcing their intentions to join the Covent Garden company. Garrick's response was to engage the attractive but comparatively inexperienced George Anne Bellamy. The stomach disorder that took him to Bath in March 1750 may have been the first grumbling of the kidney stones that plagued his last years. It was revealed at the post-mortem that Garrick was born with only one kidney, and it was through energy, stamina, and professionalism that he sustained his uncommonly demanding public career. The Garricks kept house for the Burlingtons at Chiswick through May 1750, and Garrick did some electioneering in the whig interest. Still smarting over the defections of some of his leading actors, he began the 1750–51 season in open competition with Covent Garden. For 28 September both houses announced *Romeo and Juliet*, with Garrick and Bellamy at Drury Lane challenging Barry and Cibber at Covent Garden. Honours were divided, but the spectacle was undignified, and Garrick submitted to the public will by presenting a pantomime for Christmas. Henry Woodward's *Queen Mab* was staged forty-five times in its first season and appeared in fifteen later seasons under Garrick's management. It is evidence of his capacity to compromise with his public that a pantomime was, by some way, the most frequently performed piece in Garrick's Drury Lane repertory.

Middle years of management, 1751–1765 Before the completion of the 1751 benefit performances the Garricks were in Paris, which they reached on 23 May. They were enthusiastic sightseers and theatregoers, though not yet fêted as they would be twelve years later. Jean Liotard produced portraits in pastel of both of them, Garrick looking altogether heavier than in the putative Van Loo portrait of 1741, Mrs Garrick expensively dressed and straight-backed. It was probably in this summer that Garrick met Jean Monnet, a bookseller and theatre manager, through whom he was able to keep in touch with the latest theatrical developments in Paris, and to whom he was much later indebted for the recommendation of the innovatory stage designer Jean Phillipe de Loutherbourg. The Garricks returned to London in July, in good time to prepare the theatrical programme. The Drury Lane routine was fairly well established by now: revivals until Christmas, supported sometimes by new afterpieces, pantomime into the new year, premières in February and March, benefit performances to end the season. By 1753 the Garricks were prosperous enough to plan the purchase of a house and estate in the country, something with 'taste in it', and the four requisites for 'a good Situation'—'Wood, Water, Extent, & inequality of Ground' (*Letters*, 1.193). They looked first in Derbyshire, in the vicinity of Chatsworth House, where they enjoyed the hospitality of Lord Hartington still, but the property they first rented and then, on 30 August 1754, bought was Fuller House, in Hampton-on-Thames. Garrick employed Robert Adam to supervise alterations to the house and Capability Brown to lay out

the garden. In August 1755 Adam designed for him an octagonal temple to Shakespeare in the grounds. Johann Zoffany later painted a conversation piece depicting the Garricks, two of their dogs, an unidentified boy, and a servant outside the temple, through whose open door Roubiliac's life-size statue of Shakespeare is just visible. Hampton was their summer home for the rest of their lives together, and Mrs Garrick's thereafter. The purchase price is not recorded, but on 20 April 1757 Garrick paid £13,038 for the manor of Hendon, Essex, a purely commercial speculation. Ten years later he refused to sell it for less than £20,000.

Theatre management had, inevitably, its ups and downs. On 8 November 1755 Garrick promoted at Drury Lane *The Chinese Festival*, an audacious ballet by the great Swiss choreographer Jean Georges Noverre. It was the eve of the Seven Years' War, and most of the dancers were French. Xenophobes succeeded in arousing hostile patriotism, and much damage was done to the theatre in the ensuing riots. Garrick's attempt to recompense Noverre by employing him for the 1756–7 season ended in mutual misunderstanding, but Noverre never questioned Garrick's genius as an actor. He is said to have used him as a model for his reformation of the ballet, and his description of Garrick's acting in *Lettres sur les arts imitateurs en général et sur la danse en particulier* is one of the finest known. There were compensations in friendships with remarkable men—Edmund Burke most enduringly, but also Reynolds and the much less respectable John Wilkes. Charles Churchill, whose *Rosciad* (1761) brilliantly confirmed the triumph of the Garrick revolution in acting styles, was part of Wilkes's circle, and a useful man to have on your side in the satirical newspaper campaigns of the period. Garrick was a regular contributor to newspapers, owned shares in four dailies, and was closely involved with the influential *St James's Chronicle*. In his later years he became oversensitive to criticism, but he was rarely silenced by it. Mrs Garrick excelled as a hostess, and some of the highest in the land dined at Hampton. That Garrick was gratified by his social success is less surprising than that he should have maintained his intense interest in the affairs of Drury Lane. His afterpiece *The Male Coquette* appeared there on 24 March 1757. Though light-hearted, its attack on male effeminacy reflects a constant prejudice of Garrick's. When Woodward, for whose benefit it was written, left Drury Lane in 1758, Garrick compensated for the loss of his pantomime writer by himself providing *Harlequin's Invasion* for the Christmas entertainment in 1759. His efforts to regularize the conduct of the theatre continued. He had had the support of his audience when he banished self-displaying loungers from the stage during performances and restricted their admission to the green room. But he encountered outrageous opposition during the 1762–3 season, when he attempted to abolish the custom of half-price admission after the third act of the main piece. The outcome, in January 1763, was dictated by a mob under the leadership of a man about town, Thadeus (or Thomas) Fitzpatrick. The riots that interrupted performances of *The Two Gentlemen* of *Verona* spread, in February 1763, to Covent Garden, where John Beard had similarly determined to end the custom of half-price. Garrick was mortified by his impotence in the face of mob rule, and there is a strong possibility that it was this episode that motivated him to take a holiday from the theatre. The young William Powell showed promise of filling the gap during his absence, Mrs Garrick was suffering from rheumatism, and he himself was exhausted after twenty-two unbroken years of work. Colman stood in as joint manager with Lacy.

The Garricks embarked for their grand tour on 15 September 1763 and reached Paris four days later. By 8 October Garrick was truthfully writing: 'You can't imagine, my dear Colman, what honours I have receiv'd from all kind of People here—the Nobles & the Literati have made so much of Me that I am quite asham'd of opening my heart Ev'n to You' (*Letters*, 1.387). The same applied throughout a tour that took the Garricks through Lyons and Mont Cenis to Turin, to Rome, and, through the famine of 1764, to Naples, back to Rome, to Parma, Venice, and Padua, then to Munich and Spa, and back to Paris by way of Strasbourg and Nancy. Garrick was a celebrity. He was given the freedom of the Comédie Française and entertained by its leading actors, and he mingled at salons with Diderot and the encyclopaedists. In Naples he was a guest of the expatriate nobility, especially intimate with the Spencers of Althorp (he remained in correspondence with Lady Spencer until his death). But for ill health, he would even have visited, by invitation, the great Voltaire. On the surface it was an uninterrupted triumphal progress, and one which led to enduring friendships—not least with Madame Riccoboni, whose literary cause he championed in England. Beneath the surface, though, there were constant anxieties about Mrs Garrick's health. Wherever possible she took the waters in the hope of alleviating her rheumatic pains, and then, in August 1764, as her health improved and they began the homeward journey, Garrick fell seriously ill with what was probably a severe attack of hepatitis. Warned that her husband might be dying, Mrs Garrick nursed him devotedly in the Munich inn at which he had arrived in near-delirium. While he was recuperating in Paris in November 1764 Garrick joked to Colman, 'Eight Physicians, my good friend, & still alive! & very likely to continue so' (ibid., 2.429). Convalescence was made easier after Christmas, when John Wilkes gave the Garricks the use of his comfortable lodgings in the rue Niçaise. As his health improved, Garrick's thoughts turned back to Drury Lane and his young protégé William Powell, through whom he glimpsed his own past. 'When the publick has mark'd you for a favourite', he wrote to Powell on 12 December 1764:

> (& their favor must be purchas'd with Sweat & labour) You may chuse what Company you please, and none but the best can be of service to you. … But above all, never let your Shakespear be out of your hands, or your Pocket.
> (ibid., 2.436)

After two years' absence from the stage, Garrick experienced an unfamiliar crisis of confidence as the time to return to London approached. From Paris, on 10 March 1765, he wrote to Colman: 'do the Town in general *really* wish to see me on the Stage?' (*Letters*, 2.449), and he took the extravagant precaution of sending in advance, for anonymous publication, a satirical pamphlet on his own career, *The Sick Monkey*. It was not until 25 April 1765 that the Garricks finally set foot in their Southampton Street home.

Last years of management, 1765–1776 The experience of illness, of Europe, and of Parisian culture in particular affected Garrick's personal and theatrical life. The French literati thought and wrote seriously about art, even about the 'art' of acting, but lived well and stylishly. So would he. As a young man he had written an 'Essay on acting' (1744). Now he contemplated a book (untraced, if ever started). The lighting of the Parisian stage had impressed him more than the acting. He would introduce a new technology to Drury Lane, and live to see it further advanced after 1771 by de Loutherbourg. His evident reluctance, over the summer of 1765, to return to the stage may have been a ploy to excite public demand. When he finally appeared, on 14 November 1765, as Benedick again, it was by royal command. It was one of only ten performances that season, and Garrick rarely went above thirty in his remaining years. Increasingly troubled by gout and arthritis, he was more worried by 'the Bile, which is my chief complaint. … so very uncertain in Its motions that it comes upon me like a Thief in the Night' (*Letters*, 2.507). It became his custom to take the waters in Bath during the theatre's spring benefits, prior to summer visits to country houses. Lord Camden, formerly the attorney-general, was a particularly cherished new friend and a frequent host to the Garricks at Camden Place, Kent. The major event of the 1765–6 season was the première of Colman's and Garrick's *The Clandestine Marriage*, on 20 February 1766. Colman was disappointed when Garrick chose not to act in it, though King made a success of the Garrick part of Lord Ogleby. As he acted less, Garrick wrote more for Drury Lane: two-act farces such as *Neck or Nothing* (1766), *The Irish Widow* (1772), and *Bon Ton* (1775); musical pieces such as *Cymon* (1767), *A Christmas Tale* (1773), and *May-Day* (1775); and theatrical in-jokes such as *A Peep behind the Curtain* (1767), *The Meeting of the Company* (1774), and *The Theatrical Candidates* (1775).

In terms of popular acclaim, Garrick's most successful piece was the processional entertainment *The Jubilee* (1769), a resourceful outcome of an episode that carried him to the brink of ridicule. In May 1769 Garrick received, from the corporation of Stratford upon Avon, the freedom of the borough, sealed in a box made from Shakespeare's mulberry tree. Eight days later the corporation invited him to accept the stewardship of the first Shakespeare jubilee in the town. It seemed a fitting recognition of his staging twenty-seven of Shakespeare's plays at Drury Lane, and Garrick entered into planning the September festival with almost callow enthusiasm. There would be an octagonal amphitheatre, nightly fireworks, a grand masquerade, banquets, the whole to be topped by a procession of characters from Shakespeare's most popular plays. The orchestra and most of the acting company from

Drury Lane would be there; so would the local aristocracy and many of Garrick's friends. It was a problem that Stratford had insufficient accommodation for all the visitors, but the first day, 6 September 1769, passed off in great good humour, and was pronounced a success. That night and all the next day it rained. The fireworks got wet, the amphitheatre flooded, the great procession was cancelled. It was a fiasco, and Garrick's enemies exulted in his discomfiture. But Garrick's love of Shakespeare was genuine, and he understood his audience's delight in spectacle. Loosely accommodated in a comic plot, the grand procession of Shakespearian characters (Garrick himself was always Benedick) was staged ninety-one times at Drury Lane between 14 October 1769 and the end of the season. Nothing quite like it had ever been seen. It was a triumph of showmanship.

Through the early 1770s, despite bouts of ill health, Garrick continued in effective management of Drury Lane. He continued, also, to accumulate wealth and property. In February 1771 he completed the purchase of the manor of Copford, near Colchester, and a year later, having sold the Southampton Street house, bought number 5 (later renumbered 4) in the newly built Adelphi Terrace. He was feeling his age: 'I will not stay to be Sixty with my Cap & bells', he wrote to John Hoadly on 3 January 1776 (*Letters*, 3.1063). Once his imminent retirement was made public, there was a clamour for tickets for his farewell performances in the spring of 1776. He responded with nineteen appearances in eleven different parts between 11 April and early June. They were all old favourites, even Don Felix in Mrs Centlivre's *The Wonder*, in which, rather surprisingly, he made his final bow on 10 June 1776. He had been negotiating the sale of his share of the Drury Lane patent, which was valued at £35,000, since the previous December. The first refusal was offered to George Colman, but it was the playwright Sheridan who led the group that eventually bought it. By the time negotiations were complete the Garricks were at Wilton House, as guests of the earl of Pembroke.

Retirement and death Garrick had less than three years to live when he retired from acting. Much remained the same: winters in Adelphi Terrace, summers at Hampton and on country-house visits. Garrick attended meetings of The Club, the self-selecting élite group with Dr Johnson at its centre, of which he had been a member since 1773. Sometimes he was seen at Almack's, the fashionable Pall Mall club to which he had been elected in 1773. He continued to interest himself in the fortunes of his nieces and nephews, George's children, and of his wife's niece, Elisabeth Fürst. There was no diminution in his correspondence, and only a slackening—never an abandonment—of his concern for the fortunes of Drury Lane. Clear of everyday controversy, he remained high in public esteem. There were even rumours of a baronetcy, promptly dismissed in a letter to Lady Spencer. Sir John Fielding, a zealous magistrate with whom Garrick had what was at best a strained friendship, was honest enough to summarize the general opinion when he wrote, on Garrick's retirement,

'the Chastity of Mr Garrick, as a manager of a Public Theatre, and his exemplary Life as a Man, have been of great service to the Morals of a dissipated Age' (*Letters*, 3.1117). It is doubtful whether a single actor has ever done as much as he did to raise the standing of his profession. Contemporaries recognized in his performances a new and wonderful truth to life: 'He is a little man', wrote Sylas Neville, 'but handsome and full of that fire which marks the stronger, and of the softness natural to the tender passions' (Stone and Kahrl, 336), and for William Hopkins, prompter at Drury Lane, 'suffice it to say that he was what he represented' (ibid., 28). Garrick was disarmingly open about the pleasure he took in high society: 'It is my utmost pride and ambition to deserve the kind thoughts of the great and good' (*Letters*, 2.765), and it is, perhaps, apt that the onset of his final illness coincided with a visit to the Spencers at Althorp House in the new year of 1778–9. The blockage in his kidney was too severe to be treated, and he was carried home to Adelphi Terrace, where he died on 20 January 1779.

The funeral on 1 February was a theatrical occasion in its own right. The procession took more than an hour to travel from the Adelphi to Westminster Abbey, where the actor was buried in Poets' Corner. There were crowds in the streets and upwards of fifty coaches in the cortège. The funeral service was read by the bishop of Rochester, and the pallbearers included Lord Camden, the earl of Ossory, Earl Spencer, Viscount Palmerston, and the duke of Devonshire, all aristocrats, all friends. The chief mourner was Sheridan. On 11 March 1779 Sheridan's *Monody to the Memory of Mr Garrick* was elaborately staged at Drury Lane, with music by Sheridan's father-in-law, Thomas Linley, scenery specially designed by de Loutherbourg, and the words solemnly spoken by Mary Ann Yates. Garrick's estate at death has been plausibly estimated at £100,000. It was sufficient, certainly, to keep the chief beneficiary, his widow, in comfort for the remaining forty-three years of her life. Garrick did not neglect his immediate family in his bequests, but his faithful wife came first.

Garrick's legacy While it is generally recognized that actors belong irretrievably to their own age, it must also be conceded that the impact of great actors outlives them. The young George Frederick Cooke saw Garrick perform in 1774 and vowed to emulate him. The young Edmund Kean was inspired by Cooke when many people thought Cooke a drink-sodden shadow of his former self. The extraordinary Frederick Robson (1821–1864), diminutive and terrorized by stage fright, was called a second Garrick because of his capacity to juxtapose laughter and anguish. Robson's model was Edmund Kean. More than any other single actor, Garrick changed the acting style of the nation, above all because he engineered a shift in the expectations of audiences. In place of the accuracy and control of a James Quin, Garrick gave them energy and engagement. He was most exuberantly himself when exploiting with extravagant eagerness the theatrical high points, whether comic or tragic, of a role. Like all great actors, he drew attention to himself (even so evidently unobtrusive an actor as Sir Alec Guinness did that).

Enemies might call that vanity, egotism, or exhibitionism, but these are words that translate into generosity in the present tense of performance; and Garrick was so much more a generous actor than Quin. It was his versatility that confirmed his pre-eminence for contemporaries. They found him natural and the old school artificial, but that is a judgement repeated by each new generation of theatregoers as they discard old stars in favour of new ones. Garrick did not dispense with the rhetorical style he inherited; he changed its timing. It was a subtle, not a flagrant, desecration. He was not inimitable, as Samuel Foote and Tate Wilkinson delighted to demonstrate. If he had been, his 'revolution' would have remained a personal one.

Garrick's legacy was not confined to acting. He presided over the creation of Shakespeare as the national poet and icon, always shaping the texts he admired to suit the taste of the patrons he courted. He was the first theatre manager to set about mastering the craft of public relations—but not to the neglect of in-house discipline. Neither before nor after Garrick's period of management did Drury Lane achieve such sustained supremacy. There would be nothing like it in England until Irving's reign at the Lyceum, which began a century after Garrick's death, and Irving had no other model but Garrick. The Lyceum, though, had an almost sacerdotal air: it was a temple of dramatic art. Garrick's Drury Lane, like Garrick himself, was convivial. Both performers and spectators were participants in a social act. The pubs and busy streets that bear his name are monuments to Garrick's conviviality. So, supremely perhaps (though only if you are one of its 700 members), is the Garrick Club. Founded in 1831, and housed now in one of the narrow streets actors still use on their way to Drury Lane, the Garrick Club displays its priceless collection of theatrical portraits as carelessly as postcards on a student's wall; but the food is choice and the cellar fine.

PETER THOMSON

Sources The letters of David Garrick, ed. D. M. Little and G. M. Kahrl, 3 vols. (1963) • G. W. Stone and G. M. Kahrl, David Garrick: a critical biography (1979) • C. Oman, David Garrick (1958) • A. Murphy, The life of David Garrick, 2 vols. (1801) • The private correspondence of David Garrick, ed. J. Boaden, 2 vols. (1831–2) • Boswell, Life • W. W. Appleton, Charles Macklin: an actor's life (1961) • The collected poems of Christopher Smart, ed. N. Callan, 2 vols. (1949) • R. Paulson, Hogarth, 2 (1992) • R. Cumberland, Memoirs of Richard Cumberland written by himself (1806) • Highfill, Burnim & Langhans, BDA
Archives Bodl. Oxf., corresp. • Boston PL, corresp. and papers • Folger • Garr. Club, corresp. and papers • Harvard U., Houghton L., papers • Hereford Museum and Art Gallery, papers • RA, accounts relating to property • Shakespeare Birthplace Trust RO, letters and executory papers • Staffs. RO, licences to perform, assignments, and family corresp. • Theatre Museum, London, papers relating to Drury Lane Theatre • V&A NAL, corresp. and papers | BL, corresp. with Thomas Birch, Add. MS 4308 • BL, letters to William Julius Mickle, RP251–252 [copies] • BL, letters to Countess Spencer • BL, letters to Charles Yorke, Add. MS 35350 • Chatsworth House, Derbyshire, letters to fourth duke and duchess of Devonshire • NL Wales, letters to Evan Lloyd • Sheff. Arch., corresp. with Edmund Burke • Yale U., Beinecke L., corresp. with James Boswell
Likenesses W. Hogarth, oils, c.1745, Walker Art Gallery, Liverpool • J. E. Liotard, pastel drawing, 1751, Chatsworth House, Derbyshire • T. Worlidge, oils, 1752, V&A • J. Zoffany, group portrait, oils, exh. RA 1752 (in The farmer's return), Yale U. CBA • W. Hogarth, double portrait, oils, 1757 (with his wife), Royal Collection; see illus. in Garrick, Eva Maria (1724–1822) • F. Hayman, oils, 1760, Theatre Museum, London • J. Zoffany, oils, 1762, Petworth House, West Sussex • P. Batoni, oils, 1764, AM Oxf. • A. Kauffman, oils, 1764, Burghley House, Northamptonshire • J. Zoffany, oils, c.1765, Theatre Museum, London • J. Reynolds, oils, 1767, Royal Collection [see illus.] • T. Gainsborough, oils, c.1768, Yale U. CBA • J. Scouter, miniature, 1768, V&A • T. Gainsborough, oils, exh. 1770, NPG • J. Zoffany, oils, 1770, Castle Howard, North Yorkshire • N. Dance, oils, 1771, Stratford upon Avon town council • N. Dance, pencil drawing, 1771, NPG • B. Vandergucht, oils, 1772, Althorp House, Northamptonshire • J. Reynolds, oils, exh. RA 1776, Knole, Kent • H. Webber, statue on monument, c.1797, Westminster Abbey, London • E. F. Burney, pen and wash drawing, BM • W. Hackwood, medallion (after T. Pingo, 1772), Wedgwood Museum, Stoke-on-Trent • F. Hayman, oils (with Hannah Pritchard; in a scene from The suspicious husband), Museum of London • P. J. de Loutherbourg, oils (as Don Juan in The chances), Garr. Club • J. Nollekens, marble bust, Althorp House, Northamptonshire • R. E. Pine, oils, NPG • J. Roberts, oils, BM • L. F. Roubiliac, plaster bust, NPG • J. K. Sherwin, miniature, pencil, NPG • J. Zoffany, oils (as Lord Chalkstone in Lethe), Birmingham Museums and Art Gallery • J. Zoffany, oils (as Jaffier in Venice preserved), Garr. Club • J. Zoffany, oils (as Macbeth; with Mrs Pritchard as Lady Macbeth), Garr. Club • marble bust, Royal Collection • medallion, plaster replica (after J. Tassie), Scot. NPG • oils (as Romeo; after B. Wilson), Garr. Club • photographs, BM, NPG • silhouette, Scot. NPG
Wealth at death approx. £100,000: will

Garrick [née Veigel], **Eva Maria** [performing name Violette] (1724–1822), dancer, is best-known as the wife of David *Garrick (1717–1779), whom she married on 22 June 1749. She was born into a Roman Catholic family in Vienna, the daughter of Johann Veigel, a former valet, and his wife, Eva Maria Rosina, on 29 February 1724. She became the favoured pupil of the dancing-master Franz Hilverding. At the age of ten she danced the part of Psyche in Hilverding's ballet Amour and Psyche, and her talent and delicate manners brought her frequent invitations to entertain the Austrian aristocracy. It was rumoured that the empress Maria Theresa, jealous of the emperor's interest in the graceful young dancer, encouraged her to leave Vienna. In 1746, under her stage name, Violette, she contracted to dance with the Italian Opera Company at London's King's Theatre, and was at once the talk of the town.

Violette's passage into London society was eased by the patronage of the earl and countess of Burlington, at whose artistically buzzing house in Piccadilly she lodged until her marriage to Garrick. The couple met socially, probably in 1747 when London society was pressing invitations on the city's two most celebrated performers, and they were mutually attracted, but the match was initially opposed by the countess of Burlington, who may have heard rumours of Garrick's earlier liaisons and who had higher aspirations for her protégée. In 1746–7, while Violette was dancing at Drury Lane, Garrick was at Covent Garden, and in the following season, when Garrick began his long association with Drury Lane, she was at Covent Garden. The marriage settlement, when it was reached, was a virtual guarantee of prosperity for Violette. Not only

Eva Maria Garrick (1724–1822), by William Hogarth, 1757 [with her husband, David Garrick]

did she receive £10,000 from Garrick, together with £70 per year, but also the annual interest on Lady Burlington's estates in Lincolnshire. There followed thirty years of contented marriage and forty-three of dignified widowhood. Eva Maria was Garrick's constant companion at home and abroad, his supporter and adviser in theatrical affairs, a gracious hostess on social occasions, and a welcome guest in the grand houses the couple visited. Garrick's social aggrandizement is inconceivable without her. Her taste and intelligence are discernible in the books and paintings they bought, in the way they furnished their houses, and between the lines of Garrick's voluminous correspondence. The Garricks were childless, but there was maternal generosity in Eva Maria's quiet care for Garrick's difficult protégé, Samuel *Cautherley, and in her relationship with the children of Garrick's brother George. She was less at ease with her own siblings and with her widowed mother, all of whom were tempted to take advantage of her. Fluent in French and Italian, she spoke English with a trace of an Austrian accent, and wrote it stiltedly.

After Garrick's death in 1779, Eva Maria maintained their house in Adelphi Terrace and the large house and estate in Hampton that was her summer resort. Perhaps to save her from exploitation by her family, Garrick had stipulated in his will that she would forfeit the greater part of his legacy if she ceased to live in England, but there is no evidence that she wished to do so. Widowhood gave her time to develop her interest in mesmerism and alchemy. She continued to purchase books and to worship according to the forms of Roman Catholicism. After refusing two proposals from the extraordinary Lord Monboddo in 1782, she settled into a semi-reclusive way of life, happiest with friends and acquaintances when speaking of her dead husband or displaying mementoes of their time together. She died suddenly, on 16 October 1822 and in her ninety-ninth year, in the Adelphi Terrace house, and was buried beside her husband in Westminster Abbey nine days later. Of a multiplicity of detailed bequests in her will, many were to charities. PETER THOMSON

Sources G. W. Stone and G. M. Kahrl, *David Garrick: a critical biography* (1979) · Highfill, Burnim & Langhans, *BDA* · *The letters of David Garrick*, ed. D. M. Little and G. M. Kahrl, 3 vols. (1963)
Archives BL · Folger, papers, incl. diary · Garr. Club | Theatre Museum, London, Forster collection
Likenesses J. E. Liotard, pastels, 1751, Chatsworth House, Derbyshire · W. Hogarth, double portrait, oils, 1757 (with her husband), Royal Collection [*see illus.*] · N. Dance, pencil drawing, 1771, NPG · J. Reynolds, double portrait, oils, exh. 1773 (with her husband), NPG; copy, NPG · R. Cruikshank, engraving, 1820, Harvard TC · C. Read, portrait, Garr. Club; copy, miniature · photograph (after J. Zoffany, *c*.1755), Harvard U., Fogg Museum
Wealth at death under £100,000; house in Adelphi Terrace, villa in Hampton; also books, paintings

Garrod, Sir **Alfred Baring** (1819–1907), physician, was born at Ipswich on 13 May 1819, the second child and only son of the five children of Robert Garrod, founder of a firm of auctioneers and estate agents, and his wife, Sarah Enew, *née* Clamp. Garrod was educated at Ipswich grammar school, and after being apprenticed to Charles Hammond, surgeon to the East Suffolk Hospital, studied medicine at University College Hospital, London, from which he graduated MB in 1842 and MD in 1843, gaining the gold medal in medicine at both examinations.

In November 1842 the hospital decided to practise chemical pathology to supplement mere study of the appearance of diseased organs. Garrod was appointed chemical assistant to the clinical department; his task was to study blood or fluid from diseased tissue sent to him by the medical officers (Merrington, 218). On 15 July 1845 Garrod married Elizabeth Ann (*d*. 1891), daughter of Henry Colchester and Elizabeth Sparrow, of the Ancient or Sparrow House in Ipswich. Charles Keene of *Punch* and Meredith Townsend of *The Spectator* were her first cousins. They had four sons and two daughters, and three of their children survived him. The eldest son, Alfred Henry *Garrod (1846–1879), and the fourth son, Archibald Edward *Garrod (1857–1936), were, like their father, fellows of the Royal Society. Archibald Garrod became famous for his recognition of inborn errors of metabolism which constituted the birth of biochemical genetics and human individuality. The third son, Herbert Baring, was general secretary of the Teachers' Guild of Great Britain and Ireland from 1886 to 1909.

In 1846 Garrod was appointed assistant physician to University College Hospital; he became full physician, professor of materia medica and therapeutics, and a professor of clinical medicine in 1851. He became a licentiate, and in 1856 a fellow, of the Royal College of Physicians, where he was Goulstonian lecturer in 1857. He was elected FRS in 1858. Garrod surprised his colleagues by resigning his posts at University College Hospital in 1862. A good lecturer and popular teacher, he was elected physician to King's College Hospital and its professor of materia medica and therapeutics; on his retirement in 1874 he was elected consulting physician. He was knighted in 1887 and in 1890 became physician-extraordinary to Queen Victoria, and was elected an honorary member of the Verein für Innere Medizin in Berlin. In 1891 he was honoured by the first award of the Royal College of Physicians' Moxon medal for distinguished research and observation in clinical medicine. His appearance was described by a former student, Dr Talfourd Jones, who noted Garrod's 'fine and broad forehead, his abundant and curly hair, his habitual spectacles, and his genial look' (Jones, 121).

Garrod, a follower of Prout and Bence Jones, devoted himself to chemical pathological investigation of the problems of disease. He is remembered for his ingenious discovery in 1847 that in gout the blood contains an increased quantity of uric acid. Taking a small sample of blood and placing it in a watch-glass into which he placed a cotton thread, he noted that, overnight, crystals of uric acid assembled on the cotton thread. He announced his discovery in 1848 to the Royal Medical and Chirurgical Society (of which he became vice-president in 1880–81). Garrod is also remembered for having distinguished rheumatoid arthritis from gout, with which it had previously been confused. At the Medical Society of London, of which he was orator in 1858 on 'Diabetes', and president in 1860, Garrod gave in 1857 the Lettsomian lectures 'On the pathology and treatment of gout'.

Garrod long enjoyed an extensive practice, but when old age diminished his work as a consultant he returned with ardour to his chemical investigations. He frequently referred his patients to Aix-les-Bains to take the waters. In recognition of Garrod's appreciation the council of the city named a road in his honour—rue Sir Alfred Garrod.

Garrod was the author of two standard works. His *Treatise on Gout and Rheumatic Gout* (1859) went to a third edition in 1876, and was translated into French and German. His textbook *Essentials of Materia Medica and Therapeutics* (1855), the first of its kind, went to a thirteenth edition by 1890. He also contributed articles on gout and rheumatism to Russell Reynolds's *System of Medicine* (1866, vol. 1).

Garrod lived in London at 84 Harley Street, and later at 10 Harley Street. He had not been seen in public for some years before he died at his home, 10 Harley Street, on 28 December 1907; he was buried in the Great Northern London cemetery, Southgate.

H. D. ROLLESTON, *rev.* ALEXANDER G. BEARN

Sources A. G. Bearn, *Archibald Garrod and the individuality of man* (1993) · J. H. Talbott, *A biographical history of medicine* (1970) · *BMJ* (4 Jan 1908), 58–9 · T. Jones, 'The late Sir Alfred B. Garrod', *BMJ* (11 Jan 1908), 121 [letter] · Suffolk RO, Ipswich, parish registers, parish rate books, census records, wills, poll books, newspapers · W. R. Merrington, *University College Hospital and its medical school: a history* (1976), 218 · Munk, *Roll* · *CGPLA Eng. & Wales* (1908) · IGI

Likenesses portrait, c.1859; formerly in possession of Dr Oliver Garrod · H. von Herkomer, oils, 1882, RCP Lond. · Elliott & Fry, photograph, 1887, repro. in *The Lancet*, 1 (1908), 67
Wealth at death £84,551: probate, 14 Feb 1908, *CGPLA Eng. & Wales*

Garrod, Alfred Henry (1846–1879), zoologist, was born in Charterhouse Square, London, on 18 May 1846, the eldest child of Sir Alfred Baring *Garrod (1819–1907), physician, and his wife, Elizabeth Ann Colchester (d. 1891). He was educated at University College School, and entered University College in October 1862. Following a course which included lectures in physiology, mathematics, and mechanics, in October 1864 he entered King's College, as a medical student. He gained a Warneford scholarship at entrance, the medical scholarship in three successive years, and in 1868 he became a licentiate of the Society of Apothecaries. However, an interest in the natural sciences, and the winning in 1868 of an exhibition in the subject at St John's College, Cambridge, led to further university studies.

During his Cambridge course Garrod made several interesting researches on the causes of the varying temperature of the human body and on the circulation of the blood, and made some improvements in the sphygmograph. In 1870 he was elected to a foundation scholarship at St John's, and in December 1871 he was placed senior in the natural sciences tripos. He was elected to a fellowship at St John's in November 1873—the first natural scientist to be so distinguished.

In June 1871 Garrod was elected prosector to the Zoological Society, a position which involved much work in the dissecting room of the zoological gardens at Regent's Park, and which drew him into almost exclusively zoological work. He became particularly interested in the anatomy of birds and he was soon able to work out on a more extensive scale many of Nitzsch's observations on pterylography (skin patterns of the development of feathers) and to add many new facts, especially in the area of muscle structure and function.

In 1874 Garrod was elected professor of comparative anatomy at King's College, London, and in the following year was also appointed Fullerian professor of physiology at the Royal Institution. As Fullerian professor he gave three lecture courses between 1875 and 1878. The courses were illustrated by models and experiments of his own devising; their ingenuity made the lectures very popular. In 1875 he also delivered several of the Davis lectures at the zoological gardens. For several years he acted as one of the sub-editors of *Nature*, writing many articles and reviews on biological subjects. In 1876 he was elected a fellow of the Royal Society, and undertook to write a comprehensive work, aided by a government grant, on the anatomy of birds. Unfortunately, only a portion of it was completed at his death and it seems never to have been finished, although W. A. Forbes (1855–1883) certainly intended to complete it.

In 1876–8 Garrod was examiner in zoology in the Cambridge natural sciences tripos. In June 1878 he was seized with severe pulmonary haemorrhage, but continued to

Alfred Henry Garrod (1846–1879), by unknown engraver, pubd 1879 (after Elliott & Fry)

work indefatigably. After conducting the tripos examination in December 1878, he wintered in the Riviera, but returned to London unrelieved. He continued to work as much as possible, occupying himself at last, when too ill to go to the gardens, with dissecting and comparing the trachea in different groups of birds. He died of phthisis at his home, 10 Harley Street, London, on 17 October 1879, aged thirty-three.

Garrod was highly esteemed by a large circle of friends, and his rooms at the Zoological Society were a base from which he was ever ready to provide assistance or to direct study. He was cheerful and unselfish, with a strong and energetic character and a wide range of information and interest. His work was of considerable value. His most important paper on mammalian anatomy, *On the Visceral Anatomy and Osteology of the Ruminants*, was read before the Zoological Society in 1877. It developed important points in the classification of the group, and suggested the adoption of a new system of nomenclature. His great energy enabled him to take full advantage of the exceptional opportunities of dissecting animals during his prosectorship; he dissected no fewer than five rhinoceroses belonging to three different species and wrote valuable papers on his findings. At the time of his death he was considered one of his generation's pre-eminent experts on birds. His scientific papers were collected by a committee of zoologists, and published in one large volume in 1881, edited with a biographical notice by W. A. Forbes, his successor in the prosectorship at the zoological gardens. Garrod also contributed the important section 'Ruminantia' to Cassell's *Natural History*, and edited (with

valuable notes) the translation of Johannes Müller's celebrated paper on the vocal organs of passerine birds (by Professor F. J. Bell), published in 1879.

G. T. BETTANY, *rev.* CLEMENCY THORNE FISHER

Sources W. A. Forbes, 'Biographical notice to Garrod's papers', *The Ibis*, 4th ser., 5 (1881), 1–32 · *The Ibis*, 4th ser., 4 (1880), 146–52 · private information (2004) [Michael Palmer, Zoological Society, London] · *CGPLA Eng. & Wales* (1880)
Likenesses wood-engraving (after photograph by Elliott & Fry), NPG; repro. in *ILN* (8 Nov 1879) [*see illus.*]
Wealth at death under £500: administration, 28 April 1880, *CGPLA Eng. & Wales*

Garrod, Sir Archibald Edward (1857–1936), physician and biochemist, was born in London on 25 November 1857, the fourth and youngest son of Sir Alfred Baring *Garrod (1819–1907), physician to King's College Hospital and an authority on diseases of the joints, and his wife, Elizabeth Ann (*d.* 1891), daughter of Henry Colchester and Elizabeth Sparrow of Ipswich. Garrod was educated at Marlborough College, where he was only a fair student, and at Christ Church, Oxford, where he blossomed and obtained a first class in natural science in 1880. He received his medical training in London at St Bartholomew's Hospital, where he qualified, and afterwards he paid a visit to Vienna.

Shortly after returning to England Garrod was appointed to the medical staff of St Bartholomew's, becoming casualty physician in 1888 and assistant physician in 1903. He also joined the visiting staff of the West London Hospital, the Hospital for Sick Children, Great Ormond Street (where he became full physician in 1899), and the Alexandra Hospital for Children with Hip Disease. Promotion at St Bartholomew's was slow on account of the unusual amount of talent there at the time, and it was not until 1912, at the age of fifty-five, that he was appointed full physician. Garrod took an active part in the First World War, in which he served first on the staff of the 1st London General Hospital at Camberwell; later, in 1915, he was promoted to the rank of temporary colonel in the Army Medical Service and went to Malta, where he was consulting physician to the Mediterranean forces until 1919. For his services he was appointed CMG in 1916 and KCMG in 1918.

On returning to St Bartholomew's in 1919 Garrod became the first director of the new medical unit, but less than a year later in 1920 he was nominated regius professor of medicine at Oxford in succession to Sir William Osler; here he remained for seven years. Garrod had married in 1886 Laura Elisabeth (*d.* 1940), eldest daughter of Sir Thomas *Smith, first baronet, surgeon to St Bartholomew's Hospital. The war exacted a most grievous personal tragedy on the Garrods. Two of their three sons, both medical men, were killed in action, and the youngest son died of influenzal pneumonia at Cologne in 1919, during the months immediately following the war. They had one daughter, Dorothy Annie Elizabeth *Garrod (1892–1968), who became Disney professor of archaeology at Cambridge.

In 1900 Garrod gave the Bradshaw lecture to the Royal

College of Physicians, entitled 'Urinary pigments in their pathological aspects'; and to the same college in 1908 he delivered the epoch-making Croonian lectures, dealing with the incidence and heredity of inborn errors of metabolism; these were published in a revised version in 1909. To the Medical Society of London he read the Lettsomian lecture on glycosuria in 1912; he was Linacre lecturer at Cambridge in 1923, and in 1924 he gave the Harveian oration to the Royal College of Physicians, entitled 'The debt of science to medicine'. At Charing Cross Hospital in 1927 he gave the Huxley lecture on diathesis; this seminal work was published in fuller form as *The Inborn Factors in Disease* (1931). In this book he emphasized in particular the role of individual genetic susceptibility in human disease—a concept that also placed the nature–nurture controversy on a scientific basis.

Garrod's other works include *An Introduction to the Use of the Laryngoscope* (1886) and *A Treatise on Rheumatism and Rheumatoid Arthritis* (1890). His earlier works were mainly clinical, whereas his later books were concerned more with biochemistry. Despite the profound impact of Garrod's work on the subsequent one gene–one enzyme hypothesis of George W. Beadle and Edward Tatum and the pivotal role that genes play in determining protein structure, Garrod always considered himself as a physician interested in chemical pathology and as an investigator of metabolic diseases. Although his work greatly influenced the development of human genetics he never regarded himself as a geneticist.

Osler's high opinion of Garrod was shown by his invitation to Garrod in 1907 to join the editorial board of the *Quarterly Journal of Medicine* (on which he remained until 1927) and to help in the formation of the Association of Physicians of Great Britain. Garrod was co-editor in 1913 with F. E. Batten and Hugh Thursfield of the first edition of *Diseases of Children*, to which he contributed three articles. He also wrote for the *Journal of Pathology* and the *Proceedings* of the Royal Society. He joined the British Medical Association in 1888 and in 1922 was vice-president of the section of medicine. He was a member of the Medical Research Council from 1923 to 1928.

Garrod received many distinctions besides those already named. In 1910 he was elected a fellow of the Royal Society, of which he was vice-president from 1926 to 1928. He received honorary degrees from the universities of Aberdeen, Dublin, Glasgow, Malta, and Padua.

After leaving Oxford, Garrod spent some years in Suffolk; he then moved to Cambridge, to be close to his daughter. He died there on 28 March 1936 at his home, 1 Huntingdon Road, after a short illness and was buried at Melton, Suffolk.

J. D. ROLLESTON, rev. ALEXANDER G. BEARN

Sources F. G. Hopkins, *Obits. FRS*, 2 (1936–8), 225–8 · A. G. Bearn, *Archibald Garrod and the individuality of man* (1993) · *CGPLA Eng. & Wales* (1936) · election certificate, RS
Archives RS
Likenesses photographs, 1910, RS · W. Stoneman, photograph, 1918, NPG · portrait, priv. coll.
Wealth at death £19,204 5s. 7d.: probate, 2 June 1936, *CGPLA Eng. & Wales*

Garrod, Dorothy Annie Elizabeth (1892–1968), archaeologist and prehistorian, was born on 5 May 1892 at 9 Chandos Street, London, the second of four children and only daughter of Sir Archibald Edward *Garrod (1857–1936), physician, later first professor of medicine at St Bartholomew's Hospital and regius professor of medicine at Oxford, and his wife, Laura Elisabeth (d. 1940), daughter of Sir Thomas Smith, first baronet, surgeon. She was initially educated at home, where her governess, Isabel Fry, was the first in a series of inspirational teachers. Birklands School, St Albans, prepared her for entrance to Cambridge University; she read history (1913–16) at Newnham College, with which she began a lifelong association. During the First World War two brothers and her (unofficial) fiancé were killed; her youngest brother died of influenza in 1919 before demobilization. Her own war service (1917–19) with the Catholic Women's League (she converted to Roman Catholicism in 1913) took her to France and Germany, then after the armistice to Malta, where her father was head of war hospitals. It was his suggestion that she occupy her mind among the island's spectacular prehistoric antiquities.

The family's move to Oxford enabled Dorothy Garrod to study for the university diploma in anthropology, gained with distinction in 1921, under the legendary R. R. Marett, who regarded the study of prehistory as no longer an amateur pastime but a branch of science in its own right. She had pledged to compensate her bereaved parents by achieving a life worthy of the family's formidable intellectual tradition (Caton-Thompson, 341). She now found her goal, to be a prehistorian of the palaeolithic, the Old Stone Age.

Through Marett, Dorothy Garrod met the great men of French prehistory and saw the wonders of the painted caves; at Count Bégouën's house, the Abbé Henri Breuil agreed to take her as his pupil at the Institut de Paléontologie Humaine in Paris (1922–4). During these years she gained fieldwork experience at palaeolithic sites including La Quina with Henri Martin, Les Eyzies (Denis Peyrony), and in Corrèze (Jean Bouyssonie). At this time also she attracted the notice of George Grant MacCurdy of Yale University, then planning the creation of his American School of Prehistoric Research (ASPR). With Breuil's encouragement she gathered material for her first book *The Upper Palaeolithic in Britain* (1926), hitherto unsynthesized, for which she was awarded a BSc degree from Oxford.

To Breuil also Garrod owed her own first major excavation at the Devil's Tower, Gibraltar, discovered by him during wartime missions to Spain. Here she found the middle palaeolithic Mousterian flint industry known from her French studies, thereafter a central interest, and five skull fragments of a Neanderthal child. Though she was not a woman given to sentiment, this discovery made a deep impression. She gave the child the resonant name Abel, recording the date of his disinterment, age at death, and probable age before present (22,000 years) in her private photograph album. The rare ability shown in the digging and publication (1928) of the site established her

Dorothy Annie Elizabeth Garrod (1892–1968), by Elliott & Fry, 1920s

place in palaeolithic studies. She was appointed—the only woman and youngest member—to the international commission charged in 1927 with investigating the notorious Glozel affair. The commission considered that artefacts of a supposed ancient civilization found at Glozel (near Vichy) were fraudulent, though counter-claims were made, some—unjustly—against Dorothy Garrod herself. She considered the whole affair absurd, although belief in a 'Glozelian civilization' has proved curiously persistent.

The years 1928–37 were largely concerned with western Asia and determined Garrod's lasting reputation. Prehistoric archaeology in Palestine under British mandate, though still in its infancy, showed signs of great potential. The patronage of MacCurdy and Sir John Linton Myres, both anxious to explore this field of research, was among the factors which led to her excavation in the Judaean cave of Shukba, in the Wadi en-Natuf, for the British School of Archaeology in Jerusalem. Overlying a Mousterian occupation level were human remains associated with a previously unknown mesolithic culture she named—after the wadi—Natufian. Later in 1928 she excavated two caves in southern Kurdistan, Hazar Merd (Mousterian) and Zarzi (late upper palaeolithic). The area, unexplored in prehistoric terms, was as troubled then as later; this apparently held no fears for her, though her small team worked under armed police escort. In Palestine further work at Shukba was abandoned in favour of the need to

excavate a group of caves in the Wadi el-Mughara, Mount Carmel, recently reprieved from destruction by quarrying. Dorothy Garrod was appointed director of the Anglo-American expedition which began work in spring 1929. The series of seven seasons' work at Mount Carmel (1929–34) was to prove the most important in her archaeological career.

At El-Wad cave Garrod found again the distinctive Natufian culture first identified at Shukba, but here in a far richer phase of decorated burials with a complex tool kit of worked stone and bone. Flint blades hafted into bone sickles persuaded her that the Natufians were practising an early form of agriculture. The deepest (Mousterian) of seven archaeological levels in El-Wad corresponded to the uppermost undisturbed level of a further seven in Tabun cave nearby, extending down to a pre-handaxe stone industry at the deepest level. By skilled typological analysis of tens of thousands of stone implements recovered from the Carmel caves she established an almost unbroken cultural sequence, now known to span some 600,000 years or more of human activity, thus imposing order on the hitherto incoherent archaeology of the Levant. In addition to the Natufian burials, the caves contained older human remains. In Tabun cave an adult Mousterian female with Neanderthal characteristics was found, while under her direction T. D. McCown found at Skhul cave a virtual cemetery of ten Mousterian individuals with features more similar to modern humans.

The young Jacquetta Hawkes, at Mount Carmel during the 1932 season, remembered the personal and professional qualities of her director:

> Small (5 ft. 2 in.), composed and neat beside her fellahin workers—girls in brightly ballooning skirts and a few lusty pick-men—her command of them was absolute. When a builder tried to cheat her she overwhelmed him, thumping the table, her normally calm eyes glaring. In the cool peace of the evening after a good dinner there were a few classical records to be played or she might take up her flute. Her talk (low-pitched) was sometimes witty, always congenial.   (DNB)

By the final season (1934) the excavation's surviving daily journal shows how these qualities were tested by the immensity of the task, as anxieties over funding, sickness among her workers, and the privations of daily living all drew on her reserves of courage and humour.

Garrod had begun the Mount Carmel excavation as a research fellow at Newnham College (1929–32); she finished it as director of studies (1933–42). She now returned to Cambridge to prepare her final report (including the faunal analysis by D. M. A. Bate). The Stone Age of Mount Carmel, 1 (1937) established a new standard for its time, recognized by the award of the degree of DSc by Oxford University.

Garrod's continuing interest in palaeolithic migration patterns underlay a survey in Anatolia undertaken for the ASPR in 1938. When bureaucratic delays proved unacceptable, she moved on to Bulgaria, then another largely unexplored area. A short excavation in Bacho Kiro cave established the first prehistoric sequence in eastern Europe, with possible evidence of a westward movement by modern humans across the continent in the early upper palaeolithic. Described as calm, self-assured, perfectly confident, and authoritative, Garrod is remembered by an expedition member, Bruce Howe, as 'unique, rather like a glass of pale fine stony French white wine' (private information, Howe).

On 6 May 1939 Dorothy Garrod was elected Cambridge University's Disney professor of archaeology, becoming the first woman to hold a chair at Cambridge or Oxford. No hint of controversy surrounds this important election. Renowned for her excavations, Garrod was clearly chosen for her qualifications. Although women became eligible for all Cambridge University teaching offices and for membership of faculties and faculty boards in 1926, in 1939 they were still not admissible to degrees, were not yet full members of the university, and thus could not become members of its governing bodies. Garrod's election as professor highlighted this inherent contradiction, accentuated the need for administrative change, and added weight to the argument that women should be allowed to graduate from Cambridge. The event was greeted with joy by the women's colleges and was heralded by the wider community as an immense step towards complete equality with men. Full membership for women in the university followed in 1948.

In 1942 Garrod was recruited to the RAF Medmenham unit for photographic interpretation, where she served as a section officer, mapping the effects of allied bombing: she was remembered as superbly efficient. Returning to Cambridge in 1945, she gained a reputation as a conscientious, hard-working administrator with a strong distaste for petty politics. In 1946 she proposed that archaeology became part of the full Cambridge tripos. Her endless committee labour resulted in the institutionalization of the desired curriculum and full degree in 1948.

Fieldwork was maintained during Garrod's professorial years by excavation in France during long vacations with her closest friends, Germaine Henri-Martin at Fontéchevade (Charente) and Suzanne de St Mathurin at Angles sur l'Anglin (Vienne). On retirement in 1952 she settled permanently in France. Now free to resume her own research, she began the long-postponed task of relating the prehistoric sequence of the Levant with that of Europe. Her plan (before absolute dating methods became available) was to correlate the Quaternary sea levels of the eastern Mediterranean with the periodic glaciations in Europe; the ancient beaches and caves of the Lebanese coast provided evidence no longer existing in Palestine. Five years (1958–63) of strenuous excavation were necessary to produce the correlation she sought, with a relative succession which—though greatly extended by modern dating methods—remains valid. Nevertheless her health was overtaxed in the process and continued to decline. In June 1968, while writing up her Lebanese work for publication and shortly after receiving—again as the first woman—the gold medal of the Society of Antiquaries, she suffered a stroke from which she did not recover. She died at the Hope House (Catholic) nursing home in Cambridge on 18 December 1968. Her ashes were buried in her parents' grave at Melton, Suffolk.

Dorothy Garrod's reputation, and appreciation of her pioneering work in prehistoric archaeology, has increased as research in her subject has grown during the years since her death. The excavation techniques of her day enabled her to see long stratigraphic sequences and define basic frameworks on which her successors could safely build. Through her work in the Levantine caves, she identified and addressed crucial questions that still preoccupy prehistorians: the appearance of modern humans and extinction of Neanderthals during the middle palaeolithic, and the later mesolithic transition from nomadic hunter-gathering to settlement and agriculture. Her publications were prompt, thorough, and prolific (over one hundred academic papers and articles), and showed her continual readiness to revise her opinions and to learn. Her election as professor at Cambridge came to be celebrated as a milestone in the struggle to gain access to higher education for women in England. Using her degree plan, Cambridge has become a world centre for prehistoric studies.

In addition to her MA (Cantab.) and DSc (Oxon.) degrees Garrod received honorary doctorates from Toulouse and Poitiers. She was a fellow of the British Academy (1952), the Royal Anthropological Institute (Huxley memorial medal, 1962), and the Society of Antiquaries (gold medal, 1968). She was appointed CBE (1965). She was unmarried.

JANE CALLANDER

Sources G. Caton-Thompson, 'Dorothy Annie Elizabeth Garrod, 1892–1968', *PBA*, 55 (1969), 338–61 · O. Bar-Yosef and J. Callander, 'Dorothy Annie Elizabeth Garrod', *Women in archaeology: the first generation, the pioneers*, ed. G. M. Cohen and M. S. Joukowsky [forthcoming] · P. J. Smith, 'From "small, dark and alive" to "cripplingly shy": Dorothy Garrod as the first woman professor at Cambridge', *Antiquity*, 74 (2000), 131–6 · P. J. Smith, J. Callander, P. G. Bahn, and G. Pinçon, 'Dorothy Garrod in words and pictures', *Antiquity*, 71 (1997), 265–70 · *DNB* · private information (2004) [B. Howe, F. Mason, P. J. Smith] · B. Boyd and W. Davies, 'Dorothy A. E. Garrod: a provisional bibliography', *Dorothy Garrod and the progress of the palaeolithic*, ed. W. Davies and R. Charles (1999), 277–82 · d. cert.

Archives Bibliothèque du Musée des Antiquités Nationales, St Germain-en-Laye, France, Fonds Suzanne Cassou de St Mathurin · U. Oxf., Pitt Rivers Museum, photographs (mainly negatives) taken during excavations |FILM BFI NFTVA |SOUND BL NSA

Likenesses photograph, *c.*1913, Newnham College, Cambridge · Elliott & Fry, photograph, 1920–29, NPG [*see illus.*] · photograph, 1928, Musée des Antiquités Nationales, St Germain-en-Laye, France · photograph, *c.*1942, priv. coll. · photograph, 1960–69, priv. coll.

Garrod, Sir (Alfred) Guy Roland (1891–1965), air force officer, was born in London on 13 April 1891, the third son of Herbert Baring Garrod, barrister-at-law of Hampstead, London, and his wife, Lucy Florence Colchester. Among his immediate forebears were no fewer than three fellows of the Royal Society: his grandfather, Sir Alfred Baring Garrod, and two uncles, Sir Archibald Edward Garrod KCMG and Alfred Henry Garrod, all three of whom were distinguished physicians. He was educated at Bradfield College and University College, Oxford, where he held an open classical scholarship. He obtained a second class in classical moderations in 1912 and a third in *literae humaniores* in 1914. His outside interests included the Officers' Training Corps (OTC) and the Oxford Union Dramatic Society.

At the outbreak of the First World War, Garrod joined the army. Helped no doubt by his OTC experience and his skill as a rifle shot, which gained him a bronze and a silver medal at Bisley, he was commissioned into the Leicestershire regiment in August 1914. He was wounded near Ypres in November 1914 and invalided to the United Kingdom. Later he learned to fly and was seconded to the Royal Flying Corps in 1915. He spent most of his wartime service overseas. He was thrice mentioned in dispatches and awarded the DFC and MC. On 23 August 1918 he married Cicely Evelyn Bray ARRC (*d.* 1960), a nursing sister, the daughter of John Bray, estate agent, of St Leonards, Sussex. They had a son and a daughter.

When war ended, Garrod planned a career in industry, but Sir Hugh Trenchard, who was at this time assembling the elements of the peacetime Royal Air Force, persuaded him to return, and in August 1919 he accepted a permanent commission in the Royal Air Force. Between the wars he filled a wide variety of posts. He was a natural selection for Staff College appointments and was a student at the Royal Naval Staff College, Greenwich (1921–2), the Imperial Defence College (1933), and the Royal Air Force Staff College (1923–7), where he was a member of the directing staff. From 1928 to 1930 he was chief instructor to the air squadron at Oxford University; he was a staff officer in Iraq (1931–2) and he became deputy director of organization at the Air Ministry in 1934. He was promoted to air commodore in 1936.

By the outbreak of the Second World War, Garrod, now an air vice-marshal, was serving in the Air Ministry as director of equipment, the duties of which included ensuring that hundreds of thousands of items of technical and other equipment (from barrack stores to complete engines and airframes) were available in due proportion to Royal Air Force units all over the world. In July 1940 Garrod succeeded to the appointment which was undoubtedly the climax of his service career—that of air member for training, a new post on the Air Council created to run the vitally important programme of air force training. In 1934 the personnel strength of the Royal Air Force was 30,000. By September 1939 it had grown to 174,000 and by the end of the war the total, including dominion and allied personnel, came to well over 1 million. Most of these men and women were trained to exacting standards, and nearly 200,000 of them were aircrew. This was a massive achievement which played a significant part in the allied victories in the air. Of course the programme was too vast to be confined to Britain; it involved, for example, creating no fewer than 300 flying training schools. So from the start the training programme was conceived as a Commonwealth effort, with flying schools in Canada, Rhodesia, South Africa, and Australasia. As air member for training on the Air Council, Garrod played a leading role in these developments.

In 1943 Garrod was posted overseas, where his appointments included deputy allied air commander-in-chief, south-east Asia, and (briefly) at the end of the war, commander-in-chief, Royal Air Force, Mediterranean and Middle East. After the war Garrod served as Royal Air Force military representative on the military staff committee of the United Nations and head of the Royal Air Force delegation, Washington. He retired in 1948 with the rank of air chief marshal.

Garrod went on to hold several business posts, wrote extensively on Royal Air Force subjects, and joined the advisory panel on official military histories of the war. He became warden of his old school, Bradfield College (1959), an honorary fellow of University College, Oxford (1947), and an honorary steward at Westminster Abbey. The University of Aberdeen awarded him an honorary LLD. He was appointed OBE in 1932, GBE in 1948, CB in 1941, and KCB in 1943.

Garrod was a man of many parts. As a young man he was an excellent athlete, winning his half blues at Oxford for cross-country running and rifle shooting. He was a shot of international class, representing Britain in competitions in the early 1920s. He had an abiding interest in music and was an excellent violinist.

In appearance, Garrod was of average height, softly spoken, with a distinctly academic air, though there was nothing academic about his military activities. He was approachable to the young and was an enthusiast for pressing new ideas to practical conclusions. He made a great success of his career as an airman but would have been equally at home as an academic or as a professional man. In conversation Garrod was restrained, friendly, and courteous. After his first wife's death in 1960 he married in 1961 Doris Eleanor Baker, the widow of Samuel J. Baker. He died on 3 January 1965 at his home in Lea Sling Lane, Malvern, Worcestershire, survived by his second wife.

M. J. DEAN, *rev.*

Sources *The Times* (5 Jan 1965) · *The Times* (8 Jan 1965) · *The Times* (12 Jan 1965) · private information (1981) · Burke, *Peerage* (1959) · *CGPLA Eng. & Wales* (1965)
Archives FILM IWM FVA, actuality footage
Likenesses R. R. Thomson, oils, 1943, IWM
Wealth at death £30,562: probate, 9 March 1965, *CGPLA Eng. & Wales*

Garrod, Heathcote William (1878–1960), literary and classical scholar, was born at Wells, Somerset, on 21 January 1878, the fifth of six children of Charles William Garrod, solicitor, and his wife, Louisa Ashby. From Bath College he went with an exhibition to Balliol College, Oxford, where in 1899 he gained a first class in honour moderations and won the Hertford scholarship and a Craven scholarship; in 1900 he won a Gaisford prize and in 1901 a first class in *literae humaniores*, the Newdigate prize, and a prize fellowship at Merton College. He did some classics teaching at Corpus Christi College (1902–4) until he was elected to a tutorial fellowship at Merton. With a few short breaks he lived in Merton from 1904 until his death.

During the early part of his career Garrod concerned

himself in the main with classical scholarship. He published editions of Statius (1906) and of the second book of Manilius's *Astronomicon* (1911), and the *Oxford Book of Latin Verse* (1912), together with many contributions to learned periodicals. He was for many years an editor of the *Journal of Philology*. During the First World War he served in the Ministry of Munitions from 1915, and then for the last few months of the conflict in the Ministry of Reconstruction; his efforts were highly praised by his superiors in the civil service. He was appointed CBE in 1918.

On his return to Merton, although he continued his teaching for classical honour moderations, Garrod became increasingly interested in English literature, and in 1925 resigned his tutorship for a research fellowship in English. His *Wordsworth: Lectures and Essays* (1923) won him much esteem in wider circles and led directly to his election to the professorship of poetry at Oxford (1923–8), which fell vacant on the death of W. P. Ker. Thereafter he published several critical studies and collections of essays and lectures on various English authors: *The Profession of Poetry* (1929, lectures delivered during his professorship); *Poetry and the Criticism of Life* (1931, lectures delivered at Harvard while he was Charles Eliot Norton professor); *Keats: a Critical Appreciation* (1926); and *Collins* (1928). His chief contribution to English scholarship came in 1939 with the publication of his edition of Keats in the series Oxford English Texts; the second edition of this work, issued in 1958, remains an indispensable book for Keats scholars.

As well as this critical output Garrod produced original work: *Oxford Poems* (1912); *Worms and Epitaphs* (1919); *Poems from the French* (1925); *Epigrams* (1946); and in 1950 a slim volume of *belles-lettres* entitled *Genius loci*. His learned interest in Renaissance scholarship enabled him to do valuable work on the muniments, the library regulations, and the ancient painted glass of Merton. It culminated in his completion, with Mrs Helen Mary Allen, of an edition by her late husband Percy Stafford Allen, the *Letters of Erasmus*.

In his early years Garrod delighted in daring and ingenious emendations of classical texts which did not always win acceptance. The solid worth of his scholarship shows itself in his editions of Statius and Manilius, although the latter was severely criticized by A. E. Housman in volume 5 of his own edition of Manilius in 1930. The *Oxford Book of Latin Verse* brought Garrod wide acclaim, and his subsequent editing of the *Letters of Erasmus* brought into play his qualities of sustained scholarship and his profound learning; it is likely to have more enduring value than his classical work.

Garrod, who remained through his life a devoted disciple of Wordsworth and Matthew Arnold, brought to his literary criticism great seriousness of judgement. He rejected what he thought artificial and pretentious, and poetry which made no claims on the deepest human feelings had no appeal for him. Yet the strong moral influence of Wordsworth and Arnold, which ran through all his work, was tempered by an irresistible tendency to mischief and impish witticisms. Garrod was never dull. His style, which perhaps owed something to Hazlitt, a critic whom he held in high esteem, was lively and alert, and was full of idiosyncrasies and tricks, daring colloquialisms, and obtrusive parentheses. His chief passion was good poetry and he liked to praise it, but his admiration always had what he called 'bone and gristle'. It never sprawled. He could moreover be highly critical of work that seemed to him to be based on falseness of feeling or shallowness of thought. A notable example of this was his lecture on A. E. Housman, included in *The Profession of Poetry*, where he derided 'the false pastoralism' of *A Shropshire Lad*. In his own poetry there was the same mixture of moods as was to be found in his prose: his epigrams were neat and witty; his lyrics romantic and emotional; in both he achieved considerable technical skill. The variety of his learning and the liveliness of his manner were well illustrated in a collection of essays brought together after his death by John Jones and published in 1963 under the title *The Study of Good Letters*. In this judicious selection the severity of Garrod's scholarship was tempered by his wit and humanity, while beneath the bantering cleverness of his light-hearted essays were persistent undertones of his moral sensibility. The differing elements in Garrod's personality—the cleverness, the caustic wit, the profoundly Romantic and moral feeling, the respect for exact scholarship—which sometimes seemed at war with one another, achieved a true harmony in his edition of Keats. Here all his powers were deployed, and alongside the exact scholarship is a profound depth of feeling for the subject, which informed the whole work.

For more than fifty years Garrod lived as an unmarried Oxford don, never away from Merton for long. He took great delight in holidays with Merton friends, young and old, mainly in the Lakes, in Devon, and in Dorset. In Oxford the meadows saw him on most days exercising a succession of much loved and much spoilt dogs. Otherwise he rarely moved further afield than Blackwell's bookshop; there his figure was well known, standing firm upon small pointed feet, of medium stature, a slight tendency to obesity, his impressive head crowned with a trilby hat worn back to front, cigar held between the first two fingers of his right hand, intent upon a book. More than most Oxford dons, however, he seemed at home in any kind of company, and understood what went on in the world. In his own college he was a presiding genius, and in friendship he was generous and unselfish, asking nothing in return. Other dons, undergraduates, Merton men of all generations, and friends from wider circles were drawn irresistibly to his rooms as to the centre of the college.

Garrod received the honorary degrees of DLitt at Durham (1930) and LLD at Edinburgh (1953). He was elected FBA in 1931 and an honorary fellow of Merton in 1955. He died at the Acland Nursing Home, Oxford, on 25 December 1960.　　　GEORGE MALLABY, *rev.* MARK POTTLE

Sources *The Times* (28 Dec 1960) · *List of the writings of H. W. Garrod* (1947) · *Postmaster* (Dec 1961) · J. Jones, 'Heathcote William Garrod, 1878–1960', *PBA*, 48 (1962), 357–70 · personal knowledge (1971) · private information (1971) · *CGPLA Eng. & Wales* (1961)
Archives Merton Oxf., papers · Yale U., Beinecke L., materials collected, incl. notes, for his work on Keats | U. Birm. L., corresp. with C. T. Onions

Likenesses W. Stoneman, photograph, 1932, NPG · R. Moynihan, oils, 1947, Merton Oxf. · M. Bone, portrait
Wealth at death £6639 7s. 6d.: probate, 10 March 1961, CGPLA Eng. & Wales

Garrod, Lawrence Paul (1895–1979), bacteriologist, was born on 7 December 1895 at 71 Mountview Road, Stroud Green, Hornsey, London, the younger son (there were no daughters) of Cubbitt Garrod, draper, of Exeter, and his wife, Gertrude Dwelley Davey. He was descended from a Suffolk farming family that produced a number of distinguished physicians, including Sir Alfred Baring *Garrod, Alfred Henry *Garrod, and Sir Archibald Edward *Garrod. His brother died in childhood and he was brought up as an only child. He was educated at Sidcot School and left in 1913 to spend several months in Germany, where he founded his grasp of the language, before going up to King's College, Cambridge, in 1914. He entered St Bartholomew's Hospital (Bart's) as a clinical student in 1916 but interrupted his studies to serve as a surgeon sub-lieutenant with the Royal Naval Volunteer Reserve, in 1917–18.

Returning to Bart's after the war, Garrod completed his clinical studies with distinction, winning the senior prize, the Brackenbury scholarship in medicine, in 1919. He graduated BA from Cambridge in 1918, MRCS and LRCP in 1920, and MA MB and BChir in 1921. In 1922 Garrod married Marjorie, daughter of Bedford Pierce MD FRCP, medical superintendent of The Retreat at York. They had a daughter, who spent the war years working in his department, and three sons.

Garrod worked in clinical medicine for five years, passing the MRCP in 1923, before his interests turned decisively to bacteriology. His MD thesis on the use of inhibitors in selective culture media was written in 1932 (he gained the degree in 1938), before the momentous discovery of prontosil in 1935 opened the era of effective antimicrobial chemotherapy. This was the subject with which Garrod quickly became identified and on which, during almost fifty years of dramatic advances, he was the premier British authority. He spent almost the whole of his professional life at Bart's, and became senior demonstrator of pathology in 1925, reader in bacteriology in 1934, and professor of bacteriology in 1937. He was elected FRCP in 1936. After his retirement in 1961, when he became emeritus professor, he held the part-time post of honorary consultant in chemotherapy at the Royal Postgraduate Medical School.

Early in his career Garrod's investigations centred on antiseptic agents, about which comparatively little was then known. He elucidated their action and efficacy and developed a new test which was rapidly adopted as a British standard method. During the Second World War, Bart's was evacuated to Hill End Hospital and there Garrod conducted important work on hospital cross-infection, particularly with streptococci, in the large unit for plastic surgery and burns.

However, it is for his work on antibiotics that Garrod is best remembered. When the therapeutic properties of penicillin were first recognized, Bart's was one of the first four hospitals outside Oxford to pioneer its study. It was a time of unusual effort, reward, and excitement, as patients recovered from previously incurable infections. Garrod was a member of the original Medical Research Council committee on clinical trials of penicillin. He later became chairman of the Medical Research Council committee on clinical trials of antibiotics, and he served on several expert committees on antimicrobial chemotherapy of the World Health Organization and of the Department of Health and Social Security. From 1965 to 1970 he was chairman of the antibiotics panel of the committee on medical aspects of food policy.

Garrod was a skilful writer and his output was prodigious. In addition to his books with various co-authors—*Recent Advances in Pathology* (1932), *Hospital Infection* (1960), and *Antibiotic and Chemotherapy* (1963)—he wrote some 200 scientific papers and over 600 unsigned editorials for the *British Medical Journal*. His pungent comments, wit, and style were instantly recognizable. From 1951 to 1957 he was editor of the *British Journal of Experimental Pathology*.

At the time he retired in 1961 Garrod had been bacteriologist to St Bartholomew's Hospital since 1934, bacteriologist of the City of London since 1936, and consultant in antibiotics to the army since 1948. He was president of the pathology section of the Royal Society of Medicine from 1954 to 1956 and president of the Institute of Medical Laboratory Technology from 1949 to 1953. He also served as vice-president of the British Medical Association.

While he was warm and generous to those who knew him well, Garrod's tall figure presented a forbidding aspect to the world at large and his ability to deliver devastating dismissals may have had something to do with the paucity of conventional honours he received. Some acclaimed his worth: he was a Lister fellow of the Royal College of Physicians of Edinburgh, an honorary alumnus of the University of Louvain, an honorary LLD of the University of Glasgow (1965), and an honorary fellow of the Royal College of Pathologists (1979). He died on 11 September 1979 at the Royal Berkshire Hospital, Reading, Berkshire.

FRANCIS O'GRADY and PAMELA M. WATERWORTH, rev.

Sources BMJ (22 Sept 1979) · Nature (14 Feb 1980) · personal knowledge (1986) · private information (1986)
Archives Wellcome L., corresp. with Sir Ernst Chain
Wealth at death £90,189: probate, 20 Dec 1979, CGPLA Eng. & Wales

Garrow, Sir William (1760–1840), barrister and judge, was born on 13 April 1760 at Monken Hadley, Middlesex, the youngest son of David Garrow (1715–1805), an ordained minister of the Church of England who maintained a boarding-school at Monken Hadley, and his wife, Sarah Lowndes, of Camberwell, Surrey. He was educated at his father's school until, aged fifteen, he was articled to a London attorney named Thomas Southouse, of Milk Street, Cheapside. Three years later, in November 1778, he was admitted a student of Lincoln's Inn. He was called to the bar on 27 November 1783. About 1780 Garrow entered into a relationship with Sarah Dore (d. 1808). It was a connection formed 'somewhat irregularly', a contemporary was later to say (Farington, *Diary*, 11.4017). Indeed, they were not to be married until 17 March 1793, a decade after Sarah had borne two children: David William (1781–1827) and Eliza Sophia (1783–1857). They also raised a son (William Arthur Dorehill) from Sarah's earlier relationship with Arthur William Moyes Hill, later second marquess of Downshire.

Garrow came to prominence early in his career. He had trained himself for criminal as well as civil practice by regular attendance at the Old Bailey, and he enjoyed immediate success. His ability as defence counsel to undermine what appeared to be unassailable prosecution cases by effective cross-examinations was soon noticed in the London press: one paper predicted after a particularly notable success that he would go 'rapidly onwards in his profession' (*London Chronicle*, 15 Dec 1784). He was also admired for his ability to prosecute felony cases and to present evidence clearly and coherently through examinations in chief. One of his first cases as prosecuting counsel, in January 1784, two months after being called to the bar, was to be recalled in obituaries and memoirs after his death for the 'cogent and luminous' quality of the argument he made on a complex point of law against two of the leading barristers of the day (*The Times*, 7 Nov 1840). At the same time Garrow had developed a reputation as a persuasive speaker at the meetings of the debating societies that flourished in London in the early 1780s. Despite his youth and inexperience, these evident legal and oratorical skills—and his whig political sympathies—led to his being selected by Charles James Fox to represent him before the House of Commons in his petition to be allowed to take his seat as member for Westminster following the election of 1784. Garrow's two-hour speech on that occasion was widely praised as being 'to the advantage of his clients as to his own honour and credit' (*Parliamentary History*, 858).

Garrow was fortunate in the timing of his entry into the profession in that, as well as building a career in the civil courts, he was able to develop a practice at the Old Bailey and on the home circuit because opportunities for barristers to prosecute and to act for defendants in felony cases increased in the 1780s, half a century after lawyers had first been allowed to act in criminal cases but in which few accused and even fewer victims had chosen to seek their services. By the 1780s increasing numbers of prosecutors and defendants were seeking the assistance of barristers. What those lawyers could do for their clients, especially those acting for the defence, was limited by a rule of court that prevented them speaking directly to the jury: they were allowed to examine and cross-examine witnesses, but defendants were still required to make their own defence. These constraints emphasized the importance of defence counsel's cross-examination as a way of uncovering weaknesses in prosecution evidence and of probing the credibility of hostile witnesses. Within a few years Garrow replaced John Silvester as leader of the fledgeling Old Bailey bar because the promise of his early career was amply fulfilled, particularly the skill with which, as a defence counsel, he was able to exploit the opportunities

to undermine prosecution cases provided by the rules governing the trial of felons. He was by all accounts a commanding presence in the courtroom, and the speed of his mind, the power of his speech, and his aggressive advocacy of his clients' rights made him a formidable opponent. He showed himself willing in cross-examining to do bruising battle with prosecutors and recalcitrant witnesses, particularly with those who stood to earn reward money by the conviction of his clients. His aggressiveness and what some observers considered the coarseness of his language helped to promote the new tone and intention that had been emerging in the defence of prisoners in the criminal courts since the middle decades of the century, an alteration in the conduct of trials that rested on a more active commitment to advocacy on the part of defence counsel. Over time their interventions on behalf of their clients encouraged an elaboration of the law of evidence and a clearer sense of the rights of men and women on trial for felonies, including their right to be presumed innocent until convicted by a jury beyond reasonable doubt.

In the vast majority of his cases at the Old Bailey in the decade 1783–93 Garrow acted for the defendant, and much of his reputation was based on his revealing cross-examinations. He was no less skilled, however, as a prosecutor and he was to draw on those talents most emphatically after 1793, when he was named king's counsel and ceased to practise regularly at the Old Bailey. He continued his profitable career in the civil courts, but in the tumultuous last decade of the century, with Britain at war with France and radicalism challenging at home, Garrow's legal career took on a more political character. He had begun ten years earlier as a friend of Charles James Fox; with the onset of the war against the French republic, he followed Burke and other whigs into support for the Pitt administration. His appointment as KC was a consequence of that, and the government often employed him in prosecuting alleged treasonable activities; he was counsel for the crown in the prosecutions of Thomas Hardy and John Horne Tooke, for example, and in other treason cases in the 1790s.

In 1805 Garrow was brought into parliament by the administration as the member for Gatton and, at the election in the following year, for Callington. He made no mark in those parliaments, but his political connections and his skill as an advocate brought him continuing advancement in the legal profession. In 1806 he was appointed solicitor-general to the prince of Wales and advanced to attorney-general in the following year, thanks to the recommendation of Thomas Erskine, a leading lawyer of the age, who said of Garrow on this occasion that 'he knows more of the real justice and policy of everything connected with the criminal law than any man I am acquainted with' (*Correspondence of George, Prince of Wales*, 7.268). Further advancement came under the Regency, when he was named successively solicitor-general (1812–13) and attorney-general (1813–17). He was also returned to parliament during those years for the borough of Eye. In

1817 he was named as a puisne baron of the court of exchequer.

Garrow did not distinguish himself either as a parliamentarian or as a law officer of the crown. He remained implacably opposed to any reform of the criminal law at a time when its heavy reliance on capital punishment was coming under attack by Sir Samuel Romilly and others. Nor was he to be a great success as a judge, except at the Old Bailey and on the crown side of the assize courts. He had never mastered the deeper complexities of the civil law, and his career on the bench was marred by stories of his failures and inadequacies. It is striking that at his retirement from the bench in 1832 and after his death, what was recalled most vividly in memoirs and obituaries was his skill as a barrister. In a sketch of his life the *Law Review* found a good deal to criticize in his work as a law officer and as a judge, but recalled his career as 'a great, a very great advocate' who had 'reached the lead of the Old Bailey practice and domineered without a competitor at the bar' (*Law Review*, 1, 1844, 318–20).

Garrow died on 24 September 1840 at home at Pegwell Cottage, near Ramsgate, Kent. He was buried in the churchyard of St Lawrence, Thanet. A generation later, when he had been entirely forgotten, Garrow's skill in the courtroom became evident to Robert Louis Stevenson and his wife, Fanny, when, wanting to learn something about eighteenth-century trials, they read large numbers of the Old Bailey sessions papers from the 1780s. They became absorbed, Mrs Stevenson reported later, 'not so much in the trials as in following the brilliant career of a Mr. Garrow … whose subtle cross-examination of witnesses and masterly, if sometimes startling, methods of arriving at the truth seemed more thrilling to us than any novel' (Stevenson, prefatory note).   J. M. BEATTIE

Sources *The correspondence of George, prince of Wales, 1770–1812*, ed. A. Aspinall, 8 vols. (1963–71) • Farington, *Diary* • T. Hague, *A letter to William Garrow* (1808?) • *Law Review*, 1 (1844–5), 318–28 • 'Judicial characters, no. V: Sir William Garrow', *Legal Observer*, 3 (1831–2), 253–6 • A. Polson, *Law and lawyers, or, Sketches and illustrations of legal history and biography*, 2 vols. (1840), 1.216–8 • *The proceedings on the king's commission of the peace* [Old Bailey sessions papers] • *Parliamentary history of England*, 24 (1815) • R. L. Stevenson, *Kidnapped* (1993) • HoP, *Commons, 1790–1820*, 4.5–7 • *The Times* (7 Nov 1840) • J. M. Beattie, 'Scales of justice: defense counsel and the English criminal trial in the eighteenth and nineteenth centuries', *Law and History Review*, 9/2 (1991), 221–67 • S. Landsman, 'The rise of the contentious spirit: adversary procedure in eighteenth-century England', *Cornell Law Review*, 75/3 (1990), 498–609 • J. H. Langbein, 'The criminal trial before the lawyers', *University of Chicago Law Review*, 45/2 (1978), 263–316 • J. H. Langbein, 'Shaping the eighteenth century criminal trial: a view from the Ryder sources', *University of Chicago Law Review*, 50/1 (1983), 1–136 • D. Lemmings, *Professors of the law* (2000) • A. N. May, 'Reluctant advocates: the legal profession and the Prisoner's Counsel Act of 1836', *Criminal justice in the old world and the new*, ed. G. T. Smith, A. N. May, and S. Devereaux (Toronto, 1998), 183–207 • DNB • LMA, microfilm roll X096/231

Likenesses J. Purden, stipple, pubd 1801, BM, NPG • R. Dunkarton, mezzotint, pubd 1810 (after A. W. Denis), NPG • G. Harlow, oils, Lincoln's Inn, London • G. Hayter, group portrait, oils (*The trial of Queen Caroline*, 1820), NPG • G. Hayter, sketch, NPG • stipple, BM, NPG

Garry [*née* Campbell], **Flora Macdonald** (1900–2000), broadcaster and poet, was born on 30 September 1900 at Mains of Auchmunziel, New Deer, Aberdeenshire, the second of the four children of Archibald William Campbell (1869–1947) and his wife, Helen Mary, *née* Metcalfe (1873–1955). The Campbells were of farming stock, but 'they weren't really meant to be farming people at all, they were both writers' (Garry and Olson, 32). Archie Campbell was farming columnist for the Aberdeen *Press and Journal* and Helen Campbell was a writer of radio plays.

Flora Campbell was 'steeped in farming tradition', including the Buchan dialect. While it was so different from classroom English that she 'had to speak two languages' she nevertheless lived happily in 'two worlds', 'in whatever one I happened to be in at the time' (Garry and Olson, 30). Farm life lacked electricity and piped water but not culture: 'We liked to know the prevailing climate of opinion … we devoured the daily and weekly papers' (*Collected Poems*, 76). Discussion was in Scots, which the young Flora was encouraged to speak.

From New Deer school and Peterhead Academy, Campbell went to Aberdeen University, where she graduated, with honours, in English in 1922. After teaching practice at New Deer and Peterhead she taught at Dumfries Academy and at Strichen, Aberdeenshire, before marrying the distinguished physiologist Robert Campbell Garry (1900–1993) on 6 July 1928. Marriage meant leaving schoolteaching, but she continued to give talks on cultural subjects to varied audiences. From the early 1920s she broadcast these talks and her own stories, and acted in radio dramas written by her mother and herself.

Flora Garry began writing and publishing poetry in the 1940s, but full recognition came only in 1974, when her poems first appeared in book form as *Bennygoak and other Poems*. Women played an important part in the tradition of Scotland's north-east regional poetry and Garry's work continues a line that began with Mary Symon and Violet Jacob. Her vigorous Buchan Scots captures local landscapes and weather, most vividly in 'Ae Mair Haist' and 'Spring on a Buchan Farm'. She deals unsentimentally with country folk and their ways, depicting the reticence bred of generations of struggle with the land. Women's changing experience and consciousness are central interests. Though no longer resigned to the narrowness of their lives her female speakers cannot yet break free of it. In 'Bennygoak' a daughter sacrifices herself unwillingly for her widowed mother, while in 'Suffie, Last of the Buchan Fishwives' the fisher-women bait lines, tramp the country selling fish, and, afraid for their men folk in bad weather,

> harken tull the heerican at midnicht
> Caul' wi dreid.

The traditional antipathy of the farming community to fishing people here turns to admiration for a specifically female kind of heroism. 'Figures Receding' is elegiac, lamenting the passing of kinds of awareness—of land, weather, plants, animals—that do not depend on schooling or literacy but on 'yer finger-eyns, yer instincts an yer een'. Such 'lear o anidder kind' has been especially important in Scotland, since much that is characteristic in the culture has been preserved and transmitted through popular tradition and vernacular speech.

Garry's *Collected Poems* was published in 1995, and she was awarded an honorary degree by Aberdeen University in 1999. She died on 16 June 2000 at Dalginross House Nursing Home, Comrie, in Perthshire. She was cremated at Perth on 26 June, and her ashes buried at the cemetery atop the hill of Culsh, New Deer, on 30 September.

COLIN MILTON

Sources F. Garry and E. Olson, interview, 4 Jan 1986, U. Aberdeen, MS 3620/I/41 [interview for Aberdeen University oral history archive] · private information (2004) [Elizabeth Bell, granddaughter] · *Flora Garry: collected poems* (1995) · D. Kynoch, 'The art of Flora Garry', *Leopard* (Feb 1993) · R. C. Garry, *Life in physiology*, ed. D. Smith (1992) · F. Garry, *Bennygoak and other poems* (1975) · b. cert. · m. cert. · d. cert. · gravestone [A. W. Campbell] · gravestone [H. M. Campbell]

Archives priv. coll., personal and literary MSS · U. Aberdeen, transcript of interview by Elizabeth Olson

Likenesses photographs (aged thirteen and twenty-five), priv. coll.; repro. in *Flora Garry: collected poems*, 10, 12

Garscadden, Kathleen Mary Evelyn (1897–1991), radio broadcaster, was born on 18 February 1897 at 13 Nithsdale Gardens, Crossmyloof, Glasgow, the daughter of George Garscadden, accountant and businessman, and his wife, Maggie Jane Vint. She was educated at Hutchesons Girls' Grammar School, Glasgow, before moving to London to train as a professional singer under Sir Henry Wood. She did not pursue her goal of becoming an opera singer and returned to Glasgow.

Garscadden's broadcasting career began when she acted as a singer, pianist, and announcer on her father's amateur radio station (5MG), located at 141 Bath Street, Glasgow. This station was later bought by the BBC when opening its first Scottish station (5SC) on 6 March 1923 at 202 Bath Street, the location of her father's business premises. Garscadden was invited by Herbert Carruthers (the BBC's first station director in Scotland, and organist in the church choir in which she sang) to join the BBC as a programme assistant in 1923. She sang in concerts and was involved in schools broadcasting, but the primary outlet for her talents was *Children's Hour*, which was broadcast daily at 5 p.m. BBC local stations were also opened in Edinburgh, Aberdeen, and Dundee, transmitting their own children's programmes. Broadcasting was local because of the limited power of the transmitters.

In the early years BBC staff became the friendly unseen 'aunts' and 'uncles' to young listeners. Garscadden was originally referred to as Auntie Cyclone by her fellow broadcasters because she sometimes read the weather forecasts. She was accompanied by Uncle Bert (Herbert Carruthers), Uncle Mungo (Mungo Dewar), and Uncle Alex (A. H. S. Paterson). She recalled that the BBC disapproved of her being called Auntie Cyclone because it was thought this might confuse children, and so she later became known simply as Auntie Kathleen. Her popularity turned her into a public celebrity. Crowds gathered at the studio to obtain her autograph, and she received a large volume of correspondence from listeners.

Garscadden retained vivid recollections of the excitement at hearing her voice transmitted from the studio in Bath Street. She produced serial plays, including the Scottish version of *Toytown*, and was also involved in the Radio Circle, a forerunner of Children in Need, which helped children's charities and kept the BBC in contact with its young listeners. On 1 November 1928 the Edinburgh and Dundee stations began to take *Children's Hour* from Glasgow, which Garscadden presented. The programme became an important fixture in the programme schedules because the BBC recognized that young listeners constituted its future adult audience. Garscadden believed in the Reithian concept that radio could be used to inform and educate, not just to entertain the audience. The coverage of music, literature, history, art, geography, and natural history was certainly appreciated by the programme's young and not so young audience—in many homes the family listened together.

Following the outbreak of the Second World War regional programme services disappeared and were replaced by a single Home Service from London, in which Scotland contributed material to *Children's Hour*. In 1940 Garscadden was appointed as *Children's Hour* organizer for Scotland, a post she held until her retirement. Favourite serials first broadcast during the war years included *Tammy Troot* and *Down at the Mains*. A separate fifty-minute Scottish *Children's Hour* was restored after the war with the introduction of the Scottish Home Service on 29 July 1945. Programme output was wide-ranging and included dramatized adaptations of classics, outside broadcasts, features on famous Scots, and music from the Glasgow Orpheus Choir. Wireless created many radio personalities, and Garscadden gave opportunities to aspiring actors, musicians, comedians, and entertainers. Many went on to become household names within and beyond Scotland. They included the actors Gordon Jackson, Fulton MacKay, John Grieve, Molly Weir, and Tom Conti; singers such as Moira Anderson and Sydney Devine; the entertainers Stanley Baxter, Jimmy Logan, and Rikki Fulton; and the impressionist Janet Brown. Andrew Stewart, an early participant on *Children's Hour*, went on to become controller of BBC Scotland in 1957.

Garscadden retired in June 1960 after thirty-seven years' service with the BBC. On 1 July members of the Broadcasting Council for Scotland placed on record their warm appreciation of her outstandingly fine record of service. She left the BBC at a time when children's programmes on radio were being scaled down because of television's increasingly powerful counter-attraction. She returned to give a talk about her childhood in the final *Children's Hour* programme in 1964. She continued to sing and give piano lessons to children in her small flat at Victoria Place, Station Road, Milngavie, and also took part in occasional programmes. She was presented to the queen in 1983 at the diamond jubilee of BBC children's broadcasting.

Garscadden was unusual in having worked during her long career as a presenter, broadcaster, programme organizer, and producer. She helped to inform, inspire, and stimulate that boundless world of the imagination in children fostered by the intimacy of radio. Her vast programme output complemented the formal work of the classroom. She conveyed her love of children over the years, and was a natural broadcaster who adhered to high professional standards. She was a legendary character in Scottish broadcasting, discovering many well-known personalities and endearing herself to generations of young listeners. She died of haematemesis at the Western Infirmary, Glasgow, on 20 February 1991 and was cremated at Clydebank crematorium, North Dalnottar, on 27 February. She was unmarried. W. H. McDOWELL

Sources Children's hour, radio files, BBC WAC · W. Grevatt, BBC Children's hour: a celebration of those magical years (1988) · Scotland's radio times, BBC Radio Scotland, 2–3 March 1998 · Scotland's Home Service, BBC Radio Scotland, 6 March 1998 · The Scotsman (22 Feb 1991) · Glasgow Herald (22 Feb 1991) · Tuned in: 75 years of broadcasting by the BBC in Scotland, BBC 1 Scotland, 15 March 1998 · W. H. McDowell, The history of BBC broadcasting in Scotland, 1923–1983 (1992) · R. Goring, ed., Chambers Scottish biographical dictionary (1992) · Glasgow Herald (20 Feb 1897) · Glasgow Herald (25 Feb 1991) · The Times (11 March 1991) · The Independent (26 Feb 1991) · The Independent (4 March 1991) · b. cert. · d. cert. · private information (2004) · NA Scot., SC/CO 511/113
Archives BBC WAC, radio files, Children's hour programmes | SOUND BL NSA
Likenesses photograph, repro. in The Independent (26 Feb 1991) · photograph, repro. in The Times
Wealth at death £20,893.14: confirmation, 29 April 1991, NA Scot., SC/CO 511/113

Garside, Charles Brierley (1818–1876), Roman Catholic priest, was born on 6 April 1818 at Manchester, the only son of Joseph Garside (1790–1868), a surgeon and distinguished ornithologist, and his wife, Mary Ann, daughter of Thomas Pearson. He was educated at Manchester grammar school and Brasenose College, Oxford, which he entered as an exhibitioner in 1838. He gained one of the Somerset scholarships and in 1840 became Hulme divinity exhibitioner. He graduated BA on 28 May 1841 and MA in 1844. Ordained in 1842 by the bishop of Gloucester, he became curate, first at Tetbury, Gloucestershire, next at Christ Church, Albany Street, Regent's Park, London, and then, in 1847, at Margaret Street Chapel, Marylebone, under William Richards.

At the time of the Gorham case Garside lost faith in the established church of England and was received into the Roman Catholic church, at St Leonards, on 15 August 1850. After theological studies at the Collegio Romano he was ordained priest at Rome by Cardinal Patrizi on 23 December 1854. He was appointed domestic chaplain to Bertram, the last Roman Catholic earl of Shrewsbury, in April 1855, and served as assistant priest at St Mary's, Cadogan Street, Chelsea, in 1857, and at St Aloysius', Somers Town, London, in May 1861. He was the author of several works of devotional piety, including The Preaching of the Cross (1869) and The Sacrifice of the Eucharist (1875). Garside died at Posilippo, near Naples, on 21 May 1876.

THOMPSON COOPER, rev. G. MARTIN MURPHY

Sources The Tablet (27 May 1876), 686 · E. G. K. Browne, Annals of the Tractarian movement, 3rd edn (1861), 174 · J. Gordon, Les récentes conversions de l'Angleterre (1851), 233 · Foster, Alum. Oxon. · W. E. A.

Axon, ed., The annals of Manchester: a chronological record from the earliest times to the end of 1885 (1886), 357 · Gillow, Lit. biog. hist. · CGPLA Eng. & Wales (1876)
Wealth at death under £1000: probate, 1 July 1876, CGPLA Eng. & Wales

Garson, (Eileen Evelyn) Greer (1904–1996), film actress, was born on 29 September 1904 at 88 First Avenue, Manor Park, Essex, the daughter of George Garson (1865–1906), a commercial clerk, and his wife, Nancy Sophia (Nina), née Greer (d. 1958), who claimed descent from Rob Roy McGregor. Her father died when she was two and as her mother was preoccupied with managing a row of inherited townhouses the sickly child spent much time in the care of her aunt, Alexina Logie, and her maternal grandparents in Castlewellan, northern Ireland; hence the popular misconception that she was Irish. Always a loner at both Essex Road elementary school and East Ham secondary school, she entered the University of London in 1921 after her mother refused her permission to apply for the Royal Academy of Dramatic Art. She considered herself 'The Girl Least Likely to Succeed' (Troyan, 3), although she was listed in a college yearbook as 'a unique blend of La Belle Dame Sans Merci and Goldilocks' (ibid., 19). An academic career seemed likely until she began acting in amateur productions while studying at the University of Grenoble.

After a spell working in Lever Brothers' advertising department Garson made her professional stage début in the Birmingham Repertory production of Elmer Rice's Street Scene on 30 January 1932. She was billed as Greer Garson for the first time in George Bernard Shaw's Too Good to be True at the New Theatre, London, in September 1932, stirring the playwright to opine she would be 'the new Ellen Terry! Never leave the theatre. I shall be very disappointed indeed if you go to Hollywood to work with magic lanterns' (Troyan, 30). On 28 September 1933 she married Edward Alec Abbott Snelson (1904–1992), then a junior judge in India, only to realize on honeymoon that she had made a mistake. (The marriage ended in divorce in 1940.) Remaining in London, she continued to act, finally making her name opposite Laurence Olivier in Sylvia Thompson's The Golden Arrow (1935). Despite being of the opinion 'she is so piss-elegant that it hurts. Too mannered. Too old. Too tall. And her voice is too deep' (ibid., 51), Noël Coward offered her the lead in Mademoiselle in 1936 and prevented her from accepting Douglas Fairbanks Jr's offer of a film contract.

Garson broke into television with Twelfth Night in May 1937, becoming the medium's highest-paid star when she earned about £100 to appear in How she Lied to her Husband that July. But it was Hollywood that beckoned, after MGM boss Louis B. Mayer saw her in Keith Winter's Old Music at the St James's Theatre in August 1937. An instant fan, he later wrote: 'if she were a man, she could be prime minister of England' (Troyan, 367). Yet she refused the many supporting roles Mayer suggested, before finally agreeing to play Kathie in Goodbye, Mr Chips (1939), a performance that brought her an Oscar nomination and prompted Time

(**Eileen Evelyn**) **Greer Garson** (1904–1996), by unknown photographer

magazine to describe her as 'a goddess sculptured in butterscotch' (ibid., 169). A spinal injury sustained in a riding accident caused MGM to cancel her contract, but it was swiftly restored after she received the nomination.

A reunion with Olivier in *Pride and Prejudice* (1940) was followed by a second Oscar nomination for *Blossoms in the Dust* (1941). Yet it was the lead in *Mrs Miniver* (1942) that secured the Garson legend. Winston Churchill considered her performance as a village housewife surviving the blitz to be worth more than six divisions, while Queen Elizabeth thanked her for making 'us feel more brave than we actually were' (Troyan, 1). Greer Garson dolls sold healthily, and she was voted 'the woman we'd like to spend the rest of our lives in the nose of a bomber with' (ibid., 151) by British troops. An Oscar duly followed, only for her to gain an unwanted place in the award's history by giving the longest-ever acceptance speech, at an unscripted five and a half minutes. *Miniver* had other consequences, including an introduction to her second husband, the actor Richard Ney, whom she married on 24 July 1943. Moreover, it established her screen partnership with Walter Pidgeon, with whom she would co-star in a further seven features, landing Oscar nominations for *Madame Curie* (1943) and *Mrs Parkington* (1944).

Further Oscar-nominated performances in *Random Harvest* (1942) and *The Valley of Decision* (1945) reinforced Garson's reputation as a statuesque sophisticate whose red hair betrayed a deeper passion. Yet she was keen to debunk this wholesome image and nicknamed herself 'the walking cathedral' and 'Metro's Golden Mare' (Troyan, 176). She longed to do comedy or play a villain, but instead found herself saddled with Clark Gable's postwar return to movies, *Adventure* (1945), which bore the grisly advertising slogan 'Gable's Back and Garson's Got Him'—although this was infinitely preferable to the alternative, 'Gable Puts the Arson in Garson' (ibid., 194).

The disappointing box-office showing of *The Miniver Story* (1949) convinced MGM that Garson's star was waning. Moreover, her second marriage having ended in divorce in 1947, on 15 July 1949 she married the Texan oil billionaire Colonel Elizah E. (Buddy) Fogelson (1908–1987), and became more interested in cattle, with her 'white short-horned Greers' becoming a prize-winning crossbreed. She also later successfully bred racehorses. Disillusioned with the new MGM regime of Dore Schary, she left the studio in 1954. Few of her freelance films were worthy of her talent, although she did draw her seventh Oscar nomination for playing Eleanor Roosevelt in *Sunrise at Campobello* (1960). Taking only occasional stage and television assignments, she retired after starring in *The Madwoman of Chaillot*, at the Greer Garson Theatre, Santa Fe, in June 1975. Poor health dogged her following a heart attack in 1980 and she lived quietly in Dallas until her death, at the Dallas Presbyterian Hospital, from congestive heart failure, on 6 April 1996. She was buried at the Sparkman Hillcrest Memorial Park, Dallas, on 9 April. She was survived by a stepson from her third marriage. She had been appointed honorary CBE in 1993.   DAVID PARKINSON

Sources M. Troyan, *A rose for Mrs Miniver: the life of Greer Garson* (1999) · M. Wald, 'Greer Garson: blue ribbon winner', *Close-ups: the movie star book*, ed. D. Peary (New York, 1978) · D. Thomson, *A biographical dictionary of film*, 3rd edn (1994) · *WWW* · *The Times* (8 April 1996) · *The Independent* (8 April 1996)
Archives College of Santa Fe, Santa Fe, New Mexico
Likenesses photographs, 1929–62, Hult. Arch. · photograph, repro. in *The Times* · photograph, repro. in *The Independent* · photograph, Rex Features Ltd, London [*see illus.*] · photographs, Kobal Collection, London · photographs, Ronald Grant Archive, London · photographs, Huntley Archive, London

Garstang, John Burges Eustace (1876–1956), archaeologist, was born in Blackburn, Lancashire, on 5 May 1876, the sixth child of Walter Garstang, consulting physician, and his wife, Matilda Mary Wardley. His eldest brother, Walter, was from 1907 to 1933 professor of zoology at Leeds. Educated at Blackburn grammar school, Garstang was early interested in the classics and in astronomy; but circumstances forced him to specialize in mathematics, for which in 1895 he obtained a scholarship at Jesus College, Oxford. While at school he often paid nocturnal visits to the observatory at Stonyhurst College, and as he passed the ruins of the Roman camp at Ribchester (Roman name Bremetenacum) his interest in archaeology was aroused. He conducted excavations there, publishing the results in 1898. Already in contact with F. J. Haverfield, then the leading scholar of Romano-British archaeology, Garstang was encouraged to take up archaeology. He

John Burges Eustace Garstang (1876–1956), by Elliott & Fry, 1950

devoted his vacations as an undergraduate to excavating, first at Melandra (Ardotalia) in Derbyshire in 1899, then in 1903 nearby at Brough-on-Noe (Navio), and at Richborough (Rutupiae) on the south coast of England in 1900.

After taking a third in mathematics (1899), in 1900 Garstang joined Flinders Petrie at Abydos in Egypt, where he had leisure to explore the vicinity. His work included excavations at Abmyeh (1900) and Beyt Dawd (1901–2), and having discovered the great tomb at Beyt Khallaf (1901) he was provided with funds for its excavation. A visit from Archibald Henry Sayce was the beginning of a lifelong friendship.

Appointed honorary reader in Egyptian archaeology at Liverpool in 1902, Garstang used this appointment to raise funds single-handedly for the creation of an institute of archaeology in 1904; he remained honorary secretary of the institute for over forty years, after which it was incorporated within the university. During the next few years Garstang led expeditions to the Egyptian sites of Negadeh (1902–4), Beni Hasan (1902–4), Hierakonpolis (1904–5), and Esna (1905–6). Through his friendship with Sayce he became interested in the Hittites, and in 1904 he undertook a journey of archaeological exploration in Asia Minor. In 1907 a permit was secured for the excavation of the Hittite capital of Boghazköy by a British expedition under Garstang's leadership; but on arrival at Constantinople he was disappointed to learn that the permit had

been transferred to Hugo Winckler at the personal request of the German emperor. He therefore made a second exploratory journey through Asia Minor, visiting Winckler at Boghazköy, and in the following year he selected the late Hittite site of Sajke-geuzi for excavation, while in the winter months he continued his explorations of the tombs of Abydos. He published a valuable topographical study of the Hittite monuments in 1910 under the title *The Land of the Hittites* (later rewritten as *The Hittite Empire* in 1929).

In 1907 Garstang was appointed to the newly founded professorship in the methods and practice of archaeology at Liverpool, a post which he held until 1941. There he took a leading part in organizing the Institute of Archaeology and a new journal, the *Annals of Archaeology and Anthropology*. He married in 1907 Marie Louise (d. 1949), daughter of Étienne Bergès, of Toulouse; they had one son and one daughter.

Largely at the instigation of Sayce, Garstang transferred his activities in 1909 to Meroe in Sudan, and there conducted excavations every winter until the outbreak of war in 1914. The finds included a bronze head of Augustus, later placed in the British Museum. Of particular interest to Garstang was a graffito showing primitive astronomical apparatus.

After serving during the First World War with the Red Cross in France, Garstang took charge of the newly created School of Archaeology in Jerusalem (1919–26); and as director (1920–26) of the department of antiquities for the mandatory government of Palestine he found time for much archaeological exploration of the country. His discovery of the site of Hazor was a notable achievement. Subsequent research on the topography of Palestine resulted in the publication of *Joshua Judges* (1931) and *The Heritage of Solomon* (1934). His most important archaeological work in Palestine, however, was the excavation of Jericho where, under the patronage of Sir Charles Marston, he worked from 1930 until 1936, when political conditions obliged him to transfer his activities to another country.

It was to Turkey that Garstang returned in autumn 1936 with an expedition sponsored by Francis Neilson. After a survey and soundings in the Cilician plain in 1938 he selected Yümük Tepe near Mersin for a full-scale excavation; but only two winter seasons were possible before war broke out. In the early months of the Second World War, however, he was again in Turkey in charge of administration of earthquake relief. After returning in 1946 Garstang completed in 1948 his interrupted work at Yümük Tepe and the results were published in *Prehistoric Mersin* (1953). While at Mersin he conceived the idea of a British institute of archaeology at Ankara, and in 1948, with the full support of the Turkish government, the institute was formally opened, with Garstang as its first director; he retired the following year, to assume the presidency of the institute.

Garstang was appointed a chevalier of the Légion d'honneur (1920), received the honorary degree of LLD from Aberdeen (1931), and was made a corresponding member of the Institut de France (1947), and CBE (1949). His death occurred on a cruise, at Beirut, on 12 September 1956. His study of the geography of the Hittite empire, on which he had spent many of the later years of his life, was published posthumously in 1959.

With his trim beard, his deep musical voice, slow speech, and air of abstraction, Garstang, especially after middle age, gave an impression of great learning. A prolific publisher of the results of his archaeological work, he also wrote histories of the county of Lancashire and Blackburn grammar school. Yet his effective training was as a field archaeologist, and it is in this essentially practical field, as well as in that of organization, for which he had a natural gift, that his permanent achievements are to be found. He was a sensitive, lovable character, with a boyish enthusiasm which never failed to infect those who worked with him.

O. R. GURNEY, rev. P. W. M. FREEMAN

Sources A. H. Sayce, *Reminiscences* (1923) · J. Shore, unpublished history of the School of Archaeology, Classics and Oriental Studies, University of Liverpool, 1985, University of Liverpool, School of Archaeology, Classics and Oriental Studies [typescript] · personal knowledge (1971)
Archives Palestine Exploration Fund, London, field notebooks, drawings, papers, and photographs · U. Lpool, fieldwork notes, etc. | Bodl. Oxf., corresp. with J. L. Myers
Likenesses G. H. Heale, oils, 1906, Blackburn grammar school · H. E. D. Bate, bust, c.1950, priv. coll. · Elliott & Fry, photograph, 1950 [see illus.] · photograph, U. Lpool, School of Archaeology, Classics and Oriental Studies

Garstin, (Mary) Alethea Dochie (1894–1978). *See under* Garstin, Norman (1847–1926).

Garstin, Norman (1847–1926), landscape and genre painter, was born on 28 August 1847 at Cahirconlish, co. Limerick, the only child of an Anglo-Irish army officer, Colonel William Garstin (1806–1861), of the 83rd regiment of foot of the Irish army, and his wife, Mary Hastings Moore (1823–1871). His father committed suicide when Garstin was young and, as his mother suffered from muscular paralysis, he was brought up by relatives (mainly an aunt at Fetard) in co. Limerick. He was sent to school in Jersey, where he attended the Victoria College, St Helier, and lived with another relative, Dr Norman Garstin.

Garstin studied engineering briefly at Queen's College, Cork, and then architecture, entering an architect's office in London. However, he found the profession of little interest, and in 1872 he set sail for the diamond mines of South Africa. He spent four years in Kimberley, where he shared a tent with Cecil Rhodes, and was employed for some of the time by the government secretary, Frederick St Leger. Later he went to Cape Town where he worked for St Leger as sub-editor on the newly established *Cape Times*. He returned to Ireland in 1877.

Soon after his return Garstin was blinded in one eye in a riding accident, although this incident did not deter him from his decision to become an artist. He studied in 1878–9 in Antwerp, under Charles Verlat, and then between 1880 and 1883 in Paris in the studio of Carolus Duran. The influence of the northern tradition is reflected in the sombre palette of his early works, and his oils and watercolours include many canal and street scenes of such places as Delft and Bruges, as well as scenes of everyday life in Breton towns, in which he depicted local women in peasant costume. In Paris Garstin had the opportunity of seeing the work of the French impressionists: he is said to have met Degas, and in 1884 he wrote a critical appraisal of Edouard Manet for the *Art Journal*.

Garstin exhibited widely in Britain from the early 1880s: at the Walker Art Gallery, Liverpool, in 1882, at the Royal Academy for the first time in 1883, when he showed *Philomene*, in Birmingham, Manchester, and Glasgow, and in many London galleries, including the Fine Art Society, the Walker Gallery, and the Grosvenor Gallery. He exhibited with the New English Art Club in 1887. During this time Garstin travelled extensively. In 1882 he painted in Brittany, a place popular with English painters and where Jules Bastien-Lepage encouraged his fellow artists in *plein air* painting. The following year he went to Hyères in the south of France, in 1884 to Italy (including Venice), and in 1885 to Morocco and Spain. The experience of these journeys found expression not only in the subject matter of Garstin's paintings of the 1880s but also in a developing interest in colour and the effects of sunlight and shadow, and in the creation of scenes with atmospheric effects, mystery, and mood. He also painted scenes of London in a free, sketchy style while staying there in the 1880s.

After his marriage to Louisa Fanny (Dochie) Jones on 14 July 1886, Garstin settled in Newlyn, Cornwall, welcomed by the colony of artists who, like himself, had trained on the continent, and who were also influenced by the work of Bastien-Lepage. He rented one of the new glass-covered studios on the Meadow (a plot of land bought for development to meet the needs of the growing number of artists), which he shared with his friend Frank Wright Bourdillon. Garstin and his wife later moved to Penzance, where they lived at 4 Wellington Terrace with their two sons, Crosbie (b. 1887) and Denys (b. 1890), and daughter, Alethea [see below]. Garstin was a friend of Stanhope Forbes, leader of the *Newlyn school, who described him as 'a distinguished looking Irishman with a delightful wit … tall and imposing and with a fine artistic insight' (*Norman and Alethea Garstin*, 23). He became the intellectual mentor of the Newlyn artists, forward looking and refreshingly free of dogmatic ideas, believing in the freedom of expression of the individual as opposed to the hidebound conventions of other Victorian painters. However, Garstin was dogged by his impoverished financial circumstances, which forced him to combine painting with writing articles for journals and teaching. From 1899 he took sketching parties abroad, to such places as Quimperlé, Delft, and Normandy. Eventually he opened his own school—the Penzance and District Art Students School, where Harold Harvey was a pupil.

Garstin's work followed two directions: anecdotal, studio paintings executed for large exhibitions such as the Royal Academy and lively, impressionistic oil studies painted from nature on small panels. He was inspired by the avant-garde work of Walter Sickert and J. A. M. Whistler, as well as by Japanese art with its sense of assymetry. *Woman Reading a Newspaper* (1891; Tate collection) is powerfully evocative in the manner of Sickert, while *Mounts Bay from Trewidden* (Tate collection) follows the Japanese compositional style. His most important work, *The Rain it Raineth every Day* (1889; Penzance Museum and Art Gallery), is strongly atmospheric and has a powerful sense of depth and space. *Her Signal* (exh. RA, 1892; Royal Cornwall Museum, Truro) is an anecdotal painting with a dual light source, one of Garstin's favourite devices. Many of Garstin's paintings, in both oil and watercolour, show a powerful interplay of sunlight and shadow reminiscent of the French impressionists. The reviewer of an exhibition held at the Walker Gallery, Bond Street, in 1909 encapsulated this aspect of the artist's work, saying: 'His directness of statement and freshness of handling give to his studies of nature a definite significance as frank records of simple facts, and make them decoratively pleasing without diminishing their value as realities' ('Studio talk', 227). His later works were more anecdotal and included scenes of upper-class life—for example, *The Last Dance*—and were designed to have greater saleability. Garstin remained in Penzance for the rest of his life, although he visited Canada in 1892, when he painted the opening of the Canadian Pacific Railway. He died at Wellington Terrace on 22 June 1926, survived by his wife.

(Mary) Alethea Dochie Garstin (1894–1978), landscape painter, was born Mary Dochie Garstin on 1 June 1894, the third child of Norman Garstin and his wife, Louisa. She was trained as a painter by her father and accompanied him on many of his trips abroad, travelling round France with him as a child on the handlebars of his bicycle. She also painted with her friend the Cornish painter Dod Proctor.

Garstin's first Royal Academy exhibit was hung when she was eighteen and so impressed the president, Edward Poynter, that he asked to meet her. Thereafter she exhibited regularly in the 1920s and 1930s. Although she was based in Penzance until 1960, she travelled to northern France, Italy, Morocco, Kenya, and the Caribbean. She had a very fine tonal sense and accurately reproduced the hot, intense colours of Morocco and the West Indies in contrast to the cooler, more muted tones of scenes of Cornwall or Brittany. She worked directly on to the canvas with a freedom of brushstrokes and light touch, using square hogs' hair brushes.

In 1960 Garstin moved to the Old Poor House, at Zennor, on the Penwith north coast. She was one of the major painters of the Cornish school in the first half of the twentieth century. She died at her home on 23 January 1978, just before a major exhibition of her work and that of her father, entitled 'Two Impressionists, Father and Daughter', was held in St Ives. Her work is represented in Bristol City Art Gallery and Plymouth City Art Gallery.

DIANA BASKERVYLE-GLEGG

Sources C. Fox and F. Greenacre, *Artists of the Newlyn school, 1880–1900* (1979) • *Norman and Alethea Garstin* (1978) [exhibition catalogue, Penwith Society of Arts, 1978] • C. Fox, *Stanhope Forbes and the Newlyn school* (1993) • J. Campbell, *The Irish impressionists* (1984) [exhibition catalogue, NG Ire.] • T. Cross, *The shining sands: artists in Newlyn and St Ives, 1880–1930* (1994) • *The Times* (24 June 1926) • private information (2004) • 'Studio talk', *The Studio* (15 April 1909), 227 • m. cert. • d. cert. • b. cert. [Alethea Garstin] • d. cert. [Alethea Garstin]

Likenesses F. Hall, caricature, 1890, Tate collection • W. Wainright, caricature, Forbes Collection, New York

Wealth at death £3490 18s. 8d.: probate, 10 Nov 1926, CGPLA Eng. & Wales

Garstin, Sir William Edmund (1849–1925), civil engineer, was born in India on 29 January 1849, the second son of Charles Garstin, of the Bengal civil service, and his wife, Agnes Helen, daughter of W. Mackenzie, of the East India Company's service. He was educated at Cheltenham College (1864–6) and at King's College, London, where he studied engineering. In 1872 he entered the Indian public works department.

In 1885, while still in the Indian service, Garstin was invited by Colin Campbell Scott-Moncrieff, under-secretary of state in the ministry of public works at Cairo after the British invasion of Egypt in 1882, to join William Willcocks and Murdoch MacDonald in transforming the hydrology of the Nile to improve agriculture, to control flooding, and to improve navigation as part of the British plan to establish and consolidate control in the area. Garstin was placed in charge of irrigation in the eastern part of the Nile delta before he became inspector-general of irrigation in Egypt in May 1892, at the same time definitely retiring from the Indian service. In the following September he became under-secretary of state in the ministry of public works.

Garstin's first task was to transform the traditional system of basin irrigation, in which water and silt were trapped in the flood season only, into one of perennial irrigation in which water would be available all year round and larger areas could be brought under cultivation. This work had already begun, but many installations were so poorly designed and constructed that they were of little use. Garstin carried out extensive works on the Nile which, when completed after his retirement, formed an integrated system of water storage and control. This in turn allowed a great increase in crop yields per acre, particularly in cotton, the main cash crop. The construction of a reservoir at Aswan had been suggested in William Willcocks's *Report on Perennial Irrigation and Flood Protection for Egypt* (1894). Garstin referred the question to a commission which approved the plan. Four years later Garstin recommended acceptance of Ernest Joseph Cassel's offer to advance the necessary money and the dam, built to Willcocks's design, was finished in 1902 at a cost of £2.4 million. Protective works downstream were completed in 1906, Willcocks having failed to provide concrete aprons below the sluices to prevent scour. As early as 1904, however, demand outstripped supply for water stored at Aswan. In that year Garstin published his report on the basin of the upper Nile, in which he recommended the heightening of the Aswan Dam, although Willcocks thought the idea a waste of money. The work, undertaken between 1907 and 1912, increased the cubic capacity of the

Sir William Edmund Garstin (1849–1925), by unknown photographer

storage lake by about two and a half times. As both the construction and the subsequent raising of the Aswan Dam involved the complete submersion of the temples on the island of Philae, a short distance above Aswan, from January to July, they were extremely controversial. Garstin made some effort to underpin the temples and obtained a grant for an archaeological survey of the affected part of the Nile valley.

Between 1898 and 1902 Garstin superintended the construction of the Asyut barrage halfway between Cairo and Aswan; between 1901 and 1902 he constructed the Zifta barrage on the lower Nile, and between 1906 and 1908 built another barrage across the Nile immediately north of Esna town. All were intended to regulate flow and improve irrigation.

In 1899 Garstin reconnoitred the upper Nile area and reported that many channels were made impassable by blocks of vegetation which should be cleared immediately. The arduous and often unpleasant work of clearing vegetation was begun in autumn 1899 by Egyptian prisoners and British soldiers. Its aim was to restore navigability and to secure British control of the Nile waters and in turn to allow British control of the southern Sudan, to which the Congo Free State had aspirations. On his trip up the White Nile in 1902–3 Garstin gathered further information about the hydrology of the Nile system. He recommended the creation of a separate Sudanese irrigation service, but instead Sudanese irrigation was organized as an extension of the Egyptian service. Had Garstin's scheme been adopted there might have been fewer conflicts

between the Sudanese and Egyptian administrations' claims to the Nile waters. Collins attributes to Garstin the fundamental guiding idea of the late twentieth-century Nile management, that is, the need to see the Nile system as a whole and to store water in Sudan and the equatorial lakes for use along the whole length of the river (Collins, 130–31).

Garstin's hydrographical work was recorded in the Foreign Office blue book (*Egypt, No. 2*) and in his *Report upon the Basin of the Upper Nile with Proposals for the Improvement of that River* (1904). These 'magisterial' works, unequalled in the history of Nile hydrography, reveal the 'Olympian sweep of Garstin's imagination', combining as they do a firm grasp on the scientific questions and the imperial aspirations of the British (Collins, 89). The proposals in the latter report and in 'Some problems of the upper Nile' (*Nineteenth Century and After*, September 1905) were undertaken from 1913.

As under-secretary in the department of public works Garstin also had responsibility for the buildings and antiquities of Cairo. New buildings for the National Museum of Egyptian Antiquities at Cairo opened in 1902 as a result of his efforts to house the ever-increasing collections. In 1896 on his recommendation, a geological reconnaissance of Egyptian territory, later the geological survey, was begun. In 1905 the public works service was reorganized and Garstin became adviser to that department. He retired in 1908 but often went back to Egypt to give advice on hydrological questions and to act as a director of the Suez Canal Company. He was created CMG in 1894, and advanced KCMG in 1897, and GCMG in 1902. He was also a chevalier of the Légion d'honneur and held the grand cordons of the Mejidiye and Osmanie orders. During the First World War he worked with the St John Ambulance and on the council of the Red Cross Society, for which he was made GBE in 1918.

If Garstin's life was marked by professional success, his personal life was marred by unhappiness and scandal. In 1888 he married Mary Isabella, daughter of Charles Augustus North and granddaughter of Brownlow North (1810–1875). She accompanied her husband during his service in Egypt and she there began a passionate and ill-concealed affair with Charles à Court *Repington, an army officer stationed there. In October 1899 Repington signed an affidavit promising Garstin and his (Repington's) wife not to see Mary again. Despite this the affair was renewed and Garstin divorced his wife in 1902, the revelations of the case being the subject of much gossip. Mary subsequently lived with Repington and they had a daughter. She changed her surname in 1903 to Repington, but his wife's refusal to grant him a divorce prevented their marrying. Mary published an account of the affair as *Thanks for the Memory* in 1938, after her husband's and partner's deaths. Garstin's personal unhappiness was not confined to relations with his wife: the son and daughter of the marriage both predeceased him.

Garstin died at his home—17 Welbeck House, Wigmore Street, London—on 8 January 1925. He and his fellow engineers transformed the hydrology of the Nile. The principles of ever larger, technologically more complex, and more expensive interventions which guided his work went unchallenged until the late twentieth century, when the ecological, economic, human, and archaeological costs associated with them cast a shadow over his work. His writings and his engineering show his science to have been at all times at the service of British expansionism, but his scientific vision was such that even Egyptian nationalists described him as 'the treasure of Egypt' (quoted in Collins, 108).   ELIZABETH BAIGENT

Sources *The Times* (9 Jan 1925) · *Nature*, 115 (1925), 92–3 · D. R. Headrick, *The tentacles of progress: technology transfer in the age of imperialism, 1850–1940* (1988) · H. E. Hurst, *The Nile* (1957) · T. Waterbury, *Hydropolitics of the Nile valley* (1979) · E. W. C. Sandes, *The royal engineers in Egypt and the Sudan* (1937) · R. L. Tignor, *Modernization and British colonial rule in Egypt, 1882–1914* (1966) · R. O. Collins, *The waters of the Nile: hydropolitics and the Jonglei Canal, 1900–1988* (1990) **Archives** U. Durham L., corresp. with Sir Reginald Wingate **Likenesses** photograph, NPG [*see illus.*] **Wealth at death** £23,085 1s. 2d.: administration with will, 25 Feb 1925

Garter, Bernard (*fl.* 1565–1579), poet, who describes himself on his title-pages as citizen of London, was, according to Hunter, the second son of Sir William Garter of London, and the father of a Bernard Garter of Brigstocke, Northamptonshire. But in the 1633–5 visitation of London, 'Barnerd Garter of Brikstocke', Northamptonshire, was described as the son of Thomas Garter, the husband of Elizabeth Catelyne, and the father of George Garter, who was living in 1634 (*Visitation*, 1.303). He is described as a clerk of the Blacksmiths' Company in an Elizabethan chancery suit involving the company and Joseph Preston (PRO, C Pp.8.55).

Garter wrote *The Tragicall and True Historie which Happened betweene Two English Lovers*, published by Tottell in 1565, though licensed first to Alexander Lacy, an imitation in ballad metre of Arthur Broke's 'Romeus and Juliet', 1561. He also wrote commendatory verses for William Page's *Pasquin in a trance, a Christian and learned dialogue contayning wonderfull and most strange newes out of heaven, purgatorie, and hell* (1565), a translation from Celius Secundus Curio. The year 1566 saw Garter print several poems, including *A Strife between Apelles and Pigmalion*, and *A Dittie to the Worthie Praise of a High and Mighty Prince*, a panegyric addressed to Thomas Howard, fourth duke of Norfolk. But after this little is known about his activities until August 1578, when Garter was in Norwich with Henry Goldingham and Thomas Churchyard, preparing spectacles and entertainments for the visit of Queen Elizabeth. Back in London he published an account of them in *The Joyfull Receavinge of the Quenes Majestie into Norwiche* (1578), dedicated to Sir Owen Hopton.

In 1579, he printed his last known work, *A new yeares gifte, dedicated to the popes holinesse and all Catholikes addicted to the sea of Rome: prepared the first day of Januarie* [1579] *by B. G., citizen of London*. This work, wrongly ascribed by Ritson to Barnabe Googe, contains, besides verses against the Catholics, a reprint of a letter sent in 1537 by Cuthbert Tunstall, bishop of Durham, and John Stokesley, bishop of London, to Cardinal Pole, maintaining the royal supremacy; lives of Alexander II and Gregory VII; an account of the frauds of Elizabeth Barton, Maid of Kent; and 'invectives against the pope'. 'A New Yeres Geyfte Made by Barnarde Garter' was licensed for printing to Alexander Lacy in 1565, but no copy of so early a date has been met with.

Warton also claims for Garter a now-lost 'ballet of Helen's Epistle to Paris from "Ovid", in 1570, by B. G.' (*History of English Poetry*, 3.422).

SIDNEY LEE, *rev.* MATTHEW STEGGLE

Sources J. Nichols, *The progresses and public processions of Queen Elizabeth*, new edn, 2 (1823), 133–78 · *Thomas Warton's History of English poetry*, ed. D. Fairer, 4 vols. (1998), vol. 3, pp. 422–3 · *STC, 1475–1640* · *The visitation of London, anno Domini 1633, 1634, and 1635, made by Sir Henry St George*, 1, ed. J. J. Howard and J. L. Chester, Harleian Society, 15 (1880), 303 · BL, Add. MS 24488, fol. 318 [J. Hunter, 'Chorus Vatum']

Garth, John (*bap.* 1721, *d.* 1810), musician, was born in Harperley, near Witton-le-Wear, near Bishop Auckland, co. Durham, and was baptized at Witton-le-Wear on 27 December 1721. He was fifth of the six children of William Garth (*bap.* 1672, *d.* 1726) of Harperley, but the first with his second wife, Elizabeth.

Nothing is known of Garth's early life, but in September 1745 and August 1746 he promoted single concerts in Stockton. By the time of the second of these he was living in Durham city, where he had organized a concert in June that year. Durham proved to be receptive ground, and he promoted concert series there through to 1772, selling tickets from his house. From 1746 to 1751 this was in Sadler Street, but by 1752 he had moved to the North Bailey, where he lived until after 1791. It appears that the Durham concerts were in alternate weeks to those organized by Charles Avison in Newcastle, and that the two men combined forces. Garth featured at times in these concerts as a cellist and as an accompanist; and he appeared in the latter capacity at York in August 1753.

Garth had competition as a concert organizer in Durham. In November 1752 Dean Spencer Cowper referred to hostilities between 'the Newcastle party' (*Letters*, 159) and the Durham Cathedral musicians who themselves had been promoting concerts in Durham for some years. Cowper described Garth as a cellist, as did the London-based sons of Durham prebendary Thomas Sharp in 1758.

Garth's musical talents were in demand throughout the north of England. In 1752 he was music teacher to the family of Henry Vane, first earl of Darlington, who lived at Raby Castle in co. Durham. In 1779 he gave harpsichord lessons to Judith Milbanke at Seaham, and in 1785 to her niece Sophia Curzon; in 1784 he was well enough known to dine with the Yorkes of Bewerley Hall, near Ripon. About 1760 he was organist at Sedgefield; and he gave the opening recitals on new organs at Stockton (in 1759), Wakefield (1767), and Kirkleatham, Yorkshire (1770). From Michaelmas 1792 to Michaelmas 1793 he received a salary of 10 guineas from the bishop of Durham, presumably for acting as his organist.

He is chiefly remembered for his eight-volume edition

with English text of *The First Fifty Psalms Set to Music by Benedetto Marcello* (1757–65). To this edition his friend Charles Avison contributed at least the introductory section. Garth composed one set of cello concertos (op. 1, 1760) and five sets of harpsichord sonatas (opp. 2, 4–7, 1768–82) in which the two violins and cello duplicated the keyboard. Of these, op. 2 proved to be the most popular, with five editions between 1768 and 1790. He also composed one set of organ voluntaries (op. 3, 1771) and 30 collects (1794). All these works were published in London. Three anthems by him were copied into the Durham Cathedral music manuscripts between 1783 and 1804.

Late in life, and described as 'of Wolsingham', he married at Darlington, by licence on 20 July 1794, Nancy (Nanny) Wrightson (1749/50–1829), heir of William Wrightson of Cockerton, Darlington. He died at his home, Cockerton Hall, Cockerton, Darlington, on 29 March 1810 and was buried on 5 April 1810 in the churchyard of St Cuthbert's, Darlington. His will, which was proved twice, first at Durham on 30 May 1810 and then at London on 20 June 1810, named his wife as his sole executor and principal heir. She established at Cockerton three almshouses (demolished in 1944) in his memory, and died on 1 December 1829.

BRIAN CROSBY

Sources *Monthly Magazine and British Register* (1 May 1810) • parish register, Witton-le-Wear, St Philip and St James, 27 Dec 1721 [baptism] • parish register, Darlington, St Cuthbert, 5 April 1810 [burial] • Garth wills, *c.*1600–1810, U. Durham L. • R. Scarr, 'Georgian musician who lived at Cockerton', *Darlington & Stockton Times* (25 June 1960) • *Newcastle Courant* (1745–80) [concert advertisements] • *Newcastle Chronicle* (1745–80) [concert advertisements] • G. G. Androux, *Six trios for two German flutes or two violins with a thorough bass* [n.d., *c.*1760] [list of subscribers] • U. Durham L., archives and special collections, Auckland Castle episcopal records, box 36 [Group no. 4]—*temp. ref.* • *Letters of Spencer Cowper, dean of Durham, 1746–74*, ed. E. Hughes, SurtS, 165 (1956) • Glos. RO, Lloyd-Baker papers, (D3549, 7/2/15) • M. Elwin, ed., *The Noels and the Milbankes: their letters for twenty-five years, 1767–1792* (1967) • *Music and theatre in Handel's world: the family papers of James Harris, 1732–1780*, ed. D. Burrows and R. Dunhill (2002) • S. Sadie, 'Garth, John', *New Grove* • R. Southey, 'Secular music-making in the eighteenth-century north-east' (proposed title), PhD diss., U. Newcastle, [forthcoming]

Wealth at death no value given: will, 11 Jan 1808, U. Durham

Garth, Sir Richard (1820–1903), judge in India, was born at Morden, Surrey, on 11 March 1820, the eldest son in the family of six children of Richard Lowndes, afterwards Garth (1790–1862), educated at Eton College and Trinity College, Cambridge, rector of Farnham, Surrey, and his wife, Mary, daughter of Robert Douglas, rector of Salwarpe, Worcestershire. His father was the second son of William Lowndes of Brightwell Baldwin, Oxfordshire, and his wife, Elizabeth, daughter and heir of Richard Garth of Morden, Surrey, and assumed the name and arms of Garth on 20 March 1837 on succeeding to his mother's property. In due course Richard became lord of the manor of Morden.

Garth was educated from 1835 at Eton, where he played in the cricket elevens of 1837–8, and at Christ Church, Oxford, of which he was a student from 1839 to 1847; he graduated BA in 1842, and proceeded MA in 1845. He was a member of the university cricket eleven from 1839 to 1842, and captain in 1840 and 1841. Admitted a student of Lincoln's Inn on 9 July 1842, he was called to the bar there on 19 November 1847. On 27 June 1847 Garth married his cousin Clara (d. 1903), second daughter of William Loftus Lowndes QC; they had six sons and three daughters.

Garth joined the home circuit; he was popular in the profession, and gained especial repute in commercial cases heard at the Guildhall. For many years he was counsel to the Incorporated Law Society. He was made queen's counsel on 24 July 1866 and two days later was elected a bencher of his inn. At a by-election in December 1866 he was elected a Conservative MP for the electorally corrupt small borough of Guildford. He favoured moderate reform and 'an adjustment of the church-rate question' so as to secure 'civil and religious liberty' (*WWBMP*, 153). During the 1866 election Garth made a speech attacking John Bright, alleging that his employees disliked him and that he had not subscribed to the Lancashire cotton famine relief fund. Bright answered Garth's allegations and asserted, 'There are many men who go "through dirt to dignities", and I suspect you have no objection to be one of them' (*Public Letters*, 127). In January 1867 in Rochdale meetings were held supporting Bright and protesting against Garth's 'libels'. Garth was defeated at the 1868 general election.

In 1875 Garth was appointed chief justice of Bengal and was knighted (13 May). A bluff, genial, fresh-complexioned man, he looked more like a country squire or a naval officer than a judge. Popular in Calcutta, he reportedly tried to bring the European and Indian communities into closer social contact. His judicial decisions were reportedly marked by learning, patience, and practical good sense, and were rarely reversed by the judicial committee of the privy council.

Garth frequently came into conflict with the Indian and Bengal governments. The Liberal Lord Ripon, viceroy from 1880 to 1884, described Garth as 'a prejudiced second rate Tory lawyer with strong party feelings to which he is apt to give way' (Gopal, 119). The views of the high court were then systematically sought on legislative proposals, and Garth framed confidential minutes. But he often publicly expressed pronounced opinions about the proposed legislation. The most notable example was his vigorous propaganda against Ripon's 1883 Bengal Tenancy Bill, designed to give the ryots (cultivators) in the permanently settled areas defined and transferable occupancy rights, and passed after much controversy in 1885. In his published *Minute* (1882) he declared it to be ruinous for the zamindars (landlords) and to embody a policy of confiscation. His sincerity was unquestioned, but it was improper for the chief justice to engage in partisan controversy over legislation which he would probably have to interpret judicially. He showed some sympathy with Indian aspirations. He promoted the Legal Practitioners Act of 1879, and he insisted that one of the three additional judges appointed to the Bengal high court in 1885 should be an Indian. Nevertheless, in 1882 when Garth intended going on leave and heard that Ripon intended to appoint an

Indian judge, Romesh Chandra Mitter, as acting chief justice, he wrote angrily protesting and declaring that rather than see an Indian judge appointed he would give up his leave, but he gave way. In 1883 Garth was hostile to Ripon's controversial Criminal Procedure Code Amendment Bill (known as the Ilbert Bill) whereby Europeans could be tried by Indian judges. In May, Garth sentenced Surendranath Banerjea to two months' imprisonment for making an unfounded allegation in his *Bengalee* against Justice Norris of the Calcutta high court. Norris was a known opponent of the Ilbert Bill and Banerjea's imprisonment caused protests in and beyond Bengal.

Ill health led to Garth's retirement in March 1886, shortly before he had qualified for full pension. He was named of the privy council in February 1888, but was not appointed to the judicial committee. A supporter of the Indian National Congress, he wrote *A Few Plain Truths about India* (1888), largely in advocacy of its views. His vigorous reply (1895) to some criticisms of the movement by General Sir George Chesney was repeatedly quoted by the Congress politicians (see *Indian National Congress*, Madras, 1909, 2.24). Garth promoted in July 1899 a memorial to the India Office from retired high court judges for the separation of executive and judicial functions in the administrative organization of districts.

Garth died at his residence, 10 Cedar House, Cheniston Gardens, Kensington, London, on 23 March 1903, and was buried at Morden, Surrey. A portrait of Garth by John Collier was in the Calcutta high court.

F. H. BROWN, *rev.* ROGER T. STEARN

Sources J. Foster, *Men-at-the-bar: a biographical hand-list of the members of the various inns of court*, 2nd edn (1885) · *Englishman Weekly Summary* (23 March 1886) · *Englishman Weekly Summary* (30 March 1886) · *Friend of India and Statesman Weekly* (26 March 1903) · *India* (23 March 1903) · *India* (3 April 1903) · *Wisden* (1904), lxxx · private information (1912) [Richard Garth] · personal knowledge (1912) · Burke, *Peerage* (1894) · Foster, *Alum. Oxon.* · Kelly, *Handbk* (1891) · Venn, *Alum. Cant.* · *WWW*, 1897–1915 · H. E. C. Stapylton, *The Eton school lists, from 1791 to 1850*, 2nd edn (1864) · *The public letters of the Right Hon John Bright, M.P.*, ed. H. J. Leech (1885) · G. B. Smith, *The life and speeches of the Right Hon. John Bright, M.P.*, 2 (1881) · G. M. Trevelyan, *The life of John Bright* (1913) · S. Gopal, *The viceroyalty of Lord Ripon, 1880–1884* (1953) · *WWBMP* · D. Argov, *Moderates and extremists in the Indian nationalist movement, 1883–1920* (1967) · A. Denholm, *Lord Ripon 1827–1909: a political biography* (1982) · P. Spear, *The Oxford history of modern India, 1740–1947* (1965) · J. M. Brown, *Modern India: the origins of an Asian democracy*, 2nd edn (1994)

Archives BL, letters to Lord Ripon, Add. MS 43610

Likenesses J. Collier, oils, 1888; formerly in the high court, Calcutta

Wealth at death £2324 10s. 5d.: administration, 29 May 1903, CGPLA Eng. & Wales

Garth, Sir Samuel (1661–1719), physician and poet, was born at Bowland Forest in the West Riding of Yorkshire, the eldest son of William Garth of Bolam. He was educated at Ingleton and in 1676 was admitted to Peterhouse, Cambridge, where he proceeded BA in 1679 and MA in 1684. On 4 September 1687 he matriculated in physic at Leiden; on 7 July 1691 he was created MD at Peterhouse. Garth then settled in Covent Garden, London, where he

Sir Samuel Garth (1661–1719), by Sir Godfrey Kneller, *c.*1705–10

practised for the rest of his life. He was admitted a candidate of the Royal College of Physicians on 25 June 1692, became a fellow on 26 June 1693, and served as censor during 1702. He and his wife, Martha (d. 1717), daughter of Sir Henry Beaufoy, of Emscote, Warwickshire, had one daughter, Martha, who eloped to marry Colonel William Boyle, a younger son of Colonel Henry Boyle.

Throughout his career Garth remained active as a practising physician, a conscientious member of the Royal College of Physicians, and a man of letters. Known for his wit, poetry, and love of classical literary models, rather than expertise in experimental philosophy, Garth was among the first English physicians to make a substantial contribution to its imaginative literature. Garth was also active in medical politics as a whig, and his early career spans a divisive period in the college as well as among the English healing professions. Although officers of the Royal College of Physicians asked Garth to publish his 1694 Goulstonian lectures 'De respiratione', he declined. In September 1697, however, when he delivered the college's annual Harveian oration, he consented to its prompt publication in Latin. Garth's oration mostly follows Harvey's precise testamentary directive that the oration commemorate all college benefactors by name. Harvey also wished the oration to promote collegial concord; in addition to an extended panegyric to William III, Garth included a penultimate paragraph entreating unity over an issue that had divided college members for two decades: the form and substance of college sponsorship of charitable medical care in London and its environs. Garth's assent to publication of his Harveian oration may reflect the fact that he was an active supporter of the college's proposal made on 22 December 1696 for a members' subscription of £10 to establish a dispensary for free medical advice and discounted medicines for the sick poor, the first in England. Intra-college debate divided those licentiates and fellows who dispensed medicines—apothecary physicians and their supporters—from the majority, who denigrated them for engaging in trade. Meanwhile, London apothecaries had been pressing their case for professional autonomy, including the privilege to dispense medical advice, through pamphlets and petitions to the Commons since the plague of 1665-6. By the 1690s attempts at reaching a compromise between apothecaries and the college had failed. Apothecaries adamantly opposed establishment of the dispensary, fearing that it would enable the college to displace them professionally. College opponents of the dispensary included the eminent physicians John Radcliffe, Sir Richard Blackmore, Hugh Chamberlen, and Thomas Sydenham.

Garth's most noted literary work, *The Dispensary, a Poem*, first published in 1699, celebrates the opening of the college dispensary in the winter of 1697-8. Composed of six cantos, the poem's first five employ Ovidian conceits to describe a mock Homeric battle between physicians and apothecaries, with William Harvey finally being sought in canto 6 in the Elysian fields to give advice to settle the war. Deploring that the controversy interferes with useful researches and the nation's health, Harvey dispatches 'Atticus' (Garth's fellow Kit-Cat Club member Lord Somers, the prominent whig lawyer) to restore concord. Ridiculing the apothecaries and their allies in the college in its first five cantos, the poem illustrates Garth's sense of humour, attachment to classical literary models, and convictions about the medical profession and apothecaries. Following his friend and poetic mentor John Dryden's published advice in Dryden's *Discourse Concerning the Original and Progress of Satire* (1693) to adopt a verse of ten syllables as the metre best suited to 'manly satire', Garth used the French poet Nicolas Boileau-Despréaux's 1674 poem, *Le lutrin* (rev. 1683) as his specific model, so much so that Garth's opponents criticized him freely for verging on plagiarism. *The Dispensary* appeared in three editions by the end of 1699. A fourth edition appeared in 1700, a sixth in 1706, and a tenth in 1741. Garth omitted and changed lines in the editions published during his lifetime.

The Dispensary cemented Garth's reputation as a poet and whig wit. In the early 1700s the Kit-Cat Club, a dining group, comprised approximately thirty prominent whig talents who included Addison, Dorset, and John Churchill, duke of Marlborough, as well as Garth and Somers. Garth contributed humorous verses that were inscribed on the club's drinking glasses, and these are recorded in Dryden's *Miscellanies*. Garth continued to publish verse and prose in English and Latin throughout his life. In 1711 he wrote a Latin dedication for an edition of Lucretius dedicated to the future George I, then elector of Brunswick. In 1715 he wrote *Claremont*, a poem on Lord Clare's villa, and in 1717 an English translation of Ovid's *Metamorphoses*. Also, he wrote a verse dedication of Ovid's *Art of Love* to Richard, earl of Burlington, and one for Ovid's *Epistles* to Lady Louisa Lenox. Pope, whom Garth encouraged to publish *Rape of the Lock*, wrote the prologue and Garth the epilogue to Addison's tragedy *Cato*. Garth also wrote serious poems dedicated to the earl of Godolphin and the duke of Marlborough when they were out of favour politically.

Garth was knighted upon George I's accession to the throne in 1715 and was appointed physician-in-ordinary to the king and physician-general to the army. Garth's friends valued his loyalty and thoughtfulness. For example, the poem to Marlborough laments the latter's disgrace and voluntary exile. When Dryden died destitute in May 1700, Garth arranged for his corpse to be brought to the Royal College of Physicians and for a burial procession from there to Westminster Abbey. Garth died in London on 18 January 1719 and was buried four days later beside his wife at St Mary's Church, Harrow on the Hill, Middlesex. Garth bequeathed his entire estate to his daughter. Responding, perhaps, to widespread belief in Garth's lack of Christian faith, Pope wrote to a friend on 12 December 1719 that Garth was the best natured of men, and that

> his death was very heroical, and yet unaffected enough to have made a saint or philosopher famous. But ill tongues, and worse hearts, have branded even his last moments, as wrongfully as they did his life with irreligion. You must have heard many tales on this subject; but if ever there was a good Christian, without knowing himself to be so, it was Dr. Garth.

ROBERT L. MARTENSEN

Sources A. Kippis and others, eds., *Biographia Britannica, or, The lives of the most eminent persons who have flourished in Great Britain and Ireland*, 2nd edn, 5 vols. (1778-93) • Munk, *Roll* • private information (2004) [G. C. R. Morris] • R. I. Cook, *Sir Samuel Garth* (1980) • C. C. Booth, 'Sir Samuel Garth, FRS: the dispensary poet', *Notes and Records of the Royal Society*, 40 (1985-6), 125-45 • H. Cushing, 'Dr Garth: the Kit-kat poet', *Bulletin of the Johns Hopkins Hospital* (1906), 1-17 • *DNB*
Archives BL, the key to his dispensary and letters to Sir Hans Sloane, Sloane MSS 629, fols. 265-268b, 4059, fols. 27-47b • BL, corresp. and papers, Add. MSS 27989, 32685, 35335, 40060, 47126, 61284, 61475; Stowe MS 155
Likenesses G. Kneller, oils, *c*.1705-1710 (Kit-Cat Club), NPG [see illus.] • oils, *c*.1705-1710, NPG • oils, *c*.1705-1710, Knole, Kent • J. Faber junior, mezzotint, 1733 (after G. Kneller), BM, NPG, Wellcome L. • J. Houbraken, line engraving, 1748 (after G. Kneller), Wellcome L. • J. June, line engraving, 1764 (after G. Kneller), Wellcome L. • J. Golder, line engraving, 1786 (after G. Kneller), Wellcome L. • F. Sansom, line engraving, 1795 (after G. Kneller), Wellcome L. • B. Granger, stipple, 1798 (after W. H. Brown; after G. Kneller), Wellcome L. • R. Newton, stipple, 1823 (after G. Clint; after G. Kneller), Wellcome L. • J. Caldwell, line engraving (after G. Kneller), Wellcome L. • T. Cook, line engravings (after G. Kneller), Wellcome L. • Hogarth, drawing • G. Kneller, portrait, RCP Lond. • J. Simon, mezzotint (after G. Kneller), BM, NPG, Wellcome L. • engravings (after G. Kneller), Wellcome L.

Garthshore, Maxwell (1732-1812), physician accoucheur, was born at Kirkcudbright on 28 October 1732, the son of Barbara Gordon and her husband, George Garthshore (1687/8-1760), for fifty years minister in Kirkcudbright. After being educated at the Kirkcudbright grammar school he was apprenticed to a surgeon apothecary in

Edinburgh at the age of fourteen, and attended medical classes in the university. Before proceeding to his degree Garthshore, then aged twenty-two, entered the army as surgeon's mate to Richard Hick-Saunders, in Lord Charles Hay's regiment. In 1756 he settled at Uppingham, Rutland, succeeding (through the aid of his cousin Robert Maitland, a prosperous London merchant) to the practice of John Fordyce. On 11 November 1759 at Anworth, Kirkcudbright, he married Elizabeth, daughter of William Blair McGuffoch, who brought him the small estate of Ruscoe in Kirkcudbrightshire; she died in 1765, leaving him one son surviving. After practising successfully at Uppingham for eight years, Garthshore was encouraged to move to London, and to improve his chances there he graduated MD at Edinburgh on 8 May 1764, and was admitted a fellow of the Royal College of Physicians of Edinburgh. He was admitted a licentiate of the Royal College of Physicians on 1 October 1764. He developed a large practice as an accoucheur, was appointed physician to the British Lying-in Hospital, became FRS (1775) and FRSE (1792), and was also a fellow of the Antiquarian Society. He was a formal, fashionable physician, a sincere orthodox Christian, and extremely generous to the poor, although parsimonious in his personal expenditure. It is said that on one occasion he gave in a single donation more than his entire annual income (GM, 387–8). The widow of the surgeon John Hunter also received financial assistance from him.

Garthshore bore a striking resemblance to the first earl of Chatham, and was once pointed out in a debate in the House of Commons as the earl, whom everyone believed to be present (GM, 391). His only publications were his inaugural dissertation at Edinburgh, De papaveris usu ... in parturientibus ac puerperis (1764); two papers read before the Society of Physicians in 1769, and published in the fourth and fifth volumes of Medical Observations; 'Observations on extra-uterine cases, and ruptures of the tubes and uterus', published in the London Medical Journal (1787); and 'A remarkable case of numerous births' (PTRS, 1788, 78). As an accoucheur Garthshore was judged to be:

> extremely patient, as long as patience was a virtue; and in cases of difficulty or extreme danger, he decided with quickness and great judgement; and he always had a mind sufficiently firm to enable his hands to execute that which his head dictated. (GM, 390)

On 17 May 1795 he married Elizabeth Murrell, widow of William Murrell; she died some years before him. Garthshore died on 1 March 1812 at St Martin's Lane, London, and was buried in Bunhill Fields cemetery, where a monument was erected to his memory. He died worth about £35,000. Garthshore derived the greater part of his wealth from his son, causing him to remark 'My son, when living, made me poor. At his death, he made me rich' (GM, 300).

William Garthshore (1764–1806), politician, Garthshore's son by his first marriage, was born in London on 28 October 1764. He was educated at Hampstead, Westminster School, and Christ Church, Oxford, where he graduated BA (1786) and MA (1789) and became a tutor. He afterwards was tutor to the marquess of Dalkeith, and made an extensive tour in Europe with him. Returning in 1792, he 'declined payment from Dalkeith's father, the 3rd Duke of Buccleuch, preferring the latter's patronage for his diplomatic career' (Ingamells, 393). The duke recommended him to Henry Dundas, who appointed him his private secretary in 1794. On 24 May 1794 Garthshore married Sarah Jane, daughter of John Chalié, wealthy wine merchant. Garthshore was elected MP for Launceston in January 1795, and for Weymouth and Melcombe Regis in September of the same year, and retained his seat until his death. He was also elected FRSE in 1745. In 1801 he was appointed a lord of the Admiralty by Addington, holding the post until 1804; before then, however, he had suffered the deaths of his father-in-law, his wife, and his only child within a few days of one another (5 and 9 August 1803). Garthshore retired to Worthing but never recovered from these events. He died on 5 April 1806, having 'been in a melancholy state of mind for a considerable time ... so as to render an application to the Court of Chancery and a Commission of lunacy necessary' (HoP, Commons).

G. T. BETTANY, rev. MICHAEL BEVAN

Sources M. P., 'Memoirs of the late Dr Maxwell Garthshore', GM, 1st ser., 82/1 (1812), 387–91 · GM, 1st ser., 82/1 (1812), 300, 673 · 'Garthshore, William', HoP, Commons · IGI · Munk, Roll · J. Ingamells, ed., A dictionary of British and Irish travellers in Italy, 1701–1800 (1997) [William Garthshore] · Foster, Alum. Oxon., 1715–1886 [William Garthshore] · G. Grieg, The death of believers precious in the sight of Jehovah: a discourse [on Psalm cxvi.15] occasioned by the death of M. Garthshore ... to which are added, notes, biographical, devotional, and miscellaneous (1812) · The record of the Royal Society of London, 4th edn (1940) · F. Bennet and M. Melrose, Index of fellows of the Royal Society of Edinburgh: elected November 1783 – July 1883, ed. H. Frew, rev. edn (1984)

Archives Lpool RO, papers relating to French prisoners of war

Likenesses attrib. T. West, coloured etching, 1803, Wellcome L. · Collyer, engraving (after Slater) · Slater, portrait

Wealth at death under £35,000: GM, 673

Garthshore, William (1764–1806). See under Garthshore, Maxwell (1732–1812).

Garthwaite, Anna Maria (1688–1763?), textile designer, was born on 14 March 1688 at Harston, Leicestershire, the second of the three daughters of the Revd Ephraim Garthwaite (d. 1719), rector of Grantham, Lincolnshire, and his wife, Rejoyce, née Henstead. The first forty years of her life were spent in Lincolnshire where her father was a well-connected Anglican clergyman with family associations with the City of London. After his death in 1719 it is probable that she went to live with her elder sister, Mary, the wife of Robert Dannye, rector of Spofforth, Yorkshire. In 1729 or 1730 Dannye died, and both sisters then went to London, where they eventually settled in Princes Street (now 2 Princelet Street) in the parish of Christ Church, Spitalfields. Their choice of residence may have related to a connection to the locality via the Bacon family, but germane to Anna Maria's professional life was the significance of Spitalfields as the centre of the quality eighteenth-century silk industry in England.

The Garthwaite daughters, to each of whom their father left a legacy of £500 as well as his library, were probably well educated in a conventional manner, Anna Maria having had particular aptitude for design and botanical drawing. Her interest in textile design was apparent by 1726, when she collected and annotated a series of textile designs, 'by diverse hands', which included technically innovative and high-quality French work. Her first drawing, inscribed 'sent to London before I left York', was competent but simple. The largest series of her work, comprising many hundreds of drawings of silk designs and patterns, some of which are still enrolled in their contemporary arrangement covering the period from 1726 to 1756, has survived and is in the collection of the Victoria and Albert Museum in London. It is clear that, at a time when the English silk industry vied with French manufacturers for the quality home and export market, she was one of the foremost designers of 'flowered', or brocaded, silks.

The V&A collection shows that Garthwaite was capable of working within all the stylistic trends of the period. Her designs with a floral emphasis have particular grace and individuality, and her work demonstrates considerable ability in placing these against the fashionable formal background. Noteworthy is her interest in some rare exotics. Her output was at its highest in the 1730s and 1740s, when such patterns were most fashionable, and at her peak she was producing eighty designs a year. In the early 1750s the numbers declined sharply and by 1756 she had varied her range to include a flowered gauze and a carpet pattern. Silks of her design have been found not only in the United Kingdom but also in Europe and North America.

The enrolled lists and the annotations, probably in her own hand, show her to have been working for silkmen at the top level of the market concerned with textiles which were time-consuming to weave and costly to manufacture. She displayed a noteworthy grasp of textile technique, including technical direction as necessary. Surviving silks show how well her designs adapt to form and function. Garthwaite point paper, imprinted with squares for drafting designs in the early nineteenth century, may be a retrospective tribute to her expertise. The basis for her technical knowledge can only be conjectured, though Robert Campart, a Spitalfields ribbon weaver of Huguenot extraction, is named as a beneficiary, together with his wife, in Garthwaite's will.

Since the status of silk designers was high, and their role in the export trade crucial, it is unfortunate that the female silk designer so favourably referred to in the *Gentleman's Magazine* for 1749 (*GM*, 319) and adversely criticized in F. Rouquet's *L'état des arts en Angleterre* of 1755 (Rouquet, 111) is not named. However, P. K. T. Thornton has made a convincing case for Garthwaite's authorship of 'Of designing and drawing of ornaments, … for the use of the flowered silk manufactory, embroidery and printing (of the various kinds of flower'd silks)' in the 1759 edition of G. Smith's *The Laboratory or School of Arts*. Knowledgeable, lucid, and amusing, it sheds a somewhat jaundiced light on the role of the English silk designer as opposed to the French, at a time when the English silk industry was about to enter a period of crisis. The heartfelt comments that 'a new pattern drawer will come into vogue and the old experienced one will be discarded. These ungenerous proceedings I have experienced myself' (Garthwaite) may have oblique reference to Garthwaite's diminishing output after 1750.

It is not known where or exactly when Garthwaite died, but on 24 October 1763, at Princes Street in the parish of Christ Church, the 1758 will of Anna Maria Garthwaite, spinster, in which she left a fairly modest estate of about £600, was proved. Bequests imply a friendly, well-provided household but there is no mention of designs, though these were valued tools of the trade. Her sister, Mary Dannye, in whose Yorkshire estate she was to have an interest, predeceased her. Their niece, Mary Baron, was the main beneficiary.   M. GINSBURG

Sources N. Rothstein, *Silk designs of the eighteenth century: in the collection of the Victoria and Albert Museum, London, with a complete catalogue* (1990) · P. K. T. Thornton, 'A silk designer's manual', *Bulletin of the Needle and Bobbin Club*, 42/1–2 (1958) · A. M. Garthwaite, 'Of designing and drawing of ornaments, … for the use of the flowered silk manufactory, embroidery and printing (of the various kinds of flower'd silks)', in G. Smith, *The laboratory or school of arts* (1759) · N. Rothstein, *The Victoria & Albert Museum's textile collection: woven textile design in Britain to 1750* (1994) · N. Rothstein, *The Victoria & Albert Museum's textile collection: woven textile design in Britain from 1750 to 1850* (1994) · *GM*, 1st ser., 19 (1749), 318–19 · F. Rouquet, *L'état des arts en Angleterre* (1755), 111 · bishop's transcripts, 1582–1936 (birth), parish church of Harston, Leicestershire · will, PRO, PROB 11/892, sig. 471 · IGI

Wealth at death approx. £600: will, 1758, PRO, PROB 11/892, sig. 471

Garton, Sir Richard Charles (1857–1934), chemist and brewer, was born at 11 Richmond Place, Bedminster, Somerset, on 8 October 1857, the eldest of five sons of William Garton (1832–1905) a brewer, and his wife, Ellen Miller, *née* Littleton. William Garton's company, Garton Hill, pioneered the production of saccharin, or invert sugar, at Southampton in 1855. Richard was educated at Owens College, Manchester, and at Marburg University, Germany, where he studied the problems of fermentation in brewing. He made an early study of chemistry, and later became involved in the application of modern chemistry to the brewing and sugar industries. He was a pioneer in the manufacture of liquid glucose (corn syrup), the development of which, in the confectionery trade, he did much to foster. A practical brewer of great ability, his knowledge and advice were sought by many companies. He provided financial assistance to institutions founded to advance the science and practice of brewing, such as the Institute of Brewing, of which he was vice-president, the School of Brewing at the University of Birmingham, and the Sir John Cass Institute of London. He provided financial support and gave advice to the council of the Brewers' Society and the National Trade Defence Association, and encouraged brewery companies to adopt a policy of public-house reform. In 1902, when the brewing industry was experiencing difficulties, Garton was invited to join the board of Watney, Combe, Reid & Co. Ltd as a director. He was appointed deputy chairman in 1924 and chairman in 1928, but ill health forced him to relinquish the post in 1932, though he remained on the board. He was also a director of E. Lacon & Co., a brewery in Great Yarmouth, permanent governing director of Garton, Sons & Co., and a director of Manbré and Garton Ltd, brewing-sugar manufacturers of Battersea. Considered a financial expert, he was for some years a director of Lloyds Bank Ltd.

In 1900 Garton unsuccessfully contested Battersea as a Conservative. A staunch unionist, he was president of the Haslemere branch of the Unionist Association, and of the Constitutional Club. In 1912 he established the Garton Foundation for the study of international relations, especially the relation of military and political power to social and economic advantage. Knighted in 1908, he was created a GBE for his war services in 1918. Although he took a minor role in the public life of Haslemere, he was a generous supporter of local organizations and institutions. Garton had married in 1883 Nellie (d. 1925), daughter of Andrew Durrant of Bishops Hall, Chelmsford. They had two daughters. In memory of his wife he built the children's ward of Haslemere Hospital, and later added a nurses' hostel. He presented the town with a steam fire engine, which he later replaced with a motorized one.

Sir Richard was one of the founders of the British Empire Cancer Campaign. His gift of £20,000 set the campaign up in 1923 and he thereafter served as its honorary secretary and chairman of its finance committee. In 1928 he paid for the entire cost of the International Conference on Cancer, which was attended by over 600 delegates. In connection with his investigations into cancer, he established the Garton prize of £500 and medal in 1931. He was honorary secretary and treasurer of the King's College for Women department of household and social science in the University of London.

Sir Richard made a hobby of collecting seventeenth- and eighteenth-century drinking glasses, which were exhibited at the Educational Museum, Haslemere, in 1932. Yachting and horse-racing were his chief sports, and he later devoted much time to the breeding of racehorses. Not long before his death he took over the Brook stud at Newmarket, intending to breed on a large scale, but he became very ill and died at his home, Lythe Hill, Haslemere, on 22 April 1934, survived by his daughters. He was buried at Haslemere parish church on 25 April.

FIONA WOOD

Sources *Journal of the Institute of Brewing* (June 1934), 261–2 · *Brewing Trade Review* (May 1934), 268 · *Brewers' Journal* (15 May 1934), 277 · *Red Barrel Magazine* (May 1934) · H. H. Janes, *The red barrel: a history of Watney Mann* [1963] · *WWW* · J. L. Garbutt, *Manbré and Garton Ltd, 1855–1955: a hundred years of progress* (1955) · T. Corran, 'Garton, Sir Richard Charles', *DBB* · *The Times* (24 April 1934), 5a, 16b · *The Times* (26 April 1934), 9e · *The Times* (27 April 1934), 17a · d. cert. · b. cert. · *CGPLA Eng. & Wales* (1934)
Likenesses photograph, Brewers' Society, London; repro. in *Brewing Trade Review* · photograph, Brewers' Society, London; repro. in *Brewers' Journal* · photograph, Brewers' Society, London; repro. in *Journal of the Institution of Brewing* · picture, repro. in *Red Barrel Magazine*
Wealth at death £2,641,364 19s. 7d.: probate, 22 June 1934, *CGPLA Eng. & Wales*

Gartside, Thomas Edmund [Tommy] (1857–1941), cotton spinner, was born at Park Lane, Royton, 2 miles north of Oldham, on 9 February 1857, the only son of Alice Gartside. His birth occurred at a most propitious time, since Oldham became the world's leading mill town during the 1860s, and so opened up opportunities for the young and enterprising. Gartside went to the Methodist school in Royton and later took evening classes at Royton Temperance Seminary. He began work at the age of twelve and gained experience in half a dozen different posts, rising from shop assistant in 1869 to clerk in 1876, and to company secretary in 1889. In 1883 he married Harriet (1855–1937), daughter of William Travis, a waste dealer; they had two sons and two daughters. Only when he became a director of the Shiloh Spinning Company in 1891, and its manager in 1894, did Gartside embark on his real business career. The seal was set upon his ascent in 1891, when he became a member of the Manchester Royal Exchange, and so joined the élite of the cotton world in the largest of markets for cotton yarn and cotton cloth.

Gartside's first task was to restore Shiloh to financial health and to a position befitting its auspicious name. Founded during the boom of 1874 as one of Oldham's limited-liability spinning companies, it had proved to be one of the least successful of ventures. Its dividend record was appalling and its debit balance had trebled in the decade from 1885 to 1894. Gartside infused a new spirit into the administration of the company, pursued a shrewd financial policy, and established tight control over the purchase, spinning, and sale of yarn. He liquidated the debit balance by 1897, and so restored the confidence of investors. He raised the proportion of loan capital to 76 per cent of the total capital by 1902. Not merely did he resume the payment of dividends from 1899, for the first time since 1885, but he also raised their level by paying a low fixed interest to the loanholders. He endowed Shiloh with a new mill (1899–1901) and installed mules manufactured by Platts, which proved more productive than those from Asa Lees. He depreciated his plant at the same high annual rate of 6 per cent as his fellow businessman John Bunting (1839–1923). He bought cotton cheaply and in bulk, and enlarged his storage facilities in order to avoid being held to ransom by speculators in the raw cotton market. Shiloh joined the élite of the 'Oldham limiteds' in 1906 when it ceased to publish accounts, and so passed from the realm of public scrutiny to semi-private status, its shareholders remaining content with the regular payment of 10 per cent dividends for the twenty-two years from 1904 to 1926.

The abilities of Tommy Gartside were recognized by his appointment, by 1899, as a director of three other companies, by which time he had laid the foundation for the construction of a group of associated companies. The formation of that group took place in two phases, during the Edwardian boom of 1904–8, and during the years 1916–23. Between 1904 and 1908 he became the chairman of three companies, including Shiloh itself in 1907. From 1908 he was attending the regular weekly meetings of eight different boards of directors. By 1914 his three core companies controlled six mills, with 284,325 spindles. By 1923 he had become the chairman of nine companies, with fourteen mills and 962,780 spindles, some 44 per cent of the total number in Royton. The construction of the Gartside group was complete. Until 1922 all the companies were located in Royton itself, so easing the task of supervision. All save two had built new mills rather than operating the old mills favoured by Bunting. Gartside himself confined his interests to the cotton trade, becoming a director of the local board of the London and Lancashire Insurance Company and of John Hepworth & Co., yarn agents. In 1914 he became a member of the committee of the Oldham Master Cotton Spinners' Association and of the Federation of Master Cotton Spinners' Associations, both bodies which Bunting shunned. In 1919 he served as one of Oldham's five delegates to the World Cotton Conference in New Orleans. In 1923 he became vice-president of the Oldham Master Cotton Spinners' Association.

During the boom of 1919–20 Gartside avoided the temptation to recapitalize his companies in the extravagant mode adopted by other limiteds. He undertook a conservative recapitalization of Shiloh in 1920, but used the opportunity to end its reliance on loan capital. The group registered its best performance for the year 1925 when Shiloh paid a dividend of 12.5 per cent and the rest of the group averaged 31 per cent, an abnormally high level caused by the 115 per cent distributed by the group's Grape Mill. The performance of Shiloh was indeed outclassed by that of the other Gartside mills for twelve years from 1921. In 1916 Gartside had first introduced high-speed ring spinning into the Park and Sandy Lane Mill, but he remained loyal to the Lancashire mule, the proportion of ring spindles in his mills averaging only one-third the proportion in the Oldham district as a whole. He built the Elk Mill in 1926–7 out of Shiloh's reserve funds and equipped it with 107,000 mule spindles supplied by Platts. That mill, together with the Holden Mill built at Astley Bridge to the north of Bolton, were the last mule mills to be built in Lancashire: both were built by cotton magnates who had begun their working lives in their shirt-sleeves. The year 1926 marked the climacteric of the textile industry in Lancashire and in the world. Thereafter dividends declined, especially after 1931, to reach a nadir in 1934–5, and averaged during the 1930s only one-third of their level in the 1920s. The price of Shiloh shares sank below par from 1930 and did not rise above par until 1939.

The mills of Royton spun coarse counts of yarn, or Royton counts, for the home trade, and successfully preserved their independence, while other mills were reluctantly forced by their dependence on loans into large combines. Gartside remained fiercely independent and declined to join the Cotton Yarn Association formed in 1927. In 1933 he did negotiate with his local rival, Will Cheetham (1869–1942), the Royton coarse counts agreement, which was the first price-fixing agreement reached within the industry since 1909. He refused to join the Lancashire Cotton Corporation which had been formed in 1929 in order to rationalize the American spinning trade

by closing down mills. Nor would he conform to its policies for regulating the market: 'He is an impossible fellow … He will creep under the general price just so long as he is allowed to' (minutes of the board of directors, Lancashire Cotton Corporation, 30 May 1934, 4). Thereby Gartside performed a valuable social service: he excluded outside influence from Royton and maintained local employment opportunities when they were shrinking elsewhere. Two of the Gartside companies, the Roy and the Willow Vale, ceased to pay dividends after 1922, but were kept in operation as machines for processing cotton and for paying wages. Even burdened by such millstones, the Gartside group averaged a dividend for the years 1908–41 of 8.9 per cent, while Shiloh itself paid one of 8.6 per cent (1902–41), or one quarter higher than the Oldham average. By 1941 Shiloh was paying a dividend of 20 per cent and its shares stood at a premium of 35 per cent. Thus Gartside fulfilled his responsibilities to Royton as well as to his shareholders: in return he secured the intense loyalty possible only within a small community. He also served as vicar's warden at St Paul's Church, Royton, from 1903, as a Lancashire magistrate from 1913, and as a Liberal councillor on Royton urban district council (1906–15). The whole of Royton mourned his passing when he died, at the age of eighty-three, on 8 January 1941, at his home, Highlands House, Royton. He was buried at Royton cemetery on 11 January.

Gartside was succeeded at Shiloh first by his son, Colonel J. B. Gartside (1897–1964) and then, from 1965, by his grandson, Edmund Gartside. Under that dynasty the Shiloh group achieved a unique status within Lancashire. First, it survived through the pursuit of a shrewd policy of product diversification, while other groups disintegrated and disappeared. It successfully preserved its independence of the giant corporations which invaded Lancashire during the 1960s. Second, it remained under the administration of the same family for three generations, in flat defiance of the local proverb 'From shirt-sleeves to shirt-sleeves takes three generations'. Third, it maintained a highly effective paternalist tradition which created 'the Shiloh breed' of workpeople and integrated the members of 'the Shiloh family' into the service of a continuing enterprise.

D. A. FARNIE

Sources *Oldham Chronicle* (11 Jan 1941) · *Oldham Chronicle* (13 Jan 1941) · 'Cotton mill share investments, XIV. Shiloh Mills Ltd, Royton', *The Textile Weekly* (23 June 1933), 432 · D. J. Jeremy, 'Gartside, Thomas Edmund', *DBB* · [E. Gartside], *The Shiloh story, 1874–1949* (privately printed, London, 1949) · [E. Gartside], *The Shiloh story, 1874–1974* (privately printed, Royton, 1974) · D. A. Farnie, 'The emergence of Victorian Oldham as the centre of the cotton spinning industry', *Bulletin of the Saddleworth Historical Society*, 12/3 (autumn 1982), 41–53 · b. cert. · d. cert. · *CGPLA Eng. & Wales* (1941) · U. Warwick Mod. RC, Lancashire Cotton Corporation, minutes of the board of directors

Archives Shiloh plc, Holden Fold, Royton, Oldham, minute books of the Shiloh Mills Ltd and of the member companies of the Shiloh Group | SOUND BBC WAC

Likenesses photograph, repro. in J. Middleton, *Oldham past and present* (1903), 185

Wealth at death £237,496 11s. 1d.: resworn probate, 3 March 1941, *CGPLA Eng. & Wales*

Garvey, Amy Ashwood (1895/1897–1969), pan-African organizer and feminist, is variously recorded as having been born on 18 January 1895 and on 10 January 1897, in Port Antonio, Jamaica. She was the only daughter among three children of Michael Delbert Ashwood, businessman, and his wife, Maudriana Thompson. She was taken to Panama as an infant but returned in 1904 to Jamaica, where she attended the Westwood High School for Girls.

In 1914 Amy met Marcus Mosiah *Garvey (1887–1940), who was just back from England, and within days she had become a member of his new Universal Negro Improvement Association (UNIA), which was to become the largest pan-African mass movement. Marcus Garvey's dream was to unite the African race through his association. Amy Ashwood worked closely with him, first as friend and later as fiancée. He left for the United States in 1916 but was reunited with Amy in 1918 in New York, by which time he had re-established the UNIA in Harlem. Together they travelled around North America, and Amy became a director of the UNIA's Black Star Line Steamship Corporation. In October 1919 she helped to save Marcus Garvey's life from a would-be assassin, and on Christmas day of that year they married. The union was substantially over within three months, leaving the couple embroiled in divorce and related lawsuits. Marcus Garvey later married his former wife's chief bridesmaid, Amy Jacques.

Amy visited England and Europe from 1921 to 1924. In London she founded the Nigerian Progress Union, a precursor to the important West African Students' Union. In 1924 she returned to New York, where she produced musical comedies in collaboration with Trinidad calypso musician and her lifelong companion, Sam Manning. Amy and Manning toured the Caribbean (1929–1931) with a musical show, on the heels of Marcus Garvey, who had been deported to Jamaica in 1927.

From 1935 to 1938 Amy lived in England. She ran a restaurant and club in London's West End and was an active member of radical organizations led by C. L. R. James and George Padmore. She and Manning again collaborated on musical shows. Marcus Garvey was also in London at this time and the former lovers had a chance encounter in 1938. Amy spent some time in New York in 1939 before returning to Jamaica, where she remained from 1940 to 1944; there she formed the short-lived J. A. G. Smith Political Party.

Back in Harlem, Amy became a fixture at radical gatherings. She associated with the West Indies National Council and Paul Robeson's Council on African Affairs; she also campaigned for Adam Clayton Powell jun., African America's first congressman from Harlem. Because of these activities she was kept under FBI surveillance. She returned to England in 1945 in time for the fifth Pan-African Congress, and chaired its first session. Also at this time she thwarted, via a legal injunction, an initiative by Marcus Garvey's second wife to have his remains repatriated to Jamaica.

In 1946 Amy travelled to west Africa, and in Liberia she began a long-lasting love affair with President William V. S. Tubman. In the Asante kingdom she was able to trace

Amy Ashwood Garvey (1895/1897–1969), by unknown photographer

her roots to the village of Juaben, and she was welcomed home as a long-lost daughter by the Asantehene, King Prempeh II. In Nigeria she did extensive research into the condition of women and lectured to women's groups.

In 1949 Amy was back in England and was able to welcome the post-war influx of Caribbean immigrants. In 1953 she toured the Caribbean for seven months, addressing women's groups. In the same year she established the Afro Peoples Centre at 1 Bassett Road, Ladbroke Grove, London. This building, which became a well-known community centre, was purchased for her by an English MP, Sir Hamilton Kerr. Following the Notting Hill riots of 1958 she worked to obtain justice for Caribbean immigrants. In another important initiative she helped to found the Association for the Advancement of Coloured People; this had influential support from Dr David Pitt and Fenner Brockway MP, who both served as vice-presidents.

Amy returned to Africa in 1960 but was back in London four years later, when the Jamaican government renewed its efforts to repatriate Marcus Garvey's remains. This time she was persuaded to co-operate, and she spent the next three years mostly in Jamaica and Trinidad. In 1967–8 she was in the United States, where the black power generation rediscovered her. There she produced a gramophone record celebrating Marcus Garvey's work.

Amy returned to Jamaica in 1968 with failing health, and died in Kingston on 3 May 1969. Though she had wished to be buried in Liberia this was beyond the slender resources of her few friends, and she was buried instead, on Sunday 11 May 1969, in Kingston's Calvary cemetery. Despite never attaining the historical prominence of her famous associates Amy Ashwood Garvey was an important figure during several decades of pan-African endeavour. TONY MARTIN

Sources Amy Ashwood Garvey papers [formerly in the possession of Lionel M. Yard of Brooklyn, New York; present whereabouts unknown] · priv. coll., London, Amy Ashwood Garvey papers · National Library of Jamaica, Kingston, Amy Ashwood Garvey papers · T. Martin, *Amy Ashwood Garvey: pan-Africanist, feminist and wife no. 1* (1988) · T. Martin, 'Discovering African roots: Amy Ashwood Garvey's pan-Africanist journey', *Comparative Studies of South Asia, Africa and the Middle East*, 17/1 (1997) · L. M. Yard, *Biography of Amy Ashwood Garvey, 1887–1969* [n.d., 1987?] · T. Martin, *The pan-African connection* (1983) · private information (2004) [I. Constable Richards]

Archives priv. coll., papers | FILM NYPL, Schomburg Center for Research in Black Culture, interview
Likenesses photograph, Amy Ashwood Garvey Archive [*see illus.*]
Wealth at death practically nothing: private information (2004) [I. Constable Richards]

Garvey, Edmund (1740–1813), landscape painter, was born at Kilkenny, Ireland, in 1740, the son of a painter. According to Farington, Garvey's father had been a pupil of Richard Carver (*d.* 1754) and Edmund studied under Carver's son Robert (*d.* 1791). Garvey was in London before 1764 and visited Italy when young. On his return he took up residence in Bath, where he remained until the late 1770s. Garvey first exhibited at the Free Society of Artists in 1767, where he showed views of Italy and Switzerland. His works had a mixed reception; one reviewer commented that 'this artist is not without great share of merit; but a disagreeable sameness at colouring reigns throughout his whole paintings, and his figures are without one spark of life' (*GM*). His landscapes depicted, predominantly, foreign scenery and gentlemen's seats, and though Garvey was reasonably adept at imitating nature, his paintings were dry and hard in manner.

Garvey first exhibited at the Royal Academy in 1769, being awarded a premium of 20 guineas. He exhibited annually until 1808, first from Bath and after 1778 from various London addresses. Garvey became an associate of the Royal Academy in 1770 but it was not until 1783 that he was elected a full academician, presenting *A View of Rome* as his diploma piece. Garvey's election was controversial as he was chosen over Joseph Wright of Derby, receiving ten votes to his rival's eight. Farington claims that Thomas Gainsborough canvassed in favour of Garvey and that Sir Joshua Reynolds had favoured a candidate resident in London, who could carry out the duties of an academician.

Garvey was back in Rome by March 1792 and in 1793 was sharing lodgings at the strada Gregoriana with the painter Henry Howard. He returned to England some time before November 1795. During the peace of Amiens he visited Paris with John Flaxman, Henry Fuseli, and Farington. He died in London on 28 May 1813 a relatively wealthy man, leaving between £4000 and £5000 to his sister. He was buried at St Paul's, Covent Garden, London on 3 June. A collection of Garvey's pictures was sold at auction in 1816.

L. H. CUST, *rev.* DEBORAH GRAHAM-VERNON

Sources Farington, *Diary* · J. Ingamells, ed., *A dictionary of British and Irish travellers in Italy, 1701–1800* (1997) · W. G. Strickland, *A dictionary of Irish artists*, 2 vols. (1913); repr. with introduction by T. J. Snoddy (1989) · Waterhouse, *18c painters* · W. Sandby, *The history of the Royal Academy of Arts*, 2 vols. (1862); facs. edn (1970) · Redgrave, *Artists* · W. T. Whitley, *Artists and their friends in England, 1700–1799*, 2 vols. (1928) · *The exhibition of the Royal Academy (1769–1808)* [exhibition catalogues] · Graves, *RA exhibitors* · *GM*, 1st ser., 37 (1767), 240
Likenesses G. Dance, drawing, RA · H. Singleton, group portrait, oils (*Royal Academicians, 1793*), RA

Wealth at death £4000–£5000: Farington, *Diary*

Garvey, John (*c.*1515–1595), Church of Ireland archbishop of Armagh, was the son of John Garvey or O Garvey of Murrisk, co. Mayo, 'marshal and sergeant under the Lord O'Malley', and his wife, Fionnghuala Butler, from the same area. The belief that he was born in Kilkenny is apparently derived from a mistaken speculation by Anthony Wood that he was a member of the well-known Garvey family of that city, but a genealogy written down before his elevation to the episcopate in 1585 gives a detailed account of his ancestry in Mayo for four generations (TCD, MS 663, 96). The date of 1527 given for his birth in later sources is irreconcilable with his being called an 'old man' by Sir Henry Sidney (himself born in 1529) in 1576 and 'very aged' by Archbishop Loftus in 1586. He is said by Wood to have graduated at Oxford in the reign of Edward VI, although his name does not appear in the university's register, and he is described in 1561 as 'Sir John Garvey', or 'John Garvey, chaplain', showing that he had not graduated MA.

It may have been in England that Garvey came to the attention of Thomas Radcliffe, earl of Sussex and lord lieutenant of Ireland, whose servant and chaplain he became. His first ecclesiastical appointment, so far as is known, was the deanery of Ferns, to which he was appointed by Sussex between November 1558 and March 1559. He seems to have resigned it on being appointed, on 14 July 1560, to the archdeaconry of Meath with its annexed rectory of Kells. In the following months he acted as one of the negotiators between Sussex and Shane O'Neill. About this time he received the additional preferment of one of the two prebends of Tipperkevin in St Patrick's Cathedral, Dublin, obtaining on 27 January 1561 a grant of 'English Liberty' on account of the old statutes prohibiting Gaelic Irishmen from holding such benefices. On 8 April 1565 he was appointed to the rich deanery of Christ Church, Dublin, with permission to retain his other benefices, and in November 1566 was made a member of the Irish council. About this time he married his parishioner at Kells, Margaret, daughter of Christopher Plunket of Taterath, a marriage which linked him, a Gaelic outsider, to the upper gentry of the pale. They had five sons and three daughters, but she does not seem to have been the mother of his eldest son, Sir Christopher, who must have been by an earlier, unrecorded, marriage.

In October 1567 Garvey was recommended for the vacant archbishopric of Armagh by Hugh Brady, bishop of Meath, who extolled him as 'grave and well-learned, a sharp preacher in the Irish tongue' (Shirley, 315), but he was not appointed. In October 1572 he was recommended to the queen for the bishopric of Ardagh, with permission to retain his existing benefices, but although the matter dragged on until July 1573 he was again denied promotion. In the spring of 1576 he was sent into Connaught by Sir Henry Sidney, lord deputy, 'to sound the disposition of the potentates and great ones of that province' ahead of Sidney's own visit; in praising his service on this errand Sidney urged the queen to send an individual letter of thanks to 'the old man' (PRO, SP 63/55, no. 34). Recommendations by the Irish council that he be made bishop of Kildare (February 1583) and, once more, archbishop of Armagh (May 1584), were again unsuccessful, but on 20 January 1585 he was appointed bishop of Kilmore, with dispensation to retain his existing benefices, and was consecrated on 25 April following. A proposal that he be transferred to the richer see of Ossory in March 1586 was unsuccessful.

In January 1589, a new vacancy having arisen in the archbishopric of Armagh, Garvey wrote to Burghley and Walsingham seeking the appointment, and citing his thirty years 'daily service' to the queen. His appeal was backed by Sir Nicholas White, another Irish protestant, who praised his lifestyle, his knowledge of the Irish language and his record as a councillor, although admitting that he no longer preached (perhaps hardly surprising in view of his age). Although alternative New English candidates were put forward by the lord deputy and by Archbishop Loftus, he was nominated as archbishop by the queen on 21 March 1589 (again with the right to retain his deanery and archdeaconry) although he was still not yet consecrated on 10 May. He was subsequently, on 12 July 1591, remitted the payment of £137 13s. 1d. first fruits. In the interval between his nomination for the archbishopric and his appointment he had served as a member of the commission sent to investigate the complaints made against the oppressions and misgovernment of Sir Richard Bingham as governor of Connaught; the commission's report, delivered on 4 May 1589, was very unfavourable to Bingham, and seems to have brought Garvey into collision with his own son, Christopher, who was one of Bingham's lieutenants.

Although Garvey was described by Loftus in 1586 as 'one justly suspected to incline to papistry, if he have any religion at all' (Ford, 32-3), his early career suggests that he was, at that time at least, a sincere protestant. As a native Irish speaker of unimpeachable loyalty, he was a useful member of the Irish council of which he was a hard-working and diligent attender, but, although his own inclination was certainly towards a moderate and conciliatory policy, the evidence suggests that he supported the policies of whatever lord deputy happened to be in power. Most, if not all, of his children were subsequently Roman Catholics, but the same is true of others of his contemporaries of whose protestantism there is no doubt. His sons Sir Christopher and Anthony amassed a large landed estate in their ancestral co. Mayo, of which all but a small part was to be lost in the Commonwealth confiscations.

Garvey died in Dublin on 2 March 1595 and was buried in Christ Church. He had married as his third wife Rose, daughter of Alderman Thomas Ussher of Dublin and widow of John Money, and was succeeded in his archbishopric by his brother-in-law Henry *Ussher. The attribution to Garvey of a tract on the conversion to protestantism (in 1589) of a Franciscan friar, Philip Corwine or Curwen, published by Robert Ware in 1681, is certainly fictitious, and the alleged original has not been located.

K. W. NICHOLLS

Sources TCD, MSS 663, 1212, 6404 · PRO, SP 63 · *CSP Ire., 1509–92* · J. Morrin, ed., *Calendar of the patent and close rolls of chancery in Ireland, of the reigns of Henry VIII, Edward VI, Mary, and Elizabeth*, 1 (1861) · J. Morrin, ed., *Calendar of the patent and close rolls of chancery in Ireland, of the reigns of Henry VIII, Edward VI, Mary, and Elizabeth*, 2 (1862) · *The Irish fiants of the Tudor sovereigns*, 4 vols. (1994) · E. P. Shirley, ed., *Original letters and papers in illustration of the history of the church in Ireland during the reigns of Edward VI, Mary and Elizabeth* (1851) · Wood, *Ath. Oxon.*, new edn, 2.838 · A. Ford, *The protestant Reformation in Ireland, 1590–1641* (1985)
Wealth at death very substantial

Garvey, Marcus Mosiah (1887–1940), pan-African nationalist leader, was born on 17 August 1887 in St Ann's Bay, Jamaica, the last of two surviving children of Malcus Mosiah Garvey, stonemason (1838–1920), and Sarah Jane Richards (1847/1852–1908), a farmer and domestic servant. His father was a descendant of the maroons, fugitive Africans from the era of slavery. Marcus (baptized Malcus) received a good elementary education. He became apprenticed to printer Alfred E. Burrowes in his early teens, later moving to Kingston where by eighteen he was the youngest foreman printer in Jamaica. His activities expanded into journalism, public speaking, trade unionism, and politics. In 1910 he came third in an all Jamaican oratorical contest. In 1908 Garvey led a pioneering printers' strike. He became assistant secretary of the important National Club. In 1910 he travelled to Central and South America, where he mixed work with travel and political activism. He published newspapers in Costa Rica and Panama.

Garvey toured Europe in 1912–14, visiting Scotland, Ireland, France, Italy, Spain, Austria, Hungary, and Germany. He settled in London, speaking regularly at Hyde Park's speakers' corner, labouring on the London docks, frequenting the public galleries of the House of Commons, attending law lectures at Birkbeck College, and working for the *Africa Times and Orient Review*, edited by an African, Duse Mohamed Ali, a leader of London's Muslim community. Garvey's peripatetic lifestyle and slender resources brought him to the verge of destitution, but he was able to avoid repatriation as a pauper and departed for home on 17 June 1914. He arrived in Jamaica on July 8 and started the Universal Negro Improvement and Conservation Association and African Communities (Imperial) League (usually rendered UNIA), days later. The UNIA emerged from Garvey's realization, enhanced by his travels, that African peoples were everywhere in dire straits and in need of organized uplift. Stories relayed to him on board ship by a Jamaican returning home from southern Africa filled him with a sense of urgency. His simultaneous reading of the United States educator Booker T. Washington's autobiography, *Up from Slavery*, convinced him that self-reliance should be the key to reversing the fortunes of his suffering race.

The fledgeling UNIA articulated both Jamaican and international objectives. The former included the provision of education and jobs and the rehabilitation of fallen women. International objectives included helping to develop Africa and the establishment of a powerful central African nation. The organization immediately

Marcus Mosiah Garvey (1887–1940), by unknown photographer, *c*.1920

became a quasi-literary society with debates, recitations, and oratorical contests. It fed the hungry and visited the sick. It sought employment for the unemployed. Plans to set up an industrial school modelled after Washington's Tuskegee Institute led Garvey into correspondence with Washington and a fund-raising tour of the United States.

Garvey arrived in Harlem, New York, on 23 March 1916. Within a year he had toured the country and returned to Harlem. There he built a following as a street corner orator. He then moved his meetings indoors and by 1918 had made his decision to shift UNIA headquarters to New York. In 1918 Garvey began the *Negro World*, by the early 1920s the world's most widely circulated African newspaper. In 1918 the Negro Factories Corporation appeared, to found and run several UNIA businesses. The Black Star Line Steamship Corporation, the most spectacular of UNIA businesses, was launched in 1919. The UNIA acquired its own meeting place, Liberty Hall, on 138th Street, Harlem. Attendance at weekly meetings sometimes ran into the thousands. UNIA auxiliaries included the Black Cross Nurses, the paramilitary Universal African Legions, and the women's military unit, the Universal African Motor Corps. Children were organized into the UNIA Juveniles.

The organization divided the world into districts run by commissioners, with organizers criss-crossing each district. By the early 1920s membership was estimated by Garvey in the millions. There were about 1200 branches in more than forty-one countries. The UNIA attracted not only masses of people, but also many prominent persons. These included *Negro World* editors T. Thomas Fortune and John Edward Bruce, two of African America's most distinguished journalists; landowner Isaiah Morter from British Honduras (Belize), who bequeathed the UNIA $100,000; Adelaide Casely-Hayford, outstanding Sierra Leone educator; several leaders of the African National Congress in South Africa; the top leadership of the Trinidad Workingmen's Association; Gabriel Johnson, mayor of Monrovia, Liberia; *Negro World* editor, William H. Ferris, graduate of Harvard and Yale; and others.

In the United States the UNIA continued to complement its political work with extensive cultural activity. Garvey's movement is one of the principal originators of the Harlem renaissance of the 1920s, with the *Negro World* an important outlet for poetry, literary criticism, book reviews, and the like. Augusta Savage, major African American sculptor and UNIA member, did a bronze bust of Garvey. In the midst of this activity Garvey was married to Amy Ashwood (1895/1897–1969) [*see* Garvey, Amy Ashwood], lecturer and activist, on 25 December 1919, not long after an attempt on his life. The marriage was short-lived. In 1922 he married Amy Euphemia Jacques (1896–1973), journalist and author. Both women were Jamaicans.

Garvey's movement represented the nationalist wing of the pan-African struggle. He accordingly advocated 'race first', which insisted that Africans must put their racial self-interest first in historical writing, literary criticism, religion, self-reliance, and nationhood, or political self-determination. The culminating point in Garvey's early rush to prominence was his First International Convention of the Negro Peoples of the World, held in August 1920. The opening night's ceremonies in New York hosted 25,000 people from around the African world. The delegates adopted a declaration of rights of the black peoples of the world and a universal Ethiopian anthem, and declared red, black, and green to be the colours of the race.

By 1920 Garvey was probably the world's best-known person of African descent and his UNIA had become the largest pan-African movement ever. Success, however, engendered great hostility. Integrationists such as W. E. B. DuBois of the National Association for the Advancement of Colored People (who preferred interracial organization to the all-black UNIA) and communists (who preferred class first to race first), worked assiduously for his downfall. The most powerful opposition came from the governments of the United States and Europe. British and French administrations banned the *Negro World* in Africa and the Caribbean, imprisoned Garveyites and denied Garvey entry into such places as Bermuda and the Bahamas. They collaborated with Liberia in thwarting Garvey's efforts to relocate his headquarters there. Despite this, some governors and presidents extended to Garvey the courtesies of a head of state on his travels. Garvey's most devastating setback came with his imprisonment in the USA in 1925 on a politically motivated charge of mail fraud. His sentence was commuted by President Calvin Coolidge in 1927, followed by immediate deportation to Jamaica.

It was during the litigation and imprisonment that Amy Jacques Garvey edited her husband's most important work, *The Philosophy and Opinions of Marcus Garvey, or, Africa for the Africans*. This was originally published in two separate volumes in 1923 and 1925 but later became available in a single volume. *The Tragedy of White Injustice* and *Poetic Meditations of Marcus Garvey* appeared in 1927; both were collected, together with Garvey's other poetry, in *The Poetical Works of Marcus Garvey*. Garvey's secret course of instruction for his top organizers in 1937 was published only in 1986, as *Message to the People: the Course of African Philosophy*.

Garvey arrived back in Jamaica in December 1927 to the most massive welcome accorded anybody in Jamaica's history up to that time. There he published *The Blackman* and *New Jamaican* newspapers and the *Black Man* magazine. He ran an entertainment business, wrote plays, and held international conventions in 1929 and 1934.

The Garveys spent five months in England in 1928. After being turned away by fifty hotels in London they secured lodgings at Castleton Road, West Kensington. From here Garvey established a close relationship with Ladipo Solanke and the West African Students Union (WASU), for whom he rented a hostel in West Kensington. Jomo Kenyatta, later independence ruler of Kenya, was among the hostel's residents. From London the Garveys journeyed to France, Belgium, and Germany. At Geneva, Garvey delivered a petition to the League of Nations.

In 1929 Garvey founded the People's Political Party. He was jailed by judges in Jamaica at the start of his campaign for the legislative council. They alleged that he compromised the dignity of the judiciary by promising to end unfair judgments motivated by bias. Garvey lost his bid for this council (elections to which were based on undemocratic colonialist arrangements which disfranchised most of his followers). He was, however, elected to the Kingston and St Andrew corporation council from gaol in 1929.

Garvey emigrated to London in 1935 and lived there until his death in 1940. He hoped that a presence in a major world capital would make it easier to revitalize a movement weakened by his absence from the USA. From his office at 2 Beaumont Crescent, West Kensington, he published the *Black Man*, visited Canada in 1937 and 1938, and toured the Caribbean in 1937. He again spoke regularly at Hyde Park, where he was heckled by younger Marxist activists like C. L. R. James and George Padmore. Amy Jacques joined him from 1937 to 1938 with their two young sons, Marcus jun. and Julius, both born in Jamaica.

Garvey died at 2 Beaumont Crescent, West Kensington, on 10 June 1940 after a series of strokes. Wartime conditions made it impossible to ship his body home so it was placed in a vault in catacomb no. 317, Kensal Green Roman Catholic cemetery, London. Amy Jacques's efforts to repatriate the remains at the war's end were thwarted by Amy Ashwood, who obtained a court injunction. His remains were finally shipped home for burial in Kingston in 1964 for ceremonies making him Jamaica's first national hero.

Though Garvey's name was expurgated from history books for many years, popular interest in him remained strong. Jamaica's Rastafarian religion made him a prophet. With the black power movement in the 1960s came a great upsurge of popular and scholarly interest. Some of those who joined or sympathized with Garvey's movement in their youth were now leaders of independence and civil rights struggles. These included Kwame Nkrumah of Ghana and Elijah Muhammad of the USA. Children of Garveyites, among them Malcolm X and congresswoman Shirley Chisholm, were now leaders of the post-Garvey generation.

In 1956 the Kingston and St Andrew corporation erected a bust of Garvey, and in 1957 independent Ghana named its Black Star Square in his honour. In ensuing years Garvey was celebrated on stamps, currency, plaques, and statues by the Cameroon and Jamaican governments and the Organization of American States. Statues were erected in St Ann's Bay and San Fernando, Trinidad. The London borough of Tottenham dedicated a Marcus Garvey Library in 1987.

The Garvey centenary commemoration of 1987 saw a proliferation of popular and governmental celebrations all over the world, probably unmatched by the acclaim extended to any other pan-African historical figure.

TONY MARTIN

Sources *Negro World* [newspaper] (1918–33) • A. J. Garvey, ed., *The philosophy and opinions of Marcus Garvey*, first pub. 1923 and 1925 in 2 vols. (1986) • T. Martin, *Race first: the ideological and organizational struggles of Marcus Garvey and the UNIA* (1976) • T. Martin, *Literary Garveyism: Garvey, black arts and the Harlem renaissance* (1983) • T. Martin, *The pan-African connection* (1983) • R. A. Hill and C. A. Rudisell, eds., *The Marcus Garvey and UNIA papers*, 1 (1983) • M. Garvey, *Message to the people: the course of African philosophy*, ed. T. Martin (1986) • T. Martin, *Marcus Garvey, hero: a first biography* (1983) • *The poetical works of Marcus Garvey*, ed. T. Martin (1983) • A. J. Garvey, *Garvey and Garveyism* (1963) • private information (2004) • Fisk University, Marcus Garvey memorial collection

Archives Fisk University, memorial collection • National Library of Jamaica | National Archives and Records Administration • NYPL, Schomburg Center for Research in Black Culture, UNIA Central Division (New York) files • PRO | FILM BFI NFTVA, 'Colonial madness: Marcus Garvey and the question of colour', Mirus Productions, 26 Sept 1987 • BFI NFTVA, news footage

Likenesses photographs, *c*.1920–1925, Hult. Arch. [*see illus.*] • A. Savage, bust, *c*.1920–1929

Wealth at death apparently died without substantial accumulation of wealth: Garvey, *Garvey and Garveyism*

Garvice, Charles Andrew (1850–1920), writer, was baptized on 18 September 1850 at St Dunstan and All Saints' Church in Stepney, London, the son of Andrew John Garvice, and his wife, Mira. Little else is known of his family origins and personal life. Obscurity envelops the formative phase in the career of an author who became a publishing phenomenon—'the most successful novelist in England', according to Arnold Bennett in 1910. There is no record of his marriage, although he had married by 1873, when he dedicated his début publication, *Eve: and other Verses*, to his wife; they had two sons and five daughters. Possibly, Garvice had married abroad, as in the preface to *Eve* he says that he 'scribbled on foreign steam-boats and

in railway carriages'. He also alludes to a struggling existence, including, perhaps, a bereavement: 'Most of them
[the verses] were written at midnight when the hand was
too weary to write and the brain to forge stronger work;
some few were born under the cloud of a heavy sorrow.'.

From *Eve* and his first published novel, *Maurice Durant*
(1875), it may be surmised that Garvice had lived in Italy,
perhaps also in the American West, although the circumstantial detail is not such as to make this supposition completely convincing; and among later Garvice stories were
also Australian bushranger tales. *Maurice Durant* was dedicated to the actor Henry Irving, 'with the warmest admiration and esteem'; and it contained a preface addressed
from The Retreat, Cookham, in Berkshire. The text and
chapter epigraphs indicate something of Garvice's education: an acquaintance at least with Greek, Roman, and
English classical literature. A hero of the story is Chudleigh Chichester, a baronet's son; and this unusual forename was given by the author to a son of his own who was
born on 12 January 1875 and who joined the Royal Dublin
Fusiliers in 1896. Chudleigh Garvice was made DSO in the
Second South African War; afterwards, in Egypt, he rose to
major and was commandant of police at Alexandria when
he died on 23 March 1921. *Maurice Durant* is revealing too
about Charles Garvice's politics, which may be captioned
as tory democrat. A centrepiece of the story involves a parliamentary election in which Chudleigh Chichester is victorious on account of his 'outspoken determination to
uphold the British throne and constitution' and to act as
'the working man's friend by voting for the reduction of
taxes and the labour time'. His opponents are a self-made
Manchester millionaire who cheerfully advocates 'rampant liberalism', and an alternative 'labourers' friend'
who has large red hands and 'greasy shock head', spouts
revolutionary balderdash, and organizes roughs to break
up Chudleigh's meetings. This was an immature story, but
the politics stuck. Later Garvice would serve as Conservative county councillor for the Northam district of north
Devon; he joined the Primrose League and Freemasons;
and a socially conservative philosophy formed the bed-
rock of all his tales—that there was nothing really wrong
with the world that could not be fixed by good hearts beating in honest men and virtuous women.

Maurice Durant was published first in periodical serialization, where it had a fair amount of success. The book
version did not, and Garvice explained its failure in marketing, not literary, terms: it was overlong and overpriced
for popular sales. Astuteness as a businessman of letters
would become Garvice's trademark, and for the next
twenty years he published no more books, only stories for
fiction magazines on both sides of the Atlantic. He was
editor as well as chief contributor for one of the periodicals of the American publisher George Monro, which sold
for 7*d.* in England. Garvice was sufficiently well paid to
buy Moorlands, a dairy farm at Little Silworthy in north
Devon, about which he wrote in *A Farm in Creamland* (1911).
He began to farm directly in 1903, though he had owned
the property earlier; more extraordinarily, he became
president of the Farmers' and Landowners' Association,

though he described himself still as an amateur farmer. It
was at a debating society at neighbouring Bideford that
Garvice discovered his talent for public speaking. In those
pre-broadcasting days, lecturing was a remunerative sideline for an author. A favourite on the circuit, Garvice
became president of the Institute of Lecturers.

Garvice's literary career had been relaunched at the end
of the 1890s, when the stranglehold over publishing practices exerted by Mudie's and Smith's circulating libraries
had been broken, and the format for new novels was the
single volume, price 6*s.*, rather than the three-decker selling for a guinea and a half. There was not one but several
reading publics, however; Garvice's embraced those possessed of pennies rather than shillings: the mass reading
public, comprising people educated to elementary level
following the 1870 act. It was the sixpenny paper-covered
Garvice, not the 6*s.* hard-backed Garvice, which emerged
'as numerous in the shops and on the railway bookstalls as
the leaves of Vallombrosa'. This description was by Eve-
leigh Nash, whose literary agency included Garvice
among its first clients and negotiated the simultaneous
publication of four of his novels, *Nance*, *A Coronet of Shame*,
Her Heart's Desire, and *The Outcast of the Family*, in 1900. Nash
and, after him, the literary agency of A. P. Watt, deserve
some credit for accelerating the Garvice vogue, but the
original discovery was made in America, where *Just a Girl*
(1898) had sold 100,000 copies. The publicity it received
there attracted reviewers in England, who assured readers
that here was a born story writer of thrilling romances
and pulsating adventures which were healthy in tone.
This last was important for a church- and chapel-going
audience who still retained suspicions that novel reading
was sinful; and it was notable that Garvice's novels were
strongly commended by Robertson Nicoll in the *British
Weekly* and by other religious periodicals—the *Methodist
Times*, *The Baptist*, the *Christian World*, and *Church Family
Magazine*—as well as by the national and provincial dailies
and the decidedly secular *Sportsman* and *Referee*. 'Round a
large kiosk at a popular seaside place', observed *T. P.'s
Weekly* in 1911, 'Garvice's love stories fairly dominated its
shelves. A dozen of them at least were displayed in the
best places, and in provident quantity'.

Between 1900 and 1920 over fifty novels flowed from
Garvice's pen—more correctly, from his secretary's typewriter because, thorough professional that he was, he
took to dictating his work, pipe smoking all the while.
These tales were not all the product of a fifty- and sixty-
year-old imagination, but recycled from his long apprenticeship of writing *feuilleton*. Garvice originally sold his
stories outright but, as his wealth increased, 'I got them
back by the simple expedient of buying the periodical,
lock, stock and barrel in which they appeared; and I am
glad to be able to state that I hold now the copyright of
everything I have written', he told Douglas Sladen in 1913.
Sladen, the first editor (1897–9) of *Who's Who*, was a friend
and neighbour of Garvice who, in his prime, resided at 4
Maids of Honour Row, by the palace at Richmond, as well
as keeping the Thatch Cottage, Hambledon, near Henley-
on-Thames. Garvice had, Sladen recorded in 1914, 'the

largest sales of any one in the world. I have seen the figures. Last year's sales alone amounted to 1,750,000 copies—books of all prices' (Sladen). The *Daily Chronicle*'s estimate in 1911 was that his readership was 6 million; nor did the First World War slow his popularity, and the final computation must result in a staggering sum.

Riding, fishing, and cycling were among the recreations Garvice listed in 1905; and the first two persisted, the cycling being overtaken by motoring with advancing age and riches. Garvice was clubbable, a member of the Garrick, Whitefriars, and Authors', indeed chairman of the last, whose fortunes he restored after 1908 when it had appeared doomed to closure. He was made a fellow of the Royal Society of Literature, although intellectual types joked that he 'did not strain himself to write Literature; he just lured away Ford Madox Ford's secretary, for he felt sure that, working so much with Ford, she must have caught it from him' (Jepson). Garvice was not dim or humourless—*The Scribblers' Club* (1909) is a clever set of droll short stories about the literary world—but he was unpretentious. He saw nothing wrong in brightening the lives of millions of readers with a string of unsophisticated romances, which careered along pell-mell and tumbled over all sorts of obstacles before reaching that always satisfying terminus where villainy is defeated and virtue rewarded. Garvice joined sympathy to vitality. He was the 'kindest, most self-effacing' man, thought Baroness Orczy, who served with him in 1914–15 on a committee of the Society of Authors which dispensed relief to impoverished colleagues. Garvice's own fortune was vast: his will, made in 1917 and proved at £71,049 6s. 9d., mentioned his wife, Elizabeth, and indicated that he had already made extensive provision for his surviving children. Garvice died on 1 March 1920 at his home in Richmond, from cerebral haemorrhage, after lying in a coma for eight days.

PHILIP WALLER

Sources WWW · *The Times* (2 March 1920) · D. Sladen, *Twenty years of my life* (1914) · E. Nash, *I liked the life I lived* (1941) · E. A. Jepson, *Memories of a Victorian* (1933) · d. cert. · IGI
Archives BL, corresp. with Society of Authors, Add. MSS 56768–56769 · Richmond Local Studies Library, London, corresp. with Douglas Sladen
Likenesses G. Newnes, photograph, Richmond Local Studies Library · photograph, Richmond Local Studies Library · photograph (in old age), repro. in *Evening Standard* (2 March 1920)
Wealth at death £71,049 6s. 9d.: probate, 28 May 1920, CGPLA Eng. & Wales

Garvie, Alfred Ernest (1861–1945), Congregational minister and theologian, was born on 29 August 1861 at Zyrardow, a Polish town under Russian rule, the son of Peter Garvie and Jane Kedslie (d. 1865). His parents were of Scottish descent, their families having emigrated in the 1820s and worked in the linen and flour trades. Garvie was the fifth in a family of six surviving children; a further three died in infancy, and his mother died when he was four. Plagued by illness as a child, he was left with defective sight after a serious eye inflammation, but during his long periods of convalescence he developed a passion for study, and became fluent in English, German, and Russian. Later he attributed his characteristic preoccupations to childhood influences: the experience of Russian hegemony engendered his instinctive dislike of tyranny and his strong sense of personal liberty. He maintained that his proudly Scottish and reformed upbringing 'may explain why my Scottish and British patriotism has always been qualified by internationalism, and my congregational loyalty by ... ecumenicity' (Garvie, 53).

Sent to Edinburgh to complete his education, Garvie attended George Watson's College (1874–8) before his four-year apprenticeship as a draper in Glasgow. He attended United Presbyterian church services, committing much of his time to street-mission, but his calling to ministry was hampered by doctrinal difficulties with Presbyterianism and reservations about the Westminster confession. He studied Latin, Greek, and philosophy at Glasgow University (1885–9), gaining the Logan gold medal as the most distinguished arts graduate in 1889, and, having discovered that creed subscription was not a prerequisite for Congregational ministry, changed his church membership and took first-class honours at Mansfield College, Oxford (1889–92). In 1893 he married Agnes Gordon (d. 1914) of Glasgow. His first pastorates were in Macduff (1893–5) and Montrose (1895–1903). Chairman of the Scottish Congregational Union in 1902, he became professor of the philosophy of theism, comparative religion, and Christian ethics at Hackney College and New College, Hampstead, in 1903. He was principal of New College from 1907 and of Hackney College from 1924. When the two merged in 1924, he continued as principal of the institution later known as New College, London. The death of his wife in 1914 was a considerable blow, ameliorated only by devotion to his two daughters.

In 1896 Garvie published his first book, *The Ethics of Temperance*, reflecting a lifelong aversion to alcohol and tobacco. A work of considerable intellectual power and theological influence, his *The Ritschlian Theology* (1899), a critique of the works of A. Ritschl, W. Herrmann, J. W. M. Kaftan, and A. Harnack, excited some interest in German theology on the normally insular British scene. He criticized Ritschl's failure to give pre-eminence to the scriptures, but applauded his emphasis on the experiential, insisting that 'The experience of the apostolic Church must be relived in order that its doctrine may again be rethought' (*Ritschlian Theology*, 390–91). This assertion epitomized his self-styled 'liberal evangelical' approach to theology, further developed in popular works such as *A Guide to Preachers* (1906) and *The Evangelical Type of Christianity* (1916), and in the three volumes of his systematic theology, *The Christian Doctrine of the Godhead* (1925), *The Christian Ideal for Human Society* (1920), and *The Christian Belief in God* (1932). He reacted against Barthianism, describing the doctrine of original sin as a 'grievous burden on the Church', and saw the role of the Christian theologian as being to synthesize the 'absolute eternal values' latent in the world's religions

into one Christian monotheistic faith ... so that the common brotherhood of man, the goal towards which human evolution points, may be sustained and sublimated by the one Fatherhood of God, as revealed in history by Christ, and realised in experience by His Spirit.　(*Christian Belief*, 411, 191)

His theology was increasingly cruci-centric and trinitarian.

Garvie's academic career was complemented by consistent social action and ecumenicity. During his pastorate at Montrose he incurred displeasure by announcing his pro-Boer sympathies, and during the First World War he vigorously defended the rights of conscientious objectors. As vice-chairman of the interdenominational Conference on Politics, Economics and Citizenship he chaired its report *Christianity and War* (1924), but felt that its potentialities for peacemaking were thwarted by arguments about absolutist pacifism. Further ecumenical commitments included the Edinburgh Missionary Conference (1907), and the faith and order, and life and work movements. He was co-president of the latter with Bishop George Bell of Chichester, and also developed friendships with churchmen of such varying outlooks as A. Deissman, C. Gore, and C. G. Lang. At the Stockholm conference in 1925 Garvie and Bell wrote a pacifying message to the churches on Germany and 'war guilt'. In 1927 he was deputy chairman of the Lausanne conference, and became moderator of the Free Church Federal Council in 1928. He received three honorary doctorates: from Glasgow (1903), Berlin University (1930), and New College, London.

Widely respected for his cheerful personality and genuine flair for peacemaking, Garvie's intellectual and pastoral life was, as was recognized at Berlin University, marked by his 'devotion in evangelical love and faith to the unity of the Church of Christ' (Garvie, 220). After his retirement in 1933 he remained an active public figure in British Christianity until his death at the Hendon Cottage Hospital on 7 March 1945.　　　　　GILES C. WATSON

Sources A. E. Garvie, *Memories and meanings of my life* (1938) · R. Tudur Jones, *Congregationalism in England, 1662–1962* (1962) · *DNB* · *CGPLA Eng. & Wales* (1945) · *WWW*
Archives DWL, corresp. and papers · LPL, corresp. and papers relating to Reunion | LPL, letters to Tissington Tatlow
Likenesses G. E. Butler, oils, New College, London; on loan to DWL · photograph, repro. in Garvie, *Memories and meanings of my life*, frontispiece
Wealth at death £2651 8s. 10d.: probate, 14 July 1945, *CGPLA Eng. & Wales*

Garvin, James Louis (1868–1947), journalist and newspaper editor, was born on Easter Sunday, 12 April 1868, at 117 St Anne Street, Birkenhead, the second of two children of Michael Garvin (1832–1870), labourer, and his wife, Catherine Fahy (*d*. 1917). Both his parents were Irish, Catholic, and poor. His father, who had moved from co. Tipperary because of the potato famine, died at sea in 1870. Garvin was raised by his mother, whose family, originally from co. Cork, had lived in Birkenhead for some years. To provide for her young family Catherine Garvin took in washing and, with the support of her relatives as well as the tightly knit Irish Catholic community around the St Laurence church and school in Birkenhead, ensured a loving and supportive, though spartan, upbringing for her

James Louis Garvin (1868–1947), by Alvin Langdon Coburn, 1913

two sons. The elder, Michael (1865–1914), became a schoolmaster, and his success in securing teaching positions meant family moves to Hull (1884) and Newcastle (1889).

Had Catherine Garvin had her way, James, as the younger son, would have become a priest. Although he added Louis, after the crusading king of France, to his name at confirmation, Garvin had a growing discomfort with Catholicism. His precocious and prodigious reading, together with extensive retentive powers, pointed him in other directions well before he left school at thirteen. He was a polymath and his library, which housed more than 25,000 volumes at his death, was but one measure of his eclectic learning. He taught himself French, German, and Spanish and, until his mid-twenties, regularly took evening classes in a wide range of practical subjects. As a boy he delivered newspapers and day-dreamed about being an editor. Upon leaving school he worked as a messenger and then in various clerical jobs. In 1887 he failed in the annual competition for clerical work in the civil service and was too old to sit the examinations the next year. After the collapse of his clerical employment in Newcastle in 1891 Garvin determined to become a full-time journalist.

Journalism in Newcastle and London While in Hull, Garvin was active in the local branch of the Irish National League, turning out the Irish vote, as directed by Parnell, for the Conservatives in the 1885 general election and for the Liberals less than a year later. Home rule had become Garvin's first public cause and, heartened by the personal encouragement of its editor, the young J. A. Spender, he regularly canvassed the issue through letters and articles in the *Eastern Morning News*. He also contributed to the *Dublin Weekly Freeman* and then was the north of England correspondent for *United Ireland*, a Dublin weekly supporting Parnell. Thus, when Garvin approached Joseph Cowen, the proprietor of the *Newcastle Daily Chronicle*, for employment his cuttings book was voluminous. He was offered a position as a proof-reader at 28s. a week, as well as the chance to write unpaid short editorial notes, and his first contribution appeared on 11 September 1891. A month later he demonstrated, through a 2000-word article on Parnell's funeral cabled from Dublin, that he was a journalist of uncommon talent. For the next eight years Garvin honed his skills as a journalist and received an intensive education in history and politics from a man whose political experience reached back to the revolutions of 1848. Twelve years a Liberal MP, Cowen described himself in *Who's Who* as 'an old radical, imperialist and anti-socialist'. An independent thinker with a cross-bench mind, he was far more than Garvin's employer; he was a mentor and father figure whose influence ran very deep.

While Cowen played a remarkably positive role in Garvin's development as a journalist, the reach of the *Newcastle Chronicle* was too limited for his soaring ambitions. Contrary to the myth he later perpetuated that no one in journalism should go to London until the age of thirty, London was always Garvin's immediate objective. While he was in Newcastle two offers to work in London foundered over his salary requests, and in 1898 he made desperate but futile attempts to join no fewer than four London papers. By mid-decade he had found a way to have a national but anonymous voice when an unsolicited article of his on Irish politics was prominently published in W. L. Courtney's *Fortnightly Review*. For the next sixteen years, eleven of them as Calchas, the famous Greek prophet of the Trojan war, Garvin contributed well over 100 articles to the *Fortnightly*. In 1899 he began to write for the *National Review* and eight years later for the *North American Review*. Ultimately it was his connection with Courtney, an editorial writer for the *Daily Telegraph*, that brought Garvin to London in 1899 as a leader writer for that paper. By then his writing on politics, foreign affairs, and literature, the latter much inspired by his friendship with Wilfrid and Alice Meynell and their London literary circle, made it clear that Garvin possessed great range, prolixity, and a mastery of vivid phraseology.

The *Observer* and pre-1914 politics In the decade and a half before the First World War, Garvin's journalism had a remarkable and, on occasion, quite discernible impact on British politics. Increasingly fearful of the threat posed by Germany, he campaigned ceaselessly for the strengthening of Britain's military resources—working closely with Lord Roberts and Admiral Sir John Fisher. In Fisher, Garvin found a partner who shared his deepening fear of Germany, his passion for naval matters, and his love of behind-the-scenes manoeuvring. Their joint intrigues to strengthen the navy were remarkably successful; similar efforts with the politically naïve Roberts to sound the alarm about the inadequacy of the army largely failed. The political salvation of the nation and the empire

Garvin found in another of his heroes, Joseph Chamberlain, and his campaign for tariff reform. As editor of the pro-tariff weekly *The Outlook* from late 1904 to 1906, then from 1908 as editor of *The Observer*, and in his voluminous *Telegraph* and periodical writing, Garvin applied his distinctive wordsmithing to the task of making ready Britain for the inevitable struggle with Germany. *The Observer* was at the epicentre of a successful campaign to encourage the Lords to reject David Lloyd George's 1909 budget and in the following year, after the death of Edward VII, called unsuccessfully for a 'truce of God' and a constitutional conference to break the political deadlock created by the actions it had advocated. This was to be the first of Garvin's many efforts to promote a national government. On the divisive question of Irish home rule he put aside his family background and youthful political experiences as an Irish nationalist, and sought a federal solution.

Garvin's pre-war editorship of *The Observer* at a time of political near paralysis in national politics as well as within the tory party gave him both great influence and a remarkable profile. As a radical tory he clearly set his stamp on both party thought and organization and was, as many of his contemporaries acknowledged, the *de facto* leader of the opposition.

When Lord Northcliffe made Garvin editor, manager, and one-fifth owner of *The Observer* in 1908 he inaugurated a unique chapter in the history of British journalism. Within eighteen months Garvin had nearly tripled the circulation of the paper to 57,000, made it a paying proposition, and added a distinctive, largely Unionist, but occasionally cross-bench, voice to political journalism. A quarrel with Northcliffe in 1911 over food taxes occasioned a proprietorial split with his close friend. Generously given time to find a new owner for *The Observer*, Garvin interested Waldorf Astor in the paper. Recently elected as a tariff reform Unionist MP with a strong interest in social issues, Astor was then looking for an editor for his father's paper, the *Pall Mall Gazette*. On condition that Garvin edit both papers and give up his part ownership of *The Observer*, William Waldorf Astor bought the paper for £45,000. Four years later, frustrated with unsuccessful attempts to sell his newspapers, the elder Astor abruptly gave them to Waldorf as a birthday present. The *Pall Mall Gazette* was soon sold and Garvin happily reverted to his *Observer* pulpit, relieved at not having lost his beloved paper to potential close control by Unionist Party officials. In Astor he found a proprietor with whom he was able to work in relative harmony for more than a quarter of a century.

The First World War and after The First World War was a watershed for Garvin. As editor of *The Observer* his influence rose steadily as he pressed relentlessly for decisive leadership of Britain's war effort. Herbert Asquith's lethargy alarmed him and he thus contributed to, and welcomed, the emergence of the first coalition government in May 1915, although it ended the career of Fisher and abruptly checked the rise of another of his heroes, Winston Churchill. Eighteen months later Lloyd George was prime minister, Waldorf Astor was one of his parliamentary secretaries, and *The Observer* was now at the service of the government's war effort. With a circulation of 200,000 (a level which held until 1939), with the editor's passionate leaders providing informed and lengthy commentary on the war and politics, and with a remarkable network of contacts, Garvin's *Observer* was, in many ways, at the height of its influence during this period.

On the personal level, however, the First World War was the low point of Garvin's life. His only son, Gerard Roland (1895–1916), was killed on the Somme, a loss that Garvin never got over; his remembrance day editorials in *The Observer* spoke to that pain for years. A few months later his mother, who had lived with his family since his marriage in 1894, also died. On Christmas eve 1918 the third blow fell when his wife of twenty-four years, Christina Ellen Wilson (1876–1918), mother of Gerard and four daughters, died of heart failure. She was the daughter of Robert Wilson, superintendent of police, of Newcastle upon Tyne. For many years the marriage had been troubled. Garvin's enormous absorption in his work, especially after the move to London, together with the strains of sharing the same home with her mother-in-law for more than two decades, had pushed Tina into serious problems with drink and, ultimately, with her health.

Garvin's deeply personal experience of the war, especially the sacrifice of his son, haunted him and led him to press repeatedly for an enlightened peace settlement. In less than four months he wrote a massive 574-page tome making the case for an inclusive League of Nations, the fullest possible Anglo-American co-operation, and moderate German reparations. Published in March 1919, *The economic foundations of peace, or, World partnership the truer basis of the League of Nations* immediately sold out. But it was in his weekly *Observer* editorials that Garvin had his immediate impact. The most powerful of a relentless series appeared on 11 May after presentation of the peace terms to the Germans. In 'Peace and dragon's teeth', with its allusion to Greek mythology, Garvin wrote:

> All the Treaty—apart from the incorporated and saving Covenant of the League—scatters Dragon's teeth across the soil of Europe. They will spring up as armed men unless the mischief is eradicated … Nothing is more clear and certain … and we are bound to state it.

Here was the dominant idea which was to shape his writing on foreign affairs for most of the next two decades.

By the mid-1920s Garvin had completed a gradual move from London to Beaconsfield, Buckinghamshire, where he lived at Gregories, the bailiff's home on Edmund Burke's estate. Except for his time at the *Pall Mall Gazette*, Garvin had always edited from home. But now his base was no longer London and, with the exception of increasingly irregular attendance at the weekly *Observer* lunch, Garvin was rarely in the city. Visits to Cliveden, the Astors' nearby country estate, and convivial open Sunday lunches at Gregories did enable him to maintain some direct contacts in the wider world. In his early years Garvin had sought out his contacts; now they had to come to him and, over time, fewer and fewer did. This physical isolation was

partially compensated for by a massive flow of correspondence, written in a spidery hand on both sides of distinctive blue stationery that went on for pages when often paragraphs would do. A direct telephone line to *The Observer* office and intensive reading of the reputed forty newspapers and periodicals that arrived daily at Gregories kept Garvin in touch with the office and the world. His work for *Encyclopaedia Britannica*, beginning with a 200-page contribution to *These Eventful Years: the Twentieth Century in the Making* (1924) also kept him well informed. He then edited a three-volume supplement of the *Encyclopaedia* which became the thirteenth edition, and was the editor of the twenty-four-volume fourteenth edition (1929). A need for money and a profound conviction that the *Encyclopaedia* was essential to the Anglo-American relationship led him to assume this major burden. Fealty to a powerful memory had led also to a crushing and ultimately destructive commitment to write the biography of Joseph Chamberlain. Three volumes were produced (1932–4), but the project was never completed by a Garvin who saw himself living in an era of political pygmies longing 'for the big ideas of big men worthy of a big people. I don't understand anything else' (Garvin to Astor, 25 Feb 1929, Astor MSS).

So deeply rooted was Garvin in the events and personalities of the early decades of the century that little changed in his outlook after 1922. Never an orthodox Conservative, he found Stanley Baldwin devoid of vision and he had no rapport with Neville Chamberlain. Among Labour politicians he gave occasional *Observer* support to Ramsay MacDonald, especially over his efforts to improve Anglo-American relations before and during the London naval conference of 1930. Like many journalists of the time Garvin was briefly intrigued by Oswald Mosley. As he had done for years, Lloyd George regularly bedazzled and infuriated Garvin. In foreign policy Garvin's *Observer* ceaselessly promoted the Anglo-American relationship, was long critical of French attitudes towards Germany, and was an apologist for Mussolini's Abyssinian adventure. By then, however, Garvin knew that another war was a distinct possibility; in his mind Italy was a necessary counterweight to Germany. A perceptive and repetitive visionary about air power, he used *The Observer* to advocate British rearmament.

The breach with Astor When war came in 1939 Garvin, then aged seventy-one, inevitably viewed it through the lens of 1914–18. Delighted by Churchill's return to the Admiralty, he was unwaveringly loyal to his old friend after he became prime minister in 1940. In February 1942, however, Garvin's determination to assert his editorial independence in commentary about Churchill collided with his ageing proprietor's increasing alarm at the overwhelming authority being invested in one man. Astor declined to renew Garvin's contract, and the remarkable association of Garvin with *The Observer*, and of *The Observer* with Garvin, came to an end. What had been foreshadowed thirty years earlier, when Northcliffe decided to sell *The Observer*, was confirmed in 1942. Garvin may have been, in his mind and that of the readers, *The Observer*; in fact, although he had finally become a minority shareholder in 1938, control clearly rested with his proprietor. The last of the great Edwardian editors was gone from his pulpit.

Garvin's *Observer* revolutionized Sunday journalism and, as one contemporary noted, made the sabbath almost bearable as he set out to make *The Observer* half a newspaper and half a magazine. By creating the 'Week end' pages in 1926 he institutionalized and separated the 'views' side of the paper from the 'news' side. At the core of the paper was Garvin's signed 1500- to 4000-word editorial in which he gave his readers not necessarily what they wanted but what they ought to have, leaving them, in Beachcomber's telling phrase, 'browsing on the southern slopes' of his article (*New Statesman and Nation*, 1 Feb 1947). His leader writing was inescapable for friend or foe. Beginning his scrutiny of the Sunday papers with *The Observer*, Baldwin asked Tom Jones in 1923: 'What madness is Garvin up to today?' (T. Jones, *Whitehall Diary, 1914–1925*, 1969, 244). His writing was passionate, based on encyclopaedic knowledge, and full of the self-assuredness of one who knew he was read by those who mattered. 'As you know' he told one interviewer, 'I am the greatest authority on foreign affairs in this country' (*Time and Tide*, 1 Feb 1947). The conceit was breathtaking but valid for much of his career. As a tribute to his skills this 24- to 36-page newspaper, which generated an average pre-tax profit of £25,000 per annum, was produced by a permanent full-time staff of no more than thirty, of whom only six to eight worked on the editorial side. Before 1930 there was only one full-time reporter; the bulk of the content of the paper came from contributors whose talents and influence were unmatched in the Sunday press until the mid-1930s. Public recognition of Garvin's leadership in journalism included honorary degrees from Durham (1921) and Edinburgh (1935) universities, and senior roles in several press organizations. He declined honours from both Lloyd George and MacDonald but willingly acceded to Churchill's request and became a Companion of Honour in 1941.

In person, as on paper, Garvin's personality filled all available space. Tall and thin, with bulging eyes accentuated by glasses, he loved music, poetry, and vigorous tramps in the countryside with his beloved dogs. His fingers always in danger of being burnt as matches were struck to relight the ever-present cigar which had died out in a torrent of one-sided conversation, Garvin never failed to leave an impression on those whom he had met. His imagined epitaph said it well:

> Here rests
> (for the first time)
> J. L. Garvin
> a bad party man:
> a good journalist:
> a better patriot:
> And a most unswerving friend.
> (Garvin to Beaverbrook, 26 May 1930, Beaverbrook MSS)

Garvin's departure from *The Observer* did not end his career in journalism. He was immediately hired by Lord Beaverbrook to write a weekly column for the *Sunday Express*. In early 1945 when Garvin was told he could no longer write about the war, his friend Brendan Bracken secured his return to the *Daily Telegraph*. His final years were spent writing for his old paper and in the company of his second wife, Viola Taylor Woods (*b.* 1882), writer, whom he married in 1921 after her divorce from Maurice Woods. Garvin died of double bronchial pneumonia at his Beaconsfield home on 23 January 1947. A memorial service was held on 6 February at St Martin-in-the-Fields, London.

JOHN O. STUBBS

Sources D. Ayerst, *Garvin of The Observer* (1985) • K. Garvin, *J. L. Garvin: a memoir* (1948) • A. M. Gollin, *The Observer and J. L. Garvin, 1908–1914* (1960) • J. Stubbs, 'Appearance and reality: a case study of *The Observer* and J. L. Garvin, 1914–1942', *Newspaper history: from the seventeenth century to the present day*, ed. G. Boyce, J. Curran, and P. Wingate (1978), 320–38 • J. Stubbs, *Observer: read all about it!* (1979) • Ransom HRC, Garvin MSS • U. Reading L., Astor MSS • *DNB* • *The Times* (7 Feb 1947) • J. L. Garvin, correspondence with Lord Beaverbrook and related papers, HLRO

Archives Ransom HRC, corresp. and papers | BL, letters to G. K. Chesterton and other household members, Add. MS 73195, fols. 70–85 • BL, letters to Albert Mansbridge, Add. MS 65259 • BL, corresp. with Lord Northcliffe, Add. MSS 62236–62237 • BL OIOC, letters to Lord Reading, MSS Eur. E 238, F 118 • BL OIOC, corresp. with John Simon, MSS Eur. F 77 • Bodl. Oxf., corresp. with Sibyl Colefax • Bodl. Oxf., corresp. with Lord Simon • Bodl. Oxf., letters to E. J. Thompson • CAC Cam., letters to Lord Fisher • CAC Cam., letters to W. T. Stead • CUL, corresp. with Sir Samuel Hoare • Durham RO, letters to Lady Londonderry • HLRO, corresp. with Lord Beaverbrook and related papers • HLRO, letters to Ralph Blumenfeld • HLRO, corresp. with Andrew Bonar Law • HLRO, letters to David Lloyd George • HLRO, letters to Lord Samuel • HLRO, corresp. with John St Loe Strachey • JRL, letters to the *Manchester Guardian* • King's Lond., Liddell Hart C., corresp. with Sir B. H. Liddell Hart • LUL, corresp. with Emile Cammaerts • Mitchell L., Glas., Glasgow City Archives, letters to J. P. Smith • NA Scot., corresp. with Lord Elibank • NA Scot., corresp. with Lord Lothian • News Int. RO, letters to *The Times* • NL Ire., letters to John Redmond • Norfolk RO, corresp. with Henry Massingham • PRO, corresp. with James Ramsay MacDonald, PRO 30/69/6/106 • U. Birm. L., corresp. with Austen Chamberlain and Mary Chamberlain • U. Birm. L., letters to W. H. Dawson • U. Reading, corresp. with Nancy Astor | FILM BFI NFTVA, home footage

Likenesses A. L. Coburn, photogravure, 1913, NPG [*see illus.*] • W. Stoneman, photographs, 1942, NPG • D. Low, drawing, repro. in *New Statesman* (15 May 1926) • B. Partridge, pencil drawing, NPG; repro. in *Punch* (25 April 1928) • A. P. F. Ritchie, caricature, Hentschel-colourtype, NPG; repro. in *VF* (13 Sept 1911)

Wealth at death £27,048 16s. 8d.: probate, 31 May 1947, *CGPLA Eng. & Wales*

Garway [Garraway], **Sir Henry** (*bap.* 1575, *d.* 1646), merchant and politician, was baptized at the church of St Peter-le-Poer, Broad Street, City of London, on 17 April 1575, the son of Sir William Garway, merchant and tax farmer, and his wife, Elizabeth, *née* Anderston. He was one of seventeen children and was brought up in the City of London where his family had long resided. Sir William was one of a number of prominent merchants who were farmers of the 'great customs' during the reign of James I. A leading Levant merchant and foundation member of the East India Company, the source of his wealth attracted hostile comment: he was 'known to be a very poor man when he entered upon the customs yet left great treasures behind him' (Ashton, *City*, 25).

As a young man Garway travelled, according to his own

account, 'in all parts of Christendom' (Heywood, dedication). He afterwards carried on an extensive trade with the Netherlands, France, Italy, the East Indies, Greenland, Russia, and Turkey. He played a prominent role in the great mercantile companies that traded with those regions: his involvement in commerce with the eastern Mediterranean brought him the governorship of the Levant Company, 1635–43. He was also an important figure in trade with the East Indies, and served as deputy governor, 1636–9, and then governor, 1641–3. Garway was also governor of the Greenland and Russia companies, until he was deposed from these offices on account of his royalist sympathies.

Garway inherited his father's interest in the 'great farm' of the customs in 1621 (retaining it until 1625), and was also a member of the syndicates of traders in currants and of French and Rhenish wine farmers. In October 1637 he bid unsuccessfully to farm both the great and the petty customs for £30,000. One of his associates was an even more spectacular figure, Sir Maurice Abbot. His marriage to Margaret (d. 1656), daughter of Henry Clitherow, a London merchant, brought ten children, including the politician William *Garway, of whom the last three died in childhood. Garway lived in Broad Street, near Drapers' Hall, and in 1616 he petitioned the company for a lease of his own and another house adjoining its hall, offering to rebuild them in a substantial manner. This he did at a cost of over £1000, erecting a frontage of brick and stone, and in 1628 the company granted him a seventy-year lease at an annual rent of £9.

Garway's forebears had been connected with the Drapers' Company since the time of Queen Elizabeth. He was admitted a liveryman of the company by patrimony in 1607, serving as warden in 1623 and as master in 1627 and 1639. In 1638–9 he was on a government commission appointed to reform abuses in the drapery trade. He became sheriff in 1627 and afterwards alderman of Vintry ward, removing to Broad Street ward in 1638. In 1637 he served as one of the commissioners for buildings, ordered to investigate complaints of poor workmanship in the repairs to city churches.

Garway was elected lord mayor of London on Michaelmas day 1639. His shrievalty and mayoralty were kept at his newly built mansion, the Drapers' Company giving him sums of money on each occasion towards its further embellishment. His inauguration pageant was written by the dramatist Thomas Heywood and entitled *Londini status pacatus, or, London's Peacable Estate* (1639). The company bore the expenses of the pageant, the mechanical devices, or 'triumphs', being executed by John and Mathias Christmas.

Garway's year as lord mayor was, however, anything but peaceable. In the autumn of 1639 Charles, having quarrelled with parliament, turned to the City for a war loan and, when faced by their hostility, threatened to depose Garway, who at that time, unlike the majority of the Drapers, was a royalist. He later persuaded the aldermen to provide a loan, though the Drapers continued to resist. On 4 April 1640, in obedience to the king's letter and the

council's instructions for impressing 200 soldiers to reinforce the garrison of Berwick, Garway had about one hundred idle persons rounded up from taverns, inns, and alehouses and held in Bridewell. This ill-assorted regiment was, however, released in compliance with subsequent orders.

When the London apprentices attacked Laud's palace at Lambeth on 9 May, Garway effectively suppressed the tumult, imprisoning the promoters and executing the ringleaders. In the same month the council ordered him to double the watch in the City and to call out the trained bands when he should think it necessary. Another order from the council in the same month required the lord mayor to raise a regiment of 4000 men for the king's service in the north. After some debates, common council refused either to raise or to equip the force and Garway was left to raise the men by his own exertions. Also in May Garway and the aldermen were asked by the king to furnish a list of the richest inhabitants of their wards, classed according to wealth. Garway hesitated to comply, and Charles ordered him to resign his sword and collar of office, but quickly restored them. Finally, four aldermen were sent to prison for refusing to aid the king.

Garway was nevertheless knighted by the king at Whitehall on 31 May 1640. In June 1640, when Charles made his last attempt to raise ship money in the City, Garway and the sheriffs led a house-to-house search. However, 'their zeal, if zeal it was, did not save them from a sharp rebuke from the monarch for their failure to collect the loan' (Ashton, *City*, 188). Garway unsuccessfully proposed a loan and present for the king in August 1640.

In the autumn of 1640 the king made every effort to secure the election of a new lord mayor favourable to his cause, but found himself blocked by the precedent which forbade him to overrule the citizens' choice except on the ground of poverty or infirmity. Garway was not elected but nevertheless worked to prevent the final rupture between the City and the king. He himself asserted in 1642 that he was often a member of the House of Commons, but there is no record of the constituency which he represented and he may have simply attended from time to time.

A common hall was held on 13 January 1643 to receive the king's answer to the City's petition asking the monarch to call a parliament. It was attended by John Pym and others who wished to prevent the City's reconciliation with Charles. The meeting was adjourned to 17 January; it then took place, and a speech which Garway was supposed to have made in answer to Pym was published under the title *The Loyal Citizen Revived* (1643). Garway's arguments, if indeed they were his, reflected widespread fear of religious radicalism, an important factor in influencing the attitude of the City fathers during 1640–42. By the time of the common hall fears of social disruption had begun to seem to many in the City establishment a much greater threat than royal aggression. The speech by Garway was said to have completely silenced the radical supporters of parliament:

I am not willing to speak slighly of any persons gotten into authority; only we may say there be some amongst us, we did not think two years ago to have met here ... before God, I have no more authority in the city, than a porter ... If to be governed by people whose authority we know not, and by rules which no body ever heard of, or can know, be a sign of arbitrary power, we have as much of it as we can wish. (Ashton, *City*, 219)

However, the cause of parliament prevailed at the meeting.

Garway and the master and wardens of the Merchant Taylors' and Grocers' companies were subsequently summoned to appear before both houses. Although he had complied in providing arms for the parliamentary forces, the House of Commons dismissed Garway from his office of governor of the Turkey and other companies on 10 April 1643, and he was expelled from the court of aldermen. On 5 November the trained bands arrested many of the wealthiest royalists in the City, including Garway and his brother, for not contributing to parliament's demands for money, and other misdemeanours; thereafter 'he was tossed as long as he lived from prison to prison, and his estate conveyed from one rebel to another' (Lloyd, 633). He was, however, still governor of the Russia Company on 1 June 1644 when the House of Commons ordered his discharge from that office, and at the same time imprisoned him in Dover Castle during its pleasure. However, Garway did not die in prison, but 'of a grievous fit of the stone' (ibid.) in the parish of St Mary Magdalen, Milk Street, and he was buried on 24 July 1646 in the church where he had been baptized.

Garway left large estates in Sussex, Kent, Devon, Northumberland, Westmorland, and Yorkshire to his three sons, which they seem to have obtained after his death without interference from parliament, but the commissioners for sequestrations raised difficulties about some of his property in Cornwall. They alleged that Garway died a delinquent in prison for assisting the king against parliament, and that all his family were known enemies of parliament, a statement which John and Thomas Garway vehemently denied.

ANITA MCCONNELL and ROBERT BROWN

Sources A. H. Johnson, *The history of the Worshipful Company of the Drapers of London*, 5 vols. (1922), vol. 3 · R. R. Sharpe, *London and the kingdom*, 3 vols. (1894), 2.122–5, 181 · D. Lloyd, *Memoires of the lives ... of those ... personages that suffered ... for the protestant religion* (1668), 633 · T. Heywood, *Londini status pacatus, or, London's peacable estate* (1639), dedication · *CSP dom.*, 1635, 87; 1637, 218; 1638–9, 355; 1640, 31–2; 1640–41, 90, 101, 103–4; *addenda, 1625–49*, 300 · R. Ashton, *The city and the court, 1603–1643* (1979) · R. Ashton, *The crown and the money market, 1603–1640* (1960) · *DNB*

Garway [Garraway], **William** (*bap.* 1617, *d.* 1701), politician, was baptized on 10 April 1617 at St Peter-le-Poer, London, the eldest of the ten children of Sir Henry *Garway (*bap.* 1575, *d.* 1646), draper and lord mayor of London in 1639–40, of Broad Street, London, and his wife, Margaret (*d.* 1656), daughter of Henry Clitherow, merchant of London. He was educated at Pembroke College, Cambridge, where he was admitted in 1632. Garway's father was one of the staunchest royalists in the City during the civil war

and Garway himself fought in the royal army as a captain of foot before being captured in November 1644.

Garway's activities after the death of his father in 1646 are obscure, although he may have succeeded to some of Sir Henry's Levantine business interests. In 1656 he inherited land in Sussex and in 1661 was returned to parliament for Chichester. Garway soon acquired a reputation for independence from the court, coupled with understanding of public finance. He became associated with a group around Sir John Vaughan including Sir Thomas Littleton and Sir Richard Temple, which established itself as the most consistent critic of the government. In 1663 he was involved in the efforts of Temple and George Digby, second earl of Bristol, to remove Edward Hyde, first earl of Clarendon, from power. With his allies he had opposed in 1664 aspects of the government's financing plans for the Second Dutch War, and during the session of 1666–7 Garway was in the forefront of the group's demands for scrutiny of war expenditure, proposing a statutory committee to examine the accounts of the money which had been given for the war with the Dutch. Despite the failure of the bill to give effect to the committee Garway was one of the government's critics who were included in the royal commission on public accounts appointed during the following prorogation. With the fall of Clarendon and the rise to power of George Villiers, second duke of Buckingham, an ally in the session of 1666–7, Garway was appointed in 1668 to the committee of trade. Nevertheless, throughout 1669, often in concert with Sir Thomas Lee, he continued to press for further investigation of corrupt practices in government accounts, to argue for limits to the supply granted to the king and against the new assessment and excise taxes.

In 1671, however, Garway accepted a commissionership of the customs, and in February 1673 he and Sir Thomas Lee (who later admitted to receiving money from the government) supported the court in its request for £1.2 million in order to carry on the war with the Dutch. Despite this, though, Garway continued to articulate suspicions of the court, and particularly its connections with popery. He criticized the French war and joined the attack on the members of the cabal. In 1675 he attacked the granting of money for rebuilding the navy. At the end of the autumn session that year he was dismissed from his position as customs commissioner.

By the session of 1677 Garway was one of the most influential country voices in the Commons, demanding a hostile stance against France, but rejecting most of the policies advanced by the government to achieve it. But he maintained his distance from the most prominent of the government's opponents, Anthony Ashley Cooper, first earl of Shaftesbury, and Buckingham; during the Exclusion parliaments, in which he sat for Arundel, he demanded 'expedients'—measures against popery, frequent parliaments, the disbandment of the army, and the uniting of protestants—as an alternative to the exclusion of the duke of York. Garway's resistance to exclusion perhaps earned him the respect of the government of James II. He was returned again to the 1685 parliament, and in

1688 was approved as deputy lieutenant and JP. Nevertheless he greeted the revolution with relief: in the Convention Parliament he was among the first to support William's coup, although he saw it as crucial to take the opportunity to make England's liberties more secure. As the new government consolidated itself Garway returned to his more customary role as the watchdog of the nation's purse: in 1689–90 he was active in pursuing miscarriages in the supplying of the troops in Ireland. In the election of 1690 Garway finally lost his seat at Arundel. Although he lived for eleven more years he did not stand again.

The roots of Garway's country politics are not clear: Sir William Coventry told Pepys in 1666 that he had 'not been well used by the court, though stout to death' (Pepys, 7.310). But Garway's attitude and deep suspicion of successive Restoration administrations were tempered by an acknowledged expertise in public finance and a well thought out moderation on constitutional issues. He never married and died on 4 August 1701. He was buried at Ford, Sussex.

PAUL SEAWARD

Sources B. M. Crook and B. D. Henning, 'Garway (Garraway), William', HoP, *Commons, 1660–90* · P. Seaward, *The Cavalier Parliament and the reconstruction of the old regime, 1661–1667* (1989) · M. Knights, *Politics and opinion in crisis, 1678–81* (1994) · Pepys, *Diary* · CSP *dom.*, 1661–90 · Venn, *Alum. Cant.*

Gascar, Henri (1634/5–1701), portrait painter, was probably born in Paris. He was perhaps the son of an obscure French artist, Pierre Gascard. He is known to have been in Rome in 1659, where he may have studied with Pierre Mignard. In 1671 he was *agréé* at the Académie Royale in Paris but the next year that body rejected his *morceau de réception*, a portrait of Louis de Bourbon, the grand dauphin. Perhaps as a reaction to the unfavourable response to his reception piece, he soon left France for England.

Bainbrigg Buckeridge reported that Gascar had come to England, 'encourag'd … by the Dutchess of Portsmouth, whose Picture he came over to draw' (Buckeridge, 421). Certainly Louise de Kéroualle, duchess of Portsmouth, seems to have been his most assiduous patron (his best portraits of her, all *c*.1675, are in private collections in England and Sweden); he also painted her with her son Charles, duke of Richmond (*c*.1676; priv. coll.). Vertue reported that Gascar's portrait of Philip Herbert, earl of Pembroke, was painted 'at the appointment of the Dutches of Portsmouth … by stealth' (Vertue, *Note books*, 4.61). Her steady patronage, however, did not preclude him from working for a varied court clientele: among others, Barbara Villiers, duchess of Cleveland (*c*.1675; formerly Ditchley Park, Oxfordshire); Frances Jennings, duchess of Tyrconnell (*c*.1677; priv. coll.); and Elizabeth Percy, duchess of Somerset, as a child (*c*.1675; priv. coll.). His success in England was reportedly so great that during his sojourn 'our wise Nation … [could not] see the difference between him and his Contemporary Sir Peter Lely'; at his departure he was said 'to have carry'd above 10000 Pounds out of England' (Buckeridge, 421).

Gascar's most accomplished work is arguably the elaborate full-length portrait of James II when duke of York (*c*.1673; Greenwich Hospital collection, on permanent loan to NMM). This painting is probably that mentioned in the inventory of James II's collection ('Gaskar the Kings picture when he was duke. or Gascar more likely,'; Vertue, *Note books*, 4.93). Depicting James in his role as lord high admiral of the navy, it was most likely painted prior to March 1673 since in that month the passage of the Test Act forced the duke of York, who was by that time an openly practising Catholic, to resign from office. Two other full-length portraits of a similar scale are still in England, *Henrietta Anne, Duchess of Orléans, in the Guise of Diana* and *Frances Teresa Stuart, Duchess of Richmond, in the Guise of Minerva* (both priv. coll.); these are likely to date to this same period, the former being a posthumous portrait of its sitter.

Gascar's style strikes the modern viewer as mannered and decorative. Certainly, his meticulous attention to details of embroidery, lace, shot silks, and other decorative elements belies an inadequate mastery of human form (the arms and hands of his sitters frequently have a metallic, lifeless, and almost tubular quality). His tendency to use what Buckeridge termed 'ornament' to mask his artistic inadequacies led the biographer to dub his style a 'gay cap-and-feather manner' (Buckeridge, 421). One early twentieth-century critic unfavourably assessed the Frenchman's style as corresponding 'exactly with the type of feminine animation and allurement preferred by makers of wax dummies for modistes and coiffures' (Baker, 2.4), and his work has also been described as the 'nadir of decadent French court portraiture in the earlier years of Louis XIV' (Whinney and Millar, 175). Only later in the century did these negative judgements give way to more measured assessments of Gascar who, at his best, provided sitters with a sparkling and decorative alternative to the less frilly and subtler styles of Sir Peter Lely and Sir Godfrey Kneller.

Although he established his reputation in England as a portrait painter in oils, Gascar made perhaps his most significant contribution to artistic culture in England through his association with the nascent art of mezzotint engraving. He was, without doubt, one of the first artists whose work was consistently engraved in mezzotint, although it remains uncertain whether he himself scraped the plates or whether another artist executed them from his paintings. At the very least, he is likely to have initiated and supervised their production in an effort to promote himself. In addition to being some of the first examples of this medium, the mezzotints of his portraits both serve as confirmation of his otherwise elusive *œuvre* and provide identifications for many of his sitters who, due to his difficulty with human anatomy and his adherence to fashion, might otherwise remain anonymous, for example, *Madame Ellen Groinn and her Two Sons, Mrs. Jenny Middleton, My lady Anne Barrington and my lady Mary Sanion* [Saint John], and *George Fitzroy, Earle of Northumberland*.

Gascar left England about 1678, possibly owing to strong anti-French and anti-Catholic sentiment sparked by the Popish Plot and Exclusion crisis. By 1680 he had returned to Paris, where he was *reçu* by the Académie Royale on 26

October that year. In 1681 he left France once again, going this time to Italy, where he lived and worked mainly in Rome (his altarpiece in Santa Maria dei Miracoli is still *in situ*). Buckeridge reported that 'by a prevailing Assurance, customary with his Nation, he … imposed upon the Italian Noblesse, as he did on those of England' (Buckeridge, 421). He died in Rome on 18 January 1701, and was buried there in San Lorenzo in Lucina.

JULIA MARCIARI ALEXANDER

Sources [B. Buckeridge], 'An essay towards an English school of painters', in R. de Piles, *The art of painting, and the lives of the painters* (1706), 398–480, esp. 421 • Thieme & Becker, *Allgemeines Lexikon*, 13.224–5 • Vertue, *Note books*, 1.33, n. 87; 2.92; 4.17, 61, 91, 93, 136 • A. Griffiths and R. A. Gerard, *The print in Stuart Britain, 1603–1689* (1998), 217–22 [exhibition catalogue, BM, 8 May – 20 Sept 1998] • J. C. Smith, *British mezzotint portraits*, 2 (1879), 522–8 • H. Walpole, *Anecdotes of painting in England: with some account of the principal artists*, ed. R. N. Wornum, new edn, 3 vols. (1849); repr. (1876); repr. in 4 vols. (New York, 1969), vol. 2, p. 464 • D. Brême, 'Gascar, Henri', *The dictionary of art*, ed. J. Turner (1996) • E. K. Waterhouse, *The dictionary of British 16th and 17th century painters* (1988), 97 • C. H. C. Baker, *Lely and the Stuart portrait painters: a study of English portraiture before and after van Dyck*, 2 (1912), 4–5 • M. Whinney and O. Millar, *English art, 1625–1714* (1957), 7, 175, 184 • L. Dussieux, *Les artistes français à l'étranger*, 3rd edn (Paris, 1876), 72, 166, 266–7, 477 • Bryan, *Painters* (1903–5), 2.217 • J. D. Champlin and C. C. Perkins, eds., *Cyclopedia of painters and paintings*, 4 vols. (1888), 2.111 • Bénézit, *Dict.*, 4th edn • E. Coquery, ed., *Visages du grand siècle: le portrait français sous le règne de Louis XIV, 1660–1715* (1997), 63, 206, 226, 271, 273, 280 • C. Macleod and J. M. Alexander, eds., *Painted ladies: women at the court of Charles II* (2001) [exhibition catalogue, NPG, 11 Oct 2001–6 Jan 2002; Yale U. CBA, 25 Jan – 17 March 2002]

Gascoigne, Sir Bernard [Bernardo Guasconi] (**1614–1687**), royalist army officer and diplomat, was born Bernardo Guasconi in Florence in April or May 1614, the son of Giovambatista Guasconi (*d.* 1614) and his wife, Clemenza Altoviti (*d.* 1634). His father having died four months after his birth, Bernardino, as he was known, was raised by various uncles and grew up with the Medici princes. He seems to have received a thorough academic education and training in arms.

The English civil wars Guasconi's later reputation as a ladies' man might explain how he contracted certain enmities in Florence that caused him to find it prudent to go to Germany in the suite of Prince Matthias de' Medici, alongside whom he fought for three years. After the prince's departure in 1637 Guasconi continued raising troops there until he entered service with the Spaniards, for whom he showed bravery at the siege of Turin in 1639. By the spring of 1641 he was having trouble getting paid, and he left Milan a year later, 'andare a cercare mia fortuna ad altera parte' ('to go and seek my fortune in other parts'; Guasconi to Soliti, 13 March 1642, Biblioteca Nazionale Centrale Firenze, Gonnelli MS 15, no. 40). He took service in France in 1642 but soon moved on to fight for the royalists in the English civil war. In August 1644, as 'an Italian, who troopes with Colonel [Richard] Nevil' (R. Symonds, *The Marches of the Royal Army*, ed. C. E. Long, CS 74, 1859, 48), Gascoigne (as he was now known in England) earned

renown for a daring raid on Lord Mohun's house outside Oxford.

The end of the first civil war saw Gascoigne return to France, where he stayed in Paris with the exiled court, by now, apparently, having received a knighthood. As early as August 1646 he was already discussing terms for returning to service in England, and by September 1647 he was with the king at Hampton Court. However, with no immediate fighting he complained to a friend, 'che tanto ho perso tempo in questo paese possi vedere' ('you can see how much time I've wasted in this country'; Guasconi to Soliti, 22 Oct 1647, Biblioteca Nazionale Centrale Firenze, Gonnelli MS 15, no. 44). On 4/14 November 1647 he sent to Ferdinando II an account of events that year from the handing over of the king by the Scots to just before the king's escape. Gascoigne's view was that the army council, believing that its men should be paid and realizing their strength, deliberately challenged parliament. It was because they wanted to use the sentiments and actions of the rank and file as a cover that they sent a low-ranking officer like Joyce to take the king from Holmby. Some of his account is clearly first hand. For instance, he describes seeing the army drawn up on Hounslow Heath. It made a striking impression on Gascoigne, who, though a highly experienced soldier, was awed by the troops' appearance and discipline. Consequently it is not surprising that as he headed for Kent in June 1648 Gascoigne was intensely pessimistic about the poor quality of troops being raised, and perceived that the royalist cause would be 'in peggior stato che mai' ('in a worse state than ever'; Salvetti to Gondi, Archivio di Stato di Firenze, Mediceo del Principato MS 4202, fol. 646r).

Sidestepping Fairfax's army, the royalists crossed the Thames and occupied Colchester, where they surrendered, after a long siege, on 28 August. Three leading officers were ordered to be shot, but, with Sir Charles Lucas and Sir George Lisle dead, and his doublet already removed in preparation for sharing their fate, Gascoigne was suddenly reprieved. It was said that this was due only to Fairfax's last-minute realization that Gascoigne was a foreigner, and that he did not want to damage relations with Tuscany. Imprisoned in Windsor, Gascoigne was freed on parole through the offices of Lord Culpepper and the Florentine resident, Salvetti; but he did not leave England immediately, even after being threatened with rearrest, and retired abroad only on 13/23 January 1649.

On 3 December 1649 Gascoigne was granted a £1000 pension for his services by Charles II. This was obviously meaningless at the time, and the records of the 1660s to 1680s are littered with efforts on Gascoigne's part to collect his due, the success of which is unclear but seems to have been partial at best.

While still representing royalist interests in Tuscany Gascoigne was busy in the 1650s building a successful mercantile operation, which appears to have had some focus on tobacco and wine. Based in Livorno and Florence, he travelled widely in Tuscany and also to Rome, where he was cup bearer to Cardinal Gian Carlo de' Medici. Gascoigne still led a military life also, but this seems to have been much scaled down. Following duties as a cavalry captain in the Val d'Arno, he received a commission from Ferdinando II in September 1657 as captain of the cuirassiers of Montalcino.

The Restoration At the restoration of Charles II, Gascoigne talked of returning to England as early as June 1660 with his house guest in Florence, Sir Lewis Dyve, a former royalist comrade-in-arms. But only after his old colonel, Richard Neville, wrote 'Your companye … is earnestly desyered by all this nation from the King to the beggar. The King talkes much of you' (Neville to Gascoigne, 18 Nov 1660, Crinò, *Fatti e Figure*, 176) did he make the journey, arriving the following January. The denization granted Gascoigne on 18 October 1661 facilitated a double life. Trading in both England and Tuscany he travelled frequently between the two until his death.

As a pensioner of Spain for whom the secretary of state, Henry Bennet, earl of Arlington, had 'a most particular friendship' (Finch to Arlington, 8 June 1669, PRO, SP 98/10, fol. 226r), Gascoigne was an open and active enemy of France. He was widely regarded as having been central to enlisting the men in the service of the Spanish ambassador, who gave their French counterparts a drubbing on the streets of London in 1662 and caused scandal across Europe as a result. When in Tuscany Gascoigne wrote regularly to Arlington and did what he could to supply news, arranging both newsletters and intelligencers in various European cities.

The outbreak of war with the Dutch in 1664 was embarrassing for all Florentines because, although they were friendly with the English, their trading interests were intimately linked with the Netherlands. Indeed Gascoigne had two cousins in Amsterdam who ran a successful trading and banking house. It is not surprising, therefore, that Gascoigne withdrew from England for the duration of the war and based himself in Tuscany, though ships of his sailing from the Netherlands were granted protection. Almost immediately he claimed to be weary of Italy, and wrote later that 'Io vivendo in Fiorenza mi chiamo in esilio … per che il mio Genio, mi fa piu amar lingilterra' ('Living in Florence, I call myself an exile, because my spirit makes me love England more'; Gascoigne to Charles II, 30 Aug 1664, PRO, SP 98/5, unfoliated). Yet it was not until peace was in the air that Gascoigne returned to England. Lucky to survive a storm that claimed many of his belongings, he landed at Dover on 1 May 1667, along with his acquaintance Aphra Behn.

At Henry Howard's nomination Gascoigne was elected a fellow of the Royal Society on 20 June 1667. He brought the society into contact with several luminaries of Florence's recently extinguished but vastly significant Accademia del Cimento, including Lorenzo Magalotti and Paolo Falconieri when they visited England first in 1668.

Diplomat and matchmaker On 29 October 1667 Gascoigne took oaths preparatory to naturalization, but his name does not appear in any act. Nevertheless, he represented England diplomatically, sailing for Spain in June 1668. Though John Werden was officially managing English affairs in Madrid pending ambassador Godolphin's arrival, Gascoigne also produced credentials to negotiate. In one notable meeting he provoked Peñaranda to a rage which he withstood so calmly that the count was reduced to giving him a hearing. Returning to England that December, Gascoigne brought news that Ferdinando II's son Cosimo (later Cosimo III) intended to visit incognito on the second of his grand tours. The prince arrived in March 1669, and Gascoigne was in constant attendance during his three-month stay.

Among Gascoigne's personal papers are some extraordinary love letters, most in draft, some returned, that corroborate other evidence of his activities as an enthusiastic pursuer of women, who included the dowager countess of Lincoln. When compared with his more official papers, they indicate an instance in which he had an apparently undeclared interest in settling a suit in chancery in May 1669. Gascoigne acted ostensibly in the earl of Essex's behalf, yet he was clearly intimate enough with the other party, Mary Biggs, for her to have expected him to marry her. She returned his final letter to her in which he pleaded, 'madam my misfortune ist only this, that you are persuaded that I am Rich wen I am a Power fellowe' (Gascoigne to Biggs, undated, BL, Add. MS 34077, fol. 38). Gascoigne nevertheless remained unmarried.

The most famous example of Gascoigne's fun-loving side was the occasion on which he drove a horse and cart with the queen and two duchesses behind him, all dressed as peasants, to a fair near Audley End in October 1670. In view of Gascoigne's atrocious pronunciation of English, it should be no surprise that their disguises were quickly penetrated by an over-enthusiastic crowd, and the soldier and ladies had to beat a disorderly retreat.

Soon after this Gascoigne left for Florence, taking with him Samuel Cooper's miniature of Cosimo III. On 19 March 1671 Sir Thomas Clifford's son, also Thomas, who had travelled with him, died at Gascoigne's house in Florence, attempts at bringing in a priest to administer the last rites being foiled by Sir John Finch, the English resident.

The death of his wife, Anne Hyde, in 1670 rendered James, duke of York, eligible for marriage again. Cosimo III was eager to make his second cousin, the Habsburg infanta Claudia Felice, the duke's bride. Gascoigne returned to London in November 1671 with the archduchess's portrait and, as fresh hostilities between the Dutch and the English loomed, Arlington sent Gascoigne in February 1672 to negotiate the marriage. Gascoigne met the infanta that April, and by October it seemed as if the match would happen. However, the sudden death of the empress in Vienna meant that Leopold I took Claudia Felice for himself, and Gascoigne returned to London in August 1673. A description of the imperial diet that Gascoigne wrote after his visit was published posthumously in Tom Brown's *Miscellanea Aulica* (1702). It is noteworthy that while Gascoigne was representing England in Vienna his cousin Marcantonio Altoviti (1624–1679) was Florentine resident in Venice.

After another stay in Florence Gascoigne again undertook marriage brokership on Cosimo's behalf in 1677. The grand duke hoped to marry his son Ferdinando to the Princess Anne, but the Popish Plot put paid to these efforts. Indeed, at this time, even as well-established a figure at court as Gascoigne was berated in the House of Commons for his catholicity.

Death and assessment In his final years Gascoigne kept up an active social life, be it dining with John Evelyn or losing at cards to Robert Hooke. He continued to befriend Italians in England, for instance securing both an audience and a gift in 1681 for Gregorio Leti. In early summer 1682 Gascoigne travelled to Florence, and he made a will there in 1684. But it was at his house in the Haymarket, London, that he took to his bed on 25 December 1686, drawing up an English will the following day, to which he added various *ad hoc* codicils. His last days were somewhat sad and pathetic, darkened by paranoia and almost comical in his fleeing for a night to the clean air of Richmond, dressed only in his nightgown. He died at Haymarket, London, on 20 January 1687 os and was buried two days later at a private, Catholic ceremony in the royal chapel of St James's Palace. His many legatees included several members of the Boyle family, particularly Lord Clifford, to whom he had often lent money, as well as two of the Berties and various titled ladies. Nevertheless Terriesi, the Florentine resident who tended Gascoigne to the last, described his will as laughable, 'ridiculoso' (Terriesi to Bassetti, Archivio di Stato di Firenze, Mediceo del Principato MS 4245, 565). This was because Gascoigne had no idea of his liabilities, so his bequests may have been more valuable in the sentiment they expressed than in the material benefit they conferred.

Gascoigne's heroism at Colchester and steadfastness of service to the English crown seem to have imbued him with considerable prestige and social cachet in both England and the state of his birth. The quintessential Anglo-Italian, he was referred to often in contemporary literature both seriously and humorously, be it in Rochester's *Signior Dildo* (lines 51–5) or Butler's *Hudibras* (canto 1, pt 3, lines 1170–74). The hapless John Doddington was only one of many Englishmen to be grateful for Gascoigne's 'singular Friendshippe & Goodnesse' (Doddington to Temple, 1 Jan 1672, Hunt. L., MS STT 680). An 'excellent officer' according to Clarendon (Clarendon, *Hist. rebellion*, 4.359), and 'a recht courtier infatigable in solicitinge his bussinesse' (Donellan to Arlington, 19/29 Sept 1672, PRO, SP 80/13, fol. 45r), Gascoigne was widely recognized as mentally agile, physically energetic, eloquent, and charming. When it came to his adeptness with women, Magalotti understated: 'non è un' oca' ('he's no fool'; Magalotti to Leopold, 29 June 1668, in A. Fabroni, *Lettere inedite d'uomini illustri*, 1773, 1.308). The guarded Venetian diplomat Giavarina described him as 'a man of ability, sharp and very off-handed' (Giavarina to doge and senate, 1 Sept 1662, *CSP Venice, 1661–4*, 182), while Gregorio Leti found him 'generoso, magnanimo e cortese' ('generous, magnanimous and courteous'; Leti, *Il teatro brittanico*, 5.352). Gascoigne himself neatly summed up the tenor of his life:

'I will be merrye evere were; and lett the worlde say wath the Please' (Gascoigne to Williamson, 20 June 1664, PRO, SP 98/5, unfoliated). RODERICK CLAYTON

Sources G. Gargani, *Relazione della storia d'Inghilterra* (Florence, 1886) • A. M. Crinò, *Fatti e figure del Seicento anglo-toscano: documenti inediti sui rapporti letterari, diplomatici e culturali fra Toscana e Inghilterra* (Florence, 1957) • G. Leti, *Il teatro brittanico*, 2nd edn, 5 vols. (Amsterdam, 1684), vol. 5 • Gascoigne correspondence, BL, Add. MSS 34077, 38850, 63729; Egerton MS 3810 • Archivio di stato, Firenze, Mediceo del principato MSS 4202, 4213, 4232, 4245 • state papers foreign, holy Roman empire, 1672–5, PRO, SP 80/13 • state papers foreign, Tuscany, 1664– 6, 1667, 1669, 1670–71, PRO, SP 98/4-5, 8, 10, 12–13 • Biblioteca Nazionale Centrale, Florence, MS Gonnelli 15; Carteggi Vari 99 • Clarendon, *Hist. rebellion* • *CSP dom.*, 1649–87 • *CSP Venice, 1660–75* • A. M. Crinò, ed., *Un principe di Toscana in Inghilterra e in Irlanda nel 1669* (Rome, 1968) • L. Passerini, *Genealogia e storia della famiglia Altoviti* (Florence, 1871) • R. D. Waller, 'Un Anglo-Fiorentino alla corte di Carlo II', *Bollettino degli Studi Inglesi in Italia … dell' Istituto Britannico*, 4/2 (April 1935) • Cassiobury papers, BL, Add. MS 40630 • *Calendar of treasury boooks, 1660–85* • A. Fabroni, ed., *Lettere inedite di uomini illustri*, 2 vols. (Florence, 1773–5)
Archives BL, corresp. and papers, Add. MS 63729 • BL, letters and papers, Add. MS 38850 | Biblioteca Nazionale Centrale, Florence, MS Gonnelli 15 • BL, corresp. mainly relating to marriage of James, duke of York, Add. MS 34077
Likenesses drawing (after unknown portrait), Royal Collection; repro. in C. H. Hartmann, *Clifford of the cabal* (1937), facing p. 182
Wealth at death sizeable landholdings in Italy and Lincolnshire: will, PRO, PROB 11/386, fols. 164v–167r

Gascoigne, Charles (1738?–1806), ironmaster, was the son of Captain Woodroffe Gascoigne, a member of the Gascoigne family of Parlington, Yorkshire, and his wife, the Hon. Grizel Elphinstone, eldest daughter of Lord Elphinstone. His father was involved in the highland settlement of 1746, but nothing is known about Gascoigne's early life or education. On 22 July 1759, at St Martin's, Birmingham, he married Mary, daughter of Samuel *Garbett, ironmaster. They had three daughters, one of whom, Anne, became countess of Haddington.

Gascoigne joined the Carron ironworks, near Falkirk, Stirlingshire, where his father-in-law was a partner, quickly established a reputation as an iron-founder, and became managing director. The Carron Company first produced iron cannon in 1761 and from it the Russian admiralty college ordered, in February 1772, 1000 tons of iron cannon. The first consignment of forty-five guns reached Kronstadt in June 1772 and further orders were sent later in 1772 and in 1773. Difficulties under proof were found with many of the guns and no further orders were dispatched until 1785, by which time the famous carronades, first introduced in 1779, were being manufactured. In addition the Carron Company supplied Russia with a Newcomen steam engine, improved by John Smeaton, for pumping duty at Kronstadt. Both these enterprises led to the emigration of skilled British workers to Russia and established a long tradition of technological transfer. A major problem was that the workers had neither the managerial skills nor the social standing to carry out any major breakthrough. Unsuccessful attempts were made to recruit the engineer James Watt, and also William Small, the latter being a friend of the manufacturer

Matthew Boulton and Thomas Jefferson's teacher. The solution to this dilemma proved to be the 'seduction' of Charles Gascoigne.

The recruitment of Scots to the Russian navy, both as officers and as educationists, together with a growing colony of instrument makers and other skilled artisans in St Petersburg, created a suitable environment for the diffusion of technology to Russia. The negotiations for Gascoigne's recruitment were carried out, in great secrecy, through the agency of Admiral Sir Samuel Greig, at the instigation of Count A. A. Bezborodko. At the British end the agents were the Russian ambassador, Count S. R. Vorontsov, and the shipbuilder Mikhail Stepanov. Suspicion already existed in the minds of Garbett, Boulton, and others about Russian intentions because of the export of cannon, a copy of Smeaton's model for testing waterpower, and other machines from the Carron Company. Nevertheless, the British government, anxious to establish good relations with Russia, allowed these exports to go forward. A few workers were taken off Russian ships and returned to Scotland, but it was with the British government's tacit approval that, in May 1786, Gascoigne and twelve skilled men, including his chief assistant, Adam Armstrong, embarked for Russia.

The move to Russia was also fortuitous for Gascoigne, who had personally become bankrupt and whose shares in the Carron Company were held by creditors. In England he was strongly criticized by Garbett, Boulton, and others, though Boulton's position was always suspect, since he himself was angling for Russian business, first in the ormolu trade and later in the provision of a steam-powered mint for St Petersburg. From the Russian point of view, preparing for a war against Turkey, the provision of cannon that would not explode in the faces of their Russian operators was essential. Greig celebrated Gascoigne's arrival in St Petersburg by writing to Vorontsov to say that he was the man they needed more than anyone else.

Gascoigne was placed in charge of the Olonets factories, near Lake Onega, north-east of St Petersburg. He was to direct the Aleksandrovsk textile manufacture and to establish the Koncherzersky iron foundry. His salary was to be £2500 (25,000 gold roubles) p.a., plus a percentage of the profits from the Olonets complex; he was also to be given complete control of the enterprises. His position at that time, as a private contractor to the Russian government, afforded him excellent opportunities for amassing a fortune.

Within three years Gascoigne was awarded the order of St Vladimir, followed by the order of St Anna (second and then first class). In 1789 a Russian barony was bestowed on him. Not surprisingly, he met with a good deal of envy and suspicion. His second wife was Anastasia-Jessye, daughter of Dr Matthew Guthrie, physician to Tsar Paul; Count F. Golovkin claimed that she became the mistress of Procurator-General P. V. Lopuklim, father of the tsar's favourite (Bartlett, 'Charles Gascoigne', 355).

The establishment of Henry Cort's process of iron-founding in Britain made it possible to use increased amounts of scrap iron. In 1789 Gascoigne introduced at Kronstadt a foundry using scrap metal, and it was later transferred to St Petersburg to become the basis of the Peterburgsky Liteiny Zavod. Several years later the increased danger of war with Turkey and the need to strengthen Russian defences led to Gascoigne establishing the Lugansk foundry, which began smelting in 1797. As Russia was also interested in the British invention of copper sheathing for the hulls of wooden ships, Gascoigne wanted to learn about the rolling mills that Boulton was bringing over in the 1790s for the steam-powered mint at St Petersburg, as well as the Boulton and Watt steam engines. Every move that 'the Baron' made was regarded with suspicion by Boulton's agents, despite the fact that Boulton had promised the disclosure of every part of the mint machinery to the Russian government.

In 1796 Gascoigne established a factory at Petrozavodsk to make buttons for military uniforms, a typical Birmingham manufacture. In 1803 he reorganized the admiralty's Izhora works at Kolpino, south-east of St Petersburg. William Hastie, the architect, was involved in drawing up the plans, as he was for the first metal bridge erected in St Petersburg, also by Gascoigne. In 1805 Gascoigne was made technical director of the Aleksandrovsk manufacture and installed its first steam engine. When John Quincy Adams visited the textile factory in 1810 he found three steam engines there, but it may have been Alexander Wilson, Gascoigne's assistant and successor, who was responsible for them. Much of the ornamental ironwork on buildings in St Petersburg was created in factories directed by Gascoigne. He was a consultant to N. Mordvinov in the 1790s in the reconstruction of the docks at Nikolayev. He also played a large part in the introduction of a new Russian statute on weights and measures, setting the English inch as the basis of the Russian *arshin*.

Despite later problems with the collapse of the dam at Kolpino and a violent quarrel with A. N. Olenin over the St Petersburg mint, Gascoigne retained government support. The steam engine at the mint, built by George Sheriff under his direction, had to be replaced by Boulton and Watt engines, but such failures were outweighed by Gascoigne's many successes in bringing Russia into the era of industrialization through the introduction of new machines and processes and the attraction of skilled British labour, including Adam Armstrong, George Sheriff, and Charles Baird.

Gascoigne was ambitious, unscrupulous, and self-seeking but he was also energetic, entrepreneurial, and effective. He died at St Petersburg on 1 August 1806 leaving a large fortune.

ERIC H. ROBINSON

Sources R. H. Campbell, *Carron Company* (1961) · A. F. Steuart, *Scottish influences in Russian history, from the end of the 16th century to the beginning of the 19th century* (1913) · E. H. Robinson, 'The transference of British technology to Russia, 1760–1820', *Great Britain and her world, 1750–1914*, ed. B. M. Ratcliffe (1975) · E. A. Jones, 'The enticement of Scottish artificers to Russia and Denmark in 1784 and 1786', *SHR*, 18 (1920–21), 233–4 · R. P. Bartlett, 'Scottish cannon-founders and the Russian navy, 1768–1785', *Oxford Slavonic Papers*, new ser., 10 (1977), 51–72 · R. P. Bartlett, 'Charles Gascoigne in Russia: a case study in the diffusion of British technology, 1786–1806', *Russia and the west in the eighteenth century*, ed. A. G. Cross (1983), 354–

67 • A. G. Cross, 'By the banks of the Thames': Russians in eighteenth-century Britain (1980) • Ia. A. Balagurov, Olonetskia gornye zavody v doreformennyi period (1958) • R. Gladkikh, 'Privatne Delo', Kraeved Karelii, ed. V. Verkhogliadov (1990), 68–87 • P. S. Bebbington, 'Samuel Garbett, 1717–1803, a Birmingham pioneer', MCom diss., U. Birm., 1938

Archives Birm. CL, Boulton and Watt MSS • NA Scot., Carron Co. MSS • PRO, FO 65/110 Consular • Russia Arkiv Grafov Mordvinovykh, St Petersburg, letter books • Tsentral'nyi Gosudarstvennyi Istoricheskii Arkhiv SSSR, St Petersburg

Gascoigne, George (1534/5?–1577), author and soldier, was the eldest of three children of Sir John Gascoigne (b. in or before 1510, d. 1568) of Cardington, Bedfordshire, and his wife, Margaret (d. 17 Oct 1575), daughter of Sir Robert Scargill of Thorpe Hall, Richmond, Yorkshire. Knighted in 1541, Sir John served as sheriff for Bedfordshire and Buckinghamshire, 1542–3; MP for Bedfordshire, 1542, 1553, and 1558; commissioner of the musters, 1546; justice of the peace, 1546 until his death; and almoner at the coronations of Edward VI and of Mary. Gascoigne's grandfather, Sir William Gascoigne (d. 1540) of Cardington, the namesake of his great-grandfather, the chief justice, served as treasurer of Cardinal Wolsey's household, 1523–9; MP for Bedfordshire, 1529 and 1536; justice of the peace in several counties; and almoner at the coronations of Henry VIII and of Anne Boleyn.

Early and middle years The details of Gascoigne's early life are obscure, and more is known about his last five years than about any earlier period. A birth date of 1534 or 1535 depends on a deposition, of 15 February 1569, in which Gascoigne gives his age as thirty-four (Eccles, 55), but an inquisition post-mortem says that at the time of his father's death, 4 April 1568, Gascoigne was twenty-six years old 'et amplius' ('and more'; Prouty, 287). An aside in a dedicatory letter to Queen Elizabeth—'suche English as I stale in westmerland' (Gascoigne, 2.477)—suggests that he spent some of his childhood with his mother's Yorkshire relatives, who owned property on the border of Westmorland. In one poem Gascoigne states that he attended Cambridge (Gascoigne, 2.168), and in another he refers to Stephen Nevynson as his master (Gascoigne, 1.180). Nevynson was tutor at Christ's College, from about 1544 to 1547, and at Trinity College in 1547–8. There is, however, no college or university record of Gascoigne's attendance. He was admitted to Gray's Inn in 1555 and was made an ancient in 1565.

Sir John owned part of the barony of Bedford and was recorder of the town, which Gascoigne represented in parliament in 1558 and 1559. At the time of Elizabeth's coronation, Gascoigne's father was ill and deputed his son to serve as almoner. It is not known whether Gascoigne frequented the court before this, but he does say, after studying law, that he ruined himself financially while trying to make his way at court (Gascoigne, 1.67–8, 349). He wrote two poems from Fontainebleau (ibid., 331), but when he visited the Valois court is unknown.

Presumably seeking to mend his fortune, Gascoigne married Elizabeth Boyes, née Bacon (d. c.1585), a wealthy widow, on 23 November 1561, at Christ Church Greyfriars. Sir Nicholas Bacon, lord keeper of the great seal, was her

George Gascoigne (1534/5?–1577), by unknown engraver, pubd 1576

distant cousin and supervisor of her father's will. Elizabeth's first husband was William Breton; the couple married in 1545 and had five children, including the poet Nicholas Breton. Within months of her husband's death on 12 January 1559, Elizabeth married Edward Boyes of Nonington, Kent. In a 1566 chancery bill Elizabeth's sons refer to the 'colour of a pretended marriage' (Prouty, 299), so Elizabeth may not have considered herself married to Boyes when she married Gascoigne. In any event, her marriages led to more than legal disputes. In his diary for 30 September 1562 Machyn records 'a grett fray in Redcrosse stret betwyn ii gentyllmen and ther men, for they dyd mare [marry] one woman, and dyvers wher hurtt; thes wher ther names, master Boysse and master Gaskyn gentyllmen' (Diary of Henry Machyn, 293). After lengthy legal proceedings, Elizabeth was divorced from Boyes. In 1566 Gascoigne, Elizabeth, and her sons were still trying to recover substantial property from Boyes. In that year Gascoigne and his wife appropriated property belonging to her children contrary to the terms of Breton's will.

In May 1562 Gascoigne leased a manor in Willington, Bedfordshire, for an unsuccessful experiment at farming. Also during that month he was a servant of the countess of Bedford. Elizabeth Gascoigne had inherited from her first husband a house on Red Cross Street, St Giles Cripplegate, and in 1563 Gascoigne was assessed on an income of £67 per annum. The couple probably lived in Willington from 1563 to 1565, at which time Gascoigne returned to Gray's Inn. To join the 'fellowship' of five members of the inn, Gascoigne wrote a series of poems on Latin mottoes furnished by them (Gascoigne, 1.62–70). For the revels of 1566 he translated and adapted two plays: *Supposes*, from Ariosto's *I suppositi*, and, with Francis Kinwelmersh, *Jocasta*, purportedly from the Greek of Euripides' *Phoenician Women* but actually from Lodovico Dolce's Italian adaptation/translation of Euripides.

Gascoigne was never called to the bar but had ample opportunity to use his legal training, usually to no avail. In addition to lawsuits stemming from his marriage and his wife's inheritance, he was involved in suits concerning his lease of the manor at Willington and a dispute with the earl of Bedford, among others. The least edifying of these legal battles concerned the lease of the parsonage of Fenlake Barnes. Left to Gascoigne's brother John in their father's will (PRO, Prob 11/50/12), which was probated on 1 June 1568, this lease had already been, according to Gascoigne, purchased by him from his father. Gascoigne brought a complaint against his brother for stealing tithe lambs due to the parsonage; John countered that he was recovering lambs which Gascoigne had stolen from their mother; Gascoigne denied the charge and alleged his mother's 'unnaturalness' towards him. John eventually won the rights to Fenlake Barnes. The episode helps to explain why Lady Margaret did not mention Gascoigne in her will (PRO, PROB 11/50/4), which was probated on 10 March 1576, and which he unsuccessfully contested.

Later years Disappointed by the terms of his father's will, if not actually disinherited, and embroiled in lawsuits that were going against him, Gascoigne found himself in a desperate financial situation. On 13 June 1569 Gray's ordered him to pay his debts or 'be put out of the fellowshipp of the house' (Fletcher, 3); there is no evidence that he resided there again. On 21 April 1570 he was in Bedford gaol for debt. An anonymous, undated petition to the privy council declares

> he is indebted to a great number of personnes for the which cause he hathe absented him selfe from the citie and hathe lurked at villages neere unto the same citie by a longe time, and nowe beinge returned for a burgesse of Midehurste in the countie of Sussex, doethe shewe his face openlie in the despite of all his creditors.　(PRO, SP 12/86/59; Prouty, 61)

Gascoigne was probably elected MP for Midhurst, which was controlled by Anthony Browne, first Viscount Montagu, for the double wedding of whose children he wrote a masque later in the year. Gascoigne's name was crossed out on a list of MPs, probably drawn up before the opening of parliament in May 1572 (PRO, C 193/32/10); on another list, tentatively dated to the week before parliament opened, his name does not appear (PRO, C 193/32/8). He did not take his seat because he was brought into the house on 9 June to give evidence concerning his father.

At this juncture Gascoigne, presumably to escape his creditors and to repair his fortune, joined Sir Humphrey Gilbert's expedition to prevent the French from holding Flushing and to assist the revolt of the Netherlands against Spanish rule. The English reached Flushing on 10 July 1572 and returned to England towards the beginning of November, after unsuccessful attempts to take Sluis and Bruges in Flanders and to besiege Goes on the island of South Beveland. The account of these events by Gascoigne in 'The fruites of warre' (Gascoigne, 1.160), as well as that of another participant, Roger Williams, in *The Actions of the Lowe Countries* (108–21), stresses the incompetence of the leaders and the ineffectualness of the English.

Gascoigne wrote a lively narrative of his second voyage to the Netherlands, on 19 March 1573, which almost ended in shipwreck (Gascoigne, 1.354–63), but he was probably back in England for the funeral of Reginald Grey, fifth earl of Kent, on 17 April. He served as a captain in various efforts to capture Middelburg in August, quarrelling with his colonel, and went to the prince of Orange in Delft. In that city he was suspected of treachery by the Dutch. While at The Hague in July, Gascoigne had given his portrait to 'a worthie dame'. After The Hague fell to the Spanish on 30 October, she sent her maid to Gascoigne with 'a loving letter' (ibid., 165), which was stopped at the gates of Delft. Orange apparently did not share the Dutch suspicions of the Green Knight, the name they bestowed upon Gascoigne, for the prince provided him with a hoy to help prevent the Spanish efforts to relieve Middelburg at the end of January 1574. After the surrender of that town on 18 February, Orange gave Gascoigne 300 gulden above his pay. Assuming the captaincy of a company of English volunteers who arrived in March, Gascoigne tried to fortify Valkenburgh, 3 miles from Leiden. The Dutch suspected Gascoigne and the other English captains of treachery and would not admit their troops into the city. The English surrendered to the Spanish at the end of May, and Gascoigne returned to England after approximately four months in prison in Haarlem.

In the winter of 1572–3, between his two stints of military service, Gascoigne was invited to hunt by Arthur, fourteenth Lord Grey of Wilton, and wrote 'Gascoignes Wodmanship', a much-admired poem in which he turns his shooting awry at the deer into an appeal for patronage. The last four years of his life saw numerous attempts to secure patronage through writing. His first attempt shot spectacularly awry: *A Hundreth Sundrie Flowres* (1573), a collection of his writings under the guise of an anthology of works by diverse gentlemen, assembled by one of their friends and surreptitiously published by another. Instead of demonstrating Gascoigne's resourcefulness as a writer and mastery of courtly indirection the book was deemed lasciviously offensive and 'written to the scandalizing of some worthie personages' (Gascoigne, 1.7). This last phrase comes from one of the three prefatory letters which Gascoigne prefixed to the second edition, *The Posies of George Gascoigne Esquire* (1575). In these letters Gascoigne adopts the stance of a reformed prodigal, whose early errors 'might yet serve as a myrrour for unbrydled youth, to avoyde those perilles which I had passed'. Despite these efforts to control the damage caused by the first edition the book was confiscated for reasons that remain obscure.

On 13 August 1576, 'by appointment of the Q. M. Commissioners', Richard Smith, the bookseller, returned 'half a hundred of Gascoignes poesies' to the Stationers' Hall (Greg and Boswell, 86–7).

The sincerity of Gascoigne's 'reformation' has been questioned, but no one disputes that he was presenting himself as fit for service to the state. The title-page of *The Posies* bears the motto which Gascoigne was to use for the rest of his life, *Tam Marti, quam Mercurio* ('As much for Mars as for Mercury'), signifying his desire for employment as a soldier and/or a writer. Two of the prefatory letters advertising Gascoigne's reformation were dated January 1575, and his next work, dedicated to Sir Owen Hopton, 26 April, adopts an unremittingly austere moral stance: *The glasse of governement: a tragicall comedie so entituled, bycause therein are handled aswell the rewardes for vertues, as also the punishment for vices*. His next work, however, was *The Noble Arte of Venerie or Hunting*, largely a translation of treatises by Jacques du Fouilloux and Gaston de Foix, with a prefatory letter dated 16 June 1575. 'Noble' indicates the desire for a courtly audience, and woodcuts of Queen Elizabeth, who was very fond of hunting, suggest an effort to attract her attention and patronage. The translation was published anonymously, perhaps because it did not further the image of a reformed Gascoigne.

In July 1575 Gascoigne was one of the authors employed by the earl of Leicester to devise masques, pageants, and speeches for Elizabeth's visit to Kenilworth. As the queen returned from hunting, Gascoigne appeared before her 'clad like a Savage man, all in Ivie' (Gascoigne, 2.96) and made a direct plea for royal patronage. When the savage man, as a sign of submission, broke his tree and threw the top of it away, it startled Elizabeth's horse, but she graciously called out, 'no hurt no hurt' (R. Langham, *A Letter*, ed. R. J. P. Kuin, 1983, 46). The posthumous 1587 edition of Gascoigne's *Works* includes *The Princelye Pleasures at the Courte at Kenelworth*, which was published anonymously in March 1576, and it has been assumed that Gascoigne was responsible for editing that collection. In any event, Gascoigne was present at Woodstock when the queen proceeded there in September 1575. As a new year's gift for 1576, Gascoigne, advertising his skill with languages and thus his fitness for foreign service, translated into Latin, Italian, and French an entertainment which had pleased her, 'The Tale of Hemetes the Heremyte'. The manuscript includes his famous drawing of himself, 'A Poett with a Speare' (Gascoigne, 2.473), kneeling to present his book to the enthroned Elizabeth. His prefatory letter is an extended plea for patronage, professing repentance for his 'youthfull pranks' (ibid., 475).

The plea did not bring Gascoigne immediate employment, and the first months of 1576 witnessed the publication of several works. His epistle to the reader, on 12 April, to *A Discourse of a Discoverie for a New Passage to Cataia* by his former colonel, Sir Humphrey Gilbert, professed to publish the discourse against Gilbert's wishes. Three days later Gascoigne dedicated *The Steele Glas* to Lord Grey with the by now familiar regret for his misspent youth and a prayer for 'speedy advauncement' (Gascoigne, 2.137). On 2 May Gascoigne dedicated *The Droomme of Doomes Day* to the earl of Bedford. The first part of this longest and most religious of Gascoigne's works, 'The view of worldly vanities', is a translation of Innocent III's *De miseria condicionis humane*, and the other parts are equally sombre: 'The shame of sinne', 'The needels eye', and 'Remedies against the bitternes of death'. A much shorter tract, *A Delicate Diet, for Daintiemouthde Droonkardes*, was published with a dedicatory letter dated 22 August to Lewis Dive.

The long-sought government employment finally came that autumn. On 15 September and 7 October Gascoigne wrote to Burghley about the effect of news from the Netherlands on the French court (*CSP for.*, 1575–7, 70/139, fol. 169; 70/140, fol. 23). He proceeded to Antwerp, where he witnessed the Spanish sack of the city, and returned to London on 21 November with letters for Walsingham, including praise of his 'humanitie' from the governor of the English merchants at Antwerp (Prouty, 95). Gascoigne's vivid anonymous account, *The Spoyle of Antwerpe*, was published at the end of the month.

For new year's day 1577 Gascoigne prepared another manuscript for the queen, 'The Grief of Joye', four songs on 'the uncerteine joyes of men' (Gascoigne, 2.514). The tone of the dedication of this work is much less urgent than in 1576, thanking Elizabeth for her 'undeserved favor' (ibid.) and offering his services once again. The songs, full of praise for the queen, imagine an intimacy between them and express confidence in her indulgence. Despite the confident tone, however, Gascoigne was once again in financial straits. On the same day he sent Nicholas Bacon a charming letter with an emblematic drawing of a colt being broken and ridden. Gascoigne concluded with an appeal for support,

> my colltyshe and jadishe trickes have longe sythens broughte me so owte of fleashe, as withowte some spedye provysione of good provender I shall never be able to endure a longe jorneye, and therfore am enforcede to neye and braye unto your good Lordship. (*Papers of Nathaniel Bacon*, 2.3)

In his letter to the earl of Bedford the previous May Gascoigne had described himself as 'in weake plight for health' (Gascoigne, 2.215). Nothing is known about the last year of his life other than that he died, after an illness of three months, in Stamford, Lincolnshire, on 7 October 1577, and was buried six days later in St Mary's parish, Stamford. No will has been discovered. Letters of administration were granted to John Campion of Woodford, Essex, on 2 December 1578, but on 7 May 1597 they were revoked and replaced by a grant to Gascoigne's brother John (PRO, PCC, admonition act book, 1578, fol. 158; 1597, fol. 208). Elizabeth Gascoigne survived her husband for approximately eight years; her eldest son, Richard Breton, received letters of administration in 1585. The couple's only child, William, died without issue on Drake's expedition to the West Indies in 1585–6.

Historical significance Although Gascoigne is remembered as an author, he published his writings primarily as a means of seeking preferment. He admits that it pleased him 'To heare it sayde there goeth, the *Man that writes so* well' (Gascoigne, 1.381), but when he asserts that he did not claim title to 'the name of an English Poet' (ibid., 1.5), it is probably not just false modesty (a common rhetorical convention). Some of his writings date from the early 1560s, but none appeared in print until 1573, and all of them appeared between that year and 1576. Aside from the two new year's gifts for Elizabeth, the only manuscript known from his lifetime contains *Jocasta*, in 1568 in the possession of Roger, second Lord North, so his works may not have circulated extensively in manuscript.

Ever since N. R.'s commendatory poem in *The Steele Glas*, Gascoigne has been praised for the variety of his works: '*Gascoigne* doth, in every vaine indite' (Gascoigne, 2.138). *Supposes* is the first prose comedy in English, and *Jocasta*, in blank verse, introduces Greek tragedy to the English stage. *The Glasse of Governement* imports Dutch prodigal-son drama. The masque for the Montagu–Dormer double marriage, one of the earliest extant masques, includes an account of the siege of Famagusta and the battle of Lepanto. Gascoigne's poems are as varied as his dramatic productions: a translation of Psalm 130; 'The fruites of warre', 207 stanzas of rhyme royal that expound the adage 'dulce bellum inexpertis', and then offer an account of Gascoigne's military service in the Netherlands; *The Steele Glas*, an estates satire which is also the first original non-dramatic poem in blank verse in English; and love poems of many shapes and sizes. Heavily influenced by Chaucer's *Troilus and Criseyde*, *A Discourse of the Adventures Passed by Master F. J.* is a masterpiece of Elizabethan fiction and Gascoigne's most discussed work. In its first edition G. T. sets out to explain the occasions of his friend F. J.'s poems about an adulterous affair, but the rambling, chatty discourse threatens to overwhelm the poems and to become a narrative in its own right. Alarmed by the scandal of its reception, Gascoigne stripped the second edition of its narrative complexity and produced a moral fable of what one ought to avoid. The rest of Gascoigne's prose is nonfiction: 'Certayne notes of instruction concerning the making of verse or ryme in English', the first treatise of its kind in English, as well as the already mentioned moral tracts, hunting treatise, and military reporting.

From shortly after his death until the present Gascoigne's reputation as the foremost poet of his generation and as a precursor of the great Elizabethans has remained constant. Commenting on Spenser's *Shepheardes Calender* in 1579, E. K. called Gascoigne 'a wittie gentleman, and the very chefe of our late rymers' (E. Spenser, *Poetical Works*, ed. J. C. Smith and E. de Selincourt, 1912, 463). Ten years later Thomas Nashe observed, 'Maister *Gascoigne* is not to bee abridged of his deserved esteeme, who first beate the path to that perfection which our best poets have aspired to since his departure' (T. Nash, *Works*, ed. R. B. McKerrow, rev. F. P. Wilson, 1958, 3.319). Shakespeare did Gascoigne the honour of taking the subplot for *The Taming of the Shrew* from *Supposes*.   G. W. PIGMAN III

Sources *The complete works of George Gascoigne*, ed. J. W. Cunliffe, 2 vols. (1907–10) • *The papers of Nathaniel Bacon of Stiffkey*, ed. A. H. Smith and G. M. Baker, 2: *1578–1585*, Norfolk RS, 49 (1983) • G. Whetstone, *A remembraunce of the wel imployed life, and godly end, of George Gaskoigne esquire, who deceased at Stalmford in Lincolne Shire the 7. of October. 1577* (1577) • G. W. Pigman, 'Biographical introduction', in G. Gascoigne, *A hundreth sundrie flowres*, ed. G. W. Pigman (2000) • C. T. Prouty, *George Gascoigne: Elizabethan courtier, soldier, and poet* (1942) • *The diary of Henry Machyn, citizen and merchant-taylor of London, from AD 1550 to AD 1563*, ed. J. G. Nichols, CS, 42 (1848) • R. Williams, *The works*, ed. J. X. Evans (1972) • M. Eccles, *Brief lives: Tudor and Stuart authors* (1982) • E. L. Brooks, 'The burial place of George Gascoigne', *Review of English Studies*, new ser., 5 (1954), 59 • W. W. Greg and E. Boswell, eds., *Records of the court of the Stationers' Company, 1576 to 1602, from register B* (1930) • R. J. Fletcher, ed., *The pension book of Gray's Inn*, 1 (1901) • G. Austen, 'The literary career of George Gascoigne: studies in self-presentation', DPhil diss., U. Oxf., 1997 • G. W. Pigman, 'George Gascoigne', *The Cambridge bibliography of English literature*, ed. J. Shattock, 3rd edn, 4 (1999) • J. L. Mills, 'Recent studies in Gascoigne', *English Literary Renaissance*, 3 (1973), 322–6 • B. M. Ward, 'George Gascoigne and his circle', *Review of English Studies*, 2 (1926), 32–41 • G. Ambrose, 'George Gascoigne', *Review of English Studies*, 2 (1926), 163–8 • F. Flournoy, 'William Breton, Nicholas Breton, and George Gascoigne', *Review of English Studies*, 16 (1940), 262–73 • J. Drakard, *The history of Stamford* (1822), 447
Likenesses engraving, 1575, BL, Royal MS 18 A xlviii; repro. in Gascoigne, *Complete works*, 2 (1910), 472 • woodcut, NPG; repro. in G. Gascoigne, *The steele glas* (1576), frontispiece [see illus.]

Gascoigne, John (*fl.* **1376–1381**), canon lawyer, was possibly the 'Jo. Gascoigne, cler.' who is named in a seventeenth-century pedigree as brother to Sir William *Gascoigne, the chief justice, and to Richard Gascoigne of Hunslet, who is said to have been father of Thomas Gascoigne, chancellor of the University of Oxford. John Gascoigne was a member of Oxford University and became a doctor of canon law, in which capacity he was called to give evidence before a commission of five bishops, appointed on 20 June 1376 to examine into certain controversies between the masters of arts and the faculty of law at Oxford. In 1381 he was one of the twelve Oxford doctors who unanimously assented to the judgment of William Berton, chancellor of the university, condemning the doctrine of Wycliffe touching the sacrament. Possibly on the strength of this, for there is no further available evidence, Konrad Gesner and, following him, John Pits attributed to Gascoigne a treatise *Adversus Wiclevi dogmata* as well as a life of St Jerome, the latter being really the work of Thomas Gascoigne. In a manuscript in the Royal Collection there are notes on his 'Lectura de officio et potestate delegati' (BL, Royal MS 9 E.viii, fol. 174). He also compiled a *Repertorium de judiciis* (PRO, C 115/L2/6692, fols. 151–166*v*), which can be dated to 1376.

R. L. POOLE, rev. F. DONALD LOGAN

Sources Emden, *Oxf.* • H. B. Workman, *John Wyclif*, 2 vols. (1926) • C. Gesner, *Bibliotheca universalis*, 2 vols. (Zürich, 1545–55) • J. Pits, *Relationum historicarum de rebus Anglicis*, ed. [W. Bishop] (Paris, 1619) • Tanner, *Bibl. Brit.-Hib.* • R. Thoresby, *Ducatus Leodiensis, or, The topography of … Leedes*, ed. T. D. Whitaker, 2nd edn (1816) • D. Wilkins, ed., *Concilia Magnae Britanniae et Hiberniae*, 4 vols. (1737) • *CPR, 1374–7*, 290–91 • [T. Netter], *Fasciculi zizaniorum magistri Johannis Wyclif cum tritico*, ed. W. W. Shirley, Rolls Series, 5 (1858)
Archives BL, Royal MS 9 E.viii, fol. 174 • PRO, C 115/L2/6692, fols. 151–166*v*

Gascoigne, Richard (*bap.* **1579**, *d.* **1661×4**), antiquary, was baptized on 27 May 1579 at St Mary the Virgin, Shenfield, near Brentwood, Essex, the fourth son of George Gascoigne (1531?–1620), barrister, at one time of Old Hurst in

Huntingdonshire, and Mary, daughter of John Stokesley. He was admitted pensioner at Jesus College, Cambridge, on 21 October 1594, and graduated in the Lent term of 1599. Gascoigne later claimed that if failing health had not compelled him to leave in September of that year he would have obtained a fellowship. For many years he lived in Bramham Biggan, in the West Riding of Yorkshire, moving towards the end of his life to lodgings in Little Turnstile, Lincoln's Inn Fields, London. During his lifetime he appears to have suffered from poverty and incarceration in debtors' prisons, which in his will he blamed on his ward John, the son of his elder brother Sir Nicholas Gascoigne. The date of his marriage to Elizabeth Colles is not known; she probably predeceased him, as there is no mention of her in his will made on 23 August 1661 in London.

Gascoigne spent his time and money collecting antiquarian documents, and compiling pedigrees of his Yorkshire kinsmen and neighbours. As a pedigree maker he charged high fees, which he appears, on occasion, to have found difficulty in collecting, complaining in his will of Sir Thomas Darby's failure to pay him £100 for a pedigree. He kept the documents as security, and finally pawned them to his landlady for £30.

A memorandum Gascoigne produced in 1658, at the age of seventy-nine, attests to his erudition. This is held by Jesus College, Cambridge, to which he bequeathed his printed books, a total of fifty-seven titles, with special instructions for their preservation. He particularly mentioned his copy of Augustine Vincent's 1621 correction of Ralph Brooke's work on the English nobility as of great value. The heavily annotated copy was part of his bequest. He left his pedigrees and seals to his cousin Thomas, son of Sir Thomas Gascoigne, and his picture of Lord Strafford to his executor. The chief part of Gascoigne's collection, his manuscripts, books, and transcripts, were acquired by William, the second earl of Strafford, who preserved them in his house at Wentworth-Woodhouse until his death in 1695. They then passed to Thomas Watson-Wentworth, son of the earl's sister, Anne. He died in 1723 and his son, of the same name, when about to be created Baron Malton, deliberately burnt the greater part of Gascoigne's manuscripts. William Oldys, antiquarian and Norroy king-at-arms, who in his diary, published in 1862, gave details of the esteem felt for Gascoigne by his contemporaries, witnessed this act of vandalism, which he attributed to Lord Malton's attorney, fearing that some of the material may have been damaging to his client's claim to the Wentworth-Woodhouse estates. Oldys managed to salvage a few rolls and associated manuscripts from the 'six or seven great chests' full of Gascoigne's collection. Some few have survived, and are preserved in Yorkshire, London, and Oxford. Gascoigne died in London between 23 August 1661, the date of his will, and its probate on 24 March 1664.

R. E. O. PEARSON

Sources will, PRO, PROB 11/313, sig.30 • F. S. Colman, *A history of the parish of Barwick-in-Elmet in the county of York*, Thoresby Society (1908) • *A literary antiquary: memoir of William Oldys … together with his diary*, ed. J. Yeowell (1862) • parish register, Shenfield, St Mary the Virgin [baptism], 27/5/1579 • donors' records, Jesus College, Cambridge, MS R.2.25 • Gascoigne family tree, R. Thoresby, *Ducatus Leodiensis, or, The topography of … Leedes*, ed. T. D. Whitaker, 2nd edn (1816) • Venn, *Alum. Cant.* • Burke, *Gen. GB* (1937) • *The life, diary, and correspondence of Sir William Dugdale*, ed. W. Hamper (1827)

Archives BL, antiquarian notes and collections, Add. MSS 6118, 40008–40009; Egerton MSS 3053, 37770–37771 • Bodl. Oxf., transcripts of antiquarian notes • Northants. RO, genealogical notes and papers • W. Yorks. AS, Leeds, MSS, antiquarian and literary MSS | Bodl. Oxf., heraldic and antiquarian notes copied by Roger Dodsworth • Coll. Arms, Vinant Collection, antiquarian notebooks, etc. • Sheff. Arch., book of Wentworth arms

Gascoigne, Richard (d. 1716), Jacobite conspirator, was of an Irish Catholic gentry family. Little is known of them other than that Gascoigne's grandfather had been killed fighting for Charles I in the civil wars, and that his father served in James II's army at the siege of Limerick (October 1691) and died soon afterwards.

Gascoigne succeeded to the estate, worth £200 a year; but the penal laws drove him to sell it and settle in England. Crooked London gamblers soon stripped him of his fortune and sums extracted from his mother and sisters. He was obliged to turn professional gamester himself, became 'an Artist in the Profession he had newly taken up' (*The Case of Richd Gascoigne*, 6), and, whether by skill or sharping, helped ruin several other foolish gentlemen. His later fellow sufferer Henry Oxburgh was a friend. His life was debauched. Yet, 6 feet 8 inches tall, handsome, and elegantly dressed, a brilliant, charming, and educated conversationalist, and even-tempered, he moved easily in London and Bath in the highest tory social circles, knowing James Butler, second duke of Ormond, Henry St John, first Viscount Bolingbroke, and Sir William Wyndham.

Gascoigne, a zealous Jacobite, was involved in 1715 in the plans for a west country rising, which were disrupted by Ormond's flight to France. However, as nearly all the Jacobite archives and the government's confidential papers on this episode have disappeared, knowledge of his role depends on the disputed evidence at his trial. In late September 1715 he took messages from Ormond in France to the duchess of Ormond and, presumably, the conspirators. He retreated to Bath, a centre of the planned rising, although he was convinced that only Wyndham's reappearance to lead it could prevent ruin. The Jacobites had many weapons, even artillery, hidden there; but some arms boxes marked 'R. G.', which convinced the government that Gascoigne's role was central, were probably intended for the Bristol slaver *Royal George*. After Major-General George Wade and his regiments entered the town in mid-October, many Jacobites, including Gascoigne, fled; a warrant for his arrest was issued on 26 October. He slowly moved towards Lancashire, where a Jacobite force was advancing south. Once he tried to go passively into hiding; once a JP arrested but mysteriously freed him, possibly because Gascoigne was already travelling with a leading Huntingdonshire Jacobite, Robert Cotton of Little Gidding, and his mounted party, which one source claimed was a hundred strong. Gascoigne joined the Jacobites at Preston about 10 November 1715—his splendid appearance made many assume that he was an important personage—and fought bravely in the battle.

Gascoigne was taken to London with the other captured gentry, and was committed to Newgate on 9 December 1715. The ministers pressed him to testify against more important Jacobites, particularly Wyndham and George Granville, Baron Lansdowne, but he denied any damning knowledge. He wrote to many generals asking their opinion as to whether a surrender on discretion, such as the Jacobites had made at Preston, did not by a military convention accepted across Europe guarantee their lives, and several assented. He understood the likely consequences for himself, and devoted himself to repentant piety.

On 9 May 1716, after several prisoners' escapes from Newgate, close confinement, including double irons, was ordered for Gascoigne only. He was tried on 17 May in the court of exchequer, Westminster Hall, largely conducting his own defence. As the government wished to keep secret its strongest evidence against him, from spies and intercepted letters, some witnesses exaggerated their testimony. Gascoigne was allowed by contemporary convention to deny their allegations in his last paper, although they were founded on truth. He wrote protesting to the dukes of Marlborough and Argyll over the terms of surrender. Hanged at Tyburn on 25 May, he died religiously and 'with the greatest Unconcernedness of any of the unfortunate rebels' (Patten, 151). His quartered body was given to his friends, and was presumably buried in London later in the month. His last paper emphasized that loyalty and duty, not Catholicism, had led him to fight for the Stuart cause. He was survived by his mother and sisters. He was unmarried.

PAUL HOPKINS

Sources *The case of Richd Gascoigne, esq.; executed at Tyburn for high treason on Friday, the 27th [sic] of May, 1716* (1716) [only recorded English copy in the Gascoigne papers, W. Yorks. AS, Leeds] • A. Boyer, *The political state of Great Britain*, 11 (1716) • *The history of the press-yard, or, A brief account of the customs … that are put in practice … in … Newgate* (1717) • *The manuscripts of the Marquess Townshend*, HMC, 19 (1887) • secretaries of state: state papers: warrant books, PRO, SP 44/79A, 80, 118 • R. Patten, *The history of the late rebellion*, 2nd edn (1717) • C. Petrie, 'The Jacobite activities in south and west England in the summer of 1715', *TRHS*, 4th ser., 18 (1935), 85–106 • P. K. Monod, *Jacobitism and the English people, 1688–1788* (1989) • S. H. Ware, ed., *Lancashire memorials of the rebellion, 1715* (1845) • *The Weekly Journal, or, British Gazetteer*, 420 (26 May 1716) • *The secret history of the rebels in Newgate*, 3rd edn (1717) • *VCH Huntingdonshire*

Likenesses line engraving, NPG • line engraving (of Richard Gascoigne?), BM, NPG; repro. in J. Caulfield, *Portraits, memoirs, and characters, of remarkable persons* (1819)

Gascoigne [Gascoygne], **Thomas** (1404–1458), theologian and university administrator, was the only son of Richard Gascoigne (d. 1422) and Beatrix, his wife. He was born on 5 January 1404 at Hunslet, near Leeds, where his father owned the manor. He had two sisters of whom the elder, Alice, married and carried the estate into the Neville family. The younger, Joan, married Sir Robert Roos of Ingmanthorpe. Gascoigne's father died in 1422, leaving enough to finance his son for the rest of his life, though not without occasional difficulties.

Life and career As an only son Gascoigne would probably have entered a secular career had he not suffered from ill health. Instead, he looked to the church. He started at Oxford, almost certainly Oriel College, between 1416 and 1420. In 1427 he was ordained priest by Bishop Richard Flemming of Lincoln in Thame church, Oxfordshire. In July 1433, perhaps thanks to Sir Robert Roos, he was appointed to the rectory of Kirk Deighton, close to his manor at Hunslet. He also continued at Oxford, obtaining a licence to attend an English university for three years on 22 February 1434. On 14 June 1434 he incepted as DTh, having fulfilled the academic requirements for the degree within a year. He then enjoyed a lifelong scholarly and administrative career, mainly in Oxford. At some time between 1434 and 1445 he was chaplain to Henry VI. On 26 November 1445 he was appointed to the rectory of St Peter's Cornhill, in London; he resigned less than three months later. On 7 February 1449, upon becoming a canon of Wells, he accepted the prebend of Combe Decima, worth 12 marks (£8) a year. On 8 February 1449 Oriel College granted him the use of his room rent-free for the rest of his life. He died on 13 March 1458 and was buried in the ante-chapel of New College, Oxford (the text of his memorial brass is recorded by Anthony Wood). His will was dated 12 March 1458 and proved on 22 March 1458.

Chancellor of Oxford Gascoigne embodies some of the most striking paradoxes of his age: he was a medieval schoolman who loved gossip, an old-fashioned moralist who collected material things, and a pious preacher who wanted to be remembered in this world. He has also been well described as

> one of the earliest of a new type of Oxford master who, while sharing the general interests of contemporaries involved in ecclesiastical or secular business, was prepared to commit his whole adult life to teaching in and administering the university. (Catto, 'Scholars and studies', 773)

He did most of his administering in the earlier part of his career. He first appears in the record as chancellor's commissary (vice-chancellor) in the month of his inception, again appearing as such in July and September of the same year, and in July 1439. By 15 May 1442 he was *cancellarius natus* (the senior doctor of divinity acting as chancellor during a vacancy), again appearing as such on 13 and 21 March 1444. And on 14 March 1444 he was for the first time elected chancellor of the university (that he appears as *cancellarius natus* a week later was probably because of some administrative complication).

Gascoigne seems to have valued being chancellor, and to have done what he could to extend the scope of the office. He nevertheless resigned on 7 April 1445, and hesitated about returning even when the university immediately re-elected him. His worries were probably financial, as on 18 April 1445 the university asked the king to help Gascoigne continue serving. It must have been then that the king wrote to the abbot of Westminster recommending his 'trusty and welbeloved chapeleyn' to a vacancy at the church of St Magnus the Martyr, at the foot of London Bridge (Monro, 53). Gascoigne, perhaps encouraged by the hope of a living within reach of Oxford, resumed office as chancellor on 5 June 1445. He served until November of the same year when he was admitted not to St Magnus, which seems never to have had a vacancy, but to St Peter's. He nevertheless continued to reside in Oxford. In 1448 he served on a committee for raising money to help build the new divinity schools. In 1450 he was appointed to deliver the Lenten sermon in St Martin's Church in Carfax, when he pleaded for a simple preaching style on the model of St Augustine. On 4 November 1452 he arbitrated in an appeal brought by Philip Uske DCL. In May 1453 he was again *cancellarius natus*. On 11 April 1455 he witnessed Bishop John Carpenter's grant of Bedell Hall to Oriel College. And in 1456 he arranged the thanksgiving service for the deliverance of Belgrade from the Turks (22 July 1456), and preached at St Frideswide's in commemoration of the event.

Gascoigne could surely have solved any financial worries he might have had by collecting more benefices like St Peter's. But he considered non-residency and plurality to be the main causes of the church's failings, and only ever held two such appointments for any length of time. The first was the rectory of Kirk Deighton, which he resigned before 1443 to Thomas Eborall because he thought Eborall well placed for preaching around York diocese. The second was the prebend of Combe Decima, which he held until death. All his other appointments he seems either to have refused outright or to have given up as soon as he realized he could not serve their needs. The rectory of St Peter's he gave up on 24 February 1446, when it became clear that continuing ill health would prevent his regularly travelling to London. And in July 1452 he refused the profitable chancellorship of York Cathedral, partly because its revenues were derived from the tithes and rents of impropriated churches.

Preacher and bibliophile Upon finally resigning as chancellor, Gascoigne must have returned with some relief to his other scholarly pursuits, especially preaching. He is probably the most visible of a self-consciously orthodox group of theologians who believed that preaching, and especially preaching by graduates, held the key to reform. He accordingly devoted a good deal of time to preparing a preachers' aid, the *Dictionarium theologicum*, or *Veritates collectae ex s. scriptura et aliorum sanctorum scriptis in modum tabulae alphabeticae*, also known as the *Liber veritatum*, a collection of theological excerpts under alphabetically (or roughly alphabetically) arranged headings accompanied by a good deal of moral, topical, and often autobiographical commentary of his own. He also made sure he preached in several places a year. His preaching probably did not compare either in frequency or effectiveness with that of certain other graduate preachers—Dr William Lichefeld at All Hallows-the-Great (1425–48), for example. But on 28 April 1436 he was specially commended by the university for his sermons on Easter Sunday and on the Tuesday after Easter. And by 1456 he could claim that he had preached in various churches in York and London, in all the churches in Oxford, in churches in Oxfordshire, in Pontefract, Doncaster, Leeds, Coventry, Nottingham, and Evesham, in Sussex, at Sheen Charterhouse in Surrey, and Syon Monastery in Middlesex.

Gascoigne's *Dictionarium* occupied him throughout his career; in the version that still survives (an incomplete two-volume copy, now Oxford, Lincoln College, MSS 117 and 118) its most recent material describes the condemnation of Reginald Pecock's writings on 17 December 1457. It differs from similar predecessors above all in the extent to which it reflects the personality of its compiler; it is indeed because Gascoigne so determinedly wrote himself into the work that much of the information available about him exists. It also differs in the extent to which it derives from primary rather than intermediate sources; they mainly include the Bible, the fathers, and especially Jerome, all of whose works Gascoigne had read and whom he quotes more than 2000 times, Robert Grosseteste, who was Gascoigne's favourite post-patristic author, and Hugues de St Cher; they also include Duns Scotus, Aquinas, the *Glossa ordinaria*, Bonaventure, Guillaume d'Auvergne, Stephen Langton, Bede, Rabanus, Clement of Llanthony, and the anti-Wycliffite polemicists William Woodford and Thomas Netter. Many of these were available in Oxford, where Gascoigne worked especially in the library of the Greyfriars. But he had to track down some in collections as far apart as Worcester, Peterborough, and Canterbury, as he indicates himself in his many semi-autobiographical comments. In his pursuit of these books and book collections, Gascoigne was substantially moved by the passion of a collector. Sometimes he actually acquired the books he used, and in such cases showed himself very concerned to provide them with a secure future. But usually he satisfied himself with collecting excerpts into his highly personal *Dictionarium*. Yet even then he left his mark on the books he consulted, annotating them with his semi-autobiographical comments, and writing a distinctive 'Jesus-Maria' at the heads of many of their pages. More than seventy manuscripts that passed through his hands can still be identified: as a reader, at least, he did not intend to be forgotten.

If Gascoigne took steps not to be forgotten as a reader, he also wanted to be remembered as a collector. His interest in providing his collections with a secure future reveals itself perhaps most clearly in instructions he left in his will that the monks of Syon transcribe his paper *Dictionarium* onto parchment and then keep both copies in their library. But he also gave generously to several of the corporate institutions whose facilities he had enjoyed. As early as 1429, when he rented a room in Exeter College, he gave the college 3s. 4d. for chaining books. He gave books and a sizeable collection of relics to New College, as well as books and 5 marks towards the building of its library to Oriel, and books to All Souls, Balliol, Lincoln, and possibly Durham colleges. He also gave books to St Paul's Cathedral and the Augustinian canons at Osney, as well as his remaining papers to Syon Monastery at his death.

Writings and influence John Bale credits Gascoigne with six named works 'and several others': *Dictionarium theologicum*, *Hieronymi illius vita*, *Septem flumina Babylonie*, *Veritates ex scripturis*, *Ordinariae lectiones*, and *Sermones evangeliorum*. Of these, by far the most important is the *Dictionarium*. Early records of the library at Syon reveal that the Lincoln College manuscript is not the copy made there by the monks; rather, it seems to represent a working copy started under Gascoigne's supervision. Contemporary or near contemporary sigla draw attention to Gascoigne's unusually personal commentary; it is tempting to regard these as being ultimately the work of the compiler, and as originating, at least in part, in Gascoigne's desire to bequeath a lasting version of himself to posterity.

That Gascoigne wanted to create such a version of himself is further suggested by part of a notebook which he compiled with the help of various amanuenses (now Bodl. Oxf., MS Lat. theol. e.33). Like the *Dictionarium*, though in a less organized way, it records Gascoigne's reading, this time in the form of bibliographical notes about St Bridget of Sweden followed by patristic authorities and extracts from the writings of Grosseteste. But also like the *Dictionarium* it contains autobiographical notes. And this time Gascoigne even writes in his own obit, leaving a space for the year in which this would take place.

Of the other works by Gascoigne that Bale names, only the *Septem flumina Babylonie* and the life of St Jerome are certainly extant. The first appears in the *Dictionarium* (between *Exposicio scripture* and *Fides*); it allegorizes the waters of Babylon as seven abuses in the church. The second, transcribed in 1439 by John Digoun, a recluse at Sheen, is extant in Magd. Oxf., MS 93. Also extant are some works by Gascoigne that Bale left unnamed: a sermon about the persecution of Christians (in Cambridge, Trinity College, MS B.4.23); what seems to be a theological lecture in which Gascoigne tries to reconcile true contrition with papal indulgences (in BL, Royal MS 8 G.vi); a letter about the Council of Florence of 1439 (in Cambridge, Trinity College, MS B.4.23); entries often accompanied by his 'Jesus-Maria' in the records of the university administration; and so partisan an account of Archbishop Richard Scrope's execution in 1405 as to suggest that Gascoigne's own politics were strongly Yorkist (in Oxford, Lincoln College, MS liv, supplemented by Bodl. Oxf., MS Auct. D.4.5). And he is known to have compiled a vernacular life of St Bridget for the nuns of Syon. He also caused John Raynton to compile a *Tractatus de ordinali Sarum* (extant in BL, Add. MS 25456).

Had Gascoigne's views more directly anticipated those of the Reformation he would doubtless have had a greater impact on later generations. But his *Dictionarium* was not entirely without influence. At least four versions must have existed shortly after his death: one he had made about 1455 when he arranged for his papers to be copied and bound in one volume, his own paper version, the copy transcribed from this by the monks of Syon, and the version that still exists. It is likely, too, that more copies once existed, as extracts are contained in BL, Cotton MS Vitellius C.ix, and BL, Harley MS 6949. Francis Bigod, executed for treason in June 1537, also used it in his *Treatise Concerning Impropriations of Benefices*.

Historical significance As commentators have repeatedly observed, it would be difficult to write of the mid-fifteenth century in England without referring to Gascoigne. He is a major source of information about the church and university, as well as about all kinds of other happenings, how Archbishop Arundel died by choking because he had tied up the tongues of preachers, for example, or how in 1457 people bled to death through the very body parts they had invoked when swearing. He also provides important information about the resources available to scholars before the dissolution of the monasteries. His main significance today may well lie less in any information he provides, however, than in his having been a man who helps bridge the gap between better-known persons and events. He does this especially in relation to the church. He was passionately orthodox, and in many ways a typical representative of a piety the church had encouraged partly as a means of countering Wycliffism. Yet he vehemently deplored the prevalent clerical abuses of his time, and many of his emphases echo those of Wyclif and his followers. His method, like theirs, was one of historical enquiry, of seeking the purer doctrine of the church through the literal sense of the Bible and the careful study of the fathers. And like the Wycliffites he believed in preaching, to the extent that he was very critical of Archbishop Arundel's all-embracing attempts to silence heretical preachers early in the century. But he looked to the pope as well as to the king to implement reform. He thereby denied himself the lasting influence he might otherwise have had.

CHRISTINA VON NOLCKEN

Sources Emden, *Oxf.*, 2.745–8 · W. A. Pronger, 'Thomas Gascoigne', *EngHR*, 53 (1938), 606–26; 54 (1939), 20–37 · T. Gascoigne, *Loci e libro veritatum*, ed. J. E. Thorold Rogers (1881) · J. I. Catto, 'Theology after Wycliffism', *Hist. U. Oxf.* 2: *Late med. Oxf.*, 263–80 · J. I. Catto, 'Scholars and studies in Renaissance Oxford', *Hist. U. Oxf.* 2: *Late med. Oxf.*, 769–84 · *Letters of Queen Margaret of Anjou and Bishop Beckington and others written in the reigns of Henry V and Henry VI*, ed. C. Monro, CS, 86 (1863), 52–3 · *DNB* · Bodl. Oxf., MS Lat. theol. e.33 [and Bodl.'s typewritten description] · Bale, *Cat.*, 1.596 · A. Wood, *The history and antiquities of the colleges and halls in the University of Oxford*, ed. J. Gutch (1786), 207 · H. E. Salter, ed., *Registrum cancellarii Oxoniensis, 1434–1469*, 2 vols., OHS, 93–4 (1932) · H. Anstey, ed., *Epistolae academicae Oxon.*, 1, OHS, 35 (1898) · G. C. Richards and H. E. Salter, eds., *The dean's register of Oriel, 1466–1661*, OHS, 84 (1926), 369–71 · R. W. Southern, *Robert Grosseteste: the growth of an English mind in medieval Europe* (1986), 313–15 · J. Gairdner, *Lollardy and the Reformation in England*, 1 (1908), 228–64 · N. R. Ker, *Books, collectors and libraries: studies in the medieval heritage*, ed. A. G. Watson (1985)
Archives BL, Cotton MS Vitellius C.ix · BL, Harley MS 6949 · BL, Royal MS 8 G.vi · Bodl. Oxf., MS Auct. D.4.5 · Bodl. Oxf., MS Lat. theol. e.33 · Lincoln College, Oxford, MS liv · Lincoln College, Oxford, MSS 117, 118 · Trinity Cam., MS B.4.23 | Magd. Oxf., MS 93
Wealth at death bequest of books and papers to Syon Monastery; additional books; other belongings of little value: will, *Registrum cancellarii*, 406–7

Gascoigne, Sir Thomas, **second baronet** (1596–1686), accused conspirator, was born on 26 April 1596, the eldest son of Sir John Gascoigne (c.1556–1637) of Barnbow in the West Riding of Yorkshire, and his wife, Anne (c.1560–1637), daughter of John Ingleby of Lawkland Hall, also in the West Riding. In 1635 his father became the first Englishman to be made a Nova Scotian baronet. The family was Roman Catholic and paid recusancy fines continuously from 1605 until 1642. Three of Sir John's sons took orders in the Roman Catholic church. John (1598–1681) entered the Benedictine order and became abbot of Lambspringe in Germany, Francis was a priest, and Michael (1603–1657) was a missioner at Welton in Northumberland. His daughters Catherine and Justina entered the Benedictine convent at Cambrai, and Justina was prioress of the convent at Paris when she died on 17 May 1690.

About 1620 Thomas Gascoigne married Anne (c.1600–1661), daughter of John Symonds of Brightwell, Oxfordshire. He succeeded to the baronetcy and family estates on his father's death on 3 May 1637 (his mother died on 20 June). He continued his father's policy of improving the estates by enclosing wastes and commons, draining land, quarrying and mining, and acquiring more property. He was said to have raised £4000 by the sale of land formerly belonging to the Oglethorpe family, neighbours of the Gascoignes, while retaining land and manorial rights worth £170 per annum. The annual value of the Gascoigne estates rose from £1000 in 1608 to £1700 by the 1640s. Gascoigne was a benefactor to the Franciscan community at Mount Grace and in 1678 endowed with £90 per annum a convent of the Institute of the Blessed Virgin at Dolebank near Fountains Abbey, of which his daughter Tempest was a patron.

Between 1676 and 1678 Gascoigne employed Robert Bolron as steward of his coalmines. In 1679 Bolron, with Thomas Mowbray, who had joined Gascoigne's household as a servant in 1674, claimed that meetings had been held at Gascoigne's house, Barnbow Hall, at which a conspiracy to kill the king and establish the Roman Catholic faith had been discussed. They implicated several others in this alleged Yorkshire plot, including Gascoigne's son Thomas, his daughter Tempest, Sir Miles Stapleton, and John Middleton of Stockhill Hall. Bolron and Mowbray also claimed that 'the Papist's Bloody Oath of Secrecy' had been forced upon them by Gascoigne. In the climate created by the Popish Plot their accusations could not be ignored, even though Gascoigne was an unlikely conspirator; he was eighty-three years old, was infirm, partially deaf, and had not been south of the River Trent for thirty years. Nevertheless he was arrested on 7 July 1679 and taken to London, where he was examined by the privy council on 18 July and committed to the Tower. Bolron and Mowbray gave their depositions before the lord mayor of York on 27 October and Gascoigne was arraigned for high treason in the king's bench on 24 January 1680. His request for a jury of Yorkshire gentlemen was granted.

The trial took place on 11 February before the lord chief justice, Sir William Scroggs, and three other judges, although Scroggs left part of the way through the proceedings to sit at a *nisi prius* court at Guildhall. Bolron and Mowbray, who were the only prosecution witnesses, repeated their allegations, largely based on conversations allegedly overheard at Barnbow Hall, adding some plausibility by claiming that the conspirators had planned to set fire to London and York, an assertion that could be linked to the conflagration in Southwark in 1676. Seventeen protestant Yorkshire gentry testified on Gascoigne's behalf and it emerged that Bolron and Mowbray had grounds for resentment because of their dismissal for dishonesty. Gascoigne was acquitted. His daughter Tempest was tried at the summer assizes at York and acquitted, and the trial of Sir Miles Stapleton, held over until the following year, also ended in his acquittal. No charge was brought against Thomas Gascoigne because he had been abroad when the alleged meetings had taken place. The only victim of the Yorkshire plot was Thomas Thwing, a priest, who was executed.

After his acquittal Gascoigne retired to the monastery at Lambspringe, where he was visited by William Carr, English consul at Amsterdam. Carr described him as a good and harmless gentleman, who had more integrity and piety than to be guilty of even thinking of the offences of which he had been accused. Gascoigne died at Lambspringe priory on 3 May 1686 and was buried there. He was survived by three sons and five daughters. The eldest son, Thomas (1623–1698), married Elizabeth, daughter of William Sheldon of Beoley, Worcestershire, and died childless. The title passed to Thomas, the eldest son of George, Gascoigne's second son, who had died in 1669, and his wife, Anne, daughter of Ellis Woodroffe of Helperley, Yorkshire.   STEPHEN PORTER

Sources State trials, 8.959–1044 • J. Raine, ed., *Depositions from the castle of York relating to offences committed in the northern counties in the seventeenth century*, SurtS, 40 (1861), 242–4 • J. Kenyon, *The Popish Plot* (1972), 25, 197–9 • J. T. Cliffe, *The Yorkshire gentry from the Reformation to the civil war* (1969), 34, 60, 149–50, 205, 208, 213–15, 220, 225, 228 • GEC, *Baronetage*, 2.407 • DNB
Archives Leeds Central Library, Gascoigne of Barnbow MSS

Gascoigne, Sir William (c.1350–1419), justice, the eldest son of William Gascoigne and his wife, Agnes, the daughter of Nicholas Frank, was born at Gawthorpe, Yorkshire. The Gascoignes were a gentry family of long standing. Gascoigne had at least two brothers who survived to adulthood; a seventeenth-century family memoir states that he was the eldest of five brothers. He is said to have studied at Cambridge and the Inner Temple, and he is included in Segar's list of readers at Gray's Inn, although the date of his reading is not given. From the year-books it appears that he argued a case in Hilary term 1374, although he does not begin to appear in chancery records as a feoffee and commissioner until the 1380s. He was created a serjeant-at-law, with seven others, in the 'call' of serjeants in October 1388. Following his creation he was commissioned as a justice of assize and gaol delivery on the East Anglian circuit. He was one of the king's serjeants in 1389 and again between 1396 and 1399. During the 1390s Gascoigne was retained by Henry Bolingbroke, the future Henry IV. He was appointed chief justice of the palatinate of Lancaster in 1397, and was mentioned as a feoffee in the will of John of Gaunt, duke of Lancaster, in 1399. He was also retained by the dean and chapter of York, Selby Abbey, and Thomas Holland, duke of Surrey. He was appointed by letters patent attorney to Bolingbroke on his banishment, and he also held an estate in Yorkshire in trust for him. His patent of king's serjeant was renewed when Henry IV became king in 1399, and he was created chief justice of the king's bench on 15 November 1400. He was a trier of petitions in parliament between 1400–01 and 1403–4. In July 1403 he was commissioned to raise forces against the insurgent earl of Northumberland. At about the same time he was appointed justice of assize and gaol delivery for the northern circuit, which included Yorkshire and Northumberland, the main centres of rebel activity. In April 1405 Gascoigne was appointed to receive the submission of the earl's adherents, with power to impose fines.

One of the leaders of the rebellion of 1405 was Richard Scrope, archbishop of York, who was later convicted of treason before a military court presided over by the earl of Arundel and Sir Thomas Beaufort and, in one of the most notorious acts of Henry IV's reign, executed. Some chronicle sources assert that Gascoigne was appointed to the court that was to try Scrope, but that when called upon by King Henry to pass sentence of death on the archbishop he refused, warning the king that a secular court had no power to do so. Modern scholars have generally accepted this account of Gascoigne's principled stand against the king, confirming as it does Gascoigne's posthumous reputation as an exemplar of judicial independence and integrity. The fact that the main source for the story, Clement Maidstone's narrative (Wharton, 2.169–72), is directly associated with Gascoigne's nephew Thomas Gascoigne (d. 1458), the theologian, may cast doubt on its accuracy. On the other hand, because of his close ties with York Gascoigne may indeed have been reluctant to become directly involved in the trial, and it seems likely that he did not participate in Scrope's conviction.

Chief Justice Gascoigne was a man around whom legend gathered. Most famous is the story, immortalized by Shakespeare, of his imprisonment of the prince of Wales, the future Henry V, for contempt of court in attempting to rescue one of his servants from the bar of king's bench. This legend, which is undoubtedly apocryphal, first appeared in print in Thomas Elyot's *Boke Named 'The Governour'* in 1531. Elyot's source, which he presumably obtained through his father, Sir Richard Elyot (d. 1522), who was a justice of common pleas, was the chief justice's address at the creation of serjeants-at-law, probably in 1521. The origin of the legend thus lies within the judiciary itself, and may stem from York legal circles close to the Gascoigne family. In 1459 Guy Fairfax of Steeton, Yorkshire, a justice of king's bench from 1478 to 1495, was bequeathed a 'great register' formerly belonging to William Gascoigne by John Dawtry, a York ecclesiastical lawyer. Guy's son William Fairfax was also a royal justice, and sat alongside Richard Elyot in the court of common pleas between 1500 and 1514.

The appearance of the legend in Elyot may therefore represent the emergence into print of an oral legal tradition concerning Gascoigne's relations with the prince. The legend may contain a kernel of truth, in suggesting that Gascoigne clashed with the prince as the latter sought to wrest power from his father at the end of Henry IV's reign. Certainly Gascoigne's appointment as chief justice was not renewed on Henry V's accession in 1413. He was replaced by William Hankeford on 29 March 1413, a

week after the new king's accession. In 1414, however, he received a grant of four bucks and does annually from the forest of Pontefract for the term of his life.

Gascoigne died on 17 December 1419. His will, dated 'Friday after St. Lucy's day' (15 December) 1419, was proved in the prerogative court of Yorkshire on the 23rd of the same month. His considerable wealth, including a large quantity of silver plate, was divided up among his family. He left his widow, Joan, 500 marks, several items of plate, and the manor of Wheldale in dower. He gave his three granddaughters £100 each, and assigned £40 for the marriage of the younger daughter of his brother Nicholas. Most of the remainder of his moveable wealth went to his son Sir William, who also inherited the family estates at Gawthorpe and five other Yorkshire manors, as well as property in York. Gascoigne was buried in the parish church of Harewood, Yorkshire, under a monument representing him in his robes and hood, his head resting on a double cushion supported by angels, a lion couchant at his feet. The monumental inscription giving the date of his death has been lost.

Gascoigne married first Elizabeth, daughter of Alexander Mowbray of Kirklington, Yorkshire, and second Joan, daughter of Sir William Pickering, and widow of Sir Ralph Greystoke. Joan outlived Gascoigne, dying in 1426. With his first wife he had one son, William, who married Jane, daughter of Sir Henry Wyman. Their son, Sir William Gascoigne, served with distinction under Henry V in his French campaigns. He was knighted by 1419 and was killed in action in 1422, leaving two sons and three daughters. A descendant, Sir William Gascoigne, held the manor of Gawthorpe in the reign of Elizabeth; but on his death without male issue, it devolved on his heir, Margaret, who by her marriage with Thomas Wentworth, high sheriff of Yorkshire in 1582, became the grandmother of Thomas Wentworth, earl of Strafford. The will of Gascoigne's second wife, Joan, mentions four sons and a daughter, but since Gascoigne's own will refers to no children other than Sir William, it seems likely that they were the children of her previous marriage. The seventeenth-century Gascoigne family memoir contains a highly coloured account of the accidental killing by Gascoigne's son from his first marriage of a stepson from the second marriage. This no doubt apocryphal tale is used by the author of the memoir to provide another illustration of Gascoigne as a paragon of justice.

EDWARD POWELL

Sources *Chancery records* · C. Rawcliffe, 'Gascoigne, Sir William', HoP, *Commons* · Baker, *Serjeants* · N. L. Ramsay, 'The English legal profession, *c*.1340–1450', PhD diss., U. Cam., 1985, xc · [J. Raine], ed., *Testamenta Eboracensia*, 4, SurtS, 53 (1869), 390–95 · E. F. Jacob, *The fifteenth century* (1961), 61–2 · T. Elyot, *The boke named 'The governour'* (1531) · R. Gough, *Sepulchral monuments in Great Britain*, 2/2 (1796), 37 · [H. Wharton], ed., *Anglia sacra*, 2 (1691), 169–72 · 'Records and evidences belonging to the descents of the Gascoignes', W. Yorks. AS, Leeds, Leeds District Archives, GC/F5/1
Likenesses tomb effigy, All Saints, Harewood, Yorkshire
Wealth at death see Surtees Society, *Testamenta Eboracensia* IV, 390–95 (1836)

Gascoigne, William (1612?–1644), inventor of optical instruments, was the son of Henry Gascoigne of Thorpe on the Hill, Rothwell, near Leeds, Yorkshire, and his first wife, Margaret Jane, daughter of William Cartwright. No precise record of his birth survives. It was claimed that he was descended from Sir William Gascoigne, chief justice to Henry IV (Rigaud, 2.34). Though Gascoigne made references to Oxford in his letters, his name is not recorded in the matriculation registers of the university. In a letter to William Oughtred in 1641, probably in February (Rigaud, 2.35), he claimed to be fluent only in English (though he displayed a familiarity with the Latin writings of contemporary European astronomers), and to have become interested in scientific matters only after returning home from Oxford and London. On 2 December 1640, he told Oughtred: 'I bestow only part of that time on these studies, which other gentlemen, our neighbours, spend in hunting' (ibid., 2.33–4). Almost certainly, Gascoigne belonged to the Roman Catholic gentry of Yorkshire. John Aubrey, indeed, believed him to have been educated by the Jesuits, and to have been taught 'a way of Flying' by them (*Letters … and Lives*).

Charles Townley, writing to Ralph Thoresby on 16 January 1699, mentions that Gascoigne was a correspondent of Jeremiah Horrocks and William Crabtree. Gascoigne was one of the 'Three North-Country Astronomers', along with Crabtree and Horrocks, who were innovative in developing both practical instrumentation and planetary theory. He experienced considerable difficulties in purchasing good lenses for his instruments, and it was possibly this inconvenience which led him to devise methods of grinding his own. A letter from Gascoigne to Oughtred in early 1641 revealed his thorough knowledge of optics. In it he described how he solved the problem which troubled Galileo and others; namely, how to insert a marker-point into the field of a telescope so that it could be used as a sighting instrument. Gascoigne had set up a telescope of the Keplerian type, with convex objective and eyepiece lenses, when he noticed that a spider had spun a line across the common focal point of the lenses. The line stood out sharply in the field of the telescope. When two webs were formed into a cross in the field of view, they provided an ideal measuring point. Gascoigne then attached the telescope, with its webs, onto the sighting arm of a 4 foot radius astronomical sextant, and used it to make angular measurements that were much more accurate than was possible when the sextant was sighted with the naked eye alone. This was the telescopic sight.

Gascoigne's other invention was the eyepiece micrometer. This instrument, which must have postdated the telescopic sight, measured the linear size of the prime-focus image produced by the object glass of a telescope as seen through the eyepiece. It used a pair of movable pointers, visible in the telescope's field of view, to enclose the diameter of the moon, or the distance between a pair of stars. The position of the pointers was controlled by a fine-pitched screw, which itself formed a tangent to a circle, the centre of which was the telescope object glass. By knowing the pitch of the screw in inches, the number of full and part turns necessary to enclose the object, and the exact focal length of the lens which formed the image

being measured, the user could compute the object's angular diameter to a few arc seconds. The telescopic sight and the micrometer were of great significance in the development of practical astronomy, as they made possible the measurement of small angles from which demonstrations of the earth's motion around the sun, and other aspects of celestial mechanics, could be made.

Gascoigne's inventions had probably been made by 1639. In that year his friend Crabtree, living in Salford, informed Horrocks, then residing at Much Hoole, Lancashire, of a visit to Yorkshire. Crabtree reported being shown a large telescope 'amplified and adorned with new inventions of his own', whereby Gascoigne could measure angles down to an arc second (Sherburne, 92, 114). The instruments, and especially the micrometer, also figured in correspondence between Gascoigne and Crabtree from 1638 to 1642, and on 30 October 1640, Crabtree asked: 'Could I purchase it with travel or procure it with Gold?' (*Philosophical Transactions*, 30, 1717, 607). Gascoigne's instruments were significant to the work of Horrocks, who needed precision measurements of the lunar diameter to test his discovery of the elliptical shape of the moon's orbit, though Horrocks may never have corresponded with Gascoigne directly, only via Crabtree. It is unlikely that Horrocks ever possessed a Gascoigne instrument, for the former's account of the transit of Venus observation, made on 26 November 1639, contains no reference to telescopic sights or micrometers being used. But forty years later, when John Flamsteed, the first astronomer royal, was developing demonstrations of Horrocks's astronomical ideas, he found the telescopic sight and micrometer to be essential instruments for accurate data collection.

Gascoigne fell on the royalist side at the battle of Marston Moor in Yorkshire on 2 July 1644. Aubrey's erroneous assertion (*Letters … and Lives*, 2.355) that at the time of his death he was 'about the age of 24 or 25 at most' has been frequently repeated. Gascoigne is said to have left a manuscript treatise on optics ready for the press.

Gascoigne's work remained largely unknown outside a small circle until the 1660s, when Auzout and Picard in Paris announced their independent attempts to use telescopes for measuring purposes. The newly established Royal Society of London then began to advance the claims of Gascoigne, as Richard Townley, Sir Jonas Moore, Robert Hooke, and somewhat later William Derham, drew attention to his inventions and began to publish his surviving letters. John Flamsteed was deeply indebted to Gascoigne; he first studied his papers at Townley Hall, Lancashire, in 1671–2, and incorporated telescopic sights and micrometers into the design of the original set of instruments at the Royal Observatory, Greenwich, after 1676. Flamsteed began his *Historia coelestis Britannica* (1725) with the publication of some of Gascoigne's and Crabtree's correspondence, which he saw as the starting point of British observational astronomy. ALLAN CHAPMAN

Sources S. P. Rigaud and S. J. Rigaud, eds., *Correspondence of scientific men of the seventeenth century*, 2 (1841), 33–59 • E. Sherburne, *The sphere of Marcus Manilius: made an English poem with annotations and an astronomical appendix* (1675); suppl. *A catalogue of the most eminent*

astronomers (1675), 92, 114 · R. Towneley, 'An extract of a letter written to Dr. Croon', *PTRS*, 2 (1667), 457–8 · W. Derham, 'Observations upon the spots that have been upon the sun', *PTRS*, 27 (1710–12), 270–90, esp. 280–89 · W. Derham, 'Extracts from Mr. Gascoigne's and Mr. Crabtrie's letters', *PTRS*, 30 (1717–19), 603–10 · J. Bevis, 'A letter to Mr. James Short', *PTRS*, 48 (1753), 190–02 · *Letters written by eminent persons … and 'Lives of eminent men' by John Aubrey*, ed. J. Walker, 2 (1813), 355 · *Aubrey's Brief lives*, ed. O. L. Dick (1949) [Jonas Moore] · *GM*, 3rd ser., 15 (1863), 760–62 · *Annual Register* (1761), 196 · C. Knight, ed., *The English cyclopaedia: biography*, 3 (1856) · R. V. Taylor, ed., *The biographia Leodiensis, or, Biographical sketches of the worthies of Leeds* (1865), 86–7 · 'Gascoygne', *Supplement to the penny cyclopaedia of the Society for the Diffusion of Useful Knowledge*, 1 (1845) · J. Flamsteed, *Historia coelestis Britannica*, 1 (1725), 1–5 · *The preface to John Flamsteed's Historia coelestis Britannica, or, British catalogue of the heavens*, ed. A. Chapman, trans. A. D. Johnson (1982) · F. Baily, *An account of the Revd John Flamsteed, the first astronomer-royal* (1835) · *The diary of Ralph Thoresby*, ed. J. Hunter, 1 (1830), 357, 387 · [J. Hunter], ed., *Letters of eminent men, addressed to Ralph Thoresby*, 1 (1832), 349–51, 352–4 · [J. Hunter], ed., *Letters of eminent men, addressed to Ralph Thoresby*, 2 (1832), 302 · S. B. Gaythorpe, 'A Galilean telescope made about 1640 by William Gascoigne', *Journal of the British Astronomical Association*, 39 (1928–9), 238–41 · A. Chapman, *Dividing the circle: the development of critical angular measurement in astronomy, 1500–1850* (1990), 35–45

Archives Royal Greenwich Observatory Archive, John Flamsteed's MSS, Lord Macclesfield MSS [copies]

Gascoyne, Bamber (*bap.* **1725**, *d.* **1791**), politician, the eldest son of Sir Crisp *Gascoyne (*bap.* 1700, *d.* 1761), a brewer and lord mayor of London in 1752–3, and his wife, Margaret (*d.* 1740), the daughter and coheir of John Bamber MD, of Bifrons, Barking, was baptized at All Hallows Staining, London, on 22 February 1725. He went to school at Felsted and then, in 1743, to Queen's College, Oxford. Having decided on a legal career, he entered Lincoln's Inn in 1745 and was called to the bar in 1750, but his ambition was to be a country gentleman and to enter parliament. He was inclined towards the tory side, and in 1761 he contested Maldon in that interest and was returned at the head of the poll, aided by his opponents' shortage of cash and his own youthful zeal and energy. He was already showing a 'well-nigh obsessionist persistence and perseverance' (HoP, *Commons*) which marked him throughout his life, and in the Commons he spoke frequently on the government side 'in a voice rather audible, than melodious' (Malmesbury MSS). He attracted attention accordingly, but professed independence of ministers. He declined a seat at the Board of Trade in 1762 from Bute, but accepted one the following year from Grenville on terms of independence, declaring himself to Pitt a supporter 'upon principle, gratitude, and respect' (*Correspondence of William Pitt*, 2.204–6). Fox thought he would be useful in the house as a tough and aggressive speaker, but to Gascoyne's lasting dismay and resentment he was defeated at the next election at Maldon by an American adventurer, even after spending far more than he could afford on the ungrateful electors. He fulminated on 'hypocrisy and ingratitude' (Strutt MSS) and vindictively pursued a series of lawsuits which eventually resulted in the revocation of the borough charter and the destruction of the corporation. He was not a man to trifle with, never forgot a wrong, and was constantly engaged in litigation, but as a result he was

Bamber Gascoyne (*bap.* 1725, *d.* 1791), by Benjamin Wilson [detail]

never popular with his neighbours and was dissuaded from standing for the county in 1763.

Gascoyne pressed Grenville to secure him a seat in parliament and in 1765 was returned for Midhurst by the somewhat reluctant nomination of Henry Fox, now Lord Holland, on the grounds of an earlier pledge. He was also giving a good deal of attention to building up an interest at Liverpool, where he had acquired consequence from his marriage on 24 January 1757 at Westminster Abbey to Mary, the daughter and coheir of Isaac Green of Childwall Abbey and Hale Hall in Lancashire, a substantial estate which passed to the Gascoynes on Green's death. The couple had five children, four sons and one daughter. Gascoyne was unsuccessful in establishing his electoral influence for the time being, but his eldest son, also named Bamber (1757–1824), gained a seat representing Liverpool from 1780 to 1796 and was a noted defender of the slave trade, in the interests of his constituents but also, it seems, from conviction. His third son Isaac *Gascoyne was also later elected to this seat. In the meantime Gascoyne made it his chief preoccupation to become a country squire at his estate at Bifrons, and devoted himself to hunting in the morning and cards at night and to county business in Essex. Nevertheless, he failed to secure the nomination for the county in 1768. He typically attributed his failure to ill will and misrepresentation of his private life by others, and expressed some grim satisfaction when the tory candidates, whom he had loyally supported, were defeated at the polls. He was now out of parliament for two years, until in December 1770 he secured the nomination at Weobley by the patron, Lord Weymouth: on his re-entry he professed himself a changed man, prepared to be 'sparing in my speech, cautious in my words, and cool in my temper' (Strutt MSS)—new year's resolutions which soon went the way of most others. He again became a frequent speaker, specializing in matters concerned with trade, where he was something of an expert among a gathering of amateurs, and devoting much time to local affairs. He was diligent in attending meetings of the Board of Trade and had some influence on American matters. One of the under-secretaries for the colonies, John Pownall, referred to him as 'minister for America at the Board of Trade' (*Various Collections*, 6.110). In 1779 he was promoted to a seat at the Admiralty board and devoted himself to his new department's business, but he left office with Lord North in 1782, opposed the Rockingham whigs and the Fox–North coalition, and settled into support of Pitt in 1784, in line with his lifelong attitude of loyalty towards the king in politics and professed dislike of 'faction'. In 1784 he was returned for the Cornish pocket borough of Bossiney through the assistance of the Treasury, half of his expenses being contributed by the secret service fund, and resumed his regular support of the government in speaking and in the lobbies. In April 1786 he was appointed receiver-general of customs and left parliament.

Gascoyne's political career was a chequered one. He never succeeded in establishing a personal electoral interest and was always obliged to purchase his seats, though sometimes with government assistance. In return he gave steady support to the administrations of the day, excepting when they were whig, but he never rose above minor office and his frequent interventions in debates on a miscellany of subjects did not enhance his reputation as a speaker. Wraxall declared that he had:

> strong common sense, which he expressed with force and freedom … he possessed a clear and sound understanding, with a most convivial disposition, though not a very cultivated mind, nor highly polished manners. Rough, frank, and manly, he was not intimidated by Burke's eloquence. (*Historical and Posthumous Memoirs*, 2.361–2)

He also attacked those who 'stimulated the inferior orders of people … to throw the nation into a ferment' (ibid., 2.445). He was something of a rough diamond in the polite world of eighteenth-century society, self-centred and aggressive in manner: he resented the dislike of others and showed it. Nevertheless, his wealth and property and his services to his neighbourhood were widely recognized, and, if he never achieved the national prominence which his abilities and early promise seemed to foretell, locally his death was greatly mourned. Gascoyne died at Milsom Street, Bath, on 27 October 1791, 'of a total decay' (*GM*, 1066). His body lay 'in state' at Bifrons, where he had been known as the 'king of Barking', and was buried in November 1791 in the family vault 'amidst the greatest concourse of people that has assembled there for some

years', attended by eight pallbearers and followed by ten gentlemen in scarves with 'a numerous train of the principal persons in the parish' (ibid.), while the shipping in the harbour flew their flags at half mast. He left entailed estates in Essex and Lancashire worth altogether nearly £4000 per annum to his eldest son, who later cut off the entail, pulled down the house at Bifrons, and sold the park.

E. A. SMITH

Sources HoP, *Commons* · H. Walpole, *Memoirs of the reign of King George the Third*, ed. G. F. R. Barker, 4 vols. (1894) · *The historical and the posthumous memoirs of Sir Nathaniel William Wraxall, 1772–1784*, ed. H. B. Wheatley, 5 vols. (1884) · Terling Place, Essex, Strutt MSS · *Correspondence of William Pitt, earl of Chatham*, ed. W. S. Taylor and J. H. Pringle, 4 vols. (1838–40) · *GM*, 1st ser., 61 (1791), 1066 · *Parliamentary papers of John Robinson, 1774–1784*, ed. W. T. Laprade (1922) · 'Parliamentary memorials of James Harris', Hants. RO, Malmesbury papers [transcript, History of Parliament Trust, London] · *DNB* · *Report on manuscripts in various collections*, 8 vols., HMC, 55 (1901–14), vol. 6 · IGI

Archives BL, letters to Sir Frederick Haldimand, Add. MS 21709 · Terling Place, Essex, Strutt MSS

Likenesses J. Sayers, caricature etching, pubd 1782, Hatfield House, Hertfordshire, NPG · B. Wilson, portrait, priv. coll. [*see illus.*]

Wealth at death c. £4000 p.a.: *GM*

Gascoyne, Sir Crisp (*bap.* 1700, *d.* 1761), local politician, was born at Chiswick and baptized in the parish church there on 26 August 1700, the youngest son of Benjamin and Anne Gascoyne. He set up in business as a brewer in Gravel Lane, Houndsditch, and lived at Barking between 1733 and 1738 with his wife, Margaret, the daughter and coheir of Dr John Bamber. The couple had several children, four of whom were baptized at Barking between 1733 and 1738. His wife was buried at Barking on 10 October 1740.

Gascoyne was admitted as a freeman of the Brewers' Company on 17 December 1741, took the clothing of the livery on 8 March 1744, and was elected an assistant on 11 October 1745 and master of the company for 1746–7. He was elected alderman of Vintry ward on 20 June 1745 and sworn into office on 2 July. In 1747–8 he served as sheriff of London and Middlesex, and in December 1748 took a prominent part, as head of the committee of city lands, in passing an act for the relief of the orphans of the City of London, whose estates, vested in the guardianship of the corporation, had been ruined during the seventeenth century.

Gascoyne became lord mayor in 1752 and was knighted soon after (22 November), on the occasion of presenting an address to the king. His term of office is of interest for three reasons. He was the first chief magistrate to occupy the present Mansion House, the building of which had begun in 1739. Owing to the introduction of the Gregorian calendar in September 1752, the date of the mayoralty procession was that year altered from 29 October to 9 November. Finally, Gascoyne presided at the celebrated trial of the two women accused of kidnapping and torturing Elizabeth Canning in 1753. Gascoyne remained sceptical of Canning's story, which was finally proved false. His stand was in contrast to that of Henry Fielding, who championed her cause, supported by an eager news-sheet readership, some of whom attacked Gascoyne's coach and threatened his life. Gascoyne justified himself in an address to the liverymen of London, an abstract of which was printed in the *London Magazine*, and received a vote of thanks from the common council at the end of his year of office.

Gascoyne was also a verderer of Epping Forest, in which office he was succeeded by his eldest son. In 1755 he was described as of Mincing Lane, where he probably lived in his father-in-law's house, though he continued to maintain the brewhouse at Houndsditch. He also purchased large estates in Essex, including the buildings and grounds of a hospital and chapel at Ilford. He died on 28 December 1761 (his will was dated 20 December 1761), and was buried on 4 January 1762 in Barking church. He was survived by four children, Joseph, Ann, Margaret, and Bamber *Gascoyne.   PHILIP CARTER

Sources DNB · A. B. Beaven, ed., *The aldermen of the City of London, temp. Henry III–[1912]*, 2 vols. (1908–13) · *London Magazine*, 23 (1755) · J. Traherne, *The Canning enigma* (1989) · *London Magazine*, 32 (1763)
Likenesses monument, after 1761, Barking church, Essex · W. Keable, oils, Hatfield House, Hertfordshire

Gascoyne, Isaac (*c*.1763–1841), army officer and politician, third son of Bamber *Gascoyne the elder (*bap.* 1725, *d.* 1791), of Bifrons, Barking, Essex, and his wife, Mary, daughter of Isaac Green of Childwall Abbey and Hale Hall, Lancashire, and grandson of Sir Crisp *Gascoyne, was educated at Felsted School, Dunmow. On 8 February 1779 he was appointed ensign in the 20th foot, from which he was transferred to the Coldstream Guards in July 1780. His promotions were to lieutenant and captain on 18 August 1784, captain and lieutenant-colonel on 5 December 1792 (both in the Coldstream Guards), brevet colonel on 3 May 1796, lieutenant-colonel in the 16th foot on 7 June 1799, major-general on 29 April 1802, colonel in the 7th West India regiment on 10 October 1805, lieutenant-general on 25 April 1808, colonel 54th foot on 1 June 1816, and general on 12 August 1819. He was with the guards in most of the engagements in Flanders in 1793–4, and was wounded in the brilliant action at Lincelles in 1793, and again, in the head—a wound from which he suffered for the rest of his life—when covering the retreat of Sir Ralph Abercromby's corps from Mouvaix to Roubaix in 1794.

Gascoyne commanded the Coldstream battalion in the brigade of guards sent to Ireland at about the end of the 1798 uprising, and acted as a major-general on the staff there and elsewhere, a position he held in the Severn district before his promotion to lieutenant-general in 1808. He married on 1 July 1794, Mary, daughter and coheir of John Williamson, brewer, of Roby Hall, and they had one son.

Gascoyne, whose seat, Roby Hall, was near Liverpool, was in 1796 elected an MP for Liverpool for which his eldest brother, Bamber Gascoyne the younger (1757–1824) had sat from 1780 to 1796. MP for thirty-five years and nine successive parliaments, Gascoyne became a familiar figure in the house, as well as on the turf at Newmarket. He was a staunch conservative, from Pittite to ultra. Liverpool was the leading Atlantic and slave-trade port, and Gascoyne, like his brother before him, strongly opposed abolition of the slave trade, advocated by William Wilberforce and others; but he failed to defeat the 1807 abolition bill, and hoped the act would be repealed. He was also against abolition of bull-baiting—leading the opposition to a bill which was defeated in May 1802—parliamentary reform, sinecure reform, and Roman Catholic relief, on which he was one of the ultras who opposed Wellington and Peel in 1829. He spoke repeatedly on behalf of Liverpool and West India interests. He advocated ending the East India Company's trade monopoly, in 1813 alleging Indians were worse off than the slaves. He was supported by the Liverpool corporation and, he claimed, brought in and carried more than two hundred local bills. Concerned for the welfare of his fellow army officers (though not, apparently, for that of the rank and file), he tried to increase officers' half pay, and opposed attempts to reduce allowances to deceased officers' families. At his suggestion the mess allowance in lieu of wine duty exemption was increased from £5 to £25 per company.

Liverpool, with its large and venal freeman electorate, had some vigorously contested and expensive elections; hostile propaganda characterized Gascoyne as 'Squinting Isaac' and 'Hopper-arsed Isaac'. He was re-elected in all elections from 1802 to 1830, including that of 1812 when the tories, reportedly spending £20,000, defeated Henry Brougham. From 1812 to 1822 the other Liverpool MP was George Canning; John Gladstone tried to replace Gascoyne but failed. Like other ultras after Catholic emancipation, Gascoyne favoured some parliamentary reform. In 1830 he supported enfranchisement of Leeds and Manchester, arguing that the parliamentary local business of such large towns necessitated their direct representation. In March 1831 the Grey ministry's Reform Bill proposed to reduce the number of MPs and the number of English constituencies. This was unpopular and Gascoyne proposed that each part of the kingdom retain its proportionate share of the representation. The opposition groups agreed an amendment against reduction in the number of MPs for England and Wales, which Gascoyne moved on 18 April. The government was narrowly defeated (20 April) and so decided on dissolution and another general election. Gascoyne was defeated (3 May), bottom of the poll in the pro-reform landslide, and retired from parliamentary life. He died at his residence, 71 South Audley Street, London, on 26 August 1841, of 'inflammation in his bowels' (*GM*, 542), and was buried on 2 September in a vault in the catacombs of the Kensal Green cemetery, Harrow Road, Kensal Green, Middlesex.

H. M. CHICHESTER, *rev.* ROGER T. STEARN

Sources *Army List* · *Parliamentary Debates*, 1796–1831 · *GM*, 2nd ser., 16 (1841) · M. H. Port, 'Gascoyne, Isaac', HoP, *Commons, 1790–1820* · M. Brock, *The Great Reform Act* (1973) · E. Porritt and A. G. Porritt, *The unreformed House of Commons*, 1 (1909) · J. Pollock, *Wilberforce* (1977) · R. Coupland, *Wilberforce* (1923) · C. Bolt and S. Drescher, eds., *Anti-slavery, religion and reform: essays in memory of Roger Anstey* (1980) · S. G. Checkland, *The Gladstones: a family biography, 1764–1851* (1971) · H. P. Brougham, *The life and times of Henry, Lord Brougham*, ed. W. Brougham, 2 (1871)

Gascoyne, Joel (*bap.* 1650, *d.* 1705), chart maker and cartographer, was baptized in Holy Trinity parish, Hull, on 31 October 1650, the younger child and only son of Thomas Gascoyne or Gaskin, master mariner. The family had since 1605 been prominent in Hull and especially in the Hull Trinity House. Joel Gascoyne was apprenticed for a period of seven years from 21 October 1668 to John Thornton. Thornton was one of a group of manuscript chart makers who, since the early seventeenth century, had plied their trade as members of the Drapers' Company in shops lining the streets and alleys down-river from the Tower of London. Under Thornton, Gascoyne learned the skills of chart making, engraving, and surveying, an unusual combination for the period.

In 1675 Gascoyne established himself in business as a chart maker at 'The Signe of the Platt neare Wapping Old Stayres three doares below the Chappell' (Ravenhill and Johnson, 1). As a full member of the Drapers' Company and with apprentices indentured to him he produced manuscript and engraved charts. He built up a considerable reputation in chart making, his advice being sought in 1680 and again in 1685 by Samuel Pepys, secretary to the Admiralty. Notable works were a 1678 portolan chart for Captain John Smith of the east coast of North and Central America and the West Indies and 1682 and 1685 maps of Carolina.

Gascoyne's last payment of dues to the Drapers' Company was recorded in February 1689 and from this date his energies were directed mainly, but not exclusively, towards land surveying. This may have been because he, like other manuscript chart makers, was suffering competition from the publishers of printed charts, or because of the death of his patron the second duke of Albemarle. In 1691 Gascoyne mapped the estates of James Cecil, third earl of Salisbury; the following year he mapped Sayes Court, Deptford, Kent, which was owned by John Evelyn who had there laid out a fine garden (BL, K xviii 18.0 18p). In 1692 he was directed by Samuel Travers, surveyor of land revenue to King William and Queen Mary, to make a survey of the 'Mannor of East Greenwich in Kent' (PRO, CREST 2 60/1642) following the grant by the monarchs of 'the house at Greenwich to be a hospital for wounded seamen' (*CSP dom.*, 1691–2, 481). Gascoyne produced a fine map on vellum (now at the PRO).

Travers introduced Gascoyne to his native county of Cornwall where he did his most important work. He produced two large atlases of estate maps; the Stowe Atlas of thirty-three manuscript maps on vellum, detailing estates owned by the Grenville family around Kilkhampton (Cornwall RO, DD X273), and the Lanhydrock Atlas of four large volumes containing 258 manuscript maps on vellum, compiled between 1694 and *c.*1699, of properties scattered widely over the county belonging to the Robartes family (Lanhydrock House, Bodmin). At the same time Gascoyne took the opportunity of surveying the whole of Cornwall. As a result of this new fieldwork a map, dedicated to Charles Bodville Robartes, second earl of Radnor and lord lieutenant of Cornwall, was published on 27 March 1699. It is a fine map and on what was for the period the large scale of almost 1 inch to the mile, making Cornwall the first major English county to be mapped on this large scale. In 1700 Gascoyne issued proposals to produce a similar map for Devon but, probably through lack of support following a succession of deaths in the family of his patrons, this did not materialize. Such failures were typical of the times and Gascoyne returned to London that year. In 1700 he produced maps and a report on Enfield Chace for the chancellor of the duchy of Lancaster. He continued surveying for the earl of Radnor at Great Haseley and Latchford, Oxfordshire, in 1701 (copy Bodl. Oxf. (E) C 17: 49 (58); original in private hands) and for the earl of Salisbury in Hertfordshire, among others. Between 1702 and 1703 he was commissioned by the vestry to survey the parish of Stepney, producing manuscript and printed maps of the whole parish and of the individual 'hamlets' to help in the administration of this rapidly growing area.

Gascoyne died in London on 13 February 1705 leaving a wife, Elizabeth. He was undoubtedly a pioneer in his specifications for county maps and initiated the eighteenth-century remapping of England on large scales.

WILLIAM RAVENHILL, *rev.* ELIZABETH BAIGENT

Sources W. L. D. Ravenhill, 'Joel Gascoyne: a pioneer of large-scale county mapping', *Imago Mundi*, 26 (1972), 60–70 • W. L. D. Ravenhill and O. J. Padel, eds., 'Joel Gascoyne, a map of the county of Cornwall, 1699', *Devon and Cornwall Record Society*, new ser., 34 (1991) • W. L. D. Ravenhill and D. J. Johnson, 'Joel Gascoyne's engraved maps of Stepney, 1702–04', *London Topographical Society*, publication 150 (1995) • W. L. D. Ravenhill, *Joel Gascoyne and the mapping of Sayes Court in the parish of Deptford, 1692* (1975) • W. L. D. Ravenhill, 'The mapping of Great Haseley and Latchford: an episode in the surveying career of Joel Gascoyne', *Cartographic Journal*, 10 (1973), 105–11 • J. B. Harley and W. L. D. Ravenhill, 'Proposals for county maps of Cornwall (1699) and Devon (1700)', *Devon and Cornwall Notes and Queries*, 32 (1971–3), 33–9

Gaselee, Sir Alfred (1844–1918), army officer, was born on 3 June 1844 at Little Yeldham, Essex, the eldest son of the Revd John Gaselee (*b. c.*1806), rector of Little Yeldham, and his wife, Sarah Anne Mant. He entered Felsted School in 1853 and Sandhurst in 1861. Gaselee received a commission as ensign in the 93rd regiment (Sutherland Highlanders) on 9 January 1863, and almost immediately had experience of active service, taking part in the campaign on the north-west frontier of India in that year. He was promoted lieutenant on 11 October 1866, transferred to the Bengal staff corps, and joined the 4th Punjab infantry on 27 September 1867. He went with the Indian force to Abyssinia, where he acted as assistant to the director-general of transport and was present at the capture of Magdala (13 April 1868). He took part in the expedition against the Bisatis in 1869, and was thanked by the government of India. He was promoted captain on 9 January 1875, and served with the Jowaki expedition of 1877–8. In the Anglo-Afghan War of 1879–80 he was a deputy assistant quartermaster-general, and accompanied Roberts on the march from Kabul to the relief of Kandahar. He was made brevet major on 2 March 1881.

In 1882 Gaselee married Alice Jane, daughter of the Rt Hon. William Edward *Baxter, from whom he obtained a divorce in 1893. He married Alice Margaret, daughter of Gartside Gartside-Tipping of Rossferry, co. Fermanagh, on 20 August 1895; she survived her husband. There were no children from either marriage.

Meanwhile, Gaselee continued to serve on the north-west frontier, and accompanied the Zhob valley expedition of 1884 and the Hazara (Black Mountain) expedition of 1891. He was promoted major on 9 January 1883 and lieutenant-colonel on 9 January 1889, and received the CB on 19 November 1891. On 27 September 1892 he was promoted to the command of the 1st battalion, 5th Gurkha rifles. On 1 February 1893 he was promoted colonel and appointed aide-de-camp to Queen Victoria. He served in the Isazai expedition (1892), the Waziristan field force (1894–5), and the Tirah campaign (1897–8). For his services in Tirah Gaselee was created KCB on 20 May 1898. From 25 July 1898 to 3 June 1901 he served simultaneously as quartermaster-general at Simla and brigadier-general commanding Bundelkhand district. He was promoted major-general on 3 July 1900.

In the summer of 1900, when the Boxer uprising in China was at its height, Gaselee was chosen to command the British element in the international expeditionary force. A large force was to have been assembled under the German commander, Count Von Waldersee, consisting, in addition to British, of Japanese, Russian, Italian, French, American, and German troops. Before Von Waldersee's arrival news broke that the foreign legations in Peking (Beijing) were still holding out. Gaselee was therefore put in command of a smaller force of 20,000 men, mostly Japanese and Russian, but including 3000 British and Indian troops, which set out for Peking immediately. The 7th Rajputs, under Gaselee himself, were the first troops to enter Peking, reaching the legations on the afternoon of 14 August 1900. The international rivalries between the component parts of the relieving forces might have given rise to the most serious complications. Gaselee showed tact and firmness in his handling of a very delicate situation. As a reward for his services he was created GCIE on 24 July 1901.

Gaselee was promoted lieutenant-general on 30 June 1903 and full general on 30 June 1906. From 30 June 1903 to 29 June 1908 he was commander of the forces in Bengal. He then retired to Guildford. He was created GCB on 25 June 1909 and was colonel of the 54th Sikhs from 13 May 1904 until his death, which took place at Grove End, Pit Farm Road, Guildford, on 29 March 1918.

R. J. BEEVOR, rev. ALEX MAY

Sources *Army List* · *Indian Army List* · *The Times* (1 April 1918) · private information (1927) · J. G. Elliott, *The frontier, 1839–1947* (1968) · L. E. Bodin, *The Boxer rebellion* (1979) · H. L. Nevill, *Campaigns on the north-west frontier* (1912) · H. D. Hutchinson, *The campaign in Tirah, 1897–1898: an account of the expedition against the Orakzais and Afridis* (1898) · R. O'Connor, *The Boxer rebellion* (1974) · P. Fleming, *The siege at Peking* (1959) · Burke, *Peerage* · *CGPLA Eng. & Wales* (1918)
Archives NRA Scotland, priv. coll., letters to his sister-in-law from Peking | NAM, corresp. with Kitchener, Minto, and others, NAM 6001/67, 6001/68 · PRO, private corresp. with Sir Ernest Satow, PRO 30/33/9/18

Wealth at death £12,444 1s. 1d.: probate, 13 Aug 1918, *CGPLA Eng. & Wales*

Gaselee, Sir Stephen (1762–1839), judge, was the son of Stephen Gaselee, an eminent surgeon at Portsmouth, and his wife, of whom little is known. He was admitted as a student at Gray's Inn on 29 January 1781, but was not called to the bar until 20 November 1793. He had the advantage of being a pupil of Sir Vicary Gibbs, under whose instruction he became a skilful special pleader.

Gaselee joined the western circuit, and was so much respected as a careful and well-informed junior, that when, after twenty-six years' practice, he was made a king's counsel in Hilary term 1819, his professional income was probably diminished. Although he was neither a particularly distinguished orator nor leader of his circuit, his reputation for legal knowledge soon secured him a judgeship. On the resignation of Sir John Richardson, he was selected on 1 July 1824 to supply the vacant justiceship in the common pleas, became a serjeant-at-law on 5 July 1824, and was knighted on 27 April 1825. He sat in the court of common pleas for nearly thirteen years and was regarded as a knowledgeable, painstaking, and upright judge. He was a vice-president and an active member of the Royal Humane Society, and was said to have been the model for the irascible Judge Stareleigh who presided over the trial of *Bardell* v. *Pickwick* in Charles Dickens's *Pickwick Papers* (1837). He was married to Henrietta Harris with whom he had several children. Their eldest son, Stephen *Gaselee, was a serjeant-at-law. Gaselee retired from the bench in 1837 and died two years later at 13 Montagu Place, Russell Square, London, on 26 March 1839.

G. C. BOASE, rev. SINÉAD AGNEW

Sources E. Foss, *Biographia juridica: a biographical dictionary of the judges of England … 1066–1870* (1870) · *Legal Observer*, 17 (1838–9), 450–51 · *GM*, 2nd ser., 12 (1839), 315 · J. Foster, *The register of admissions to Gray's Inn, 1521–1889, together with the register of marriages in Gray's Inn chapel, 1695–1754* (privately printed, London, 1889), 391

Gaselee, Stephen (1807–1883), serjeant-at-law, eldest son of Sir Stephen *Gaselee (1762–1839), judge, and his wife, Henrietta, daughter of James Harris of the East India Company's Service, was born at 77 Upper Guilford Street, Russell Square, London, on 1 September 1807, and educated at Winchester College. He matriculated from Balliol College, Oxford, on 4 June 1824 and graduated second class in classics in 1828, when he took his BA degree; he proceeded MA in 1832.

Gaselee was called to the bar at the Inner Temple on 16 June 1832, and practised on the home circuit. On 2 November 1840 he became a serjeant-at-law, and at the time of his decease he was the oldest surviving serjeant, though he had not practised for many years. On 21 July 1841 he married Alicia (or Alma) Mary (1814–1886), eldest daughter of Vice-Admiral Sir John Tremayne Rodd, KCB, at Marylebone in London.

Gaselee unsuccessfully contested the boroughs of Bridgwater in 1847, Portsmouth in 1855, and Oxford in 1857. However, on 13 July 1865, he was elected Liberal MP for Portsmouth, though he lost the seat at the general election in 1868. For many years he was also a director of the

London and South Western Railway, and he was counsel in the Marshalsea court and a magistrate for the county of Middlesex. He sometimes presided as assistant judge at the Middlesex sessions, and he became treasurer of Serjeants' Inn, in succession to Serjeant James Manning, in 1866. He died at his home, 2 Cambridge Square, Hyde Park, London, on 20 October 1883.

G. C. BOASE, rev. BETH F. WOOD

Sources Solicitors' Journal, 27 (1882–3), 802 · Law Times (27 Oct 1883), 435 · The Times (23 Oct 1883), 10 · WWBMP · Boase, Mod. Eng. biog. · Foster, Alum. Oxon.

Wealth at death £46,976 7s. 9d.: probate, 14 Dec 1883, CGPLA Eng. & Wales

Gaselee, Sir Stephen (1882–1943), librarian and scholar, was born in Brunswick Gardens, Kensington, London, on 9 November 1882, the elder son of Henry Gaselee (1842–1926), fellow of King's College, Cambridge, from 1863 to 1882 and a distinguished equity draftsman and conveyancer, and his wife, Alice Esther, daughter of the Revd George Frost, second master of Kensington grammar school. His great-grandfather was Sir Stephen Gaselee, justice of the court of common pleas.

After attending Temple Grove School in East Sheen, in 1896 Gaselee entered Eton College, where he was elected (second in the list) a King's scholar. A gifted student, he edited the Eton College Chronicle, won prizes for Latin verse, was awarded the Newcastle medal, and in 1901 he was elected a scholar of King's College, Cambridge. Gaselee obtained a first class in part 1 of the classical tripos (1904) and a second class in part 2 (1905). He left Cambridge in that year and, as tutor to Prince Leopold of Battenberg (later Lord Leopold Mountbatten), travelled widely, attaining an experience of foreign countries and courts that was to stand him in good stead for his later duties. In 1907 he returned to Cambridge and as editor of the Cambridge Review was an enthusiastic promoter of the work of the poet Rupert Brooke. After failing, to the surprise of his friends, to win (by his dissertation on Petronius) a fellowship at King's in the following year, he accepted two months later the post of Pepys librarian at Magdalene College, which he held until 1919. After moving there in the autumn he was elected in 1909 into a fellowship which he held for thirty-four years.

Gaselee mastered his Pepysian duties and published an account of The Spanish Books in the Library of Samuel Pepys (1921). He then concentrated on Coptic studies, cataloguing the Coptic manuscripts in the Cambridge University Library, lecturing on Coptic dialects, and publishing a series of texts, edited with a Latin translation and commentary, entitled Parerga Coptica. In 1918 he published a popular selection of Stories from the Christian East. From 1903 he had steadily pursued his study of Petronius, adding to his original fellowship dissertation a handlist, and a preface and Latin text of the Satyricon to face the translation by William Burnaby of 1694 which was privately printed by Ralph Straus in 1910. In 1915 he edited a collotype facsimile of a fifteenth-century manuscript in the Bibliothèque Nationale in Paris (Lat. 7989). For the Loeb

Classical Library he reprinted an amended version of William Adlington's Apuleius (1915), Parthenius (1916), and Achilles Tatius (1917).

Gaselee contributed a brief preface (1922) to the anonymous 1588 translation, Sixe Idillia, of Theocritus, with woodcut illustrations by Vivien Gribble; he edited (with H. F. B. Brett-Smith) Caxton's translation of books 10–15 of Ovid's Metamorphoses from a manuscript in the Pepys Library (1924); and he wrote for the Tudor Translation series an introduction to John Frampton's Joyfull Newes out of the Newe Founde Worlde, a translation of 1577 from the Spanish of Nicolas Monardes (2 vols., 1925). The printers and publishers with whom he chose to work usually shared his fastidious taste in book production. In 1925 Gaselee published An Anthology of Medieval Latin, in 1928 The Oxford Book of Medieval Latin Verse, and in 1938 he edited for the Roxburghe Club, of which he was a member, the 'Costerian' Doctrinale of Alexander de Villa Dei.

In 1916 Gaselee entered the Foreign Office and was rewarded for this war service in 1918 by appointment as CBE. By Michaelmas term 1919, however, he was back in Cambridge, lecturing on Coptic, but his outstanding qualities had not been lost upon the Foreign Office and on 1 January 1920 he was made librarian and keeper of the papers. He was appointed KCMG in 1935, and served the crown until his death.

In 1917 at All Saints, Margaret Street, London, Gaselee married May Evelyn (1894–1990), daughter of E. Wyndham Hulme, librarian, of the Patent Office. The couple were introduced by the writer A. C. Benson, and they had three daughters. A high Anglican, Gaselee's convictions were strengthened by the width and profundity of his knowledge, and included a commitment to ecumenism.

Sir Stephen Gaselee was strikingly more than his career or his literary output. The value of his department was enhanced, partly by the extent and profundity of his knowledge and experience, and partly by his conception of its duties. He improved and enlarged the Foreign Office library from insignificance to 80,000 books, missing no single publication, in whatever language, which bore usefully upon foreign affairs; he also ensured that diplomatic missions abroad were likewise appropriately provided, not infrequently at his own expense. In 1935 he compiled and published a useful list of libraries and sources of information in government departments. He was widely and constantly consulted not only by his colleagues at home and abroad, but also by foreign scholars, diplomatists, and public institutions. After Gaselee's death it proved impossible to find a substitute, and he was succeeded by the director of research, with whose responsibilities those of the librarian were henceforth merged.

At Cambridge, Gaselee had been both as undergraduate and don a noteworthy figure, with a remarkable variety of unusually combined interests. To his eminence as Latinist, Coptologist, medievalist, palaeographer, liturgiologist, and hagiographer he added later that of president of the Bibliographical Society (1932) and honorary librarian of the Athenaeum from 1928. As an undergraduate, his bibliographical interests had been nurtured by Francis

Jenkinson and in 1920 he published a list of the incunabula and other early printed books in his possession. In 1934 he presented to the Cambridge University Library 300 early printed books, to which he subsequently added his rare and large collection of early sixteenth-century books and his *Petroniana*. Many of these had been chosen with advice from the London bookseller E. P. Goldschmidt, a near contemporary at Cambridge. But as a bibliographer he remained conservative, and clashed publicly with W. W. Greg.

The personality of this dignified traditionalist was enhanced by a gentle serene manner, a clear tenor voice, and by the archaic originality of Gaselee's broadcloth cutaway tailcoat, his spats, red socks, and Old Etonian bow tie. A dilettante in the best sense of the word, he dispensed a distinguished hospitality, and was noted for his wise counsel. Gaselee's honours included the honorary degree of LittD from the University of Liverpool (1933), the honorary fellowship of King's College (1935), the Sandars readership in bibliography at Cambridge (1935), the presidency of the Classical Association (1939) and the Egypt Exploration Society (1941), and the fellowship of the British Academy (1939). Sir Stephen died at his home, 24 Ashburn Place, London, on 16 June 1943. After cremation his ashes were scattered at Golders Green crematorium, Middlesex.

RONALD STORRS, rev. DAVID MCKITTERICK

Sources A. S. F. Gow, 'Sir Stephen Gaselee, 1882–1943', *PBA*, 29 (1943), 441–61 · A. B. Ramsay, *Cambridge Review* (23 Oct 1943), 25–6 · R. Storrs, *Orientations* (1937) · T. A. Layton, *Restaurant roundabout* (1944) · J. C. T. Oates, *A catalogue of the fifteenth-century printed books in the University Library, Cambridge* (1954) · private information (2004) · *CGPLA Eng. & Wales* (1943)
Archives CUL, corresp. · UCL, school of Slavonic and east European studies, corresp. relating to Anglican committee on eastern churches | BLPES, letters to Sir C. K. Webster · Bodl. Oxf., corresp. with J. L. Myres; letters to Sir Horace Rumbold · CUL, Cambridge University Archives, letters to Cambridge University librarian relating to purchase and donation of books · King's AC Cam., letters to Oscar Browning; letters to G. H. W. Rylands · LPL, corresp. with J. A. Douglas · Royal Society of Literature, letters to the Royal Society of Literature
Likenesses W. Stoneman, photograph, 1936, NPG · J. Innes, oils, c.1944 (posthumous; after photograph), Magd. Cam. · photograph, repro. in Gow, 'Sir Stephen Gaselee, 1882–1943'
Wealth at death £52,714 12s. 6d.: probate, 19 Aug 1943, *CGPLA Eng. & Wales*

Gashry, Francis (1702–1762), naval administrator and politician, was born on 14 November 1702, the son of Francis Gascherie, a perfumer in Lamb's Street, Stepney, Middlesex, and his wife, Susanna. His parents were Huguenots from La Rochelle, and Francis was baptized on 13 December at the French Huguenot church of La Patente, Spitalfields. Whatever calling or profession he may have followed as a young man, Gashry owed his advancement in the public service very largely to a connection he formed with Admiral Sir Charles Wager. During Wager's term as first lord of the Admiralty (21 June 1733 to 19 March 1742) Gashry served as his secretary, combining that post from 1738 with that of assistant secretary to the Admiralty board. From 8 December 1738 until 7 March 1741 Gashry

also occupied the office of clerk of the journals, which involved inspecting and making abstracts from captains' journals received in the Admiralty. He was the first and only holder of this office, which commanded a £200 annual salary. In 1737 he had also been appointed commissioner for the sick and wounded on the Navy Board, and he took the post of senior member, at a salary of £400 p.a. when the sick and hurt board (a wartime institution) was reconstituted in 1740 following the outbreak of war with Spain in the previous year.

Following the death on 6 March 1741 of George Purvis, controller of the treasurer's accounts and another of the first lord's protégés, Wager's influence secured Gashry the vacant seat on the Navy Board as an extra commissioner, a post he held from 21 March 1741 to 7 June 1744. He also inherited Purvis's seat in parliament as the member for Aldeburgh in Suffolk. Gashry sat for Aldeburgh only from 30 March to 27 April 1741, but in the general election the same year he took the seat of East Looe in Cornwall, which he held for the rest of his life. In this, too, Wager had been instrumental, exerting his influence over the local magnates, the Trelawny family. Edward Trelawny, who was to become a powerful connection and friend of Gashry's after Wager's death, described him as 'one recommended by the ministry, so as they should be obliged to us for [his] being chosen', rather than one 'coming in by [his] own interest or at the desire of our family' (Cruickshanks).

Along with the secretary of the Admiralty, Josiah Burchett, Gashry seems to have been one of Wager's chief advisers, and there is some indication that in his old age Wager came to depend on his secretary: a correspondent of the duke of Bedford said of the first lord that 'tho a good sort of man [he] was not thought by every body fit for such a post … [and] saw everything through the Eyes of his Servant Gashry' (Baugh, *British Naval Administration in the Age of Walpole*, 67). In 1742 Gashry was called to give evidence to the secret committee investigating Robert Walpole's administration, concerning the abuse of secret-service money for Wager's election campaign the previous year.

Possibly much earlier, in which case it might even explain his connection with Wager, but more probably at about this time, Gashry married Martha Bolton, the aunt of Philip Goldsworthy MP, sister of Burrinton Goldsworthy (British consul at Leghorn and Cadiz) and the widow of Wager's nephew, Charles Bolton. The marriage, in any case, appears to have taken place before 1747. Whether this marriage was his route to or the reward for his close association with Wager, it was materially advantageous to Gashry, bringing him the manors of Rotherhithe and, after the death of Wager's widow in 1748, Kilmenath near Looe.

It was again the death of the incumbent, in this case John Fawler, which made room for Gashry to move up the hierarchy to the position of comptroller of the victualling accounts on 7 June 1744—this time without the assistance of Wager, who had died the previous year. In his will Wager described Gashry as 'my very good friend', and in 1747 Gashry had a monument to his 'Great Patron' erected in Westminster Abbey (Cruickshanks).

Under the Place Act of 1742 membership of the Navy Board became incompatible with holding a seat in the Commons, so on 19 June 1747 Gashry resigned from the board in order to remain in parliament. He 'served as agent for the Treasury for its two controlled constituencies of East and West Looe, and was believed to control personally three votes in the House of Commons' (Valentine, 1.357). In this capacity he acted as intermediary between the Treasury and Edward Trelawny when the latter was appointed governor of Jamaica. Gashry was also, it appears, a manager of minor Admiralty patronage. In 1749 he became a director of the South Sea Company, which had commercial interests in the West Indies; and then, in 1751, he was appointed treasurer and paymaster of the ordnance, a post which offered to a shrewd speculator the potential for greater rewards than just the £500 annual salary.

Although a member of parliament for twenty-one years, Gashry is not recorded as ever having spoken in the house. Having 'long been in a declining state' (BL, Add. MS 32934, fol. 490), Gashry died on 19 May 1762, and was buried in the churchyard of All Saints', Fulham. Of presumably humble origins, Gashry lived a life that provides a fine instance of the combination of successful public service and personal advancement through the cultivation of powerful interest and judicious marriage.

RANDOLPH COCK

Sources E. Cruickshanks, 'Gashry, Francis', HoP, Commons, 1715–54, 2.60 • D. A. Baugh, British naval administration in the age of Walpole (1965) • A. Valentine, The British establishment, 1760–1784 (1970) • L. Namier, The structure of politics at the accession of George III, 2nd edn (1960) • J. M. Collinge, Navy Board officials, 1660–1832 (1978) • J. C. Sainty, ed., Admiralty officials, 1660–1870 (1975) • W. C. Ford, List of Vernon-Wager manuscripts in the Library of Congress (1904) • D. A. Baugh, ed., Naval administration, 1715–1750, Navy RS, 120 (1977) • BL, Add. MS 32693, fol. 391; Add. MS 32893, fol. 481; Add. MS 32937, fol. 225; Add. MS 32934, fol. 490; Add. MS 19038, fols. 44–5, 48–9, 50–51 • will, PRO, ADM 3/45, 48, 57 • M. E. Matcham, A forgotten John Russell (1905)
Archives BL, Add. MSS 19038, fols. 44–5, 48–9, 50–51; 32693, fol. 391; 32893, fol. 481; 32934, fol. 490; 32937, fol. 225 • L. Cong., Vernon-Wager MSS

Gask, George Ernest (1875–1951), surgeon, was descended from a family of Lincolnshire smallholders. His father, Henry, walked to London to seek his fortune, in which he and his brother succeeded by establishing a drapery business in Oxford Street; Henry married Elizabeth Styles and settled in Dulwich, where George, the youngest of four sons, was born on 1 August 1875. Gask went to Dulwich College and also studied at Lausanne, Freiburg, and Baden universities before entering the medical school of St Bartholomew's Hospital in 1893 (where he was active in the students' Christian Union); he thus gained a working knowledge of German and French, some experience of continental methods of education, and a realization of the benefits of foreign travel, which had a lasting effect on his subsequent career.

Gask qualified LRCP and MRCS in 1898 and became house surgeon to John Langton; he proceeded FRCP in 1901. A period of training as a demonstrator of pathology and as surgical registrar led to his appointment in 1907 as assistant surgeon to Power, whose researches into the history of medicine were at once a stimulus and an example to Gask (who ultimately became expert in the history of military surgery). He thus embarked on the life of a surgical consultant and teacher, and for five years was warden of the residential college at St Bartholomew's.

In 1912 the younger surgeons at the hospital formed a study group which they called the Paget Club, and in the light of subsequent events it is significant that at their second meeting Gask read a paper on the methods of teaching surgery in England, Germany, and America. In the previous year he had visited several of the university medical schools in the United States, and he advocated the incorporation of certain features of the foreign systems into British schools, though he concluded that such innovations were hindered by the burden of routine work in the hospitals. Clearly he had the advantages of 'whole-time' academic units in mind, but he had to wait until after the war of 1914–18 for a chance to translate his ideas into practice. During the war he distinguished himself in the surgery of chest wounds, and was appointed DSO in 1917 and CMG in 1919 for his services as consulting surgeon to the Fourth Army.

As soon as he returned from France, Gask set about forming the surgical professorial unit at St Bartholomew's, manifesting from the outset an important attribute of a professor—good judgement in the choice of assistants. He brought Thomas Dunhill from Melbourne as his deputy. The unit gradually gained the confidence of the rest of the hospital staff, who appreciated Gask's unselfish idealism and trusted him not to interfere with their work. A further evidence of his good judgement was his selection of subjects for research, and in due course significant contributions were made to thyroid surgery, to the use of radium for breast cancer, and to the surgery of the sympathetic nervous system. Gask was quick to appreciate the help he could obtain from his scientific colleagues, and the collaboration of F. L. Hopwood in physics, H. H. Woollard in anatomy, and Mervyn Gordon in virology was invaluable. Gask was a model director who provided ideas and encouraged younger doctors to do the work. Even when teaching he tried to make the students find out things for themselves instead of telling them the answers; the undiscerning thought 'Uncle George' was merely lazy. Although not a brilliant operator his technique was gentle and based on sound principles. He organized a group called the Pilgrim Surgeons, who travelled widely to see the great masters at work, and he also arranged that in alternate years a leading surgeon should become temporary director of the surgical unit at St Bartholomew's.

Gask, who retired in 1935, was called upon to serve on several bodies outside his own medical school: at the Royal College of Surgeons he was on the council from 1923 until 1939; he gave the Vicary and Bradshaw lectures, and was twice a Hunterian professor; he was an original member of the Radium Trust, and served on the Medical Research Council from 1937 to 1941; and he took a leading part in planning the postgraduate medical school at Hammersmith and was an active member of its governing body. Gask succeeded Lord Moynihan as chairman of the editorial committee of the *British Journal of Surgery*. His own writings included a pioneer study, *The Surgery of the Sympathetic Nervous System* (with J. Paterson Ross, 1934), and *Essays in the History of Medicine* (1950). During the war of 1939–45 he acted as a temporary surgeon to the Radcliffe Infirmary, and greatly appreciated the consequent associations with the University of Oxford and the medical services in the Oxford region.

In 1913 Gask had married Ada Alexandra, daughter of Lieutenant-Colonel Alexander Crombie, of the Indian Medical Service (IMS); they had one son, John, who became a general practitioner.

A likeable and even-tempered person of fine physique, Gask in his younger days was a distinguished mountaineer. Latterly he suffered from coronary disease and he died at his home, Hatchmans, Hambleden, near Henley-on-Thames, Oxfordshire, on 16 January 1951, his wife surviving him.   J. P. Ross, *rev.*

Sources *BMJ* (27 Jan 1951), 193–4 · *BMJ* (3 Feb 1951), 253–4 · *BMJ* (17 Feb 1951), 358
Likenesses M. Ayoub, group portrait, oils, *c.*1927–1929 (*Royal College of Surgeons council, 1926–27*), RCS Eng. · M. Ayoub, portrait (study for *Royal College of Surgeons council, 1926–27*), priv. coll.
Wealth at death £38,410 1*s.* 4*d.*: probate, 29 June 1951, *CGPLA Eng. & Wales*

Gaskell [*née* Stevenson], **Elizabeth Cleghorn** (1810–1865), novelist and short-story writer, was born on 29 September 1810 in Belle Vue House, then part of Lindsey Row (now Cheyne Walk), Chelsea, London. She was the second surviving child of William *Stevenson (*bap.* 1770, *d.* 1829), writer and minor Treasury official, and his first wife, Elizabeth (1771–1811), daughter of Samuel and Mary Holland, of Sandlebridge Farm, near Knutsford in Cheshire.

Family background and early life Both of Elizabeth Stevenson's parents were Unitarians and this faith was a central force in her life, combined with a firm belief in social duty and reform. Her family background, and the settings of her parents' lives, also found a place in her fiction. William Stevenson, the son of a naval captain from Berwick-on-Tweed, studied for the Unitarian ministry at Manchester Academy. After his marriage in 1797 he turned first to teaching at Manchester College, expressing his radical ideas in *Remarks on the Very Inferior Utility of Classical Learning* (1796), and then tried scientific farming at Saughton Mills, East Lothian, Scotland. Here the Stevensons' son John (1798–1828) was born, while a local friend is remembered in their daughter's second name, Cleghorn. In Scotland Stevenson was one of the earliest contributors to the *Edinburgh Review* in 1802, and edited the *Scots Magazine* from 1803 to 1806. He then moved to London, where he was given a post in the Treasury and wrote articles on subjects from topography and experimental agriculture to naval history.

Elizabeth's mother also came from an old dissenting

Elizabeth Cleghorn Gaskell (1810–1865), by George Richmond, 1851

family. The Hollands of Cheshire had farming, professional, and mercantile interests; Elizabeth's uncle Peter was a doctor whose son, Sir Henry Holland, became physician to Queen Victoria, and was also a well-known travel writer. Another uncle, Samuel, was a Liverpool trader and north Wales quarry owner, while a third, Swinton, became a London merchant, with a large estate in Gloucestershire. The Hollands were linked by marriage and friendship to other prominent Unitarian families, including the Wedgwoods, Darwins, and Turners.

By early 1811 the Stevensons had moved to 3 Beaufort Row, Chelsea, but in October 1811 Mrs Stevenson died, and so at the age of thirteen months Elizabeth was taken to Cheshire to live with her mother's sister Hannah Lumb (1767–1837). Mrs Lumb was legally separated from her husband, who had not only been declared insane but also had another, unacknowledged family; her own daughter, Marianne, was disabled and died in 1812, aged twenty-one. Hannah Lumb's large house, The Heath, was later shared with another Holland sister, Abigail.

In 1814 William Stevenson married Catherine Thomson, the sister of Anthony Todd Thomson, the doctor who had delivered Elizabeth. They had two more children but Elizabeth stayed in Knutsford, visiting her father and stepmother rarely. She was '*very, very* unhappy' on such visits, she later wrote, adding that were it not for the comfort of the river, and some local friends, 'I think my child's heart would have broken' (*Letters*, 797–8). She grew up keenly aware of family breakdown and tragedy, and with the difficulties and strengths of extended families, themes which she would later explore in depth in her fiction.

Elizabeth Stevenson was educated at home, by her aunts and occasional outside tutors, and at the Sunday school of Brook Street Chapel, until 1821. From her family and the chapel she imbibed the tenets of Unitarianism, which rejected as unknowable mystical doctrines such as the Trinity and the divinity of Christ, and placed great stress on human rather than divine responsibility for society. The church emphasized freedom of thought and rationality, believing in social progress aided by scientific discovery. But it also recognized the existence of suffering and oppression, and called on its adherents to speak out against them. The tension is reflected in her later fiction in the movement between optimism and intense awareness of pain, and in the drive to expose hypocrisy, in family, community, and nation. In the 1840s and 1850s, influenced by James Martineau and the Christian socialists, she seemed drawn to a more emotional form of worship, and often attended Anglican services. Her only antipathy, she declared, was 'to the Calvinistic or Low Church creed' (*Letters*, 648).

At eleven Elizabeth was sent away to the school run by the Byerley sisters, from October 1821 at Barford, Warwickshire and then, from May 1824, at Avonbank, Stratford upon Avon. The school had been partly funded by a loan from Josiah Wedgwood (a relation and partner of the sisters' father) and their pupils included both Unitarians and Anglicans. The curriculum was conventional: English, geography, history, French, dancing, music, drawing, and writing, with arithmetic at the end of the list. Unitarians tended to champion girls' education, but not women's full independence; *Domestic Duties* (1825), by one of the sisters who ran the school, Fanny Parkes, both advises young women to 'suffer and be still' and stresses their rights as well as their responsibilities. Another sister was Katherine Thomson, wife of Dr Anthony Todd Thomson and thus sister-in-law to the second Mrs Stevenson. A published novelist and talented journalist, she provided Elizabeth with a model of the way in which literary production could be combined with domestic life.

Family loss and widening circles, 1826–1831 Elizabeth left school in June 1826, returning to Knutsford and staying with Holland relations in Wales and Liverpool. Her letters suggest that she was already writing stories, but no early work survives. Her brother John had joined the merchant navy in 1820 (she retained vivid memories of going to London to see him off on one voyage). His graphic letters stimulated her imagination and in 1827 he directly encouraged her to write, but the following year he disappeared on a voyage to India, a haunting loss that may be remembered in her descriptions of the return of men feared drowned (like Charley Kinraid in *Sylvia's Lovers*) as well as the brother's surprise return from India in *Cranford*.

At this point Elizabeth went to Chelsea to live with her father and stepmother, but on 22 March 1829 William Stevenson died. After his death Elizabeth's base remained

Knutsford, but she also stayed with different Holland relations in Gloucestershire, Liverpool, and Wales, and spent much of the next two years at the home of the Revd William Turner, a relation and the famous Unitarian minister of Hanover Chapel, Newcastle upon Tyne. Turner was a founder of the Literary and Philosophical Society, a scientific lecturer, and tireless campaigner for social causes: the emancipation of Catholics and Jews, the abolition of the slave trade, and the support of charity and Sunday schools. Humane, generous, and eccentric, he undoubtedly influenced her moral, humanitarian, and political outlook and his character is suggested in her portrayal of Mr Benson in *Ruth*.

In 1830 Elizabeth visited Edinburgh with Turner's daughter Anne, renewing links with Scottish family acquaintances, a circle evoked in the fictional frame to the collection *Round the Sofa* in 1859. At twenty Elizabeth was effervescent and well read, more interested in gossip of marriages than religious controversies or political causes. A neoclassic bust made about 1829 by the Newcastle-based sculptor David Dunbar shows a strong-featured, assured young woman. In 1832 she was also painted by William John Thomson, her stepmother's brother; his fine miniature (Manchester University Library) suggests the alert gaze of her blue-grey eyes, but is a more romantic portrayal than the bust, showing her glancing over her shoulder, with soft brown hair falling from a coil on top of her head.

Marriage and early writing In Manchester in 1831 Elizabeth met William *Gaskell (1805–1884), assistant minister at the Unitarian Cross Street Chapel, a powerful centre of reform, with a congregation largely composed of the families of prosperous manufacturers and professional men. They were engaged by mid-March 1832 and were married on 30 August at St John's parish church, Knutsford. They shared a faith and a love of literature and music but often seemed a contrast in appearance and temperament. While Elizabeth was of medium height, tending to plumpness (especially in later life), with an open smile, a constant flow of talk, and a distinct romantic streak, William was extremely tall and thin and apparently austere, with a dry sense of humour and an infinite capacity for hard work. Yet the marriage appears to have been extremely close, despite Elizabeth's many absences from home in later years.

After a honeymoon in north Wales the Gaskells set up home at 14 Dover Street, Manchester. The city had suffered badly from the trade depression of 1829, followed by strikes, lock-outs, and riots, and from the 1832 cholera epidemic. This directed sharp attention to the plight of local workers, illustrated by *The moral and physical condition of the working classes employed in the cotton manufacture in Manchester* (1832) by James Kay (later Kay-Shuttleworth). A ring of slums, factories, and polluted canals surrounded the city centre, separating it from the suburbs. Some sense of the shock of a country-bred young woman coming to live there is expressed by Margaret Hale's first impressions of Milton in *North and South*: the dark cloud of smoke, the 'long, straight, hopeless streets of regularly built houses', the jostling crowds, hard-faced men and independent mill girls.

Although Gaskell roundly resisted her time being taken up with the duties of a minister's wife, her husband's work continually drew her into direct contact with the Manchester poor. Helping the District Provident Society, she distributed soup tickets, food, and clothing, and later worked with the Sunday school children, visiting their homes, and inviting groups of girls to her house. Some of the most harrowing descriptions in *Mary Barton* echo the reports of the Mission to the Poor, produced by the Manchester Domestic Mission, based at Cross Street.

In July 1833 Gaskell's first child, a daughter, was born dead, and three years later she wrote a poignant sonnet, 'On Visiting the Grave of my Stillborn Little Girl'. Her first surviving daughter, Marianne, was born on 12 September 1834 (d. 1920) and her daughter's first years are recorded in Gaskell's detailed, comic, and touching maternal diary: 'She will talk before she walks I think. She can say pretty plainly "papa, dark, stir, ship, lamp, book, tea, sweep" &c—leaving poor *Mama* in the back ground' (Chapple and Wilson). Another daughter, Margaret Emily (Meta), was born on 5 February 1837 (d. 1913), but Hannah Lumb, whom Gaskell called 'my more than mother', died in Knutsford in May. Worn out by pregnancy and her aunt's death, Gaskell recuperated on holiday in Wales.

In these early years of marriage literary interests were not forgotten. Since 1832 William Gaskell had lectured at the Salford Mechanics' Institute and elsewhere on 'Poets of humble life', an interest fostered by Southey's *Lives and Works of the Uneducated Poets* (1831) and Carlyle's discussion of Ebenezer Elliott's *Corn-Law Rhymes* (*Edinburgh Review*, 1832). Local poets such as Samuel Bamford and Elijah Ridings were known to the Gaskells, and her husband's lasting interest in local writing and in dialect influenced Gaskell's writing, particularly *Mary Barton* (she attached his 'Two lectures on the Lancashire dialect' to the 1854 edition) and *Sylvia's Lovers*, which was often criticized for its oblique dialect forms.

This interest in artisan writing and local life paralleled that of the Quaker writers Mary and William Howitt, with whom Gaskell began to correspond, particularly on vanishing rural customs. In 1836 she was continuing her own study of poetry, especially the Romantics, and attempting to link it to contemporary life. In January 1837 a poem, 'Sketches among the Poor', by Mr and Mrs Gaskell, appeared in *Blackwood's Edinburgh Magazine*, 'rather in the manner of Crabbe' as she later told Mary Howitt (*Letters*, 33). In 1838 she sent William Howitt her atmospheric, neo-Gothic description of a schoolgirl's outing, 'Clopton Hall', possibly written at school at Avonbank, which Howitt included in his revised edition of *Visits to Remarkable Places* in 1840.

Between 1838 and 1840 Manchester was riven by clashes between Chartists and anti-corn law leaguers, while a new depression in 1840 caused widespread destitution, bringing exhausting relief work. In 1841, escaping the city, the Gaskells visited the continent, touring the Rhine country (where they met the Howitts), which would become the

setting for some of her stories such as 'The Grey Woman' and 'Six Weeks at Heppenheim'.

But the real centre of Gaskell's life was now her family. One heartbreak of these years—mentioned only once in her surviving correspondence—was the death of 'a little son while yet a baby'; his name and dates are still unknown (letter to Harriet Andersen; *Gaskell Society Journal*, 71). Then on 7 October 1842 Florence Elizabeth (d. 1881) was born and soon the family moved to a larger house at 121 Upper Rumford Street, Manchester, and began the enduring habit of taking annual holidays at Silverdale on Morecambe Bay in Lancashire. On 23 October 1844 came the birth of the Gaskells' son William. This bright, red-headed baby brought Elizabeth intense joy, but at ten months he caught scarlet fever at Ffestiniog, north Wales, and died at Porthmadog in August 1845. After this Elizabeth sank into a deep depression which did not really dissipate until her last daughter, Julia Bradford (1846–1908), was born.

Intellectual circles, early stories, and *Mary Barton*, 1846–1848
In 1846 William Gaskell was appointed professor of history, literature, and logic at Manchester New College. The college brought new contacts, including the new professor of philosophy, the charismatic James Martineau, brother of Harriet. In contrast to dry, traditional Unitarianism, Martineau energetically promoted a more emotional faith, insisting that 'the unconscious affections' underlay belief more than rational judgement, an emphasis that resembles the current of feeling in Gaskell's fiction. Another highly unconventional new friend who also stressed the intuitive basis of faith was Francis Newman, professor of classics, brother of the future cardinal John Henry Newman.

Theological debate was intense, as Unitarian connections also extended to Germany and the United States: Elizabeth Gaskell corresponded frequently with the Boston minister John Pierpont, and reviewed Emerson's Manchester lectures for *Howitt's Journal* in 1847. Since 1840 her husband's membership of the Literary and Philosophical Society had also introduced Gaskell to new scientific ideas and arguments. This ferment of ideas, too, resonates in her work, most notably in *Wives and Daughters*. Her circle of personal friends also widened to include younger women like the future writers and translators Catherine and Susanna Winkworth, and the Essex Unitarian and feminist Annie Shaen.

Gaskell's first stories began to appear in 1847. The first was 'Libbie Marsh's Three Eras', published anonymously in 1847 in *Howitt's Journal*, which also carried 'The Sexton's Hero' and 'Christmas Storms and Sunshine' in 1848. During her long depression after her son's death, William had encouraged her to write. She had first planned a story set on the Yorkshire borders in the eighteenth century but then, as she wrote in her 'Preface', 'I bethought me how deep might be the romance of those who elbowed me daily in the busy streets of the town where I resided'. The result was *Mary Barton: a Story of Manchester Life*.

The novel was finished by late 1847 and sent to several publishers before William Howitt negotiated terms with

Chapman and Hall. When it was published in October 1848 Gaskell's 'state of the nation' tale of Chartism, strikes, murder, and prostitution, misery and redemption prompted praise from concerned men as different as Samuel Bamford and Thomas Carlyle. Charles Kingsley applauded it in *Fraser's Magazine* (April 1849), as explaining the unrest and Chartism to the threatened, uncomprehending middle classes:

> Do they want to know why poor men, kind and sympathising as women to each other, learn to hate law and order, Queen, Lords and Commons, country-party and corn law leagues, all alike—to hate the rich in short? then let them read *Mary Barton*.

In contrast, Manchester manufacturers (including many Cross Street Chapel members) felt they had been unfairly, and ignorantly, represented. The *Manchester Guardian* accused Gaskell of maligning the employers (28 February and 7 March 1849), and a stinging review from W. R. Greg in the *Edinburgh Review* that April denounced her ignorance of economics. The book appeared anonymously, but her authorship was soon known and she justified herself openly by her nonconformist belief that she had to 'speak the truth' and to urge antagonistic groups to communicate, in the hope of averting a crisis.

Despite her distress at exposure, Gaskell also enjoyed the fame, or notoriety. Visiting London in April 1849, she met Charles Dickens, John Forster, Anna Jameson, Jane Carlyle, and others. She also forged close friendships with her relations Fanny and Hensleigh Wedgwood, and with Eliza (Tottie) Fox, the artist daughter of the radical minister W. J. Fox. New Manchester friends included J. A. Froude and his wife and (less warmly) the novelist Geraldine Jewsbury. On holiday at Skelwith, near Ambleside in the Lake District, she met the Arnold family and Mary Fletcher, and her hero, Wordsworth.

Widening circles, 1849–1852 In 1849 two more of Gaskell's stories appeared, already revealing her command of different modes: 'Hand and Heart' in the *Sunday School Penny Magazine*, and in *Sartain's Literary Magazine*, 'The Last Generation of England', whose whimsical memory of village eccentricities anticipates *Cranford*.

In 1850 the Gaskells moved to a large house which would be their permanent home, 84 Plymouth Grove, Manchester; summer holidays were spent in the Lake District and at Silverdale. Domestic life engrossed her but Gaskell's letters show that the new house made her more self-analytical, divided, and restless. She felt, as she told Tottie Fox, that she had several 'Mes':

> and that's the plague. One of my mes is, I do believe, a true Christian—(only people call her socialist and communist), another of my mes is a wife and mother, and highly delighted at the delight of everyone else in the house … Now that's my 'social' self I suppose. Then again I've another self with a full taste for beauty and convenience whh is pleased on its own account. How am I to reconcile all these warring members? (*Letters*, 108)

Gaskell's joking distress was linked to conflicts typical of women of the time, between family duty and the need for self-expression. She resolved this by seeing her writing as the proper use of a God-given talent, and emphasizing her

social concerns: in response to an invitation from Dickens to contribute to *Household Words*, she sent 'Lizzie Leigh', a story about a Manchester prostitute, which appeared in the first issue, on 30 March 1850. (She had first contacted Dickens the previous winter—knowing his interest in the subject—for advice concerning the emigration of a young girl in prison for prostitution, an incident clearly linked to her second novel, *Ruth*.)

'Lizzie Leigh' was quickly followed by 'The Well of Pen Morfa' and 'The Heart of John Middleton' for *Household Words*, and Gaskell's long novella *The Moorland Cottage* was also published as a separate book in 1850. She began to see herself as a professional writer, and welcomed the chance of friendship with Charlotte Brontë, whom she met in August 1850 at the Kay-Shuttleworths' summer home, Brierley Close, on Lake Windermere. Gaskell's avid curiosity about the identity of Currer Bell, and keen gathering of Charlotte's own words, mingled with gossip, already laid the foundation for her later biography. Brontë paid a return visit the following June, on her way back from the Great Exhibition, and became fond of the Gaskell children and of Elizabeth, whom she described as 'a woman of whose conversation and company I should not soon tire. She seems to me kind, clever, animated and unaffected' (1 July 1851, *The Brontës: their Lives and Correspondence*, ed T. J. Wise and J. A. Symington, 1933, 3.255). In July 1851 Gaskell herself visited the exhibition in London, and sat for her portrait to Richmond (National Portrait Gallery).

Gaskell's wide network of acquaintances added richness to her fiction. She was interested in all classes: mill workers and agricultural labourers, small shopkeepers, tradesmen and clerks; doctors, and lawyers and ministers; landowners and politicians and duchesses. Unitarian connections linked her with scholars and reformers in Britain, Europe, and America, from refugee supporters of Garibaldi to young, independent-minded women like Bessie Parkes and Barbara Bodichon. Gaskell, however, was never a wholehearted radical or feminist; while she treated controversial subjects, she elevates sympathy and communication above radical change. In this she resembles Marian Evans (George Eliot), ten years her junior. The two novelists had never met, and at first Gaskell supported the cause of Joseph Liggins as the author of *Adam Bede*. When she learned the true identity of the author she was dismayed but fascinated, begging Charles Bosanquet for a full account 'of what she is like &c &c &c &c,—eyes, nose, mouth, *dress* &c' (*Letters*, 587). Although Gaskell remained distressed that Evans could not legally marry G. H. Lewes, their correspondence was warm, and Evans spoke of their 'fellow-feeling', describing her as 'one of the minds which is capable of judging as well as being moved' (*The George Eliot Letters*, ed. G. S. Haight, 1954, 3.198–9).

Short stories, *Ruth* and *Cranford*, 1851–1853 At the start of the 1850s came a rush of short stories by Gaskell: the comic, Cranfordian 'Mr Harrison's Confessions' in the *Ladies Companion*, 1851, and 'Bessy's Troubles at Home' in the *Sunday School Penny Magazine* in 1852. *Cranford* (not originally conceived as a novel) appeared in batches of episodes in *Household Words* between 13 December 1851 and 21 May 1853. Over the next few years *Household Words* published a string of atmospheric sketches and stories including 'Traits and Stories of the Huguenots', 'Morton Hall', 'My French Master', and 'The Squire's Story' (1853); 'Modern Greek songs' and 'Company Manners' (1854); 'An Accursed Race' and 'Half a Lifetime Ago' (1855); 'The Poor Clare' (1856) and 'My Lady Ludlow', 'The Sin of a Father', and 'The Manchester Marriage' (1858).

As the first *Cranford* episodes appeared, Gaskell was already planning her next novel, *Ruth*; she gave an outline to Charlotte Brontë in April 1852, and the book itself appeared in January 1853. (Brontë postponed *Villette* slightly in the vain hope of avoiding comparisons.) Causing even more uproar than *Mary Barton*, *Ruth* tells the story of a fifteen-year-old seamstress who is seduced and has an illegitimate son. Taken in by a Unitarian minister, Mr Benson, she is passed off as a widow, making a new life until she is exposed and publicly denounced, before finally 'redeeming' herself as a nurse in a fever epidemic. A brave attack on current hypocrisy, the novel was attacked not only for the sexual theme but because of Benson's 'lie'; a copy was even burnt by members of William Gaskell's own congregation. Reviews were either equivocal or, like the influential *Blackwood's*, openly hostile: even some time later, the *Anglican Observer* (July 1857) was horrified at the idea that a woman who 'has violated the laws of purity' should be accepted by society. On the other hand several readers condemned the heroine's death as authorial cowardice. 'I am grateful to you as a woman for having treated such a subject', wrote Elizabeth Barrett Browning, but 'Was it quite impossible but that your Ruth should *die*?' (15 July [1853], JRL, MS 730/9).

Cranford, published in volume form in June, caused no such controversy. The episodic tale of two sisters, Deborah and Matty Jenkins, and their genteel circle of women friends has always been valued for its humour, while its clever experiment with narrative voice and structure have won increasing recognition and its profound analysis of 'community' and of women's lives has recently been reappraised by feminist critics.

North and South, 1854–1855 Gaskell's second Manchester novel, *North and South*, outlined a clash of social philosophies through its depiction of the relationship between the 'southern' Margaret Hale and the northern mill owner John Thornton. After the furore surrounding the publication of *Mary Barton*, friends had suggested that she respond to criticisms of bias towards the workers by writing a more sympathetic portrait of the masters. At first she resisted, saying that 'whatever power there was' in her novel, 'was caused by my feeling strongly on the side which I took' (*Letters*, 119). However, by 1854 industrial strife had eased and experiments in caring for the workforce, like those of her factory owner friends Samuel Greg and Salis Schwabe, made her think again.

Gaskell's new novel set out to be conciliatory. By cleverly exploiting the conventions of a romance blocked by preconceptions and misunderstandings (an industrial *Pride and Prejudice*) Gaskell brilliantly conveys the tensions of her society, and her own deep-held belief, stated by her heroine, that 'God hath made us so that we must be mutually dependent'. Employing a network of interlinked contrasts—between men and women, country and city, royalist and roundhead, evangelical, Anglican and freethinker, Norse and oriental myth—this powerful and inventive novel is at once a guardedly optimistic 'protest novel', a fierce questioning of authority, and an intimate study of a young woman's growth to self-knowledge.

North and South first appeared as a weekly serial in *Household Words* from 2 September 1854 to 27 January 1855. This was a mode of publication that Gaskell found hard to handle: her refusal to accept Dickens's editing, and a miscalculation of length, as well as her own perpetual lateness in delivering copy, made their relationship extremely tense. She regarded the abrupt ending of the serial version as 'mutilated'—'like a pantomime figure with a great large head and a very small trunk' (to Maria James, n.d. [1854], U. Leeds, Brotherton L.)—and expanded it for volume publication in 1855.

In 1854 William Gaskell became the senior minister of Cross Street Chapel, but, despite her current preoccupation with Manchester in her novel, from this point Elizabeth Gaskell herself spent less and less time in the city. In 1854 she visited France with her daughter Marianne, forming a lasting friendship with Mary Clarke Mohl, with whom she and her daughters often stayed in future years. While writing *North and South*, she also stayed with the Nightingale family at Lea Hurst, Derbyshire, meeting Florence Nightingale just before she set off to the Crimea. Gaskell admired Nightingale, but found her tendency to put causes before individual relationships 'jarring': 'She has no friend—and wants none. She stands perfectly alone, half-way between God and His creatures' (*Letters*, 319). While the strong heroines of her novels often reflect the determination and the trials of contemporary women, ultimately they value feeling and sympathy above male structures of power.

The Life of Charlotte Brontë, 1856–1857 The insistence on women 'speaking out' is the point at which Gaskell comes closest to Charlotte Brontë, whom Gaskell recognized as the more powerful writer. Their friendship was close, although based only on occasional visits. In April 1853 Brontë stayed in Manchester again, while Gaskell visited Haworth from 19 to 23 September, after a summer which included a stay in Paris and a visit to Normandy. The following May Brontë paid her last visit, shortly before her marriage to Arthur Nicholls. The two authors did not meet again, perhaps, Gaskell thought, because Nicholls's strict Anglicanism made a Unitarian friend unwelcome.

In 1855 Gaskell returned from a Paris holiday to learn that Charlotte had died on 31 March, and in June Patrick Brontë asked her to write his daughter's life, to offset inaccurate versions. Much of the next two years was spent in gathering letters, collecting information, and compiling the life: the manuscript (JRL) shows that her daughters helped with transcription, and her husband with style. In

May 1856 she went to Brussels, where she met Constantin Heger (the model for Paul Emmanuel in *Villette*) and read Charlotte's passionate letters to him. Yet Gaskell suppressed the true relationship with Heger in her desire to save Brontë from the allegations of 'coarseness' made in her lifetime. To compensate, and explain Charlotte's despair in 1845, she emphasized the moral disintegration of Branwell Brontë and the sisters' isolation.

To escape the storm that was bound to accompany publication of *The Life of Charlotte Brontë* on 24 March 1857, Gaskell left in February for three months on the continent with her two eldest daughters and Catherine Winkworth. In Rome she stayed with the family of the American sculptor William Whetmore Story, whom she had met at the Mohls in 1854, and also formed a close and enduring attachment to the young Charles Eliot Norton, soon to become editor of *The Nation*. She went on to visit Venice before returning home via Paris.

In her absence William Gaskell had to deal with the many complaints of misrepresentation, helped by her publisher, George Smith and the Gaskells' solicitor, William Shaen. When threats of libel writs came from Lady Scott (who as Lydia Robinson was blamed by Gaskell for Branwell Brontë's disgrace), unsold copies of the biography were withdrawn and a formal letter of apology placed in *The Times*. Fierce criticism and more legal threats came from supporters of W. Carus Wilson, founder of Cowan Bridge, the school blamed for the deaths of the elder Brontë sisters. Individual complaints came from many individuals, including Harriet Martineau, G. H. Lewes and, most particularly, Patrick Brontë. All were dealt with in the revised third edition. Faced with such criticism, Gaskell took refuge in the justification used of *Mary Barton* and *Ruth*: 'I *did so try* to *tell the truth*, & I believe now I hit as near the truth as any one *could* do. And I weighed every line with all my whole power & heart' (*Letters*, 454).

Above all, Gaskell's biography had recognized the split that the creative life involved for women, something that she herself experienced. Describing the publication of *Jane Eyre*, Gaskell wrote: 'Henceforward Charlotte Brontë's existence becomes divided into two parallel currents—her life as Currer Bell, the author; her life as Charlotte Brontë, the woman. There were separate duties belonging to each character, not impossible, but difficult to be reconciled' (*Life of Charlotte Brontë*, part 2, ch. 2).

Censored and shaped as it was, *The Life of Charlotte Brontë* was none the less a landmark in biography, creating a new, feminine form which linked emotional and domestic life and suffering to creativity. At the end of the century the novelist Margaret Oliphant remembered its impact, suggesting that Gaskell had shattered the notions of 'delicacy' regarded as 'the most exquisite characteristic of womankind', and had 'originated in her bewilderment a new kind of biography … *The Times* blew a trumpet of dismay; the book was revolution as well as revelation' (*Women Novelists of Queen Victoria's Reign*, 1897, 118). However, many have since blamed Gaskell for creating a myth of Brontë as suffering victim, rather than active agent.

The arguments still rage, and even late in the twentieth century, the *Life* was described as 'a persuasive and powerful polemic which has never been seriously challenged' (J. Barker, *The Brontës*, 1994, xviii).

Shorter fiction and *Sylvia's Lovers*, 1858–1863 The next few years saw the height of Gaskell's achievement as a storyteller. 'The Doom of the Griffiths' appeared in *Harper's Magazine* in 1858; in March 1859 'My Lady Ludlow' and several short pieces were collected in *Round the Sofa*, while one of her greatest stories, 'Lois the Witch' appeared in Dickens's new magazine, *All the Year Round*, in October. This journal also carried other Gothic tales: 'The Crooked Branch' (1859), 'The Grey Woman' (1861), 'A Dark Night's Work', and 'Crowley Castle' (1863). Dismayed by Dickens's treatment of his wife after their separation, and his declaration on that matter, published in *Household Words*, in 1860 Gaskell was hunting for new outlets in which to present her fiction. In that year she published 'Curious but True' in the rival *Cornhill Magazine*, edited by Thackeray and published by George Smith.

Stories were a good source of ready cash. Although Gaskell maintained that her husband had quickly buttoned up her first cheque from *Household Words* in his pocket (a teasing action that has since won him an undeserved reputation for stern patriarchal repression), most of her earnings seem to have been in her direct control, channelled through the family solicitor, William Shaen. She never earned as much as her great contemporaries (receiving £2000 from the *Cornhill* for *Wives and Daughters* in 1864, for example, compared to £7000 paid to George Eliot for *Romola* in 1862). Many of her short works were written quickly, in order to pay for holidays. At times, it seemed, she had a passionate desire to be anywhere but Manchester. She visited relations in Scotland, London, and Gloucestershire and friends in the south of England. In 1857 she made her first trip to Oxford, where her friends included the family of Benjamin Brodie, professor of chemistry. She also went to Germany and Paris with Meta and Florence in 1859, and revisited France in 1860 and 1862, when she toured Normandy and Brittany, planning a memoir of Mme de Sevigné. (Her interest can be seen in the delightful articles on French life published in *Fraser's Magazine* in 1864.) In 1863 she stayed with the Mohls before continuing to Rome with three of her daughters, returning for the wedding of her youngest daughter, Florence, to Charles Crompton.

Gaskell did not detach herself completely from Manchester, however, and she was certainly intensely active there in 1862, when a collapse in the cotton trade, brought on by the American Civil War, created widespread distress. In this crisis she set up sewing workshops to provide part-time employment for women, sought Florence Nightingale's help to see if former mill women might train as nurses, and canvassed support from local philanthropists. Exhausted by the work, both Gaskell and her daughter Meta collapsed, and stayed with the Brodies in Worthing to recuperate.

Yet Gaskell still wrote on. Since a visit to Whitby in 1859 she had been working on a historical story set largely in this small whaling port in the 1790s. *Sylvia's Lovers*, which she felt was the saddest story she ever wrote, was eventually published in February 1863. A haunting, experimental mixture, its complex plot sets personal dramas and betrayals against wider debates about responsibility and torn loyalties: in business life, in the relation of family to state, and the 'nation' to the 'people', even in the tension between divine and human law. Beneath the surface lie the inexplicability of human pain, and Gaskell's unspoken sense that neither religion nor the new evolutionary science afforded much consolation.

Wives and Daughters, 1864–1866 *Sylvia's Lovers* looked back to an era before industrialization and the coming of the railways. The pressures of that change, felt in all Gaskell's fiction, haunt the background of *Cousin Phillis*, a Turgenev-like pastoral tale of young love and paternal misunderstanding. There is also an element of personal nostalgia in this story, the setting of which, Heathbridge, was based on memories of Sandlebridge, the farm owned by Gaskell's grandfather Samuel Holland. *Cousin Phillis* was published by George Smith in four episodes in the *Cornhill*, from November 1863 to February 1864. The story's abrupt ending, forced by the deadline, gives a slightly false, if moving, sense of uncertainty, since Gaskell seems to have planned that her heroine would find some ease for personal pain in social work.

By mid-1863 Gaskell was planning her next novel, *Wives and Daughters*. Here she turned triumphantly to the time of her own youth, the late 1820s. This brilliant and touching novel combines a comedy of manners with the parallel tales of adolescent growth to self-knowledge of Molly Gibson and Cynthia Kirkpatrick. Through humour and the suggestive imagery of science, medicine, and exploration, Gaskell excavated the personal, social, and political values that formed her own generation: in a way the novel forms a study of the evolution of a society, and some aspects of the hero Roger Hamley were drawn directly from Gaskell's relation Charles Darwin.

Wives and Daughters began to appear in the *Cornhill* in August 1864, proving an immediate success. That summer, anxious about the health of her daughter Meta, she took her to the Alps, and in March 1865 they visited the Mohls in Paris. Deadlines were still a problem, 'I *am* so badly behind hand' she wailed (*Letters*, 937), but somehow she managed to send the text episode by episode to the supportive George Smith. Smith also helped her in her determination to buy a house in the south, to be near Florence, now living in London, and Marianne, who had long been engaged to her cousin Thurstan Holland.

In June 1865, without viewing it herself, Gaskell bought The Lawn, Holybourne, near Alton in Hampshire: she had borrowed money from George Smith, and the purchase was kept a secret from William Gaskell, despite the fiction that the house was for him 'to retire to'. By mid-August she was ill with strain—but still fitted in a lively visit to Lord Houghton (Monckton Milnes) at Fryston. She was rushing through the final chapters of *Wives and Daughters* and also sending 'Columns of gossip from Paris' to the *Pall Mall Gazette*, as well as five instalments of 'A Parson's Holiday',

comic fictional letters about a dissenting minister trying to escape his congregation. In September and October, worn out, she herself took a quick holiday in Dieppe.

On her return, Gaskell at last saw her new house. Ten days later, at tea there with her family on 12 November 1865, she collapsed suddenly with a massive heart attack and died almost instantly. She was buried on 17 November in the cemetery of Brook Street Chapel, Knutsford, where William Gaskell was later buried beside her in 1884. *Wives and Daughters* remained unfinished. The last episode appeared in January 1866, with a note rounding off the story from the *Cornhill's* editor, Frederic Greenwood. It was published in two volumes later that year.

Literary reputation Elizabeth Gaskell was an immensely lively personality and a writer of varied talents and moods. This has made her hard to classify and readers have tended to identify her with one or other of her novels: the humorous, subtle reporter of village life and spinster habits in *Cranford*; the social protest novelist of *Mary Barton*, *Ruth*, and *North and South*; the vivid historian of *Sylvia's Lovers*; the wise analyst of parental tension and female longing in *Wives and Daughters* and *Cousin Phyllis*. She is also one of the great, and still underrated, Victorian short-story writers. Often thought of as artless, or as a 'natural story-teller', she was in fact a skilled and self-conscious artist, revelling in the possibilities of genres, playing with narrative stance and ambivalence and literary reference. Her awareness of the different languages (religious, political, economic, scientific) applied to contemporary problems is reflected in her aim as a fiction writer to mediate between discourses and to break down barriers of communication between classes and individuals.

The basis of Gaskell's vision is realistic, displaying an acute observation of domestic detail and a marvellous ear for dialogue—from Manchester tenements to Paris salons. She was also a shrewd psychologist, but beyond that, realism often gives way to more symbolic writing. Dreams and supernatural elements, particularly in the shorter works, offer a method of exploring power and weakness, the potential for horror, oppression, distress, and redemption.

Largely because of concentration on single aspects of her varied work, Gaskell's reputation has probably undergone more revisionist critical swerves than that of any other major nineteenth-century author. After her death a collected edition of Gaskell's works was published in 1873, and the 'Knutsford' edition, edited by A. A. Ward appeared in 1906. By then, however, she had fallen out of fashion, although *Cranford* remained a staple text, read in a spirit of nostalgia by travellers and expatriates, and by soldiers in the trenches in the First World War. In the inter-war years her feminine, pastoral aspect was stressed and critical opinion was tellingly summed up by Lord David Cecil's highly misleading formulation of her in *Early Victorian Novelists* (1934) as 'a dove': 'she was all a woman was expected to be; gentle, domestic, tactful, unintellectual, prone to tears, easily shocked. So far from chafing at the limits imposed on her activities, she accepted them with a serene satisfaction'.

Not until the 1950s were Gaskell's social concerns fully recognized, first by Kathleen Tillotson in *Novels of the Eighteen-Forties* (1954) and then by Marxist critics like Arnold Kettle in *From Dickens to Hardy* (1958) and Raymond Williams in *Culture and Society* (also 1958). Now she was classed with Dickens, Disraeli, and Kingsley as a critic of industrial society. *Mary Barton* and *North and South* were singled out in Williams's terms, for their sensitive observation and attempt at imaginative sympathy, but her critique of industrialism was also felt to have weaknesses and her endings were attacked as melodramatic and escapist.

More recently, critics have acknowledged that Gaskell's structural breaks and vacillation of tone are related to a refusal to give easy answers to social and spiritual dilemmas, and to her desire to 'feminize' traditional values and forms. An early work placing Gaskell in the context of the contemporary women's movement was Aina Rubenius's *The Woman Question in Mrs Gaskell's Life and Works* (1950) but Gaskell as social novelist remained the main focus until the 1980s, with some attempts to place her in the different traditions of the provincial novel, and the fiction of dissent.

Following the 1980s 'rediscovery' of women's fiction Gaskell was ranged not only with Dickens and Kingsley but with contemporary women critics of society such as Frances Trollope, Harriet Martineau, and Charlotte Elizabeth Tonna. Feminist criticism of the 1990s explored her subtle extension of female, maternal values from the domestic to the public sphere, her dramatization of the tension between old and new systems of values, and the relation between her experience as a woman writing for male editors, and that of the industrial workers she described. In the process, the powerfully subversive elements of Gaskell's shorter fiction have received belated recognition.

Outside academe, Gaskell has always found devoted readers. In the late twentieth century their numbers increased and she acquired a high reputation in unexpected places—Italy and Japan, for example, produced a surprising number of Gaskell fans. At the same time, in Britain, her works became rich material for adaptations, or modern versions like David Lodge's novel *Nice Work* (1988), a colourful reworking of the sexual and cultural battles of *North and South*. In 1997–8 a radio dramatization of *North and South* was followed by radio readings of her short stories, while one of the last BBC television 'classic serials' of the twentieth century, screened in November and December 1999, was Andrew Davies's superb adaptation of Gaskell's final, greatest novel, *Wives and Daughters*.

JENNY UGLOW

Sources *The letters of Mrs Gaskell*, ed. J. A. V. Chapple and A. Pollard (1966); new edn (1996) • J. Uglow, *Elizabeth Gaskell: a habit of stories* (1993) • N. S. Weyant, *Elizabeth Gaskell: an annotated bibliography* (1991) • J. Chapple, *Elizabeth Gaskell: the early years* (1997) • J. A. V. Chapple and A. Wilson, eds., *Private voices: the diaries of Elizabeth Gaskell and Sophia Holland* (1996) • J. A. V. Chapple, *Elizabeth Gaskell: a portrait in letters* (1980) • *Gaskell Society Journal*, 6 (1992), 71 • J. G. Sharps, *Mrs Gaskell's observation and invention* (1970) • A. Eassan, ed., *Elizabeth Gaskell: the critical heritage* (1992) • E. H. Chadwick, *Mrs Gaskell: haunts, homes, and stories* (1910) • P. Stoneman, *Elizabeth Gaskell* (1987) • W. Gerin, *Elizabeth Gaskell* (1976)

Archives Harvard U., MSS • Hunt. L., letters • JRL, corresp., literary MSS, and papers • JRL, letters • Man. CL, Manchester Archives and Local Studies, letters • NRA, priv. coll., MSS • Princeton University Library, New Jersey, letters and literary MSS • U. Leeds, Brotherton L., letters and literary MSS, incl. MS of *Sylvia's lovers* | BL, letters to F. J. Furnivall, Add. MS 43798 • CUL, letters to John Malcolm Ludlow • Lancs. RO, letters to Lady Kay-Shuttleworth • NL Scot., letters to George Smith and Mrs Smith • Trinity Cam., letters to Lord Houghton • U. Birm. L., letters to Harriet Martineau

Likenesses D. Dunbar, bust, c.1829, University of Manchester • W. J. Thomson, miniature, 1832, University of Manchester Library • G. Richmond, pastel drawing, 1851, NPG [*see illus.*] • S. Lawrence, pastel drawing, 1854, priv. coll. • A. McGlashon, carte-de-visite, 1862–3, NPG • photograph, c.1864, JRL • W. H. Thornycroft, marble bust, 1895 (after D. Dunbar), University of Manchester Library • C. A. D'Orsi, bronze plaque, Mrs Gaskell Memorial Tower, Knutsford

Gaskell, Holbrook (1813–1909), chemical manufacturer, was born on 5 March 1813 in Wavertree, near Liverpool, the eldest son (there was also at least one daughter) of Roger Gaskell, manager of the commercial branch of a Warrington sailcloth firm, and his wife and cousin, Anne Hunter. Educated at a private school in Norton near Sheffield, Gaskell was apprenticed as a clerk to Yates and Cox, Liverpool iron merchants and nail makers, in 1827. In 1836 he joined James Nasmyth as a partner with responsibility for commercial and financial operations at the Bridgewater foundry at Patricroft near Manchester. On 28 December 1841 Gaskell married Frances Ann, daughter of Henry Bellhouse, of Victoria Park, Greenhayes, Manchester. They had three sons and three daughters. All three sons became partners in the family firm; one of them, also Holbrook Gaskell (b. 1878), a director of ICI, was knighted in 1942. The physiologist Walter Holbrook Gaskell was his nephew.

Gaskell's business acumen placed Nasmyth, Gaskell & Co. among the leading engineering firms in Britain, but in June 1850 ill health forced him to retire. In June 1855, his health restored, he entered into a second partnership, this time with Henry Deacon, industrial chemist and former apprentice of Nasmyth. At first Gaskell supported Deacon's plans to manufacture alkali by the new Solvay process, but later persuaded him for financial reasons to employ the older Leblanc method. In the 1860s Gaskell, Deacon & Co. was among the largest and most successful chemical works in Widnes, owing to Gaskell's commercial management and Deacon's method of recovering chlorine for bleaching powder manufacture. Gaskell was actively involved with the firm until the 1870s, after which he remained a director until November 1890, when it was absorbed into the United Alkali Company. He was then appointed to a vice-presidency in recognition of his services to the chemical industry.

Gaskell had wide interests in the north-west. Inspired by a sense of private and public duty, he served as a magistrate in Widnes for many years. In politics he was an active liberal, and after 1886, Liberal Unionist, a member of the Liverpool Reform Club, and a supporter of radical causes, including the extension of the franchise. Interested in education, he donated nearly £6000 towards the endowment of a chair of botany and the provision of chemistry laboratories at University College, Liverpool. He presented Widnes with public baths in 1889 and supported convalescent homes in Heswall and Southport. He was a proprietor of the *Liverpool Daily and Weekly Post and Echo* and became chairman when the *Daily Post* and *Liverpool Mercury* amalgamated in 1904. An art connoisseur, Gaskell owned one of the finest collections of paintings in the north of England, including works by J. M. W. Turner and John Constable. The collection was loaned to the Walker Art Gallery, Liverpool, in 1885. He died at his home, Woolton Wood, Much Woolton, Lancashire, on 8 March 1909.

N. G. COLEY, rev.

Sources J. Cantrell, 'Gaskell, Holbrook', *DBB* · *Liverpool Weekly Post* (10 March 1909) · D. W. F. Hardie and R. Dickinson, 'Gaskell Deacon 1853–1953', ICI Ltd · *General Chemical Division News* (Aug 1953) · D. W. F. Hardie, *A history of the chemical industry in Widnes* (1950) · m. cert. · d. cert.
Archives Salford Museum and Art Gallery, Salford City Archives, corresp., Salford AC Misc U313
Wealth at death £433,251 5s. 1d.: probate, 28 May 1909, *CGPLA Eng. & Wales*

Gaskell, James Milnes (1810–1873), politician, was born on 19 October 1810, the only child of Benjamin Gaskell (1781–1856), of Thornes House, Yorkshire (which he inherited in 1805 from James Milnes, MP for Maldon), and his wife, Mary, *née* Brandreth. The Gaskells were Presbyterians by origin. James attended Dr Roberts's school at Mitcham from 1821 until 1824, when he went to Eton College. There he was a prominent member of those revitalizing the Society of Literati ('Pop') and was the close friend of Arthur Henry Hallam and William Ewart Gladstone. Obsessive about the minutiae of politics and an expert on division lists and whipping, Gaskell was an important influence on his Eton generation, several of whom were prominent in British politics for much of the rest of the century. His letters from that time, published posthumously as *Records of an Eton Schoolboy*, edited by C. M. Gaskell with a preface by Francis Doyle (privately printed in 1883) are a sparkling source. Gaskell matriculated at Christ Church, Oxford, in 1829. He was three times secretary of the Oxford Union but left without taking a degree. In 1832 he married Mary (d. 1869), second daughter of Charles Watkin Williams *Wynn, MP; they had two sons and two daughters. A moderate tory who supported the passing of the Reform Bill, Gaskell inherited Egremont House from a Mr Milnes. The possibility of standing for Maldon or for Wakefield came to nothing (in the latter case he withdrew in favour of his uncle, Daniel Gaskell), but his father-in-law found him a seat at Wenlock for which he was elected in 1832.

Gaskell was a whip in Peel's administration of 1841–6, resigning in January 1846 and making a strong attack in the Commons on 12 February on Peel's conduct, especially his inconsistency over the corn laws. Gaskell voted against the government on corn law repeal on 15 May and abstained in the Irish vote on 25 June 1846 which terminated the ministry.

Gaskell never established a clear enough political position for his career to revive. He was said to have declined office in Derby's tory government of 1852. His nonconformist background made his position in the tory party uneasy, or so his obituarist in *The Times* (probably Francis Doyle) felt. After 1856 he usually supported Palmerston on Canningite grounds. His health was poor in 1868 and he did not stand for re-election. He died from disease of the bladder on 5 February 1873 at 28 Norfolk Street, Park Lane, London.

H. C. G. MATTHEW

Sources *The Times* (8 Feb 1873) · *The Times* (21 March 1873) · J. M. Gaskell, *Records of an Eton schoolboy*, ed. C. M. Gaskell (privately printed, 1883) · Gladstone, *Diaries* · H. C. G. Matthew, *Gladstone*, 2 vols. (1986–95); repr. in 1 vol. as *Gladstone, 1809–1898* (1997) · N. Gash, *Sir Robert Peel: the life of Sir Robert Peel after 1830* (1972) · R. G. Thorne, 'Gaskell, Benjamin', *HoP, Commons* · d. cert.
Archives BL, letters to W. E. Gladstone, Add. MS 44161
Wealth at death under £40,000: *The Times* (21 March 1873)

Gaskell, Walter Holbrook (1847–1914), physiologist, was the third child and younger twin son of John Dakin Gaskell, barrister of the Middle Temple, and his wife (and cousin), Anne, daughter of Roger Gaskell. He was born on 1 November 1847 at Naples, where his parents were residing for the winter. Brought up in Highgate, he attended Sir Roger Cholmeley's School until he was seventeen. In 1865 he entered Trinity College, Cambridge, where he became a scholar and was twenty-sixth wrangler in the mathematical tripos of 1869. With the intention of taking a medical degree he attended the lectures of Michael Foster on biology, and in 1872 (the year in which he proceeded MA) went to University College Hospital. However, an interest in physiology led to his interrupting his formal medical studies; in October 1874 he went to work under Karl F. W. Ludwig, professor of physiology at Leipzig, on problems in vascular innervation.

Gaskell returned to Cambridge in 1875 and married Catherine Sharpe, daughter of Reginald Amphlett Parker, solicitor; they settled in Grantchester so that he could work in the Cambridge Physiological Laboratory. He proceeded to the degree of MD in 1878, but he was by then already a career physiologist. Following his return from Germany he had continued his investigations into vascular innervation, and he subsequently devised an ingenious method of watching the blood-flow in the mylohyoid muscle of the frog during stimulation of its nerve. He next turned his attention to the heart, and demonstrated by many beautiful experiments the inherent rhythm of cardiac muscle and the influence on it of nervous impulses and drugs. He proved that the normal beat starts in the sinus and is propagated by way of the muscular tissue of the auricle to the ventricle. This work led to his being elected a fellow of the Royal Society in 1882. In the following year he was appointed university lecturer in physiology, and, in 1889, was elected to a fellowship at Trinity Hall.

In the course of his researches Gaskell discovered that the vagus nerve of the frog contains two sets of fibres, which not only produce an opposite effect on the action of the heart, but differ in structure and in their origin from the central nervous system. He therefore extended his enquiry to viscera other than the heart. The movements of these organs were generally thought to be governed by a 'vegetative nervous system', which lay outside and was largely independent of the brain and spinal cord. Gaskell revealed on broad lines the true plan of their relationship to the central nervous system, and showed that, like the heart, they are all supplied by peculiar motor and inhibitory nerves arising from specially restricted areas of the same nerve-axis as that which governs the ordinary muscles of the body.

Gaskell then passed on to enquiries of a still wider scope, the consideration of function from its developmental aspect. It had been taught that one set of nerves quickened and another stopped the heart; Gaskell's aim was to discover not only the mechanical means by which this was brought about, but how these functions arose. This method of considering physiological problems had a profound effect on scientific medicine. Gaskell revolutionized current ideas of the action of the heart, and, consequently, of cardiac disease. He laid bare both the structure and the functions of the involuntary nervous system: never content simply to record a new fact, he always asked the meaning of the phenomena which he described.

From these studies Gaskell was led to consider the mode by which vertebrate animals derived from an invertebrate ancestry. In 1889 he put forward the first indications of his theory that the vertebrates are descended from an arthropod stock, of which the king crab is the nearest living example. He accounted for the obvious differences in the relation of the principal organs by supposing that the gut of the arthropod, surrounded by its chain of ganglia, had been transformed into the central canal of the spinal cord. This theory raised a vehement storm of protest from certain zoologists, which grew in volume as new points were brought forward by Gaskell in paper after paper. Finally, when he published *The Origin of the Vertebrates* in 1908, the work passed almost unnoticed. This book is written in a fascinating manner, clear, simple, and concise, and contains innumerable original observations marshalled with unusual skill. Shortly before his death he completed the manuscript of a small book, embodying the results of all his researches, which was published in 1916 under the title of *The Involuntary Nervous System*.

Gaskell's robust frame, sanguine complexion, and abundant dark hair and beard, which never went entirely white, gave him the appearance of a man whose occupation was in the open air—indeed, digging and the care of his garden formed his principal recreation. The clarity and half-veiled enthusiasm of his exposition, together with his somewhat slow and emphatic utterance, made him an enthralling teacher for senior students. He always treated them as if they were worthy to participate in the researches which occupied him at the moment. He was ever ready to turn aside to give counsel or encouragement, and no one was more frequently consulted by the

younger physiologists. Those who came under his influence never forgot his transcendent sincerity, his gift of sympathetic attention, and the unfailing wisdom of his advice. He received numerous honours, including the gold medal of the Royal Society and honorary LLDs from Edinburgh (1894) and McGill (1897) universities.

After having lived for a few years in Cambridge, in the early 1890s Gaskell built The Uplands, at Great Shelford, where he died from a cerebral haemorrhage on 7 September 1914. He was survived by one son and two daughters.

HENRY HEAD, *rev.* PETER OSBORNE

Sources WWW · Venn, *Alum. Cant.* · private information (1927) · personal knowledge (1927)
Archives Oxf. U. Mus. NH, letters and postcards to E. B. Poulton
Likenesses photograph, NPG
Wealth at death £29,408 13s. 10d.: probate, 9 Jan 1915, *CGPLA Eng. & Wales*

Gaskell, William (1805–1884), Unitarian minister, was born in Latchford, Warrington, on 24 July 1805, the eldest of four sons and seven children born to William Gaskell (1762–1819), a sail-cloth manufacturer from an old Warrington family, and his wife, Margaret Jackson (1780/81–1850), also of Warrington; in 1822 the widowed Mrs Gaskell married the Revd Edward Dimock (1795?–1876), Unitarian minister there and later in Rivington.

The younger William was educated privately by the Revd Joseph Saul (d. 1846), perpetual curate of Trinity Church, Warrington, and later chaplain and classical tutor at a school near Carlisle. In 1820 he matriculated at the University of Glasgow, graduating MA in 1825, and then entered Manchester College, York. In 1828 Gaskell became junior minister to the Revd John Gooch Robberds (1789–1854) at Cross Street Chapel, Manchester, a congregation notable for its complement of merchant princes and civic leaders. Robberds was unhappy about the appointment, apparently because of some student scrape in which Gaskell had been involved, but whatever ill feeling there was did not persist. Both men were eloquent and compelling preachers, and neither was a doctrinaire Unitarian; they enthusiastically supported the chapel's schools and the Manchester Domestic Mission.

On 30 August 1832 Gaskell married Elizabeth Stevenson (1810–1865) [*see* Gaskell, Elizabeth Cleghorn], the daughter of William *Stevenson (*bap.* 1770, *d.* 1829), a former Unitarian minister, writer on geographical and naval subjects, and keeper of records in the Treasury. Although Gaskell was reserved and scholarly and his wife spirited and intuitive, the marriage proved remarkably congenial; it was also unusual for its time, notably in the couple's long separate holidays. While sharing interests in literature, congregational activities, and the welfare of the town's poor, each recognized the other's need for autonomy. Privately, Gaskell had a fine sense of humour (he was an incorrigible punster), and family life was warm and relaxed. Their first child, a daughter, was stillborn, and a son died at just under a year of age in 1842; one married daughter died in 1881 and three others, one married, survived their father. Gaskell's poetic bent led to extensive hymn writing and to the publication of *Temperance Rhymes*

(1839). Following the death of their son, he encouraged his wife to write, and the publication of *Mary Barton* in 1848 launched her career as one of the major novelists of the century. He was her closest adviser and critic—*Mary Barton* reflects his scholarly interest in Lancashire dialect—and the increased income made possible the maintenance of a large house in Plymouth Grove in Manchester. The almost twenty years that followed her sudden death in 1865 he spent in extensive congregational, educational, and denominational activity.

It would be difficult to overestimate the pivotal part William Gaskell played in nineteenth-century Unitarianism. For most of his career the denomination was seriously divided between the Unitarianism inherited from the late eighteenth century and the reconstruction proposed after 1833 by Gaskell's York contemporary James Martineau (1805–1900), who abandoned the older emphasis on natural religion and biblical evidences for an introspective grounding of religious impulses. That Gaskell's instinctive sympathies lay with the former school, dominant in the college at York, is suggested by the couple's closest friendships, by a few surviving sermons of biographical importance, such as his fiftieth-anniversary sermon at Cross Street, and in the *Unitarian Herald*, a weekly newspaper established in 1861 by Gaskell, with John Relly Beard (1800–1876), Brooke Herford (1830–1903), and John Wright (1824–1900), as a counterpoise to the London-based *Inquirer*, by then inclining to the Martineau camp. Gaskell's leading articles, which can be identified for two of the paper's early years, were generally conservative but also eirenic and open to new understandings.

After Manchester College returned from York in 1840 it was renamed Manchester New College. In 1846 Gaskell became clerical secretary and later professor of history, literature, and logic; from 1859 until his death he served as visitor of the college, then in London. In 1854, in Manchester, John Relly Beard founded the Unitarian Home Missionary Board to train ministers of humbler background; from the start, Gaskell taught there and served as principal after 1876. He played an important part in establishing Memorial Hall, opened in Albert Square, Manchester, in 1865 to commemorate the origin of dissent in the St Bartholomew's day ejections of 1662. It is suggestive of the respect and affection accorded him that he was the only minister invited three times to preach before the British and Foreign Unitarian Association, in 1844, 1862, and 1875.

Although he took little part in politics, Gaskell was active in the flourishing culture of Manchester through the Literary and Philosophical Association, the Portico Library, and charitable and educational work, notably his lectures to working men. On his fiftieth anniversary as a minister in 1878 a subscription of £2200 became the basis of a scholarship for students from the Home Missionary Board (later Unitarian College, Manchester) at the new Owens College, later the University of Manchester. Gaskell's health failed early in 1884, and he died in his house in Plymouth Grove on 11 June 1884 of 'senile decay' and bronchitis. The funeral and burial took place on 14 June at the Unitarian chapel in Brook Street, Knutsford, Cheshire, the town where his wife had grown up and where she was buried.   R. K. WEBB

Sources B. Brill, *William Gaskell, 1805–1884: a portrait* (1984) • *The Inquirer* (14 June 1884) • *The Inquirer* (21 June 1884) • *Christian Life* (14 June 1884) • W. Gerin, *Elizabeth Gaskell, a biography* (1980) • *The letters of Mrs Gaskell*, ed. J. A. V. Chapple and A. Pollard (1966) • R. K. Webb, 'The Gaskells as Unitarians', *Dickens and other Victorians: essays in honour of Philip Collins*, ed. J. Shattock (1988), 144–71 • minute books, *Unitarian Herald*, 1861–3, DWL • J. G. Robberds, letter to Mrs Robberds, 22 Oct 1827, Harris Man. Oxf. • d. cert. • d. cert. [Margaret Dimock, mother]
Archives Harris Man. Oxf., Manchester College archives
Likenesses photograph, *c*.1869, Cross Street Chapel • photograph, *c*.1871, Central Reference Library, Manchester, Bing Cuttings • W. Percy, oils, 1872, Unitarian College, Manchester • R. Potter, photograph, 1876–9 (double portrait with Beatrix), repro. in Brill, *William Gaskell*, p. 93 • G. W. Swynnerton, marble bust, 1878, Portico Library, Manchester • R. Hooke, oils, Harris Man. Oxf. • R. Potter, photograph, NPG • A. L. Swynnerton, oils, Portico Library, Manchester; on loan from Man. City Gall. • engraving, Central Reference Library, Manchester, Print Collection • photograph, repro. in Cross Street Chapel, *Commemoration of the Rev. William Gaskell's fifty years' ministry* (1878) • portraits, repro. in Brill, *William Gaskell*
Wealth at death £48,133 15s. 8d.: resworn probate, Dec 1884, CGPLA Eng. & Wales

Gaskin, Arthur Joseph (1862–1928). *See under* Gaskin, Georgie Evelyn Cave (1866–1934).

Gaskin, George (1751–1829), Church of England clergyman and religious society administrator, was born at Newington Green, Islington, Middlesex, son of John Gaskin, leatherseller of London (1709/10–1766), and his wife, Mabel (1706/7–1791). Educated at a classical school in Woodford, Essex, he entered Trinity College, Oxford, as a commoner in 1771, graduating BA in 1775, MA in 1778, and BD and DD in 1778.

Gaskin was ordained deacon in 1774 by the bishop of Chester, and priest by the bishop of Rochester, as curate of St Vedast, Foster Lane, London. In 1778 he became curate of Stoke Newington and in 1779 also lecturer of Islington parish church. He married Elizabeth, daughter of Thomas *Broughton, rector of All Hallows, Lombard Street, London, and of Wotton, Surrey, and secretary of the Society for Promoting Christian Knowledge (SPCK). In 1783 he succeeded his father-in-law in the position of secretary. He was presented to the rectory of Sutton and Mepal in the Isle of Ely, which he exchanged for St Benet Gracechurch in London in 1791, as more convenient for his curacies and the SPCK.

In 1784 Gaskin looked after the three American priests sent to London to be consecrated for the new dioceses in the United States. His active interest in the Episcopal church in the USA continued. In 1821 he published an edition of the sermons of the American bishop Theodore Dehon, and in 1823 he acted as a trustee of the funds to endow a diocese of Ohio. His 1791 SPCK report looked forward to the establishment of a native church in India, with its own bishops, priests, and deacons. He was actively involved in the attempt to gain the support of the English bishops for a bill for the legal toleration of episcopal clergy in Scotland in 1791 which failed. A second attempt in 1792, led by Samuel Horsley, then bishop of St David's, secured an act removing the prohibition of episcopal clergy from ministering in Scotland, provided they subscribed to the Thirty-Nine Articles, but disbarring them from holding preferment or ministering in England. Gaskin continued his involvement with Scottish episcopal affairs, serving on the 'English committee' of the duke and duchess of Buccleuch's fund for augmenting the incomes of episcopal bishops and clergy. In 1796 he visited the Isles of Scilly on behalf of the SPCK, to review the needs for schools and teachers there. Van Mildert described Gaskin in 1799 as 'a rising star of the Old High Church firmament' (Mather, 158). He was closely associated with the Hackney Phalanx.

During Gaskin's secretaryship of the SPCK its income and expenditure increased tenfold; district committees were established on the model of the British and Foreign Bible Society, more than doubling the membership and establishing it as a national rather than a London society; the National Society for Promoting the Education of the Poor in the Principles of the Established Church in England and Wales was established to manage the society's educational interests; a diocese in India was successfully lobbied for; and committees were established in India and New South Wales. However Gaskin, who was deeply suspicious of institutional reform, resisted these developments. Joshua Watson referred to 'all the fears and prejudices of our willing Secretary' (Clarke, 155). In opposing attempts to allow district committees to make recommendations to the society's board, he was defeated by Watson, Norris, and Christopher Wordsworth. The separation of the educational work of the SPCK into the National Society was, in fact, an attempt to avoid another battle with Gaskin.

In 1822 Archbishop Manners-Sutton asked the bishop of Ely to give Gaskin a prebendal stall so he might resign the secretaryship of the society and the lectureship of Islington parish church, where he had given the Sunday afternoon lecture for forty-four years. He resigned on 4 March 1823, and was succeeded at the SPCK by his son-in-law, William Parker.

He died from 'a rapid succession of epileptic fits' on 29 June 1829 at the rectory, Stoke Newington. His wife had predeceased him.   W. M. JACOB

Sources DNB · Foster, *Alum. Oxon.* · *GM*, 1st ser., 99/2 (1829), 91, 183–6, 280–82 · W. K. L. Clarke, *A history of the SPCK* (1959) · E. A. Varley, *The last of the prince bishops: William Van Mildert and the high church movement of the early nineteenth century* (1992) · H. Cnattingius, *Bishops and societies: a study of Anglican colonial and missionary expansion, 1698–1850* (1952) · F. C. Mather, *High church prophet: Bishop Samuel Horsley (1733–1806) and the Caroline tradition in the later Georgian church* (1992)

Archives LMA, annotated agenda | CUL, SPCK Archive

Likenesses S. W. Reynolds, mezzotint, pubd 1820 (after W. Owen), BM, NPG · oils, Holy Trinity Church, London, Society for Promoting Christian Knowledge

Gaskin [*née* France], **Georgie Evelyn Cave** (1866–1934), designer, was born on 8 December 1866 at Cliff Cottage, Belle Vue, Shrewsbury, the elder daughter of William

Georgie Evelyn Cave Gaskin (1866–1934), by William Smedley-Aston

Hanmer France, contractor's agent, and his wife, Frances Emily Cave-Brown-Cave. **Arthur Joseph Gaskin** (1862–1928), artist, designer, and teacher, was born on 16 March 1862 at 169 Great Lister Street, Birmingham, the second son of Henry Gaskin, journeyman decorator, and his wife, Harriet Brassington.

Little is known about Georgie France until 1888, when as a student at Birmingham Municipal School of Art she began to win prizes with designs for needlework, wallpaper, and metalwork. Her work reflected a new emphasis on decorative art in the teaching of the school, an emphasis by which the city council hoped to raise standards of design in local industries. It also reflected the enthusiasm of young Birmingham artists for the medievalizing themes and craft revival of the arts and crafts movement. Arthur Gaskin, who had studied at the school and taught there from 1885, was one of these artists. The careers of Georgie and Arthur Gaskin depended on this fruitful coincidence between the city's forward-looking civic ideals and the backward-looking romanticism of the arts and crafts movement.

Arthur Gaskin began to work as a decorative artist about 1890, when he took up black and white illustration, inspired by woodcuts of *c*.1500. He developed a linear, decorative style that is seen at its best in *The Shepheardes Calender*, printed at William Morris's Kelmscott Press in 1896. His work encouraged a flowering of book illustration at the school, and Georgie France's illustrations in the early 1890s followed his style. But with *Divine and Moral Songs for Children* (1896) she changed to a more distinctive style that suited the Kate Greenaway world of her imagination, with doll-like children in smocks and bonnets, drawn in fine outline and often in colour.

Arthur Gaskin and Georgie France were married on 21 March 1894. In *Divine and Moral Songs* Georgie wrote that the pictures were dedicated to her husband 'by his pupil and wife'. But she was not his pupil in the marriage. He was a shy man who loved teaching—tradesmen did not always escape the Gaskin household without a drawing lesson. She was grander socially, more intellectual, and more in control of the family, and she dressed their two daughters, Joscelyne (*b.* 1903) and Margaret (*b.* 1907), in the style of her illustrations, sometimes to their embarrassment. The Gaskins were a thoroughly artistic couple and their marriage embraced a working relationship.

Arthur and Georgie worked together and apart. For a few years about 1900 Arthur painted in tempera but found the paintings difficult to sell. About 1898 he started designing enamelwork; Georgie took some to London in January 1899. In summer 1899 Georgie and he started producing jewellery. Georgie did all the designing, Arthur contributed enamelwork, and they both made the pieces with assistants. About 1900 Arthur started designing metalwork, and in 1903 he was appointed headmaster of the Vittoria Street School for Jewellers and Silversmiths, a branch of the school of art in the jewellery quarter, where the mass of Birmingham's (and thus Britain's) decorative metalwork was made. His task was to improve taste in the skilled but commercialized quarter and, as emblems of this task, he designed several pieces of presentation silver which were then executed by colleagues skilled in damascening, niello, and other techniques. Meanwhile in the south-eastern suburbs of Birmingham Georgie was at work on the jewellery on which their reputation mainly rests. At first it consisted of silver wirework set with coloured stones and enamel, graceful and technically unambitious. Gradually the scrolls of wire were encrusted with colour and detail, flowers in enamel, tiny birds cast in silver, and, by the time of the First World War, her work was often richly set with gems, resembling seventeenth- and eighteenth-century work. (The largest collection of the Gaskins' work in all media is in Birmingham Museum and Art Gallery.)

In 1924 Arthur resigned from Vittoria Street and he and Georgie retired to Chipping Campden, in the Cotswolds. Arthur returned to wood-engraving and painting in tempera; Georgie designed jewellery until a few months before her death. Arthur Gaskin died on 4 June 1928 in Chipping Campden. Shortly afterwards Georgie moved to West Malling, in Kent, where she died at her home, the White Cottage, on 29 October 1934. They are both buried in Chipping Campden.   ALAN CRAWFORD

Sources *Arthur & Georgie Gaskin* (1981) [exhibition catalogue, Birmingham Museum and Art Gallery] • A. Crawford, ed., *By hammer and hand: the arts and crafts movement in Birmingham* (1984) • *Memorial exhibition: Arthur Joseph Gaskin, A.R.E. (1862–1928)* [1929] [exhibition catalogue, Birmingham Museum and Art Gallery] • T. Hunt, ed., *Finely taught, finely wrought: the Birmingham School of Jewellery and Silversmithing, 1890–1900* (1990) [exhibition catalogue, Birmingham Museum and Art Gallery, 19 Sept 1990 – 13 Jan 1991] • *The collected letters of William Morris*, ed. N. Kelvin, 4 vols. (1984–96), vols. 3–4 • W. S. Peterson, *The Kelmscott Press: a history of William Morris's typographical adventure* (1991) • *Birmingham gold and silver, 1773–1973* (1973) [exhibition catalogue, Birmingham Museum and Art Gallery] • *Joseph Southall, 1861–1944: artist-craftsman* (1980) [exhibition catalogue, Birmingham Museum and Art Gallery] • V. Benson, diaries, 15 Jan 1899, priv. coll. • b. cert. [A. J. Gaskin] • b. cert. [G. E. C. France] • d. cert. [G. E. C. Gaskin] • CGPLA Eng. & Wales (1928) [A. J. Gaskin] • CGPLA Eng. & Wales (1934) [G. E. C. Gaskin]

Archives Birmingham Museum and Art Gallery, corresp. and artworks

Likenesses A. Gaskin, self-portrait, *c.*1880 (Arthur Gaskin), priv. coll. • group portrait, photograph, 1887–8 (with Arthur Gaskin), University of Central England, Birmingham, Birmingham School of Art archives • A. Gaskin, portrait, 1898, priv. coll. • W. Smedley-Aston, group portraits, photographs, *c.*1900–1913 (with Arthur Gaskin and their children), Birm. CL • A. Gaskin, portrait, 1902, priv. coll. • A. Gaskin, portrait, *c.*1910, priv. coll. • W. Smedley-Aston, photograph, Birm. CL [*see illus.*]

Wealth at death £14,306 10*s.* 2*d.*: probate, 11 Dec 1934, CGPLA Eng. & Wales • £9211 2*s.* 1*d.*—Arthur Joseph Gaskin: probate, 18 Aug 1928, CGPLA Eng. & Wales

Gaspars, John Baptist (1620?–1691), portrait painter, was born in Antwerp where he trained under Thomas Willeborts Bossaerts, a pupil of Van Dyck. He was admitted to Antwerp's Guild of St Luke in 1641 or 1642 and shortly after moved to England. Along with a number of other England-based artists such as Emanuel de Critz, Peter Lely, John Michael Wright, Remigius van Leemput, and Balthasar Gerbier, Gaspars was a buyer at the dispersal of Charles I's art collection, purchasing some fifty-five pictures, including Van Dyck's *Margaret Lemon* and Palma Vecchio's *Virgin and Child with SS Catherine and John the Baptist*, for a total of £1073. During the Commonwealth he worked for, and it is alleged taught, the former parliamentarian General Lambert, an amateur watercolourist. At the Restoration in 1660 he began a long-term association with Charles II's principal painter, Peter Lely, which was to earn him the nickname of 'Lely's Baptist' (Vertue, *Note books*, 2.135). Lely employed Gaspars to paint postures and drapery in his large Covent Garden studio. Reputedly a 'greate Judge of Painting' (Buckeridge, 400), and clearly familiar with Lely's style and method of working, Gaspars and fellow artist Parry Walton were hired by Lely's executors following Lely's death in 1680 and each paid £2 3*s.* to value Lely's collection and any works by him or his assistants which remained in the studio. Unlike his earlier purchases at Charles I's sale, Gaspars appears not to have bought any pictures at Lely's sale, only spending small amounts of money on pigments and studio-prop pieces of material. Largely known now as a posture painter for other artists, after Lely's death he subsequently painted postures for Godfrey Kneller and John Riley; he also produced several portraits of his own including a *Charles II* (Painter–Stainers' Hall, London), and *Thomas Hobbs*, presented by the antiquarian John Aubrey to Gresham Hospital (Royal Society, London), as well as portraits of aristocratic sitters such as Henry, first earl of Stamford (priv.

coll.) and Sir Justinian Isham (priv. coll.). His portrait of Catherine of Braganza was engraved by Edward le Davis in 1683 as part of a series of five full-length portraits of the royal family published by Moses Pitt between 1682 and 1684. Gaspars's draughtsmanship was much praised by contemporaries (interestingly, one of his purchases at Charles I's sale was a small set of mechanical instruments, possibly for drawing) and he produced what many considered to be some excellent designs for tapestries—he was described by Buckeridge as 'eminent for his Designs for Tapistry' (ibid.)—and a number of copies after Lely, usually in two colours, for the mezzotinter Jan van Somer. His pencil copy of Van Dyck's *Lords John and Bernard Stuart* (print room, BM) was engraved by the engraver and printseller Richard Tompson. In keeping with the short-lived fashion for etching in the early 1650s, Gaspars also made a few prints of his own; in 1653 he etched four plates for John Davies' translation of Charles Sorel's *The Enchanted Shepherd* and a large etching of *The Banquet of the Gods* (print room, BM).

Acclaimed as a 'good painter of the Flemish school' Gaspars died in London in 1691 and was buried in St James's, Piccadilly.

DIANA DETHLOFF

Sources Vertue, *Note books*, 2.135 · [B. Buckeridge], 'An essay towards an English school of painters', in R. de Piles, *The art of painting, and the lives of the painters* (1706), 398–480, esp. 400 · D. Dethloff, 'The executors' account book and the dispersal of Sir Peter Lely's collection', *Journal of the History of Collections*, 8 (1996), 15–51, esp. 47 · A. Griffiths and R. A. Gerard, *The print in Stuart Britain, 1603–1689* (1998) [exhibition catalogue, BM, 8 May – 20 Sept 1998] · E. K. Waterhouse, *The dictionary of British 16th and 17th century painters* (1988) · W. L. F. Nuttall, 'King Charles I's pictures and the Commonwealth sale', *Apollo*, 82 (1965), 30 · A. Macgregor, ed., *The late king's goods* (1989) · Ex-Gildebroeder, *De Gilde van St. Lukas en Tael en Kunst: Open Brief aen de Maetschappyen deelgenooten van de feesten op 21 en 22 Augusty 1854, te Antwerpen, door een Ex-Gildebroeder* (Antwerp, 1854)

Gaspey, Thomas (1788–1871), novelist and journalist, born at Hoxton on 31 March 1788, was the son of William Gaspey, a lieutenant in the navy. While a youth he wrote verses for yearly pocket books, and when about twenty contributed to *Literary Recreations*, a monthly publication edited by Eugenius Roche of the *Morning Post*. Soon afterwards he was engaged as parliamentary reporter on the *Morning Post*, contributing also dramatic reviews, clever political parodies, and reports of trials for treason. In this paper he wrote an 'Elegy on the Marquis of Anglesey's Leg', which, however, was mistakenly attributed to Canning. He was employed on the *Morning Post* for sixteen years, followed by three or four years on the *Courier*, a government paper, as sub-editor. Meanwhile, he had married Anne Camp in 1810 or 1811, and begun his own publications with a novel, *The Mystery* (1820), followed by *Calthorpe, or, Fallen Fortunes* (1821), *The Lollards, a Tale* (1822), and other works.

In 1828 Gaspey bought a share in the *Sunday Times*, and raised its tone as a literary and dramatic organ with the help of Horace Smith, the Revd T. Dale, Alfred Crowquill, E. L. Blanchard, Gilbert à Beckett, and other contributors.

His novels and other publications continued with *The Pictorial History of France* (1843), written in conjunction with G. M. Bussey, *The Life and Times of the Good Lord Cobham* (2 vols., 1843), *The History of England from George III to 1859* (4 vols., 1852–9), *The Political Life of Wellington* (1853), and several other works.

Gaspey was for many years the senior member of the council of the Literary Fund. He was a very kindly man, genial, witty, and an excellent mimic. The last twenty years of his life were spent quietly on his property at 4 Ordnance Terrace, Shooter's Hill, Kent, where he died on 8 December 1871, aged eighty-three, and was buried at Plumstead, Kent.

Gaspey was survived by his wife, who died on 22 January 1883. His son Thomas W. Gaspey PhD, of Heidelberg, who died on 22 December 1871, became well known in his own right as the author of works on the Rhine and Heidelberg, and of several linguistic handbooks. Another son, William Gaspey (who was born at Westminster on 20 June 1812 and died at Brixton on 19 July 1888), was also a prolific writer in prose and verse.

C. W. SUTTON, rev. NILANJANA BANERJI

Sources Allibone, *Dict.* · private information (1889) · catalogue [BM] · catalogue, Advocates' Library, Edinburgh
Wealth at death under £300: probate, 22 Dec 1871, *CGPLA Eng. & Wales*

Gasquet, Francis Neil [*name in religion* Aidan] (1846–1929), cardinal and historian, was born on 5 October 1846 in Somers Town, north London, the third son of the six children of Raymond Gasquet, a physician whose family had emigrated from Toulon during the French Revolution, and his wife, Mary Apollonia, daughter of Thomas Kay of York. He was educated from 1862 at Downside School, Stratton on the Fosse, near Bath, a small Catholic boarding-school attached to the Benedictine priory of St Gregory the Great, which he entered as a monk in 1866. His ecclesiastical studies took place from 1866 to 1870 at Belmont Priory, Hereford, then the central noviciate of the English Benedictines. Before his ordination to the priesthood on 19 December 1874 he had established himself at Downside as an energetic and competent teacher of history and mathematics. He had no formal university education, but was an enthusiast for the learned tradition of Benedictinism, and in the 1870s worked on the first complete catalogue of the Downside Library. In 1878 he was elected prior of the Downside community, which made him both superior of the monastic community and headmaster of the school.

Gasquet's seven years as prior were crucial for Downside's future growth. The community, driven from Douai in France in 1794, had settled in reduced circumstances at Downside in 1814. By the 1870s its buildings and facilities, especially its church (a pastiche Gothic creation of 1823), seemed inadequate, and Gasquet, who combined a medievalist's romanticism with a Victorian love of progress, liked to think big. He began the construction of a new church, the transepts of which were opened in 1882. It was the beginning of a conventual church which was to become, by the time of its consecration in 1935, England's

Francis Neil Gasquet (1846–1929), by James Russell & Sons

largest post-Reformation abbey church. He attempted to expand and improve the curriculum of the school and open both monastery and school to a wider world. In the *Downside Review*, which he co-founded in 1880, he hoped to inaugurate a tradition of scholarship.

In July 1885, after eighteen months of unsatisfactory health, Gasquet resigned the priorship, apparently a broken and exhausted man. In the years that followed, with the patronage of Cardinal Manning, to whom he was related by marriage, Gasquet (resident in London first with his mother and later in Great Ormond Street and Harpur Street), began a wide reading of monastic history and source material in the British Museum and the Public Record Office. He sought, from the personal perspective of a monk, to reassess the history of the English monasteries, especially in the crucial years before the Henrician dissolution. He also endeavoured to present his fellow English monks with a model of monastic life based on large resident communities under an abbot, which had not been possible during the years of persecution when monks spent most of their life on missionary work. His publications came fast and furious, beginning with the two-volume *Henry VIII and the English Monasteries* (1888–9), which became a historical best-seller. This was followed by *Edward VI and the Book of Common Prayer* (1890), which he produced in collaboration with Edmund Bishop, a scholar of deep erudition.

Gasquet was awarded a DD by Pope Leo XIII in 1891, but

his reputation as a historian, based on a solid narrative style and an intuitive ability to discover new sources, was largely undermined by the Cambridge medievalist G. G. Coulton and, in a celebrated lecture after Gasquet's death, by his monastic confrère, Dom David Knowles. Coulton regarded Gasquet as doubly suspect, both as an unusually inaccurate scholar, and as a devious agent of Roman priestcraft. Knowles regarded Gasquet's capacity for carelessness as amounting almost to genius. Although later scholarship, in its revisionist way, endorsed some of Gasquet's findings about the more positive features of late medieval monasticism, his writings are flawed by the weaknesses his critics identified. His *Lord Acton and his Circle* (1906), though a useful introduction to that subject, is marred by misdatings and poor transcriptions. Nevertheless Gasquet was the first historian of the dissolution of the monasteries to explore methodically the papers of Thomas Cromwell and the court of augmentations, as well as the pension list of Cardinal Pole. He was also the first to appreciate the value of using medieval books as evidence of the tastes and interests of their scribes and to use medieval sermon notes.

In 1896, when his reputation for scholarship was at its height, Gasquet went to Rome as a member of the special commission to study the question of Anglican orders; its findings led to 'Apostolicae curae' (13 September 1896), Pope Leo XIII's encyclical condemning Anglican orders as invalid. This was to usher in the final part of Gasquet's career, his time in the papal curia. He combined his activities in Rome with the position of abbot president of the English Benedictine congregation, which he held from 1900 to 1919. Following the papal bull *Diu quidem* (1899), the three priories of the congregation, including Downside, became independent abbeys. At this time he was also titular abbot of St Albans. In 1903 he came close to becoming fourth archbishop of Westminster in succession to Cardinal Herbert Vaughan, when his name appeared on the terna submitted to Rome. In 1907 he was made president of the Vulgate Commission by Pope Pius X; this body was charged with a revision of the text of the Vulgate Bible. In May 1914 he was created cardinal-deacon of San Giorgio in Velabro and, in December 1915, cardinal-deacon of Santa Maria in Campitelli. He became a cardinal-priest in 1924. He took part in the conclave of 1914 which elected Pope Benedict XV, an occasion overshadowed by the beginning of the First World War. Gasquet was fiercely anti-German; he pressed the British cause, fearing a German bias in Rome, and took a leading part in the negotiations which led to the appointment of a British minister to the Vatican in December 1914. The first minister, Sir Henry Howard, was a near contemporary of Gasquet's at Downside, and his appointment mitigated Gasquet's isolation as the only English high curial council official. Gasquet's years as a curial cardinal, resident in the Vulgate Commission at the Palazzo San Calisto in Trastevere, were dominated in the early years by the war, but later he was able to return to more congenial scholarly interests. In 1917 he became prefect of the archives of the Holy See, and in 1919 librarian of the Holy Roman church. Many practical improvements, including reshelving many of the books, were made in the organization of the library during his time. He played a full part in the Roman Congregations and was at the centre of English life and influence on Rome. In 1924 he received King George V and Queen Mary at the Vatican Library in great state.

Gasquet had an elegant courtly bearing, an upright carriage, and a handsome demeanour, which even Coulton, seeing him working at his books, acknowledged. He was of medium height, 5 feet 6 inches, and developed a full head of grey hair. His tendency to pomposity was ameliorated by his sense of humour. He particularly delighted in Irish jokes and was a skilled raconteur. He was, despite his paternal ancestry, John-Bullish in his manner and attitudes, patriotic, and bluff. During the First World War Cardinal Hartmann, archbishop of Cologne, reflected to Gasquet: 'Eminence I will not insult you by talking of the war.' 'Eminence,' replied Gasquet, 'I will not mock you by talking about peace.' He had a slight stroke shortly after his eightieth birthday from which he never fully recovered. He died at the Palazzo San Calisto, Rome, on 5 April 1929 from pneumonia, having suffered for many years from a weak heart. He was buried on 15 April in the abbey church at Downside, where a vast and exotic monument designed by Sir Giles Gilbert Scott was erected to his memory.

DOMINIC AIDAN BELLENGER

Sources *The Times* (6 April 1929) • *Downside Review*, 47 (1929), 124–56 • S. Leslie, *Cardinal Gasquet: a memoir* (1953) [incl. passages from Gasquet's unpubd autobiography] • D. Knowles, 'Cardinal Gasquet as a historian', in D. Knowles, *The historian and character and other essays*, ed. C. N. L. Brooke and G. Constable (1963), 240–63 • D. A. Bellenger, 'Cardinal Gasquet's papers at Downside', *Catholic Archives*, 4 (1984), 40–47 • N. J. Abercrombie, *The life and work of Edmund Bishop* (1959) • G. G. Coulton, *Fourscore years: an autobiography* (1943) • M. Anderson de Navarro, *A few more memories* (1936)
Archives Downside Abbey, corresp. and papers | CUL, corresp. with Lord Acton • NL Ire., letters to John Redmond • U. St Andr., corresp. with Wilfred Ward
Likenesses J. Crealock, portrait, 1924, Downside Abbey • E. Carter Preston, tomb effigy, 1933, Downside Abbey • S. Elwes, charcoal drawing, Downside Abbey • J. Russell & Sons, photograph, NPG [*see illus.*] • A. Savage, portrait, Downside School

Gass, Ian Graham (1926–1992), geologist, was born on 20 March 1926 at 273 Whitehall Road, Gateshead, co. Durham, the son of John George Gass, mechanical engineer, and his wife, Lilian Robinson, *née* Peacock. Because his father worked abroad Gass was brought up by an aunt in Gateshead until the family returned to England at the beginning of the Second World War and settled in Huddersfield. He was educated at the Royal Grammar School, Newcastle upon Tyne, transferring to the Free Grammar School of King James, Almondbury, Huddersfield, before joining the Royal Navy in 1944. The war ended before he finished his training as a Fleet Air Arm pilot, and he spent the next two years in Malaya in the Royal Army Service Corps, leaving with the rank of captain. He entered the University of Leeds, where William Quarries Kennedy was professor of geology, and after graduating with a BSc in geology in 1953 he joined the staff of the Sudan geological survey. On 2 July 1955 he married (Florence) Mary Pearce (b. 1930/31), secretary, and daughter of Arthur Pearce,

farmer, of Bamford, near Rochdale, Lancashire; they had a daughter, Katherine, and a son, Graham. He spent the next five years working for the Cyprus geological survey until the growth of the EOKA movement made field mapping dangerous: his work in the Troodos Mountains formed the basis of his Leeds PhD, awarded in 1960.

In 1960 Gass was appointed assistant lecturer at the University of Leicester, returning to Leeds in 1961 as a lecturer. He led the Royal Society expedition in 1962 to investigate the eruption of the volcanic island of Tristan da Cunha, and another Royal Society expedition to investigate volcanoes in southern Arabia in 1964: he published his findings in a chapter in *African Magmatism and Tectonics* (1970), which he co-edited, dedicated to Kennedy, who had set up the Research Institute of African Geology at Leeds in 1955. In 1963 he became a member of the Royal Society volcanology subcommittee, which he chaired from 1971 to 1979. His discovery that the Troodos complex in Cyprus was oceanic made a significant contribution to the theory of plate tectonics, which in the 1960s revolutionized ideas of the formation of the earth's crust, and he went on to investigate areas of similar rocks in Oman, bringing together the results in *Ophiolites and the Ocean Lithosphere* (1984).

In 1969 Gass was appointed foundation professor of earth sciences at the Open University, set up by the Labour government to provide distance learning. He prepared the earth sciences section of the science foundation course, first offered in 1971, and with his team wrote the introductory text, *Understanding the Earth* (1971), the first textbook on earth sciences to be published after the plate tectonics revolution: this was widely used in British universities, and the third edition was published in 1992, with a new preface written by Gass. He developed three Open University courses in the 1970s: the introductory course, 'Geology', first offered in 1972, for which all students were sent thousands of specimens of rocks, and plaster casts of fossils, together with a collapsible microscope; 'The earth's physical resources' (1974); and 'Oceanography' (1977). He chose the University of Leeds as the venue for the very popular Open University summer schools in earth sciences, and when the Open University Geological Society, one of the largest student societies, was set up he was invited to become president. Very successful at attracting funding for advanced analytical equipment he was able to build up a research centre with an international reputation, especially for volcanological studies, and the department of earth sciences became one of the leading departments of the Open University. In 1982 he gave up his position as head of department, accepting a personal chair, in order to devote more time to research. He retired in 1991.

Gass was elected a fellow of the Royal Society in 1983, and was president of the International Association for Volcanology and Chemistry of the Earth's Interior from 1983 to 1987. He was awarded the Prestwich medal of the Geological Society of London in 1979, and the Murchison medal in 1988. He underwent a coronary by-pass operation in 1981 and suffered a stroke in 1987, from which he gradually recovered; he died on 8 October 1992 in Bedford General Hospital, following another stroke and was buried eight days later. He was survived by his wife and their two children.   ANNE PIMLOTT BAKER

Sources K. G. Cox, *Memoirs FRS*, 41 (1995), 171–82 • *The Independent* (17 Oct 1992) • *Annual report of Open University Geological Society* (1992) • WWW • b. cert. • m. cert. • d. cert.
Likenesses photograph, 1981, repro. in Cox, *Memoirs FRS*, 170 • photograph, repro. in *The Independent*
Wealth at death £17,068: probate, 8 Dec 1992, CGPLA Eng. & Wales

Gassiot, John Peter (1797–1877), electrician, was born in London on 2 April 1797. He went to school at Lee and was for a few years a midshipman in the Royal Navy. He married, on 6 February 1819, Elizabeth Scott, and had nine sons and three daughters; six of his children survived him. Gassiot was a member of the firm of Martinez, Gassiot & Co., wine merchants, of London and Oporto. He was a generous promoter of science. His house on Clapham Common was always open to his fellow workers, and was provided with the best apparatus for scientific experiments. One of those workers was James Clerk Maxwell, who carried out experiments aimed at establishing the unit of electrical resistance at Gassiot's laboratory during the later 1860s.

Gassiot, along with William Sturgeon and others, was one of the founding members of the London Electrical Society in 1837. He remained the society's treasurer until 1841 when he was replaced by Charles Vincent Walker who took over the whole of the society's administration for its final few years. Gassiot's electrical soirées, where invited guests were treated to spectacular displays of electrical phenomena, were famous. He became a fellow of the Royal Society in 1841 and was active within the society's reform movement during the 1840s. He was one of the founders of the Chemical Society in 1845. He was also a magistrate of Surrey.

Gassiot had a significant role to play in the Royal Society's financial affairs during the second half of the century. In 1859 he was instrumental in the foundation of the scientific relief fund for the assistance of scientific men and their families in financial difficulties. He first raised the issue at a meeting of the Philosophical Club and gained the support of the presidents of several of the specialist scientific societies before raising the issue before the council of the Royal Society. Following the British Association for the Advancement of Science's decision to discontinue their financial support for the Kew observatory, Gassiot, as a member of the Royal Society committee established to consider the matter, offered to set up a fund to finance magnetic observations at the observatory. From 1872 to 1899 it was therefore financed by the Gassiot Trust Fund under the supervision of the Royal Society's Kew committee, of which Gassiot was originally the chairman.

Gassiot wrote forty-four papers in various scientific periodicals: the first, an 'Account of experiments with voltameters having electrodes exposing different surfaces', appeared in the *Transactions of the London Electrical Society*

(1837–40); the last, 'On the metallic deposit obtained from the induction discharge vacuum tubes', was in the *British Association Report for 1869*, section 46. His work was almost entirely concerned with the phenomena of electricity.

In the *Philosophical Transactions* for 1840 and 1844, Gassiot described experiments made with a view to obtaining an electric spark before the circuit of the voltaic battery was completed. For these experiments he constructed batteries of immense power, commencing with a water battery of 500 cells, and ending with 3500 Leclanché cells. In 1844 he published perhaps his most important research—his experiments with a battery of 100 Grove's cells, specially made of glass, with long glass stems, so that each cell was effectually insulated from its neighbours. With this battery Gassiot was able to prove that the static effects of a battery increase with its chemical action, a fact which had been denied or doubted by other experimenters. Using a delicate micrometer apparatus he showed that the electric spark could be produced before contact: a powerful argument against the contact theory of voltaic electricity. In conducting a series of experiments upon the decomposition of water by electricity, Gassiot showed that when the liquid was under a pressure of 447 atmospheres it offered no extra resistance to the passage of the electric current.

In 1852 Grove discovered the dark bands, striae, or stratification, of the electric discharge; and he devoted much time and money to the study of this phenomenon. He showed that these striae accompany all electric discharges in vacuum tubes, and that they occur equally well when, as is the case when the discharge takes place in the Torricellian vacuum of a barometer, no contact breaker is employed. His researches on this matter formed the subject of the Bakerian lecture before the Royal Society in 1858. Gassiot extended this research and further proved that when vacuum tubes are exhausted of their gases beyond a certain limit, the electric discharge will not pass at all. Gassiot died at his home, St John's House, St Helens, Ryde, Isle of Wight, on 15 August 1877.

W. J. HARRISON, rev. IWAN RHYS MORUS

Sources I. R. Morus, 'Currents from the underworld: electricity and the technology of display in early Victorian England', *Isis*, 84 (1993), 50–69 • M. B. Hall, *All scientists now: the Royal Society in the nineteenth century* (1984) • JCS, 33 (1878), 227 • *Nature*, 16 (1877), 388, 399–400 • private information (1889) • d. cert. • CGPLA Eng. & Wales (1877) • IGI
Archives PRO, corresp. relating to Kew Observatory, BJ1 • Royal Institution of Great Britain, London, records of experiments | CUL, letters to Sir George Stokes • Inst. EE, archives, corresp. with Sir Francis Ronalds • RS, letters to Sir John Herschel • RS, letters to Sir John Lubbock
Wealth at death under £250,000: probate, 7 Sept 1877, CGPLA Eng. & Wales

Gast, John (c.1772–1837), trade unionist and radical, was born in Bristol, the son of Robert Gast, a seller of milk. He had at least two brothers, and at some time married Elizabeth, who outlived him, but nothing else is known of his family. Soon after finishing his apprenticeship he left Bristol, and after a short spell at Portsmouth Royal Dockyard in 1797, where he acted as the workers' spokesman in complaints against one of the quartermen, he went to London. He worked there in the Thames dockyards for the rest of his life. He was a leader in the great shipwrights' strike of 1802, of which he wrote and published a remarkable account; he also became a publican between 1810 and 1812, and was for a time a dissenting preacher in Deptford. In 1814 he was imprisoned for fortune-telling.

As a political reformer, Gast organized support for Sir Samuel Romilly in his candidacy at Bristol in the 1812 general election, but voted for both Romilly and the more radical Henry Hunt, whose ally he became. In 1818 he led the formation of the Philanthropic Hercules, a very early attempt at a general union of trades, a cause he supported for the rest of his career. He also became a leading member of the group of radical revolutionaries led by James Watson and Arthur Thistlewood that eventually in 1820 organized the Cato Street conspiracy, although it is unclear how far Gast was involved in this. He then took the leading role in organizing artisan support for the great campaign in favour of Queen Caroline against her husband, George IV.

In 1824 Gast was one of the leaders of the new Thames shipwrights' union, which organized a great strike in 1825. Gast also formed a committee of trades' delegates in 1825 to campaign against the move to repeal the legalization of trade unions the previous year. This committee went on to establish the world's first trade union paper, the *Trades' Newspaper*, of which Gast was manager. In the later 1820s he formed a new general trades organization, and was also one of the leaders in a campaign that in 1828 secured the defeat of a bill to control friendly societies; they went on to draw up a bill of their own, which was passed into law in 1829. In 1830 he was active in the new co-operative movement, and a deist lecturer in a group of radicals, freethinkers, Spenceans, and Owenites that met at various places during the next few years. He was also a prominent member of the National Union of the Working Classes between 1831 and 1833, and in 1836 was a founder member of the London Working Men's Association that drew up the famous People's Charter.

Gast died of a cerebral haemorrhage at Rotherhithe on 5 November 1837, after a long and exceptionally full career that made him one of the outstanding working-class leaders of his time and a pioneer of the labour movement.

IORWERTH PROTHERO

Sources I. J. Prothero, *Artisans and politics in early nineteenth-century London: John Gast and his times* (1979) · S. J. Webb and B. P. Webb, *The history of trade unionism, 1666–1920* (1919) · E. P. Thompson, *The making of the English working class* (1963) · J. Gast, *Calumny defeated, or, A compleat vindication of the conduct of the working shipwrights during the late disputes with their employers* (1802) · d. cert.
Archives BL, letters to Francis Place, Add. MSS 27803, 27829, and set 57

Gast, Luce of (*supp. fl. c.*1230), supposed writer and translator, appears as knight and lord of the castle of 'Gat' (variously 'Gast', 'Galt', 'Gaut', 'Gant', 'Gad', 'Gait') near Salisbury (no identification has ever been made), and as the ostensible translator of the *Tristan en Prose* according to the prologue contained in many manuscripts of the work.

His language he says is not the French of France, but the insular variety, since he was born in England. In fact, his language is not at all Anglo-Norman. It is said elsewhere in the work that he abandoned his labours through death and that the completion is due to Hélie de Boron, which appears to be a pseudonym (through the influence of Robert de Boron) representing an entirely fictional person.

There is disagreement about what is meant to be credited to Luce and whether or not he existed as a real person. R. L. Curtis argues that Luce commenced a biography of Tristan and that Hélie, desiring to produce a much broader 'roman de la Table Ronde', substituted his own plan more or less at the point where Tristan and Kaherdin leave Brittany, and continued the work to its conclusion. For E. Baumgartner, on the other hand, Luce, which she regards as a *senhal* or poetic pseudonym, wrote a complete romance of Tristan, now lost, and Hélie in writing his own romance refers to this at various points, in the same way that the *Lancelot en prose* refers to *le conte* ('the tale'). The *Tristan en Prose* survives in over eighty manuscripts comprising four principal redactions from the period 1240–1340. The earliest form, representing the combination of Luce and Hélie, is dated to *c.*1230.   TONY HUNT

Sources R. L. Curtis, 'The problem of the authorship of the prose *Tristan*', *Romania*, 79 (1958), 314–38 · R. L. Curtis, 'Who wrote the prose *Tristan*? A new look at an old problem', *Neophilologus*, 67 (1983), 35–41 · E. Baumgartner, 'Luce del Gat et Hélie de Boron: le chevalier et l'écriture', *Romania*, 106 (1985), 326–40

Gaster, Moses (1856–1939), scholar and rabbi, was born in Bucharest, Romania, on or about 16 September 1856, the eldest son of Abraham Emanuel Gaster (d. 1926), then the commercial attaché of the Netherlands consulate in that city, and his wife, Phina Judith Rubinstein. Gaster was educated at the universities of Bucharest and Leipzig. After graduation from Bucharest he proceeded to the rabbinical seminary in Breslau, at which he was ordained as a rabbi in 1881, but the same year he returned to Bucharest as a lecturer specializing in the history of Romanian literature and in comparative mythology. Gaster also found employment as a school inspector and a member of the council for the examination of teachers. However, he incurred the wrath of the Romanian political leadership through his activities on behalf of Romanian Jews, who had become entitled to Romanian citizenship under the treaty of Berlin (1878); this right had been obtained only after considerable pressure from Disraeli, acting at the behest of Jewish leaders such as the Rothschilds in Britain and France. Gaster was expelled from Romania in 1885; he never returned. Instead he sought refuge in England, where he had friends and was naturalized in 1893; he spent the rest of his life there. In 1890 Gaster married Leah Lucy, the only child of Michael Friedlander (1833–1910), principal of Jews' College, London. There were seven sons and six daughters of the marriage.

Gaster's subsequent career falls into several interconnected spheres. He was a man of outstanding intellect, a most accomplished linguist—speaking, reading, and writing many European and Near Eastern languages (the Gaster papers, now housed at University College, London, are in ten languages), and a leading scholar in many fields. In 1886 he accepted an invitation to deliver at Oxford the Ilchester lectures, on Graeco-Slavic literature (published 1887); he was reappointed Ilchester lecturer in 1891. In purely Jewish subjects he was responsible for the first translation of the Jewish liturgy into Romanian (1883); additionally he published a number of monographs on subjects as diverse as Hebrew illuminated bibles of the ninth and tenth centuries and early Jewish magic. He also wrote in the fields of mythology and folklore (on which he became an internationally acknowledged authority) and on the Samaritans. In 1891 he published a two-volume study of Romanian language and literature which came to be regarded as the standard work on the subject. His intellectual eminence was publicly recognized through (for example) his election as vice-president of the Royal Asiatic Society and of the English Folklore Society, of which he became president. In 1930 he was elected a fellow of the Royal Society for Literature. Meanwhile, the authorities in Romania had become, after a fashion, reconciled with him. In 1929 he became an honorary member of the Romanian Academy and he was also invested with the Romanian orders of the Crown and Bene Merenti.

In 1887 Gaster accepted an invitation to fill the historic office of *haham* of the Spanish and Portuguese Jews in England, which had remained vacant since the death of Rabbi Benjamin Artom eight years previously. The *haham*—meaning, literally, 'wise man'—was in effect the chief rabbi of the Spanish and Portuguese Jews, who followed the Sephardi ritual and who had constituted the first Jewish community of the Cromwellian resettlement in the mid-seventeenth century. By the end of the eighteenth century they were far outnumbered by the Ashkenazi, or German and Yiddish-speaking Jews, who had come to Britain from central Europe. But the Sephardim, led for much of the nineteenth century by Sir Moses Montefiore, regarded themselves as the senior of the two Jewish 'nations' in Britain, and stubbornly refused to place themselves under the ecclesiastical authority of the Ashkenazi chief rabbinate, an office filled from 1845 until his death in 1890 by Nathan Marcus Adler, and from 1891 until 1911 by his son Hermann Adler.

Gaster was not, of course, Sephardi. That did not bother the elders of the Spanish and Portuguese Jews, who needed a strong figure to stand up to the presumed authority of the Adlers. And it certainly did not bother Gaster. He relished and exulted in the role of underdog, which might have been made for him, and used the majesty of his office (an image which in a sense he created) to make the voice of Sephardi distinctiveness heard in every corridor of power to which he could gain access. He had no hesitation in turning personal prejudices into religious principles, a task made easier by Hermann Adler's comparative ignorance of Talmudic matters. So, for example, while Adler used his influence discreetly on behalf of the Conservatives in the general election of 1906, Gaster was publicly outspoken in his support for Liberalism. While Hermann Adler denounced before the royal commission on divorce (1910) the activities of foreign-born rabbis who

insisted on their right to conduct religious marriages on their own authority, Gaster in turn denounced Adler. In 1929 Gaster helped undermine the attempt of Adler's successor, J. H. Hertz, to have the Ashkenazi chief rabbi recognized as the sole authority competent under English law to certify Jewish slaughterers of cattle and poultry.

If the Spanish and Portuguese leadership hoped that Gaster would put the Sephardim back on the map of Anglo-Jewry, they were certainly not disappointed. But Gaster fell out with this leadership, just as he fell out with most other people with whom he came into contact. Gaster was (and had already in Romania been) a confirmed Zionist, a believer in the right of Jewish national self-determination, and an espouser, therefore, of the view that Jews did indeed constitute a separate nationality. He was one of the earliest supporters in England of the founder of political Zionism, the Austrian Jewish journalist Theodor Herzl. When, on 13 July 1896, Herzl had made his first public speech on political Zionism (just a few months after the publication of his seminal pamphlet *Der Judenstaat*), the meeting had been chaired by Gaster at the Jewish Working Men's Club, Whitechapel. Gaster helped found the English Zionist Federation (of which he later became president) in 1899, and it was at his house in London that the dialogue was initiated between leading Zionists and the representative of the British Foreign Office, Sir Mark Sykes, which resulted in the promulgation of the Balfour declaration in 1917.

Gaster was immensely proud of his part in the triumph of Zionism. But the Sephardi leadership became increasingly angry and alarmed over his activities, which they viewed as compromising, undermining, and perverting his ecclesiastical position—and also their status as British citizens. Gaster's claim (in a volume of essays edited by the Manchester Zionist Harry Sacher in 1916) that those who regarded themselves simply as 'Englishmen of the Jewish persuasion' were guilty of 'an absolute self-delusion' enraged the Sephardi elders. Other causes of friction added to their list of complaints. Chief among these were his management of the Judith Montefiore Theological College, Ramsgate (which was closed in 1896), and his defence of the right of foreign-born Jews not to be conscripted into the British armed forces during the First World War. There was, additionally, a feeling that Gaster had come to put his national profile before his purely parochial obligations. When the Zeppelin raids over London were launched by the Germans, Gaster took refuge in Brighton. This provided the pretext for his dismissal in 1918. But he continued for the next two decades to harry the Anglo-Jewish establishment at every opportunity. Gaster died of heart disease on 5 March 1939 at The Gables, Appleton, Berkshire, and was buried in the Hendon cemetery of the Spanish and Portuguese Jews, north-west London.

GEOFFREY ALDERMAN

Sources A. M. Hyamson, *The Sephardim of England: a history of the Spanish and Portuguese Jewish community, 1492–1951* (1951) · G. Alderman, *Modern British Jewry* (1992) · C. Bermant, *Troubled Eden* (1969) · L. Stein, *The Balfour declaration* (1961) · CGPLA Eng. & Wales (1939) · DNB · d. cert. · personal knowledge (2004)

Archives BLPES, corresp. · JRL, collection of Hebrew and other codices · UCL, corresp. and papers
Likenesses M. Maimon, oils, Spanish and Portuguese Synagogue, London · photographs, Spanish and Portuguese Jews' Congregation, London · portraits, Spanish and Portuguese Jews' Congregation, London
Wealth at death £3218 5s. 8d.: probate, 5 July 1939, *CGPLA Eng. & Wales*

Gastineau, Henry (1790/91–1876), landscape painter, was born in London to a family with Huguenot origins. After serving an apprenticeship to an engraver, he made his public début as the engraver of a plate entitled *Fountain Cottage, Camberwell Grove*, for volume fourteen of John Britton's *Beauties of England and Wales*, published in 1811. The direction of Gastineau's career quickly changed, however: following study at the Royal Academy Schools, he began to exhibit landscapes there in 1812, and, from 1816, at the British Institution. Some of these early works were oils, but it was as a watercolourist that he increasingly found employment, initially as a supplier of views for the print trade, and, after his début at the Society of Painters in Water Colours in 1818, as a successful exhibiting artist. Indeed, Gastineau's association with the society was to dominate his long career: he became an associate member in 1821, full membership followed in 1823, and he showed with the society for fifty-eight years continuously, including eleven exhibits when aged eighty-five. In all, he exhibited about 1300 works, including about 200 sketches, and his support for the society extended to all aspects of its affairs.

Given Gastineau's productivity, it is not surprising to find a certain sameness among his works. Throughout his career he portrayed a familiar round of architectural subjects and attractive views of the home counties, the southern coast, Yorkshire, Scotland, and Wales. From 1829, however, he did branch out, showing continental scenes following visits to Italy, Germany, and Switzerland, some of which were said to have taken place in the company of his friend J. M. W. Turner. Once his career was established, Gastineau remained faithful to the style pioneered in the early years of the Society of Painters in Water Colours. Although this increasingly seemed old-fashioned, his work was never less than technically competent and at his best, as in works such as *Carrick-y-Rede* (exh. Society of Painters in Water Colours, 1839; Birmingham Museum and Art Gallery), painted after a visit to Ireland, he could create large-scale, highly finished landscapes full of drama. Gastineau's landscape sketches, lightly worked in wash over pencil, showed that he could also work outside the rather tired picturesque conventions of the day.

Despite his popularity as an artist, Gastineau relied heavily on teaching, both privately and at various schools, and this income was further supplemented by the regular contribution of drawings to topographical publications. These included eighteen subjects for T. K. Cromwell's *Excursions in the County of Kent* (1822), thirteen scenes for W. H. Ireland's *History of Kent* (4 vols., 1829–30), numerous views for Jones & Co.'s *Wales Illustrated in a Series of Views* (2 vols., 1830–31), and, as late as 1860, he contributed nineteen works to John Tillotson's *Picturesque Scenery in Wales*.

Gastineau's works were mainly reproduced by steel-engraving, but lithography was also used, and he himself occasionally drew subjects on stone. His works are held in the British Museum and the Victoria and Albert Museum in London, the Birmingham Museum and Art Gallery, and a large variety of other provincial galleries in England, Wales, and Ireland.

On 7 July 1819 Gastineau married Mary Knaggs (d. 1861), and in the early 1820s he built for himself a house, Norfolk Lodge, in Cold Harbour Lane, Camberwell, where he continued to live until his death there on 17 January 1876. One of his daughters, Annie Jane, married a steel tube millionaire named Hills. His second daughter, **Maria Gastineau** (bap. 1827, d. 1890), landscape painter, was baptized at St Matthew's, Brixton, Surrey, on 24 October 1827. She also worked in watercolours, developing a style close to her father's. She exhibited at various institutions from 1855 to 1889, and she was a member of the Society of Female Artists. The exhibition in 1867 of an Italian scene suggests that she may well have accompanied her father on some of his foreign travels. She died on 27 September 1890 at Llantysilio, Llangollen, in north Wales, apparently of exhaustion on a mountain walk. GREG SMITH

Sources J. L. Roget, *A history of the 'Old Water-Colour' Society*, 1 (1891), 507–8; 2 (1891), 207–9 · A. Rose, *Henry Gastineau, 1792–1876: centenary exhibition* (1976) [exhibition catalogue, Birmingham Museums and Art Gallery] · Mallalieu, *Watercolour artists*, 2nd edn, 1.140 · Graves, *RA exhibitors* · IGI · *Art Journal*, 38 (1876), 106 · Bankside Gallery, London, Royal Watercolour Society MSS · DNB
Likenesses carte-de-visite, c.1860–1869, NPG · photograph, c.1863, Bankside Gallery, London, Royal Watercolour Society archive · wood-engraving, repro. in *ILN* (5 Feb 1876)
Wealth at death under £5000: resworn probate, Nov 1876, *CGPLA Eng. & Wales*

Gastineau, Maria (bap. 1827, d. 1890). *See under* Gastineau, Henry (1790/91–1876).

Gastrell, Francis (1662–1725), bishop of Chester and writer on theology, was born at Slapton, Northamptonshire, on 10 May 1662, the second son of Henry Gastrell, gentleman, and Elizabeth Bagshaw, his wife. Following attendance at Westminster School (1677–80), where he came under the tutelage of Dr Richard Busby, Gastrell matriculated at Christ Church, Oxford, on 17 December 1680, subsequently graduating BA in 1684, MA in 1687, BD in 1694, and DD in 1700. Having been ordained deacon on 29 December 1689 and priest on 25 June 1690, in 1694 he was elected preacher at Lincoln's Inn and six years later was nominated as chaplain to Robert Harley, the newly appointed speaker of the House of Commons. With Harley's patronage, he was installed as a canon of Christ Church in January 1703, and seven months later was married at St Helen's, Bishopsgate, to Elizabeth Mapletoft (d. 1761). In 1711 he served as proctor in convocation for the Christ Church chapter and in the same year was appointed chaplain to Queen Anne. Finally, in 1714, after years of loyal service to Harley (now lord treasurer), he was at last rewarded with the see of Chester, vacant upon the translation of Sir William Dawes to the archdiocese of York, and

Francis Gastrell (1662–1725), by George Vertue, 1728 (after Michael Dahl, *c*.1720)

on 14 April 1714 was consecrated bishop at Somerset House chapel, thereupon resigning the preachership of Lincoln's Inn but continuing to hold *in commendam* his canonry of Christ Church.

While still at Westminster, Gastrell met and entered upon a lifelong association with a group of gifted contemporaries, several of whom, including Francis Atterbury and George Smalridge, would also become canons of Christ Church. Indeed, between 1698 and 1700, Atterbury spent most of his time in Gastrell's lodgings at Lincoln's Inn, researching and writing his refutation of *The Authority of Christian Princes over their Ecclesiastical Synods* (1697), William Wake's controversial assault on the autonomous powers of convocation. As yet close friends with careers in the church to make, both were eager to establish their reputations in the theological and ecclesiastical controversies of the day. As early as 1696, Gastrell had published anonymously *Some Considerations Concerning the Trinity* and in the following year was invited by Archbishop Tenison to give the Boyle lectures, which he published as *The Certainty and Necessity of Religion in General … Establish'd in Eight Sermons* (1697). As well as asserting his orthodoxy by defending the doctrine of the Trinity against its Socinian critics, he became a keen supporter of the charity schools movement and, in 1708, launched an assault upon the tenets of deism with a volume subsequently reprinted in four separate editions during the 1720s. As a scholar and theologian, though, Gastrell's lasting reputation depended primarily on his *Christian Institutes*, a volume of precepts collected from the Old and New testaments, first published in 1707 and reprinted at regular intervals

between 1721 and 1832. He is also remembered for a comprehensive survey of the parishes in his sprawling Chester diocese, known as the *Notitia Cestriensis*.

Yet Gastrell was not simply a scholar. Augustan England was a society torn by bitter political as well as religious divisions in which, propelled by his ambition, Gastrell played a full and sometimes factious part. In 1709 he allowed his lodgings to be used for a clandestine meeting between Atterbury and Harley over the politically charged convocation issue, and thereafter served as a facilitator of further meetings and correspondence between them. However, two years later, as the tory party began to splinter, he would find himself forced to choose between his patron and his friend. By 1711, Harleian influence in Oxford was well established, with Gastrell and fellow canon Dr William Stratford both clearly identified as the lord treasurer's agents. Atterbury, on the other hand, now dean of Christ Church, was engaged to build up a rival tory connection for Lord Keeper Harcourt and Secretary of State St John and soon became locked in a bitter feud with canons Gastrell, Stratford, and Smalridge; indeed, by the end of 1712, the dean and Gastrell had almost come to blows. The animosity generated by these rivalries only began to abate when, in June 1713, under strong pressure from Harcourt, the lord treasurer finally persuaded Queen Anne to accept Atterbury's appointment to the diocese of Rochester and the deanery of Westminster; ten months later, Gastrell and Smalridge were themselves installed as bishops of Chester and Bristol respectively.

Having thus earned their elevation, it came as a matter of general surprise when both of these hitherto loyal Harleians abandoned the government in the Lords and joined with Bishop Robinson of London in opposition to a motion suggesting that fears of the protestant succession being in danger were groundless. And though Gastrell subsequently voted for the Schism Bill, he also preached a sermon affirming the duty of reconciliation before Queen Anne herself, adopting Romans 14: 18 as his text: 'For he that herein serveth Christ is well-pleasing to God, and approved of men'. For increasingly puzzled onlookers, though, the acid test of his loyalty came in November 1715, when, with the Pretender's army marching south into England, the archbishop of Canterbury promulgated a declaration supported by the greater part of the episcopal bench in which he sought to dissuade Anglicans from giving succour to the rebels. Upon being asked to add his own name to this document, Gastrell declined even to read it, saying that 'it was his fixed principle not to sign any public engagements but what the law required' (*Portland MSS*, 7.213). His public reputation would henceforth be that of a crypto-Jacobite.

For the last seven years of his life, Gastrell was enmeshed in almost continuous controversy and subsequent litigation over the validity of degrees awarded by faculty at Lambeth for purposes of ecclesiastical preferment. Prior to the presentation of Samuel Peploe as warden of Manchester College in 1717, the bishop had already proposed that this office should be annexed to the see of Chester, in order both to augment the meagre diocesan revenues and to provide a more convenient administrative centre. He now responded to the situation by, first, attempting for as long as possible to prevent the 'Manchester cause' from coming to trial; and, second, by launching himself into print, thereby earning a vote of thanks from convocation at Oxford for upholding the rights of the universities. In August 1722, the case was at last brought into court at Lancaster assizes on a writ of *quare impedit* and a finding returned in favour of the plaintiffs. Gastrell again refused Peploe admission, had his counsel offer a bill of exceptions to the general decision, and appealed the case to the court of king's bench, which in May 1725 ruled definitively against him.

For his part, Peploe became convinced that the bishop's obstinacy was political rather than legal in its motivations. 'No small rejoyceings have been made by some on this occasion; not to say scandalous reflections on their superiors', he told Archbishop Wake in April 1722, referring to a further delay in the trial proceedings. 'I believe … that this has been made a Party Cause on one side from the beginning' (Christ Church Wake MSS, Arch. W. Epist., 9/182). Although he clearly underestimated Gastrell's genuine concern for the privileges of the universities, Peploe was able to cite other evidence which suggested that the bishop was not above intruding party bigotry into the exercise of his episcopal functions. It was alleged, for example, that in the autumn of 1720 Gastrell had denied letters dimissory to a candidate for holy orders, for no better reason than the man's assertion of 'the King's title against one who advanced certain propositions which manifestly subverted it' (ibid., 8/296; Peploe to Wake, 13 Sept 1720). Neither, by all accounts, was this an isolated instance. Although seemingly parochial and petty at first sight, such obstructionist tactics were perceived as a great boost to battered tory morale in his diocese.

But was Gastrell in any real sense a Jacobite? In the opinion of some local whigs he was not without complicity in what subsequently became known as the Atterbury plot, and at the bishop of Rochester's trial in 1723 he was the only tory prelate able and willing to speak in Atterbury's defence. Yet though he subsequently visited his old friend and sometime adversary in the Tower, in order to receive the latter's thanks before he went into exile, Gastrell's own involvement in the plot itself was incapable of proof and he remained in his diocese until the end of his life. He died from gout on 24 November 1725 at Christ Church, Oxford, where he was also buried.

STEPHEN W. BASKERVILLE

Sources G. V. Bennett, *The tory crisis in church and state: the career of Francis Atterbury, bishop of Rochester* (1975) · F. Gastrell, *Notitia Cestriensis, or, Historical notices of the diocese of Chester*, ed. F. R. Raines, 1, Chetham Society, 8 (1845); F. R. Raines, introduction, 2/2, Chetham Society, 21 (1850) · Christ Church Oxf., Wake MSS Arch. W. Epist. 7–10 · *The manuscripts of his grace the duke of Portland*, 10 vols., HMC, 29 (1891–1931), vols. 4–5, 7 · L. Colley, *In defiance of oligarchy: the tory party, 1714–60* (1982) · Foster, *Alum. Oxon.* · S. Hibbert Ware, *Lancashire memorials of the rebellion*, 2 pts in 1, Chetham Society, 5 (1845) · *N&Q*, 6 (1852), 529–30 · *N&Q*, 2nd ser., 1 (1856), 318–19 · *DNB*

Likenesses G. Vertue, line engraving, 1728 (after M. Dahl, *c*.1720), BM, NPG [*see illus.*] · oils (after M. Dahl), Christ Church Oxf.

Gatacre, Thomas (1531/2–1593), member of parliament and Church of England clergyman, was born at Gatacre Hall in the parish of Claverley, Shropshire, third son of William Gatacre (*d.* 1577) and his wife, Eleanor, née Mytton (*d.* after 1533). His family, settled there since the time of Edward the Confessor, remained zealous Catholics. His father intending him for the law, Gatacre was admitted to the Middle Temple, probably in 1553, where he became a friend of John Popham, afterwards lord chief justice.

The accession of Mary brought both father and son into parliament, Thomas sitting for Gatton, Surrey, in that of April 1554 and William as knight of the shire for Shropshire in that of November 1554. Simeon Ashe related that during his years as a law student Gatacre was impressed by the constancy of protestants at whose interrogations, while visiting relatives 'then high in place and power', he was present (Ashe, 41). He was perhaps also influenced by his fellow member for Gatton, Thomas Copley, a convinced protestant. In an attempt to confirm him in the old faith his parents sent him to the English College in Louvain in 1558–9, settling on him an estate worth £100 a year as an inducement. Since his name does not disappear from the Middle Temple records until November 1558 his final conversion and consequent confrontation with his parents presumably occurred at the very end of Mary's reign.

Finding him confirmed in his protestantism Gatacre's father recalled him from Louvain after six months, demanded the revocation of the settlement and thereupon disowned him. According to Ashe, Gatacre found friends who supported him at Oxford until 1564 and then for four years at Magdalene, Cambridge. These may have included Robert Dudley, earl of Leicester, chancellor of Oxford University, whose chaplain he subsequently became.

Ordained deacon on 24 August 1568 by Edmund Grindal, bishop of London, Gatacre described himself as BA, recently scholar of Magdalene, and aged thirty-six. Since he was ordained priest on the following 28 October as 'lately of St Edmund Lombard Street', a city parish in the archbishop of Canterbury's gift, it would seem that he had been immediately appointed, perhaps on Grindal's recommendation, to serve there during a vacancy (London, Guildhall Library, MS 9535/1, fol. 139r).

Gatacre evidently proved satisfactory, since on 19 February 1570 Archbishop Parker presented him to the rectory. His activities during the following months, however, are mysterious and confused. For unknown reasons he was not instituted to St Edmund's until 21 June 1572. On 16 February 1573 Parker's register again records letters of presentation on his behalf, yet the London register lists no reinstitution. It must be surmised that he seriously compromised himself in some way in the wake of the *Admonition to Parliament* of 1572, for at the end of 1573 Gatacre was one of those whom the ecclesiastical commissioners pressed for unqualified subscription to the Book of Common Prayer in an effort to enforce conformity in the capital. His submission survives at the Inner Temple Library (Petyt MS 538/47, fol. 594).

At about this time Gatacre married Margaret Piggott of Hertfordshire: their eldest son, Thomas *Gataker, was born in the parish of St Edmund in September 1574. On 25 January 1577 he was instituted vicar of Christ Church Greyfriars, granted to him on 12 May 1576 by the master and commonalty of St Bartholomew's Hospital. Although he had resigned by January 1579, he continued to lecture there.

Gatacre's early militancy appears to have been replaced by a moderate evangelical stance. Not known to have resisted Archbishop Whitgift's renewed demands for conformity in 1584, he received Whitgift's faculty, on 19 December that year, as Leicester's chaplain and a preacher licensed by the archbishop, to hold St Edmund in plurality with Newington, Surrey, a peculiar of Canterbury. Three days later he was instituted rector on the crown's presentation, the living being in the lord chancellor's gift during the vacancy of the see of Worcester.

Following John Aylmer's visitation of London diocese in 1586, Gatacre was cited for allowing unlicensed preachers to occupy the pulpit at St Edmund's. By the time of the visitation of 1589 he was clearly living wholly at Newington. Although the churchwardens stated that St Edmund's was well served, they knew of no hospitality kept in the parish. Gatacre himself failed to appear at the visitation, later claiming that he had not been informed of the correct date. To the registrar's evident surprise he then left court without petitioning for release from the excommunication which his absence had automatically incurred.

Gatacre was not listed at St Edmund's at all in the visitation of 1592 and in his will of the following year he described himself only as 'parson of Newington'. His slender assets were left wholly to Margaret for the bringing up of their children. His books were to be sold and the profits divided between his three sons. He calculated that they would each therefore receive £15. His Geneva Bible went to Margaret, his 'best' Bible to Thomas, and other bibles to his younger sons, George and Henry, and to his daughters, Anna and Elizabeth. The will was dated 8 January 1593 and his successor at Newington, where Gatacre was probably buried, was instituted eight days later. Margaret was granted probate on 2 April 1593.   BRETT USHER

Sources S. Ashe, *Gray hayres crowned with grace* (1655) • HoP, *Commons, 1509–58*, 2.195–6 • GL, MS 9535/1, 138v, 139r • Inner Temple Library, London, Petyt MS 538 • S. Clarke, *The lives of thirty two English divines*, in *A general martyrologie*, 3rd edn (1677), 248 ff • LMA, DL/C/334, fols. 221v–222r • LMA, DL/C/616, 354 • register of John Whitgift, LPL, 1, fol. 457v; 2, fol. 316v • P. S. Seaver, *The puritan lectureships: the politics of religious dissent, 1560–1662* (1970) • registered will, PRO, PROB 11/81, sig. 27, fol. 217r–v • G. Hennessy, *Novum repertorium ecclesiasticum parochiale Londinense, or, London diocesan clergy succession from the earliest time to the year 1898* (1898) • *Registrum Matthei Parker, diocesis Cantuariensis, AD 1559–1575*, ed. W. H. Frere and E. M. Thompson, 3 vols., CYS, 35–6, 39 (1928–33)
Wealth at death approx. £45 in books: will, 1593, PRO, PROB 11/81, sig. 27

Gatacre, Sir William Forbes (1843–1906), army officer, born at Herbertshire Castle, near Stirling, on 3 December 1843, was the third son of Edward Lloyd Gatacre (1806–1891) and his wife, Jessie, second daughter of William Forbes of Callendar House, Falkirk, Stirlingshire. Their second son was Major-General Sir John Gatacre. The father was squire of Gatacre in the parish of Claverley, Shropshire, a manor held by his ancestors from the time of Henry III, and was high sheriff of Shropshire in 1856.

Educated at Mr Hopkirk's school, Eltham, Kent, and at Sandhurst from August 1860 to December 1861, Gatacre was commissioned on 18 February 1862 as ensign in the 77th foot (later 2nd battalion Middlesex regiment), then stationed in Bengal. He was promoted lieutenant (by purchase) on 23 December 1864. He went to Peshawar with the regiment in November 1866, and in 1867 he spent six months' leave alone in the upper valleys of the Indus, shooting and exploring. He was invalided home with fever soon afterwards, and the 77th returned to England in March 1870. In November, disobeying regulations, he briefly visited the Franco-Prussian War. He was promoted captain (by purchase) on 7 December.

In February 1873 Gatacre entered the Staff College and, after two years there, was four years at Sandhurst (1875–9) as instructor in surveying. In 1876 Gatacre married Alice Susan Louisa, 'a charming and beautiful girl' (Gatacre, 35), third daughter of Anthony La Touche Kirwan, dean of Limerick, and they had three sons. In August 1880, after a year's service on the staff at Aldershot, he went back to India with his regiment. In January 1881 his baby son died of cholera. He was promoted major on 23 March 1881, and lieutenant-colonel on 29 April 1882. He was then serving on the staff of Sir Harry Prendergast at Rangoon; he returned to regimental duty in 1883 in Rangoon, and succeeded to the command of the regiment at Secunderabad on 24 June 1884.

From 17 December 1885 to 30 September 1889 Gatacre was deputy quartermaster-general of the Bengal army. He was promoted brevet colonel on 29 April 1886. In the spring of 1886 he accompanied the commander-in-chief, Sir Frederick Roberts, on two long tours, but he did not become one of Roberts's 'ring'. In the successful Hazara expedition of 1888 he was chief staff officer, and showed his capacity for activity and endurance. He was mentioned in dispatches and awarded the DSO. After temporary command of the Mandalay brigade for twelve months (1889–90) engaged in counter-insurgency operations and serving on the Tonhon expedition, he was made adjutant-general of the Bombay army at Poona, with the substantive rank of colonel and temporary rank of brigadier-general (25 November 1890).

Gatacre's wife left him for another man, and in 1892 he divorced her; the divorce was undefended. An enthusiastic jackal hunter with the Bombay Jackal Club, he was himself bitten by a jackal. Becoming temporarily deranged, he had his bungalow windows barred to prevent jackals jumping in.

Gatacre was in command of the Bombay district from January 1894 to July 1897, but from March to September of

Sir William Forbes Gatacre (1843–1906), by Elliott & Fry

1895 he was engaged in the Chitral expedition. He commanded the 3rd brigade of the relief force under Sir Robert Low, and on 20 April his brigade was sent forward as a flying column to relieve the besieged Chitral garrison. It reached Chitral on 15 May, after an arduous passage of the Lowari Pass, but the garrison had already been relieved by Colonel J. G. Kelly's force from Gilgit. Gatacre was made CB.

In the winter of 1895–6 Gatacre went to England for three months. On 10 November 1895 he married Beatrix Davey, daughter of Horace, Baron Davey; she survived him without issue. During the summer of 1896 he was in temporary command at Quetta, and during the first half of 1897 he was fighting the plague at Bombay. Plague deaths there in January rose to over 300 a day. Gatacre not only took care of his own troops but, appointed by the governor, was chairman of the plague committee. He repeatedly visited the houses of plague victims to ensure their removal to hospital, and, due largely to his energy and tact, the outbreak was well under control by July, when he left India to take command of a brigade at Aldershot. In 1900 the gold medal of the kaisar-i-Hind order was awarded him for this service.

Gatacre was a brave, dedicated, hard-working, if unoriginal, professional soldier. As his wife wrote, 'It was the soldiering that he loved' (Gatacre, 118). He was a small, lean man with a bristling moustache. Conan Doyle wrote of 'his gaunt Don-Quixote Face, and his aggressive jaw', but questioned whether he 'possessed those intellectual gifts which qualify for high command' (Conan Doyle, 167). Restless, energetic, a physical fitness enthusiast proud of his feats of endurance, Gatacre drove himself and his subordinates hard.

In January 1898 Gatacre went to Egypt, with the local rank of major-general, to command the British brigade in Kitchener's advance up the Nile to reconquer the Sudan. He was criticized for driving his men too hard, and they nicknamed him 'General Backacher'. Believing their rifle ammunition ineffective, he ordered them to dum-dum 3 million rounds, using files. On 8 April Kitchener's army attacked the Mahdist forces under the Emir Mahmud in their entrenched camp on the Atbara. Gatacre himself led his brigade's attack on the zariba. His flag-bearer was fatally wounded, but Gatacre survived the fighting unscathed. He was promoted major-general on 25 June. In the operations, which ended with the capture of Omdurman (2 September), he commanded a division of two British brigades. He was mentioned in dispatches, made KCB (15 November), and received the Mejidiye (second class). The Sudan War brought his reputation to its peak; a friend wrote to him that he was 'becoming more famous every day' (Gatacre, 213).

On 8 December 1898 Gatacre took over command of the eastern district, with headquarters at Colchester. On 21 October 1899 he embarked for South Africa, to command the 3rd division of the army corps sent out under Sir Redvers Buller. Most of his division went to Natal to save Ladysmith, while Gatacre himself remained in Cape Colony, charged with the defence of the railway from East London to Bethulie and the country on each side of it. On 2 December Buller asked Gatacre if he could not close with the enemy, or otherwise hinder their advance southward. Gatacre decided to capture Stormberg railway junction by a night march and dawn attack. Due to mismanagement his men—two infantry battalions, mounted infantry and field artillery—were tired when, on 9 December, they started the night march. The Cape police guides misunderstood, Gatacre was confused, and the exhausted force blundered, lost, towards the Boer positions. In a confused 1½ hour battle his force was repulsed; the men retreated, demoralized and in disorder. They were lucky the Boers failed to counter-attack. Gatacre was unaware he had left behind about 600 men who had not been given the order to retreat. They and stragglers from the retreat surrendered. The defeat resulted from 'a most extraordinary combination of bad management and bad fortune' (Amery, 2.381). After it Gatacre continued confused: the map drawn to accompany his dispatch placed the battle 4 miles north of its actual location.

The Stormberg 'disaster'—one of the defeats of 'black week'—destroyed Gatacre's reputation with the government and military in Britain. Wolseley wanted him relieved of his command and restricted to lines of communication. Lansdowne cabled Buller to sack him, but Buller did not. Roberts wrote that Gatacre had shown 'a want of care, judgment, and even of ordinary military precautions' (Gatacre, 286), which disqualified him from serving where serious fighting was likely.

By Roberts's orders Gatacre acted on the defensive for the next three months, except for reconnaissances on 23 February and 5 March 1900. On 15 March he crossed the Orange River at Bethulie with his division, numbering 5000 men, and came in touch with the main army, which was at Bloemfontein. He was placed in charge of the lines of communication. After vague orders from Roberts, Gatacre detached a small force, five infantry companies (about 600 men) under Captain Robert M'Winnie, to Dewetsdorp. Following de Wet's successful offensive Roberts ordered their withdrawal. Gatacre passed on the order, but failed to warn of the danger from de Wet's force. Attacked by the Boers on 3 April, M'Winnie's force fought near Reddersburg. Gatacre set out to save them, but delayed and was too late. M'Winnie's force surrendered on 4 April and Gatacre failed to follow up de Wet. Roberts held Gatacre responsible, and on 10 April relieved him of his command and ordered him back to England. Bitter and resentful, he returned. Though still popular with the public, his military career had effectively ended.

Gatacre resumed command of the eastern district at Colchester, and remained there until 8 December 1903. He was placed on the retired list on 19 March 1904, but was employed for some months in connection with remounts and the registration of horses. In 1905, invited by Sir Lepel Griffin, he joined the board of the Kordofan Trading Company. Late in 1905 he went out, for the company, via the Sudan, to explore rubber forests in Abyssinia. He caught fever, apparently from camping in a swamp, died at Iddeni on 18 January 1906, and was buried in the Abyssinian Christian cemetery at Gambeila. A brave soldier, Gatacre's successful career of colonial campaigning ended when he was inadequate, though also unlucky, in his actions against the Boers. He was thereafter a disappointed man.

E. M. LLOYD, rev. ROGER T. STEARN

Sources *The Times* (6 March 1906) · B. Gatacre, *General Gatacre* (1910) · A. C. Doyle, *The great Boer War: a two years' record, 1899–1901*, 15th edn (1901) · G. J. Younghusband and F. E. Younghusband, *The relief of Chitral* (1895) · G. W. Steevens, *With Kitchener to Khartum* (1898) · J. F. Maurice and M. H. Grant, eds., *History of the war in South Africa, 1899–1902*, 4 vols. (1906–10) · T. Pakenham, *The Boer War* (1979) · L. S. Amery, ed., *The Times history of the war in South Africa*, 2 (1902) · L. S. Amery, ed., *The Times history of the war in South Africa*, 4 (1906) · *Hart's Army List* (1882) · Burke, *Gen. GB* · C. N. Robinson, *Celebrities of the army*, 18 pts (1900) · B. Farwell, *The great Anglo-Boer war* (New York, 1976); repr. as *The great Boer War* (1977)
Likenesses Bourne & Shepherd, photograph, repro. in Gatacre, *General Gatacre*, facing p. 74 · Elliott & Fry, photograph, NPG [*see illus.*] · Whitlock, photograph, repro. in Robinson, *Celebrities of the army* · photograph, repro. in Amery, ed., *Times history of the war in South Africa*, vol. 2, facing p. 370 · prints, NAM
Wealth at death £14,041 16s. 11d.: resworn probate, 25 April 1906, CGPLA Eng. & Wales

Gataker, Charles (bap. 1613, d. 1680). *See under* Gataker, Thomas (1574–1654).

Gataker [*formerly* Gatacre], **Thomas** (1574–1654), Church of England clergyman and scholar, was born on 4 September 1574 in his parents' house in Lombard Street, London, the son of Thomas *Gatacre (1531/2–1593), rector of St Edmund the King, Lombard Street, and his wife, Margaret

Piggott. In later life he changed the spelling of his name to Gataker 'to prevent miscalling' (Ashe, 41).

Education and life in London to 1611 Subject from childhood to migraine, Gataker was nevertheless so addicted to study that according to Simeon Ashe, who preached his funeral sermon, 'he needed a bridle rather than a spur' and exhibited 'a lovely gravity in his young conversation'. He matriculated at St John's College, Cambridge, in 1590. His father's death in 1593 left him 'not wholly destitute' but he was able to continue his studies only with the financial aid of friends (Ashe, 42–3); he graduated BA in 1594, and proceeded MA in 1597.

Cambridge set the pattern of Gataker's life. He attended the Greek lectures of John Bois (delivered from his bed at 4 a.m.) and was profoundly influenced by his tutors, Henry Alvey and Abdias Ashton, and by his older contemporary Richard Stock, with whom he formed a lifelong friendship. In 1596 he accepted a fellowship at newly endowed Sidney Sussex College but while college buildings were being constructed acted as tutor in the household of William Ayloffe of Great Braxted, Essex, teaching Hebrew to Ayloffe and preparing his son for entry to Cambridge. According to his own account he was ordained by John Sterne, suffragan bishop of Colchester, a relative of Mrs Ayloffe, who while visiting Great Braxted was impressed by Gataker's learning and urged him to enter the ministry. After some initial hesitation he accepted Sterne's overtures. There is, however, no record of the event in the London diocesan ordination book.

Gataker took up residence at Sidney Sussex in 1599. Since the college buildings were still incomplete he offered accommodation in his rooms to William Bradshaw, also a foundationer fellow. This act of courtesy resulted in another enduring friendship. For reasons which remain obscure Gataker spent little time in Cambridge thereafter, subscribing to the scheme of Ashton and William Bedell for the provision of preachers in neglected parishes in the vicinity of Cambridge. He undertook Sunday duties at Everton, on the borders of Huntingdonshire and Bedfordshire, resigning his fellowship six months later on Ashton's advice. This step seems to have happened after Bradshaw's retirement following his troubles for espousing the cause of John Darrell the exorcist.

Gataker returned to the environs of his native city about the end of 1600, becoming tutor to the family of Sir William Cooke of Charing Cross, whose wife, Joyce, was a relative. He preached occasionally at St Martin-in-the-Fields and was described, as he wryly recalled, as 'a prettie pert Boy' who nevertheless 'made a reasonable good Sermon' (Gataker, 34–5). James Montagu, first master of Sidney Sussex, attempted to lure him back to Cambridge with the offer of a lectureship in Hebrew which Lord Harington of Exton was prepared to finance. Finding him unwilling, Montagu used his influence instead to obtain for Gataker the lectureship at Lincoln's Inn, a post he took up in 1601. His initial salary was a modest £40 and until his marriage he continued to live with the Cookes, spending his vacations at their estate in Northamptonshire and for some years enjoying an annuity of £20 from the family. After his marriage—some five years after his appointment 'or thereabouts'—the benchers raised his stipend to £60 'without anie motion of mine' (ibid., 35).

Gataker proceeded BD in 1604 but in 1609, and subsequently, he refused to proceed to the degree of DD on the grounds that his income was insufficient to maintain the dignity 'and also because, like Cato the censor, he would rather have people ask why he had no statue than why he had one'. He declined the lectureship at the Rolls Chapel, Chancery Lane, worth twice his existing stipend, as well as livings offered by Sir Roger Owen, Sir William Sedley, and Robert Rich, third Lord Rich. He later stated that following the Hampton Court conference of 1604 he had preferred to rest content 'with a small portion in a priviledged place' than by moving to a better-endowed living 'to attract more distraction, and expose my self to the hazard of greater disturbance' (Gataker, 38). He resisted attempts to have him appointed a prebendary of St Paul's or an episcopal chaplain but accepted the honorary office of chaplain to Sir Henry Hobart, then attorney-general and a loyal patron throughout his life.

Rotherhithe, marriage, and early writings Gataker married the widow of William Cooper (her first name is unknown), becoming stepfather to two girls to whom he became so devoted that many assumed they were his own daughters. It was perhaps his new family responsibilities which in 1611 finally prompted him to accept a benefice, the rectory of Rotherhithe, Surrey. He resigned from Lincoln's Inn, although continuing as guest preacher both there and at Serjeant's Inn, where he had powerful friends. His first marriage ended in his wife's death following the birth in 1611 or 1612 of their only child, Thomas (d. 1639), but there is no record of her burial at Rotherhithe. His second wife, Margery, daughter of a clergyman, Charles Pinner, likewise died following the birth of an only child, Charles [see below]. Charles was baptized, and Margery buried, at Rotherhithe on 26 August 1613.

Remaining for some years afterwards, 'in a disconsolate solitude' (Ashe, 50), Gataker found time for study and for correspondence with such contemporaries as James Ussher and Samuel Ward, in 1617 publishing an edition of Ward's *Balme from Gilead*. During July and August 1620 he travelled through the Netherlands with a nephew and some friends in order to ascertain the present condition of Dutch protestantism, whose interests he believed imperilled by recent developments in English foreign policy.

Dedicated to Sir Henry Hobart and other leading lawyers, Gataker's first extant work, *Of the Nature and Use of Lots* (1619), defended the lawfulness of lots when not used for divination. This exposed him to attack as an advocate of games of hazard, and in 1623 James Balmford reprinted his 1594 diatribe against card-playing, adding criticisms of Gataker's work. The latter immediately issued a spirited restatement of his views, against the 'Imbecillitie' of Balmford's arguments in *A Just Defence of Certain Passages in a Former Treatise* (1623).

Altogether Gataker published no fewer than twenty-four tracts and sermons between 1619 and 1627, including his funeral sermon for Richard Stock, preached in April 1626 and published the following year as *Abrahams Decease*. This sustained spate of eloquence may have owed something to the fact that after his return from the Netherlands he married again; with his third wife, Dorothy, sister (according to Ashe) of Sir George and Sir John Farwell, he had three children: John (September 1622 to March 1627), Elizabeth (*bap*. 15 January 1624), and Esther (January 1625 to January 1627).

In early 1625 Gataker became an unwitting victim of court manoeuvres evidently designed to discredit the archbishop of Canterbury's chaplain Daniel Featley, a close friend of his. On the orders of King James himself, two books by Edward Elton, licensed for publication by Featley with an uncontentious commendatory preface by Gataker, were in February consigned to the flames at Paul's Cross as seditious and subversive. As a result Gataker endured a short term of imprisonment in the Fleet, from where, in the king's absence, he was released by Henry Montagu, first earl of Manchester, then president of the council. But 'afterward by his Majesties special command [I was] for a longer time confined to my house, and so restrained from my pastoral employment ...' (Gataker, 53).

The silent years, 1628–1637, and re-emergence Having survived the plague year of 1625, when the Rotherhithe register records more than 200 burials, Dorothy Gataker is said by Ashe to have died of consumption in 1627. She was buried at Rotherhithe on 15 August. It could be argued that imprisonment and house arrest at the personal behest of the king, and then the deaths of a bosom friend, two infant children, and a third wife within the space of only sixteen months, would have been enough to reduce any man to a state of temporary reclusiveness. There follows, however, a gap of no less than ten years in the sequence of Gataker's published writings. In his funeral sermon Ashe glides over it in silence but that it initially coincides with William Laud's rule as bishop of London (1628–33) suggests that Gataker was forced, or else chose, to maintain a low profile and to observe as an impotent, muzzled bystander Charles I sliding to disaster.

Within months of Dorothy's death Gataker married his fourth wife, Elizabeth (d. 1652), a citizen's widow 'whose comfortable conversation he enjoyed twenty-four years' (Ashe, 50). Perhaps they were the Thomas Gataker and Elizabeth Carlton married at St Peter-le-Poer on 12 August 1628. They had no children but for her sake he bought a private house so that if she survived him she would not be 'subject to anothers curtesie for removal' from the rectory house at Rotherhithe (Ashe, 50).

Gataker returned to print with a vengeance in 1637. Folio volumes of his collected sermons—all printed by John Haviland, but with numerous variants on behalf of several different publishers—reached the London bookstalls during the succeeding months. Between then and his death a further two dozen or so tracts, sermons, and learned editions left the London presses, several of them in Latin. With Charles I and parliament moving ever closer to outright conflict the claims of godly preaching were evidently high on the agenda. When in 1641, for example, George Walker raked up in print an old theological dispute with Anthony Wotton, Gataker vigorously defended Wotton in two separate tracts, as well as supplying a preface and postscript to one by Wotton's son, Samuel. He did this in the face of another personal tragedy: on 8 October 1639 his eldest son, Thomas, was buried at Rotherhithe. He had 'seen the most parts of the world wherewith we keep commerce' and 'returned home to his Father to die in peace' (Ashe, 50). Perhaps Gataker derived some consolation from celebrating, on 2 June 1640, the marriage of his only surviving daughter, Elizabeth, to William Draper.

The Westminster assembly Like James Ussher, Gataker had come to favour a judicious mixture of episcopacy and presbyterianism and in 1643 he was nominated to the Westminster assembly. In 1644 and 1645 he was placed on the committees appointed to examine ministers; to select scholars for the translation of the directory into Welsh; and to draft a confession of faith. During the deliberations of the latter he differed from the majority over justification, securing a less rigid definition which he accepted for the sake of unity. Meanwhile he had refused an offer of the mastership of Trinity College, Cambridge, from Edward Montagu, second earl of Manchester.

In the summer of 1645, however, Gataker's public career came to an abrupt end. He had suffered a near-fatal fit of 'Wind-Colic' in 1642 and a violent, second attack at this juncture meant that he was never able to return to the assembly (Gataker, 57). It was perhaps to offer its profound regrets that the assembly dispatched Jeremiah Whitaker and Cornelius Burgess to visit him on 5 August 1645. Gataker was nevertheless able to carry out a limited schedule of pastoral work and continued to write vigorously, on both classical and biblical subjects. In 1645 he published not only a Latin treatise on the tetragram but also *Gods Eye on his Israel*, a sermon inveighing against antinomianism. He returned to the latter theme in 1646 with *A mistake, or misconstruction, removed … In way of answer to … a Treatise of Mr John Saltmarsh*. The assembly offered him formal thanks for his 'pains' in composing it (Mitchell and Struthers, 444). Saltmarsh, however, promptly hit back and Gataker equally promptly countered with *Shadowes without Substance*, having first submitted it to the assembly for approval. He duly received thanks on 14 September 1646 for his 'great respect' towards them (ibid., 281). The dispute rumbled on and he later reissued *A Mistake* as *Antinomianism Discovered and Confuted* (1652).

Final years, 1649–1654, and influence Gataker signed the first address against the trial and execution of Charles I on 18 January 1649. His wife, Elizabeth, was buried at Rotherhithe on 21 August 1652, and in 1654 he published his last exercise in popular polemics, *A Discours Apologetical*. This was a comprehensive onslaught upon William Lilly for his 'shameless slanders' against himself in his quasi-astrological maunderings (Gataker, title-page). It is of particular value to the historian because of the many autobiographical references Gataker uses to bolster his arguments.

Gataker entered his last illness at the beginning of July 1654—Ashe provides a blow-by-blow account—and died of fever, probably at Rotherhithe, on 27 July, only a few weeks short of his eightieth birthday. He was buried in Rotherhithe parish church on 1 August when, at Gataker's own final insistence, Simeon Ashe preached his funeral sermon, published as *Gray Hayres Crowned with Grace* (1655). He had drawn up his will, with a typically godly preamble, on 17 July. Two codicils were added (19 and 21 July). It argues a man in full possession of his faculties and indeed Ashe declared that his mind was strong until the end. Running to six pages in a registrar's closely written transcript, it mentions a bewildering number of relatives and their families, including those of his stepdaughters, Mrs (Francis) Taylor and Martha Barnard (now deceased), and that of his daughter, Elizabeth Draper. He carefully renounced any remaining legal claim he may have had to the annuity which he had once received from the Cooke family and drew up a schedule of legacies to be handed over to his last wife's relations out of the remains of her marriage portion. Considering 'the iniquity and distraction of the tymes' he left £5 each to ten poor ministers and to eight poor ministers' widows, specifically naming Katherine Bradshaw. He also remembered two of Bradshaw's sons, as well as his daughter Sarah and her husband, a tenant of his. His property in Rotherhithe and four messuages in the City parish of St Thomas were left to his son Charles and a tenement in Plumstead, Kent, to Elizabeth and William Draper. The residue went to Charles, his sole executor. In the second codicil Gataker distributed ten copies of 'Mr Baxter's rest handsomely bound' to a sister, Mistress Carleton, to Lady Whitlocke, and to eight named cousins. Altogether monetary bequests amounted to at least £250, and his servants all received six months' wages. Charles was granted probate on 31 July.

Gataker combined some of the best qualities of the contemporary godly preacher, of the dedicated humanist scholar and, when occasion required it, of the rollicking, satirical pamphleteer. As his spirited onslaughts on Saltmarsh and Lilly show, he was not averse to a good scrap in public and many a turn of phrase suggests that he was fully acquainted with the effusions of Martin Marprelate which, as an undergraduate, he had presumably read with horrified fascination. Although there is an occasional suggestion of self-regard (if not actually self-righteousness) and, in his last works, a tendency to harp on his status as valetudinarian, he never pontificates, preserving 'a pleasing middle course' between a plain, homely style and that of the more witty, courtly preachers of his day (Emerson, 202). Although he was addicted to sprinkling his texts with classical references some of his asides could have come straight out of Shakespeare's best prose passages. Upbraiding Saltmarsh, for example, he observes: 'For my yeers, Sir, scof not at *old age*: you may live, if God pleas, to come to it your self' (*Shadowes without Substance*, 15).

But it was above all for his profound scholarship that Gataker impressed posterity. His edition of Marcus Aurelius, on which he worked for over forty years, was admired by Henry Hallam as the first classical text published in England with original, scholarly annotations. His *Opera critica*, handsomely edited by the Dutch theologian Herman Witsius, was published in Utrecht in 1698. The German classical scholar Morhoff doubted whether any critic of his age was to be preferred to Gataker 'for diligence and accuracy' (Emerson, 201).

Like many a godly preacher Gataker was touchy when his probity was called into question. Criticized for not resigning Rotherhithe to a more active incumbent in his last years he retorted that there was difficulty in finding a successor to suit both patron and parishioners, defending himself by going minutely into his receipts and expenditures in order to prove that he was not 'gripple' (grasping), spending most of his income on reparations and upon a stipend for a worthy curate. He further defended his 'wilful silencing' of himself at the Westminster assembly by expatiating upon his poor health (Gataker, 55–7).

The dedications which preface his many published sermons reveal that Gataker was a trusted member of a wide-flung godly network in the City, embracing senior lawyers, the Haberdashers' Company (of which he had been made free) and the East India Company, in the shape of Sir Thomas Smith. As well as the Cookes, his influential kinsmen included Richard Taylor, recorder of Bedford, and Sir Robert and Lady Brilliana Harley, at whose marriage he had preached.

Charles Gataker (*bap.* 1613, *d.* 1680), Church of England clergyman, only son of Gataker and his second wife, Margery, was admitted on 11 March 1629 to Sidney Sussex College, Cambridge, from where he graduated BA early in 1633. He transferred to Pembroke College, Oxford, from where he proceeded MA on 30 June 1636. For a time he served as chaplain to Viscount Falkland, before becoming in 1647 rector of Hoggeston, Buckinghamshire. By that year he had married; his wife's name was Anne, and the couple were probably the Charles Gataker and Anne Jones who married on 21 September 1647 at St Peter Paul's Wharf, London. Six sons of Charles and Anne were baptized at Hoggeston between August 1648 and April 1657.

Gataker conformed in 1662. In 1670 he published his father's *An Antidote Against Errour, Concerning Justification*, with his own attempt to reconcile the apparently conflicting standpoints on the issue of St Paul and St James. He also entered the fray against Catholics, with *Five Captious Questions* (1673) (revealing that he had debated the papacy with Falkland), and Quakers, with *An Examination of the Case* (1675). He died at Hoggeston on 20 November 1680, and was succeeded as rector there by his son Thomas (*d.* 1701).   BRETT USHER

Sources T. Gataker, *A discours apologetical* (1654) · S. Clarke, *The lives of thirty two English divines*, in *A general martyrologie*, 3rd edn (1677) [incl. Gataker's 'Life and death of Mr William Bradshaw'] · S. Ashe, *Gray hayres crowned with grace: a sermon preached … at the funerall of … Mr Thomas Gataker* (1655) · E. H. Emerson, *English puritanism from John Hooper to John Milton* (1968) · A. F. Mitchell and J. Struthers, eds., *Minutes of the sessions of the Westminster assembly of divines* (1874) · Venn, *Alum. Cant.* · J. T. Cliffe, *The puritan gentry: the great puritan families of early Stuart England* (1984) · P. S. Seaver, *The puritan lectureships: the politics of religious dissent, 1560–1662* (1970) · C. Hill, *Economic problems of the church* (1956) · parish register, Rotherhithe, LMA, P71/MRY/006 [baptism: Charles Gataker; burials: Margery Pinner, second wife; Dorothy Gataker, third wife] · parish register, Rotherhithe, LMA, P71/MRY/007/01 [burial: Elizabeth Gataker, fourth wife] · will, PRO, PROB 11/241, fols. 344v–347r · P. Lake, *The boxmaker's revenge* (2001) · private information (2004) [P. Lake] · IGI

Wealth at death over £250 in monetary bequests; plus property in Rotherhithe, City of London, and Plumstead, Kent: will, PRO, PROB 11/241, fols. 344v–347r

Gatenby, James Brontë (1892–1960), zoologist, was born at Wanganui, New Zealand, on 10 October 1892, the younger son of Robert McKenzie Gatenby, pharmacist, and his wife, Catherine Jane Brontë, a granddaughter of John Brontë of Down. He was educated at Wanganui Collegiate School, St Patrick's College, Wellington, New Zealand, and Jesus College, Oxford, of which he was an exhibitioner. He graduated with first-class honours in zoology in 1916, was demonstrator in forest zoology and human embryology in 1916–19, lecturer in histology in 1917, and senior demy of Magdalen in 1918. In 1919 he was senior assistant in zoology and comparative anatomy at University College, London, and was lecturer in cytology there in 1920. He was appointed professor of zoology and comparative anatomy at Trinity College, Dublin, in 1921. Later he became professor of cytology, a research chair specially created in 1959. He was MA, PhD (Dublin), DPhil (Oxford), and DSc (London). Gatenby married in 1922 Enid Kathleen Mary (Molly; *d.* 1950), daughter of C. H. B. Meade, barrister, of Dublin. They had two daughters and two sons, of whom the elder, P. B. B. Gatenby, became professor of clinical medicine at Trinity College. In 1951 he married Constance Harris, daughter of Captain W. W. Rossiter, of co. Wicklow.

As a boy Gatenby was fascinated by insects and collected butterflies. As a research worker he soon became interested in the structure of cells. The germ cells and early development of parasitic hymenopterans (insects with four transparent wings—including bees, wasps, and ants) attracted him first but he reverted at intervals to the study of insectan cytology. He was a cytologist in the classical descriptive style and his technique was superlative. He concentrated on the Golgi bodies, mitochondria, and other cytoplasmic structures, and studied these in many animals, from protozoans to humans. His description of the processes involved in fertilization of sponges was notable, as was his joint work with J. P. Hill on the corpus luteum of the platypus. He criticized new cytochemical techniques until they were proven, and was involved in many controversies. Yet he used modern methods when opportunity offered and he was convinced of their value, as witnessed by the enthusiasm with which he turned to the electron microscope in his later years. Much of his work on the structure of the germ cells, using classical methods, proved, in the light of later findings, to be nearer the mark than that of some of his rivals.

Gatenby took over a department in Dublin which was moribund. He laboured to build it up, but it was only after the Second World War that even the essentials of staff and equipment were forthcoming. As a teacher he inspired interest and enthusiasm; the knowledge he could impart was limited by his facilities but the inspiration was lasting. Several of his pupils occupied university chairs of zoology, among them his successor in Trinity College.

Gatenby was generous and warm-hearted and loved social contacts. He was apt to like, or dislike, a person almost at first sight, and liking soon developed into warm and lasting friendship; he sometimes attributed to imagined intrigue honest actions of which he did not approve.

Gatenby enjoyed travel; was visiting professor at Alexandria and visiting lecturer at Louvain; and went twice to the United States: as Theresa Seessel fellow of Yale (1930–31) and as visiting research fellow to the Argonne National Laboratory (1958). But long residence had made him Irish in outlook, and he was glad to return to fly-fishing its rivers and lakes, in which art he was skilled. He was an honorary fellow of the Royal Microscopical Society and of the Academy of Zoology of India and an honorary member of the Royal Society of New Zealand and of the International Society for Cell Biology. He died on 20 July 1960 while on a fishing holiday in Galway. He was survived by his second wife.

F. W. ROGERS BRAMBELL, rev. V. M. QUIRKE

Sources *The Times* (27 July 1960) · *Irish Times* (27 July 1960) · *Nature*, 187 (17 Sept 1960) · *Trinity*, 12 (1960) [Michaelmas 1960] · *Journal of the Royal Microscopical Society*, 53/1 (1961) · personal knowledge (1971) · *CGPLA Eng. & Wales* (1960) · *WWW*, 1951–60
Likenesses H. W. Addison, oils, TCD
Wealth at death £786: probate, 28 Oct 1960, *CGPLA Éire*

Gater, Sir George Henry (1886–1963), educational administrator and civil servant, was born in Southampton on 26 December 1886, the son of a solicitor, William Henry Gater (1855–1942) and his wife, Ada Mary Welch (1859–1939). After attending Winchester College and New College, Oxford, where he gained a fourth in classical moderations (1907) and a second-class degree in modern history (1909), and took the diploma in education, he joined Nottinghamshire county council in 1912 as assistant director of education under B. W. L. Bulkeley. He thus belonged to the generation of public-school men who sought to develop secondary education by county councils, which under the 1902 act replaced local school boards. Two years in Nottingham before the outbreak of the First World War gave him sufficient experience to apply for posts in other counties after an awe-inspiring period of military service as an infantry officer with the 9th Sherwood Foresters, the 6th Lincolnshire regiment, and the 62nd infantry brigade. His reputation as a former young brigadier preceded him wherever he went. Serving at Gallipoli and in Egypt as well as on the western front in France, he was wounded twice, mentioned in dispatches four times, awarded a DSO and bar, made a commander of the Légion d'honneur,

awarded the Croix de Guerre, and made CMG (1918). On completion of service, in January 1919, he was granted the honorary rank of brigadier-general.

In 1919 Lancashire county council, with 4000 teachers and 118,000 children, appointed Gater as director of education. He learned how to handle diplomatic relations between district committees with delegated powers and between the county council and the major county boroughs in the north-west which often dominated the discussions of the professional associations then being formed. In 1924 the breadth of his experience led the London county council (LCC), with 480,000 children in its schools, to invite him to succeed Robert Blair, who had been its first director of education. Two years later he married Irene (1896–1977), the daughter of John Bowyer Buchanan Nichols; one of her brothers was the poet Robert Malise Bowyer Nichols. They had one son.

At the time of Gater's directorship the Labour Party in the LCC, faced by a Municipal Reform majority, was working to promote equality of educational opportunity through the introduction of free secondary education, and to recruit support through the National Association of Labour Teachers. The LCC maintained secondary, trade, and central schools for children beyond the school leaving age of fourteen, but the majority of pupils in secondary schools were fee-payers. Councillors were asked to consider whether to increase the provision of secondary places and how to introduce a system of secondary selection which did not penalize the children of poor parents. Gater administered the reorganization of schools in the three-year plan for 1925–8, a slow recovery after the Geddes axe of 1921, and handled the cuts made after the 1931 economies. He used his public-school contacts to open up the range of candidates coming forward for teaching posts in the capital, and was keen on the promotion of new secondary schools. He was closely involved with the development of the Bloomsbury site for the University of London, and expressed a strong interest in the Survey of London which recorded the historic buildings. He was also respected for his judicious chairmanship of meetings on delicate questions, such as mental testing; he recommended no change in the system of secondary examinations.

Councillors were sufficiently impressed by Gater's skills to invite him, in 1933, to succeed Sir Montagu Cox as clerk to the LCC, an unusual career move because the post was normally held by a lawyer. He was knighted in 1936. The success of the Labour Party in gaining a working majority after the elections of 1934 placed Gater at the centre of its plans for progressive reform in such fields as housing, special services, and the designation of a green belt, and brought him into close contact with Herbert Morrison, the majority party leader. It drew him also to the attention of Malcolm MacDonald, a National Labour member of the National Government under Chamberlain and the son of the former Labour prime minister, who having become secretary of state for the colonies in May 1938 found himself dissatisfied with the style of his permanent secretary, Sir Cosmo Parkinson.

In July 1939 MacDonald secured permission to transfer Parkinson to the Dominions Office and to bring in Gater as his new permanent secretary. The senior civil servants in the Colonial Office were taken aback by this unconventional move, of which they first learned through the newspapers. Gater, however, had no time to build up confidence among his new colleagues. Indeed, he was unable to take up the post as arranged, because he was asked instead to support Sir John Anderson at the new Ministry of Home Security where his knowledge of local government was deemed invaluable. Gater went to the Colonial Office on 1 February 1940, but on 25 May he was again taken away, this time to the Ministry of Supply by his former chief, Herbert Morrison, with whom he returned to home security in October.

Gater finally took up his post at the Colonial Office on 13 April 1942, having missed some of the key meetings on post-war planning. He became responsible for the department's forward policy, which was announced by the secretary of state to the House of Commons on 13 July 1943. The delay in his arrival meant that he inherited the expansion in the size of the department and in the responsibilities of its subject divisions negotiated by Parkinson to handle post-war reconstruction. He served four secretaries of state during his five years as permanent secretary: Viscount Cranborne, Oliver Stanley, who served both the coalition and the caretaker administrations, and George Hall and Arthur Creech Jones, the ministers in Attlee's Labour government. All found him particularly sensitive to parliamentary opinion, partly as a result of his experience with elected members in local government. He conducted a number of negotiations with American representatives, stressing the importance to Britain of American public opinion, and he administered the ending of the Palestine mandate. He had a short sick leave in 1943–4 because of trouble in one eye, of which he subsequently lost the sight. He was appointed KCB in 1941 and promoted to GCMG in 1944.

Gater earned great respect from his contemporaries for his ability to concentrate on the essentials of administration and to show sympathy for those who brought problems to him from all levels. He had prestige without vanity and never allowed attention to detail to obscure a common purpose. In addition he was an excellent chairman, which meant that he remained in great demand after his retirement in 1947. A substantial proportion of his energies was devoted to the business of Winchester College, of which he was warden from 1951 to 1959, having become a fellow in 1936, and to the Polish Education Committee of which he was chairman. He, his father, and his son were all Wykehamists. As warden he supervised the appeal for funds for a new hall, and secured the appointment of Desmond Lee as headmaster. Although he and his wife moved to live near Oxford, he continued to have a *pied-à-terre* in London from which to fulfil his many obligations. In the mid-1950s he held seven chairmanships, including those of the special overseas appointments committee, the Schools' Broadcasting Council of the United Kingdom, and the Building Apprenticeship and Training Council.

On behalf of the Board of Trade he chaired the film studio committee in 1948 and the working party on film production costs in 1949. He was a member of the five-man committee on intermediaries in 1949, which investigated the risks of corruption after the Lynskey tribunal on the conduct of certain ministers. The University Grants Committee in 1956–7 invited him to chair the subcommittee on the methods used by universities in contracting, and in recording and controlling expenditure. He died at St Joseph's Nursing Home, Boars Hill, Sunningwell, near Abingdon, Berkshire, on 14 January 1963, and his ashes were deposited in Winchester College cloisters. His wife, Lady Gater, survived him; she had run the National Gallery canteen and midday concerts during the Second World War, and was appointed MBE in 1946.   J. M. LEE

Sources *The Times* (15 Jan 1963) · *The Wykehamist*, 1110 (12 Feb 1963), 100 · *Winchester College register, 1930–1975* (1992) · J. D. Marshall, ed., *History of Lancashire county council, 1889–1974* (1977) · G. Sutherland and S. Sharp, *Ability, merit and measurement: mental testing and English education, 1880–1940* (1984), 263–4 · A. Saint, ed., *Politics and the people of London: the London county council, 1889–1965* (1989), 147–65 · J. Dancy, *Walter Oakeshott: a diversity of gifts* (1995) · LCC minutes, 1933, LMA, 806–7 · J. M. Lee and M. Petter, *The colonial office, war & development policy* (1982), 67–8

Archives priv. coll. | FILM BFI NFTVA, news footage

Likenesses photograph, *c*.1935, repro. in *The London Headteachers' Association, 1888–1938*, London Headteachers' Association (1938) · photograph, *c*.1938 (with his son), repro. in Saint, ed., *Politics and the people*, pl. 16c · W. Stoneman, photograph, 1941, NPG · photograph, repro. in *ILN* (26 Jan 1963)

Wealth at death £3201 19s. 0d.: probate, 9 April 1963, *CGPLA Eng. & Wales*

Gater [*née* Rogers], **Sarah** (*bap.* 1605, *d.* 1656), merchant, was baptized on 19 June 1605 in the parish of St Michael, Cornhill, London, the daughter of John Rogers (*d.* 1615), a clothworker, of Whitechapel, and his wife, Elizabeth. Sarah's share of her father's estate was an annuity of £8 for twenty-one years. She married, on an unknown date, William Gater (*d.* 1624), who had been admitted to Emmanuel College, Cambridge, in 1612, and graduated BA in 1616 and MA in 1619; he was ordained in 1616. Gater was lecturer at St Andrew Undershaft and a freeman of the Merchant Taylors' Company, by redemption dated 18 February 1623. The couple had one son, William, who died abroad in 1646. Widowed in her nineteenth year, Sarah Gater carried on a retail trade in her deceased husband's company until her own death. During her brief marriage she lived in Leadenhall Street in the parish of St Andrew Undershaft, but by at least 1630 she had moved to the parish of St Michael, Cornhill. There she established a modest residence and business, with several female servants, one or two apprentices, and, by the time of her death, one journeyman clothworker. Although never prosperous, she was a 'subsidyman', and was in 1642 rated at £10 as the contribution of one-twentieth of her estate for the parliamentary wartime assessment. At her death she owned her residence and held a lease of a garden situated in the parish of St Botolph without Bishopsgate. She appears to have outlived all five of her brothers, possibly as early as 1625, when she was appointed administrator for the estate of her deceased brother Peter; this act suggests her own leading role within her family at a youthful age. The first apprentice she took on in her own right as a widow was Gerrard Winstanley (1609–1676), bound on 25 March 1630, the future leader of the Diggers: Winstanley took his company freedom on 21 February 1638.

Sarah Gater was an educated individual. Her will of 14 September 1654 demonstrated a keen interest in medicine and theology. She owned both books and manuscript 'notes' on physic and surgery (which she passed on in matriarchal succession to her widowed sister), although the only volume cited by name was an edition of the popular *Herbal* by John Gerard. In addition to her own holdings in divinity, she acquired, and retained to her death, a large proportion of the library of her relative Henry Mason BD, rector of St Andrew Undershaft and prebendary of St Paul's Cathedral, possibly secured in 1641 when Mason departed London for his native Wigan. Before the civil war Gater was apparently an Anglican, probably influenced by Mason, in whose parish she had resided as a married teenager, from whom she received her treasured Bible, and with whom she remained close. He was an orthodox divine who owed his ecclesiastical preferment, and acknowledged an intellectual debt, to Bishop John King of London.

Gater was buried on 16 April 1656 in the churchyard of St Michael, Cornhill. The cause of death was given as 'aged'. One overseer of her will was her 'dear cousin' the poet and religious biographer Izaak Walton, of Worston Place, Staffordshire. In the absence of business or personal papers, much of Gater's life remains obscure. None the less, she is of interest for maintaining a commercial concern over three decades, her learning, and her intersection with some of the most original intellects of the seventeenth century, figures as distinctive and contrasting as Winstanley and Walton. Surrounded by a number of female and male friends and relatives, and employing in her establishment kin of both sexes, she reveals the lifestyle and intellectual interests of a woman who achieved economic and domestic independence following the early separation by death from father, husband, and male siblings.

J. D. ALSOP

Sources PRO, PROB 11/125, sig. 26 [John Rogers] • PRO, PROB 11/193, sig. 86 [Thomas Grinsell] • PRO, PROB 11/254, sig. 123 • consistory court of London, will register, 1621–41, LMA, fols. 5v–6 • consistory court of London, vicar-general's book, LMA, vol. 13 [unfoliated] • J. L. Chester, ed., *The parish registers of St Michael, Cornhill, London*, Harleian Society, register section, 7 (1882), 104–5, 108, 133, 215, 219, 240, 248 • J. D. Alsop, 'A high road to radicalism? Gerrard Winstanley's youth', *Seventeenth Century*, 9 (1994), 11–24 • GL, MS 4063/1, fol. 136 • Merchant Taylors' Company presentment book, 1629–37, GL [unfoliated] • Merchant Taylors' Company apprentice binding book, 1623–8, 11 • Merchant Taylors' Company apprentice binding book, 1629–35, GL, 91, 434 • Merchant Taylors' Company apprentice binding book, 1635–9, GL, 99 • Merchant Taylors' Company court minute book, 1619–30, GL, fol. 233 • archdeaconry court of London, act book, 1611–26, GL [unfoliated] • PRO, E 179/147/568 • PRO, E 179/147/577, fols. 24–8 • PRO, PROB 6/19, fol. 20 [William Gater] • Venn, *Alum. Cant.* • H. Mason, *Christian humiliation* (1625), sig. A3–A4, p. 37

Gates, Bernard (1686–1773), musician, was born on 23 April 1686 at The Hague, Netherlands, the second son of

Bernard Gates (1686–1773), by unknown artist

Bernard Gates (d. 1718?) and his wife, Maria (d. 1725?). His father accompanied William III to England in 1688 and subsequently served as page of the presence to Mary II: his will, as Bernard Gates, gentleman, of St Margaret's, Westminster, was proved on 21 May 1718. Bernard junior was a chorister of the Chapel Royal from 1697 to 1705, where he received his training under John Blow. He was appointed to a temporary place as gentleman of the Chapel Royal from 1 January 1708, and moved to a permanent place following the death of John Howell on 15 July. He received a second place at the chapel early in 1738, the combined places requiring his attendance throughout the year. In 1711 he also became a lay vicar at Westminster Abbey. He was chosen as clerk at St George's Chapel, Windsor, on 4 November 1714, probably sharing a place with George Laye, but he only served there for about a year. He married Elizabeth (c.1689–1737) before 1717, since on 6 June of that year his eldest child, a daughter named Atkinson, was buried in the north cloister of Westminster Abbey. This unusual forename, which was also borne by another daughter of Gates (buried in 1736), was derived from a Mrs Atkinson, launderer to Queen Anne, who had brought up Elizabeth Gates and made her her heir.

In 1727 Gates succeeded to two offices following the death of William Croft: he was appointed tuner of the regals, organs, virginals, and flutes on 21 August and master of the children of the Chapel Royal on 4 September. On 23 February 1732 Handel's *Esther* was performed at Gates's house in James Street, Westminster, by the children of the Chapel Royal and others, thus initiating a series of events which led Handel to introduce the work towards the end of his opera season at the King's Theatre, and beginning his career in English oratorio at the London theatres.

Gates himself had a long association with Handel's music, singing as a bass soloist in various works between the 'Utrecht' music of 1713 and the 'Dettingen' music of 1743, and supplying the treble voices for Handel's oratorio performances. In 1726 Gates was one of the founder members of the Academy of Vocal Music, but in 1734 he seceded from the academy, taking the children of the chapel with him. On 10 March 1737 Mrs Gates died, but Bernard continued as master of the children of the Chapel Royal and added the similar post of master of the boys at Westminster Abbey from Michaelmas 1740. In 1757 he resigned from these posts (from the Chapel Royal by 18 March, and from Westminster Abbey by 29 September), although he retained his singing places as sinecures, and he moved to North Aston, Oxfordshire. He died there on 15 November 1773 and was buried in the north cloister of Westminster Abbey on 23 November. His will, dated 5 October 1772, was proved on 28 November 1773. Failing the issue of a nephew, Bernard Downes, to whom the estate at North Aston was left, he bequeathed his property to Dr Thomas Sanders Dupuis, who had been his pupil, with a further remainder to Dr Samuel Arnold. He directed that his chaise horse should be kept on his estate at Aston without working, that it should never be killed, and that when it died naturally it should be buried without mutilation of any kind. Hawkins said that in Gates's singing there was such an exaggeration of the shake as to destroy the melody altogether, and that the boys of the chapel had adopted the same habit. He also said that Gates introduced into the chapel the system, then lately revived by J. C. Pepusch, of solmization by the hexachords. Gates was a minor composer of church music: his surviving works include substantial solo passages for his trebles. A tablet to his memory was put up in the church of North Aston at the expense of his pupil, Dupuis.

J. A. F. MAITLAND, *rev.* DONALD BURROWS

Sources *Public Advertiser* (20 Nov 1773) • A. Ashbee, ed., *Records of English court music*, 9 vols. (1986–96) • PRO, 'Old' and 'New' MS cheque-books of the Chapel Royal up to 1714, LC/3, LC/5 • Westminster Abbey, monument in the north cloister, registers, and treasurer's accounts • St George's Chapel, Windsor, chapter acts and treasurer's accounts • BL, register of the Academy of Vocal Music, Add. MS 11732 • C. Burney, *An account of the musical performances … in commemoration of Handel* (1785), 100–01 • J. Hawkins, *A general history of the science and practice of music*, new edn, 3 vols. (1853), 735, 832, 885 • Burney, *Hist. mus.*, new edn, 2.775–6 • Highfill, Burnim & Langhans, *BDA*, vol. 6 • Westminster Abbey, muniments 60020 and 61228B [choir accounts and registers] • FM Cam., Chapel Royal pension fund book, MS 1011

Likenesses stipple, pubd 1784, BM • attrib. T. Hudson, oils, repro. in *British paintings, 1500–1850* (1900) [sale catalogue, Sothebys, London, 16 May 1990] • oils, U. Oxf., faculty of music [*see illus.*]

Wealth at death will implies substantial property in North Aston; several individual bequests: will

Gates, Geoffrey (*fl.* 1566–1580), soldier and polemicist, was the eldest son and heir of Geoffrey Gates; his mother was a Pascall of Essex. His uncle was the Essex gentleman Sir John *Gates (1504–1553), captain of the guard of Edward VI and chancellor of the duchy of Lancaster. Geoffrey married Joane Wentworth and had one son, Peter. Little is known of his career. He was admitted a member of

the Society of Lincoln's Inn in March 1566. From 1578 to 1580 he fought as a gentleman volunteer under Sir John Norreys in the Netherlands. While there he became friends with William Blandy, whose book *The Castle, or, Picture of Policy* (London, 1581) takes the form of a narrative between Blandy and Gates. Gates had published his own book already, *The Defence of the Militarie Profession* (London, 1579). Many Elizabethan veterans wrote about their experiences, but this is one of the most remarkable works of its type.

Gates was related by marriage to the zealous reformer Sir Anthony Denny and, through him, to Lord Grey of Wilton and the Champernownes, all notable protestant warriors. His own convictions—Calvinist and apocalyptic—burn through the pages of *The Defence*. A rambling and at times almost incoherent work, it still has a power to move the reader because of its author's intense zeal and commitment to his cause. Gates's chief purpose is to praise 'the speciall martialists of the Lord God of hostes' and:

> [God's] Cheefteynes of courage, fayth, and Militarie prudence, fitte for the wars of Jacob. … above them al, William, Earle of Nassau, the vertuous, good, and happie Prince of Orange. By vertue of the fayth, industry, and prowesse of these sacred martialists, is the gospell, and kingdome of Christ Jesus … freely preached to the world, an inspeakable comfort & richnes to al mankinde, and that specially to the elect children of God, to whom be prayse. (Gates, 42)

Gates seeks to impart his own fiery ardour to his readers and encourages Englishmen everywhere to join in the 'fight with Sathan in plain battell, for the recoverie of [God's] holy Sanctuary, … trodden under the feete of Antichrist'. He emphasizes that 'as all Souldiers of worthinesse and knowledge are to bee highly esteemed and maintened, so are the gentlemen, and worthie people of our nation that have pursued the defensory warres in the lowe Countrie, specially to be praised' (ibid.). Many other writers, including Blandy, Barnaby Rich, and Thomas Churchyard, praised these soldiers to their fellow countrymen, but only Gates has such obvious apocalyptic fervour. Whether he died in the Netherlands, or whether, having served his time, he returned home, is unknown, but *The Defence of the Militarie Profession* remains a remarkable monument to his obscure yet passionate life.

D. J. B. TRIM

Sources W. C. Metcalfe, ed., *The visitations of Essex*, 2, Harleian Society, 14 (1879), 574 • Venn, *Alum. Cant.*, 1/2.200 • W. P. Baildon, ed., *The records of the Honorable Society of Lincoln's Inn: admissions*, 1 (1896), 73 • *DNB* • W. Blandy, *The castle, or, Picture of pollicy* (1581) • G. Gates, *The defence of the militarie profession* (1579)

Gates, Sir Henry (*b.* before 1523, *d.* 1589). *See under* Gates, Sir John (1504–1553).

Gates, Horatio (1727?–1806), revolutionary army officer, was the son of Robert Gates (*d.* 1766), a Thames waterman, and his wife, Dorothy Reeve (*d.* 1768), housekeeper to Peregrine Osborne, second duke of Leeds. The circumstances of his birth remain controversial: even the date is uncertain, and while his birthplace is traditionally given as Maldon in Essex, the alternative location of Old Malden, close to the Leeds estates at Wimbledon, Surrey, is more logical (Mintz, *The Generals of Saratoga*, 15). Another suggested birthplace is Greenwich, Kent, near Leeds's house at Deptford. According to Gates's godfather Horace Walpole, his mother was considerably older than her husband; this encouraged persistent but unproven rumours that Horatio was in fact the illegitimate son of the duke of Leeds. In 1729, following the duke's death, Dorothy and Robert Gates both entered the service of Charles Powlett, third duke of Bolton, at Greenwich. The patronage of their new employer proved decisive for the Gateses' family fortunes; in 1741 Bolton's influence secured Robert the respectable post of surveyor of customs at Greenwich, and four years later launched Horatio upon what would prove to be a lengthy and chequered military career.

Like other noblemen, Bolton raised his own regiment to counter the threat posed by the Jacobite rising of 1745; in October, the teenaged Gates was appointed to a lieutenancy within it. Though reduced with Bolton's corps in June 1746, he returned to the army in 1748 as quartermaster, and subsequently ensign, in the 20th foot. In November that year, following the treaty of Aix-la-Chapelle, he was placed upon the half-pay list of disbanded officers. Gates sought fresh employment by volunteering to accompany the expedition dispatched to establish the naval base of Halifax, Nova Scotia, in 1749. He served as an aide-de-camp to the settlement's commander, Colonel Edward Cornwallis. That same year he secured the rank of captain-lieutenant in the 45th foot; promotion to captain followed in the summer of 1750. With poor prospects for further advancement at Halifax, Gates returned to London in January 1754. Increasing friction between the French and British in the Ohio valley raised the prospect of war: on 13 September, with backing from Cornwallis, Gates purchased a captain's commission in one of the independent companies of regular troops at New York; his motives for quitting the 45th for the same rank in a less prestigious unit remain obscure, though the chance to join a formation deemed likely to see active service may have been a factor.

On 20 October 1754, after returning to Nova Scotia, Gates married Elizabeth Phillips (*d.* 1783); they had one child, Robert. In the following year his company was sent to join the expedition against Fort Duquesne under the command of Major-General Edward Braddock. On 9 July 1755 Braddock's column was routed by French-led Native Americans on the Monongahela River: Gates was among the many officers wounded. Upon his recovery, Gates rejoined his company on the New York frontier. Subsequent stints of garrison duty gave the ambitious Gates little opportunity for advancement. His luck changed in 1759 with his appointment as brigade major to Brigadier-General John Stanwix, the commander of the southern department at Fort Pitt (the former Fort Duquesne); in the following spring, Stanwix was replaced by Robert Monckton, who had distinguished himself as James Wolfe's second in command at Quebec. In 1761, when Monckton was appointed major-general to command an expedition against Martinique, he took the dependable Gates with

him as an aide-de-camp. Following the capitulation of the island's key citadel of Fort Royal in February 1762, Gates was awarded the honour of carrying the victory dispatches to London; the mission earned Gates promotion to major in his old regiment, the 45th foot (24 April 1762), and enough cash to buy his next step on the promotion ladder should the opportunity arise.

However, the hopes raised at Gates's triumphant return to London were swiftly dashed by the onset of peace. The frustrating decade that followed saw him denied the further promotion he craved and seeking consolation in alcohol, gambling, religion, and republicanism. In 1769 he sold his army commission and three years later moved with his family to farm an estate in Virginia's Shenandoah valley. Although Gates had at first remained largely aloof from the escalating quarrel between Britain and her North American colonies, by 1775 he was openly opposed to any reconciliation with the mother country. At the eruption of hostilities that year he made it clear that despite his past as a soldier of the king he was now willing to offer his services to congress. On 17 June 1775 his organizational skills gained him the rank of brigadier-general and appointment as adjutant-general in the fledgeling continental army. That winter Gates served on the staff of General George Washington at the siege of Boston. Both men had campaigned under Braddock twenty years before but they had little else in common: besides their marked differences in background and temperament, Gates was a vocal supporter of the amateur militia, while Washington called for a standing army of regular troops.

Gates proved keen to cultivate influential friendships within congress. Promotion to major-general, which brought appointment to a field command, followed on 16 May 1776. As an increasingly radical advocate of American independence, in June 1776 Gates was given command of the patriot forces that had previously been sent on a fruitless expedition against Canada. These troops were now within the northern department commanded by Major-General Philip Schuyler, who refused to relinquish his authority over them. It was the beginning of a lengthy dispute between the two generals that continued despite the growing threat of a major British invasion from Canada. Gates finally prevailed on 4 August 1777: his position was bolstered by Schuyler's conspicuous failure to preserve the crucial bastion of Fort Ticonderoga from General John Burgoyne's advancing forces. Now placed in command of the northern department, Gates prepared to contest Burgoyne's effort to march down the Hudson valley to Albany. Burgoyne's attempts to outflank the American defences led to fierce fighting at Freeman's Farm on 19 September and at Bemis Heights (7 October). When the frustrated Burgoyne withdrew, Gates mounted a cautious pursuit. Short of rations and hounded by prowling rebel militias, the beleaguered Burgoyne was obliged to capitulate at Saratoga on 17 October. Many commentators have attributed Burgoyne's defeat to Gates's fiery subordinate Benedict Arnold; they have accused Gates of failing to afford the future turncoat sufficient recognition in his dispatches. On balance it was probably a combination of

Gates's careful planning and Arnold's inspired battlefield leadership that secured victory. Beyond doubt is the fact that Saratoga marked a turning point in the American War of Independence: the elimination of a major British force encouraged direct French intervention and thereby transformed colonial rebellion into a global conflict.

Saratoga also brought Gates immense prestige; indeed, his clear-cut success was in marked contrast to the fortunes of Washington, whose inconclusive campaigning against General Sir William Howe had failed to prevent British occupation of Philadelphia. Washington's supporters now began to suspect that the triumphant Gates coveted their own idol's position of commander-in-chief. Such fears were not without some foundation: they were reinforced by Gates's failure to inform Washington directly of events at Saratoga, and culminated in accusations that Gates was party to the notorious 'Conway cabal' that supposedly planned to appoint him in Washington's stead.

That winter Gates served as president of the board of war at York, Pennsylvania, before returning to the Hudson command in April 1778. Gates now hoped to orchestrate a fresh invasion of Canada: this obsession led him to disregard orders from congress to mount an expedition against the Seneca and Cayuga Indians. The plan continued to occupy his thoughts after he was sent to Boston in October to command the eastern department. Washington, who feared a diversion of resources, opposed the Canadian venture; by January 1779, when congress finally abandoned Gates's cherished scheme, relations between him and the commander-in-chief had deteriorated to the extent that they threatened a dangerous rift in the revolutionary ranks. Indeed, that April, Washington informed John Jay, the president of congress, that Gates's initial 'symptoms of coldness and constraint' towards him had now degenerated into continual incidents of 'malevolence and opposition' calculated to undermine his credibility (*Writings*, 14.385).

Following the British capture of Charles Town in May 1780, Gates was chosen by congress to restore American fortunes as head of the southern department. In marked contrast to his cautious strategy against Burgoyne three years earlier, Gates now advocated a rapid advance to contest the approach of crown troops under Charles Cornwallis, second Earl Cornwallis. Gates's strategy was reckless: his hopes of fighting another advantageous defensive action were baffled when he unexpectedly encountered Cornwallis at Camden on 16 August. Cornwallis's veteran redcoats made short work of the motley militia and continentals that Gates ranged against them, and inflicted an overwhelming defeat. Before the fighting was over Gates rode from the field: his intention was to rally the remaining patriot forces at Hillsborough, but the general's critics were quick to place a less flattering interpretation upon his actions.

For Gates the body blow of Camden was compounded by the recent death of his son. While he sought to recover the perilous situation in the south, congress demanded a court of inquiry into his conduct and permitted Washington to replace him with his own trusted subordinate, Major-General Nathanael Greene. To Gates's chagrin the court was never convened and it was almost two years before he was permitted to rejoin the army. During the war's final winter of 1782–3, Gates served as second in command to Washington at Newburgh. Here Gates was once again embroiled in controversy through his involvement in the abortive 'Newburgh conspiracy' by which disgruntled army officers threatened mutiny in an attempt to secure arrears of pay. Gates finally left the continental army in March 1783, and returned home to his terminally ill wife. For the bereaved and discredited Gates, the immediate post-war years proved both lonely and bitter. However, on 31 July 1786 he gained a fresh lease of life when he married Mary Valens (1740–1810), a Maryland landowner, the second surviving daughter of Joseph Valens, a Liverpool merchant, and former companion of the republican clergyman Bartholomew Booth. They subsequently moved to Rose Hill Farm, Manhattan, New York. Gates backed the new constitution and in old age proved a vigorous partisan of Thomas Jefferson. In 1800 Gates was elected to the New York state legislature, where he served a single term. Noted for his generosity to fellow veterans of the revolutionary war—a struggle in which he had played an important if sometimes controversial part—Gates died at Rose Hill Farm on 10 April 1806, and was buried in New York later that month. The total value of his estate is unknown, but he left stock worth $9500 in the Bank of New York.

STEPHEN BRUMWELL

Sources P. D. Nelson, *General Horatio Gates: a biography* (1976) · M. M. Mintz, *The generals of Saratoga: John Burgoyne and Horatio Gates* (1990) · G. A. Billias, 'Horatio Gates: professional soldier', *George Washington's generals*, ed. G. A. Billias (1964), 79–108 · J. S. Pancake, *1777: the year of the hangman* (1977) · M. M. Mintz, 'Horatio Gates, George Washington's rival', *History Today*, 26 (1976), 419–28 · R. H. Kohn, 'The inside story of the Newburgh conspiracy: America and the coup d'état', *William and Mary Quarterly*, 27 (1970), 187–220 · *The writings of George Washington from the original manuscript sources, 1745–1799*, ed. J. C. Fitzpatrick, 39 vols. (1931–44) · H. Walpole, *Journal of the reign of King George the Third*, ed. Dr Doran, 2 vols. (1859) · J. K. Martin, *Benedict Arnold, revolutionary hero: an American warrior reconsidered* (1997) · *DNB* · P. D. Nelson, 'Gates, Horatio', *ANB* · *DAB* · M. Whitehead, 'Wealth creation, ethics and education: the career of Joseph Valens of Liverpool', *Transactions of the Historic Society of Lancashire and Cheshire*, 145 (1995), 203–13 · *IGI*

Archives Chicago Historical Society, collection · National Archives and Records Administration, Washington, DC, letters · New York Historical Society, papers · North Carolina Division of Archives and History, Raleigh, letters · NYPL, papers

Likenesses C. W. Peale, oils, 1782, Independence National Historical Park Collection, Philadelphia · J. Trumbull, group portrait, oils, 1787–9 (*The surrender of General Burgoyne at Saratoga*), Yale U. Art Gallery · G. Stuart, oils, 1794, Metropolitan Museum of Art, New York · J. Peale, oils, 1799, Maryland Historical Society, Baltimore · J. A. O'Neill, stipple (after G. Stuart), NPG · J. Trumbull, drawing, Metropolitan Museum of Art, New York · two line engravings, NPG

Wealth at death estate incl. stock valued at $9500 in Bank of New York

Gates, Sir John (1504–1553), courtier, was born into an Essex gentry family, his grandfather William Gates having purchased the manor of Garnetts in High Easter; this remained the property of his descendants until 1582, and it was where John was born. John's father, Sir Geoffrey Gates (d. 1526), was a JP for Essex and served as sheriff of the county. With his wife, Elizabeth, daughter of Sir William Clopton, he had three sons, of whom John was the eldest, and a daughter, Anne, who married Thomas Darcy, uncle of Thomas, Lord Darcy of Chiche, vice-chamberlain of Edward VI's household.

Having trained as a lawyer at Lincoln's Inn from 1523, John Gates became a groom of Henry VIII's privy chamber in 1533. He may have owed his advancement to Anthony Denny, whose sister Mary he married. In January 1535 he was one of the commissioners who drew up the *valor ecclesiasticus* for Essex, and in October the following year was directed to keep the peace in that county during the Pilgrimage of Grace. On 10 October 1537 he became a page of the wardrobe of robes. A member of a closely knit circle of royal servants, Gates was Denny's deputy within the privy chamber and in charge of the king's coffer. Licensed to retain ten men in his livery, in addition to bailiffs and other servants, he supplied sixty soldiers to the French expedition of 1544, and even commanded 3073 men remaining with the king at Boulogne. It is a sign of his growing importance that on 20 September 1545 he should have been authorized to authenticate all official documents with the king's dry stamp, an appointment which gave Gates and Denny substantial political influence in the last twelve months of the reign. He was a witness to Henry's will on 30 August 1546 and received a bequest of £200 from the king.

Gates probably first sat in parliament in 1542, for Chipping Wycombe, while in 1545 he was MP for New Shoreham. Elected for Southwark in 1547, he became a knight of the shire for Essex in 1551. In Edward VI's reign he was also made knight of the Bath (20 February 1547) and in 1549 sheriff of Essex. In the latter capacity he was ordered to act against Princess Mary's plans to escape to the continent in the summer of 1550. In the same year he became one of the four chief gentlemen of the privy chamber (designated principal knights in 1552), while in the following year he was appointed successively vice-chamberlain of the household and captain of the guard (8 April), a privy councillor (10 April), and lord lieutenant of Essex (14 April). On 7 July he was made chancellor of the duchy of Lancaster, and on 14 December he was entrusted with the king's signet. On 19 April 1552 he was licensed to have twenty-five retainers. As well as being actively involved in raising money by selling chantry lands, he was appointed to the revenue commission of 1552, and to commissions to 'demande alloawances for the fall of … monie' and for the sale of crown lands.

Gates's increasing prominence reflects his closeness to the duke of Northumberland. He became implicated in the latter's conspiracy to alter Henry VIII's will in order to transfer the succession to the throne away from Princess Mary in favour of Jane Grey, the daughter of the duke of Suffolk, who was Northumberland's daughter-in-law. But he was not the young king's confidant, even though he had close access to Edward's person, and he did not, as has

been claimed, mastermind the 'Devise' for the alteration of the succession. Nor, although he was regarded by Nicholas Ridley and others as an educated and God-fearing man, and died professing his faith in scripture, does he seem to have been primarily influenced by religious motives. Probably it was because he was a conscientious and capable man of affairs that he wished to carry out his superior's orders and therefore joined Northumberland's expedition against Mary. None the less, Mary was proclaimed queen and Gates was arrested with his patron and executed on 22 August 1553. He seems to have been singled out for the scaffold less for his complicity in Northumberland's rebellion than for his acting against Mary in 1550 and also preventing her from attending mass.

Gates acquired several valuable monastic properties, starting in 1537, and came to possess manors in Essex, Hertfordshire, Norfolk, and Northamptonshire, and also at Westminster, where he was granted the site of St Stephen's College. The capital value of the properties he acquired under Edward VI was said to have amounted to more than £13,600, and he also received £147 3s. 10d. per annum from sinecures and held three wardships. Following his attainder and execution most of his properties were confiscated by the crown, a judgment which even John Strype, who regarded Gates as covetous, thought 'somewhat hard and unjust' (Sil, 'King's men', 269).

Sir John Gates's younger brother **Sir Henry Gates** (b. before 1523, d. 1589) sat with his brother in parliament as the other MP for New Shoreham in 1545, had become a gentleman pensioner by 1546, and as a protestant flourished during the protectorate of the duke of Somerset, who knighted him in Scotland on 28 September 1547. MP for Bridport in the latter year, in 1551 he became a gentleman of Edward VI's privy chamber, and was also appointed controller of the petty custom at the port of London and receiver-general of the duchy of Cornwall. Like his elder brother, Sir Henry became involved in Northumberland's conspiracy against Mary, and was arrested and condemned to death. But though he lost his government offices he was soon pardoned and restored to favour, being entrusted with a command for the defence of the north during the Anglo-French war of 1557. Although he was MP for Bramber in 1559, he became increasingly settled in Yorkshire, where he acquired an estate at Seamer, and was MP for Scarborough in 1563 and 1572, and a knight of the shire for Yorkshire in 1571 and 1586. He became a member of the council of the north and gave valuable service against the northern rising of 1569, when he risked being murdered during an official mission to Scotland. Sir Henry Gates married twice. His first wife, Lucy Knyvet, with whom he had four sons and four daughters, died in 1577, and by 1584 he had married Katherine Vaughan, who survived him. When he died, on 7 April 1589, his heir was his eldest son, Edward.

NARASINGHA P. SIL

Sources N. P. Sil, 'The rise and fall of Sir John Gates', *HJ*, 24 (1981), 929–43 · N. P. Sil, 'King's men, queen's men, statesmen: a study of the careers of Sir Anthony Denny, Sir William Herbert, and Sir John Gates, gentlemen of the Tudor privy chamber', PhD diss.,

University of Oregon, 1978 • N. P. Sil, *Tudor placemen and statesmen: select case histories* (2002) • D. E. Hoak, *The king's council in the reign of Edward VI* (1976) • W. K. Jordan, *Edward VI, 2: The threshold of power* (1970) • W. K. Jordan, *Edward VI, 1: The young king* (1968) • R. C. Braddock, 'The royal household, 1540–1560', PhD diss., Northwestern University, 1971 • HoP, *Commons, 1509–58*, 2.197–9 • HoP, *Commons, 1558–1603*, 2.173–5 • *N&Q*, 148 (1925), 350, 394 • *CSP Spain, 1553* • *CSP for., 1569–71* • *CSP dom., 1547–80*, with *addenda, 1566–79* • *CPR, 1547–58* • C. Sharp, ed., *Memorials of the rebellion of 1569* (1840); repr. with foreword by R. Wood as *The rising in the north: the 1569 rebellion* (1975) • J. Strype, *Ecclesiastical memorials*, 3 vols. (1822) • P. Morant, *The history and antiquities of the county of Essex*, 2 vols. (1760–68)

Archives BL, Lansdowne MS 205, fols. 56, 152–3 • BL, Harley MS 284, fols. 127–8 • BL, Harley MS 6164, fol. 58

Wealth at death £13,600—property: Strype, *Ecclesiastical memorials*

Gates, Reginald Ruggles (1882–1962), botanist and geneticist, was born on 1 May 1882 near Middleton, Nova Scotia, the eldest son of Andreas Bohaker Gates and his wife, Charlotte Elizabeth Ruggles. The Gates family was descended from Stephen Gates of Higham, Essex, who emigrated to Massachusetts in 1638. Earlier ancestors included Sir John Gates (1504–1553) who served in the courts of both Henry VIII and Edward VI. Gates had antecedents on the loyalist side during the American War of Independence. He was related to Major-General Horatio Gates (1728–1806) and through his mother to Brigadier-General Timothy Ruggles. The latter was forced to flee the colony and secured a large land grant in Nova Scotia. Gates was to be greatly influenced by the loyalist traditions of his family.

Gates's father managed a large farm and orchard outside Middleton and manufactured a herbal medicine with considerable local notoriety. His mother was a teacher and botanist who schooled Gates at home and awakened his early interest in natural history. In 1891 he went to Middleton high school, and in 1899 he entered Mount Allison University in Sackville, Nova Scotia, graduating with first-class honours in science in 1903. His first scientific paper, published in 1902, examined the fungi in the area around Middleton. After graduation he spent a year at McGill University as demonstrator in botany.

Gates went to the United States in 1905, where he worked on plant genetics at the Marine Biology Station, Woods Hole, Massachusetts. He received a research fellowship to the University of Chicago and studied genetics and cytology with Wilson, Conklin, and Lillie. He was awarded a PhD in 1908 for research examining heredity in *Oenothera*, the evening primrose. His work at Chicago, and subsequently at the Missouri Botanical Garden in St Louis (1908–10), produced a remarkable series of findings which would elucidate genetic mechanisms applicable to many organisms, including humans.

Gates found changes in the chromosomes of *Oenothera* which correlated with hereditary changes in different plant lines. As early as 1908 he observed one mutant species that had chromosomes which divided unequally, a process termed nondisjunction. Another line had an extra chromosome; it was aneuploid. A third line had tetraploidy, twice the number of chromosomes as the parent species. These mechanisms for genetic change were

Reginald Ruggles Gates (1882–1962), by Lafayette, 1929

later confirmed in *Drosophila* and other species of plants and animals.

In 1910, at a meeting of the American Association for the Advancement of Science, Gates met Marie Charlotte Carmichael *Stopes (1880–1958), then active as a palaeobotanist. The couple married in Montreal on 18 March 1911 and soon settled in London. However, despite Gates's reputation (he received the Mendel prize in 1911 and the Huxley medal and prize in 1914), he had trouble finding a suitable post. He worked at Imperial College for a year, followed by two years at St Thomas's Hospital, where he taught biology. He taught heredity and cytology at Oxford in 1914 before spending two years at the University of California teaching zoology. He then returned to England and served the remainder of the First World War as a gunnery instructor for the Royal Flying Corps. Gates summarized his early research work in the book *The Mutation Factor in Evolution* (1915). He argued that genetic change could occur by two mechanisms. There could be a physical rearrangement of the chromosomes, or change could result from a chemical alteration in the components of the genetic material itself.

During the war, in 1916, the marriage between Gates and Stopes was annulled. Whatever the truth behind their acrimonius parting Stopes convinced the court that the marriage had never been consummated and that she had learned about sex only from reading the books then kept in the 'cupboard' at the British Museum reading room. Gates on the other hand later claimed that Stopes was not sexually ignorant; she had not been a virgin when he met her, and during their marriage had had numerous sexual relationships with other men. It was a matter about which he remained bitter until his death.

After the war Gates was appointed reader in botany at King's College, London. In 1921 he was elected professor of botany and embarked on a highly productive career as teacher, administrator, and researcher. He and his students greatly expanded the work done in cytology and genetics at the college. The quality of his work was recognized by his being elected FRS in 1931. A colleague said of him:

> He was most assiduous in the supervision of his many research students, paying a daily visit to the research laboratory and seeing every one of them, and the daily meetings around the tea table were always lively and stimulating affairs. (DNB)

The onset of the Second World War forced the evacuation of King's College from London in 1942. Gates was appointed research fellow at Harvard and worked there in collaboration with E. A. Hooton. He returned to England in 1957, where he lived for the remainder of his life.

Gates's research never focused solely on the genetics of plants. From an early age he sought to apply the principles of heredity to many different species. In 1909 he published a note on hybridization in dogs and a report on heredity in a medical journal. In the 1920s he began a series of field trips to study local variation in plant species. He travelled widely throughout North and South America, Africa, and Asia. These expeditions would continue until his death, and while travelling he collected data on local peoples which he thought could be used to study human heredity and evolution. He studied physiognomy, hair texture, skin colour, and blood types as representative markers of genes which varied in human populations. *Heredity and Eugenics* (1923) was one of the first books to draw anthropology and genetics together in order to explain human evolution. He expanded this work to include inherited abnormalities and diseases for the purpose of educating medical professionals on the importance of inheritance in their daily practices. *Heredity in Man* (1929) and its next edition in two volumes entitled *Human Genetics* (1946) were the most comprehensive works on the topic in English at that time.

The genetic data collected by Gates suggested to him that the crossing of human races was undesirable from a eugenic point of view. Some critics called him a racist. However, by the 1930s he was convinced that there was no simple correlation between physical characters and hereditary make-up. It was clear that many genes often contributed to the production of a particular character, and that single genes often had multiple effects on the organism. He attended the anthropological congresses in Europe during this era and was convinced that the simplistic hereditary theories of the Fascists and Nazis were political rhetoric rather than rigorous science. He noted: 'To say all men are equal has not got us very far. It is more accurate to say all men are different, and then to respect each other's differences' (DNB).

Gates's active research continued until the end of his life. In his seventies, he investigated men with hairy ears and demonstrated that this trait segregated as a Y-linked human character. He published thirteen papers on human evolution and genetics in his last two years; eight others were published posthumously. He received many academic honours including an honorary LLD from Mount Allison University and a DSc from London University. He was elected fellow and served as vice-president of both the Linnean Society and the Royal Anthropological Institute.

Following the annulment of his first marriage, Gates married twice more. He married an American, Miss J. Williams, in 1929, but this marriage was also set aside. In 1955 he married another American, Laura Greer, widow of Samuel Greer of Texas. She was a skilled sociologist and photographer. This union proved ideal, and they worked together on scientific expeditions until the very end of his life. Gates died on 12 August 1962 in London. He was survived by his third wife.   ALAN R. RUSHTON

Sources J. A. F. Roberts, *Memoirs FRS*, 10 (1964), 83–106 · *DNB* · *DSB*, 5.293–4 · private information (2004)
Archives King's Lond., corresp. and papers · RBG Kew, corresp. | Bodl. Oxf., corresp. with C. D. Darlington and relating to the John Innes Institute · CUL, corresp. with C. C. Hurst
Likenesses Lafayette, photograph, 1929, NPG [*see illus.*] · A. Connors, oils, 1940, Mount Allison University, Sackville, Nova Scotia, Canada · photograph, repro. in Roberts, *Memoirs FRS*

Gates, Sir Thomas (*d.* in or before **1632**), colonial governor, was born in Colyford, Devon. Nothing is known of his parents, or of his life prior to 1596, when he was knighted by Elizabeth I for his service in the military expedition against Spain at Cadiz. He entered Gray's Inn on 14 March 1598 but was apparently never called to the bar and eventually abandoned the law in favour of diplomatic and military activities. In July 1604 he went to the Netherlands with Sir Henry Wotton, and then proceeded to Vienna to serve as an ambassador for England at the court of the Holy Roman emperor. Subsequently, he served with Captain Thomas Dale at the English garrison in Oudewater, Netherlands.

In April 1608 Gates requested and received a one-year leave of absence from the Dutch states general in order that he might accept a commission from James I to travel to the Virginia colony. The English settlement at Jamestown, Virginia, had been struggling due to famine, lack of supplies, and poor organization, and James therefore granted the colony a new charter, dated 23 May 1609, giving the Virginia Company wider powers and more extensive privileges to establish the colony. Among the company's chief officers were Gates as lieutenant-governor, Lord De La Warr as governor, Sir George Somers as admiral, and Sir Thomas Dale, Gates's companion at Oudewater, as high marshal. The involvement of such influential individuals as Sir Francis Bacon and the earl of Salisbury brought prominence and respectability to the Virginia Company, which succeeded in raising a large sum of money and attracted over 500 Englishmen and -women as migrants to the colony. At the end of May 1609 a squadron of nine ships, under the direction of Gates, Somers, and Captain Christopher Newport, left England and sailed for Virginia.

Of the nine vessels that sailed, only seven completed the Atlantic crossing. Gates's ship, the *Sea Venture*, became separated from the rest of the fleet during a hurricane at the end of July, in the course of which 'the violent Working of the Seas' (Jourdain, 4) was so great that the ship was driven aground and stranded between two great rocks on the island of Bermuda. The approximately 150 passengers managed to get themselves and most of their supplies onto the island, where they remained for nearly ten months. Two passengers, William Strachey and Silvester Jourdain, wrote accounts of the hurricane and the landing at Bermuda which were later published in London.

Six of the passengers from the *Sea Venture* died in the course of their stay upon Bermuda, but the remainder salvaged beams from their wrecked ship which they used, in combination with island timber, to build two pinnaces, which they named *Patience* and *Deliverance*. At the end of April 1610 they set off on the 700 mile voyage to Virginia, where they made a successful landing at Jamestown just two weeks later, on 10 May 1610. They found the fledgeling colony in a wretched condition; the colonists had failed to maintain social order or a regime of labour in Jamestown, and many had fallen victim to disease, famine, or Native American attacks. Shocked by the miserable appearance of the settlement, Gates decided to take the surviving colonists and sail for the English settlement at Newfoundland, but before he could do so Lord De La Warr arrived with new colonists and supplies, and Gates's party opted to remain in Jamestown and attempt to rejuvenate the colony. In order to prevent the new settlers from falling into the same bad habits as their predecessors, Gates, with the assistance of Thomas Dale, drew up a series of 'Laws Divine, Morall and Martiall' by which to govern the colony. The laws were 'mostly martial, and they set the colonists to work with military discipline and no pretense of gentle government' (Morgan, 79). Under Gates's rule, those settlers who were lazy, disorderly, or lawless would suffer stern correction.

Towards the end of 1610 De La Warr sent Dale and Gates back to England in order to purchase more supplies. Upon arriving in London, Gates found that the treasurer and council of the Virginia Company had heard bad tidings of Jamestown and were inclined towards abandonment of the endeavour. Gates's report of the changes he, Dale, and De La Warr had initiated revived the company's hopes and prompted it to continue to support the project. Although some influential supporters decided to withdraw from the company, Gates's enthusiasm and determination were effective enough to recruit several hundred new settlers. In March 1611 Dale departed England for Virginia with three ships bearing a year's supplies, and that June Gates followed him with a further six vessels, carrying more supplies and approximately 300 settlers, including his wife and two daughters. Gates's wife's name and when they married are unknown, but they had at least four children. Mrs Gates died in the course of the voyage and the daughters were sent back to England. Gates's squadron arrived at Virginia in August, at which time he succeeded Dale as the colony's governor. In that capacity he established the authority of the Church of England and created a new settlement at Henrico, named for James I's son Prince Henry.

Gates returned to England again in 1614 and attempted to maintain the morale and commitment of the Virginia Company, whose shareholders had yet to gain any financial rewards from their venture. He considered returning to Virginia, but after the death of his patron, De La Warr, the company appointed Captain Yeardley instead as captain-general and governor. Some time after 1614 Gates went to the Netherlands, from which he had taken a leave of absence more than six years before, and succeeded in getting the states general to pay him immediately the arrears of his salary. Nothing more is known definitely of his subsequent life or of his death. Captain John Smith claimed in a speech of 1621 that Gates had voyaged to the East Indies and died there, but no further references have been found to such a voyage. In 1623 he was listed as having fifty great shares in the Virginia Company, amounting to 5000 acres of land in Virginia. It appears from two petitions by his daughters to the privy council concerning their inheritance that Gates had died by November 1632, either in the Low Countries or in Virginia. Despite an investigation ordered by the privy council, Gates's daughters seem not to have recovered the estate and by 1636 claimed to be destitute.   NATALIE ZACEK

Sources DNB · E. S. Morgan, *American slavery, American freedom* (New York, 1975) · W. Meade, *Old churches, ministers and families of Virginia*, 2 vols. (1878) · P. A. Bruce, *Institutional history of Virginia in the seventeenth century*, 2 vols. (Gloucester, Mass., 1964) · S. Jourdain, *A discovery of the Barmudas* (1610); facs. edn (1940) · J. Fiske, *Old Virginia and her neighbours*, 2 vols. (1897) · B. W. Sheehan, 'Gates, Sir Thomas', *ANB* · J. Foster, *The register of admissions to Gray's Inn, 1521–1889, together with the register of marriages in Gray's Inn chapel, 1695–1754* (privately printed, London, 1889), vol. 1 · W. M. Billings, J. E. Selby, and T. W. Tate, *Colonial Virginia: a history* (1986) · C. Bridenbaugh, *Jamestown, 1544–1699* (1980) · W. L. Grant and J. F. Munro, eds., *Acts of the privy council of England: colonial series, 1: 1613–80* (1908)

Gatford, Lionel (*d.* 1665), Church of England clergyman, was a native of Sussex; his parents' names are unknown. He was admitted as a scholar to Jesus College, Cambridge, in 1618, graduated BA in 1622, and proceeded MA and was elected a fellow of his college in 1625. He was ordained a deacon at Peterborough on Christmas eve 1626, and elected junior proctor of the university in 1632. The following year he proceeded BD and was appointed vicar of St Clement's, Cambridge. He reacted strongly against Eleazar Duncon's DD thesis of March 1633 commending bowing at the altar and asserting the efficaciousness of good works, writing critically and at length on the subject to Lord Goring on 22 July. He enjoyed the patronage of Goring and of Sir John Rous throughout his career, and having resigned his fellowship in 1638 was presented by Rous in 1641 to the rectory of Dennington, Suffolk. About this time, or soon after, he married Dorcas, whose other name is unknown.

Soon after the outbreak of the civil war Gatford was ejected from his parish. He then went to Cambridge to supervise the printing of a pamphlet he had written concerning 'the Right, Power, Honour and Dignity, of Kings … and the loyalty and obedience due to them from all their Subjects' (Gatford, *Exhortation*, A2v). On the night of 26 January 1643 Oliver Cromwell seized the manuscript and those sheets which had already been printed, and arrested Gatford in his bed at Jesus College. He was sent to London, and on 30 January the Commons ordered that he be imprisoned in Ely House, Holborn. He spent seventeen months in custody, during which he wrote an attack on puritan preachers, *An Exhortation to Peace* (1643), before he was exchanged on 7 May 1644 for a puritan clergyman imprisoned by royalists at Oxford. After his release Gatford travelled to the royalist headquarters at Oxford, where he lodged in the house of the mayor, Thomas Smith, and wrote a pamphlet, *Logos àlexifarmakos, or, Hyperphysicall Directions* (1644), which dealt with the spiritual and bodily causes and effects of the outbreak of plague in the city.

On 18 February 1645 the committee for plundered ministers authorized a payment to his wife, but Gatford himself was that year appointed chaplain to the royalist garrison at Pendennis Castle in Cornwall. In the summer he drafted an address 'to the valiant and loyal Cornish men' urging them to rise up in support of the royal cause (Ogle and others, 1.271–2). He was taken prisoner at the surrender of Pendennis Castle in August 1646, and may have been exiled from England at this time. By March 1647, at the latest, he was with the royalists in Jersey and had become chaplain to Sir Edward Hyde. In *Englands Complaint* (1648), Gatford urged those who had been seduced by 'the Devil and Devilish men' to repent of rebellion. This pamphlet argued that the Jesuits were behind the attacks on the Church of England and warned that the execution of the king would lead to the shedding of the blood of more protestants than had 'been shed since the Reformation' (Gatford, *Englands Complaint*, 1648, 4, 14, 36).

It is not clear when Gatford returned to England, but he may have been in the country when his *A Petition for the Vindication of the … Book of Common Prayer* appeared in September 1654. This argued that the Book of Common Prayer had been an integral part of the most perfect church 'that ever yet saw light in the Christian world' (Gatford, *Petition*, sig. Aa4r). After his return to England, Gatford lived at various addresses in Norfolk, Middlesex, and Kent and his 'poverty of condition' evidently forced him to take boarders (ibid., sig. A2r). He was 'much tormented by the county committees' (*DNB*) because of his continued adherence to the traditional rites of the Church of England, but continued to publish, his *Publick Good without Private Interest* appearing in 1657.

After the Restoration, Gatford was created DD by royal mandate and restored to the parish of Dennington. In 1661 he petitioned the king for appointment as vicar of Plymouth in Devon because the chancel and parsonage

house of his old parish in Suffolk were in ruins and he could not afford to have them rebuilt. In August 1662 the nonconformist minister of Plymouth was ejected, but the corporation elected Roger Ashton as his successor and Gatford never took up his position. In 1661 he addressed a petition *To the most Reverend, the Archbishops and Bishops* in convocation for the relief of the large number of impoverished royalists, in which he claimed to be 'Chaplain to his Sacred Majesty'. In the same year he penned a vigorous defence of his patron, Sir John Rous, from puritan charges of drunkenness, *A True and Faithfull Narrative of the … Death of Mr William Tyrrell* (1661). In 1663 he was appointed curate of Great Yarmouth on the recommendation of Sir Edward Hyde, now earl of Clarendon. He died there of the plague in 1665 and the corporation of the town presented his widow, Dorcas, with £100 in consideration of his services to the cure.   JASON MᶜELLIGOTT

Sources Venn, *Alum. Cant.* · *Walker rev.*, 334 · *Calendar of the Clarendon state papers preserved in the Bodleian Library*, ed. O. Ogle and others, 5 vols. (1869–1970) · L. Gatford, *An exhortation to peace* (1643) · L. Gatford, *A petition for the vindication of the publique use of the Book of Common Prayer* (1655) · *JHC*, 2 (1640–42), 953 · *CSP dom.*, 1633–4, 150, 279 · *DNB*
Archives BL, Add. MS 5870, fol. 172

Gatley, Alfred (1816–1863), sculptor, was born at Kerridge, near Macclesfield, Cheshire, the second son of William Gatley, a quarry owner, and his wife, Betty (or possibly Hannah) Henshaw (d. 1823). His father was a yeoman who owned and worked two small quarries in the Kerridge hills, an occupation with which the family had long been connected.

After the death of his mother, Alfred was sent to a local dame-school and afterwards attended a day school at Rainow. In his youth he was employed in his father's yards, where early works included a bust of Milton (Kerridge stone, 1833; priv. coll.) and stone statuettes of Tam O'Shanter and Souter Johnnie (1833), after James Thom's celebrated figures. He was befriended at this time by the Revd James Sumner, vicar of Pott Shrigley, who encouraged his artistic talents and furthered his education. Sumner arranged for his protégé to work for a sculptor in London, and in 1837 Gatley joined the studio of E. H. Baily.

Gatley studied anatomy and obtained permission to copy in the British Museum; in 1839 he was admitted to the Royal Academy Schools. There he obtained silver medals for models in the antique academy and life academy in 1841, 1842, and 1844. His first exhibit at the academy was in 1841, and in 1843 he became an assistant to the sculptor M. L. Watson. In the same year he gained his first success with his bust of Hebe (exh. RA, 1843) was chosen by one of the prizewinners of the Art Union of London, the leading art lottery of the time. The work was subsequently cast in bronze by the firm of J. A. Hatfield and editions were distributed to other prize holders. Leaving Watson about 1847, in the following years Gatley made a precarious living as a sculptor of portrait busts. Several were executed for patrons in Cheshire, for example his bust of John Sumner, bishop of Chester (afterwards archbishop of

Canterbury) (exh. RA, 1848), commissioned following a local subscription. He also made busts of the theologian Richard Hooker (1851; Temple Church, London) and General Espartero, duke of Vittoria and Morella, ex-regent of Spain (exh. RA, 1846). Gatley's church memorials include those to Bridget Downes (1840; Pott Shrigley, Cheshire) and George Lockwood (d. 1854; Lambourne, Essex).

Seeking to improve his prospects, Gatley went to Rome in 1852. He took a studio near the Porta Pinciana and soon met the sculptor John Gibson, whose enthusiasm for Greek art he is said to have shared. He produced several 'ideal' works at this time, including figures of Echo (marble, 1853; version priv. coll.) and Night. In 1855 he received his most important commission, from Samuel Christie-Miller MP, for a large bas-relief for the mausoleum of the book collector William Henry Miller, at Craigentinny, near Edinburgh. The subject was *Pharaoh and his Army in the Red Sea* (1855–61). It was followed by a second order for a companion relief representing *The Song of Moses and Miriam* (1857–63) (both *in situ*). These works attracted universal admiration in Rome: their epic proportions, complex figuration, and detailed rendering of costume and physiognomy—based on a study of fifth-century Greek and ancient Egyptian relief sculpture—were rarely seen at that time. Gibson is said to have considered them to be 'modelled in the true sculptural style of bas-relief' (Sumner, 730) and *The Queen* magazine thought them 'among the noblest productions of modern art' (July 1863). He also carved a group, A Greek Hero Leading a Bull to Sacrifice (marble, 1861; Salford Art Gallery) and a series of animal studies which earned him the title 'the Landseer of sculpture'.

Gatley visited England in 1862, when he contributed nine works—including the *Pharaoh* relief, *Echo*, *Night*, and some statuettes of lions—to the London International Exhibition of that year. He had hoped to establish his reputation in England with these, but despite many favourable notices in the press he received no commissions. He returned to Rome bitterly disappointed to complete the *Song of Miriam* relief. In June 1863 he was taken ill with dysentery; after an apparent recovery he deteriorated and died, unmarried, on 28 June 1863, aged forty-seven. He was buried in the protestant cemetery in Rome. Despite the great success of his *Pharaoh* and *Miriam* reliefs, Gatley received few commissions during his career and he barely made a living from his sculpture. Though conscientious and well-liked, he was said to have been highly sensitive, diffident, and 'utterly unable to push himself forward in any way' (Sumner, 733). In appearance he was 'considerably below middle height … and extremely thin', though 'his face and head were fine' and 'his laughter was most hearty and infectious' (ibid., 726, 731).

R. E. GRAVES, rev. MARTIN GREENWOOD

Sources M. S. S. [M. S. Sumner], 'Our sculptor–friend: a biographical sketch', *Aunt Judy's Annual Volume* (1885), 722–36 • A. Reaney, 'Landseer of sculpture', *Cheshire Life*, 34/5 (May 1968), 54–5 • R. Gunnis, *Dictionary of British sculptors, 1660–1851* (1953); new edn

(1968) • *Art Journal*, 25 (1863), 181 • Graves, *RA exhibitors* • *The Athenaeum* (25 July 1863), 117 • *The Queen* (18 July 1863) • F. T. Palgrave, ed., *Official catalogue of the fine art department* (1862), 145, 269 [exhibition catalogue, International Exhibition, London, 1862] • private information (2004)
Archives priv. coll., diaries and corresp.
Likenesses J. Adams-Acton, exh. RA 1860 • M. da Tuna, portrait, 1862, priv. coll. • Da Silva, portrait; formerly in family home at Kerridge, Cheshire
Wealth at death under £200: probate, 13 Nov 1863, *CGPLA Eng. & Wales*

Gatliff, James (1765–1831), army officer and Church of England clergyman, the son of James Gatliff of Manchester, a man of leisure, was born in Manchester on 21 December 1765. Educated at the Manchester grammar school until the age of eleven, and then at a succession of private schools, he was commissioned into the 52nd foot as an ensign in January 1782. His memoirs provide a vivid impression of military life, initially in camp at Epsom and subsequently on tours of duty in India and China. Enthusiasm for hunting and gaming, combined with a quick temper, led him into a succession of quarrels and duels, in one of which his adversary was killed. On returning to England he left the army with the rank of captain-lieutenant and lived for some time by private means, pursuing his interests in sport and rose growing. His skill as a botanical draughtsman was commended by Sir Joseph Banks, but this activity was never more than an amateur diversion. After marrying Margaret Firth, of Norwich, sister of the first attorney-general for Canada, he resided first at Llawhaden House near Narberth in Pembrokeshire and later in Devon and on the Isle of Man.

In 1801, compelled by shortage of money and prompted by his wife, Gatliff was ordained by Bishop Creigan of Sodor and Man, and in 1802 he obtained the stipendiary curacy of Gorton Chapel near Manchester through the influence of his brother, John Gatliff, a fellow of the Manchester collegiate church. In 1803 he succeeded to the perpetual curacy of St Thomas's Chapel, Heaton Norris, and in 1808 he returned as incumbent to Gorton. Throughout this period he lived beyond his means, and repeated attempts to retrieve his fortunes by gambling on the lottery all ended in disappointment. A venture into publishing produced a new edition of William Wogan's *Essay on the Proper Lessons with a Memoir of the Author* (4 vols., 1818). The essay was considered unusual on account of its author's inclinations towards visionaryism. Far from proving profitable, its publication involved Gatliff in further pecuniary embarrassment and imprisonment for debt in the Fleet from January to July 1818.

At this point the bishop of Chester, George Henry Law, moved also by reports of Gatliff's heterodoxy, sequestered the living of Gorton. Gatliff, in protest, published a statement of his own case in 1820 with the curious title *A firm attempt at investigation, or, The twinkling effort of a falling star to relieve the Cheshire full moon*. Such behaviour exhausted the bishop's patience, and although Gatliff eventually returned to Gorton in 1826, he was obliged to resort to the expedient of dealing in books and pictures for a period before securing a temporary preaching appointment at Brechin, where he compiled his memoirs and perfected his skills as a fly-fisherman. He died in April 1831 at Gorton and was buried in the chancel of his chapel there.

RICHARD SHARP

Sources H. E. Gatliff, ed., *Stations, gentlemen! Memoirs of James Gatliff* (1938) • J. F. Smith, ed., *The admission register of the Manchester School, with some notes of the more distinguished scholars*, 3 vols. in 4 pts, Chetham Society, 69, 73, 93, 94 (1866–74) • J. Higson, *The Gorton Historical Recorder* (1852)
Likenesses portrait, repro. in Gatliff, ed., *Stations, gentlemen!*

Gatti family (*per.* 1847–1981), restaurateurs, theatre owners, and entrepreneurs, came to prominence with **Carlo Gatti** (1817–1878), who was born into a patrician family in the *frazione* (district) of Marogno in Dongio, Val di Blenio, Ticino, Switzerland, on 27 July 1817, the youngest of four sons and three daughters of Stefano Gatti (1776–1842) and his wife, Apollonia de Righetti. Fleeing a rough and rudimentary education from his oldest brother, Giacomo (1804–1863), parish priest of Castro in the same valley, in 1829 he walked, supposedly with only 25 francs in his pocket, to Paris. Though his family were partners in the wholesale chestnut importing business of Righenzi et Gatti, Carlo eventually went his own way. He plied a variety of trades, particularly selling hot chestnuts and light pastry *goffres*, returning to Ticino in the summers. In 1839 he married, at Castro, Maria Marioni (1814–1868), with whom he had five daughters and a son, Stefano (1840–1849). He enjoyed little success before his arrival in England in July 1847.

Within a few months Gatti had earned enough from selling *goffres* in Battersea Fields and from a stall or shop in Hatton Wall, in the Italian quarter of London, to open a French-style café in the great hall of Hungerford Market. Further cafés there and at 129 Holborn Hill and a chocolate factory at 122 Holborn Hill had opened by 1849. The cafés were the first of their kind in Britain. They created a stir with their elegant marble tables, plate-glass mirrors, red velvet seating, small string orchestras, high quality, and moderate prices. In the course of the 1850s Carlo became the first mass manufacturer of ice cream, previously an aristocratic delicacy. By 1858 he claimed to have sold up to ten thousand penny ices a day. In the same years he opened other cafés in Hungerford Market (including the so-called 'Hungerford Hall') and in central London. Under pressure from his clientele, by the end of the decade some began to provide 'chops and chips' and heavier fare, thereby becoming 'Swiss café-restaurants'. They were often run in partnership with fellow Bleniesi, notably Battista Bolla, Giuseppe Monico, Carlo's cousin Agostino Gatti, and his older brothers Giuseppe (1807–1873) and Giovanni (1809–1876), who had arrived in London from Paris by 1852, though Giovanni seems soon afterwards to have returned to Paris, where he remained. In 1857 Carlo, who had owned ice wells off the Regent's Canal for some years, formed a company, based in New Wharf Road, King's Cross, to import ice from Norway.

Though not the first, by the 1870s it had become the largest such concern in the country, with more than sixty ice wagons, and constituted Carlo's principal source of income.

In 1862, when Hungerford Market was demolished to make way for Charing Cross Station, Carlo and his brothers were amply compensated and opened a restaurant (1862) and in 1864 a music-hall (Gatti's Palace of Varieties, alias Gatti's-in-the-Road, alias Gatti's-over-the-Water) at 212–14 Westminster Bridge Road. In 1866 Carlo returned to the site of Hungerford Market where, in the arches supporting the station at 10–12 Villiers Street, he opened large billiard rooms, Gatti's Charing Cross Music-Hall (alias Gatti's-under-the-Arches), and the Café Restaurant de la Confédération Suisse. This was soon bringing in far greater profits than Gatti's-over-the-Water. In addition, Carlo and his brothers formed part of a syndicate, Variety Theatres Consolidated, that owned a string of other music-halls throughout London. The brothers also owned a chocolate company, Gatti Brothers (1852), based in Acton Street, Haggerston, and a steam works manufacturing hydraulic lifts in Little George Street near the Minories. Carlo personally owned a patisserie, run by one of his daughters, at 52 Strand and, from 1870, the 60 acre Renters Farm in Hendon. From the 1850s he also had profitable investments in Piedmont.

Gatti acted as a semi-official honorary consul to his fellow Ticinese, offering them employment and arranging accommodation, tickets, and loans for those emigrating to Australia and America. Through loans and renting premises he also enabled many families from the Val di Blenio and its neighbouring valley, the Valle Leventina, as well as several Italian nationals, to set up their own café-restaurants in London, its suburbs and, from the later 1850s, beyond. His brothers and nephews followed his lead and by 1900 'Swiss restaurant-cafés' of varying sizes, often advertising themselves on their fascias as 'from Gattis' or even, simply, as 'Gattis' (a practice understandably resented by the family) were to be found throughout the United Kingdom.

Despite naturalization in 1858, Carlo Gatti played an active part in Ticinese affairs. Between 1872 and 1877 his donations and low-interest loans made possible the construction of a carriage road over the Lukmanier Pass into the Val di Blenio. Between 1867 and 1875, he served as a councillor for the *circolo* of Malvaglia on the Ticinese *gran consiglio*. He was a regular attender, though not a speaker. Initially a conservative, his views grew increasingly radical until in 1875, following his definitive return to Switzerland, he stood as a liberal. This caused divisions in his family, and his nephew Stefano stood against him as a conservative. His failure to be elected embittered him towards his home village and contributed to the decision that, in his reputed words, if Dongio had had his goods, it would not have his bones. He was buried in Bellinzona on 10 September 1878 following his death four days earlier as a result of a fall from a loft. His grandiose tomb, erected in 1883, which incorporates a portrait bust by Giovanni Chierici, professor at the Accademia di Belle Arti at Parma, survives. Though Gatti was rumoured to have died a millionaire, he left less than £60,000 of personal property in England.

Thick-set and bearded, self-confident, genial, uncouth, energetic, and garrulous, Il Gatton (Big Cat) or Milord never lost the demeanour of the peasant or learned to spell correctly in Italian or English. He was an excellent self-publicist, however, and kept close control over his businesses. He was frequently to be found, even at the height of his fortune, chatting beside a large restaurant grill (which he claimed to have pioneered), on a stool by the cash desk, or in a horse-drawn cart with a daughter by his side, collecting rent from tenant cafés. His first wife died in 1868, and in 1871 he married the 23-year-old Marietta Andreazzi. Though this marriage was childless he had at least two illegitimate children, including a posthumous son. His eldest daughter and principal heir, Rosa (1845–1927), inherited all her father's energy but none of his sociability. She first married her cousin, Giuseppe's son, Giuseppe (1836–1870), who had taken over the management of his father's London concerns following the latter's return to Ticino in 1866. After his death she married Giacomo Corazza. Though originally from Dongio, the Corazzas had established themselves in Parma and their workforce increasingly stemmed from that region.

The leading members of the next generation were **Agostino Gatti** (1841–1897) and **Stefano Gatti** (1844–1906), the sons of Carlo's brother Giovanni Gatti and his first wife, Maria, *née* Gatti (1813–1854). Agostino was born in Paris on 29 March 1841 and Stefano in Dongio on 29 December 1844. Educated in commercial schools in France and, after 1852, in England, they began work as waiters in their uncle's cafés in Hungerford Market in their teens. From the very first the two brothers were inseparable. In May 1862, with Hungerford Market's demolition imminent, Agostino Gatti and Giacomo Monico (also of Dongio) opened their own, initially rather small, café at the Royal Adelaide Gallery at 7–9 Adelaide Street off the Strand. Stefano Gatti became a partner a few years later and Giacomo Monico left in 1872, eventually to found a major café-restaurant at the intersection of Piccadilly Circus and Shaftesbury Avenue.

An offshoot of the music provided in the Gattis' cafés were the autumn Promenade Concerts which Agostino and Stefano organized between 1873 and 1880 at the Covent Garden Theatre, and the pantomimes mounted there in the winters of 1878–80. They showed how profitable such popular entertainments could be and gave vent to the creative side of Stefano's character. In 1879 Agostino and he took on the lease of the Adelphi Theatre and the neighbouring restaurant, popularly known as the Marble Halls. They purchased the building outright in 1881, rebuilding it in 1887. In 1892 they bought the Vaudeville Theatre a few doors away, reopening it after refurbishment in 1896. The brothers were actively involved in the management of both theatres, the emphasis being on melodrama at the Adelphi and light comedy at the Vaudeville.

By 1880 Agostino and Stefano were running their restaurants and theatres in competition with those of Carlo Gatti's heirs. After 1882, and presumably utilizing the enormous profits from their Promenade Concerts, the brothers more than doubled the ground space and redeveloped the interior of the Adelaide Gallery to create a café-restaurant and beer hall with entrances onto the Strand, William IV Street, and Adelaide Street. By the 1890s the Adelaide Gallery was employing between 180 and 200 predominantly Ticinese waiters and forty chefs in enormous subterranean kitchens, and had a reputation as 'the most popular restaurant in London' (Pascoe, 1887, 51). In spite of their growing wealth, the brothers were to be found most nights at a table in the restaurant checking the quality of the food and the honesty of their waiters.

In 1882 Agostino and Stefano had installed an electricity sub-station in the cellars of the Royal Adelaide Gallery. In 1885, finding that no company would supply their theatre with electric light because it was illegal to lay electric cables in the Strand in daytime, they opened another sub-station in Maiden Lane and laid cables along the Strand themselves at night. The Adelphi became the first London theatre to be lit with electric light. In 1889 they created the Charing Cross and Strand Electricity Supply Corporation Ltd. By 1900 it was providing the City and most of Westminster with electricity.

Alongside these activities, and although they had been naturalized as British subjects in 1868, the Gatti brothers continued to take a close interest in Swiss affairs. Agostino served as a conservative member of the Swiss federal assembly for the Sopraceneri from 1873 to 1893, and Stefano as a member, also conservative, of the Ticinese *gran consiglio* for Blenio from 1875 to 1893. Though they attended when they could (usually in June and December), neither was active. They probably owed their nominations to their family's wealth and influence in the Val di Blenio. Their opponents regularly accused them of transporting their waiters to Switzerland to vote for conservative candidates. Political as well as philanthropic considerations may have influenced Stefano, in 1874, in expanding a pension and sickness fund for Gatti employees, created four years earlier, into a mutual benefit society, the Unione Ticinese, for the Ticinese colony in England. In 1885 he founded a short-lived Conservative club, Il Ticino.

Numerous contemporaries commented on the sociability, amiability, and integrity of Agostino and Stefano, their circle of friends ranging from composers, actors, and playwrights to Lord Salisbury. Agostino, nicknamed Angostura (a bitter aperitif), thickset, balding, and with heavy dark eyebrows and moustache, was more the businessman while Stefano (Stephanotis or Gattin or 'Little Cat'), small, thin, delicate, possibly a homosexual, and with a love of travel, was more an aesthete. Their pronounced Catholic piety found expression in philanthropy in England, where they were benefactors of Corpus Christi Church, Maiden Lane, Covent Garden, and in Switzerland. Despite Agostino's marriage in 1866 to Giulia Bonzanigo of Bellinzona (1847–1925), with whom he had three sons and four daughters, the two brothers always lived together, initially over the Royal Adelaide Gallery, then in Beckenham, and from 1879 at 10 Bedford Square. It was there that Agostino died on 14 January 1897 of kidney disease, leaving his whole estate, valued at £168,278 11s. in Great Britain, to his brother. Stefano died of cancer in the same house on 12 October 1906, leaving £220,415 19s. 3d. in Great Britain. Both were buried in the family mausoleum in Kensal Green Roman Catholic cemetery.

The leading member of the next generation was Agostino's oldest son, **Sir John Maria Emilio** [*formerly* Joannes Maria Aemilius] **Gatti** (1872–1929). He was born in Dongio on 13 August 1872 and Italian was spoken at home. He was particularly attached to his younger, bachelor brother Rocco Joseph Stefano (1874–1950), who bore a striking physical resemblance to their father. From Stonyhurst College John proceeded to St John's College, Oxford, and the Inner Temple, qualifying as a barrister in 1894. In 1897 he married Lily Mary (*d.* 1964), an amateur artist and poet, and daughter of Dr Samuel Lloyd; they had four sons and three daughters.

In 1897 John Gatti took over his father's businesses. Leaving the management of the restaurants to Rocco, he dutifully pursued his business interests in the theatre and, with more enthusiasm, in electricity, which continued to expand through a series of mergers with other companies and the building of new power stations. The latter aroused his interest in London's infrastructure and led him to embark on a political career in London. A Westminster councillor from 1906, he served as mayor of Westminster in 1911–12. In 1918 he was elected to the London county council, serving as chairman of the finance committee from 1920 to 1927 and as chairman in 1927–8. A Conservative, he was described as 'a moderate Progressive rather than a Municipal Reformer' (*The Star*, 10 March 1927), but his relative radicalism is said to have obstructed a national career.

John Gatti severed his links with Dongio in 1911, selling his family's estate to create a charitable trust. Yet contemporaries still thought that 'there is some suggestion of Italy about him, though he is a most patriotic Englishman' (*Liverpool Post*, 12 March 1927) and a sister and one of his daughters were to die in Ticino. 'Small grey-haired and swarthy with a mild manner and quiet mental grip evincing considerable grasp' (ibid.), he was always elegant and had a penchant for Ticinese Brissago cigars. Although interested in the arts and literature and a collector of antiquarian books, prints, and bindings, he was of a practical bent. He was knighted in 1928. He died of a heart attack on the Littlestone golf course on 14 September 1929, leaving £265,689 0s. 6d. He was buried in Kensal Green.

John Gatti was succeeded in his businesses by his eldest son, John (Jack) Agostino Stefano Gatti (1898–1972). The Royal Adelaide Gallery closed in 1939, and the electricity company was nationalized in 1948, though Jack's brother, Stephen Geoffrey Gatti (*d.* 1958), remained involved until 1957. Jack Gatti sold the Adelphi Theatre in 1955 and the Vaudeville in 1969. Carlo Gatti's Charing Cross Music-Hall closed in 1903, to be followed shortly afterwards by his restaurants. The family chocolate factory, which had been owned after 1876 by Giuseppe's descendants, the Peduzzis, and was known in its last years as C. P. Ducie, closed in the late 1920s. At about the same period, the music-hall on Westminster Bridge Road was sold and converted into a cinema. Carlo Gatti's Corazza descendants continued to run his ice business, in its final incarnation as United Carlo Gatti, Stevenson and Slaters Ltd, until 1981. Carlo Gatti's family house in Villiers Street was finally sold only in 1988.

PETER BARBER

Sources P. Peduzzi, *Pioneri Ticinesi in Inghilterra: la saga della famiglia Gatti, 1780–1980* (1985) • F. Kinross, *Coffee and ices: the story of Carlo Gatti in London* (1991) • 'The self-made men of our times: Carlo Gatti', *Chimney Corner* (17 Dec 1870), 26 • account ledgers for Carlo Gatti, Coutts Bank Archives, London • registro della popolazione, Dongio, Archivio cantonale, Bellinzona, Switzerland • family papers, priv. coll. [Stefano Gatti and Sir John Gatti] • private information (2004) • Boase, *Mod. Eng. biog.* • *London of To-day* [C. E. Pascoe] (1885–1907) • *The Post Office London directory* (1847–1980) • BM • GL, Philip Norman collection • quarter session records, Middlesex licensing sessions, LMA • *Il Gottardo* [Switzerland] (11 Sept 1878) • *CGPLA Eng. & Wales* (1878) [Carlo Gatti] • WWW, 1929–40 • hearings into opening of Hungerford Bridge, 1858, HLRO • P. Barker and P. Jacomelli, *Continental taste: Ticinese emigrants and their café-restaurants in Britain 1847–1981* (1997) • P. Barker and others, *Vita Ticinese a Londra: 125 years of the Unione Ticinese* (1999) • F. Ferrari, ed., *Lo Zampino dei Gatti* (1996)

Archives priv. coll., family papers

Likenesses photographs, *c.*1875 (Agostino, Stefano), priv. coll.; repro. in Barker and Jacomelli, *Continental taste* • G. Chierici, bust (Carlo Gatti), Bellinzona cemetery • photograph (Agostino in old age), repro. in *ILN* (Jan 1897) • photographs (Carlo, Giuseppe, Agostino, Stefano, Sir John, Rocco Gatti), repro. in Peduzzi, *Pioneri Ticinesi in Inghilterra* • portrait (Carlo Gatti), priv. coll.; repro. in Ferrari, *Lo Zampino dei Gatti*

Wealth at death under £60,000—Carlo Gatti: probate, 1878, *CGPLA Eng. & Wales* • £168,278 11s.—Agostino Gatti: probate, 1897, *CGPLA Eng. & Wales* • £220,415 19s. 3d.—Stefano Gatti: probate, 1906, *CGPLA Eng. & Wales* • £265,689 0s. 6d.—Sir John Gatti: probate, 1929, *CGPLA Eng. & Wales*

Gatti, Agostino (1841–1897). *See under* Gatti family (*per.* 1847–1981).

Gatti, Carlo (1817–1878). *See under* Gatti family (*per.* 1847–1981).

Gatti, Sir John Maria Emilio (1872–1929). *See under* Gatti family (*per.* 1847–1981).

Gatti, Stefano (1844–1906). *See under* Gatti family (*per.* 1847–1981).

Gattie, Henry (1774–1844), actor and singer, was born near Bath and brought up to the trade of a wig maker, but very early in life acquired a liking for the theatre. At the age of nineteen he had become well known at some musical associations. His first appearances on the stage were in singing parts, such as Frederick in *No Song No Supper*, Valentine in *The Farmer*, and Captain Macheath in *The Beggar's Opera*. On 7 November 1807 he made his début at Bath as Trot in Thomas Morton's comedy *Town and Country*, and was next seen as Paul in J. Cobb's *Paul and Virginia*, but he soon settled down into playing, as a general rule, old men, Frenchmen, and Irishmen.

Having been introduced by the comedian William Lovegrove to Samuel James Arnold, the proprietor of the Lyceum Theatre, Gattie made his first appearance in London on 14 July 1813, in Moore's new comic opera entitled *MP, or, The Blue Stocking*, in which he took the character of La Fosse, and afterwards played Sir Harry Sycamore and other old-men characters and footmen's parts. From this house he migrated to Drury Lane, where he was first seen on 6 October 1813 as Vortex in Morton's *A Cure for the Heartache*. He remained at Drury Lane until his retirement in 1833, filling up his summer vacations at the Haymarket, the Lyceum, and other houses. At Drury Lane, where he was paid £7 a week, he was frequently the substitute for Joseph S. Munden, William Dowton, Daniel Terry, and Charles Mathews, to none of whom, however, he was equal in talent. In August 1815 he took the part of the justice of the village in *The Maid and the Magpie* at the Lyceum Theatre. His most celebrated and best-known impersonation was Monsieur Morbleu in William Moncrieff's farce *Monsieur Tonson*, which was first played at Drury Lane in September 1821. His acting in this piece was much commended by George IV, who had commanded its performance soon after its first production. Other characters in which he was popular were Dr Caius in *The Merry Wives of Windsor* and Moses in Sheridan's *The School for Scandal*. After a career of twenty-six years as an actor and comedian, Gattie retired from the stage in 1833 and opened a cigar shop at Oxford, which became the resort of many of the students, by whom his dry humour was much appreciated. He was married, but had no family. His death occurred at Reading on 17 November 1844, in his seventieth year.

                                          G. C. BOASE, rev. NILANJANA BANERJI

Sources *The Era* (24 Nov 1824) · Adams, *Drama* · 'Memoir of Mr Gattie', *Oxberry's Dramatic Biography*, 4/51 (1826), 36–46 [incl. sketch by Sharpe] · *The biography of the British stage, being correct narratives of the lives of all the principal actors and actresses* (1824) · *Era Almanack and Annual* (1892) · Hall, *Dramatic ports.* · Genest, *Eng. stage* · *GM*, 2nd ser., 22 (1844), 645 · [Clarke], *The Georgian era: memoirs of the most eminent persons*, 4 (1834), 569

Likenesses R. Cooper, stipple engravings, pubd 1822–5 (after M. W. Sharpe), NPG · Dean, stipple, pubd 1823 (after T. G. Wageman), NPG · Rogers, stipple and line engraving, pubd 1826 (after M. W. Sharpe), NPG · J. Kennerlay, stipple and line engraving (as Monsieur Morbleu in *Monsieur Tonson*; after M. W. Sharpe), NPG · four prints (of Gattie?), Harvard TC · portrait, repro. in *New English drama* (1823) · portrait, repro. in D. Terry, *British theatrical gallery: a collection of whole length portraits* (1825) · portrait, repro. in 'Memoir of Mr Gattie', *Oxberry's Dramatic Biography*

Gatty, Alfred (1813–1903), Church of England clergyman and author, born in London on 18 April 1813, was the second surviving son of Robert Gatty, solicitor, of Angel Court and Finsbury Square, London, and his wife, Margaret, daughter of Edward Jones of Arnold, Nottinghamshire. The family originally came from Cornwall, where it had been settled since the fifteenth century. After receiving preparatory schooling at Temple Grove, East Sheen, Gatty entered Charterhouse in 1825, and Eton in 1829. For a time he prepared for the legal profession, but on 28 April 1831 he matriculated from Exeter College, Oxford, and graduated BA in 1836, proceeding MA in 1839 and DD in 1860. Gatty was ordained deacon in 1837 and priest in the

following year. From 1837 to 1839 he was curate of Bellerby, a small chapel of ease in the North Riding of Yorkshire. He was married, on 8 July 1839, to Margaret [see Gatty, Margaret (1809–1873)], youngest daughter of Alexander John *Scott, with whom he had six sons (two of whom died in infancy) and four daughters.

Upon his marriage Gatty was nominated by his wife's uncle Edward Ryder to the vicarage of Ecclesfield, near Sheffield, which he held until his death. In *A Life at One Living* (1884) he described how he found the large medieval church and its churchyard in a sad state of neglect and the parish 'rude and rough, notoriously so'. A moderate high-churchman, he was determined to see the church 'beautified' and restored to its former dignity. This was largely achieved between 1858 and 1879. He was active in subdividing his enormous parish and in building new churches and schools. He was appointed rural dean in 1861 and became subdean of York Minster the following year. After the death of his first wife, he married, on 1 October 1884, Mary Helen, daughter of Edward Newman, solicitor, of Barnsley, Yorkshire; they had no children, and she died in 1919. Gatty died at Ecclesfield vicarage on 20 January 1903 and was buried in the churchyard. His parishioners erected the Gatty Memorial Hall as a village social centre.

Of the children of his first marriage, Gatty's daughter Juliana *Ewing shared her mother's fame as a children's writer. His eldest surviving son, Revd Reginald Alfred Gatty (1844–1914), acquired a reputation as a field archaeologist and local historian; the second, Sir Alfred Scott Gatty (1847–1918), became Garter king of arms. The third son, Sir Stephen Herbert Gatty (1849–1922), became chief justice of Gibraltar, and the youngest, Charles Tindal Gatty (b. 1851), a convert to Roman Catholicism, had a varied career as a museum curator, newspaper editor, and private secretary to Lord Bute.

Gatty was a regular lecturer at the Sheffield Literary and Philosophical Society and published his writings on a wide range of subjects from an early age. While still an undergraduate he wrote *The Fancies of a Rhymer* (1833). He and his first wife published *Recollections of the Life of the Rev. A. J. Scott, DD, Lord Nelson's Chaplain* (1842) *Travels and Adventures of the Rev. Joseph Wolff* (1860), a descriptive tour of Ireland entitled *The Old Folks from Home* (1861), and *The Book of Sundials* (1872; 4th edn, 1900). Gatty also wrote *The Bell: its Origin, History, and Uses* (2nd edn, 1848) and *Key to Tennyson's 'In Memoriam'* (1881; 5th edn, 1894). Between 1846 and 1858 he published four volumes of sermons. He never responded to charges that he wrote anonymous political articles for a Sheffield paper of Conservative persuasion. His most substantial works, however, were in the field of local history. In 1869 he published a folio edition of Joseph Hunter's *Hallamshire*, a greatly enlarged version of the original work, which had been published fifty years earlier. The Gatty edition of *Hallamshire* was for many years highly regarded by local historians, though inevitably its approach became dated. In 1873 he published a popular history, *Sheffield, Past and Present*. A brief history of Ecclesfield church and priory is contained in his *A Life at One Living* (1884).

Gatty was a venerable figure in Ecclesfield, where he was vicar for sixty-four years. His granddaughter, Christabel Maxwell, wrote:

> Dr. Gatty, as I remember him was a distinguished-looking old man, with white whiskers who was never to be seen without a black-velvet skull-cap. He was a person whom we instinctively avoided, as he had a testy way of expressing himself when there were children about … He played innumerable games of patience in his chair by his fireside … and as he shuffled the cards with his elegant fingers he usually had a glass of port by his side. He was surrounded (so it seemed to us) by a host of elderly and middle-aged females who tended to his wants, and who to our minds all looked alike. (Maxwell, 55)

DAVID HEY

Sources *The Times* (21 Jan 1903) · A. Gatty, *A life at one living* (1884) · C. Maxwell, *Mrs. Gatty and Mrs. Ewing* (1949) · D. Hey, *The village of Ecclesfield* (1968) · *Men and women of the time* (1899) · **Archives** Sheff. Arch., lecture notes relating to Yorkshire history · U. Reading, letters to George Bell, publisher · **Likenesses** S. E. Waller, portrait; formerly in possession of Reginald Gatty, rector of Hooton Roberts, Yorkshire, 1912 · **Wealth at death** £1484 12s. 9d.: probate, 28 Feb 1903, CGPLA Eng. & Wales

Gatty [*née* Scott], **Margaret** (1809–1873), writer on natural history and children's writer, was born on 3 June 1809 in Burnham, Essex, the second daughter of the Revd Alexander John *Scott (1768–1840) and his wife, Mary Frances Ryder (1785–1811). Her father, a linguist and scholar, had been chaplain to Horatio Nelson; although he had hoped for greater preferment, he held the livings of Southminster, Essex, and Catterick, Yorkshire. Margaret and her sister Horatia had a lonely childhood, their mother having died when they were very young. Educated in their father's library, they learned several languages, sketched avidly, and wrote for a family literary club. Much influenced by her German reading, Margaret translated German and Italian poetry. Despite encouragement from Margaret Hodson, she gave up poetry, however, after a rejection from *Blackwood's*. Margaret's youth was much occupied with a demanding grandfather, an erratic sister, and a father frequently ill, and in pain. In 1837 the Scotts began an acquaintance with a local curate and antiquarian, Alfred *Gatty (1813–1903), but Dr Scott refused Margaret permission to marry him. Unlike her own parents, who had eloped in similar circumstances, Margaret submitted. In due course her father relented, and they were married on 8 July 1839. Margaret's uncle Edward Ryder presented them with the living of Ecclesfield, near Sheffield, where they spent the rest of their lives.

For the next dozen years Margaret Gatty was occupied chiefly with household cares and eight children. Shortly after her father's death she and her husband published *Recollections of the Life of the Rev. A. J. Scott* (1842), but it did not bring either the attention or the income they had hoped for. After a breakdown in 1848, she spent the winter in Hastings, and there began her lifelong passion for the collection and classification of seaweeds. A network of scientific friends, including W. H. Harvey of Trinity College, Dublin, and George Johnston of Berwick upon Tweed, shared her enthusiasm and their expertise.

In 1851, Margaret Gatty wrote some didactic fairy-stories; George Bell published them as *The Fairy Godmothers*, paying the author in books on marine botany. A varied writing career ensued: a clerical story (*The Poor Incumbent*, 1858), an account of an Irish holiday (1861), and moral tales (*Proverbs Illustrated*, 1857; *Legendary Tales*, 1858; *The Human Face Divine*, 1860). Fascinated by Joseph Wolff, a European Jew and world traveller who had become a Church of England clergyman, she and her daughters collaborated on his autobiography (*Travels and Adventures of the Rev. Joseph Wolff*, 1860). 20 guineas induced her to translate Jean Macé's *History of a Bit of Bread* (1864), a children's introduction to anatomy and physiology; a lifelong private interest resulted in *The Book of Emblems* and *The Book of Sundials* (both 1872).

More enduring, however, were the domestic stories based upon Margaret Gatty's family, especially those centring upon her daughter Juliana, who as Juliana Horatia *Ewing (1841–1885) was eventually to eclipse her mother's reputation as a writer for children. Juliana was the family story-teller in *Aunt Judy's Tales* (1859) and *Aunt Judy's Letters* (1862). *Domestic Pictures and Tales* (1865) drew upon Margaret's own childhood. Her reputation in this field encouraged Bell to establish *Aunt Judy's Magazine* under her editorship; this monthly periodical published stories, natural history, songs, and miscellany by Juliana and others, including Lewis Carroll. Even more popular than these stories, however, were the five series of *Parables from Nature*, produced between 1855 and 1871, in which Margaret Gatty used natural history to teach moral and religious lessons, including the overriding lesson that God and nature need not be at strife. Appealing to both adult and child, the *Parables* remained in print, in some form at least, through most of the twentieth century. Among their admirers was Tennyson, whom the Gattys visited several times. In addition, Margaret Gatty published a *History of British Seaweeds* (1863), a guide for serious amateurs.

Margaret Gatty's literary and scientific accomplishments are the more remarkable for having been achieved despite family and parochial responsibilities, and increasing ill health. Afflicted by an intermittent muscular paralysis, she maintained her interests to her death, at the vicarage in Ecclesfield, on 4 October 1873. She was buried on 9 October in Ecclesfield churchyard, and like her daughter was commemorated by a memorial window in the church there.

SUSAN DRAIN

Sources C. Maxwell, *Mrs. Gatty and Mrs. Ewing* (1949) · J. H. Ewing, 'In memoriam, Margaret Gatty', *Aunt Judy's Magazine*, 12 (1874), 3–7; repr. in *Miscellanea* [1896], 179–87 · J. H. Ewing, 'Margaret Gatty', in M. Gatty, *Parables from nature* (1879), ix–xxi · records, Sheff. Arch., Hunter Archaeological Society · George Bell & Co. correspondence, U. Reading · private information (2004) · S. Drain, 'Margaret Gatty', *Victorian Britain: an encyclopedia*, ed. S. Mitchell (1988), 323 · S. Drain, 'Marine botany in the nineteenth century: Margaret Gatty, the lady amateurs, and the professionals', *Victorian Studies Association of Ontario Newsletter*, 53 (1994), 6–11 · W. Katz, *The emblems of Margaret Gatty: a study of allegory in nineteenth-century children's literature* (1993) · A. Rauch, 'Parables and parodies: Margaret Gatty's audiences in the *Parables from nature*', *Children's Literature*, 25 (1997), 137–52 · *Canada home: Juliana Horatia Ewing's Fredericton letters, 1867–1869*, ed. M. H. Blom and T. E. Blom (1983)

Archives Boston PL, corresp. · Sheff. Arch., corresp., diaries, and papers · Sheffield Central Library, corresp. and papers · U. Leeds, Brotherton L., musical commonplace book · U. St Andr. L., albums · Wordsworth Trust, Grasmere, Cumbria, letters | Bodl. Oxf., letters to C. S. Erskine · U. Reading L., letters to George Bell & Sons
Likenesses wood-engraving, pubd 1873 (after an unknown artist), NPG · Elliott & Fry, carte-de-visite, NPG · photograph, repro. in Maxwell, *Mrs. Gatty and Mrs. Ewing* · wood-engraving (after photograph), NPG; repro. in *ILN* (18 Oct 1873)

Gau, John. *See* Gaw, John (d. c.1553).

Gauden, John (1599/1600?–1662), bishop of Worcester, was born at Mayland, Essex, the son of John Gauden (*b. c.*1571, *d.* in or before 1625), the vicar there. Educated at Bury St Edmunds School he matriculated as a sizar from St John's College, Cambridge, at Michaelmas 1619, probably aged nineteen. He graduated BA in 1623 and proceeded MA in 1626. Four years later he accompanied Francis and William Russell, the two eldest sons of Sir William Russell of Chippenham, Cambridgeshire, when they went to Wadham College, Oxford; the boys matriculated aged fourteen and thirteen in January 1631. Gauden proceeded BD from Wadham in 1635.

By August 1638 Gauden was household chaplain to Robert Rich, earl of Warwick. In March 1640 he was presented by his former pupil, now Sir Francis Russell, to the vicarage of Chippenham. About this time he married Russell's sister Elizabeth (*d.* 1671), widow of Sir Edward Lewknor of Denham, Suffolk, and already the mother of a daughter; the Gaudens' eldest son, Lewknor, matriculated at university in 1661. On 29 November 1640 Gauden preached before the House of Commons a sermon published as *The Love of Truth and Peace* (1641). In July 1641 he proceeded DD. His continuing obligations to the Rich family were acknowledged in the dedication to Warwick of *Three Sermons Preached upon Several Occasions* (1642). Perhaps the earl had been behind his nomination in 1641 by the Commons to a royal peculiar, the deanery of Bocking, Essex, which came directly under the control of the province of Canterbury. Gauden obtained collation from the then imprisoned Archbishop William Laud, and was admitted to the living and title on 1 April 1642.

While the political and religious stance of Warwick and the later career of his young brother-in-law Russell as an army officer and Cambridgeshire MP might indicate that Gauden had parliamentarian sympathies, his views and activities in the 1640s and 1650s appear rather chameleon-like, and it seems that his ambitious nature allowed him to be a player for both sides; and as the Restoration came closer he seems to have engaged in an exercise of re-imaging this period of his life. He claimed that he had been nominated in 1642–3 to the Westminster assembly, but that his episcopal convictions had led to his name being dropped; certainly he was not on the final nominated list, though others of stronger episcopal conviction—such as Henry Hammond—had been nominated, and were on the final list. He seems to have taken the solemn league and covenant, but later denied having done so. He did persist in using the Book of Common Prayer

John Gauden (1599/1600?–1662), by John Hoskins, 1655

longer than many, but gave in to pressure from some of the neighbouring godly presbyterian clergy. Indeed, he seems to have co-operated with these clergy and remained in active ministry throughout the interregnum. It may be that Gauden had genuine moderate episcopalian sympathies, but was also a staunch royalist. Certainly in 1648–9, like many of the moderates, he had serious misgivings about the course of events, and he published *Religious and loyal protestation of John Gauden, D.D., against the present purposes and proceddings of the army and others about the trying and destroying our sovereign lord the king; sent to a colonell to bee presented to the Lord Fairfax*. He also wrote a tract attacking Cromwell for the king's execution, not published until 1660; entitled *Cromwell's Bloody Slaughter-House* it had all the invective and vocabulary of the Old Testament prophets.

There has been some debate over the part Gauden played in the *Eikon basilike* of Charles I. In a letter of January 1661 he referred to some secret service which he had undertaken, namely, as ghost writer of the monarch's work. According to Gilbert Burnet, Charles II and the duke of York considered that he had fulfilled this task; both Elizabeth Gauden and Anthony Walker, curate at Bocking, confirmed his involvement. On the other hand royalist writers claimed that Charles had begun the work at Theobalds in March 1641 and that the manuscript, lost at Naseby, was recovered by Major Huntington of Cromwell's regiment. However, this document was almost certainly Sir Edward Walker's 'Memorials', given by the author to Charles, then lost at Naseby, and later restored to the king. The likelihood is that Gauden had a significant responsibility for *Eikon basilike*, but that his many enemies sought to deny it.

Through the 1650s, although Gauden published trenchant defences of a traditional Church of England, he offended many strong episcopalian royalists by espousing some compromise with the presbyterian clergy on the lines suggested by Archbishop James Ussher for the reduction of episcopacy. *The Case of Ministers Maintenance by Tithes* (1653), arguing a common episcopalian–presbyterian cause, was accompanied by *Hieraspistes: a defence by way of apology for the ministry and ministers of the Church of England* (1653) and followed by *Christ at the Wedding: the Pristine Sanctity and Solemnity of Christian Marriage* (1654), in which he was critical of the provision for civil marriage. He returned to the troubles of the clergy in *A petitionary remonstrance presented to O[liver] P[rotector] Feb 4 1655 … in behalf of many thousands of his distressed brethren* (1656), but his reputation was probably further damaged in some quarters when on 5 March 1658 he delivered *Funerals Made Cordials* (1658), a sermon at the burial of Warwick's grandson and heir Robert Rich, who had only recently married Cromwell's daughter Frances. His *Hiera dakrya, ecclesiae Anglicanae suspira* (1659) is a defence of episcopacy and the Church of England against presbyterianism and Independency. This work included a large illustration of a tree of the Catholic church, with side shoots representing presbyterian and Independent polities, described in the text as 'low shrubs'. Episcopacy is defended as being primitive and catholic. In this work Gauden also defended Archbishop Laud but hinted at the shortcomings which had made him unpopular. Gauden also defended the liturgy of the Church of England, and in a reference to the Westminster directory for worship complained of 'the late *ramblings*, barrenness and confusion of some mens sad and *extemporary rhapsodes*, their rude and rusticall devotions'. However, it is clear that the episcopacy he defended was of a distinct, 'primitive' kind. His funeral sermon for the late bishop of Exeter, Ralph Brownrigg, preached at the Temple Church on 17 December 1659 and published with a memoir in 1660, praised this Calvinist prelate in illuminating terms. The dedication, dated 1 January, celebrated him 'for his conformity to his blessed Saviour, for his loyalty to sovereign power, for his love to his Country, for his zeal to the Reformed Religion'.

For a while this must have seemed a promising platform for future religious settlement. In February 1660 Gauden was chosen to deliver *A Sermon Preached in St Pauls … before the Lord Mayor and Common Council* (1660) in thanksgiving for the restoration to parliament of the secluded members. However, once the restoration of the monarchy had been effected the initiative was in the hands of those such as Gilbert Sheldon, soon bishop of London, who thoroughly distrusted Gauden's brand of compromise. Gauden was made a chaplain to the king and on 3 November, despite Sheldon's opposition, was elected bishop of Exeter, but Gauden complained that the revenues were only about £500 a year and asked in vain to be advanced to the vacant see of Winchester. One of the episcopal representatives at the Savoy conference, he showed himself the most obviously ready to negotiate with presbyterians.

In his *Considerations Touching the Liturgy of the Church of England* (1661) Gauden defended the integrity of the Church of England prayer book rites, arguing (as opposed to the Westminster directory) that a set liturgy defended true doctrine, advanced unity, and was helpful to simpler Christians. Gauden's earlier liaison with parliamentary persons and preachers meant that he knew at first hand the lengthy debate on infant baptism ignited by the exchange between John Tombes and Stephen Marshall in 1643. In this work Gauden defended infant baptism, appealing to the reformed covenant theology, and argued that the Church of England baptismal rite needed no change. In baptism original sin is removed, because regeneration is imputed to infants. Passive regeneration is sufficient for the removal of original sin, but after actual sin, it must have the active work of regeneration, which is to 'performe the Evangelical Conditions of actual faith and repentance'. In his work *The Whole Duty of a Communicant* Gauden defined sacraments as holy seals annexed to the word. The Lord's supper was a renewal of the covenant, mystical union with, and incorporation into, Christ. The sacramental elements, he taught, were signs and seals which really conveyed the power of Christ to the believer. In this work Gauden complained about the irreverence of certain ministers using the Westminster directory during the interregnum:

> I knew one Minister, (and he no small one in *vulgar esteem*,) would add to his delivery of the elements, such most uncharitable sarcasms as these: *Here, Darest thou take it! To another Take this and love Christ's Ministers better*, so to a *third, Here take it and leave your lying*; to a *fourth, Take heed the Devil enter not into thee*, and the like: Good God, are these fit decoys of mens *private passions* and *fancies*, to win *Common-people* to the Sacraments.   (J. Gauden, *The Whole Duty of a Communicant*, 1688, 21)

There was little that was controversial here, but his misreading of the political situation is seen in his life of Richard Hooker, and in his comments on the unfinished, or unpublished, book, *Of the Lawes of Ecclesiasticall Politie*, published in January 1662. Gauden added little to what was already known of Hooker's life, but failed to make his account hagiographical. Indeed, Hooker and the pre-civil war Church of England are shown to have had weaknesses. He failed to mitigate Hooker's dull preaching style, and of the church in the 1640s wrote that

> the strength of the Church of England was much decayed and undermined, before it was openly battered; partly by some superfluous, illegal, and unauthorized innovations in point of Ceremony, which some men affected to use in publique, and impose upon others, which provoked people to jealousie and fury.

He made eirenic remarks about moderate nonconformists and presented Hooker as a counterweight to extremes. Episcopacy was hardly elevated; rightly managed, it 'is manifested to be the great Interest of Gods glory, and our saviour's honor, as they have precepts and examples constituted a visible Church, regular Flock, and orderly Family in this world'. The immediate result was that Sheldon commissioned Izaak Walton to write a replacement life, in which Hooker was the paradigm for the Restoration Church of England.

In his last months Gauden experienced mixed fortunes. He had a hand in the revision of the prayer book which took place in convocation in November 1661, but failed in his attempt to have the Act of Uniformity modified to accommodate those of presbyterian convictions within the Church of England. He got his new bishopric, but had to settle with election to Worcester in May 1662. Enthroned by proxy on 9 August he did not live long enough to make any impact on the diocese or enjoy its revenues. He died of 'the stone and strangury' on 20 September. His widow petitioned the king for the half-year's profits of Worcester to cover removal expenses, but this was refused. He was buried in Worcester Cathedral and a monument (a bust) was erected to his memory. His will, dated 10 September 1662, left his lands and goods to his wife, Elizabeth, during her natural life, with power to divide it among their four sons, 'Lukenor', Charles, John, and William; his daughter, Anne, and step-daughter, Lady Townshend, also received small legacies.

BRYAN D. SPINKS

Sources will, PRO, PROB 11/310, sig. 26 · Venn, Alum. Cant. · Foster, Alum. Oxon. · C. J. Sisson, The judicious marriage of Mr Hooker and the birth of 'The laws of ecclesiastical polity' (1940) · J. Spurr, The Restoration Church of England, 1646–1689 (1991) · V. D. Sutch, Gilbert Sheldon: architect of Anglican survival, 1640–1675 (The Hague, 1973) · D. Novarr, The making of Walton's 'Lives' (Ithaca, New York, 1958) · Fasti Angl., 1541–1857, [Ely] · Fasti Angl. (Hardy), 1.380–81 · Essex RO, Branston MSS, 7/B211/1 [39]
Archives CUL, preparatory thoughts · LPL, preparatory thoughts on communion; private devotions · NL Wales, preparatory thoughts · U. Birm. L., notebook
Likenesses J. Hoskins, miniature, 1655; Sothebys, 4 Nov 1968, lot 188 [see illus.] · T. Cross, double portrait, print (with Charles I), BM; repro. in J. Gauden, Hieraspistes (1653) · oils, LPL; copy, Fulham Palace, London · relief bust on monument, Worcester Cathedral

Gaugain, Thomas (*bap.* 1756?, *d.* 1810?), engraver and painter, has been claimed as a native of Abbeville, France, but was almost certainly the John Thomas Gaugain, son of Philip John Gaugain and his wife, Mary Anne, *née* Malherbe, who was baptized at St Anne's, Soho, London, in April 1756. He entered the Royal Academy Schools in 1771, when his date of birth was given as 24 March 1756. Gaugain exhibited at the academy between 1778 and 1782, showing oil paintings of literary genre and portraits, and in 1783 he exhibited colour-printed stipples after his own designs with the Free Society. Between 1780 and 1783 Gaugain made a number of prints to be printed in colours from several plates in the manner of Jean-François Janinet in France. They were executed in mixed methods involving aquatint, rocker work, and machine tools and were probably printed by Peter Gaugain (*b.* 1762), who shared his elder brother's dwelling at 4 Little Compton Street, Soho, and who was named as printer on some plates. Thomas Gaugain rapidly established himself as an engraver and publisher of stipples with a business geared to the export market. He moved to Denmark Street in 1786, insuring his stock for £500, and then, about 1791, to Chelsea. Publications of 1804 were issued from Five Fields Row, Chelsea, and 4 Little Compton Street, so the Soho property was evidently retained.

Gaugain's own designs are attractive, and his ability as an interpretative engraver may be seen in such sensitive stipples as *Lady Catherine Manners*, after Reynolds. During the 1780s he formed associations with several contemporary designers, notably James Northcote, William Redmore Bigg, and George Morland. Gaugain engraved at least nine of Northcote's designs in the 1780s, and in the mid-1790s they worked together on Northcote's grand ten-plate Hogarthian series *Diligence and Dissipation*. He worked with Morland on several occasions. The remarkable foreign demand for the pair *Dancing Dogs* and *Guinea Pigs*, of which 'five hundred pair were sold in a few weeks', astonished Morland's contemporary biographer George Dawe (Dawe, 41). The collapse of the European market in the wake of the revolutionary wars and the failure of *Diligence and Dissipation* hit Gaugain hard, and he was reduced about 1800 to working for other publishers. A series of plates after Richard Westall was engraved for John Raphael Smith and the Boydells. Gaugain's last-known dated plate, of *Lt-Col. Disbrowe*, was published in November 1809, and he probably died soon afterwards.

TIMOTHY CLAYTON

Sources parish register, St Anne's, Soho, City Westm. AC [baptism] · S. C. Hutchison, 'The Royal Academy Schools, 1768–1830', Walpole Society, 38 (1960–62), 123–91 · Waterhouse, 18c painters · G. Dawe, George Morland (1807) · T. Clayton, The English print, 1688–1802 (1997) · studio sale, 1793 · D. Alexander, Angelica Kauffman: a continental artist in Georgian London, ed. W. Roworth (1992)

Gaule [Gall], **John** (1603/4–1687), Church of England clergyman and author, was born in Lincolnshire. Nothing is known about his parents. He matriculated from Magdalen College, Oxford, where he is recorded as Gall, on 16 November 1621, graduated BA from Magdalene College, Cambridge, in 1624, and was ordained at Peterborough in 1625. Gaule was in the service of Robert, earl of Lindsey, the lord chamberlain, for a while and also became chaplain to Baptist Hicks, Viscount Campden, whose funeral sermon he preached in 1629 and published in 1630 as *A Defiance to Death*. In 1632 he was presented to the vicarage of the church of St Andrew in Great Staughton, Huntingdonshire, by Lady Campden. Between 1628 and 1630 he published several collections of 'votive speculations' on biblical episodes and a study of 'holy madnesse'. From his 'The practique theorists panegyrick', a sermon preached at Paul's Cross on 7 September 1628, there developed an interest in witchcraft, magic, and astrology, which later inspired more substantial works on the subject.

Gaule's signing of the protestation in 1641 offers little indication of other than traditional political views; he apparently continued in his living throughout the 1640s, 1650s, and 1660s. About 1646 his parish was threatened by a visit from the witch finders Matthew Hopkins and John Stearne as part of England's only major witch panic. Gaule, who believed in witchcraft in principle, was nevertheless highly critical of their investigative methods and the way they capitalized on popular fears. First in sermons and then in his *Select Cases of Conscience Touching Witches and Witchcrafts* (1646), a book that had the puritan John Downame's approval and was dedicated to Cromwell's brother-in-law Valentine Walton (as the local MP), Gaule argued that witchcraft was a greatly exaggerated phenomenon, with every woman who had 'a wrinkled face, a furr'd brow, a hairy lip, a gobber tooth, a squint eye, a squeaking voyce, or a scolding tongue' being accused of it (pp. 4–5). Further studies followed in 1652 and 1657.

Gaule managed to give an assize sermon in Huntingdon in March 1648, published in 1649 as *A Sermon of the Saints*, without making a single topical religious or political allusion. At some point, however, he was imprisoned for a while by Cromwell for declaring the war against Charles I unlawful. One New Model Army colonel, Edward Whalley, apparently wanted him shot by firing squad 'but a soldier prevented it' (*CSP dom.*, 1660–61, 346). The stance is in line with a tract entitled *An Admonition Moving to Moderation* that Gaule published in 1660 dedicated to Charles II and attacking all forms of what he called 'immoderate' belief and action during the 1640s and 1650s. In 1660 he also petitioned Valentine Walton's estate for arrears on the grounds that the local regicide had seized the benefits of his living, valued at £400 p.a., while he was detained. Gaule died in 1687. It is not known if he ever married.

STUART CLARK

Sources Venn, *Alum. Cant.* · *Transactions of the Cambridgeshire and Huntingdonshire Archaeology Society*, 3 (1914), 37–8 · *Transactions of the Cambridgeshire and Huntingdonshire Archaeology Society*, 5 (1937), 364, 367 · *VCH Huntingdonshire*, 2.358 · *CSP dom.*, 1660–61, p. 346 · J. Sharpe, *Instruments of darkness: witchcraft in England* (1996)

Gaultier [Gautier], **Jacques** (*fl.* 1617–1652), lutenist, of whose family nothing is known, does not seem to have been related to any of the other French lutenists named Gaultier. He was the foremost solo lutenist in England during the reign of Charles I. He is mentioned by Robert Herrick in several of his poems, and all subsequent writers on lute music in England such as Thomas Mace and the anonymous author of the *Burwell Lute Tutor* single Gaultier out as the most influential lutenist at the English court at this time.

Gaultier's career was punctuated by scandal and incidents of violence. Never far from trouble, he had to flee to England from France in 1617 after being accused of murder, and was imprisoned in the Tower of London in March 1618. He was not returned to France, owing to the protection of the duke of Buckingham. The *Burwell Lute Tutor* credits Gaultier with the introduction and success of the distinctive double-headed twelve-course lute. An engraving by Jan Lievens shows him holding such a lute; here Gaultier has full hair, large eyes, and a goatee beard and moustache similar to those of Charles I.

By 1622 Gaultier had been drawn into the circle of Sir Robert Killigrew (*d.* 1633), who was a close friend of Buckingham at this time. Here he made a lifelong friend and correspondent in Constantijn Huygens de Zulichem, the polymath, amateur musician, and secretary of the United Provinces, who praised Gaultier's playing in a Latin poem. The first mention of Gaultier in royal accounts dates from 1623, when he was paid £40 'towards the defreyeng of his Journey into Spayne' in connection with the visit by Buckingham and Prince Charles to woo the infanta (Ashbee,

IACOBO GOVTERO INTER REGIOS MAGNÆ BRITANNLÆ ORPHEOS ET AMPHIONES LYDLÆ DORLÆ PHRYGLÆ TESTVDINIS FIDICINI ET MODVLATORVM PRINCIPI HANC E PENICILLI SVI TABVLA IN ÆS TRANSSCRIPTAM EFFIGIEM IOANNES LÆVINI FIDÆ AMICITLÆ MONIMENTVM I. M.CONSECRAVIT.

Jacques Gaultier (*fl.* 1617–1652), by Jan Lievens

4.227). Gaultier visited Madrid and played on his 'most excellent lute' in the cabinet of the king (Laurencie, 36). He may have sat for Van Dyck, as the Prado has a fine painting entitled *El musico Jacob Gaultier* (Prado, Madrid, no. 1487). Gaultier gained an annuity for life of £100 on 28 November 1625 and, judging from a letter of 28 August 1649 to Huygens, remained in royal service until that date without interruption (BL, Add. MS 15944, fols. 46*r*–47*v*). Exchequer accounts after 1625 always list Gaultier as lutenist to Queen Henrietta Maria, whom he taught for a while, and with whom it was rumoured he was having an affair in the winter of 1626–7, an accusation which occasioned a second visit to the Tower. By 1635 he was married.

Comments made by Mace and Huygens show that Gaultier was an authority on old lutes and also dealt in lutes. His surviving music is in the new French *style brisé* but with a clear separation between treble and bass. Comments in the *Burwell Lute Tutor* refer to his thundering play and an emphasis on the long bass strings of the twelve-course lute that he championed. The last mention of Gaultier is in a diary of Lodewijck Huygens, son of Gaultier's long-standing friend Constantijn Huygens, written while visiting England. Here there are several references to Gaultier between the months of February and July 1652, from which it is known that he was still resident in London, that he was surviving by teaching the lute, and that (according to Gaultier) his wife was insane (L. Huygens, 24, 49, 71, 85, 93, 94, 108, 149, 151).

MATTHEW SPRING

Sources L. de la Laurencie, 'Le luthiste Jacques Gaultier', *La Revue Musicale*, 5/3 (1924), 33–9 · I. Spink, 'Another Gaultier affair', *Music*

and Letters, 45 (1964), 345–7 • A. Ashbee, ed., Records of English court music, 9 vols. (1986–96) • The Burwell lute tutor (1974) [facs. with an introduction by R. Spencer] • M. C. Jones, ed., 'Old Herbert papers at Powis Castle and in the British Museum collections', Montgomeryshire Collections (1886) • L. Huygens, The English journal, 1651–1652, ed. and trans. A. G. H. Bacharach and R. G. Collmer (1982) • T. Mace, Musick's monument (1676) • Société pour l'histoire musicale des Pays-Bas: musique et musiciens au XVII siècle, correspondance et oeuvres musicales de Constantin Huygens, ed. W. J. A. Jonckbloet and J. P. N. Land (Leiden, 1882) • J. D. Alsop, 'The medical casebook of Joseph Binnes, a London surgeon', Journal of the American Musicological Society, 32 (1979), 367 • BL, Add. MS 15944, fols. 46r–47v • CSP dom., 1625–6

Archives BL, Add. MS 15944, fols. 46r–47v • PRO, IND 6746 • PRO, SO 3/7

Likenesses A. Van Dyck, oils, c.1635, Prado, Madrid • J. Lievens, etching, BM, NPG [see illus.]

Gaunt, Elizabeth (d. 1685), conspirator and convicted traitor, and her husband, William, were both deeply involved in London whig and dissenting politics in the early 1680s, when they emerge from obscurity. They were residents of the parish of St Mary, Whitechapel, and well known about Wapping, which at that time lay in the parish. Elizabeth kept a tallow chandler's shop, though by September 1683, when she was living in lodgings at the upper end of Old Gravel Lane, Wapping, she appears to have given it up. In Bishop Burnet's History of his Own Time, Elizabeth is portrayed as a charitable woman who 'spent a great part of her life in acts of charity, visiting the gaols, and looking after the poor of what persuasion soever they were' (Bishop Burnet's History, 3.61).

But Elizabeth and William Gaunt's activities went beyond mere acts of charity. In the early 1680s they were also agents, linking the growing refugee community of whigs and dissenters in the Netherlands with London. They conveyed secretly men and women as well as messages and money between London and Amsterdam. In 1682 London authorities believed that they had acted as the earl of Shaftesbury's brokers, enabling him to leave London for Amsterdam. In Amsterdam Elizabeth was referred to by the refugee community as Mother Gaunt, where she was one among several 'mothers', who provided aid and shelter, and carried messages for radicals between the Netherlands and England (BL, Add. MS 41818, fol. 77v). In spring 1685, as the preparations for the duke of Monmouth's invasion began, Elizabeth Gaunt was in Amsterdam staying with Mrs Ann Smith, a wealthy English widow, who helped fund both Monmouth's and the earl of Argyll's rebellions. Monmouth sent Elizabeth and the whig barrister, Edward Norton, back to England to instruct the earl of Macclesfield to be ready to act in Cheshire. A few weeks later Elizabeth was back in Amsterdam to find out why Monmouth had been delayed.

Elizabeth Gaunt had returned to London by July 1685. Following the defeat of Monmouth's army at Sedgemoor she and her husband reverted to arranging passage overseas for fleeing rebels. One such rebel was James Burton. The Gaunts knew Burton. In 1683 he had been outlawed for his part in the Rye House plot. Elizabeth had then helped hide Burton in September, given him money, and procured for him a boat which took him to Gravesend,

where he took ship to Amsterdam. In 1685 Burton was among Monmouth's original band that landed in Lyme Regis. After Sedgemoor he fled to London and stayed with his wife in Wapping for two nights. Frightened by his presence, she arranged for him to stay at the house of a neighbour, John Fernley, a barber who was also a constable. On 2 August, while waiting for the Gaunts to arrange his passage to the Netherlands, Burton was arrested at Fernley's house, trying to escape through the chimney. Fernley was indicted as a traitor for harbouring Burton. Elizabeth Gaunt was indicted for treason against Charles II, for conspiring with others to rebel against the government, and for harbouring a traitor. The government's chief witness against both Fernley and Gaunt was Burton, who turned king's evidence and won himself a pardon.

Gaunt's trial took place on 19 October 1685 at the Old Bailey. James Burton, his wife, Mary, and his widowed daughter, Mary Gilbert, all testified against her. Burton claimed that Mrs Gaunt was anxious to assist his flight overseas in 1683 because she knew about her husband's role in the Rye House plot. Elizabeth did not deny knowing Burton, but she swore that she did not 'contrive to send him away' (State trials, 11.419). There were no witnesses in Gaunt's defence and nothing disloyal proved against her other than that she had assisted Burton. She was convicted of high treason along with John Fernley. Alderman Henry Cornish was tried and convicted that same day by the same judges and jury. On 23 October, the same day that Cornish was hanged, drawn, and quartered at Cheapside, London, she was burnt to death at Tyburn, the penalty for treason inflicted on common women. She was not strangled first as was sometimes done out of mercy, but she was literally burnt alive as ordered. Gaunt made a powerful and provocative dying speech at the stake. According to Roger Morrice, Gaunt held up the Bible and claimed that she had aided Burton's wife and children 'in obedience to the contents of this book' (Morrice, 'Ent'ring book', DWL, 487). William Penn, who also witnessed Cornish's execution that day, saw the death of Gaunt and told Burnet that 'she died with a constancy, even to a cheerfulness, that struck all that saw it'. Penn reported that she calmly arranged the straw around her to hasten her burning and that she 'behaved herself in such a manner that all the spectators melted in tears' (Bishop Burnet's History, 3.62). Both the whig printer John Dunton and the presbyterian preacher Thomas Jolly reported that 'a dreadful storm, which terrified both man and beast', erupted upon the death of 'compassionate Mrs. Gaunt' and Alderman Cornish (Fishwick, 73; Dunton, 113). Gaunt's dying speech, written by herself from her gaol cell, was later published in both English and Dutch. It too struck a defiant note. She died, as the Marian martyrs had before her, not for any criminal offence, but because of her faith. She quoted scripture throughout and ended her speech by laying her blood at the door of the 'furious judge and unrighteous jury' (Mrs … Gaunt's last Speech).

Gaunt's arrest and trial are probably best understood in the context of her activities in Amsterdam. In summer 1685 the government received numerous intelligence reports from the Netherlands repeatedly stating that 'if she be brought to confession', Mother Gaunt could reveal much about several eminent persons both in exile and in England (BL, Add. MS 41818, fol. 77v). Yet these agents also believed that she would prove obstinate and be less than forthcoming in her testimony. This may well have been the case: that Burton's arrest had given the government cause to arrest and interrogate Gaunt and that she had revealed little or nothing and was thus tried without mercy.

Elizabeth Gaunt was the last woman in England to be executed for treason. William Gaunt was excepted from James II's general pardon of March 1686 but was later pardoned on 31 March 1687.   MELINDA ZOOK

Sources State trials, 11.382–454 • Bishop Burnet's History, 3.61–2 • BL, Add. MS 41812, fol. 223; 41817, fols. 181, 219, 225; 41818, fols. 77, 112v • T. B. Macaulay, The history of England from the accession of James II, new edn, ed. C. H. Firth, 6 vols. (1913–15), vol. 2, pp. 656–8 • J. Ralph, The history of England: during the reigns of K. William, Q. Anne and K. George I, 2 vols. (1744–6), vol. 1, pp. 889–90 • N. Luttrell, A brief historical relation of state affairs from September 1678 to April 1714, 1 (1857), 361 • M. S. Zook, Radical whigs and conspiratorial politics in late Stuart England (1999), 2, 35, 137, 140 • R. L. Greaves, Secrets of the kingdom: British radicals from the Popish Plot to the revolution of 1688–89 (1992), 301, 415 • The autobiography of Sir John Bramston, ed. [Lord Braybrooke], CS, 32 (1845), 209 • E. Parry, The bloody assize (1929), 267–9 • J. Dunton, The life and errors of John Dunton ... written by himself (1705), 113 • The note book of the Rev. Thomas Jolly, AD 1671–1693, extracts from the church book of Altham and Wymondhouses, AD 1649–1725, and an account of the Jolly family of Standish, Gorton, and Altham, ed. H. Fishwick, Chetham Society, new ser., 33 (1894), 73 • Mrs Elizabeth Gaunt's last speech, who was burnt at London, Oct 23 1685 [1685] • R. Morrice, 'Ent'ring book', DWL, Morrice MS P, 483, 486–8
Likenesses portrait, repro. in J. Tutchin, The western martyrology, or, Bloody assizes, 5th edn (1705)

Gaunt, Maurice de. See Gant, Maurice de (c.1185–1230).

Gauntlett, Henry (1762–1833), Church of England clergyman, was born at Market Lavington, Wiltshire, on 15 March 1762, and educated at the grammar school of West Lavington under the care of the Revd Mr Marks. After leaving school he was idle for some years until, on the advice of the Revd Sir James Stonhouse, he decided to enter the Church of England. After three years' preparation he was ordained in 1786 and became curate of Tilshead and Imber, villages about 4 miles from Lavington. He remained in this neighbourhood, adding to his income by taking pupils, until 1800, when he married Arabella, the daughter of Edward Davies, rector of Coychurch, Glamorgan, and moved to the curacy of Botley, near Southampton. He left Botley in 1804 for the curacy of Wellington, Shropshire, which he occupied for a year, and then took charge of a chapel at Reading, Berkshire, not under episcopal jurisdiction. Two years later he moved to the curacy of Nettlebed and Pishill in Oxfordshire, and thence in 1811 to Olney in Buckinghamshire. In 1815 the vicar of Olney died and Gauntlett obtained the living, which he held until his death in 1833.

Gauntlett was a close friend of Rowland Hill and an important supporter of the evangelical revival in the English church, in company with his predecessors at Olney,

John Newton and Thomas Scott. He published several sermons during his lifetime, and in 1821 An Exposition of the Book of Revelation, which quickly passed through three editions and brought its author the sum of £700. The second edition contained a letter in refutation of the opinion of Basilicus, published in the Jewish Expositor, that during the millennium Christ would personally reign. In 1836 the Revd Thomas Jones published an abridgement of this refutation entitled The interpreter: a summary view of the Revelation of St John ... founded on ... H. Gauntlett's exposition. After Gauntlett's death a collection of his sermons, in two volumes, was published in 1835, together with a lengthy memoir by his daughter Catherine. The appendix reprints sections of a rare work on the career of John Mason of Water Stratford, Buckinghamshire, and thirty-eight letters written by William Cowper to Teedon. Gauntlett published several collections of hymns for his parishioners. Henry John *Gauntlett, the church composer, was his son.   RONALD BAYNE, rev. H. C. G. MATTHEW

Sources C. T. Gauntlett, 'Memoir', in H. Gauntlett, Sermons, 2 vols. (1835)
Likenesses M. Gauci, lithograph (after A. Rippingille), BM; repro. in Gauntlett, Sermons

Gauntlett, Henry John (1805–1876), organist, organ designer, and composer, was born at Wellington, Shropshire, on 9 July 1805. He was the second son and fourth child of the Revd Henry *Gauntlett (1762–1833), originally from Wiltshire, and from 1815 vicar of Olney, Buckinghamshire, and his wife, Arabella, the daughter of the Revd Edward Davies, vicar of Coychurch, Glamorgan. Henry John Gauntlett incorporated Deane, from his maternal grandmother, into the family name.

After sojourns at Reading (1805–7) and Nettlebed and Pishill (1807–11), the family settled at Olney, where Gauntlett confounded his father's intention that his sisters should have charge of the new church organ by learning to play it himself. He was formally appointed organist in 1815, and remained until 1825. To celebrate George IV's accession in 1820 he trained the singers and copied the parts for his own performance of Handel's Messiah. His tenure as organist is commemorated in the church by a stained-glass window and an engraving on the glass front of the organ console.

In 1821 Gauntlett's father took him to London to see the distinguished musicians William Crotch and Thomas Attwood. Nevertheless, he declined Attwood's offer to teach his son, at no expense, with a view to his becoming Attwood's successor as organist of St Paul's Cathedral. In 1826, after a short stay in Ireland as a private tutor, Gauntlett was articled to a London solicitor, and qualified as a lawyer in 1831. During this period his reputation as an organist was enhanced by church appointments in London and by tuition from Samuel Wesley and a meeting with Mendelssohn. His career as composer, arranger, and music journalist also began to develop.

In 1827 Gauntlett was appointed organist at St Olave's, Southwark, where he remained for twenty years. Additionally, in 1836 he was appointed evening organist at Christ Church Greyfriars, at a salary of 2 guineas per

Henry John Gauntlett (1805–1876), by Maull & Co., c.1870

annum. From that year he campaigned in favour of enlarging the compass of the organ pedals at Christ Church so that the more elaborate works of J. S. Bach could be played. After much opposition the organ was expanded in time for Mendelssohn's 1837 visit. Gauntlett researched continental organs, including that at Haarlem, and used the knowledge gained as the basis for his own imaginative ideas on organ design, in partnership with the organ builder William Hill from the 1840s. Between 1838 and 1845 Gauntlett was directly involved in the design of at least fourteen organs, and evidence for seven more has recently been discovered. His influence was widespread, reaching church organs in London, Liverpool, Calcutta, and St Petersburg, as well as the instruments at Edinburgh Music Hall and Birmingham town hall. His innovative ideas included enlarging manuals as well as pedals from G compass to C compass, extending the principal choruses, and in 1852 patenting the use of electricity for organ actions. He attempted to use this means to enable all the organs at the Great Exhibition to be played simultaneously from one console. The mechanism proved defective, but the idea was central to the development of pneumatic organ action with magnets and armatures. Gauntlett's transformation of organ design was probably his most significant, and certainly his most enduring, contribution to music.

On 5 October 1841 Gauntlett married Henrietta Gipps Mount (1819–1891) in All Saints' Church, Canterbury. She was the daughter of William Mount, a local magistrate and deputy lieutenant of Canterbury. The couple had eight children, six of whom survived into adulthood. By 1843 Gauntlett's contribution to church music was widely acknowledged. In that year the archbishop of Canterbury conferred on him the Lambeth degree of Doctor of Music, the first since that conferred on John Blow in 1677. On 3 August 1843, at Christ Church Greyfriars, Gauntlett performed organ works by John Bull for the king of Hanover, who gave him permission to style himself his organist. Honours like these meant much to Gauntlett, for whom lack of early formal musical training was a source of frustration and regret. His ability transcended this perceived shortcoming. For example, when chosen by Mendelssohn as organist for the first performance of *Elijah* at Birmingham town hall in 1846, Gauntlett had to reduce the part from the full score at sight, since the written-out organ part had been lost. He did so to Mendelssohn's complete satisfaction, yet his payment for this was less than one-fifth of that of a vocal soloist. By 1846 Gauntlett had ceased work as a lawyer, and was consequently dependent on music for a living. In 1847 he sold his extensive library, which was remarkably wide-ranging, including sixteenth-century manuscripts of Italian and English musical treatises and compositions. In the same year his first child, Henry Chrysostom Deane, was born.

After relinquishing his appointment at St Olave's, Southwark (1847), Gauntlett held organist's appointments sporadically at other London churches: Union Chapel, Islington (1853–61), All Saints, Notting Hill (1861–3), and St Bartholomew-the-Less, Smithfield (1872–6). His performance style was forthright almost to the point of eccentricity, and his organ registration practice was a novelty in its day. He was in demand as a recitalist: as early as 1843 his inaugural performance on the Edinburgh Music Hall organ was commended for the orchestral approach in his playing of variations and transcribed pieces, using a wide variety of soft stops. However, satirists ridiculed his frequent changes of stops, as well as his habit of jerking his head while playing.

The brevity of Gauntlett's later organist's appointments was perhaps a reflection of his character, and of his unsettled formative years clouded by bereavement and career frustration. As a whole, his life's work seems to have been fragmented and diffuse. He was a creative, highly original person, yet he was difficult to relate to, self-important, and at times insensitive to the feelings and needs of others. For example, he wrote to John Bacchus Dykes, precentor of Durham Cathedral and a distinguished church musician, with a lengthy, pedantic, and pretentious analysis of Dykes's hymn tune 'Hollingside', criticizing the latter's choice of harmony and supplying an 'improved' version with what he termed the correct harmony.

Gauntlett's own output of hymn tunes is said to have exceeded 10,000, though there is little evidence for so great a number, roughly equal to one tune per day for over twenty-seven years. 'St Fulbert', 'Laudate dominum', and 'St Albinus' are still sung, as well as some of his Anglican psalm chants. His best-known tune is 'Irby', indissolubly wedded to the Christmas hymn 'Once in royal David's city' and the basis for numerous harmonizations and arrangements, some of which detract from the directness and restraint that characterize the composer's hymn tunes. He published many anthologies of tunes which included original works by him. These included books of psalm tunes, Christmas tunes, and harmonizations of Gregorian plainchant for use in English services. Gauntlett was a firm advocate of the use of plainchant, a practice supported by the Tractarian movement in the Anglican church. In some of his collaborative compilations he did not receive the recognition due to him. However, his appointment in 1853 as organist of the nonconformist Union Chapel, Islington, was the start of a fruitful partnership with its minister, the Revd Dr Henry Allon. Their joint publication, *The Congregational Psalmist*, went through numerous editions and revisions, and it may have been the edition of 1864 (containing 7000 tunes) that led to the belief that Gauntlett had composed all these and more.

In addition to his contributions to collections, Gauntlett composed several anthems and organ transcriptions. His songs included a set of twelve entitled *The Song of the Soul*: the style and relative mediocrity of texts and music do not commend them to a later generation, although the choice of texts (by Felicia Hemans, Longfellow, Wordsworth, Coleridge, and others) conveys something of Gauntlett's deeply troubled nature. As a music journalist and writer, Gauntlett was important in his day. He wrote a set of *Notes, Queries, and Exercises in the Science and Practice of Music* (1859), intended as aids to church officials in choosing organists, but some of the contents are musical conundrums and unanswerable questions, scarcely relevant to the task. He edited and wrote for three periodicals (the *Church Musician*, the *Musical World*, and the *Morning Chronicle*) and contributed extensively to several more, writing authoritatively on Gregorian plainchant, Beethoven, and Bach, as well as on other musical and non-musical matters.

With his fearless and outspoken views, Gauntlett often aroused controversy and was disinclined to embrace the approval and admiration of his contemporaries. His self-importance was sometimes a cause of ridicule and alienation. However, his more perceptive associates (including Mendelssohn) looked beyond his difficult personality, recognizing the true value of his contribution to music. Gauntlett died of heart disease at his home, 15 St Mary Abbotts Terrace, Kensington, on 21 February 1876 and was buried at Kensal Green cemetery four days later.

TERENCE CROLLEY and JUDITH BLEZZARD

Sources N. Thistlethwaite, *The making of the Victorian organ* (1990) • N. Thistlethwaite, 'The Hill–Gauntlett revolution: an epitaph', *British Institute of Organ Studies Journal*, 16 (1992), 50–59 • J. Bishop, 'A frustrated revolutionary: H. J. Gauntlett and the Victorian organ' [unpublished lecture, Royal College of Organists, 1971] • H. Gauntlett, *Sermons, with a memoir of the author by his daughter* (1835) • C. Gauntlett, *The gathered lily: a brief memoir of Lydia Gauntlett* (1838) • H. J. Gauntlett, 'English ecclesiastical composers of the present age', *Musical World*, 18 (Aug 1836) • H. J. Gauntlett, 'The ecclesiastical music of this country', *Musical World*, 17 (July 1836), 49–52 • *ILN* (11 March 1876) • A. H. King, *Some British collectors of music* (1963) • J. Werner, *Mendelssohn's 'Elijah'* (1965) • 'Dr Gauntlett: his centenary', *MT*, 46 (1905), 455 • W. Pole, *Some short reminiscences of events in my life and work: abbreviated from manuscript notes* (privately printed, London, 1898) • parish register, All Saints, Wellington, Shropshire • m. cert. • d. cert. • *The Times* (25 Feb 1876)

Likenesses J. D. Sharp, oils?, *c*.1840, Royal College of Organists, London • Maull & Co., photograph, *c*.1870, NPG [*see illus.*] • C. E. Fry & Sons, photograph, NPG • Maull & Co., cartes-de-visite, NPG • Victoria Photographic Co., carte-de-visite, NPG

Wealth at death under £300: administration, 10 June 1876, *CGPLA Eng. & Wales*

Gauvain, Sir Henry John (1878–1945), children's orthopaedic surgeon, was born in Alderney on 28 November 1878, the second son of William Gauvain, receiver-general for the island, and his wife, Catherine Margaret, daughter of Peter Le Ber, jurat of Alderney. He was educated at Tonbridge high school, King's College, London, and St John's College, Cambridge, where he was a scholar. In 1902 he went to St Bartholomew's Hospital as senior science scholar. He qualified in 1906 and proceeded to graduate MD and MCh (Cambridge) in 1918. He married in 1913 Louise Laura (*d*. March 1945), daughter of Surgeon-Major William Butler, formerly of the Indian Medical Service (IMS). They had one son, who predeceased his father, and a daughter who entered the medical profession.

In 1908 Sir William Treloar founded a 220-bed home at Alton, Hampshire, primarily for children who had suffered as a result of tuberculosis of the bones and joints. Gauvain was offered the post of resident medical officer. By 1914 the institution was known as the Lord Mayor Treloar Cripples' Hospital and College, and Gauvain was designated medical superintendent. Gauvain's treatment regime at Alton was subsequently to give him and his institution an international reputation. Treatment then in vogue for tuberculosis of the lungs, the commonest form of the disease, included fresh air, rest, and exercise, at a sanatorium. Gauvain applied similar principles to tuberculosis of the bones and joints (commonly known as 'surgical tuberculosis'). Claiming that surgical tuberculosis was a generalized and not a local infection, his approach was more holistic than that prevailing. He opposed radical surgical treatment, explaining that incising infected lesions resulted in high mortality and also caused much suffering from sepsis and 'deplorable and unavoidable crippling' (*Transactions*, 109–11). His treatment included 'climatic, hygienic, dietetic, drug, educational and other general measures' (ibid.). Immobilization of the bones and joints was an important part of the treatment, and Gauvain was inventive in devising plasters and splints, including his famous 'wheelbarrow' splint for children with Pott's disease. Sunlight therapy or 'heliotherapy' formed another essential component. An artificial substitute for heliotherapy had been devised in Denmark in the 1890s, and Gauvain boasted that Alton was the first country hospital in England and Wales to have a properly equipped light department. His belief in the importance of sunlight and fresh air in the treatment of tuberculosis led him to open a marine branch of the hospital at Sandy Point, Hayling Island, Hampshire, in 1919. He also favoured remoteness from towns as it prevented 'interference from outside visitors' (ibid.). In 1912 the hospital school at Alton became the first in the country to be recognized by the Board of Education for the education of physically handicapped children, and certified teachers were employed. A college was added to the hospital, for the technical training of disabled boys aged fourteen to eighteen.

In 1925 Gauvain opened the Morland Hall clinics for private patients. He wrote numerous papers on surgical tuberculosis, hospital design, and heliotherapy. He was consulting surgeon to the King Edward VII Welsh National Memorial Association for the treatment of tuberculosis, to the London, Essex, and Hampshire county councils, and to King George's Sanatorium for Sailors, Bramshott. He was president of the sections on electrotherapeutic and diseases of children at the Royal Society of Medicine, and vice-president of the National Association for the Prevention of Tuberculosis. In 1920 he was knighted for his services to disabled children. He was elected FRCS in 1927, and in 1936 he was awarded the distinguished service gold key of the American Congress of Physical Therapy. In 1935 while president of the section of public medicine at a British Medical Association meeting in Australia, he received the honorary degree of MD from Melbourne University.

Gauvain was a man of abundant kindness and charm, and was beloved by his patients and his staff. He died at Morland Hall, Alton, Hampshire, on 19 January 1945, and his wife died two months later.

W. J. BISHOP, rev. LINDA BRYDER

Sources BMJ (3 Feb 1945), 167 · The Lancet (3 Feb 1945) · W. P. Treloar, 'The Lord Mayor Treloar Cripples' Hospital and College, Alton', Tuberculosis Year Book and Sanatoria Annual, 1 (1913–14), 338–9 · The Lancet (4 July 1925) · The Lancet (13 April 1929) · The Lancet (16 Nov 1918)
Likenesses C. Pibworth, bronze bust, priv. coll. · F. O. Salisbury, oils (posthumous), Lord Mayor Treloar Orthopaedic Hospital, Alton, Hampshire · photographs, Lord Mayor Treloar Orthopaedic Hospital, Alton, Hampshire
Wealth at death £84,345 2s. 2d.: probate, 17 July 1945, CGPLA Eng. & Wales

Gaveston, Piers, earl of Cornwall (d. 1312), royal favourite, was a younger son of the Gascon knight Arnaud de Gabaston and his wife, Claramonde de Marsan. Claramonde had shared in the substantial estate of her father, Arnaud-Guillaume de Marsan, with her brother, Fortaner de Lescun. An inquest taken by Edward I in 1273/4 reveals that in right of his wife, Arnaud de Gabaston owed homage to the duke of Aquitaine for the castles of Louvigny, Roquefort de Marsan, Montgaillard des Landes, Hagetmau, and St Loubouer. In addition he served as a jurat of Béarn as lord of Gabaston and was a faithful servant of Edward I, fighting in Wales in 1282–3, serving as a hostage to Alfonso III of Aragon in 1288 and to Philippe IV of France in 1294, and serving in other capacities in Gascony, England, and Scotland until his death some time before 18 May 1302.

Youth and early court connections Piers Gaveston first appears in the records in 1297, when he served in the army of Edward I in Flanders, following which he became a yeoman in the king's household. He served in Scotland in 1300—as did his father, Arnaud, and his brother Arnaud-Guillaume de Marsan—and by late in the year he had been transferred to the household of the prince of Wales. A contemporary chronicle explains that Edward I was impressed by his courteous manner, and Geoffrey Baker describes Gaveston as 'graceful and agile in body, sharp witted, refined in manners, … [and] well versed in military matters' (Chronicon Galfridi le Baker, 4). He may well have been selected by the king himself to serve as a role model for Edward of Caernarfon, the future *Edward II. Proximity to the prince brought opportunities for advancement to Gaveston, but also risks. In June 1305 the prince was cut off from the royal household in consequence of a dispute with Walter Langton (d. 1321), bishop of Chester and treasurer of Edward I. Moreover, Gaveston and Gilbert de Clare were temporarily excluded from the prince's own household. A reconciliation was effected between father and son in October 1305, and in the following spring the prince of Wales was knighted by his father on Whitsunday in anticipation of another Scottish campaign. Gaveston was knighted four days later, on 26 May 1306, along with many other young men.

Although the ensuing campaign went well initially, it was to be marred by the desertion of twenty-two well-known knights, including Gaveston, who left their winter quarters in order to attend tournaments in foreign parts. Order was given that the deserters be arrested and their lands seized, although Edward I later pardoned them all, in January 1307, at the instance of Queen Margaret. Soon afterwards, however, Gaveston was sent into the first of his three exiles. While the story of Walter of Guisborough, in which the occasion for Gaveston's exile was the prince's request through the treasurer Langton that Gaveston be given the county of Ponthieu, may be discounted as apocryphal, there can be little doubt that the growing favouritism shown to the young Gascon by Prince Edward was at the root of this exile, which was very likely viewed by Edward I more as a punishment for the prince than for Gaveston. On 26 February 1307 at Lanercost Gaveston was ordered to abjure the realm before 30 April. It is worth noting that the ordinance of banishment provided for an annuity of 100 marks sterling 'for as long as he shall remain in parts beyond the sea during the king's pleasure and waiting recall' (CClR, 1302–1307, 526–7).

The king's favourite Contemporary chronicles describe the prince of Wales's love for Gaveston in such terms as 'immoderate', 'excessive', and 'beyond measure', and it has been generally assumed that the two men developed a homosexual relationship. Recently, however, it has been suggested that they had entered into a compact of adoptive brotherhood. The extant records will bear either interpretation, although neither can be proved; in any case it is clear that by early 1307 the future Edward II was emotionally bound to Piers Gaveston more deeply than he was ever to be to any other person. This bond of affection was to have grave consequences for both men, and for the kingdom as a whole.

Almost immediately after the death of Edward I Gaveston was recalled from his exile in Ponthieu—the Lanercost ordinance had specified Gascony as his destination—and received a grant of the earldom of Cornwall and of all lands belonging to Edmund, late earl of Cornwall (d. 1300). Although the charter is dated 6 August 1307 at Dumfries, it may well have been written some time later. The original is decorated with the royal arms of England and the arms of both Gaveston and Clare, although Gaveston's marriage to Margaret de *Clare, sister of the earl of Gloucester and niece of Edward II himself, did not take place until 1 November 1307. The charter was witnessed by seven of the eleven earls, apparently indicating their acquiescence to, if not their support for, Gaveston's elevation to the peerage.

The period following Gaveston's marriage seems to have been crucial in shaping opposition to the royal favourite. First of all, on 2 December a tournament was held at Wallingford, in which Gaveston's entourage defeated a company that included the earls of Arundel, Hereford, and Warenne. The victory, which some chronicles attributed to duplicity, seems to have been a genuine cause of enmity between Gaveston and at least Warenne. More importantly, on 26 December 1307 Gaveston was appointed *custos regni* (regent) in anticipation of the king's absence at his impending wedding to Isabella of France. Although his regency did not prove to be an occasion for the abuse of power, Gaveston's mere appointment was remarkable enough in the eyes of his contemporaries, and pointed to his control of the flow of royal patronage. Worse was to follow at the coronation, on 25 February 1308, in which Gaveston played an extremely prominent role. He immediately preceded the king, bearing the crown of St Edward the Confessor. He also redeemed the Curtana sword and fastened the spur on the king's left foot. His ostentatious dress and behaviour at the banquet that followed is said to have disgusted and insulted the king's new brothers-in-law, Charles de Valois and Louis d'Évreux, who left the banquet in indignation. Such ostentation and arrogance, rather than any political ambition or agenda, was ultimately to be his undoing. As the judicious author of the contemporary *Vita Edwardi secundi* remarked, 'I therefore believe and firmly maintain that if Piers had from the outset borne himself prudently and humbly towards the magnates of the land, none of them would have opposed him' (*Vita*, 15).

As early as January 1308 baronial dissatisfaction with the governance of Edward II had been apparent in the so-called 'Boulogne declaration', setting out the need for reform. By the spring of 1308 opposition to the Gascon favourite, upon whom Edward's shortcomings were blamed, had come into the open. The earl of Lincoln, the most senior of the earls, is credited with leading this opposition, and with drawing up the three articles presented at the parliament of April 1308, to which the barons had come armed, calling for Gaveston's exile. The threat of civil war was clear—Edward and Gaveston seem

to have had little support apart from the earls of Lancaster and Richmond, and some of the household barons and knights, including the elder Hugh Despenser (d. 1326)—and the magnates also had the support of Queen Isabella's father, Philippe IV, king of France. Edward had little choice but to capitulate, which he did on 18 May. Gaveston was to abjure the realm on 24 June, and Archbishop Winchelsey pronounced him excommunicate should he return.

Second and third exiles At once Edward set about efforts to gain Gaveston's recall, while compensating him for the loss of Cornwall which his exile entailed. Meanwhile, on 16 June, Edward II appointed Gaveston king's lieutenant in Ireland, although Richard de Burgh, earl of Ulster (d. 1326), had been appointed to the same position on the previous day. A comparison of the two grants reveals Edward's intentions in providing a safe and honourable haven for his favourite. Unlike de Burgh, Gaveston was given authority to remove any royal official in Ireland and replace him with his own man. He also had the power to issue letters of presentation and collation to vacant churches and benefices in Ireland. As Edward's Irish lieutenant, Gaveston would also be able to authorize letters under the great seal of Ireland. What had been meant as a source of embarrassment and humiliation by the magnates had become an opportunity for the exercise of substantial power, and in 1311 his enemies would be careful to ensure that Gaveston was forced to abjure not only the realm but all English possessions. Yet in 1308 little if any opposition was voiced to his Irish lieutenancy, and, as was also the case when he served as regent in 1307–8, Gaveston did not abuse his power. His administrative acts were few and generally uncontroversial, while his military activity in the Wicklow Mountains was clearly successful.

By the spring of 1309 Edward had managed to effect Gaveston's recall from exile, but once again it proved to be to little effect. According to the chroniclers Gaveston returned to England as arrogant as ever, and it is during this period that he is alleged to have dubbed his fellow earls with slanderous nicknames: the earl of Lincoln was 'Burst-belly'; Lancaster was 'the Fiddler', 'the Actor', or 'the Churl'; Pembroke was 'Joseph the Jew'; and Warwick was 'the Black Dog of Arden'.

The growing discontent with king and favourite led to a confrontation which resulted in Edward II's agreeing on 16 March 1310 to the election of the lords ordainer, a body of prelates, earls, and barons empowered to provide measures for the well-being of the royal household and the realm. Edward did his best to avoid the consequences of this capitulation by organizing a Scottish campaign during 1310–11, and on 1 October 1310 he appointed Gaveston justice of the forest north of Trent as well as keeper of Nottingham Castle—in open disregard of the ordinances. Gaveston wintered at Roxburgh, but by January had moved north to Perth in pursuit of Robert I. The Scots, however, refused to engage the superior English forces. Although he was appointed king's lieutenant in Scotland in July 1311, by August Gaveston had moved south to Bamburgh to await the outcome of the king's confrontation with the ordainers. The result was his third and final exile. Clause 20 of the ordinances of 1311 called for his perpetual exile not only from England but from all English possessions. He was to leave from Dover by 1 November 1311 under pain of excommunication.

Final return and death As it turned out, Gaveston's final exile was not long in duration. After spending no more than two months abroad he returned to England, most probably meeting the king at Knaresborough on 13 January 1312. From there the two immediately proceeded to York. The best explanation for this foolhardy return has less to do with the king or the ordinances than with Gaveston himself. His wife, Margaret, had given birth to a daughter, Joan, probably on the previous day, and both king and favourite remained in York throughout the countess of Cornwall's confinement. She was churched in the house of the Friars Minor in York on 20 February 1312, as indicated by the lavish payment of 40 marks to 'King Robert' and other minstrels for entertaining on that day. Although the king proclaimed Gaveston's return and reinstatement on 18 January, the latter was publicly excommunicated in March by Archbishop Winchelsey in accordance with the ordinances. The baronial opposition, now led by the earl of Lancaster, raised forces to oppose king and favourite. After barely escaping from a force led by Lancaster, Henry Percy, and Robert Clifford at Newcastle on 5 April, Gaveston established himself in Scarborough Castle while the king returned to York. Scarborough was besieged by the earls of Pembroke and Warwick, Percy, and Clifford, and on 19 May Gaveston agreed to terms. He would surrender to the besiegers on condition that, if a negotiated settlement with the king could not be reached by 1 August, he was to be returned to Scarborough. Pembroke, Percy, and Clifford guaranteed his security. After an initial meeting in York Gaveston was taken south in the custody of the earl of Pembroke.

On 9 June Gaveston was lodged in the rector's house at Deddington in Oxfordshire, while Pembroke went on to his manor of Bampton. But before dawn on the following day Gaveston was seized by the earl of Warwick who conveyed him back to his own castle of Warwick. After hastily convened deliberations among the magnates, notably the earls of Warwick, Lancaster, and Hereford, Gaveston was condemned to death. On 19 June 1312 he was led along the road to Kenilworth until he reached Blacklow Hill, which was on the land of the earl of Lancaster. There his head was cut off. The body was removed by the Dominican friars to Oxford, where it remained for over two years until Edward II had it taken to Kings Langley, where Gaveston's remains were finally laid to rest on 2 January 1315 in the Dominican house there.

The *Vita Edwardi secundi* reports that the king had proposed first to avenge Gaveston's death, and then to consign his body to the grave. Although his vengeance had to wait, Edward continued to nurture his grievance, and this certainly had an impact on the broader political history of the reign. At the siege of Berwick in 1318 the king is reported to have said, 'When this wretched business is over, we will turn our hands to other matters. For I have

not forgotten the wrong that was done to my brother Piers' (*Vita*, 104). And four years later, in the aftermath of the battle of Boroughbridge, the execution of the earl of Lancaster was seen by contemporaries as the inevitable retribution exacted by the king for Gaveston.

Gaveston left at least one daughter, and possibly a second, the latter presumably illegitimate. His daughter Joan, born in 1312, was brought up in the convent at Amesbury along with the king's niece, Eleanor of Hereford, with whom she received a joint allowance of 100 marks. A marriage arrangement with Thomas Wake fell through, and was followed by another by which Joan was to marry John, son of Thomas Multon, lord of Egremont. Unfortunately Joan died before the marriage could take place, one day after her thirteenth birthday, on 13 January 1325. Gaveston may also have been the father of Amie or Amice Gavaston, who is referred to in one contemporary document as 'Amie filie Petri de Gaveston'. She became a damsel of the chamber of Queen Philippa, wife of Edward III, and later married (by 1338) John Driby, a yeoman at various times of John of Gaunt, duke of Lancaster, Lionel, duke of Clarence, and Edward III himself.

J. S. HAMILTON

Sources J. S. Hamilton, *Piers Gaveston, earl of Cornwall, 1307–1312: politics and patronage in the reign of Edward II* (1988) • P. Chaplais, *Piers Gaveston: Edward II's adoptive brother* (1994) • J. R. Maddicott, *Thomas of Lancaster, 1307–1322: a study in the reign of Edward II* (1970) • J. R. S. Phillips, *Aymer de Valence, earl of Pembroke, 1307–1324: baronial politics in the reign of Edward II* (1972) • T. F. Tout, *The place of the reign of Edward II in English history: based upon the Ford lectures delivered in the University of Oxford in 1913*, rev. H. Johnstone, 2nd edn (1936) • N. Denholm-Young, ed. and trans., *Vita Edwardi secundi* (1957) • W. Stubbs, ed., *Chronicles of the reigns of Edward I and Edward II*, 2 vols., Rolls Series, 76 (1882–3) • PRO • GEC, *Peerage* • *Chancery records* (RC) • Rymer, *Foedera*, 3rd edn, vols. 1/2–2/1 • *Galfridi le Baker de Swinbroke chronicon Angliae temporibus Edwardi II et Edwardi III*, ed. J. A. Giles, Caxton Society, 7 (1847) • patent rolls, PRO, C 66/138, m. 3

Wealth at death wealth confiscated; Cornwall lands valued at £4000 p.a. in February 1308: Hamilton, *Piers Gaveston*; PRO, C 66/138, m.3

Gavin, Antonio (*fl.* 1716–1726), Church of England clergyman and religious controversialist, was born in Saragossa, Spain; there he was educated at the university and graduated MA. Before he was twenty-three he received ordination as a secular priest in the church of Rome. Having subsequently determined to embrace protestantism he escaped from Spain, disguised as an officer in the army, and reached London, where he was civilly received by James, first Earl Stanhope, whom he had met in Saragossa. On 3 January 1716 he was licensed to officiate in a Spanish congregation by John Robinson, bishop of London, to whom he had made his recantation.

For two years and eight months Gavin preached, first in the chapel in Queen Square, Westminster, and afterwards in Oxenden's chapel, near the Haymarket. His first sermon (on Deuteronomy 30: 9–10), which was dedicated to Lord Stanhope, was published as *Conversion de las tres potencias del alma, explicada en el primer sermon* in 1716. Stanhope, wishing to obtain for Gavin some settled preferment in the Church of England, advised him to accept the chaplaincy of the man-of-war *Preston*, in which capacity he would have had ample leisure to master English. The ship having been put out of commission he went to Ireland '*on the Importunity of a Friend*' (Gavin, 2nd edn, 1.vi) and while there he heard of the death of Stanhope at London on 5 February 1721. Through the influence of William Palliser, archbishop of Cashel, and of Dean Percival, Gavin obtained the curacy of Gowran, near Kilkenny, which he served for nearly eleven months. He then went to Cork, where he served the cure of a nearby parish for almost a year, sometimes preaching at Cork, Gortroe, and Shandon.

Gavin became well known as the author of a savage, and sometimes scurrilous, anti-Catholic tirade attacking Romish doctrine and practices, and popes and priests; he published it in 1724 with the title *A master-key to popery. Containing … a discovery of the most secret practices of the secular, and regular Romish priests in their auricular confession* and dedicated it to Lord Viscount Shannon, commander-in-chief of the crown's forces in Ireland, and to the officers serving there. Encouraged by the work's success he published a second edition, '*carefully corrected from the Errors of the First, with large Additions*', in three volumes (1725–6); a French translation by François-Michel Janiçon appeared in 1726–7. In the preface to the second edition's third volume Gavin wrote:

> in less than two Years 5,000 *of my First and Second* Volumes, *are dispersed among the Protestants of* Great Britain *and* Ireland … *I shall assiduously apply myself to finish the* Fourth Volume, *which shall be a* Master-Key *both to* Popery *and to* Hell. (Gavin, 2nd edn, 3.viii)

He wished his readers to infer that he was undeterred by the violent threats of the pope's emissaries. The concluding volume, which never appeared, was to have been entitled, according to the advertisement on the last page of volume three, 'Dr. Gavin's *Dreams, or the Master-piece of his Master-Key*'. As a former Catholic priest in a pronouncedly anti-Catholic state Gavin was correct in anticipating the considerable appeal of his work. It is not known when or where he died.

GORDON GOODWIN, *rev.* COLIN HAYDON

Sources A. Gavin, *A master-key to popery* (1724); 2nd edn in 3 vols. (1725–6)

Gavin, Ethel (1866–1918), educationist and headmistress, was born on 2 April 1866, at Elgin, Moray, the elder daughter of John Gavin, coffee planter of Craigellachie, Banffshire, Kandy, Ceylon, and Wester Elchies near Elgin, and Mary Isabella Macandrew. She was educated at a private school in Switzerland and from the age of fourteen at the Maida Vale high school in London. From there she went up to Girton College, Cambridge, in 1885 as Russell Gurney scholar. She was placed in the second class, division three, of the classical tripos in 1888 and returned in the same year to her old school of Maida Vale as assistant mistress. Ethel Gavin had a meteoric career: headmistress of the Shrewsbury high school in 1893 at the age of twenty-seven, she was appointed to Notting Hill high school at thirty-four, on the retirement of the first headmistress, Harriet Morant Jones, in 1900. She took her MA at Trinity College, Dublin, by incorporation in 1905 (Cambridge did not concede degrees to women until 1948). In 1908 she transferred to another of the Girl's Public Day School Company's schools in London, Wimbledon, where she remained until her early death in March 1918. At Notting Hill high school she was appointed in preference to the senior mistress, Mrs M. Withiel, who had long been expected to succeed to the headship. Her appointment brought resignations and some difficulties, with Mrs Withiel leaving to join the inspectorate. The girls, too, sensed a certain tension between the headmistress and her staff, and seemed shocked rather than captivated by her youth, her vigorous actions, and her modern dress, for she wore a blouse and tie and ankle-length (rather than full-length) skirt.

There was no doubt, however, that Ethel Gavin was a gifted teacher, assessed at Notting Hill by the inspectors as 'an able teacher' whose work was done 'efficiently and successfully' (Sayers, 128). At Wimbledon the inspectors (now including Mrs Withiel) found her teaching, which amounted to not less than nineteen lessons a week in all parts of the school, excellent in the field of religious instruction (she also taught Latin and history). However, the opinion was expressed that she might 'do well to spare more time … for supervising the work of her assistants, some of whom in a large staff … will necessarily be lacking in experience', though the inspectors noted that she was a 'capable and experienced headmistress' (Archives, Wimbledon high school, report of inspection, 1912). The belief was also expressed by one of the Wimbledon pupils that Miss Gavin was disloyal to her staff: the schoolgirls 'noticed and deplored … the way she would sometimes speak to a mistress sharply in a classroom or when passing through the hall instead of in the seclusion of her study' (Sayers, 129).

Ethel Gavin played an important part, not only in the Girls' High Schools movement, but also in the Headmistresses' Association, the Wimbledon educational authority, and Surrey county council's district committee for higher education. She was on the council of the Classical Association and was a member of the Simplified Spelling Society. On the outbreak of the First World War in 1914 she was detained for some weeks in Germany while on a visit to observe the teaching at the modern language college at Lichterfelde (a suburb of Berlin). The Ethel Gavin prize at Girton College was founded in her memory, as was a fine library at Wimbledon high school. Her health was not good, and she died of cancer at 117 Ridgway, Wimbledon, on 2 March 1918 at the early age of fifty-one, not long after the fire which destroyed the high school, in the aftermath of which she had shown characteristic organizing powers.

JANE E. SAYERS

Sources staff registers, inspectors' reports, correspondence, school magazines, Notting Hill and Ealing high school archives, London · staff registers, inspectors' reports, correspondence, school and trust magazines, Wimbledon high school archives, Surrey · student records and prizes, Girton Cam. · K. T. Butler and H. I. McMorran, eds., *Girton College register, 1869–1946* (1948) · *Girton Review* (March 1888) · *Girton Review* (July 1888) · J. E. Sayers, 'Second generation, 1900–01', *The fountain unsealed: a history of the Notting Hill*

and Ealing high school (privately printed, Broadwater Press, 1973), 126–47 · d. cert.
Archives Girton Cam. · Notting Hill and Ealing high school archives, London, staff registers, inspectors' reports, corresp., school magazines · Wimbledon high school archives, Surrey, staff registers, inspectors' reports, corresp., school and trust magazines

Gavin, Robert (1826–1883), genre painter, the second son of Peter Gavin, merchant, and Jane Strachan, was born in South Leith, Midlothian, on 21 June 1826. He was educated at Leith high school and, at the age of about twenty-one, enrolled at the Trustees' Academy in Edinburgh where he studied mainly under Thomas Duncan. He also attended the life school of the Royal Scottish Academy between 1848 and 1852. Gavin's early paintings included landscapes, portraits, and narrative subjects based on literary themes. These he exhibited at the annual exhibitions of the Royal Scottish Academy from 1846 to 1882 and at the Royal Academy in London from 1855 to 1871. Described as 'fancy pictures', these were eagerly bought up by a London dealer, and as a mark of his early success he was elected an associate of the Royal Scottish Academy in 1855. However, in 1857 he became dissatisfied with his artistic progress and he entered partnership with a wine merchant; the venture lasted only a year and he afterwards returned to painting.

In 1868 Gavin sailed to the United States and visited New Orleans. Fascinated by the exoticism of the varied racial types he made studies of black and mixed-race Americans, such as *'Mulatto Flower-Girl'* (exh. Royal Scottish Academy, 1871). In the mid-1870s he again travelled, this time to Europe and north Africa. He settled in Tangier and produced a series of portraits and figure paintings of Moorish life. In 1879 he was elected a full academician of the Royal Scottish Academy. He deposited a Tangier painting as his diploma work, *The Moorish Maiden's First Love* (1879, Royal Scottish Academy). The subject is a tribal girl with her Arab horse, and in its details of costume it combines a love for the exotic with accurate observation of racial features and a strong dose of sentimentality. Ill health forced Gavin to return to Scotland and he died, unmarried, at his home, Cherry Bank, Newhaven Road, Leith, on 5 October 1883. He was buried in Warriston cemetery in Edinburgh on 9 October.   JOANNA SODEN

Sources *Annual Report of the Council of the Royal Scottish Academy of Painting, Sculpture, and Architecture*, 56 (1883), 13–14 · *The Scotsman* (8 Oct 1883) · C. B. de Laperriere, ed., *The Royal Scottish Academy exhibitors, 1826–1990*, 4 vols. (1991), vol. 2. pp. 117–19 · Graves, *RA exhibitors*, 3 (1905), 217 · R. Brydall, *Art in Scotland, its origin and progress* (1889), 406–7 · W. D. McKay, *The Scottish school of painting* (1906), 351–2 · J. Wallace, *Further traditions of Trinity and Leith* (1990), 70–71 · Bryan, *Painters* (1909–10), 2.221 · P. J. M. McEwan, *Dictionary of Scottish art and architecture* (1994), 224 · b. reg. Scot. · papers, Royal Scot. Acad., 1848–52, 1870–83 · d. cert.
Archives Royal Scot. Acad., corresp., letter collection | Royal Scot. Acad., life school records
Wealth at death £780 14s. 6d.: confirmation, 6 Dec 1883, CCI · £644 18s. od.: additional inventory, 7 May 1885, CCI

Gaw, John (d. c.1553), protestant reformer, is of obscure origins, and it is no more than an assumption that he was related to the family of Gaw in Perth, whose ranks included prominent merchants. His contemporary and probable kinsman Alexander Gaw, a priest and notary public, was chaplain at Abernethy, 8 miles from Perth. John Gaw is customarily identified with the student of that name who was incorporated in St Salvator's College in St Andrews University in 1509, became a determinant or bachelor of arts in the session 1510–11, and graduated master of arts in 1512. Yet there is reason to believe that the early reformer may not have been a graduate: at Copenhagen in 1551 he was styled 'dominus', not 'magister' (though so, too, in the same document was Erasmus, himself a doctor). One John Gaw was already a student at St Andrews as early as 1507, and 'sir' John Gaw (a non-graduate priest) appears on record as a witness in 1513 at Kilwinning Abbey in Ayrshire.

It seems probable that Gaw was one of the protestants seeking exile in the aftermath of Patrick Hamilton's execution in St Andrews for protestant heresy in 1528—an execution denounced as 'cruel' in *The Richt Vay*. Gaw may have acted as chaplain to the community of Scottish merchants at Malmö in Sweden, then in the Danish king's possession. His book, *The Richt Vay to the Kingdom of Hevine*, the first known protestant work to be printed in Scots, was published there in October 1533. In 1536 Gaw married Brigit, an inhabitant of Malmö, who died in 1551, and with her had a daughter, born in 1544, and twins, born a few years later. Later Gaw served as Lutheran chaplain in the church of Our Lady in Copenhagen where his fellow countryman John MacAlpine, formerly Dominican prior at Perth and a convert to Lutheranism, taught theology at Copenhagen University from 1542. In his book Gaw briefly alluded to his conversion to protestantism where he acknowledged how, in his 'blindness', he had held many errors—'the devil's doctrine'—until 'the father of light' brought him and many others out of the darkness of Egypt by the light of scripture.

Gaw's work, designed as an aid to devotion, was not an original composition but rather a Scots translation and adaptation of a Danish treatise by Christiern Pedersen entitled *Den rette vey till hiemmerigis rige*, first published at Antwerp in 1531, and itself based on a German work, published at Augsburg in 1523, by Urbaus Rhegius, the reformer of Augsburg, who utilized material from Luther's own writings. Gaw had evidently sufficient command of Danish by 1533 to undertake his translation into Scots, and he anticipated that his book would circulate readily among layfolk, whom he hoped would read it daily. It offered an exposition of the ten commandments, the twelve articles of the apostles' creed, the Lord's prayer, and Ave Maria. It condemned 'skaithful bukis and fals doctrine' which had deceived the people for many years; it stressed the supremacy of scripture as the rule of faith and obedience; it recognized the right of the laity to read the vernacular Bible; it examined humanity's fall from grace, corrupt nature, and the need for redemption, and the provision of redemption by the incarnation, the work and passion of the eternal son of God, justification by faith alone, and sanctification by the Holy Spirit. The Christian church is the congregation of the faithful throughout the world, gathered by the Word and governed by the Holy Spirit; headship of the church belongs to no sinful mortal, whether pope or patriarch; all are merely members; Christ gave the keys of the kingdom to all Christians and not to Peter alone; all have power to bind and loose, not just bishops, priests, or monks; ministers of the keys should be chosen by Christian congregations; pilgrimages to holy places and journeys to Rome for papal pardons are unnecessary; instead of intercessory prayer to the saints, Christ alone should be worshipped as he uniquely made 'perfit satisfactione for al our sinnis and wil mercifullie forgif ws thaime of his awne gracious guidnes'; Christ's body and blood are 'contenit veralie in the sacrament of the alter onder the forme of breid and vine'. The work closes with a letter to the Scottish nobles and barons in which false preaching, 'dremis and fablis and the tradicions of men' are contrasted with biblical teaching and the example of Patrick Hamilton, martyred for confessing Christ. Gaw died in Copenhagen, where he was buried, about 1553.   JAMES KIRK

Sources J. Gau, *The richt vay to the kingdom of hevine*, ed. A. F. Mitchell, STS, 8 (1888) · J. M. Anderson, ed., *Early records of the University of St Andrews*, Scottish History Society, 3rd ser., 8 (1926) · A. I. Dunlop, ed., *Acta facultatis artium universitatis Sanctiandree, 1413–1588*, St Andrews University Publications, 56 (1964) · *Liber protocollorum M. Cuthberti Simonis* (1875) · *Protocol book of Sir Alexander Gaw* (1910)

Gawain Poet (*fl. c.*1375–1400), author, is the name now given to the unknown author to whom most scholars ascribe the four alliterative poems *Sir Gawain and the Green Knight*, *Pearl* (though *Gawain* has some rhyming lines in each stanza, *Pearl* is alone in using rhyme throughout its alliterating stanzas), *Patience*, and *Cleanness* (or *Purity*), preserved only in BL, Cotton MS Nero A.x, Art. 3; most today reject the inclusion in his œuvre of *St Erkenwald*, another alliterative poem, preserved uniquely in BL, Harley MS 2250. The date of the Cotton manuscript is *c.*1400, and its language (reckoned not significantly different from that of the author) has been localized in south-east Cheshire, close to the Staffordshire border. Though the author's name and life are unknown, his cultural milieu must have included the Cheshire gentry in the reign of Richard II; the Stanley family of Storeton and Hooton in Cheshire and Stanley in Staffordshire has been suggested as being involved in the patronage of the Gawain Poet.

The poet was well read in English romances and probably in French ones, too; he drew extensively on the Vulgate in three of his poems, and had a general awareness of Christian exegesis and of sermons, though specific debts have not been established. The only book he cites by name is Jean de Meun's *Roman de la rose* in *Cleanness*, in which he also makes use of *Mandeville's Travels* (in perhaps the English as well as the French text [see Mandeville, Sir John]). Some terms used in *Pearl* to define a mystical state are found elsewhere in this context only in Walter Hilton's *Scale of Perfection*. Some have detected echoes of Dante in *Pearl*, but these cannot be regarded as certain. It cannot even be ascertained whether the poet was a layman or a priest. His extensive command of the technical vocabularies of courtesy (*Gawain* and *Pearl*), hunting and

Gawain Poet (*fl. c.*1375–1400), manuscript painting [as the father in *Pearl*]

armour (*Gawain*), feasts (*Gawain* and *Cleanness*), mysticism (*Pearl*), and ships (*Patience*) is compatible with either.

Though the poems can be assigned to genres—romance (*Gawain*), elegiac dream-vision (*Pearl*), and biblical paraphrase (the book of Jonah in *Patience* and various biblical accounts of moral uncleanness in *Cleanness*)—the blurring of boundaries between them is frequent: moral and religious issues in *Gawain*, courtly love and its language transposed to a grieving father and his daughter in *Pearl*, parody of the romance hero setting forth in *Patience*, reminiscence of sermons in *Patience* and *Cleanness*, biblical paraphrase in *Pearl*, the romance taste for *meruaylez* ('marvels') in all four poems. In theme, there is a common preoccupation on the one hand with total moral perfection and on the other with an awareness of how man, the best as well as the worst, falls short of it; an admiration for the beauty of holiness is more than matched by a profound sensitivity to the blemishes of sinfulness: Gawain triumphantly survives a beheading game with the Green Knight but ends in despair over what to everyone else seems a mere ungentlemanly sleight; the *Pearl* narrator's magnificent vision of the New Jerusalem is brought to an abrupt end by his impatient wish to join his daughter in the city; the reader learns of patience not through the exemplary Job but through the impatient Jonah; the celebration of the purity of Christ's life shines briefly amid the lengthy and darksome narratives of man's filth. The distinctive flavour of the author's mind is the combination of moral *gravitas* with drama, psychological realism, elegance, wit, ingenuity, paradox, and, above all, surprise—as he says in *Gawain*, 'þe forme to þe fynisment foldez ful selden' ('the beginning is very seldom like the end').

EDWARD WILSON

Sources *The poems of the Pearl manuscript: Pearl, Cleanness, Patience, Sir Gawain and the Green Knight*, ed. M. Andrew and R. Waldron (1978) • A. McIntosh and others, *A linguistic atlas of late mediaeval English*, 4 vols. (1986), vol. 3, pp. 26, 37–8 [linguistic profile for Cheshire] • E. Wilson, '*Sir Gawain and the Green Knight* and the Stanley family of Stanley, Storeton, and Hooton', *Review of English Studies*, new ser., 30 (1979), 308–16 • M. J. Bennett, *Community, class and careerism: Cheshire and Lancashire society in the age of 'Sir Gawain and the Green Knight'* (1983) • E. Wilson, *The Gawain-Poet* (1976) • T. Turville-Petre, *The alliterative revival* (1977) • D. Lawton, ed., *Middle English alliterative poetry and its literary background: seven essays* (1982) • A. C. Spearing, *The Gawain-Poet: a critical study* (1970) • W. A. Davenport, *The art of the Gawain-Poet* (1978) • D. Brewer and J. Gibson, *A companion to the Gawain-Poet* (1997)
Archives BL, Cotton MS Nero A.x, Art. 3 • BL, Harley MS 2250
Likenesses manuscript painting, BL, Cotton MS Nero A.x, fol. 37 [*see illus.*]

Gawdy family (*per. c.*1500–1723), gentry, rose to prominence in Norfolk in the third quarter of the fifteenth century thanks to successful careers in the law and to a series of multiple marriages which brought dowries in land as well as in cash. Early training at the inns of court led to useful contacts with officials and courtiers who could forward the family's interests when necessary.

Beginnings The speed with which the family rose to prominence in Tudor Norfolk was due to three half-brothers, Thomas Gawdy (*c.*1476–1556/7), bailiff of Harleston, Sir Thomas *Gawdy (*d.* 1588), created a justice of queen's bench in 1574, and Sir Francis *Gawdy (*d.* 1605), created chief justice of common pleas in 1605. The eldest brother, Thomas the bailiff, in spite of a career less brilliant than those of his half-brothers, founded a line that was to influence his native county more profoundly than did the descendants of the London-based judges.

In the early years of the sixteenth century Norfolk was dominated by great landowning magnates whose influence was only gradually diluted by the rise of newly wealthy families. The land market of the 1530s provided investment opportunities and brought forward new men who could be called upon to assume local leadership. Such a one was **Thomas Gawdy** (*d.* 1556), eldest son of Thomas the bailiff and his wife, Elizabeth Hellows. He, too, had been trained in the law at the Inner Temple, and on returning to Norfolk had become influential throughout the county as high steward of the third duke of Norfolk's estates and as a JP. He was recorder of King's Lynn (1545), and of Norwich (1550), and in 1553 was elected to parliament as a burgess of Norwich, when he so successfully opposed the Charities Act that the guild lands of King's Lynn were returned to the town by the crown. His religious convictions were reformed, and this precluded his subsequent return to parliament. His standing as a lawyer, however, was enhanced by his elevation to the rank of serjeant-at-law in 1552, while the fortunes accrued by his marriages, first to Anne Bassingbourne, who died after 1533, then to Elizabeth Staynings (*née* Harris), who died

after 1537, enabled him to establish himself with a mansion house in Norwich and estates in East Anglia, Hertfordshire, and the west country. His third and last marriage, to Katherine, daughter of Sir Robert Lestrange and widow of Sir Hugh Hastings of Elsing, under a settlement of 9 July 1554, brought him and his family a secure position among the long-established gentry of Norfolk. When Thomas Gawdy died in 1556 his will divided his estates and properties equitably between his children and stepchildren and he had remembered to make provision for his old, blind father, who outlived him by five months, and to leave £10 to 'Megge the bastard' (PRO, PROB 11/38, fol. 105*r*).

Alliances and rivalries Bassingbourne Gawdy (*c.*1532–1590) was the second son of Thomas Gawdy's first marriage. He was well qualified to follow his father's example of public service. His first wife, Anne Wootton, was twice widowed and childless when they married on 26 September 1558 in the Gawdy family parish of Redenhall, near Harleston. She was heir to her mother's estate at West Harling near Thetford, centred on a great house, Berdewell Hall, which became the home of her family and their descendants. As a young man Bassingbourne Gawdy went to the Inner Temple after a time at Trinity Hall, Cambridge, and while in London had secured the post of gentleman waiter to the queen, a position with advantageous contacts. His religious convictions, like his father's, were puritan, and once back in Norfolk he found a congenial niche in the circle of the Bacons of Redgrave and Stiffkey. A dispute over his purchase from Sir Nicholas Bacon of Redgrave of the manor of Eccles laid the foundation of a protracted quarrel with the Lovells of East Harling, a family as closely aligned with religious conservatives in the county as the Gawdys were with 'the godly'. Between these two factions there was a constant struggle over control of the county. Nevertheless, when Bassingbourne Gawdy became sheriff for 1578–9 family solidarity obliged him to apply to the privy council and the bishop of Norwich for the release from close imprisonment in Bury St Edmunds gaol of his brother-in-law Henry Everard, a persistent recusant, so that he could attend his wife on her deathbed. Arrangements were duly made, and Gawdy later undertook the maintenance of some of Everard's thirteen motherless children. It was characteristic of the Gawdy family through the generations to fulfil the wish of an earlier Thomas Gawdy that they should be 'loving, faithfull, frendlie and trustie to one another in all ther necessities' (Norfolk RO, Jagges 192).

As sheriff, Bassingbourne Gawdy was widely recognized to be a source of wise counsel as well as a conscientious officer of the crown. His letter-book gives a précis of all his business, and the copies of his replies to a wide range of petitioners and officials substantiate his reputation as a man of integrity. He had been a member of the Suffolk bench since the 1570s and by 1581 he was also a Norfolk magistrate. With the backing of Sir Nicholas Bacon of Redgrave he became MP for Eye in 1584, after a rebuff from Thetford where he had earlier reproved the leading townsfolk for their lukewarmness in religion. This additional responsibility added to his consequence in the county, to the chagrin of Sir Thomas Lovell and other local rivals and opponents. The last years of Bassingbourne's life were clouded by illness. On 20 January 1590 he died at Berdewell Hall and was buried on the 25th in the Lady chapel in the parish church of West Harling.

Advancement in country and court His son, **Sir Bassingbourne Gawdy** (1560–1606), succeeded to the West Harling estate and, with almost the same ease, to his father's position in the county, being appointed to the bench in 1590. The old feud with the Lovells showed no sign of diminishing: 'Malice was his mother, and envy nursed him, and hate brought him into the world and never will forsake him till he leave world and all' (*Letters*, ed. Jeayes, 47) was the comment of Philip Gawdy, the younger Bassingbourne's courtier brother. It is not easy to disentangle the generations of a prolific family whose members entered into multiple marriages. **Philip Gawdy** (1562–1617) was some eight years younger than his uncle **Anthony Gawdy** (c.1554–1606), son of Thomas Gawdy (d. 1556) and his second wife. They were close friends; together at Clifford's Inn they lived the carefree life of young men about town. Philip Gawdy wrote home about his activities:

> I have been marvelously troubled with the common dysease of payne in the eyes which you knowe must neades be some hynderaunce to my study and for which indeed I durst not muche look of a booke but only tend playing the lute. (ibid., 6)

Constantly writing home for funds, Philip and Anthony Gawdy became familiar figures on the fringe of the court, until the need for a reliable member of the family to act as agent at West Harling obliged Anthony Gawdy to leave London in 1587. Philip Gawdy remained at court to forward the family's interests and to pick up a living to augment his meagre allowance as a younger brother of the heir. In 1591 he went to sea with Sir Richard Grenville, setting off in the *Revenge* for the Azores to intercept the Spanish fleet. There he transferred to Lord Thomas Howard's flagship and so avoided being caught up in the action that sank the *Revenge*. Nevertheless, he was captured and imprisoned in the castle at Lisbon until £200 arrived from his brother to ransom him.

As MP for Eye (1595–7), for Thetford (1597–1601), for Sudbury (1601–3), and subsequently for Dunwich (1604, 1614), Philip Gawdy was a living example of the power of patronage, exercised largely by the Bacons. In 1597 he married Bridget ('my Bidd'), daughter of Bartholomew Strangman of Chilton near Hadleigh, Suffolk, a lady as improvident as her husband. Their eight children were handed round the families to be brought up by generous relatives while the parents returned to London, ever fighting off penury and cheerfully soliciting and receiving support from their Gawdy relations. When Anthony Gawdy died in 1606 he left all his property, with the exception of some small bequests to friends and servants, to his close friend and nephew Philip Gawdy. Philip died in 1617 after a short illness, described as a 'surfett'.

In the meantime the younger Bassingbourne Gawdy was advancing in importance. With the support of the Bacons he twice became MP for Thetford, in 1593 and 1603–4; in 1593 and 1601 he was sheriff, and in 1606 was elected knight of the shire. He made an advantageous first marriage to Anne, daughter and heir of Sir Charles Framlingham of Debenham, Suffolk. This marriage strengthened still further Bassingbourne Gawdy's ties with the godly of East Anglia, as his wife was granddaughter to Sir Clement Heigham of Barrow, a prominent puritan justice and landowner in west Suffolk. Their eldest son, Framlingham Gawdy, on whom his maternal grandfather's estates were entailed, was born in 1589. Anne Gawdy died in 1594 and Bassingbourne advanced into the first rank of Norfolk society through his marriage to Dorothy, daughter of Sir Nicholas Bacon of Redgrave. He was knighted in 1597. The six children of this marriage inherited less of their mother's family's sobriety and financial acumen than of the high spirits and improvidence of their Gawdy relations.

Staying afloat Sir Bassingbourne died in 1606, and in the same year his heir, Framlingham *Gawdy (1589–1655), inherited the fortune and property of his maternal grandfather. All may have seemed well, with an assured line of succession of Gawdys of West Harling, but an examination of their finances and landholdings indicates that for many years consumption had outstripped income. Anthony Gawdy had lacked the training and expertise needed to cope with the fluctuations of land and food prices. The inventory of Berdewell Hall taken immediately after Sir Bassingbourne's death gives a picture of a house where elegance and comfort was offset by a multiplicity of rooms used for the storage of ancient junk, from tapestry hangings, Turkey carpets, and velvet-cushioned high-backed chairs to 'Twoe Ancientes [ensigns] of blewe and yellowe with either of them a red crosse and one with a tortue [the family arms] … in the Halle a hawkes perke, three mapps in the Parlor and Sir Bassingbourne's armor'. The total value, 'besides the Crown lease of lands in Suffolk not valued', was £2312 3s. 11d. and 5000 sheep, all of which descended to Framlingham Gawdy.

From the first, Framlingham Gawdy had the charm and insouciance of his forebears, as witness a letter to his father, written on carefully ruled lines when he was eleven years old: 'When i am a better Scholar youe shall have a better letter. Your loving son' (BL, Add. MS 5522, 50). After being frustrated in his hopes of marrying one of the waiting-women at Berdewell Hall, in 1608 he married Lettice, daughter of Sir Robert Knowles, to whom he was in wardship, not in a church but at Sir Robert's London house, The Vinefields, in the parish of St Margaret, Westminster. The ceremony was performed under a special licence. After Lettice's death in 1630, George Gawdy, a member of a collateral branch of the family, challenged the validity of the marriage in the hope of obtaining all the West Harling and Framlingham inheritances, but without success. Several times an MP, Framlingham wrote a valuable account of events in the early years of the Long Parliament. When he was not in London on business, he seems to have been locally famous as a great flock-master. The family letters reveal a cheerful, easy-going man, devoted to his children and grandchildren, to whom 'the boys Fram, Bass and Charles' wrote constantly from Cambridge and London:

> I would entreate you to send me 5s. Because I stand in great need of money ... I shall be boulde to begge of you, it is a sword which is here to be sould, the price of it is fortie shillings, it is a very handsome one. (BL, Add. MS 27396)

His second son, another Framlingham Gawdy, was a competent lawyer, and from 1635 undertook all the family's legal business. In January 1653 the elder Framlingham married his cousin Dorothy Gawdy, who had acted as housekeeper at Berdewell Hall after Lettice's death. In his last illness he was attended by Sir Thomas Browne of Norwich, the famous physician and philosopher. He died at West Harling on 25 February 1655.

Last generations All six of the elder Framlingham Gawdy's sons had started their education locally at the grammar schools at Bury St Edmunds and Thetford. All but one made careers in the law or attending to county or family business. The eldest of them, **Sir William Gawdy**, first baronet (*bap.* 1612, *d.* 1669), married Elizabeth, daughter of John Duffield of East Wretham, a Norfolk neighbour; they had a family of four sons and a daughter. Elizabeth died in 1653 and William Gawdy left the care of the family estates in the hands of his brother Charles and moved into lodgings in Bury St Edmunds. The only county office he appears to have held was that of major of militia foot, to which he was appointed in 1660. In the same year he travelled to The Hague and became one of the entourage of the returning Charles II. But this was a year of personal tragedy for him. Two of his sons, William and Bassingbourne, and their cousin Framlingham, students together at the Inner Temple, died there of smallpox within six days of one another. It can have been of small comfort to him to be created baronet in 1663. His two remaining sons, Sir John *Gawdy (1639–1709) and Framlingham, were both deaf mutes, and his only daughter, Mary, suffered from exophthalmic goitre, exacerbated by an unsightly skin condition on her face. Both sons were clearly intelligent and their father did his utmost to make their lives as fulfilling as possible. John was placed in the workshop of the Bury St Edmunds miniaturist, Matthew Snelling, an associate of Samuel Cooper. Both brothers studied in the studio of Sir Peter Lely and were in touch with their student relatives at the Inner Temple. Framlingham and Mary lived with their relations at Crows Hall, Debenham, under the special care of their uncle Framlingham, Sir William's brother, who had made his home there since 1637, and who in 1661 as the family lawyer negotiated the marriage of his nephew John to Anne, daughter of Sir Robert de Grey of Merton, Norfolk. The wedding took place in St James's Church, Bury St Edmunds, in 1662. Sir William Gawdy died in 1669 at Barton Mills, Suffolk, and was buried at West Harling.

Sir John Gawdy and his wife continued to live in Bury St Edmunds. Sir William's will had made good provision for his surviving children with settlements for Framlingham of an annuity of £100 and for Mary an annuity of £80 until she reached eighteen and lands in trust to give her a marriage portion of £2500. Mary's disability caused great anxiety to her brothers and uncle Framlingham, and the most eminent doctors were consulted. Mary herself had little confidence in her physicians but a touching faith in the efficacy of the monarch's power over diseases. She wrote:

> I heare that the King have cut his heare and if hee have, pray Sr, gett me sum of it, if you can, to weare about my necke, for Mrs Franklen have a daughter that had such a swelling in her neck as I have and she gott a lock and wore it about her neck and it have almost cured her, and they think it was that. (BL, Add. MS 27396/271)

But, on a visit to London in 1671, like her two brothers before her, she contracted smallpox and died, aged twenty-two. She was buried in the Temple Church where a mural tablet commemorates the four young Gawdys.

Sir John Gawdy and his wife had four children, two of whom died in infancy. His family took its place in Suffolk society and were welcome guests. Sir John continued to paint as a pastime and became known as an accomplished portraitist. He died in 1709 and was succeeded by his son **Sir Bassingbourne Gawdy**, third baronet (1667–1723). Bassingbourne showed little interest in education after the preliminaries at Thetford grammar school but all the Gawdys' enthusiasm for rash adventure. He held a commission in the militia and was a close friend of Oliver Le Neve, husband of his sister Anne, in whose rackety exploits he often participated. A notable sportsman, he died unmarried, on 10 October 1723, following a hunting accident, and was buried at West Harling. The Gawdy property and Berdewell Hall were sold by the Le Neves who had inherited them in the right of Anne Le Neve. The aisle of the lady chapel in the parish church of West Harling in which so many generations of Gawdys had been baptized and buried, was demolished by the new owner of Berdewell Hall, as was the great house itself.

JOY ROWE

Sources P. Millican, *The Gawdys of Norfolk and Suffolk* (1938) · *Letters of Philip Gawdy, 1579–1616*, ed. I. H. Jeayes (1906) · A. Hassell Smith, *County and court: government politics in Norfolk, 1558–1603* (1974) · *Report on the manuscripts of the family of Gawdy, formerly of Norfolk*, HMC, 11 (1885) · J. Hasler, 'Gawdy, Bassingbourne I', 'Gawdy, Bassingbourne II', HoP, *Commons, 1558–1603*, 176–7 · F. Blomefield and C. Parkin, *An essay towards a topographical history of the county of Norfolk*, [2nd edn], 11 vols. (1805–10), vol. 3 · A. Harvey, ed., 'Bury St Edmunds grammar school list, 1550–1900', *Suffolk Green Books*, 13 (1908) · Bodl. Oxf., MS Tanner 241 · BL, Add. MSS 27395–27399, 36989, 36990 · BL, Egerton MSS 2713–2722, 2804 · BL, Add. Rolls, 10549, 1606 · will, PRO, PROB 11/38, fol. 105r [Thomas Gawdy, d. 1556] · probate will register, Norfolk RO, Jagges 192 · R. Virgoe, 'Gawdy, Thomas I', R. J. W. Swales, 'Gawdy, Thomas II', HoP, *Commons, 1509–58*, 199–201, 201–2

Archives BL, deeds, family and household papers, Add. Ch 53512–53518, Add. MSS 27395–27399, 36989–36990, Egerton MSS 2713–2722 · Norfolk RO, deeds and papers · Norfolk RO, family corresp. mainly relating to financial and legal affairs [copies] · Norfolk RO, further papers · Norfolk RO, Norfolk magistracy papers, etc.

Likenesses circle of G. Jackson, oils (Bassingbourne Gawdy, 1560–1606), repro. in sale catalogue, Sothebys, 1995

Wealth at death £2312 3s. 11d. plus crown leased Suffolk lands; also 5000 sheep—Sir Bassingbourne Gawdy (1560–1606): BL, Add. Roll 10549, 1606

Gawdy, Anthony (c.1554–1606). *See under* Gawdy family (*per. c.*1500–1723).

Gawdy, Bassingbourne (c.1532–1590). *See under* Gawdy family (*per. c.*1500–1723).

Gawdy, Sir Bassingbourne (1560–1606). *See under* Gawdy family (*per. c.*1500–1723).

Gawdy, Sir Bassingbourne, third baronet (1667–1723). *See under* Gawdy family (*per. c.*1500–1723).

Gawdy, Framlingham (1589–1655), politician and parliamentary diarist, was born on 8 August 1589 at Berdwell Hall, West Harling, Norfolk, the eldest son of Sir Bassingbourne *Gawdy (1560–1606) [see under Gawdy family] and his first wife, Anne, daughter and coheir of Sir Charles Framlingham of Crow's Hall, Debenham, Suffolk. Gawdy remained at Berdwell Hall until he was sixteen, when, after an affair with a serving maid, he was sent to live in London with his uncle, Philip Gawdy. Philip Gawdy was an esquire to the body to King James and he introduced Gawdy to life at court, where the young man proved a popular figure and entertained the notion of becoming a courtier himself. He retained his youthful high spirits throughout his life, often enjoyed playing bowls at Buckenham, Norfolk, and was usually present at East Anglian hunts; he also bet his uncle £60 that the latter could not undertake a journey to Jerusalem and return with proof that he had visited the city.

When his father died Gawdy inherited substantial estates in Norfolk and Suffolk but as he was still under age his guardianship was entrusted to Sir Robert Knollys. He lived with Knollys in London until 1609, when on 16 February he married Knollys's daughter, Lettice (d. 1630), and returned to West Harling. Although he frequently travelled to London, and was admitted to Gray's Inn in 1624, he mainly busied himself with running the family's foldcourse sheep farming business which brought in a large income of over £1000 per annum during the 1630s. Commensurate with his family's status in East Anglia, he served as a JP for Norfolk from 1614 and on numerous other local commissions. In 1626 he was appointed as a captain of the foot militia in Norfolk and the following year he was a commissioner for the forced loan. In 1642 he was made a deputy lieutenant for Norfolk.

Gawdy was elected to his first parliament as an MP for Thetford in 1614, and he subsequently served as one of its MPs in 1621, 1624, 1625, and 1626 and in the Short and Long parliaments of 1640. His influence within the county is evident from the fact that, while Thetford's elections were almost always contested, he never failed to gain a place. The only parliament for which he did not stand for election was that of 1628, when he was pricked as sheriff for Norfolk and thus technically ineligible to stand. Despite his long parliamentary service, he was rarely appointed to committees and throughout the period he was never recorded as speaking. However, in 1641 and 1642 he kept a daily account of events in the Commons, which are preserved in the British Library (Add. MSS 14827–14828) and have subsequently been published (W. H. Coates, A. S. Young, and V. F. Snow, eds., *Private Journals of the Long Parliament*, 3 vols., 1982, 1987, 1992). Gawdy's political views are not apparent from his diaries, and his notes reveal an interest in the procedure of the house rather than any overt political motives. However, included among them is a detailed account of the trial of the earl of Strafford, although Gawdy left London before the final debates.

Gawdy was a moderate parliamentarian who did not sit in parliament after Pride's Purge in 1649, and after the execution of King Charles I he was removed from local commissions. After the death of his first wife in 1630 he was encouraged by many friends to marry a rich widow but he resisted the temptation of remarriage until on 28 January 1653 he married a cousin, Dorothy Gawdy (d. 1659), who had cared for him after Lettice's death. Gawdy died at Berdwell Hall on 25 February 1655. He and his first wife had had six sons and two daughters; there were no children from his second marriage. The bulk of his estate was left to his eldest son, William, who was created a baronet by Charles II and continued the family tradition by serving as an MP for Thetford in the Cavalier Parliament.

CHRIS R. KYLE

Sources HoP, *Commons* [draft] · P. Millican, 'The Gawdys of Norfolk and Suffolk', *Norfolk Archaeology*, 26 (1936–8), 335–90 · W. H. Coates, A. Steele Young, and V. F. Snow, eds., *The private journals of the Long Parliament*, 3 vols. (1982–92) · BL, Add. MSS 14827–14828 · *Letters of Philip Gawdy*, ed. I. H. Jeayes, Roxburghe Club, 148 (1906) · Thetford Town Council, King's House, T/C2/3,4 · *Report on the manuscripts of the family of Gawdy, formerly of Norfolk*, HMC, 11 (1885) · R. W. Ketton-Cremer, *Norfolk in the civil war: a portrait of a society in conflict* (1969), 106, 109, 114, 117–18, 144, 152, 357 · *JHC*, 1 (1547–1628) · BL, Harleian MS 6395, fol. 82 · BL, Add. MS 36990, fols. 100–104 · J. Foster, *The register of admissions to Gray's Inn, 1521–1889, together with the register of marriages in Gray's Inn chapel, 1695–1754* (privately printed, London, 1889)

Archives BL, personal and family MSS, Add. MSS 14826–14827, 27395–27399, 56103 · Norfolk RO, family accounts, and accounts as treasurer of maimed soldiers and Norfolk treasurer of king's bench and Marshalsea | Norfolk RO, corresp. [copies]

Gawdy, Sir Francis (d. 1605), judge, was the third and most successful son of Thomas Gawdy (c.1476–1556/7) of Harleston, Norfolk; his mother was Elizabeth Shires (d. 1563). His eldest half-brother, Thomas (d. 1556), was a serjeant-at-law; the second half-brother, also Thomas *Gawdy (d. 1588), was a judge of the court of king's bench; Francis became chief justice of the court of common pleas. Like his father and half-brothers, he was baptized Thomas, but changed his name to Francis at his confirmation, thereby establishing the legal rule permitting the change of baptismal name at confirmation. He may have studied at Trinity Hall, Cambridge, where a Thomas Gawdy is recorded as having matriculated in 1545, but proceeded to the Inner Temple in 1549, where he was a bencher by 1558 and treasurer in 1571. Gawdy served as reader at Lyon's Inn in 1561, and was Lent reader in the Inner Temple in 1566 and 1571. He had a brief and undistinguished parliamentary career, representing Morpeth in the parliament of 1571, but his legal practice continued to flourish. He was created serjeant-at-law in 1577; and as queen's serjeant (1582–8) he opened the prosecution of Mary, queen of Scots, in 1586. In 1588 he succeeded his brother as judge of the court of king's bench, continuing to play his part in the major state trials of the period. The last of these was the trial of Sir Walter Ralegh in 1603; Gawdy is reputed to have regarded his conviction as an affront to justice. He was knighted the same year. He seems to have had some expectation of appointment as chief baron of the exchequer in succession to Sir William Peryam, but he was informed by King James in 1603 that he was being saved for a better place when it became available and Sir Thomas Fleming was appointed in his stead. In 1605 the necessary opening arose, and in August Gawdy was appointed chief justice of the common pleas. Contemporary gossip had it that he had paid well for the position; but if so it proved a bad investment, for he died of apoplexy four months later, on 15 December 1605, at Serjeants' Inn.

Gawdy was a first-rate lawyer; he had the intellectual sharpness and the moral courage to hold his own on the late Elizabethan bench, and in contemporary reports of judicial discussions he stands out as a firm-minded man capable of grounding his conclusions on well-formulated legal arguments. Though the Gawdy family in general leaned towards puritanism, Francis may have harboured Catholic sympathies. As justice of assize on the midland circuit in the 1590s he seems to have been curiously blind to the activities of Roman Catholics centred around the earl of Shrewsbury; he was on good terms with Sir Christopher Hatton, a reputed harbourer of recusants, who led the dancing at the marriage of his nephew and heir to Gawdy's daughter in 1589; and he opposed the marriage of his granddaughter Frances to the puritan Sir Robert Rich. He seems to have had an unhappy family life. Sir Henry Spelman describes his wife, Elizabeth Coningsby, whom he had married in 1563, as 'to him for many years a perpetual affliction' (Spelman, 141), though the cause of this may have been the perhaps well-justified belief that her husband had cheated her out of her interest in her ancestral Norfolk home, Eston Hall, Wallington. His daughter died soon after her marriage, and he broke off relations with his granddaughter after her marriage to Rich in 1604. When Gawdy died intestate, letters of administration of his estate were taken out by Rich, who took rather less interest in his corporal remains. Gawdy was buried on 27 February 1606; the circumstances are described by the Norfolk historian Blomefield:

> The judge was suddenly stricken with an apoplexy, and died without male issue, ere he had continued in his place one whole Michaelmas term, and having made his appropriate parish church a hay house, or a dog kennel, his dead corps being brought from London to Wallington, could for many days find no place of burial, but growing very offensive, he was at last conveyed to the church of Rungton, and buried there without any ceremony, and lyeth yet uncovered (if visitors have not reformed it) with so small a matter as a few paving stones. And indeed no stone or memorial was there ever for him, and if it was not for this account it would not

have been known, that he was there buried. (Blomefield, 7.412)

DAVID IBBETSON

Sources P. Millican, *The Gawdys of Norfolk and Suffolk* (1939) · HoP, *Commons, 1558–1603* · Baker, *Serjeants*, 513 · F. A. Inderwick and R. A. Roberts, eds., *A calendar of the Inner Temple records*, 1 (1896) · Sainty, *Judges* · J. S. Cockburn, *A history of English assizes, 1558–1714* (1972) · BL, Add. MSS 27395–27399, 36989–36990; Egerton MSS 2713–2722, 2804 · *Report on the manuscripts of the family of Gawdy, formerly of Norfolk*, HMC, 11 (1885) · *Letters of Philip Gawdy*, ed. I. H. Jeayes, Roxburghe Club, 148 (1906) · *State trials*, vols. 1–2 · *The letters and life of Francis Bacon*, ed. J. Spedding, 7 vols. (1861–74) · *Reports from the lost notebooks of Sir James Dyer*, ed. J. H. Baker, 1, SeldS, 109 (1994) · inquisition post mortem, PRO, C142/305/136 · PRO, PROB 6/7 fol. 24v [administration] · F. Blomefield and C. Parkin, *An essay towards a topographical history of the county of Norfolk*, [2nd edn], 11 vols. (1805–10) · H. Spelman, *The history and fate of sacrilege* (1698) · E. Coke, *The first part of the institutes of the lawes of England, or, A commentarie upon Littleton* (1628)
Archives BL, family MSS, Add. MSS 27395–27399, 36989–36990; Egerton MSS 2716–2722, 2804 · Norfolk RO, corresp. [copies] | BL, letters to B. Gawdy, etc., Egerton MSS 2713–2715
Wealth at death wealthy: PRO, C 142/305/136; administration, PRO, PROB 6/7, fol. 24v

Gawdy, Sir John, second baronet (1639–1709), painter, born on 4 October 1639, was the second son of Sir William *Gawdy, baronet (d. 1669) [see under Gawdy family], of West Harling, Norfolk, and his wife, Elizabeth (d. 1653), daughter and heir of John Duffield of East Wretham in the same county, and grandson of Framlingham *Gawdy. He was a deaf mute, and became a pupil of Sir Peter Lely, intending to follow portraiture as a profession. However, on the death of his elder brother, Bassingbourne, in 1660, he became heir to the family estates, and thereafter painted only for amusement. He took a prominent part in county affairs; the manuscripts of the Gawdy family give an interesting description of the social life of the period. Sir John Evelyn, who met him in September 1677, described him as 'a very handsome person … and a very fine painter; he was so civil and well bred, as it was not possible to discern any imperfection by him' (*Diary and Correspondence*, 2.111). He married Anne, daughter of Sir Robert de Grey, of Merton, Norfolk, with whom he had one son, Bassingbourne, and one daughter, Anne. Two other children died in infancy. Gawdy died in 1709. His son remained unmarried, and upon his death on 10 October 1723 the baronetcy became extinct.

GORDON GOODWIN, *rev.* SUSAN COOPER MORGAN

Sources Vertue, *Note books*, 4.14; 5.45 · Redgrave, *Artists* · *Diary and correspondence of John Evelyn*, ed. W. Bray, new edn, ed. [J. Forster], 4 vols. (1850–52), vols. 2–3 · F. Blomefield and C. Parkin, *An essay towards a topographical history of the county of Norfolk*, [2nd edn], 11 vols. (1805–10) · B. Burke, *A genealogical history of the dormant, abeyant, forfeited and extinct peerages of the British empire*, new edn (1866) · *Report on the manuscripts of the family of Gawdy, formerly of Norfolk*, HMC, 11 (1885) · J. Burke and J. B. Burke, *A genealogical and heraldic history of the extinct and dormant baronetcies of England, Ireland and Scotland*, 2nd edn (1841); repr. (1844) · E. K. Waterhouse, *The dictionary of British 16th and 17th century painters* (1988)
Archives BM, letters · Courtauld Inst., Witt Library, MSS

Gawdy, Philip (1562–1617). *See under* Gawdy family (*per. c.*1500–1723).

Gawdy, Thomas (*d.* 1556). *See under* Gawdy family (*per. c.*1500–1723).

Gawdy, Sir Thomas (*d.* 1588), judge, was the second of three sons of Thomas Gawdy (*c.*1476–1556/7) of Harleston, Norfolk, by different wives; each son was given the baptismal name Thomas, and each was a successful lawyer. The mother of this Thomas was Anne Bennett. His elder half-brother was created serjeant-at-law in 1552 and died in 1556; the younger, who took the name Francis *Gawdy at his confirmation, was chief justice of the court of common pleas from August 1605 until his death in December of that year. A member of the Inner Temple, Thomas was called to the bench in 1550, appointed Lent reader in 1560, and elected treasurer of the inn in 1562. A writ to create him serjeant-at-law was issued in October 1558, but it lapsed on the death of Queen Mary one month later. He was excluded, perhaps at his own request, from the first general call of Queen Elizabeth in 1559, but renominated in 1567. Seven years later he was made a judge of the court of king's bench, which place he occupied until his death. He was knighted in 1578.

Gawdy made the most of his East Anglian connections. As a young lawyer he came under the patronage of the earl of Arundel—it was no doubt through this that he came to represent Arundel in the parliament of 1553—but the main focus of his activities was Norwich, which he represented in the parliament of 1557 and where he was recorder between 1558 and 1574. In 1548 he married Audrey Knightley (*d.* 1566?), the daughter of a wealthy attorney of the city, who brought to him substantial property in the area, and his professional success enabled him to build around this nucleus. He was not above taking advantage of members of his family who had fallen upon hard times, reputedly using money brought to him on his second marriage in 1567 (to Frances, daughter of Henry Richers of Swannington) to purchase Gawdy Hall and other family estates around Redenhall and Harleston. He died at Gawdy Hall on 5 November 1588, and was buried in the family chapel at Redenhall church on 12 December.

Gawdy had a good reputation as a lawyer, though his earliest appearance in the reports is as defendant in an action brought against him for permitting the escape of a prisoner when he was deputy to the earl marshal. He sat in several state trials, including that of Mary, queen of Scots. Sir Edward Coke, the nephew of his first wife, described him as 'a most reverend judge and sage of the law, of ready and profound judgement, and of venerable gravity, prudence, and integrity' (*Le quart part*, 54). His widow, Frances, died in 1622.

DAVID IBBETSON

Sources P. Millican, *The Gawdys of Norfolk and Suffolk* (1939) • HoP, *Commons, 1509–58* • Baker, *Serjeants,* 513 • F. A. Inderwick and R. A. Roberts, eds., *A calendar of the Inner Temple records,* 1 (1896) • Sainty, *Judges* • J. S. Cockburn, *A history of English assizes, 1558–1714* (1972) • BL, Add. MSS 27395–27399, 36989–36990; Egerton MSS 2713–2722, 2804 • *Report on the manuscripts of the family of Gawdy, formerly of Norfolk,* HMC, 11 (1885) • *Letters of Philip Gawdy,* ed. I. H. Jeayes, Roxburghe Club, 148 (1906) • *State trials,* vol. 1 • *Reports from the lost notebooks of Sir James Dyer,* ed. J. H. Baker, 2 vols., SeldS, 109–10 (1994) • *Le quart part des reports de Sr. Edw. Coke* [*Fourth report of Sir Edward Coke*] (1697), 54 • inquisition post mortem, PRO, C 142/223/59

Archives BL, family MSS, Add. MSS 27395–27399, 36989–36990; Egerton MSS 2713–2722, 2804
Likenesses oils; in possession of Peter Le Neve in eighteenth century
Wealth at death wealthy: PRO, C 142/223/59

Gawdy, Sir William, first baronet (*bap.* 1612, *d.* 1669). *See under* Gawdy family (*per. c.*1500–1723).

Gawen, Thomas (1612–1684), religious writer and traveller, son of Thomas Gawen, a Church of England minister of Bristol city, was born at Marshfield, Gloucestershire. He was admitted a scholar of Winchester College in 1625. In 1632 he was made perpetual fellow of New College, Oxford. In 1639, after taking degrees in arts, and holy orders, he travelled in France and Italy, where he became acquainted with Milton. In the course of this journey he improved himself 'in the languages, and customs of the countries, through which he pass'd' (Dodd, *Church History,* 3.275). In 1642, after his return to England and having left his fellowship, he became chaplain to Dr Curl, bishop of Winchester, who appointed him tutor to his son, then a commoner of Magdalen College, Oxford. The bishop also gave him the rectories of Exton (1641), Bishopstoke (1643–5), and Fawley in Hampshire and gave him a prebendship in the church of Winchester in 1645, 'he being much valued for his learning' (Wood, *Ath. Oxon.,* 4.130).

Upon completion of his tutorship of Mr Curl and, according to Dodd, foreseeing the ruin of the Church of England, Gawen travelled again to Rome and other parts of Italy accompanied by his new pupil, the son of Henry Pierrepont, the royalist marquess of Dorchester. They were entertained in Rome by George Bisset, rector of the Scots College. On their return home through France in 1658 they stayed in Paris at the house of James Mouat, the Scots banker and host to numerous Catholic exiles. During this time Gawen was introduced to Dr Stephen Goffe, chaplain to Henrietta Maria, by an acquaintance who noticed 'some Romish dye in his discourse' (Wood, *Ath. Oxon.,* 4.130).

It is unclear when exactly Gawen converted. In writing to Bisset from Paris in August 1658 Gawen was equivocal in his commitment to Catholicism (Blairs papers, Scottish Catholic Archives). Wood suggests that he was already a Catholic at this stage but avoided the court of Henrietta Maria for fear of being discovered 'so that he might gain some profit from the Church of England' (Wood, *Ath. Oxon.,* 4.130). According to Dodd, Gawen 'spun on the time, till the restoration of king Charles II, when he was restored to his fellowship in New College' (Dodd, *Church History,* 3.275), but later had a return of his scruples concerning religion and, giving up these positions in England, became a Catholic and returned to France, where Goffe and Abbot Walter Montague introduced him into the household of Henrietta Maria. On her death in 1669 Gawen returned to Rome for a third time. Here he married an Italian woman and they had a child. He eventually returned to England for the last time, leaving his wife and child behind in Rome. According to Ralph Sheldon, a contemporary diarist, he pretended to desert his wife because she had no fortune, but the true reason was that Gawen had wealth and wished to leave it to the Jesuits on his death (Sheldon, 'Diary', Bodl. Oxf., MS Wood B. 14, fol. 63). In his will, however, Gawen is very clear that his two houses in Bloomsbury, and another in Pall Mall, should go to his brother William Gawen, and that in consideration of this bequest William should give £400 to his own son when he reached twenty-one years of age, with other bequests to his brother's children. Thomas's books were bequeathed to Richard Allibone of Gray's Inn (PROB 11/372, fol. 269r).

Gawen spent the remainder of his life in London, and died at his house in Pall Mall on 8 March 1684. He was buried in the church of St Martin-in-the-Fields on 10 March. He published a number of devotional treatises and was the author of an unprinted Latin version of John Cleveland's poem 'The Rebel Scot' and a translation from the Italian of the life of Vincent Caraffa (1585–1649), seventh general of the Jesuits.   RUTH JORDAN

Sources E. Chaney, *The grand tour and the great rebellion* (1985), 389–92 · *Dodd's Church history of England*, ed. M. A. Tierney, 5 vols. (1839–43); repr. (1971); vol. 3, p. 275 · Wood, *Ath. Oxon.*, new edn, 4.130–31 · R. Sheldon, 'Diary', Bodl. Oxf., MS Wood B. 14, fol. 63 · Foster, *Alum. Oxon.*, 1500–1714, 2.553 · T. F. Kirby, *Winchester scholars: a list of the wardens, fellows, and scholars of … Winchester College* (1888), 171 · C. Dodd, *Certamen utriusque ecclesiae* (1724) · *DNB* · W. Kennett, *A register and chronicle ecclesiastical and civil* (1728), entry for 6 Sept 1662
Archives Scottish Catholic Archives, Edinburgh, Blair papers, letters

Gawler, George (1795–1869), colonial governor, the only child of Samuel Gawler, captain in the 73rd regiment, and his wife, Julia Russell, was born in Devon on 21 July 1795. After education at a school in Islington, London, and at the Royal Military College, Sandhurst, he became an ensign in the 52nd regiment in October 1810. He served with distinction in Portugal, where he was promoted lieutenant, in Spain and France, and at Waterloo. During the peace he became a fervent evangelical Anglican and in 1820 married Maria (*d.* in or after 1869), daughter of John Cox of Derby; they had twelve children. When the 52nd regiment was stationed in Ireland in 1820–23 and New Brunswick in 1823–5, Gawler devoted much time to charitable and religious work. He was gazetted captain in 1825, purchased his majority in 1830, and left the regiment in 1834, an unattached lieutenant-colonel. He wrote many articles for newspapers and military periodicals, and produced pamphlets on *The Close and Crisis of Waterloo* (1833) and *The Essentials of Good Skirmishing* (1837). He was appointed KH in January 1837.

In 1838 Gawler applied successfully for appointment as governor of South Australia. The administration of the colony had suffered because power had been divided between a governor, responsible for peace, order, and general administration, and a resident commissioner in charge of land sales and immigration. Gawler was given both offices. With his wife and their five surviving children he arrived in South Australia on 12 October 1838. He found the Treasury empty, civil servants unpaid, and a population dependent upon imported food. Because the land surveys were badly in arrears, more than half the 6000 immigrants who had arrived since 1836 were camping on the Adelaide parklands, unemployed and often destitute. The chief occupation of those with some capital was speculation in subdivisions of town and suburban acres. Gawler's instructions had stipulated that no public works were to be undertaken except in cases of pressing emergency, but he saw that an emergency existed. Land purchasers could not begin farming, or hiring the agricultural labourers, stockmen, and shepherds who had been attracted to the colony by free sea-passages and the promise of work, until they could gain possession of their sections and pastoral leases.

Gawler spent heavily accelerating the survey, with most beneficial results. 7000 square miles were mapped, 500,000 acres were made available to buyers, and much land was brought into production. Meanwhile, another 8000 assisted immigrants arrived. Gawler saved many from starvation by putting them to work making a road between Adelaide and its port, 8 miles away, making roads into what were to become the agricultural districts, and erecting public buildings, including government offices, customs houses, a wharf, a hospital, and a gaol. He also established a police force and temporarily put a high duty on the export of foodstuffs. James Stephen, at the Colonial Office, approved of his conduct and, for eighteen months, so did the South Australian colonization commissioners in London. But he financed most of his expenditure by drawing bills on the commissioners, who had frittered away on publicity and less worthy purposes two-thirds of the £300,000 they had raised by selling orders for South Australian land. The commissioners procrastinated until mid-1840, when their chairman, Robert Torrens, remembered Edward Gibbon Wakefield's theory that, in South Australia, roads and other public works could be constructed by the co-operative efforts of the colonists, without any need for government to take a lead or spend money on such things. In December 1840, Gawler received a letter recommending that the colony become self-supporting, but it was not until April 1841 that he received orders to stop billing the commissioners. It was too late. By then he had drawn bills for £200,500. The news that he had been recalled arrived with his successor, on 15 May 1841.

After a select committee on South Australian affairs found that Gawler's expenditure had been necessary, parliament agreed to meet most of the debt. The statute which had reconstituted the South Australian colonization commission was repealed, and the Colonial Office took full control. Nevertheless, Gawler was the butt of a flood of public criticism from Wakefield's disciples and was refused further public employment. His only serious error had been to accept the advice of Mr Justice Cooper, of the Supreme Court, that when Aboriginal people committed 'atrocities' against the immigrants they were placing themselves in a state of war with the white community and could therefore, under the articles of war, be punished summarily. As a result, two Aborigines had been hanged without trial. Apart from that incident, his benevolence towards the Aborigines was remarkable.

In South Australia, Gawler and his wife had continued their religious and charitable work, and this occupied the remainder of their lives. He actively supported resettlement of the Jews in Palestine. Promoted colonel in 1847, he resigned from the army in 1850. He died of pneumonia at Southsea, Hampshire, on 7 May 1869, and was buried at Portsmouth.

P. A. HOWELL

Sources AusDB · D. Pike, *Paradise of dissent: South Australia, 1829–1857* (1957) · 'Select committee on South Australia', *Parl. papers* (1841), vol. 4, nos. 119, 394 · P. A. Howell, 'One hundred years after: reassessing lives for the *New DNB*', *Voices*, 5/3 (1995), 6–15 · *CGPLA Eng. & Wales* (1869) · J. Statton, ed., *Biographical index of South Australians, 1836–1885*, 2 (Marden, South Australia, 1986)
Archives State Records, Adelaide, South Australia, corresp. and papers | BL, corresp. with William Siborn and others · Lpool RO, letters to the fourteenth earl of Derby · NRA, priv. coll., letters to Lord Seaton · PRO, CO13/11/41
Likenesses H. W. Pickersgill, oils, Art Gallery of South Australia, Adelaide, Australia · oils, Adelaide City Council Chamber, Australia
Wealth at death under £800: probate, 10 June 1869, *CGPLA Eng. & Wales*

Gawler, John. See Ker, (John) Bellenden (1764–1842).

Gawler, William (1750–1809), organist and composer, was born in Lambeth, Surrey, the son of a schoolmaster. His sister married Dr Pearce, lecturer at St Mary's, Lambeth, master of the academy at Vauxhall and afterwards sub-dean of the Chapel Royal. Gawler's op. 2, a collection of varied pieces for harpsichord or piano, with instructions, was published by Preston in the Strand in 1780. *Harmonia sacra*, containing psalm tunes, anthems, hymns, and a voluntary, appeared in 1781. In 1784 he was appointed organist (with a salary of £63) to the Asylum for Female Orphans, Lambeth, for whose chapel he composed music to Dr Watts's *Twelve Divine Songs* (op. 16), and published *Hymns and Psalms* (1785) in use there. He also composed two sets of organ voluntaries and some patriotic songs. Before 1798 he had become a music publisher, at 19 Paradise Row, Lambeth. He was parish clerk at Lambeth for many years, and died there on 15 March 1809.

L. M. MIDDLETON, rev. K. D. REYNOLDS

Sources F. Kidson, 'Gawler, William', Grove, *Dict. mus.* (1927) · T. Allen, *The history and antiquities of the parish of Lambeth* (1827) · *The history and antiquities of the parish of Lambeth, in the county of Surrey* (1786), no. 39 [2/6] of *Bibliotheca topographica Britannica*, ed. J. Nichols (1780–1800) · will, PRO, PROB 11/1494, fols. 256v–257r · parish registers, Lambeth, LMA

Gawsworth, John. See Armstrong, Terence Ian Fitton (1912–1970).

Gawthern [née Frost], **Abigail Anna** (1757–1822), diarist and lead manufacturer, was born on 10 July 1757, probably in Nottingham, the second surviving child of Thomas Frost (1719–1798), a grocer and tallow chandler of Nottingham, and his first wife, Ann (1721–1761), daughter of the Revd John Abson, rector of St Nicholas's Church, Nottingham. She was named after her paternal grandmother, Abigail Anna Frost *née* Secker, sister of the Revd Thomas Secker, archbishop of Canterbury from 1758 to 1768. This relationship was a major influence on the younger Abigail's family, both in a social and a material sense, as most

of the archbishop's fortune passed to Thomas Frost and his daughter; indeed following Secker's death in 1768 Frost, not content with a substantial bequest, contested the will and managed to lay claim to an additional £11,000 intended to be 'devised to charitable uses' (Dickinson, 170–71).

Abigail was educated in private academies in Nottingham and Surrey until she was thirteen. At the age of twenty-five she married her first cousin, Francis Gawthern (1750–1791), at St Peter's Church, Nottingham, on 6 March 1783. Her contribution to the marriage settlement was £6700. Her husband ran his family's white lead manufactory in Nottingham, which specialized in the production of high quality white paint. In 1763 the firm was supplying the Worcester Porcelain Company. Abigail moved into the Gawtherns' handsome town house, built in 1733 (subsequently 26 Low Pavement, Nottingham). However at the age of thirty-four she found herself a widow left with two children (two others had died young) and a considerable fortune.

Abigail Gawthern continued to conduct the family business, aided (and sometimes frustrated) by managing clerks, for a further sixteen years; she also engaged in considerable property transactions in and around her rapidly expanding home town, including the enclosure and redistribution of land in Basford parish. Her son Francis came of age in 1807 and, presumably receiving the legacy of £2000 mentioned in his father's will, he also assumed control of the leadworks. The following year, however, the works 'were discontinued, notwithstanding the Nottingham lead very deservedly continued to retain its reputation to the last', the process having been superseded by more economic forms of production using molasses and tanners' bark (*Diary*, 15).

From an early age Abigail had kept a record of notable local and personal events in a series of annual pocket books, but in the early 1800s she copied the entries into a folio volume. The diary, which covers the years 1751–1810, is thus a retrospective compilation, with some entries made with the benefit of hindsight. Although it has no literary merit it is a valuable record of life in upper middle-class society in an English provincial town during the late Georgian period. The author was herself engaged in trade but she possessed considerable landed property in the region and had numerous relatives in the Anglican church. Her circle of relatives and friends were typical of the urban (or 'pseudo') gentry, ranging from junior members of titled families, the county gentry, the clergy, and visiting army officers, to attorneys, physicians, and affluent tradesmen, all of whom constituted Nottingham county society at the time. However in one respect her family were atypical, for they supported the tory and Anglican causes during a period when the greater part of the influential Nottingham tradesmen, who controlled the closed corporation, were whigs and dissenters.

Abigail's main interests lay in the social round—in the local assemblies, plays, concerts, balls, race meetings, and private card parties—and in visits to fashionable resorts. She describes at length visits to London in 1802 and to Bath and Weymouth (where she saw the royal family) in 1805. Although many of her entries are taken up with social gossip, especially notices of births, marriages, and deaths, they give an insight into the social mores of the time, as well as into aspects such as the operation of the provincial marriage market and the short life expectancy even of the better off. She also records details of local events such as the hotly contested parliamentary elections, and the many riots prompted by a variety of economic and political causes for which Nottingham, with its economy based on a volatile domestic hosiery industry, became notorious in and around the 1790s.

Abigail Gawthern died at her home, Low Pavement, Nottingham, on 7 January 1822, aged sixty-four, 'after a long and painful illness, which she bore with Christian fortitude' (*Diary*, 16). She was buried in St Mary's Church, Nottingham, on 15 January. ADRIAN HENSTOCK

Sources *The diary of Abigail Gawthern of Nottingham, 1751–1810*, ed. A. Henstock, Thoroton Society Record Series, 33 (1980) • *Nottingham Journal* (12 Jan 1822) • W. Dickinson, *Antiquities … of Southwell* (1817), 170–1 • parish register, Nottingham, St Mary's
Archives Notts. Arch., M. 23, 904–13 | LPL, Secker MSS, 1719, 1729, 2165 and Secker Sr 25
Wealth at death owned substantial property, but mostly in trust

Gawthorpe, Mary Eleanor (1881–1973), suffragist and socialist, was born at 5 Melville Street, Leeds, on 12 January 1881, the third of the five children of John Gawthorpe, leather worker and sometime political agent, and Anne Mountain, needlewoman. Mary Gawthorpe attended St Michael's national school, Buslingthorpe. She was apprenticed as a pupil teacher there at the age of thirteen, after which she took a post as assistant mistress at St Luke's Boys' School, Beeston Hill. She completed the government teachers' certificate examinations in 1902, becoming a fully certificated assistant schoolmistress in 1904.

At about this time at the Leeds Arts Club, Mary Gawthorpe encountered A. R. Orage, subsequently editor of the *New Age*, and heard lecturers such as George Bernard Shaw. After her introduction to socialism she moved rapidly to the fore in local radical politics and trade unionism, becoming vice-president of Leeds branch of the Independent Labour Party in 1906. When she began to gain notice outside her own locality as an effective speaker and political organizer, she left teaching to pursue this new career.

In 1906 Mary Gawthorpe became for a short time the first secretary of the Women's Labour League, formed by Margaret MacDonald. In the previous year she had also become an active member of the Leeds branch of the National Union of Women's Suffrage Societies, but found herself increasingly drawn to the militants of the Women's Social and Political Union (WSPU). In the autumn of 1906 she was appointed a WSPU organizer, becoming one of its most popular figures, liked and respected by constitutional suffragists as well as militants. When some militants split away in 1907 to form the Women's Freedom League, she remained loyal to the

Mary Eleanor Gawthorpe (1881–1973), by unknown photographer, *c*.1908

WSPU leadership and was placed on the WSPU's national committee. In this year she also wrote *Votes for Men*, comparing women's militancy to the earlier actions of men to gain enfranchisement.

Mary Gawthorpe first went to prison for the suffrage cause in October 1906, and in subsequent imprisonments adopted the hunger strike. Although she was never forcibly fed, the pace of suffrage campaigning, combined with a violent assault during the general election campaign of January 1910, left her in poor health. By 1911 she was also associated with women who increasingly advocated a different route to female equality, through sexual emancipation. With a former WSPU colleague, Dora Marsden, she helped to establish *The Freewoman*, a journal which promoted open discussion of varieties of sexuality, and which argued against marriage as an especially oppressive institution for women. She resigned as a WSPU organizer, but subsequently also sought to distance herself from Dora Marsden's attacks on the Pankhursts by resigning from *The Freewoman*. Still in poor health, she had largely withdrawn from active service in the cause by mid-1912.

In January 1916 Mary Gawthorpe travelled to the United States, where she returned to suffrage and labour organizing. After the war she took an active role in the formation of the Farmer–Labor Party, and campaigned on behalf of Parley Parker Christenson, its presidential candidate in the election of 1920. In 1922 she retired into private life, a retirement that may have been occasioned by her marriage to an American, John Sanders (1882/3–1963) on 19 July 1921. Throughout her life she retained her single name. She made a brief return to Britain in 1933, and was also in contact with the Suffragette Fellowship in these years. Little is known of her life after this date, though some of her surviving correspondence from the 1950s and 1960s shows that she remained keenly interested in political issues, and was still in touch with movements in Britain, including the Campaign for Nuclear Disarmament. In 1962 Mary Gawthorpe published *Up Hill to Holloway*, the story of her life up to her release from prison in November 1906. She died in the USA, perhaps at her home in Long Island, New York state, on 12 March 1973.

SANDRA STANLEY HOLTON

Sources M. E. Gawthorpe, *Up hill to Holloway* (1962) · *Reformer's Year Book* (1908) · S. S. Holton, *Suffrage days: stories from the women's suffrage movement* (1996) · T. Steele, *Alfred Orage and the Leeds Arts Club, 1893–1923* (1990) · J. Hannam, *Isabella Ford* (1989) · L. Garner, *A brave and beautiful spirit: Dora Marsden, 1882–1960* (1990) · *The young Rebecca: writings of Rebecca West, 1911–17*, ed. J. Marcus (1982) · E. S. Pankhurst, *The suffragette movement: an intimate account of persons and ideals* (1931); repr. (1977) · m. cert. · NYPL
Archives Museum of London, Suffragette Fellowship MSS, book of the suffragette prisoner, Mary Gawthorpe, 60. 15/10 [microform, 1983] | Harvard U., Radcliffe Institute for Adavanced Study, letters to Mary Dreier, Box 7 folder 110
Likenesses photograph, 1907, repro. in Gawthorpe, *Up hill to Holloway* · photograph, c.1908, Museum of London [*see illus.*] · Gothard, photograph, repro. in *Reformers' year book*, 232 · oils, Guildhall, London, Fawcett Library · photographs, Guildhall, London, Fawcett Library

Gay, John (1685–1732), poet and playwright, was born in Barnstaple, north Devon, on 30 June 1685, probably in the High Street, the last of the five children of William Gay (d. 1695) and Katherine Hanmer (d. 1694). The Gays had been both powerful and numerous in the town's history and the poet's great-grandfather Anthony Gay was mayor in 1638; but by the time of the poet's birth, both the town and the family's role in it had declined. Gay recalled, in *Rural Sports*, that he 'ne'er … brighten'd plough shares in paternal land' and seems to have had a deep sense of this lost patrimony. His parents had both died by the time he was ten, and he and the other children were looked after by their uncles.

Gay attended Barnstaple grammar school where he soon came under the influence of the vainglorious but charismatic Robert Luck. The poet's uncle John Hanmer, an inspired and gifted preacher, was the leader of the Castle Meeting; but Gay had little interest in divinity. Luck fired his enthusiasm for drama which Hanmer, and those who ran the town, thoroughly deplored; the borough accounts show 20s. 'paid to players to rid the town of them' (*North Devon Athenaeum*, 3792, no. 229/5) but Luck encouraged the boys at the school to read and imagine acting in the plays of Terence and Plautus. Among Gay's schoolfellows at Barnstaple were Aaron Hill and William Fortescue, both of whom played a part in his later life. After leaving school Gay did not go to university, unlike many of his family, as there was no money to send him

John Gay (1685–1732), by Francis Kyte (after William Aikman)

there. Instead he entered the drapery trade which his family knew well; he left Barnstaple to become apprentice to the silk mercer John Willet in the New Exchange, London.

Early years in London and first publications Apart from one letter sent to his kinsman Nicholas Dennis, very little is known about Gay's early years in London, but he did not flourish in the drapery trade. The next time there is more definite information about him is May 1708 when he published the poem *Wine*, full of a sharp juvenile wit in parodying the parody of Milton, John Philips's poem *The Splendid Shilling*. 'He can only hope to be considered as the repeater of a jest' was Johnson's comment, but the poem offers a lively indication of the way Gay's wit worked. As a literary mentor he relied on Aaron Hill who was currently running the periodical question and answer sheet the *British Apollo*. Gay appears to have toiled away on the paper for about two years, contributing a promotional poem 'To the learned ingenious Author of *Licentia Poetica Discuss'd*', (fellow contributor William Coward) which even modest hints at mockery do little to revive.

On 3 March 1711 Gay published *The Present State of Wit*, displaying a genuine pleasure in reproving himself for having 'quite forgot' the *British Apollo*; this, he explains, is a journal known only in 'the city', not Westminster, where the present pamphlet is self-consciously printed. With its conspicuous praise for Addison and Steele *The Present State of Wit* bears all the hallmarks of a name-dropping literary neophyte, a style he repeated six months later in his dedicatory verses 'On a Miscellany of Poems'. Also in Bernard Lintot's *Miscellany* he published his translation 'The Story of Arachne' which suggests some personal associations.

Arachne he presents as, like himself, a humble provincial ('No famous town she boasts, or noble name'; 1.11), who, in the images she weaves, presents the violence and deceit of power. Furious at her presumption, Pallas transforms her into a spider, which was to become an image of Gay's life. 'It is a miserable thing to live in suspense' wrote Swift, 'it is the life of a spider' (Swift, *Journal*, 2.508–9).

The first mention of Gay in Pope's correspondence is in 1711, and from the start he adopted a proprietorial tone. 'Gay they would call one of my *eleves*' he later boasted, ignoring the fact that he was actually three years younger than his 'pupil'. Gay was always willing to assist in Pope's literary feuds, and the first instance occurred that summer, with Dennis's *Reflections on Pope's 'Essay on Criticism'* which included a section referring to Pope as a 'hunchbacked toad'. Gay immediately wrote *The Mohocks*, a one-act tragicomical farce, dedicated 'To Mr D***' who had pronounced *Paradise Lost* 'the greatest poem that was ever written by man' (J. Dennis, *The Grounds of Criticism in Poetry*, 1704). Gay happily parodies Milton in this 'play', which appears never to have been designed for a performance, and includes mocking imitations of Dryden, Shakespeare, and contemporary newspapers. It is his first attempt to create a literary freak show, and is interesting, though few of the jests now work. He returned to the Mohock theme in a contemporary parody 'A Wonderful Prophecy' aimed at the French Camisards.

Lintot paid Gay £2 10s. for the copyright of *The Mohocks*, which indicates the kind of meagre income he could then expect. Accordingly, in the autumn of 1712 he took a position as the secretary and domestic steward to the elderly duchess of Monmouth, whose first husband had been beheaded in 1685. The duties of the post were not onerous, and Gay was able to continue with his writing, producing *Rural Sports* in January 1713; but one article in the terms of his employment was humiliating, namely that he was forced to wear the household livery of blue cloth laced with silver loops. In the prologue to *The Shepherd's Week* he affects to ridicule this, but the shame of it was real.

Dedicated to Pope, *Rural Sports* is the first of Gay's mature poems to adopt the ambiguity of tone which was to become characteristic of his work. While ostensibly a 'peace' poem, written to celebrate the treaty of Utrecht, it finds, beneath the apparent calm of a rural landscape, any number of scenes of natural warfare. Scenes of killing, performed as part of the rural lore, predominate, and, in the 1720 version of the poem, are even increased. Concentrating on such details as the fisherman's artful lures, Gay takes deceit as his subject, and tenderly dissects it to reveal a predatory instinct as deeply rooted in the country as the town. Back in London in the spring he contributed part of the essay on an 'Obsequium Catholicon' to Steele's newly founded *Guardian*, for which Steele thanked him a few weeks later by writing an enthusiastic puff for his play *The Wife of Bath*. Pope had the previous December published his own modernization of *The Wife of Bath's Prologue*, and a smutty fondness for Chaucer was something that he and Gay shared. Unfortunately the play lacked animation,

and ran for only one, two, or three performances (there is some dispute about which). In 1730 Gay had another attempt at the play, producing a much smoother version which this time had some success. Lintot paid him £25 for the copyright of the first version of the play, and £75 more for its 1731 update; this, together with the £56 6s. Gay had taken on his benefit night represented quite a haul. But by this time Gay had tasted wealth with his *Beggar's Opera*, and such sums did not satisfy him. He always referred to *The Wife of Bath* as his 'damned play'.

The failure of *The Wife of Bath* at its first outing may partly be accounted for by the furore that surrounded Addison's *Cato*, which preceded it on the stage at Drury Lane. Thereafter, though often depending on Addison and Steele for work, Gay usually managed to mingle some satire within whatever he was writing. In his next major poem, *The Fan*, he artfully animates Addison's mock-serious tone in *The Guardian*. Discussing female fashion, Addison had confessed that he 'could scarce forbear making use of my hand to cover so unseemly a sight' (*The Guardian*, 100) when faced by a pair of female breasts. Gay takes this and gives it life in *The Fan*, describing how Cephalus, provoked by the wanton display of Aurora's charms 'his modest hand upon her bosom *warms*' (2.158); the satire is in the apparently innocent verb. It has been suggested that Gay may have taken his hostility further, and while contributing verses like 'A Thought on Eternity' to Steele's *Poetical Miscellany*, was also writing anonymous satires from a tory perspective, in *The Examiner*. The case cannot be proved, but it is very like this man who always hated the dependence that he lived on.

The middle years In the spring of 1714 the Scriblerus Club began to meet, a small like-minded group of friends including Gay, Pope, Swift, John Arbuthnot, the queen's physician, Thomas Parnell, the Irish poet, and Lord Oxford, the lord treasurer. Here, for the first time, Gay found himself at the heart of the literary and political establishments, and psychologically it had a profound effect. In April he published *The Shepherd's Week*, one of his poems that retains its sense of surprise and glee for a modern age. The 'Proeme' and part of the poem are concerned with maintaining the ridicule of Ambrose Philips which Pope had begun in *The Guardian*, no. 40; Gay insists on writing in a pseudo-archaic dialogue, which is 'explained' in a glossary, at the foot of each page. These glosses are masterpieces of false learning: the gloss on 'quient' for example, which is used, he says, 'in the same Sense, as *Chaucer* hath done in his *Miller's Tale* … (by which he means *Arch* or *Waggish*) and not in that obscene Sense wherein he useth it in the Line immediately following' (*Monday*, 1.79). The use of fake archaic and dialect terms, pedantically annotated; the coy erotic hints; the pseudo-folklorish superstitions; the banal repetitions and pretentious glossary are all deliberately chosen to draw attention to the false simplicity of Philips's verses. Yet amid all this Gay inserts some genuinely lyrical moments, before bathetically undermining them, reminding us of the rhythmic beauty of the country, quite separate from the town and its ambitions.

The Shepherd's Week was Gay's best work so far, but dedicating it to Bolingbroke proved a disastrous error. At the end of July, Bolingbroke seized power from the earl of Oxford, but only four days later Queen Anne died, and with her perished tory hopes of power. 'What a world is this', complained Bolingbroke, 'and how does fortune banter us' (*Correspondence of Jonathan Swift*, 2.101). Meanwhile Gay had left the duchess of Monmouth and was in Hanover, where he acted as secretary to the earl of Clarendon. He owed this position to Swift, and such was his speed of departure that Swift cynically suspected that his money would be 'put off till the day after he went'. Arbuthnot however wrote on 26 June that 'Gay had a hundred pounds in due time, [and] went away a happy man' (ibid., 2.36). In this appointment Gay transcribed Clarendon's official correspondence, made friends with Henrietta Howard, and wrote to Arbuthnot earnestly to send over some copies of his books to show Princess Caroline, or else 'I shall lose my credit' (*Letters of John Gay*, 13). He had no time to establish himself, however, for with Queen Anne's death his embassy was over. Swift and Pope hurried to leave London, where Oxford was arrested, and Bolingbroke fled to France to lead the Jacobite conspirators.

Pope urged Gay to write 'something' on the new royal family to gain some patronage, but his *Letter to a Lady* was not published until November, long after he and they were in England. As a poem it is a comic failure, so obsessed with the thought of 'preferments' that 'scarce I could produce a single strain' (1.128). Lintot paid him £5 7s. 6d. for the copyright, and the poem went through four editions that year. But by Christmas he told Charles Ford that he still had 'not been interrupted by any place at court' (*Letters of John Gay*, 16). His next work, *The What d'ye Call it*, is one of his happiest performances, an afterpiece which revels in its own freakishness. Subtitled 'a Tragi-Comi-Pastoral Farce' it is a magnificent hybrid which received twenty performances that year, and made him over £100. Making use of the 'play-within-a-play' structure, it is set in a country justice's hall and uses that setting for a comic of mock-tragic forms. There are parodic attacks on Ambrose Philips, Thomas D'Urfey, Nicholas Rowe, Joseph Addison, and many other current playwrights; but whereas Rowe liked it, and happily used this afterpiece for his own lampooned plays, Addison resented its attack and (it appears) used his position as secretary to the council of regents to prevent Gay's advancement. *The What d'ye Call it* is fast, assured, and wonderfully funny; though neglected for two centuries, it was frequently revived in the twentieth century. 'I hope my performance may please the Dean' (that is, Swift), Gay wrote to Parnell in Ireland (*Letters of John Gay*, 21). Replying, Swift was moved to ask whether Gay had ever thought of 'a Newgate pastoral, among the whores and thieves there?' It was a dozen years before Gay took up the hint.

Gay's next poem, *Trivia*, was published on 26 January 1716; Lintot paid him £43 for the copyright, and Pope reckoned that the poem 'may be worth £150 to him in the whole'. This poem, a walk through the streets of London,

strikes an ambivalent tone. The poem's subject is a fearless 'walker', yet, as Swift wrote to Gay much later 'A coach and six horses is the utmost exercise you can bear'; Gay offers fastidious advice for maintaining a cleanly image, yet depicts filth and waste as the mythological source for a flourishing industry. *Trivia* is a town georgic and its 'hero' is a bootboy with whom Gay found a certain amount in common; for though he attended the levees of the Hanoverian placemen, laughed at their witticisms, and flattered them with verses, he never felt at home. Throughout the spring of 1716 he and Pope enjoyed the fellowship of the earl of Burlington, and Gay wrote (but did not publish until 1720) his comical *Epistle to Burlington*, subtitled *A Journey to Exeter*, which is full of informal details about his life: his woeful attempts at portraiture, and his ecstasy when dressed, for a night, in the maid's dowlas smock. A letter that he wrote at much the same time to the Blount sisters takes further his habit of comical self-abasement, being curiously written in the persona of an emasculated horse. Becoming involved, through Pope, with Lady Mary Wortley Montagu, he wrote *The Toilette*, an utterly inoffensive 'court poem' filled with deft and gentle ironies; but when Lady Mary's attitude to Pope shifted to overt hostility, he suffered for it.

Gay's next major work, the play *Three Hours after Marriage*, opened at Drury Lane on 16 January 1717 to a barrage of criticism, most of it intended not for Gay, or for the play itself. Ten days before it opened the rumour was that 'Pope is coming out with a play in which every one of our modern poets are ridiculed' (*Letters of Thomas Burnet*, 119–20), and between January and March at least eight pamphlets appeared attacking the play's alleged obscenity and vindictiveness. Naïvely Gay had admitted, in the advertisement, receiving 'the assistance' of 'two of my friends' (Pope and Arbuthnot); when the storm broke, he wrote Pope a fulsome apology, promising his 'obstinate silence' about his role. But the damage had been done, and the play effectively damned. Only recently, on re-reading all these pamphlets, has it been possible to determine that there was a deliberate attempt to damn the play as Pope's work. The fact that it ran to packed houses for seven nights was not sufficient to save it at the time, but has been enough to guarantee it respectable modern productions. Dennis figured in act I as Sir Tremendous, 'the greatest critic of our age', while John Woodward, the natural scientist, was burlesqued throughout in the role of Fossile. Two suitors (Plotwell and Underplot) to Townley, Fossile's new wife, disguise themselves as a crocodile and mummy in order to have access to her, while Phoebe Clinket attempts to write a play on Deucalion's Flood. The eight pamphlets provide a stage history that proves the play was anything but a flop. Plotwell, played by Colley Cibber, didn't realize that the part ridiculed himself, and Penkethman, in the role of the crocodile, caused a riot of hilarity. The chief pamphlet attacking the play, *The Confederates* by J. D. Breval, contains several allegations, including the rumour (almost certainly false) that Gay received £400 from the maids of honour not to sacrifice it the first night. In fact he received £16 2s. 6d. from Lintot on 4 May as copy money for the three-act version of the play, a five-act version being printed for W. Whitestone in 1758.

Gay strove to make up his income by translating part of book IX of Ovid's *Metamorphoses* for Sir Samuel Garth, a task which he should have found easy to judge by his copy of Mattaire's *Horace* in the Forster collection of the Victoria and Albert Museum. For a more settled life he cultivated the friendship of William Pulteney, who, having just resigned from government, promised a continental jaunt. A sudden parliamentary assault occurred, with William Pulteney and Walpole attacking William Cadogan, and it seems probable that Gay used the pseudonym James Baker to aid his new patron. But the assault failed and by the summer of 1717 Gay was travelling with the Pulteneys in France.

Pulteney was repaid for the trip to France by a rhymed epistle, which takes as its theme the superiority of all things English to all things French. At much the same time Gay amused himself writing a poem on William Lowndes, 'author' of the Land Tax Bill, in which he ironically reckons Lowndes the most successful writer of the age, given that his compositions rake in over £1 million per year. The following year he joined Pope in a visit to Stanton Harcourt, near Oxford, and joined him in sentimentally describing two young lovers killed by lightning, though he might privately have taken a more cynical view. Living as a perpetual nomad, as the house guest of others, he had the habit of ingratiation, and his own views are hard to judge. He wrote the libretto of *Acis and Galatea* at this time, and several miscellaneous verses, but the essential texture of his life is difficult to gauge as he proved very dilatory about keeping letters received. In the summer of 1719 he was in Dijon where he had gone, in part, on a remedial cure for the colical disorder which troubled him for the rest of his life. In a letter from there to Mrs Howard he relates how, the name of 'Gay' being mentioned, he disowned all knowledge of himself—an indication of the isolation he experienced. While away he wrote his five-act pastoral tragedy *Dione* which, according to the lord chamberlain's records, he had ready for the Drury Lane managers on 16 February 1720. But the play was never staged and is best remembered now for Johnson's comment that 'a pastoral of an hundred lines may be endured, but who will hear of sheep and goats, and myrtle bowers and purling rivulets, through five acts?' Gay was in a grim mood, and about this time he wrote his epitaph:

Life's a jest; and all things show it.
I thought so once; but now I know it.

Gay now had recourse to his old friends, and under Pope's management 'cabals were formed our Johnny's debts to clear'. *Poems on Several Occasions*, the subscription edition of his poems which resulted, indicates that he had many friends among the great, headed by the prince and princess of Wales. Of the 364 names Burlington and Chandos both subscribed for fifty copies, followed by Pulteney who took twenty-five. Bathurst, Henry Pelham, the earl of Warwick, and James Craggs all took ten copies, Walpole took two, the duke of Newcastle took two, and Spencer Compton, speaker of the House of Commons,

took three. Suddenly wealthy, Gay invested in the South Sea Company and saw his money rise and rise. By the end of June he was even cherishing the dream of becoming a landowner in Devon. He wrote *Mr Pope's Welcome from Greece* to congratulate his friend on completing his six-year labour of translating the *Iliad*, and to thank the friends who had subscribed to his poems, yet for some reason preferred not to publish it. Among poems first appearing in *Poems on Several Occasions* are his 'Epistles' to William Pulteney and to Paul Methuen, and several minor poems, including the charming sea shanty 'Sweet William's Farewell to Black-Ey'd Susan'.

On 18 July the lords Burlington and Bruce were attacked and robbed, whereupon Burlington applied to Jonathan Wild. Within a few months Wild identified and tracked down James Wright, and received £25 for his trouble, all of which was observed by Gay. Meanwhile in September, South Sea stock began to slide, and by the end of the month had crashed. Gay was severely hurt by the fall of stock and, in October, replied with some asperity to a dunning letter from his publishers. By the autumn, however, it appears that, thanks to Pope's intervention, he had not lost everything, and for his original investment of £1000 it seems that, a year later, Gay was able to realize something over £400. His *Panegyrical Epistle to Mr Thomas Snow*, published on 8 February 1721 (before these rescue packages were finalized), demonstrates him viewing the episode not with the rancour of a ruined man but the wry humour of a stoic comedian.

Gay spent much of the spring and early summer at Chiswick, reporting that 'I live almost altogether with my Lord Burlington', and passed the late summer at Bath, treating his 'colical humour' and becoming very melancholy at the death of the young earl of Warwick; 'I lov'd him', he told a friend (*Letters of John Gay*, 39). Warwick's death, without leaving a will, was a serious disappointment to Gay, who set about finding another aristocrat to protect him. By September he had found the duchess of Queensberry, who was to be a loyal ally for the rest of his life. Back in London he wrote *An Epistle to her Grace Henrietta, Duchess of Marlborough*, an entirely formulaic panegyrical exercise which indicates his hunger for some kind of court patronage. He spent the summer of 1722 again at Bath, and was able to resume his lodgings at the earl of Burlington's property in Piccadilly in November. Swift invited him to move to Dublin where he might live more cheaply, but just at that time his hopes of patronage paid off. He was made a commissioner of the state lottery, which brought him £150 a year, and also obtained free lodgings at Whitehall. Feeling much happier he spent the summer at Tunbridge Wells again as a guest of the Burlingtons. He sent amusing letters to Mrs Howard and wrote *The Quidnuncki's*, drawing familiar comparisons between statesmen and baboons. On 15 January 1724 his new play *The Captives* opened at Drury Lane, thanks largely to Mrs Howard's influence, and though the play had few points to recommend it, ran for seven nights. This brought Gay an estimated £1000; together with his £150 from the lottery, his free lodgings, and his habit of travelling as the guest of aristocratic friends, this meant that he was at last financially secure. But he had made a lot of compromises to achieve such security, and, as he wrote to Mrs Howard, 'I have not and fear never shall have a will of my own' (*Letters of John Gay*, 47).

The Beggar's Opera, and after In June the following year Gay joined a house party at Lord Bathurst's place at Riskins Park, and proved a less proficient fisherman than his pronouncements in *Rural Sports* might have suggested. He was angling for bigger fish, however, and spent the summer hovering near the court hoping for a place. In the summer of 1725 he resolved to make a final bid by writing a book of *Fables* for the four-year-old Prince William (later the 'Butcher of Culloden'). Meanwhile, in the spring of 1726 Swift sailed back to England bearing the manuscript of *Gulliver's Travels*, and at once there was a new earnestness among the tory forces. But Swift had not the energy for all this excitement, and eventually settled with Gay for a short period in August; this marked a turning point in Gay's career. From this time Gay not only abandoned light courtly verse in favour of the major works on which his reputation now depends; he also changed his pattern of correspondence, and almost three-quarters of his surviving letters for the last six years of his life were written to Swift.

Gay's *Fables*, much delayed by waiting for Wootton and Kent to print the plates, were finally published in March 1727, and have had long-running success, going through more than 350 editions, mostly before 1900. Their popularity relies less on ironic wit than on their anthropomorphic and proverbial charm, but at court his female friends were delighted. Mrs Howard promised that 'by my consent you shall never be a *hare* again' (*Letters to and from Henrietta*, 1.284), a reference to *Fable L*, the last one, in which Gay symbolically represents himself as a female hare, threatened by baying hounds. Swift arrived in England again that summer, and was immediately surrounded by a frenzy of tory hopes as George I died at Osnabruck in June and was succeeded by George II. But Walpole's cunning quickly re-asserted the whig position and Swift was troubled both by deafness and by news of Stella's fatal illness. He left on 18 September and, within the week, Gay had his long promised reward, the position of gentleman usher to the two-year-old Princess Louisa.

Gay was deeply disappointed to be offered such an ignominious position, and declined it. To Pope he wrote 'there is now what Milton says is hell, "darkness visible". O that I had never known what a court was!' To Swift he said 'now all my expectations are vanished; and I have no prospect, but in depending wholly upon myself' (*Letters of John Gay*, 65–8). In the same letter to Swift he refers to his next effort, the famous *Beggar's Opera*, which, he says, is 'already finished' (ibid.). Swift was glad, but advised Gay to treat the opera carefully; 'I beg you will be thrifty and learn to value a shilling', he counselled. 'Get a stronger fence about your £1,000, and throw the inner fence into the heap' (*Correspondence of Jonathan Swift*, 3.250). The *Beggar's Opera*, which finally opened at Lincoln's Inn Fields on 29 January 1728, was a phenomenal success, enjoying a run of sixty-two nights in its opening season, and inspiring a host of imitations, parodies, and Beggar-mania bric-à-brac, ranging from playing cards to fans and fire screens. Such fame has generated many stories, from the *Universal Spectator*'s confident assertion that 'Mr Gay was not the sole author of *The Beggar's Opera*' to Charles Macklin's comment in his *Memoirs* that 'there was no music originally intended to accompany the songs' (1804, 60). However, the very originality of the opera's hybrid form should convince us that it was Gay's own work; one of the best-known accounts, which insists the audience reaction was uncertain until Lavinia Fenton, in the part of Polly, sang 'O ponder well!' in act I, sounds reasonably credible. She went on to become the duke of Bolton's mistress at £400 a year (according to a jaundiced Gay), and Hogarth painted one of the opera's prison scenes (III.xi) with her gazing into her admirer's eyes. Gay made £693 13s. 6d. from the production of *The Beggar's Opera*, together with 90 guineas for the copyright of that and *The Fables*; he treated the money wisely, although his friends all asserted that he would waste it. Three years later he boasted to Swift that his fortune amounted to 'above three thousand four hundred pounds', which was a vast amount.

The Beggar's Opera had several consequences, one of which was the death of the vogue for Italian opera in England. This was not Gay's intention, as he had many friends for whom opera was a way of life; but it may point to a significant breakup of his relationship with Burlington, the chief shareholder and leading figure-head of the Royal Academy of Music. Four years later Gay wrote to Swift that he had 'not been admitted' within Burlington's walls 'this year and a half' and his claim 'for what reason I know not' (*Letters of John Gay*, 72) is less than candid. His circumscribed use of operatic music in *The Beggar's Opera* is not a wholesale rejection, however: almost a third of its airs are taken from Purcell, Handel, Giovanni Bononcini, and Richard Leveridge, and he does not enter into the disputes between Handel and Faustina Bononcini, or between the rival singers Faustina and Francesca Cuzzoni. But his main sources are the ballads and folk-songs collected by D'Urfey in his *Wit and Mirth* (1719–20) which cast a far more beguiling light on the vanities of life. Similarly, the opera has always been taken to be a satire on Walpole; Swift wrote to Gay from Dublin 'Does W[alpole] think you attended an affront to him in your opera? Pray God he may'. But though Gay may have revelled in the notoriety this reputation gave him, it is not clear that any of the characters in the opera satirize the prime minister. Hazlitt's comment on the opera is more succinct: 'The moral of the piece was to show the *vulgarity* of vice' (W. Hazlitt, *Works*, 1930–34, 4.65–6).

Removal to the country, and death, 1730–1732 From this time Gay's relationship with Pope, who remained on good terms with Burlington, becomes more distant. 'Mr Pope talks of you as a perfect stranger' wrote Swift in 1730 (*Correspondence of Jonathan Swift*, 3.380). Gay spent the summer in Bath working on *Polly*, which he referred to as the 'second part of the *Beggar's Opera*', and which grew to have a very dangerous reputation among the opposition. But the government had other plans, and, once Gay was back in London, he learned on 12 December that *Polly* 'was not allowed to be acted, but commanded to be suppressed'. There was much protest among the *Craftsman* group of politicians, and Gay boldly took the step of publishing the opera unperformed, having some 10,000 copies printed at his own expense. His gamble paid off; he made a total of £1200 and the duchess of Queensberry was banished from court for soliciting subscriptions there, among them from the young duchess of Marlborough, who gave £100. In the event, *Polly* is not a dangerous opera, but innocuous and largely conventional, though its surroundings were deeply disturbing. Gay was ejected from his Whitehall lodgings and simultaneously became severely ill. He was taken to the Queensberrys' house in Burlington Gardens where Arbuthnot declared, only partly facetiously, that he was 'one of the obstructions to the peace of Europe' and 'the darling of the city'.

From this point on Gay lived mainly with the Queensberrys in rural isolation. In January 1730 he tried out his redrafted *Wife of Bath* on the stage at Lincoln's Inn Fields, but was disappointed by the result. 'My old vamped play got me no money, for it had no success' (*Letters of John Gay*, 88), he told Swift in March. Thereafter he continued to write, producing *Achilles*, *The Distressed Wife*, and *The Rehearsal at Goatham*, but made little serious attempt to have them staged, writing now for private satisfaction and not public renown. He made perfunctory efforts to purchase a house, at Marble Hill, and to marry a wife, Anne Drelincourt (*d*. 1775), heir of the wealthy dean of Armagh (she brought £30,000 when she married Viscount Primrose in 1739), but these were only pipe dreams, and gradually he settled into a pampered life as a permanent house guest of the Queensberrys at Burlington Gardens in London, or Amesbury, Wiltshire. 'A state of indolence is what I don't like' (ibid., 93), he told Swift, yet he made little serious endeavour to change it, and, writing again in March 1731 admitted 'I am very happy in my present independency' (ibid., 105). Throughout the summer he occupied himself with a new volume of *Fables*, though most of them 'are of a political kind; which makes 'em run into a greater length than those I have already published' (ibid., 122). Significantly, in these last *Fables* corrupt ministers, their pimps, spies, and placemen, are usually exposed and vanquished, but Gay made little effort to complete them, and they were finally published, under Pope's direction, in 1738. Swift spoke of making a visit in 1732 which led to a certain excitement, but he fell and strained his leg, leading him to rage at Gay's 'rooted laziness' (ibid., 120). Goaded by this constant refrain, Gay determined to ride to Sir William Wyndham's Somerset estate and back on horseback, but unfortunately this had no good effect on his medical condition. He made a last journey to London early in November to deliver the manuscript of *Achilles* to the Covent Garden playhouse, but was pessimistic about its likely success: 'I don't expect much encouragement' (ibid., 132) he told Swift in his last letter. On 1 December 1732 he caught a sudden fever, and three days later he was dead. He left approximately £6000, which was divided between his two sisters, Katherine Baller and Joanna Fortescue.

Reputation Gay was buried on 23 December with much pomp in Westminster Abbey, his pall carried by six people, including Pope, and the funeral attended by many persons of distinction. *Achilles* opened in February, the princess of Wales attended on the second night, and it received nineteen performances that season. Gradually Pope in particular fashioned an image of Gay, as he wrote on the epitaph, 'In wit, a man; simplicity, a child'. Swift agreed that 'nothing more be published of his that will lessen his reputation' (*Correspondence of Jonathan Swift*, 4.133), and together they sought to promote the image of Gay as an innocent child of nature. Partly this was justified by Gay's own indecisiveness; 'What will become of me I know not', he once wrote to a female friend, 'for I have not and fear I never shall have a will of my own' (*Letters of John Gay*, 47). In 1736 Pope wrote to dissuade Richard Savage from publishing information about Gay's early career. 'As to that of his being apprenticed to one Willet, etc', he protested, 'what are such things to the public? Authors are to be remembered by the works and merits, not accidents of their lives' (*The Correspondence of Alexander Pope*, ed. G. Sherburn 5 vols., 1956, 4.38). Pope spoke from a defensiveness, and a care for the reputation of his friend, but his words remain true.

The Beggar's Opera in particular has kept Gay's memory green. It was performed nearly every year until the 1880s. Revived in 1920 by Nigel Playfair at the Lyric, Hammersmith, it ran without a break for 1463 performances, the longest run of any opera. More famously, it supplied the plot for Brecht's and Weill's *Die Dreigroschenoper* (*The Threepenny Opera*), first performed in Berlin in 1928. Post-war versions of *The Beggar's Opera* include those by Benjamin Britten (1948) and Arthur Bliss (for a 1953 film); another film version, by Jiri Menzel, from a play by Vaclav Havel, appeared in 1991. Gay's text continues to be performed worldwide.

DAVID NOKES

Sources D. Nokes, *John Gay: a profession of friendship* (1995) • *Dramatic works*, ed. J. Fuller, 2 vols. (1983) • *John Gay: poetry and prose*, ed. V. A. Dearing and C. E. Beckwith, 2 vols. (1974) • *The letters of John Gay*, ed. C. F. Burgess (1966) • *The poetical works of John Gay*, ed. G. C. Faber (1926) • *Three hours after marriage*, ed. J. H. Smith (Los Angeles, 1961) • *The correspondence of Jonathan Swift*, ed. H. Williams, 5 vols. (1963–5) • S. Johnson, *Lives of the English poets*, [new edn], 2 vols. (1906); repr. (1964–8) • J. Swift, *Journal to Stella*, ed. H. Williams, 2 vols. (1948) • R. Steele and others, *The Guardian*, ed. J. C. Stephens (1982) • *Letters to and from Henrietta countess of Suffolk*, ed. J. W. Croker, 2 vols. (1824) • *The letters of Thomas Burnet to George Duckett, 1712–1722*, ed. D. N. Smith (1914)
Archives BL, Stowe MS 242, fols. 161–3
Likenesses G. Bickham, line engraving, pubd 1729 (after W. Aikman), BM • M. Dahl, oils, *c*.1729, Knowle, Kent • J. M. Rysbrack, relief medallion on monument, 1736, Westminster Abbey • W. Aikman, Scot. NPG • G. Kneller, oils, NPG • F. Kyte, mezzotint (after W. Aikman), BM [*see illus.*] • sculpture, Tate collection
Wealth at death £6000

Gay, John (1699–1745), writer on philosophy, was born at Meeth, Devon, the second son of James Gay (1655–1720), rector of Upton Pyne, near Exeter, and his wife, Elizabeth

(d. 1732), daughter of Nicholas Hooper of Fulbrook, Braunton, Devon. The poet John Gay was his cousin. He was educated at Torrington School and Tiverton grammar school, and entered Sidney Sussex College, Cambridge, on 7 November 1717. He was elected Blundell scholar on 12 January 1718, and graduated BA in 1721 and MA in 1725. On 24 January 1724 he was elected a fellow. While in residence he held the offices of Hebrew lecturer, Greek lecturer, and ecclesiastical history lecturer. He was held in high esteem by his contemporaries at Cambridge, Edmund Law, future bishop of Carlisle, remarking that no one could rival his knowledge of the Bible and of the works of John Locke.

In 1731, when Law published his English translation of William King's *Essay on the Origin of Evil*, a short dissertation by Gay entitled 'Concerning the fundamental principle of virtue or morality' was included as an introduction. Originally anonymous, the introduction was acknowledged to be Gay's work in a fourth edition of *Essay on the Origin of Evil* which appeared in 1758. Although elements of Gay's position in this short treatise can also be found in Locke's *Essay Concerning Human Understanding* (bk 2, chap. 20) and in Francis Hutcheson's *Illustrations on the Moral Sense*, it provided the first systematic exposition of utilitarian morality, arguing that happiness was pleasure and avoidance of pain, and that virtue was therefore conformity to a rule of life which directs the promotion of the happiness of others. It had a wide impact, prompting the mechanistic philosopher David Hartley to embark on his theory of association, and strongly influencing the writings of Abraham Tucker and William Paley.

In 1730 Gay resigned his fellowship and was presented to the vicarage of Wilshampstead in Bedfordshire, to which he added the nearby living of Haynes in 1739. With his wife, Elizabeth (d. c.1795), he had two sons and four daughters. He died at Wilshampstead on 18 July 1745, and was buried at Wilshampstead church on 22 July.

JONATHAN HARRIS

Sources F. A. Blaydes, ed., *Bedfordshire Notes and Queries*, 3 vols. (1886–93), 2.278 • Venn, *Alum. Cant.* • J. L. Vivian, ed., *The visitations of the county of Devon, comprising the herald's visitations of 1531, 1564, and 1620* (privately printed, Exeter, [1895]), 394 • *N&Q*, 3 (1851), 424 • *N&Q*, 4 (1851), 388–9 • *N&Q*, 5 (1852), 36 • W. Paley, 'Life of Edmund Law', *The history of the county of Cumberland*, ed. W. Hutchinson, 2 (1794), 636 • D. Hartley, *Observations on man, his frame, his duty and his expectations*, 2nd edn (1791), 1.iii • D. L. Lemahieu, *The mind of William Paley* (1976), 124 • PRO, E331/Lincoln/23, fol.21, and E331/Lincoln/25, fol. 24

Gay, John (1812–1885), surgeon, was born at Wellington, Somerset, on 26 September 1812, the son of John Gay, a carrier, and his wife, Mary (*née* Timewell). After studying at St Bartholomew's Hospital, London, he became MRCS in 1834 (FRCS in 1843), and in 1836 was appointed surgeon to the newly established Royal Free Hospital, with which he was connected for eighteen years. In 1856 he became surgeon of the Great Northern Hospital, of which he was senior surgeon until his death. On 12 October 1860 he married Elizabeth (*née* Elworthy). Gay was also consultant surgeon to Earlswood Idiot Asylum.

Besides contributions to the medical press and an elaborate article, 'Cleft palate', in William Costello's *Cyclopaedia of Practical Surgery* (1841–3), Gay wrote several important works: *On Femoral Rupture, its Anatomy, Pathology and Surgery* (1848) described a new method of operating, modified from that of John Luke, which proved to be important in the treatment of crural hernia; *On Indolent Ulcers and their Surgical Treatment* (1855) introduced considerable improvements in the treatment of chronic and indurated ulcers of the leg; and his Lettsomian lectures, *On Varicose Disease of the Lower Extremities and its Allied Disorders* (1867) and *On Haemorrhoidal Disorder* (1882), also exhibited intelligence, study, and practical skill. Gay also advocated and successfully practised the free incision of acutely suppurating joints, and this came into general use.

Gay's career was briefly shaken in 1853 when he was dismissed from the Royal Free for his involvement in a publication praising his role at the hospital. However, the profession was divided and his reputation soon recovered. In person Gay was of short stature, active, enthusiastic, and somewhat impetuous; he was also principled and popular socially. He died at his home, 51 Belsize Park, London, on 15 September 1885, leaving a widow, a daughter, and two sons.

G. T. BETTANY, rev. CHRISTIAN KERSLAKE

Sources *The Lancet* (26 Sept 1885) • *Medical Times and Gazette* (26 Sept 1885), 449–50 • V. G. Plarr, *Plarr's Lives of the fellows of the Royal College of Surgeons of England*, rev. D'A. Power, 2 vols. (1930) • *Medico-Chirurgical Transactions*, 69 (1886), 13–15 • *London and Provincial Medical Directory* (1860) • *CGPLA Eng. & Wales* (1885)
Likenesses E. Edwards, photograph, 1868, Wellcome L. • W. H. Kemp, marble bust, 1878, RCS Eng. • T. H. Maguire, lithograph, Wellcome L. • photograph, repro. in T. H. Barker, ed., *Photographs of eminent medical men* (1967–8)
Wealth at death £23,306 0s. 1d.: resworn probate, Jan 1886, *CGPLA Eng. & Wales* (1885)

Gay, Maisie [*real name* Daisy Munro-Noble] (1883–1945), actress and singer, was born on 7 January 1883 in London, the daughter of Peter Munro-Noble and his wife, Elizabeth. She was educated in Germany and at the North London Collegiate School for Girls, in Canons Park, Edgware. A chance conversation with a chorus girl on a bus made her enthusiastic about a theatrical career, and she made her first stage appearance, in the chorus of *The Cherry Girl* by Seymour Hicks, in Blackpool in November 1903. The following year she joined the company of theatre manager George Edwardes on tour in J. T. Tanner's musical play *A Country Girl*, later playing the leading part of Nan over 1000 times between 1904 and 1907. She toured in other Edwardes productions as well as those of the company of playwright and theatre manager George Dance. In April 1908 Gay made her début in the West End at the Hicks Theatre as Fifi in *A Waltz King*, followed by Clementine in George Grossmith's *The Girls of Gottenberg*. The latter led to her being cast as Mrs Farquhar, 'an impecunious woman of fashion', in the hugely successful musical by J. T. Tanner, *Our Miss Gibbs*, a role she played for almost two years. This also marked her first appearance at the Gaiety Theatre which, with the Adelphi, was where she appeared most often.

In 1911 Gay toured as Madame Blum in Tanner's *The Quaker Girl*; she played the same part in London, then in New York and across the United States—in 160 towns in 266 days. Back in London in 1913 she appeared in Tanner's musical farce *The Girl on the Film* before going again to America, appearing in *Phyllis* in Boston, as Adelaide Fontaine in *High Jinks*, by Frederick Lonsdale, touring through 1914 and 1915, and in *Sybil*, by Harry Graham, in New York. She also appeared in the 1915 American film *The Siren's Song*. In London in 1916 she followed a reprise of her role in *High Jinks* by starring in a successful series of musical comedies (*The Boy*, by Fred Thompson, *The Beauty Spot*, adapted from the French by Arthur Anderson, and *Soldier Boy*, by Rida Johnson Young) and, especially, revues. Her revue début was in 1919 in *The Whirligig*, by Albert de Courville, followed by his *Pins and Needles* in 1921 (reprised in New York the following year). Next came *A to Z*, by Dion Titheradge and *Snap*, by Ronald Jeans and Titheradge, both in 1922 (introducing the song 'March with Me' in the former, and touring the provinces with the latter). She also appeared in Noël Coward's *London Calling!* in 1923, *Charlot's Revue of 1924* and *Charlot's Revue of 1925*, both by R. Jeans, and Coward's *This Year of Grace!* in 1928. In 1929 Gay appeared in the last named in Melbourne and toured major cities in Australia. The following year she was in *Cochran's 1930 Revue*, by Beverley Nichols. Cochran later wrote in tribute that 'in her particular genre Maisie Gay was unique and irreplaceable' (*The Times*). Later musical comedies included *Better Days* in 1925, *Wildflower* in 1926, and *White Birds* and *Peggy-Ann*, both in 1927.

In December 1930, at the Winter Garden, Gay succeeded Sophie Tucker as Georgia Madison in *Follow a Star*. Also that year she made her first sound film, *To Oblige a Lady*, written by Edgar Wallace from his play, in which she again sang her song from *London Calling!*, 'What Love Means to Girls Like Me'. She then appeared as Mrs Harris, the charlady, in Wallace's play *The Old Man*, subsequently appearing in the film version in 1932. Her last appearance on the London stage was the same year at the Queen's Theatre as Bibbo in *Caravan* before ill health forced her premature retirement. She suffered from severe arthritis; at times she had had to use the downstairs dressing-room with the chorus girls instead of that upstairs for the principal because of the great difficulty she had in using stairs.

According to an early biographer of Noël Coward, 'Maisie Gay was plump and her pop-eyed face as round as a full moon' (Cole Lesley, *The Life of Noël Coward*, 1967, 77). Gay wrote an autobiographical volume *Laughing through Life* in 1931. Upon her retirement she had built a small house, Kingsdown, at Box in Wiltshire, a few miles north-east of Bath. However, she was practically bedridden and her activity was limited largely to reading and listening to the radio. She did, though, give a series of talks for invalids for BBC radio in 1941. Gay died, unmarried, at her home, Kingsdown, on 13 September 1945. ROBERT SHARP

Sources WWW · *The Times* (15 Sept 1945), 6f · K. Gänzl, *The British musical theatre*, 2 vols. (1986) · F. Gaye, ed., *Who's who in the theatre*, 14th edn (1967) · S. Green, *Encyclopaedia of the musical* (1977)

Likenesses two photographs, 1926–35, Hult. Arch. · caricature, repro. in C. Castle, *Noël* (1972) · photograph, repro. in M. Gay [D. M. Noble], *Laughing through life, etc.* (1931)

Gay, Noel [*real name* Reginald Moxon Armitage] (1898–1954), composer and lyricist, was born on 15 July 1898 at Park Terrace, Leeds Road, Chetwood, Wakefield, the son of Harry Armitage, a colliery clerk, and his wife, Charlotte Elizabeth Moxon. Musically precocious, he joined the Wakefield Cathedral choir school at the age of eight and subsequently often deputized for the choirmaster. His original ambition was to obtain a choral appointment in a cathedral, but at the age of fifteen, in 1913, he took up a scholarship at the Royal College of Music in London, where he studied with Sir Frederick Bridge and Walter Parratt. By the time he was eighteen he was already director of music and resident organist at St Anne's Church in Soho.

Armitage then went up to Christ's College, Cambridge, to study composition, again with a view to joining a cathedral, and graduated four years later with an MA and a BMus. At Cambridge, however, his interests had begun to turn more secular, specifically towards the world of undergraduate revues, to which he contributed many popular songs in the chirpy, colloquial style which became his hallmark.

After coming down from Cambridge, Armitage began to contribute songs to such mid-1920s West End revues as *Stop Press* with such success that the impresario André Charlot invited him to write all the words and music for his 1926 revue. He took his *nom de plume*—Noel Gay—from a sign he read on a London bus in 1924: 'NOEL Coward and Maisie GAY in a new revue'. He also began writing for the successful husband-and-wife musical comedy team of Jack Hulbert and Cicely Courtneidge. On 26 April 1927 Armitage married Amy Marshall, daughter of Walter Marshall, a liquorice refiner.

Altogether, Gay wrote the music for twenty-six London shows, twenty-eight feature films, and forty-five songs, one of which, 'Tondeleyo', was the first ever to be used in a British talking picture. His song hits included 'The Lambeth walk', 'Run rabbit run', 'There's something about a soldier', and 'Let the people sing', all of which bear the distinctive features of his work: an absolute simplicity of lyrical thought, the refusal to use a polysyllabic word if a monosyllable would do ('Run, rabbit, run, rabbit, run, run, run'), and the gift of a cheery melodic line which implanted itself almost involuntarily in the memory of its audiences (to that extent he was the closest Britain ever came to a local Irving Berlin).

Like such near-contemporaries as Noël Coward and Ira Gershwin, Gay combined a solid classical musical training with a passion for Gilbert and Sullivan and an ability to write readily accessible songs with catchy lyrics. He later provided the music for such hit musical comedies as *Clowns in Clover* (1927), by Ronald Jeans, *Hold my Hand* (1931), by Stanley Lupino, *She Couldn't Say No* (1932), *That's a Pretty Thing* (1933), and *Love Laughs* (1935). The most remarkable of all was *Me and My Girl*, written by L. Arthur Rose and

Noel Gay (1898–1954), by Howard Coster, 1932

Douglas Furber, which included Gay's celebrated 'Lambeth walk' number.

Gay afterwards described how he deliberately employed 'everyday homely symbols, with simple repetitions, or otherwise new angles on old situations' (McKibbin, 407). The central figure, Bill Snibson, a cockney who inherits an earldom but still lives as a cockney, was played by Lupino Lane. He organizes a grand party, attended by 'toffs' as well as old friends. However, when Snibson begins to sing 'The Lambeth walk' the social classes intermingle: 'there is a terrific effect of social breakdown, everyone joins in and shouts "Oi!" and the Duchess finally goes into dinner on Bill's arm, wearing his bowler on her head' (ibid.).

The musical first opened in 1937 at the Victoria Palace, London. It was by no means an overnight success, but it was broadcast on radio by the BBC on 13 January 1938, live from the theatre, and this helped turn its fortunes around. Despite being bombed out of two different theatres, the show ran for five more years as the greatest of all Second World War London hits. A revival of *Me and My Girl* in 1985, with its book revised by Stephen Fry, ran for more than seven years and made stars of Emma Thompson and Robert Lindsay on both sides of the Atlantic.

Gay continued to write through the rest of the war and into the 1950s, but his later songs never lived up to the success of those in *Me and My Girl*—arguably the most successful London musical of the mid-twentieth century. The 1985 revival incorporated such other hit songs of Gay's as 'The sun has got his hat on', 'Love makes the world go round', and 'I'm leaning on a lamp post', the old George Formby hit. Among other leading performers for whom Gay wrote hit songs were Jessie Matthews, Sonnie Hale, the Crazy Gang, and Gracie Fields. But he had been going prematurely deaf for several years, and in the early 1950s his writing slowed down; the fashion for his especial kind of cheery London cockney song was also now on the wane. His last score was for the pantomime *Aladdin* at Richmond in 1949–50, and he died from cancer at his London home, 48 Portland Place, on 4 March 1954, aged only fifty-five.

A successful businessman, Gay established the Noel Gay Agency; run by his son Richard Armitage, this became one of the leading British and European musical and talent agencies. While one of his grandsons, Alex Armitage, masterminded the revival of *Me and My Girl*, another, Charles Armitage, looked after the equally successful music-publishing division of the agency.

Gay never achieved the musical fame of such West End contemporaries as Noël Coward, Ivor Novello, or Vivian Ellis, but he rivalled them in terms of the colloquial, populist, and streetwise tenor of his songs.

SHERIDAN MORLEY

Sources A. Lamb, 'Gay, Noel', *New Grove* · E. Rogers and M. Henessy, *Tin Pan Alley* (1964) · *The Times* (5 March 1954) · K. Gänzl, *The British musical theatre*, 2 vols. (1986) · R. McKibbin, *Classes and cultures: England, 1918–1951*, pbk edn (2000) · b. cert. · m. cert. · d. cert. · will, 15 July 1927

Likenesses H. Coster, photograph, 1932, NPG [*see illus.*] · photograph, 1941, Hult. Arch. · H. Coster, photographs, NPG

Wealth at death £6470 10s. 5d.: probate, 2 June 1954, CGPLA Eng. & Wales

Gayer, Arthur Edward (1801–1877), ecclesiastical commissioner, was born on 6 July 1801 near Newcastle under Lyme in Staffordshire. He was the eldest son of Edward Echlin Gayer, major in the 67th regiment, and his wife, Frances Christina, the only daughter of Conway Richard Dobbs MP, of Castle Dobbs, Carrickfergus, co. Antrim. He was educated at a private school near Moneymore, co. Londonderry, and then at Durham and Bath grammar schools. In October 1818 he entered Trinity College, Dublin, where he obtained honours in both science and classics, graduating BA in 1823 and proceeding LLB and LLD in 1830. After studying at Lincoln's Inn he was called to the Irish bar in 1827, and was admitted an advocate in the ecclesiastical and admiralty courts in 1830. In November 1844 he was called within the bar as queen's counsel. He was appointed chancellor and vicar-general of the diocese of Ossory in 1848, of Meath in January 1851, and of Cashel, Emly, Waterford, and Lismore in June 1851. In March 1857 he stood a stiffly contested election for the University of Dublin, when, after a five-day poll, he was defeated by Anthony Lefroy, eldest son of Chief-Justice Lefroy. On 8 June 1859 he was chosen one of the ecclesiastical commissioners for Ireland, an office which he held in conjunction with his three vicar-generalships, until the disestablishment of the Irish church in July 1869. He wrote a number of pamphlets on disestablishment, including one, *Fallacies and Fictions Relating to the Irish Church Establishment Exposed* (1868), which went into twelve editions.

Gayer helped to found the Dingle and Ventry Mission Association and was made its honorary secretary; he was also an honorary secretary of the Hibernian Temperance Society for many years (during two of which he edited the *Irish Temperance Gazette*), and then of the Italian Church Reformation Fund. He was also one of the founders of the Night Asylum for the Houseless Poor in Dublin, and of the protestant reformatory schools. In 1851 he also helped to start a new newspaper in Dublin, the *Catholic Layman*, whose object was to discuss points of difference between the Anglican and Roman Catholic traditions. He was for several years the sole editor, but received contributions and help from some of the most eminent priests in the Irish church. The periodical reached a circulation of 16,000 in 1858 but was discontinued because of Gayer's increasingly poor health. In 1859 he was presented with a silver plate worth 500 guineas in honour of his editorship, and in 1862 the existing volumes were published, with a general index, in eight volumes, under his name. He published a number of lectures, most of which had been delivered to the Dublin Young Men's Christian Association, and wrote the *Memoirs of the Family of Gayer: Compiled from Authentic Sources Exclusively for Private Distribution among Friends and Relatives* (1870) and *Papal Infallibility and Supremacy Tried by Ecclesiastical History, Scripture, and Reason* (1877). He died at his home, Abbotsleigh, Upper Norwood, Surrey, on 12 January 1877, leaving children from two marriages.

GORDON GOODWIN, rev. DAVID HUDDLESTON

Sources A. E. Gayer, *Memoirs of the family of Gayer* (1870) · Burtchaell & Sadleir, *Alum. Dubl.* · [J. H. Todd], ed., *A catalogue of graduates who have proceeded to degrees in the University of Dublin, from the earliest recorded commencements to … December 16, 1868* (1869), 217 · Burke, *Gen. GB* (1875) · W. H. Rennison, ed., *Succession list of the bishops, cathedral and parochial clergy of the dioceses of Waterford and Lismore* (1920), 115 · *CGPLA Eng. & Wales* (1877)
Wealth at death under £7000 (in England): probate, 30 Jan 1877, *CGPLA Eng. & Wales* · £47 3s. 11d.: probate, 5 March 1877, *CGPLA Ire.*

Gayer [née Jones], **Henrietta** (d. 1814), Methodist leader, was the daughter of Valentine Jones of Lisburn, co. Antrim; her date of birth and her mother's name are unknown. In 1758 she married Edward Gayer (d. 1799) of Derryaghy, near Lisburn, clerk to the Irish House of Lords. Vivacious, sociable, and worldly, Mrs Gayer was described as 'remarkably attractive in her appearance and manner, a charming singer and highly accomplished, the life and soul of a highly respectable and fashionable circle of friends' (Crookshank, *Memorable Women*, 117). Following her marriage Mrs Gayer's 'ardent temperament' was increasingly directed towards spiritual fulfilment (ibid.). A scrupulous member of the established church, she sought guidance from a clergyman, who advised her to 'travel, go more into society, and engage more frequently in fashionable amusements' (ibid.). Still dissatisfied, she embarked on a rigorous regime of fasting and prayer, while maintaining her social activities, and allegedly once took her prayer book to a ball at Dublin Castle 'and after each dance retired and read a portion of it' (ibid.).

About 1772 Mrs Gayer came into contact with Methodism, which had established itself in Ulster's 'linen triangle', of which Lisburn was a part, during the previous decade. Although attracted to the movement she hesitated to become a member, 'being unwilling to act contrary to the prejudices of her husband against Methodists and Methodism' (Crookshank, *Memorable Women*, 119). Shortly afterwards, however, she was invited by Jane Cumberland, a baker's wife and leader of Methodism in Lisburn, to attend a meeting in her house. She did so, bringing with her her thirteen-year-old daughter, Mary.

Both were converted and subsequently became members of the society.

When John Wesley visited Lisburn in 1773 he was introduced to Mrs Gayer, and on the following day visited her and preached at Derryaghy. Mr Gayer's hostility to Methodism was overcome by Wesley's 'culture and gentlemanly deportment', and Derryaghy subsequently became a centre of Methodism (Crookshank, *Memorable Women*, 120). A room, known as 'the Prophet's Chamber', was set aside in the Gayers' house and used for many years by itinerant preachers as a resting place (Crookshank, *History of Methodism*, 1.277). Wesley himself visited Derryaghy on a number of occasions, and in 1775 was nursed there through a serious illness. Following her conversion Mrs Gayer devoted herself to the promotion of Methodism in her locality and social circle, and was instrumental in attracting a number of new members, among them her niece Mrs Agnes Smyth, who herself became an effective proponent of the movement. Mrs Gayer was also instrumental in having a chapel built at Lisburn, facilitating the expansion of Methodism in the district.

Widowed in 1799, Mrs Gayer continued to take an active leadership role in her local congregation. Her outstanding traits were her humility and her zeal, described by Crookshank as 'remarkable' but regarded by other observers as 'excessive'; the Revd Henry Moore remarked of her that he 'never was acquainted with a person more dead to the world' (Crookshank, *Memorable Women*, 122). Charitable giving was an essential tenet of her faith, undertaken with characteristic fervour: according to Crookshank,

she … curtailed her personal expenses in every possible way, sometimes depriving herself of even the necessaries of life, that she might have more to give to those in greater need. She often said that, as she received all her mercies from God, it would be very ungrateful if she did not give back a part to Him in His poor. (ibid., 122)

In March 1814 her health began to decline and she died on the 25th. Giving instructions for her funeral, which took place at Derryaghy, where was buried at Christ Church, she directed that no unnecessary expense be incurred, 'so that all that could be spared might be given to the poor' (ibid., 124). In fact her various charities had entirely dissipated her fortune and she died 'without having one shilling to leave to any person or for any purpose whatever' (ibid., 123–4).

ROSEMARY RAUGHTER

Sources C. H. Crookshank, *Memorable women of Irish Methodism in the last century* (1882) · C. H. Crookshank, *History of Methodism in Ireland*, 1 (1885) · D. Hempton and M. Hill, 'Born to serve: women and evangelical religion', *Evangelical protestantism in Ulster society* (1992), 129–42 · D. Hempton, 'Methodism in Irish society, 1770–1830', *TRHS*, 5th ser., 36 (1986), 117–42 · W. Smith, *A consecutive history of the rise, progress and present state of Wesleyan Methodism in Ireland* (1830)
Wealth at death died 'without having one shilling to leave': Crookshank, *Memorable women*, 123–4

Gayer, Sir John (*bap.* 1584, *d.* 1649), merchant, was baptized on 16 March 1584 at St Andrew's Church, Plymouth, the eldest son of the merchant John Gayer (d. 1593) and Margaret, daughter of Robert Trelawny of Tideford, Cornwall. He was apprenticed to a London merchant and became prominent in the Levant and East India trades, serving frequently on the governing body of the Levant Company between 1617 and 1636 and on that of the East India Company between 1626 and 1649. Elected alderman of Aldgate ward, he achieved civic prominence as sheriff in 1635–6, when he was active in the collection of ship money, and was prime warden of the Fishmongers' Company in 1638, and a colonel of the trained bands in the same year. Gayer's moderate reforming sympathies found expression in his support for a citizens' petition of grievances which met with the disapproval of the court of aldermen in the summer of 1640, while in May he and three other aldermen were imprisoned for refusing to assess the inhabitants of their wards towards a loan for the king. He was a popular, though unsuccessful, candidate for the mayoralty in September. However, his subsequent career graphically illustrates how the course of events in the 1640s could turn erstwhile moderate reformers into dyed-in-the-wool conservatives. An early straw in the wind is probably his being knighted by Charles I on 3 December 1641 along with some other members of a City deputation attending the king, who was anxious to win back the support of the City. Nevertheless, at the beginning of the civil war Gayer was, nominally at least, a parliamentarian rather than a royalist. Having been appointed as a somewhat unenthusiastic member of the newly created City committee of safety in March 1642, he was removed in September, 'having wholly deserted the said service'. In the same year he ceased to be a colonel of the trained bands. In December 1643 he refused to contribute to a loan to parliament, and he had earlier been arrested and roughly treated for refusing to pay his contribution to the monthly assessment. Nevertheless, in February 1645 he was appointed to the City committee for raising this assessment.

Gayer's election as lord mayor in September 1646 was welcomed neither by the Independents nor by high presbyterians. One Independent pamphleteer charged that Gayer 'maliciously circumvents men that he may like the devil take them in a snare contrary to law' (Wilbee, 10). To the London Independent Thomas Juxon, Gayer, 'a man Competently wise … but not over well affected to ye Parliament' (DWL, MS 24.50, fols. 91–91b), was at least preferable to his nearest competitor, Alderman John Langham, the favoured candidate of London high presbyterians and of their Scottish mentor Robert Baillie. Baillie described Gayer as 'a greater malignant than sectarie' (*The Letters and Journals of Robert Baillie*, ed. D. Laing, 1841–2, 2.400), and he was certainly not the sort of presbyterian for whom religious scruples would impose insuperable obstacles to reaching agreement with the king. During his mayoralty his close alliance with like-minded parliamentary presbyterians such as Holles and Stapleton culminated in the summer of 1647 in the attempted counter-revolution against the Independents and the army. Its main features in the City were the reconstitution of the London militia committee following a parliamentary ordinance of 4 May; the purging of Independent officers from that militia; the

recruitment of a counter-revolutionary force in association with the parliamentary committee of safety; and, following the parliamentary rescission of the militia ordinance of 4 May at the behest of the army, a tumult of apprentices, disbanded soldiers, and others invading parliament on 26 July. The rioters forced parliament to rescind the new militia ordinance and to invite the king to London to negotiate a settlement.

Whether or not the blame attaching to Gayer and his aldermanic associates for this outrage extended further than their failure to preserve order and protect parliament, they clearly had sympathy with the rioters' objectives. The speakers of both houses and many Independent MPs fled to the army, and for the next eleven days parliament was virtually a presbyterian rump. Both Edward Massey and Sir William Waller, commanders of the London defence force authorized by parliament, were later to criticize Gayer and his City associates for what they regarded as their spineless capitulation in allowing the army to occupy London on 6 August without offering even a token show of resistance. Nevertheless, on 2 September Gayer and his principal associates were sent to the Tower to await impeachment for high treason, and in the same month the Independent John Warner succeeded Gayer as lord mayor. It was not until the following 13 March that the articles of impeachment were sent up from the lower house to the Lords. When brought before the upper house on 10 April, Gayer defiantly refused to kneel at the bar and demanded trial by jury. He was fined £500 for contempt and returned to the Tower, notwithstanding a reported plot to rescue him *en route*. On 23 May Lord Mayor Warner, obviously with reluctance and under pressure from more conservative City fathers, petitioned the House of Commons for the release of Gayer and his colleagues, and on 6 June all charges against them were dropped. This astonishing volte-face should probably be seen as part of a policy of conciliation designed to prevent a recurrence of the tumultuous events of the previous summer, but now in the far more dangerous context of renewed civil war and an imminent Scottish invasion. Nevertheless, Gayer's day was past, and the failure of the treaty of Newport, which he had supported, simply underlined this fact. Following the establishment of the Commonwealth, he was formally deprived of his aldermanry on 7 April 1649 and he died in London on 20 July. He was buried on 14 August in the City church of St Katherine Cree. His wife, Katharine, daughter of Sampson Hopkins of Coventry, had died earlier, but six of their children (two sons and four daughters) survived him. The bequests specified in his will (excluding land, houses, and most of his personal goods) amounted to about £10,000. They included £200 to endow an annual sermon—the so-called lion sermon—to be preached in St Katherine Cree, 'in memory of his deliverance from the paws of a lion in Arabia', and a number of charitable bequests for the poor in London, Surrey, Coventry, and Plymouth. Plymouth had already benefited from his generosity both to its Orphan Boys' Asylum in 1626 and as co-founder of a new almshouse and workhouse in 1630. In 1648 Gayer had become president of Christ's Hospital in

London, to which he had donated £500 and which he also remembered in his will with an additional bequest of £25, 'to make them a dinner in the day of my funerall'.

ROBERT ASHTON

Sources journals, CLRO, court of common council, 40 · repertories of the court of aldermen, CLRO, 55–6, 58 · *JHC*, 5 (1646–8) · *JHL*, 9–10 (1646–8) · J. Rushworth, *Historical collections*, new edn, 8 vols. (1721–2), vols. 6–7 · *State trials*, vol. 4 · Cobbett, *Parl. hist.*, vols. 16–17 · will, Plymouth and West Devon Record Office, Plymouth, 745/57 · *CSP col.*, vols. 6, 8 [East Indies] · E. B. Sainsbury, ed., *A calendar of the court minutes … of the East India Company*, [1–2]: 1635–43 (1907–9) · [A. Wilbee], *Plain truth without feare or flattery* (1647) · *Vox civitatis, or, The cry of the city of London* (1647) [Thomason tract E 409(10)] · *A declaration of the lord maior* (1647) [Thomason tract E 400(29)] · *The declaration of Generall Massey and Colonell Generall Poyntz* (1647) [Thomason tract E 401(12)] · *Vindication of the character and conduct of Sir William Waller* (1793) · C. H. Firth and R. S. Rait, eds., *Acts and ordinances of the interregnum, 1642–1660*, 1 (1911) · A. B. Beaven, ed., *The aldermen of the City of London, temp. Henry III–[1912]*, 2 vols. (1908–13) · T. Juxon, journal, DWL, MS 24.50, fols. 91–911b · R. Ashton, *Counter-revolution: the second civil war and its origins, 1646–8* (1994) · will, PRO, PROB 11/209, fols. 119r–121v

Likenesses Lely, portrait; known to be at Stockton House, Wiltshire, in 1870

Wealth at death minimum of £10,000, apart from houses and personal goods not bequeathed: will, copy in Plymouth and West Devon RO, MS 745/57

Gayer, Sir John (*d.* 1711), administrator in India, was one of the two sons and three daughters of Humfrey Gayer, a merchant of Plymouth, Devon (the fourth son of John Gayer, who died in 1593), and his wife, whose maiden name was Sparke, of the same town. He was the nephew of Sir John Gayer (*d.* 1649), lord mayor of London, who bequeathed to him the sum of £100. At an early age he entered the service of the East India Company, and rose to be a sea captain. On being appointed by the owners commander of the ship *Society*, Gayer was admitted into the freedom of the company on 7 April 1682.

On 3 June 1692 Gayer was chosen governor of the port and island of Bombay. On 18 March 1693 he was knighted, and on 10 April in that year was appointed 'our Lieutenant-Generall, Governour of Bombay, and Directore-in-Chief of all our Affaires and Factoryes … next and under Our Generall Sir John Goldsborough', whom he was to succeed in case of death. Gayer departed for India in December 1693 as governor of Bombay and general, and arrived at Calicut on 5 March 1694, where, on hearing of the death of Goldsborough, he immediately took charge. Gayer's prolonged tenure of office was much troubled by difficulties with the unchartered 'interlopers' and the growth of the rival New (or English) East India Company, which had been established in 1698. He also suffered from repeated bouts of ill health at Bombay, and pleaded with the company to allow him to return to England. However, in 1699 Sir Nicholas Waite (a dismissed agent of the old company) arrived as the new company's president at Surat and king's consul. The servants of the old company refused to recognize the new men or even the authority of Sir William Norris, who came out as King William's ambassador to the Mughal emperor Aurangzeb on 10 December 1700. Waite conspired unscrupulously against the old company, not even hesitating, it would

appear, to engineer Mughal hostility against it by blaming the old company for the breakdown of the protection of Mughal shipping against the depredations of English pirates such as the notorious Captain John Avery. The Mughal government was ready enough to take advantage of these rivalries. A contest in bribery began between the agents of the two companies, and Gayer made the mistake of leaving his stronghold at Bombay to go to Swally, the roadstead of Surat, ostensibly to mediate in the disputes in which the governor of Surat was involved. There he was arrested by the Mughal governor of Surat, in consequence apparently of Waite's charges. Along with his wife and some of his council, he was taken to Surat by a body of Indian troops, and confined to the factory under a form of house arrest. He was still a prisoner at the beginning of 1709, when the old and new companies had been amalgamated. Despite their confinement, Gayer and his council were still able to send dispatches home, and in their letters to the court from Surat, dated 31 March and 25 April 1706, they give a vivid description of the anarchy that prevailed in Gujarat and the country between Surat and Ahmadabad prior to Aurangzeb's death.

Eventually, the old company, in a letter to Gayer dated 20 April 1708, intimated that Waite had finally been removed from office, although his perverse violence had driven his council previously to confine him; and, as Gayer's captivity disqualified him from succeeding, William Aislabie, deputy governor at Bombay, had been appointed general in his place. They also hinted that Gayer might have gained his freedom sooner had he not stood so much on the punctilios of release. Yet they retained their faith in him, writing that they had 'great dependence on his fidelity and experience' (*Diary of William Hedges*, 2.cxlviii). He was certainly released by 5 October 1710, for on that day he made his will in Bombay Castle. He left India for England in 1711, but died of wounds received during a battle with the French *en route*.

Gayer was twice married, but left no children. His first wife, a Miss Harper, whom he had married some time before 1695, had died before 1710 in India, and he desired, should he himself die there, to be buried in her tomb at Bombay. His will was proved at London by his second wife, Mary, on 17 April 1712. After making liberal bequests to his relatives and friends, he left £5000 for the benefit of young ministers and students for the ministry, especially desiring that the recipients should be of the same principles as the nonconformist minister Richard Baxter.

As a contemporary observer, Alexander Hamilton, concluded, 'Sir John Gayer was a Man not vitious in his temper, yet he had some slips in his Government that proved prejudicial to his Character, tho', in Matters of common Commerce, he acted pretty regularly' (Hamilton, 1.134).

GORDON GOODWIN, rev. ANDREW GROUT

Sources *The diary of William Hedges … during his agency in Bengal; as well as on his voyage out and return overland (1681–1687)*, ed. R. Barlow and H. Yule, 2, Hakluyt Society, 75 (1888), cxxxvii-clv · H. Furber, *Rival empires of trade in the Orient, 1600–1800* (1976) · A. Hamilton, *A new account of the East Indies*, 1 (1727); new edn, ed. W. Foster (1930) · J. L. Vivian and H. H. Drake, eds., *The visitation of the county of Cornwall in the year 1620*, Harleian Society, 9 (1874), 172 · *The visitation of*

London, anno Domini 1633, 1634, and 1635, made by Sir Henry St George, 1, ed. J. J. Howard and J. L. Chester, Harleian Society, 15 (1880) · CSP dom., 1629–31, 152 · N. Luttrell, A brief historical relation of state affairs from September 1678 to April 1714, 5 (1857), 97 · will, PRO, PROB 11/526, fols. 190v–191v

Archives BL OIOC, factory corresp. · Bodl. Oxf., Rawlinson MSS, A.302 · Bombay RO, Bombay, India, Secretariat outwards or order books no. 7 · Bombay RO, Bombay, India, Surat presidency and factory diaries of chief in council, no. 2 · GL, ALSs Gayer-Evance, MS 1525 (box 12)

Wealth at death bequests to family and friends, plus £5000 to the ministry for young ministers and students: will, PRO, PROB 11/526, fols. 190v–191v

Gayre [formerly Gair], **George Robert** (1907–1996), racial theorist and specialist in heraldry, was born George Robert Gair at 4 Woodland Villas, Rathmines, Dublin, on 6 August 1907, the son of Robert William Gair (d. 1957) and his wife, Clara, née Hull. He was schooled in Bristol and Yorkshire. On 23 September 1933 he married Nina Mary (d. 1983), daughter of Louis and Margaret Terry; they had one son. Gair graduated from Edinburgh University in 1934 with a second-class MA in geography. He had a lifelong interest in racial theories, believing that humanity is divided into separate races with different mental abilities and that racial factors explain the crucial questions of history and anthropology. Such theories flourished in Nazi Germany, which he visited regularly, making contacts with Nazi race theorists such as Hans Günther. Gair drew upon Günther's work for his book Teuton and Slav on the Polish Frontier (1944), which discussed ways to make European nations more 'racially homogeneous'.

During the Second World War, Gair served in the British army. In 1943 he was appointed educational adviser in Italy with the aim of re-establishing the Italian educational system. He wrote about his experiences in his book Italy in Transition (1946), which also contained remarks about 'racial types' and criticisms of 'negro' soldiers.

Gair's type of racial theorizing was increasingly rejected by mainstream academics after the war. He was briefly professor of anthropology at the University of Saugor in India (1954–6), but otherwise remained outside conventional academic circles. His many subsequent books on topics such as race, heraldry, and Scottish genealogy were privately published or issued by small presses.

In the post-war years Gayre (who legally changed the spelling of his name in 1957) moved within two secretive worlds: that of chivalric orders and that of race theorists. He founded the British branch of the order of St Lazarus and enthusiastically collected titles from international chivalric orders. At the same time he was in contact with race theorists through various eugenic societies, which were devoted to promoting biological interpretations of social issues. Gayre even had contacts with the Northern League, a so-called cultural organization that included race theorists like Hans Günther and members of post-war fascist groups. In 1968, following a request from A. K. Chesterton, the founder of the British fascist group the National Front, Gayre spoke as a defence witness on behalf of five racist activists who were prosecuted under the new Race Relations Act. He also contributed financially to their defence fund. Gayre wrote extensively in support of the apartheid regime in South Africa, which he frequently visited.

In 1960 Gayre established the journal Mankind Quarterly as a quasi-academic forum for racial theories. Mankind Quarterly's editorial board included old 'race-scientists', such as von Verschuer, the former supervisor of the Nazi war criminal Josef Mengele, as well as younger academics interested in using IQ tests to demonstrate the supposed lower intelligence of blacks. Gayre edited the journal from its foundation in 1960 until 1978, when he became honorary editor-in-chief. He appointed Roger Pearson, the founder of the Northern League, as his editorial successor.

Gayre's own voluminous writings have had no impact on contemporary anthropology, which has rejected his type of racial speculation and unsystematic folklorism. He was extremely litigious, and sued the Sunday Times for defamation in 1973 after it questioned his expertise in anthropology. Gayre lost the case.

Gayre's significance, however, rests with Mankind Quarterly rather than with his own writings. The journal is part of a network of conservative and far-right organizations. This network includes American foundations which have had high-level contacts in the Reagan and Bush (senior) administrations and which have financed the sort of racial research that Mankind Quarterly publishes. In 1994 a best-selling American book, The Bell Curve, argued that poverty is genetically determined. This well-publicized book, much admired by senior American conservatives, drew upon material from contributors to Mankind Quarterly. In this way Gayre's journal contributed to perpetuating and developing racial theory.

Gayre spent his last years in the seclusion of Minard Castle, Argyllshire. He died there on 10 February 1996.

MICHAEL BILLIG

Sources M. Billig, L'internationale raciste (1981) · WW · W. H. Tucker, The science and politics of racial research (1994) · A. Winston, 'Science in the service of the far right: Henry E. Garrett, the IAAEE and the liberty lobby', Journal of Social Issues (1998) · C. Lane, 'The tainted sources of The bell curve', New York Review of Books (1 Dec 1994) · R. Littlewood, Anthropology Today, 11/2 (1965) · J. Lomas, Current Anthropology, 2/4 (1961) · Gayre of Gayre and Nigg, An autobiography (1987) · CGPLA Eng. & Wales (1996) · b. cert. · d. cert.
Archives Royal Anthropological Institute, London, material compiled for libel action
Likenesses photograph, repro. in Gayre, Autobiography · photograph, repro. in The Times (23 Nov 1994)
Wealth at death £523,170.71: confirmation, 1996 · £606,810.57: eik to confirmation, 2001

Gayton, Clark (c.1720–c.1787), naval officer, is of unknown parentage. After serving as a midshipman in the Squirrel with Captain Peter Warren on the coast of North America, and subsequently as a lieutenant in the West Indies, he was promoted by Commodore Charles Knowles to command the storeship Bien Aimé on 12 August 1744. On 6 July 1745, being then at Boston, he was posted by Commodore Peter Warren to command the Mermaid, in which he went home in the following March in charge of convoy. He continued to command the *Mermaid* on the home station until September 1747. On 10 July 1754, applying for employment, he described himself as a man with a large family and seven years on half pay, and on 3 February 1755 he added that before that almost his whole life had been spent at sea.

In the following May, Gayton commissioned the *Antelope*, which he commanded on the home station until August 1756, when he was moved into the guardship *Royal Anne* at Spithead, and in April 1757 into the *Prince*, for service in the Mediterranean, as flag captain to Admiral Henry Osborn. In his entertaining *Journal*, Augustus Hervey asserts that Gayton would have made a better boatswain than a captain. But, as a captain, Gayton was certainly popular with his men, who deserted back to him from other ships (PRO, Adm 1/5299, fol. 667). On Osborn's return home, in the summer of 1758, Gayton was appointed to the *St George*, in which he went out to the West Indies, and joined the squadron under Commodore John Moore at the unsuccessful attack on Martinique and the reduction of Guadeloupe in January 1759. Towards the close of the year the *St George* returned to England, and continued until the peace attached to the Grand Fleet in the Bay of Biscay.

In 1769–70 Gayton commanded the guardship *San Antonio* at Portsmouth. In October 1770 he became a rear-admiral, and in May 1774 he left England, with his flag in the *Antelope*, to take command of the Jamaica station, where, during 1776 and 1777, he had frequent and troublesome correspondence with the French commodore at Cap François, or with the French governor, concerning right of search and alleged breaches of neutrality. Like his fellow station commanders on the American coast, Gayton lacked the number of ships required to stop supplies from reaching the American revolutionaries. In April 1778 he returned to England, after which he had no further service. He had been advanced to vice-admiral in February 1776, and in April 1782 was raised to the rank of admiral. In December 1778 he was one of the admirals who signed the memorial protesting against the court martial of Admiral Augustus Keppel. During his last years he was very infirm and lived in retirement at Fareham in Hampshire, where he died about 1787.

J. K. LAUGHTON, *rev.* RUDDOCK MACKAY

Sources PRO, Admiralty MSS · W. L. Clowes, *The Royal Navy: a history from the earliest times to the present*, 7 vols. (1897–1903); repr. (1996–7), vol. 3 · N. A. M. Rodger, *The insatiable earl: a life of John Montagu, fourth earl of Sandwich* (1993) · [earl of Bristol], *Augustus Hervey's journal*, ed. D. Erskine (1953) · R. F. Mackay, *Admiral Hawke* (1965) · PRO, PROB 11/1127, fol. 214
Archives PRO, corresp., PRO 30/20 | PRO, Admiralty records
Likenesses J. S. Copley, oils, 1779, NMM

Gayton, Edmund (1608–1666), physician and hack writer, was born at Little Britain, London, on 30 November 1608, the son of George Gayton. In 1623 he entered Merchant Taylors' School, London, from where he was elected a scholar of St John's College, Oxford, in 1625. He was awarded a BA on 30 April 1629. On 9 May 1633 he received the degree of MA and was elected a fellow of his college. In the same year he was appointed superior beadle in arts and physic to the university. On 30 August 1636 he was one of the principal actors in *Love's Hospital, or, The Hospital for Lovers*, a comedy performed in the college refectory before the king and queen when they were Laud's guests at the college.

During the royalist occupation of Oxford, Gayton served as a captain in the duke of York's company and, after the surrender of the city, he accompanied James to Uxbridge where he took his leave of the prince. Gayton was clearly proud of his military record, and many years later described himself as 'at once a *Captain*, a *Physitian*, and a *small Poet*' (E. Gayton, *The Religion of a Physician*, 1663, sig. A4). On 1 February 1648 he was awarded the degree of bachelor of physic. In the same year the parliamentary delegates expelled him from his beadleship. After the Restoration, in a bid to attract the patronage of the duke of York, Gayton stressed the hardships he had to endure as a known royalist and fugitive. He 'was in a *Brown study* in the *City*, and at many a dangerous *Forrage* in the *Countrey*' (ibid., sig. A4). Besides what can be deduced from his own writings, Anthony Wood is the chief source for an account of Gayton's life, and his version is decidedly more prosaic. He writes that Gayton 'lived afterwards in London in a sharking condition, and wrote trite things merely to get bread to sustain him and his wife'. Of Gayton's works, he concludes that they are 'fit to be buried in oblivion' (Wood, *Ath. Oxon.*, 3.756).

Gayton presumably tried to earn a living as a physician, evidently without much success. In 1654 there appeared his *Pleasant Notes upon Don Quixot*, a digressive and anecdotal commentary in four books, in both prose and verse, 'which', writes Wood (with barely concealed sarcasm), 'is accounted our author's master-piece' (Wood, *Ath. Oxon.*, 3.756). He displayed his medical training in *Hymnus de febribus* (1655), a manual for the diagnosis and treatment of fevers in Latin verse, and *The Art of Longevity, or, A Dieteticall Institution* (1659), which is in rhyming couplets. During the interregnum he also wrote numerous poems commemorating the feast days of saints and other events of the liturgical year. He called them his 'dispersed Poems' (*The Religion of a Physician*, sig. A4) as he distributed copies of them to his friends at a time when the Anglican liturgy was officially proscribed. He published these poems in 1663 as *The Religion of a Physician*, although he disclaims any comparison with the *Religio medici* of Sir Thomas Browne.

The Mercers' Company commissioned Gayton to supply some verses for the pageant of Mayor Dethicke, which took place on 29 October 1655, the first pageant allowed since Cromwell's seizure of power. Gayton was in debtors' prison on the day of the show. In 1659 he was transferred to the king's bench, and when released, he moved to Suffolk in the same year. At the Restoration he was restored to his beadleship and continued to write broadside verses, including *Epulae Oxonienses* (1661), a 'jocular relation' of the 1636 royal visit to Oxford and the banquet whose centrepiece was a marzipan model of the convocation of the university, and the *Poem upon Mr. Jacob Bobard's Yew-Men of the Guards to the Physic Garden* (1662). He edited, and probably to some extent fabricated, *Henry Martens Familiar Letters to his Lady of Delight* (1663). He died in his lodgings at Cat Street, Oxford, near the public schools, on 12 December 1666 and was buried in St Mary's Church. Three days later, at the convocation for the election of a new beadle, the vice-chancellor, John Fell, mounted an attack on Gayton's reputation, claiming that he was 'such an ill husband, and so improvident, that he had but one farthing in his pocket when he died, &c' (Wood, *Ath. Oxon.*, 3.758). Gayton apparently liked to use the Latin name 'de Speciosa Villa' ('of the noble mansion'; Wood, *Ath. Oxon.*, 3.756)—a nicely ironic sobriquet for someone who presumably lived in an attic.   IAN WILLIAM MCLELLAN

Sources Wood, *Ath. Oxon.*, new edn, 3.756 · DNB

Gaywood, Richard (*fl.* 1644–1668), etcher, was the most prolific individual working in this medium for the London print trade in the years between the beginning of the civil war and the Restoration. Only two documents have so far been found that relate to his life: in 1658–9 he was paying tithes in the parish of St Sepulchre in the City of London, while on 17 July 1664 his daughter was baptized in the same church. George Vertue mentions him only once, in a list of followers of Wenceslaus Hollar, and states that under some of his plates are found the words 'quondam discipulus', that is, a former pupil of Hollar. Although these plates have never been seen since, there is no reason to doubt the truth of Vertue's assertion, for Gaywood was Hollar's most prolific and competent imitator. The great bulk of his large production, which no one has yet attempted to catalogue, consists of portraits. Most of these are too small to have been used as frontispieces to books, and must have been sold as single-sheet prints; some were probably private plates. One series of heads is copied from Anthony Van Dyck's *Iconography* (*c.*1632–44). Other plates were on a larger size, among them a folio of *The most Magnificent Riding of Charles the II to Parliament* of 1661.

Gaywood's abilities as a draughtsman were small, and most of his plates, and all his more ambitious ones, seem to have been copied from other prints: such is certainly the case with a print of a husband beating his wife, which is copied from Abraham Bosse, and one of Democritus and Heraclitus, which is taken from Jan van Vliet. In other cases Gaywood was supplied with designs by Francis Barlow. This is probably the case with the 1661 print mentioned above, and the collaboration between the two men is documented in the case of a 1656 etching of *Venus with the Organist* after Titian. The plate is signed by Gaywood, but is dedicated to John Evelyn by Barlow. A letter from Barlow to Evelyn of 22 December 1656 explains that 'the drawing after the originall paynting I did, and the drawing and the outlines of this plate', but that 'Mr Gaywood my friend' finished it 'which desyeres his name might be to it for his advantage in his practice, soe I consented to it' (*Diary and Correspondence*, 3.81–3). A small portrait etching of Evelyn by Gaywood is dated 1657.

Although Gaywood published a few plates himself,

much of what he produced was made for the publisher Peter Stent, and Alexander Globe's 1985 catalogue of Stent's output gives a good insight into the range of Gaywood's work.   ANTONY GRIFFITHS

Sources A. Globe, *Peter Stent, London printseller circa 1642–1665: being a catalogue raisonné of his engraved prints and books* (1985), 204–5 · A. Griffiths and R. A. Gerard, *The print in Stuart Britain, 1603–1689* (1998), 169–72, 194 [exhibition catalogue, BM, 8 May – 20 Sept 1998] · *Diary and correspondence of John Evelyn*, ed. W. Bray, rev. edn, ed. [J. Forster], 4 vols. (1859–62), 3.81–3

Geach, Charles (1808–1854), banker, was born on 1 May 1808 probably in St Austell, Cornwall, and baptized there on 4 September. He was the sixth child and second son of George Geach (1772–1850) and his wife, Grace, *née* Guichard (1776–1839). Little is known of his early years, but at fifteen he left school and became a clerk with a draper in St Austell.

Geach's banking career began in 1826 when he was elected to a clerk's position at the Bank of England. This post was probably obtained through the influence of his maternal uncle, mayor of Penryn, Cornwall, and friend of the borough's MP, J. W. Freshfield, solicitor to the Bank of England. Another relative, an aunt, provided Geach with lodgings in Paddington. He made good progress in the bank and in 1828 he was chosen to go to Birmingham with Sir George Nicholls (1781–1865) to establish a branch of the bank there. Working his way through the ranks in the new Birmingham branch, he became second inspector in 1831. His progress did not match his personal ambitions, however, as he later complained of the reluctance of the directors to promote to a high level those who had joined the bank at its lower levels. During these years he nevertheless acquired a thorough knowledge of both banking practice and the Birmingham business community. Geach married, in 1832, Eliza Lucy Skally (1816–1876), the daughter of a schoolmaster in whose house he first lodged in Birmingham.

In 1836 Geach advised a group of manufacturers in Birmingham on the establishment of a new joint-stock bank, the Birmingham Town and District Bank. Against expectations, he was not offered the managership of the new bank. A second group of businessmen then approached him to form another bank and this time he was promised, and obtained, the position of manager. The confidence that the promoters of the bank had in Geach must have been considerable: he was only twenty-eight, had never managed a bank before, and would be faced with stiff rivalry from the Bank of England and other banking institutions operating in Birmingham. In his favour, he had established a reputation for outstanding ability, industry, and 'singularly agreeable good manners' (Edwards, 130).

The new Birmingham and Midland Bank (the Midland) opened for business in Union Street, Birmingham, on 22 August 1836. The first year was dominated by discussions with the Bank of England over the capital structure of Midland and about its relationship with the Bank. Geach shrewdly negotiated with his former masters to gain the best terms for Midland: in return for Midland circulating the Bank's notes rather than issuing its own, the Bank would give preferential rates. The decision to restructure the capital base of Midland in 1837 was a condition laid down by the Bank and was instrumental in its survival; many of Midland's contemporaries later collapsed due to inadequate capitalization. Midland's business was primarily of a commercial nature, especially the discounting of bills of exchange. Geach set strict rules as to the quality and security of bills that the bank would discount, and these measures prevented the young bank falling prey to bad debts.

As well as overseeing the financial basis of the new bank, Geach was also called upon to protect the physical security of the bank building. In 1839 during Birmingham's Bull Ring riots it seemed likely that an advancing mob would attack the bank. Geach mounted his staff on the roof, armed with missiles, and himself rode through the mob to fetch support from the barracks.

Geach's own business affairs were characterized by the same shrewdness and courage that had made Midland a success. In 1838 he led a group of Birmingham businessmen in purchasing the patents and works of an iron-axle manufacturer in Wednesbury. The company was reconstructed and in 1844 Geach bought out his partners. In the railway boom that followed the Patent Shaft and Axle Tree Company was transformed by the increase in demand from a small-scale operation to a large and thriving business. Similarly, in 1842 Geach bought the Parkgate Company, a failing iron manufacturing business in Rotherham. When iron prices were driven up two years later due to the demand for iron rails, the new company benefited. Geach was also an active promoter and director of the Manchester, Sheffield and Lincolnshire Railway, and of the Shrewsbury and Birmingham Railway.

Geach was a Liberal, and his entry into politics coincided with the agitation for the repeal of the corn laws, with which he was heavily involved. He became an alderman of the Birmingham corporation in 1844 and mayor in 1847, his main contribution being an overhaul in the corporation's accounts and bookkeeping procedures. His civic duties forced him to resign as manager of Midland in 1847. Although relieved of responsibility for the day-to-day running of the bank, he joined the board as managing director, and thus retained an executive role. In 1851, following nomination by the National Parliamentary and Financial Reform Association, he was elected MP for Coventry. He seldom spoke in parliament, but was acknowledged as an authority on financial matters. On his election the family, including the six children, moved to Park Street, Westminster. However, Geach's parliamentary career was to be short-lived, as he died at home on 1 November 1854, after a short illness. The cause of death was stated to be a combination of chronic physical disorders, and the after-effects of a kick from a hansom cab horse. He was buried in Kensal Green cemetery. SARA KINSEY

Sources A. R. Holmes and E. Green, *Midland: 150 years of banking business* (1986) · E. Edwards, *Personal recollections of Birmingham and Birmingham men* (1877) · W. F. Crick and J. E. Wadsworth, *A hundred years of joint stock banking* (1936) · *The Times* (2 Nov 1854) · *Coventry Licensed Victuallers Weekly Diary* (6 Nov 1854) · 'Memoir of the late Mr Charles Geach', *Bankers' Magazine*, 14 (1854), 721–4 · T. W. Whitley, *The parliamentary representation of the city of Coventry* (1894) · HSBC Group Archives, London, Midland Bank archives · St Austell Parish Records

Archives HSBC Group Archives, London, Midland Bank archives

Likenesses J. Partridge, oils, 1850, HSBC Group Archives, London, Midland Bank archives · medallion, 1854, HSBC Group Archives, London, Midland Bank archives

Gear, William (1915–1997), artist, was born on 2 August 1915 in Methil, Fife, the first of the two children of Porteous Gordon Gear (1881–1965), coalminer, and his wife, Janet, *née* Inglis (1886–1955). The family lived in East Wemyss, Fife, where Gear grew up in the Scottish ethos of self-improvement by education and hard work, enlivened by the visual stimulus of his father's fondness for flowers and experimental photography, practised at the pit face. He was educated at East Wemyss primary school and Buckhaven secondary school. Having decided in his teens to become an artist, he won scholarships to Edinburgh College of Art (1932–6) and the University of Edinburgh (1936–7), where his studies included art history with David Talbot Rice. In 1937–8, with a travelling scholarship, he spent five months in Paris as a pupil of Fernand Léger, then visited Italy, Greece, Serbia, Istanbul, and Albania. On his return he took a teaching course at Moray House Training College (1938–9) and briefly taught art near Dumfries.

Early in 1940 Gear was called up and posted to the Royal Corps of Signals. He served in Egypt, Palestine, Cyprus, and Italy, where he managed consistently to paint and exhibit, first in Jerusalem and lastly in Florence. In 1945 he volunteered to serve in Germany and was posted to the monuments, fine art, and archives section of the Allied Control Commission, with the rank of major. He lived, with a studio, in Schloss Celle near Hanover, where the Berlin art collections were housed. As well as organizing exhibitions, he helped avant-garde German artists and was a member of an international committee that visited Bergen-Belsen with a remit to devise a memorial.

Shortly after demobilization in April 1947 Gear moved to Paris and took a studio at 13 quai des Grands Augustins, working part-time as an announcer for the English section of Radiodiffusion Française to supplement his gratuity. Ambitious, determined, and immensely hard-working, Gear, who was also highly sociable and a witty companion and raconteur, became friendly with many of the radical artists of the École de Paris. However, his most enduring professional links were with the members of the Cobra group. He was one of the two British artists to take part in the first Cobra exhibition at the Stedelijk Museum, Amsterdam, in 1949, when he also showed at the Betty Parsons Gallery, New York, fortuitously at the same time as Jackson Pollock. In 1949 he married an American dental assistant, Charlotte Chertok (1920–1988); their son David was born that year in Paris.

In October 1950 Gear and his family moved to England, to live in an isolated Buckinghamshire cottage. There Gear painted *Autumn Landscape* (oil on canvas 1950), his best-known work, commissioned by the Arts Council for its Festival of Britain exhibition, 'Sixty paintings for '51'. It won one of five purchase prizes, but its dynamic abstract forms were immensely controversial: a vituperative correspondence in the press was followed by a parliamentary question on the proper use of public money. By 1949 he had abandoned the figure groups and representational scenes of his early years and developed a consistent, abstract imagery, indebted both to Léger and Byzantine art, with jewel-like patches of colour arranged in a heavy black armature, which were gradually replaced with a softer focus and structure, or fan-like pleats which unfolded across the canvas. Titles such as *Gay Landscape* and *Summer Garden* indicate the natural origin of his paintings, which have been compared with the abstract landscape painting of his French contemporaries. His work changed only in the mid-1950s, when he experimented briefly with heavily impasted, near-monochrome canvases, inspired by his friend Nicolas de Staël. As a pioneer of post-war abstract painting, Gear received less critical attention than his contemporaries in St Ives, though his contribution to modernist landscape-related art was no less innovatory. His most radical period occurred early and his career outside painting and his allegiance to continental European rather than American models left him somewhat isolated, despite his international affiliations.

In 1951 a second son, Robert, was born and in 1953 the family moved to the Old Brewery House in Littlebourne, Kent. Although Gear was able to sell his work, in order to supplement his income he made prints; designed fabrics and wallpapers; worked on a project for stained glass; and even designed sets and costumes for a production of *Weir of Hermiston*. Though he always had time to spend with his children, he was a prolific artist. He maintained a strenuous exhibiting schedule, with group shows at home and abroad, often with the British Council, interspersed with regular one-man exhibitions at Gimpel Fils. In 1958 he became curator of the Towner Art Gallery in Eastbourne, where he built up a notable permanent collection of contemporary art, despite entrenched opposition from the purchasing committee and councillors which taxed his always limited patience.

Gear's appointment as head of the faculty of fine art at Birmingham College of Art in 1964 was a welcome change, though he was happy to retire in 1975. He lived in Birmingham for the rest of his life, travelling widely to visit museums and galleries, which were often the focus of family holidays. Despite the sadness of his wife's death in 1988, he participated with delight in the Cobra revival, which began earlier in the decade. In 1995 he was belatedly elected a Royal Academician. He died of cancer at the Queen Elizabeth Hospital, Edgbaston, Birmingham, on 27 February 1997, and was cremated on 12 March 1997 at Lodge Hill crematorium in Birmingham. He was survived by his two sons.   MARGARET GARLAKE

Sources S. Wilson, 'Cosmopolitan patternings: the painting of William Gear', *William Gear, 75th birthday exhibition: paintings and works on paper* (1990) [exhibition catalogue, Redfern Gallery, London, 11 Sept – 12 Oct 1990] • W. Gear and T. Sidey, interview, BL NSA, National Life Story Collection, Artists' Lives • A. Lewis, 'British avant garde painting, 1945–1956, part 1', *Artscribe* (March 1982), 17–33 • R. Tilston, 'Aspects of abstract painting in England, 1947–56', MA diss., Courtauld Inst., 1977 • *25 from '51: 25 paintings from the Festival of Britain, 1951* (1978), 3–9, 13–14, 25–5 [exhibition catalogue, Mappin Art Gallery, Sheffield, 17 May – 2 July 1978, and elsewhere] • *William Gear and Cobra* (1998) [exhibition catalogue, Aberdeen Art Gallery, 15 Nov 1997 – 10 Jan 1998] • *The Times* (1 March 1997) • *The Independent* (10 March 1997) • *Daily Telegraph* (4 March 1997) • *The Guardian* (3 March 1997) • *The Scotsman* (3 March 1997) • *William Gear: retrospective exhibition* (1961) [exhibition catalogue, Gimpel Fils, London, Feb 1961] • *William Gear: a retrospective exhibition from the artist's studio* (1982) [exhibition catalogue, Edinburgh and Birmingham, May–Sept 1982] • speeches at memorial event, Birmingham, 1997 • M. Garlake, *New art, new world: British art in post-war society* (1998) • private information (2004) [D. Gear] • WWW • d. cert.

Archives priv. coll. | SOUND BL NSA, National Life Story Collection, Artists' Lives

Likenesses J. Chillingworth, photograph, April 1952, Hult. Arch. • photograph, repro. in *The Times* • photograph, repro. in *The Guardian* • photograph, repro. in *The Scotsman* • photograph, repro. in *Daily Telegraph* • photograph, repro. in *The Independent* • photographs, repro. in Wilson, 'Cosmopolitan patternings'

Wealth at death £908,365: probate, 27 April 1998, *CGPLA Eng. & Wales*

Geare, Allan (1622–1662), clergyman and ejected minister, was born at Stoke Fleming near Dartmouth in Devon, the son of Allan Geare of Stoke Fleming. His parents were not wealthy, but managed to arrange for him to become the clerk of Francis Rous, afterwards the provost of Eton College. In 1636 Geare, with Rous's recommendation, became clerk to Sir Alexander Carew of Antony, near Plymouth, in Cornwall, and his learning was owed to the tutelage of Carew. With the burgeoning religious and political crisis, in 1640 Geare was sent to the Netherlands as the guardian of Carew's grandson. On 30 September 1643 he enrolled at the University of Leiden as a student in philosophy; his degree from there saw him created MA at the University of Oxford on 15 April 1648. While in the Netherlands he became acquainted with John Canne, the pastor of the English church at Amsterdam; he married Canne's daughter, Mary, about 1645.

In 1649 Geare was called to take pastoral charge at the London parish of St Benet Paul's Wharf and was ordained by the presbytery of the first London classis under the presidency of Matthew Poole. While at St Benet's, Geare proved to be a follower of the city presbyterians. He worked with lay elders in his parish, was scribe to the first London classis, and was a delegate at the London provincial assembly. However, London's unsanitary conditions played havoc with his health and so he resigned his charge at St Benet's on 8 May 1654, accepting the invitation of the earl of Bedford to become curate at Woburn in Bedfordshire. On 10 September 1656 the local magistracy of Dartmouth offered him the cure of Townstall with St Saviour's in Dartmouth. Major-General Desborough confirmed him and John Flavell, his fellow minister, as the ministers of Dartmouth on 7 August 1656. While at Dartmouth, Geare joined the godly clergy of Devon in setting up the Devon Association.

At the Restoration, Geare refused to conform and was deprived of his living on 3 October 1662 by order of the bishop of Exeter. Calamy notes that he became ill as a result of attending the hearings of the ecclesiastical commission at Exeter and died in Dartmouth in December 1662, possibly from influenza. He was buried, despite local opposition, at St Saviour's on 17 December 1662. His wife and five children survived him: Joseph, Mary (b. 1651), Elizabeth (b. 1653), Allan (b. 1656), and Benjamin (d. 1663).

E. C. VERNON

Sources *The nonconformist's memorial ... originally written by ... Edmund Calamy*, ed. S. Palmer, 2 (1775), 16–18 • minutes of the London provincial assembly, DWL, MS 201.12 • records of St Benet, Pauls Wharf, GL, MS 877/1 • *Calamy rev.*, 219 • Foster, *Alum. Oxon.*

Wealth at death £331 19s. 9d.: Calamy rev., 219

Geary, Sir Francis, first baronet (1709/10–1796), naval officer, was born in Cardiganshire. Details of his parents and early life are obscure; however, it is known that in his youth he was an accomplished bellringer and a member of the Ancient Society of College Youths. In 1726 and 1727 he took part in new and record-breaking peals at St Bride's, Fleet Street, London. In 1727 he entered the navy on the *Revenge* (70 guns, Captain Coningsbury Norbury); he served in the Baltic and then at Gibraltar, and was made lieutenant on 19 March 1734. On 27 May 1739, at the start of the war with Spain, Geary was first lieutenant of the *Adventure* (40 guns), and on 4 July he became sixth lieutenant in the *Namur* (90 guns); he was promoted fourth lieutenant and on 14 April 1740 was given the same rank in the *Victory* (100 guns), which for the next two years was in the channel under Sir John Norris.

On 30 June 1742 Geary was promoted to command the *Squirrel* (20 guns), and on 10 February 1743 he captured a very valuable Spanish prize off Madeira. He was appointed to the *Dolphin* (20 guns) in December 1743 and in the following February moved to the *Chester* (50 guns) in the channel. Again, he captured several rich French and Spanish prizes. Geary was sent out to Louisbourg in the *Chester* in early 1745, joined Commodore Warren on 10 June, took part in the capture of the garrison, and after leaving his ship on station was immediately sent home by Warren with dispatches; he left on 4 July, and arrived in London on 28 July. He was fortunate to be appointed to the *Culloden* (74 guns), then being built at Deptford, though for a short time in the winter of 1746–7 he commanded the *Prince Frederick* (64 guns) in the channel. On 20 September 1747, his fortune established, Geary married Mary Bartholomew (d. 1778) of Oxen Hoath, Kent, daughter of Admiral Philip Bartholomew; and he purchased Polesden (later rebuilt as Polesden Lacey) in Surrey, which he owned until his death. He commanded the *Culloden*, launched on 9 September 1747, in the channel under Rear-Admiral Sir Edward Hawke until the end of the War of the Austrian Succession in 1747.

In February 1755 Geary was appointed to the *Somerset* (64 guns), one of the fleet sent to North America under Vice-Admiral Edward Boscawen; he sailed on 22 April 1755 and returned before the year's end. In 1756 he cruised in the channel, first in January under Vice-Admiral Henry Osborne, then, by March, under Hawke, next under Boscawen in the summer, and finally under Vice-Admiral Charles Knowles in November. In July 1757 Geary was senior officer in command of a squadron of four ships sent out to Halifax, North America to strengthen the squadron under Vice-Admiral Francis Holbourne in the effort to take the fort at Louisbourg again, though he arrived too late to make any difference to the unsuccessful attempt on the garrison.

From September 1757 Geary was senior officer at the Nore, based mostly in the *Princess Royal* (90 guns), but on 2 June 1758 he moved into the *Lenox* (74 guns), in the Channel Fleet under Anson; in the following year he served on the same station in the *Resolution* (74 guns) and then from late August 1759 in the *Sandwich* (90 guns). It was under Hawke that Geary hoisted his flag as rear-admiral on 5 June 1759, but it was also his misfortune that after many months on station the *Sandwich* was forced to Plymouth for repairs for a few days, and he missed the decisive victory at Quiberon Bay on 20 November 1759. For another year he commanded detached squadrons in the *Sandwich* in the channel, but he was moved to the less active post of commander-in-chief at Portsmouth on 4 March 1761. Here he remained until 30 October 1762, although for some of this time he retired to Polesden when Vice-Admiral Holbourne took over the command. Geary was made vice-admiral on 21 October 1762.

Geary was on half pay for the rest of the 1760s until, on 2 December 1769, at the time of the Falkland Islands mobilization, his old commander Admiral Hawke, by now first lord, re-appointed him commander-in-chief at Portsmouth, where he dispatched business punctually and diplomatically. On 6 January 1771, when the rush was over, Geary again retired to the countryside. His promotion to admiral came on 31 March 1775 in the middle of another long period on half pay.

On 22 May 1780, just under twenty years after he was last at sea, and at the age of seventy, Geary was appointed at very short notice by Lord Sandwich to be commander-in-chief of the Channel Fleet. The circumstances were remarkable. Admiral Sir Charles Hardy had been the commander-in-chief in 1779, when the combined Franco-Spanish fleet, bent on invasion, had dominated the channel, caused panic in the civilian population of Plymouth, and shaken the government. Hardy commanded a fleet which had low morale and in which the senior officers were driven by political and personal differences. On 18 May 1780, just as the fleet of thirty ships of the line was about to sail, he died on board the *Victory*. Sandwich had experienced extreme difficulty in filling the post in the previous year and Hardy, though slightly younger than Geary, had himself been taken out of semi-retirement. In 1780 the younger admirals, with Samuel Barrington the most obvious choice, once again refused to serve. In the event Geary did not hesitate to accept command and went to sea with Barrington as his second-in-command and Richard Kempenfelt as captain of the fleet. Intelligence was not good and Geary's instructions were vague: to remain at sea for as long as possible, intercept enemy squadrons, and protect British merchant vessels.

Geary and his fleet of twenty-three ships of the line sailed on 8 June 1780, took station off Ushant, and remained there until 27 June, before moving south to the middle of the Bay of Biscay in an effort to find the French or Spanish fleets. The fleet was at sea for seventy-six days and Geary captured twelve ships in a convoy, fog preventing a far bigger total. However, this success has to be set against the far bigger loss of the British convoy to the East Indies under Captain John Moutray, captured by the Spanish fleet, and just missed by Geary's fleet; this was a great blow and brought peace negotiations with Spain to an end. By the end of August, 2000 seamen were to be found to have scurvy. Geary returned to Spithead on 18 August and nine days later requested sick leave. Worn out rather than ill, he reluctantly gave up the command. Barrington again refused to serve and Vice-Admiral George Darby succeeded to the command on 7 September 1780.

Geary's contribution towards the end of his professional life has been written off by historians because he was not perceived to have improved the situation. He did, however, hold the Channel Fleet together at the navy's lowest point in the second half of the eighteenth century; moreover, it is difficult to imagine two more difficult subordinates than Barrington and Kempenfelt. Clearly not a great commander, Geary was apolitical and notably popular. He was much trusted by Hawke as a second-in-command and there were few others to whom Sandwich could have turned, given the paucity of talent or spirit among the fifty-year-old admirals. Geary was made baronet on 3 August 1782 and died at Polesden on 7 February 1796; he was buried in Great Bookham parish church. His son William (1756–1825) succeeded to the baronetcy and was MP for Kent (1796–1806 and 1812–18).

ROGER KNIGHT

Sources J. Charnock, ed., *Biographia navalis*, 5 (1797) · warship histories index, PRO, ADM 8 · NMM, Geary MSS, GEA/1–3 · lieutenants' logs, *Victory*, 1740, NMM, ADM L/v/60 · N. A. M. Rodger, *The insatiable earl: a life of John Montagu, fourth earl of Sandwich* (1993) · D. Syrett, *The Royal Navy in European waters during the American revolutionary war* (1998) · G. Callender, 'With the grand fleet in 1780', *Mariner's Mirror*, 9 (1923), 258–70 · P. Mackesy, *The war for America, 1775–1783* (1964) · R. F. Mackay, *Admiral Hawke* (1965) · *The Hawke papers: a selection, 1743–1771*, ed. R. F. Mackay, Navy RS, 129 (1990) · *The Royal Navy and North America: the Warren papers, 1736–1752*, ed. J. Gwyn, Navy RS, 118 (1975) · H. W. Richmond, *The navy in the war of 1739–48*, 3 vols. (1920) · *Letters and papers of Charles, Lord Barham*, ed. J. K. Laughton, 1, Navy RS, 32 (1907) · *The private papers of John, earl of Sandwich*, ed. G. R. Barnes and J. H. Owen, 3, Navy RS, 75 (1936) · Geary family pew, memorial plate, West Peckham parish church, Kent · PROB 11/1272
Archives BL, letter- and order books, Add. MSS 40857–40858 · NMM, letter- and order books
Likenesses style of F. Cotes, oils, *c*.1780, NMM · G. Romney, oils, 1782–3, NMM
Wealth at death very considerable; annuities totalling £500; balance (incl. Polesden) to son: will, PRO, PROB 11/1272

Ged, William (1684/5–1749), goldsmith and stereotype founder, was probably born in Dunfermline, son of William Ged, said to have been a member of the family of Ged of Baldridge in Fife. He was apprenticed to Robert Inglis, goldsmith, in Edinburgh in 1696, and his own mark was entered with the Incorporation of Goldsmiths in 1706. The extant pieces of his work, including a silver bowl for

the Royal Company of Archers (1720), show that he was a highly skilled craftsman.

Ged was once thought to be the inventor of printing 'each Page of a Book upon a single Plate, instead of a Type for every Letter, as used in the Common Way of Printing', as he put it in his proposal of 1736; the process was later named stereotyping. It is now certain that Johann Müller, a German living in the Netherlands, made stereotype plates from which books were printed at the beginning of the eighteenth century. Ged was ignorant of his work and was the first in Britain to make stereotype plates.

In 1725 a printer told Ged that there was a shortage of type in Scotland because there were no letter-founders. Ged responded that it would be easier to make plates from complete pages composed from movable types than to make single pieces of type. He used plaster of Paris to make the intermediary mould and experimented to find the best metal for the plate: by 1727 he had settled on a composition similar to type metal. He encountered opposition from the Edinburgh printers, and in 1729 moved to London where he went into partnership with William Fenner, stationer, Thomas James, typefounder, and John James, architect. To advertise his method Ged accepted a challenge to produce a stereotype block in eight days in competition with the typefounder William Caslon. Ged's victory was pyrrhic: the typefounders and compositors, afraid of being put out of work and now fully aware of its practicality, were hostile to him.

In 1731 the partnership obtained a licence to print Bibles and prayer books for the University of Cambridge. Some printing from stereotype plates was done there, but the licence was surrendered in 1737. Ged had returned to Edinburgh in 1733. Three years later he issued a proposal for a stereotype edition of Sallust. It appeared in duodecimo in 1739, his son James having set the type, and a second edition from the same plates appeared in 1744. On the title pages of both editions he described himself as 'Aurifaber Edinensis', but there is no evidence that he worked as a goldsmith after 1725. He made stereotype plates for two editions of Henry Scougal's *The Life of God in the Soul of Man*, both printed in Newcastle in 1742.

Ged presented a demonstration plate of ten consecutive pages of the Sallust to the Society of Advocates in 1739. It was later housed in the National Library of Scotland. Plates of the Sallust which could have been used for printing survived in the National Museums of Scotland and Glasgow University Library.

The identity of Ged's wife is not known but their son, James (d. 1760), was a Jacobite who took part in the 1745 rebellion as a captain in the Duke of Perth's regiment. He was imprisoned until 1748. William Ged died in Leith or Edinburgh on 19 October 1749 when he was about to join James in London. James issued proposals for stereotype printing in 1751 and set up as a master printer in London: his name appears on a number of works published in 1752 and 1753. Later, he emigrated to Jamaica, where his brother William (d. 1767) was in business as a printer.

JOHN BURNETT

Sources J. Carter, 'William Ged and the invention of stereotype', *The Library*, 5th ser., 15 (1960), 161–92 · J. Carter, 'William Ged and the invention of stereotype: a postscript', *The Library*, 5th ser., 16 (1961), 143–5 · J. Carter, *The Library*, 5th ser., 18 (1963), 308–9 [corrections] · [J. Nichols], ed., *Biographical memoirs of William Ged* (1781) · J. S. Gibb, 'Notes on William Ged & the origins of stereotyping', *Proceedings of the Edinburgh Bibliographical Society*, 1/8, 25 (1890–95) · W. H. J. van Westreenen van Tiellandt, *Verslag der naspooringen omtrent … der stereotypische drukwijze* (1833) · P. Gaskell, *A new introduction to bibliography* (1972), 201 · E. Beveridge, *A bibliography of works relating to Dunfermline and the west of Fife* (1901), 150–52

Gedde [Geddy], **John** (*fl.* 1647–1697), apiculturist, was born in St Andrews, Fife, the second son of Michael Geddy, bailie of St Andrews, and Catherine Avery. In 1649, two years into a four-year apprenticeship to William Henderson, writer to the signet, he was appointed steward clerk to the steward of Fife, James Murray, earl of Annandale, a post he retained when John Murray, earl of Atholl, succeeded as steward in 1661. During Charles II's campaign in Scotland in 1650/51 Gedde was clerk to the committee of war. He married Anne (*d.* 1691), daughter of an Ayr schoolmaster, William Wallace, in 1657. Elected a bailie of Falkland in 1665, Gedde generally resided there until his death.

Gedde's presbyterianism brought him into conflict with the crown after the Restoration. He was reported to the privy council of Scotland for attending field conventicles and entertaining outed ministers, and in 1678 refused to sign assurances to desist. Religious scruples, reflected in the precocious piety of his daughter Emelia *Geddie (1665–1681), lost him his clerkship. It also undermined ten years litigation with Patrick Telfer, who in 1678 excluded the family from their property in Falkland and felled Gedde's woods, plantations, and nurseries. Telfer defended these actions by maintaining that Gedde was 'knowne to be a most seditious persone, disaffected with the government and one who for his principles and practeisses hath been inter commoned severall years' (Bryden, 205). Gedde refused to sign the Test Acts introduced under James VII which 'necessitated him, his wife and family to abandon his native country until King William's accession' (Mylne, 341). Returning to Falkland, Gedde recovered part of his fortune, having taxable property valued at £330 in 1695. In 1697 his London publisher described him as 'an ancient Gentleman of the Scottish Nation' (Walker, 306).

Gedde's apicultural interests were awakened through observation of wild bees in the royal park at Falkland. In 1672, without acknowledgement, Sir Robert Moray presented to the Royal Society 'a bee hive of a peculiar contrivance, sent out of Scotland … made up of several pieces, to take off one; whereby bees are kept from swarming, by adding a new box for every swarm' (T. Birch, ed., *The History of the Royal Society of London*, 4 vols., 1756–7, 3.60), given wider publicity by Henry Oldenburg in the *Philosophical Transactions* for 1673. Gedde travelled to London, claimed credit for design and operating instructions, and applied for fourteen-year monopoly rights, duly granted in 1675. English partners managed the patent, selling licences to regional manufactures who marketed sets of supered hives complete with a bee colony. His book

A New Discourse of an Excellent Method of Bee-Houses and Colonies was published in London in 1675.

In fact, the design for a supered hive with observation windows had been published by Samuel Hartlib during the interregnum and by 1655 such hives, credited to Gloucestershire cleric William Mew with improvements by Christopher Wren, were in use at Wadham College. In retrospect, the originality in Gedde's design lay only in the insertion of a removable frame in each super. This, with honeycomb attached, could be removed causing little disturbance to the colony. Gedde's apicultural protocols ran counter to traditional management of bees in straw skeps. Suggestions of plagiarism, together with the restrictions implicit in the patent, caused further adverse comment. Nevertheless, extended editions of his book were published in 1676, 1677, and 1697. In 1679 the hive design, openly acknowledging Gedde's patent, was central to the bee-keeping book written by Moses Rusden, successfully recommended by John Evelyn for appointment as bee master to Charles II. Gedde's apicultural ideas were further promulgated through the 1721/2 reprinting of his 1675 text as part of a composite work, in turn the source of a German translation published in Leipzig (1727, 1729, 1752, 1755). In the nineteenth century, when the life cycle of *Apis mellifera* was better understood, the potential of the supered hive with removable frames was fully exploited to actively manage bees and optimize honey harvested. D. J. BRYDEN

Sources R. Mylne, 'Memoir of John Geddy', *Miscellanies of the Abbotsford Club*, 1 (1837), 327–51 [ed. version of 'The descent probative, branches and relations of R Mylne esq engraver in Edinburgh, Feb 1728', NL Scot., MS 2094] · D. J. Bryden, 'John Gedde's bee-house and the Royal Society', *Notes and Records of the Royal Society*, 48 (1994), 193–213 · J. H. O. Walker, 'John Geddy of Hilltown, Falkland', *British Bee Journal*, 50 (1992), 265–7, 306–7, 401–2 · H. M. Fraser, *History of beekeeping in Britain* (1958), 35–42 · J. Hog, *Some choice sentances and practices of Emelia Geddie* (1717)
Wealth at death £300, value of taxable property in 1695: Bryden, 'John Gedde's bee-house', 212 n.54

Geddes, Alexander (1737–1802), Roman Catholic priest and biblical scholar, was born on 4 September 1737 in the parish of Rathven, Aberdeenshire, the son of Alexander Geddes and Janet Mitchel, small tenant farmers at Arradowl, Rathven, on the borders of the Gordon estates. Perhaps unusually for a Roman Catholic home in Scotland at the time the King James Bible was read attentively in the Geddes household, so that Alexander was to look back in 1790 and comment: 'before I had reached my eleventh year, I knew all its history by heart'. At the age of seven he began his formal elementary schooling, among a group of boys of similar background, under the tutorship of James Shearer and then under various teachers and Catholic priests enjoying the protection of the Gordon family. A particular influence on him from 1748 was James Grant, the priest in charge of the Catholics of Rathven, and so he entered the minor seminary of Scalan in the Braes of Glenlivet in 1751. He stayed at Scalan until he was twenty-one, when he entered the Scots College at Paris, where he attended lectures at the Collège de Navarre and came top

Alexander Geddes (1737–1802), by Samuel Medley, exh. RA 1802 [detail]

of his class in rhetoric, which he studied under Professor Vicaire. Subsequently he studied Hebrew at the Sorbonne under Jean Baptiste de L'Advocat and, excelling also in Greek and Latin, was encouraged by L'Advocat to settle in Paris and become a scholar. Bound by his commitment to serve the Scottish mission, however, he returned to Scotland in 1764, where he spent several months ministering in Dundee before being appointed chaplain to Traquair House, Peeblesshire, home of one of the leading Catholic families in Scotland.

Geddes spent four years at Traquair, with its well-stocked library, able to spend much of his time in biblical study and conceiving a plan for a new translation of scripture designed to fill a need, particularly, for British Catholics. In 1768, at the request of the dowager countess of Traquair, he was removed from his post, having fallen in love with one of the ladies of the house and having been known to criticize the higher authorities in his church. Bishop George Hay, who removed him, was a man with whom he was to stand in lifelong antipathy.

After a brief return to Paris, Geddes spent the years from 1769 to 1781 as a popular parish priest at Auchinhalrig, 50 miles from Aberdeen. During this period his efforts in maintaining the chapels under his care, which included also that at Preshome, next to his own parish, brought him into great debt. In 1779 his financial fortunes improved when he earned £100 for his *Select Satires of Horace Translated into English Verse*. Admired by Samuel Johnson and by many of the Enlightenment scholars of Aberdeen University, including the philosopher and poet James Beattie, who had developed a friendship with Geddes, this publication secured for him in 1780 the degree of LLD. About the same time, however, Bishop Hay secured his resignation as parish priest by threatening him with suspension from his divine office after Geddes, a man always intrigued by other preachers, had attended an Episcopalian service at the invitation of the earl of Findlater.

In 1781 Geddes left Scotland for London, where he became briefly a chaplain in the Imperial Chapel in Portman Square. Thereafter he enjoyed the patronage of Lord Petre, a member of the leading Catholic family in England. With a pension endowed by Petre, Geddes was able to work on his *Idea of a new English Catholic edition of the holy Bible for the use of the Roman Catholics of Great Britain* (1782) and on his *Prospectus of a New Translation of the Holy Bible* (1786). With the publication of the latter Geddes abandoned his idea of a specifically Catholic Bible and instead conceived a much wider project, re-examining the manuscript and textual sources of the Old Testament. In this work he was encouraged and materially supported by the Anglican bishop of London, Dr Robert Lowth, and inspired by the work of such exegetes as Dr Benjamin Kennicott, pioneer British scholar of Hebrew, and by German orientalist studies.

Geddes's work on the Old Testament attempted to draw clear lines between the mythic and the historical. Amid this process he argued that the contemporary search for the real garden of Eden was of no import, was probably an impossible historical quest, and that this paradise did not even need to have actually existed. The 'golden age' scenario of the prelapsarian condition of humanity required simply an ideal, pastoralized setting and this is what the ancient Hebrew mythologizers had provided. Geddes's search for actual historical credibility, on the other hand, led him to the conclusion that the absolutely divine inspiration of the decalogue, or the ten commandments, through the person of Moses was suspect.

Increasingly from the mid-1780s Geddes was widely perceived in both Catholic and Anglican circles to be a rather dangerous iconoclast. His motivation in criticism of scripture, however, was consistent with his insistence that divine authority as transmitted or embodied through human agency was perfect only in the case of Christ. This position perhaps explains why he increasingly found friendship among Unitarians such as Joseph Priestley, who became an intimate in the 1790s, and why he became less active in any kind of Catholic priestly ministry, given his own church's traditional insistence upon the sanctity of its own institutional authority. He continued to retain the material support of the Petres and the moral, though sometimes questioning, support of his cousin Bishop John Geddes (1735–1799) in Scotland, with whom he frequently corresponded. His own text used on the monument at his grave, erected to his memory by Lord Petre in 1804, sums up his attitude well:

> Christian is my name, and Catholic my surname. I grant, that you are a Christian, as well as I; And embrace you, as my

fellow disciple in Jesus: And if you are not a disciple of Jesus, Still I would embrace you as my fellow man.

In *A Modest Apology for the Roman Catholics of Great Britain* (1800) Geddes's ecumenical and catholic mindset is evident when he writes:

it should be granted that the whole Church of Christ, that is the aggregate of all Christians is in some sense *infallible* or, to speak more properly *indefectible*; it by no means follows that any particular Church or partial collection of Churches is that indefectible Catholic church *against which the gates of Hell shall not prevail.*

In the absence of Catholic emancipation his views on church authority were, while entirely sincere, also a strategy toward securing greater tolerance for Roman Catholicism in a Britain that remained deeply suspicious of the dispensing power of the pope. Geddes was frustrated by the superstition and phobia that he saw in both Catholicism and protestantism, and his *The holy Bible, or, The books accounted sacred by Jews and Christians; otherwise called the books of the old and new covenants* (1792) provoked a reactionary backlash when a fellow priest, the Revd John Milner, urged Geddes's area Catholic bishop, John Douglass, to excommunicate its author. Resisting such full rigour, Douglass did suspend Geddes from holy orders on 27 June 1793.

Geddes's radicalism in his approach to scripture was matched by radicalism in politics. His primary logic as an exegete was to counter as flawed history, or to relocate in the province of inadequately interpreted mythology, instances of a seemingly unjust God. So too in politics Geddes opposed perceived injustices. His *Apology for Slavery* (1792) is a well-written satirical pamphlet in which he applied the principles of Thomas Paine in aid of the abolitionist cause. Many of his essays in the *Analytic Review*, the *Sunday Review*, and elsewhere are critical of Britain's politics and foreign policy, as is a large body of his poetry (much of it published anonymously) in the radical press of the day, most especially in the *Morning Chronicle*. His boldest political stance is found in relation to the French Revolution. He was a member of the society for constitutional reform that was inspired by events in France, and he may have been co-author of Joel Barlow's important radical document *Address to the National Convention of France*. Geddes's poetic sequence *Carmen seculare pro Gallica gente tyrannidi aristocraticae erepta* (1790), published in Latin with parallel English translation, was intended to be read in French to the assembly of deputies in Paris as an exercise in assuring the assembly of continuing international intellectual support for the revolution. The poem demonstrated Geddes's radical whig, Foxite credentials, for its watchword was 'liberty', which, Geddes argued, Britain had a long and proud record in defending.

Geddes inspired the Catholic radical David Downie, a Friend of the People who was tried for high treason in Edinburgh in 1794. Geddes's activities in this instance particularly embarrassed the Scottish Catholic church, which was beginning to enjoy greater freedom in return for supporting the war against France. Henry Dundas, secretary for war, wrote to Geddes on 19 June 1794, assuring

him that he had no doubts about the loyalty of the Catholics of Great Britain. The most logical reading of this letter is that it was a response to a letter from Geddes avowing his allegiance, like that of other Catholics, to George III. This exchange represents a not easily explained turn of events and perhaps shows Geddes playing a double game where pressure had been placed upon him, possibly by his cousin Bishop John Geddes, not to endanger the increasing liberty that the Catholic community was then enjoying. Geddes's anonymously published radical poetry, which continued unabated throughout the 1790s, remained severely critical of the war-time curtailment of traditional legal practices (as, for example, in 'Trial by Jury', 1795) and of the freedom of the press (as in 'The Blessings of a Free Press', 1795). His most dangerous note is sounded in 'The Irish *Ca ira*' (1798?), which may never have been published, in which he suggests that the Irish ought to be inspired by events in France to rebel against British rule. Geddes was one of the circle of Joseph Johnston, who published much of his work, and was intimate with many of the most revolutionary whigs, as well as with the most radical romantic artists, especially William Blake and Samuel Taylor Coleridge. Jerome McGann has demonstrated that Geddes's reading of the Bible is a very strong and hitherto overlooked influence upon Blake's incorporation of ideas of heaven, hell, and scripture in his poetry.

Geddes's fame for at least part of the nineteenth century rested not only upon his Bible—though his exegetical legacy was not properly appreciated until the twentieth century—but upon his skill as a philologist. His linguistic aptitude is demonstrated in his *Three Scottish Poems with a Previous Dissertation on the Scoto-Saxon Dialect*, published by the Scottish Society of Antiquaries in 1792. Here he shows his skill in analysing the changing condition of the Scots language in a way that has excited belated notice by professional students of Scots in the late twentieth century. With his dissertation Geddes includes translations of ancient pastoral poetry into Scots, which show a striking skill that might have developed further, had he been exclusively interested in poetry. His virtuosity with language is seen again in his prose satire *The Book of Zaknim*, posthumously published in 1963.

Geddes died in London, about four o'clock in the morning on Friday 26 February 1802, after a short but completely debilitating illness, having received absolution the day before from a French émigré priest, the abbé de St Martin. He was buried in St Mary's churchyard, Paddington. A fellow priest, Dr Belasyse, urged Bishop Douglass to permit a requiem mass for Geddes, but the bishop refused and, though attended by a large number of people, the precise nature of the funeral service remains unknown.

GERARD CARRUTHERS

Sources R. C. Fuller, *Alexander Geddes, 1737–1802: a pioneer of biblical criticism* (1984) • B. Aspinwall, 'The last laugh of a humane faith: Dr Alex. Geddes, 1737–1801', *New Blackfriars*, 58 (July 1977), 333–40 • W. Mckane, *Selected Christian Hebraists* (1999) • J. J. McGann, 'The idea of an indeterminate text: Blake's bible of hell and Dr Alex. Geddes', *Studies in Romanticism*, 25 (1986), 303–24 • W. J. Anderson, 'David Downie and the "Friends of the people"', *Innes Review*, 16 (1965), 165–79 • G. Carruthers, 'Alexander Geddes and the Burns "lost poems" controversy', *Studies in Scottish Literature*, 31 (1999) • C. Jones, *A language suppressed* (1995) • J. M. Good, *Memoirs of the life and writings of the Reverend Alexander Geddes* (1803) • W. J. Anderson, 'The book of Zaknim', *Innes Review*, 14 (1963) • *DNB*

Archives Essex RO, papers, mainly poems • NL Scot., letters • Scottish Catholic Archives, Edinburgh, letters and papers

Likenesses portrait, *c.*1770, repro. in Fuller, *Alexander Geddes* • G. Chalmers, portrait, 1785, repro. in Fuller, *Alexander Geddes* • S. Medley, oils, exh. RA 1802, DWL [*see illus.*]

Geddes, Andrew (1783–1844), painter and etcher, was born on 5 April 1783 at St Patrick Street, Edinburgh, and baptized on 16 April at St Cuthbert's Church, Edinburgh, the second of the six children, and only son, of David Geddes (who died at 18 Buccleuch Place, Edinburgh, on 15 March 1803), deputy auditor of excise, and his second wife, Agnes Boyd (who also died at Edinburgh, on 11 January 1828). He received a classical education at the high school and the University of Edinburgh, acquiring fluency in French, and in 1803 became a clerk in the Excise Office. His father was a connoisseur and collector of prints (auctioned by Thomas Philipe in London in 1804); Geddes was so strongly drawn to art that he spent his leisure in sketching and copying engravings, and, when he was free to choose his own way of life, he resolved—fortified by the advice of John Clerk, afterwards Lord Eldin—in 1806 to proceed to London and study as a painter. In the same year he exhibited his first picture, *St John in the Wilderness*, at the Royal Academy, the schools of which he attended for a year, having enrolled on 15 January 1807. In 1810 he opened a studio in York Place, Edinburgh, and soon had a good practice as a portrait painter. Four years later he visited Paris with the engraver John Burnet, and traces of the Venetian masters whom he studied in the Louvre appear in his *Ascension*, an altarpiece executed after his return for St James Garlickhythe, London. His next important picture was the *Discovery of the Regalia of Scotland in 1818*, with full-length portraits of all the commissioners appointed for its search. After Geddes's death the picture was cut up, the portrait heads being sold individually (Laing, 15–16). It had been exhibited in the academy in 1821, and formed the chief feature in the collected exhibition of seventy of his works which he brought together in Waterloo Place, Edinburgh, in December of the same year, and which comprised portraits, sketches from the old masters made in Paris, and 'pasticcio compositions' in the manner of Rembrandt and Watteau. Before 1823 he had finally established himself in London, for in that year he declined the suggestion of his artist friends in the north that he should return to Edinburgh with the view of filling the place of leading Scottish portrait painter, vacant by Raeburn's death. On 5 May 1827 he married in London Adela (1791–1881), youngest daughter of the miniaturist Nathaniel *Plimer [*see under* Plimer, Andrew], members of whose family he had painted in 1812–15. A few months later her sister married a wealthy corn-dealer and collector, Andrew James (1791/2–1854), who shared with Geddes a passion for the works of Watteau. Geddes also became a collector and influenced other collector friends such as Alexander Oswald (1777–1821) and John Sheepshanks (1787–1863). In 1832 he unsuccessfully urged the

British Institution to buy Sir Thomas Lawrence's old master drawings.

In 1828 Geddes started for the continent, where he resided, mainly in Italy, until the beginning of 1831, copying in the galleries, and at Rome painting portraits of Cardinal Weld, the ladies M. and G. Talbot (afterwards princesses of Doria and Borghese), John Gibson RA, and James Morier. After a rebuff in 1821, he was elected an associate of the Royal Academy in 1832, disappointed at not achieving greater recognition. In 1839 he visited Holland for purposes of artistic study. He died on 5 May 1844 of consumption, first manifested in 1830, at 15 Berners Street, London, where he had lived since 1832 with his wife, who died childless in her ninetieth year on 26 February 1881 and was buried alongside him at Kensal Green cemetery.

Geddes began the systematic practice of art comparatively late, and his works occasionally show defects of form; but he improved himself by a study of the great masters, especially Rembrandt, and from the first his sense of colour and tone was unerring. He is best represented in the National Gallery of Scotland. His *Portrait of the Artist's Mother* is entitled to rank as the painter's masterpiece, and forms the subject of one of his finest etchings. The portraits of George Sanders, miniature painter, and of David Wilkie (Scot. NPG), one of his keenest admirers, are good examples of his cabinet-sized full-lengths, in which both the figures and the interiors in which they are placed are rendered with the most scrupulous finish of crisp detail. As a painter he never bettered these early portraits; his portrait groups, histories, and fancy pictures were less successful. His copies from the old masters were once quite highly valued. One of them, a full-sized transcript of Titian's *Sacred and Profane Love*, belongs to the Royal Academy, London.

As an etcher Geddes ranks higher than as a painter; his plates may be regarded as among the very earliest examples in modern British art of the brilliancy, concentration, and spirited selection of line proper to a 'painter's-etching'. His dry-points and etchings include portraits, landscapes, and a few copies from the old masters. He published ten of them himself in 1826; fifty are catalogued by Campbell Dodgson. The verdict on Geddes of B. R. Haydon—'A man of pure taste but no power'—seems just (B. R. Haydon, *Diaries*, ed. W. B. Pope, 5.372).

J. M. GRAY, rev. SELBY WHITTINGHAM

Sources D. Laing, *The etchings of Sir David Wilkie, R.A., ... and Andrew Geddes, A.R.A., with biographical sketches* (1875) • A. Geddes, *Memoir of the late Andrew Geddes, esq., A.R.A.* (1844) • C. Dodgson, *The etchings of Sir David Wilkie and Andrew Geddes: a catalogue* (1936) • K. Sanderson, 'Engravings after Geddes', *Print Collector's Quarterly*, 16 (1929), 109–31 • 'An Edinburgh citizen's account-book', *The Scotsman* (27 Sept 1913) • W. Martin, 'Andrew Geddes', *The Connoisseur*, 95 (1935), 334–8 • C. Campbell, 'De etsen van Andrew Geddes', *De Kroniek van het Rembrandthuis*, 29/1 (1977), 10–19 • *Catalogue of Mr Geddes's pictures* (1821) [exhibition catalogue, Bruce's Great Room, Waterloo Place, Edinburgh, 1821] • *Catalogue of the valuable collection of pictures and drawings by old masters ... formed by Andrew Geddes* (1845) [sale catalogue, Christie and Manson, London, 8–13 April 1845] • T. Philipe, *Catalogue of the valuable collection of prints by the great ancient and modern masters of all the schools formed ... during a period of forty years, by*

David Geddes, esq., of Edinburgh, deceased (1804) • P. J. M. McEwan, *Dictionary of Scottish art and architecture* (1994) • H. Smailes, *Andrew Geddes, 1783–1844, painter–printmaker* (2001) [exhibition catalogue, NG Scot., 15 Feb – 29 April 2001]

Archives NL Scot., corresp. • priv. coll. | U. Edin., David Laing MSS

Likenesses A. Geddes, self-portrait, oils, 1812, Scot. NPG • A. Geddes, self-portrait, oils, 1816, Royal Scot. Acad. • A. Geddes, etching (after his earlier work), NPG • A. Geddes, self-portrait, oils, Scot. NPG • A. Geddes, self-portrait, oils, priv. coll.

Geddes, Auckland Campbell, first Baron Geddes (1879–1954), politician and businessman, was born in London on 21 June 1879, the second of three sons of Auckland (originally Acland) Campbell Geddes (1831–1908), civil engineer, and his wife, Christina Helen Macleod Anderson (1850–1914). He had four sisters, of whom two survived into adulthood. His siblings included Sir Eric Campbell *Geddes, Irvine Geddes, chairman of the Orient Steam Navigation Company, and Dr Mona Chalmers-*Watson, who was the first woman awarded an MD by Edinburgh University.

At birth Geddes suffered haemorrhages in both eyes, and problems of sight shaped his career at decisive moments. He was educated at George Watson's College, Edinburgh, where his study of the defence of empire was nurtured, and Edinburgh University, where he became a medical student in 1898. He hoped to join the Army Medical Service, where eyesight tests were less stringent than for the ordinary service. He joined the university rifle volunteers and wrote marching songs which were, subsequently, published in the *British Student's Song Book*. Attempts to enlist for military service during the Second South African War were unsuccessful, until militia units started to require junior volunteer officers. He sailed for South Africa as a second lieutenant in the 3rd battalion, Highland light infantry, late in 1901. It was converted into mounted infantry and he saw active service, but was disappointed not to be rewarded with a regular commission after failing the medical examination.

Geddes resumed his medical studies, and graduated in 1903. He undertook three years of postgraduate study in anatomy at Edinburgh, London, Freiburg, Paris, Bern, and Vienna. He also visited hospitals in Canada and the United States on a four-month tour. In May 1906 he became demonstrator and assistant professor of anatomy at Edinburgh University and later that year (3 September) he married Isabella Gamble (d. 1962), daughter of W. A. Ross, who originated from Belfast but had settled in New York. He proceeded to his MD in 1908, gaining the university gold medal. In the following year he became fellow of the Royal Society (Edinburgh) after presenting a paper on the embryology of the penguin. While in Edinburgh he continued his voluntary military service, and his ideas on officer training at universities were used by R. B. Haldane, secretary of state for war, who was a distant relative. On the creation of the Territorial Force in 1908 he formed the Second Scottish General Hospital unit. In 1909 he wrote articles for the *Scotsman* promoting preparedness for European war through compulsory military service. Like many volunteers, Geddes had concluded that national efficiency

Auckland Campbell Geddes, first Baron Geddes (1879–1954), by Olive Edis, 1916

required the military training of the young and administrative reform at the War Office.

Isabella Geddes did not find the Scottish climate or Edinburgh University social life to her liking, and in 1909 Geddes accepted the chair of anatomy at the medical school of the Royal College of Surgeons, Dublin, where he established a territorial medical unit. In the autumn of 1913 he took up the appointment as professor of anatomy at McGill University, Montreal, where his inaugural lecture warned that the medical profession would have to prepare for war. On the outbreak of war his wife and children—they had four sons and one daughter—remained in Nova Scotia, while he returned to Britain at the earliest opportunity as a combatant officer, with the rank of major.

Geddes was attached to the 17th (service) battalion, Northumberland Fusiliers, which was raised by his brother Eric, assistant general manager of the North Eastern Railway Company. Auckland Geddes soon became second-in-command, but a bad fall from his horse rendered him unfit for general service. However, he was passed fit for staff duties and he was posted to British general headquarters, France, where he rose to assistant adjutant-general with the rank of lieutenant-colonel. He analysed casualty lists, allocated padres to units, and dispatched drafts for depleted divisions after the battle of Loos, efficiently mastering the procedures of manpower supply and its deployment on the western front.

In 1916 Geddes made the remarkable ascent to the rank

of brigadier-general with the role of director of recruiting at the War Office. Lord Derby, secretary of state for war, valued his ability to represent the War Office in conferences on labour supply with other government departments, industrial employers, and trade unions. In an attempt to establish clear principles Geddes insisted, according to Lloyd George, that 'the only rational basis for recruiting is on an occupation and not an age basis' (House of Lords RO, Lloyd George MSS, F/7/1/2, Lloyd George to Neville Chamberlain, 20 July 1917). It offered Lloyd George, prime minister, a way out of the chaos of voluntary national service. The director general of national service, Neville Chamberlain, finally resigned in August 1917 after months of interdepartmental strife, and Geddes became minister of national service with responsibility for military recruiting *and* the retention of skilled men in vital war industries. Lloyd George observed that it would be inappropriate for a figure active in recruitment to revert to his civilian title, doctor, and, soon afterwards Geddes was appointed KCB (military division) and sworn of the privy council. At a by-election in October 1917 he was returned unopposed as Unionist MP for Basingstoke, a seat he held until March 1920. As adviser to the war cabinet on the supply and allocation of manpower, his quest for rational, systematic procedures, and tireless industry and independent mind sometimes understated the political context of executive decision making.

During 1917–18 Geddes refined the schedules of protected occupations, judiciously regulating the release of young men for the army while ensuring that priority was given to the labour needs of merchant shipbuilding and munitions output. On 14 January 1918 he criticized the 'thoughtless waste of life' resulting from British military plans (*Hansard 5C*, 101.58–86). In April 1919 he told Lloyd George:

> Many duties which I have done I have hated and none more perhaps than the duty which you laid on me of administering the Military Service Acts although paradoxically I enjoyed the doing of that work in the circumstances of that time.   (Lloyd George MSS F/17/5/32, A. Geddes to D. Lloyd George, 26 April 1919)

In November 1918 Geddes became president of the Local Government Board to prepare for the creation of a reforming Ministry of Health. However, in January 1919 Lloyd George intended to appoint him chancellor of the exchequer, but illness prevented him from accepting the post and he was given the caretaking jobs of winding up the ministries of National Service and Reconstruction. In March 1919 the choice of developing a political career or returning to university life appeared to be decided when McGill University appointed him principal. He never got to Montreal for in May 1919 he was appointed president of the Board of Trade at the same time as his brother took responsibility for transport. The survival of the Geddes brothers in government reflected Lloyd George's reconstructionist intent, but the restoration of financial orthodoxy and party discipline made them vulnerable to political attack as technocratic outsiders who knew little

of parliamentary life. The railway strike in September 1919 exemplified the renewal of antagonism between labour and government. An inflexible negotiating approach exacerbated tension with the National Union of Railwaymen, but Geddes was not alone in imagining that a revolutionary working class was about to seize power through industrial militancy. At the Board of Trade he ignored the advice of his labour advisers, and K. O. Morgan concluded that he 'presided over a disastrous period of mutual incomprehension between unions and government' (Morgan, 50). Among Unionist back-bench MPs there was little sympathy for Lloyd George's leading hustlers as wartime controls were dismantled. Businessmen in government returned to their enterprises.

In March 1920 the appointment of Geddes as British ambassador in Washington caused some surprise at a delicate moment in Anglo-American relations. On being asked for a farewell message by journalists he telegrammed, 'The prayers of the congregation are desired' (Clark, 195). In a quiet self-effacing way he played a part in easing the strained relationship, assisted by the ending of the Anglo-Japanese alliance. In November 1921 he was a full British delegate at the Washington conference on the limitation of armaments, where conciliatory discussion enabled both powers to accept naval parity. He was appointed GCMG in 1922. He also took part in the negotiations for the settlement of British war debts with the United States, 1922–3. He was awarded a medal by the National Institute of Social Sciences, and honorary degrees by many American universities. In May 1923 eye trouble recurred, and in July he returned to England, with no vision in one eye and peripheral vision in the other.

In 1924 Geddes was appointed chairman of the royal commission on food prices. In November 1924 he joined the board of the Rio Tinto Company at the suggestion of his erstwhile ministerial colleague and friend Lord Milner, and Lionel Rothschild, with whom he had liaised on recruiting issues which affected finance houses during the war. On Milner's death in May 1925 Geddes became chairman. He quickly undertook a detailed inspection and reorganization of the Rio Tinto copper and sulphur mines in Spain, and launched ambitious schemes, including a dynamic acquisitions policy, the formation of exploration subsidiaries, and the reduction of market instability in the pyrites trade through controlled competition with powerful commercial rivals. The declining demand for pyrites, as fertilizer manufacturers looked elsewhere for sulphur, and political unrest in Spain during the second republic provided the context for diversification after 1931.

This development was deeply controversial inside the company, but proved to be far-sighted as it struggled to remain solvent during the years of civil war and nationalist rule, in which pyrites supplies were effectively requisitioned for Germany. In extensive correspondence on the subject with the Foreign Office in 1937–8 Geddes unsuccessfully demanded diplomatic and naval intervention to forestall shipments to Germany. Ultimately, investment in the Northern Rhodesian (Zambian) copperbelt sustained the Rio Tinto mines during the 1930s and 1940s. Following discussions in 1928 with Stanley Baldwin, prime minister, who emphasized the importance of retaining British control over copper and cobalt supplies in Africa, Geddes and Sir Ernest Oppenheimer founded Rhokana Corporation Ltd which merged three development companies and acquired substantial copperbelt holdings to halt American control of mineral resources in Northern Rhodesia. Geddes became chairman and its main advocate in the city of London.

Initially Geddes expressed little enthusiasm for the business world and referred to 'daily-breading' (Geddes, 336). Later he drew parallels between the activities of a company chairman and a general who plans and directs a military campaign. In January 1930 his basic salary was increased from £10,000 to £20,000 per annum, by which time the company had operating staff in 22 countries and involvement in metallurgy and chemical processes. He had also forged a partnership with the Silica Gel Corporation to promote the commercial use of this new chemical absorbent outside the United States. Under Geddes's chairmanship the Rio Tinto Company adopted a dual identity as a mining house and an investment holding company. Reforms in management structure, involving full-time directors from outside and precisely defined roles, reliable data on production, and forecasts arising from systematic investigation, allowed the emergence of high-order entrepreneurial activity at board level which gave the company access to business growth, even if the momentum faltered in the 1930s.

In the months between the Munich crisis (1938) and the outbreak of the Second World War, Geddes urged the creation of a ministry of national service to ensure that essential naval, air, and civil defence needs were met and the idea of a vast conscript army avoided (*The Times*, 8 Nov 1938 and 13 Oct 1938). He supported compulsory training, not for military service, but in a variety of skills for factories, fields, and fire fighting, and urged that the lesson of 1916–18 should be learned, namely, that in exceptional circumstances 'we only sent conscripts in the later reinforcements, and I am of the opinion that by doing so we added little to the effective sum of our military effort' (*The Times*, 16 Nov 1938). In June 1939 he was appointed regional commissioner for civil defence for the south-eastern region. In 1941 he steadily lost his vision and resigned. An operation restored sight in his right eye and he became commissioner for the north-western region until failing eyesight forced his resignation in June 1942; he suffered a further haemorrhage from fragments from a blast at his home in Rolvenden, which was in the V-1 'bomb alley' in 1944. He was created Baron Geddes of Rolvenden in the new year honours of 1942.

The onset of total blindness forced Geddes's departure from the chairmanship of the Rio Tinto Company in 1947. He was presented with a tape recorder by the board, which enabled him to dictate a family history, later published as *The Forging of a Family* (1952). In it he explored the 'family gene bank' to fathom the relationship of cultural

transmission and physical heredity. It revealed his interest in spiritualism and extra-sensory perception; he recounted periods of heightened consciousness, informed by 'psychic streams', which arose on three occasions of near-death experiences, and he argued that his family's history contained examples of the paranormal reception of knowledge and memory from previous generations. Among the book's autobiographical fragments is a precise and moving account of the slow onset of blindness as it affected a busy man who enjoyed sport and travel. As one 'prohibition' followed another he noted 'Talk and ideas became vastly important' (Geddes, 355). He also wrote a play with Cecil Madden, board member of the Rio Tinto Company and Rothschilds, entitled *Through the Veil—a Thrilling Psychic Drama* which he partly financed and which briefly ran in the West End in 1931. Geddes died at the Royal West Sussex Hospital, Chichester, on 8 June 1954. His wife survived him.   KEITH GRIEVES

Sources A. C. Geddes, *The forging of a family* (1952) · D. Avery, *Not on Queen Victoria's birthday: the story of the Rio Tinto mines* (1974) · C. E. Harvey, *The Rio Tinto Company: an economic history of a leading international mining concern, 1873–1954* (1981) · A. C. Geddes, correspondence with Lloyd George, HLRO, Lloyd George papers · Lord Derby, correspondence with Lloyd George, HLRO, Lloyd George papers · K. Grieves, *The politics of manpower, 1914–1918* (1988) · J. Shakespear, *A record of the 17th and 32nd service battalions, Northumberland fusiliers, N.E.R. Pioneers, 1914–1919* (1926) · B. W. E. Alford and C. E. Harvey, 'Copperbelt merger: the formation of the Rhokana Corporation, 1930–1932', *Business History Review*, 54 (1980), 330–58 · *The Scotsman* (9 Jan 1954) · *The Times* (9 Jan 1954) · Burke, *Peerage* (1931), 2687 · Burke, *Peerage* (1947), 817–18 · *A good innings: the private papers of Viscount Lee of Fareham*, ed. A. Clark (1974) · CAC Cam., A. Geddes MSS · K. O. Morgan, *Consensus and disunity: the Lloyd George coalition government, 1918–1922* (1979) · P. Fraser, *Lord Esher: a political biography* (1973) · C. E. Harvey, 'Geddes, Auckland Campbell', *DBB* · *CGPLA Eng. & Wales* (1954)

Archives CAC Cam., personal and family corresp. and papers | BL OIOC, corresp. with Lord Curzon, MSS Eur. F 111–112 · HLRO, corresp. with Andrew Bonar Law · HLRO, corresp. with J. C. C. Davidson and Andrew Bonar Law · HLRO, corresp. with David Lloyd George, etc. · King's Lond., Liddell Hart C., corresp. with Sir B. H. Liddell Hart · PRO, MSS relating to relations between the British government and Rio Tinto Company in Spain, FO 371/21303, FO 371/22673 · RTZ Corporation, London, Rio Tinto Company archives, incl. board minute book, letter-books and staff books

Likenesses O. Edis, three photographs, 1916, NPG [*see illus.*] · W. Stoneman, two photographs, 1917, NPG · O. Edis, photograph, 1920, NPG · P. Bryant Baker, bust, priv. coll. · O. Edis, autochrome photograph, NPG

Wealth at death £67,801 4s. 4d.: probate, 22 Sept 1954, *CGPLA Eng. & Wales*

Geddes, Sir Eric Campbell (1875–1937), politician and businessman, was born at Agra, India, on 26 September 1875, the second of five children of Auckland Campbell Geddes, civil engineer, of Edinburgh and his wife, Christina Helen Macleod, daughter of the Revd Alexander Anderson, of Old Aberdeen.

Education, early career, and marriage Geddes was placed in a succession of public schools which included Merchiston Castle School, Edinburgh, and Oxford Military College, Cowley, where he passed the preliminary examination in

Sir Eric Campbell Geddes (1875–1937), by Howard Coster, 1936

preparation for entry into Woolwich and the Royal Engineers. However, he demonstrated more interest in rugby football than in study and was required to leave most of the schools he attended. In 1892 he sailed on a passenger liner for New York with an introduction to family friends in Pittsburgh, but spent the following two years in a sequence of jobs. He scraped a living as a Remington typewriter salesman, a labourer at Carnegie's steel works, and as a lumberman in west Virginia. In relation to his later career Geddes's experience as a brakeman on freight trains and as an assistant yard master on the Baltimore and Ohio Railway was more significant. In later life Geddes highlighted his origins as a railway porter as part of his 'self-made' mythologizing, and he deliberately emphasized his failure, in early life, to have 'climbed the ladder' of a successful career. He also extolled the benefits of experiencing life as a machine hand to gain insight of the working man's perspective, for any young man who was born to manage.

On Geddes's return home with little more money than he had taken, family contacts secured him a post with Carew & Co. to manage forest land in the Himalayan foothills. Subsequently he managed 50 miles of the Powayan steam tramway which the company controlled. His management of the tramway impressed the agent of the Rohilkhand and Kumaon Railway, who had worked under his father, and Geddes joined the company in 1899 and became its traffic superintendent two years later.

Geddes married Alice Gwendoline, daughter of the Revd Arthur Stokes, schoolmaster in India in 1900. The couple had three sons. He took home leave in 1903 to seek employment with a British railway company; and on his return to India he organized the transport of military forces on the railway, during a sharp deterioration in Anglo-Russian relations in 1904, which impressed Lord Kitchener as commander-in-chief. Later that year Geddes joined the North Eastern Railway (NER)—one of the largest transport enterprises in Britain—under its traffic apprenticeship scheme, and he became chief goods manager three years later. During this time his energy, focus on the larger issues, and clear judgement were identified as ideal executive qualities which were, increasingly, sought by other railway companies. In particular, his rigorous attention to statistical data to improve the volume of traffic and control operating costs was an impressive example of the NER's expertise in operating efficiency. In 1911 Geddes became deputy general manager on a salary of £5000 per annum with the promise of the general managership (in 1916) as a way of forestalling further overtures for his managerial skills. He benefited from an induction into the most innovatory management-conscious railway company in Britain.

Munitions and military railways In September 1914 Geddes became a raiser of manpower to ensure the availability of men with railway experience in an identifiable unit. His 17th (service) battalion, Northumberland Fusiliers (NER pioneers) was an unusual expression of local patriotism which took the form of an entire company-sponsored battalion. As government control of the railways became more centralized the prospect of vital war work at the NER diminished. In December 1914 Geddes was summoned to meet Lord Kitchener, then secretary of state for war, to discuss railway facilities in France, but it was not until Lloyd George founded the Ministry of Munitions in May 1915 that businessmen became temporary civil servants to supervise the enlarging industrial functions of the state. Geddes became the pre-eminent example (and survivor) of Lloyd George's 'man for the job' approach. As a deputy director of munitions supply he became responsible for the supply of rifles, machine guns, field guns, motor lorries, field kitchens, and innumerable other items, relishing his unorthodox interventionist 'comptroller' role. He investigated machine gun output and, in December 1915, became responsible for the new national filling factories. Geddes headed a semi-autonomous organization of managers and statisticians, many of whom were NER staff. As head of the gun ammunition department he earned a knighthood in 1916 and the undying gratitude of Lloyd George for improving shell output in time for the opening of the Somme offensive.

Lloyd George became secretary of state for war in July 1916 and he asked Geddes, 'will you come and put Transport right in France?' During a two-day visit at general headquarters Geddes impressed Haig who demanded his appointment as director-general of transportation in France, as his fourth principal staff officer. Geddes was already director-general of military railways at the War Office. This dual appointment, and the rank of major-general, quickly became a source of amazement. The transport base at general headquarters became known as Geddesburg and offended regular army opinion, but Haig relished Geddes's large-scale planning and his access to additional resources for the construction of an extensive light railway system to ensure that shells were rapidly transported to front-line artillery positions. Geddes noted, 'War is made up of the use of men, with munitions and movement as handmaids' (Geddes to Lloyd George, 8 Aug 1918, Lloyd George MSS P/18/2/8). In addition to tackling the problem of railway congestion, detailed surveys were made of port facilities, inland waterways, and roads so that traffic flow proceeded on a more integrated basis. In March 1917 Geddes's responsibilities expanded further with his appointment as inspector-general of communications in all theatres of war. However, he remained in France and was consulted by Haig on the timing of the Arras attack on 4 April 1917 because the light railways were a crucial feature of the timetabled supply system.

Geddes and Haig attached great importance to their Scottish identities and regretted the ending of their working partnership. In reflecting on the war years in 1920 Geddes described his period at general headquarters as 'the happiest time of my life' (Lloyd George MSS, G/252). His younger brother Auckland, later Lord Geddes, noted that during this period Eric 'radiated capacity' and it was his 'noontide hour' (Geddes, 240). Haig noted his 'quick intuition of requirements and his powers of drive and energy' (Haig to Lord Derby, 22 Nov 1917, Lloyd George MSS F/14/4/78). The pioneering role of Sir Eric Geddes as a civilian to rectify a supply problem in the military sphere was widely discussed during 1917 as one of the more notable, if unorthodox, achievements of civil–military relations in the war. It was remembered by Winston Churchill in August 1941 who in one of his 'Action this day' notes to the War Office stated, 'If you do not give me your very best man and one thoroughly capable of doing the work, I will look for a civilian of the Eric Geddes type, and have him invested with the necessary military rank' (M. Gilbert, *W. S. Churchill: Finest Hour, 1939–41*, 1983, 1152). Lloyd George's 'civilianizing' approach to malfunctioning aspects of the war effort was extended into the naval sphere in May 1917 when he appointed Geddes controller of the navy with responsibility for Admiralty dock facilities and shipyards. Geddes was required to adopt naval rank and was briefly both vice-admiral and major-general at the same time, which invoked many cartoon responses.

Geddes at the Admiralty Lloyd George wanted to create a separate supply department for the Admiralty, similar to the relationship of the Ministry of Munitions to the War Office as the relationship of ship construction rates to tonnage sunk deteriorated. However, Geddes and his (NER) staff—characterized in the Admiralty as 'bright people full of new ideas from the north' (W. James, *A Great Seaman*, 1956, 158)—obtained less than full control of shipyards in the three months that he grappled with the problem after May 1917. Lloyd George suspected intransigent naval custom and complacent organization throughout

the Admiralty and on 6 July 1917 replaced Carson as first lord of the Admiralty with Geddes. As political head of the Admiralty he became Unionist member of parliament for Cambridge University and, subsequently, was sworn of the privy council. As head of a fighting department, but not, initially, a member of the war cabinet, without political experience and more remote from the security of Lloyd George's personal supervision, organizational change and ministerial control were difficult to obtain at the Admiralty. His dismissal of the first sea lord, Admiral Sir John Jellicoe, to remove resistance to the convoy system, was a bruising experience in December 1917 for it was made without much ministerial support. Consequently, Geddes lobbied for an appointment as allied transport 'supremo' for all movements of manpower and material on the western and Italian fronts.

In 1918 Geddes found the admirals less difficult to work with but the clashes between an improviser *par excellence* and age-old naval traditions continued to highlight the problems which confronted administrators as they stepped into the political limelight without a sufficient 'hardening process'. During 1918 Geddes enjoyed opportunities to lead troubleshooting missions to Italy, north Russia, and the United States to review aspects of the naval war effort. As the war came to an end Geddes was anxious to ensure that the role of the British navy and mercantile marine was publicized to convey the point that the national contribution to victory did not merely comprise the armies on the western front. During 1918 the Admiralty board reorganization schemes were implemented in a more constructive context of mutual respect between the first sea lord, Admiral Sir Wester Wemyss, and commander-in-chief Grand Fleet, Admiral Sir David Beatty. In some ways the firmer determination to assert British offensive maritime power was illustrated by the Zeebrugge raid in April 1918. It was some recompense for the nagging feeling expressed by Geddes that he had become a politician against his better judgement.

Geddes and transport In January 1919 Beatty wrote to Geddes to regret his departure from the Admiralty. Geddes was firmly resolved on this course of action, but from October 1918 he was extremely unsettled about postwar prospects. Four posts of increasing significance had drawn him away from the NER, but the prospect of a political career was an insufferable idea. After the coalition manifesto was signed on 12 November, Lloyd George quickly appealed to Geddes to remain available 'for the organization of the immense questions of transportation' (Lloyd George MSS, F/18/2/26) during the further two years of government control of the railways. The coalition programme appeared to express national unity and social harmony and Geddes's imagination was captured by the 'priceless opportunity' (S. W. Roskill, *Hankey: Man of Secrets*, vol. 2) of organizing a state subsidized integrated transport network which he assumed would be a consensual, indeed depoliticized, scheme. As a couponed Unionist candidate at the general election Geddes came under pressure to clarify his position on 'making Germany pay' and on 9 December 1918 he said 'we will get everything out of her that you can squeeze out of a lemon and a bit more' (*The Times* 10 Dec 1918), which did not represent the gist of his early electioneering speeches. As there was no immediate prospect of legislation for a transport ministry Geddes co-ordinated demobilization and industrial rehabilitation in December 1918 which suggested the continuing relevance of wartime improvisers to rectify the immediate problems of peace. Large scale demobilization was another problem entirely without precedent but, more noticeably, the transforming power of business-men–ministers was less evident in conditions of peace.

Non-interventionist economic orthodoxy and issues of private ownership undermined plans for transport reorganization and by August 1919, when the Ministry of Transport was established, the idea of a 'supreme co-ordinating authority' had given way to the financial complexities of preparing the railways for decontrol. In the absence of the state's commitment to enhancing the national infrastructure, Geddes declared his opposition to nationalization and promoted the idea of private ownership with amalgamations in his cabinet paper 'Future transport policy' of 9 February 1920. Standardized wages and conditions of service and the settlement of 'incomprehensible' wartime railway agreements were hard-won achievements as the Railways Act of 1921 turned the Ministry of Transport into a watchdog, and the priority became financial stability in the industry and the savings which the department secured for the state. After over six years of close association with Lloyd George, Geddes departed as the last businessman-in-government in August 1921. In the years 1919–21 he was given a further troubleshooting role as chairman of the supply and transport committee (STC) and assumed a firm place in Labour's demonology as co-ordinator of the government's strike-breaking organization. His involvement was probably a case of practical transport experience rather than ideological fervour. He often seemed intent on narrowing the focus of the STC's contingency plans in the absence of cabinet agreement on the scenarios which would cause it to intervene. In September 1921 he noted that the STC should be disbanded, and although the power of trade unions worried Geddes, he was not a typical representative of a homogeneous political élite.

The Geddes axe As chairman of the committee on national expenditure in August 1921 Geddes participated in the dissolution of reconstructionist ideas. It was a final service to Lloyd George in the delivery of a highly publicized quest for retrenchment which acknowledged the failure of reconstruction. It also gave Geddes a reputation for fiscal management prior to his return to industry. Like many businessmen, he did not respect education expenditure but the main reason for the Geddes axe lay not with the chairman's desire for public economy, but with Lloyd George's attempts to sustain Conservative support for his premiership. It was confirmation of the assertion of Treasury control and the return to normality. In this way the partnership of Lloyd George and Geddes highlighted the political continuities and economic coherence of the

years 1915–21. Thereafter Geddes tended to assert the separateness of politics and business.

Later business career Geddes left the House of Commons in February 1922 and joined three months later the board of directors of Dunlop Rubber Company Ltd. In December 1922 he became chairman and his commitment to Dunlop was his largest business interest in his remaining years. In 1924 he became part-time chairman of Imperial Airways Ltd on a one day per week basis, although this commitment grew in later years. Dunlop's financial crisis represented a formidable business challenge which became clear in the Whinney report in September 1923. After 1924 he initiated a policy of acquisitions to diversify the product range beyond tyres to general rubber products. The productive capacity of Fort Dunlop near Birmingham was greatly extended in the years 1925–8 and Geddes paid particular attention to manufacturing layout, time and motion studies, and the exploration of management ideas. He was always interested in the latest 'American practice' and in his visits to the United States he sought opportunities to discuss work study while remaining sceptical of theoretical models of explanation. Instead, accountancy was an important aid to centralized control at Dunlop in the 1920s; and it became one of the most measured companies in Britain as the NER had been in the Edwardian era. In addition, he was fully aware that Dunlop's place in the market depended on the constant application of technological innovation. He was, frequently, the first critical consumer of Dunlop's newly marketed lines. Alongside the importance of scientific research he recognized the revolutionary impact of mass production, for example, on the debate on protective tariffs, such as the McKenna duties. Geddes had a combative approach to the defence of Dunlop's interests in dialogue with governments and tributes to his energy and vision in 1937 mentioned the same qualities of commitment and purpose which were noted at the end of his ministerial career in 1922.

As part-time chairman of Imperial Airways, Geddes used the same purposeful approach, contributing to the development of a commercial air service and the promotion of 'air-mindedness'. His knowledge of transport and his experience of Whitehall were vital qualities, as continuous contact with the Air Ministry was an inevitable feature of managing a subsidized 'chosen instrument' of the government's civil air policy. Under Geddes's chairmanship empire routes were negotiated and the hostility towards the overland flight paths was confronted. To publicize the flying boat Geddes undertook an aerial cruise on Britain's western seaboard in 1928. In 1929 he visited Australia to promote an extension of the weekly service between Britain and India and he participated fully in the inter-governmental agreements which led to the first air-mail flight to Australia in 1934. He undertook a tour of inspection of the Cape to Cairo link in 1932 and having negotiated with all the governments en route he drafted the first law of the air. The long haul scheduled 'flying hotel' services served the all-up empire airmail scheme for which Imperial Airways were paid a tightly negotiated fee. The financial structure drew increasing controversy but the original conception became an exciting visual expression of imperial unity in the 1930s. Much was expected of the state-subsidized airline and criticism in parliament in 1936 brought the monopolistic phase of British commercial aviation to an end. By this stage a full-time chairman was needed to direct the business, not least because the airline was more obviously a national and strategic asset. To use his own phrase Geddes led the 'steady, conservative building-up of the Company' (Geddes to Hoare, 5 Aug 1929, Templewood MSS, TEM V:4) during experimental years of low capacity and high maintenance costs.

Assessment and death Lloyd George concluded that Geddes was 'one of the most remarkable products of the great War' (tribute, 23 June 1937, Lloyd George MSS, G/8/7/21). His work provided evidence that total war in the early twentieth century was as much a matter of continuous supply and organizational elasticity as it was of mobilization and operational planning. He offered systematic plans and had to confront the assumptions which separated civil and military spheres of the war effort. The participation in Lloyd George's coalition government of businessmen–ministers proved contentious as party politics returned to normality and the active spending state was dissolved. Geddes was president of the Federation of British Industries in the years 1923–5 and expressed frustration with adverse trading conditions in Europe. He sought to influence government policy on specific issues but usually saw the spheres of politics and industry as separate after 1922. He remained in contact with few politicians, with the exception of Lloyd George.

Geddes had a reputation for 'pushful' force, impatience, independent thought, and unremitting toil and it was a measure of his significance as a 'captain of industry' or 'superman' that he was asked by the Bank of England to advise the board of the Lancashire Cotton Corporation from October 1931 to August 1932. He was a hard-working, technically proficient Scot of large stature whose respect for innovation in the transport sphere knew few equals. He was enthusiastic and often inspirational but his managerial approach did not always make for harmony.

After Geddes's knighthood in 1916 he was subsequently appointed KCB (military) in 1917, GBE in the same year, and GCB (civil) in 1919; he declined a peerage unless it could be for his life only; the honorary degree of LLD was conferred on him by Sheffield University in 1920 and he was president of the Institute of Transport in 1919–20. His wife's health had deteriorated and after 1912 she became, in effect, permanently invalided, which his brother Auckland noted as his 'inner sorrow'. Geddes died at his country house, Albourne Place, near Hassocks, Sussex, on 22 June 1937 after a long illness, his wife dying in 1945. After cremation his ashes were placed on an Empire flying boat of Imperial Airways and scattered in the English Channel off the Isle of Wight.   KEITH GRIEVES

Sources private information (2004) • A. C. Geddes, *The forging of a family* (1952) • D. Lloyd George, *War memoirs*, 6 vols. (1933–6) • *The Times* (23 June 1937) • K. Grieves, *Sir Eric Geddes: business and government in war and peace* (1989) • P. K. Cline, 'Eric Geddes and the "experiment" with businessmen in government, 1915–22', *Essays in anti-labour history*, ed. K. Brown (1974), 74–104 • K. Grieves, 'Improvising the British war effort: Eric Geddes and Lloyd George, 1915–18', *War and Society*, 7 (1989), 40–55 • K. Grieves, 'Sir Eric Geddes, Lloyd George and the transport problem, 1918–21', *Journal of Transport History*, 3rd ser., 13 (1992), 23–42 • *DNB* • S. Armitage, *The politics of decontrol of industry: Britain and the United States* (1969) • R. Bell, *Twenty-five years of the North-Eastern Railway, 1898–1922* (1951) • J. C. W. Reith, *Into the wind* (1949) • S. W. Roskill, *The period of Anglo-American antagonism, 1919–1929* (1968), vol. 1 of *Naval policy between the wars* • S. W. Roskill, 'The dismissal of Admiral Jellicoe', *Journal of Contemporary History*, 1 (1966), 69–83 • R. Storrs, *Dunlop in war and peace* (1946) • C. Tennyson, *Stars and markets* (1957) • Lord Riddell, *Intimate diary of the peace conference and after, 1918–23* (1933) • R. Higham, *Britain's imperial air routes, 1918 to 1939* (1960) • M. J. Daunton, *Royal Mail: the Post Office since 1840* (1985) • Lord Beaverbrook, *The decline and fall of Lloyd George* (1963) • *CGPLA Eng. & Wales* (1937) • HLRO, Lloyd George papers • CUL, Templewood MSS

Archives PRO, corresp. and papers relating to ministry of munitions, SUPP 12 • PRO, corresp. as first lord of the admiralty, ministry of transport and supply and transport committee, air ministry and cabinet, ADM 116/1804–10; MT49; AIR 19; CAB 24 | BL, corresp. with Arthur James Balfour, Add. MSS 49709, *passim* • BL OIOC, corresp. with Sir John Anderson, MS Eur. F 207 • CAC Cam., corresp. with his brother Baron Geddes • HLRO, corresp. with Andrew Bonar Law • HLRO, corresp. with J. C. C. Davidson and Andrew Bonar Law • HLRO, corresp. with David Lloyd George, etc. • IWM, corresp. with Sir Henry Wilson • NA Scot., corresp. with A. J. Balfour • NMM, corresp. with Katherine Furse • U. Warwick Mod. RC, corresp. with W. G. Granet | FILM BFI NFTVA, documentary footage • BFI NFTVA, news footage, 4 Feb 1919 • BFI NFTVA, news footage, 7 March 1918 • BFI NFTVA, news footage, 16 June 1922

Likenesses W. Stoneman, photograph, 1917, NPG • group portrait, photograph, 1918 (with members of the royal family), IWM • H. Oliver, oils, 1919, Gov. Art Coll. • J. Guthrie, oil study, c.1919–1921, Scot. NPG • O. Edis, autochrome photograph, c.1920–1929 • R. G. Eves, oils, c.1922, Dunlop Group of Companies, London • J. Guthrie, group portrait, oils, c.1924–1930 (*Statesmen of World War I*), NPG • F. May, gouache caricature, 1935, NPG • H. Coster, photograph, 1936, NPG [*see illus.*] • B. Partridge, watercolour and pen-and-ink caricature (as Mrs Partington), NPG; repro. in *Punch Almanack* (1922)

Wealth at death £100,432 0s. 7d.: probate, 3 Aug 1937, *CGPLA Eng. & Wales*

Geddes, James (1710–1749), author, was born in the county of Peeblesshire, the son of James Geddes of Rachan. He was educated at home and at the University of Edinburgh, where he distinguished himself in mathematics. He afterwards practised with success as an advocate. Andrew *McDouall, Lord Bankton, married his sister Isobel. In 1748 his *Essay on the Composition and Manner of Writing of the Antients, Particularly Plato* was published at Glasgow. A German translation appeared in the third and fourth volumes of *Sammlung vermischter Schriften zur Beförderung der schönen Wissenschaften* (1759). Geddes died of consumption in 1749.   GORDON GOODWIN, rev. PHILIP CARTER

Sources J. Geddes, preface, *An essay on the composition and manner of writing of the antients, particularly Plato* (1748)

Geddes, Jenny (*fl.* **1637**), supposed religious activist, is traditionally credited with having begun the demonstrations against Charles I's new Scottish prayer book when it was used for the first time in St Giles's, Edinburgh, on 23

July 1637. Her parentage is unknown, and indeed it is not entirely certain that she existed at all. There is no doubt that the riot in St Giles's was started by women, and a near-contemporary anonymous satire mentions a woman who 'did cast a stoole' at the dean of St Giles's, James Hannay, as he read from the new book (Rothes, 199). The caster of the stool is not identified until 1670, when she is referred to as 'Jane (or Janot) Gaddis (yet living at the time of this relation)' (Baker, 478). In the light of this reference, sense can be made of an allusion in a 1661 pamphlet *Edinburgh's Joy for his Majestie's Coronation in England*. It satirically describes celebrations in Scotland of Charles II's Restoration, including the deeds of 'the immortal Jenet Geddis, Princess of the Tron Adventurers', a seller of vegetables who dominated women of a similar status. Geddes's 'immortality' evidently lay in her being alleged to have been the first to resort to violence in the events that led to Britain's civil wars: and the moral of the pamphlet of 1661 is that she had repented and rejoiced at the return to royal government. However, no other sources mention Geddes's name. James Kirkton wrote in 1679 that 'First, ane unknown obscure woman threw her stool' (Lothian, 24–5), while an English source of 1694 calls her 'the old Herbswoman at Edinburgh' (ibid., 26). Robert Wodrow in 1705 suggested another name, recording it as 'the constant believed tradition' that the first stool thrower was Barbara Hamilton, the wife of Robert Mean, a well-known presbyterian sympathizer (Wodrow, 1.64).

However, it was Geddes who survived in popular tradition, as is shown by *The History of the Most Famous and Most Renowned Janny Geddes* (1730s?), which indicates that 'a scolding woman mad' was known as 'a Janny Geddes':

So—when a scolding woman mad is,
She's called, e're since, A JANNY GEDDES.
(Lothian, 25)

Reference to Geddes in Sir Walter Scott's *Tales of a Grandfather* (1830) was influential in preserving her fame, which was also celebrated in a poem by John Stuart Blackie. A plaque placed in St Giles's in 1886 also commemorates her deed according to 'constant oral tradition', and a bronze stool was added in 1992 (Lothian, 27). Robert Burns was less reverential, calling his old mare Jenny Geddes.

Jenny was used as a generic name for Scottish women, the equivalent of Jock for men, and a satirical Scottish 'litany' of about 1640 asks for deliverance:

From Gutter Jennie, pulpit Jockie,
From all such head-controlling tayles
(Maidment, 57)

It may be that the generic Gutter Jenny evolved into the heroic Jenny Geddes to create a symbolic individual commemorating the major role played by women demonstrators in the early months of the covenanting movement.

DAVID STEVENSON

Sources M. Lothian, *The cutty stool* (1995) · *DNB* · John, earl of Rothes, *A relation of proceedings concerning the affairs of the Kirk of Scotland*, Bannatyne Club, 37 (1830) · R. Baker, *Chronicle*, continuation to 5th edn (1670) · R. Wodrow, *Analecta, or, Materials for a history of remarkable providences, mostly relating to Scotch ministers and Christians*, ed. [M. Leishman], 4 vols., Maitland Club, 60 (1842–3) · J. Maidment, *A book of Scottish pasquils* (1868)

Geddes, John (1735–1799), coadjutor vicar apostolic of the lowland district, was born on 29 August 1735 at the Mains of Corridoun in the Enzie of Banffshire, the son of John Geddes (*d.* 1747) and his wife, Marjory Burgess (*d.* 1753), both of whom were probably farm workers and certainly Catholics. He started school at Rathven, Banffshire, in 1742, living during the week with his great-uncle John Burgess. Following the frustration of a 'scheme of adoption and education in the Protestant religion' (Anderson, 'Autobiographical notes', 41), in November 1743 he moved to a school at Cairnfield, where he was joined by his cousin Alexander Geddes, the future biblical scholar. He left Cairnfield in 1745, and was educated at home, at Rathven, and Litchiestown until Alexander Godsman established his school at the Preshome mission in 1748. From there Geddes was sent to the Scots College, Rome, in 1749, entering in 1750. He appears to have considered and rejected entering the Society of Jesus in 1752. At Rome he became a friend of the future vicar apostolic of the lowland district George Hay. Geddes was ordained priest in March 1759 and returned to Scotland that August; he was based at the Shenval mission in Banffshire, where he lived alongside the Jacobite vicar apostolic of the highland district, Hugh Macdonald.

In 1762 Geddes became superior of the small seminary at Scalan, also in Banffshire. He renewed the sub-tack on the land, and was able to raise a new stone building for the seminary. It was completed in 1767, when Geddes left for the mission at Preshome.

Two years later Geddes was given the task of re-establishing the Scottish seminary in Spain. This had been founded in Madrid by the soldier and courtier William Sempill in 1623 with the stipulation that the college be administered by Jesuits, and had lapsed following the expulsion of the Jesuits from Spain in 1767. Geddes arrived in Spain in April 1770. The effects of the college had already been recognized as the property of the secular clergy, but a petition from the Scottish bishops had been misinterpreted, and the Spanish government had merged the Scots College with its Irish counterpart at Alcalá. Geddes secured new premises for the college in the former Jesuit college of San Ambrosio, Valladolid, and was able to admit a deacon and three boys transferred from Douai and Paris in December 1770. Geddes himself moved to Valladolid in March 1771. He continued to display diplomatic acumen, negotiating the college's royal charter and permanent establishment at Valladolid, obtained in 1778. He was less successful in attempts to gain Spanish government support for the Scottish mission, although in 1780 he was awarded a pension of £106 p.a. for life. He was a controversial rector, allowing his students greater freedom to mingle with each other and with townspeople than the Scottish bishops thought proper, but his friendships with local administrators and Scottish businessmen in Spain helped integrate Valladolid into the intellectual and economic geography of Scottish and Spanish religious life.

In 1779, in the wake of the riots at Edinburgh against the Scottish Catholic Relief Bill, Bishop Hay offered Geddes the position of coadjutor vicar apostolic of the lowland district. On 30 November 1780 Geddes was ordained bishop of Morocco *in partibus*, and he arrived in Edinburgh in May 1781. It was probably hoped that the gregarious Geddes would provide a face for Scottish Catholicism that non-Catholics would find unthreatening, while applying his diplomatic experience to the problems of Catholics in a Scotland undergoing economic and social upheaval. He familiarized himself with the district through a series of arduous walking tours which did not restrict themselves to Catholic areas, observing and gathering information that could help adapt the requirements of the lowland mission to a Catholic population increasing through migration from the highlands and from Ireland. Between 1781 and 1793 he paid regular visits to Glasgow, where the Catholic congregation grew from five to about 300 during the period, and worked towards establishing a permanent Catholic chapel there with a resident minister. The congregation in Edinburgh also increased; in 1784 he moved to a new residence and chapel at 35 Blackfriars Wynd, but it proved necessary to maintain the old chapel on the same street. Geddes was not a controversialist, but it was widely known or suspected that he thought it possible to reach salvation without outward communion with the church, a position opposite to that expressed by Bishop Hay in *The Sincere Christian*. Geddes was too mindful of the security of the Scottish church to publish his reservations. He had a friendly relationship with his cousin Alexander Geddes, and in their correspondence pressed the historian to be more respectful towards scholarly tradition and Catholic teaching.

Geddes was an active participant in the intellectual life of Scotland. He was elected a member of the Scottish Society of Antiquaries soon after his return, and was a frequent guest at the 'learned suppers' held by the judge James Burnett, Lord Monboddo. He contributed to the *Encyclopaedia Britannica*, through which he became a friend of the Scottish episcopalian clergyman George Gleig, a controversial connection as many leading episcopalians at the time were opposed to Catholic relief. At one point Geddes's relations with the episcopalians were so close that it was suggested the Edinburgh Catholics share the episcopalians' new chapel, an offer Geddes declined. Geddes's circle also included some leading Church of Scotland figures, such as the historian and minister William Robertson. He also befriended Robert Burns, who borrowed Geddes's copy of his poems between August 1787 and February 1789, writing new verse on fourteen of the blank leaves. This 'Geddes Burns' was subsequently acquired by the Huntington Library, San Marino, California. Geddes also wrote a treatise against duelling and *The Life of Saint Margaret, Queen of Scotland* (1794); in the preface to the latter the ever sensitive Geddes apologized to non-Catholic readers for the Catholic sentiments expressed throughout the book. He began preparing a New Testament in English for the use of Scottish Catholics in 1790, to be based on Bishop Richard Challoner's edition, but this, like his projected history of Scottish Catholicism, was overtaken by events. The material he collected for the history was subsequently placed in the Scottish Catholic Archives, Edinburgh.

Geddes visited France between October 1791 and May 1792 in an unsuccessful attempt to resolve the friction between the Scots College, Paris, and the Scottish bishops, complicated by the national assembly's moves against the involvement of the church in education. At Hay's urging Geddes carried out with little difficulty the negotiations which secured the Act for the Relief of Roman Catholics in Scotland in 1793. This could be regarded as a triumph for his sociable approach to the coadjutorship, where he had made great progress in persuading Scottish opinion to accept Catholicism once more as part of the mainstream of Scottish culture, but it proved to form the end of his active career.

Since the previous summer Geddes had been suffering from a gradual paralysis in his left arm which began to spread across his body. In an attempt to restore his health, he moved to Scalan in July 1793, but there it became clear he would need better care and facilities and he travelled on to Aberdeen, where he was nursed by his nephews John Gordon and Charles Gordon, both priests. Hay took over in Edinburgh and also managed Geddes's financial affairs; as a bishop, Geddes rarely kept proper accounts, and between 1793 and 1799 his debts were reduced from £900 to £150. After November 1794 he was bedridden, although his mind remained active. An additional coadjutor, Alexander Cameron, his successor at Valladolid, was appointed in 1797. Geddes died at the Chapel House, Aberdeen, on 11 February 1799 and was buried on 15 February in the Snow churchyard, near King's College, Old Aberdeen.

MATTHEW KILBURN

Sources J. A. Stothert, 'George Hay, 1769–1811', *The Catholic church in Scotland*, ed. J. F. S. Gordon (1869), 12–453 · 'John Geddes', *The Catholic church in Scotland*, ed. J. F. S. Gordon (1869), 454–8 · W. J. Anderson, 'The autobiographical notes of Bishop John Geddes', *Innes Review*, 18 (1967), 36–57 · M. Taylor, *The Scots College in Spain* (1971) · J. Darragh, *The Catholic hierarchy of Scotland: a biographical list, 1653–1985* (1986) · R. C. Fuller, *Alexander Geddes, 1737–1802: a pioneer of biblical criticism* (1984) · A. MacWilliam, 'The Glasgow mission, 1792–1799', *Innes Review*, 4 (1953) · '*Ambula coram Deo*: the journal of Bishop Geddes for the year 1790', ed. D. McRoberts, *Innes Review*, 6 (1955), 46–68, 131–43 · *The letters of Robert Burns*, ed. J. de Lancey Ferguson, 2nd edn, ed. G. Ross Roy, 2 vols. (1985), vol. 1, pp. 366–7 · P. J. Anderson, ed., *Records of the Scots colleges at Douai, Rome, Madrid, Valladolid and Ratisbon*, New Spalding Club, 30 (1906), 136, 203–8 · J. F. McMillan, 'Development, 1707–1820', *The Scots College Rome, 1600–2000*, ed. R. McCluskey (2000), 43–66

Archives Scottish Catholic Archives, Edinburgh, journals, notebooks, and papers | Scottish Catholic Archives, Edinburgh, corresp. with J. P. Coghlan

Likenesses portrait, *c.*1780, Scots College, Valladolid, Spain; repro. in Taylor, *Scots College*, facing p. 112 · Fraser?, portrait, Blairs Museum, Aberdeenshire; repro. in Geddes, '*Ambula coram deo*', facing p. 48 · engraving, repro. in Stothert, 'George Hay', facing p. 454

Wealth at death approx. £150 in debt: Taylor, *Scots College*

Geddes, Michael (*c.*1647–1713), Church of England clergyman, was born in Scotland, the son of Robert Geddes of 'Cornhill in Marcy's' (probably Cornhill, Aberdeenshire), gentleman. He was educated at the University of Edinburgh, where he graduated MA in 1668. He matriculated at Oxford on 13 December 1669, aged twenty-two, at Gloucester Hall (now Worcester College) and was incorporated from Balliol College on 11 July 1671. Not much is known of Geddes's life at Oxford, except that he met Anthony Wood there.

In 1678 Geddes went to Lisbon to take up a post as chaplain of the English factory there. In 1686 the Inquisition forbade him to continue his work despite a privilege negotiated by treaty which never before had been called into question. The English merchants complained to Henry Compton, who as bishop of London was responsible for the church beyond the seas, but before action could be taken, Geddes was suspended by James II's ecclesiastical commission and forced to wait for the English envoy, Mr Scarborough, who was to take over all responsibility in matters of religion. Geddes returned to England in May 1688 and was rector of Farmington, Gloucestershire, which he exchanged in 1693 for that of Compton Bassett, Wiltshire. In 1691 his fellow Scot Gilbert Burnet made him chancellor of the diocese of Salisbury after the latter's promotion to that see. Geddes's wife was Elizabeth, possibly the Elizabeth Packer, or Parker, of Groombridge, Kent, who married a Michael Geddes at St Mary Somerset, London, on 27 March 1696; together they had three sons, Gilbert, Michael, and John.

Burnet remembered Geddes as:

> a learned and a wise man; he had a true notion of popery, as a political combination, managed by falsehood and cruelty, to establish a temporal empire in the person of the popes. All his thoughts and studies were chiefly employed in detecting this; of which he has given many useful and curious essays in the treatises he wrote, which are all highly valuable. (G. Burnet, *History of the Reformation*, ed. N. Pocock, 7 vols., 1865, 3.306)

The history of the church of Malabar, from the time of its being discover'd by the Portuguezes in the year 1501, giving an account of the persecutions and violent methods of the Roman prelates, to reduce them to the subjection of the church of Rome (1694) was more than an exercise in the black legend of popish cruelty. It sought to show how the existence of this ancient church served to prove, 'That there has always been a considerable visible Church upon Earth, that never believed the doctrines of the Pope's supremacy, purgatory, transubstantiation, adoration of images, auricular confession, &c.' (sig. *3r).

In 1695 Geddes was awarded a Lambeth LLD. His next work, *The Church-History of Ethiopia* (1696), was similarly intended as:

> the history of a Church that was never at any time under the papal yoke, and which when its princes, instead of being nursing fathers, struggled hard of late years to have brought its neck under it; never rested until it had both broke that insupportable yoke asunder, and secured it self from ever having the like attempts made again upon its liberty. (sig. A2r)

This was an apt subject for the Church after 1688, and dedicated to Bishop Compton who had provided the first check to James II's attempt to impose the papal yoke on England. Geddes's third work, *The Council of Trent No Free Assembly* (1697), pursued the anti-popish theme, providing a translation by leading participants which he had been asked to translate from Spanish by Bishop Edward Stillingfleet, and putting Trent into the historical perspective of the bondage into which the papacy had brought the general councils of the church. His three-volume *Miscellaneous Tracts* went through several editions (1702–06, 1709–14, and 1730). *Several Tracts Against Popery* (1715) and *The most Celebrated Popish Ecclesiastical Romance, being the Life of Veronica, of Milan* (1716), a translation which Geddes began but was unable to complete, were published posthumously.

On 3 October 1710 Geddes became rector of East Hendred, Berkshire. He seems to have moved to his new parish and erected a charity school in the village in 1711. He died there on Sunday 12 April 1713, aged sixty-five, and was buried on the 18th in St Augustine's parish church at East Hendred. A memorial stone was erected in the south wall of the tower. In his will, dated 28 March 1712, he bequeathed the yearly interest of shares worth about £1500, invested in Bank of England stock and a mortgage to the City of London, to his wife. He also left £20 to his brother Henry and 20s. for a mourning ring and the choice of six books from his library to Gilbert Burnet. His Bank of England stock was to go to his son Gilbert after his wife's death, and the rest of his estate was to be divided between his sons Gilbert and John, to be paid out to them when they reached the age of twenty-one. His other son, Michael, had presumably died before the drawing up of the will. On 10 June 1713 probate was granted to his wife, whom he had appointed executor. His library was sold on 10 May 1714 at Exeter Exchange in the Strand, London.

MARJA SMOLENAARS

Sources A. L. Humphreys, *East Hendred: a Berkshire parish historically treated* (1923) · Foster, *Alum. Oxon.* · *DNB* · will, PRO, PROB 121/533, sig. 134 (fol. 303v)
Wealth at death approx. £1600: will, PRO, PROB 121/533, sig. 134

Geddes, Sir Patrick (1854–1932), social evolutionist and city planner, was born at Ballater, west Aberdeenshire, Scotland, on 2 October 1854, the youngest son of Alexander Geddes (1808–1899), and his wife, Janet Stivenson. His father was a quartermaster in the Black Watch; his mother came from a family of strict Presbyterian covenanters.

Early life and education Geddes' youth was spent near Perth and he attended the Perth Academy until he was sixteen. He was an able student but his early passions were not so much for scholarship as for vigorous outdoor activity, especially long country rambles and gardening, both activities which he undertook with his father. They inspired in him a deep love of nature and a desire to study the relatively recent concept of evolution. His mother wished her much-loved youngest son to enter the church but he had lost his faith. Geddes was typical of his generation in rejecting religion as the key to understanding the universe, and seeking to replace it with science. His

Sir Patrick Geddes (1854–1932), by Lafayette, 1931

father, though, did not approve of Geddes' idea of attending the University of Edinburgh to study natural sciences. Instead, he wanted him to follow in the footsteps of his more successful older brother (Geddes had two surviving brothers and one sister, all much older than he) and have a career in banking. Geddes managed a compromise. He would become a bank clerk for a year and if he still did not wish to pursue that career, his father would permit him to enrol at the University of Edinburgh. He worked in a bank for eighteen months between 1871 and 1873 before his father relented. Thus, in 1874, at the age of twenty, he was finally permitted to go to Edinburgh.

Despite having waited so long for the chance to study, Geddes left Edinburgh University at the end of his first week. His natural impetuosity had led him to this quick rejection—he wanted to study evolution and not the course that was offered. He thus became determined to study under Thomas Huxley, the greatest proponent of Darwinian evolution, who was then teaching a four-month intensive course in the natural sciences at the Royal School of Mines in London (within a training programme for engineering students). Huxley was kind to this dedicated and bright Scottish student, who had to wait eight months in London before the short course started and showed himself to be both enthusiastic and talented in his pursuit of the subject. Huxley subsequently employed him as a demonstrator on the course. He also sent him for further scientific training to his friend Professor Lacaze-Duthiers of the Sorbonne, Paris,

when Geddes needed a period of convalescence after illness in the summer of 1878. Geddes went to the marine station of the University of Paris, which was located at Roscoff in Brittany. As a result, he became passionate about the efficacy of marine stations as educational tools for the teaching of natural sciences and he had an introduction to French life and culture (as he went back to Paris in the autumn of 1878 with the Sorbonne students) which was to influence him deeply. Back in London, Huxley tried to obtain for Geddes some form of employment but Geddes had no degree and, despite his gratitude and admiration for the master, he sometimes ignored Huxley's advice.

What had begun to obsess Geddes was what he had found in Paris. He had met Edmond Demolins of the Le Playist Société d'Economie Sociale and had been introduced to the attempts being made to develop a Le Playist social science dedicated to securing peaceful social evolution in the future. This interested Geddes intensely—he saw it as the mission to which he wanted to devote his life. With Le Play's formula for studying society—'lieu, travail, famille' ('place, work, folk')—Geddes began his quest to relate the natural sciences to the social sciences. His interests were pushed further in this direction after 1880 when, on a field trip to Mexico, he suffered a temporary blindness which ruled out a career as a microbiologist (as microscopal work would strain his eyesight); his mother had become blind through overstraining her eyes and that was enough to deter Geddes. Besides, he had already begun his own mission towards finding a way of using the insights of evolution science to understand modern society. He was convinced that the only possible method was the same as in microbiology—observation. However, instead of looking down a microscope, he needed to observe human society. He thus began a lifelong interest in cities (arguably the most complicated human environment) and spent much time travelling and walking around them. In this way he became deeply interested in the study of the manner in which modern conditions interacted with city development.

First contributions to the social sciences Geddes chose Edinburgh as the context for his research. As a boy, he had visited Scotland's ancient capital with his father. Now he gained a living as a demonstrator in zoology at the university and a demonstrator at the medical school. During the 1880s he was also to engage in voluntary work in the city, though always with the ultimate purpose of studying city development in his mind. In 1867 the lord provost of Edinburgh had launched an improvement scheme to demolish the worst areas of the Old Town and to regenerate it with new buildings. In this context, Geddes learned at first hand about the problems of urban renewal. As a scientist he was aware of the importance of context and history in evolution and he worked on a voluntary basis to save the old houses of Edinburgh from demolition as a matter of urgency, preserving the best of the past to influence the development of the best in the future. He undertook rehabilitation schemes in the Royal Mile with the help of teams of volunteers, mostly students, whom he inspired.

Urban renewal and the preservation of historic buildings were related in his thinking with a new way of developing the evolutionary potential not just of place but also of people, including the students of Edinburgh University.

Geddes ordered his ideas into a theory of 'civics' which was related to current theories of citizenship but had a more immediate purpose of training young people to understand their environment so that they could cherish it for the benefit of future generations. Civics was applied sociology—the way in which enlightened individuals could work for their local city. As part of his educational work in Edinburgh he purchased the old camera obscura building near the castle in 1892 and set it up as a museum, called the Outlook Tower. The work he did there, inventing ways of looking at the city based on geographical, historical, and sociological perspectives, was a major part of his contribution to the evolution of social sciences in Britain. A number of Edinburgh students were to continue this work, including Victor Branford, who became a businessman but used his money both to support Outlook Tower activities and to set up the British Sociological Society (in 1903); A. J. Herbertson, who was recruited by H. J. Mackinder when he set up the first institute of geography at a British university in Oxford in 1899; and T. R. Marr, who went to Manchester, after a period of running the Outlook Tower, to work as the warden of the university settlement there. There were many others. Geddes' mode of operation was to inspire others while he himself continued his never-ending study of evolution within civic society. He even invented his own graphical method for charting his ideas which he called his 'Thinking Machines'. Yet his personal museum, the Outlook Tower, for all the vitality he poured into it and the inspiration it gave to many who visited it, was a failure. Its expenses always outran its income and Geddes' volunteer helpers found it hard to keep up with his next idea.

In the 1880s Geddes had not yet given up the idea that he should pursue an academic career at the University of Edinburgh, and he undertook research for his first monograph with one of his students, J. Arthur Thomson, who became another of his lifelong admirers. Together they produced *The Evolution of Sex*, which was published in 1889. The work made his reputation, though the subject was of a controversial nature at that time. This was especially so in this case as Geddes wrote his chapters speculating about the ways in which sex in nature could help an understanding of sex in human society. Geddes based his ideas on the then fashionable cell theory: masculinity and femininity were decided by cell structure. His view on the women's movement was that 'what was decided among the prehistoric protozoa cannot be annulled by acts of parliament' (*The Evolution of Sex*, 269). Yet he was a revolutionary conservative. He promised the many women who flocked to help him in his voluntary schemes that the reward for their labours to promote favourable evolutionary environments would, at the same time, lead to their own heightened personal individuality. As such they would become outstanding people able to experience to the full all human emotions. He even hinted that this would increase their chances of developing the deepest and most satisfactory sexual relationships with their future spouses. These ideas were to make Geddes and Thomson influential nationally and internationally for a decade. Women particularly came to the annual summer schools that he began in 1885 at the Granton Marine Station of the University of Edinburgh (which he had helped to set up). These initially were designed to help schoolteachers acquire the necessary knowledge to teach the natural sciences, especially in elementary schools. (Geddes and Thomson were to campaign successfully to have the subject included in the Scottish school code of 1899.) After Geddes had acquired the Outlook Tower in the 1890s, his summer schools became more ambitious and more directly related to his primary objective—the study of evolution in society. Women still made up a good proportion of those who attended, and the schools reached a peak of popularity with about 120 students in 1896.

Geddes met his future wife through his voluntary work in Edinburgh. Anna Morton (1857–1917) was the daughter of a Liverpool merchant of Irish descent who had gone to Edinburgh to visit her sister, married to James Oliphant, an Edinburgh schoolmaster. Oliphant had helped Geddes form his first little Environment Society in 1884. Geddes and Anna were married in April 1886. They had a family of three children: Norah (1887–1967), Alasdair (1891–1917), and Arthur (1895–1968). Anna worked tirelessly to free Geddes from the cares of everyday life and to help him in his peripatetic role as urban troubleshooter. She provided the stability and back-up which enabled him to sustain many of his schemes. Although he was not to secure a position at the University of Edinburgh, the success of *The Evolution of Sex* gained him a chair in botany at the University of Dundee in 1889, endowed especially for him by a benefactor, J. Martin White of Perth. Geddes had known White since boyhood and had accompanied him as a tutor–companion on a continental tour just before his marriage. The Dundee chair was to be the only regular source of income in Geddes' life for the next thirty years, until he transferred to the University of Bombay in 1919 (having worked in India since 1914) where he was given a similar contract. He enjoyed special conditions. He was only required to teach for three months each year; for the rest of the time he was free to devote himself to the double task of earning extra income and continuing his researches on city development—usually managing to combine the two.

Achievements of his middle years It took Geddes two decades to find a role as a sociological town planner. That was because 'town planning' was not yet a recognized activity in the modern sense and indeed the first housing act in Britain which included the term was not passed until 1909. In any event, Geddes was not interested in just the physical layout of new town extension schemes (the subject of the 1909 legislation). He was concerned with social evolution and the role cities played in this as repositories of the key cultural influences of past and present. In the 1890s the focus of his attention was Edinburgh, where he lived at Ramsay Gardens, a romantic and yet modern block of flats that he managed to get built on a co-operative basis on the best site of the Old City, on the Castle Esplanade, in 1893. His activities revolved round three major areas: the rehabilitation of medieval houses in the Old City, which he transformed into student halls of residence for the university which, hitherto, had had no such facility; the further development of the summer schools as a means for exploring the role of culture and civilization in forming the present; and the Outlook Tower, which he wanted to be a regional and national museum.

Geddes was a pioneer of regionalism and as such wanted a unit for study which could contain all the elements of human society. His answer was the 'valley section', a diagrammatic representation of a region based on a river, from source in the mountains to mouth at the sea. This unit thus encompassed every type of occupation from hunters and foresters in the mountains and farmers on the plains, to the citizens and seafarers at the port. In cultural terms he believed, as a scientific social evolutionist, that regional study had a double function which both made possible a sense of personal identity and provided the means for understanding the world. (The sense of self in a particular context was the equivalent of the evolutionist's equation: Environment/function/organism = Organism/function/environment, i.e., Efo = Ofe.) Geddes' ideas on regionalism made him a pioneer of environmental education, but he wanted more than just an academic outcome. In 1913 he formed the International Regional Survey Association, which was unable to thrive because of the outbreak of the First World War. However, during the hostilities, Geddes preached the importance of regionalism as an antidote to conflict. War was the outcome of the machinations of national governments based in capital cities; regional centres, on the other hand, were dedicated to peaceful exchanges of goods and ideas. During the First World War, together with Victor Branford, Geddes published a series of volumes under the title The Making of the Future, which included in his own works a plea for what he called 'The Third Alternative'—the way to peaceful social evolution through regionalism.

Since his youth, the alternatives for the future had seemed to be either capitalism or socialism. Geddes had not wanted to opt for either. For him they were both too abstract—after the revolution, what then? What concerned him more was the practical result of the change. As a young man seeking to make his reputation, he had written a number of pamphlets in the 1880s including On the Conditions of Progress of the Capitalist and of the Labourer (1886). He argued that for both modern life was

> decidedly a poor affair. ... For both, life is equally bland at present; the capitalist in his big ugly house is no happier than the labourer in his little ugly one; if one has more fatigue, the other has more worry. (On the Conditions of Progress, 36)

Much more effort was needed to understand and control the effects of the physical manifestations of change. The well-being of society depended on a harmonious interaction of people with their environment. That interaction did not preclude extra-regional dimensions such as nationalism. Indeed, Geddes consciously fostered a sense of Scottish identity at the Outlook Tower in an overtly nationalistic manner and he has been subsequently regarded as one of the pioneers of modern Scottish nationalism. His argument, though, was not a narrow one. The purpose of reviving a nationalistic consciousness was both apolitical and cultural. The obverse side of the coin of Geddes' form of nationalism was cosmopolitanism. The security of a Scottish identity was the passport to understanding the nationalities of the world. In India after 1914, he was able to step over national and imperialistic boundaries when helping his friend Sir Jagadis Bose found his own scientific institute in Calcutta. Geddes was the only European present at the opening ceremony, and wore Indian-style clothes.

Geddes marked the end of the nineteenth century by taking his Edinburgh summer school to Paris for the duration of the Paris Centennial Exhibition of 1900. This earned him an international reputation, but it also marked the beginning of the end of his attempts to found a new kind of museum movement of which the Outlook Tower was but a part. In Paris the pavilions of the major countries of the world provided him with the most amazing raw material for his interpretation of future developments. He made an almost successful bid to save the exhibition as the basis for a world museum, but problems of cost brought his efforts to nothing. Subsequent efforts to persuade the Royal Geographical Society to set up a new complex of national museums and locate them in Edinburgh also came to nothing. The impetus which was to take him forward from this into the arena of the nascent town-planning movement came about almost by accident. In 1904 he received a commission from the Carnegie Dunfermline Trust to help lay out Pittencrieff Park in Dunfermline, which it had recently purchased. He used this as an invitation to promote all his ideas on how to preserve historic towns, on urban renewal, and on rehabilitation. He also promoted his regional ideas and, by suggesting the development of a number of cultural institutions in the park itself, the need to develop the evolutionary potential of citizens, ideas published in his City Development: a Study of Parks, Gardens, and Culture Institutes. A report to the Carnegie Dunfermline Trust (1904). As usual, Geddes failed to give the trustees exactly what they wanted but the volume he published became a landmark for those interested in the problems of urban development. Far away in America the young Lewis Mumford read the work a decade later and determined to visit Britain to find the author, a desire which was to have considerable consequences for both of them.

However, the most important step to Geddes' newly defined role was the position he was given by Raymond Unwin at the first international town-planning conference organized by the Royal Institute of British Architects in 1910, held to mark the passing of the 1909 Housing and Town Planning Act. Unwin, as currently the most eminent British architect–planner, was the chair of the conference committee. It was considered important to mount an exhibition in conjunction with the conference and Geddes' collection at the Outlook Tower was by far the largest collection of suitable material in Britain. Geddes was asked to be the director of what was designated the Cities and Town Planning Exhibition; he made a great success of this, and it proved to be exactly the kind of activity which suited his way of working. After the end of the conference Geddes decided to make the exhibition a peripatetic one and offered his services to any municipality who wanted to learn about the latest developments in planning. He received recognition from a city where he had laboured largely unrewarded for three decades when Edinburgh invited him to take the exhibition there. It was seen by Lord Pentland, then secretary of state for Scotland, before he became governor of Madras. (Geddes was offered a knighthood at this time but declined it on the grounds of insufficient income; he accepted a knighthood in 1932, the year of his death.)

In 1911 Pentland recommended Geddes to his in-laws, Lord and Lady Aberdeen, the former then viceroy of Ireland; Lady Aberdeen was to invite Geddes to Dublin between 1911 and 1913. He enjoyed his most successful years between 1910 and the First World War, working on planning in Ireland with Raymond Unwin and taking the exhibition to Ghent, Belgium, as part of an international congress on cities organized by Paul Otlet and Henri La Fontaine, leaders of the European peace movement. He produced the only general monograph he ever wrote on cities (mostly written between 1911 and 1913 though not published until 1915), *Cities in Evolution*. This is a curious volume, idiosyncratic in the extreme and aimed at arousing interest in city development rather than offering specialist training. By then, Geddes was already approaching sixty. He was to have one last chance to promote his ideas, and he seized it with both hands: in 1914 he was invited by Pentland to take his Cities and Town Planning Exhibition to India where he worked for ten years and wrote more than fifty town-planning reports.

The later years: India, Palestine, and France Geddes' work in India brought together all his interests and it provides the best illustration of his ideas. He found a continent on the brink of a period of rapid industrialization. He went to India for two reasons: to test his ideas on city development in a totally different cultural context and to try to save Indian people from the same fate which had befallen the British during the process of urbanization. In 1914 the level of urbanization in India was not high, and Geddes hoped it might be possible to avoid the process of deterioration and decay. His first major target was the imperial British. Two problems faced British administrators of Indian cities—public health and transport. In the absence of a western-style infrastructure in terms of sewage disposal, water supply, and roads, there were few restrictions on building. Cities such as Calcutta were famous for their acres of streetless slums. The most common solution used by British engineers (mostly army trained) was to demolish great swathes of poor housing and build wide roads in their place. For Geddes this had echoes of Edinburgh all

those decades ago. He sought instead to try and understand the evolution of Indian cities.

The first task was to survey. Geddes had worked out a training programme for town planners which was based on three-pronged action: survey, diagnosis, and (finally) plan. H. V. Lanchester, architect and vice-president of the Royal Institution of British Architects, had gone to India to work with Geddes, and had co-ordinated the effort made in Britain to send material for Geddes after the latter's original Cities and Town Planning Exhibition was lost at sea on its way to India. Lanchester carried out an economic and social survey of Madras and Geddes used this work to demonstrate exactly what he meant by survey. He then discovered that towns in south India had been shaped by their ancient Dravidian origins and that their plans were dictated by religious considerations. Road widths had been fixed in the past to allow the passage of religious processions. Here was a cultural factor which could be revived to control and sustain street widths. Many Indian cities in the north still had their city walls. Geddes tried to persuade the Indians to keep them, unlike in Europe where such walls had been destroyed. His argument here was that the walls would preserve the historic core of the city and people would be able to continue to live there. Expansion could take place beyond the walls and traffic would be kept out of the city centre. His most passionate campaign was to save the great water tanks attached to temples. The British had discovered that the mosquito was the cause of malaria, and engineers were busy filling in the tanks. Geddes was furious, as the tanks had many social and cultural functions of great importance, and suggested the use of fish and ducks to eat the mosquito larvae.

In India, Geddes was to demonstrate his most famous planning technique, which he called 'conservative surgery' (Tyrwhitt, 40–60). It was his answer to city 'improvers' bent on destruction. Geddes advocated a survey of all buildings in the designated area: those past repair should be pulled down; those repairable should be saved. The gaps left by the lost properties could be made into small open spaces which would enhance the quality of the environment for all inhabitants. Geddes' Indian reports, and those he went on to write for the new towns and old cities in Palestine, remain the most important repository of his ideas. As ever, they are couched in the language and the concerns of the time and the modern reader has to work to understand them. Geddes' work thus remains relatively obscure, to be discovered and rediscovered from time to time as different generations find enormous inspiration in his special perspective on city development and his understanding of environmental issues.

Immediately after the Second World War, when Britain at last instituted a national system of planning, there were two key regional plans for Scotland. One was headed by Geddes' son-in-law, Frank Mears; the other, the Clyde valley plan, the most successful in Britain, employed a number of planners who had learned a great deal from Geddes. One, Robert Grieve, acknowledged that he had learned from Geddes' ideas on 'conservative surgery' a crucial lesson: 'that we should not so much be so concerned about the degradation of our environment as the degradation of our people' (R. Grieve, *Grieve on Geddes: Professor Sir Robert Grieve's Appreciation of the Effect of Sir Patrick Geddes' Thinking on his Planning Work in Scotland*, c.1992, 40). Grieve became first professor of town planning at the University of Glasgow, in 1965, and he, and others who had come to understand Geddes' ecological perspective through practical experience, passed the lesson on to their students: Geddes could not have hoped for a better legacy.

In his old age, Geddes moved to Montpellier in France for the sake of his health. He made a second marriage, to Lilian Brown (d. 1936), the heir of a cotton manufacturer from Paisley, Renfrewshire, in 1928, when he was seventy-three and she was in her fifties. With the help of her money he built his last effort, the Collège des Écossais on the garrigue above Montpellier. He dreamed of bringing young people of every nation to learn about his ideas on social evolution. He did raise the money for a second 'Collège des Indiens', but the whole project was really an old man's pipe dream. He had visited America in 1923 for the first time on the invitation of Lewis Mumford and met the small group of the Regional Planning Association of America. He hoped Mumford would take the place of his son Alasdair, killed in 1917, and carry on his work, but the former could not take on such a task even though he knew he had learned much from Geddes. He contented himself by promoting at least the name of Geddes. Geddes died at his college in Montpellier on 17 April 1932. His remains were cremated at Marseilles.

Ten years after Geddes' death, in the dark hours towards the end of the Second World War, Lewis Mumford wrote an emotional eulogy of Geddes as the best possible guide to present and future. Yet Mumford admits that Geddes was 'obscure in his lifetime, hardly better known today. … What he was, what he stood for, what he pointed toward will become increasingly important as the world grows to understand both his philosophy and his example' (L. Mumford, *Condition of Man*, 1944, 382). Why this obscurity if what Geddes was saying was so important? The reasons have to do with aspects of his character, the context in which he worked, and the particular approach he adopted to develop his ideas. By nature immensely energetic, Geddes quickly became bored and was always more interested in the next idea than in following the last one to the point where he could write a monograph about it. Thus he worked in a context in which his ideas were not rigorously tested at the time, nor could they be transmitted to the future except through the work of others.

HELEN MELLER

Sources H. Meller, *Patrick Geddes: social evolutionist and city planner* (1990) • P. Boardman, *The works of Patrick Geddes: biologist, town-planner, re-educator, peace-warrior* (1978) • P. Kitchen, *A most unsettling person: an introduction to the life and ideas of Patrick Geddes* (1975) • P. Geddes, *Cities in evolution: an introduction to the town-planning movement and the study of cities* (1915) • P. Geddes, *City development: a study of parks, gardens, and culture institutes. A report to the Carnegie Dunfermline Trust* (1904) • P. Geddes, *Town planning towards city-development: a report to the Durbar of Indore*, 2 vols. (1918) • P. Mairet, *A pioneer of sociology: life and letters of Patrick Geddes* (1957) • J. Tyrwhitt, ed., *Patrick Geddes in India* (1947) • C. Barnett, *The ideal city*, ed. H. E. Meller (1979) • *Lewis Mumford and Patrick Geddes: the correspondence*, ed. F. G. Novak (1995) • W. I. Stevenson, 'Patrick Geddes, 1854–1932', *Geographers: biobibliographical studies*, 2, ed. T. W. Freeman and P. Pinchemel (1978), 53–65 • H. Meller, 'Cities in evolution: Patrick Geddes as an international prophet of town planning before 1914', *The rise of modern urban planning, 1890–1914*, ed. A. Sutcliffe (1980), 199–223

Archives Central Zionist archives, Jerusalem, municipal archives, MSS · NL Scot., corresp. and papers • PRO, official papers, MT 49 · University of Strathclyde, Glasgow, corresp. and papers | Keele University Library, Branford MSS, personal papers and corresp. • U. Edin. L., corresp. with Charles Sarolea • University of Toronto Library, letters to James Mavor

Likenesses D. Chute, pencil drawing, 1930, Scot. NPG • oils, c.1930, Scot. NPG • Lafayette, photograph, 1931, NPG [*see illus.*] • C. J. Pibworth, bronze head (modelled 1907; cast 1936), Scot. NPG • photographs, priv. coll. • photographs, repro. in Boardman, *Works of Patrick Geddes*

Wealth at death £3805 15s. 10d.: confirmation, 9 Nov 1932, *CCI*

Geddes, Wilhelmina Margaret (1887–1955), artist, was born on 25 May 1887 on her maternal grandparents' farm at Drumreilly, co. Leitrim, Ireland, the eldest of four children of William Geddis (c.1852–1916), a site engineer with the Sligo/Leitrim and North Counties Railway, and Eliza Jane (1863–1955), daughter of John Stafford, farmer, and his wife, Mary Anne Bleakley, both British. In 1888 her father moved to Belfast where he set up a thriving business as a building contractor. Her earliest (mostly life) drawings date from c.1891, executed when on a family summer outing to Ayrshire, where her lifelong love of Scottish border ballads was kindled. From an early age her (mostly unpublished) black and white book illustrations reflected her love of reading, while her literary skills included writing verse and stories. After attending the Methodist college, Belfast, between 1898 and 1902, she entered the Municipal Technical Institute of Belfast at the age of fifteen, spending eight years drawing from the antique and from life, while participating in Greek drama and suffragist meetings at Queen's University, Belfast, and winning a number of prizes for her assured graphic work, book illustrations, poster designs, and draughtsmanship. As early as 1906 her designs were declared 'too modern' (W. M. Geddes, MS diary, 18 May 1906; priv. coll.), a criticism sometimes levelled against her subsequent stained glass.

In 1910 Geddes's watercolour *Cinderella Dressing the Ugly Sister* (Hugh Lane Gallery, Dublin) was exhibited at the Arts and Crafts Society of Ireland and attracted the attention of Sarah Purser (1848–1943), the Irish painter and founder of An Túr Gloine, the Dublin stained-glass co-operative. Purser, recognizing a strong, expressive line, rich colour, and original imagery, bought it and invited Geddes to join her workshop.

Back in Belfast, Geddes made an initial conventional stained-glass panel (*Sir Walter Raleigh*) before embarking in

1911 on a travelling scholarship to London and subsequently life classes with Sir William Orpen at the Metropolitan School of Art, Dublin. Her first, entirely original, work in stained glass, *Episodes from the Life of St. Colman Macduagh* (Hugh Lane Gallery, Dublin), a triptych of three small panels, revealed her lifelong vocation. By the end of 1912 she had become a member of An Túr Gloine, receiving tuition from its manager, Alfred Child, trained in the London studio of the English arts and crafts stained-glass master Christopher Whall, and designed and made her first, remarkably mature, full-scale church window, *The Angel of Resurrection* (Inishmacsaint, co. Fermanagh).

Geddes's small frame and spirited expression belied the solemn, monumental drama with which she imbued the fluidly modelled, introspective, and increasingly commanding figures that filled the thirty or so windows, swathed in colours of unimaginable depth and intensity, that she made throughout her life. Her love of archaic, Romanesque, and Assyrian sculpture informed the treatment of her always figurative designs, while her innate feeling for the lead calmes as an integral part of the orchestration of glass, light, colour, and painting revealed her understanding of medieval glass even more than her arts and crafts training.

In 1925 Geddes moved to London, to a studio in the Glass House in Fulham, which remained her working base for the rest of her life. Her best-known windows are HRH the duke of Connaught's war memorial to his Canadian officers in the governor general's church of St Bartholomew, Ottawa (*The Welcoming of a Slain Warrior by Soldier-Saints, Champions and Angels*, 1919), *The Crucifixion with the Virgin Mary and St. John, Moses, Joseph of Arimathea, and the Deposition* (1922; St Luke's, Wallsend upon Tyne), and the Royal Air Force memorial rose window to King Albert of the Belgians in the rebuilt cathedral of St Martin, Ypres (*Te Deum*, 1938). In 1955 she collapsed in the street, and died at University College Hospital, St Pancras, London, on 10 August. She was unmarried. She was buried at Carnmoney, co. Antrim.   NICOLA GORDON BOWE

Sources N. Gordon Bowe, 'Wilhelmina Geddes, 1887–1955: her life and work—reappraisal', *Journal of Stained Glass*, 18/3 (1988), 275–301 • D. Gaze, ed., *Dictionary of women artists*, 2 vols. (1997) • N. Gordon Bowe, 'Wilhelmina Geddes', *Irish Arts Review*, 4/3 (1987), 53–9 • N. Gordon Bowe, D. Caron, and M. Wynne, *Gazetteer of Irish Stained Glass* (1988) • N. Gordon Bowe and E. S. Cumming, *The arts and crafts movements in Dublin and Edinburgh* (1998) • W. M. Geddes, 'Making stained glass windows', *Belfast News-Letter* (25 Sept 1930) • S. Gwynn, 'The art of Miss W. M. Geddes', *The Studio*, 84 (1922), 208–13 • N. Gordon Bowe, 'Wilhelmina Geddes (1887–1955): stained glass designer', *Women designing: redefining design in Britain between the wars*, ed. S. Worden and J. Seddon (1994) [exhibition catalogue, University of Brighton Gallery, 7–31 March 1994] • N. Gordon Bowe, '"Cats are my favourite animals": Wilhelmina Geddes (1887–1955)', *New perspectives: studies in art history in honour of Anne Crookshank*, ed. J. Fenlon, C. Marshall, and N. Figgis (1987) • P. Cormack, *Women artists of the arts and crafts movement* (1985) • N. Gordon Bowe, 'Wilhelmina Geddes, Harry Clarke and their part in the arts and crafts movement in Ireland', *Journal of Decorative and Propaganda Arts*, 8 (1988), 58–79 • N. Gordon Bowe, 'Women and the arts and crafts revival in Ireland, c.1886–1930', *Irish women artists: from the eighteenth century to the present day* (1987) [exhibition catalogue,

NG Ire., the Douglas Hyde Gallery, TCD, and the Hugh Lane Municipal Gallery of Modern Art, Dublin, July–Aug 1987] • private information (2004) [family]
Archives NL Ire. | NL Ire., Sarah Purser MSS | SOUND BBC Television archive, London
Likenesses photograph, repro. in Bowe, 'Wilhelmina Geddes', 296 • photograph, repro. in S. Worden and J. Seddon, eds., *Women designing: redefining design in Britain between the wars* (1994), 64
Wealth at death £4143: certificate, Belfast probate office

Geddes, William (c.1630–1694), Church of Scotland minister and writer, was born in Moray. He entered King's College, Aberdeen, about 1646, graduating MA in 1650. On 13 November 1650 he became schoolmaster of Leith, Edinburghshire. In 1652 he was governor to Hugh Ross of Kilravock; receipts indicate that he remained in this employment until at least 1654. He was ordained minister of Wick, Caithness, on 23 November 1659. Before 1 June 1664 he married Katherine, daughter of John Dunbar of Hempriggs, because on that day the minister, James Dunbar, was censured for celebrating the marriage without the usual proclamations. Both Charles Seton, earl of Dunfermline, and Alexander Livingston, earl of Callendar, appear to have presented Geddes to Urquhart in Moray, and he was translated there on 3 June 1677. He resigned in 1682 on refusing to take the Test.

In 1683 Geddes published *The Saint's Recreation*, dedicated to the countess of Perth, the countess dowager of Wemyss, and to three female members of the Ross family (another version includes the duchess of Hamilton). This was the only one of Geddes's literary projects which was completed and published, although he told the Scottish privy council in March 1683 that another work (*Memoriale historicum*) was in press and that he intended to publish four more works ('Geographical and arithmetical memorials', 'Memoriale Hebraicum', 'Vocabularium Latino-Hebraicum', and 'Familiae famigeratae'). As Geddes had 'been at great care, pain, diligence and expence, in compiling' these books the privy council granted him the copyright for nineteen years. He continued to work on his books for in June 1684 Alexander Brodie of Brodie noted, 'Mr William Geddes came here with some of his books. I had promised him some encouragement' (*Diary*, ed. Laing, 491). Following the re-establishment of presbyterian discipline within the Church of Scotland, Geddes was readmitted to Wick in 1692, and died in 1694, aged about sixty-four.   STUART HANDLEY

Sources *Fasti Scot.*, new edn, 6.409; 7.141 • C. Innes, ed., *Fasti Aberdonenses … 1494–1854*, Spalding Club, 26 (1854), 467, 514, 543 • J. B. Craven, *A history of the episcopal church in the diocese of Caithness* (1908), 121–6 • *The diary of Alexander Brodie of Brodie … and of his son James Brodie*, ed. D. Laing, Spalding Club, 33 (1863), 491 • *A genealogical deduction of the family of Rose of Kilravock*, Spalding Club (1848), 349 • L. Shaw, *The history of the province of Moray* (1827), 376 • *Geographical collections relating to Scotland made by Walter MacFarlane*, ed. A. Mitchell, 1, Scottish History Society, 51 (1906), 1.162 • W. Geddes, *The saints recreation, upon the estate of grace* (1683)

Geddes, Sir William Duguid (1828–1900), classical scholar, was born on 21 November 1828, the son of John Geddes, a farmer of Fenar, Huntly, and his wife, the daughter of Peter Maconochie, farmer, of Keithmore, Banffshire. He was educated at Elgin Academy until 1842, when he entered University and King's College, Aberdeen, graduating MA in March 1846, when he was only seventeen. In the same year he was appointed parish schoolmaster of Gamrie, and in 1848 classical master at Aberdeen grammar school. He became rector of the grammar school in 1853, and in 1855 was elected professor of Greek at University and King's College. In the same year he published a *Greek Grammar*, which reached a seventeenth edition in 1883. On 28 April 1859 he married Rachel Robertson, daughter of William White, merchant, of Aberdeen.

In 1860, when the unification of Aberdeen took place, Geddes became professor of Greek in the united university. He held this post until 1885, and was largely instrumental in reviving and reforming the study of Greek in Scottish universities. He was a popular and influential lecturer, nicknamed Old Homer by his pupils. In 1885 he was elected principal and vice-chancellor of Aberdeen, in succession to Dr W. R. Pirie. The chief achievements of his tenure were the restoration of the chapel in 1891 and the extension of the buildings on the Marischal College site to house the faculties of science and medicine.

Geddes was created LLD of Edinburgh in 1876 and LittD of Dublin in 1893, was knighted in 1892, and died at the Chanonry Lodge, Old Aberdeen, on 9 February 1900. His wife survived him, with an only daughter, Rachel Blanche, who in 1887 married John Harrower, who succeeded Geddes as professor of Greek at Aberdeen.

Besides the *Greek Grammar*, Geddes published in 1878 *The Problem of the Homeric Poems*, which developed a theory similar to that of George Grote: Geddes postulated an original *Archilleid* consisting of books i, viii, and xxi–xxii of the present *Iliad*, which was enlarged by the author of the *Odyssey*. His work was commended by W. E. Gladstone and E. A. Freeman. Among his other works was a scholarly edition of Plato's *Phaedo* (1863).

A. F. POLLARD, rev. RICHARD SMAIL

Sources *The Times* (10 Feb 1900) · *The Athenaeum* (17 Feb 1900), 208–10 · W. D. Simpson, ed., *The fusion of 1860* (1963) · J. E. Sandys, *A history of classical scholarship*, 3 (1908), 428 · *WWW*
Wealth at death £3064 4s. 11d.: confirmation, 30 March 1900, CCI · £255: additional estate, 20 April 1900, CCI

Geddie, Emelia [Emilia] (**1665–1681**), child prophet and exemplar of godliness, was born at Hilltown of Falkland, Fife, one of three children (her two brothers died young) of John *Gedde of Hilltown of Falkland (*fl.* 1647–1697), steward clerk of Fife, and Anne Wallace (*fl.* 1657–1691), daughter of William Wallace, schoolmaster of Ayr; she was named after Lady Emelia, daughter of John Stanley, earl of Derby. Both parents were staunch presbyterians, and their daughter was precociously pious from her earliest years. By the age of three she was composing her own grace before meals and chiding sabbath-breaking servants. Popular presbyterian belief held that such unusual religious development was a sign of God speaking through the child. This excited an almost superstitious regard for her sayings among those who encountered her. In the highly charged religious atmosphere of Restoration Scotland, where members of her denomination were persecuted, there was great interest in prophecy, signs, and

wonders. As a result, she exerted influence far beyond her years. Her sayings were carefully noted down and she was often invited to pray at clandestine prayer meetings. Emelia was also much sought after as a spiritual counsellor. Several adults ascribed the cure of their spiritual problems to her intervention, and she knew large sections of the Bible by heart. Her family hid covenanting field preachers at great risk to themselves, and this gave the child the opportunity to confer with ministers such as Donald Cargill and John Welwood, who held her in high esteem. She was in some respects a kind of covenanting Pet Marjory (Marjory Fleming, (1803–1811), the diarist). Her youth gave her the opportunity to rebuke social superiors for complying with episcopacy, and she insisted to her father that she would rather go into service than see him forced to take the declaration oath to keep his place.

Emelia's piety was also greatly influenced by her schoolmistress Katherine Collace, the autobiographer and covenanting activist. Katherine wrote down many of her pupil's sayings, including prophetic intimations which she had in prayer concerning the church and the persecution of the presbyterians. In 1675 Emelia went with her father and mother to London, where she learned to write at a private school. On her return to Scotland she attended presbyterian meetings, and was often asked by ministers to give her opinions on weighty matters, such as the defeat of the presbyterian party at Bothwell Bridge in 1679. She died at Hilltown of Falkland on 2 February 1681, aged sixteen, of a continued flux and a gravel, and was buried at the new burial place, Falkland.

Emelia's influence continued after her death. Her sayings were collected by James Hogg, minister of Carnock, and first published in 1717 as *Some Choice Sentences and Practices of Emilia Geddie, Daughter to John Geddie*, though it seems that they circulated in manuscript before this. The account of her life was published and republished as an example to the young, going through several editions. In 1741 it was printed with a recommendation by George Whitefield, and in 1821, as *The Life of Emilia Geddie*, it crossed the Atlantic and was printed in a first edition of 6000 for the New England Tract Society. Her life was also featured by seceding divine John Brown in his *The Young Christian, or, The Pleasantness of Early Piety Exemplified*, published in Glasgow in 1782.

L. A. YEOMAN

Sources *Life of Emelia Geddie, recommended by the Reverend George Whitefield* (1805) · K. C. Ross, 'Memoirs or spiritual exercises of Katherine Ross with memoirs of Jean Collace', NL Scot., Adv. MS 32.4.4 [incl. letters of J. Welwood] · *Miscellany of the Abbotsford Club*, vol. 1, ed. J. Maidment (1837), item 21 · commonplace book, NL Scot., MS 10700

Geden, John Dury (**1822–1886**), Wesleyan Methodist minister, the son of John Geden, Wesleyan minister, was born at Hastings on 4 May 1822. He was educated at Kingswood School, near Bath, from 1830 to 1836. When he left school he devoted himself to study and teaching. In 1844 he became a candidate for the Wesleyan ministry, and was sent to Richmond College, Surrey. After three years Geden was appointed assistant tutor at the college. By the conference of 1851, which met at Newcastle upon Tyne, Geden was stationed in that town, having William Morley Punshon as one of his colleagues. After a year each in this and the neighbouring circuit of Durham, he moved to Manchester, where he spent three years in the Oxford Road circuit. His ministry was appreciated by some of the most educated congregations of his church.

On the death of Jonathan Crowther in January 1856 Geden was requested to fill provisionally the vacant post of tutor in the sacred and classical languages at Didsbury College, Manchester, and by the conference of the same year was formally appointed Crowther's successor. Geden's favourite field of study was oriental literature and philology, but he also explored various branches of philosophy and natural science. Soon after his appointment to Didsbury he became joint editor of the *London Quarterly Review*, established in 1853, and contributed to its pages many valuable papers, among them a review of the sermons of F. W. Robertson of Brighton (October 1861). Meanwhile Geden's services as an occasional preacher were in request over a wide surrounding district, and his reputation became established as one of the leading thinkers and writers of Methodism, though he was not often a prominent figure in public meetings or church committees. Geden was married twice, first to Elizabeth, daughter of Solomon Mease, JP, of South Shields, and secondly to Eliza Jane, daughter of Robert Hawson of Scarborough. From the first marriage there were two sons and a daughter. The younger son, Alfred (1857–1936), became a missionary to India, where he was principal of Royapettah College, Madras, from 1886–9, and was later professor of Old Testament languages and literature at Richmond College.

In the autumn of 1863 Geden made a journey to the Middle East, and passed through parts of Egypt, the Sinai peninsula, and the Holy Land. A dangerous attack of dysentery at Jerusalem permanently damaged his health. He subsequently wrote an account of his journey in the *City Road Magazine* during 1871–3. In 1870 Geden was invited to become a member of the Old Testament Revision Committee, then first formed, and for many years he regularly attended its meetings at Westminster. When no longer able to travel to London, Geden still made many suggestions to his colleagues; he was specially anxious to preserve the dignity and rhythm of the Authorized Version. In 1874, at the Wesleyan Methodist conference held at Camborne, Geden delivered the fifth of the Fernley lecture series. He chose as his subject 'The doctrine of a future life as contained in the Old Testament scriptures', vigorously opposing the view that the doctrine is not to be found in the Old Testament. The lecture was published by the Wesleyan conference office. In 1878 Geden published his fifteen *Didsbury Sermons*, which combine vividness of expression with strict orthodoxy.

In 1883 failing health compelled him to retire. In January 1885 he received the honorary degree of DD from the University of St Andrews. After prolonged suffering, patiently endured, he died on Tuesday 9 March 1886 at Didsbury College.   A. J. FRENCH, *rev.* TIM MACQUIBAN

Sources W. Hill, *An alphabetical arrangement of all the Wesleyan-Methodist ministers, missionaries, and preachers*, rev. J. P. Haswell, 9th edn (1862) · *Minutes of the Methodist conference* · N. B. Harmon, ed., *The encyclopedia of world Methodism*, 2 vols. (1974) · personal knowledge (1889) · private information (1889)
Wealth at death £1733 14s. 9d.: probate, 31 March 1886, *CGPLA Eng. & Wales*

Gedge, Sydney (1802–1883), Church of England clergyman, was born on 3 April 1802, the youngest son of Peter Gedge, journalist, of Bury St Edmunds in Suffolk. He was educated at Bury St Edmunds grammar school, whence he proceeded to St Catharine's College, Cambridge, in 1820. He graduated BA in 1824, coming out fourteenth wrangler and in the first class in classics. In the following year he was elected a fellow of his college. For a short time he read in chambers at Lincoln's Inn, but threw up his intention of being called to the bar and took holy orders.

From 1827 until 1835 Gedge was curate of North Runcton in Norfolk, also taking pupils. In 1835 he was appointed second master of King Edward's School, Birmingham, where he remained until 1859. He was an enthusiastic supporter of the Church Missionary Society and held the post of honorary secretary in Birmingham during the whole of the time he was there. In 1859 he was presented by Lord Overstone to the vicarage of All Saints', Northampton, which he held, with the rural deanery, until his retirement from active parochial work in 1875. He then chiefly occupied himself in advancing the cause of Christian missions by speaking and preaching for the Church Missionary Society. His acute reasoning power and independence in action won him much influence in Birmingham and Northampton. His readiness, especially in later years, to believe in the purity of motive of those from whom he differed in opinion gained him the warm regard of all with whom he came in contact. In politics he was a Liberal.

Gedge died on 29 August 1883 at Edinburgh House, Cromer, after a few days' illness, having enjoyed to the last full vigour of body and mind. He was survived by at least two sons. Four of his sermons were published separately.

S. F. GEDGE, *rev.* H. C. G. MATTHEW

Sources *The Times* (3 Sept 1883) · *The Guardian* (5 Sept 1883) · Venn, *Alum. Cant.* · E. Stock, *The history of the Church Missionary Society: its environment, its men and its work*, 4 vols. (1899–1916) · d. cert. · *CGPLA Eng. & Wales* (1883)
Archives Herts. ALS, letters to first Baron Bulwer-Lytton and second Baron Bulwer-Lytton
Wealth at death £13,123 9s. 3d.: probate, 27 Sept 1883, *CGPLA Eng. & Wales*

Gedney [Brodyng], **John** (*d.* 1449), draper and mayor of London, is of unknown origins. In a petition to parliament in 1419 he styled himself John Brodyng, alias Gedney. He may have been related to two other John Gedneys recorded in early fifteenth-century London, one a clothworker, the other a grocer.

Gedney was trading in London by 1407, when he was already a man of substance. He sold cloth worth £417 to the Grocers' Company for livery gowns and hoods between 1412 and 1422, and by 1420 supplied the royal wardrobe, often on long credit. By 1440 he was owed nearly £490 for cloth by Henry VI. Gedney never plunged deeply into crown finance. In 1417 he lent £20 for the French war. His later loans were mainly on this scale, but in 1431 he was one of four prominent citizens guaranteeing a loan of £2000 on the security of the clerical subsidy. Gedney traded in Calais as well as in London, had links with Venetians and Genoese over the luxury trade in mercery, and imported woad through Southampton. Already a leading member of his livery by 1408, when he helped to acquire land for the new Drapers' Hall, he pledged £20, the second largest amount, for the new building in 1419. In 1427–8 he served as a warden, and, after the company received its charter in 1439, Gedney was the first master; he was again master in 1447–8. Gedney arbitrated in many commercial disputes, but seems to have been drawn into the drapers' quarrel with the tailors in the 1440s to only a limited extent.

Gedney was returned to parliament in 1414 and 1432. His rise in city politics began in 1415. Elected alderman of the ward of Farringdon Without, Gedney took the oath only on threat of penalties, but remained an alderman until his death, for Coleman Street ward (1416–35), and for Cornhill ward (1435–49). He was a tax collector in 1416 and 1421, and auditor of London in 1419–20. Gedney was elected sheriff in 1417–18, and mayor for the first time in 1427–8. He was one of only nine men to serve twice as mayor before 1545, his second term of office being in 1447–8. Evidently an accomplished committee man with an interest in public works, he often attended the court of aldermen, and was present at eight parliamentary elections. In the 1440s he was an auditor of London Bridge's finances, and an adviser on the new granary being built in Leadenhall market. In 1445 he pledged a legacy of 200 marks (£133 6s. 8d.) for the new conduit.

Most of Gedney's London property lay in the parish of St Christopher-le-Stocks in Cornhill and Broadstreet wards. By 1407 he held a reversionary interest in a messuage in Cornhill. In 1415 he obtained the Leaden Porch in Cornhill, described by John Stow in the sixteenth century as a fair, large house, together with shops. The purchase of a tavern, the Cock and Star on the Hoop, with six other messuages, shops, solars, and cellars, and an alley in the same parish, was finalized in 1437, but Gedney and his son, another John Gedney, who predeceased his father, were already enjoying the profits in 1436, when the income from Gedney's properties in London and Middlesex was assessed at the handsome sum of £120.

Gedney's great prize in Middlesex was Tottenham Manor. He acquired the first of four sub-manors in 1427. By the 1440s he held the whole and ran the estate at a profit, consolidating the demesne, increasing rents, building two fulling mills, and founding a brickworks. Surpluses of over £100 per annum are recorded in all surviving accounts for the manor between 1443 and 1449, showing its declared annual value of nearly £60 at Gedney's death to have been a considerable underestimate. Gedney often acted as a trustee for Cardinal Beaufort and others, and this probably explains his interest in manors in Essex and property in Cambridgeshire and Huntingdonshire.

Gedney was married three times, first to Alice (surname unknown), second to Elizabeth, sister of John Clopton, esquire, of Long Melford, Suffolk, and third, by 1444, to Joan Large (d. 1462). Joan was three times a widow. Her third husband, Robert Large, mercer, mayor of London and William Caxton's master, died in 1441. Gedney was a friend and business associate of Large, and one of his executors. The scandal caused by the marriage is recorded in a London chronicle under the year 1443–4, in a version followed by Stow. Joan Large, perhaps for sound financial reasons, had broken her vow of chastity (no doubt undertaken to protect her late husband's inheritance) to marry Gedney; for this they were 'put to penance both he and she' by the church authorities (Bodl. Oxf., MS Digby Roll 2). Gedney's undertaking in 1445, to the bishop of London to fund four poor scholars at Oxford and Cambridge for nineteen and a half years, may be related to the marriage.

Gedney died on 12 February 1449. He was buried in the newly built lady chapel on the north side of St Christopher-le-Stocks, and Joan Large beside him. His will is lost, but some provisions are known. Besides money for the conduit, Gedney left 100 marks for glazing the west window of Guildhall chapel. The lavish perpetual chantry he wished to found in St Christopher's for himself, his three wives, and his dead son, was not yet in existence in 1483. John Clopton, one of Gedney's executors, included Gedney's portrait in stained glass among those he commissioned in Long Melford church, where it still survives.

JENNY STRATFORD

Sources C. Rawcliffe, 'Gedney, John', HoP, Commons, 1386–1421, 3.170–73 [see also John Knyvet, Richard Turnaunt, and John Walden] • M. C. Erler, 'Three fifteenth-century vowesses', *Medieval London widows, 1300–1500*, ed. C. M. Barron and A. F. Sutton (1994), 171–6 [and sources] • E. Freshfield, ed., *Wills, leases, and memoranda in the book of records of the parish of St Christopher le Stocks in … London* (privately printed, 1895), 9–13, 27–8 • RotP, 4.119 • PRO, chancery, inquisitions *post mortem* Henry VI, C 139/134/18 • S. L. Thrupp, *The merchant class of medieval London, 1300–1500* (1948) • Bodl. Oxf., MS Digby Roll 2 • J. Stow, *A survay of London*, rev. edn (1603); repr. with introduction by C. L. Kingsford as *A survey of London*, 2 vols. (1908); repr. with addns (1971)
Archives BL, Add. charters, manor of Tottenham • Bruce Castle Museum archives, MR 10; MR 24
Likenesses glass, Long Melford church, Long Melford, Suffolk
Wealth at death £120 from property in London and Middlesex: 1436, Thrupp, *Merchant class*; PRO, E 179/238/90 • £59s. 2d. from property in Middlesex: 1449, PRO, C 139/134/18

Gedy, John (*fl.* 1370–1401?), abbot of Arbroath, is first recorded in 1370, when he already held the abbacy of Scotland's greatest Tironensian house. Nothing is known of his earlier career. In 1371 he attended Robert II's coronation. When the monastic church was struck by lightning and suffered severe damage from fire in 1380, the monks had to be transferred elsewhere while money was raised and repairs carried out; the abbot was closely involved in this process, which was still in progress in the mid-1390s. On 2 April 1394 Gedy made an agreement with the burgesses of Arbroath whereby the latter would co-operate with the monks in constructing a port at Arbroath, which was suffering acutely for lack of a harbour for shipping. No doubt this measure was prompted by the charter of 4

May 1392 in which Robert III granted the abbey a proportion of the customs levied on wool, skins, fells, and hides in the port. In that year the monastery received just over £7 as a result of the king's grant, and presumably the inadequacies of the harbour were felt to be restricting the abbey's gains, though hopes of higher returns seem to have been disappointed.

In 1396 Benedict XIII conferred the privileges of a mitred abbot on Gedy, who was still in office on 2 May 1399; it was probably he who in March 1401 secured from Robert III confirmation of an ancient grant of 4 merks yearly to maintain lights round the tomb of William the Lion, the founder of Arbroath. But all that can be said for certain is that he had been succeeded as abbot by 11 December 1411. It is likely that both his death and burial took place at Arbroath Abbey. It is possible, though there is no evidence to support the conjecture, that Gedy's harbour-building at Arbroath lay behind Robert Southey's poem *The Inchcape Rock* (completed in 1798, published in 1802). It tells how 'The good old abbot of Aberbrothoc' attaches a bell to a buoy floating by the deadly Inchcape Rock, some 12 miles south-east of Arbroath, to give warning to mariners, and how the wicked Sir Ralph the Rover, in order to spite the abbot, cuts the bell from the buoy, only to be himself sunk and drowned by the rock several years later.   HENRY SUMMERSON

Sources C. Innes and P. Chalmers, eds., *Liber s. Thome de Aberbrothoc*, 2 vols., Bannatyne Club, 86 (1848–56) • BL, Add. MS 33245 [Arbroath Register] • G. Burnett and others, eds., *The exchequer rolls of Scotland*, 3 (1880), 297–8 • APS, 1124–1423, 181 • R. Southey, *The Inchcape rock* (1907)

Gedye, (George) Eric Rowe (1890–1970), journalist, was born at Clevedon, Somerset, on 27 May 1890, the eldest son of George Edward Gedye, a provisions merchant of Bristol, and his wife, Lillie Rowe. He was educated at Clarence School, Weston-super-Mare, and Queen's College, Taunton, and matriculated at London University. After an unsuccessful start as a would-be journalist and author he was gazetted in August 1914 from London University Officers' Training Corps to the 12th battalion of the Gloucestershire regiment, and served from November 1915 on the western front. He was wounded on the Somme in September 1916. In May 1918 he joined the intelligence corps and was mentioned in dispatches. During the advance into Germany he was attached to the cavalry, and served on the British military governor's staff in Cologne and on the inter-allied Rhineland high commission until 1922.

In that year Gedye's real life-work began. As he himself put it, 'Lord Northcliffe came to Cologne, had a nervous breakdown and appointed me local correspondent there of *The Times* and the *Daily Mail*'. He had a flying start. In January 1923 the French occupation of the Ruhr was extended because of a German default in coal deliveries, and Gedye was on the spot. Within a few days he was promoted from an obscure local correspondent to the well-paid post of 'our special correspondent' on the staff of *The Times*. During the next two years his dispatches from the Rhineland describing the French plans for the establishment of separatist states 'led' the paper for a longer period

than any foreign correspondent had ever achieved, and he came to be regarded by the French as one of the main obstacles in the way of their intrigues to establish what Gedye called 'government by desperadoes'. His most famous scoop was his eyewitness account of the assassination by young German nationalists of Heinz, given by the French the title of 'president of the Autonomous Palatinate', in the Hotel Wittlesbacher Hof in Speyer. Gedye afterwards described this period in *The Revolver Republic* (1930), an exciting piece of contemporary history which perhaps remains his best book. He noted wryly that, while the German press regarded his dispatches at that time as 'objective', when he turned his attention to manifestations of extreme German nationalism in the Rhineland his lack of 'objectivity' was immediately deplored. This provides an important clue to Gedye's character throughout his life. He was always passionately opposed to extremism and violence wherever he found them—and he found them often enough in the central Europe of the 1920s and 1930s, which he continued to interpret vividly for the readers of a variety of newspapers until the outbreak of war in 1939.

In 1925 *The Times* sent Gedye as its central European correspondent to Vienna, which became his home for the next thirteen years. In 1926 he moved to the *Daily Express* and in 1929 to the *Daily Telegraph*. From 1929 he also represented the *New York Times*. His experience of central Europe was summed up in his book *Heirs to the Hapsburgs* (1932), a study of political, economic, and social conditions in an area which, as he rightly foresaw, would be a source of increasing trouble in the years to come. In these years he also produced a charming guidebook to his beloved Austria, *A Wayfarer in Austria* (1928). He covered the darkening scene in Vienna, the suppression of the socialists, and the murder of Dollfuss, but his coverage of the most tragic events of all, the Nazi invasion of Austria and the proclamation of the *Anschluss*, was rudely cut short. In 1938 he was expelled from Austria by the Gestapo at three days' notice. When he left Vienna by rail, seen off on the platform by a mixed crowd of colleagues and Gestapo officials, his dachshund was seen at the window with its paw raised in the Nazi salute. Gedye moved his base to Prague, but worked for the *Daily Telegraph* for only a few months longer. In 1939 he published another book of contemporary history, *Fallen Bastions*, in which he severely criticized Chamberlain's appeasement policy. Rather surprisingly, for the *Daily Telegraph* was anything but enthusiastic about appeasement, the paper considered the book so partisan that he could not credibly carry on as an 'impartial' correspondent. The editor announced that he had resigned by 'mutual consent'. 'That', commented Gedye, 'is correct. It is equally correct that Herr Hitler invaded Czechoslovakia by "mutual arrangement" with President Hácha.'

When the Germans marched into Prague in March 1939 Gedye, with two other British correspondents, took refuge in the British embassy to avoid arrest under a Gestapo warrant, and was allowed to leave the country with a safe conduct a week later. He then became Moscow correspondent of the *New York Times*, for which he had continued to work in Prague after the break with the *Daily Telegraph*, and from 1940 to 1941 correspondent in Turkey. He was employed on special military duties in the Middle East from 1941 until the end of the war, when he returned to Vienna, first of all for the *Daily Herald*, and then for *The Observer* and the *Manchester Guardian*. In 1946 he was appointed MBE. In 1954 he became head of evaluation for Radio Free Europe. He retired and returned to England in 1961 and settled in Bath.

That Gedye was the greatest British foreign correspondent of the inter-war years can hardly be disputed. By his style and personality he contributed a great deal to the aura of romance which surrounded the profession at that period. He was brown-haired, thin, grey-eyed, and electrically energetic. Among other foreign correspondents he was the best of colleagues and companions.

In 1922 Gedye married Elisabeth Bremer of Cologne; she died in 1960. His second wife, whom he married in 1948, was Alice Lepper of Vienna, daughter of Bernard Mehler, a factory owner. They had one son. Gedye died on 21 March 1970 in Bath. In retirement he started work on an autobiography. The few chapters he completed are in the Imperial War Museum. HUGH GREENE, *rev.*

Sources *The Times* (24 March 1970) · personal knowledge (1981) · *WWW* · *CGPLA Eng. & Wales* (1970)
Archives IWM, corresp. and papers · News Int. RO, papers | JRL, letters to the *Manchester Guardian*
Wealth at death £21,512: probate, 3 Nov 1970, *CGPLA Eng. & Wales*

Gee, Edward (1565/6–1618), Church of England clergyman, was the son of Ralph Gee of Manchester. He matriculated from Merton College, Oxford, on 22 February 1583 aged seventeen, graduated BA from Lincoln College on 12 October 1586, and was admitted to a fellowship at Brasenose College in 1588, where he proceeded MA on 23 June 1590. He was appointed a university proctor in 1598, and was awarded a BD degree on 14 April 1600. On 19 September the previous year he had been instituted to the rectory of Tedburn St Mary near Exeter. In 1603 Gee resigned his Brasenose fellowship, probably on the occasion of marriage to his wife, Jane, whose death on 21 September 1613 inspired the rector to compose, and to have placed in the church, an epitaph in which he sadly compared himself to 'a turtle which hath lost his dear mate' (Polwhele, 2.59).

At an unknown date Gee became a chaplain-in-ordinary to King James. On 9 July 1616 he was awarded his doctorate by the University of Oxford. On 20 July that year one Richard Everleigh was collated to a canonry of Exeter Cathedral but, on 28 August, Arthur Lake, bishop of Bath and Wells, wrote to his brother, the influential Sir Thomas Lake, recommending Gee for the next vacant residentiary at Exeter: Gee was collated by the crown and installed in place of Everleigh. He was also appointed a fellow of the newly founded Chelsea College and served the lord chancellor, Thomas Egerton, as a chaplain. Wood reports that he was 'a person well known for his sincerity in conversation, generality of learning, gravity of judgement and

soundness of doctrine' (Wood, *Ath. Oxon.*, 2.258–9). Edward Gee died in the winter of 1618; he had married again and his second wife, Mary, survived him. In 1620 Gee's *Two Sermons* was published posthumously by his brothers John (*d.* 1631) and George (*d.* 1636), who were both clergymen. This John Gee was the father of another John *Gee (1595/6–1639), the religious controversialist.

C. W. SUTTON, *rev.* STEPHEN WRIGHT

Sources Foster, *Alum. Oxon.* · Wood, *Ath. Oxon.*, new edn · J. Le Neve, *Fasti Ecclesiae Anglicanae*, ii · E. Gee, *Two sermons* (1620) · *DNB* · *CSP dom.*, 1611–18 · J. E. Bailey and H. Fishwick, *N&Q*, 6th ser., 2 (1880), 71–2 · R. Polwhele, *The history of Devonshire*, 3 vols. (1793–1806)

Gee, Edward (*bap.* 1612, *d.* 1660), Church of England clergyman and writer, was baptized on 1 November 1612 at Banbury, Oxfordshire, the son of George Gee, minister of Newton in Manchester parish, Lancashire. He was probably educated at Banbury and Newton, and subsequently matriculated from Brasenose College, Oxford, as a commoner on 26 October 1626. After graduating BA on 16 December 1630 he continued his studies at Brasenose, and became committed to promoting the cause of godly living. He proceeded MA on 8 July 1636, having entered the ministry by that date. Upon leaving university Gee returned to Lancashire and became chaplain to Dr Richard Parr, bishop of Sodor and Man and the rector of Eccleston parish, Lancashire. At Eccleston, he married Elizabeth Raymond (*fl.* 1640–1656) on 22 June 1640, a match which produced eight surviving children.

Following the outbreak of the civil wars Gee became a zealous supporter of the parliamentarian cause. His allegiance was rewarded in 1643 when the living of Eccleston, then in the hands of the prominent parliamentarian Viscount Saye and Sele, became vacant. After a vote among parishioners Gee was nominated rector of Eccleston, a position which he held for the remainder of his life. On 13 December 1644 he was appointed a commissioner for the ordination of ministers in Lancashire, and thereafter he used his influence to agitate vigorously for the implementation of godly rule. Following the establishment of presbyterianism in Lancashire in early 1647 Gee quickly became a leading figure within local church government. He was elected a member of the sixth classis at Preston, and later acted as scribe to the classes at Manchester and Bury. During the late 1640s and throughout the 1650s he preached widely across the county, and was thought by the Lancashire MP William Ashhurst to hold 'the approbation of all honest and good ministers' (*DNB*).

In 1648 and 1649 Gee signed several pamphlets which sought to consolidate presbyterianism in Lancashire and expressed a solidarity with London brethren. At the same time, however, he also acquired a reputation for an uncompromising adherence to the Scottish model of presbytery and an intolerance of Independency in any form. In 1650 he became involved in the dispute over the engagement, the oath of allegiance to the Commonwealth imposed on all men aged eighteen or over. Gee wrote a number of pamphlets against the oath, entering a bitter print debate with the Cheshire Independent minister Samuel Eaton. He asserted the basic presbyterian argument that any new oaths of allegiance must be consistent with the solemn league and covenant of 1643, which had bound takers to protect the life and person of the king. Indeed, the minister Adam Martindale remembered Gee as a 'great knocker for disputation' with the Lancashire presbyterians Richard Heyrick and Richard Hollinworth concerning the problems which the engagement posed for some ministers (Parkinson, 91). Such was his dissatisfaction that in the following year he was rumoured, along with several other discontented Lancashire ministers, to have conspired with Charles II and the Scots. After an order of the council of state on 2 September 1651 Gee was arrested and imprisoned, first in Liverpool and then in Ormskirk, Lancashire. Eventually, after several weeks, he was released without charge; he subsequently concentrated upon recording his religious experiences, which were published as *A Treatise of Prayer and Divine Providence as Relating to it* (1653). Although deeply affected by his imprisonment, he continued to play a prominent role in presbyterian circles, was appointed as an assistant to the Lancashire ejectors in 1654, and preached the funeral sermon of Richard Hollinworth in 1656.

In 1658 Gee published *The Divine Right and Originall of Civil Magistrates from God Illustrated and Vindicated*. The tract alluded to a presbyterian settlement under a restored monarchy and was signalled out for attack by some of his fellow brethren, most notably in Richard Baxter's *A Holy Commonwealth* (1659). Gee devoted the remainder of his life to his parishioners in Eccleston and lived to see the restoration of Charles II in 1660. However, he may have been suffering from a long-term illness, as he died suddenly at Eccleston on 27 May 1660. He was buried at Eccleston parish church two days later, and left a fortune of some £632 10s. 4d. to his family.

S. J. GUSCOTT

Sources *DNB* · Foster, *Alum. Oxon., 1500–1714*, 1.535 · J. Arrowsmith, ed., *Registers of the parish church of Eccleston, christenings, burials and weddings, 1603–1694* (1903) · *The life of Adam Martindale*, ed. R. Parkinson, Chetham Society, 4 (1845), 91 · W. A. Shaw, ed., *Minutes of the Manchester presbyterian classis*, 3 vols., Chetham Society, new ser., 20, 22, 24 (1890–91) · R. Halley, *Lancashire: its puritanism and nonconformity* (1872), 246, 263, 273, 278, 290 · Q. Skinner, 'Conquest and consent: Thomas Hobbes and the engagement controversy', *The interregnum*, ed. G. E. Aylmer (1972), 79–98 · inventory, 1 July 1679, Lancs. RO

Wealth at death £632 10s. 4d.: inventory, 1 July 1679, Lancs. RO

Gee, Edward (bap. **1657**, d. **1730**), dean of Lincoln, was born in Manchester, where he was baptized at the collegiate church on 29 August 1657, the son of George Gee, a shoemaker. He attended Manchester grammar school and was admitted as a sizar to St John's College, Cambridge, in May 1676; he graduated BA in 1680 and MA in 1683. Gee was incorporated at Oxford in March 1684 and in February 1695 was created DD by the archbishop of Canterbury. At some point he travelled on the continent. From 1685 to 1688 he was vicar of Great Wilbraham, Cambridgeshire, and from 1688 to 1706 he was rector of St Benet Paul's

Wharf, London. He was also chaplain-in-ordinary to William and Mary. Gee was made a prebendary of Westminster Abbey in 1701 and in 1707 became rector of Chevening, Kent; he retained both positions until his death. Appointed dean of Peterborough late in 1721, Gee resigned the next year to become dean and prebendary of Lincoln, and in 1724 he was made rector of St Margaret's, Westminster, positions which he also held until his death.

During the reign of James II, Gee became involved in the literary debate with Roman Catholic authors over church doctrine. His first publication, *Veteres vindicati* (1687), responded to the Putney minister Edward Sclater's justification of his conversion to Roman Catholicism. Gee directed his next work, *An Answer to the Compiler of Nubes testium* (1688), at another English Catholic writer, John Gother, refuting the Roman Catholic doctrines of invocation of saints, transubstantiation, and papal supremacy; in a postscript to this tract Gee took issue with a sermon preached before the king in 1687 by James's chaplain, the Jesuit Lewis Sabran. This, and three subsequent pamphlets Gee published in 1688 in the form of *A … Letter to Father Lewis Sabran*, contested Sabran's claim that the church fathers had promoted a belief in the intercession of the Virgin Mary. Two of Gee's works, criticizing papal image worship and rebutting the belief in seven sacraments, were contained in a collection of writings entitled *Popery not Founded on Scripture* (1688). These publications, and several others from 1688 in his ongoing debate with Sabran and Gother (*A Vindication of the Principles of the Author*; *The Primitive Fathers No Papists*; *A Letter to the Superiours*), constructed arguments and evidence by compiling passages from early Christian authorities, but also always included an endorsement of the doctrine and practices of the Church of England.

Gee continued on this anti-papal theme in the early years of William and Mary's rule with *The Jesuit's Memorial* (1690), which outlined papal, political, and religious designs against England in the late sixteenth- and early seventeenth-century writings of the Jesuit Robert Parsons. He also published *Of the Improvement of Time* (1692), a sermon which he preached before Queen Mary.

Gee was licensed to marry Jane Limbrey (1667–1733), from Upton Grey in Hampshire, at Lambeth on 25 January 1703. Of their children at least two, Elizabeth and Henry, died in infancy, but three others, Edward, Ann, and Martha, were minors living when their father composed his will in 1727. Gee died in London on 1 March 1730, and was buried on 6 March in Westminster Abbey near the north door by the monuments, where his predeceased children had been interred, and where his wife and his daughter Martha were later buried. He left an estate with a value of more than £7500. His will provides a commentary on the commitment to his church which had shaped his life and his writings; blessing God that he had been born a member of the Church of England, Gee rejoiced:

> In her Bosome I was educated and in her Communion I hope to dye being fully convinced in Judgement by study and by my observation dureing my travells abroad that the Church

of England is the very best and safest Communion to live and dye in of any now on Earth.   (PRO, PROB 11/636, fol. 364r)

WARREN JOHNSTON

Sources Foster, *Alum. Oxon.* • Venn, *Alum. Cant.* • will, PRO, PROB 11/636, sig. 94, fols. 363v–364v, 9 June 1727 • E. Gee, *The catalogue of all the discourses published against popery, during the reign of King James II* (1689), 18–22, 22–4, 30, 31 • *DNB* • J. L. Chester and J. Foster, eds., *London marriage licences, 1521–1869* (1887), 535 • J. L. Chester, ed., *The marriage, baptismal, and burial registers of the collegiate church or abbey of St Peter, Westminster*, Harleian Society, 10 (1876), 47 n.5, 78 n.8, 79 n.8, 258, 267, 327 n.8, 333 n.5, 339 n.1 • *Fasti Angl.* (Hardy), 2.36, 232, 540
Wealth at death approx. £7500; plus furnishings and books: will, PRO, PROB 11/636, sig. 94

Gee, Henry Simpson (1842–1924), shoe manufacturer and businessman, was born on 6 April 1842 at Lowerhead Row, Leeds, the eldest son of George Walker Gee, linen draper, and his wife, Ellen, née Simpson. He was educated privately at Grange School, Thorp Arch, near Leeds. After working briefly for his father, in 1863 he joined the successful leather tanning and dressing business of Stead and Simpson, which had been founded in 1834 by Edmund Stead and Gee's uncle, Edward Simpson.

Gee's appointment coincided with significant technological innovations in the footwear industry, notably the application of sewing and riveting machines, which facilitated the rapid expansion of factory production of ready-to-wear boots and shoes in the last third of the nineteenth century. Recognizing the importance of this, the firm had opened new boot factories in Leicester and Daventry, and in 1864 Gee moved to Leicester to oversee them. Under his control the business expanded rapidly. By the mid-1880s the Leicester factory alone was producing 30,000 pairs per week, and the firm employed over 1750 workers on various sites. In 1889 the partnership was converted into a private company, Stead and Simpson Ltd, with Gee as chairman, and after closing the original leather processing works in 1892 it concentrated entirely on footwear production and distribution.

By this time Gee had diversified into retailing to secure outlets for the firm's products, opening a network of more than 100 shops by as early as 1889. These adopted pioneering marketing strategies common to other emerging multiples of the time—using central locations, vigorous selling methods, low prices, and minimal fixtures. By the end of the century, therefore, Gee was responsible for one of the largest vertically integrated footwear businesses in the country. He was also personally involved with other leading firms, notably Freeman, Hardy, and Willis, of which he was a board member and later deputy chairman; its chairman, Edward Wood, was a member of Stead and Simpson's board.

Gee's interests, however, extended well beyond the footwear industry. He was 'a master of management well nigh in every field of industry and speculation' (*Leicester Mail*, 24 July 1924), and 'by far the most prominent and interesting personality in local commercial circles for nearly half a century' (*Shoe and Leather News*, 25 July 1924).

From 1874 he was chairman of the Leicester Horse Tramway Company and, in 1886, successfully negotiated its takeover by the corporation. He was elected to the board of the Leicestershire Banking Company in 1878, became its chairman in 1890, and was instrumental in initiating and conducting negotiations which led to its amalgamation with the London City and Midland Bank Ltd (later the Midland Bank) of which he also became a director. He was also chairman of the Bagworth Colliery Company and of Richard Hornsby & Sons Ltd, agricultural engineers of Grantham. As a commercial magnate he acquired a reputation for being able to turn round struggling businesses, which led to numerous directorships in fields as diverse as engineering, grocery, dress, drapery, and shipping. As a businessman Gee had a reputation for being something of an autocrat who did not relish challenges to his authority, and this occasionally led to bitter boardroom battles. Nor did he suffer fools gladly or sadly, sweeping the slacker and trifler from his presence 'without the slightest regard to their position or connections' (*Leicester Mail*, 21 July 1924).

Gee's involvement in local affairs was restricted to spheres in which he had particular interests. He was briefly Liberal town councillor for the North St Margaret's ward between 1878 and 1881, but he resigned due to pressure of business. In 1889 he became JP for the city and county of Leicester. He was a passionate advocate of vocational education, promoting the Leicester technical schools and leaving £20,000 in his will, the largest single bequest, to the endowment fund of the Leicester, Leicestershire, and Rutland College, later the University of Leicester. He was also president of the Leicester Trade Protection Society, the Leicester chamber of commerce, and the board of governors of the Royal Infirmary. He was firmly discriminating in his support of charities, approving in particular the work of the Charity Organization Society. Initially a Liberal, he became a unionist as a result of the home rule crisis, but he remained a committed free-trader. His political conversion was mirrored by his religious affiliation, for he abandoned the Wesleyan Methodism of his youth to become a staunch Anglican.

Gee was married three times: on 5 May 1870 to Isabella Gorham, daughter of John Gorham, surgeon, of Tonbridge; then to Mary Blanche, daughter of James Dalton of Fillingham Manor, near Lincoln; and finally to the widow of Mr S. R. Wykes, who survived him. He had four sons, all of whom eventually joined the board of directors of Stead and Simpson: Harry Percy, George Cecil, Ernest Gorham, and Charles Dalton. He also had four daughters, one of whom married Dr Astley V. Clarke, a prominent promoter of university education in Leicester.

Gee died on 20 July 1924 at his fashionable residence of Knighton Frith at Knighton, near Leicester, aged eighty-two. His funeral service was held on 24 July at St John the Baptist Church, Leicester, and he was interred at St Mary's, Knighton.   MICHAEL WINSTANLEY

Sources K. Brooker, 'Gee, Henry Simpson', *DBB* • *Leicester Mail* (21 July 1924) • *Leicester Mail* (24 July 1924) • *Leicester Mercury* (21 July 1924) • *Leicester Mercury* (29 Sept 1924) • *Shoe and Leather Record* (25

July 1924) • *Shoe and Leather News* (25 July 1924) • *The Times* (30 Sept 1924) • b. cert. • m. cert. • d. cert. • *CGPLA Eng. & Wales* (1924) **Archives** HSBC Group Archives, London, Leicester Banking Co. minutes, K 9–14 **Likenesses** Ouless, portrait • photograph, repro. in *Leicester Mail* (21 July 1924) • photograph, repro. in *Leicester Mercury* (21 July 1924) **Wealth at death** £659,699 19s. 11d.: probate, 24 Sept 1924, *CGPLA Eng. & Wales*

Gee, John (1595/6–1639), Church of England clergyman and religious controversialist, was the eldest son of John Gee (d. 1631), vicar of Dunsford, Devon, and his first wife, Grace (1575/6–1611). He was the grandson of Ralph or Raphe Gee (d. 1598) of Manchester, and nephew of two more ministers, George Gee (d. 1636) and Edward *Gee (1565/6–1618). He matriculated at Brasenose College, Oxford, on 13 July 1612 but migrated to Exeter College, where he graduated BA on 28 February 1617 and proceeded MA on 17 October 1621. He took orders before his master's degree and by 1619 had begun his career as a curate of Newton in Makerfield (Newton-le-Willows), in the parish of Winwick, Lancashire. Gee married Jane about 1621. They had five children; the eldest son, and heir, John Gee, was born in 1622. In an attempt to improve his financial position Gee undertook a series of illegal activities such as conducting clandestine, possibly Catholic, marriages and holding a disciplinary court. As a result John Bridgeman, bishop of Chester, suspended Gee from preaching in August 1623. A decade later, when, in a Laudian climate, the 'puritan' Bridgeman's financial legislation was scrutinized by royal commissioners it was alleged that during the period 1620 to 1623 Gee had acted as a kind of rural dean or informal local administrator on behalf of the bishop.

During the same period Gee had become involved with the Stanleys, the recusant gentry of Winwick, who presented him as a contestant for the incumbency of the rich and largely recusant parish. Gee appeared to be a willing instrument in an unsuccessful attempt to displace the embattled puritan rector of Winwick, Josiah Horne, who brought the issue to the Star Chamber court in December 1623. Later (in 1626) Gee pleaded guilty to writing and distributing libellous articles against Horne. Meanwhile he had established contacts with London Catholics. On 26 October 1623 he attended a Catholic evensong read by the Jesuit Robert Drury in a gatehouse adjoining the French embassy in Blackfriars. During this event, which became known as the 'fatal vespers', supporting beams gave way and the congregation fell through two floors. About ninety-five people were killed and many were injured. Gee escaped with only a bruised arm but was summoned by George Abbot, the archbishop of Canterbury, to explain his presence at a Catholic gathering. Abbot and his chaplains, Thomas Goad and Daniel Featley, wished to exploit the story of this foolhardy 'apostate' minister as a signal instance of divine judgment.

A newly resolved penitent, now living in London, Gee produced his account of the Blackfriars disaster in *The Foot out of the Snare* (1624). Above all, the tract investigated the

'ensnaring' proselytizing activities of the Catholic priesthood, wishing to expose the underground mission in England between 1621 and 1624. *The Foot* appeared in four editions in one year and was dedicated to Abbot and the new parliament. Gee claimed that he had inclined to Catholicism for about a year but had never converted. Besides the standard anti-popery polemic and the variety of anecdotes and stories—for which he ransacked such works as Samuel Harsnett's *A Declaration of Egregious Popish Impostures* (1603)—Gee's work contained historically valuable material: a catalogue of Catholic books printed abroad, and lists of Catholic priests, publishers, printers, and physicians. Though Gee was seen to act as an informer (Westminster archives), it is likely that he was given much information already available to the government.

In *New Shreds of the Old Snare* (1624) and in *Hold Fast* (1624), his recantation sermon at Paul's Cross, Gee published similar anti-Catholic materials which he had not been able to fit into his first tract. In addition he published two prayer books, the popular *Steps of Ascension unto God* (1625), possibly by his uncle Edward Gee, and *The Christian Store-House* (1631). Soon after the publication of *The Foot*, the archbishop secured Gee the living of Chislet, Kent, which he held from 1624 to 1628. Gee settled down in Kent as a reputable minister of Old Romney (1628), St Mary in the Romney Marshes (1634), and finally of Tenterden (1634–9). He died at Tenterden in July 1639 and was buried in the parish church on 20 July. His will was proved by his wife on 18 October 1639.

John Gee's half-brother, **Sir Orlando Gee** (bap. 1620, d. 1705), office-holder and benefactor, was baptized on 6 February 1620 at Dunsford, Devon, the third of the six children of John Gee (d. 1631) and his second wife, Sarah. He was steward to Algernon Percy, tenth earl of Northumberland, through whose influence he became registrar of the high court of Admiralty in 1660, and was knighted on 18 August 1682. He married, on 17 or 18 May 1662, Elizabeth Barker, daughter of Sir William Maxey. After her death he married, on 7 August 1682, Ann Chilcot (d. c.1704), daughter of Robert Chilcot of Isleworth, Middlesex. Sir Orlando was a benefactor to the parish church of Isleworth, in which he was buried on 16 June 1705.

THEODOR HARMSEN

Sources T. H. B. M. Harmsen, *John Gee's Foot out of the snare (1624)* (1992) • PRO, STAC 8/175/19 [*Josiah Horne v. John Gee etc.*, 1623–6] • bishop's act book, consistory court book, consistory court papers, visitation correction book, Ches. & Chester ALSS, MS EDA 1/4, fols. 61–2; EDC 1/45, 5/1623, nos. 29, 48; EDV 1/24, fol. 136 • A. Freeman, 'John Gee and the exploitation of disaster', in A. Freeman, *Elizabeth's misfits: brief lives of English eccentrics, exploiters, rogues and failures, 1580–1660* (1978), 50–87 • M. C. Questier, 'John Gee, Archbishop Abbot, and the use of converts from Rome in Jacobean anti-Catholicism', *Recusant History*, 21 (1992–3), 347–60 • R. C. Richardson, *Puritanism in north-west England: a regional study of the diocese of Chester to 1642* (1972) • T. S. Willan, *Elizabethan Manchester* (1980) • J. E. Bailey, *Mr. Beamont's history of Winwick; Charles Herle and the Gee family* (1877) • W. Beamont, *Winwick: its history and antiquities*, 2nd edn (1878) • J. P. Earwaker, ed., *Local gleanings relating to Lancashire and Cheshire*, 2 vols. (1875–8) • J. L. Chester and J. Foster, eds., *London marriage licences, 1521–1869* (1887) • J. G. Chilcott, 'Sir Orlando Gee', *N&Q*, 4th ser., 4 (1869), 21–2 • T. Cogswell, *The blessed revolution:*

English politics and the coming of war, 1621–1624 (1989) • P. Milward, *Religious controversies of the Jacobean age* (1978) • J. Limon, 'An allusion to the alleged Catholicism of some Jacobean players in John Gee's *New shreds of the old snare* (1624)', *N&Q*, 230 (1985), 488–9 • PRO, PROB 11/181; 11/483 sig. 138 • C. W. Boase, ed., *Registrum Collegii Exoniensis*, new edn, OHS, 27 (1894), 120 • W. A. Shaw, *The knights of England*, 2 vols. (1906) • E. Hasted, *The history and topographical survey of the county of Kent*, 2nd edn, 12 vols. (1797–1801); facs. edn (1972)

Archives Ches. & Chester ALSS, MS EDA 1/4, fols. 61–2; EDC 1/45, 5/1623, nos. 29, 48; EDV 1/24, fol. 136 • PRO, STAC 8/175/19 • PRO, SP 16/234/24, 27; SP 16/236/38, 42, 63; SP 16/237/85, 86; SP 16/240/50 and 244/13 | Staffs. RO, John Bridgeman's corresp., MSS D 1287/18/2 • Staffs. RO, earl of Bradford (Weston Park) MSS

Likenesses F. Bird, marble bust, 1705 (Orlando Gee), Isleworth church, Middlesex

Wealth at death besides his own house, owned four houses in parish of Tenterden, which he bequeathed to his children; Tenterden valued in 1640 at £120 p.a. (600 communicants): will, PRO, PROB 11/181; 11/483, sig. 138; Hasted, *History*, vol. 3, p. 102

Gee, Joshua (*fl.* **1713–1748**), writer on trade, is a figure known only through his publications. He is often described as a merchant, and according to J. R. McCulloch was 'extensively engaged in trade'. He published the work that made him famous, *The Trade and Navigation of Great Britain Consider'd*, in London in 1729. It went through many editions (4th edn, 1738) and was frequently reprinted during the eighteenth century, notably by Robert and Andrew Foulis of Glasgow in 1755 and in a French translation in 1750. Gee's most famous work presented its overview of British trade both historically and by national areas, and commented on specific problems of trade (for example devoting chapter 12 to 'French *fashions pernicious to England*'). However, the greater part of the work was concerned with suggesting remedies: in particular solving the colonial labour problem by transporting domestic convicts and the unemployed poor and the creation of free ports at Gibraltar and Port Mahon; and, more generally, the encouragement of foreign import-replacing production in the plantations. In 1742 Gee published two further works, both related to the woollen trade, namely, *An Impartial Enquiry into the Importance and Present State of the Woollen Manufactures of Great Britain* and *The Grazier's Advocate, or, Free Thoughts of Wool and the Woollen Trade*.

Gee is widely thought to have been, in 1713–14, an important contributor to the twice-weekly issues of the *British Merchant*, and a collaborator with Henry Martin in arguing the protectionist case against the treaty of commerce with France proposed at Utrecht. The *British Merchant* was set up in opposition to the *Mercator, or, Commerce Retrieved*, which defended the idea of such a treaty. Gee has been described as a 'staunch protectionist' (Johnson, 145) and as 'the spokesman for the wool manufacturers as well as a merchant enemy of the India Company' (ibid., 348). Whether he was therefore a merchant writing now and again on trade or just a writer on trade is not clear. The latter seems to have been David Hume's opinion:

> The writings of Mr. Gee struck the nation with an universal panic, when they saw it plainly demonstrated, by a detail of particulars, that the balance was against them for so considerable a sum as must leave them without a single shilling in five or six years. But luckily, twenty years have since elapsed, with an expensive foreign war [1739–48]; yet it

is commonly supposed, that money is still more plentiful among us than in any former period. (Hume, 61–2)

In his *Lectures on Jurisprudence* Adam Smith cited Hume's opinion approvingly, but in addition poked considerable fun at Gee's balance of trade data showing all the nations of Europe as having a favourable balance with Britain, with the exceptions of Spain, Portugal, and Ireland, as well as the American (but not West Indian) plantations. Although Gee's works did contain much of the protectionist content with which they were charged, they provided no clues as to the life of the author. It is not known when he died.   PETER GROENEWEGEN

Sources J. R. McCulloch, *The literature of political economy: a classified catalogue* (1845), 45–6 • E. S. Furniss, *The position of the laborer in a system of nationalism* (1957), 53 • D. Vickers, 'Joshua Gee', *The new Palgrave: a dictionary of economics*, ed. J. Eatwell, M. Milgate, and P. Newman (1987) • D. Hume, *Writings on economics*, ed. E. Rotwein (1955), 61–2 • Adam Smith, *Lectures on jurisprudence*, ed. R. L. Meek, D. D. Raphael, and P. G. Stein (1978), 392–3, 506–7, 513, 516 • E. A. J. Johnson, *Predecessors of Adam Smith* (1937), 145, 348n. • C. Knight, ed., *The English cyclopaedia: biography*, 6 vols. (1856–8) [suppl. (1872)]

Archives LUL, memorials and related papers relating to colonial trade

Gee, Sir Orlando (*bap.* **1620**, *d.* **1705**). *See under* Gee, John (1595/6–1639).

Gee, Samuel Jones (**1839–1911**), physician, was born at 359 Oxford Street, London, on 13 September 1839, the only surviving child of William Doddrell Gee (1804–1891), dealer in china and glass, and his wife, Lydia Sutton. He always held high regard for his parents, his father as a businessman and his mother who educated him for the first eight years of his life. From her care he went in 1847 to a school at Enfield and afterwards to University College School (1852–4). He passed the matriculation examination of the University of London in May 1857 and the following October entered as a student at University College Hospital where he graduated MB in 1861 and MD in 1865. He served as house surgeon both at the University College Hospital and at the Hospital for Sick Children, becoming in April 1865 a member of the Royal College of Physicians; he was made assistant physician at Great Ormond Street in 1866. It was through the efforts of Thomas Smith that Gee was elected assistant physician at St Bartholomew's Hospital on 5 March 1868. Dr Francis Harris had been ill and Sir Thomas Smith persuaded him to give Gee an opportunity. Though Harris resented him they then became great friends, and Gee often stayed at his home at Lamberhurst. He married, on 2 December 1875, Sarah, daughter of the late Emmanuel Cooper. Robert Bridges was his best man, reflecting his love of poetry. The Gees were blissfully happy in their married life, and two daughters were born to them.

On 24 October 1878 Gee was elected physician and on 22 September 1904 consulting physician, continuing in the post until his death. In St Bartholomew's medical school he was demonstrator of morbid anatomy (1872–4) and lecturer on the principles and practice of medicine (1878–93). In addition he became an expert on the diseases of children at Great Ormond Street, and was invited to deliver the

Goulstonian lectures in 1871 entitled 'The heat of the body', the Bradshaw lectures, 'The signs of acute peritoneal diseases', in 1872, and the Lumleian lectures, 'The causes and forms of pulmonary emphysema and asthma', in 1899. He was censor at the Royal College of Physicians in 1893–4 and senior censor in 1894. Gee had a considerable private practice and in 1901 was appointed physician to the prince of Wales (later George V).

For thirty years Gee was one of the characters of medicine in London. His short, almost diminutive stature, his manner of speech, his dry wit, the intonation of his voice, his aloofness, and punctilious habits made him a living legend. A case in point is the story of his leaving his home at 31 Upper Brook Street for the hospital when a patient detained him. The door of the carriage was closed but not fastened. It soon swung open and hit a lamppost. The door was taken off its hinges, and Gee ordered his coachman to drive on without the door so that he could arrive on time.

A prolific writer, Gee's earliest works were on chickenpox, scarlet fever, and tubercular meningitis, and appeared in Russell Reynolds's *System of Medicine* vols. 1 and 2 (1866, 1868). Forty-six other papers were published in the *St Bartholomew's Hospital Reports*. His *Auscultation and Percussion together with other Methods of Physical Examination of the Chest* (1870) was used by generations of students, reaching its fifth edition in 1906. His other best-seller was *Medical Lectures and Aphorisms*, which appeared in 1902 and went into three editions in four years. It contains fourteen lectures (including his Royal College of Physicians lectures) and 272 aphorisms collected by his house surgeon, T. J. Horder, which represent the style of clinical teaching at the bedside of his patients. Its dogmatic method he had learned from Sir William Jenner, but his knowledge he gathered from his vast library of the history of medicine, philosophy, metaphysics, and English literature. Gee was librarian of the Royal Medical and Chirurgical Society from 1887 to 1889; he read Montaigne often, and immersed himself in the writings of Sydenham, Heberden, Milton, Phineas Fletcher, and Hobbes. His favourite politician was Oliver Cromwell.

Gee was considered one of the most brilliant clinical teachers of the Victorian era, the first to identify coeliac disease as well as splenic cachexia in children. He died suddenly on 3 August 1911 of extensive atheromatous degeneration of the aorta and its valves, at Keswick Hotel, Keswick, while on a visit with his daughter. Cremated at Golders Green, Middlesex, on 8 August, his urn was placed next to those of his wife and his deceased daughter in the columbarium at Kensal Green cemetery.

D. BEN REES

Sources D. Power, *The Lancet* (19 Aug 1911), 554–5 · N. Moore, *St Bartholomew's Hospital Reports*, 47 (1911), 21–7 · *St Bartholomew's Hospital Journal*, 19 (1911–12), 12–13, 25–7 · *DNB* · *BMJ* (19 Aug 1911), 411–12; (16 Sept 1911), 642 · *St Bartholomew's Hospital Reports*, 71 (1938), 229–79 · Munk, *Roll*, 4.183–4 · b. cert. · m. cert. · d. cert.
Archives RCP Lond., corresp. and papers
Likenesses G. Jerrard, photograph, 1881, Wellcome L. · C. Vigor, oils, *c*.1900, RCP Lond. · miniature, RCP Lond. · photograph, repro. in Moore, 'In memoriam' · photomechanical print, Wellcome L.

Wealth at death £34,981 19s. 2d.: probate, 9 Sept 1911, *CGPLA Eng. & Wales*

Gee, Thomas (1815–1898), newspaper publisher and politician, was born at Denbigh on 24 January 1815, the second son of Thomas Gee (1780–1845), printer, and Mary Foulkes of Hendre'r-ŵydd, Denbighshire. He was educated at Grove Park School, Wrexham, and Denbigh grammar school; at fourteen he was apprenticed to his father, though he continued to attend the grammar school to read Greek and Latin with the masters there. In 1836, having finished his apprenticeship, he spent two years in London working at the offices of the publishers Eyre and Spottiswoode, before returning to his father's business in Denbigh in 1838.

At this time Gee seriously contemplated a career as a preacher. In 1837 he wrote to his parents 'it is my wish to employ my talent (which I know is but very small) to the glory of God' (Gwynn Jones, 54) and began to preach with the Calvinistic Methodists. In 1838 he became a member of this connection's Denbighshire monthly meeting, of which he was to remain a member for the rest of his life, taking an especial interest in education and Sunday schools. Any thoughts Gee might have had of a career in the ministry, however, were terminated in 1845 when his father died, leaving him in sole charge of the family business. On 11 October 1842 he had married Susannah (*b.* 1817), daughter of John Hughes, Plas Coch, Llangynhafal, Denbighshire. They had six daughters, including Sarah Magdalene *Matthews, and three sons.

Gee's success as a publisher was the basis for the great influence he enjoyed in nineteenth-century Wales. His success was based on expansion of the business—he was described as a 'publisher–wholesaler, printer, binder, newspaper proprietor, stationer and retail book-seller' (P. H. Jones, 30)—and stemmed from a number of factors. In part, he was able to exploit his denominational connections: for example, he published the official hymnbook used by all Calvinistic Methodists before 1876. However, he was also alert to developments in the market for Welsh-language texts, and put himself in a position to supply it with a wide range of general religious books, collections of sermons by famous preachers, and poetry. Although his methods did not make him popular with everyone—he fell out badly with some of his authors—his motivation was by no means the simple pursuit of profit. From early publishing ventures such as the innovative quarterly *Y Traethodydd* (which he published from 1845 to 1854), to the massive Welsh-language encyclopaedia *Y Gwyddioniadur* (1858–78), the total cost of which exceeded £20,000—Gee aimed deliberately to educate his compatriots through the medium of their native tongue.

Perhaps Gee's most successful publishing venture, however, came in 1857, when he saw an opening in the market for a weekly Welsh-language newspaper. He told a friend that he planned a family paper 'of a superior class … of a distinctly religious character … and as liberal in its politics as you please' (P. H. Jones, 110). On 4 March 1857 *Baner Cymru* (known as *Baner ac Amserau Cymru* after its merger with the Liverpool-based title *Yr Amserau* in October 1859)

Thomas Gee (1815–1898), by Maull & Fox, c.1860

was launched. *Baner*, with its highly talented staff, among whom were such luminaries of mid-Victorian Welsh politics as John Griffith (Y Gohebydd), became the most authoritative newspaper in the Welsh language—what one contemporary called 'the mightiest regenerating engine in our country' (J. Davies to T. Gee, 24 July 1865, NL Wales, Gee MSS, 3305 D/41). Gee's influence pervaded its pages, and it was said that he checked all copy before it went to press, as well as writing many of the leading articles. Under his editorship *Baner* defined the agenda of Liberal politics in Wales for a generation: vote by ballot, the disestablishment of the Anglican church in Wales, the abolition of tithes (especially during the so-called 'tithe war' of 1886–9, in which Gee played a leading part), Welsh home rule, and even, in the 1890s, land nationalization were all key issues backed by the paper.

If, on occasion, *Baner* overstepped the mark in its enthusiasm, as in 1868, when Gee was successfully sued for having libelled a Conservative candidate at the general election, the paper helped make Gee 'the ruling power of all the great Liberal Party of North Wales' (reminiscence of Lady Watkin Williams [1913], NL Wales, Gee MSS 8319E). Yet he remained personally unambitious, and asked few favours from either the party or from the individuals whose popularity his newspaper did so much to promote. Though offered several chances to stand as a candidate for

parliament himself, notably at Cardiganshire in 1867 and South Caernarvonshire in 1885, he preferred to remain in his native town, where he could keep a close eye on his business interests. His political activism was confined to the affairs of the region. He was a familiar figure on the platform at Liberal political meetings across north Wales, and he also took a leading role in the municipal affairs of Denbigh. And alongside his political activities, he always remained an active member of the Calvinistic Methodists.

Gee died in Fronallt, Denbigh, on 28 June 1898, and was buried in the new graveyard at Denbigh. As a businessman, he played a part in nearly all the important developments in the Denbighshire economy after 1850, having, in addition to his publishing business, interests in mining and slate quarrying, the Ruthin Soda Water Company (of which he was a director), and both the Vale of Clwyd Railway and the North Denbighshire Building Society (of which he was the first president in 1866). Yet his fame and posthumous reputation ultimately rested on his political role. To Welsh politicians of the generation before the First World War Gee was 'one of the Pioneers of Welsh liberty' (O. Williams to T. Gee [1892], NL Wales, Gee MSS 3809D); to his first biographer and former employee, T. Gwynn Jones, writing in 1913, Gee 'was the one man who practically made modern Wales what it is politically' (T. Gwynn Jones to Miss Gee, 12 Sept 1911, NL Wales, Gee MSS 3811D). MATTHEW CRAGOE

Sources *DWB* · T. Gwynn Jones, *Cofiant Thomas Gee* (1913) · P. H. Jones, 'A nineteenth century Welsh printer: some aspects of the career of Thomas Gee (1815–98)', fellowship diss., Library Association, 1977 [2 vols.] · *Baner ac Amserau Cymru* (1858–98)
Archives NL Wales, corresp. and papers · NL Wales, family MSS | NL Wales, letters to J. Gwynoro Davies; letters to Lewis Edwards; letters to T. C. Edwards; letters to T. E. Ellis; letters to John Ceiriog Hughes; letters to David Lewis; corresp. with Sir J. H. Lewis; letters to David Lloyd George
Likenesses Maull & Fox, photograph, c.1860, repro. in Gwynn Jones, *Cofiant Thomas Gee* [*see illus.*] · photographs, repro. in Gwynn Jones, *Cofiant Thomas Gee* · portrait, repro. in *ILN*, 113 (1898), 507

Geeran, Thomas (d. 1871), impostor, was, according to his own story and that of two of his biographers, born at Scarriff, co. Clare, on 14 May 1766, the son of Michael Geeran, farmer. Geeran's account of his life gave him a military career, enlisting in March 1796, travelling to Madras, joining the 71st highlanders, and taking part in the siege of Seringapatam in 1799. After serving in Egypt, he claimed to have fought at Waterloo and returned to Britain in 1819, being discharged from the army without a pension. After working as a sawyer, he settled in Brighton, where he became something of a local character, living on his military reminiscences. He died in the infirmary of the Brighton poor-law union on 28 October 1871, aged, by his own account, 105 years and 6 months. His death certificate, witnessed by the mark of Mary Ann Cooper, an illiterate inmate of the workhouse, gives his age as 105 years.

Research by W. J. Thomas showed, however, that Geeran's account was mythical, except that a Michael Gearyn or Gayran enlisted on 3 March 1813 and deserted a month later on 10 April, which, if this was the same person, would make Geeran perhaps eighty to eighty-five years old at the time of his death. Geeran's almost certainly duped biographers were H. R. Williams (*Life of Thomas Geeran, a Centenarian*, 1870) and an anonymous writer (*Longevity, with Life, Autograph, and Portrait*, 1871).

H. C. G. MATTHEW

Sources *The Times* (20–27 Nov 1871) · R. T. Massy, 'Autopsy of a centenarian', *Medical Times and Gazette* (25 Nov 1871), 642–3 · *DNB* · W. J. Thoms, *Human longevity* (1873) · d. cert.
Likenesses photograph, repro. in H. R. Williams, *Life of Thomas Geeran* (1870)

Geffery [Geffrey], **Sir Robert** (*d.* 1704), merchant, came from Cornwall, but his precise ancestry is uncertain. A Robert Geffery, the son of Robert of Tredennach, was baptized at Landrake on 24 May 1613, but this may have been another member of the Geffery or Geffrey family, several members of which were born and married at Landrake. It has been said that his father came from Truro and that Geffery was born in 1622.

On 23 September 1651 Geffery married Presilla (Priscilla; 1633–1676), the daughter of Luke Cropley, a lawyer, of London. The *London Visitation Pedigrees, 1664* mentions a daughter of the London merchant Robert Geffryes, called Sarah, who married another London merchant, Richard Lant, and died in 1682, but there is no certainty that this was the same Geffery. He does not seem to have been related to the Jeffries clan whose numerous branches provided several important London merchants in the Levant and American tobacco trades and with whom Sir Robert is easily and frequently confused. He certainly knew and, while lord mayor, entertained the infamous George Jeffries, but there is little hard evidence that they were more than acquaintances.

All that is known of Geffery's business is that he was free of the Ironmongers' Company and lived at Lime Street in the City of London. He is listed among the original charter members of the Royal Africa Company, in 1672, and he held £400 of stock, which qualified him to become an assistant in 1691, but he is not known to have traded overseas. Ironmongery may indeed have been his real as well as his nominal trade. His loans to the government were comparatively modest. On 28 September 1689 he subscribed £500 to a loan secured on the 12*d*. Aid, a levy of 12*d*. in the pound to raise money for defence, and the Treasury books record a similar subscription of £1000 in March 1690, 1693, and 1694.

Although he did not enter national politics, Geffery rose to high office in his livery company and in the City. He was elected warden of the ironmongers in 1664 and master in 1667 and 1685, common councilman for Lime Street in 1660–62, deputy from 1663 to 1667 and from 1669 to 1676, sheriff in 1673–4, receiving a knighthood in 1673. He was alderman of Cordwainer ward from 22 June 1676 to 16 August 1687, and from 3 October 1688 to 6 February 1704, by which time he had become, as senior alderman, father of the City. He held office as lord mayor in 1685–6. In 1670–71 he was deputy governor of the Irish Society and in 1673–5 auditor. In 1681 he was also colonel of a regiment of

Sir Robert Geffery (*d.* 1704), attrib. Sir Godfrey Kneller

trained bands, and on 1 and 9 March 1690 he was commissioned deputy lieutenant and lieutenant of the City. He was president of Bridewell and Bethlem hospitals from 1688 to 1690 and from 18 March 1693 to 1704, but on 20 February 1691 he failed to succeed Sir John Lawrence as president of St Thomas's Hospital, a post which fell to the whig Sir Robert Clayton.

Geffery was one of six ironmongers appointed to represent the company at the entertainment at Guildhall for Charles II on 5 July 1660. It was he who presented the company's petition of submission to the king when Charles II seized the company's charter in 1683 by the process of *quo warranto*. Under the new charter granted by James II he was appointed master in the place of William Hinton, who had been elected by the company in the usual manner. But he was dismissed along with twenty-one other assistants on 25 September 1685 until the previous charter was restored.

Geffery was an Anglican tory who was sued, along with others, for reviling Gilbert Nelson, another London merchant, by calling him rogue and for inciting the lord mayor to commit him to Newgate. He specified Anglican orthodoxy in his endowment of schools and prayers, and he refused to compromise with the Catholic policies of

James II in order to retain office. Bramston mentions that Geffery took action, when lord mayor, to suppress an alleged mass set up in a house in Lime Street, his own neighbourhood, and he was turned out of his aldermanry by James in 1687.

Geffery died on 26 February 1704. His wife had predeceased him and there were no children. His personal estate was probably about £10,000, a conventional sum for a successful domestic merchant, but well below the wealth of the élite of overseas merchants and financiers. He made many bequests to relatives and friends, and to the Ironmongers' Company, which received £200 and silver plate. The bulk of his estate, however, went to a wide variety of charities. His philanthropy took a somewhat old-fashioned form and included a gift of £400 to the church of St Dionis Backchurch, to endow the reading of prayers twice daily, together with a velvet carpet for the communion table, a pulpit cushion, and the Book of Common Prayer. A school at Landrake, Cornwall, was endowed with £520 and an annuity was allocated to the school of Bishop's Stortford, Hertfordshire, both of which were put into the hands of the Ironmongers. Relief was provided for the poor of Landrake and London and 10s. per annum for dowries for twenty poor maids. Among other beneficiaries were hospitals and the widows of clergymen. The residue of his estate was left in trust to be administered by the Ironmongers' Company. He specified that his assets be sold and reinvested in real property. The Ironmongers were to purchase land in or near London as a site for almshouses and provide pensions of £6 per annum plus 15s. for gowns. There were sufficient funds in the trust to enable the company to purchase for £200 on 25 March 1712 a plot of land in the country (now Kingsland Road, Hackney) and to erect fourteen almshouses and a chapel in 1715 for £4500. On 29 March 1716 further land was acquired for £20 as a burial-ground. In 1910 the almshouses were moved to Mottingham and the original site was purchased by the London county council for a museum of furniture and cabinet-making, called the Geffrye Museum, which opened in 1914.   RICHARD GRASSBY

Sources N. Luttrell, *A brief historical relation of state affairs from September 1678 to April 1714*, 6 vols. (1857) • *The autobiography of Sir John Bramston*, ed. [Lord Braybrooke], CS, 32 (1845) • *CSP dom.* • J. B. Whitmore and A. W. Hughes Clarke, eds., *London visitation pedigrees, 1664*, Harleian Society, 92 (1940) • W. A. Shaw, ed., *Calendar of treasury books*, [33 vols. in 64], PRO (1904–69) • J. R. Woodhead, *The rulers of London, 1660–1689* (1965) [has several misprints] • K. G. Davies, *The Royal Africa Company* (1957) • A. B. Beaven, ed., *The aldermen of the City of London, temp. Henry III–[1912]*, 2 vols. (1908–13) • J. Nicholl, *Some account of the Worshipful Company of Ironmongers* (1851) • 'Report to the twentieth general meeting, 12 April 1860', *Transactions of the London and Middlesex Archaeological Society* [London and Middlesex Archaeological Society], 2 (1859–64), 64–74 • [E. Hatton], *A new view of London*, 2 vols. (1708) • S. Lee, ed., *A collection of the names of the merchants living in and about the City of London* (1677) • J. Polsue, *A complete parochial history of the county of Cornwall*, 4 vols. (1867–72) • *The Geffrye Museum* (1952) [handbook] • J. L. Chester, ed., *The reiester booke of Saynte De'nis Backchurch parishe … begynnynge … 1538*, Harleian Society, register section, 3 (1878) • *IGI* • will, PRO, PROB 11/475, sig. 63

Archives BL, Harleian MS 2263 • CRO, Repertories

Likenesses J. van Nost, lead statue, 1723; copy, 1912, Geffrye Museum, London • J. van Nost, statue, 1723, almshouses, Mottingham, Kent; formerly at almshouses, Kingsland Road, Hackney • T. Athow, watercolour (after R. Phillips), GL • attrib. G. Kneller, portrait, priv. coll. [*see illus.*] • R. Phillips, portrait, Ironmongers Hall, London • Trotte, engraving (after portrait attrib. Kneller), Bridewell Hospital, Witley, Surrey

Wealth at death approx. £10,000—aggregated charitable bequests

Geiger, Hans [*formerly* Johannes Wilhelm] (1882–1945), physicist, was born on 30 September 1882 in Neustadt in the Rhine Palatinate, Germany, the eldest of the five children of Wilhelm Geiger (1856–1943) and Marie Plochmann (1858–1910). His father was a philologist, first at secondary school (*Gymnasium*) in Neustadt and Munich and from 1891 as professor at the University of Erlangen. Geiger grew up in Erlangen and finished school (took his *Abitur*) there in 1901. After one year's military service he began to study physics and mathematics at the universities of Erlangen and Munich. Eilhard Wiedemann in Erlangen became his teacher, supervising Geiger's thesis on 'Strahlungs-Temperatur- und Potentialmessungen in Entladungsröhren bei starken Strömen' (1906). The dissertation involved experiments with and measurements of electrical discharges and made Geiger familiar with experimental skills that were of great importance for his later work on the development of electrical methods for the detection of nuclear particles. With the recommendation of his teacher Geiger went as a postdoctoral researcher to Arthur Schuster at the University of Manchester. He had planned to stay in Manchester for only a year, but remained for more than six years. Schuster's successor, Ernest Rutherford, made the talented German his assistant and educated him in radioactivity research. Geiger's scientific work centred on the development of electrical methods and instruments for detecting and counting atomic particles, and on their use for the investigation of atomic structure. In 1908, together with Rutherford, he invented an electrical technique (based on an ionization chamber) for counting single alpha particles, and was able to show the equivalence of the new technique with the common optical scintillation detector. Using the counter Geiger proved in 1908 the statistical character of radioactive decay. This result was important not only for radioactivity itself but for the further development of atomic physics and quantum theory, since it was a key for the general understanding of emission and absorption as a statistical process. Later, Geiger and Rutherford estimated the total number of alpha particles emitted per second from 1 gram of radium and also the half-life period for radium. With this number they could also determine the value of the elementary charge and that the alpha particle was a double charge particle.

In 1910 Geiger investigated the linear relationship between the radius of action (R) and the third power of velocity (v) for alpha particles from various radioactive materials (Geigersche Reichweitegesetz R ~ v^3) and in 1911 the relation between the half-value period (η) and the radius of action (R) (Geiger-Nuttall rule ln η ~ ln R). During this period Geiger had also observed that some alpha particles were scattered in a thin metal foil in a way which was inappropriate to a statistical scattering based upon multiple scattering. This observation, made together with E. Marsden in 1909, led to Rutherford's nuclear model of the atom (1911) and the so-called Rutherford's scattering formula, which was verified by Geiger and Marsden in 1911–12. Geiger earned such a large reputation in this new field of physics at Manchester that in 1912 he was appointed head of the new laboratory for radioactivity of the Physikalisch-Technische Reichsanstalt (PTR—Physical-Technical Institute) in Berlin and during the following years he made it one of the leading centres in radioactivity and early nuclear physics.

It was during this Berlin period that Geiger carried out a great deal of metrological work in connection with the establishment of a radium standard and improved his Geiger counter to establish the so-called point counter. This was a detector which made possible much more rapid counting, not only of alpha particles but also of beta particles as well as other types of radiation. With the help of the new counter James Chadwick, who came as Rutherford's student to Geiger in 1913, was able to demonstrate the continuous beta spectrum. After the war Geiger developed, together with Walther Bothe, the coincidence method, the combination of two point counters for the detection of simultaneous events. Using this new precision technique they could test the exact validity of classic conservation principles for single atomic events (1925), which were then called into question by the Compton effect and its statistical interpretation by N. Bohr, H. A. Kramers, and J. Slater. Max von Laue stated that with this work Geiger and Bothe 'turned the course of physics from the path of error' (Laue, 153). In 1920 Geiger married Elisabeth Heffter (1896–1982), daughter of a famous Berlin family of scientists; they had three sons, born in 1921, 1924, and 1927.

In 1925 Geiger accepted the chair of physics at the University of Kiel. In 1928 he and his student Walther Müller developed the counting device for which Geiger is still best known: the Geiger–Müller counter. It combined the virtues of the Geiger counter with that of the point counter and became the most important device in nuclear physics and related fields. During the following years Geiger endeavoured to improve this instrument in many studies and applications—for instance for investigations in cosmic ray physics—and led the way in making it a very commonly used piece of equipment. In 1928 Geiger moved to Tübingen as professor of physics. In 1935 he returned to Berlin as director of the Institute of Physics at the Technical University.

Besides his scientific work Geiger was a talented and fascinating teacher and also found time for a great deal of literary work: between 1926 and 1933 he was the editor of the *Handbuch der Physik* (with K. Scheel) and from 1936 he edited the *Zeitschrift für Physik*. Geiger was a member of several scientific societies and academies (Leipzig, 1932; Leopoldina, 1935; Berlin, 1936); in 1929 he was honoured with the Duddell medal of the Physical Society and in 1938 with

the Hughes medal of the Royal Society of London. Further, in 1954 Walther Bothe, Geiger's closest colleague at the PTR, was awarded the Nobel prize for the coincidence method of counting particles that Geiger and Bothe had developed together in the mid-1920s. The outbreak of the Second World War and a painful rheumatic condition soon led to a cessation of his research activities. His poor health and the chaotic events of 1945 (his home was damaged by bombs and later occupied by the allies in connection with the Potsdam conference) were instrumental in his early death, on 24 September 1945 in Potsdam. He was buried on 29 September at Neuer Friedhof, Potsdam.

DIETER HOFFMANN

Sources H. Geiger, 'Memories of Rutherford in Manchester', *Nature*, 141 (1938), 244 • H. Geiger, 'Some reminiscences of Rutherford during his time in Manchester', *The collected papers of Lord Rutherford*, ed. J. Chadwick (1963), 2.295–8 • W. Bothe, 'Die Geigerschen Zählmethoden', *Die Naturwissenschaften*, 30 (1942), 593–9 • M. von Laue, 'Nachruf auf Hans Geiger', *Jahrbuch der Deutschen Akademie der Wissenschaften* (1950), 150–58 [with bibliography] • J. Chadwick, 'The Rutherford memorial lecture, 1953', *PRS*, 224A (1954), 436–447, esp. 441–3 • T. J. Trenn, 'Geiger, Hans', *DSB* • T. J. Trenn, 'The Geiger–Müller counter of 1928', *Annals of Science*, 43 (1986), 111–35 • F. G. Rheingans, *Hans Geiger und die elektrischen Zählmethoden 1908 bis 1928* (1988) • E. Swinne, *Hans Geiger: Spuren aus einem Leben für die Physik* (1988) • D. Hoffmann, ed., *Hans Geiger: Studien zu Leben und Werk* (1998)

Archives Akademie der Wissenschaften zu Berlin Brandenburg, Berlin • Berlin University • Kiel University • Tübingen University • U. Cam., Rutherford MSS

Likenesses portrait, Akademie der Wissenschaften zu Berlin Brandenburg, Berlin • portrait, University of Manchester

Geikie, Sir Archibald (1835–1924), geologist and historian, was born in Edinburgh on 28 December 1835, the eldest son of James Stuart Geikie, a shop proprietor and subsequently professional musician, and Isabella Thom. James Murdoch *Geikie (1839–1915) was his younger brother. Geikie was educated in Edinburgh, first at Mr Black's preparatory school, then at the high school (1845–8), studied classics at Edinburgh University (1854–5), and also took private classes in mineralogy and chemistry. Due to some misdemeanour of Geikie's brother William his family got into financial difficulties, and Geikie left university without graduating. However, he had already begun geological fieldwork and had carried out independent investigations round Edinburgh and in the Hebrides, and he made the acquaintance of local scientists and naturalists, especially Hugh Miller (1802–1856). Youthful manuscripts show that Geikie was extremely devout when young and an admirer of the theologian Thomas Chalmers (1780–1847), but early religious zeal later gave way to the character of a determined bureaucrat and to conventional religious observance.

Introduced to Andrew Ramsay (1814–1891) in 1853, and with a recommendation from Miller to Sir Roderick Murchison (1792–1871), Geikie was appointed to the new Scottish branch of the geological survey in 1855, and remained with the organization until his retirement in 1901. His survey work began near Edinburgh, a region well endowed with volcanic rocks. Following in the tradition of James Hutton and John Playfair, Geikie became an acknowledged authority on igneous rocks, and devoted much of his career to their study—in Britain, on the continent, and in the United States. He also accepted the ideas of Ramsay and others on glacial theory, and the 'fluvialism' of Hutton. This was well illustrated by Geikie's account of the Sgùrr of Eigg, visited in 1864, which he construed as a remnant of a lava that had flowed down a valley eroded into a previously extruded lava sheet. Thus the effects that could be achieved by the slow processes of erosion over great lengths of time were exemplified, in accordance with the doctrines of gradualism and 'uniformitarianism'—a term that Geikie later deftly characterized by the aphorism 'the present is the key to the past' (Geikie, *Founders*, 299). He had learned to reason in this way in geology from Miller.

In 1860 Geikie was called to accompany the ageing Murchison on an important reconnaissance survey in the north-west highlands. Together they formulated the theory that there was a regular ascending sequence: from the 'Fundamental Gneiss' of the west coast, to the Moine Schists of the central part of north Scotland, and on to the Old Red Sandstone of the east coast. Some limestones to the west of the Moines were identified by their fossils as Silurian, and on this basis the Moines were also designated Silurian, being regarded as metamorphosed *in situ*. This pleased Murchison, as it allowed large areas of Scotland to be mapped in the colour representing 'his' Silurian system. Thus supporting Murchison, Geikie was appointed to the directorship of the Scottish branch of the survey (1867), and conjointly to the new Murchison chair at Edinburgh (1871). Geikie subsequently published a substantial biography of his former chief (1875), and several other important studies in the history of geology, notably his influential *Founders of Geology* (1897), but in 1883–4 the Murchison–Geikie theory of the highlands was shown by Charles Lapworth and others, including Geikie's own surveyors, to be illusory. Even so, by 1882 Geikie had already achieved his life ambition, being appointed director general of the survey in succession to Ramsay. He worked zealously and efficiently in this role, but he was not universally popular, and not all the staff felt that he defended their interests sufficiently. In 1871 he had married Anna Maria Alice Gabrielle Pignatel (1851–1916), from Lyons, who was generally known as Alice. They had four children: Lucy, Roderick, Elsie, and Gabrielle. Lady Geikie was related by marriage to Alexander Macmillan of the well-known publishing house, which published several of Geikie's books. Geikie and Macmillan were old friends from student days in Edinburgh.

Geikie's career was outstandingly successful. He served as president of the Geological Society (1890–92 and 1906–8), and as president of the British Association (1892). Elected fellow of the Royal Society in 1865, he served as foreign secretary (1889–93), secretary (1903–8), and president (1908–12), the only geologist ever to have occupied this position. He was also active in the work of the early international geological congresses. He was knighted in 1891, created KCB in 1907, and appointed to the Order of Merit and received the cross of the Légion d'honneur in 1913. He held honorary degrees from most British and many foreign universities and was a corresponding member of numerous learned academies. He received medals from the Geological Society of London, the Royal Geographical Society of Scotland, the Royal Society of Edinburgh, and the Royal Society of London.

Geikie's success was due in considerable measure to his great industry, tenacious memory, and splendid gifts as a writer. (He was also an accomplished artist.) Even his technical works, of which his *Ancient Volcanoes of Great Britain* (1897) was the most important, were highly readable. Geikie greatly enhanced the study of geology in Britain with his *Text-Book of Geology* (1882), and he also wrote widely used school texts. His popular writings in geology, notably his *Scenery of Scotland* (1865), *Geological Sketches at Home and Abroad* (1882), and *Landscape in History* (1905), are enduring contributions to geological literature. He wrote interestingly about the relationship between landforms and rock types and human history and character. As an educationist, besides having a successful tenure in the Murchison chair at Edinburgh, where his student field excursions were greatly appreciated, Geikie served, for example, as a governor of Harrow School and a trustee of the British Museum. He also played an important role in the activities of the Haslemere Educational Museum.

Though an extremely experienced geologist, Geikie did not make important theoretical advances. He often relied on the support of his subordinates to corroborate his views, and was known to publish under his name work that was chiefly carried out by his staff. Among his most important investigations was his study of the Scottish deposits of Old Red Sandstone, which he subdivided into an upper and lower series, each characterized by its particular fish-fauna and separated from one another by unconformity. This supposedly allowed correlation between exposures in different regions and temporarily superseded the earlier tripartite subdivision of Murchison. But after Geikie's retirement from the survey the trichotomy was restored on the basis of palaeobotanical evidence.

Following the idea of John Fleming and Henry Godwin-Austin that the Old Red sediments were lacustrine in origin, Geikie hypothesized several large lakes in the region of northern Britain in Devonian times, with 'Lake Orcadie' occupying the region north of the Grampians up to the Shetlands. The model subsequently received acceptance, the idea being that the deposits were laid down in sometimes saline basins adjacent to mountainous areas. Geikie's investigations of Carboniferous and Permian volcanics in Scotland also found favour, but his rejection of Precambrian rocks in Pembrokeshire involved him in controversy and has not been sustained.

Following a visit to the United States in 1879, when he observed lava flows of the Snake River region of Idaho, Geikie applied von Richthofen's idea of fissure eruptions to the 'plateau basalts' of the Hebrides, and in so doing became involved in a heated controversy with John Judd about the granites and gabbros of Skye. Helped by his subordinates, and apparently vindicated by the subsequent mapping of Alfred Harker, Geikie 'won' this debate, though later observers now see merit in Judd's pioneer work also. Today, Geikie is perhaps more highly regarded as a pioneer historian of geology than as geologist. His excellent autobiography, *A Long Life's Work* (1924), crowned his achievement as author, and well revealed the art of building a successful scientific career. He went to live at Haslemere, Surrey, in 1913, and died at his home there, Shepherd's Down, Hill Road, on 10 November 1924. He was buried in St Bartholomew's churchyard, Haslemere.

DAVID OLDROYD

Sources E. Cutter, 'Sir Archibald Geikie: a bibliography', *Journal of the Society of the Bibliography of Natural History*, 7 (1974–6), 1–18 · A. Geikie, *A long life's work: an autobiography* (1924) · D. R. Oldroyd, *The highlands controversy: constructing geological knowledge through fieldwork in nineteenth-century Britain* (1990) · B. N. Peach and J. Horne, *Proceedings of the Royal Society of Edinburgh*, 45 (1924–5), 346–61 · J. H. [J. Horne], *PRS*, 111A (1926), xxiv–xxxix · G. W. Tyrrell, 'Sir Archibald Geikie', *Zeitschrift für Vulkanologie*, 9 (1926), 149–55 · A. S. [A. Strahan], 'Anniversary address of the president', *Proceedings of the Geological Society of London*, 81 (1924–5), lii–lx · C. Keyes, ed., *Pan-American Geologist*, 43 (1925), 1–14 · A. Geikie, 'Autobiographical notes', Haslemere Educational Museum, Surrey · A. Geikie, *The founders of geology* (1897); 2nd edn (1905); repr. (1962) · *Nature*, 114 (1924), 758–60

Archives BGS, corresp. · GS Lond., corresp. and papers · Haslemere Educational Museum, Surrey, field notebooks, letters, drawings · Museum of Scotland, Edinburgh, notebook · U. Edin. L., corresp. and papers · U. Lpool, letters | BGS, letters to Benjamin Peach · BGS, letters to T. Reeks · BGS, letters to Frederick Rudler · BL, corresp. with Macmillans, Add. MS 55212 · Elgin Museum, letters to George Gordon · Falconer Museum, Forres, letters to Sir Joseph Prestwich and Lady Prestwich · GS Lond., letters to Roderick Impey · King's Cam., letters to Oscar Browning · NL Scot., letters to Henry Cadell · NL Scot., corresp. with Henry Drummond · NL Scot., corresp. with John Bartholomew and Son · NL Scot., corresp. incl. Sir Patrick Geddes · NL Wales, letters to Sir Andrew Ramsay and Lady Ramsay · U. Edin. L., corresp. with Sir Charles Lyell

Likenesses P. Merimée, caricature, 1860 (with Murchison), NL Scot. · group portrait, photograph, 1868 (with survey colleagues), BGS · group portrait, photograph, 1897, repro. in Keyes, ed., *Pan-American Geologist*, facing p. 4 · R. G. Eves, oils, *c*.1915, RS · E. Lantéri, marble bust, *c*.1916, Geological Museum, South Kensington, London · W. Stoneman, photograph, 1917, NPG · R. G. Eves, pencil drawing, Scot. NPG · photograph, repro. in Peach and Horne, 'The scientific career of Sir Archibald Geikie', 347 · photograph, repro. in 'Eminent living geologists, no. 6: Professor Archibald Geikie', *Geological Magazine*, 7, decade 3 (1890), pl. 2 · photographs, Haslemere Educational Museum, Geikie archive · photographs, repro. in Geikie, *A long life's work*, frontispiece, facing p. 408

Wealth at death £16,595 16*s*. 9*d*.: probate, 15 Jan 1925, *CGPLA Eng. & Wales*

Geikie, James Murdoch (1839–1915), geologist, was born on 23 August 1839 in a house between Bristo Street and George Square in Edinburgh, the third son and third of eight children of James Stuart Geikie and his wife, Isabella Thom, the daughter of a Dunbar sea captain. He disliked the name Murdoch and dropped it as a child. His father was evidently in the perfume trade, but the family preferred to have him remembered as an amateur musician and music critic for *The Scotsman*. His uncle was the artist Walter Geikie and his eldest brother was the geologist Sir Archibald *Geikie. He was educated at the Edinburgh high school (1850–53) and as a schoolboy he joined in the geological rambles of his brother Archibald and John Young, the future professor of natural history at Glasgow University. In August 1850 he conducted some strangers to the summit of Arthur's Seat without realizing that they were Queen Victoria, Prince Albert, and four of the royal children. In 1854 he was apprenticed to the printer and publisher Thomas Constable, but disliked both the work and the indoor confinement. He renounced his apprenticeship in 1858 and resolved to follow his eldest brother into the ranks of the geological survey. While awaiting a vacancy he enrolled in the natural history class at Edinburgh University under George James Allman.

In October 1861 Geikie joined the local branch of the geological survey as assistant geologist. He was promoted geologist in 1867, when the branch was reorganized as the geological survey of Scotland with Archibald Geikie as its director, and he was promoted district surveyor in 1869. With the survey he was in his element. He loved both the outdoor life and the companionship of genial and talented colleagues. He was a hardy, enthusiastic, and capable field geologist, the superficial deposits being his chief interest. For the survey he mapped in Fife and the Lothians, in the southern uplands, and in the Ayrshire and Lanarkshire coalfields, while from 1875 until 1882 his station was at Perth. It was in 1875, on 8 July, that he married Mary Simson, daughter of John Somerville Johnston of Crailing Hall, Jedburgh. They later had four sons and a daughter. While at the survey Geikie achieved an international reputation as a student of the Quaternary and his book *The Great Ice Age* (1874; later editions in 1877 and 1894) became a classic, not least because of his advocacy of the reality of interglacial periods. Among his other texts, *Outlines of Geology* (1886) and *Structural and Field Geology for Students* (1905) both appeared in several editions.

In 1882 Archibald Geikie was appointed director-general of the geological survey and moved to London, leaving vacant the directorship of the Scottish survey and the Murchison chair of geology at Edinburgh University, which he had held concurrently with his survey post. Geikie was his brother's obvious successor in both posts, but Archibald announced first that for the moment he would himself retain control of the Scottish survey and second that he would not sanction the holding of the Murchison chair by any survey geologist. Forced to choose between the survey and the chair, James Geikie chose the latter. It was a decision which he regretted for some years, although within the university he proved an effective teacher in both the classroom and the field and he was dean of the faculty of science from 1894 until 1913. He resigned his chair in June 1914.

A hearty, plain-spoken man, Geikie lacked his brother's wide-ranging talents but was by far the more popular of the two. He was elected FRS in 1875 and was much involved in the affairs of the Royal Society of Edinburgh (president 1913–15) and the Royal Scottish Geographical Society, of which he was a co-founder and president in 1904–10. He travelled widely in Europe and he visited

North America twice. Geikie died suddenly in Edinburgh from a heart attack on 1 March 1915. He was survived by his wife. GORDON L. HERRIES DAVIES

Sources M. I. Newbigin and J. S. Flett, *James Geikie: the man and the geologist* (1917) • 'Eminent living geologists: James Geikie', *Geological Magazine*, new ser., 5th decade, 10 (1913), 241–8 • W. E. Marsden, 'James Geikie, 1839–1915', *Geographers: biobibliographical studies*, 3, ed. T. W. Freeman and P. Pinchemel (1979), 53–62
Archives BGS, corresp. and papers • NHM, lecture notes • RGS, letters to publisher • U. Edin. L., lecture notes | BGS, letters to Benjamin Peach • ICL, letters to Sir Andrew Ramsay • NL Scot., corresp. with Sir Patrick Geddes
Likenesses four portraits, repro. in Newbigin and Flett, *James Geikie* • portrait, repro. in 'Eminent living geologists'
Wealth at death £436 4s. 3d.: confirmation, 9 June 1915, CCI

Geikie, John Cunningham

Geikie, John Cunningham (1824–1906), religious writer, was born on 26 October 1824 in Edinburgh, the second son of Archibald Geikie, Presbyterian minister in Toronto, Canada, and at Canaan, Connecticut, USA. Geikie received his early education in Edinburgh, and then studied divinity for four years at Queen's College, Kingston, Ontario. He was ordained a Presbyterian minister in 1848, and undertook missionary work in Canada. In 1849 he married Margaret, daughter of David Taylor of Dublin. They had two sons. From 1851 to 1854 he was Presbyterian minister at Halifax, Nova Scotia. In 1860 he returned to Britain, where he was Presbyterian minister in Sunderland until 1867, and at Islington Chapel from 1867 to 1873.

In 1876 Geikie was ordained deacon in the Church of England and priest the following year. He was curate of St Peter's, Dulwich (1876–9), rector of Christ Church, Neuilly, Paris (1879–81), vicar of St Mary's, Barnstaple (1883–5), and vicar of St Martin-at-Palace, Norwich (1885–90). In 1871 he was made an honorary DD of Queen's College, Kingston, Ontario, and in 1891 honorary LLD of Edinburgh University. In 1890 he retired to Bournemouth.

Geikie was well known as a writer of popular books on biblical and religious subjects. Scholarly, imaginative, and lucid, his books dealt on orthodox lines with historical and practical rather than with theological themes. His most ambitious work was *Hours with the Bible, or, The Scriptures in the Light of Modern Discovery and Knowledge* (10 vols., 1881–4; new edn 1893, 1896, 1915). *The Life and Words of Christ* (1877) sold nearly 100,000 copies. He was interested in the exploration of Palestine by Claude Régnier Conder and visited the country several times, gathering material for *The Holy Land and the Bible: a Book of Scripture Illustrations Gathered in Palestine* (1887). Among Geikie's other works are *Old Testament Portraits* (1878), *The English Reformation* (1879), a popular history from an ultra-protestant standpoint, and *Landmarks of Old Testament History* (1894). He also contributed regularly to religious magazines.

Geikie died at 58 Southcote Road, Bournemouth, on 1 April 1906, and was buried in Barnstaple. He was survived by his wife. W. F. GRAY, rev. ANNE PIMLOTT BAKER

Sources Allibone, *Dict.* • P. Schaff and S. M. Jackson, *Encyclopedia of living divines and Christian workers of all denominations in Europe and America: being a supplement to Schaff-Herzog encyclopedia of religious knowledge* (1887) • *The Scotsman* (3 April 1906) • Crockford
Archives LPL, corresp. with A. C. Tait and related papers

Wealth at death £8710 5s. 9d.: probate, 28 July 1906, CGPLA Eng. & Wales

Geikie, Walter

Geikie, Walter (1795–1837), painter and printmaker, was born in Charles Street, Edinburgh, on 9 November 1795, the son of Archibald Geikie, a pharmacist. Before he was two, according to his early biographer, Sir Thomas Dick Lauder, Geikie suffered 'a nervous fever' which left him deaf and dumb. He then became a pupil of Thomas Braidwood, pioneer teacher of the deaf (Dick Lauder, vi). This must have been when he was very young as Braidwood died in London in 1806 shortly after leaving Edinburgh. Notably another of Braidwood's pupils, Charles Sheriff, also became an artist.

In 1812 Geikie enrolled in the Trustees' Academy in Edinburgh, where John Graham, who had been David Wilkie's teacher, was master. According to Dick Lauder, however, it was Graham's successor, Andrew Wilson, who taught Geikie to paint (Dick Lauder, x). The style of his paintings supports this and, although he is principally known for his figure subjects, he did produce and exhibit picturesque landscapes very like Wilson's. Geikie's strong and simple drawing style using a pencil to record directly his observations of life in the streets of Edinburgh and notably also the appearance of Edinburgh closes and tenement kitchens (drawings, NG Scot. and Edinburgh City Library) closely resembles that of Alexander Nasmyth, Wilson's teacher, who ran an informal drawing academy. It was Wilkie's early style, however, that was the dominant influence on Geikie's art with its humour and its concern with the observation of expression and gesture.

Geikie first exhibited in 1815 at the Edinburgh Exhibition Society. From 1821 he exhibited regularly in Edinburgh at the Association for the Promotion of the Fine Arts and later at the Scottish Academy, where he became an associate in 1831 and an academician in 1834. (The academy did not get its royal charter until 1837.) His obituary records that 'owing to a natural defect his eye was less sensible to beauties of tone and colour' (*Caledonian Mercury*), implying that he was colour-blind. Dick Lauder makes a similar observation (p. xi), as do David and Francina Irwin (Irwin and Irwin, 195). He is certainly best-known for his work as a printmaker and draughtsman, but the ambitious *Hallow Fair* (Hopetoun House, near Edinburgh), though damaged by fire, and many other smaller works seem wholly successful as paintings.

According to Dick Lauder, Geikie made his first etching in 1825 for a book of Scottish ballads by the antiquarian and collector David Laing (Dick Lauder, xi). This is an illustration to the ballad 'John Barleycorn' which Laing included in his *Early Metrical Tales*, published the following year. One of the artist's few surviving letters is also to Laing concerning an etching illustrating the poem 'Christ's kirk on the green' (NL Scot. n.d.) and the antiquarian formed a collection of 'about thirty fine drawings' by Geikie which was sold after his death in 1879 (*Catalogue of the collection of rare and curious drawings, … the property of a … Scottish collector, recently deceased* [David Laing]: *including about 30 fine works by Wm.* [sic] *Geikie … an interesting collection of drawings of old Edinburgh … which will be sold by auction by*

Messrs. T. Chapman & Son … December 22 & 23, 1879 … T. Chapman & Sons at their Great Rooms, 11 Hanover St, Edinburgh, 22 and 23 December 1879 at 12 o'Clock).

From 1826 to 1829 Geikie published in parts a set of eighty-seven etchings under the imprint of R. Nimmo. These are mostly comic scenes of the street life of Edinburgh and he did clearly draw from life in the street. He also produced engravings and published a collection of lithographs, demonstrating a range of printmaking skills that he could only have learned from a professional. The most likely candidate is the leading Edinburgh engraver William Lizars, who did in fact engrave several of Geikie's landscapes for various topographical publications and who on the occasion of the disastrous fire in Edinburgh in 1824 also worked in the street. Overall Geikie produced more than 100 etchings. Eighty were published in the 1841 collection with Dick Lauder's biography and an anonymous commentary on the plates. The etchings included here are almost all from the humorous 1826–9 set, however. The book was republished several times during the nineteenth century, but its popularity also confirmed the impression given by Dick Lauder and repeated in very unkind terms by Robert Brydall (Brydall, 211) that Geikie's art was limited by his disability to this humorous vein. In 1831, however, H. Paton, an Edinburgh printseller, published a second set of eighteen etchings which are much less familiar, but which have a frank and simple dignity that at times approaches grandeur. Some of these compositions also survive as paintings, notably *Our Gudeman's a Drucken Carle* (priv. coll.), which shows a drunk man led home by two sympathetic friends. Geikie's later drawings, such as *May Rennie Peeling Potatoes* (NG Scot.), also etched in this series, have this same quality and are quite outstanding in the art of their time. His interest in expression is confirmed by his contributing illustrations to Alexander Morison's *Physiognomy of Mental Diseases* (1840), though it was published after his death. Geikie was a good mimic, though necessarily only in mime, and in spite of his disability was a lively and entertaining member of the Scottish Academy. He dealt in prints and also ran a prayer meeting for the deaf and dumb. He died in his brother's house at 11 Charles Street, Edinburgh, on 2 August 1837.

DUNCAN MACMILLAN

Sources *Caledonian Mercury* (10 Aug 1837) · T. Dick Lauder, biographical introduction, in *Etchings illustrating Scottish character and scenery executed after his own designs by the late Walter Geikie Esq. R.S.A.* [1841] · A. Morison, *Physiognomy of mental diseases* (1840) · R. Brydall, *History of art in Scotland* (1889) · D. Irwin and F. Irwin, *Scottish painters at home and abroad, 1700–1900* (1975) · D. Macmillan, *Walter Geikie (1795–1837): Scottish life and character* (1984) [exhibition catalogue, U. Edin., Talbot Rice Gallery] · D. Macmillan, *Painting in Scotland: the golden age* (1986) [exhibition catalogue, U. Edin., Talbot Rice Gallery, and Tate Gallery, London, 1986] · D. Macmillan, *Scottish art, 1460–1990* (1990)

Gelasius. *See* Gilla meic Liac (1087–1174).

Geldart, Edmund Martin (1844–1885), Unitarian minister, was born in Norwich on 20 January 1844, the second son and second child of six of Thomas Geldart and his second wife, Hannah Martin (1819/20–1861), second daughter

of Simon Martin (*d*. 1840), a partner in the eminent Norwich banking firm of Gurney. From 1847, when Thomas Geldart became secretary of the Country Towns Mission, the family lived in or near London; from 1856 to 1874 he was secretary of the Manchester City Mission, the family residing chiefly in Bowdon, Cheshire. Under the penname Hannah Ransome (her mother's maiden name), Hannah Geldart was a much-published writer of religious books, primarily for children. The elder Geldarts were evangelicals but sat rather loosely to denominational affiliation; Thomas was a Baptist who attended an Independent chapel when he could, and Hannah Geldart, born into Quakerism, became a Baptist and latterly attended the Anglican church.

Known in his family as Martin, Geldart was educated briefly at Merchant Taylors' School in London and subsequently at the Manchester grammar school, where in 1863 he was the first student to win an open scholarship to Balliol College, Oxford. At Oxford he was able to cultivate a strong amateur interest in entomology. He also formed a friendship with his Balliol contemporary the future Jesuit and poet Gerard Manley Hopkins (1844–1889), although Hopkins was appalled by Geldart's 'full haggard hideousness' (letter to Kate Hopkins, 22 April 1863, Hopkins, 11). His philological and classical interests were primarily influenced by Friedrich Max Müller (1823–1900) and Benjamin Jowett (1817–1893). Geldart was later scathing about the deficiencies of Oxford theology but informally kept abreast of the currents of higher criticism that swept over the university and the church following publication of *Essays and Reviews* (1860) and gradually abandoned his inherited evangelicalism.

After taking his BA in 1867 he became an assistant master at his old school in Manchester but suffered a breakdown through overwork and went to Greece to recover. There he mastered modern Greek and developed the somewhat eccentric scholarly position set out in *The Modern Greek Language in its Relation to Ancient Greek*, published by the Clarendon Press in 1870, in which he argued the close identity of the two languages. He returned to Manchester grammar school in 1869 and was ordained deacon. On becoming a priest in 1870 he added to his teaching duties a part-time curacy at Chorlton-cum-Medlock and in 1871 became curate at St George's, Everton, in Liverpool, where he came into close contact with an impressive Unitarian community. On 26 June 1868 he had married Charlotte Frederika Sophia Andler (1841–1923), the daughter of William Joseph Andler, a government official in Württemberg; they had two children, one of whom, William Martin Geldart (1871–1922), also an amateur entomologist and accomplished classicist, became a law tutor and later Vinerian professor at Oxford.

Geldart's advancing heterodoxy, possibly encouraged by his wife, led the incumbent of St George's to request his resignation. He declined an offer to become dean to J. W. Colenso (1814–1883), the schismatic South African bishop. Formally joining the Unitarians in 1872, he taught for a time at St Paul's School, Stony Stratford, Buckinghamshire. There he formed a friendship with a science master,

William Rossiter (*d.* 1897), who, after training as a portmanteau maker, had attended the London Working Men's College and become a high-church socialist. Having taken the MA in 1873, Geldart became minister of the distinguished Unitarian congregation in Hope Street, Liverpool; he had been deeply affected by James Martineau (1805–1900), whose continuing influence at Hope Street was a factor, along with Geldart's defection from Anglicanism, in an appointment surprising for one with so little dissenting or ministerial experience. The congregation prospered in the early period of his tenure but later fell off; his stipend suffered accordingly. He resigned in 1877 and the next year succeeded the Revd R. R. Suffield (1821–1891) at the Free Christian Church, Croydon.

By the early 1880s Geldart's religious orientation, tinged with pantheism and agnosticism, had become increasingly tenuous, and he turned wholeheartedly to socialism as a kind of surrogate religion, becoming active in the Social Democratic Federation at both the local and the national level. Some members of the Croydon congregation agitated for his resignation, which he eventually submitted late in March 1885. He fell ill: Hopkins's description of him as 'a selftormentor' (letter to A. W. M. Baillie, 24 April 1885, Hopkins, 207) gains credibility from the strange recollection at the beginning of his autobiography of his childish fascination with death and (even allowing for evangelical moral-pointing) from his mother's harrowing account, in *Strength in Weakness, or, Early Chastened, Early Blessed* (1860), of the long death of her eldest son, William, and of his fervent dying adjurations to the younger Martin. On the night of 10 April Geldart left Newhaven to visit a friend in Paris and was lost on the voyage—this was presumably suicide. The circumstances of his death gave a colour of martyrdom to the outpouring of admiration from leading members of the 'new school' of Martineau and his friends, with whom Geldart had been identified.

Writing as Nitram Tradleg in *A Son of Belial: Autobiographical Sketches* (1882), Geldart confers disguised but mostly penetrable identities on many of his teachers and colleagues. But the quasi-fictional form, compounded by some imprecision and much archness and strained wit, makes the book a difficult source for an odd, sad life that reflected the centrifugal nature of Unitarianism, and of religion generally, at the end of the nineteenth century.

R. K. WEBB

Sources A. B. Downing, 'From Max Müller to Karl Marx: a study of E. M. Geldart, scholar of Balliol', *Transactions of the Unitarian Historical Society*, 14 (1967–70), 171–89 · N. Tradleg [E. M. Geldart], *A son of Belial: autobiographical sketches* (1882) · C. B. Upton and P. H. Wicksteed, *Two discourses in memory of Edmund Martin Geldart … with a brief memoir* (1885) · *Gerard Manley Hopkins: selected letters*, ed. C. Phillips (1990) · B. Marshall, *Emma Marshall: a biographical sketch* (1900) · Hope Street Church, Liverpool, minute book, 1873–6 · H. Geldart, *Strength in weakness, or, Early chastened, early blessed* (1860) · m. cert. · *CGPLA Eng. & Wales* (1885)
Wealth at death £5,457 10s. 1d.: probate, 22 Dec 1885, *CGPLA Eng. & Wales*

Geldart, James William (1785–1876), jurist, was born on 15 February 1785 at Swinnow Hall, Wetherby, Yorkshire, the eldest son of the Revd James Geldart (1760–1839), rector of Kirk Deighton, Yorkshire, and his first wife, Sarah (*bap.* 1759, *d.* 1791), daughter of William Williamson of Linton Spring, Wetherby, and his wife, Ann. Educated at Beverley grammar school, Geldart was admitted a pensioner at Trinity College, Cambridge, on 2 September 1799. He migrated to Trinity Hall on 5 May 1800, and there became a scholar in December 1803. He took the degree of LLB in 1806, and on 16 February 1808 was elected a Skirne fellow of St Catharine's College, where his brother Richard held a Skirne scholarship. Ordained priest on 24 September 1809, Geldart returned to Trinity Hall as fellow and tutor on 4 October of the same year and held those offices until 1821; from 1812 until 1821 he also acted as vicemaster. He was created LLD on 2 March 1814, having been admitted to the degree on 24 November 1813.

Following the death of Joseph Jowett, Geldart was appointed regius professor of civil law on 11 December 1813 on the nomination of the earl of Liverpool; he subscribed to the articles on 28 January 1814. In contrast to the situation in Oxford, Geldart's more recent predecessors in the regius chair of civil law at Cambridge had given lectures. Geldart maintained this practice, giving as many as fifty lectures in a year, which he based upon the *Analysis of the Civil Law* (1774) of his predecessor Samuel Hallifax, which followed a comparative method. A new edition of Hallifax's *Analysis* in 1836 was Geldart's only published work, but he took early steps towards the reform of legal education at Cambridge. An attempt to introduce written examinations for the LLB by grace of the senate had failed in 1811, but from 1815 Geldart required on his own authority that candidates for the LLB pass written examinations based upon his lectures before performing the statutory disputation. Continued by his successors, the results of the examinations, known as the civil law classes, were published annually until their replacement in 1858 by the new 'law tripos', under university regulations. Geldart attended the University Press Syndicate regularly between 1816 and 1846, and served frequently on the *caput senatus*.

On 4 August 1836 Geldart married Mary Rachel (1808–1890), daughter of William Desborough of Hemingford Grey, Huntingdonshire, and his wife, Elizabeth. They had two sons: James William Geldart, who became rector of Kirk Deighton, and Henry Charles Geldart, who was sheriff of Cambridgeshire and Huntingdonshire between 1887 and 1888. Geldart resigned as regius professor in 1847, to be succeeded by Henry Maine. After the death of his father, and on his own presentation, Geldart had become rector of Kirk Deighton in 1840, and he held the benefice until his death there, of old age, on 16 February 1876. He was buried in Kirk Deighton churchyard on 19 February 1876.

N. G. JONES

Sources Grace Books Λ and M, CUL, department of manuscripts and university archives · CUL, department of manuscripts and university archives, Faculty of Law MSS, CUR 28.3 · subscriptions book, 1617–1874, CUL, department of manuscripts and university archives, subsc. Add. 1 · G. E. Kirk, *The parish church of All Saints, Kirk*

Deighton, Yorkshire (1938) · *The Times* (19 Feb 1876) · Trinity Hall Archives, Cambridge, folder 42, C14, C59, C60, C76, C77 · *Cambridge University Calendar* (1858) · 'Royal commission on … the university and colleges of Cambridge', *Parl. papers* (1852–3), 44.77–9, no. 1559 · E. C. Clark, *Cambridge legal studies* (1888), 77–8 · *LondG* (11 Dec 1813) · W. H. S. Jones [W. H. Samuel], *A history of St Catharine's College, once Catharine Hall, Cambridge* (1936), 204 · Ely, diocesan records, EDR/G1/15, 465, 468 · admissions book, 1787–1805, Trinity Cam., fol. 49v · d. cert. · parish register, Thorp Arch, Yorkshire, 17 Sept 1786 [birth] · parish register, Sunninghill, 4 Aug 1836, Berks. RO, D/P 126/1/6 [marriage] · parish register, Kirk Deighton church, Yorkshire, 19 Feb 1786 [burial]

Likenesses T. Uwins, costume plate, 1814 (of Geldart?), repro. in R. Ackermann, *A history of the University of Cambridge*, 2 (1815), following p. 312 · photograph, All Saints Church, Kirk Deighton, Yorkshire

Wealth at death under £30,000: probate, 13 March 1876, *CGPLA Eng. & Wales*

Geldorp, George (d. 1665), portrait painter, was probably born in Antwerp and was the son of the painter Geldorp Gortzius (1553–1616). In 1610 he was admitted master of the guild of St Luke in Antwerp and also became a member of the Violieren guild. On 5 February 1613 he married Anna, daughter of Willem de Vos, the painter, and from 1615 to 1620 they resided in a house called De Keyser on De Meir, subsequently moving to the Happartstraat before leaving Antwerp for England in 1623. In 1628 a return was ordered of the names, qualities, and conditions of all recusants resident in London; among the names was 'George Geldropp, a picture-drawer'.

The portraits that Geldorp painted during his early years in England are in an Anglo-Netherlandish style similar to that of his contemporaries Daniel Mytens, Cornelius Johnson, and Paul van Somer. This can be seen in his full lengths of William Cecil, second earl of Salisbury, and his wife, Catharine (both 1626; Hatfield House, Hertfordshire). Geldorp's original receipt for the paintings, frames, and gilding reveals that the gilding was done by his wife. Other sitters during his long career included Sir Arthur Ingram (City Art Galleries, Leeds) and Thomas, Lord Bruce of Kinloss, first earl of Elgin (Hardwick Hall, Derbyshire). Geldorp is known to have employed Peter Lely when the latter first came to England. As a painter Geldorp was much decried by his contemporaries, and J. von Sandrart wrote that he drew so badly that he used the drawings of others to make his portraits, pinning them over his own canvas and tracing through with prepared chalk. In his later career he particularly specialized in copies of works by Van Dyck and in June 1653 Richard Symonds saw an 'Abundance of Coppyes of Ritrattos of Vandyke' in Geldorp's house (BL, Egerton MS 1636, fol. 93v).

By the early 1630s Geldorp had obtained royal patronage, and had some share in the charge of the royal collections. From the crown he rented a large house and garden in Drury Lane, London, and Mr Rose, son-in-law of Richard Gibson the dwarf, told Vertue that Geldorp 'was mighty great with people of Quality in his Time, & much in their favour, he used to entertain Ladies and Gentlemen with wine & hams & other curious eatables, & carryd on intreagues between them' (Vertue, *Note books*, 1.116). After the king's death Geldorp moved to a house in Archer Street, Westminster.

From the mid-1630s Geldorp increasingly involved himself with picture dealing. In January 1636, for example, he and Van Dyck were paid for pictures and frames by the tenth earl of Northumberland, son-in-law of his earlier patron William Cecil. Furthermore, in 1637–8 Geldorp was employed by the great Cologne art patron Everhard Jabach, to negotiate with Rubens for the altarpiece the *Martyrdom of St Peter* (St Peter's, Cologne). At the time of the Commonwealth he also acted as the London agent for Cardinal Mazarin, no doubt dealing in the flood of paintings brought onto the market by the sale of Charles I's collection following the king's execution.

During the interregnum, Geldorp, along with Peter Lely and Sir Balthazar Gerbier, proposed a series of paintings for Whitehall on the theme of the achievements of the Long Parliament. Despite this apparent enthusiasm for the Commonwealth, prior to the Restoration Geldorp was one of the leading figures in the attempt to reassemble the dispersed Royal Collection, and according to Vertue numbers of these works were stored for safety in his house. For this he was appointed picture-mender and cleaner to Charles II. Geldorp died in London on 14 November 1665 and was buried in the parish of Westminster.

An interesting figure, Geldorp's career reflects the decline of the Anglo-Netherlandish style during the mid-seventeenth century under the pervasive influence of Van Dyck.

L. H. CUST, rev. P. G. MATTHEWS

Sources *Joachim von Sandrarts Academie der Bau-, Bild-, und Mahlerey-Künste von 1675*, ed. A. R. Peltzer (Munich, 1925) · O. Millar, 'Notes on British paintings from archives: III', *Burlington Magazine*, 97 (1955), 255–6 · E. K. Waterhouse, *The dictionary of British 16th and 17th century painters* (1988), 99 · E. Auerbach and C. Kingsley Adams, *Paintings and sculpture at Hatfield House* (1971), 27, 84–6 · C. H. C. Baker, *Lely and the Stuart portrait painters: a study of English portraiture before and after van Dyck*, 2 vols. (1912), vol. 1, pp. 66–70; vol. 2, p. 112 · M. Whinney and O. Millar, *English art, 1625–1714* (1957), 75–6, 81, 173 · E. Waterhouse, *Painting in Britain, 1530–1790*, 4th edn (1978), 66, 92, 96 · Vertue, *Note books*

Likenesses A. Bannerman, double portrait, line engraving, pubd 1765 (with J. van Belcamp), NPG

Gell, Anthony (d. 1583), law reporter, was the first son of Ralph Gell (c.1491–1564) and his first wife, Godeth, daughter of Nicholas Ashby of Willoughby on the Wolds. The Gell family had owned Hopton Hall near Wirksworth, Derbyshire, for many generations, but Anthony seems to have been the first member to obtain a grant of arms. He became a student at Clement's Inn, and his notes of the lectures given there in 1543–4 by his Derbyshire neighbour Richard Blackwall (d. 1562) are now in Cambridge University Library. Blackwall may well have been his patron. In 1545–6 Gell served as principal of the inn—an office frequently held by a young man, elected by his peers—and was by this time practising as an attorney of the common pleas. The following year he was specially admitted to the Inner Temple, where he was later called to the bar.

Gell's printed and manuscript law books remained in the library at Hopton Hall until the twentieth century, but they have become partly dispersed. They include a copiously annotated copy of the 1537 edition of Fitzherbert's *Natura brevium*. Two of the manuscripts contain a unique series of law reports from the common pleas, written in Gell's hand and probably, for the most part, of his own taking. The first, now in the Library of Congress, begins with the year books of 13 Richard II, 18–19 and 26–7 Henry VIII, as in print, and then a series in the same style as the printed year books of Henry VIII running from 1541 to 1555, with a few later additions. The second volume, now in the Derbyshire Record Office, continued the series from 1557 to 1562. Gell seems to have kept these reports to himself, and they were not copied or cited by contemporaries. They include the earliest known reported case on the doctrine of consideration.

Gell became a bencher of the Inner Temple in 1559 but paid 40 marks to be excused from reading in 1563. He died, unmarried, on 29 June 1583, and was buried in Wirksworth church, where there is a bearded effigy in a long gown of flowered damask and an inscription describing him as 'sapiens jurisque peritus' ('wise and skilled in the law'). Part of his gains from the law went to found and endow the grammar school and almshouses at Wirksworth. His nephew Thomas (1595–1657) was recorder of Derby and also became a bencher of the Inner Temple. The Gell family remained at Hopton Hall until the 1970s.

J. H. BAKER

Sources F. A. Inderwick and R. A. Roberts, eds., *A calendar of the Inner Temple records*, 1 (1896) • J. C. Cox, *Churches of Derbyshire* (1877), 2.558–9; 4.521 • J. H. Baker and J. S. Ringrose, *A catalogue of English legal manuscripts in Cambridge University Library* (1996), 641–52 • L. Cong., manuscript division, law MSS 15, 29 • *Ninth report*, 2, HMC, 8 (1884), 385 • *The reports of Sir John Spelman*, ed. J. H. Baker, 2, SeldS, 94 (1978), 2.169 • PRO, CP 40/1127, m. 626d • *The Antiquary*, 11, pl. 31 [pedigree of Gell family] • W. H. Cooke, ed., *Students admitted to the Inner Temple, 1547–1660* [1878], 3 • J. H. Baker and S. F. C. Milsom, eds., *Sources of English legal history: private law to 1750* (1986) • tombstone, Wirksworth church, Derbyshire

Archives CUL, Add. MSS 8935–8949 • L. Cong., law MSS 15, 29 | Derbys. RO, Hopton Hall deposit, MSS

Likenesses alabaster effigy on monument, *c.*1583, Wirksworth church, Derbyshire

Gell, Sir James (1823–1905), lawyer and judge, was born at Kennaa, Isle of Man, on 13 January 1823, the second son of John Gell. The family of Gell had held land at Kennaa for more than four centuries. After education at Castletown grammar school and King William's College, at sixteen Gell was articled to the clerk of the rolls, John McHutchin, in Castletown, and was admitted to the Manx bar on 16 January 1845. He enjoyed a large and important practice, and became known as the chief authority on Manx law and custom. On 17 December 1850 he married Amelia Marcia (*d.* 1899), daughter of William Gill, vicar of Malew and a member of another ancient Manx family. They had four sons and three daughters. In 1854 Gell was appointed high bailiff of Castletown, and in May 1866, the year of the Manx Reform Act, became attorney-general. He filled that office for over thirty-two years. He drafted nearly all the acts which came into operation during the period. From

1898 to 1900 he was first deemster (judge), and from 1900 until his death clerk of the rolls.

Gell temporarily filled the post of deputy governor in 1897, acting governor in July 1902, and deputy governor in November 1902. He was a member of the legislative council and of the Tynwald court for thirty-nine years. An intensely patriotic Manxman, he championed all the rights and privileges of the island. He took an active part in educational and religious work. He was chairman of the insular justices from 1879, a trustee of King William's College, and chairman of the council of education from 1872 to 1881. For many years he was chairman of the Manx Society for the Publication of National Documents, and in 1867 he edited volume 12 of Parr's *Abstract of Laws of the Isle of Man*. He was also editor for the insular government of the statute laws of the island from 1836 to 1848, and he supervised and annotated a revised edition of the statutes dating from 1417 to 1895.

An earnest churchman, Gell was for the greater part of his life a Sunday school teacher, and was one of the church commissioners, the trustees of Manx church property. He was knighted in 1877. He was acting governor when King Edward VII and Queen Alexandra paid a surprise visit to the island in 1902, and he was created CVO. He died at Castletown on 12 March 1905.

WILLIAM CUBBON, *rev.* CATHERINE PEASE-WATKIN

Sources *The Times* (13 March 1905) • *Men and women of the time* (1899)

Gell, Sir John, **first baronet** (*bap.* 1593, *d.* 1671), parliamentarian army officer, was born at Hopton Hall, Derbyshire, and baptized at nearby Carsington church on 2 July 1593. He was the eldest son of Thomas Gell (1532–1594) of Hopton, and Millicent, daughter of Ralph Sacheverel of Stanton by Dale, Derbyshire. His father died in 1594 just before the birth of his brother Thomas. His mother then married John Curzon of Kedleston, to whose house she took her sons in 1598, and she bore their stepbrother, Sir John Curzon.

John Gell married Elizabeth Willoughby (1593/4–1644), the sixteen-year-old daughter of Sir Percival Willoughby of Wollaton, near Nottingham, on 22 January 1610 (just possibly 1609). He matriculated a commoner at Magdalen College, Oxford, in 1610, but soon returned to Kedleston where three of his daughters and two sons were baptized between 1611 and 1617. He had taken residence at Hopton Hall by 1620, when his last daughter was baptized at Carsington. He was among the richest gentry in Derbyshire, his family's wealth having been derived from sheep farming, lead mining (where his claims to lead tithes brought him into prolonged conflict with local miners), and legal office. Gell was a captain of the county's trained bands (1624–30) and may have seen brief service in the Low Countries in 1627. Although he contributed £10 on the king's request for a loan in 1625, by 1630 his loyalty was waning and he refused to contribute to the mustering and exercising of the trained bands. Nevertheless in 1632 he was appointed a receiver for the honour of Tutbury (duchy

Sir John Gell, first baronet (*bap.* 1593, *d.* 1671), by unknown artist

of Lancaster) and in 1635 he was pricked sheriff of Derbyshire and charged with collecting the first ship money in the county. In doing so he vented his spite on the recalcitrant Sir John Stanhope of Elvaston and distrained his cattle. Stanhope's wife, Mary (*d.* 1653), and his brother Philip, earl of Chesterfield, took their case to the privy council and lost. Sir John died in 1638, but Gell's feud with the family continued into the civil war.

In 1632, presumably for his outspoken puritanism, Gell was summoned to appear before the archbishop of Canterbury at Lambeth. Nevertheless the crown continued to load him with local offices—JP in 1638, deputy lieutenant of Derbyshire and commissioner for the militia in 1642. In the latter year he was created a baronet. Yet when Charles I raised his standard at Nottingham in 1642 and marched into Derby Gell was absent at Northampton receiving a commission from the earl of Essex to raise a regiment of foot and secure Derbyshire for parliament. He then proceeded to Hull to enlist a company of London greycoats to serve as the nucleus of his regiment. On moving to Sheffield he secured the town and castle for parliament and found his house at Hopton plundered by the royalists. The earl of Chesterfield twice called on him to leave Derbyshire but Gell made Derby his base and recruited a regiment of horse and a small train of artillery.

Chesterfield had seized nearby Lichfield where he was besieged by Lord Brooke. When the latter was killed in 1643 Gell took over the command, captured the city, and dispatched Chesterfield to London in chains. He then united with Sir William Brereton's Cheshire forces to repel a relief force under the earl of Northampton. At Hopton Heath a drawn battle was fought in which Gell lost his artillery and in response removed the dead body of the earl of Northampton to Derby; after the earl's son refused to return the cannon which Gell had lost and the money which Gell had paid to embalm the body, the corpse was paraded through Derby before its burial.

Gell was now made commander-in-chief of parliament's forces in Derbyshire, Staffordshire, and Warwickshire and was the sole exception in the king's pardon to the disaffected in Derbyshire. In 1644 the earl of Essex

commissioned him governor of Derby. His successful fortification of the town thwarted successive royalist threats from the queen, Prince Rupert, the earl of Newcastle, and the earl of Loughborough.

At the height of Gell's military achievement his wife, Elizabeth, died in October 1644. Thereafter his influence within the parliamentarian cause began to decline. Amazingly he married Mary Stanhope, Sir John's widow and daughter of Sir John Radcliffe of Ordsall, Lancashire, in December 1647, a marriage that dissolved within a year. By threats and cajolery he dominated the Derbyshire county committee and the corporation of Derby, placing relatives and friends in important positions. He protested vehemently to parliament about his lack of pay and compensation while secretly enjoying income from royalist lands. Quarrels broke out in the Derby regiments and his opponents protested to parliament. Gell opposed the formation of the New Model Army and resented the occupation of north Derbyshire by Sir Thomas Fairfax. When summoned to bring his midland forces to join Fairfax at Naseby he procrastinated and allowed the king to slip away to Newark. For this he was castigated by Cromwell.

Gell's rebellious command was ended by parliament in 1646 following his part in the siege of Tutbury Castle. Here he secretly offered the royalists his own favourable terms of surrender in opposition to those of his fellow commander, Sir William Brereton. Gell resigned his commission and left for London to answer charges and fight for his arrears. As a precaution he had made over his Derbyshire estate to his son, John, keeping an annuity of £1100. In 1648 he tried to secure his pardon from Charles I, imprisoned on the Isle of Wight, where he lent the king some £900 in gold. By 1650 he was implicated in a plot by Eusebius Andrews and some Derbyshire royalists to help restore Charles II. Gell was found guilty of misprision of treason by the high court of justice and sent to the Tower of London for life. He petitioned for release on grounds of rapidly declining health, was released in 1652, and pardoned under the great seal in 1653. Thereafter he resided in St Martin's Lane, Westminster. Charles II pardoned him in 1660 and created him a gentleman of his privy chamber. He died at his house on 26 October 1671 and was taken back to St Mary's, Wirksworth, Derbyshire, for burial. By provision in the will of his son and heir, John, his mural monument was erected there.

TREVOR BRIGHTON

Sources R. Slack, *Man at war: John Gell in his troubled time* (1997) • T. Brighton, 'The Gell family in the 16th and 17th centuries: a case of the rising gentry', *Journal of the Bakewell District Historical Society*, 7 (1980), 4–34 • T. Brighton, *Royalists and roundheads in Derbyshire*, Bakewell and District Historical Society (1981) • T. Brighton, 'Sir John Gell and the civil war in Derbyshire (Sept 1642 to March 1643)', *Journal of the Bakewell and District Historical Society*, 8 (1981), 37–63 • T. Brighton, 'Sir John Gell, governor of Derby, 1642–46', *Journal of the Bakewell and District Historical Society*, 9 (1982), 1–54 • A. Polkey, *The civil war in the Trent valley* (1992) • A. Wood, *The politics of social conflict: the peak country, 1520–1770* (1999) • G. Turbutt, 'The early Stuarts and the civil war', *A history of Derbyshire*, 4 vols. (1999), vol. 3, chap. 14, 1027–1107 • Derby House committee, treasurers' accounts, PRO, SP 28/153 • transcripts of papers of Major Sanders of Sir John Gell's regiment, CUL, Add. MSS 226 and 731 • *The letter books of Sir William Brereton*, ed. R. N. Dore, 2 vols., Lancashire and

Cheshire RS, 123, 128 (1984–90) • W. Brereton, corresp. with Sir John Gell, BL, Stowe MS 155 • royalist account of the battle of Hopton Heath, Bodl. Oxf., MS Clarendon 23

Archives Derbys. RO, Matlock, papers | Birm. CL, Sir William Brereton's letter-book incl. corresp. with Sir John Gell, MS 595611 • BL, Sir William Brereton's corresp. with Sir John Gell, Stowe MS 155 • BL, Sir William Brereton's letter-books, incl. corresp. with Sir John Gell, Add. MSS 11331–11332 • Derbys. RO, Matlock, Dakeyne MSS, Derby committee treasurers' accounts, D9 • Derbys. RO, Matlock, corresp. and papers re Thomas Sanders • Derbys. RO, Matlock, corresp. with members of the parliamentary forces, incl. Lord Thomas Fairfax and Lord Ferdinand Fairfax, various Derbyshire commanders

Likenesses R. Graves, line engraving, BM • oils, Newnham Hall, Daventry, Northamptonshire • portrait; Christies, 11 July 1994, lot 202 [*see illus.*]

Wealth at death small; he had made over his Derbyshire estate to his son John in 1646, reserving for himself £1100 for life; minor bequests to friends, servants, etc.: will, 4 May 1671, Derbys. RO, D258/67/7c

Gell, John (*c*.1740–1806), naval officer, was probably a younger son of John Eyre and his wife, Isabella Jessop. John Eyre, upon inheriting from an uncle the Hopton estates, became head of the old Derbyshire family of Gell of Hopton Hall, and took that name. The future admiral's elder brother seems to have been Philip Gell (*d.* 1793), whose three children appear in John's will as nephews and nieces. The first record traced of John's naval service relates to his joining the *Prince* on 2 September 1757, but, as he was at once rated a midshipman, it seems that he must have had previous sea experience, especially as he was promoted lieutenant to the *Conqueror* in the Mediterranean by Admiral Thomas Brodrick as soon as 6 January 1760; shortly afterwards he was moved to the *Guernsey*, also in the Mediterranean. On 14 October 1762 he was appointed commander of the storeship *Grampus*, but she soon after paid off. On 4 March 1766 he became captain of the *Launceston*, flagship of Vice-Admiral Durell on the North American station. Although Durell died in August, the ship completed her full commission. After some years on half pay Gell was appointed in 1776 to the frigate *Thetis*, at first on the North American station, then engaged in the search for John Paul Jones's ships in the Irish Sea, but later having a near escape from capture by two French line-of-battle ships in the Strait of Gibraltar, while running supplies into Gibraltar. In 1780 he was appointed to the *Monarca* (70 guns), a fine ship, captured from the Spaniards by Sir George Rodney on 16 January 1779. Towards the close of the year he was ordered to the West Indies, under the command of Sir Samuel Hood; but the ship was dismasted on 11 December and ordered back to Plymouth, whereupon she was dispatched with urgent information to the East Indies to warn Sir Edward Hughes of the approach of the French squadron under Suffren. Hughes commended Gell for his fast passage (18 April to 4 October). Subsequently, as one of the squadron under Hughes, the *Monarca* took part in each of the five indecisive engagements with the French under Suffren. In 1784 she returned to England, and was paid off. During the Spanish armament in 1790 Gell commanded the *Excellent* for a few months; and on 1 February 1793 he was advanced to the

rank of rear-admiral. He was then ordered out to the Mediterranean, with his flag in the *St George*, in command of a squadron of four ships of the line and a frigate. On the way, off the coast of Portugal, they fell in with and captured a French privateer, the *Général Dumouriez*, convoying a Spanish treasure-ship, the *Santiago*, which she had taken a few days before. The prizes were sent home, and, after some doubt in respect to the *Santiago*, both were condemned. The Spanish ship was of immense value, and her condemnation, under the circumstances, caused much dissatisfaction in Spain, and is said to have been one of the principal causes of the total change of Spanish policy and of the war with England.

Gell's squadron was the advanced division of the fleet which, in several detachments, went out to the Mediterranean, and which, by the end of June, was collected at Gibraltar under the command of Lord Hood. As a junior flag-officer Gell was present with this fleet at the occupation of Toulon, and in October was sent with a small squadron to Genoa, where his ships took possession of the French frigate *Modeste*. The British capture of the *Modeste* was followed by the murder of the crew of the merchant brig *Peggy* by French forces in 1794. In April 1794 Gell was compelled by ill health to resign his command, and in doing so ended his active service. He became a vice-admiral on 4 July, admiral on 14 February 1799, and died of an apoplectic seizure on 24 or 28 September 1806 at his home at Crickhowell, Brecknockshire. Gell appears to have died unmarried; he left bequests of over £4000 to nephews and a niece, the children of Philip Gell, and to friends, with the residue to his two sisters Maria Catherine and Isabella, although only the former survived him. One of the nephews, Sir William Gell, was a noted archaeologist and traveller. J. K. LAUGHTON, *rev.* A. W. H. PEARSALL

Sources *The private papers of John, earl of Sandwich*, ed. G. R. Barnes and J. H. Owen, 1, Navy RS, 69 (1932), 272–3; 3, Navy RS, 78 (1938), 171 • H. W. Richmond, *The navy in India, 1763–1783* (1931) • W. James, *The naval history of Great Britain, from the declaration of war by France, in February 1793, to the accession of George IV in January 1820*, 5 vols. (1822–4), vol. 1, pp. 97, 100 • J. Charnock, ed., *Biographia navalis*, 6 (1798), 579 • *GM*, 1st ser., 76 (1806), 984 • *Naval Chronicle*, 16 (1806), 515 • PRO, ADM 1/1839–40; 2/110; 2/1339; 36/5648, 5684, 5864

Likenesses J. Reynolds, oils, 1786, NMM, Greenwich Hospital collection

Wealth at death over £4100 in bequests; plus some landed property: will

Gell [*née* Packer], **Katherine** (*bap.* 1624, *d.* 1671), religious patron, was baptized at Westminster Abbey on 11 March 1624, the third daughter, in a family of five sons and three daughters, of John *Packer (1572–1649), administrator and politician, and his wife, Philippa Mills (*bap.* 1590, *d.* 1665). Her father's career flourished under the patronage of the duke of Buckingham, whom he served as secretary until the latter's assassination in 1628; the wealth that he had amassed was such that he could afford to give his youngest daughter a marriage portion of £4000. Katherine also grew up in a godly household. John Packer knew by heart the New Testament, the Psalms, and the book of Proverbs; he frequently attended sermons and personally subsidized clergymen to preach the word in the dark corners of the land. 'I was', she later recalled, 'brought up under such Parents as took great care to educate me well (my father being a man of Eminent holines) whereby I was as formall as any & as constant in duties till neere 20 years of age' (Keeble and Nuttall, 1.185). John Packer supported parliament during the first civil war and Katherine married John Gell (*bap.* 1612, *d.* 1689), later second baronet, the eldest son of parliament's commander in Derbyshire, Sir John *Gell of Hopton, near Wirksworth. Their first child, Katherine, was baptized in Westminster Abbey on 22 April 1645. In all they had four sons and three daughters, of whom one died in infancy. As Sir John made over his Derbyshire estates to his son in 1646, Hopton Hall became her home for the rest of her life.

Katherine Packer had married into a family which shared the Packers' puritan sympathies. Sir John was also a patron of godly ministers. The younger John Gell did not serve during the civil war, but sat in the protectoral parliaments of 1654, 1656, and 1659. At the Restoration he was regarded as 'the most rigid Presbyterian in the county' and was not restored to the county bench until after his father's death (HoP, *Commons, 1660–90*, 2.384). To Roger Morrice, who was ejected from a Derbyshire living in 1662, he was a religious, wise, and worthy gentleman. In the late 1660s he kept the ejected minister Francis Tallents as a chaplain at Hopton Hall. In 1669 it was reported that, while conventicles were held in his house, John Gell remained a regular attender of Anglican services. William Bagshaw, the nonconformist minister who became known as the Apostle of the Peak, primarily presented the Gells, husband and wife, in such public roles, emphasizing their assiduous maintenance of household worship and godly chaplains: 'Was not that great house a Bethel, an house of God?' (Bagshaw, 57).

Bagshaw, however, paid tribute to Katherine Gell as a godly exemplar in her own right. She 'was no little the promoter of God's Work in Derby-shire. Did she not in the qualifications proper to her sex, match with those of her husband?' (Bagshaw, 58). In the household her voice was raised loud in the singing of psalms and her concern for the spiritual welfare of her servants was such that she released them from their duties early each evening to allow them time for prayer and meditation. At the Restoration, although she had serious reservations about the re-imposed Anglican liturgy, 'she managed 'em modestly, and consulted with the best ministers, and shunned the way of rigid separation' (Bagshaw, 59). Bagshaw touched on her relations with local clergy: she had preserved and passed on to him the spiritual confession of Anthony Buxton. He also noted her private spirituality:

> The Lord only knew (though his servants guessed at it) how sweet and satiating the communion was, which she had with the Lord in secret, where the choicest books were read, and meditated on. Might she not say, she was never less alone, than when alone? (Bagshaw, 59)

However, the survival of Katherine Gell's correspondence with the great puritan casuist Richard Baxter, while confirming Bagshaw's portrait of her meditating and

reading religious works, provides a depth and sense of spiritual struggle absent from the latter's somewhat hagiographic account. Katherine made the first move in July 1655 by introducing herself to Baxter as a distressed soul. At the age of almost twenty, she told Baxter, she had been spiritually awakened by a sermon of Stephen Marshall, the puritan minister. This had produced 'many sad brambles in my soule & raised many thoughts within which I concealed' and two years later she wrote to Marshall and was comforted by his advice. Baxter's great work, *The Saints Everlasting Rest* (1650), however, had set standards for her which she could not sustain: the sense of her own failings (which included a belief that her bashfulness had prevented her from adequately fulfilling her duty of promoting the spiritual welfare of her household) had convinced her that she was not in a state of grace. She therefore sought reassurance from him and apologized for her English style: she was only a woman. A month later, she described to him the effects upon her a year previously of the death of her seventeen-week-old child. For a day and night it lifted her to an unprecedented pitch of assurance. Three days later, however, she was oppressed by the contrary conviction that 'god had taken him away in anger throwne him into hell and I shall shortly follow'. At the time of writing she had achieved some kind of balance, but a fragile one. She was happier about her own condition but uncertain about the salvation of her child (Keeble and Nuttall, 1.191). Baxter's letter of 7 June 1656 was a plea to her not to overdo the introspection: 'in this life, even Grace itselfe doth usually worke according to this way of nature' (Keeble and Nuttall, 1.214)—an epitome of the central message in Baxter's first controversial anti-Calvinist work, *The Aphorismes of Justification* (1649). While it is true that hypocrites can content themselves with a 'seeming assurance' of salvation 'once they are past the fears of damnation', and she should be congratulated for aiming higher, that very aim revealed in itself her 'high degree of Grace' (DWL, Baxter correspondence, vol. 5, fol. 217). There is an extraordinary parallel in the exchanges between Baxter and another tormented lady, Mary Rich, countess of Warwick, as recorded in her diary (BL, Add. MS 27354, fol. 95).

In April 1657 Katherine Gell could report to Baxter how she had followed his advice and buried herself in family matters. But there was a downside to this in the sense that such activities left little room for good thoughts as well as bad ones: 'I had rather locke my selfe up in a room alone amongst my books, for meditation' (Keeble and Nuttall, 1.249). Baxter's memoir of his wife had actually revealed similar tensions within his own marriage: he would prefer a good book to a clean house (R. Baxter, *A Breviate of the Life of Margaret*, 1681, 80). Katherine explained that her fears were not for herself (she could face martyrdom) but for her children, and had been recently prompted by a smallpox outbreak in the locality. Baxter, a month later, was upbeat: 'most women are of more sensible passionate dispositions than men' (DWL, Baxter correspondence, vol. 5, fol. 11). Too much should not be expected of prayer: he instanced his own fear of the dark until the age of twenty. He offered her a case study, of his dear friend Lady Rous, 'as far from over much passionate sensibility as most woemen that ever I knew', who fell into a fever on the report of her husband's illness. She died, while he recovered. Katherine could report to Baxter, on 10 November 1657, that she was getting over her depression, but she too had a fear of the dark: 'Every little noise doth of late soe affright me that it makes me start from the place' (Keeble and Nuttall, 1.273). Baxter rejoices, a month later, in her recovery, but wants her to put her present feelings down in writing as a prevention against future lapses. He had not overlooked the significance of her quickness in copying his anecdote about the dark: 'I perceive that your nature hath that melancholy disposition still'. He admitted that he still had some fear of the dark, but nothing to what it formerly was. Reason and faith helped, but Baxter thought that 'some change in my temperature by age' might have been more decisive. So Katherine should avoid the dark and wait—with age—for the time of deliverance. If the Devil appear to her in person, it would be a tribute to her piety: she was an adversary worth fighting. Diary-keeping (she had told him of the spiritual diary she had kept for the past two years) was a good activity but that too could be overdone (did he know the existence of the countess of Warwick's profuse self-analysis?). When her scruples extended to usury, Baxter was evasive (Keeble and Nuttall, 1.280; DWL, Baxter correspondence, vol. 5, fol. 183).

Six months on, and prayer is still not working for Katherine Gell. She could only look forward to another thirty years of unrelieved suffering; she was prepared to die. She had sought the private counsel of her minister but, in the eyes of her neighbours, when this got out this was worse than 'gaming or mixed dancing or bare breasts'. These same people would consult physicians, lawyers, or bishops: the ordinary clergy were beneath them. 'Most of the gentry of England are now come to be of this strane', and their anti-clericalism worsened her depression (DWL, Baxter correspondence, vol. 5, fol. 5). Baxter, a week later, was sympathetic to that point: 'they know not it is the Ministers office to oversee each member of the flock, and to be a stated Director for mens salvation for all to goe to in their needs, as Physicians care for mens health and lives'. Baxter had made a gift to her of George Herbert's poems: as he had hoped, they had put her 'into a very good praying frame'. He responded to her request for a bibliography of his writings, but wanted her not to waste time on the ensuing controversies they had provoked (DWL, Baxter correspondence, vol. 5, fol. 9).

The correspondence dries up on 27 December 1658 with Katherine's thanks to Baxter for his 'chiding', and his recognition that her melancholia might have a physical cause. The loss of her godly minister at Wirksworth, Martin Topham, was lamented by 'all the ministers of our Classis in a day of humiliation at our house' (Keeble and Nuttall, 1.367–8). One Baxter correspondent would criticize Baxter in 1690 for the emphasis he had placed, in the memoir of his wife, on the perils of over-intensive introspection: 'What Ugly Conceit have you of God, the Beautie

of Angells and Immortal Souls' (DWL, Baxter correspondence, vol. 1, fol. 119). The chance survival of his exchanges with Katherine Gell reveal why indeed they were central to his pastoral concerns. When Katherine Gell died in 1671 her death called forth letters of condolence from local ministers. The presbyterian John Otefield wrote to one of her daughters that 'such a Mother is a losse indeed ... shee though dead yet speaketh, her instructions may yet live in your heart ... by following her steps you may hope to enjoy her again in a blessed eternity' (Cliffe, 71).

WILLIAM LAMONT

Sources DWL, Baxter correspondence, vol. 5 · *Calendar of the correspondence of Richard Baxter*, ed. N. H. Keeble and G. F. Nuttall, 1 (1991) · W. Bagshaw, *De spiritualibus Pecci* (1702) · J. T. Cliffe, *The puritan gentry besieged, 1650–1700* (1993) · G. D. Squibb, ed., *The visitation of Derbyshire, begun in 1662*, Harleian Society, new ser., 8 (1989) · E. R. Edwards, 'Gell, Sir John', HoP, *Commons, 1660–90* · J. L. Chester, ed., *The marriage, baptismal, and burial registers of the collegiate church or abbey of St Peter, Westminster*, Harleian Society, 10 (1876), 65–7 · T. Brighton, 'The Gell family in the 16th and 17th centuries: a case of the rising gentry', *Journal of the Bakewell District Historical Society*, 7 (1980), 4–34 · J. C. Cox, ed., 'The minute book of the Wirksworth classis, 1651–1658', *Journal of the Derbyshire Archaeological and Natural History Society*, 2 (1880), 135–222 · W. M. Lamont, *Richard Baxter and the millennium: protestant imperialism and the English revolution* (1979) **Archives** Derbyshire RO, Matlock, family papers | DWL, Baxter corresp., vol. 5

Gell, Robert (1595–1665), Church of England clergyman, was born on 19 February 1595 at Frindsbury, Kent, the son of William Gell, vicar of Frindsbury, who was related to the Gell family of Hopton, Derbyshire. He was educated for eight years at Westminster School, where he was a king's scholar. Having matriculated as a sizar from Christ's College, Cambridge, in April 1615, he graduated BA in 1618, proceeded MA in 1621, was elected a fellow in 1623, and proceeded BD in 1628. Spending a total of about twenty-seven years in the college, as he recalled in his will, he held several college offices and preached frequently before the university.

On 27 January 1641 Gell was presented to the rectory of St Mary Aldermary, a rich London parish. The same year he proceeded DD and on 7 November married Elizabeth Lawrence (d. 1668) at Pampisford, Cambridgeshire. They had two children baptized at Pampisford: John on 20 October 1644 and Elizabeth on 5 June 1648. In 1645 Gell survived an attempt by some of his parishioners to have him removed from his rectory. Evidently not a presbyterian, he was able to present himself as orthodox at the Restoration, but in the interim was associated with some decidedly unorthodox views. Two sermons delivered to the Society of Astrologers on 1 August 1649 and 8 August 1650 were published respectively as *Stella nova: a New Starre Leading the Wisemen unto Christ* (1649) and *Aggelokratia theon, or, A Sermon Touching God's Government of the World by Angels* (1650). Gell admitted in his preface to *Stella nova* that it had resulted in accusations that he 'had defended Conjurers and Jugglers' (sig. A3v); he also called for the reformation of doctrine to be given precedence over the reformation of discipline. On 7 August 1655 he preached before the lord mayor and Drapers' Company a sermon published as *Noahs Flood Returning* (1655). Writing from London on 24

August 1658, Matthew Poole, the presbyterian rector of St Michael-le-Querne, told Richard Baxter that he had heard Gell 'once or twice & I find him run much upon Arminian and some Popish errours & that way of Allegorizing Scripture miserably'. He had heard 'from good hands hee is a familist'; his audience were 'divers of them Astrologers, some Seekers others well willers to the Quakers like him'. Having once called on him to register his disapproval, Poole 'found him not to bee able to make out what he had asserted' (Keeble and Nuttall, 1.335). In his lengthy preface to his even lengthier *An Essay toward the Amendment of the Last English Translation of the Bible* (1659), Gell spoke out against 'those men who now for many years, have rendered me odious unto such as know me not, and have endeavoured to smother me, like a Rat behind the Hangings'; they had traduced him 'as a man of erroneous judgement; a dangerous man; one who turns the Scriptures into Allegories' (sig. d1v). His present work, in which he acknowledged the assistance of his friends Dr Thomas Drayton, William Parker, and Richard Hunt, was a detailed discussion of the Pentateuch which he hoped would confound his critics.

Undisturbed in his rectory at the Restoration, Gell published in 1660, under a pseudonym and describing himself as a 'presbyter and professor of the more ancient doctrine', *Eirenikon, or, A Treatise of Peace between the Tow Visible Parties*. He urged readers to forget their religious differences and live together peacefully. Subsequently he served as a chaplain to Archbishop Gilbert Sheldon. He died on 25 March 1665 at Pampisford and was buried there. His will, dated 21 July 1661, left much of his estate to his only surviving child, Elizabeth; it was proved by his widow on 3 September 1668, just nine days before she died. The preface to *Gell's Remaines, or, Several Select Scriptures of the New Testament Opened and Explained* (1676) praised Gell's ability to make the Bible accessible and easily understandable, by writing 'in a plain, modest and humble stile, and so much the better, Truth needs no paint'.

LOUISE HILL CURTH

Sources parish register, Pampisford, Cambs. AS, P130/1/1 [marriage] · Wood, *Ath. Oxon.*, new edn, 3.562 · BL, Sloane MS 1707 · G. Hennessy, *Novum repertorium ecclesiasticum parochiale Londinense, or, London diocesan clergy succession from the earliest time to the year 1898* (1898), 299–300 · R. Newcourt, *Repertorium ecclesiasticum parochiale Londinense*, 1 (1708), 426 · Venn, *Alum. Cant.* · will, PRO, PROB 11/316, sig. 37 · J. Peile, *Christ's College* (1900), 137 · *N&Q*, 2nd ser., 6 (1858), 374 · *Calendar of the correspondence of Richard Baxter*, ed. N. H. Keeble and G. F. Nuttall, 2 vols. (1991) · Tai Liu, *Puritan London: a study of religion and society in the City parishes* (1986) · *Old Westminsters*, 1.369

Gell, Sir William (1777–1836), classical archaeologist and traveller, born on 1 April 1777 at Hopton, Derbyshire, was the younger son of Philip Gell of Hopton and his wife, Dorothy, who was the daughter and coheir of William Milnes of Aldercar Park. After Philip Gell died in 1795, Dorothy married Thomas *Blore, the topographer, who had been Philip's estate manager. William Gell's paternal grandfather, John Eyre, had assumed the name of Gell from his mother's family, the Gells of Hopton. Gell was educated at Derby School and matriculated from Emmanuel College, Cambridge, in 1793, graduated BA and was

Sir William Gell (1777–1836), by Cornelius Varley, 1816

elected to the fellowship in 1798, and proceeded MA in 1804. His books are mostly illustrated from his own sketches, sometimes with the aid of the camera lucida. While these show no great artistic power, they have been praised for their exactness and minuteness.

The first portion of Gell's scholarly career was based on extensive travels in the eastern Mediterranean during the early years of the nineteenth century. In 1801 he visited the Troad, where he made numerous sketches and fixed the site of Troy at Burnabashi. He published the *Topography of Troy* (1804), a work to which Byron alluded in his *English Bards* (1809):

Of Dardan tours let dilettanti tell,
I leave topography to classic Gell.

After a diplomatic mission to the Ionian Islands in 1803, Gell began a journey in the Morea and then visited Ithaca in company with Edward Dodwell, the traveller. He afterwards published the *Geography and Antiquities of Ithaca* (1807), the *Itinerary of Greece, with a Commentary on Pausanias* (1810), *Itinerary of the Morea* (1817), *Narrative of a Journey in the Morea* (1823), and *Itinerary of Greece* (1827). Byron wrote an elaborate article on the *Ithaca* and *Itinerary of Greece* in the *Monthly Review* for August 1811. From 1811 until 1813 Gell led the Society of Dilettanti's second Ionian expedition, the results of which were published by the society in *The Unedited Antiquities of Attica* (1817) and the revised editions of *Ionian Antiquities* (1821 and 1840).

Gell was knighted on 11 May 1814 for his services in the eastern Mediterranean. Later that year when Princess (afterwards Queen) Caroline left England for Italy, Gell accompanied her as one of her chamberlains. When he left her service in 1815 she granted him a pension of £200 per annum for life, which was abruptly terminated after her death in 1821. Gell testified effectively for her on 6 October 1820 at her trial before the House of Lords, although in letters and conversation he often retailed little bits of scandal about the queen. His papers contain several dozen of her letters to him: 'What curious things they are,' he wrote, 'and how rightly it would serve the royal family, supposing they had not quarrelled with her to publish their wife and cousin's correspondence, as they have cheated me out of my pension!' (Madden, 1.377).

The pension from Princess Caroline enabled Gell, who was not wealthy, to establish himself in Italy and devote the second portion of his career to studying Italian antiquities and producing some of his best-known archaeological work. His *Pompeiana* (2 vols., 1817–19) was the first account of Pompei in English. J. P. Gandy (later J. P. Deering) helped to prepare the work, which ran to several editions. Gell had obtained from the government special facilities for visiting the excavations, and made very numerous sketches (reproduced in the volumes) of objects which he declared would otherwise have perished unrecorded. He collaborated with Professor Antonio Nibby to produce *Le mura di Roma* in 1820, and in 1834 he published the *Topography of Rome and its Vicinity*. He had been a member of the Society of Dilettanti since 1807, and was appointed 'Resident minister-plenipotentiary' of the society in Italy in 1830 and regularly forwarded reports. He was also a fellow of the Society of Antiquaries, of the Royal Society, a member of the Royal Academy of Berlin, and of the Institut de France.

In Italy Gell lived in Rome and Naples, making his home exclusively in the latter city during the closing years of his life. He was intensely active in society. His house, which attracted a constant stream of distinguished visitors, was described as 'the resort of all ranks, ages, and sexes, and [the] mornings one continued levée' (Madden, 1.331–2). Notable literary visitors included Sir Walter Scott, about whose visit Gell wrote a detailed memoir, and Bulwer Lytton, who dedicated his novel, *The Last Days of Pompeii*, to his host. Gell also maintained a wide correspondence, some character of which may be derived from Lady Charlotte Bury's *The Diary of a Lady-in-Waiting* (1908) and R. R. Madden's *The Literary Life and Correspondence of the Countess of Blessington* (1855). But all accounts indicate that Gell's wit shone most brilliantly in conversation, particularly at his dinner parties with the archbishop of Tarentum, Francis Augustus Hare, and Sir William Drummond. The poet Walter Savage Landor, who occasionally joined them as a youth, later remembered,

> I miss the tales I used to tell
> With cordial Hare and joyous Gell.
> (M. Elwin, *Landor*, 1958, 224–5)

Gell's aptitude for scholarship, correspondence, and conversation combined to bear fruit in what is arguably his greatest contribution: his role as intellectual intermediary. He actively worked to bring together the right people and ideas, a particularly useful function before the formalization of the modern academic disciplines. 'I glory in communicating all the new discoveries', he declared (J. Leitch, ed., *Miscellaneous Works of … Thomas Young*, 3, 1855, 407). His activity is evident in a number of fields, but especially in the nascent science of Egyptology where he followed developments closely and became acquainted with such pioneers as Thomas Young and Jean François Champollion. Gell, who once referred to himself as 'purveyor-general to the hieroglyphics' (ibid., 3.408), was a virtual clearing-house of Egyptological information and inspired several individuals to study the field. He particularly influenced Sir Gardner Wilkinson, one of the founders of Egyptology in Great Britain, who afterwards acknowledged his debt to Gell on many occasions.

From about 1815 until his death Gell suffered severely from gout and rheumatism, or more likely from rheumatoid arthritis, though he was always cheerful. When he became seriously ill in 1835, he was tended kindly by his great friend Keppel Craven. He died in Naples on 4 February 1836 and was buried in the English burial-ground at Naples in the tomb of Craven's mother, the margravine of Ansbach—a monument in the shape of an Ionic temple. Gell was unmarried. By his will he left his house and gardens at Naples to the English congregation there. His plate and carriage, almost his only other property, he left to his servants. All his papers were bequeathed to Craven, who presented them to his (Craven's) Italian secretary, Pasquini. The original drawings, nearly eight hundred in number, made by Gell during his travels, were also left to Craven and were bequeathed by him to the British Museum. Unfortunately, most of Gell's other papers were subsequently dispersed; some have been recovered, but many more have apparently been lost.

Gell represented the culmination of the literary topographical tradition. Written when Greece and even Italy were comparatively little known to English travellers and classical students, his works were for some time regarded as standard treatises, and much of the information they contain is still of value. He once expressed an ideal of creating topographical background so that 'a student reading the account of any battle may be certain that here stood such a height & there ran such a brook' (*Gell in Italy*, 59).

W. W. WROTH, rev. JASON THOMPSON

Sources *Sir William Gell in Italy: letters to the Society of Dilettanti, 1831–1835*, ed. E. Clay and M. Frederiksen (1976) • W. Gell, *Reminiscences of Sir Walter Scott's residence in Italy, 1832*, ed. W. Rollinson (1957) • *The diary of a lady-in-waiting, by Lady Charlotte Bury*, ed. A. F. Steuart, 2 vols. (1908) • R. R. Madden, *The literary life and correspondence of the countess of Blessington*, 2 vols. (New York, 1855) • M. R. Bruce, 'A tourist in Athens, 1801', *Journal of Hellenic Studies*, 92 (1972), 173–5 • E. Clay, 'Rhodes: Sir William to Sir Walter', *Journal of the Warburg and Courtauld Institutes*, 33 (1970), 336–43 • H. R. Hall, 'Letters of Champollion le jeune and of Seyffarth to Sir William Gell', *Journal of Egyptian Archaeology*, 2 (1915), 76–87 • H. R. Hall, 'Letters to Sir William Gell from Henry Salt, (Sir) J. G. Wilkinson, and Baron von Bunsen', *Journal of Egyptian Archaeology*, 2 (1915), 133–67 • J. Thompson, *Sir Gardner Wilkinson and his circle* (1992) • M. I. Wiencke, 'Fauvel's model of the Parthenon and some drawings of Gell from the time of the Elgin mission, 1801–03', *American Journal of Archaeology*, 78 (1974), 184–5 • W. Gell, *A tour of the Lakes made in 1797 by William Gell*, ed. W. Rollinson (1968) • L. Cust and S. Colvin, eds., *History of the Society of Dilettanti* (1898) • *Hansard 2* (1820), 3.318–63 • Derbys. RO, Gell papers • *LondG* (14 May 1814), 1007 • Venn, *Alum. Cant.*

Archives BL, corresp., Add. MS 50135 • BL, corresp., Add. MSS 63617–63619 • BM, department of Greek and Roman antiquities, classical notebooks • Bodl. Oxf., record of dreams • Bodl. Oxf., notebooks and sketches of travels in Greece and Italy • Cumbria AS, Barrow, sketchbook and account of tour of lakes • Derbys. RO, corresp. • McGill University, McLennan Library, notebook • NL Scot., notes on Rhodes • Suffolk RO, Bury St Edmunds, Scottish travel journal • U. Oxf., Griffith Institute, notebooks • University of Bristol Library, special collections, diaries of tours through Germany, Austria, north Italy, Greece, the Morea, and the Aegean Islands • Yale U., Beinecke L., journal in Germany, Switzerland, and Italy | BL, corresp. with John Peter Deering, Add. MS 63617 • Bodl. Oxf., corresp. with Sir J. G. Wilkinson [incl. some copies] • NL Scot., corresp. with Robert Liston

Likenesses C. Varley, pencil drawing, 1816, NPG [*see illus.*] • T. Uwins, pencil drawing, 1830, NPG • Fenner Sears & Co., stipple, pubd 1832 (after T. Uwins), BM, NPG • T. Uwins, portrait (after engraving), repro. in W. Gell, *Pompeiana* (1832) • busts

Wealth at death see will, Madden, *The literary life*, 2.500

Gellibrand, Henry (1597–1637), mathematician, was born in the parish of St Botolph, Aldersgate, London, on 17 November 1597, the eldest son of Henry Gellibrand (*d.* 1615), fellow of All Souls College, Oxford, and of St Paul's Cray, Kent. He matriculated at Trinity College, Oxford, on 22 March 1616 and took the two degrees in arts, BA (on 25 November 1619) and MA (on 26 May 1623). He took holy orders, and had a curacy at Chiddingstone, Kent, but was led to devote himself entirely to mathematics by one of Sir Henry Savile's lectures. He settled at Oxford and became a friend of Henry Briggs, on whose recommendation he was chosen professor of astronomy at Gresham College in London on 2 January 1627. When Briggs died in 1630 he left his unfinished *Trigonometria Britannica* to Gellibrand who published the completed work in 1633.

Gellibrand held puritan meetings in his rooms, and encouraged his servant, William Beale, to publish an almanac for 1631, in which the Catholic saints were superseded by those in Foxe's book of martyrs. Laud, then bishop of London, brought them both into the high commission court. They were acquitted on the ground that similar almanacs had been printed before, and this prosecution was used against Laud at his own trial in 1643.

Gellibrand devoted much time to searching for a solution to the longitude problem. In 1631 he arranged an experiment with Captain Thomas James, who was leading an expedition in search of the north-west passage, to observe simultaneously the lunar eclipse due on 29 October. The time difference enabled him to establish the difference in longitude between Gresham College and Charlton Island in James Bay, Canada. An account was published as 'An appendix concerning longitude' in James's book *The Strange and Dangerous Voyage of Captaine Thomas James* (1633).

Gellibrand was also investigating the phenomenon of the magnetic variation of the compass, which led to his discovery of secular variation. Measurements of the magnetic variation taken at Deptford in 1634 were found to differ from those taken in 1622 by Edmund Gunter by more than two degrees. Later experiments showed the variation to have diminished still further. This discovery contradicted the categorical statement of William Gilbert in *De magnete* that the magnetic variation in a particular place was constant. Gellibrand published his findings in *A discourse mathematical of the variation of the magneticall needle together with its admirable diminution lately discovered* (1635).

In 1636 Gellibrand retired to Mayfield, Sussex. He died in London of a fever on 16 February 1637, and was buried in the church of St Peter-le-Poer, Broad Street, London. His main concern had been to improve methods of navigation and much of his work consisted of investigating the ways in which mathematics could help navigators to establish their position. His most popular work was his *Epitome of Navigation*, which was published posthumously in 1674 and appeared in several further editions. If not a particularly original thinker Gellibrand was nevertheless an able mathematician and textbook writer.

GORDON GOODWIN, rev. H. K. HIGTON

Sources E. G. R. Taylor, *The mathematical practitioners of Tudor and Stuart England* (1954) • *DSB* • Foster, *Alum. Oxon.* • J. Ward, *The lives of the professors of Gresham College* (1740)

Gellibrand, Sir John (1872–1945), army officer, was born at Ouse, Tasmania, on 5 December 1872, son of Thomas Lloyd Gellibrand (*d.* 1874), a sheep farmer, and his wife Isabella (*née* Brown), and grandson of Joseph Tice Gellibrand, the first attorney-general of Tasmania.

After John's father's death in 1874 his mother took her seven children to Europe where John was educated at Crespigny House, Aldeburgh, Suffolk; Frankfurt am Main, Germany; and King's School, Canterbury (1888–9). He graduated from the Royal Military College, Sandhurst, in 1892, and was commissioned in the 1st South Lancashire regiment, with which he fought in the Second South African War at the relief of Ladysmith. In May 1900 he transferred, as captain, to the Manchester regiment, and in 1907 passed a Staff College course at Camberley. In 1908–12 he was deputy assistant adjutant and quartermaster-general in Ceylon. When his battalion was disbanded in 1912 he resigned his commission and returned to Tasmania where he became an orchardist at Risdon, near Hobart. On 27 July 1894 he had married Elizabeth Helena (*d.* 1949), daughter of Charles Frederick Alexander du Breul, shipping merchant, of Shortlands, Kent; they had one son and two daughters.

In 1914 Gellibrand was appointed to the 1st Australian division, Australian Imperial Force, and in 1915 he was twice wounded during the Gallipoli campaign. After serving on the staffs of the 1st and 2nd divisions during that campaign he was appointed to command first the 12th battalion (1915–16) and then the 6th infantry brigade, which he took to France. He was wounded again and became known as a commander of devoted courage, sardonic but kindly humour, and supreme ability in training, especially of young officers. Unconventional, dressing and living like his men, he turned his brigade into a most formidable fighting instrument. After taking a prominent part in many battles, especially second Bullecourt (May

1917), he commanded the 12th brigade, and following a term as director of training at the Australian Imperial Force depots in England, he commanded the 3rd Australian division through the victories of 1918. For his services in the field he was appointed DSO (1916), with bar (1917), and CB (1917), and promoted KCB in 1919; in the same year he was appointed officer of the Légion d'honneur, received the French Croix de Guerre, and the United States DSM. He was mentioned six times in dispatches and once in French army orders.

Back in Australia Gellibrand became successively public service commissioner of Tasmania (1919–20) and commissioner of police in Victoria (1920–22), and then (1925–8) Nationalist member for Denison (Tasmania) in the federal parliament. His independent spirit, exemplified by his dislike of being overruled and an inability to compromise, made him unsuited to public life, and he returned to his orchard. In 1937 he became a grazier at Murrindindi, near Yea in Victoria, mainly to be near his son. In Tasmania he had founded the Remembrance Club—the forerunner of the important Legacy clubs of Australia—to continue the wartime comradeship of all ranks and care for the widows and children of ex-servicemen. From 1938 he interested himself in the state of Australia's defence, which had suffered from years of neglect. He was consulted by prime ministers J. A. Lyons and R. G. Menzies, wrote articles in the press in a nationwide campaign to double the size of the militia, and spoke at numerous recruiting meetings. Recurrent ill health, however, forced him to give up this work in 1940. He died of cerebro-vascular disease at Balaclava, Murrindindi, on 3 June 1945 and was buried in Yea cemetery.

Gellibrand was a close friend of C. E. W. Bean, the official Australian war historian. Their long correspondence (1916–45) reveals a conscious attempt by Gellibrand to influence Bean's assessment of his performance as a commander as well as the *Official History* itself. But Bean certainly needed no prompting when he wrote in volume 1, *The Story of Anzac*, concerning the second tense struggle at Bullecourt: 'if ever a fight was won by a single brain and character' this battle was won by John Gellibrand (Bean 1.81).

With standards which seemed at times impossibly high, Gellibrand was a great leader—as Bean affirms—but a sensitive and often difficult subordinate. He was fortunate in serving under a commander and chief of staff who were aware of his rare qualities of mind and moral courage.

GERALD WALSH

Sources AusDB · C. E. W. Bean and others, *The official history of Australia in the war of 1914–1918*, 12 vols. (1921–43) · P. S. Sadler, *The Paladin: a life of Major-General Sir John Gellibrand* (South Melbourne, 2000) · Australian War Memorial, Canberra, J. Gellibrand MSS · J. Monash, *The Australian victories in France, 1918* (1920) · M. Lyons, *Legacy: the first fifty years* (1978) · L. M. Newton, *The story of the twelfth* (1925) · CGPLA Eng. & Wales (1946) · b. cert. · m. cert. · d. cert.
Archives Australian War Memorial, Canberra, diaries and papers | FILM IWM FVA, actuality footage
Likenesses W. Stoneman, photograph, 1919, NPG · J. P. Quinn, oils, Australian War Memorial, Canberra, Australia

Wealth at death £1013 12s. 8d.: probate, Melbourne · £313 17s. 11d.—in England: Australian probate sealed in England, 22 Aug 1946, CGPLA Eng. & Wales

Gellner, Ernest André (1925–1995), social philosopher and anthropologist, was born on 9 December 1925 in Paris, the elder of two children of Jewish parents, Rudolf Gellner (1897–1987), a lawyer, and his wife, Anna, *née* Fantl (1894–1954), both from Czechoslovakia. The family returned to Prague, where he attended the English grammar school, but in 1939 they fled the German occupation to England, where Gellner attended St Albans county grammar school, winning a scholarship at seventeen to Balliol College, Oxford. After a year at Balliol he served with the Czech armoured brigade in northern France. He returned to Prague in 1945 and spent half a term at Prague University, but, foreseeing the communists' takeover, he returned to England and Oxford as an undergraduate. He read philosophy, politics, and economics, and obtained a first in 1949. After two years lecturing in philosophy at Edinburgh University, he moved to the London School of Economics (LSE) to teach philosophy in the sociology department, but was attracted to the ideas, though not to the cult, of Karl Popper and to anthropology, in the Malinowskian tradition, in which he wrote a doctoral thesis, doing fieldwork among the Berbers in Morocco. In 1954 he married Susan Ryan (b. 1926), with whom he had two sons and two daughters. He stayed at the LSE for thirty-three years, becoming professor of philosophy in 1962, moving in 1979 to the philosophy department. In 1984 he became professor of social anthropology at Cambridge but returned to Prague in 1991 as director and resident professor of the Centre for the Study of Nationalism at the Central European University.

Gellner was brilliant, forceful, irreverent, mischievous, sometimes perverse, with a biting wit and love of irony, while abundantly generous with his time, support, and energy, all the more impressively given a chronic bone disease from which he suffered. He was an intellectual whose impact extended across the world and beyond the various academic disciplines on whose frontiers he flourished. He engaged in vivid academic polemics, in an aphoristic and knockabout satirical style, but always in defence of bold philosophical and substantive positions. These cohered within an overall vision: an anti-relativist defence of Enlightenment ideals and insistence upon the difference between the agrarian religious world and the industrial scientific one, the need to explain the transition from the one to the other, and the cognitive and technological superiority of the second. That vision was most fully set out in his reflections on 'the structure of human history' in his *Plough, Sword and Book* (1988).

The first such polemic was *Words and Things* (1959), Gellner's notorious onslaught on contemporary Oxford linguistic philosophers, much influenced by the later Wittgenstein, forever his particular *bête noire*. He attacked them for idealism and relativism, for assuming that philosophy must 'dissolve' philosophical problems by endorsing the ordinary language conventions of existing communities. Bertrand Russell wrote the preface, but Gilbert

Ernest André Gellner (1925–1995), by Geoff Howard, 1979

Ryle, the editor of *Mind*, refused to have it reviewed. Subsequent polemical targets included the 'churches' of French structuralism, 'Frankfurter' neo-Marxism and the psychoanalytic movement, the 'anti-Orientalist' analyses of Edward Said, the 'meta-twaddle' of postmodernism, and, within anthropology, the highly influential writings of Clifford Geertz for denying that knowledge beyond culture is possible and thereby influencing his fellow anthropologists towards the very idealism and relativism to escape which he had originally turned to anthropology.

Gellner's major positive contributions within anthropology began with important contributions to debates about kinship and rationality. Then in *Saints of the Atlas* (1969) he applied 'segmentary lineage theory' to analyse the role played by charismatic religious specialists in maintaining political order in the absence of state power; he also incorporated a cyclical model of tribal–urban interaction derived from Ibn Khaldun. He developed this analysis into a general model for Islamic polities, in *Muslim Society* (1981), which, though criticized, was an important stimulus to scholars of Islam. But his best-known and most influential contribution was his theory of nationalism, expounded in *Thought and Change* (1965) and *Nations and Nationalism* (1983). This theory focused on the 'requirements' of industrialism which, with its need for labour mobility, entailed a measure of egalitarianism and institutions to promote a homogeneous culture to enable communication. Industrialism's uneven spread meant that the élites of backward areas had an incentive to foster nationalism and separate off to become bigger fish in a smaller pond. This model was also criticized, especially in

relation to nationalism outside Europe, yet it remains the best general theory of nationalism yet proposed.

Gellner also turned his attention to Soviet-style socialism in eastern Europe and the Soviet Union. He had a keen eye for its corrupting mechanisms and inability to fulfil its promises, combining native understanding and linguistic facility with anthropological expertise, spending a year in Moscow in 1989–90. He interpreted Soviet ethnographers' use of Marxist theories for the light they shed on Soviet realities, in *State and Society in Soviet Thought* (1988). In his last years he put to work the concept of 'civil society' in *Conditions of Liberty: Civil Society and its Rivals* (1994), contrasting it with traditional segmentary and totalitarian societies, while arguing for guarantees that would protect citizens from the tyranny of the market. A striking study of Wittgenstein and Malinowski, *Language and Solitude* (1998), appeared posthumously, relating their contrasting viewpoints to conditions of life and thought under the Habsburg empire.

Gellner was a provocative and exciting but schematic thinker who liked, as he once admitted, 'neat, crisp models'. These should be seen as 'ideal types' for generating theories that have the Popperian virtue of being falsifiable. He offered sketches of the big picture of large-scale social processes, while admiring and encouraging those committed to the detailed understanding of local concepts and ideas but fiercely opposing those who fashionably argued that local knowledge is all the knowledge there is. He was a passionate universalist in both his thought and his life. He built up an extraordinary range of international contacts, but his incessant travels finally caught up with him. On 5 November 1995 he died of a heart attack in Prague after flying back from a meeting in Budapest. He was cremated in Chichester, Sussex. Gellner was survived by his wife and four children.

STEVEN LUKES

Sources *The Independent* (8 Nov 1995) · *The Independent* (9 Nov 1995) · *The Independent* (15 Nov 1995) · *The Times* (7 Nov 1995) · *The Guardian* (8 Nov 1995) · 'It's out there, like Mount Everest: thoughts on the Gellner legacy', *Cambridge Anthropology*, 19/2 (1996–7), 35–48 · J. Davis, 'An interview with Ernest Gellner', *Current Anthropology*, 32/1 (Feb 1991), 63–72 · C. Hann, 'Gellner, Ernest', *International encyclopedia of the social and behavioral sciences*, ed. N. J. Smelser and P. B. Baltes (2001) · WWW, 1991–5 · CGPLA Eng. & Wales (1996) · private information (2004) [David Gellner]
Archives BLPES, papers | McMaster University, Hamilton, Ontario, corresp. with Bertrand Russell
Likenesses G. Howard, photograph, 1979, Camera Press Ltd, London [*see illus.*] · photograph, repro. in E. Gellner, *Language and solitude* (1998), frontispiece · photograph, repro. in E. Gellner, *Spectacles and predicaments*, pbk edn (1991), cover · photograph, repro. in J. A. Hall and I. C. Jarvie, eds., *Transition to modernity: essays on power, wealth and belief* (1992), jacket · photograph, repro. in *The Times* · photograph, repro. in *The Independent* (8 Nov 1995)
Wealth at death under £145,000: probate, 29 April 1996, CGPLA Eng. & Wales

Gem, Thomas Henry (1819–1881), lawyer and tennis player, was born in Birmingham on 21 May 1819, the eldest son of William Henry Gem (*d.* 1856), a well-known Birmingham solicitor and one of the clerks to the Birmingham magistrates. He was educated under Dr Major at

King's College, London, and articled at the age of sixteen to H. M. Griffiths, solicitor of Birmingham. On admission in 1841 he commenced practice in his native town. Though he built up an extensive private practice and acquired numerous legal and public appointments, 'Harry' Gem, as he was widely known, was principally known for his sporting, literary, and other public activities.

Gem was an active sportsman throughout his life, enjoying cricket, horse-riding, athletics, and 'pedestrianism', yet it was the game of lawn tennis for which he was known in the midlands. His part in the development of the rules of the game went largely unrecognized, save by his contemporaries in Birmingham and Leamington Spa. In the 1850s Gem was a keen racket player and leading spirit of the local club, but his enthusiasm was blunted by the necessity for expensively constructed courts. With his friend J. B. A. Perera, a Birmingham merchant, he drew up rules for a game named 'pelota' and later 'lawn rackets', with an emphasis placed upon simplicity and athleticism. The first game was played in the garden of Perera's Edgbaston residence about the year 1865. In 1872 Gem and Perera moved to Leamington Spa where they established a club and the name changed again to 'lawn tennis'. Consequently, this predates the claims of Major Walter C. *Wingfield to be the inventor of lawn tennis, the publication of his book on sphairistike, and the debate on the origin of the game in 1874–5.

In 1859, to the detriment of his other activities, Gem had thrown himself into the cause of the volunteer movement. He initiated the attempts to establish a local corps in Birmingham, holding the position of honorary secretary to the founding committee. At the time of his death Gem held the rank of major in the 1st Warwickshire (Birmingham) rifles. However, the movement made little progress in Birmingham and the waning of interest led to Gem's renewed preoccupation with tennis.

Gem was a prolific author. He wrote on numerous subjects and in a variety of forms, the majority of his works being for private or limited circulation. He contributed regularly to Baily's Magazine on a wide range of subjects, such as pugilism, horses, bull-baiting, and other sporting matters. Other material included election squibs (he was a staunch Conservative), songs, poems, verses (for example, on tennis), and a history of the Birmingham rifle corps. His major piece, completed shortly before his death, was a dramatization, in verse, of the Bardell v. Pickwick trial scenes from Charles Dickens's Pickwick Papers. In addition to writing for the stage, Gem was considered an accomplished performer of light comedy in local amateur productions. He was the first president of the Birmingham Dramatic Club and a member of the Birmingham Amateur Dramatic Association.

Gem also gained prominence locally as a result of his legal posts. On the death of his father in 1856 he succeeded to the office of clerk to the Birmingham magistrates. In addition, he held appointments as magistrate's clerk to the Kings Heath and Balsall Heath petty sessions and clerk to the commissioners of taxes for the hundred of Hemlingford.

Gem died at 21 Portland Place, Leamington Priors, Warwickshire, from 'paralysis' on 4 November 1881. He was survived by his wife, Ellen Maria Gem.

ANDREW ROWLEY

Sources Edgbastonia, 1 (1881), 126–31 · Birm. CL, T. H. Gem MSS, no. 150861 · Solicitors' Journal, 26 (1881–2), 114 · CGPLA Eng. & Wales (1882) · d. cert.
Archives Birm. CL
Likenesses drawing, repro. in Edgbastonia, facing p. 126
Wealth at death £2113 16s. 8d.: probate, 7 Jan 1882, CGPLA Eng. & Wales

Gemini [Geminus, Lambrit], **Thomas** (fl. 1540–1562), engraver, printer, and instrument maker, was the publisher of a compendium of anatomy entitled Compendiosa totius anatomie delineatio (1545), whose own copper-engravings were copied from the De humani corporis fabrica libri septem and De humani corporis fabrica librorum epitome, both published by Oporinus for Andreas Vesalius in Basel only two years earlier. The famous Vesalian plates in the larger work had been executed in woodcut after designs by Jan van Calcar, and were the basis of most of Anatomie delineatio. These copper-engravings of Gemini were the first of any artistic significance to be published in England. The first edition of the work was inspired by and dedicated to Henry VIII and signed by 'Thomas Geminus Lysiensis, Londini Quarto Calendas Octobres Anno 1545'. Lysiensis signifies 'Leighe nighe unto Marke Wesett within the bishopryke of Leuke in the partes of beyonde the Sea', according to his will. This is probably Lexhe or Lixhe, a village some 2 miles west of Vise and about 8 miles north of Liège. Nearby are Vise'-le-Mach'e, and Val-St Lambert, from which Lambrit may derive. Thomas bequeathed his property to a brother, Jasper Lambrit.

Thomas probably learned the art of copper-engraving at Louvain, then a centre of instrument making and other trades based on copper. The strong similarity between the engraving hands of Gemini and Gerard Mercator, who was making scientific instruments at Louvain, suggests a connection between the two men, and Gemini may possibly have been a pupil of Mercator. He may also have known Vesalius there, according to Robert Karrow, as Vesalius's brother Franciscus was later to complain of an 'English' plagiarist who had lived with them once in Louvain.

The English editions of Gemini's Anatomie delineatio, 1553 and 1559, were dedicated to Edward VI and Elizabeth I respectively, and confirm Gemini's Flemish birth as well as his status in England, 'lyvinge and beeinge here in your realme of England under your graces protection'. His text had been translated into English (and supplemented with non-Vesalian material) by others, 'for as muche as I am not of myselfe so perfete and experte in the Englysshe toonge that I dare warrant or trust myne owne douinges, I have used the studious paynes, first of Nicolas Udall and certen other learned men, and now lastly of master Richard Eden' (1559). From his published work we can infer that Gemini worked in England from 1540 to 1559—an edition of Vesalius using Gemini's plates but under the name of Jacques Grevin appeared in 1564, which must have been published with the permission of Gemini's executors.

Gemini was attached to the court and in receipt of an annuity of £10 during the king's pleasure from 1546; following the death of Henry VIII he seems to have received a salary from Edward VI in 1547. The only other official record bearing on his life is an entry for 21 July 1555 in the register of the Company of Stationers, a receipt for a fine of 12 pence from 'thomas Gemyne, stranger, for transgressynge the ordinaunces of this howse, callynge a brother of the companye a flasse [false?] knave'. Gemini was established as a printer in the Blackfriars by 1555, but the 1559 fifth edition of the *Anatomie delineatio* was the first he printed himself. The two other books he printed were both by Leonard Digges, *Prognostication of Right Good Effect* (1555, an almanac with astronomical tables added, especially for seamen) and a *Boke Named Tectonicon* (1562), a work on mensuration. The imprint of the *Tectonicon* advertised that Gemini 'is there ready exactly to make all instrumentes apperteyninge to this Booke'. Gemini was probably a maker of surgical as well as mathematical instruments. We can certainly attribute to him seven known mathematical instruments. They include an engraved astrolabe, now in the possession of the Royal Belgian Observatory, Brussels, which bears the arms of the duke of Northumberland, Sir John Cheke, and Edward VI. A second signed planispheric astrolabe made for Elizabeth I in 1559 is in the Museum of the History of Science at Oxford; a horary quadrant is at the British Museum. All his astrolabes and a quadrant in the Istituto e Museo della Scienza, Florence, bear witness to the influence of the workshops of Louvain. An unsigned and undated (c.1581) astrolabe at the National Maritime Museum and a sundial in the Science Museum are probably attributable to him.

In engraving his copies of the Vesalian plates Gemini made no secret of his debt to one whom he acknowledged as by far the most skilled of his contemporaries in delineating the human body according to its parts. Gemini says that he published his engravings for the use of students, and the project was a consequence of the formal unification of the Company of Barbers and the Fraternity of Surgeons into the united Company of Barber–Surgeons, accomplished by act of parliament in 1540, and commemorated in the well-known Holbein group portrait. By the same act a regular course in anatomy was instituted, supervised by a reader of anatomy, and Gemini's work was in effect a manual of anatomy for this course. In dedicating the book to Henry VIII Gemini acknowledged the king's role in arranging for physicians and surgeons to acquire knowledge of the correct arrangement of the human body, and more specifically, in requesting Gemini to publish the Vesalian figures before Henry left England for the siege of Boulogne on 14 July 1544. The text of the book was a secondary concern, and in the first Latin edition Gemini published only extracts from the *Fabrica* together with a truncated version of the *Epitome*. Not surprisingly Vesalius, who had gone to considerable trouble to obtain privileges for the publication of his works, was

angry at the plagiarism, and attacked the engravings as inept in his China Root epistle of 1546.

In fact Gemini's copies, though omitting the background to Vesalius's figures, are very competent technically. Perhaps the best tribute to this competence is the speed with which his copperplates were in turn themselves plagiarized by continental publishers. His skill as an engraver is less convincingly witnessed by the two portraits of Elizabeth I which he completed. One was inserted in the title page of the fifth edition of the *Anatomie delineatio* (1559), and a second larger plate is known only by the impression originally found in the Storer Granger at Eton College. As early portraits of Elizabeth these are of considerable interest—but their lack of resemblance to other portraits have led some scholars to see them as portraits of Queen Mary hastily adapted to the new monarch. Gemini's other known engravings include the title page and twenty-eight plates of ornament design found in a single remaining copy of *Morysse and damashin renewed and encreased very profitable for goldsmythes and embroiderars by Thomas Geminus at London anno 1548*. The only other engravings securely identified with Gemini are maps of Spain and the British Isles, both dated to 1555. The former was well enough known to be mentioned by Ortelius as Gemini's map in the *Theatrum orbis terrarum* (1570), though it is a copy of a map by Hieronymous Cock. At one time Gemini was associated with some of the plates in Roesslin's *The Byrth of Mankynde, Otherwyse Named the Womans Booke*, edited by Thomas Raynald and published in 1545. But both on the grounds of dating (Gemini claimed the *Anatomie delineatio* was his first anatomical work) and of technique, this association cannot be upheld. Gemini probably died early in 1562; his will was proved on 7 May that year.

PETER MURRAY JONES

Sources G. L'E. Turner, *Elizabethan instrument makers: the origins of the London trade in precision instrument making* (2000), 12–20 • C. D. O'Malley, 'Introduction', in T. Geminus, *Compendiosa totius anatomie delineatio*, ed. C. D. O'Malley (1959) • A. M. Hind, *Engraving in England in the sixteenth and seventeenth centuries*, 1 (1952), 39–58 • S. V. Larkey, 'The Vesalian compendium of Geminus and Nicholas Udall's translation', *The Library*, 4th ser., 13 (1932–3), 367–94 • E. G. R. Taylor, *The mathematical practitioners of Tudor and Stuart England* (1954); repr. (1970) • *STC, 1475–1640*, vol. 3 • H. Michel, 'Gemini', *Biographie nationale*, 31, suppl. 3 (Brussels, 1961) • R. T. Gunther, 'The astrolabe of Queen Elizabeth', *Archaeologia*, 86 (1937), 65–72 • R. W. Karrow, *Mapmakers of the sixteenth century and their maps: bio-bibliographies of the cartographers of Abraham Ortelius, 1570* (1993), 250–54 • private information (2004) [Koenraad van Cleempoel, of the Warburg Institute] • will, PRO, PROB 11/45, fol. 96
Wealth at death property left to brother: will

Geminiani, Francesco Saverio (1687–1762), composer and music theorist, was born in Lucca, Italy, probably on 3 December 1687 (the feast day of St Francis Xavier), two days before his baptism, the fourth son of Giuliano Antonio Geminiani (*fl.* 1681–1707) and his wife, Angela. Although the precise details of Geminiani's musical training are unknown, he almost certainly received his first musical instruction from his father, a violinist in the Cappella Palatina at Lucca, and it is likely that he studied with the illustrious Arcangelo Corelli and Alessandro Scarlatti for a short period in Rome at some time between April

1704 and December 1706. Thereafter he performed in Naples (without complete success, according to Charles Burney) before returning to Lucca and taking over his father's position in 1707. A short cantata for soprano, *Nella stagione appunto*, the only vocal piece Geminiani is known to have written, probably dates from his time in Rome or Naples. He stayed in Lucca until September 1709 and departed for London in 1714.

Given the prestige afforded a disciple of Corelli and the lack of competition from the generally neglected native artists, Geminiani was able to flourish and move among the highest echelons of society in England. In 1716 he published his op. 1 sonatas in London, dedicated to his patron Baron Johann Adolf von Kielmansegge, who was married to the countess of Darlington, half-sister of George I. The sonatas, heavily influenced by his teacher, achieved great success in five different versions. His profile and estimation as a composer, teacher, and violin virtuoso remained high, although his public performances were rare. He joined societies, including the Queen's Head masonic lodge (which funded the publication of his arrangements of works from Corelli's op. 5 sonatas in 1726) and the Academy of Vocal Music, and assisted with the appointment of an organist for St George's Church in 1725. According to Sir John Hawkins, Handel was his fellow judge. He also became a sought-after teacher; prominent among his pupils were Matthew Dubourg, Charles Avison, Michael Festing, Cecilia Young, William Savage, Joseph Kelway, and Robert Bremner. The last two were independently involved in the distribution of Geminiani's works later in the century as a vendor and publisher respectively, and a letter from Geminiani to Kelway is his sole extant autograph.

In 1728 Geminiani was offered the position of master and composer of the state music in Ireland through the influence of William Capel, third earl of Essex, a former pupil who was a gentleman of the bedchamber to George II. He declined, possibly because of his Catholic beliefs, and his pupil Dubourg took up the post. Rather than the relative financial security this position could have offered, Geminiani was henceforth destined to experience economic hardship and fluctuating professional fortunes. A subscription series of twenty concerts over five months at Hickford's Room, London, beginning in December 1731, made possible the publication of the op. 2 and op. 3 concerti grossi, long established in the repertory, in 1732. These two sets, infused with Roman stylistic traits, secured his reputation during his lifetime and have endured to the present day; however, they mark the onset of decline in his personal circumstances.

From London Geminiani travelled to Paris, whence he returned on 20 September 1733, accompanied by his Irish patron, Charles Moore, second Baron Moore of Tullamore, and from London he went to Dublin, arriving on 6 December 1733. His first public concert there took place just over a week later, and he went on to open what became known as 'Geminiani's great room', a concert-hall in Dame Street, Spring Gardens. This venue was used for selling pictures, and points to Geminiani's activities as an art dealer, which

surfaced during his visit to Paris in 1733. His involvement with the art world, along with the publication of his own music, helped him to avoid the private and institutional patronage upon which so many other musicians were dependent. However, it was the source of other problems, at one point landing him in 'the prison of the Marshalsea' (Hawkins, 2.847) before he was extricated by the earl of Essex.

Following concerts in the spring of 1734, Geminiani left for London. He returned to Dublin in 1737 and remained there until a trip to Paris in 1740, which resulted in French editions of some of his works. By about a year later he was back in London, and he was performing at the Haymarket Theatre on 19 March 1742 by command of Frederick and Augusta, prince and princess of Wales; Frederick was the dedicatee of the concerto grosso arrangement of his second set of violin sonatas (op. 4) published in 1743. Geminiani remained productive, directing concerts and issuing cello sonatas and concerti grossi (op. 5 and op. 7 respectively, both engraved in the Netherlands, which Geminiani visited in 1746), as well as several treatises and various new arrangements and editions during the 1740s. However, his ventures were less successful than before, and he decided to turn away from composition and concentrate mainly on theoretical writings.

In 1748 came Geminiani's *Rules for Playing in a True Taste* and in 1749 *A Treatise of Good Taste in the Art of Musick*, in which the correct use of ornamentation appears as the most important ingredient of 'tasteful' performance and musical expression. His *The Art of Playing on the Violin*, published in 1751, was both popular and critically acclaimed among contemporaries (even by Burney). It is a significant work, standing alone as an instrumental treatise from the period that is of English origin but also of international and enduring importance, especially in its treatment of vibrato, bowing, metric accent, and shifting. It is the first ever violin treatise with contents aimed primarily at advanced performers, predating Leopold Mozart's *Violinschule* by five years. In addition to its intrinsic value and the foreign editions it enjoyed, the treatise influenced numerous subsequent native pedagogical works for the instrument. It was followed by the *Guida armonica* (c.1752), a kind of 'dictionary' of harmonic passages, *The Art of Accompaniment* (c.1756), focusing on the realization of figured bass, and *The Art of Playing the Guitar or Cittra* (1760), for the 'English guitar'.

In spring 1745 Geminiani was living in Dufour's Court, Broad Street, Soho, and he directed the orchestra at Drury Lane on 11 April 1750. He continued to travel and to eschew permanent positions, returning to Paris probably the following year and again in 1754 for a performance of his music for the unsuccessful pantomime *The Inchanted Forest*. Although back in London about two years later, he then proceeded to Ireland, where he became music master to Charles Coote, later earl of Bellamont, at Coothill in 1759. In November he moved to Dublin, possibly at the invitation of his old pupil Dubourg. Soon after, according to Hawkins, the 'elaborate' treatise on music on which he had been working was stolen from his residence on College Green by a female servant. Geminiani's last public appearance took place on 3 March 1760 at the Great Musick Hall in Fishamble Street. He died at College Green, Dublin, on 17 September 1762, and was buried two days later at the church of St Andrew nearby.

During his long career in England and Ireland Geminiani had been widely acknowledged as the equal of Handel and Corelli and a positive influence on native violinists. His later works, in particular the op. 5 sonatas, represent a more individual approach and distance themselves somewhat from the Corellian legacy. However, this compromised their popularity among British audiences, and criticism (thanks largely to Burney) has focused on their perceived 'irregularities' of rhythm in composition and performance ever since. In addition, suspicion surrounded Geminiani's dealing in paintings and the 'reheating' of old works for financial gain. More recent appraisal has sought to provide a more balanced assessment of his achievements. It is now possible to assert that his contribution, primarily as a violinist and theorist, was significant and was felt by a wide circle of British musicians long after his death, remaining important today.

DAVID J. GOLBY

Sources E. Careri, 'Geminiani, Francesco (Saviero) [Xaviero]', *New Grove*, 2nd edn [incl. list of works] • E. Careri, *Francesco Geminiani (1687–1762)* (1993) [incl. full bibliography and thematic catalogue and complete listing of Geminiani's extant MSS, 290–93] • Highfill, Burnim & Langhans, *BDA* • Burney, *Hist. mus.*, new edn • J. Hawkins, *A general history of the science and practice of music*, new edn, 2 (1853), 847–50, 915–17 • D. J. Golby, 'The violin in England, c.1750–c.1850: a case-study in music education', 2 vols., DPhil diss., U. Oxf., 1999
Archives BL, letter to 'Mr Kalloway', Add. MS 21520
Likenesses W. Hoare, portrait, c.1735, repro. in Careri, *Francesco Geminiani* • Lathern, portrait, 1737 • Bettelini, engraving, c.1805 (after L. Scotti) • P. Aveline, engraved medallion (after E. Bouchardon), repro. in Careri, *Francesco Geminiani* • C. Grignion, engraving (after J. Macardell), repro. in Hawkins, *General history*, facing p. 847 • Howard, portrait • attrib. T. Hudson, portrait, Royal College of Music; repro. in Careri, *Francesco Geminiani* • J. Macardell, mezzotint (after T. Jenkins), NPG, Royal College of Music, earl of Wemyss collection

Gendall, John (*bap.* 1791, *d.* 1865), watercolour painter, was baptized on 2 January 1791 at St Edmund's Church, Exeter, the son of John and Frances Gendall. When later employed as a domestic servant some of his drawings were seen in the shop of W. Cole, High Street, Exeter, by a salesman of Rudoph Ackermann, the London publisher and printseller who was later to provide him with permanent employment. About 1811 he joined Ackermann, initially in charge of artists' stock and later as a house artist. The first of his many drawings to be engraved was *Great Room of Rugby* published in Ackermann's *Colleges and Public Schools* (1816) and in that year he began to assist Ackermann in his experiments in lithography. He first exhibited at the Royal Academy in 1818, a watercolour *North-East View of Westminster Abbey*, which Ackermann published as an aquatint by J. C. Stadler in a major series of London views which included Gendall's *St Paul's*, *Westminster Hall*, and *The Tower of London*. Ackermann also published

Gendall's views of Dover and Calais (1820), the River Seine (1821), Hastings (1822), Edinburgh (1823), and fifty-eight country seats in *The Repository of Arts* between 1824 and 1828.

One of the leading topographical painters in pure watercolour, Gendall displayed exact draftsmanship, brilliance of colouring, and competent figure drawing in his work. He also worked in oils and in 1824 executed a fine large painting, *The Thames below London Bridge*, which was exhibited at the Exeter Art Exhibition. In that year he left Ackermann's employment in London and returned with his wife, Maria, *née* Havell, a native of Eton, whom he had married on 19 January 1824 at St Martin-in-the-Fields, Westminster, to Exeter. There they resided until his death. By the end of 1825 Gendall had become a partner of W. Cole, selling paintings and drawings and executing carving, gilding, and framing. Cole's shop was at the heart of the artistic life in Exeter and Gendall, with his high professional reputation and wide commercial experience, was the ideal partner for the older Cole. He quickly gained the reputation, which he never lost, for being 'an agreeable, honest, little man' (J. H. Anderdon MSS, Royal Academy Library). Although the partnership ended with Cole's approaching retirement and financial difficulties, Gendall continued in the same line of business from 1832 in the Cathedral Yard, Exeter, where he also opened a successful art school at his own premises, Mols Coffee House. His pupils included the writer Richard Ford and the sculptor Edward Bowring Stephens. He continued to execute many private commissions, including work for Ackermann's successors, and between 1846 and 1863 at the Royal Academy he regularly exhibited views of the Devon countryside both in watercolour, and now with increasing use of gouache and oils.

Gendall played a central role in the cultural life of Exeter, and from 1862 to 1864 served as the first curator of the Royal Albert Memorial Museum. Towards the end of this period he was injured in a railway accident, suffering partial paralysis of his right hand. He died on 1 March 1865 in the Cathedral Yard, and was buried in St Bartholomew's burial-ground, Exeter. He was survived by his wife, Maria. Fifty-four of Gendall's watercolours of Exeter Cathedral monuments are in the Westcountry Studies Library, Exeter.

L. H. CUST, rev. JOHN FORD

Sources *John Gendall, 1789–1865: 'Exeter's forgotten artist'* (1979) [exhibition catalogue, Royal Albert Memorial Museum, Exeter, 11 July – 16 Oct 1979] • G. Pycroft, *Art in Devonshire: with the biographies of artists born in that county* (1883) • J. Ford, *Ackermann, 1783–1983: the business of art* (1983) • J. R. Abbey, *Scenery of Great Britain and Ireland in aquatint and lithography, 1770–1860* (1952) • R. V. Tooley, *English books with coloured plates, 1790–1860* (1954) • *CGPLA Eng. & Wales* (1865) • F. Owen, 'Gendall, John', *The dictionary of art*, ed. J. Turner (1996) • *IGI*
Likenesses J. P. Knight, oils, 1835, Royal Albert Memorial Museum, Exeter
Wealth at death under £4000: resworn probate, Nov 1866, *CGPLA Eng. & Wales*

Genée [married name Isitt], **Dame Adeline** [real name Anina Margarete Kirstina Petra Jensen] (1878–1970), ballet dancer, was born on 6 January 1878 in the Jutland village of

Dame Adeline Genée (1878–1970), by Bassano, 1916

Hinnerup, Århus, Denmark, the survivor of twins and younger of two daughters of the Danish farmer Peter Jensen and his wife, Kirsten. She was baptized Anina Margarete Kirstina Petra. The family loved music and her parents recognized in Anina a natural love of dancing; thus she was adopted in 1886 by her uncle, Alexander (Peter's younger brother who had taken his stage name from the composer Richard Genée) and his wife, a Hungarian ballerina, Antonia Zimmermann. Zimmermann had been trained by Gustav Grantzow and became Alexander Genée's partner on stage and off; they married in 1877 in Russia. Alexander Genée ran his own small ballet company touring in central Europe. Following her adoption Anina was given the name Adeline, after the great opera star Adelina Patti, for whom Alexander Genée had once arranged dances in *Carmen*.

Training and early performances Genée's formal training and upbringing were supervised by her uncle and aunt as she toured with her uncle's ensemble in Scandinavia, making her début at the age of ten in a *demi-caractère* solo, *Polka à la Picarde*, at Christiania (Oslo), Norway. Alexander Genée then accepted a position as ballet master and manager of the Centralhallen Theatre, Stettin, where Genée learned a wide range of *corps de ballet* and solo roles in a repertory that included the well-known ballets *Giselle* and *Sylvia*, and opera ballets such as *La favorite* and *Robert le diable*.

From Stettin Genée progressed south through Germany and a clear indication of her potential was shown when in 1896, aged eighteen, she was invited to replace Antonietta Dell'Era, the powerful ballerina of the Berlin Opera, in *Die Rose von Schiras* while Dell'Era took her summer vacation. Genée's performance was well received but she realized that in Berlin she would be in the prima ballerina's shadow for years. Nevertheless one variation she had danced in *Die Rose von Schiras* became a signature dance. She inserted it into *Monte Cristo* when she made her London début and frequently added it into ballets when she needed to make a strong impression. It was common practice in the late nineteenth century for leading dancers to insert favourite solos into any ballet where they needed to be seen to advantage.

At the London Empire In autumn 1896 Genée travelled to Munich, where she danced Swanilda in *Coppélia* (a role with which she would become closely associated). She auditioned for the ballet in Vienna but there were no vacancies for principal dancers. It was here that she received a telegram from London offering a six-week contract from November 1897 at the Empire Theatre, an engagement that proved so satisfactory that she remained there as ballerina for the next decade, becoming London's best-loved dancer. A 'palace of varieties' was a demanding place at which to work; at the Empire Genée had to dance six nights a week all year round while at opera houses a ballerina would perform only occasionally and in a more varied repertoire. Genée's decision to remain at the Empire certainly limited the development of her career but it enabled her to become the Porcelain Rogue with whom countless men fell in love over the footlights. In turn this fame and her own impeccable standards in her professional and private life enabled her to raise the quality of dance teaching and enhance the position of dancers in public estimation in her adopted country. She raised the dancers' status in society in the way Henry Irving had achieved for actors.

By the time that Genée made her London début the Empire, following the lead of its close neighbour in Leicester Square, the Alhambra, had put ballet at the core of its programme. Usually two ballets were performed with a wide range of other acts preceding and between them, the programme finishing with a selection from the bioscope. Sometimes, however, there would be just one longer work and supporting programme. The popularity of the ballets is indicated by the fact that an individual ballet could remain in performance for over a year. The theatre's ballet mistress, Katti Lanner, with her collaborators, the composer and musical director Lépold Wenzel, and designer C. Wilhelm (professional name of William John Charles Pitcher), quickly recognized the strengths of their new star and gradually the roles she danced showed more of her versatility as a soubrette actress as well as classical ballerina. Initially Genée danced only classical variations. It was typical of the ballets created by Lanner at this time that the ballerina played little part in the action but represented an ideal. In inserted variations ballerinas engaged for short periods could be easily accommodated. Once Genée was established with the company, her roles became more developed.

Genée first danced at the Empire on 22 November 1897

in the jewel scene of *Monte Cristo* (inspired by Alexandre Dumas's novel), a ballet already well established by the time Genée took over the role of the Diamond. This was followed on 14 February 1898 by *The Press*, a work planned before her arrival. *The Press* was typical of the pageant-style of ballets that emphasized the charm of Wilhelm's costume designs and Lanner's clever arrangements of groups over narrative or original choreography. Genée's role was simply that of the Liberty of the Press. It was in *Round the Town Again* (1899), as a charming French maid, Lizette, that Genée had the opportunity to play a more rounded character. This was the type of role that would be choreographed for her: a Dresden shepherdess in *Old China* (1901), Coquette, the naïve country girl in the hat shop who develops into a sophisticated woman, in *The Milliner Duchess* (1903), and the title role in *Cinderella* (1906). As Margaret in *High Jinks* (1904) Genée had the opportunity to perform a variety of dances; the hunting dance to 'John Peel' (which became a popular work in her divertissement repertory), a cakewalk, and an appearance as Marguerite in a burlesque of *Faust*. When the Empire closed for improvements in 1905 Genée appeared at Daly's Theatre as the ballerina Mlle St Cyr, specially introduced into André Messager's comic opera *The Little Michus*. The publicity this generated clearly emphasized the status she had attained in British theatre. It must be noted that almost all the repertory Genée performed was tailor-made to her own abilities; the ballets and her variations were created by her uncle, Katti Lanner, or, later in her career, by herself. At the Empire Genée was most frequently partnered by a woman *en travesti* but, with the exception of her appearance in *The Bugle Call* (1905), she rarely took such parts herself.

Genée as a dancer Genée was a pretty, petite, blonde ballerina of great charm. She was noted for her light, precise footwork, her pirouettes, jumps, *brisées*, and *bourrées*, and also for her characterization through mime. She performed in both classical and *demi-caractère* work. Her training had been in the Franco-Danish school which unlike the rival Italian school did not place an emphasis on obvious virtuosity. Towards the end of her career, after the companies of Anna Pavlova and Serge Diaghilev were established in Britain, it was noted that Genée's dancing was less exotic and sensual than that of the Russians. Many critics tried to compare Genée with Pavlova and Tamara Karsavina but D. G. MacLennan noted that 'they waste their time; they were never comparable. Pavlova was poetry, Karsavina the artist of the ballet, but Genée was prose—vivid, precise, brilliant prose. Her feet twinkled, so did her mind. Her tragedy was she was never "stretched"'.

Genée's personality and dancing appealed to an audience (particularly in London and the United States of America) who were unaware of the finer points of ballet technique but she was also admired by the informed audiences. In 1902 she was invited to guest in Copenhagen with the Royal Danish Ballet in *Coppélia* and in an extract from August Bournonville's *Flower Festival in Genzano*. The ballet master, Hans Beck, was so impressed by Genée's

technique that he insisted all the company be present at a rehearsal to see her entrechats six (which Danish dancers did not then attempt) and her double pirouettes. It should be noted that she also worked hard to adopt the Bournonville style for *Flower Festival*, even though it appeared old-fashioned and unspectacular next to the choreography in which she usually danced. A decade later Diaghilev sang her praises and tried, without success, to persuade her to join his company. In Britain there were few critics who understood the art of ballet but among them was S. L. Bensusan, who in '"The belle of the ball": the art of Adeline Genée' in *The Sketch* (2 October 1907) placed Genée alongside the romantic ballerinas of the 1845 *pas de quatre*:

> She has more than the gift of a dancer's grace, the charm of exquisite balance, the power of passing quickly and without apparent effort from a sudden movement to a pose that suggests the sculptor at his best. She has taken the somewhat stiff and formal movements of the orthodox mime, and by an infusion of her own gracious personality endowed them with the life they refuse so often to reveal in the interpretation of less sympathetic artists. (p. 396)

Queen Alexandra should be placed among the connoisseurs of dancing. She was present when Genée danced in Copenhagen and in January 1905 Genée was invited to dance before the king and queen at Chatsworth, an unprecedented honour for a ballerina.

Although for much of her dancing career she remained under her uncle's domination, Adeline revealed a strong will of her own. When in a position to renew her contract at the Empire she negotiated her own terms including the right to approve music for her solo variations. She had a sense of own status and was determined to ensure the roles she danced were worthy of her talent. Most famously in 1906 she refused to renew her contract until the management agreed to allow her uncle to mount *Coppélia* for her.

In many respects Genée's productions looked back to creations earlier in the nineteenth century. Both *Coppélia* and the ballet from Meyerbeer's *Robert the Devil*, also produced by Alexander Genée, were already heritage works. The ballets she created for herself also derived from romantic ballet traditions; she favoured slight divertissements such as the pastoral *The Dryad*, in which an imprisoned wood nymph fails to find the human love needed to release her, and *A Dream of Roses and Butterflies*, in which Genée repeated Taglioni's trick of balancing on point on the centre of a flower (securely nailed to the floor) giving the illusion of weightlessness. Other productions animated the history of ballet. Collaborating with the designer Wilhelm and the composer Dora Bright, Genée choreographed a series of dances including *La Camargo* and *La danse*. These productions were on a much smaller scale than the huge Empire productions with casts of more than 100 dancers but were convenient to perform on tours and for short seasons at the London Coliseum, which became a second home for her after 1911.

Later career and retirement From 1908 Genée interspersed her performances in London with six tours in the United States of America, initially in musical productions. In 1913 she also toured Australia and New Zealand with what was billed as the Imperial Russian Ballet. Genée (advertised as 'The World's Greatest Dancer') was partnered by the Russian *danseur noble* Aleksandr Volinin. By this time international audiences were excited at the prospect of seeing Russian ballet and the group's repertory combined works from or inspired by those of the Ballets Russes including *Les sylphides* and oriental fantasies, with Genée's own favourites, *Coppélia*, *The Dryad*, and *La danse*. There were also older works from the St Petersburg Imperial Ballet, notably the Polka Comique from *Les millions d'Arlequin*.

Genée's retirement from the stage was more gradual than originally intended. She began her farewell season in March 1914 but the war, with its inevitable charity galas to help relieve suffering, resulted in her continuing until 1917. This may have been one reason why, although in December 1916 she announced in the *Dancing Times* her intention to open a school, this never happened. Instead she devoted a great deal of time to working with leading British-based teachers from all the recognized 'schools' and Philip Richardson, editor of the *Dancing Times*, to systematize and improve the quality of dance training. They established the Royal Academy of Dancing (originally the Association of Operatic Dancing—founded 1920) of which Genée was the first president, a position she held for thirty-four years. She personally secured the academy's royal charter and patronage as well as establishing standards of dance teaching, launching and developing syllabuses and examinations. Genée travelled extensively in Britain (and in Canada in 1940) superintending the academy's examinations and concerning herself with the quality of teachers, dancers, and their working conditions.

On 11 June 1910 Genée married Frank S. N. Isitt at All Saints' Church, Margaret Street, London. Isitt was a London businessman, a founder of a firm of surveyors, adjusters and valuers, freeman of the City of London, and a member of Lloyd's of London. Together they made their home at 5 Hanover Terrace, Regent's Park, London, until his death on 8 December 1939. Isitt shared Genée's interest in theatre and music and supported her lifelong work to promote Anglo-Danish relationships. In 1931 she became president of the Anglo-Danish Society and in 1932 was able to arrange for a group of British dancers to be seen in Denmark during the British Industries Fair. This drew on the work of the Camargo Society (of which she was a founder) and the young Vic-Wells Ballet. Genée, partnered by Anton Dolin, returned to the stage to perform *Love Songs*, which was also televised on 15 March 1933. Thus her performing career in Britain spanned Queen Victoria's diamond jubilee to one of the earliest BBC transmissions.

As her friend and colleague at the academy, Kathleen Gordon, acknowledged in the *Dancing Times* after her death:

> [Genée] was not a 'simple' woman in any sense of the word; sometimes the working of her mind was very devious and difficult to comprehend. At the same time there was a certain artlessness—a childlike quality—that was both

unexpected and endearing. She had an iron will linked to a streak of obstinacy which stood her in good stead during the inevitable ups and downs of her professional life. She had enormous integrity and a deep religious faith, and through it all, like the bright threads in one of her own pieces of exquisite embroidery, was a wit, and an impish sense of fun that rendered her adorable to friends. (*Dancing Times*, June 1970)

Genée received many honours, including an honorary doctorate of music of the University of London in 1946, and became a DBE in the 1950 new year honours list for services to dancing. She was honoured by the king of Denmark ('Ingenio et Arti') in 1923; and became a commander of the order of Dannebrog in 1953 (only the second time this honour was conferred on a woman). In 1967 the Adeline Genée Theatre at East Grinstead was named after her and annual awards in her name are presented by the Royal Academy of Dancing.

Genée, who had no children of her own, died on 23 April 1970 at the home of her nephew, Goodwyn Isitt, The Willows, The Green, Esher, Surrey, and was cremated at Golders Green.

JANE PRITCHARD

Sources I. Guest, *Adeline Genée: a pictorial record* (1978) · K. Gordon, 'Obituary: Dame Adeline Genée-Isitt, D.B.E.', *Dancing Times* (June 1970), 467–9 · M. E. Perugini, *The art of ballet* (1915) · CGPLA Eng. & *Wales* (1970) · P. Bedells, *My dancing days* (1854) · S. L. Bensusan, '"The belle of the ball": the art of Adeline Genée', *The Sketch* (2 Oct 1907) · C. Caffin and C. H. Caffin, *Dancing and dancers of today* (1912) · J. E. C. Flitch, *Modern dancers and dancing* (1912) · I. Guest, *Adeline Genée: a lifetime of ballet under six reigns* (1958) · I. Guest, *The Empire ballet* (1962)

Archives Royal Academy of Dancing, archive · Theatre Museum, London, costumes and ephemera

Likenesses W. Funk, portrait, 1904, repro. in Guest, *Adeline Genée* · U. Troubridge, bronze statuette, 1905, repro. in Guest, *Adeline Genée* · Bassano, photograph, 1916, NPG [*see illus.*] · C. Avery, sketches · photographs, Royal Academy of Dancing, London

Wealth at death £26,023: probate, 4 Aug 1970, *CGPLA Eng. & Wales*

Genest, John (1764–1839), theatre historian and Church of England clergyman, was the second son of John Genest of Dunkeswell, Devon. He was educated at Westminster School, London, was entered on 9 May 1780 as a pensioner at Trinity College, Cambridge, and graduated BA in 1784 and MA in 1787. While at Cambridge he became a close friend of Richard Porson. Genest took holy orders, and was for many years curate of a village in Lincolnshire. Subsequently he became private chaplain to the duke of Ancaster. Compelled to retire, owing to ill health, he went to Bath for the benefit of the waters.

While in Bath, Genest wrote *Some Account of the English Stage from the Restoration in 1660 to 1830* (10 vols., 1832), a work of great labour and research, illustrated with portraits and engravings; he 'spent the whole of his life in the task of collecting materials' according to the flyleaf of the first volume. It is a remarkably thorough and uncommonly accurate work, but does not make easy reading, as the author was given to long sentences broken up with whole series of dashes. Genest is justifiably hard on his predecessors, who followed one another in error. The index to the book is, however, inadequate by modern standards: the entries list only dates and not page, nor even volume, references. William Davenant and John Webster, though discussed, are among the names not indexed.

After nine years of great suffering, Genest died at his Bath residence in Henry Street on 15 December 1839. He was buried in St James's Church, Bath.

JOSEPH KNIGHT, rev. BRIAN BAILEY

Sources *N&Q*, 2nd ser., 9 (1860), 65, 108–9, 231 · R. Manvell, *Sarah Siddons* (1970) · *GM*, 2nd ser., 13 (1840) · d. cert.

Geneville [Joinville], **Geoffrey de**, **first Lord Geneville** (1225×33–1314), soldier and administrator, came from Champagne, and styled himself lord of Vaucouleurs. He was a younger son of Simon de Joinville (d. 1233) and his wife Béatrice (fl. 1226×1233), daughter of Étienne, count of Burgundy and Auxonne; his eldest brother was Jean de Joinville, biographer of Louis IX of France (r. 1226–70). Geoffrey came to England in 1251. His half-sister was the wife of Peter of Savoy, earl of Richmond (d. 1268), one of the queen's uncles, and he was linked to a powerful group of Savoyards at court. He was closely associated with the heir to the throne, the future Edward I, and was with him in Gascony in 1255. Through marriage between 1249 and 1252 to Matilda de Briouze, widow of Pierre de Genevre, and a granddaughter and coheir of Walter de Lacy, Lord Lacy (d. 1241), he acquired lands in the Welsh marches, at Ewyas Lacy and Ludlow, and in Ireland, where he and his wife held half the county of Meath. His power there was centred on the great castle at Trim, which he held at the king's pleasure.

Edward, the heir to the throne, used the Geneville castle at Ludlow in the days after his escape from custody in 1265. Geneville also provided important assistance in Ireland in that year. He showed great political skill in reconciling Montfortian and royalist supporters, enabling Edward to receive significant support from Ireland in the campaign that culminated in victory at Evesham.

There was a strong crusading tradition in the Geneville family, extending back to the mid-twelfth century: Geoffrey and his brother William duly accompanied Edward on crusade in 1270, but returned before him. Geoffrey was then appointed justiciar of Ireland in 1273, a post he held until 1276. He was given wide powers, and every effort was made to keep him supplied with money. But his years in office can hardly be regarded as successful, and he was heavily defeated by the Irish in 1274 and 1276. He served in Edward's Welsh wars, but his interests increasingly centred upon Ireland: in 1283 he granted his English lands to his son Peter. Later in Edward I's reign Geneville and his wife had a series of disputes with the Dublin government. They had been successful in the 1250s in recovering the original franchisal rights, as they had existed under Henry II, in their liberty of Trim. In 1293, however, the liberty of Trim was taken into the king's hands, following a dispute over a case of imprisonment. The liberty was restored two years later in recognition of Geneville's service in Wales. It was confiscated again in 1302, but eventually, after a long struggle, he succeeded in maintaining his palatine

rights. Geneville was fortunate in having the support of the king in his arguments with royal officials in Ireland.

Geoffrey de Geneville was an experienced diplomat: he took part in negotiations with the Welsh prince Llywelyn ap Gruffudd (d. 1282) in 1267, and in 1280 he acted as Edward's proctor in Paris. In 1290 and 1300 he went on missions to the papal curia, and in 1298 and 1299 took part in Anglo-French peace negotiations. His major role in domestic politics came in 1297, when he supported the king in the crisis caused by royal demands for men and money for the French war. Edward summoned troops to London, and demanded that Roger (IV) Bigod, earl of Norfolk (d. 1306), and Humphrey (VI) de Bohun, earl of Hereford (d. 1298), enrol them, in their capacities as marshal and constable. This the earls refused to do, so the king replaced them in their offices with Geneville and Thomas de Berkeley respectively. Geoffrey's appointment was appropriate, as he had been assistant to the marshal in the Welsh war of 1282. Once the crisis was over, the office reverted to the earl of Norfolk. Between February 1299 and November 1306 Geneville received a number of personal summonses to parliaments.

Geoffrey de Geneville outlived his wife, who died on 11 April 1304, and their two sons, Geoffrey and Peter, and died on 21 October 1314, far from his native Champagne and advanced in years, at the Dominican priory of Trim, to which he had retired in 1308, and where he was to be buried. His heir, his granddaughter Joan, married Roger Mortimer, earl of March (d. 1330), lover of Queen Isabella.

MICHAEL PRESTWICH, rev.

Sources Rymer, *Foedera*, new edn · GEC, *Peerage* · M. Prestwich, *Edward I* (1988) · G. J. Hand, *English law in Ireland, 1290–1324* (1967) · R. Frame, 'Ireland and the barons' wars', *Thirteenth century England: proceedings of the Newcastle upon Tyne conference* [Newcastle upon Tyne 1985], ed. P. R. Coss and S. D. Lloyd, 1 (1986), 158–67 · S. D. Lloyd, *English society and the crusade, 1216–1307* (1988) · T. W. Moody and others, eds., *A new history of Ireland*, 2: *Medieval Ireland, 1169–1534* (1987); repr. with corrections (1993)

Geninges, John. *See* Gennings, John (c.1576–1660).

Gennari, Benedetto (bap. 1633, d. 1715), painter, was baptized in the parish of S. Biagio, at Cento in Emilia-Romagna, Papal States, on 19 October 1633. His father, Ercole Gennari (1597–1658), and grandfather were also painters, and his mother, Lucia Barbieri, was a sister of Guercino. In 1643 the family moved to Bologna, where Guercino was already established and where Gennari received his early training from his father and his uncle; his early paintings clearly show the latter's influence. He remained in Bologna until the age of thirty-eight, producing portraits for some of the noble families and religious works for the local churches and convents.

From April 1672 to September 1674 Gennari lived in Paris where his connection with Guercino secured him a favourable reception. (During this time he began to keep a complete list of all his pictures.) He then moved to England, where James, duke of York, had recently married an Italian princess, Mary of Modena. The duchess and her husband became Gennari's most important patrons, but his first important commission was from Catherine of

Braganza, who asked him to produce new paintings for the Queen's Chapel at St James's Palace in 1675.

Gennari lived in England for over fourteen years and produced a total of 138 pictures, divided roughly equally between portraits, religious works, and profane subjects. Most of his pictures were commissioned by members of the royal family, though he was also employed by various Portuguese and Italian courtiers and a small group of ministers and household officials. His most important commissions were from Charles II, for whom he provided mythologies for the new apartments at Windsor Castle, and James II, for whom he decorated the new Catholic chapel at Whitehall in 1686–7. Gennari never held an official court appointment, but he seems to have been informally given the position of first painter by the duke of York, an arrangement that continued when the duke succeeded as James II in February 1685.

The revolution of 1688 brought an end to Gennari's career in England. His position was perhaps eased during the crisis itself because, exceptionally, he was working at the time on two pictures for a leading whig, the earl of Devonshire. Once they had been finished, he left the country on 28 January 1689 and never returned. This was not the end of his connection with England, however, because he joined the Jacobite court in exile at St Germain-en-Laye in February 1689, and continued to enjoy the protection of Mary of Modena for a further three years, employed almost exclusively on portraits, which comprise twenty-six of the thirty-two pictures included in his list. Gennari is the only artist to have left us with a visual record of the Stuart court both at Whitehall and in exile.

Gennari returned to Italy in the spring of 1692, when James II was preparing to invade England. He probably had no desire to resume his work in London in the event of a restoration and saw little prospect of obtaining commissions in France outside the Jacobite court. Before he left, he was finally granted a formal warrant by James II acknowledging him as his first painter; the warrant was renewed by his son James Stuart in December 1701. Gennari remained in Bologna for the rest of his life. He continued to be prolific and finally stopped painting at the age of seventy-six in 1709. The following year he became a founding member of the Accademia Clementina and devoted himself to teaching, being nominated direttore della scuola de nudo. He died at home in the via S. Alò, Bologna, on 19 December 1715 and was buried in the church of S. Nicolò degli Albari, Bologna.

Gennari was content to work within the tradition established by Guercino, of whose drawings he possessed over two and a half thousand. His style is easily recognizable, in part because of the monumentalism of his figures. But he was also influenced by the paintings of Pierre Mignard and incorporated some of the latter's grace and softness into his works. About a quarter of the pictures that he produced in London and St Germain have survived, most notably in the Royal Collection at Hampton Court. Gennari worked for a restricted number of patrons and was overshadowed as a court portraitist by Godfrey Kneller, but he was a more versatile painter. It is unfortunate that the fall of James II not only abruptly terminated his career in England but also led to the destruction of the Catholic chapels in London that he had decorated. EDWARD CORP

Sources P. Bagni, *Benedetto Gennari e la bottega del Guercino* (1986) · D. C. Miller, 'Benedetto Gennari's career at the courts of Charles II and James II, and a newly discovered portrait of James II', *Apollo*, 117 (1983), 24–9 · E. T. Corp, 'Benedetto Gennari', *La cour des Stuarts*, ed. [E. T. Corp and J. Sanson] (Paris, 1992), 107–8, 136, 173, 185–6 [exhibition catalogue, Musée des Antiquités Nationales de Saint-Germain-en-Laye, 13 Feb – 27 April 1992]
Likenesses B. Gennari, self-portrait, oils, 1686, Uffizi Gallery, Florence; repro. in Bagni, *Benedetto Gennari*, 103
Wealth at death 95,000 lire: Bagni, *Benedetto Gennari*, 127

Gennings, Edmund [St Edmund Gennings] (**1566–1591**), Roman Catholic priest and martyr, was born in Lichfield, Staffordshire, possibly the son of John Gennings (*fl.* 1555–1579), innkeeper and bailiff, and his wife (*fl.* 1566–1581). He was brought up as a protestant and was 'of modest behaviour in childhood, little given to play, much delighted to view the heaven and stars' (Gennings, 'Life and death'). He claimed to see visions in the night sky. He had a brother, John *Gennings (*c.*1576–1660).

On his schoolmaster's recommendation, a gentleman, Richard Sherwood, who was passing the inn in Lichfield, took Gennings, who was about fourteen at the time, as his page. He secretly carried messages between Sherwood and James Layburne, a Catholic imprisoned in Lancaster, after smuggling pen, paper, and ink to the latter. Influenced by Sherwood's plans, Gennings decided to join him in studying for the priesthood at Rheims. For safety, Sherwood sent the young man on ahead, with a letter to William Allen, founder of the English seminary colleges at Douai and Rheims. Gennings was admitted to Douai College on 12 August 1583, aged seventeen. Always delicate physically, and of a sensitive nature, he made himself ill with study. Apparently consumptive, he was sent home, but at Le Havre, Normandy, while reluctantly waiting for a ship, he prayed continuously to be cured. The night before his intended departure he made a sudden recovery, and he returned to Douai. He also worked in the infirmary there. The intensity of his meditations on the responsibilities of priesthood induced a shaking of his body like a palsy that remained with him all his life, yet he spoke constantly of his hope of becoming a martyr. He was ordained on 18 March 1590, by papal dispensation because, at twenty-three, he was still under canonical age.

In April 1590 Gennings set off for England with two other priests, Alexander Rawlins and Hugh Sewell. They had a difficult passage and were robbed and briefly imprisoned by Huguenots, shot at by pirates, and caught in a storm before finally landing by night under a cliff at Whitby, Yorkshire. While recovering at an inn they were questioned by a local officer but convinced him that they were travellers from Newcastle, driven off course by the tempest. Gennings went to Lichfield but found all his family dead except for his younger brother, who had moved to London. He worked in and around Lichfield for about six months before going to London in search of John Gennings. After several months he twice met him by chance in the street but John Gennings, realizing he was a priest, refused to acknowledge him.

Gennings worked as a priest in London. On 2 November 1591 he was celebrating mass with Polydore Plasden in an upper room of Swithin Wells's house in Holborn when Richard Topcliffe and his men burst in. In the struggle to defend the priests until the mass was finished, Topcliffe was thrown down the stairs, cutting his head. He did not forget it. The priests surrendered quietly and were taken to Newgate prison with their congregation, Gennings still wearing his priestly vestments. The next day Wells, who had not been present, tried to get his wife released but was also arrested. They were all tried at Westminster Hall on 4 December and found guilty, the priests of high treason, the lay people of felony. During the trial Gennings was forced to wear a fool's coat found in Wells's house. On their return to Newgate Topcliffe offered Gennings his life if he conformed; when he refused he was put into 'little ease', unable to stand or stretch his arms, and remained there until his execution.

On 10 December Gennings and Wells were dragged on a sledge to a scaffold set up outside the latter's house. Once again Gennings refused to conform or admit treason. This infuriated Topcliffe, who ordered him to be immediately hung, drawn, and quartered, giving him leave to say no more, and scarce to recite the Pater noster. With Gennings 'crying upon St. Gregory his patron to assist him, the hangman astonished said with a loud voice, "God's wounds! His heart is in my hand and yet Gregory is in his mouth"' (Gennings, 'Life and death').

Gennings's courage during his execution impressed many but particularly his brother, who had been, in his own words, 'a perverse Puritan'. At first glad at his brother's death, a few nights later he converted to Catholicism and wrote an account of his life that was published in 1614. Several miracles have been attributed to Gennings, and he was canonized in 1970.   CHRISTINE J. KELLY

Sources J. G. [J. Gennings], 'Draft of life and death of Edmund Geninges by his brother John, 1610', Archives of the British Province of the Society of Jesus, London, MSS Collectanea, M. 186–187 · [J. Gennings], The life and death of Mr. Edmund Geninges (1614) · T. F. Knox and others, eds., The first and second diaries of the English College, Douay (1878) · beatification of E. Geninges, Archives of the British Province of the Society of Jesus, London · Catholic Record Society, 12 (1913), 204–8, 292 · The letters and despatches of Richard Verstegan, c. 1550–1640, ed. A. G. Petti, Catholic RS, 52 (1959), 39, 42 · G. Anstruther, The seminary priests, 4 vols. (1969–77)
Archives Archives of the British Province of the Society of Jesus, London, papers relating to his beatification | Stonyhurst College, Lancashire, MSS Anglia vi, 117 · Stonyhurst College, Lancashire, MSS Collectanea, M. 186–187
Likenesses M. Bas, line engravings, repro. in Gennings, Life

Gennings [Geninges], **John** (c.1576–1660), Franciscan friar, was born at Lichfield and was brought up a protestant, but became a Catholic after the execution of his elder brother, the priest Edmund *Gennings (1566–1591). He probably went to the English College at Douai and then entered the English College, Rome, in 1598 and was ordained priest there in 1600. He was sent on the mission in May 1601 and in 1611, under the alias of Perkins, was imprisoned in Newgate. In 1614 or 1615 he was admitted into the order of St Francis by William Staney, one of the last survivors of the Marian Franciscan revival. In 1616, in his capacity of vicar and custos of England, he assembled at Gravelines about six of his brethren, including novices, but this was an unsuitable site and within three years he succeeded in establishing at Douai the monastery of St Bonaventure, of which he was the first vicar and guardian. In 1621, with the assistance of Father Christopher Davenport, he founded the convent of St Elizabeth at Brussels for English nuns of the third order of St Francis. On the restoration of the English province of his order he was appointed its first provincial, in a chapter held at Brussels on 1 December 1630. He was re-elected provincial in the second chapter held at Greenwich on 15 January 1634, and again in the fourth chapter at London on 19 April 1643. He wrote The life and death of Mr Edmund Genings priest crowned with martyrdome at London, the 10 day of November in the year MD.XCI, published at St Omer in 1614. He also wrote Institutio missionariorum (Douai, 1651). He died at St Bonaventure's Monastery, Douai, on 12 November 1660 and was buried in the church of St Bonaventure there.

THOMPSON COOPER, rev. G. BRADLEY

Sources Father Thaddeus [F. Hermans], The Franciscans in England, 1600–1850 (1898) · Gillow, Lit. biog. hist., 2.419–23 · Angelus à Sancto Francisco [R. Mason], Certamen seraphicum provinciae Angliae pro sancta Dei ecclesia (1649) · P. Guilday, The English Catholic refugees on the continent, 1558–1795 (1914), 284–306 · [J. Gennings], The life and death of Mr. Edmund Geninges (1614); [new edn] (1960) · J. Berchmans Dockery, Christopher Davenport: friar and diplomat [1960] · G. Anstruther, The seminary priests, 1 (1969), 128 · W. Kelly, ed., Liber ruber venerabilis collegii Anglorum de urbe, 1, Catholic RS, 37 (1940)
Archives St Antony's Friary, Forest Gate, London, archives of the English Province of Friars Minor, Acta Capitulorum, Reg. 1.A
Likenesses M. Bas, line engraving, BM; repro. in W. F. L., Life and death of Ven. Edmund Geninges (1614) · oils, St Antony of Padua Church, 56 St Antony's Road, Forest Gate, London

Gent, Thomas (c.1530–1593), judge, was the first son of William Gent and his second wife, Agnes, daughter and heir of Thomas Carr of Thurlow, Suffolk. The Gent family had been seated at Steeple Bumpstead, Essex, since the fourteenth century, and so this William Gent is seemingly to be distinguished from the attorney of that name who practised in Northamptonshire in the 1530s and 1540s. The judge's family owned the manor house of Moyns Park, which he himself was to rebuild about 1580. Thomas was probably the 'Gent' who matriculated as a pensioner of Christ's College, Cambridge, in 1548. He was admitted to the Middle Temple about 1550, and was duly called to the bar. Among his clients were the seventeenth earl of Oxford, who appointed him steward of all his courts in 1571, and the town of Maldon. He became recorder of Maldon in 1569 and represented the borough in the parliament of 1571.

Gent's marriage with Elizabeth (d. 1585), daughter and heir of John Swallow of Bocking, Essex, produced at least nine children; some sources give the number as twelve or thirteen. In 1586 he married Elizabeth Robyns, widow of Robert Hogeson of London. Gent agreed to serve as reader of the Middle Temple in 1569 but deferred office until 1574, and it is uncertain that he ever performed. He was created serjeant-at-law by himself at the end of June 1584, which was an unprecedented procedure save in the case of men chosen for the bench. The explanation is doubtless that he was already intended for the court of exchequer, to which he was appointed one year later. One of the offices of junior baron had become vacant in May 1584, about a week before Gent received his serjeant's writ, but in the event Gent's expectations were defeated and Edward Flowerdew was appointed. Gent was appointed to the next vacancy on 28 June 1585. As an assize judge for eight years he accompanied Chief Justice Anderson on the western circuit. Gent died intestate on 12 August 1593 and was buried at Steeple Bumpstead. J. H. BAKER

Sources HoP, *Commons, 1558–1603*, 2.182 • Baker, *Serjeants*, 174, 513 • Sainty, *Judges*, 123 • P. Morant, *The history and antiquities of the county of Essex*, 2 (1768), 354 • All Souls Oxf., MS 156, fol. 10 • C. H. Hopwood, ed., *Middle Temple records*, 1: *1501–1603* (1904) • W. C. Metcalfe, ed., *The visitations of Essex*, 2 vols., Harleian Society, 13–14 (1878–9) • Cooper, *Ath. Cantab.*, 2.263 • PRO, PROB 6/5, fol. 65

Gent, Thomas (1693–1778), printer, was born in Ireland on 4 May 1693 to, he later wrote, 'meek and gentle parents … rich in grace, tho' not in shining ore' (*Life*, 23). Gent's father, also Thomas, was an Englishman descended from a Staffordshire family (he had a brother, Ralph, who was a baker in Uttoxeter), and described by Gent as 'of an honest trade', elsewhere identified as a saddler (ibid., 29). Gent's parents, who had given him a Presbyterian baptism, saw to it that he learned reading, writing, arithmetic, and Latin, and that he read his Bible and was God-fearing. On 25 March 1707 Gent was apprenticed to Stephen Powell, printer in Fishamble Street, Dublin: 'a tyrant' and 'a Turk' who beat his apprentices 'furiously'. Gent later wrote:

a wretch so furious in his wrathful ire
as filled us all with heat, and set our souls on fire.
(ibid., 25–6)

Gent 'strove to live' with Powell for over three years (ibid., 26). Partly to be free of his cruel master, partly to escape the unwanted attentions of his master's maidservant who accused him of promising marriage, and partly at the suggestion of a former playmate, Richard Arnold, on 9 August 1710 Gent absconded from his master, stowing away on a ship bound for England and arriving at Park Gate on the Wirral four days later. Travelling via Chester and St Albans, he arrived in London and found employment with Edward Midwinter of Pie Corner, Smithfield, a printer of ballads and broadsides, to whom he was bound apprentice on 2 October 1710.

After almost four years in London Gent appears to have been reckoned (taking into account his time with Powell) to have completed a seven-year apprenticeship and by the age of twenty was 'smouting' or doing jobbing work for other printers. As early as 1711 he had printed 'The Royal Martyr, or, The Bloody Tragedy of King Charles the First', a single-sheet ballad, and in 1713 he had printed for him, or printed himself, *The Efficacy of Christian Perseverance in Time of Trouble*, a sixteen-page condensed version of Henry Sacheverell's highly popular sermon *The Christian Triumph*.

In 1714, on the verge of returning to Dublin to see his parents, Gent received an offer through Midwinter of a year's work with the York printer John White. Accordingly, he left London on foot on 20 April 1714, arriving at White's six days later. White worked Gent hard but was generally fair, and White's wife, Grace, was exceptionally kind to him; Gent also seems to have been particularly taken with White's maidservant, Alice Guy. Following the expiration of his contract, Gent left York on 15 May 1715 and travelled to Dublin. Here he found temporary employment with the printer Thomas Hume or Humes, but his old master Powell sought to seize Gent for breaking his original indentures. An offer of compensation by Gent was refused, and on 8 July he left for England.

Gent returned to offers of employment from both Midwinter and White, but the prospect of seeing Alice Guy again persuaded him to return to York. However, his stay in York seems to have been cut short by White's death on 10 January 1716. White left his printing equipment and materials jointly to his widow and his grandson Charles Bourne. Bourne was not yet of age, so Grace carried on the business alone, but she produced nothing substantial until 1718—and therefore probably had no need to employ a journeyman such as Gent. Certainly by 1716 he was back in London working for Midwinter. On 7 October the following year he was freed as a member of the London Stationers' Company, and shortly afterwards Powell finally accepted £5 compensation for Gent's uncompleted apprenticeship. Gent left Midwinter and, after some jobbing work for various printers, worked for the whig printer William Wilkins, for whom he set Bishop Benjamin Hoadly's *An Answer to the Representation Drawn up by the Committee of the Lower-House of Convocation* (1717–18). He followed this with a spell working for the printer John Watts, the partner of Jacob Tonson and later the employer of Benjamin Franklin.

In 1718, after turning down an offer to work at Norwich, Gent went to Ireland for a time, doing some work once again for Hume. On his return to London he resumed work with Watts, and shortly afterwards was induced to take employment with Francis Clifton, a Roman Catholic printer with whom Gent paid a mysterious visit to Dr Francis Atterbury at Westminster about some illicit printing. In 1719 Clifton issued a satirical piece which Gent had written on his fellow workmen entitled 'Teague's Ramble'; a ballad, *God's Judgments Shewn unto Mankind: a True and Sorrowful Relation of the Sufferings of the Inhabitants of the City of Marseilles*, printed in 1720 or 1721, may also be by Gent. Resuming employment with Midwinter about this time, Gent set up an abridgement, probably made by himself, of Defoe's *The Life and Most Surprizing Adventures of Robinson Crusoe* which was published in 1722 with thirty crude woodcuts cut by himself. Although Gent fell under suspicion at this time with Clifton and Midwinter for printing seditious libels, no action seems ever to have been taken against him (unlike the other two printers, both of whom later suffered imprisonment). Gent opened a workshop in Fleet Street, next to the prison, working on occasion for noted printers such as Henry Woodfall and Samuel Richardson, helping them print part of an unidentified 'learned Dictionary … composed of English, Latin, Greek, and Hebrew' (*Life*, 140, 143). Besides popular ballads, topical pieces, and other verse compositions of his own, Gent also produced some books on his own account including *A Collection of Songs*, *The Bishop of Rochester's Effigy*, and 'observations in nature of a large speech … on the few dying words … of Counsellor Layer' (ibid., 140); few of these works, however, survive. A secret list of printers in London and Westminster presented by the disaffected printer Samuel Negus to Lord Townshend in 1724 enumerates 'Gent, Pye-Corner', among those 'said to be high-flyers', that is, high-churchmen or tories (Nichols, *Lit. anecdotes*, 1.303). In that year Gent printed a Latin ode on the return of George I from Germany, and *Divine Entertainments, or, Penitential Desires, Sighs of the Wounded Soul*, a book of emblems based on Herman Hugo's *Pia desideria* (1624), with woodcuts crudely copied from Hugo's. This last work was published jointly with the bookseller Matthew Hotham, and was the last work of any consequence that Gent did in London.

During his time in London Gent had invested in a little press and two founts of pica, intending to set up in business on his own account and be in a position to marry Alice Guy. However, she had grown impatient and in June 1721 married Bourne, who had taken over the business after Grace White's death in early 1721. The event moved Gent to compose sixty-four lines of verse entitled 'The Forsaken Lover's Letter to his Former Sweetheart' which was printed in thousands of copies, none of which appear to survive. The death of Bourne in August 1724, however, offered an opportunity for Gent, who hastened to York and on 10 December married Alice in the Minster, obtaining the freedom of the city by purchase before the end of the year. The couple had only one child, Charles, who died aged eight months on 12 March 1726 and was buried in the church of St Michael-le-Belfry.

Gent's marriage to Alice brought with it her former husband's printing business; indeed Gent was active as a printer in York even before the marriage, issuing on 23 November 1724 the first number of the *York Journal* (previously entitled the *York Mercury*), which he published under various titles to 1741: the *York Journal, or the Weekly Courant* (1725); the *Original York Journal, or Weekly Courant* (1727); and the *Original Mercury, York Journal, or Weekly Courant* from 1728. As the sole printer in the city and county of York, he now had a fair prospect of commercial success; Newcastle was the only other English town north of the Trent to possess a printing press and local newspaper. However, he met considerable opposition from John White junior, son of his former employer, who had been active as a printer and bookseller in Newcastle at least since 1711. Resentful that Gent rather than himself had eventually succeeded to his father's business, White set up as a rival printer in York in 1725, although Gent seems to have suffered at the hands of White's temper rather than financially.

Gent was active as a printer in York for nearly fifty years. He printed a wide range of works including sermons, school texts, classical works, literary works, and playbills for the York theatre, but was most notable for his topographical publications. The first of these—and Gent's first substantial publication—was his own *The Antient and Modern History of the Famous City of York*, which appeared in 1730 in an unusually large edition of 1000 copies; proposals had been circulated the previous year, and a list of about 170 subscribers obtained. *The Antient and Modern History of the Loyal Town of Rippon*, accompanied by accounts of several other towns and villages in Yorkshire, with seventy-eight woodcuts and advertisements of his other publications, appeared in 1734. In the following year Gent's history of Hull, *Annales regioduni Hullini*, was published. These works, each of which is the earliest printed account of the city or town concerned, are not mere compilations from earlier writers, but are full of minute examples of personal observation and research, and contain many descriptions of objects now lost. Gent also made an exceptionally early attempt to establish a magazine in a country town: *Miscellaneae curiosae, or, Entertainments for the Ingenious of Both Sexes* was a quarterly devoted to enigmas, paradoxes, and mathematical questions which ran to only six numbers between 1734 and 1735. In addition, he printed official publications for the corporations of York and Doncaster.

In 1741 Gent published his quaint *Historia compendiosa Anglicana, or, A Compendious History of England*, accompanied by a second volume giving the history of Rome. One of the pieces appended to this was a poem of his own on the life and merits of Charles Howard, sixth earl of Carlisle, who had died in 1738, and his works at Castle Howard; this was separately reprinted by Gent as *Pater patriae: being an Elegiac Pastoral Dialogue*, which was kindly received although Gent's poetry is generally beneath criticism.

Despite some entrepreneurial ventures such as the short-lived establishment of a printing office at Scarborough about 16 June 1734 to be run by his nephew and apprentice Arthur Clarke, and the printing of keepsakes on an improvised light printing press on the frozen River Ouse in January 1740, Gent's business was failing by the 1740s, owing at least partly to the increased competition of other printers in the city. On 11 November 1742, having lost the lease of his premises in Stonegate, York, he moved to a nearby house in Petergate, where the first work produced was a long poem of his own, *The Holy Life and Death of St. Winefred*. In 1744 he wrote a manuscript account of his life which provides an unusually detailed insight into the career of an eighteenth-century printer; the manuscript, now in York Minster Library along with Gent's own musical commonplace book, was published in an expurgated form in 1832.

With the move to Petergate, Gent's output dropped significantly, and he produced only about eight further books before 1760. The last twenty years of his life were one long struggle against poverty and illness. In 1761 he was reduced to pronouncing a prologue (which he printed and sold) and epilogue at two benefit performances of the tragedy *Jane Shore*. His wife died on 1 April and was buried in St Olave's churchyard, and in 1762 he published—with some difficulty—his least impressive topographical work, *The Most Delectable, Scriptural, and Pious History of the Famous and Magnificent Great Eastern Window … in St. Peter's Cathedral, York*, which included a large number of wretched woodcuts, many cut down from blocks used previously. About 1766 he issued proposals for printing a revised second edition of his history of York Minster but it never appeared; at this time he was living as a beneficiary of Allen's charity, probably through the kindness of his rival historian of York, Dr Francis Drake. His last publication appears to have been *Divine Justice and Mercy Displayed … in the … Life … of … Judas Iscariot* (1772), 'originally written in London at the age of 18, and late improved at 80' (title-page). In the same year he printed a few copies, never published, of his own verse translation of Dean Heneage Dering's *Reliquiae Eboracenses*, a Latin poem on the early history of Yorkshire. Gent died at his house in Petergate on 19 May 1778, and was buried in the church of St Michael-le-Belfry, York.   H. R. TEDDER, *rev.* C. BERNARD L. BARR

Sources The life of Mr Thomas Gent … written by himself, ed. J. Hunter (1832); repr. (1974) · 'Of the life of Thomas Gent, printer', 1744, York Minster Library, York Minster Archives, MS Add. 31 · R. Davies, *A memoir of the York press* (1868); repr. with introduction by B. Barr (1988) · T. Gent, *The contingencies, vicissitudes or changes of this transitory life* (1761) · H. R. Plomer and others, *A dictionary of printers and booksellers who were at work in England, Scotland, and Ireland from 1668 to 1725* (1922) · H. R. Plomer and others, *A dictionary of the printers and booksellers who were at work in England, Scotland, and Ireland from 1726 to 1775* (1932) · W. K. Sessions and E. M. Sessions, *Printing in York from the 1490s to the present day* (1976) · D. F. McKenzie, ed., *Stationers' Company apprentices*, [3]: *1701–1800* (1978), 234 · M. Pollard, *A dictionary of members of the Dublin book trade 1550–1800* (2000) · F. Collins, ed., *The registers of St. Michael-le-Belfrey, York*, Yorkshire Parish Register Society, 11/2 (1901), 180, 240 · D. F. Foxon, *English verse, 1701–1750*, 2 vols. (1975) · R. M. Wiles, *Freshest advices: early provincial newspapers in England* (1965) · Nichols, *Lit. anecdotes*, 1.288–312 · R. G. [R. Gough], *British topography*, [new edn], 2 (1780), 422–3, 428, 443, 446 · W. Upcott, *A bibliographical account of the principal works relating to English topography*, 3 vols. (1818); repr. (1978), vol. 3, pp. 1356, 1376, 1411 · C. Knight, *Shadows of the old booksellers* (1865) · G. Ohlson, 'Life of Gent', in *Gent's history of Hull (Annales regioduni Hullini)* (1869), 11–27 · C. A. Federer, *Yorkshire chap-books* (1889) · J. Marshall, E. Hailstone, and J. T. F., 'Thomas Gent', *N&Q*, 7th ser., 1 (1886), 308, 356–7, 436, 471 · W. Blades and E. Hailstone, 'MSS of Thomas Gent', *N&Q*, 7th ser., 2 (1886), 149, 218 · A. C. S., 'Portrait of Thomas Gent', *N&Q*, 7th ser., 2 (1886), 329 · [F. Drake], *The history and antiquities of the city of York*, 3 (1785), 129

Archives York Minster Library, York Minster Archives, commonplace book, MS Add. 66 · York Minster Library, York Minster Archives, 'Life', MS Add. 31

Likenesses V. Green, mezzotint, pubd 1771 (after oil painting by N. Drake), BM, NPG · N. Drake, oils, W. Yorks. AS, Leeds, Yorkshire Archaeological Society

Gentileschi [*married name* Stiattesi], **Artemisia** (1593–1652/3), painter, was born in via di Ripetta, Rome, on 8 July 1593, daughter of the painter Orazio *Gentileschi (1563–1639) and Prudenzia Montoni (1575–1605). Her initial artistic training almost certainly took place in the surroundings of her father's studio, he having already been influenced by the new caravaggesque style at that time. In any case she proved to be an independently minded artist early on, as is demonstrated by the painting *Susanna e i*

Artemisia Gentileschi (1593–1652/3), self-portrait, 1638–9 [*Self-Portrait as the Allegory of Painting (L'allegoria della pittura)*]

vecchioni ('Susanna and the Elders'; Schloss Pommersfelden, Germany), signed 1610, in which association with Orazio—but also signs of great personal talent—are evident, and reaffirmed by the more or less contemporary *Madonna col bambino* ('Madonna and child'; Galleria Spada, Rome) and by the first of her versions of *Giuditta che decapita Oloferne* ('Judith Slaying Holofernes'; Museo di Capodimonte, Naples), which probably can be dated about 1610–12. In all these works the painter adopts a caravaggesque naturalism, within which she expresses a strong character that does not deny the most brutal themes in subjects such as Judith, Salome, Jael and Sisera, and Cleopatra but rather conveys them with particular bluntness.

In February–March 1612 Orazio denounced Agostino Tassi (*c*.1580–1644), with whom he had collaborated in notable decorative projects (for example, the ceiling of the sala del Concistoro in the Palazzo del Quirinale, Rome, in 1611 and the Casino delle Muse, Palazzo Rospigliosi, Rome, in 1611–12), for the rape of Artemisia in May 1611 (of which he had only just been informed). There followed a long trial, with numerous testimonies and conflicting versions of events, which ended in Tassi's conviction but also had serious repercussions for Artemisia's reputation and her promising career, only just begun. Hence Orazio organized a sort of reparative marriage for his daughter with a family friend, the Florentine Pierantonio Stiattesi, and the new couple soon left Rome for Florence, perhaps already by the end of 1612. On 21 September 1613 Giovanni

Battista, Artemisia's first son, was baptized in Florence, where she also gave birth to Cristofano (8 November 1615), Prudenza (2 August 1617), and Lisabella (13 October 1618), who died less than a year afterwards, on 9 June 1618. It seems that at least two of the other children died very young because at Easter 1621, when Artemisia was once again in Rome, she is reported as living in via del Corso with her husband and an only daughter, Palmira (Prudenza).

In Florence, Artemisia Gentileschi had notable professional success and developed relations with Michelangelo Buonarroti the younger (for whom she painted the panel *L'Inclinazione*, 1615–16) and with the Grand Duke Cosimo II—several of her paintings are registered in the collections of the grand dukes, to which belong *Maddalena* ('The penitent Magdalen'; Galleria Palatina, Florence) and *Giuditta che decapita Oloferne* ('Judith Slaying Holofernes'; Galleria degli Uffizi, Florence). Belonging also to the Florentine period is *L'Autoritratto come suonatrice di liuto* ('Self-Portrait as Woman Playing a Lute'), which turned up at an auction at Sothebys in London in 1998. On the basis of this portrait, which presents the face of a beautiful woman with a proud gaze and a distinctive nose, we can identify further images of the painter in others of her works: in *Salome* (Musée d'Histoire et d'Art, Geneva); in the aforementioned *Maddalena*; in *Santa Martire* (Newhouse Galleries, New York); and in *Santa Caterina d'Alessandria* (Galleria degli Uffizi, Florence).

Gentileschi is recorded as being in Rome, in via del Corso, with her daughter and a servant, from 1621 to 1626 (from 1623 her husband, of whom she soon lost all trace, no longer lived with her). In 1622 she completed her portrait masterpiece, *Ritratto di gonfaloniere* ('Portrait of a gonfaloniere'; Collezioni Comunali d'Arte, Bologna), and a few years later another, innovative version of *Giuditta e Oloferne* (Institute of Arts, Detroit), which places her among the most significant and avant-garde painters of the late 1620s. From 1627 (possibly even the close of 1626) to 1628 she is recorded as being in Venice, her fame and prestige confirmed by poems dedicated to, and numerous writings about, her. In her latter years in Rome and those spent in Venice she was acquainted with distinguished individuals such as Nicolas Lanier (1588–1666), master of the king's musick and art agent to Charles I, who must have been more than a friend to her.

Perhaps as early as 1629 Gentileschi moved to Naples, where *L'annunciazione* ('The Annunciation'; Palazzo Reale, Naples) was completed in 1630; there she developed important epistolary contacts and work-related contacts with patrons such as Cassiano Dal Pozzo (1588–1657), who was in Rome, and Don Antonio Ruffo, of Messina. Among her most significant paintings realized in the 1630s were the three canvases for Pozzuoli Cathedral (held today in the Museo di Capodimonte) and the *Natività del Battista* ('The Birth of St John'), executed for the count of Monterey, viceroy of Naples, to decorate—along with another five canvases by Massimo Stanzione—the Cason del Buon Retiro in Madrid (today the painting is in Madrid's Museo

del Prado). From this period (1635) dates a letter that testifies to Gentileschi's friendship with Galileo Galilei, one that began during her time in Florence. In her Neapolitan period, when she was closely linked to artists such as Massimo Stanzione and Bernardo Cavallino, she took on a new subject, *Betsabea* ('Bathsheba'; there are versions in Potsdam; Conversano; Columbus, Ohio; Galleria degli Uffizi, Florence; and Gosford House, Scotland).

Gentileschi's stay in London falls in the late 1630s, although she was already in negotiations with the court of Charles I (who requested her services) in 1635. What must have prompted the move in early 1638 was the bad state of health of her father, a painter for the king for more than ten years, who died in London on 7 February 1639. It is possible that Artemisia had no direct contact with her father after 1612; if so an air of final reconciliation would have been lent to the journey, but it is also highly likely that the stay was prompted by her search for new, prestigious commissions. From the London period certainly belong *L'Allegoria della pittura* (*The Allegory of Painting*; Royal Collection) and her participation in completing the panels for the Queen's House at Greenwich (which today decorate the ceiling of Marlborough House in London), which had been commissioned from her father. The abundance of activity at the English court, which ended for Gentileschi in her departure in 1641 or 1642 (there is no documentary evidence to establish an exact date), is corroborated by at least eight works by her listed in later inventories of the royal household (1639 and 1649) and by the role of portrait painter that she developed at court.

Very little is known of the last years of Gentileschi's life, which were spent in Naples; she does not reappear in records until 5 September 1648 (a payment from Don Fabrizio Ruffo for a painting on which she was working). About Christmas 1651 there is news of her being ill, but it is not known whether this illness caused her death, which occurred in 1652 or 1653, when Giovanfrancesco Loredan and Pietro Michiele published an epitaph for her.

GIANNI PAPI

Sources R. Longhi, 'Gentileschi padre e figlia', *L'Arte*, 19 (1916), 245–314 • A. Banti, *Artemisia* (1947) • A. Moir, *The Italian followers of Caravaggio* (1967), 1.99–101; 2.73–4 • R. W. Bissell, 'Artemisia Gentileschi: a new documented chronology', *Art Bulletin*, 50 (1968), 153–68 • E. Borea, *Caravaggio e caravaggeschi nelle gallerie di Firenze* (Florence, 1970), 71–80 [exhibition catalogue, Pitti Palace, Florence, 1970] • R. E. Spear, *Caravaggio and his followers* (1971), 96–9 [exhibition catalogue, Cleveland Museum of Art] • A. S. Harris, 'Artemisia Gentileschi', *Women artists, 1550–1950* (New York, 1976), 118–24 [exhibition catalogue] • M. Gregori, 'Artemisia Gentileschi', *Civiltà del Seicento a Napoli*, ed. E. Bellucci and others, 1 (Naples, 1984), 146–50, 304–6 [exhibition catalogue, Museo di Capodimonte, 24 Oct 1984 – 14 April 1985, and Museo Pignatelli, 6 Dec 1984 – 14 April 1985] • M. D. Garrard, *Artemisia Gentileschi: the image of the female hero in Italian baroque art* (1989) • R. Contini and G. Papi, *Artemisia* (Florence, 1991) [exhibition catalogue, Casa Buonarotti, Florence, 18 June – 4 Nov 1991] • E. Cropper, 'New documents for Artemisia Gentileschi's life in Florence', *Burlington Magazine*, 135 (1993), 760–61 • M. D. Garrard, 'Corisca and the satyr', *Burlington Magazine*, 135 (1993), 34–8 • G. Papi, 'Artemisia: senza dimora conosciuta', *Paragone*, 529–33 (1994), 197–202 • G. Pagliarulo, 'Artemisia: la

Betsabea di Gosford House', *Nuovi Studi*, 1 (1996), 151–6 · G. Papi,
'Un David e Golia di Artemisia Gentileschi', *Nuovi Studi*, 1 (1996),
157–60 · A. Lapierre, *Artemisia: un duel pour l'immortalité* (1998) ·
R. W. Bissell, *Artemisia Gentileschi and the authority of art* (1999) ·
G. Papi, 'Artemisia Gentileschi and the authority of art', *Burlington
Magazine*, 142 (2000), 450–53 [review] · K. Christiansen and J. Mann,
Orazio and Artemisia Gentileschi (2001) [exhibition catalogue, Museo
del Palazzo di Venezia, Rome, 15 Oct 2001 – 6 Jan 2002, Metropol-
itan Museum of Art, New York, 14 Feb – 12 May 2002, and Saint
Louis Art Museum, 15 June – 15 Sept 2002]
Likenesses A. Gentileschi, self-portrait, 1615–20; Sothebys, 9
June 1998, lot 68 · A. Gentileschi, self-portrait, oils, 1638–9
(*L'allegoria della pittura*), Royal Collection [*see illus.*] · Adem, pen and
ink, and wash drawing, NPG · A. Gentileschi, self-portrait, oils,
Althorp, Northamptonshire · A. Gentileschi, self-portrait, oils,
Royal Collection

Gentileschi, Orazio (1563–1639), painter, was born in Pisa
and baptized in San Biagio alle Catene, Pisa, on 9 July 1563,
the third son of Giovanni Battista di Bartolomeo Lomi (*d.*
1575), a goldsmith from Florence, and his wife, Maria Gentileschi. He probably trained as a goldsmith, and as late as
1593 was practising as a medallist. Both his older brothers,
Baccio Lomi and Aurelio Lomi (*b.* 1556, *d.* after 1623), were
painters. Orazio, who used his mother's surname, moved
to Rome in 1576 or 1578 and found employment in the
large workshops executing decorative cycles in the Biblioteca Sistina and in the basilicas of Santa Maria Maggiore
and San Giovanni Laterano. Gentileschi's works from the
1590s, mostly frescoes, are painted in a conventional late
mannerist style.

Gentileschi's style changed radically after 1600 thanks
to his contact with Caravaggio, whose adherence to natural appearances and dramatic use of light offered a
powerful and distinctive alternative to the timid conformity of his own art. Gentileschi began making greater use of
the model, the lighting in his pictures became more varied, and he brought the figures closer to the picture plane.
Caravaggio admired Gentileschi's skill as a painter and
they shared studio props. Gentileschi's Caravaggism was
highly refined and lyrical in character, as may be seen in
his *St Francis Supported by an Angel* (Museo del Prado,
Madrid), dating from the early 1600s.

In 1605 Gentileschi's wife, Prudentia di Ottaviano Montoni (*b. c.*1575), died, leaving him with four children under
the age of twelve—Artemisia *Gentileschi (1593–1652/3);
Francesco (*b.* 1597, *d.* after 1665); Giulio (*b.* 1599, *d.* after
1642); and Marco (*b.* 1604, *d.* after 1639). During the first
decade of the century, however, he enjoyed a successful
career, producing designs for mosaics in the dome of St
Peter's and painting several altarpieces, including *The Baptism of Christ* (1607) for the church of Santa Maria della Pace
in Rome and *St Michael Overcoming the Devil* (*c.*1607–8) for
the church of San Salvatore at Farnese. In 1611–12 he
painted frescoes in the Casino delle Muse for Cardinal Scipione Borghese, the nephew of Pope Paul V, showing figures around a balcony in an elaborate fictive architecture
executed by the Florentine Agostino Tassi (1578–1644). He
also executed exquisite cabinet pictures on alabaster and
copper, for example, *St Christopher Bearing the Christ Child*

Orazio Gentileschi (1563–1639), by Sir Anthony Van Dyck

(Gemäldegalerie, Berlin), which show the influence of
Adam Elsheimer's precious landscape and light effects.

In spring 1611 Tassi raped Gentileschi's daughter, Artemisia (who became a distinguished painter in her own
right, and worked in a style similar to her father's). There
followed Tassi's trial and brief imprisonment, but
Gentileschi's prosecution of the case and the intervention
of Tassi's powerful friends seem to have seriously compromised his own prospects in Rome. Over the course of
the 1610s, therefore, he took on several commissions for
the wealthy churches and monasteries of the Marches. In
1612 he wrote to the grand duchess of Tuscany in the hope
of obtaining employment in Florence, and in 1617 he was
seeking the support of the Medici to obtain a commission
to paint in the Palazzo Ducale in Venice. His contact with
Artemisia, after her marriage to Pietro Antonio Stiattesi in
1612, became much less frequent. In 1621 Gentileschi was
invited to Genoa by the nobleman Giovanni Antonio Sauli
and there began a new and highly successful phase in his
career. In Genoa his style acquired a more stately and theatrical character, evident in, for example, *Lot and his Daughters* (J. Paul Getty Museum, Los Angeles). From Genoa he
sent works to Duke Carlo Emanuele I of Savoy at Turin,
and in 1624 he entered the service of Queen Marie de'
Medici in Paris. Among the works he painted during the
two to three years he spent at the French court are the allegorical figure of *Public Felicity* (Louvre, Paris), which is
remarkable for its superb rendition of draperies and
jewels, and two paintings, *The Rest on the Flight to Egypt* and
The Penitent Magdalene (Kunsthistorisches Museum,

Vienna), which were acquired for the collection of George Villiers, first duke of Buckingham, the favourite and chief minister of Charles I.

Gentileschi travelled to London at the end of September 1626, accompanied by his three sons, at the invitation of Buckingham, and was provided with richly furnished rooms in York House. He received a pension of £100 per annum from Charles I (seemingly paid only three times) but was principally active in the service of Buckingham (for whom he painted a mythological ceiling in York House, now lost) and, after the latter's death in 1628, for Queen Henrietta Maria. Several of his most important English pictures were assembled in the Queen's House in Greenwich, including another *Lot and his Daughters* (1628; Museo de Bellas Artes, Bilbao), *The Finding of Moses* (early 1630s; priv. coll.), and *Joseph and Potiphar's Wife* (early 1630s; Royal Collection). These are large sumptuous works influenced by the Venetian sixteenth-century artist Paolo Veronese, whose paintings were much admired at the Stuart court. The ceiling canvases he painted for the Great Hall of the Queen's House, showing *An Allegory of Peace and the Arts* (1635–8), constitute his most significant English commission. They survive in a mutilated state at Marlborough House, London.

Gentileschi encountered opposition from local artists and found himself overshadowed at court first by Rubens, who was in London in 1629–30, and then by Van Dyck, who settled in the city in 1632. His arrogant and vindictive character may also have compromised his prospects at the court. His intention to return to Tuscany is signalled in a letter of 1633. He painted a second version of *The Finding of Moses* (1632–3; Museo del Prado, Madrid), which he sent to Philip IV of Spain in the hope of obtaining his support in making an honourable homecoming. In the event he stayed on in London, where he died on 7 February 1639. He was buried in the Queen's chapel at Somerset House. Van Dyck's black chalk portrait of Gentileschi (mid-1630s) is in the British Museum and characterizes him as a stern individual of haughty bearing. The drawing was made into a print by Lucas Vorsterman, as part of Van Dyck's *Iconographie*. Other examples of Gentileschi's work may be seen in the Galleria Nazionale di Palazzo Barberini and the Galleria Spada, Rome; the Pinacoteca di Brera, Milan; the National Gallery of Art, Washington; and the National Gallery of Ireland, Dublin.   GABRIELE FINALDI

Sources R. Ward Bissell, *Orazio Gentileschi and the poetic tradition in Caravaggesque painting* (1981) [The standard monograph on the artist, with a register of documents and catalogue raisonné] · G. Finaldi, ed., *Orazio Gentileschi at the court of Charles I* (1999) [exhibition catalogue, National Gallery, London] · A. Weston-Lewis, 'Orazio Gentileschi's two versions of *The finding of Moses* reassessed', *Apollo*, 145 (June 1997), 27–35 · R. Soprani, *Vite de' pittori, scultori e architetti Genovesi* (Genoa, 1674) · W. N. Sainsbury, *Original unpublished papers illustrative of the life of Sir Peter Paul Rubens* (1859) · W. N. Sainsbury, 'Artists' quarrels in Charles I's reign', *N&Q*, 2nd ser., 8 (1859), 121–2 · R. Longhi, 'Gentileschi padre e figlia', *L'Arte*, 19 (1916), 245–314 · K. Christiansen and J. Mann, *Orazio and Artemisia Gentileschi* (2001) [exhibition catalogue, Museo del Palazzo di Venezia, Rome, 15 Oct 2001 – 6 Jan 2002, Metropolitan Museum of Art, New York, 14 Feb – 12 May 2002, and Saint Louis Art Museum, 15 June – 15 Sept 2002] · J. Wood, 'Orazio Gentileschi and
some Netherlandish artists in London: the patronage of the duke of Buckingham, Charles I and Henrietta Maria', *Simiolus*, 28/3, 103–28

Archives Archivio di Stato, Florence, letters, Mediceo 4232, inserto 15 · Biblioteca Civica, Turin, autografi, Lascito Cossilla · PRO, state papers, SP 16/133, no. 29 · PRO, state papers, SP 16/139, no. 88 · PRO, state papers, SP 16/141, no. 35 · PRO, state papers, SP 16/174, no. 33
Likenesses A. Van Dyck, black chalk drawing, BM [*see illus.*] · L. Vorsterman, line engraving (after drawing by A. Van Dyck, c.1632), BM; repro. in A. Van Dyck, *Iconographie*, 2 vols. (1759)

Gentili, Alberico (1552–1608), jurist, was born on 14 January 1552 in Castello di San Ginesio (prefecture of Macerata, in the march of Ancona), Italy. He was the eldest son of Matteo Gentili (1517–1601), physician, descendant of the Gentili Rossi and Gentili Bianchi lines, and Lucretia Petrelli (d. 1591). Matteo and Lucretia were married in 1549 and had six other children: Manillo, Antonio, Nevida, Vincenzo, Scipio, and Quinto.

Early years—Italy The young Gentili was tutored at home by both parents (his father is reputed to have been well versed in philosophy and philology). In 1569 he matriculated at the strongly Bartolist faculty of law at the University of Perugia from which he graduated with a doctorate on 22 September 1572.

Gentili was appointed as praetor in Ascoli, where his father had practised since 1571, and gained experience in both criminal and civil law. In 1574 he and his father moved back to San Ginesio, and a year later Alberico began what was to prove an impressive career by undertaking to revise the local laws of his native town, in his capacity as municipal lawyer. He resigned from that post as soon as he completed his task, on 22 September 1577, in order to devote more time to his legal studies. Nevertheless he continued to contribute to municipal matters until the inquisition forced him to follow his father and his younger brother Scipio into exile.

Exile—first years in England Matteo Gentili's Reformist ideas and possible Zwinglian leanings had already offended many of his Catholic compatriots. When he insisted that several influential fellow members of the ancient brotherhood of SS. Tommaso e Barnabà be expelled on grounds of irregularities, the enemies he made were quick to take their revenge by putting the inquisition on his track. About 1579 Matteo, Alberico, and Scipio, fearing for their lives, fled to Laibach, Austria, where Matteo (probably assisted by his brother-in-law, the influential jurist Nicolò Petrelli) was appointed chief physician for the duchy of Carniola. However, the inquisition's influence reached as far as Austria and, as a precaution, early in 1580 Matteo sent Scipio to Tübingen, where he became professor of law and an acclaimed poet, while Alberico fled to London (to be followed later on by Matteo himself) via Cologne, Tübingen, Heidelberg, Neustadt, and Hesse, reaching London about August.

Several eminent religious refugees had already sought a safe haven in England, among them Queen Elizabeth's Italian tutor, the physician Giambattista Castiglione, to whom Gentili first turned for assistance. It was through Castiglione that he met his benefactor, Tobie Matthew, then vice-chancellor of Oxford University, later bishop of Durham and archbishop of York. Thanks to Matthew's efforts Gentili became a protégé of the powerful Robert Dudley, earl of Leicester. As chancellor of Oxford, Leicester asked that the university incorporate Gentili, 'a stranger and learned and an exile for religion' (letter of 24 Nov 1580, *Reg. Oxf.*). His recommendation was accepted by the senate on 14 December 1580 and Gentili was formally received as a member of the university on 14 January 1581. He was offered lodgings at New Inn Hall and was appointed tutor for law at St John's College. On 6 March 1581 Gentili was officially appointed professor of Roman law; he went on to become 'the grand ornament of the university in his time … and … the flower of the university for his profession' (Wood, *Ath. Oxon.*, 2.90).

The work that inaugurated Gentili's prolific career in England was *De juris interpretibus dialogi Sex* (1582, dedicated to the earl of Leicester), a critique of the humanist school led by Cujas. This was followed swiftly by a collection of lectures and letters entitled *Lectionum et epistolarum quae ad ius Civile Pertinent, libri I–IV* (1583–4). The dedications in these works (to, among others, Thomas Henning and Horatio Pallavicino) brim with a sense of gratitude towards England, where he had found a new home and his talents and erudition were amply acknowledged. Gentili could not return home. Several male members of the Gentili family narrowly escaped imprisonment, while the inquisition issued life sentences to the 'heretics' *in absentia* and confiscated their property. Matteo's and Alberico's names were struck from the town register and, in Alberico's case, from the legal code he had revised. In 1581 Matteo too joined his son in England, never to return to Italy.

In 1584 Gentili and John Hotman were consulted by the privy council in the case of the Spanish ambassador Don Bernardino de Mendoza. Both legal experts concluded that, as an ambassador, Mendoza enjoyed diplomatic immunity, the charges of conspiracy against the queen notwithstanding. The privy council respected their verdict, however reluctantly, and Mendoza was unceremoniously dispatched back to Spain rather than to the executioner's block. Out of this high-profile case Gentili produced the first coherent study on diplomatic law: his views on the legal aspects of embassies (first delivered at the church of St Mary the Virgin, Oxford, on the occasion of the annual conferment of degrees) were published in 1585 as *Legalium comitiorum Oxoniensium actio*. The work subsequently expanded to *De legationibus libri tres* (1585, dedicated to Sir Philip Sidney), a book that scandalized as much as it impressed because of Gentili's laudatory remarks on Machiavelli.

In the summer of 1586, perhaps because of the antagonism aroused by *De legationibus libri tres*, or simply because he grew restless, Gentili left England to accompany the ambassador Horatio Pallavicino to Saxony with the view, it seems, of settling there, not far from his brother Scipio. However, his stay in Saxony proved unexpectedly short. In November he was approached by Sir Francis Walsingham, principal secretary—a staunch protestant, sympathetic to refugees from Catholic countries—who offered him the position of regius professor of law at Oxford. Gentili was officially appointed to the chair on 8 June 1587 and retained his seat until his death. Having published two works in the interim, *De diversis temporum appellationibus liber* and the brief *De nascendi tempore disputatio* (both 1586), Gentili returned to England and duly dedicated his next work, *Disputationum decas prima* (1587), to Walsingham.

A year later, at the height of the Anglo-Spanish crisis, Gentili delivered a lecture on justice in the context of war before the *comitia* at Oxford. The lecture was published in three parts as *De jure belli commentatio prima* (1588), *Commentatio secunda* (1589), and *Commentatio tertia* (1589). Thoroughly revised and expanded to five times its original length over the following decade, it served as the basis of Gentili's *magnum opus*, *De jure belli libri tres* (1598) dedicated to Robert Devereux, second earl of Essex.

De jure belli In *De jure belli* Gentili grappled with issues of great currency, born of the increasing complexity of international commerce, as well as the conflicts of religious allegiance and civic loyalty, which were echoed in the raging debates between humanists and theologians. Regarding the former, Gentili took the view that the jurisdiction of sovereign states extended to the high seas and argued for the regulation of navigation. This idea began to take hold once the activities of Dutch fishing fleets near England's shores began to pose a threat to English interests. Regarding the latter, Gentili made systematic efforts to dissociate international law from theology, taking pains to separate *jus divinum* ('divine law') from *jus humanum* ('human law'), and temper the prevalence of canon law in jurisprudence. While there is no substance to the accusation of 'Italus Atheus' ('atheist Italian'; van der Mollen, 254) that was raised against Gentili by later commentators, his qualified reverence for Augustinian ideas did little to appease his Catholic detractors. In a Europe where the pope no longer reigned supreme, Gentili's argument, that religious authority rested in the word of God (the holy scriptures), not with God's earthly representatives, and that rulers had duties to their people, as well as rights over them, had immense political significance. Though Gentili did not accept that a ruler's decisions in religious matters could be challenged by the people, in *De jure belli* he examined whether a subject could lawfully fight against a ruler of his own faith; more specifically, whether it was justifiable for a Catholic subject to fight against papist forces on behalf of the queen.

The question of what is legally justifiable in war lies at the core of *De jure belli*. Even though in *De armis Romanis* (written in the 1590s) Gentili draws amply on Roman sources in order to examine the concept of 'just' war in a historical perspective, his primary concerns in *De jure belli*, as in most of his works, are practical. Rather than tackle the legitimacy of war as such, he focuses on what constitutes legitimate practice in war, accepting (as many of his contemporaries did) that war was sometimes necessary to regulate the balance of power among rival states. The idea that alliances based on race or religion made it lawful, indeed imperative, for third parties to offer military assistance to belligerents reflected largely the need for solidarity among protestant states before the threat of papist opponents, but could be equally applied to the need for Christian nations to join forces against the Ottoman expansion, as well as to the legitimation of colonial expeditions.

In the same pragmatic spirit, Gentili undermined his own argument, that a war can be 'just' on both sides, by counter-arguing that infidels, such as the Ottoman Turks, and people given to 'unnatural' practices (such as cannibalism and bestiality, which were thought to be common among native tribes of the American continent) excluded themselves from the international society and its laws. In effect, this meant that Christian states were not legally bound to respect any treaties struck with Ottoman rulers, nor was there any legal or moral impediment in aggressing against the inhabitants of the new colonies, with a view to instilling in them Christian principles.

Nevertheless, Gentili rejected religious difference alone as a just cause of war, and (moved, perhaps, by his personal experience) objected strongly to the execution of heretics. Throughout *De jure belli*, he remained true to the principle that war was a means of attaining or preserving peace. He reasoned that reprisals should be strictly proportionate to the damage inflicted by the enemy and, where not only women and children, but also libraries, works of art, and manuscripts were concerned, acts of violence should be altogether avoided. He argued that from a moral point of view prisoners of war should be treated humanely, although he conceded that from a political point of view their execution could be justified.

Regarding the question of whether it was lawful to enslave peoples whose conduct was seen as contrary to the precepts of civilization, Gentili's pragmatism led him to make similar concessions. In theory he agreed that the notion of a universal 'natural law' was not sustainable in the face of enormous cultural diversity, and even made references to Montaigne. None the less, in a difficult act of balance, Gentili effectively upheld interventionism, stopping just short of accepting the notion of natural slavery. He was aware that legitimizing warfare against people who refused to engage in commercial interaction (a common issue for Europeans in their dealings with the native peoples of the newly discovered America), and condoning the colonization of vacant lands out of necessity, often served as an excuse for expansionist wars, and was critical of the Spanish (at a time of intense rivalry with the English on that account).

Gentili's defence of acting In 1593 Gentili expanded his legal repertory with the publication of two essays, dedicated to his friend Tobie Matthew: a legal commentary on magicians and astrologers, entitled *Ad titulum codicis de maleficis et mathematicis*, and *Commentatio ad legem III codicis de professoribus et medicis*, a defence of poetry and drama written in response to a dispute between William Gager, Oxford lawyer, dramatist, and poet, and the erudite John Rainolds, scholar of divinity. Rainolds had condemned drama in general on theological grounds, and Gager's

plays in particular on the grounds that the character of Momus satirized his person.

Whether Gentili had contributed his legal opinion to some of the arguments Gager raised against Rainolds remains unclear. In a letter to Rainolds dated 7 July 1593 Gentili enclosed a copy of his *Commentatio* stressing that the lecture that had inspired it predated the dispute between Rainolds and Gager. Rainolds—an old enemy who had, apparently, objected to Gentili's appointment to the professorship on account of his Italian origin and personality—was offended regardless. In any event, the two men engaged in a heated correspondence on the propriety and lawfulness of acting, which was published several years later as *De actoribus et spectatoribus* and *De abusu mendacii* (both 1599).

In his *Commentatio* Gentili argued that poetics benefited morals, that from a strictly legal point of view university actors could not be accused of corruption as they were not paid, that even indecorous acting could improve morals; further, that the injunctions of Deuteronomy 22: 5 forbidding cross-dressing were to be interpreted metaphorically—a point that Rainolds (in line with those theologians who feared the stage as a source of propaganda and considered drama pernicious to Christian morals) interpreted literally. In his response to the rest of Gentili's points Rainolds invoked an impressive array of religious texts to condemn all drama as an abomination and a threat to the university's moral standing.

In the frenzied debate that ensued, the elaborate theological and legal arguments of the two men were laced with a good deal of personal animosity, with each side accusing the other of vice, ignorance, and barbarity. It is more than likely that Gentili used the controversy as a vehicle for a broader argument about the bounds between law and theology, which—he never tired of repeating—were absolute, and as an opportunity to settle old scores between Rainolds and himself. In a letter indicative of the deeply personal issues which were at stake in this debate, Gentili wrote to Rainolds:

> Why do you, who now hinder me from treating the sacred books out of a papist spirit, make me out to be guilty of immodesty? ... Do you not see that you act tyrannically with him who despised the power of the Pope and was banished from his country and the entire papal realm? ... Theology is the teacher of faith and life, but not of all life. Nor is every part of the word of God completely yours. (*Latin Correspondence*, 39)

The London years In 1589 Gentili married a fellow religious refugee from France, Hester de Peigne (or Peigni) (*d.* 1648), whose sister Jaël became the second wife of Sir Henry Killigrew. Their first child, Robert, was born on 11 September 1590. About this date the couple moved to London; in 1590 Gentili's lectures were delegated to a deputy. In this year he also published *De injustitia bellica Romanorum actio*. The couple's second child, Anna, born in 1592, was baptized at the French church, Threadneedle Street, and their next two children at St Helen, Bishopsgate. Anna died in infancy and her name was given to a daughter born in 1598. *De jure belli libri tres* came out in its final form that same year, and a year later *De actoribus* and *De armis Romanis et injustitia bellica Romanorum libri II* (written in the 1590s) were published. They were followed by *Ad primum Maccabaeorum disputatio* in 1600.

Gentili spent the last years of his life in London. England acted as mediator in the war that ensued after the uprising of the Dutch provinces against their Spanish overlords, and many legal disputes between the Dutch and the Spanish were brought to the admiralty court in London. Gentili's involvement in the defence of Spanish affairs against the Dutch led him to devote increasing amounts of time to his legal practice. By the time he was admitted to Gray's Inn (14 August 1600) he was seen at Oxford only during royal visits and at the *comitia*. His spectacular rise in academic and political circles as well as his involvement in theological disputes prompted some of the enemies he had inevitably made to try and implicate him in the rebellion of Robert Devereux, second earl of Essex, in 1601. Their efforts came to nothing and Gentili's scholarly output and family continued to grow: 1601 was marked by the publication of his treatise on matrimony and divorce, *Disputationum de nuptiis libri VII*, the birth of his daughter Hester, the death of his father Matteo (on 4 June 1601), and the execution of Essex, after whom Robert (Essex's godson) had been named. The birth of the youngest child, named Matteo, in 1603 coincided with the publication of *Lectiones Virgilianae*: not, in fact, a legal work but a method for teaching Virgil to young pupils which Gentili had devised himself for the sake of Robert, who graduated BA in early July of the same year from Jesus College, Oxford.

In 1604 Gentili published three more works: *Ad I Maccabaeorum disputatio, et de Linguarum mistura*; *De si quis principi ed ad Leg. Jul. disp. decem*; and *De Latinitate vet. bibl. vers. male accusata*. They were followed by another four in 1605: his personal tribute to the universities of Perugia and Oxford (*Laudes academiae Perusinae et Oxoniensis*), a discourse on the thorny issue of the union between England and Scotland (*De unione Angliae et Scotiae discursus*), and two collections of essays entitled *Disputationes tres* and *Regales disputationes tres*, part of which Gentili had urged Robert to dedicate to the principal of Brasenose College, Oxford, Dr Singleton, in a rather clumsy attempt at promoting his son's interests. It is speculated that Gentili may also be the author of another work that was published in 1605, the satire *Mundus alter et idem*, though Joseph Hall is a more likely candidate. Also in 1605 Gentili was appointed advocate to the Spanish embassy, a post that he held until his death, without being troubled by any apparent misgivings about defending Catholic interests against a protestant state—a question he had explored on a broader scale in *De jure belli*. Gentili justified his controversial decision to accept the post by arguing that the judge who dealt with the cases (almost certainly Thomas Crompton) was prejudiced; however, this apparently noble motive did not convince his critics who accused him of opportunism. His legal work in that capacity was not published until 1613 by his brother Scipio, under the title *Hispanicae advocationis libri Duo*.

At the close of his career Gentili worked almost exclusively at the admiralty bar. The last volume he published was *In titulos codicis si quis imperatori maledixerit* in 1607 (*De libro Pyano* which came out in 1606 had been written three years earlier). In the same year, aged barely seventeen, Robert became a probationer fellow at All Souls, Oxford, where he eventually took a degree in civil law. Both Hester and Alberico Gentili had fostered a lot of time and care on their precocious son and such a prestigious appointment might suggest that their efforts were about to be amply repaid. In truth, Robert's achievements seem to owe less to his own industry and more to his father's exertions on his account: the fellowship at All Souls had been backed by considerable pressure from Alberico's influential contacts, and Robert had been repeatedly encouraged by Alberico to dedicate some of his illustrious father's works in his own name to high-ranking patrons in order to gain their favour—a practice that met with considerable disapproval among Gentili's peers. Despite all the care that Gentili lavished on his son, Robert turned out to be a 'rake-hell' and 'king of the beggars for a time, and so much given up to sordid liberty, if not downright wickedness, that he … spent all that he could get from his father (whom he would often abuse) … [and] from his mother' (Wood, *Ath. Oxon.*, 3.394) and did his best, it seems, to live up to the model of the proverbial prodigal son.

Gentili took his eldest child's behaviour to heart. 'If he will I doe forgive him all faltes which he hath comitted against me since he was borne', he wrote bitterly in his will, drafted on 14 June 1608, and in a harsher tone continued: 'I doe not thincke that he will desire one fardinge of myne'. Indeed, Robert may have well been effectively disinherited, if Hester Gentili and her coexecutor, Gentili's 'syster' (probably Jaél Killigrew), heeded his last wishes: he desired that his wife 'be Mistris' of his fortune 'for shee will well knowe howe to dispose boath of hers and myne, which I doe leave her for the benefitt of those my three little ones. The first hath hadd to much.' He commended his three youngest children, especially Matteo ('because he beares the name of my father'), to the care of his brother Scipio, who was also assigned the task of burning all Alberico's books 'bycause they are to much imperfecte', except for the *Hispanicae advocationis*. Clearly Scipio chose not respect this latter wish and saw to it instead that Alberico's works were preserved for posterity. He did, however, fulfil his brother's desire that he be buried 'as deepe and as neare' his father as possible: Alberico Gentili died in London on 19 June 1608 and he was buried two days later in the churchyard of St Helen, Bishopsgate, London. His widow died in 1648 in Rickmansworth, Hertfordshire, where their daughter Anna married Sir John Colt of Woodoaks Manor.

Overview of Gentili's work Though Gentili's ideas do not seem to have had significant effect on colonial policy, they are representative of an era that saw the transformation of European naval powers to colonial empires. Gentili's brilliance consists in his astute appreciation of trends and developments that impacted on interstate relations in a dramatic way, and in his response to those changes by forging an essentially modern concept of international law. His ability to mould the ideas that he drew from a wealth of sources (including classical and canonical texts, as well as the works of his predecessors, such as Vitoria, Ayala, Justus Lipsius, and Tacitus) into a body of law that was immediately applicable to current events is precisely what led the nineteenth-century jurist T. E. Holland to discern Gentili as an innovator.

Holland's reappraisal was crucial to the gradual acknowledgement of Gentili as a major legal thinker. Gentili was certainly one of the most eminent professors of law at Oxford. He was highly regarded by his contemporaries, and many of his pupils were distinguished in the legal profession. Though he was never quite forgotten, until Holland no one had seriously challenged Hugo Grotius's reputation as the founder of international law. Grotius himself built many of his theories on Gentili's *De jure belli* and borrowed heavily from Gentili's examples without checking the original sources (thus duplicating several of Gentili's own misquotations). Though in his *De jure belli ac pacis libri tres* (Paris, 1625, para. 38) Grotius names Gentili as one of the worthiest legal theorists on war, in general he was rather remiss in acknowledging Gentili's influence on his own work.

The main criticism levelled at Gentili is that though his arguments are weighty they lack coherence. Gentili's admirers (including Holland) agree that his ideas lack the systematic approach and sound theoretical basis of Grotius's works, but they point out that it was Gentili who first conceived of a body of international regulations that would supersede the arbitrary practices (such as pledges and oaths) on which interstate relations were hitherto based.

His critics point out that Gentili's total rejection of humanist jurisprudence and his unyielding objections to Catholic commentaries on canonical texts have more to do with the trauma of persecution than with legal opinion. Indeed, the complications of Gentili's religious affiliation were to persist beyond his death: when Professor P. S. Mancini joined Holland as a champion of Gentili's reputation and sought to have a monument erected in San Ginesio, he and the Italian committee who backed him met with staunch opposition. This was partly because in Italy Gentili's reinstatement was politicized by both the anti-clerical faction and members of the Catholic clergy. The prestigious committee of distinguished statesmen and jurists, with Professor Mancini as president and Prince Umberto, later king of Italy, as honorary president, was unable to overcome the objections of the anti-Gentilian lobby. Although in 1885 the technical institute of Macerata was renamed Istituto Tecnico Alberico Gentili and memorial tablets in his honour were placed both there and, in 1890, at the University of Perugia, the ultra-Catholic press did not cease to inveigh against Gentili, even labelling him an 'apostate'. His statue was not erected until 1908, thirty-one years after the committee founded in England had erected a monument to Gentili in St Helen, Bishopsgate. The Centro Internazionale di Studi

Gentiliani at San Ginesio was founded in 1981 by a local committee determined to bestow appropriate honour upon the memory of their once famous compatriot. An inaugural lecture was held in 1983 and since then the centre has organized several conferences and overseen a number of publications on Gentili; it also holds a unique collection of resources on him.

ARTEMIS GAUSE-STAMBOULOPOULOU

Sources G. H. J. van der Mollen, *Alberico Gentili and the development of international law* (1937) · T. E. Holland, *Studies in international law* (1898), 1–39 · *Hist. U. Oxf.* 3: *Colleg. univ.*, 261–93, 360–61 · W. B. Bannerman, ed., *The registers of St Helen's, Bishopsgate, London*, Harleian Society, register section, 31 (1904), 264, 271 · Foster, *Alum. Oxon., 1500–1714*, 2.557 · Wood, *Ath. Oxon.*, new edn, 2.90–93; 3.393–4 · *Latin correspondence by Alberico Gentili and John Rainolds on academic drama*, trans. L. Markowicz (1977) · J. W. Binns, 'Alberico Gentili in defence of poetry and acting', *Studies in the Renaissance*, 19 (1972), 224–72, esp. 224–8 · L. Markowicz, 'Background to the correspondence', in *Latin correspondence by Alberico Gentili and John Rainolds on academic drama*, trans. L. Markowicz (1977), 1–14 · R. Tuck, *The rights of war and peace: political thought and the international order from Grotius to Kant*, pbk edn (2001), 9–127 · G. I. A. D. Draper, 'Grotius's place in the development of legal ideas about war', *Hugo Grotius and international relations*, ed. H. Bull and others (1990), 178–207 · P. Haggenmacher, 'Grotius and Gentili: a reassessment of Thomas E. Holland's *Inaugural lecture*', in H. Bull and others, *Hugo Grotius and international relations* (1990), 133–76 · C. Philipson, 'Introduction', in A. Gentili, *De jure belli libri tres*, ed. J. B. Scot, trans. J. C. Rolfe, new edn, 2 (1933), 15a–51a [based on 2nd edn of 1612] · B. Kingsbury, 'Confronting difference: the puzzling durability of Gentili's combination of pragmatic pluralism and normative judgement', *American Journal of International Law*, 92/4 (Oct 1998), 713–23 · *Reg. Oxf.*, 2/1.149 · M. G. Forsyth and others, eds., *The theory of international relations: selected texts from Gentili to Treitschke* (1970) · Wijffels, 'Civil law in the practice of the high court of admiralty at the time of Alberico Gentili', PhD diss., U. Cam., 1993 · K. R. Simmonds, *Alberico Gentili at the admiralty bar, 1605–1608* (1958) · K. R. Simmonds, *The contribution of Alberico Gentili to the pre-Grotian literature of the law of nations* (1955) · G. Del Vecchio, 'The posthumous fate of Alberico Gentili', *American Journal of International Law*, 50/3 (July 1956), 664–5 · will, PRO, PROB 11/128, fol. 4425 · *DNB* · monument, St Helen, Bishopsgate, London

Likenesses statue, repro. in Gentili, *De jure belli libri tres*, 1 (1933)

Wealth at death see will, 1616, PRO, PROB 11/128, fol. 4425

Gentili, Luigi [Aloysius] (1801–1848), Roman Catholic missionary, was born at Rome on 14 July 1801, the son of a solicitor of Neapolitan descent, Giuseppe Gentili, and his wife, Anna Maria Gnaccarini. After completing his studies at the Sapienza in Rome, he took the degree of doctor of civil and canon law, and began to practise as an advocate. The death of his patron, Cardinal Consalvi, successively auditor of the rota and secretary of state, destroyed his hopes of advancement. He turned to languages, and acquired a fluency particularly in English. He was artistic and musical with a good speaking and singing voice. His arresting appearance (he was tall with blue eyes) and his enthusiastic manner commanded attention, and were remarked upon throughout his life. He became popular as a teacher of Italian to foreigners. In 1829 a meeting with Antonio Rosmini led to his joining the Institute of Charity. Having been ordained priest in 1830, he was sent in 1831 to the first house of the institute, on Monte Calvario, near Domodossola, and was appointed master of the novices.

Luigi Gentili (1801–1848), by unknown artist

In 1835 Gentili's knowledge of English prompted Rosmini to send him and two other missionaries to Prior Park, near Bath. Differences arose with Bishop Baines of the western district over educational matters and the introduction of Italian devotions, and Gentili was first demoted from the position of superior over his companions, then sent into exile, and eventually returned to Italy. At the request of Ambrose Phillipps de Lisle of Grace Dieu Manor, Leicestershire, Gentili became his chaplain in 1840, but there was another clash of personalities. In 1842 he found his niche in the mission at Loughborough, and his talents and success as a preacher led to his being appointed itinerant missionary. He began this new career in company with Father Furlong in 1845 and gave missions in all the large towns of England and Ireland with a zeal and dedication that were regarded as heroic. His reputation for lack of moderation was officially redeemed in 1847 when he was commanded by Cardinal Franzoni, prefect of *propaganda fide* in Rome, to send reports on the state of the Roman Catholic church in England, and on its bishops and priests. Gentili wrote fourteen reports (70,000 words) in sixteen months, information which was subsequently used in the establishment of the English Roman Catholic hierarchy in 1850; those planning the establishment took account of Gentili's reports in dividing the country into Roman Catholic sees, the appointing of bishops, and the retention of missionary status for the Roman Catholic church in England. Gentili died at Dublin on 26 September 1848 of typhus fever, exhausted, it was said, by his labours and extreme asceticism.

THOMPSON COOPER, rev. MARGARET PAWLEY

Sources G. B. Pagani, *Life of the Rev. Aloysius Gentili L.L.D., Father of Charity and missionary apostolic in England* (1851) · C. R. Leetham, *Luigi Gentili, a sower for the second spring* (1965) · C. R. Leetham, *Rosmini* (1957)

Archives Centro Internazionale di Studio Rosminiani, Stresa, Italy · Rosminian English Province Archives, Wonersh, Surrey | Quenby Hall, Hungarton, Leicestershire, de Lisle Archives

Likenesses drawings, 1840–49, Rosminian English Province, Wonersh, Surrey · death mask, 1848, Rosminian English Province, Wonersh, Surrey · oils, Grace Dieu Rosminian School, Coalville, Leicestershire [*see illus.*]

Gentilis [Gentili], **Robert** (*b.* **1590**, *d.* in or after **1655**), translator, was born on 11 September 1590 in London, the eldest of the five children of Alberico *Gentili (1552–1608), jurist and regius professor of civil law at Oxford, and his wife, Hester (*d.* 1648), of the Huguenot family of de Peigne, sister-in-law of Sir Henry Killigrew. He was named after his godfather, the second earl of Essex. His father's first language being Italian and his mother's French, Robert grew up exposed to these languages as well as to English; he was also taught Latin and Greek by his father. He was admitted to Christ Church, Oxford, at the age of eight, spending part of his time reading through Virgil with his father. These lessons formed the basis of Alberico's *Lectiones Virgilianae* (1603), a philological and jurisprudential commentary on the *Eclogues*, published with a Latin dedication which had been written by Robert on his tenth birthday. Robert graduated BA as a member of Jesus College in 1603, when he was twelve, and he was appointed in the next year to the influential university office of collector by William Laud. These precocious academic beginnings were the result of his own talent, his father's teaching, and his father's exertion of considerable influence on his behalf. Over the next couple of years, he wrote dedications—to the heads of three Oxford colleges and to James I—for more of Alberico's books, and in 1607 he was elected, while below the statutory age, to a fellowship of All Souls College. His father had campaigned vigorously for this, enlisting the personal intervention of the king and devising the legal quibble that, just as a debt that is seventeen days and one minute overdue may be regarded as eighteen days overdue, so Robert, who was seventeen and a fraction years old, should be regarded as in effect eighteen, and therefore of the statutory age after all (BL, Add. MS 12504).

By 1608 something was already going wrong in Robert Gentilis's life. Alberico's will, made in that year, says that Robert 'hath hadd to much, and yett hath to muche to mayntayn himselfe' and that 'I hope that my death will cause him to remember himselfe' (Holland, 30). It did not; Anthony Wood records that although Robert took his BCL in 1612 he 'turned a rake-hell, became king of the beggars for a time', and was 'given up to sordid liberty, if not downright wickedness' (Wood, *Ath. Oxon.*, 3.394). Robert left All Souls, went abroad, and disappeared for twenty-five years. He may have left a first wife behind on his emigration since one Alice, 'wife of Robert Gentilis', was buried in London in 1619; he married Mary, widow of Richard Simpson, in London on 4 January 1638. Wood believed that hereafter Robert 'was a retainer to the royal court, and received a pension from the king' (ibid.), and Robert himself acknowledged 'manifold obligements wherewith I am everlastingly tied unto you' in a dedication of 1650 to the daughters of the first earl of Strafford (V. Malvezzi, *Considerations upon the Lives of Alcibiades and Coriolanus*, 1650, sig. A4v), pursuing further Strafford patronage in a dedication to their brother five years later.

Part of Gentilis's income certainly came from writing: in his youth he had translated Isocrates' *Ad demonicum* from Greek into Latin, Italian, French, and English (Bodl. Oxf., MS D'Orville 600, fols. 191–213), and this linguistic versatility now enabled him to work as a professional translator, employed for the most part by Humphrey Moseley and his partner Nicholas Fussell. His translation *History of the Inquisition* (from the Italian of Paolo Sarpi) appeared in 1639, followed by *Antipathy between the French and the Spaniard* in 1641 and *Annotations upon the Holy Bible*, the product of 'neere two yeares labour and paines' (sig. A4v) in 1643 (versions of Carlos Garcia's Spanish work and Giovanni Diodati's Italian work respectively). In 1647 he translated *Chief Events in the Monarchy of Spain in the Year 1639* from the Italian of Virgilio Malvezzi, following this with *Considerations upon the Lives of Alcibiades and Coriolanus* (also from Malvezzi) in 1650, *Natural and Experimental History of Winds* from Bacon's Latin in 1652, an anonymous *Discourse for the Attaining of the Sciences* from French in 1654, *Discourse of Constancy* from Lipsius's work in Latin in the same year, and Giovanni Francesco Biondi's *Coralbo* from Italian in 1655. On 16 August 1655 Moseley entered 'a booke entityled The Anatomy of profane love, written in Italian … & translated into English by Ro: Gentilis' in the Stationers' register; he subsequently advertised this translation as by 'I. S.', and the book seems never to have appeared (Eyre, 2.8). It is possible that Gentilis died before completing it; he refers to a recent dangerous illness in the dedication of *Coralbo* (sig. A2r). There is no evidence for the date of his death beyond this argument from silence.

JOHN CONSIDINE

Sources T. E. Holland, 'Alberico Gentili', *Studies in International Law* (1898), 1–39 · Wood, *Ath. Oxon.*, new edn · Arber, *Regs. Stationers* · G. E. B. Eyre, ed., *A transcript of the registers of the Worshipful Company of Stationers from 1640 to 1708*, 3 vols. (1913–14) · C. H. J. van der Molen, *Alberico Gentili and the development of international law*, 2nd edn (1968) · D. B. Morhof, *Polyhistor literarius, philosophicus et practicus*, 4th edn (1747) · J. W. Binns, *Intellectual culture in Elizabethan and Jacobean England: the Latin writings of the age* (1990)
Archives All Souls Oxf. · Bodl. Oxf., D'Orville MSS

Gentleman, Francis (1728–1784), playwright and essayist, was born on 23 October 1728 in York Street, Dublin, the son of a British army captain. The details of his early life and ancestry are obscure, but it is known that he was educated at the grammar school in Digges Street, Dublin, from the ages of ten to fifteen. He was then (as he saw it) unlucky enough to gain a commission in his father's regiment, and he remained in the army until 1748. Gentleman saw little or no active service during his military career, and, having made the mistake first of transferring into a temporary regiment in 1745 and then buying promotion, he was left on reduced pay with few prospects. In 1749 he

was employed by Thomas Sheridan, manager of Dublin's Smock Alley Theatre, as Aboan in Thomas Southerne's *Oroonoko*, and afterwards in minor supporting roles. He then unexpectedly inherited £800 from an uncle in the East Indies, which was, according to its beneficiary, reduced by three-quarters by his lawyers; this was to establish a pattern of thwarted expectations, financial insecurity, and debt which would continue for the rest of his life. He temporarily suspended his indifferent acting career and headed for London. Having settled briefly in Richmond, he embarked upon his true vocation as a man of letters. In 1751 he published his adaptation of Ben Jonson's *Sejanus*, the first of many such revisions of Jonson, Shakespeare, and others, in line with the tastes of eighteenth-century audiences. Around this time he wrote a tragedy, *Osman*, which was produced in Bath in 1754. Ready to turn his hand to any form or genre in the hope of financial reward, he sustained a competent but mediocre literary output, as well as a considerable body of literary and theatrical criticism and an itinerant career as a supporting actor, moving between London, Scotland, and the north of England, and, finally, Dublin, over the next three decades. His poetry, prose, and drama have been relegated to obscurity, although his farce *The Tobacconist* (based on Jonson's *The Alchemist*, and first produced in 1760) remained popular on the London stage for a considerable period.

Gentleman's most significant work, however, was one of criticism, *The Dramatic Censor*, which was published in two volumes in 1770. Addressing the increasingly literate theatregoing public of the late eighteenth century, this was a playgoer's guide which attempted to adjudicate between scholarly criticism and the demands of popular taste, particularly in relation to the theatrical adaptation of Shakespeare. The key figure for Gentleman was David Garrick, with whom he had been associated since 1751, and whose self-identification with Shakespeare he enthusiastically endorsed. Even though Gentleman was fulsome to the point of extravagance in his praise of the actor in his writing, *The Dramatic Censor* is of interest for its accounts of Garrick's major Shakespearian roles, including Macbeth, Romeo, and Richard III. Gentleman's other enduring legacy to the history of criticism and performance lay in his editorial contributions to the 'acting edition' of Shakespeare's plays published by G. K. Bell & Sons in 1772, in the form of the introduction and notes. Gentleman celebrated a Shakespeare who is identified morally and temperamentally with the works themselves, while his notes to the text are frequently justifications of cuts or adjustments correcting lapses of dignity, taste, and sense on Shakespeare's part in the interests of contemporary standards of sexual, social, and semantic propriety. Gentleman's opinions, naturally enough, bear the moralizing imprint of the ruling critical ideas of his time, in that a neo-classical concern with order and just proportion, combined with the developing interest in natural genius and spontaneity, provide the categories within which taste is defined and judgement exercised. Garrick's Shakespearian acting, in Gentleman's account, offered a harmonious, well-regulated, and decorous synthesis of cultivated craft and innate artistry, and in this respect the actor constituted an appropriate apostolic successor to the national poet himself. In a rhetorical manoeuvre which foreshadowed later debates over the competing authorities of literary criticism and theatrical performance, Gentleman declared Garrick to be Shakespeare's most astute commentator.

Gentleman's eulogizing of Garrick is hardly surprising in view of the latter's domination of the eighteenth-century London stage. Even so, his occasionally blatant sycophancy reflects an opportunism which (given not only Gentleman's increasingly desperate personal circumstances but also the prevailing conditions of literary production and patronage within which he operated), while predictable, gave rise to a number of instances of (ultimately self-destructive) personal disloyalty which offended a number of his contemporaries, Garrick among them. Although Garrick had repeatedly given him financial support from the mid-1750s onwards, Gentleman unwisely became embroiled in the feud between the actor and his rival Samuel Foote, and joined Foote's company at the Haymarket in 1770. In 1771 he published (under a pseudonym) *The Theatres: a Poetical Dissection*, which fiercely attacked both managers; in the same year he wrote to Garrick insinuating that he had plagiarized Gentleman's masque 'On the institution of the garter'—a charge Garrick emphatically rejected. Yet by 1775 he was ready to resume his begging letters to Garrick, having failed to win patronage from the marquess of Granby. The bad luck which had characterized his life was compounded by personal tragedy: in 1770 one of his sons died; his wife, Ruth, whom he had married in 1764, died three years later. He spent the final decade of his life in sickness, near destitution, and considerable bitterness, and died in George Lane, Dublin, on 21 December 1784.

ROBERT SHAUGHNESSY

Sources Highfill, Burnim & Langhans, *BDA* · *The private correspondence of David Garrick*, ed. J. Boaden, 2 vols. (1831–2) · D. Thomas, ed., *Restoration and Georgian England, 1660–1788* (1989) · B. Vickers, ed., *Shakespeare: the critical heritage*, 5: 1765–1774 (1979) · P. Fitzgerald, *The life of David Garrick* (1899)

Gentleman, Robert (1745–1795), Presbyterian minister, was born near Whitchurch, Shropshire, and baptized at Doddington on 7 October 1745, the son of Robert Gentleman (1701/2–1757), a Scot. His early education was by dissenters, as his father was a supporter of the Presbyterian chapel at Doddington. Early in life Gentleman came under the influence of Job Orton, minister at Swan Hill Presbyterian Chapel, Shrewsbury, of which he became a member in January 1762. In 1763 he entered Daventry Theological Academy under Caleb Ashworth to prepare for the ministry, supported by the Presbyterian Fund.

In 1765 Orton resigned his ministry and there was a split in the congregation. The theologically conservative faction led by Orton first met in a malthouse on 12 October 1766, at which Gentleman preached although still a student; later the same month they asked him to become their first minister. He took up the post the following

June, opened the new chapel in Shrewsbury on 10 September 1767, and was ordained on 6 April 1768. He married Frances Hatton (*d.* 1791) on 29 June 1767 at St Alkmund Church, Shrewsbury; all their six children survived them.

Gentleman was a popular and practical preacher, and soon gained a reputation for learning. To supplement a meagre income he opened a school for boys in Hill's Lane, Shrewsbury, in 1775. In 1778 he declined an invitation to the ministry of Weigh House Chapel, London. In 1779 he left Shrewsbury to head the academy maintained by the Presbyterian Fund at Carmarthen (situated at nearby Rhyd-y-gors). In theology Gentleman had changed his views and become an Arian, although his assistant Benjamin Davis was an anti-trinitarian. Theological dispute was rife among the students, leading to the turbulence that was common in residential dissenting colleges at this time, 'of the 23 students receiving exhibitions at the college from the Presbyterian Board (under Gentleman and Davis), at least 12 were or became anti-Trinitarian' (Jeremy, 66). Gentleman was probably forced out of his post in 1784, when the academy was moved to Swansea.

In a repeat of the events at Shrewsbury, Gentleman went to Kidderminster in June 1784 as first minister of the New Meeting, a group of Arian seceders from the Old Meeting. He continued at the New Meeting until his death at Kidderminster on 10 July 1795; he was buried on 12 July alongside his wife in St Mary's churchyard, Kidderminster.

Gentleman published several works, the most well known being *The Young English Scholar's Complete Pocket Companion*, *Plain Addresses to Youth*, and *A Short Exposition of the Old Testament etc.* in six volumes taken from Orton's manuscripts. He was an able minister caught up in the theological maelstroms of the late eighteenth century. His successor at the New Meeting, William Severn, was an anti-trinitarian, a path which Gentleman may well have taken had he lived longer.

ALAN RUSTON

Sources T. Watts, 'Robert Gentleman', *Congregational History Circle Magazine*, 2/7 (1991–2), 25–39 · E. D. P. Evans, *A history of the New Meeting House, Kidderminster, 1782–1900* (1900), 43–8 · E. Elliott, *History of Congregationalism in Shropshire* (1898), 22–3 · W. D. Jeremy, *The Presbyterian Fund and Dr Daniel Williams's Trust* (1885), 66 · *IGI* · *Protestant Dissenter's Magazine*, 2 (1795), 312 · W. Wilson, *The history and antiquities of the dissenting churches and meeting houses in London, Westminster and Southwark*, 4 vols. (1808–14), vol. 1, pp. 192, 201 · T. Belsham, 'A list of students educated at the academy at Daventry [pt 2]', *Monthly Repository*, 17 (1822), 195–8, esp. 195 · J. Williams, *Memoirs of the late Reverend Thomas Belsham* (1833), 421 · C. G. Bolam and others, *The English presbyterians: from Elizabethan puritanism to modern Unitarianism* (1968), 227 · *GM*, 1st ser., 65 (1795), 621 · *DNB* · will, PRO, PROB 11/1300, fols. 221r–223r

Archives Shrops. RRC, records of High Street Chapel, letters and completion of registers · Worcs. RO, records New Meeting, Kidderminster, letters and completion of registers

Wealth at death see will, 1798, PRO, PROB 11/1300, fols. 221r–223r

Gentleman, Tobias (*fl.* 1567–1614), mariner and writer, was a younger son of Thomas (*c.*1511–1609) and Joan Gentleman or Jentelman, of Southwold, where Thomas was bailiff in 1564, 1572, and 1604, and, according to

Tobias, died aged ninety-eight. Thomas was the elder son of William and Elizabeth (later Suckling) of Southwold, merchants and shipowners, and the clerk who entered his burial on 30 July 1609 added that 'he lived above fourscore years in perfect sight and memorie, and in his flourishinge time for building of shipps and many other commendable parts he continued in his place unmatchable' (Southwold parish register).

Tobias, by his own account, was 'borne a Fisherman's sonne by the Sea-side, and spent [his] youthful time at Sea about Fisher affaires, whereby now [he was] more skilfull in Nets, Lines and Hookes than in Rethoricke, Logicke, or learned bookes' (Gentleman, 3). In his youth he sailed to Iceland with his father in one of the four barques from which they fished by line for ling and cod. Probably because his older brother Thomas was taking over the Southwold business from Thomas senior, Tobias left that 'naughty Harbour' (ibid., 44) and moved to Yarmouth, which he later praised above all other east coast ports for 'brave buildings' (ibid., 26). Every year each of the two bailiffs there had the right to nominate a freeman, and in September 1588 the merchant John Yonges presented Tobias. Tobias never held office in the town, but occasionally came to prominence. In 1595 the bailiffs were required by the lord high admiral to produce Gentleman and five others at the shire house in Cambridge on a charge of sending a ship into Scotland 'against the Statute'. In 1600 Tobias received a bounty on a 200-ton ship. At the assembly in February 1611 John Wheeler, alderman and member of parliament for the town, 'delivered in the newe mapp of this Towne made by Tobye Jentleman' (Norfolk RO, Y/C 19/5, fol. 86), an indication of another of his skills.

Gentleman's experience in the fisheries attracted the attention of the early economist John Keymer, who consulted him about ways to stimulate the herring trade. Several writers urged Britain to follow the example of the Dutch, whose prosperity was apparently based on their exploitation of the herring fishery, which profited also the shipbuilding, cooperage, and salt trades. When by 1614 no more had been heard of Keymer's initiatives, Gentleman went ahead with a slim quarto pamphlet published for him by Nathaniel Butter of London. It was dedicated to Henry, Lord Howard, earl of Northampton and warden of the Cinque Ports, and titled *England's way to win wealth, and to employ ships and marriners, or, A plain description what great profite, it will bring unto the Commonwealth of England, by the erecting, building, and adventuring of busses, to sea, a-fishing. With a true relation of the inestimable wealth that is yearely taken out of his majesties seas, by the Hollanders, by their numbers of busses, pinkes and line-boates … and also a discourse of the sea-coast townes of England*. Gentleman calculated the costs of voyages to Iceland for cod and in the North Sea for herring, with running expenses and profit levels detailed. His concerns about Dutch incursions into English fisheries caused a considerable stir, right up to the privy council. As early as 1581 Robert Hitchcock of Caversfield, Oxfordshire, had sounded the same alarm, and his and Gentleman's efforts were both praised by Thomas Mun in

chapter 19 of *England's Treasure*. Gerard Malynes quoted Gentleman at some length in chapter 47 of his *Lex mercatoria*.

Gentleman wrote in a lively, direct style, describing 'the very good Breed of Fisherman' brought up in the neighbouring towns of Southwold, Dunwich, and Walberswick, where he then counted 'of North Sea boats, some 20 saile, and of Iseland Barks some 50 saile' (Gentleman, 25). He asserted that the Dutch view was that 'his Majestie's seas is their chiefest, principall and onely rich treasury' (ibid., 5), fishing our waters intensively, selling the catch to Yarmouth traders, and taking the gold back to enrich their country. They even bought fish a second time after it had been smoked for export, and Gentleman claims that their taunts included 'yon English, we will make you glad for to weare our old shoes' (ibid., 44). In *The Trades Increase*, a similar pamphlet published in 1615, the author, I. R. (Robert Kayll), probably referring to the bulky build of their herring busses, complained that the Dutch 'swimme like elephants, we wading like sheepe' (I. R., 38). Gentleman argues that if Britain built a fishing fleet to compete, it would 'bring wealth to the nation, train up hardy mariners fit for any service, and give employment to numbers of the poor' (Gentleman, 3). It is not known when Gentleman died, and no record of a marriage or burial has been traced.

J. M. BLATCHLY

Sources T. Gentleman, *England's way to win wealth* (1614) • G. Malynes, *Lex mercatoria* (1622) • I. R. [R. Kayll], *The trades increase* (1615) • R. Hitchcock, *A pollitique platt for the honour of the prince* (1580) • T. Mun, *England's treasure by forraign trade* (1664) • parish register, Southwold, Suffolk RO • will of Elizabeth Suckling, 1560, Suffolk RO, IC/AA1/18/122 • will of William Gentleman, 1562, Suffolk RO, IC/AA1/18/440 • grant of freedom, 1588, Norfolk RO, Yarmouth assembly books, Y/C 19/4, fol. 156v • 'Mappe', Norfolk RO, Yarmouth assembly books, Y/C 19/5, fol. 86 • Charles, Lord Howard of Effingham, writ to the bailiffs of Yarmouth (copy), Norfolk RO, Y/C 36/17/10 • J. O. Appleby, *Economic thought and ideology in seventeenth century England* (1978)

Gentry, Amy Constance (1903–1976), oarswoman, was born on 26 July 1903 at 111 White Hart Lane, Barnes, Surrey, the first of the two children of Carl Otto Gentry (1871–1949), book publisher's representative, and his wife, Amy Carr Wright (1868–1955). Born near to the River Thames, she had a great love of the river from an early age; she first took part in dinghy-racing at the locally organized gymkhanas of 1909 and 1910. In 1919 Weybridge Rowing Club introduced a ladies' four-oared race into the Victory regatta and Amy Gentry was one of the sixteen girls coached to take part in the event. The success of this innovation led to the formation of a women's section of the club, which soon became well enough known to be invited to send a crew to the royal charity regatta of 1925 in Brussels. She was a member of the crew, which defeated crews from France, Belgium, and the Netherlands. In 1926 the women established their own club, the Weybridge ladies' rowing club, of which she became captain and soon afterwards chair, a position she retained until her death fifty years later. In 1928 she was stroke of the Weybridge eight which won the women's head of the river race rowed between Putney and Mortlake on the Thames. During the 1930s she was a successful sculler and was British single sculls champion in 1932, 1933, and 1934 before retiring undefeated. With her brother Frank she won the mixed double sculling championship of the Thames in 1924, 1925, and 1926.

As one of the early members of the Women's Amateur Rowing Association, Amy Gentry was invited to become secretary and held the position from 1926 to 1938. She chaired the association until 1963, when it became the women's committee of the Amateur Rowing Association, and continued as chair of that body until her retirement in 1968. In 1960 she achieved perhaps her greatest success for women's rowing by persuading the International Rowing Federation to stage the women's European championships on the Welsh Harp in London, where the borough of Willesden annually sponsored a 1000 metre multi-lane regatta. These championships marked the beginning of the acceptance of women's rowing at international level, which culminated with the sport's inclusion in the Olympic games for the first time in 1976. In 1969 she was appointed OBE for services to women's rowing. By then there were fifty affiliated women's clubs functioning in the United Kingdom.

Amy Gentry was employed as a secretary by Vickers Armstrong in Byfleet, Surrey, and became personal secretary to Barnes Wallis, the chief designer at Vickers Aviation, during the time (1941–3) when he was developing the 'bouncing bomb'. On occasions she accompanied him to trials of the device on nearby Burwood Park Lake, turning up at the rowing club at 8 a.m. after working all night. She was also an accomplished singer, and took part in Gilbert and Sullivan operas with local operatic societies and in 'old-time' variety shows; her starring role in the latter productions was invariably a stirring rendition of 'Don't dilly dally on the way'. Amy Gentry, who was unmarried, died at Ashford Hospital, Stanwell, Middlesex, on 11 June 1976.   NEIL WIGGLESWORTH

Sources British Rowing Almanack, 29 (1977) · Rowing (July 1976) · private information (2004) · b. cert. · d. cert.
Likenesses statue, bronze, River and Rowing Museum, Henley on Thames, Oxfordshire
Wealth at death £15,882: probate, 8 Sept 1976, CGPLA Eng. & Wales

Geoffrey (d. 1093), bishop of Coutances and magnate, belonged to the energetic and warlike baronage of western Normandy who did so much to restore the Norman church after the viking raids and civil wars of the tenth and early eleventh centuries, and were among the most prominent counsellors and supporters of William the Conqueror after 1066. He was certainly of noble stock, connected with the family of Montbray (Mowbray), and was probably the brother or half-brother of Roger de Mowbray, who went to England with the Conqueror. The family resources ran to providing property for his sister as well as buying a bishopric for Geoffrey. Nothing is known of his parents, or of his early life. His later military exploits suggest that, like many Norman younger sons, he trained as a knight before entering the church.

Geoffrey was elected bishop of Coutances and consecrated at Rouen on 12 March 1049. The following October his election was challenged as simoniacal in the council held at Rheims by the reforming pope, Leo IX; but he cleared his name by claiming that his brother had given money without his knowledge or consent, and the council confirmed his consecration. He left immediately for Italy, and attended the Rome synod of April 1050. But his main purpose was to seek resources for the restoration of his bishopric, which was in a sorry state. After the destruction of the first cathedral by viking raiders, the bishops and many of the canons had resided first at Rouen, and then at St Lô. Bishop Robert (c.1026–1048) had begun the rebuilding of a new cathedral at Coutances, aided by gifts from the Duchess Gunnor; but most of the estates of the bishop and canons had been dissipated and the work could not proceed far. The family of Hauteville, whose castle was near Montbray, were establishing themselves in Apulia and Calabria, and from them and kinsmen of his own Geoffrey was able to collect gold, silver, precious gems, and other treasure, much of which must have been looted from Greek churches. This, augmented by gifts from the ducal family, enabled him to complete the rebuilding of his cathedral, which was consecrated in the duke's presence on 8 December 1056. He also built a bishop's palace, with a fine hall and stabling, and enclosed a spacious park. Throughout his life he attached equal importance to the dignity of a bishop, who needed to maintain baronial status and support a numerous retinue, and to the beauty and dignity of the liturgy.

His care for the welfare of the canons and the upkeep of his church won Geoffrey the respect of the cathedral clergy, including the author of the treatise known as De statu [Constantiensis] ecclesiae. Its author was a canon, John, son of Peter the Chamberlain. Peter had been dean in Geoffrey's time, and had often acted as vicar during Geoffrey's long absences. It describes his work in raising money, increasing the number of prebends for the canons, and appointing new dignitaries, among them a master of the schools. These schools were important in training clergy to serve as parish priests in the churches of the diocese, for Geoffrey had to restore the whole diocesan organization, and to provide a clergy with sufficient education for their duties. An archdeacon appears for the first time under him. He insisted on appointing canons for merit, refusing to accept nominations from secular lords. Unlike Odo of Bayeux, who provided a nursery for future bishops in his schools, Geoffrey aimed at training clergy for the work of his own diocese.

Geoffrey's career falls into two parts. Up to 1066 most of his attention went to his diocese. He appears occasionally in the ducal court, and attended church councils at Rouen in 1055 and 1063. His practical ability appears in his shrewd management of the property of his church; he saw the importance of urban development and revenues from trade. After he provided a stone bridge at St Lô, the improvement in the routes raised the revenues from tolls from 15 to 220 livres. Duke William certainly regarded him highly before 1066.

The second part of Geoffrey's life began when he accompanied William's army to England. According to the duke's chaplain and biographer, William of Poitiers, Geoffrey supported the combatants with prayers, but did not himself fight. He had an important role in William's coronation at Westminster on Christmas day, 1066. He returned briefly to Normandy with the king in 1067, but from 1068 until 1075 he was very active in England, where he had the dual status of bishop and baron.

The estates worth about £788 given to him by the king made him one of the ten wealthiest tenants-in-chief. Orderic Vitalis stated that he received 280 'manors', a figure supported by modern calculations (c.265–9) made from Domesday Book. On these estates he established vassals from the Cotentin and the Bessin, who had accompanied him to fight at Hastings. These men and others followed him in 1069, when he went to the relief of Montacute Castle, besieged by rebels from Somerset and Devon. The territories granted him show his special responsibilities in the south-west; in both Somerset and Devon he received possessions worth more than £80. His other most important estates were in central England. The increase in value by 8 per cent of the estates he kept in demesne is a further example of the financial and administrative skills already shown in Normandy. The reconstruction of his Norman diocese had been completed before 1066; his new wealth enabled him to send valuable gifts to his cathedral, and to add the manor of Winterbourne, Gloucestershire, to its endowment.

In the king's service Geoffrey appeared prominently as a judge and as the head of commissions. He presided over the great lawsuit held on Penenden Heath to settle the claims of Lanfranc, archbishop of Canterbury, against Odo of Bayeux. He took a leading part in the Ely land pleas and presided over the commission that settled the claims of Wulfstan, bishop of Worcester, against the abbot of Evesham. Between 1066 and 1087, he received more mandates than any other Norman lord, and only Roger de Montgomery witnessed more royal charters than him. In his baronial capacity he attended church councils in 1072 and 1075. During the king's absence in Normandy in 1075 he himself, with William (I) de Warenne and Robert Malet, led troops against the rebel earls of Hereford and Norfolk and besieged Norwich Castle. After the surrender of the castle, he remained with substantial forces to ensure the peace of the region. Geoffrey's role may have been confined to leading the men without taking part in the fighting. Orderic Vitalis commented that he was more skilled in training knights to fight than clerks to sing psalms; but though his military activities were noticed, they were not condemned.

Geoffrey was with King William in Normandy and Maine between 1078 and 1080. Back in England he served as a Domesday commissioner in East Anglia. He was in Normandy in September 1087, when he attended the king's funeral in Caen. From that time his position was complicated by the temporary separation of England and Normandy. As bishop of Coutances, his loyalty was to Duke Robert Curthose, to whom he had sworn fealty.

Being reluctant to accept William Rufus as king of England, he took part in the baronial revolt of 1088 and held the castle of Bristol for the rebels. After the revolt collapsed he was able to make his peace with the king and retain his estates; but from that time he played a minor role in England. He appeared among the barons taking part in the trial of William of St Calais, bishop of Durham, where he intervened unsuccessfully to protest that the bishop should not have been required to obey the royal summons until his episcopal lands had been restored. His last years were spent in his diocese, where he lived long enough to oversee the repairs to his cathedral, damaged in an earthquake, and to watch the new gilded weathercock being set in place on the central tower. He died at the bishop's palace in Coutances on 2 February 1093 and was buried the next day, probably in the cemetery against the wall of the apse. All his English estates were regarded as his personal property, and passed to his nephew, Robert de *Mowbray, who forfeited them for treason a few years later.

Geoffrey was well suited by his character and ability to fill the dual role of bishop and baron in a turbulent time. Less wealthy than Odo of Bayeux, and probably less ambitious personally, he preserved a balance of loyalty in his double role. Although living in episcopal state, he was on terms of familiarity with the more austere Wulfstan of Worcester. His qualities of pragmatism, legal and administrative competence, and military experience enabled him to restore order in his war-torn diocese, before ably seconding King William in England after the conquest.

MARJORIE CHIBNALL

Sources 'De statu Constantiensis ecclesiae ab anno 836 ad 1093', *Gallia Christiana in provincias ecclesiasticas distributa*, 11, ed. P. Henri and J. Taschereau (1759), cols. 217–24 • J. Le Patourel, 'Geoffrey of Montbray, bishop of Coutances, 1049–93', *EngHR*, 59 (1944), 129–61 • M. Chibnall, 'La carrière de Geoffroi de Montbray', *Les évêques normands du xi^esiècle*, ed. P. Bouet and F. Neveux (1995), 279–93 • M. Fauroux, ed., *Recueil des actes des ducs de Normandie de 911 à 1066* (Caen, 1961) • *Reg. RAN*, vol. 1 • Ordericus Vitalis, *Eccl. hist.* • *The Gesta Guillelmi of William of Poitiers*, ed. and trans. R. H. C. Davis and M. Chibnall, OMT (1998)

Geoffrey [Geoffrey (I) of Dunfermline] (d. **1154**), abbot of Dunfermline, is of unknown but presumably Anglo-Norman origins, since in 1125 or 1126 he became prior of Christ Church, Canterbury. In 1128, at the personal request of David I (r. 1124–53) and with the agreement of William de Corbeil (d. 1136), archbishop of Canterbury, he was blessed in Scotland as abbot of Dunfermline by Robert (d. 1159), bishop of St Andrews. The king's need for a new abbot was part of a focused effort, involving the confirmation and enhancement of its possessions, to revive the abbey. From c.1130 to c.1150 Geoffrey regularly witnessed many royal and episcopal *acta*, dealing with both secular and church affairs; as head of the oldest and wealthiest royal abbey in Scotland, he normally took precedence over other abbots. In his long rule Dunfermline flourished. It was already the burial place of the kings of Scots of the Canmore line, and Geoffrey's enduring legacy was a larger abbey church rebuilt in the then current Norman Romanesque style. His new church, truly fit for kings, was dedicated in 1150. Little is known of him after that. He was no doubt present at the burial of David I at Dunfermline in the summer of 1153, and he died about a year later, on 9 June 1154. He was probably buried in his abbey. His nephew *Geoffrey (II) (*d.* 1178) succeeded him as abbot. W. W. SCOTT

Sources A. O. Anderson, ed. and trans., *Early sources of Scottish history, AD 500 to 1286*, 2 (1922) · G. W. S. Barrow, ed., *Regesta regum Scottorum*, 1 (1960) · *Fasti Angl., 1066–1300*, [Monastic cathedrals] · A. C. Lawrie, ed., *Early Scottish charters prior to AD 1153* (1905) · E. Fernie, 'The Romanesque churches of Dunfermline Abbey', *Medieval art and architecture in the diocese of St Andrews*, ed. J. Higgit (1994)

Geoffrey [Geoffrey (II) of Dunfermline] (*d.* **1178**), abbot of Dunfermline, was the nephew of *Geoffrey (I) (*d.* 1154), whom he succeeded as abbot on the latter's death. Soon after, the abbey's possessions were confirmed by Malcolm IV (*r.* 1153–65). From *c.*1160 Geoffrey regularly witnessed *acta* of Arnold (*d.* 1162) and Richard (*d.* 1178), bishops of St Andrews, and of Malcolm IV, usually of grants or confirmations to churches, and, like his uncle, he took precedence over other abbots. In May/June 1163 he was probably at the council held at Tours by Pope Alexander III (*r.* 1159–81), who confirmed the abbey's possessions on 7 June 1163. Likewise he was probably present when Malcolm IV was buried at Dunfermline.

After witnessing three early *acta* of William the Lion, king of Scots (*r.* 1165–1214), Geoffrey disappeared from the royal circle until 1174, when Scottish clerics negotiated the release of the king from his imprisonment in Normandy; he was one of those who, in the treaty of Falaise in December 1174, granted that the church in England should have 'the right in the church in Scotland which it lawfully should' (Stones, 2). He probably attended the council at York in August 1175, when the convention was confirmed, and also the council of January 1176 at Northampton, where Scottish clerics collectively refused obedience to Archbishop Roger of York (*d.* 1181). Geoffrey witnessed *acta* of Richard, bishop of St Andrews, in the mid- to late 1170s, and died on 14 October 1178. He was probably buried in Dunfermline Abbey. W. W. SCOTT

Sources A. O. Anderson, ed. and trans., *Early sources of Scottish history, AD 500 to 1286*, 2 (1922) · G. W. S. Barrow, ed., *Regesta regum Scottorum*, 1–2 (1960–71) · W. Bower, *Scotichronicon*, ed. D. E. R. Watt and others, new edn, 9 vols. (1987–98), vol. 4 · T. Thomson, ed., *Liber cartarum prioratus Sancti Andree in Scotia*, Bannatyne Club, 69 (1841) · E. L. G. Stones, ed. and trans., *Anglo-Scottish relations, 1174–1328: some selected documents*, OMT (1965) · J. Stevenson, ed., *Chronica de Mailros*, Bannatyne Club, 50 (1835)

Geoffrey (1151?–1212), archbishop of York, was the illegitimate son of Henry II. He was probably named after his paternal grandfather, Geoffrey of Anjou (*d.* 1151).

Family and youth Geoffrey's date of birth is suggested by indirect evidence. Gerald of Wales, who wrote his life, says that Geoffrey was barely twenty when elected to Lincoln in 1173 and about forty when consecrated archbishop of York in 1191. The identity of his mother is uncertain. According to Walter Map, the only contemporary writer

Geoffrey (1151?–1212), seal

to mention her name, she was a harlot called Ykenai who foisted her son on the gullible young king. Map is a hostile witness: Henry acknowledged Geoffrey unquestioningly and brought him up with his legitimate children. Nevertheless, Map's account may have some factual foundation. Early authorities linked Geoffrey with Rosamund Clifford, 'Fair Rosamund', the destruction of whose shrine at Godstow so enraged him in 1191, and although later historians stress that she was a *puella* (girl) in 1174, Gerald of Wales may have been using the term disparagingly. 'Ykenai' resembles Acquigny (Eure), and Acquigny Castle was held by the Tosny family, who in Domesday also held Clifford Castle in Herefordshire which almost certainly passed to Rosamund's family by marriage. Moreover, William (II) Longespée (perhaps Geoffrey's full nephew) claimed Akeny land in 1228. Geoffrey's mother perhaps received a pension from the bishopric of Lincoln in 1180–81, and Geoffrey displayed particular affection for Godstow throughout his life, attempting when archbishop of York to appropriate Clementhorpe Priory to that house.

Archdeacon and bishop-elect of Lincoln (1170/71–1181/2) Archdeacon of Lincoln by 1170/71, Geoffrey also held the prebend of Mapesbury (attached to St Paul's) until 1173. However, apart from acting occasionally as papal judge-delegate, there is little evidence that he showed anything but a financial interest in either office. Perhaps he was studying: Gerald of Wales linked him with the law schools of Northampton, and Egasse du Boulay listed him among the masters at Paris at this time. about May 1173 he was elected to Lincoln on Henry II's orders, but Pope Alexander III, probably conscious of his youth, did not confirm him in that office until 1175, and then only under duress. By then, the young elect had already acquired fame, though not in the ecclesiastical sphere. In 1173 the Young King's revolt in France forced Henry II into a war on two fronts. Immediately Geoffrey supported his father by fighting a brilliant campaign across northern England whose success led to the eventual capture of the king of Scots and the compulsion of a vacillating Hugh du Puiset, bishop of Durham, into swearing fealty to the crown.

When father and son met at Huntingdon in 1174 after hostilities ceased, Geoffrey more than deserved Henry's joyful praise. 'My other sons are the real bastards', Henry is said to have exclaimed, embracing Geoffrey fervently. 'This is the only one who's proved himself legitimate!' (*Gir. Camb. opera*, 4.368).

In October Henry and Geoffrey crossed to Normandy; in July 1175, perhaps following a visit to Alexander III, Geoffrey's election was confirmed by the archbishop of Canterbury, and on 1 August he was solemnly received at Lincoln. Henry now sent him to Tours to study, which may explain why his surviving Lincoln *acta* are sparse in comparison with those of his predecessor Robert de Chesney, and why his personal seal appears to depict a young man holding a stylus and a wax tablet, the tools of scholarship. He certainly filled his cathedral with masters and numbered Peter of Blois, who later dedicated to Geoffrey his life of St Wilfrid, among his friends. He also gave Lincoln two great bells, redeemed church ornaments pledged for £300 to Aaron of Lincoln, made other unspecified gifts, and recovered some diocesan lands. In March 1178 he crossed from Southampton to Normandy with Prince John, spent Christmas with Henry II at Winchester, and about 1180 'not like a shepherd but with violence' taxed his diocese harshly (Map, 497). This, according to Walter Map (whose church of Ashwell owed 4 marks), earned him a severe reprimand from his father. Early in 1181 Henry and Geoffrey were at Argentan, and the pope protested that Geoffrey should either be consecrated or resign. Despite gaining a further delay Henry chose the latter course and made his son chancellor instead.

Royal chancellor (1181/2–1189) Two resignation ceremonies took place, one in France in February 1181 and one before the English bishops at Marlborough at Epiphany (6 January 1182). This latter was recorded by Walter Map (among others) who noted that Geoffrey mumbled in execrable French. He succeeded Ralph de Warneville as chancellor, also inheriting Ralph's archdeaconry of Rouen and treasurership of York, and he was given besides the castles of Baugé (Anjou) and Langeais (Touraine) and ecclesiastical and secular estates worth 500 marks a year in England and as many in Normandy. However, despite his considerable patrimony, Geoffrey's appearances as chancellor are sparse, and the fact that Walter de Coutances acted as his *sigillifer* (seal-keeper) implies that Geoffrey spent most of his time on other activities. He was with Henry spasmodically in 1182 and 1185, but not for two years does he again appear in contemporary documents. Perhaps he spent some time in Italy or Palestine, after magnates from those lands offered to Henry or one of his sons the crowns of their respective countries. A letter of Peter of Blois records that Geoffrey's goodness and diligence made several men consider him a likely candidate, and it may be significant that Simon de Apulia, later chancellor and dean of York, first appeared in England about 1189 as his clerk. About May 1187 when war broke out again in France, Henry gave Geoffrey command over a quarter of his army, and in June 1189 father and son were driven from Le Mans as it was burned by the French. They were together when

Tours fell. Henry, already ill, submitted to Philippe Augustus at Colombières, but Geoffrey could not bear to see his father's humiliation. Escorting him afterwards to Chinon, he nursed Henry devotedly, fanning away the flies which buzzed round his dying father's head. Here, learning of John's treachery, Henry gave Geoffrey a gold ring engraved with a *pantera* (perhaps a leopard of Anjou) and a costly sapphire ring having the qualities of a talisman, and expressed a last wish to see him bishop of Winchester or archbishop of York. Geoffrey actually presumed on the latter advancement, confessing later that he had used the royal seal to make three York appointments after Henry's death on 6 July (which would seem to contradict Gerald of Wales's flattering account of Geoffrey's secret hopes of a throne). Having accompanied the corpse to Fontevrault for burial, he met Richard I and resigned the seal. Eleven days later Richard nominated him to York, and on 10 August he was elected archbishop.

Archbishop of York: first quarrels (1189–1191) Accounts of events following Henry's death are contradictory. Gerald of Wales describes Geoffrey's modest reluctance to accept office; Benedict of Peterborough states that he swiftly sent his clerks to seize the estates of the archbishopric. Certainly Richard seems to have been apprehensive about the ambitions of his turbulent half-brother, and when a minority of the York chapter appealed to the pope that their absence and that of the dean (Hubert Walter) and bishop of Durham (Hugh du Puiset) invalidated Geoffrey's election, on 30 August at Windsor the new king—perhaps hoping to deny Geoffrey even his archbishopric—restored Walter's rights over York, retained the lucrative temporalities, and delayed confirming Geoffrey's appointment until 16 September at the Council of Pipewell. Here, Richard made Henry Marshal dean of York, Burchard du Puiset (Hugh's nephew) treasurer, and Roger of London abbot of Selby, men who were to become Geoffrey's dedicated opponents. When Geoffrey objected, Richard confiscated both his archiepiscopal estates and his lands abroad, thus forcing him to take priest's orders to avoid losing everything. Geoffrey moved fast. Defying Archbishop Baldwin of Canterbury, he was ordained at Southwell on 23 September by his newly consecrated suffragan, John, bishop of Whithorn, and inducted at York where, supported by many of the York chapter, he refused to install the new treasurer until his own election had been papally confirmed. Intercepting Geoffrey's urgent letters to Rome, Richard sent him north in November to act as escort to William the Lion, who was to pay homage to the English king at Canterbury, but here in early December the papal legate Giovanni di Anagni, dismissing all appeals against Geoffrey, ratified his appointment. Before Geoffrey could regain his estates, though, he had to promise Richard £2000, ratify his hostile appointments to York, confirm Durham privileges, and stomach the consecration by Hugh du Puiset of Roger, abbot of Selby.

Further difficulties followed at York. At Epiphany 1190, after an undignified fracas during vespers the previous evening, Geoffrey suspended minster services and excommunicated the ringleaders, Henry Marshal and Burchard du Puiset. Richard then summoned Geoffrey to Normandy and demanded his £2000, but Hugh du Puiset, left in England as justiciar, had prevented Geoffrey from raising the money. Richard therefore ruthlessly confiscated his estates, increased his fine, and made him promise not to return to England for three years. On 7 March the pope confirmed Geoffrey's election, thus forcing Richard's hand, but not until June were the brothers reconciled at Tours, and not until July at Vézelay, whence Richard set off on crusade, were Geoffrey's estates restored, following a payment of 800 marks.

In May 1191 on Queen Eleanor's intervention, surprisingly at Richard's prompting (from Messina), the new pope Celestine III finally authorized Geoffrey's consecration by Bartholomew, archbishop of Tours. Geoffrey's reaction following the ceremony was predictable. After receiving his pallium on 18 August from Abbot Geoffrey of Marmoutier, the new archbishop, defying the king's ban, landed at Dover on 14 September. The English bishops, stupefied at the slight to Canterbury implied by Geoffrey's consecration at Tours, appealed to the pope. The chancellor William de Longchamp, now also legate, ordered his arrest. However Geoffrey, forewarned and with Count John's blessing, escaped in disguise to St Martin's Priory, whence Longchamp's servants, after a five-day siege, violated sanctuary to drag him from the altar after mass, still dressed in his archiepiscopal vestments. Imprisoned in Dover Castle for eight days, he was finally freed on the intervention of the bishops of London and Norwich. Bishop Hugh of Lincoln excommunicated the perpetrators of the outrage, the chancellor subsequently fled the country, and Geoffrey processed to London via Becket's tomb at Canterbury amid general rejoicing, arriving on 2 October.

Quarrels at York Geoffrey was now the highest ecclesiastic in the land (Archbishop Baldwin had died on crusade in November 1190) and on All Saints' day (1 November) he was enthroned at York. However, he now provoked further dispute by pursuing a prolonged and seemingly personal vendetta against Hugh du Puiset over the question of authority, excommunicating him, after appeal, before Christmas, and at Candlemas (2 February 1192) extending anathema to all who consorted with him. Appeals flew to Rome from all sides, including one from Prioress Alice of Clementhorpe, who objected to Geoffrey's proposal to subject her house to Godstow. Celestine III, Queen Eleanor, Walter de Coutances, and Hugh of Lincoln all intervened, and Geoffrey exacerbated the situation by carrying his cross erect in the New Temple in the province of Canterbury. The other bishops, horrified at this, refrained from breaking his cross into pieces only because he was the son and brother of a king, and a new archbishop. In October the papal delegates allowed Hugh of Durham not to obey him. John's attempted usurpation in the spring of 1193 united Geoffrey and Hugh: showing shades of earlier military prowess, Geoffrey fortified Doncaster and attempted to assist Hugh's siege of John's castle of Tickhill. However, when Geoffrey sold a large proportion of the York treasury later that year to help towards Richard's

ransom, this infuriated his chapter, who also objected to his attempted intrusion of his brother Peter (in Paris) as dean of York, then (as a temporary stopgap for Peter) of the chancellor of York, Simon de Apulia, and finally (when Simon refused to give up the post) of Philip of Poitou, a royal clerk. Defiantly the chapter elected Simon themselves. Geoffrey appealed to Rome: Simon proceeded to Germany, where Richard forbade the appeal and summoned Geoffrey.

Prevented from departing by disturbances in York instigated by the recalcitrant canons, who suspended minster services and locked him out, Geoffrey reacted with characteristic vigour. On 1 January 1194 he dismissed and excommunicated the ringleaders and appointed new clerks. But Simon, proceeding to Rome, was invested by Celestine on 17 May, whereupon the canons, emboldened, accused Geoffrey of simony, extortion, violence, and neglect of duties, and Roger of Selby and eleven other Premonstratensian abbots also testified against him. Celestine ordered restoration of Geoffrey's unlawful confiscations within forty days and on 16 June took the entire church of York under his protection. Meanwhile, when Geoffrey and Hubert Walter (by then archbishop of Canterbury) met Richard at Nottingham in March, Walter carried his cross illegally in the diocese of York, protesting that he was the primate of all England. Richard, needing Geoffrey's offer of 3000 marks plus 100 marks per year for the shrievalty of Yorkshire, did not censure Geoffrey when he responded by carrying his cross at Waltham in April, and subsequently even restored his confiscated Angevin estates and reconciled him with Longchamp. But when Richard left for France on 12 May, Hubert Walter remained behind as justiciar, and that summer sent a commission of royal judges to York to investigate Geoffrey's controversial activities. They imprisoned his servants, and when Geoffrey scorned to appear before them, they confiscated all his manors except Ripon, where he was residing, and appointed two custodians of his shrievalty. At Michaelmas the excommunicated canons, on Celestine's orders, were restored to York by Bishop Hugh of Durham.

Quarrels with Richard I Geoffrey, appealing against the papal sentences, attempted to intrude first his brother Peter, and then Peter de Dinan, into the archdeaconry of the West Riding, then went to see Richard in Maine and presented him with 1000 marks and promised 1000 more. Immediately Richard restored his lands and pardoned his illegal use of Henry II's great seal, but allowed the three beneficiaries, who had now turned against Geoffrey, to buy back for £100 each the offices to which their archbishop had presented them. In January 1195 a papal commission at York headed by Hugh of Lincoln cited Geoffrey to appear in Rome on 1 June on pain of suspension. By February relations had become so bad that Geoffrey's own servants were accused of attacking Simon de Apulia when he returned to York with his letters of appointment, and on Maundy Thursday (30 March) the York canons threw the chrism consecrated by Bishop John of Whithorn on the dungheap, and unsuccessfully applied for it instead to

Hugh of Lincoln. Forbidden by Richard to proceed to Rome, moreover, Geoffrey did not appear in June, and when he expressed his grievances to the king, Richard disseised him for his insolence, leaving him virtually powerless when Hubert Walter triumphantly held a legatine council at York on 14–15 June. Geoffrey's clerks in Rome gained a postponement for his deadline until 1 November, but when he did not appear even then, Celestine ordered Hugh of Lincoln to suspend him. Hugh protested that he would rather be suspended himself, but on 23 December Celestine enforced the sentence personally and increased Simon de Apulia's authority in York.

This measure finally forced Geoffrey's submission. In 1196 he went to Rome and faced his detractors. Dramatically, their case collapsed and Celestine restored him. Heading for England through France, Geoffrey returned to Rome when he found that 'he could not find favour in the king's sight' (*Chronica … Hovedene*, 4.8), and may even have remained there until Celestine's death, while his officials, Master Honorius and Master Ralph of Kyme, administered the see. Not until 1198 did Richard meet Geoffrey, perhaps alarmed by a rumour that he had been made a legate by the new pope Innocent III, but old quarrels resurfaced when Simon de Apulia joined them in Normandy in May. When Geoffrey refused to confirm the presentations which the king had made in his absence, Richard revoked Geoffrey's recent grant of the archdeaconry of Richmond to Master Honorius and intruded his own clerk, Roger of St Edmund's, whom Simon invested at York. When Innocent urged Richard to be reconciled with Geoffrey on pain of ecclesiastical censure, the king sent the bishops of Durham, Ely, Winchester, Worcester, and Bath to arrange a compromise. If the archbishop would ratify the royal presentations within the church of York, Richard would restore him to his archbishopric. Geoffrey agreed on condition that the bishops would stand by their judgment before the pope, and returned to Rome when they refused. Innocent ruled on 28 April 1199 that Geoffrey's temporalities should be restored when he had paid the money owed to Richard, that royal clerks intruded into York should either resign or defend themselves within six months, on pain of interdict, and that he would adjudicate future quarrels concerning York. Before the letter was written, John had become king.

Further quarrels at York John restored York's temporalities to the archbishop's servants pending his return, many of Richard's appointees resigned, and the brothers met on friendly terms at Rouen on 24 June 1199 (Geoffrey against the pope's advice). Innocent also sent back advisers with Geoffrey, among these Master Pierre de Corbeil and Master Columbus. Master Stephen Langton, later archbishop of Canterbury, appears on a few of Geoffrey's charters at this time. Archbishop and chapter promised (Geoffrey on pain of a fine of 200 marks) to abide by the decision of papal judges-delegate, but when the high-handed attitude of Geoffrey's officials prompted the chapter to demand their fine, John decided to keep Geoffrey with him. After August 1199 they appear together regularly in sources,

and they were both in York in March 1200. The papal delegates reconciled Geoffrey with his chapter, but squabbles over authority and finance soon destroyed the truce with John and may partly explain his frequent visits to the north. In October 1200 Geoffrey was dispossessed for refusing to let John's servants collect the carucage (tax levied on ploughland), and he subsequently excommunicated James of Poterne, sheriff of Yorkshire. His estates were restored after he attended Hugh of Lincoln's funeral in November, but when he absented himself from John's negotiations with France, and continued to withhold the carucage, peace was again shattered.

John demanded the 3000 silver marks owed to the crown under Richard, and ordered the arrest of Geoffrey's men when he visited Beverley in January 1201. The archbishop consequently absolved his enemies in March, and in May obtained pardon, restitution, and the release of his servants when he promised £1000 to the king; but hostilities erupted again when the dean and chapter of York, supported by John, gave the archdeaconry of Cleveland to Canon Hugh Murdac, rather than to Geoffrey's candidate, Master Ralph of Kyme. The inevitable appeals and litigation followed, and Geoffrey excommunicated Hugh, previously one of his few allies at York. Although Ralph eventually became precentor instead, Geoffrey also failed to obtain the provostship of Beverley for his half-brother Morgan, and became embroiled with Master Honorius over the archdeaconry of Richmond. It must have been a chastened archbishop who later in that year respectfully received at York the fiery Abbot Eustace of Fly, then preaching the crusade in England.

Disputes continued, but with Geoffrey subsequently enjoying slightly more success. In October 1201 Innocent supported him in a quarrel with Philip of Poitou, bishop of Durham. A prolonged dispute, involving many judges-delegate, over the right of presentation to the mastership of St Peter's Hospital, York, in 1201, followed the familiar pattern of the archbishop and the dean and chapter providing rival nominees, but this time the brothers of the hospital unanimously elected Geoffrey's candidate in 1204, and although the post finally went to Ralph of Nottingham because Geoffrey had acted after appeal, it was a victory of sorts for the archbishop. The religious houses of the diocese also took a leading part in disputes. In March 1202 Geoffrey quarrelled with Guisborough Priory, and by the end of May complaints against him had become so frequent that Innocent, ordering an inquiry at York into whether he was equal to the duties of his office, summoned Geoffrey and the dean and chapter to Rome. In June the pope took the church of Scarborough under his protection, and in December ordered an inquiry into complaints by the prior and monks of Durham that Geoffrey was delaying institutions to their benefices in order to enjoy the revenues himself. He also ordered Geoffrey to institute all presentees more than four months overdue, and to allow the Durham monks to enjoy the fruits in the meantime. Other disputes involved the monks of Meaux over tithe exemption, Peter Thebert (Philip of Durham's nephew) whom Geoffrey refused to institute to Howden in 1203, and the canons of Kirkham. In November 1203 Geoffrey and the York clergy joined Philip, bishop of Durham, on Innocent's orders, to protect Fountains Abbey, and in the spring of 1204 he entertained the king at York before quarrelling with him once again. Later that year two of his servants were in the king's prison, and John subjected him to threatening measures and selective disseisins in October for being in arrears with scutage payments.

Quarrels with King John Royal harassment continued until at least 29 May 1205, by which time Geoffrey seems to have moved to Southwell, but by April 1205 Southwell was interdicted by the dean and treasurer of York for Geoffrey's non-payment of debt, and Geoffrey was also at loggerheads with neighbouring Thurgarton Priory. His charters, however, reveal that he pressed on with his diocesan duties, constituting vicarages, issuing confirmations, and even obtaining the provostship of Beverley for Alan, his chaplain. In early January 1206 his possessions were finally restored following his submission to John, on 25 January he was received back into royal favour, on 12 February he was with John at York, on 14 February he paid him 700 marks at Knaresborough, and on 16 February at Bowes he regained his archiepiscopal rights over the forest of Nottingham. But royal favour had its price. Almost immediately the king presented some of his own clerks to York livings. When in 1207 he levied a tax of a thirteenth on all clerical rents and movables, however, Geoffrey stood firm, excommunicated all who attempted to collect it in his province, and, supported by the bishop of Durham, begged John to reconsider. In response, the king only mocked him and attacked his property. Geoffrey appealed to Innocent, who threatened immediate interdict of the province of York unless the king compensated Geoffrey. John either refused or ignored the threat. On 27 May 1208 Innocent wrote again to John, but to no avail. Geoffrey, realizing that his position was hopeless, had fled to France with other dissident English bishops. His temporalities were immediately confiscated again, and Geoffrey of Coldingham wrote that he was seen as a martyr by the whole English church.

Archiepiscopal administration Geoffrey's long absences from York after 1194 militated against any systematic administration of his diocese: indeed, almost every known aspect of his administration is overshadowed by dispute. Constant quarrels with the dean and chapter and, at various times, the archdeacons of York, Cleveland, and Richmond probably explain why canons of Southwell, Ripon, and Beverley are so often found in his entourage, and many of the religious houses of his diocese appealed to the pope against him. However, there are some positive aspects. New features appeared, such as the office of chancellor (for Simon de Apulia in 1189), and Geoffrey's consistent (and legitimate) description of himself after 1191 in his charters as primate of England. In the face of hostility from Durham, the archbishop made extensive use of his suffragan, John, bishop of Whithorn, until about 1195, and may even have considered claiming the Isle of Man as

a suffragan see in 1201, when Bishop Michael occasionally witnessed in his company, while Innocent III's translation of Bernard of Ragusa to the see of Carlisle in 1203 clearly filled a gap in diocesan administration during Geoffrey's frequent absences.

However, the situation was obviously unstable, and the handful of men who witnessed Geoffrey's charters most consistently seem to have been merely personal academic friends, some perhaps masters from Northampton and Tours, who travelled with him and enjoyed his enduring favour. Their loyalty spans his archiepiscopate, as does that of Alan, his chaplain and most constant companion, who was rewarded with a canonry of Ripon and, in 1205, the provostship of Beverley. Diocesan administration in York itself was largely taken over, during the archbishop's absences, by his officials, and by the dean and chapter who, under Simon de Apulia, chancellor and later dean, and Hamo, precentor and later treasurer, became increasingly organized and effective. These men seem to have witnessed none of the archbishop's later charters. Meanwhile, Geoffrey himself seems to have attempted to control his diocese from Southwell or Ripon. His charters, which are witnessed by fifty or more masters, among others, follow on the whole an established pattern of confirmations, with occasional and relatively insignificant grants, but there is a notable increase in the number of vicarages established by him, especially in his later years in office.

Last years: a career of conflict Perhaps Geoffrey entered a French monastery during the last years of his life. He died in Normandy on about 18 December 1212. Henry II had wished to be buried at Grandmont: it was Geoffrey who was interred in the tiny Grandmontine house of Notre Dame du Parc which his father had founded about 1156 just outside Rouen. A. C. Ducarel recorded the inscription on his tomb, in 1767. The most striking feature of Geoffrey's archiepiscopate was his capacity to arouse conflict. This stemmed partly from his temperament and partly from the awkwardness of his position as the favoured but illegitimate son of a king. Few bishops had such formidable adversaries as Richard and John, few archbishops such hard-headed and assertive suffragans as Hugh du Puiset. But Geoffrey also displayed charm and obstinate loyalty, particularly to his father, to his illegitimate brothers, and to his clerks. His archiepiscopal charters suggest a deliberate policy to gather around himself an expert *familia*, particularly (with the help of Innocent III) after 1199; his patronage of scholars is noteworthy, and his bravery in 1173–4 and in leading the English bishops against John in 1207 was typical. His relatively numerous archiepiscopal charters also suggest a sustained interest in his diocese despite conflict and exile, although he made no substantial ecclesiastical benefactions. His faults were those of impetuosity and lack of judgement: but the enmity of Walter Map and Simon de Apulia should be set alongside the friendship of Hugh of Lincoln and the patient support of Innocent III.   MARIE LOVATT

Sources *Gir. Camb. opera*, esp. vols. 4, 8 [bibliography ends in 1191] · *Chronica magistri Rogeri de Hovedene*, ed. W. Stubbs, 4 vols., Rolls Series, 51 (1868–71) · W. Stubbs, ed., *Gesta regis Henrici secundi Benedicti abbatis: the chronicle of the reigns of Henry II and Richard I*, AD 1169–1192, 2 vols., Rolls Series, 49 (1867) · *Radulfi de Diceto … opera historica*, ed. W. Stubbs, 2 vols., Rolls Series, 68 (1876) · W. Map, *De nugis curialium / Courtiers' trifles*, ed. and trans. M. R. James, rev. C. N. L. Brooke and R. A. B. Mynors, OMT (1983) · *The letters of Pope Innocent III (1198–1216) concerning England and Wales*, ed. C. R. Cheney and M. G. Cheney (1967) · D. M. Smith, ed., *Lincoln, 1067–1185*, English Episcopal Acta, 1 (1980) · 'Petri Blesensis epistolae', *Patrologia Latina*, 207 (1855) · W. Holtzmann and E. Kemp, *Papal decretals relating to the diocese of Lincoln in the twelfth century*, Lincoln RS, 47 (1954) · M. Lovatt, 'The career and administration of Geoffrey Archbishop of York, ?1151–1212', PhD diss., U. Cam., 1974–5 [incl. extensive bibliography] · M. Lovatt, ed., *York, 1189–1212*, English Episcopal Acta, 27 [forthcoming] · A. C. Ducarel, *Anglo-Norman antiquities considered in a tour through part of Normandy* (1767) · K. Norgate, *England under the Angevin kings*, 2 vols. (1887) · L. C. Loyd, *The origins of some Anglo-Norman families*, ed. C. T. Clay and D. C. Douglas, Harleian Society, 103 (1951) · R. W. Eyton, *Antiquities of Shropshire*, 12 vols. (1854–60), vol. 5 · *Pipe rolls* · I. J. Sanders, *English baronies: a study of their origin and descent, 1086–1327* (1960) · D. Douie, 'Archbishop Geoffrey Plantagenet and the chapter of York', *St Anthony's Hall Publications*, 18 (1960) · Geoffrey of Coldingham, 'Liber Gaufridi sacristae de Coldingham de statu ecclesiae Dunelmensis', in *Historiae Dunelmensis scriptores tres: Gaufridus de Coldingham, Robertus de Graystanes, et Willielmus de Chambre*, ed. [J. Raine], SurtS, 9 (1839) · *Close rolls of the reign of Henry III*, 1, PRO (1902), 64 · C. E. Du Boulay, *Historia universitatis Parisiensis*, 6 vols. (Paris, 1665–73) · *Francisci Godwini primo Landavensis dein Herefordensis Episcopi De praesulibus Angliae commentarius*, ed. G. Richardson (1743), 677

Likenesses archiepiscopal seals, Prior's Kitchen, Durham · seal, LUL; taken from Fuller Charter · seal, U. Durham L., Durham Cathedral muniments, 2.1.Archiep.30 [*see illus.*]

Geoffrey, duke of Brittany (1158–1186),

Geoffrey, duke of Brittany (1158–1186), prince, the fourth son of *Henry II and *Eleanor of Aquitaine, was born on 23 September 1158. From extreme youth he was destined to represent Plantagenet hopes for domination of neighbouring Brittany, of which he became duke *iure uxoris*. For while Geoffrey was a traditional family name and the Angevins had for several generations been extending their domination over the Bretons, his birth shortly after the death of his uncle, Geoffroy, count of Nantes (July 1158), and the continuing dependence on Henry II's support of Conan (IV), duke of Brittany (1156–71), who recognized Plantagenet claims to Nantes less than a week after Geoffrey's birth, provided ideal circumstances in which Geoffrey's interests in the duchy could be promoted. His prospects were further improved when Conan and his wife, Margaret of Scotland, who were married in 1160, produced only one child, *Constance of Brittany (*d*. 1201), who became their sole heir. Exploiting numerous baronial revolts in Brittany for his own ends, Henry II was able in 1166 to demand her hand for Geoffrey. They were betrothed, while at the same time Conan, exhausted and disillusioned by perennial opposition, transferred the duchy's administration to the king, retaining for life only the lordship of Guingamp and his earldom of Richmond in England. After more baronial unrest, increasingly aimed against Angevin attempts to exert effective control, Henry II and Louis VII agreed on 6 January 1169 that Geoffrey should perform homage for the duchy to *Henry (*d*. 1183), his elder brother. The latter was in his turn to perform homage to the French king for both Brittany and Anjou.

Geoffrey's first recorded visit to the duchy quickly followed. In May 1169 he received at Rennes the homage of some Breton barons reconciled to the proposed match with Constance. He spent the following Christmas at Nantes with his father, whom he then accompanied on an extended tour of the duchy in January 1170 during which further homages were received from barons absent in the previous May. Real power in the duchy remained, however, in the hands of the king and his nominees, many of them non-Bretons appointed to high civil and ecclesiastical positions. In August 1170, while on his sickbed at Domfront, Henry planned to divide his lands among his sons: as already arranged Geoffrey was to marry Constance and receive Brittany, though it was now recognized that the duchy might be held of Louis VII. The death of Conan on 20 February 1171 did not signal any weakening of Henry's control—indeed his grip strengthened since he now had custody of Constance. At Pontorson in May 1171 Henry accepted the submission of one of the most unruly Breton barons, Guihomar de Léon, and in 1172 he paid a further visit to the duchy. Geoffrey himself spent most of the period from April 1170 to March 1171 at Northampton, although he attended the young Henry's coronation at London in June 1170, and was probably later present at a celebrated feast held at Bur near Bayeux in 1171 when, according to Robert de Torigni, over a hundred knights named William were entertained by the Young King as a tribute to William Fitzhamon, Henry II's chief representative in Brittany, who accompanied Geoffrey to the festivities.

It was early in 1173 that Geoffrey first began to participate in the quarrels which notoriously split the Plantagenet family. In March Queen Eleanor sent him and his brother, the future *Richard I, from Aquitaine, to join the Young King then in revolt against his father in northern France. Geoffrey joined the siege of Driencourt in July and quickly gained a reputation for martial skill as well as for eloquence and duplicity. The rebels agreed not to make peace with their father without the consent of Louis VII. Warfare was widespread both on the continent and in England. Normandy was invaded; Henry ordered the reinforcement of his castles in Brittany, and in August launched a powerful attack on Raoul de Fougères, a leading Breton rebel. An attempt at mediation in September 1173 at Gisors, when Henry II offered to release Constance's land when her marriage to Geoffrey received papal consent, broke down when Louis VII refused his assent. Military action filled much of the following year, and in June 1174 Henry II once more laid waste parts of Brittany.

Eventually negotiations between the king and his sons were resumed. An accord was reached at Montlouis near Tours on 30 September 1174, confirmed in October at Falaise, by which Henry agreed that Geoffrey should be given half the revenues of Brittany in cash until his marriage and received his son into homage. In December

Geoffrey was still at Falaise when peace terms were agreed with the Scots. He was then dispatched to Brittany by Henry II, in the company of Roland de Dinan, a former rebel now reconciled and newly appointed as Henry II's representative in the duchy, just before Easter (13 April) 1175. Efforts were made to cultivate the goodwill of Breton lords, although some former rebels, including Eudes de Porhoët, were dispossessed. A year later Geoffrey and Richard returned to England to report to a welcoming father on their respective administrations, and the royal family celebrated Easter at Winchester. Geoffrey went back to Normandy but was in England again for the next Christmas court at Nottingham in 1176. A sign of his father's favour was the release to him of Cheshunt, part of the honour of Richmond, otherwise kept tightly in the king's hand. In January 1177 the relics of St Petroc were stolen from Bodmin Priory and carried to the abbey of St Méen in Brittany. On the orders of Henry II and Geoffrey they were recovered by Roland de Dinan. Geoffrey, however, remained in England where in March 1177 he witnessed the arbitration by his father at London of a dispute between the kings of Castile and Navarre.

When Geoffrey returned to the continent in late August 1177, crossing to Normandy with the king, he was sent to bring Guihomar de Léon, once more in revolt, to heel before rejoining the royal court at Angers for that year's Christmas celebrations. On 6 August 1178 he was knighted by his father at Woodstock, and a brief sojourn in Normandy followed, during which Geoffrey displayed his chivalric prowess in feats of arms, probably inspired by fraternal rivalry, but he was back at Winchester for 25 December. The pattern of earlier years was almost exactly repeated in 1179; he crossed to Brittany shortly after Easter (1 April) and, on Henry II's orders, marched once more against Guihomar de Léon, inflicting on him another crushing defeat, dispossessing him of virtually all his estates, forcing a division of them among his heirs, and leaving the chastened rebel little option but to undertake a pilgrimage to the Holy Land.

On 1 November 1179 Geoffrey attended the coronation of Philip Augustus at Rheims, where he did homage for Brittany and struck up a personal friendship with the French king which eventually soured relations with Henry II, as Philip skilfully exploited the divisions between Henry and his sons. It may have been on this occasion that Geoffrey took part in a tournament at Lagny-sur-Marne mentioned in the *Histoire de Guillaume le Maréchal*. No records survive for Geoffrey's actions in 1180, but in 1181 his alliance with Philip was manifested in the armed support he and his brothers gave the French king in campaigns against the counts of Sancerre and Flanders, the duke of Burgundy, and the countess of Champagne. Probably in July of this year Geoffrey at long last married Constance, and Henry II finally devolved control of Brittany to him, although he retained Richmond until 1183.

In conformity with Angevin practice elsewhere, Henry II had created an administration for Brittany which was effective over most of the duchy. Geoffrey was the beneficiary of this. He began to appoint his own officers and, probably in 1182, dispossessed the legal heir of the county of Tréguier on the death of his father, Count Henry. Extant charters issued by Geoffrey and Constance witnessing to routine matters in the duchy date from this time onwards, but their number remains disappointingly small (less than thirty are known); most relate to the privileges of monastic houses. One famous secular document exists, however, issued with the duchess's consent, after extensive consultation with the leading barons at Rennes in 1185. This was the assize of Count Geoffrey, which lay at the base of aristocratic privilege in the later medieval duchy, since it regulated baronial and knightly successions by establishing primogeniture, controlled the inheritance and marriage of heiresses, and determined relations with cadets. Other additional evidence for the critical importance and independent nature of Geoffrey's rule in the duchy may be found in central financial and judicial developments and the creation of firmer local administrative units, but it has usually been the disruptive aspects of his last years that have attracted most attention.

The concord that had existed largely uninterrupted between Henry II and Geoffrey since 1175 was still evident in June 1182, when Geoffrey accompanied the king to Grandmont Abbey, and when they later went to the aid of Richard, besieging rebels in Périgueux. The ageing king and his sons were also together the following Christmas at Caen, but it was for the last time, since Richard revolted shortly afterwards, holding Le Mans by force against young Henry. In order to restore amity Henry II required Geoffrey and Richard to perform homage to their elder brother. This Geoffrey did but Richard refused, provoking another major military and political crisis. With a force including many Brabançons collected in Brittany, Geoffrey led his troops into Poitou in February 1183 and occupied Limoges, where he was joined by young Henry, and the abbey of St Martial was plundered in March. Fearing that Richard would be crushed by the Young King and Geoffrey, Henry II attempted to restrain them by besieging Limoges, which was finally relieved in May. The death of the Young King on 11 June 1183 opened the way for an uneasy peace. Geoffrey was brought to heel in July, when he was deprived of fortresses in Brittany, though he was otherwise left at liberty.

Relations with Richard remained hostile, however, as Geoffrey tried to enlarge his territories. Probably in June 1184 he joined with his younger brother *John in an attack on Richard, who retaliated by invading Brittany before Geoffrey reciprocated with a new raid on Poitou in August. The warring brothers were summoned back to England by their father, who attempted to reconcile them before sending Geoffrey to Normandy in December 'to govern it'. Back in his father's favour, he may even have been considered as his possible successor. Charters in favour of the abbeys of Bonrepos, Beaulieu (Pont-Pillard), and Savigny, confirmation of an accord between the priory of St Cyr and Geoffroy de la Guerche, the foundation of an anniversary mass in Rouen Cathedral for Henry, the

Young King, funded by revenues from the mills of Guingamp, as well as the assize of Count Geoffrey witness to his current domestic preoccupations, but military action against Richard also continued in the spring of 1185, when the latter inflicted a serious reverse on Geoffrey, who failed to gain control of Anjou, possession of which was now the major bone of contention between them.

It was probably in pursuit of these Angevin ambitions that early in 1186 Geoffrey renewed contact with Philip Augustus, who recognized him as seneschal of France when he visited Paris. After a final sojourn in his duchy Geoffrey returned again to Paris where he died on 19 August 1186, either from wounds received in a tournament, subsequent complications arising from such wounds, or the effects of an unrelated illness, which Gerald of Wales called a fever and Roger of Howden a bowel complaint. He was buried with great pomp in the choir of Notre Dame, where according to some accounts a distraught Philip Augustus had to be forcibly prevented from throwing himself into the grave; he later endowed masses in Geoffrey's memory.

During Geoffrey's marriage to Constance, two daughters, *Eleanor and Matilda, were born, and on 29 March 1187 the duchess gave birth to a posthumous son, *Arthur, duke of Brittany. During the latter's minority and brief and tragic reign Brittany struggled to retain its identity under constant pressure from the senior branch of the Plantagenet family, as Richard I and John continued the interventionist policies long pursued by their father. Geoffrey himself was remembered in hostile fashion by Gerald of Wales as 'overflowing with words, smooth as oil, possessed by his syrupy and persuasive eloquence, of the power of dissolving the apparently indissoluble, able to corrupt two kingdoms with his tongue, of tireless endeavour and a hypocrite in everything' (Gir. Camb. opera, 8.177-8), while the usually more reliable Roger of Howden, yet more outspokenly, called him 'that son of perdition … that son of iniquity' (Chronica … Hovedene, 2. 277).

MICHAEL JONES

Sources J. C. Holt and R. Mortimer, eds., Acta of Henry II and Richard I (1986) • A. de Boüard, 'Diplôme de Philippe Auguste instituant deux chapellenies pour l'âme de Geoffroy, comte de Bretagne', Le Moyen Age, 35 (1924–5), 63–70 • J. H. Round, ed., Calendar of documents preserved in France, illustrative of the history of Great Britain and Ireland (1899) • J. Everard and M. Jones, eds., The charters of Duchess Constance of Brittany and her family, 1171–1221 (1999) • Chronica magistri Rogeri de Hovedene, ed. W. Stubbs, 4 vols., Rolls Series, 51 (1868–71) • W. Farrer and others, eds., Early Yorkshire charters, 12 vols. (1914–65), vol. 4 • M. Planiol, ed., La très ancienne coutume de Bretagne (Rennes, 1896); repr. (Paris and Geneva, 1984) • P. H. Morice, Mémoires pour servir de preuves à l'histoire ecclésiastique et civile de Bretagne, 1 (Paris, 1742) • Radulfi de Diceto … opera historica, ed. W. Stubbs, 2 vols., Rolls Series, 68 (1876) • L. Delisle and others, eds., Recueil des actes de Henri II, roi d'Angleterre et duc de Normandie, concernant les provinces françaises et les affaires de France, 4 vols. (Paris, 1909–27) • W. Stubbs, ed., Gesta regis Henrici secundi Benedicti abbatis: the chronicle of the reigns of Henry II and Richard I, AD 1169–1192, 2 vols., Rolls Series, 49 (1867) • R. Howlett, ed., Chronicles of the reigns of Stephen, Henry II, and Richard I, 4 vols., Rolls Series, 82 (1884–9), vols. 1–2; vol. 4, pp. i–ii • The letters of John of Salisbury, ed. and trans. H. E. Butler and W. J. Millor, rev. C. N. L. Brooke, OMT, 2: The later letters, 1163–1180 (1979) [Lat. orig. with parallel Eng. text] • P. Grosjean, ed.,

'Vies et miracles de S. Petroc', Analecta Bollandiana, 74 (1966), 131–88, 470–96 • D. M. Owen, 'An early Boston charter', Lincolnshire History and Archaeology, 23 (1988), 77–8 • Pipe rolls • A. Le M. de La Borderie, ed., Recueil d'actes inédits des ducs et princes de Bretagne (XIe, XIIe, XIIIe siècles) (Rennes, 1888) • Gir. Camb. opera • J. Boussard, Le gouvernement d'Henri II Plantegenêt (1956) • GEC, Peerage, new edn, 10.794–7 • M. Craig, 'A second daughter of Geoffrey of Brittany', BIHR, 50 (1977), 112–15 • J. Gillingham, Richard the Lionheart (1978) • R. W. Eyton, Court, household, and itinerary of King Henry II (1878) • M. Jones, 'La vie familiale de la duchesse Constance: le témoignage des chartes', Bretagne et pays celtiques, langues, histoire, civilisation: mélanges offerts à la mémoire de Léon Fleuriot, 1923–1987, ed. G. le Menn and J.-Y. le Moing (Rennes, 1992), 349–60 • J. Le Patourel, 'Henri II Plantagenêt et la Bretagne', Mémoires de la Société d'Histoire et d'Archéologie de la Bretagne, 58 (1981), 99–116; repr. in J. Le Patourel, Feudal empires: Norman and Plantagenet (1984) • J. Le Patourel, 'Plantagenet rule in Brittany to 1205', c.1970, U. Leeds, Brotherton L. [unpublished MS] • B.-A. Pocquet du Haut-Jussé, 'Les Plantagenets et la Bretagne', Annales de Bretagne, 53 (1946), 1–27 • W. L. Warren, Henry II (1973) • P. Meyer, ed., L'histoire de Guillaume le Maréchal, 3 vols. (Paris, 1891–1901) • J. Everard, Brittany and the Angevins: province and empire, 1158–1203 (2000)

Geoffrey (d. 1235), prior of Coventry, is probably identical with the Geoffrey who in 1214 appears among the Coventry monks giving their assent to the election of William of Cornhill as their bishop. By 7 July 1216 he had himself been elected prior of the Benedictine cathedral priory of St Mary. He worked to strengthen his house's cathedral status, obtaining confirmation charters in 1221 and 1227—on the latter occasion the rights confirmed included the annual St Leger fair. On 7 July 1223 he was appointed a justice of assize in Warwickshire. Bishop Cornhill died in August that year, and by 29 November the Coventry monks, anxious to exercise their electoral rights, chose Geoffrey to be bishop. Ever since 1102, when the see of Lichfield was transferred to Coventry, the secular canons of Lichfield had disputed the right to elect the bishop with the monks of Coventry. The Lichfield canons now objected to Geoffrey's election, and Archbishop Langton quashed it. The monks appealed to Rome, and Honorius III nominated an outsider, Alexander of Stainsby, who was consecrated on 14 April 1224. Both monks and canons assented, but the dispute continued, erupting again in 1227—hence the licence granted to Geoffrey to go to the curia in August that year.

The bishop of Coventry, as titular abbot of the cathedral monastery, claimed the right of visitation there. However, when Bishop Stainsby attempted to exercise this right in 1232, Geoffrey resisted him, on the grounds that he was not required to accept a non-Benedictine visitor. For this Geoffrey was suspended, and although he appealed against the judgment, and in 1233 went to Rome to prosecute his case, he was unsuccessful. Nevertheless, in 1235 Stainsby agreed that he would only visit with the monks' consent. In May 1233 Geoffrey was one of three arbitrators appointed to try to settle a dispute between Westminster and Pershore abbeys. In 1235 he was pardoned a fine of 25 marks for failing to send knights to serve in the king's army in Wales. He died between 16 August and 19 September 1235—the election of his successor received royal assent on the latter date. References in Dugdale's *Antiquities of Warwickshire* to a 'chronicle' by Geoffrey most probably relate to his sworn statement concerning elections to the see of Coventry in the twelfth century; this survives as BL, Cotton MS Ch. xiii 26, and was printed by Dugdale in his *Monasticon*.   BRENDA M. BOLTON

Sources H. E. Savage, ed., *The great register of Lichfield Cathedral known as Magnum registrum album*, William Salt Archaeological Society, 3rd ser. (1924, [1926]) · [H. Wharton], ed., *Anglia sacra*, 1 (1691), 4335–8, 464 · *Ann. mon.*, 1.88; 3.90 · *VCH Warwickshire*, 2.52–60 · *CEPR letters*, 1.84–591 · W. Dugdale, *The antiquities of Warwickshire illustrated*, rev. W. Thomas, 2nd edn, 2 vols. (1730), 160–61 · Dugdale, *Monasticon*, new edn, 3.183; 6.1242–4 · N. Vincent, 'Master Alexander of Stainsby, bishop of Coventry and Lichfield, 1224–1238', *Journal of Ecclesiastical History*, 46 (1995), 615–40 · *Chancery records* [PRO and RC] · J. Greatrex, *Biographical register of the English cathedral priories of the province of Canterbury* (1997), 356 · R. Sharpe, *A handlist of the Latin writers of Great Britain and Ireland before 1540* (1997)
Archives BL, Cotton MS Ch. xiii 26
Likenesses seal, 1223, repro. in *VCH Warwickshire*, 2.59

Geoffrey de Geneville. *See* Geneville, Geoffrey de, first Lord Geneville (1225x33–1314).

Geoffrey de Muschamp. *See* Muschamp, Geoffrey de (d. 1208).

Geoffrey fitz Peter, fourth earl of Essex (d. 1213), justiciar, was the son of Peter, forester of Ludgershall, Wiltshire, under Henry II, and the younger brother of Simon, Henry II's sheriff of Northamptonshire, Buckinghamshire, and Bedfordshire. His mother's name was Matilda or Maud. The family was one of local royal officials who were minor landholders. In the survey of 1166 Geoffrey held lands of mesne lords: of Girard Giffard a knight's fee at Cherhill in Wiltshire, and, together with Hugh de Diva, another knight's fee of the countess of Clare, and a third of a knight's fee with the wife of Adam son of John son of Guy, held of Walter of Beck.

Royal service Geoffrey made his way in royal service. In 1184 he accounted for the farm of Kinver before the itinerant justices in Oxfordshire. A year later he was sheriff and local justiciar of Northamptonshire, and he heard the pleas of the forest in an extensive circuit, while being custodian of Robert fitz Bernard's land at Newton in Berkshire and of Herbert fitz Herbert's manors in Surrey. He may have achieved this emergence into some prominence as the clerk of the royal justice Thomas fitz Bernard, whom he succeeded as guardian of the heir of Gilbert de Monte in the two hundreds of Sutton, Northamptonshire. At the same time he held the custodies of the land and heir of William de Chauz at Elton in Buckinghamshire and of Burton, Norfolk, which Roger Caperon held of Hugh, earl of Chester. More importantly, he was given custody of Saham in Norfolk which had belonged to William de Say, with the wardship of his two daughters. William's father had married Beatrice de Say, sister of Geoffrey de Mandeville, earl of Essex, and her granddaughter, another Beatrice, was the ward whom Geoffrey fitz Peter married in 1184 or 1185. She was coheir to the Mandeville barony, an

extensive complex of lands across the East Anglian counties of Essex, Suffolk, and Cambridge, the neighbouring counties of Hertfordshire, Northamptonshire, and Buckinghamshire, and the counties of Surrey, Middlesex, Berkshire, and Warwickshire. The Mandeville honour owed the service of 113 knights in Henry II's time. Earl William de Mandeville was one of the justiciars whom Richard I appointed to rule England during his absence on crusade in 1189, but he died before the end of that year, leaving no children.

Geoffrey fitz Peter then claimed the barony in the right of his wife against her uncle Geoffrey de Say. The justiciar, William de Longchamp, at the wish of Say's grandmother Beatrice, awarded the barony to him for a relief of 7000 marks, which he failed to pay. For 3000 marks Geoffrey fitz Peter was then given the barony. He paid only £200 at once, but received seisin of the lands and the third penny of the county of Essex, although not the title of earl. His wife died before April 1197 and was buried at Chicksand, later being transferred to Shouldham Priory, which Geoffrey fitz Peter founded as holder of the barony. He had become a great magnate in 1190, though he had already been rewarded for his service by Henry II with a knight's fee at Cherhill, the house of Master Thomas Brown in Winchester, four knights' fees that a previous justiciar, Richard de Lucy, had held of the honour of Boulogne, and four held of Earl Roger.

As justiciar When Richard I became king in 1189, Geoffrey fitz Peter had taken a vow of crusade, but in the arrangements the king made in 1190 for the government of England Geoffrey was one of the named colleagues of the justiciar, as a baron of the exchequer and a royal justice. Consequently he was one of those whom the king, by papal permission, released from his vow. By 1190 he had sufficient administrative experience, and by his marriage baronial status, to be a prominent figure, side by side with William Brewer, Hugh Bardolf, and William (I) Marshal, among those left to serve as colleagues of the justiciar. He was one of those excommunicated for his part in removing Longchamp in 1191, but he became a colleague of the new justiciar, Archbishop Walter de Coutances, and he remained sheriff of Essex and Hertfordshire where many of his own lands lay. He was also an important colleague of Archbishop Hubert Walter, who became justiciar in 1193, and under whom royal administration showed marked innovation.

Under Hubert Walter's justiciarship Geoffrey's name appeared at the head of the justices before whom final concords were made at Westminster. With Hubert Walter he went on circuit in the midlands and East Anglia. Together they tallaged Norwich in 1198. He accompanied the justiciar on his Welsh expedition in the same year. And when Hubert resigned the justiciarship in July 1198, the king appointed Geoffrey as his successor, for by then he was a justice of considerable experience, who had begun his career in the days of Glanville when Henry II's assizes were being worked out. Indeed, he, as well as Hubert Walter, has been suggested as the author of the treatise on the laws which bears Glanville's name. Geoffrey had had similarly long experience as a baron of the exchequer, and as a local royal officer. Like William Marshal he had become a great magnate by marriage. When, on Richard I's death, there was discussion, and perhaps doubt, about the succession, Geoffrey was said to have secured the barons' allegiance for John at a council at Northampton in 1199; and at John's coronation feast he was girded with the sword of earl.

As justiciar Geoffrey fitz Peter was at first in the shadow of Hubert Walter who, although archbishop of Canterbury, became the new king's chancellor at the beginning of the reign. Nevertheless, when John was in France, before the loss of Normandy in 1204, and when he was in Ireland in 1210, government ran in Geoffrey fitz Peter's name as regent. He presided over the exchequer, and was the authority to whom the barons looked for instruction even when the king was in England. From 1200 a scutage was levied almost annually, and in 1202 and 1203 the money raised by tallages, and the profits of justice, went through the exchequer audit in the same year, which suggests that he was making a determined attempt to collect and deliver as much as he could as quickly as possible. In 1204 he was himself sheriff of seven counties, with other curial officers holding other shrievalties, which points to a reorganization of the exchequer machinery, under the justiciar's supervision.

As a justice Geoffrey was no less active. He organized three eyres in the later summer and early autumn of 1199, and himself led the justices who visited Warwickshire, Leicestershire, and Northamptonshire. In 1202 there was a general eyre, as extensive as those of 1194 and 1198, and he led the justices in Surrey, Kent, Berkshire, Wiltshire, Hampshire, and Sussex. He regularly presided over the bench at Westminster, and in his absence pleas were adjourned for consultation with him, even though there had emerged a group of regular and experienced justices who could maintain the legal fiction of the justiciar's presence.

While Hubert Walter remained chancellor until 1205, it is not certain how much he or Geoffrey fitz Peter was the driving force behind royal administration. Some scholars have spoken of Walter's 'genius' as distinct from Geoffrey's 'competence'. Matthew Paris uses the same unreliable story of both men at their deaths. Of Geoffrey he has the king say: 'when he arrives in Hell, let him greet there Hubert Walter, whom no doubt he will find' (Paris, *Chron.*, 2.559); but in another work he transfers his sentiment to Hubert Walter: 'by God's feet, now at last I am king and lord of England' (Paris, *Historia Anglorum*, 2.104). There is no evidence that Geoffrey was anything other than a loyal servant who furthered the king's interests in the administration of justice and finance, and also served him as a soldier, when he campaigned against the Welsh in 1206 and 1210. The king's presence in England after the loss of Normandy, the disappearance of chancery enrolments between 1210 and 1212, and the cessation of pleadings in the bench after 1210, give the appearance of a diminished role for the justiciar, but there is no evidence of royal distrust of him, nor of a breach between them. The justiciar could always have been dismissed, but Geoffrey held his office until his death.

Wealth and death After the loss of Normandy he had, indeed, been rewarded by the king. He was granted the castle and honour of Berkhamsted at a fee farm of £100 p.a. in May 1205, its income being £400 p.a., with the right of succession to the children of Geoffrey and his second wife, Aveline. The honour included twenty-two knights' fees held of the honour of Mortain. Geoffrey had married Aveline before 29 May 1205; she was the widow of William de Munchensi; of Swanscomb, Kent, and Gooderstone, Norfolk, and a daughter of Roger de Clare, earl of Hertford. Geoffrey also received from the king a significant part of the lands forfeited by Normans, being granted those of Robert fitz Ernis which included the manors of Hatfield Peverel and Depden in Essex, and other land in Norfolk and Suffolk, in all worth over £100 p.a. In 1208 he was given Queenhithe, and fairs and markets at his manors of Kimbolton and Morton, and in the same year he had custody of the land and heir of Werresius de Valognes. In 1211 his offerings to the king of 30 marks and two Norwegian hawks for the land of Jordan de Ros, and of 20 marks and a palfrey for the land and heir of William of Streetly, were accepted. The only indication of any strained relations with King John comes from 1212, when the king allowed Geoffrey de Say to claim the Mandeville barony in his court, but the case was not determined. Two of the sons of Geoffrey fitz Peter and Beatrice de Say were married to the two daughters of Robert Fitzwalter, who was prominent among the king's baronial enemies, but the Mandeville barony descended in turn to both Geoffrey and his brother William as earls of Essex in succession to their father, both of them dying without heirs. Geoffrey fitz Peter's third son of his first marriage, Henry, was a clerk, while his daughter Maud married Henry de Bohun, earl of Hereford. With his second wife, Aveline, who survived to a date between 22 November 1220 and 4 June 1225, Geoffrey had a son, *John fitz Geoffrey, who succeeded to Berkhamsted. Geoffrey himself died on 2 October 1213, but his burial place is unknown, though he had founded Shouldham Priory, Norfolk, before 15 June 1198, and a hospital at Sutton de la Hone, Kent, and was a benefactor of the hospital of St Thomas of Acre in London.

F. J. WEST

Sources PRO · Pipe rolls · Chancery records (RC) · *The historical works of Gervase of Canterbury*, ed. W. Stubbs, 2 vols., Rolls Series, 73 (1879–80) · *Chronica magistri Rogeri de Hovedene*, ed. W. Stubbs, 4 vols., Rolls Series, 51 (1868–71) · D. M. Stenton, ed., *Pleas before the king or his justices*, 4 vols., SeldS, 67–8, 83–4 (1952–67) · D. M. Stenton, ed., *Rolls of the justices in eyre*, 3 vols., SeldS, 53, 56, 59 (1934–40) · *Curia regis rolls preserved in the Public Record Office* (1922–) · W. L. Warren, *King John* (1961) · F. J. West, *The justiciarship in England, 1066–1232* (1966) · B. Wilkinson, ed., *Angevin England, 1154–1377* (1978) · H. Hall, ed., *The Red Book of the Exchequer*, 3 vols., Rolls Series, 99 (1896) · Paris, *Chron.*, 2.559 · *Matthaei Parisiensis, monachi Sancti Albani, Historia Anglorum, sive … Historia minor*, ed. F. Madden, 3 vols., Rolls Series, 44 (1886–9), 2.104

Wealth at death see Hall, ed., *Red Book*

Geoffrey of Gorham. *See* Gorham, Geoffrey de (*c*.1100–1146).

Geoffrey Rufus (*d.* 1141), administrator and bishop of Durham, is of unknown parentage. It is not known to what circumstances he owed his surname. In 1114 he may have been a household clerk and protégé of Bishop Roger of Salisbury (*d.* 1139), and by 1116 he was possibly a chaplain in the royal household. In 1123 he was appointed royal chancellor, an office he held probably until his consecration as bishop of Durham. While chancellor, he was regularly in attendance on the king, although his attestations to royal charters show that he frequently remained in England when Henry I went to Normandy. In 1129–30 he was responsible for more royal custodies than any other royal official. While serving in the royal household he became a patron and tutor of William Cumin (*d.* 1160), who later became chancellor of King David of Scotland, and he was also a patron of Lawrence, prior of Durham (*d.* 1154).

Geoffrey was nominated as bishop of Durham after 14 May 1133, and consecrated at York on 6 August 1133. In the early part of his episcopate he dealt severely with the monks of St Cuthbert's, but later became more generous towards them, granting them certain liberties, customs, and privileges. In his time the chapter house of the monks was completed. He granted the monks property in several vills, and (at his death) valuable ornaments. He was also a benefactor of Newminster Abbey.

After 1135, although he apparently accepted Stephen as king, Geoffrey kept his distance from the royal court. He may have adopted a position of neutrality in the succession dispute of Stephen's reign, in the hope of limiting its impact on his bishopric. The first peace agreement between King Stephen and King David was made at Durham in February 1136. After his castle of Norham surrendered to David in 1138, the bishop incurred great ignominy for failing to defend it as well as he might have done. However, he rejected David's suggestion that he should abandon his allegiance to Stephen in return for the restoration of Norham, and suffered the destruction of the town as a result. Geoffrey appears to have offered practical support to neither the English nor the Scots in the Scottish invasion which was repulsed at the battle of the Standard in August 1138, and he may have helped to negotiate the peace between Stephen and David which was agreed at Durham in April 1139. Shortly after entertaining William Cumin as his guest at Durham, Geoffrey died there, on 6 May 1141, after which Cumin tried to seize the bishopric. Cumin's supporters, who may have included Geoffrey's relatives, concealed Geoffrey's death while Cumin sought the support of King David for his scheme. Geoffrey was buried at Durham. He had a daughter, who was married to Robert of Amundeville.   PAUL DALTON

Sources Symeon of Durham, *Opera*, 1.141–3; 2.285, 300, 309, 316 · *Reg. RAN*, vols. 2–3 · J. Hunter, ed., *Magnum rotulum scaccarii, vel, Magnum rotulum pipae, anno tricesimo-primo regni Henrici primi*, RC (1833) · R. Hexham, 'De gestis regis Stephani et de bello standardi', *Chronicles of the reigns of Stephen, Henry II, and Richard I*, ed. R. Howlett, 3, Rolls Series, 82 (1886), 3.156–9 · H. S. Offler, ed., *Durham episcopal charters, 1071–1152*, SurtS, 179 (1968) · *Dialogi Laurentii Dunelmensis monachi ac prioris*, ed. J. Raine, SurtS, 70 (1880) · J. A. Green, *The government of England under Henry I* (1986) · E. B. Fryde and others, eds., *Handbook of British chronology*, 3rd edn, Royal Historical Society Guides and Handbooks, 2 (1986), 241 · A. Young, *William Cumin: border politics and the bishopric of Durham, 1141–1144*, Borthwick Papers, 54 (1979) · J. T. Fowler, ed., *Chartularium abbathiae de novo monasterio*, SurtS, 66 (1878) · C. W. Hollister, *Monarchy, magnates, and institutions in the Anglo-Norman world* (1986)

Archives Durham Cath. CL, Charters MSS, cartuarium vetus, cartuarium secundum, cartuarium tertium, prior's register II, Misc. 7195, 4.1.Pont. 16, 4.1.Pont. 15, 4.1.Pont. 17, 2.1.Finch. 1

Geoffrey the Grammarian (*fl.* 1440), lexicographer and Dominican friar, is the identity attached by tradition to the compiler of the Anglo-Latin dictionary known as the *Promptorium parvulorum*. In a Latin preamble the compiler says of himself only that he is 'fratrem predicatorem reclusum Lenne Episcopi', and that he completed the work in 1440. It has been widely accepted that this means that, like the spiritual adviser who encouraged Margery Kempe on her pilgrimage more than twenty years earlier, the compiler was an anchorite attached to the Dominican friary in Bishop's Lynn (now King's Lynn). The writer admits familiarity with the dialect of Norfolk alone, and this association is confirmed both by details of the language of the text (*werd*, 'world'; *crowd*, 'wheelbarrow') and by the predominantly East Anglian distribution of the surviving manuscripts. Three names have been associated with him: Galfredus Grammaticus, from a handwritten note in the Cambridge University Library copy of Pynson's print of 1499 and from sixteenth-century bibliographic tradition; Richard Frauncis, reported by Thomas Hearne, also from a copy of Pynson's edition; and the surname Starkey, from annotations to a copy of the *Medulla grammatice* (with which the *Promptorium* has been confused) in Lincoln Cathedral Library, MS 88. None of these attributions is at all secure. The name Richard Frauncis is that of a contemporary Bishop's Lynn merchant.

The text is preserved in six manuscripts (in the British Library, King's College and St John's College, Cambridge, and Winchester Cathedral Library) and two fragments (in BL, Harley MS 2274, and in the binding of a printed book in the library of Emmanuel College, Cambridge). The manuscripts of the work contain various versions of its name, of which the most likely to have been correct is *Promptuarium parvulorum clericorum* ('A storeroom for young scholars'). Although nominally intended for novices, this earliest Anglo-Latin dictionary was more widely used, and a bishop was among its owners. It was printed after Pynson (1499) by Julian Notary (1508) and repeatedly by Wynkyn de Worde (1510–28).

As an innovation in medieval lexicography, the work commands respect. The compiler explains something of the principles of his work and proceeds with considerable consistency. He cites his sources in his preamble, and these include most of the major medieval Latin dictionaries. His text is organized alphabetically, but within each letter division he distinguishes first the *nomina* (which consists of all word classes except verbs) and then the *verba* (but past participles are considered to be *nomina*).

Thorn (þ) and yogh (ȝ) are placed last in the order. A typical noun entry begins with the English headword followed by an English explanation and then the nominative and genitive of the Latin followed by a note on gender and declension and then the source of the entry.

It is evident that the work has proceeded in conformity with the material found in Latin dictionaries, sometimes by the reversal of entries found in Latin–English sources. Many of the English headwords are in fact phrases which translate single Latin forms. Thus 'gronyn or grutchyn privyly *quod dicitur* þe devylis pater noster' ('grousing') is rendered by Latin *mutio*; 'fylþ of mannys fete' by *petor*; and 'cammyd or schort nosyd' by *simus*. In a few cases, the English headword becomes an encyclopaedic entry for a Latin cultural concept: 'Pley þat be-gynnyth with myrth and endyth with sorow: Tragedia, -ie; Fem., prime, "catholicon".'

Latin grammatical gender and lexical structures may also influence the presentation. Two entries for *eme* ('uncle') reflect a semantic distinction made in Latin but not in English: 'Eme, fadiris brodyr: patruus, -i; Masc., 2, "catholicon" / Eme, modiris brodyr: Auunculus, -i, -o; Masc., 2 decl.' And an explanatory phrase is needed when English lacks a common term found in Latin: 'Fader and moder in j word: Parens, -tis; commune 2orum gen., 3.'

A sequence of entries is found with the verbal operator *growyn*, suggested by Latin verbs with the derivational suffix *-esco* ('Growyn rede: Rubesco, -is, -re'). But the inclusion of headwords is not always determined by Latin. The lengthy sequence using the operator *make* is only occasionally modelled on Latin words formed on *facere*, and indeed a number of words even lack Latin equivalents entirely. The author demonstrates scholarly independence too in his entry for *walnote*, where he reports disagreement between his sources on the appropriate Latin rendering.

The compiler is well aware of the problems caused by the varying competence of his audience in an English language which was still lexicographically uncharted and orthographically unsettled. In the case of words he thinks unfamiliar or polysemous, he often adds some note about their meanings or domain of use: 'Indytyd, as clerkly speche: Dictatus, -a, -um: / Luminnyd, bokys: Elucidatus, -a, -um.' Homonyms and polysemous words are separately entered according to distinct Latin senses.

Formal variants and synonyms are often handled by cross-reference, so that the headword *have* gives only a cross-reference to the form *han*. Four distinct entries are given for the different senses of the verb *strekyn*, and the last of these is cross-referenced to *smytyn*. Apart from cross-reference, a second presentational device is common. This is explained in a colophon to one surviving manuscript (Cambridge, King's College, MS 8), which warns continuators not to distribute variants such as *hande* / *honde* or *kaye* / *keye* through the text, but to present them instead as alternatives under a single heading. It is a method also employed by the compiler for both formal variants and synonyms.   J. D. BURNLEY

Sources The 'Promptorium parvulorum': the first English Latin dictionary, ed. A. L. Mayhew, EETS, extra ser., 102 (1908) • A. Way, ed., Promptorium parvulorum sive clericorum, 3 vols., CS, 25, 54, 89 (1843–65) • G. Stein, The English dictionary before Cawdrey (1985) • D. Thomson, A descriptive catalogue of Middle English grammatical texts (1979) • D. M. Owen, The making of King's Lynn: a documentary survey (1984) • R. Beadle, 'Prolegomena to a literary geography of later medieval Norfolk', Regionalism in late medieval manuscripts, ed. F. Riddy (1991), 89–108 • L. Voigts and F. Stubbings, 'Promptorium parvulorum: manuscript fragments at Emmanuel College and their relation to Pynson's Editio princeps', Transactions of the Cambridge Bibliographical Society, 9 (1986–90), 358–71 • The book of Margery Kempe, ed. S. B. Meech and H. E. Allen, EETS, 212 (1940)
Archives BL, Harley MS 2274 • Emmanuel College, Cambridge • King's Cam., MS 8 • St John Cam. • Winchester Cathedral Library

George [St George] (*d. c.*303?), patron saint of England, is a figure whose historicity cannot be established with certainty. However, an inscription at Shaqqa in the Hauran, in the south-west of present-day Syria, which commemorates 'the holy and triumphant martyrs, George and the saints who [suffered martyrdom] with him' (Budge, 16), and which can be plausibly dated to the mid-fourth century, bears witness to the existence of a cult by that time, while the fact that the name George, from the Greek word for peasant or farmer, is not known to occur before the fourth century, makes it impossible to date the origins of that cult to the third century or earlier. It therefore seems very likely that there was a martyr George, and that he suffered in the persecution of Christians which began on the orders of Diocletian in 303. But later efforts to identify him with the unnamed man who according to Eusebius was executed after tearing down the decree in which the emperor proscribed Christianity, and to locate his martyrdom at Nicomedia, where this act of defiance took place, rest on pure speculation. The earliest locus for George's cult was Diospolis or Lydda, present-day Lod, in Palestine, where it was flourishing by the early sixth century.

By the last quarter of the fifth century the story of George, however it had first been told, had been subjected to a fantastical hagiographical elaboration, which itself survives in several forms. Shared elements are George's occupation as an army officer, his defiance of paganism and its representatives, up to and including the emperor 'Dadianus', and his protracted sufferings for his faith, lasting for seven years. During that time he is subjected to an appalling series of torments and is killed and resurrected three times, before being finally executed by beheading. His exemplary courage and devotion prompt thousands of conversions, the empress 'Alexandra' among them. In this highly embellished form the *passio* of George both reflected and helped to create his standing as one of the great martyr–saints of the eastern Mediterranean. Further west it aroused misgivings through its sheer extravagance, and in the sixth century the Roman church, in decretals later inaccurately attributed to Gelasius I (*r.* 492–6), purged the story of many of its details, attributing them to heretics, and declared that George was one of the saints who were rightly reverenced by men, but whose deeds were known only to God.

Early cult in western Europe and Britain The intervention of Rome had little effect. No modified version of the *passio* of George is recorded in western Europe, where the saint's cult was already beginning to circulate—it is recorded at several places in sixth-century Francia. Thus Gregory of Tours professed to know several stories of miracles wrought by St George, and associated two with relics preserved in the Limousin and Maine. But not until the late seventh century did accounts of George reach Britain, beginning with the arrival of the Frankish bishop Arculf on Iona about 683. Arculf had been a pilgrim in the Near East between 679 and 682, and visited Constantinople. Two miracle stories concerning St George which he heard there were recorded by Abbot Adomnán in his *De locis sanctis*, composed shortly after Arculf's visit. Bede, who reports Adomnán's giving a copy of his book to King Aldfrith of Northumbria, was clearly unimpressed by what it says of George, for he makes no mention of the saint in any of his works (George was added by later hands to Bede's *Martyrology*). But Willibald, a native of Wessex who visited the Holy Land in the 720s, was less critical, and in his *Hodoeporicon*, dictated in his old age as bishop of Eichstätt to the nun Hugeburc, he recorded the impact made upon him by the cult he observed at Diospolis.

The cult of St George seems ultimately to have spread into England from Francia rather than from Scotland, especially through the links between Benedictine monasteries. Hence the saint's commemoration in the ninth-century Old English martyrology, and in all the surviving pre-conquest kalendars; his feast day is always 23 April. In the late tenth century he appears among the saints whose lives were recorded, primarily for the benefit of monks, by Ælfric of Eynsham. Ælfric shows himself aware that doubts have been expressed about the cult:

> Heretics have written falsehoods in their books
> About the holy man who is called George.
> Now we will tell you that which is true about him.
> (*Aelfric's Lives*, 307)

But what he provides is essentially a pared-down version of the *passio* in its original form, and it was clearly this which circulated in England. George's inclusion among the saints whose lives are narrated by Ælfric is only one indication how far his cult had become established in England about the end of the first millennium, in the north as well as in the south. At the beginning of the tenth century he was honoured in the Durham *rituale*. Towards its end a chapel was dedicated to him at Winchester under Bishop Æthelwold, and by the mid-eleventh century there were relics of him there and at Exeter. A monastery founded at Thetford during the reign of Cnut was dedicated to St George, as was Doncaster church in 1061. The death of Æthelred the Unready, on 23 April 1016, is recorded in every surviving version of the Anglo-Saxon Chronicle as occurring on St George's day. He was still a very long way from being in any sense a national saint, but by the time of the Norman conquest the martyr George was at least well on the way to becoming a nationally known one.

Inconsistent observances, 1066–c.1275 The cult of St George has never been confined to England. He is revered in many other countries, and not only in Christian ones. The cult which had established itself in England by the mid-eleventh century originated in the eastern Mediterranean, and it continued to develop there. By the ninth century George had become one of the great Byzantine soldier-saints and, along with other holy warriors, he also came to be reverenced in that guise in western Christendom, where hitherto he had been primarily honoured as a martyr. By about 1000 there existed a German *ordo* for giving arms to a knight, who is blessed by a bishop in the names of saints Maurice, Sebastian, and George. Following the Norman conquest this enhanced cult crossed the channel. In a set of *laudes* composed at Canterbury, probably between 1084 and 1095, for the acclamation of either William I or William II, the same three saints are invoked to bring safety and victory to the English army. Orderic Vitalis records that the chaplain of Hugh d'Avranches, earl of Chester for the last thirty years of the eleventh century, in his efforts to reform the manners of the earl's household 'told them vivid stories of the conflicts of Demetrius and George, of Theodore and Sebastian, of the Theban legion and Maurice its leader, and of Eustace, supreme commander of the army and his companions, who won the crown of martyrdom in heaven' (Ordericus Vitalis, *Eccl. hist.*, 3.217).

This militarization of the image of St George began independently of the crusades, but is likely to have been advanced by them. Both William of Malmesbury and Orderic tell how St George was among the 'ancient martyrs who had been knights in their own day' who were seen fighting on behalf of the crusading army at the siege of Antioch in 1098 (William of Malmesbury, *Gesta regum*, 1.639). The impression made by his intervention was given visual form very soon afterwards in the tympanum of Fordington church, Dorset, where George (the patron of the church) is shown as a mounted knight striking down Saracens with his lance, while Christian soldiers kneel in prayer, and subsequently in the wall paintings at Hardham, Sussex, datable to about 1135 and possibly made for the monks of Lewes, which represent both George's martyrdom and his exploits on behalf of the crusade. But there is little sign of a widespread cult in England at this time—very few monasteries were dedicated to George in the years on either side of 1100, for instance—suggesting that the impact of the crusade on his cult was ultimately ephemeral. English involvement in the third crusade in 1190–92 did little to promote it. It has been claimed that it was from this time that English soldiers fought under the red cross on a white ground, identified as the banner of St George, but the chronicler Roger of Howden, who participated in the crusade, states unambiguously that it was the French soldiers who wore red crosses, and that the English had white ones. Nor is there any evidence that Richard I had a particular devotion to St George—his favourite saint was St Edmund.

The claim that St George's day appears in a list of feasts recommended for nationwide observance drawn up in 1222 similarly rests on insecure foundations—all that can confidently be said of the list is that it predates 1329.

Thomas of Chobham, writing in the early thirteenth century, places St George's day among feasts of purely local celebration, and this is confirmed by the uneven record of its observance. At Osney Priory, whose canons had earlier been granted the college dedicated to St George in Oxford Castle, the saint's day was a major festival by 1238, when a serious riot was apparently sparked off by attempts to celebrate it. But a set of diocesan statutes issued for London between 1245 and 1259 names the day only as one on which it was lawful to work after mass, and in several dioceses its celebration went unremarked. That the cult still had only a limited appeal in England is also suggested by the infrequency with which the name George is recorded there, either of people or of ships. In the early south-English legendary, datable to the third quarter of the thirteenth century, the story of George's martyrdom is recounted without any nationalist *parti pris*, but with Gregory the Great it is another matter:

Bidde we þanne þene holie man: apostle of Engelonde
þat he bi-fore ihesu crist: ore neode ounder-stonde.
(Horstmann, 359)

The English should pray to Gregory as their apostle, to intercede for them with Christ.

Kingship, chivalry, and nationalism, c.1272–1377 The association of St George with the English nation is indissolubly linked with the purposes of the English crown, above all in war. In the civil wars of the 1260s the soldiers in royalist armies led by the future Edward I wore red crosses (those of Simon de Montfort had white ones), and it may have been as a result of that association that in 1277 the same arms, now specifically associated with St George, were made for the pennoncels and bracers (little flags and protective armbands) of the footsoldiers and archers in Edward's armies in Wales. The banners which Edward displayed at the siege of Caerlaverock in 1300 included that of St George, while three such banners were made for his son in 1322. The same cult was taken up by other members of the royal family. Edward II's cousin Thomas, earl of Lancaster, is represented standing alongside St George in the Douce Hours of the 1320s (Bodl. Oxf., MS Douce 231), and he owned at least one relic of the saint, a bone which he gave to Thomas Beauchamp, eleventh earl of Warwick, at the latter's baptism. The young Edward III was likewise devoted to St George from the beginning of his reign. An illumination in the 'Milemete treatise' of about 1327 (Christ Church, Oxford, MS 92) shows him receiving his shield from the saint.

The links he had already established with the warrior saint help explain why, in the context of the early years of the Hundred Years' War, Edward III chose St George as the spiritual focus for his military endeavours, in preference to less warlike figures such as St Edmund, St Gregory the Great, and St Edward the Confessor, who had all hitherto enjoyed the status of English national saints. In 1344 he had planned a chivalric fraternity modelled on King Arthur's Round Table, as a means of uniting his foremost magnates and soldiers in loyalty to himself. But this proposal was abandoned, to be replaced in 1348 by the Order

of the Garter, a fraternity of identical purpose whose patron was to be St George. It met for the first time a year later. Its physical locus was Windsor Castle, where, significantly, the chapel of St Edward the Confessor was rededicated to St George and the Virgin. A statue of George in armour, to stand by the high altar, was paid for in February 1351. When fighting against the French at Calais in 1349, Edward is said to have drawn his sword with the words 'Ha Sant Edward, Ha Sant George' (*Historia Anglicana*, 1.274), but it was the latter to whom his devotion was increasingly given. When the walls of St Stephen's chapel in Westminster Palace were redecorated about 1350, George was shown kneeling before the altar, alongside Edward and his sons. On 13 August 1351 the saint was acclaimed as 'the blessed George, the most invincible athlete of Christ, whose name and protection the English race invoke as that of their patron, in war especially' (*CPR, 1350–54*, 127).

By the fourteenth century the image of George as a man of war had been reinforced by the increasing circulation of the most famous myth associated with him, that of his slaying a dragon and rescuing a princess. Yet again this had originated in the Byzantine world. The story was known in western Christendom in the late twelfth century, but owed its popularity above all to the *Golden Legend* of Jacobus de Voragine, completed by 1265. It tells how George, a military tribune of Cappadocian origins and a Christian, comes to 'Silena' in the province of 'Lybia', where a dragon has been terrorizing the populace. Appeased at first by offerings of sheep, it has latterly been fed men and women as well, chosen by lot, which has now fallen on the king's daughter. George arrives in time to defeat the dragon, and tells the princess to lead it into the city, where he promises to kill it if the people become Christians. They do, their former scourge is dispatched, and George departs, to undergo his protracted martyrdom. The addition enriched the symbolism of George's cult by presenting his victory as a clear-cut analogy for the victory of good over evil, the latter being equally easily identified with foes spiritual or earthly. The point was explicitly made in the fourteenth-century English prayer which invokes George as simultaneously a martyr, albeit one pre-eminent in soldiership, and the saviour of 'a royal child in sorrow before the wicked dragon', and begs for deliverance from enemies visible and invisible (BL, Arundel MS 341, fol. 19r–v). The memorial brass of Sir Hugh Hastings, an experienced soldier who died in 1347 immediately after being appointed seneschal of Gascony, shows him spearing a humanoid figure with a dragon's head. Loyalty, familiarity, and national feeling all served to promulgate George's cult. By the 1330s ships were coming to be named after the saint in south- and east-coast ports. Froissart several times records how English forces went into battle in France or Spain under the banner of St George and with such war-cries as 'God and St George' and 'St George for Guienne'. Fraternities and guilds were dedicated to the saint. Tellingly, a guild was founded at Chichester in 1368 'to the honour of the holy Trinity and of its glorious martyr George, protector and patron of England' (Dawson, 16–17).

The defender of the crown and nation, 1377–1536 From the late fourteenth century the observance of the cult of St George in England steadily intensified. This was a development found at every level of society, including the topmost, for St George remained the patron of the monarchy and of the activities associated with it. It was on St George's day 1377 that the elderly Edward III knighted his heir apparent, Richard of Bordeaux. However, Richard II seldom aspired to military glory, and his attitude to the saint who had become so closely linked with English prowess on the battlefield seems to have been ambivalent and unconventional. By 1384 the relic collection at Windsor contained part of an arm of St George, in a silver-plated reliquary which was repaired in October 1388, and in 1394 repairs were carried out on 'a table on which is painted the story of St George' (Bond, 97). But although the king of Aragon had reported a year earlier that a Gascon adventurer had obtained the saint's head at Levadhia in central Greece, and hoped to sell it to King Richard, if he did approach the English king no sale resulted. Richard seems to have been more interested in the red cross of St George, which he saw as a symbol of the nation, and one which could in turn be identified with himself. When he prepared for his only large-scale military venture, an invasion of Scotland in 1385, every soldier was ordered to wear 'un signe des armes de seint George large' (Twiss, 1.456), and ninety-two standards of St George accompanied the army. When Richard faced rebellion at the end of 1387, his troops fought under 'the royal standard and that of St George' (Hector and Harvey, 221–3). Most strikingly of all, in the Wilton diptych of the late 1390s, one of the angels surrounding the Virgin and Child before whom Richard kneels holds the red cross flag, surmounted by a tiny orb on which is painted an island representing Britain.

Richard II's idiosyncratic linking of national cult with an unusually pacific style of kingship may have aroused discontent, or at any rate raised eyebrows. No sooner had he been deposed than on 6 October 1399 the clergy petitioned Archbishop Thomas Arundel for the nationwide observance of the feast of St George, 'who is the spiritual patron of the whole soldiery of England' (Wilkins, 3.241). Under the Lancastrian kings, and especially under Henry V, there was no danger of the saint's losing his associations with war. At the battle of Agincourt on 25 October 1415 Henry is said to have ordered his men to attack with the cry 'In the name of Almyghti God and Saynt George avaunt banarer! and Saynt George, this day thyn help!' and stories circulated afterwards that the saint had 'halpe hym to fighte, and was seyne aboven in the eyre, that day they faught' (Brie, 2.337–8, 557). On the king's return to London a statue of George formed part of the pageants which greeted him, while on 4 January 1416 Archbishop Chichele ordered that throughout the southern province the feast of St George should be a 'greater double', a day on which no one should work, as that of 'the special patron and protector of the said nation … by whose intervention, we unhesitatingly believe, the army of the English nation

is directed against enemy attacks in time of wars' (*Register of Henry Chichele*, 3.9). In 1422 the northern province followed suit, with even more fervent praise for the saint as military intercessor. Meanwhile, in 1416 the emperor Sigismund had visited England, bringing with him as a gift for King Henry the heart of St George, which Henry had kept at Windsor, and where it featured prominently in Garter processions. The emperor also gave a portion of the saint's skull. In 1419 it was ordered that all Frenchmen in conquered Normandy must proclaim their submission by wearing the cross of St George. Banners of St George were prominent at Henry's exequies three years later.

Henry V's brother, John, duke of Bedford, was no less devoted to St George. He owned relics and images of him, and is represented in his book of hours kneeling before the saint, who wears the robes and other insignia of the Order of the Garter. Other Englishmen who fought in fifteenth-century France similarly reverenced George. A book of hours prepared for Sir William Oldhall, who served there almost continuously between 1415 and the mid-1440s, shows him and his wife kneeling on either side of the dragon-slaying saint, while an anonymous poet commemorating Robert, sixth Baron Willoughby of Eresby, who likewise fought long and hard in France, acclaims him, too, as an ardent devotee of St George:

> Now holy St George, myne only avower,
> In whom I trust for my protection;
> O very Chevalier of the stourished Flower
> By whose Hands thy Sword and Shield hast wone.
> (Dugdale, 2.85–6)

By the time Willoughby died, in 1452, the English conquests in France had been almost entirely lost under the unwarlike Henry VI. The latter, despite his military incompetence, also cultivated St George. He spent no less than 2000 marks on 'a tabernacle w^t an image of Seynt George of gold garnysshed w^t dyvers stonys & perles' (Palgrave, 102), and in 1458 had an image of George on horseback made for St George's Chapel, Windsor. But the fact that Henry was no warrior may have fostered the development of another side of St George's cult, one foreshadowed in the devotions of Richard II. Not only was he a supernatural associate in foreign war, his links with the monarchy also made him a plausible upholder of another of the king's responsibilities, namely the well-being of the nation at home. John Lydgate, writing about 1430, acclaimed George as:

> protectour and patroun,
> þis hooly martir, of knighthood loodsterre,
> To Englisshe men booþe in pees and werre.
> (*Minor Poems*, 145)

An anonymous fifteenth-century Latin hymn, addressing George as the glorious knight who is protector of England, calls on him 'graciously to cause those at variance to be brought back to concord'—possibly a reference to the Wars of the Roses but more likely, since the hymn also alludes to the 'clamorous populace', to disturbances like that led by Jack Cade (Bodl. Oxf., MS Arch. Selden B.26). As government crumbled, the saint's intercession was coming to be looked for in England rather than in France.

The Yorkists who deposed Henry VI were no less fervent in their reverence for St George, whose cult was perceived as a valuable prop for monarchic authority. Although the name George was never widely used in medieval England, Edward IV's younger brother bore it, as did one of Edward's own sons. Edward himself was a lavish patron of the Order of the Garter, financing the building of a magnificent new chapel of St George at Windsor, and making provision for his own burial there. Unlike his predecessor, moreover, he seems to have seen George as a saint who might be called upon for victory in battle, so that when fighting to recover the throne in 1471 he could be plausibly described as appealing 'To oure lady and to saynt George, and other seyntes moo' (Wright, 275). When Prince Edward, the future Edward V, visited Coventry in 1476 he was greeted by pageants which included one of St George and the dragon, in which the saint claimed for himself and the Virgin 'proteccion perpetual' of England, 'Hit to defende from enemyes ferre & nere' (Bulley, 25–6). St George had remained the protector of England, and he had clearly also recovered all his former militancy. In his translation of the *Golden Legend*, published in 1483, William Caxton describes the saint as 'patrone of this royame of Englonde and the crye of men of warre', and concludes with the injunction: 'Thenne let us praye unto hym that he be specyall protector and defensor of this royame' (Barclay, 118).

The broadening of the cult of St George, to serve the cause of domestic peace as well as of continental war, was maintained under the Tudors. Henry VII claimed the protection of the saint from the very beginning of his reign (the red-cross banner was one of three under which his victorious army entered London in 1485) and he had visible form given to George's protection for his dynasty, in the panel from an altarpiece which survives in the Royal Collection, showing Henry and his queen kneeling in prayer, flanked by their children, while behind them St George overthrows the dragon. When he visited Hereford in 1486 he was greeted by a pageant of St George, who promised to 'be your Helpe, unto your Lives Fine [end], To withstonde your Enemyes with the Help of that blessed Virgin' (Leland, 4.197). Though the saint was invoked for Henry's invasion of France in 1492—'Sent Iorge protector, be hys good gyd!' (Robbins, 96)—the enemies referred to in 1486 were essentially domestic ones: dynastic rivals and unreconciled Yorkists. The disguising staged on twelfth night 1494 at Westminster, in which St George defeated 'a Terryble & hughe Rede dragun', which 'spytt ffyre at hys mowth' (Streitberger, 27–9), furnished, like the altarpiece panel, an obvious symbolism for Henry's pursuit of security.

Henry VII's devotion to St George became well known outside England. In 1504 he was presented either by the king of the Romans or by Georges d'Amboise, cardinal of Rouen, with 'a legg of Seynt George Inclosid in sylvyr parcellis Gylt' (Thomas and Thornley, 328–9), which was carried before him in procession through London, and which he bequeathed to St Paul's Cathedral in his will. The identification of the saint with the well-being of the monarch could be extended to advance the latter's policy. In 1495 the parliament of Ireland, in an attempt to curtail the violence provoked by that country's magnates, enacted that their retainers should no longer use such expressions as 'Cromabo, Butlerabo, or other words like … but to call only on St George, or the name of his Sovereign Lord the King of England' (*Statutes … of Ireland*, 1.55). The saint was similarly exploited for pacific purposes in Wales, where in 1507 a magnificent tournament staged at Carew Castle by Sir Rhys ap Thomas, one of King Henry's most influential supporters, culminated with St George embracing St *David. Henry VII's aspirations for Anglo-Welsh co-operation could hardly have been more clearly expressed. During the early years of Henry VIII's reign, too, the saint's cult continued to serve royal ends, most notably in 1526, when the reform of the currency led to the issue of a new coin, the George noble, a gold piece which on the reverse showed George mounted and killing the dragon with his lance (another issue represented him with sword in hand). Henry also took a close interest in the Order of the Garter (he reformed its statutes), and it may have been during his reign that the practice developed whereby its members unable to be present at Windsor on 23 April observed the patronal feast in appropriate style wherever they happened to be. In the early decades of the sixteenth century the cult of St George was a significant link binding the ruling classes of England to one another and to the monarch.

Popular cults in the later middle ages Where kings and nobles led, their subjects soon followed. St George did not, in fact, always appear in sanctified isolation. It is not surprising to find him associated with St Michael, as his fellow dragon-killer, for instance in paintings on the altar screen at Ransworth, Norfolk, and he is also several times referred to as linked with the Virgin, and in particular as 'our lady's knight', in fifteenth-century verses. This may have owed something to chivalric culture—it would not be remarkable if the saint who saved a princess also came to be seen as devoted to the queen of heaven—while the fact that the Virgin, too, was perceived as the defender of England, as on the Wilton diptych, may also have reinforced the connection. Nevertheless St George was increasingly seen as the principal patron of the whole nation, and not just of its ruling classes, a development reflected in late medieval illuminations showing the rebellious peasants of 1381 mustered round banners bearing the saint's arms. Such was the reverence in which those arms had come to be held that the Northumbrian chronicler John Hardyng associated them with figures from Britain's legendary past, with King Lucius, who after his conversion in 184 'bare of sylver a crosse of gowles [gules] in fourme of seynt Georges armes' (BL, Lansdowne MS 204, fol. 47v), and with Sir Galahad, who bore them on a shield made by Joseph of Arimathaea.

Meanwhile guilds like that of Chichester had begun to proliferate, particularly in East Anglia: Bury St Edmunds c.1369, Bishop's Lynn in 1376, Great Yarmouth and Lincoln in 1377, Littleport in 1378. The most notable of these fraternities was that of Norwich, probably founded in 1385. The Norwich guild was typical in its purposes of honouring the saint and his feast day, while offering prayers for its dead and living brothers and sisters, but was ultimately uncommon in the closeness of its ties to the government of the city. In the early fifteenth century 23 April was already marked by a long and magnificent procession in which the clergy and members of the guild were joined by an armed man representing the saint and by a representation of the dragon, the latter made as lifelike as possible; in 1429 another man received 2s. 4d. 'for playing in the dragon with gunpowder' (Grace, 17). From 1452, when a dispute which had bitterly divided the citizens was resolved, the fraternity became effectively part of the government of Norwich, the St George's day celebrations a hierarchically organized expression of civic unity, involving the mayor and aldermen as well as the humbler members of the guild.

Elsewhere processions (often known as 'ridings') and plays featuring St George increasingly provided the means for expressions of communal pride and religious devotion. Although they continued to be concentrated in the south and east of England, by 1437 there were plays at Chester, by 1478 at Salisbury, by 1511 at Newcastle, and by the mid-1520s at Leicester, where one may in fact have been staged sixty years earlier. A St George's day pageant has been claimed for Dublin c.1490, while in Scotland the saint appeared in Corpus Christi pageants at Jedburgh after 1488, and at Aberdeen from 1530. At Jedburgh the pageants must have been largely the work of the canons of the Augustinian abbey, just as an enactment of St George and the dragon was the responsibility of the Augustinian canons at Woodbridge in Suffolk after c.1475. The diffusion of the cult was the work of many agencies, and its consequent spread remained geographically uneven. In London the guild of armourers received a charter in 1453 incorporating them as the guild or fraternity of St George, and in 1521 the midsummer celebrations included 'St George, choking the dragon and delivering St Margaret' (Lancashire, no. 969), but although the saint featured in pageants like that which welcomed Henry V in 1415, his cult seems to have put down few roots in the city, where there was only one church dedicated to him, in Botolph Lane. And although it expanded into the midlands and north, its incidence is only thinly recorded there. Such apparent indifference to St George in some regions may, however, have been partly counteracted by the influence of the nobility, and especially of those who were Garter knights. Thus 'Sainte-George-Tide' was one of the 'Principal Feestes' for the household of the fifth earl of Northumberland, who himself attended a requiem mass on the day after the feast 'for the saullis of all the Knightes of th'Order of the Garter Departede to the Mercy of God ...' (Percy, 160, 324), and in the far north-west the Dacres, who had a chantry dedicated to the saint in Lanercost Priory, may likewise have done something to spread awareness of his cult; hence, perhaps, the carving of St George and the dragon in Carlisle Castle, executed about 1500.

Relics of St George are recorded as far afield as Haltemprice, a small Augustinian priory in the East Riding of Yorkshire, which claimed to have an arm (one of several). But most were found further south. The guild chapel in Norwich Cathedral also claimed to have an arm, and other relics were recorded at Lincoln, Yarmouth, London, and Salisbury, as well as Windsor, where there was a notable collection and where pilgrims could apparently obtain cheap badges representing the saint in combat with the dragon. The pattern of distribution is in keeping with evidence which suggests that on the whole the cult of St George intensified in the south and east of England in the later middle ages—in the areas, that is, which contributed most to, and were most affected by, Anglo-French conflict—rather than spreading into areas in which it was previously little known. It may be significant that it was in faraway Manchester that in 1421 Thomas, fifth Baron de la Warr, 'being partly a French man and partly an Englishman', was said to have converted St Mary's Church into a college dedicated 'to S. Dionyse, the patron of France, and S. George, the patron saint of England' (Arnold-Foster, 513). It is hard to imagine so eirenic a dedication closer to the battlelines.

Plays seem to have played an important part in spreading the cult of St George. In 1490 the chaplain of the guild of St George at New Romney went to Lydd in order to inform himself about the latter town's play of the saint (staged since at least 1456), so that it could be performed at home, while in 1511 no fewer than twenty-eight Cambridgeshire townships united to stage a play of St George at Bassingbourn. Plays and processions continued well into the 1530s, just as images of the saint went on being refurbished or replaced. In 1531 the churchwardens of Morebath in Devon recorded their contract with Thomas Glasse, how 'he schall make us a new iorge & a new horse: to our dragon to hys one proper coste & charge' (Wasson, 208–9). By this time the saint's name had long been given to inns as well as ships, starting no later than 1402, when the Byzantine emperor's ambassadors were entertained at the sign of St George in Lombard Street, London. In 1524 the third earl of Kent died in this same inn. Forty years earlier a hostelry named 'le George' had been recorded in St Albans. The foundation in 1537 of a guild of St George at Chester for the encouragement of shooting suggests that by then the saint's cult had become a secure, and increasingly familiar, element in England's social and religious life.

The Reformation and St George By the 1530s, however, the cults of all non-scriptural saints were beginning to come under pressure from humanist disdain and Reformist criticism, either as pre-Christian survivals or as unwarranted additions to the sum of religious practice. Their existence was often challenged, their intercessory role rejected. Erasmus denounced soldiers who called on St George, comparing them with pagan devotees of Hercules, while Martin Luther later regarded the saint as an allegorical rather than a historical figure. It was hardly to be expected that St George would be proscribed while Henry

VIII was king—the posthumous inventory of his possessions records pictures, effigies, and embroideries of the saint, often richly wrought, for instance 'a Table of wall nuttree with the picture of Seyncte George on horsebacke raised with liquid golde and silver' (Starkey, 238). In 1536 St George's day was preserved as a high holy day. Nevertheless there were signs of diminishing reverence, ominous for the future. At Canterbury, for instance, the traditional St George's day procession was prohibited in 1538 for contravening that year's royal injunctions against 'feigned images … abused with pilgrimages or offering of anything made thereunto' (*English Historical Documents, 1485–1558*, 812), and order was given for the destruction of the saint's image, albeit in the teeth of protests by the churchwarden. Elsewhere, however, the cult still attracted devotion, as at Norwich, where in 1543 the old celebrations persisted, with agreement 'that the Georg' shalhave xs. & the berer of the dragon ijs. this yeer for ther' ffeez' (Grace, 149). Perhaps at this point it helped St George that he had increasingly come to be perceived as a destroyer of idols, as well as a dragon-slayer.

But with the death of Henry VIII in 1547, St George was left largely without earthly defenders in England. It was a sign of things soon to come that when the young Edward VI processed through London to his coronation he was met at the Little Conduit in Cheap by the saint on horseback, ready to deliver a speech promising to defend the new king as he had protected his ancestors, 'but for Lacke of Time it could not be done, his Grace made such Speed' (Leland, 4.319). Although it may have been Edward's advisers who on this occasion decided that St George's intercession was not worth having, the king himself soon came to share their views. On 23 April 1550, according to the evangelical Edward Underhill, he asked the Garter knights assembled at Greenwich, 'My Lords, I pray you what saint is S. George that we heere so honour him?' Lord Treasurer Winchester responded with a paraphrase of the *Golden Legend*, telling how George 'out with his sword, and ran the dragon through with his speare', to which the king, barely able to speak for laughter, rejoined '"I pray you, my lord, and what did he with his sword the while?" "That I cannot tell your Majestie", said he. And so an end of that question of good S. George' (Nichols, *Narratives*, 323–4).

By this time the traditional cults of saints like George were withering throughout England, as the evangelically inspired governments of the dukes of Somerset and Northumberland successively applied themselves to purging the realm of popish superstitions. In this they were increasingly influenced by the radical theology of Geneva, and to John Calvin St George was not even an allegory, but rather a spectre or even a 'bug'. In August 1547 royal injunctions forbade all processions, and so ended the 'ridings' in which the saint had so often appeared. The Chantries Act at the end of that year abolished the fraternities which had supported his cult. At Leicester the churchwardens of St Martin's sold for 12d. the horse on which George had ridden. At Ludlow the image of the saint fetched 18d., the dragon just 7d. At York the corporation was incredulous that the government should intend to abolish the guild dedicated to the national saint, and made ineffective representations to Westminster. At Norwich the fraternity of St George was saved from dissolution by a charter of Henry V making it a perpetual community, but its character changed markedly; it became instead the 'company and citizens of St George', a name chosen to distance it from the now proscribed doctrine of purgatory, while its annual festivities were severely curtailed. The reformers were determined that the saints should not receive the reverence due to God and Christ alone, and in 1548, in a treatise on the ten commandments published at Zürich, the radical John Hooper rejoiced accordingly 'that Englishmen hath resigned St George's usurped title to the living God, the God of battle' (Hooper, 314).

The saints still had defenders, but the latter did not always do much to advance their cause. In May 1547 Stephen Gardiner, the conservative bishop of Winchester, defending images as an aid to the unlettered, observed how 'he that cannot read the scripture written about the King's great seal, yet he can read St George on horseback on the one side, and the King sitting in his majesty on the other side'. Gleefully Somerset pointed out how 'As the image testifieth, the King's image is on both the sides … If it were St George, my lord, where is his spear and dragon?' Gardiner's lame response, that 'I uttered the common language I was brought up in, after the old sort', though it bears witness to popular perceptions of St George, would only have confirmed the protector in his belief that the saint was a superstitious icon best dispensed with (Nichols, *Literary Remains*, 594–5). St George's day still had red-letter status in the kalendar of the 1549 Book of Common Prayer, but was demoted to black letters in that of 1552, when Bishop Nicholas Ridley also successfully prohibited its observance in London. Even at Windsor, where the Order of the Garter had long held a place at the very centre of the English cult of St George, the latter's position was steadily undermined. His images and relics in the Royal Collection were sold in instalments, like the 'Little plate of golde where in Sainct George's harte', sold in 1548/9, and the 'Ymage of Sainct George' disposed of a year later (Bond, 203, 205). And in 1550/51 the king himself drafted new statutes effectively ending the saint's association with the order. To prevent the honour due to God being given to 'a creature', the order's name was to be formally changed from that of St George to 'th'ordre of the gartier or defence of the trueth', while its emblem was no longer to be a representation of the saint, but 'a horsman graven, holding in one hand a sweard, pearsing a boke, on wich shall be written *Verbum Dei*' (Nichols, *Literary Remains*, 521–3). Not all the proposed details survived reconsideration, but when revised statutes were finally promulgated on 17 March 1553, the Garter was no longer under the protection of St George.

Edward VI's new statutes for the Garter, like his reforms in religion generally, were quickly abrogated after the accession of Mary in 1553. The former St George's day cere-monies were revived at such places as Chester, York, and Norwich (though on a different day at the last), images restored in churches in several counties. On 23 April 1554 the queen herself processed with the knights of the Garter, in a ceremony which concluded with the election of her future husband, Philip of Spain, to their number. Twelve months later she 'lokyd out of a cassement' while Philip and the other knights 'went in their robes, on procession, with three crosses', at Hampton Court (*Diary of Henry Machyn*, 85). But in 1558 Mary's death once more called the status of St George into question. It was in keeping with Elizabeth I's cautious position on religion that he should have been a red-letter saint in the 1559 reissue of the prayer book, and that his feast should have been named as a holy day in a list promulgated in 1560. But a year later, as the cause of reform prevailed, he was again reduced to black lettering. In the calendar which John Foxe composed for the 1563 edition of his *Acts and Monuments*, however, St George retained a place, albeit now surrounded by Reformist luminaries like Wyclif, Erasmus, and Luther—he and Mary Magdalene were the only non-apostolic saints from the Catholic calendar to do so. It is hard not to believe that it was his role as national saint that had preserved his standing.

Survivals and divergencies, 1558–1660 In the years after Elizabeth's accession, attitudes to St George developed along lines which lasted for centuries. Increasingly under pressure from the 1530s onwards, the late medieval cult effectively broke in two; the trappings of religion continued to support a court cult focused on the monarch and the Order of the Garter, while nationalist feeling and secular narratives inspired the development of an image of George as an essentially lay representative of England. But between the images of St George shaped respectively by royal policy and popular culture there lay a theological battleground, for the Catholic religion which before the Reformation had held these elements together now served instead to keep them apart, as the spokesmen for a new church establishment continued to attack the remains of its predecessor. In the eyes of militant protestants, intent on purging the realm of the relics of popery, George's traditional position as patron of England was irrelevant, while efforts to promote him as a way of enhancing the image of the monarch merely associated the crown with superstition and worse. The connection was to be ultimately disastrous for king and saint together. Attempts to bridge the religious gap, and to give St George a new standing as a specifically protestant saint, usually enjoyed only limited and temporary success.

For Queen Elizabeth, the Garter and St George, like much else, were primarily aids to her own glorification. Garter feasts were celebrated in lavish style, but ceased to be merely private ceremonies for courtiers and aristocrats; held at Greenwich or Whitehall instead of Windsor, the processions of the knights became magnificent public rituals which drew large crowds, and in the process exalted the image of the ruler who was sovereign of the order—about 1575 Elizabeth had herself portrayed in that capacity. It remained customary, moreover, for knights of the order who were unable to attend the annual Garter feasts to celebrate St George's day, with all the splendour at their disposal, wherever they happened to be (the earl of Essex did so at Dublin in 1599), thereby further advertising the greatness of the monarch and her association with the saint. Such a development chimed well with the self-conscious revival of chivalry at court, proclaiming Elizabeth to be a ruler of time-honoured qualities, not least in being sustained by religion and by the valour and devotion of her subjects. One of her roles was that of leader of a protestant nation in war, and here she could associate her own image with that of St George the dragon-slayer (perhaps influenced by contemporary Dutch engravings of William the Silent in the same role), quelling an enemy easily identified with militant Catholicism. It was in this context that the writer George Whetstone, who served in the Netherlands against Spain in the mid-1580s, addressed *The Honorable Reputation of a Souldier* (1585) to 'the right valiant gentlemen & souldiers, that are, or shalbe Armed under the Ensigne of Sainct George', and urged on his countrymen in verses which begin:

> God with S. George, Allon, brave Gentlemen,
> Set Speares in rest, renew your auncient fame.
> (sig. Aiiii)

It was against this background that St George made his first and arguably only appearance in a major work of creative literature. Book 1 of Edmund Spenser's *The Faerie Queene* (1590, revised edition 1596) is largely devoted to the adventures and misadventures of the Red Cross Knight, specifically identified by Contemplation, in the guise of an aged holy man, with St George:

> thou Saint George shalt called bee,
> Saint George of mery England, the signe of victoree.
> (canto 10.61)

Although he drew on earlier sources, most obviously the *Golden Legend*, Spenser presents George as a native Englishman, stolen at birth by 'a Faerie'. But there the similarities with contemporary romances end, as Spenser develops his learned and many-layered allegory. The Red Cross Knight is indeed St George, but he is many other things too, for the allegory is enriched as well as complicated by its kaleidoscopic quality, making it possible to see the knight, variously or simultaneously, as the type of the true-born Englishman, as Everyman, as Christian knighthood defending the church, as holiness, and even as Christ. Similarly the adventures in which he is assailed by the forces of sin and death represent at one and the same time the resistance of protestant righteousness to Catholic aggression and the tests faced by the Christian soul in pursuit of salvation, for either of which the knight's overthrow of the great dragon on the third day of their fight provides an appropriate conclusion.

References to Queen Elizabeth, who herself appears in several allegorical guises, and to the Order of the Garter, and sometimes to the two of them together, as when Una describes how, hearing of:

That noble order hight of Maidenhed,
Forthwith to court of Gloriane I sped,
Of Gloriane great Queene of glory bright,
(canto 7.46)

further associate Spenser's poem with the world of
courtly chivalry, of which St George formed an emblematic part. After 1603 he continued in that role. Shortly
before James VI became king of England, he compared the
unruliness of his Scottish subjects with the security of
English government: 'Saint george surelie rydes a
towardlie rydding horse, quhaire I ame daylie burstin in
daunting a wylde unrulie coalte' (Bruce, 31–2). Once
safely mounted alongside St George, James I presided over
ever more lavish Garter celebrations, while the saint's
association with them became still closer. The subtitle of
Tristram White's *The Martyrdome of Saint George of Cappadocia* (1614) describes the latter as 'Titular patron of England
and of the most Noble Order of the Garter'. In public ceremonies away from court, too, George appeared as a friend
of monarchy. With other knights and a dragon he took
part in May pageants at Wells in 1607, and again six years
later in entertainments provided for Queen Anne. At
Chester, where there had been plays of St George in the
early fifteenth century, he appeared with a lively dragon
in a procession staged to greet Prince Henry, and was
saluted by 'Rumor', in verses provided by Richard Davies,
as the symbol of military valour:

So Britaines, when they fight with cheere, they say,
'God and Saint George for England!' to this day.
(Nichols, *Progresses*, 2.30–31)

After 1625 St George became wellnigh overtly the patron of Charles I. In keeping with the latter's more cere-
monious style of kingship, the Garter feasts became less public; moved back to Windsor, they were conducted in an
ordered style akin to Laudian church ritual. In the same
spirit St George was given a place in the calendar of *Collections of Private Devotions* (1627), a primer devised by John
Cosin for the use of court ladies. The monarch's personal
identification with the saint received spectacular visual
expression in Sir Peter Paul Rubens's *Landscape with St
George and the Dragon* of 1629/30 (Royal Collection), in
which the victorious George, an idealized representation
of King Charles, presents his sword to a no less romanti-
cized Queen Henrietta Maria after overthrowing the
dragon on the banks of the Thames. So close did the connection between saint and king become that impugning
the one was commonly regarded as derogatory by the
other. Thus in 1634, according to John Aubrey, the controversialist Daniel Featley was 'brought upon his knees'
before Archbishop Laud for having denied the existence
of St George (Aubrey, 68–9), and a similar charge was
brought against William Prynne.

The multiplication of such attacks called forth the first
English defence of St George, in Peter Heylyn's *History of
that Most Famous Saynt and Souldier of Christ St George of Cappadocia* (1631, enlarged edition 1633); significantly it had
two dedications, one to King Charles and the other to the
Order of the Garter. In a work of wide-ranging learning,
drawing upon classical, patristic, and contemporary

sources, Heylyn is principally concerned to establish the
historicity of St George, against those who proclaim him a
mythical or allegorical figure. This determination sometimes leads him into strange positions; thus he concedes
that the story of George and the dragon, as narrated by
Jacobus de Voragine, is so close to that of Perseus and
Andromeda as told by Ovid, 'that were the names
changed, and the occasion altered; we might with good
reason affirme it for the same', yet declines to rule out the
possibility of a dragon, because 'that in times before us,
there have been Dragons, Serpentine creatures of excessive bulke, and no lesse danger, is a thing evident in the
best writers' (Heylyn, 14–16, 19). But though he concedes
that the legend of the saint 'hath in it many vaine and
grosse absurdities' Heylyn argues steadfastly that this is
no good reason for declaring that George is himself fictitious (ibid., 56). Many leading English clergymen and theologians would have disagreed. John Boys, dean of Canterbury, and the famous Cambridge theologian William Perkins were among those whom Heylyn assailed, but the
most formidable of his antagonists was certainly the radical puritan John Rainolds, whose *De Romanae ecclesiae
idolatria* had appeared in 1596. For Rainolds, following Calvin, George is merely a figure of fantasy, at best an allegory. The arguments for his existence propounded by Cardinal Robert Bellarmine, which largely anticipated those
of Heylyn, are dismissed as fallacious. In so far as there
had ever been a historical George, he was no orthodox
martyr but rather the Arian bishop of Alexandria lynched
by his flock in 363. Several later writers followed Rainolds
in rejecting the saint, though more often on theological
than historical grounds. Thus for the poet George Wither
in 1623, 'Jesus Christ is the true Saint George' (Wilson,
116–17).

Puritan hostility to St George was apt to make itself felt
outside the worlds of the court and of theological debate.
That the May games staged round London in 1559 featured
George and the dragon is a sign that the saint had retained
a place in popular culture, albeit one largely shorn of formal religious affiliations. Even before the Reformation
George seems to have been celebrated in towns and villages at least as much as a hero of romance, the dragon-
killer who rescued a princess, as a Christian martyr. At
Bassingbourn, where in 1511 he appeared in both capacities, the existence of playbooks (also attested at Lydd in
1532/3) helps to explain how the legend was transmitted.
The *Satires* of Joseph Hall attest its survival in the late
1590s, with a list of 'forworne tales' including:

Saint Georges Sorrell, or his crosse of blood,
Arthurs round Board, or Caledonian wood,
Or holy battels of bold Charlemaine.
(Hall, 93–4)

Earlier in that decade Shakespeare had alluded to celebratory bonfires—'Bonfires in France forthwith I am to make,
To keep our great Saint George's feast withal' (*1 Henry VI*,
I.i, 153–4)—and also to inn-signs—'Saint George that
swinged the dragon, and e'er since Sits on's horseback at
mine hostess' door' (*King John*, II.i, 288–9). Such signs had
so proliferated that 'Saint George on horseback' had

become a synonym for immobility, and by inference, use-lessness: 'An idle justice of the peace is like the picture of Saint George upon a signe-post with his sword drawne to no purpose' (Tilley, 581). But the saint's patriotic associ-ation, already given expression by Whetstone, survived such disrespectful treatment, to be memorably encapsu-lated in the war-cry 'God for Harry! England and Saint George!' (*Henry V*, III.i, 34).

Internal evidence dates *Henry V* to 1599. By then there had appeared the book that more than any other recast the legend of St George into the form in which it was thereafter transmitted in popular culture. Despite its title, *The Famous Historie of the Seaven Champions of Christendome* (1596–7) by Richard Johnson is primarily concerned with the deeds of St George, later assisted by his sons. The evi-dence suggests that Johnson drew on earlier romances, both of the saint and of other legendary figures like Tris-tan, but took the shape of his narrative primarily from the early fourteenth-century tale of Bevis of Hampton, a lengthy saga of aristocratic adventure in foreign parts which was first printed in 1500. In Johnson's remarkably unsubtle narrative his George, like Spenser's, is an Eng-lishman, born by caesarean section at Coventry to Albert, lord high steward of England, and his royal wife. Having escaped from the witch who stole him at birth, George sets out on a career of knight-errantry. He soon kills a dragon in Egypt and rescues the Princess Sabra, but declines to marry her before he has fulfilled his chivalric mission, a process entailing several years of mayhem and slaughter over much of central Europe and the Middle East. His victims include a number of giants and wild beasts, but are more often either black men or pagans, sometimes both. But although Johnson several times describes George as the champion of Christendom, the latter's religious zeal is less in evidence than his anxiety to protect virgins from rape, a threat sometimes described in near-pornographic detail. Eventually George returns to England, where he succumbs to the sting of a dragon he has killed on Dunsmore Heath outside Coventry, where-upon the king decrees his commemoration on 23 April, 'naming it S Georges day, upon which day he was most solemnly interred in the Citie where he was borne', and also 'that the Patron of the Land should be named S George, our Christian Champion' (Johnson, sig. Cc *verso*).

The saint who was acclaimed at Chester in 1610 as a native Englishman, and as renowned not for his martyr-dom but for killing the dragon and quelling the heathen, could have derived from either Johnson or Spenser. Nor is it possible to say whether it was tradition or monarchism which after 1603 led to the gilded figure of the saint mak-ing intermittent appearances in civic pageants at Nor-wich, after he had been excluded from them since 1558, or to the mysterious custom reported from Morpeth in Northumberland for a young man chosen to represent the saint to come to church, suitably attended, on 23 April, and at the creed 'stand up and draw his sword' (Lanca-shire, no. 1190). But there can be no doubt that, away from the court, it was Johnson's lurid romance, as transmitted

through plays and chapbooks, which did most to main-tain the position of St George in popular culture. There may have been a play of 'St George for England' by Went-worth Smith as early as 1603; there was certainly a drama-tization of Johnson's book by John Kirke no later than 1638. Chapbooks containing massively abridged versions of the *Seaven Champions*, and sometimes a ballad of St George as well, circulated in huge numbers, and were surely the source of the story which John Bunyan later rebuked himself for having enjoyed in his misspent youth: 'give me a Ballad, a News-Book, George on horse-back or Bevis of Southampton' (Spufford, 7). In this format Johnson's romance provided the basis for still further popularization of St George, for it has been convincingly argued that chapbooks were the principal source of the later mummers' plays.

Despite such varied support, St George's standing remained precarious. Among puritans and intellectuals his allegorical treatment by Spenser may well have helped to undermine respect for him as a historical figure, and his identification with crown and court was potentially equally damaging as the Stuart monarchy faced increas-ing hostility, in both England and Scotland. An engraving of Queen Elizabeth from the 1620s or 1630s, representing her with the accoutrements of St George against the back-ground of the Spanish Armada, shows how the images of the queen and saint together could be manipulated to attack the Stuarts for their unwillingness to assist the protestant cause in Europe. But while the memory of Elizabeth was increasingly cherished, St George was more likely to be attacked. In 1609 he appeared side by side with St *Andrew in London in the lord mayor's pageant, but around 1634 a tract entitled *A Comparison between St Andrew and St George* praised the apostolic patron of Scotland at the expense of his mythical English equivalent. Nor were the crown's critics likely to be any more sympathetic towards George as a figure in popular culture. Without a basis in scripture, he was readily associated with popish or heathen superstitions. Thus in his *Anatomy of Melancholy* Robert Burton placed 'St George for England' in 'a rable of Romish Deities' (Burton, 3.384). Unsurprisingly, such asso-ciations led to his cult being attacked, and where possible suppressed, by parliament and its supporters during and after the civil wars. His images were not spared by puritan iconoclasts. William Dowsing destroyed several of them, recording, for instance, how on 26 January 1643 'We pulled down St George and the Dragon' at St Catharine's College, Cambridge (*Journal*, ed. Cooper, 166). Then in 1645 the celebration of his feast day was formally prohibited through the *Directory for the Publique Worship of God* which brought an end to the annual celebrations at places like Norwich: there, and no doubt elsewhere, there was to be 'no standard with the George thereon' (Hutton, *Merry Eng-land*, 208). But though the saint was proscribed his flag sur-vived, if without his name—in 1649 the council of state ordered that 'Ships at Sea in service of the State shall onely beare the red Crosse in a white flag' (Perrin, 62–3).

Monarchs, mummers, and mockers, 1660–1837 The associ-ation of St George with the English monarchy survived the civil wars, and to outward appearances was strengthened by the return of the Stuarts. General George Monck was likened to the saint at the time of the Restoration which he did so much to bring about, and Charles II, James II, and Anne all chose to have themselves crowned on 23 April, making it entirely appropriate for Thomas Lowick to dedicate to Charles his *History of the Life & Martyrdom of St George, the Titular Patron of England* (1664). But the break with the past had arguably been too great for monarchy and saint to continue to buttress one another as in the past. Only a modest number of parishes marked 23 April with bonfires—an estimated 13 per cent under Charles, rising to 20 per cent under his brother. The saint's day was celebrated at Chester in 1660, but such festivities continued only until 1678. At Norwich the annual civic processions no longer found room for St George, although the dragon, 'a magnificent reptile, all glittering in green and gold', took part every year until 1835 (R. Chambers, 1.541). Samuel Pepys attended Charles's coronation in 1661, but without noting in his diary that it took place on St George's day, and in subsequent years he usually recorded either saint's day or coronation day only if it coincided with a Garter feast. Among churchmen and scholars doubts about the saint's existence persisted. In 1676 Edward Stillingfleet observed of those who reverenced saints like Christopher and George, that 'the wisest among them cannot to this day tell, whether they were *Saints* or *Allegories*' (Wilson, 149). Sir Thomas Browne was no more certain: 'That such a person there was, we shall not contend' (Browne, 1.411). John Aubrey shared their doubts, leavened with a characteristically wry humour: 'I will conclude this paragraph with these following verses, that I remember somewhere':

To save a Mayd, St George the Dragon slew,
A pretty tale, if all is told be true:
Most say, there are no Dragons: and tis sayd,
There was no George; pray God there was a Mayd.
(Aubrey, 68–9)

A new element of flippancy was beginning to colour attitudes to St George, perceptible in the facetiously long-winded poem, *St George for England: the Second Part*, which John Grubb, of Christ Church, Oxford, wrote in 1688 as a continuation of an earlier ballad, to gain admission to a university club which met on St George's day and all of whose members were to be named George.

In the year that Grubb wrote his poem Anthony Wood recorded that bonfires were lit and bells rung all over Oxford on St George's day. Perhaps this was to be expected in a city traditionally loyal to the Stuarts. But the decades immediately after the deposition of James II saw regard for St George at a low ebb. Attacks on his historicity continued. In 1704 the Revd Thomas Salmon, the musicological rector of Meppershall, published *A New Historical Account of St George for England, and the Original of the Most Noble Order of the Garter*, in which he argued, without the least plausibility, that the original patron of the nation was the eighth-century papal legate George of Ostia, later supplanted by the eastern intruder through the machinations of monks. There are hints that St George, whoever

he was conceived to be, retained a traditional respect among soldiers and sailors. In 1704 the chaplain of the *Ranelagh* recorded that on 23 April the ship was 'dress'd very fine with all the colours and penants' (Taylor, 137–8), while on the same day two years later, according to the New England puritan Samuel Sewall, the governor came to Boston with an escort of troops, and conducted obstreperous celebrations—'Because to drinking Healths, now the Keeping of a Day to fictitious St. George, is plainly set on foot' (Holford-Strevens and Blackburn, 169). Later in the eighteenth century a number of leading towns on the American coastline established societies of St George to provide assistance to English immigrants. For many of the English who stayed at home, however, the saint seems to have become primarily associated with drinking and sex. About 1700 there were sixty-three inn-signs in London representing the saint, and 'riding St George', or 'the dragon upon St George', had become the name popularly given to the sexual act when the woman took the upper position.

As far as attitudes to St George were concerned, the establishment of a new dynasty in 1714 was important at first principally for the names borne by its first four monarchs, making it possible for the loyal, the ambitious, and the sycophantic to acclaim the one by celebrating the other, as was particularly apparent in the years immediately after the accession of George I. Thomas Dawson, who had published his erudite *Memoirs of St George the English Patron* by the end of 1714, with a dedication to the new king, was unusually quick off the mark. A number of church dedications reflect the same development, for instance that of St George's Church built in London's aptly named Hanover Square between 1721 and 1724. The fact that the Society of Antiquaries of London, founded in 1717, was dedicated to St George may likewise have owed something to a wish to cultivate the Hanoverian monarchy, though it may also been due to the fervent admiration felt for the saint by the eccentric but influential Browne Willis, one of the society's founder members.

For much of the eighteenth century attitudes to St George seem to have varied among the classes of society. Although Sir Joshua Reynolds painted the youthful fifth duke of Bedford and other children enacting St George and the dragon (exhibited 1777, since destroyed), there is little evidence of aristocratic interest in the saint, for whom it seems likely that the nobility felt much the same condescension that they usually extended to the monarchy. The intelligentsia, outside the established church, tended to remain sceptical, and was prepared to make fun of St George, directly or by implication. The principal target of Henry Cary's burlesque opera *The Dragon of Wantley* (1737) was the conventions of Italian opera, but the fate of the eponymous dragon, dispatched by Moore of Moore Hall by a kick up the backside, was hardly reverential towards the national saint either. In the mid-1750s John Byrom wrote a facetious poem (published in 1779) suggesting that St George had been confused with Pope Gregory the Great, and when the elder Samuel Pegge responded with a defence of George's historicity in the pages of *Archaeologia* he was ridiculed by Horace Walpole, who described Pegge's article as 'despicable. All his arguments are equally good for proving the existence of the dragon' (Lewis and Wallace, 2.163–4). A far more telling attack on the saint—deadlier, indeed, for the Olympian disdain with which it was delivered—was that of Edward Gibbon, who having described the misdeeds and violent death of Archbishop George of Alexandria, concluded:

> The odious stranger, disguising every circumstance of time and place, assumed the mask of a martyr, a saint, and a Christian hero; and the infamous George of Cappadocia has been transformed into the renowned St. George of England, the patron of arms, of chivalry, and of the Garter. (Gibbon, 1.903)

In a footnote Gibbon acknowledged that 'This transformation is not given as absolutely certain, but as extremely probable.' He was being disingenuous. His sole source was an unsupported assertion among a French scholar's posthumous *pensées*, and he certainly knew of Heylyn's riposte to Rainolds, whose arguments for a confusion of Georges had largely anticipated Gibbon's own, for he cited it in the very next footnote, but in such a context mockery was more effective than scholarship. John Milner's rejoinder of 1792, though learned, was laborious by comparison.

The figure of St George received more respect at humbler levels of society. The story of the dragon fight was savoured. In 1757 Bishop Richard Pococke, travelling in Wiltshire, was told by 'peasants' that 'Dragon's Hill' near Highworth was the site of George's victory, and that grass would not grow where the dragon's blood had been spilt. But among working people George became prominent above all in mummers' plays. The early history of these entertainments is obscure. The fact that George takes a leading part in most of them supports the argument that they derived principally from chapbooks and ballads for which Johnson's *Seaven Champions* was a major source, and which continued to circulate in large numbers well into the nineteenth century. But evidence for their early development is meagre. A Dublin manuscript of *c*.1800 contains an account from about 1685 of:

> the drollest piece of mummery I ever saw in or out of Ireland. There was St George and St Dennis and St Patrick in their buffe coats and the Turk likewise and Oliver Cromwell, and a Doctor and an old woman who made rare sport till Beelzebub came in with a frying pan upon his shoulder and a great flail in his hand. (Helm, 7)

It is not said when in the year the Dublin play was staged, but at Exeter by 1737 it was customarily associated with Christmas, as it has usually been ever since:

> With less Decorum Christmas Mummer struts,
> Than on He bears his goodly Grace of Guts,
> Though that same Mummer England's Heroe plays
> And Dragon with his Whineard's Flourish slays.
> (Bede, 464)

A similar play was recorded in Cheshire in 1788, while in 1811 'a kind of short piece about St George and the Dragon and the Holy Land which ended in a sham fight' was reported at Halifax in Nova Scotia (Helm, 8). Direct references to the dragon are in fact rare in mummers' plays outside the challenge with which George usually opens

the play, but it is likely that his principal antagonist, commonly named 'Slasher', is in fact a transmogrification of George's monstrous foe, hence his boast:

> My head is made of iron
> My body is made of steel
> My arms and legs of beaten brass;
> No man can make me feel.
> (E. K. Chambers, *English Folk-Play*, 177–8)

The princess very seldom has any part in the plays, although she, too, is mentioned in George's challenge. Her absence was probably due to the mummers' plays having acquired a shadowy but potent undercurrent of symbolism, one to which they owed a good deal of their staying power but from which the feminine element was largely excluded. An essential component of the substructure of the plays upon which the cast of stock characters traditionally improvises its comic business is the theme of death and resurrection, either of the adversary whom George kills or of George himself. In this respect George is a fertility figure, a role once attributed to him, as 'Green George', across much of eastern Europe, where he was 'a spirit of trees or vegetation in general' (Frazer, 2.343). In England he takes on a similar function in a song from the Padstow hobby-horse procession:

> Where is St George, where is he, O,
> He is out in his longboat all on the salt sea, O,
> And in every land, O, the land that ere we go,
> And for to fetch the summer home,
> The summer and the May, O,
> For summer is acome and winter is ago.
> (Hulst, 113)

It is easy to see how George's association with the generation of crops and livestock, arising from his springtime feast day, could be transferred with equal appropriateness to the season of the turning of the year. The figure of St George as he appeared in mummers' plays was also enriched by a patriotic component which may have developed, at least in part, through an association with the monarchy resulting from a coincidence of names. In the plays George very often proclaims himself to be 'King George' or 'Prince George', or more precisely to be George III or even George IV, though in all cases he then goes on to describe how he slew the dragon and won the king of Egypt's daughter. The connection gave added force to an image of the saint as the champion of England, and as such the embodiment of national superiority, as he claims to be in the sword dance from the Shetland Islands, recorded by Sir Walter Scott and dated by him to about 1788:

> In England, Scotland, Ireland, France, Italy, and Spain,
> Have I been tried with that good sword of steel.
> Yet I deny that ever a man did make me yield;
> For in my body there is strength,
> As by my manhood may be seen;
> And I, with that good sword of length,
> Have oftentimes in peril been,
> And over champions was I king.
> (Scott, *The Pirate*, 501–2)

The late 1780s saw attempts at other levels of society to exploit, or develop, an image of St George as a patriotic icon. Probably these should be seen in the context first of attempts to rebuild national self-confidence after the loss of the American colonies in 1783 and then of war with France from 1792. Between 1787 and 1789 Benjamin West's paintings for the king's audience chamber at Windsor Castle included one of St George and the dragon for the overmantel, and paintings by Matthew Wyatt for the royal apartments, executed about 1805, included episodes from the life of the saint. In 1789 a play called *St George's Day, or, Britons Rejoice* was staged at Covent Garden. Later on, the wellnigh demonic qualities attributed to Napoleon in England made it appropriate for a cartoon of 1805, entitled *St George and the Dragon*, to show George III as the saint, in the act of dealing its death blow to a dragon with the French emperor's head, and for Walter Scott, in *The Field of Waterloo* (1815), to exclaim:

> Now, Island Empress, wave thy crest on high,
> And bid the banner of thy patron flow,
> Gallant St George, the flower of Chivalry,
> For thou hast faced, like him, a dragon foe,
> And rescued innocence from overthrow,
> And trampled down, like him, tyrannic might.
> (Girouard, 33)

For Scott himself the image would have been given additional force by his fascination with medieval art and culture, which he did much to promote. In his novel *Ivanhoe* (1820), set in late twelfth-century England, nearly everyone, from Richard I downwards, swears by St George, sometimes with Merry England thrown in; at the novel's climactic moment, when Ivanhoe challenges the villainous Brian de Bois-Guilbert, he invokes the aid 'of God, of Our Lady, and of Monseigneur Saint George, the good knight' (chap. 43). In 1822 *St George and the Dragon, or, The Seven Champions of Christendom*, was performed at the Royal Amphitheatre in London. The cult of chivalry had not yet reached its apogee, however, and the influence of the ancient world remained potent in public culture. In 1816 St George appeared on the English currency for the first time since the reign of Henry VIII, in a handsome engraving for the gold sovereign by Benedetto Pistrucci in which the dragon-slaying saint closely resembles Greek carvings of Perseus. But however it was expressed, a connection with St George was clearly becoming one worth cultivating, as George IV showed when he ordered that his own birthday should be celebrated on 23 April instead of 12 August; whether out of respect for the saint or disrespect for the monarch, however, the royal command was ignored.

Victorian visions, 1837–1914 At the accession of Queen Victoria in 1837 St George probably enjoyed a wider appeal in England than at any time since the mid-seventeenth century. He had still to recover from the loss of much of his standing as a specifically religious figure at the Reformation, and arguably never fully did so, but during the nineteenth century he gained strength instead from a growing association with the combined forces of English nationalism and imperial expansion. Like the empire itself, this development was slow. In 1853 George was eulogized in an almost impenetrable rhapsody by the eccentric occultist Hargrave Jennings, telling how:

> his goodly cross of red, which shone a very beacon in the conflicts with the Paynim, hath, of itself, passed, and been eagerly transmitted from land to land, and hath served as the rallying light for a hundred, (but for it), to all Christian and humane tendencies, benighted generations.   (Jennings, 3–4)

Churches and missions were an essential part of that process of enlightenment, and cathedrals were at various times dedicated to St George at Madras in India (where Fort St George had been the nucleus of the English settlement since the mid-seventeenth century), at Cape Town and Grahamstown in South Africa, at Kingston in the Windward Islands, and at Georgetown in British Guiana. The Anglican cathedral in Jerusalem, too, was dedicated to him, as were the churches of the English chaplaincies in Livorno, Lisbon, Paris, Berlin, and the Azores, and one of the English churches in Cannes. In 1897 his flag's association with empire, and the latter's perceived benevolence, were acclaimed together in Edward Elgar's 'ballad' *The Banner of St George*, with words by Shapcott Wensley, in which George, having vanquished the dragon, bids farewell to Princess Sabra and tells how:

> Where the strong the weak oppress,
> Where the suffering succour crave,
> Where the tyrant spreads distress,
> There the cross of George must wave!
> (p. iv)

The last verse of the epilogue (marked *largamente e grandioso* by Elgar) saluted Queen Victoria. She too celebrated St George, if less bombastically. As a girl she recorded enjoying the spectacular show of *St George and the Dragon* put on at Drury Lane in the 1830s by Andrew Ducrow, while in 1908 it was reported how:

> Until a few years ago an old ballad called 'St George for England' was sung at Windsor on 23 April by the choirboys of St George's Chapel, and from the time of George I until the reign of the late Queen Victoria, a golden rose decorated the royal dining-table on the same day.   (Bulley, 30–31)

In 1896 she became the patron of the Society of St George, founded for patriotic purposes two years earlier (the society acquired its royal prefix under Edward VII). The Church of England once more felt able to reverence St George, on the evidence of a 'supplementary collect' published by the bishop of Salisbury in 1899, invoking him, however, as a martyr and soldier rather than as a dragon-killer—'O Lord God of hosts, Who didst give grace to Thy servant George to lay aside the fear of man and to confess thee even unto death' (Wordsworth, 323). Six years earlier, when the Roman Catholic church had proposed that the Virgin and St Peter should become the patrons of England, Cardinal Herbert Vaughan wrote reassuringly to *The Times*, upholding George's traditional role of 'military protector' of England, and declaring that 'Catholics, at all events, are not likely to forget the historic and national cry and prayer, "St George for England"' (Arnold-Foster, 465).

The towns and villages of England continued to encounter St George principally through chapbooks, ballads, and mummers' plays, all of which proliferated, or at least are recorded as proliferating, during the nineteenth century.

References to mummers' plays become suddenly plentiful, and show that they were performed in industrial towns and cities as well as in the countryside, perhaps more often in the midlands and north than in the southern counties. In Northern Ireland, mummers staged a play in Belfast in the 1890s apparently remarkably similar to that put on in late seventeenth-century Dublin—St George appeared with St *Patrick and Oliver Cromwell as well as with such stock characters as the Turky Champion, Beelzebub, Little Devil Doubt, and a Doctor. The words attributed to St George in such productions show that here, too, he often struck a robustly patriotic note, sometimes British, in the company of Sts Patrick, David, and Andrew, and sometimes for England alone. In a play recorded at Lutterworth at Christmas 1863, for instance, he announces himself as the king of England's only son:

I am Prince George, a worthy knight;
I'll spend my blood for England's right.
England's right I will maintain;
I'll fight for old England once again.
(E. K. Chambers, *Medieval Stage*, 2.276–9)

The fact that he continued to be often referred to as Prince or King George can only have accentuated his Englishness.

St George achieved this apotheosis despite opposition. As before, there were those who doubted his existence. The study of comparative religion, which was beginning to have momentous effects for attitudes to the Bible, also had corrosive implications for the national saint; thus for Anna Jameson he was no more than a 'mythic allegory by which was figured the conquest achieved by beneficent power over the tyranny of wickedness … this time-consecrated myth transplanted into Christendom' (Jameson, 2.398), while for Sabine Baring-Gould he was 'a Semitic god Christianized' (Baring-Gould, 291). In 1853 George was attacked by Ralph Waldo Emerson in terms borrowed directly from Gibbon. Some twenty years later John Ruskin replied to Emerson in a defence of George's historicity explicitly derived from Heylyn. But in the 1870s Ruskin was interested in George less as a historical figure than as a moral symbol, at a time when he was increasingly concerned with social reform, and it was for that reason that he invited his followers to join him in what at first he called 'my St George's Company', eventually the guild of St George, which met for the first time in 1879. Ruskin was willing to accept the mythico-allegorical derivation of George's combat with the dragon because he saw the mission of his own guild in allegorical terms, a war waged on behalf of traditional Christian values, represented by the saint, against the disruptive forces of industrial capitalism, embodied in 'the Lord of Decomposition, the old Dragon himself' (Ruskin, 1.332).

As an institution the guild of St George failed. But the ideas behind it proved influential. Among Ruskin's disciples was Edward Carpenter, an early socialist who in 1908 published *St George and the Dragon: a Play in Three Acts for Children and Young Folk*, dedicated to the Independent Labour Party and Socialist Sunday Schools. Its message is all that Ruskin might have wished, for after an opening lament for a time 'when all was gladness in this land and men and women sang at their work, and rejoiced in their strength and in the goodly stores they won by their labour from the soil', St George kills a dragon explicitly identified as Greed, who 'slays the souls Of men, as well as takes their bodies' toll', after which he and the princess he has saved are chosen by the people to be their rulers, in the place of 'such as consult their own ease and safety first and leave their people to perish' (pp. 4, 12–13, 15). Ruskin might have regretted that a play about St George made no mention whatever of Christianity, or any other religion, but he could not have charged Carpenter with lack of seriousness. There must have been many of his contemporaries, however, for whom the saint remained little more than an inn-sign, like the George and the Dragon noticed in London, with the inscription below, 'Entertainment for man and horse' (Brand, 2.357–8), or the cheerful sign painted in 1876 by the artist John Evan Hodgson and a friend for the George and the Dragon at Wargrave, Berkshire, showing the fight on one side, and the victorious saint reviving himself with beer on the other.

A similarly light-hearted note is struck by Kenneth Grahame's *The Reluctant Dragon*, first published in *Dream Days* (1899). In this engaging fable a dragon appears on the downs, where he befriends a small boy, shows an unexpected talent for poetry, and settles down to a quiet life—'Meanwhile the dragon, a happy Bohemian, lolled on the turf, enjoyed the sunsets, told antediluvian anecdotes to the Boy, and polished his old verses while meditating on fresh ones' (Grahame, 135). His idyllic existence is disturbed by the arrival of St George, whom he is eventually compelled to fight by the machinations of the locals, who are betting on the outcome. By now George is no more eager for the fray than the dragon, but the unenthusiastic combatants finally agree that George shall enjoy a bloodless triumph in the third round. The day concludes with a banquet, at which the dragon, having 'won popularity and a sure footing in society … proved the life and soul of the evening' (ibid., 149).

Others continued to take St George with the utmost seriousness. One such was Robert Baden-Powell, founder of the Boy Scouts, for whom the saint was the embodiment of chivalry, and as such 'the patron saint of cavalry and scouts all over Europe', on whose day 'all good scouts wear a rose in his honour and fly their flags' (Baden-Powell, 210). He was treated no less reverently in the children's play *Where the Rainbow Ends* by Mrs Clifford Mills and Reginald Owen (the latter under the pseudonym John Ramsey), first performed on 21 December 1911 and published as a novel by Mrs Mills in the following year. Here two children, Crispin and Rosamund, desperate to be reunited with their absent parents and possessing a magic carpet which can take them to 'the land where all lost loved ones are found', successfully call on St George to accompany and assist them. They are opposed by their Uncle Joseph, a Hampstead liberal before his time who mocks the Union Jack and is eventually eaten by hyenas, and by his abettor the Dragon King. The latter reflects on the children's ally:

This saint, the champion of England, who spoke to the hearts not the greed of his countrymen, who demanded from those who fought his country's battle the sacrifice of self purpose and the clean hand to wield the sword, to what heights had he not led Englishmen in the past, to what greater heights would not his lofty spirit lead them in the future? (Mills, 70)

The story culminates in George's last-minute appearance to save the children from death, and his challenge to the Dragon King: 'Once more we meet, arch-enemy', he cried, 'to fight the everlasting fight of good and evil' (ibid., 154). Good prevails in the apocalyptic struggle, and all ends happily.

The association of St George with the forces of righteousness, and of both with England, is explicit throughout *Where the Rainbow Ends*, but equally apparent is an undertone of menace, even pessimism. In an analogy Ruskin would have appreciated, the saint represents not only England but also the heroic qualities needed to defeat the forces of materialism and greed which threaten the nation's soul, forces symbolized by the dragon. The outcome of their conflict cannot be taken for granted. When he first appears, wrapped in a cloak, the children do not recognize St George, mistaking him for one of the unemployed, to which he responds with the admission that 'I am … one of England's unemployed ideals … I am no longer wanted here, men do not war with the dragon nowadays, and the maidens prefer to fight their own battles'. But when Rosamund calls on him for aid, the saint is utterly transformed, into 'the St George they knew and honoured—a noble knight in shining armour. Tall, slender and muscular, yellow-haired, English of the English' (Mills, 41–3). The change was doubtless such as was looked for by those concerned for the moral health of England. George's physical appearance, English or otherwise, was in fact seldom illustrated in the high art of the Victorian age, though his legend inspired paintings by Dante Gabriel Rossetti and Edward Burne-Jones, and the image evoked by Mrs Mills probably derived from children's books and from the illustrations of the numerous studies of the saint published in the years on either side of 1900. Those studies in turn reflect the public position George had increasingly come to occupy as a patriotic as well as a moral symbol. In 1899 it was estimated that there were over 190 churches dedicated to him in England, with at least one in every county except Huntingdonshire, Hertfordshire, and Rutland. By this time his feast day was being widely celebrated. In 1902, for instance, children near Dunstable were given a holiday from school, while in 1914 the townspeople of Kidderminster flew flags and held a church service. Ignorance, indifference, and mockery no doubt continued, but to outward appearances St George was not only English himself, he had become part of the English cultural landscape.

Images of war and peace, 1914–2000 The beginning of the First World War in 1914 quickly led to a revelation of St George's significance as a patriotic icon, albeit in an oblique fashion. Among the literary responses to the outbreak of war was Arthur Machen's story 'The bowmen', published in London's *Evening News* on 29 September 1914, telling how during the retreat from Mons an English soldier repeats the inscription calling on St George which he remembers having seen on a plate in a vegetarian restaurant. A line of figures promptly materializes, the pursuing Germans fall under a hail of arrows, and although the saint himself does not appear, 'the man who knew what nuts tasted like when they called themselves steak knew also that St George had brought his Agincourt Bowmen to help the English' (Machen, 66). Machen's patriotic fantasy made a startling impact, and within months the overwrought public imagination had transformed his dimly perceived archers, originally 'a long line of shapes, with a shining about them', so that 'the Bowmen of my story have become "the Angels of Mons". In this shape they have been received with respect and credence everywhere, or almost everywhere' (ibid., 18–19). St George is similarly but more explicitly represented in John Hassall's painting of 1915, *Vision of St George over the Battlefield* (IWM), where his appearance over the trenches, mounted and armed as a medieval crusader, brings terror to the Germans. At Thaxted in Essex, the vicar, Conrad Noel, turned an aisle of the parish church into a wartime shrine, with a picture of St George defeating the dragon surrounded by the flags of Britain's allies, while Jessie Pope explicitly equated the soldiers in the trenches with the English national saint:

Of gallant St Georges to-day we've a legion,
As sturdy and game as the knights of Romance;
They are fighting their fight in that shell-battered region
That bears the vague pseudonym—'Somewhere in France' …
(Parker, 226)

Whether the troops themselves valued the association is open to question, although it was with the signal 'St George for England' that Admiral Roger Keyes led a daring raid against Zeebrugge on 23 April 1918.

As the war ended G. F. Raggett concluded a short book which he entitled *An Essay on the Life of St George the Martyr, Patron Saint of England* (1919). Though eventually dedicated to Keyes, it had been begun before the Zeebrugge raid, 'to be a guide, although very imperfect, to the vast number of English people who know nothing whatever about our Saint' (p. 3). By the time Raggett's book appeared his fellow countrymen (whose ignorance he probably exaggerated) were being widely familiarized with the form of St George through the medium of public war memorials. The saint is nearly always represented as a medieval knight victorious over the dragon, most strikingly in Adrian Jones's powerful cavalry memorial, now in London's Hyde Park; Eric Gill's memorial at Trumpington, near Cambridge, is exceptional in showing George as a soldier of the trenches. Sometimes he was set upon memorials in places where he already had a particular local appeal, as at Newcastle upon Tyne, where he had long featured on the regimental cap-badge of the Northumberland Fusiliers, but the wide distribution of such figures seems more often to have stemmed simply from his constituting an appropriately warlike and patriotic image, albeit one capable of conveying more than one message.

In some cases the saint appears as a transcendental image of good overcoming evil, as at Lawrence Sheriff School, Rugby, where the memorial represents George killing his traditional adversary above the inscription: 'There are dragons still. 1914–1918'. And he was also envisaged as embodying the values for which the war had been fought and the qualities by which it had been won. The duke of York (later King George VI), when unveiling the memorial at the Leys School, Cambridge, said of its central image of St George: 'It will stand for all time, a pivot of the school's history and tradition and the inspiration of those ideals of chivalry, self-sacrifice, and patriotism which are essential to the highest conduct and character' (Borg, 100–01). There could be no sectarian monopoly of such ideals, and in London memorial chapels commemorating the victims of the 1914–18 war were dedicated to St George in both the Roman Catholic Westminster Cathedral and the Anglican Westminster Abbey, while a stained-glass window served the same purpose in Wesley's Chapel.

No doubt it was at least partly due to his commemorative association with the war dead that between 1918 and 1939 St George's day continued to be fairly widely observed. He was promoted by the Royal Society of St George, which had 20,000 members by 1920, and by the Boy Scouts, and 23 April was often marked by church services and the flying of flags, and sometimes by a show or fête, which might include a pageant of the saint and the dragon. It was on St George's day that George V opened the British Empire Exhibition at Wembley in 1924. Although in this context George remained an essentially backward-looking patriotic symbol, he was also capable of being used for progressive purposes. In *Vision of England, '38*, the young radical poet George Barker tells of encountering the saint in a vision set at Brighton, where he emerges from the sea to denounce capitalism in terms Ruskin would have approved—'I killed an enormous monster, but the brute Still rules England with its scales of gold'—and then imagines him rising in the north to free 'The national man and woman, who groan!' (Barker, 68, 75). But when war with Germany broke out again in 1939, George once more became an emblem of valour and resistance, though not always to the same end. Soldiers fighting in the western desert constructed a chapel dedicated to him, making bells from shell cases and altar furnishings from gun parts. And acts of civilian bravery on the home front were marked by the award of the George Medal, under a royal warrant of 24 September 1940 which stipulated that the reverse should show 'St George slaying the dragon on the coast of England' (Henderson, 106). But shortly afterwards the saint's name and military role were invoked for very different purposes by the traitor John Amery, a fanatical anti-communist who defected to the Nazis and tried to persuade British prisoners of war to enlist in what he called the Legion of St George, to fight alongside the Germans against the Russians. The name of the English national saint had no appeal, for only about thirty men enlisted, and when Amery left Berlin at the end of 1943 the tiny force was handed over to the SS, who renamed it the British Free Corps.

Although Amery's venture can hardly be held responsible, there are signs that even before war ended the appeal of St George as a heroic warrior-saint was beginning to wane in England. The chivalric qualities he could still be seen as embodying in the early decades of the twentieth century had little meaning to people enduring rationing and the blitz, and he was easily identified with retrograde inter-war social attitudes by those who now looked forward to the welfare state, and for whom empire and military glory had lost their appeal. In 1943 23 April fell on Good Friday, and St George's day was therefore celebrated on 3 May instead. The move had the support of the archbishop of Canterbury but was not a success. A year later a BBC producer declared that 'nine out of ten people haven't the least idea who St George was and don't care anyway' (Weight, 56). He may have been over-freely attributing his own views to the nation at large, but there is no doubt that the years following 1945 saw a steady decline in interest in the saint. He again featured in a number of war memorials—the chapel of remembrance at RAF Biggin Hill was dedicated to St George—but less often in new statuary (the names of the dead of 1939–45 were usually added to existing memorials) than in stained-glass windows in churches, where they inevitably made less impression on the public at large. The general decline in churchgoing, too, contributed to the growing indifference, as did the coincidence of St George's day with the day of William Shakespeare's death (and possible birth). The national saint lost ground to the national poet, and by 1947 the author and artist Laurence Whistler could comment that 'The celebration of "the Birthday" is now the main feature of St George's Day' (Whistler, 133). In John Masefield's verse drama *A Play of St George* (1948), set in the reign of Diocletian, George's links to the land of his future tutelary role are confined to a passing reference to 'A place called Londinium in South Britain' (p. 48).

During the 1950s and 1960s the Royal Society of St George (which received a royal charter of incorporation in 1963) worked to maintain interest in and knowledge of the English national saint, against a background of widespread apathy which the Roman Catholic church's demotion of George's cult to one of purely local observance in 1969 can have done nothing to dispel. He retained his traditional place in mummers' plays, but also his equally traditional confusion with King George, which can only have obscured his status. Thus in a performance recorded at Antrobus, Cheshire, on 12 November 1974, he announced himself at the outset:

> In come I, King George, the champion bold,
> I won ten thousand pound in gold.
> 'Twas I that fought the fiery dragon and brought it to a
>   slaughter,
> And by these deeds won the King of Egypt's daughter.
> (Green, 144–5)

Two years earlier, however, the United Kingdom's entry into the European Economic Community (31 December 1972) had helped to fuel emotions which did much to recast the image of St George, albeit in an overtly militaristic and xenophobic mould which found little space for traditional associations with chivalric gallantry. Here a leading role was taken by the League of St George, founded in 1975, which was overtly hostile to outsiders and foreigners of all kinds, and made much of the threat allegedly posed to Britain's (as much as England's) national identity by immigration. The incongruity of the choice of name, given that George is also widely honoured on the continent (for instance as the patron of Catalonia and of the Greek army) and in the Middle East, by both Eastern Orthodox and Coptic Christians and by Muslims, was overlooked.

The impact of the League of St George was never more than local and ephemeral, but in the 1990s the saint's cause was taken up again, now with the support of sections of the media—in 1998 *The Sun* launched a campaign to revive the observance of St George's day. The decade 1984–94 saw a substantial increase in the number of boys given the first name George (from 804 to 3907), and in 1995 it became possible to buy cards marking 23 April—50,000 were being sold each year by the end of the century. The principal force behind these developments was less religion, however, than continued anxiety over national identity, now fuelled not only by racism but also by hostility towards the European Union (as the European Economic Community became in 1992) and fears that it aimed to create a European 'superstate', and perhaps, too, by concerns for England's place in the United Kingdom at a time when its long-established primacy seemed to be threatened first by demands for, and then by the enactment of, Welsh and Scottish devolution. Indeed, despite the decision of its general synod in 1996 that St George's day should be one of the Church of England's twenty-eight major festivals, in the 1980s and 1990s the saint himself was less in evidence as a patriotic symbol than his banner, which became all too often associated with the violence of football hooligans and extreme nationalists. To some extent this was in keeping with popular perceptions of St George as above all a soldier and dragon-killer, his initial status as a martyr having been almost entirely forgotten. Yet despite this warlike image, he has also continued to be linked by name to beneficent institutions of all kinds, to hospitals and charities as well as churches, and thus to functions in keeping with those gentler aspects of his legend which tell of his rescuing an imperilled princess and saving heathen souls. That this should be so illustrates the extent to which that legend has over the centuries gathered a rich variety of elements, which in their turn have enabled St George to show himself a protean figure, capable of continuous adaptation. At the beginning of the twenty-first century there is every reason to suppose that this process will continue.   HENRY SUMMERSON

Sources BL, Arundel MS 341 • BL, Lansdowne MS 204 • Bodl. Oxf., MS Arch. Selden B.26 • Gregory of Tours, *Glory of the martyrs*, trans. R. Van Dam (1988) • *Adomnan's De locis sanctis*, ed. D. Meehan, Scriptores Latini Hiberniae, 11 (1958) • *Aelfric's Lives of the saints*, ed. W. W. Skeat, EETS, orig. ser., 76 (1881) • Ordericus Vitalis, *Eccl. hist.* • William of Malmesbury, *Gesta regum Anglorum / The history of the English kings*, ed. and trans. R. A. B. Mynors, R. M. Thomson, and M. Winterbottom, 2 vols., OMT (1998–9) • Jacobus de Voragine, *The Golden Legend*, ed. W. G. Ryan, 2 vols. (1993) • C. Horstmann, ed., *The* early south-English legendary, EETS, orig. ser., 87 (1887) • *CPR, 1350–54* • Thomae Walsingham, *quondam monachi S. Albani, historia Anglicana*, ed. H. T. Riley, Rolls Series, 28 (1863–4) • L. C. Hector and B. F. Harvey, eds. and trans., *The Westminster chronicle*, OMT (1982) • J. Froissart, *Chronicles of England, France, Spain, and the adjoining countries*, trans. T. Johnes, 2 vols. (1874) • T. Twiss, ed., *Monumenta juridica: the Black Book of the admiralty*, 1, Rolls Series, 55 (1871) • D. Wilkins, ed., *Concilia magnae Britanniae et Hiberniae*, 4 vols. (1737) • *The minor poems of John Lydgate*, ed. H. N. MacCracken, EETS, extra ser., 107 (1911) • E. F. Jacob, ed., *The register of Henry Chichele, archbishop of Canterbury, 1414–1443*, 3, CYS, 46 (1945) • F. W. D. Brie, ed., *The Brut, or, The chronicles of England*, 2 vols., EETS, 131, 136 (1906–8) • F. Palgrave, ed., *The antient kalendars and inventories of the exchequer*, 2 (1836) • J. Stratford, *The Bedford inventories* (1993) • T. Wright, ed., *Political poems and songs relating to English history*, 2 vols., Rolls Series, 14 (1859–61) • R. H. Robbins, ed., *Historical poems of the fourteenth and fifteenth centuries* (1959) • A. Barclay, *The life of St George*, ed. W. Nelson, EETS, original ser., 230 (1955) • M. Grace, ed., *Records of the gild of St George in Norwich, 1389–1547*, Norfolk RS, 9 (1937) • J. Leland, *Collectanea*, ed. T. Hearne (1770), vol. 4 • A. H. Thomas and I. D. Thornley, eds., *The great chronicle of London* (1938) • W. R. Streitberger, *Court revels, 1485–1559*, Studies in Early English Drama, 3 (1994) • *The statutes at large passed in the parliaments of Ireland*, 1: 1310–1612 (1765) • D. Starkey, ed., *The inventory of King Henry VIII* (1998) • M. F. Bond, ed., *The inventories of St George's Chapel, Windsor Castle, 1384–1667* (1937) • I. Lancashire, *Dramatic texts and records of Britain: a chronological topography to 1558* (1984) • J. M. Wasson, ed., *Records of early English drama: Devon* (1986) • *English historical documents*, 5, ed. C. H. Williams (1967) • J. G. Nichols, ed., *Narratives of the days of the Reformation*, CS, old ser., 102 (1858) • *Literary remains of King Edward the Sixth*, ed. J. G. Nichols, 2, Roxburghe Club, 75 (1857) • J. Nichols, *The progresses, processions, and magnificent festivities of King James I, his royal consort, family and court*, 4 vols. (1828) • *Early writings of John Hooper*, ed. S. Carr, Parker Society, 15 (1843) • *The diary of Henry Machyn, citizen and merchant-taylor of London, from AD 1550 to AD 1563*, ed. J. G. Nichols, CS, 42 (1848) • G. Whetstone, *The honorable reputation of a souldier* (1585) • E. Spenser, *The faerie queene*, ed. A. C. Hamilton (1977) • R. Johnson, *The famous historie of the seven champions of Christendome* (1616) • J. Bruce, ed., *Correspondence of King James VI of Scotland*, CS, old ser., 78 (1861) • J. Rainolds, *De Romanae ecclesiae idolatria* (1596) • R. Burton, *The anatomy of melancholy*, ed. T. C. Faulkner and others, 3 (1994) • *The collected poems of Joseph Hall*, ed. A. Davenport (1949) • *The journal of William Dowsing*, ed. T. Cooper (2001) • Pepys, *Diary* • T. Browne, *Pseudodoxia epidemica*, ed. R. Robbins, 2 vols. (1981) • J. Aubrey, *Remaines of Gentilisme and Judaisme*, ed. J. Britton, Folk Lore Society, 4 (1881) • *The poems of John Byrom*, ed. A. W. Ward, Chetham Society, new ser., 30 (1894) • W. S. Lewis and A. D. Wallace, eds., *Horace Walpole's correspondence with the Rev. William Cole*, 2 (1937) • E. O. Gordon, *Saint George: champion of Christendom and patron saint of England* (1907) • C. S. Hulst, *St George of Cappadocia in legend and history* (1909) • M. H. Bulley, *St George for Merrie England* (1908) • D. S. Fox, *Saint George: the saint with three faces* (1983) • S. Riches, *St George: hero, martyr, myth* (2000) • P. Heylyn, *The history of that most famous saynt and souldier of Christ Jesus St George of Cappadocia*, 2nd edn (1633) • T. Salmon, *A new historical account of St George for England, and the original of the most noble Order of the Garter* (1704) • T. Dawson, *Memoirs of St George the English patron, and of the most noble Order of the Garter* (1714) • E. A. W. Budge, *George of Lydda* (1930) • S. Braunfels-Esche, *Sankt Georg: Legende, Verehrung, Symbol* (1976) • F. J. W. Harding, *The legend of St George and literature in England* (1965) • F. Arnold-Foster, *Studies in church dedications, or, England's patron saints*, 2 (1899) • C. Hole, *English folk-heroes* (1948) • R. Hutton, *The rise and fall of merry England: the ritual year, 1400–1700* (1994) • R. Hutton, *The stations of the sun: a history of the ritual year in Britain* (1996) • L. Holford-Strevens and B. Blackburn, *The Oxford book of days* (2000) • J. Brand, *Observations on the popular antiquities of Great Britain*, rev. H. Ellis (1882) • R. Chambers, ed., *The book of days: a miscellany of popular antiquities in connection with the calendar*, 2 vols. (1863–4) • E. Partridge, *The Penguin* *dictionary of historical slang* (1972) · A. R. Wright, *British calendar customs*, ed. T. E. Lones, 2; Folk Lore Society, 102 (1938) · S. Baring-Gould, *Curious myths of the middle ages* (1869) · J. Hill, 'St George before the conquest', *Report of the Society of the Friends of St George's and the Descendants of the Knights of the Garter*, 6 (1979–89), 284–95 · O. De Laborderie, 'Richard the Lionheart and the birth of a national cult of St George in England: origins and development of a legend', *Nottingham Medieval Studies*, 39 (1995), 37–53 · J. L. André, 'St George the martyr, in legend, ceremonial, art, etc.', *Archaeological Journal*, 57 (1900), 204–23 · S. Pegge, 'Observations on the history of St George', *Archaeologia*, 5 (1779), 1–32 · J. Barron, 'The Augustinian canons and the University of Oxford: the lost college of St George', *The church and learning in later medieval society: essays in honour of R. B. Dobson*, ed. C. M. Barron and J. Stratford (2002), 228–54 · J. Bengtson, 'St George and the formation of English nationalism', *Journal of Medieval and Early Modern Studies*, 27 (1997), 317–40 · J. Fellows, 'St George as romance hero', *Reading Medieval Studies*, 19 (1993), 27–53 · M. C. McClendon, 'A moveable feast: Saint George's day celebrations and religious change in early modern England', *Journal of British Studies*, 38 (1999), 1–27 · E. C. Williams, 'Mural paintings of St George in England', *Journal of the British Archaeological Association*, 12 (1949), 19–36 · J. E. Matzke, 'Contributions to the history of the legend of Saint George', *Publications of the Modern Language Association of America*, 17 (1902), 464–535 · J. E. Matzke, 'Contributions to the history of the legend of Saint George', *Publications of the Modern Language Association of America*, 18 (1903), 99–171 · J. B. Aufhauser, *Das Drachenwunder des Heiligen Georg* (1911) · T. H. Wilson, 'Saint George in Tudor and Stuart England', MPhil. diss., U. Lond., 1976 · H. Delehaye, *Les légendes grecques des saints militaires* (1909) · A. P. Kazhdan, ed., *The Oxford dictionary of Byzantium* (1991), vol. 2 · C. Erdmann, *The origin of the idea of crusade*, trans. M. W. Baldwin and W. Goffart (1977) · H. E. J. Cowdrey, 'The Anglo-Norman Laudes Regiae', *Viator*, 12 (1981), 37–78 · C. R. Cheney, 'Rules for the observance of feast-days in medieval England', *BIHR*, 34 (1961), 117–47 · C. Tyerman, *England and the crusades, 1095–1588* (1988) · W. Dugdale, *The baronage of England*, 2 (1676) · H. E. L. Collins, *The Order of the Garter, 1348–1461: chivalry and politics in late medieval England* (2000) · J. Anstis, ed., *The register of the most noble order of the Garter*, 2 vols. (1724) · J. Selden, *Titles of honour*, ed. D. Wilkins (1726) · E. K. Chambers, *The medieval stage*, 2 vols. (1903) · E. K. Chambers, *The English folk-play* (1933) · H. F. Westlake, *The parish gilds of medieval England* (1919) · N. Morgan, 'The significance of the banner in the Wilton diptych', *The regal image of Richard II and the Wilton diptych*, ed. D. Gordon, L. Monnas, and C. Elam (1997), 179–88 · W. G. Perrin, *British flags* (1922) · H. A. Percy, *The regulations and establishment of the household of Henry Algernon Percy, the fifth earl of Northumberland*, new edn, ed. T. Percy (1905) · E. Duffy, *The stripping of the altars: traditional religion in England, c.1400–c.1580* (1992) · J. Simons, ed., *Guy of Warwick and other chapbook romances* (1998) · H. C. White, *Tudor books of saints and martyrs* (1963) · J. N. King, 'Spenser's religion', *The Cambridge companion to Spenser*, ed. A. Hadfield (2001), 200–16 · M. P. Tilley, *A dictionary of the proverbs in England in the sixteenth and seventeenth centuries* (1950) · J. A. Dop, *Eliza's knights: soldiers, poets, and puritans in the Netherlands, 1572–1586* (1981) · R. Strong, *The cult of Elizabeth* (1977) · R. Strong, *Portraits of Queen Elizabeth I* (1963) · J. Larwood and J. C. Hotten, *English inn signs* (1951) · M. Spufford, *Small books and pleasant histories* (1981) · G. Taylor, *The sea chaplains* (1978) · E. Gibbon, *The history of the decline and fall of the Roman empire*, ed. D. Womersley (1994), vol. 1 · J. Milner, *An historical and critical inquiry into the existence and character of Saint George* (1792) · F. G. Stephens and M. D. George, eds., *Catalogue of political and personal satires preserved … in the British Museum*, 8 (1947) · W. Scott, *The pirate* (1846) · W. Scott, *Ivanhoe* (1820) · C. Bede, 'Christmas at Exeter in 1737', *N&Q*, 2nd ser., 10 (1860), 464–5 · A. Helm, *The English mummers' play*, mistletoe ser., Folk Lore Society, 14 (1981) · A. Brody, *The English mummers and their plays* (1970) · A. E. Green, 'Popular drama and the mummers' play', *Performance and politics in popular drama*, ed. D. Bradby, L. James, and B. Sharratt (1980), 139–66 · J. G. Frazer, *The golden bough: the magic art*, 3rd edn, 2 (1936) · *Standard catalogue of British coins: coins of England and the United Kingdom*, 37th edn (2002) · H. Jennings, *St George: a miniature romance* (1853) · C. M. Yonge, *The Christmas mummers* (1858) · A. Jameson, *Sacred and legendary art*, 9th edn, 2 vols. (1883) · C. Wordsworth, ed., *Ceremonies and processions of the cathedral church of Salisbury* (1901) · E. Carpenter, *St George and the dragon: a play in three acts for children and young folk* (1908) · M. Girouard, *The return to Camelot: chivalry and the English gentleman* (1981) · P. Barnes, *St George, Ruskin, and the dragon* (1992) · J. Ruskin, *Fors clavigera*, ed. W. G. Collingwood, 4 vols. (1891) · *The banner of St George: a ballad for chorus and orchestra, the words written by Shapcott Wensley, the music composed by Edward Elgar* (1897) · *Official year-book of the Church of England* (1892) · K. Grahame, *The reluctant dragon* (1936) · R. Baden-Powell, *Scouting for boys*, 2nd edn (1910) · Mrs C. Mills, *Where the rainbow ends* (1912) · A. Machen, *The bowmen and other legends of the war*, 2nd edn (1915) · J. Wolffe, *God and Greater Britain: religion and national life in Britain and Ireland, 1843–1945* (1994) · A. Wilkinson, *The Church of England and the First World War* (1978) · P. Parker, *The old lie: the Great War and the public school ethos* (1987) · A. Borg, *War memorials from antiquity to the present* (1991) · D. Boorman, *At the going down of the sun: British First World War memorials* (1988) · G. F. Raggett, *An essay on the life of St George the Martyr, patron saint of England* (1919) · L. Whistler, *The English festivals* (1947) · G. Barker, *Collected poems*, ed. R. Fraser (1987) · D. V. Henderson, *Dragons can be defeated: a complete record of the George Medal's progress, 1940–1983* (1984) · D. Boorman, *For your tomorrow: British Second World War memorials* (1995) · R. West, *The meaning of treason* (1982) · J. Masefield, *A play of St George* (1948) · R. Weight, *Patriots: national identity in Britain, 1940–2000* (2002) · E. Merry, *First names* (1995)

George, duke of Clarence (1449–1478), prince, was the fifth son, the third who survived infancy, of *Richard, duke of York (1411–1460), and Cecily Neville (d. 1495), the youngest daughter of Ralph *Neville, first earl of Westmorland. Although of the highest nobility, with many influential relatives, he had no hereditary expectations.

Early life and dukedom George was born at Dublin during his father's residence as lord lieutenant of Ireland on 21 October 1449 and was baptized in St Saviour's Church. During the 1450s, when his elder brothers had a separate establishment, George and his younger siblings probably resided with their mother. In 1459 all were placed in the custody of the duchess of Buckingham following their father's flight. After the victory of the Neville earls his mother housed them at Fastolf Place in Southwark in September 1460. George and his brother Richard were sent for safe keeping in Utrecht in January 1461, returning only after their brother's accession as Edward IV. As next brother, George was Edward's heir, his male heir until 1471, and thus of instant importance. Still only eleven years of age he was knighted, on 29 June created duke of Clarence (a title that recalled the house of York's title to the crown), elected a knight of the Bath, appointed lord lieutenant of Ireland in 1462 and JP in many counties, and granted extensive estates, including very briefly the whole county of Chester. He was also nominally steward of England both at his brother's coronation and in 1465 at that of the queen. Being only a child, he neither enjoyed the income from the lands nor exercised his offices in person, but lived mainly with his brother Richard, duke of Gloucester, and sister Margaret at Greenwich Palace. Initially an offshoot of the royal household funded by Edward IV's cofferer, Clarence's establishment included a chancellor (John Tapton) in 1462, a surveyor of his livelihood in 1463, and was described as a multitude early in 1466, by when the duke was leading a more public life. He was not yet seventeen when his minority was terminated by his homage on 10 July 1466 and he embarked on his career as royal duke and great magnate.

Estates and marriage Clarence set off at once for Tutbury Castle in Staffordshire, centre of his most important complex of estates, which he seems to have made his principal seat. He started new buildings at the castle, retained local gentry, sued poachers and defaulting ministers, and arbitrated and took sides in local disputes. Henceforth he officiated on some of the commissions to which he was appointed and attended parliament. In 1468 he approved an ordinance that would have made his household the largest and most expensive known for any medieval nobleman. There were to be 399 staff, 188 in the riding household, and the annual cost was £4500. This was considerably grander even than Edward IV's lavish endowment, so much more generous than that of earlier kings towards their brothers. The 1467 Act of Resumption reserved for Clarence 5500 marks a year and a further 1000 marks in reversions, three times the minimum qualification for a duke, but clearly insufficient to support Clarence's plans which, if implemented, must have left him short of money. Clarence was certainly more interested in an heiress as his duchess than the continental princess fitfully projected by his brother's diplomacy. From 1467 or perhaps even 1464 he wished to marry Isabel Neville (1451–1477), eldest daughter of Richard *Neville, earl of Warwick, and related to him in several degrees, but the king forbade the match. Neither Clarence nor Warwick accepted his prohibition, continuing secret negotiations at the papal curia through Edward's own representative for a dispensation, which was granted on 14 March 1469. Clarence and Isabel were married at Calais on 11 July 1469 in a splendid ceremony attended by five knights of the Garter and solemnized by Warwick's brother Archbishop Neville.

Rebellion against Edward IV After 1466 Clarence was not the ally for which Edward IV had presumably hoped. He embroiled himself in a dangerous feud in the north midlands and associated himself politically with Warwick, who graduated from direction of Edward's affairs in the early 1460s to outright opposition. Clarence's motives can only be deduced: disappointed if unrealistic ambition, symbolized by his unsatisfactory income and thwarted marriage, evidently played a part. Immediately after the marriage Clarence and the Nevilles landed in Kent and identified themselves with the manifesto of the Yorkshire rebel Robin of Redesdale, which denounced Edward's evil government and his favourites and proposed reform. Following the rebel victory at Edgcote, the execution of the earls Rivers, Pembroke, and Devon, and Edward's arrest and imprisonment, Clarence was an unsuccessful peacemaker in East Anglia, where his intervention failed to prevent the duke of Norfolk's siege and capture of Caister Castle (Norfolk). Following his release Edward excluded

Clarence and Warwick from power, but was evidently convinced by them of their loyalty at a great council in November. Presumably fearful of future punishment, they orchestrated a further rebellion in Lincolnshire led by Sir Robert Welles, apparently with a view to making Clarence king, concealing their involvement and even persuading the king to grant them a commission to array troops in his support. The defeat of the rebels at Losecote Field (Empingham, Rutland) on 12 March, where correspondence incriminating Clarence was found, their own inability to recruit, and the king's decisive countermeasures forced them to retreat northwards to Lancashire and then to take flight to the south-west, whence they fled from Dartmouth on 9 April into exile. Clarence's duchess gave birth to a short-lived son at sea off Calais, where they failed to secure admission; they eventually took refuge at Harfleur in Normandy about 1 May 1470.

The penalty for failure In retrospect, Edward erred in refusing to temporize and in offering only justice, since it forced Clarence to join in an invasion to depose his brother, not in his own favour, but instead to make Henry VI king once more. Clarence was treated with honour during the negotiations, but it was Louis XI of France, Warwick, and Queen Margaret who were the principal parties. Clarence had to abandon his immediate title to the throne, though a reversionary right on the death of Henry VI and his son may have been accepted. He was to surrender Tutbury at once and could expect to lose any lands formerly forfeited by Lancastrians, but would be compensated. Probably he was recognized as heir to the duchy of York. His sister-in-law Anne Neville, Warwick's second daughter, was married to Henry VI's son and heir, Edward of Lancaster. He shared in Warwick's successful invasion, landing on 13 September and attending Henry VI's emergence from the Tower of London on 15 October, and attended both sessions of the readeption parliament, residing at the bishop of Salisbury's house in Dowgate from October 1470 to February 1471. Unfortunately the parliament roll is lost: it is not certain whether he was recognized as reversionary heir to the crown or to the duchy of York. Probably Clarence was not associated with Warwick as king's lieutenant, as Polydore Vergil suggested. He was confirmed as lieutenant of Ireland and, against Lancastrian opposition, retained possession of the honour of Richmond.

Reconciliation with Edward IV The new regime combined unnatural allies against a common enemy, Edward IV. Once he had been deposed, old rivalries revived. Clarence and the Nevilles, as principal beneficiaries from Lancastrian defeat and forfeitures, were bound to lose property and political importance, particularly after the arrival of Queen Margaret and her son. Hence when the women of the house of York proposed reconciliation, as recounted in *The Arrivall*, they found Clarence receptive, and he secretly agreed to revert to his former allegiance. On 17 February he was at Salisbury, remaining in the west country until 2 April, when he led 4000 men into Edward IV's army at Coventry, having earlier persuaded Warwick not to deploy his numerical superiority against Edward in the expectation that the duke would be joining him. He mediated unsuccessfully between Edward IV and Warwick in the hope of saving both and fought on the king's side at Barnet, where he was wounded, and at Tewkesbury, where Prince Edward of Lancaster apparently appealed to him in vain, and thus contributed substantially to Edward IV's triumphant return. There is no convincing evidence that he was involved in any of the ineffective plotting over the next few years involving Archbishop Neville and the earl of Oxford.

Whatever King Edward's private feelings, he was reconciled with Clarence, who seems initially to have been influential at court, interceded on behalf of the city of Bristol, and attended parliament regularly. Clarence was one of those who swore allegiance to Edward's son as prince of Wales in 1471, led one of the largest contingents to invade France in 1475, and shared in the ceremonial reinterment of his father at Fotheringhay in 1476. Following Warwick's death at Barnet, and even before Tewkesbury, Clarence was allowed as husband of Warwick's elder daughter to enter all the earl's lands except the tail male Neville estate in the north, which was granted to Gloucester. Already lieutenant of Ireland, he recovered Tutbury, was appointed great chamberlain of England, and was compensated for lands that he had lost with most of the forfeited Courtenay estates in the south-west. It was at this stage of his career that he had most lands and most wealth, the equal certainly of any contemporary; he resided regularly at Tutbury, Warwick, Tewkesbury in Gloucestershire, and Tiverton in Devon. The birth in 1475 of his son Edward, to whom the king was godfather, assured the succession.

The Warwick inheritance Unfortunately the reconciliation was short-lived and domestic politics in 1471–5 were dominated by the Warwick inheritance dispute between Clarence and his brother Gloucester. Clarence's title to Warwick's lands was insecure and ambiguous. Most of it belonged in strict right to the countess of Warwick, who was in sanctuary at Beaulieu Abbey; his duchess was only one of Warwick's two daughters; and Warwick himself had died a traitor and was liable to attainder and forfeiture. To secure his position Clarence took custody of the widowed younger daughter, Anne, sought to prevent her marriage and inheritance, and may indeed have disguised her as a kitchen maid. Clarence's brother Gloucester determined to marry her and even before doing so sought her share of the inheritance, which Clarence resisted. Gloucester won a debate before the royal council in March 1472, at which partition of the whole inheritance including the Neville lands was agreed. Clarence was created earl of Warwick and Salisbury and provisionally assigned the midland and southern estates, Gloucester those in the north and Wales, to the disappointment of both dukes. Clarence however resisted a formal partition and transfer in the summer of 1473, perhaps by force, but he was restrained by a royal progress and was forced to submit by the parliamentary resumption of all his lands. Parliament implemented the division in two acts of 1474–5 that

excluded the countess of Warwick and the earl's heir male in preference to attainting Warwick. As punishment, Clarence lost Tutbury, which, the Crowland continuator reports, he strongly resented.

Judicial murder of Ankarette Twynho After 1473, when he lost Tutbury, Clarence resided mainly on his wife's estates and modelled his conduct on that of earlier earls. He extended and modernized Warwick Castle, dedicated the Beauchamp chapel in Warwick College, retained members of families traditionally associated with the earldom, arbitrated local disputes, and planned the advancement of local interests. It has been suggested that his authority declined as the decade progressed. Apparently he broke with some long-standing retainers, such as Sir Roger Tocotes, who may however have deserted him only after his arrest. It was nevertheless to Warwick that he abducted Ankarette Twynho from Somerset in April 1477, where he had her indicted, convicted, and executed in a single day on false charges of poisoning his duchess, who had died, actually from the after-effects of childbirth, on 22 December 1476. This is one of the classic instances of abuses of power by an over-mighty subject.

Arrest and trial for treason Although the Warwick inheritance dispute had not been Clarence's fault, for Gloucester was the aggressor and does not seem ever to have contracted a legal marriage with Anne Neville, the king was exasperated with Clarence's obstruction and increasingly took Gloucester's side. Clarence resented the loss of Tutbury and was further frustrated in 1477 when, following the death of his duchess, the king decisively vetoed his projected marriage first to Mary of Burgundy, 'the greatest heiress of her time', proposed by his sister Margaret, duchess of Burgundy (Ross, 251), and then to a Scottish princess. Still only twenty-seven Clarence was bound to marry again. Duke and king alike complained of one another in their households and their remarks were relayed from one to the other, understandably stimulating their mutual hostility. Clarence was not directly implicated in May 1477 in the trial, for imagining the king's death by necromancy, of his retainer Thomas Burdet of Arrow (Warwickshire), but unwisely he had Burdet's declaration of innocence on the scaffold read to the royal council. The king was not present, but was enraged. Clarence's action was the immediate cause for his summons to Westminster where, in the presence of the corporation of London, the king denounced him for 'most serious [misconduct] … in contempt of the law of the land and a great threat to judges and jurors of the kingdom' and prompted his imprisonment (*The Crowland Chronicle Continuations*, 145). It was apparently later that the king learned of the judicial murder of Ankarette Twynho.

The contemporary continuator of the Crowland chronicle does not suggest that at Clarence's arrest a trial on charges of treason was then intended, but that is what occurred in January and February 1478 at a parliament especially summoned, packed, and stage-managed for this purpose. Clarence was duly tried, convicted, and executed on 18 February 1478. The surviving act of attainder, which bears the king's sign manual, refers to the Burdet trial, to Clarence's supposed intention of sending his heir abroad, to his supposed retention of an exemplification of his Lancastrian title to the crown, to indentures of retainer that did not reserve allegiance to the king, to his claim that Edward was a bastard, and to his railing against the king. Although long, it is insubstantial and imprecise, and it is questionable whether many of the charges were treasonable; some were covered by earlier pardons, others seem improbable, none is substantiated, and certainly no accomplices were named or tried. It does not implicate Clarence in known treasons committed since 1471. The Crowland continuator was apparently an eye-witness to the trial. He was shocked by the spectacle of the king and duke in dispute, by the procedures, in which witnesses doubled as prosecutors, and was not convinced by the verdict. Neither were later commentators, almost all of whom ignore the act of attainder and search instead for explanations in court factions, especially the queen's. It is certainly true that the trial was very carefully prepared in the autumn of 1477, apparently by the queen's family, that the compliance of the duke of Gloucester was assured by a series of grants at Clarence's expense that anticipated his death and in some cases the trial itself, that efforts were made to secure a compliant House of Commons, and that the appearance of a united royal family was secured by the simultaneous marriage of the king's younger son. Any suspicion that Edward may have had of his unreliability would have been heightened by Clarence's explicit expression of resentment over the execution of Burdet, and by his judicial murder of Twynho.

Death by malmsey The king certainly led the prosecution of his brother. Edward may, however, have later repented: he had to be pushed into proceeding with Clarence's execution; he provided for an expensive funeral, monument, and chantry foundation at Tewkesbury Abbey; and he is alleged to have bewailed Clarence's death. One modern study regards Clarence's death as a judicial murder organized by the family of the queen, who persuaded King Edward to participate against his better judgement. If the queen really regarded Clarence as a threat to the succession of her son, certainly his removal substantially strengthened the king's authority over his greater subjects, as the Crowland continuator alleged.

There is no doubt that Clarence was executed for treason in the Tower of London on 18 February 1478. It appears, however, that he was neither hanged nor beheaded, as was normal, but was drowned in a butt of malmsey wine (sweet wine imported from Greece). This strange story occurs in the earliest reports, of Jean de Roye and Mancini, and was evidently known to the Crowland continuator, who declares himself uncertain. No chronicler suggests any other mode of death.

Reputation and progeny History's view of Clarence has traditionally been shaped by Shakespeare's treatment of him in 3 *Henry VI* and especially in *Richard III*. His sources, Holinshed and Hall, relied mainly on the non-contemporary accounts of Polydore Vergil and Sir Thomas

More, which he drastically reshaped both for the politics of 1464–71 and for Clarence's fall and death, which are wrongly located in 1483. Shakespeare attributes Clarence's arrest to a prophecy, probably apocryphal, that Edward IV would be succeeded by someone whose name began with G (that is, Gloucester). He has Clarence murdered rather than executed at the instigation of Gloucester: his Clarence admits to many earlier offences and is dismissed as 'false, fleeting, perjur'd Clarence'. If there is some justice in such charges, and he was certainly a failure, Clarence was not so incorrigible as the memorable phrase suggests. There is some consistency and logic to his career. He has also been accused of incompetence and (by Lander) of insanity. His actions cannot all be fully explained, but far from accusing him of madness, the Crowland chronicler pays tribute to his ability and dangerous popularity as 'an idol of the multitude' (*The Crowland Chronicle Continuations*, 133, 147). Clarence carried ambition to unreasonable extremes. On the other hand he did not merely back his retainers in their quarrels, but made serious and fairly successful attempts to arbitrate them. Rous reports that he was a great alms-giver and he was certainly a generous benefactor of the church: 'Thanks be to God', observed the Salisbury Cathedral chapter, 'who has given such a benevolent and devout prince into the tutelage of the church' (Salisbury chapter act book, 13.214). Apparently he was genuinely saddened by the death of his duchess, taking great pains over her exequies, and by the death of Thomas Burdet.

Clarence had four children. The first, unnamed, was born and died at sea off Calais in 1470 and the fourth, Richard, lived only briefly in 1476. His son and heir, *Edward, earl of Warwick, was born in 1475 and was executed for treason, unmarried, and without having been allowed to succeed to his estates in 1499. His daughter Margaret [see Pole, Margaret], born in 1473, later countess of Salisbury and mother of Cardinal Pole, was executed in 1541. Unlike his brothers, Clarence is recorded as having no mistress or bastards.

MICHAEL HICKS

Sources M. A. Hicks, '*False, fleeting, perjur'd Clarence*': George, duke of Clarence, 1449–78, rev. edn (1992) • M. A. Hicks, *Richard III and his rivals: magnates and their motives in the Wars of the Roses* (1991) • M. C. Carpenter, 'The duke of Clarence and the midlands: a study in the interplay of local and national politics', *Midland History*, 11 (1986), 23–48 • C. Ross, *Edward IV* (1974) • N. Pronay and J. Cox, eds., *The Crowland chronicle continuations, 1459–1486* (1986) • K. Dockray, ed., *Three chronicles of the reign of Edward IV* (1988) • *Thys rol was laburd and finished by Master John Rows of Warrewyk*, ed. W. Courthope (1859); repr. as *The Rous roll* (1980) • *RotP* • *Chancery records* • P. de Commynes, *Mémoires*, ed. J. Calmette and G. Durville, 3 vols. (Paris, 1924–5) • Salisbury chapter act book 13

Likenesses J. Rous, BL, Add. MS; repro. in *The Rous roll* • manuscript drawing, BL, Cotton MS Julius E.iv, art. 6, fol. 28; *see illus. in* Neville, Richard, sixteenth earl of Warwick and sixth earl of Salisbury (1428–1471) • portrait, Brocket Hall, Hertfordshire, Brocket collection

Wealth at death £4500 p.a.

George, prince of Denmark and duke of Cumberland (1653–1708), consort of Queen Anne, was born, according to an inscription on his coffin plate, at Copenhagen on 2 April 1653, the second son of Frederick III (1609–1670),

George, prince of Denmark and duke of Cumberland (1653–1708), by Sir Godfrey Kneller, 1702–8

king of Denmark, and Sophia Amalia (1628–1685), daughter of George, duke of Brunswick-Lüneburg. After a course of tuition from Otto Grote, his governor from 1661 to 1665, George travelled through France, Germany, and Italy, and accompanied the grand duke of Tuscany on his official visit to England in April 1669. In 1674 he was put forward as a candidate for the crown of Poland. The diet, however, objected to his Lutheranism, and elected John Sobieski instead. In 1677 George fought alongside his brother, King Christian V of Denmark, against the Swedes at the battle of Landskrona.

England, 1683–1688 Following an earlier visit to England in 1681, on 28 July 1683 George married Princess Anne (1665–1714) [see Anne], second daughter of James, duke of York [see James II and VII]. The marriage was a diplomatic coup for the French king, who had actively promoted it, countering that of Anne's elder sister Mary to the Dutch William of Orange, as both France and Denmark were opposed to the Dutch. Anne's husband had precedence over Mary's, which led William to refuse to visit England, even to attend James II's coronation. A principal agent in negotiating the marriage from the English side was

Anne's uncle, the earl of Rochester. He drove a hard bargain, insisting that the prince's household should be staffed exclusively by English servants and forcing his confidant Christian Siegfried von Plessen to retire to Denmark to manage George's estates there. After the marriage Anne and George took up residence in the Cockpit in Whitehall Palace. They were also given Wandsworth manor house in Surrey. John Evelyn noted in his diary that the thirty-year-old prince 'had the Danish Countenance, blound … seemed somewhat heavy; but reported Valiant' (Evelyn, 4.332). Lord Dartmouth also observed that George 'had given great proofs of bravery in his own country, where he was much beloved'; but otherwise his comments were all critical. 'Prince George of Denmark was the most indolent of all mankind', he claimed; 'King Charles the second told my father he had tried him, drunk and sober, but "God's fish" there was nothing in him' (*Bishop Burnet's History*, 3.49n.). Charles nevertheless made the prince a knight of the Garter in 1684.

When James II became king in 1685 he promoted George to the privy council, and thereafter George met every Sunday with the cabinet council, which considered foreign affairs. Apart from this, however, the prince never enjoyed any influence in James II's reign. Burnet was convinced that he 'committed a great error in not asking the command of the army' at the time of the Monmouth rebellion, 'for the command, how much soever he might have been bound to the counsels of others, would have given him some lustre; whereas his staying at home in such time of danger brought him under much neglect' (*Bishop Burnet's History*, 3.49). His staunch protestantism backed up his wife's determination to resist attempts to convert her to Catholicism. 'Luther was never more earnest than this Prince' asserted Father Petre, 'He has naturally an aversion to our society [the Jesuits] and this antipathy does much to obstruct the progress of our affair' (Gregg, 43). The prince and princess subsequently withdrew from court.

In June 1687, following an attack of smallpox, George, whose asthma had become chronic since his residence in England, went back to Denmark to try to recover his health. After his return to England on 15 August he and Anne again withdrew from court. George was aware of William of Orange's plans to invade England in 1688, and refused to accept any command in James II's army, foreseeing serious disaffection in its ranks when the Dutch invasion occurred. He attended the extraordinary meeting of the privy council in October where witnesses testified that the queen had given birth to a son, and accompanied the king to Salisbury in November. Anne, however, assured William on 18 November that George would desert to him, adding: 'I am sure will do you all the service that lyes in his power' (Dalrymple, 2/2, 334).

On 24 November George deserted James and went over to William of Orange. He had apparently been in the habit of exclaiming 'Est-il possible?' ('Is it possible?') at the news of every defection, and when he himself added to the number of defectors the king apparently dismissed his action with 'So "Est-il possible" is gone too' (Clarke, 2.225).

The Danish ambassador, however, reported to Christian V, 'Your Majesty can not imagine the King of England's consternation at this news' (Gregg, 64). George wrote James a letter justifying his conduct on the grounds that he was defending protestantism against a concerted attack by its Catholic enemies backed by Louis XIV. He might have been encouraged in his stance by the fact that one of the protestant princes who he claimed were united against France was the king of Denmark, who supplied troops for William of Orange's invading army. George joined his wife, who had also deserted James and fled to Nottingham, when she reached Oxford on 15 December, and he returned with her to London on 19 December.

Uneasy royal relations, 1689–1701 George's desertion to William was rewarded after the revolution of 1688. On 20 March 1689 he was ennobled as baron of Ockingham, earl of Kendal, and duke of Cumberland; and on 3 April an act of parliament received the royal assent naturalizing him as an English subject. The 'honeymoon' between the new monarchs, William III and Mary II, and the prince and princess of Denmark was, however, short-lived. The two sisters soon quarrelled over the princess's financial settlement. The prince too came to dispute with the king over finance. In July 1689 William was involved in peace negotiations between Sweden and Denmark, and put pressure on George to yield mortgages on some of his Danish lands to the duke of Holstein to ease the process. Although George was promised compensation, he never received it in full. The king did not pay his share of the deal until 1699. George's resentment at his treatment by the king was increased by the coldness with which William dealt with him when they went to Ireland in 1690. The prince was present at the battle of the Boyne but got no thanks from William, who 'treated him with the utmost contempt' (*Bishop Burnet's History*, 3.49). After their return to England George told William that he wished to join the navy as a volunteer. The king at first offered no objection but later changed his mind, and on departing for the continent in January 1691 left instructions that George was not to be allowed to serve in the navy and forbade him to join the ship to which he had already consigned his baggage. The prince and princess spent that summer away from court at Tunbridge Wells. In August George wrote to the king to request that the earl of Marlborough, his wife's favourite, should be admitted to the Order of the Garter, stressing that this was the only request he had ever made to William. The king took no action to grant it. Later that year Marlborough came under suspicion of Jacobitism, which led to a rupture between Mary and her sister Anne. George found himself in the invidious position of go-between, as he continued to attend meetings of the privy council. Some pressure was placed on him to play this role by his brother King Christian V of Denmark, in hopes of effecting a reconciliation between the quarrelling parties. They were not reconciled while Mary was alive, but when she died in 1694 the prince and princess re-established formal relations with the king. Informally, however, they remained as distant as ever. William continued to show coldness towards George, excluding him from the councils of regency which were set up when the king left England on his annual visits to Holland.

How George coped with his wife's frequent miscarriages, which left her devastated, can only be surmised. The death in July 1700 of their only child to survive babyhood, William, duke of Gloucester, affected him as deeply as it did Anne. They both withdrew to Windsor and saw nobody except their most intimate acquaintants. The loss of the heir to the throne reopened the question of the succession. To avoid the exiled Pretender, James Stuart, succeeding to the throne parliament passed the Act of Settlement in 1701 to provide for the accession of the house of Hanover. During the debates in the House of Lords the marquess of Normanby moved that George should be given the title of king, with precedence over the Hanoverians should he survive Anne, but this was dismissed.

Prince consort, 1702–1708 The idea of recognizing George's regal status was apparently revived after Anne's accession in 1702, when a joint monarchy similar to that of William and Mary was mooted by some tories, but was never put before parliament, which would almost certainly have rejected such 'a patent device for evading the Act of Settlement' (Holmes, 90). It is possible that the queen herself encouraged such a scheme, since she showed herself to be very ambitious for her husband. Two days after her accession she indicated to the Dutch envoys that she wished him to be elected as captain-general of the United Provinces. Anne even wrote to the states general urging his election, while the earl of Marlborough also raised the issue with Dutch officials. No doubt to his relief, the request was diplomatically ignored. Although Marlborough was appointed captain-general of the forces abroad, Anne gave George the grandiloquent if rather empty title of generalissimo on 17 April 1702. On 20 May he was also appointed lord high admiral. This too was a symbolic appointment, the real work of the Admiralty being conducted by a council headed by George Churchill, Marlborough's brother. This device of having George as admiral assisted by the so-called 'prince's council' was a constitutional anomaly. The prince was not entirely a figurehead, for he regularly attended meetings of the cabinet, which were usually held every Sunday with the queen presiding. It is nevertheless significant that he was not a member of the 'lords of the committee', which drew up the agenda for the cabinet, while the 'prince's council' did attend their meetings whenever they involved Admiralty business, and were called into cabinet meetings to discuss it even though George himself was present. He did, however, take an interest in navigation and seafaring and the welfare of seamen, and as a fellow of the Royal Society from 1704 he made arrangements for the publication of the *Observations* of the royal astronomer, John Flamsteed.

The prince's lack of aptitude for administration was compounded by the increasingly debilitating effects on his health of his chronic asthma. He suffered a severe attack in August 1702, which led him to seek relief at Bath. The waters were not efficacious, however, for after his return to Windsor in October his illness was still regarded as very serious. He recovered sufficiently to take part in December in the debates on the Occasional Conformity Bill. Ironically the prince's many offices under the crown, which included the lord wardenship of the Cinque Ports, meant that he had occasionally to take communion in the Church of England in order to qualify for them, but he usually worshipped in the Lutheran chapel in St James's. Yet he voted in the House of Lords, where he sat by virtue of being duke of Cumberland, in favour of the bill outlawing the practice whereby dissenters took communion in the established church in order to qualify for office and then frequented their own conventicles. As he did so he reportedly said to one of the whig tellers, 'my heart is vid you' (Stanhope, 80). The broken English fits in with Burnet's assertion that 'he spoke acquired languages ill and ungracefully' (*Bishop Burnet's History*, 5.391). When the tories offered to put in the bill a clause exempting the prince from its provisions he declined the offer, saying that if his conscience did not permit him to communicate with the established church he would renounce all his offices. The tories expressed their appreciation of the prince's political stance by supporting a resolution to vote him an annual income of £100,000 should he survive the queen. The whigs, on the other hand, led by the earl of Sunderland in the House of Lords, opposed a clause in a bill to enact the measure exempting George from the ban imposed by the Act of Settlement on naturalized subjects sitting in parliament, which was to come into effect on Anne's death. After strenuous exertions by the Marlboroughs the bill passed the upper house by four votes.

In the debates on the second Occasional Conformity Bill in 1703 George declined to participate, some observers attributing this to the queen's growing lukewarmness towards the measure, while others maintained that he was determined not to play the hypocrite a second time. The prince was certainly more comfortable than Anne herself with the move towards the whigs which the Marlboroughs and Lord Treasurer Godolphin insisted was essential for the queen's service. He exerted his influence as lord warden of the Cinque Ports in several parliamentary boroughs in Kent and Sussex on behalf of whig candidates in the general election of 1705. And he supported the choice of a whig speaker in the ensuing parliament to the extent of dismissing George Clarke, the secretary of the prince's council, in the lobby of the House of Commons after he voted for the tory candidate. The composition of the council itself was brought into line with changes in the ministry as they moved from high-church tory to moderate whig in the middle years of the reign. This made the continued service of George Churchill as the head of the council more and more of an anomaly. The junto whigs marked him down for destruction in their drive to gain office, and the Admiralty therefore became a prime target for their parliamentary attacks. In May 1707 there was even a rumour that the prince's council was to be wound up and that George would have the earl of Orford, a member of the junto, as his vice-admiral. These rumours apparently persuaded the prince to go along with Robert Harley's schemes to resist further encroachment of the whig

leaders. 'It was said that the prince was brought into the concert, and that he was made to apprehend that he had too small a share in the government' (*Bishop Burnet's History*, 5.335-6).

The whigs stepped up their attack in the parliamentary session of 1707-8. They not only accused the Admiralty of gross incompetence, which was an easy charge after the naval disasters of the summer, but even challenged the legality of the prince's council. Both George and Anne regarded this as an assault on their authority. It concluded in February 1708 with a blistering address from the Lords which held the prince's council, though not George himself, responsible for the mismanagement of naval affairs. Although the fall of Harley removed one obstacle in the junto's path, the whig lords were not immediately taken into the ministry, which was patched up with moderate whigs, some of them associated with the prince. The junto kept up their pressure throughout 1708, their hand strengthened by the results of the general election of that spring which produced a whig majority. Anne was determined to resist them, but the death of her husband on 28 October, at Kensington Palace, took the fight out of her and she conceded cabinet posts to lords Somers and Wharton. The prince died a week after his asthma developed complications, and was buried in the vault made for Charles II at Westminster Abbey on 13 November. 'Nature was quite worn out in him', noted Godolphin, 'and no art could support him long' (*Marlborough–Godolphin Correspondence*, 2.1142).

Prince George is usually dismissed as a boneheaded nonentity. Even his chaplain, John Tribbeko, who preached his funeral sermon, found little to say about his role in public affairs, and his private activities were likewise obscure. Yet despite Burnet's claim that 'he meddled little in business' (*Bishop Burnet's History*, 5.391) his influence behind the scenes has been underestimated.

W. A. SPECK

Sources *Bishop Burnet's History* · J. Dalrymple, *Memoirs of Great Britain and Ireland*, 2 vols. (1771-3) · R. Harley, cabinet memoranda, BL, Add. MSS 70334–70338 · E. Gregg, *Queen Anne* (1980) · G. S. Holmes, *British politics in the age of Anne* (1967) · DNB · Evelyn, *Diary* · [N. Hooke], *An account of the conduct of the dowager duchess of Marlborough ... in a letter from herself to my lord* (1742) · W. A. Speck, *The birth of Britain: a new nation, 1700–1710* (1994) · J. Tribbeko, *A funeral sermon on the death of ... Prince George of Denmark ... now translated into English* (1708) · P. H. Stanhope, Earl Stanhope, *History of England, comprising the reign of Queen Anne until the peace of Utrecht* (1870) · *The Marlborough–Godolphin correspondence*, ed. H. L. Snyder, 3 vols. (1975) · *The life of James the Second, king of England*, ed. J. S. Clarke, 2 vols. (1816) · J. L. Chester, ed., *The marriage, baptismal, and burial registers of the collegiate church or abbey of St Peter, Westminster*, Harleian Society, 10 (1876) · [H. Lyons], *The record of the Royal Society of London*, 4th edn (1940), 389

Archives BL, household papers, Egerton MS 380 | BL, Blenheim MSS · BL, Harley MSS

Likenesses G. Galton, oils, 1680, Gripsholm, Denmark · W. Wissing, oils, 1684, Reedtz-Thot Collection, Denmark · J. Riley, oils, c.1687, Royal Collection; version, NPG · M. Dahl, oils, c.1690–1704, Royal Collection · G. Kneller, oils, 1702–8, Drumlanrig Castle, Dumfriesshire [*see illus.*] · G. Kneller, oils, c.1704, NMM · by or after M. Dahl, oils, c.1705, NPG · G. Kneller, double portrait, oils, 1705 (with George Clarke), All Souls Oxf.; *see illus.* in Clarke, George (1661–1736) · P. Schenck, mezzotint, 1705 (after G. Kneller), BM, NPG · C. Boit, double portrait, enamel on copper miniature, 1706 (with Queen Anne), Royal Collection · J. Smith, mezzotint, 1706 (after G. Kneller, 1704), BM, NPG · I. Beckett, mezzotint (after W. Wissing), BM, NPG · G. Bower, medal, BM · M. Roeg, medal, BM · J. Smith, mezzotint (after M. Dahl), BM, NPG · K. von Mander, oils, Frederiksborg Castle, Denmark, Nationalhistorische Museum · mezzotint (after J. Huysmans), BM, NPG

George, Prince, second duke of Cambridge (1819–1904), army officer, was born George William Frederick Charles, the only son of *Adolphus Frederick, first duke of Cambridge (1774–1850), the youngest son of *George III. His mother was Augusta Wilhelmina Louisa (1797–1889), daughter of Frederick, landgrave of Hesse-Cassel. He was born at Cambridge House, Hanover, on 26 March 1819 and, being then the only grandchild of George III, his birth was formally attested. Prince George spent his childhood in Hanover, where his father was the governor-general, until 1830, when he was sent to live with William IV and Queen Adelaide in England. He was privately tutored by the Revd Henry Harvey, by Mr Welsh, who went mad and threatened to kill him, and by the Revd John Ryle Wood, who had sole charge of his education from 1831 to 1836. At Wood's insistence, he began to keep a diary from the age of fourteen and continued until a few months before his death. Made a knight of the Order of the Garter in August 1835, he rejoined his parents in Hanover in 1836, with his tutor replaced by a military governor, Lieutenant-Colonel William Henry Cornwall of the Coldstream Guards. Having held the rank of colonel in the Jäger battalion of the Hanoverian guards since he was nine years old, Prince George now began to learn regimental duty both as a private and an officer.

Marriage On the accession of Prince George's first cousin, Queen Victoria, in June 1837, the kingdom of Hanover passed to the duke of Cumberland. The duke of Cambridge returned with his family to England, and on 3 November 1837 Prince George was made a brevet colonel in the British army. In September 1838 he went to learn garrison duties and drill with the 33rd foot in Gibraltar. After spending six months there and another six months travelling in the south of Europe, he returned home to undertake a two-year attachment with the 12th lancers in England and Ireland. On the queen's wedding day, 10 February 1840, he met the beautiful actress and dancer Miss Sarah, usually known as Louisa, Fairbrother (1816–1890), daughter of Robert Fairbrother, a London theatrical printer. They began an affair and had two children (George William Adolphus on 27 August 1843 and Adolphus Augustus Frederick on 30 January 1846) before marrying on 8 January 1847, in defiance of the Royal Marriages Act. Known as Mrs FitzGeorge, Louisa lived in 6 Queen Street and bore the prince another son, Augustus Charles Frederick, on 12 June 1847.

Military promotion The prince's military career progressed rapidly. On 15 April 1842 he was appointed as a

Prince George, second duke of Cambridge (1819–1904), by Frank Holl, 1883

lieutenant-colonel in the 8th light dragoons and ten days later transferred to the 17th lancers as its colonel. He commanded the regiment during the industrial disturbances in Leeds during August and assisted the magistrates in restoring order. On 20 April 1843 he was appointed colonel on the staff in the Ionian Islands, and after two years' service there received the GCMG on Lord Seaton's recommendation. On 7 May 1845, at the age of twenty-six, he was promoted major-general, and later held a six-month command at Limerick before being appointed to the command of the Dublin district. He disliked Ireland, but never doubted the ability of the military and the local constabulary to maintain order, not least after the arrest of William O'Brien, a rebel leader, in 1848. While holding this command for five and a half years, he demonstrated his interest in military education by accepting appointments as commissioner for the Royal Military College, Sandhurst, and the Duke of York's School in 1850. On 1 April 1852 he was appointed inspector-general of cavalry, and in this post wrote several memoranda criticizing the current state of the army and advocating a divisional organization, annual manoeuvres for all three arms, and a system of retirement for senior officers which would permit younger men to assume senior commands. The subsequent camp held at Chobham in 1853 confirmed the prevalence of many shortcomings within the army's organization.

When his father died on 8 July 1850 the prince became the second duke of Cambridge and received from parliament an income of £12,000 a year. Made a knight of the Order of St Patrick on 18 November 1851, he was also awarded the order of the Black Eagle by the king of Prussia. He commanded the troops at the funeral of the duke of Wellington, and on 28 September 1852 was transferred as colonel from the 17th lancers to the Scots Fusilier Guards.

Commanding in the Crimea When war erupted with Russia the duke was eager to serve, and in February 1854 he was chosen to command the first division in the army destined for the Crimea. At thirty-five years of age, he was the youngest of the divisional commanders due to serve under Lord Raglan. On 10 April he accompanied his commander-in-chief to Paris, before travelling on to Vienna with a letter from the queen for Emperor Francis Joseph. He left Vienna on 1 May and reached Constantinople on the 10th. Promoted lieutenant-general on 19 June, he accompanied his division (composed of guards and highlanders) to Varna and thereafter to the Crimea. At the battle of the Alma (20 September 1854) his division was deployed in the second line behind the light division. Although personally brave, the duke had never served in battle before and lacked any experience of field command. At one point in the battle he actually considered withdrawal, but Brigadier-General Sir Colin Campbell stiffened his resolve. Exhorted by Sir George De Lacy Evans, one of the hard-pressed, front-line commanders to advance, and ordered by Raglan to do so, the duke responded in a slow, deliberate, and hesitant manner. Having halted his forces on the other side of the river, he had to be pressed again by Sir Richard Airey, the quartermaster-general, to resume the advance. Once he ordered his men forward, they moved to the front, scaled the slope first, and led the successful assault on the Russian redoubt. At the battle of Inkerman (5 November 1854), the duke led the brigade of guards to the assistance of the 2nd division and retook 'Sandbag Battery'. He had a horse shot from under him and found himself left with about a hundred men, while the remainder pushed down the slope. In trying desperately to hold the high ground, he found himself nearly cut off by an advancing Russian column and had to gallop back to his lines with his aide-de-camp. The guards lost 622 officers and men out of 1361 engaged.

Two days after Inkerman the duke was ordered to rest, as he had succumbed to dysentery and typhoid fever and was exhausted by the rigours of field command. He had taken great care of his men, and was fondly regarded by them, but was utterly dejected by the slaughter of the guards. He sought recuperation on the HMS *Retribution* but was even more alarmed when a thunderbolt struck the frigate on 14 November and nearly sank it. The duke left the Crimea on 25 November and a medical board invalided him home on 27 December. Broken 'in body and mind' (St Aubyn, 92), he was showered with honours—twice mentioned in dispatches, thanked by parliament, awarded the medal with four clasps, the Turkish medal, the grand cross of the Légion d'honneur, and the GCB (5 July 1855). As soon as he had recovered his spirits, the duke repeatedly pressed the authorities to sanction his return to the Crimea, even to succeed General Sir James Simpson when he resigned as Raglan's successor in November 1855. Lord Panmure, the secretary of state for war, rejected the proposal, doubting that the duke would display sufficient 'self-control' (Douglas and Ramsay, 1.283), and offered him instead the governorship of Gibraltar, which the duke rejected. In January 1856 the duke was sent to Paris to participate in a conference about the future conduct of the war but the peace agreed in March rendered the conference superfluous.

Commander-in-chief and army reform On 15 July 1856 the duke succeeded Lord Hardinge as general commanding-in-chief. He was promoted general and sworn of the privy council on 28 July. The duke had attained office at a time when the military administration was split between his own headquarters in Horse Guards and the war department, wherein the secretary of state for war exercised overall responsibility for the efficiency and civil administration of the army. The duke, representing the crown, had responsibility for command, discipline, appointments, and promotions. He gradually acquired a wider remit, assuming the military duties of the inspector-general of fortifications in 1859 and responsibility for the artillery and engineers when the Board of Ordnance was abolished. The duke was appointed as colonel of these two corps on 10 May 1861, and gained general control of the troops serving in India when the European troops of the East India Company were amalgamated with the army of the crown in 1862.

The duke wrote regularly to many officers in India and took a close interest in all senior appointments and promotions there. This occasionally proved irksome for the commander-in-chief in India, Lord Roberts, who managed to minimize his disagreements with the duke and to prevail over his objections by adroitly outmanoeuvring him. In pressing for the accelerated promotion of Sir George White, Lord Roberts briefed the editor of *The World* on an unattributable basis about White's services in Upper Burma, and his relative merits compared with the 222 colonels senior to him. In promoting the introduction of an army corps system within India (and the consequent abolition of the presidency armies), he overcame the recalcitrance of the duke by securing the endorsement of his scheme by the duke of Connaught, the queen's adored son.

By contrast with his subsequent reputation as an arch-conservative, resolutely opposed to many army reforms, the duke was a proponent of many improvements in his early years as the general commanding-in-chief. He took a keen interest in military music and founded the school of military music at Kneller Hall in 1857. He favoured improvements in military education and the training of men for the commissariat and for staff duties. He supported the creation of a department of military education, helped to found the Staff College in 1858, and pressed the case for annual military manoeuvres. When the volunteer movement arose in 1859 he proffered tacit support for it, even if he had little faith in the movement and opposed the award of a capitation grant. He assumed the colonelcy of the 1st City of London brigade on 24 February 1860 and the presidency of the National Rifle Association, which was founded in 1859. In 1862 he was made governor of the Royal Military Academy at Woolwich, and on the death of the prince consort exchanged the colonelcy of the Scots Fusilier Guards for that of the Grenadier Guards. On 9 November 1862 he was made a field marshal. During the first thirteen years of command, he worked effectively with successive secretaries of state, especially Sidney Herbert, who held office from 1859 to his death in 1861. Nevertheless, the duke always opposed reductions in military expenditure, advocated increases in the size of the army, and defended the system of promotion by purchase as effective in practice, if indefensible in theory.

The duke found it much more difficult to work with Edward Cardwell when he became secretary of state in December 1868. Cardwell, supported by W. E. Gladstone as prime minister, embarked upon a series of wide-ranging reforms which undermined many of the traditions cherished by the duke. In the first place, Cardwell reduced the army estimates by nearly halving the number of men deployed in colonial garrisons, cutting the stores vote, and reducing the size of the infantry battalion cadres retained at home. The duke deplored these measures, fearing that the home units were now too small, once their raw recruits were deducted, to serve in Ireland or elsewhere, and that the remaining overseas battalions would soon become much less effective once disease and dissipation had taken their toll. Cardwell then prepared the way for further reforms by removing the so-called 'dual government' of the army which had preserved a costly and cumbersome bureaucracy. By the War Office Act of 1870 the general commanding-in-chief was definitely subordinated to the war minister, and became one of three departmental chiefs charged respectively with military, supply, and financial matters. To underpin the reform, the duke was required to remove his offices from Horse Guards to the War Office in Pall Mall. He deeply resented the reorganization, regarding it as one which undermined the sovereign's rights and his own status within the army. Although the queen interceded on his behalf, her ministers were resolute and the duke had to move, only extracting the concession that he could address his letters from the 'Horse Guards, Pall Mall'.

Thereafter Cardwell introduced short-service enlistments (with accompanying measures to form an army reserve), the abolition of purchase, and the linking of infantry battalions and their localization within specific territorial districts in which militia battalions and volunteers were also located. The duke opposed all these measures as liable to undermine the regimental system and the virtues of the old army composed of long-service

soldiers. He feared the consequences of abolishing promotion by purchase and, when forced by the government to support the proposal in the House of Lords debate, spoke inaudibly and without conviction. After the Lords rejected the abolition bill, and the government abolished purchase by royal warrant, the duke insisted that he would approve promotions thereafter only on the basis of seniority tempered by selection. If the duke's ill-concealed indignation encouraged many officers to believe that the reforms of 1870–72 could be reversed, his concerns, particularly about the short-term utility of the reserve, were largely apposite. He feared that the reserve, whose accumulation could not begin until 1876, would not meet the requirements of small colonial conflicts, and that expeditionary forces could be formed only by raiding the home-based battalions for fit and experienced men. In spite of this difficulty, and a growing imbalance between the battalions stationed at home and abroad (which augmented the strains on the home-based units), successive governments retained the system, and in 1881 the secretary of state, H. C. E. Childers, welded the linked battalions into double battalions within territorial regiments. The duke regarded the consequent loss of the historic regimental numbers and the facings on uniforms as a further blow to *esprit de corps*.

Nor was the duke impressed by the readiness of Sir Garnet Wolseley to endorse the Cardwell system, to form his expeditionary forces by finding volunteers from home-based battalions, and to select particular officers to serve on his campaign staffs. The duke feared that Wolseley's 'ring' of officers was likely to prove divisive within the army, and maintained that Wolseley had an exaggerated reputation as a commander. He contended that Wolseley had advanced his career by manipulating the press, advocating reform, and exploiting his connections with Liberal politicians. Although he periodically applauded Wolseley's achievements, especially the victory at Tell al-Kebir (13 September 1882), the duke desperately tried to block his career, even threatening to resign over Wolseley's appointment as adjutant-general. Personal relations between the men never really improved, but they were able to work together on certain issues: they both sought to dilute civilian control of the army, to advocate the creation of a larger and better-equipped army for home defence, and to denounce the channel tunnel concept as a grave risk to national security. They both favoured the retention of the duke's office, which the queen had elevated on 26 November 1887 (after the duke had completed fifty years' service in the army) by appointing him as commander-in-chief by patent.

Persuaded to retire However, the office of commander-in-chief had become increasingly controversial. After the complaints about supply and transport during the Nile campaign had been upheld by a royal commission chaired by Sir James Fitzjames Stephen in 1887, the office of surveyor-general of the ordnance was abolished on 21 February 1888. This left the duke with responsibility for all matters of military personnel and *matériel*, including the collection of intelligence and the construction and maintenance of fortifications. The administration, in all matters save finance, had now become excessively centralized, with the subordinate heads of departments able to advise the secretary of state only informally. In June 1888 another royal commission, headed by Lord Hartington, began an inquiry into naval and military administration, and in May 1890 it recommended that the office of commander-in-chief should cease to exist when the duke retired, and that a chief of the staff should be appointed. Sir Henry Campbell-Bannerman, who became war minister in 1892, dissented from the majority recommendation and opposed the creation of a chief of staff, but he still favoured enhancing the degree of civilian control by establishing a board of advisers with equal and direct access to the secretary of state. Unable to implement this reform until the duke retired, the government pressed for the duke's resignation in May and June 1895. The duke, though seventy-six years of age, felt fit and able to remain in office; he resolutely opposed all pressure until the queen reluctantly at last advised him to resign. On 31 October he issued his farewell order and handed over command to Lord Wolseley. As a consolation the queen appointed the duke as her chief personal aide-de-camp and colonel-in-chief to the forces, with the right to hold the parade on her birthday.

In announcing the duke's impending retirement to the House of Commons on 21 June, Campbell-Bannerman alluded to his attractive personality, his devotion to the interests of the army, and his knowledge of its traditions and requirements. He also emphasized that the duke had a fund of common sense and a deeply rooted respect for constitutional proprieties. The duke was immensely popular within the army. An excellent after-dinner speaker, he was known to be kindly and considerate, a staunch upholder of military traditions, and a keen sportsman. He was also fondly regarded by those who appreciated his thorough knowledge of drill and his outspoken comments at field days and inspections. A series of banquets at military clubs and messes marked the duke's retirement, and for several years he kept in close touch with the army, presiding at regimental dinners and riding in Queen Victoria's diamond jubilee procession of 1897 and at the Salisbury manoeuvres of 1898.

Other activities, decline, and death In spite of his considerable weight, which rigorous dieting could reduce to just under 16 stones, the duke was energetic and undertook a wide range of royal duties. In 1862 he opened an international exhibition, entertaining the foreign commissioners and distributing the prizes. He also took a real interest in several charities and presided over the London Hospital, Christ's Hospital, and the Royal Female Orphan Asylum for fifty years. When elected as the president of Christ's Hospital on 23 March 1854, he was the first president who was not an alderman of the City of London. Thereafter he worked enthusiastically for it, and in his later years championed the opposition to the proposed removal of the school to Horsham. He even described that prospect as 'the most *wanton* thing that ever was undertaken' (Sheppard, 2.322). He was much in demand as a chairman and speaker at charitable meetings and dinners, since he often established a good rapport with his audience.

Personally the duke appeared to be the embodiment of the bluff, hearty English gentleman with a penchant for field sports and good living. Yet he also had artistic and musical interests and was an emotional man, devoted to his mother, who lived until 6 April 1889, and to his wife. Louisa sometimes suspected that he spread his affections and favours rather too widely, but he was distraught by her death on 12 January 1890. He led the mourning at her burial in Kensal Green cemetery, and regularly marked the anniversary of her death.

The duke had rooms at St James's Palace from 1840 to 1859 but then moved to Gloucester House, Park Lane, left to him by his aunt, the duchess of Gloucester. On the death of the duchess of Cambridge the queen granted him Kew Cottage for the rest of his life. He had been made ranger of Hyde Park and St James's Park in 1852, and of Richmond Park in 1857. In addition to the orders already mentioned, he received the usual plethora of British and foreign orders, colonelcies, honorary degrees, and civic distinctions awarded to royalty by royalty and others; these included the Thistle in 1881.

Cambridge's strength and hearing began to fade in his later years. He was unable to ride at the queen's funeral and had to attend in a carriage. He paid his last visit to Germany in August 1903. On 17 March 1904 he died at Gloucester House of a haemorrhage of the stomach, and on the 22nd he was buried, in accordance with his wishes, beside his wife at Kensal Green. The first part of the service was held at Westminster Abbey with Edward VII as the chief mourner. He was survived by three sons: Colonel George William Adolphus FitzGeorge; Rear-Admiral Sir Adolphus Augustus Frederick FitzGeorge, who became equerry to his father in 1897; and Colonel Sir Augustus Charles Frederick FitzGeorge, who was his father's private secretary and equerry from 1886 to 1895.   EDWARD M. SPIERS

Sources W. Verner, *The military life of H.R.H. George, duke of Cambridge*, 2 vols. (1905) · G. St. Aubyn, *The royal George* (1963) · J. E. Sheppard, *George, Duke of Cambridge: a memoir of his private life*, 2 vols. (1906) · *The Panmure papers, being a selection from the correspondence of Fox Maule*, ed. G. Douglas and G. D. Ramsay, 2 vols. (1908) · B. J. Bond, 'The retirement of the duke of Cambridge', *Journal of the Royal United Service Institution*, 106 (1961), 544–53 · H. Strachan, *The reform of the British army, 1830–1854* (1984) · E. M. Spiers, *The late Victorian army, 1868–1902* (1992) · A. Bruce, *The purchase system in the British army, 1660–1871*, Royal Historical Society Studies in History, 20 (1980) · A. R. Skelley, *The Victorian army at home: the recruitment and terms and conditions of the British regular, 1859–1899* (1977) · J. Sweetman, *War and administration* (1984) · *Roberts in India: the military papers of Field Marshal Lord Roberts, 1876–1893*, ed. B. Robson (1993) · A. E. Sullivan, 'The last commander-in-chief: George Duke of Cambridge', *Army Quarterly*, 61/1 (Oct 1950) · K. M. Wilson, *Channel tunnel visions, 1850–1945: dreams and nightmares* (1994) · GEC, *Peerage* · *The Times* (18 March 1904), 7

Archives CUL, corresp. · Royal Arch., military papers; royal MSS | Balliol Oxf., letters to Jonathan Reel and Lady Alice Reel · Balliol Oxf., corresp. with David Urquhart · BL, corresp. with Sir Henry Campbell-Bannerman, Add. MSS 41209 · BL, corresp. with

W. E. Gladstone, Add. MSS 44192–44760 · BL, corresp. with Lady Holland, Add. MS 52113 · BL, corresp. with Sir Stafford Northcote, Add. MS 50013 · BL OIOC, corresp. with Lord Napier · Bodl. Oxf., letters to Michael Bruce · Bodl. Oxf., letters to Lord Kimberley · Bodl. Oxf., letters to Samuel Wilberforce · Borth. Inst., corresp. with Lord Halifax · Bucks. RLSS, letters to duke of Somerset · CAC Cam., corresp. with Lord Randolph Churchill · Chatsworth House, Derbyshire, letters to Lord Hartington · CKS, letters to Aretas Akers-Douglas · CKS, letters to Edward Stanhope · CKS, letters to Lord Stanhope · CUL, corresp., incl. letters to Sir Richard Airey · CUL, Royal Commonwealth Society collection, corresp. with Hugh Childers · Glos. RO, letters to Sir Michael Hicks Beach · Gwent RO, Cwmbrân, letters to Lord Raglan · Herefs. RO, letters to Lord Airey · Hove Central Library, Sussex, letters to Lord Wolseley · LPL, corresp. with A. C. Tait · Lpool RO, corresp. with fifteenth earl of Derby · Lpool RO, letters to fourteenth earl of Derby · NA Scot., corresp. with Lord Panmure · NAM, letters to Colonel T. Barker · NAM, letters to Sir Frederick Haines · NAM, corresp. with Lord Raglan · NAM, letters to Lord Roberts · NAM, letters to Sir H. J. Warne · New Brunswick Museum, corresp. with Sir W. F. Williams · NL Scot., corresp. with Sir George Brown · NL Scot., corresp., incl. to Lord Rosebery · NRA Scotland, priv. coll., letters to duke of Argyll · NRA Scotland, priv. coll., letters to Lord Campbell · priv. coll., FitzGeorge MSS · PRO, corresp. with Lord Cardwell, PRO 30/48 · PRO, corresp. with Lord Carnarvon, PRO 30/6 · PRO, letters to Lord Cowley, FO 519 · PRO, corresp. with Lord Granville, PRO 30/29 · PRO, corresp. with Sir Edward Malet, FO 343 · PRO, corresp. with Lord John Russell, PRO 30/22 · Royal Arch., letters to Lord Westmorland · Som. ARS, letters to Lady Waldegrave · St Deiniol's Library, Hawarden, letters to duke of Newcastle · Suffolk RO, Ipswich, letters to Lord Cranbrook · U. Durham, corresp. with Charles Grey · U. Southampton L., corresp. with Lord Palmerston · U. Southampton L., corresp. with W. F. Cowper-Temple · W. Sussex RO, letters to fifth duke of Richmond and sixth duke of Richmond · Wilts. & Swindon RO, corresp. with Sidney Herbert

Likenesses H. W. Dawe, mezzotint, pubd 1830 (after Tielemann), BM, NPG · W. Behnes, marble bust, 1831, Royal Collection · J. Lucas, oils, 1836, Royal Collection · S. F. Diez, pencil and wash drawing, 1841, Staatliche Museen zu Berlin, Germany · J. P. Knight, oils, exh. RA 1866, Christ's Hospital, Horsham, Sussex · F. Sargent, pencil drawing, 1870–80, NPG · Gleichen, marble bust, exh. RA 1883, Army and Navy Club, London · F. Holl, portrait, 1883 (as a field marshal), Royal Collection [*see illus.*] · H. von Herkomer, oils, 1893, Royal Engineers, Chatham, Kent · R. Lehmann, drawing, 1893, BM · A. S. Cope, oils, 1897; formerly at United Service Club, London, in care of Crown Commissioners · F. J. Williamson, marble bust, exh. RA 1897, Corporation of London · A. Jones, statue, 1907, War Office, Whitehall · Aτη [A. Thompson], caricature, chromolithograph, NPG; repro. in *VF* (23 April 1870) · H. J. Brooks, oils, Staff College, Camberley, Surrey · J. Clarck, photograph, NPG · W. & D. Downey, photographs, NPG · A. J. Dubois Drahonet, group portrait, Royal Collection · Fenton, photograph, NPG · A. Jones, bronze statue, Whitehall, London · Maull & Polyblank, photograph, NPG · H. H. Voigt, photograph, repro. in Verner, *Military life* · Walery, photograph, NPG · F. X. Winterhalter, oils, Royal Collection · group portraits, Royal Collection · group portrait, sepia photograph, NPG · memorial window, St Paul's Cathedral, chapel of St Michael and St George · oils, NAM · oils, Kneller Hall, Twickenham · oils, Gov. Art Coll. · photograph, NAM · photographs, BM, NPG · prints, BM, NPG

Wealth at death under £121,000: GEC, *Peerage*

George, Prince, first duke of Kent (1902–1942), naval and air force officer, was born George Edward Alexander Edmund at York Cottage, Sandringham, on 20 December 1902, the fifth child and fourth son of *George V (1865–1936) and Queen *Mary (1867–1953). After several years (1912–16) at St Peter's Court, Broadstairs—being, with his

Prince George, first duke of Kent (1902–1942), by Dorothy Wilding, 1934

brother Prince Henry, the first sons of a British monarch to attend preparatory school—Prince George in October 1916 joined the Royal Naval College at Osborne. Throughout his education he was harried by his father in a way only too familiar to his elder brothers. 'Being at the bottom of the term I consider a disgrace, as you passed in half way up, you have only got to make up your mind to try your best and all will be right', wrote the king sternly (23 Jan 1917, Royal Archives). In fact he was perfectly correct; Prince George was intelligent and quick-witted, but he disliked concentrating on matters that did not absorb him and was easily beguiled into more agreeable if less meritorious pursuits.

The naval college at Dartmouth followed Osborne in 1917, and in May 1920 Prince George joined HMS *Temeraire*. For the next seven years he led the life of a normal naval officer, serving mainly with the Mediterranean Fleet but passing through the Royal Naval College at Greenwich in 1924 and, as a lieutenant, joining HMS *Hawkins* at Shanghai. During these years he grew close to his mother, with whom he shared many tastes. 'I've been sight-seeing with Mama and seen various cathedrals and abbeys and old houses, but I don't think that it would have amused you', he told the king (24 Aug 1923, Royal Archives). He acquired a particularly keen eye for furniture and became, initially in a modest way, something of a collector. He was an enthusiastic pianist, preferring popular music but capable of grappling competently with the classics. He was also a good shot, relishing stalking in the highlands, rode courageously to hounds, and was a zealous golfer.

From 1927 Prince George's association with the Royal Navy became more desultory. He spent the first half of that year travelling around Europe, and in July accompanied his brother, the prince of Wales, on a visit to Canada. He briefly rejoined the Atlantic Fleet, but by 1929 was serving in the western department of the Foreign Office, dealing chiefly with Spain, Portugal, and the League of Nations. Subsequently he spent a period in the Home Office, where he specialized in working conditions in factories, a concern which remained with him all his life.

These were difficult years. Prince George was exceptionally good-looking, taller than most of his family, athletic in build, and with piercingly bright blue eyes; and his charm, coupled with his royal birth, made him irresistibly attractive to many women. By temperament he was enquiring, adventurous, and dangerously ready to sample any delight that might be offered him. He fell into the grasp of an American adventuress, drank too much, experimented with drugs, and had to be rescued by the prince of Wales. By November 1930, however, the worst was past; when George V appointed him his representative at the celebration of King Haakon's jubilee in Oslo, he wrote with satisfaction that 'this dismal chapter of your life is now over' (25 Nov 1930, Royal Archives). In fact Prince George was still to give his parents a fright or two, until in 1934 he became engaged to Princess *Marina (1906–1968), daughter of Prince Nicholas of Greece. Shortly before his marriage (on 29 November 1934), he was created duke of Kent, earl of St Andrews, and Baron Downpatrick.

Prince George had justly been criticized for his choice of friends, but his selection of a wife was impeccable. Princess Marina was beautiful, intelligent, and resolute, and she gave her husband a new sense of purpose and commitment. He began to take on increasingly important roles, in 1935 being appointed lord high commissioner to the general assembly of the Church of Scotland. The abdication crisis of 1936 caused him much distress, since he felt particularly close to Edward VIII and got on well with Mrs Simpson, but he never doubted that his loyalty to the country and the institution of monarchy must outweigh his affection for his brother. He did not attend the wedding of the duke of Windsor and caused still more offence when he accepted the views of his wife and mother and refused to call on the duke in the course of a European holiday.

In 1935 the duke inherited from his aunt, Princess Victoria, a country house, Coppins, near Iver, in Buckinghamshire. Here he installed his by now distinguished collection of furniture and paintings, and he and his wife brought up their three children: Prince Edward George Nicholas Paul Patrick (b. 1935), Princess Alexandra Helen Elizabeth Olga Christabel (b. 1936), and Prince Michael George Charles Franklin (b. 1942). In 1938 he was designated governor-general of Australia, a task which he would have performed with tact and style; but the Second World War began before he could take up the appointment. Instead, in 1939 he succeeded his great-uncle, the duke of Connaught, as grand master of the freemasons,

and in the same year returned to the navy. He was attached to the intelligence division of the Admiralty with the rank of captain (later rear-admiral).

In April 1940 Kent transferred to the Royal Air Force, renouncing his honorary rank of air vice-marshal on the grounds that it would have made him senior to many men of incomparably greater experience. He was appointed group captain in the Training Command and was given responsibility for supervising welfare work at the larger air force stations—a task which involved a great deal of travel, both in the United Kingdom and abroad. On 25 August 1942, shortly after being promoted air commodore, he set out to inspect Royal Air Force establishments in Iceland. His plane crashed at the Eagle's Rock, near Dunbeath, in Caithness, and all on board were killed. The duke was buried at St George's Chapel, Windsor, and later at a private burial-ground at Frogmore, Windsor. His elder son, Prince Edward, succeeded to his titles.

PHILIP ZIEGLER

Sources private information (2004) · Royal Arch. · *Daily Telegraph* (26 Aug 1942) · *The Times* (26 Aug 1942)
Archives Royal Arch. | Norfolk RO, letters to E. G. Buxton | FILM BFI NFTVA, documentary footage · BFI NFTVA, news footage
Likenesses F. Salisbury, black chalk drawing, 1922, Courtauld Inst., NPG · D. Wilding, chlorobromide print, 1934, NPG [*see illus.*] · P. A. de Laszlo, two oil paintings, 1934–5, Courtauld Inst. · C. Beaton, photographs
Wealth at death £157,735 4s. 1d.: probate, 27 Jan 1943, *CGPLA Eng. & Wales*

George I (1660–1727), king of Great Britain and Ireland and elector of Hanover, was born Georg Ludwig (George Lewis) at Hanover on 28 May 1660, the first of the seven children who survived of the marriage in 1658 of Ernst August (1629–1698) of Brunswick-Lüneburg to *Sophia (1630–1714), youngest daughter of Frederick V of the Palatinate, Winter King of Bohemia, and of *Elizabeth, daughter of James I of England. At the time of the marriage, and still in 1660, Ernst August was not a ruling prince. He had the expectation of becoming the next protestant prince–bishop of Osnabrück, but that was a non-hereditary position which, under the terms of the settlement of 1648, alternated between Roman Catholic and protestant incumbents. Moreover, as the youngest of the four sons of the junior branch of the dukes of Brunswick, his chances of becoming the ruling prince of either of the two duchies into which the Brunswick-Lüneburg inheritance had been divided under the will of his father, Duke Georg (1582–1641), were remote.

Nor did they become much more certain when, on 21 April 1658, Ernst August's brother Georg Wilhelm, as amends for the slight he had done Sophia and the Palatinate house, and for the dishonour he had brought upon his own house by reneging on a solemn contract to marry Sophia, entered into an agreement with him never to get married. There was still no guarantee that Ernst August would succeed to either of the two duchies and anyway, given the track record of Georg Wilhelm in breaking promises, the agreement might not be honoured. Still, it was the best deal available, and it did at least offer Ernst

George I (1660–1727), by Sir Godfrey Kneller, 1716 [replica; original, 1714]

August improved odds in the race for an inheritance. Mortality among his competitors greatly improved his chances. In 1661 he achieved independent status as prince–bishop of Osnabrück, which gave him an army and the capacity to perform a minor role on the stage of European power politics. In 1665 his eldest brother, Christian Ludwig, died without children. In 1679 another brother, Johann Friedrich, died without a male heir, and Ernst August succeeded him as duke of Calenberg (Hanover). If the engagement of 1658 remained in place then Ernst August was now within sight of reuniting the Brunswick-Lüneburg duchies, and closer to realizing the long-cherished dream of the dukes of Brunswick-Lüneburg of obtaining from the emperor elevation to the prestigious, influential, and financially rewarding rank of elector by creating a ninth, Hanoverian, electorate. Georg Ludwig and his prospects now became central to Ernst August's designs.

Early years and preparations for becoming elector of Hanover 1660–1698 As the eldest son of an ambitious father who was fearful that he might die young or in battle, Georg Ludwig's early education and experience had been shaped to prepare him for the vital role he would be called upon

to play. His early years seem to have been happy and conventional. Sophia was a good and devoted mother to all her children: Georg Ludwig, if not the best loved, was much loved. He seems to have been in his mother's eyes dutiful, conscientious, and anxious to please, capable of jollity, but in the eyes of others reserved, even cold. He received a formal education from a governor and a preceptor until 1675. Although never as good at languages as his mother, and never possessing anything but the most rudimentary knowledge of English, he was no mean linguist. His education and a cosmopolitan court enabled him to gain a good command of French and German, the languages with which he grew up, as well as Latin, some Italian, and Dutch. But his interests seem to have been practical. From an early age he showed that liking for things military which was to become a dominating passion throughout the rest of his life. It was a liking which his father shared and encouraged. Father and son were also companions in riding and hunting. Georg Ludwig developed into a good horseman, and riding and hunting remained his abiding pleasures. In 1675 he received his first taste of military combat, accompanying his father in operations against the French in the so-called Dutch War, showing personal bravery at the battle of Conzbrücke. He participated in three more campaigns in that war, in 1676, 1677, and 1678, developing into a capable officer. More serious preparations for his future as a ruling prince took place from 1679, after Ernst August became duke of Hanover.

A suitable marriage for Georg Ludwig was one preparation. Ernst August's long-settled choice of a bride for his eldest son seems to have been *Sophia Dorothea, born in 1666, the only child of Georg Wilhelm and his Huguenot wife, formerly his mistress. Georg Wilhelm's marriage in a church ceremony in 1676, which of course broke his promise of 1658, not only removed retrospectively the stigma of illegitimacy from their daughter, but meant that any future sons would be legitimate. The marriage therefore placed at further risk the prospects of Ernst August for himself and his family. The risk increased, or became more evident, when in 1675 Sophia Dorothea became engaged to the son and heir of the prestigious elder branch of the house of Brunswick. That particular danger proved temporary and was removed the following year with the death of the prospective bridegroom at the siege of Philippsburg. But the alarm was heeded by Ernst August: any bridegroom for Sophia Dorothea other than Georg Ludwig posed too much of a risk to plans and prospects so long and carefully nurtured. But there seemed no harm, and possibly some leverage in negotiations with Georg Wilhelm, in allowing it to be thought that other possibilities were being considered, or were not excluded.

This is the context in which must be judged the visit Georg Ludwig made to the court of Charles II in December 1680, a visit made upon the prompting initially of Sophia's brother Prince Rupert. There is no evidence that Georg Ludwig was empowered to make any overtures of marriage to Princess Anne (later Queen Anne), the younger daughter of the duke of York, or indeed that any matrimonial proposal concerning them was ever considered at any point in the entire course of Georg Ludwig's visit, which lasted until March 1681 and included a visit to the University of Oxford to receive an honorary degree. Nor does there seem to be any substance in the charges made later that the incident excited in Anne and Georg Ludwig feelings of humiliation and rejection which affected their subsequent relations with each other and between Hanover and England, sowing in Anne the seeds of her later enmity towards Hanover, and causing Georg Ludwig to bear a grudge against England and the English. But it did cause Ernst August to resume more seriously negotiations for the hand of Sophia Dorothea, which concluded with the celebration of her marriage with Georg Ludwig on 22 November 1682.

Sophia Dorothea was aged sixteen, Georg Ludwig was twenty-two. Probably Georg would have accepted any bride in the service of his house, even a 'cripple', as his mother delicately put it, but initially he does not seem to have actively disliked his bride. Sophia Dorothea for her part did what was primarily expected of her. In November 1683 she presented Georg Ludwig with their first child, baptized Georg August (George Augustus), the future *George II. Since primogeniture had just recently been decreed by Ernst August for his dominions, though it had yet to be accepted by all members of his family, an undivided succession into a second generation was within reach. The marriage and primogeniture together also strengthened Ernst August's bid for the electoral cap: it made more certain that on the death of Georg Wilhelm, Celle, his dukedom, would be joined to Hanover, while the size and strength of the combined lands might help to convince the emperor that here was a force worth cultivating, and worthy of the electoral cap.

Further evidence of the availability and value of that force was soon forthcoming. Georg Ludwig and his brother Friedrich August were dispatched as volunteers with a small body of cavalry to take part in Sobieski's raising of the siege of Vienna in 1683, as a pledge, and as the first instalment, of further and more significant Hanoverian involvement, once the electoral cap had been secured. In 1684 and 1685 Georg Ludwig, his brothers, and Hanoverian forces saw further service in campaigns against the Turks in Hungary. What clinched matters, however, was Ernst August's promise of full and formal Hanoverian participation in the so-called Palatinate War between the emperor and Louis XIV, which had broken out in 1688, on condition that the emperor agree to Hanover's becoming the ninth electorate. Hard pressed militarily and under pressure from his principal ally, William III, the emperor gave way. In December 1692 Ernst August became elector, though Hanover's introduction into the electoral college remained to be negotiated, and proved a difficult and lengthy process.

By now Georg Ludwig and Sophia Dorothea had a five-year-old daughter as well as a son. The daughter, another Sophia Dorothea, was born in 1687, and became the queen of Frederick William I of Prussia. By now too the couple,

who were ill matched, had grown apart, having been separated for long stretches while Georg Ludwig had been on his campaigns. Separation had encouraged indifference, and indifference had developed into mutual repugnance and infidelity. Not later than 1691 Georg Ludwig took a lover seven years his junior, Ehrengard Melusine (Melusina) von der *Schulenburg, later duchess of Kendal, who gave him a daughter (the first of three) in January 1692. In 1692 Sophia Dorothea and a Swedish count, Philipp Christoph von Königsmarck, a colonel in the Hanoverian army, became lovers. If Sophia Dorothea had been discreet she might have avoided her wretched fate, but she was not, and neither was her lover. Warnings that the affair must cease were ignored. When elopement seemed likely, the love affair became a matter of state, which had to be terminated.

Georg Ludwig seems to have played no part in the killing of Königsmarck on 1 July 1694, at the hands, it is thought, of Hanoverian courtiers, with Ernst August an accessory either before or after the count's death. He was perhaps deliberately kept out of the way and in ignorance of the planned assassination. He may not have insisted on divorce from Sophia Dorothea but he did not resist it, and nor did Sophia Dorothea: indeed, initially she warmly embraced it. On 28 December 1694 the marriage was dissolved, on the grounds of Sophia Dorothea's refusal to cohabit. Sophia Dorothea spent the rest of her life a virtual prisoner at Ahlden, near Celle. While alive she was a focus for diplomatic intrigues against Hanover as long as Hanover's admission into the electoral college remained in the balance, and after 1715 she was a focus for Jacobite conspiracies, which helps to explain her position until her death on 3 November 1726.

During her confinement Georg Ludwig saw to it that Sophia Dorothea's financial circumstances were well managed. For the most part, however, he tried to act as if she did not exist and, by making the divorce a forbidden subject between himself and his children, encouraged them to do the same. Whether he succeeded in respect of his son Georg August is a matter for speculation, as is the argument that Georg Ludwig's hatred for his son is to be explained largely in terms of the latter's regard for his mother. Hatred of father for son seems to have run in the family, as it did in other royal families of the period. The rising son was rarely a pleasant sight.

The elector of Hanover and the claiming of the English and protestant succession, 1698–1714 Shortly after the divorce the health of Ernst August began to fail, and he died on 23 January 1698, to be succeeded as elector by Georg Ludwig. From 1694 Georg Ludwig had taken over the day-to-day government of the electorate. With his father's death he assumed full responsibility for electoral policy. The campaign of 1693, in which he had narrowly avoided death at the battle of Neerwinden, proved to be the last engagement in which he participated during the course of the Palatinate War. Henceforth Hanover became the seat of his activities, and the security of its newly won status his main concern. The domestic affairs of the electorate were largely a matter of routine, but its foreign affairs in the second half of the 1690s required and received careful and decisive action, and were concentrated on countering a number of threats from opponents of Hanover's ninth electorate.

The English succession does not seem to have occasioned Georg Ludwig's personal intervention until 1698. As long as Ernst August had been alive, Sophia had been allowed great freedom in the handling of English affairs, and naturally so. There had been little to show for her activities. In 1688–9 she had failed to persuade William III and the English parliament to include in the Bill of Rights provision for a contingency that then seemed remote, by designating Sophia and her descendants as next in the line of succession, after Mary and Anne, and the heirs of their bodies, and in the event of there being no heirs of William III by another marriage. After the birth in July 1689 of a son, William (later duke of Gloucester), to Princess Anne, there had seemed no point, and some risk, in taking up the issue again, and it had been allowed to rest. But it was not forgotten.

Early in 1698 Georg Ludwig cautiously sought to get the matter aired again, using the duchess of Celle, the mother of Sophia Dorothea, as his intermediary, to remind William III of the claims of Sophia, himself, and his son to the English and protestant succession. It is a reminder too that Georg Ludwig was not personally indifferent to the English succession. If he was usually content to allow his mother to set the pace, it was not simply out of filial respect, but was done in the conviction that their purposes were the same. When Sophia's actions seemed to endanger those purposes, as they did in 1706, Georg Ludwig moved swiftly to make sure that this would not happen again.

What effect, if any, Georg Ludwig's initiative had in 1698 is not clear. What is certain is that the death in July 1700 of the duke of Gloucester reopened the question of the English succession. It became plain to William III and the English parliament that the provisions made for the succession in the Bill of Rights of 1689 were no longer sufficient. The choice of a successor in the line of succession established in 1689 was not difficult. That successor had to be a protestant—no Roman Catholic would have been considered—and of Stuart descent, a combination which automatically excluded over fifty claimants with a closer hereditary claim. The person who united these qualifications was Sophia. The Act of Settlement of June 1701 settled the English succession (in so far as this could be achieved by act of parliament) in favour of Sophia and the heirs of her body, being protestant, in default of direct heirs of Anne and William. In August 1701 an English embassy arrived in Hanover to present Sophia with a copy of the Act of Settlement, and to invest Georg Ludwig with the Order of the Garter, the highest English honour the crown could bestow.

Meanwhile, in Europe Georg Ludwig was gathering honours of a different sort. In 1699 he took charge of the army which helped to effect the restitution to the duke of Holstein-Gottorp of lands and rights seized by Denmark. The following year, at the treaty of Travendal, Denmark agreed to return the lands and rights she had seized, and not to oppose Hanover's electoral title. In 1701 Hanover and Celle joined the second grand alliance against France. In joining the grand alliance Georg Ludwig sought to advance both his Hanoverian and his English interests, for the alliance committed its signatories to securing the English succession and enforcing recognition of Hanover's ninth electorate upon Louis XIV. In 1702 Georg Ludwig made another significant political gain, and displayed considerable military skill, in invading Wolfenbüttel. The purpose of the operation was to pre-empt the plans of its co-regent, Duke Anton Ulrich, to seize the duchy of Celle. The operation was successful and almost bloodless, and was conducted with tact and moderation, as well as military skill. In 1705 Georg Ludwig received his due reward. Anton Ulrich, returned from temporary exile and now sole regent of Wolfenbüttel, accepted the Hanover–Celle merger, and in 1706 formally recognized the ninth electorate.

It was immediately after the Wolfenbüttel episode, and in the aftermath of the death of William III, that the suggestion was made that Georg Ludwig might be appointed commander-in-chief of the army of the United Provinces. One such proposal came from a Dutch diplomat who had spent some time at the court of Hanover, Albert van der Meer. It is worth detailing because of the picture it provides of Georg Ludwig. According to van der Meer, Georg Ludwig was a prince much concerned with his reputation, yet not a slave to mere ambition; of great application to affairs of state; of solid understanding and judgement, who did not allow his attention to be distracted by trifles; a brave and experienced soldier, with a liking for war, and with the capacity to become a great general, who kept good discipline among his troops and good order in his finances, and whose high birth and rank would command obedience from generals of other nations; a man not given to losing his temper, indeed, usually very calm by temperament; concerned to be just; reserved but kindly; one whose zeal for the common cause could be counted upon, because it was in his interests as elector of Hanover and as future king of England to see France diminished (*Briefwisseling van Anthonie Heinsius*, 55).

Of course, van der Meer had an axe to grind: he was concerned to advance the claims of Georg Ludwig to be considered the most useful and best-qualified candidate for the position of commander-in-chief of Dutch forces. Yet what is striking about his description of Georg Ludwig is its close correspondence with the more familiar picture drawn almost contemporaneously by John Toland, a member of the English embassy to Hanover in 1701, who had returned to Hanover in 1702 to record his impressions of Sophia, Georg Ludwig, and the Hanoverian court, and published them in 1705. Toland described Georg Ludwig as a popular prince, equitable in administration, frugal and punctual in his payments, a perfect man of business, but spending much time with his mistresses; very knowledgeable about military affairs, and personally courageous; passionate about hunting to the exclusion of other diversions; very reserved in manner; unsurpassed in his 'zeal against the long intended project of universal monarchy of France', and 'most hearty for the common cause of Europe' (Boyer, 8.209–12). Granted that, like van der Meer, Toland had an axe to grind—he was an enthusiastic advocate of the Hanoverian succession in England, and was concerned primarily to win over English opinion—he had quite independently of van der Meer identified the same central qualities in Georg Ludwig.

Toland's advocacy of the Hanoverian succession found a receptive audience. Van der Meer's promotion of Georg Ludwig as commander-in-chief of the Dutch army fell on deaf ears, as did later advocacy from others of a similar kind. The pleas were unrealistic. Compared with the maritime powers, Hanover did not carry sufficient military clout, and compared with Marlborough and Prince Eugene, Georg Ludwig did not possess sufficient experience in commanding large-scale military operations. In any case, Marlborough and Eugene were disinclined to give way, having their own ambitions to fulfil. Finally, Georg Ludwig's own ambitions were more modest, and were restricted to achieving an independent command of a part of the allied army. Even this limited ambition was effectively frustrated.

Georg Ludwig performed well in the campaign of 1707 in Germany. He was rewarded by being offered the position of imperial field marshal, which he accepted in July 1707 before taking command the following September. What attracted him to the post, which was something of a bed of thorns in that the imperial army lacked money and men, was the prospect of making it a force capable of taking offensive action, and being allowed to do so. In the event, Georg Ludwig raised the finances, only to find them diverted elsewhere. Without the money the men were not forthcoming. More than that, Marlborough and Eugene were determined that Georg Ludwig's operations should be subordinated to their own, and deceived him as to their intentions. In 1708 and 1709 the imperial army was sidelined, and performed badly. Georg Ludwig was made the scapegoat. In 1710 he came to the conclusion that he had had enough. He resigned his imperial command and never went on active service again.

One political gain came to Hanover as result of Georg Ludwig's acceptance of the post of imperial field marshal. Since the electors had made it clear that they wanted his services, they proved ready to pay a price. The price was Hanover's admission to the electoral college of the imperial diet. This occurred in 1708. In 1710 the archtreasurership of the empire was conferred on Georg Ludwig.

By 1710, however, Georg Ludwig's attentions were focused upon the British succession. Effectively he had been the directing force on British affairs since the so-called invitation crisis of 1705–6. Then Sophia, keen to reside in England, had allowed herself to become enmeshed in British party politics by sanctioning the publication of a pamphlet which made clear her support for the tory motion to parliament to invite her over, and her criticism of the whigs for having opposed it. Georg Ludwig had no wish to see his mother or his son reside in England, where they might be manipulated into open opposition to Queen Anne. He saw the tory invitation as a move to cause trouble between the Hanoverian and British courts, and to weaken the common cause in Europe. He therefore moved rapidly to defuse the situation by banning from the electoral court the supposed author of the pamphlet and ordering the Hanoverian resident in London to dissociate himself from the pamphlet. Anne too did her bit to repair relations, and to reaffirm her support for the protestant succession. In April 1706 the electoral prince, Georg August, was awarded the Garter. In November of the same year, in response to overtures from Hanover, Anne made him duke of Cambridge, somewhat warily, since she feared that it might prove a handle to reopen the invitation issue; and so it did.

In April 1714 the Hanoverian resident in London, Baron Schütz, on behalf of Sophia but with the knowledge of Georg Ludwig, together with the encouragement of whigs and Hanoverian tories, visited the lord chancellor of the then tory administration to ask 'whether the electoral prince, the duke of Cambridge, should not have a writ enabling him to take his seat in the House'. As there proved to be no legal grounds for denying the writ, it was duly issued, though Anne made clear to Sophia, Georg Ludwig, and the electoral prince her displeasure, and reiterated her adamantine refusal to allow any member of the electoral family to enter England while she was alive. Georg Ludwig took heed of the warning and of the strictures: he did not send over Georg August, and he recalled Schütz.

Probably Georg Ludwig never intended to dispatch his son without the queen's invitation. That he should have been prepared to give the impression that he was, and to risk the certain wrath of Anne, is a measure of the extent to which relations between Britain and Hanover had cooled since the advent of a tory ministry and a tory parliament in 1710, and of the felt dangers to the protestant and Hanoverian succession. The making by Britain of a separate peace in 1713 had alarmed and angered Georg Ludwig. As elector of Hanover, he had openly opposed the Utrecht settlement, and he continued to wage war against Louis XIV until Louis XIV made peace with the empire in 1714, which brought at last French recognition of Hanover's ninth electorate. He viewed with deep and ineradicable distrust those tory ministers who had made the peace, and suspected them, as did others, of hostility to the protestant and Hanoverian succession. The question of the appropriateness of issuing a writ of summons to the duke of Cambridge to take his seat in the House of Lords may have soured relations between Hanover and Anne, but it also brought benefits to the Hanoverian cause in Britain. For it helped to focus, and to give force and urgency, to the efforts of Hanover's supporters in Britain to persuade parliament that the protestant and Hanoverian succession was in danger, and that countervailing measures were necessary to protect it. On 12 April 1714, the same day that Schütz had visited Lord Chancellor Harcourt, the House of Lords resolved that a request be made to the queen to issue a proclamation offering a reward to anyone who apprehended and brought to justice James Francis Edward Stuart (the Pretender) in case he landed or attempted to land in Great Britain or Ireland. On 21 June 1714 Anne issued the proclamation, offering a reward of £5000 out of her own pocket, and on 23 June the Commons resolved *nemine contradicente* to offer an additional £100,000. Meanwhile, Sophia had died on 8 June 1714, so that Georg Ludwig became Anne's direct heir, and the immediate beneficiary of these measures. Less than two months later, on 1 August 1714, at 7.45 a.m., Anne died.

Accession and Jacobite rising, 1714–1716 Immediately upon Anne's death there came into play the mechanisms and procedures set out in the Act of Regency of 1706 to address the perils of the hiatus expected to ensue after Anne's death, and until the arrival of the new monarch in England. The privy council met at Kensington Palace to disclose the regency nominations of the new king, to establish the regency council, and to swear in the lords justices. At 4 p.m. the proclamation of George, king of Great Britain and Ireland, began at St James's Palace. Henceforth Georg Ludwig always signed himself *George R.*, thus Anglicizing his first name, and sacrificing the second to bring himself into line with the uninominal style of British rulers. At 6 p.m., notwithstanding that it was a Sunday, and that the speaker of the House of Commons was in the country, parliament met at Westminster. On 6 August this overwhelmingly tory-dominated parliament proclaimed unanimously its loyalty to the new king in his 'undoubted right to the imperial crown of this realm, against the Pretender, and all other persons whatsoever'. More significantly, and again unanimously, parliament settled upon the king the same revenue that Anne had enjoyed, and guaranteed it, which meant that George I came to enjoy a more generous and a more certain civil list than either of his two predecessors, though it was still insufficient to avoid periodic insolvency.

Not until 18 September 1714, however, did George I arrive in England, a measure of the efficacy of the measures taken by parliament in Anne's reign to ensure a peaceful and orderly transition to a Hanoverian monarchy. The king landed at Greenwich at 6 p.m. Accompanied by his son, many nobility and gentry, and great crowds, he then took his first public walk on British soil, to the Queen's House in the park, where he stayed overnight. The following day he held his first royal reception there. It was a very crowded court, notable in that the king made clear his friendly regard for the whig lords in attendance, and notable for his hostility towards Lord Oxford, formerly Robert Harley. Oxford, who was introduced to the king in French, was publicly snubbed; he was allowed to kiss the king's hand but no words were exchanged. On 20 September the king, with the prince of Wales at his side, made his royal entry into London from 12 noon, and arrived at St James's Palace between 7 and 8 p.m.

The accession of George I had thus been effected according to plan, with dispatch, vigour, an impressive display of parliamentary unity, and expressions of popular acclaim. George I had played the waiting game well, by showing steadiness of purpose but keeping a prudent distance from British party politics until the perceived threat to the Hanoverian cause had dictated otherwise. But formidable difficulties still faced him in converting a bloodless accession into a settled succession.

Trouble began with the appointment of a ministry in September and October 1714. George I did not lack advice, but if he took it, it was because it accorded with views he already held, or with decisions he had already taken. What he valued above all was loyalty. Proven loyalty to the Hanoverian succession had determined his choice of regents to form an interim government until his arrival in England, and it was his paramount consideration in appointing a ministry, just as it was his paramount consideration in 1714 in making appointments to the highest and most personal posts in his British court. The whigs had proved their loyalty to the Hanoverian succession over a long period. It was natural therefore that they should have been rewarded when George I formed his first ministry, and natural too that they should have dominated it. Of the seven *ex officio* regents appointed under the Regency Act of 1706, only two remained in their offices after the formation of George I's first ministry, and both were whigs. In the major offices of state only one Hanoverian tory of the four George I had nominated under the Regency Act survived: Nottingham, who had commended himself to the king by his opposition to the peace and by his loyalty to the Hanoverian succession, and who had experience in a high office of state. Offers of employment were made to William Bromley and Sir Thomas Hanmer, both moderate tories also with experience of high office, but the positions were rejected out of party loyalty, on the grounds that more places should have been made available to tories and that the offers were in any case a whig manoeuvre to neutralize tory opposition in the Commons. Whatever hopes George I may have entertained of forming a balanced administration—and they were always slim, given his priorities, his predispositions, and the intensity of party conflict in England—they were now dashed. However, if most members of George I's first ministry were whigs, its most significant members all possessed either previous experience of important office or previous diplomatic experience. For George I prized efficiency as well as loyalty.

Evidence was soon forthcoming that the king stood also for strong government. The need for it was dramatically demonstrated on 20 October 1714, coronation day. Disturbances were then reported in many towns and villages, and there followed several months of rioting. Most of the riots seem to have been high-church demonstrations directed against dissenters. There is little evidence that they were intended as a prelude to insurrection, though it is easy to understand why this should have been thought likely. But they are best understood as the opening shots in the general election bound to come within six months of Anne's death. An appeal to high-church feeling, with the cry of the church in danger, seemed the only way to those displaced and discontented, and their adherents, of counteracting the influence that the crown had made clear it would exercise at the general election in favour of those who had demonstrated fidelity to the protestant and Hanoverian succession: which was longhand for the whigs.

Until the election had taken place there was little that could be done to restore order, though George I quickly made clear his preference for bringing rioters to speedy justice, even if it meant having recourse to special commissions and overruling ministers. With the return of a parliament with a whig majority, it became possible to take a series of strong measures to safeguard George on the throne. The impeachments of Viscount Bolingbroke, the earl of Oxford, and the duke of Ormond, the Riot Act of 1715, the suspension of habeas corpus, the arrest of a trio of peers and of half a dozen MPs, and a strengthening of the army all made it clear that the Hanoverian and protestant succession would be defended with strength and vigour.

There is no reason to suppose that any of these measures received anything other than wholehearted support from the king. In no short time, it is true, the impeachments became a great, eventually an intolerable, political burden. But that did not prevent George I from keeping open the possibility of a resumption of the impeachment proceedings against Oxford—dropped in 1717 because of a dispute between the two houses—by acceding in July 1717 to an address from the House of Commons to except Oxford from the Act of Pardon of 1717. George I was a good hater, and for Oxford he cherished a deep and abiding hostility, contempt, and distrust.

On the strengthening of the army, it is possible to speak more positively about the personal role of George I. For it is clear that on all military matters, from the very beginning of his reign and throughout it, George took a close personal interest. He began his reign with a purge of colonels, dismissed because of their Jacobite leanings. As someone not inexperienced in military management, he quickly made clear his determination to take a lead in the management of the British army, with the secretary at war relegated to the role of a carrier of royal orders (or finding it convenient to let it be thought that such was his role). George I held strong opinions, which he expressed forcibly, on the importance of experience, merit, and length of service as criteria for promotion, on the evils of buying and selling commissions and of patronage, on the need for uniformity in drill and in the design of the army's firearms, and on the need for regular, ultimately annual, inspections of all regiments at home, with all reports going to the king himself, and with the king personally present at many of the inspections. In short, in army affairs George I wished to be a reformer and an innovator. If his achievements finally fell far short of what he had hoped to achieve, he had by the end of his reign brought under better control, and into closer questioning, some of the established interests and practices most obviously harmful to the cohesion and efficiency of the army he had inherited.

If the early months of George I's reign had shown the need for strong government, and the king's determination to provide it, the aftermath of the Jacobite rising of 1715 showed also his determination to be strong within the constitutional limits prescribed by his coronation oath, in which he had sworn to govern 'according to the statutes in parliament agreed'. The defeat of the rising did not prove to be a difficult operation. Its aftermath was perhaps more onerous because it threw up the problem of what to do with those rebels, gentry, and nobles who had been captured.

A particular problem arose from the capture at Preston of the seven Scottish lords, impeached and sentenced to death in 1716. The Act of Settlement had stated that 'no pardon under the Great Seal of England be pleadable to an Impeachment by the Commons in Parliament' (Costin and Steven Watson, 95). The act had said nothing about the king's right to pardon an impeached person after he had been sentenced. It was widely held that the king could not pardon in such circumstances. The Commons in resolving to impeach the Scottish lords accepted the assurance of the solicitor-general that if the Scottish peers were convicted they could not be pardoned by the king. Nevertheless, friends of the Scottish earls at court and in the Lords pressed the king to grant a pardon. It is clear that the king was embarrassed and angered by the pressure, mindful that if he did nothing the odium of executing the condemned lords would fall upon him. But he was mindful too of the need to keep to the law, as recently redefined. A solution of sorts came from the House of Lords, which resolved that the king had the right to reprieve, and besought the king in an address to reprieve such of the condemned lords as he considered deserving of the same, for such time as he thought fit. George I was not pleased with the address, which still left the decision with him, and still exposed him to charges of vindictiveness, or weakness, depending on the course he took. In the event leniency was tempered by prudence. Two of the Scottish lords were executed and three were reprieved, to be pardoned eventually not by royal clemency but by act of parliament.

On the whole George I came out of the affair well, or better than he might have expected. His conduct was taken as evidence of resolution, of a determination not to let justice be deflected by public clamour, and of fitness to govern. What is clear is that his conduct conformed scrupulously to the prevailing interpretation of the crown's prerogative powers in respect of the right to pardon in cases of impeachment.

There is a footnote to the case of the Scottish lords. Nottingham, who in cabinet and in the House of Lords had urged the king to pardon the condemned lords, was dismissed on 27 February 1716. It is further proof of the importance attached by George I to loyalty and to gratitude from his servants. It is also worth mentioning that George I showed concern that the defeat of the rising should not be made the occasion for religious triumphalism: he is reported as saying, in explanation of his opposition to attending a thanksgiving service for the defeat of the rising, that he did not consider it fitting that he should render thanks for having vanquished his own subjects (Hatton, *George I*, 291 and 370, n. 43).

George I and the Church of England Upholding 'the statutes in parliament agreed' soon presented George I with larger and more lasting problems than those identified in the case of the Scottish lords in 1716. But in one respect at least, and it was a crucial respect, George I had no difficulty in keeping to the statutes agreed. The Act of Settlement had required that the successor to Anne and her issue should join in communion with the Church of England. The requirement seems to have presented as few difficulties for George I as it had for Sophia. Sophia had been brought up a Calvinist, but seems to have attached little importance to forms of worship. George was a practising Lutheran but latitudinarian and tolerant, or at least no persecutor. Both had indicated their readiness to observe the required religious proprieties before George's accession, and were wise to do so.

The Lutheranism of the Hanoverians had been a tender point in England among high-churchmen at the time of the Act of Settlement and remained so in 1714 and afterwards. Prominent among the criticisms made of George I upon his accession was that as a Lutheran he was incapable of understanding the Anglican church. It was also charged against him that as the father of 'devout Calvinists', and as the tool of whigs, he was likely to become a conduit of presbyterianism.

That the charges were felt to have force is indicated first by the attention devoted to refuting them over several years by loyalist propagandists, who stressed the piety and zeal of the king, as well as the regularity of his conformity to Anglican observances. His various religious identities, it was argued, did not betoken a coolness towards Anglicanism or constitute a danger to it; they should be seen rather as the embodiment of protestant union, and as an inspiration to a divided protestantism. The king's Lutheranism, it was asserted, was no bar to his conformity to the Anglican church, or to his role as defender of the (Anglican) faith. A detailed comparison of the Augsburg confession would show there to be complete doctrinal harmony between the two.

But George I too was required to do his bit to combat the charges of his critics, and to live up to the picture his propagandists had drawn of him. He was certainly long-suffering; he went to church on Sundays and listened to sermons by divines whose language he did not understand. If his attention at services wandered sometimes, and it seems sometimes that it did, and if his behaviour at services was sometimes less than decorous, and it seems sometimes that it was, he was apparently soon pulled up for it by ministers, and was quick to offer his regrets, even if he was also sometimes quick to reoffend. It was a recognition by the king that being a good Anglican, or at least being seen to be a regularly conforming Anglican, went with the job of being a British monarch, was indeed the indispensable and unavoidable requirement of the job description, unavoidable even in Hanover. When George I visited his electorate, he was always accompanied by a royal chaplain. His Anglican devotions while there formed a regular item of news in the contemporary accounts of his visits published in the English press.

For George I, however, compliance with Anglicanism meant compliance with, and deference to, the particular form of low-church Anglicanism favoured by the whigs, and ultimately to a conservative consensus within Anglicanism to which Walpolean whigs subscribed, that stood for only limited concessions to dissenters. For the most part George I accepted the promotions recommended to him by his ministers: the clerics promoted, and those clerics closest to him, were good whigs and reliable pro-Hanoverians.

But if the king adopted the ecclesiastical policy of his ministers, it was not always out of mere compliance, or without demur. He strongly supported the repeal of the Occasional Conformity and Schism Acts in 1719, which belatedly honoured the promise he had given immediately upon his accession to take all protestants under his protection, because he was convinced that repeal was just and prudent. He seems to have placed a higher priority upon repeal of these acts than he did upon another measure on which he had set his heart. A universities bill was bruited in 1716. Its declared intention was to root out disloyalty in the universities—especially in Oxford, where Jacobite sentiment was strong, vocal, and provocative on the king's accession—and to transform them into nurseries of loyalty, by vesting authority in the crown, via a body of commissioners, for nominations and appointments to all university and college posts. In truth the bill, which would have attacked a vast body of property and patronage, stood little chance of being enacted. The king accepted reality, falling in with the resolve of ministers to postpone the initiative, which effectively meant its abandonment, until repeal of the Occasional Conformity and Schism Acts had been secured. Indeed, in his eagerness to assist dissenters, George I seems to have been ready to repeal the sacramental clauses of the Test Act, which legally confined the rights of full citizenship to Anglicans, in so far as they affected protestant dissenters. Here again he deferred reluctantly to advice from ministers that there was no hope of carrying such a measure.

Very occasionally George I seems to have stood his ground against the Anglican church, when it threatened his pleasures. One of these was attending masquerades, much in vogue at the beginning of his reign, but viewed by the church as a corrupting and enslaving French diversion. Propriety caused him quickly to apologize in 1718 to William Wake, the archbishop of Canterbury, for the fact that he had attended a masquerade at which a bishop had been impersonated, but he failed to respond to pressures from Wake and the majority of bishops in 1724 to ban masquerades altogether. He was much more touchy and difficult to move where hunting was concerned. For hunting was more than a pleasure: it was his passion, to which even major matters of policy were sometimes subordinated. When in the autumn of 1717 Daniel Ernst Jablonski, the religious counsellor of the king of Prussia and advocate of a protestant ecclesiastical union, arrived in Hanover to press his proposals upon George I, he was told that the king had gone to his hunting estate at Gohrde, where he was expected to stay for six weeks, and that it would not be advisable to follow him. Jablonski heeded the advice, and his mission came to an abrupt and unsuccessful conclusion.

George I bears some responsibility for the failure in 1717, and subsequently, to bring about a protestant union, or at least for a failure to advance its progress, and not simply by making himself scarce at a crucial moment. His personal dislike and mistrust of the Prussian king, whose co-operation was vital, played a part. So did his Lutheranism: as a Lutheran, he seems to have shared, or deferred to, Lutheran coolness in Hanover towards the project. Also, as king of Britain, he had to respond to what seemed higher priorities in domestic and foreign policy. In any case, British opinion was not enthusiastic about the chances of a union, and was even hostile in some respects. More importance was attached to securing a common front against a resurgent Catholicism in Germany. A move towards protestant union was held likely to aggravate disputes within European protestantism, and thus make a common front more difficult. Held up by propagandists in Britain as the embodiment of religious unity, and as an inspiration to it, George I failed to give the venture any significant support.

Much the same comment might be made of George I's alleged role as the champion of European protestantism against Catholic persecution. He was quick to make representations on behalf of persecuted protestants in Europe, whether Huguenots or the protestants of Poland, but political circumstances beyond his control, or the higher necessities of foreign policy, meant that little success was obtained. His response to the so-called massacre of protestants in the Polish town of Thorn in 1724, for example, was strong on rhetoric but of little practical help. On the other hand, his response to the more familiar and more easily alleviated sufferings of Huguenots in France was not confined to representations on their behalf. One of the earliest acts of his reign, in December 1715, was to grant an annual sum of £15,000 out of the civil list for the relief of those Huguenots who accepted exile in Britain.

Attitudes to Hanover There was nothing especially generous about the sum provided for Huguenot relief, certainly nothing unprecedented: the same sum had been made available first by William and Mary, and then by Anne. Indeed, it could be regarded as not just generosity, but as also a fitting and timely reward for the pledges of financial and armed support for the securing of the Hanoverian succession given by the Huguenot community in Britain in the dying days of Anne's reign. It could also be regarded as a continuation by George I of the policy of support for the Huguenots which he had displayed as elector of Hanover by building a church for its small Huguenot community and taking into the service of a cosmopolitan Hanoverian court Huguenot artists and craftsmen.

Nevertheless, generosity to strangers at the beginning of his reign, at a time when popular resentment at foreign immigration had been recently refuelled by the disastrous failure of the Palatine migration of 1709, was not the best way for George I to endear himself to British opinion, particularly as he himself was something of a stranger in 1715, and was often decried as such. His accession, and the Hanoverian following he brought with him, further embittered, and provided a new focus for, an already existing and heated controversy about foreigners and foreign immigration. The Hanoverians could be regarded—were regarded—by contemporaries as another descent of battening foreigners, extravagantly favoured by a Hanoverian king. There was a good deal of hyperbole and mischief-making in these contemporary charges.

In the first place few Hanoverians came to Britain and fewer stayed for long. In 1714, upon his state arrival and concerned exceptionally to cut a grand figure, as seemed to befit the grandeur of the occasion and the dignity of his electorate, George I brought with him, or there followed quickly in his wake, about ninety ministers, courtiers, and servants. Of these, fifteen were members of what came to be known as the Hanoverian chancery in London, the office through which the king–elector conducted the affairs of his German lands while in Britain. The other seventy-five were the king's personal household servants, including a complete kitchen staff of thirty to minister to the king's considerable appetite for food, and for the typical dishes of his homeland. Most of these personal household servants had returned to Hanover by 1716—to the great comfort, it was said, of people in Britain—though the Hanoverian cooks not only remained but were increased. After 1716 George I's Hanoverian servants, apart from his chancery staff, seem never to have exceeded twenty-five.

In terms of numbers, the king's personal Hanoverian household in Britain was small, especially compared with his British household, which numbered about 1000. None the less, its very existence was something of a political liability, especially during the opening years of his reign. In the first place, by providing the king with a retreat into the kind of privacy and informality he preferred, it made him seem to his subjects not merely remote, but positively reclusive, and it reinforced his perceived 'strangeness'. This was undesirable, and potentially dangerous, at a time when the new monarchy needed to make itself visible, accessible, and attractive to its new subjects, and especially to its most influential subjects. The fact that the prince and princess of Wales were prepared, even keen, to take on the kind of public role which the king found irksome, may have helped to make the Hanoverian monarchy seem less alien in its early years, and may have suited George I himself initially, but it soon set up, or exacerbated, tensions within the royal family, between the king and his son, which quickly brought to an end their unspoken and unwritten disposition of roles.

If the size of the Hanoverian household was often exaggerated then so too were the accusations of Hanoverian greed for British money, which came from ministers as well as from the monarchy's opponents. It is true that British money provided by the exchequer for the privy purse was used to pay the expenses of the German court in London. But the sum involved was small—about £15,000 a year—and the payment could be defended in terms of the need to compensate electoral courtiers and ministers for the loss of Hanoverian income consequent upon transfer to London, where the cost of living was much higher than in Hanover. It is true also that some Hanoverian courtiers profited greatly in financial terms by acting as conduits of patronage, easing the way to royal access and to royal favour for British petitioners. To the king this seemed quite normal courtly behaviour, simply a case, as he reminded Robert Walpole when the latter sought to reproach him with it, of 'German ministers' doing what British ministers usually did. That of course was the rub. But it was not just a matter of sour grapes on the part of British ministers. For them patronage, because it was an essential element in political power, must be kept in the hands of British ministers, and they fought, ultimately successfully, to keep things that way. There is the further point that though greasing Hanoverian palms may have helped petitioners for office, and was certainly felt by them to be a necessary lubricant, the gift of office still lay with the king, who needed to be persuaded of the merits of the person being put forward for office, and sometimes was not.

There was certainly nothing illegal, or unconstitutional, or even unusual in this form of Hanoverian money-grubbing. Given that the Act of Settlement of 1701 rendered the Hanoverians—or those of them not naturalized before the accession of George I—incapable of receiving office, or land, or hereditary title, money-grubbing from the royal bounty, or from acting as the facilitators of patronage, remained the most obvious and legal means of making a quick financial gain. Indeed, it was almost the only means remaining to Hanoverians of making a swift killing, for in respect of titles, land, and hereditary peerages, the king kept strictly to the letter of the Act of Settlement. So far as titles to Hanoverians were concerned, hereditary peerages were granted only to the king's youngest brother, Ernst August, who was made duke of York in 1715, and to his grandson Frederick, made duke of Gloucester in 1716. Both satisfied the requirements of the Act of Settlement, since they had become naturalized British subjects as a result of the Act of Naturalization (1706) of Sophia and her issue.

The only other honours which went to Hanoverians were the life peerages conferred after naturalization on three Hanoverian royal ladies: Melusine von der Schulenburg, mistress of George I, was made duchess of Munster in the Irish peerage in 1716 and duchess of Kendal in the British peerage in 1719; her daughter and the natural daughter of George I, Petronilla Melusina von der Schulenburg [see Stanhope, Petronilla Melusina, under Stanhope, Philip Dormer], was made countess of Walsingham in 1722; and Sophia Charlotte von *Kielmansegg, half-sister and reputed mistress of George I, was made countess of Leinster in the Irish peerage in 1721 and countess of Darlington in the British peerage in 1722. As life peerages, these did not conflict with the Act of Settlement's proscription of hereditary peerages for those not British-born, or not naturalized before George I's accession.

Royal prerogative and the Act of Settlement So far as the granting of peerages for native British subjects was concerned, George I was much more forthcoming. In the course of a thirteen-year reign he created twenty-eight new peerages and promoted another thirty-three. If, in total, this did little more than make good the gaps created by death, it was nevertheless a good deal more than Anne had done in a reign only slightly shorter (forty-five new titles, of which thirty were new peerages and fifteen were promotions of existing members) and proportionately it was a great deal more than was done by George II, who in a thirty-three year reign conferred only four more titles than George I.

Significantly, three-quarters of the new titles conferred by George I were created in the first two years of his reign, and went to faithful whigs to help in the process of bedding down the Hanoverian succession. As a party ploy, in their scale as well as in their intention, these creations are scarcely less remarkable than Anne's creation of twelve peers in 1712, though they excited much less outrage.

What created much more outrage was the attempt by George I, or to be precise the attempt by some of his ministers, from whom the initiative seems to have come, in the Peerage Bill of 1719 to restrict for the future, or at least for the king's successors, the crown's prerogative of creating new peers. Just why George I was prepared to see one of the cynosures of the crown's prerogative taken away in this manner is a matter for conjecture. Of course, in the short term, far from submitting to a restriction in prerogative, the king would have enjoyed a massive enhancement of his powers in that the Peerage Bill would have allowed him to create at least another thirty-one peers: twenty-five hereditary Scottish peers to replace the sixteen representative peers guaranteed by the Act of Union, and six further English peerages, apart from replacements to peerages becoming extinct. A future king, George II, would then have had his hands tied. Given the poisonous relations which existed at the time between George I and his son, that option may have seemed attractive to the king, and was certainly attractive to his British ministers, as a form of insurance against the day when a new king might seek to replace them, and would need to be able to reward his followers in order to do so. What seems certain too is that George I's Hanoverian ministers were not in favour of the Peerage Bill and worked against it. It is worth noting that their opposition to the bill was not sufficient to prevent its introduction, and was not crucial to its defeat. Curiously, despite the failure of the Peerage Bill, George I for the rest of his reign behaved in respect of English peerages as if it had passed. Only four new peerages were created after 1719 in George I's reign, which suggests that once the exceptional political requirements of the early years of his reign had been met, the king's preference was for a more sparing exercise of the royal prerogative.

Not so in the conduct of foreign affairs, which George I, in common with other monarchs, regarded as the fairest jewel of the royal prerogative. According to the constitution, foreign policy lay unambiguously in the crown. Though the revolution settlement of 1688–9 had imposed certain limitations upon William III, it had not touched the crown's prerogative in foreign affairs. Indeed, in practice, William enjoyed almost total freedom in the conduct of foreign policy until the end of his reign, a freedom which parliament came to believe had resulted in the subordination of English interests to those of the Dutch republic during the 1690s. Hence the stipulation in the Act of Settlement that, in the event of the crown's coming to someone who was not a native of England, England (or now Britain) would not be obliged to go to war, without the consent of parliament, in defence of lands not belonging to the crown of England. The stipulation carefully did not formally breach the crown's prerogative in foreign affairs, and it was also a statement of the long obvious, in that well before 1689 it had become clear that if the crown wished to wage war at the public expense—and it could wage war in no other way—it would have to get the consent of parliament. Nevertheless it served a useful purpose. A future monarch of Britain—an elector of Hanover—was certain to have interests, and might have quarrels, from the pursuit of which England might wish to keep aloof. It was a warning, therefore, that English involvement in the Hanoverian concerns of a future monarch was not to be regarded as automatic, and would need to be justified to parliament.

A further clause in the Act of Settlement made a much more explicit statement of parliament's determination in 1701 to keep in check, and under its constant scrutiny, the involvement of a future monarch in the concerns of his continental lands. This was the requirement that a future (Hanoverian) monarch would need to secure the consent of parliament before going out of the British Isles.

There were good reasons for parliament's anxiety about royal absenteeism, especially at a time when there existed a threat to national security from a Stuart Pretender who might enlist foreign aid, but not for the particular remedy parliament sought to apply. As elector of Hanover, George I had duties to his electorate which he was determined to discharge: to do this effectively required his regular presence in Hanover. Visiting Hanover also gave him great pleasure and, according to his Hanoverian doctors, was good for his health, since it enabled him to take the cure at Pyrmont, in whose spa waters George placed great faith. The restriction, indeed, was intolerable to the king, and would have proved incurably embarrassing to ministers and parliament. Rather than face the possibility of annual nightmares, this restrictive clause of the Act of Settlement was repealed in 1716, before it had come into operation.

George I made immediate use of his newly granted freedom. In July 1716 he made the first of his six visits to Hanover, and was away for twenty-eight weeks. Further visits occurred in 1719, 1720, 1723, 1725–6, and 1727. In total George I spent about two and three-quarter years of his thirteen-year reign in Hanover, or at any rate out of Britain. This was about half the time spent abroad by William III in his thirteen-year reign, and about half the time spent abroad by George II in a reign of over thirty-three years, both of whom of course were involved as kings of Britain in major European wars. In British eyes—in the estimation of some British ministers, and probably in the estimation of British tradesmen, for whom the absence of the court, a huge consumer, must have meant a substantial financial loss—George I's visits to his electoral lands seemed too frequent and too long. They were also fraught with dangers. On the king's return to England in January 1726 a most violent storm, which lasted thirty-six hours, scattered the royal fleet, left the royal yacht on its own, save for the company of one ship, and placed all in the utmost danger. Nor, from a British perspective, were the dangers of a royal visit to Hanover confined to the perils of the sea. A more frequent and ever present danger was that once in Hanover the king and the British minister who invariably accompanied him might 'go native', become too Hanoverian. For George I was naturally intent on using his position as king of Great Britain and Ireland to advance his Hanoverian interests, and did so as soon as he could.

Hanover had long had designs on the Swedish duchies of Bremen and Verden. In 1713, as elector of Hanover, George had demanded as his price for entering the anti-Swedish coalition a guarantee that at a peace the duchies would become Hanoverian possessions. The price had then seemed to the coalition too high. It became a price worth paying when, as king of Great Britain, George I gave verbal assurances to Sweden's opponents that British men-of-war in the Baltic would be used to assist in the 1715 campaign to conquer Pomerania. The king, it was further understood, would endeavour to continue with naval help until Sweden had complied with the terms of the treaties the elector had signed with Prussia, Denmark, and Russia before his declaration of war against Sweden in October 1715. The British navy was so used in 1715 and in subsequent years, to the undoubted advantage of Hanoverian interests.

Strictly speaking, what George I had promised to do, and did, was not a breach of the Act of Settlement. George I, as king of Great Britain, did not wage war against the king of Sweden on behalf of his Hanoverian lands. He did not need to: the mere presence of a British fleet in the Baltic, appropriately deployed, proved sufficient for Hanoverian ends. Nevertheless, it seems clear from the king's determination not to give any written engagement to his allies about providing a Baltic squadron, and from the care taken to provide the admirals in charge of the Baltic squadron with written instructions that would bear parliamentary scrutiny (but which were at odds with their verbal instructions), that George I was aware that his actions might be construed as a breach of the Act of Settlement, as indeed they were in Britain.

Yet, though George I persisted in using the British navy to advance specific Hanoverian interests, despite knowing that in doing so he might be acting unconstitutionally, that is not to say that his actions did not serve at the same time British interests: they did. A British squadron was necessary in the Baltic to protect British merchantmen plying the vital trade in naval stores with Russia and as a deterrent against the fear, unfounded but felt strongly in

1716 and 1718, that Charles XII of Sweden, whose capacity for rashness and unpredictability seemed unbounded to contemporaries, might offer military and naval support to the Pretender.

The same might be said more generally. Even where Hanoverian interests tended to dictate George I's foreign policy, as they did in northern affairs between 1715 and 1718, their pursuit did not significantly deflect the main course of British policy or seriously damage British interests. Indeed, it has been argued persuasively that George I was well fitted to undertake what was the overriding task of British foreign policy in 1715, that of repairing relations with Britain's erstwhile allies the Dutch Republic and the Habsburg monarchy, and contributed much to the process of reconciliation which was effected in 1715 and 1716.

More than that, however, George I's initiatives, and his family relationship to Philippe, duc d'Orléans, the regent of France after the death of Louis XIV, contributed to the most novel and influential diplomatic departure of his reign, the conclusion in 1717 of the triple alliance between Britain, France, and the Dutch Republic. The alliance was intended to serve, and in fact did serve, both British interests and the electoral interests of Hanover. Under it the contracting powers renewed their guarantee to maintain the clauses of the Utrecht settlement in regard to the succession in Britain and France, while France gave a pledge to remove the Pretender from Avignon, and recognized Hanover's acquisition of the duchies of Bremen and Verden.

The biggest prize for Britain, however, came in 1718, with the so-called 'Treaty of Quadruple Alliance'. The treaty owed much in its genesis, manner of negotiation, and ultimate formulation to the desire of George I, as elector of Hanover, to please the emperor, from whom alone could come the investiture of the duchies of Bremen and Verden. Nevertheless, it emphatically served long-established British ends, by providing for the first time a guarantee from the emperor of the Hanoverian succession as established by parliament, and a system of interlocking guarantees of the successions in Britain, France, and the Habsburg monarchy. George I thus brought to fruition the design of William III for a scheme of collective security for western Europe. So far as Britain specifically was concerned, he had completed the European defences of the Hanoverian succession. The defences were not perfect, but they proved sufficient to meet the challenges posed in George I's reign by the exiled Stuarts.

But if George I had won security for the Hanoverian succession in Britain, and for Hanover's territorial gains against Sweden, he had paid a political price. This came initially in terms of the loss of previously close and trusted British ministers, and ultimately in terms of the sidelining of his oldest and closest Hanoverian advisers from British foreign affairs.

Political disputes and relations with the prince of Wales What developed into the first major political crisis of George I's reign began in December 1716 with the dismissal of Charles, second Viscount Townshend, from the post of secretary of state for northern affairs, a post which he had occupied since September 1714, and which had been George I's first ministerial appointment. Townshend was dismissed because he had come to be seen by George I as insufficiently attentive, even obstructive, to Hanoverian interests. He was suspected by the king and James Stanhope, secretary of state for southern affairs, of dragging his feet in the treaty negotiations with France, which George I was anxious to see expedited for Hanoverian reasons. He also seemed to George I not to take sufficiently seriously Hanoverian fears of a threat to Hanover itself, and to the future development of the duchies of Bremen and Verden, from the presence in the winter of 1716–17 of a Russian army in the adjoining duchy of Mecklenburg. Townshend even went so far as to suggest that, in the interests of making a balanced peace in the north, George might give up some of his gains against Sweden.

It seems clear, however, that in removing Townshend from his post as secretary of state for northern affairs, George I still hoped to retain his services in another ministerial post, and to preserve the ministry. At any rate, in February 1717 Townshend was offered, and pressed into accepting, the lord lieutenancy of Ireland. The post was something of a political oubliette in the eighteenth century, and was perceived as a clear relegation in the political pecking order. To sweeten the pill, Townshend was assured by the king that he need not visit Ireland, that he could retain his place in the cabinet, and that his relegation was only temporary.

The arrangement preserved the ministry for only a short while. Personal rivalries between, on the one hand, Stanhope and Charles Spencer, third earl of Sunderland, who had replaced Townshend as secretary of state for northern affairs, and, on the other, Townshend and Robert Walpole, not only continued unabated, but daily became more heated. The cabinet, indeed, became something of a bearpit. On one occasion Stanhope and Walpole were on the point of throwing candlesticks at each other. It was not the sort of behaviour George I had been accustomed to as elector of Hanover; he did not like it, and it may have been a contributory factor in his withdrawal from meetings of the cabinet council in April 1717. The absence, however, does not seem to have been permanent. The king apparently returned to cabinet council meetings. Perhaps significantly, when he is recorded as having done so, it was to a ministry to which harmony had largely been restored.

What brought an already volatile situation to actual explosion in April 1717 was the involvement of the prince of Wales. Relations between George I and his son were naturally bad. They further deteriorated when it became necessary to make arrangements to carry out the government of Britain during the king's absence in Hanover, which began in July 1716. The king at first designed to appoint his son regent in his absence, exercising powers with several others in a commission. Upon being told that there was no precedent, he made his son not regent but guardian of the realm, for which there was a precedent, in that the post had been held by the Black Prince. As guardian of the realm, the prince of Wales was hedged about with restrictions, which effectively left all major matters to be determined by George I.

There was much to be said for the arrangement, but the prince of Wales took it badly that his powers were so restricted, as an expression of a lack of trust on the part of the king, which in part it was. It must also have seemed insulting to the prince, aged thirty-three in 1716, that the title given to him of guardian of the realm had been given first to an eight-year-old. He began to develop an interest of his own in parliament independent of the king's, and encouraged his followers to vote against the ministry. More dramatically, he began to stay away from meetings of the cabinet council.

The impact of the prince's absence from the council was probably minimal in terms of the effective conduct of government business. It was obviously useful to the king that his son had a sound knowledge of English, when his own grasp of the language was rudimentary, and always remained so. But business could always be conducted in French, the king's preferred language and the language of the British court. The king's closest British ministers had good French, and Sunderland had German, though Robert Walpole's knowledge of French seems to have been confined to the ability to read it with the aid of a dictionary: in the royal presence Walpole needed an interpreter, or may have had recourse to Latin.

But if the withdrawal of the prince of Wales did not inhibit the course of government business, it did highlight divisions at the heart of government. Matters came to a climax early in April 1717. Townshend, notwithstanding his position as a member of the government, continued to criticize its policies, and was dismissed on 5 April. On the 6th Robert Walpole resigned, followed by some of his associates. On the 8th the government just scraped home in a vote in the House of Commons on its northern policy, and it became clear that followers of Robert Walpole (though not Walpole himself) and those of the prince of Wales had joined the opposition. The rupture between the king and his son had become open, as had the divisions within the whig party. Stanhope became the head of a reconstructed administration which lasted until 1720.

Relations between George I and his son became much worse before they became any better. On 20 October 1717 the princess of Wales gave birth to a son, George William, who died in infancy. In accordance with alleged precedents, the duke of Newcastle, as lord chamberlain, was appointed as one of the child's godfathers. The prince seems to have been incensed at his father's insistence on appointing Newcastle, and at Newcastle for agreeing to act against his, the prince's, will in this matter.

There was, indeed, a clash of royal wills. George I might invoke precedents, but what was at issue was his determination, shared by his ministers, both British and Hanoverian, to bring the prince of Wales to what was regarded as the proper respect owed by a son and a subject to his father and to his king.

The cumulative tensions, mutual dislikes, and fears between the king and his son found their most dramatic expression on the evening of 28 November 1717, after the baptism ceremony. The prince verbally insulted Newcastle, who thought the prince had challenged him to a duel. On receiving confirmation from the prince that he had in fact used abusive words, George I ordered him, in writing, to leave St James's Palace and to leave his children in the king's care. The prince and princess of Wales set up their own court early in 1718 in Leicester House, which remained their permanent home until the death of George I, and became the haunt of opposition MPs. George I made it clear that those attending the court of the prince and princess of Wales would not be welcome at his own court, and he even sought to make access to the prince and princess by prelates in spiritual matters conditional upon their formal request and his final pleasure.

Court style The public quarrel between George I and his son did more than intensify the hostility between two rival and now mutually exclusive courts, and reinforce the existing political divide. It also had the effect of producing something of a cultural divide in the life of the king's court, and more generally. In a spirit of competitive and grudging conviviality, forced upon him by the need to give visible support to his ministers and to counter the attraction of his son's court, George I abandoned his former and preferred seclusion and, doubtless with gritted teeth, adopted a more active, more visible, and more sociable court style.

While at his British summer residence of Hampton Court in July 1717, George I began to dine in public daily, watched by visitors to the court and usually in the company of between a dozen and twenty (but sometimes as many as fifty) invited guests, made up of foreign ambassadors, members of the nobility, and 'other persons of distinction', including his British gentlemen-in-waiting. He took to walking in the gardens with them and with visitors. In the evenings during the summer at Hampton Court there were balls several times a week and sometimes a concert, always cards and billiards. The king regularly attended the evening receptions and mixed freely with visitors. More to his taste, and in accordance with his new determination to make himself more visible and accessible to a wider section of his people, he went hunting several times, near Hampton Court and in Windsor Forest, and combined the hunt with visits to the nearby country houses of several of the whig nobility. He went to Windsor in September 1717 and, after visiting the castle, met the mayor and aldermen of Windsor, together with the principal inhabitants of the corporation. More spectacularly, he made a carefully orchestrated journey to Cambridge in October 1717.

After setting out from Hampton Court at 7 a.m. on 2 October, he passed first through Southwark, where he left tokens of his benevolence and charity to the prisoners of the Marshalsea, and then through the City, before arriving at Newmarket in the evening. He paused at Newmarket to attend the races on 3 and 4 October, and to indulge in more hunting, before accepting an invitation to dinner from the 'loyalist' University of Cambridge, which was presented to him by the vice-chancellor and many heads of colleges. On 6 October, attended by various dukes, a marquess, several earls, a viscount or two, the lord bishop of Norwich, and 'other persons of distinction', he was met at some distance from the town by the mayor and aldermen and the rest of the corporation on horseback. Proceeding along Regent's Walk, lined with scholars, who saluted him with cries of 'Vivat Rex', he was received by the duke of Somerset, the chancellor, attended by the whole body of the university. After a speech from the chancellor, and a reply of a few words from the king, apparently in French, there followed the creation of some doctors of divinity in the king's presence, divine service in King's College chapel, and a visit to the library—to which in 1715 George I had made a gift of the large and valuable library of the late Bishop John Moore of Ely—followed by dinner at King's College and evening service in Trinity College chapel. The king left Cambridge by coach at 7 p.m. to return to Newmarket, where he was met by a large welcoming concourse of people from all the neighbouring parts of the county. The following day he returned to Hampton Court.

Given his distaste for public life, and the fact that during the summer of 1717 he was suffering from a painful attack of piles and a suspected anal fistula, the king's efforts in 1717 to make his court a centre of sociability, and to make himself a more sociable animal, were striking, almost heroic: a measure both of the gravity of the political crisis and of his dislike for his son.

Nor was there any immediate let-up for the king in what was for him the distasteful round of socializing. True, he did not make another extended journey into the south of England until the end of August 1722. This was amid the Atterbury plot, when it seemed vital for the king to show himself to his people, or to some of them, and to gather professions of support for the Hanoverian succession. It was the only proper progress of his reign, and in five days took the king as far west as Salisbury before taking in Winchester, Portsmouth, Chichester, and Guildford on the return journey to Kensington Palace. Some indication of its status, and of the importance attached to it by government, is that an official account was published 'by authority'.

George I continued to make himself more visible and more sociable to a section of his people after 1717. Indeed, if anything, entertainment at Hampton Court in the summer of 1718 was more lavish than it had been in the previous year. There was more dining in public; there were more guests, more musicians, more balls, and—for the first time—plays in a specially erected theatre in the Great Hall.

The last was George I's response to the theatre the prince and princess of Wales had set up in their summer house at Richmond in August 1718. Patronizing the theatre in this way did not betoken a disinterested love of the theatre by the royal family. It was simply a way of enabling the king and his son to continue to indulge their pleasure in the theatre while avoiding each other's company. It also helped to compensate performers for the lack of the usual royal support for the London theatre. The king attended the theatre in London only twice in 1717, and did not attend any theatrical performances in London between 19 December 1717, when he was present at the first performance of Colley Cibber's anti-Jacobite play *The Non-Juror*, and 22 November 1718, when he sat through another Cibber play, *Love Makes a Man*. Nor was there a royal command performance at a London theatre between July 1717 and November 1718. The prince too kept away from the theatre in London once he had left St James's Palace. When he did resume attendance at the London theatre in April 1718, he had to run the gauntlet of the king's displeasure. According to Edward Harley junior, he decided not to attend a performance of Dryden's *The Indian Emperor* at Drury Lane on 22 April on learning from the players that the king had threatened them with the sack if they performed in front of the prince.

That kind of public humiliation does not seem to have been inflicted again. In the course of 1719 the king and the prince of Wales resumed their attendances at London theatres, though carefully continuing to avoid each other's company. The only occasions on which they were together publicly during their period of public estrangement seem to have been at the state opening and closing of sessions of parliament.

Reconciliation, or, to be exact, the formal submission of the prince of Wales to his father, eventually came on 23 April 1720, St George's day. Relations between the two remained noticeably frosty, but they did at least resume theatre-going together. On 11 May 1720 George I, the prince and princess of Wales, 'and a prodigious number of the nobility' attended the opera at the King's Theatre for a performance of Handel's *Radamistus*. In time, and with the birth of another son to the prince of Wales in 1721, baptized William, relations improved, without there ever being genuine reconciliation.

Relations with Hanover and final years Such reconciliation as existed between George I and the prince of Wales owed much to the efforts of Townshend and Robert Walpole, who quickly reaped their reward. On 11 June 1720 both ministers were readmitted to the ministry, Townshend as lord president of the council and Walpole as paymaster-general of the forces. The reconciliation was soon cemented by Walpole's skilful handling of the crisis in the affairs of the South Sea Company, of which the king was a governor and in which he and his mistresses had speculated in shares. On the death on 4 February 1721 of Stanhope, a victim of the South Sea Bubble crisis, Townshend was restored on 10 February to his old post as secretary of state for northern affairs, and on 3 April 1721 Walpole was made chancellor of the exchequer.

This time George I was easier to please and to manage, largely because Hanover's circumstances had changed. With the making of peace in northern Europe between 1719 and 1721, and with the ratification in treaties with Sweden of Hanover's acquisitions, Hanover became a more or less satisfied power, territorially speaking. George I's Hanoverian ministers, including those he trusted most, such as Andreas Gottlieb von Bernstorff and Hans Kaspar von Bothmer, counted for less. In these changed circumstances, where there was less need for George I to be actively Hanoverian, it became easier for him, at least for a time, to allow his role as king of Great Britain and Ireland to count for more.

That is not to say that the elector of Hanover was ever completely transformed into the king of Great Britain, or became British, save in a very restricted sense in the field of foreign affairs, or that Hanoverian interests ever ceased to be of account to George I. Indeed, it was in the pursuit of primarily Hanoverian interests that George I returned in 1719 and 1720 to a consideration of the dissolution of the dynastic union between Great Britain and Hanover. He first addressed this issue in a will he had drawn up in February 1716. It was written, therefore, in the immediate aftermath of the Jacobite rising, and when George had already experienced difficulties with his British ministers over the use of the British fleet in the Baltic to further Hanoverian objectives, and over his proclaimed determination to pay regular visits to his electorate.

What was provided for in the will was a future dissolution of the personal union, but one which preserved the rights his son and his grandson had been given to expect would be theirs. Thus, it was stipulated that if his grandson Frederick should have more than one son, the first-born should inherit the royal crown and the second the electoral cap. If Frederick had only one son, that son should become king of Great Britain, while the electorate would pass into the Brunswick–Wolfenbüttel branch of the house of Brunswick.

In 1719 George I brought the matter to the attention of British ministers, who referred it to a committee of legal experts under the chairmanship of the lord chancellor, Lord Macclesfield. The committee came to the conclusion that, far from strengthening the Hanoverian succession in Britain, the proposal in the will would expose it to new dangers. Judging from the arguments used to reject the proposal, the committee's assumption seems to have been that its sole concern was to strengthen the Hanoverian succession in Britain. That was not the case. While genuinely convinced that a dissolution would strengthen the Hanoverian succession by making it seem less Hanoverian, and while acknowledging in his proposal that Britain had first claim upon the family of Hanover, George was also fearful of a threat to Hanover from the British connection once Hanover's possession of the duchies of Bremen and Verden had been made secure, as they had been by 1719.

In 1719 a prospect beckoned for George I and his Hanoverian ministers in which British interests would dictate foreign policy to the exclusion, even to the detriment, of the interests of Hanover. That such a prospect seemed real to George I is indicated by the fact that, even after his proposal for dissolution had been rejected by expert opinion in Britain, he continued to give it his solemn support by signing a codicil in 1720 confirming the will. The fears that lay behind the will and the codicil were not misplaced,

and they materialized in the diplomatic crisis of the years 1725-7.

Visiting Hanover also continued to give George I the greatest pleasure. Indeed, the visits of 1723 and 1725-6 were the longest of his reign. On both occasions negotiations took place which involved his electoral as well as his British concerns. In 1723 British and Hanoverian interests were in harmony, and found expression in the conclusion of a defensive alliance between Britain and Prussia, the treaty of Charlottenburg, which included the German dominions of George I, and of an informal agreement for a double marriage between the Prussian crown prince, Frederick (later Frederick the Great), and Anne, the eldest granddaughter of George I, and between Frederick ('Poor Fred'), the elder son of the prince of Wales, and his cousin the Prussian Princess Wilhelmine.

Harmonizing British and Hanoverian interests proved much more difficult in 1725-6. George I's visit to Hanover from June 1725 to January 1726 lasted over thirty weeks: it was the longest of his visits, a longer period spent abroad than by William III in any of his annual excursions to Europe, and exceeded only twice by George II. Unusually, this visit was encouraged by George I's British ministers, and was prompted by Britain's need to find a response to the threat to the European balance of power and to specific British interests thought to arise from the surprising and sinister alliance in April and May 1725, in the treaties of Vienna, of Spain and the Habsburg monarchy, hitherto apparently irreconcilable enemies. In September 1725 in Hanover a counter-alliance was signed, consisting initially of Britain, France, and Prussia. In signing up to the alliance of Hanover, albeit reluctantly and with justifiable misgivings, George I embarked upon a course that threatened to bring about an invasion of Hanover, and the ban of the empire upon himself, for the sake of largely British interests.

In short, in foreign affairs at the end of George I's reign, the elector of Hanover subordinated himself to the king of Great Britain, and to the advice of his British ministers. It was something of a reversal of roles as compared with the early years of the reign, when the elector of Hanover had sought to determine the agenda of British foreign policy, and had partially succeeded. It is also something of an irony that the dominant British minister in charge of foreign affairs during the crisis of 1725-7, whose advice was most influential in leading George I to sign the alliance of Hanover and thus to place Hanover at risk of invasion, was Charles Townshend, dismissed in 1717 for being insufficiently Hanoverian. It is a measure of the distance George I had travelled since 1714 in accommodating himself to the responsibilities of his royal office, and to the realities of contemporary British political life, which required the king to find ministers who possessed the confidence of parliament.

The king was travelling still, on his way to Hanover again, apparently in good health, and in good humour, when he reached Delden in the Netherlands on the evening of 8 / 19 June 1727. He complained the next morning of a bad night and of stomach pains, which he put down to an excess of strawberries and oranges at supper the previous evening, but insisted on continuing the journey. After setting out from Delden at 7 a.m. on 9 / 20 June, in the company of his Dutch guard, a couple of Hanoverian courtiers, and a Hanoverian surgeon brought along to tend to the ailments of the courtiers, he suffered a stroke at about 8.30 a.m. He recovered consciousness briefly—long enough according to the *Historical Register* to utter as his last words, 'C'est fait de moi'—but died in the early hours of 11 / 22 June 1727, at Osnabrück, at the bishop's palace of his brother *Ernest Augustus (Ernst August), the sole surviving relative of his own generation. He was aged sixty-seven and had reigned, as the *Historical Register* further noted, for twelve years, ten months, and ten days (p. 24). He was buried in Hanover, near his mother, in the Leineschloss church.

Character and reputation To the majority of his British subjects George I was always something of a distant presence who spent long periods in Hanover and, while in Britain, was visible on a regular basis only to what was usually a very restricted population of London and its environs. He was widely regarded as a stranger, as indeed he was. Nor did he make much effort to make himself less of a stranger when it came to learning the language of his British subjects, or at least to speaking it. He may have acquired a smattering of spoken English, but there is no convincing evidence that he acquired a growing command of it. If he did, he certainly concealed it from Westminster. His speeches to parliament were a regular reminder of his shortcomings in this respect. Each began with a brief sentence in English, which varied slightly according to whether he was opening or closing a session, after which it was passed over to the lord chancellor, who read it for him. This was little more than budgerigar English, and contrasted bleakly with the practice of William III and George II, both of whom themselves read their speeches to parliament. He must surely have understood something of what was said to him in English—he certainly attended a small number of plays in English—but so far as reading the language was concerned, he seems to have preferred, even to the end of his reign, to get others to do it for him. From 1724 to 1727 at least he paid for English lessons for his two Hanoverian pages, with the duty, it seems, to keep him in touch with the reportage of British newspapers. If this weakens the argument for the notion that George I did not care about English affairs—and there is no certainty that it does, given that most of the reports in contemporary British newspapers were foreign news—it strengthens the argument that he showed little inclination to learn the language of his British subjects. As has been noted, in terms of the conduct of government business, the king's lack of spoken English and his minimal understanding of it were of little account. But in terms of image it counted for a great deal. That it was a very touchy point in parliament, and to the political nation, is underlined by parliament's immediate and brutal reaction to the charge made in December 1717 by the Jacobite MP William Shippen that the king was 'unacquainted with our

language and our constitution' (Torbuck, 15). Shippen was clapped in the Tower for the rest of the session.

If Shippen was largely on target when he charged the king with being unacquainted with English, he was wide of the mark in charging him with being unacquainted with 'our constitution'. Even when Shippen uttered the remark, George I was well aware of the extent and limits of the powers conferred upon him, and for the most part he operated within these. He sailed close to the wind in his early years in the field of foreign policy, but he quickly, if painfully, learned what was possible and what was not, and the importance of carrying parliament in whatever he did. In this respect he made a much better fist of accommodating himself to the British constitution than William III had done. The achievement is the greater when it is recalled that George I was fifty-four at his accession, then the oldest occupant upon accession of the British crown. At any rate he was of an age when it might have been supposed that it would have been difficult to learn new tricks, especially as he brought with him, as elector of Hanover, long experience of a very different polity, not absolutist but less limited than monarchy in Britain. Yet he did.

Culture and royal patronage George I also made some effort to be seen to participate in the favoured social leisure pursuits of some of his British subjects. Apart from hunting and riding, and the occasional visit to the races, he also attended the London theatre. His preference in terms of straight theatre seems to have been for the classical French theatre of Corneille, Racine, and Molière, which he was able to indulge occasionally in Hanover. However, despite his difficulties with the English language, he attended fourteen performances of English plays at London theatres in the course of his reign, though none after 1723. For the most part, the plays were those of contemporary or near contemporary whig playwrights, and the players most favoured by the king, those of the noisily whig and devotedly Hanoverian company of Sir Richard Steele and others at Drury Lane. In other words, George I's attendance at English plays may say less about his understanding of English than about his wish to make a political point, even a party political point. Royal command performances reveal the same pattern of theatrical loyalties: most of the plays favoured by royal command were those of contemporary or near contemporary whig playwrights, and the company at Drury Lane was much better favoured than the politically suspect company at Lincoln's Inn Fields.

But George I's much stronger preference, so far as the performing arts were concerned, was for opera, and specifically for opera in the Italian tongue. His taste for it, and a taste for it in England, had been formed long before his accession to the British throne, and neither changed when he became king of Great Britain. He attended the opera and related musical events frequently: not as often as is sometimes alleged, but much more frequently than he attended the theatre. He attended thirty-two performances of Italian opera, of which seventeen were performances of operas by Handel. George I had been a patron of

Handel before he became king. In 1710 Handel had been made kapellmeister to the court of Hanover. As king of Great Britain, however, George I contributed much to the process of making Handel something of a national institution. His contribution was not confined to attending Handel's operas and to showing publicly his pleasure in them, and that of the whole royal family. As was the way, royal patronage rubbed off, in the sense of attracting other patrons for Handel. More than that, George I granted him an annual pension of £200. This was in addition to the £200 Handel had been given for life by Queen Anne as reward for his birthday ode of 1713 and his Te Deum for the peace of Utrecht. There was also extra money for acting as music teacher to George I's granddaughters. Above all, however, George I contributed significantly, by way of a subscription of £1000, towards the establishment of the so-called Royal Academy of Music in 1719–20. A business enterprise in the form of a joint-stock company, it attracted a variety of other subscribers, including the prince of Wales, officials of the court, members of the whig aristocracy, whig military officers, and whig MPs. Its specific object was to further opera at the King's Theatre, Haymarket (with Handel as one of the three principal musical directors). This it succeeded in doing in George I's lifetime. Singers and instrumentalists of international calibre were attracted to London, and Handel himself benefited greatly, with over half of the academy's 487 performances of opera being performances of his operas. With the king's death, however, and having fallen on difficult financial days, the academy was wound up in 1728. The only ambitious cultural innovation with which George I can be associated proved short-lived.

It has been claimed that George I was in tune with the ideas of the early Enlightenment (Hatton, *George I*, 290). In support of this view attention has been drawn to the fact that on his accession George I dropped the practice of touching for the king's evil, which does not seem wholly convincing evidence, and might point to something other than the view that he held the practice to be superstitious. More convincing arguments might be given. George I had more than a passing interest in contemporary Newtonian science, and this was not confined to trying to find an amicable resolution to the calculus controversy between Newton and Leibniz. According to the Paduan savant, mathematician, and poet the Abbé Antoine Schinella-Conti, who visited England in April 1715 to witness the solar eclipse and to talk with Newton, the king was 'feru des sciences', smitten with science (Simon, 33). He was, Conti continued, eager to understand the principles of physics, and to have 'phenomena' explained to him, and insisted only on being enlightened in French. This created difficulties. The court's mentor on scientific matters at the time was Samuel Clarke, Boyle lecturer and favourite divine of the princess of Wales, who could speak only English and Latin. Conti therefore agreed to act as interpreter. Things must have been easier linguistically for George I in 1716. He then invited to Hampton Court the French-speaking Huguenot refugee John Theophilus Desaguliers,

fellow of the Royal Society and one of the foremost popularizers of Newtonian science, to demonstrate some experiments on friction and weight, and seems to have enjoyed the experience. The experiments formed part of Desaguliers's *A Course of Experimental Philosophy*, and George I was among its subscribers. He also subscribed a small sum in 1721 to help the mathematician William Whitson find a way of discovering longitude at sea. At the end of his reign, in May 1727, he accepted the invitation of the Royal Society to become its patron. It had been a long time coming. The council of the Royal Society had agreed to invite the king to become its patron at the very beginning of the king's reign. Unfortunately it entrusted the bearing of the invitation to Newton, its president, who was 'desired to wait upon the King'. Newton, through inertia, or with characteristic bloodymindedness, chose not to wait upon the king, ignored council's request, and thus effectively blackballed the king for more than a decade. Not until Newton died in 1727, and the presidency of the Royal Society was assumed by Sir Hans Sloane, was the invitation presented to the king, accepted by him, and by the fellowship as a whole. Henceforth, the 'office' of royal patron became firmly established in the society's ceremonial hierarchy.

It was in the same year, in January 1727, that George I received Voltaire, made him a present of about £250, and allowed his name to be placed at the head of subscribers to Voltaire's *Henriade*, which was published in London, dedicated to the princess of Wales (now Queen Caroline), another subscriber, in the first week of March 1728. The episode has been cited to counter the common assertion, which finds support in the kind of books that George is known to have bought for himself, that the king knew little of literature and cared little for it, and to support the picture of an 'enlightened ruler'. It may be conceded that George I knew more of French literature than has been allowed for. But his generous welcome to Voltaire and to his work says nothing about the king's liking for literature or his enlightened credentials. It was essentially a matter of politics, of the politics of the Anglo-French alliance. The *Henriade* was seen by the regency in France, and by Britain's ministers in France, as a piece of useful propaganda in favour of the Anglo-French alliance. Ministers in Britain were persuaded of that too, and so, it appears, was George I. His generosity to Voltaire was no more than a measure of the value he attached to the Anglo-French alliance. In the visual arts George supported the choice in October 1714 of James Thornhill to commemorate pictorially the protestant succession in the Great Hall at Greenwich, perhaps less for artistic reasons than as a recognition of the strength of feeling in favour of a native, protestant artist. But he seems to have taken to Thornhill: he made him his royal history painter in 1718 and knighted him in May 1720, the first English-born painter to be so honoured. He also retained Godfrey Kneller as principal painter and made him a baronet in 1715. It is said that when Kneller died in 1723, George I blocked the appointment as his successor of the Swedish-born Michael Dahl in favour of an inferior artist, Charles Jervas, who had the patronage of Robert Walpole, because of a slight Dahl had offered on being invited to paint the two-year-old duke of Cumberland. George I built no great palaces, or indeed any palaces at all in Britain. In this sphere he was no more than a repairer and an improver. Three state rooms—the king's drawing-room, the cupola or cube room, and the privy chamber—and new courtyards were added to Kensington Palace, where the king usually spent the spring months, to cater for his extended German family. William Kent was called in to decorate the new state rooms, and also assisted in the relandscaping of the grounds of the palace, which the king used for relaxation and for exercise (he was an energetic walker) and to which the public was allowed limited access. A new stable block was erected at St James's Palace.

It is small beer, even compared with some of the petty principalities of Europe. George I was never a great patron of the arts, though he was less miserly in this respect than has often been allowed. The advent of limited monarchy in Britain meant the advent of restricted royal patronage in this area. Granted, however, that he was strapped for cash, George I remains responsible for his choices: he spent considerably more on the upkeep of his horses during his reign than he did on the theatre, music, and payments to writers combined.

An elusive character As a person, George I remains somewhat elusive. In private he displayed some appealing features. His letters to his daughter Sophia Dorothea, queen of Prussia (always addressed as 'ma Chere Fillie'), written in very free French, reveal a genial and affectionate parent ('George I's letters to his daughter', 492–9). Likewise, he showed a lively and affectionate interest in his granddaughters. In the more private and relaxed atmosphere of his inner court he showed a capacity for pleasantry, even for wit, and a liking for bawdy table talk and the *double entendre*. In public, however he was uneasy and awkward with the formality and splendour required of him as a king. He was stiff and withdrawn, and even seemed sullen. His appearance and bearing didn't help. Shortish and thickish in stature, though well proportioned for his age, with a countenance that gave the impression of being wooden, he seemed lacking in majesty, and something of a blockhead.

Yet for a man who was sometimes taken by contemporaries for stupid, and has often been so taken by historians, George I showed remarkably good political sense. In his pursuit of the Hanoverian succession he avoided the pitfalls of over-eagerness and over-confidence. Once king, he showed prudence in the treatment of his enemies and in his choice of political friends and, after some initial hiccups, he had the sense to work with the grain of the constitution as defined by the revolution settlement and the Act of Settlement. The securing of the revolution settlement was seen by contemporaries, and has been seen by historians, as his central achievement, though one he shared with others, and as outweighing his personal defects and the inconveniences of the Hanoverian connection. On his accession the future of the protestant and Hanoverian succession was precarious, at risk from enemies within and without. At his death its future seemed and indeed proved secure, even when challenged. One measure of this achievement—of the sufficiency of the defences George I had built to protect it and of the extent to which under his leadership the Hanoverian succession had been made secure in Britain—is the easy, untroubled, and gladsome accession of George II. In a macabre sense this was a very personal achievement of George I. He had wanted a sudden death, and he got his wish, though he was afflicted with the attentions of doctors, which he had hoped to avoid. It proved also to be his last service to his kingdom, important and fitting. For the very suddenness of his death wrong-footed the Jacobites and found them unprepared, divided, and disorientated.   G. C. GIBBS

Sources DNB · R. M. Hatton, *George I: elector and king* (1978) [incl. comprehensive bibliography of MS sources and pubd works] · R. M. Hatton, 'In search of an elusive ruler: George I as an English and a European figure', *The triumph of culture: eighteenth-century perspectives*, ed. P. Fritz and D. Williams (1972), 191–209 · R. M. Hatton, 'New light on George I of Great Britain', *England's rise to greatness, 1660–1763*, ed. S. B. Baxter (1983), 213–56 · R. M. Hatton, 'England and Hanover, 1714–1837', *England und Hannover/England and Hanover*, ed. A. Birke and K. Kluxen, *Prinz-Albert-Studien/Prince Albert Studies*, 4 (1986), 17–32 · R. M. Hatton, *Diplomatic relations between Great Britain and the Dutch republic, 1714–1721* (1950) · J. M. Beattie, *The English court in the reign of George I* (1967) · A. W. Ward, *The electress Sophia and the Hanoverian succession*, 2nd edn (1909) · A. W. Ward, *Great Britain and Hanover: some aspects of the personal union* (1899) · *De briefwisseling van Anthonie Heinsius, 1702–1720*, ed. A. J. Veenendaal and others, [17 vols.] (The Hague, 1976–) · G. M. Trevelyan, *England under Queen Anne*, 3 vols. (1930–34) · G. S. Holmes, *British politics in the age of Anne* (1967) · E. Gregg, *Queen Anne* (1980) · M. A. Thomson, *A constitutional history of England, 1642–1801* (1938) · W. C. Costin and J. Steven Watson, eds., *The law and working of the constitution: documents, 1660–1914*, vol. 1, 1660–1783 (1952) · G. Holmes, *The making of a great power: late Stuart and early Georgian Britain, 1660–1722* (1993) · G. Holmes and D. Szechi, *The age of oligarchy: pre-industrial Britain, 1722–1783* (1993) · W. A. Speck, *Stability and strife: England, 1714–60* (1976) · A. Boyer, *The political state of Great Britain*, 60 vols. (1711–40), vols. 8–34 · *JHC*, 17–21 (1714–27) · *JHL*, 19–23 (1714–27) · *Diary of Mary, Countess Cowper*, ed. [S. Cowper] (1865) · *The diary of Dudley Ryder, 1715–1716*, ed. W. Matthews (1939) · J. J. Cartwright, ed., *The Wentworth papers, 1705–1739* (1883) · G. C. Gibbs, 'English attitudes towards Hanover and the Hanoverian succession in the first half of the eighteenth century', *England und Hannover/England and Hanover*, ed. A. Birke and K. Kluxen, *Prinz-Albert-Studien/Prince Albert Studies*, 4 (1986), 33–51 · K. Wilson, *The sense of the people: politics, culture, and imperialism in England, 1715–1785* (1995) · J. Hayes, 'The royal house of Hanover and the British army, 1714–60', *Bulletin of the John Rylands Library Manchester*, 40 (1957–8), 328–57 · J. A. Houlding, *Fit for service: the training of the British army, 1715–1795* (1981) · L. Colley, *In defiance of oligarchy: the tory party, 1714–60* (1982) · L. Colley, *Britons: forging the nation, 1707–1837* (1992) · N. W. Wraxall, *Historical memoirs of my own time*, 3rd edn, 3 vols. (1818), vol. 3 · N. Sykes, *Edmund Gibson, bishop of London* (1926) · N. Sykes, *William Wake, archbishop of Canterbury 1657–1737*, 2 vols. (1957) · *The London diaries of William Nicolson, bishop of Carlisle, 1702–1718*, ed. C. Jones and G. Holmes (1985) · 'Von der Schulenburg MSS: letters written by Friedrich Wilhelm von der Schulenburg, 1717–20' [transcripts of the originals in French made by Hatton from Graflich Gortzisches Archiv, Darmstadt] · B. Williams, *Stanhope: a study in eighteenth-century war and diplomacy* (1932) · G. M. Townsend, 'Religious radicalism and conservatism in the whig party under George I: the repeal of the occasional conformity and schism acts', *Parliamentary History*, 7 (1988), 24–44 · P. Langford, 'Tories and Jacobites, 1714–51', *Hist. U. Oxf.* 5: 18th-cent. Oxf. · A. S. Turberville, *The House of Lords in the eighteenth century* (1927) · J. Cannon, *Aristocratic century: the peerage of* *eighteenth-century England* (1984) • C. Jones, 'The House of Lords and the growth of parliamentary stability, 1701–1742', *Britain in the first age of party, 1680–1750: essays presented to Geoffrey Holmes*, ed. C. Jones (1987) • J. F. Naylor, ed., *The British aristocracy and the peerage bill of 1719* (1968) • E. B. Fryde and others, eds., *Handbook of British chronology*, 3rd edn, Royal Historical Society Guides and Handbooks, 2 (1986) • G. C. Gibbs, 'Parliament and foreign policy in the age of Stanhope and Walpole', *EngHR*, 77 (1962), 18–37 • M. A. Thomson, 'Self-determination and collective security as factors in English and French foreign policy, 1689–1718', *William III and Louis XIV: essays 1680–1720 by and for Mark A. Thomson*, ed. R. Hatton and J. S. Bromley (1968), 271–86 • J. H. Plumb, *The making of a statesman* (1956), vol. 1 of *Sir Robert Walpole* • J. H. Plumb, *The king's minister* (1960), vol. 2 of *Sir Robert Walpole* • J. H. Plumb, 'The organization of the cabinet in the reign of Queen Anne', *TRHS*, 5th ser., 7 (1957), 137–57 • W. Coxe, *Memoirs of the life and administration of Sir Robert Walpole, earl of Orford*, 3 vols. (1798) • E. L. Avery, ed., *The London stage, 1660–1800, pt 2: 1700–1729* (1960) • *Historical Register* (1727) • J. Torbuck, *A collection of the parliamentary debates in England (1668–1741)*, 21 vols. (1739–42), vol. 7 • U. Daan, *Hanover and Great Britain, 1740–1760* (1991) [for a useful account of the Hanoverian polity] • J. Brewer, *The pleasures of the imagination: English culture in the eighteenth century* (1997) • H. Weinstock, *Handel* (1946) • R. A. Streatfeild, *Handel* (1909) • R. S. Westfall, *Never at rest: a biography of Isaac Newton* (1980) • L. R. Stewart, *The rise of public science: rhetoric, technology, and natural philosophy in Newtonian Britain, 1660–1750* (1992) • J. T. Desaguliers, *A course of experimental philosophy*, 2 vols. (1734–44), vol. 1 • R. Simon, *Nicolas Freret, academicien*, ed. T. Besterman, Studies on Voltaire and the Eighteenth Century, 17 (Geneva, 1961) • *The record of the Royal Society of London*, 3rd edn (1912) • A. Ballantyne, *Voltaire's visit to England, 1726–1729* (1893) • Voltaire, *La Henriade*, 1, Studies on Voltaire and the Eighteenth Century, 38 (Geneva, 1965) [incl. notes and introduction by O. R. Taylor] • I. Pears, *The discovery of painting: the growth of interest in the arts in England, 1680–1768* (1988) • 'George I's letters to his daughter', ed. R. L. Arkell, *EngHR*, 52 (1937), 492–9 • John, Lord Hervey, *Some materials towards memoirs of the reign of King George II*, ed. R. Sedgwick, 3 vols. (1931), vol. 1 • R. Halsband, *The life of Lady Mary Wortley Montagu* (1961) • H. M. Imbert-Terry, *A constitutional king: George I* (1927)

Archives Niedersächsisches Hauptstaatsarchiv Hannover, Hanover, papers • NYPL, letters and papers • Royal Arch., papers and letters on plan to dissolve by a will the dynastic union, 53017 | BL, Egmont papers, journal and corresp. of Sir John Percival, first earl Egmont, 47028–47029 • BL, letters to Abraham Stanyan • Hunt. L., letters to earl of Loudoun • Niedersächsisches Hauptstaatsarchiv Hannover, Hanover, Calenberg Brief Archive • Royal Arch., wardrobe account, Geo. 57581–57583 • V&A NAL, Forster collection, an account of the misunderstanding between George, elector of Hanover, and his lady

Likenesses J. van Somer, mezzotint, 1680 (after G. Kneller), NPG • R. Tompson, mezzotint, 1680 (after G. Kneller), BM, NPG • attrib. G. Kneller, portrait, *c*.1680–1681, Herrenhausen Palace, Hanover; repro. in Hatton, *George I* • C. Weigel, engraving, *c*.1692, Historisches Museum am Hohen Ufer, Hanover; repro. in Hatton, *George I* • H. H. Quiter, portrait, 1705, Blenheim Palace, Oxfordshire • J. Smith, mezzotint, 1706 (after J. L. Hirschmann), BM, NPG • portrait, *c*.1707–1710, repro. in Hatton, *George I*; priv. coll. • studio of G. Kneller, portrait, *c*.1714, Houghton Hall, Norfolk • coronation medal, 1714, BM; repro. in *The correspondence of Isaac Newton*, vol. 6: *1713–1718*, ed. A. R. Hall and L. Tilling (1976) • oils, *c*.1714 (after G. Kneller), NPG • studio of G. Kneller, oils, *c*.1714–1718, NPG; version, Royal Collection • attrib. M. Dahl, portrait, *c*.1714–1727, Burghley House, Northamptonshire • J. Croker, silver medal, 1715, Scot. NPG • J. Smith, mezzotint, 1715 (after G. Kneller), NPG • G. Kneller, oils, 1716 (replica; original, 1714), Beningbrough Hall, North Yorkshire [*see illus.*] • Delvaux, statue, 1717, repro. in Hatton, *George I* • E. Seeman, portrait, 1717, Middle Temple, London • J. M. Rysbrack, terracotta bust, *c*.1720–1735, NPG • J. Faber, two mezzotints, 1722 (after D. Stevens), NPG • J. Faber junior, mezzotint, pubd 1722 (after D. Stevens), BM, NG Ire. • G. W. La Fontaine, portrait, 1725–7, Royal Collection • J. Vanderbank, portrait, 1726, Royal Collection • G. W. Monguibert, line engraving, 1733 (after G. W. La Fontaine), BM • J. Croker, bronze medal, Scot. NPG • J. Croker, copper medal, Scot. NPG • J. Croker, medals, BM • attrib. I. Gosset, wax profile medallion, V&A • E. Hannibal, gold medal, BM • G. Kneller, portrait, repro. in Hatton, *George I*; priv. coll.; Kneller studio, copy, NPG • B. Lens, mezzotint (after Seaghley, *c*.1702), BM • D. le Marchand, ivory bust, V&A • T. A. Prior, line print (after oils by G. Kneller and T. Worlidge, 1716), NG Ire. • J. M. Rysbrack, marble bust, Christ Church Oxf. • bronze equestrian statuette, V&A • medallion, plaster replica (after J. Tassie), Scot. NPG • portrait, Rathaus, Osnabrück • portrait, Scot. NPG

George II (1683–1760), king of Great Britain and Ireland, and elector of Hanover, son of Georg Ludwig, prince of Hanover (electoral prince 1692, elector 1698, king of Great Britain and Ireland from 1714) [*see* George I (1660–1727)], and *Sophia Dorothea (1666–1726), daughter of Georg Wilhelm, duke of Lüneburg-Celle, was born at Herrenhausen on 10 November 1683 NS, a year after his parents' marriage, and baptized Georg August. His only sister, Sophia Dorothea, later queen of Prussia, was born in 1687. The disaster of his boyhood was the disgrace and divorce of his mother over her liaison with Count Königsmarck in 1694 and her subsequent banishment to Celle. George never saw her again and is reported to have been deeply attached to her memory. His upbringing was then entrusted to his grandparents Ernst August (1629–1698) and *Sophia (1630–1714), the granddaughter of James I of England. When he was seventeen the Act of Settlement changed his prospects dramatically by establishing the probability that he would succeed to the throne of England, since William III was in poor health and Princess Anne, though only thirty-six, was unlikely to have more children.

On 2 September 1705 NS George married *Caroline (1683–1737), daughter of Johann Friedrich, margrave of Brandenburg-Ansbach, an intelligent and handsome woman eight months his elder. Though far from faithful, George was devoted to her: their eldest son, *Frederick Lewis, was born in January 1707. Their eighth child was *Mary, landgravine of Hesse-Cassel. Queen Anne was extremely reluctant to invite her Hanoverian heirs to visit England, but George's position was recognized by the Garter in June 1706 and a peerage as duke of Cambridge in November. His reputation soared when he fought on the allied side under Marlborough's direction as a cavalry commander at Oudenarde in 1708, had a horse killed under him, and acquitted himself with outstanding bravery. Immediately afterwards, some of the whigs proposed to invite a member of the Hanoverian family to England, partly as a guarantee against Jacobite intrigues. Anne reacted angrily, telling Marlborough that it would be a 'mortification' to her and begging him to 'contrive some way to put any such thoughts out of their heads' (Brown, 253–4). The Hanoverian family was therefore reduced to watching, while in England the tories gained a great majority at the general election of 1710 and began negotiating with France for a separate peace. In April 1714, when the Electress Sophia instructed her envoy Schütz to

George II (1683–1760), by Thomas Hudson, 1744

request a writ of summons for the prince to take his seat in the Lords, the queen exploded with a volley of sharp letters. To the elector she warned that she was 'determined to oppose a project so contrary to my royal authority', and to the prince that 'nothing can be more disagreeable to me' (ibid., 413–15).

Prince of Wales Within two months both electress and queen were dead. The arrangement for the Hanoverian succession went into effect with remarkable smoothness. George accompanied his father to England, landing at Greenwich on 18 September 1714, and four days later was created prince of Wales. First impressions of him were very favourable. At the age of thirty-one he was short but comely, less reserved than his stolid father, and spoke English volubly, though with a thick German accent. A page at court reported that 'I find all backward in speaking to the king, but ready enough to speak to the Prince', and at a ball to celebrate his birthday Lady Cowper thought that the princess danced well, but the prince 'better than anybody'. George expressed himself enchanted with his new country—an opinion he later revised—and showed marked interest in the ladies-in-waiting, promising them 'a very gay court' (Trench, 41; Cowper, 11, 99–100;

Westmorland MSS, 13.417). He is reported to have said, rather implausibly, before leaving Hanover, that he had no drop of blood that was not English.

The next few years were difficult. Though the prince took his seat in the Lords and could attend the council, he had no formal share in government. He established his court at first at St James's and, after the quarrel with his father in 1717, at Leicester House. His chief political adviser in the early months was his groom of the stole, the duke of Argyll, a brave warrior, but hardly a stable confidant. The prince was appointed guardian of the realm during the king's visit to Hanover from July 1716 to January 1717, but his powers were carefully circumscribed.

The regency, which might have helped to cement relations between the prince and his father, inflamed them. George Augustus spent the summer at Hampton Court, where he entertained lavishly. In December 1716 he gained applause, first by helping to suppress a fire in London, then by coolness when facing an assassination attempt at Drury Lane. Alarmed at his son's popularity the king, on his return, increased his own hospitality, though visitors noted that the two men remained on cold terms. The threatened explosion occurred in December 1717 and had an element of farce. At the christening of his young son, George William, the prince quarrelled violently with the duke of Newcastle, appointed as godfather by the king, hissing at him 'You are a rascal, but I will find you'. The duke, easily terrified, took the words to be 'fight you', and complained that he had been challenged to a duel. Though the prince was induced to offer two letters of decent apology, the king's reaction was disproportionate and betrayed pent-up resentment. The prince was ordered out of St James's, deprived of his guards, and courtiers were warned that they must choose between father and son. The open breach was made worse by a split between the whig ministers, with Robert Walpole and Viscount Townshend going into opposition to James, Viscount Stanhope, and the third earl of Sunderland. The king saw in the quarrel the outlines of a plot to depose him, while the prince believed that he might be disinherited. The public scandal was a great encouragement to the Jacobites, and Walpole's drift into opposition brought into play once more the tories, who had suffered so bad a defeat at the general election of 1715. The animosity was very great. Though the story that Sunderland or Stanhope advised the king to have the prince kidnapped and taken off to some distant land where he would never be heard of again may be dismissed as a Gothic fantasy, it is certain that in January 1718 the king consulted the judges to what extent he could control the education of his grandchildren, and was assured by ten votes to two that he had absolute authority. Stanhope's Peerage Bill, which Walpole, in particular, helped to prevent, was acceptable to the king primarily because the limitations on the royal prerogative of creating peers were to apply not to him, but to the reign of his son. Not until April 1720, when Walpole and Townshend resumed office, was the breach healed, and even then a cold and taciturn audience was the best that could be managed. George I made four more visits to Hanover during his lifetime, but his son was never again appointed regent.

In one respect the estrangement was of some service to George Augustus. In 1715 the South Sea Company had hastened to elect the prince as governor in place of Lord Oxford, with Argyll as a director. Immediately after the quarrel, the prince was replaced by the king, and Argyll removed. Consequently, when the 'bubble' burst in the autumn of 1720, though the prince had invested heavily he was not in the exposed position of the king. He would have been even safer had he listened to his advisers and declined the governorship of one of the bubble companies. After the public reconciliation, the prince's political behaviour was discreet. His advisers were Sir Spencer Compton, speaker of the House of Commons and his treasurer, and Lord Scarbrough, master of the horse. Compton stood for compromise, worked closely with Walpole, and in 1722 was rewarded with the lucrative office of the paymastership. The prince also kept in friendly touch with the tories through Sir Thomas Hanmer, thus keeping his options open and reducing the temptation for them to move into Jacobitism. But, unlike his son twenty years later, he made little attempt to develop an electoral interest and, with the king aged sixty in 1720, he could afford to wait.

The succession Death caught up with George I near Osnabrück in June 1727. George II's first instructions were to place Compton at the head of his government. The story that Compton made a hash of the draft speech to parliament may be doubted: the speech was a routine matter which any experienced politician could have drawn up, and Compton was notoriously fond of forms and ceremonies. It is more probable that, not a ready speaker and deprived of practice by twelve years in the chair, he did not relish the possibility of an opposition led by Walpole, a consummate parliamentarian. John Scrope, secretary to the Treasury, wrote at the time that Compton was 'frighted with the greatness of the undertaking' (HoP, *Commons, 1715–54*, 1.568; *Buckinghamshire MSS*, 516). He was compensated with elevation to a barony in 1728 and an earldom in 1730, and continued employment in high office for the rest of his life. It is probable that at this crisis the attention Walpole had always shown to the princess paid off and that she used her influence on his behalf, and Walpole's cause cannot have been harmed by the generous financial settlement he persuaded parliament to make. There were few casualties. Even the duke of Newcastle, the prince's old enemy, remained in post. Lord Carteret, who had remained on good terms with the prince, was reappointed to the viceroyalty, and Lord Chesterfield, one of the prince's gentlemen of the bedchamber, was brought in as ambassador to The Hague. Disappointment was shared by the tories, who had to be content with increased representation as justices of the peace, and by the Jacobites, who failed to take advantage of the opportunity, save for a mournful protest from the Old Pretender.

An early embarrassment for the new king was that the archbishop of Canterbury produced at council George I's will. George II pocketed it, never to be seen again, and took steps to recover the other two copies which his father had lodged with the emperor and with the duke of Wolfenbüttel. Horace Walpole, presuming that the will contained legacies which George II refused to honour, called it 'an indelible blot on his memory' (Walpole, *Memoirs*, 1.116; Walpole, *Reminiscences*, 54–6). Modern research has established that the will contained George I's instructions that the succession to Hanover and Britain be separated after the death of Prince Frederick, with Britain going to the elder son. At law George I had dubious right to dispose of his territories: the British succession was governed by the Act of Settlement and could be modified only by another act of parliament. Though the proposal for a separation had much to commend it for both countries, George II may well have favoured a different solution, with Hanover going to Frederick and Britain to his younger son, *William. George II's action, at first sight indefensible, may have arisen from a desire to avoid public discussion of what was certain to be a contentious and divisive issue.

Installed once more in St James's Palace, George's life soon fell into a regular routine, described at length by Lord Hervey in malicious and entertaining detail. Though the king retained mistresses, Henrietta *Howard, countess of Suffolk, and Mary *Scott, countess of Deloraine, there was little excitement, and decorum was observed. At one point the queen intervened to prevent Lady Suffolk being banished by the king as old and deaf, while the king's opinion of Lady Deloraine ('a pretty idiot' according to Walpole) was that she stank of Spanish wine. Though he enjoyed music, he had little interest in art or literature and complained of Caroline, who read books and conversed with men of learning, that she was more like a schoolmistress than a queen. His uncertain temper made court life tense:

> His Majesty stayed about five minutes in the gallery, snubbed the Queen, who was drinking chocolate, for being always stuffing, the princess Emily for not hearing him, the princess Caroline for being grown fat, the Duke for standing awkwardly, Lord Hervey for not knowing what relation the Prince of Sultzbach was to the Elector Palatine, and then carried the Queen to walk, and be re-snubbed in the garden. (Hervey, 490)

Cards were the main resource and the standard of wit was not high, judging from Walpole's report that Lady Deloraine was in disgrace for pulling the king's chair from under him. George was punctual to the point of meticulousness:

> his time of going down to Lady Suffolk was seven in the evening: he would frequently walk up and down the Gallery looking at his watch for a quarter of an hour before seven, but would not go till the clock struck. (Walpole, *Corr.*, 31.421)

The king's conversation was liberally bespattered with oaths—'rogue', 'puppy', and 'scoundrel'—but occasionally achieved a savage humour, as when he called Bishop Hoadly 'a canting hypocritical knave to be crying "The kingdom of Christ is not of this world" at the same time that he receives £6,000 or £7,000 a year'. To Princess

*Anne, who in 1734 declared her resolution to marry Prince William of Orange even if he were a baboon, the king retorted 'Well, then, there is baboon enough for you!' (Hervey, 499; Walpole, *Memoirs*, 1.139).

The vividness of Hervey's portrait of George's domestic life, coupled with the disappearance of most of the king's papers, has encouraged the belief that he was a weak and ineffective ruler, 'a king in toils'. This view was strengthened by George's tendency to bluster. But there is much evidence on the other side, and Lord Waldegrave's view was that George's lack of intellectual resource and his restlessness meant that business was 'almost his only amusement' (Clark, *Waldegrave*, 147). Fortunately a number of letters from Townshend to the king, with George's comments, have survived and suggest, at least, a competent supervising mind: 'this letter can be of no use at all'; 'in the letter to Chavigny, I believe it will be better to leave out the whole paragraph … there are several points about which I must speak to you before it goes'; 'with the alteration I have made, this article may pass'. Of course it was inevitable that the king should be particularly concerned with foreign affairs, but it should be remembered that they formed, at this time, the greater part of governmental activity and of parliamentary debate. George's opinions in other areas were clear and to the point: of the place bill of 1730 he wrote: 'the sooner it is thrown out the better' (Coxe, *Robert Walpole*, 2.526, 531, 535, 537). George regarded the army as his special responsibility, though as Sir Robert Walpole was told by his brother in 1740, 'he does not understand anything of military matters' (*Beaufort MSS*, 40, 53). Likewise the duke of Newcastle was warned not to interfere in questions of the bedchamber, 'which is a personal service about myself, and I won't suffer anybody to meddle in' (Yorke, 2.224–5). The king did not share Caroline's taste for theology, but he had strong views on church patronage. He developed a dislike for John Potter, created archbishop of Canterbury in 1737, denounced him as 'a man of a little dirty heart', and twice refused him audiences (Sykes, *Gibson*, 379). In 1750 he insisted that Joseph Butler be translated from the bishopric of Bristol to Durham. When Butler died in 1752 the king lost to Newcastle, who carried the promotion of Richard Trevor—'a high-church fellow, a stiff, formal, fellow and nothing else', in the king's opinion—but in 1757 the king carried the elevation of Matthew Hutton to the archbishopric of Canterbury. A royal chaplaincy was a sure road to promotion. John Thomas, son of a drayman, became chaplain at Hamburg, talked German to the king, and was made dean of Peterborough in 1740 (against Newcastle) and bishop of Lincoln in 1744. His namesake, John Thomas, was a royal chaplain in 1742, bishop of Peterborough in 1747, of Norwich in 1752, and Salisbury 1757.

The Walpole years The early years of George's reign were comparatively peaceful. The war with Spain, which had broken out in February 1727, was brought to a conclusion in 1729 and the siege of Gibraltar lifted. The Anglo-French understanding, one of the main planks of Walpole's diplomacy, survived for a time, though Sir Robert had an awkward debate in the Commons in February 1730, when the opposition sprang their surprise that the French were refortifying Dunkirk in violation of the treaty of Utrecht. The king's first political crisis arose in part from foreign policy issues, when Townshend in 1730 quarrelled with his brother-in-law Walpole and tendered his resignation. Walpole moved in Lord Harrington and took the opportunity to dismiss Carteret from his viceroyalty, much against the king's will. Family matters were forming an ominous and predictable pattern. In December 1728 Prince Frederick, aged twenty-one, was brought over from Hanover and created prince of Wales the following year. The welcome from the public was warmer than from the king, who was already on bad terms with his son for wishing to marry Wilhelmina, daughter of Frederick William of Brandenburg-Prussia, whom George detested. As soon as the prince was established in England the king left for Hanover, appointing not the prince but Queen Caroline as regent.

The resignation of Townshend demonstrated the strength of Walpole's position, re-established in the confidence of the crown. George II had resented the terms of the reconciliation negotiated in 1720, believing that Walpole had gained more from it than he had, but like many monarchs he grew comfortable with ministers he knew. But there was also a possible weakness that, by his monopoly of power, Walpole was building a potential coalition of the excluded. Townshend did not go into opposition but retired from public life to concentrate on turnips. Carteret advertised his intentions by moving an opposition amendment at the earliest opportunity in January 1731, and with William Pulteney, another erstwhile Walpole ally, in the Commons, and Viscount Bolingbroke co-ordinating the attacks of *The Craftsman*, the foundations of a formidable opposition were laid. George, not fond of opposition unless he was himself leading it, struck Pulteney's name off the privy council in 1731. The king's strong support was essential to Walpole during the protracted excise crisis of 1733, and particularly in disciplining and dismissing the rebels afterwards.

Townshend's resignation had been on foreign policy questions, and it was there that Walpole's relations with the king needed particular care. Carteret's intervention in January 1731 had deplored the aggressive attitude of the ministers towards the emperor and was intended, perhaps, as a signal to the king that there were alternatives to Walpole's approach. As elector, George was anxious to remain on good terms with the emperor and suspicious of French designs on Germany. Disentanglement formed a major plank of Walpole's strategy, partly because war involved heavy taxation and alienated support, but also to avoid a situation in which foreign powers would pick up the Jacobite stick. The issue became important in 1733 when the War of the Polish Succession broke out, with France and the emperor supporting rival candidates. The king wished to support the emperor, and Walpole's position was rendered more delicate by the fact that his staunch ally, the queen, was also belligerent. Fortunately for him the war was of short duration and by 1734 he was able to make his famous boast of 50,000 men slain in Europe and not one Englishman (Hervey, 361).

Relations between Frederick, prince of Wales, and his parents did not improve on closer acquaintance. In April 1736 the prince married *Augusta of Saxe-Gotha and, dissatisfied with his financial allowance, forced his friends to raise the matter in parliament. Carteret in the Lords was well beaten, but in the Commons Pulteney lost by only 234 to 204. This was the prelude to a public quarrel. Princess Augusta was reported to be pregnant, which the queen doubted, suspecting some plot to bring in a baby and deprive her younger son, *William Augustus, the duke of Cumberland, of his hopes of the succession. That the allegation was absurd merely underlines the astonishing hatred expressed by Caroline, George, and the princesses towards Frederick. But when Augusta fell into labour at Hampton Court, the prince bundled her into a coach and drove pell-mell for St James's, where she was delivered of a girl. The king shouted at the queen that it was all her fault: 'there is a false child will be put upon you'. The prince was turned out of St James's, deprived of his guards as his father had once been, and the breach was not healed, even formally, until after Walpole's downfall.

In November 1737 Caroline died after a painful and protracted illness. The king hovered round her deathbed, offering advice and protesting undying devotion. This was the occasion for his famous reply to her kindly suggestion that he should marry again, when he sobbed, 'Non, non, j'aurai des maîtresses'. In the context of the day and in the relations of this strange pair it was a moving reply, and observers expressed surprise at the depth of the king's feelings. Though he bullied and snubbed her, his admiration for and reliance upon her was great. His unpleasant relations with his father and the scandal about his mother had left him emotionally isolated and even his intimates found him lacking in warmth. Chesterfield, after his death, commented that the king had no friends, lacking 'expansion of heart'. Though he could, on occasion, be courteous and agreeable, he was too self-occupied to feel much sympathy or to understand the problems of others. Amalie von *Wallmoden was brought over from Germany within the year to meet the king's physical needs and granted a title as countess of Yarmouth, but she had little political influence and offered George companionship rather than affection. His instructions were that at his burial the side of his coffin should be removed so that his remains would mingle with those of Caroline.

Carteret and Dettingen It was felt by many that Caroline's death would weaken Walpole's hold on power, but the king's support for his minister remained strong. His fall was brought about by the outbreak of war with Spain, which he could neither avoid nor control. Sir Robert achieved one last great triumph when an ill-considered opposition motion calling on the king to dismiss him was overwhelmingly defeated in the Commons by 290 votes to 106, the tories refusing to support it as an infringement of the royal prerogative. After the general election of 1741 his majorities crumbled, and he tendered his resignation in February 1742. For the king the most mortifying aspect of

the episode was that the prince of Wales had played a critical role. He had built up a parliamentary following, based largely upon his influence in the duchy of Cornwall, and commanded some twenty-one votes. It is a sign of George's anxiety to retain Walpole that, before the final vote, he authorized an approach to the prince, offering to pay his debts and raise his allowance by £50,000 p.a. in exchange for support. The prince's reply had been a flat refusal, at which, according to Sir John Shelley, the king fell into 'great passions, flinging off his wig' (*Egmont Diary*, 3.238–41). In other respects the king came out of the crisis well. His favourite, Lord Wilmington, in whom he perceived political wisdom undetected by most others, took the Treasury and became titular head of the ministry. Pulteney, whom the king disliked, obligingly ruled himself out of taking office, though he accepted an earldom (Bath) and a place at the cabinet table. Chesterfield and Pitt, both of whom George detested, were passed over, and a solid core of old ministers—Henry Pelham, and lords Newcastle, Harrington, and Hardwicke—remained to prevent any witch-hunt against Walpole. One secretaryship went to Carteret, for whom the king had great respect. Above all Walpole, as the earl of Orford, took an important part in constructing the new ministry and continued to advise the king privately. The prince soon received his improved allowance and made his appearance at the royal levee at St James's, where the king managed to ask if the princess was well (Walpole, *Corr.*, 17.337).

The composition of the ministry made it improbable that any of the reform measures proposed by the opposition to Walpole would be implemented. Repeal of the Septennial Act, a pensions bill, and a place bill were all voted down within a week, the first in the Commons, the last two in the Lords. A greater shift of policy was in foreign affairs, where Carteret was undoubtedly more interventionist than Walpole had been. In 1740 Frederick of Prussia had attacked Maria Theresa, with the assistance of the French and the Bavarians. The king's desire to fulfil the terms of the 'pragmatic sanction' and come to Maria Theresa's aid was neutralized by fear that France and Prussia would invade Hanover. The complex solution, while remaining neutral towards France, was to subsidize the Austrians and to urge them to split their assailants by coming to terms with Frederick. In addition, a 'pragmatic army', consisting of British, Hessian, Hanoverian, and Dutch troops, was put into the field as an auxiliary to the Austrians. In the summer of 1743 George decided to rekindle past glories by taking personal charge of the army, and on 16 June he gained a notable defensive victory over the French at Dettingen. The king, in his sixtieth year, was exposed to great danger and won vast credit. But though his courage was hardly disputed, there was criticism of his strategy as unimaginative; his senior commander, Lord Stair, resigned two months later complaining that his advice was neglected, and accusations that the king had shown undue favour to his Hanoverian troops provided William Pitt, Lord Chesterfield, and the opposition with the opportunity for vituperative xenophobic speeches.

In the midst of the Dettingen campaign, a ministerial

reshuffle became inevitable with the death of Lord Wilmington. This occasioned a power struggle between the component parts of the ministry. The earl of Bath, regretting his decision of 1742 not to take office, begged Carteret, who was with the king in Germany, to urge his claims, while the 'old corps' whigs insisted that Henry Pelham, Walpole's trusted lieutenant, had been promised the reversion. The delay in reporting any decision broke Pelham's nerve and he presumed treachery from Carteret. To Henry Fox, Pelham wrote: 'that man is a madman that has any confidence in him, and I own freely to you that nothing shall ever persuade me to trust him out of my sight again' (Ilchester, *Letters of Henry Fox*, 1). The king had little admiration for Pulteney and resolved in favour of Pelham. Carteret wrote a frank and handsome letter to Pelham, explaining the obligation he was under to Bath, but promising to 'cement an union with you'. Nevertheless the affair rankled, and Orford, in his comment, referred to Carteret as 'that great man abroad' (Yorke, 1.337; Coxe, *Pelham*, 1.91–3).

In the course of 1744 the ministry fell to pieces. Carteret was well established in the king's confidence, but his policy, which for a time had appeared so successful, ran into increasing difficulties. The treaty of Worms, bringing Sardinia to the assistance of the Austrians, was regarded as a master stroke (September 1743), but was cancelled the following month by an understanding between France and Spain. France declared war in March 1744, and the union of the French and Spanish fleets offered the chance of an invasion of Britain and a renewal of Jacobite activity. For good measure Frederick of Prussia, alarmed at the revival of Austria's fortunes, re-entered the conflict in August 1744. In parliament Carteret came under strong and incessant attack as a minister who had sold out to Hanover, while Pelham and Newcastle were increasingly irritated by his nonchalant attitude towards the problem of raising funds to support his subsidy schemes.

Throughout 1744 the ministers were at loggerheads. With the war taking a bad turn, policy differences developed over the role of the Dutch. The king and Carteret wished to approach them gently lest the Dutch should demand to know why, if they took the brunt of French attacks, Hanover should remain neutral. When the Pelhams begged the king not to go abroad with the army again, he acquiesced with obvious resentment. When the 'pragmatic army' in the summer of 1744 did nothing, the king claimed that he could have animated it, and poured out his wrath on Newcastle. 'No man can bear long', wrote the duke, 'what I go through every day in our joint audience in the Closet' (Yorke, 1.357). Pelham told Devonshire that 'our master is barely civil' (Owen, *Rise of the Pelhams*, 232). On 1 November Newcastle delivered what was in effect an ultimatum to the king to dismiss Carteret. George sounded out lords Chesterfield and Gower, who would not serve with Carteret, and when he appealed for advice to Orford he was told to agree to the Pelhams' demands. By the end of the month Carteret had resigned. The way was now clear for the 'broad-bottom administration' as a kind of government of national unity. To the king's disgust Chesterfield was brought in as viceroy, but Pitt's attacks on Hanover and even on the king's courage made it impossible for the Pelhams to recommend him. To reinvigorate the 'pragmatic army' the king's younger son, Cumberland, was given the command, with a senior general to guide him.

The Pelham ministry The king gave way with bad grace and fierce explosions in the closet continued. To Harrington in February he declared that Carteret was 'a man of the greatest abilities this country ever bred: you have forced him from me; and I am weary of you all' (Owen, *Rise of the Pelhams*, 274). 'Worse than ever', wrote Newcastle to Hardwicke in April 1745 (*Lonsdale MSS*, 125). Nor did the war prosper. In May Cumberland was beaten by the French at Fontenoy and the following month the Young Pretender set out on his daring voyage to Scotland. Even this imminent danger did not bring the king and his ministers together. In September, with the Jacobite rising gathering strength, the king tried, without success, to tempt Harrington to form a ministry. Only the continuation of the rebellion prevented the ministers from demanding a showdown, as Chesterfield from Dublin constantly urged. George was confident that the Jacobite invasion would not succeed and that Cumberland, brought over from the continent, could deal with it. By 6 December Prince Charles Edward had begun his retreat from Derby, and the way was open early in 1746 for the ministers to resume political warfare.

On 14 February 1746 the ministers began tendering their resignations, and the king asked Bath and Carteret to form a government. It did not get very far, since neither man had much of a parliamentary following. A lord privy seal was found and a first lord of the Admiralty, but there recruitment stopped, and the City of London made its support for the Pelhams clear by withdrawing a £3 million loan it had offered. Critical was the inability to find anyone to lead the Commons in the face of Pitt, Pelham, and Henry Fox, once Winnington had refused. After two days the fledgeling ministry was at an end, Carteret confessing cheerfully that it had been mad. The recalled ministers insisted that Bath be removed from the cabinet, Carteret's private influence ended, and some office found for William Pitt.

From February 1746 onwards the king moved into calmer waters. The Jacobites were crushed at Culloden in April 1746. The Pelham administration took root, and at length the king came to feel confidence in it. In 1747 at the general election the ministry did well, with, according to Newcastle, some 341 supporters against 216. Even better, from the king's point of view, was that the prince's electoral following did badly. In 1748 the peace of Aix-la-Chapelle brought the long war to a close and removed many of the issues in relation to Germany and Hanover that had dogged previous administrations. In 1748, at the age of sixty-five, the king was tiring. Soon after the collapse of the Bath–Carteret ministry he is reported as saying that:

> he was resolved to be quiet, and let them do what they
> thought fit … that it signified nothing, as his son, for whom

he did not care a louse, was to succeed him, and would live long enough to ruin us all.   (Rose, 1.181, 187)

But in March 1751, at the age of forty-four, the prince of Wales died, it was said as the result of a blow from a cricket ball. His son, and heir to the kingdom, was Prince George, twelve years old, and for a few years the king's position was strengthened by the absence of a reversionary interest.

Once Pelham had settled in, the king was able to win some political tricks. Part of the surrender terms in February 1746 had been a post for Pitt, but George kept him at arm's length as joint vice-treasurer to Ireland. In May 1746 on the death of Winnington he became paymaster, a lucrative but minor post, with the king still refusing to grant him audiences. Harrington, whom the Pelhams had pushed over the top to lead their co-ordinated resignations, had incurred the king's displeasure, and it was only eight months before policy differences and the king's treatment forced him to resign. Lord Chesterfield, whom the king had never trusted, took his place as secretary, but found Newcastle impossible to work with and resigned in February 1748, to be replaced by the duke of Bedford. He also found the Pelhams difficult colleagues and resigned in June 1751. His successor, the earl of Holdernesse, had been a lord of the bedchamber for ten years (1741–51) and was something of a royal favourite: 'he was originally thought of and named by the king', wrote Newcastle (Walpole, *Memoirs*, 1.132 n. 6). But the most surprising development was that Newcastle, old enmities obliterated by newer resentments, began to reflect kindly upon his former colleague Carteret and press Pelham to approach him. Bedford's retirement was the opportunity for a ministerial reshuffle, in which Carteret became lord president of the council, a post he held for the rest of George's reign. 'Here is the common enemy returned', he announced jauntily (ibid., 1.131). Though George's miscalculation in February 1746 had put him at a disadvantage, it did not last long, nor was it possible, in eighteenth-century conditions, for a determined monarch to be kept from intervening and asserting himself.

The death of the prince of Wales, when the king was approaching seventy, made arrangements for a regency inevitable. The difficulty was that Cumberland, young Prince George's uncle, now captain-general, was extremely unpopular and believed to be capable of a coup: a fly-by-night broadsheet entitled *Constitutional Queries* warned the public to ponder the case of Richard Crookback. The outcry made it impossible to appoint Cumberland as regent, so the Princess Augusta was nominated, with a council of elder statesmen to advise her and restrictions upon her powers. Cumberland was to serve as chairman of the council. The arrangements for a regency were never tested, but the education of the princes caused anxiety. In 1753 Earl Harcourt, the princes' governor, complained that other members of the prince's court were filling the boys' heads with Jacobite or tory notions. The king took a relaxed view of the accusations that some of the prince's tutors may have been Jacobites in their youth: 'it is of very little importance to me what the parties accused

may have said, or done, or thought while they were little more than boys' (Trench, 250). An inquiry established that the accusations were groundless, and Harcourt was replaced by Waldegrave as governor.

The Seven Years' War On 6 March 1754, just before the general election, Henry Pelham died: 'now I shall have no more peace', observed the king (Coxe, *Pelham*, 2.302). George played the matter very correctly, writing to Lord Chancellor Hardwicke that he had 'no favourite for this succession', and asking him to sound out the cabinet. He added that he 'hoped they would not think of recommending to him any person who has flown in his face', by which he meant William Pitt (Yorke, 2.206). Sensible consultation was accompanied by reserving the final decision to the monarch. Once the duke of Devonshire had declined to serve as first minister, Newcastle became the obvious choice, but the crucial question was who was to have the lead in the Commons. The duke's failure to deal with it adequately produced a protracted crisis. When William Murray ruled himself out to concentrate on his legal career, the outstanding candidates were Henry Fox and William Pitt. The latter, incapacitated at Bath, presumed that Fox would be the man and waived his own pretensions: 'I am so tired I cannot hold my head down to write any longer. A fine Secretary of State I should make' (Smith, 1.116). Whether his protestations deceived even himself may be doubted. Fox, on the other hand, was out early in the morning knocking on doors. The king liked Fox as a friend of Cumberland, but Hardwicke and others feared a military government. Fox's behaviour scarcely confirmed his reputation as a strong man. After accepting the secretaryship, he gave up within the week on discovering that Newcastle was to retain election matters and patronage in his own hands, and resumed his old post. There was much recrimination and several versions about what had been promised, and opinion hardened against Fox. But the difficulties of working with Newcastle as a colleague were well known, and Hardwicke had written 'If the power of the Treasury, the secret service and the House of Commons is once settled in safe hands, the office of Secretary of State of the Southern Province will carry very little efficient power along with it' (Yorke, 2.208). At the king's suggestion the secretaryship was then given to Sir Thomas Robinson, a sound diplomat but a poor debater, and Henry Legge put in as chancellor of the exchequer. The new government did not have to face parliament until after the general election in April 1754, but it was asking for trouble to go into the new session with the two leading House of Commons men deeply discontented.

The general election produced a handsome majority for the new administration. The summer of 1754 was devoted to inconclusive jockeying for position by the more prominent politicians, and in September the king asked Newcastle 'who is to take the lead in the House of Commons? I know it is Sir Thomas Robinson's place, and rank, but he does not care for it' (Clark, *Dynamics of Change*, 90). Before parliament met, news came that Colonel Washington had been obliged to surrender in America: reinforcements were dispatched and Britain moved one step nearer to a major war. When parliament assembled on 14 November, signals were soon flashing. In a discussion of bribery at Berwick, William Pitt took the opportunity to deplore the decline in authority of the House of Commons, which was in danger of 'serving no other purpose than to register the arbitrary edicts of one, too powerful, subject'—taken by most members to be an arrow for Newcastle. On an election dispute at Reading, Pitt and Fox joined forces to disparage their ministerial colleague Robinson, kindly begging the house to overlook his inexperience. These were no more than skirmishes, but they were enough to agitate Newcastle. The king sent for Fox on 2 December and urged him to resume negotiations. The outcome was that Fox was given a cabinet place. In these complex manoeuvres, George II took an active and informed part.

In April 1755 the king left for his last visit to Hanover, accompanied by Lady Yarmouth and Lord Holdernesse. In view of the possible need for speedy military decisions, Cumberland was put at the head of the lords justices. On 8 June two French men-of-war were seized off the coast of Canada, but the following month General Braddock, leading the reinforcements, was defeated and killed outside Fort Duquesne. The king was, as usual, greatly concerned for the security of Hanover and responded by negotiating a number of subsidy treaties for its protection should the colonial skirmishing spread to Europe. These revived many of the issues of the previous war. The first of Newcastle's shaky team to wobble was Henry Legge, his chancellor of the exchequer, who pointedly refused to authorize payment of the Hesse subsidy. This persuaded Newcastle to reopen discussions with Pitt. They did not get far, since not only was Pitt hostile to the treaties but he had staked out a new line by coming to an understanding with Leicester House, where young Prince George and his tutor the earl of Bute had decided to set up as a political interest. George consequently returned from Hanover in September 1755 to find yet another political crisis, with the government looking in bad shape for the new parliamentary session and an unpredictable reversionary interest emerging. One response to the second was to attempt to divert Prince George from politics into matrimony by dwelling on the charms of Princess Sophia Caroline of Brunswick-Wolfenbüttel: indeed, added the king characteristically, were he twenty years younger he would marry her himself (Clark, *Waldegrave*, 165). Prince George's mother, with some justice, objected that it was premature and that her son was 'shy and backward', adding that Sophia Caroline's mother was 'the most intriguing, meddling and also, the most satirical, sarcastic person in the world' (*Political Journal of … Dodington*, 317–18). The proposal foundered.

With Legge and Pitt certain to oppose when parliament met, Fox came into play once more. According to Walpole, Newcastle confronted the king with the problem the moment he returned (Walpole, *Memoirs*, 2.60). Fox settled for the secretaryship of state; Robinson was shunted back to the mastership of the great wardrobe, better suited to his talents, and given an annual pension of £2000. Legge and Pitt launched their attacks as expected, with the latter

prophesying that the subsidies would ruin the nation: 'within two years His Majesty would not be able to sleep in St James's for the cries of a bankrupt people' (ibid., 2.72). Newcastle's majority held firm with 311 votes to 105, and within the month Pitt and Legge were dismissed. The reinforcements brought in to face the gathering storm were not formidable—George Bubb Dodington, a superannuated placeman stolen from Leicester House, and George Lyttelton, a prosy poet extracted from the Pitt–Grenville connection to take over from Legge as chancellor of the exchequer.

The year 1756 opened disastrously. Britain's understanding with Prussia in the convention of Westminster, part of Newcastle's subsidy strategy, prompted the French to come to terms with the Austrians in the reversal of alliances. European war was inevitable. On 3 June Minorca was surrendered to the French after John Byng had failed to relieve it, and in August 1756 Fort Oswego in America was overrun and its garrison massacred. The outcry against Byng was shattering, and ministers swayed in the gale. It was inevitable that the king should be in the midst of the controversy, since the court martial which sentenced Byng to death added a recommendation for mercy. George was unlikely to respond. A brave man himself, he would not tolerate flinching, and it was reported that on reading one of Byng's early reports, outlining the difficulties he faced, the king dashed it to the ground exclaiming 'This man will not fight' (Walpole, *Memoirs*, 2.157–8). He complained, with some justice, that the court martial had shuffled its responsibility on to him. That the case for Byng was put by Pitt and Earl Temple may not have done him much good, and the admiral was shot on his own quarter-deck in March 1757, dying with conspicuous courage.

Meanwhile the disasters had brought about yet another ministerial upheaval. Pitt enjoyed an agreeable summer, watching his rivals in disarray. If one saw a child driving a go-cart towards a precipice, he asked the house, was one not under an obligation to take the reins from his hands? (Yorke, 2.289–92) First to falter as the storm clouds gathered was Fox. The removal of Murray from the Commons to take the lord chief justiceship left him even more bereft of support in debate. With the usual catalogue of complaints that he had not been consulted, Fox resigned in October 1756. George II complained bitterly to Carteret of Fox's ingratitude and ambition, and asked if he should take Pitt, adding 'Pitt will not do my business'—by which he meant Germany. At an audience on the 18th the king did not try to talk Fox out of going. In discussions Pitt refused to serve with either Newcastle or Fox, and Newcastle resolved to resign. The meeting of parliament was postponed while a government was being formed, and Horace Walpole, with his usual taste for melodrama, talked of civil war. But in the end a strange administration was formed, with Devonshire at the head, Pitt and Holdernesse as secretaries, Bedford as viceroy, the great seal in commission, and Temple as first lord of the Admiralty.

Horace Walpole gave the new ministry six months, which was not a bad guess. It had very little support in the

Commons and even less in the closet. The first Pitt tried to combat by wooing the tories, especially with his Militia Bill, and by continuing his understanding with Lord Bute at Leicester House. This made it even harder to capture the confidence of the king, who retained his mistrust of tories and was still sore at being obliged to appoint Bute as groom of the stole to the young prince. He was uncommunicative with his new ministers and he retained as lord president his old favourite Carteret, and through him links with Fox and Cumberland. To Bute, Pitt reported that his first audience on 1 December had been 'favourable, considering the long impressions against me, and longer than I expected, for it lasted some minutes' (Pares and Taylor, 116–17). A difficult tactical problem for ministers was how to please their patriot support by appearing to repudiate Hanover without making their relations with the king even worse. Just before parliament met, it was discovered that the Lords' reply to the royal address thanked the king for bringing over Hanoverian troops when an invasion had threatened: Pitt and Temple were horrified, but Devonshire brushed aside their objections, expressing concern lest the new venture be 'demolished on a point of this sort'. Temple had to be content with a one-man protest in the Lords.

The storms in the closet did not subside as Pitt had hoped they might. Instead the king poured out to Lord Waldegrave his dissatisfaction. Temple he found peculiarly offensive, pert, insolent, and incompetent, while Pitt lost him in elaborate and convoluted expositions: 'before they could ever finish their exordium', wrote Waldegrave, 'His Majesty had both forgot the subject, and lost his patience'. Waldegrave was dispatched to tell Newcastle that 'I do not look upon myself as king while I am in the hands of these scoundrels' (Clark, *Waldegrave*, 188–90). Cumberland fed the king's anger, urging him to dismiss Pitt before he left for Hanover to take up command of the army of observation. Newcastle, true to form, remained irresolute, anxious to return but worried by the responsibility. In March the king sounded out Fox again. This collapsed, with only the ever willing Dodington stepping forward. Before he could put together a new ministry the king dismissed Temple, and when Pitt refused to resign in protest he was pushed out. The moment had come to reshuffle the old pack of cards.

From early April until late June 1757 the search for a viable administration continued, while the duke of Devonshire presided over a shrunken caretaker ministry. In addition to reconciling the claims of Fox, Pitt, and Newcastle in a way acceptable to the king, Bute and Leicester House, now actively engaged in politics, had to be kept in mind. On 11 June a Fox-led ministry with Waldegrave as nominal head got as far as the ante-chamber before it was cancelled. Chesterfield and then Hardwicke were sent out to see if a Pitt–Newcastle coalition could be formed. In the end Newcastle resumed as first lord of the Treasury, with Pitt and Holdernesse as secretaries, Temple as lord privy seal, and Fox, whose ambitions were shrinking, as paymaster. In this inauspicious fashion was constructed what became the most successful ministry in British history.

Though it gave little pleasure to the king to see Pitt and Temple back so soon, he salvaged several things from the episode, including Carteret (Granville), who continued as lord president, Lord Anson back at the Admiralty, and a Garter by way of reward to Waldegrave for all his efforts.

Since the country was engaged in global warfare, forming a government was only the first problem solved. Many of the strategic decisions turned on Europe and Hanover, and kept the king in the centre of events: though his ailments increased with age, his grip on events remained strong. He had emphatic views on the appointment of commanders and did not hesitate to express them. The prospects were not good. On 18 June Frederick of Prussia was badly beaten by the Austrians at Kolin, and a month later Cumberland's army was defeated by the French at Hastenbeck, only 30 miles from Hanover. Cumberland withdrew north to the Elbe to keep open his lines of communication but left Hanover open to invasion, and in September signed the convention of Kloster-Zeven, whereby his Hanoverians were immobilized and the remaining German mercenaries sent home. George II reacted in fury, repudiating the convention and recalling his son: in a curious reversal of roles Pitt tried to defend Cumberland, pointing out that he had been given '*full powers*, Sir, very *full powers*'. A month later, when Cumberland arrived at Kensington, he found the king playing cards: 'there is my son', declared George, 'who has ruined me and disgraced himself'. Cumberland resigned all his military appointments and never served again (Walpole, *Memoirs*, 2.282; Yorke, 3.170–82).

There was not at first very much to offset these disasters. The expedition sent to Canada in 1756 had been unable to assault either Louisbourg or Quebec. The attack upon Rochefort in September 1757 had been totally mishandled: 'I shall never get Rochefort off my heart', Pitt confided to Bute, his present ally (Pares and Taylor, 134). The most encouraging news came from Germany, where Frederick of Prussia, revealing astonishing resilience, defeated his opponents in quick succession at Rossbach and at Leuthen. One difficulty that George had foreseen—that Pitt would not do his German business—did not materialize. With the effortless effrontery that was his hallmark, Pitt performed a complete volte-face, forgetting that he had once described Germany as a millstone and an ocean of gore and discovering that it was there that his great colonial ambitions would be underpinned.

Under these circumstances Pitt's over-cordial rapprochement with Bute came to an end and the florid exchange of compliments ceased. Prince George's letters marked the change, with Pitt becoming first 'the Great Orator' and then 'a true snake in the grass'. Though relations between the prince and the king remained decent, Leicester House waited impatiently for his death. Late in 1758 the prince noted that despite a serious illness the king might last until the summer; by July 1759 he was 'ashamed of being his grandson'; and at length his references to his monarch and grandfather were 'this old man'. A request in July 1759 for some military employment—assuring the king rather optimistically that the prince's name alone would be a terror to the enemy—received a diplomatically bland reply (*Letters ... to Lord Bute*, nos. 23, 60, 22, 34, 49, 33).

It was not to be expected that the new coalition would be free from strain. Newcastle took office determined that Pitt 'shall not be *my superior*' and was soon contemplating resignation. Hardwicke, who had given up office but continued without portfolio, remained the recipient of the duke's piteous letters, but was provoked to warn that he had no wish to become 'perpetually the middle man'. Newcastle also considered himself a middleman, complaining in turn that he was 'cut to pieces' between the king and Pitt. By January 1758 George was complaining that Holdernesse was incompetent and toyed with the idea of dismissing Pitt and trying yet again a Fox-led ministry. Fox, he remarked was 'a brave fellow', but when Newcastle passed on the opinion to Hardwicke, his friend observed laconically that there had not been much evidence of that recently (Yorke, 3.39, 40, 42, 46, 48). A long-running sore was that Temple, Pitt's brother-in-law, demanded the Garter, which the king maintained was in his personal gift. Under pressure George retreated into sulkiness and would not talk to Pitt, telling him, 'Do as you please'. In September 1759 he told Newcastle he wished he had stayed in Hanover in 1755. When ministers tried to approach him indirectly through Lady Yarmouth, it made matters worse: 'why do you plague her? What has she to do with these things? The only comfortable two hours I have in the whole day are those I pass there, and you are always teasing her with these things'. The issue rumbled on, with George protesting, 'I am to be *wheedled* sometimes, *forced* sometimes ... I am nothing and wish to be gone'. In November 1759 Temple resigned, but a compromise was patched up: he wrote a letter of submission, resumed office, and obtained his promise of the Garter (ibid., 3.57, 60, 61, 63; Smith, 1.331–2). Discontent then moved back to Holdernesse, who had 'sneered' at Newcastle and irritated the king. Chesterfield, one of the godfathers of the coalition, summed it up: 'the duke of Newcastle and Mr Pitt jog on like man and wife; that is, seldom agreeing, often quarrelling, but by mutual interest, upon the whole, not parting' (*Letters*, ed. Dobrée, 5.2302). By the autumn of 1760 relations between Newcastle and Pitt were better, though the king continued testy. Hardwicke counselled patience: 'some allowance must be made for the infirmities of great old age. A prince, naturally vivacious and passionate, brusque and emporté, when young, will of course increase in these qualities as he grows older' (Yorke, 3.110).

The fortunes of war slowly improved. In July 1757 Chesterfield was declaring 'we are no longer a nation. I never yet saw so dreadful a prospect' (*Letters*, ed. Dobrée, 5.2232). The balance began to tip in Germany where Ferdinand of Brunswick, who had replaced Cumberland, won an important victory over the French in June 1758 at Crefeld: George, now deaf and blind in one eye, was in high spirits. Pitt's raids on the coasts of France did little real damage, though he claimed that they caused a great dispersal of

French resources. The colonial endeavours were more successful. A small expedition to Africa took Fort Louis in Senegal and a second one added Goree in December 1758. A force against Martinique in the West Indies found it too strong, but occupied Guadeloupe in May 1759 as an alternative. In the spring of 1759 Ferdinand won a second encounter at Minden, a victory marred only by the conduct of Lord George Sackville, who was court-martialled for disobedience, thereby making him a persecuted hero in the eyes of Leicester House. In autumn 1759 news of General James Wolfe's capture of Quebec was followed by Admiral Sir Edward Hawke's great naval victory at Quiberon Bay, which put an end to any threat of invasion. In January 1760, in the almost self-contained struggle for India, Sir Eyre Coote's victory at Wandiwash, which led to the capture of Pondicherry, completed the work started by Robert Clive at Plassey in 1757. In all of this the king was involved—questioning strategies, accepting or rejecting admirals and generals. He was persuaded not to take command himself after the disgrace of Cumberland and was talked into appointing Ligonier. News of Hanover's deliverance at Minden prompted him to quote scripture—a rather rare occurrence—'that God Almighty sent out a destroying Angel'. When Newcastle objected to Pitt's proposal to give the command in Canada to Wolfe on the grounds that he was mad, the king is said to have retorted, 'Mad? I wish he would bite some of my other generals'.

Death and reputation George died at Kensington Palace at seven in the morning on 25 October 1760, after drinking his chocolate and retiring to his close-stool. Horace Walpole, long his critic, gave him an elegiac farewell: 'what an enviable death! In the greatest period of the glory of this country, and of his reign, in perfect tranquillity at home, at seventy-seven, growing blind and deaf, to die without a pang' (Walpole, *Corr.*, 21.442–4). He was buried at Westminster Abbey on 11 November.

Contemporary verdicts on George II were, for the most part, cautiously respectful. The most sympathetic came from Lord Waldegrave, who saw him at close range. He credited the king with 'a good understanding, though not of the first class', and defended him from the charge of rudeness and irritability: 'I never knew a Person of high rank bear contradiction better, provided the intention was apparently good, and the manner decent'. He quoted George's own defence:

> we were angry because he was partial to his Electorate, though he desired nothing more to be done for Hanover, than what we were bound in honour and justice to do for any country whatsoever, when it was exposed to danger entirely on our own account. That we were indeed a very extraordinary people, continually talking of our constitution, our laws and own liberties. That as to our constitution, he owned it to be a good one, and defied any man to produce a single instance wherein he had exceeded his proper limits; that he never would attempt to screen or protect any servant that had done amiss, but still he had a right to choose those who were to serve him. (Clark, *Waldegrave*, 146–7, 207)

Chesterfield's assessment was much less friendly but

still perceptive. George had 'all the weaknesses of a little mind ... He was generally reckoned ill-natured, which indeed he was not. He had rather an unfeeling than a bad heart'. A blunder by a valet at the levee would upset him so much that onlookers were sure news of some national disaster must have been received. Though he was well bred, 'it was in a stiff and formal manner, and produced in others the restraint which they saw he was under himself' (Franklin, 98–100). Horace Walpole's assessment was even less charitable and marred by tedious antithesis. Like most people he accused George of avarice and vanity, sneered at his reputation for courage, and offered a characteristically back-handed compliment—'his understanding was not near so deficient as it was imagined' (Walpole, *Memoirs*, 1.116–20; 3.117–20). Lord Charlemont called him 'a man of strict honour ... His temper was warm and impetuous, but he was good-natured and sincere. Unskilled in the royal talent of dissimulation, he always was what he appeared to be. He might offend, but he never deceived' (*Charlemont MSS*, 1.13–14).

Horace Walpole suggested that there had been a 'diminution of majesty' during George II's reign, and for many years this view prevailed. But few historians still believe that he was the captive of his ministers, even though George himself sometimes said so. No minister ever took him for granted and many found him intimidating. To a very late stage he maintained his active role in government, approving, modifying, rejecting: in January 1756 Ligonier reported that the king 'struck off with his own hand' three of the army officers on a list of possible commanders, and within a few days of his death Pitt reported him 'violently for' the expedition against Belle Île (*Stopford-Sackville MSS*, 1.53; Walpole, *Corr.*, 21.438 n. 3). Though his initial reaction was often fierce, his considered opinion was usually restrained. His favourites—Wilmington, Carteret, and Fox—were, after all, no mere courtiers or private companions but very experienced politicians. The three 'crises' of his reign—1727, 1746, and 1757—do not bear out any deep decline in the influence of the crown, and were each followed by ministries of remarkable stability and achievement—those of Walpole, Pelham, and the Pitt–Newcastle coalition, which between them accounted for the greater part of his reign. The bizarre episode of 1746 did not, in itself, do much to weaken the crown. In view of the mass resignations, while civil war still raged, the king could do little save send for Carteret and Bath; they were men of some standing and the error of judgement was more theirs, in believing they could form a ministry, than the king's. The episode lasted two days and produced few ill effects. It is true that George was obliged to give way to Pitt in 1757, but he had kept him at bay for fifteen years and was by no means the only man to think him a charlatan, while Pitt's personal attacks on him had been idiotically offensive. In naming the choice of ministers, George rightly identified the key constitutional issue and one which could scarcely be solved by any general formula. He was handicapped by the extent to which the tories were out of consideration,

partly because George himself distrusted them as Jacobites and partly because of their own lack of ability. Nevertheless, he defended stoutly the prerogatives he had inherited and was, for example, resolute not to damage the standing of the nobility by too liberal creation of honours. His reign saw the Jacobite threat reduced to nothing, the Hanoverian succession securely established, and his country transformed into a great world power.

JOHN CANNON

Sources DNB · John, Lord Hervey, *Some materials towards memoirs of the reign of King George II*, ed. R. Sedgwick, 3 vols. (1931) · C. C. Trench, *George II* (1973) · R. Hatton, *George I, elector and king* (1978) · *Diary of Mary, Countess Cowper*, ed. [S. Cowper] (1864) · C. Franklin, *Lord Chesterfield: his character and 'Characters'* (1993) · W. Coxe, *Memoirs of the life and administration of Sir Robert Walpole, earl of Orford*, 3 vols. (1798) · *Memoirs of Horatio, Lord Walpole*, ed. W. Coxe, 2 vols. (1802) · W. Coxe, *Memoirs of the administration of the Right Hon. Henry Pelham*, 2 vols. (1829) · P. C. Yorke, *The life and correspondence of Philip Yorke, earl of Hardwicke*, 3 vols. (1913) · *Correspondence of John, fourth duke of Bedford*, ed. J. Russell, 3 vols. (1842–6) · *The Grenville papers: being the correspondence of Richard Grenville ... and ... George Grenville*, ed. W. J. Smith, 4 vols. (1852–3) · *The letters of Philip Dormer Stanhope, fourth earl of Chesterfield*, ed. B. Dobrée, 6 vols. (1932) · *Correspondence of William Pitt, earl of Chatham*, ed. W. S. Taylor and J. H. Pringle, 4 vols. (1838–40) · H. Walpole, *Memoirs of King George II*, ed. J. Brooke, 3 vols. (1985) · Walpole, *Corr.* · J. C. D. Clark, ed., *Memoirs and speeches of Lord Waldegrave* (1985) · J. D. G. Davies, *A king in toils* (1938) · J. B. Owen, 'George II reconsidered', *Statesman, scholars and merchants: essays in eighteenth century history presented to Dame Lucy Sutherland*, ed. A. Whiteman (1973), 113–34 · J. B. Owen, *The rise of the Pelhams* (1956) · J. M. Beattie, *The English court in the reign of George I* (1967) · J. Carswell, *The South Sea Bubble* (1960) · *Lord Hervey and his friends, 1726–38*, ed. earl of Ilchester [G. S. Holland Fox-Strangways] (1950) · Earl of Ilchester [G. S. Holland Fox-Strangways], *Henry Fox, first Lord Holland, his family and relations*, 2 vols. (1920) · *Letters of Henry Fox*, ed. earl of Ilchester [S. Fox-Strangeways], Roxburghe Club (1915) · B. Williams, *Stanhope, a study in eighteenth century war and diplomacy* (1932) · N. Landau, *Justices of the peace, 1679–1760* (1984) · J. Campbell, *Lives of the lord chancellors*, 4th edn, 10 vols. (1856–7) · R. Pares and A. J. P. Taylor, eds., *Essays presented to Sir Lewis Namier* (1956) · *The papers of George Wyatt, esquire, of Boxley Abbey in the county of Kent*, ed. D. M. Loades, CS, 4th ser., 5 (1968) · J. H. Plumb, *Walpole*, 2 vols. (1956–60) · A. W. Ward, *The Electress Sophia and the Hanoverian succession*, 2nd edn (1909) · *Letters of Henrietta Howard, countess of Suffolk*, ed. J. W. Croker, 2 vols. (1824) · J. J. Cartwright, ed., *The Wentworth papers, 1705–39* (1883) · W. H. Wilkins, *Love of an uncrowned queen*, rev. edn (1903) · H. Walpole, *Reminiscences*, ed. P. Toynbee (1924) · J. H. Plumb, *Chatham* (1953) · G. H. Rose, *A selection of the papers of the earls of Marchmont*, 3 vols. (1831) · *The political journal of George Bubb Dodington*, ed. J. Carswell and L. A. Dralle (1965) · J. C. D. Clark, *The dynamics of change: the crisis of the 1750s and the English party systems* (1982) · *Letters from George III to Lord Bute, 1756–1766*, ed. R. Sedgwick (1939) · R. Wright, *Life of Major-General James Wolfe* (1864) · *The letters and diplomatic instructions of Queen Anne*, ed. B. C. Brown (1935) · Cobbett, *Parl. hist.*, vols. 7–15, 36 · N. Sykes, *Edmund Gibson* (1926) · N. Sykes, *Church and state in England in the XVIII century* (1934) · *The manuscripts of his grace the duke of Portland*, 10 vols., HMC, 29 (1891–1931), vols. 5–10 · *The manuscripts of the earl of Carlisle*, HMC, 42 (1897) · *Report on the manuscripts of Mrs Stopford-Sackville*, 2 vols., HMC, 49 (1904–10) · *Manuscripts of the earl of Egmont: diary of Viscount Percival, afterwards first earl of Egmont*, 3 vols., HMC, 63 (1920–23) · *The manuscripts of the earl of Lonsdale*, HMC, 33 (1893) · *Report on the manuscripts of Lord Polwarth*, 5 vols., HMC, 67 (1911–61) · *The manuscripts and correspondence of James, first earl of Charlemont*, 2 vols., HMC, 28 (1891–4) · *The manuscripts of the earl of Westmorland*, HMC, 13 (1885); repr. (1906) · *The manuscripts of the earl of Buckinghamshire, the earl of Lindsey ... and James Round,*

HMC, 38 (1895) · *The manuscripts of the duke of Beaufort ... the earl of Donoughmore*, HMC, 27 (1891) **Archives** BL, establishment book, Dep. 9904 · BL, letters to Lord Holland, Add. MS 51375 · Herrenhausen, MSS · Hunt. L., letters to earl of Loudon · Royal Arch., MSS · U. Nott. L., corresp. · Yale U., Farmington, Lewis Walpole Library, letters to C. H. Williams | BL, Newcastle and Hardwicke papers **Likenesses** J. Vaillant, group portrait, oils, *c.*1690, Bomann-Museum, Celle; *see illus. in* Sophia Dorothea (1666–1726) · J. Smith, mezzotint, 1706 (after J. Hirschmann), BM, NPG · attrib. G. Kneller, oils, before 1714, Niedersächsiche Landesgalerie, Hanover, Germany · J. Thornhill, oils, *c.*1714–1715, Royal Collection; version, NPG · J. Thornhill, double portrait, *c.*1715 (with his son), Royal Naval College, Greenwich · portrait, *c.*1716 (after G. Kneller), NPG · studio of C. Jervas, oils, *c.*1727, NPG · E. Seeman, oils, *c.*1730, Royal Collection · J. Highmore, oils, 1730–39, Walker Art Gallery, Liverpool · J. M. Rysbrack, marble bust, 1738, Royal Collection · D. Morier, oils, *c.*1743, Royal Collection · T. Hudson, oils, 1744, NPG [*see illus.*] · B. du Pan, chalk drawing, *c.*1746, Marble Hill House, London · attrib. J. V. Haidt, group portrait, oils, *c.*1752–1754 (group associated with Moravian Church), NPG · W. Hogarth, group portrait, oils, *c.*1753 (*The family of George II*), Royal Collection · by or after T. Worlidge, oils, *c.*1753, NPG · J. Wootton, double portrait, oils, *c.*1754 (with the duke of Cumberland), NAM · J. Wootton, oils, *c.*1754, priv. coll. · J. Highmore, portrait, 1755, Mayor's Parlour, York · J. Shackleton, oils, *c.*1755, Scot. NPG · J. Reynolds, oils, *c.*1756, Bishopthorpe, York · R. E. Pine, oils, 1759, Audley End House, Essex · L. von Lücke, ivory bust, 1760, V&A · J. M. Rysbrack, bust, 1760, V&A · W. Dickinson, mezzotint, pubd 1766 (after oil painting by R. E. Pine, 1759), NG Ire. · J. Heath, steel engraving, pubd 1830 (after W. H. Bartlett), NG Ire. · C. W. White, stipple, pubd 1971 (after T. Worlidge), NG Ire. · J. Faber junior, mezzotint (after G. Kneller, 1716), NG Ire. · W. Faithorne, mezzotint (after L. Fontaine, *c.*1701), BM, NPG · I. Gosset, wax medallion, Royal Collection · E. Hannibal, medal, BM · J. Highmore, oils, Goodwood House, West Sussex · R. Honston, mezzotint (after T. Worlidge, *c.*1753), NG Ire. · C. Jervas, oils, Blickling Hall, Norfolk · J. Kirk, copper medals, Scot. NPG · attrib. C. Philips, oils, Marble Hill House, London · L. F. Roubiliac, marble bust, Royal Collection · J. Shackleton, portrait, Pruitt Collection · J. Wootton, oils, Blickling Hall, Norfolk · T. Worlidge, double portrait, line engraving (with George I; after G. Kneller, 1716), NG Ire. · plaster replica (after medallion by J. Tassie), Scot. NPG

George III

George III (1738–1820), king of the United Kingdom of Great Britain and Ireland, and king of Hanover, was the second child and eldest son of *Frederick Lewis, prince of Wales (1707–1751), and his wife, *Augusta (1719–1772) of Saxe-Gotha. He was the first prince of Wales to be born in England since Charles II in 1630, which he turned to advantage in his accession speech of 1760, 'glorying in the name of Britain'. Both his parents had been educated in Germany and spoke German as their native tongue. Since his father had been forbidden St James's Palace in 1737, after the quarrel over the birth of his first child, Princess Augusta, George was born in the duke of Norfolk's house in St James's Square, on 24 May 1738. He was privately baptized by the bishop of Oxford at 11 p.m. on the day of his birth as there were doubts whether he would live; he was publicly baptized George William Frederick at Norfolk House on 21 June. At the age of ten he appeared in a family performance of Addison's *Cato*, and spoke a new prologue: 'What, tho' a boy! It may with truth be said, A boy in *England* born, in England bred'.

Princely dreams Estimates of George's ability have varied. Horace Walpole was responsible for the story that he

George III (1738–1820), by Allan Ramsay, 1761–2

could not read English at the age of eleven, but Walpole cherished a deep dislike of the prince and his mother (Walpole, *Memoirs*, 1.56). George's father complained that he did not sufficiently care to please—no unusual remark for a father—and in a long conversation in 1752 with George Bubb Dodington the princess confessed that 'she wished that he was a little more forward, and less childish, at his age', and that all his affection was focused on his younger brother Edward (*Diary of ... Dodington*, 151). Romney Sedgwick thought that there were signs of mental retardation, but John Brooke produced evidence that the prince could read and write English and German by the age of eight, and that from the age of eleven he received systematic schooling from George Lewis Scott. The truth seems to be that he was a boy of average ability, rather reserved, and surrounded by tutors like Lord Harcourt and the bishop of Norwich, who were not particularly stimulating. In another conversation with Dodington in 1755 the princess admitted that her son was 'shy and backward ... but, with those he was acquainted, applicable and intelligent' (*Diary of ... Dodington*, 317). But in later life he spoke French and German, was keenly interested in astronomy and clocks, drew and painted well, was fond of chess, and was a great collector of books. He was devoted to music, played the flute and harpsichord, and confided to Fanny Burney that he found it as strange to meet people who had no ear for music as to meet people who were dumb. The most detailed analysis of his character was made by Lord Waldegrave, who took over as governor from Harcourt and was obliged to resign in 1752 after complaining that George was being brought up on Jacobite, in other words autocratic, notions. 'His parts', wrote Waldegrave, 'tho' not excellent, will be found very tolerable'. He was 'uncommonly indolent' and had 'a kind of unhappiness in his temper' which led him to become 'sullen and silent', and to retire to his room 'to indulge the melancholy enjoyment of his own ill humor' (*Memoirs and Speeches*, 148–9). Some of these characteristics disappeared as he grew older. Indolence was replaced by restless activity, and inattention by meticulousness—his letters and memos dated to the precise minute. But an attribute which did remain was a tendency to censoriousness—'his religion', wrote Waldegrave, 'is not of the most charitable sort: he has rather too much attention to the sins of his neighbour' (ibid., 148–9)—and he frequently complained that it was his misfortune to live in peculiarly wicked times (ibid., 176–7).

The death of his father when George was twelve was unfortunate, less because Frederick might have been a good influence on him than because it meant that the burdens of state would fall on him early in life. Frederick left a political testament for his son, drafted in 1749. He was advised to separate Hanover from England, as George I had suggested, practise economy, and reduce the national debt. It concluded by advising George to 'convince the nation that you are not only an Englishman born and bred, but that you are also this by inclination'. There was no suggestion that royal authority must be strengthened or that parties should be eradicated. But the extirpation of parties was something of a commonplace at the time. Bolingbroke had denounced them in a *Dissertation upon Parties* (1733–4) and in *The Idea of a Patriot King* (1749), and Frederick had promised to eradicate them in his contract with the tories in 1747.

Waldegrave's welcome at Leicester House in 1752 wore thin, and by 1756 he was glad to give way. His influence had already been replaced by that of Lord Bute, lord of the bedchamber to Prince Frederick in 1750, but he was retained by the princess after her husband's death to help plan Kew Gardens. Prince George was given his own establishment in 1756, but insisted on remaining with his mother, and succeeded in appointing Bute as groom of the stole. Bute had already begun to act as adviser to the prince: 'the prospect of serving you and forming your young mind', he wrote to the prince, 'is exquisitely pleasing to a heart like mine' (*Letters … to Lord Bute*, liii). Great hopes were pinned on the young man. In 1758 he gave £50 to John Home, author of the play *Agis*, and visited the performance at Drury Lane three times. Home's dedication to the prince observed that 'the serious cares and princely studies of your youth, the visible tenor of your generous and constant mind, have filled the breasts of all good men with hopes of you'. Garrick delivered a patriot prologue, drawing the parallel with the Spartan Agis: 'the widow'd mother shewed her parting son, The race of glory which

his sire had run'. Mrs Pritchard's epilogue drove the point home—'France shall yet tremble at the British sword, And dread the vengeance of her ancient Lord' (*The Works of John Home*, ed. H. Mackenzie, 1822 1.185–286). To Bute, George wrote, 'I can't praise enough the noble generous sentiments that run through the whole play' (*Letters … to Lord Bute*, 9, no. 10).

Bute was savagely handled by contemporaries and has found little favour with historians, but it is to his credit that he established warm personal relations with the prince where previous governors had notably failed. The prince not merely responded to Bute's advice, but developed for his 'dearest friend' an unbounded admiration and affection: 'I esteem your friendship above every earthly joy', he declared (*Letters … to Lord Bute*, 38, no. 47). Should Bute set him adrift, he would renounce the crown and 'retire to some distant region where in solitude I might for the rest of my life remain' (ibid., 14, no. 18). This was romantic and charming, if rather an unrealistic suggestion from a prince of Wales. There is no evidence that Bute took advantage of his position to instil autocratic or prerogative notions into George—nor, indeed, that he possessed them himself—but he undoubtedly reinforced certain unfortunate tendencies, towards suspiciousness, self-righteousness, and a taste for meaningless melodrama. Far from seeking to subvert the constitution, he and George saw themselves as defending it against a possible military coup by George's uncle, the duke of Cumberland:

> my friend is attacked in the most cruel and horrid manner, not for anything he has done … but because he is my friend, and wants to see me come to the throne with honor and not with disgrace, and because he is a friend to the blessed liberties of his country and not to arbitrary notions. (ibid., 3, no. 3)

The merest criticism by Bute—in this case of George's sloth—was enough to plunge him into agonies of remorse. He would throw off that 'incomprehensible indolence, inattention and heedlessness' that Bute had charged him with: 'nothing but the true love you bear me could have led you to remain with me so long' (ibid., 13–14, no. 18).

Bute's plan to eradicate party was easier said than done. In a parliamentary system parties have a remarkable capacity for splitting and re-forming as the great issues change. The early eighteenth-century questions, such as 'the church in danger', were giving way to fresh issues, such as relations with the colonies. In the late 1750s, as George waited for his grandfather to die, the Seven Years' War was fast becoming the dominant issue. Though undoubtedly glorious, it was also undeniably expensive, and it involved the career of William Pitt, the organizer of victory. Though formal relations between the prince and the court were maintained—which they had not been under his father or grandfather—George increasingly adopted a political stance, and the reversionary interest gained adherents. In 1755, when Pitt had been dismissed for his attacks upon the duke of Newcastle, he had moved towards an understanding with Leicester House. During

Pitt's first term as secretary of state under the duke of Devonshire, relations with Bute had remained good. In the summer of 1757, when he came to terms with Newcastle, Pitt wrote to his 'truly noble and generous friend' Bute of the sacrifice he had made in agreeing to work with such a wretch. But as the new coalition ministry established itself and the tide of war began to turn Bute became uneasy, disliking the extent to which Pitt was being pulled into reinforcing Britain's contribution to the war in Germany. By 1758 the prince was talking of the 'infamous and ungrateful part' Pitt was taking, and wrote to Bute that 'he seems to forget that the day will come, when he must expect to be treated according to his deserts' (*Letters ... to Lord Bute*, 18–19, nos. 24–5). By 1760 Pitt was 'the blackest of hearts' and 'a true snake in the grass' (ibid., 45, 47, nos. 57, 60). With Legge, the chancellor of the exchequer, the prince was 'incens'd'. Since the prince was also convinced that Fox and Cumberland were 'mirmidons of the blackest kind', planning a military coup, and had no great opinion of Newcastle, the number of leading politicians who did not measure up to his demanding standards was considerable. Luckily he still had Bute: 'in what a pretty pickle I should be in a future day if I had not your sagacious councils' (ibid., 11, no. 14).

Meanwhile, the old king was anxious to see his grandson married before his accession. In 1759 a proposal on behalf of Caroline of Brunswick-Wolfenbüttel was revived; despite George II's assurance that the princess was 'très aimable de toute sa personne', the prince expressed dislike of the pride of petty German courts, and refused (*Letters ... to Lord Bute*, 23, no. 30). In 1759 he offered his services in a military capacity, explaining that he would prove 'a terror to the enemy'. Since he had no military experience of any kind the offer was politely deferred, leaving the prince to fume that he was ashamed to be the grandson of George II, to whom he began referring as 'the old man' (ibid., 25, 40–41, nos. 33–4, 49, 51).

Bute and marriage As the prince's moment drew near, his aspirations remained extremely vague, but his list of potential victims long and specific. His dependence upon Bute was still total. In November 1759, about to be admitted to the House of Lords, he wrote to Bute: 'I am desirous to know whether I am not to put on my hat on taking my seat' (*Letters ... to Lord Bute*, 33, no. 42). The clash with Pitt came on 25 October 1760, the very first day of George III's reign as king of Great Britain and Ireland and elector of Hanover. The declaration to the privy council, drafted by Bute, referred to the 'bloody and expensive war' in progress. Pitt bridled, and the resulting formula—'expensive but just and necessary war'—showed how hard it had been to keep the domestic peace. Bute replaced Holdernesse as secretary of state for the north, the new king arguing sensibly that he would otherwise be denounced as a favourite and a minister behind the curtain. The duchess of Northumberland offered a friendly portrait of the new monarch:

He was in his person tall and robust, more graceful than genteel ... with an unparalleled air of majestic dignity. There was a noble openness in his countenance, blended with a cheerful good-natured affability. He was fair and fresh coloured and had now and then a few pimples out. His eyes were blue, his teeth extreamly fine. His hair a light auburn ... his voice was strong, melodious and clear. (*Diaries of a Duchess*, 35)

At once the search for a suitable bride was resumed. Bute had succeeded late in 1759 in steering George away from Lady Sarah Lennox, Henry Fox's sister-in-law, insisting that he must marry a foreign princess, and the prince, despite incoherent protestations of rapture for Lady Sarah, had himself suggested looking through an almanac for possible German candidates. The princesses of Darmstadt and of Swedt were ruled out after reports that they were 'stubborn and ill-tempered to the greatest degree' (*Letters ... to Lord Bute*, 53, no. 67). The princess of Saxe-Gotha was said to be of a philosophical turn, which George did not relish. In the end, without vast enthusiasm, he settled on *Charlotte of Mecklenburg-Strelitz (1744–1818), then aged seventeen. Three separate reports denied her beauty, but she was reputed sensible, and although a Lutheran had no objection to the Anglican creed. The marriage took place at St James's Palace on 8 September 1761. The bride and groom met at three in the afternoon and were married at nine at night. Horace Walpole, who had not yet learned to despise the king, wrote that he looked 'very handsome, and talked to her continually with great good humour' (Walpole, *Corr.*, 38.117). A fortnight later, on 22 September 1761, they celebrated their coronation in Westminster Abbey. That year, the king bought Buckingham House (the nucleus of the present Buckingham Palace) and in 1775 he settled it on the queen. It became the usual royal residence in London, all the royal children, save George, being born there.

Parts of the king's programme were effected with little difficulty. Newcastle was dismayed to be told that there would be no secret service money for the general election—though in later years George reverted to the practice of his forebears. To bring the tories back into the political fold as a means of eradicating party several of them were appointed to bedchamber posts and tories were welcomed at the levee. But the real author of this policy was Pitt, whose rapprochement with the tories had continued since he took office in 1757. 'The extinction of parties' wrote Horace Walpole, 'had not waited for, but preceded, the dawn of his reign' (Walpole, *Memoirs*, 1.5). Nor were the consequences what the king hoped. The obscuring of party battle lines helped to produce a confused political situation in which ministries came and went in swift succession, and soon parties were re-forming on different principles.

George's determination to appoint Lord Bute and to wind up the war also contributed to the political instability which lasted until Lord North took over in 1770. From the moment that George succeeded to the throne it was clear that the days of Pitt and Newcastle were numbered. Since one was a national hero and the other commanded a large parliamentary following, and together they had presided over one of the most successful of all administrations, their removal would cause a stir. George was not deterred, since he had Bute on his side. In November 1760 he wrote that unless Pitt behaved, he would 'show him that aversion which will force him to resign', and in September 1761 that 'we must get rid of him in a happier minute than the present one' (*Letters … to Lord Bute*, 50, no. 63; 63, no. 87). Of the duke, he wrote in April 1762 that 'the more I know of this fellow, the more I wish to see him out of employment' (ibid., 94, no. 129). Pitt obligingly resigned in October 1761 when the cabinet refused to endorse a preemptive declaration of war against Spain. Newcastle was at odds with the king, who wished to wind down the German war: in April 1762 George wrote that if Newcastle resigned Bute, 'void of his [Newcastle's] dirty arts', must take the helm (ibid., 93, no. 127). In May 1762 Newcastle went; Bute took his place as first lord of the Treasury and the following day received the Garter. In response to an attack of nerves by Bute, George wrote 'Vigour and the day is ours' (ibid., 109, no. 148).

The promotion of Bute and the debate on the peace settlement produced a storm which unnerved Bute and caused the king much uneasiness. Pitt denounced the treaty as inadequate, but Henry Fox was brought in to push it through parliament. Though George was upset at the employment of a man who was, to his mind, associated with corruption and the old gang, Fox did the job, and the treaty was carried in the Commons by 319 votes to 65. But the peace was unpopular. Bute was caricatured as a Scottish favourite, hanged in effigy, assaulted in the streets, and his name was linked with the princess dowager in countless squibs and verses. In this crisis he revealed, as a friend put it, 'more than ordinary sensibility to unmerited reproach and abuse' (J. A. Cannon, *Parliamentary Reform, 1640–1832*, 1973, 58). It was soon his turn to pine for the uninhabited cavern: 'I would retire on bread and water', he wrote in February 1763, 'and think it luxury, compared with what I suffer' (*Lonsdale MSS*, 132). The king tried desperately to dissuade him from retirement but Bute, feeling himself on the brink of a precipice, insisted on resignation. George was most reluctant to accept his suggestion that Henry Fox be offered the Treasury—'in the case of Mr Fox I fear we shall never think alike'—and in the end, without enthusiasm, gave the post to George Grenville (*Letters … to Lord Bute*, 197, no. 278). The king wrote sadly 'Tho young, I see but too much that there are few very few honest men in this world … I shall therefore support those who will act for me and without regret change my tools whenever they act contrary to my service' (ibid., 220, no. 309). Yet in his disagreement with Bute over Fox and Shelburne there were signs that the king, as he gained experience and his marriage prospered, was liberating himself. It was a slow process though, and in the three weeks of April subsequent to Bute's resignation George addressed more than thirty letters to him.

Turbulent years, 1763–1770 The Grenville ministry was a nightmare for the king. At an audience on 4 April, George explained to Grenville that he was Bute's choice, and that there must be no negotiation with Newcastle or Pitt—'I would rather quit my Crown' (*Letters … to Lord Bute*, 210, no. 294). There were few disagreements on policy. They agreed on a strong attitude towards the American colonies and were resolved to treat John Wilkes firmly for his attacks on the government in the *North Briton*. But George found Grenville intolerable—unbelievably prolix and much inclined to stand on his dignity. In less than three weeks the king was complaining to Bute of Grenville's 'tiresome manner' and 'ill humour' (ibid., 231, no. 326; 233, 328). On 1 June the king asked Bute to sound out Newcastle and his friends, who refused to join the ministry. In August when Egremont, secretary of state and Grenville's brother-in-law, died suddenly Bute was instructed to approach Pitt. At an audience with the king Pitt's demands were unacceptably high and his language lofty—'he saw the boat was sinking, that what he proposed was merely to keep it afloat' (W. J. Smith, 2.199). The breakdown in negotiations left the king stranded, and Grenville resumed office on condition that Bute withdrew completely from active politics. Bute accordingly resigned the last position he retained—that of keeper of the privy purse—and retired to his house at Luton Hoo. On 8 September 1763, at the audience, the king told Grenville 'let us not look back, let us only look forward, nothing of that sort shall ever happen again' (ibid., 2.205).

The reconciliation did not last long. By the end of the month Grenville and the king had a sharp exchange over the disposal of the keepership, which the king wanted to give to Sir William Breton, a follower of Bute, and Grenville wanted for himself. The conversation became heated and the king finished with 'Good God! Mr Grenville, am I to be suspected after all I have done?' (W. J. Smith, 2.210). There were reports that Bute had seen Beckford, Pitt's right-hand man, at Luton, which turned out to be true. These difficulties set the tone for the rest of Grenville's ministry. 'No office fell vacant in any department', wrote the king in a memo, 'that Mr Grenville did not declare he could not serve if the man he recommended did not succeed' (*Correspondence*, ed. Fortescue, 1.164, no. 139). The following year there was another quarrel over the appointment of a successor to Hogarth as court painter. The king thought Grenville insolent: 'if men presumed to speak to me on business without his leave … he would not serve an hour' (ibid., 1.164, no. 139). Bute's return to London in the spring of 1764 revived all Grenville's old suspicions, and since Bute's brother, James Stuart Mackenzie, continued to serve as lord privy seal for Scotland, there were further disputes over Scottish patronage.

This constant bickering with his ministers had a serious effect on the king's health and for much of early 1765 he was very unwell. In May he tried once more to escape by appealing through Cumberland to Pitt, but again the great man refused. Grenville and his allies, thinking their position impregnable, imposed severe terms, including the dismissal of Mackenzie, though George pleaded that he had personally promised him the post for life. 'Not able to remove them', wrote the king, 'I could not be so wanting to myself as to treat them otherwise than as Jailers' (*Correspondence*, ed. Fortescue, 1.166, no. 139). The illness produced yet another crisis when the king decided that arrangements for a regency would be prudent. Though the obvious person in the event of the king's death was the queen, George reserved the right to nominate at a later stage. Grenville presumed that this was in order to name the princess dowager and thus restore Bute's influence, though in fact it was because the king did not wish to give the position to his brother the duke of York, whom he thought would be unsuitable. 'My very sleep', the king wrote to Bute, 'is not free from thinking of the men I daily see ... excuse the incoherency of my letter; but a mind ulcer'd by the treatment it meets with from all around is the true cause of it' (*Letters ... to Lord Bute*, 241, no. 336). For a king who had come to the throne determined not to be held in toils, as he insisted his grandfather had been, George was not doing very well. There were demons, at least for the time being, worse than Newcastle and Pitt.

It was inevitable that George III would seek once more to escape from this intolerable situation. The difficulty was that neither Pitt nor Newcastle and his friends were any more willing than Grenville to find themselves in Bute's shadow. In June, despite an audience with the king, Pitt declined once more to come to the rescue, pleading his ally Temple's refusal to take the Treasury. The king consequently authorized Cumberland to begin discussions with Newcastle, and after complicated negotiations the marquess of Rockingham took office as first lord of the Treasury with Newcastle as lord privy seal. Grenville was dismissed at an audience on 10 July 1765, still arguing. He protested that he was utterly ignorant why he had forfeited royal favour, to which the king replied that 'when he had anything proposed to him, it was no longer as counsel, but what he was to *obey*' (W. J. Smith, 3.213).

The Rockingham ministry also expected a similar assurance from the king that 'my lord Bute should not be suffered to interfere in the least degree in any public business whatever' (Bateson, 30–31). They refused categorically to reinstate Mackenzie or to offer him any alternative place. But at least the king had different gaolers.

The Rockingham ministry was not strong and was weakened in October 1765 by the death of its sponsor and supervisor, the duke of Cumberland. Several of its leading members, particularly the duke of Grafton, were anxious to enlist the help of Pitt. Fresh approaches were made in January 1766, but Pitt was ambivalent and unresponsive. In a letter to Bute on 10 January the king made it clear that though he had no great opinion of his ministers' talents, he felt himself committed to support them. He was determined not to negotiate himself with Pitt, 'which I think would for ever stain my name' (*Letters ... to Lord Bute*, 245, no. 337). But the main proposal of the ministry, to repeal the Stamp Act, caused great trouble, not only from the hardliners on America, but from those who were concerned at such fluctuations in imperial policy. When some of Bute's friends warned the king that they could not support repeal and tendered their resignations he persuaded them to continue. On 6 February 1766 Bute's intervention in debate convinced many that the king was hostile to repeal, and the ministers lost by 59 votes to 54. Rockingham then insisted on authority from George III that he favoured repeal, and the following day in the Commons

the ministry won by 274 votes to 134. This victory gave a deceptive impression of the government's strength, and may have made Rockingham overconfident. In April, Grafton told the king that he had to resign since Pitt would not join the ministry. Convinced that no alternative ministry could be formed Rockingham refused to negotiate either with Pitt or with Bute's former supporters. Meanwhile Pitt hardened his attitude towards the administration, with violent denunciations, while his references to Bute and his group became kinder. At the same time the king's gratitude towards the men who had rescued him from Grenville waned. The duke of Richmond, who replaced Grafton as secretary of state, was not a man George liked. On 3 May 1766 the king wrote to Bute: 'I can neither eat nor sleep: nothing pleases me but musing on my cruel situation ... if I am to continue the life of agitation I have these three years, the next year there will be a Council of Regency to assist in that undertaking' (ibid., 248–9, no. 338). In his desperation he swallowed his pride and approached Pitt once more, and at an audience on 12 July he agreed to serve. George's letter to Bute showed how much he had learned: he had parted with the Rockinghams, he wrote, without a quarrel, 'for it is very unpleasant to be afterwards obliged to appear forgetting what one has suffered' (ibid., 253–4, no. 339). Since Temple was again unwilling to serve, Grafton was put in as a nominal first lord of the Treasury, while Pitt, ennobled as Lord Chatham, became lord privy seal and superintending genius. Rockingham and Newcastle went out, but many of the ministers remained. Since Pitt agreed with the king on the paramount need to destroy party, it looked as if, at length, some of the king's youthful hopes were about to be realized. The fifth government in the first six years of his reign took office.

George III certainly bore little blame for the disaster which overcame this ministry. He gave Chatham full and total support, continuing to do so long after it had become apparent that the great man was a broken reed. To Chatham he transferred some of the respect he had felt for Bute. The negotiation to bring in Chatham produced the final breach between the king and Bute, who was greatly hurt that though his brother, James Stuart Mackenzie, had been restored as lord privy seal for Scotland for life, Bute had not been consulted in the matter by Pitt, and Bute's follower Fletcher Norton had not been given office. He wrote in the autumn of 1766 to beg the king that their private friendship should not be terminated: 'I have for ever done with this bad public, my heart is half broke and my health ruined, with the unmerited barbarous treatment I have received' (*Letters ... to Lord Bute*, 256, appx 1). His political following disintegrated, and at last Bute withdrew completely from public life and access to the monarch.

The foundation for a successful ministry appeared to have been laid. Bute's influence was finally removed; an experienced and admired statesman was at the helm who shared the aspirations of the king, and who, in addition, possessed at least in theory, a most exalted view of the dignity of the crown. In fact, the Chatham ministry was one of the greatest political catastrophes in British history. From October 1766 Chatham was stricken by a severe nervous breakdown which rendered him not only incapable of public business but of all human contact. Grafton coped as best he could, but on his appointment had protested that he was unfit to fill the office; he could not deal with America and John Wilkes, and had no control over his effervescent colleague Charles Townshend. Ministers repaired to Chatham when they could obtain permission, only to find him distressingly vague and incoherent. The king treated Chatham with quite remarkable patience. For nine weeks over Christmas 1766 Chatham retired to Bath, and on the way back was marooned at the Castle inn, Marlborough, for another three weeks. When he did reach London in March 1767 the king wrote: 'now you are arrived in town every difficulty will daily decrease' (*Correspondence*, ed. Fortescue, 1.462, no. 490). In fact they multiplied, and Chatham withdrew into complete seclusion, sitting for hours in a darkened room. The restoration of his health must be the only consideration, wrote the king. When in May 1767 Grafton did obtain permission for a visit, George wrote: 'I already look on all difficulties as overcome'. Unfortunately Grafton found Chatham in a pitiful condition, 'nerves and spirits affected to a dreadful degree' (ibid., 1.478, no. 519; *Autobiography … of Grafton*, 136–9). The king offered to visit Chatham, sent him advice on physicians, and constantly encouraged him: 'when you are able to come out all the difficulties that have been encountered will vanish' (*Correspondence*, ed. Fortescue, 1.491, no. 535). But Chatham did not come out, and Grafton's problems mounted with the return of Wilkes as MP for Middlesex in 1768. The king's attitude to Wilkes was uncompromising, despising him as a rake and demagogue and fearing the power of the mob. 'The expulsion of Mr Wilkes appears to be very essential and must be effected', he wrote to North on 25 April 1768; he urged strong action against the rioters, and in January 1769 described the expulsion of Wilkes as 'a measure whereon almost my Crown depends' (ibid., 2.21, no. 613; 2.75, no. 693).

In October 1768 Chatham tendered his resignation. George replied: 'I think I have a right to insist on your remaining in my service, for I with pleasure look forward to the time of your recovery' (ibid., 2.57, no. 669). Chatham insisted that his health was broken and implored the king to accept his resignation; should he ever recover every moment of his life would be devoted to the king's service. He went, and Grafton soldiered on, but there was one last twist. In January 1770, miraculously restored, Chatham reappeared in the House of Lords, denounced his former colleagues, and declared that his ministry had been undermined by the baneful influence of the earl of Bute: 'he had been duped when he least suspected treachery … at the time when he was taken ill' (Cobbett, *Parl. hist.*, 16, 1770, 842). His intervention was enough to bring down Grafton's shaky ministry, and the king approached Lord North as a forlorn hope: 'you must easily see that if you do not accept, I have no peer at present … to place in the Duke of Grafton's employment' (*Correspondence*, ed.

Fortescue, 2.126, no. 745). As it happened, the years of instability were at an end and George had, at last, backed a winner. North's ministry lasted twelve years, longer than all George's previous ministries put together.

North's ministry, 1770–1782 By this time George had changed considerably from the inexperienced youth who had inherited the crown. He was still inclined to censoriousness and though he frequently paid tribute to his own good intentions found it harder to perceive those of others. But the vicissitudes of his first ten years, though highly disagreeable, had left him more circumspect and more inclined to distance himself. Villains had become saviours, and saviours villains, in bewildering combinations. Bute, once a man of unsurpassed wisdom, had, in the end, seemed much like other politicians; Henry Fox, whom George despised as a man of corruption, had had to be employed to carry the peace; his uncle Cumberland, the ogre of George's Leicester House days, had saved him from Grenville. Pitt had moved from a scoundrel in the 1750s into a mentor and friend in the 1760s, only to revert to 'that perfidious man' in the 1770s (*Correspondence*, ed. Fortescue, 4.59, no. 2224). Not surprisingly, the king told North in 1778: 'I have had enough of personal negotiations' (ibid., 4.58, no. 2221). The reign of virtue had not been abandoned but it would be a long road.

As well as being head of state George became, on the death of his grandfather, head of the royal family. With his mother, the princess dowager, he remained on cordial terms, and the misunderstanding over her initial exclusion from the Regency Bill was the last straw in his relations with Grenville. His marriage to Charlotte proved both affectionate and—as George had fervently hoped—fruitful. The queen preferred a quiet domestic life, shared her husband's love of music, and had no wish to play a political role. For the first time since the reign of Charles I there were no mistresses at court to complicate private or public matters. Their first son, George (*George IV) was born after eleven months of married life on 12 August 1762, and was followed by eight more sons and six daughters [see George III, daughters of (*act.* 1766–1857)], the last, Amelia, born in 1783. By May 1770, when Elizabeth was born, there were seven children in the royal nursery. The king was an affectionate father: when Prince Octavius died in 1783 at the age of four, George declared 'Heaven will be no Heaven to me if Octavius is not there'. It is doubtful whether the king read widely, particularly in later life when his eyesight was giving trouble, but his long audiences with Dr Johnson, James Beattie, Charles Burney, and others suggest a cultivated mind and a gift for pleasant conversation. To Johnson he paid an elegant compliment, and his remark—no doubt obvious enough—that Johnson ought to attempt a literary history bore fruit in the most delightful of Johnson's works, the *Lives of the Poets*.

The king's brothers and sisters provided a variety of problems. At the accession his brother Edward was twenty-one, William seventeen, Henry fifteen, and Frederick ten; his elder sister Augusta was twenty-three, Louisa eleven, and Caroline nine. His sister Elizabeth, a bright girl, who had been born with a deformity, had died of appendicitis in 1759 at the age of eighteen; his brother Frederick died of tuberculosis in 1765. Prince Edward, once his favourite companion, became a cause of anxiety. His way of life was raffish and self-indulgent, he showed signs of dabbling in opposition politics, and in May 1767 was said to be 'in great disgrace at court' (Walpole, *Corr.*, 22.524). He died suddenly in Monaco in September 1767. Princess Augusta, the king's eldest sister, married in January 1764 Charles, duke of Brunswick, but her husband was unfaithful, the marriage did not prosper, and by 1765 Rigby reported 'their living very ill together' (*Correspondence of … Bedford*, 3.318). Another sister, Louisa, small and pretty, died of tuberculosis in May 1768. The king's troubles continued in the 1770s. Henry, duke of Cumberland, his third brother, was successfully sued for damages in 1770 over his relations with Lady Grosvenor, and his fervent but ungrammatical love letters were read out in court. In January 1772 came news that George's youngest sister, Caroline, married to Christian VII of Denmark, had been arrested for adultery and her lover executed; though George negotiated for her an honourable retirement to Celle, she died in 1775. The princess dowager died in February 1772 after a long and painful cancer of the throat. Disentangled from Lady Grosvenor the duke of Cumberland hastily made a secret marriage to Anne Horton, a widow, and was told bluntly by the king that he had 'irretrievably ruined himself' (Brooke, *King George the Third*, 273). To prevent any repetition of such *mésalliances* the king insisted on the passage of the Royal Marriages Act in 1772, which forbade the marriage of any member of the royal family under twenty-five without the monarch's approval. No sooner had this become law than the duke of Gloucester, to whom the king had confided his outrage at Cumberland's behaviour, confessed that he had been secretly married for the past six years to Lady Waldegrave, an illegitimate daughter of Sir Edward Walpole. Neither duchess was ever received at court. At times the king must have turned with relief to politics.

Until overwhelmed by the American troubles, North's ministry gave the king some respite from political difficulties. North and George were on good terms, and the prime minister was given the Garter within eighteen months. Government majorities were quickly restored, opposition withered, the Wilkes issue was defused, and war with Spain, which would have brought a demand for the recall of Chatham, averted. The king was content to play a less prominent political role, following North's lead: 'you are my sheet anchor', he wrote in November 1775 (*Correspondence*, ed. Fortescue, 3.279, no. 1742).

By that time the waves were rolling high again. The origin of the American crisis lay in the cost of the Seven Years' War, which made it imperative for ministers to raise more revenue from the colonists. It is possible that the repeal of the Stamp Act, though accompanied by the Declaratory Act reaffirming parliamentary authority, might have averted a clash, had not Charles Townshend, during Chatham's illness, rekindled agitation with his miscellaneous duties. The defeat of the government's land tax proposals in February 1767—'a thing almost unknown in Parliament'—by an opposition led by Grenville made it all the more urgent to raise additional revenue from America (*Correspondence*, ed. Fortescue, 1.453, no. 473). Townshend's sudden death in September 1767 meant that the problem passed to North. Although his own instincts were conciliatory, he had little room for manoeuvre, since parliament, beset by Wilkite rioters at home and organized resistance in the colonies, was in no mood to truckle to violence. Two months after taking office in 1770 North proposed to withdraw the Townshend duties, 'which had given umbrage to the Americans', retaining only a small tax on tea at 3*d*. in the pound (Cobbett, *Parl. hist.*, 16, 1770, 853). He had some difficulty in persuading his followers to agree. The gesture lost much of its point since the same day the Boston massacre took place, inflaming American opinion. In June 1772 American patriots seized the revenue cutter *Gaspée*, wounded the captain, and burnt the ship. In 1773 the Boston Tea Party, accompanied by the tarring and feathering of a customs officer, persuaded most Britons that the Americans were incorrigible. Even the friends of America, Chatham and Rockingham, condemned the outrage and agreed that Britain must protect its officials and their property. The decision to close the port of Boston as a reprisal passed without opposition.

Since it was the view of almost all members of parliament that strong measures should be taken against the colonists, it is not surprising to find the king taking a similar line. In *Common Sense*, Tom Paine denounced him as 'the royal brute', and the Declaration of Independence credited him with a settled plan to enslave his American subjects. In fact, until the crisis, like most Britons, he showed little interest in America. Once resistance flared he insisted that it was his duty to uphold the authority of the imperial parliament: 'I am fighting the battle of the legislature', he wrote, 'therefore have a right to expect an almost unanimous support' (*Correspondence*, ed. Fortescue, 3.256, no. 1709). When the Americans co-ordinated their resistance in the summer of 1774 through the Philadelphia Congress, his attitude hardened. 'The New England governments are in a state of rebellion', he wrote in November 1774: 'blows must decide whether they are to be subject to this country or independent' (ibid., 3.153, no. 1556). It is not easy to see what other attitude a constitutional monarch could have adopted, even setting aside the improbability that an eighteenth-century ruler would be sympathetic towards rebels.

Once rioting developed into warfare after the first shots at Lexington in April 1775, the king took little part in strategic discussions, though he was greatly exercised in raising and reviewing troops and building men-of-war. His main contribution was to stiffen the resolve of his ministers, retain the important services of Lord North, and head off any negotiations with the parliamentary opposition. After the first severe setback in October 1777, when Burgoyne surrendered at Saratoga, North warned the king that 'some material change of system' was needed, and that a national coalition might be necessary (*Correspondence*, ed. Fortescue, 3.504, no. 2095). The following month he complained that the disaster had deprived him of his memory and understanding, and confessed his own incapacity for the office he held. In February he begged leave to approach Chatham as 'of all the opposition, the person who would be of most service to his Majesty' (ibid., 4.38, no. 2193). George III was extremely reluctant: 'No advantage to this country nor personal danger can ever make me address myself for assistance either to Lord Chatham or any other branch of the opposition honestly I would rather lose the crown I now wear than bear the ignominy of possessing it under their shackles' (ibid., 4.59, no. 2221). He was forced to agree to an approach, but added: 'I do not expect Lord Chatham and his crew will come to your assistance' (ibid.). Chatham, as usual, insisted on an audience and demanded full powers. The king refused to have him as 'Dictator', and hinted to North that he could find himself Chatham's first victim. In a phrase that might have recalled Bute, North retorted that capital punishment would be better than the mental agony he suffered. From this dilemma both men were rescued by news of Chatham's final collapse in the House of Lords on 7 April 1778. The king was too honest to pretend to grief he did not possess: 'may not the political exit of Lord Chatham', he enquired briskly of North the following day, 'encline you to continue at the head of my affairs?' (ibid., 4.102, no. 2284).

Though the danger from Chatham had gone North still pined for release, particularly when the parliamentary session drew near or the news from America was bad. The entry into the war of France and Spain in 1778 and 1779, though making it more popular, placed an enormous strain on the country's resources, particularly its naval strength. Opposition in parliament, though few in numbers, was vigorous and highly personal: Edmund Burke was not the only member to threaten North with impeachment and the block. Under these circumstances retaining his first minister was a major consideration for the king, since North's conciliatory attitude and parliamentary skill were valuable assets. George paid off North's personal debts in 1777 and for some years kept up a private correspondence with Charles Jenkinson and John Robinson, who monitored the first minister's state of mind. This has been seen as a sinister example of backstairs influence and each man acquired a reputation for intrigue, but since the arrangement was intended not to undermine North but to encourage and support him, it appears scarcely objectionable. Nor did the king flinch from emotional blackmail: 'are you resolved, agreeable to the example of the Duke of Grafton', he wrote to North in the spring of 1778, 'at the hour of danger to desert me?' (*Correspondence*, ed. Fortescue, 4.72, no. 2240).

It has often been suggested that by his obstinacy George III protracted the American war. But no eighteenth-century ruler would contemplate tamely surrendering the greater part of his empire, nor is it clear why Frederick the Great's resistance in the Seven Years' War should be regarded as heroic, yet George's resistance in America

foolhardy. Until after Yorktown it was not certain that the outcome must be defeat. As late as 1781 there was mutiny in the American army, and George Washington wrote that there was 'not a single farthing in the military chest' (*The Writings of George Washington*, ed. J. C. Fitzpatrick, 39 vols., 1931–44, 21.55); in France, Vergennes conceded that it was 'a war of hard cash, and if we drag it out, the last shilling may not be ours' (Mackesy, 386). Admiral Rodney's great naval victory off the Saints in 1782, and General Elliott's magnificent defence of Gibraltar enabled better terms of peace to be obtained than had seemed likely.

Political crisis, 1782–1784 After Yorktown the king's resolve held but North's parliamentary majority melted away, until on 15 March 1782, on a vote of no confidence, it stood at only nine. Even then the king was most unwilling to contemplate a change of ministry. 'If you resign before I have decided what I will do', he warned North, 'you will certainly for ever forfeit my regard' (*Correspondence*, ed. Fortescue, 5.397, no. 3567). North reminded the king sharply:

> The torrent is too strong to be resisted; Your Majesty is well apprized that, in this country, the Prince on the Throne, cannot, with prudence, oppose the deliberate resolution of the House of Commons … Your Majesty having persevered, as long as possible, in what you thought right, can lose no honour if you yield at length.   (ibid., 5.395, no. 3566)

The crisis which followed was as painful to the king as those of the 1760s. He drafted an abdication speech expressing his sorrow that he 'finds he can be of no further utility to his native country', and declaring his intention to retire to Hanover (ibid., 5.425, no. 3601). It was never delivered. He was obliged to accept Rockingham, leader of the largest opposition group, but installed the earl of Shelburne, the least objectionable of his opponents, as a check and counter-balance to the new first minister. He was forced to agree not only to recognition of American independence, but to the programme of economical reform to which the new ministers were pledged.

The influence of the crown, which Dunning's motion of 1780 had declared to be increasing, was more the influence of government than of the monarchy itself. Nevertheless, the king was deeply offended at the proposal to reform his household by act of parliament. Ministers conceded that the household should be reformed by internal regulation and the king sent a message to parliament to that effect. A number of sinecure officers such as the master of the stag hounds and the master of the harriers were abolished, but the effect was slight, and one unforeseen consequence was an enhancement in the importance of honours.

A struggle for power between Shelburne and Rockingham began in the first week of the new ministry and continued until the latter's death on 1 July 1782. The king gave Shelburne full support, grooming him for the succession, and at once invited him to form an administration. Charles James Fox, the second secretary of state, and a number of his colleagues resigned, protesting that they could not serve under Shelburne. The balance between the contending factions was held by Lord North, who had retained a sizeable following. Despite his parting protest-ations of devotion to the king's service, his decision depended primarily upon the terms of the peace treaty which Shelburne was negotiating, and the nature of the approaches made to him by the other two parties. In August the king, anxious to buttress Shelburne's position before parliament met, addressed a personal appeal to North, begging him to give 'the most cordial support' to Shelburne's ministry and to use his great influence with the country gentlemen (*Correspondence*, ed. Fortescue, 6.97, no. 3872). North's reply was circumspect, provoking the king to remark that loyalty did not last long. When the terms of the settlement became known the neglect of the American loyalists made it very difficult for North to advise acceptance, he closed with Fox's offer of a coali-tion, and in February 1783 Shelburne was forced to resign.

George was distracted at the thought of once more employing Charles James Fox, whom he despised on both personal and public grounds, as the son of Henry Fox, as a gambler and a libertine, an evil influence on the prince of Wales, and a politician whose avowed aim was to strike 'a good stout blow' at the influence of the crown. His abdica-tion speech was brought out and revised. For six weeks he refused to surrender to the coalition, until the total absence of an alternative ministry obliged him to yield. Portland became first minister, Fox and North the secre-taries of state. He had been forced to give way, the king told Lord Temple, to:

> the most unprincipled coalition the annals of this or any other nation can equal. I have withstood it till not a single man is willing to come to my assistance … I trust the eyes of the nation will soon be opened as my sorrow may prove fatal to my health if I remain long in this thraldom.
> (*Correspondence*, ed. Fortescue, 6.329–30, no. 4272)

The coalition ministry was living on borrowed time. The king retired into sulky seclusion, refusing to grant peer-ages as a demonstration of hostility. A very sharp dispute over the proposed allowance for the prince of Wales nearly brought about a crisis. George thought the provi-sion suggested by the ministers was far too lavish and expressed his 'utter indignation and astonishment' at this attempt to 'gratify the passions of an ill-advised young man … the public shall know how well founded the prin-ciples of economy are in those who have so loudly preached it up' (Cannon, *Fox–North Coalition*, 96). Fox and his friends prepared to 'die handsomely' (ibid., 97), but Temple and others advised the king that a family dispute was not a good issue for a public showdown. The king made a sudden retreat, apologizing profusely to Portland, and explaining that the American war had 'soured and ruined his temper' (ibid., 98).

The pivotal position was that of young William Pitt, who had been sounded out in the spring of 1783, but had declined to form a ministry. Ironically, this meant that the king's hopes of rescue depended upon the Grenvilles—since Temple was Pitt's first cousin and the son of George Grenville—the very people he had detested in the 1760s.

But one difficulty was that the king was uncertain to what extent Pitt felt himself pledged to further measures of economical reform and to parliamentary reform—his maiden speech in 1781 had, after all, been made on the need to reduce the influence of the crown. The opportun-ity for which the king had waited came with the decision of ministers to bring forward an India Bill, yet another attempt to frame an adequate administrative structure for the vast territories which could no longer be left to the unchecked rule of the East India Company. Since any pro-posal must involve intervention in the company's affairs and could be represented as an invasion of its charter, there was bound to be scope for powerful opposition. The duke of Manchester, a coalition supporter to whom the outlines of the scheme were sent in September 1783, saw at once the potential political danger:

> His Majesty perhaps might be induced to acquiesce without being thoroughly convinced of the fitness of the measure, and should he coldly support it in the outset, means at the same time might be found to thwart it before it could be brought to maturity.   (*Eighth Report*, HMC, 2.134)

George III seems to have offered no objection to the draft, and the bill passed the Commons with a comfortable majority of 229 votes to 120. Unless the king intervened the bill would almost certainly go through the Lords with-out difficulty. On 1 December Thurlow, lord chancellor until 1782, acting in conjunction with Temple, had an audience in which he suggested that the king should make his disapproval of the bill known. But any alterna-tive ministry would still need a Commons leader, for whom North, Fox, Burke, and Sheridan would prove for-midable adversaries. In a secret negotiation authorized by the king, Pitt agreed to serve, provided that 'the Great Pat-riot's' hostility to the bill was made clear. In an audience with Temple, the king declared that 'whoever votes in the House of Lords for the India Bill is not *his* friend' (*Aberga-venny MSS*, 62). Amid scenes of great excitement the bill was rejected by 87 votes to 79. Three days later Fox, North, and Portland, at a midnight conclave, received from the king terse notices of dismissal, 'as audiences on such occa-sions must be unpleasant' (*Correspondence*, ed. Fortescue, 6.476, no. 4546).

Pitt took office in a minority administration, with Tem-ple as his secretary of state. On 17 December a motion that to report any opinion of the monarch in order to influence voting was a 'high crime and misdemeanour' was carried in the Commons by 153 votes to 80 (*JHC*, 39, 1783, 842). Temple's resignation after only three days was a blow which nearly shattered the enterprise at the outset, and George wrote that he felt himself on the edge of a preci-pice. But the Christmas recess gave the chance for Pitt and his friends to proselytize. The engines of patronage were turned on: 'they are crying peerages about the streets in barrows', wrote Horace Walpole, with pardonable exag-geration (Walpole, *Corr.*, 33.430). By the time parliament reassembled in January 1784 the coalition's majority was down to 39. The king urged a dissolution: 'we must be men; and if we mean to save the country, we must cut those threads that cannot be unravelled. Half measures are ever puerile' (Stanhope, 1.appx, v). Again he threatened to abdicate. The ministers struggled on, and on 8 March the coalition's majority was down to one vote—191 against 190. The king recognized the significance of the figures. Pitt's letter conveying the news was, he wrote, 'the most satisfactory I have received for many months': Pitt would 'be ever able to reflect with satisfaction that in having supported me he has saved the Constitution, the most perfect of human formations' (ibid., 1.appx, x). The subsequent general election endorsed the king's detestation of the coalition and placed Pitt firmly in power. The results, wrote the king, were 'more favourable than the most sanguine could have expected' (ibid., 1.appx, xii). After two years of turmoil the king was once more in clear waters.

The Pitt ministry The loss of America, finally acknowledged in September 1783, though a humiliating blow, had compensating advantages. Britain's economic and financial recovery was remarkably swift, and the disappearance of the American problem removed a factor which had unsettled the political scene since the earliest years of George III's reign. To the new American ambassador, John Adams, the king managed to give a dignified welcome in June 1785:

> I will be free with you. I was the last to consent to the separation; but the separation having been made and having become inevitable, I have always said, as I say now, that I would be the first to meet the friendship of the United States as an independent power. (*Works of John Adams*, 8.255–7)

Pitt held office for the next sixteen years, and by the time he resigned in 1801 the king was an elderly man in uncertain health. Relations between the two were correct rather than cordial, but each understood how much the other depended on the other. It was clear to Pitt how greatly the absence of the king's confidence had weakened the coalition ministry, while the king realized that only Pitt could hold Charles James Fox at bay. There were, of course, occasional disagreements, sometimes sharp, and some residual suspicion on both sides to be removed. The king regretted Pitt's continued commitment to parliamentary reform, and when the issue came up in 1785 Pitt was concerned lest his own position be undermined by secret influence: 'there is but one issue of the business', he warned the king, 'to which he could look as fatal ... that is the possibility of the measure being rejected by the weight of those who were supposed to be connected with government' (*Later Correspondence of George III*, 1.139, no. 182). George III assured him that, though he disapproved of the measure, he had kept his opinion to himself, but added 'there are questions men will not by friendship be biased to accept' (Barnes, 203). Nothing could save Pitt's bill, fewer than half the placemen voted with him, and he went down to defeat by 248 votes to 174. Though it was a mortification, Pitt's government was in no danger. George's note acknowledging Pitt's account of the debate shows how tactful he could sometimes be. Ignoring the subject matter, he passed on Lord Camden's opinion that

Pitt's speech had been 'a masterly performance' (Stanhope, 1.appx, xvii). The most cogent and scholarly attempt to establish that Pitt was in thrall to the king has not won widespread support (Barnes). There was no dramatic change in the constitutional relationship betwen the king and his first minister, but certain long-term factors were beginning to operate against the personal supervision of the monarch—the growing complexity of public business, the growth of party allegiance, the expansion of public opinion, and the development of cabinet solidarity. In addition, a factor which had strengthened George's position in the 1760s—his youth and expectations—no longer operated: in the 1780s his prime minister was in his twenties, while the king was approaching fifty and had a grown-up son.

That son, George, prince of Wales, was, with his brothers, a source of great anxiety to the king. It had not been easy to find governors for the prince and his brother Frederick, and they had not been very successful: one of them, Lord Holdernesse, had been reduced by illness to taking a long recuperation abroad before resigning in 1776, explaining that he had not obtained that share of the princes' confidence which would enable him to be of use. In August 1780 the king had written to the prince that he had not made the progress in his studies that had been anticipated, and begging him to lead a devout and decent life. But the prince had already made considerable progress in other respects. In 1779 he had persuaded Perdita Robinson, the actress, to become his mistress. She had extracted from him a guarantee of £20,000 when he succeeded, and in 1781 was threatening to print his love letters, written under the signature Florizel. Apprised of the affair, the king had to find £5000 to redeem the letters, adding, characteristically, 'I am happy at being able to say that I never was personally engaged in such a transaction' (*Correspondence*, ed. Fortescue, 5.269, no. 3396). The prince immediately plunged into another affair with a Mme Hardenberg, confessing to his brother that he was spitting blood and thought his brain would split. The injured husband took his wife off to Brussels. The following month the prince wrote to his brother that 'the king is excessively cross and ill-tempered, and uncommonly grumpy' (*Correspondence of George, Prince of Wales*, 1.73, no. 50). The prince's political attachment to Fox and the dispute in 1783 over his allowance did nothing to improve relations.

The prince's lavish lifestyle ensured that he was well provided with debt. The acrimonious settlement of 1783 had paid off £23,000, and given him the use of Carlton House. The prince promised instant reformation and the king total forgiveness. The prince at once commenced large-scale alterations to Carlton House, ran once more into debt, and declared in the spring of 1784 that he would be obliged to live abroad. From the 'unruly passions' of his son, complained the king, 'every absurdity and impropriety may be expected' (*Later Correspondence of George III*, 1.85, no. 114). The king was forced to send urgently to Brighton, as a father and a sovereign, to forbid the prince from leaving the country. The prince's debts, he remarked, amounted to £100,000, 'which in one year and without gaming seems hardly credible' (ibid., 1.89, no. 120). A further reason for the prince's continental plans was that he had fallen madly in love with a widow, Mrs Fitzherbert, and was determined to follow her to the Netherlands and marry her. Under the terms of the Act of Settlement this would forfeit his succession to the throne, and by the Royal Marriages Act it would be invalid. In July 1784, in a frenzy of passion, he had stabbed himself, not very deeply.

George III was already in financial difficulties, partly because of his growing family, partly because he had taken on an election debt of £23,000 incurred during Lord North's ministry. Colonel Hotham, the prince's treasurer, was asked to make a new assessment of the prince's debts, a task which he confessed to be impossible: at a rough estimate they had reached £150,000. To compound his difficulties and after abandoning a scheme to escape to America, the prince went through a secret marriage in December 1785 with Mrs Fitzherbert, conducted by a clergyman set free from the Fleet prison for the occasion. The following year he purchased a farmhouse at Brighton and began building the Pavilion. By that time his debts had reached £270,000, which he attributed to the 'incompetency' of his income. In 1787 the whole question was laid before parliament, which voted £161,000 for redemption of debt and £60,000 for the completion of Carlton House. When a member raised the matter of the prince's marriage, Fox, speaking on personal authority, declared the rumours quite untrue. The following day he was told privately that the prince had deceived him.

The prince's brothers, Frederick and William, were aged twenty-one and nineteen in 1784. Frederick had been placed in the army, despite the fact that from the age of six months he had been bishop of Osnabrück, and was serving in Germany. He shared his brother's pursuit of women and was addicted to gambling, but had more sense and understood the damage which a public rift would do to the royal family. Prince William was in the navy. Frederick reported from Hanover that he was given to swearing, a habit he retained, and did not much care how he behaved. In August 1784, the king wrote to reproach him for 'forecastle' manners and his love of improper company (*Later Correspondence of George III*, 1.77, no. 104). The four youngest princes were too young to have started to run up debt. The princesses lived quiet lives under the watchful eye of Queen Charlotte. In 1791 the princess royal, still unmarried at twenty-five, confided to the prince of Wales 'the tiresome and confined life' she was forced to live, and the 'violence and caprice of her mother's temper'. Any marriage would be 'preferable to the misery she was a slave to at present' (*Correspondence of George, Prince of Wales*, 2.162, no. 591). In 1797 she accepted an offer from the duke of Württemberg, lived in Germany, and never saw her father again.

George's court was sober and respectable. The king and queen were good Anglicans, and paid attention to their religious duties without ostentation. Fanny Burney has left a vivid description of the formality and punctiliousness of court life. The king was not fond of St James's,

Kensington, or Hampton Court palaces, and had purchased Buckingham House to develop as a family residence. For country air he used Kew Palace or Windsor, which he increasingly enjoyed. 'I certainly see as little of London as I possibly can', he wrote in 1785, 'and am never a volunteer there' (Brooke, *King George the Third*, 287). Audiences, correspondence, and the levees took up much of his time. He enjoyed riding and hunting, preferred family dinners to entertaining, visited the theatre and concerts regularly, and enjoyed cards and domestic music in the evenings. His preference for frugal meals and his sober habits became a source of fun for the graphic satirists.

One of the remarkable features of George's way of life was his comparative lack of interest in travel. He never visited his Hanoverian dominions, though they were, at least in theory, very dear to him. He gloried in the name of Britain, but knew little about it. Scotland, Wales, and Ireland were ignored. So was most of England. The royal family visited Weymouth for sea bathing, and when at Cheltenham in 1788, the king and queen saw Gloucester, Worcester, Tewkesbury, and a few nearby manor houses like Matson and Croome. But the midlands and north were a closed book, as was the south-west and Cornwall. He never visited the University of Cambridge, nor the great cathedrals at York, Lincoln, Norwich, or Wells. The explanation seems to be a certain lack of intellectual vitality, the problem of conveying court and family, and the king's preference for a routine and familiar existence.

Regency crisis, 1788–1789 This pleasant and relatively undemanding way of life was shattered late in 1788 by the onset of a severe illness. Physically strong, abstemious in diet and conduct, taking regular exercise, George was often agitated by political difficulties, his opinions strongly held and frequently expressed with vigour. John Brooke and other historians have denied that there were any traces of derangement in his illness of 1765, though on 18 March George Grenville noted 'the king's countenance and manner a good deal estranged' (W. J. Smith, 3.122). This may have been caused, or at least exacerbated, by the presence of Grenville himself, whom the king disliked intensely. But the king's determination, once he had recovered, to make provision for a regency suggests that his indisposition was severe. At other periods he was much agitated: in 1783 William Grenville reported him highly excited and talking incessantly. The 1788 illness began in the summer with unpleasant stomach pain. The visit to Cheltenham, though a great success socially, did not put an end to it. By October the king was seriously unwell, sleeping badly, hoarse with relentless talking, unsteady on his feet, mentally confused, and occasionally violent. These alarming symptoms lost nothing in the retelling. In December Dr Francis *Willis, a mad-doctor, was brought in; his implements included a strait-jacket and a restraining chair—which the king referred to ruefully as his 'coronation chair'. The king's conversation was at times indecent, he declared a violent passion for Lady Pembroke, and talked against the queen.

The political implications of the king's illness were dramatic. If the incapacity became permanent the prince of

Wales must become regent. In that case he would certainly dismiss Pitt and install in office Fox and the remnants of the coalition. The opposition insisted that the regent should have full powers, including the granting of peerages. Pitt and his friends argued that, certainly at first, the regent's powers should be limited and defined. A number of government supporters, among them Thurlow, prepared to shuffle. The piquancy of the reversal of roles, Pitt arguing for parliamentary sanctions, Fox for the prince's prerogative, was not lost on observers. A further complication was that the Irish House of Commons rebelled against the lord lieutenant and addressed the prince to assume the government at once. The prospect of the component parts of the British Isles moving in different directions, as Scotland and England had briefly done in the 1700s, began to loom. But on 17 February, three days before the Regency Bill was due to take effect, it was announced that the king was convalescent. A thanksgiving service was held at St Paul's on 23 April and medals were struck commemorating the king's recovery.

The nature of the king's illness was much discussed. Of the severe mental disturbance, albeit intermittent, there can be no doubt, and the treatment of lunatics in that period was so brutal that the king's fears and resentments are easily understood. The contemporary explanation by the medical consultants was old fashioned and bizarre: George's condition was, in their opinion, caused by a 'humour' in the legs, which the king's own imprudence (omitting to change wet stockings) 'drove from thence into the bowels' (Buckingham, 2.6–7). Nineteenth-century historians, few of them sympathetic to the king, were content to accept his illness as lunacy, either an inherited defect or the result of external pressures. In the 1920s, under the influence of Freud, it became fashionable to regard the derangement as the product of severe sexual repression, and the king's attitude to Lady Pembroke and the queen was deemed peculiarly significant. In 1969 Ida Macalpine and Richard Hunter pointed out that many of the symptoms, particularly purple urine, suggested that the illness was porphyria, a rare but acknowledged hereditary illness, which often produces neurological damage and mental instability.

The consequences of the illness were considerable. It did little good for the opposition, some of whom, like Burke, had expressed their case extravagantly, appearing to gloat over the king's condition. The prospect of a return to power by Fox and his friends sobered a number of people. The rift between the Irish and British parliaments meant that the possibility of a union, mooted after the beginning of Grattan's parliament in 1782, moved to the forefront of people's minds, and especially that of Pitt. But most marked was a great rise in the reputation and standing of the king himself. The 'Farmer George' image and the 'Father of his People' description gained greater popularity in this period, and newspapers, circulating more widely than ever before, began to devote increasing space to stories and anecdotes about him. In part this was the natural result of pity, reinforced by the contrast between the homely virtues of the king and the self-indulgence of the prince. But the change preceded his illness. On their visit to Cheltenham the royal family had been gratified at the large and enthusiastic crowds which turned out to welcome them. George III had shaken off the burden of Hanover, which had dogged his grandfather and great-grandfather. He was the first king in living memory whose domestic life was beyond reproach. His stand against the Americans, which won him few friends among nineteenth-century liberal historians, was popular with most of his subjects, who disliked the ambivalent attitude of the opposition towards national defeats. One result of the loss of America, though short-lived, was to foster a mood of insularity and conservatism, which could easily identify with the king. He also gained great applause for the composure he showed on several occasions when his life was in danger—when stabbed by Margaret Nicholson in 1786, stoned in the state coach on his way to parliament in the dark days of 1795, or shot at by James Hadfield at Drury Lane Theatre in 1800.

Such a severe illness, and his advancing years, was bound to reduce the king's political activity. For some time afterwards he complained of tiredness, and on 23 February 1789 he wrote to Pitt that for the remainder of his days he would 'only keep that superintending eye which can be effected without labour or fatigue' (Stanhope, 2.appx, vii). But, as Pitt soon discovered, that eye remained vigilant, and within days the king was writing to remind him to see to the translation of the bishop of Gloucester to St Asaph. The number of court days was reduced and the royal family henceforth took regular holidays at Weymouth. There was less necessity for the king's intervention since on most issues he saw eye to eye with Pitt, and the ministry was securely established. At the general election of June 1790 the opposition lost ground: it did not divide on the address in November 1790, and in December, in the division on the Spanish convention, it was beaten by 123 votes to 247. Pitt's authority within his cabinet was unchallenged. In May 1792, when relations between him and Lord Chancellor Thurlow broke down, the prime minister wrote simply that the king must choose between them. Despite the 'affection' (ibid., 2.150) he felt for Thurlow, George had no hesitation in dismissing him.

French Revolution Meanwhile developments in France were taking place which shaped the rest of George III's reign. The most immediate effect was to weaken Fox and the opposition still further, as first Burke, then Loughborough, and finally Portland and Windham moved over to support the government. In March 1792 came an echo from the past when the king coolly acknowledged the news of Lord Bute's death. Embarrassed at his youthful infatuation, George ultimately wrote it out of his mind, confiding to George Rose in 1804 that at his accession Bute had insisted on taking office, much against the king's will. The events of the French Revolution, which many in Britain had watched at first with detached interest and some satisfaction, became menacing with the execution of

Louis XVI and Marie Antoinette in 1793 and the declaration of war by the French. The king denounced the executions as the work of savages and welcomed war against 'that unprincipled country whose aim at present is to destroy the foundations of every civilised state' (*Later Correspondence of George III*, 2.xiv). But though he followed the progress of the war with great attention and offered suggestions, the king's role was not central, nor did Pitt need the constant encouragement that North had sought twenty years earlier.

One problem which did not abate was that of George III's family. Indeed, almost the first communications George received after his recovery in 1789 were from princes Frederick and William warning him of the inadequacy of the financial provision made for them: 'I think it my duty not to incur the risk of deceiving Your Majesty', wrote the latter, 'by giving expectations that I can live within the present income' (*Later Correspondence of George III*, 1.417, no. 518). The conduct of the prince of Wales and of Prince Frederick during their father's illness had been very equivocal and relations afterwards were strained. A meeting with the king passed off without mishap, but political and public questions were studiously avoided. In 1791 Prince Frederick married the princess royal of Prussia. The princess royal of Britain was safely married in 1797 to the duke of Württemberg, though she was dismayed at seeing him, since he was even fatter than the prince of Wales, who was a mere 17 stone. The rest of the royal princes provided excellent copy for the more scurrilous newspapers. Lord Melbourne, explaining their behaviour to the young Queen Victoria, blamed it on the Royal Marriages Act, which 'sent them like so many wild beasts into society, making love everywhere they went, and then saying that they were very sorry they couldn't marry them' (*Later Correspondence of George III*, 2.xxxviii). Prince William settled down with Mrs Jordan, a popular actress, and began producing a large family of FitzClarences; his offer of naval service during the war was politely declined. Prince *Edward (eventually father of the future Queen Victoria), confessed in 1787 a substantial debt and like his brothers promised immediate reformation; it did not last and he was subjected to one of the king's, by now, routine letters of reproach. He then found a French lady, Mme de St Laurent, and set up home with her. Prince Augustus Frederick was of a more serious cast of mind and was said to be contemplating holy orders. But in December 1793 a gentleman giving his name as Mr Augustus Frederick and dressed 'like a common shopkeeper' was privately married at St George's, Hanover Square, to an eight-months pregnant Lady Augusta Murray. This impenetrable disguise sufficed for a whole month, until *The Times* revealed the marriage of 'a young gentleman of very high rank' to 'the daughter of a northern peer'. The marriage was declared void in July 1794 under the terms of the Royal Marriages Act. The behaviour of the prince of Wales was so hard to defend that it would have threatened Pitt's large parliamentary majority had not the opposition had its own reasons for palliating his conduct. By 1795 his debts had reached £630,000, and since friends could no longer

oblige and bankers were unwilling to make loans, the only escape was into matrimony, which would enable a fresh application to be made to parliament. The prince broke with Mrs Fitzherbert and suggested marriage with his cousin Princess Caroline of Brunswick, though enquiries reported that among her defects was an unfortunate lack of interest in personal cleanliness. Pitt's proposal that the prince's income should be more than doubled to £121,000, a further £77,000 granted for wedding and domestic expenses, and the establishment of a sinking fund to repay his debt within twenty-seven years, was badly received. There was a rebellion of several of the government's most trusted supporters, and Pitt was obliged to inform the king that it could not be carried. Meanwhile the opposition hinted that the king himself could be more generous. The amount set aside for the redemption of debt had to be increased. The marriage, which took place on 8 April 1795, was in all other respects an unmitigated disaster, though Princess Charlotte was conceived on what was said to be the first and last nuptial night, and born on 7 January 1796. Three days later the Prince made a will leaving all his property (largely debt) to Maria Fitzherbert, 'my wife, the wife of my heart and soul' (*Correspondence of George, Prince of Wales*, 3.133, no. 1067). In February the prince was forced to beg the king to prevent bailiffs moving into Carlton House, and in March he announced his intention of separating from the princess. To compound matters, Queen Charlotte wrote to the king on 15 April 1796 that she could no longer pay her tradesmen.

Ireland and the breach with Pitt Meanwhile war against revolutionary France raged. The main political problem concerned Ireland. Strategically it was a point of weakness since a French landing might expect considerable Irish support, but Ireland was potentially a great source of recruitment to the British armed forces if the population was loyal. In 1782 the volunteers had done more to promote Irish interests than to frighten the enemy and Pitt was not anxious for a repetition. An early concession in 1793 was an Irish Act allowing Catholics to vote, to hold certain restricted and defined public appointments, and to attend Trinity College, Dublin. Since legislative independence had been granted in 1782 it did not need British ratification, though Pitt's cabinet was in full support. There is no evidence that George III opposed the concession—indeed he gave a courteous welcome to a Catholic committee deputation and the Catholics in turn voted £2000 for a statue of the king in Dublin—but the measure was certain to raise expectations of full emancipation: the right to sit in parliament. On that question the king certainly had an opinion.

The issue touched on in 1793 exploded in 1795. Westmorland, the lord lieutenant, had been appalled at the British government's concessions and had carried them in the Irish parliament with great reluctance. He was recalled in 1795 and his successor, Lord Fitzwilliam, one of the Portland whigs, primed by Burke, undertook an abrupt reversal of policy, favouring Catholic emancipation and dismissing many of the office-holders, who appealed to Pitt for redress. The ensuing crisis nearly wrecked the newly formed coalition. Fitzwilliam's head-strong conduct raised undue expectations, Pitt was not prepared to abandon responsibility in so important an area, and when George III belatedly learned what was intended he was horrified. He protested his 'greatest astonishment' at the 'total change of the principles of government, which have been followed by every administration in that kingdom since the abdication of King James the Second' (Stanhope, 2.appx, xxiii). He pointed out that his family had been invited to the throne specifically to protect the protestant state, and warned that the subject was beyond the authority of the cabinet to determine without wider consultation. There was no confrontation, however, between the monarch and the cabinet because Fitzwilliam's colleagues also concluded that he had badly overplayed his hand. They resolved on Fitzwilliam's recall after only seven weeks in Dublin.

Irish affairs dominated much of the remainder of George III's active political life, against the background of the war against revolutionary and then Napoleonic France. After 1795 discontent in Ireland increased, demonstrating to the conservatives that the Irish were incorrigibly disloyal, and to the Liberals that the reforms had been inadequate. Pitt had for some time considered that a union of Ireland with Britain might be desirable; after the great rebellion of 1798, which had been belatedly assisted by French troops, the case seemed overwhelming. Catholic emancipation could then be granted for the Westminster parliament in the knowledge that Catholic MPs in a United Kingdom would remain a small minority. With the general principle of union the king was in agreement. It came into effect on 1 January 1801, with George proclaimed king of the United Kingdom of Great Britain and Ireland. The old claim to be king of France was at last abandoned. George had been asked whether he wished to be known as 'Emperor of the British Isles', but replied that he was satisfied with the title of king (*Later Correspondence of George III*, 3.435n., no. 2274).

But if he had been hostile to Catholic emancipation in Ireland in 1795, he was unshakeably opposed to it for Britain as a whole, regarding it as a breach of his coronation oath. In January 1799 he had warned Pitt that 'though a strong friend to the Union of the two kingdoms, I should become an enemy to the measure if I thought a change in the situation of the Roman Catholics would attend this measure' (*Later Correspondence of George III*, 3.186 n. 2, no. 1914). Pitt, harassed and unwell, neglected to inform George what the cabinet was contemplating, leaving others to draw it to his notice. It was a subject on which George felt most strongly. On 28 January 1801, at his levee, he approached Dundas 'in a loud voice and agitated manner', asked him what was going on, and declared that he would regard as his personal enemy any man who proposed Catholic emancipation to him (Ehrman, 3.503). Pitt called a cabinet at once, postponed the opening of parliament, and wrote to the king that his own opinion in favour of emancipation was 'unalterably fixed'. George replied that his coronation oath did not allow him to consent to a measure 'no less than the complete overthrow of

the whole fabric' of the constitution in church and state, but if Pitt agreed not to urge the proposal, the king would keep his opinions to himself (Stanhope, 3.appx, xxvi, xxix). He then approached Addington, speaker of the House of Commons and a friend of Pitt, to form a new administration. The whole crisis was over in a week. No one could argue that Pitt had not had fair warning or that it was not a matter so close to the prerogative and status of the monarchy that the king had a right to be consulted. The tactic of using the king's name against his ministers was a startling repetition of the events of December 1783 which had overthrown the Fox–North coalition and brought Pitt to power, yet Pitt and the king parted with great regret and expressions of mutual esteem.

The Catholic question It is not easy to know whether the next and ominous development was a cause or a consequence of the political upheaval. But on 13 February 1801, amid the crisis, the king was unwell, and by the 17th he was excited, talkative, and hoarse. On the 21st he told Thomas Willis, who had succeeded his father as a mad-doctor, 'I have prayed to God all night, that I might die, or that he would spare my reason' (Brooke, *King George the Third*, 370). This bout of illness lasted some four weeks, ending before plans for a regency could be put into effect, though it took longer for the king to extricate himself from his doctors. It left George thinner, exhausted, and less resilient, and his eyesight was also causing concern. Worst of all, under the severe strain his relations with the queen had deteriorated. She was terrified of a return of violence and perhaps upset by his obscene language in delirium. Her temper worsened, much of it directed at the princesses, and she locked her bedroom door against her husband. 'It is a melancholy circumstance', remarked Lord Hobart, 'to see a family that had lived so well together, for such a number of years, completely broken up' (*Journal and Correspondence of … Auckland*, 4.214).

Pitt made a formal pledge to the king that he would not again raise the question of Catholic emancipation, and at first gave strong support to his successor, Addington. The king agreed to peace negotiations being opened, though he had never thought that any understanding with republican France was likely, and he described the treaty of Amiens, signed in 1802, as an 'experimental peace'. The experiment failed, and the renewal of the war in May 1803 made the recall of Pitt only a matter of time. The country braced itself for a Napoleonic invasion, and the king wrote to Bishop Hurd in November 1803 in heroic terms: 'should his troops effect a landing, I shall certainly put myself at the head of mine … to repel them' (Jesse, 3.330). It was not very practical but entirely in character. But early in the new year there were signs of a recurrence of his illness, with continuous talking and hurry. Though the regime of the Willises gave way to that of Dr Samuel Simmons, the strait-jacket was still employed. The severe attack lasted only a week, but recovery was protracted and intermittent. George was at once confronted with another political crisis arising from the negotiations for Pitt's return. The king parted from Addington with great reluctance, wishing to reward 'the best friend he has in the world' (Ziegler, 222–3) with an earldom and pension. At an audience on 7 May 1804 Pitt found the king remarkably composed and in total command of the situation. Pitt repeated his promise not to raise the Catholic question. The king had already vetoed the inclusion of Charles Fox, though suggesting, perhaps sardonically, that he might be offered an ambassadorship. Grenville refused to serve without Fox, and Pitt's hope for 'a strong and comprehensive government, uniting the principal weight and talents of public men of all descriptions' to deal with the French menace did not materialize.

Pitt's second ministry survived until his death in January 1806. It was fraught with difficulties. The third coalition against France was destroyed by Napoleon's victories at Ulm and Austerlitz, though Nelson's triumph at Trafalgar in October 1805 removed the last threat of a French invasion. The king's position was very odd. He was no longer under restraint after February 1804 but was easily disturbed and in need of constant attention. On 16 May 1804 his new prime minister and Lord Chancellor Eldon wrote to beg him, on medical advice, 'to avoid too frequent or protracted audiences and conversations' (Stanhope, 4.appx, xv). In December 1804 he expressed his joy that Pitt and Addington were reconciled, and Addington joined the government in January 1805 as lord president of the council. But the disgrace and impeachment of Dundas, now Viscount Melville, long one of Pitt's closest friends, caused the prime minister great distress, and led to Addington's resigning once more. Grenville and Fox, in opposition, were short of numbers, but watchful and persistent. In May 1805 they moved to exploit the Catholic difficulty by proposing a committee on the subject. To the king's satisfaction they were defeated in the Lords by 178 votes to 49, and in the Commons by 336 votes to 124. The king's attitude towards Pitt remained friendly, but he was increasingly unpredictable, particularly over court appointments, and Pitt's awareness that a regency would probably mean his own dismissal, curbed his powers of remonstrance. In January 1805 there was a very sharp quarrel, with raised voices, over the vacant archbishopric of Canterbury. The king carried his candidate, Manners-Sutton, against Pitt's former tutor Tomline, even though Pitt hinted at resignation and warned the king how much it must weaken his position. But the king's precarious state of health meant that the situation was quite abnormal and, paradoxically, gave him a temporary advantage. Moreover, in the light of so many discussions on the relationship of church and state, arising from the Catholic issue, the king was certain to be sensitive on ecclesiastical matters, and regarded the appointment as well within the remit of his royal authority.

Pitt's death on 23 January 1806 opened the way for the 'ministry of all the talents' which he had failed to construct in 1804. The king had little choice of prime minister. The cabinet met immediately and decided that it could not form the basis for a new administration and that resort to the opposition must be had. Addington had clearly demonstrated that he was not the man to lead a great national struggle for survival, though the king was reported to have approached him and also to have sounded out Lord Hawkesbury. George sent for Lord Grenville, knowing that this would mean accepting Fox as a minister, though he had once declared that he would rather risk civil war. Addington was brought back as lord privy seal while the rest of the Pittites moved into opposition. At the inescapable audience with Fox, who took the ministry for foreign affairs, the king was composed and conciliatory: 'Mr Fox, I little thought you and I should ever meet again in this place. But I have no desire to look back upon old grievances, and you may rest assured I shall never remind you of them' (Jesse, 3.474). He found Fox's manner perfectly acceptable though, in the event, he did not have to accept it for long: by June 1806 Fox was gravely ill and he died in September. His hopes of peace with Napoleon had gone, but his other great objective—abolition of the slave trade, about which the king was unenthusiastic—was in good shape. He was replaced by Lord Howick, the future prime minister Earl Grey.

The issue of Catholic emancipation was avoided at the foundation of the 'ministry of all the talents', but the Irish Catholics had no reason to be equally circumspect, and in January 1807, much to the irritation of Grenville and his colleagues, they prepared to submit a petition. This threatened both the unity of the cabinet, where Sidmouth was strongly opposed to concessions, and its relations with the monarch. The duke of Bedford, lord lieutenant of Ireland, suggested that some small concessions might persuade the Catholic committee to hold its fire. Grenville's original intention was merely to extend the 1793 Irish Act to Britain, thus taking account of the union, and allowing British Catholics to hold commissions up to staff rank. It would have the additional advantage of encouraging recruitment at a time of manpower shortage. The cabinet was well aware that it would not be easy to persuade the king to accept even this modest concession, but after protest he did so, Grenville writing to Dublin Castle that royal approval had been obtained with difficulty, but 'with proofs of temper and good will … Beyond this, I am perfectly satisfied he will not go' (Fortescue MSS, 9.37). But Bedford, Elliot, and Buckingham warned him that so slight a concession would do nothing to buy off the Irish Catholics. Indeed, there was no reason why it should, since it benefited only British Catholics and protestant dissenters. The government therefore changed the terms, agreeing that the concession must apply to all ranks, including staff appointments—which the 1793 act had not. The day before the revised measure was due to be presented to parliament by Howick, the king complained that the concessions were far greater than he had been led to believe and threatened to use his veto if the bill passed. Grenville agreed to withdraw the measure on the condition that his cabinet reserved the right to express their opinions on the Catholic question. George III refused to concede this and looked for an alternative administration. Portland then formed his second ministry out of the remnants of the Pitt survivors, with Spencer Perceval as leader in the Commons.

Recriminations and accusations of bad faith abounded,

and the episode went down in whig legend as a stab in the back by the crown. The crisis blew up quickly out of Irish affairs, the king and ministers had many other matters to consider, and the legislation was rushed. Howick admitted rather lamely that he had 'not sufficiently attended to the distinction between it and the Irish Act' (*Hansard 1*, 9, 1807, 267–8). But the fact that the legislation had started life as a mere amendment to the Mutiny Bill and was then brought forward as a bill in its own right indicates a significant shift in the ministers' position. They had already been warned, in unmistakable terms, that the original concession was as far as the king would go, and they decided to attempt to slide the change past George III. The most careful and scholarly study of the episode concluded that the whigs were engaged in 'a sort of juggle' (Roberts, 32), which the king saw through. Two later studies, the biographies of Lord Grey by John Derry and E. A. Smith, concurred—the ministers attempted to 'smuggle' (Roberts, 22) the extended bill past the king. Fortunately for the whigs their dismissal enabled them to present themselves as deeply injured men, martyred in the cause of toleration and progress.

Darkness With the advent of Portland's government, George III's political problems were almost at an end, though the outcome of the war remained in the balance and the Spanish campaign caused great anxiety in 1808 and 1809. Portland's conservative anti-Catholic ministry was close to the king's own views and one of its first moves was to obtain a dissolution (the second within eight months) and win a handsome victory at the general election. Portland was in bad health when he took office—'I have often been with him when I thought he would have died in his chair', wrote Malmesbury—but he survived until the autumn of 1809 (*Diaries and Correspondence*, 4.413). His successor, Spencer Perceval, steady, experienced, and a staunch Anglican, was entirely acceptable to George, and he saw out the king's effective reign.

George's family difficulties did not diminish. The continuing rift between the prince and princess of Wales caused acute embarrassment, and the rumours that the princess had had an illegitimate son led to the establishment of the 'delicate investigation' of 1806. Though the report declared that there was 'no foundation whatever' for the allegation, it added that the princess's conduct had been such as to encourage 'very unfavourable interpretations' (*Correspondence of George, Prince of Wales*, 5.403–4, no. 2196). The king was less critical of the princess than some of his family, but recriminations rumbled on, with Caroline asking for accommodation in Carlton House and for assistance with her mounting debts. In 1809 Colonel Wardle's accusation in the House of Commons that the duke of York, the king's favourite son and commander-in-chief, was guilty of corruption in selling commissions through his mistress, Mary Anne Clarke, forced the duke's resignation in March. At the same time there was growing concern over the health of the king's youngest and favourite daughter, Princess Amelia, who spent two months at Weymouth in the autumn of 1809 in search of recovery. The arrangements for the king's jubilee—the entrance to

his fiftieth year on the throne, on 25 October 1809—though the occasion for widespread popular celebrations, were overshadowed for the royal family by these personal misfortunes. On 31 May 1810, another son, the duke of Cumberland, was found covered in blood, with his valet, Sellis, dead in a nearby room. The jury found that Sellis had attacked the duke and then committed suicide, but insinuations circulated that the duke himself had been the aggressor. By the summer of 1810 it was apparent that Princess Amelia was dying.

The last public appearance of the king was at a reception at Windsor on 25 October 1810, the anniversary of his succession. He appeared flustered and excited. Within days his former symptoms had returned and recourse was had to the strait-jacket. Princess Amelia died on 2 November 1810 and a regency was declared on 7 February 1811.

Many people this time expected a fairly speedy recovery, attributing the king's illness to concern for his daughter. But though at first there were lucid intervals his condition worsened, and the last ten years of his life were spent in a twilight world. His eyesight deteriorated until he was completely blind and he was increasingly afflicted by deafness. Deprived for the most part of the stimulus of visitors, conversation, and outings, he took refuge in the past, sometimes real, often invented, talking to Lord North, long dead, and inspecting imaginary parades. 'In short' wrote Dr Heberden, 'he appears to be living in another world and has lost almost all interest in the concerns of this' (Macalpine and Hunter, 160–61). Towards the end he was a detached observer of his own misfortunes. One of his remaining pleasures was to play the harpsichord which had once belonged to Handel, hammering at the keyboard in an effort to hear; to his attendant he confided that it was a favourite piece of the late king, when he was alive. He died at Windsor on 29 January 1820, and was buried in St George's Chapel, Windsor, on the evening of 15 February.

George III had an important influence on national cultural life. On ascending the throne he determined to add to the library given by his royal predecessors to the British Museum. In the course of his reign he assembled 'one of the finest libraries ever created by one man' (Miller, 125). He was advised in this process by his librarian, Sir Frederick Barnard, and by Samuel Johnson, among others; by the time of his death it consisted of 65,250 volumes, 19,000 tracts and pamphlets, and the first large British collection of maps and charts. The king was also interested in typography and the design of books, establishing a royal bindery at Buckingham House. The royal collection was organized in three or more series, stored chiefly at Windsor and Buckingham House. After George III's death his son George IV offered the library to the nation, and after protracted and complex negotiations it entered the British Museum, becoming known as the King's Library and acting as a valuable stimulus to the extension of the museum in the form of 'a proper building for the reception of the Royal Library' (Miller, 128). For a century and a half the King's Library was the oldest and most elegant part of the British Museum. It now forms the visual centre of the British Library at St Pancras.

The king was also an important art collector, as well as being a competent architectural draughtsman. His accession was 'a watershed in the history of the royal collection' (Millar, xi). In 1762 he bought the large collection of Joseph Smith, British consul in Venice, to put into Buckingham House, which he had just acquired. He commissioned portraits and other works of art from a number of contemporary artists, including a series of portraits of the royal family from Gainsborough, and he played an important part in the establishment of the Royal Academy in 1768, providing it with accommodation and with some initial funding, though he became notorious for his interference in appointments and art patronage. George III's state portrait was by Allan Ramsay (1761), with the king full length, in his coronation robes, and an accompanying portrait of the queen in hers. Ramsay also provided the king's profile for the new coinage. In 1781 Gainsborough painted a further and much admired full-length pair of the king and queen, the king's being regarded by Horace Walpole as 'very like, but stiff and raw' (Millar, xx). George III commissioned portraits of the queen and various members of his family from Sir Thomas Lawrence, but did not commission one of himself.

Historical judgements It is not immediately apparent why George III became one of the most controversial and criticized monarchs in British history. Liberals disliked his hostility to parliamentary reform and Catholic emancipation; Americans condemned him as an oppressor of their country. There is little in this. Monarchs are not often found in the vanguard of reform and those who are, like Joseph II of Austria, were not conspicuously successful. The Americans' quarrel was with parliament, though they skilfully dramatized and personalized it by blaming the king. One reason for such widespread condemnation is that many of the early printed sources, greatly used by nineteenth-century historians, were hostile to George III. Much of the historical writing of the twentieth century was devoted to scraping away accumulated layers of myth and distortion. Burke's *Thoughts on the Cause of the Present Discontents* (1770) popularized the idea that George governed through a double cabinet—a set of secret advisers—though there is scant evidence to support it and the theory was little more than an attempt to excuse the Rockinghams' remarkable lack of success. Not only would such a system have been extremely difficult to operate in a small political circle, in which all major politicians were watched, but it would have sat oddly with the constant changes in the official and avowed personnel. Horace Walpole, whose *Memoirs of the Reign of King George the Third* were first published in 1845, wove a gothick romance around an attempt by the king, encouraged by his scheming mother and her paramour Lord Bute, to achieve prerogative and absolute power. Lord John Russell, an apostolic whig, whose edition of the correspondence of the duke of Bedford came out in 1846, insisted that 'the project of restoring to the crown that absolute direction and control which Charles I and James II had been forced to relinquish

... was entertained and attempted by George III' (*Correspondence of … Bedford*, 3.xxix). For this there is no evidence at all. One of George's earliest schoolroom essays praised the revolution of 1688 as the foundation of British religion and liberty, and for saving the country from arbitrary power. If George III had any desire to increase the power of the crown, it was within the context of the revolution settlement, not against it. Despite the fact that J. W. Croker, in his brilliant review of Walpole's *Memoirs*, warned against 'pertinacious attempts to poison history', the hostile interpretation of George continued to hold the field (J. W. Croker, 'Review of *Memoirs of the Reign of King George III* by Horace Walpole', *Quarterly Review*, 77, 1845–6, 274). Sir George Otto Trevelyan declared in 1880 that the king 'invariably declared himself upon the wrong side in a controversy' (Trevelyan, 122), and W. E. H. Lecky in 1882 wrote of George that 'it may be said without exaggeration that he inflicted more profound and enduring injuries upon his country than any other modern English king' (Lecky, 3.14). As late as 1937 this view was expressed, in its crudest form, in a review of Vulliamy's *Royal George*, which suggested that the king made 'the last attempt to foist a dictatorship on Britain' (Barnes, vii).

Magisterial judgements went out of fashion in the mainstream of twentieth-century historiography. In his Ford lectures for 1934 L. B. Namier began the process of reassessment, arguing that in 1760 the king's right to choose his own ministers was not a provocation but a commonplace. Sedgwick, in his edition of George III's letters to Lord Bute of 1939, denied G. M. Trevelyan's contention that there was a break in 'the smooth development of our constitutional history in 1760', and attributed any enhanced influence of the crown after 1760 to the fact that for twenty years there was no rival reversionary interest (Sedgwick, introduction, *Letters … to Lord Bute*, xvi). Pares, in the Ford lectures for 1951, took an intermediate position: there was no fundamental difference in the situations of George II and George III, but the latter's more conscientious personality meant 'a more active royalty' (Pares, 61–2). Namier had a chance to restate his own position in 1953 with his Academy of Arts lecture, 'King George III: a study of personality', concluding that 'in reality the constitutional practice of George III differed little from that of George I and George II', and calling him a 'much maligned ruler' (Namier, *Personalities and Powers*, 43, 58). J. B. Owen, attacking the problem from the other end in 'George II reconsidered', denied that George II was a weak or ineffective ruler, and maintained that the theory of the pivotal importance of 1760 was 'an accident of historiography' (Whiteman, 118).

Yet though to explode myths is an important part of the historian's task, it is not the only one, and something must be put in their place. In his critique of Namier, Herbert Butterfield remarked that he and his associates came close to denying George III any views at all. Several of his ambitions were clear, and not necessarily contentious. His desire to discourage vice and to set an example of duty and respectability was welcomed by many of his subjects, particularly in the middle class of society. His aspiration to eradicate party was highly predictable. It was the ambition of most monarchs, attracted by the concept of national unity, as well as the increased flexibility which a non-party approach offered; many of George's contemporaries were still profoundly ambivalent towards party, regarding it as self-seeking and factious. His wish to eliminate corruption may have been pious and ill-defined—a mere parrot phrase of the patriot opposition of the 1730s—but such ideas can strike root, and the elimination of pensions and sinecures was to become a very popular programme in the later eighteenth century. In this instance, liberal historians failed to identify George as 'on the right side'.

But an important explanation of George's difficulties is that the revolution settlement, which he admired so greatly, while establishing the broad framework for limited monarchy, left many everyday questions unresolved. There was ambiguity at the heart of the eighteenth-century system, even if commentators dignified it as balance. The practical working of the constitution was being decided in the politics of the period, not in theoretical discussions or in legislation, but in the daily struggles for power. In a reign of fifty active years, in so fluid a situation, almost all of the undecided issues of the revolution settlement came into discussion, and produced sharp confrontations.

The precise powers of the crown were far from clear. The formal limitations which the revolution settlement, reinforced by the Act of Settlement, imposed on monarchs were important, but few. They could not be Catholics nor marry a Catholic. They could not use the suspending power, or the dispensing power as it had been used of late. They could not dismiss judges, nor maintain an army in peacetime without parliamentary approval. To that extent the door had been bolted against popery and autocracy. What they positively could do was not spelled out. The veto was not employed after Anne's reign, but nobody could say whether it had become obsolete, and its use was considered in 1783 and again in 1807. It was agreed that the monarch must choose ministers, but the effective use of this prerogative depended upon alternative men being available. This was not the case in March 1783 or January 1806, but was in January 1770 and December 1783. Peers had an undisputed right to private audience and to offer advice, but this sat awkwardly with the theory of responsible ministers. The acceptance of the propriety of opposition—perhaps the key element in the idea of parliamentary government—was a plant of slow growth in the eighteenth century, tainted by treason as long as an active Jacobite cause survived, but remaining something that many men were uneasy with for decades after Culloden. By position and temperament George III found opposition peculiarly hard to come to terms with: 'I have no wish but for the prosperity of my dominions', he wrote angrily in November 1782, 'therefore must look on all who will not heartily assist me as bad men as well as ungrateful subjects' (*Correspondence*, ed. Fortescue, 6.151, no. 3973). The lord chancellor retained a special position as the

king's man in the cabinet and the keeper of the royal conscience, yet when he clashed with the first minister, as Thurlow did with Pitt in 1792, he was forced out. The office of first minister was developing, from an unpleasant term of abuse directed at Sir Robert Walpole, through characteristic evasion by North, to an avowed and formal exposition of its necessity by William Pitt in 1803. It was a development which militated strongly against the powers remaining to the monarch. Parliamentary government evolved as a means of resolving conflict peacefully, and to that extent disagreement was built into the system, but the nineteenth-century method of finally deciding such matters by means of a general election had not yet come about. The king chose and dismissed ministers, and it was therefore inescapable that what he decided could be greatly resented. The constitution which George III admired so much avoided civil war and *coups d'état*, but it functioned with creaks and groans.

It is scarcely surprising that George III found, at times, so delicate and shifting a position difficult to understand and to operate. It called for much compromise, conciliation, and tact. Patronage and honours questions—another grey area between the monarch and his ministers—provided a never-ending source of discontent and irritation, to say nothing of more profound issues of war and peace. In the middle of the American crisis George declared that he would take refuge in his closet and see no one, not because of military disasters, but because he could not face quarrels about peerage promotions.

Yet it would be both unprofitable and misleading to attempt to trace the many difficulties to which these ambiguities gave rise in a long reign, since it would mean an undue concentration on the malfunctioning of the constitution. But four episodes in which the king's conduct was much criticized may briefly be mentioned. The elevation of Lord Bute in 1760 was clearly an error of judgement. But it was neither unconstitutional nor unusual. Monarchs usually brought their friends forward at the outset of their reigns. Anne had elevated the Marlboroughs on her 'sunshine day'; George I had dismissed the tories and called in the whigs; George II intended to promote his favourite Sir Spencer Compton, and it had been the intention of Frederick, prince of Wales, to place power in the hands of Lord Egmont. Indeed, George III insisted upon Bute's taking office to counter any complaint that he was a minister behind the curtain. It should be remembered that Bute was supported in parliament by large majorities and, despite inexperience, his performance in the House of Lords was far from foolish—certainly compared with that of Lord Rockingham. The other three episodes, in 1783, 1801, and 1807, were superficially similar in character, involving accusations that the king had deliberately deceived his ministers. But in practice they were very different. The king's intervention against the Fox–North coalition in December 1783 does not seem to have been preceded by any warning to Portland that he disapproved of the India Bill, nor was the use of the king's name easy to reconcile, as Fitzwilliam and North argued, with responsible government. The extraordinary nature of the king's action is confirmed by the fact that nobody tried to defend it: Pitt, who had insisted on it as a *sine qua non* before taking office, pretended that the rumours were 'the lie of the day' (Cobbett, *Parl. hist.*, 24, 1783, 202). George's reply would have been that so unnatural a coalition, depriving him of any choice of ministers, was tantamount to a breach or breakdown of the constitution, and justified him in using the means he did to free himself; they were not his ministers but men who had forced themselves on him. His belief was endorsed by national opinion at the election of 1784. Pitt's resignation in 1801 was quite different. The king had no wish to part with his minister and did so with sincere expressions of regret and esteem. His outburst to Dundas at the levee seems to have been unpremeditated, the result of his conscientious scruples over his coronation oath. It would be hard to argue that the monarch of a dynasty brought in specifically and only because it was protestant should not have the right to object to concessions to the Catholics. Nor can one deny that there was a plausible case for George's belief that concessions to the Catholic Irish, far from bringing reconciliation and loyalty, would merely promote fresh demands and pave the way for independence. In the third example, of 1807, the evidence suggests strongly that the proposed legislation had not been adequately explained to the king, that he had given a very deliberate warning of his disapproval, but that he used the occasion to part with a ministry which he had accepted with reluctance and now mistrusted.

One charge repeatedly made against George III—and strangely at odds with his popular image as a plain, honest gentleman—was that of duplicity. It was a favourite accusation of Wilkes and Junius, and erected by Horace Walpole into a 'habit of dissimulation' (Walpole, *Memoirs*, 1.16). But none of them (assuming that Sir Philip Francis *was* Junius) knew the king well enough to make his opinion of much value, and these remarks may be dismissed as general political abuse. Chatham, after his comeback in 1770, complained that he had been undermined by secret influence, and Shelburne, briefly a royal favourite in 1782, believed afterwards that he had been betrayed by the king, of whom he spoke bitterly as a man who 'obtained your confidence, procured from you your opinion of different public characters, and then availed himself of this knowledge to sow dissension' (J. Nicholls, *Recollections and Reflections, Personal and Political, as Connected with Public Affairs, during the Reign of George III*, 1820, 1822, 1.389). There was little need for the king to sow dissension in the Chatham or Shelburne ministries—it grew of its own accord. But although George had done his best to sustain and encourage each of them, it suited them to suspect treachery and cry 'foul'. The reality is rather the reverse. Far from being a master of dissimulation the king, a man of strong feelings and with an excitable nature, found it hard to dissemble, and might have had an easier life had he cared less deeply about his duty and been more willing to give way with good grace. Namier, ruminating on a lifetime devoted to George's early reign, concluded: 'what I have never been able to find is the man arrogating power to

himself, the ambitious schemer out to dominate, the intriguer dealing in an underhand fashion with his Ministers' (Namier, *Personalities and Powers*, 57). But another explanation of the charge was the ambiguity of George's position as both head of society and active politician. Most monarchs develop defences against importunity: Charles II is said to have walked very fast, while George II's temper was enough to keep most petitioners at bay. George III found the stylized routine of court life rather difficult, and his famously repeated interjections—'What? What?'—were attempts to fill awkward gaps and silences. He replaced his initial shyness by bland and vague assurances, which others sometimes mistook, or pretended to mistake, for promises. His conservative attitude and liking for a routine life made him prefer ministers whom he knew and was comfortable with, and if he subsequently turned against them, it was not that he was ruthless and unfeeling, but that often the ministers, like Chatham, North, Shelburne, and Pitt, had drifted into opposition. George III, like many men in public life, found it hard to distinguish political from personal friendship and, as a result, often felt betrayed. Even Bute had, in the end, disappointed him.

The reign of George III saw a long and unspectacular decline in the power of the monarchy. This was to some extent masked from contemporaries by the difficulty they experienced in distinguishing between the crown and the government in a period in which the two were so closely related. Dunning's motion of 1780—'that the influence of the crown has increased, is increasing, and ought to be diminished'—was a political slogan not an impartial analysis, and a commentary on the government rather than on the monarchy's share in it. The causes of the crown's decline were many and insidious, but included the great growth in public opinion (manifested in newspapers and petitions), the consolidation of party loyalties which ultimately diminished the crown's choice of ministers, the financial debility of the monarchy, the decline in crown patronage, the rise in the power of the first minister, and the growing complexity of public business—the last of which also sounded the knell for the amateur gentleman in politics. George III fought a steady and not unsuccessful rearguard action for the rights of the monarchy, conscious of his duty, determined to remain briefed and informed, but increasingly handicapped by age and ill health. As he must have suspected, his son had neither the stamina nor the character to preserve the position his father handed on to him in 1810. In the course of George III's reign the monarch had been increasingly forced on to the defensive; he could object, frustrate, delay, and obstruct, but he no longer had much power of initiative. He could keep Charles James Fox out, but he could not keep Bute, Grafton, North, and Addington in. His two most controversial actions were, significantly, negative ones—against the India Bill and against Catholic emancipation. In each case he was supported by the voters, at the general elections of 1784 and 1807. But in the event of hostile public opinion the king would have been dangerously exposed.

In some respects George's reign was a dress rehearsal for the even longer reign of his granddaughter, Queen Victoria. Probably unwittingly, George had shown the way out of the ambiguities of the monarch's role, moving to a position less prominent politically, and substituting a concept of the monarchy as the symbol of the nation, a pattern of duty and respectability—'the head of our *morality*' in Walter Bagehot's phrase—which Victoria, Albert, and their descendants were to develop (*Collected Works*, 5.235). George was an unlucky man whom life treated badly and whose talents did not quite fit the situation in which he found himself. But he cannot be faulted for want of effort. 'I do not pretend to any superior abilities', he wrote, 'but will give place to no one in meaning to preserve the freedom, happiness and glory of my dominions and all their inhabitants, and to fulfill the duty to my God and my neighbour in the most extended sense' (J. Brooke, frontispiece, *King George the Third*, new edn, 1985).

JOHN CANNON

Sources *The correspondence of King George the Third from 1760 to December 1783*, ed. J. Fortescue, 6 vols. (1927–8) • *Letters from George III to Lord Bute, 1756–1766*, ed. R. Sedgwick (1939) • *The later correspondence of George III*, ed. A. Aspinall, 5 vols. (1962–70) • J. Brooke, *King George III* (1972) • S. Ayling, *George III* (1972) • H. Butterfield, *George III and the historians* (1957) • R. Pares, *George III and the politicians* (1955) • H. Walpole, *Memoirs of the reign of King George the Third*, ed. D. Le Marchant, 4 vols. (1845) • *The memoirs and speeches of James, 2nd Earl Waldegrave, 1742–1763*, ed. J. C. D. Clark (1988) • Walpole, *Corr.* • J. H. Jesse, *Memoirs of the life and reign of King George the Third*, 2nd edn, 3 vols. (1867) • L. B. Namier, *Personalities and powers* (1955) • *The diary of the late George Bubb Dodington*, ed. W. P. Wyndham (1809) • *The diaries of a duchess: extracts from the diaries of the first duchess of Northumberland (1716–1776)*, ed. J. Greig (1926) • *Additional Grenville papers, 1763–1765*, ed. J. R. G. Tomlinson (1962) • *The Grenville papers: being the correspondence of Richard Grenville … and … George Grenville*, ed. W. J. Smith, 4 vols. (1852–3) • *Correspondence of John, fourth duke of Bedford*, ed. J. Russell, 3 vols. (1842–6) • *Memorials and correspondence of Charles James Fox*, ed. J. Russell, 4 vols. (1853–7) • Earl Stanhope [P. H. Stanhope], *Life of the Right Honourable William Pitt*, 4 vols. (1861–2) • Duke of Buckingham and Chandos [R. Grenville], *Memoirs of the court and cabinets of George the Third*, 4 vols. (1853–5) • H. R. Vassall, Lord Holland, *Memoirs of the whig party during my time*, ed. H. E. Vassall, Lord Holland, 2 vols. (1852–4) • *The Jenkinson papers, 1760–1766*, ed. N. S. Jucker (1949) • *Diary and letters of Madame D'Arblay*, ed. [C. Barrett], 7 vols. (1842–6) • *The correspondence of George, prince of Wales, 1770–1812*, ed. A. Aspinall, 8 vols. (1963–71) • D. G. Barnes, *George III and William Pitt, 1783–1806: a new interpretation based upon a study of their unpublished correspondence* (1939) • *The diaries and correspondence of the Right Hon. George Rose*, ed. L. V. V. Harcourt, 2 vols. (1860) • *The journal and correspondence of William, Lord Auckland*, ed. [G. Hogge], 4 vols. (1861–2) • *Diaries and correspondence of James Harris, first earl of Malmesbury*, ed. third earl of Malmesbury [J. H. Harris], 4 vols. (1844) • I. R. Christie, *Myth and reality in late-eighteenth-century British politics, and other papers* (1970) • J. W. Derry, *The regency crisis and the whigs, 1788–9* (1963) • P. Langford, *The first Rockingham administration, 1765–1766* (1973) • J. Cannon, *The Fox–North coalition: crisis of the constitution, 1782–4* (1969) • P. Ziegler, *Addington: a life of Henry Addington, first Viscount Sidmouth* (1965) • N. Gash, *Lord Liverpool* (1984) • I. Macalpine and R. Hunter, *George III and the mad-business* (1969) • M. Roberts, *The whig party, 1807–12* (1965) • *Autobiography and political correspondence of Augustus Henry, third duke of Grafton*, ed. W. R. Anson (1898) • J. W. Derry, *Charles, Earl Grey* (1992) • E. A. Smith, *Lord Grey, 1764–1845* (1990) • G. O. Trevelyan, *The early years of Charles James Fox* (1881) • L. Colley, 'The apotheosis of George III: loyalty, royalty, and the British nation, 1760–1820', *Past and Present*, 102 (1984), 94–129 • *The collected works of Walter Bagehot*, ed. N. St

John-Stevas, 5 (1974) • W. E. H. Lecky, *A history of England in the eighteenth century*, 8 vols. (1879–90) • L. B. Namier, *Crossroads of power* (1962) • *A narrative of changes in the ministry, 1765–1767*, ed. M. Bateson, CS, new ser., 59 (1898) • E. N. Williams, ed., *The eighteenth-century constitution, 1688–1815* (1960) • P. Mackesy, *The war for America, 1775–1783* (1964) • K. W. Schweizer, ed., *Lord Bute: essays in re-interpretation* (1988) • J. Brooke, *The Chatham administration, 1766–1768* (1956) • P. D. G. Thomas, *Lord North* (1976) • A. Whiteman, ed., *Statesmen, scholars and merchants: essays in eighteenth century history presented to Dame Lucy Sutherland* (1973) • J. Ehrman, *The younger Pitt*, 1: *The years of acclaim* (1969) • J. Ehrman, *The younger Pitt*, 2: *The reluctant transition* (1983) • J. Ehrman, *The younger Pitt*, 3: *The consuming struggle* (1996) • *The manuscripts of the marquess of Abergavenny, Lord Braye, G. F. Luttrell*, HMC, 15 (1887) • *Eighth report*, 2, HMC, 7 (1910) • *The manuscripts of the earl of Lonsdale*, HMC, 33 (1893) • *The manuscripts of J. B. Fortescue*, 10 vols., HMC, 30 (1892–1927) • HoP, *Commons, 1754–90* • HoP, *Commons, 1790–1820* • Cobbett, *Parl. hist.*, vol. 16, 1770; vol. 24, 1783 • *The works of John Adams, second president of the United States*, ed. C. F. Adams, 10 vols. (1850–56) • C. E. Vulliamy, *Royal George: a study of King George III* (1937) • C. Hibbert, *George III: a personal history* (1998) • P. D. G. Thomas, 'George III and the American Revolution', *History*, new ser., 70 (1985), 16–31 • P. D. G. Thomas, 'Thoughts on the British constitution by George III in 1760', *Historical Research*, 60 (1987), 361–3 • I. R. Christie, 'George III and the historians: thirty years on', *History*, new ser., 71 (1986), 205–21 • H. Butterfield, 'George III and the constitution', *History*, new ser., 43 (1958), 14–33 • J. H. Plumb, 'New light on the tyrant George III', *The American experience: the collected essays of J. H. Plumb* (1989), 50–60 • *GM*, 1st ser., 8 (1738), 323 • *GM*, 1st ser., 90/1 (1820), 172–6 • C. Lloyd, *The quest for Albion: monarchy and the patronage of British painting* (1998) • M. Levey, *The later Italian pictures in the collection of her majesty the queen* (1964) • O. Millar, *The later Georgian pictures in the collection of her majesty the queen*, 2 vols. (1969) • *A king's purchase: King George III and the collection of Consul Smith* (1994) • E. Miller, *That noble cabinet: a history of the British Museum* (1974) • Burke, *Peerage*

Archives BL, letters, Add. MS 50825 • Royal Arch., corresp. and papers • Royal Arch., household accounts | BL, letters to Lord Barrington, Dep 9389 • BL, corresp. with Lord Chichester, Add. MS 33115 • BL, letters to Henry Seymour Conway, Egerton MS 982 • BL, letters to Henry Dundas, Add. MSS 40100–40102 • BL, letters to Charles James Fox, Add. MS 51457 • BL, corresp. with Lord Grenville, Add. MSS 58855–58864 • BL, letters from George Grenville; addresses and petitions, draft speeches, Add. MS 57833 • BL, corresp. with Richard Grenville, Add. MSS 70956–70983, 70992–70997 • BL, letters to Lord Holland, Add. MS 51375 • BL, corresp. with earls of Liverpool, loan 72 • BL, letters to Lord Mountstuart • BL, corresp. with Lord North, Add. MS 61860 • BL, corresp. with John Robinson, Add. MSS 37833–37835 • BL, letters to the second Earl Spencer • BL, corresp. with Charles Philip Yorke, Add. MSS 35644, 45035 • Bucks. RLSS, corresp. with Richard Grenville • Bucks. RLSS, letters to Lord Hobart • CKS, letters to Jeffry Amherst; corresp. with Lord Camden • CUL, corresp. with Spencer Perceval • Devon RO, corresp. with Lord Sidmouth • Hunt. L., letters to Grenville family, letters to Lord Sydney • NA Scot., corresp. with Lord Melville • NMM, corresp. with Lord Barham; letters to Lord Sandwich • NRA, priv. coll., letters to Lord Eldon • priv. coll., corresp. with Spencer Perceval, etc. • priv. coll., letters to Lord Shelburne • PRO, letters to Lord Chatham, PRO30/70, 30/80 • PRO, letters to William Pitt, PRO30/8 • PRO NIre., corresp. with Lord Castlereagh • Sandon Hall, Staffordshire, Harrowby Manuscript Trust, corresp. with Lord Harrowby • Sheff. Arch., corresp. with Lord Rockingham • Suffolk RO, Bury St Edmunds, letters to duke of Grafton • U. Durham L., archives and special collections, corresp. with Lord Grey • U. Hull, Brynmor Jones L., letters to Sir Charles Hotham-Thompson • U. Nott. L., corresp. with duke of Portland • Wilts. & Swindon RO, corresp. with Lord Pembroke

Likenesses J. B. van Loo, group portrait, oils, 1739? (*Augusta, princess of Wales, with members of her family and household*), Royal Collection • B. Du Pan, group portrait, oils, 1746 (*The children of Frederick,* *prince of Wales*), Royal Collection • G. Knapton, group portrait, *c.*1751 (family of the Princess Dowager), Hampton Court • R. Wilson, double portrait, oils, *c.*1751 (with Edward, duke of York), NPG • J. E. Liotard, miniature, *c.*1753; Christies, 21 Oct 1997 • J. E. Liotard, pastel drawing, *c.*1753, Royal Collection • J. Reynolds, oils, 1759, Royal Collection • J. Reynolds, oils, 1759, Royal Collection • D. Morier, portrait, *c.*1760 (scene with Ligonier), Royal Collection • D. Morier, four oil paintings, *c.*1760–1765, Royal Collection • J. Reynolds, group portrait, oils, 1761, Royal Collection • J. Reynolds, portrait, 1761, NPG • A. Ramsay, oils, 1761-2, Royal Collection [*see illus.*] • A. Ramsay, portrait, *c.*1762, NPG • A. Carlini, plaster statue, 1769, RA • N. Dance, oils, *c.*1769, Drapers' Company, London • N. Dance, portrait, *c.*1770, Uppark, Sussex • J. Zoffany, group portrait, oils, 1770 (with family), Windsor • J. Zoffany, group portrait, oils, 1770 (*George III, Queen Charlotte and their six eldest children*), Royal Collection • J. Zoffany, oils, 1771, Royal Collection • J. Zoffany, oils, 1771, NPG • M. F. Quadal, group portrait, oils, 1772 (*George III at a review*), Royal Collection • A. Carlini, marble bust, 1773, RA • J. Bacon sen., marble bust, 1775, Royal Collection • P. Jakob or P. J. de Loutherbourg, group portrait, oils, exh. RA 1779 (*Warley camp: The mock attack*), Royal Collection • J. Reynolds, oils, *c.*1779, RA • B. West, oils, 1779, Royal Collection • W. Beechey, oils, *c.*1779–1800, Royal Collection • P. Jakob or P. J. de Loutherbourg, group portrait, oils, 1780 (*Warley camp: The review*), Royal Collection • T. Gainsborough, oils, exh. RA 1781, Royal Collection • T. Gainsborough, portrait, 1781, NPG • T. Gainsborough, oils, 1782, Royal Collection • B. West, double portrait, oils, 1789 (with Queen Charlotte) • T. Lawrence, oils, exh. RA 1792, Windsor • T. Lawrence, oils, 1792, St Mary's Guildhall, Coventry • W. Beechey, portrait, 1793, NPG • G. Dupont, oils, probably exh. RA 1794, Royal Collection • G. Dupont, oils, *c.*1795, Royal Collection • H. Singleton, group portrait, oils, 1795 (*The marriage of George, prince of Wales*), Royal Collection • W. Beechey, group portrait, oils, 1797–8 (*George III at a review*), Royal Collection • P. Stroehling, oils, 1807, Royal Collection • T. Lawrence, portrait, 1809, St James's Palace • P. Turnerelli, marble bust, 1809, NPG • P. Turnerelli, marble bust, *c.*1810, V&A • F. Chantrey, marble statue, *c.*1812, Guildhall, London • F. Chantrey, marble bust, 1814, RCS Eng. • J. Lee, portrait, 1819, Windsor • F. Hardenberg, statuette, 1820, NPG • S. W. Reynolds, mezzotint, pubd 1820, BM, NPG • R. Westmacott, statue, 1822, Monument Place, London Road, Liverpool • R. Westmacott, statue, 1824-30, Windsor Great Park • H. P. Briggs, group portrait, oils, 1828 (*Visit of George III and Queen Charlotte to Howe aboard his flagship, 26 June 1794*), NMM • J. Bacon sen., statue on monument, Somerset House, London • J. Meyer, miniature, Royal Collection • J. Nollekens, marble bust, Royal Collection • studio of A. Ramsay, portrait, Scot. NPG • J. Tassie, medallion, Scot. NPG • attrib. J. Wootton, group portrait, oils (*George III's procession to the Houses of Parliament*), Royal Collection • medallions (after J. Tassie), Scot. NPG • miniature, NPG

George III, daughters of

George III, daughters of (*act.* 1766–1857), were born over a period of seventeen years to *George III (1738–1820) and Queen *Charlotte (1744–1818). The six daughters in the family of fifteen children lived predominantly secluded and undistinguished lives; the reluctance of their parents to allow them to marry denied them even the dynastic significance generally accorded to the daughters of royal houses.

Charlotte Augusta Matilda, princess royal (1766–1828), queen of Württemberg, consort of Friedrich I, was the eldest daughter and fourth child, born at Buckingham House, London, on 29 September 1766. After the birth of a fourth son, the queen's sixth and seventh children were **Princess Augusta Sophia** (1768–1840), born on 8 November 1768, and **Princess Elizabeth** (1770–1840), landgravine of Hesse-Homburg, consort of Friedrich VI, born on 22 May 1770. In the next five years Queen Charlotte bore

Daughters of George III (*act.* 1766–1857), by Thomas Gainsborough, 1784 [the three eldest princesses: (left to right) Charlotte, princess royal, Augusta, and Elizabeth]

three sons; **Princess Mary**, duchess of Gloucester (1776–1857), was born on 25 April 1776, **Princess Sophia** (1777–1848), the next year, on 3 November. **Princess Amelia** (1783–1810), the youngest daughter and last child, made her appearance on 7 August 1783, between the deaths of her two youngest brothers, Alfred (1780–1782) and Octavius (1779–1783).

Family life The family life of the daughters of George III was not, prior to the king's first serious illness in 1788, an unhappy one. They were spared the strict educational regime and harsh discipline which fell to the lot of their brothers, and under the supervision of a well-loved governess, Lady Charlotte Finch, received lessons in English, French, geography, music, and art. In art Princess Elizabeth shone: her series of pictures 'The Birth and Triumph of Cupid' (1795) was engraved by Tomkins and published at the king's expense, and reissued as 'The Birth and Triumph of Love' in 1796. Twenty-four of her sketches, 'The Power and Progress of Genius', were issued in 1806. The princesses were allowed to play sports and boisterous games with their brothers, to whom they were close: the prince of Wales in particular was idolized by his sisters, and he was to prove their lifelong friend and protector.

Despite (or perhaps because of) the size of her family Queen Charlotte was not benignly maternal, and her daughters were scared of her, while the king was highly emotionally attached to them, preferring them to his sons, and was reluctant for them to marry and leave home. The king's illness in 1788–9, which resulted in frightening bouts of mental aberration and delusions, cast a long shadow over the lives of the young princesses. He was to experience further attacks in 1801 and 1804, and it became increasingly difficult for the question of the marriage of any of his daughters to be broached. The queen feared that any such discussion would precipitate a breakdown in his health, and she was herself determined to keep her daughters about her. Thus it was that the sisters, eager to marry and attractive in youth (the elder three inherited the family tendency to corpulence), were kept at home in the 'Nunnery'.

Escaping the Nunnery A succession of foreign princes made tentative attempts to become suitors to the princesses, but most of their offers were repelled by the queen, and many were not even passed on to the potential brides. Charlotte, the princess royal, whom the queen held responsible for the conduct of her sisters (who in turn regarded her as a 'tell-tale'), was the first to succeed in marrying. In 1796 an offer was made by Prince Friedrich of Württemberg (1754–1816), a 42-year-old widower whose first wife had died in suspicious circumstances; the king gave reluctant consent to the match, and the wedding took place on 18 May 1797. The groom was extremely fat, and the wits and cartoonists of the day had great fun with the 'Great Belly-gerent' and his plump bride. The marriage was happy, but the only child, a daughter, was stillborn. Friedrich succeeded as duke of Württemberg later in 1797, and assumed the title of elector in 1803 and king in 1806: Charlotte enjoyed her new status as consort to a ruler, addressing her mother as 'Ma très chère Mère et Soeur' ('My dearest Mother and Sister'). When Württemberg became a satellite of the French empire its queen was technically an enemy of her native country until her husband adroitly, if belatedly, switched sides again in December 1813.

The princess royal's escape from the Nunnery did not open the way to marriages for her sisters. As all, except perhaps Princess Mary, were warmly sexual by nature, and wished for children, their position was unenviable. In their confined world they sought romance with the few men that they met frequently, principally courtiers and equerries. A pattern developed of clandestine love affairs, which caused rumours of secret marriages and illegitimate children. Having seen her potential suitors turned away, Princess Augusta, the most extrovert of the sisters, fell in love with an equerry, Major-General Sir Brent *Spencer (1760–1828); she revealed her feelings to the prince of Wales, and in 1812, after he had become regent, attempted to gain his support for a private marriage. It has been suggested that this marriage did take place, but there is no evidence supporting the assertion. Princess Amelia, the king's favourite daughter, was always in poor health: from the age of fifteen it was clear that she had tuberculosis. In 1801 she was sent to Weymouth for her health; there she was attended by another of the king's equerries, Colonel Charles Fitzroy (1762–1831), second son of Lord Southampton. She quickly fell in love with him, and thereafter never gave up hope of marrying him. She told her brother, the duke of York, that she considered herself married, and took to using the initials A. F. R. (Amelia FitzRoy). Her own death intervened to thwart her plan of marrying Fitzroy after the king's death.

Princess Sophia, denied the opportunity to marry, became greatly attached to yet another equerry, Major-General Thomas Garth (1744–1828). He was aged fifty-six, and his face was disfigured by a large purple birthmark, but she was soon infatuated with 'the purple light of love', as her sister Mary unkindly remarked of him. It is possible that they went through some form of marriage, but they never lived together openly; a child was born of their liaison late in the summer of 1800. Allegations that the child was the result of an incestuous union with Sophia's brother Ernest, the duke of Cumberland, were malicious slander, aimed principally at the unpopular duke. The child, also called Thomas Garth, was acknowledged by his father, and brought up at Weymouth. (In 1829 the son attempted to blackmail the royal family by producing incriminating papers he had obtained from his father.)

The stout Princess Elizabeth (known to her sisters as Fatima), whose great love of children made it all the more sad that she did not marry until she was forty-eight, sought the support of George, prince of Wales [see George IV] in her desire to marry and escape her family. In 1808 she desperately wanted to accept the offer of marriage made by the duke of Orléans (later King Louis Philippe of France), but her hopes were confounded by his Catholicism and the queen's opposition.

Regency and revolt The sisters frequently called on the prince of Wales to assist them in finding husbands, in marrying their lovers, or simply in escaping from the confined life they lived in the queen's household. The help he could offer was limited before the regency: Princess Amelia's death after two years of permanent invalidity on 2 November 1810 came too early for him to be able to help her marry Colonel Fitzroy. (Indeed, it was the harrowing news of his daughter's last illness and death which seems to have contributed to the final collapse of the king's health, thus precipitating the regency.) On becoming regent the prince of Wales improved the position of his four remaining unmarried sisters by increasing their allowances, and supporting their wish to be allowed out into society. The princesses themselves planned a revolt against their restricted way of life under their mother's authority: Princess Augusta took the lead in April 1812 when they sent four letters to their mother asking for more freedom. The queen's reaction was one of horror and outrage, and it took all the prince regent's tact to effect a reconciliation between mother and daughters which gave the latter some degree of independence.

This enhanced independence resulted in two further marriages, those of Mary and Elizabeth. Princess Mary was perhaps the most physically attractive of the sisters, with an affectionate, rather than an actively sexual, nature. 'Dearest Minny' had been the devoted nurse and companion of Princess Amelia during her last illness, and no rumours or scandals had attached themselves to her name. Like her sisters she resented the restrictions of her mother's household, and her marriage on 22 July 1816 to her cousin Prince *William Frederick, second duke of Gloucester (1776–1834), should be seen in this light. Despite early assurances from the princess that she was content, their married life at Bagshot Park does not seem to have been entirely happy. Gloucester proved to be something of a domestic tyrant, while his political radicalism made relations with Mary's beloved brother, the regent, difficult. They had no children. Marriage for Princess Elizabeth in 1818 seemed unlikely; but in that year she was informed of an offer made by Prince Friedrich of Hesse-

Homburg (1769–1829) (he had been suggested as a husband for Princess Augusta fourteen years earlier). She could no longer hope for children, but wished to have her own home, and thankfully accepted the prince, although he was a less than prepossessing figure. Queen Charlotte, after much grumbling, ungraciously gave her consent, and the wedding took place on 7 April 1818 at St James's Palace. The marriage appears to have been a great success. The princess's jointure enabled the couple to repair the dilapidated castles of Hesse-Homburg, and in 1820 Friedrich succeeded his father as landgrave.

Final years The death of Queen Charlotte in November 1818 liberated her two remaining unmarried daughters, Augusta and Sophia, but their freedom came too late, and neither married. Augusta attended her mother during her final illness, and on her father's death she moved into Frogmore House, near Windsor, which she had been given. She remained close to her brothers, frequently visiting both *George IV and *William IV, and was a companion to the latter's wife, *Adelaide, during the early years of her widowhood. Princess Augusta lived into the reign of her niece *Victoria, who spoke affectionately of her. She died at Clarence House, St James's, on 22 September 1840. Princess Sophia lived in Kensington Palace after Queen Charlotte's death, in close proximity to the duchess of Kent and the young Princess Victoria. Like the duchess she fell under the influence of Sir John Conroy, who took over her finances; this friendship alienated her from Victoria, who thought her a spy. Following her death at her house in Vicarage Place, Kensington, on 27 May 1848, it became apparent that Conroy had embezzled most of her money.

The married sisters, Charlotte, Elizabeth, and Mary, all survived their husbands by some years. The king of Württemberg died in 1816, and the Dowager Queen Charlotte remained in his kingdom, visiting England only in 1827, when, grotesquely fat, she came in search of medical treatment for dropsy, and was entertained by George IV at Windsor. She died in Württemberg, at Ludwigsburg, on 6 October 1828, of an apoplectic seizure. The landgrave of Hesse-Homburg died in 1829, and his widow, Elizabeth, thereafter divided her time between Homburg and Hanover; she visited England in 1835–6, and in her last years spent much of her time at spas. She died at Frankfurt am Main on 10 January 1840. Princess Mary, the duchess of Gloucester, was the last survivor of George III's children, living on until 30 April 1857. Following her death at Gloucester House, Piccadilly, Queen Victoria wrote: 'Her age, and her being a link with bygone times and generations … rendered her more and more dear and precious to us all, and we all looked upon her as a sort of grandmother' (Martin, 4.27).

The lives of these unexceptional but warm-hearted sisters had undoubtedly been marred by the possessiveness of George III, by the family calamity of his long illness, and by the selfishness of their mother, Queen Charlotte. Members of a family and social structure which gave them the sole function of marriage and childbirth, between them the six sisters produced only one living child, and he was illegitimate. The dull misery caused by the restriction of their lives at Windsor was summed up by Princess Elizabeth, on a kindness from the regent: 'tho' I do not expect to be *happy*, believe me, I shall be *content*' (*Correspondence of George, Prince of Wales*, 8.317).

A. W. PURDUE

Sources J. Van der Kiste, *George III's children* (1992) · D. M. Stuart, *The daughters of George III* (1939) · L. Iremonger, *Love and the princess* (1958) · C. Hibbert, *George IV, 1: Prince of Wales* (1972) · C. Hibbert, *George IV, 2: Regent and king* (1973) · A. McNaughten, *The book of kings: a royal genealogy*, 3 vols. (1973) · J. Brooke, *King George III* (1972) · *The correspondence of George, prince of Wales, 1770–1812*, ed. A. Aspinall, 8 vols. (1963–71) · *Burke's guide to the royal family* (1973) · T. Martin, *The life of … the prince consort*, 4 (1879)

Archives BL, estate corresp. and papers, Add. MSS 31134–31135 [Amelia] · BL, music album, Add. MS 56469 [Augusta Sophia] | BL, corresp. with Mrs Warren Hastings, Add. MSS 39073, 39076 [Mary] · BL, corresp. with Mrs Warren Hastings, Add. MSS 39873, fols. 84–97, 106 · BL, corresp. with Susan O'Brien and William O'Brien, Add. MS 51352 [Mary] · BL, letters to T. Willis, Add. MS 41694 [Elizabeth] · Bodl. Oxf., North MSS [Elizabeth] · Bucks. RLSS, corresp. with Sir W. H. Fremantle [Augusta Sophia] · Derbys. RO, Fitzherbert MSS [Elizabeth] · Dorset RO, letters to Fanny Williams [Amelia] · Dorset RO, letters to Fanny Williams [Elizabeth] · Dorset RO, letters to Fanny Williams [Mary] · Gwent County RO, Cwmbrân, letters to Lord Raglan [Mary] · Keele University, letters to Charlotte Sneyd [Mary] · NA Scot., Hepburne-Scott MSS [Elizabeth] · NA Scot., letters to Lady Polwarth [Mary] · Niedersächsisches Hauptstaatsarchiv, Hannover, letters to duke of Cumberland [Augusta Sophia] · Niedersächsisches Hauptstaatsarchiv, Hannover, letters to duke of Cumberland [Mary] · Northumbd RO, letters to Lady Melville [Charlotte Augusta Matilda] · NRA, priv. coll., letters to Lady Jane Dalrymple-Hamilton [Mary] · PRO, Pitt MSS [Elizabeth] · Royal Arch., letters to George III [Amelia] · Royal Arch., letters to George III [Mary] · Sheff. Arch., letters to Lady Erne [Mary] · Sheff. Arch., Montagu-Stuart MSS [Mary] · Staffs. RO, letters to Lady Dartmouth [Mary] · Warks. CRO, letters to Sir J. A. Waller [Mary] · Wilts. & Swindon RO, corresp. with Herbert family [Amelia] · Wilts. & Swindon RO, corresp. with countesses of Pembroke [Augusta Sophia] · Wilts. & Swindon RO, corresp. with countesses of Pembroke [Charlotte Augusta Matilda] · Wilts. & Swindon RO, corresp. with countesses of Pembroke [Mary]

Likenesses F. Cotes, double portrait, oils, 1767 (Charlotte with her mother), Royal Collection · F. Cotes, double portrait, pastel, 1767 (Charlotte with her mother), Royal Collection · O. Humphrey, miniature, 1769 (Charlotte), Royal Collection · J. Zoffany, double portrait, oils, *c*.1770 (Charlotte with Prince William), Royal Collection · J. Zoffany, group portrait, oils, 1770 (*George III, Queen Charlotte and their six eldest children*), Royal Collection · J. Zoffany, group portrait, oils, exh. RA 1773 (*Queen Charlotte with members of her family*), Royal Collection · B. West, group portrait, oils, 1776 (*The children of George III and Queen Charlotte*), Royal Collection · oils, 1776 (Charlotte), Royal Collection · B. West, group portrait, oils, 1779 (*Queen Charlotte with her children*), Royal Collection · T. Gainsborough, oils, 1782 (Augusta), Royal Collection · T. Gainsborough, oils, 1782 (Elizabeth), Royal Collection · T. Gainsborough, oils, 1782 (Mary), Royal Collection · T. Gainsborough, portrait, 1782 (Charlotte), Royal Collection · T. Gainsborough, group portrait, oils, 1784, Royal Collection [*see illus.*] · J. Hoppner, oils, exh. RA 1785 (Amelia), Royal Collection · J. Hoppner, oils, exh. RA 1785 (Mary), Royal Collection · J. Singleton Copley, group portrait, oils, exh. RA 1785 (*The three youngest daughters of George III*), Royal Collection · W. Ward, stipple, pubd 1788 (Elizabeth; after H. Ramberg), BM, NPG · T. Lawrence, oils, exh. RA 1790 (Amelia), Royal Collection · W. Beechey, oils, exh. RA 1797 (Amelia), Royal Collection · W. Beechey, oils, exh. RA 1797 (Augusta), Royal Collection · W. Beechey, oils, exh. RA 1797 (Mary), Royal Collection · W. Beechey, oils, exh. RA 1797 (Elizabeth), Royal Collection · W. Beechey, oils, *c*.1797–1800 (Charlotte), Royal Collection · W. Beechey, portrait, *c*.1800 (Sophia),

Royal Collection · W. Beechey, oils, exh. RA 1802 (Augusta), Royal Collection · R. Cosway, miniature, 1802 (Amelia), V&A · H. Edridge, drawing, 1802–4 (Elizabeth), Royal Collection · P. E. Stroehling, oils, c.1805 (Amelia), Royal Collection · A. Robertson, miniature, c.1807 (Elizabeth), Royal Collection · P. E. Stroehling, oils, 1807 (Amelia), Royal Collection · P. E. Stroehling, oils, 1807 (Augusta), Royal Collection · P. E. Stroehling, oils, 1807 (Elizabeth), Royal Collection · P. E. Stroehling, oils, 1807 (Mary), Royal Collection · P. E. Stroehling, oils, 1807 (Sophia), Royal Collection · J. S. Agar, stipple, pubd 1811 (Amelia; after A. Mee), BM, NPG · A. Robertson, miniature, 1811 (Amelia), Royal Collection · W. Beechey, oils, probably exh. RA 1819 (Augusta), Museum of Fine Art, Baltimore, Maryland · T. Lawrence, oils, exh. RA 1824 (Mary), Royal Collection · J. G. P. Fischer, miniature, 1827 (Charlotte), Royal Collection · R. J. Lane, lithograph, pubd 1840 (Augusta; after W. C. Ross), BM, NPG · T. H. Maguire, lithograph, pubd 1851 (Mary; after F. X. Winterhalter), BM, NPG · R. Cosway, miniature (Amelia), Royal Collection · R. Cosway, miniature (Mary), Royal Collection · H. Edridge, drawing (Mary), Royal Collection · H. Edridge, drawings (Augusta), Royal Collection · H. Edridge, pencil and wash (Amelia), Royal Collection · G. Engleheart, miniature (Charlotte; after R. Cosway?), Wallace Collection, London · E. Miles, miniature (Charlotte), Royal Collection · J. Roberts, pencil and watercolour (Amelia; as a child), Royal Collection · A. Robertson, miniature (Augusta), Royal Collection · J. Slater, pencil and wash (Amelia), Royal Collection · P. W. Tomkins, chalk (Charlotte), BM · B. West, group portrait, Royal Collection · oils (Augusta; after W. Beechey, c.1815), Royal Collection

Wealth at death £1607—plus few shares of little value; Sophia

George IV (1762–1830), king of the United Kingdom of Great Britain and Ireland, and king of Hanover, was born at St James's Palace, London, on 12 August 1762. The eldest son of the fifteen children of *George III (1738–1820) and Queen *Charlotte (1744–1818), daughter of the duke of Mecklenburg-Strelitz, he was by right of birth duke of Cornwall, duke of Rothesay, earl of Carrick, and baron of Renfrew. In addition to eight brothers George had six sisters [see George III, daughters of (act. 1766–1857)]. He was created prince of Wales and earl of Chester on 17 August, and baptized under the names of George Augustus Frederick by the archbishop of Canterbury, Thomas Secker, on 8 September, crying 'most lustily' throughout the ceremony (*Diaries of a Duchess*, 51).

Education George was placed in the care of the royal governess, Lady Charlotte Finch, 'a woman of remarkable sense and philosophy' (*The Last Journals of Horace Walpole*, ed. A. F. Steuart, 1, 1910, 125), who was provided with an establishment including an assistant governess, a wet-nurse, a dry-nurse, a necessary woman, a sempstress, and two rockers of the cradle. In the care of these women the child prospered. At the age of four, while lying in bed with the curtains drawn after a smallpox inoculation, he precociously replied to a remark about the tedium of his condition, 'Not at all, I lie and make reflections' (*Diaries of a Duchess*, 63). A year later he had mastered the rudiments of English grammar and was able to write in a neat, round hand. When he was six he was reported to be making good progress in all his lessons; and, although he was rather hot-tempered and lacking in determination, it was hoped that these and other flaws of character would be eradicated by a secondary, more rigorous stage in his education which the king now ordained for the prince and his brother *Frederick at the Dutch House, Kew. Rigorous this

George IV (1762–1830), by Sir Thomas Lawrence, 1822

education certainly was: the boys were kept at their lessons, or at some form of closely supervised recreation, from early in the morning until eight at night. The king insisted that they must be screened from the temptations of the outside world, taught the virtues of simplicity, hard work, punctuality, and regularity, and, at the first sign of laziness, laxness, or untruthfulness, they must be severely beaten. This injunction was obeyed. One of their sisters later recalled how she had seen them 'held by their tutors to be flogged like dogs with a long whip' (A. M. Murray, *Recollections from 1803 to 1837*, 1868). Despite the perceived need for such chastisement, the prince of Wales was described by his preceptor as 'an extremely promising pupil' (F. Kilvert, *Memoirs of the Life and Writings of Richard Hurd*, 1860, 130). He was proficient in the classics, and was instructed in mathematics, natural philosophy ('sacred', 'profane', and 'modern'), and 'polite literature'. He could speak French and had a good grasp of both German and Italian. He was taught to play the cello, and received drawing lessons from Alexander Cozens, and boxing and fencing lessons from Henry Angelo; he had a pleasant singing voice. In his own garden at Kew he was taught the elements of agriculture. He sowed and harvested a variety of crops and even baked his own bread. One of his mother's German attendants wrote of his attractive personality when he was sixteen, of his 'elegant person', his 'engaging and distinguished manners' and 'affectionate disposition' (*Court and Private Life*, 1.132–3, 144).

The undutiful son, 1779–1789 This high opinion of his son was not shared by the king, from whose affection the prince felt increasingly excluded as he grew older. His father accused him of not making the required progress in his studies, particularly in German. His attitude towards his religious duties showed that he was deficient in gratitude to 'the Great Creator'. Above all his 'love of dissipation' had for months, even at his present age, been 'trumpeted in the public papers' (*Court and Private Life*, 1.91; Royal Archives, RA41774–41775).

The prince himself admitted that he was 'rather too fond of wine and women' (George III, *The Later Correspondence of George III*, ed. A. Aspinall, 5, 1962–70, 22). There were rumours of affairs with the slatternly wife of a groom as well as with a maid of honour to the queen. He professed his undying passion for the duke of Hamilton's great-granddaughter, to whom he sent a lock of his abundant light brown hair and numerous letters, seventy-five of which survive; and, by the end of 1779, he had fallen violently in love with the beautiful and notoriously exhibitionist young actress Mary (Perdita) *Robinson (1756/1758?–1800), who gave up her career on the stage to become his mistress when promised a fortune of £20,000 to be paid upon his coming of age. The prince soon tired of her, however, and she was dismissed with a capital sum of £5000 and an annuity of £500.

A succession of other mistresses, or supposed mistresses (among them Elizabeth Bridget *Armitstead), took her place. The prince caused further offence to his father by keeping the company of rakes and wastrels and such whig politicians as Charles James Fox, notoriously *persona non grata* at court. The prince is generally believed to have been the father of the politician George *Lamb. Prince Frederick urged his brother to try to get on better terms with his parents: 'It really is of so much consequence to yourself', he wrote, 'that it appears to me quite ridiculous that you do not attempt it' (*Correspondence of George, Prince of Wales*, 1.76). But the prince of Wales could not bring himself to follow his brother's advice. The king was always so 'excessively cross, ill-tempered and uncommonly grumpy', as well as being 'so stingy' that he would 'hardly allow [his eldest son] three coats in a year' (ibid., 1.75). It was as though his parents' dull, domestic way of living, and their constant criticism of his extravagance, incited him to further dissipation and expenditure. It seemed, indeed, to the prince that his father was jealous of him as his successor, and that he disliked him as his heir. Certainly it was never suggested that the prince should occupy himself in some capacity that might fit him for his future state. As the bishop of Llandaff put it to the duke of Queensberry, 'he was a man occupied in trifles, because he had no opportunity of displaying his talents in the conduct of great concerns' (*Memoirs of … Wraxall*, 5.363).

That the prince had talents could not be denied. Not all his friends were dissolute, and it was generally agreed by the less frivolous among them that 'Prinny's' conversation when sober was as intelligent as it was entertaining. A master of anecdote, he had an excellent memory, while, as the duke of Wellington said, he possessed 'a most extraordinary talent for imitating the manner, gestures, and even the voices of other people, so much so that he could give you the exact idea of anyone however unlike they were to himself' (*A Portion of the Journal Kept by Thomas Raikes*, 1, 1856, 191). According to George Brummel, had his lot fallen that way, he could have been 'the best comic actor in Europe' (C. Macfarlane, *Reminiscences of a Literary Life*, 1917, 102). William Beckford found him 'graciousness personified' (J. W. Oliver, *The Life of William Beckford*, 1932, 108); George Canning, upon meeting him for the first time, was 'charmed beyond measure' and 'far beyond' his expectation with 'the elegance of his address and the gentlemanliness of his manner'. Even that mordant gossip Samuel Rogers thought him 'very agreeable' (*Reminiscences of the Table Talk of Samuel Rogers*, ed. A. Dyce, 1856, 36); while Edmund Burke suggested that, should he ever resolve to quit a course of life in which he found 'little more than disgust', he might even 'become a great king' (*The Manuscripts and Correspondence of James, First Earl of Charlemont*, 2, 1891–4, 98).

As for the prince's appearance, the discriminating duchess of Devonshire thought him 'very handsome', though inclined to be too fat and too much like 'a woman in men's cloaths' (*Third Report*, HMC). All agreed that as an amateur connoisseur of the visual arts he had few equals.

'Torrents of debts' The prince's taste was well displayed in the decoration and furnishing of his fine mansion on the south side of Pall Mall, Carlton House. This residence had come into his possession as part of the financial arrangements which were settled, with much difficulty, after his twenty-first birthday. The government had suggested to the king in 1783 that the prince should be granted an income of £100,000 a year. His majesty was horrified: he had had 'little reason to approve of any part of his son's conduct for the last three years'; his neglect of every religious duty was 'notorious', while 'his want of even common civility' to his parents was 'not less so' (*Correspondence of George, Prince of Wales*, 1.113). The outrageous idea of granting an income of £100,000, so long as the prince remained unmarried, was 'a shameful squandering of public money besides an encouragement of extravagance' (ibid., 1.117). Eventually, with the help of Fox, who persuaded the prince to keep the peace within the royal family, the prince agreed to accept £50,000 and the duchy of Cornwall revenues, amounting to a further £12,000 a year, on the understanding that he would also receive a capital sum of £60,000. Thus comfortably provided for, the prince instructed the architect Henry Holland to make Carlton House as grandly imposing as possible.

Month after month the work continued at what even the prince himself admitted was 'enormous' cost. Without regard to this expense, and in defiance of the king's known wishes, more and more splendours were gradually added to Carlton House. Adjoining houses were bought and demolished to make way for new wings. Craftsmen of all kinds were brought over from France. Agents were sent to China to buy furniture for the drawing-room, for which the mercer's bill alone amounted to £6817 and for which £441 was spent on lanterns. The sale rooms and dealers' shops of Paris and London were scoured for tapestries and clocks, bronzes, girandoles, and looking-glasses. Walls were decorated with pictures by Van Dyck and Vernet, Claude and Greuze. Suites of new rooms appeared, some Gothic, others Corinthian. A fan-vaulted Gothic conservatory was designed in the manner of a small cathedral. The prince's treasurer, called upon to calculate the amount of his debts, discovered that they were 'beyond all kind of calculation whatever'. Apart from the enormous sums being spent on Carlton House, there was the 'amazing expense' of the prince's stables, which alone were costing £31,000 a year (ibid., 1.162, 167; Royal Archives, RA41822–41823).

Gratified as the king was to learn that, faced by these 'torrents of debts', the prince had decided to practise 'a system of economy', he was distressed beyond measure to be told in August 1784 that his son intended to do so abroad (*Correspondence of George, Prince of Wales*, 1.155; Royal Archives, RA16379). He would have been even more distressed had he known the real reason for his son's desire to leave England. For the prince had fallen in love again and had made up his mind to marry the object of his passion, Mrs Maria *Fitzherbert (1756–1837), a handsome, charming, and sedate Roman Catholic widow of twenty-eight, six years older than himself, who had fled to France after the prince had stabbed himself in a frenzied effort to prevent her doing so.

Marriage, debts, and Brighton The marriage which the prince proposed was in defiance of the Royal Marriages Act of 1772, which provided that no member of the royal family could marry without the king's consent. It was also a marriage that would require him to forfeit all rights to the throne, since the Act of Settlement of 1701 excluded those married to Roman Catholics from the succession. Undeterred by these considerations, the prince dispatched letter after frantically passionate letter to Mrs Fitzherbert, one of them extending to forty-two pages, until she at last consented to return to England. They were illegally married in her drawing-room on 15 December 1785 by an Anglican clergyman brought from the Fleet prison for the purpose, the prince writing out a certificate and giving it to his bride for her to keep in a safe place. Her brother, John Smythe, and her uncle, Henry Errington, were present.

Happy as the prince was with Mrs Fitzherbert, his mounting debts, which had risen to the astonishing sum of £269,878 6s. 7¼d., were a constant source of worry to him. It was suggested to him that some arrangements might be made to settle them if he were to marry a suitable foreign princess, a proposal that provoked him to declare that he would 'never marry'. It was also suggested that the king might prove less intractable if the prince were to abandon his open support of the whig opposition. This, however, was equally impossible: he would never 'abandon Charles' and his other friends (Harris, 2.130).

Announcing that he was firmly determined 'not to appear again in public' until he could do so with that 'dignity and splendour' to which his rank in life entitled him (*Correspondence of George, Prince of Wales*, 1.236), the prince closed down Carlton House and went to live with Mrs Fitzherbert quietly in Brighton, a move which further annoyed the king, who protested that his son was flaunting his poverty to draw attention to his father's meanness. Certainly the prince was hoping to win public sympathy for his plight; and, having been strongly advised not to borrow money in France, he trusted that parliament might help him. It was, however, difficult to raise the subject of the prince's finances in the House of Commons without questions being asked about his rumoured marriage to a Roman Catholic; and when Fox rose to deny the truth of the rumours, on the strength of the prince's assurances, he so distressed Mrs Fitzherbert (who considered that the denial of the marriage injured her moral reputation) that she threatened to break off all connection with her husband and for a time refused to see him. By the time a financial settlement had at last been reached, however, she and the prince were reconciled. Carlton House, for the completion of which parliament had granted £60,000, was opened up again; and, having also received £161,000 to pay his debts and a further £10,000 a year from the king out of the civil list, the prince began work on the Marine Pavilion at Brighton, a house originally designed in a Graeco-Roman style by Henry Holland, which was to be transformed at immense cost by John Nash into the fabulous palace, the style of which—'a mixture of Moorish, Tartar, gothic and Chinese, and all in stone and iron'—Dorothea Lieven, the wife of the Russian ambassador, was at a loss to describe, but which remains a chief memorial of the Regency period.

The regency crisis, 1798 While the prince's works at Brighton were in progress, disturbing news came from Windsor: the king was suffering from some kind of mental collapse, talking endlessly and making little sense. The prince drove over to Windsor where, at dinner, the king suddenly rose from his chair, seized his son by the collar, and hurled him against the wall. The queen fell into violent hysterics, and the prince burst into tears.

It appears that the king was suffering from a virulent form of a rare metabolic disorder known as porphyria, but to observers at the time he was clearly going mad; and the questions to be answered by the several doctors called in to report upon his condition were whether or not he would recover and, if he were to recover, how soon that recovery might take place. They were at least agreed upon the necessity of removing him to Kew, where he might take exercise in the garden in privacy. But at Kew he became 'almost unmanageable', attacking his pages, swearing, and uttering strange indecencies. They tied him to his bed, blistered him, and eventually placed him in a strait-jacket.

While the doctors argued and squabbled at Kew, the political quarrels intensified in bitterness in London, where the government lived in fear that the king would be declared incurably insane and that they would consequently be dismissed as soon as his son assumed power. The prime minister, William Pitt, reconciled himself to the likelihood of his ministry's fall, the installation of the prince's whig friends in its place, and his return to a career in the law.

The prince, who had behaved well enough when his father was first taken ill at Windsor, could not disguise his excitement at the prospect of influence and money after he had become regent. He and his supporters, notably Fox and R. B. Sheridan, eagerly discussed and argued about the allotment of offices when a whig government was formed under the probable leadership of the duke of Portland. Pamphleteers and caricaturists, journalists and newspaper publishers were paid large sums of money by both sides to denigrate their opponents: the prince was attacked by supporters of the government as a 'Papist or married to a Papist', a man unfit to be regent by reason of his 'friendships of the card table and the attachments of the turf', and at the same time was lauded in whig publications as 'a true genius', 'the first young man in Great Britain' (Derry, 34–6). 'The acrimony is beyond anything you can conceive,' Lord Sydney told Lord Cornwallis. 'The ladies are as usual at the head of the animosity.' Supporters of the king and government wore 'constitutional coats', the prince's friends 'regency caps' decorated with three feathers and inscribed 'Ich Dien'.

In the Commons the debates were long and heated, Fox arguing that the prince had 'as clear, as express a right' to assume the exercise of royal power as he would have done if the king were dead, Pitt slapping his thigh in triumph at the opposition's expression of so high a tory doctrine and declaring that he would 'un-Whig' Fox for the rest of his life. In the end a Regency Bill passed the Commons on 12 February 1789. It was, however, a bill in which the regent's powers were very much restricted; and, in any event, before it passed the Lords news arrived from Kew that the king was on the mend. The prince emerged from the regency crisis with his reputation still further impaired, and on his way to a thanksgiving service in St Paul's Cathedral his coach was greeted with jeers and catcalls.

Marriage to Princess Caroline, 1789–1809 Spurned by his father, whom he took no steps to placate, and bitterly disappointed by his failure to gain any sort of responsible command in the army, in which his younger brother Frederick (now duke of York) had reached the highest rank, the prince was condemned in *The Times* as a hard-drinking, swearing, whoring man who 'at all times would prefer a girl and a bottle to politics and a sermon'; his only states of happiness were 'gluttony, drunkenness and gambling' (*Correspondence of George, Prince of Wales*, 2.2–3). The more he was accused of being such a wastrel, the more he felt inclined to behave like one, and the more, indeed, he did behave like one. He was 'little respected' any more, the duke of Portland had to confess; while Sir Gilbert Elliot was of the opinion that if anything could make a democracy in England it was the behaviour of the prince and his tiresome brothers (*Life and Letters*, 1.327). He took a selection of new mistresses. He abandoned Mrs Fitzherbert for the clever, sensual, and rather heartless wife of the earl of Jersey; and, largely in order to arrange a settlement of new

and alarming debts, he agreed to marry his cousin *Caroline (1768–1821), daughter of the duke of Brunswick, though of all the women he might have chosen she was, while undeniably cheerful and good-natured, one of the least likely to suit him, being gauche and boisterous, tactless, talkative, and none too clean. On embracing her for the first time he withdrew to the far corner of the room and asked Lord Malmesbury, who had brought her over from Brunswick, to get him a glass of brandy. On the night of the wedding, which took place at the Chapel Royal on 8 April 1795, he fell, insensible with drink, into the fireplace of their bedroom. In the morning he had recovered sufficiently to climb into bed with his wife, who gave birth to their daughter, *Charlotte, exactly nine months later. By then they were living apart; and by the summer of 1800 the prince and Mrs Fitzherbert were once more inseparable.

The number of the prince's illegitimate children is uncertain. He seems to have accepted the paternity of three sons, to one of whom, so he told Lord Eldon when discussing the provisions of his will in 1823, he thought himself bound to give a legacy of £30,000. The other boys were provided for less generously. Mrs Fitzherbert, whose miniature portrait was found hanging in a diamond locket around his neck at his death, never denied having had children. Her relative, Lord Stourton, suggested that she might write on the back of her marriage certificate, 'No issue from this marriage'. To this, so Lord Stourton said, 'she smilingly objected on the score of delicacy'. The year before her death in 1837, however, she wrote a paper which ended with the words, 'I, Maria Fitzherbert, testify that my union with George, Prince of Wales, was without issue.' But, although she indicated a space where the document was to be signed, she never did sign it.

There was a story that her adopted niece, Mary Anne Smythe, supposed to have been the illegitimate daughter of her brother John Smythe—who, according to family tradition, had no children—was in reality her daughter by the prince. It was also rumoured that another girl she took into her care, Mary Seymour, daughter of her friends Lord Hugh and Lady Horatia Seymour, was, in fact, her own child. In later years Mary Seymour intimated that Mrs Fitzherbert had had more than one child by the prince. There was talk of a boy born in 1793 at Lille where Mrs Fitzherbert had gone after a quarrel with the prince, and of another boy brought up by Sir James Harris and given his name. However, no references to any children that there may have been of the marriage survived the destruction of most of her papers by her executors; nor are there any references to children of hers in the Royal Archives.

The king's relationship with his eldest son became more uneasy than ever. There were occasional *rapprochements*; but when his father suffered from a recurrence of his malady in 1804, the prince took to giving large dinner parties for the government's enemies at Carlton House, where he talked at inordinate length on all manner of subjects, political and otherwise. On his recovery, the king was as much annoyed to hear of this as the prince was exasperated by his father's visits to Princess Caroline's house at

Blackheath, where George III professed himself delighted with his granddaughter, 'the perfect little creature', Princess Charlotte (*Correspondence of George, Prince of Wales*, 3.148).

Disturbing stories of Princess Caroline's eccentric and flirtatious behaviour at Blackheath reached the prince in the summer of 1805, and—after hearing of allegations that she had had an illegitimate child there—he felt obliged to have her conduct investigated. The commissioners appointed to carry out this 'delicate investigation' concluded that, while her extraordinary behaviour was indiscreet to the point of recklessness, there was no positive proof of adultery. The investigation also revealed that she had become 'a female political', asking to her house as many of her husband's political opponents as would accept her invitations (Jennings, 2.89). They were now in opposition since, after Pitt's death in 1806, the so-called 'ministry of all the talents', composed largely of friends of Fox, had given the prince a chance to exercise some influence. But the transfer of the power of the crown from St James's to Carlton House, as Lord Melville put it, was short-lived; the 'ministry of all the talents' fell in March 1807, and in the administration that succeeded it there were many of the princess's friends, including George Canning, who the prince believed had been her lover.

The prince as regent, 1811–1819 The prince, once more on the political sidelines, occupied himself with his private concerns and with his new mistress, the marchioness of Hertford, a very rich, handsome, stately, and formal woman of ample though well-corseted proportions, whose attraction for the prince was a mystery to those who did not understand his need to be dominated by an authoritarian woman older than himself.

In October 1810, however, politics once more absorbed the prince as the king lapsed into the illness from which he was not to recover. As in 1788 the government, now led by Spencer Perceval, held fast to hopes of the king's recovery, trusting that he would be better before a regency bill became necessary and fearing that such a bill would result in their dismissal in favour of the prince's whig friends. Indeed, by the end of January 1811, after lengthy discussions between the prince and these friends, the composition of a whig government had more or less been decided. But the whigs were to be disappointed. When the prince was sworn in as regent on 5 February 1811 he decided to keep the tories in office. He had been urged to do so by his persuasive, arch-conservative brother the duke of Cumberland, as well as by the duke of York and Lord and Lady Hertford. He did not like change and was too lazy to provoke it. Nor, when he had to settle down to it, did he like the work that being regent imposed upon him. 'Playing at King', he said, daunted by the amount of papers to which he was expected to attend, 'is no sinecure' (*The Farington Diary*, ed. J. Greig, 1922–8, 7.22). George Tierney, member for Knaresborough, reported on 20 July:

> The Prince is very nervous, as well he may be at the prospect before him, and frequent in the course of the day in his applications to the liquor chest. I much doubt, however, whether all the alcohol in the world will be able to brace his nerves up to the mark of facing the difficulties he will soon have to encounter. (*Correspondence of George, Prince of Wales*, 8.52)

First of all there was the indignation of the whigs, annoyed by the prince's hostility to the political emancipation of Roman Catholics. Their indignation became particularly rancorous after the murder of Spencer Perceval in 1812 and the appointment of Lord Liverpool as prime minister in a reorganized tory administration after a prolonged political crisis in which the prince's hostility to his erstwhile friends became fully apparent. Then there was his ever increasing unpopularity, so hard to bear when compounded by the cheers which still greeted the appearance of his detested wife. Eventually Princess Caroline decided to go to live abroad; but their difficult daughter, Princess Charlotte, talkative, hoydenish, and rather coarse, was left behind to worry him. He wanted her to marry the prince of Orange, but she made objections and was soon clandestinely meeting the wholly unsuitable Prince Augustus of Prussia. Her father had her servants dismissed and herself removed to Cranbourne Lodge in Windsor Forest. On 2 May 1816 she was married to Prince Leopold of Saxe-Coburg-Saalfeld; but she died less than two years later, having given birth to a stillborn son. The distressed regent, who had been seriously ill himself, was accused of not sharing the general grief, even of being in some way responsible for the death of a young woman who had been so much better liked in the country than himself. The regent was also widely held responsible for the repressive measures that the government introduced to combat the intermittent outbreaks of violence, the revolutionary gatherings, and threats against the established order which had been troubling the country since the conclusion of the war with France. In August 1819 he was 'hissed by an immense mob' around his front door after he had written, at the home secretary's request, to approve the action of the Manchester magistrates who had authorized the use of force to disperse a largely peaceful crowd of demonstrators at St Peter's Field, several of whom had been killed.

King, 1820, and the problem of Queen Caroline Within a few months of the Peterloo massacre, the regent had to face an adversary far more destructive of his peace of mind than demonstrators in Manchester and jeering mobs in London. For, on 29 January 1820, his father died. At fifty-seven he was king himself at last; and his wife announced her intention of coming back to England to claim her rights as queen.

Ever since her arrival on the continent Caroline had been providing Europe with scandalous stories about her astonishingly imprudent behaviour; and her husband, who had employed agents to report upon her activities, had good grounds for supposing that she had committed adultery with her major-domo, Bartolomeo Bergami. His agents' reports were, therefore, sent by the king to parliament in the hope that the queen might not only be divorced but tried for high treason. But, since Bergami was Italian and not subject to English law, and since the alleged offences had not taken place in England, it was impossible to institute a trial for high treason; moreover, the king's own conduct had rendered an ecclesiastical divorce unobtainable. The only option was to introduce a bill of pains and penalties, a parliamentary method of punishing a person without resort to a trial in a court of law.

The proceedings in the House of Lords, which opened on 17 August 1820, did not go as well for the king as he had hoped. No impartial observer of the evidence presented—and of the evidence which would have been presented had certain witnesses not been too frightened to come to England to give it—could reasonably doubt that the queen was guilty. But the result of the voting on the bill was so close that, as Lord Grey commented, it was 'tantamount to a defeat' (Quennell, 70–71); and the government, having accepted the impossibility of getting the bill through the Commons, was forced to conclude that it would have to be withdrawn.

Throughout the trial, as the proceedings were generally known, the king was execrated and the queen adulated as a persecuted victim of his malevolence. Immense crowds gathered in the streets to shout their support of her and to insult her husband. 'The fermentation increases much', Coutts, the banker, was told. 'It has got amongst the soldiery who skirmish in their barracks' (4 July 1820; Royal Archives, Coutts MS Y 56/57). Lord Grey feared 'a Jacobin Revolution more bloody than that of France' (E. T. Lean, *The Napoleonists*, 1970, 118). By God, the queen declared, she would blow her husband off the throne. It was a possibility that Henry Brougham, for one, considered not at all unlikely (C. Bury, *The Diary of a Lady-in-Waiting*, 2, 1908, 94). Indeed, when the government decided to withdraw the bill, the king apparently spoke of retiring to Hanover and leaving the British throne to the duke of York.

Coronation and popularity Less than a year later, however, the mood of the country had entirely changed. At the king's coronation—for the celebration of which parliament had voted no less than £243,000—George IV was the improbable and unexpected hero of the day. His past was forgotten in the splendour of the occasion, while the queen, who had unsuccessfully tried to gain entrance to Westminster Abbey, was jeered as she was driven away. The popularity of that 'Bedlam Bitch of a Queen', as Walter Scott called her (*The Letters of Sir Walter Scott*, ed. H. J. C. Grierson, 1932–7, 6.505), was now on the wane, while that of the king was increasing. The queen died less than three weeks later.

Satisfied to find himself so comparatively well liked in England, the king was quite as gratified by his reception when, in this early period of his reign, he visited Ireland, Hanover, and Scotland, the last a notable excursion in August 1822 organized by Sir Walter Scott which, almost for the first time, made a Hanoverian monarch popular in Scotland. He was also pleased to be on far better terms than he had been in the past with the often irritable prime minister, Lord Liverpool; and when the foreign secretary, Lord Castlereagh, committed suicide in 1822 and he was obliged to accept his former *bête noire*, Canning, as Castlereagh's successor, he was soon on the best of terms with

the tactful and amusing Canning, both as foreign secretary and, after Liverpool's resignation, as prime minister in a government which had to rely heavily on whig support.

Yet, for the monarchy, the crisis provoked by Canning's appointment as prime minister in 1827 proved cataclysmic. Throughout the king's reign the power of the crown had been declining. In the past the monarchy had been sustained by the support of the tories; but the king's dislike of several of Liverpool's colleagues, his indiscreet talk about their principles and measures, his brilliant and needlessly wounding mimicry of their idiosyncrasies and mannerisms, his discussions with advisers beyond their control and influence, and his indolent character and aversion to uncongenial work all served to undermine their confidence in him, despite the fact that most tories agreed with George IV in opposing the political emancipation of Roman Catholics. By turning to Canning (regardless of Canning's support for Catholic emancipation) and to those whigs who supported him, the king lost for good the confidence of the tories, who now abused him, so Lady Cowper said, 'a thousand times worse than the Whigs ever did' (*Letters of Lady Palmerston*, ed. T. Lever, 1957, 165). Yet, by spurning the tories in 1827 he did not regain the trust of the whigs whom he had rejected in 1812. For the first time, the monarch was without significant support or personal influence in either party.

The king, the duke, and Catholic emancipation, 1827–1829 In the event, the king's pleasant relationship with his prime minister was soon brought to an end by Canning's early death in August 1827, and after the brief premiership of the lachrymose Lord Goderich, the king had to deal with the duke of Wellington, whom he found far less companionable and whom he exasperated by taking a perverse pleasure in pretending that he had fought at Waterloo and had helped to win the battle of Salamanca, 'when things looked very black indeed', by leading a magnificent charge of dragoons, disguised as General Bock. Really, the duke declared, he sometimes thought that the king was mad (Quennell, 111).

His majesty had certainly never appeared in such 'an agitated state' as when the duke attempted to persuade him of the necessity of passing a Roman Catholic Relief Act, in addition to the repeal of the Test and Corporation Act to which the king had reluctantly agreed in 1828. The king at first roundly declared that he was, like his 'revered father', categorically opposed to such an act; and on several occasions worked himself up into such a state of turbulent emotion on the subject that tears poured from his eyes and he rambled on inconsequentially for hours on end, once talking almost continuously for five and three-quarter hours, sipping brandy the while (*Greville Memoirs*, 1.301; Ellenborough, 1.377). Wellington shrewdly persuaded him on 29 January 1829 to sign the cabinet minute which committed the cabinet to an emancipation bill, and the bill was introduced in parliament.

The king grew increasingly peevish and fretful, constantly disputing with the government about his rights of patronage, which he had been allowed to indulge in the days of Canning and Goderich, threatening to dismiss his ministers from office as though they were his footmen, and protesting his determination not to give royal assent to Roman Catholic relief. Under pressure from the duke of Cumberland, whose prejudice against Catholics was fanatical, the king became 'the most Protestant man in his dominions' (Ellenborough, 1.139).

Lady Holland heard that he 'worked himself up into a fury whenever the subject was mentioned', declaring that he would go abroad and never return to England if he were made to give way, and that his subjects would then get a 'Catholic' king in the shape of the duke of Clarence, who had come round to declaring himself in sympathy with the bill. The king's frenzied agitation became even more extreme when it was made clear to him that most of his household did not support him in the stand he was taking. The cabinet reminded him that he had signed his assent to the policy and, when he again refused, resigned on 4 March. Next day he repented, the ministry remained, and the bill made its way. When at last in April 1829 George IV was finally obliged to submit on the issue, he was found in a 'deplorable state', lying on a sofa utterly worn out (Ellenborough, 1.376–7, 384–5). The duke was 'King Arthur' now, he said; he himself was merely a 'Canon of Windsor' (*Letters of Dorothea, Princess Lieven*, ed. L. G. Robinson, 1902, 187).

Last years The king had little more than a year to live. In the over-heated rooms of the Marine Pavilion at Brighton and at Windsor Castle in the company of his latest and last intimate friend, Elizabeth *Conyngham, Marchioness Conyngham, and his influential keeper of the privy purse, Sir William Knighton, he passed his days in extraordinary self-indulgence, exacerbating his ill health by drinking immoderately and dosing himself with as many as 250 drops of laudanum a day. He was frequently 'tortured by gout' and suffered other ills, including arteriosclerosis, inflammation of the bladder, and, possibly, porphyria. He submitted to having leeches applied around the pelvis for the pain in his bladder; but his doctors had little control over their difficult patient, who alarmed them exceedingly by his habit of opening veins himself when they considered he had been bled quite enough and by his dreadful spasms of breathlessness. At first there would be a gurgling in his throat, then not only his face but even the ends of his swollen fingers would turn black as he struggled to get his breath. Yet as soon as he felt better he would drink a large glass of brandy and go for a ride round the park in his phaeton.

The king's mode of living was 'really beyond belief', so the duke of Wellington's friend Harriet Arbuthnot said. One day in April 1830:

> at the hour of the servants' dinner, he called the page in and said, 'Now you are going in to dinner. Go downstairs and cut me off just such a piece of beef as you would like to have yourself … and bring it me up.' The page accordingly went and fetched an enormous quantity of roast beef, all of which he ate, and then slept for five hours. (*Journal of Mrs Arbuthnot*, 2.352)

For breakfast a few days earlier, according to the duke of Wellington, he had consumed:

> a pigeon and beef steak pie of which he ate two pigeons and three beef-steaks, three parts of a bottle of Mozelle, a glass of champagne, two glasses of port and a glass of brandy! He had taken laudanum the night before, again before this breakfast, again last night and again this morning.
> (G. Wellesley, ed., *Wellington and his Friends*, 1965, 70)

'He will have all these things and nobody can prevent him,' Mrs Arbuthnot added. 'No wonder he is likely to die.'

Dorothea Lieven said the king looked 'ghastly'. His once handsome features were overblown and heavy, much flattered in the portraits by Thomas Lawrence and David Wilkie and the statues by Francis Chantrey and John Flaxman for which he delighted in sitting. The expensive oils and ointments, creams and unguents which he bought, with characteristic extravagance, in such immense quantities from his perfumers, were applied so assiduously to his almost copper-coloured skin that it looked wax-like rather than youthful. His corsets and expertly cut clothes could not disguise the fact that he was extremely fat. His grey eyes were watery; the flesh beneath his chin sagged into the folds of his immensely high neckcloth.

'A most magnificent patron' After George IV's death at Windsor on 26 June 1830 and his burial in St George's Chapel, Windsor, on 15 July, obituarists had little good to say of this 'Leviathan of the *haut ton*'. *The Times* on 29 June 1830 went so far as to suggest that 'there never was an individual less regretted by his fellow-creatures than this deceased King', who was as roundly condemned for his 'most reckless, unceasing and unbounded prodigality' as he was for his 'indifference to the feelings of others'.

This assessment of the character and career of George IV prevailed throughout the nineteenth century: his biographer in the *Dictionary of National Biography*, J. A. Hamilton, lapidarily summed him up in terms of unmeasured condemnation:

> There have been more wicked kings in English history, but none so unredeemed by any signal greatness or virtue. That he was a dissolute and drunken fop, a spendthrift and a gamester, 'a bad son, a bad husband, a bad father, a bad subject, a bad monarch and a bad friend', that his word was worthless and his courage doubtful, are facts which cannot be denied, and though there may be exaggerations in the scandals which were current about him, and palliation for his vices in an ill-judged education and overpowering temptations, there was not in his character any of that staple of worth which tempts historians to revise and correct a somewhat too emphatic contemporary condemnation.

Hamilton's view that 'in substance this is likely to be the judgement of posterity' has proved in the long run to be too harsh: George IV has, it is true, been much neglected by historians (with the exception of the magnificent, multi-volume edition of his correspondence by Arthur Aspinall), but his personal life has been a focus of popular interest (including a BBC serial in 1979), and the period which bears his name has inspired countless works of romantic fiction. It is, however, among art historians and students of patronage that his reputation has been rehabilitated.

Very few of the king's contemporaries saw fit to give thanks for the treasures which had been bestowed upon the nation by this greatest royal patron since Charles I, and which were his true memorial. Friend of Walter Scott, patron of Jane Austen and Robert Southey, bestower of knighthoods upon Humphry Davy, William Herschel, and William Congreve, George IV had enthusiastically encouraged John Nash in his development of Regent Street and Regent's Park. He had bought fine works by Rembrandt and Rubens, Dou, Steen, and De Hooch, and had welcomed Canova to London and immediately commissioned sculptures from him; he had also commissioned paintings from almost every commendable British artist of the day, including Gainsborough and Reynolds, Stubbs and Beechey, Hoppner, Cosway, and Constable. In opening his collections to public view he had declared that he had not formed them for his 'own pleasure alone' but 'to gratify the public taste' (Buckingham, 1.277). At the same time he had been largely instrumental in establishing the National Gallery in Trafalgar Square.

George IV persuaded the government to build a splendid palace on the site of his parents' relatively modest Buckingham House, and had insisted that John Nash be appointed its architect; and, at even greater cost, he had supervised the transformation of Windsor Castle by Jeffry Wyatville into one of the most distinctive monuments in the world, becoming so absorbed in the work that, as the duke of Wellington complained, he appeared 'not to be the least interested in public affairs' (*Journal of Mrs Arbuthnot*, 1.295). Yet, in the end, the duke was forced to recognize that, tiresome and evasive as the king was when political matters had to be discussed, the nation would always have cause to be grateful to a man who had been 'a most magnificent patron of the arts in this country, and in the world'. Moreover, with the king's bad qualities went many good: 'he was, indeed, the most extraordinary compound of talent, wit, buffoonery, obstinacy and good feeling' that the duke had seen in any character in his life (*A Portion of the Journal Kept by Thomas Raikes*, 1, 1856, 92).

CHRISTOPHER HIBBERT

Sources C. Hibbert, *George IV, 1: Prince of Wales* (1972) · C. Hibbert, *George IV, 2: Regent and king* (1973) · *The correspondence of George, prince of Wales, 1770–1812*, ed. A. Aspinall, 8 vols. (1963–71) · *The letters of King George IV, 1812–1830*, ed. A. Aspinall, 3 vols. (1938) · *The Greville memoirs, 1814–1860*, ed. L. Strachey and R. Fulford, 8 vols. (1938) · *The Creevey papers*, ed. H. Maxwell, 2 vols. (1903) · *The diaries of a duchess: extracts from the diaries of the first duchess of Northumberland (1716–1776)*, ed. J. Greig (1926) · *Court and private life in the time of Queen Charlotte, being the journals of Mrs Papendiek*, ed. V. D. Broughton, 2 vols. (1887) · *The autobiography and correspondence of Mary Granville, Mrs Delany*, ed. Lady Llanover, 1st ser., 3 vols. (1861); 2nd ser., 3 vols. (1862) · J. Brooke, *George III* (1972) · *The journal of Mrs Arbuthnot, 1820–1832*, ed. F. Bamford and the duke of Wellington [G. Wellesley], 2 vols. (1950) · C. Langdale, *Memoirs of Mrs Fitzherbert* (1856) · *The historical and the posthumous memoirs of Sir Nathaniel William Wraxall, 1772–1784*, ed. H. B. Wheatley, 5 vols. (1884) · *Diaries and correspondence of James Harris, first earl of Malmesbury*, ed. third earl of Malmesbury [J. H. Harris], 4 vols. (1844) · *The private letters of Princess Lieven to Prince Metternich, 1820–1826*, ed. P. Quennell (1937) · E. Law, Lord Ellenborough, *A political diary, 1828–1830*, ed. Lord Colchester, 2 vols. (1881) · *Life and letters of Sir Gilbert Elliot, first earl of Minto, from 1751 to 1806*, ed. countess of Minto [E. E. E. Elliot-Murray-Kynynmound], 3 vols. (1874) · *The Croker papers: the correspondence and diaries of … John Wilson Croker*, ed. L. J. Jennings, 3 vols. (1884) · duke of Buckingham, *Memoirs of the court of George IV*, 2 vols. (1859) · J. Derry, *The regency crisis and the whigs, 1788–9* (1963) · R. Fulford, *George IV* (1935) · P. Fitzgerald, *George IV*, 2 vols. (1881) · *The reminiscences and recollections of Captain Gronow*, 2 vols. (1892) · S. Leslie, *Life and letters of Mrs Fitzherbert*, 2 vols. (1939–40) · J. Richardson, *George IV: a portrait* (1966) · S. David, *The prince of pleasure: George IV and the making of the regency* (1998) · J. Prebble, *The king's jaunt: George IV in Scotland, August 1822* (1988) · *Third report*, HMC, 2 (1872) · Royal Arch.

Archives BL, establishment book, Add. MS 44843 · Royal Arch., corresp. and papers | Archives, Sheffield, letters to Earl Fitzwilliam · BL, corresp. with Lord Bathurst, loan 57 · BL, letters to Charles James Fox, Add. MSS 47560, 47601, 51457 · BL, corresp. with Lord Grenville, Add. MSS 58865–58867 · BL, corresp. with Lord Holland, Add. MSS 51520–51521 · BL, corresp. with Princess Leiven, Add. MS 47347 · BL, corresp. with Lord Liverpool, loan 72 · BL, corresp. with Lord North, Add. MS 51518 · BL, corresp. with Sir Robert Peel, Add. MSS 40299–40300 · BL, letters to Lord Spencer · BL, corresp. with Charles Philip Yorke, Add. MS 45035 · Chatsworth House, Derbyshire, letters to the duke of Devonshire · CUL, corresp. with Spencer Perceval · Devon RO, corresp. with Lord Sidmouth · Hove Central Library, letter to Mrs Fitzherbert · Lambton Park, letters to Lord Durham · NA Scot., corresp. with Lord Melville · NRA, priv. coll., letters to Lord Eldon · priv. coll., letters to Sir Walter Farquhar · priv. coll., corresp. with Spencer Perceval, etc. · PRO, letters to Lord Keith, PRO 30/70 · RA, corresp. with Thomas Lawrence · Royal Arch., letters to George III · Strand, London, Coutts MSS · Stratfield Saye House, Hampshire, Wellington MSS · U. Durham L., corresp. with Lord Grey · U. Southampton L., letters to the duke of Wellington · Warks. CRO, Ragley MSS · Warks. CRO, corresp. with Lord Hugh Seymour · Leeds, Canning MSS

Likenesses A. Ramsay, group portrait, oils, *c*.1764 (*Queen Charlotte with her two eldest sons*), Royal Collection · R. Brompton, oils, *c*.1770, Royal Collection · J. Zoffany, double portrait, oils, *c*.1770 (with Prince Frederick), Royal Collection · J. Zoffany, group portrait, oils, 1770 (*George III, Queen Charlotte and their six eldest children*), Royal Collection · B. West, double portrait, oils, 1777 (with Prince Frederick), Royal Collection · R. Cosway, miniature on ivory, *c*.1780–1782, NPG · T. Gainsborough, oils, 1782, Royal Collection · T. Gainsborough, oils, exh. RA 1782, Waddesdon Manor, Buckinghamshire · G. Stubbs, oils, *c*.1782, Royal Collection · J. Reynolds, oils, exh. RA 1785, Tate collection · C. Lochée, Wedgwood medallion, 1787, Castle Museum, Nottingham · J. Reynolds, oils, exh. RA 1787, Arundel Castle, West Sussex · C. J. Robinson, group portrait, oils, 1787 (*The fencing match between the chevalier de Saint George and the chevalier D'Éon*), Royal Collection · C. J. Robinson, oils, 1787, Royal Collection · J. Sayers, etching, pubd 1788 (after his earlier work), NPG · M. Brown, oils, *c*.1789–1791, Royal Collection · R. Dighton, oils, *c*.1790, Royal Collection · J. Barry, etching and line engraving, pubd 1791 (after his oil mural, 1777–84), NG Ire. · G. Stubbs, oils, 1791, Royal Collection · R. Cosway, miniature on ivory, 1792, NPG · J. Gillray, coloured etching, 1792 (*A voluptuary under the horrors of digestion*), NPG · J. Russell, oils, exh. RA 1792, Royal Collection · H. de Jauvry, miniature, 1793, NPG · W. Beechey, portrait, *c*.1794, Royal Collection · J. Hoppner, oils, exh. RA 1796, Royal Collection · W. Beechey, group portrait, oils, 1797–8 (*George III at a review*), Royal Collection · W. Beechey, oils, 1803, Royal Collection · T. R. Poole, wax medallion, 1804, Royal Collection · J. Hoppner, oils, *c*.1807, Walker Art Gallery, Liverpool · J. J. Copley, equestrian group portrait, exh. RA 1810, Museum of Fine Arts, Boston · W. Say, mezzotint, pubd 1812 (after J. Hoppner), BM, NPG · T. Lawrence, oils, *c*.1814, NPG · P. Fischer, miniature on ivory, 1815 (after T. Lawrence), NPG · J. Nollekens, marble bust, 1815 (after model, *c*.1807), Belvoir Castle, Leicestershire · T. Wyon junior, Waterloo medal and ribbon, 1815 (after T. Lawrence), NPG · etching, pubd 1815 (after unknown artist), BM, NPG · T. Lawrence, oils, exh. RA 1818, NG Ire. · J. L. Marks, engraving, pubd 1820 (*How to get unmarried*),

NPG • Irish school, line with watercolour, pubd c.1820 (after Irish school), NG Ire. • H. Brocas the elder?, stipple, pubd c.1821 (after his earlier work), NG Ire. • T. Lawrence, oils, 1821, Royal Collection • S. W. Reynolds, mezzotint, pubd 1821, BM, NPG • bronze bust, c.1821, Royal Collection • W. Bain, bronze medal, 1822, Scot. NPG • W. Bain, copper medal, 1822, Scot. NPG • W. Bain, silver gilt, 1822 (*George IV's visit to Edinburgh, 1822*), Scot. NPG • T. Lawrence, oils, 1822, Wallace Collection, London [*see illus.*] • D. Wilkie, group portrait, pencil and watercolour drawing, 1822 (*An incident during the visit of George IV to Edinburgh, 1822*), Scot. NPG • D. Wilkie, portrait, 1822, Royal Collection • English school, lithograph, pubd 1822 (after drawing by T. Hammond), NG Ire. • pewter medal, 1822, Scot. NPG • D. Wilkie, group portrait, oils, 1822–30 (*The entrance of George IV at Holyrood House*), Royal Collection • D. Dighton, watercolour on paper, 1823 (*The entrance of George IV into Edinburgh, 14 Aug 1822*), Scot. NPG • T. Woolnoth, stipple prints, pubd 1823 (after A. Wivell), BM, NPG • T. Lupton, mezzotint, pubd 1824 (after A. Wivell the elder), NG Ire. • S. W. Reynolds, mezzotint, pubd 1825 (after F. Chantrey), BM; NPG • F. Chantrey, marble bust, 1826–30, Royal Collection • J. Phillips, engraving, pubd 1827 (*The king commander in chief*), NPG • W. Turner de Lond, oils, c.1828, Scot. NPG • plaque, plaster replica, 1829 (after F. Chantrey), Scot. NPG • F. Chantrey, bronze equestrian statue, 1834, Trafalgar Square, London; commissioned by the king in 1829 • F. Chantrey, sketches, NPG • R. Cosway, miniature, Royal Collection • D. Dighton, watercolour on paper (*The procession of George IV to Edinburgh Castle, 1822*), Scot. NPG • D. Dighton, watercolour with some pencil, Scot. NPG • C. Doyle, satirical drawings, BM • P. Fischer, miniature, NPG • W. Hamilton, group portrait, oils (*The marriage of George, prince of Wales, 1795*), Royal Collection • G. Jones, group portrait, oils (*The banquet at the coronation of George IV, 1821*), Royal Collection • R. J. Lane, lithograph (after T. Lawrence), BM, NPG • T. Lawrence, oils, Windsor • T. Lawrence, oils, Scot. NPG • studio of T. Lawrence, oils, NPG • T. Lawrence, unfinished oil painting, NPG • T. R. Poole, double portrait, wax relief (with duke of York), NPG • J. Rogers, mixed-method engraving (after A. Huffam), NPG • L. Sailliar, stipple (after R. Cosway), NG Ire. • W. Turner de Lond, oils (*George IV, king of England, entering Dublin, 1821*), NG Ire. • double portrait, silhouette (with duke of York), NPG • English school, lithograph (after T. Hammond), NG Ire. • mezzotints, BM, NPG • watercolour, Scot. NPG

George V (1819–1878), king of Hanover, was born George Frederick Alexander Charles Ernest Augustus in Berlin on 27 May 1819, and was thus three days younger than his cousin, Queen Victoria. He was the only child of *Ernest Augustus (fifth son of George III), first duke of Cumberland and Teviotdale (1771–1851), and his wife, Friederike Caroline Sophia Alexandrina of Solms-Braunfels (1778–1841). Ernest Augustus succeeded his brother, William IV, as King Ernst August of Hanover in 1837. Most of Prince George's boyhood was spent at Kew where, in March 1833, he lost the sight of both eyes after an unexplained accident. On 18 February 1843 he married Princess Marie Alexandrina (1818–1878), daughter of Joseph, duke of Saxe-Altenburg. They had a son and two daughters. Prince George acceded to the throne of Hanover upon his father's death, on 18 November 1851, whereupon he also became second duke of Cumberland and Teviotdale in the British peerage.

Bismarck, received in audience two years later, left a vivid, pitiless account in his memoirs of the blind king's handling of government business, without a minister in attendance, in a study 'littered with every imaginable kind of public and private papers'. In 1866 loyalty to the German confederation made George V side with Austria and oppose Prussia in the contest for German primacy. He was present when his troops repelled the Prussians at Langensalza but, within a few days, his kingdom was overrun and he escaped to Austria. From Hietzing he protested in vain at Prussia's annexation of Hanover and the sequestration of his estates. He never abdicated.

The king's last years were spent in Paris, the tedium of exile relieved by the pleasures of music; he died there suddenly on 12 June 1878, after a drive through the Bois de Boulogne. To avoid political embarrassment Queen Victoria had discouraged her cousin from settling in England but, as a prince of Great Britain, he was buried at St George's Chapel, Windsor, where his Garter banner had hung since 1835. His only son, Ernest Augustus William Adolphus George Frederick (1845–1923), resumed the title of duke of Cumberland and Teviotdale, as third duke; but as an officer in the Austrian army he was considered to have borne arms against the United Kingdom during the First World War, and lost his peerage in 1919 under the terms of the Titles Deprivation Act (1917).

ALAN PALMER, rev.

Sources E. Rosendahl, *König Georg V von Hannover* (1928) • G. M. Willis, ed., *Hannovers Schicksalsjahr 1866 im Briefwechsel König Georgs V mit der Königin Marie* (1966) • A. Palmer, *Crowned cousins: the Anglo-German royal connection* (1985) • Burke, *Peerage* • GEC, *Peerage*

George V (1865–1936), king of Great Britain, Ireland, and the British dominions beyond the seas, and emperor of India, was born at Marlborough House, London, on 3 June 1865, the second child of the prince and princess of Wales, later *Edward VII (1841–1910) and Queen *Alexandra (1844–1925). He was baptized at Windsor Castle on 7 July by the names of George Frederick Ernest Albert. The prince's elder brother, Prince *Albert Victor Christian Edward (later duke of Clarence), was, after his father, heir to the throne should Queen Victoria die. Though much beloved in the family, Prince Albert Victor had a variety of difficulties which encouraged his parents to bring Prince George to the fore. From an early stage George was the dominant of the two brothers. The prince of Wales was determined to avoid for his sons the over-pressured intellectual education which he had been required to undergo, especially as he was aware in his own case of its lack of success. The family was based chiefly at Sandringham, and from an early age George acquired the values of the Norfolk squirearchy which so moulded his contribution to the British monarchy in the twentieth century. The boys' tutor from 1871 was the Revd John Neale Dalton (1839–1931), with whom Prince George formed a close, if sometimes awkward, bond which lasted much of his life; on his marriage he made Dalton his domestic chaplain. Dalton's chief responsibility was to educate the heir to the throne, and the lessons to which Prince George accompanied his brother were directed to that end. Dalton was not as heavy-handed as some of the prince of Wales's tutors had been, and he was not being constantly urged by the parents to make his pupils work. With Queen Victoria keeping a distant but characteristically watchful eye, Dalton gave his charges a limited education: exceptionally among European royalty, the future George V could barely

George V (1865–1936), by Sir John Lavery, 1913 [*The Royal Family at Buckingham Palace, 1913*; left, with (left to right) Princess Mary, Edward, prince of Wales, and Queen Mary]

speak French or German, and could not read those languages.

An active seaman From an early stage Prince George was intended for the navy. It was clear that Prince Albert Victor could not do without him, and in 1877 the two boys were sent to HMS *Britannia*, the Royal Navy's training ship, with Dalton in attendance. This was followed, again with Dalton on board, by three years in HMS *Bacchante*, captained by Lord Charles Scott, in which the princes went round the world (1880–82); this was the third of their three voyages on the *Bacchante*, the first being to the West Indies (1879), the second to Spain and Ireland (1880). In an age when naval disasters were almost commonplace, placing both male heirs in one ship was a risk (as the cabinet pointed out), and indeed between South Africa and Australia the *Bacchante* was adrift rudderless for several days and several members of the crew were killed. The toughness of the conditions gave Prince George a point of reference to which he returned throughout his life. No member of the royal family had been exposed to such harsh physical and mental conditions since the youth of William IV. The voyage was recorded in *The Cruise of HMS Bacchante, 1879–1882* (2 vols., 1886), which Dalton presented as being edited by himself from the journals and letters of the princes, but was in fact largely his own work (Nicolson, *King George*, 20). On their return the princes were confirmed by Archbishop Tait in Whippingham church on 8 August in the presence of Queen Victoria. George throughout his life was a middle-of-the-road Anglican.

Thus far, Prince George had been with his brother and

tutor. In 1883 his naval career and independence advanced when as a sub-lieutenant he was posted to HMS *Canada* sailing in the north Atlantic; during this posting he visited Canada, where his Aunt Louise was wife of the governor-general (Lord Lorne), and on his return he was made KG by Queen Victoria. He then attended the Royal Naval College, Greenwich, and HMS *Excellent*, the shore-based school at Portsmouth, to complete his training. *Excellent's* captain was J. A. Fisher, later the admiral. George failed his pilotage but passed the rest, being promoted lieutenant. Prince Albert Victor had begun a life of dissipation and, unlike his father, had given worrying signs of being unable to control its extent. In July 1889 Prince George took command of HMS *Torpedo Boat no. 75*, and in 1890 a gunboat, HMS *Thrush*, being promoted commander in August 1891. These were no token or chaperoned commands, and a royal prince in a naval command was necessarily in a very exposed position. Kenneth Rose notes: 'Soon after Prince George's twenty-first birthday, the smile disappears from his much photographed face, to be replaced by the familiar bearded stare that scarcely changed for the next half-century' (Rose, 19).

Duke of York and marriage In August 1891 Prince Albert Victor became engaged to Princess Mary of Teck in an arranged marriage (his own preference, Princess Hélène d'Orléans, having been turned down as a Roman Catholic). In November 1891 Prince George, usually of exemplary health except for seasickness, suffered a serious bout of typhoid. He had barely recovered when Prince Albert Victor died of influenza and pneumonia. On 14 January 1892 Prince George thus became the second in line to the throne and in due course was encouraged, especially by his grandmother, to propose to his dead brother's fiancée. He mourned his brother, with whom his youth had been so closely intertwined; but had Prince Albert Victor lived to ascend the throne in 1910 Prince George would have had the miserable role of trying to shield a hapless monarch from an unforgiving nation.

In 1892 the queen created Prince George duke of York, earl of Inverness, and Baron Killarney, and he took his seat in the House of Lords in June. His active naval career ended after a brief command of the cruiser *Melampus*, though he was promoted captain. He resisted the queen's wish that he should promote to first the last of his names, Albert. Almost wholly without direct political experience, he began the political round. His father, much more liberal on many topics than his grandmother, had taken care to insulate him from the extreme Unionism of Queen Victoria's court, and had even taken him and his brother to visit Gladstone in 10 Downing Street in August 1882 (when the Liberals were in exceptional royal disfavour). In February 1893 York dined with the aged premier, who found him 'not only likeable but perhaps loveable' (Gladstone, *Diaries*, 16 Feb 1893); George attended the introduction of the Government of Ireland Bill in February 1893, and with his father underwent the queen's fury when they acted as pallbearers at Gladstone's funeral in 1898. Both the atmosphere of the Wales's household and the naval context of the prince's early adult experience were much less politically partisan than the Conservative army circles to which his brother had been sent after his navy years.

On 3 May 1893 York became engaged to Princess Mary of Teck [see Mary (1867–1953)], their marriage in the Chapel Royal, St James's, following rapidly on 6 July. The Yorks settled happily into life on the Sandringham estate, where they lived in York Cottage. They quickly fulfilled their duty in perpetuating the succession, with the first of their six children born on 23 June 1894, the future *Edward VIII, known in the family as David, his seventh name. Sensitivity to the nations of the United Kingdom was shown by the inclusion of the names of all the patron saints in their first son's names. The Yorks had five more children in quick succession: Prince George [see George VI (1895–1952)]; Princess *Mary, later the princess royal; Prince *Henry William Frederick Albert, later duke of Gloucester (1900–1974); Prince *George Edward Alexander Edmund, later duke of Kent (1902–1942); and Prince John Charles Francis (1905–1919).

Within three years the fortunes of the house of Saxe-Coburg and Gotha had been transformed: the duke of York removed severe doubts as to the quality of the succession, and by his marriage and children provided a further generation of monarchs (in fact, through George VI, until 1952). These years, chiefly spent at Sandringham, were the calmest of the duke of York's life. Shooting was his chief pleasure, and he became one of the best shots in the empire. He enjoyed filling in his game book as much as his diary. In the 1890s he also developed his other major pastime, the collection of postage stamps. Though predecessors in the nineteenth century had begun the collection, the royal philatelic collection was in effect his creation. From 1906 he concentrated largely on the unused stamps of Britain and the empire, usually spending three afternoons a week on the collection; by the time of his death it comprised over a quarter of a million stamps in 325 volumes. From 1894 he was instructed in naval and constitutional history by J. R. Tanner, under whose guidance the prince made an abstract from Walter Bagehot's *English Constitution*, listing the crown's powers and obligations under the headings 'its *dignified* capacity' and 'its *business* capacity' (an interesting change from Bagehot's term, 'efficient'; Nicolson, *King George*, 62).

Despite the domesticity of these years, the duke's behaviour to his wife—then and subsequently—often seemed abrupt and off-hand. She, in turn, felt excluded from significant aspects of her husband's life. Neither of the Yorks found it easy to bring up small children. The duke failed to perceive that his wife's intelligence needed more than the simple respect he undoubtedly felt for her, or that she longed for something more than the country *longueurs* of Sandringham life. He failed to protect her from his relatives' jealousy. On the other hand, he was scrupulously and contentedly monogamous, and his wife never had to suffer the indignities of Queen Alexandra.

The duke of York was not expected to perform many duties, but in 1900 a journey to Australia was planned to open the new commonwealth parliament there. The death of Queen Victoria in January 1901 made York heir to the throne and the new king was reluctant for him to go. On A. J. Balfour's insistence the successful royal visit went ahead, the prince travelling as duke of Cornwall and York (the new dukedom having come with the duchy of Cornwall's income at the time of his father's succession). The duke, with the duchess, travelled via Aden, Ceylon, and Singapore and opened the Australian parliament in Melbourne on 9 May 1901. The royal party then visited Brisbane and Sydney, and then New Zealand. They next went to Mauritius and South Africa, where the duke presented medals (the Second South African War was still being fought). Canada was reached on 16 September and was crossed and recrossed by the Canadian Pacific Railway. This was much the most substantial imperial tour hitherto made by a future monarch and its timing at the start of the century was appropriate, for it pointed to what for the next hundred years was to be a principal duty of the monarchy.

Prince of Wales On his return to Britain the duke was met by Edward VII, and on 9 November 1901 was created prince of Wales and earl of Chester. On 5 December the prince caught the national mood for the first time with his remarks at Guildhall: he reported that in the empire many thought 'that the old country must wake up'. (Often rendered 'Wake up, England!', this phrase became a hallmark of the prince's bluff, commonsensical manner.)

The prince was thirty-six when he became prince of Wales. His father's coronation was delayed by an operation, and the new prince was unlikely to spend as much time as heir apparent as his father (the longest-serving prince of Wales). The new reign was accompanied by vastly improved relations between the monarch and the heir apparent. Edward VII and the prince of Wales enjoyed close and friendly ties. On the prince's side, expression of affection was restricted by his natural reticence and by his respect for his father, but this was a restriction by the prince and not, as with Queen Victoria, an exclusion by the monarch. Edward VII ensured that his son saw important foreign dispatches and (from 1903) the daily telegrams. In due course he also saw cabinet papers. The prince of Wales's imperial experience was extended by a visit to India from 19 October 1905 to 8 May 1906. As with his father in 1875–6, he was struck by the complacent sense of superiority of many of the white civil servants, and on his return made a speech calling for 'a wider sympathy' on the part of the Indian Civil Service. On his return he also took an active interest in imperial defence and naval reform and was encouraged by his father to attend the House of Lords regularly. In the bitter dispute over naval policy, he took the side of Lord Charles Beresford against Sir John Fisher (thus differing from his father). Wales had visited Berlin in 1902 and in March 1908 returned thither. In July 1908 he again briefly visited Canada. He had quite frequent contacts with members of the Liberal cabinet, and became well known in high political circles for salty remarks at dinner parties, notably his comment that though he trusted H. H. Asquith he thought him 'not quite a gentleman' and, to the head of the Treasury, that he could not think how he could 'go on serving that damned fellow Lloyd George' (Rose, 71). Such comments were reported to Asquith and Lloyd George and, though not necessarily reflecting hostility to Liberalism, did not foster a constructive relationship. As king, he regretted having said them.

Early reign On Friday 6 May 1910 Edward VII died, his son having told him that his horse had won the 4.15 p.m. race at Kempton Park. The prince of Wales thus ascended the throne as George V, emperor of India, and his wife as Queen Mary. He was aged forty-four. He led the mourners at his father's funeral at Windsor—the last great gathering of international royalty before 1914. He ascended the throne more thoroughly prepared for his reign than his father or his grandmother had been for theirs, and the view often stated that he was a political novice had little substance. There was, however, an element of naïvety in his intellect, and he lacked the intellectual sharpness of his two predecessors. He also lacked their cosmopolitan character and European experience. However, he had an exceptional memory for figures and details, whether of uniforms, politics, or relations. He had always had difficulty with foreign languages, to the extent that his trips abroad were far less frequent than those of his father, in part because when in France or Germany he was expected to be able to speak in the relevant language. But he also had little interest in 'abroad': for George V, Norfolk was his emotional home in the sense that France had been for his father.

George V seemed scandal free, and in fact was domestically much the most respectable of British kings from George III until the accession of George VI. Yet his reign opened with an extraordinary episode, the prosecution in February 1911 for criminal libel of E. F. Mylius for the claims, stated in his article 'Sanctified bigamy', published in Paris in *Liberator*, that the new king was a bigamist with three children from a marriage in 1890 in Malta to Mary Culme-Seymour, daughter of Admiral Sir Michael Culme-Seymour. Mylius, who was repeating a rumour which had been in circulation in certain circles from the early 1890s, was found guilty and imprisoned for a year, and his attempt to subpoena the king was rejected. Sir John Simon, who as solicitor-general prosecuted the case, used the conclusion of the trial to make a strong statement of the king's innocence. The trial was well timed, encouraging popular support for the new king, who had clearly been wronged.

The king opened parliament for the first time on 6 February 1911, for which occasion the obligatory anti-Roman declaration of his protestant faith was statutorily amended to a simple declaration that he was a protestant and would uphold the protestant succession. His coronation by Randall Davidson, archbishop of Canterbury, was on 22 June 1911. In July the king and queen visited Ireland (his sole visit as monarch) and Scotland, and on 11 November they embarked for India for a great durbar held in Delhi on 12 December, the most spectacular ceremony in the history of the British empire. The king–emperor declared Delhi the new capital and laid its foundation-stone (soon after moved when New Delhi was re-sited). The durbar was followed by an elaborate shooting expedition in Nepal and a visit to Calcutta. The royal party reached Portsmouth on 5 February 1912. This was the first visit (other than to Mediterranean colonies) by a ruling British monarch to an imperial territory, and it completed the ceremonial inauguration of George V's reign.

Domestic politics George V's reign began at one of the few moments in the development of the modern British constitution when the powers of the crown, so often regarded as dormant, were required to be alive and active. The budget of 1909 had been rejected by the Lords, and the general election of January 1910 had been won by the Liberals, though now dependent on Irish and Labour support for their majority in the Commons. Asquith had opened his election campaign with a remark taken to mean that he had secured Edward VII's agreement to create peers if the Lords again resisted the budget, though the king had later made clear that he would require a further Liberal success at the polls before doing so. The Lords passed the budget on 28 April 1910 without a division, but the government was now moving forward with the Parliament Bill, intended to curtail the Lords' powers by statute. Asquith introduced the bill on 14 April with a rather opaque reference to the terms the government would request from the crown should a further general election on the Lords be necessary. Behind the parliament stood the question of Irish home rule and other constitutional reforms. Asquith, who was on holiday aboard the Admiralty yacht when Edward VII died, had been careful not to harry the king and to avoid pressing him into an alliance between the crown and the aristocracy of the sort many of the peers expected. He was likewise cautious about appearing to force the hand of George V—but the Parliament Bill was already making its way through the Commons, backed by a large majority of MPs.

Just before his death Edward VII had discussed with A. J. Balfour, the leader of the Unionist opposition, the possibility of Balfour's forming a government should Asquith resign if the king refused to appoint peers. This exchange was not revealed to George V until 1913. The new king initially had two private secretaries: Sir Arthur Bigge, who had been his secretary when prince of Wales, and Francis Knollys, Viscount Knollys, Edward VII's private secretary, whom George V appointed side by side with Bigge. Knollys, who withheld the exchange between Edward VII and Balfour from the king, was a well-known Liberal; Bigge's position was less well tried, but he was soon shown to be as Unionist as Knollys was Liberal. Asquith suggested private talks with the opposition, which began on 17 June 1910 and continued spasmodically until November, with no resolution of the central predicaments. On 11 November Asquith requested a dissolution of parliament, which the king granted. Three days later Asquith alarmed the king and his secretaries by requesting that George V 'should give guarantees *at once* for the next Parliament'

(Rose, 116). The king refused to give contingent guarantees. The cabinet sent a minute, ambiguous in certain respects but clear enough in its general drift, stating that in order to dissolve, it would require a private guarantee of royal action to support government policy (assuming a Liberal government was again supported by a majority in the Commons). Knollys supported the cabinet's request; Bigge urged the king to reject it. On 16 November the king 'agreed most reluctantly to give the cabinet a secret understanding … I disliked having to do this very much, but agreed that this was the only alternative to the Cabinet resigning, which at this moment would be disastrous' (George V's diary, Rose, 121).

If George V had known of Balfour's possible willingness to take office in such circumstances, he might have acted differently. If he had, he would have placed the monarchy in a perilous position. Bigge's recommendation, that the king decline his cabinet's advice on a central and well-matured constitutional question, would similarly have placed the monarchy at the centre of political controversy. George V long resented the cabinet's treatment of him, but that his government needed a guarantee that he would follow its advice was as much a comment on the monarchy as on the cabinet with its large Commons majority—a majority which the election of December 1910 confirmed. Asquith continued to give the king as much elbow room as he could and, when the Lords passed wrecking amendments to the Parliament Bill in July 1911, agreed to the king's request not to be required to create peers immediately but to allow a further negotiation between the two houses. The king's pledge was made public, so that the peers should have full knowledge of the consequence of their actions. On 7 August, at the king's request, Lord Crewe said in the Lords that the king's guarantee was given in November only with 'natural and legitimate reluctance', a remark which was taken by the last-ditch peers as encouraging. Lord Morley made it clear on 10 August, the day of the vote, that the king definitely would create peers if the bill was defeated: it passed by seventeen votes.

One purpose of the Parliament Act was to enable the passing of a Government of Ireland Bill. In 1912 the Liberals duly brought forward the third Home Rule Bill, which was rejected by the Lords in January 1913. On 9 June 1913 Asquith again introduced the bill in the Commons and the process for passing it under the Parliament Act began. In September 1911 Andrew Bonar Law replaced Balfour as Unionist leader and astonished the king in May 1912 by asserting that, as the Lords had lost its power of permanent veto and had moreover not been reformed (as the Parliament Act intended), the king's personal veto (dormant since the reign of Queen Anne) had again become an efficacious arm of the constitution. Bonar Law's implication was that Unionists expected the king to use his veto to prevent the enactment of the bill once passed under the Parliament Act. This was a desperate move on the part of Bonar Law and reflected the Unionist view that they dictated British affairs whether they could gain a majority in the Commons or not. The king was of course under no obligation to seek or take advice from an opposition leader, but the Unionists' attempt to use the monarch in this way greatly angered and distressed the king.

In February 1913 the king retired Knollys, leaving himself with Stamfordham (as Bigge had become) as his private secretary. This was a dangerous move, for Stamfordham's Unionism was becoming, if anything, more strident. Asquith countered the influence of Bonar Law and Stamfordham—embodied in memoranda from the king to Asquith of 11 August and 23 September 1913 in effect putting the Unionist case for a dissolution of parliament—by a memorandum of his own reminding the king of his constitutional relationship to his ministers. In return, the king reminded Asquith that as head of the army the sovereign could not avoid concern about the possibility of civil strife in Ireland. He also returned to the suggestion he had made earlier of a conference at which he would try to ensure that the opposition acted 'in a reasonable and conciliatory spirit'.

During his visit to Balmoral in October 1913 Asquith proposed to Bonar Law that there be a conference. A variety of conversations were held between October and January 1914. George V was personally much upset by the 'Curragh mutiny' in March 1914, especially, perhaps, because his requests to Asquith to exclude Ulster from the Home Rule Bill had had some success, and the 'mutiny' thus, if anything, made the exclusion of Ulster from the bill more difficult. The king played a part in the process by which the government, on its side, accepted that home rule could not apply to the whole of Ireland; the opposition, for its part, accepted that home rule for much of Ireland was inevitable. The king hoped this gradual convergence could be consolidated by a conference held at Buckingham Palace from 21 July. The king attended the opening session and privately encouraged all parties. Such direct monarchical political involvement was unprecedented since the reign of George III. The curious mixture of formal powers and informal commission of those powers to the cabinet—what F. W. Maitland called 'our careful conservation of forms'—made a degree of royal involvement unavoidable. The various parties, by the time the conference ended inconclusively on 24 July, were in fact close to agreement, with the definition of boundaries the outstanding issue, and it cannot be known if civil war would have followed the enactment of the statute accompanied by an amending act: though as Stamfordham remarked 'It is obvious that Civil War cannot be permitted on the subject of the delimitation of a county' (Rose, 157).

George V's unavoidable involvement in the political and constitutional crisis of 1910 until the outbreak of war in August 1914 was by a long distance the most testing constitutional experience for a British monarch since the early years of the reign of George III. George V played his part manfully. In strict interpretation of the constitution, as Asquith implied, he leaned too far towards the Unionists (and he was reluctant to see that the Parliament Act eased the role of the monarch). But the extent to which Unionism had been institutionalized in the armed forces, the army, and the House of Lords meant that the king could not avoid responding, more than his prime minister, to so powerful a force.

The First World War The constitutional crisis of 1909 to 1914 had shown the king to be an active and needed element in the resolution of political difficulties. He was much less active than his father or grandfather in foreign affairs. He had entertained the Kaiser at the opening of the Victoria memorial in the Mall in May 1911 (the king was so pleased with it that he drew his sword and knighted the architect, Sir Thomas Brock, on the spot), on which occasion Wilhelm II mentioned in passing possible German action in Morocco and later claimed that the king's courteous but uncritical reply constituted British acceptance of the German initiative. In 1913 George V visited Berlin for the marriage of the Kaiser's daughter, a private family occasion, at which the tsar of Russia was also present.

In 1914 the European-wide connection of Queen Victoria's descendants was able to play little part in avoiding war. Indeed family relationships were as much a hindrance as a help. On 28 July 1914 Prince Henry of Prussia told his brother, the Kaiser, that at Buckingham Palace on 26 July George V had told him 'We shall try all we can to keep out of this and shall remain neutral'; the king's memorandum of the conversation notes that he told Prince Henry: 'I hope we shall remain neutral' (Nicolson, *King George*, 245–6). Ever prone to exaggeration, the Kaiser made more of this than it deserved, but in the context of the delicate negotiations about Britain's reaction to an invasion of Belgium, it was not a helpful conversation. On Saturday 1 August Asquith woke the king at 1.30 a.m. to ask him to approve a direct appeal for restraint to the tsar. Next day the king showed a sharp appreciation of the likely course of events: 'At this moment public opinion here is dead against our joining in the War but I think it will be impossible to keep out of it as we cannot allow France to be smashed' (Rose, 168). On 4 August he noted: 'Warm, showers and windy ... I held a Council at 10.45 to declare War on Germany, it is a terrible catastrophe but it is not our fault' (ibid.).

George V was well placed to respond to the extraordinary course of the First World War. Like his prime minister, Asquith, he was intent on both winning the war and maintaining the peacetime values which the British believed they were fighting to safeguard. The king normally wore uniform during the war and resided in Buckingham Palace, his lifestyle, never extravagant, being even more frugal than usual. He was eager to encourage, and in the course of the war made 450 visits to troops, 300 to hospitals, and almost as many to shipyards and munitions factories. He initially signed all officers' commissions, though this soon became impossible, and he personally gave 50,000 awards for gallantry. He first visited the western front in December 1914. During a visit to the First Army at Labuissière the king was thrown by the mare he was riding, fractured his pelvis, and suffered severely from pain and shock. The injuries, and his need to recover quickly from them so as to resume his role, left a lasting strain. Given his naval experience, the king was a skilful

visitor to forces in the field. His lack of bombast, his straightforward manner, and his able appreciation of military positions were unusual and attractive qualities. As was already the case with the sons of a number of cabinet members, the king's son Prince Albert (later George VI) was a serving officer and saw action in HMS *Collingwood* at the battle of Jutland in May 1916. That the royal family was thus directly committed was an important bond between George V and his people. (As heir to the throne, the prince of Wales was not permitted to serve in a fighting capacity, but he was an energetic presence as a non-combatant officer on the western front.)

George V was already accustomed, in the various meetings between politicians in 1910–14, to working together with both party leaderships. He was good at encouraging his ministers—an important support for men isolated and working in a quite unprecedented and exceptionally stressful context. He came to value Asquith's qualities more than in peacetime. Perhaps surprisingly, he found Lloyd George's effervescent enthusiasm initially attractive, and was drawn by him into declaring what became known as the 'king's pledge' of teetotalism from 6 April 1915. He encouraged Asquith when forming a coalition government in May 1915 to create a separate Ministry of Munitions under Lloyd George.

A German on the throne? The need to accept the replacement of his first cousin by marriage, Prince Louis of Battenberg, as first sea lord in October 1914 had early alerted the king to the problems of xenophobia; but many felt his reluctance to remove the eight enemy knights of the Garter from the Garter roll went too far the other way (they were struck off in May 1915, though their brass plates in St George's Chapel remained). George V reluctantly agreed that the titles of foreign members of the royal family should be considered by the Bryce committee of the House of Lords on foreign titles. This led to the Titles Deprivation Act of 1917, though the titles were not actually removed until March 1919, after the war had ended. Allied to this question, and at a time when the monarchy was being widely criticized in early 1917, was the name of the Saxe-Coburg dynasty (as the royal house was conventionally if erroneously called—the College of Heralds in 1917 was unable to provide a certain name). George V spoke English with no foreign accent (the first monarch since 1830 to do so) and resented aspersions on his patriotism. Yet he recognized the problem and on 17 July 1917, by royal proclamation approved by the privy council, the king announced that all descendants of Queen Victoria should bear the name of Windsor. He also renounced for himself and his successors further use of the titles of princes of Saxe-Coburg and Gotha, but not the succession to those duchies. At the same time he defined and limited the use of royal titles such as royal highness, prince, and princess.

In the same year, on the advice of Lord Esher, the king created the order of the Companion of Honour (with sixty-five members) and the Order of the British Empire; the latter had five classes, and in 1918 was divided into civil and military divisions. The Order of the British

Empire quickly established itself as a popular decoration, with its bottom two classes (officers and members) quite different in membership from the élitist tone of other orders and decorations. By the end of 1919 there were about 25,000 recipients, including trade unionists and syndicalists, some of them among the monarchy's critics. The order linked well to the democratic aspirations of post-war reconstruction, while at the same time playing on the traditional English liking for recognition of merit by according status: 'as a tool to instil deference and dish republicanism it was a masterstroke' (F. Prochaska, ed., *Republic of Britain*, 2000). Moreover, the inclusion of women in all classes, including the creation of the rank of dame to equal that of knight, was a striking innovation, anticipating the extension of the franchise to women in 1918.

Cautious, perhaps as a result of Unionist behaviour in 1910–14, the king was careful not to be drawn into Conservative criticism of Asquith or into the various political plots of 1916 against Asquith. In December 1916 the king noted in his diary that he accepted Asquith's resignation 'with great regret. … It is a great blow to me & will I fear buck up the Germans' (Nicolson, *King George*, 288). He then sent for Bonar Law, following one view of the precedents, and to Law's annoyance declined to agree to a dissolution until Law asked him in the capacity of prime minister (anticipating Law's request, the king had equipped himself with Haldane's advice). In circumstances of some confusion, on Balfour's advice the king called a conference of leading politicians of all British parties (including Labour) at Buckingham Palace on 6 December 1916. The upshot was that Law declined the king's offer, and the king then sent for Lloyd George, who formed a government which saw out the war.

The king found Lloyd George much less easy to deal with than Asquith as prime minister, and did not fall for his charm. Though he admired Lloyd George's energy he disliked his lack of method, which the king saw as epitomized by the prime minister's ceasing to provide handwritten reports of cabinet meetings and by the haphazard selection of printed cabinet minutes received from the new cabinet secretariat. Moreover, the king was drawn into military politics far more than before by his long-standing friendship with Douglas Haig, commander of the British armies in France. The king defended Haig. His defence of Haig was important and its effect was hard to measure, for royal support was almost always indirect and was very rarely directly challenged or even exposed. Even so, it should probably not be seen as critical to Haig's survival, which was the result not of royal support but of the absence of genuine prime ministerial determination to replace him.

Uncertainty about the tone of popular politics played an important part in George V's reaction to the suggestion that Britain offer a place of refuge to the Russian royal family, following the tsar's abdication in March 1917. Initially, the king did not demur to his cabinet's suggestion to respond favourably to a request from the provisional government, but soon, strongly encouraged by Stamfordham, he requested Balfour as foreign secretary to withdraw the offer, and the British ambassador was instructed to say nothing more, with the implication that a further request would be rejected (though a number of Russian princes were rescued by cruiser). The king attended the tsar's memorial service in July, and apparently never regretted his judgement in this matter. In his biography Kenneth Rose believed this may have been because he had not been as inactive or hostile as appeared, perhaps encouraging unsuccessful plans for the British Secret Service to effect a rescue.

George V found it difficult to maintain his spirits about the war. Affected by his accident, worried about his children, wearied by the constant slaughter, he was observed to have aged. This was hardly surprising as, unlike his ministers and generals who were from time to time replaced, he was the only person in British politics in the same position at the end of the war as at its start, and was almost the only monarch in Europe to retain his throne.

The king visited the front twice in 1918, first in March–April to encourage troops facing the start of the formidable German spring offensive, and again on 7 August 1918, the day when the British army at last broke through the German line and the war was in effect won. On 11 November, the day of the armistice, the king wrote in his diary: 'Today has indeed been a wonderful day, the greatest in the history of the Country' (Rose, 222).

Post-war politics The armistice celebrations were a brief caesura for George V. He and the queen appeared on the balcony of Buckingham Palace, the noise too great for his intended speech to be heard. On five successive days they drove through the streets of London and attended various formal celebrations in St Paul's Cathedral and at Westminster, with similar ceremonies a little later in Edinburgh. The king reviewed disabled soldiers and sailors in Hyde Park and the fleet in the Firth of Forth. In November he visited Paris (where one of the main boulevards was named after him) and on 19 November he addressed both houses of parliament. He received President Wilson of the USA in London in December. The king and queen's return to Sandringham was saddened by the death, following an epileptic attack, of their youngest son, Prince John, on 18 January 1919. Post-war ceremonials were completed by a victory parade in London on 19 July 1919, after the peace treaties had been signed and a national act of remembrance established in November 1919, the king supporting the suggestion of two minutes' silence at 11 a.m. on 11 November. On 11 November 1920 the king unveiled Lutyens's cenotaph in Whitehall and walked to Westminster Abbey for the burial of the Unknown Soldier.

The king failed to persuade Lloyd George not to request an immediate general election, which was requested the week before the armistice; this was the start of a tetchy peacetime relationship, soon exacerbated by Lloyd George's failure to consult the king about his plan for a trial of the Kaiser. The king faced the prospect of losing a significant part of his kingdom through the secession of the Irish Free State—the first such loss of territory to the

English crown since the Danes were expelled in the ninth century—though the king helped to keep the free state within the empire as a dominion. The king personally on 22 June 1921 opened the first session of the Northern Ireland parliament, established in Belfast by the Government of Ireland Act (1920). His speech, drafted by E. W. M. Grigg and influenced by General Smuts, contained eirenic comments with respect to Ireland as a whole and expressed the hope that the south of Ireland would establish the reciprocal parliament provided for in the act. However, the time had passed for Ulster to be offered as a role model for the rest of Ireland. In July 1921 the king was reported as having told Lord Northcliffe with respect to the British government and the activities of British troops in Ireland: Lloyd George 'must come to some agreement with them [the Irish]. This thing cannot go on. I cannot have my people killed in this manner' (Nicolson, *King George*, 347; Rose, 240). Apparent royal intervention on such a subject caused a sensation: the interview was forsworn by Wickham Steed, the editor of *The Times*, and by Lloyd George in the Commons on behalf of the king. In fact the interview was less of a fabrication than was made out at the time, and the king was distressed at the slow resolution of the Irish question (*History of The Times*, vol. 4, pt 2, 806ff.; Rose, 241). A treaty establishing the Irish Free State as a dominion was signed on 6 December 1921. The king believed 'that now after seven centuries there may be peace in Ireland' (Nicolson, *King George*, 361), but in fact the treaty led to civil war.

George V's inclination at the end of the war was, like that of many of his wealthier subjects, for a 'return to normalcy'. He recognized that post-war austerity required an absence of display. His excellent system of intelligence (independent of the government's) alerted him to those elements of working-class opinion which criticized the monarchy as a way to advance a more general critique of the governing class. However, though recognizing that more appearances in working-class areas were desirable and though concerned at the potential impact on the monarchy of extensive unemployment, the king did not see this as the moment for any fundamental reconsideration of the monarchy's role. He even helped to restore some traditional but abandoned ceremonies, such as the distribution of Maundy money (brought back in 1921). Though he was not opposed to some pragmatic changes, the king and his secretary, Stamfordham, were ill-equipped for any such reconsideration (though Clive Wigram, the junior secretary, did have plans for closer relationships with the newspaper press, and a full-time press secretary was appointed in 1918, the position lapsing between 1931 and 1944).

One consequence of this was that the king was at the mercy of those, like Lloyd George, who had their own views and methods about uses to which the court might be put—namely the sale of political honours, each of which had to be bestowed with the king's personal encomium. The king was unable to counter Lloyd George's habit—unthinkable to earlier prime ministers—of offering titles without first having obtained royal approval.

The use of honours by Lloyd George and others in the post-war years was not wholly new, but its flagrant disregard for the usual niceties was new. The king protested about some of the proposed honours—such as the barony for William Vestey, of the meat-importing family, whose skill at evading income tax had become a matter of national comment—but he made little headway against the prime minister's will. Lloyd George's honours played on a national cult of snobbery which the king and his father, for all their rather egalitarian behaviour in private, had done nothing to diminish. The royal commission on honours was established partly as a result of the king's requests. On its recommendation the political honours scrutiny committee was set up as the Honours (Prevention of Abuses) Act passed in 1925, and honours in due course returned to their traditional decorum, at least as far as the public was aware.

Politics in the 1920s Lloyd George's resignation on 19 October 1922, following a meeting of Conservative MPs at the Carlton Club, brought to an end the complex manoeuvres of the wartime coalitions, but it began a series of important political decisions for George V, which he and Stamfordham handled adroitly. The king requested Bonar Law—not technically the Conservative leader (that being Austen Chamberlain, who had supported Lloyd George at the Carlton Club meeting)—to form a government which, after prevarication, he did. Bonar Law's reserved, matter-of-fact manner pleased the king, but ill health forced his resignation in May 1923. In circumstances almost as confusing as those surrounding the formation of the Lloyd George coalition in December 1916 (and with Balfour again playing an important role behind the scenes), the king asked Stanley Baldwin to form a government, which he successfully did. George V appears to have been guided by a simple rule: that, given the complex political circumstances of the time, the prime minister should be in the Commons. The good sense of this was seen in the next year, as the Labour Party came to the fore. To have had Lord Curzon as prime minister (the alternative to Baldwin and about whose personal qualities for the premiership the king probably had doubts, as did almost everyone except Curzon himself) might have made a delicate situation even more awkward.

Against the king's advice Baldwin obtained a dissolution in November 1923 and lost the consequent general election. It appeared to be for the king to decide who had won, for no party had an absolute majority, and Labour came second to the tories, and ahead of the Liberals. The king asked Baldwin to meet the new House of Commons without resigning. That Ramsay MacDonald became the first Labour prime minister was in fact largely Asquith's decision, for, in deciding not to support Baldwin, Asquith left MacDonald as the person whom the king would by precedent invite. A Labour government was also the outcome favoured by the king. He noted in his diary for 22 January 1924, the day of MacDonald's appointment: 'Today 23 years ago dear Grandmama died. I wonder what she would have thought of a Labour Government' (Rose,

326). That George V dealt amiably with a Labour government which was at least in intention socialist in its ideology was in part a tribute to his own quality of businesslike commonsense. It also marked Labour's moderation in approach, and the decline of Unionist partisanship by the court (eased by the loss of most of Ireland). Court society was by no means progressive in tone, but it had become, like the king, rather apolitically conservative, certainly relative to the last decades of Victoria's reign. Indeed, it would not be going too far to say that the king's behaviour in the 1920s showed considerable mistrust of the Conservatives' confidence that their party represented in some unique way the national interest. J. C. C. Davidson later recorded his view that the king 'was very right-wing and he knew where his friends really lay, and that the Conservative Party was the King's Party and a radical party was not', which was certainly how tories liked to see their relationship to the monarchy (*Memoirs of a Conservative*, 177). But George V was skilful at distinguishing between the conventional, slightly old-fashioned views which he personally held as to society and social behaviour, and the dangers of eliding social preferences with political positions. Moreover the king had concluded, he told Ramsay MacDonald in 1930, that the British had been 'fools ... not to have accepted Gladstone's Home Rule Bill' (Rose, 242); the basic premiss of Unionism since 1886 was thus, in George V's later view, fallacious. With much of Ireland lost to the United Kingdom, it was not surprising that he was cautious about a simple association of Unionism with the national interest.

MacDonald's minority government was short-lived, Asquith withdrawing support in October 1924. George V tried to avoid a general election, which might be as inconclusive as the last, but neither Asquith nor Baldwin would form another minority government. The election, fought in the context of the Zinoviev letter (of whose authenticity the king was sceptical), resulted in a substantial overall Conservative majority. 'I like him and have always found him quite straight' wrote the king of MacDonald when the latter resigned on 4 November 1924 (Nicolson, *King George*, 403). The accommodation of a Labour government into the processes of the British constitution looks easy in retrospect, but it was a considerable achievement on the king's part, among others, that friction was minimal. The king, though usually a stickler for dress conventions and court etiquette, proved easy-going on the question of court dress for his Labour privy councillors, a matter of considerable importance with respect to the public presentation of Labour in power.

The experience had considerable impact on a king and a court assumed to be Conservative in politics. Industrial relations were to play a significant role in Baldwin's government and the king, though suspicious of the practice of picketing, was very careful to distinguish the national interest from that of the government in his approach to the trade union question between 1925 and 1927.

The king was concerned at the deteriorating relations between employers and employees in the coalfields in 1925, and requested Baldwin by the autumn 'to put before the country some definite policy to deal with, and if possible avert, the dangerous state of things with which we shall otherwise be confronted in the coming winter' (Stamfordham to Baldwin, 12 June 1925, Nicolson, *King George*, 414). Baldwin's solution of July 1925—some financial assistance to the industry and a royal commission—prevented a strike at that time and was greeted with relief by the king, though not by Stamfordham, who regretted that the government had been driven into concession. Stamfordham fairly consistently took a harder line than the king, but this does not seem to have precluded an excellent inter-war working relationship between monarch and secretary. The existence of this difference of view, however, shows how far George V took his own line and stuck to it.

During the general strike in May 1926 the king stayed in London, receiving frequent bulletins on developments. He criticized the *British Gazette* (Churchill's emergency tabloid) for announcing that the armed forces would receive full support 'in any action ... to aid the Civil Power' (Nicolson, *King George*, 418), and at the end of the strike told the prime minister to beware of 'being rushed by some of his hot-headed colleagues into legislation which might have disastrous effects' (Barnes and Middlemas, 415), a remark which shows how successfully Baldwin had presented himself as the moderate leader of a belligerent cabinet, when in fact he himself directed the cabinet's policy.

The post-war empire Though George V set great store by the empire and valued its role in the war, he surprisingly did not visit its dominions and colonies after that war, though he sent the prince of Wales out to do so. His inability to complete the tour of the empire begun by the Indian visit after his coronation was initially because British politics were unstable, but this was less of an obstacle after the war. The prince's tours were extremely successful. Though the king disapproved of many of his son's egalitarian innovations, he perhaps felt that this was the sort of thing his imperial subjects expected, and which he certainly could not emulate.

Balfour's formula for imperial development and devolution was accepted by the Imperial Conference of 1926, confirmed by the conference of 1930, both of which the king hosted, and implemented by the Statute of Westminster in 1931. The changes involved the king in several ways. By the conference of 1926 and the statute, the royal title was modified (to the form stated at the head of this article) with the intention of providing a title usable in all parts of the empire (including Ireland). This was a relief to the king, who had dreaded the possibility that each dominion parliament might legislate individually on the royal title and succession. The title question continued to cause difficulties for the rest of his reign, with South Africa passing its own acts in 1934. Behind this question lay the complex matter of the dominions' relationship to the British government and crown—a matter especially raised with respect to the governor-generalship of Australia in 1930, when the Australian prime minister wished to make a direct recommendation of an Australian to the king. There was a real tension between imperial devolution and the wish of the British government and, on the whole, of the king, to act as a single power in such matters. As Nicolson observes, 'The resolutions of 1926 and 1930 and the Statute of Westminster itself left King George with a number of loose ends. He did not like loose ends' (Nicolson, *King George*, 488). The king's good relations with dominion representatives, over which he took considerable time, were important when imperial relations were evolving in the context of the British hope, successfully realized in 1939, that the dominions would still see themselves as part of a worldwide pattern of defence and foreign policy led and co-ordinated by the British.

Family and friends George V saw himself as a family man. Whereas the public had associated his father with cosmopolitan life tempered by scandal, and a wide circle of internationally known friends, George V seemed to embody the virtues of the Norfolk squirearchy from whose ranks several of his small group of cronies were drawn. Certainly the Sandringham estate, with Balmoral as a summer alternative, was where he felt most at ease. Yet accounts of the royal children's upbringing are closer to Rudyard Kipling's alarming stories of his own youth than to George V's cheery, sometimes even playful relationship with his easy-going father. Unlike Edward VII, George V did not particularly enjoy being king, and the sense of duty which kept him so assiduously at his boxes and his letter-writing informed his view of his children's development. Though he sensed the narrowness of his own naval education (undertaken, of course, when he was not expected to become king), he imposed the same tough regime on his sons as he himself had undergone, sending three of them (Edward VIII, George VI, and the duke of Kent) to the Royal Naval College at Osborne and then to Dartmouth (another, Henry, duke of Gloucester, went to preparatory school and Eton College, followed by Sandhurst, while John was educated at home). The absence of a chaperon tutor at Osborne and Dartmouth was a change from his own experience, allowing the boys a more 'normal' experience, but exposing them to bullying. On the other hand, the king rather abruptly sent his eldest son to Oxford University, as his father had been sent—though to Magdalen College rather than Christ Church—the experience proving as liberating for the future Edward VIII as it had been for the future Edward VII.

George V has received poor marks from historians for his record as a father: as Kenneth Rose remarks, he 'has passed into history as a heavy-handed father' (Rose, 305). Certainly, George V displayed little of his father's expansive affection, and he treated his children, even when adult, as naval ratings rather than as close relatives; gruff rebukes about errors of dress and punctuality were humiliatingly administered before cabinet ministers and courtiers. Though he was a very regular correspondent with his children, his letters sometimes read unfeelingly. On the other hand, as Frances Donaldson points out, the notion that George V was deliberately brutal towards his children is a fiction. The coldness they felt and the high early expectations that were required of them were not dissimilar to those recorded in scores of memoirs by children of the propertied classes reared in this period. A monarch, exceptionally, cannot choose for the heir to the throne an education simply to suit the personal needs and character of the child. Despite the absence of affection in their upbringing, both Edward VIII and George VI, in their very different ways, showed in their adult lives considerable public capacity. None of the children of George V and Queen Mary was problematic in the sense that Prince Albert Victor (George V's elder brother) or Prince Leopold (Edward VII's younger brother) had been.

Much more problematic was the king and queen's management of the succession, in a hereditary monarchy a vital responsibility of the monarch. George V was the last British monarch to experience a thoroughly managed marriage. His dependence on Queen Mary throughout their marriage was considerable, but the circumstances of his engagement to her could not be called those of romantic love (though, at least on his side, their relationship came to be so). The twentieth century brought an expectation on the part both of the public and of royalties that 'falling in love' would play a central part in royal marriages. The prince of Wales (later Edward VIII) fell in love, but not with someone who—as future king—he could marry, and George V died leaving the question of his successor's consort unknown, though his three other surviving sons made successful marriages to acceptable spouses. The king and queen's abrupt and censorious handling of the prince of Wales's relationships with married women was at the least unsympathetic. The consequence was that the prince told his parents as little as possible about his 'private' life, so they could not help him in his search for a wife and future queen.

During the 1920s George V recovered something of the bonhomie which many felt the war years had blunted. His middle-brow remarks became something of a hallmark of his peacetime reign, with the peppery comments which so often upset his offspring. When as a Royal Academician he was asked to sign Augustus John's diploma, he remarked: 'What, that fellow! I've a damned good mind not to sign it' (Rose, 318). The king knew his own reputation, and was probably not above adding to it. Many of his *bons mots*, though not uncharacteristic, seem to have gained in the telling, and Frances Donaldson is surely correct in seeing one of his most famous—'My father was frightened of his mother; I was frightened of my father, and I am damned well going to see to it that my children are frightened of me'—as at least improbable (Donaldson, 10). With respect to the story about Augustus John, it is striking that the king clearly knew who the young artist was. The king's visits to galleries were field days for the collectors of these *bons mots* (and perhaps for their creator). He stood before a French impressionist painting and called out to the queen: 'Here's something to make you laugh, May'. He told the director of the National Gallery, 'I tell you what, Turner was *mad* ... My grandmother always said so' (K. Clark, *Another Part of the Wood*, 1974, 237). He shook his stick at a Cézanne. On the other hand, he suggested a tax on works of art being exported from Britain, so as to preserve the national collection (Rose, 317–18). His conservative taste was sometimes usefully deployed: he prevented the illustration of postage stamps (a favoured ploy of the Post Office to raise money) and told Kenneth Clark: 'We invented the postage stamp—all it had on it was the sovereign's head and Postage and its value. That's all we want' (Clark, 238).

George V, Kenneth Rose remarks, 'liked a book with a plot, a tune he could hum and a picture that told a story' (Rose, 312); but within those limits he was industrious and quite knowledgeable. He read a book a week and recorded his reading. This included much political biography and novels by such as John Buchan and C. S. Forester, but also R. S. Lambert and H. L. Beales's *Memoirs of the Unemployed* (1933) and Giles and Edmund Romilly's *Out of Bounds* (1935). He was determined to harness the ability of the young Kenneth Clark, and in 1934 bullied him into becoming surveyor of the king's pictures. The king's taste was prescient: on the walls of his writing room, in which he normally spent most of the morning, the pictures were David Wilkie's *Letter Writer of Seville* and W. P. Frith's *Ramsgate Sands* (the latter a favourite picture). Even so, and despite the best efforts of Clark and others, there was no return to the days when the royal family were the nation's leading patrons of art. The king enjoyed listening to the gramophone, though his taste in music was conservative (a special favourite was 'The Departure of the Troopship', which ended with the national anthem and all in the drawing room standing to attention). He also enjoyed the cinema, but complained to the headmaster at Eton that the boys there had been shown Eisenstein's *Battleship Potemkin*. Travelling theatre appealed to him, and a company was often invited to Balmoral.

In addition to his stamp collection (the king's especial enthusiasm), George V was an energetic patron of a variety of sports. In terms of personal participation, shooting was to the outdoors what philately was to the study. The king was one 'of the first ten game-shots of his day at grouse and pheasants … and a very notable driven-partridge shot' (Gore, 233), dedicated to the practice of the sport rather than the social ambiance which surrounded it. The king always shot with hammer guns, though they slowed him up. On a day at the end of the last shooting season before the war, he fired 1760 cartridges—representing, his biographer John Gore observed, 'the high-water mark of superabundance in his sporting career' (ibid., 230). It was said that during the years of his head keeper F. W. Bland over 1 million head of game were killed at Sandringham, the record being on 18 December 1913, when 3937 pheasants were shot by the king and his guests. The king's closest companions were, in addition to the navy friends whom he appointed to court offices, the shooting gentry of Norfolk such as George Brereton. After his illness in 1928 he used a pair of specially made light twelve-bore guns, but never had to use spectacles except for reading. George V balanced this pastime by developing the royal pigeon lofts; he was a frequent and successful competitor in this predominantly working-class sport. Despite rumours to the contrary circulating at the start of his reign, George V was a keen attender at horse races, especially Ascot and Goodwood, but though he nurtured the royal stud at Sandringham he was a much less successful owner than his father. Indeed, though a good judge of a horse, his attitude to racing was the reverse of his view of shooting: he chiefly enjoyed the ambiance. His only classic was the One Thousand Guineas with Scuttle in 1928. It was with his attempt to win the Derby that one of the most famous episodes of royal racing occurred: in 1913 the suffragette Emily Wilding Davison died after throwing herself under the king's horse Anmer; attempting to disrupt the race, she had miscalculated the speed of the horses. The king's other participation in sport was yachting. He inherited *Britannia* from his father; he initially used her as a pleasure boat, but in 1913 re-rigged her as a racing cruiser and raced her regularly. Between 1893 and 1934 she sailed in 569 races, winning 231 and taking prizes in 124 more (Rose, 323). In 1935 George V was asked if he would like a replacement as a jubilee gift from yachtsmen. He declined this offer and requested that *Britannia* be scuttled after his death. In July 1936 she was sunk off the Isle of Wight.

The king enjoyed the new spectator sports and established the tradition of a regular royal presence at their chief occasions: the association football cup final at Wembley and before, test matches at Lord's, tennis at Wimbledon, the Derby at Epsom, the summer meetings at Goodwood and Ascot, and, less frequently, international rugby matches at Twickenham. Indeed the emergence of a national canon of certain sports over others (in addition to horse racing) owed something to his patronage. He was the most eclectic of Britain's sporting royals.

George V in later life: appearance, illness, and the National Government George V had a trim figure. Except between 1898 and 1900, when he put on half a stone, he was usually within a pound of 10 stone 5 pounds. Sir Owen Morshead, his librarian, thus described him: he

> was slightly below the middle height, neatly made, and impeccably dressed in the style before last. His voice was strong and resonant, his prominent eyes arrestingly blue. Moderate in diet, he drank hardly at all but smoked heavily. His mode of life was of an extreme regularity, his occupations being predictable to the day, indeed almost to the hour … Although not pietistically inclined, the King was all his life a sound churchman and early formed the habit of daily Bible reading. He attended Sunday morning service wherever he might be; when travelling in India his train used to be stopped for the purpose. (DNB)

The king's smoking had begun when he was a youth, with cigarettes given to him by Dalton, his former tutor. Both his sons smoked heavily, George VI fatally. George V, Harold Nicolson observed, spoke just like George VI: 'Very virile, rather bronchial, very emphatic. I notice the closed "o" as in "those"; it is what the B.B.C. would call "off-white", meaning slightly cockney' (Nicolson, *Diaries*, 208).

In November 1928 the king fell ill with a chest infection, confirmed by radiology. By December his heart was weakened and the blood generally infected. On 12 December he was almost dead when Lord Dawson, his doctor, found the abscess with his needle and drew off the poison. Further drainage and the removal of a rib ended the decline. Dawson was much criticized for not consulting experts, but, whether by luck or good clinical experience, his patient recovered and was able, from February 1928, to convalesce at Craigweil, Sir Arthur du Cros's house at Bognor. One version of the king's most famous but unfortunately perhaps apocryphal expletive is that as he prepared to leave Bognor a deputation of its citizens requested the renaming of the town as Bognor Regis to mark its new royal association. 'Bugger Bognor' was said to have been the royal reply (but the town was so renamed). The king went from Bognor to Windsor, but in May 1929 suffered a further abscess. His illness was the longest suffered by a monarch since the accession of Queen Victoria. On 4 December the king signed a warrant nominating six councillors of state to act in his place during his illness. This followed the precedent of the hiatus in Queen Victoria's reign after the death of the prince consort. The prince of Wales and the duke of York were both councillors, but a regency does not seem to have been seriously contemplated. The illness, accompanied by bulletins, attracted wide sympathy. Churches were kept open day and night for prayer. The king attended a service of thanksgiving in Westminster Abbey, his wound still unhealed. He subsequently laughed so hard at J. H. Thomas's ribald jokes that the wound split and a further rib had to be removed. The king was not an equable patient and his temper showed. Sister Catherine Black proved good at managing him (sometimes assisted by the duke of York's elder daughter, later Elizabeth II); Sister Black remained his nurse for the rest of his life. Popular sympathy supported the king for the rest of his reign, but his illness left him a weakened man.

When he was partially recovered the king had to deal, on 4 June 1929, with the resignation of Stanley Baldwin following the Conservatives' defeat in the general election (unlike 1923, Baldwin resigned without meeting parliament). The king sent for Ramsay MacDonald, who on 4 June kissed hands for the second time. To the surprise of both—for this was a second minority government—MacDonald was to be prime minister almost until the king's death: his longest-serving premier and for nearly a quarter of the reign. The king was encouraging to the government, supporting MacDonald and Snowden as they respectively negotiated the three power settlement for the navy and the Dawes plan. But the government was soon facing not merely the chronic unemployment of the later 1920s but what was said to be the imminent collapse of the financial system. The king was depressed by the deaths of his sister, the princess royal, in January 1931 and of his oldest friend, Sir Charles Cust, the same month. Moreover, Stamfordham, his secretary since his accession, died in March 1931 (the king appointed Clive Wigram to the post). George V thus faced the political crisis of 1931 uneasily. Wigram suggested to him at an early stage that 'Your Majesty might be asked to approve a National Government' (Nicolson, *King George*, 449). After departing for Balmoral on 22 August the king had to return that night. At 10 a.m. on 23 August MacDonald came to the palace to resign. Baldwin, the Conservative leader, could not be

found, but Herbert Samuel, as temporary leader of the Liberals, advised the king at noon that day that the preference should be for a continuing Labour government administering retrenchment or, failing that, for a national government. Wigram later noted 'It was after the King's interview with Sir Herbert Samuel that His Majesty became convinced of the necessity for the National Government' (ibid., 461). The king then saw Baldwin and asked him not if he would form a government, but whether he would serve in a national government under MacDonald; Baldwin agreed to do anything necessary to assist. Next day MacDonald visited the palace to tell the king that his cabinet had resigned and that consequently he must resign also. He had also mentioned to the cabinet his intention to recommend the king to summon a conference of himself (MacDonald), Baldwin, and Samuel. This he did, the king summoning the conference for 24 August. It was known to MacDonald, but perhaps not to the king, how hostile many members of the Labour cabinet were to accepting severe retrenchment and reduction of the welfare benefits. At this meeting the king pressed on MacDonald his view that the prime minister who was attempting to resign 'was the only man to lead the country through the crisis' (ibid., 464). Both men—the king in his personal appeal to MacDonald as an individual rather than as a party leader, MacDonald with his suggestion of a conference of party leaders—had moved significantly towards the formation of a national government. The king noted in his diary:

> I held a Conference here in Indian room with the Prime Minister, Baldwin & Samuel & we discussed the formation of a National Government composed of all three Parties, with Ramsay MacDonald as P. M. … The Prime Minister came at 4.0 and tendered his resignation. I then invited him to form a National Government, which he agreed to do.   (ibid., 465)

The government was to be 'a temporary measure' to meet the crisis, followed by a dissolution with the parties acting separately in the consequent general election. MacDonald's exceptional position and his separation from the former Labour government was marked by the fact that he again kissed hands, though there had been no intervening attempt to form a government and he had not resigned.

This was the most energetic use of royal prerogative since Edward VII's unauthorized sallies into foreign policy. The king had not merely been asked to approve a national government, as Wigram had predicted: he had been the most active agent in creating one. It is hard to avoid the view that, but for royal pressure, MacDonald would have resigned the premiership and the Labour Party would not have split. Some have seen that as a skilful ploy on the king's part to destroy, at least for the time being, the party of British socialism. But, as we have seen, the king was not hostile to Labour governments. His action is more likely to be explained by his underestimating, especially at the time of his first interview with MacDonald, the Labour Party's unwillingness to join the National Government. It is also of importance that it was MacDonald who advised the king to call a conference of the three party leaders: an unprecedented suggestion from a prime minister at the point of resignation, and one with a strong implication of inter-party co-operation. Wigram may well have been playing a deeper game, and his role in the crisis is hard to assess.

Last years, jubilee, and death   The National Government stabilized politics and proved anything but a short-term interlude. The king found its attempt at non-politics reassuring. He stiffened MacDonald's resolve to continue as prime minister, and the phrase 'Your majesty's government' became something more than a well-worn formula. The king encouraged MacDonald in his dotage and seemed undisturbed by his premier's diminishing grasp of public affairs. George V approved of the government's policies, including its controversial legislation for India. In 1931, during the second round-table conference, he received Gandhi and other Congress Party delegates at Buckingham Palace. He was 'disgusted' when the Indian princes denounced proposed legislation for a central federation in 1935 and said that it would be better if the princes improved conditions in India rather than attended his jubilee. MacDonald was determined to continue in office beyond the king's jubilee, which was held on 6 May 1935—marked by a service in St Paul's Cathedral, an address next day in Westminster Hall, and a series of banquets and processions in glorious weather. The king noted in his diary: 'The greatest number of people in the streets that I have ever seen in my life. The enthusiasm was indeed most touching' (Nicolson, *King George*, 524), and MacDonald recorded of the service:

> We all went away feeling that we had taken part in something very much like a Holy Communion. ... This Jubilee is having a miraculous effect on the public mind & on the King himself. He is finding confidence & is showing the Prince of Wales's aptitude for saying the right popular thing & feeling the popular mind. But with it all he retains the demeanour and the status of a King & does not step down to get on a lower level.   (Marquand, 775)

Contact between the king and his subjects in the British Isles and throughout the empire had been dramatically enlarged by the introduction of a royal Christmas broadcast from Sandringham in 1932 (John Reith had suggested such a broadcast as early as 1923). The king's speech opening the British Empire Exhibition at Wembley in 1924 was thought to have been heard by 10 million people, and marked the popular arrival of the new medium as well as selling many wireless sets. The first Christmas broadcast was drafted by Rudyard Kipling; those for 1933–5 by Archbishop Lang.

On 7 June 1935 MacDonald resigned as prime minister, George V telling him (according to MacDonald's diary): 'I hoped you might ha[ve] seen me through, but I now know it is impossible ... You have been the Prime Minister I have liked best' (the king persuaded MacDonald to stay in the government as lord president; Marquand, 777). It was Stanley Baldwin who was to see George V out. Baldwin's third premiership began in the midst of the Abyssinian crisis. The king supported, in general terms, the government's approach to foreign policy. His dislike of war was strong. He quite often made comments suggesting the abolition of capital ships and of submarines. On the other hand, in April 1934 the king gave a strong warning to the German ambassador that, if Germany 'went on at the present rate, there was bound to be a war within ten years' (Nicolson, *King George*, 521), and he warned the British ambassador in Berlin in January 1935 'that we must not be blinded by the apparent sweet reasonableness of the Germans, but be wary and not taken unawares' (letter from Wigram, Nicolson, *King George*, 522). He reacted sharply when hearing, through the medium of Lady Snowden, of a German proposal for action by 'the two Germanic nations'; the king deplored any suggestion of abandoning the French. In 1935, as the Abyssinian crisis developed, the king told Lloyd George: 'I will not have another war. *I will not* ... I will go to Trafalgar Square and wave a red flag myself sooner than allow this country to be brought in' (Rose, 387). The Abyssinian crisis caused the king to wake in the night, though during the day his constricted arteries were by the end of 1935 causing him to doze off. The king's ambivalence, between profound suspicion of Hitler and Mussolini, and a pronounced wish to avoid war, placed him foursquare with his government and most of his subjects.

By the start of 1936 George V was, at just over seventy, a man close to his end, as he himself sensed. The final diary entry written by the king, on 17 January, reads: 'Dawson arrived this evening. I saw him & feel rotten' (Nicolson, *King George*, 530). On 20 January members of the privy council gathered in the king's bedroom at Sandringham and a proclamation constituting a council of state was with great difficulty initialled by the king. Dawson drafted a lapidary bulletin: 'The King's life is moving peacefully to its close.' In the course of the evening, the king asked Wigram 'How is the Empire?' and attempted to discuss political developments. A variant on the story about his earlier remark about Bognor became common after his death. It is said that one of the doctors tried to cheer him with the suggestion that he might soon again be convalescing in Bognor. That the king responded 'Bugger Bognor' is hard to substantiate, but it soon became the most famous of his many *bons mots*. With Dawson easing his patient's pain, and perhaps timing his death to suit the quality papers, George V died that evening, 20 January, just before midnight (though by Sandringham time he died at 12.25 a.m. on 21 January, for the king kept all the Sandringham clocks half an hour fast, the prince of Wales ordering them to be corrected, perhaps to avoid exactly this confusion).

George V lay in state in Westminster Hall for four days before his funeral in St George's Chapel, Windsor, on 28 January. His four sons kept vigil on the last evening. His body was later placed in a tomb in the nave of St George's Chapel, with an effigy by Sir William Reid Dick. The king's death occasioned considerable national and imperial mourning, with that individual but widespread sense of loss which a monarch, personally unknown in any direct way to most of his subjects, can provoke. The psychoanalyst W. R. D. Fairbairn interestingly recorded the profound effect of the king's death on some of his patients (see 'The effect of the king's death upon patients undergoing analysis', 1936, in W. R. D. Fairbairn, *Psychoanalytic Studies of the Personality*, 1952).

Iconography George V's trim figure made him a much less exotic subject for artists than his two predecessors. His state portrait by Sir Luke Fildes (1912) is at Windsor Castle, a work of little distinction. He disliked sitting to artists, and many of his portraits were largely done from photographs. Of his many portraits, the group portrait of the royal family by John Lavery (1913, NPG) is by some way the most distinguished, with that by John Berrie for the King's Liverpool regiment (1935?) an attractive likeness. The king's appearance lent itself to photography, and the *Illustrated London News* jubilee supplement (4 May 1935) gives a good pictorial portrait of the reign. The king's head for the coronation medal and for the coinage was the work of E. Bertram Mackennal, a sculptor much liked by the king; he also carved marble statues for Madras and Delhi. In London, George V's statue outside the east end of Westminster Abbey is by William Reid Dick, by whom other sculptures or effigies were done for Sandringham, Crathie, and St George's Chapel, Windsor.

Reputation George V was fortunate in being the subject of two among the best-written biographies of constitutional monarchs. Harold Nicolson's official life was published in 1952; Nicolson followed Sidney Lee's official life of Edward VII in giving as candid an account of the king's life as reasonable discretion permitted (an easier task for Nicolson than for Lee). Nicolson's account of the king's role in the politics of the reign was particularly sharp. Kenneth Rose in 1983 took Nicolson's account a good deal further, especially on the domestic and family side, and brought out, more than it had been appropriate for Nicolson to do, the full flavour of the king's slightly off-beat personality in private life. The king had already been the subject of an unusual personal memoir by John Gore (1941), with access to the king's diaries and other papers. John Buchan's *The King's Grace* was written for the jubilee and, though it had a vast sale, was not one of Buchan's best books.

George V left the throne certainly no weaker, and perhaps stronger, than he found it at his accession. His was the busiest service of any nineteenth- or twentieth-century British monarch. He dealt with a remarkable and arduous series of crises: the reaction of the Unionists to the Parliament Bill and the home rule crisis, the complex coalition-forming of the First World War, the incorporation of the Labour Party into the working of constitutional government, the replacement of orthodox politics by a national government. George V's assiduous and non-partisan approach smoothed the process of political change which these crises represented. The significance of the royal prerogative in such cases is hard to separate from the personal force of the monarch. George V guarded the royal prerogative carefully. He did not try to use it aberrantly, as had his father in his foreign policy expedition, or to attempt to frustrate policy, party, or persons approved by the electorate, as had his grandmother.

He worked with the grain of representative government politics, but he was capable of giving his own finish to the wood. When he acted, he did so decisively, but within a well-prepared context and in a way which made the outcome seem natural—a great skill in a monarch. Deeply conservative by nature and personal behaviour, George V had moved with the times, and faster than the times in certain respects. In an epoch when many of the older European monarchies were abolished, this was an achievement of substance. Though the British showed little sign of anti-monarchism, wrong steps by the king could have quickly changed their view. Compton Mackenzie wrote of him (intending criticism) that he 'had all the talents but none of the genius of monarchy'; the crises with which George V dealt were exactly those in which attempts at 'genius' would have been disastrous. The nature of the British constitution requires monarchic action at certain points, almost always in moments of crisis in which each participant looks to a different precedent. George V experienced these in abundance and enabled the constitution to work. He was also important in the new style he brought to royal life: unstuffy and unpretentious, but combining with these a sharp and rather self-conscious sense of separateness that his otherwise more egalitarian tone perhaps required. His father had started the Sandringham style among the royals, but had balanced it with Paris and the continent: George V made the county habits and dress of the Norfolk gentry central to the royal style, and brought the British royal family closer to the English country gentry than had the earlier European, cosmopolitan attitudes of the Victorian and Edwardian royal family. George V thus set the tone for the rest of the century.   H. C. G. MATTHEW

Sources H. Nicolson, *King George V: his life and reign* (1953) · K. Rose, *King George V*, pbk edn (1984) · J. Gore, *King George V: a personal memoir* (1941) · J. Van der Kiste, *Edward VII's children* (1989) · J. Van der Kiste, *George V's children* (1991) · J. Buchan, *The king's grace, 1910–1935* (1935) · F. E. G. Ponsonby, *Recollections of three reigns* (1951) · M. Brice, *The king's dogs: the sporting dogs of His Majesty King George V* (1935) · J. Pope, *The tour of their royal highnesses the duke and duchess of Cornwall and York through the dominion of Canada in the year 1901* (1903) · J. W. Day, *King George V as a sportsman* (1935) · D. Judd, *The life and times of George V* (1973) · F. Donaldson, *Edward VIII* (1974) · H. H. Asquith: letters to Venetia Stanley, ed. E. Brock and M. Brock (1985) · D. Marquand, *Ramsay MacDonald* (1977) · J. Barnes and K. Middlemas, *Baldwin* (1969) · H. Nicolson, *Diaries and letters, 1945–1962*, ed. N. Nicolson (1968) · *Memoirs of a Conservative: J. C. C. Davidson's memoirs and papers, 1910–37*, ed. R. R. James (1969)
Archives Royal Arch. | BL, corresp. with Arthur James Balfour, Add. MS 49686 · BL OIOC, corresp. with Lord Brabourne, MS Eur. F 97 · BL OIOC, corresp. with Lord Chelmsford, MS Eur. E 264 · BL OIOC, letters to Lord Curzon, no. 1146 · BL OIOC, corresp. with Lord Goschen, MS Eur. D 595 · BL OIOC, corresp. with Lord Halifax, MS Eur. C 152 · BL OIOC, corresp. with Lord Lytton, MS Eur. F 160 · Bodl. Oxf., corresp. with Herbert H. Asquith · Bodl. Oxf., corresp. with Lord Selborne · CAC Cam., corresp. with Lord Egham · CAC Cam., corresp. with Lord Esher · CAC Cam., letters to Sir Bryan Godfrey-Faussett · CAC Cam., letters to Lord Fisher · CAC Cam., corresp. with Reginald McKenna · CCC Cam., letters to Lady Derby · CUL, corresp. with Lord Hardinge · HLRO, corresp. with Lord Cadogan · HLRO, corresp. with David Lloyd George · HLRO, corresp. with Andrew Bonar Law · LPL, corresp. with Randall Thomas Davidson, archbishop of Canterbury · Lpool RO, corresp.

with Lord Derby · NA Scot., corresp. with Lily Langtry · NL Aus., corresp. with Lord Novar · NL Scot., corresp. with Lord Haldane · NL Scot., letters to Lord Minto · NL Scot., corresp., incl. Lord Rosebery · NRA, corresp. with Lord Durham · NRA, priv. coll., letters to Lily Langtry · PRO, corresp. with James Ramsay Macdonald, PRO 30/69/1/197 627 · U. Nott. L., letters to Lady Galway · U. Southampton L., corresp. of George V and other members of the royal family with J. H. Hertz · U. Wales, Swansea, letters to Sir Robert Meade · Wilts. & Swindon RO, letters to earls of Pembroke | FILM BFI NFTVA, 'The coronation procession of his majesty King George V, Gaumont, 22 June 1911; actuality footage · BFI NFTVA, 'George the beloved: the nation, the empire, the world mourns the passing of a great king', newsreel compilation, 22 Jan 1936 · BFI NFTVA, The Windsors, 25 May 1995 · BFI NFTVA, current affairs footage · BFI NFTVA, documentary footage · BFI NFTVA, news footage

Likenesses K. W. F. Bauerle, group portrait, oils, c.1871, Royal Collection · J. Sant, group portrait, oils, c.1872 (Victoria with three of her grandchildren), Royal Collection · J. Sant, oils, 1872, Royal Collection · F. J. Williamson, marble statue and bust, 1877, Royal Collection · Count Gleichen, bronze statuette, 1878, Royal Collection · Judd & Co., lithograph, 1879, NPG · C. Sohn junior, oils, 1882, Royal Collection · L. Tuxen, group portrait, oils, 1887 (The royal family at the time of the jubilee), Royal Collection · H. von Angeli, oils, 1893, Royal Collection · L. Fildes, oils, 1893, Royal Collection · L. Tuxen, group portrait, oils, 1893, Royal Collection · L. Tuxen, group portrait, oils, 1896 (Marriage of Princess Maud and Prince Charles of Denmark), Royal Collection · W. Q. Orchardson, pencil drawing, c.1897, Royal Collection · W. Q. Orchardson, group portrait, oils, c.1897–1899 (Four generations), Royal Agricultural Society, London · W. Q. Orchardson, oil study, c.1897–1899 (Four generations), NPG · M. Beerbohm, caricature, 1899, AM Oxf. · Chancellor of Dublin, panel print, 1899, NPG · J. Collier, oils, 1900, Trinity House, London · H. de T. Glazebrook, oils, c.1901–1908, Royal Marines Museum, Eastney barracks, Southsea, Hampshire · J. H. F. Bacon, group portrait, oils, 1903, NPG · E. A. Abbey, group portrait, oils, 1904 (The coronation of King Edward VII, 1902), Royal Collection · A. Drury, marble bust, 1906, Bradford City Art Gallery · W. H. Thornycroft, bronze bust, 1907, National Gallery of Canada, Ottawa · M. Beerbohm, pencil and watercolour caricature, 1911, NPG · J. H. F. Bacon, group portrait, oils, 1912, Royal Collection · L. Fildes, oils, 1912, Royal Collection · A. S. Cope, oils, c.1912–1913; formerly at United Service Club, London · G. Frampton, marble bust, 1913, Guildhall, London · J. Lavery, group portrait, oils, 1913, NPG [see illus.] · J. Lavery, oils, 1913, Royal Collection · L. Calkin, oils, c.1914, NPG · S. J. Solomon, oils, 1914, NPG · A. T. Nowell, oils, 1920, Leys School, Cambridge · F. O. Salisbury, group portrait, oils, 1920 (Burial of the unknown warrior), Palace of Westminster, London · A. J. Munnings, group portrait, oils, 1925 (Their majesties return from Ascot), Tate collection · A. S. Cope, oils, 1926, Royal College of Music, London · R. Jack, oils, 1926, Royal Collection · A. S. Cope, oils, 1928, RA · O. Birley, oils, 1928–34, NMG Wales · O. Birley, oils, 1928–34, Lincoln's Inn, London · O. Birley, oils, 1928–34, Royal Collection · O. Birley, oils, 1928–34, NPG · F. Whiting, oils, 1930–39, NPG · W. R. Dick, marble bust, 1933, Royal Collection · J. Lavery, group portrait, oils, 1933, NPG · C. Beaton, pen, brush, and ink drawing, 1935, NPG · J. A. A. Berrie, portrait, 1935?, King's Regiment · K. Kennet, head, c.1935, Royal Collection · J. St H. Lander, oils, 1935, Victoria College, Jersey; version, Canada House, London · F. O. Salisbury, group portrait, oils, 1935 (Thanksgiving service of the king's silver jubilee), Guildhall, London · F. O. Salisbury, group portrait, oils, 1935 (Jubilee service), Royal Collection · F. O. Salisbury, oils, c.1935, National Gallery of Art, Washington, DC · F. Weiss, bronze bust, 1935, NPG · S. Mrozewski, wood-engraving, after 1936, NPG · A. J. Munnings, oils, c.1936, Ipswich Corporation · W. R. Dick, marble tomb effigy, 1937, St George's Chapel, Windsor · Ape Junior, mechanical reproduction, NPG; repro. in VF (21 June 1911) · C. Sims, oils, Scot. NPG · Spy [L. Ward], caricature, lithograph, NPG; repro. in VF (24 May 1890) · double portrait, lithograph (with the duke of Clarence),

NPG; repro. in Whitehall Review (16 Aug 1879) · photographs, NPG, Royal Collection

George VI (1895–1952), king of Great Britain, Ireland, and the British dominions beyond the seas, and sometime emperor of India, was born at York Cottage, Sandringham, Norfolk, on 14 December 1895. He was the second of the five sons and one daughter of the duke and duchess of York, who became prince and princess of Wales in 1901 and *George V and Queen *Mary in 1910. His birthday fell on the same day as the anniversary of the deaths of Prince Albert, the prince consort, in 1861 and Princess Alice in 1878, which upset his great-grandmother, Queen Victoria. The queen had failed to persuade the Yorks to give their first child (later *Edward VIII) Albert as the first of his forenames but her request with respect to the second child was anticipated by the duke of York's father, the prince of Wales (later *Edward VII), whose suggestion it was that the baby's first name be Albert and that the queen be his godmother (with six other royals). The baby was baptized at Sandringham on 17 February 1896 as Albert Frederick Arthur George, and was known in the family as Bertie.

Youth and education Prince Albert was brought up at York Cottage—his home until 1923 with his elder brother, Prince Edward (later Edward VIII), and his sister, Princess Mary [see Mary (1897–1965)]. He was shy and sensitive and from about the age of seven developed a severe stammer, possibly compounded by being made to write with his right hand though he was naturally left-handed. His stammer emphasized the contrast with his outward-going elder brother, and it left him defenceless when his father dressed him down. He was knock-kneed, like his father and brothers, and was made to wear splints, initially by day and night. When the splints interfered with his school work, he was allowed to wear them at night only. Prince Albert attended the classes provided by Henry Peter Hansell, hired mainly for his sporting abilities. Though his only pupils were the royal children, Hansell's aim was to reproduce the atmosphere of a school, with the oldest child as 'captain'. None made good progress. Prince Albert was slow to develop the resistance and determination needed for survival. His mathematics was especially poor. With his stammer, his splints, his gruff father, his distant mother, and his showy brother, it was not surprising that he was frequently in tears. The departure in 1907 of Prince Edward for the Royal Naval College at Osborne eased matters and in 1908 Prince Albert himself passed the entrance examination, including mathematics (a vital subject for naval officers), though Mr Hansell thought he had 'failed to appreciate his position as "captain"' in the Sandringham school (Wheeler-Bennett, 32). However, his French was good, and there were signs of development in his character. At Osborne and Dartmouth (1909–12) Prince Albert, like his brother, received the education of a naval officer. Prince Edward was heir to the throne from 1910, but Prince Albert was expected to follow a naval career, as his father had done. After taking some time to settle down, Prince Albert found friends and with them his stammer almost disappeared. Like his father, but unlike

George VI (1895–1952), by Sir Gerald Kelly, c.1941

his brother Prince Edward, Prince Albert's naval friends from his cadet days were important to him in his later career.

Though personally more at ease, Prince Albert was never more than a mediocre student, sixty-eighth out of sixty-eight in the final examinations at Osborne. While at Dartmouth he took part in his father's coronation on 22 June 1910. He received a stern written warning from the new king about lack of effort in his academic work, and he gained something of a reputation at Dartmouth for sky-larking, on one occasion receiving a beating of six strokes. He passed out sixty-first out of sixty-seven. While at Dartmouth Prince Albert developed stomach problems, which he did not report. He also gained a strong affection for the Church of England, being confirmed at Sandringham on 18 April 1912; he later wrote 'I have always remembered that day as one on which I took a great step in life' (Wheeler-Bennett, 57). He was throughout his life a convinced Christian, and later also an enthusiastic freemason.

Naval service and the First World War Prince Albert began his time at sea with a training course on HMS *Cumberland* in 1913, during which he visited the West Indies and Canada. Though he suffered from seasickness, he enjoyed being free of the family context and tried to avoid publicity: he was happy to let his elder brother be the focal point of media attention. On his return he was appointed midshipman on HMS *Collingwood* in the Home Fleet and toured the Mediterranean. He was serving on *Collingwood* when war was declared on 4 August 1914 and he served in the Royal Navy until 1917, being actually at sea for twenty-two months. Late in August 1914 the gastric problems from which he had spasmodically suffered intensified, and his appendix was removed. On his return to *Collingwood* he undertook the normal duties of a senior midshipman, but a further bout of gastric pains soon required his transfer to the hospital ship HMS *Drina*. The king and the prince were both determined that the latter should not be invalided out (as he could have been), for the prince's presence in the navy was an important aspect of the monarchy's relationship to the war—and the prince much wished to remain with his ship and his comrades.

During his convalescence Prince Albert undertook some public duties before returning to *Collingwood* as an acting sub-lieutenant in May 1916, just in time to take part, in a turret of the *Collingwood*, in the battle of Jutland, the chief naval battle of the war. This was an important experience for the prince personally and for the monarchy nationally, George V on his visit to the Grand Fleet after the battle declaring: 'I am pleased with my son.' The prince of Wales—confined to minor duties behind the trenches—ached for this sort of activity and praise. It was symbolic of the brothers' developing relationship that it was Prince Albert who achieved his objective. In August 1916 he was diagnosed as suffering from a duodenal ulcer. Rest alleviated the symptoms and the prince returned to sea duties in May 1917 on HMS *Malaya* as acting lieutenant. He had been made KG on his twenty-first birthday. His persistence with naval service finally had to end in July 1917 when his stomach and other symptoms of debilitation brought him near collapse. The ulcer was successfully operated on, on 29 November 1917. He had been posted—at his own suggestion—to the Royal Naval Air Service station (HMS *Daedalus*) at Cranwell earlier that month. He was thus one of the first officers (as Flight-Lieutenant Prince Albert) when the Royal Air Force was instituted in April 1918, and a royal presence was a handy political advantage for the new service. He was officer commanding boys (about 2500 of them). In October 1918 he was posted to General Trenchard's staff in France and witnessed the armistice on 11 November. At his father's request, he represented the king when the allies entered Brussels. Though he disliked flying, he trained as a pilot (though forbidden to fly solo) and qualified on 31 July 1919, next day being gazetted squadron leader.

Through frequent illness and two operations, Prince Albert had shown considerable determination during his time in the forces. His presence at Jutland gave him a status and confidence which he later found of great value, and his experience with boys' education in the RAF pointed him towards his chief subsequent innovation, his work with boys.

Prince Edward had spent several terms at Oxford before the war to no great purpose. Prince Albert (aged twenty-three) and his brother Prince Henry were sent to Trinity College, Cambridge, in October 1919. Like other post-war servicemen, they found college and academic life both frustrating and liberating. Prince Albert was tutored by the historians R. V. Laurence, J. R. M. Butler, and D. H. Robertson; he showed special interest in constitutional history. His equerry at Cambridge was Louis Greig (1880–1953), by whom he had been taught at Osborne; Greig, with whom the prince won the RAF tennis doubles in 1920, was an important influence in encouraging this still rather immature, somewhat gauche and uncertain young man, who had a good deal of his father's temper, to treat life with equanimity. George V permitted his son only three terms at Cambridge and, in a mark of paternal favour, on 3 June 1920 conferred on him the titles he himself had been given, Baron Killarney, earl of Inverness, and duke of York.

The duke and duchess of York: 'very different to dear David'
George V made it clear to his second son that when he came down from Cambridge he would not resume his career in the forces but would take on royal duties: the prince of Wales would look after the empire, the duke of York would help chiefly on the home front. In 1920 the duke met Lady Elizabeth Angela Marguerite Bowes-Lyon (1900–2002), the ninth of the ten children of Claude George Bowes-*Lyon (1855–1944) and his wife Nina Cecilia, *née* Cavendish-Bentinck (*d.* 1938), cousin of the sixth duke of Portland. Lady Elizabeth, recently launched into London society from her Scottish origins at Glamis Castle, hoped to avoid an early marriage and was reluctant to respond to the duke of York's attempts at courtship. The duke for his part had as little experience of women as his elder brother had much, and was unsure how to proceed, though it would seem certain from an early stage that he wished to do so. He adhered to the view that a king's son could not propose, lest he be refused. J. C. C. Davidson, the tory *éminence grise*, advised him in 1922 to make a direct proposal none the less; on what was said to be the third attempt, he was accepted. The couple were married in Westminster Abbey on 26 April 1923; he was the first royal prince to be married there since Richard II. George V strongly approved of his son's bride and his letter of congratulation to him ended: 'I feel that we have always got on very well together (very different to dear David)' (Wheeler-Bennett, 154). The duke of York was different in a variety of (but not all) respects from his elder brother, and in making a happy marriage approved of by his family and the British establishment he had fulfilled one of the chief duties of a royal prince. He and his wife secured the succession to the end of the twentieth century with the births of their daughters Princess Elizabeth Alexandra Mary (from 1952 Elizabeth II), born at 17 Bruton Street, London, on 21 April 1926 (George V approved the names and the omission of Victoria) and Princess Margaret Rose, born at Glamis on 21 August 1930 (*d.* 9 February 2002).

By all accounts the duke of York was greatly altered by his marriage: 'It transformed him, and was the turning point of his life' (Rhodes James, 96). It is usually said that the Yorks had no expectation of the throne, but Wheeler-Bennett remarks:

> as the years passed and the Prince [of Wales] remained a bachelor, there came an ever-increasing acceptance of the fact that, in the nature of things, the Duke and Duchess of

York would one day become King and Queen.   (Wheeler-Bennett, 156)

Initially the Yorks lived at White Lodge in Richmond Park, which they found too large and expensive; in 1926 they moved to 145 Piccadilly, in London. Royal Lodge in Windsor Great Park became their country house in 1931.

Philanthropy, recreation, and travel In public the duke of York became quite a prominent philanthropist. His Industrial Welfare Society gained him knowledge of a wide range of industrial developments and discussions and he met trade unionists on something approaching a business footing, certainly more so than any previous prince. Within the royal family he became known as 'the Foreman' because of his interest in labour questions. Building on his RAF experience, he developed a special interest in education and from 1921 he played the leading part in the experiment in social integration known as the Duke of York's Camps, in which he was encouraged and in the early days financed by Sir Alexander Grant, the biscuit manufacturer. These camps brought together boys of working-class and public-school backgrounds in games, competitions, and discussions. The camps were held annually until 1939 (except for 1930), attended in all by about 6000 young men (R. R. Hyde, *The Camp Book*, 1930). The duke attended each camp (as 'Great Chief') except that of 1934, which he missed through illness. As an experiment in social integration in a period of social deprivation, high unemployment, and class tension, the camps were a bold move. It was an innovation for a royal prince to show such sustained interest in a cause of this sort. Film footage shows the duke relaxed and happy in what he, at least, found the sort of family atmosphere he hoped to encourage, and his joining in the camp song, 'Under the Spreading Chestnut Tree', with its accompaniment of cumulative body gestures, showed genuine camaraderie.

The duke of York also became well known for sport. In 1926, partnered by Greig, he played in the men's doubles championship at Wimbledon, being heavily defeated in the first round. The duke was embarrassed and never played tennis in public again (one member of the crowd shouted to the left-handed prince: 'Try the other hand, Sir'; Bradford, 129). In September 1930 he played himself in as captain of the Royal and Ancient Golf Club at St Andrews, acquitting himself well in the nerve-wracking opening drive from the first tee; the caddies, recalling the prince of Wales's dismal effort a few years earlier, stood, a local paper noted, 'disloyally close' (ibid.). But the duke found that golf brought out his bad temper, and he gave it up for gardening. He also rode to hounds and was, like his father, an excellent shot.

The Yorks had little of the prince of Wales's restless enthusiasm for travel, but equally they did not follow George V in simply disliking 'abroad'. They visited the Balkans in 1923 and in 1924–5 east Africa and Sudan. On their return the duke of York made the speech closing the British Empire Exhibition at the new Wembley stadium in north London. His father's opening speech had been one of the first to be broadcast; the duke's brief remarks exposed his stutter to the listening nation as well as the immediate audience. From October 1926 he was treated by Lionel Logue (1880–1953), an Australian speech therapist practising in London, who made good progress where others had failed. Under Logue's influence, the duke's confidence increased and his stutter diminished (though it by no means disappeared: on several occasions, film of speeches taken for newsreels was withdrawn). The duke and duchess visited New Zealand and Australia in 1927, travelling in HMS *Renown* via the Pacific. The duke was in Melbourne for Anzac day (25 April) and opened the new parliament building in Canberra on 9 May. His speeches on both occasions were considered great successes. Despite a major fire on *Renown*, the Yorks returned to Britain on 27 June.

The serious illness of George V in the winter of 1928–9 reminded his four sons that the accession of the prince of Wales might follow soon, with consequences for each of them, and particularly the duke of York, who would become heir presumptive. The years 1929 to 1935 saw the Yorks engaged in quiet domesticity, with no major foreign expeditions. This domesticity gave them a deceptive view of what was to be their role, for in the 1920s the duke had been much more publicly prominent as his father's representative.

The reign of Edward VIII George V's death on 20 January 1936 put the duke's brother on the throne. Edward VIII's uncertain and unsettled view of the monarchy was, from the duke's point of view, reflected in a wounding absence of consultation and, unlike Lord Louis Mountbatten, the duke and duchess of York were certainly not regularly included in the king's circle which met at Fort Belvedere, nor would they have wished to be (they do appear in swimming costumes in one of the well-known photographs of the Fort Belvedere circle). They had a very limited acquaintance with Wallis Simpson, the king's mistress, and the duke, at least, seems not to have appreciated the seriousness of the developing constitutional and thus personal crisis. Edward VIII's secretary, Sir Alexander Hardinge, warned the duke on 20 October 1935 of Mrs Simpson's impending divorce and on 28 October told the duke he believed the king might abdicate. In such circumstances, the Yorks' policy of uninvolvement was wise: it was also a strong indication that in this case, at least, they placed national before family priorities. The duke wrote to his brother several times in early November offering help, but does not seem to have gone to see him. The Yorks were not a party to the complex discussions which might have enabled Edward VIII to marry Mrs Simpson and remain king. On 17 November the king told his brother of his intention to marry Mrs Simpson. If the duke of York did not seek out his brother to assist him, neither did the latter seek assistance or advice from the person closest to him in the family. This was apparently their only private meeting during the crisis until two days before the abdication, and the king's news had already been told to Queen Mary and Stanley Baldwin, the prime minister. On 10 December the duke of York with his brothers witnessed

Edward VIII's instrument of abdication and on 11 December he became king when Edward VIII assented to the statute enabling his own abdication. 'When D and I said goodbye we kissed, parted as freemasons & he bowed to me as his King' (George VI's account of the abdication, Wheeler-Bennett, 287). Freemasonry rather than religion or a common view of family had been a bond between the brothers, but it was not a bond that endured.

George VI The abdication crisis was traumatic for George VI, the title the duke of York chose for himself. He had clearly underestimated the intensity and the speed of the crisis that led to his accession: when he visited his mother to tell her it was imminent, 'I broke down and sobbed like a child' (Wheeler-Bennett, 286). Even so, he dealt expeditiously and decisively with his elder brother's anomalous position, creating him duke of Windsor at his accession council. A good deal has been made of his statement to his friend Lord Louis Mountbatten: 'I'm quite unprepared for it. David has been trained for this all his life. I've never even seen a State Paper. I'm only a Naval Officer, it's the only thing I know about' (Wheeler-Bennett, 294). But this was a considerable exaggeration made in the immediate aftermath of the crisis. In fact George V had prudently (and possibly intentionally) prepared his second son for the kingship to a much greater extent than in previous analogous cases. The new king did not like publicity—he was that rare being, a genuinely shy monarch—but he was well used to deputizing for his father. It was in the behind-the-scenes aspects of monarchy that he was inexperienced, but not much more so at the time of his accession than any other monarch since George III. Even here, he learned quickly and always went through his cabinet boxes with something of the assiduity of his father.

Publicly, the new king had the advantage of a government with a large majority and no anticipation of domestic political crises; privately, he was happily married, with two daughters and a queen who acted as confidante to a greater extent than had been enjoyed by any recent British king. The emphasis on family happiness was an innovation in the twentieth-century monarchy: George V had often been photographed with his sons, usually in uniform or with shotguns, but the domestic element which George VI's young daughters brought to photographs and visits was homely and appealing. In broadcasts and public appearances he skilfully used this family aspect of his life to associate himself with the common experience of his subjects.

The 'royal family' no longer included the duke and duchess of Windsor; of that George VI was quite clear, and as late as 1941 he referred in his diary to his sister-in-law as 'Mrs. S[impson]'. The revelation that the duke had failed to disclose assets material to his financial settlement hardened the king's resolve to exclude her, characterized by the legally dubious denial of the title 'her royal highness' to the duchess of Windsor. So also did the Windsors' irresponsible visit to Hitler in October 1937. The king probably overestimated how far the abdication endangered the stability of the monarchy—the events of 1936 in fact showed the crown in parliament acting with rapid and conclusive effectiveness—but in the pre-war years his treatment of his brother was prudent. It was soon generally understood that George VI sat on the throne through a sense of duty; this effectively countered the implication of Edward VIII's action, that occupation of the throne was a voluntary matter, with personal preferences in certain circumstances being given greater weight than the obligations of sovereignty.

George VI retained Sir Alexander *Hardinge, private secretary to Edward VIII and before him George V. He afforced him with Sir Alan *Lascelles (who had also served both previous monarchs) and Sir Michael *Adeane, grandson of George V's secretary Lord Stamfordham. The secretariat thus embodied experience and tradition, though the secretaries' complaint was that the king too often disregarded them. Robert Rhodes James observes: 'The myth that the Queen, Hardinge, Lascelles and Wigram [briefly private secretary in 1936] ran the monarchy and dominated a weak King, is amusing to the constitutionalist because the exact reverse was the case' (Rhodes James, 132). The king retained something of the temper he had shown as a child, and he certainly had much of his father's will. The queen was noted for her ability to calm her husband, just as she had her father-in-law.

George VI was crowned on 12 May 1937 (the date planned for Edward VIII) and with his coronation in an important sense both passed and demoted his brother, who was not only the sole monarch since 1688 to abdicate, but also the only one to fail to be crowned. The coronation was broadcast by the BBC to a world and empire-wide audience, the king's wish prevailing against considerable opposition, but the coronation service was not televised (the element of intrusion into a religious ceremony rather than the smallness of the potential audience being the objection), though the procession was. The king's broadcast that evening was delivered almost faultlessly and the many rumours—that his stammer had worsened, that he suffered epileptic fits, that he would barely be able to undertake monarchic duties—were scotched.

Foreign policy and the onset of war Neville Chamberlain's succession to Baldwin as prime minister in May 1937 required no initiative or choice on the king's part. Much less straightforward, in personal or policy terms, was foreign policy. As the Conservative Party divided into factions, so the king risked being drawn into the argument which came to be seen as pro- and anti-appeasement. His inexperience in this area eased him into his role as constitutional monarch, for its effect was that he did not interfere (though he was much put out by Chamberlain's failure to brief him in February 1938 that Anthony Eden's resignation was imminent). Thus he supported Chamberlain more because Chamberlain was his prime minister than because he approved of his German policy. Whatever view one takes of appeasement, George VI's conduct was correct. He did not initiate, as Edward VII had done, and he did not unilaterally interfere, as Queen Victoria had done.

On the other hand, George VI did at one important moment associate himself with Chamberlain's policy in a most unusual and public way, probably without appreciating the implications. The king's intended contribution to foreign affairs in 1938 was a message to Hitler, 'from one ex-Serviceman to another', which he suggested he send during Chamberlain's first visit to Germany in 1938 (he also offered to write in similar terms to King Victor Emmanuel of Italy and Emperor Hirohito of Japan). Lord Halifax, who had just succeeded Eden as foreign secretary on the latter's resignation, discouraged the idea, suggesting a later approach might be more appropriate. Nothing came of this, though the king returned to the idea in September 1938, shortly before Chamberlain's journey to Munich. But when Chamberlain returned from Munich on 30 September 1938, the king asked him to come 'straight to Buckingham Palace, so that I can express to you personally my most heartfelt congratulations on the success of your visit to Munich' (Wheeler-Bennett, 354). Chamberlain's visit to the palace was not unusual, but the king's appearance with his prime minister on the palace's balcony was an exceptional association of the monarchy with the government's foreign policy. The king followed this up with a message to his people on 2 October, praising Chamberlain's 'magnificent efforts' (Wheeler-Bennett, 355). Queen Victoria had made Beaconsfield a knight of the Garter when he returned from Berlin in 1878 bearing 'peace with honour', the phrase Chamberlain repeated in his speech in Downing Street after returning from the palace. George VI also wished to honour his prime minister, but Chamberlain, who immediately regretted his use of the famous phrase, declined and thus saved the king considerable subsequent embarrassment. The close association of the king with the government's policy of appeasement and rearmament was intended to be further shown by a royal announcement of a system of voluntary national service but Chamberlain, not the king, made the broadcast (not because the monarchy should not be involved in the implementation of policy, but because a royal message might be too alarming to the stock exchange).

George VI, influenced by Lord Halifax (who with his wife, a lady-in-waiting, regularly dined privately with the king and queen) and Lord Cranborne, appears to have moderated his position during the winter of 1938–9. His secretary, Hardinge, had always been hostile to Chamberlain's foreign policy. Unqualified evidence of Hitler's aggressive character and of the failure of 'appeasement' provided by the annexation of the rest of Czechoslovakia in March 1939 thus left the king in a somewhat uncertain relationship to his prime minister, though in this he shared the ambivalence of much of the cabinet.

Happily for George VI a tour of Canada, which was suggested in 1937 and planned from 1938, provided an alternative focus of royal activity. A visit to the USA and the Roosevelts, suggested by the president in 1938, was associated with it. The king had already made an important state visit to France in July 1938. The king and queen sailed on 5 May 1939 on the Canadian Pacific liner *Empress of Australia* on what had become, given the deteriorating international situation, a royal tour of much more than usual importance. The support of the dominions for a second war in Europe could by no means be taken for granted, and the USA was still quite strongly isolationist. President Roosevelt, who proposed the visit with the deliberate intent of encouraging British–American co-operation at the personal level of head of state as well as at the diplomatic, showed much greater prescience than the British Foreign Office. Carefully choreographed by John Buchan (who as Lord Tweedsmuir was governor-general of Canada), the Canadian visit was a great success. This was, remarkably, the first visit by a British sovereign to a dominion. The royal party crossed Canada by train, welcomed by almost the entire populations of the little towns at which they stopped. They returned to Niagara Falls and there crossed into the United States, the first British sovereign to do so. A visit to Washington, accompanied by Mackenzie King, the Canadian premier, on 8 and 9 June 1939 was followed by a private visit at the Roosevelts' country house, Hyde Park. The royal party returned to Canada, sailing for Britain on 15 June. The king's notes of his talk with Roosevelt are an important source for the president's views at this time; so important did George VI consider these talks that he carried his handwritten notes of them in his briefcase throughout the war.

Royal visits are habitually described as successful; this visit to North America was, in diplomatic terms, second in importance in the twentieth century only to Edward VII's visit to Paris in 1903. Edward VII's initiative was an intended change of direction sponsored by the monarch. George VI's was not a personal initiative in that sense, nor did it reflect a change in direction; but it was effective all the same.

George VI and the Second World War George VI was forty-three when war was declared on 3 September 1939. He began a diary which he kept through the war. That night he broadcast to the empire, and it was intended that a copy of his message be circulated to each household in the UK (a plan abandoned because of its cost). In 1914 George V had played no public role in the nation's adaptation from peace to war. The development of radio and film meant that the public role of the monarchy in this war would be prominent. The king had discontinued his father's Christmas broadcasts, but in 1939 reluctantly agreed to make one. He had been sent a book of poems, *The Desert* (privately printed, 1908), by Minnie Louise Haskins, a lecturer at the London School of Economics, and from it he included at the end of his message lines which immediately became famous:

> I said to the man who stood at the Gate of the Year,
> 'Give me a light that I may tread safely into the unknown'.

The broadcast followed well-publicized royal visits to the fleet at Invergordon and the British expeditionary force in France and placed the fit and energetic monarch at the forefront of the national effort, in contrast to his prime minister, who was aged seventy and looked it. The king believed a national government was desirable but, while he made this clear to Chamberlain, he did not undermine his prime minister, though the latter was the chief obstacle to its achievement. In the political crisis of 1940 the king personally hoped Chamberlain would continue as prime minister or, failing him, Lord Halifax. The king's secretaries, sensing an impending crisis, consulted constitutional authorities about the details of procedure, establishing, somewhat dubiously, that the king was not required to ask an outgoing premier's advice on his successor. On 8 May 1940 the Conservative government's majority fell from about 200 to 81 in the vote on the conduct of the Norway campaign. Meetings between the government and the Labour Party established that the latter would join a coalition, but not one led by Chamberlain. Halifax in effect removed himself from consideration for the premiership. Hardinge told the king that when Chamberlain offered his resignation the out-going premier would also '*without hesitation* recommend Mr Churchill' (Rhodes James, 191). The king's abstinence from the process of cabinet-making at this time was highly beneficial, as the new national government led by Churchill emerged through the efforts and negotiations of its members, rather than as the result of royal encouragement.

When the king saw Chamberlain on Friday 10 May 1940, he accepted his resignation, and, according to his diary, told him 'how grossly unfairly I thought he had been treated' and learned in 'an informal talk over his successor' that Halifax would not serve. The king noted in his diary that he:

> was disappointed … as I thought H. was the obvious man … Then I knew that there was only one person whom I could send for to form a Government … & that was Winston. I asked Chamberlain for his advice, & he told me Winston was the man to send for … I sent for Winston & asked him to form a Government.   (Wheeler-Bennett, 444)

Churchill had emerged from a political process of elimination, despite the king's preference for Halifax, and the monarch at this dramatic moment in fact played no more of a part in that process than was usual, and certainly less than his father had played in the making of the First World War coalitions. George VI's account of his discussions at this time shows a very sensitive understanding of constitutional proprieties, with careful distinction drawn between conversation and formal request for advice. He floated Halifax at Chamberlain informally, and asked formally for advice only once that option was eliminated. He was careful to avoid being the recipient of advice which he was not ready to accept, and was also careful, at such an important moment in the nation's history, to be seen as ready to accept his new prime minister, Winston Churchill. Churchill now rapidly took on the role of leader of the war effort, in a way that Chamberlain could not do, leaving the king to a more symbolic role. The king soon appreciated Churchill's capacity for this, recognizing the effectiveness of the combination which they provided of baroque bravado and homely dignity.

The king's role was to encourage the war effort by morale-boosting visits to bombed towns, cities, and factories, while at the same time providing a sense that normal life had not altogether disappeared. Thus the king and queen lived in Buckingham Palace (with their daughters living at Windsor) until the palace—virtually unprotected—was bombed on 9 September 1940: the bomb did not immediately explode and the king worked in his study just above it. At 1.25 a.m. next day it exploded, but with no casualties since that part of the palace had been evacuated. The palace was again bombed three days later (and altogether was hit nine times during the war). Subsequently the king and queen slept at Windsor, commuting to London each day. This German bombing was a great advantage to the British monarchy. It diminished the slightly paternalist tone of the royal visits to bombed areas in London and elsewhere. It was a good card to play in the USA. It gave the royal family greater confidence: the queen famously observed: 'I'm glad we've been bombed. We can now look the East End in the face' (Wheeler-Bennett, 470). The remark emphasized the difference as well as the advantage. No one else would have welcomed being bombed—indeed the king suffered some subsequent trauma—and it was of course the case that the royal family lived differently from 'ordinary' citizens in wartime as they did in peacetime. But their spartan existence, with their clothes and food subject to rationing, was relatively closer to ordinary life than at any time in the history of the monarchy. Although even Churchill was not told how close the escape from the first set of bombs had been, enough was known nationally for the point to be taken. The result of the bombing of the palace was, according to a Mass-Observation survey, that one-third of the king's appearances on newsreels were interrupted by applause in the cinema, as opposed to one-seventh before the bombing (Richard and Sheridan, 213).

The bombing of the palace occurred just as the full force of the blitz began, ordered by Hitler's directive of 5 September 1940. During the blitz the king and queen assiduously visited bombed areas, often on their own initiative and with little prior notice. The king was in Coventry on 16 November 1940, the day after its destruction. Similar visits were made to Southampton, Birmingham, and Bristol. The absence of notice meant that the usual disruptions of a royal visit were largely avoided. The king was aware that a royal visit in such circumstances could be awkward as well as encouraging, and noted in his diary: 'I feel that this kind of visit does do good at such a moment & it is one of my main jobs in life to help others when I can be useful to them' (Wheeler-Bennett, 479). Some felt that these visits could be intrusive—'too busy cleaning up and one thing and another' was sometimes the comment (T. Harrisson, *Living through the Blitz*, 1976, 164). But the absence of the sovereign from areas of devastation would have caused far more adverse comment than his presence. Clara Milburn of Burleigh, Warwickshire, wrote in her diary on 11 September 1940:

> Their Majesties have visited the heavily-bombed areas today and, as an air raid warning was sounded, they went into a police station and had tea with A. R. P. workers and others ... many remarked that Hitler couldn't have gone out visiting like that—he would have needed an armed bodyguard. Pah!! (*Mrs Milburn's Diaries*, ed. P. Donnelly, 1979, 55)

The king emphasized the importance of the home front by creating, on his own initiative and with his own design, the George Cross and George Medal, announced in his broadcast of 23 September 1940. They developed from his observation of civilian work following air raids. It proved difficult and sometimes divisive to select particular acts of civilian bravery, and many of the awards went to servicemen. The work of the king and queen on the home front, and especially in 1940–41, constitutes an exceptional moment in the history of the monarchy. The timing of the visits was largely at royal initiative and, though there was no palace press secretary until 1944, so was their management and presentation. Much of the detail was handled by the assistant private secretary, Sir Alan Lascelles, with whom the king formed a close bond. When in 1943 Sir Alexander Hardinge, the private secretary, resigned through ill health following a row with Lascelles, the king accepted the resignation with alacrity and would not allow Hardinge to withdraw it. The king—who felt of Hardinge that 'he was doing me no good'—noted in his diary: 'It was difficult for me to have to do this but I know that I should not get the opportunity again ... I feel happier now it is over' (Rhodes James, 248). Lascelles became George VI's private secretary, holding the post until the king's death and into the next reign. He was simultaneously keeper of the Royal Archives.

George VI worked well with Churchill once the latter became accustomed to his post. They met for lunch each Tuesday at Buckingham Palace. The first of over 200 lunches was on 10 September 1940, the day the palace was bombed, and continued until the end of Churchill's premiership. They met without advisers or secretaries present. The king found these talks invaluable for keeping in touch, though his staff regretted the absence of the memoranda that George V habitually dictated immediately following such meetings. Churchill also seems to have found them useful, and they ensured that there was no court influence on strategy other than via the prime minister (Churchill perhaps recalled the importance to Field Marshal Haig of palace support in 1916–18). Their mutual respect and affection was reflected in an exchange of telegrams following the axis surrender in north Africa in May 1943, an exchange unusually released for public information; the king's simple message and Churchill's florid reply neatly represent the differences between the two men (Wheeler-Bennett, 564–5). On Tuesdays, before the prime-ministerial lunch, George VI held investitures, for which he prepared himself very thoroughly; in 1945 he calculated that during the war he had personally bestowed over 44,000 medals and decorations (Rhodes James, 230).

The possibility of the death or assassination of the prime minister concerned the king, who at a Tuesday lunch on 16 June 1942—with Churchill about to leave for Washington—asked his advice on his successor. On the king's request, Churchill by letter that day confirmed that he recommended Anthony Eden. When Churchill and Eden travelled together in 1945, the king returned to the point, Churchill recommending Sir John Anderson, an independent MP, as prime minister in the event of Churchill and Eden's both being killed.

George VI, like many of his subjects, found the slow pace of the war frustrating. He longed to visit his troops, but, apart from a visit to the British expeditionary force in France in December 1939, there was no suitable occasion until 1943, after the defeat of the axis powers in north Africa. Travelling as General Lyon, he left for north Africa on 11 June, was prevented by fog from refuelling at Gibraltar, and reached Algiers on 12 June. He travelled 6700 miles in two weeks visiting camps and former battlefields. As well as his fear of flying, George VI suffered from a phobia about inspecting lines of troops and on at least one occasion was only with difficulty persuaded to leave his tent. 'The real gem of my tour', the king reported, was his entrance into Valletta harbour, Malta, on 20 June 1943 when, suffering quite severely from dysentery, he took the salute from the bridge of HMS *Aurora*. On his own imaginative initiative he had on 15 April 1942 awarded the people of Malta the George Cross for their heroism during a period of sustained siege and assault.

Encouragement to the government and people of the United States after they had entered the war was uncontroversial, and was developed by George VI in a series of letters and by the reception of Eleanor Roosevelt in London in October 1942. More complex were the United Kingdom's relations with the Soviet Union. Here the king played a characteristically straightforward role. He wished to honour the citizens of Stalingrad in the same way as he had honoured those of Malta, and incidentally associate the monarchy with the very popular pro-Russian sentiments of the working class. The award of a British medal to Stalingrad was thought inappropriate (though George V had awarded the Military Medal to French cities in the First World War) and it was decided instead to award a sword of honour, the personal gift of the king, 'to the steel-hearted citizens of Stalingrad'. This the king played an active part in designing; the sword was displayed in British cities prior to being taken by Churchill to the Casablanca conference early in 1943 for presentation to Stalin, the high point of Anglo-Russian fraternity.

The end of the war   George VI made one of his rare strategic suggestions when in 1943, encouraged by Smuts, he encouraged Churchill to reconsider operation Overlord (the D-day landings) in favour of further attack via Italy. Churchill sent the king's letter to the chiefs of staff and, after a dinner attended by the king, Churchill, and Smuts, plans for D-day went ahead, though some extra attention was paid to Italy. The king attended the conference in London on 15 May 1944 at which senior staff were briefed on the landings, and he brought it to a conclusion with a brief and effective unscheduled speech of exhortation. The king, now thoroughly enthused about operation Overlord, visited each of its assault forces in its port of assembly, and conceived the notion of accompanying the invasion in person, as, separately, did Winston Churchill: 'W. cannot say no if he goes himself, & I don't want to have to tell him he cannot', the king noted in his diary

(Wheeler-Bennett, 601). The queen encouraged her husband to go, but his secretary, Lascelles, wisely persuaded him out of what would have been a dangerous prank and a deflection of important resources since the king and prime minister would both have had to be guarded. Reluctantly the king agreed not to go and with considerable difficulty he persuaded Churchill not to go either (the king eventually had to tell Churchill he would personally drive to Portsmouth to prevent the premier embarking on HMS *Belfast*).

On the evening of D-day, 6 June 1944, the king broadcast to his subjects and on 16 June visited the Normandy beaches for the day, returning to find London bombed for the first time by V1 rocket weapons: Buckingham Palace, though not directly hit, suffered constant indirect effects in the subsequent assaults, and several bombs fell in close proximity. From 23 July until 3 August the king was in Italy with his troops, and in October 1944 he visited recently liberated Belgium (just as in 1918 he had represented his father for the same purpose). Churchill vetoed the king's plan to follow up these visits with a tour of the Far East, and especially India. The king prepared carefully for the long-anticipated VE (Victory in Europe) day, but disagreements between the allies about the timing of the announcement somewhat spoilt his plans. However, on 8 May 1945 the king received the war cabinet and the chiefs of staff to congratulate them and that evening made a broadcast. The royal family and Churchill made repeated appearances on the balcony of Buckingham Palace. In subsequent days the king and queen drove in state through east and south London and attended services at St Paul's and St Giles' cathedrals. On 17 May the king made an affecting speech in Westminster Hall to members of both houses, his voice faltering only at the end when he referred to his brother, the duke of Kent, killed on active service in a plane accident in 1942. At the end of the speech, Churchill waved his top hat and called for three cheers for the sovereign. He was wise to do so. The war ended with the monarchy on a high note, and clearly more popular than the rest of the upper class; as Ross McKibbin observes: 'the exceptional popularity of the monarchy throughout the war—a lucky escape, given George VI's commitment to Chamberlainite Conservatism—did much to shield the old élites' (McKibbin, 534).

Towards peacetime   The king was noticeably tired in 1945 but not apparently ill. During the war his health seemed to hold up well. He drank moderately but smoked heavily. It was not suspected that he had only six years to live. During the war, however, he requested parliament to amend the Regency Act so as to permit his daughter, Princess Elizabeth, though still a minor, to be included among the counsellors of state if necessary. The king ignored suggestions, including those of the cabinet, that she be made princess of Wales on her eighteenth birthday (for that, the king argued, would make her husband, once she had one, prince of Wales, the normal title of the heir to the throne; this was in fact an erroneous argument, for women never confer titles on their husbands by marriage alone). A public announcement was made that there would be no change at that time to the princess's style and title. According to Robert Rhodes James, who had access to exceptional sources, both written and oral, the king was 'seriously irritated' by his cousin, Lord Louis Mountbatten, for 'his constant promotion of the virtues of his nephew Prince Philip of Greece'. The king 'liked the dashing young naval officer, and invited him to Balmoral on leave, but Mountbatten's pushiness annoyed him, seeing only too clearly what his cousin's motives and ambitions were' (Rhodes James, 254). The king and queen had handled their daughters' upbringing much more sensitively than any of their recent predecessors. For the first time since 1760, a calm, straightforward, uncomplicated succession to the throne was assured (that of 1910 had been straightforward, but only by the fortuitous early death of George V's elder brother). This in itself was a striking achievement. Much less satisfactory, from George VI's point of view, was the position of his elder brother and sister-in-law. Churchill in 1944 had raised the question of the Windsors' status, suggesting the duchess be received in London, and proposing other posts for the duke, who was bored with governing the Bahamas. Churchill moved too early and too insistently, and by conflating the question of the recognition of the duchess with that of a post for the duke made a complex situation more so. The queen and Queen Mary were unwilling to receive or even meet the duchess (Rhodes James, 164). The exile of the Windsors—whether imposed or self-imposed—was not ended during the king's reign, and the unwelcome flurry of activity about them in 1944–5 delayed rather than encouraged a rehabilitation which might have occurred once the war had ended safely.

Politics and the end of the war In 1918 a general election had immediately followed the armistice. In 1945 there had been no general election since 1935. Churchill hoped the national government formed in 1940 would continue until the end of the Japanese war (thought to be still some time off), a view with which the king sympathized. The king and Churchill knew of the atomic bomb, and plans to use it, but C. R. Attlee, the Labour leader and deputy prime minister, did not. The Labour Party conference in May 1945 opposed maintenance of the coalition beyond the autumn. Churchill was hostile to such a brief extension, and on 23 May 1945 resigned his posts and, by inference, those of his cabinet. The king declined to accept his resignation, and asked him to return later that day. At the second audience, the king accepted Churchill's resignation and asked him again to form a government. Churchill then at once asked for a dissolution of parliament, which was granted. The effect of this constitutional quadrille was that the Labour members of the national government went out of office. Churchill had not been leader of the tory party when appointed prime minister in 1940, but had been careful to be so elected in October 1940, after Chamberlain's death. As the tories were the largest party in the Commons, the king was right to ask Churchill to form another government, even though he had just resigned as a result of his inability to maintain the national government. Churchill resigned on 26 July, the

day the counting of the votes revealed the overwhelming victory of the Labour Party in the general election held on 5 July. The king, according to his diary, asked if he should send for Attlee (an innovation, in that the sovereign by convention asked for advice, rather than proposed a name) and Churchill agreed. 'We said good bye & I thanked him for all his help to me during the 5 War Years', the king noted in his downbeat way (Wheeler-Bennett, 636). George VI regretted Churchill's departure as he had that of Chamberlain five years previously. The king offered him the Garter but not, it would seem, the customary peerage. Churchill would, in fact, have had to recommend himself for the Garter, for it was only in July 1946 that, by agreement with the party leaders, the patronage of the Garter and the Thistle became, like the Order of Merit, non-political and at the personal disposal of the monarch (the prime minister being consulted but his or her advice not being necessary). The king then revived various aspects of the Garter chapter, which had not met since 1911.

The post-war monarchy The king's enthusiasm for the Garter and similar ceremonies cut across the tone of his new Labour government. In May 1940 the king had sent the Foreign Office a proposal for a voluntary federation of European states at the end of the war and had encouraged the subsequent ministerial committee to develop a plan of social post-war reconstruction. This was squarely in line with the king's interests when duke of York, but they were not interests to which he gave prominence during the rest of the war, even though in 1940 the TUC had presented him with its Gold medal. Churchill's regular lunches drew the king into a close interest in military strategy and tactics and kept him somewhat distant from the development of home policy represented by the Beveridge report and its aftermath. The king summoned Beveridge when the report was published, but, according to Lady Beveridge, wanted to know, not about national insurance, but about the 'queer people' at the London School of Economics (J. Harris, *Beveridge*, 1977, 426). Even so, the king in 1945 at once played an important part in Labour politics by suggesting to Attlee that Ernest Bevin would be preferable as foreign secretary to Hugh Dalton (Attlee's suggestion). The king had never got on well with Dalton, the son of his father's tutor. It is hard to know how heavily the king's advice weighed with Attlee in his decision to make Bevin foreign secretary, and, as a stickler for form, the new prime minister said nothing about the king's advice to his colleagues, including Bevin (it was the king who, somewhat naïvely, revealed his suggestion to Bevin at their first audience, thus making the crown quickly controversial in certain sections of the Labour Party).

On 15 August the king opened parliament and that evening appeared on the balcony of Buckingham Palace to take part in the celebrations marking the surrender of Japan and the final end of the war. The Labour government and party embarked on their great programme of legislative innovation, which extended into most aspects of British home life. At the same time the king's cousin, Lord Mountbatten, oversaw what became the partition of the Indian subcontinent, the subsequent establishment of India, Pakistan, and Burma as independent republics, and the ending of George VI's title emperor of India. This great turning point in the world role of Britain, linked as it was to the rise of the domestic welfare state, might have been the occasion for some fundamental reconsideration of the role of the monarchy. George V had undertaken just such a reappraisal in the last two years of the First World War. But George VI did not think in such bold terms. Moreover, the Labour government had no modernizing plans for the monarchy, beyond some modification of the civil list, and Clement Attlee was quite conservative in his approach to the institution of monarchy, as well as being deferential to the monarch. Though the Parliament Act of 1949 reduced the power of the House of Lords, that was the extent of Labour's interest in the constitution (George VI made it clear to the tories that they should not look for resistance from him on this question). The instinct of the palace was a return to 'normalcy'. But the inter-war normalcy to which the palace by degrees returned ignored the change which the Labour government represented, even though that government did not propose any changes for the role of the crown or the monarch. While the king's personal life was never ostentatious, and while a few minor changes of court style were made, he did not reappraise his role or that of the palace with respect to British domestic life.

George VI never had what could be called a normal period of rule. In the aftermath of the abdication the king, his family, and the court were accommodating of the fact that the king had not expected to be on the throne; when that accommodation was complete, preparations for war began; the war itself was followed by a period of post-war hardship and reconstruction in the latter part of which the king was ill. George VI thus was never in a position to take part in the usual round of royal duties in a settled situation. For much of his reign the sporting events which his father had used as a means of regular royal association with the British calendar were suspended or held in unusual circumstances and places. The royal palaces were restored or reopened after the war; there was not much time or money for the exercise of royal patronage of the arts and architecture; nor was this an area in which the king wished to take an especial interest, leaving picture collecting to the queen (she assembled a fine private collection). He took much interest in the restoration of the Royal Collection after the war, but did not see it as his role to add to it. The exhibition 'The King's Pictures', held at the Royal Academy in 1947 and arranged by the new surveyor of the king's pictures, Anthony Blunt (appointed in 1945), was the first great post-war exhibition held in London. Blunt set the royal collections on a fresh footing and started their *catalogue raisonné*, preparatory work having been done by Ben Nicholson while deputy surveyor during the war. Like his father, George VI had middlebrow tastes in music, art, the theatre, cinema, and literature. When John Piper completed his brooding series depicting Windsor Castle (commissioned by the queen), the king is said to have remarked to him 'You've been pretty unlucky

with the weather, Mr Piper.' The king's equivalent to George V's stamp collection was a collection of medals, on which he became a considerable authority. Also like his predecessors, he was a stickler for correct dress and turnout.

The war even affected royal iconography. Gerald Kelly was commissioned to paint the state portraits of the king and queen in their coronation robes and had begun to do so when war intervened. The king disliked wearing the full panoply of silk tights and court dress for the picture, but characteristically agreed to be so portrayed. The architectural background to the portraits was designed by Lutyens. Kelly resided at Windsor Castle for two years during the war to work on the portraits. It was said that Kelly rose early each day to paint out the changes imposed on him the previous afternoon. The portraits, now at Windsor Castle, were finished in 1945 in time for the Royal Academy exhibition.

In external affairs the king strongly supported the Labour government's policies and played an important part in encouraging the development of the Commonwealth. Having been encouraged by Smuts during his wartime visits to London, the king and queen and their daughters visited South Africa in 1947, sailing from Portsmouth in HMS *Vanguard* on 1 February, just as the full rigours of the appalling British winter of 1947—one of the coldest and snowiest of modern times—were reaching their height (the king considered shortening the tour because of the home situation, but was advised by Attlee not to). The southern African visit was demanding and exhausting. The king opened parliament in Cape Town on 21 February and in Salisbury, Southern Rhodesia, on 7 April. The choice of South Africa as the dominion first to be visited after the war was questionable and the king was necessarily drawn into the politics of a deeply divided polity: the National Party boycotted most of the events at which its members would normally have been expected to be present and though apartheid was not yet official policy, the question already dominated South African politics. The king was not allowed to shake hands with African servicemen when he invested them with medals. The royal party felt itself much more at ease in the surrounding colonies than in the dominion.

Ironically, for the tour was intended to highlight the importance of the Commonwealth and was marked by Princess Elizabeth's broadcast on her twenty-first birthday in which she dedicated herself to it, the king's absence from London removed him from the details of the negotiations and discussions as the Indian subcontinent moved towards independence: by the time he returned from South Africa in May 1947 partition had become unavoidable. The king signed himself 'G. R. I.' for the last time on 15 August 1947 (except for the final India honours list of 1 January 1948). He asked for the last of the union flags flown at the residency at Lucknow in 1857, and this was recovered for him.

Thus the brief Indian empire ended. The question of the change of title (which required the permission of all members of the Commonwealth) was tidied up at the

Commonwealth heads of government meeting in London in April 1949, by the India (Consequential Provisions) Act of 1949, and, after the king's death, by the Royal Titles Act of 1953. India and Pakistan remained among the king's dominions but both were set on republican courses, becoming republics within the Commonwealth in 1950 and 1956 respectively. Burma left the Commonwealth on becoming an independent republic in 1948; in the same year the Irish Free State declared itself a republic outside the Commonwealth, the position being regularized on the British side by the Ireland Act of 1949, though Ireland was not modified to Northern Ireland in the royal title during the king's lifetime. The late 1940s thus saw a significant modification of the formal authority and title of the monarch. George VI showed none of the *amour propre* with respect to his position which would have been expected from Queen Victoria, Edward VII, or George V. His absence of complaint has sometimes been taken for weakness. But for busy politicians it must have been a relief not to have to cope with royal interventions fundamentally irrelevant in the face of unavoidable changes.

While the royal family was in southern Africa, the protracted question of the naturalization of Prince Philip (*b.* 1921), which had implications for Greek politics, was resolved, the prince taking his mother's family name, Mountbatten. The king had been cautious about Lord Mountbatten's energetic promotion of his nephew, and still, as his biographer observed, 'found it difficult to believe that his elder daughter had really fallen in love with the first young man she had met' (Wheeler-Bennett, 751). George VI later hoped he had not seemed 'hard-hearted'. However, the engagement of Princess Elizabeth to Lieutenant Philip Mountbatten was announced on 10 July 1947, with their wedding in Westminster Abbey being solemnized on 20 November 1947. Just before the wedding the king made his daughter, and a few days later, his prospective son-in-law, KG. He created Philip a royal highness (but not a prince, though he was popularly known as Prince Philip), and duke of Edinburgh.

Final years George VI did not much like the domestic legislation of the Attlee government, but he maintained a stoically proper public front, and concentrated on the Commonwealth, the arena which the king and his advisers increasingly saw as a valuable new area of royal activity. In March 1948 it was announced that the king, the queen, and Princess Margaret would visit Australia and New Zealand in 1949. In the course of 1948, however, the king's health declined; as in his Dartmouth days, however, he was reluctant to report his condition to his doctors. In October he was examined but, with remarkable lack of urgency, it was not until 12 November that the recommended specialist, Sir James Learmonth, saw him. Learmonth diagnosed severe arteriosclerosis with the possible need for the amputation of his right leg. The royal tour was deferred from 1949. On 12 March 1949 Learmonth operated, making a right lumbar sympathectomy. He recommended that the king live effectively as an invalid, and greatly reduce his smoking. At his final examination, the king remarked to his surgeon: 'You used a knife on me,

now I'm going to use one on you', and, producing a sword, knighted him on the spot (Wheeler-Bennett, 768). The king resumed limited official duties, and a scaled-down royal tour was rescheduled for 1952, to follow the Festival of Britain in 1951.

In the general election of 1950 the Labour Party obtained its largest popular vote, but saw its number of seats reduced to an overall majority of about eight. Lascelles, the private secretary, in an anonymous letter to *The Times* signed Senex, claimed a good deal of latitude for the sovereign in granting a dissolution; George VI's view is not known, and the issue did not immediately arise. The king opened the Festival of Britain from the steps of St Paul's on 3 May, but at subsequent public events that month it was clear that he was not well. His condition deteriorated and on 16 September an exploratory operation showed he had cancer of the lung. He was not told of this conclusion, and believed the operation performed by Mr Price Thomas on 23 September was to remove his lung to free his bronchial tube. This series of operations was far more public than George V's somewhat similar illness in 1928–9, and occasioned intense public interest. It seemed unfair that one who had led so well in the war should not share in the post-war recovery which the Festival of Britain so effectively represented.

In October 1951 the Conservative Party won the general election with a small majority and Attlee, who had been the king's minister for eleven continuous years, resigned, the king conferring on him the Order of Merit. Churchill thus for the third time became prime minister. On 2 December there was a day of national thanksgiving for the king's recovery.

On Christmas day 1951 George VI made what turned out to be his final Christmas broadcast, having just celebrated his fifty-sixth birthday. The speech, always an ordeal for the king despite the value he had come to attach to it, was for the first time recorded. He told the nation he had come through his illness. He also planned a convalescent private visit to South Africa (remarkably, as the National Party was now in power). Princess Elizabeth and the duke of Edinburgh departed on 31 January 1952 for east Africa, the first stage of the postponed tour of Australia and New Zealand on which they were taking the king and queen's place. On the tarmac at London airport, the king, hatless, windblown, haggard but cheery, led the royal party in waving farewell. On the morning of 6 February, after a happy day's shooting, his valet found him dead in bed at Sandringham. The new queen and her husband returned rapidly from Kenya. Public mourning was extensive but restrained; the king's death was marked by just that quiet dignity that he himself had shown in his life. George VI's body lay in state for three days in Westminster Hall, about 300,000 people filing by to pay their respects, and was buried in St George's Chapel, Windsor, on 15 February, where a memorial chapel was built and dedicated in 1969.

Assessment George VI was a plain, straightforward, though sometimes in private tempestuous man who was fortunate in his years of kingship, his life intimately intertwined with his subjects' experience of war and suffering.

He did his duty without fuss when national circumstances required his subjects to do the same. This gained him exceptional respect, as did his lifelong struggle with his speech impediment. He worked well with each of his four prime ministers; between them they covered a large spectrum of political style and ideology, from the florid Churchill to the phlegmatic Attlee. Like his father in the First World War, George VI's down-to-earth absence of flamboyance well suited the 'see it through' attitude of his subjects to the Second World War. When the king had tea in a bomb shelter during an air raid, his presence seemed natural and unforced. Royal visits during the war were the least formal since Queen Victoria ceased her practice of calling unannounced on Scottish cottagers. Though he kept an eye on the royal prerogative—even in his last illness preventing Churchill from describing Eden as deputy prime minister—George VI in practice allowed the prerogative to become more latent. Though he disliked some of its legislation, he made no attempt to circumscribe the Attlee government's great programme of social reform.

George VI embodied homely virtues in a violent age. He remarked in his final Christmas broadcast, echoing Macaulay, that in:

an age which is often hard and cruel … I think that, among all the blessings which we count today, the chief one is that we are friendly people … I wonder if we realize just how precious this spirit of friendliness and kindness is.

H. C. G. MATTHEW

Sources DNB · J. W. Wheeler-Bennett, *King George VI: his life and reign* (1958) · R. Rhodes James, *A spirit undaunted: the political role of George VI* (1998) · S. Bradford, *King George VI* (1989) · *King George VI to his peoples, 1936–1951: selected broadcasts and speeches* (1952) · F. Donaldson, *Edward VIII* (1974) · K. Rose, *George V* (1983) · D. Morrah, *The royal family in South Africa* (1947) · K. McLeod, *Battle royal* (1999) · M. Gilbert, *Winston S. Churchill, 7: Road to victory, 1941–1945* (1986) · J. Richard and D. Sheridan, *Mass-Observation at the movies* (1987) · H. Jennings, *May the twelfth: Mass-Observation day-surveys, 1937* (1937) · R. Allison and S. Riddell, eds., *The royal encyclopedia* (1991) · *In royal service: the letters and journals of Sir Alan Lascelles, 1920–1936*, ed. D. Hart-Davis (1989) · O. Millar, *The queen's pictures* (1977) · R. McKibbin, *Classes and cultures: England, 1918–1951* (1998) · G. Greig, *Louis and the prince* (1999) · V. Bogdanor, *The monarchy and the constitution* (1995) · B. Pimlott, *The queen* (1996) · P. Ziegler, *King Edward VIII* (1990)
Archives Royal Arch. | BL OIOC, corresp. with Lord Brabourne, MS Eur. F 97 · BL OIOC, corresp. with Lord Linlithgow, MS Eur. F 125 · Bodl. Oxf., corresp. with Lord Monckton · Durham RO, corresp. with Lord Londonderry · Lpool RO, corresp. with seventeenth earl of Derby · NRA, priv. coll., related material in papers of private secretary · U. Birm. L., corresp. with Joseph Chamberlain · Wilts. & Swindon RO, letters and telegrams to Herbert family, earls of Pembroke | FILM BFI NFTVA, 'George VI: a retrospective of the king's life', *British news*, 29 March 1937 · BFI NFTVA, *The Windsors*, 1 June 1994 · BFI NFTVA, *Reputations*, BBC2, 10 May 1999 · BFI NFTVA, 'The Queen Mother: her reign in colour, ITV, 10 Aug 2001 · BFI NFTVA, documentary footage · BFI NFTVA, news footage
Likenesses photographs, 1902–43, NPG · F. O. Salisbury, group portrait, oils, 1920 (*Burial of unknown warrior*), Palace of Westminster, London · R. G. Eves, oils, 1924, NPG · M. Frampton, oils, 1929, NPG · F. O. Salisbury, group portrait, oils, 1935 (*Jubilee service for George V*), Royal Collection; related portrait, Guildhall, London · K. Kennet, bronze bust, *c*.1935–1937, Royal Collection · S. Elwes, oils, 1936, Cavalry and Guards Club, London · L. Underwood, bronze figure, 1937, NPG · F. Hodge, oils, *c*.1938, RCS Eng. · F. O.

Salisbury, group portrait, oils, 1938 (*Coronation*), Royal Collection · O. Birley, oils, 1939, Royal Agricultural Society, London · H. Rayner, etching, 1939, NPG, V&A · G. Kelly, oils, *c*.1939–1945, Royal Collection · G. Kelly, oils, *c*.1939–1945, Trinity Cam. · G. Kelly, oils, *c*.1941, NPG [*see illus.*] · O. Birley, oils, *c*.1945, Royal Naval College, Greenwich · D. Fildes, oils, 1948, Staff College, Camberley, Surrey · E. Seago, oils, 1948, RAF College, Cranwell, Lincolnshire · D. Fildes, oils, 1949, Inner Temple, London · M. Codner, oils, 1951, Honourable Artillery Company, Armoury House, London · W. R. Dick, bronze bust, Royal Collection · J. Gunn, group portrait, oils (*Conversation piece at the Royal Lodge, Windsor, 1950*), NPG · W. MacMillan, bronze statue, The Mall, London · photographs, Royal Collection · photographs, Hult. Arch.

George, David (*c*.1743–1810), Baptist preacher, was born a slave in Sussex county, Virginia, to African-born parents, John and Judith. Their owner regularly abused his slaves, publicly stripping and brutally whipping George and the other members of his family, including his mother. To avoid further beatings George ran away in 1762, when he was about nineteen years old. He fled south but was relentlessly pursued by his owner's son, who found him living as a slave among the Creek Indians. George escaped before he could be reclaimed and went further south to live as a slave with the Natchez, who sold him to a white trader, George Gaulphin, in Silver Bluff, South Carolina.

About 1770 George married Phillis, another slave, and they started a family. Having been introduced to Christianity by a fellow black person, George began attending the Baptist services conducted periodically on the plantation by his long-time friend George Liele, a former slave, as well as by Wait Palmer, a white itinerant Baptist evangelist from Connecticut. Under Palmer, George was one of the founding members in the early 1770s of the Silver Bluff Baptist Church, probably the first exclusively African-American church. As a church elder he preached in the absence of Liele and Palmer. George acquired a spelling book and took lessons from the white children at school on the plantation in order to learn to read the Bible.

In 1778 Gaulphin abandoned his plantation and its slaves in the face of advancing British troops. George chose to enlist with them as a black loyalist soldier, fortifying Savannah, Georgia, when it was unsuccessfully besieged by rebel American forces in 1779. He supported his family by keeping a butcher's stall in Savannah. He also, along with Liele, preached to the other black people behind the British lines. At the end of the war in 1783 George and his family went to Charles Town to join the three thousand other former slaves evacuated from the colonies by the British and resettled in Nova Scotia, Canada.

George preached the Baptist word throughout Nova Scotia and New Brunswick to both black and white audiences, often meeting resistance not only from white, but also from fellow black congregations belonging to rival Anglican and Methodist denominations. Consequently George was a strong supporter of the Sierra Leone Company's project to establish a colony of free black people in Africa at Freetown, Sierra Leone. He helped the company's white representative, John Clarkson, recruit black loyalists for the settlement of twelve hundred people in 1792, among them George, his wife, and their four children. George, one of the settlement's three superintendents, established the first Baptist church in Africa. Amid the settlers' growing resentment of white supervision, George accompanied Clarkson to England in 1792 to meet fellow Baptists and to gather funds to support his African mission. In the following year the *Baptist Annual Register* published 'An account of the life of Mr David George' and in 1798 printed letters written from George after his return to Sierra Leone. Back in Africa his continued unwavering support for company policies cost him some of his influence among his fellow settlers. George attended to maintaining his alehouse, proselytizing neighbouring Africans, and ministering to his congregation in Freetown until his death in 1810.   VINCENT CARRETTA

Sources J. Rippon, ed., 'An account of the life of Mr David George, from Sierra Leone in Africa; given by himself in a conversation with Brother Rippon of London, and Brother Pearce of Birmingham', *The Baptist Annual Register*, 1 (1793), 472–84 · V. Carretta, ed., *Unchained voices: an anthology of black authors in the English-speaking world of the eighteenth century* (1996) · C. Fyfe, ed., *Our children free and happy: letters from black settlers in Africa in the 1790s* (1991) · G. Gordon, *From slavery to freedom: the life of David George, pioneer black Baptist minister* (1992) · C. Fyfe, *A history of Sierra Leone* (1962) · J. W. St G. Walker, *The black loyalists: the search for a promised land in Nova Scotia and Sierra Leone, 1783–1870* (1976) · E. G. Wilson, *The loyal blacks* (1976) · J. W. St G. Walker, 'George, David', *DCB*, vol. 5
Archives BL, Add. MSS 41262A, 41262B, 41263, 41264 · Hunt. L., Zachary Macaulay MSS · PRO, CO 217/63, 267/25, 270/2–4, 270/13; WO/1/352 · Public Archives of Nova Scotia, MG1, 219; MG4, 140–41, 143; MG100, 220, #4

George, David Lloyd, first Earl Lloyd-George of Dwyfor (1863–1945), prime minister, was born at 5 New York Place, Chorlton upon Medlock, Manchester, on 17 January 1863, the second child and elder son of William George (1820–1864), schoolmaster, and his wife, Elizabeth (1828–1896), daughter of David Lloyd, shoemaker and Baptist pastor, of Llanystumdwy, Caernarvonshire. Failing health led his father to return to farm in his native Pembrokeshire, and he died there in 1864. The family were then brought back to Llanystumdwy by Elizabeth's unmarried brother, Richard Lloyd, a master shoemaker. The children soon numbered three—Mary Ellen, the eldest, David, and a second son, William, born posthumously in 1865. Richard Lloyd proved to be a towering influence on the infant David. An autodidact of broad culture, he was also a strong Liberal politically and a lay preacher in the local church of the Campbellite Baptists, a radical offshoot of the main Baptist denomination. His role guided David Lloyd George's early steps in the law and politics. Indeed 'Uncle Lloyd' remained an influence in the shadows down to his death at the age of eighty-three in February 1917. By that time, his nephew David was prime minister of Great Britain.

Early years: the road to Westminster The boy David's political ascent was almost pre-ordained. At the age of five he was carried on his uncle's shoulders at meetings during the dramatic Liberal victories in Caernarvonshire and elsewhere in Wales at the 'great general election' of 1868.

David Lloyd George, first Earl Lloyd-George of Dwyfor (1863–1945), by George Charles Beresford, 1908

Lloyd George went to the local village school at Llanystumdwy, where he stayed until July 1878 when he was fifteen. He was admirably taught mathematics and geography by the headmaster, David Evans. But even here politics intruded. The school was an Anglican foundation and when the children were invited to recite the catechism before a local landowner, Ellis Nanney, Lloyd George led a strike by the pupils. When his brother, William, broke the silence by intoning 'I believe', according to legend (later denied) he received a thrashing from his elder brother. Ellis Nanney was destined to be Lloyd George's opponent at his first parliamentary election in Caernarfon Boroughs. In 1878 Lloyd George was attached to a solicitor's firm in nearby Portmadoc, Breese, Jones, and Casson. In 1884 he passed the Law Society final examinations with honours. He could now set up practice on his own in Cricieth (brother William was shortly to join him there), a platform for a future political career.

It was a time of great political excitement in Wales. The impact of democracy after the Reform Acts of 1867 and 1884 fired campaigns by radical Liberals against landlordism and the established status of the Church of England in Wales. They fought for civic equality for nonconformists, social equality for tenant farmers and labourers—and increasingly national equality for Wales. Lloyd George plunged into political life while still in his teens. He took part in the debates of the Portmadoc debating society and spoke in local temperance and foreign mission gatherings. He proved to be a naturally graphic and compelling speaker with a rare gift of imagery. His political ambitions were kindled by a visit to London in 1881 at which he saw the House of Commons for the first time. He noted in his diary for 12 November 1881 (W. R. P. George, *Making of Lloyd George*, 101), 'I will not say but that I eyed the assembly in a spirit similar to that in which William the Conqueror eyed England on his visit to Edward the Confessor, as the region of his future domain. Oh, vanity!' By 1885 he had established a reputation as a fiery young orator on Liberal platforms. He took some part in the Merioneth contest in the general election of November 1885, and made a particular impact in a brilliant performance on a platform in Blaenau Ffestiniog in January 1886 when the main speaker was the Irish nationalist and land leaguer Michael Davitt. He was already spoken of as an MP in the making even though he was only just twenty-three.

A major crisis for Lloyd George, as for many others, was the Liberal split over Gladstone's Irish Home Rule Bill in 1886. He veered towards the opposing faction under his boyhood hero, Joseph Chamberlain. Legend has it that the accident that he missed a train in May 1886 which would have taken him to the inaugural meeting of Chamberlain's Radical Union was decisive. At any rate, he remained in the Gladstonian fold, even though his enthusiasm for Irish home rule remained equivocal. It was an early sign of the looseness of his political attachments, to be demonstrated so graphically later on in 1910, 1916, 1918, and other key phases of his career. At all events after the Liberals' heavy defeat at the 1886 general election, he rose rapidly to political prominence. His diary (4 September 1887) spelt out the calculated strategy that he would pursue to promote himself as a politician. He took a vigorous part in campaigns against the payment of tithe to the established church, to reform the land system, and above all to disestablish the church. He was also a forceful delegate to the North Wales Liberal Federation. A legal case which made him famous was the Llanfrothen burial case when he successfully defended some local nonconformists who dared to bury their dead in the parish churchyard.

There was also an important personal milestone—marriage on 24 January 1888 to Margaret (Maggie) Owen (1866–1941) of Mynydd Ednyfed. She was the daughter of a prosperous Methodist farmer who disapproved of her wish to marry the radical young Baptist attorney. But Lloyd George won him over in the end. They settled in Criccieth at first, where a son, Richard, was born in 1889. He was followed by Mair in 1890 (who was to die young in 1907), Olwen in 1892, Gwilym [*see* George, Gwilym Lloyd-] in 1894, and later Megan [*see* George, Lady Megan Arfon Lloyd] in 1902. But Margaret's reluctance to live in London and Lloyd George's inclination to seek consolation elsewhere foreshadowed the later strains of their relationship. It was from the first made brutally clear to Margaret that her husband was driven by dominating political ambition. 'My supreme idea is to get on. To this idea, I shall sacrifice everything—except, I trust, honesty. I am prepared to thrust even love itself under the wheels of my Juggernaut if it obstructs the way' (David Lloyd George to Margaret Owen, *c*.1885, NL Wales, D. Lloyd George MS 20,404C). The next half-century was to provide graphic commentary on this candid self-analysis.

First steps in parliament In 1890 Lloyd George found his base in parliament. He had been nominated in 1888 for the small Caernarfon Boroughs constituency, then held by the Conservatives. He cultivated support in the area, including contributions to the press and a short-lived Welsh National Newspaper Company. He also became a 'boy alderman' on the first Caernarvonshire county council. Then in 1890 the sitting Caernarfon MP died and Lloyd George had to fight a fierce by-election against the Conservative squire Ellis Nanney. With the Anglican cathedral in Bangor, it was one of the few really marginal seats in Wales, there was much local pressure from the more nationalistic Liberals, and Lloyd George scraped home by just eighteen votes. Although he was to remain member for Caernarfon Boroughs for the next fifty-five years, it was a safe seat for him only from 1906 onwards. But the career of a great parliamentarian had been forged.

In his first ventures in parliament, Lloyd George showed himself to be a radical of distinctive style and outlook. This came out in a dashing maiden speech on the familiar theme of temperance. He was, like Tom Ellis and other young colleagues, strongly Welsh in his radicalism, deeply involved with the politics of the nonconformist chapel, with land and temperance reform, and with campaigning for the special needs and status of Wales. As throughout his career, he viewed the London establishment—crown, court, civil service, the armed services, high society—as a self-made Welsh nonconformist outsider. On the other hand, he was something of an outsider in the ranks of Welsh radicalism too. He took little part in the campaign for higher education which led to the University of Wales being created on a federal basis in 1893. After all, he had left school himself at fifteen. Again, while he battled for the civil rights of nonconformists, he viewed their creed privately with scepticism, even contempt. He loathed the moralism and the hypocrisy of wealthy deacons in the 'big pews' of the chapels; he told his wife how he hated 'being cramped up in a suffocating malodorous chapel listening to some superstitions I had heard thousands of times before' (David Lloyd George to Margaret Lloyd George, 13 Aug 1890, NL Wales, D. Lloyd George MS 20,407C). He was also a young politician of unusual independence of outlook, casual over party affiliations and orthodoxies. He ventured to irritate Gladstone himself in attacks on the Clergy Discipline Bill, though it probably added to his radical reputation. In the 1892 general election he increased his majority to 196. But the Liberal majority overall was only forty and that dependent on the support of the Irish nationalists.

Lloyd George's main concern, in a parliament dominated by Gladstone's second Irish Home Rule Bill, was to press for priority for Welsh disestablishment. This campaign reached a new level of rebelliousness in April 1894.

With the succession of the imperialist aristocrat Lord Rosebery as prime minister after Gladstone's resignation, Lloyd George joined three other Welsh Liberals, Herbert Lewis and Frank Edwards from rural Wales, and D. A. Thomas (later Lord Rhondda) from the industrial south, in a short-term revolt against the party whips. When a Welsh Disestablishment Bill came before the Commons in May 1895 Lloyd George engaged in complex manoeuvres to try to get a form of Welsh home rule tacked on to the disendowment parts of the measure. When the government resigned after defeat on the trivial 'cordite' vote in June, there were those who blamed Lloyd George and his freelance activities. The home secretary responsible for the Welsh Church Bill, Herbert Asquith, believed Lloyd George to be guilty of disloyalty and remembered these events long after. At the ensuing general election, Lloyd George was somewhat fortunate to scrape home by less than 200 votes.

Lloyd George's involvement with Welsh national issues now reached a crisis. In 1894 he had launched the so-called *Cymru Fydd* League (popularly known as Young Wales). The object was to take over the Liberal federations of north and south Wales in order to promote home rule for Wales. He made headway in the Welsh-speaking north and west. But *Cymru Fydd* ran into fierce opposition from the south Wales Liberals, and their leader, Lloyd George's former ally, D. A. Thomas. A crusading lecture tour by Lloyd George in the industrial valleys had only limited impact. At a fateful meeting of the south Wales Liberals at Newport in January 1896, Lloyd George met with the indignity of being howled down by the Anglicized mercantile representatives of the southern ports of Swansea, Cardiff, and Newport. *Cymru Fydd* promptly collapsed, as did hopes of Welsh self-government for almost another hundred years. Condemned by the 'Newport Englishmen', Lloyd George had suffered a serious defeat.

This coincided with much anxiety in Lloyd George's private life, leading to his suffering from a kind of nervous exhaustion, a feature of his career at moments of extreme crisis, as later on in December 1916. He had been earlier involved in a futile venture of investing in alleged gold deposits in Patagonia, losing significant sums of money on his shares, and had continual financial problems. They were only partially relieved by his starting a new law partnership in London in 1897. His marriage too was not altogether happy, with his wife Margaret still reluctant to move to London and Lloyd George himself seeking female company elsewhere. In 1897 he was mentioned in a paternity suit, when Catherine Edwards, the young wife of a Montgomeryshire doctor, alleged (unsuccessfully in the end) that Lloyd George had fathered her illegitimate child. As Lloyd George recovered from these various torments and his political defeat over *Cymru Fydd*, one thing became clear—that henceforth his political horizon would encompass far more than simply the local politics of Wales.

Second South African War and the progressive advance In fact, Lloyd George bounced back as a leading Liberal spokesman, being eventually given a front bench role. He denounced the government's bills on agricultural land rating (1896) and education (1897), which gave him scope to develop assaults on landlordism and the church. Then his career was transformed in the course of 1899. In April, the untimely death of the chief whip, Tom Ellis, gave Lloyd George an unchallenged ascendancy in Liberal Wales. More importantly, the outbreak of the Second South African War in October made him prominent, or notorious, throughout British public life. He was on a visit to Canada when the war broke out, but from the start he was implacable in his opposition. Though not in principle hostile to the idea of empire, he put himself at the head of the 'pro-Boer' or 'Little England' opponents of the war. During the early British disasters in Natal, he became a devastating critic. In particular, he trained his fire on his old hero Joseph Chamberlain who, he believed, had not only connived at the war on behalf of capitalists on the Rand, but was personally profiting through his links with armaments firms. Lloyd George was fiercely attacked— his eldest son had to leave his school because of bullying. Even in Caernarfon Boroughs there were 'jingo' mobs threatening to assault him. In the 'khaki' election of October 1900 he did well to retain his seat by a somewhat increased majority.

But Lloyd George remained a target for imperialists. In December 1901 he had to flee for his life from Birmingham town hall when an anti-war meeting was broken up by a Chamberlainite mob. According to legend, he escaped by dressing up in the uniform of a (much taller) policeman. But it was to Lloyd George that the ultimate victory went. The war became increasingly unpopular as Boer guerrillas kept the British army at bay, and thousands of Boer women and young children died in concentration camps on the veldt. Campbell-Bannerman, the Liberal leader, denounced the 'methods of barbarism' with which the war was being prosecuted. Lloyd George had become a major, nationally recognized politician now, prominent in rebuilding the Liberal Party by keeping his links with both pro-Boer and Liberal Imperialist politicians. He also ensured that the Liberal *Daily News* changed its politics to become an anti-war newspaper, by persuading the Quaker cocoa magnate George Cadbury to purchase it. Then as always, the press was vital for Lloyd George's advancement. When the war came to an end with the peace of Vereeniging in May 1902, his public standing had been transformed.

Lloyd George's reputation continued to grow rapidly with the Liberal revival from 1902. The new Education Bill introduced by Arthur Balfour in April 1902 offered him new opportunities. While in many ways he approved of the new structure created for primary and secondary education, he led nonconformist resistance to the public financing of Anglican and Roman Catholic schools. He recalled from his own childhood the social resentment provoked among dissenters in Anglican 'single-school areas'. There was individual passive resistance by nonconformists in England. In Wales, by contrast, Lloyd George seized the initiative by leading a collective revolt by the Welsh county councils which would have to administer the bill; by February 1904 all of them were under Liberal control. He offered a solution by which the act would be operated but on condition that the religious and other demands of nonconformists over the running of the schools be met. Several councils were declared to be in default. There remained an impasse until the autumn of 1905 by which time the Balfour government was in dire straits.

Labour issues were another priority for Lloyd George, not least after the three-year strike of the Bethesda slate quarrymen in his own constituency against their auto-cratic employer, Lord Penrhyn. He also warned of the dangers to trade unionism from 'free labour', using the example of so-called 'Chinese slavery' on the Rand in South Africa. He took a leading part also in the Liberal defence of free trade in the face of Joseph Chamberlain's campaign for an imperial tariff reform in 1903. He urged that pensions and other social measures should be paid for with redistributive taxation, not through protectionist food taxes. On the other hand, he was never the most dog-matic of free-traders, and he recognized the problems of foreign competition. Free trade was a means, not an end for him, then and always. As over Irish home rule or edu-cation, he was always an independent spirit, not a dog-matic adherent of the party line.

President of the Board of Trade In the autumn of 1905 Lloyd George was recovering in Italy after a minor operation. Then it was announced that the Unionist government of Balfour had resigned and the elderly Liberal leader, Campbell-Bannerman, became prime minister. The Lib-erals were confirmed in power in January 1906 with a mas-sive landslide majority. Lloyd George, with no previous experience of ministerial responsibility, found himself in the cabinet as president of the Board of Trade. It launched a career of nearly seventeen unbroken years at the pinn-acle of power in peace and in war. His style as a minister was from the first unconventional. He was never one to be bogged down in official boxes, always preferring to obtain information orally from the widest range of contacts, however unorthodox. Some civil servants thought him lazy, but his free-ranging, intuitive style often led to their being by-passed in the interests of swift decision making. It was clear that his stage was now a British, if not an inter-national one. He continued to be a powerful voice for Welsh Liberalism. In 1906 he was curiously involved with trying to tack on a Welsh educational council to the gov-ernment's abortive Education Bill, which was thrown out in the Lords. Welsh disestablishment continued to engage him as a front-line issue. At the Treasury from 1908 he found new funding for the Welsh National Museum and National Library, and he was faithful in attendance at chapel and eisteddfod.

But as president of the Board of Trade Lloyd George made a far wider impact as a vigorous and dynamic execu-tive minister. He showed especial skill and subtlety in his personal contacts, notably in handling deputations of businessmen and industrialists, flattering them, listening carefully, and probing for weak links. More, he passed a remarkable series of important legislative measures to defend British commerce—the Merchant Shipping Act (1906), the Patents Act (1907), the Port of London Authority Act (1908), and a new census of production. Contempor-aries noted that this pugnacious and eloquent free-trader was perhaps something of a protectionist. Certainly he was no doctrinaire free-trader. The government, as a whole, frustrated by the Lords in obstructing its bills, had in this area at least a record of major legislative achieve-ment. It was one acknowledged by his Unionist opponent on the floor of the house, Andrew Bonar Law, with whom Lloyd George struck up an unlikely but most important political friendship.

At the Board of Trade, too, Lloyd George developed his skills in another crucial area—the handling of labour. Here he proved to be remarkably interventionist. He negotiated his way successfully through major disputes in the cotton and coal industries. Praise was lavished on him (perhaps to excess) at the settlement of a threatened national railway strike in October 1907 via a conciliation board to review wage agreements. It created new links between him and the trade unions; his special relation-ship with the labour movement (though not the Labour Party) was a main theme in his career down to 1919 or even 1922. Popular with the classes, Lloyd George was now something of a hero with the masses as well. He had also to endure a devastating personal ordeal—the death from appendicitis of his favourite daughter, Mair, in November 1907 at the age of seventeen. Perhaps through kindling a sense of guilt, it seems somehow to have pushed him on towards new campaigns for social reform. The old Liberal of Welsh chapel politics was becoming the leading new Liberal of his time.

A reforming chancellor In April 1908 Asquith succeeded Campbell-Bannerman as prime minister. Lloyd George followed him as chancellor of the exchequer. It was in some ways a risky appointment. Lloyd George had no spe-cialist knowledge of public finance, and his handling of statistics was always cavalier or perhaps romantic. His civil servants at the Treasury found him unconventional in methods of work: he seemed to have an aversion to paperwork and his command of detail was often hazy. But his vision now ranged far beyond narrow arcane financial details. After his earlier limited views on social questions, he sought to make the Treasury the powerhouse of long-term sustained reform. Already he had been in contact with his friend Winston Churchill, who succeeded him at the Board of Trade, to promote the new Liberalism of social welfare, to combat poverty, unemployment, ill health, and malnutrition, in place of the old Liberalism of Gladstonian days. This programme would deal with immense issues of human and social deprivation; it would also outflank the socialism of the Independent Labour Party while showing the Unionists that social reform could be financed in a free trade country through direct taxation. He had an early taste of reforming activity by taking over the passage of old-age pensions, launched by Asquith at the Treasury, which for the first time gave old people a state-financed pension of 5s. a week. In commit-tee, Lloyd George accepted an amendment to remove the reduction of pension for a married couple: this cost perhaps an extra £400,000 a year. Elderly citizens would collect it at their post office: some exclaimed 'God bless Lord [*sic*] George.' His passion for social welfare was taken further during a significant visit to Germany in August 1908 when he looked in detail at the Bismarckian legacy of social insurance and labour exchanges—and also for the first time engaged in serious discussions on foreign affairs, and Anglo-German relations in particular.

The main landmark of Lloyd George's social programme, which turned out to be an immense constitutional landmark as well, was the so-called 'People's Budget' of April 1909. It was one of the most momentous in British history, and was very much the chancellor's work presented to a somewhat sceptical cabinet. In a lengthy, somewhat rambling budget speech of over four hours on 29 April, he declared that it was a 'war budget' to 'wage implacable warfare against poverty and squalidness' (*Hansard 5C*, 4.548). It would do this through new direct taxation on spirits, on estates, on higher incomes (with a 6*d*. in the pound 'supertax' on incomes over £5000 a year) and, most sensationally, through various taxes on land, notably on the 'unearned increment' on the value of land enhanced by the effort of the community. It was subsequently claimed that Lloyd George deliberately framed a budget which the House of Lords would be compelled to reject. But there seems no evidence for this. His main need was for vastly more money—to pay for the new dreadnought battleships and to meet the £16 million cost of the new old-age pensions. It would also deal with a growing crisis in the finances of local government. But it was also an explicit attempt, through income tax and other direct taxation, to create a new platform for social advance—national development, road building, afforestation, and public works generally. It would seize the political initiative. If the Lords wanted to reject it, they would do so at their peril. The 'great assize of the people' would decide.

In the summer and autumn it became clear that the Lords would indeed reject the budget, the first time since the revolution of 1688. In retaliation, Lloyd George delivered a series of fiery speeches, notably at Limehouse and Newcastle, to drive them on to new heights of fury. The Lords, he declared at Newcastle on 9 October 1909 (*The Times*, 10 Oct 1909), in language that terrified King Edward VII, were only 'five hundred ordinary men chosen at random from amongst the unemployed', chosen on the principle of 'the first of the litter'. The chancellor seemed to be preaching class war. After the Lords rejected the budget, a general election was held in January 1910 at which the Liberals held on to power, though with a majority of only two over the Unionists, leaving them dependent on the support of Labour and the Irish nationalists.

Throughout the next eighteen months, Lloyd George urged his colleagues that there should be no surrender. He strongly backed a new Parliament Bill which would permanently limit the powers of the Lords by giving the Commons primacy on all certified money bills and by limiting the Lords' delaying power to only two years. That would open the way for Irish home rule and Welsh disestablishment both to become law. Lloyd George urged more conservative colleagues like Haldane and Grey that, rather than embark on the quagmire of reforming the composition of the upper house, it was the powers of the Lords on which they should focus. Asquith himself handled the constitutional crisis over the Parliament Bill with judicial skill. Another general election was won in December 1910 with a very similar result. The People's Budget, land taxes and all, became law in 1910, and in August 1911, threatened with mass creation of new Liberal peers by the king if they resisted, the Lords narrowly passed the Parliament Act as well. Lloyd George's standing as a radical tribune had never seemed more secure.

Yet, in fact, during the height of the Parliament Bill crisis in the summer of 1910, soon after the accession of the new king, George V, an extraordinary episode had taken place. It showed that alongside Lloyd George the bitter partisan was a different figure, a man who envisaged national government through a coalition. He proposed this to colleagues such as Grey and Churchill on the Liberal side and to Balfour, the Unionist leader (with whom he struck up a surprising friendship). Lloyd George suggested that most of the controversial issues of the day—free trade, Irish home rule, Lords' reform, or Welsh disestablishment—were in fact 'non-controversial' and could be passed on to fact-finding independent commissions. A new national administration could focus on the supreme needs of the day—social reform or 'national efficiency', and, to a lesser degree, national defence. To promote the latter, he suggested selective national service on the Swiss model. Coalition appealed to free spirits like Churchill and Smith. But the party regulars, Asquith on the Liberal side, men like Austen Chamberlain among the Unionists, felt that the roots of party could not be erased by the magical touch of a Welsh outsider. The dream of a national coalition perished in 1910—although the idea was to remain part of Lloyd George's scheme of things henceforth.

The troubles of Liberal England Lloyd George's next and even greater achievement reflected both his new Liberal zeal for social reform and his ability to work out strategic alliances to gain a broad base of support. This was his National Insurance Act of 1911, the zenith of his career as a social reformer. He had limited help in the cabinet. Ministers such as Haldane were frankly sceptical, while Churchill had moved to the right in the face of violent labour disputes in the mines and railways, and had become reviled among the working class for sending in troops to quell disturbances in the Welsh mining valleys around Tonypandy. Lloyd George's new allies were a wider group—lesser ministers such as Sir Rufus Isaacs, the Jewish attorney-general, and a radical reformer, C. F. G. Masterman, a kind of Christian socialist. On the back benches, health insurance drew him to Dr Christopher Addison, a distinguished anatomist newly returned for an East End constituency: 'we encourage each other to dream dreams but to base them on existing reality', the latter observed (C. Addison, *Four and a Half Years*, 1, 1934, 22). Among the intelligentsia

Lloyd George received guidance from figures such as the sociologist Seebohm Rowntree and W. H. Dawson, an authority on German social policy. The press provided another range of support, notably that zealous reformer, C. P. Scott of the *Manchester Guardian*, and George Riddell, owner of the *News of the World*, who bought the impecunious chancellor both a home at Walton Heath near his favourite golf course, and one of the new motor cars. But among the patrician Liberal Party leadership, Lloyd George was still the pushy, lower-middle-class Welsh Baptist on the outside looking in.

For all that, Lloyd George's National Insurance Act of 1911 was a triumph, Britain's most important measure of social reform prior to the Beveridge report of 1942. He used the familiar insurance principle, known to all householders, to underlie a system of state-assisted contributory social insurance broadly on the German model, as interpreted by W. H. Dawson. Contributors to the national health insurance scheme would pay 4*d.* and the state and employers together pay 5*d.*—'ninepence for fourpence', a bargain in anybody's language. There would also be a limited programme of unemployment insurance, to include construction and shipbuilding. His measure was fiercely attacked, in some cases rightly, since many of the basic financial principles were unclear. Trade unions were unenthusiastic about insurance contributions which would be a levy on the hard-pressed working man and his family. Insurance companies and friendly societies were worried about their own insurance schemes. An extraordinary campaign by duchesses and their housemaids declared they would never lick stamps for Lloyd George. Most damaging of all, the medical profession, who would man the panels under the health scheme, feared for their incomes. Lloyd George handled them all with great skill. With the aid of Dr Addison, he outmanoeuvred the doctors just as another Welshman, Aneurin Bevan, was to do over the National Health Service in 1948. The Labour Party was won over when the use of the trade unions as approved agencies led to greatly increased membership for both unions and party.

In the end, Lloyd George received all-party acclaim for a brilliant legislative coup. A major blow had been struck against Victorian poor-law ideas of 'less eligibility' and on behalf of the idea of social citizenship. The basis for a new public medical system had been set out, with key provision also for medical research. A nationwide machinery had been set up to run the system, with important public servants like Arthur Salter and Thomas Jones. It was a major advance towards a welfare democracy; overseas, admirers such as former president Theodore Roosevelt in the United States hailed Lloyd George's achievement.

This was a heady period in Lloyd George's public life. At the end of the great debate on national insurance, in April 1912 Lloyd George won yet more acclaim for his negotiating a settlement of a national miners' strike by creating the basis for a minimum wage. He seemed to be promoting the government's more radical programme almost on his own. Yet this also marked one of the great troughs of his career. His long-running difficulty with his marriage was reinforced in the summer of 1912 when Frances Stevenson (1888–1972) [see George, Frances Louise Lloyd], a young woman brought in as tutor in French for his daughter, Megan, entered his life. She was soon his long-term mistress. She became his second wife on 23 October 1943; her memoirs, *The Years that are Past* (1967), noted that 'their real marriage' had taken place thirty years before.

More publicly damaging, by far, was a serious charge of corruption in the Marconi case. As over Patagonian gold in the 1890s, Lloyd George was seen to lack judgement in money matters. It emerged that he and the attorney-general, Sir Rufus Isaacs, had bought shares in the American Marconi company from Isaacs's brother, just when the British Marconi company was about to enter into a highly profitable deal with the British government to build telegraphy stations across the empire. The part played by radio during the sinking of the liner *Titanic* underlined the importance of long-range telegraphic communication. Lloyd George argued that he had lost money on the shares purchased, and that in any case American and British Marconi companies were quite distinct. But it looked like a case of major sleaze by ministers of the crown. There were overtones of antisemitism in the attacks on the roles of the Isaacs brothers and Herbert Samuel, while Unionists sought to get even with 'the little Welsh attorney' who had tormented them for so long. After a select committee reported on strictly party grounds, Asquith and the government took a simple partisan point of view, and Lloyd George narrowly escaped. But his reputation was undeniably tarnished by the stain of Marconi.

Politics were not going Lloyd George's way altogether at this time either. The government was under fire from many directions. There were long and often violent strikes in many major industries, with some loss of life. Ireland was a constant torment. In addition, the women suffragettes turned their wrath on the government, after fierce handling of demonstrators by the Home Office. Lloyd George himself was actually known to be a supporter of votes for women, but he found himself under attack from them for being insufficiently zealous—literally so when angry suffragettes blew up part of his new house being built at Walton Heath. In late 1913 he tried to find another great radical cry to rouse the Liberal masses, by raising again the old cry of the land. A national campaign was mounted in the autumn for rural and urban land reform, including the taxing of site values, and schemes for publicly supported housing were linked with it. It was launched with a major speech at Bedford on 11 October, and for a brief moment threatened to regain the political initiative for the beleaguered Liberal government. But somehow the new land campaign fell rather flat. In an increasingly urbanized world, it seemed out of date, a replay of the issues of Lloyd George's Welsh youth. His strident anti-landlord rhetoric failed to strike the chord that it once had done. Elsewhere he became caught up in a massive political battle with his old ally Churchill over the 1914 naval estimates and there was talk of his resignation. But in the event he came out the loser.

Lloyd George turned to another massive budget initiative to boost himself and the government in the spring of 1914, including more radical taxes than in 1909, an increased income tax, a new supertax, and further proposed land charges even though the land taxes of 1909 seemed to be yielding little or nothing. But the budget proved to be a great procedural mess, and was actually ruled by the speaker not to be a 'money bill' as interpreted by the Parliament Act. Again Lloyd George was frustrated. Charles Masterman described him in May 1914 as 'jumpy, irritable, overworked and unhappy' (Masterman to Arthur Ponsonby, 30 May 1914, Bodl. Oxf., Ponsonby papers). He was becoming detached from his roots in Wales, yet not finding many allies in London politics either. His two households, his wife in Cricieth, Frances Stevenson in London, testified to his divided existence.

Of course, Lloyd George was still the government's leading voice. He was frequently in conclave with radical allies such as Addison planning new initiatives for 1915, education, or housing, or perhaps a kind of national health service, all of them gaps in the armoury of the new Liberalism. He was still an important figure in labour matters, settling the great railway strike of 1911 as well as the miners' strike a year later. He saw the historic issue of Welsh disestablishment passed through parliament a first time in 1912. Under the Parliament Act this old radical objective could now take effect at the end of 1914. He himself delivered a slashing attack (16 May 1912) on aristocratic Anglican opponents of disestablishment. They denounced disendowment; yet, as a result of the land settlements after the Tudor Reformation, their own hands were 'dripping with the fat of sacrilege' (*Hansard 5C*, 38.1326). He was also an important intermediary, for the first time, in Irish affairs. By 1913–14 Irish home rule had reached a grave impasse. It passed the house as had Welsh disestablishment in 1912; there was no permanent obstacle that the Lords could offer in future to prevent Ireland achieving self-government. As always on Irish matters, Lloyd George had his doubts. He attempted a major modification in March 1914 under which the application of home rule to the six mainly protestant countries of north-east Ulster would be suspended for up to six years. But this too failed amid the historic antagonisms of Irish politics. A civil war between Ulster and the south, with gun-running on both sides, seemed a real possibility. Lloyd George had failed here too, and by comparison with his high noon of 1911 he was still somewhat in the shadows.

The road to war Then Lloyd George's entire career, and the history of his country, was transformed by the coming of world war in August 1914. Usually thought of as an essentially domestic politician, he had in fact been involved with foreign policy to an increasing degree since 1908. He had met Kaiser Wilhelm II in 1907 and had discussed foreign relations with Bethmann Hollweg during his visit to Germany in 1908; he was deeply concerned at aggressive German naval rivalry. He was no longer the neo-pacifist little Englander that people had suspected him of being in South African War days. He served on the committee of imperial defence and would undoubtedly have been briefed on the prospects of a German attack through Belgium and the channel ports. In July 1911 he shook the political world with a speech delivered during the Agadir crisis with Germany in Morocco in which he appeared to threaten the Germans with military or naval retaliation. He was never a peacemonger thereafter in public or in private. He showed some enthusiasm for the Balkan wars of 1912–13 since they involved set-backs for his old Gladstonian bugbear, the Turks, always 'unspeakable' to him.

On the other hand, on issues such as the naval estimates Lloyd George seemed to be in the 'peace party'. The Liberals' anti-war foreign affairs group saw him as a friend. It was known that he had been an opponent of Churchill's demands for increased naval estimates since 1912. He spoke of warmer relations with Germany in the early summer of 1914. At the Mansion House on 17 July 1914, well after the murder of Archduke Franz Ferdinand at Sarajevo on 28 June, he declared that internationally the sky had seldom seemed to be so relatively blue. As events moved towards war on 1–3 August 1914, he seemed to be among those playing down Britain's territorial commitment to help France through the military links established within the entente. 'I am moving through a nightmare world these days' he wrote to his wife (David Lloyd George to Margaret Lloyd George, 3 Aug 1914, NL Wales, D. Lloyd George MS, 20,433C). Yet he had long foreseen a German invasion of Belgium, another 'small nation', with the direct threat to British national security, and there was never any real prospect of his resigning along with Viscount Morley and John Burns. Pro-war friends such as Churchill were pushing at an open door. After a moment of doubt on 3 August, he committed himself to Britain's going to war. Unwittingly, he had taken the decisive step that would lead him to the premiership.

Lloyd George at war After the tensions of the pre-war years, Lloyd George now found a new buoyancy. The party truce he had visualized back in 1910 had now come about, with Irish home rule suspended for the duration of the war. He could now throw himself into vigorous executive action. Faced with the challenge of salvaging the national finances during total war, he reacted with remarkable confidence, working with Cunliffe, governor of the Bank of England. The 'flapping penguins' among the bankers, hoarding gold and calling in loans from the discount market, were given backbone by the chancellor's decisiveness. By 10 August, the immediate financial crisis was over. A bank moratorium was declared, the suspension of specie payments was avoided, new £1 and 10s. notes were issued by the Treasury as legal tender, banks were guaranteed against bad debts made on pre-war bills of exchange. Economists, including the new Treasury official John Maynard Keynes, previously scornful of Lloyd George's grasp of financial technicalities, now sang his praises. More questionable was his war budget that November which included a doubling of income tax and an increase in tea and beer duties but was generally too cautious.

Lloyd George followed up with further vigorous action on the home front, though with mixed results. He sought to reduce the impact of the drinking of beer and spirits on war production, a theme congenial to an old nonconformist advocate of temperance. The strength of beer was reduced, opening hours were cut, measures were taken to deter munitions workers from consumption of alcohol and the unfortunate King George V later agreed to 'the king's pledge' to abstain from consuming alcoholic drink for the duration of the war. There was even an ambitious attempt to nationalize the drink trade in the spring of 1915, but that collapsed, leaving only the unique state-run pubs of the 'Carlisle experiment'. More effective was a high-profile Treasury agreement concluded by Lloyd George with Arthur Henderson and the other members of the TUC in March 1915, the high point of his special relationship with organized labour. The unions agreed to accept the 'dilution' of the workforce in munitions factories (this would allow for women workers) and for the suspension of strikes in return for a vague promise to check wartime profiteering and a firmer guarantee of union rights of collective bargaining during the war. At a time when his fellow Liberals were viewing him with greater suspicion, over civil liberties or the prospect of military conscription, his standing with both sides of industry and with the general public seemed to rise ever upwards.

Inevitably, for so prominent a member of the Asquith cabinet, Lloyd George would be involved in debate on the conduct of the war. In the first few weeks, in fact, immersed as he was in the affairs of the Treasury, he made no public pronouncement and this led to much speculation in the press. However, in a stirring speech to a large audience of London Welshmen at the Queen's Hall on 19 September 1914, he made a strong commitment to all-out war, a 'fight to a finish' (*The Times*, 20 Sept 1914). Germany was condemned as 'the road hog of Europe'; the allies would advance 'from terror to triumph'. It was, Lloyd George proclaimed, a just war, a war for liberal principles including the defence of small nations against German and Austrian aggression. There was much sentimental reference to 'the little five-foot-five nations', gallant little Belgium, Serbia, Montenegro—and, by implication, gallant little Wales. Floods of enthusiastic letters poured thereafter into his office. He was also at odds with the mighty Kitchener, secretary of state for war during early wartime disasters. There was a small but significant clash over the admitting of nonconformist chaplains to the British army and to the creation of a Welsh division in France, a battle which Lloyd George won. More seriously in the early months of 1915, Lloyd George was attacking Kitchener for responsibility for the shortage of shells and other military supplies on the western front.

Increasingly now Lloyd George turned his attention to wider strategic issues. On 1 January 1915 he launched a fierce attack in cabinet on the hopeless war of attrition in the trenches in France, extending from the channel ports to the Swiss borders. He joined Churchill in calling for a more flexible strategy and for assaults on the enemy's 'under-belly' in the Balkans and eastern Mediterranean—what critics called 'side-shows'. Battle was joined in the government between 'westerners' who included generals such as Haig and Robertson, and mainly civilian 'easterners' among whom Lloyd George was conspicuous. He was certainly among those who approved of the sending of the expedition to the Dardanelles although when it collapsed in bloody failure it was noticeable that it was on Churchill that the main blame then fell. Asquith's government was now in serious disarray, the more so when Turkey entered the war on the side of Germany and Austria–Hungary. Lloyd George responded with calls for the dispatch of British forces to the Balkans and also for diplomatic initiatives to enlist the support of Greece, Romania, and Bulgaria.

On 17 May 1915 a week-long political crisis began at home, triggered off by a dispute between Churchill and admiral of the fleet Lord Fisher, when the Unionists declared that they could no longer support Asquith in a party truce. On 17 May Bonar Law had a meeting with Lloyd George at which there was some talk of Lloyd George's becoming prime minister. But he was not the agent of the Liberal government's collapse. Rather was it Asquith, saddened by personal circumstances and wartime set-backs, who seized the initiative to create a coalition with the Unionists and also Labour. An old Liberal ally such as Haldane was sacrificed to anti-German feeling while Reginald McKenna, an old rival of Lloyd George's, succeeded him at the Treasury. Lloyd George himself was the pivotal figure. His agreement to move to the newly created Ministry of Munitions, with Addison as his assistant, was decisive in Asquith's remaining prime minister. The Liberals still dominated the wartime coalition. Asquith's wife, Margot, often a critic, wrote 'L. G. has come grandly out of this—he has the sweetest nature in the world' (Margot Asquith to St Loe Strachey, 27 May 1915, HLRO, Strachey papers). On the other hand, if he were to succeed in his new ministry, Lloyd George would clearly advance his power to new heights.

Minister of munitions   Going to munitions was a great gamble. But from the start Lloyd George proved to be a spectacularly effective executive minister. He sensed that in total war Britain must be turned into a war economy. New controls were imposed on the supply and allocation of raw materials. The engineering, chemical, and other industries were effectively taken over in the service of the war effort. Younger businessmen such as G. M. Booth carried out the minister's demands into the factories and workshops. They became popularly known as 'men of push and go', a term first used by Lloyd George himself in a speech on a new Defence of the Realm Act on 9 March 1915. Munitions factories also became laboratories of change in the improvement of working conditions. The agreement with the trade unions ensured that the workforce in arms factories was much expanded, including the employment of tens of thousands of women workers, in itself a notable landmark in the social emancipation of women. On the other hand, labour relations remained a complex and contentious area. There were many disputes in the engineering trades, especially in Clydeside, and Lloyd George attempted to quell a major strike by skilled workers there in a difficult address to them in Glasgow on Christmas day 1915.

Despite these problems, there is no question that the supply of munitions of all kinds vastly expanded. When Lloyd George left the ministry in July 1916, supplies which had taken a year to produce in 1914–15 were now assembled within three weeks. Supplies of shells and ammunitions grew massively, mortars and especially machine-guns (Lewis and Vickers guns) were manufactured in vast numbers. The British expeditionary force became a big-gun army. Highly significant for the future, fifty armoured gun-carrying tanks came into service by early 1916. Perhaps all this was Lloyd George's supreme contribution to the ultimate winning of the war. Unquestionably his high-profile and inspirational activity added even further to his reputation.

Lloyd George's location in politics was also notably different. He was drifting away from his fellow Liberals, especially when his ally Churchill was dropped from the government. Disaster followed disaster in France, under first General French, then Haig. There came a serious set-back at Loos, the collapse of the Dardanelles expedition, the bleeding white of the French army at Verdun, massive losses (142,000) in four days at Arras. This drove Lloyd George seemingly closer towards the Conservatives. He now built up contacts with the imperialist followers of Lord Milner; several of them, notably Philip Kerr, were later to become his closest supporters. Meanwhile, at sea the Grand Fleet was badly mauled by the German navy at Jutland. A bloody climax was to be reached on 1 July 1916 at the start of the battle of the Somme, a disaster which saw 60,000 British casualties on the very first day, 20,000 of them killed. Lloyd George outspokenly condemned the dilatory approach of generals and government, even in a major speech in the Commons on 20 December 1915 which caused a sensation: 'Too late in moving here! Too late in the mocking spectre of "Too late"!' (*Hansard 5C*, 87.121).

The focal point of Lloyd George's criticisms was the issue of military conscription. It was known that the Liberals were divided, with their traditional commitment to civil liberties, while Unionists such as Curzon, Long, Lansdowne, and the Irishman Edward Carson felt that in a total war it was essential. Lloyd George seemed to join them in the preface to a book of war speeches, *From Terror to Triumph*, published on 13 September 1915, when he called openly for a compulsionist view towards military recruitment. Throughout that winter, Asquith's cabinet was torn by arguments about conscription, with Lloyd George central to them. Many Liberals were unhappy: the home secretary, John Simon, resigned. At one point in November 1915 Lloyd George appeared almost to be offering his resignation. At the end of December, Asquith wearily conceded the main point—the military conscription of all single men between the ages of eighteen and forty-five, subject to exclusions for key industrial workers and others. But the issue continued to rage and to tear the coalition almost apart. Eventually in May 1916 Asquith had to concede universal male conscription for married men as well.

There was much speculation at this point about Lloyd George's future. Some historians have subsequently seen the conscription issue as Lloyd George's 'bid for power'; evidence for this has been seen in the formation of a pro-Lloyd George Liberal war committee of Liberal MPs, including men such as Alfred Mond, Freddie Guest, William Sutherland, and others later among his closer allies. But the majority of Liberals still remained loyal to Asquith, while Unionists in general still viewed the mercurial munitions minister with much distrust. The government seemed to be failing almost everywhere. In Ireland, Asquith's maladroit response to the Easter rising by a small group of republicans in Dublin served only to maximize Irish disaffection and to trigger off the rise of Sinn Féin at the expense of the old nationalist party of Redmond. Lloyd George remained discontented, frequently contemplating resignation.

Secretary of state for war Then the situation was transformed in early June 1916 by the drowning of Kitchener at sea on a somewhat mysterious mission to Russia. Asquith had no option but to offer the crucial post of secretary of state for war to Lloyd George. After a month's ominous uncertainty, Lloyd George took it on 4 July 1916. He was now the central figure in the prosecution of the war. But at first he was embroiled in the ancient tribal animosities of Ireland. Asquith, tired and with his reputation tarnished after the Easter rising and the execution of republican leaders, asked Lloyd George to try to resolve somehow the endless impasse over Irish home rule. For three weeks he appeared to be within reach of a remarkable political triumph. It involved simultaneous but separate sets of discussions with both the Irish nationalists under their leader, John Redmond, and with the Unionists, Edward Carson and Walter Long, friendly Irishmen such as T. P. O'Connor MP acting as intermediaries. But the essential stumbling-block concerned the six mainly protestant counties of north-east Ulster which Lloyd George proposed to exclude from a home rule settlement. Was this exclusion to be temporary only for a period of years, or would Ireland be permanently partitioned? This circle could never be squared. Lloyd George had to admit failure at the end of July. Yet Asquith's very decision to hand over an Irish solution to him seemed only to confirm his indispensability to the government.

As secretary of state for war, even with the vast additional supplies of munitions, Lloyd George saw things go from bad to worse. The British offensive at the Somme had run into the sands with enormous loss of life, while a Russian offensive in Poland and another new offensive by the entente powers' new ally, Italy, also resulted in failure. Lloyd George was particularly disturbed by the failure to act in the Balkans which saw the defeat of Romania in October 1916. Depressed and angry, he spoke frequently of resignation and going to the country to tell the truth about the cause of failures. In early November, he had several meetings with Sir Maurice Hankey, observing, 'We are going to lose this war' (Roskill, 1.312 ff.).

These troubles were resolved in dramatic fashion in a complex series of events between 20 November and 9 December 1916, events that are still vigorously, even bitterly, debated. The fact that Max Aitken, Lord Beaverbrook, was both their major historian and a significant participant added passion to the controversy. The outcome was the permanent split of the Liberal Party and Lloyd George supplanting Asquith at 10 Downing Street. In fact, the crisis began with a threat to the leadership of the Unionist Bonar Law by his own back-benchers after a debate on Nigerian assets. The future of the coalition was now in real doubt. From 20 November, Lloyd George entered into private discussions with Bonar Law and the Irish Unionist Sir Edward Carson about remodelling the government. Asquith was kept informed of the existence of these talks, but it was clear that a lack of confidence in the present method of government lay behind their discussions. The subtle mediation of Aitken, a close ally of Bonar Law's and an open admirer of Lloyd George, added to the sense of unease.

On 1 December they sent a draft to Asquith which the prime minister rejected. Here was a crisis. Lloyd George rallied Bonar Law with a famous note—'The life of the country depends on resolute action by you *now*' (Lloyd George to Bonar Law, 2 Dec 1916, HLRO, Bonar Law papers, 117/1/30). However, on 3 December Asquith did accept a revised scheme, which would set up a supreme war cabinet of three men, but would also retain Asquith himself as prime minister. Despite the mass of rumours in the press, the crisis appeared to be over. Then Asquith unexpectedly threw out the agreement after discussions with McKenna and other Liberal colleagues, and a naked struggle for power broke out.

In the next thirty-six hours it emerged that not only had Asquith lost the confidence of the Unionist Party, but also that many Liberals openly favoured Lloyd George as a leader who would win the war. Lloyd George and Bonar Law both resigned, and Asquith himself had to surrender the seals of office on 5 December. Bonar Law predictably turned down the offer of the premiership and on the evening of 7 December Lloyd George kissed the king's hand to become prime minister. By 9 December he had won the support not only of the Unionists but also, by the narrowest of majorities, of the Labour Party. Even more remarkably, over 100 Liberal MPs, many of them of the second rank, had endorsed his premiership. On 19 December, a stirring speech in the Commons confirmed his authority and his unflinching commitment 'to the rescue of mankind from the most overwhelming catastrophe' (*Hansard 5C*, 88.1357–8).

No part of his career has aroused more intense controversy. Lloyd George has been freely accused of blatant disloyalty, of mounting a conspiracy via Aitken and others behind his leader's back, to grasp the supreme office. In fact, attempts to show that he was building up a kind of anti-Asquith faction among his own back-benchers are not convincing, while it was Asquith who broke off negotiations and provoked the final trial of strength. Only after that, from the morning of 4 December, could Lloyd George amass the strength to create a viable government. On the other hand, the effect of his proposals was clearly to undermine Asquith's authority. At every stage it was Lloyd George who emerged with enhanced strength, while the press offered open support. In the end, perhaps the explanation for the events of December 1916 is not so much political as psychological. Lloyd George simply looked like the vigorous, dynamic leader who could win the war, while the faltering, weary Asquith, so dominant in peacetime, did not. Lloyd George emerged through intricate manoeuvres among secret cabals at Westminster. But, just like Churchill in May 1940, he was the people's choice and their confidence proved not to be misplaced.

Lloyd George as wartime premier Lloyd George's regime as wartime prime minister was without precedent. It marked a political and constitutional revolution as a new leviathan of state power was created. Lloyd George, after all, was a prime minister detached from his party. Most Liberals in the Commons stayed loyal to the fallen Asquith, and Lloyd George was dependent on the mercies of his old opponents, the Unionists. At least until May 1918 the survival of his government, as it lurched from crisis to crisis through the fortunes of war and rumour-mongering in the London press, seemed in doubt.

In part, the controversy his premiership aroused was purely personal. He was the Welsh Baptist outsider, a 'ranker' as prime minister who had not passed through the training of a university (although admittedly Wellington and Disraeli were at least two notable previous examples). His household at 10 Downing Street was austere and frugal, with occasional relaxation in Welsh singing around the hearth. The bleakness of Downing Street was underlined by Margaret Lloyd George's decision still to remain largely in Cricieth. The existence of an alternative household in Frances Stevenson's flat in central London (about which the journalists kept remarkably quiet) added to tension with his wife—and also his eldest son, Richard. The family, however, kept up appearances. Lloyd George frequently returned to Cricieth for partial relaxation, while his Thursday orations at the Welsh national eisteddfod were powerful events—none less so than the 1916 Aberystwyth eisteddfod when Lloyd George compared the singing of the Welsh people during war to the nightingale singing at the darkest hour of the night. But he was drifting away from Wales. The snapping of the links was symbolized by the death of old Uncle Lloyd in February 1917. One of the great mass leaders of his day, Lloyd George survived in lonely eminence.

The controversy surrounding Lloyd George's role in Downing Street concerned mainly the nature of his authority. He seemed to be turning the premiership into something like the American presidency, with power radiating uniquely from the man at the centre. He created at once a supreme war cabinet of five men to run the war. The others were Bonar Law, the Unionist leader, now chancellor; Curzon, another Unionist; Arthur Henderson, leader of the Labour Party; and, most remarkably, the old imperialist Lord Milner. Over them, Lloyd George's authority was unquestioned. His former Liberal ally Churchill was excluded until mid-1917. Beyond the war cabinet, Lloyd George appointed individual executive ministers to run specific departments. Most were businessmen such as Sir Joseph Maclay (shipping), Sir Eric Geddes (transport), and lords Devonport and Rhondda (food). The traditional cabinet system seemed to be dissolving. Further signs of change was the bringing into the cabinet in June 1917 of General Jan Smuts from South Africa, an important influence on the premier, and the creation of an imperial war cabinet.

The centralization of wartime government and the personal ascendancy of the premier was underpinned by two further innovations. The Cabinet Office, under Sir Maurice Hankey with, as his deputy, the influential Welshman Thomas Jones, added to the authority of no. 10. It became a formidable machine of government, extending the control of the prime minister to all departments, civilian and military. In Thomas Jones's famous phrase (Thomas Jones to Eirene Theodora Jones, 12 Dec 1916, NL Wales, Thomas Jones papers), they were 'fluid persons moving amongst people who matter'. They had their own role in policy making, too. Hankey was a frequent operator in post-war diplomacy while Jones had much to do with the Irish settlement in 1921. Beyond them were a cabinet secretariat of talented young Milnerite imperialists such as Mark Sykes, Leo Amery, and Lionel Curtis, pushing government in a collectivist, perhaps imperialist, direction.

There was yet another novelty, the prime minister's own personal secretariat at Downing Street, popularly called the 'Garden Suburb' because it first met in huts in the gardens of no. 10. It consisted at first of five members, Waldorf Astor, a tory newspaper owner, and David Davies, a Liberal MP (who soon left), both wealthy businessmen; Professor W. G. S. Adams, an imperially minded professor from All Souls, Oxford; Sir Joseph Davies, a commercial statistician; and, most important of all, Philip Kerr, a Milnerite imperialist again of visionary outlook whose specialism was foreign affairs, an active figure in Lloyd George's summit diplomacy on the eastern front in 1917–18. These personal advisers underlined how presidential the traditional system of British cabinet government was becoming. Beyond this there were other aides, many of them Welsh. There were two principal private secretaries, J. T. Davies and the ever present Frances Stevenson; other assistants like John Rowland; and Lloyd George's personal link to the press, active in providing or withholding information and using patronage or censorship as appropriate, Sir William Sutherland, popularly known as Bronco Bill. At the parliamentary level, an important go-between was Captain Freddie Guest, the government's Liberal chief whip, active in the soliciting of political funding. The entire atmosphere seemed to many alarming, even sinister, with figures like Basil Zaharoff or the trafficker of honours, Maundy Gregory, hovering around the throne. But a war had to be won, and it was perhaps no time for constitutional niceties.

Wartime leadership The crucial test was, of course, the winning of the war, which continued to go badly. A massive encouragement came with the entry of the United States as a belligerent in April 1917, whereas the virtual removal of Russia as a belligerent in the course of 1917 after the revolution there in March was another blow. But the news on sea and land continued to be mostly depressing, for all the prime minister's brave speeches. A major factor was the deep political antagonism between Lloyd George and leading figures among the military and naval high command. The prime minister had particularly bad relations with General Haig and the chief of staff, Robertson, after the disaster of Passchendaele. He used the press, even the French and the American military commanders, to undermine their authority. The generals for their part played politics quite openly, consorting with Conservative politicians, press lords, and soliciting sympathy even from the king. This profound clash, renewed with immense and unforgiving vigour in Lloyd George's war memoirs in the 1930s, was a massive complication in trying to delineate a successful war strategy.

One early victory for Lloyd George was over the navy. Alarmed at growing losses to German U-boats, he urged the need for the navy to adopt the convoy system. In a much debated episode in April 1917, he visited the Admiralty in person. By the year's end he had the convoy system accepted. The first sea lord, Jellicoe, whom he felt had been defeatist after Jutland, was removed from office. 'It is a good thing', observed Lloyd George (*Lord Riddell's War Diary, 1914–1918*, 1933, 301). The generals were a far tougher obstacle. Lloyd George pressed his broad objectives that allied resources be pooled, that the front lines from Flanders to Mesopotamia be treated as one, and that there should be unity of command on the western front. But there was military resistance, notably from Haig. Lloyd George's authority was weakened by his having given backing, at the London conference in January 1917, to a new French offensive under General Nivelle. This was a great failure, led to mutinies among the French troops, and almost removed them as participants.

Lloyd George was, therefore, unable to prevent a new offensive conducted by Haig in Flanders. Despite his deep misgivings, all his cabinet, Smuts prominent among them, gave Haig's plan their backing, and Third Ypres, more usually called the battle of Passchendaele, began on 31 July 1917. It was a terrible failure, with the British handicapped by heavy rain, quite apart from entrenched German defences. In three weeks, over half a million British troops were lost in advancing just a few miles, many of them drowned in the Flanders mud. The British army was unable to mount a major offensive for months to come. For Lloyd George, it confirmed his view that Haig's judgement could not be trusted, and he followed the risky policy of limiting the reserves available to him, lest he fritter away yet more lives. He would have removed Haig had there been an obvious successor. An unexpected British success at Cambrai in November, with a dramatic breakthrough for the new tanks, was some consolation. Meanwhile he again urged a peripheral strategy, 'knocking the props away' from the enemy in the Balkans and the eastern Mediterranean.

However, at the darkest crisis, Lloyd George remained buoyant. At an allied conference at Rapallo in November 1917 he pressed strongly the need for a unified command, using the Italian disaster at Caporetto as a justification: he had previously elaborated the idea to the Italians and the Americans. He proposed a new supreme allied war council at Versailles. The intended target was clearly Robertson, chief of the general staff, to whom he was now implacably opposed. He found the key at the war council meeting at Versailles on 21 January 1918 when it was agreed to create a mobile general reserve under an executive war board over which the French General Foch would preside. Robertson opposed this challenge to his power. In a major crisis in February 1918, pressure was put on him by the government to move to the new council in Versailles. He chose to stay put. But in the event, the Asquithian Liberals in the Commons failed to defend Robertson; the 'cocoa slop' from anti-government Liberal newspapers was ignored; Derby, the war minister, gave way; even Haig backed off. Robertson had to resign and the earthy figure of General Sir Henry Wilson replaced him. The so-called 'X committee' of Lloyd George, Milner, and Wilson oversaw high strategy from that time. With the military and economic resources of the United States coming on stream in early 1918, the prospects for an ultimate allied victory now seemed that much less bleak.

The personal domination of the prime minister over wartime diplomacy was always evident. Lloyd George was dominant in the supreme war council at Versailles, and in stiffening the resolve of the Italians after defeat at Caporetto. A constant priority was pressure on the United States to speed up its military contribution to the war in Europe. His influence also lay behind wartime peace treaties which would give Britain a dominant role in the Middle East including Mesopotamia with its oil supplies when war ended. He was involved in peace feelers with the new Bolshevik regime in Russia after October 1917. At home he worked to conciliate radical sentiment, encouraged by events in Russia, among the workers. In a notable speech to the trade unions at Westminster Hall on 5 January 1918, intended to counteract the damaging effect of news of the secret wartime peace treaties now published by Lenin's government in Russia, he appealed to labour and radical opinion as a lifelong Liberal intent on freeing mankind from exploitation and class rule, a world of economic co-operation and national self-determination for all peoples. The publication of Woodrow Wilson's 'fourteen points' shortly afterwards reinforced Lloyd George's appeal.

In the main, Balfour the foreign secretary played a subordinate role—his policy was 'a free hand for the little man' (B. Dugdale, *Arthur James Balfour*, 2, 1936, 196). However, it was Balfour who directed another momentous wartime decision, his declaration in November 1917 to set up a national home for the Jewish people in Palestine. Lloyd George was a generally philosemitic politician. While at munitions he had struck up a relationship with Chaim Weizmann, a chemistry professor and also leader of the Zionist movement. The premier now endorsed warmly a proposal that would, among other things, strengthen Britain's position in the eastern Mediterranean and the Suez Canal area. But it left a tangled web of promises or commitments to Zionist Jews and native Arabs alike that bequeathed a violent legacy to the region for the remainder of the twentieth century.

The ending of the war In the spring of 1918 events at the front reached a critical point. On 21 March the Germans launched a huge assault on the British Fifth Army near Amiens; within a week the situation was critical and the French feared for the safety of Paris. A crucial conference at Beauvais on 3 April, attended by Lloyd George, Haig, and Foch, and with the American generals Pershing and Bliss also present, made the vital decision to entrust Foch with 'the co-ordination of the action of the Allied Armies on the Western Front' and the 'strategic direction of military operations' (D. Lloyd George, *War Memoirs*, 2, 1938, 1749). At last Lloyd George had won the unified command for which he had long striven. However, at no other time in the war were his will-power and qualities of inspirational leadership more fully tested. He brought back reinforcements from Italy, Egypt, and Salonika, and speeded up the use of American troops, to be merged with allied divisions in France. There was gloomy news elsewhere, on the Italian front, in Russia, in Ireland, in German U-boat attacks on allied shipping. At home there were food shortages and the terrifying phenomenon of air raids by German zeppelins on British homes. But by the start of May it was clear that the German offensive had failed to break through; by a narrow margin, the Anglo-French line held.

There was an important political consequence. In a letter to the newspapers published on 7 May General Frederick Maurice alleged that Lloyd George and Bonar Law had made seriously inaccurate statements in the house and that Haig had been deliberately starved of reinforcements on the western front in the six months after Passchendaele. Asquith decided to move a vote of censure and the press seethed with rumours that the government would fall. But in the debate on 9 May Lloyd George launched a brilliant counter-attack and achieved one of his most remarkable parliamentary triumphs. He used figures which seemed to show that British military strength was greater in January 1918 than a year earlier. Further, if Haig had been starved of troops Maurice himself was partly responsible since the figures of personnel came from his own department. The opposition largely collapsed and Lloyd George won a large majority in the Commons debate. The accuracy of his figures has been hotly contested since; Frances Stevenson later wrote of a draft of the correct figures being found by herself and J. T. Davies, unknown to Lloyd George, and being deliberately burnt. What is indisputable is the political outcome. The 106 MPs who voted against the government in the Maurice debate included 98 Liberals. The campaign against them by the government whips marked the beginning of a permanent split among the Liberal Party. It also meant that, for the rest of the war, Lloyd George had total control of the Commons as well as of the country.

Elsewhere, Lloyd George's pre-war social radicalism was still very much in evidence. His government was responsible for major reforms at home. Fisher's Education Act of 1918 substantially extended the base of state education, elementary and secondary, and made some provision for part-time education. The Representation of the People Act hugely extended the electorate from 8 million to 21 million by enfranchising not only all adult men over twenty-one but, dramatically and with relatively little debate, all women aged thirty and over (assuming they were local government electors or wives of such electors). With over 8 million women enfranchised, it was a massive step towards gender equality. There were also major wartime reforms in housing, agriculture, and health; Addison's Ministry of Reconstruction planned a new Ministry of Health. There was talk of creating a land fit for heroes when hostilities ended.

Less successful by far was policy in Ireland which had lapsed into disarray after the failure of Lloyd George's diplomatic efforts in the summer of 1916. The old Irish nationalists were rapidly being overtaken by the militant republicans of Sinn Féin, their charismatic leaders (currently in British gaols) such as Arthur Griffith, Michael Collins, and Eamonn de Valera far more aggressively nationalist than the traditional nationalist parliamentarians. Lloyd George threw himself personally into trying to achieve a new settlement. He set up an abortive convention in May 1917 to try to find a home rule solution, and responded to its ending in April 1918 with an attempt to link the granting of home rule to the whole of Ireland with the imposing of military conscription. It had disastrous results. Southern Irish opinion turned massively towards Sinn Féin; relations between Britain and Ireland deteriorated alarmingly; and martial law was imposed in Ireland. Alongside his triumphs in the war must be set Lloyd George's failures in Ireland, a crucial factor in his later difficulties and decline.

But what mattered above all was the course of the war on the front. In the summer the news at last appeared better. Allenby's advance in Palestine and then Syria against the Turks was gaining momentum; on the western front, the German offensive had been rebuffed, and American troops were now coming into active deployment in large numbers. Lloyd George continued to appeal with charismatic effect to national morale. To mark the fourth anniversary of the war, an inspirational message from him was read out in theatres and cinemas across the land. A similar declaration was made to the Commons three days later.

Then on 8 August 1918 Haig launched a massive assault at Amiens, with the aid of Canadian and Anzac troops. This time he broke through the seemingly impregnable German 'Hindenburg line'. Enemy resistance rapidly collapsed and there were riots and much social unrest in Germany. On 5 October it was learned that Prince Max of

Baden, the German chancellor, had approached Woodrow Wilson to discuss the restoration of peace. Austria–Hungary signed an armistice on 3 November. In tense discussions on the peace terms to be presented to Germany, Lloyd George insisted on important modifications of Wilson's fourteen points—'freedom of the seas', a key British proviso relating to the right of search, and compensation for invaded territories with stern treatment of Germany on whom the stigma of war guilt would be uniquely placed. Without these, Lloyd George and Clemenceau of France declared they would continue the fighting, and Wilson had to give way. On 11 November Lloyd George announced in the Commons that an armistice had been signed that day with Germany, to take effect at 11.00 a.m. He received an unprecedented ovation in the house. Honours rained on him. He received the Order of Merit from the king, the grand cordon of the Légion d'honneur in France, the freedom of cities. He was hailed as 'the man who won the war'.

Even at his moment of greatest triumph, however, the political instincts of David Lloyd George were ever alert. After all, his post-war political future had been totally obscure. He was a prime minister with no real party base, in power for the duration of the war alone. He was constantly at odds with the press, where much of the political debate of the time took place, and developed an implacable feud with Northcliffe, owner of *The Times*, when the latter failed to receive the Air Ministry. In a swift coup, the opposition-minded *Daily Chronicle* was bought up by a pro-government syndicate, and its editor, Robert Donald, a former golfing companion, was cast into oblivion. Elsewhere, Lloyd George's hold over public opinion, in much of Ireland and in the world of labour, excited by the revolution in Russia, was indeed fragile. Relations with Labour were further soured when their leader Arthur Henderson quarrelled with Lloyd George after a visit to Petrograd in Russia prior to attendance at a socialist peace conference at Stockholm. After the famous 'doormat incident', according to legend, he left the government in August 1917.

Somehow, the prime minister had to create a political base. There had been talks during 1917, involving Dr Addison, Waldorf Astor, the American owner of *The Observer*, and the ever-busy Beaverbrook, about creating a 'Lloyd George party'. But after the Maurice debate in May 1918 had opened up a massive schism in Liberal ranks, Captain Guest, Addison, and others took steps to create a pro-Lloyd George coalition Liberal party. Two months later, talks with the Unionists led to a list of pro-government candidates for the next election being drawn up (at that time, it was assumed it would be a wartime election) with 150 approved Liberal candidates. This was the origin of the notorious 'coupon' or signed letter of approval at the general election that followed. In October 1918 a draft manifesto with the Unionists laid down a basis for post-war policy: old Liberal priorities like free trade, Irish home rule, Welsh disestablishment, and social reform would all be there, especially the last, but in modified form. There were hopes that Labour might join the government again, but at its conference on 14 November Bernard Shaw successfully urged the delegates, 'Go back to Lloyd George and say—"Nothing doing!"' (*The Times*, 15 Nov 1918).

On 12 November the Liberal ministers, including Churchill, agreed on fighting the election as a coalition. A half-hearted offer of the lord chancellorship to the fallen Asquith was refused. At the subsequent election, Lloyd George dominated the campaign. It was an election later much denounced by Keynes and others as marked by chauvinistic, anti-German rhetoric about hanging the Kaiser and 'squeezing Germany until the pips squeaked'. There was indeed much of this, including Lloyd George's own aggressive speech at Bristol on 11 December in which he departed from his text to urge that Germany should pay the uttermost cost of the war. The remainder of his campaign speeches were in fact moderate statements of the need for major post-war social reconstruction, 'a country fit for heroes to live in' (speech at Wolverhampton, *The Times*, 24 Dec 1918) in the much touted phrase. At any rate, the outcome was a huge majority for the coalition, with over 520 supporters, largely Unionist but including 136 Coalition Liberals and a handful of coalition Labour. The Labour Party, despite a strong poll, won only 57 and the Asquithian Liberals (or 'Wee Frees') a mere 26.

The future seemed uncertain. Politics had been transformed by the war, and with them Lloyd George's role. The old issues of his youth, land reform, the chapels, even free trade, had lost their priority. Instead politics were shaped by the all-purpose term 'reconstruction'. There was a background of chauvinist and anti-alien right-wing reaction. The post-war world would be dominated by the giant clash between capital and labour, with Lloyd George now in alliance with right-wing 'anti-Bolsheviks' using red scare techniques. Abroad, Europe from the Pyrenees to the Urals was shattered and in revolutionary chaos. Beyond dispute, however, was the overwhelming personal ascendancy of David Lloyd George. Bonar Law observed to Beaverbrook, 'He can be prime minister for life if he likes' (Beaverbrook, 325).

Post-war premiership: Versailles and after Lloyd George's domination after the 'coupon' election seemed complete. He was the most powerful prime minister since the younger Pitt, perhaps ever. The wartime cabinet system was retained until October 1919. Ministers who departed from the government line were fiercely slapped down—Milner, even Churchill who was repeatedly chided for his doctrinaire attitude towards Soviet Russia. The constitution seemed to be cast aside by a presidential prime minister backed up by his Cabinet Office and a cabinet itself dissolving into *ad hoc* 'conferences of ministers'. The point was emphasized in September 1921 when the cabinet met not in Downing Street but in Inverness town hall. The 'Garden Suburb' of private prime ministerial advisers, many of them Milnerite imperialists headed by Philip Kerr, aroused particular hostility. Even more did the activities of Sir William Sutherland in undercover deals with the press and in the trafficking of titles and honours in return for contributions to government or party funds. Critics quoted Dunning's famous resolution against Lord North's government in 1780 that the power of the prime minister had increased, was increasing and ought to be diminished.

The premier was initially wholly absorbed with the peace conference at Paris which began on 18 January 1919. Bonar Law held the fort in the Commons while the prime minister, along with Wilson and Clemenceau, changed the world. On the initiative of Lloyd George, the original unwieldy council of ten was reduced to the council of four (including the Italian prime minister, Vittorio Orlando) in March. There followed months of hectic negotiations, Lloyd George being variously assisted not only by close aides such as Hankey and Kerr, but ministerial colleagues such as Balfour, Milner, and for a time the South African General Smuts. Eventually the treaty was signed, most reluctantly, by the German delegates in the hall of mirrors in the Palace of Versailles. Lloyd George's defence of its terms was given an overwhelming majority in the House of Commons.

Lloyd George's role over the Versailles treaty is central to the ways in which his career and purposes were later viewed. J. M. Keynes's slashing attack on the treaty in *The Economic Consequences of the Peace* that autumn helped to create a mood of hostility towards an unjust and self-defeating settlement. He condemned the 'coupon' election as encouraging the spirit of vengeance of a Carthaginian peace. His later sketch of Lloyd George in his *Essays in Biography*, partly through the brilliance of his writing, did more than any other critique to create a view of the prime minister as ruthless and unprincipled, 'a vampire and a medium in one', a man 'rooted in nothing' (J. M. Keynes, *Essays in Biography*, 1961 edn, 36).

Certainly Lloyd George had his full share of responsibility for the harsher features of the treaty. He took a strongly nationalist position on issues deemed to be affecting Britain's national security or other interests. He fought to maintain Britain's right of search of naval vessels on the high seas in the face of American demands for 'the freedom of the seas'. He pressed for extending the empire, notably in the Middle East where new British-mandated territories such as in Mesopotamia were to reflect the massive oil supplies discovered there. At the same time, French claims to Syria under wartime secret treaties were resisted. He also upheld Britain's claims to German colonies in Africa, notably in German East Africa (Tanganyika). Over Germany, he joined Clemenceau in taking the harsh view, calling for the trial of the Kaiser, urging that war guilt be attached to Germany in clause 231, and imposing long-term reparations payments in compensation for the damage done to allied territories and supplies. It was this last that especially led to Keynes's bitter criticism.

Yet Lloyd George was also the most flexible of the peacemakers, sometimes taking an intermediate line between the nationalism of Clemenceau and the sometimes high-flown generalities of Woodrow Wilson, a zealot for the new League of Nations which in the end the American

GEORGE, DAVID LLOYD 904

senate was to refuse to join. Lloyd George was always aware of wider themes—the devastation of European trade and industry, the problems of simple starvation in Germany and elsewhere, the dangerously fluid situation in eastern Europe where a civil war was taking place between the Bolsheviks and White Russians, the impossibility of a stable long-term international settlement based on a one-sided policy of revenge.

Lloyd George's thinking was set out in a document of 25 March, the Fontainebleau memorandum, worked out with Hankey, Kerr, and especially Smuts. This called for realism in German reparations payments, based on the facts of Germany's capacity to pay. More vigorously, the memorandum condemned the subjecting of German-speaking populations to French or Polish rule. Lloyd George fiercely, though unavailingly, condemned decisions such as the so-called Polish corridor, the Saarland, or placing the Sudeten Germans under the regime of the new hybrid Czechoslovakia: Lloyd George never held much regard either for this new creation, or for the main Czech spokesman, Eduard Benes, as was to emerge in the Munich crisis twenty years later. He urged the dangers of creating a sense of mass grievance at a time when Russia and perhaps Europe were gripped by 'the spirit of revolution' (D. Lloyd George, *The Truth about the Peace Treaties*, 1, 1938, 407). Germany should be admitted to the League of Nations. The memorandum, however, withered on the vine in the face of French opposition.

Lloyd George, however, did have some successes at Paris, notably the placing of German-speaking Danzig under the League of Nations, and achieving a plebiscite for Upper Silesia (which in 1921 resulted in a massive vote for that territory to be restored to Germany). To meet Clemenceau's demand for occupation of the left bank of the Rhine, he and Wilson offered a guarantee of military aid to France against unprovoked aggression—an offer which the American senate's failure to ratify the treaty caused to lapse. On reparations he had the issue handed over to a non-partisan and supposedly objective reparations commission which might in time delay or even scale down to close to zero effective payments by Germany. In a later book, *The Truth about Reparations and War Debts* (1932), he called, in effect, for reparations to be abandoned altogether. It would not, he argued, be a breach of the peace treaty. On the contrary, such a policy would embody its proper intentions.

On his return, Lloyd George hailed a peace with honour which had fulfilled the aspirations of British Liberals for the principles of economic freedom and national self-determination. Nevertheless, both in terms of frontier settlements and of reparations, the Versailles treaty appeared harsh and vindictive to many observers. The 'stab in the back' could lead to a nationalist backlash in Germany. There were still peace treaties to be concluded with Austria and Bulgaria, and a final settlement with Turkey. For the remainder of his premiership he sought to redress major features of the peace settlement to bring Germany and the other former enemies within the comity of nations and to produce a more stable and productive

economic order. The revision of the injustices of the peace treaties, for which he was partly responsible, was his overriding objective right down to the onset of a second world war in 1939.

The peacetime premiership at home Freed from the strains of peacemaking at Paris, however, Lloyd George now threw himself for a time into domestic affairs. His constitutional role seemed ever more unusual. He stood aloof, it seemed, not only from party politics but from parliament itself from which for long periods he absented himself. He acted as a kind of minister of all departments, interfering in policy issues at will either directly or through intermediaries such as Kerr. Yet for a time the energies of the pre-war new Liberalism were revived. The economy remained buoyant until May 1920 when the post-war inflation gave way to a sudden and lasting depression and growing unemployment. There were progressive reforms such as Fisher's Education Act and Addison's Housing and Town Planning Act of 1919 which began the principle of publicly subsidized housing provided by the local authorities—though at what soon appeared to be an unacceptable financial cost. There was also a new minister of health, a position which Addison himself filled. Thomas Macnamara, minister of labour, began a remarkably generous nationwide system of unemployment insurance. Women now had the vote; one of them, Lady Astor, entered the Commons. There was also at least one nostalgic gesture to his Welsh past—the passage of Welsh disestablishment in June 1919, although by now few cared.

Lloyd George's major test at home, however, lay in the challenge from Labour. The British trade unions, having doubled in size during the corporate arrangements of wartime, were in militant mood. In major industries, especially the railways and the coalmines, class passions built up. The period from 1919 to 1921 was the worst for days lost through industrial strike action that Britain had ever known. Ministers talked of Bolshevist subversion. Even the police went on strike. Violent clashes in George Square in Glasgow seemed to suggest that a British revolution was at hand. Lloyd George was prepared to use the full resources of the state in response. He contemplated starving the striking railwaymen into submission in the autumn of 1919. Much use was made of the army, the navy, and even (for surveillance) the air force, along with MI5, in suppressing the strikers. The Emergency Powers Act of 1920 created a permanent anti-strike apparatus, both civil and military. But even in these years, Lloyd George's skills in handling the unions and negotiating his way through industrial crises were in evidence.

The main crisis arose in the mines. The Sankey royal commission in 1919 called, by a narrow majority, for the nationalization of the coal industry. The failure of the government to respond led to a national miners' strike in 1920. In the spring of 1921 there was a real prospect of a general strike by the 'triple alliance' of miners, dockers, and railwaymen. But on 'black Friday' (15 March 1921) Lloyd George managed to persuade or bamboozle Frank Hodges, the general secretary of the Miners' Federation, to accept the principle of a wages pool. The triple alliance broke up and the great post-war strikes diminished thereafter, especially as mass unemployment began to spread. Lloyd George in part was able to show the Trade Union Council that its ideological position was untenable. If there were a general strike, the unions would have to become the government. 'We are at your mercy', declared Lloyd George. Robert Smillie of the Miners' Federation, in Bevan's later account, reflected that at that moment the unions were beaten 'and we knew we were' (A. Bevan, *In Place of Fear*, 1976 edn, 41). But Lloyd George's role as a perceived champion of labour was now effectively destroyed. He was seen henceforth as a man who had lied over the Sankey commission, and allied himself with capitalist bosses like the hated coal owners and red-baiting politicians of the far right. Worse still, promises of a land fit for the heroes back from the war seemed to be betrayed.

Lloyd George lost more credibility in another major area—Ireland. In 1919 violence spread throughout the island, between the Irish Republican Army under Michael Collins and the British army. Murders occurred everywhere and the government engaged in a policy of reprisals against the IRA. When the Government of Ireland Act in 1920 partitioned the island at least for the moment, by setting up a Northern Ireland parliament in Belfast (later in Stormont), southern Irish republicans ignored it. Hatred was stoked up by the army's being reinforced by the auxiliary and quite undisciplined 'Black and Tans'. Episodes such as the Black and Tans' firing indiscriminately into a football crowd at Croke Park, Dublin, on 'bloody Sunday' (21 November 1920) or the hunger strike which led to the death of the mayor of Cork, Terence MacSwiney, shocked the conscience of the world.

Lloyd George was too absorbed with other priorities to focus on Ireland until the spring of 1921. His pronouncements were hawkish: the IRA was dismissed as 'the murder gang' (*The Times*, 11 Oct 1920). His own life was thought to be in danger at the hands of Irish assassins. When he did turn to Ireland, policy rapidly changed. Before, he had seriously miscalculated the strength of and support for Sinn Féin and the IRA. Now secret contacts began with Sinn Féin. The king delivered a remarkably conciliatory speech when opening the new Northern Ireland parliament in Belfast. From July 1921 Lloyd George began a lengthy series of face-to-face meetings with the Sinn Féin leader, Eamonn de Valera, at 10 Downing Street. The talks made slow progress, though Lloyd George used his Celtic background to persuade de Valera that neither in Irish nor Welsh was there a word for 'republic'. Full-scale talks began in October in London. The British delegation, headed by Lloyd George and also including Austen Chamberlain, Lord Birkenhead, and Churchill, wrestled endlessly with Arthur Griffith and Michael Collins, the chief Sinn Féin delegates, over the precise relationship of a free Ireland to the British empire, finance and defence issues, and the oath of allegiance to the crown. In the background was the problem of Ulster, protestant and loyalist, dedicated to the historic call of 'no surrender'.

On 5 December 1921 Lloyd George brought the discussions to a head. He threatened the Sinn Féiners with an immediate resumption of hostilities unless they accepted the terms already agreed, including a future boundary commission to settle the problem of the territory of Ulster. He brandished two telegrams in the air—'Which letter am I to send? … We must know your answer by ten pm tonight' (F. Pakenham, *Peace by Ordeal*, 1972 edn, 239–40). It was a colossal bluff. But, helped by the good personal relations of Griffith with him and his Welsh aide, Thomas Jones, Lloyd George carried the day. By 3 to 2, the Sinn Féiners accepted terms. A month later, the treaty was endorsed by the Irish Dáil in Dublin by 64 to 57.

It was an ambiguous achievement. The future of Ulster was left in abeyance pending a boundary commission; in practice Ireland was to remain partitioned, at the cost of massive internal conflict in the north, for the remainder of the century. Appalling episodes such as the killing of Field Marshal Sir Henry Wilson in Eaton Square by IRA gunmen in 1922 showed that Irish violence was still a political reality. But still it was a settlement. The twenty-six counties of southern Ireland—the 'Irish Free State'—were granted dominion status within the empire and became effectively a sovereign state. Lloyd George could claim to have solved the Irish question where Pitt, Peel, Gladstone, and Salisbury had all failed. Yet it was achieved at grave cost. Liberal and Labour opinion had been appalled by the government's counter-violence in the troubles in Ireland. On the other hand, many Unionists resented an ultimate surrender to Sinn Féin/IRA violence. The prime minister responsible would have to go.

Even after his coup over Ireland, therefore, Lloyd George remained an isolated titan. Public spending on social policies aroused the opposition of the right-wing 'anti-waste' movement. Other Unionists opposed surrender in Ireland or the dismissal of General Dyer in India after the shooting of hundreds of Sikhs in the Amritsar massacre in 1919. On the left, Labour was largely alienated after the Sankey report and 'black Friday', while many Liberals were downcast by the Black and Tans and the undermining of free trade. In March 1920 there had been a scheme to organize the fusion of the unionist and the Coalition Liberal parties behind Lloyd George, who recalled as a parallel the unity of command between the French and British armies on the western front during the war. But the Unionists were hostile, and in the end so were the Coalition Liberals as well. They and their leader continued in a kind of political no man's land, their political future unpredictable and precarious. The 'man who won the war' had yet to establish himself anew in time of peace.

Lloyd Georgian diplomacy Lloyd George's detachment from home politics was emphasized by the priority he gave to trying to modify the peace settlement at Versailles and create a stable post-war international structure. Conference after conference was held: the new foreign secretary, Lord Curzon, was treated by Lloyd George, it seemed, almost with contempt at times. Further treaties were concluded. The treaty of Sèvres in August 1920 managed an imposed settlement with the Turks by giving the Greeks, a favourite people of Lloyd George's, large areas of territory in Asia Minor, including the great port of Smyrna, but it proved a cause of massive future conflict. The treaty of Rapallo (12 November 1920) reached agreement with Italy over Fiume. But the main issue of contention was always Germany and particularly the question of reparations. The San Remo conference (19–26 April 1920) began the process of scaling down French claims. The French were persuaded to accept lump-sum figures for payment over the next thirty-five years. Further reductions were agreed in Anglo-French conferences at London and Boulogne. Clearly, some of Germany's alleged obligations would never be paid.

Lloyd George also paid much attention to French demands for security on its eastern frontiers; after all, Germany had invaded them twice, in 1870 and 1914. At Cannes in January 1922, he seemingly came close to agreeing with the French radical prime minister, Aristide Briand, a Breton and therefore another Celt, a new settlement of German indemnities alongside a permanent guarantee of French frontiers through a long-term continental commitment of support by the British government. This dramatic departure from British traditions towards continental Europe was, however, frustrated by the fall of the Briand government following photographs of a fateful golf match with Lloyd George on the Cannes links. Briand was succeeded by the intransigent right-wing Lorrainer, Raymond Poincaré, no friend of a settlement with Germany. But Lloyd George still felt that progress had been made in restoring the pariah enemy to the comity of nations.

The other great pariah proved unexpectedly more amenable. Soviet Russia was a massive problem for the British in 1919 since they had troops committed to aid the White Russians there during the civil war. In fact, despite pressure from Churchill and the political right, Lloyd George managed to wind up all British military involvement in Russia by early in 1920. Threatened assistance to the Poles in a brief war with the Russian Bolshevik government did not materialize either. Although there were threats of strikes by British trade unions, the decisive factor was that the Polish army managed to defeat the Russian invaders on its own. Lloyd George now strove to bring Russia also into the international community, mindful of the value of its huge markets to British industry still struggling after the war. His tactical skills evoked the admiration of Lenin who even dedicated a book to him as the most gifted political leader in the capitalist world. An Anglo-Russian trade agreement was signed in March 1921, and there seemed a real prospect of full *de facto* recognition of the Soviet Union being achieved early in 1922.

Lloyd George aimed to combine both a German and a Russian settlement in a massive international conference held at Genoa in April–May 1922. This might also afford him a platform for a political recovery at home and a new appeal to the voters. In fact, Genoa was undermined even before it began. Poincaré would countenance no concessions. The recognition of the Soviet Union was undermined by Churchill and right-wing critics at home. Disastrously, the German Weimar government and the Soviet Union concluded a private treaty at Rapallo before the

conference even met. Genoa was a slow, long-running failure, with nothing agreed on the main issues. A face-saving conference of experts at The Hague brought no settlement on the issue of Russian debts incurred by the tsarist regime and repudiated by the Soviet government. Europe after Genoa was as unstable as before. Lloyd George, assailed by the Northcliffe press and the Unionist right wing, no longer looked like an international messiah.

More difficulties occurred in another sphere, that of Greek–Turkish relations. In his other diplomatic policies, Lloyd George had been a conciliator and a peacemaker. Here it was very different. His enthusiastic backing for the Greek premier Venizelos after the treaty of Sèvres led to conflict. The post-war Turkish leader, Mustafa Kemal, refused to accept the treaty or the surrender to Greece of large parts of Asia Minor including Smyrna. Finally, after belligerent speeches by Lloyd George backing up Venizelos's claims in Asia Minor, the Turks attacked and smashed through the Greek armies there in late August 1922. Smyrna was put to fire and sword, with over 100,000 Greeks perishing. The British post at Chanak on the Dardanelles was now threatened with attack. A new crisis threatened to rock finally the unstable and unpopular coalition.

The downfall of Lloyd George The crisis in Asia Minor came at a time when Lloyd George's position at home was slowly crumbling. Liberals of various persuasions were losing faith, especially after the one truly radical minister, Dr Addison, was sacked from the government in July 1921 after the expensive and inflationary outcome of his housing subsidies. Another Liberal, Edwin Montagu, followed in March 1922. There resulted serious cuts in social expenditure, the so-called Geddes 'axe' in 1922, which further reduced support among Liberal opinion. More serious, however, was Unionist disaffection over domestic, Irish, and foreign policy. Press attacks were remorseless; Lloyd George hit back after Northcliffe's death by suicide with an abortive attempt to purchase *The Times* as a pro-government organ. The retirement of Bonar Law through ill health had left leadership of the Unionists in the less effective hands of Austen Chamberlain. Then Law returned to politics, still loyal, but perhaps an alternative leader in waiting.

Right-wing criticism reached a new level of venom in June 1922 in the so-called 'honours scandal'. Lloyd George's aides such as Guest and Sutherland, along with sinister figures such as Maundy Gregory, had been trading honours and peerages, it appeared, in London's clubland and elsewhere in return for contributions to party funds (Unionist as well as Liberal, though this was less commonly emphasized). The award of a peerage to a corrupt South African businessman led to attacks on the government in both houses of parliament. The prime minister was accused of dishonesty. In fact, Lloyd George was careless about honours himself; the purpose of the sale of honours was simply to raise a war chest for a premier without a party base. He was still a relatively poor man, and remained so until he made money after his fall from office through a lecture tour in America in 1923 and then through the sale of United Newspapers in 1927 which brought him perhaps £2.5 million. But the episode underlined for critics his role as a rogue elephant, trampling roughshod on the ethical standards of British life.

The crisis with Turkey brought these problems to a head. As the Turkish army advanced towards General Harington's British forces at Chanak, war seemed close at hand. But the public were weary of fighting; Keynes had taught them it was pointless anyhow. Bonar Law unexpectedly wrote a letter to *The Times*, published on 7 October 1922 observing that Britain could not alone act as 'policeman of the world'. Lesser Unionist ministers rebelled. On 17 October it was known that they were to be joined by the obscure Stanley Baldwin at the Board of Trade and even Lord Curzon, the foreign secretary. The French were pro-Turk; no member of the empire offered any assistance other than New Zealand. Lloyd George seemed oblivious to the danger he faced, and delivered a furiously anti-Turk speech at Manchester on 14 October. On 19 October at a meeting of Unionist MPs at the Carlton Club called by Austen Chamberlain, the coalition was voted down by 185 to 88. Baldwin described Lloyd George as a 'dynamic force' which he declared was 'a very terrible thing' (*The Times*, 20 Oct 1922). The party regulars had had their revenge for 1916. Later that day, in good humour, Lloyd George left Downing Street. Many, though, felt he would return.

The record of the Lloyd George coalition in the period 1919–22 has been severely criticized subsequently, perhaps for its tone as much as its policies, its atmosphere of intrigue and corruption captured in Arnold Bennett's novel *Lord Raingo*. In some ways, it was not a bad government. It passed measures of social reform, it brought eventual peace to Ireland, it promoted naval disarmament, it extended some self-government to India and to Egypt, it tried to defuse labour unrest, it sought peace in foreign affairs. Liberals such as the education minister, H. A. L. Fisher, felt they could remain in office without shame. It provided some basis for a stable Britain in the inter-war years when many other European nations plunged into dictatorship.

In the end, the coalition's basic instability, moral, and political, brought it down. In addition, a post-war world which saw growing mass unemployment at home, and renewed instability overseas meant that the government's legacy was an unsuccessful one. Above all, Lloyd George's highly personal ascendancy, exemplified by novelties like the 'Garden Suburb' (promptly abolished after his fall) was appropriate only for emergency wartime circumstances. His presidential style now appeared anomalous, even dangerous. Politicians, like businessmen, hankered for the 'normalcy' of the world they had lost. So Lloyd George retired to the wings from centre-stage. He sought consolation less from Dame Margaret in Cricieth than from Frances Stevenson, for whom he had just built a new house, Bron-y-de, at Churt in Surrey, to face the imponderable challenges of his fall from power.

Liberalism in the 1920s Lloyd George had lost office and was in search of a role. The Conservatives under Bonar Law won the general election in November 1922, with Lloyd George's Liberals winning only 57 seats, a few less than Asquith's followers. The Liberal Party remained bitterly divided, especially over Lloyd George's huge war chest of money, the notorious 'Lloyd George fund'. Labour under MacDonald was anxious above all to ensure that they replaced the Liberals as the main opposition to the tories. In September 1923 Lloyd George left for a major lecture tour in the United States and Canada, appealing for clemency towards Germany—and also earning much needed money for himself. Then the situation changed in October when Baldwin, the new premier, declared for protection of the home market as the way to combat unemployment. At once Asquithian and Lloyd George Liberals reunited to defend free trade. At the next general election, called by Baldwin in December 1923, the Conservatives lost their majority. The Liberals joined Labour in voting them down in the Commons and the first Labour government, headed by Ramsay MacDonald, took office. But they were a minority dependent on the support of the 157 MPs of the reunited Liberal Party. However, the few months of Labour government were an unhappy time for the Liberals with endless acrimony within the party. At the general election in October 1924 their MPs fell alarmingly to only 40. Distrust between Lloyd George and Asquith continued. After they differed over the general strike of May 1926, towards which Lloyd George was far more sympathetic, Asquith resigned as party leader. Lloyd George now for the first time became Liberal leader, but of a rump third party only, engaged in endless internal rows over the Lloyd George fund and its master.

However, there was a far more characteristic aspect of Lloyd George's activities in the 1920s—a crusade to galvanize Liberal policies, and thereby to give a creative stimulus to British politics as a whole. Charles Masterman, recently a bitter opponent, told his wife, 'When Ll. G. came back to the party, ideas came back to the party' (L. Masterman, *C. F. G. Masterman*, 1939, 345–6). He made use of the annual Liberal summer school begun by Ramsay Muir in the 1920s as a forum of new ideas. He assembled a kind of general staff of advisers, some of them pre-war new Liberals such as Rowntree, others younger economists such as Lionel Robbins, Hubert Henderson, and Walter Layton. They worked out new schemes to promote industrial and agricultural recovery. Most remarkable of all was Keynes, a fierce opponent over Versailles, but now reconciled with Lloyd George in advocating schemes for massive public works and counter-cyclical spending policies promoted by central government, instead of the deflation and Treasury orthodoxy that prevailed under the Conservatives. Both Keynes and Lloyd George condemned Churchill's return to the gold standard at the pre-war parity in 1925.

A series of multi-coloured policy books followed, dealing variously with land, industry and power, coal and power, and unemployment. They were highly radical in their proposals. The 'green book', *The Land and the Nation* (1925), which advocated a kind of nationalization of cultivable land, drove Sir Alfred Mond into the Conservative

Party forthwith. The 'yellow book', *Britain's Industrial Future* (1928), set out comprehensive proposals for regenerating the economy. It was popularized in the 'orange book', *We can Conquer Unemployment* (1929), which urged that tens of thousands of unemployed men could be given work on national enterprises such as road building, housing, and land drainage. In a supportive document, *Can Lloyd George do it?*, Keynes and Henderson spelt out, almost for the first time, the 'multiplier effect' for employment of planned public spending.

It was a dynamic, novel programme which captured many of the headlines in the 1929 general election. Baldwin and MacDonald seemed almost united in trying to ensure that Lloyd George did not return to power. Baldwin called for 'Safety First', MacDonald for 'no monkeying'. But in fact the Liberals made only scant progress in the election. Their vote rose by nearly 2.5 million but their tally of MPs only from 40 to 59. Labour won 287 seats and MacDonald formed a second minority government, this time as head of the largest party. The years of this government, from 1929 to August 1931, were a dismal time for the Liberals. They were squeezed between the two large parties as an enfeebled third force. A few right-wing Liberals, headed by Simon and Runciman, moved over to the Conservatives. Lloyd George remained in touch with MacDonald through Addison, now a Labour cabinet minister, and there were talks about his joining the government in March 1931, but to no effect.

When a massive financial crisis in August 1931 led to the collapse of MacDonald's government and his re-emergence as head of a coalition National Government Lloyd George was convalescing after a serious prostate operation. However, he made it clear that he strongly disapproved of the National Government and of Samuel, the acting Liberal leader, joining it. The subsequent general election in October was won by the National Government with a colossal majority amid political hysteria which saw Labour almost wiped out. The Liberals were divided into three—Simon's pro-tory National Liberals, Samuel's main grouping, and a Lloyd George family rump of four Welsh members—himself, his daughter Megan (MP for Anglesey), his son Gwilym (MP for Pembrokeshire and briefly a junior minister in the National Government), and his family relative Goronwy Owen (MP for Caernarvonshire). The Welsh outsider was now almost alone.

The 1930s and 1940s: the end Lloyd George was now an elderly man, entering his seventies. He spent much of his time at Churt, partly in farming and growing fruit, notably a famous strain of raspberries. His main and exhausting task, however, was the writing of massive works of reminiscence, his *War Memoirs* (1933–6) and *The Truth about the Peace Treaties* (1938). They were written with the aid of advisers, notably Liddell Hart. These volumes, especially the *War Memoirs*, are a remarkable achievement, which bear comparison with Churchill's later. Based on a vast array of private materials, in them Lloyd George refought the old battles of wartime with zest, to confound critics

and justify himself. There are vivid portraits of individuals such as Grey, Kitchener, and Wilson, and many brilliant insights. The purpose was in large measure polemical, to heap criticism on Haig, Robertson, Jellicoe, and other old adversaries, to argue the case relentlessly for a more peripheral military strategy, and to denounce the sterile bloodbath of the trenches. These volumes are central to the long, ongoing debate on the strategy and ethics of the First World War. They were also implicitly arguing the case for a totally different approach towards Germany and international affairs in the 1930s. Their purpose was the present as much as the past.

Even in his seventies, Lloyd George remained vigorous in domestic politics. Early in 1935, he launched a final crusade, the Council of Action for Peace and Reconstruction, or Britain's New Deal, calling again for active intervention in the economy, public works, and a presidential style of national government. Much was made of reviving agriculture, perhaps an echo of his old rural radicalism. MacDonald and Baldwin invited him to outline his ideas: there was talk of his entering the government, but it came to nothing. In the 1935 general election, the non-government Liberals, Samuelite and Lloyd Georgeite, won a mere 21 seats. The last bid for power had failed. Lloyd George now seemed a rudderless old man, as in his attacks on greater self-government for India and his support for Edward VIII after his abdication in December 1936.

Lloyd George's main preoccupation now was trying to reverse the effects of Versailles and the other peace treaties. As Germany fell into totalitarian dictatorship under Hitler, Lloyd George renewed his attacks on the reparations and unjust frontiers imposed on the defeated Germans. He was critical of the league and the failure to disarm as laid down in the peace treaties, and highly censorious of the French. Once again, he urged that frontier concessions be made to Germany over the Saar, Danzig, the Polish corridor, and the Rhineland. Hitler's occupation and remilitarization of the Rhineland on 7 March 1936, in flat defiance of the Versailles treaty, did not seem to distress him: indeed he urged that a non-aggression pact was possible. Fatefully, in August 1936 he went with Thomas Jones and others on a visit to Germany, which included a widely publicized meeting with Hitler in Berchtesgaden. Against the Wagnerian background of the Bavarian Alps, Hitler gave Lloyd George a signed photograph, addressed to 'the man who won the war'. Lloyd George expressed warm enthusiasm both for Hitler personally and for Germany's public works schemes. He did not mention the treatment of the Jews. When he returned, he wrote ecstatically of Hitler as 'the greatest living German', 'the George Washington of Germany' (*Daily Express*, 17 Sept 1936). It was a serious miscalculation, partly influenced by his later biographer Thomas Jones, a key member of the All Souls group of appeasers, and did him much harm.

Lloyd George pursued a curiously schizoid approach thereafter. He continued to argue the case for a revised peace agreement with Germany. Even the Munich pact brought a somewhat mixed response. He saw the justice of the case of the Sudeten Germans and was savagely critical of the Czech leader, Benes, 'that little swine' (Cross, diary, 5 Oct 1938, Cross, 219). On the other hand, he also urged the vital need to end appeasement and to promote a vigorous policy of rearmament, especially for the air force. He passionately denounced the government's craven failures over Abyssinia and the Spanish Civil War. He argued for an alliance with the Soviet Union, and had private meetings with Maysky, the Soviet ambassador. On 3 April 1939 in the Commons he devastatingly criticized the British guarantee to Poland: without Russia it was an empty gesture. Through this time, he attracted a variety of politicians and journalists, younger tory MPs such as Robert Boothby and Brendan Bracken, editors such as Garvin of *The Observer*, military and economic experts of all kinds. Right down to September 1939 he was a major political player.

When war broke out, Lloyd George remained relatively silent. He was believed to favour the idea of a possible negotiated peace. He made one last great Commons speech, on 8 May 1940, when his devastating attack on Neville Chamberlain helped to bring the prime minister down and led to the succession of Winston Churchill. There was much speculation that Churchill might bring his old comrade into his government, even at the age of seventy-seven. But discussions in June were inconclusive: Churchill perhaps suspected that Lloyd George had defeatist tendencies. Again that November, when Philip Kerr, Lord Lothian, the ambassador to Washington, died, Lloyd George, remarkably, was offered the post, but he turned it down. His appearances in parliament were now increasingly rare. A pessimistic speech on 7 May 1941 led Churchill to compare him, woundingly, with the venerable Pétain in France. He cast his last vote in the Commons on 18 February 1943 as one of the 121 MPs (97 Labour) condemning the government for its failure to back the Beveridge report. Appropriately, his final vote was in defence of the welfare state which he had helped to create.

Lloyd George's life now went into decline. He was deeply upset by the death of his wife Dame Margaret in January 1941; heavy snowdrifts prevented his getting to her bedside before she died. In October 1943, aged eighty, he married Frances Stevenson, his secretary-mistress for thirty years, in Guildford register office, causing severe tension with his daughter, Megan, and other members of the family. He viewed the course of the war with pessimistic resignation and was fearful of German air raids. One of his few pleasures was listening to the broadcasts of William Joyce, Lord Haw-Haw. Increasingly in his late years his characteristic political courage gave way to physical timidity and hypochondria. He continued to attend Castle Street Baptist Chapel in London, and to preside over the national eisteddfod at its Thursday session each summer. At the end, he returned to Wales. In September 1944, he and Frances left Churt for Tŷ Newydd, a somewhat bleak farming property near his boyhood home in Llanystumdwy. He was now weakening rapidly and his voice failing. He was still an MP but learned that wartime changes in the constituency meant that Caernarfon Boroughs

might go Conservative at the next election. In the honours list of 1 January 1945 it was learned that Wales's great commoner would become Earl Lloyd-George of Dwyfor. It did not enhance his reputation among his admirers. On 26 March he died of cancer in Tŷ Newydd, Frances and his daughter, Megan, at the bedside. Four days later, in a simple service, he was buried beside the River Dwyfor in Llanystumdwy. A great boulder marks his grave. There is no inscription.

A historical assessment David Lloyd George is not only one of the most important but also one of the most controversial of British statesmen. In his earlier years, perhaps down to the end of the First World War, biographers and other authors treated him as a great popular hero, a kind of British Abraham Lincoln, the simple 'cottage-bred boy' who tore down privilege and injustice in peacetime, and who then showed himself one of the great war leaders of history. But after 1918—perhaps indeed after the mysterious events of December 1916 which made him premier—treatment of him became almost universally hostile. Conservatives denounced him as an unprincipled dictator, tarnished for ever by the Lloyd George fund. Labour saw him as the ally of reactionaries who betrayed hopes of a land fit for heroes. Fellow Liberals condemned him for the destruction of their great party through the 'coupon' election and treachery to his Liberal past. Keynes's famous essay of 1933 marked him down as an unprincipled adventurer. He appeared almost to have become a national scapegoat, responsible for the downfall of Liberalism, perhaps the decline of Britain itself. Even generally favourable books on him like his official biography by Thomas Jones in 1951 were guarded. As late as 1966, the historian Trevor Wilson's *Downfall of the Liberal Party* placed the blame on Lloyd George alone. Closer to home, Lloyd George's son Richard, the second earl, wrote a book in 1960 in which he depicted his father as an unfeeling libertine. Novelists from Arnold Bennett to Joyce Cary followed this hostile tone.

Since the 1960s, however, historical opinion has changed significantly. In part, it may result from generational change, as older Asquithian enemies disappeared, and the 'permissive society' demolished Victorian puritanism. The opening up of the Lloyd George archives in the Beaverbrook Library in 1967, under A. J. P. Taylor, generated a flood of monographs and biographies, almost all of them emphasizing the greatness of Lloyd George's achievement in peace and in war, his inspirational qualities of leadership, his visionary grasp of the forces of change at home and abroad. Taylor himself in 1974 called him Britain's greatest leader since Oliver Cromwell (introduction to K. O. Morgan, *Lloyd George*, 8). Many commentators bracketed Lloyd George and Churchill as giants kept in the wings in the 'locust years' of the 1930s while Britain languished under the 'pigmies and second-class brains' of the National Government. As a result, both the assessment of historians and of the wider public has become increasingly sympathetic; his heroic status seems to have returned. There was in the 1990s a campaign to install a statue of him in Parliament Square, and in 2001 a new bust of him was unveiled in the smoking room of the Reform Club. Labour prime ministers, Wilson, Callaghan, and especially Blair (speech to Fabian conference, 5 July 1995), paid tribute to him as a great social reformer and pioneer of the British progressive tradition. A millennial poll of historians on 31 December 1999 placed Lloyd George a strong second to Churchill as the outstanding prime minister of the twentieth century.

To a remarkable degree, earlier attacks focused on Lloyd George's personality and his private life. His sexual proclivities have aroused obsessive enquiry reserved for no other prime minister. The biography by his son Richard depicted his father as an oversexed philanderer. And, of course, with his secretary and mistress, Frances Stevenson, he maintained an alternative household over three decades. He was almost certainly the father of Frances's child Jennifer, born in 1927. He was always attracted to pretty young women; he never felt shackled by the marital vows and admitted as much to Maggie Owen when they were courting. Apart from the case of Mrs Kitty Edwards and a later story in a French newspaper (in both of which he was exonerated) he certainly had affairs with the wives of three Liberal MPs, Timothy Davies, Sir Charles Henry, and Sir Arthur Crosfield, with rumours of many others. He was immensely attractive to women, with his beguiling charm, bright blue eyes, fashionably long hair, and neat figure and feet. His personality was hypnotic: it was said that 'he could charm a bird off a bough'. At the same time, the abuse directed at him now seems overdone, as moral standards in society have changed: contrasted with the private activities of several American presidents, Lloyd George's peccadillos appear almost mundane. He was after all an intensely committed professional politician with great ideals to pursue. Nothing should get in the way of that. As regards his relationships with Margaret Lloyd George and Frances Stevenson, both responded to different facets of his make-up. Margaret, reluctant to join him in the metropolis, kept him in contact with the values of Welsh village democracy in which he was brought up. Frances Stevenson offered him more sophisticated assurance in the world of high politics in London. Her diary gives insights into a deeply human side of Lloyd George the critics tend to ignore. He loved two women, and perhaps needed them both.

It has also been claimed that Lloyd George was a man incapable of friendship. 'He had no friends and did not deserve any', A. J. P. Taylor once wrote (A. J. P. Taylor, *English History, 1914–1945*, 1965, 74). Like all politicians who reach the top, Lloyd George had a ruthless streak towards those who crossed him, as Addison, Mond, Montagu, and others discovered. On the other hand, he forged lasting friendships with many honourable figures too—C. P. Scott of the *Manchester Guardian*, the historian H. A. L. Fisher, the social scientist Seebohm Rowntree, a Christian socialist such as Charles Masterman, decent Welsh colleagues such as Herbert Lewis or the preacher-poet Elfed. In many ways, he seems to have been a warmer, more outgoing man than many of his patrician, better-educated contemporaries.

He was usually splendid company, full of fun, a good listener, at ease with monarchs and working people alike, and always happy with children. Not a man of great literary or cultural interests, he relished the interplay of ideas in personal communication. His capacity for absorbing new ideas and for visionary insight was extraordinary. He had a lively, if romantic, interest in history, while his own historical volumes remain of immense value; perhaps in some ways they are more reliable than the more celebrated literary works of Winston Churchill.

Criticisms of Lloyd George's financial improprieties also need to be viewed with caution. Episodes like Marconi arose because he was a comparatively poor man. The trafficking of honours was to provide funding for political objectives. Better to sell titles than to sell policies, he said. He was not personally corrupt. He was very casual in his attitude to political funding, and the Lloyd George fund proved to be a huge public embarrassment, but it was acquired to pursue wider objectives. Public life not personal greed led him into the darker by-ways of the relationship between politics and business. He was, however, greatly remiss in not observing the harm they did to his career and the way they diminished his public reputation. One major cause for the downfall of his government in 1922 was its reputation for corruption.

As a politician Lloyd George was clearly in the front rank among British prime ministers, with a war reputation comparable to that of Churchill and a more creative record of reform during years of peace. He was one of the great mass leaders of his day, a superb orator in harmonious command of voice and gesture, full of spontaneous eloquence, native wit, and poetic imagery that could touch an audience, yet also uniquely effective in the Commons. In key crises such as the Maurice debate, his ascendancy over the house was to save the day. Many of his speeches have a universal quality that transcends time and place. Yet he was equally effective in handling smaller groups, and especially persuasive in face-to-face negotiation. His public style was a product of the pulpit and the Victorian music-hall; the mysteries of the 'wireless' he had still to master at his death.

As an executive minister Lloyd George was highly unorthodox, preferring face-to-face contact and oral information, substantiated or not, gleaned at private meetings, at discussions over breakfast, or perhaps on the golf course, to official material derived from red boxes or blue books. The statistician Sir Joseph Davies observed that Lloyd George tended to use statistics 'from a buoyant—not to say romantic—angle' (J. Davies, *The Prime Minister's Secretariat*, 1951, 153). This could plunge him into difficulties as in the Maurice debate in May 1918, while his flouting of constitutional convention added to the unpopularity of the post-war coalition from 1919 onwards. He would say of himself that, in government as in warfare, he preferred to avoid 'costly frontal attacks if there were a way around'. At his frequent best, though, in peace and in war, he was a minister of astonishing capacity, speed of thought, and inspirational power, notably at the Ministry of Munitions in 1915. In a succession of key ministerial and prime ministerial posts between 1905 and 1922, he could show a remarkable record of legislative and executive achievement. The American envoy Walter Hines Page in February 1917 noted Lloyd George's change-ability which he attributed to his Welshness—'a Scotchman's truth is a straight line, a Welshman's is more or less of a curve'. But he added 'he is the one public man here who has an undoubted touch of genius' (Harvard U., Houghton L., W. H. Page MSS, b MS Am 1090.5 (2)).

The legacies of Lloyd George's career are many and far-reaching. He was clearly one of the makers of the modern world. In his early career he helped to ensure that Wales was regarded as a political reality: he was a forerunner of devolution. At the Treasury he launched the welfare state and was a pioneer of Britain's 'middle way' of social democracy. In wartime he showed genius at munitions, and as prime minister he offered inspirational leadership that led the nation to victory, while achieving lasting changes in spheres ranging from Palestine to the enfranchisement of women. As peacetime prime minister his legacy was far more mixed, and his reputation in his unproductive final twenty years was thus a tarnished one. He was partly responsible for many of the worst features of the Versailles peace treaty. Yet even here were notable achievements such as the Irish Free State treaty. In the inter-war years his was a powerful voice calling for new policies to combat industrial depression and, to some degree, urging a reversal of the policy of appeasement. He was always a man with major long-term objectives. Where he was most open to severe criticism was in the means by which he sought to achieve them. He was never a pliant party man, not in 1910, 1918, nor in the 1930s. His loyalties were casual, and his friendships often flags of convenience. The lure of a government of 'national unity' too often ensnared him. He was condemned for fatally dividing the Liberal Party at the end of the First World War, and the 'coupon' election was certainly a major factor in this, although historians now observe that socio-economic and religious changes were weakening Gladstone's old party at the base even before 1914. It could be added that in welfare policies during the pre-war new Liberalism or in quasi-Keynesian planning programmes in the 1920s and 1930s he galvanized an old Victorian party with new life.

Lloyd George's political style, personalized, quasi-presidential, unpredictable, autocratic, went against the grain of British party politics. Perhaps he would have done better as an American politician, another Theodore or Franklin Roosevelt. But in the light of later transformations in the British political and constitutional system, the erosion of the social structure and received authority, changing perceptions of morality, and changing interactions between politicians, media, and people, he seems an increasingly contemporary, classless figure. Despite massive errors of judgement, as over Versailles, Ireland, or the meeting with Hitler, he remains a giant whose stamp is indelible on modern British history. As Churchill observed at the time of his death (*Hansard 5C*, 409.1377–80), later generations would see how much Great Britain,

in peace and in war, owed to the Welsh outsider from the shoemaker's cottage in Llanystumdwy, and how he had changed their world.   KENNETH O. MORGAN

Sources W. Davies, *Lloyd George, 1863–1914* (1939) • T. Jones, *Lloyd George* (1951) • F. Owen, *Tempestuous journey: Lloyd George, his life and times* (1954) • M. A. Beaverbrook, *Men and power, 1917–1918* (1956) • W. George, *My brother and I* (1958) • A. J. P. Taylor, *Lloyd George: rise and fall* (1961) • A. J. P. Taylor, ed., *Lloyd George: twelve essays* (1971) • K. O. Morgan, *The age of Lloyd George* (1971) • K. O. Morgan, *Lloyd George* (1974) • K. O. Morgan, *Consensus and disunity: the Lloyd George coalition government, 1918–1922* (1979) • J. Grigg, *The young Lloyd George* (1973) • J. Grigg, *Lloyd George: the people's champion, 1902–1911* (1978) • J. Grigg, *Lloyd George: from peace to war, 1912–1916* (1985) • J. Grigg, *Lloyd George: war leader, 1916–1918* (2002) • D. M. Cregier, *Bounder from Wales: Lloyd George's career before the First World War* (1976) • C. J. Wrigley, *David Lloyd George and the British labour movement: peace and war* (1976) • C. J. Wrigley, *Lloyd George and the challenge of labour: the post-war coalition, 1918–1922* (1990) • B. B. Gilbert, *David Lloyd George: a political life, 1: The architect of change, 1863–1912* (1987) • B. B. Gilbert, *David Lloyd George: a political life, 2: The organizer of victory, 1912–1916* (1992) • P. Rowland, *Lloyd George* (1976) • J. Campbell, *Lloyd George: the goat in the wilderness, 1922–1931* (1977) • M. Pugh, *Lloyd George* (1988) • *David Lloyd George, the Llanystumdwy lectures* (1997) • T. Jones, *A diary with letters, 1931–1950* (1954) • T. Jones, *Whitehall diary*, ed. K. Middlemas, 3 vols. (1969–71) • S. W. Roskill, *Hankey, man of secrets*, 3 vols. (1970–74) • F. Stevenson, *Lloyd George: a diary*, ed. A. J. P. Taylor (1971) • *My darling pussy: the letters of Lloyd George and Frances Stevenson, 1913–1941*, ed. A. J. P. Taylor (1975) • *Lloyd George family letters, 1885–1936*, ed. K. O. Morgan (1973) • C. Cross, ed., *A. J. Sylvester: life with Lloyd George* (1975) • W. R. P. George, *The making of Lloyd George* (1976) • W. R. P. George, *Lloyd George, backbencher* (1983) • M. Gilbert, ed., *Winston S. Churchill*, companion vol. 4/1–3 (1977)

Archives Gwynedd Archives, Caernarfon, corresp. and papers • HLRO, corresp. and papers • Lloyd George Museum, Highgate, Llanystumdwy, memorabilia, papers, and photographs • NL Wales, corresp., diaries, papers, incl. letters to his brother; political and family corresp.; letters, papers, and family corresp.; family corresp. and papers; letters and notes for speeches • NL Wales, items, mainly invitations and souvenir programmes • NL Wales, political and business letter-book, incl. letters relating to liberal campaign in Caernarfon boroughs; letters to Annie Hughes Griffiths and Peter Hughes Griffiths • NL Wales, papers relating to proposed memorial • NL Wales, personalia, incl. many illuminated addresses • PRO, papers as minister of munitions, MUN 9 | BL, corresp. with Arthur James Balfour, Add. MS 49692, *passim* • BL, corresp. with J. H. Bernard, Add. MS 52781 • BL, corresp. with John Burns, Add. MS 46282 • BL, letters to Sir Henry Campbell-Bannerman, Add. MSS 41207, 41237–41240 • BL, corresp. with Lord Cecil, Add. MS 51076 • BL, corresp. with Lord Northcliffe, Add. MS 62157 • BL, corresp. with A. J. Spender, Add. MS 46388 • BLPES, corresp. with the Tariff commission • Bodl. Oxf., corresp. with Viscount Addison • Bodl. Oxf., corresp. with Herbert Asquith • Bodl. Oxf., letters to Geoffrey Dawson • Bodl. Oxf., corresp. with H. A. L. Fisher • Bodl. Oxf., corresp. with H. A. Gwynne • Bodl. Oxf., Ponsonby papers • Bodl. Oxf., corresp. with Lord Selborne • CAC Cam., Churchill papers • CAC Cam., corresp. with Reginald McKenna • CAC Cam., corresp. with Sir Edward Spears • CUL, corresp. with Hilton Young • CUL, corresp. with Sir Leo Money • Flintshire RO, Hawarden, letters to Sir J. H. Morris-Jones • HLRO, Beaverbrook papers • HLRO, corresp. with Lord Beaverbrook and related papers • HLRO, corresp. with Andrew Bonar Law • HLRO, corresp. with Herbert Samuel • HLRO, Strachey papers • IWM, corresp. with Sir Henry Wilson • Joseph Rowntree Foundation Library, York, corresp. with B. Seebohm Rowntree • JRL, Guardian archives, letters to the *Manchester Guardian* • King's Lond., Liddell Hart C., corresp. with Sir B. H. Liddell Hart • Lpool RO, corresp. with seventeenth earl of Derby • NA Scot., corresp. with A. J. Balfour and G. W. Balfour • NA Scot., corresp. with Lord Lothian • NL Scot., letters to Sir William Robertson Nicoll · NL Wales, letters to D. R. Daniel · NL Wales, letters to John Gwynoro Davies · NL Wales, letters to T. E. Ellis · NL Wales, letters to Sir Ellis Ellis-Griffith · NL Wales, letters to Sir Samuel Evans · NL Wales, letters to Thomas Gee · NL Wales, letters to his wife, Margaret, and his children · NL Wales, speech notes and letters to Megan Lloyd George · NL Wales, corresp. with Lady Julia Henry · NL Wales, corresp. with E. T. John · NL Wales, Thomas Jones papers · NL Wales, Herbert Lewis papers · NL Wales, corresp. with Sir J. H. Lewis · NL Wales, corresp. with Edward Owen relating to burial place of Owain Glyn Dŵr · NL Wales, letters to W. J. Parry · NL Wales, Stuart Rendel papers · NL Wales, J. Bryn Roberts papers · NL Wales, Sylvester papers · NL Wales, D. A. Thomas, Viscount Rhondda papers · Norfolk RO, corresp. with H. W. Massingham · NRA Scotland, priv. coll., letters to Lord Aberdeen · PRO, cabinet papers; treasury papers · PRO, corresp. with Lord Kitchener, PRO 30/57; WO 159 · PRO, corresp. with Lord Middleton, PRO 30/67 · PRO NIre., corresp. with Edward Carson · TCD, corresp. with Erskine Childers · Trinity Cam., Montagu papers · U. Birm. L., corresp. with Francis Brett Young · U. Newcastle, Robinson L., corresp. with Walter Runciman · U. Warwick Mod. RC, corresp. with Sir William Granet · University of Sheffield, corresp. with W. A. S. Hewins · West Glamorgan Archive Service, corresp. with Winifred Coombe Tenant and her journals of meetings with Lloyd George; notes for speeches | FILM BFI NFTVA, 'Lloyd George resigns', *Topical budget*, 25 Oct 1922 · BFI NFTVA, *Timewatch*, BBC2, 6 Oct 1998 · BFI NFTVA, documentary footage · BFI NFTVA, news footage · BFI NFTVA, record footage | SOUND BL NSA, '23 years ago', 6 Dec 1939, M4523R BD1 · BL NSA, documentary recordings · BL NSA, news recordings · BL NSA, oral history interview · BL NSA, performance recordings · Lloyd George Museum, Llanystumdwy, recordings

Likenesses H. Furniss, ink caricature, 1890–99, NPG · B. Stone, photographs, 1902, NPG · Spy [L. Ward], caricature, 1907, NPG; repro. in *VF* (13 Nov 1907) · M. Beerbohm, pencil and wash caricature, 1908, NPG · G. C. Beresford, photograph, 1908, NPG [*see illus.*] · B. Partridge, caricatures, watercolour, 1908–45, NPG · B. Partridge, pen-and-ink caricatures, 1908–45, NPG · L. Fildes, oils, 1909, Law Society, London · B. Stone, photograph, 1909, NPG · W. Adams, bromide print, *c*.1913, NPG · C. D. Williams, portrait, *c*.1914, National Liberal Club · A. John, oils, 1916, Aberdeen Art Gallery · O. Edis, photograph, 1917, NPG · C. D. Williams, oils, 1917, NMG Wales · A. L. Coburn, photograph, 1918, NPG · H. A. Olivier, oils, 1919, Gov. Art Coll. · W. Orpen, group portrait, oils, *c*.1919 (*A peace conference at the Quai d'Orsay*), IWM · E. R. Pinches, bronze plaque, 1919, NMG Wales · J. Guthrie, oils, *c*.1919–1921, NPG · J. Guthrie, oils, *c*.1919–1921, Scot. NPG · W. Goscombe John, bronze head, 1921, NMG Wales · W. Stoneman, photograph, 1921, NPG · K. Kennet, bronze bust, *c*.1923, IWM, NMG Wales · J. Guthrie, group portrait, oils, *c*.1924–1930 (*Statesmen of World War I*), NPG; study, Scot. NPG · print, pubd 1926 (after D. Low), NPG · W. Orpen, oils, 1927, NPG · P. A. de Laszlo, oils, 1931, Gov. Art Coll. · H. Coster, photographs, 1934, NPG · J. Lavery, oils, 1934?, Dublin Municipal Art Gallery · J. Lavery, oils, 1935, NMG Wales · F. Man, photograph, *c*.1940, NPG · M. Rizzello, bust, 2001, Reform Club, Pall Mall, London · G. C. Beresford, photographs, NPG · T. Cottrell, cigarette card, NPG · J. Epstein, plaster head (posthumous), NMG Wales · F. C. Gould, ink caricature, NPG; repro. in *Pall Mall Gazette* · R. Guthrie, chalk drawing, NPG · D. Low, caricature, National Liberal Club, London · H. Lund, lithograph, IWM · M. Milward, bronze head, NMG Wales · H. L. Oakley, silhouette, NPG · H. L. Oakley, silhouette, NPG · D. Olfsen, bust, NMG Wales · W. Orpen, group portrait, oils (*The signing of peace in Versailles, 28th June 1919*), IWM · A. P. F. Ritchie, cigarette card, NPG · bust, House of Commons · cigarette card, NPG · oils, NPG · statue, Caernarfon Castle Square, Cardiff

Wealth at death £141,147 12s. 6d.: administration, 23 Jan 1946, *CGPLA Eng. & Wales* [cessate] · £139,855 8s. 2d.: probate, 31 July 1946, *CGPLA Eng. & Wales*

George [*née* Gordon], (**Mary**) **Dorothy** (1878–1971), historian, was born at Cheam, Surrey, on 14 July 1878, the daughter of Alexander Gordon (*d.* 1888), barrister, and his wife, Harriet Emily (*d.* 1939), the daughter of the Revd Robert Stammers Tabor. She was educated at St Leonards School, St Andrews, and Girton College, Cambridge. The choice of school and college were decided upon by her father after he saw the Du Maurier cartoon in *Punch* (July 1887), celebrating Agnata Ramsay's achievement of the highest first class in the classical tripos at Cambridge. Alexander Gordon decided that his daughter would follow her to St Leonards and Girton. He died in the following year, but his widow ensured that his wishes were carried out. Mary Dorothy Gordon arrived at Girton at Easter 1896, in her own words 'a quite exceptionally raw schoolgirl' (*Girton Review*, 23). The college was 'no longer a place of pioneers' and she was only loosely supervised by the redoubtable Ellen MacArthur (ibid., 24). Left to her own devices, she attended the lectures of Lord Acton, William Cunningham, and J. R. Tanner, and overcame a 'depressing atmosphere' (ibid.) to gain a first class in the historical tripos of 1899.

Gordon spent the next nine years with her family abroad, with the exception of a single year, 1901–2, when she was persuaded to teach history at Wycombe Abbey School. In 1909 she trained in palaeography at the London School of Economics, and she proceeded to doctoral research there as the Girton College J. E. Cairns scholar, 1910–13. Her dissertation on early Stuart finances, which was supervised by Lilian Knowles, was near to completion when she became engaged to Eric Beardsworth George (1881–1961), a portrait and figure painter, the son of Frederick Beardsworth George, iron merchant. They married on 4 October 1913 in the parish church of St Luke, Chelsea, and lived in London; there were no children. While they were away on honeymoon the sole manuscript of Dorothy George's dissertation was lost. She managed to salvage two articles on the seventeenth-century exchequer, but the dissertation itself was not to be resurrected.

During the First World War, Dorothy George worked in the intelligence department of the War Office, where she was engaged in counter-espionage with MI5 from 1915 to 1919. She afterwards resumed her academic career, making a fresh start in the social and economic history of the eighteenth century. She became a research scholar at the London School of Economics and in 1925 published *London Life in the Eighteenth Century*, an important and widely read work. Partly on the strength of its success the trustees of the British Museum invited her, in 1930, to complete the monumental *Catalogue of Political and Personal Satires Preserved in the Department of Prints and Drawings*, the first five volumes of which had been published by Frederic George Stephens (1870–83). Stephens's volumes had covered the period 1320–1770. To Dorothy George fell the years 1771–1832, when English caricature was at its most profuse. She included nearly 13,000 items in her seven volumes, giving a precise description of each print and, where necessary, an elucidation of its historical context. She also provided in each volume a detailed index of persons, titles, subjects, artists, and printsellers.

Dorothy George began this great work on 14 October 1930 and produced her first volume in 1935. A new volume then appeared every three to five years. During the Second World War the whole project was moved to the shelter of the National Library of Wales at Aberystwyth. On the publication of the final volume in 1954 *The Times* hailed a remarkable feat of scholarship, which Dorothy George had accomplished 'with a persistence equalled only by her learning' (*The Times*, 27 Nov 1954). She was appointed OBE that year. In 1959 she published a companion to her *magnum opus*: *English Political Caricatures, 1793–1832*, tracing the evolution of political caricature, a theme illustrated in the pictorial representation of John Bull himself. Her later study of Welsh caricatures may have been inspired by her friendship with Mary Gwladys Jones, another Girtonian scholar of the eighteenth century.

Among Dorothy George's other notable works were *England in Johnson's Day* (1928) and *England in Transition* (1931). She also contributed numerous articles to learned historical journals, among them a seminal essay on the combination laws, which forbade trade unions and strikes. Originally published in 1927, her argument was intended as a critique of the writings of J. L. Hammond and B. Hammond on the British state in the industrial revolution. She contended, contrary to received opinion, that the Combination Act of 1800 was virtually a dead letter: 'in practice a very negligible instrument of oppression' ('The combination laws', *Economic History Review*, April 1936, 177). Her thesis has featured significantly in the debate on politics and society during the French wars, being challenged among others by E. P. Thompson in *The Making of the English Working Class* (1963).

The scholarship of Dorothy George's later years was interrupted by her husband's long illness. After his death in 1961 she resumed her research, and in her ninetieth year she published *Hogarth to Cruikshank: Social Change in Graphic Satire* (1967). Growing deafness accentuated her retiring nature, and she lived quietly at her home, 51 Paultons Square, Chelsea, London, where she died on 13 September 1971. Dorothy George was awarded an MA degree by Cambridge University in 1927, and a LittD degree in 1931. In 1955 she was made an honorary fellow of Girton College. Self-effacing, courteous, and shy, she carried 'the inescapable air of authority that marks a great scholar' (*Girton Review*, 24).　　　　　MARK POTTLE

Sources K. T. Butler and H. I. McMorran, eds., *Girton College register, 1869–1946* (1948) · *Girton Review*, 187 (1972), 23–4 · *The Times* (27 Nov 1954), 7c–d; (15 Sept 1971), 17h · M. Berg, *A woman in history: Eileen Power, 1899–1940* (1996) · WWW · b. cert. · m. cert. · d. cert. · *Punch, or, The London Charivari*, 2399 (2 July 1887), 326 · J. Johnson and A. Greutzner, *The dictionary of British artists, 1880–1940* (1976), vol. 5 of *Dictionary of British art* · G. M. Waters, *Dictionary of British artists, working 1900–1950* (1975) · *Who's who in art* (1929) · E. P. Thompson, *The making of the English working class* (1963) · J. Rule, ed., *British trade unionism, 1750–1850: the formative years* (1988) · J. V. Orth, *Combination and conspiracy: a legal history of trade unionism, 1721–1906* (1991)
Likenesses H. Coster, photograph, NPG
Wealth at death £135,471: probate, 25 Oct 1971, CGPLA Eng. & Wales

George, Sir Ernest (1839–1922), architect, was born at 9 Portland Place, Southwark, London, on 13 June 1839, the second of three sons of John George (1806–1886), ironmonger, and Mary Elizabeth (*b*. 1811), daughter of William Higgs, a wholesale ironmonger of Streatham. John George, in Ernest's words 'a man of Kent', had entered partnership with Higgs about 1840, and in 1851 moved with his family into an old house adjoining the warehouse and yard at 179 Borough High Street, Southwark. In 1854 the family moved to 36 Albert Square, Kennington, and the business moved to new premises at the corner of Cannon Street and College Hill, in the City. Ernest was educated at schools in Clapham and Brighton. Apparently afflicted with bronchitis, he was transferred to William White's school at Reading. Here his marked aptitude for sketching was encouraged not only by White, but also by his father. George persuaded his parents to allow him to become an architect and from 1856 to 1860 he was articled to Samuel Hewitt, a 'rising', but short-lived architect of Buckingham Street, Adelphi, London. In 1857 George joined the Royal Academy Schools, where he won the gold medal in 1859. After a few months in the office of Allen Boulnois (1823–1893) at 6 Waterloo Place, George undertook a sketching tour of France and Germany, doubtless to perfect his accomplished penmanship. On his return in November 1861 he set up partnership with fellow Royal Academy student Thomas Vaughan (1839?–1875) in Cannon Street. Another office in Croydon was opened briefly, but in 1869 they succeeded to the business of the architect Frederick Hering (1799–1869) at 11 Argyll Street. Having established his practice, George married on 22 September 1866 Mary Allan Burn (1842/3–1877), daughter of Robert Burn, ironmonger, of Epsom, and moved from his parents' home (since 1862), 4 Manor Park Terrace, Mitcham Lane, Streatham, to 7 Grecian Cottages, Crown Hill, Lower Norwood, Surrey. They had four sons and three daughters. In 1887 he moved to Redroofs, the house he built for himself on Streatham Common, where his sister Mary acted as housekeeper and cared for his young children.

Vaughan concentrated on the business side of the practice, while George undertook the 'more artistic branch of the profession' (*Building News*, 12 March 1875, 308). By the early 1870s they had not only established a sound practice, designing commercial, domestic, and some ecclesiastical work, principally in London and Kent, but had attracted the attention of the second duke of Wellington, for whom they designed a villa and bodegas in Granada, Spain (1870). In 1874 they made their country house début with Rousdon, Devon, for Henry William Peek (1825–1898), the first of a long series of great country houses, which were to make their designer's name almost, if not quite, as well known as that of his contemporary Richard Norman Shaw.

In March 1876, exactly a year after the early death of Vaughan, George entered into partnership with Harold Ainsworth Peto (1854–1933), fifth son of the celebrated public works contractor Sir Samuel Morton Peto (1809–1889). A modest and gentle man, George favoured architectural partnerships, believing 'the complete architect is

Sir Ernest George (1839–1922), by Sir Hubert von Herkomer, 1910

hardly to be found in one individual' (George, 622). Peto was 'not a draughtsman, but he had all the feeling of an artist' (E. George, *Builders' Journal*, 24 June 1896, 317), and his taste and business acumen were invaluable to the long-lasting partnership, the most successful of George's long and prolific career. The scope of the practice widened dramatically, with many commissions emanating from the Peto family's connections with the worlds of art, commerce, and construction. George and Peto enjoyed spectacular success throughout the late 1870s and 1880s, and in 1883 they moved to 18 Maddox Street. Commissions ranged from the picturesque Queen Anne premises for Thomas Goode & Co. in South Audley Street (1875–6) to the Ossington Coffee Palace, Newark-on-Trent, Nottinghamshire (1881–2), and the village of Buscot, Berkshire (1892). George's artistic sense alerted him to the potential of colour in building, witnessed by his imaginative use of terracotta, notably at Woolpits, Ewhurst, Surrey (1885–8), for Sir Henry Doulton.

It was the timely Peto Brothers speculation in Harrington and Collingham Gardens (1880–88) which was to establish George and Peto's reputation as advanced domestic architects. Their superbly conceived designs represent the extreme point of late Victorian individualism and were inspired by the old Flemish and German town houses, sketched and painted in watercolour so stylishly and evocatively by George on his frequent tours in northern Europe. Special interest attaches to 39 Harrington Gardens, built for the dramatist W. S. Gilbert. Country

house design, however, was the partnership's métier, and their works ranged in style from Queen Anne, Elizabethan, Jacobean, and Tudor to neo-Georgian, the best-known examples of which are Buchan Hill, Crawley, Sussex (1882–4), Batsford Park, Gloucestershire (1887–8), Shiplake Court, Oxfordshire (1889–91), Poles, Ware, Hertfordshire (1890–92), Motcombe House, Shaftesbury, Dorset (1892–4), West Dean Park, Sussex (1891–3), and North Mymms, Hertfordshire (1893–8).

Over a period of thirty years a continuous flow of talented architects, including Edwin Lutyens, Herbert Baker, E. Guy Dawber, Arnold Mitchell, and J. J. Joass passed through the office either as articled pupils or assistants, attracted by its fashionable reputation. The first two women members of the Royal Institute of British Architects, sisters Ethel Mary Charles (1871–1962) and Bessie Ada Charles (1869/70–1931), were trained by E. G., as George was invariably known in the office. His son Allan (1874–1961) joined the firm c.1895, but left in 1911 to practise in Canada. Peto retired through ill health in 1892 to concentrate on landscape gardening and interior design. That year George entered into his final partnership, with Alfred Bowman Yeates (1867–1944), an improver at Maddox Street since 1889. The domestic practice continued to flourish with large country house commissions including Crathorne Hall, Yarm-on-Tees, Yorkshire (1903–6), Eynsham Hall, Witney, Oxfordshire (1904–8), Ruckley Grange, Shifnal, Shropshire (1904), and the partial rebuilding of Welbeck Abbey, Nottinghamshire, after the fire in 1902. They were almost the last of their kind; soon afterwards the Liberal Party came into power, and fear of higher taxation brought an end to this side of George's practice. Other work, however, came to occupy the place of great country houses. The Royal Exchange buildings, Cornhill, London (1906–9), the Royal Academy of Music in Marylebone (1910–11), Southwark Bridge (1908–21), and Shiapur Palace in India (1914–15) are among the more notable of his later commissions.

In 1896 George was awarded the royal gold medal for architecture; he became ARA in 1910 and RA in 1917. He was knighted in 1911. An associate of the Royal Institute of British Architects in 1861, and a fellow in 1881, he served as president from 1908 to 1910. In 1903 George moved to 36 Lancaster Gate, London, and in 1914 to Inverness Terrace, Hyde Park. He retired in 1920 and died on 8 December 1922 at his home at 71 Palace Court, Bayswater. His funeral was conducted by his son-in-law Canon C. H. Robinson and he was cremated on 18 December at Golders Green crematorium, which he had designed in 1901.

George was not in any sense a theoretical artist, but rather an intuitive designer, keenly sensitive to the pictorial, the scenic side of architecture. One of the finest architectural draughtsmen and watercolourists of his time, he was able to transfer to paper with the utmost sureness and rapidity the first transient idea for a design. Essentially a picturesque architect, this almost certainly explains his lack of success when he attempted, as he occasionally did, the larger forms of monumental architecture. He was, however, a first-class designer of houses, whose understanding of the mechanism of life as lived in great households informed his building and planning. He published six volumes of etchings, but it was his personal style of perspective drawing in pen and sepia wash which was most influential. Examples of his drawings are to be found in the RIBA Drawing Collection, and several of his sketchbooks are deposited at the Victoria and Albert Museum.

HILARY J. GRAINGER

Sources *DNB* · H. J. Grainger, 'The architecture of Sir Ernest George and his partners, c.1860–1922', PhD diss., U. Leeds, 1985 · E. George, 'An architect's reminiscences', *The Builder*, 120 (1921), 622–3 · G. [J. W. Gleeson-White], 'The revival of English domestic architecture: the work of Mr Ernest George [pts 1–3]', *The Studio*, 7 (1896), 147–58; 8 (1896), 27–33, 204–15 · T. A. D. Braddell, 'Architectural reminiscences [pt 1]', *The Builder*, 168 (1945), 6–7 · T. A. D. Braddell, 'Architectural reminiscences [pt 2]', *The Builder*, 168 (1945), 27–9 · G. Aitchison, 'Presentation of the royal gold medal to Mr Ernest George', *RIBA Journal*, 3 (1895–6), 469–71 · P. Waterhouse, 'The late Sir Ernest George', *RIBA Journal*, 30 (1922–3), 107 · H. H. Wigglesworth, 'The late Sir Ernest George RA: an appreciation', *Architects' Journal* (20 Dec 1922), 855 · 'The work of the late Sir Ernest George', *Architects' Journal* (20 Dec 1922), 857–60 · E. G. Dawber, *The Builder*, 123 (1922), 903 · *Building News*, 123 (1922), 389 · 'A note on Sir Ernest George's life with a list of his principal works', *RIBA Journal*, 30 (1922–3), 106 · *The Architect* (15 Dec 1922) · *The Times* (9 Dec 1922) · b. cert. · m. cert. · d. cert. · will, PRO, 1886, F–G, 301 [John George]
Likenesses H. von Herkomer, oils, 1910, RIBA [*see illus.*] · photograph, priv. coll. · photograph, NPG
Wealth at death £32,019 6s. 6d.: probate, 29 Jan 1923, *CGPLA Eng. & Wales*

Frances Louise Lloyd George, Countess Lloyd-George of Dwyfor (1888–1972), by Olive Edis, 1917

George, Frances Louise Lloyd [*née* Frances Louise Stevenson], **Countess Lloyd-George of Dwyfor** (1888–1972), political secretary, was born at 62 Doddington Grove, Kennington Park, Surrey, on 7 October 1888. She was the eldest in the family of three daughters and one son of John Stevenson (d. 1945), the secretary to a firm of French import agents who was descended from Lanarkshire farmers of sternly religious outlook, and his wife, Louise Augustine Armanino, the daughter of a Genoese who had lived in the Latin quarter of Paris and married a French woman. Puritan and bohemian strains thus mingled in Frances Stevenson. She was an intelligent girl who read widely, became an accomplished pianist, and developed a keen interest in gardening; her grandmother ensured that she became a fluent French speaker. Her father sent her to Clapham high school (1901–6). Her friends there included Mair Lloyd George, the eldest daughter of her future husband, destined to die young while she was still at school. Frances went on to study classics at Royal Holloway College, London, where she graduated in 1910, and to take up a post at a girls' boarding-school in Wimbledon. At this time, she was a strong Liberal and an ardent supporter of the suffragette movement, much influenced by H. G. Wells's study of an emancipated young woman, *Ann Veronica*.

The turning point in Frances Stevenson's life came in July 1911, when she was invited to act as private tutor in French and music to Megan, the younger daughter of David Lloyd *George (1863–1945), then chancellor of the exchequer. The impact that Lloyd George at once made

upon her was dramatic. She felt 'a magnetism which made my heart leap and swept aside my judgement, producing an excitement which seemed to permeate my entire being' (*Years that are Past*, 42). Soon she and Lloyd George were becoming intimately friendly; he gave her a copy of a biography of Charles Stewart Parnell by his mistress, Kitty O'Shea. When he became embroiled in the crisis of the Marconi shares affair in 1912 she realized that she could not part with him. In January 1913 she made 'her final commitment'. She accepted his frank proposal that she should stay on with him as personal secretary 'on his own terms', even though it conflicted with her Victorian upbringing. Her relationship as secretary–mistress scandalized both her parents; inevitably it led to prolonged tension with Lloyd George's wife, Margaret, who usually preferred to remain in north Wales. Nevertheless, despite private pressures and the threat of public scandal, Frances Stevenson remained the person closest to Lloyd George from the time of their 'real marriage' (in her own words) on 21 February 1913 until his death in 1945.

When war began in 1914, Frances Stevenson was now installed as Lloyd George's personal secretary, jointly with J. T. Davies. She worked closely with Lloyd George when he moved to the new Ministry of Munitions in May 1915 and then to the War Office in July 1916. When he became prime minister in December 1916, she became his joint principal private secretary, the first woman to hold that post, although she never formally joined the civil service. She travelled with Lloyd George to Italy in the autumn of

1917 after the Italian army's disastrous defeat at Caporetto; she was valuable not only as a secretary but as a translator when Lloyd George met French politicians such as Albert Thomas. She also helped marshal Lloyd George's case when he was attacked by General Sir Frederick Maurice in May 1918 for withholding reinforcements from the western front. She and J. T. Davies later destroyed a damaging document which had emerged and appeared to undermine Lloyd George's argument. At the Paris peace conference in 1919 she worked with the British delegation there, sharing a hotel room with Lloyd George's daughter Megan, who did not yet realize that Frances was her father's mistress; she also went to the conference at San Remo in 1920. Throughout the trials of Lloyd George's peacetime premiership in 1918–22, she was his faithful confidante; indeed, their affection steadily deepened. In 1921 they arranged to purchase 60 acres at Churt, in Surrey, on which they built a house named Bron-y-de. Later Frances built for herself a small house, Avalon, on land adjacent to Lloyd George's Surrey estate. At Churt they shared many common interests, including the development of the farm and experiments in horticulture.

But Frances Stevenson's life continued to be geared to Lloyd George's public career. She declined the suggestion made by Sir Warren Fisher when Bonar Law became prime minister that she should stay on in the civil service. Instead, despite some difficulties with the former premier's other private secretary, Albert James *Sylvester, she now headed Lloyd George's personal secretariat from 1922 onwards, years which saw his leadership of a reunited Liberal Party after 1924 and his final bids for power in 1929 and 1935. After the creation of the National Government in 1931, formed at a time when Lloyd George was seriously ill, she was deeply involved in the research and writing of his War Memoirs (6 vols., 1933–6). At the outbreak of the Second World War, Lloyd George's dependence on her increased, especially after the death of Dame Margaret in January 1941. On 23 October 1943, at Guildford register office, she became Lloyd George's second wife. She had had a daughter, Jennifer Mary, born in October 1929. The birth certificate does not name the father, but many historians (and indeed the young Jennifer) were convinced that Lloyd George was the father, even though Frances had herself been caught up in a passionate affair a little earlier with a married man, the Liberal Party organizer, Colonel T. F. Tweed, a relationship which had led to frequent tensions between her and Lloyd George. After their marriage Frances returned with her husband to Wales, and they lived briefly at Tŷ Newydd, near Cricieth, during which time he became Earl Lloyd-George of Dwyfor on 1 January 1945. But he was a dying man now, and on 26 March 1945 he died in the presence of his wife and of his daughter, Megan. The aftermath was a bitter one, with endless quarrels with Lloyd George's four surviving children, disputes over a memorial fund and the small museum set up at Llanystumdwy, and arguments over Lloyd George's statue in the House of Commons. She soon left Wales and lived quietly in Surrey with her sister Muriel for the rest of her life. She had sold her private papers to the Beaverbrook Foundation but published an attractive and generous work of reminiscence (which does not, however, mention her daughter), The Years that are Past, in 1967. A. J. P. Taylor edited and published her diary, covering the period 1914–44, in 1971, a year before the dowager Countess Lloyd-George's death at her home in Farm Cottage, Churt, Surrey, on 5 December 1972. She had been appointed CBE in 1918.

Frances Stevenson's long association with Lloyd George openly flouted current moral conventions. It led to much tension not only with Lloyd George's wife and children but sometimes between the couple themselves. As early as 1915, Lloyd George proposed to Frances that, as a pure formality, she marry a young Welshman, Captain Hugh Owen, as a camouflage for their relationship, but she refused. The mid-1920s were another tense period, with trouble over an offer for Frances to serve on the board of the Daily Chronicle, and Lloyd George apparently offering Dame Margaret a divorce in 1926. There were many rows resulting from Frances's affair with Colonel Tweed. Yet her enduring relationship with the great statesman fulfilled a vital need for them both. Just as Dame Margaret kept him in touch with his Welsh roots, Frances, with her charm, intelligence, and social poise, was at ease in the world of high politics. She was always sympathetic and unusually responsive to male (but also to female) company. She was a cultured and capable person, with shrewd political judgement, and deeply loyal to Lloyd George. Despite their occasional quarrels, the relationship remained unshaken to the end. Her life, and the records she has left, are testimony to a unique political partnership.   KENNETH O. MORGAN

Sources HLRO, Lloyd George papers · NL Wales, David Lloyd George papers · R. Longford, Frances, Countess Lloyd George: more than a mistress (1996) · F. L. Lloyd George, The years that are past (1967) · F. Stevenson, Lloyd George: a diary, ed. A. J. P. Taylor (1971) · My darling pussy: the letters of Lloyd George and Frances Stevenson, 1913–1941, ed. A. J. P. Taylor (1975) · Lloyd George family letters, 1885–1936, ed. K. O. Morgan (1973) · C. Cross, ed., A. J. Sylvester: life with Lloyd George (1975) · O. Carey Evans, Lloyd George was my father (1985) · The Times (7 Dec 1972) · b. cert. · m. cert. · d. cert.
Archives HLRO, corresp. and papers · NL Wales, corresp. and papers | HLRO, corresp. with Lord Beaverbrook · King's Lond., Liddell Hart C., corresp. with Sir B. H. Liddell Hart · U. Birm. L., corresp. with Francis Brett Young; letters to Jessica Brett Young
Likenesses O. Edis, photograph, 1917, NPG [see illus.] · P. Rasmussen, portrait, priv. coll.
Wealth at death £11,672: probate, 15 Feb 1973, CGPLA Eng. & Wales

George, Georgina [known as Mrs Oldmixon] (d. 1835), singer and actress, was born in Oxford, the daughter of Tobias George. She was sometimes described as coming from the pipe office, Oxford, so her father may have been a clerk employed in connection with the sheriff's accounts for Oxfordshire. She made her début at the Holywell Music Room, Oxford, on 11 February 1779 and sang regularly in Oxford concerts for four years. In November 1780 her father was involved in an acrimonious dispute between the cellist G. Monro and her teacher, Dr Philip Hayes, over her non-appearance at Monro's benefit, from which it is clear that her father was not a clergyman as has been stated. She moved to London in 1783 to sing at the Haymarket Theatre in the summer and began a three-year engagement at Drury Lane that autumn. She made her stage début as Rosetta in the pasticcio *Love in a Village* and then sang Euphrosyne in Thomas Arne's *Comus* and the taxing role of Mandane in his *Artaxerxes*. She became a great favourite at the Haymarket in light musical pieces composed by Samuel Arnold, William Shield, and Charles Dibdin, singing there each summer (except for 1788, when she was ill) until 15 September 1789, when she made her last London appearance. She was less successful in the larger, more demanding Drury Lane Theatre, where she was criticized in the press for laughing and talking on stage when in the chorus of singing witches in *Macbeth*. Her contract was not extended beyond 1786, and she worked at the Brighton Theatre that autumn. When Mary Ann Wrighten left Drury Lane for the USA the *Gazetteer* of 3 January 1787 suggested that since one star had left, the wandering but brilliant 'Georgium Sidus' might be employed. (This flattering use of Herschel's name for his recently discovered planet Uranus has led to modern reference books describing Georgina George as '*née Sidus*'.) Miss George was a soprano soloist in the Lent oratorios at Drury Lane in 1784–8 and also sang at Ranelagh. She moved to the Edinburgh Theatre in spring 1788 and to Dublin that autumn, and returned to Edinburgh for the first few months of 1789, when she also fitted in a week with Tate Wilkinson's company in York, playing seven leading roles to fashionable and crowded houses. In Dublin in 1790–91 she sang at the Rotunda concerts and at the Crow Street Theatre, where in November 1790 she played Lucy to Elizabeth Billington's Polly in John Gay's *The Beggar's Opera*. After Mrs Billington had been applauded for singing her verse of their duet in the second act with sweetness and expression,

> Miss George in reply, availing herself of her extraordinary compass of voice, and setting propriety at defiance, sang the whole of her verse an octave higher, her tones having the effect of the high notes of a sweet and brilliant flute. (Parke, 128)

At Cork the following year their relationship on stage 'could compare to nothing but St. George and the Dragon' (*Hibernian Chronicle*, 20 Oct 1791).

While performing in John Palmer's new Royalty Theatre in east London in winter 1787–8, Miss George sang in *Apollo Turn'd Stroller* by Sir John Morella Oldmixon (1758?–1818), a man of fashion and army officer whom she appears to have married between 1788 and 1793. They were in financial difficulties by May 1793, when she was recruited by Thomas Wignell for his new theatre in Philadelphia, Pennsylvania, USA. As Mrs Oldmixon, she made her début at the Chestnut Street Theatre as Clorinda in Shield's *Robin Hood* on 14 May 1794. She began to take non-singing roles, such as Richard Brinsley Sheridan's Mrs Malaprop in *The Rivals* and Mrs Candour in *The School for Scandal*. When she appeared at the Park Theatre, New York, in 1798–9, she was the highest-paid performer 'engaged for

the first comic singing characters, and her choice of serious ones—the best comic old women, and the best chambermaids' (Ireland, 181). Mrs Oldmixon also performed in the pleasure gardens, and many songs, including several by American composers, were published as sung by her. The Oldmixons had separated by January 1809, when a New York paper called her 'a widow with seven children dependent on a mother's professional talents for support' (Porter, 223). Sir John died in eccentric obscurity in 1818. As late as May 1810 the New York theatrical correspondent of the *Mirror of Taste* described her as 'the only female singer among us!' Mrs Oldmixon retired from the stage in 1814 and settled in Philadelphia, where she ran a ladies' academy with two of her daughters. She died on 3 February 1835.   OLIVE BALDWIN and THELMA WILSON

Sources C. B. Hogan, ed., *The London stage, 1660–1800*, pt 5: 1776–1800 (1968) • *Oxford Journal* (3 Jan 1787) • *Gazetteer* (22 May 1793) • J. H. Mee, *The oldest music room in Europe* (1911) • J. Jackson, *The history of the Scottish stage* (1793) • W. T. Parke, *Musical memoirs*, 2 vols. (1830) • T. J. Walsh, *Opera in Dublin, 1705–1797: the social scene* (1973) • B. Boydell, *Rotunda music in eighteenth-century Dublin* (1992) • T. Wilkinson, *The wandering patentee, or, A history of the Yorkshire theatres from 1770 to the present time*, 4 vols. (1795) • A. Pasquin [J. Williams], 'The children of Thespis', *Poems*, 2 [1789] • *The Euterpeaid*, 2 (16 March 1822), 202 • *Mirror of Taste and Dramatic Censor*, 1 (1810), 416–17 • J. R. Parker, *A musical biography* (1825) [repr. 1975] • J. Bernard, *Retrospections of America, 1797–1811*, ed. B. Bernard (1887) • J. N. Ireland, *Records of the New York stage, from 1750 to 1860*, 1 (1866) • W. Dunlap, *A history of the American theatre*, 2 vols. (1832) • G. O. Seilhamer, *History of the American theatre*, 3 vols. (1888–91), vol. 3; repr. (1968) • S. L. Porter, *With an air debonair: musical theatre in America, 1785–1815* (1991) • O. G. Sonneck, *Early concert-life in America, 1731–1800* (1969) • D. W. Krummel, 'The displaced prima donna: Mrs Oldmixon in America', *MT*, 108 (1967), 25–8 • *GM*, 1st ser., 88/2 (1818), 478 • *GM*, 2nd ser., 3 (1835), 671

Likenesses Russell, pastel drawing, exh. London 1780–89 • D. Orme, engraving (after miniature by S. Howell, 1787), Harvard TC • print (after engraving, after miniature by S. Howell, 1787), Harvard TC

George, Gwilym Lloyd-, first Viscount Tenby (1894–1967), politician, was born at Criccieth, Caernarvonshire, on 4 December 1894, the younger son and the fourth of the five children of David Lloyd *George (1863–1945) and his wife, Margaret (1866–1941), daughter of Richard Owen, a substantial farmer of Mynydd Ednyfed, Criccieth. Lady Megan Lloyd *George was his younger sister. He was educated at Eastbourne College and at Jesus College, Cambridge. After the outbreak of the First World War he served, first, in the 38th (Welsh) division on the western front in France. Later he commanded a battery of artillery on the Somme and at Passchendaele, rose to the rank of major, and was mentioned in dispatches. His letters written in Welsh to his father in 1917–18, with their references to 'the Hun', show that he shared to the full the 'patriotic' emotions of the time.

After the armistice Lloyd George became almost inevitably involved in the career of his father, then prime minister and apparently at the zenith of his popularity and authority. He attended the Paris peace conference with the British delegation in 1919 and took an active interest in foreign policy questions over the next three years. On 14 June 1921 he married Edna Gwenfron (d. 1971), daughter of David Jones of Gwynfa, Denbighshire; they had two sons. Inexorably he became involved in Liberal politics in Wales, and in the 1922 general election he was elected to parliament as National Liberal member for Pembroke-shire (the native county of his grandfather) with a major-ity of 11,866 over Labour. He retained his seat in 1923, against Conservative and Labour opposition, and was made a junior Liberal whip but was narrowly defeated by a Conservative in the 1924 election. However, this rebuff did not deflect him from continuing to take an active part in Liberal politics, especially in his father's campaigns for land reform and for combating unemployment with a public works programme.

In 1925 his father made Lloyd George managing director of United Newspapers, which included the *Daily Chronicle*. He also became a junior trustee, in May 1925, of the National Liberal Political Fund (as the Lloyd George Fund had now been rechristened). In 1945 the remnants of the fund were to be transferred to his sole possession. His father privately attacked him for indolence, and he resigned his directorship in 1926. But he still maintained a warm relationship with his father and largely escaped the family bitterness that was kindled by the growing estrangement of his parents as a result of his father's rela-tionship with his private secretary, Frances Stevenson.

In the 1929 general election Gwilym Lloyd George returned to parliament, having regained the Pembroke-shire seat in a three-cornered contest; he was to retain it for the next twenty-one years. He was a loyal supporter of his father in the turmoil that afflicted the parliamentary Liberal Party during the period of the second Labour gov-ernment in 1929–31. However, when the National Govern-ment was formed in 1931 under J. Ramsay MacDonald, Gwilym Lloyd George served briefly (September–October) as parliamentary secretary to the Board of Trade. But, like his father and his sister Megan (then member for Angle-sey), he turned against the government after the decision to call a 'doctor's mandate' election. He particularly objected to any proposal to introduce tariffs, and resigned from the government on 8 October. After the general elec-tion, which saw the National Government victorious by a huge majority, he joined his father, sister, and his relative Goronwy Owen in a four-member party of Welsh inde-pendent Liberals opposed to the government.

Throughout the 1930s Lloyd George was a loyal sup-porter of his father's domestic and foreign policies. He accompanied him on his notorious visit to Hitler at Berch-tesgaden in the summer of 1936. However, when war broke out again, in September 1939, it was confirmed, as in 1931, that Gwilym Lloyd George was far less hostile to Conservatism than were either his father or his sister Megan. He again became parliamentary secretary at the Board of Trade and served there, under first Chamberlain and then Churchill, until February 1941, when he became parliamentary secretary to the Ministry of Food. He was now carving out a new career of his own, and this was con-firmed in June 1942, when he was appointed to the vital new post of minister of fuel and power, an office he held until the 1945 general election.

Here Lloyd George proved to be an able and tactful min-ister. He devised an effective system of fuel rationing and persuaded domestic consumers to exercise economy. He helped to stimulate the miners into vastly increased coal production. He worked closely with Ernest Bevin, minis-ter of labour, in starting the 'Bevin boys' scheme to increase the labour force, and in instituting a national minimum wage for miners, fixed at a higher rate than in other industries. Most important of all, in October 1943 he implemented some wide-ranging changes in the manage-ment of the coal industry. He recognized that the private enterprise system was inefficient and totally inadequate for raising coal production. In a memorandum to the cabi-net on 7 October 1943 (WP446) he proposed that the gov-ernment secure operational control over the mines and become the direct employer of the various managements for the duration of the war. Although Churchill's personal veto prevented outright nationalization, sweeping changes were instituted which saw the setting up of a National Coal Board with wide powers over production targets and industrial relations. Lloyd George's major achievement was to secure a dramatic increase in the nation's fuel supplies during the wartime period. He was, however, unsuccessful in an attempt to turn the electri-city supply industry into a public corporation, a scheme advocated by himself and by Herbert Morrison.

After his father died in March 1945 Lloyd George went on to confirm both his steady drift towards the Conserva-tives and his new stature as a politician in his own right. He narrowly (by 168 votes) held Pembrokeshire in the 1945 general election, standing as a National Liberal and Con-servative. He insisted in public speeches that no major issues now divided the Liberals and the Conservatives and that the fight against the 'socialist menace to liberty' was paramount. It was noticeable that he adopted the hyphen-ated form Lloyd-George, and also that he declined the chairmanship of the parliamentary Liberal Party after the defeat of Sir Archibald Sinclair. In the February 1950 general election he was defeated in Pembrokeshire by a Labour candidate, Desmond Donnelly, but in October 1951 he was comfortably returned for Newcastle upon Tyne (North) instead. He thus preserved the Lloyd George trad-ition in the Commons, as his sister Megan had been nar-rowly defeated at Anglesey at the same time. Churchill had spoken for him at Newcastle and had a high regard for his administrative abilities and conciliatory approach. He appointed Lloyd-George to the sensitive post of minister of food in October 1951 and he remained there for three years, presiding successfully over a difficult transitional period which saw the ending of food rationing in 1954, and savings in the bill for food imports. The previous year had seen him elected an honorary fellow of his former col-lege, Jesus, Cambridge.

Lloyd-George's success saw him promoted, in October 1954, to home secretary, an office which he combined, appropriately, with the new ministry of Welsh affairs. He retained these portfolios when Eden succeeded Churchill as prime minister in 1955. His most important achieve-ment at the Home Office was to pilot what became the

1957 Homicide Act through the Commons. This modified the severity of the law in murder cases, although Lloyd-George was now firmly opposed to the abolition of capital punishment (having been an abolitionist as recently as 1948). When Harold Macmillan became prime minister in January 1957 Lloyd-George was one of those removed from office, ostensibly to make way for younger men, though his successor at the Home Office was the scarcely youthful R. A. Butler.

Lloyd-George then went to the House of Lords as Viscount Tenby. He continued to play a part in public life. He served as chairman of the Council on Tribunals in 1961, a body created to scrutinize administrative tribunals and ministerial inquiries. This council helped to add to the safeguards for individual citizens against omissions and errors by departmental officials. He also remained active in his native Wales, serving as president of the University College of Swansea, president of the London Welsh Rugby Football Club, and president of the Football Association of Wales. In 1961 he succeeded Lord Birkett as president of the Fleming Memorial Fund for Medical Research.

Gwilym Lloyd-George was notable for forging a career for himself, independently of his distinguished father; he had a far happier and more fulfilling career than do the sons of many great men. He also avoided the storms that beset his father's political and personal life. Although increasingly a somewhat conservative, almost squirearchical, figure himself he remained on the best of terms with his father, mother, and sisters. A warm-hearted, humorous man, who was an excellent mimic, he was especially well liked in the House of Commons, where his knowledge of parliamentary procedure led some to speculate that he might have been nominated as speaker. He was an able, if not outstanding, minister in a variety of departments. His work at the Ministry of Fuel and Power during the war was a significant contribution to victory through the building up of the nation's energy supplies. Although a popular, placid figure he made his own distinctive contribution to the Lloyd George political tradition. He died at St Thomas's Hospital, London, on 14 February 1967. He was succeeded in the title of Viscount Tenby by his elder son, David (1922–1983).　　KENNETH O. MORGAN, rev.

Sources NL Wales, Lloyd George papers · MSS, priv. coll. · *The Times* (15 Feb 1967) · *The Guardian* (15 Feb 1967) · *Western Mail* [Cardiff] (15 Feb 1967) · *CGPLA Eng. & Wales* (1967)
Archives NL Wales, MSS · NL Wales, family corresp. | CAC Cam., corresp. with Sir E. L. Spears · King's Lond., Liddell Hart C., corresp. with Sir B. H. Liddell Hart · NL Wales, corresp. with Huw T. Edwards | FILM BFI NFTVA, news footage
Likenesses W. Stoneman, photograph, 1942, NPG · M. Codner, oils, exh. 1955 · pen-and-ink drawing, U. Wales, Swansea
Wealth at death £64,647: probate, 3 April 1967, *CGPLA Eng. & Wales*

George, Hereford Brooke (1838–1910), historian and geographer, born at Bath on 1 January 1838, was the eldest of the three children (two daughters and a son) of Richard Francis George, a surgeon, and his wife, Elizabeth Brooke. He entered Winchester College as a scholar in 1849, and was elected to a fellowship at New College, Oxford, in

Hereford Brooke George (1838–1910), by unknown photographer

1856. He obtained first classes in both classical and mathematical moderations in 1858, a second class in the final classical school in 1859, and a second class in the final mathematical school in 1860. He graduated BA in 1860 and proceeded MA in 1862. Having been called to the bar at the Inner Temple on 6 June 1864, he practised on the western circuit until 1867, when he returned to New College as tutor in the combined school of law and history. He was ordained in 1868, but never undertook parochial work.

After the separation of the law and history schools at Oxford in 1872 George became history tutor of New College; he retained that post until 1891, and remained a fellow of New College until his death. He was active in reorganizing the work of the university, and played a prominent part in the establishment of the system of inter-collegiate lecturing and in the business of the local examinations delegacy. He was also a reformer in college matters, and his participation there is described in his *New College, 1856–1906* (1906). He was one of the first members of the Oxford University volunteer corps, and was a leader of the university *Kriegspiel* (war-games) Club, of which Halford Mackinder was also a member. His writing and teaching were concerned mainly with military history (in which he was a pioneer at Oxford), and the relations between history and geography, especially in the British empire. He lectured on geography in the modern history school at Oxford. He was elected a fellow of the Royal Geographical Society, and took an active interest in its affairs.

George's major publications include *Battles of English History* (1895), *Napoleon's Invasion of Russia* (1899), *The Relations of Geography and History* (1901), *Historical Evidence* (1909), *The Historical Geography of the British Empire* (1904), and *Genealogical Tables Illustrative of Modern History* (1874). These were works of synthesis, showing an erudite and critical mind though little research into original or documentary sources. In *The Relations of Geography and History* (1901) his view is mildly environmentally deterministic, and emphasizes strategic aspects of geographical conditions as experienced in the Khartoum campaign and the Second South African War.

George's *Historical Geography of the British Empire* was first published in 1904, and had reached a seventh edition by 1924; revisions of the work after his death in 1910 were undertaken by R. W. Jeffery, fellow of Brasenose College, Oxford. It reviews the geographical and historical contexts of the development of the British empire, and is written with a confident view of the manifest destiny of Britain's power and position in the world, describing imperial growth as spontaneous, albeit fed by international rivalry and commercial opportunity. He stresses the heterogeneity and flexibility of the British imperial administrative system, and confidently asserts the justifiability of the British empire and robustly and jingoistically rebuffs criticism by Britain's opponents.

George was a pioneer climber and alpinist from 1860, having first visited Switzerland in that year, when he met Leslie Stephen at Zermatt and they climbed up to the Riffel by the Gorner glacier. He joined the Alpine Club in 1861 and edited the first three volumes of the *Alpine Journal* (1863–7). He accompanied Stephen in 1862 on the first ascent of the Jungfrau Joch, and was also on the first ascent of the Gross Viescherhorn, and of the Col du Tour Noir in 1863 with Christian Almer as guide. This shed light on the relative positions of the heads of the Argentière, Tour, and Salène glaciers. In 1866 he published *The Oberland and its Glaciers*. He was a founder of the Oxford Alpine Club.

George inherited a moderate fortune from his father, and was director of the West of England and South Wales Bank, though he took no active part in its management. The bank failed in 1880, which not only injured him financially, but also involved him and his fellow directors in an abortive trial for irregularities in keeping the accounts. In 1870 he married Alice Bourdillon (d. 1893), the youngest daughter of William Cole Cole of Exmouth; they had two sons. George died at his home, Holywell Lodge, Oxford, on 15 December 1910.   R. S. RAIT, rev. ROBIN A. BUTLIN

Sources A. O. P., 'In memoriam: H. B. George', *Alpine Journal*, 25 (1911), 530–36 · *GJ*, 37 (1911), 325–6 · R. A. Butlin, 'Historical geographies of the British empire', *Geography and imperialism, 1820–1940*, ed. M. Bell, R. Butlin, and M. Heffernan (1995), 151–88 · C. Oman, *Memories of Victorian Oxford and some early years* (1941) · B. W. Blouet, *Halford Mackinder: a biography* (1987) · R. Symonds, *Oxford and empire: the last lost cause?* (1986) · D. I. Scargill, 'The RGS and the foundations of geography at Oxford', *GJ*, 142 (1976), 438–

61 · *Hist. U. Oxf.*, vols. 6–7 · F. W. Maitland, *The life and letters of Leslie Stephen* (1906)
Archives King's Cam., letters to Oscar Browning
Likenesses photograph, Alpine Club, London [*see illus.*]
Wealth at death £682 15s. 7d.: resworn probate, 24 Jan 1911, CGPLA Eng. & Wales

George, John (1776/7–1842). *See under* Cato Street conspirators (*act.* 1820).

George, John (1804–1871), judge, was born in Dublin on 18 November 1804, the eldest son of John George of Dublin (d. 1837), merchant, and his wife, Emily Jane, daughter of Richard Fox. After attending the Frascati School, Dublin, he matriculated at Trinity College, Dublin, in 1818. He graduated BA in 1823 and MA in 1826. He was admitted a student of Gray's Inn, London, on 19 November 1822, and in 1826 he was called to the bar at King's Inns, Dublin. On 16 May 1827 he was also called to the bar at Gray's Inn in London. He then practised in Ireland and in 1832 married Susan Rosanna D'Olier; they had several children. On 2 November 1844 George took silk. His first wife died in 1847; the following year he married Mary Carlton L'Estrange, on 10 August 1848.

George represented Wexford county in parliament as a Conservative from 1852 to 1857, and again from May 1859 to 1866. He acted as solicitor-general for Ireland under Lord Derby from February to July 1859. In 1849 he became a bencher of King's Inns and in 1866 a member of the Irish privy council. In November 1866 he was appointed a judge of the court of the queen's bench, Ireland.

George was highly esteemed as an upright and independent judge and remembered as a kindly country gentleman. He died at his home, 45 Fitzwilliam Square West, Dublin, on 15 December 1871.

G. C. BOASE, rev. SINÉAD AGNEW

Sources *ILN* (23 Dec 1871), 618 · Boase, *Mod. Eng. biog.* · J. S. Crone, *A concise dictionary of Irish biography*, rev. edn (1937), 76 · Burtchaell & Sadleir, *Alum. Dubl.* · J. Foster, *The register of admissions to Gray's Inn, 1521–1889, together with the register of marriages in Gray's Inn chapel, 1695–1754* (privately printed, London, 1889), 426 · *The Times* (16 Dec 1871) · *The Times* (18 Dec 1871) · CGPLA Ire. (1872)
Wealth at death under £30,000: probate, 6 March 1872, CGPLA Ire.

George, Lady Megan Arfon Lloyd (1902–1966), politician, was born in Criccieth, Caernarvonshire, on 22 April 1902, the third daughter and youngest of the five children of David Lloyd *George (1863–1945) and his wife, Margaret Owen (1866–1941). Her early years were overshadowed by her father, who entered the Liberal government in 1905 and finally became prime minister in December 1916. Megan was brought up in a strongly political atmosphere, first at no. 11 then at no. 10 Downing Street. Since the death of the eldest daughter, Mair, in 1907, Megan had succeeded her as foremost in her father's affections. She was at first tutored privately, notably by Frances Stevenson [*see* George, Frances Louise Lloyd], her father's long-term secretary and mistress. Later she was educated at Garratt's Hall, Banstead, and at a finishing school in Paris. She stayed with her father during the Paris peace conference in 1919 and accompanied him to subsequent international

Lady Megan Arfon Lloyd George (1902–1966), by Bassano, 1923

conferences, often acting as his hostess. After his fall from office, she went with him to the United States in 1923; afterwards, she spent a year in India as the guest of Lord Reading. On her return in 1925 she had to have an emergency operation for appendicitis, but she made a rapid recovery.

By her mid-twenties Megan Lloyd George was widely regarded as her father's likely political heir. In 1928 she secured the Liberal nomination for Anglesey and was returned to parliament in the 1929 general election. She showed considerable gifts as a parliamentarian, and soon built up a reputation in her own right. She made a sparkling maiden speech in 1930 on rural housing. In later sessions she made notable interventions on agriculture, unemployment, and Welsh affairs. She also delivered powerful public speeches on foreign affairs and disarmament, as befitted an executive member of the League of Nations Union. Throughout the 1930s, she faithfully followed her father's radical line. She opposed Ramsay MacDonald's National Government and was one of the family group of four Welsh independent Liberal members led by Lloyd George after the 1931 general election. She often urged co-operation between the Liberals and Labour; even at this early period there were rumours of her joining the Labour Party. But her father kept her faithful to Liberalism. She was a forceful supporter of his 'new deal' programme in 1935 for combating unemployment. She also followed her father in foreign policy and accompanied him on the visit to Germany in 1936 during which, to her

apparent embarrassment, they met Hitler. However, Megan was an uncompromising critic of appeasement from the Abyssinia crisis onwards. She remained a fierce opponent of Chamberlain's government after the outbreak of the war, and played a major part in persuading her father to speak, with devastating effect, in the debate of 7–8 May 1940, which led to Chamberlain's resignation.

During the war, Megan emerged more distinctly as an independent public figure. Her father was now ageing rapidly and died in March 1945. Shortly before, his earldom had led to her becoming Lady Megan. She served on wartime consultative committees for the ministries of Health and Labour and National Service, and on the salvage board for the Ministry of Supply. She was a member of the speaker's conference on electoral reform in 1944. But she was most prominent as a leading figure on the unofficial, non-party woman power committee, concerned with the wartime employment of women and with women's rights. She also campaigned hard for equal pay. A member of the pressure group Radical Action, she was now apprehensive of the post-war policies to be adopted by the Liberal Party. With such colleagues as Dingle Foot, she urged that the Liberals align themselves unambiguously on the left. She rejected any possible alliance with the Simonite 'National Liberals'. In the event, she hung on to her seat at Anglesey with a much reduced majority over her Labour opponent at the 1945 general election.

Lady Megan was now foremost among those striving to prevent the Liberals drifting to the right. She feared that the emergence of Clement Davies as the party's leader in 1945 meant a further erosion of its radicalism. When made deputy leader of the Liberal parliamentary party in January 1949 she demanded that the party shed rightwing elements, and often clashed with Asquith's daughter, Lady Violet Bonham Carter. In the parliament of 1950–51, with two other Liberals, she was criticized for often voting with the Labour government in defiance of official party policy. She was on friendly personal terms with the prime minister, Attlee. The Conservatives put up a candidate against her in Anglesey in the general elections of 1950 and 1951; in the latter, she was defeated by her Labour opponent after more than twenty-two years in the house.

After 1951 Lady Megan was much involved with Welsh affairs. She was president of the Parliament for Wales campaign, which attracted over a quarter of a million signatures. In 1952 she declined invitations both to continue as Liberal candidate for Anglesey and to seek re-election as vice-president of the Liberal Party. She did so in terms which suggested that the parting of the ways was not far off. In April 1955 she finally announced that she was joining the Labour Party, as it now seemed to be the essential voice of British radicalism: it was a decision she had taken privately two years earlier. She played an active part in the following general election; Labour saw her as a major force in winning over former Liberal voters. Her opportunity to return to the house came in a by-election at Carmarthen in February 1957, just after the Suez crisis. In a fiercely fought contest she defeated her Liberal opponent by over 3000 votes. In three subsequent general elections she built up her majority to over 9000. She now took part in debates mainly on Welsh questions and agriculture, but was never asked to speak from the opposition front bench. She did not receive office when Labour returned to power in 1964. The March 1966 general election was fought in her absence through ill health. Soon afterwards, on 14 May 1966, at her Criccieth family home, Bryn Awelon, she died of cancer. She was buried four days later in Criccieth. Just before her death she had been appointed CH. In the resulting by-election, a Welsh Nationalist was returned for the first time.

Lady Megan never married, but her private life was tempestuous. She had several close men friends, notably Geoffrey Crawshay, and a traumatic twenty-year relationship with Philip Noel-*Baker (1889–1982), a leading Labour politician who was himself married. From 1936 onwards Megan was his mistress, and the relationship brought her long periods of happiness. But when Noel-Baker's wife died in 1955, his cold rejection of the idea that they should now marry was emotionally devastating for Megan. With her father, her relationship was even stormier. He was always her model and inspiration. But, although devoted to him, she was much opposed to his second marriage, to Frances Stevenson, in 1943, and the family feud continued after her father's death, even at the funeral. She also differed from her brother, Gwilym Lloyd-*George, who moved over to the Conservatives as she herself moved left, but with her older sister, Olwen Carey Evans, her relationship was always close and affectionate. In almost thirty years in the Commons, she never attained office. She was a back-bencher when she died. But she brought rare gifts to British political life. She was a sparkling speaker in Welsh or English. Her speeches in the house, while somewhat infrequent, powerfully focused attention on such issues as rural housing and regional unemployment. She was a regular and effective broadcaster: her many outside interests included membership of the BBC advisory council. A devoted Welsh patriot, she became a bard of the national eisteddfod in 1935 and the first woman member of the Welsh church commissioners in 1942, supervising a church her father had disestablished. She was a woman of vivacity and charm, with a wide range of friends inside and outside politics. Her particular loves were the theatre and ballet; she was also a keen tennis player. With her animated gestures and eager wit, she embodied much of the Lloyd George magic. She was in many ways ideally equipped to serve as the heir to her father's brand of independent radicalism, but her talents were largely unused.   KENNETH O. MORGAN

Sources NL Wales, Lady Megan Lloyd George papers · NL Wales, David Lloyd George papers · NL Wales, William George papers · NL Wales, A. J. Sylvester papers · HLRO, Lloyd George papers · M. Jones, *A radical life: the biography of Megan Lloyd George* (1991) · *Lloyd George family letters, 1885–1936*, ed. K. O. Morgan (1973) · F. Stevenson, *Lloyd George: a diary*, ed. A. J. P. Taylor (1971) · *My darling pussy: the letters of Lloyd George and Frances Stevenson, 1913–1941*, ed. A. J. P. Taylor (1975) · C. Cross, ed., *A. J. Sylvester: life with Lloyd George* (1975) · *The Times* (16 May 1966) · *The Guardian* (16 May 1966) · *Western Mail* [Cardiff] (16 May 1966) · d. cert.

Archives HLRO, letters · NL Wales, corresp. and papers; family corresp.; diary | CAC Cam., corresp. with Attlee · NL Wales, letters to her secretary Helen Dightam; letters to Thomas Iorwerth Ellis; papers, incl. scrapbooks relating to her political career · PRO, corresp. with colonial secretary, CO 967, 959 · West Glamorgan Archive Service, corresp., incl. with Winifred Coombe-Tennant |FILM BFI NFTVA, news footage · BL NSA, party political footage · NL Wales, Audio-visual archive |SOUND BBC Sound Archive

Likenesses Bassano, photograph, 1923, NPG [*see illus.*] · H. Lamb, oils, exh. RA 1953

Wealth at death £87,180: probate, 1966, *CGPLA Eng. & Wales*

George, Thomas Neville (1904–1980), geologist, was born on 13 May 1904 in Swansea, the only son and elder child of (Thomas) Rupert George (1873–1933), a schoolteacher originally from Port Eynon, Glamorgan, and his wife, Elizabeth Evans (1875–1937), a schoolteacher, of Swansea. His paternal grandfather was also a schoolteacher and this background influenced his lifelong interest and dedication to education.

George was educated at Morriston boys' elementary school (1910–14), and from 1914 to 1919 at Swansea municipal secondary school (later Dynevor School). From 1919 to 1920 he attended Swansea grammar school, whence he entered University College, Swansea, with a senior scholarship as one of its first students. In 1924 he was the first student to obtain in Swansea a first-class honours BSc (Wales) in geology. He published two research papers while an undergraduate.

As a student George was called 'TN', a name by which he was known for the rest of his life. Following graduation he stayed on at Swansea and obtained his MSc (1926) under Arthur E. Trueman. He then went to St John's College, Cambridge, where he studied spiriferid brachiopods under Henry Woods, obtaining his PhD in 1928. That year he returned to Swansea as a demonstrator in geology.

George remained in Swansea until 1930 when he was appointed to the Geological Survey of Great Britain and set to work mapping the English midlands. While working for the survey he began writing the first editions of the British Regional Geology handbooks *North Wales* (1935) with Bernard Smith and *South Wales* (1937) with J. Pringle. These proved to be enormously popular and he undertook several revisions over four decades. In 1932 George married the teacher and university lecturer Sarah Hannah Davies MA PhD, though she continued to use her maiden name. Her father was Joseph Davies, a writer and draper, and her mother was Florence Annie Roberts, a schoolteacher. There were no children.

In 1933, at the age of only twenty-nine, George was appointed to the chair of geology and geography at University College, Swansea, which had been vacated by Trueman. In 1946 Trueman resigned from a subsequent position as chair of geology at Glasgow University, and in 1947 George again succeeded him, remaining at Glasgow until his retirement in 1974.

George ruled this department absolutely; not the smallest expenditure could be incurred without his permission and he alone determined the syllabus and content of lectures. George himself was an excellent lecturer, appreciated both in the university and abroad. He possessed a high reputation as an examiner and acted for almost half the geology departments in Britain at one time or another and for many abroad. George published forty-two articles while in Swansea and about a hundred during his time in Glasgow. Most were single-authored. His more important contributions were in synthesizing British landscape evolution, and Carboniferous stratigraphy and palaeontology.

George carried a very heavy load of committee work both within and without the university. Adult education was a lifelong interest. He loved debate, and had a puckish sense of humour and a brisk manner. He was rather ascetic, being an abstainer from alcohol and tobacco and he rarely took lunch. He worked very hard and consistently right up to his death. Even after partial paralysis in 1977 he continued to teach and write from a wheelchair.

George received many honours: the Lyell medal of the Geological Society of London (1963); the Clough medal of the Edinburgh Geological Society (1973); the Neill prize of the Royal Society of Edinburgh (1978); the medal of Charles University, Prague; the Kelvin prize of the Royal Philosophical Society of Glasgow (1975); an honorary DSc of Rennes (1956); and an honorary LLD of Wales (1970). He was a corresponding member of the Geological Society of Belgium. He was president of, among others, the Association of University Teachers (1959–60), the Geological Society of London (1968–70), and the Palaeontological Association (1962–4). He received the DSc (Wales), the ScD (Cambridge), and was elected FRS in 1963. George died on 18 June 1980 at 1 Princes Terrace, Glasgow.

BERNARD ELGEY LEAKE

Sources private information (1986) · personal knowledge (2004) · B. E. Leake, 'Thomas Neville George', Year Book of the Royal Society of Edinburgh (1979–80), 14–20 · B. E. Leake, Memoirs FRS, 37 (1991), 197–217

Archives NMG Wales · U. Glas., Archives and Business Records Centre · U. of Wales, Cardiff · University of Bath, National Catalogue Unit for the Archives of Contemporary Scientists

Likenesses photographs, 1947–74, U. Glas., Department of Geology and Applied Geology, Geological Society of Glasgow Archives · photograph, 1974, repro. in Memoirs FRS, 198

George, Walter Goodall (1858–1943), athlete, was born on 9 September 1858 at the Market Place, Calne, Wiltshire, the second of the seven children of Frederick Benjamin George, chemist and druggist, of Calne, Wiltshire, and his wife, Elizabeth Smith. In 1874, aged fifteen, George became 'apprenticed to chemistry' at the Worcestershire sauce firm of Lea and Perrins, where he was often obliged to work a fourteen-hour day. He grew up to a lithe 5 feet 11¼ inches and 10½ stone. His earliest sporting interests were as a co-founder of the Worcester Rugby Football Club and as a penny-farthing cyclist in 1876. In 1878 he became the joint winner in Birmingham of a handicap walking race over 1 mile with a 45 yard handicap.

At this time the fastest anyone had yet covered the English mile distance had been set by the Welsh professional runner William Richards, at 4 min. 17¼ sec. in Manchester on 19 August 1865. On 1 June 1878 the nineteen-year-old George wrote down his thoughts on how some 10 yards a lap (5.7 seconds of the total time) could be knocked off the

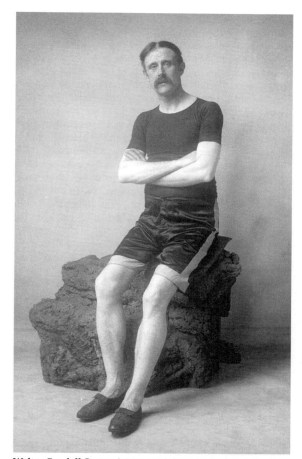

Walter Goodall George (1858–1943), by unknown photographer, c.1884

then world standard. He proclaimed his plan to much mirth. The deed, he said, could be done with laps of 59, 63, 66, and 64 seconds. Remarkably, more than seven years later he ran laps of 58½, 63½, 65¾, and 66 seconds at Lillie Bridge, London, on 23 August 1886 to establish a world's best time of 4 min. 12¾ sec., which was unbeaten anywhere for the next twenty-eight seasons and was unbeaten by a Briton for forty-nine years, until Sydney Wooderson (b. 1914) returned 4 min. 12.7 seconds, running in Glasgow on 3 August 1935.

George won the English championship for the mile and the 4 miles in 1879 and the same distances at the inaugural Amateur Athletic Association (AAA) championships at the Lillie Bridge grounds, West Brompton, London, which were open to the world in the following year. In 1882 at Stoke-on-Trent and in 1884 at Aston, Birmingham, he performed the feat of taking the ½ mile, 1 mile, 4 mile, and 10 mile championships. His dominance was such that few dared challenge him. In 1882 his 4 mile title was a walkover, and in both his ½ mile and 10 mile triumphs in 1884 there was only one other finisher.

George was a moderate smoker and his favourite meal before a race was a glass of beer and a hunk of bread and cheese. He was, however, often racked by asthma and suffered much from hay fever. He became unbeatable over the middle distances in an era before training became scientific. One of his training runs over a mile was timed at 4 min. 9.8 sec. but the absence of opposition and official timekeepers rendered the mark unofficial. He won more than 1000 cups and prizes as an amateur, setting records ranging from 1000 yards (in 2 min. 18 sec.) to 12 miles. Additionally he won the English national cross-country title in 1882, 1883, and 1884 in the colours of Moreley Harriers.

George resigned from the harriers and turned professional in 1886. He was thus able to confront over a mile the leading pedestrian of the Victorian age—William Jeffrey Cummings (1858–1919) of Paisley, Renfrewshire. The police, who were overwhelmed, estimated that 30,000 people converged on the red-brick dust track at Lillie Bridge, West Brompton, London, to bet on the outcome of the gladiatorial duel between George and Cummings. Only after he finished in his world's best time of 4 min. 12¾ sec. did George learn that the tenacious Scot had collapsed 60 yards from the tape and had fallen on the grass infield. Because he recorded this time as a professional, it was not recognized by the governing bodies of the sport. George made five journeys to the United States, both as an amateur and as a professional, and proved himself to be the world's greatest middle-distance runner, so starting a British tradition which was continued by Wooderson, Roger Bannister, Derek Ibbotson, Steve Ovett, Sebastian Coe, and Steve Cram. George also pioneered the '100-up' athletic training exercise, on which he published a short book in 1913.

At St Nicholas's Church, Worcester, on 11 October 1887, George married Ada Annie, younger daughter of George Grainger, the proprietor of the Royal Worcester porcelain works. In the early inter-war years he worked as a park-keeper and groundsman in south London. He received some financial support during hard times from sports journalists. The senior officials of the AAA revered his achievements, but felt inhibited by the strict amateur code of the day from offering more formal and practical recognition to one who had joined the ranks of the professionals. Only his local club, Mitcham athletics club, afforded him true celebrity status. George died at the age of eighty-four, at his home, 21 Frimley Gardens, Mitcham, Surrey, on 4 June 1943, with Ada George, his wife of fifty-five years, by his side. They had one daughter and a son, Walter Gordon, who was shot dead in an industrial fracas in San Francisco in March 1932.   NORRIS MCWHIRTER

Sources P. H. Lovesey, *The kings of distance* (1968) • A. F. H. Newton and others, *Running* (1935) • W. G. George, *Athletics and kindred sports* (1902) • W. G. George, *The '100-up' exercise* (1913) • b. cert.
Likenesses photograph, c.1884, Hult. Arch. [*see illus.*]

George, William (1697–1756), dean of Lincoln, was the son of a mercer of George Street, London. He was admitted to Eton College on 1 July 1712, and entered King's College, Cambridge, as a scholar, on 17 April 1716. He proceeded BA in 1719/20, MA in 1723, and DD in 1728. He was elected a fellow of King's in 1719, resigning in 1728. He became an assistant master at Eton in 1720. He was ordained deacon

in 1725 and priest on 17 July 1726 by the bishop of Ely. In November 1728 he married the daughter of Dr Bland, headmaster of Eton and subsequently dean of Durham, whom he succeeded as headmaster that year, and was appointed a chaplain to the king. George and his wife had a daughter, Margaret, and a son, Robert, who both died in infancy.

When a rebellion broke out at Eton College in 1729 the earl of Bristol alleged that 'the whole government of the school was in a state of anarchy' and described George's conduct as 'so weak as to invite another rebellion' (Hollis, 130). Following the rebellion there was a serious decline in numbers of boys. A Mr Pratt, writing in 1743, thought George was miscast as headmaster, appearing 'not only foolish, but proud, ill mannered and brutal' (Nichols, *Illustrations*, 1.564). However, George's pupils included the earl of Lincoln, nephew and heir of the duke of Newcastle, whose tutor, John Hume, described a strict and academically demanding regime at the school. Neither Horace Walpole nor Thomas Gray, who were at Eton under George, complained of cruelty, and both seem to have been happy there. For Gray, Eton under George seems to have been the happiest period of his life, reflected in his 'Ode on a Distant Prospect of Eton College'. Sir Robert Walpole, as a distinguished son of Eton, took a strong interest in the school. In 1731 George became a canon of Windsor, and in 1742 Walpole adopted George as his candidate for provost of its sister foundation, King's College, Cambridge, against Dr J. Chapman. In a hard-fought contest George secured the provostship by twenty-eight votes to ten. At King's he was described as 'the delight of the Society' (ibid.). He was elected vice-chancellor of Cambridge University in November of the same year. In 1747 he was an active supporter of the duke of Newcastle in his successful campaign for election as chancellor of the University of Cambridge. In 1748 George was appointed prebendary of Thorngate in Lincoln Cathedral and he succeeded as dean Dr Cheyney, who was appointed dean of Winchester. He resigned his other preferments, except the provostship of King's and his royal chaplaincy. He was personally installed as dean and he carefully observed an annual period of residence during the summer and autumn months, and took his turn with the residentiaries to serve as master of the fabric and auditor of the chapter accounts. He played his part in the life of the cathedral and the city, offering hospitality to the residentiaries, and preaching a charity school sermon in 1752. In 1755 the dean and chapter commissioned an architect to draw up a plan to dress, clean, and polish the walls, columns, and arches of the cathedral, and agreed to appropriate a tenth of their incomes, and the fines arising from their capitular estates, to a repair fund.

George was reckoned to have been an admirable classical scholar, and a good Latin poet. His poem on the death of Frederick, prince of Wales, in the collection *Musae Etonenses* (ed. J. Prinsep, 2 vols., 1755, vol. 2) is said to have been commended by Pope Benedict IV. Two Latin poems of his, 'Camera obscura' and 'Omnia vanitas', were included anonymously in *Musae Anglicaniae* (vol. 3, 1741). His 5000 volume library was bought on his death by Earl Spencer; many volumes were subsequently purchased by the John Rylands Library, Manchester. He died on 21 September 1756, and was buried in a side chapel of King's College chapel, Cambridge.   W. M. JACOB

Sources Venn, *Alum. Cant.* · C. Hollis, *Eton: a history* (1960) · R. A. Austen-Leigh, ed., *The Eton College register, 1698–1752* (1927) · T. Harwood, *Alumni Etonenses, or, A catalogue of the provosts and fellows of Eton College and King's College, Cambridge, from the foundation in 1443 to the year 1797* (1797) · dean and chapter of Lincoln, chapter act book, 1731–61, Lincoln Cathedral · Nichols, *Illustrations*, vol. 1 · memorial slab, King's Cam.

Archives King's AC Cam., printed sermons and MSS, funeral sermon

Likenesses portrait (as a boy), Eton

George-Brown. For this title name *see* Brown, George Alfred, Baron George-Brown (1914–1985).

Gerald of Wales [Giraldus Cambrensis, Gerald de Barry] (*c*.1146–1220×23), author and ecclesiastic, was the son of William de Barry, a knightly vassal of the earls of Pembroke, and Angharad, daughter of Gerald of *Windsor, constable of Pembroke.

Family, education, and early career Gerald was born in his father's castle at Manorbier, his father being the son of Odo de Barry, who had possibly served as sheriff of Pembroke and died in or shortly before 1130. His mother brought him family ties not only with Gerald of Windsor's numerous descendants (the ancestors of the Fitzgeralds) but also with the native Welsh princes, for her mother was Nest, daughter of *Rhys ap Tewdwr of Deheubarth. Gerald was thus kinsman both to the leading Anglo-Norman families settled in south-west Wales and to *Rhys ap Gruffudd, the Lord Rhys, who was a grandson of Rhys ap Tewdwr and the chief representative of the Deheubarth line in the later twelfth century.

Gerald had at least one sister, two full brothers, Philip of *Barry and Robert of *Barry, and a half-brother, Walter, who was killed in battle in Wales some time before 1189. His brothers were all raised as knights but Gerald's own destination, as the youngest son, was clear from childhood, when he supposedly built sand-churches instead of sand-castles and was referred to by his father as 'my bishop'. His clerical training and promotion were to be furthered by his uncle, *David fitz Gerald, bishop of St David's (1148–76). His very earliest education seems to have been entrusted to Bishop David's clerks and he was then taught by Master Haimo at St Peter's Abbey, Gloucester, during the abbacy of Hamelin (1148–79).

Gerald's further education took place in the schools of Paris. According to his own testimony, he spent three periods of several years in Paris studying the liberal arts and eventually was himself a teacher of the trivium, winning especial praise for his talents in rhetoric. This period cannot be dated precisely, but he was certainly in Paris in the summer of 1165 when the future Philip Augustus of France was born. During this time he was supported financially by the tithes from the wool and mills of several of his relatives, which they diverted to him.

Upon his return to Wales, it was again tithes that figured

in Gerald's career. During the period 1174–6, with a legatine commission from Richard, archbishop of Canterbury, he undertook to enforce payment of the tithe of wool and cheese in the diocese of St David's. This brought him into conflict with the Flemish settlers in the county of Pembroke. Soon thereafter he was embroiled with the sheriff, who, however, had to give way and submit to corporal penance. Gerald's visitation continued with the suspension of the archdeacon of Brecon for concubinage. On his return to the archbishop, accompanied by his uncle, Bishop David, Gerald was himself appointed archdeacon of Brecon. With this new authority, he continued his campaign in the diocese of St David's, enforcing the payment of tithes, reclaiming appropriated ecclesiastical revenues and asserting his rights even against physical opposition. It was during this time that Gerald's uncle, Bishop David, died (8 May 1176). His own account of the following proceedings relates how the canons of St David's agreed to nominate their four archdeacons, expecting that the king would choose Gerald, but that Henry II was outraged at this apparent pre-emption and refused to have him, even rejecting the recommendation of Archbishop Richard on the grounds that Gerald was too well connected with the great men of south Wales. In the event Peter de Leia, prior of Much Wenlock, was elected bishop and consecrated on 7 November 1176.

Perhaps disappointed at this outcome, but certainly with the firmer financial backing of his prebends and benefices (he held Angle, Laugharne, and Mathry at this time and accumulated others later), Gerald now returned to Paris, where he proceeded to the higher studies of civil law, canon law, and theology. These occupied him for three years (1176–9) and he eventually lectured privately on Gratian's *Decretum*. He bore the title *magister* ('master') throughout the rest of his life. Upon his return to Wales, he was at first appointed administrator of the diocese of St David's while Bishop Peter resided in England, but soon fell into a fierce dispute with him, although this was finally settled. About this time, in 1183, Gerald made his first visit to Ireland, with his brother Philip. Gerald's kinsmen were among the earliest Anglo-Norman settlers in Ireland and Philip had been enfeoffed with a lordship in Munster by his uncle, *Robert fitz Stephen.

Court service Shortly after this, probably in the summer of 1184, a major change took place in Gerald's life, one which was to have important implications for his literary career. While Henry II was in the Welsh march negotiating with the Lord Rhys, he took Gerald into his service as a royal clerk. For the next twelve years or so Gerald was actively involved in royal service. He describes a conversation he had with King Henry at Clarendon in the spring of 1185, during the visit of the patriarch Heraclius of Jerusalem; he accompanied the king's son, John, to Ireland in 1185 and stayed on there as associate of Bertram de Verdon, whom he calls 'seneschal of Ireland'; in 1188 he went with Archbishop Baldwin to preach the crusade in Wales (he himself took the cross, but was absolved from his vow in late 1189); and on several occasions he served as royal envoy to the princes of Wales, notably after Henry II's death when, according to his own report, he 'pacified the country by his arrival and intervention' (*Gir. Camb. opera*, 1.84). Like other court clerks of the Angevin kings, such as Walter Map, he was a critic as well as a beneficiary of court life and he left vivid portraits of those unpredictable, energetic, and self-willed rulers. He also became embroiled in the bitter resentments and antagonisms that court service seemed to breed, engaging in a feud with the Cistercian monk William Wibert, who accompanied Gerald on some of his diplomatic missions and sought to undermine him by accusing him of treachery.

Despite the pressure of business and the distractions of court, it was during this period of royal service that Gerald composed his first and most remarkable literary works, the *Topographia Hibernica* (1186–7), which he read aloud in public at Oxford, the *Expugnatio Hibernica* (1189), *Itinerarium Cambriae* (*c*.1191), and *Descriptio Cambriae* (*c*.1194). These four books are remarkable not only for the detailed narratives they provide of such events as the establishment of English lordship in Ireland in the years after 1169, but also for their acute comments on social customs. Indeed, in the *Descriptio Cambriae* Gerald virtually reinvented the ethnographic monograph, a genre that had largely lapsed since antiquity.

The exact circumstances of Gerald's retirement from court, probably in 1196, are not entirely clear. He claims that he decided 'it was empty foolishness to follow the court', but also seems to have been moved by the fact that 'promotions were empty foolishness, unworthy and not according to merit' (*Gir. Camb. opera*, 1.89). It seems to have been specifically his failure to obtain an English bishopric (although he says he was offered and declined Welsh and Irish ones) that soured Gerald the courtier. This disappointment about patronage may conceivably have been tied to other political factors. Gerald was an interested and opinionated observer of court politics, as his *Vita Galfridi archiepiscopi Eboracensis* ('Life of Geoffrey, archbishop of York') of *c*.1193 shows, with its partisan viewpoint on the infighting of 1189–93, and it may be that his political association with John made a retirement from court at the time of King Richard's return from captivity in 1194 opportune. He was not, however, in disgrace, for he continued to receive payments from the exchequer, at the rate of 5*d*. per day, until 1202.

At any event, Gerald went to Lincoln, where a former Paris acquaintance, William de Montibus, was now chancellor. There he spent several years in study. Works composed in this time include saints' lives; the *Gemma ecclesiastica*, a handbook on the sacraments and morals addressed to his clergy and heavily dependent on the work of the Parisian theologian Peter the Chanter; and probably also a first version of the *De principis instructione*.

The St David's case, 1198–1203 The death of Peter de Leia, bishop of St David's, on 16 July 1198 initiated a long period in which Gerald was completely preoccupied with the attempt to become not only bishop, but archbishop of St David's. His failure to do so turned his ingrained sense of dissatisfaction into bile and bitterness that were with him for the rest of his life.

Gerald had the support of the canons of St David's, but Hubert Walter, archbishop of Canterbury (and from 1199 chancellor), made it clear from the outset that he was quite unacceptable as a candidate. The grounds for this, as Gerald records them, were political: Gerald was too closely associated with the Welsh. It is possible, however, that his marcher ties were at least as important an objection in Hubert Walter's eyes. Moreover, the prospect of Gerald's reviving the claim of St David's to be a metropolitan see and thus of the Welsh church to be independent of Canterbury would obviously rouse the opposition of any archbishop. Gerald was indeed elected by the canons of St David's on 29 June 1199 with the understanding that he would seek consecration directly from the pope and that he would revive the St David's claims.

It is impossible to give a full account here of the intricate negotiations, court hearings, gambits, and manoeuvrings of the next four and a half years, although they are recorded in often painful detail in Gerald's own writings. The prosecution of his case involved him in three trips to Rome (1199–1200; 1201; 1202–3), where he found Innocent III not unsympathetic, though unable to offer him much. Gerald's arguments for his case drew partly on an earlier attempt to establish the autonomy of St David's by Bishop Bernard (1115–48). He also became increasingly strident in his assertion of the distinctive identity of the Welsh and his condemnation of the oppressive treatment they had received at the hands of the English. In response the native Welsh princes gave him their support. This naturally made his English opponents yet more determined. Hubert Walter received the backing of King John, who was otherwise personally favourable towards Gerald, but who now brought pressure to bear on him and his supporters. Declared an 'enemy of the lord king', Gerald found himself disavowed by the canons of St David's (*Gir. Camb. opera*, 3.201). In April 1203 Innocent III quashed his election and ordered another one, and in November and December of that year a settlement was reached in which Hubert Walter's candidate, Geoffrey of Henlaw, became bishop of St David's and Gerald promised never to raise the metropolitan issue again, while he was allowed to resign his archdeaconry of Brecon in favour of his nephew and namesake.

Later years Gerald lived for almost twenty years after the formal renunciation of his case. He spent two years (1204–6) in Ireland with his relatives and made a fourth visit to Rome, purely as a pilgrimage, in 1206. Thereafter he probably lived mainly in Lincoln. During this time he continually went over the St David's case in his mind and produced a substantial polemical–apologetic literature on the subject (*Invectiones*, *De rebus a se gestis*, *De jure et statu Menevensis ecclesie*) and a similarly self-justifying work on his quarrel with his nephew that dragged on for many years from 1208 to *c*.1213 (*Speculum duorum*). This period also saw the composition of his life of Hugh of Lincoln and completion of the *De principis instructione* and *Speculum ecclesie*. He was also continually revising his earlier works, for example issuing a third redaction of the *Itinerarium Cambriae* *c*.1214. He was thus busily engaged in writing as well as squabbling throughout these years. The attempt in 1216 by Louis of France, in alliance with the rebel barons, to replace King John was warmly supported by Gerald, who wrote a poem welcoming the French prince. He was still active in 1220, for the preface to the *Speculum ecclesie* refers to a papal bull of November 1219, but was dead by 1223, when his benefice of Chesterton, Oxfordshire, was filled. Certification of his death on that occasion was given by the dean of Hereford and it thus may have been in that city (where he held a prebend) that he ended his days.

Gerald's literary works Gerald's *œuvre* is large, running to about ten volumes in modern printed editions, and covers a great variety of subjects. He produced poems, letters, and saints' lives, as well as polemic and treatises. It has also been suggested that Gerald was responsible for a surviving schematic map of Europe based on a portion of a contemporary *mappa mundi*. His style was something he justly prided himself on. His Latin is vigorous, fluent, and often striking; the influence of Roman authors is pronounced and his prose is full of citations from them (although his use of anthologies has also been amply demonstrated). Horace, Ovid, and Virgil are the most commonly cited Roman poets; Cicero, Caesar, Sallust, and Seneca figure prominently among the prose authors; and there are many quotations from patristic authors, notably Augustine. Gerald criticized the tendency apparent in his own day for literary training to be neglected in favour of logic and he belongs to the world of *belles-lettres* rather than that of systematic thinking. His general observations are always veering off into anecdote, a form at which he excelled.

Gerald was sharp, critical, and occasionally savage. His vanity and his disappointed ambitions could make him solipsistic and obsessional. In Powicke's words, 'Gerald lived every day an existence of dramatic egotism' (Powicke, 114). A large part of his output was dedicated either to proving himself right or to castigating the vices of others. Sometimes this was in the context of his own quarrels, as in the works on the St David's case or on his dispute with his nephew. Sometimes he adopted a moral, quasi-pastoral stance, as in the *Gemma ecclesiastica* or the *Speculum ecclesie*, which was concerned primarily with criticisms of the monastic orders. In the *De principis instructione* it was the Angevin kings who were the targets of Gerald's vitriol, as he created an image of damned and violent rulers whose replacement by the serene Capetians of France would be a blessing for England.

Yet the enduring impression left by reading Gerald is of that of a man with a powerful and curious eye, who was willing to focus his attention on new subjects and record them with an unusual preciseness and concrete detail. The works on Ireland and Wales reveal more of the natural and the human patterns of those countries in his time than can usually be extracted from medieval authors. The *Expugnatio Hibernica* is, of course, written from the viewpoint of the conquerors—or at least of one party of them, Gerald's relatives—but its vivid and credible picture of twelfth-century warfare and colonial expansion means that it is much more than propaganda. The *Itinerarium Cambriae*, framed by the tale of Gerald's journey through Wales in 1188, is a rich and diverse picture of that half-conquered region, where groups of different languages and traditions lived side by side. The *Topographia Hibernica* and *Descriptio Cambriae* contain not only important observations on the terrain and fauna of Ireland and Wales but also sustained and perceptive characterizations of the native Irish and Welsh, the former admittedly less sympathetic than the latter, but both full of an alert interest in the social patterns and behaviour of other peoples that can only be called ethnographic. Gerald notices everyday details, such as the way the Welsh clean their teeth, but also has a sense of the coherence of the societies he describes, noting the genealogical pride, rough egalitarianism of the warrior class, and political disunity of the Welsh, creating a credible image of their society and social psychology. In the case of both the Welsh and the Irish, it is, in Gerald's view, their pastoral way of life that marks them out most distinctly from their more agrarian and urbanized neighbours, and he is even ready to interpret this in the framework of evolutionary stages—they have remained in the pastoral stage, while other peoples have moved on. Gerald's observations on the language, warfare, music, and social customs of the Welsh and Irish form one of the most significant bodies of source material for medieval Irish and Welsh history. The concluding chapters of the *Descriptio Cambriae*—'How this people may be conquered', 'How they may be ruled when conquered', and 'How they may effectively resist and rise up'—represent very well both Gerald's powerful skill as an analyst of geography, military affairs, and social organization, and the complex and unresolved pattern of his identities and loyalties.

As the manuscript evidence reveals, the four books on Wales and Ireland were Gerald's most successful and widely read works. The same is true today: he is remembered not as a vain and disgruntled clerical careerist but as a pioneering observer of the Celtic lands and peoples.

ROBERT BARTLETT

Sources *Gir. Camb. opera* · Giraldus Cambrensis, *Expugnatio Hibernica / The conquest of Ireland*, ed. and trans. A. B. Scott and F. X. Martin (1978) · Gerald of Wales, *Speculum duorum*, ed. Y. Lefèvre, R. B. C. Huygens, and M. Richter (1974) · *The autobiography of Giraldus Cambrensis*, ed. and trans. H. E. Butler (1937) · Gerald of Wales, *The history and topography of Ireland*, trans. J. J. O'Meara, rev. edn (1982) · Gerald of Wales, 'The journey through Wales' and 'The description of Wales', trans. L. Thorpe (1978) · R. Bartlett, *Gerald of Wales, 1146–1223* (1982) [handlist of MSS, 213–21] · F. M. Powicke, 'Gerald of Wales', *The Christian life in the middle ages and other essays* (1935), 107–29 · J. C. Davies, 'Giraldus Cambrensis, 1146–1946', *Archaeologia Cambrensis*, 99 (1946–7), 85–108, 256–80 · M. Richter, *Giraldus Cambrensis: the growth of the Welsh nation*, 2nd edn (1976) · B. F. Roberts, *Gerald of Wales* (1982) · E. E. Best, 'Classical Latin prose writers quoted by Giraldus Cambrensis', PhD diss., University of North Carolina, 1957 · G. J. E. Sullivan, 'Pagan Latin poets in Giraldus Cambrensis', PhD diss., University of Cincinnati, 1950 · M. Lapidge and R. Sharpe, *A bibliography of Celtic-Latin literature, 400–1200* (1985), 22–8 · A. A. Goddu and R. H. Rouse, 'Gerald of Wales and the *Florilegium angelicum*', *Speculum*, 52 (1977), 488–521 · R. W. Hunt, 'The preface to the *Speculum ecclesie* of Giraldus Cambrensis', *Viator*, 8 (1977), 189–213 · W. P. W. Phillimore and others, eds., *Rotuli Hugonis* *de Welles, episcopi Lincolniensis*, 3 vols., CYS, 1, 3–4 (1907–9) • *Pipe rolls* • G. R. Coone, *Early maps of the British Isles, A.D.1000– A.D.1579* (1961) [for National Library of Ireland, MS 700]

Geraldo. *See* Bright, Gerald Walcan- (1904–1974).

Gerard (*d.* 1108), bishop of Hereford and archbishop of York, was a member of a notable ecclesiastical family, being the nephew of Walkelin, bishop of Winchester (1070–98), and of Simeon, abbot of Ely (1082–94). His parents, Osbert and Anna, and his brother, Peter, were commemorated by the monks of Canterbury Cathedral priory. In his early career Gerard held the position of precentor of the cathedral church of Rouen, and he may also have been archdeacon there. In England he rose to prominence as a royal clerk, and the balance of evidence suggests that he held the office of royal chancellor under William I and William II. He appears to have been succeeded in that office by Robert Bloet by about 1091, but he evidently remained a trusted servant of William Rufus, for in 1095 he was sent with William de Warelwast, later bishop of Exeter, on a mission to Rome on behalf of the king. Their purpose was to inquire into the state of the Roman church and the claims of the rival popes, and, without naming Anselm, to persuade the pope to send the king the pallium for the archbishop of Canterbury. In this way William would be able to bestow the pallium on Anselm, or on another candidate, should Anselm continue to oppose him. Gerard and Warelwast met the pope, probably at Cremona, and then returned to England (May 1096) with the papal legate, Cardinal Walter of Albano, to whom the pallium had been entrusted. Later in 1096 the king appointed Gerard to be bishop of Hereford, even though, according to Eadmer, he was not yet a deacon. He was ordained deacon and priest on the same day and, with Bishop Samson of Worcester, was consecrated on the following day (15 June 1096) in London by Anselm. He duly made his profession of obedience to the archbishop of Canterbury.

At Hereford it is likely that Gerard was the man responsible for the introduction of the rite of the cathedral church of Rouen. His presence is recorded at the consecration of Gloucester Abbey, on 15 July 1100, and at the coronation of Henry I (5 August 1100), although there is no evidence, as alleged by Walter Map, that Gerard himself crowned the king; the ceremony was performed by Bishop Maurice of London. Walter Map is also the source of the unsubstantiated statement that Henry promised Gerard the next vacant archbishopric. However, within a few months (December 1100) the king had indeed translated Gerard to the archbishopric of York, vacant since the death of Thomas of Bayeux (18 Nov 1100). Gerard did not require consecration, and so attempted to sidestep the issue which had caused so much trouble for his predecessor, that of Canterbury's demand that the archbishop of York make written profession of obedience to the southern metropolitan. When Anselm demanded a written profession, Gerard refused. However, he required letters from Anselm if he were to go to Rome to seek his pallium from the pope, and in order to obtain these, he promised that on his return he would make the profession sought by Anselm.

In 1101 Gerard set out for Rome with a double purpose; he was able to combine his own quest for the pallium with his embassy, as one of three envoys of Henry I, in the dispute between the king and Anselm over investitures. The party reached Rome in 1102, and Gerard used his evident diplomatic skills on behalf of the king, according to Hugh the Chanter impressing the papal curia with his eloquence. The pallium was duly granted to Gerard by Pope Paschal II. Nevertheless when he and his companions, the bishops of Chester and Norwich, returned to England shortly afterwards they carried letters for the king and the archbishop which upheld the papal ban on investitures. Gerard is alleged by Eadmer to have intimated to Henry that the pope would overlook a continuation of the practice whereby the king invested bishops with the symbols of their office should Henry make good appointments. This was strongly denied by the pope.

While in Rome, Gerard had secured papal bulls for York, including one that commanded the Scottish bishops to obey York as their metropolitan, and another that confirmed the settlement of the disputed claims to jurisdiction over the diocese of Lincoln. On his return to England Gerard restored Ranulf Flambard to the see of Durham following his reconciliation with the king (1101) and the two archbishops. Gerard avoided making profession to Canterbury, and continued to uphold the dignity of York: when he attended Anselm's reforming council held at Westminster in September 1102, he defended there the equality of the sees of Canterbury and York by refusing to accept a seat placed lower than that accorded to Anselm. As a result of this defiance Anselm wrote to Pope Paschal asking him to order Gerard to comply with his request for a profession of obedience (December 1102). Gerard ignored a letter from the pope, and the following year he threatened further to embarrass the senior archbishop. Anselm had refused to consecrate the bishops of Salisbury and Hereford on the grounds that they had been invested by the king with the symbols of their office. The king now turned to Gerard for support, and Gerard agreed to his request that he, rather than Anselm, should consecrate the bishops. However, when Gerard attempted to perform the ceremony one of the bishops, Reinhelm of Hereford, refused to accept consecration at his hands, alleging that it would constitute an unwarranted attack on the authority of Canterbury. William Giffard, bishop-elect of Winchester who was also to be consecrated, interrupted the service by refusing to allow himself to be consecrated by Gerard, and the proceedings had to be abandoned.

In his capacity as metropolitan Gerard attempted to assert the authority of York over Scotland: he consecrated Roger, bishop of Orkney, but refused to perform the ceremony for Turgot, prior of Durham and bishop-elect of St Andrews, because of his unwillingness to profess obedience to York. He secured five churches from royal manors for the church of York, one of which, Driffield, formed the nucleus of a prebend. Gerard himself established one prebend, that of Laughton-en-le-Morthen. He afforded his protection to the Benedictine monasteries of the diocese, granting the church of Snaith to the monks of Selby Abbey, and issuing a charter of confirmation for St Mary's Abbey, York. Despite his hostility to Canterbury over the question of the primacy he was, by 1105, willing to concede that for the sake of the English church Anselm should return from the exile in which his opposition to the king had resulted. Accordingly, with the bishops of Chester, Norwich, Chichester, and Worcester, Gerard wrote to the archbishop to entreat him to end his exile. On Anselm's return Gerard made profession of obedience at London (on about 3 August 1107): placing his hand in Anselm's he promised to maintain the obedience he had pledged as bishop of Hereford. He thus avoided making explicit profession as archbishop of York. A week later (11 August), at Anselm's request, he attended the consecration of five bishops at Canterbury.

Gerard had clearly been impressed by Anselm's moves towards reform, for he attempted to make changes in the York chapter in line with the canons of the council of Westminster of 1102. A letter that he wrote to Anselm revealed his concern about the refusal of the York canons to give up their wives and concubines, and to proceed from minor orders to the priesthood. In it he envied Anselm his chapter of co-operative, and celibate, monks, and asked Anselm to rule that the York canons should have no contact with women, that those who had been ordained but had failed to make their profession should do so without delay, and that those who refused to be ordained should be compelled. Moreover Gerard revealed his dilemma about having made a simoniacal appointment: he had taken money from the son of an archdeacon for a prebend, and when, realizing his error, he had tried to reverse the appointment, the prebendary had refused to surrender his office. According to Hugh the Chanter, Gerard's successor, Thomas (d. 1114), was later to complain that Gerard had impoverished the see of York, though no precise reasons were given.

Gerard was described by Hugh the Chanter as 'a clerk second to none, or few, in his time for learning and eloquence' (Hugh the Chanter, 21). His erudition was also commented upon by William of Malmesbury and later recorded by William of Newburgh; both, however, added that Gerard was lewd and lustful. The author of the early twelfth-century law books Leges Henrici primi and Quadripartitus has been plausibly associated with Gerard, whose scholarship also stretched to an interest in Hebrew; he owned a Hebrew psalter, and Maurice of Kirkham later claimed that it was under the archbishop that he himself had acquired his knowledge of Hebrew. Gerard's interests were mistaken by some for an interest in the occult. William of Malmesbury, certainly, linked Gerard's sudden death on 21 May 1108 with an unhealthy preoccupation with the black arts. The archbishop was on his way to the council summoned at London by Anselm and had halted for the night at the archepiscopal manor of Southwell. He had, according to William, sent away his attendants and sat down in a garden adjoining the house in order to rest. When his clerks returned they found him dead,

although he had been suffering from only a minor illness. Beneath the pillow on which he rested was found a copy of a book by the astrologer Julius Firmicus. The canons of York refused to accept Gerard's body for burial in the cathedral church because he had died without the last rites. Their hostility stemmed less perhaps from his supposed unhealthy intellectual interests than from his attempts to reform their lifestyle. Gerard's body was carried back to York without ceremony; none of the clergy came to accompany the cortège, and on the journey boys allegedly threw stones at the bier on which his body was conveyed. The canons of York showed their contempt by laying Gerard to rest in a grave outside the porch of York Minster where the body remained until it was moved by his successor, Thomas, into what he considered to be a more worthy location within the cathedral church.

In his short career at York, Gerard failed to win the affection of his chapter, but nevertheless had shown himself a champion of the cause to uphold York's independence from Canterbury. Although conservative in his attitude towards investitures, and thus opposed to Archbishop Anselm of Canterbury on two issues, namely Anselm's stand against the king on investitures and the question of the primacy, Gerard attempted to initiate reform in the cathedral church at York in line with the changes proposed by Anselm's councils.   JANET BURTON

Sources Hugh the Chanter: the history of the church of York, 1066–1127, ed. and trans. C. Johnson, rev. edn, rev. M. Brett, C. N. L. Brooke, and M. Winterbottom, OMT (1990) · Eadmeri Historia novorum in Anglia, ed. M. Rule, Rolls Series, 81 (1884) · Willelmi Malmesbiriensis monachi de gestis pontificum Anglorum libri quinque, ed. N. E. S. A. Hamilton, Rolls Series, 52 (1870) · 'Epistolae Anselmi', ed. F. S. Schmitt, S. Anselmi Cantuariensis archiepiscopi opera omnia, 3–5 (1938–61) · R. Howlett, ed., Chronicles of the reigns of Stephen, Henry II, and Richard I, 1, Rolls Series, 82 (1884) · J. E. Burton, ed., York, 1070–1154, English Episcopal Acta, 5 (1988) · J. Barrow, ed., Hereford, 1079–1234, English Episcopal Acta, 7 (1993) · 'Historia regum', Symeon of Durham, Opera, vol. 2 · Florentii Wigorniensis monachi chronicon ex chronicis, ed. B. Thorpe, 2 vols., EHS, 10 (1848–9) · V. H. Galbraith, 'Girard the chancellor', EngHR, 46 (1931), 77–9 · D. Nicholl, Thurstan: archbishop of York, 1114–1140 (1964) · F. Barlow, The English church, 1066–1154: a history of the Anglo-Norman church (1979)

Gerard of Cornwall [Girardus Cornubiensis] (supp. fl. c.1350), supposed historian, is credited with two works, known only through citation by the late fourteenth-century Liber monasterii de Hyda (associated with Hyde Abbey, Winchester) and by the fifteenth-century writers John Lydgate and Thomas Rudborne. The Liber cites one, De gestis regum West Saxonum, for information on the death of King Alfred, the exploits of his daughter Æthelflæd, the 'revival of the University and the establishment of public schools' (Liber monasterii de Hyda, 111) at Cambridge by Edward the Elder, and an account of the legendary Guy of Warwick, who is said to have defeated the Danish champion Colbrand outside Winchester in the reign of Æthelstan. The latter account is also extant at the end of Oxford, Magdalen College, MS 147 (whence it was printed by Thomas Hearne in 1733). The main part of this manuscript is a text of the Polychronicon of Ranulf Higden which in 1449 belonged to St Sepulchre's, Newgate, London. This may be where, about 1450, John Lydgate found the source for his poem on Guy, which he states he had translated 'out of the Latyn … of Girard Cornubyence' (Bodl. Oxf., MS Laud misc. 683, fol. 77v). Other parts of Gerard's work on the kings of the West Saxons were quoted by Rudborne in his *Historia major* for the revolt against King Æthelwulf in 855, for an account of King Æthelbald and Bishop Swithun, for the seventh-century 'third foundation' of a monastic community at Winchester Cathedral, for the viking attack on Winchester in 867 (*recte* 860), and for the burning of St Frideswide's, Oxford, in 1015 (*recte* 1002). This work is also cited in the *Epitome* of Rudborne's *Historia major*.

The latter is the sole authority for Gerard's second work, *De gestis Britonum*, which Rudborne cited for the legendary first and second 'foundations' of a monastic community at Winchester Cathedral in 164 and 293. It has been suggested by Gransden that the works of Gerard may have been forgeries and that he was a fictional source, invented by Rudborne and given a name of similar type to that of Gerald of Wales. However, whatever their degree of respectability as sources, citation of Gerard's works by the earlier *Liber monasterii de Hyda* and also by Lydgate indicates both an earlier and a wider currency than just Rudborne for them, and allows the possibility that Gerard actually existed. As the monks of St Swithun's, Winchester, made no reference to either of Gerard's works when they expounded their version of the earlier history of their community during their dispute with the bishop in the late thirteenth and early fourteenth centuries, they were presumably not written by then.

ALEXANDER R. RUMBLE

Sources A. Gransden, *Historical writing in England*, 2 (1982), 493–4 · E. Edwards, ed., *Liber monasterii de Hyda*, Rolls Series, 45 (1866), 62, 111, 118–23 · [H. Wharton], ed., *Anglia sacra*, 1 (1691), 180–81, 186, 189, 201, 204–5, 227 · H. O. Coxe, ed., *Catalogus codicum MSS qui in collegiis aulisque Oxoniensibus hodie adservantur*, 2 (1852), 71 · *Registrum Johannis de Pontissara, episcopi Wyntoniensis* AD MCCLXXXII–MCCCIV, ed. C. Deedes, 2, CYS, 30 (1924), 609–12 · *The universal chronicle of Ranulf Higden*, ed. J. Taylor (1966), 157 · *Chronicon … prioratus de Dunstaple*, ed. T. Hearne, 2 vols. (1733), 2.825–32 · DNB

Archives Magd. Oxf., MS 147

Gerard, Alexander (1728–1795), Church of Scotland minister and university professor, was born on 22 February 1728 at Chapel of Garioch, Aberdeenshire, the eldest son of Gilbert Gerard (*d*. 1738), Church of Scotland minister, and his wife, Marjory Mitchell (*d*. 1785), the daughter of Alexander Mitchell of Colpnay. Following his father's death on 3 February 1738 the family moved to Aberdeen, where Gerard attended the grammar school. He entered Marischal College, Aberdeen, in 1740, and before taking his MA in 1744 was apparently taught by David Fordyce. He then studied for the ministry at Marischal, and was licensed to preach by the presbytery of Garioch on 26 April 1749. While studying divinity he joined a theological society founded by George Campbell, who became a lifelong associate and, slightly later, struck up a friendship with Thomas Reid which lasted until Reid left Aberdeen for Glasgow in 1764.

Through the academic year of 1750–51 Gerard substituted at Marischal for David Fordyce, who had embarked on the grand tour. When Fordyce died at sea in September 1751 Gerard was reappointed to teach during the following session, and was chosen to replace Fordyce as regent on 18 May 1752. His appointment was confirmed on 7 July 1752, and two months later he was caught up in a move to revamp the curriculum at the college, which culminated in sweeping reforms, unanimously agreed by the Marischal faculty on 11 January 1753. Gerard and his colleagues restructured the sequence in which subjects were to be taught, and adopted the professorial system of instruction, with Gerard becoming the first professor of moral philosophy and logic on 21 August 1753. As one of the leading architects of the reforms, Gerard defended the changes instituted at Marischal in his *Plan of Education in the Marischal College and University of Aberdeen* (1755), a tract which synthesized the educational ideas of Bacon, Locke, Hume, Fordyce, and George Turnbull, and which subsequently influenced pedagogical thinking in Germany and the American colonies.

As professor Gerard discussed six main branches of philosophy in his course. After a methodological preamble in which he argued that the study of human nature was an empirical science akin to natural philosophy, he began with a detailed analysis of the powers of the mind and summarized the basic conclusions of natural theology. He then turned to ethics, before moving on to jurisprudence, economics, politics, and finally logic, where he first outlined some of the ideas that were later to appear in his *Essay on Genius* (1774). Although much of what Gerard had to say was derivative, his lectures are nevertheless significant historically because they mark an early stage in the emergence of the philosophy of common sense developed collectively by Gerard, Campbell, Reid, and Gerard's protégé, James Beattie.

Outside the classroom Gerard was elected a member of the Aberdeen Philosophical Society shortly after it was founded in 1758. During the fifteen years of its existence, he canvassed topics ranging from agricultural improvement to political theory. In 1758 he was also awarded a gold medal by the Edinburgh Society for the Encouragement of Arts, Sciences, Manufactures, and Agriculture for an essay on taste which was published in London in 1759. In its original form, *An Essay on Taste* contained Gerard's own text, plus translations of brief works on the subject by Voltaire, D'Alembert, and Montesquieu which signalled his absorption of the French tradition in aesthetics. But the *Essay* was also distinctively Scottish in character, for Gerard blended the ideas of Hutcheson, Hume, and his Aberdeen contemporaries, and grounded his discussion of the principles of taste on the science of human nature. Moreover, in the third edition of the *Essay* (1780) he replaced the translations with a lengthy discourse, written largely in the winter of 1778–9, in which he argued that standards of taste could be established using empirical methods analogous to those employed by natural philosophers. Because of its wide readership the *Essay* popularized the philosophical approach to the arts developed by Scots moralists in the early eighteenth century, and it quickly became a canonical text in the literature on taste.

In addition the late 1750s saw important changes in Gerard's personal and professional life. On 14 June 1757 he married Jane Wight (d. 1818), with whom he had at least seven children. Ecclesiastical affairs also began to figure more prominently in his activities. He regularly attended the general assembly of the Church of Scotland and, through his visits to Edinburgh, cemented his ties with members of the moderate party in the kirk, including Alexander Carlyle, who visited Gerard in Aberdeen in 1765. In October 1759 Gerard was selected as moderator of the synod of Aberdeen. The following month he reflected on Britain's involvement in the Seven Years' War in the sermon *National Blessings: an Argument for Reformation*, and he subsequently delivered a withering attack on the writings of David Hume in a sermon preached on 8 April 1760, *The Influence of the Pastoral Office on the Character Examined*, which was published shortly thereafter. This sermon was the first of a series of apologetic works which culminated in *The Corruptions of Christianity Considered as Affecting its Truth* (1792), in which Gerard sought to stem the tide of infidelity by demonstrating the reasonableness of Christianity and, more specifically, to refute the heterodox ideas of Hume, whom he regarded as being the most acute of all the critics of religion.

Gerard's stock within church circles rose further when he transferred to the Marischal chair of divinity. Supported by the town council he was elected on 24 May 1759 and, after being ordained on 5 September 1759, he was finally admitted as professor and preacher at Greyfriars Church on 11 June 1760. Recognition soon followed from neighbouring King's College, which awarded Gerard the degree of doctor of divinity on 1 October 1761, and from the general assembly, which elected him to succeed William Robertson as moderator in 1764. Gerard pursued his apologetic aims in his theology classes as well, as can be seen in the work published by his grandson in 1828, *A Compendious View of the Evidences of Natural and Revealed Religion*, which contains the heads of lectures initially given by Gerard and then recycled by his son Gilbert *Gerard (1760–1815), who took over Gerard's chair at his death.

On 19 June 1771 Gerard was elected professor of divinity at King's College, where he remained a dedicated teacher. He regularly gave a course on the study of the scriptures, and his annual lectures on practical divinity were posthumously published as *The Pastoral Care* (1799). Having earlier advocated uniting the two Aberdeen colleges, Gerard now steadfastly opposed the union schemes proposed in the 1770s and 1780s, and his attempts to block the plans earned him a place among the 'Sapient septemviri' satirized in a print by John Kay.

Gerard's sermon *Liberty: the Cloak of Maliciousness*, published in 1778, shows that his engagement with kirk politics continued unabated after his move, for whereas the members of the popular party were sympathetic to the American cause, Gerard and his moderate allies questioned the legitimacy of the colonists' actions. The parties were at odds, too, over the contentious issue of Catholic relief. Although widespread popular unrest eventually put an end to the initiative in Scotland, in 1778–9 Gerard convinced a hostile presbytery of Aberdeen to endorse the moderates' call to grant Catholics limited rights. His success in doing so attests to his managerial skills, and to his moral standing within the church, which had been reinforced by his appointment as a chaplain-in-ordinary to the king in 1777. His status as a clergyman was additionally enhanced by the appearance of two volumes of sermons in 1780 and 1782, and by his election as a fellow of the Royal Society of Edinburgh in 1783.

Like most of the moderates Gerard was alarmed by the French Revolution, but he did not live to see all of the drama played out in France, for he died of cancer in Aberdeen on 22 February 1795, and was buried in the Old Machar churchyard. His wife survived him.

PAUL WOOD

Sources G. D. Henderson, 'Aberdeen divines: being a history of the chair of divinity in King's College Aberdeen', 2 vols., U. Aberdeen, MS 3411 [typescript] · G. D. Henderson, 'A typical moderate', *The burning bush: studies in Scottish church history* (1957), 163–79 · P. B. Wood, *The Aberdeen Enlightenment: the arts curriculum in the eighteenth century* (1993) · H. L. Ulman, ed., *The minutes of the Aberdeen Philosophical Society, 1758–1773* (1990) · *Fasti Scot.*, new edn · P. J. Anderson and J. F. K. Johnstone, eds., *Fasti academiae Mariscallanae Aberdonensis: selections from the records of the Marischal College and University, MDXCIII–MDCCCLX*, 3 vols., New Spalding Club, 4, 18–19 (1889–98) · minutes of Marischal College, 1729–90, U. Aberdeen, MS M.41 · burgess register, 4 April 1690–17 Dec 1760, Aberdeen city archives · G. Campbell, *Lectures on ecclesiastical history*, 2 vols. (1800) · R. B. Sher, *Church and university in the Scottish Enlightenment: the moderate literati of Edinburgh* (1985) · *DNB*

Archives NL Scot., corresp., MS ACC 10662 · U. Aberdeen, contributions to the Aberdeen Philosophical Society, AUL MS 3107/1/3; MS on university matters in AUL MS 3107/7/7 · U. Aberdeen, corresp., MS CT Box 43 · U. Aberdeen, personal cash book, AUL MS K. 68 · U. Edin., corresp., EUL MS La.iii.352

Likenesses J. Kay, caricature, etching, 1786, NPG; repro. in J. Kay, *A series of original portraits and caricature drawings … with biographical sketches and illustrative anecdotes*, ed. [H. Paton and others], new edn [2nd edn], 1 (1842) · portrait; formerly at U. Aberdeen, now lost

Gerard, Alexander (1792–1839), surveyor and explorer, was born in Old Machar parish, Old Aberdeen, on 19 February 1792, the second of the five sons of Gilbert *Gerard DD (1760–1815), of Rochsoles, Lanarkshire, professor of Greek at the University and King's College, Aberdeen, and his wife, Helen, daughter of John Duncan, provost of Aberdeen. He was a grandson of Alexander *Gerard DD (1728–1795), and brother of James Gilbert *Gerard (1793–1835) and Patrick *Gerard (1794–1848). In 1808, at the age of sixteen, Gerard graduated MA from King's College, Aberdeen, and took up a cadetship in the 13th native infantry of the East India Company's Bengal army. In 1812 he surveyed the routes from Delhi to Lahore and from Ludhiana to Bareilly.

In 1814 Gerard was promoted lieutenant and appointed to conduct a survey of Saharanpur district in the upper Ganges–Jumna Doab. He was recalled to regimental duties during the Anglo-Nepal War but returned to Saharanpur in December 1815, completing the survey in February 1819. It had been commissioned as an aid to the more efficient collection of revenue, and Gerard included in it a minutely detailed study of a single village in order to show the revenue potential of his work. In 1819 he was transferred to the Sirmur battalion (later the 2nd Gurkha rifles) based at Dehra Dun.

Gerard's health suffered in the plains and each summer he retreated to Sabathu or Kotgarh in the hills, where his brothers were stationed, to draw up his survey maps. In the summer of 1817, accompanied by Dr George Govan (1787–1865), he embarked from Sabathu on the first of several expeditions to the Sutlej valley in the Himalayas, an area then relatively unknown to Europeans. His route book of this expedition, 'Journal of a survey from Soobathoo to Rarung, 1817', was published posthumously by his editor, George Lloyd, in *Account of Koonawur, in the Himalaya* (1841). The eponymous text of this work, a descriptive account of the narrow strip of inhabited land straddling the upper Sutlej, was written by Gerard in 1831.

In September 1818 Gerard and his brother James set out from Sabathu on a two-month journey across the Sutlej and northwards up the Spiti River to Shipki. As with all of Gerard's expeditions, the two were laden with expensive surveying equipment—perambulators, theodolites, sextants, thermometers, and numerous barometers—in the use of which both brothers excelled. Aware of the suspicion aroused by survey work, Gerard attempted to take measurements unobtrusively, although this often meant setting up his equipment in the sub-freezing temperatures of first light. Three versions of Gerard's account of this expedition, written up in August 1819, were eventually published: 'Journal of a journey from Shipké to the frontier of Chinese Thibet' appeared in the *Edinburgh Journal of Science* (1, 1824, 41–52, 215–25), 'Narrative of the journey in 1818' in George Lloyd's *Account of Koonawur* (1841), and 'Journey from Subathoo to Shipké in Chinese Tartary' in the *Journal of the Asiatic Society of Bengal* (11, 1842, 363–91).

In June 1821 Gerard, initially accompanied by James, departed from Sabathu on his longest Himalayan journey. On 8 June they ascended the treacherous Shatul Pass (where in the previous year two of James's servants had frozen to death in a snowdrift), detoured to visit Yusu Pass in the east and then travelled on to the Borendo Pass (approximately 15,100 feet). The cold was extreme and the local guides refused to camp at altitude, leaving Gerard and his brother huddled in a tent with their ten servants, whom they had brought from the plains, smoking hookahs and drinking cherry brandy. From the Borendo Pass they crossed over to the Baspa valley before, on 23 June, James was obliged to return to duty. After exploring the ridges to the south of the Sutlej, on 24 July Gerard crossed the Keobarang Pass (18,313 feet), but just before Bekhur was prevented by Tibetan frontier guards ('Chinese Tartars') from penetrating further east into Tibet, Lake Manasarowar, source of the Sutlej, having been his object. Turned back at two more points by courteous but unyielding Tibetan officials, Gerard then travelled back down the Sutlej, crossed the Manirang Pass and, this time heading north-west, reached Manes, on the road to Leh, capital of

Ladakh, on 31 August. Here too he was refused permission to proceed, whereupon he began his return journey, reaching Kotgarh on 24 September.

Disappointed at not having entered Tibet, Gerard had nevertheless amassed a vast amount of geographical information which he converted into beautifully drawn maps. His narrative of the expedition, 'Captain Alexander Gerard's account of an attempt to penetrate by Bekhur to Garoo and the Lake Manasarowara', was published by George Lloyd in 1840 as the second volume of a work by Lloyd's father, Sir William Lloyd, entitled *Narrative of a Journey from Caunpoor to the Boorendo Pass in the Himalaya Mountains*. Gerard's diary of the 1821 expedition served as the basis for Henry Colebrooke's memoir 'On the valley of the Setlej river, in the Himalayan mountains', published in the *Transactions of the Royal Asiatic Society of London* (1, 1827, 343–80).

In November 1822, his health apparently stable, Gerard returned to the plains to undertake a survey of Malwa and Rajputana, but although he completed measurements at Agra, Gwalior, Bhopal, Kotah, and Neemuch, he was dogged throughout by sickness. In 1824 he was appointed acting political agent at Bangur and afterwards at Nasirabad near Ajmer, and did not become available again for survey work until September 1826. In the following August, crippled by rheumatic pain and fever, he was forced to surrender the survey altogether. He never fully recovered his health and in 1836 he retired from the army and returned to Scotland. Gerard never married. He died of fever in Aberdeen on 15 December 1839, a few weeks before the narrative of his 1821 expedition was published.

KATHERINE PRIOR

Sources R. H. Phillimore, ed., *Historical records of the survey of India*, 4 vols. (1945–58) · W. Lloyd, *Narrative of a journey from Caunpoor to the Boorendo pass in the Himalaya mountains*, ed. G. Lloyd, 2 vols. (1840) · BL OIOC, Cadet MSS · P. J. Anderson, ed., *Roll of alumni in arts of the University and King's College of Aberdeen, 1596–1860* (1900) · Burke, *Gen. GB* (1894) · *DNB* · *GM*, 2nd ser., 13 (1840), 324–5
Archives U. Nott., Bentinck MSS

Gerard, Anne, countess of Macclesfield. *See* Brett, Anne (1667/8–1753).

Gerard, Charles, first earl of Macclesfield (c.1618–1694), royalist army officer, was the eldest of at least three sons of a relatively obscure south Lancashire gentleman, Sir Charles Gerard of Halsall, and Penelope, sister and coheir of Sir Edward Fitton of Gawsworth, Cheshire. His parents were licensed to marry at Chester on 3 January 1612, but from later references to his age his birth seems to have occurred about 1618.

Early life Nothing is known of his upbringing until he matriculated at Leiden University on 23 March 1633. He was also said later to have been tutored in France by an Oxford scholar, John Goffe of Magdalen College. This was a remarkably cosmopolitan education for the age, and especially for the heir of a protestant north country squire; it may be suggested that it was intended to equip him for a military career in foreign service, and indeed he is said to have served as a captain in the Dutch forces before 1639, when he must still have been an adolescent.

Charles Gerard, first earl of Macclesfield (*c*.1618–1694), by William Dobson, *c*.1645

From there he returned to take up the same rank in Charles I's wars against the Scots in 1639 and 1640.

Royalist officer, 1642–1644 This precocious record of military experience explains why he rapidly became one of the senior commanders in the army raised by the same king at the opening of the English civil war. In the late summer of 1642 he was commissioned to recruit and command a foot regiment, which turned out to be one of the largest in Charles's field force, ten companies in distinctive blue coats having been raised by the time that the campaign opened, from Lancashire, Cheshire, and north-east Wales. The recruiting drive in the region seems virtually to have been a family business, Charles's uncles Sir Gilbert Gerard and Sir Edward Fitton raising and leading another foot regiment each, and both of his known brothers, another of his uncles, and three of his cousins also becoming royalist officers. The money needed for these efforts would have been beyond the resources of the Gerards and Fittons alone, and it is a reasonable assumption that much of it, and moral support in the work, was provided by the magnate who led the local royalist war effort, the earl of Derby. His seats lay close to the Gerard family home of Halsall, and he may well have proposed Charles and his relatives as commanders of the soldiers to be sent to join the king.

Join him they did, the Lancashire regiments catching up with the royal army in Warwickshire in mid-October, a few days after it had commenced its march on London. They played a crucial part at the battle of Edgehill upon the 23rd, where Charles, despite his youth, was given command of a 'tercia' of foot regiments totalling about 2000 men, stationed on the right hand of the royalist centre. It

was the steadiness of this brigade that prevented a parliamentarian breakthrough and so probably saved the day for the king, turning the action into a drawn one. Gerard himself was clearly in the thick of the fighting, because he was badly wounded in it. He recovered during the winter, in time to take part in the siege of Lichfield in April 1643, and to be wounded again while encouraging a working party. Once more he recuperated, and at the siege of Bristol in July he was given command of the left wing of horse regiments, covering the eastern approaches to the city. In that position he seems to have been spared any direct involvement in the storm, and was chosen instead as the agent sent to negotiate the terms of surrender with the garrison. It was noted that he was 'willing to condescend to any reason in favour of the city but pinching as hard as might be on the soldiers' (Warburton, 2.259). He was already getting a reputation as a hard man as well as a brave and steady one. He was noted for the courage of his performance at the first battle of Newbury on 20 September, and played another prominent part in the relief of Newark during March 1644. There he was clearly well to the fore again, because he received another wound, and was pulled from his horse and made a prisoner, only to regain his freedom almost immediately as his captors were themselves surrounded and obliged to surrender.

General in south Wales, 1644–1645 By now he had good reason to have acquired a fine reputation as a royalist soldier, but to gain higher rank he needed a powerful patron, and this also he had achieved. The actions at Lichfield, Bristol, and Newark had been directed by the king's nephew Prince Rupert, and Gerard clearly caught his eye and so became one of the group of officers whom the prince preferred to regional commands as part of his policy of strengthening the local war effort and increasing his own power over it. In the spring of 1644 the royalist position in south-west Wales had collapsed in the face of a parliamentarian breakout from Pembroke, and an expeditionary force was urgently required to restore it. Gerard was at Bristol in April, presumably convalescing from his latest injury, when he learned that he had been appointed to lead it, at the recommendation of Rupert.

He returned to the royalist capital of Oxford, and commenced his march from there on 8 May, taking his foot regiment and one of horse. His commission has not survived, but it clearly made him lieutenant-general in the six counties of south Wales and in Monmouthshire. The western third of this region had been completely lost to the enemy, and Gerard halted in the eastern part to recruit further strength, rapidly increasing his field force to 1000 foot, 700 horse, and 200 dragoons. Although small, this local army outnumbered that at the disposal of the parliamentarians, and his campaign was literally a walkover, as his opponents slowly retreated before him until by August they stood at bay in Tenby and Pembroke. These were two strongly fortified seaports, which could be regularly supplied and reinforced by parliament's navy. To besiege them was futile under these circumstances, as had already been proved in the spring, and Gerard set to work instead to hem them in with local royalist garrisons. To install and maintain these required heavy pressure upon the resources of the region, and this its new general was both officially empowered and personally ready to apply. When the local gentry protested that they could not afford the money and manpower necessary for the effort, he replaced them as governors of the fortresses in their counties with experienced soldiers brought in from England by himself, and answerable only to him. In this manner he put garrisons into every town and castle in Cardiganshire and Carmarthenshire, and laid waste Pembrokeshire with a savagery which provoked horror in the parliamentarian press, to starve his enemies of local supplies and create a scorched-earth zone between them and his royalist cordon sanitaire. In September he received orders to bring his field force eastward to join the royal army for its march on London, and began his journey in October.

The result was a triumph, for having left west Wales apparently secure, he was able to meet the king with an augmented marching army of about 3000. This came up with the royal forces in Berkshire on 5 November, and assisted them in the stand-off four days later, sometimes called the third battle of Newbury, in which they offered battle to the main parliamentarian army and outfaced it. After this Gerard and his men retired to Oxford with the rest of the king's soldiers, and then went on to Monmouthshire to repair its defences after a parliamentarian thrust from Gloucester had been pushed back from the county in mid-November. From these winter quarters he was ordered northward in March 1645, to join Rupert and some of the royal army in opposing further advances by the enemy in Cheshire and Shropshire.

The union of the two forces took place at Bridgnorth on the 9th, and they advanced across Shropshire, reasserting royalist supremacy in the field. On the 15th they were further reinforced at Ellesmere, and went on to relieve Chester and Beeston Castle and to quarter and refresh in western Cheshire. After about a week Gerard marched his own army into Montgomeryshire, to pin the parliamentarians there into their castles, arrest collaborators, and rest and re-equip his men for a second campaign in the west. There the Pembrokeshire parliamentarians had broken through his cordon of garrisons, taking Laugharne Castle in October and Cardigan in November, and established contact with their comrades in Montgomeryshire. By basing his own force at Newtown, Gerard severed this contact, and also gave his men a fortnight in what was now enemy territory to conscript recruits and levy supplies, once again provoking complaints of brutality unusual for a local field commander. After that time had elapsed he was ready to strike westward and did so, catching the Pembrokeshire parliamentarian forces by surprise outside Newcastle Emlyn on 23 April. He totally routed them, and the next day pressed on to Haverfordwest and stormed it. This cut off the outlying enemy garrisons such as Cardigan, which had to be evacuated by sea. The following day he stormed Picton Castle, and four days later took Carew Castle in turn. Within a week, therefore, he had recovered all of the territory lost since his departure from the region in the previous autumn.

Once again he faced the problem of having to keep his opponents penned into Pembroke and Tenby even when they were reinforced by a hostile navy which dominated the coasts. His solution was the same as before, but this time he moved forward his cordon of fortresses much closer to the enemy bases, by garrisoning Haverfordwest and the two castles very strongly and so bottling the parliamentarians into southern Pembrokeshire. He then settled down to recruit again, and by mid-May 1645 was able to leave his garrisons in place under chosen officers while marching to rejoin the royal field army once more, with a mobile force of 2000 foot and 700 horse. He had repeated his success of 1644, in a quarter of the time.

Most of the fruits of this success were thrown away by the destruction of the royal army at Naseby on 14 June, so that it was the king who ran into Gerard in the course of his headlong flight towards safety in Wales with the remnant of his forces. When they met at Hereford in late June, Gerard's field force was broken up to meet the needs of the emergency, the foot being shipped over to Bristol to reinforce it against an anticipated attack and the horse united with those remaining from the king's army. Gerard himself was kept with the royal entourage as Charles settled down in Glamorgan and Monmouthshire to recruit a new body of infantry from Wales and its borders. This effort, however, proved to be too much for the hitherto loyal local communities of south Wales. Observing that the subtraction of Gerard's soldiers had deprived him of the mechanism with which he had enforced royal demands upon them hitherto, they went into mutiny, led by their gentry, on 31 July. Their first demand was the removal of Gerard from his regional command and of his officers from command of its garrisons. The king agreed to this, compensating Gerard himself with the promise of a peerage and of command of the foot soldiers in a future royal field army.

The first promise was kept, although apparently not until 8 October, when a patent was signed to award him the title of Baron Gerard of Brandon. The second could not be, because the body of foot concerned was never recruited. Instead, Gerard found himself in control of the largest troop of horse in the king's life guard and the largest brigade of cavalry in a royal army now virtually reduced to horse soldiers, almost certainly representing those who he had himself led out of Wales. With them, he accompanied Charles on the desperate series of marches which commenced when the king left south Wales on 5 August and took them in zigzags from there to Yorkshire and the east midlands and so back to the Welsh border again, always seeking a plan of action. He fought in the action at Rowton Heath, outside Chester, on 23 September, when the king's horse were defeated by a pursuing parliamentarian army. He was reported to have been wounded in it, although the truth seems impossible to establish. At any rate he was still with his monarch as Charles made his way eastward again to Newark after the action and settled there for a month. Gerard and his horse were quartered around Belvoir Castle.

Royalist quarrels, 1645–1646 It was here, on the heels of the belated award of his peerage, that Gerard's loyalties became divided. In September the king had dismissed Prince Rupert after the latter's surrender of Bristol, believing him to have become untrustworthy. The prince arrived at Newark on 15 October with a body of followers and demanded a hearing. Charles awarded his nephew a formal court martial, at which he was exonerated for the loss of Bristol. On the 20th, however, the king replaced the governor of Newark, who had been one of Rupert's many military protégés, with another man. The prince took this as a further slight, and an illustration of the continued ascendancy over Charles of Rupert's bitter enemy Lord Digby. He and his followers promptly confronted the king in a stormy and unruly interview which broke Charles's patience and caused him to dismiss all of them from his service.

Gerard had plainly never forgotten that he had owed his own promotion to Rupert's favour. Although he had apparently made no objection to the prince's disgrace in September, he had shown his sympathies when Rupert approached Newark, in defiance of his uncle's orders, by leading out his horsemen to escort the prince into the town. In the fracas of the 20th he was well to the fore, shouting that Digby was a traitor, and the king sacked him with all the others. He retired with Rupert and his 400 followers to Worton House, and then to Belvoir Castle again, from where on the 29th they applied to parliament for passes to leave the country.

These were eventually granted, but not until after a long interval, occasioned by a demand from parliament that they swear never again to fight against it. Being unwilling to betray their royal master so completely, they temporized and were allowed to march into Worcestershire, where they all spent the midwinter in limbo, under royal displeasure but unable to persuade parliament to withdraw its condition. This was ended in January 1646, when Charles forgave them and allowed them to return to Oxford and assist in its preparation for the final siege. Gerard was put in command of a horse troop, with which he raided into the surrounding region, and was still with Rupert in the city when it surrendered on 24 June. At some point in the second half of the year he was granted his pass and went overseas. He had won himself a general's baton and a peerage, only to lose his employment, his family lands, and his country; and he was still not yet thirty years of age.

Exile, 1646–1660 For a time his movements are as hard to trace as those of many royalist exiles at this period. He is recorded at The Hague on 27 December 1646 and with Rupert at the queen's court at St Germain-en-Laye in September 1647. He next appears in Dutch territory in November 1648, being appointed vice-admiral—significantly under Rupert—of the royalist fleet laid up in the harbour at Helvoetsluys. For some reason he did not sail with it and the prince in January 1649, but remained at The Hague, where before April he had been appointed a gentleman of the bedchamber to the newly succeeded

Charles II. As such, he followed this king from the Netherlands to Jersey later in the year, and back again in 1650. In May of that year another distinguished exile, Sir Edward Nicholas, described him as 'the gallantest, honestest person now about the king' (*Nicholas Papers*, 171). What this meant was that Gerard opposed the treaty which Charles had agreed with the Scottish covenanters at Breda in April, as a betrayal of the episcopalian Church of England. As a result, he was left behind when Charles sailed to Scotland in June. He attached himself to the cabinet council of the king's brother James, and by September was in Paris with that prince. By November it had been agreed that Gerard would command the Kentish section of an English royalist uprising planned to coincide with a Scottish invasion led by the king. This invasion never occurred; instead, the English republic conquered Scotland and Charles was forced to flee back into exile in 1651. Gerard, having wandered between France and the Netherlands during that year, with James, rejoined the king in Paris during the following winter and was appointed captain of the royal guard in May 1652.

His favour at court waned thereafter, first because of his involvement with a bungled and unauthorized attempt on Oliver Cromwell's life by his cousin John Gerard, and then because of his part in an attack on Charles's counsellor Sir Edward Hyde. He left the court in June 1654, in a classic historical double-take, after the king had quarrelled with Rupert. He joined the French royal army, and served at the relief of Arras in August. For unknown reasons he dropped out of French employment in turn, and spent the rest of the 1650s moving between the exiled royal court, itself peripatetic, and Paris, Brussels, Antwerp, and The Hague, engaging in successive fruitless schemes for royalist uprisings in England. He commanded a troop of Horse Guards in the small royalist army in Flanders during the summer of 1657. It was during this restless and obscure phase of his life that he married Jane (*d.* 1671), daughter of Pierre de Civelle, a Frenchman who served as equerry to the queen mother, Henrietta Maria. They first appear as husband and wife on 1 December 1656, and produced two sons, Charles *Gerard and Fitton, and three daughters, Elizabeth, Charlotte, and Anne.

Later career, 1660–1694 Gerard rejoined the king at Breda in April 1660, and accompanied him from there to England as he was restored. He now reaped his share of the windfall of rewards due to leading royalist exiles. Both his former offices, of gentleman of the bedchamber and captain of the Royal Life Guard, were confirmed to him, and he led the guard during the king's formal entry to London on 29 May. On 13 September his forfeited estates were restored by the convention parliament. On 29 July he was granted the reversion of the office of remembrancer of first fruits and tenths, on 15 May 1661 he was made ranger of Enfield Chase, and in 1662 he received a pension charged on the customs. In the same year he briefly served as envoy-extraordinary to the French court, and his wife was made a lady-in-waiting to the new queen, Catherine of Braganza. His property was much augmented by his acquisition of the major Fitton property of Gawsworth, claimed through his mother, in 1663. In 1667, the year of threat of invasion from the Dutch, he returned to military service, being appointed to oversee the defences of Hampshire and the Isle of Wight, and command their militia, on 5 January. He carried out these duties energetically, and when the Dutch raided Kent instead he was made a colonel in the field army briefly raised to guard southern-eastern England in June. He also invested in trade, becoming in 1663 a member of the Royal Adventurers, later the Royal African Company.

All this seems glorious enough, but the same events were attended by difficulties and frustrations. His title as ranger of Enfield Chase first involved him in litigation with two subordinate officials whose patents he would not recognize, and then with the earl of Salisbury, who claimed a prior right to his office. He won against the former, but it is not known if he also saw off the earl. His acquisition of Gawsworth was made at the cost of another lawsuit, with his kinsman Alexander Fitton, and involved a squalid incident in which the latter published a tract accusing Gerard of intimidating a key witness. His wife lost her post with the queen in 1663, for telling her details of the king's affair with the countess of Castlemaine. In 1668 Charles persuaded him to resign his command of the life guard in favour of the king's son, the duke of Monmouth, and although he was handsomely bought out, the move pushed him further into an effective retirement from public affairs.

Little is known of him during the 1670s, save that his wife died on 28 September 1671, but the exclusion crisis returned him to the forefront of national affairs. He became a classic case of the old royalist turned whig, a pattern which may variously be related to his continuing loyalty to Rupert (the greatest example of such a political trajectory), or to his friendship with Monmouth, or to a personal detestation of the duke of York, or to that rigid Anglicanism which made him oppose Charles II's alliance with the covenanters. At the opening of the crisis he became one of the handful of peers to request that York be excluded from the king's counsels and presence, and the most intemperate, claiming that the people had long been unsure of who was truly the monarch. Thereafter he staunchly supported the moves to remove York from the succession. Charles tried to buy him off by promoting him to the earldom of Macclesfield on 23 July 1679, as part of a sequence of moves to regain support for the court. This one failed, and the new earl voted for the Exclusion Bill on 15 November 1680 and subsequently shared in the vicissitudes of the defeated whig leaders.

In July 1681 he was one of the group who offered bail for the imprisoned earl of Shaftesbury, and was punished in August with dismissal from his office as gentleman of the bedchamber. This seemed to bring him to heel, for he submitted to the king in April 1682, but he had changed his mind again by 29 May, when he encouraged a whig demonstration in London by supplying it with trumpets and kettledrums. On 5 September he defiantly entertained Monmouth at his Cheshire home during the latter's tour of the region. The exposure of the Rye House plot made him vulnerable to reprisals, and on 17 September 1683 he was one of a list of Cheshire whig grandees presented as seditious by the county grand jury and subsequently bound over by Judge Jeffreys. At the same time he faced a renewed challenge to his possession of Gawsworth. The old soldier's response was to counter-attack. In 1684 he won the case over Gawsworth, and he sued for libel the printer of the declaration of the grand jury. The action commenced in the court of exchequer on 24 November, and ended in defeat for Macclesfield as the jury was pronounced to be immune from legal process.

The accession of James II and Monmouth's rebellion sealed his fate. He remained passive during the rising itself, but Monmouth had certainly expected him to co-operate, and on 7 September 1685 his arrest was ordered on suspicion of treason. He fled abroad, and moved around the Netherlands and Germany for three years, only to make a second triumphant return to England in the entourage of William of Orange, whose life guard he commanded at the entry to London in December 1688, just as he had done at that of Charles II. Fresh rewards came his way in February 1689: the offices of privy counsellor, president of the council of Wales and the marches, and lord lieutenant of every Welsh county and of Gloucestershire, Herefordshire, and Monmouthshire. Once again, however, he seems to have vitiated royal favour upon a point of conscience, by opposing the Abjuration Bill in the Lords on the grounds that such oaths only provoked opposition. His last known public service was upon the commission appointed in July 1690 to inquire into the naval defeat off Beachy Head. He died suddenly on 7 January 1694, in a fit of vomiting, presumably in London, as he was buried in the Exeter vault of Westminster Abbey.

Soldier and politician Gerard's Welsh campaign of April 1645 represents a textbook example of fine tactical and strategic thinking, but he never found another opportunity to display his abilities as a general. Thereafter he features as a minor figure of the royalist exile and a second-rank whig leader, in many ways a shadow of his mentor Prince Rupert. His character emerges strongly as that of a brave, energetic, pugnacious, and ruthless man, with a fierce loyalty to certain individuals and issues of principle. RONALD HUTTON

Sources NL Wales, MS LI/MB/17, fols. 44–85 · William Salt Library, Stafford, Salt MS 517 · *Mercurius Aulicus* (1644–5) · *A Perfect Diurnall* (1644–5) · BL, Egerton MS 787, fol. 73 · Bodl. Oxf., MS Carte 14, fol. 609 · Bodl. Oxf., MS Carte 130, fols. 14f–62 · *Memoirs of Prince Rupert and the cavaliers including their private correspondence*, ed. E. Warburton, 3 vols. (1849) · *The Nicholas papers*, ed. G. F. Warner, 1, CS, new ser., 40 (1886) · *Diary of the marches of the royal army during the great civil war, kept by Richard Symonds*, ed. C. E. Long, CS, old ser., 74 (1859), 147–271 · Bodl. Oxf., MSS Clarendon 46–47 · Thurloe, *State papers* · N. Luttrell, *A brief historical relation of state affairs from September 1678 to April 1714*, 1 (1857) · E. Peacock, *Index to English speaking students who have graduated at Leyden University* (1883) · GEC, *Peerage* · *State trials*, 10.1330

Archives PRO, Lancashire estate book, C 103/175 | NL Wales, corresp. with Sir Edward Mansell

Likenesses W. Dobson, oils, c.1645, Dunedin Public Art Gallery, New Zealand [*see illus.*] · oils, Longleat, Wiltshire

Gerard, Charles, second earl of Macclesfield (*c*.1659–1701), army officer, diplomat, and divorcé, was born in Paris, the elder son of Charles *Gerard, first earl of Macclesfield (*c*.1618–1694), and his French wife, Jane (*d*. 1671), whose father, Pierre de Civelle, was an equerry to Queen Henrietta Maria. He served as a volunteer with Condé's French army in the 1670s, and on 17 May 1676, in a drunken temper, killed a footboy in St James's Park. Although he absconded he was soon granted a pardon and was naturalized by act of parliament the following year.

Gerard was elected to parliament for Lancashire in the three exclusion parliaments and was identified as a staunch whig and supporter of exclusion. In June 1680 he was a member of the Middlesex grand jury that presented James, duke of York, as a recusant, and in summer 1682 he entertained the duke of Monmouth during his progress through Cheshire. On 8 July 1683, following the Rye House plot, he was sent to the Tower, but was released on 28 November and acquitted the following February.

Following Monmouth's rebellion a warrant was issued for the arrest of Gerard and his father, and he was committed to the Tower on 31 July 1685. He was tried for treason before the court of king's bench between 14 and 25 November and, owing largely to the evidence of Lord Grey of Warke, was convicted of complicity in the Rye House plot. He was sentenced to death on 28 November, but was reprieved, released (January 1687), and pardoned (31 August 1687). He then vigorously supported James II's policies, especially over the dispensing power, was granted his father's forfeited estates as a result, and in 1688 even took the field for James, having been restored in October to the position of colonel of Lord Gerard's horse that he had briefly held in 1679. However, he quickly mended his bridges with William, was returned to parliament for Lancashire once more, in January 1689, and also became lord lieutenant of the same county. He was appointed additionally to the new board of general officers created in 1689 to oversee the running of the army in England.

Following his father's death on 7 January 1694 Gerard succeeded as second earl of Macclesfield and took his seat in the Lords. He was restored to his colonelcy shortly afterwards and was then promoted to major-general on 15 April, in which capacity he served in the disastrous attack at Camaret Bay on 8 June, although he did not go ashore. Following the death of the commanding general, Talmash, Macclesfield succeeded to the chief command, and remained in that capacity aboard the fleet for the remainder of the summer's campaign. As a senior officer he tried to insist on his subordinate cavalry officers possessing military experience, but was still responsible for the appointment for political reasons of the militarily ignorant and slightly unhinged Goodwin Wharton as his lieutenant-colonel.

Macclesfield was appointed lord lieutenant of north Wales on 10 March 1696. In 1698 he met and offended the visiting tsar, Peter the Great, who objected to Macclesfield coming to gawp at him as he ate and left the room in anger (the tsar had an aversion to being stared at). In June 1701 Macclesfield was accredited an envoy-extraordinary to Hanover in order to present the dowager electress Sophia with a copy of the Act of Settlement, and to invest the elector George with the Garter. The composition of the embassy was controversial at the time and since, consisting as it did of an atheist (John Toland) and two murderers (Macclesfield's friend and fellow envoy, Charles Mohun, Lord Mohun, had been tried for murder in 1694). The ambassadors left in July, were liberally entertained at Hanover, and returned in October. Macclesfield caught a fever almost immediately and died in London on 5 November, being buried in Westminster Abbey nine days later.

Macclesfield's greatest claim to fame, both in his own lifetime and subsequently, was not his somewhat opportunistic and unprincipled political career, nor his mediocre record as an army officer, nor his rather mixed dealings with heads of state, nor even his penchant for random violence—it was his central role in perhaps the most sensational divorce of the age. On 18 June 1683, at St Lawrence Jewry, Viscount Brandon (his courtesy title since his father had been created earl) had married Anne Mason [*see* Brett, Anne (1667/8–1753)], aged about fourteen, the daughter of Sir Richard Mason of Sutton, Surrey. The marriage had been a disaster, and on 2 March 1685 Gerard wrote a long letter in which he ordered his wife not to return. He defended vigorously his own conduct:

> Your youth and folly did long plead your excuse, but when I saw ill nature in you and ill will (not to say malice) in your mother join against me, I then had reason to despair of your amendment … [I sought] not to make a prey of you, as you have often upbraided me withal, and that I had no such mercenary thoughts … you would have the world believe that I have used you ill, and that I have beaten you, a thing so base that, as you know it to be false yourself, so you will never be able to persuade the world that it is true. I have governed my passions under great and frequent provocation, either by silence or by avoiding your company.

His indulgence had now reached its limit, however:

> You have often-times spoken with scorn and contempt of me and my family to my face, and expressed that you did not care to have any children by me, but always pretended yourself with child whenever I went out of town from you … And now, Madam, I am resolved to give you the satisfaction you have often asked, in parting with me, which you may have cause to repent at leisure.   (*House of Lords MSS*, 3.65–7)

In 1689 Anne made an unsuccessful attempt to reclaim some of the lands involved in her marriage settlement. Later, in 1695 and then in January 1697, the countess was delivered of two children, respectively a girl and a boy; when the earl learned of this he applied to the court of arches for a divorce. In December 1697 he additionally opened proceedings in the House of Lords—an unprecedented action, as no marriage had been dissolved by parliament prior to a decree from an ecclesiastical court. The case led to a pamphlet war. Macclesfield and his apologists were damning about the countess's 'notorious open adultery, having had children begotten on her body in adultery, and using vile practices to have her spurious issue imposed and obtruded upon him' (*Reasons for the Earl of Macclesfield's Bill*, 20). 'Though the children have not happened till ten years after living apart from her husband, 'tis well known she did not live virtuous so long', sneered another pamphlet, determined to disprove the suggestion of the countess's apologists 'that her husband ought to keep another man's bastards' (*Further Considerations*, 1-2).

The case was debated by the Lords between 15 January and 3 March 1698 with much airing of salacious detail. Servants and midwives recounted the comings and goings to and from the countess's room of 'a tall gentleman', the births of the two children, and the countess's desperate attempts to conceal their births, even to the extent of wearing a mask throughout most of the birth of the elder child (*House of Lords MSS*, 3.57-67). In the event, the act received the royal assent on 2 April. It illegitimated the countess's children, settled an annuity on her, indemnified Macclesfield against her debts, and allowed the earl to marry again. In 1700-01 it was widely reported that he was about to marry Letitia Harbord, the daughter of the prominent whig MP William Harbord, but this seems not to have taken place. However, in his will Macclesfield bequeathed her 'my great diamond shaped like a heart'; a diamond necklace and pair of diamond pendants went to his niece, Elizabeth, duchess of Hamilton (PRO, PROB 11/462, fols. 91-2). The belief that Macclesfield's attainder, a consequence of his alleged role in the Rye House plot, had never been reversed, led the crown to claim his estate, provoking a lengthy legal battle with his executor and eventual heir, Lord Mohun (Gerard's successor in the estates; his brother Fitton, last Gerard earl of Macclesfield, survived him by barely a year). Although Mohun won the case a subsequent lawsuit over the Macclesfield inheritance between himself and the duke of Hamilton culminated in the fatal duel between the two in 1712. As for the disgraced countess of Macclesfield, she married Colonel Henry Brett and lived until 11 October 1753.

J. D. DAVIES

Sources *The manuscripts of the House of Lords*, 4 vols., HMC, 17 (1887-94), vol. 2 · *The manuscripts of the House of Lords*, new ser., 12 vols. (1900-77), vols. 1, 3 · N. Luttrell, *A brief historical relation of state affairs from September 1678 to April 1714*, 6 vols. (1857) · V. Stater, *High life, low morals: the duel that shook Stuart society* (1999) · J. C. R. Childs, *The Nine Years' War and the British army, 1688-1697: the operations in the Low Countries* (1991) · *Reasons for the earl of Macclesfield's bill in parliament for dissolving the marriage between him and his wife, and illegitimating her spurious issue* (1697) · *Further considerations for the earl of Macclesfield's bill* (1697) · will, PRO, PROB 11/462, fol. 92 · I. Cassidy, 'Gerard, Hon. Charles', HoP, *Commons, 1660-90* · J. K. Clark, *Goodwin Wharton* (1984) · GEC, *Peerage* · *The manuscripts of his grace the duke of Portland*, 10 vols., HMC, 29 (1891-1931), vol. 3 · registers of Westminster Abbey

Archives HLRO, manuscripts of the House of Lords

Wealth at death estates and properties to Lord Mohun; bequests of £30 to £500 to individual servants and friends, and a year's wages to all of his servants; £100 bequeathed to the poor of St Ann's parish; pair of diamond pendants and a diamond heart to niece; 'a great diamond shaped like a heart' to Letitia Harbord; a ring worth £100 to Captain James Tyrrell: PRO, PROB 11/462, fols. 91-2

Gerard, Dorothea Mary Stanislaus (1855-1915). *See under* Gerard, (Jane) Emily (1849-1905).

Gerard [*married name* de Laszowska], **(Jane) Emily** (1849-1905), novelist, was born on 7 May 1849 at Chesters, Jedburgh, Roxburghshire, Scotland, the eldest daughter of

Colonel Archibald Gerard (1812-1880) of Rochsoles, Lanarkshire, and his wife, Euphemia Erskine (1818-1870), eldest daughter of Sir John *Robison (1778-1843), the distinguished inventor. She was also directly descended from Gilbert Gerard (1760-1815), Church of Scotland minister and theological writer, Alexander Gerard (1728-1795), philosophical writer, and Archibald Alison (1757-1839), Scottish Episcopalian minister and writer. Her sister **Dorothea Mary Stanislaus Gerard** [*married name* Longard de Longgarde] (1855-1915), novelist, was born at New Monkland, Lanark, Scotland, on 9 August 1855. They had two other sisters and three brothers, including General Sir Montagu Gilbert *Gerard (1842-1905).

The family lived in Vienna from 1863 to 1866, and moved in aristocratic émigré circles. Emily, who had been educated at home until she was fifteen, took lessons with, and became a lifelong friend of, Margarita of Parma, niece of the Bourbon pretender to the French throne and later wife of Don Carlo VII, pretender to the Spanish throne. Emily finished her education studying European languages for three years in the convent of the Sacré Coeur at Riedenburg, near Bregenz, Austria, and Dorothea spent four years in the convent of the Sacré Coeur in Graz. Although their family background was Scottish Episcopalian, their mother had converted to Catholicism in 1848, and both sisters were raised in that faith.

On 14 October 1869 Emily married Chevalier Miecislas de Laszowski (d. 1904), a member of an old Polish noble family and an officer in the Austrian army, and moved with him to Brzezum, in what later became Poland, where she was joined by her sisters following the death of their mother in 1870. She had two sons. Dorothea married Julius Longard de Longgarde, who eventually became a field marshal lieutenant, also in the Austrian army, in 1886. They lived in Galicia and had one daughter.

Despite residing in Austria and other central European countries for most of their adult lives, the sisters, who used the name Gerard professionally, became active participants in the later nineteenth-century British literary community, both independently and as collaborators. Emily Gerard wrote a number of stories for *Blackwood's Magazine* (which were later reprinted in *Bis*, 1890, and *An Electric Shock and other Stories*, 1897), and reviews of contemporary French and German fiction, both for *Blackwood's* and for *The Times* (London), whose obituary notice praised her as 'an able critic of German literature'. She began to write fiction in 1879, collaborating with her sister Dorothea on their first major work, *Reata*, about a Mexican girl adapting to European customs, which was published as a serial in *Blackwood's Magazine* (beginning in April 1879), as were a number of their subsequent novels. *Beggar My Neighbour* (1882), a story of feuding brothers, *The Waters of Hercules* (1885), and *A Sensitive Plant* (1891), dedicated to Margarita of Parma, concerning a timid young girl coming to terms with a ruthless mother and her beautiful unruly daughter, were published under the collective pseudonym E. D. Gerard, or E. and D. Gerard. They stopped writing together after Dorothea's marriage but a number of their individual works cross-refer: a character in

Dorothea's *A Queen of Curds and Cream* (1892) appears in Emily's *A Foreigner* (1896).

In her fiction Emily Gerard frequently employed central European characters and settings, and it is likely that *A Foreigner* (1896), which featured a cross-cultural marriage, was shaped by her own experiences. She also wrote about the Transylvanian culture and landscape, drawing on the knowledge of the area, particularly of Hermannstadt and Kronstadt, gained during the two years (1883–5) that her husband had been posted there. She wrote on the vampire myth in 'Transylvanian superstitions', an article that Bram Stoker used for research when writing *Dracula* (1897), and where he discovered the term 'nosferatu'. While these articles appeal to a taste for anecdotes about what were, in nineteenth-century Britain, exotic and little-known regions, they also include some consideration of wider political matters. In 'Transylvanian peoples' published in the *Contemporary Review* (1887), for example, Emily Gerard concludes by suggesting that central European cultures might eventually become important in wider European affairs, giving British audiences reason to learn about them. She collected her observations in *The Land beyond the Forest: Facts, Figures and Fancies from Transylvania* (1888).

Even though Emily Gerard wrote six novels of her own in addition to reviews and short stories, it was Dorothea who became the better-known writer. She was more prolific, publishing at least thirty-seven books of her own and some shorter magazine pieces. Her work, also influenced by her European experiences, often touches on potentially controversial or unconventional topics. She opens *Orthodox* (1888), for example, with a depiction of the reflexive antisemitism of a Polish army officer, and *The Million* (1901) features a radical, discontented Polish villager as a central character. But on the whole her fiction is more escapist than polemical, and explorations of larger social issues such as antisemitism or, as in *A Queen of Curds and Cream* (1892), the cultural gaps between English and central European characters, are subordinated to sentimental romance plots. She was praised for this conventionality at the time; *The Churchman* recommends her novel *The Rich Miss Riddell* (1894) as 'clean, interesting, and wholesome' entertainment (Gerard). *One Year* (1899), a novel about love and suicide set in Galicia, is often considered to be her most powerful work, however.

Both *The Athenaeum* and *The Times* comment on Dorothea's wider appeal in their articles on Emily's death, *The Times* observing that Emily 'had not won equal popularity with that of her sister' (p. 7), despite Emily's being 'a capable novelist, with an excellent gift for telling a story' as *The Athenaeum* pointed out (p. 86). Yet Dorothea's greater popularity did not mean that she won more critical respect; in its obituary for Dorothea, *The Times* coolly described her as being 'hardly a novelist of the first order', although it conceded that she 'could write naturally and with spirit … in her own straightforward and fluent style' (*The Times*, 18 Nov 1915, 11).

Emily Gerard died on 11 January 1905 in Vienna, where she was buried two days later; she and her husband had made their home there following his retirement from active service. Dorothea Gerard, who had also settled in Vienna, and had lived the last few years of her life as a recluse, died there on 29 September 1915.

PAM PERKINS

Sources *The Times* (13 Jan 1905), 7 · *The Times* (18 Nov 1915), 11 · *The Athenaeum* (21 Jan 1905), 86 · *DNB* · *WW* (1907–15) · D. Gerard, *Miss Providence* (1897) · *The Times* (12 Jan 1905) · *IGI*

Gerard, Sir Gilbert (*d.* 1593), judge, was the eldest son of James Gerard of Astley and Ince, Lancashire, and his wife, Margaret, daughter of John Holcroft of Holcroft in the same county. Having spent some time at Cambridge without taking a degree, Gerard was admitted to Gray's Inn in 1537 and called to the bar in 1539. He became an ancient of the inn in 1547, was autumn reader in 1553, and treasurer, jointly with Nicholas Bacon, on 16 May 1556. A surviving commonplace book from these years suggests that he was a diligent attender at readings and moots and that, like others of his generation, he learned the law by immersing himself in the fifteenth-century year-books.

Gerard's public career developed quickly. His selection as MP for Liverpool in 1545, and for Wigan in 1553 and 1555, attests to his standing in Lancashire; his election for Steyning, Sussex, in 1554 may have owed something to the patronage of the earl of Arundel. Already on the commissions of the peace for Bedfordshire, Buckinghamshire, Cambridgeshire, Cheshire, and Huntingdon, he was named in the writ calling new serjeants-at-law that was issued on 27 October 1558, but which abated on the death of Queen Mary. When Elizabeth came to the throne, Gerard was not again named a serjeant but immediately appointed attorney-general instead. According to a credible but unverified tradition retailed by Dugdale more than a century later, Elizabeth chose Gerard because he had ably represented her when she was questioned on one occasion by the Marian privy council. Whatever the truth of this, it is probably no less important that he appears to have been a long-time friend of Lord Keeper Bacon and also acted as legal counsel for Edward Stanley, third earl of Derby.

Attorney-general for over twenty years, Gerard was evidently a trusted administrator, but the surviving evidence suggests that he played only a small role in policy making. In 1560 he was sent to Ireland to reform the procedure of the court of exchequer, and drew up certain 'orders and articles for the better collecting the queen's rents, revenues, and debts' (BL, Sloane MS 4767, fol. 22). In 1561 he was made counsel to the University of Cambridge, and in May 1563 commissioner for the sale of crown lands. As attorney-general he was responsible for putting forward cases in the queen's name in courts such as Star Chamber, and he sat as a judge in many notable trials, including that of John Hales in 1564. In 1565 he rode the home assize circuit, and on 23 July was entertained with other judges at a banquet given by Archbishop Parker at his palace in Canterbury. On 12 June 1566 he was appointed one of the special commission for hearing causes within the bounds of the palace or any other place where the queen might be residing. He seems to have been a member of the ecclesiastical commission in 1567, when he assisted Archbishop Parker in reforming Merton College, Oxford.

During a great part of 1570 Gerard was on a special commission that sat at York and Durham to try participants in the northern uprising. In January 1571 he received a letter of thanks from the senate of Cambridge University for his services in connection with the passing of the statute 13 Eliz. c. 29 confirming the charters and privileges of the university, and for services rendered in connection with other statutes. The probable author of the interrogatories administered in October 1571 to the duke of Norfolk concerning his intrigues with the bishop of Ross and Ridolfi, Gerard was present at the examinations and signed the depositions. On 16 January 1572 he seconded the queen's serjeant, Nicholas Barham, in the prosecution of the duke on the charge of conspiring to depose the queen, arguing that if Norfolk planned to marry the queen of Scots then he was bound to maintain her title to the English throne, and therefore to 'imagine' treason against Elizabeth. The following February he took part in the prosecution of Robert Higford, the duke's secretary, for the offence of adhering to and comforting the queen's enemies, and on 5 May he examined Thomas Bishop, another of the duke's dependants. The same day he sent Lord Burghley the depositions of the bishop of Ross, taken on interrogatories prepared by himself two days before, and remarked on the bishop's obstinacy. In the following June he drew up the interrogatories for the examination of the earl of Northumberland.

Having married Anne, daughter and heir of Thomas Ratcliffe of Winmarleigh, Lancashire, with whom he subsequently had three sons and four daughters, Gerard established his country seat in what Dugdale described as a 'stately quadrangular fabric of stone' (*DNB*) that he built at Gerrard's Bromley in Staffordshire, but he continued to own property in Lancashire and to hold important positions there. He was steward of several manors attached to the honour of Clare (from 1573), as well as being steward of the manor of Rochdale and bailiff of West Derby hundred. From about 1571, as vice-chancellor, he acted as judge in the chancery court of the county palatine of Lancaster while still undertaking many tasks in London. In 1573, for instance, he was a commissioner for gaol delivery for the Marshalsea and on the commission of oyer and terminer for Middlesex. In 1576 he was a member of the ecclesiastical commission, and in the same year Lord Deputy Sidney asked the privy council to send him to Ireland to advise on legal questions, although it is uncertain whether he went or not.

Despite being knighted at Greenwich on 5 July 1579, Gerard was evidently passed over when the lord keepership of the great seal was given to Solicitor-General Bromley in the same year, but on 30 May 1581 he was made master of the rolls, the second in command in the court of chancery. In addition to Rolls House in Chancery Lane, the post, which Gerard held until his death, brought with it £1000 p.a. and a considerable amount of patronage over appointments in the court bureaucracy. Gerard's tenure

has generally not been considered a success, but it is not altogether clear how far this should be put down to his own failings in either ability or application. Chancery suffered in these years from administrative difficulties caused by increases in its business and from a rapid turnover in lord keepers and chancellors. Gerard himself must frequently have been otherwise occupied in both Lancashire and London. He was returned as knight of the shire for Lancashire in November 1584, although a by-election was called in the following January to replace him on the grounds that, as master of the rolls, he would be required to assist the House of Lords in their proceedings. Between December 1583 and June 1585 he was a member of a commission that tried John Somerville, William Parry, and William Shelley for the offence of conspiring the queen's death. On 23 June 1585 he was one of the judges who assembled in Star Chamber to take the inquest on the death of the earl of Northumberland, who had committed suicide in the Tower three days before. He was a member of the tribunal that on 28 March 1587 tried Secretary William Davison for misprision and contempt in laying the death-warrant of the queen of Scots before the council, and of that which on 18 April 1589 tried the earl of Arundel, who was charged with having for some years carried on treasonable intrigues with Roman Catholics on the continent. On 26 July 1591, at the Sessions House, Newgate, Gerard tried and convicted three fanatics—Hackett, Copinger, and Arthington—for the crime of libelling the queen and defacing the royal arms.

On the death of Lord Chancellor Hatton on 20 November 1591, Gerard was made chief commissioner of the great seal in the interim before the appointment of Sir John Puckering in the following May. He evidently found it a difficult task, complaining that some of the other judges on the commission were challenging the finality of his rulings. His last state trial appears to have been that of Sir John Perrot, who was arraigned on 27 April 1592 on the charge of having imagined the death of the queen in 1587, when he was lord deputy of Ireland. Gerard died on 4 February 1593, probably at Gerrard's Bromley, and was buried in the parish church of Ashley in Staffordshire, having been incapacitated by ill health for much of the previous year. His wife and two of his daughters were Catholics, but although an anonymous letter of 1586 described him as a 'protestant at London and a papist in Lancashire' (HoP, *Commons, 1558–1603*, 2.184), there is no evidence that Gerard wavered in public from the church established by law. In the lengthy statement with which he began his will he described himself as:

> [a] sinfull creature conceyved and borne in synne and have in this my naturall life many thinges throughe evell temptatcons transgressed the precepts and comandementes of God. … There is nothinge in any of my Workes or deedes whereby I can or may challenge or atteyne unto everlasting life yet being nowe by godes goode grace penytente and hartely sorry for al the offences by me committed, I doe onlie appeale unto godes great and infinite mercie.

CHRISTOPHER W. BROOKS

Sources DNB · HoP, *Commons, 1558–1603*, 2.183–4 · W. J. Jones, *The Elizabethan court of chancery* (1967) · G. Gerrard, commonplace book,

c.1540–1555, CUL, MS Ee.6.15 • reading, 1553, CUL, MS Gg.6.18, fol. 59v • *State trials* • R. Tittler, *Nicholas Bacon: the making of a Tudor states-man* (1976) • *Reports from the lost notebooks of Sir James Dyer*, ed. J. H. Baker, 2 vols., SeldS, 109–10 (1994) • J. H. Baker, *An introduction to English legal history*, 2nd edn (1979), 106, n. 18 • J. H. Baker and J. S. Ringrose, *A catalogue of English legal manuscripts in Cambridge University Library* (1996) • will, PRO, PROB 11/81, fols. 224v–227v
Archives JRL, letters to Sir Piers Legh and Peter Legh
Wealth at death wealthy, but sum not quantifiable: will, PRO, PROB 11/81, fols. 224v–227v

Gerard, Gilbert (1760–1815), Church of Scotland minister and theological writer, was born at Aberdeen on 12 August 1760, the son of Alexander *Gerard (1728–1795) and his wife, Jane (d. 1818), the eldest daughter of Dr John Wight of Colnae. He studied at Aberdeen and Edinburgh universities. On being licensed as a clergyman he became minister of the Scottish church in Amsterdam. During his residence there he gained a considerable knowledge of modern languages and literature, which he turned to account in contributions to the *Analytical Review*, for which he edited the literature section. He also started a journal called *De recensent*. On 3 October 1787 he married Helen, daughter of John Duncan and his wife, Margaret Wight. The couple had five sons and five daughters.

In 1791 Gerard returned to Aberdeen to fill the chair of Greek in King's College. On his father's death in 1795 he succeeded him in the chair of divinity, and in 1811 he added to his professorship the second charge in the collegiate church of Old Aberdeen. He published *A Compendious View of the Evidences of Natural and Revealed Religion* (1828), based on his own and his father's divinity lectures. His only other theological publication was the *Institutes of Biblical Criticism* (1808), in which he discussed the interpretation of the scriptures. Questions concerning the language of scripture, the text, the versions, and the ordinary rules of interpretation were considered, but the work did not anticipate any of the advances of later nineteenth-century biblical criticism. Gerard was also a king's chaplain, and served as moderator of the general assembly in 1803. He became minister of Old Machar, Aberdeenshire, on 19 September 1811, and died there on 28 September 1815. Three of his sons, Alexander *Gerard (1792–1839), James Gilbert *Gerard (1793–1835), and Patrick *Gerard (1794–1848), became well known as Indian explorers.

W. G. BLAIKIE, rev. ROSEMARY MITCHELL

Sources *Fasti Scot.* • Chambers, *Scots.* (1855) • Anderson, *Scot. nat.*

Gerard, James Gilbert (1793–1835), East India Company military surgeon and surveyor, son of Gilbert *Gerard, DD (1760–1815) and his wife, Helen, daughter of John Duncan, provost of Aberdeen, and brother of Alexander *Gerard and Patrick *Gerard, was born in the parish of Old Machar, Aberdeenshire, on 13 February 1793. He graduated from King's College, Aberdeen, as an MA in 1811. In 1814 he became a member of the Royal College of Surgeons, and in November of the same year was appointed assistant surgeon in the Bengal army. In 1815 he took medical charge of the 1st Nasiri battalion, based at Sabathu in the foothills of the Himalayas. He was promoted to surgeon in May 1826.

Gerard was a competent surveyor, especially skilled in barometrical calculations, and with his brother Alexander undertook several Himalayan expeditions. Their journey up the Spiti River in 1818 was the basis for his 'Observations on the Spiti valley and the circumjacent country within the Himalaya', published in *Asiatic Researches* (18, 1833), an account which not only illustrates his passion for exotic landscapes but also reveals his antagonism to the cultures they produced—the Tibetans he characterized as wantonly ugly and barbaric. A letter written by Gerard in 1822 while making an ascent of the Shatul Pass appeared posthumously in Sir William Lloyd's *Narrative of a Journey from Caunpoor to the Boorendo Pass* (1840).

In January 1832, though in poor health, Gerard accompanied Alexander Burnes on his expedition through Afghanistan to Bukhara. They reached Bukhara in June and then pushed on across the Oxus to Persia. Gerard collected what geographical information he could without exciting the suspicions of their various hosts, but by September recurrent bouts of fever had overwhelmed him and he parted company with Burnes at Mashhad. Extremely ill, he nevertheless documented his return journey with meticulous measurements, which when he finally reached Sabathu in April 1834 enabled his brother Alexander to construct a route map from Herat to the Indus. The army of the Indus relied on the map in the First Anglo-Afghan War (1838–42), and Alexander wrote with fraternal pride in his notebook (now lost) that they had found the positioning of the roads 'wonderfully correct, considering the distances were estimated by time and the bearings taken with a small pocket-compass'. Gerard survived for less than a year after his return. He died, unmarried, at Sabathu on 31 March 1835, and was buried next day in the old cemetery there.

H. M. CHICHESTER, rev. KATHERINE PRIOR

Sources M. Irving, *A list of inscriptions on Christian tombs or monuments in the Punjab, North-West Frontier Province, Kashmir, and Afghanistan*, ed. G. W. de Rhé-Philipe, 2 (1912), 124 • R. H. Phillimore, ed., *Historical records of the survey of India*, 3 (1954), 40–41, 204, 451–2 • D. G. Crawford, ed., *Roll of the Indian Medical Service, 1615–1930* (1930), 67 • P. J. Anderson, ed., *Roll of alumni in arts of the University and King's College of Aberdeen, 1596–1860* (1900), 117 • W. Lloyd, *Narrative of a journey from Caunpoor to the Boorendo pass in the Himalaya mountains* (1840) • East India Company records, BL OIOC • *DNB*
Archives BL, Napier MSS
Wealth at death see will, 1825, BL OIOC, East India Company records

Gerard, John (c.1545–1612), herbalist, was born at Nantwich, Cheshire, of unknown parentage; his family was possibly connected with the Gerards of Ince, as indicated by the coat of arms he used in his *Herball*. He went to school at Willaston, 2 miles from Nantwich. In 1562 he was apprenticed to Alexander Mason, a surgeon of the Barber–Surgeons' Company, in London, and he was admitted to the freedom of the company on 9 December 1569. Probably he travelled in Scandinavia and Russia, as he frequently refers to these places in his writing. In 1586 the College of Physicians decided to establish a physic garden and Gerard was appointed its curator. He was well known as a skilled herbarist in 1595, when the Barber–

John Gerard (*c*.1545–1612), by William Rogers, 1598

Surgeons elected him to the court of assistants. He was superintendent of the gardens of William Cecil, Lord Burghley, in the Strand, and at Theobalds in Hereford-shire. In 1596 Gerard suggested that the Barber–Surgeons should keep a garden for the cultivation and study of medicinal plants. A piece of land at East Smithfield was selected, but although the scheme was still under discussion on 2 November 1602, when 'the committee for Mr. Gerrard's garden' held a meeting, no active steps were taken.

Gerard was married to Anne or Agnes (*d.* 1620) and probably had five children of whom only one, Elizabeth, survived her parents. Gerard lived all his adult life in Holborn, close to Barnards Inn, between Chancery Lane and Fetter Lane, probably in a tenement with garden belonging to Lord Burghley. He frequently referred to this garden in his *Herball* and he published a plant list of it in 1596 (*Catalogus arborum, fruticum, ac plantarum tam indigenarum, quam exoticarum, in horto Johannis Gerardi … nascentium*). The only known copy of this first edition, reputed to be the first complete catalogue ever published of the plants in one garden, public or private, is in the Sloane collection in the British Library. A second edition, this time in folio, with English names as well as Latin in opposite columns, was brought out in 1599 by John Norton, the queen's printer, who also published Gerard's major work, *The Herball, or, Generall Historie of Plants Gathered by John Gerarde of London* (1597), dedicated to Lord Burghley. The *Herball* is by far the most famous of Gerard's works, although he was condemned for using a translation begun by Dr Priest of Dodoens's *Stirpium historiae pemptades sex* without acknowledgement. The *Herball* contained more than 1800

woodcuts, only sixteen of which were original, the majority being those used by Bergzabern (better known as Tabernae-montanus) in his *Eicones plantarum* of 1590, which Norton had procured from Nicolas Bassaeus of Frankfurt. The *Herball* contains many of Gerard's own remarks, such as localities in various parts of England for scarce plants, and many allusions to persons and places now of high antiquarian interest. Many friends, among them Jean Robin, director of the Jardin Royale at the Louvre, sent him specimens and information. In his own garden Gerard raised many exotic plants such as the potato. His illustration of that plant is the first to appear in any herbal, although his naming of the plant as the 'Virginian potato' caused some confusion. Jean l'Ecluse (Clusius) had correctly identified the origin as Peru. Gerard is shown holding some potato foliage in his portrait for the first edition of the *Herball*. Despite the many errors and repetition of folklore, such as the story of the barnacle tree from which geese were supposed to be hatched, Gerard's *Herball*, being in the English vernacular, is still one of the best-known English herbals. In 1633 Thomas Johnson edited a new, more scholarly, edition which was so well received that it was reprinted in 1636. Johnson used illustrations from the stock of Antwerp's famous printer Plantin. The genus *Gerardia* was founded by Linnaeus in commemoration of John Gerard.

On 15 January 1598, and again on 20 July 1607, Gerard was appointed an examiner of candidates for admission to the freedom of the Barber–Surgeons' Company (then controlling the surgeons practising in London) and on 17 August 1607 he was chosen master. In 1604 he was granted a lease of a garden adjoining Somerset House by Anne of Denmark, consort of James I, but in 1605 he parted with his interest in it to Robert, earl of Salisbury, second son of Lord Burghley. In the legal document connected with this lease Gerard is described as 'herbarist' to James I. He made his will on 11 December 1611, leaving his books 'of phisick & surgerie' to his son-in-law Richard Holden and most of his estate (valued at over £550) to his wife, who died in 1620. He died in February 1612 and was buried in St Andrew's Church, Holborn, on 18 February.

MARJA SMOLENAARS

Sources B. Henrey, *British botanical and horticultural literature before 1800*, 1 (1975) · M. Edmond, 'John Gerard, herbalist', *Genealogist's Magazine*, 14 (1962), 137–45 · E. S. Rohde, *The old English herbals* (1971) · R. Salaman, *The history and social influence of the potato*, rev. edn (1985); repr. (1989) · Arber, *Regs. Stationers* · J. Gerard, *The herball, or, Generall historie of plantes* (1597) · St Andrew's Church, Holborn, registers · PGC wills
Archives BL, Sloane MSS · BL, Lansdowne MSS
Likenesses W. Rogers, coloured line engraving, 1598, Bodl. Oxf., NPG [*see illus.*] · J. Payne, line engraving, BM; repro. in J. Gerard, *The herball* (1633) [enlarged and amended by T. Johnson]
Wealth at death £550: Edmond, 'John Gerard'

Gerard, John (1564–1637), Jesuit, was born on 4 October 1564 at Etwall, Derbyshire, the second son of Sir Thomas Gerard (*d.* 1601) of Bryn, Lancashire, and Elizabeth, eldest daughter and coheir of Sir John Port of Etwall. His early life was spent at Etwall and Bryn. He matriculated at Exeter College, Oxford, on 3 December 1575. About Easter 1576 he left Oxford because he refused to go to church, and returned to Bryn. In August 1577 he arrived at the English College in Douai, migrating with it to Rheims the following March. In 1580 he transferred to Collège de Clermont, Paris, 'to see from close hand what Jesuit life was like and at the same time to get a better grounding in Latin and philosophy' (*Autobiography*, 2). For reasons of health he withdrew from Clermont after a year. In late 1581 he accompanied the Jesuit Thomas Derbyshire to Rouen to visit Robert Parsons to discuss his intention to join the Society of Jesus.

To improve his health and to settle various financial matters Gerard decided to return to England. He did so, it seems, in spring 1583. He was captured at Dover and sent to London as he attempted to return to the continent the following November. Although he confessed his Catholicism he was not arrested but was committed to the custody of a maternal uncle, most likely George Hastings, who succeeded his brother as earl of Huntingdon in 1595. Despite Hastings's failure to convince Gerard to conform he petitioned the privy council for his nephew's full release. Instead, on 5 March 1584 Gerard was sent to Marshalsea prison. The following year friends obtained his release by providing sureties in cash. With the approval of Anthony Babington, who thus forfeited his surety, Gerard left England for France around May 1586. He then accompanied William Holt, recently returned from Scotland, to Rome, where Holt was to become rector of the English College.

Gerard arrived at the English College on 5 August and remained for eight days. After seven months as a convictor he was received into the college on 5 April 1587. Ordained in the Lateran on 17 July 1588 with a papal dispensation because he was under the canonical age, he entered the Society of Jesus in Rome on 15 August 1588. He and Edward Oldcorne were dispatched almost immediately for England. Arriving in Rheims on 21 September they departed for England via Eu on the 26th. At Eu they awaited further instructions because of increased danger after the failure of the Armada. Oldcorne and Gerard decided to proceed, embarking in late October or early November. Much to the annoyance of the Jesuit superior, Henry Garnet, Gerard travelled through East Anglia without reporting immediately to London. After he had secured a residence at the house of Edward Yelverton at Grimsto, near King's Lynn, he finally journeyed to London in December to return to Grimston before Christmas. Gerard was dressed as a

> gentleman of moderate means ... [because it] was thus that I used to go about before I became a Jesuit and I was therefore more at ease in these clothes than I would have been if I had assumed a role that was strange and unfamiliar to me.
> (*Autobiography*, 17–18)

Thus attired, he avoided capture and moved freely among recusant gentry, directing many through the spiritual exercises and fostering many vocations.

Gerard's success in eluding pursuivants ended with his apprehension on 23 April 1594 at a house in Holborn. Confined first in the Counter, where he made the spiritual exercises from memory, he was transferred to the Clink in the summer of 1594 through the intercession of friends. There he developed a thriving ministry hearing confessions and ministering to other prisoners. He established a chapel in a room above his cell where he conducted six or seven men through the spiritual exercises. Until his transfer to the Tower of London in April of 1597 his cell was an apostolic centre.

In the Tower, Gerard coincidentally occupied Henry Walpole's former cell. That provided Gerard with no small amount of comfort as he rested before being tortured anew in an attempt to extract information. He was often suspended by his wrists for hours on end. Despite his weakened condition and severely damaged hands he and John Arden dramatically escaped from the Tower on 5 October by swinging on a rope over the Tower ditch. Until his departure from England on 3 May 1606, the day of Garnet's execution, Gerard travelled between rented houses in London and country residences. Because many of his friends were indicted for involvement in the Gunpowder Plot the government pursued Gerard relentlessly and publicly proclaimed him traitor. 'Seeing it was a time for lying quiet, not for working' (*Autobiography*, 207) Gerard departed for the continent in the entourage of the Spanish and Flemish ambassadors.

During his time in England, Gerard was directly or indirectly responsible for *An Epistle or Exhortation of Iesus Christ to the Soule* (1592–3, translated from the Latin of Johann Justus Lanspergius by Philip Howard, earl of Arundel) and *The Spiritual Conflict* (pre-1606, translated from the Italian of Lorenzo Scupoli). Commonly attributed to Gerard is 'An answere to a comfortable advertisement' (Oscott College, MS E. 5. 16), an attack against the practice of church popery (occasional conformity by Catholics to avoid fines and penalties).

Gerard remained in the Low Countries, possibly at St Omer but probably in Brussels, until his departure for Rome some time around September. In early 1607 he was appointed English confessor at St Peter's. Most likely during this sojourn he wrote his narrative of the Gunpowder Plot, later edited by John Morris and published in 1871. Gerard was back in Brussels by 3 May 1609 when he was professed of the four vows. For the next few years he was assistant to the novice master in Louvain. On 23 November 1613 the father-general appointed Gerard rector and novice master at Liège, to where the noviciate had recently moved, positions he held until 28 August 1621.

Gerard's wholehearted support of Mary Ward and her controversial new institute at Liège led to his temporary assignment to Rome, where he sought to defend these women against their vehement opposition. In 1623 he was appointed tertian director in Ghent. In 1627 he returned to Rome, to the English College, to serve as consultor, admonitor, and confessor. In 1630 Richard Smith, bishop of Chalcedon and vicar apostolic, revived accusations of

Gerard's involvement in the Gunpowder Plot as an example of Jesuit mismanagement of the English mission. Gerard sought to clear his name and the affair died when Smith withdrew to France in August 1631. Gerard died in Rome on 27 July 1637.   THOMAS M. MCCOOG

Sources T. M. McCoog, *English and Welsh Jesuits, 1555–1650*, 2 vols., Catholic RS, 74–5 (1994–5) · T. M. McCoog, ed., *Monumenta Angliae*, 1–2 (1992) · H. Foley, ed., *Records of the English province of the Society of Jesus*, 7 vols. in 8 (1875–83) · G. Anstruther, *The seminary priests*, 1 (1969) · T. F. Knox and others, eds., *The first and second diaries of the English College, Douay* (1878) · W. Kelly, ed., *Liber ruber venerabilis collegii Anglorum de urbe*, 1, Catholic RS, 37 (1940) · J. Morris, *The life of John Gerard of the Society of Jesus*, 3rd edn (1881) · *John Gerard: the autobiography of an Elizabethan*, trans. P. Caraman, 2nd edn (1956) · A. F. Allison and D. M. Rogers, eds., *The contemporary printed literature of the English Counter-Reformation between 1558 and 1640*, 2 vols. (1989–94) · A. F. Allison, 'John Gerard and the Gunpowder Plot', *Recusant History*, 5 (1959–60), 43–63 · Burke, *Peerage* · Foster, *Alum. Oxon.* · *The Elizabethan Jesuits: Historia missionis Anglicanae Societatis Jesu (1660) of Henry More*, ed. and trans. F. Edwards (1981) · A. Walsham, *Church papists: Catholicism, conformity and confessional polemic in early modern England* (1993) · *The condition of Catholics under James I: Father Gerard's narrative of the Gunpowder Plot*, ed. J. Morris (1871) · H. Peters, *Mary Ward: a world in contemplation* (1994)
Archives Archives of the British Province of the Society of Jesus, Stonyhurst College, Lancashire · Archivum Romanum Societatis Iesu, Rome · Oscott College, Birmingham · Stonyhurst College, Lancashire, narrative of the Gunpowder Plot, autograph letters · Westm. DA

Gerard, John (1632–1654), royalist conspirator, was the son of Ratcliffe Gerard (b. c.1584, d. in or before 1670) of Halsall, Lancashire, and his wife, Jennet (b. c.1588), daughter of Edward Barrett of Pembrokeshire. His brothers were Ratcliffe, Charles, and Gilbert, who was created a baronet in 1666, and his first cousin was Charles Gerard, first Baron Gerard of Brandon. The family actively supported the royalist cause in the civil war. Gerard's father served as lieutenant-colonel in the foot regiment of his twin brother, Gilbert Gerard. He was in Raglan Castle at its surrender in 1646, was in arms again in 1651, when he was captured at Wigan, and was noted in 1658 as a non-Catholic royalist activist in Lancashire. John Gerard served as an ensign in the royalist army and by the early 1650s was associating with clandestine royalist groups in London. On 21 November 1653, at the New Exchange, he quarrelled with Don Pantaleon, the Portuguese ambassador's brother, who was so affronted that he returned the next day with a group of armed attendants seeking revenge. He mistook another man for Gerard and during the brawl that ensued the man was killed and others were hurt. Don Pantaleon was arrested and subsequently convicted for the murder.

Gerard attended meetings, which began in November 1653, of a group led by Roger Whitley, a brother-in-law of Lord Gerard, and Captain Richard Dutton. This was not linked to the Sealed Knot, the royalist organization supported by Sir Edward Hyde, but was directed by a rival faction at the exiled court that included Lord Gerard and Sir Edward Herbert. The plan was to foment a riot by apprentices and seize London during the confusion. The plot

came to light at the Ship tavern in Old Bailey in February 1654 and many of the conspirators were arrested.

Gerard left England after the plot had been discovered and went to Paris. Here plans were laid for another royalist conspiracy and Gerard returned to London in late April 1654. The objective of this scheme, the Gerard plot, was the murder of Oliver Cromwell as he travelled in his coach from Whitehall to Hampton Court on Saturday 13 May, with attacks on the guards at the Tower and St James's and an uprising of apprentices in the City. A proclamation was circulated that offered a reward of £500, a knighthood, and a colonelcy to anyone who killed Cromwell. The government may have had knowledge of the plot by early May. On the appointed day Cromwell went to Chelsea by boat and not by coach. The plotters then planned to kill him in chapel on Sunday 21 May, but on that day Gerard and five fellow conspirators were seized, and others were arrested later. He, Peter Vowell, and Somerset Fox were brought before the high court of justice on 30 June. Fox admitted his guilt, but Gerard and Vowell denied any knowledge of the plot. Gerard claimed that his visit to Paris had been on private business, but his brother Charles was one of the witnesses and gave a summary of the plot. On 6 July all three were convicted of treason and condemned to death by hanging. Gerard asked the court if, as a soldier, he could be beheaded or shot and accordingly a petition was presented to Cromwell. His request was granted and he was beheaded on 10 July 1654 on Tower Hill, admitting on the scaffold only that he had known of the plot. Don Pantaleon was then executed on the same scaffold. Vowell was hanged on the same day and Fox was reprieved. Cardinal Mazarin's personal envoy Baron de Baas was implicated in the plot and was expelled. In 1660 Gerard's father and his brother, Gilbert Gerard, petitioned the House of Lords that those involved in Gerard's conviction should be excluded from the Act of Indemnity.   STEPHEN PORTER

Sources D. Underdown, *Royalist conspiracy in England, 1649–1660* (1960), 97–104 · *State trials*, 5.517–40 · *Mercurius Politicus* (1–8 June 1654), 3539–40 · *Mercurius Politicus* (29 June–6 July 1654), 3599–604 · *Mercurius Politicus* (6–13 July 1654), 3612–15, 3619 · Clarendon, *Hist. rebellion*, 5.292–7 · S. R. Gardiner, *History of the Commonwealth and protectorate, 1649–1656*, new edn, 4 vols. (1903); vol. 3, pp. 144–9 · P. R. Newman, *Royalist officers in England and Wales, 1642–1660: a biographical dictionary* (1981), 152 · A. Fraser, *Cromwell, our chief of men* (1973), 493–6 · GEC, *Peerage*, 8.328 · GEC, *Baronetage*, 4.38 · *Seventh report*, HMC, 6 (1879), 111 · *Calendar of the Clarendon state papers preserved in the Bodleian Library*, 2: *1649–1654*, ed. W. D. Macray (1869), vol. 2, p. 388 · *DNB*

Gerard, Sir Montagu Gilbert (1842–1905), army officer, born at Edinburgh on 29 June 1842, was the second son in a family of three sons and four daughters of Archibald Gerard (1812–1880) of Rochsoles, near Airdrie, Lanarkshire, and his wife, Euphemia Erskine (1818–1870), eldest daughter of Sir John *Robison. He was a great-grandson of Alexander Gerard, philosophical writer, and of Archibald Alison, father of the historian. The family was originally Scottish episcopalian, but the mother joined the Roman

Catholic church in 1848, the father a little later, and the children were brought up as Roman Catholics. Montagu's eldest brother became Father John Gerard SJ, and his eldest sister was (Jane) Emily *Gerard. He was educated at Stonyhurst (from 1850), Ushaw College (1855–9), and the Royal Military Academy, Woolwich (1860–64).

Gerard was commissioned lieutenant in the Royal Garrison Artillery on 19 April 1864, and served duty at Gibraltar. In 1866, on being transferred to the Royal Field Artillery, he was stationed in the central provinces, India. In 1867–8 he was employed on the transport train during the Abyssinian expedition, and was mentioned in dispatches. In 1870 he joined the Bengal staff corps, and was attached to the Central India horse. Promoted captain on 19 April 1876, he acted as brigade major throughout the Second Anglo-Afghan War (1878–80), and had his horse wounded at the action of Deb Sarak. He took part in the second Bazar valley expedition and in the defence of Jagdalak. In December 1879 he accompanied General Charles Gough's brigade to Sherpur, took part in Roberts's march from Kabul to Kandahar, and was engaged at the battle of 1 September 1880. He was mentioned in dispatches, and received brevets of major (22 November 1879) and of lieutenant-colonel (2 March 1881). He served in the Egyptian campaign of 1882. Appointed deputy assistant adjutant and quartermaster-general of the cavalry division, he was at the battles of Qassasin and Tell al-Kebir, and the surrender of Arabi Pasha. He was mentioned in dispatches and created CB and the Mejidiye (third class). He became major on 19 April 1884 and brevet colonel on 2 March 1885.

Gerard had other qualities besides those of the successful soldier. In 1881 and in 1885 he was sent on secret missions to Persia. After serving as district staff officer in Bengal, he took charge of the tour which the tsarevich (afterwards Nicholas II) made in India (December 1890 to February 1891), and his success resulted in his appointment in 1892 as British military attaché at St Petersburg. He had an important role in the negotiations on the Pamirs boundary dispute, and when in March 1895 an agreement was signed between Great Britain and Russia for the delimitation of their spheres of influence in central Asia, Gerard was sent out to the Pamirs at the head of a British commission. He met the Russian mission under General Shveykovsky in June at Lake Victoria, and from that point eastwards to the Chinese frontier demarcated the line which from that time divided Russian from British interests. He married on 19 September 1888 Helen Adelaide, third daughter of Edward Richard Meade, a grandson of John Meade, first earl of Clanwilliam; she survived him with one son.

In 1896 Gerard was nominated to the command of the Hyderabad contingent, and in 1899 was promoted to the command of a first-class district in Bengal. He was created CSI in 1896, KCSI in 1897, and KCB in 1902. He was promoted major-general on 1 April 1897, lieutenant-general on 12 September 1900, and general on 29 February 1904. A keen killer of big game, he published *Leaves from the Diaries*

of a Soldier and a Sportsman, 1865–1885 (1903). On the outbreak of the Russo-Japanese War in 1904 he went to Manchuria as chief British attaché with General Kuropatkin's army; but his health succumbed to the rigours of the campaign, and he died of pneumonia at Irkutsk, Siberia, on 26 July 1905 on his way home from Kharbin. He was buried at Airdrie, Scotland, on 8 September.

G. S. WOODS, rev. JAMES FALKNER

Sources *The Times* (28 July 1905) · *The Times* (22 Aug 1905) · *The Times* (9 Sept 1905) · *Army List* · *Hart's Army List* · *Stonyhurst Magazine* (Oct 1905) · private information (1912) · H. B. Hanna, *The Second Afghan War*, 3 (1910)
Wealth at death £3822 14s. 4d.: confirmation, 30 Oct 1905, *CCI*

Gerard, Patrick (1794–1848), geographer, was the son of Gilbert *Gerard (1760–1815), theologian, and Helen Duncan; the grandson of Alexander *Gerard (1728–1795); and the brother of Alexander *Gerard (1792–1839) and of James Gilbert *Gerard (1793–1835). He was born on 11 June 1794, probably in Aberdeen, one of six sons and five daughters. He probably entered King's or Marischal College, Aberdeen, in 1808, and received a Bengal cadetship in 1812. In the 8th Bengal native infantry he was appointed ensign on 19 August 1812, lieutenant therein on 16 December 1814, and brevet captain on 19 August 1827.

Like his brothers, also army officers with a remarkable interest in geography, Gerard was a keen and meticulous observer of his surroundings. His particular interest was climate and its effect on agriculture. Despite difficulties in obtaining reliable instruments, he made numerous systematic meteorological observations recorded in a manuscript in the British Library and published in *Asiatic Researches* (1825) and in the *Edinburgh Journal of Science* (1828). He also wrote on mineralogy for the *Delhi Medical Journal* (1844). In 1821 with his brother Alexander—in whose memoir a full account is given—he journeyed to remote and inaccessible parts of the Himalayan mountains, many never before visited by Europeans. The brothers described part of the journey in the *Edinburgh Philosophical Journal* (1824) in which their barometrical and trigonometrical observations helped establish the heights of several locations and their observations on the geomorphology, climate, and language of the areas through which they travelled were recorded.

Gerard became captain in the 9th native infantry on 11 April 1828, and was placed on the invalid establishment in India on 8 August 1832. He died at Simla on 4 October 1848. His contribution to the geography of India and of the Himalayas was slight compared with that of his brother, but they shared the same concern to record precise information about little known regions.

H. M. CHICHESTER, rev. ELIZABETH BAIGENT

Sources BL OIOC · private information (1888) · Sir W. Lloyd, *Account of a journey from Caunpoor to the Boorendo pass* (1840) · A. Gerard, *Account of Koonawur in the Himalaya*, ed. G. Lloyd (1841)
Archives BL, meteorological journal in India, Add. MSS 24017–24022

Gerard, Richard (1613–1686), royalist army officer, was born in October 1613, the third of ten children of Sir Thomas Gerard (1594/5–1630), knight and second baronet, of Bryn, Lancashire, and his wife, Frances Molyneux (d. 1614), daughter of Sir Richard Molyneux, baronet, of Sefton, Lancashire. Both Richard's grandfathers had been created baronet at the institution of the order in May 1611, and his father inherited the title in 1621; his maternal uncle was Sir Richard Molyneux, from 1628 first Viscount Molyneux of Maryborough. The large Gerard estates consisted of demesnes, mills, and coal mines. As Roman Catholics they were legally disqualified from royal service, but like other Catholic gentry in Lancashire, the Gerards seem to have been treated leniently when it came to discriminatory taxes against recusants. At a time when one Thomas Gerard was lord of the manor of St Clements in Maryland, Richard Gerard is said to have spent a year in the colony soon after the landing of the planters in 1634. Gerard returned to England in 1635.

About 1638 Gerard raised a foot company to recruit one of the English regiments in the service of Spain. This was posted to Flanders, where Gerard served until 1642, in which year he entered the service of Henrietta Maria at The Hague, as an officer of the queen's guard, which escorted her on her return to England. Here he was commissioned lieutenant-colonel of the queen's foot guards. The queen wrote from Newark, on 22 June 1643, that her marching army was under the command of Henry Jermyn, 'as colonel of my Guard' with the foot under Sir Alexander Lesley, 'and Gerrard the horse' (Rushworth, pt 3, 2.274). Richard Gerard was wounded in the action leading to the capture of Burton upon Trent on 2 July. His regiment became part of the garrison of Oxford, billeted at Merton College and kitted out with red coats. The issue of shovels, spades, pickaxes, and hoes to the regiment shows that the men were employed in finishing the works and clearing the outskirts. In June 1644 the regiment was sent to join the king at Banbury, on the eve of the battle of Cropredy Bridge, but it appears not to have arrived in time. When Jermyn accompanied the queen to France in July Gerard took command of the regiment, and in October joined Colonel Henry Gage to relieve Banbury Castle. Thereafter his service seems to have been limited to garrison duties.

In May 1646 Gerard was one of 25 signatories of a rather bombastic protest against the treaty of surrender of Oxford, declaring that the lords of the council had forced it upon the governor. Negotiations continued and were concluded on 20 June. The treaty provided that members of the garrison should be admitted to composition. Gerard lost no time in applying to compound, and was fined £100, which he paid in September 1648.

Little firm evidence exists as to Gerard's later years. He is said to have waited on Charles I at Hurst Castle and to have carried letters from the king to the queen in France. At the Restoration he was appointed cupbearer in ordinary and waiter to Henrietta Maria. The herald's visitation of 1665 records that he was married twice: first to Frances Hansby, the daughter of Sir Ralph Hansby of Tickhill, Yorkshire, and afterwards to Judith Steward, daughter of Sir Nicholas Steward of Pattishall, Northamptonshire. He appears

to have lived on his brother's estates at Bryn and Garswood, where Roger Lowe the diarist was an occasional visitor, but he settled eventually at Ince in south-west Lancashire, where he died on 5 September 1686. He was buried at Wigan parish church. PAUL H. HARDACRE

Sources W. Dugdale, *The visitation of the county palatine of Lancaster, made in the year 1664–5*, ed. F. R. Raines, 2, Chetham Society, 85 (1872), 116–17 • B. G. Blackwood, *The Lancashire gentry and the great rebellion, 1640–60*, Chetham Society, 3rd ser., 25 (1978) • J. Rushworth, *Historical collections*, 2nd edn, 3/2 (1692), 274 [letter of Henrietta Maria, 22 June 1643] • E. J. Parsons, *Some proclamations of Charles I* (1936) • I. Roy, ed., *The royalist ordnance papers, 1642–1646*, 2 vols., Oxfordshire RS, 43, 49 (1964–75) • M. Toynbee, ed., *The papers of Captain Henry Stevens, waggon-master-general to King Charles I*, Oxfordshire RS, 42 (1962) • P. R. Newman, *Royalist officers in England and Wales, 1642–1660: a biographical dictionary* (1981), 153 • E. Walker, *Historical discourses upon several occasions* (1705) • M. Toynbee and P. Young, *Strangers in Oxford: a side light on the first civil war, 1642–1646* (1973) • F. J. Varley, *The siege of Oxford: an account of Oxford during the civil war, 1642–1646* (1932) • J. H. Stanning and J. Brownbill, eds., *The royalist composition papers … related to the county of Lancaster*, 7 vols., Lancashire and Cheshire RS, 24, 26, 29, 36, 72, 95, 96 (1891–1942) • *The diary of Roger Lowe*, ed. W. L. Sachse (1938) • GEC, *Peerage*, new edn, 1.21–3

Gerard, Thomas. See Garrard, Thomas (1498–1540).

Gerard, Thomas (1592–1634). *See under* Coker, John (d. 1631/1635).

Gerard, Sir William (d. 1581), administrator, was the son of Gilbert Gerard of Ince, Lancashire, and his wife, Eleanor, daughter of William Davison, alderman of Chester. He was a cousin of Sir Gilbert *Gerard, master of the rolls. He married Dorothy, daughter of Andrew Barton of Smithills, Lancashire; they had two sons and four daughters, one of whom, Sidney, married the antiquary Sir John *Wynn of Gwydir. He entered Gray's Inn in 1543, was called to the bar in 1546, and served as queen's attorney in Wales and the marches from 1554 to 1559. He was recorder of Chester from about 1554 to 1574 and sat as MP for Chester in 1555, 1558, 1559, 1563, 1571, and 1572, but played only a minor part in the affairs of the House of Commons.

In 1559 Gerard was made a justice of the great sessions for the Brecknock circuit and in the following year he entered the council in the marches of Wales, which became his principal arena of activity for the next sixteen years. Together with Sir Henry Sidney, the lord president, and Sir John Throckmorton, justice of Chester, Gerard was one of the dominant group within the council; he was made vice-president in 1562 when Sidney was sent on missions to France and Scotland. In January 1576 Gerard sent Walsingham two 'discourses' on the council. In part they were a reply to a fierce attack on the government of Wales by Dr David Lewis, a native of Abergavenny and a commissioner of the admiralty, who urged the need for greater severity. Gerard set out to demonstrate the necessity of the council for good government and to provide remedies for its defects. The first of his discourses opened with a careful analysis of the history of Wales from the Edwardian conquest to his own day and proceeded with a diagnosis of the present problems. Where Lewis had insisted that disorder was rife and severity essential, Gerard advocated moderation: 'at this day it is to be affirmed, that in Wales universally, are as civil people and obedient to law, as are in England. Throughout Wales in every respect justice embraced' (Thomas, 148). Unfortunately the respect for law had led to a multiplication of suits and the overburdening of the council, and Gerard concluded with a set of orders to reduce the number of unnecessary suits. He also criticized some members of the council and recommended that the councillors travel more frequently throughout Wales. While he was writing his discourses Gerard, fearing opposition from his fellow councillors, asked Walsingham for a letter of support, of which he provided a draft. Walsingham obliged, complaining of the high cost of the council and the grievances of its subjects, and pointing out that the queen intended reforms. This seems to have had the desired effect in the marches, where the councillors began to consider changes of their own. Gerard's recommendations were put into effect later in 1576 with a new book of orders issued by the privy council.

By then Gerard had entered the next and most important phase of his career. In April of that year he had been appointed lord chancellor of Ireland, probably at the instigation of Sir Henry Sidney, who wrote of him: 'I ever found him the sufficientest man both for judgement and diligence, that ever I found attend that house [the council in the marches]' (Collins, 1.143). Shortly after Gerard's arrival the Dublin government was faced with serious opposition from the landowners of the pale to its proposed levy of the cess, a form of purveyance, for the support of the army. Three of the palesmen went to England to petition the privy council, and in July 1577 Gerard was sent to court to defend Sidney's policy against their claims. By this time he was coming to accept their complaints about abuses of government, while firmly defending the crown's prerogative right to levy the cess; and he accepted their offer of a compromise. Sidney was understandably furious; but by then the end of his government was in sight. Gerard in effect helped, perhaps unintentionally, to destroy his policy with a long report on the state of Ireland which he presented to the earl of Leicester in May 1578. In it he implicitly criticized Sidney for the expense of his rule and urged a less ambitious and less costly approach to the problems of Ireland. We should not 'wade further to gain territories' and should use the law rather than the sword: 'it is the rod of justice that must scour out those blots' (McNeill, 96). He followed with a set of detailed proposals: above all, the crown should not attempt to settle the whole of Ireland at once, but should begin with the pale and proceed gradually from there. The way to do this was by the appointment of judges from England, copying the procedure used to good effect in Wales. Gerard returned to Ireland after writing his report and was knighted there in 1579 by Lord Justice Pelham, 'for well discharging of the trust committed unto him, and ... in one or two causes for border actions ... also a disposition to have adventured his life if the case so required' (Hogan and O'Farrell, 212). Gerard came back to England

in October 1579, and was made a master of requests. After a further short visit to Ireland in the summer of 1580 he returned to England for the last time in January 1581. He died in Chester on 1 May of that year.

Gerard's will, written on 16 February 1581, shows him to have been a strong protestant. 'Prostrate in tears before the throne of heavenly grace with inward remorse and bleeding repentance at my former wicked life', he prayed that through God's mercy he might 'be placed with Him in the heavenly Jerusalem provided ... for all his elect (amongst which number I faithfully believe I am one)' (will, fol. 208v). He instructed his elder son, Gilbert, to take special care of his mother, who had been several times afflicted with 'such sickness as bereaveth her from all sense and understanding' (ibid.), and made careful provision for the upkeep of her household: she was to have two maidservants and two menservants. Much of the will is devoted to recovering the debts owed to him by the crown and to renewing the licence for the export of yarn on which his family must depend. He requested that William Garrett, son of the earl of Kildare, currently in his custody, be handed over to Sir Francis Walsingham. He asked the earl of Leicester and Walsingham to further his petition to the queen over the yarn licence. Among many small legacies, he left his best falcon to Sir John Huband, a ring to Sir John Perrot, his best hobby to Leicester, and 'my well paced nag' to Walsingham. To Arthur, Lord Grey of Wilton, the new lord deputy of Ireland, he gave 'the treasure of a true heart' together with all his notes and collections on the state of Ireland (ibid., fol. 210).

Gerard was a conscientious and intelligent public servant. Attentive to history, he analysed carefully the background to the problems of Wales and Ireland, making cogent recommendations to remedy the defects of government. His approach in both countries was moderate, rejecting extreme solutions and basing himself always on the law rather than excessive severity or military action. His proposals for reform of the council in the marches were largely accepted and his comments on Irish government led the crown to adopt a more cautious and economical policy until the Munster rebellion made that impossible.

PENRY WILLIAMS

Sources P. Williams, 'The council in the marches of Wales in the reign of Elizabeth', DPhil diss., U. Oxf., 1955, 462–6 • P. Williams, *The council in the marches of Wales under Elizabeth I* (1958) • *DNB* • D. L. Thomas, 'Further notes on the council in the marches', *Y Cymmrodor*, 13 (1900), 97–163 • will, PRO, PROB 11/63, fols. 208v–210r • C. McNeill, ed., 'Lord Chancellor Gerard's ... report on Ireland', *Analecta Hibernica*, 2 (1931), 93–291 • J. S. Brewer and W. Bullen, eds., *Calendar of the Carew manuscripts*, 2: *1575–1588*, PRO (1868) • C. Brady, *The chief governors: the rise and fall of reform government in Tudor Ireland, 1536–1588* (1994) • S. G. Ellis, *Tudor Ireland: crown, community, and the conflict of cultures, 1470–1603* (1985) • J. G. Crawford, *Anglicizing the government of Ireland: the Irish privy council and the expansion of Tudor rule, 1556–1578* (1993) • H. Sydney and others, *Letters and memorials of state*, ed. A. Collins, 2 vols. (1746) • J. Hogan and N. McNeill O'Farrell, eds., *The Walsingham letter-book, or, Register of Ireland, May 1578 to December 1579*, IMC (1959) • T. Helsby, introduction, in G. Ormerod, *The history of the county palatine and city of Chester*, 2nd edn, ed. T. Helsby, 1 (1882), 194–5 • J. Foster, *The register of admissions to Gray's Inn, 1521–1889, together with the* *register of marriages in Gray's Inn chapel, 1695–1754* (privately printed, London, 1889), 16

Archives Bodl. Oxf., D Rawl. 657 · PRO, state papers, domestic Elizabeth I (SP 12), esp. SP 12/107/10, 21

Wealth at death complained of being owed money by the crown: will, PRO, PROB 11/63, fols. 208v–210r

Gerarde, Derrick (*fl.* 1550–1590), composer and copyist, was probably of Flemish origin. Although virtually nothing is known of his life, there is strong circumstantial evidence for believing that he spent some time in England. Almost his entire musical output is contained in manuscripts now in the Royal Appendix sequence of the British Library. The fact that so many of these can be traced back to the library established by Henry Fitzalan, twelfth earl of Arundel (1512–1580), and his son-in-law John, Lord Lumley (1534–1609), suggests that Gerarde had personal contact with their household. Both men were sympathetic patrons of the arts, and their country residence at Nonsuch, Surrey, was a flourishing centre of continental music and culture. Two sets of partbooks emanating from Nonsuch contain a work with English text—'Yf Phebus Stormes' and 'Lorde be my judge'—apparently by Gerarde. He copied Royal Appendix 57 (the only surviving partbook of another Nonsuch set) using printed music paper thought to have been produced in England in the 1560s. A textless chanson or instrumental piece, 'Chera la fountayne', is attributed to 'Gerardus' in British Library, Add. MS 31390, a manuscript of English provenance, and his motet *Sive vigilem* appears in Oxford, Christ Church, MSS 979–983, a collection that, with one exception, contains music by British composers or foreigners working in Britain. However, there is no documentary proof that Gerarde ever directly enjoyed the patronage of either Arundel or Lumley, and it has even been suggested that they acquired some of his manuscripts secondhand. While admitting this as a possibility, it seems more likely that he was employed at Nonsuch in some capacity.

Gerarde's manuscripts constitute one of the largest collections of polyphony by a single composer to have survived from the Elizabethan era. A number of these are autographs and preserve reworkings of his pieces, often in the form of new staves pasted over the old versions, which afford a fascinating insight into the compositional processes of a Renaissance musician. His large and varied output is international in scope, with instrumental pieces, Italian madrigals and villanellas, chansons, liturgical pieces for four to ten voices, and a number of secular motets. His finely crafted music is typical of the generation of Lassus, with smoothly flowing lines and declamatory passages occasionally enlivened by touches of chromaticism. The style is seen at its best in his *Dulces exuviae*, a setting of Dido's final words from book 4 of Virgil's *Aeneid*, which achieves a remarkably powerful effect for all its technical restraint.

Nothing is known of Gerarde's career before coming to England, and attempts to identify him with one of the many musicians of that name working on the continent have produced only speculative results. He may have arrived in England as early as the reign of Queen Mary, when Arundel was in the Low Countries as ambassador to Philip of Spain, or in the mid-1560s as a musician acquired by the earl on his visit to the baths at Padua. After Arundel's death Gerarde may have sought alternative employment, and he is possibly the 'Gerrard Direck' alias 'Direck Gerrerd' who was a singing man at York Minster from about 1590 until his death in 1604. Conceivably, he may also be the 'Derrick' whose English service music appears in early seventeenth-century manuscripts at Cambridge and Durham, and the composer of 'Mr Dethicks Pavin' in British Library, Add. MSS 30826–30828, another Cambridge source.   DAVID MATEER

Sources J. A. Owens, *Composers at work: the craft of musical composition, 1450–1600* (1997) · P. Holman, *Four and twenty fiddlers: the violin at the English court, 1540–1690*, new edn (1993) · J. Milsom, 'The Nonsuch music library', *'Sundry sorts of music books': essays on the British Library Collections presented to O. W. Neighbour on his seventieth birthday*, ed. C. Banks, A. Searle, and M. Turner (1993), 146–82 · I. Fenlon and J. Milsom, '"Ruled paper imprinted": music paper and patents in sixteenth-century England', *Journal of the American Musicological Society*, 37 (1984), 139–63 · C. W. Warren, 'Music at Nonesuch', *Musical Quarterly*, 54 (1968), 47–57 · J. Milsom, 'Gerarde, Derrick', *New Grove*, 2nd edn · S. Jayne and F. R. Johnson, eds., *The Lumley library: the catalogue of 1609* (1956) · D. Epps, 'The life and work of Deryck Gerarde', DMus diss., U. Edin., 1964 · C. W. Warren, 'The music of Derick Gerarde', PhD diss., Ohio State University, 1966 · C. W. Warren, 'The music of Royal Appendix 12–16', *Music and Letters*, 51 (1970), 357–72

Gerbier, Sir Balthazar (1592–1663/1667), art agent, miniature painter, and architect, was born on 23 February 1592 at Middelburg in the Netherlands, the son of Antonie Gerbier and Radigonde Blavet, who were Huguenot émigrés. Gerbier later styled himself Baron d'Ouvilly, or Doully. Little is known about his early upbringing or education, and Gerbier's own claims invite scepticism. He certainly studied drawing and penmanship while in the Netherlands, perhaps with Hendrik Goltzius in Haarlem. In 1620 Gerbier published a verse lament on Goltzius's death (*Eer ende claght-dicht*) which evokes an imaginary procession of grieving artists led by Peter Paul Rubens.

Gerbier's surviving works are miniatures and pen-and-ink portraits datable to 1616–19. He introduced the table-book leaf (a sheet of card, prepared with gesso on each side, used as a backing for vellum) into England. Several of Gerbier's portraits of the Dutch nobility are dated after he left the Netherlands and so were not made from life. Nevertheless, Gerbier kept an eye on the house of Orange and in 1658 presented a volume of calligraphy (Koninklijke Bibliotheek, The Hague) to Princess Mary for the education of the young William III.

Keeper of the York House collection In 1616 Gerbier accompanied Noël de Caron, ambassador from the states general, to London. According to William Sanderson he lettered the ten commandments in Austin Friars, 'his first rise of preferment' (*Graphice*, 1658, 15). He joined the household of George Villiers, marquess of Buckingham (later first duke), in 1619, becoming his factotum, agent, and the keeper of the picture collection. In July of that year he went to Hainault, where he bought nine paintings by Veronese from the collection formed by Charles de

Sir Balthazar Gerbier (1592–1663/1667), by Paulus Pontius, 1634 (after Sir Anthony Van Dyck)

Croy, duc d'Aarschot. Gerbier travelled to Italy in 1621 where he acquired a number of sixteenth-century pictures for Buckingham, among them Titian's large and important *Ecce homo* (Kunsthistorisches Museum, Vienna) which cost the huge sum of £275, as well as works by living artists, notably Guido Reni. Gerbier showed great expertise as an art agent and was allowed to act independently by Buckingham.

In 1624–5 Gerbier supervised the remodelling of York House, Buckingham's mansion on the Strand. His work, which incorporated a marble fireplace and gateway presented by Dudley Carleton, Viscount Dorchester, was said by Gerbier to have disconcerted Inigo Jones (Goodman, 2.360). He may also have designed the Water Gate (sometimes attributed to Nicholas Stone) which survives in Embankment Gardens, London. Although Gerbier was versatile and increasingly indispensable, his position in the household was sometimes troubled. In 1628 he feuded with Orazio Gentileschi (an Italian artist employed by Buckingham) who would not endorse the 'merritt and vallue' of pictures that Gerbier had bought (PRO, SP 133/29, fols. 44r–45r).

Art and diplomacy abroad Gerbier was trusted with Buckingham's ciphers, and was sent on a diplomatic mission to Brussels in 1622, although at this time he was more the duke's creature than the king's. In 1623–4 he accompanied Buckingham and the prince of Wales on their visit to

Madrid to woo the Spanish infanta. When Giambologna's *Samson Slaying a Philistine* (V&A) was presented to the prince of Wales (who in turn gave it to Buckingham), Gerbier arranged its transportation to London where it was installed in the gardens at York House.

Gerbier travelled to Paris late in 1624 for the proxy marriage of Charles I and Henrietta Maria. During the visit he used unscrupulous methods to force Nicolas Chevalier, président of the chambre des comptes, to part with works from his collection, but met with resistance from duc Henri II de Montmorency who would not relinquish Michelangelo's *Slaves* (Louvre Museum, Paris). In 1625 Gerbier met Rubens in Paris, perhaps for the first time, and they were to remain in intermittent contact until the artist's death in 1640. Gerbier returned to Paris in 1627 bearing letters from Buckingham to Richelieu. He then travelled to Delft where he met Rubens on 21 July. The two men used the purchase of Rubens's collection by Buckingham as cover, but were in reality negotiating what Sir John Coke called 'delusory treaties' between Britain and Spain (R. Lockyer, *Buckingham*, 1981, 395).

After the assassination of Buckingham in 1628, Gerbier reminded the king of his devotion by becoming a British national and taking the oaths of allegiance and supremacy. The lord treasurer, Richard Weston (first earl of Portland), then succeeded Buckingham as Gerbier's patron to some extent. Between 1628 and 1632 Gerbier directed the rebuilding of Weston's house, Putney Park at Roehampton (dem. *c*.1775). Gerbier also supervised two sculptural commissions for him: a bronze equestrian statue of the king for the gardens at Roehampton made by Hubert le Sueur in 1629–30 (Trafalgar Square, London) and Weston's monument in Winchester Cathedral designed by Isaac Besnier.

Rubens visited London from May 1629 to February 1630 in the hope of negotiating a truce between England and Spain. In his own words Gerbier acted as 'innkeeper' (Sainsbury, *Original … Papers*, 144) but was paid handsomely by the king for his pains. Rubens may have begun a group portrait of Gerbier's wife, Debora Kip (*b.* 1601), whom he had married in 1618, with four of their children at this time, although the best surviving version (National Gallery, Washington) raises problems of authorship and dating. Their eldest son, George Gerbier *D'Ouvilly, became a playwright and translator. Gerbier later commissioned an enlarged version from an artist in the circle of Rubens (Royal Collection) which included his portrait. Before Rubens's departure, Gerbier sold a diamond ring and hatband to the king for £500 for presentation to the artist.

Agent in Brussels, 1631–1641 In 1631 the king appointed Gerbier as his agent in Brussels, where he was soon occupied with matters political and artistic. He had frequent dealings with artists, including Van Dyck, who restored a damaged *Vitellius* by Titian (lost) for the king. In 1631 Gerbier bought a *Mystic Marriage with St Catherine* (identification uncertain) for Weston. It was sold by Solomon Nobliers as an original by Van Dyck, but, for reasons unknown, the artist chose to repudiate the work and embarrass Gerbier.

Gerbier was involved with two major decorative projects for the royal palaces. From 1634 onwards he arranged the dispatch of Rubens's ceiling paintings for the Banqueting House in Whitehall, and tried to obtain payment for the artist. From 1639 Gerbier, together with Edward Norgate and the Abbé Cesare Alessandro Scaglia, were involved in obtaining a series of pictures for the cabinet in the Queen's House, Greenwich, depicting the story of Cupid and Psyche. Gerbier favoured Rubens, but Jacob Jordaens got the job and delivered the first picture in May 1640. Following Rubens's death in the same month Gerbier translated the inventory of his collection, the *Specification*, and sent it to the king.

Gerbier's achievements as a diplomat were less substantial. He implemented the king's policy of supporting those Flemish aristocrats who resented the Spanish ascendancy in Brussels, but then sold their names to the Archduchess Isabella for 20,000 crowns. Despite this duplicity Gerbier retained the confidence of the king and was knighted on 22 October 1638.

Return to London, 1641–1643 Gerbier returned to London and became master of ceremonies in April 1641. He proposed the creation of an international bank and pawnbrokers, a scheme which was wisely ignored. In June Gerbier disgraced himself in the House of Lords by accusing Lord Cottington of his own betrayal of the king's plans in Brussels. He was described as 'utterly lost' (*CSP dom.*, 1641–3, 36) and Charles Cotterell became *de facto* master of ceremonies in July. Adding insult to injury, Gerbier (who was no papist) saw his house ransacked and his pew in the local parish church destroyed. He was now a discredited figure and departed for France in 1643, but scandal followed him to Paris where his daughter Elizabeth converted to the church of Rome and took refuge in a convent.

Gerbier and the Commonwealth It was only after the king's execution in 1649 that Gerbier felt able to return to London, where he busied himself writing pamphlets and devising preposterous schemes. While abroad, he had inherited a house in Bethnal Green from his father-in-law, Willem Kip, a jeweller and engraver, who died in 1646. This enabled him to open an academy for young gentlemen, which was effectively a school for spies since the curriculum included horsemanship, foreign languages, cosmography, and the construction of military fortifications. It opened in July 1649 and closed in August 1650.

On 20 April 1653 Gerbier, together with George Geldorp and Peter Lely, offered to paint a series of pictures at Whitehall of 'the most remarkablest Battails' of the civil war (BL, Stowe MS 184, fol. 283). In similar vein, Gerbier was the anonymous author of *The None-Such Charles his Character* (1651), a hypocritical attack on the king and his purchase of 'old rotten pictures', but he had no qualms in acquiring Van Dyck's *Equestrian Portrait of Charles I* (National Gallery, London) and Titian's *Charles V with a Hound* (Museo del Prado, Madrid) at the dispersal of the king's goods, quickly selling them at a profit.

In the 1650s Gerbier's stratagems became increasingly desperate. Briefly considered of use to the Commonwealth, he was sent as an agent to The Hague in August 1652, and again in 1658 to spy on royalists in exile, but lacked all credibility. He then persuaded the states general to support an expedition to Guiana in search of gold, embarking in August 1659. His daughter, Catherine, was murdered during a mutiny on 7 May 1660, and Gerbier returned to Amsterdam where, in a spate of pamphlets, he declared himself the victim of conspiracy.

The Restoration and architecture Gerbier, together with Peter Mills, designed the triumphal arches that welcomed Charles II into London in 1661. He tried to regain the post of master of ceremonies but was immediately suspended. In the face of royal disdain, Gerbier turned to architecture and entered the service of William, first earl of Craven, remodelling his house at Hampstead Marshall in Berkshire (destr. 1718) for which a number of drawings survive (Bodl. Oxf.). Gerbier was assisted by Captain William Winde who continued the work after his death. Gerbier was uncharacteristically reticent about his practice as architect, thinking it beneath him, but he published *A Brief Discourse Concerning the Three Chief Principles of Magnificent Building* in 1662, and the *Counsel and Advise to All Builders* in 1663. Gerbier died at Hampstead Marshall either in 1663 (according to a petition to the king from his daughters who asked for £4000 in unpaid salary) or in 1667 (according to Gerbier's monument in the local church). He was also buried there. The earlier date limits the work he could have achieved at the house and implies a more substantial role for Winde.

According to William Sanderson, Gerbier 'had little of Art or merit' (*Graphice*, 1658, 15), and Samuel Pepys said one of his books was 'not worth a turd' (Pepys, *Diary*, 28 May 1663). Gerbier's main achievement was the creation of the picture gallery at York House, and it is this aspect of his career which has received most attention in recent years. As a diplomat Gerbier was at least a credible negotiator with Rubens but his period of service as agent in Brussels was lamentable, even by the low standards of Charles I's ambassadors. The stratagems of Gerbier's later years reveal the desperation of a courtier deprived of a court, but the Restoration created opportunities in country house architecture which were cut short by his death.

JEREMY WOOD

Sources W. N. Sainsbury, *Original unpublished papers illustrative of the life of Sir Peter Paul Rubens, as an artist and a diplomatist, preserved in H. M. State Paper Office* (1859) · C. Ruelens and M. Rooses, eds., *Correspondance de Rubens et documents épistolaires concernant sa vie et ses œuvres*, 6 vols. (Anvers, 1887–1909) · L. R. Betcherman, 'The York House collection and its keeper', *Apollo*, 92 (1970), 250–59 · P. McEvansoneya, 'Some documents concerning the patronage and collections of the duke of Buckingham', *Rutgers Art Review*, 8 (1987), 27–38 · I. G. Philip, 'Balthazar Gerbier and the duke of Buckingham's pictures', *Burlington Magazine*, 99 (1957), 155–6 · G. Goodman, *The court of King James the First*, ed. J. S. Brewer, 2 vols. (1839) · W. N. Sainsbury, 'Artists' quarrels in Charles I's reign', *N&Q*, 2nd ser., 8 (1859), 121–2 · W. H. Carpenter, *Pictorial notices consisting of a* memoir of Sir Anthony Van Dyck (1844) • H. R. Williamson, Four Stuart portraits (1949) • E. Croft-Murray and P. H. Hulton, eds., Catalogue of British drawings, 1 (1960) • J. Murdoch, Seventeenth-century English miniatures in the collection of the Victoria and Albert Museum (1997) • D. Freedberg, 'Fame, convention and insight: on the relevance of Fornenbergh and Gerbier', The Ringling Museum of Art Journal: papers presented at the international Rubens symposium, April 14–16, 1982 (1983), 236–59 • O. Hill and J. Cornforth, English country houses: Caroline, 1625–1685 (1966) • Colvin, Archs. • M. J. Power, 'Sir Balthazar Gerbier's academy at Bethnal Green', East London Papers, 10 (1967), 19–34

Archives PRO, state papers, Flanders, entry books with drafts of letters and dispatches, SP 105/7–18 • Wellcome L., papers | BL, declaration of loyalty to Commonwealth, addressed to O. Cromwell and B. Whitelocke, Add. MS 32093 • Bodl. Oxf., Gough drawings • Koninklijke Bibliotheek, The Hague, Aenmerckingen ende doen van keysers, coningen, coninginnen, prinsen, princessen ende doordluchtinge mannen • PRO, state papers, Flanders, SP 77 • University of Sheffield, letters to S. Hartlib, bundle X.2 and XXXVI • University of Sheffield, letters relating to proposed academy for gentlemen's sons • Warks. CRO, letters to Lord Feilding

Likenesses circle of P. P. Rubens, group portrait, oils, c.1629–1638 (Balthazar Gerbier and Debora Kip with their family), Windsor Castle • P. Pontius, line engraving, 1634 (after A. Van Dyck), BM, NPG [see illus.] • E. Harding, wash drawing (after unknown artist), Scot. NPG

Gere, Charles March (1869–1957), artist, was born on 5 June 1869 in Gloucester. His father, Edward Williams Gere, a member of an American family long settled in Massachusetts, was a partner in the firm of Hayden, Gere & Co., brass-founders, of Haydenville, Massachusetts. After the death of his first wife he sold his share of the business and came to England, where in 1868 he married Emma March of Gloucester. Charles was their only child.

Educated at a school in Windsor, Gere received his first artistic training at the Gloucester School of Arts and Crafts. He continued his training at the Birmingham School of Art and taught there under E. R. Taylor, who kept the arts and crafts movement very much alive. Gere practised portrait painting, and designing for stained glass and embroidery. He went to Italy to study tempera painting and learned to speak Italian fluently. For a time associated with William Morris, among the books he illustrated for the Kelmscott Press were the Fioretti of St Francis, Dante, and the Morte d'Arthur. He was responsible for the view of Kelmscott Manor used as the frontispiece to Morris's News from Nowhere, the most frequently reproduced of any Kelmscott Press image. Later he worked with St John Hornby at the Ashendene Press.

At his studio at Bridge End, Warwick, Gere gradually became known as a painter of landscapes with figures in oil, tempera, and watercolour. He was a member of both the New English Art Club and the Royal Watercolour Society. He also exhibited with the Royal Academy. In 1904, with his half-sister Margaret Gere (1878–1965), herself a distinguished artist, he settled at Painswick, then a quiet village in the unspoilt Cotswolds between Stroud and Gloucester. He became a member of the Cheltenham Group of Artists and was its president in 1945; and a member of the Gloucester diocesan advisory committee. He was elected an associate of the Royal Academy in 1934 and

Royal Academician in 1939. In 1941 he exhibited at the academy a striking battle scene, The Last Stand at Calais.

Gere's early figure paintings were in the manner of the early Italian painters. An extraordinarily accurate and careful draughtsman, he trained his memory for landscape by making methodical notes of the subject on the spot in sketchbooks, afterwards completing the work in the studio in oil or tempera on silk or thin canvas. His surviving sketchbooks are in the Victoria and Albert Museum, London and Cheltenham Art Gallery and Museum.

The best period of Gere's art was when he was inspired by the Cotswold countryside. The small landscapes he then painted show that he was deeply conscious of the charm of the simple life and the sacramental significance of everyday actions; his holidays in northern Italy and Wales provided him with rich and glowing subjects. These have a freshness of colour, and innocence of feeling and vein of lyricism, which, though gentler and more subdued, stand in the direct line of descent from the ecstatic poetic landscapes of Edward Calvert and Samuel Palmer. His productions of landscapes in oil on a larger scale for the Royal Academy were not always so successful. Although the structure of the hilly escarpments and broad sketches of the Severn valley bathed in sunlight were realized with great fidelity, as in Tidal Severn and Mouth of Severn, his pictures were in fact open windows with the subject cut by the frame instead of being composed in relation to it. His paintings are in the collections of the Walker Art Gallery, Liverpool, the City of Birmingham Museum and Art Gallery, the Cheltenham Art Gallery and Museum, and the Tate collection. Throughout his long life he painted exquisite watercolour portraits of children.

Gere was a man of great personal charm and urbanity whose New England ancestry gave an austerity to his personality which strengthened the weight of his opinions. His level-headed kindliness of manner made him an excellent committee man and his advice was often sought by students and his many friends. He died, unmarried, at the Royal Hospital, Southgate Street, Gloucester, on 3 August 1957. As well as the family group entitled The Tennis Party, there is a self-portrait in the Cheltenham Art Gallery and Museum.   E. R. PAYNE, rev.

Sources personal knowledge (1971) • private information (2004) [C. Gere] • CGPLA Eng. & Wales (1957)

Likenesses F. Dodd, drypoint etching, 1927?, NPG • F. Dodd, pencil drawing, 1929, NPG • C. M. Gere, self-portrait, oils, c.1939, Cheltenham Art Gallery, Cheltenham • Lafayette, photograph, NPG

Wealth at death £17,409 16s. 7d.: probate, 31 Oct 1957, CGPLA Eng. & Wales

Geree, John (1599/1600–1649), Church of England clergyman, was born in Yorkshire. On 21 June 1616, aged sixteen, he matriculated from Magdalen Hall, Oxford, from where he graduated BA on 27 January 1619 and proceeded MA on 12 June 1621. Subsequently appointed rector of Tewkesbury, Gloucestershire, he became one of the prominent nonconformist ministers in the county. On 17 November 1631 he appeared before the court of high commission to answer the charge that his preaching was so powerful that Hickes, a churchwarden, 'threw himself into a well and drowned himself' (Gardiner, 244). Because of his continuing nonconformity, Geree was eventually suspended by Bishop Geoffrey Goodman in 1634. In 1637 he promised Goodman that he would leave the diocese for ever so the suspension was lifted, but he continued to preach from the pulpits of Nathaniel Wight, another Gloucestershire preacher, and Walter Fones, a curate of Tredington. He reportedly paid the latter £4 annually for the use of his pulpit, and this led Goodman to reinforce the suspension. It appears, however, that Geree remained active in the county and he is found supporting the nomination of a Mr Stephens of Sudbury for the elections to the Short Parliament of 1640. It was at this time that John Allibond observed his activities and in a letter to Peter Heylin he provides a physical description of Geree as 'the canny mumping fellow with the red head whom you sometime knew at Magdalen Hall, likewise suspended and deprived' (*CSP dom.*, 1639–40, 582).

Geree was restored to his living at Tewkesbury in 1641 by the Long Parliament's committee for religion. He immediately published *Judah's Joy* (1641) supporting the protestation, issued by parliament in the same year, which required all office holders in church and state to defend the true religion against popery and papist innovations. Attached to this work was Geree's reply to Henry Burton's *The Protestation Protested*, in which he defended the presbyterian position. In *Vindiciae ecclesiae Anglicanae* (1644) he argued against separatism. On 31 January 1645 he moved to the abbey church in St Albans and during this time he entered into controversy with his old friend John Tombes over the issue of infant baptism. This prompted him to publish not only *Vindiciae paedo-baptismi* (1646), but also the small tract *The Character of an Old English Puritane or Nonconformist* (1646), which presents a picture of pre-civil war puritanism as a movement of order and sobriety and one which accepted the importance of ecclesiastical and secular authority. The tract lays great stress on the spiritual and devotional activity of the 'old English puritan', at a time when the radical religious sects were appearing with their subversive doctrines. Despite his adherence to royal supremacy, Geree vehemently opposed the institution of episcopacy and, in one of his more famous tracts, *A Case of Conscience Resolved* (1646), urged the king that it was lawful for him to break his coronation oath and agree to its abrogation.

In 1647 Geree became involved in the London provincial assembly and was appointed moderator of the first classis, and in the same year received his first appointment in London as preacher of St Faith's under Paul's. During the proceedings of the treaty of Newport Geree was asked by William Gouge and Cornelius Burgess to preach in London a sermon on peace, which was subsequently published as *The Red Horse, or, The Bloodines of War* (1648). Following Colonel Pride's wholesale expulsion of MPs in 1648, Geree joined those who were preaching fiercely against the violation of parliament and, in a lengthy polemic, *Might Overcoming Right* (1649), he attacked John Goodwin, who was contending that the purge was necessary to secure England's liberties. The story is told by Richard Baxter that Geree died at the news of the king's death in 1649. Having made his will on 7 February, when he described himself as weak in body, he was buried in London later that month. Probate of his will was granted to his widow, Comfort, on 12 March; their two eldest daughters, Susanna and Comfort, were to receive land in Yorkshire.

Stephen Geree (1593/4–1664), Church of England clergyman and elder brother of John, was born in Yorkshire. On 22 November 1611, aged seventeen, he matriculated from Magdalen Hall, Oxford, where he graduated BA on 5 May 1615. He was instituted as vicar of Wonersh, Surrey, on 22 December 1629. Ten years later he preached there a funeral sermon for Elizabeth Macrell, subsequently published as *The Ornament of Women, or, A Description of the True Excellency of Women* (1639). His *The Doctrine of the Antinomians … Confuted* (1644) was a scorching attack on Tobias Crisp's theory on the doctrine of free grace. In 1645 Geree was appointed to the church of Holy Trinity in Guildford by the parliamentary commissioners but he never held the rectory. On 9 June 1646 he was examined by the Westminster assembly for his suitability to take up the cure of Abinger, Surrey, and was subsequently appointed. He was still there when he published in 1656 *The Golden Mean*, a work arguing 'for a more full, and frequent administration of, yet not free admission unto, the sacrament of the Lord's Supper'. He died in 1664 and was buried on 9 February in that year.   KENNETH GIBSON

Sources Foster, *Alum. Oxon.* · D. C. Beaver, *Parish communities and religious conflict in the vale of Gloucester* (1998) · S. R. Gardiner, *Reports of cases in the courts of star chamber and high commission*, CS, 39 (1886) · C. E. Surman, *The records of the provincial assembly of London, 1647–1660* (1957) · *CSP dom.*, 1639–40 · H. Denny, *A brief history of the parish church of St. James, Abinger* (1931) · H. E. Maden, 'Rectors and vicars of Surrey parishes', *Surrey Archaeological Collections*, 27 (1914), 88–102 · O. Manning and W. Bray, *The history and antiquities of the county of Surrey*, 2 (1809) · will, PRO, PROB 11/207, sig. 9
Wealth at death see will, PRO, PROB 11/207, sig. 9

Geree, Stephen (1593/4–1664). *See under* Geree, John (1599/1600–1649).

Gerhard, Roberto Juan Rene (1896–1970), composer, was born on 25 September 1896 in Valls, Catalonia, Spain, son of a Swiss-German father, a wine merchant by trade, and a French mother. His teenage years were spent in Germany and in Switzerland, where in 1908 he embarked on training for a career in commerce at the school in Zofingen at the insistence of his parents. He transferred to Neuchâtel three years later, but by 1913 he had switched to studying music with the Lausanne-based musician Hugo Strauss. At the outbreak of the First World War he was studying the piano at the Munich Academy and taking private composition lessons from Walter Courvoisier. Gerhard returned to the Catalonian capital of Barcelona in 1914 and continued his studies with his eminent countrymen Enrique Granados and Felipe Pedrell. In 1923 he was accepted as a pupil of Arnold Schoenberg, with whom he studied first

Roberto Juan Rene Gerhard (1896–1970), by Erich Auerbach, 1964

in Vienna and then at the Prussian Academy of Arts in Berlin.

Despite such an international approach to his academic studies, Gerhard was deeply committed to retaining, promoting, and developing a distinctive Catalan cultural identity. He returned to Barcelona in 1929 and in the following year married Leopoldina (Poldi) Fiechtegger (d. 1994), whom he had met in Vienna. In 1931 he was appointed professor of music at the Escola Normal de la Generalitat, Barcelona. By this time he was already a significant figure in the cultural life of Catalonia, promoting the works of Schoenberg, Anton Webern, and Hanns Eisler, with his own compositions promoted by the Associacio de Musica Catalana and a number of articles and translations published. His interests ranged across the arts, and in 1932 he co-founded the organization Amics de l'Art Nou (Friends of New Art) with Salvador Dalí, Lluis Montanya, and Sebastia Gasch. Gerhard was then appointed head of the music section at the Biblioteca de Catalunya in Barcelona, where he edited works by the eighteenth-century Spanish composers V. M. y Soler and D. M. B. Terradellas. From 1937 to 1938 he was adviser to the ministry of fine arts in the Catalan government and on the Central Musical Council of the republican government. The defeat of the republicans in 1938, while Gerhard was in Warsaw as a member of the jury of the International Society of Contemporary Music, precipitated his life as an émigré. He did not return home but instead took refuge with the painter Joan Miró (with whom he had collaborated on the ballet *Ariel* in 1934) and Josep Lluis Sert in Paris. In 1939 Gerhard secured a fellowship at King's College, Cambridge, thanks to the intervention of Professor Edward J. Dent. He subsequently made Cambridge his permanent home, accepting British citizenship in 1960.

Even after the move to Cambridge, Gerhard's works remained overtly nationalistic, being infused with Iberian folk melodies and rhythms; but his wider European experience had brought him into contact with serial techniques, and it is the fluctuation between Mediterranean ebullience and German tradition that makes them so distinctive. Neither of these qualities endeared him to the conservative musical establishment of Britain in the decade following the Second World War. The remarkable dodecaphonic operetta *The Duenna* (1945–7), which was not staged until 1992, and the ballet *Don Quixote* (1947–9) mark the peak of this nationalist period, after which his music became increasingly concerned with the abstract potential of sound. Described by the composer–conductor Antal Dorati as 'a very shy, retiring, modest man', Gerhard stayed on the periphery of Cambridge academic life, earning his income mainly through writing incidental music for thirty-eight theatre, radio, and television productions. In 1943 he also made several arrangements of popular Spanish music at the behest of the BBC Theatre Orchestra under the pseudonym Juan Serrallonga (the name of a seventeenth-century Catalan fighter against Castilian oppression).

Gerhard was an avid collector of sounds on tape and was described in *The Guardian* as 'a connoisseur of unfamiliar, delicious and unexpected sounds'. This talent, combined with his literary interests, produced spectacularly atmospheric scores for works by authors and playwrights as varied as Salvador de Madariaga, Cervantes, Albert Camus, Shakespeare, J. B. Priestley, Jean Rhys, Schiller, Wyndham Lewis, Lorca, Chekhov, Gogol, Hoffmansthal, Robert Graves, Hemingway, and Dorothy L. Sayers. Gerhard had met Edgar Varèse, the American pioneer of electronic music, in Catalonia in 1933. Working in a tiny studio in his new home in Cambridge, Gerhard became one of the first composers in Britain to experiment with taped sounds. In 1955 he composed an electronic score for Peter Brook's staging of *King Lear* in Stratford which no doubt contributed to the notoriety of this production. That he is not better known may perhaps be because such a significant proportion of his work is incidental music and therefore remains unpublished.

In the late 1950s Gerhard began to benefit from a decision by Sir William Glock, head of the Third Programme, to extend the patronage of the BBC to commissions for concert works. In an obituary of Gerhard, Glock stated:

> At present we are apt to seize on the high ratio of brilliance and sheer impetuous movement in his works, and on his instrumental mastery. The other qualities—of nobility, restraint, of a poetry which rejects any borrowed world of emotion and is itself severely disciplined in every chord, every progression—will grow on us. And perhaps the brilliance itself will be more deeply understood. (*The Listener*)

The freedom to try out new techniques of structure and orchestration in the incidental scores undoubtedly informed Gerhard's concert works, which develop groups of characteristic intervals into contrasting textural episodes. His music was criticized by contemporary critics for its lack of motivic development and for being merely a succession of cleverly balanced aural events. Perhaps this opinion is valid in some of the larger-scale orchestral works: the first two of the four symphonies, *Epithalamion*, and the concerto for piano. What is so striking and perturbing about Gerhard's compositions, however, is his ability to create radical sonic structures using serial means.

> Of all the atonal composers of stature, Roberto Gerhard … is the most likely to disarm the listener suspicious of serial techniques. His music has two characteristics immediately attractive to any audience—incisive wit and propulsive rhythmic drive, qualities either lacking in the works of the great Viennese atonalists or else so deeply embedded as to be imperceptible to the average listener.   (*The Guardian*)

Where this fusion of means undoubtedly works is in the single-movement compositions *Nonet* (1957), *Concert for Eight* (1962), *Hymnody* (1963), and *Concerto for Orchestra* (1965) and the three 'horoscope' pieces *Gemini* (1966), *Libra* (1968), and *Leo* (1969). Such innovative works still reveal their Catalan roots, however, with allusions to flamenco rhythms and guitar strumming. Most haunting, however, is the simple and beautiful folk-like clarinet tune that closes *Leo*, significantly named after Gerhard's own zodiacal sign and his last completed composition.

Gerhard was invited to the United States of America twice: in 1960 as visiting professor of composition at the University of Michigan, where he wrote his symphony no. 3 (*Collages*), and in 1961 as composition tutor at the Berkshire Music Center, Tanglewood, Massachusetts. He was made a CBE in 1967 and was awarded an honorary doctorate of music by the University of Cambridge and a fellowship of University College, London, in 1968. He died at his Cambridge home, 14 Madingley Road, on 5 January 1970.

A revival of nationalist interest in Catalonia in the post-Franco era and the opportunity for promoters to highlight Gerhard's music in the centenary year of his birth in 1996 has led to increased recognition and critical acclaim, as foretold by Sir William Glock. In 1992 *The Duenna* received a triumphant stage première at the Teatro Lírico Nacional in Madrid, at the Gran Teatre del Liceu in Barcelona, and subsequently on tour in the UK with the British company Opera North, all conducted by Antoni Ros Marbà. Many of the concert works are now available on quality commercial recordings, and the chamber pieces, especially the 'horoscope' trilogy, are in the repertory of many of the specialist contemporary music ensembles in Europe.

Gerhard's posthumous reputation is that of a composer who successfully wove together fragmenting elements of twentieth-century musical styles—nationalism, electronic music, new formal structures, new instrumentations—without ever resorting to the 'mix and match' of post-modernism. The music, like the composer's life, is eclectic and quixotic but drawn together by a vigorous intellectual coherence and integrity.

HELEN C. THOMAS

Sources www.roberto-gerhard.com [accessed 30 June 2001] • *New Grove*, vol. 7 • programme book, Schoenberg–Gerhard concert series, London Sinfonietta (1973) • D. Drew, *MT*, 111 (1970) • C. Mason, 'Roberto Gerhard', *Music in Britain* (spring 1965) • 'Roberto Gerhard: a survey', *Tempo*, 139 (Dec 1981) • J. Homs, *Roberto Gerhard and his music* (2000) • A. Orga, 'Roberto Gerhard', *Music and Musicians* (Oct 1970), 36–62 • *The Guardian* (21 Oct 1964) • d. cert. • *CGPLA Eng. & Wales* (1970) • *The Listener* (12 Feb 1970)

Archives Bodl. Oxf., Society for Protection of Science and Learning, corresp. • CUL, corresp. and papers

Likenesses E. Auerbach, photographs, 1946, Hult. Arch. • E. Auerbach, photograph, 1964, NPG [*see illus.*] • Y. Sonnabend, pencil and charcoal drawing, 1965, NPG

Wealth at death £2109: administration with will, 5 March 1970, *CGPLA Eng. & Wales*

Gerhardie, William Alexander (1895–1977), novelist, was born at St Petersburg, Russia, on 21 November 1895, the fifth of six children (one son died in childhood) of Charles Alfred Gerhardi (1864–1925), a British industrialist settled in Russia, and his wife, Clara Annie (1869–1948), daughter of John Wadsworth.

William Gerhardi, their youngest son, was educated at the Sankt Annenschule and Reformierte Schule in St Petersburg from 1906 until 1912. He was sent to London to train for a commercial career, either in banking or by way of marrying a rich bride. These plans, and his own dreams of taking by storm the London theatre with a melodrama, *The Haunting Roubles*, were interrupted by the First World War in which, as a trooper, he joined the Royal Scots Greys. To improve his English he had been studying Oscar Wilde, arriving at the cavalry barracks in York with an elegant cane, languid expression, and longish hair under a bowler hat. He applied for a commission and was posted to the staff of the British embassy in Petrograd (1916–18) and, having provided himself with an enormous sword bought second-hand in Charing Cross Road in London, was greeted as an old campaigner. From Petrograd he observed—through a monocle—several stages of the Russian Revolution which was to ruin his father, who, escaping to Bolton in Lancashire hidden in a barrel, owed his life to being identified as the famous British socialist Keir Hardie. In 1918 Gerhardi was attached to the Scots Guards and sent on the British military mission in Siberia, being demobilized two years later, retaining the rank of captain. He was made an OBE, and awarded the order of St Stanislav of Imperial Russia and the Czechoslovak war cross.

After travelling round the world, Gerhardi went to Worcester College, Oxford. There he obtained a BA (shortened course, in Russian, 1922), wrote a book on Anton Chekhov (1923), and his first novel, *Futility* (1922), which was sponsored in Britain by Katherine Mansfield, who found a publisher for it, and in the United States by Edith Wharton, who wrote an introduction. The critical acclaim he gained with this novel on Russian themes increased after the publication of his next novel, *The Polyglots* (1925), which remained the most celebrated of his books and was described by Anthony Powell as 'a classic'.

Over the next fifteen years Gerhardi was prolific. Among his best fiction were *Pretty Creatures* (1927), a collection of short stories; *Pending Heaven* (1930), a novel based on his friendship with the writer Hugh Kingsmill; *Resurrection* (1934), a complex and ambitious semi-autobiographical book that uses an occult experience as an illustration of future life; and *Of Mortal Love* (1936), a novel charting the progress of love erotic into love imaginative, which was based on his attachment to Vera

Boys, in whose divorce he had been named as co-respondent.

Up to the early 1930s Gerhardi had travelled widely through Europe, India, and the United States. In 1931, at the age of thirty-five, he published his autobiography, *Memoirs of a Polyglot*, and moved into a flat in Rossetti House, in Hallam Street behind Broadcasting House in London, where he lived for the rest of his life. His last book published in his lifetime was *The Romanovs* (1940), a massive and unorthodox study of the Russian dynasty. In 1942 he joined the BBC, first as a sub-editor in the Czechoslovak section, then as a scriptwriter for its European productions. The following year he helped to start English by Radio, a project which eventually fell 'just short of fatuous', the cheerful vacuity of which left him feeling bewildered and helpless. On 31 March 1945 he resigned, returning with relief to a solitary life of contemplation and literary work.

During the 1920s Gerhardi had been one of the most talked about literary figures of his day. H. G. Wells roared his praises; Arnold Bennett called him a genius; Evelyn Waugh acknowledged having learned 'a great deal of [his] trade from [Gerhardi's] novels'. He was taken up by Lord Beaverbrook, who makes several bows in his work as Lord Ottercove and whom he attempted to repay with a written invitation to collaborate on a musical comedy. His novels of the 1930s, which, Graham Greene wrote, 'fulfil all the fine promise of his earlier books and showed him to be a poet as well as a wit', indicate that his chief literary influence had passed from Chekhov to Marcel Proust: from the comic agonies of procrastination to the imaginative power of time regained. It was perhaps as a symbol of this preoccupation with the past that he reverted to an ancestral spelling of his name by adding an 'e' to Gerhardi. This name appears for the first time on the title-pages of the second collected edition (in ten volumes) of his work issued from 1970 to 1974. Although his reputation has declined since those heady days between the wars, the intermittent reprintings and translations of *Futility* and *The Polyglots*, and the publication of an excellent biography by Dido Davies (1990), have ensured that his name is not forgotten.

Over the last thirty-seven years of his life Gerhardi lived in increasing obscurity, a hermit in the West End of London, his only link with the outside world a telephone line and the remembrance of things past. Although his entry in *Who's Who* lengthened fantastically over these years and, in 1975, he was made a fellow of the Royal Society of Literature, he published no new book—merely broadcasting occasionally, writing a few essays (of which the most interesting is 'My literary credo', appearing at the beginning of the 1947 edition of *Futility*), and experimenting with various unpromising plays with promising titles (such as *English Measles* and *The Private Life of a Public Nuisance*). He was rumoured to have long been at work on another novel, a tetralogy entitled 'This present breath', the two concluding chapters of which, Gerhardie-style, had been published in Neville Braybrooke's *The Wind and the Rain* (1962). But after he died, in the Middlesex Hospital, London, on 15 July 1977, though he had left an astonishingly elaborate card index for a work of fiction, no consecutive narrative was uncovered, and, it was concluded, there was no novel. Instead, an original work of non-fiction in several drafts was found, a biography of the age 1890–1940 called *God's Fifth Column*, which plotted the view of men of action versus men of imagination over this period. This was edited for publication by Michael Holroyd and Robert Skidelsky and published posthumously (1981). The scattering of his ashes in Regent's Park in London by a ramshackle band of his admirers, including the novelists Olivia Manning and J. G. Farrell, as well as the founder and director of the Foundation for Business Responsibilities, and a strip-tease dancer reputed to be writing a thesis on his work, enriched the meaning of the word Gerhardiesque.   MICHAEL HOLROYD

Sources W. Gerhardie, *Memoirs of a polyglot* (1931) · D. Davies, *William Gerhardie: a biography* (1990) · B. Gunnarsson, *The novels of William Gerhardie* (1995) · *The revised definitive edition of the works of William Gerhardie*, [8 vols.] (1970–74) [prefaces by M. Holroyd] · personal knowledge (2004) **Archives** CUL, corresp. and papers | BBC WAC, corresp. with BBC staff · HLRO, corresp. with Lord Beaverbrook · University of Bristol Library, Penguin Books files | FILM 'Arena', BBC2 film portrait, 1971 · film portrait by Kenneth Tynan's Tempo, c.1965 | SOUND BL NSA, recording of a film portrait of him, BBC2 'Arena' series, 1971 **Likenesses** Bianca, princess of Loewenstein, sculptured bust, priv. coll. · Fergusson, drawing, repro. in *Financial Times* (21 April 1990) · photograph, repro. in *The Independent* (21 April 1990) · photograph, repro. in *London Review of Books* (24 May 1990), 9 · photograph, repro. in *The Spectator* (28 April 1990), 24 · photographs, repro. in Gerhardie, *Memoirs*, facing p. 353 · photographs, repro. in Davies, *William Gerhardie* **Wealth at death** £13,133: probate, 27 Sept 1977, *CGPLA Eng. & Wales*

Gérin [*née* Bourne; *other married name* Lock], **Winifred Eveleen** (1901–1981), biographer, was born on 7 October 1901 in Hamburg, Germany, the youngest of four children of Frederick Charles Bourne, director of Nobel's Chemical Industries, and his wife, Katherine Hill. Upon their return to England Winifred was raised in South Norwood, London, and educated at Sydenham High School for Girls in Croydon. Her mother had studied music in Hamburg and both parents encouraged artistic expression in their children. Winifred played the piano, sang (later with the London Philharmonic Choir), and wrote poetry; her sister, Nell Bourne, became a painter. At the age of nineteen Winifred entered Cambridge, graduating from Newnham College in 1923 with a degree in English and modern languages. She was fluent in French, German, and Spanish. Her romantic nature took her to Paris, where she began writing poetry, and in 1930 she published her first volume, *The Invitation to Parnassus*. In Paris she met Eugène Gérin (1897–1945), a Belgian poet, who was a professional cellist with the Monte Carlo Symphony. They were married in Croydon, England, in September 1932. At the beginning of the war they were trapped in France for two years, during which time they courageously helped refugees escape. For the remainder of the war, they worked in political intelligence in London. Eugène Gérin died in 1945 at the age of forty-eight.

From 1945 until 1955 Winifred Gérin lived with her sister, Nell, in Kensington, London. She turned to playwriting and wrote seven plays; the most significant, *My Dear Master* (staged in Leeds in 1955), focused on Charlotte Brontë's attachment to her Belgian tutor, M. Heger. Winifred had very early been drawn to the Brontës, their untameable spirits, and the 'illimitable moors' of their Haworth landscape (W. Gérin, *Charlotte Brontë*, 1967, xvi). One of her earliest recollections was of her mother reading *Jane Eyre* to her. On a visit to Haworth in 1954 she met John Lock (1918/19–1998), who was writing a biography of Patrick Brontë, and in October 1955 they were married in London. For the next ten years they lived in Haworth, where they bought a house on the edge of the Haworth Moor within sight of the Brontë parsonage and began their lifelong work on the Brontës. Developing an intimate familiarity with the subject's landscape became a significant aspect of Gérin's biographical credo. As she declared in her first biography, *Anne Brontë* (1959), she hoped that 'By such close contacts has something of the spirit of that family and of this place … enter[ed] into the composition of this book' (p. viii).

Winifred Gérin is known as the biographer of the Brontës. Between 1959 and 1971 she published individual biographies on the four famous Brontë children. Following *Anne Brontë*, the first full-length biography to appear on Anne, was *Branwell Brontë* (1961). *Charlotte Brontë: the Evolution of Genius* (1967) is Gérin's most accomplished work and she herself thought it her best, most rounded biography. The trademarks of her approach, empathy for her subject and extensive research into her subject's physical and cultural landscape, were brought to fulfilment in this biography. Her move to Oxford University Press necessitated a more scholarly style, but she was still criticized for her use of the Brontë fiction as a biographical resource and for her 'sensational approach', which she defended as a deliberate technique for creating necessary 'warmth' for the subject (Oxford University Press archives). *Charlotte Brontë* was highly distinguished by three major awards: the James Tait Black memorial prize for the best biography of the year; the Royal Society of Literature Heinemann prize for English literature; and the Rose Mary Crawshay prize for English literature. It became the standard biography on Charlotte Brontë for over twenty years and remains a respected source.

Of all the Brontës, Emily was Gérin's favourite, and it was her picture which hung over the fireplace in her home. Like Emily, Gérin had a passionate interest in literature and art and, as John Lock noted, a 'mystical love of nature' (private information). Gérin felt, though, that Emily's mysticism had been overplayed in previous biographies and offered a more balanced portrait, showing, as well, her womanly, practical self. *Emily Brontë* (1971) remains the most popular of her Brontë biographies. Her commitment to Brontë studies is evidenced by her edition

of five of Charlotte Brontë's early fictional pieces (*Five Novelettes*, 1971), her introductions to Elizabeth Gaskell's *Life of Charlotte Brontë* (1971) and Anne Brontë's *The Tenant of Wildfell Hall* (1979), and her lectures on the Brontës and their influences.

Gérin's other biographies include *The Young Fanny Burney* (1961), a slim novelistic biography written for teens, and *Horatia Nelson* (1970), written in an attempt to break out of her Brontë mould. With *Elizabeth Gaskell: a Biography* (1976), which won the Whitbread literary award for biography, and *Anne Thackeray Ritchie: a Biography* (1981), published just prior to her death, she returned to figures associated with the Brontës and to personalities warm and enthusiastic like her own. Her biographies, noted for their considerable research, are personalized by an expressivist style. The words she chose, in her final biography, to describe Anne Thackeray Ritchie can equally be ascribed to herself: 'She brought to her portraits of the well-known faces a new expression that her kindling enthusiasm could alone call up' (p. viii).

For her contributions to Brontë research and to the field of biography Gérin received two notable distinctions: she was made a fellow of the Royal Society of Literature in 1968 and in 1975 an OBE. During the last few years of her life, she carried on energetically, overcoming the effects of an earlier stroke, and devotedly looking after her ailing sister. Winifred Gérin died of a stroke at her London home, 2 Marlborough Court, Pembroke Road, Kensington, on 28 June 1981. Her remains were cremated on 7 July at Kensal Green crematorium. BARBARA MITCHELL

Sources B. Mitchell, 'Winifred Gérin', *Twentieth-century British literary biographers*, ed. S. Serafin, DLitB, 155 (1995), 96–105 · DNB · private information (2004) [John Lock; Irene Lock] · Oxford University Press, archives, Winifred Gérin MSS · J. M. P., 'Winifred Gerin', *Newnham College Roll Letter* (1983), 55–6 · WWW, 1981–90 [Gérin, Winifred Eveleen (Mrs John Lock)] · *The Times* (1 July 1981) · *Brontë Society Transactions*, 18 (1981)

Archives CUL, letters to G. E. Moore · Oxford University Press, Winifred Gérin MSS

Likenesses photographs, 1955–81, *Keighley News* offices, Keighley, Yorkshire, Gérin file · photographs, Royal Society of Literature, London

Wealth at death £157,656: probate, 6 Nov 1981, CGPLA Eng. & Wales

Germain [*née* Berkeley], **Lady Elizabeth** [Betty] (1680–1769), courtier and art collector, was the second daughter in the family of four sons and three daughters of Charles Berkeley, second earl of Berkeley (1649–1710), and his wife, Elizabeth (*d.* 1719), daughter of Baptist *Noel, third Viscount Campden (*bap.* 1611, *d.* 1682). She spent her childhood at Berkeley Castle, Gloucestershire. Lady Betty's friendship with the satirist Jonathan Swift began when Berkeley went to Ireland as a lord justice in 1699, taking Swift with him as chaplain and secretary. Swift spent much of his time in Dublin Castle with the family, playing cards, and reading aloud to Lady Betty. Nearly thirty years later, in a letter to Swift (19 September 1730), she recalled a line of a poem which he had written in Ireland in 1701, 'The Humble Petition of Frances Harris':

Lord help me, said Mary, I never stirred out of this place!
Nay, said I, I had it in Lady Betty's Chamber, that's a plain
   Case.
(J. Swift, *The Poems of Jonathan Swift*, ed. H. Williams, 2nd edn,
1958, 1.70)

Swift returned to England with Berkeley in 1701. During his visit to Berkeley Castle in 1702 Lady Betty added a final stanza to a poem he was writing, 'A Ballad on the Game of Traffick':

With these is Parson Swift,
Not knowing how to spend his time,
Does make a wretched shift,
To deafen 'em with puns and rhime.
(ibid., 1.75)

Lady Betty Berkeley was a lady-in-waiting to Queen Anne in the years before her marriage to Sir John *Germain (1650–1718), a Dutch soldier and gambler rumoured to be the illegitimate son of Prince William II of Orange (and hence half-brother of King William III). Germain had moved to England in 1688; he fought in William III's campaigns in Holland and Flanders, and received a baronetcy in 1698. His first wife, Lady Mary Mordaunt, daughter and heir of the second earl of Peterborough, had died childless in 1705, leaving her family estates, including the manor of Drayton, in Northamptonshire, to her husband. Germain met Lady Betty while she was taking the waters at Bristol Hotwells in the company of her cousin Lionel Sackville, earl (later duke) of Dorset, and his future wife, the daughter of Lieutenant-General Walter Colyear, an old friend of Germain's from the Dutch service. Sir John and Lady Betty were married in 1706, and although they had three children, two sons and a daughter, all died in childhood. Charles, third earl of Peterborough, the second earl's nephew, who had inherited the title, disputed Germain's ownership of Drayton, but withdrew his lawsuit when Germain died in 1718, leaving Drayton to Lady Betty.

On his deathbed Germain asked Lady Betty to remarry and have children who could inherit the property, but she remained a widow, spending the rest of her life with the duke and duchess of Dorset at Knole, in Kent, where she had her own apartments. She made occasional visits to Drayton, where she kept up the old house and the formal Dutch gardens created by her husband exactly as they had been in his lifetime. She redecorated the chapel in 1725, and according to tradition many of the beeches in the park came from seedlings from Knole. A collection of oriental china begun by Sir John Germain and continued by Lady Betty was kept at Drayton. It included a few examples from the Ming dynasty, but was mainly Chinese porcelain from the Kangxi period, including celadon vases, a collection of small *blanc-de-Chine* figures, decorated blue and white vases, a set of tall cobalt jars decorated with gold, and a vase decorated with a panel containing baskets of flowers in *famille verte* colours. In 1763 Horace Walpole described Drayton as 'covered with portraits, crammed with old china, furnished richly' (*Letters*, 4.100). Lady Betty also maintained a London house in St James's Square, where she entertained politicians of all parties.

Lady Betty Germain continued her friendship with Swift, who dined with her frequently on his visits to England, and there are several references in his *Journal to Stella* to heated political discussions: 'Lady Betty Germain and I were disputing Whig and Tory to death this morning' (17 October 1711), and 'I have been so teased with Whiggish discourse by … Lady Betty Germain' (19 November 1711) (Swift, *Journal*, 2.385–6, 417). During the 1730s Swift, in Ireland, and Lady Betty exchanged many letters, a correspondence started by Swift in the hopes of her using her influence on his behalf. In 1733 they disagreed violently over the character of Henrietta Howard, countess of Suffolk, the mistress of George II and a close friend of Lady Betty, whose brother Lord George Berkeley she later married. Swift disliked the countess mainly because she did nothing for him. The correspondence continued to be acrimonious at times—'My Lady Elizabeth Germain uses me very ill in her letters' wrote Swift to the duke of Dorset on 15 April 1735 (*Correspondence of Jonathan Swift*, 4.324)— and stopped altogether in 1737. But Lady Betty remained fond of Swift, and a portrait of him which belonged to her still hangs in her apartments at Knole.

Lady Betty Germain died on 16 December 1769 at her house in St James's Square, London, and was buried at Lowick in Northamptonshire. In accordance with her husband's wishes that in the absence of an heir she should leave her property to a younger son of the duke of Dorset, she left Drayton House to Lord George Sackville, the duke's youngest son, together with £20,000 and half the residue of her wealth, on condition that he change his name to Germain; this he did by act of parliament in 1770. She left most of the rest of her estate to her niece Lady Vere.

ANNE PIMLOTT BAKER

Sources *The correspondence of Jonathan Swift*, ed. H. Williams, 5 vols. (1963–5) · I. Ehrenpreis, *Swift: the man, his works and the age*, 3 vols. (1962–83) · V. Sackville-West, *Knole and the Sackvilles* (1922) · C. J. Phillips, *History of the Sackville family*, 2 [1930], 183–7 · G. Jackson-Stops, *Drayton House, Northamptonshire* (1978) · V. Glendinning, *Jonathan Swift* (1998) · J. Swift, *Journal to Stella*, ed. H. Williams, 2 vols. (1948) · *The letters of Horace Walpole, earl of Orford*, ed. P. Cunningham, 9 vols. (1857–9) · N. W. Wraxall, *Historical memoirs of my own time*, 2nd edn, 2 (1815), 576–80 · *GM*, 1st ser., 39 (1769), 609 · HoP, *Commons, 1715–54* · Burke, *Peerage* (1931) · B. Burke, *A genealogical history of the dormant, abeyant, forfeited and extinct peerages of the British empire*, new edn (1866) · *VCH Northamptonshire*, 3.231–43 · *Ninth report*, 3, HMC, 8 (1884) [Mrs Stopford Sackville MSS; incl. letters to and from Lady Betty Germain] · *DNB*
Likenesses C. Philips, oils, 1731, Knole, Kent · D'Agar, portrait, Drayton House, Northamptonshire · W. Hoare, pastels, Knole, Kent · G. Kneller, portrait, Drayton House, Northamptonshire
Wealth at death £120,000; also Drayton House; china collection; collection of gems: *DNB*

Germain, George Sackville [*formerly* George Sackville], **first Viscount Sackville (1716–1785)**, army officer and politician, was born on 26 January 1716 at his father's house in the Haymarket, Westminster, the third and youngest son of Lionel Cranfield Sackville, seventh earl and first duke of Dorset (1688–1765), and his wife, Elizabeth (1687–1768), the daughter of Lieutenant-General Walter Colyear.

Early life and career Sackville was educated at Westminster School and at Trinity College, Dublin (BA 1733, MA

George Sackville Germain, first Viscount Sackville (1716–1785), by Thomas Gainsborough, c.1783–5

his middle thirties, with clear blue eyes, a prominent nose, and a protruding lower lip. On 3 September 1754 he married Diana (1730/31–1778), the second daughter and coheir of John Sambroke and the niece of Sir Jeremy Sambroke. They had two sons and three daughters; the eldest son, Charles (b. 1767), eventually succeeded to Sackville's viscountcy and in 1815 to the Dorset dukedom. Diana died of measles on 15 January 1778.

With war again approaching, Sackville was promoted major-general with the command of a brigade at Chatham. He developed about now political links with the court of George, prince of Wales (later George III), at Leicester House, and seemed a certain candidate for high office in the next reign. Although George II resented his attachment to the rival court and refused Pitt's wish to appoint him secretary at war, Pitt nevertheless made him lieutenant-general of the ordnance, thereby adding a skilful speaker to the ministry and giving Leicester House a stake in the government.

After sitting on the board which reported unfavourably on Sir John Mordaunt's conducting of the Rochefort expedition in 1757, Sackville took part the following year in the raid led by Charles Spencer, third duke of Marlborough, on St Malo. It was a fiasco, and the disgusted Sackville vowed that he would go buccaneering no more, and applied to Pitt to be sent as second in command to Marlborough with an expedition which a change of strategy was embarking for Germany.

The Minden scandal The expedition landed in the Ems in August 1758 and marched to join the German forces defending Hanover. In October Marlborough's unexpected death at Münster left Sackville in command of the British contingent. His supremo, Prince Ferdinand of Brunswick, was a field marshal in the Prussian service with a distinguished record. His royal blood qualified him for the international command, and, though he wrote to Frederick the Great in French, he corresponded regularly with George II in German. If he fell out with his British general, the king would not support Sackville; and Sackville's impatient temperament and arrogant manner would not promote easy relations.

Some friction soon arose, though Sackville praised Ferdinand's professional skills. But the decisive collision did not occur until the battle of Minden, on 1 August 1759. Ferdinand, whose confidence had been shaken by a severe reverse at Bergen in April, faced a critical situation to which he responded at first with hesitation. However, prompted by his chief of staff, he devised a daring plan to lure the French out of their unassailable position and attack them. For the coming operation the British contingent was split, and, while Sackville commanded the cavalry of the right wing (twenty-four squadrons, of which ten were German), his six battalions of British infantry were in the neighbouring column commanded by General Spörcken.

Ferdinand's written instructions were no more than a bare order of march and his secret plan immediately began to miscarry. Delayed intelligence allowed the French to occupy part of his intended line of deployment.

1734). On 23 April 1737 he was appointed clerk to the council in Dublin and in July 1737 captain in Lord Cathcart's horse (later the 6th dragoon guards). In 1740 he was promoted lieutenant-colonel of the 28th foot (Bragg's). The following year he was returned to parliament for Dover, the borough for which he sat continuously until 1761 (his father being lord warden of the Cinque Ports).

In April 1743 Bragg's embarked for the war in Flanders. Sackville appears to have been present at the battle of Dettingen, and a few days later, on 27 June 1743, he was appointed one of George II's aides-de-camp. At Fontenoy on 11 May 1745 he was shot in the breast while advancing with his regiment, which he commanded. On news of the Jacobite rising Bragg's was ordered home, and Sackville's commander-in-chief, the duke of Cumberland, wrote that he was sorry to lose him, as he had 'not only shown his courage, but a disposition to his trade which I do not always find in those of higher rank' (DNB). Bragg's was sent to Ireland, but on 9 April 1746 Sackville was appointed colonel of the 20th foot, which he joined at Inverness just after the battle of Culloden. After returning to Flanders in 1747, he was sent in 1748 by Cumberland on a mission to the French commander Marshal Saxe. Following the peace of 1748 he was transferred to the colonelcy of the 12th dragoons and then to the 3rd dragoon guards. Of his leaving the 20th, Major James Wolfe commented that, with one exception, 'no possible successor can in any measure make amends for his loss' (ibid.).

His father now resumed the lord lieutenancy of Ireland, and Sackville re-entered Irish politics as a contentious chief secretary. He was by now a tall, rather heavy man in

On the right Sackville advanced in good order at the head of his 3300 horse and deployed in front of the hamlet of Hahlen, which was already in enemy hands, while infantry pickets prepared to clear it. His right was secured by marshland, while on his left a long belt of woodland at a right angle to the front hid the rest of the army from his view. Moreover the wood was impassable for cavalry in tactical order, except opposite his second line, commanded by John Manners, marquess of Granby. Sackville had been led by Ferdinand to expect that he was to advance beyond Hahlen until he was clear of the wood and to form in the Minden plain, possibly behind allied infantry.

In the meantime Ferdinand, beyond the wood, had been disconcerted by the sight of the British infantry suddenly advancing towards the enemy. Anticipating disaster, he ordered Captain Winzingerode to fetch Sackville's cavalry, which he intended to form in support behind the infantry. What Winzingerode said to Sackville was later disputed, but he used the word 'advance'; Sackville assumed that the cavalry were to march to their front, as he had been led to expect. A flank march to their left seemed improbable: it would expose the right flank of the army and throw the cavalry into confusion as they threaded their way through the trees. It was later alleged that Granby began to move the second line to his left but was stopped by Sackville; in fact he had begun to close his line towards the front as if preparing to advance.

By now Ferdinand's situation was changing. The French cavalry had charged Spörcken's infantry and had been shattered by their volleys, and there was an opportunity for Sackville's cavalry to complete the destruction. Ferdinand sent off Captain Edward Ligonier to hasten the cavalry. Again the orders delivered were ambiguous, and Sackville set the cavalry in motion towards their front. Ligonier maintained that he rode alongside Sackville and told him he was meant to march to his left; but Sackville and his staff denied that they had heard him. At this moment there appeared an excited and breathless youth of twenty-two, Colonel Charles Fitzroy, who told Sackville he was to move the *British* cavalry to his left. To divide the cavalry in face of the superior enemy cavalry made no sense. Neither Fitzroy nor Ligonier could say which of them had brought the latest order.

Eventually Sackville rode off through the wood to speak to Ferdinand, and the British cavalry followed. But the opportunity had passed. The French were in full retreat to their strong original positions, and it was too late to achieve much more. Nevertheless Sackville's deliberate pace, halting frequently to correct his 1300 yard line, failed to rise to the occasion.

Ferdinand's revenge was both cunning and shabby. In a general order after the battle he declared that, if Granby had commanded the cavalry of the right wing, the victory would have been more complete. Thus, without complaining to the British government, he made Sackville's position untenable. He refused Sackville's appeal for a hearing and suggested unfairly that the latter's tactical responsibility in the battle had included his British infantry, which had formed part of a separate column commanded by a German general. 'I never knew anything so unfair, so unjust, and I must say so wicked', wrote Sackville (Mackesy, *The Coward of Minden*, 149). It was impossible for him to lie low and wait for the cloud to pass. His disgrace was public, his position undermined. He sent home an aide-de-camp with a letter of resignation to the king, to be delivered only on the advice of John Stuart, earl of Bute, the leader of the Leicester House connection. At the same time Sackville attempted to vindicate himself in the army, which allowed Ferdinand to demand his dismissal.

Sackville relied on Leicester House to protect him, but his decision to serve in Germany had offended their bluewater strategic principles. Before Ferdinand's complaint reached the king, Bute had passed on Sackville's letter of resignation to the ministry, which rapidly decided that Sackville's was an unpopular cause. He was sent leave to come home, and arrived in London on 7 September, five weeks after the battle, to find that he was the current hate-object of the press. London was flooded with pamphlets accusing him of crimes ranging from cowardice to sodomy. The only way to establish the truth was by court martial, which he demanded with the conviction that it would clear him. The ministry prevaricated, while the king dismissed him from all his military appointments by royal prerogative, a dubious procedure for which the only precedent was the disreputable dismissal of Richard Temple, Viscount Cobham, by Walpole in 1733.

The ministers enquired whether Sackville, now a civilian, could still be tried by court martial, and for a military offence committed outside the king's dominions. The law officers pronounced that it was lawful in the case of a capital offence; and the ministers resorted to another delaying tactic, asking Sackville to name the capital charge for which he wished to be tried. Sackville stood firm, demanding to know of what Ferdinand had accused him; rather than give him free rein to attack Ferdinand outside the control of a courtroom, the cabinet issued a warrant on 26 January 1760 to try him for disobedience.

The trial opened before fourteen generals on 29 February, and on 5 April the verdict and sentence were agreed. Sackville was found guilty of disobedience, which vindicated Ferdinand. But what was the sentence? The popular guess was death; but the prime minister, Newcastle, feared embarrassment. The king had indicated that he would confirm a death sentence—and he had allowed Admiral John Byng to be shot three years earlier in spite of the court's unanimous recommendation of mercy. Sackville's judges avoided that risk by a sentence which affirmed that the king's dismissal of Sackville had been justified, yet came as close as possible to an acquittal. He was 'adjudged to be unfit to serve his Majesty in any military capacity whatever' (*DNB*). 'Unfit' did not even amount to 'incapable', the usual wording. The trial had come close to justifying Sackville, and it had established a verbatim record by which others could judge him.

Rehabilitation The king did everything in his power to humiliate the victim. He personally struck Sackville's name from the list of privy councillors and had the fact reported in the *London Gazette*; and he had the sentence published in army orders and read out on parade—an unprecedented act except in the case of a flogging or execution. An embellishment to the order, condemned as unjust by a later lord chancellor, reflected on 'censures much worse than death to a man who has any sense of honour' (*DNB*).

Sackville resumed his place in society and in the House of Commons. Six months after the sentence was announced George II died, but Sackville's reinstatement in public office had to wait for the end of the war in 1763 and the reshaping of politics in the new reign. In 1765 he was given the lucrative post of vice-treasurer of Ireland in the Rockingham ministry and was restored to the privy council. In 1770 he assumed the surname Germain under the provisions of the will of Lady Elizabeth Germain, who had left him a fortune and the estate of Drayton in Northamptonshire, and in December that year he demonstrated personal courage in a pistol duel with 'Governor' George Johnstone, who had insulted him in the Commons.

Lord North formed his ministry in 1770, and Germain, shaking loose from the Rockingham clique, proved his usefulness to the new ministry with speeches described by Horace Walpole as 'full of pith, matter, irony and satire' (Mackesy, *The Coward of Minden*, 250). As the American crisis intensified he allied himself with the hardliners, and in November 1775, a few months after the outbreak of fighting, he was appointed secretary of state for the American colonies.

The office was of recent origin. Germain's two predecessors had not been regarded as secretaries of state in the full sense but had been confined to colonial matters. Germain was given parity with the secretaries for the northern and southern departments, as 'one of his Majesty's Principal Secretaries of State'. This status was crucial, for the secretaries of state exercised a general authority outside their departmental responsibilities, issuing instructions to execute cabinet decisions. In wartime this was especially significant. Germain, in the absence of forceful secretaries in the other departments, provided the will and the force to impart momentum to cabinet war plans. The elder Pitt had performed the role in harness with Newcastle at the Treasury; Germain was to perform it in harness with the unwarlike North. As American secretary he had direct responsibility for operations in the North American and West Indian theatres, but he also had constitutional authority to co-ordinate the work of the Admiralty and the Navy Board, of the slothful Board of Ordnance, of the army departments, and of the Treasury. He became the driving force in the execution of global strategy.

Directing the global war Germain's rehabilitation was complete, and, although his opponents harassed him in the house with gibes about Minden, he remained firmly in office until 1782. He had not proved himself as a tactical commander in the field, but his gifts perhaps fitted him better for the higher direction of war. In Germany his strategic grasp and administrative drive had had to be subordinated to maintaining good relations with the German supremo, but at Westminster these qualities quickly showed their worth. Germain's under-secretary Richard Cumberland was immediately impressed by his precision and clarity, his unequivocal instructions, and his punctuality.

Germain has been blamed for interfering in far-off military operations, undermining the autonomy of theatre commanders. He certainly recognized the problem. 'The distance from the seat of government necessarily leaves much to the discretion and resources of the General', he had recently observed (Marlow, 175). His problem was the political weakness of the ministry, which inhibited it from replacing failed commanders. Only when Howe and Carleton had failed him and Clinton had shown his irresolution did Germain begin to press operational plans on his generals.

The strategy which Germain inherited, and approved, was to strike with large forces from New York and the St Lawrence in order to control the Hudson valley and thus isolate the supposed heart of rebellion in New England. This aim was sustained through two campaigning seasons, until John Burgoyne's capitulation at Saratoga in October 1777 and the consequent intervention of France.

The first evidence of Germain's energy was the assembling in harsh winter weather of a small relieving force for Quebec, besieged by Richard Montgomery and Benedict Arnold. The expedition was got away on 22 February 1776, and its arrival saved British Canada. In the meantime preparations were driven on for the major expeditions which in the summer of 1776 brought 10,000 British and German reinforcements to Sir Guy Carleton in Canada and 16,000 to Lord Howe near New York—an administrative achievement across 3000 miles of ocean on a scale without previous parallels. The failure to reach a decision in 1776, after initial successes on both fronts, was due more to failings on the part of the generals than to flaws in the strategic concept. The same is true of the disastrous campaign of 1777. Howe diverted his major effort from the Hudson to the Chesapeake, leaving Burgoyne, advancing from Canada, to be trapped on the upper Hudson. There is no truth in Lord Shelburne's allegation that Germain had failed to inform Howe of Burgoyne's intentions.

The intervention of France in the spring of 1778 expanded the colonial rebellion into a global war. Spain joined France in 1779, to be followed by the Netherlands in 1780, and fighting on land and sea spread to the Caribbean, Florida, and Honduras, and even to India, while England itself was threatened with invasion. From America troops were transferred to the West Indies, where much of the subsequent conflict was fought, and for the next two years the American theatres stagnated without reinforcements, while the battles for maritime command and the mastery of the sugar islands were decided.

But in 1780 Germain initiated a new phase of the

American struggle. He had learned from the opening campaigns that containing George Washington's continental army was not enough to secure victory. Reoccupied territory had still to be consolidated in the face of rebel militias and guerrillas. Hitherto, when the British regulars moved on from reoccupied areas, the rebels had been able to reassert their control. Germain's new concept required Henry Clinton at New York to neutralize the continental army on the Hudson, while the colonies were successively reoccupied and then consolidated by systematic counter-insurgent warfare, using organized loyalist militias and fortified villages to protect the inhabitants and flying columns to hunt down guerrilla bands.

The experiment began in the south, with the capture of Charles Town in May 1780, and expanded northwards under Charles, second Earl Cornwallis, until all Georgia and South Carolina had been cleared of American regulars. Whether Germain's plan of pacification could then have succeeded is a question still in contention. South Carolina was reduced to ferocious civil war and reciprocal terror; yet against determined opponents guerrillas could not ultimately succeed without external support. This was forthcoming. At New York Clinton allowed Washington to detach to the south a force under Nathanael Greene, which gave the guerrillas the support they needed. Cornwallis, with diminishing forces, was lured northwards, ultimately to Virginia and Yorktown, while Greene in his absence recovered most of South Carolina. Germain's imaginative rethinking of counter-insurgency was thus denied a fair trial.

In global strategy Germain was an advocate of boldness and the retention of the initiative, using his authority as secretary of state to intrude into the work of the Admiralty and its first lord, John Montagu, fourth earl of Sandwich. In every theatre command of the sea was the prerequisite of success, and Germain resisted the Admiralty's tendency to over-insure in home waters at the expense of overseas theatres. But for his pressure the French navy would have been allowed to dominate the American coast in 1778 and the Caribbean in the winter season which followed. His faith in boldness had the support of the king. Together they contrived to retain some share of the strategic initiative in the dark years 1779–81, prevailing over Sandwich and the commander-in-chief, Jeffrey, first Baron Amherst. Without Germain's pressure it is unlikely that Admiral Sir George Rodney in the Caribbean would have been allocated the superiority of force which was to win the battle of the Saints in 1782 after Germain's resignation.

These interventions caused some serious clashes with the first lord; for unless Germain was prepared to 'give the orders yourself instead of leaving it to Lord Sandwich to make them out from a minute of Cabinet' (Mackesy, *The War for America*, 441), the Admiralty could not be relied on to execute decisions with vigour.

Resignation and last years Cornwallis's capitulation at Yorktown, of which news arrived on 25 November 1781, was the result of an operational surprise inflicted within the theatre on Rodney and Clinton by the French and the Americans. It marked the end of active operations to recover the American colonies. But Germain, like the king, could not agree to give them up: 'We can never continue to exist as a great or powerful nation after we have lost or renounced the sovereignty of America' (Mackesy, *The War for America*, 461). It was not an irrational view, though hindsight makes it seem so. Germain wanted to retain the surviving British footholds in America by an *uti possidetis* settlement with the Americans while fighting on in the West Indies against the French, who were reaching the end of their resources.

Recognizing, however, that the temper of parliament was against these views, Germain asked the king before Christmas to accept his resignation. The king would have released him, yet insisted on retaining his policy, while Lord North, abandoning the policy, would have retained the man. It took six weeks to settle the matter, and on 9 February 1782 Germain left office, having borne for six and a half years the main burden of a great war. He had directed it with courage and considerable imagination, maintaining balanced priorities in a global conflict.

Germain retired with a peerage as Viscount Sackville, recovering the family name under which he had stood trial for Minden. In the House of Lords a Minden claque led by Peregrine Osborne, marquess of Carmarthen, opposed his admission as derogatory to the honour of the house. It was, wrote Richard Cumberland, 'one of the last and most painful trials of his life' (Cumberland, *Character of the Late Lord Sackville*, 20). The motion was rejected, but Carmarthen renewed it eleven days later when Sackville took his seat. His reply was temperate and generous, but he never forgave Carmarthen.

Sackville lived only three years longer. He often visited his house in Pall Mall and spoke regularly in the House of Lords, but in the country at Stoneland Lodge in Sussex (now Buckhurst, near Withyham, Tunbridge Wells) he lived the life of an old-fashioned squire, taking an interest in the welfare of his tenants and cottagers and reproving the singing of the village choir. He had suffered for many years from the stone, and as the end approached he seemed anxious that his composure in the face of death should be noted. He died at Stoneland on 26 August 1785, aged sixty-nine.

Historians seeking a scapegoat for the loss of America naturally turned on Sackville as the director of the war and used the Minden episode to vilify his character and denigrate his competence. Sackville seems in reality to have been a man of great capacity, undermined by faults of temperament; a capable leader who did not inspire devotion, as his successor in Germany Lord Granby could do; loyal to his inferiors, but easily moved to rancour against his equals; courteous and agreeable in private life though not convivial, but in public unable to resist employing a wounding irony. He was often described as arrogant, though that trait may have concealed an underlying insecurity. The relentless malice of Lord Shelburne's characterization of the man is puzzling, but may reflect contemporary attitudes to Sackville's reputed homosexuality, a reputation for which there appear to be foundations.   PIERS MACKESY

Sources P. Mackesy, *The coward of Minden: the affair of Lord George Sackville* (1979) · P. Mackesy, *The war for America, 1775–1783* (1964) · A. Valentine, *Lord George Germain* (1962) · L. Marlow, *Sackville of Drayton* (1948) · *The trial of the Rt. Hon. Lord George Sackville at a court martial* (1760) · R. Cumberland, *Memoirs of Richard Cumberland written by himself*, 2 vols. (1806–7) · R. Cumberland, *Character of the late Lord Sackville* (1785) · *DNB* · *Report on the manuscripts of Mrs Stopford-Sackville*, 2 vols., HMC, 49 (1904–10) · GEC, *Peerage*
Archives Derbys. RO, corresp. relating to Ireland · Derbys. RO, letters · Drayton House, Northamptonshire, MSS · U. Hull, Brynmor Jones L., corresp. · U. Mich., Clements L., corresp. and MSS | BL, corresp. with Lord Amherst, etc., Add. MSS 21697–21704 · BL, corresp. with William Eden, etc., Add. MSS 34413–34417, *passim* · BL, letters to Sir William Hamilton, Add. MS 39779 · BL, corresp. with Lord Holdernesse, Egerton MSS 3435, 3443 · BL, corresp. with Lord Liverpool, Add. MSS 38198–38201, 38306–38309 · BL, corresp. with duke of Newcastle, Add. MSS 32733–32984, *passim* · CKS, Sackville MSS, letters to duke of Dorset · Hunt. L., letters to Lord Percy · JRL, letters to Sir James Caldwell · NMM, letters to Lord Sandwich · Norfolk RO, corresp. with earl of Buckinghamshire · PRO, corresp. with Lord Amherst, WO 34 · PRO, corresp. with Lord Cornwallis, PRO30/11 · PRO, letters to Admiral Rodney, PRO 30/20 · U. Mich., Clements L., corresp. with Richard Howe · U. Nott. L., Newcastle MSS · U. Nott. L., letters to Henry Pelham and Sir Henry Clinton
Likenesses J. Reynolds, oils, *c.*1759, Drayton House, Northamptonshire · N. Hone, miniature, 1760, NPG · line engraving, pubd 1760 (after unknown portrait), NPG · F. Cotes, oils, 1769, NPG · J. Jacobé, mezzotint, pubd 1780 (after G. Romney), BM, NPG · G. Romney, oils, *c.*1780, Drayton House, Northamptonshire · G. Stuart, oil sketch, 1782–7, NMM · T. Gainsborough, oils, *c.*1783–1785, Knole, Kent [*see illus.*] · J. Sayers, etching, pubd 22 July 1785, NPG · W. Beechey, oils, 1792–3, NMM · J. de Vaere, Wedgwood medallion, 1798, BM · D. Pellegrini, oils, 1806, NMM · J. Hoppner, oils, 1809, Royal Collection · S. W. Reynolds, mezzotint, pubd 1820 (after J. Reynolds), BM, NPG · oils, *c.*1822–1823, NMM · studio of L. F. Abbott, oils, NPG · W. Beechey, oils, Guildhall Art Gallery, London · W. Beechey, oils, NPG · Bouch, pencil drawing, NPG · F. Chantrey, bust, AM Oxf. · F. Chantrey, bust on monument, St Michael's Church, Stowe, Staffordshire · J. S. Copley, group portrait, oils (*The collapse of the Earl of Chatham in the House of Lords, 7 July 1778*), NPG; on loan from Tate collection · J. Macardell, mezzotint (after J. Reynolds), BM, NPG · line engraving, BM, NPG; repro. in *European Magazine* (1785) · plaster medallion (after J. Tassie), Scot. NPG
Wealth at death wealthy; owned Drayton and Stoneland

Germain, Sir John, first baronet (1650–1718), army officer and politician, was born in May 1650, probably at The Hague, the son of John Germain and his wife, Mary Moll. His father was a private officer in the Dutch army and his mother reputedly a mistress of Prince William II, hence Germain's adoption of a red cross on his seal and armorial bearing to suggest royal parentage, and his relationship with William III.

In 1685 Germain became the lover of Mary *Howard, duchess of Norfolk (1658/9–1705), the wife of Henry Howard, seventh duke of Norfolk, and heir of Henry Mordaunt, second earl of Peterborough. Norfolk discovered them together in the summer of 1685, when Germain apparently escaped through a window. The duchess was sent to a monastery in France, but returned to England and took up residence with Germain in London. In the summer of 1688 Germain was lodging at the Golden Ball in London, and on 16 August he received letters of denization. At some point he returned to the Netherlands, as he was a member of William of Orange's invasion force later that year. He took up residence near to the Cockpit, where the duchess (who had left England at the revolution and returned there following her father's incarceration in the Tower) lived with him for two months, before being installed in a house in Vauxhall. Germain was naturalized by act of parliament in January 1690, taking the sacrament at St Mary Aldermary on 26 March. He was in Ireland for four months in the summer of 1690, and in Brussels in May 1691. As well as soldiering he soon became an important player in English financial circles, lending money to the crown and using his contacts in the exchequer to cash tallies he had purchased at a discount.

In January 1692 Norfolk introduced a bill into the House of Lords to divorce his wife, the first such bill to do so without a separation first being obtained through the church courts. The bill failed owing to opposition from the bishops and to the absence of two key witnesses, servants of Germain, who had been spirited out of the country to the Netherlands, and no doubt because Norfolk himself had a mistress. However, the bill did attract a lot of attention: William III attended the debate on 26 January incognito. Norfolk's next step was to sue Germain for £100,000 damages in king's bench. Although Germain pleaded a Statute of Limitations for the offence the jury found him guilty, but awarded only 100 marks (£66) damages, plus costs. Armed with this verdict Norfolk introduced a second divorce bill into the Lords in December 1692, which was narrowly lost by six votes in January 1693.

Germain was knighted on 26 February 1698 and created a baronet on 25 March following. In the same month John Evelyn characterized him as 'a Dutch gamester of mean extraction, who had gotten much by gaming' (Evelyn, 5.393–4). Norfolk's third divorce bill passed in 1700, but with the important addition to the earlier bills that the duchess should receive back her portion of £10,000. By that date Germain may well have favoured a divorce: in 1697 Lady Mary became *suo jure* Baroness Mordaunt upon the death of her father, inheriting his substantial estates, and marriage may have been an attractive proposition. Norfolk died on 2 April 1701, and on 15 September following Germain was licensed to marry Lady Mary. She died childless on 17 November 1705, 'in her 47th year' (Bridges, 2.248), leaving Germain as heir to Drayton and the Mordaunt fortune; this led one contemporary to write in 1714 that 'the chief promotion of him was occasioned by his being a stallion to the Lady Mary Mordaunt' (Lucas, 178). Germain had to defend his inheritance against the claims of Lady Mary's cousin, Charles Mordaunt, third earl of Peterborough; he continued the suit he had begun against her, only abandoning it on Germain's death.

In mid-September 1706 Germain was reported to be on his way to marry Lady Elizabeth (1608–1769), daughter of Charles Berkeley, second earl of Berkeley [*see* Germain, Lady Elizabeth]. He took as a present the £700 he had won at the tables, and in return for a portion of £6000, he settled on his wife £500 per annum pin money and a jointure of £1200 per annum, out of the Drayton estate. On 26 October 1706 Luttrell reported that the wedding had taken place 'some days since' (Luttrell, 6.101). Their three children, two sons and a daughter, all died in infancy.

Germain attempted to make an interest at Weobley, Herefordshire, at a by-election in December 1708, and was an assistant of the Royal African Company in 1709 and 1711–12. He gave evidence 'in his ill English' (Cartwright, 259) to the Commons on behalf of the duke of Marlborough on 24 January 1712, asserting that the allowances claimed by Marlborough 'were customary perquisites of the commander-in-chief in Flanders' (Boyer, 3.26–7), and had been allowed to Prince Walbeck, under whom Germain had served. He was returned to parliament at the 1713 election for Morpeth, and although he did not stand in 1715 he was returned for Totnes in a by-election of 22 April 1717, serving until his death. He died at his house in St James's Square, London, on 11 December 1718, of 'a mortification of his back' (*Remarks*, 4.265) and was buried on 17 December at Lowick, near Drayton, where his monument records his age as sixty-eight years and seven months.

Germain's will revealed the extent of his wealth. His bequests to the poor totalled £350, £200 of which went to the Dutch church in London. He left his brother Daniel and sister Judith (the wife of Mr Persode) £15,000 each, and £20,000 to his brother Philip. The main beneficiary of his will was his wife, who survived until 16 December 1769. According to Germain's dying wish she then left the estate to a younger son of the first duke of Dorset, who had married the daughter of Lieutenant-General Walter Colyear, his military comrade: Lord George Sackville duly took the name Germain.   STUART HANDLEY

Sources D. W. Hayton, 'Germain, Sir John, bart.', HoP, *Commons, 1690–1715* [draft] · S. R. Matthews, 'Germain, Sir John, 1st bt', HoP, *Commons, 1715–54*, 2.61 · will, PRO, PROB 11/566, fols. 256r–257 · GEC, *Baronetage* · W. A. Shaw, ed., *Letters of denization and acts of naturalization for aliens in England and Ireland, 1603–1700*, Huguenot Society of London, 18 (1911), 210, 222 · J. Bridges, *The history and antiquities of Northamptonshire*, ed. P. Whalley, 2 (1791), 222, 248 · *The manuscripts of the House of Lords*, 4 vols., HMC, 17 (1887–94), vol. 4 · *The manuscripts of the House of Lords*, new ser., 12 vols. (1900–77), vol. 5 · *State trials*, 12.883–948; 13.1283–370 · N. Luttrell, *A brief historical relation of state affairs from September 1678 to April 1714*, 6 vols. (1857) · *GM*, 1st ser., 39 (1769), 609 · A. Boyer, *The political state of Great Britain*, 60 vols. (1711–40), vols. 3–4, 26–7 · *Remarks and collections of Thomas Hearne*, ed. C. E. Doble and others, 6, OHS, 43 (1902), 265–6 · J. J. Cartwright, ed., *The Wentworth papers, 1705–1739* (1883), 246, 259 · T. Lucas, *Memoirs of the lives, intrigues, and comical adventures of the most famous gamesters and celebrated sharpers in the reigns of Charles II, James II, William III and Queen Anne* (1714), 178–82 · Evelyn, *Diary*, 5.393–4 · *The manuscripts of his grace the duke of Portland*, 10 vols., HMC, 29 (1891–1931), vol. 5, p. 329 · R. Weil, *Political passions: gender, the family and political argument in England, 1680–1714* (1999), 129–38 · L. Stone, *Road to divorce: England, 1530–1987* (1990), 313–17 · *The historical and the posthumous memoirs of Sir Nathaniel William Wraxall, 1772–1784*, ed. H. B. Wheatley, 5 vols. (1884), vol. 3, pp. 131–3
Wealth at death very wealthy; bequests of over £57,000: will, PRO, PROB 11/566, fols. 256r–257

German, Sir Edward [*formerly* German Edward Jones] (1862–1936), composer, was born German Edward Jones

Sir Edward German (1862–1936), by Flora Lion, c.1912

at St Mary's Street, Whitchurch, Shropshire, on 17 February 1862, the second child and elder son of John David Jones, a liquor merchant, and his wife, Betsey (Elizabeth) Cox (d. 1901). The family income came from a brewery and the wine and spirits trade. German began life in The Vaults, an old public house, but, surprisingly in view of the conflicts between drink and nonconformity, the Dodington Congregational Chapel was the primary interest of his parents. John David was the organist and a fervent local preacher, Betsey a teacher of the Bible class for young women. Family piety was, however, enlivened with home-made entertainments above his uncle Ted's grocer's shop. As his talents grew, German gained a reputation for comic songs in local village halls. His elder sister, Ruth, with whom he played piano duets in public, died when he was fifteen, and he himself had to leave his boarding-school in Chester after a serious illness. During his enforced convalescence he taught himself the violin to a level at which he could lead the town orchestra. He impressed the conductor of the Whithurch choral society, Walter Hay, a former military bandsman but a serious musician, who encouraged him to enter an examination for the Royal Academy of Music. German lived for nine months in Shrewsbury with Hay, studied his scores, and had professional tuition on the organ and violin.

German entered the academy in 1880 with the intention of becoming an organist, but his horizons were greatly widened. He was an enthusiastic participant in prize competitions. Because there were two other students named Jones, the name J. Edward German began to appear under his compositions in the academy programmes. (In his family circle he was always known as Jim). He won the

Lucas medal for composition in 1885 with a Te Deum for soloists, choir, and organ. He was briefly engaged to a fellow student, Ethel Boyce, who came from a wealthy Chertsey family, but the engagement was broken off; and both remained single. Fellow students encouraged German to write a symphony, which was performed at the academy in 1886, where he was then a sub-professor of the violin. In 1890 he conducted it in a more polished version at the Crystal Palace. He also wrote a short comic opera, *The Two Poets*, which was well received by the opera class at the academy and was taken on tour to Whitchurch and other market towns with success.

German's decision to attempt a career as a composer was bold, for he had no private income or patron, and there was no great demand for English music. Years of attempting to win the favour of managements and conductors followed. After teaching at Wimbledon School he had a chance meeting with the conductor Alberto Randegger on the steps of the Royal Academy of Music which led to his appointment as musical director for the American actor–manager Richard Mansfield at the old Globe Theatre. There was a vogue in the 1890s for lavish stage productions with incidental music, as employed later in films and drama on television. German's score for *Richard III* (1889) received critical acclaim and led to a commission by Henry Irving in 1892 for music for *Henry VIII* at the Lyceum Theatre. The dances from this score became popular concert pieces throughout the land: Elgar told friends that he could never hear 'The Shepherds Dance' without feeling a lump in his throat. Even finer was the music for Forbes Robertson's *Romeo and Juliet* (1895) at the Lyceum, especially the overture. For other actor–managers of the time, Herbert Beerbohm Tree and George Alexander, German wrote atmospheric pages and graceful dances for *As You Like It* (1896) and *Much Ado about Nothing* (1898), as well as for some modern plays. The 'Nell Gwyn' dances from Anthony Hope's *English Nell* (1900) rivalled those from *Henry VIII* in popularity.

Simultaneously, German was building a reputation as an orchestral composer for provincial festivals. For Norwich he wrote a second symphony (1893) and a suite *The Seasons* (1899); for Leeds a suite (1895); and for Birmingham a symphonic poem, *Hamlet*, conducted by Hans Richter in 1897. For Brighton in 1902 he wrote a stirring *Rhapsody on March Themes* using material he had contributed to a fantasia for the diamond jubilee; and for Cardiff an acclaimed *Welsh Rhapsody* (1904). Always sensitive to criticism, he abandoned the symphonic form when the 'Norwich' symphony was treated harshly by some London critics; but his orchestral writing is imaginative and finely crafted. These works deserve to be restored to the repertory.

There was something of a loss to serious music when German was invited to complete *The Emerald Isle*, an operetta which Sir Arthur Sullivan had left unfinished at his death in 1900. The D'Oyly Carte management and public hailed him as Sullivan's successor. Basil Hood, the librettist, swiftly produced the text for *Merrie England*. This opened at the Savoy Theatre on 2 April 1902 and gave German his greatest triumph. Although he was never a folk-song collector, his music for *Merrie England* breathed an air of pastoral innocence and countryside revels. Much of the score was written in Shropshire, to which he had returned after his mother's death. The work is set in the forest of Windsor, and involves Queen Elizabeth I and her courtiers. One of the greatest English melodists, German produced such memorable solos as 'The English Rose', 'O Peaceful England', and 'The Yeomen of England'. The work was frequently revived, and the songs remained popular down to the mid-twentieth century.

No new Savoy tradition ensued, however. Hood's next offering, *A Princess of Kensington* (1903), suffered from an absurd plot and, despite its musical worth, had no sequels. In 1907 an operetta based on Henry Fielding's novel *Tom Jones* was devised by a team of writers brought together by the impresario Robert Courtneidge on the occasion of the Fielding bicentenary. German wrote a score of the highest quality, and following its success in London he conducted it in New York, and also a performance of his *Welsh Rhapsody* in Carnegie Hall. Unfortunately, a collaboration with the elderly W. S. Gilbert, *Fallen Fairies*, a satirical fantasy, made him disillusioned with the theatre. Gilbert tried to embroil him in litigation over the casting; and German became nervous and unhappy over the clash of personalities. Although German was commissioned to write the coronation march and hymn for George V and Queen Mary, no further major works appeared until after the First World War. His *Theme and Six Diversions* for orchestra was performed at the Queen's Hall on 26 March 1919, and *The Willow Song*, a short symphonic poem inspired by *Othello*, for the Royal Academy of Music centenary celebration on 19 July 1922.

German continued to arrange and conduct his music and gave vigorous support to the Performing Right Society. He made some early recordings and took an intense interest in the frequency and performances of his works on the new medium of radio. In 1928 German was knighted, and he was awarded the gold medal of the Royal Philharmonic Society in 1934; but efforts to persuade him to produce new masterpieces failed. He jokingly referred to himself as the Hermit of Maida Vale, but he had circles of friends, enjoyed many hours watching cricket at Lord's, and devoted much time to correspondence with a sister, Rachel. His appearance had once been unusually boyish. He was called 'the young composer' even in his thirties. By contrast, his health in old age was poor. He lost the sight of an eye in 1927, and this affected his editing of scores. He died of cancer on 11 November 1936 at his home, 5 Biddulph Road, Elgin Avenue, Maida Vale, London, and after cremation at Golders Green crematorium on 13 November his ashes were interred in Shropshire at Whitchurch cemetery. A tribute on radio by Sir Landon Ronald, and the playing of 'The Shepherds Dance', heard in the evening of an Armistice day, had a poignancy for countless homes, where musical appreciation had first been nurtured by songs such as 'Glorious Devon' or piano arrangements of his graceful and evocative music. BRIAN REES

Sources B. Rees, *A musical peacemaker: the life and work of Sir Edward German* (1987) · W. H. Scott, *Edward German: an intimate biography*

(1932) • A. Lamb, 'German, Sir Edward', *New Grove* • private information (2004) [family papers belonging to Mrs Winifred German, niece-in-law] • *DNB* • b. cert. • d. cert. • K. Gänzl, *The encyclopedia of the musical theatre*, 2 vols. (1994)

Archives priv. coll. | SOUND BL NSA, documentary recording • BL NSA, *Music weekly*, B1502/2 • BL NSA, performance recordings
Likenesses F. Lion, lithograph, *c.*1912, NPG [*see illus.*] • Bailey, group photograph, 1922, NPG • Bailey, photograph, *c.*1922, NPG • H. L. Oakley, silhouette, NPG • Vandyk, double portrait, photograph (with Sir A. C. Mackenzie), NPG • photographs, Performing Right Society, London • photographs, Hult. Arch. • photographs, priv. coll.
Wealth at death £57,117 2*s.* 3*d.*: probate, 31 Dec 1936, *CGPLA Eng. & Wales*

German Princess, the. *See* Carleton, Mary (1634x42–1673).

Germanus [St Germanus] (*d. c.*437/448), bishop of Auxerre, was papal envoy to Britain in 429–30. No full contemporary account of Germanus's life survives and certain facts about him are few. Soon after his death he became the object of a cult and stories of his miraculous powers quickly accumulated. About 480, several decades after his death, his life was written by Constantius, priest of Lyons and friend of another aristocrat-bishop, Sidonius Apollinaris. The life was dedicated to the then bishop of Auxerre, Censorius, and aimed to promote Germanus as the patron saint of all Gaul, to rival and perhaps displace the Aquitainian Martin of Tours.

Germanus was born at Auxerre to 'very distinguished parents' (Constantius of Lyons, i), named in an unreliable later tradition as Rusticus and Germanilla (Hericus of Auxerre, i.19). He was educated in the schools of Gaul in the liberal arts and moved to Rome to study law and practised advocacy in the courts of the prefect of the city. There he married a rich, well-born, and virtuous lady. He returned to Gaul as a military commander (*dux*), perhaps of the *tractus Armoricanus et Nervicanus* (roughly equivalent to modern Brittany and Normandy). He was unanimously chosen to succeed Bishop Amator at Auxerre in 418. His change of career fits a pattern which became increasingly widespread as Roman power in western Europe declined. Members of local élites, who, under the empire, had combined power in their own communities with occasional forays into imperial office, now perpetuated their influence in their cities by asserting control of the episcopate, along with other positions of leadership. Germanus provided an effective role model for bishops to come because, unlike Martin of Tours, his previous career qualified him to combine the gifts of an aristocrat for secular leadership with the saintly lifestyle of the holy man.

Germanus's sanctity was advertised by his ascetic lifestyle and his ability to perform miracles. His diet was frugal, his dress simple, and his bed was exceptionally hard. A supporter of the cult of St Maurice, to whom he dedicated an oratory on his own estates, he also actively promoted monasticism at Auxerre and founded a community of monks on the far side of the River Yonne, separated from, but in full view of, the city. In line with his hagiographical purpose, Constantius reports public demonstrations of Germanus's powers as a worker of miracles, in which he exorcized demons and healed the sick: a demon

was expelled from a hardened thief, who openly admitted his crime; and a ruin haunted by the unquiet spirits of two dead criminals left unburied, who frightened travellers by hurling showers of stones, was cleansed when the bones were discovered by the bishop and given proper funeral rites. His previous career gave Germanus skill in diplomacy and debate, and he had friendly relations with other bishops. Although not known to have visited the famous island monastery of Lérins, Germanus was on close terms with a number of bishops of good family associated with Lérins, notably Lupus of Troyes, with whom he visited Britain, Hilary of Arles, and Eucherius of Lyons.

In 429 Germanus was sent with Lupus to Britain by Pope Celestine on a mission to suppress the Pelagian heresy, which was fashionable among a section of the nobility there. Having calmed a storm in the channel, Germanus and Lupus landed in Britain and held a series of public meetings to spread the orthodox word through the rural districts. After some hesitation, the Pelagians emerged for a public confrontation, resplendent in the costly attire characteristic of late Roman public display, and attended by large bands of supporters. The Pelagians spoke first, but were refuted on every point by Germanus and Lupus. A subsequent visit by the two bishops to the shrine of the martyr St Alban suggests that the debate took place at or near Roman Verulamium. Archaeological evidence lends support to the tradition; the site seems to have been under continuous occupation as an urban centre well into the second half of the fifth century and the community showed some confidence in itself and its future, through investment in public works, long after the Roman government had abandoned the island to its fate in 409. Moreover, Germanus's reported healing of a military tribune's little daughter may point to the continued existence of a military garrison there.

Germanus is also shown encouraging the Britons to confront the raiders menacing what remained of Roman Britain. Adopting the role of warlord, he inspired the heavily outnumbered Romano-Britons to confront and defeat an invasion of Saxons and Picts; after a baptismal service, the Romano-Britons terrified the enemy by charging at them with cries of 'Hallelujah!'. On this, or a later visit with Bishop Severus of Trier (which may be a literary doublet of the first), Germanus reinforced his prestige by publicly healing the young son of a local noble, Elafius, and his mission ended triumphantly with the condemnation and exile of the Pelagians.

This was not the end of Germanus's connection with Britain. The mission of 429 had been prompted by Celestine's deacon, Palladius, who was to be designated in 431 as 'the first bishop of the Irish Christians' (Prosper of Aquitaine, s.a. 431) and the seventh-century life of Patrick asserts that Patrick had been Germanus's disciple at Auxerre and was persuaded by Germanus to take up missionary activity in Ireland after Palladius's failure and death.

Germanus's last journey was to the imperial court at Ravenna. The traditional date accepted for this journey is 448 but some scholars (for example, E. A. Thompson) make a case for a date in the mid-430s. His mission resulted from a revolt of dissidents (the Bacaudae) in the territory of Auxerre (which could be dated either to 435–7 or to 448). The imperial government had summoned a war band of Alans under their king, Goar, to suppress the rebels, but the bishop intervened and personally halted the king's advance. Germanus then set out to the imperial court at Ravenna to intercede for all parties concerned. His route was marked by further miracles of healing at Alesia, Autun, and Milan. At Ravenna, Germanus set prisoners free by his prayers, exchanged gifts with the empress Galla Placidia, and once again exhibited his healing powers. Although the main purpose of his mission was frustrated by a further revolt in northern Gaul, Germanus's prestige was unaffected and his death at Ravenna after a short illness was publicly mourned by the empress and other courtiers. The return of his funeral cortege to Gaul inspired frenzied relic hunting. He was buried on 1 October at Auxerre, where his tomb became a focus for many miraculous happenings.

The cult soon became widespread and the tradition on Germanus was enriched by numerous fictitious accretions. His fame in British tradition is based on memories of the British visit recorded by Prosper of Aquitaine, whose *Chronicle* was known to early medieval writers, on the incorporation by Bede of Constantius's life into his *Historia ecclesiastica*, and on the many legends which connect him to Celtic Christianity in Britain and Ireland.

JILL HARRIES

Sources 'Prosperi Tironis epitoma chronicon', *Chronica minora saec. IV. V. VI. VII.*, ed. T. Mommsen, 1, MGH Auctores Antiquissimi, 9 (Berlin, 1892), 341–499, 429, 431 · Constantius of Lyons, 'Vita Germani episcopi', *Passiones vitaeque sanctorum aevi Merovingici*, ed. B. Krusch and W. Levison, MGH Scriptores Rerum Merovingicarum, 7/2 (Hanover, 1920), 247–83 · Constantius of Lyons, *Vita s. Germani*, ed. and trans. R. Borius (Paris, 1965), 247–83 · *Sidonius: poems and letters*, ed. and trans. W. B. Anderson, 1 (1936), 8.15.1 · Gregory of Tours, 'Liber in gloria confessorum', in B. Krusch, *Gregorii Turonensis opera*, ed. W. Arndt, MGH Scriptores Rerum Merovingicarum, 1/2 (Hanover, 1885), esp. 40 · *Gregorii Turonensis opera*, ed. B. Krusch and W. Levison, MGH Scriptores Rerum Merovingicarum, 1/1 (Hanover, 1937–52), 2.20, 10.31 · Gregory of Tours, 'De passione et virtutibus s. Juliani', *Gregorii Turonensis opera*, ed. W. Arndt and B. Krusch, MGH Scriptores Rerum Merovingicarum, 1/2 (Hanover, 1885), 29 · Murchiu, *Life of Patrick*, ed. and trans. A. B. E. Hood, History from the Sources (1978), 6, 8 · Hericus of Auxerre, *De miraculis Sancti Germani*, 1207–70 · Bede, *Hist. eccl.*, 1.17–21 · Nennius, 'British history' and 'The Welsh annals', ed. and trans. J. Morris (1980) · K. F. Stroheker, *Der senatorische Adel in spätantiken Gallien* (1948), 177–8 · J. R. Martindale, *The prosopography of the later Roman empire*, 2: AD 395–527 (1980), 504–5 · E. A. Thompson, *Saint Germanus of Auxerre and the end of Roman Britain* (1984) · G. Le Bras and others, *Saint Germain d'Auxerre et son temps* (1950) · P. Salway, *Roman Britain* (1981)

Gernsheim, Helmut Erich Robert (1913–1995), photographer and historian, was born in Munich on 1 March 1913, the third son of Karl Gernsheim, a historian of literature at Munich University, and his wife, Hermine, *née* Scholz. He was educated at St Anne's College, Augsburg, and began a degree course in art history at Munich University in 1933, but soon realized he was unlikely to complete it in the prevailing political climate: he feared being drafted into Hitler's army, and in any case he was partly

Helmut Erich Robert Gernsheim (1913–1995), by Ida Kar

Jewish. He decided to move to London, where his brother ran an art gallery, but the latter advised him to acquire a practical skill first (on the grounds that he would make no living as an art historian in Britain). So in 1934 he enrolled in the Bavarian State School of Photography in Munich, where he studied for two years, emerging with a first-class diploma. In 1937 he moved to London and set up as a freelance photographer; he became a British citizen in 1946.

Gernsheim's outlook on photography and his own practice as a photographer were influenced by *Neue Sachlichkeit* (new objectivity), which characterized much radical German art and design in the 1920s. *Neue Sachlichkeit* was suppressed in Nazi Germany (Gernsheim became properly conscious of it only from books he bought in London during the war), but by the 1930s its influence on German photography was irrevocable. This is evident in Gernsheim's photographs of the details and surfaces of objects, often in close-up and isolated from their usual contexts.

Gernsheim was a man of strong opinions and a justified faith in his own taste and judgement, and his criticisms could be trenchant (the British, he declared 'are not a visually minded nation'). However, they were rarely groundless. He pronounced the generality of 1930s British photography 'antiquated, fuzzy, sentimental, sugary ... an artificial world one associates with chocolate and soap boxes' (Hill and Cooper, 166). It is certainly true that British taste and practice were at odds with Gernsheim's *Neue Sachlichkeit* approach. Many British photographers remained influenced by the pictorialism of Victorian and Edwardian photography, drawing their aesthetic from painting, and employing printing techniques to impart a more 'painterly' quality to their work. Gernsheim saw the Royal Photographic Society (RPS) as a bastion of this approach, and felt frustrated in his attempts to convert the society to his views, eventually resigning his RPS fellowship in 1952.

In 1940 Gernsheim was interned as an enemy alien, and he ended up in a camp in Australia. His photographic training came to his rescue, and in 1941 he was permitted to return to Britain to work for the National Buildings Record, photographing buildings of national importance ahead of anticipated war damage. While waiting for clearance to undertake this work, Gernsheim revised some lectures he had given during his internment in Australia, and in 1942 they were published as his first book, *New Photo Vision*. The book lays down 'a challenge to those photographers for whom photographic means are not "artistic" enough' (*New Photo Vision*, 3), illustrating the point with his own photographs.

New Photo Vision also initiated Gernsheim's friendship with Beaumont Newhall, the American photo-historian. It was Newhall who persuaded Gernsheim of the need for a photo-historian also to be a collector. Gernsheim recounts finding his first Julia Margaret Cameron prints 'more or less by accident', at a dealer where they were in danger of being used for packing 'because of their stout cardboard' (Hill and Cooper, 182). He amassed a collection of great importance, and made two especially significant discoveries. He rediscovered Charles Dodgson (Lewis Carroll) as a photographer, and found what is considered the earliest extant photograph, Niépce's image of a view from a window, taken in 1826 or 1827 with an exposure of eight hours.

Gernsheim collaborated closely with his wife, Alison, *née* Eames (*c*.1911–1969), whom he met in 1942 and married in 1946; indeed, his most significant work was produced during their marriage. He published prolifically, adopting an approach whereby research and writing were closely dependent on the fruits of his collecting. Alison, a historian by training, undertook the historical research, and she is named as his collaborator in a number of his publications. He wrote more than twenty monographs on subjects including Julia Margaret Cameron (1948), Lewis Carroll (1949), and Roger Fenton (1954). In 1955 he published *The History of Photography*, a monumental work of photo-history which appeared in an enlarged edition in 1969, and out of which came the very popular *Concise History of Photography* (1965).

The Gernsheims selected works from their collection for a ground-breaking exhibition held in 1951 at the Victoria and Albert Museum, entitled 'Masterpieces of Victorian Photography'. They envisaged their collection forming the basis of a British national collection of photography, with Gernsheim as director. However, a suitable home was not forthcoming, partly due to widespread ignorance about the need for such a museum, but also on account of Gernsheim's very particular specifications. The collection (33,000 photographs, together with cameras and Gernsheim's library) was ultimately sold to the University of Texas in 1963, though the Gernsheims finally decided against moving to Texas with it. They moved instead to Castagnola, Lugano, Switzerland, from where Gernsheim continued to work, though his output

decreased after Alison's death on 27 March 1969. In 1971 he married Irène Guénin of Geneva. Gernsheim died in Switzerland on 20 July 1995, survived by his second wife.

Gernsheim's importance to photography cannot be overstated. The Gernsheim collection immeasurably enriches our photographic inheritance, and the scholarship that he built upon the collection was instrumental in establishing the academic credibility of photo-history.

HELEN BARLOW

Sources P. Hill and T. Cooper, 'Helmut Gernsheim', *Dialogue with photography* (1979), 160–210 • M. Harker, 'Helmut Gernsheim: an appreciation', *Photographic Journal* (Oct 1995), 366–7 • photography and film, www.hrc.utexas.edu/collections/photography/, 30 Jan 2002 • 'Gernsheim', *The dictionary of art*, ed. J. Turner (1996) • S. Wolff, 'Professor Helmut Gernsheim', *Photographic Collector*, 5 (1986), 345–9 • A. Hopkinson, *British Journal of Photography* (16 Aug 1995), 9 • *The Independent* (5 Aug 1995) • *The Times* (25 July 1995) • *Daily Telegraph* (30 Aug 1995) • *The Guardian* (9 Aug 1995) • *New York Times* (12 Aug 1995) • *The Times* (7 April 1969) • WW
Archives Ransom HRC, collection
Likenesses I. Kar, photograph, NPG [*see illus.*] • photograph, repro. in *The Independent* • photograph, repro. in *The Times* (25 July 1995) • portrait, repro. in Hill and Cooper, 'Helmut Gernsheim', 160 • portrait, Ransom HRC • portrait, repro. in Wolff, 'Professor Helmut Gernsheim' • portrait, repro. in Harker, 'Helmut Gernsheim'

Gerontius (*d*. 411), Roman general, was commander-in-chief (*magister militum*) successively of the usurpers Constantine III and Maximus. Gerontius was a native of Britain; his name is Greek, but since the third century it had been popular in Rome's western provinces, and has survived in Welsh as Geraint. His wife's name, Nunechia ('prudence'), is also Greek, but is so unusual in the Latin-speaking West that it may indicate a non-British origin. She was a Christian. Gerontius's religion is unknown, likewise his career before 407; but since he is said to have been brave, experienced, and a firm disciplinarian, he was presumably an officer in the British garrison which proclaimed Constantine III. After the legitimate emperor Honorius's general, the Goth Sarus, had killed his first joint commanders-in-chief, Constantine replaced them with Gerontius and Edobichus (a Frank). Together they drove Sarus out of Gaul.

Now that he controlled Britain and Gaul, Constantine in 408 appointed his son Constans as his deputy (Caesar) and sent him with Gerontius and an army to Spain, where they soon crushed the local resistance. Leaving Gerontius in charge, Constans returned to his father's capital at Arelate (Arles) on a visit. Gerontius seized this opportunity to rebel and proclaim an emperor of his own, a dependant called Maximus. He is also said to have incited 'the barbarians in Gaul' against Constantine (Zosimus, vi 5.2), but they need not be identified with the Vandals, Alans, and Sueves *before* they invaded Spain; on balance, Gerontius's rebellion should be connected with the disaster of October 409 (dated by the Galician chronicler Hydatius to a Tuesday, either that of 28 September or 12 October), when these tribes crossed the Pyrenees. Gerontius may have feared supersession when Constans returned with a general called Justus, or he may have simply usurped authority in a crisis, like Constantine himself in Britain.

When Constantine sent reinforcements to Spain, promoting Constans to full emperor (Augustus), the men went over to Gerontius, and Constans took refuge in Vienna (Vienne on the River Rhône). Here he was killed by Gerontius, who then besieged Constantine at Arelate; but when (in summer 411) the army of Honorius's commander-in-chief, the future emperor Constantius III, approached, Gerontius was forced to retreat because many of his men deserted. This made the Spanish army despise him, and it too rebelled. Gerontius was trapped by rebels in a house where he resisted heroically with a few followers, but when the house had been set on fire he first killed Nunechia at her own request, and then himself. His nominee Maximus was deposed.

Gerontius's defection was fatal to Constantine and his regime in Gaul and Britain, for his resulting inability to defend them against the invaders from across the Rhine:

> forced the inhabitants of Britain and some of the tribes in Gaul to secede from Roman rule and to be independent, obeying Roman laws no longer. And so the Britons took up arms, and risked their lives to free their own cities from the barbarians who were attacking them; and the whole of Armorica [Brittany] and other Gallic provinces copied the Britons by freeing themselves in the same way, expelling the Roman officials and establishing whatever government they wished.   (Zosimus, vi 5.2)

Since Roman rule was never restored, the formal end of Roman Britain can thus be dated to 409 or 410 and was indirectly caused by the Briton Gerontius in Spain.

R. S. O. TOMLIN

Sources Zosimus, *Historia nova: the decline of Rome*, ed. and trans. J. J. Buchanan and H. T. Davis (1967), vi. 2–5 · Olympiodorus, *Fragments, The fragmentary classicizing historians of the later Roman empire*, ed. and trans. R. C. Blockley, 2 (1983), 152–210, no. 16 · Orosius, 'Historiarum libri septem', *Patrologia Latina*, 31 (1846) · Hydatius, *Chronicle*, ed. R. Burgess (1995) · Sozomen, *Kirchengeschichte*, ed. J. Bidez and G. C. Hansen (Berlin, 1960), ix, 13 · J. R. Martindale, *The prosopography of the later Roman empire*, 2: AD 395–527 (1980), 508, 744–5 · J. Matthews, *Western aristocracies and imperial court, AD 364–425* (1975), 308–12

Gerrald, Joseph (1763–1796), political reformer, was born on 9 February 1763 in St Kitts, West Indies, the only child of Joseph Gerrald (d. 1775), a planter from a wealthy Irish family, and his second wife, Ann Rogers, of English descent. His parents moved to England in 1765, apparently on account of his mother's desire for a cooler climate, residing first at Hanover Square and then at the corner of St Swithin's Lane, Lombard Street, London. Shortly afterwards Gerrald's mother died, and his father returned to the West Indies to manage his business affairs. At this time, Gerrald was living with a Mrs Crudge, a friend of his mother, before being sent to the boarding-school of a Mr Allen at Hammersmith, where he remained until the age of eleven. His father died in the West Indies in 1775 and Gerrald was placed under the guardianship of his maternal uncles and sent to the academy of Dr Samuel Parr at Stanmore to further his education. Gerrald excelled at his studies of Latin, French, Greek, geography, and art, but Parr was still apparently forced to expel him for 'extreme indiscretion' (*DNB*). Despite the unhappy end to his schooling years, Gerrald developed during this time a

Joseph Gerrald (1763–1796), by Samuel William Reynolds senior, pubd 1795 (after Charles Smith, 1794)

close personal relationship with Parr and reputedly became acquainted with Richard Brinsley Sheridan and William Pitt.

In 1780 Gerrald returned to the West Indies in order to settle his inheritances. His father's extravagances during his lifetime, however, had reduced the family fortunes considerably and Gerrald's own impulsions on taking possession of the bequest diminished the estate further. Soon after arriving in the West Indies, Gerrald hurriedly married a woman by the name of Brothers, with whom he had one son and one daughter. She died within a short period of time, leaving Gerrald in ill health, relatively impoverished, and with two children to support. He then decided to move to the United States, where he was admitted to the bar and for several years practised in the courts of Pennsylvania. Early in 1788 he returned to England, travelling through several parts of the country before settling in London, where his attention was devoted to a lawsuit in relation to his former West Indian properties. In London Gerrald lodged first at Furnival's Inn, Holborn, before moving to Southampton Buildings, and then to premises close to where his family first resided, at 40 Swallow Street, Hanover Square.

Gerrald was not a man of particularly imposing stature, with one contemporary describing him as 'about five feet, eight inches in height; of a slender make, and puny constitution' (*Gerrald a Fragment*, 16), and his health was even more delicate at the time of his arrival in London. Indeed, in 1789 Gerrald seemed determined to move to Bath on his physician's advice that the capital was 'too noisy and full of company for a sick man' (*Authentic Biographical Anecdotes*, 17). By this time, however, Gerrald was intrigued by politics, apparently writing a series of anonymous letters on the subject in 1788 and subsequently joining the reformist Society for Constitutional Information and later the more radical *London Corresponding Society. He quickly became a popular and prominent figure in radical circles, not least because of his oratory and temperament. As one contemporary observed: 'His eloquence had equally the power to charm and astonish; and the brilliancy of his imagination was not inferior to the terrors of his invective. ... He was placable and generous to an extreme' (*Gerrald a Fragment*, 22). As a member of the London Corresponding Society he drafted a reform petition in March 1793 and canvassed signatures from inmates of the king's bench prison, and that same year he published a pamphlet entitled *A Convention the Only Means of Saving Us from Ruin* (1793). Gerrald's reputation as a firm advocate of reform saw him elected on 24 October 1793 as delegate, along with Maurice Margarot, of the London Corresponding Society to the British Convention, then convening in Edinburgh. Following his arrival in Edinburgh on 6 November, Gerrald set out on a quick tour of the Scottish countryside to promote reform, returning to Edinburgh by 19 November. Seeking universal suffrage and annual parliaments, the convention was seen by the authorities as subversive. Gerrald was twice arrested on 5 and 6 December 1793 and, along with several other delegates, subsequently charged with sedition. He was released on bail to attend to private matters in London, during which time Margarot and William Skirving, secretary to the convention, were sentenced to transportation. These convictions were a sure warning of Gerrald's fate and his friends implored him to leave England, including Parr, who promised to reimburse Gerrald's bondsmen. Nevertheless, Gerrald returned to Edinburgh for trial during the first two weeks of March 1794. Despite an eloquent and impassioned speech in his own defence Gerrald was found guilty, and an order for fourteen years' transportation to Australia was given on 30 December 1794.

Gerrald was initially detained in the Tolbooth, Edinburgh, for several weeks before being removed to Newgate prison until October 1794 and then to the New Compter, Giltspur Street, London. During his imprisonment he was allowed the companionship of his young daughter and friends. In spite of a subscription being raised to help him during these months Gerrald's physical appearance had 'degenerated into a sloven' (*Authentic Biographical Anecdotes*, 21). On 2 May 1795 he was removed, under guard and shackled, to Gosport, where he was placed on board the convict ship *Sovereign* to await transportation to New South Wales. While Gerrald was being kept on board, Parr had taken custody of Gerrald's son and arranged for books, money, personal items, and a farewell letter to be conveyed to his former pupil, but none of this was received by Gerrald. After nearly six months at sea, he arrived in Sydney on 5 November 1795 suffering from advanced tuberculosis. Gerrald was permitted to purchase a house and garden at Farm Cove, but his illness forced him to move early in 1796 to the home of fellow radical exile, Thomas Fyshe Palmer, where he was

attended by the surgeon George Bass. Gerrald, however, died from consumption on 16 March 1796 and was buried in his garden at Farm Cove. To perpetuate his memory as one of the so-called Scottish Martyrs an obelisk was erected on Calton Hill, Edinburgh, in August 1844 and another monument built at the Nunhead cemetery in Surrey during February 1851.   MICHAEL T. DAVIS

Sources DNB · *Gerrald a fragment: containing some account of the life of this devoted citizen* [1795] · *Authentic biographical anecdotes of Joseph Gerrald, a delegate to the British convention in Scotland from the London Corresponding Society* (1795) · *The trial of Joseph Gerrald ... with an original memoir, and notes* (1835) · 'Memoirs and trials of the political martyrs of Scotland; persecuted during the years 1793-4-5', *Tarr's Edinburgh Magazine*, 4 (1837), 1-20 · E. P. Thompson, *The making of the English working class* (1963) · E. T. Kosberg, 'Gerrald, Joseph', *BDMBR*, vol. 1
Archives Harris Man. Oxf., Shepherd MSS · State Library of New South Wales, Sydney, Samuel Parr MSS
Likenesses J. Kay, etching, 1794, NPG · S. W. Reynolds senior, mezzotint, pubd 1795 (after C. Smith, 1794), BM, NPG [*see illus.*]

Gershon, Karen. *See* Tripp, Kathleen (1923–1993).

Gertler, Mark (1891–1939), painter, was born on 9 December 1891 at 16 Gun Street, Spitalfields, London, the youngest of the five children of Louis Gertler (*c*.1858–1917), master furrier, and his wife, Kate (Golda) Berenbaum (*c*.1862–1932). In 1893 the family returned to their native Przemyśl in Galicia, Austria–Poland, for three years while the father, after a series of unsuccessful business ventures, sought work in the United States. In 1896 they were reunited in the East End of London and Gertler spent his formative years in the poverty and unity of the Jewish community, attending schools in Settles Street and Deal Street (1897–1906). He showed precocious artistic talent (making his first drawing at the age of three) and, inspired by pavement artists, advertising posters, and the autobiography of the painter William Powell Frith, resolved to become a professional artist.

Gertler began classes at the Regent Street Polytechnic in 1906, but a year later was forced through poverty to begin an apprenticeship at Clayton and Bell, glass painters, next door to the school, though he continued to attend art classes in the evenings. His early pictures were modelled on the old masters and showed great precision and accuracy. In the summer of 1908 he won a bronze medal for painting in a national art competition, and applied to the Jewish Educational Aid Society for support. On the advice of the artist William Rothenstein he attended the Slade School of Fine Art, University College, London, from 1908 to 1912 and studied under Henry Tonks, winning a Slade art scholarship (1909), first prize in head painting and second prize in painting from the cast (1910), and leaving with a British Institution scholarship in 1912. Fellow student Paul Nash described Gertler riding high 'upon the crest of the wave' (Nash, 90) with his contemporaries Stanley Spencer, William Roberts, Edward Wadsworth, and Christopher Nevinson, who considered Gertler 'the genius of the place' (Nevinson, 25). At the Slade he also

Mark Gertler (1891–1939), self-portrait, 1920

met and fell in love with a young student, Dora de Houghton *Carrington (1893–1932), who would become his confidante and muse, and the object of his unrequited passion for the next ten years.

In the early years (1907–11) Gertler painted his own family repeatedly, and after 1910 he attended the Slade part-time in order to concentrate on Jewish subjects. His mother became the focus of these portraits, and through her he sought to express a vision both 'barbaric and symbolic' (*Selected Letters*, 55). By 1913 the naturalistic style of his *Portrait of the Artist's Mother* (1911) had evolved into a bold use of colour and simplification of form which heightened the emotive intensity of these portraits. He exhibited with the New English Art Club from 1911 to 1916 (he became a member in 1912) and joined the London Group in 1915.

St John Hutchinson described Gertler in his youth as 'a Jew from the East End with amazing gifts of draughtsmanship, amazing vitality, … a sense of humour, and of mimicry unique to himself—a shock of hair, [and] the vivid eyes of genius and consumption' (Hutchinson, 18–22). These qualities impressed the collector Edward Marsh, who in 1914 offered Gertler a subsidy in return for paintings, and the writer Gilbert Cannan, whose novel *Mendel* (1916) is based on Gertler's early struggles and his difficult affair with Carrington. Through Marsh, Gertler found himself plunged into society and his reaction was deeply ambivalent. He wrote to Carrington in December 1912:

By my ambitions I am cut off from my own family and class and by them I have been raised to be equal to a class I hate! They do not understand me nor I them. So I am an outcast. (*Selected Letters*, 49)

These feelings reached a pitch in 1911, when he refused an offer from the Jewish Educational Aid Society to study abroad, and would also characterize his future testy relations with patrons. However, his relationship with the society hostess Lady Ottoline Morrell, who later purchased his *Fruit Sorters* (1914, Leicestershire Museum and Art Gallery, Leicester) in her capacity as buyer for the Contemporary Arts Society, quickly developed into an enduring friendship when it became clear that she understood this ambivalence. At her London salon he met the painter Walter Sickert, and later at her Garsington home near Oxford he mixed with a wide circle of artists and writers, including many members of the Bloomsbury set.

Gertler settled in Hampstead in January 1915, but his attempt to shake off his roots and become 'neither Jew nor Christian' (*Selected Letters*, 81) was never fully achieved and lay at the root of his insecurity. During the First World War his pacifism caused him to break with Marsh and his subsidy, and his 1916 painting *The Merry-Go-Round* (Tate collection) combines a pacifist vision of cultural disintegration with one of personal despair at his unhappy affair with Carrington. Shortly after he completed the painting she briefly became his lover, before developing a lifelong attachment to the homosexual writer Lytton Strachey, with whom she set up house. D. H. Lawrence revered in the painting a quality he called 'the great articulate extremity of art' (ibid., 129) and used Gertler as the model for the sculptor Loerke in his novel *Women in Love* (1921). Friendships with other writers resulted in further fictional portraits: the painter Gombauld in Aldous Huxley's *Crome Yellow* (1921) and the writer Raoul Duquette in Katherine Mansfield's short story 'Je ne parle pas français' in *Bliss and other Stories* (1920).

Gertler's post-war work was profoundly influenced by post-impressionism. A debt to Cézanne is apparent in his studies of bathers executed in 1917–18, and he exhibited briefly with Roger Fry's Omega workshops in 1918. On frequent visits to Paris in the 1920s, he developed an admiration for the work of Renoir, reflected in a series of sumptuous nudes, of which *The Queen of Sheba* (1922) is a fine example. By 1924, however, he found Renoir 'too refined …', declaring 'we must have something more brutal today' (*Selected Letters*, 210–11), and he returned to a final portrait of his mother to express this. The 1920s were Gertler's most successful period commercially. He had five one-man shows at the Goupil Galleries (1921–6) and was a leading member of the London Group, but after collapsing with tuberculosis in 1920 he was often confined to sanatoriums (1925, 1929, and 1936), where he learned to paint landscapes from his window with a claustrophobic intensity. Forced to organize his life to a strict regime, he held weekly meetings for a group of friends, which included the Russian translator S. S. Koteliansky and the poet Ralph Hodgson, and which became known as 'the Thursdays'.

In his last years Gertler was an increasingly isolated figure. Although he had five shows at the Leicester Galleries between 1932 and 1939, financial worries led him to begin teaching part-time at the Westminster School of Art in 1931. The elaborate and highly coloured still-lifes of the late twenties were succeeded by semi-cubist compositions suggesting an imposition of order and design, which he also struggled hard to achieve in his private life. His friendship with Marjorie Greatorex Hodgkinson (1902–1979), a former Slade student, led to marriage on 3 April 1930 and the birth of a son, Luke, in 1932, but he was unable to reconcile his feelings of family responsibility with his longing for detachment. 'There are two creatures in me—the painter and the man' he wrote. 'It is the painter in me that causes difficulties' (*Selected Letters*, 247). In his last years he began to redefine his concept of the female nude, simplifying and intensifying his earlier vision, but, depressed over his ill health and uncertain about the direction of his work, he attempted suicide in 1936. A final fictional portrait by Greville Texidor, *These Dark Glasses* (1949), captures the tension of his failing marriage, which together with the failure of his final exhibition at the Lefevre Gallery in 1939, compounded his acute feelings of isolation. He gassed himself in his studio at 5 Grove Terrace, Highgate Road, London, on 23 June 1939 and was buried four days later in Willesden Jewish cemetery, London.   SARAH MacDOUGALL

Sources S. MacDougall, *Mark Gertler* (2002) · S. MacDougall, *Mark Gertler: a new perspective* (2002) · S. MacDougall, 'A catalogue raisonné of the works of Mark Gertler' [unpubd manuscript] · *Mark Gertler: selected letters*, ed. N. Carrington (1965) · *Mark Gertler: paintings and drawings* (1992) [incl. essays and biographical information; exhibition catalogue, Camden Arts Centre, London] · F. Spalding, 'Mark Gertler: the early years', in N. Carrington and others, *Mark Gertler: the early and the late years* (1982) [exhibition catalogue, Ben Uri Art Gallery, London, 30 March – 27 May 1982] · R. Shone, 'Mark Gertler: the late years', in N. Carrington and others, *Mark Gertler: the early and the late years* (1982) [exhibition catalogue, Ben Uri Art Gallery, London, 30 March – 27 May 1982] · St J. Hutchinson, 'Introduction', in Redfern Gallery, London, *The Montague Sherman collection of French and English paintings* (1940), 18–22 · J. Woodeson, *Mark Gertler: biography of a painter, 1891–1939* (1972) · P. Nash and H. Read, *Outline: an autobiography and other writings* (1949) · C. R. W. Nevinson, *Paint and prejudice* (1937) · b. cert. · census returns, 1891 · register of deaths, General Register Office for England [Louis Gertler and Kate (Golda) Gertler] · PRO · University of Westminster, London, Archive Services · UCL, Slade archive · private information (2004) · *Daily Mirror* (3 April 1930) · b. cert. [Marjorie Greatorex Hodgkinson] · electoral registers

Archives Bodl. Oxf. · Tate collection, corresp. [photocopies] | BL, letters to S. S. Koteliansky, Add. MSS 48969–48970 · NYPL, Berg collection, Marsh MSS · Ransom HRC, Dora Carrington collection · Ransom HRC, Mary Hutchinson collection · Ransom HRC, Ottoline Morrell collection · Tate collection, letters to Richard Carline · U. Leeds, Dobrée MSS · UCL, Slade archive

Likenesses M. Gertler, self-portrait, pencil, c.1908–1911, NPG · M. Gertler, self-portrait, oils, 1909, priv. coll. · J. Currie, group portrait, tempera, 1912 (*Some later primitives and Mme Tisceron*), City Museum and Art Gallery, Stoke-on-Trent · J. Currie, oils, 1913, City Museum and Art Gallery, Stoke-on-Trent · M. Gertler, still life with self-portrait, oils, 1918, Leeds City Art Gallery · M. Gertler, self-portrait, oils, 1920, Arts Council, London [*see illus.*] · M. Gertler, self-portrait, oils, 1920, Edgar Astaire collection · M. Gertler, self-portrait, oils, 1921, repro. in *The Arts* (Nov 1926), 193 · M. Gertler, self-portrait, oils, c.1921, repro. in *Sotheby's* (3 Nov 1982), 78 · M. Gertler, self-portrait, oils, 1922 · photograph, c.1930, repro. in *Mark Gertler: paintings and drawings*; priv. coll. · M. Gertler, self-portrait, oils, c.1938 · portrait, repro. in Carrington, ed., *Mark Gertler: selected letters* · portraits, repro. in Woodeson, *Mark Gertler*

Gervase of Canterbury. *See* Canterbury, Gervase of (*b.* c.1145, *d.* in or after 1210).

Gervase of Chichester. *See* Chichester, Gervase of (*d.* in or before 1197).

Gervase of Tilbury. *See* Tilbury, Gervase of (*b.* 1150s, *d.* in or after 1222).

Gervase, John (*d.* 1268), bishop of Winchester, probably came of an Exeter family. In 1234 he served as a royal messenger to Ireland; in the following year he received royal letters of protection without term, and in 1240 a gift of timber in Hampshire. In 1247 he was presented by the monks of Ware to the church of Byfield, and at some time between 1248 and 1251 was promoted chancellor of York Minster, holding the prebend of Fenton from 1256, and from 1258 the prebend of Warthill. In Yorkshire he was also rector of Wawne. By 1251 he had been presented by Richard of Cornwall (*d.* 1272) to the church of Mixbury in Oxfordshire. As Master John of Exeter, physician, he was granted timber by the king in 1246, and in papal letters of 1248 he is described as learned in the physical sciences. In the years around 1250 he probably spent much of his time teaching in Paris, since it was there that a settlement over his tithes at Mixbury was drawn up in 1251, sealed at his request by various Parisian and English dignitaries. In 1255 he is recorded serving as a papal judge-delegate at Oxford, and by March 1256 had been appointed papal chaplain, when he travelled to Rome as a representative of the chapter of York over the election of an archbishop. In 1262 he was again at the papal curia, giving evidence in the canonization process for Richard of Wyche, bishop of Chichester (*d.* 1253), who seems to have been a close associate.

Following the exile and death of Aymer de Lusignan, bishop-elect of Winchester (*d.* 1260), the Winchester monks failed to agree on the election of a successor, so the see came under papal provision. John Gervase, who had been unsuccessfully postulated to the see of Carlisle by the archbishop of York in 1257, was provided as bishop by Pope Urban IV on 22 June 1262, consecrated on 10 September, and enthroned at Christmas, the temporalities being restored to him on 18 October by the king in return for an enormous fine of £2000. Gervase had already borrowed at least 12,000 marks from various Italian merchants, and the financial difficulties that ensued were compounded by accusations that he had in effect committed simony, having purchased his see from the pope and the papal vice-chancellor. His years as bishop were marked by a prolonged dispute with his cathedral convent over the election of their prior, and were overshadowed by the political crisis of 1264–5 in which Gervase lent tentative support to the baronial party. He refused military service to Henry III before the battle of Lewes, and in the aftermath failed to dissociate himself from Simon de Montfort, being engaged in fruitless attempts to obtain arbitration from the court of France late in 1264. In France he sought absolution for his support of the rebels from the papal legate, the future Pope Clement IV (r. 1265–8), but failed to publish a sentence of excommunication passed by the legate against the English barons. As a result, after Montfort's defeat at Evesham in 1265, Gervase was censured by Pope Clement, and in 1266 he was suspended from office and forced to travel to Rome. Custody of the see of Winchester was entrusted to the papal legate, Ottobuono, and Gervase was burdened with yet further debt, being fined 1000 marks for the king's grace. He died at the papal court at Viterbo on 19 or 20 January 1268, and was buried there. On his deathbed he surrendered to the monks of Winchester his right to nominate their prior. As bishop he issued a new set of statutes for the diocese of Winchester, and appears to have carried out one of the earliest episcopal visitations of the cathedral convent of St Swithun. However, it is for his political misfortunes and for burdening his successors with debt that he deserves chiefly to be remembered.

C. L. KINGSFORD, rev. NICHOLAS VINCENT

Sources Chancery records • Emden, Oxf. • Report on manuscripts in various collections, 8 vols., HMC, 55 (1901–14), vol. 4 • CEPR letters, vol. 1 • Fasti Angl., 1066–1300, [St Paul's, London; Monastic cathedrals; Lincoln; Salisbury] • C. T. Clay, ed., York Minster fasti, 2 vols., Yorkshire Archaeological Society, 123–4 (1958–9) • Ann. mon. • The historical works of Gervase of Canterbury, ed. W. Stubbs, 2 vols., Rolls Series, 73 (1879–80) • F. N. Davis, ed., Rotuli Roberti Grosseteste, episcopi Lincolniensis, CYS, 10 (1913) • F. N. Davis and others, eds., Rotuli Ricardi Gravesend, diocesis Lincolniensis, CYS, 31 (1925) • A. W. Goodman, ed., Chartulary of Winchester Cathedral (1927) • J. Heidemann, Papst Clement IV (1903) • P. L. Hull, ed., The cartulary of Launceston Priory (Lambeth Palace MS. 719): a calendar, Devon and Cornwall RS, new ser., 30 (1987) • V. C. M. London, ed., The cartulary of Canonsleigh Abbey: Harleian MS no. 3660, a calendar, Devon and Cornwall RS, new ser., 8 (1965) • M. Howell, Regalian right in medieval England (1962), 230

Likenesses episcopal seal

Gery [Geary], **John** (1637/8–1722), Church of England clergyman and land agent, was the son of John Gery of Coventry (d. c.1653), and his second wife, Anne, daughter of Richard Butler of the Charterhouse near Coventry. He matriculated at Magdalen College, Oxford, on 9 December 1653, and graduated BA.

Having been ordained at Lincoln on 1 May 1661, Gery became rector of Swepstone, Leicestershire, in 1662, replacing an ejected nonconformist minister, with whom, however, he maintained cordial relations for thirty years. He married, probably before 1665, Anne (d. 1681), daughter of Richard Morrice of Burbach, Leicestershire, and had at least one child, George. In 1672 he was incorporated at Pembroke College, Cambridge, and proceeded MA.

From at the latest the date of his first extant letter in February 1674, Gery exercised a detailed but unsalaried superintendence over the Leicestershire estates of Theophilus Hastings, seventh earl of Huntingdon. He drew up leases of farms, mills, warrens, and coal mines, advised on prospective tenants, hired gamekeepers and gardeners, and audited the steward's accounts. He counted the passing cart teams spoiling the ground in the park; he counted and recounted the deer; he advised which mares to cover, which colts to geld, what trees to buy and where to plant them, and when to transfer fish between the various ponds. He oversaw repairs to weirs, watermills, farmhouses, the market house in Loughborough, and the chancel and Hastings family monuments in the church at Ashby-de-la-Zouch. He mediated in marriage negotiations, and his wife attended to the needs of Huntingdon's infant daughter Lucy. 'As you have made me', he wrote on 5 December 1684, 'So command me in everything' (Hunt. L., HA 3973). During the proceedings of the 1680s against borough charters, he acted as the earl's agent in inducing the corporation of Leicester (partly by judicious gifts of sack to the wives of the aldermen) to surrender their charter without a resistance which would have reflected badly on Huntingdon's attempts to reassert his family's traditional standing in the town and then, in a well-judged compromise, urged Huntingdon that his influence would be better maintained by not allowing country gentlemen to be intruded onto the remodelled corporation.

On the earl's recommendation, Gery obtained a string of clerical preferments. Having become rector of Stoney Stanton, Leicestershire, in 1676, he became archdeacon, first of Stowe in 1683 and then of Buckingham in 1684. In 1687 he obtained a long sought-after prebend at Lincoln, and further gratification came in November, when Huntingdon obtained a royal mandate to Queens' College, Cambridge, to elect Gery's son to a fellowship. The college did not comply, even though warned in March 1688 not to oppose the royal prerogative.

By 1688 Gery was sitting in loyal isolation on the justices' bench at the assizes. He soon stood out equally among the clergy by reading the king's declaration of indulgence in his two churches, and ordering, if fruitlessly, a return of where it had and had not been read in his archdeaconry. In August the chancellor of Lincoln diocese urged Huntingdon to recommend him as successor to the bishop in case of a vacancy. But the revolution ended Huntingdon's influence, and with it Gery's prospects.

Gery's wife had died on 8 January 1681; his former patron died in 1702. He lived on until his eighty-fifth year, died at Swepstone on 9 August 1722, and was buried there. William Bromley, reporting to Robert Harley on his reputedly large collection of books and manuscripts, found a mere handful.   CHRISTINE CHURCHES

Sources correspondence between Gery and Huntingdon, Hunt. L., Hastings, earls of Huntingdon archives • J. Nichols, The history and antiquities of the county of Leicester, 3/2 (1804), 1038–41 • Venn, Alum. Cant. • J. Twigg, The University of Cambridge and the English Revolution, 1625–1688 (1990), 280, fn. 32 • Report on the manuscripts of the late Reginald Rawdon Hastings, 4 vols., HMC, 78 (1928–47), vol. 2, p. 188 • The manuscripts of his grace the duke of Portland, 10 vols., HMC, 29 (1891–1931), vol. 7, pp. 366–7 • VCH Leicestershire, 4.114–18 • P. D. Halliday, Dismembering the body politic: partisan politics in England's towns, 1650–1730 (1998), 189–190

Archives Hunt. L., letters to Hastings

Gestetner, David (1854–1939), inventor of duplicating machinery and industrialist, was born on 31 March 1854 in Csorna, Hungary, the first son of the four children of Sigmond Gestetner, a small businessman, and his wife, Theresa Figdor. He left school at the age of thirteen and in 1871 moved to Vienna to work in the office of a stockbroker before emigrating to the USA in 1873. He struggled to make ends meet in a variety of occupations in both New York and Chicago before returning to Vienna and entering into a partnership making equipment for hectographs (apparatus for copying documents using a gelatin plate). This partnership was dissolved in 1879 and he moved to London where he became an assistant at Fairholme & Co., stationers, in the City. Gestetner had an inventive frame of mind and was preoccupied with the problems associated with copying from his original days in Vienna. In 1879, in London, he filed the first of his many patents in connection with copying. His most fundamental patent, filed in 1881, was concerned with the invention of the Cyclostyle, a pen with a small, sharp-toothed, rotating wheel at its tip which could be used to write and draw by perforating a new kind of stencil; the latter was based on a Japanese tissue with which he was familiar from a period during which he sold kites in Chicago. The pen and the stencil used in conjunction enabled office duplicating to be done for the first time in quantity, at speed, and with good quality results, and Gestetner can with justification be called the founder of the worldwide office copying and duplicating industry.

On 18 August 1885 Gestetner married Sophie Lazarus (1862–1893), daughter of Ralph Lazarus, a government store contractor. They had one son and six daughters. His main interests were his business and his family. At different stages he employed his brother, his brother-in-law, various cousins, nephews, and nieces, as well as his son, three sons-in-law, and several grandchildren. He was a devout Jew who devoted any spare time to communal activities, especially connected with a congregation of like-minded believers he had been instrumental in founding. He never retired and continued to be involved in the firm he founded until his death, going daily to his laboratory in the main factory. The only exception to this routine was an annual two-month winter break in the south of France, from whence he communicated on a regular basis with his assistants in London. He died in the Hotel Ruhl, Nice, on 8 March 1939, during one of these breaks, and was buried in Nice.   DAVID GESTETNER

Sources W. B. Proudfoot, *The origin of stencil duplicating* (1972) · *Gestetner's Bulletin* (Nov 1933) · S. David, private notes on David Gestetner, Gestetner Holdings PLC · C. Shaw, 'Gestetner, David', *DBB* · private information (2004) · register of births, Csorna, Hungary · m. cert.
Likenesses photograph, repro. in Shaw, 'Gestetner, David'
Wealth at death £67,071: probate, Principal Registry of the Family Division, London

Gethin [*née* Norton], **Grace**, Lady Gethin (1676–1697), essayist, was probably born at Abbotsleigh in Somerset. Her parents, Sir George Norton (1647/8–1715) and Frances

Grace Gethin, Lady Gethin (1676–1697), by William Faithorne the younger, pubd 1699 (after A. Dickson)

*Norton (1644–1731), had two other children, George and Elizabeth, both of whom died young. She was educated by her mother, and the fruits of this education can be seen in the collection of twenty-nine short essays published from her papers after her death as *Reliquiae Gethinianae* (1699); however, the publishers of this compilation appear to have been unaware that about a quarter of the pieces reproduced therein as Lady Gethin's own work were simply notes on, or abridgements of, essays by Francis Bacon. She married Sir Richard Gethin, of Gethin-Grott in Ireland, but the couple had no children. She died aged twenty-one on 11 October 1697 and was buried at Hollingbourn in Kent; her funeral sermon, preached by Peter Birch, was printed in 1700. Monuments to her were erected at Hollingbourn and in Westminster Abbey, where a sermon in her memory was founded to be preached every year on Ash Wednesday. An engraving of Lady Gethin's monument in Westminster Abbey was reproduced along with a verse eulogy from William Congreve (praising her as 'Some Angel-mind with Female Form endu'd') in the 1703 edition of the *Reliquiae Gethinianae*, depicting Lady Gethin kneeling and clasping a book, flanked by her mother, Lady Norton, and her friend Lady Bloemburgh, under the motto 'Death is Swallow'd up in Victory'.   DAVID WILSON

Sources G. Ballard, *Memoirs of several ladies of Great Britain* (1752), 363–5 · P. Birch, *A funeral sermon preached on the decease of Grace Lady Gethin* (1700) · *DNB*

Likenesses W. Faithorne the younger, engraving (after A. Dickson), BM, NPG; repro. in P. Birch, *Reliquiae Gethinianae, or, Some remains of the most ingenious … Grace Gethin* (1699), frontispiece [*see illus.*] · marble figure on monument, Westminster Abbey, London

Gething, Richard (1585?–1652?), writing-master, was born in Herefordshire and moved to London some time before 1616. No details are known of his early life, except that, while still in Hereford, he studied under the noted poet and writing-master John Davies (1565?–1618). According to John Bagford's 'MS catalogue of copy books', by 1616 Gething had established a writing school at the sign of the Hand and Pen in Fetter Lane, where his students included a Mr Topham, who would eventually take over his school. It was also from this address that he published his first copybook, entitled *A Coppie Book of the Usuall Hands Written* (1616), but this first venture seems to have gone largely unnoticed until it was republished, in 1619, with two additional plates and a distinctive engraved frontispiece portrait of Gething juxtaposed with a penman's hand and the penman's motto 'Vive la Plume' in highly ornate characters. In this new edition Gething's work, comprising twenty-six engraved quarto plates, was retitled *Calligraphotechnica* (1619) and dedicated to Sir Francis Bacon, who had just been knighted.

In the following years it is probable that Gething continued to teach at his writing school, which evidently flourished, as after his death it was taken over by the writing-master John Goodyear and remained a landmark name within the community of writing-masters up to the early eighteenth century. Gething himself did not venture into the public arena again until the appearance of his *Chirographia* (1645), a publication which concentrated on promoting the Italian hand and in which he styled himself 'master of the pen'. His skill as a penman is visible in this work, despite his characteristic restraint; he has recently been described as 'a somewhat austere practitioner in an age of baroque endeavour' (Whalley, 21). The work itself must have been something of a success, as a posthumous edition was published under the indicative title *Gething redivivus* (1664). His celebrity as a penman is confirmed in the comments of William Massey, who compared him to '*Bales*, *Davies*, and *Billingsley*, those heads and fathers … of our *English* calligraphic tribe' (Massey, 2.60).

LUCY PELTZ

Sources A. Heal, *The English writing-masters and their copy-books, 1570–1800* (1931) · W. Massey, *The origin and progress of letters: an essay in two parts* (1763) · *Engraved Brit. ports.* · J. I. Whalley, *The pen's excellencie: calligraphy of western Europe and America* (1980) · Wood, *Ath. Oxon.*, new edn, 2.261 [John Davies]
Likenesses J. Chantry, line engraving, BM, NPG; repro. in R. Gething, *Calligraphotechnia* (1619), frontispiece

Getsius, John Daniel [*formerly* Johann Daniel] (1591/2–1672), Church of England clergyman and writer, was born at Odernheim in the Rhine palatinate, a descendant of the ancient family of the barons of Goetz, who had been driven from France during the persecution of the Albigensians. His father died while Getsius was a boy, and his mother put him under the strictly Calvinist tutelage of the Huguenot exile and eminent theologian Daniel Toussaint (Tossanus). He gained a degree in philosophy at Marburg in 1618. After the outbreak that year of the Thirty Years War and the Bavarian invasion of the Palatinate his family moved to their estates in Hesse, and Getsius himself moved to his mother's brother Justus Baronius in Vetera Castra (now Xanten, near Düsseldorf). However, Baronius was a vehement convert to Roman Catholicism and the two soon fell out over religion.

After a short stay in the United Provinces, Getsius proceeded to London, and then, at the end of 1619, to Cambridge. Here he studied under Dr John Preston for over two years and took a BA. In 1623 he went to The Hague to petition King James's son-in-law Frederick, the deposed and exiled elector palatine and king of Bohemia, for (presumably) patronage or employment. All he seems to have obtained from Frederick is a letter of recommendation, but this helped secure him four years' funding (at £18 a year) from Oxford University to study at Exeter College. He remained for some six years, further supporting himself by giving private lessons in Hebrew and other subjects. He obtained another BA on 19 June 1628.

From 1629 to 1636 Getsius was a preacher at Dartmouth, and thenceforth at nearby Stoke Gabriel, all the while continuing to offer private tuition to gentlemen's sons. One of his pupils, Valentine Greatrakes, rewarded him with a small life annuity.

Getsius wrote, but did not publish, some of his own pedagogic material, including an abstract of the Bible in Latin heroic verse and a dictionary of New Testament Greek. He had married Elizabeth (buried 27 October 1667) by the late 1630s; they had four sons, John, Daniel, who in 1660 petitioned for and subsequently received the rectory of Bigbury, Devon, Walter, who also followed their father into the church, and Samuel (1642–1661), and a daughter, Elizabeth.

After securing a royalist victory at Dartmouth, Prince Maurice commissioned Getsius to preach an anti-parliamentarian sermon, 'The ship in danger', in October 1643 (it was never published). Partly as a result of the sermon Getsius was subsequently arrested and narrowly investigated for 'malignancy' by the Commonwealth authorities, and feared banishment from England. However, after the intervention of Sir Arthur Upton, an old friend from Oxford days and justice of the peace in Devonshire, he was sent back to his parish with an admonition to 'live quietly' and meddle no further in politics (Wood, *Ath. Oxon.*, 2.510). In 1658 he published the short tract *Tears Shed in the Behalf of his Dear Mother the Church of England*. Intended for the instruction of commoners, this is an exhortation to obedience and unity within the established church, directed against the radical sects of the Commonwealth period, especially the Anabaptists, but avoiding discussion of any issues that divided the Church of England itself. He was suspected of presbyterianism, but his son Walter strongly denied this (Wood, *Ath. Oxon.*, 2.510). His only other surviving work is a life in German of Lord Chancellor Jeffries, published posthumously in (probably) 1689 (Wing, *STC*).

Getsius died at Stoke Gabriel on 24 December 1672 and was buried two days later in his church there. He left a very meagre estate to his four surviving children.

JOHN T. YOUNG

Sources Wood, *Ath. Oxon.*, 2nd edn, 2.508–10, 565 · Foster, *Alum. Oxon.* · Venn, *Alum. Cant.* · V. Greatrakes, *A brief account of Mr Valentine Greatrak's* (1688), 16–17 · Wing, *STC* · *CSP dom.*, 1660–61, 174 · parish registers, Stoke Gabriel, Devon RO · will, proved, 14 Feb 1673, Devon RO [transcript]
Wealth at death left very meagre estate to four surviving children

Gex, Sir John Peter De (1809–1887), legal writer, was born in London, the eldest son of John De Gex, hotel-keeper, of Leicester Place, London, who came from Switzerland but settled in England about the beginning of the century. He matriculated from Jesus College, Cambridge in 1827, graduated BA in 1831, and proceeded MA in 1834, when he also became a fellow of his college. In 1874 he was elected to an honorary fellowship. Having entered Lincoln's Inn on 4 November 1831, he was called to the bar there in January 1835. His name first appears in the *Law List* in 1837. For many years he had next to no practice, and devoted himself to reporting. He collaborated with Basil Montagu and Edward Deacon to produce three volumes of *Cases in Bankruptcy* (1842–5). In 1852 he published a further volume of cases in bankruptcy, reported by himself alone. At the same time he was reporting cases in chancery, in conjunction with John Smale, which were published in five volumes (1849–53). With Steuart Macnaghten he wrote reports of *Cases in the Court of Appeal in Chancery*, known as 'De Gex, Macnaghten, and Gordon's reports' (1851–7). Subsequently he wrote on the same subject in collaboration with H. Cadman Jones, F. Fisher, and R. Horton Smith.

De Gex took silk in 1865, in company with Joshua Williams and George Jessel, afterwards master of the rolls. On 19 April following he was elected a bencher of his inn. In 1867 in conjunction with R. Horton Smith he published *Arrangements between Debtors and Creditors under the Bankruptcy Act, 1861*, which consisted of a collection of precedents of deeds of arrangement, with an introduction and notes, and a digest of cases. Supplements appeared in 1868 and 1869. In 1871 De Gex became a director of the Legal and General Insurance Office, of which he had been appointed auditor in 1867.

For many years De Gex had an extensive practice in bankruptcy. However in 1869 he played a leading part in the case of the duke of Newcastle against Morris, which belongs as much to constitutional as to private law. The question was whether the duke of Newcastle, not being engaged in trade, was exempt from the operation of the law of bankruptcy on the ground of his being a peer. The bankruptcy court held that he was exempt. The case was elaborately argued before the Court of Appeal, De Gex being the leading counsel for the appellant, and Sir Roundell Palmer representing the duke. Lord Justice Giffard decided in favour of the appeal. In 1882 De Gex was elected treasurer of Lincoln's Inn, and in December of the same year he was knighted on the occasion of the opening of the new lawcourts. He had then recently retired from practice. In 1880 he married Alice Emma, eldest daughter of Sir John Henry Briggs. De Gex died on 14 May 1887 at his residence, 20 Hyde Park Square, London, and was buried on 19 May at Kensal Green cemetery. He was survived by his wife. J. M. RIGG, rev. CATHERINE PEASE-WATKIN

Sources *The Times* (18 May 1887) · *Law Times* (28 May 1887) · *Solicitors' Journal*, 31 (1886–7), 481 · *Inns of Court Calendar* (1878) · J. Foster, *Men-at-the-bar: a biographical hand-list of the members of the various inns of court*, 2nd edn (1885) · Venn, *Alum. Cant.* · *The records of the Honorable Society of Lincoln's Inn: the black books*, 5, ed. R. Roxburgh (1968)
Likenesses F. Theed, marble bust, 1887, Lincoln's Inn, London
Wealth at death £123,338 15s. 5d.: resworn probate, Nov 1887, CGPLA Eng. & Wales

Gheeraerts, Marcus, the elder (b. c.1520/21, d. in or after 1586), painter and etcher, was born in Bruges, Flanders, the son of Egbert Gheeraerts, painter, who joined the Guild of St Luke at Bruges in 1516, at which date he was apparently childless, and Antonine van der Weerde (d. 1580). On his death in December 1521 he left a son named Marcus; his widow married another painter, Simon Pieters. Marcus Gheeraerts did not join the Bruges guild until 31 July 1558, becoming a member of its council as *vinder*, or dean's assistant, on 10 September. This unusually late age of joining suggests that he may have trained elsewhere—perhaps in Antwerp, a city with which he was later to be associated.

On 3 June 1558 Gheeraerts married Johanna Struve (d. before 9 Sept 1571) according to the rites of the Roman Catholic church. He was described as a painter by profession, and aged about thirty-six. On 10 September 1559 he was awarded a contract to work on the tombs of Mary of Burgundy and Charles the Bold in Onze-Lieve-Vrouwekerk in Bruges. On 6 January 1564 he took on an apprentice in Bruges named Melchior d'Assoneville, and on 4 March 1566 he was commissioned to carry out further work associated with the tombs; this work was subsequently completed by Simon Puseel. During the 1560s Gheeraerts also worked on a large triptych for the same church; although this survives, it was blown up in the iconoclasm of 1566 and was entirely repainted by others, making Gheeraerts's work no longer discernible in it.

In 1562 Gheeraerts etched an immense bird's-eye view of Bruges, almost 6 feet long. About 1566 he produced his etching *The Image Breakers*, which referred to the anti-Catholic iconoclasm of August in that year. Gheeraerts published Edewaerd de Dene's Flemish version of Aesop, *De warachtighe fabulen der dieren*, in Bruges in 1567, himself etching the title-page and 107 illustrations. This work has been seen as his major achievement, and its illustrations were to prove extremely influential. The duke of Alva's harsh repression of Calvinists and other dissidents in the Low Countries from August 1567 led many to flee abroad. Gheeraerts was a member of the Bruges Calvinist council. He did not appear in court when proceedings were taken against him, and on 1 December 1568 he was banned from the country and his property confiscated. He had evidently already left for England, with his son Marcus *Gheeraerts the younger (1561/2–1636), who also became a painter. His wife Johanna, still a Catholic, remained in Bruges and contested the sale of her share of his property; an inventory of his possessions at this time survives in the Brussels archives. His daughter Hester also emigrated to London, perhaps after her mother's death.

Gheeraerts thus went to London for reasons of religion. Initially the family lived in the parish of St Mary Abchurch, but by May 1571 they had moved to the parish of St Stephen, Coleman Street. His first wife must have died by 9 September 1571 when, at the Dutch church in Austin Friars, London, Gheeraerts married Susanna de Critz, sister of the future painter John de Critz. The couple had four children: Rachel, baptized in September 1573, and Tobias, baptized in November 1576, both died young; Sara (1575–1605) became the second wife of the miniaturist Isaac Oliver; and Susanna, not baptized at the Dutch church and whose date of birth is unknown, married the sculptor Maximilian Colt in London in 1604. At her marriage Susanna was described as 'v. Antwerpen', suggesting that her parents may have been in Antwerp rather than London at the time of her birth.

In London Gheeraerts was part of a group of intellectual Netherlandish émigrés, including Emanuel van Meteren (to whom he became related through his second marriage), Lucas de Heere, and Abraham Ortelius. It has been suggested (Hodnett, Gheeraerts, 12) that they were all sympathizers with the Family of Love, followers of the Dutch mystic, Hendrik Niclaes. The community spirit of the Familists appealed to humanists, but government bans meant that they had to keep their allegiance to their austere beliefs secret. In July 1576 the Gheeraerts family were recorded in the return of aliens in the parish of St Dionis Backchurch. Gheeraerts the elder appears to have returned to the Netherlands shortly afterwards, as 'Marcus Geeraert, Schilder [painter]' was received in the Guild of St Luke in Antwerp in 1577. On 30 January 1578 he wrote in the friendship book of Johannes Vivianus of Antwerp (although where he was when he did so is not known). In a list of those who contributed to the expenses of the guild between 26 September 1585 and 30 September 1586 his name occurs as 'Marcus Geraerts (de oude) schilder'. Various engravings produced in Antwerp during the 1580s can be associated with him. He must have been back in London by 14 August 1586, however, when he stood as godfather there to Emanuel van Meteren's thirteenth child, presenting a christening gift of 4 gold angels 'to buy something' for the boy (Hodnett, Gheeraerts, 20).

Few works survive from Gheeraerts's English years. An etching, in the form of a lengthy multi-sheet strip, entitled Procession of the Knights of the Garter, is signed and dated 1576 (BM). A small whole-length Elizabeth I on panel (priv. coll.) is signed MGF, which must stand for 'Marcus Gheeraerts fecit', as a similar MG monogram appears on his drawings. It is thus the only surviving painting (not overpainted) that can be attributed to him with certainty. The costume worn by the queen in this work dates from c.1580–85, but the circumstances in which the painting was produced are now wholly unknown. Although small,

it is one of the most refined of all images of the queen, setting her next to a throne-like chair in an enclosed garden, with small courtly figures in the background. Gheeraerts may also have portrayed the diplomatist Daniel Rogers, for in 1578, while representing Elizabeth I in the Low Countries, Rogers referred in a letter to Ortelius to a picture 'as large as Marcus has painted me' (Hodnett, Gheeraerts, 15). Karel van Mander, in the brief account of Gheeraerts's life published in his Schilder-boeck of 1604, said that he was 'well experienced in everything, whether in figures or landscape, architecture, composition, drawing, etching, miniature and all that art might embrace … He also drew for … stained-glass makers' (Mander, 290).

Gheeraerts died after 14 August 1586 when he stood godfather to Emanuel van Meteren's thirteenth child in London. No will of his has been found in Britain. A Susan Garrett, who was living alone in Lymestreet Ward in London when she paid the subsidy required of aliens in October 1599, may have been his widow. Karel van Mander stated that Gheeraerts had died in England, adding that 'I would have liked to have obtained his dates and his age from his son, but he did not care to oblige me, feeling that it was not up to him to convey anything honourable about his father' (Mander, 290).   KAREN HEARN

Sources M. J. P. Martens, ed., Bruges and the Renaissance (Ludion, 1998), 231–8, 260–73 · M. J. P. Martens, ed., Bruges et la Renaissance: notices (Ludion, 1998), 156–9, 175–83 · E. Hodnett, Marcus Gheeraerts the elder (Utrecht, 1971) · R. Poole, 'Marcus Gheeraerts, father and son: painters', Walpole Society, 3 (1913–14), 1–8 · A. Schouteet, Marcus Gerards (Bruges, 1941) · E. Hodnett, Aesop in England (Virginia, 1979), 6–8 · K. Hearn, ed., Dynasties: painting in Tudor and Jacobean England, 1530–1630 (1995), 86–7 [exhibition catalogue, Tate Gallery, London, 12 Oct 1995 – 7 Jan 1996] · M. Aston, The king's bedpost (1993), 168–71 · D. Piper, 'Some portraits by Marcus Gheeraerts II and John de Critz reconsidered', Proceedings of the Huguenot Society, 20 (1958–64), 210–29 · K. van Mander, The lives of the illustrious Netherlandish and German painters, ed. H. Miedema, 1 (1994), 290 · R. W. Goulding, Catalogue of the pictures belonging to his grace the duke of Portland, ed. C. K. Adams (1936), 49–50 · J. Becker, 'Een tropheum zeet groot? Zu Marcus Gheeraerts Portrat von Willem van Oranje als St. Georg', Bulletin van het Rijksmuseum, 1 (1986), 4–35 · A. M. Hind, Engraving in England in the sixteenth and seventeenth centuries, 1 (1952), 104–23 · J. Sandrart, Academia Nobilissimae Artis Pictoriae, 1 (1683), 261
Archives National State Archives, Brussels, manuscript inventory of his possessions, Copien vanden goedinghen ghemaect binnen der stede van Brugghe vanden persoonen die hemlieden gheabsenteert hebben ende werderomme ghecommen zynde … Ander copie vanden inventaris vanden goedinghen van Maerck Gheeraerts schildere, archives of the council of troubles 249, fol. 36r–38v
Likenesses A. Bannerman, line engraving (after W. Hollar), NPG · W. Hollar, etching (after M. Gheeraerts), Royal Collection

Gheeraerts, Marcus, the younger (1561/2–1636), painter, came as a boy to London from his birthplace Bruges in 1568 with his protestant father, the painter Marcus *Gheeraerts the elder (b. c.1520/21, d. in or after 1586). They were escaping the religious persecutions of the duke of Alva, but his mother Johanna, née Struve (d. in or before 1571), who was a Catholic, remained behind. Initially the family lived in the parish of St Mary Abchurch, but by May 1571 they had moved to the parish of St Stephen, Coleman Street. In July 1576 the two Gheeraerts, father and son, living in the same house, were noted in the return of aliens

MARCVS GARRARDVS *Pictor*, *Illustrisimis & Serenissimis Principibus Beatæ memoriæ* Elizabethæ *&* Annæ *magnæ* Brittaniæ Franciæ *&* Hiberniæ Reginis *Servus, & Præstantissimo Artifici* Marco Garrardo Brugensis Flandriæ *filius, ubi natus erat*   *Obyt* Londini   Ianuary 19. *Anno Domini* 1635 *Ætatis suæ* 74.

hic ipse Marcus depinxit Ao 1627.   *Wenceslaus Hollar Bohe. fecit Londi 1644*

Marcus Gheeraerts the younger (1561/2–1636), by Wenceslaus Hollar, 1644 (after self-portrait, 1627)

in the parish of St Dionis Backchurch. It is not known where the younger Gheeraerts received his training, but presumably some of it may have been with his father; he could also have passed some time in the Netherlands, but no definite evidence for this survives.

On 19 May 1590, at the Dutch church in London, Gheeraerts the younger married Magdalen de Critz (*d.* in or before 1636), who was the sister of his stepmother, Susanna de Critz, as well as of the painter John de *Critz [*see under* Critz, John de]. The couple's first three children—Maria (*b.* 1591), Daniel (*b.* 1594), and Elizabeth (*b.* 1599)—all seem to have died young. The fourth, Marcus Gheeraerts III (*b. c.*1602), became a painter too; he died about 1654. A further son, Henry, was born in 1604, and his baptism was witnessed by Gheeraerts's major patron, Sir Henry Lee, who had been champion of Elizabeth I's accession day tilts. Henry Gheeraerts lived until August 1650, but the couple's final child, Susanna, born in 1611 and whose baptism was witnessed by the miniature painter Isaac Oliver, seems also to have died in childhood.

In 1594 and 1595 the young family were living in Lothbury and from 1599 to 1636 they lived in the parish of Christchurch, Newgate Street. It is not clear when the elder Marcus Gheeraerts died, or indeed where, as he had spent some years back in Flanders. He was certainly dead

by 1604, when Karel van Mander described his career in his *Schilder-boeck*, and stated that Gheeraerts had died in England, adding that 'I would have liked to have obtained his dates and his age from his son, but he did not care to oblige me, feeling that it was not up to him to convey anything honourable about his father' (p. 290). It is not clear how this reluctance should be interpreted: Eva Tahon (Martens, *Bruges and the Renaissance*, 232) suggests that Marcus may have been upholding the strict standards of personal modesty of the Family of Love, with which his father's name has been linked.

In the royal accounts for 1596–8 Marcus Gerarde was repeatedly mentioned in connection with decorative work on—among other things—coaches, carriages and steps (Auerbach, 115). In his *Wits Commonwealth*, 2 (1598) Francis Meres mentioned 'Marcus' in his list of English painters who could rival those of antiquity. This is generally presumed to be the younger Gheeraerts.

The earliest known paintings by the younger Marcus Gheeraerts date from the early 1590s. These are the half-length portrait *Mary Rogers, Lady Harington* (1592; Tate Collection) and—perhaps Gheeraerts's most celebrated work—the large and iconographically complex 'Ditchley' *Queen Elizabeth I* (NPG). This portrait is thought to have been commissioned by Sir Henry Lee, who entertained the queen at his house at Ditchley, Oxfordshire in 1592. The full-length of Sir Henry's cousin, *Captain Thomas Lee* (1594; Tate Collection) is one of the earliest full-length English paintings to have a landscape background. A number of portraits by Gheeraerts of Sir Henry himself also survive.

George Vertue referred to a letter (now lost) written about 1597 by Sir Robert Sidney, later first earl of Leicester, asking his wife to pay 'Mr. Gerrats' for the picture of herself and their children, which had long been completed and not yet paid for (Vertue, *Note books*, 5.75). This seems to be the large group portrait *Barbara Gamage, Lady Sidney, and her Six Children*, dated 1596, which is still in the family's collection at Penshurst Place, Kent.

Gheeraerts seldom signed his canvases. When, on rare occasions, he did so, he sometimes took the opportunity to allude to his origins in Bruges—for example, on the full-length portrait *Louis Frederick, Duke of Württemberg* (Royal Collection), presumably painted on the sitter's visit to London in 1608, which is signed 'Gerardi Brugiense fece'. This suggests that being of foreign birth was considered an asset for a painter working in England.

Gheeraerts seems to have become the favoured large-scale painter of James I's queen, Anne of Denmark; a half-length of her (*c.*1611–14; Royal Collection) and related versions survive. In 1609 the royal accounts record a payment to Gheeraerts for a posthumous portrait of Philip II of Spain. In 1611 an entry in the accounts of the treasurer of James I's chamber refers to Gheeraerts as 'His Ma[jes]ties Paynter'; it relates to four portraits, depicting the king, the queen, Princess Elizabeth, and the future Charles I, for which he was paid £79 (Edmond, 138). There are further payments for royal portraits up to 1618. Gheeraerts was listed among the artificers who attended Anne of Denmark's funeral in 1619. As Gheeraerts's brother-in-law John de Critz was the official serjeant painter to James I, it has been suggested that the two artists may have worked in collaboration, although no sure evidence for this survives.

In 1618 the return of aliens recorded Gheeraerts as living in Farringdon Within as 'noe free denizen picture drawer to his Majesty, professing the Apostolick faith taught & held by the Church of England' (Poole, 7). On 26 February 1619, however, Gheeraerts did gain denization, which was a form of naturalization. By this date he was clearly being supplanted in royal favour by the new wave of Netherlandish-trained portraitists who arrived at the Jacobean court between 1616 and 1618, most notably Paul van Somer and then Daniel Mytens.

From about 1620 onwards, Gheeraerts's sitters were progressively less exalted: examples are his signed head-and-shoulders portrait of the scholar William Camden of about 1620, and a full-length portrait of Sir Henry Savile, provost of Eton, formerly inscribed on the back as painted by Gheeraerts in 1621 (both Bodl. Oxf.), and a pair of full-lengths, *Sir William Russell* and *Lady Russell*, the latter signed and dated 1625 (both priv. coll.). His latest extant signed work is the three-quarter-length *Mrs Anne Hoskins* (1629; ex Christies, 20 April 1990, lot 6, repr. in colour). His self-portrait of 1627 is now known only from the engraving made after it in 1644, which bears a Latin caption which may be translated thus:

> Marcus Garrardus the painter, in the service of the most illustrious and serene princes, Elizabeth and Anne, of blessed memory, queens of Great Britain, France, and Ireland, was the son of the outstanding artist Marcus Garrardus of Bruges in Flanders, where he was born. He died in London on 19 January 1636 at seventy-four. Marcus himself produced this painting in 1627, which was engraved by Wenceslaus Hollar of Bohemia in 1644.

Following his denization Gheeraerts is thought to have become a freeman of the London Painter–Stainers' Company, because a Ferdinando Clifton, who himself became a freeman on 24 February 1627 had had 'Mr Marcus Garrett' as his master (Edmond, 139, and 205 n.343).

Gheeraerts died in the parish of Christchurch, Newgate Street, London on 19 January 1636. The date of his wife's death is not known. Gheeraerts had apparently named her as his executor, but records show that his will was proved by his elder son Marcus (III) on 21 March in the same year, suggesting that Magdalen must by then have died. The will itself does not survive.   KAREN HEARN

Sources M. P. J. Martens, ed., *Bruges and the Renaissance* (1998), 231–3 · R. Strong, 'Elizabethan painting: an approach through inscriptions: Marcus Gheeraerts the younger', *Burlington Magazine*, 105 (1963), 149–59 · O. Millar, 'Marcus Gheeraerts the younger', *Burlington Magazine*, 105 (1963), 533–41 · K. Hearn, 'A fatal fertility? Elizabethan and Jacobean pregnancy portraits', *Costume: The Journal of the Costume Society*, 34 (2000), 39–43 · K. Hearn, 'Insiders or outsiders? Overseas-born artists at the Jacobean court', *From strangers to citizens*, ed. R. Vigne and C. Littleton (Brighton and Portland, 2001), 117–26 · E. Auerbach, *Tudor artists* (1954), 115, 134, 164–5 · R. Poole, 'Marcus Gheeraerts, father and son: painters', *Walpole Society*, 3 (1913–14), 1–8 · K. Hearn, ed., *Dynasties: painting in Tudor and Jacobean England, 1530–1630* (1995), 89–90, 176–80, 192–6 [exhibition catalogue, Tate Gallery, London, 12 Oct 1995 – 7 Jan 1996] · D. Piper, 'Some portraits by Marcus Gheeraerts II and John de Critz reconsidered', *Proceedings of the Huguenot Society*, 20 (1958–64), 210–29 · E. Hodnett, *Marcus Gheeraerts the elder* (1971) · K. van Mander, *The lives of the illustrious Netherlandish and German painters*, ed. H. Miedema, 1 (1994), 290 · M. Edmond, 'Limners and picturemakers', *Walpole Society*, 47 (1978–80), 60–242, esp. 134–9, 205n., 343

Likenesses W. Hollar, engraving, 1644 (after lost self-portrait, 1627), BM, Royal Collection [*see illus.*]

Ghent, Simon (*c*.1250–1315), bishop of Salisbury, is of obscure origins, but possibly he was a member of a London merchant family that had recently migrated from the Low Countries. The *Flores historiarum* gives Westminster as his birthplace. In 1268 the archbishop of York, Walter Giffard, granted him Wilford church (Nottinghamshire) *in commendam*, because of the expenses entailed by his studies. At that time he was probably reading the arts course at Oxford, and he was *magister* by 1280. Between 1284 and 1297 he held the archdeaconry of Oxford. During that period he studied theology, and was regent doctor when elected chancellor of the university on 17 December 1291. On Ash Wednesday 1293 he preached a university sermon on penitence in which he referred to the moral dangers of student life. By November he had vacated the chancellorship. As archdeacon, Ghent was in demand as a man of independent judgement. Thus he was among those put forward by the bishop of St Asaph in 1288 for the resolution of his dispute with Bishop Swinfield of Hereford, and in the following year he acted as arbitrator in Godfrey Giffard's dispute with the Worcester chapter. Elected bishop of Salisbury on 2 June 1297, he was consecrated by Archbishop Winchelsey, at whose Oxford inception he had been respondent in the disputation.

An outspoken prelate and conscientious diocesan who in 1302 complained to Pope Boniface VIII about the intrusion of outsiders into the dignities and prebends of his cathedral, Ghent protested (unsuccessfully) when Cardinal Raimond de Fargis was provided to the Salisbury deanery. In defiance of current practice he endeavoured to force beneficed royal clerks to undertake residence and appropriate orders, and desisted only when forced by specific mandate under the great seal. He seized the opportunity, provided by Boniface's constitution *Cum ex eo* (1298), to foster an educated clergy. This constitution permitted dispensation for absence to be granted to rectors for up to seven years, provided that they undertook study and appropriate orders. By such means he licensed men to attend the arts course or to study theology or canon law, mainly at Oxford, but also at Cambridge, Orléans, and Paris, as well as locally. Between October 1298 and February 1314 more than 300 such licences are recorded in his register, and the bishop carefully monitored their use. At his cathedral he insisted on theological lectures as laid down by the Fourth Lateran Council (1215), and within his diocese he collated a substantial proportion of graduate clergy. He promoted the careers of Oxford scholars, notably the theologians William de Bosco, chancellor of Salisbury, Walter Burdon, Richard of Winchester, Roger Martival—Ghent's successor at Salisbury—and the canon lawyer Adam Orleton. In 1314 he granted tenements to the Salisbury chapter for the support of a song school with fourteen choristers and a grammar master. His plan to reform the cathedral statutes was carried out by his successor.

Ghent was equally adamant in claiming secular rights, but his attempt in 1302 to tallage the citizens of Salisbury precipitated a crisis, though a settlement favourable to the bishop was reached in 1306. He established a guildhall there and licensed the city's fortification. In 1299 Edward I employed him on a mission to secure peace with France. He was one of three bishops named by Winchelsey from whom Edward II was to choose the officiant at his coronation in 1308, the archbishop being abroad and indisposed, though Ghent was himself described as weak in body. In 1310 he was named as one of the *lords ordainer and—alone among diocesans—failed to furnish supplies for the king's Scottish expedition. He proclaimed the ordinances in St Paul's Churchyard on 27 September 1311, but by then his health restricted political activity. This fact, coupled with Winchelsey's death in 1313, seriously weakened the cohesion of the episcopate.

The chronicler Trivet praised Ghent as a man of great learning and exceptional holiness. Two manuscripts ascribe to him a brief *Meditacio de statu prelati* and he is credited with a Latin edition of the *Ancren Riwle*, written for the Cistercian nuns at Tarrant, Dorset. He died on 2 April 1315 at his house in St Bride's parish, London, and was buried in his cathedral on the south side of the presbytery, where miracles were soon reported.

ROY MARTIN HAINES

Sources *Chancery records* · W. Stubbs, ed., 'Annales Paulini', *Chronicles of the reigns of Edward I and Edward II*, 1, Rolls Series, 76 (1882), 253–370 · Canon of Bridlington, 'Gesta Edwardi de Carnarvon', *Chronicles of the reigns of Edward I and Edward II*, ed. W. Stubbs, 2, Rolls Series, 76 (1883), 25–151 · W. Stubbs, ed., 'Annales Londonienses', *Chronicles of the reigns of Edward I and Edward II*, 1, Rolls Series, 76 (1882), 1–251 · H. R. Luard, ed., *Flores historiarum*, 3 vols., Rolls Series, 95 (1890), vol. 3 · *Registrum Simonis de Gandavo, diocesis Saresbiriensis, AD 1297–1315*, ed. C. T. Flower and M. C. B. Dawes, 2 vols., CYS, 40–41 (1934) · C. Wordsworth and D. Macleane, eds., *Statuta et consuetudines ecclesiae cathedralis...Sarisberiensis* (1915) · *Snappe's formulary and other records*, ed. H. E. Salter, OHS, 80 (1924) · A. G. Little and F. Pelster, *Oxford theology and theologians*, OHS, 96 (1934) · F. M. Henquinet, 'Descriptio codicis 158 Assisii in bibliotheca communali', *Archivum Franciscanum Historicum*, 24 (1931), 91–108 · P. Glorieux, 'Le manuscrit d'Assise, Bibl. Comm. 158', *Recherches de Théologie Ancienne et Médiévale*, 8 (1936), 294 · H. Pouillon, 'Le manuscrit d'Assise, Bibl. Comm. 196', *Recherches de Théologie Ancienne et Médiévale*, 12 (1940), 347 · G. C. Macaulay, 'The Ancren riwle', *Modern Languages Review*, 9 (1914) · V. McNabb, 'The authorship of the Ancren riwle', *Modern Languages Review*, 11 (1916) · K. Edwards, 'The political importance of the English bishops during the reign of Edward II', *EngHR*, 59 (1944), 311–47 · K. Edwards, 'Bishops and learning in the reign of Edward II', *Church Quarterly Review*, 138 (1944), 57–86 · Emden, *Oxf.*, 2.759–60
Archives Biblioteca Comunale, Florence, Codex 158 Assisi · BL, Royal MS 5 C.iii, art. 18 · Bodl. Oxf., MS Laud misc. 402, art. 10 · Wilts. & Swindon RO, register · Worcester Cathedral, MS Q 46

Ghinucci, Girolamo (1480–1541), diplomat and bishop of Worcester, was most likely the illegitimate son of one of the Ghinucci, a patrician banking family of Siena. Destined for a career in the church he was sent in early childhood for education in Rome under the tutelage of Andreozzo Ghinucci, a bishop associated with the papal chancery. Girolamo studied canon law and was to become a distinguished jurist. Though appointed a canon of the cathedral of Siena, perhaps through Cardinal Todeschini Piccolomini's patronage, he remained in Rome, where on 18 December 1505 he was chosen as secretary by Julius II. The same pope on 6 August 1507 appointed him a chamber clerk, then in 1511 auditor of the apostolic chamber. Early in 1512 Julius II gave him responsibility to organize the Fifth Lateran Council and at the same time ensure English participation, so as to thwart Louis XII's rival Council of Pisa; his reward was the bishopric of Ascoli Piceno.

Ghinucci's involvement with the council (he attended sessions three to twelve) brought him into contact with English diplomats, notably Cardinal Christopher Bainbridge and Bishop Silvestro Gigli, and thereafter he was generally supportive of English as against French interests. He collaborated with Gigli in promoting Thomas Wolsey's bid for the red hat, promulgated on 10 September 1515. At that time English foreign policy as evinced by Wolsey largely coincided with Medici aspirations. Probably on 24 March 1516 the pope deposed the Della Rovere duke of Urbino and invested his nephew Lorenzo de' Medici with the papal fief. In the summer of 1517 Ghinucci successfully persuaded Wolsey to grant an English subsidy for what proved a protracted military campaign for possession.

Following the Dominican denunciation of Martin Luther's theology in June 1518, Ghinucci as auditor of the chamber unavailingly summoned Luther to Rome for a preliminary hearing; in the same capacity on 9 January 1520 he proclaimed the Elector Frederick of Saxony an enemy of the church for protecting Luther. By then the pope was deeply concerned at Lutheranism's spread and also alert to potential consequences for the Italian peninsula of a rapprochement between the English and French monarchs (which preparations for the Field of Cloth of Gold portended). Accordingly Leo X on 30 April 1520 sent Ghinucci as nuncio to England to deal with both matters. In England in May 1521 Ghinucci witnessed Wolsey's burning of Lutheran books and successfully resolved the other issue of papal concern. In 1516 the proposal that Henry VIII be awarded the papal title 'Christianae Fidei Defensor' ('Defender of the Christian faith') had received a hostile response from François I, but in 1521 Ghinucci perceived that antagonizing François could be politically advantageous to the papacy, and on 12 July he wrote to Wolsey urging that the presentation copy of the king's *Assertio* be finished and sent to the pope. The latter received the work on 2 October and issued the bull conferring the title on Henry VIII on the 25th. The bull was also a response—as Ghinucci had appreciated—to the treaty of Bruges (25 August), whereby Henry VIII and Charles V pledged themselves protectors of Leo X and of Giulio de' Medici; the cardinal feared a French-backed attack on Florence, which he then governed, from the deposed Della Rovere duke of Urbino. Leo X's sudden death on 1 December, and Adrian VI's election on 9 January 1522, necessitated Wolsey's sending Ghinucci to Spain to encounter the new pope and seek his agreement to the treaty. Ghinucci met the pope at Saragossa on 3 May; Adrian VI, unwilling to commit himself to the treaty, required Ghinucci's presence as auditor in Rome.

Ghinucci had resigned his see of Ascoli Piceno, which he had never visited, on 30 July 1518, retaining a pension on its revenues. When nuncio in England he had bid for the bishopric of Worcester, made vacant on 18 April 1521 at Gigli's death. Since Gigli died in Rome, by ancient right the pope was entitled to name the successor. Aware of this, Henry VIII wrote on 21 May offering Worcester to Cardinal Giulio de' Medici. Meanwhile Ghinucci sought through Wolsey that Cardinal Giulio (already possessed of numerous rich offices) should be persuaded to resign Worcester to him, a matter raised by Ghinucci at his meeting with Adrian VI in Spain. At a consistory held in Rome on 26 September 1522 the cardinal offered his resignation in favour of Ghinucci, reserving for himself a pension of 2000 ducats on the see's revenues. Back in Rome as auditor, in December 1522 Ghinucci heard Cardinal Soderini's lawsuit against the Medici for wrongful sequestration of his family's property and unjust exiling of family members. The following May he was one of the tribunal that examined the cardinal for supposed traitorous contact with François I. That summer Ghinucci supported Wolsey's bid to become legate for life, which Adrian VI refused.

On 10 September 1523 Clement VII (the former Cardinal Giulio de' Medici) nominated Ghinucci bishop of Malta, whereas Charles V proposed Tommaso Bosio, vice-chancellor of the order of St John. Paul III resolved the dispute in 1535 by granting Bosio a reserve on the see, resigned to him on 20 March 1538 by Ghinucci, who by then had control of several other bishoprics. After the battle of Pavia on 25 February 1525 the pope, believing English support vital for him, sent Ghinucci to England; but he was held to ransom *en route* for 1200 crowns, and returned to Rome with the mission unaccomplished. In May 1526 Wolsey sought Ghinucci's help to encourage Italian scholars to teach at Cardinal College, Oxford, and find for the college's library manuscripts and books, particularly Greek texts. On 6 September 1526 Ghinucci was sent again by the pope as nuncio in England to get support for the peace brokered between François I and Charles V. After reaching London on 3 November, he left on 28 December with what he believed were acceptable terms to take first to the French king, then to the emperor in Spain. Meanwhile on 30 April 1527 French and English representatives signed the Westminster treaty uniting their sovereigns in perpetual peace, thus rendering Ghinucci's diplomacy inconsequential.

Spared the excesses of the sack of Rome in May 1527,

Ghinucci was caught up in its consequences. In November he was with representatives of other powers at the imperial court at Burgos, attempting in vain to reach a peace settlement. On 22 January 1528 the French and English heralds jointly declared war, and at the end of February Ghinucci and the English envoy Lee were arrested and imprisoned at Pozza. Four months later Ghinucci was released and conducted to the frontier. Wolsey turned to him to further the king's divorce, and during 1530 Ghinucci sought favourable opinions from jurists of Italian universities. The following year he was still attempting to convince the pope of the justification for divorce, but Clement, faced with inflexible opposition from Charles V, consistently refused it. Unsurprisingly, from at least 1527 Henry VIII petitioned the pope to promote Ghinucci to the cardinalate. The requests were ignored, and on 21 March 1534, moreover, Ghinucci became a victim of Henry's break with Rome, when as an alien and non-resident he was deprived of his Worcester see by act of parliament backdated to the 10th. He was conceded an annual pension of 1400 ducats (infrequently paid). Even so he undertook protection of the English Hospice in Rome, which remained under royal authority until 1538. In May 1535 Ghinucci's licence to enter England was annulled when he became cardinal, but faithful to his undertaking he continued to support the custodian of the hospice, as in the case of an Englishman who spoke treasonably against the king; he was sent by Ghinucci to the galleys.

Ghinucci was held in high esteem by Paul III, who made him cardinal on 21 May 1535, his associated church eventually being San Clemente; thereon vacating the post of auditor of the chamber, he was appointed secretary of the briefs. On 25 January 1537 the pope assigned him the administration of the see of St David's, Wales, a meaningless appointment. From 12 July 1538 administration of the see of Cavaillon (Arles) brought him a pension of 120 ducats annually—he resigned on 16 July 1540. From 14 June 1538 until his death he administered the see of Tropea (Calabria) with a pension of 600 ducats annually. Increasingly from 1537 Ghinucci was involved with church reform, serving on such commissions as that investigating the legal implications of episcopal non-residence. Theologically a traditionalist, he did not favour the incipient Society of Jesus, approved by the pope on 27 September 1540. He died in Rome on 3 July 1541, being buried in the church of San Clemente near the sacristy door, commemorated by a marble monument. Family ties remained strong, for in his will he sought unsuccessfully that his brother Pietro should be given the bishopric of Cavaillon.

CECIL H. CLOUGH

Sources M. Di Sivo, 'Ghinucci, Girolamo', *Dizionario biografico degli italiani*, 53 (1999), 777–81 · E. English, 'Girolamo Ghinucci', *Contemporaries of Erasmus*, ed. P. G. Bientenholz and T. B. Deutscher, 2 (1986), 93–4 · L. Cardella, *Memorie storiche de' cardinali*, 4 (1793), 147–8 · G. Moroni, 'Ghinucci, Girolamo', *Dizionario di erudizione storico-ecclesiastica*, 30 (1845), 190 · M. Creighton, 'The Italian bishops of Worcester', in M. Creighton, *Historical essays and reviews*, ed. L. Creighton (1902), 220–27 · P. Partner, *The pope's men* (1990), 84–5, 213, 234–5 · N. H. Minnich, *The Fifth Lateran Council (1512–1517)*

(1993), item 1, 187 no.174 · W. E. Wilkie, *The cardinal protectors of England* (1974) · E. Doemberg, *Henry VIII and Luther: an account of their personal relations* (1961), 67–82 · G. de C. Parmiter, *The king's great matter: a study in Anglo-papal relations, 1527–1534* (1967) · J. F. Conwell, 'Cardinals Guidiccioni and Ghinucci faced with solemn approbation of the Society of Jesus', *Archivum Historicum Societatis Iesu*, 66 (1997), 3–50 · *The English Hospice in Rome*, 21 (1962), 175, 201–3 [*The Venerabile Sexcentenary Issue*] · C. Eubel, *Hierarchia Catholica Medii sive Summorum Pontificum, S.R.E. Cardinalium Ecclesiarum Antistitum series III*, ed. L. Schmitz-Kallenberg, 2nd edn (Münster, Westfal., 1923)

Archives BL, corresp. with James V, Royal MSS 18b vi · BL, Cotton MSS, letters to Wolsey etc. · diocesan RO, Worcester, episcopal register compiled by vicars-general · PRO, official MSS rel. to diplomatic missions on behalf of England · Vatican Secret Archives, MSS rel. to his ecclesiastical offices

Ghose, Aurobindo [*known as* Sri Aurobindo] (1872–1950), politician and spiritual leader in India, was born at 14 South Circular Road, Calcutta, on 15 August 1872, the third son of Krishna Dhan Ghose (1844–1892/3), a civil medical officer, and Swarnalata Bose or Basu (*b.* 1852). He spent his first five years in Rangpur, Bengal. Their Anglophile father did not allow Aurobindo and his brothers to learn Bengali, and in 1877 sent them to a convent school in Darjeeling. Wishing one or more of them to enter the Indian Civil Service, Dr Ghose took his family to England in 1879 and left the boys in the charge of William Drewett, a Manchester clergyman. Swarnalotta, who gave birth to a fourth son, Barindrakumar, near London in 1880 (a daughter had been born in 1877), did not rejoin her husband on her return to India. Subject from 1873 to serious emotional disturbances, she soon lapsed into incurable psychosis. In Manchester Aurobindo was educated by Drewett and his wife. He won a foundation scholarship to St Paul's School, London, in 1884, a senior classical scholarship to King's College, Cambridge, in 1889, and passed the Indian Civil Service entrance examination in 1890. Two years later he was awarded a first class in the classical tripos, and passed the Indian Civil Service final, but feeling no call to the civil service, failed to attend the riding test and was rejected.

Aurobindo returned to India in 1893, on obtaining a post in the service of the maharaja of Baroda. He worked in Baroda for thirteen years, in various administrative departments, as the maharaja's unofficial private secretary, and as a professor in the state's college. During these years he perfected his Sanskrit and Bengali, read voraciously in many languages, and wrote much poetry and prose in English. In 1901 he married a fourteen-year-old girl, Mrinalini Bose (1887–1918), in Calcutta. They spent little time together and had no children.

Aurobindo had been opposed to the British government of India since his schooldays, but had no time for the moderate politics of the Indian National Congress. Six months after his return he began a series of articles condemning the Congress's tactics, and hinting that real political change could only come about through revolution. About 1900 he and his friends began organizing secret societies in Bengal and western India, with the idea of preparing the country for a general uprising. They made little progress until, in 1905, the British partition of the Bengal presidency for political and administrative reasons created conditions conducive to radical politics and revolutionary terrorism. Quitting his job in Baroda, Aurobindo went to Calcutta, working first as principal of the National College, and later as editor of the influential English-language daily *Bande Mataram* (1906–8). Meanwhile a secret society, inspired by him but led by his brother Barindrakumar, began planning terrorist acts. Aurobindo was prosecuted for sedition in 1907 and acquitted. The next year he, Barindrakumar, and others were arrested in the wake of an unsuccessful attempt to assassinate a British judge. After a year-long trial, Aurobindo was acquitted for lack of evidence. He rejoined the national movement, speaking widely and editing the political and cultural journal *Karmayogin* (1909–10). In February 1910, warned of a planned sedition prosecution, he left Calcutta for the nearby French enclave of Chandernagore, and in April sailed for Pondicherry, the capital of French India.

In Pondicherry Aurobindo devoted himself to writing and to the practice of yoga, which he had taken up five years earlier. Now convinced that lasting social change could only come about by an individual and collective change of consciousness, he sought to put himself in contact with the 'supermind'—'the truth of that which we call God' (Sri Aurobindo, *The Life Divine*, 132)—and to make it an effective power on earth. Between 1914 and 1921 he developed his philosophy in his new monthly review, *Arya*. Grounded in Indian scriptural tradition—which he interpreted in *Isha Upanishad* (1920), *Essays on the Gita* (1922), and *The Secret of the Veda* (1956)—and influenced by European evolutionary theory, it unites an Indian recognition of the primacy of the divine with a Western concern for this-worldly perfection. In 1920 Aurobindo was joined by Mirra Alfassa (1878–1973), a Frenchwoman of Levantine Jewish extraction, whom he recognized as his spiritual equal and gave the name the Mother. In 1926 he retired from public view, placing the Mother in charge of the ashram (spiritual community) that had grown up around him. During the 1930s and 1940s he carried on an enormous correspondence (published in 1970 as *Letters on Yoga*), and revised his *Arya* works for book publication. *The Life Divine* (1939–40) was followed by *The Synthesis of Yoga* (1948), *The Human Cycle* (1949), *The Ideal of Human Unity* (1950), and *The Future Poetry* (1953). He also worked on his chief poetical production, the epic *Savitri* (1950–51). Suffering from an enlarged prostate, he developed uraemia in 1950, refused major treatment, and died at his ashram, 9 rue de la Marine, Pondicherry, on 5 December 1950. Four days later his body was placed in a vault (samadhi) in the courtyard of the ashram, his passing mourned by thousands of followers.

Fifty years later, Sri Aurobindo's influence is greater than it was during his lifetime. The Sri Aurobindo ashram is a flourishing community of 2000, with its own farms, cottage industries, schools, and research centres. Auroville, an experimental community founded by the Mother in 1968, attracts settlers inspired by his vision of a spiritually united humanity. More than a dozen of his books are continuously in print, and his complete works are being published in thirty-four volumes. His philosophy and politics are discussed in learned journals, and his teachings are an inspiration to tens of thousands of people in all parts of India and the West.   PETER HEEHS

Sources Sri Aurobindo Ashram Archives, Pondicherry, India, Sri Aurobindo MSS · Sri Aurobindo, *Sri Aurobindo on himself* (1972) · 'Biographical (alphabetical) files', Sri Aurobindo Ashram Archives, Pondicherry, India [documents relating to his family and others] · diaries and letters of Annette Beveridge (née Akroyd), BL OIOC, Beveridge MSS, MSS Eur C176 · Sri Aurobindo, Sri Aurobindo Birth Centenary Library, 30 vols. (1970–73) · Sri Aurobindo, *The life divine* (1970) · Nirodbaran, *Twelve years with Sri Aurobindo* (1972) · P. Heehs, *Sri Aurobindo: a brief biography* (1989) · U. Aberdeen
Archives Sri Aurobindo Ashram archives, Pondicherry, India | Alipore judges court, Alipore, West Bengal, Alipore bomb trial collection · Baroda RO, Baroda, India, Sri Aurobindo (Arvind Ghosh) collection · National Archives of India, New Delhi, government of India, home political department
Likenesses H. Cartier-Bresson, photographs, 1950, Sri Aurobindo Ashram Archives, Pondicherry, India · J. Hohlenberg, oils (after sketches from life, 1915), Sri Aurobindo Ashram, Pondicherry, India · portraits, Sri Aurobindo Ashram Archives, Pondicherry, India

Ghose, Manmohan (1869–1924), poet and university teacher, was born on 19 January 1869 at Bhagalpore, Bihar, India, the second son of Krishna Dhan Ghose (1844–1892/3), a civil medical officer in Bengal, and his wife, Swarnalata Basu (b. 1852), the eldest daughter of Rajnarayan Basu (1826–1899), a popular and distinguished poet and the first historian of Bengali literature. His younger brother was Sri Aurobindo (Aravinda) *Ghose (1872–1950), the politician and spiritual leader. His parents belonged to Brahmo Samaj, a Hindu reformist movement opposed to the traditional practice of suttee, and his father, who had studied at Aberdeen University, was also an Anglophile who employed an English governess and deeply admired the English character.

In 1877 Manmohan and his brothers were sent by their father to Loreto convent school at Darjeeling to be taught by Catholic nuns; Krishna Dhan Ghose wanted them to be at a distance from their mother, who as a result of repeated bouts of insanity would subject her children to extreme physical torture. In 1879 the family visited England and the boys were sent to live in Manchester in the house of the Revd William Drewett, a kind and learned Congregational minister who taught them Latin and Greek and read the Elizabethan poets with them. Manmohan, a brilliant scholar, was educated at Manchester grammar school (1881–4) and St Paul's School in London (1884–7). In London he knew Laurence Binyon, the poet, who remained his closest friend for the rest of his life. Binyon was amazed at Ghose's passion for Greek verse, his vast knowledge of English literature, and the skill and subtlety of the English poems he was writing.

Manmohan won an open scholarship to Christ Church, Oxford, which he hesitated to take up: his father, though a prosperous and philanthropic doctor, had many calls on his income, supported a great number of impoverished relations, and was harassed and distraught by the growing mental illness of his wife. Manmohan nevertheless went up to Oxford in Michaelmas 1887 with the intention of studying classics. He had almost no money and lodged among rich and fashionable undergraduates. He found himself unable to pay the tuition fees and lived a solitary and ascetic life, writing verse in his rooms and living on bread and butter. In the vacations he and his brothers stayed at 128 Cromwell Road, London, the office of the South Kensington Liberal Club, whose secretary was J. S. Cotton, editor of *The Academy*, who was born in India and sensitive to the plight of the Ghose brothers. Manmohan began work on a rich and colourful Indian story, 'Prince Pomegranate', but he was lonely in London. Sympathizing with his friend's sense of isolation, Binyon introduced him to Selwyn Image, who designed the cover for the forthcoming anthology of poems *Primavera*, and to Arthur Galton of the *Hobby Horse* circle. Ghose obtained a second class in classical moderations in 1889 but, deeply in debt to Oxford moneylenders, did not return to Christ Church in autumn 1889 and instead pursued his classical studies alone.

On 8 April 1890 Ghose met Oscar Wilde at the Fitzroy Street settlement. A little later, after several visits to Tite Street for afternoon tea with the Wildes, Ghose wrote to Binyon:

> He is a wonderful and charming being. You are inclined to think him superficial, I know, you should know him as I do then you would feel what depth and sagacity there is behind his delightful mask of paradox and irony and perversity. (Ghose to L. Binyon, 28 Aug 1890, BL)

Wilde himself was profoundly impressed with Ghose and, amused at the three-piece velvet suit in aesthetic brown in which Ghose would visit him, christened him 'the young Indian panther in evening brown' (Purani, *Sri Aurobindo in England*, 97).

Ghose's poems were published in the little anthology *Primavera* in 1890. They were praised by the reviewers (notably Wilde in the *Pall Mall Gazette* and John Addington Symonds in *The Academy*) for the music and charm of the writing and the subtle mastery of English prosody and diction. Ghose at first concealed from Wilde that he was practically destitute; when Wilde discovered the truth he gave Ghose a wealth of practical help and advice and tried to persuade him to finish 'Prince Pomegranate', so that Wilde could place it with an editor. Ghose was never satisfied with the story and it was neither completed nor published. He became a member of the Rhymers' Club and a friend of Lionel Johnson and Ernest Dowson, but his verse was not published in *The Book of the Rhymers' Club* (1892) because he could not afford to share the expenses with the other contributors.

In 1893 Ghose's father learned that the ship bringing his son Aravinda back to India had been wrecked and his son drowned. The news was untrue, but the doctor died of heart failure. Ghose returned to India in mourning and took a series of teaching posts in Patna, Bankipur, and Calcutta, enduring dullness and exhaustion for the sake of the salary. In 1897 he was appointed an assistant professor at Dacca College; here, for five years, he taught English literature, corresponded with Binyon in England, and contributed poems to the *Garland of New Poetry* (1898). In 1899 he married Malati Banerjee (*d.* 1918), the beautiful, unlettered daughter of a Dacca chemist. At this time he began work on his *magnum opus*, the epic poem 'Perseus', and published a volume entitled *Love-Songs and Elegies* (1898) with Elkin Mathews. Aided by Binyon and Herbert Horne, he made a study of Italian art and became an avid collector of prints and photographs of Renaissance painting. He became a friend and admirer of Rabindranath Tagore, whose 'Paras Pathar' he translated into English. He was made a full professor at Dacca in 1901. In the same year his first child, Mrinalini, was born. In 1903 he became an inspector of schools in the Chota-Nagpur division; this involved 200 days' travelling a year, journeying by ox-cart to remote villages. His second daughter and future biographer, Lotika, was born at this time, and shortly afterwards the family moved to Calcutta, where Ghose became a professor at Presidency College. He was widely regarded as the best teacher in the city. He filled his house with English flowers and reproductions of Italian paintings. He was extremely happy.

In 1905, however, Ghose's wife fell ill with an incurable nervous disease, which led to paralysis and loss of speech and memory. At the same time, Ghose suffered greatly from the political activities of his younger brothers Aravinda and Barindra Kumar, who settled in Calcutta with the secret intention of raising an armed revolt against British rule. Ghose, who suspected nothing of this and was a frequent visitor at their house, was put under surveillance by the intelligence services. After the detonation of a terrorist bomb, which killed two English women and for which Barindra Kumar was given a sentence of life imprisonment, Ghose himself came under suspicion as a possible associate of terrorists. Friends and relatives no longer came to his house and he became isolated and remote. During the First World War he was again put in danger of arrest and imprisonment because he was wrongly thought to be involved in a case of revolutionary arms smuggling. The government allowed him to retain his liberty on the extraordinary condition that he abandon his grandly ambitious poem 'Perseus' in case it should prove to have a concealed political motive. At this time Ghose was in anguish at what was happening in England as a result of the war and was writing deeply patriotic verse to the country he regarded as his home.

Restored to favour after a decade in which his salary had been frozen by the authorities, Ghose was promoted to a class I post in the Indian education service, with a specially enhanced grade of pay. Ghose's wife, whom he 'worshipped', died in October 1918, and his own health broke down following the long years of devoted care with which he had nursed her while also caring for two infant daughters. He aged prematurely. In 1921 he lost the sight of one eye and could see little with the other. There followed a period of renewed poetic composition, inspired by his grief for his dead wife. The blind Ghose dictated to his daughters two series of elegiac lyrics, 'Immortal Eve' and

'Orphic Mysteries', which were published posthumously in 1926 as *Songs of Love and Death*, with a moving memoir by Binyon. W. B. Yeats, moved to tears on reading 'page after page of majestic lines', described the volume as 'one of the most lovely works in the world' (Ghose, *Selected Poems*, 253). John Freeman compared the poems to *The Angel in the House* by Coventry Patmore.

For thirty years Ghose had cherished the dream of returning to England. In 1924 he booked a passage for himself and his daughters for a date in March, but he died at 275/3 Bowbazar Street, Calcutta, on 4 January 1924 after a short illness, three weeks before his retirement from Presidency College. While he lay dying his daughters read to him from Scott and Shakespeare at his request as no one was able to read to him from his beloved Greek poets. He was cremated the same day at the Keoratala burning ghat according to the rites of the Brahmo Samaj.

Between 1970 and 1977 Ghose's daughter Lotika published four of a projected five volumes of her father's hitherto unpublished writings as *Collected Poems*, garnered from scores of notebooks and mountains of loose sheets of paper lying neglected for more than half a century in the cellars of Calcutta University Library. These volumes, unnoticed in India, where they were published, also remain largely unknown to the Western world. They contain 'Perseus', abandoned after 8572 lines, and the completed lyric epic *Adam Alarmed in Paradise: an Epic of Eden during the Great War*. At 12,282 lines in trochaic trimetre, it is almost as long as John Milton's *Paradise Lost* and *Paradise Regained* put together—a splendid testimony to Ghose's devotion to poetry, his delight in difficult metre and verbal music, and his powers of concentration and learning.

GUTALA KRISHNAMURTI

Sources L. Ghose, *Manmohan Ghose* (New Delhi, 1975) · L. Binyon, memoir, in M. Ghose, *Songs of love and death* (1926) · *Manmohan Ghose: collected poems*, ed. L. Ghose, 4 vols. (1970–77) · M. Ghose, unpublished letters to Laurence Binyon, BL · M. Ghose, *Selected poems*, ed. L. Ghose (1974) · A. B. Purani, ed., *Sri Aurobindo in England* (Pondicherry, 1956) · A. B. Purani, *The life of Sri Aurobindo* (Pondicherry, 1964) · *Life—literature—yoga: some letters of Sri Aurobindo* (Pondicherry, 1962) · N. Gray, 'Friends of my father, Laurence Binyon, in the years 1890 to c.1904', *Private Library* (summer 1985), 79–91 · J. Hatcher, *Laurence Binyon: poet, scholar of east and west* (1996) · O. Wilde, review of *Primavera*, *Pall Mall Gazette* (24 May 1890) · *The Athenaeum* (21 June 1890) · J. A. Symonds, review, *The Academy* (9 Aug 1890) · E. R., review, *The Queen* (10 Jan 1891) · J. Freeman, review of *Songs of love and death*, *London Mercury* (April 1926) · J. S. Sharma, *The national biographical dictionary of India* (1972) · *Presidency College Magazine*, 10/3 (March 1924)
Archives BL, letters to Laurence Binyon
Likenesses L. Binyon, pencil drawing (aged twenty-three), repro. in *Manmohan Ghose*, ed. L. Ghose, 1 (1970), frontispiece · group portrait, photograph (with his daughters, Mrinalini and Lotika), repro. in *Presidency College Magazine*, frontispiece; priv. coll. · photograph (aged forty-two), repro. in *Manmohan Ghose*, ed. L. Ghose, 2 (1972)

Giant Haystacks. *See* Ruane, Martin Austin (1946–1998).

Giardini [Degiardino], **Felice** (1716–1796), violinist and composer, was born in Turin, Italy, on 12 April 1716, the son of a French musician named Jardin, who introduced

Felice Giardini (1716–1796), by Thomas Gainsborough, early 1760s

him to the violin. After time spent in Milan as a cathedral chorister and student of singing, composition, and harpsichord playing (under Paladini), he returned to Turin and studied the violin with G. B. Somis, a pupil of the great Italian violinist Arcangelo Corelli. Giardini quickly advanced through the ranks of various orchestras in Rome and Naples, and in 1748 embarked on a concert tour of Europe as a violin soloist. He arrived in England, via Berlin and Paris, probably in 1750 and possibly at the invitation of Frederick, prince of Wales.

Giardini's presence continued the influence of the Corellian school of violin playing in England, as epitomized formerly by Francesco Geminiani and characterized by tasteful and refined performance rather than virtuosic display. He appeared at first in private circles, enjoying immediate success and easily eclipsing the abilities of native violinists. His first public performance in London (a benefit for Francesca Cuzzoni on 27 April 1751) was a triumph. Involvement from 1762 with the concerts of Harriet Fox-Lane, Lady Bingley, his principal patron, followed, and he gained a number of gentlemen violin pupils and taught singing and harpsichord to ladies in addition to those with higher aspirations. He later taught and enjoyed the patronage of Caroline Russell, duchess of Marlborough, as well as that of William, duke of Gloucester, and Henry, duke of Cumberland, brothers of George III.

Some of Giardini's most innovative instrumental works were published during this period, including the *Sei sonate di cembalo con violino o flauto traverso*, op. 3 (1751). With the instruments treated with greater equality, these are the earliest examples of the accompanied sonata in England and are important early examples of the *galant* style in English chamber music.

Within a few years of his arrival Giardini established a morning *accademia* at his house, which provided opportunities for his students to perform. It survived until at least 1768. During the early 1750s (probably 1753 or 1754) Giardini married the Italian singer and dancer Maria Caterina Violante Vestris (*c*.1732–1791), although the marriage appears to have been short-lived.

Giardini published his own music in partnership with John Cox (until 1755) and performed widely as leader and soloist for various subscription series and benefits. After 1754 he concentrated mainly on opera and oratorio, as leader bringing higher standards to the orchestra of the Italian Opera at the King's Opera House in the Haymarket and, unusually, contributing his own operas and arias to various pasticcio productions. His connection with the Italian Opera lasted for forty years. An occasional role as impresario left him with a £602 9s. 11d. overdraft in 1764. He enjoyed greater success with the promotion of subscription series.

Giardini continued his association with high-profile musical events and influential figures during the following decades. He was involved with numerous summer or autumn festivals all round England and took responsibility for the orchestra for the Three Choirs festival (1770–76). In London he led the orchestra at the Pantheon Concerts in Oxford Street (1774–5, 1778–9), and returned to the King's Opera House as leader and music director (1776–7 and 1782–3, and possibly 1772–3). A governor of the Lock Hospital, he was associated over a long period with the numerous oratorio performances given there. *Ruth*, an oratorio originally by Giardini and Charles Avison, was performed at the hospital in 1763, and a version scored by Giardini alone appeared in most years from 1768 to 1780, making it one of the most successful oratorios apart from those by Handel. He also ran many of the concerts at the Foundling Hospital (including performances of the *Messiah*), where he was a governor (from 1770) and where the ill-fated music academy he had planned with Burney in 1774 was to have been established.

Giardini sold music and sold and repaired instruments from his Italian Musick Warehouse in the Haymarket, near Panton Street, from 1767 until 1769, in partnership with the cellist Emanuel Siprutini. Following the demise of this enterprise, Giardini's works were issued by Peter Welcker.

About this time Giardini's dominance as a violinist was seriously challenged by the German Wilhelm Cramer, who made his London début in 1773. Cramer's success may have been behind Giardini's plans to leave the country, but he stayed, playing alongside Cramer on many occasions and often performing on the viola in public. However, he performed little in public after 1779, and deliberately avoided the Handel commemoration of 1784. By this time Cramer reigned supreme and J. P. Salomon was establishing himself.

Giardini was employed as singing teacher and leader by

George, prince of Wales, from about 1782 until his departure for Italy in the summer of 1784. He travelled, via Paris, to Naples and the home of Sir William Hamilton, British envoy to the court of Naples, who had been one of his first violin pupils in London.

On 7 January 1790 Giardini made an unsuccessful return to opera in England, with Cimarosa's *Ninetta*, which he directed from the harpsichord with Cramer leading. Giardini was by this stage very much in the German's shadow and his poor physical health impaired his dexterity. He was also snubbed by the prince of Wales following an attempt to cheat him over the sale of a violin.

Giardini's last London appearance took place on 22 May 1792, in *Ruth* at Ranelagh Gardens, after which little is known of his travels. He appears to have left for Russia, possibly arriving first in St Petersburg. He certainly gave two concerts in Moscow in 1796, where he died, in poverty, of 'a neglected erysipelas of the leg' (McVeigh, *Violinist*, 193) on 8 June the same year.

Giardini was a colourful and often controversial character. He combined charm, wit, and generosity with occasional arrogance, ill temper, and even dishonesty. The anti-German feeling he often displayed was perhaps related to the success of German violinists at his expense, and even extended to Haydn. Thomas Gainsborough was a close friend of Giardini and a competent violinist, and his portrait of the Italian, bought by John Frederick Sackville, third duke of Dorset, in 1778, suggests an imposing stature.

Although a far more significant violinist than composer, Giardini's numerous chamber works, Italian arias, English songs, and glees display a particular gift for melody. Various London publishers were involved after Welcker's death. His tune 'Trinity' (now 'Moscow') can still be found in English hymnals, although his frequent association with the Russian 'Hymn to the Tsar' is inaccurate.

DAVID J. GOLBY

Sources S. McVeigh, *The violinist in London's concert life, 1750–1784: Felice Giardini and his contemporaries* (1989) · C. Hogwood and S. McVeigh, 'Giardini, Felice (de)', *New Grove* [incl. work list] · 'Memoir of Felice Giardini', *The Harmonicon*, 5 (1827), 215–17 · S. McVeigh, 'Felice Giardini: a violinist in late eighteenth-century London', *Music and Letters*, 64 (1983), 162–72 · Burney, *Hist. mus.*, 4.521–3 · C. F. Pohl, *Mozart und Haydn in London*, 1 (Vienna, 1867), 170–76
Archives Conservatorio di Musica Giuseppe Verdi, Milan
Likenesses J. Reynolds?, drawing, c.1755, AM Oxf. · T. Gainsborough, oils, 1760–64, Knole, Kent [*see illus.*] · portraits, repro. in McVeigh, *Violinist*, pp. 145, 211
Wealth at death apparently poverty: McVeigh, *Violinist in London's concert life*, 912

Gib, Adam (1714–1788), minister of the Secession church, was born on 7 April 1714 at Cowden Castle in Muckhart parish, Perthshire, the ninth son of John Gib, laird of Castletown in that parish, and his wife, Helen Bogie. He was educated at the University of Edinburgh where he studied medicine and excelled at mathematics. While at university he witnessed a public execution at the town's

Grassmarket, leading to a conversion experience confirmed by his reading of Luther's commentary on Galatians which brought assurance of the love of God. He then decided to abandon his medical studies and to devote himself to the Christian ministry.

Early in 1732 Gib attended the commission of the general assembly of the Church of Scotland where he became aware of the controversy surrounding the issue of church patronage. The previous year's assembly had seen the presentation of an overture which the majority of presbyteries believed would restrict the selection of ministers to the heritors and elders of a congregation. Despite widespread opposition the overture became law in 1732, prompting a series of criticisms like that of Ebenezer Erskine, then moderator of the synod of Perth and Stirling, on 10 October 1732. The assembly's rebuke of Erskine led, a year later, to his and his supporters'—James Fisher of Kinclaven, Alexander Moncrieff of Abernethy, and William Wilson of Perth—being suspended from the ministry and establishing the Associate Presbytery, the first secession from the Church of Scotland in December 1733. At the time of these debates Gib had taken an active part in opposing an unpopular settlement within his own parish church at Muckhart and, when the new minister—a Revd Rennie—was inducted in 1735, Gib seceded to join Erskine's secession movement. By 1742, the Associate Presbytery had twenty ministers and thirty-six congregations and, within a further three years, a synod of three presbyteries.

Having joined the Secession church, Gib moved to Perth where he studied at the Divinity Hall under the Associate Presbytery's theological tutor, William Wilson. On 5 March 1740 he was licensed to the West Kirk at Stirling and a year later was ordained as the first Secession minister in Edinburgh, with a meeting hall in Bristo Street, where he remained for much of the rest of his life. In 1742 Gib had, like other members of the Associate Presbytery, welcomed the Calvinistic Methodist minister George Whitefield to Scotland. However, Whitefield's refusal to avoid preaching in Church of Scotland pulpits led to a cooling of relations, especially in the wake of the Cambuslang revival, and prompted Gib's first publication, *A Warning Against Countenancing the Ministrations of Mr George Whitefield*, published in June 1742 in which he attacked the Methodist minister as 'Satan's Ape'.

During the Jacobite rising of 1745, with Edinburgh under the control of the Stuart army, Gib showed remarkable courage and determination by remaining in the town, where he preached to his 1200-strong congregation at several new locations (including the Jacobite garrison at Dreghorn, Colinton) against papism and in support of the Hanoverian succession. Gib's next stand came during the debate which divided the Secession church in early 1747. Central to this controversy was the legitimacy of the burgess oath (1744) which required the burgesses and burghers of Edinburgh, Glasgow, and Perth to endorse 'the true religion presently professed within this realm'. For Gib and his fellow Associate Synod member, Alexander Moncrieff, acceptance of the oath was tantamount to an acknowledgement of the legitimacy of the Church of Scotland. Others within the synod, including Ebenezer and Ralph Erskine, interpreted the oath principally as a defence of protestantism against the threat of Jacobitism and Roman Catholicism.

The result of the split was the formation of a rival to the Associate Presbytery, the General Associate Synod (Anti-Burgher), which was established by twenty-two members at Gib's home on 10 April 1747 and of which Gib became the principal leader and theologian. Strong-minded, polemical, and scornful of those who questioned his leadership, Gib aroused hostility both with erstwhile seceders and other General Associate Synod members where he was dubbed 'Pope Gib'. His *Address to the Associate Synod of 1759*, for example, offered a criticism of his fellow Anti-Burgher, Alexander Moncrieff, following his suggested appeal for assistance to George II. Further disputes were centred on the possibility of universal redemption, an idea Gib rejected in favour of his own notion of the salvation of the elect alone. Such views were prominent in one of his most significant studies, *Sacred Contemplations* (1786), which was heavily influenced by Thomas Boston's teaching on the Marrow issue. None the less, for all Gib's disputes within the synod, his many pamphlets, of which the key themes were collected in *The Present Truth: a Display of the Secession Testimony* (1774), provided a determined defence of Anti-Burgher theology.

Subsequent attempts by the Associate Presbytery to eject Gib and his congregation from the Bristo Street meeting house were vigorously resisted until he was finally forced to concede, relocating to a newly built meeting place on Nicholson Street. Gib was twice married: first at Stirling on 7 March 1743 to Hannah Erskine, and, second, on 12 December 1762 at Edinburgh to Emily McGeorge. He remained at Nicholson Street until shortly before his death in Edinburgh on 18 June 1788, followed by burial in Greyfriars kirkyard. He was succeeded by the antiquary and philologist John Jamieson.

KENNETH B. E. ROXBURGH

Sources DNB · J. M'Kerrow, *History of the Secession church*, rev. edn (1841), 845–9 · W. Mackelvie, *Annals and statistics of the United Presbyterian church*, ed. W. Blair and D. Young (1873) · R. Small, *History of the congregations of the United Presbyterian church from 1733 to 1900*, 2 (1904), 380–81, 426–28, 430–43 · S. Isbell, 'Gib, Adam', *DSCHT* · IGI
Archives U. Edin. L., lecture and sermon notes

Gibb, Sir Alexander (1872–1958), civil engineer, was born at Broughty Ferry, Scotland, on 12 February 1872, the eldest son and fourth of the eleven children of Alexander Easton Gibb, civil engineer, and his wife, Hope Brown Paton. He was descended from a long line of civil engineers: his great-great-grandfather William Gibb was a contemporary of James Brindley and John Smeaton; his great-grandfather John Gibb, an apprentice of John Rennie, became a deputy to Thomas Telford and a founder member of the Institution of Civil Engineers; his grandfather Alexander Gibb was a pupil of Telford; and his father founded the contracting firm which became Easton Gibb & Son.

Gibb was educated at Rugby School and, after a year at University College, London, was articled to John Wolfe-Barry and Henry Marc Brunel. Two years in their office were followed by work experience on the Caledonian Railway and the new Barry Dock. His pupillage completed, Gibb became Barry's resident engineer on the Metropolitan Railway extension between Whitechapel and Bow, but after two years he joined his father who was building the King Edward VII Bridge at Kew. For sixteen years he remained with Easton Gibb & Son, with whom his greatest and last contract was the construction of Rosyth naval base; through his efforts the original programme for this was accelerated so that it was brought into use during the war.

In 1916 Gibb was appointed chief engineer, ports construction, to the British armies in France with responsibility for organizing the reconstruction of Belgian ports and railway junctions which it was expected the Germans would demolish in their retreat before a British offensive. In 1918 he became civil engineer-in-chief to the Admiralty where, to counter the submarine menace, he developed the 'mystery towers' to be sunk in the English Channel. For this work he selected Major John Reith (later Lord Reith) as his assistant. The war ended before they could be used, but one of the completed towers later served as the Nab Light, an outstanding example of the durability of well-made concrete in sea water. In 1919 he became director-general of civil engineering in the newly created Ministry of Transport where the two projects which particularly engaged his attention were the channel tunnel and the Severn barrage. He always maintained that the latter, a scheme for harnessing the tidal rise and fall of the river to produce electric power, would ultimately be built. In 1900 he married Norah Isobel (d. 1940), daughter of Fleet Surgeon John Lowry Monteith RN; they had three sons.

In 1921 Gibb left government service and entered upon a career in the world of consulting engineering. In 1922 the firm of Sir Alexander Gibb & Partners was established at Queen Anne's Lodge, Westminster. The going was hard for the first ten years, and not very rewarding financially, but his friendship with C. H. Merz brought first the designs for Barking power station and later the Galloway hydroelectric development, the first major work of its kind to be linked to the national grid. Among his other notable achievements were the Kincardine Bridge, the Guinness brewery at Park Royal, the Captain Cook graving dock at Sydney, the Singapore naval base, and, in wartime collaboration, the supervision of construction of Phoenix units for the Mulberry harbours and an underground factory for aeroplane engines at Corsham. Resolved to make his firm the largest of its kind in the country, Gibb was interested in projects all over the world and by 1939 had travelled 280,000 miles and visited sixty countries.

Of particular interest was the study Gibb made of the port of Rangoon. From 1910 the navigable channel to the port had been progressively obstructed by a silt bar about 7 miles long forming at the mouth of Rangoon River. Gibb was consulted in 1929; in 1931, when the depth of the channel had become seriously reduced, he decided to build a hydraulic model to elucidate the problem. This model, installed at University College, London, reproduced a year's tidal movements in fifteen hours. The river and sea beds were initially moulded to represent conditions as they existed in 1875 and the model was then run continuously to bring its state to 1932. The agreement between the observed conditions at Rangoon and those given by the model was good; the model was then used to predict probable future conditions. The indications were that after a few more years the bar would begin to disappear and Gibb therefore recommended that no expensive remedial works were necessary. This advice was courageous when so much was at stake for the prosperity of Burma; it ran counter to established engineering practice. In 1936 the silting reached its maximum and thereafter conditions steadily improved, thus fully vindicating the study.

In the depression of the 1930s, in addition to work in heavy civil engineering, the firm directed its attention to the necessary development of industry under the direction of Hugh Beaver. By integrating architecture and mechanical services with civil engineering, the firm was able to offer to industrial clients a complete service, and was thus in September 1939 in a position to take on the design and supervision of three immense ordnance factories for the Ministry of Supply; three other smaller factories followed later.

Gibb was appointed CB and KBE in 1918 and GBE in 1920. For his services to Belgium in the First World War he was made a commander of the order of the Crown of Belgium. He was elected FRS in 1936, was president of the Institution of Civil Engineers (1936–7) and of numerous other professional bodies, received an honorary LLD from Edinburgh University, and was a member of the queen's bodyguard for Scotland (Royal Company of Archers) and of the Royal Fine Arts Commission. On other professional bodies, his presidency of the Institution of Chemical Engineers coincided with fusing the activities of laboratory chemists and works engineers. As president of the Institute of Welding he played a major part in securing the acceptance of electric welding as a means of fabricating steelwork.

The facts of Alexander Gibb's career cannot be separated from his qualities as a man: quick judgement, immense energy, humour, love of his native Scotland, utter loyalty to those he admired, a way of picking a man to trust and backing him to the limit, and impatience of sham. To a great extent these qualities became the tenets of his firm. From his family life he valued hospitality and country sports meant much to him. Gibb's health began to fail in 1937; he was rarely involved in his firm's work after 1945 and died at his home, The Anchorage, Hartley Wintney, Hampshire, on 21 January 1958. He was buried at Hartley Wintney. His eldest son, Alistair, succeeded as head of the firm after the Second World War but died after an accident in 1955. Thereafter the firm was led by Gibb's nephew, Sir Angus Paton, the work predominantly being on major civil engineering projects overseas.

A. J. S. PIPPARD, *rev.* I. P. HAIGH

Sources G. Harrison, *Alexander Gibb: the story of an engineer* [1950] · *PICE*, new ser., 10 (1957–8), 130–33 · private information (1971) · private information (1995) · G. P. Harrison and A. J. S. Pippard, *Memoirs FRS*, 5 (1959), 75–86

Archives Sir Alexander Gibb & Partners, Earley House, Earley, Reading

Likenesses W. Stoneman, two photographs, 1920–43, NPG · W. Rothenstein, oils, 1936, Inst. CE? · W. Rothenstein, drawing, *c*.1937, Inst. CE · L. Campbell Taylor?, two oil paintings, Sir A. Gibb & Partners, London · K. Loyd, oils, Sir A. Gibb & Partners, London · charcoal drawing, Sir A. Gibb & Partners, London · oils, Sir A. Gibb & Partners, London

Wealth at death £79,191 10s. 3d.: probate, 16 May 1958, *CGPLA Eng. & Wales*

Gibb, Sir Claude Dixon (1898–1959), mechanical engineer, was born at Alberton, South Australia, on 29 June 1898, the third child of John Gilbert Gibb, carrier, of Port Adelaide, and his wife, Caroline Elizabeth, *née* Dixon. He went to Alberton primary school and Lefevre high school and thence by scholarship to the South Australian School of Mines, where he studied mechanical and electrical engineering. He joined the Adelaide Cement Company as an electrician and in 1917–19 was a pilot in the Australian Flying Corps, serving in France.

After the war, Gibb obtained a post as senior research assistant to Robert Chapman at the University of Adelaide, where he took his degree in engineering and the diploma in applied science in 1923, and in 1924 won an Angas engineering research scholarship. Deciding to get experience in England, he joined C. A. Parsons in 1924 as a student apprentice. He progressed to the drawing-office and thence to the outside erection staff, where his work attracted the attention of Sir Charles Parsons (whose notice he subsequently contributed to the *Dictionary of National Biography*); Parsons made him manager first of the steam test house and later of the design and drawing offices at the Heaton works near Newcastle upon Tyne. In 1929 he became a director and chief engineer; in 1937 general manager; and in 1943 joint managing director. In 1925 Gibb married Margaret Bate Harris (*d.* 1969), daughter of William Harris, of Totnes; they had no children.

The firm's work for the navy brought Gibb into touch with Engineer Vice-Admiral Sir Harold Brown, who became director-general of munitions production at the Ministry of Supply and in October 1940 asked Gibb to join him as his assistant. Gibb became director-general of weapons and instruments production (1941) and his engineering common sense, organizing ability, firmness, and decisiveness won him a great reputation. In 1943 he became director-general of armoured fighting vehicles, and in 1944 chairman of the Tank Board, still in the Ministry of Supply. At that time British tanks were in trouble: design was dispersed in the offices of a number of manufacturers without effective co-ordination, and output was unsatisfactory. Gibb immediately decided that his department would take full responsibility for design, and reorganized production. The Centurion and all the special tank developments for infantry support were the result.

At the end of the war, despite offers from various large engineering concerns, Gibb returned to Parsons, where he became chairman and managing director in September 1945. His pride in the Parsons organization was unbounded and he wished for nothing more than to make the firm outstanding. In this he succeeded. Surmounting post-war difficulties of licences and priorities, he re-equipped first the machine shops, then the foundry and erecting shops at Heaton; his vision in forecasting the post-war trend of size and design in turbo-alternators enabled Parsons successfully to expand their output. Gibb was also chairman of Grubb, Parsons & Co., and took a close interest in their specialized optical work. In 1944 he joined the Reyrolle board, becoming deputy chairman in 1945 and chairman in 1949–58. During this period Reyrolles expanded at a greater rate than ever before and largely re-equipped their factory.

Alone among the heads of the great British electrical firms, Gibb realized the importance of the new developments in atomic energy, and in 1947–8 he collaborated with staff at the atomic energy division at Risley in preparing the first designs for a graphite-moderated gas-cooled nuclear power plant. Although the scheme evolved was clumsy, it proved the conception to be practical and formed the foundation for the design study at Harwell in 1952, which in turn provided the framework for the Calder Hall design. Gibb's engineers formed part of the Harwell team and later of the Calder Hall team at Risley. The turbo-alternators and the gas-circulating blowers at Calder Hall were supplied by C. A. Parsons.

When it was decided that the responsibility for the design and construction of nuclear power plants should be given to industrial engineering firms, Parsons was one of the four electrical firms which were asked to form consortia. Gibb brought together eight companies already skilled in nuclear engineering and formed them into the Nuclear Power Plant Company which received one of the first two orders for industrial nuclear power plants. He also formed a joint company with the Great Lakes Carbon Corporation of America and built a factory in Newcastle for the manufacture of graphite for use in nuclear reactors.

Gibb was elected FRS in 1946, was a member of the council in 1955–7, and vice-president in 1956–7. He was vice-president of the Institution of Mechanical Engineers (1945–51) and received its Hawksley medal (twice), the Parsons memorial medal, and the James Watt medal. He was president of the engineering section of the British Association in 1951; chairman of the council of the International Electrical Association, of the Athlone Fellowship committee, and of the committee on the organization and control of government research expenditure; and member of the Ridley committee on the use of coal, gas, and electricity, of the Board of Trade's informal advisory group on exports, and of the council of King's College, Newcastle upon Tyne. He received honorary degrees from London and Durham, was knighted in 1945, and appointed KBE in 1956.

Gibb loved speed, both in business and in movement. He was a good lecturer and speaker who never hesitated to state his opinions quite regardless of whether they would be unpalatable to his hearers or embarrassing to other people. As an organizer he was clear, firm, and methodical, but, like many men who are full of energy and supremely confident, he found it difficult, until his last years, to delegate responsibility. As a businessman he was astute and far-sighted. He was an engineer of a type which is unfortunately rare: at home in the design office, proud to use workshop tools and machines as a craftsman, yet having a thorough grasp of the scientific theory on which the art of engineering rests. Although at times he could be quite infuriating to his friends, he won not merely respect, but also deep affection from all those who worked for or with him. In 1948 he made a complete recovery from a severe coronary thrombosis, as he did five years later from a second and a third; but he collapsed and died at Newark airport, New Jersey, on 15 January 1959.

HINTON OF BANKSIDE, rev.

Sources C. Hinton, *Memoirs FRS*, 5 (1959), 87–94 · personal knowledge (1971) · private information (1971)
Likenesses W. Stoneman, two photographs, 1945–57, NPG · photograph, repro. in *Memoirs FRS*
Wealth at death £294,162 11s. 3d.: probate, 6 May 1959, CGPLA Eng. & Wales

Gibb, Elias John Wilkinson (1857–1901), Ottomanist, was born on 3 June 1857 at 25 Newton Place, Glasgow, the only son of Elias John Gibb (d. 1905), wine merchant, and Jane Gilmour (d. 1904). He was educated at Park School, Glasgow, and afterwards at Glasgow University, where he matriculated in 1873. He studied there until 1875, but took no degree. With strong linguistic interests, Gibb was led by an early delight in such eastern tales as the *Thousand and One Nights* to devote himself to Arabic, Persian, and, in particular, Ottoman Turkish languages and literature. Gavin Gibb, a cousin of his grandfather, who was professor of oriental languages in the University of Glasgow from 1817 to 1831, seems to have been the only connection in Gibb's family history with oriental scholarship. With singular dedication and private means sufficient to permit him the life of a gentleman scholar, Gibb quickly became a highly regarded British Ottomanist, on a par with the lexicographer Sir James Redhouse.

In 1879, when only twenty-two, Gibb published an English translation of the account of the Ottoman capture of Constantinople by the late sixteenth-century Ottoman historian Sadettin Hoca in his *Tac üt-tevarih* ('The crown of histories'). There followed his *Ottoman Poems Translated into English Verse in the Original Forms* (1882); a translation of *The Story of Jewad* by Ali Aziz, a discursive tale of mysticism and magic, in 1884; and a translation of *The History of the Forty Vezirs* by Sheyhzade in 1886. Among a few lesser writings was his entry on Turkish literature in the *Encyclopaedia Britannica*, a short summary indicative of his strongly held views on the subject.

Moving to London on his marriage to Ida Wilmot Eyre Rodriguez on 3 July 1889, and collecting a fine library of oriental manuscripts and printed books, Gibb lived the life of a scholarly recluse, rarely going further from London than Glasgow to stay with his parents. He never visited Turkey or any other part of the Ottoman empire, although he spoke and wrote Ottoman Turkish with a degree of fluency much admired by his Ottoman associates in London and Constantinople. An amiable, generous, and modest scholar, he acquired through wide reading a profound sympathy with Islamic mysticism and a deep understanding of its role in Ottoman literary expression. He joined the London-based Royal Asiatic Society about 1881, and shortly thereafter its French counterpart, La Société Asiatique de Paris.

Gibb's early, minor works established his reputation but have been almost completely eclipsed by his *magnum opus*, *A History of Ottoman Poetry* (6 vols., 1900–1909, reprinted 1958–67), on which he worked almost exclusively from about 1887 onwards. The first volume, containing an introduction to the whole subject, intended to be as useful to students of Arabic and Persian as to those of Turkish literature, and an account of the earlier period of Ottoman poetry (1300–1450), was published in 1900. In November 1901, while he was putting the final touches to the second volume, he became ill with scarlet fever, of which he died on 5 December 1901 at his home, 15 Chepstow Villas, Bayswater. He was buried at Kensal Green cemetery on 9 December, his funeral being attended by the Turkish poet ʿAbdülhak Hamid and other Muslim friends and admirers. He was survived by his wife.

On Gibb's death, the remainder of his *History of Ottoman Poetry*, although not complete, was in an advanced stage of preparation. The subsequent five volumes were brought out under the editorship of his close colleague and friend, Edward Granville Browne. Volumes two, three, and four continue the chronological discussion begun in the first volume of poets of the 'Old or Asiatic School' who wrote under the dominant influence of Persian poetic styles, creating a 'purely artificial' idiom 'entirely distinct' from the spoken language (Gibb, 1.129). Gibb's sample translations into English were consciously designed to reflect this esoteric artificiality, paralleling almost exactly the metre, rhyme, allusions, and archaisms of the Ottoman originals. In this he was at pains to demonstrate the sincerity and dexterity of Ottoman poets working within a restricted compass, whose art was considered by European and later Ottoman scholars as almost wholly imitative and therefore unworthy of serious study. Volume five, left half finished by Gibb, treats briefly of the 'New or European School' of Ottoman poetry dating from the mid-nineteenth-century Tanzimat reform era, a time in which poetry and politics alike were dominated by western European, particularly French, influences. Gibb was particularly appreciative of contemporary Ottoman verse, which had undergone a 'marvellous transformation' and 'become for the first time natural and personal' (Gibb, 1.133–4). Volume five also contains detailed indexes to the entire work. Volume six prints the Ottoman texts of all the poems translated by Gibb in the *History*.

Gibb's *History* was the first, and remains the only, study in English of the full range of Ottoman 'élite' poetry (the lesser known folk poetry lay outside his interest). Gibb's only European precursor was the Austrian Ottomanist Josef von Hammer-Purgstall, whose four-volume *Geschichte der Osmanischen Dichtkunst* (1836–8) Gibb considered a mere compendium which offered little insight into its subject. However, the first volume of *A History of Ottoman Poetry* did not meet with universal acclaim. Some reviewers were critical first of the effort spent on what they considered a largely worthless literature, and second of the chosen style of translation. Despite Gibb's defence of his subject and method in the preface to volume two, these critical reservations cast a shadow over what was otherwise regarded as a monumental achievement. A century after its first publication, Gibb's work remains a standard reference, particularly for his explanations of the wealth of cultural and mystical allusions integral to the poetry of the 'Old School'.

On his death Gibb's library was divided among the libraries of the British Museum (which received his manuscripts, approximately 325 in number), Cambridge University (which received his Arabic, Persian, and Turkish printed books, 422 in number), and the British embassy in Constantinople (which received many works on the Middle East). The E. J. W. Gibb Memorial Fund, established in 1902 through a bequest from Gibb's mother, provided a means for publication of edited texts, translations, and other scholarly studies of Arabic, Persian, and Turkish literature, and by the mid-1980s had published over seventy volumes of highly specialized material.

Christine Woodhead

Sources *DNB* • [E. G. B.], *Journal of the Royal Asiatic Society of Great Britain and Ireland* (1902), 486–9 • *The Times* (9 Dec 1901) • E. G. Browne, ed., *A handlist of the Gibb collection of Turkish and other books in the library of the University of Cambridge* (1906) • E. J. W. Gibb, *A history of Ottoman poetry*, 1 (1900); 2, ed. E. G. Brown (1902), xvi–xxi
Likenesses photograph, 1896–1899?, repro. in Gibb, *History of Ottoman poetry*, 6 (1909), frontispiece
Wealth at death £18,448 11s. 11d.: probate, 28 Dec 1901, CGPLA Eng. & Wales

Gibb [Gibbs], **Frederick** (*c.*1620–1681), writer and physician, son of Bernard Gibbs, advocate, was born in Dunfermline, Fife, and studied at the University of St Andrews. A passionate traveller, young Gibb embarked on a tour that took him to France, the Netherlands, Germany, Italy, Greece, Turkey, Syria, and Egypt. After sojourning in Rome, and in Padua, where he intended to study medicine, he made his way back to France, and is reported to have spent several years in Anduze, Languedoc. From there Gibb moved on to Nîmes where he was offered the post of professor of rhetoric at the university. An ardent protestant, he caused more than a little frisson by posting a bill which announced that in his seminar he would be lecturing on the doctrines of the orthodox religion. The Catholic clergy, furious at Gibb's effrontery, petitioned for an injunction to be issued which, among other things, sentenced Gibb's bill to incineration by the hand of the executioner; both he and his printer, Edouard Raban, were served with a subpoena. Gibb was probably forced to leave Nîmes for Valence, where he received his degree in medicine in 1651, and settled finally in Orange. In 1655 Gibb was appointed professor of rhetoric. His reputation as a polymath is said to have attracted great numbers of students to his seminars. His opening lecture, together with his poem on the arrival of the Huguenots in Orange ('Hunc centonem in ingressum serenissimi principis Auraici … animi submissione dicat et consecrat Fredericus Guibœus doctor medicus'), both printed by Raban, can be found in Barjavel (pp. 47–8).

Gibb is less known for his written works than for his erudition: he studied no fewer than ten languages and is reputed to have shown scientific insights remarkable for the time: notably, he responded to the appearance of Kirch's comet in 1680 by arguing that comets are heavenly bodies that follow specific orbits, and not, as was widely held, portents of disaster. As a writer Gibb achieved only moderate fame. His works include the *Somnium, seu, Iter ad Parnassum* and *Declamationes poeticae* (Orange, 1679), some verse in a volume of de Thou (published by Elzevir in 1678), as well as an encomium in praise of the hog, *In alimentum militis missitii D. Franc. Graverolii, Friderici Guibei porcus* (1679?), dedicated to Nîmes lawyer François Graverol and in response to the latter's *Miles missitius*; he also compiled some unpublished notes on the itinerary of Benjamin de Tudèle and on his *Symposiaca* of Plutarch and of Josephus. He may have signed some of his works by the then common pseudonym Philalethes.

Apparently Gibb was married but lost his wife to the plague. They had two sons: Henri (*b.* 1654) and Jean-Frédéric. Henri became an advocate and later succeeded his father in the chair of rhetoric at the University of Orange. Gibb's grandson Jean-Frédéric Guib also followed a career at the bar and is reported to have contributed to Pierre Bayle's dictionary. Gibb died in Orange on 27 March 1681, only a year after receiving his degree as a doctor of medicine.   ARTEMIS GAUSE-STAMBOULOPOULOU

Sources E. Haag and E. Haag, *La France protestante*, 10 vols. (Paris, 1846–59), 5.384–5 · *Nouvelle biographie générale … publié sous la direction de Dr Hoefer*, 46 vols. (1852–66), vols. 19–20 [in one], cols. 440–41 · [J. F.] Michaud, *Biographie universelle … ancienne et moderne*, new edn, 45 vols. (1843–65), 16.414 · C. F. H. Barjavel, *Dictionnaire historique, biographique et bibliographique du département de Vaucluse*, 2 vols. (1841), 2.47–8 · F. X. Michel, *Les Écossais en France, les Français en Écosse*, 2 vols. (1862) · E. Nappo, ed., *Index biographique français*, 2nd cumulated and enlarged edn, 7 vols. (1998) · *DNB* · W. J. Stankiewicz, *Politics and religion in seventeenth-century France: a study of political ideas from the Monarchomachs to Bayle, as reflected in the toleration controversy* (1960)

Gibb, Sir George Stegmann (1850–1925), railway company manager, was born on 30 April 1850 in Aberdeen, the youngest son in a family of seven children of Alexander Gibb (1804–1867), builder and engineer, and his wife, Margaret Smith, daughter of a Balmoral architect. Gibb's grandfather, John *Gibb (1776–1850), was a civil engineer who worked with Telford and specialized in harbour construction and river engineering. His nephew Sir Alexander *Gibb was the founder of a well-known firm of consulting engineers that carried his name (Sir Alexander Gibb & Partners).

Educated locally at Aberdeen grammar school and at the university of that city, Gibb chose the law as his profession and qualified as an LLB of London University. After serving as a clerk in a shipowner's office and in a maritime insurance office, he was articled to a solicitor in 1872. In 1877 he joined the Great Western Railway for three years as an assistant in the solicitor's office. He left this job to practise on his own account in London in 1880. In the following year Gibb married Dorothea Garrett Smith, the nineteen-year-old daughter of an artist, James William Smith; they had four sons and one daughter.

An election agent to the Liberal candidates for Hackney in the general election of 1880, in 1882 Gibb joined the North Eastern Railway (NER) as solicitor at an annual salary of £2000. He quickly established himself as an able assistant and adviser to the general manager, Henry Tennant, whom he succeeded in 1891 at an annual salary of £3000.

Gibb took over the reins at York at a time when diminishing returns were causing general concern in the industry, and a programme of legislation, generally considered harmful to the industry's freedom of manoeuvre in the area of railway rates, was being pushed through parliament. At the same time, railway trade unionism was expanding and the hours of work of railway labour receiving statutory attention. Over the next decade, he responded positively to the problem, changing the NER from a relatively successful if somewhat staid railway into an exemplar of advanced managerial practice, allegedly signifying his independence of mind by wearing a tweed suit to the office. Among his early and most enduring reforms was the establishment of a traffic apprenticeship scheme involving the recruitment of bright young men from the universities and the business world, such as R. L. Wedgwood and E. C. Geddes. He promoted them quickly into responsible positions in the traffic department, where Gibb needed to break the forces of conservatism and get new methods working.

Concerned by escalating operating costs, Gibb also set in motion a detailed appraisal of operating methods, organization, and information systems, and between 1900 and 1902 radically altered the company's approach in all three areas. Officers, including himself, visited America to study how things were done. He, and the contemporary statistician Sir George Paish, also joined forces to pioneer and promulgate the use of new statistical concepts for operational measurement, control, and efficiency. A traffic statistics office was set up at York under another Gibb recruit, C. P. Mossop. The office attracted officials of nearly all the large British railways as well as others from America and India. The decline in operating efficiency, especially in the management of freight, was reversed and the NER established as the managerial pace setter of the time in the British railway world.

Under Gibb's innovating and vigorous management, the company became the first main-line railway to electrify a part of its system. It also challenged orthodoxy by developing advanced systems of collective bargaining, and turning—controversially—on several occasions to the use of independent arbitration to settle disputes and pay claims. Gibb's fame spread. He served on the War Office committee of reorganization in 1901 and on the royal commission on London's transport from 1903 to 1905, for which service he was knighted.

Gibb's outstanding period of executive service with the NER ended in December 1905, when he accepted an offer, facilitated by Sir George Paish, to become deputy chairman and managing director of the Underground Electric Railway Company of London (UERL), and chairman and managing director of one of its operating units, the Metropolitan and District Railway. The salary was £8000, an increase of £3000 on what he was being paid at York. Having lost his services as general manager, the NER elected him to its board as a non-executive director.

Gibb left the NER a profitable, efficient company well positioned to benefit from the upswing in trade of 1906–14 and superbly resourced with younger managers capable of running the railway for a generation and beyond. He joined an organization close to bankruptcy and with an unsound business strategy. His reaction was to commission a searching examination of its business. He pushed ahead with changes in pricing policy, closer integration of the activities of different operating units, and restriction of competition with other suppliers. Supported by an injection of youthful managerial talent from the NER and from the USA, the UERL companies made financial progress and bankruptcy was avoided. His public image at this time was of a courtly official of great capacity and considerable charm, although behind the scenes he was at times depressive.

In May 1910 at the age of sixty, Gibb exchanged his onerous responsibilities for the underground, as well as his directorship of the NER, for the chairmanship of the newly-formed road board, at a considerably reduced salary of £3000 per annum. However, in civil service terms the pay was high (the head of the civil service received at the time £2500), and was necessary, the Treasury was told, to get 'a good man'.

Gibb's chairmanship of the road board was controversial. Its establishment had been sanctioned in 1909 as a response to the need to develop an effective road system in an age of expanding motorized transport. It was given powers to finance improvements to existing roads and to build new ones. Over 90 per cent of the moneys disbursed in its lifetime were for the former purpose. While this solved the 'dust problem', the concentration on improvement rather than network development, and the fact that the board's chairman was a former railway magnate, led to the feeling that the railway interest had captured it and prevented the building of new roads that would compete with railways. While he was defended for 'holding back' on arterial road development until research on the structure of modern road surfaces was undertaken in depth, the board was unpopular, too, because of its lack of direct accountability to parliament and the Treasury's dislike of its financial foundations, which flew in the face of established practice. With the creation in 1919 of the Ministry of Transport, it lapsed.

Although remaining road board chairman throughout the First World War, Gibb also served on the army council and as a member (and later chairman) of the government committee on production from 1915 to 1918. He was also a member of the Pacific cable board from 1914 to 1918. By late 1918, proposals for legislative reorganization of the railways caused the NER board to appoint him an adviser on their relationships with government, and on the impending amalgamations. On 1 January 1919 he was appointed at a fee of £3000 per annum, and the relationship lasted until 1922, when the new shape of the industry emerged. A short period as chairman of the Oriental Telephone Company completed his business life.

Gibb's vigorous management of the NER and his involvement in the railway reform movement around 1900 has left him an assured place in transport history. The virile organization he built at the NER proved an excellent training ground for some outstanding young railway administrators, and the management recruitment, information, and control techniques he implemented pointed the direction in which Edwardian railways needed to move to retain their edge. An independent personality, Gibb's readiness to learn from and adapt aspects of American operating practice to the British situation, as well as to promote them in the face of contemporary scepticism, was notable.

Gibb died at his home, South Corner, Alan Road, Wimbledon, Surrey, on 17 December 1925.

R. J. IRVING

Sources Records of the North Eastern Railway Company, 1854–1923, PRO, RAIL 527 · Records of the Road Board, 1910–19, PRO, TI-11257, T27-216 · T. C. Barker and M. Robbins, *A history of London Transport*, 2 vols. (1963–74) · R. Bell, *Twenty five years of the North Eastern railway, 1898–1922* (1951) · C. H. Ellis, 'The Lewin papers concerning Sir George Gibb', *Journal of Transport History*, 5 (1961–2), 226–32 · G. Harrison, *Alexander Gibb: the story of an engineer* [1950] · R. J. Irving, *The North Eastern Railway Company, 1870–1914: an economic history* (1976) · R. Jeffreys, *The king's highway: an historical and autobiographical record of the development of the past sixty years* (1949) · R. J. Irving, 'Gibb, Sir George Stegmann', *DBB* · *Railway Gazette* (25 Dec 1925) · *The Times* (18 Dec 1925) · *The Times* (19 Dec 1925) · R. J. Irving, 'Gibb, Sir George Stegmann', *DBB* · Boase, *Mod. Eng. biog.* · *CGPLA Eng. & Wales* (1926) · d. cert.

Archives priv. coll., Lewin MSS

Likenesses L. Caswall Smith, photograph, repro. in W. W. Tomlinson, *North Eastern Railway* (1967), 726 · portrait, repro. in *The Times* (18 Dec 1925) · print, repro. in 'Gibb, Sir Alexander', *DBB*

Wealth at death £46,501 3s. 3d.: probate, 12 Feb 1926, *CGPLA Eng. & Wales*

Gibb, Sir **Hamilton Alexander Rosskeen** (1895–1971),

Arabic scholar, was born on 2 January 1895 at Alexandria, Egypt, the third of the three sons and youngest of the four children of Alexander Crawford Gibb, manager of the Aboukir Dairy Company of Abu Qir, Alexandria, and his wife, Jane Anne Gardner. His father died when he was two and his mother remained in Alexandria as a teacher, but he himself was sent back to Scotland for his education at the age of five. He studied at the Royal High School, Edinburgh, from 1904 to 1912, and then at Edinburgh University; his studies there were interrupted by the First World War, during which he saw service in France and Italy in the Royal Field Artillery, but he was awarded a 'war privilege' MA. After the war he studied Arabic at the School of Oriental Studies of London University, and obtained his

MA in 1922. In the same year he married Helen Jessie (Ella), daughter of John Stark OBE; they had two children, a son and a daughter.

From 1921 to 1937 Gibb taught Arabic at the School of Oriental Studies, as lecturer, then reader (from 1929), and finally professor (from 1930) in succession to his teacher Sir Thomas Arnold. In these years his remarkable gifts as a teacher revealed themselves; more than anyone else, he formed the minds of those who were to be the teachers and scholars of the next generation. In this period also he made his reputation in the world of scholarship: he visited Egypt and other countries frequently, became one of the editors of the international *Encyclopaedia of Islam*, and wrote a number of books and articles which showed a wide range of knowledge, depth, and originality of thought, and mastery of an elegant and precise style. They included an introductory book, *Arabic Literature* (1926), a translation of selections from the travels of Ibn Battuta (1929), another translation of an Arabic chronicle of the period of the crusades (1932), a series of articles on contemporary Arabic literature, perhaps the first serious treatment of the subject by a Western scholar, and some short but penetrating articles on Islamic political theory. These works reveal two of his abiding and dominant concerns: to make the history of the Arabs available to scholars in other fields, and to understand and explain what was for him the central thread of that history, the continuous development of the *umma*, the community formed by the preaching of the prophet Muhammad, accepting the Koran as the revelation of God, articulating the deposit of faith into systems of thought and practice, protecting them against the self-interest of the holders of worldly power and the vagaries of human self-will, and transmitting them from generation to generation.

In 1937 Gibb became Laudian professor of Arabic at Oxford in succession to D. S. Margoliouth and was elected to a fellowship at St John's College. He remained in Oxford for eighteen years. They were years in which the teaching of Arabic and cognate subjects expanded, as students returned from the Second World War with knowledge of the Middle East, and others from the United States and the Middle East itself were attracted to Oxford by Gibb's growing fame. As a result of the 1947 report of a committee set up by the Treasury and chaired by the earl of Scarbrough, Oxford was given special funds to develop the teaching of Middle Eastern subjects, and the administration of the scheme was mainly in Gibb's hands. He found time, however, to continue with his own thought and writing. Together with Harold Bowen he produced *Islamic Society and the West* (vol. 1, pt 1, 1950; pt 2, 1957): a survey of Ottoman society in the late eighteenth century, before the full impact of European expansion was felt, it was intended as an introduction to a larger study of that impact. It carried further his thought on one of his central themes, the complex relationship between government and society, and between the holders of power and the men of learning who were the leaders and spokesmen of the *umma*. The same theme was developed in a number of works on Islam as a religious system, in particular *Mohammedanism* (1949),

a masterpiece of simple but subtle exposition, which was to remain for more than a generation the first book put into the hands of most students of the subject in English-speaking countries, and *Modern Trends in Islam* (1947), a penetrating analysis of the problems of the Muslim community in the modern world, with its balance and continuity threatened by external forces and by modernizing regimes and thinkers prepared to cast aside much of its heritage. It was this sense of a civilization under threat which led him also in this period to write and lecture occasionally (although more rarely as time went on) about the political problems of the day.

In 1955 Gibb left Oxford to become James Richard Jewett professor of Arabic at Harvard University and also 'university professor', a rare title given to a few scholars 'working on the frontiers of knowledge, and in such a way as to cross the conventional boundaries of the specialities'. He became director of Harvard's Center for Middle Eastern Studies, and this opened for him, at the age of sixty, a new field of activity which called out all his energy and enthusiasm; he became one of the leaders of the movement which led American universities in this period to set up centres of regional studies, bringing together teachers, researchers, and students in different disciplines to study the culture and society of a region of the world. Teaching, administration, and academic statesmanship left him less time for research, but he was able to take up again some of his earlier interests in history and literature, and in particular to undertake a complete translation of the travels of Ibn Battuta; his vast knowledge of Arabic and sensitive feeling for the nuances of literary style made him a remarkably good translator. (He had also supervised the translation of V. V. Barthold's *Turkestan Down to the Mongol Invasion* published in 1958 in the E. J. W. Gibb memorial series.) In this period, as throughout his career, teaching was central to his life, and once more he trained not only scholars for the next generation but officials for a government facing new responsibilities in the world. Once more, too, what they remembered of him was not only his great learning and skill in exposition, but the special flavour of his personality. Those who knew him well became aware, behind his mild and restrained manner and appearance, of an intellectual authority, a willingness to question received ideas, an imagination ranging among distant peoples, times and places, and a warmth of sympathy and affection: a warmth which, as a younger colleague was to write, 'came from the secure feeling of loyalty, perhaps the strongest of his qualities' (private information, 1986).

In 1964, shortly before his planned retirement, Gibb had a severe stroke, and soon afterwards returned to Oxford. His powers of speech and movement were impaired, and he had to lead a quiet life, but he was able to keep in touch with a wide circle of friends and colleagues and continue working on a reduced scale. His wife died in 1969, and in 1971 he moved to a cottage at Cherington, a village north of Oxford. He died in hospital at the neighbouring town of Shipston-on-Stour, Warwickshire, on 22 October 1971.

By the time of his death Gibb had accumulated many

distinctions. He was an honorary fellow of St John's College, Oxford (1955), a fellow of the British Academy (1944) and the Danish Academy, and a member of, among other bodies, the American Philosophical Society, the American Academy of Arts and Sciences, the Academy of the Arabic Language in Cairo, and the Institut d'Égypte. He was awarded honorary doctorates by Edinburgh, Harvard, and Algiers universities. He was knighted in 1954, and also held French and Dutch honours.

ALBERT HOURANI, *rev.*

Sources A. K. S. Lambton, *Bulletin of the School of Oriental and African Studies*, 35 (1972), 338–45 · *Journal of the American Oriental Society*, 93 (1973), 429–31 · A. Hourani, 'Sir Hamilton Gibb, 1895–1971', *PBA*, 58 (1972), 493–523 · G. Makdisi, ed., *Arabic and Islamic studies in honor of Hamilton A. R. Gibb* (1965) · private information (1986) · personal knowledge (1986) · *The Times* (23 Oct 1971) · *CGPLA Eng. & Wales* (1972)
Wealth at death £32,035: probate, 14 Jan 1972, *CGPLA Eng. & Wales*

Gibb, John (d. 1720?), founder of the Sweet Singers or Gibbite sect, was born and raised in Borrowstounness (modern day Bo'ness) in Linlithgowshire, Scotland. There he learned to sail, and was in time appointed to be the purser and master of the merchantman *The John*, which operated out of that port on regular trading voyages to the Low Countries. A strong opponent of the prelacy, Gibb was initially extremely useful to the ejected ministers of the Church of Scotland, ferrying secret correspondence and illegally printed pamphlets between the covenanter rebels and their exiled brethren in the Netherlands under the guise of conducting legitimate trading ventures on behalf of his wealthy patrons. It is entirely probable that during his frequent visits to the Low Countries he had contact with Dutch religious radicals and imbibed the Anabaptist doctrines which were so profoundly to affect the subsequent development of his own spirituality and to shape the conception of his own intensely personal, and idiosyncratic, theology. Certainly by the winter of 1680 his activities had come to the attention of the Scottish privy council, who were determined to seize both his person and his 'seditious books'. However Gibb was warned of his impending arrest, and in November 1680 jumped ship shortly before his vessel returned to port. While he headed inland, *The John* was impounded and left to rot on the shore, to the dismay and the near ruin of his former employers who went to great pains to persuade the council that Gibb was only their 'servant' and 'neither hath nor had [any] interest in the shipe' (*Reg. PCS*, 6.570, 571, 575).

Gibb now broke with Donald Cargill and the Society People, among whose ranks he had previously been numbered. He strongly believed that Cargill had broken his sacred bond of trust with the Scottish people upon his seeking the safety of a temporary exile in northern England, and moved quickly to assert his own authority over those conventicles left leaderless by this apparent desertion and by the death in action of Richard Cameron during the previous summer. Possessing a formidable charisma and a strong sexual magnetism Gibb, in the early months of 1681, built up a sizeable local following around the neighbourhood of Borrowstounness, and won over 'Twenty six Women and three Men' who were regarded, even by his enemies within the covenanter movement, as being for 'the greater Part … serious, exercised, tender, zealous [and] gracious souls' (Walker, 17). This nucleus served as the foundation of a new sect, known variously as Gibbites, after their acknowledged leader, or as Sweet Singers on account of their tearful singing of Psalms 74, 79, 80, 83, and 117, paralleling the fate of Old Testament Israel with the sufferings of the Scottish church. In April 1681 the development of the sect took a wholly new and unexpected turn, as Gibb led his followers away from their homes and families in an utter rejection of private property and all worldly authority. One group went up into the Pentland hills to wait for the imminent delivery of God's judgment, in the form of fire and tempest, upon the sinful population and city of Edinburgh; while Gibb and his closest friends sought an urgent meeting with Cargill near Clydesdale, in an attempt to gain the support of that influential preacher for their cause.

However, no agreement could be reached between the two parties and the situation was made even worse when Gibb and his companion, David Jamie, drew pistols upon a group of distraught men who had journeyed to their camp in order to beg for the return of their estranged wives. With the breach between Gibb and Cargill now complete, he was vehemently denounced as the devil incarnate by all of those field preachers still active in the south-west and took refuge, along with his followers, in the wastelands between Lothian and Tweeddale. Removed from the major centres of population, the Sweet Singers implemented a strict regime of prayer, fasting, and mourning, with both sexes preaching extempory sermons and refusing to do any manual labour on the grounds that work and all 'mechaniks' were the very 'limbs of [the] AntiChrist' (*Reg. PCS*, 7.704). Having taken to styling himself as King Solomon and rechristening his followers with similar names, such as 'Isaac … Rheoboam, Deborah, Lidiah [and] the Queen of Sheba', drawn from the pages of the Old Testament, Gibb also reiterated the excommunications and abjurations of King Charles II and the duke of York which had first been issued by Cameron and Cargill in the Sanquhar and Torwood declarations of the previous year (ibid., 7.704–5). Posing a clear threat to the established social and political order, troops were dispatched to effect Gibb's arrest, and at the beginning of May 1681 a troop of dragoons swooped upon his encampment at Woodhill Craigs, capturing him and all of his adherents without a struggle, and bringing the first period of his ministry to an abrupt and premature end. Brought to Edinburgh under guard, his followers were separated from one another, according to their gender. The women were incarcerated in the correction house, where several were bailed upon the intercession of their husbands and families, while the men were confined to the Tolbooth to await examination by the members of the Scottish privy council.

Although Gibb initially failed to impress his interrogators, his case did arouse the interest of James, duke of

York, who had recently been appointed viceroy in Scotland. The duke was keen to exploit splits within the covenanter movement and, having convinced himself that the Sweet Singers presented no military threat to his regime, spoke of them as deserving a bedlam rather than a gallows. Indeed, Patrick Walker was to allege that Gibb had received substantial sums of money from the duke of York as bribes, and that as a result he dedicated a 'most blasphemous Paper' to his new royal patron (Walker, 22). While no copies of this publication appear to be extant, it does indeed seem as though Gibb's attitude towards the monarchy and temporal authority underwent a profound change, for he was set free from the Tolbooth on 2 August 1681, having renounced those 'disloyall principalls' which he had once held (*Reg. PCS*, 7.177).

Thereafter, Gibb's career and actions become far more erratic, and harder to chart owing to the overt prejudice of mainstream Scottish presbyterian writers, while his underlying motivations are almost entirely open to conjecture. The most likely explanation for his subsequent conduct is that, during his imprisonment, he had experienced some form of nervous breakdown which led him to wilder delusions and, finally, to an utter rejection of his belief in God. Travelling west with a band of followers dramatically reduced to just three men and two women, he now railed against both the metrical psalms and the Bible itself as being no more than human inventions, and consigned his own Bible—along with those of his companions—to the flames of a bonfire raised upon the borders of Airth and Stirling. Upon his re-arrest, Gibb was once again incarcerated in the Tolbooth at Edinburgh. However, his weekly cycle of fasting, followed by sudden and violent periods of bingeing, further weakened his powers of reason and did little to endear him to the other political prisoners held alongside him. Walker writes at length of his demented howlings and ravings, which disturbed his cell mates while they were at public worship and which provoked George Jackson, a Cameronian, to physically assault him and to dash his head repeatedly against the prison wall. It was feared that this attack had killed Gibb outright, but his powerful build and enormous physical strength—which had previously earned him the nickname Meikle John—saved him, though ever afterwards he assumed the aspect of a broken and cowed man, hiding away from his fellow prisoners and stuffing his mouth with rags in order to silence his involuntary cries. Sentenced to be transported to America, on 17 May 1684 he sailed across the Atlantic in a ship chartered by merchants from Edinburgh and New York colony. Several of Gibb's erstwhile followers, transported alongside him, later found well-paid employment in the colony and it is likely that he himself spent the rest of his life in New York even after his period of indentured service had come to an end. However, his zest for preaching and prophecy had not entirely left him, and he won a great reputation for his spiritual powers among the local Native American peoples, leading them in sacrifices and ritual celebrations. It is not known if he ever married, but one of his many female followers, Isobel Bon, was described as his constant companion. Given that Gibb styled himself as King Solomon it is conceivable that the woman known as the Queen of Sheba acted as his consort, and perhaps this particular follower was synonymous with Bon. Gibb was believed to have died in 1720 and, though universally excoriated by the overwhelming majority of Scots—whether episcopalian or presbyterian—the legacy of his short-lived sect and the persuasiveness of his message continued to reinforce those eighteenth-century sectaries, such as Arden Burnell and the Muggletonians, who championed the validity of personal revelation and held that they themselves had the power to bless or damn at will.   JOHN CALLOW

Sources P. Walker, *Some remarkable passages in the life and death of … Mr Daniel Cargill* (1732) [the seminal account of Gibb and his ministry] · *Reg. PCS*, 3rd ser., vols. 6–7 · W. Scott, *Letters on demonology and witchcraft* (1884), 74–5 · M. Grant, *No king but Christ: the story of Donald Cargill* (1988), 158–64 · C. Hill, B. Reay, and W. Lamont, *The world of the Muggletonians* (1983) · R. Wodrow, *The history of the sufferings of the Church of Scotland from the Restauration to the revolution*, 2 (1722) · *A full and true account of the notorious wicked life of that grand imposter, John Taylor; one of the Sweet Singers of Israel* (1678) · W. C. Dickinson, *The Sweet Singers and other remarkable occurrents* (1953) · M. V. Hay, *Winston Churchill and James II of England* (1934) · M. V. Hay, *The enigma of James II* (1938) · *The saints jubilee, or, The fullness of joy to the Sweet Singers of Sion* (1660)
Archives BL, MSS by him and relating to him, Add. MSS 60168–60256
Wealth at death see Walker, *Some remarkable passages*

Gibb, John (1776–1850), civil engineer and contractor, was born on 13 October 1776 at Kirkcows, near Falkirk, the son of William Gibb (1736–1791), contractor. The elder Gibb died when John was fifteen and he served an apprenticeship to a mechanic. He was then employed as contractor's assistant, and later as subordinate engineer by a relative, a Mr Porteous, and next served under John Rennie on the construction of the Lancaster Canal. He then went to Leith, where he worked for Alexander Easton on construction of the docks. While there he met and married, in 1803, Easton's daughter Catherine.

Gibb began practice on his own account as a contractor, gradually establishing a reputation for professional skill. He was employed in the construction of Greenock harbour under John Rennie, where Telford's attention was drawn to his exceptional ability and great managerial tact. Telford engaged him as resident engineer at the Aberdeen harbour works. Gibb moved there in 1809, and superintended the erection of extensive piers and other details. On the temporary suspension of the works at Aberdeen, he once more turned to contracting, although he continued to report on engineering works. In addition he operated granite quarries at Rubbislaw in Aberdeenshire, supplying masonry for Sheerness Dockyard and elsewhere.

Gibb's major works included the repair of the Crinan Canal in 1817, various harbours on the east coast of Scotland, the Glasgow and Carlisle turnpike road (which involved stone bridges of extensive span), Cartland Craigs Bridge on the Lanark Road, various lighthouses for Robert Stevenson, the Dean Bridge, Edinburgh, for Telford, and Broomielaw Bridge, Glasgow, designed by Telford and built by Gibb and his son Alexander (1801–1867), who after serving a pupillage with Telford had joined his firm. Although particularly experienced in harbour construction and river engineering Gibb carried out important railway contracts, notably Victoria Bridge over the Wear on the Durham Junction Railway, and the Almond valley Viaduct on the Edinburgh and Glasgow Railway. The latter was his final work, and one on which he lost most of his fortune. His son continued his business. Gibb died at Aberdeen on 3 December 1850, being at the time one of the oldest members of the Institution of Civil Engineers, which he had joined in 1820.

JAMES BURNLEY, *rev.* MIKE CHRIMES

Sources PICE, 10 (1850–51), 82–5 · G. Harrison, *Alexander Gibb: the story of an engineer* [1950] · A. Gibb, *The story of Telford* (1935) · Irving, *Scots.* · Anderson, *Scot. nat.*, 293 · parish register (births and baptisms), 13 Oct 1776, Falkirk, Stirlingshire · parish register (proclamations of banns and marriages), 18 Dec 1803, Glasgow
Archives Inst. CE · NA Scot. · Sci. Mus. · Aberdeen Harbour records | Inst. CE, Telford MSS · Ironbridge Gorge Museum, Telford collection
Likenesses portrait, repro. in Gibb, *Story of Telford*
Wealth at death allegedly lost his fortune c.1840 on the Edinburgh and Glasgow Railway contract, but clearly retained some wealth as son continued in business

Gibb [née Harrison], **Margaret Hunter** (1892–1984), political activist, was born on 31 July 1892 at Dunston, near Gateshead, the only daughter of William Harrison, commercial traveller, and his wife, Susan Hunter. She attended Blaydon secondary school as one of its first scholarship holders, and from there trained as a schoolteacher at St Hild's College, Durham, from 1910 to 1912. It was during her years as a teacher that Margaret Harrison's political interests developed, focusing partly on opposition to the First World War. She refused, for instance, to celebrate Empire day in the schoolyard. In 1918 she began a lifetime of political commitment and activity when she joined the newly formed Dunston branch of the Labour Party and the Independent Labour Party (ILP). Before long she was vice-president of the local branch of the ILP and secretary of the women's section of Dunston Labour Party. In 1921 she was a founder member of the Durham Labour Women's Advisory Council.

In 1923 Margaret Harrison married Tom Gibb, an ILP organizer and Labour Party agent from Jarrow. When he died in July 1927 she accepted his job of agent for Central Sheffield. In 1929 she was elected to Sheffield city council and served on the education committee and four subcommittees. A year later she resigned when offered a post as organizer on the Labour Party's national staff organization, for what was then the north-east region, consisting of eighty-six constituencies in Durham, Northumberland, and Yorkshire. She held this post for twenty-seven years until her retirement in 1957.

As regional organizer, Margaret Gibb's main objective was to develop political support for the Labour Party in her region and she agreed with her fellow organizer that she would concentrate on the involvement of women in the Labour Party. She pursued this in a variety of ways, developing as varied a social and educative programme as

possible. On the social side she organized dances, family reunion evenings, galas, round table discussions, plays, sports days, and whist drives. In order to strengthen political education she set up a monthly newsletter which was sent to all the women's sections in her region, and encouraged annual 'schools' which enabled groups of women from the women's sections to attend training lectures for a week. She also started occasional 'propaganda tours' during which political literature would be distributed and which would end with a meeting.

This work continued and developed after the Second World War. An annual speakers' forum was introduced with representatives from women's sections competing for a silver shield. In 1955 the Northern Regional Women's Rest Fund was established to enable a small number of women to be sent on a fortnight's holiday each year. By the time she retired in 1957 Margaret Gibb had enabled many women in the north-east of England to become politically literate and thereby able to participate in the affairs of their local community. In 1965 she was appointed OBE for this work.

While her major preoccupation was with women's organizations, Margaret Gibb participated in a wide range of political activity. In the late 1930s she joined the Fabian Society, becoming vice-chair of the Tyneside branch and a life member. From 1951 to 1984 she was an active member of the Morpeth Labour Party. She was election agent in Berwick constituency in 1959 and 1964, and in 1968 she was made honorary life president of the Berwick constituency Labour Party. In 1977 she was a guest speaker at the Durham Labour Women's Advisory Council annual gala.

Margaret Gibb was tall, well-groomed, and distinguished looking. She brought to her work both high standards and boundless energy which she used unhesitatingly to the benefit of both the Labour Party and the women in her region. For almost the last thirty years of her life she shared a home, The Riding, in Cambo, near Morpeth, with Molly Thompson, a friend from her college days. Margaret Gibb died, after a short illness, in Hexham General Hospital on 27 January 1984 at the age of ninety-one. Her funeral was held at West End Road crematorium, Newcastle, on 6 February 1984.

SERENA KELLY

Sources M. Callcott, 'The organisation of political support for labour in the north of England: the work of Margaret Gibb, 1929–1957', *Bulletin* [North East Group for the Study of Labour History], 11 (1977) · M. Callcott, 'Gibb, Margaret Hunter', *DLB*, vol. 8 · CGPLA Eng. & Wales (1984)
Archives Northumbd RO, Newcastle upon Tyne | SOUND U. Hull, Brynmor Jones L.
Wealth at death under £40,000: probate, 3 Aug 1984, CGPLA Eng. & Wales

Gibb, Robert (1799/1800–1837), landscape painter, was a native of Dundee. Of his parents, nothing is known. He was an associate of the Royal Institution, Edinburgh, and contributed to the exhibitions of that body from 1822 to 1830. He painted in oils and watercolours. He was an original associate of the Royal Scottish Academy, became a full member in July 1829, when he received the Hope and Cockburn award for his *View of Perth* (Sandeman Library,

Perth), and contributed ninety-eight works to its exhibitions from 1830 to 1834. Of his works, which are chiefly landscapes, though he occasionally produced figure subjects, those in oil have been described as 'wholly artless' (Caw, 59), while his watercolours have been more favourably received. 'Fresh in colour and technique' (Halsby and Harris, 73) they are carefully handled and show considerable feeling for nature. McEwan noted that 'He was one of the first landscape painters in Scotland to work on location' (McEwan, 227). He is represented by eight works in the National Gallery of Scotland, including views of *Borthwick Castle* and *Craigmillar Castle*. He died in Edinburgh aged thirty-seven, in 1837. He is to be distinguished from Robert Gibb (1845–1932), portrait and figure painter, who was elected associate of the Royal Scottish Academy in 1878 and member in 1882. J. M. GRAY, rev. ANNETTE PEACH

Sources P. J. M. McEwan, *Dictionary of Scottish art and architecture* (1994) · J. L. Caw, *Scottish painting past and present, 1620–1908* (1908) · J. Halsby and P. Harris, *The dictionary of Scottish painters, 1600–1960* (1990)

Gibb, William Elphinstone [Bill] (1943–1988), fashion designer, was born on 23 January 1943 in Fraserburgh, Scotland, the eldest of the seven children of George Gibb, a farmer, and his wife, Jessie. He was brought up mainly by his maternal grandparents on a dairy farm in Pitsligo, a village 40 miles north of Aberdeen. After Fraserburgh infant school (1948–55) he attended Fraserburgh Academy (1955–62), where he was fascinated by history, costumes of the past, and the fashions that he saw around him.

Gibb developed his skills at St Martin's School of Art (1962–6), specializing in the Byzantine and Renaissance periods and extending this study of decoration and colour with explorations of folk costume in Europe and the Middle and Far East. He graduated first in his year and progressed to the Royal College of Art (1966–8), studying under Janey Ironside, who also taught Zandra Rhodes and Ossie Clark; like Gibb they revelled in the romance of fluid silhouettes and complex uses of pattern and print. Although he dropped out before graduating, the Royal College of Art provided valuable experience for Gibb. In 1967 he travelled to New York under the Yardley New Look award scheme, garnering a commission from Henri Bendell, before travelling around America for three months. He witnessed the burgeoning hippie scene, which was to inspire his later work with its sense of freedom, love of ethnic influences, and mix-and-match approach to dressing. He also met Kaffe Fassett, with whom he collaborated later on Celtic-inspired knitwear in some of his most successful collections. In 1967 he opened the Kensington boutique Alice Paul with three other students. He designed for the youth market, with clean lines that bore the imprint of contemporary trends, rather than the eclectic, romantic style that he was to evolve in the seventies. Alice Paul folded in 1969, and Gibb focused on freelance work for wholesale company Baccarat, producing hippie-inspired Gypsy dresses that were decorated in combinations of geometric designs and organic floral patterns. The willowy, neat-headed silhouette that these designs required was very popular. In 1970 he won the *Vogue* designer of the year award; one of his designs was chosen to appear at Bath Museum of Costume as dress of the year. During the same period he met Kate Franklin, who became his business partner in the ensuing decade.

In 1972, backed by the Loveable Company, Franklin and Gibb formed Bill Gibb Ltd, drawing together a close team of craftspeople. Craft, whether beading, embroidery, or knitting, was integral to his designs and enabled him to experiment with texture, combining tweeds and plaids with metallic prints, leather thong trimmings, and lavish embroidery. He used both embellishments and construction techniques from ethnic dress, for example, disguising seams with braiding in the style of Moroccan traditional dress. He became internationally renowned for his extravagant evening wear, dressing celebrities in clothes from collections with such titles as *Buddha and Moon* (1975–6) and *Byzantine* (1976), and in 1975 he opened his own boutique in Bond Street. His theatrical style lent itself well to the ballets he designed for, including Remy Charlip's *Mad River* (1972).

However, the craftsmanship that went into Gibb's garments meant that they could take three months to complete, and his clientele remained small. He faced a series of financial problems, falling prey to the recession in 1970s British fashion, as a series of backers went into liquidation or pulled funding. While he attempted a comeback in the mid-1980s, he failed to obtain enough orders, despite favourable press and a revival of his productive working relationship with Kaffe Fassett. Although he continued to work for private clients, he never repeated the splendour of his 1977 retrospective show at the Royal Albert Hall and showed his last catwalk collection in 1986. He died, unmarried, of cancer in London on 3 January 1988 and was cremated and interred in his home town, Fraserburgh. REBECCA ARNOLD

Sources C. Rew, 'Bill Gibb', *Costume*, 28 (1994), 81–96 · A. de la Haye, ed., *The cutting edge: 50 years of British fashion, 1947–1997* (1997) [exhibitition catalogue, V&A, March 1997] · 'Bill Gibb, British fashion designer', *Annual Obituary* (1988), 18–21 · E. Carter, *The changing world of fashion, 1900 to the present* (1977) · R. Martin, ed., *Contemporary fashion* (1995) · *WWW, 1981–90* · B. Polan, 'Artist of the romantic', *The Guardian* (4 Jan 1988), 11 · S. Menkes, *The Independent* (4 Jan 1988), 10 · *The Times* (4 Jan 1988), 12 · *Daily Telegraph* (4 Jan 1988), 14

Likenesses J. Bratby, portrait, priv. coll.

Gibbens, Nicholas (*fl.* 1601–1602), Church of England clergyman, was the author of *Questions and Disputations Concerning the Holy Scripture* (1601; reissued 1602). The only firm biographical information we have is the description of the author on the book's title-page: that he was a 'Minister and Preacher of the word of God'. He may be the same man as the Nicholas Gibbons who matriculated as pensioner at Clare College, Cambridge, in June 1585, graduated BA in 1589 and MA in 1592, and was incorporated at Oxford in July 1592. Despite their shared occupation he was not the Nicholas Gibbon of Heckford, Dorset, who was the father of Nicholas Gibbon, rector of Sevenoaks and of Corfe Castle: that Nicholas was a burgess of Poole.

Only the first part of the first tome of *Questions and Disputations*, covering the first fourteen chapters of Genesis in

545 pages, was ever published. In its sub-title Gibbens declared it a work 'wherein … the everlasting truth of the word of God, is freed from the errors and slaunders of Atheists, Papists, Philosphers and all Heretikes'. In the epistle dedicatory to Tobie Matthew, bishop of Durham, Gibbens called scripture an 'inestimable treasure' and lamented its neglect, especially as he feared 'church and common-wealth' were 'continually assaulted' by enemies: 'either by open invasion, or secret emission of lurking spies, intelligencers, remembrancers, seminaries, priests, Jesuits, solicitors for the church of Rome … who through the power of darkness, do work into the hearts of men' (Gibbens, epistle dedicatory, unpaginated).   CAROLINE L. LEACHMAN

Sources N. Gibbens, *Questions and disputations concerning the holy scripture* (1601) · N. Gibbens, *Questions and disputations concerning the holy scripture*, 2nd edn (1602) · Venn, *Alum. Cant.* · Wood, *Ath. Oxon.*, new edn, 2.430 · Wood, *Ath. Oxon.: Fasti* (1815), 259 · J. Hutchins, *The history and antiquities of the county of Dorset*, 3rd edn, ed. W. Shipp and J. W. Hodson, 1 (1861), 543

Gibberd, Sir Frederick Ernest (1908–1984), architect and town planner, was born in Coventry on 7 January 1908, the eldest of five children (all sons) of Frederick Gibberd, who ran a gentleman's outfitters at Earlsdon, Coventry, and his wife, Elsie Annie Clay of Nuneaton. Gibberd was educated at the King Henry VIII School in Coventry. While articled to a firm of Birmingham architects from 1925, he studied at the Birmingham School of Architecture. In 1930 he moved to London as an assistant to E. Berry Webber, before setting up his own practice in 1932. Initially he shared an office with F. R. S. Yorke, one of the pioneers of modernism in English architecture and his old room-mate in Birmingham, and the two jointly published *The Modern Flat* in 1937. By then Gibberd had already completed his first substantial building, Pullman Court, Streatham (1933–6), an elegantly designed block of modern-style flats. Unfit for active service in the Second World War, Gibberd at first occupied himself with designing air raid shelters in Hampstead, before becoming principal of the Architectural Association School of Architecture in London (1942–4). He also designed a prefabricated steel-framed, partially steel-clad house for the British Iron and Steel Federation, which was built in considerable numbers after the war.

It was as an architect–planner that Gibberd excelled, making major contributions to post-1945 reconstruction and civic design. A master plan for Nuneaton town centre, and the Somerford housing estate for Hackney council, prepared the way for his role from 1946 in the creation of Harlow New Town, one of the ring of satellite towns to be created around London. He not only drew up the master plan but served as planner and chief architect of the new town until 1980. Such was his commitment that in 1956 he purchased a property in Harlow called Marsh Lane, which he made his home for the rest of his life.

Despite his heavy workload, Gibberd also became involved in the 1951 Festival of Britain 'Live Architecture' exhibition on the Lansbury estate, Poplar. Indeed, his was the idea that an actual bomb-damaged area in the course of reconstruction should form the basis of an exhibition devoted to architecture, town planning, and building research. He was given responsibility for the market square and precinct, which provided the focus for the whole of the new estate: these were widely imitated for countless pedestrianized shopping centres and parades, as well as acting as a prototype for Gibberd's own larger market square at Harlow. Not surprisingly, between the 1950s and 1970s Gibberd and his practice were responsible for other urban design projects in Doncaster, St Albans, Hull, Leamington Spa, Bedford, Stratford upon Avon, Redcar, and Swindon.

In addition, Gibberd executed a string of important buildings after the war, including: the first terminal buildings at Heathrow airport (1950–69); power stations at Hinkley Point (1957–65) and Didcot (1964–8); the Inter-Continental Hotel at Hyde Park Corner, London (completed 1975); the reconstruction of the Coutts Bank in the Strand (a building by John Nash, for which Gibberd's glass-fronted centre, replacing a Victorian block, caused much controversy in 1969); and, as a result of architectural competitions, the Roman Catholic cathedral at Liverpool (1960–67) and the London mosque in Regent's Park (1969–77). The cathedral's circular plan and crown-like tower were original conceptions, but their total effect was, perhaps, somewhat brittle in view of their monumental purpose. Nevertheless, the cathedral added a distinctive landmark to Liverpool's townscape, providing, as intended, a counterpoint to the Anglican cathedral, and it is undoubtedly Gibberd's best-known building.

After 1945 Gibberd's work tended to conform to the idiom of the day, although at its best it retained qualities of invention and sensibility that most commercial architecture lacked. He was particularly concerned with a sense of place and sought in his work to respect and, if possible, enhance it. His housing schemes were usually low-rise mixed developments of three-storey flats and two-storey terraced houses. However, his nine-storey block of flats The Lawn, at Harlow (1949–51), is regarded as the country's first tower block of real architectural interest, and was followed by other similar blocks in the town.

Gibberd could be very persuasive and was adept at winning over committees. Crucial to his success was a willingness to work within sometimes tight budgets, and even to redesign features in order to reduce costs. Yet, in contrast to many heads of large architectural offices, he refused to become a mere administrator and insisted on spending time at the drawing-board.

Many of Gibberd's schemes benefited from his special talent for landscape, none more so than Harlow, where he devoted unremitting care and energy until the end of his life. With its green spaces penetrating the housing areas and its carefully considered planting it is probably the most successful of the post-war new towns. He was employed more specifically to landscape several new reservoirs, including Celyn Lake (designed 1959). He was also an expert and imaginative gardener, and the garden he laid out round his house at Harlow, which occupied much of his later years, was a beguiling mixture of the romantic and the monumental. It revealed qualities as a designer that circumstances had not always allowed him to display in his buildings. His aesthetic sensibility was also shown in his discriminating collection of contemporary British watercolours and drawings, including works by Edward Burra, Henry Moore, Ben Nicholson, and many other leading artists.

Gibberd was a tallish, upright man with an attractive presence. His long, wavy, swept-back hair and moustache not only gave him distinction but also expressed the artist in him, while his relaxed, well-tailored appearance signalled the successful and dedicated professional. Although delicate health prevented him from playing a greater part in affairs, he was twice vice-president of the Royal Institute of British Architects, was a hard-working president of the Building Centre, and served for twenty years on the Royal Fine Arts Commission (1950–70). He was a fellow of the Royal Institute of British Architects (1939; he had become a licentiate the previous year), of the Royal Town Planning Institute, and of the Institute of Landscape Architects, was elected RA in 1969 (having become ARA in 1961), appointed CBE in 1954, and knighted in 1967. In 1969 Liverpool University awarded him an honorary LLD, and he also won many medals and awards. Of the several books he published, the most notable was *Town Design* (1953), a well-balanced and well-illustrated survey which went through several editions.

Gibberd was twice married: first, on 21 April 1938, to Dorothy Ada Pryse Phillips (*b.* 1912/13), who was of Welsh descent and a Welsh speaker, the daughter of John Hugh Phillips, a London bank manager; they had a son and two daughters. After her death in 1970, he married, on 29 March 1972, Patricia Nanette Fox Edwards (*b.* 1926/7), the daughter of Bernard Joseph Spielman, of Bristol, who was, like Gibberd's father, a gentleman's outfitter. She particularly helped her husband on the choice of sculpture to adorn both his own garden and, more generally, Harlow New Town. Gibberd died at his home, The House, Marsh Lane, Harlow, on 9 January 1984.

JEFFREY RICHARDS, *rev.* ALAN COX

Sources biographical file, RIBA BAL · D. Sharpe, 'Sir Frederick Gibberd', *Building*, 235 (7 July 1978), 65–9 · F. Gibberd, B. Hyde Harvey, L. White, and others, *Harlow: the story of a new town* (1980) · nomination papers, RIBA BAL · S. Porter, ed., *Poplar, Blackwall and the Isle of Dogs: the parish of All Saints*, [1], Survey of London, 43 (1994), 212–46 · N. Bingham, 'A monument to modesty', *Perspectives on Architecture*, 10/2 (Feb 1995), 47–9 · *The Times* (12 Jan 1984), 12f. · private information (1990) · personal knowledge (1990) · m. certs. · *CGPLA Eng. & Wales* (1985)

Archives Bodl. Oxf., corresp. with Neville Coghill

Likenesses photograph, 1977, Hult. Arch.

Wealth at death £409,343: probate, 29 Jan 1985, *CGPLA Eng. & Wales*

PICTURE CREDITS

Freud, Sigmund (1856–1939)—Mary Evans Picture Library / Freud copyrights

Freund, Ida (1863–1914)—The Principal and Fellows, Newnham College, Cambridge

Freund, Sir Otto Kahn- (1900–1979)—British Library of Political and Economic Science

Frewen, Accepted (bap. 1588, d. 1664)—courtesy of Frewen College

Freyberg, Bernard Cyril, first Baron Freyberg (1889–1963)—© National Portrait Gallery, London

Frink, Dame Elisabeth Jean (1930–1993)—Estate of Dame Elisabeth Frink; courtesy of Fischer Fine Arts

Friswell, James Hain (1825–1878)—© National Portrait Gallery, London

Frith, Mary (1584x9–1659)—© National Portrait Gallery, London

Frith, William Powell (1819–1909)—© National Portrait Gallery, London

Frobisher, Sir Martin (1535?–1594)—© Bodleian Library, University of Oxford

Froissart, Jean (1337?–c.1404)—The British Library

Froude, James Anthony (1818–1894)—© National Portrait Gallery, London

Frowde, Henry (1841–1927)—© National Portrait Gallery, London / Oxford University Press

Frowde, James Henry (1831–1899)—V&A Images, The Victoria and Albert Museum

Fry, Charles Burgess (1872–1956)—Public Record Office

Fry, Edmund (1754–1835)—© National Portrait Gallery, London

Fry, Sir Edward (1827–1918)—The Honourable Society of Lincoln's Inn. Photograph: Photographic Survey, Courtauld Institute of Art, London

Fry, Elizabeth (1780–1845)—Norwich Castle Museum & Art Gallery / private collection

Fry, Joseph Storrs (1826–1913)—Howarth-Loomes Collection; photograph National Portrait Gallery, London

Fry, (Sara) Margery (1874–1958)—© Estate of Claude Rogers; collection National Portrait Gallery, London

Fryd, Caroline Joyce (1909–2000)—Paul Caplan / Mencap

Frye, Thomas (1711/12–1762)—© National Portrait Gallery, London

Fryer, Alfred (1826–1912)—by permission of the Linnean Society of London

Fuchs, Sir Vivian Ernest (1908–1999)—Getty Images – Hulton Archive

Fulford, Francis (1803–1868)—© National Portrait Gallery, London

Fuller, Andrew (1754–1815)—© National Portrait Gallery, London

Fuller, Francis (1807–1887)—© National Portrait Gallery, London

Fuller, Isaac (1606/1620?–1672)—© Bodleian Library, University of Oxford

Fuller, John Frederick Charles (1878–1966)—private collection; photograph National Portrait Gallery, London

Fuller, Roy Broadbent (1912–1991)—© Granville Davies; collection National Portrait Gallery, London

Fuller, Thomas (1607/8–1661)—Berkeley Castle Will Trust

Fuller, Thomas (1654–1734)—© National Portrait Gallery, London

Furneaux, Tobias (1735–1781)—Lady Juliet Townsend by descent

Furness, Christopher, first Baron Furness (1852–1912)—© National Portrait Gallery, London

Furniss, Henry [Lika Joko] (1854–1925)—© National Portrait Gallery, London

Furniss, Henry Sanderson, Baron Sanderson (1868–1939)—© Estate of Stanley Spencer 2004. All rights reserved, DACS; photographed in a private collection. Photograph: Photographic Survey, Courtauld Institute of Art, London

Furnivall, Frederick James (1825–1910)—© National Portrait Gallery, London

Furse, Dame Katharine (1875–1952)—© National Portrait Gallery, London

Fury, Billy (1940–1983)—V&A Images, The Victoria and Albert Museum; collection National Portrait Gallery, London

Fuseli, Henry (1741–1825)—V&A Images, The Victoria and Albert Museum

Fyfe, David Patrick Maxwell, earl of Kilmuir (1900–1967)—© National Portrait Gallery, London

Fyfe, Sir William Hamilton (1878–1965)—© National Portrait Gallery, London

Fyleman, Rose Amy (1877–1957)—© National Portrait Gallery, London

Gable, Christopher Michael (1940–1998)—© reserved; The Independent; photograph National Portrait Gallery, London

Gabo, Sir Naum (1890?–1977)—© Nina Williams; Tate Gallery Archive

Gabor, Dennis (1900–1979)—© reserved; collection National Portrait Gallery, London

Gadbury, John (1627–1704)—© National Portrait Gallery, London

Gadsby, William (1773–1844)—© National Portrait Gallery, London

Gage, Sir Henry (1597–1645)—© National Portrait Gallery, London

Gage, Sir John (1479–1556)—The Royal Collection © 2004 HM Queen Elizabeth II

Gage, Thomas (1719/20–1787)—Yale Center for British Art, Paul Mellon Collection

Gaikwar, Sayaji Rao, maharaja of Baroda (1863–1939)—© National Portrait Gallery, London

Gainsborough, Thomas (1727–1788)—© Royal Academy of Arts, London, 2004

Gaisford, Thomas (1779–1855)—Christ Church, Oxford

Gaitskell, (Anna) Dora, Baroness Gaitskell (1901–1989)—© National Portrait Gallery, London

Gaitskell, Hugh Todd Naylor (1906–1963)—© Estate of Hugh Gaitskell; collection National Portrait Gallery, London

Galbraith, Vivian Hunter (1889–1976)—photograph reproduced by courtesy of The British Academy

Gale, Roger (1672–1744)—Society of Antiquaries of London

Galignani, (John) Anthony (1796–1873)—© National Portrait Gallery, London

Gallacher, William (1881–1965)—© National Portrait Gallery, London

Gallenga, Antonio Carlo Napoleone (1810–1895)—© National Portrait Gallery, London

Galpin, Francis William (1858–1945)—© reserved; Galpin Society

Galsworthy, John (1867–1933)—© National Portrait Gallery, London

Galt, John (1779–1839)—© National Portrait Gallery, London

Galton, Sir Douglas Strutt (1822–1899)—courtesy of the National Physical Laboratory

Galton, Sir Francis (1822–1911)—© National Portrait Gallery, London

Gamble, John (d. 1687)—© National Portrait Gallery, London

Gambold, John (1711–1771)—© National Portrait Gallery, London

Gandhi, Indira Priyadarshini (1917–1984)—Derry Moore / Camera Press

Gandhi, Mohandas Karamchand [Mahatma Gandhi] (1869–1948)—Köln, Museum Ludwig / Rheinisches Bildarchiv Köln

Gann, Thomas William Francis (1867–1938)—© National Portrait Gallery, London

Garbett, Cyril Forster (1875–1955)—by kind permission of the Archbishop of York and the Church Commissioners

Gardiner, Alfred George (1865–1946)—© National Portrait Gallery, London

Gardiner, Allen Francis (1794–1851)—© National Portrait Gallery, London

Gardiner, Gerald Austin, Baron Gardiner (1900–1990)—© National Portrait Gallery, London

Gardiner, James (1636/7–1705)—reproduced by kind permission of His Grace the Archbishop of Canterbury and the Church Commissioners. Photograph: Photographic Survey, Courtauld Institute of Art, London

Gardiner, (Henry) Rolf (1902–1971)—© courtesy the Artist's Estate / Bridgeman Art Library

Gardiner, Samuel Rawson (1829–1902)—© National Portrait Gallery, London

Gardner, Ernest Arthur (1862–1939)—reproduced with permission of the British School at Athens

Gardner, Dame Helen Louise (1908–1986)—© National Portrait Gallery, London

Gardner, (Leslie) James (1907–1995)—© Lewis Morley, courtesy of The Akehurst Bureau; collection National Portrait Gallery, London

Gardner, Sir James Tynte Agg- (1846–1928)—© National Portrait Gallery, London

Garencières, Theophilus (1610–c.1680)—© National Portrait Gallery, London

Garfield, Leon (1921–1996)—Getty Images – Hulton Archive

Gargrave, Sir Thomas (1494/5–1579)—© National Portrait Gallery, London

Garland, Madge (1898–1990)—© Cecil Beaton Archive, Sotheby's; collection National Portrait Gallery, London

Garner, (Joseph John) Saville, Baron Garner (1908–1983)—© National Portrait Gallery, London

Garnett, Constance Clara (1861–1946)—private collection; photograph © National Portrait Gallery, London

Garnett, David (1892–1981)—© National Portrait Gallery, London

Garnett, Henry (1555–1606)—© Copyright The British Museum

Garnett, (William) John Poulton Maxwell (1921–1997)—© News International Newspapers Ltd

Garnett, (James Clerk) Maxwell (1880–1958)—© reserved; collection National Portrait Gallery, London

Garnett, Richard (1835–1906)—© National Portrait Gallery, London

Garrard, Apsley George Benet Cherry- (1886–1959)—reproduced by permission of the Scott Polar Research Institute

Garrard, Sir Samuel, fourth baronet (1651–1725)—© reserved

Garrett, George William Littler (1852–1902)—© reserved

Garrick, David (1717–1779)—The Royal Collection © 2004 HM Queen Elizabeth II

Garrick, Eva Maria (1724–1822)—The Royal Collection © 2004 HM Queen Elizabeth II

Garrod, Alfred Henry (1846–1879)—© National Portrait Gallery, London

Garrod, Dorothy Annie Elizabeth (1892–1968)—© National Portrait Gallery, London

Garson, (Eileen Evelyn) Greer (1904–1996)—Rex Features

Garstang, John Burges Eustace (1876–1956)—© National Portrait Gallery, London

Garstin, Sir William Edmund (1849–1925)—© National Portrait Gallery, London

Garth, Sir Samuel (1661–1719)—© National Portrait Gallery, London

Garvey, Amy Ashwood (1895/1897–1969)—© reserved; photograph National Portrait Gallery, London

Garvey, Marcus Mosiah (1887–1940)—Getty Images – Hulton Archive